THE UNIVERS᷃ ᷃ᴵᵀ

THE R.S.V. INTERLINEAR GREEK - ENGLISH NEW TESTAMENT

THE R.S.V. INTERLINEAR
GREEK - ENGLISH
NEW TESTAMENT

**The Nestle Greek Text
with a Literal English Translation**

by

Reverend Alfred Marshall

and a Foreword by

Canon J. B. Phillips

**also a marginal text of
The Revised Standard Version**

Marshall Pickering

Marshall Pickering
Marshall Morgan & Scott Publications Ltd
3 Beggarwood Lane
Basingstoke, Hants RG23 7LP, England

Literal English Translation © Samuel Bagster and Sons Ltd. 1958
Editorial Interlineation © Samuel Bagster and Sons Ltd. 1958
Revised Standard Version © Division of Christian Education of the
National Council of the Churches of Christ in the USA 1946 and 1971

First Published 1968
Second Edition 1973
Third Edition 1975
Fourth Impression 1985
Fifth Impression 1988

ISBN 0 85150 105 2

Printed and bound
at the University Press, Oxford

*F*OREWORD

CANON J. B. PHILLIPS

There is undoubtedly a revived interest in the reading of the New Testament today. The sales of modern versions have, I think, surprised everybody while the demand for the Authorized Version continues as before. It seems that a great many people are turning again to these inspired documents to see for themselves the foundations on which the Christian Faith is built. Naturally, to any Christian these are the most important documents in the world. If we believe with our adult minds that we live on a planet visited by God Himself in human form, the record of His life and teaching and that of the movement which He began are of supreme importance to the entire human race. Anything therefore which makes the significance and relevance of the Personal Visit clearer to the reader is to be welcomed with open arms.

As a modern translator I am delighted to see this new Interlinear Greek-English New Testament. By no means everybody knows of the quiet patient work of the textual critics who, with the utmost care and reverence, compare and revise Greek texts so that we may possess Greek as near as possible to the original documents, none of which, alas, survives. In this book we have the Greek text in its most modern revised form; it is the fruit of many years of diligent scholarship and, to my mind, should be accepted with the respect it deserves. A lot has been learned and a good deal of fresh material has been discovered since the Authorized Version was made in 1611 and indeed since the issue of the Revised Version in 1881. Here, interlined with

probably the most accurate Greek that we can arrive at, is a
literal English version. Dr. Marshall has obviously done this work
of putting the nearest English equivalents to the Greek words with
great care and skill and his work should prove of the highest value
to any student of the New Testament.

It need hardly be said that this giving of verbal equivalents
is not a full translation, but it is an essential stage in that process.
The art of translation itself is not only the transferring of words
from one language to another but also the accurate transmission
of thought, feeling, atmosphere and even of style. But no translator can do his work properly without the transitional stage
which Dr. Marshall exhibits so brilliantly in this book. Anyone
with even a small knowledge of Greek will be able to see how
and why the Authorized Version translators did their work as
they did, and will also see how and why a modern translator
produces a vastly different verbal result. The intelligent reader
cannot fail to find this transitional stage, which is here so clearly
shown, both fascinating and revealing. And if, with only a small
knowledge of Greek, he should try to make his own translation,
so much the better! He will at least be saved from over-familiarity
with extremely meaningful words and sayings; and the chances
are that the Truth will break over him afresh, as it does over any
translator, ancient or modern, professional or amateur.

Although I consider that Dr. Marshall has done his work
supremely well, it is a good thing to bear in mind that you cannot
always either give an English equivalent for a Greek word or
expression, or even always render the same Greek word by the
same English one. May I take one word, the Greek verb *ΕΚΒΑΛΛΩ*
with its basic meaning of "throwing out". Dr. Marshall renders
this word variously: it is "pluck out" (Matthew *ch*. 7, *v*. 5), "cast
out" (Matthew *ch*. 8, *v*. 12), "put out" (Matthew *ch*. 9, *v*. 25),
"expel" (Matthew *ch*. 12, *v*. 24), "puts forth" (Matthew *ch*. 12,
v. 35), and "take out" (Luke *ch*. 6, *v*. 42)! And of course there
are many other cases where absolute consistency is impossible;
for words are not static things but expressions of thought which
are inevitably modified by their context. But we must not expect
impossibilities and I for one am grateful for an alert and intelligent
literal translation wedded to the latest and most reliable Greek

Text. I am glad, for example, to see that Dr. Marshall has not missed the peculiar Greek construction in Matthew *ch.* 16, *v.* 19, where Jesus tells Peter that "what he binds on earth" will be "what has been bound" in Heaven. There is a world of difference between guaranteeing celestial endorsement of the Apostle's actions and promising that his actions guided by the Holy Spirit will be in accordance with the Heavenly pattern! Again, since I know there are many who imagine that the Authorized Version is a particularly literal and accurate translation of the Greek, it is refreshing to turn to Matthew *ch.* 27, *v.* 44 and see that not one single word of the expression "cast the same in his teeth" is in fact in the Greek! It is further made clear that the "bottles" of Matthew *ch.* 9, *v.* 17, were in reality wineskins, and that in Jesus' time people did not "sit at meat" so much as recline! (Luke *ch.* 7, *v.* 36), and naturally there are scores of further examples which are both interesting and important.

It would be unwise to omit reading Dr. Marshall's Introduction; for in it he not only explains some peculiarities of Greek construction, of which the ordinary reader may be quite unaware, but also clearly shows the rules he has set for himself in making this literal translation. Moreover, his Notes on Particular Passages are well worth our attention. In all, I have the greatest pleasure in recommending this book. It is timely because of the great contemporary interest in the New Testament. And it is profoundly interesting because we have here, combined in the most intimate fashion, the results of a great deal of textual research and the interpretation of a scholar thoroughly familiar with New Testament Greek.

INTRODUCTION

THE REVEREND ALFRED MARSHALL D.LITT

THE GREEK TEXT

THE text of the Greek New Testament has come down to us in various manuscripts, printing not being invented until the 15th century (Erasmus published his Greek New Testament in 1516). Some of these manuscripts are more important than others (age is not necessarily determinative of importance). The study of the various manuscript copies, and the assessment of their individual value in attempting to reconstruct the original as nearly as possible, constitutes the science of Textual Criticism. For those who wish to study this seriously there are many books available; it is sufficient to say here that, after Erasmus, a great number of scholars have, over a long period, applied themselves to the task of constructing a reliable text out of the mass of various readings which have arisen from copying and making copies from copies of the old manuscripts: such scholars as Mill, Stephens, Griesbach, Lachmann, Tischendorf, Tregelles, Alford, and many more.

The Revised Standard Version of the New Testament is an authorized revision of the American Standard Version, published in 1901. This was a revision of the King James Version, published in 1611, itself more a revision of older versions than a new translation.

The Greek text used in this book is that of the 21st edition of Eberhard Nestle's *Novum Testamentum Graece*, based on the study and critical research of generations of scholars, except that the passage John 7. 53, 8. 1-11 is not in that text but is relegated to the foot of the page as a critical note. It is here retained in the text. The critical notes of Nestle's work, which enable students to follow the reasons for variations in the text, have been omitted as being outside the scope of this publication. The student who requires these critical notes is referred to the Greek edition published in this country by the British and Foreign Bible Society and in Germany (Stuttgart) by Privilegierte Württembergische Bibelanstalt, by whose permission this recension is used.

In certain places in the Greek text square brackets are found; these indicate only that, according to Nestle, some editors include and others omit the word or words so enclosed. Translation has been made here in the usual way.

Avoiding interpretation, then, we give some details of how we have proceeded in the matter of a literal translation. These should be studied and understood if proper use is to be made of this attempt to promote an intelligent reading of the Greek New Testament.

THE ENGLISH TRANSLATION

The relationship between the Greek text and the interlinear English is as follows: Greek words not required in the translation into English are (a) represented by a short dash, as for example the definite article with proper names. Alternatively (b) italic type is used to show that words or even in some cases letters are not really needed for an idiomatic English rendering. 'Man' is sometimes redundant (see Matthew *ch*. 20, *v*. 1 and Acts *ch*. 2, *v*. 22) and so on. On the other hand, words supplied in English for which there is no Greek equivalent are placed in square brackets [. . .]. Naturally, there will be differences of judgment as to this practice in the passages involved.

In the interlinear translation, a comma has in a number of places been introduced after "Behold". The reason for this is as follows: the Greek ἰδού (or other form), properly an imperative of the defective verb ὁράω, is used as an exclamation, as is its English equivalent; that is to say, it is not then an active verb taking a direct object in the accusative case, but is simply exclamatory and is followed by a noun in the nominative, with its predicate or complement understood.

For example, in John *ch.* 1, *v.* 29, there is not a command to behold the Lamb of God, but, as it might be said (and as in fact a preacher was recently heard to say), "Look! [there goes] . . . " The position is different in such passages as Matthew *ch.* 28, *v.* 6 and Romans *ch.* 11, *v.* 22, where there is a command. Strangely enough, the Authorized Version inserts a comma in I. John *ch.* 3, *v.* 1, where it is not required. There is here a command as in the two passages just cited: "See what manner of love . . . ".

The modern form for the third person singular of verbs (present indicative) has been used (loves) in place of the now obsolete -(e)th (loveth); but the older 'ye' has been retained for the nominative ('you' for the oblique cases) of the second person plural pronoun; and 'thou' (thee), not 'you', for the second person singular. It is a loss that in modern English these differences have disappeared; so unaccustomed are we now to them that even the average reader of the Authorized Version misses the point of Luke *ch.* 22, *v.* 31. The loss is even more to be regretted when God is addressed as 'You'.

The subjunctive mood is dying out in English, and no attempt has been made to represent consistently the Greek mood, except by the use of the analytic form "I may . . . ", with its related optative (of which latter there are only 37 examples in the New Testament, 15 of these being the familiar γένοιτο =may it be). But such words as ἵνα and compounds of ἄν (ὅταν, ἐάν), etc., introducing a subjective or hypothetical element into a verbal idea, require to be followed by the subjunctive mood.

The Greek perfect can generally be taken as represented by an English present: a past action continuing in its effect down to the present, in contrast to an action wholly in the past. But in a literal translation the English perfect has been retained. In John *ch.* 11, *v.* 27, the Authorized Version is idiomatically correct but the Revised Version is literally so (πεπίστευκα =I have believed); *cf.* II. Timothy *ch.* 1, *v.* 12, where the Authorized Version adopts the literal equivalent. So, *e.g.*, τετέλεσται =it has been finished =it is finished. In participles, italics show that the auxiliary verbs may be dispensed with in English.

Where some word other than the strictly literal one seems to be needed in the translation, the former is printed in parentheses immediately after the latter; *e.g.*, Matthew *ch.* 10, *v.* 17, "beware from(of) men."

Occasionally it is not feasible to give a literal rendering without undue explanation; some idiomatic word or phrase has to be used. There are only a few of such passages and they are indicated by the mark †.

There are a number of Greek phrases, other than where † is used, which are not to be taken word for word, but as a whole:

ἐπὶ τὸ αὐτό = on the same = together
διὰ τοῦτο = because-of this = therefore
ἵνα μή = in-order-that not = lest
καθ' ὑπερβολήν = by-way-of excess = excessively

In familiar proper names there will appear some inconsistency, a compromise between the actual spellings preferred by Nestle and the Authorized Version; but this is of no great importance.

Εὐαγγελίζω. This and its cognate noun have been anglicized (evangelize, evangel). But while we can 'evangelize' a city, we do not 'evangelize' a person or a subject; so we must speak of 'preaching (good tidings) to' a person or of 'preaching' a subject. We can of course speak of 'evangelizing' absolutely, as in I. Corinthians *ch.* 1, *v.* 17. Ellicott on I. Thessalonians *ch.* 3, *v.* 6 has some useful information for the student.

There are five idiomatic Greek constructions which, being of frequent occurrence, call for explanation.
a. The *genitive absolute*. This is made up of a participle and a noun or pronoun, both in the genitive case and agreeing otherwise as well, but having no grammatical relation to the context. It is used to indicate time during or at which something takes place, or in some circumstances connected therewith. The close of such a Greek phrase is shown by the superior letter [a]; see Luke *ch.* 3, *v.* 1. There are variations of this. In Luke *ch.* 12, *v.* 36, two participles are used with no noun—it has to be supplied from the context.

So also II. Corinthians *ch.* 7, *v.* 15, and see the note on Romans *ch.* 9, *v.* 11 under "Notes on Particular Passages" below.

b. The *accusative* (or other case) *and infinitive.* Here what is in English the subject of the verb (the doer of the action) is put in the accusative (or other) case and the verb itself in the infinitive. A superior letter [b] closes such a phrase; see Luke *ch.* 1, *v.* 21.

c. The *dative of possession.* The possessor is put in the dative case. The idea may be grasped by comparing our English way of saying that a thing 'belongs to so-and-so'. The superior letter [c] shows this idiom; see Luke *ch.* 1, *v.* 5, 7, 14.

d. The *genitive of purpose* or *result.* The infinitive of a verb is in the genitive case, as shown by the preceding definite article. The article itself can be ignored. Again the appropriate letter [d] shows the existence of the idiom; see Matthew *ch.* 2, *v.* 13. The same idea can be shown without any article; see Matthew *ch.* 4, *v.* 1.

e. The *dative of time.* A point of time 'in' or 'at' which a thing happens is thus shown (ἐν may or may not be used). The letter [e] shows this; see Luke *ch.* 2, *v.* 43, and *ch.* 18, *v.* 35.

The constructions b and e can sometimes be combined; see Luke *ch.* 1, *v.* 8.

There is no indefinite article in Greek. The use of it in translation is a matter of individual judgment. The numeral 'one' is sometimes found; whether this means that just one, and no more, is to be understood is again open to argument. See Matthew *ch.* 21, *v.* 19 and *ch.* 26, *v.* 69. We have inserted 'a' or 'an' as a matter of course where it seems called for.

The definite article must sometimes be rendered by a pronoun or a possessive adjective. This is particularly so where parts of the body are indicated; *e.g.,* Matthew *ch.* 8, *v.* 3. Sometimes it is used 'pronominally'—that is, it must be rendered 'he' (or otherwise according to the gender) or 'they'; see Mark *ch.* 10, *v.* 4.

The ending of a Greek verb normally indicates the person (1st, 2nd, or 3rd, sing. or pl.). If the pronoun is separately expressed, this can be clearly seen in the interlinear translation.

μέν . . . δέ. These two particles, in contrasted clauses, are not translatable literally, unless "indeed . . . but" be used, as we have done in some places. But by adopting the phrases "on one hand . . . on the other" the contrast is brought out. These particles are, in fact, somewhat elusive as to their force. See John *ch.* 19, *v.* 24 and 32, where μέν has been left untranslated—an example of the difficulty of rendering it satisfactorily in a literal translation.

It has not been considered necessary always to indicate the order of a noun and its adjective; a knowledge of English is sufficient for this. But where there is any risk of ambiguity small superior figures indicate the order in which the words should be read.

A number of Greek particles are said to be 'post-positive'— that is to say, they cannot stand as the first word in a sentence, but are found in the second, third, or even in the fourth place. Such words must of course be taken first in English; but it has not been thought necessary to show this, as the construction is sufficiently obvious. They include γάρ (for), δέ (and, but, now), οὖν (there-fore; "therefore" can be post-positive in English), τις (a certain), μέν (indeed), γε (really—generally too subtle to be reproduced in English).

ὅτι as a conjunction, when meaning "that", is used to introduce spoken words as recorded; it is then known as the 'recitative ὅτι'. In English the original present tense of any verb would in such a construction ('indirect speech') be changed to the past: He said that the man was a liar. But Greek retains the original tense as actually used. What the speaker really said was "The man is a liar". The conjunction thus becomes super-fluous and the reported words would in modern usage be put within quotation marks, as above. These, however, are not used in this translation. See Matthew *ch.* 21, *v.* 3.

ἵνα is, strictly, a 'telic' particle—*i.e.,* it denotes purpose (τέλος, an end); hence a full translation is "in order that". But inasmuch as in New Testament times there was a tendency to use it where ὅτι would be expected, it sometimes means no more than the conjunction "that"; see Matthew *ch.* 5, *v.* 29. Sometimes, then, where there may be room for difference of opinion as to its precise force, or even where there is none, "*in order* that" will be found in the literal translation.

A peculiarity of Greek construction is that a neuter plural subject may take a singular verb; but this is by no means invariable, and there appears to be no rule to go by. In translating, the position is sometimes shown by the use of an italic letter for the ending of the verb ([they] commit*s*); at other times the alternative is given in parenthesis (is(are)). But there are places where neither course is possible without taking up too much space, and the matter is left to the intelligence of the reader.

Where there is more than one subject of a verb, Greek will often put the verb in the singular to agree with the nearest subject. This is not in accordance with English grammar, which requires a plural verb if there is more than one subject. In Revelation *ch*. 9, *v*. 2, "sun" and "air" call for the plural "were darkened", as in the Authorized Version. But the Greek verb is in the singular. It is sometimes typographically possible to indicate the difference of grammatical usage, but not always.

In Greek, gender belongs to the word and not necessarily to what is indicated by the word; whereas of course in English we keep the ideas of masculine, feminine, and neuter to men, women, and inanimate things respectively. (English, by the way, is the only great modern language to do so.) Allowance must be made for this in translating: sometimes it is possible to transfer the idea from one language to another, but not always. The note to Revelation *ch*. 13, *v*. 1, may be consulted.

The construction of the demonstrative adjectives is peculiar in Greek. The definite article is used as well as the demonstrative adjective in one of two possible positions: either—

οὗτος ὁ οἶκος

this *the* house

or—

ὁ οἶκος οὗτος

the house this

The definite article is of course not wanted in English, and the proper translation of the phrase is obvious—"this house".

ἐκεῖνος (that) similarly. It is sometimes possible typographically to treat the three-word phrase as a whole, with the idiomatic translation underneath.

Similarly, the definite article is used in Greek with a possessive adjective, as in Matthew *ch.* 18, *v.* 20—

εἰς τὸ ἐμὸν ὄνομα
in *the* my name

or, alternatively again, the construction may be, say—

εἰς τὸ ὄνομα τὸ ἐμόν
in *the* name *the* my

This remark applies only to the first and second persons, singular and plural, but not to the third, where the only possible construction in this respect would be "in the name of him/her/them". This has been followed literally, as the reader can always make the needful English construction for himself. Occasionally such a construction as "in the name of me" will be found, meaning the same thing.

The neuter form of an adjective may be used as an adverb. ἀληθῆ in John *ch.* 19, *v.* 35, is the neuter of ἀληθής (true) and must be rendered "truly". So πρῶτον (firstly), though "first" is quite often used in English as an adverb. Conversely, an adverb may be used as an adjective; *e.g.* νῦν, now=present.

ταῦτα=these things (neuter plural) might be rendered by the singular "this", as in the common phrase μετὰ ταῦτα=after this; but this liberty has not been taken in the present literal translation.

The gender of an adjective may demand 'man', 'woman', or 'thing' to be supplied; *e.g.* Matthew *ch.* 9, *v.* 27—"two blind men".

Greek will often use a preposition in a compound verb and then repeat it (or use one similar) before a noun in the same sentence; in such passages the preposition would not be used twice in English. But in such a phrase as εἰσέρχεσθαι εἰς οἶκον we can say 'to enter into a house' (this has a counterpart in French—*entrer dans une maison*). We can indeed say simply 'to enter a house'. Another exception would be ἀπέρχεσθαι ἀπό =to go away from. But διαφέρειν διὰ τοῦ ἱεροῦ = to carry *through* through the temple (see Mark *ch.* 11, *v.* 16).

As the negatives οὐ(κ) (categorical) and μή (hypothetical) are easily recognizable, it has not been thought necessary always to render them separately, but they are included with any verb with which they may be used. But whereas in English the negative follows the verb, in Greek it precedes; see Matthew *ch.* 3, *v.* 11. If such a phrase happens to be broken at the end of a line this course has not been feasible.

The double negative οὐ μή has been consistently rendered "by no means".

Incidentally, though of importance, these two negative particles, or their compounds, when introducing questions, expect different answers. οὐ appeals to the fact, anticipating 'Yes, it is so'; *e.g.* John *ch.* 11, *v.* 9, "Are there not twelve hours of the day?" The answer would be 'Yes, there are'. μή, on the contrary, denies the suggestion and expects the reply 'No, it is not so'; or, if not so explicit as that, doubts whether it is so; *e.g.* John *ch.* 18, *v.* 35. The form of the question in the Authorized Version and the Revised Version indicates that Pilate was asking for information, whereas he was rejecting the idea with scorn and contempt—'I am not a Jew [am I]?' The answer, if any, would be—'No, certainly not.' This distinction is largely overlooked in the English Versions. To assist to the correct nuance of thought, in such places the latter negative in the interlinear translation is italicized, and the reader must read into the original what is intended; the result is sometimes surprising.

An article in *The Bible Translator* for January, 1953, may be consulted.

While on the subject of negatives, Greek favours the use of two such, one strengthening the other. In such sentences the second negative has to be replaced in English by a positive; *e.g.* Matthew *ch.* 22, *v.* 46.

There is the *genitive of quality*, of which there are many examples in the New Testament. If in English we say "a man of courage" or "an act of kindness", this is equivalent to "a courageous man" or "a kind act" respectively. We have translated literally, with an occasional footnote where this construction is not generally recognized. The Authorized Version itself is not consistent—*cf.* Philippians *ch.* 3, *v.* 21, with Colossians *ch.* 1, *v.* 22, where surely the distinction is between "his glorious body" and "his fleshly body".

Necessity or compulsion is most frequently expressed by the use of an impersonal verb (or a verb used impersonally), with the person concerned in the accusative as the object of the verb: δεῖ με=it behoves me=I must.

As 'first' is used as an adverb as well as 'firstly' it has not been thought necessary always to print 'first*ly*'; the matter is of no great importance.

Finally, but certainly not least in importance, there are the Greek participles, to which we now give special attention.

Greek is "a participle-loving language", said the late A. T. Robertson, and it uses this part of speech much more frequently than we do, and in different ways.

To begin with, it is absolutely essential to grasp the distinction between *continuous, momentary,* and *completed* action. The first is commonly, but wrongly, spoken of as a present participle; the second as an aorist (which does not mean "past"); and the third as a perfect. (There is a rare future participle—continuous in the future.) Now—

1. A participle may be used as an adjective qualifying a noun, just as in English; *e.g.* I. Thessalonians *ch.* 1, *v.* 9—"a living God"; Hebrews *ch.* 7, *v.* 8—"dying men". This is so simple as not to need further remark.

2. A participle may be used, again as in English, as a verb to describe some action; *e.g.* Acts *ch.* 9, *v.* 39—"all the widows stood by . . . weeping and showing . . .".

3. A participle may be used, with the definite article, with, say, "one" understood, where we should use a noun or a relative phrase; *e.g.,* frequently, ὁ πιστεύων=the [one] believing=the believer *or* he who believes. Here the participle is continuous; in Luke *ch.* 1, *v.* 45, it is momentary (and, naturally, feminine in gender as referring to Mary's one act of faith at the Annunciation). If two participles are used with but one definite article, as in John *ch.* 5, *v.* 24, the meaning is that one person is doubly

described, not two persons doing two things. This feature has been preserved in our translation.

4. Very frequently indeed, where in English we use two or more finite verbs to describe associated actions, Greek will use participles and only one finite verb for the main action. But here judgment is necessary to distinguish two (or more) simultaneous actions from consecutive ones; and as we have no aorist participle in English the matter is not always free from difficulty. In Acts *ch.* 10, *v.* 34, "Peter opening his mouth said", the two actions were obviously simultaneous! So in Acts *ch.* 1, *v.* 24—"praying they said". But sometimes one action must be completed before another could begin; *e.g.* Luke *ch.* 22, *v.* 17—"having given thanks, he said . . .". Here the act of giving thanks to God would be complete before Jesus addressed His disciples; therefore the aorist participle must be represented in English by the analytic "having given thanks". That this is not unimportant is shown by Matthew *ch.* 26, *v.* 30—"having sung a hymn they went out". To translate the aorist participle here by "singing a hymn" would certainly convey the idea that the singing occurred as they went out. In Acts *ch.* 21, *v.* 14, it is not easy to see how the keeping silence and the saying could be contemporaneous: "Having said, The will of the Lord be done, we kept silence." These few examples should, we think, suffice to show the principles involved.

NOTES ON PARTICULAR PASSAGES

Mark *ch.* 10, *v.* 11.—An article by Dr. Nigel Turner in *The Bible Translator* for October, 1956, gives good reasons for understanding the verse thus, αὐτήν referring to the last woman mentioned (ἄλλην).

Mark *ch.* 14, *v.* 6.—The use of ἐν here is somewhat puzzling. The parallel in Matthew (*ch.* 26, *v.* 10) has εἰς, which would mean 'to', 'toward', or 'for'; and Mark's ἐν must then be taken as equivalent in meaning to εἰς. This may throw light on I John *ch.* 4, *v.* 16.

Luke *ch.* 7, *v.* 14.—ἐγέρθητι. It does not seem right to insist here on the passive voice; compare with *ch.* 8, *v.* 54, and, in another connection, *ch.* 11, *v.* 8. But our Lord "was raised", as are the dead generally (they do not "rise"). See I. Corinthians *ch.* 15, etc.

John *ch.* 8, *v.* 25.—"The answer of Jesus is one of the most disputed passages in the Gospel" (Godet). Nestle punctuates as a question; hence we have given what appears to be a reasonable rendering interrogatively.

Acts *ch.* 7, *v.* 46.—οἴκῳ is a manuscript variant for θεῷ. There is some uncertainty as to how this reading arose; see the Authorized Version. Has Psalm 24, *v.* 6, text and margin, any bearing on the matter?

Acts *ch.* 18, *v.* 10.—λαὸς πολύς must not be understood as meaning "many persons". λαός is the regular word for the chosen people, Israel (almost without exception). Here in Corinth was to be a new community, taking the place of the Jewish population. Translate—"a great people".

Romans *ch.* 1, *v.* 12.—That is, their faith (=confidence) in one another—Paul and his readers. "Mutual" is correct in A.V., but is generally misunderstood as being equivalent to "common", which it is not.

Romans *ch.* 9, *v.* 11.—There is no noun agreeing with the two participles. But it is nevertheless a 'genitive absolute' construction. The Authorized Version supplies the subject.

II. Corinthians *ch.* 11, *v.* 28.—There is another view of Paul's words here. ἐπίστασις occurs in the New Testament only here and in Acts *ch.* 24, *v.* 12. The related noun ἐπιστάτης (one standing over, superintendent, master) is peculiar to Luke (six times in his gospel). Then there is a variant reading in our verse, μου instead of μοι. So the meaning may be—"my daily superintendence *or* attention". This would bring it into line with the remainder of the verse.

Philippians *ch.* 3, *v.* 16.—This is, according to Burton, the only certain use in the New Testament of the 'imperatival infinitive', Romans *ch.* 12, *v.* 15 being a probable example. Moulton thinks it highly probable in Titus *ch.* 2, *v.* 1-10. The epistolary χαίρειν (Acts *ch.* 15, *v.* 23, *ch.* 23, *v.* 26; James *ch.* 1, *v.* 1) is said to be the same in origin, though a verb of bidding may be assumed, as in fact we do find in II. John *vs.* 10, 11. *Cf.* the French warning in railway carriages—*Ne pas se pencher au dehors.* In English we have such a full expression as "You are 'to do' so and so"; see

II. Thessalonians *ch.* 3, *v.* 14. If Nestle's text is accepted here, it is an additional instance to those given under Philippians *ch.* 3, *v.* 16 above, though with a negative as a prohibition. (Textus Receptus, etc., give a plain imperative.) But perhaps we may insert "so as" —"mark this man, so as not to mix with him."

II. Timothy *ch.* 4, *v.* 3.—The construction of the last three words of this verse is difficult. "Having itching ears" may be a workable paraphrase, but it cannot be said to represent literally the actual Greek. There is no word for "having"; and there is nothing corresponding to "itching" as a participial adjective qualifying "ears". τὴν ἀκοήν is accusative singular, the object of a verb—and the only verb is the participle which precedes. This is masculine plural, agreeing with διδασκάλους, and, while this latter is accusative, whereas the participle is nominative, this must be taken as an example of rational rather than grammatical concord. It is the teachers who "tickle" the ears of those concerned.

Hebrews *ch.* 2, *v.* 10.—That is, it is God who perfected Jesus Christ (the author, or captain, of our salvation) by means of sufferings, whose work it is to lead many sons to glory. This is not what the Authorized Version nor the Revised Version says, but it is demanded by the grammar: ἀγαγόντα (leading) agrees with ἀρχηγόν not with αὐτῷ (=God). Besides, there is a parallel between Joshua and Jesus, as both leaders of their peoples. (The Berkeley version adopts this view, though we were not aware of it until our own order of words had been adopted.) In fine, it is the function of a captain to lead, and Jesus is the leader here.

Hebrews *ch.* 9, *vs.* 16-17.—We are aware of the problem in regard to διαθήκη in this passage; but this translation is no place for purporting to settle a question that has divided commentators. It must suffice to say that we have translated the word consistently as 'covenant'; the idea of a legatee receiving something on the death of a testator by reason of the latter's having made a 'testament' or 'will' is, so far as we can see, quite non-biblical. The covenant victim, then, is 'the one making covenant', unless the person establishing the covenant is to be understood as identifying himself with it; and the covenant is in fact ratified over the dead body or bodies. But other views are taken of the matter.

James *ch.* 2, *v.* 1.—There are other instances of such a construction—two genitives in apposition. Colossians *ch.* 1, *v.* 18: the meaning must be 'of the body (,) *of* the Church'—the body is the Church, as verse 24 says. Colossians *ch.* 2, *v.* 2: 'of God, of Christ'. Romans *ch.* 11, *v.* 17: see note at that place. John *ch.* 8, *v.* 44: 'of the father (,) *of* the devil'—their father was the devil.

Revelation *ch.* 16, *v.* 14: 'Almighty' is not an adjective but another noun in apposition.

NOTE on Mat. 16. 3, 27. 65; Luke 12. 56; Acts 21. 37; I. Thes. 4. 4; I. Tim. 3. 5; Jas. 4. 17; II. Pet. 2. 9.

As in French, so in the Greek of the N.T., we have the idea of "to know (how) to do" a thing as being the same as "to be able to do" it. But while *savoir* only is used in this way, not *connaître*, both γινώσκω and οἶδα are found in the N.T. In fact it is the former in Mat. 16. 3 and the latter in the parallel in Luke (12. 56). So, in French, *Savez-vous nager ?* = Know you to swim? = Can you swim? In all the above passages this seems to be the meaning. It may be noted that the A.V. so renders the verbs in some passages, in others giving "know how". The James instance may be arguable. Phil. 4. 12 also may be considered, and Mat. 7. 11 = Luke 11. 13.

THE GREEK ALPHABET

A	α	Alpha	a
B	β	Beta	b
Γ	γ	Gamma	g hard, as in begin[1]
Δ	δ	Delta	d
E	ϵ	Epsilon	e short, as in met
Z	ζ	Zeta	z
H	η	Eta	e long, as in scene
Θ	θ	Theta	th as in *thin*
I	ι	Iota	i
K	κ	Kappa	k
Λ	λ	Lambda	l
M	μ	Mu	m
N	ν	Nu	n
Ξ	ξ	Xi	x
O	o	Omicron	o short, as in lot
Π	π	Pi	p
P	ρ	Rho	r
Σ	σ, final ς	Sigma	s[2]
T	τ	Tau	t
Υ	υ	Upsilon	u
Φ	ϕ	Phi	ph
X	χ	Chi	ch hard, as in lo*ch*
Ψ	ψ	Psi	ps
Ω	ω	Omega	o long, as in throne

[1] Except that before κ, χ or another γ it is nasal—ng, as in *a*nchor.
[2] Sharp as in thi*s*, but flat before β or μ, as in a*s*bestos, di*s*mal.

THE NAMES AND ORDER OF THE BOOKS OF THE NEW TESTAMENT

	Chapters	Page
Matthew	28	1
Mark	16	137
Luke	24	218
John	21	356
Acts	28	462
Romans	16	602
I Corinthians	16	656
II Corinthians	13	707
Galatians	6	741
Ephesians	6	758
Philippians	4	776
Colossians	4	789
I Thessalonians	5	801
II Thessalonians	3	813
I Timothy	6	820
II Timothy	4	834
Titus	3	844
Philemon	1	850
Hebrews	13	853
James	5	894
I Peter	5	908
II Peter	3	922
I John	5	932
II John	1	947
III John	1	949
Jude	1	951
Revelation	22	956

CHAPTER 1

THE book of the genealogy of Jesus Christ, the son of David, the son of Abraham.

2 Abraham was the father of Isaac, and Isaac the father of Jacob, and Jacob the father of Judah and his brothers, ³and Judah the father of Perez and Zerah by Tamar, and Perez the father of Hezron, and Hezron the father of Ram, ⁴and Ram the father of Ammin'adab, and Ammin'adab the father of Nahshon, and Nahshon the father of Salmon, ⁵and Salmon the father of Bo'az by Rahab, and Bo'az the father of Obed by Ruth, and Obed the father of Jesse, ⁶and Jesse the father of David the king.

And David was the father of Solomon by the wife of Uri'ah, ⁷and Solomon the father of Rehobo'am, and Rehobo'am the father of Abi'jah, and Abi'jah the father of Asa, ⁸and Asa the father of Jehosh'aphat, and Jehosh'aphat the father of Joram, and Joram the father of Uzzi'ah, ⁹and Uzzi'ah the father of Jotham, and Jotham the father of Ahaz, and Ahaz the

1 Βίβλος   γενέσεως   Ἰησοῦ   Χριστοῦ
[The] book of [the] generation   of Jesus   Christ

υἱοῦ Δαυὶδ υἱοῦ Ἀβραάμ.
son of David son of Abraham.

2 Ἀβραὰμ   ἐγέννησεν   τὸν Ἰσαάκ,   Ἰσαὰκ   δὲ
   Abraham   begat   –   Isaac,   and Isaac

ἐγέννησεν   τὸν Ἰακώβ,   Ἰακὼβ   δὲ   ἐγέννησεν   τὸν
  begat   –   Jacob,   and Jacob   begat   –

Ἰούδαν καὶ τοὺς ἀδελφοὺς αὐτοῦ, **3** Ἰούδας   δὲ
Judas and the   brothers of him,   and Judas

ἐγέννησεν τὸν Φάρες καὶ τὸν Ζάρα ἐκ τῆς
  begat   –   Phares and – Zara out of

Θαμάρ,   Φάρες   δὲ   ἐγέννησεν   τὸν Ἐσρώμ,
Thamar, and Phares   begat   –   Esrom,

Ἐσρὼμ   δὲ   ἐγέννησεν   τὸν Ἀράμ,   **4** Ἀρὰμ   δὲ
and Esrom   begat   –   Aram,   and Aram

ἐγέννησεν   τὸν Ἀμιναδάβ,   Ἀμιναδὰβ   δὲ
  begat   –   Aminadab,   and Aminadab

ἐγέννησεν τὸν Ναασσών,   Ναασσὼν δὲ ἐγέννησεν
  begat   –   Naasson,   and Naasson   begat

τὸν Σαλμών,   **5** Σαλμὼν δὲ ἐγέννησεν τὸν Βόες
  – Salmon,   and Salmon   begat   –   Booz

ἐκ   τῆς Ῥαχάβ,   Βόες δὲ ἐγέννησεν τὸν Ἰωβὴδ
out of – Rachab,   and Booz   begat   –   Obed

ἐκ   τῆς Ῥούθ, Ἰωβὴδ δὲ ἐγέννησεν τὸν Ἰεσσαί,
out of – Ruth,   and Obed   begat   –   Jesse,

6 Ἰεσσαὶ δὲ ἐγέννησεν τὸν Δαυὶδ τὸν βασιλέα.
   and Jesse   begat   –   David the   king.

Δαυὶδ   δὲ   ἐγέννησεν   τὸν Σολομῶνα ἐκ τῆς
And David   begat   –   Solomon out of the

τοῦ Οὐρίου, **7** Σολομὼν δὲ ἐγέννησεν
[one who had been the wife]– of Uriah, and Solomon   begat

τὸν Ῥοβοάμ,   Ῥοβοὰμ   δὲ   ἐγέννησεν   τὸν
  – Roboam,   and Roboam   begat   –

Ἀβιά, Ἀβιὰ δὲ ἐγέννησεν τὸν Ἀσάφ, **8** Ἀσὰφ
Abia, and Abia   begat   –   Asaph,   and Asaph

δὲ   ἐγέννησεν   τὸν Ἰωσαφάτ,   Ἰωσαφὰτ   δὲ
   begat   –   Josaphat,   and Josaphat

ἐγέννησεν τὸν Ἰωράμ,   Ἰωρὰμ δὲ ἐγέννησεν τὸν
  begat   –   Joram,   and Joram   begat   –

Ὀζίαν, **9** Ὀζίας   δὲ   ἐγέννησεν   τὸν Ἰωαθάμ,
Ozias,   and Ozias   begat   –   Joatham,

Ἰωαθὰμ   δὲ   ἐγέννησεν   τὸν Ἀχάζ,   Ἀχὰζ   δὲ
and Joatham   begat   –   Achaz,   and Achaz

father of Hezeki'ah,
10 and Hezeki'ah the
father of Manas'seh, and
Manas'seh the father of
Amos,[a] and Amos[a] the
father of Josi'ah, 11 and
Josi'ah the father of
Jechoni'ah and his
brothers, at the time of
the deportation to Baby-
lon.

12 And after the de-
portation to Babylon:
Jechoni'ah was the father
of She-al'ti-el, and She-
al'ti-el the father of
Zerub'babel, 13 and Zer-
ub'babel the father of
Abi'ud, and Abi'ud the
father of Eli'akim, and
Eli'akim the father of
Azor, 14 and Azor the
father of Zadok, and
Zadok the father of
Achim, and Achim the
father of Eli'ud, 15 and
Eli'ud the father of Ele-
a'zar, and Elea'zar the
father of Matthan, and
Matthan the father of
Jacob, 16 and Jacob the
father of Joseph the
husband of Mary, of
whom Jesus was born,
who is called Christ.[b]

17 So all the genera-
tions from Abraham to
David were fourteen
generations, and from
David to the deportation
to Babylon fourteen gen-
erations, and from the
deportation to Babylon
to the Christ fourteen
generations.

18 Now the birth of

ἐγέννησεν τὸν Ἐζεκίαν, 10 Ἐζεκίας δὲ
begat   -   Hezekias,   and Hezekias

ἐγέννησεν τὸν Μανασσῆ, Μανασσῆς δὲ ἐγέννησεν
begat   -   Manasses,   and Manasses   begat

τὸν Ἀμώς, Ἀμὼς δὲ ἐγέννησεν τὸν Ἰωσίαν,
-    Amos,   and Amos   begat   -   Josias,

11 Ἰωσίας δὲ ἐγέννησεν τὸν Ἰεχονίαν καὶ
and Josias   begat   -   Jechonias   and

τοὺς ἀδελφοὺς αὐτοῦ ἐπὶ τῆς μετοικεσίας
the   brothers   of him   at   the   deportation

Βαβυλῶνος. 12 Μετὰ δὲ τὴν μετοικεσίαν
of Babylon.   And after   the   deportation

Βαβυλῶνος Ἰεχονίας ἐγέννησεν τὸν Σαλαθιήλ,
of Babylon   Jechonias   begat   -   Salathiel,

Σαλαθιὴλ δὲ ἐγέννησεν τὸν Ζοροβαβέλ,
and Salathiel   begat   -   Zorobabel,

13 Ζοροβαβὲλ δὲ ἐγέννησεν τὸν Ἀβιούδ,
and Zorobabel   begat   -   Abiud,

Ἀβιοὺδ δὲ ἐγέννησεν τὸν Ἐλιακίμ, Ἐλιακὶμ δὲ
and Abiud   begat   -   Eliakim,   and Eliakim

ἐγέννησεν τὸν Ἀζώρ, 14 Ἀζὼρ δὲ ἐγέννησεν
begat   -   Azor,   and Azor   begat

τὸν Σαδώκ, Σαδὼκ δὲ ἐγέννησεν τὸν Ἀχίμ,
-    Sadoc,   and Sadoc   begat   -   Achim,

Ἀχὶμ δὲ ἐγέννησεν τὸν Ἐλιούδ, 15 Ἐλιοὺδ δὲ
and Achim   begat   -   Eliud,   and Eliud

ἐγέννησεν τὸν Ἐλεαζάρ, Ἐλεαζὰρ δὲ ἐγέννησεν
begat   -   Eleazar,   and Eleazar   begat

τὸν Ματθάν, Ματθὰν δὲ ἐγέννησεν τὸν Ἰακώβ,
-    Matthan,   and Matthan   begat   -   Jacob,

16 Ἰακὼβ δὲ ἐγέννησεν τὸν Ἰωσὴφ τὸν ἄνδρα
and Jacob   begat   -   Joseph   the husband

Μαρίας, ἐξ ἧς ἐγεννήθη Ἰησοῦς ὁ λεγόμενος
of Mary, of whom   was born   Jesus   the [one]   called

Χριστός.
Christ.

17 Πᾶσαι οὖν αἱ γενεαὶ ἀπὸ Ἀβραὰμ
Therefore all   the generations from   Abraham

ἕως Δαυὶδ γενεαὶ δεκατέσσαρες, καὶ ἀπὸ
until   David   generations   fourteen,   and from

Δαυὶδ ἕως τῆς μετοικεσίας Βαβυλῶνος γενεαὶ
David   until the   deportation   of Babylon   generations

δεκατέσσαρες, καὶ ἀπὸ τῆς μετοικεσίας Βαβυ-
fourteen,   and from the   deportation   of Baby-

λῶνος ἕως τοῦ Χριστοῦ γενεαὶ δεκατέσσαρες.
lon   until the   Christ   generations   fourteen.

18 Τοῦ δὲ Ἰησοῦ Χριστοῦ ἡ γένεσις
-    Now   [2]of Jesus   [4]Christ   [1]the   [5]birth

---

[a] Other authorities read Amon

[b] Other ancient authorities
read Joseph, to whom was
betrothed the virgin Mary, was
the father of Jesus who is called
Christ

Jesus Christ[c] took place in this way. When his mother Mary had been betrothed to Joseph, before they came together she was found to be with child of the Holy Spirit; [19]and her husband Joseph, being a just man and unwilling to put her to shame, resolved to divorce her quietly. [20]But as he considered this, behold, an angel of the Lord appeared to him in a dream, saying, "Joseph, son of David, do not fear to take Mary your wife, for that which is conceived in her is of the Holy Spirit; [21]she will bear a son, and you shall call his name Jesus, for he will save his people from their sins." [22]All this took place to fulfil what the Lord had spoken by the prophet: [23]"Behold, a virgin shall conceive and bear a son, and his name shall be called Emman'u-el" (which means, God with us). [24]When Joseph woke from sleep, he did as the angel of the Lord commanded him; he took his

[c] Other ancient authorities read of the Christ

οὕτως   ἦν.   μνηστευθείσης   τῆς   μητρὸς   αὐτοῦ
'thus   ¹was.   Being betrothed   the   mother   of him
= When his mother Mary was betrothed

Μαρίας   τῷ   Ἰωσήφ,   πρὶν ἢ   συνελθεῖν   αὐτοὺς
Mary*   -   to Joseph,   before to come together   them[b]
= before they came together

εὑρέθη   ἐν   γαστρὶ   ἔχουσα   ἐκ   πνεύματος
¹she was found ²in   ⁴womb   ³having of(by) [the]   Spirit
= she was pregnant

ἁγίου.   19 Ἰωσὴφ   δὲ   ὁ   ἀνὴρ   αὐτῆς,
Holy.   Now Joseph   the   husband   of her,

δίκαιος   ὢν   καὶ   μὴ   θέλων   αὐτὴν   δειγμα-
¹just   ²being   and   not   wishing   her to hold up as an

τίσαι,   ἐβουλήθη   λάθρα   ἀπολῦσαι   αὐτήν.
example,   resolved   secretly   to dismiss   her.

20 ταῦτα   δὲ   αὐτοῦ   ἐνθυμηθέντος,   ἰδοὺ
But these things   him   thinking on,*   behold
= while he thought on these things,

ἄγγελος   κυρίου   κατ'   ὄναρ   ἐφάνη
an angel   of [the] Lord   by   a dream   appeared

αὐτῷ   λέγων·   Ἰωσὴφ   υἱὸς   Δαυίδ,   μὴ
to him   saying: Joseph   son   of David,   ¹not

φοβηθῇς   παραλαβεῖν   Μαρίαν   τὴν
²fear thou   to take   Mary   the

γυναῖκά   σου·   τὸ   γὰρ   ἐν   αὐτῇ   γεννηθὲν
wife   of thee: for the thing   in   her   begotten

ἐκ   πνεύματός   ἐστιν   ἁγίου.   21 τέξεται   δὲ
²of ³[the] ⁵Spirit   ¹is   ⁴Holy.   And she will bear

υἱόν,   καὶ   καλέσεις   τὸ   ὄνομα   αὐτοῦ
a son,   and   thou shalt call   the   name   of him

Ἰησοῦν·   αὐτὸς   γὰρ   σώσει   τὸν   λαὸν
Jesus;   for he   will save   the   people

αὐτοῦ   ἀπὸ   τῶν   ἁμαρτιῶν   αὐτῶν.   22 Τοῦτο   δὲ
of him   from   the   sins   of them.   Now ²this

ὅλον   γέγονεν   ἵνα   πληρωθῇ   τὸ   ῥηθὲν
¹all has occurred in order that might be fulfilled   the [thing] spoken

ὑπὸ   κυρίου   διὰ   τοῦ   προφήτου   λέγοντος·
by   [the] Lord   through   the   prophet   saying:

23 ἰδοὺ   ἡ   παρθένος   ἐν   γαστρὶ   ἕξει
Behold   the   virgin   ²in   ³womb   ¹will have

καὶ   τέξεται   υἱόν,   καὶ   καλέσουσιν   τὸ
and   will bear   a son,   and   they will call   the

ὄνομα   αὐτοῦ   Ἐμμανουήλ,   ὃ   ἐστιν
name   of him   Emmanuel,   which   is

μεθερμηνευόμενον   μεθ'   ἡμῶν   ὁ   θεός.
being interpreted   with   us   -   God.

24 ἐγερθεὶς   δὲ   [ὁ]   Ἰωσὴφ   ἀπὸ   τοῦ
Then ²being raised   -   ¹Joseph   from   the(his)

ὕπνου   ἐποίησεν   ὡς   προσέταξεν   αὐτῷ   ὁ
sleep   did   as   bade   him   the

wife, ²⁵but knew her not until she had borne a son; and he called his name Jesus.

ἄγγελος κυρίου, καὶ παρέλαβεν τὴν
angel of [the] Lord, and took the

γυναῖκα αὐτοῦ· 25 καὶ οὐκ ἐγίνωσκεν
wife of him; and knew not

αὐτὴν ἕως [οὗ] ἔτεκεν υἱόν· καὶ ἐκάλεσεν
her until she bore a son; and he called

τὸ ὄνομα αὐτοῦ Ἰησοῦν.
the name of him Jesus.

CHAPTER 2

NOW when Jesus was born in Bethlehem of Judea in the days of Herod the king, behold, wise men from the East came to Jerusalem, saying, ²"Where is he who has been born king of the Jews? For we have seen his star in the East, and have come to worship him." ³When Herod the king heard this, he was troubled, and all Jerusalem with him; ⁴and assembling all the chief priests and scribes of the people, he inquired of them where the Christ was to be born. ⁵They told him, "In Bethlehem of Judea; for so it is written by the prophet:

⁶'And you, O Bethlehem, in the land of Judah,
are by no means least among the rulers of Judah;
for from you shall come a ruler
who will govern my people Israel.' "

2 Τοῦ δὲ Ἰησοῦ γεννηθέντος ἐν Βηθλέεμ
- Now Jesus having been born[a] in Bethlehem
=when Jesus was born

τῆς Ἰουδαίας ἐν ἡμέραις Ἡρώδου τοῦ
- of Judæa in [the] days of Herod the

βασιλέως, ἰδοὺ μάγοι ἀπὸ ἀνατολῶν
king, behold magi from [the] east

παρεγένοντο εἰς Ἱεροσόλυμα 2 λέγοντες·
arrived in Jerusalem saying:

ποῦ ἐστιν ὁ τεχθεὶς βασιλεὺς τῶν
Where is the [one] born king of the

Ἰουδαίων; εἴδομεν γὰρ αὐτοῦ τὸν ἀστέρα
Jews? for we saw of him the star

ἐν τῇ ἀνατολῇ, καὶ ἤλθομεν προσκυνῆσαι
in the east, and came to worship

αὐτῷ. 3 ἀκούσας δὲ ὁ βασιλεὺς Ἡρώδης
him. Now hearing [this] the king Herod

ἐταράχθη, καὶ πᾶσα Ἱεροσόλυμα μετ'
was troubled, and all Jerusalem with

αὐτοῦ, 4 καὶ συναγαγὼν πάντας τοὺς
him, and having assembled all the

ἀρχιερεῖς καὶ γραμματεῖς τοῦ λαοῦ
chief priests and scribes of the people

ἐπυνθάνετο παρ' αὐτῶν ποῦ ὁ χριστὸς
he inquired from them where the Christ

γεννᾶται. 5 οἱ δὲ εἶπαν αὐτῷ· ἐν
is being born. And they told him: In

Βηθλέεμ τῆς Ἰουδαίας· οὕτως γὰρ
Bethlehem - of Judæa; for thus

γέγραπται διὰ τοῦ προφήτου· 6 καὶ
it has been written through the prophet: And

σὺ Βηθλέεμ, γῆ Ἰούδα, οὐδαμῶς ἐλαχίστη
thou Bethlehem, land of Juda, ¹not at all ²least

εἶ ἐν τοῖς ἡγεμόσιν Ἰούδα. ἐκ σοῦ γὰρ
²art among the governors of Juda. For out of thee

ἐξελεύσεται ἡγούμενος, ὅστις ποιμανεῖ
will come forth a governor, who will shepherd

τὸν λαόν μου τὸν Ἰσραήλ.
the people of me - Israel.

7 Then Herod summoned the wise men secretly and ascertained from them what time the star appeared; [8]and he sent them to Bethlehem, saying, "Go and search diligently for the child, and when you have found him bring me word, that I too may come and worship him." [9]When they had heard the king they went their way; and lo, the star which they had seen in the East went before them, till it came to rest over the place where the child was. [10]When they saw the star, they rejoiced exceedingly with great joy; [11]and going into the house they saw the child with Mary his mother, and they fell down and worshiped him. Then, opening their treasures, they offered him gifts, gold and frankincense and myrrh. [12]And being warned in a dream not to return to Herod, they departed to their own country by another way.

13 Now when they had departed, behold, an angel of the Lord appeared to Joseph in a dream and said, "Rise, take the child and his

7 Τότε   Ἡρῴδης   λάθρα   καλέσας   τοὺς
Then   Herod   secretly   calling   the
μάγους   ἠκρίβωσεν   παρ'   αὐτῶν   τὸν
magi   inquired carefully   from   them   the
χρόνον   τοῦ   φαινομένου   ἀστέρος,   8 καὶ
time   of the   appearing   star,   and
πέμψας   αὐτοὺς   εἰς   Βηθλέεμ   εἶπεν·
sending   them   to   Bethlehem   said:
πορευθέντες   ἐξετάσατε   ἀκριβῶς   περὶ   τοῦ
Going   question ye   carefully   concerning   the
παιδίου·   ἐπὰν   δὲ   εὕρητε,   ἀπαγγείλατέ
child;   and when   ye find,   report
μοι, ὅπως   κἀγὼ   ἐλθὼν   προσκυνήσω   αὐτῷ.
to me, so that   I also   coming   may worship   him.
9 οἱ δὲ   ἀκούσαντες   τοῦ   βασιλέως   ἐπορεύθησαν·
So they   hearing   the   king   went;
καὶ   ἰδοὺ   ὁ   ἀστήρ,   ὃν   εἶδον   ἐν   τῇ
and   behold   the   star,   which they saw   in   the
ἀνατολῇ,   προῆγεν   αὐτοὺς   ἕως   ἐλθὼν
east,   went before   them   until   coming
ἐστάθη   ἐπάνω   οὗ   ἦν   τὸ   παιδίον.   10 ἰδόντες
it stood   over   where   was   the   child.   [2]seeing
δὲ   τὸν   ἀστέρα   ἐχάρησαν   χαρὰν   μεγάλην
[1]And   the   star   they rejoiced [with] a joy   great
σφόδρα.   11 καὶ   ἐλθόντες   εἰς   τὴν   οἰκίαν
exceedingly.   And   coming   into   the   house
εἶδον   τὸ   παιδίον   μετὰ   Μαρίας   τῆς   μητρὸς
they saw   the   child   with   Mary   the   mother
αὐτοῦ,   καὶ   πεσόντες   προσεκύνησαν   αὐτῷ,
of him,   and   falling   they worshipped   him,
καὶ   ἀνοίξαντες   τοὺς   θησαυροὺς   αὐτῶν
and   opening   the   treasures   of them
προσήνεγκαν   αὐτῷ   δῶρα,   χρυσὸν   καὶ
they offered   to him   gifts,   gold   and
λίβανον   καὶ   σμύρναν.   12 καὶ   χρηματισθέντες
frankincense and   myrrh.   And having been warned
κατ'   ὄναρ   μὴ   ἀνακάμψαι   πρὸς   Ἡρῴδην,
by   a dream   not   to return   to   Herod,
δι'   ἄλλης   ὁδοῦ   ἀνεχώρησαν   εἰς   τὴν
by   another   way   they departed   to   the
χώραν   αὐτῶν.
country   of them.

13 Ἀναχωρησάντων   δὲ   αὐτῶν,   ἰδοὺ
Now having departed   them,[2]   behold
= when they had departed,
ἄγγελος   κυρίου   φαίνεται   κατ'   ὄναρ   τῷ
an angel   of [the] Lord   appears   by   a dream   -
Ἰωσὴφ   λέγων·   ἐγερθεὶς   παράλαβε   τὸ
to Joseph   saying: Rising   take thou   the

mother, and flee to Egypt, and remain there till I tell you; for Herod is about to search for the child, to destroy him." [14] And he rose and took the child and his mother by night, and departed to Egypt, [15] and remained there until the death of Herod. This was to fulfil what the Lord had spoken by the prophet, "Out of Egypt have I called my son."

16 Then Herod, when he saw that he had been tricked by the wise men, was in a furious rage, and he sent and killed all the male children in Bethlehem and in all that region who were two years old or under, according to the time which he had ascertained from the wise men. [17] Then was fulfilled what was spoken by the prophet Jeremiah:
[18] "And a voice was heard in Ramah,
wailing and loud lamentation,
Rachel weeping for her children;
she refused to be consoled,
because they were no more."

19 But when Herod died, behold, an angel of the Lord appeared in a

---

παιδίον καὶ τὴν μητέρα αὐτοῦ, καὶ φεῦγε
child and the mother of him, and flee

εἰς Αἴγυπτον, καὶ ἴσθι ἐκεῖ ἕως ἂν εἴπω
into Egypt, and be there until I tell

σοι· μέλλει γὰρ Ἡρῴδης ζητεῖν τὸ παιδίον τοῦ
thee; for [2]is about [1]Herod to seek the child –

ἀπολέσαι αὐτό. 14 ὁ δὲ ἐγερθεὶς παρέλαβεν
to destroy[d] him. So he rising took

τὸ παιδίον καὶ τὴν μητέρα αὐτοῦ
the child and the mother of him

νυκτὸς καὶ ἀνεχώρησεν εἰς Αἴγυπτον,
of(by) night and departed to Egypt,

15 καὶ ἦν ἐκεῖ ἕως τῆς τελευτῆς Ἡρῴδου·
and was there until the death of Herod;

ἵνα πληρωθῇ τὸ ῥηθὲν ὑπὸ κυρίου
in order that might be fulfilled the [thing] spoken by [the] Lord

διὰ τοῦ προφήτου λέγοντος· ἐξ
through the prophet saying: Out of

Αἰγύπτου ἐκάλεσα τὸν υἱόν μου.
Egypt I called the son of me.

16 Τότε Ἡρῴδης ἰδὼν ὅτι ἐνεπαίχθη
Then Herod seeing that he was mocked

ὑπὸ τῶν μάγων ἐθυμώθη λίαν, καὶ
by the magi was angered exceedingly, and

ἀποστείλας ἀνεῖλεν πάντας τοὺς παῖδας
sending killed all the boy-children

τοὺς ἐν Βηθλέεμ καὶ ἐν πᾶσι τοῖς
– in Bethlehem and in all the

ὁρίοις αὐτῆς ἀπὸ διετοῦς καὶ κατωτέρω,
districts of it from two years and under,

κατὰ τὸν χρόνον ὃν ἠκρίβωσεν παρὰ τῶν
according to the time which he strictly inquired from the

μάγων. 17 τότε ἐπληρώθη τὸ ῥηθὲν διὰ
magi. Then was fulfilled the [thing] spoken through

Ἰερεμίου τοῦ προφήτου λέγοντος· 18 φωνὴ
Jeremiah the prophet saying: A voice

ἐν Ῥαμὰ ἠκούσθη, κλαυθμὸς καὶ ὀδυρμὸς
in Rama was heard, weeping and mourning

πολύς· Ῥαχὴλ κλαίουσα τὰ τέκνα αὐτῆς,
much; Rachel weeping for the children of her,

καὶ οὐκ ἤθελεν παρακληθῆναι, ὅτι
and would not to be comforted, because

οὐκ εἰσίν.
they are not.

19 Τελευτήσαντος δὲ τοῦ Ἡρῴδου, ἰδοὺ
But dying – Herod,[a] behold
= Herod having died,

ἄγγελος κυρίου φαίνεται κατ᾽ ὄναρ τῷ
an angel of [the] Lord appears by a dream

dream to Joseph in Egypt, saying, ²⁰"Rise, take the child and his mother, and go to the land of Israel, for those who sought the child's life are dead." ²¹And he rose and took the child and his mother, and went to the land of Israel. ²²But when he heard that Archela'us reigned over Judea in place of his father Herod, he was afraid to go there, and being warned in a dream he withdrew to the district of Galilee. ²³And he went and dwelt in a city called Nazareth, that what was spoken by the prophets might be fulfilled, "He shall be called a Nazarene."

Ἰωσὴφ ἐν Αἰγύπτῳ 20 λέγων· ἐγερθεὶς
to Joseph in Egypt saying: Rising

παράλαβε τὸ παιδίον καὶ τὴν μητέρα
take thou the child and the mother

αὐτοῦ, καὶ πορεύου εἰς γῆν Ἰσραήλ·
of him, and go into [the] land of Israel;

τεθνήκασιν γὰρ οἱ ζητοῦντες τὴν ψυχὴν
for have died the [ones] seeking the life

τοῦ παιδίου. 21 ὁ δὲ ἐγερθεὶς παρέλαβεν
of the child. So he rising took

τὸ παιδίον καὶ τὴν μητέρα αὐτοῦ καὶ
the child and the mother of him and

εἰσῆλθεν εἰς γῆν Ἰσραήλ. 22 ἀκούσας δὲ
entered into [the] land of Israel. But hearing

ὅτι Ἀρχέλαος βασιλεύει τῆς Ἰουδαίας
that Archelaus reigns over – Judæa

ἀντὶ τοῦ πατρὸς αὐτοῦ Ἡρώδου ἐφοβήθη
instead of the father of him Herod he feared

ἐκεῖ ἀπελθεῖν· χρηματισθεὶς δὲ κατ'
there to go; and being warned by

ὄναρ ἀνεχώρησεν εἰς τὰ μέρη τῆς
a dream he departed into the parts –

Γαλιλαίας, 23 καὶ ἐλθὼν κατῴκησεν εἰς
of Galilee, and coming dwelt in

πόλιν λεγομένην Ναζαρέθ· ὅπως πληρωθῇ
a city called Nazareth; so that was fulfilled

τὸ ῥηθὲν διὰ τῶν προφητῶν ὅτι
the [thing] spoken through the prophets[,] –

Ναζωραῖος κληθήσεται.
A Nazarene he shall be called.

CHAPTER 3

IN those days came John the Baptist, preaching in the wilderness of Judea, ²"Repent, for the kingdom of heaven is at hand." ³For this is he who was spoken of by the prophet Isaiah when he said,
"The voice of one crying in the wilderness:
Prepare the way of the Lord,
make his paths straight."

3 Ἐν δὲ ταῖς ἡμέραις ἐκείναις παραγίνεται
Now in – days those arrives

Ἰωάννης ὁ βαπτιστὴς κηρύσσων ἐν τῇ
John the Baptist proclaiming in the

ἐρήμῳ τῆς Ἰουδαίας, 2 λέγων· μετανοεῖτε·
wilderness – of Judæa, saying: Repent ye;

ἤγγικεν γὰρ ἡ βασιλεία τῶν οὐρανῶν.
for has come near the kingdom of the heavens.

3 οὗτος γάρ ἐστιν ὁ ῥηθεὶς διὰ Ἡσαΐου
For this is the [one] spoken [of] through Isaiah

τοῦ προφήτου λέγοντος· φωνὴ βοῶντος
the prophet saying: A voice of [one] crying

ἐν τῇ ἐρήμῳ· ἑτοιμάσατε τὴν ὁδὸν
in the wilderness: Prepare ye the way

κυρίου, εὐθείας ποιεῖτε τὰς τρίβους
of [the] Lord, straight make the paths

⁴Now John wore a garment of camel's hair, and a leather girdle around his waist; and his food was locusts and wild honey. ⁵Then went out to him Jerusalem and all Judea and all the region about the Jordan, ⁶and they were baptized by him in the river Jordan, confessing their sins.

7 But when he saw many of the Pharisees and Sad'ducees coming for baptism, he said to them, "You brood of vipers! Who warned you to flee from the wrath to come? ⁸Bear fruit that befits repentance, ⁹and do not presume to say to yourselves, 'We have Abraham as our father'; for I tell you, God is able from these stones to raise up children to Abraham. ¹⁰Even now the ax is laid to the root of the trees; every tree therefore that does not bear good fruit is cut down and thrown into the fire.

11 "I baptize you with water for repentance, but he who is coming after

αὐτοῦ. 4 Αὐτὸς δὲ ὁ Ἰωάννης εἶχεν
of him.   Now ²himself   –   ¹John   had

τὸ ἔνδυμα αὐτοῦ ἀπὸ τριχῶν καμήλου
the raiment of him from   hairs   of a camel

καὶ ζώνην δερματίνην περὶ τὴν ὀσφὺν
and a girdle leathern   round the   loin[s]

αὐτοῦ· ἡ δὲ τροφὴ ἦν αὐτοῦ ἀκρίδες
of him;   and the food ²was ¹of him   locusts

καὶ μέλι ἄγριον. 5 Τότε ἐξεπορεύετο πρὸς
and honey wild.   Then   went out   to

αὐτὸν Ἱεροσόλυμα καὶ πᾶσα ἡ Ἰουδαία
him   Jerusalem   and   all   –   Judæa

καὶ πᾶσα ἡ περίχωρος τοῦ Ἰορδάνου,
and   all the neighbourhood of the   Jordan,

6 καὶ ἐβαπτίζοντο ἐν τῷ Ἰορδάνῃ ποταμῷ
and were baptized in the   Jordan   river

ὑπ' αὐτοῦ ἐξομολογούμενοι τὰς ἁμαρτίας
by him   confessing   the   sins

αὐτῶν. 7 Ἰδὼν δὲ πολλοὺς τῶν
of them.   And seeing   many   of the

Φαρισαίων καὶ Σαδδουκαίων ἐρχομένους
Pharisees   and   Sadducees   coming

ἐπὶ τὸ βάπτισμα εἶπεν αὐτοῖς· γεννήματα
to the baptism   he said to them: Offspring

ἐχιδνῶν, τίς ὑπέδειξεν ὑμῖν φυγεῖν ἀπὸ
of vipers, who warned   you to flee from

τῆς μελλούσης ὀργῆς; 8 ποιήσατε οὖν
the   coming   wrath?   Produce therefore

καρπὸν ἄξιον τῆς μετανοίας· 9 καὶ
fruit   worthy of repentance;   and

μὴ δόξητε λέγειν ἐν ἑαυτοῖς· πατέρα
think not to say among [your]selves: ³[as] father

ἔχομεν τὸν Ἀβραάμ· λέγω γὰρ ὑμῖν ὅτι
¹We have – ²Abraham;   for I tell   you that

δύναται ὁ θεὸς ἐκ τῶν λίθων τούτων
²is able – ¹God out of –   stones   these

ἐγεῖραι τέκνα τῷ Ἀβραάμ. 10 ἤδη δὲ
to raise children – to Abraham.   And already

ἡ ἀξίνη πρὸς τὴν ῥίζαν τῶν δένδρων
the axe   at   the   root of the   trees

κεῖται· πᾶν οὖν δένδρον μὴ ποιοῦν
is laid; therefore every tree   not producing

καρπὸν καλὸν ἐκκόπτεται καὶ εἰς πῦρ
fruit   good   is cut down and into [the] fire

βάλλεται. 11 ἐγὼ μὲν ὑμᾶς βαπτίζω
is cast.   I   indeed you   baptize

ἐν ὕδατι εἰς μετάνοιαν· ὁ δὲ
in water   to   repentance;   but the [one]

me is mightier than I, whose sandals I am not worthy to carry; he will baptize you with the Holy Spirit and with fire. [12] His winnowing fork is in his hand, and he will clear his threshing floor and gather his wheat into the granary, but the chaff he will burn with unquenchable fire."

13 Then Jesus came from Galilee to the Jordan to John, to be baptized by him. [14] John would have prevented him, saying, "I need to be baptized by you, and do you come to me?" [15] But Jesus answered him, "Let it be so now; for thus it is fitting for us to fulfil all righteousness." Then he consented. [16] And when Jesus was baptized, he went up immediately from the water, and behold, the heavens were opened[d] and he saw the Spirit of God descending like a dove, and alighting on him; [17] and lo, a voice from heaven, saying, "This is my beloved Son,[e] with whom I am well pleased."

ὀπίσω   μου   ἐρχόμενος   ἰσχυρότερός   μού
after   me   coming   ²stronger ³[than]   ⁴I

ἐστιν,   οὗ   οὐκ   εἰμὶ   ἱκανὸς   τὰ   ὑποδήματα
¹is,   of whom   I am not   worthy   the   sandals

βαστάσαι·   αὐτὸς   ὑμᾶς   βαπτίσει   ἐν   πνεύματι
to bear;   he   ¹you   ¹will baptize   in   [the] Spirit

ἁγίῳ   καὶ   πυρί·   12 οὗ   τὸ   πτύον   ἐν   τῇ
Holy   and   fire;   of whom   the   fan [is]   in   the

χειρὶ   αὐτοῦ,   καὶ   διακαθαριεῖ   τὴν   ἅλωνα
hand   of him,   and he will thoroughly cleanse   the   threshing-floor

αὐτοῦ,   καὶ   συνάξει   τὸν   σῖτον   αὐτοῦ
of him,   and   will gather   the   wheat   of him

εἰς   τὴν   ἀποθήκην,   τὸ   δὲ   ἄχυρον   κατα-
into   the   barn,   but the   chaff   he will

καύσει   πυρὶ   ἀσβέστῳ.
consume   with fire   unquenchable.

13 Τότε   παραγίνεται   ὁ   Ἰησοῦς   ἀπὸ   τῆς
Then   arrives   –   Jesus   from   –

Γαλιλαίας   ἐπὶ   τὸν   Ἰορδάνην   πρὸς   τὸν
Galilee   at   the   Jordan   to   –

Ἰωάννην   τοῦ   βαπτισθῆναι   ὑπ᾽   αὐτοῦ.
John   –   to be baptized[d]   by   him.

14 ὁ   δὲ   διεκώλυεν   αὐτὸν   λέγων·   ἐγὼ
But he   forbade   him   saying: I

χρείαν   ἔχω   ὑπὸ   σοῦ   βαπτισθῆναι,   καὶ   σὺ
²need   ¹have   ⁴by   ⁵thee   ³to be baptized,   and   thou

ἔρχῃ   πρὸς   μέ;   15 ἀποκριθεὶς   δὲ   ὁ
comest   to   me?   But answering   –

Ἰησοῦς   εἶπεν   αὐτῷ·   ἄφες   ἄρτι·   οὕτως   γὰρ
Jesus   said   to him: Permit   now;   for thus

πρέπον   ἐστὶν   ἡμῖν   πληρῶσαι   πᾶσαν
²fitting   ¹it is   to us   to fulfil   all

δικαιοσύνην.   τότε   ἀφίησιν   αὐτόν.
righteousness.   Then   he permits   him.

16 βαπτισθεὶς   δὲ   ὁ   Ἰησοῦς   εὐθὺς   ἀνέβη
And having been baptized   –   Jesus   immediately   went up

ἀπὸ   τοῦ   ὕδατος·   καὶ   ἰδοὺ   ἠνεῴχθησαν
from   the   water;   and   behold   ²were opened

οἱ   οὐρανοί,   καὶ   εἶδεν   πνεῦμα   θεοῦ
¹the   ²heavens,   and   he saw   [the] Spirit   of God

καταβαῖνον   ὡσεὶ   περιστεράν,   ἐρχόμενον   ἐπ᾽
coming down   as   a dove,   coming   upon

αὐτόν·   17 καὶ   ἰδοὺ   φωνὴ   ἐκ   τῶν
him;   and   behold   a voice   out of   the

οὐρανῶν   λέγουσα·   οὗτός   ἐστιν   ὁ   υἱός
heavens   saying: This   is   the   son

μου   ὁ   ἀγαπητός,   ἐν   ᾧ   εὐδόκησα.
of me   the   beloved,   in whom   I was well pleased.

---

[d] Other ancient authorities add to him
[e] Or my Son, my (or the) Beloved

CHAPTER 4

THEN Jesus was led up by the Spirit into the wilderness to be tempted by the devil. [2]And he fasted forty days and forty nights, and afterward he was hungry. [3]And the tempter came and said to him, "If you are the Son of God, command these stones to become loaves of bread." [4]But he answered, "It is written,
'Man shall not live by bread alone,
but by every word that proceeds from the mouth of God.'"
[5]Then the devil took him to the holy city, and set him on the pinnacle of the temple, [6]and said to him, "If you are the Son of God, throw yourself down; for it is written,
'He will give his angels charge of you,'
and
'On their hands they will bear you up, lest you strike your foot against a stone.'"
[7]Jesus said to him, "Again it is written, 'You shall not tempt the Lord your God.'"
[8]Again, the devil took him to a very high mountain, and showed him all the kingdoms of the world and the glory of

4 Τότε   ὁ   Ἰησοῦς   ἀνήχθη   εἰς   τὴν
Then   –   Jesus   was led up   into   the
ἔρημον   ὑπὸ   τοῦ   πνεύματος   πειρασθῆναι
wilderness   by   the   Spirit   to be tempted
ὑπὸ   τοῦ   διαβόλου.   2 καὶ   νηστεύσας   ἡμέρας
by   the   devil.   And   having fasted   days
τεσσεράκοντα   καὶ   τεσσεράκοντα   νύκτας
forty   and   forty   nights
ὕστερον   ἐπείνασεν.   3 καὶ   προσελθὼν   ὁ
afterward   he hungered.   And   approaching   the
πειράζων   εἶπεν   αὐτῷ·   εἰ   υἱὸς   εἶ   τοῦ
tempting [one]   said   to him: If   Son   thou art   –   of
θεοῦ,   εἰπὲ   ἵνα   οἱ   λίθοι   οὗτοι   ἄρτοι
God,   say in order that –   stones   these   [2]loaves
γένωνται.   4 ὁ   δὲ   ἀποκριθεὶς   εἶπεν·
[1]may become.   But he   answering   said:
γέγραπται·   οὐκ   ἐπ'   ἄρτῳ   μόνῳ   ζήσεται
It has been written: Not on   bread   only   shall live
ὁ   ἄνθρωπος,   ἀλλ'   ἐπὶ   παντὶ   ῥήματι
–   man,   but   on   every   word
ἐκπορευομένῳ   διὰ   στόματος   θεοῦ.   5 Τότε
proceeding   through [the] mouth   of God.   Then
παραλαμβάνει   αὐτὸν   ὁ   διάβολος   εἰς   τὴν
takes   him   the   devil   into   the
ἁγίαν   πόλιν,   καὶ   ἔστησεν   αὐτὸν   ἐπὶ   τὸ
holy   city,   and   stood   him   on   the
πτερύγιον   τοῦ   ἱεροῦ,   6 καὶ   λέγει   αὐτῷ·
wing   of the temple,   and   says   to him:
εἰ   υἱὸς   εἶ   τοῦ   θεοῦ,   βάλε   σεαυτὸν
If   Son   thou art   –   of God,   cast   thyself
κάτω·   γέγραπται   γὰρ   ὅτι   τοῖς   ἀγγέλοις
down;   for it has been written[,]   –   To the   angels
αὐτοῦ   ἐντελεῖται   περὶ   σοῦ καὶ ἐπὶ χειρῶν
of him   he will give command   concerning thee and   on   hands
ἀροῦσίν   σε,   μήποτε   προσκόψῃς   πρὸς
they will bear   thee,   lest   thou strike   against
λίθον   τὸν   πόδα   σου.   7 ἔφη   αὐτῷ   ὁ
a stone   the   foot   of thee.   Said   to him   the
Ἰησοῦς·   πάλιν   γέγραπται·   οὐκ   ἐκπειράσεις
Jesus: Again it has been written: Not overtempt shalt thou
κύριον   τὸν   θεόν   σου.   8 Πάλιν   παρα-
[the] Lord   the   God   of the.   Again
λαμβάνει   αὐτὸν   ὁ   διάβολος   εἰς   ὄρος
takes   him   the   devil   to   a mountain
ὑψηλὸν   λίαν,   καὶ   δείκνυσιν   αὐτῷ   πάσας
high   exceedingly,   and   shows   him   all
τὰς   βασιλείας   τοῦ   κόσμου   καὶ   τὴν
the   kingdoms   of the   world   and   the

them; ⁹and he said to
him, "All these I will give
you, if you will fall down
and worship me." ¹⁰Then
Jesus said to him, "Be-
gone, Satan! for it is
written,
'You shall worship the
Lord your God
and him only shall you
serve.' "
¹¹Then the devil left him,
and behold, angels came
and ministered to him.

12 Now when he heard
that John had been
arrested, he withdrew
into Galilee; ¹³and leav-
ing Nazareth he went
and dwelt in Caper'na-
um by the sea, in the
territory of Zeb'ulun
and Naph'tali, ¹⁴that
what was spoken by the
prophet Isaiah might be
fulfilled:
¹⁵"The land of Zeb'ulun
and the land of
Naph'tali,
toward the sea, across
the Jordan,
Galilee of the Gen-
tiles—
¹⁶the people who sat in
darkness
have seen a great
light,
and for those who sat
in the region and
shadow of death
light has dawned."
¹⁷From that time Jesus
began to preach, saying,
"Repent, for the king-
dom of heaven is at
hand."

δόξαν αὐτῶν, 9 καὶ εἶπεν αὐτῷ· ταῦτά
glory of them, and said to him: These things
σοι πάντα δώσω, ἐὰν πεσὼν προσκυνήσῃς
to thee all I will give, if falling thou wilt worship
μοι. 10 τότε λέγει αὐτῷ ὁ Ἰησοῦς·
me. Then says to him – Jesus:
ὕπαγε, σατανᾶ· γέγραπται γάρ· κύριον
Go, Satan; for it has been written: [The] Lord
τὸν θεόν σου προσκυνήσεις καὶ αὐτῷ
the God of thee thou shalt worship and him
μόνῳ λατρεύσεις. 11 Τότε ἀφίησιν αὐτὸν
only thou shalt serve. Then leaves him
ὁ διάβολος, καὶ ἰδοὺ ἄγγελοι προσῆλθον
the devil, and behold angels approached
καὶ διηκόνουν αὐτῷ.
and ministered to him.

12 Ἀκούσας δὲ ὅτι Ἰωάννης παρεδόθη
Now hearing that John was delivered up
ἀνεχώρησεν εἰς τὴν Γαλιλαίαν. 13 καὶ
he departed to – Galilee. And
καταλιπὼν τὴν Ναζαρὰ ἐλθὼν κατῴκησεν
leaving – Nazareth coming he dwelt
εἰς Καφαρναοὺμ τὴν παραθαλασσίαν ἐν
in Capernaum – beside the sea in [the]
ὁρίοις Ζαβουλὼν καὶ Νεφθαλίμ· 14 ἵνα
districts of Zebulon and Naphthali; in order that
πληρωθῇ τὸ ῥηθὲν διὰ Ἡσαΐου
might be fulfilled the [thing] spoken through Isaiah
τοῦ προφήτου λέγοντος· 15 γῆ Ζαβουλὼν
the prophet saying: Land of Zebulon
καὶ γῆ Νεφθαλίμ, ὁδὸν θαλάσσης,
and land of Naphthali, way of [the] sea,
πέραν τοῦ Ἰορδάνου, Γαλιλαία τῶν ἐθνῶν,
beyond the Jordan, Galilea of the nations,
16 ὁ λαὸς ὁ καθήμενος ἐν σκοτίᾳ φῶς
the people – sitting in darkness ²light
εἶδεν μέγα, καὶ τοῖς καθημένοις ἐν
¹saw ²a great, and to the [ones] sitting in
χώρᾳ καὶ σκιᾷ θανάτου, φῶς ἀνέτειλεν
a land and shadow of death, light sprang up
αὐτοῖς.
to them.

17 Ἀπὸ τότε ἤρξατο ὁ Ἰησοῦς κηρύσσειν
From then began – Jesus to proclaim
καὶ λέγειν· μετανοεῖτε· ἤγγικεν γὰρ
and to say: Repent ye· for has drawn near
ἡ βασιλεία τῶν οὐρανῶν.
the kingdom of the heavens.

18 As he walked by the Sea of Galilee, he saw two brothers, Simon who is called Peter and Andrew his brother, casting a net into the sea; for they were fishermen. ¹⁹And he said to them, "Follow me, and I will make you fishers of men." ²⁰Immediately they left their nets and followed him. ²¹And going on from there he saw two other brothers, James the son of Zeb'edee and John his brother, in the boat with Zeb'edee their father, mending their nets, and he called them. ²²Immediately they left the boat and their father, and followed him.

23 And he went about all Galilee, teaching in their synagogues and preaching the gospel of the kingdom and healing every disease and every infirmity among the people. ²⁴So his fame spread throughout all Syria, and they brought him all the sick, those afflicted with various diseases and pains, demoniacs, epileptics, and

18 Περιπατῶν δὲ παρὰ τὴν θάλασσαν
And walking beside the sea

τῆς Γαλιλαίας εἶδεν δύο ἀδελφούς, Σίμωνα
- of Galilee he saw two brothers, Simon

τὸν λεγόμενον Πέτρον καὶ Ἀνδρέαν τὸν
- called Peter and Andrew the

ἀδελφὸν αὐτοῦ, βάλλοντας ἀμφίβληστρον εἰς
brother of him, casting a net into

τὴν θάλασσαν· ἦσαν γὰρ ἁλεεῖς. 19 καὶ
the sea; for they were fishers. And

λέγει αὐτοῖς· δεῦτε ὀπίσω μου, καὶ
he says to them: Come after me, and

ποιήσω ὑμᾶς ἁλεεῖς ἀνθρώπων. 20 οἱ
I will make you fishers of men, ²they

δὲ εὐθέως ἀφέντες τὰ δίκτυα ἠκολούθη-
¹And immediately leaving the nets fol-

σαν αὐτῷ. 21 Καὶ προβὰς ἐκεῖθεν εἶδεν
lowed him. And going on thence he saw

ἄλλους δύο ἀδελφούς, Ἰάκωβον τὸν τοῦ
other two brothers, James the [son] -

Ζεβεδαίου καὶ Ἰωάννην τὸν ἀδελφὸν
of Zebedee and John the brother

αὐτοῦ, ἐν τῷ πλοίῳ μετὰ Ζεβεδαίου τοῦ
of him, in the boat with Zebedee the

πατρὸς αὐτῶν καταρτίζοντας τὰ δίκτυα
father of them mending the nets

αὐτῶν· καὶ ἐκάλεσεν αὐτούς. 22 οἱ δὲ
of them; and he called them. And they

εὐθέως ἀφέντες τὸ πλοῖον καὶ τὸν
immediately leaving the boat and the

πατέρα αὐτῶν ἠκολούθησαν αὐτῷ.
father of them followed him.

23 Καὶ περιῆγεν ἐν ὅλῃ τῇ Γαλιλαίᾳ,
And he went about in all - Galilee,

διδάσκων ἐν ταῖς συναγωγαῖς αὐτῶν
teaching in the synagogues of them

καὶ κηρύσσων τὸ εὐαγγέλιον τῆς βασιλείας
and proclaiming the gospel of the kingdom

καὶ θεραπεύων πᾶσαν νόσον καὶ πᾶσαν
and healing every disease and every

μαλακίαν ἐν τῷ λαῷ. 24 καὶ ἀπῆλθεν ἡ
illness among the people. And went the

ἀκοὴ αὐτοῦ εἰς ὅλην τὴν Συρίαν· καὶ
report of him into all - Syria; and

προσήνεγκαν αὐτῷ πάντας τοὺς κακῶς
they brought to him all the [ones] ²ill
=those who were ill

ἔχοντας ποικίλαις νόσοις καὶ βασάνοις
¹having ²various ³diseases ⁴and ⁵tortures

paralytics, and he healed them. ²⁵And great crowds followed him from Galilee and the Decap'olis and Jerusalem and Judea and from beyond the Jordan.

συνεχομένους, δαιμονιζομένους καὶ σεληνιαζ-
¹suffering from,   demon-possessed   and   luna-

ομένους καὶ παραλυτικούς, καὶ ἐθεράπευσεν
tics   and   paralysed,   and   he healed

αὐτούς. 25 καὶ ἠκολούθησαν αὐτῷ ὄχλοι
them.   And   ²followed   ⁴him   ²crowds

πολλοὶ ἀπὸ τῆς Γαλιλαίας καὶ Δεκαπόλεως
¹many   from -   Galilee   and   Decapolis

καὶ Ἱεροσολύμων καὶ Ἰουδαίας καὶ πέραν
and   Jerusalem   and   Judæa   and   beyond

τοῦ Ἰορδάνου.
the   Jordan.

CHAPTER 5

SEEING the crowds, he went up on the mountain, and when he sat down his disciples came to him. ²And he opened his mouth and taught them, saying:

3 "Blessed are the poor in spirit, for theirs is the kingdom of heaven.

4 "Blessed are those who mourn, for they shall be comforted.

5 "Blessed are the meek, for they shall inherit the earth.

6 "Blessed are those who hunger and thirst for righteousness, for they shall be satisfied.

7 "Blessed are the merciful, for they shall obtain mercy.

8 'Blessed are the pure in heart, for they shall see God.

9 "Blessed are the peacemakers, for they shall be called sons of God.

10 "Blessed are those who are persecuted for righteousness' sake, for

5 Ἰδὼν δὲ τοὺς ὄχλους ἀνέβη εἰς
And seeing   the   crowds   he went up   into

τὸ ὄρος· καὶ καθίσαντος αὐτοῦ προσῆλθαν
the mountain;   and   sitting   him²   ⁴approached
                        =when he sat

αὐτῷ οἱ μαθηταὶ αὐτοῦ· 2 καὶ ἀνοίξας τὸ
²to him ¹the   ²disciples   ³of him;   and   opening   the

στόμα αὐτοῦ ἐδίδασκεν αὐτοὺς λέγων·
mouth   of him   he taught   them   saying:

3 Μακάριοι οἱ πτωχοὶ τῷ πνεύματι,
Blessed [are]   the   poor   -   in spirit,

ὅτι αὐτῶν ἐστιν ἡ βασιλεία τῶν οὐρανῶν.
for them   is   the kingdom   of the   heavens.

4 μακάριοι οἱ πενθοῦντες, ὅτι αὐτοὶ
Blessed [are]   the   mourning [ones],   for   they

παρακληθήσονται. 5 μακάριοι οἱ πραεῖς,
shall be comforted.   Blessed [are]   the   meek,

ὅτι αὐτοὶ κληρονομήσουσιν τὴν γῆν.
for   they   shall inherit   the   earth.

6 μακάριοι οἱ πεινῶντες καὶ διψῶντες
Blessed [are] the   hungering   and   thirsting [ones] [after]

τὴν δικαιοσύνην, ὅτι αὐτοὶ χορτασ-
-     righteousness,   for   they   shall be

θήσονται. 7 μακάριοι οἱ ἐλεήμονες, ὅτι
satisfied.   Blessed [are]   the   merciful,   for

αὐτοὶ ἐλεηθήσονται. 8 μακάριοι οἱ καθαροὶ
they   shall obtain mercy.   Blessed [are]   the   clean

τῇ καρδίᾳ, ὅτι αὐτοὶ τὸν θεὸν ὄψονται.
-   in heart,   for   they   -   ²God   ¹shall see.

9 μακάριοι οἱ εἰρηνοποιοί, ὅτι [αὐτοὶ]
Blessed [are]   the   peacemakers,   for   they

υἱοὶ θεοῦ κληθήσονται. 10 μακάριοι οἱ
sons of God   shall be called.   Blessed [are] the [ones]

δεδιωγμένοι ἕνεκεν δικαιοσύνης, ὅτι αὐτῶν
having been persecuted for the sake of righteousness, for of them

theirs is the kingdom of heaven.

11 "Blessed are you when men revile you and persecute you and utter all kinds of evil against you falsely on my account. ¹²Rejoice and be glad, for your reward is great in heaven, for so men persecuted the prophets who were before you.

13 "You are the salt of the earth; but if salt has lost its taste, how shall its saltness be restored? It is no longer good for anything except to be thrown out and trodden under foot by men.

14 "You are the light of the world. A city set on a hill cannot be hid. ¹⁵Nor do men light a lamp and put it under a bushel, but on a stand, and it gives light to all in the house. ¹⁶Let your light so shine before men, that they may see your good works and give glory to your Father who is in heaven.

17 "Think not that I have come to abolish the law and the prophets; I have come not to abolish them but to fulfil them.

ἐστιν ἡ βασιλεία τῶν οὐρανῶν. 11 μακάριοί
is   the   kingdom   of the   heavens.   Blessed

ἐστε ὅταν ὀνειδίσωσιν ὑμᾶς καὶ διώξωσιν
are ye   when   they reproach   you   and   persecute

καὶ εἴπωσιν πᾶν πονηρὸν καθ' ὑμῶν
and   say   all   evil   against   you

ψευδόμενοι ἕνεκεν ἐμοῦ. 12 χαίρετε
lying   for the sake of   me.   Rejoice

καὶ ἀγαλλιᾶσθε, ὅτι ὁ μισθὸς ὑμῶν
and   be glad,   because   the   reward   of you [is]

πολὺς ἐν τοῖς οὐρανοῖς· οὕτως γὰρ
much   in   the   heavens;   for thus

ἐδίωξαν τοὺς προφήτας τοὺς πρὸ
they persecuted   the   prophets   before

ὑμῶν.
you.

13 Ὑμεῖς ἐστε τὸ ἅλας τῆς γῆς· ἐὰν δὲ
    Ye   are   the   salt   of the   earth;   but if

τὸ ἅλας μωρανθῇ, ἐν τίνι ἁλισθήσεται;
the   salt   be tainted,   by   what   shall it be salted?

εἰς οὐδὲν ἰσχύει ἔτι εἰ μὴ βληθὲν ἔξω
for   nothing   is it strong   longer   except   being cast   out

καταπατεῖσθαι ὑπὸ τῶν ἀνθρώπων. 14 Ὑμεῖς
to be trodden down   by   –   men.   Ye

ἐστε τὸ φῶς τοῦ κόσμου. οὐ δύναται
are   the   light   of the   world.   ⁸Not   ⁵can

πόλις κρυβῆναι ἐπάνω ὄρους κειμένη·
¹a city   ⁷to be hid   ⁶on   ⁴a mountain   ²set;

15 οὐδὲ καίουσιν λύχνον καὶ τιθέασιν
   nor   do they light   a lamp   and   place

αὐτὸν ὑπὸ τὸν μόδιον, ἀλλ' ἐπὶ τὴν
it   under   the   bushel,   but   on   the

λυχνίαν, καὶ λάμπει πᾶσιν τοῖς ἐν τῇ
lampstand,   and   it lightens   all   the [ones]   in   the

οἰκίᾳ. 16 οὕτως λαμψάτω τὸ φῶς ὑμῶν
house.   Thus   let shine   the   light   of you

ἔμπροσθεν τῶν ἀνθρώπων, ὅπως ἴδωσιν
before   –   men,   so that   they may see

ὑμῶν τὰ καλὰ ἔργα καὶ δοξάσωσιν
of you   the   good   works   and   may glorify

τὸν πατέρα ὑμῶν τὸν ἐν τοῖς οὐρανοῖς.
the   Father   of you   –   in   the   heavens.

17 Μὴ νομίσητε ὅτι ἦλθον καταλῦσαι
    Think not   that   I came   to destroy

τὸν νόμον ἢ τοὺς προφήτας· οὐκ ἦλθον
the   law   or   the   prophets;   I came not

καταλῦσαι ἀλλὰ πληρῶσαι. 18 ἀμὴν γὰρ
to destroy   but   to fulfil.   For truly

¹⁸ For truly, I say to you, till heaven and earth pass away, not an iota, not a dot, will pass from the law until all is accomplished. ¹⁹ Whoever then relaxes one of the least of these commandments and teaches men so, shall be called least in the kingdom of heaven; but he who does them and teaches them shall be called great in the kingdom of heaven. ²⁰ For I tell you, unless your righteousness exceeds that of the scribes and Pharisees, you will never enter the kingdom of heaven.

21 "You have heard that it was said to the men of old, 'You shall not kill; and whoever kills shall be liable to judgment.' ²² But I say to you that every one who is angry with his brother^f shall be liable to judgment; whoever insults^g his brother shall be liable to the council, and whoever says, 'You fool!' shall be liable to the hell of fire. ²³ So if you are offering your gift at the altar, and there remember that your brother has something against you,

f Other ancient authorities insert *without cause*

g Greek *says Raca* to (an obscure term of abuse)

λέγω ὑμῖν, ἕως ἂν παρέλθῃ ὁ οὐρανὸς
I say to you, until pass away the heaven
καὶ ἡ γῆ, ἰῶτα ἓν ἢ μία κεραία οὐ
and the earth, iota one or one point by no
μὴ παρέλθῃ ἀπὸ τοῦ νόμου, ἕως ἂν
means shall pass away from the law, until
πάντα γένηται. 19 ὃς ἐὰν οὖν λύσῃ
all things come to pass. Whoever therefore breaks
μίαν τῶν ἐντολῶν τούτων τῶν ἐλαχίστων
one commandments of these the least
καὶ διδάξῃ οὕτως τοὺς ἀνθρώπους, ἐλάχιστος
and teaches thus men, least
κληθήσεται ἐν τῇ βασιλείᾳ τῶν οὐρανῶν·
he shall be called in the kingdom of the heavens;
ὃς δ' ἂν ποιήσῃ καὶ διδάξῃ, οὗτος
but whoever does and teaches, this [one]
μέγας κληθήσεται ἐν τῇ βασιλείᾳ τῶν
great shall be called in the kingdom of the
οὐρανῶν. 20 λέγω γὰρ ὑμῖν ὅτι ἐὰν μὴ
heavens. For I tell you that except
περισσεύσῃ ὑμῶν ἡ δικαιοσύνη πλεῖον
shall exceed of you the righteousness more [than] [that]
τῶν γραμματέων καὶ Φαρισαίων, οὐ μὴ
of the scribes and Pharisees, by no means
εἰσέλθητε εἰς τὴν βασιλείαν τῶν οὐρανῶν.
shall ye enter into the kingdom of the heavens.
21 Ἠκούσατε ὅτι ἐρρέθη τοῖς ἀρχαίοις·
Ye heard that it was said to the ancients:
οὐ φονεύσεις· ὃς δ' ἂν φονεύσῃ,
Thou shalt not kill; and whoever kills,
ἔνοχος ἔσται τῇ κρίσει. 22 ἐγὼ δὲ
liable shall be to the judgment. But I
λέγω ὑμῖν ὅτι πᾶς ὁ ὀργιζόμενος τῷ
tell you that everyone being angry with the
ἀδελφῷ αὐτοῦ ἔνοχος ἔσται τῇ κρίσει·
brother of him liable shall be to the judgment;
ὃς δ' ἂν εἴπῃ τῷ ἀδελφῷ αὐτοῦ ῥακά,
and whoever says to the brother of him[,] Raca,
ἔνοχος ἔσται τῷ συνεδρίῳ· ὃς δ' ἂν εἴπῃ
liable shall be to the council; and whoever says[,]
μωρέ, ἔνοχος ἔσται εἰς τὴν γέενναν
Fool, liable shall be to the gehenna
τοῦ πυρός. 23 ἐὰν οὖν προσφέρῃς τὸ
of fire. Therefore if thou bringest the
δῶρόν σου ἐπὶ τὸ θυσιαστήριον κἀκεῖ
gift of thee to the altar and there
μνησθῇς ὅτι ὁ ἀδελφός σου ἔχει τι
rememberest that the brother of thee has something

[24] leave your gift there before the altar and go; first be reconciled to your brother, and then come and offer your gift. [25] Make friends quickly with your accuser, while you are going with him to court, lest your accuser hand you over to the judge, and the judge to the guard, and you be put in prison; [26] truly, I say to you, you will never get out till you have paid the last penny.

[27] "You have heard that it was said, 'You shall not commit adultery.' [28] But I say to you that every one who looks at a woman lustfully has already committed adultery with her in his heart. [29] If your right eye causes you to sin, pluck it out and throw it away; it is better that you lose one of your members than that your whole body be thrown into hell. [30] And if your right hand causes you to sin, cut it off and throw it away; it is better that you lose one of your members than that your whole body go into hell.

κατὰ σοῦ, **24** ἄφες ἐκεῖ τὸ δῶρόν σου
against thee,　　leave　there　the　gift　of thee
ἔμπροσθεν τοῦ θυσιαστηρίου, καὶ ὕπαγε
before　　　the　altar,　　　and　go
πρῶτον διαλλάγηθι τῷ ἀδελφῷ σου, καὶ
first　be reconciled to the　brother　of thee,　and
τότε ἐλθὼν πρόσφερε τὸ δῶρόν σου.
then　coming　offer　the　gift　of thee.
25 ἴσθι εὐνοῶν τῷ ἀντιδίκῳ σου
Be　well disposed to the　opponent　of thee
ταχὺ ἕως ὅτου εἶ μετ' αὐτοῦ ἐν τῇ
quickly　while　thou art with　him　in　the
ὁδῷ· μήποτέ σε παραδῷ ὁ ἀντίδικος τῷ
way;　lest [4]thee [3]deliver [1]the [2]opponent to the
κριτῇ καὶ ὁ κριτὴς τῷ ὑπηρέτῃ, καὶ
judge and the　judge to the　attendant,　and
εἰς φυλακὴν βληθήσῃ· **26** ἀμὴν λέγω
into　prison　thou be cast;　truly　I say
σοι, οὐ μὴ ἐξέλθῃς ἐκεῖθεν ἕως ἂν
to thee, by no means shalt thou come out thence until
ἀποδῷς τὸν ἔσχατον κοδράντην.
thou repayest the　last　farthing.
27 Ἠκούσατε ὅτι ἐρρέθη· οὐ μοιχεύσεις.
Ye heard that it was said: Thou shalt not commit adultery.
28 ἐγὼ δὲ λέγω ὑμῖν ὅτι πᾶς ὁ βλέπων
But I　tell　you　that everyone　seeing
γυναῖκα πρὸς τὸ ἐπιθυμῆσαι [αὐτὴν]
a woman　with a view –　to desire　her
ἤδη ἐμοίχευσεν αὐτὴν ἐν τῇ καρδίᾳ
already committed adultery with her　in　the　heart
αὐτοῦ. **29** εἰ δὲ ὁ ὀφθαλμός σου ὁ δεξιὸς
of him.　So if the [2]eye [3]of thee – [1]right
σκανδαλίζει σε, ἔξελε αὐτὸν καὶ βάλε
[5]causes [6]to stumble [6]thee, pluck out it　and cast
ἀπὸ σοῦ· συμφέρει γάρ σοι ἵνα ἀπόληται
from thee;　for it is expedient for thee that [5]perish
ἐν τῶν μελῶν σου καὶ μὴ ὅλον τὸ
[1]one [2]of the [3]members [4]of thee and not　all　the
σῶμά σου βληθῇ εἰς γέενναν. **30** καὶ
body of thee be cast　into gehenna.　And
εἰ ἡ δεξιά σου χεὶρ σκανδαλίζει σε, ἔκκοψον
if the [1]right [2]of thee [2]hand [4]causes [6]to stumble [6]thee, cut out
αὐτὴν καὶ βάλε ἀπὸ σοῦ· συμφέρει γάρ
it and cast from thee;　for it is expedient
σοι ἵνα ἀπόληται ἐν τῶν μελῶν σου
for thee that [5]perish [1]one [2]of the [3]members [4]of thee
καὶ μὴ ὅλον τὸ σῶμά σου εἰς γέενναν
and not　all　the　body of thee into　gehenna

31 "It was also said, 'Whoever divorces his wife, let him give her a certificate of divorce.' [32] But I say to you that every one who divorces his wife, except on the ground of unchastity, makes her an adulteress; and whoever marries a divorced woman commits adultery.

33 "Again you have heard that it was said to the men of old, 'You shall not swear falsely, but shall perform to the Lord what you have sworn.' [34] But I say to you, Do not swear at all, either by heaven, for it is the throne of God, [35] or by the earth, for it is his footstool, or by Jerusalem, for it is the city of the great King. [36] And do not swear by your head, for you cannot make one hair white or black. [37] Let what you say be simply 'Yes' or 'No'; anything more than this comes from evil.

38 "You have heard that it was said, 'An eye for an eye and a tooth for a tooth.' [39] But I say to you, Do not resist one who is evil. But if any one strikes you on the right cheek, turn to him

ἀπέλθῃ. **31** Ἐρρέθη δέ· ὃς ἂν ἀπολύσῃ
go away.   And it was said: Whoever dismisses

τὴν γυναῖκα αὐτοῦ, δότω αὐτῇ ἀποστάσιον.
the   wife   of him, let him give her a bill of divorce.

32 ἐγὼ δὲ λέγω ὑμῖν ὅτι πᾶς ὁ ἀπολύων
   But I tell you that everyone dismissing

τὴν γυναῖκα αὐτοῦ παρεκτὸς λόγου
the   wife   of him apart from a matter

πορνείας ποιεῖ αὐτὴν μοιχευθῆναι,
of fornication makes her *to* commit adultery,

καὶ ὃς ἐὰν ἀπολελυμένην γαμήσῃ,
and whoever ²a dismissed [woman] ¹marries,

μοιχᾶται. **33** Πάλιν ἠκούσατε ὅτι ἐρρέθη
commits adultery. Again ye heard that it was said

τοῖς ἀρχαίοις· οὐκ ἐπιορκήσεις, ἀποδώσεις
to the ancients: Thou shalt not perjure, ²shalt repay

δὲ τῷ κυρίῳ τοὺς ὅρκους σου. **34** ἐγὼ δὲ
¹but to the Lord the oaths of thee.   But I

λέγω ὑμῖν μὴ ὀμόσαι ὅλως· μήτε ἐν τῷ
tell you not to swear at all; neither by the

οὐρανῷ, ὅτι θρόνος ἐστὶν τοῦ θεοῦ·
heaven, because [the] throne it is – of God;

35 μήτε ἐν τῇ γῇ, ὅτι ὑποπόδιόν
   nor by the earth, because footstool

ἐστιν τῶν ποδῶν αὐτοῦ· μήτε εἰς
it is of the feet of him; nor by

Ἱεροσόλυμα, ὅτι πόλις ἐστὶν τοῦ μεγάλου
Jerusalem, because city it is of the great

βασιλέως· **36** μήτε ἐν τῇ κεφαλῇ σου
King;   nor by the head of thee

ὀμόσῃς, ὅτι οὐ δύνασαι μίαν τρίχα
swear, because thou canst not one hair

λευκὴν ποιῆσαι ἢ μέλαιναν. **37** ἔστω
white *to* make or black.   ²let ⁰be

δὲ ὁ λόγος ὑμῶν ναὶ ναί, οὒ οὔ·
¹But ⁰the ⁴word ⁵of you Yes yes, No no;

τὸ δὲ περισσὸν τούτων ἐκ τοῦ πονηροῦ
for the excess of these of – evil

ἐστιν. **38** Ἠκούσατε ὅτι ἐρρέθη· ὀφθαλμὸν
is.   Ye heard that it was said: An eye

ἀντὶ ὀφθαλμοῦ καὶ ὀδόντα ἀντὶ ὀδόντος.
instead of an eye and a tooth instead of a tooth.

39 ἐγὼ δὲ λέγω ὑμῖν μὴ ἀντιστῆναι
   But I tell you not to oppose

τῷ πονηρῷ· ἀλλ' ὅστις σε ῥαπίζει εἰς
– evil;   but who thee strikes on

τὴν δεξιὰν σιαγόνα [σου], στρέψον αὐτῷ
the right cheek of thee, turn to him

the other also; ⁴⁰and if any one would sue you and take your coat, let him have your cloak as well; ⁴¹and if any one forces you to go one mile, go with him two miles. ⁴²Give to him who begs from you, and do not refuse him who would borrow from you.

43 "You have heard that it was said, 'You shall love your neighbor and hate your enemy.' ⁴⁴But I say to you, Love your enemies and pray for those who persecute you, ⁴⁵so that you may be sons of your Father who is in heaven; for he makes his sun rise on the evil and on the good, and sends rain on the just and on the unjust. ⁴⁶For if you love those who love you, what reward have you? Do not even the tax collectors do the same? ⁴⁷And if you salute only your brethren, what more are you doing than others? Do not even the Gentiles do the same? ⁴⁸You, therefore, must be perfect, as your heavenly Father is perfect.

καὶ	τὴν	ἄλλην·	**40** καὶ	τῷ	θέλοντί
also	the	other;	and	to the [one]	wishing

σοι	κριθῆναι	καὶ	τὸν	χιτῶνά σου	λαβεῖν,
thee	to judge	and	the	tunic of thee	to take,

ἄφες	αὐτῷ	καὶ	τὸ	ἱμάτιον· **41** καὶ
allow	him	also	the [outer] garment;	and

ὅστις	σε	ἀγγαρεύσει	μίλιον	ἕν,	ὕπαγε
who	²thee	¹shall impress	⁴mile	⁴one,	go

μετ'	αὐτοῦ	δύο.	**42** τῷ	αἰτοῦντί
with	him	two.	To the [one]	asking

σε	δός,	καὶ	τὸν	θέλοντα	ἀπὸ σοῦ
thee	give,	and	the [one]	wishing	from thee

δανείσασθαι	μὴ ἀποστραφῇς.	**43** Ἠκούσατε
to borrow	turn not away.	Ye heard

ὅτι	ἐρρέθη·	ἀγαπήσεις	τὸν	πλησίον σου
that	it was said:	Thou shalt love	the	neighbour of thee

καὶ	μισήσεις	τὸν	ἐχθρόν σου.	**44** ἐγὼ
and	thou shalt hate	the	enemy of thee.	²I

δὲ	λέγω	ὑμῖν·	ἀγαπᾶτε	τοὺς ἐχθροὺς
¹But	tell	you:	Love ye	the enemies

ὑμῶν	καὶ	προσεύχεσθε	ὑπὲρ	τῶν
of you	and	pray ye	for	the [ones]

διωκόντων	ὑμᾶς·	**45** ὅπως	γένησθε	υἱοὶ
persecuting	you;	so that	ye may become	sons

τοῦ	πατρὸς	ὑμῶν	τοῦ ἐν	οὐρανοῖς,
of the	Father	of you	– in	heavens,

ὅτι	τὸν	ἥλιον αὐτοῦ	ἀνατέλλει	ἐπὶ
because	the	sun of him	he makes to rise	on

πονηροὺς	καὶ	ἀγαθοὺς	καὶ	βρέχει ἐπὶ
evil men	and	good	and	rains on

δικαίους	καὶ	ἀδίκους.	**46** ἐὰν γὰρ
just men	and	unjust.	For if

ἀγαπήσητε	τοὺς	ἀγαπῶντας	ὑμᾶς,	τίνα
ye love	the [ones]	loving	you,	what

μισθὸν	ἔχετε;	οὐχὶ	καὶ	οἱ τελῶναι	τὸ
reward	have ye?	²not	³even	⁴the ⁵tax-collectors	⁶the

αὐτὸ	ποιοῦσιν;	**47** καὶ ἐὰν	ἀσπάσησθε
⁷same	¹do?	and if	ye greet

τοὺς	ἀδελφοὺς ὑμῶν	μόνον,	τί περισσὸν
the	brothers of you	only,	what excess

ποιεῖτε;	οὐχὶ	καὶ οἱ ἐθνικοὶ	τὸ αὐτὸ
do ye?	²not	³even ⁴the ⁵gentiles	⁶the ⁷same

ποιοῦσιν;	**48** Ἔσεσθε	οὖν ὑμεῖς	τέλειοι
¹do?	Be	therefore ye	perfect

ὡς ὁ	πατὴρ ὑμῶν	ὁ	οὐράνιος τέλειός
as the	²Father ³of you	–	¹heavenly perfect

ἐστιν.
is.

CHAPTER 6

"**B**EWARE of practic-
ing your piety be-
fore men in order to be
seen by them; for then
you will have no reward
from your Father who is
in heaven.

2 "Thus, when you
give alms, sound no
trumpet before you, as
the hypocrites do in the
synagogues and in the
streets, that they may be
praised by men. Truly, I
say to you, they have
their reward. ³But when
you give alms, do not let
your left hand know
what your right hand is
doing, ⁴so that your
alms may be in secret;
and your Father who
sees in secret will reward
you.

5 "And when you
pray, you must not be
like the hypocrites; for
they love to stand and
pray in the synagogues
and at the street corners,
that they may be seen by
men. Truly, I say to you,
they have their reward.
⁶But when you pray, go
into your room and shut
the door and pray to
your Father who is in
secret; and your Father

6 Προσέχετε   δὲ   τὴν   δικαιοσύνην   ὑμῶν
And take ye heed the   righteousness   of you

μὴ   ποιεῖν   ἔμπροσθεν   τῶν   ἀνθρώπων   πρὸς
not to do in front of   –   men   with a view to

τὸ   θεαθῆναι   αὐτοῖς·   εἰ   δὲ   μή   γε,   μισθὸν
– to be seen   by them;   otherwise,   reward

οὐκ   ἔχετε   παρὰ   τῷ   πατρὶ   ὑμῶν   τῷ
ye have not   with   the   Father   of you   –

ἐν   τοῖς   οὐρανοῖς.   2 Ὅταν   οὖν   ποιῇς
in   the   heavens.   ²When ¹therefore thou doest

ἐλεημοσύνην,   μὴ   σαλπίσῃς   ἔμπροσθέν   σου,
alms,   sound not a trumpet   before.   thee,

ὥσπερ   οἱ   ὑποκριταὶ   ποιοῦσιν   ἐν   ταῖς
as   the   hypocrites   do   in   the

συναγωγαῖς   καὶ   ἐν   ταῖς   ῥύμαις,   ὅπως
synagogues   and   in   the   streets,   so that

δοξασθῶσιν   ὑπὸ   τῶν   ἀνθρώπων·   ἀμὴν
they may be glorified by   –   men;   truly

λέγω   ὑμῖν,   ἀπέχουσιν   τὸν   μισθὸν   αὐτῶν.
I tell   you,   they have   the   reward   of them.

3 σοῦ   δὲ   ποιοῦντος   ἐλεημοσύνην   μὴ
But thee   doing²   alms   not
= when thou doest

γνώτω   ἡ   ἀριστερά   σου   τί   ποιεῖ   ἡ
let know   the   left [hand]   of thee   what   does   the

δεξιά   σου,   4 ὅπως   ᾖ   σου   ἡ   ἐλεημοσύνη
right of thee,   so that ⁴may be ²of thee ¹the   ³alms

ἐν   τῷ   κρυπτῷ·   καὶ   ὁ   πατήρ   σου
in   –   secret;   and   the   Father   of thee

ὁ   βλέπων   ἐν   τῷ   κρυπτῷ   ἀποδώσει   σοι.
the [one] seeing   in   –   secret   will repay   thee.

5 Καὶ   ὅταν   προσεύχησθε,   οὐκ   ἔσεσθε
And   when   ye pray,   be not ye

ὡς   οἱ   ὑποκριταί·   ὅτι   φιλοῦσιν   ἐν   ταῖς
as   the   hypocrites;   because they love   in   the

συναγωγαῖς   καὶ   ἐν   ταῖς   γωνίαις   τῶν
synagogues   and   in the   corners   of the

πλατειῶν   ἑστῶτες   προσεύχεσθαι,   ὅπως
open streets   standing   to pray,   so that

φανῶσιν   τοῖς   ἀνθρώποις·   ἀμὴν   λέγω
they may appear   –   to men;   truly   I tell

ὑμῖν,   ἀπέχουσιν   τὸν   μισθὸν   αὐτῶν.   6 σὺ
you,   they have   the   reward   of them.   ⁶thou

δὲ   ὅταν   προσεύχῃ,   εἴσελθε   εἰς   τὸ   ταμιεῖον
¹But ³when ⁴prayest,   enter   into   the private room

σου   καὶ   κλείσας   τὴν   θύραν   σου   πρόσευξαι
of thee and having shut the   door   of thee   pray

τῷ   πατρί   σου   τῷ   ἐν   τῷ   κρυπτῷ·
to the Father of thee the [one] in   –   secret;

who sees in secret will reward you.

7 "And in praying do not heap up empty phrases as the Gentiles do; for they think that they will be heard for their many words. ⁸ Do not be like them, for your Father knows what you need before you ask him. ⁹ Pray then like this:

Our Father who art in heaven,
Hallowed be thy name.
¹⁰ Thy kingdom come,
Thy will be done,
On earth as it is in heaven.
¹¹ Give us this day our daily bread;ʰ
¹² And forgive us our debts,
As we also have forgiven our debtors;
¹³ And lead us not into temptation,
But deliver us from evil.ⁱ

¹⁴ For if you forgive men their trespasses, your heavenly Father also will forgive you; ¹⁵ but if you do not forgive men their trespasses, neither will your Father forgive your trespasses.

16 "And when you fast, do not look dismal, like the hypocrites, for

ʰ Or *our bread for the morrow*
ⁱ Or *the evil one.* Other authorities, some ancient, add, in some form, *For thine is the kingdom and the power and the glory, forever. Amen.*

καὶ ὁ πατήρ σου ὁ βλέπων ἐν τῷ
and the Father of thee the [one] seeing in –

κρυπτῷ ἀποδώσει σοι. 7 Προσευχόμενοι δὲ
secret will repay thee. But praying

μὴ βατταλογήσητε ὥσπερ οἱ ἐθνικοί·
do not utter empty words as the gentiles;

δοκοῦσιν γὰρ ὅτι ἐν τῇ πολυλογίᾳ αὐτῶν
for they think that in the much speaking of them

εἰσακουσθήσονται. 8 μὴ οὖν ὁμοιωθῆτε
they will be heard. Not therefore be ye like

αὐτοῖς· οἶδεν γὰρ [ὁ θεὸς] ὁ πατὴρ
them; for ⁵knows – ¹God ²the ³Father

ὑμῶν ὧν χρείαν ἔχετε πρὸ τοῦ ὑμᾶς
⁴of you of what things ²need ¹ye have before you

αἰτῆσαι αὐτόν. 9 οὕτως οὖν προσεύχεσθε
to askᵇ him. ²Thus ¹therefore pray

ὑμεῖς· Πάτερ ἡμῶν ὁ ἐν τοῖς οὐρανοῖς·
ye: Father of us the [one] in the heavens:

Ἁγιασθήτω τὸ ὄνομά σου· 10 ἐλθάτω
Let it be hallowed the name of thee; let it come

ἡ βασιλεία σου· γενηθήτω τὸ θέλημά σου,
the kingdom of thee; let it come about the will of thee,

ὡς ἐν οὐρανῷ καὶ ἐπὶ γῆς· 11 Τὸν
as in heaven also on earth; The

ἄρτον ἡμῶν τὸν ἐπιούσιον δὸς ἡμῖν
²bread ³of us – ¹daily give to us

σήμερον· 12 καὶ ἄφες ἡμῖν τὰ ὀφειλή-
to-day; and forgive us the debts

ματα ἡμῶν, ὡς καὶ ἡμεῖς ἀφήκαμεν
of us, as indeed we forgave

τοῖς ὀφειλέταις ἡμῶν· 13 καὶ μὴ εἰσενέγκῃς
the debtors of us; and not bring

ἡμᾶς εἰς πειρασμόν, ἀλλὰ ῥῦσαι ἡμᾶς ἀπὸ
us into temptation, but rescue us from

τοῦ πονηροῦ. 14 Ἐὰν γὰρ ἀφῆτε τοῖς
– evil. For if ye forgive

ἀνθρώποις τὰ παραπτώματα αὐτῶν, ἀφήσει
men the trespasses of them, will forgive

καὶ ὑμῖν ὁ πατὴρ ὑμῶν ὁ οὐράνιος·
also you the ²Father ³of you – ¹heavenly;

15 ἐὰν δὲ μὴ ἀφῆτε τοῖς ἀνθρώποις,
but if ye forgive not – men,

οὐδὲ ὁ πατὴρ ὑμῶν ἀφήσει τὰ παραπτώ-
neither the Father of you will forgive the tres-

ματα ὑμῶν. 16 Ὅταν δὲ νηστεύητε,
passes of you. And when ye fast,

μὴ γίνεσθε ὡς οἱ ὑποκριταὶ σκυθρωποί·
be not as the hypocrites gloomy;

they disfigure their faces that their fasting may be seen by men. Truly, I say to you, they have their reward. [17] But when you fast, anoint your head and wash your face, [18] that your fasting may not be seen by men but by your Father who is in secret; and your Father who sees in secret will reward you.

19 "Do not lay up for yourselves treasures on earth, where moth and rust consume and where thieves break in and steal, [20] but lay up for yourselves treasures in heaven, where neither moth nor rust[j] consumes and where thieves do not break in and steal. [21] For where your treasure is, there will your heart be also.

22 "The eye is the lamp of the body. So, if your eye is sound, your whole body will be full of light; [23] but if your eye is not sound, your whole body will be full of darkness. If then the light in you is darkness, how great is the darkness!

ἀφανίζουσιν γὰρ τὰ πρόσωπα αὐτῶν
for they disfigure   the   faces   of them

ὅπως φανῶσιν τοῖς ἀνθρώποις νηστεύοντες·
so that they may appear –   to men   fasting;

ἀμὴν λέγω ὑμῖν, ἀπέχουσιν τὸν μισθὸν
truly I tell you, they have the reward

αὐτῶν. 17 σὺ δὲ νηστεύων ἄλειψαί σου
of them.   But thou fasting   anoint   of thee

τὴν κεφαλὴν καὶ τὸ πρόσωπόν σου νίψαι,
the   head   and the   face   of thee wash,

18 ὅπως μὴ φανῇς τοῖς ἀνθρώποις νηστεύων
so that thou appearest not –   to men   fasting

ἀλλὰ τῷ πατρί σου τῷ ἐν τῷ κρυφαίῳ·
but to the Father of thee the [one] in –   secret;

καὶ ὁ πατήρ σου ὁ βλέπων ἐν τῷ
and the Father of thee the [one] seeing in   –

κρυφαίῳ ἀποδώσει σοι.
secret   will repay thee.

19 Μὴ θησαυρίζετε ὑμῖν θησαυροὺς
Do not lay up *treasure* for you   treasures

ἐπὶ τῆς γῆς, ὅπου σὴς καὶ βρῶσις
on the earth, where moth and rust

ἀφανίζει, καὶ ὅπου κλέπται διορύσσουσιν
removes, and where thieves   dig through

καὶ κλέπτουσιν· 20 θησαυρίζετε δὲ ὑμῖν
and steal;   but lay up *treasure* for you

θησαυροὺς ἐν οὐρανῷ, ὅπου οὔτε σὴς
treasures   in heaven, where neither moth

οὔτε βρῶσις ἀφανίζει, καὶ ὅπου κλέπται
nor   rust   removes,   and where thieves

οὐ διορύσσουσιν οὐδὲ κλέπτουσιν· 21 ὅπου
do not dig through nor   steal;   [3]where

γάρ ἐστιν ὁ θησαυρός σου, ἐκεῖ
[1]for is the treasure of thee, there

ἔσται καὶ ἡ καρδία σου. 22 Ὁ λύχνος
will be also the heart of thee.   The lamp

τοῦ σώματός ἐστιν ὁ ὀφθαλμός. ἐὰν οὖν
of the body   is the   eye.   [3]If [1]therefore

ᾖ ὁ ὀφθαλμός σου ἁπλοῦς, ὅλον τὸ σῶμά
[4]be [1]the [2]eye [3]of thee single, all the body

σου φωτεινὸν ἔσται· 23 ἐὰν δὲ ὁ
of thee shining   will be;   but if the

ὀφθαλμός σου πονηρὸς ᾖ, ὅλον τὸ σῶμά
eye   of thee evil   be, all the body

σου σκοτεινὸν ἔσται. εἰ οὖν τὸ φῶς
of thee dark   will be. [1]If [1]therefore the light

τὸ ἐν σοὶ σκότος ἐστιν, τὸ σκότος
– in thee darkness is, the darkness

---

[j] Or *worm*

24 "No one can serve two masters; for either he will hate the one and love the other, or he will be devoted to the one and despise the other. You cannot serve God and mammon.

25 "Therefore I tell you, do not be anxious about your life, what you shall eat or what you shall drink, nor about your body, what you shall put on. Is not life more than food, and the body more than clothing? [26] Look at the birds of the air: they neither sow nor reap nor gather into barns, and yet your heavenly Father feeds them. Are you not of more value than they? [27]And which of you by being anxious can add one cubit to his span of life?[k] [28]And why are you anxious about clothing? Consider the lilies of the field, how they grow; they neither toil nor spin; [29]yet I tell you, even Solomon in all his glory was not arrayed like one of these. [30]But if God so clothes the grass of the field, which today is alive and tomorrow is thrown into the oven,

πόσον. 24 Οὐδεὶς δύναται δυσὶ κυρίοις
how great.   No one   can   two   lords

δουλεύειν· ἢ γὰρ τὸν ἕνα μισήσει καὶ
to serve;   for either   the   one   he will hate   and

τὸν ἕτερον ἀγαπήσει, ἢ ἑνὸς ἀνθέξεται
the   other   he will love,   or   one   he will hold to

καὶ τοῦ ἑτέρου καταφρονήσει. οὐ δύνασθε
and   the   other   he will despise.   Ye cannot

θεῷ δουλεύειν καὶ μαμωνᾷ. 25 Διὰ
God   to serve   and   mammon.   There-

τοῦτο λέγω ὑμῖν· μὴ μεριμνᾶτε τῇ
fore   I say   to you: Be not anxious   for the

ψυχῇ ὑμῶν τί φάγητε [ἢ τί πίητε],
life   of you[,]   what ye may eat   or what ye may drink,

μηδὲ τῷ σώματι ὑμῶν τί ἐνδύσησθε.
nor   for the   body   of you[,]   what ye may put on.

οὐχὶ ἡ ψυχὴ πλεῖόν ἐστιν τῆς τροφῆς καὶ τὸ
²not ³the ⁴life   ⁵more   ¹Is [than] the   food   and   the

σῶμα τοῦ ἐνδύματος; 26 ἐμβλέψατε εἰς
body [than] the   raiment?   Look ye   at

τὰ πετεινὰ τοῦ οὐρανοῦ, ὅτι οὐ σπείρουσιν
the   birds   of heaven,   that   they sow not

οὐδὲ θερίζουσιν οὐδὲ συνάγουσιν εἰς
nor   reap   nor   gather   into

ἀποθήκας, καὶ ὁ πατὴρ ὑμῶν ὁ οὐράνιος
barns,   and the ²Father ³of you – ¹heavenly

τρέφει αὐτά· οὐχ ὑμεῖς μᾶλλον διαφέρετε
feeds   them;   do not ye   more   excel

αὐτῶν; 27 τίς δὲ ἐξ ὑμῶν μεριμνῶν
them?   But who   of   you   being anxious

δύναται προσθεῖναι ἐπὶ τὴν ἡλικίαν αὐτοῦ
can   to add   to   the   stature   of him

πῆχυν ἕνα; 28 καὶ περὶ ἐνδύματος τί
cubit   one?   and concerning   clothing   why

μεριμνᾶτε; καταμάθετε τὰ κρίνα τοῦ ἀγροῦ,
be ye anxious?   consider   the   lilies   of the field,

πῶς αὐξάνουσιν· οὐ κοπιῶσιν οὐδὲ
how   they grow;   they labour not   nor

νήθουσιν. 29 λέγω δὲ ὑμῖν ὅτι οὐδὲ Σολομὼν
spin;   but I tell   you   that not   Solomon

ἐν πάσῃ τῇ δόξῃ αὐτοῦ περιεβάλετο ὡς
in   all   the   glory   of him   was clothed   as

ἓν τούτων. 30 εἰ δὲ τὸν χόρτον τοῦ
one   of these.   But if   the   grass   of the

ἀγροῦ σήμερον ὄντα καὶ αὔριον εἰς
field   to-day   being   and   to-morrow   into

κλίβανον βαλλόμενον ὁ θεὸς οὕτως
an oven   being thrown   –   God   thus

[k] Or to his stature

will he not much more clothe you, O men of little faith? ³¹Therefore do not be anxious, saying, 'What shall we eat?' or 'What shall we drink?' or 'What shall we wear?' ³²For the Gentiles seek all these things; and your heavenly Father knows that you need them all. ³³But seek first his kingdom and his righteousness, and all these things shall be yours as well.

34 "Therefore do not be anxious about tomorrow, for tomorrow will be anxious for itself. Let the day's own trouble be sufficient for the day.

ἀμφιέννυσιν,	οὐ	πολλῷ	μᾶλλον	ὑμᾶς,
clothes,	not	much	more	you,

ὀλιγόπιστοι;	31 μὴ	οὖν	μεριμνήσητε
little-faiths?	Therefore be ye not anxious

λέγοντες·	τί	φάγωμεν;	ἤ·	τί
saying:	What	may we eat?	or:	What

πίωμεν;	ἤ·	τί	περιβαλώμεθα;	32 πάντα
may we drink?	or:	What	may we put on?	²all

γὰρ	ταῦτα	τὰ	ἔθνη	ἐπιζητοῦσιν·	οἶδεν
¹for	these things	the	nations	seek after;	⁵knows

γὰρ	ὁ	πατὴρ	ὑμῶν	ὁ	οὐράνιος	ὅτι
¹for	the	⁴Father	⁵of you	–	³heavenly	that

χρῄζετε	τούτων	ἁπάντων.	33 ζητεῖτε δὲ
ye need	these things	of all.	But seek ye

πρῶτον	τὴν	βασιλείαν	καὶ	τὴν	δικαιοσύνην
first	the	kingdom	and	the	righteousness

αὐτοῦ,	καὶ	ταῦτα	πάντα	προστεθήσεται
of him,	and	these things	all	shall be added

ὑμῖν.	34 μὴ	οὖν	μεριμνήσητε	εἰς	τὴν
to you.	Therefore be ye not anxious	for	the

αὔριον,	ἡ	γὰρ	αὔριον	μεριμνήσει
morrow,	for the	morrow	will be anxious

ἑαυτῆς·	ἀρκετὸν	τῇ	ἡμέρᾳ	ἡ	κακία	αὐτῆς.
of itself;	sufficient	to the	day	the	evil	of it.

CHAPTER 7

"JUDGE not, that you be not judged. ²For with the judgment you pronounce you will be judged, and the measure you give will be the measure you get. ³Why do you see the speck that is in your brother's eye, but do not notice the log that is in your own eye? ⁴Or how can you say to your brother, 'Let me take the speck out of your eye,' when there is the log in your own eye? ⁵You hypocrite, first take the log out of your own eye, and then you will

7 Μὴ	κρίνετε,	ἵνα	μὴ	κριθῆτε·	2 ἐν	ᾧ
Judge not,	lest	ye be judged;	²with	²what

γὰρ	κρίματι	κρίνετε	κριθήσεσθε,	καὶ
¹for	judgment	ye judge	ye shall be judged,	and

ἐν	ᾧ	μέτρῳ	μετρεῖτε	μετρηθήσεται	ὑμῖν.
with what	measure	ye measure	it shall be measured to you.

3 τί	δὲ	βλέπεις	τὸ	κάρφος	τὸ	ἐν
And why	seest thou	the	chip	the	–	in

τῷ	ὀφθαλμῷ	τοῦ	ἀδελφοῦ	σου,	τὴν
the	eye	of the	brother	of thee,	²the

δὲ	ἐν	τῷ	σῷ	ὀφθαλμῷ	δοκὸν	οὐ	κατα-
¹but	²in	–	³thine	⁴eye	⁵beam	thou consider-

νοεῖς;	4 ἢ	πῶς	ἐρεῖς	τῷ	ἀδελφῷ	σου·
est not?	or	how	wilt thou say	to the	brother	of thee:

ἄφες	ἐκβάλω	τὸ	κάρφος	ἐκ	τοῦ	ὀφθαλμοῦ
Allow [that]	I may pluck out	the	chip	out of the	eye

σου,	καὶ	ἰδοὺ	ἡ	δοκὸς	ἐν	τῷ	ὀφθαλμῷ
of thee,	and	behold	the	beam	in	the	eye

σου;	5 ὑποκριτά,	ἔκβαλε	πρῶτον	ἐκ	τοῦ
of thee?	hypocrite,	pluck out	first	out of the

ὀφθαλμοῦ	σου	τὴν	δοκόν,	καὶ	τότε
eye	of thee	the	beam,	and	then

see clearly to take the
speck out of your
brother's eye.

6 "Do not give dogs
what is holy; and do not
throw your pearls before
swine, lest they trample
them underfoot and turn
to attack you.

7 "Ask, and it will be
given you; seek, and you
will find; knock, and it
will be opened to you.
[8] For every one who asks
receives, and he who
seeks finds, and to him
who knocks it will be
opened. [9] Or what man
of you, if his son asks
him for bread, will give
him a stone? [10] Or if he
asks for a fish, will give
him a serpent? [11] If you
then, who are evil, know
how to give good gifts to
your children, how much
more will your Father
who is in heaven give
good things to those who
ask him? [12] So whatever
you wish that men would
do to you, do so to them;
for this is the law and the
prophets.

13 "Enter by the nar-
row gate; for the gate is
wide and the way is easy,[1]

διαβλέψεις ἐκβαλεῖν τὸ κάρφος ἐκ
thou wilt see clearly to pluck *out* the chip out of

τοῦ ὀφθαλμοῦ τοῦ ἀδελφοῦ σου. 6 Μὴ
the eye of the brother of thee. not

δῶτε τὸ ἅγιον τοῖς κυσίν, μηδὲ βάλητε
Give the holy to the dogs, neither cast

τοὺς μαργαρίτας ὑμῶν ἔμπροσθεν τῶν
the pearls of you before the

χοίρων, μήποτε καταπατήσουσιν αὐτοὺς
pigs, lest they will trample them

ἐν τοῖς ποσὶν αὐτῶν καὶ στραφέντες
with the feet of them and turning

ῥήξωσιν ὑμᾶς. 7 Αἰτεῖτε, καὶ δοθήσεται
may rend you. Ask, and it shall be given

ὑμῖν· ζητεῖτε, καὶ εὑρήσετε· κρούετε,
to you; seek, and ye shall find; knock,

καὶ ἀνοιγήσεται ὑμῖν. 8 πᾶς γὰρ ὁ αἰτῶν
and it shall be opened to you. For every asking [one]

λαμβάνει, καὶ ὁ ζητῶν εὑρίσκει, καὶ
receives, and the seeking [one] finds, and

τῷ κρούοντι ἀνοιγήσεται. 9 ἢ τίς ἐστιν
to the knocking [one] it shall be opened. Or [1]what [2]is there

ἐξ ὑμῶν ἄνθρωπος, ὃν αἰτήσει ὁ υἱὸς
[6]of [7]you [3]man, whom [4]will ask [5]the [2]son

αὐτοῦ ἄρτον, μὴ λίθον ἐπιδώσει αὐτῷ;
[1]of him [3]a loaf, *not* a stone he will give him?

10 ἢ καὶ ἰχθὺν αἰτήσει, μὴ ὄφιν ἐπιδώσει
or also a fish he will ask, *not* a serpent he will give

αὐτῷ; 11 εἰ οὖν ὑμεῖς πονηροὶ ὄντες
him? If therefore ye [2]evil [1]being

οἴδατε δόματα ἀγαθὰ διδόναι τοῖς τέκνοις
know [3]gifts [2]good [1]to give to the children

ὑμῶν, πόσῳ μᾶλλον ὁ πατὴρ ὑμῶν ὁ
of you, how much more the Father of you

ἐν τοῖς οὐρανοῖς δώσει ἀγαθὰ τοῖς
in the heavens will give good things to the [ones]

αἰτοῦσιν αὐτόν. 12 Πάντα οὖν ὅσα ἐὰν
asking him. All things therefore as many soever as

θέλητε ἵνα ποιῶσιν ὑμῖν οἱ ἄνθρωποι,
ye wish that may do to you — men,

οὕτως καὶ ὑμεῖς ποιεῖτε αὐτοῖς· οὗτος
thus also ye do to them; [2]this

γάρ ἐστιν ὁ νόμος καὶ οἱ προφῆται.
[1]for is the law and the prophets.

13 Εἰσέλθατε διὰ τῆς στενῆς πύλης·
Enter ye in through the narrow gate;

ὅτι πλατεῖα [ἡ πύλη] καὶ εὐρύχωρος
because wide the gate and broad

---

[1] Other ancient authorities
read *for the way is wide and
easy*

that leads to destruction, and those who enter by it are many. ¹⁴For the gate is narrow and the way is hard, that leads to life, and those who find it are few.

15 "Beware of false prophets, who come to you in sheep's clothing but inwardly are ravenous wolves. ¹⁶You will know them by their fruits. Are grapes gathered from thorns, or figs from thistles? ¹⁷So, every sound tree bears good fruit, but the bad tree bears evil fruit. ¹⁸A sound tree cannot bear evil fruit, nor can a bad tree bear good fruit. ¹⁹Every tree that does not bear good fruit is cut down and thrown into the fire. ²⁰Thus you will know them by their fruits.

21 "Not every one who says to me, 'Lord, Lord,' shall enter the kingdom of heaven, but he who does the will of my Father who is in heaven. ²²On that day many will say to me, 'Lord, Lord, did we not

ἡ ὁδὸς ἡ ἀπάγουσα εἰς τὴν ἀπώλειαν,
the way – leading away to – destruction,

καὶ πολλοί εἰσιν οἱ εἰσερχόμενοι δι'
and many are the [ones] going in through

αὐτῆς· 14 ὅτι στενὴ ἡ πύλη καὶ τεθλιμ-
it; because strait the gate and made

μένη ἡ ὁδὸς ἡ ἀπάγουσα εἰς τὴν ζωήν,
narrow the way – leading away to – life,

καὶ ὀλίγοι εἰσὶν οἱ εὑρίσκοντες αὐτήν.
and few are the [ones] finding it.

15 Προσέχετε ἀπὸ τῶν ψευδοπροφητῶν,
Beware from(of) – false prophets,

οἵτινες ἔρχονται πρὸς ὑμᾶς ἐν ἐνδύμασι
who come to you in clothes

προβάτων, ἔσωθεν δέ εἰσιν λύκοι ἅρπαγες.
of sheep, but within are wolves greedy.

16 ἀπὸ τῶν καρπῶν αὐτῶν ἐπιγνώσεσθε
From the fruits of them ye will know

αὐτούς. μήτι συλλέγουσιν ἀπὸ ἀκανθῶν σταφυλὰς
them. They do not gather from thorns grapes

ἢ ἀπὸ τριβόλων σῦκα; 17 οὕτως πᾶν
or from thistles figs? So ¹every

δένδρον ἀγαθὸν καρποὺς καλοὺς ποιεῖ,
³tree ²good ⁶fruits ⁵good ⁴produces,

τὸ δὲ σαπρὸν δένδρον καρποὺς πονηροὺς
but the corrupt tree fruits evil

ποιεῖ. 18 οὐ δύναται δένδρον ἀγαθὸν
produces. ³Cannot ²tree ¹a good

καρποὺς πονηροὺς ἐνεγκεῖν, οὐδὲ δένδρον
⁶fruits ⁵evil ⁴to bear, nor ²tree

σαπρὸν καρποὺς καλοὺς ἐνεγκεῖν. 19 πᾶν
¹a corrupt ⁶fruits ⁴good ³to bear. Every

δένδρον μὴ ποιοῦν καρπὸν καλὸν ἐκκόπτεται
tree not producing fruit good is cut down

καὶ εἰς πῦρ βάλλεται. 20 ἄρα γε ἀπὸ
and into fire is cast. Therefore from

τῶν καρπῶν αὐτῶν ἐπιγνώσεσθε αὐτούς.
the fruits of them ye will know them.

21 Οὐ πᾶς ὁ λέγων μοι κύριε κύριε,
Not everyone saying to me Lord[,] Lord,

εἰσελεύσεται εἰς τὴν βασιλείαν τῶν οὐρανῶν,
will enter into the kingdom of the heavens,

ἀλλ' ὁ ποιῶν τὸ θέλημα τοῦ πατρός
but the [one] doing the will of the Father

μου τοῦ ἐν τοῖς οὐρανοῖς. 22 πολλοί
of me – in the heavens. Many

ἐροῦσίν μοι ἐν ἐκείνῃ τῇ ἡμέρᾳ· κύριε
will say to me in that – day· Lord[,]

prophesy in your name, and cast out demons in your name, and do many mighty works in your name?' [23]And then will I declare to them, 'I never knew you; depart from me, you evildoers.'

[24] "Every one then who hears these words of mine and does them will be like a wise man who built his house upon the rock; [25]and the rain fell, and the floods came, and the winds blew and beat upon that house, but it did not fall, because it had been founded on the rock. [26]And every one who hears these words of mine and does not do them will be like a foolish man who built his house upon the sand; [27]and the rain fell, and the floods came, and the winds blew and beat against that house, and it fell; and great was the fall of it."

κύριε, οὐ τῷ σῷ ὀνόματι ἐπροφητεύσαμεν,
Lord, not - in thy name we prophesied,

καὶ τῷ σῷ ὀνόματι δαιμόνια ἐξεβάλομεν,
and - in thy name demons we expelled,

καὶ τῷ σῷ ὀνόματι δυνάμεις πολλὰς
and - in thy name mighty works many

ἐποιήσαμεν; 23 καὶ τότε ὁμολογήσω
did? and then I will declare

αὐτοῖς ὅτι οὐδέποτε ἔγνων ὑμᾶς· ἀπο-
to them[.] - Never I knew you; de-

χωρεῖτε ἀπ᾽ ἐμοῦ οἱ ἐργαζόμενοι τὴν
part from me the [ones] working -

ἀνομίαν.
lawlessness.

24 Πᾶς οὖν ὅστις ἀκούει μου τοὺς
Everyone therefore who hears of me -

λόγους τούτους καὶ ποιεῖ αὐτούς,
words these and does them,

ὁμοιωθήσεται ἀνδρὶ φρονίμῳ, ὅστις ᾠκοδό-
shall be likened man to a prudent, who built

μησεν αὐτοῦ τὴν οἰκίαν ἐπὶ τὴν πέτραν.
of him the house on the rock.

25 καὶ κατέβη ἡ βροχὴ καὶ ἦλθον οἱ
And came down the rain and came the

ποταμοὶ καὶ ἔπνευσαν οἱ ἄνεμοι καὶ
rivers and blew the winds and

προσέπεσαν τῇ οἰκίᾳ ἐκείνῃ, καὶ οὐκ
fell against - house that, and not

ἔπεσεν· τεθεμελίωτο γὰρ ἐπὶ τὴν
it fell; for it had been founded on the

πέτραν. 26 καὶ πᾶς ὁ ἀκούων μου
rock. And everyone hearing of me

τοὺς λόγους τούτους καὶ μὴ ποιῶν
- words these and not doing

αὐτοὺς ὁμοιωθήσεται ἀνδρὶ μωρῷ, ὅστις
them shall be likened man to a foolish, who

ᾠκοδόμησεν αὐτοῦ τὴν οἰκίαν ἐπὶ τὴν
built of him the house on the

ἄμμον. 27 καὶ κατέβη ἡ βροχὴ καὶ
sand. And came down the rain and

ἦλθον οἱ ποταμοὶ καὶ ἔπνευσαν οἱ
came the rivers and blew the

ἄνεμοι καὶ προσέκοψαν τῇ οἰκίᾳ ἐκείνῃ,
winds and beat against - house that,

καὶ ἔπεσεν, καὶ ἦν ἡ πτῶσις αὐτῆς
and it fell, and was the fall of it

μεγάλη.
great.

28 And when Jesus finished these sayings, the crowds were astonished at his teaching, [29]for he taught them as one who had authority, and not as their scribes.

28 Καὶ ἐγένετο ὅτε ἐτέλεσεν ὁ Ἰησοῦς
And it came to pass when finished – Jesus

τοὺς λόγους τούτους, ἐξεπλήσσοντο οἱ
– words these, were astounded the

ὄχλοι ἐπὶ τῇ διδαχῇ αὐτοῦ· 29 ἦν γὰρ
crowds at the teaching of him; for he was

διδάσκων αὐτοὺς ὡς ἐξουσίαν ἔχων, καὶ
teaching them as authority having, and

οὐχ ὡς οἱ γραμματεῖς αὐτῶν.
not as the scribes of them.

CHAPTER 8

WHEN he came down from the mountain, great crowds followed him; [2]and behold, a leper came to him and knelt before him, saying, "Lord, if you will, you can make me clean." [3]And he stretched out his hand and touched him, saying, "I will; be clean." And immediately his leprosy was cleansed. [4]And Jesus said to him, "See that you say nothing to any one; but go, show yourself to the priest, and offer the gift that Moses commanded, for a proof to the people."

[5]As he entered Caper′na-um, a centurion came forward to him, beseeching him [6]and saying, "Lord, my servant is lying paralyzed at home, in terrible distress." [7]And he said to him, "I will come and heal him."

8 Καταβάντος δὲ αὐτοῦ ἀπὸ τοῦ ὄρους
And coming down himᵃ from the mountain
= as he came down

ἠκολούθησαν αὐτῷ ὄχλοι πολλοί. 2 καὶ
followed him crowds many. And

ἰδοὺ λεπρὸς προσελθὼν προσεκύνει αὐτῷ
behold a leper approaching worshipped him

λέγων· κύριε, ἐὰν θέλῃς, δύνασαί με
saying: Lord, if thou art willing, thou art able me

καθαρίσαι. 3 καὶ ἐκτείνας τὴν χεῖρα
to cleanse. And stretching out the(his) hand

ἥψατο αὐτοῦ λέγων· θέλω, καθαρίσθητι.
he touched him saying: I am willing, be thou cleansed.

καὶ εὐθέως ἐκαθαρίσθη αὐτοῦ ἡ λέπρα.
And immediately was cleansed of him the leprosy.

4 καὶ λέγει αὐτῷ ὁ Ἰησοῦς· ὅρα μηδενὶ
And says to him – Jesus: See to no one

εἴπῃς, ἀλλὰ ὕπαγε σεαυτὸν δεῖξον τῷ
thou tellest, but go thyself show to the

ἱερεῖ καὶ προσένεγκον τὸ δῶρον ὃ
priest and offer the gift which

προσέταξεν Μωϋσῆς, εἰς μαρτύριον αὐτοῖς.
commanded Moses, for a testimony to them.

5 Εἰσελθόντος δὲ αὐτοῦ εἰς Καφαρναοὺμ
And entering himᵃ into Capernaum,
= as he entered

προσῆλθεν αὐτῷ ἑκατόνταρχος παρακαλῶν
approached to him a centurion beseeching

αὐτὸν 6 καὶ λέγων· κύριε, ὁ παῖς μου
him and saying: Lord, the boy of me

βέβληται ἐν τῇ οἰκίᾳ παραλυτικός,
has been laid [aside] in the house a paralytic,

δεινῶς βασανιζόμενος. 7 λέγει αὐτῷ·
terribly being tortured. He says to him:

ἐγὼ ἐλθὼν θεραπεύσω αὐτόν. 8 ἀποκριθεὶς
I coming will heal him. answering

⁸But the centurion answered him, "Lord, I am not worthy to have you come under my roof; but only say the word, and my servant will be healed. ⁹For I am a man under authority, with soldiers under me; and I say to one, 'Go,' and he goes, and to another, 'Come,' and he comes, and to my slave, 'Do this,' and he does it." ¹⁰When Jesus heard him, he marveled, and said to those who followed him, "Truly, I say to you, not even^m in Israel have I found such faith. ¹¹I tell you, many will come from east and west and sit at table with Abraham, Isaac, and Jacob in the kingdom of heaven, ¹²while the sons of the kingdom will be thrown into the outer darkness; there men will weep and gnash their teeth." ¹³And to the centurion Jesus said, "Go; be it done for you as you have believed." And the servant was healed at that very moment.

14 And when Jesus entered Peter's house, he saw his mother-in-law lying sick with a fever;

^m Other ancient authorities read with no one

δὲ ὁ ἑκατόνταρχος ἔφη· κύριε, οὐκ εἰμὶ
But the centurion said: Lord, I am not
ἱκανὸς ἵνα μου ὑπὸ τὴν στέγην εἰσέλθῃς·
worthy that of me under the roof thou mayest enter;
ἀλλὰ μόνον εἰπὲ λόγῳ, καὶ ἰαθήσεται ὁ παῖς
but only say in a word, and will be healed the boy
μου. 9 καὶ γὰρ ἐγὼ ἄνθρωπός εἰμι
of me. ²also ¹For ²I ⁶a man ⁴am
ὑπὸ ἐξουσίαν, ἔχων ὑπ' ἐμαυτὸν στρατιώτας,
under authority, having under myself soldiers,
καὶ λέγω τούτῳ· πορεύθητι, καὶ πορεύεται,
and I say to this: Go, and he goes,
καὶ ἄλλῳ· ἔρχου, καὶ ἔρχεται, καὶ τῷ
and to another: Come, and he comes, and to the
δούλῳ μου· ποίησον τοῦτο, καὶ ποιεῖ.
slave of me: Do this, and he does [it].
10 ἀκούσας δὲ ὁ Ἰησοῦς ἐθαύμασεν
And hearing - Jesus marvelled
καὶ εἶπεν τοῖς ἀκολουθοῦσιν· ἀμὴν λέγω
and said to the [ones] following: Truly I tell
ὑμῖν, παρ' οὐδενὶ τοσαύτην πίστιν ἐν τῷ
you, from no one such faith in -
Ἰσραὴλ εὗρον. 11 λέγω δὲ ὑμῖν ὅτι
Israel I found. And I tell you that
πολλοὶ ἀπὸ ἀνατολῶν καὶ δυσμῶν ἥξουσιν
many from east and west will come
καὶ ἀνακλιθήσονται μετὰ Ἀβραὰμ καὶ
and will recline with Abraham and
Ἰσαὰκ καὶ Ἰακὼβ ἐν τῇ βασιλείᾳ τῶν
Isaac and Jacob in the kingdom of the
οὐρανῶν· 12 οἱ δὲ υἱοὶ τῆς βασιλείας
heavens; but the sons of the kingdom
ἐκβληθήσονται εἰς τὸ σκότος τὸ ἐξώτερον·
will be cast out into the darkness - outer:
ἐκεῖ ἔσται ὁ κλαυθμὸς καὶ ὁ βρυγμὸς
there will be the weeping and the gnashing
τῶν ὀδόντων. 13 καὶ εἶπεν ὁ Ἰησοῦς τῷ
of the teeth. And said - Jesus to the
ἑκατοντάρχῃ· ὕπαγε, ὡς ἐπίστευσας γενη-
centurion: Go, as thou believedst let it
θήτω σοι. καὶ ἰάθη ὁ παῖς ἐν τῇ
be to thee. And was healed the boy in -
ὥρᾳ ἐκείνῃ.
hour that.
14 Καὶ ἐλθὼν ὁ Ἰησοῦς εἰς τὴν οἰκίαν
And coming - Jesus into the house
Πέτρου εἶδεν τὴν πενθερὰν αὐτοῦ βεβλη-
of Peter he saw the mother-in-law of him having been

¹⁵he touched her hand, and the fever left her, and she rose and served him. ¹⁶That evening they brought to him many who were possessed with demons; and he cast out the spirits with a word, and healed all who were sick. ¹⁷This was to fulfil what was spoken by the prophet Isaiah, "He took our infirmities and bore our diseases."

18 Now when Jesus saw great crowds around him, he gave orders to go over to the other side. ¹⁹And a scribe came up and said to him, "Teacher, I will follow you wherever you go." ²⁰And Jesus said to him, "Foxes have holes, and birds of the air have nests; but the Son of man has nowhere to lay his head." ²¹Another of the disciples said to him, "Lord, let me first go and bury my father." ²²But Jesus said to him, "Follow me, and

μένην καὶ πυρέσσουσαν·
laid [aside] and fever-stricken;

15 καὶ ἥψατο
and he touched

τῆς χειρὸς αὐτῆς, καὶ ἀφῆκεν αὐτὴν ὁ
the hand of her, and left her the

πυρετός· καὶ ἠγέρθη, καὶ διηκόνει αὐτῷ.
fever; and she arose, and ministered to him.

16 Ὀψίας δὲ γενομένης προσήνεγκαν
And evening coming° they brought
= when evening came

αὐτῷ δαιμονιζομένους πολλούς· καὶ ἐξέβαλεν
to him being demon-possessed many; and he expelled

τὰ πνεύματα λόγῳ, καὶ πάντας τοὺς
the spirits with a word, and all the [ones]
= those

κακῶς ἔχοντας ἐθεράπευσεν·
ill having he healed;
who were ill

17 ὅπως
so that

πληρωθῇ τὸ ῥηθὲν διὰ Ἡσαΐου τοῦ
was fulfilled the [thing] spoken through Isaiah the

προφήτου λέγοντος· αὐτὸς τὰς ἀσθενείας
prophet saying: He the weaknesses

ἡμῶν ἔλαβεν καὶ τὰς νόσους ἐβάστασεν.
of us took and the diseases he bore.

18 Ἰδὼν δὲ ὁ Ἰησοῦς ὄχλον περὶ
But ²seeing - ¹Jesus a crowd around

αὐτὸν ἐκέλευσεν ἀπελθεῖν εἰς τὸ πέραν.
him commanded to go away to the other side.

19 Καὶ προσελθὼν εἷς γραμματεὺς εἶπεν
And approaching one scribe said

αὐτῷ· διδάσκαλε, ἀκολουθήσω σοι
to him: Teacher, I will follow thee

ὅπου ἐὰν ἀπέρχῃ. 20 καὶ λέγει αὐτῷ
wherever thou mayest go. And says to him

ὁ Ἰησοῦς· αἱ ἀλώπεκες φωλεοὺς ἔχουσιν
- Jesus: The foxes holes have

καὶ τὰ πετεινὰ τοῦ οὐρανοῦ κατα-
and the birds of the heaven nests,

σκηνώσεις, ὁ δὲ υἱὸς τοῦ ἀνθρώπου
but the Son - of man

οὐκ ἔχει ποῦ τὴν κεφαλὴν κλίνῃ.
has not where the(his) head he may lay.

21 ἕτερος δὲ τῶν μαθητῶν εἶπεν
And another of the disciples said

αὐτῷ· κύριε, ἐπίτρεψόν μοι πρῶτον
to him: Lord, allow me first

ἀπελθεῖν καὶ θάψαι τὸν πατέρα μου.
to go away and bury the father of me.

22 ὁ δὲ Ἰησοῦς λέγει αὐτῷ· ἀκολούθει
- But Jesus says to him: Follow thou

leave the dead to bury their own dead."

23 And when he got into the boat, his disciples followed him. [24]And behold, there arose a great storm on the sea, so that the boat was being swamped by the waves; but he was asleep. [25]And they went and woke him, saying, "Save, Lord; we are perishing." [26]And he said to them, "Why are you afraid, O men of little faith?" Then he rose and rebuked the winds and the sea; and there was a great calm. [27]And the men marveled, saying, "What sort of man is this, that even winds and sea obey him?"

28 And when he came to the other side, to the country of the Gadarenes,[n] two demoniacs met him, coming out of the tombs, so fierce that no one could pass that way. [29]And behold, they cried out, "What have you to do with us, O Son of God? Have you come here to torment us before the time?" [30]Now a herd

μοι, καὶ ἄφες τοὺς νεκροὺς θάψαι τοὺς
me, and leave the dead to bury the

ἑαυτῶν νεκρούς.
of themselves dead.

23 Καὶ ἐμβάντι αὐτῷ εἰς τὸ πλοῖον,
And embarking him⁵ in the ship,
=as he embarked

ἠκολούθησαν αὐτῷ οἱ μαθηταὶ αὐτοῦ.
followed him the disciples of him.

24 καὶ ἰδοὺ σεισμὸς μέγας ἐγένετο ἐν
And behold storm a great there was in

τῇ θαλάσσῃ, ὥστε τὸ πλοῖον καλύπτ-
the sea, so as the ship to be en-

εσθαι ὑπὸ τῶν κυμάτων· αὐτὸς δὲ ἐκάθευδεν.
veloped by the waves; but he was sleeping.

25 καὶ προσελθόντες ἤγειραν αὐτὸν λέγοντες·
And approaching they roused him saying:

κύριε, σῶσον, ἀπολλύμεθα. 26 καὶ λέγει
Lord, save, we are perishing. And he says

αὐτοῖς· τί δειλοί ἐστε, ὀλιγόπιστοι;
to them: Why fearful are ye, little-faiths?

τότε ἐγερθεὶς ἐπετίμησεν τοῖς ἀνέμοις καὶ
Then rising he rebuked the winds and

τῇ θαλάσσῃ, καὶ ἐγένετο γαλήνη μεγάλη.
the sea, and there was calm a great.

27 οἱ δὲ ἄνθρωποι ἐθαύμασαν λέγοντες·
And the men marvelled saying:

ποταπός ἐστιν οὗτος, ὅτι καὶ οἱ ἄνεμοι
Of what sort is this [man], that even the winds

καὶ ἡ θάλασσα αὐτῷ ὑπακούουσιν;
and the sea him obey?

28 Καὶ ἐλθόντος αὐτοῦ εἰς τὸ πέραν εἰς
And coming him⁴ to the other side into
=when he came

τὴν χώραν τῶν Γαδαρηνῶν ὑπήντησαν
the country of the Gadarenes met

αὐτῷ δύο δαιμονιζόμενοι ἐκ τῶν μνημείων
him two demon-possessed out of the tombs

ἐξερχόμενοι, χαλεποὶ λίαν, ὥστε μὴ
coming out, dangerous exceedingly, so as not

ἰσχύειν τινὰ παρελθεῖν διὰ τῆς ὁδοῦ
to be able anyone⁵ to pass through - way

ἐκείνης. 29 καὶ ἰδοὺ ἔκραξαν λέγοντες·
that. And behold they cried out saying:

τί ἡμῖν καὶ σοί, υἱὲ τοῦ θεοῦ; ἦλθες
What to us and to thee, Son - of God? camest thou

ὧδε πρὸ καιροῦ βασανίσαι ἡμᾶς; 30 ἦν
here before [the] time to torture us? there was

of many swine was feeding at some distance from them. ³¹And the demons begged him, "If you cast us out, send us away into the herd of swine." ³²And he said to them, "Go." So they came out and went into the swine; and behold, the whole herd rushed down the steep bank into the sea, and perished in the waters. ³³The herdsmen fled, and going into the city they told everything, and what had happened to the demoniacs. ³⁴And behold, all the city came out to meet Jesus; and when they saw him, they begged him to leave their neighborhood.

δὲ	μακρὰν	ἀπ'	αὐτῶν	ἀγέλη	χοίρων
Now	far off	from	them	a herd	pigs

πολλῶν	βοσκομένη.	**31** οἱ	δὲ	δαίμονες
of many	feeding.	And the		demons

παρεκάλουν	αὐτὸν	λέγοντες·	εἰ	ἐκβάλλεις
besought	him	saying:	If	thou expellest

ἡμᾶς,	ἀπόστειλον	ἡμᾶς	εἰς	τὴν	ἀγέλην
us,	send	us	into	the	herd

τῶν	χοίρων.	**32** καὶ	εἶπεν	αὐτοῖς·
of the	pigs.	And	he said	to them:

ὑπάγετε.	οἱ δὲ	ἐξελθόντες	ἀπῆλθον	εἰς
Go ye.	So the	coming out [ones]	went away	into

τοὺς	χοίρους·	καὶ	ἰδοὺ	ὥρμησεν	πᾶσα	ἡ
the	pigs;	and behold	rushed	all	the

ἀγέλη	κατὰ	τοῦ	κρημνοῦ	εἰς	τὴν	θάλασσαν,
herd	down	the	precipice	into	the	sea,

καὶ	ἀπέθανον	ἐν	τοῖς	ὕδασιν.	**33** οἱ
and	died	in	the	waters.	the

δὲ	βόσκοντες	ἔφυγον,	καὶ	ἀπελθόντες
But	feeding [ones]	fled,	and	going away

εἰς	τὴν	πόλιν	ἀπήγγειλαν	πάντα	καὶ
into	the	city	reported	all things	and

τὰ	τῶν	δαιμονιζομένων.	**34** καὶ	ἰδοὺ
the [things]	of the	demon-possessed [ones].	And behold

πᾶσα	ἡ	πόλις	ἐξῆλθεν	εἰς	ὑπάντησιν
all	the	city	came out	with a view to	a meeting [with]

τῷ	Ἰησοῦ,	καὶ	ἰδόντες	αὐτὸν	παρεκάλεσαν
-	Jesus,	and	seeing	²him	¹besought

ὅπως	μεταβῇ	ἀπὸ	τῶν	ὁρίων	αὐτῶν.
so that	he might remove	from	the	borders	of them.

CHAPTER 9

AND getting into a boat he crossed over and came to his own city. ²And behold, they brought to him a paralytic, lying on his bed; and when Jesus saw their faith he said to the paralytic, "Take heart, my son; your sins are forgiven." ³And behold, some of the scribes said to themselves, "This man is blaspheming." ⁴But

9 Καὶ	ἐμβὰς	εἰς	πλοῖον	διεπέρασεν,
And	embarking	in	a ship	he crossed over,

καὶ	ἦλθεν	εἰς	τὴν	ἰδίαν	πόλιν.	**2** Καὶ
and	came	into	the(his)	own	city.	And

ἰδοὺ	προσέφερον	αὐτῷ	παραλυτικὸν	ἐπὶ
behold	they brought	to him	a paralytic	on

κλίνης	βεβλημένον.	καὶ	ἰδὼν	ὁ	Ἰησοῦς
a mattress	having been laid.	And	²seeing	-	¹Jesus

τὴν	πίστιν	αὐτῶν	εἶπεν	τῷ	παραλυτικῷ
the	faith	of them	said	to the	paralytic:

θάρσει,	τέκνον,	ἀφίενταί	σου	αἱ	ἁμαρτίαι.
Be of good cheer,	child,	are forgiven	of thee	the	sins.

3 καὶ	ἰδού	τινες	τῶν	γραμματέων	εἶπαν
And behold	some	of the	scribes	said

ἐν	ἑαυτοῖς·	οὗτος	βλασφημεῖ.	**4** καὶ
among themselves:	This [man]	blasphemes.	And

Jesus, knowing[o] their thoughts, said, "Why do you think evil in your hearts? [5]For which is easier, to say, 'Your sins are forgiven,' or to say, 'Rise and walk'? [6]But that you may know that the Son of man has authority on earth to forgive sins"—he then said to the paralytic— "Rise, take up your bed and go home." [7]And he rose and went home. [8]When the crowds saw it, they were afraid, and they glorified God, who had given such authority to men.

9 As Jesus passed on from there, he saw a man called Matthew sitting at the tax office; and he said to him, "Follow me." And he rose and followed him.

10 And as he sat at table in the house, behold, many tax collectors and sinners came and sat down with Jesus and his disciples. [11]And when the Pharisees saw this, they said to his disciples, "Why does your teacher eat with tax collectors and sinners?" [12]But when

[o] Other ancient authorities read *seeing*

εἰδὼς ὁ Ἰησοῦς τὰς ἐνθυμήσεις αὐτῶν
[²]knowing – [¹]Jesus the thoughts of them
εἶπεν· ἱνατί ἐνθυμεῖσθε πονηρὰ ἐν ταῖς
said: Why think ye evil things in the
καρδίαις ὑμῶν; 5 τί γάρ ἐστιν εὐκοπώ-
hearts of you? for which is easier,
τερον, εἰπεῖν· ἀφίενταί σου αἱ ἁμαρτίαι, ἢ
to say: [⁴]are forgiven [⁵]of thee [¹]The [²]sins, or
εἰπεῖν· ἔγειρε καὶ περιπάτει; 6 ἵνα δὲ
to say: Rise and walk? But in order that
εἰδῆτε ὅτι ἐξουσίαν ἔχει ὁ υἱὸς τοῦ
ye may know that authority has the Son –
ἀνθρώπου ἐπὶ τῆς γῆς ἀφιέναι ἁμαρτίας
of man on the earth to forgive sins—
τότε λέγει τῷ παραλυτικῷ· ἔγειρε ἆρόν
then he says to the paralytic: Rise[,] take
σου τὴν κλίνην καὶ ὕπαγε / εἰς τὸν οἶκόν
of thee the mattress and go to the house
σου. 7 καὶ ἐγερθεὶς ἀπῆλθεν εἰς τὸν
of thee. And rising he went away to the
οἶκον αὐτοῦ. 8 ἰδόντες δὲ οἱ ὄχλοι
house of him. But seeing the crowds
ἐφοβήθησαν καὶ ἐδόξασαν τὸν θεὸν τὸν
feared and glorified – God the [one]
δόντα ἐξουσίαν τοιαύτην τοῖς ἀνθρώποις.
giving [²]authority [¹]such to men.
9 Καὶ παράγων ὁ Ἰησοῦς ἐκεῖθεν εἶδεν
And [²]passing by – [¹]Jesus thence saw
ἄνθρωπον καθήμενον ἐπὶ τὸ τελώνιον,
a man sitting at the custom house,
Μαθθαῖον λεγόμενον, καὶ λέγει αὐτῷ·
Matthew named, and says to him:
ἀκολούθει μοι. καὶ ἀναστὰς ἠκολούθησεν
Follow me. And rising up he followed
αὐτῷ. 10 Καὶ ἐγένετο αὐτοῦ ἀνακει-
him. And it came to pass him reclin-
=as he was reclining
μένου ἐν τῇ οἰκίᾳ, καὶ ἰδοὺ πολλοὶ
ing[ª] in the house, and behold many
τελῶναι καὶ ἁμαρτωλοὶ ἐλθόντες συνανέκειντο
tax-collectors and sinners coming reclined at table with
τῷ Ἰησοῦ καὶ τοῖς μαθηταῖς αὐτοῦ.
– Jesus and the disciples of him.
11 καὶ ἰδόντες οἱ Φαρισαῖοι ἔλεγον τοῖς
And [²]seeing [¹]the [²]Pharisees said to the
μαθηταῖς αὐτοῦ· διὰ τί μετὰ τῶν τελωνῶν
disciples of him: Why with – tax-collectors
καὶ ἁμαρτωλῶν ἐσθίει ὁ διδάσκαλος ὑμῶν;
and sinners eats the teacher of you?

he heard it, he said, "Those who are well have no need of a physician, but those who are sick. [13]Go and learn what this means, 'I desire mercy, and not sacrifice.' For I came not to call the righteous, but sinners."

14 Then the disciples of John came to him, saying, "Why do we and the Pharisees fast,[p] but your disciples do not fast?" [15]And Jesus said to them, "Can the wedding guests mourn as long as the bridegroom is with them? The days will come, when the bridegroom is taken away from them, and then they will fast. [16]And no one puts a piece of unshrunk cloth on an old garment, for the patch tears away from the garment, and a worse tear is made. [17]Neither is new wine put into old wineskins; if it is, the skins burst, and the wine is spilled, and the skins are destroyed; but

12 ὁ δὲ ἀκούσας εἶπεν·
But he hearing said:

οὐ χρείαν ἔχουσιν οἱ ἰσχύοντες ἰατροῦ
Not need have the [ones] being strong of a physician

ἀλλ' οἱ = those
but the [ones]

κακῶς ἔχοντες. 13 πορευθέντες δὲ μάθετε
ill having. But going learn ye
who are ill.

τί ἐστιν· ἔλεος θέλω καὶ οὐ θυσίαν·
what it is: Mercy I desire and not sacrifice;

οὐ γὰρ ἦλθον καλέσαι δικαίους ἀλλὰ
not for I came to call righteous [people] but

ἁμαρτωλούς.
sinners.

14 Τότε προσέρχονται αὐτῷ οἱ μαθηταὶ
Then approach to him the disciples

'Ιωάννου λέγοντες· διὰ τί ἡμεῖς καὶ οἱ
of John saying: Why we and the

Φαρισαῖοι νηστεύομεν, οἱ δὲ μαθηταί
Pharisees fast, but the disciples

σου οὐ νηστεύουσιν; 15 καὶ εἶπεν
of thee fast not? And said

αὐτοῖς ὁ 'Ιησοῦς· μὴ δύνανται οἱ
to them - Jesus: not Can the

υἱοὶ τοῦ νυμφῶνος πενθεῖν, ἐφ' ὅσον
sons of the bridechamber to mourn, so long as

μετ' αὐτῶν ἐστιν ὁ νυμφίος; ἐλεύσονται
with them is the bridegroom? [2]will come

δὲ ἡμέραι ὅταν ἀπαρθῇ ἀπ' αὐτῶν ὁ
[1]but [2]days when is taken away from them the

νυμφίος, καὶ τότε νηστεύσουσιν. 16 οὐδεὶς
bridegroom, and then they will fast. no one

δὲ ἐπιβάλλει ἐπίβλημα ῥάκους ἀγνάφου
Now puts on a patch cloth of unfulled

ἐπὶ ἱματίῳ παλαιῷ· αἴρει γὰρ τὸ
on garment an old; for takes away the

πλήρωμα αὐτοῦ ἀπὸ τοῦ ἱματίου, καὶ
fullness of it from the garment, and

χεῖρον σχίσμα γίνεται. 17 οὐδὲ
a worse rent becomes. Neither

βάλλουσιν οἶνον νέον εἰς ἀσκοὺς
do they put wine new into wineskins

παλαιούς· εἰ δὲ μή γε, ῥήγνυνται
old; otherwise, are burst

οἱ ἀσκοί, καὶ ὁ οἶνος ἐκχεῖται καὶ
the wineskins, and the wine is poured out and

οἱ ἀσκοὶ ἀπόλλυνται. ἀλλὰ βάλλουσιν
the wineskins are destroyed. But they put

[p] Other ancient authorities add much or often

new wine is put into fresh wineskins, and so both are preserved."
18 While he was thus speaking to them, behold, a ruler came in and knelt before him, saying, "My daughter has just died; but come and lay your hand on her, and she will live." ¹⁹And Jesus rose and followed him, with his disciples. ²⁰And behold, a woman who had suffered from a hemorrhage for twelve years came up behind him and touched the fringe of his garment; ²¹for she said to herself, "If I only touch his garment, I shall be made well." ²²Jesus turned, and seeing her he said, "Take heart, daughter; your faith has made you well." And instantly the woman was made well. ²³And when Jesus came to the ruler's house, and saw the flute players, and the crowd making a tumult, ²⁴he said, "Depart; for the girl is not dead but sleeping." And they laughed at him. ²⁵But when the crowd had been put outside, he went in and

οἶνον νέον εἰς ἀσκοὺς καινούς, καὶ
wine new into wineskins fresh, and
ἀμφότεροι συντηροῦνται.
both are preserved.
18 Ταῦτα αὐτοῦ λαλοῦντος αὐτοῖς,
These things him speaking[a] to them,
=As he was speaking these things
ἰδοὺ ἄρχων [εἷς] προσελθὼν προσ-
behold ruler one approaching wor-
εκύνει αὐτῷ λέγων ὅτι ἡ θυγάτηρ
shipped him saying[,] – The daughter
μου ἄρτι ἐτελεύτησεν· ἀλλὰ ἐλθὼν
of me just now died; but coming
ἐπίθες τὴν χεῖρά σου ἐπ' αὐτήν,
lay on the hand of thee on her,
καὶ ζήσεται. 19 καὶ ἐγερθεὶς ὁ Ἰησοῦς
and she will live. And rising – Jesus
ἠκολούθει αὐτῷ καὶ οἱ μαθηταὶ αὐτοῦ.
followed him[.] also the disciples of him.
20 Καὶ ἰδοὺ γυνὴ αἱμορροοῦσα
And behold a woman suffering from a flow of blood
δώδεκα ἔτη προσελθοῦσα ὄπισθεν ἤψατο
twelve years approaching behind touched
τοῦ κρασπέδου τοῦ ἱματίου αὐτοῦ·
the fringe of the garment of him;
21 ἔλεγεν γὰρ ἐν ἑαυτῇ· ἐὰν μόνον
for she was saying in herself: If only
ἅψωμαι τοῦ ἱματίου αὐτοῦ, σωθήσομαι.
I may touch the garment of him, I shall be healed.
22 ὁ δὲ Ἰησοῦς στραφεὶς καὶ ἰδὼν
– And Jesus turning and seeing
αὐτὴν εἶπεν· θάρσει, θύγατερ· ἡ
her said: Be of good cheer, daughter; the
πίστις σου σέσωκέν σε. καὶ ἐσώθη
faith of thee has healed thee. And was healed
ἡ γυνὴ ἀπὸ τῆς ὥρας ἐκείνης. 23 Καὶ
the woman from – hour that. And
ἐλθὼν ὁ Ἰησοῦς εἰς τὴν οἰκίαν τοῦ ἄρχοντος
coming – Jesus into the house of the ruler
καὶ ἰδὼν τοὺς αὐλητὰς καὶ τὸν ὄχλον
and seeing the flute-players and the crowd
θορυβούμενον 24 ἔλεγεν· ἀναχωρεῖτε· οὐ
terrified he said: Depart ye; not
γὰρ ἀπέθανεν τὸ κοράσιον ἀλλὰ καθεύδει.
for died the girl but sleeps.
καὶ κατεγέλων αὐτοῦ. 25 ὅτε δὲ
And they ridiculed him. But when
ἐξεβλήθη ὁ ὄχλος, εἰσελθὼν ἐκράτησεν
was put out the crowd, entering he took hold of

took her by the hand, and the girl arose. 26And the report of this went through all that district.

27 And as Jesus passed on from there, two blind men followed him, crying aloud, "Have mercy on us, Son of David." 28When he entered the house, the blind men came to him; and Jesus said to them, "Do you believe that I am able to do this?" They said to him, "Yes, Lord."29Then he touched their eyes, saying, "According to your faith be it done to you." 30And their eyes were opened. And Jesus sternly charged them, "See that no one knows it." 31But they went away and spread his fame through all that district.

32 As they were going away, behold, a dumb demoniac was brought to him. 33And when the demon had been cast out, the dumb man spoke; and the crowds marveled, saying, "Never was anything like this seen in Israel." 34But the Pharisees said, "He casts out

τῆς χειρὸς αὐτῆς, καὶ ἠγέρθη τὸ κορα-
the   hand   of her,   and and was raised the   girl.

σιον.   26 καὶ ἐξῆλθεν ἡ φήμη αὕτη
        And went out — report   this

εἰς ὅλην τὴν γῆν ἐκείνην.   27 Καὶ
into   all   — land   that.   And

παράγοντι ἐκεῖθεν τῷ Ἰησοῦ ἠκολούθησαν
passing by   thence   —   Jesus[e]   followed
=as Jesus passed by thence

δύο τυφλοὶ κράζοντες καὶ λέγοντες· ἐλέησον
two blind men   crying out   and   saying: Pity

ἡμᾶς, υἱὸς Δαυίδ.   28 ἐλθόντι δὲ εἰς
us,   son   of David.   And coming[e] into
                        =when he came

τὴν οἰκίαν προσῆλθον αὐτῷ οἱ τυφλοί,
the   house   approached to him   the   blind men,

καὶ λέγει αὐτοῖς ὁ Ἰησοῦς· πιστεύετε
and   says to them   —   Jesus: Believe ye

ὅτι δύναμαι τοῦτο ποιῆσαι; λέγουσιν
that I can   this   to do?   They say

αὐτῷ· ναί, κύριε.   29 τότε ἥψατο τῶν
to him: Yes,   Lord.   Then he touched the

ὀφθαλμῶν αὐτῶν λέγων· κατὰ τὴν
eyes   of them   saying: According to the

πίστιν ὑμῶν γενηθήτω ὑμῖν.   30 καὶ
faith of you   let it be   to you.   And

ἠνεῴχθησαν αὐτῶν οἱ ὀφθαλμοί.   καὶ
were opened   of them   the   eyes.   And

ἐνεβριμήθη αὐτοῖς ὁ Ἰησοῦς λέγων·
sternly admonished them   —   Jesus   saying:

ὁρᾶτε μηδεὶς γινωσκέτω.   31 οἱ δὲ
See   [2]no one   [1]let [3]know.   But they

ἐξελθόντες διεφήμισαν αὐτὸν ἐν ὅλῃ
going out   spread about   him   in   all

τῇ γῇ ἐκείνῃ.   32 Αὐτῶν δὲ ἐξερχομένων,
— land   that.   And them   going out,[a]
                  =as they were going out,

ἰδοὺ προσήνεγκαν αὐτῷ κωφὸν δαι-
behold   they brought   to him   a dumb man being

μονιζόμενον.   33 καὶ ἐκβληθέντος τοῦ
demon-possessed.   And   being expelled   the
                    =when the demon was expelled

δαιμονίου ἐλάλησεν ὁ κωφός. καὶ ἐθαύμασαν
demon[a]   spoke   the dumb man. And marvelled

οἱ ὄχλοι λέγοντες· οὐδέποτε ἐφάνη οὕτως
the crowds   saying: Never   it appeared thus

ἐν τῷ Ἰσραήλ.   34 οἱ δὲ Φαρισαῖοι
in   —   Israel.   But the   Pharisees

demons by the prince of demons."

35 And Jesus went about all the cities and villages, teaching in their synagogues and preaching the gospel of the kingdom, and healing every disease and every infirmity. [36] When he saw the crowds, he had compassion for them, because they were harassed and helpless, like sheep without a shepherd. [37] Then he said to his disciples, "The harvest is plentiful, but the laborers are few; [38] pray therefore the Lord of the harvest to send out laborers into his harvest."

ἔλεγον·   ἐν   τῷ   ἄρχοντι   τῶν   δαιμονίων
said: By   the   ruler   of the   demons

ἐκβάλλει   τὰ   δαιμόνια.
he expels   the   demons.

35 Καὶ   περιῆγεν   ὁ   'Ιησοῦς   τὰς
   And   went about   -   Jesus   the

πόλεις   πάσας   καὶ   τὰς   κώμας,   διδάσκων
cities   all   and   the   villages,   teaching

ἐν   ταῖς   συναγωγαῖς   αὐτῶν   καὶ   κηρύσσων
in   the   synagogues   of them   and   proclaiming

τὸ   εὐαγγέλιον   τῆς   βασιλείας   καὶ   θεραπεύων
the   gospel   of the   kingdom   and   healing

πᾶσαν   νόσον   καὶ   πᾶσαν   μαλακίαν.
every   disease   and   every   illness.

36 'Ιδὼν   δὲ   τοὺς   ὄχλους   ἐσπλαγχνίσθη
   And seeing   the   crowds he was filled with tenderness

περὶ   αὐτῶν,   ὅτι   ἦσαν   ἐσκυλμένοι   καὶ
concerning   them,   because   they were   distressed   and

ἐρριμμένοι   ὡσεὶ   πρόβατα   μὴ   ἔχοντα
prostrate   as   sheep   not   having

ποιμένα.   37 τότε   λέγει   τοῖς   μαθηταῖς
a shepherd.   Then   he says   to the   disciples

αὐτοῦ·   ὁ μὲν   θερισμὸς   πολύς,   οἱ δὲ
of him: Indeed the   harvest [is]   much,   but the

ἐργάται   ὀλίγοι·   38 δεήθητε   οὖν   τοῦ   κυρίου
workmen   few;   pray ye   therefore the   Lord

τοῦ   θερισμοῦ   ὅπως   ἐκβάλῃ
of the   harvest   so that   he may thrust forth

CHAPTER 10

ἐργάτας   εἰς   τὸν   θερισμὸν   αὐτοῦ.   10 Καὶ
workmen   into   the   harvest   of him.   And

AND he called to him his twelve disciples and gave them authority over unclean spirits, to cast them out, and to heal every disease and every infirmity. [2] The names of the twelve apostles are these: first, Simon, who is called Peter, and Andrew his brother; James the son of Zeb'-edee, and John his

προσκαλεσάμενος   τοὺς   δώδεκα   μαθητὰς
calling forward   the   twelve   disciples

αὐτοῦ   ἔδωκεν   αὐτοῖς   ἐξουσίαν   πνευμάτων
of him   he gave   to them   authority   of(over) spirits

ἀκαθάρτων   ὥστε   ἐκβάλλειν   αὐτά,   καὶ
unclean   so as   to expel   them,   and

θεραπεύειν   πᾶσαν   νόσον   καὶ   πᾶσαν   μαλα-
to heal   every   disease   and   every   ill-

κίαν.   2 Τῶν   δὲ   δώδεκα   ἀποστόλων
ness.   Now of the   twelve   apostles

τὰ   ὀνόματά   ἐστιν   ταῦτα·   πρῶτος   Σίμων
the   names   is(are)   these: first   Simon

ὁ   λεγόμενος   Πέτρος   καὶ   'Ανδρέας   ὁ
the [one] named   Peter   and   Andrew   the

ἀδελφὸς   αὐτοῦ,   καὶ   'Ιάκωβος   ὁ   τοῦ
brother   of him,   and   James   the [son]   -

brother; ³Philip and Bartholomew; Thomas and Matthew the tax collector; James the son of Alphaeus, and Thaddaeus;�q ⁴Simon the Cananaean, and Judas Iscariot, who betrayed him.

5 These twelve Jesus sent out, charging them, "Go nowhere among the Gentiles, and enter no town of the Samaritans, ⁶but go rather to the lost sheep of the house of Israel. ⁷And preach as you go, saying, 'The kingdom of heaven is at hand.' ⁸Heal the sick, raise the dead, cleanse lepers, cast out demons. You received without pay, give without pay. ⁹Take no gold, nor silver, nor copper in your belts, ¹⁰no bag for your journey, nor two tunics, nor sandals, nor a staff; for the laborer deserves his food. ¹¹And whatever town or village you enter, find out who is worthy in it, and stay with him

q Other ancient authorities read Lebbaeus or Lebbaeus called Thaddaeus

Ζεβεδαίου καὶ Ἰωάννης ὁ ἀδελφὸς αὐτοῦ,
of Zebedee and John the brother of him,

3 Φίλιππος καὶ Βαρθολομαῖος, Θωμᾶς
Philip and Bartholomew, Thomas

καὶ Μαθθαῖος ὁ τελώνης, Ἰάκωβος
and Matthew the tax-collector, James

ὁ τοῦ Ἀλφαίου καὶ Θαδδαῖος, 4 Σίμων
the [son] — of Alphæus and Thaddæus, Simon

ὁ Καναναῖος καὶ Ἰούδας ὁ Ἰσκαριώτης
the Cananæan and Judas — Iscariot

ὁ καὶ παραδοὺς αὐτόν. 5 Τούτους
the [one] also betraying him. These

τοὺς δώδεκα ἀπέστειλεν ὁ Ἰησοῦς
— twelve sent forth — Jesus

παραγγείλας αὐτοῖς λέγων·
giving charge to them saying:

Εἰς ὁδὸν ἐθνῶν μὴ ἀπέλθητε, καὶ
Into [the] way of [the] nations go ye not, and

εἰς πόλιν Σαμαριτῶν μὴ εἰσέλθητε·
into a city of Samaritans enter not;

6 πορεύεσθε δὲ μᾶλλον πρὸς τὰ πρόβατα
but go rather unto the sheep

τὰ ἀπολωλότα οἴκου Ἰσραήλ. 7 πορευ-
the lost of [the] house of Israel. And going

όμενοι δὲ κηρύσσετε λέγοντες ὅτι ἤγγικεν
proclaim ye saying[,] — has drawn near

ἡ βασιλεία τῶν οὐρανῶν. 8 ἀσθενοῦντας
The kingdom of the heavens. Ailing [ones]

θεραπεύετε, νεκροὺς ἐγείρετε, λεπροὺς
heal ye, dead [ones] raise, lepers

καθαρίζετε, δαιμόνια ἐκβάλλετε· δωρεὰν
cleanse, demons expel; freely

ἐλάβετε, δωρεὰν δότε. 9 Μὴ κτήσησθε
ye received, freely give. Do not provide

χρυσὸν μηδὲ ἄργυρον μηδὲ χαλκὸν εἰς
gold nor silver nor brass in

τὰς ζώνας ὑμων, 10 μὴ πήραν εἰς ὁδὸν
the girdles of you, not a wallet for [the] way

μηδὲ δύο χιτῶνας μηδὲ ὑποδήματα μηδὲ
nor two tunics nor sandals nor

ῥάβδον· ἄξιος γὰρ ὁ ἐργάτης τῆς
a staff; for worthy [is] the workman of the

τροφῆς αὐτοῦ. 11 εἰς ἢν δ' ἂν πόλιν
food of him. And into whatever city

ἢ κώμην εἰσέλθητε, ἐξετάσατε τίς ἐν
or village ye may enter, inquire who in

αὐτῇ ἄξιός ἐστιν· κἀκεῖ μείνατε ἕως ἂν
it worthy is; and there remain until

until you depart. ¹²As you enter the house, salute it. ¹³And if the house is worthy, let your peace come upon it; but if it is not worthy, let your peace return to you. ¹⁴And if any one will not receive you or listen to your words, shake off the dust from your feet as you leave that house or town. ¹⁵Truly, I say to you, it shall be more tolerable on the day of judgment for the land of Sodom and Gomor'rah than for that town.

16 "Behold, I send you out as sheep in the midst of wolves; so be wise as serpents and innocent as doves. ¹⁷Beware of men; for they will deliver you up to councils, and flog you in their synagogues, ¹⁸and you will be dragged before governors and kings for my sake, to bear testimony before them and the Gentiles. ¹⁹When they deliver you up, do not be anxious how you are to speak or what you are to say; for what you are to say will be given to you in that hour; ²⁰for

ἐξέλθητε.
ye may go out.

12 εἰσερχόμενοι δὲ εἰς τὴν
And entering into the

οἰκίαν ἀσπάσασθε αὐτήν·
house greet it;

13 καὶ ἐὰν μὲν
and if indeed

ᾖ ἡ οἰκία ἀξία, ἐλθάτω ἡ εἰρήνη ὑμῶν
be the house worthy, let come the peace of you

ἐπ᾽ αὐτήν· ἐὰν δὲ μὴ ᾖ ἀξία, ἡ εἰρήνη
on it; but if it be not worthy, the peace

ὑμῶν πρὸς ὑμᾶς ἐπιστραφήτω.
of you unto you let return.

14 καὶ
And

ὃς ἂν μὴ δέξηται ὑμᾶς μηδὲ ἀκούσῃ
whoever may not receive you nor hear

τοὺς λόγους ὑμῶν, ἐξερχόμενοι ἔξω
the words of you, going out outside

τῆς οἰκίας ἢ τῆς πόλεως ἐκείνης ἐκτινά-
- house or - city that shake

ξατε τὸν κονιορτὸν τῶν ποδῶν ὑμῶν.
off the dust of the feet of you.

15 ἀμὴν λέγω ὑμῖν, ἀνεκτότερον ἔσται
Truly I tell you, more tolerable it will be [for]

γῇ Σοδόμων καὶ Γομόρρων ἐν ἡμέρᾳ κρίσεως
[the] land of Sodom and Gomorra in [the] day of judgment

ἢ τῇ πόλει ἐκείνῃ.
than [for] - city that.

16 Ἰδοὺ ἐγὼ
Behold I

ἀποστέλλω ὑμᾶς ὡς πρόβατα ἐν μέσῳ
send forth you as sheep in [the] midst

λύκων· γίνεσθε οὖν φρόνιμοι ὡς οἱ
of wolves; be ye therefore prudent as -

ὄφεις καὶ ἀκέραιοι ὡς αἱ περιστεραί.
serpents and harmless as - doves.

17 Προσέχετε δὲ ἀπὸ τῶν ἀνθρώπων·
And beware from(of) - men;

παραδώσουσιν γὰρ ὑμᾶς εἰς συνέδρια,
for they will deliver up you to councils,

καὶ ἐν ταῖς συναγωγαῖς αὐτῶν μαστιγώ-
and in the synagogues of them they will

σουσιν ὑμᾶς· 18 καὶ ἐπὶ ἡγεμόνας δὲ καὶ
scourge you; and before leaders and also

βασιλεῖς ἀχθήσεσθε ἕνεκεν ἐμοῦ, εἰς
kings ye will be led for the sake of me, for

μαρτύριον αὐτοῖς καὶ τοῖς ἔθνεσιν.
a testimony to them and to the nations.

19 ὅταν δὲ παραδῶσιν ὑμᾶς, μὴ μεριμνή-
But when they deliver up you, do not be

σητε πῶς ἢ τί λαλήσητε· δοθήσεται
anxious how or what ye may say; ²it will be given

γὰρ ὑμῖν ἐν ἐκείνῃ τῇ ὥρᾳ τί λαλήσητε·
¹for to you in that - hour what ye may say;

it is not you who speak, but the Spirit of your Father speaking through you. 21 Brother will deliver up brother to death, and the father his child, and children will rise against parents and have them put to death; 22 and you will be hated by all for my name's sake. But he who endures to the end will be saved. 23 When they persecute you in one town, flee to the next; for truly, I say to you, you will not have gone through all the towns of Israel, before the Son of man comes.

24 "A disciple is not above his teacher, nor a servant above his master; 25 it is enough for the disciple to be like his teacher, and the servant like his master. If they have called the master of the house Be-el'zebul, how much more will they malign those of his household.

26 "So have no fear of them; for nothing is covered that will not be revealed, or hidden that will not be known. 27 What I tell you in the dark, utter in the light;

20 οὐ γὰρ ὑμεῖς ἐστε οἱ λαλοῦντες,
for not   ye   are the [ones] speaking,

ἀλλὰ τὸ πνεῦμα τοῦ πατρὸς ὑμῶν τὸ
but   the Spirit of the Father of you the [one]

λαλοῦν ἐν ὑμῖν. 21 παραδώσει δὲ
speaking in you.   And ²will deliver up

ἀδελφὸς ἀδελφὸν εἰς θάνατον καὶ πατὴρ
¹brother brother to   death and father

τέκνον, καὶ ἐπαναστήσονται τέκνα ἐπὶ
child,   and   will stand up   children against

γονεῖς καὶ θανατώσουσιν αὐτούς. 22 καὶ
parents and   put to death   them.   And

ἔσεσθε μισούμενοι ὑπὸ πάντων διὰ
ye will be being hated by all men on account of

τὸ ὄνομά μου· ὁ δὲ ὑπομείνας εἰς
the name of me; but the [one] enduring   to

τέλος, οὗτος σωθήσεται. 23 ὅταν δὲ
[the] end, this   will be saved.   But when

διώκωσιν ὑμᾶς ἐν τῇ πόλει ταύτῃ,
they persecute you in   -   city   this,

φεύγετε εἰς τὴν ἑτέραν· ἀμὴν γὰρ
flee ye   to   -   [an]other;   for truly

λέγω ὑμῖν, οὐ μὴ τελέσητε τὰς πόλεις
I tell you, by no means ye will complete the cities

[τοῦ] Ἰσραὴλ ἕως ἔλθῃ ὁ υἱὸς τοῦ ἀν-
of Israel until comes the Son - of

θρώπου. 24 Οὐκ ἔστιν μαθητὴς ὑπὲρ
man.   not is   A disciple above

τὸν διδάσκαλον οὐδὲ δοῦλος ὑπὲρ τὸν
the   teacher   nor a slave above the

κύριον αὐτοῦ. 25 ἀρκετὸν τῷ μαθητῇ
lord   of him.   Enough for the disciple

ἵνα γένηται ὡς ὁ διδάσκαλος αὐτοῦ,
that he be   as the   teacher   of him,

καὶ ὁ δοῦλος ὡς ὁ κύριος αὐτοῦ. εἰ
and the slave as the lord of him. If

τὸν οἰκοδεσπότην Βεελζεβοὺλ ἐπεκάλεσαν,
the   housemaster   Beelzebub   they called,

πόσῳ μᾶλλον τοὺς οἰκιακοὺς αὐτοῦ.
how much more the members of [the] household of him.

26 μὴ οὖν φοβηθῆτε αὐτούς· οὐδὲν γάρ
Therefore fear ye not   them;   for nothing

ἐστιν κεκαλυμμένον ὃ οὐκ ἀποκαλυφ-
is   having been veiled which will not be un-

θήσεται, καὶ κρυπτὸν ὃ οὐ γνωσθήσεται.
veiled, and hidden which will not be made known.

27 ὃ λέγω ὑμῖν ἐν τῇ σκοτίᾳ, εἴπατε
What I say to you in the darkness,   say ye

and what you hear whispered, proclaim upon the housetops. 28And do not fear those who kill the body but cannot kill the soul; rather fear him who can destroy both soul and body in hell. 29Are not two sparrows sold for a penny? And not one of them will fall to the ground without your Father's will. 30But even the hairs of your head are all numbered. 31Fear not, therefore; you are of more value than many sparrows. 32So every one who acknowledges me before men, I also will acknowledge before my Father who is in heaven; 33but whoever denies me before men, I also will deny before my Father who is in heaven.

34 "Do not think that I have come to bring peace on earth; I have not come to bring peace, but a sword. 35For I have come to set a man against his father, and a daughter against her mother, and a daughter-

ἐν τῷ φωτί· καὶ ὃ εἰς τὸ οὖς ἀκούετε,
in the light; and what in the ear ye hear,

κηρύξατε ἐπὶ τῶν δωμάτων. 28 καὶ
proclaim on the housetops. And

μὴ φοβεῖσθε ἀπὸ τῶν ἀποκτεννόντων
do not fear - the [ones] killing

τὸ σῶμα, τὴν δὲ ψυχὴν μὴ δυναμένων
the body, but the soul not being able

ἀποκτεῖναι· φοβεῖσθε δὲ μᾶλλον τὸν
to kill; but fear ye rather the [one]

δυνάμενον καὶ ψυχὴν καὶ σῶμα ἀπολέσαι
being able both soul and body to destroy

ἐν γεέννῃ. 29 οὐχὶ δύο στρουθία ἀσσα-
in gehenna. Not two sparrows of(for) a

ρίου πωλεῖται; καὶ ἓν ἐξ αὐτῶν οὐ
farthing are sold? and one of them not

πεσεῖται ἐπὶ τὴν γῆν ἄνευ τοῦ πατρὸς
will fall on the earth without the Father

ὑμῶν. 30 ὑμῶν δὲ καὶ αἱ τρίχες τῆς
of you. But of you even the hairs of the

κεφαλῆς πᾶσαι ἠριθμημέναι εἰσίν. 31 μὴ
head all having been numbered are. not

οὖν φοβεῖσθε· πολλῶν στρουθίων διαφέρετε
Therefore fear ye; ¹many ²sparrows ²excel

ὑμεῖς. 32 Πᾶς οὖν ὅστις ὁμολογήσει
¹ye. Everyone therefore who shall confess

ἐν ἐμοὶ ἔμπροσθεν τῶν ἀνθρώπων,
- me before the men,

ὁμολογήσω κἀγὼ ἐν αὐτῷ ἔμπροσθεν
will confess I also - him before

τοῦ πατρός μου τοῦ ἐν τοῖς οὐρανοῖς·
the Father of me - in the heavens;

33 ὅστις δ᾽ ἂν ἀρνήσηται με ἔμπροσθεν
and whoever denies me before

τῶν ἀνθρώπων, ἀρνήσομαι κἀγὼ αὐτὸν
- men, will deny I also him

ἔμπροσθεν τοῦ πατρός μου τοῦ ἐν
before the Father of me - in

τοῖς οὐρανοῖς. 34 Μὴ νομίσητε ὅτι
the heavens. Do not suppose that

ἦλθον βαλεῖν εἰρήνην ἐπὶ τὴν γῆν· οὐκ ἦλθον
I came to bring peace on the earth; I came not

βαλεῖν εἰρήνην ἀλλὰ μάχαιραν. 35 ἦλθον γὰρ
to bring peace but a sword. For I came

διχάσαι ἄνθρωπον κατὰ τοῦ πατρὸς
to make hostile a man against the father

αὐτοῦ καὶ θυγατέρα κατὰ τῆς μητρὸς
of him and a daughter against the mother

in-law against her mother-in-law; ³⁶and a man's foes will be those of his own household. ³⁷He who loves father or mother more than me is not worthy of me; and he who loves son or daughter more than me is not worthy of me; ³⁸and he who does not take his cross and follow me is not worthy of me. ³⁹He who finds his life will lose it, and he who loses his life for my sake will find it.

40 "He who receives you receives me, and he who receives me receives him who sent me. ⁴¹He who receives a prophet because he is a prophet shall receive a prophet's reward, and he who receives a righteous man because he is a righteous man shall receive a righteous man's reward. ⁴²And whoever gives to one of these little ones even a cup of cold water because he is a disciple, truly, I say to you, he shall not lose his reward."

αὐτῆς καὶ νύμφην κατὰ τῆς πενθερᾶς
of her and a bride against the mother-in-law

αὐτῆς, 36 καὶ ἐχθροὶ τοῦ ἀνθρώπου οἱ
of her, and [the] enemies – of a man the

οἰκιακοὶ αὐτοῦ. 37 Ὁ φιλῶν πατέρα
members of [the] household of him. The [one] loving father

ἢ μητέρα ὑπὲρ ἐμὲ οὐκ ἔστιν μου ἄξιος·
or mother beyond me is not of me worthy;

καὶ ὁ φιλῶν υἱὸν ἢ θυγατέρα ὑπὲρ
and the [one] loving son or daughter beyond

ἐμὲ οὐκ ἔστιν μου ἄξιος· 38 καὶ ὃς
me is not of me worthy; and [he] who

οὐ λαμβάνει τὸν σταυρὸν αὐτοῦ καὶ
takes not the cross of him and

ἀκολουθεῖ ὀπίσω μου, οὐκ ἔστιν μου
follows after me, is not of me

ἄξιος. 39 ὁ εὑρὼν τὴν ψυχὴν αὐτοῦ
worthy. The [one] finding the life of him

ἀπολέσει αὐτήν, καὶ ὁ ἀπολέσας τὴν
will lose it, and the [one] losing the

ψυχὴν αὐτοῦ ἕνεκεν ἐμοῦ εὑρήσει αὐτήν.
life of him for the sake of me will find it.

40 Ὁ δεχόμενος ὑμᾶς ἐμὲ δέχεται, καὶ
The [one] receiving you me receives, and

ὁ ἐμὲ δεχόμενος δέχεται τὸν
the [one] me receiving receives the [one]

ἀποστείλαντά με. 41 ὁ δεχόμενος προ-
having sent me. The [one] receiving a pro-

φήτην εἰς ὄνομα προφήτου μισθὸν
phet in [the] name of a prophet [the] reward

προφήτου λήμψεται, καὶ ὁ δεχόμενος
of a prophet will receive, and the [one] receiving

δίκαιον εἰς ὄνομα δικαίου μισθὸν
a righteous man in [the] name of a righteous man [the] reward

δικαίου λήμψεται. 42 καὶ ὃς ἐὰν ποτίσῃ
of a righteous man will receive. And whoever gives to drink

ἕνα τῶν μικρῶν τούτων ποτήριον ψυχροῦ
one – of these little [ones] a cup of cold water

μόνον εἰς ὄνομα μαθητοῦ, ἀμὴν λέγω ὑμῖν,
only in [the] name of a disciple, truly I tell you,

οὐ μὴ ἀπολέσῃ τὸν μισθὸν αὐτοῦ.
on no account will he lose the reward of him.

CHAPTER 11

AND when Jesus had finished instructing his twelve disciples, he went on from there to teach and preach in their cities.

2 Now when John heard in prison about the deeds of the Christ, he sent word by his disciples [3]and said to him, "Are you he who is to come, or shall we look for another?" [4]And Jesus answered them, "Go and tell John what you hear and see: [5]the blind receive their sight and the lame walk, lepers are cleansed and the deaf hear, and the dead are raised up, and the poor have good news preached to them. [6]And blessed is he who takes no offense at me."

7 As they went away, Jesus began to speak to the crowds concerning John: "What did you go out into the wilderness to behold? A reed shaken by the wind? [8]Why then did you go out? To see a man[r] clothed in soft raiment? Behold, those who wear soft raiment are in kings' houses. [9]Why then did you go out? To see a prophet?[s]

---

[r] Or What then did you go out to see? A man . . .

[s] Other ancient authorities read What then did you go out to see? A prophet?

---

11 Καὶ   ἐγένετο   ὅτε   ἐτέλεσεν   ὁ
And   it came to pass   when   ended   -

'Ιησοῦς   διατάσσων   τοῖς   δώδεκα   μαθηταῖς
Jesus   giving charge   to the   twelve   disciples

αὐτοῦ,   μετέβη   ἐκεῖθεν   τοῦ   διδάσκειν
of him,   he removed   thence   -   to teach[d]

καὶ   κηρύσσειν   ἐν   ταῖς   πόλεσιν   αὐτῶν.
and   to proclaim[d]   in   the   cities   of them.

2 'Ο   δὲ   'Ιωάννης   ἀκούσας   ἐν   τῷ
-   But   John   hearing   in   the

δεσμωτηρίῳ   τὰ   ἔργα   τοῦ   Χριστοῦ,
prison   the   works   -   of Christ,

πέμψας   διὰ   τῶν   μαθητῶν   αὐτοῦ   3 εἶπεν
sending   through   the   disciples   of him   said

αὐτῷ·   σὺ   εἶ   ὁ   ἐρχόμενος,   ἢ   ἕτερον
to him: Thou   art   the   coming [one],   or   another

προσδοκῶμεν;   4 καὶ   ἀποκριθεὶς   ὁ
may we expect?   And   answering   -

'Ιησοῦς   εἶπεν   αὐτοῖς·   πορευθέντες   ἀπαγ-
Jesus   said   to them: Going   report

γείλατε   'Ιωάννῃ   ἃ   ἀκούετε   καὶ   βλέπετε·
ye   to John [the things] which   ye hear   and   see:

5 τυφλοὶ   ἀναβλέπουσιν   καὶ   χωλοὶ
blind men   see again   and   lame men

περιπατοῦσιν,   λεπροὶ   καθαρίζονται   καὶ   κωφοὶ
walk,   lepers   are cleansed   and   deaf men

ἀκούουσιν,   καὶ   νεκροὶ   ἐγείρονται   καὶ
hear,   and   dead men   are raised   and

πτωχοὶ   εὐαγγελίζονται·   6 καὶ   μακάριός
poor men   are evangelized;   and   blessed

ἐστιν   ὃς   ἐὰν   μὴ   σκανδαλισθῇ   ἐν   ἐμοί.
is   whoever   is not offended   in   me.

7 Τούτων   δὲ   πορευομένων   ἤρξατο   ὁ
And these   going[a]   began   -
= as these were going

'Ιησοῦς   λέγειν   τοῖς   ὄχλοις   περὶ   'Ιωάννου·
Jesus   to say   to the   crowds   concerning   John:

τί   ἐξήλθατε   εἰς   τὴν   ἔρημον   θεάσασθαι;
What   went ye out   into   the   wilderness   to see?

κάλαμον   ὑπὸ   ἀνέμου   σαλευόμενον;   8 ἀλλὰ
a reed   by   wind   being shaken?   But

τί   ἐξήλθατε   ἰδεῖν;   ἄνθρωπον   ἐν   μαλακοῖς
what   went ye out   to see?   a man   in   soft material

ἠμφιεσμένον;   ἰδοὺ   οἱ   τὰ   μαλακὰ
having been clothed?   Behold[,]   the [ones]   -   soft material

φοροῦντες   ἐν   τοῖς   οἴκοις   τῶν   βασιλέων.   9 ἀλλὰ
wearing [are] in   the   houses   -   of kings.   But

τί   ἐξήλθατε;   προφήτην   ἰδεῖν;   ναὶ   λέγω
why   went ye out?   a prophet   to see?   Yes[,]   I tell

Yes, I tell you, and more than a prophet. ¹⁰This is he of whom it is written, 'Behold, I send my messenger before thy face, who shall prepare thy way before thee.' ¹¹Truly, I say to you, among those born of women there has risen no one greater than John the Baptist; yet he who is least in the kingdom of heaven is greater than he. ¹²From the days of John the Baptist until now the kingdom of heaven has suffered violence,ᵗ and men of violence take it by force. ¹³For all the prophets and the law prophesied until John; ¹⁴and if you are willing to accept it, he is Eli'jah who is to come. ¹⁵He who has ears to hear,ᵘ let him hear.

16 "But to what shall I compare this generation? It is like children sitting in the market places and calling to their playmates,

¹⁷'We piped to you, and you did not dance; we wailed, and you did not mourn.'

¹⁸For John came neither eating nor drinking, and they say, 'He has a demon'; ¹⁹the Son of man came eating and

---

ὑμῖν, καὶ περισσότερον προφήτου. 10 οὗτός
you, and more [than] a prophet. This

ἐστιν περὶ οὗ γέγραπται· ἰδοὺ ἐγὼ
is he concerning whom it has been written: Behold[,] I

ἀποστέλλω τὸν ἄγγελόν μου πρὸ προσώπου
send forth the messenger of me before [the] face

σου, ὃς κατασκευάσει τὴν ὁδόν σου
of thee, who will prepare the way of thee

ἔμπροσθέν σου. 11 ἀμὴν λέγω ὑμῖν,
before thee. Truly I tell you,

οὐκ ἐγήγερται ἐν γεννητοῖς γυναικῶν
there has not arisen among [those] born of women

μείζων Ἰωάννου τοῦ βαπτιστοῦ· ὁ δὲ
a greater [than] John the Baptist; but the

μικρότερος ἐν τῇ βασιλείᾳ τῶν οὐρανῶν
lesser in the kingdom of the heavens

μείζων αὐτοῦ ἐστιν. 12 ἀπὸ δὲ τῶν
greater [than] he is. And from the

ἡμερῶν Ἰωάννου τοῦ βαπτιστοῦ ἕως
days of John the Baptist until

ἄρτι ἡ βασιλεία τῶν οὐρανῶν βιάζεται,
now the kingdom of the heavens is forcibly treated,

καὶ βιασταὶ ἁρπάζουσιν αὐτήν. 13 πάντες γὰρ
and forceful men seize it. For all

οἱ προφῆται καὶ ὁ νόμος ἕως
the prophets and the law until

Ἰωάννου ἐπροφήτευσαν· 14 καὶ εἰ θέλετε
John prophesied; and if ye are willing

δέξασθαι, αὐτός ἐστιν Ἡλίας ὁ μέλλων
to receive [it or him], he is Elias the [one] about

ἔρχεσθαι. 15 ὁ ἔχων ὦτα ἀκουέτω.
to come. The [one] having ears let him hear.

16 Τίνι δὲ ὁμοιώσω τὴν γενεὰν ταύτην;
But to what shall I liken – generation this?

ὁμοία ἐστὶν παιδίοις καθημένοις ἐν ταῖς
Like it is to children sitting in the

ἀγοραῖς ἃ προσφωνοῦντα τοῖς ἑτέροις
marketplaces who calling to the others

17 λέγουσιν· ηὐλήσαμεν ὑμῖν καὶ οὐκ
say: We piped to you and not

ὠρχήσασθε· ἐθρηνήσαμεν καὶ οὐκ ἐκόψασθε.
ye did dance; we lamented and ye did not mourn.

18 ἦλθεν γὰρ Ἰωάννης μήτε ἐσθίων μήτε
For came John neither eating nor

πίνων, καὶ λέγουσιν· δαιμόνιον ἔχει.
drinking, and they say: a demon He has.

19 ἦλθεν ὁ υἱὸς τοῦ ἀνθρώπου ἐσθίων καὶ
Came the Son – of man eating and

ᵗ Or has been coming violently
ᵘ Other ancient authorities omit to hear

drinking, and they say, 'Behold, a glutton and a drunkard, a friend of tax collectors and sinners!' Yet wisdom is justified by her deeds."[v]

20 Then he began to upbraid the cities where most of his mighty works had been done, because they did not repent [21]"Woe to you, Chora'zin! woe to you, Beth-sa'ida! for if the mighty works done in you had been done in Tyre and Sidon, they would have repented long ago in sackcloth and ashes. [22]But I tell you, it shall be more tolerable on the day of judgment for Tyre and Sidon than for you. [23]And you, Caper'na-um, will you be exalted to heaven? You shall be brought down to Hades. For if the mighty works done in you had been done in Sodom, it would have remained until this day. [24]But I tell you that it shall be more tolerable on the day of judgment for the land of Sodom than for you."

25 At that time Jesus declared, "I thank thee, Father, Lord of heaven and earth, that thou hast hidden these things from the wise and under-

[v] Other ancient authorities read *children* (Luke 7. 35)

πίνων, καὶ λέγουσιν· ἰδοὺ ἄνθρωπος
drinking, and they say: Behold[,] a man

φάγος καὶ οἰνοπότης, τελωνῶν φίλος καὶ
gluttonous and a wine-drinker, of tax-collectors a friend and

ἁμαρτωλῶν. καὶ ἐδικαιώθη ἡ σοφία ἀπὸ
of sinners. And was(is) justified – wisdom from(by)

τῶν ἔργων αὐτῆς.
the works of her.

20 Τότε ἤρξατο ὀνειδίζειν τὰς πόλεις
Then he began to reproach the cities

ἐν αἷς ἐγένοντο αἱ πλεῖσται δυνάμεις
in which happened the very many powerful deeds

αὐτοῦ, ὅτι οὐ μετενόησαν· 21 οὐαί σοι,
of him, because they repented not: Woe to thee,

Χοραζίν· οὐαί σοι, Βηθσαϊδά· ὅτι εἰ
Chorazin; woe to thee, Bethsaida; because if

ἐν Τύρῳ καὶ Σιδῶνι ἐγένοντο αἱ δυνάμεις
in Tyre and Sidon happened the powerful deeds

αἱ γενόμεναι ἐν ὑμῖν, πάλαι ἂν
having happened in you, long ago –

ἐν σάκκῳ καὶ σποδῷ μετενόησαν.
in sackcloth and ashes they would have repented.

22 πλὴν λέγω ὑμῖν, Τύρῳ καὶ Σιδῶνι
However I tell you, For Tyre and for Sidon

ἀνεκτότερον ἔσται ἐν ἡμέρᾳ κρίσεως ἢ
more tolerable it will be in [the] day of judgment than

ὑμῖν. 23 καὶ σύ, Καφαρναούμ, μὴ
for you. And thou, Capernaum, not

ἕως οὐρανοῦ ὑψωθήσῃ; ἕως ᾄδου
as far as heaven wast thou exalted? as far as hades

καταβήσῃ· ὅτι εἰ ἐν Σοδόμοις ἐγενήθησαν
thou shalt descend; because if in Sodom happened

αἱ δυνάμεις αἱ γενόμεναι ἐν σοί,
the powerful deeds – having happened in thee,

ἔμεινεν ἂν μέχρι τῆς σήμερον. 24 πλὴν
it would have remained until – to-day. However

λέγω ὑμῖν ὅτι γῇ Σοδόμων ἀνεκτότερον
I tell you that for [the] land of Sodom more tolerable

ἔσται ἐν ἡμέρᾳ κρίσεως ἢ σοί.
it will be in [the] day of judgment than for thee.

25 Ἐν ἐκείνῳ τῷ καιρῷ ἀποκριθεὶς
At that time answering

ὁ Ἰησοῦς εἶπεν· ἐξομολογοῦμαί σοι,
– Jesus said: I give thanks to thee,

πάτερ, κύριε τοῦ οὐρανοῦ καὶ τῆς γῆς,
Father, lord of the heaven and of the earth,

ὅτι ἔκρυψας ταῦτα ἀπὸ σοφῶν καὶ συνε-
because thou hiddest these things from wise and intel-

standing and revealed them to babes; ²⁶yea, Father, for such was thy gracious will.ᵂ ²⁷All things have been delivered to me by my Father; and no one knows the Son except the Father, and no one knows the Father except the Son and any one to whom the Son chooses to reveal him. ²⁸Come to me, all who labor and are heavy-laden, and I will give you rest. ²⁹Take my yoke upon you, and learn from me; for I am gentle and lowly in heart, and you will find rest for your souls. ³⁰For my yoke is easy, and my burden is light."

τῶν,   καὶ   ἀπεκάλυψας   αὐτὰ   νηπίοις·
ligent men, and   didst reveal   them   to infants;

26 ναί,   ὁ   πατήρ,   ὅτι   οὕτως   εὐδοκία
yes,   –   Father,   because   thus   good pleasure

ἐγένετο   ἔμπροσθέν   σου.   27 Πάντα   μοι
it was   before   thee.   All things to me

παρεδόθη   ὑπὸ   τοῦ   πατρός   μου,   καὶ
were delivered by   the   Father   of me,   and

οὐδεὶς   ἐπιγινώσκει   τὸν   υἱὸν   εἰ   μὴ   ὁ
no one   fully knows   the   Son   except   the

πατήρ,   οὐδὲ   τὸν   πατέρα   τις   ἐπιγινώσκει
Father, neither the Father anyone fully knows

εἰ   μὴ   ὁ   υἱὸς   καὶ   ᾧ   ἐὰν   βούληται   ὁ
except the Son and [he] to whom if wills the

υἱὸς   ἀποκαλύψαι.   28 Δεῦτε   πρός   με
Son   to reveal.   Come   unto   me

πάντες   οἱ   κοπιῶντες   καὶ   πεφορτισμένοι,
all   the [ones] labouring and having been burdened,

κἀγὼ   ἀναπαύσω   ὑμᾶς.   29 ἄρατε   τὸν
and I   will rest   you.   Take   the

ζυγόν   μου   ἐφ'   ὑμᾶς   καὶ   μάθετε   ἀπ'
yoke   of me   on   you   and   learn   from

ἐμοῦ,   ὅτι   πραΰς   εἰμι   καὶ   ταπεινὸς   τῇ
me,   because meek   I am   and   lowly   –

καρδίᾳ,   καὶ   εὑρήσετε   ἀνάπαυσιν   ταῖς
in heart, and   ye will find   rest   to the

ψυχαῖς   ὑμῶν·   30 ὁ   γὰρ   ζυγός   μου
souls   of you;   for the   yoke   of me

χρηστὸς   καὶ   τὸ   φορτίον   μου   ἐλαφρόν
gentle   and   the   burden   of me   light

ἐστιν.
is.

CHAPTER 12

AT that time Jesus went through the grainfields on the sabbath; his disciples were hungry, and they began to pluck ears of grain and to eat. ²But when the Pharisees saw it, they said to him, "Look, your disciples are doing what is not lawful to do on the sabbath." ³He said to

ᵂ Or *so it was well-pleasing before thee*

12 Ἐν   ἐκείνῳ   τῷ   καιρῷ   ἐπορεύθη   ὁ
At   that   –   time   went   –

Ἰησοῦς   τοῖς   σάββασιν   διὰ   τῶν   σπορίμων·
Jesus   on the sabbath   through the   cornfields;

οἱ   δὲ   μαθηταὶ   αὐτοῦ   ἐπείνασαν,   καὶ
and the   disciples   of him   hungered,   and

ἤρξαντο   τίλλειν   στάχυας   καὶ   ἐσθίειν.
began   to pluck ears [of corn] and   to eat.

2 οἱ   δὲ   Φαρισαῖοι   ἰδόντες   εἶπαν   αὐτῷ·
But the   Pharisees   seeing   said   to him:

ἰδοὺ   οἱ   μαθηταί   σου   ποιοῦσιν   ὃ   οὐκ
Behold[,] the disciples of thee are doing what not

ἔξεστιν   ποιεῖν   ἐν   σαββάτῳ.   3 ὁ   δὲ
it is lawful to do   on   a sabbath.   And he

them, "Have you not read what David did, when he was hungry, and those who were with him: ⁴how he entered the house of God and ate the bread of the Presence, which it was not lawful for him to eat nor for those who were with him, but only for the priests? ⁵Or have you not read in the law how on the sabbath the priests in the temple profane the sabbath, and are guiltless? ⁶I tell you, something greater than the temple is here. ⁷And if you had known what this means, 'I desire mercy, and not sacrifice,' you would not have condemned the guiltless. ⁸For the Son of man is lord of the sabbath."

9 And he went on from there, and entered their synagogue. ¹⁰And behold, there was a man with a withered hand. And they asked him, "Is it lawful to heal on the sabbath?" so that they might accuse him.¹¹ He said to them, "What man of you, if he has one sheep and it falls into a pit on the sabbath, will not lay hold of it and lift

εἶπεν αὐτοῖς· οὐκ ἀνέγνωτε τί ἐποίησεν
said   to them: Did ye not read what   did

Δαυίδ, ὅτε ἐπείνασεν καὶ οἱ μετ'
David, when he hungered and the [ones] with

αὐτοῦ; 4 πῶς εἰσῆλθεν εἰς τὸν οἶκον
him;   how he entered into the house

τοῦ θεοῦ καὶ τοὺς ἄρτους τῆς προ-
- of God and the loaves of the set-

θέσεως ἔφαγον, ὃ οὐκ ἐξὸν ἦν αὐτῷ
ting forth ate, which not lawful it was for him

φαγεῖν οὐδὲ τοῖς μετ' αὐτοῦ, εἰ μὴ
to eat neither the [ones] with him, except

τοῖς ἱερεῦσιν μόνοις; 5 ἢ οὐκ ἀνέγνωτε
for the priests only? or did ye not read

ἐν τῷ νόμῳ ὅτι τοῖς σάββασιν οἱ
in the law that on the sabbaths the

ἱερεῖς ἐν τῷ ἱερῷ τὸ σάββατον βεβηλοῦ-
priests in the temple the sabbath pro-

σιν καὶ ἀναίτιοί εἰσιν; 6 λέγω δὲ
fane and guiltless are?   And I tell

ὑμῖν ὅτι τοῦ ἱεροῦ μεῖζόν ἐστιν ὧδε.
you that [than] the temple a greater [thing] is here.

7 εἰ δὲ ἐγνώκειτε τί ἐστιν· ἔλεος
But if ye had known what it is: Mercy

θέλω καὶ οὐ θυσίαν, οὐκ ἂν κατε-
I desire and not sacrifice, ye would not have

δικάσατε τοὺς ἀναιτίους. 8 κύριος γάρ
condemned the guiltless. For Lord

ἐστιν τοῦ σαββάτου ὁ υἱὸς τοῦ ἀνθρώπου.
is of the sabbath the Son - of man.

9 Καὶ μεταβὰς ἐκεῖθεν ἦλθεν εἰς τὴν
And removing thence he came into the

συναγωγὴν αὐτῶν. 10 καὶ ἰδοὺ ἄνθρωπος
synagogue of them.   And behold[,] a man

χεῖρα ἔχων ξηράν· καὶ ἐπηρώτησαν αὐτὸν
¹[his] hand ²having ³withered; and they questioned him

λέγοντες· εἰ ἔξεστιν τοῖς σάββασιν
saying: If it is lawful on the sabbaths

θεραπεῦσαι; ἵνα κατηγορήσωσιν αὐτοῦ.
to heal?   in order that they might accuse him.

11 ὁ δὲ εἶπεν αὐτοῖς· τίς ἔσται ἐξ
So he said to them: ¹What ²will there be ⁶of

ὑμῶν ἄνθρωπος ὃς ἕξει πρόβατον ἕν,
⁵you   ³man who will have sheep one,

καὶ ἐὰν ἐμπέσῃ τοῦτο τοῖς σάββασιν
and if ²fall in ¹this on the sabbaths

εἰς βόθυνον, οὐχὶ κρατήσει αὐτὸ καὶ
into a ditch, will he not lay hold of it and

it out? ¹²Of how much more value is a man than a sheep! So it is lawful to do good on the sabbath." ¹³Then he said to the man, "Stretch out your hand," And the man stretched it out, and it was restored, whole like the other. ¹⁴But the Pharisees went out and took counsel against him, how to destroy him.

15 Jesus, aware of this, withdrew from there. And many followed him, and he healed them all, ¹⁶and ordered them not to make him known. ¹⁷This was to fulfil what was spoken by the prophet Isaiah:
¹⁸"Behold, my servant whom I have chosen,
my beloved with whom my soul is well pleased.
I will put my Spirit upon him,
and he shall proclaim justice to the Gentiles.
¹⁹He will not wrangle or cry aloud,
nor will any one hear his voice in the streets;
²⁰he will not break a bruised reed
or quench a smoldering wick,
till he brings justice to victory;
²¹ and in his name will the Gentiles hope."

ἐγερεῖ; **12** πόσῳ οὖν διαφέρει ἄνθρωπος
raise? By how much then surpasses a man
προβάτου. ὥστε ἔξεστιν τοῖς σάββασιν
a sheep. So that it is lawful on the sabbaths
καλῶς ποιεῖν. **13** τότε λέγει τῷ ἀνθρώπῳ·
well to do. Then he says to the man:
ἔκτεινόν σου τὴν χεῖρα. καὶ ἐξέτεινεν,
Stretch forth of thee the hand. And he stretched forth,
καὶ ἀπεκατεστάθη ὑγιὴς ὡς ἡ ἄλλη.
and it was restored healthy as the other.
14 ἐξελθόντες δὲ οἱ Φαρισαῖοι συμβούλιον
And going out the Pharisees counsel
ἔλαβον κατ' αὐτοῦ, ὅπως αὐτὸν ἀπολέ-
took against him, so as him they might
σωσιν. **15** Ὁ δὲ Ἰησοῦς γνοὺς ἀνε-
destroy. - But Jesus knowing de-
χώρησεν ἐκεῖθεν. καὶ ἠκολούθησαν αὐτῷ
parted thence. And followed him
πολλοί, καὶ ἐθεράπευσεν αὐτοὺς πάντας,
many, and he healed them all,
16 καὶ ἐπετίμησεν αὐτοῖς ἵνα μὴ φανερὸν
and warned them that ²not ⁴manifest
αὐτὸν ποιήσωσιν· **17** ἵνα πληρωθῇ τὸ
⁵him ¹they ³should ⁴make; that might be fulfilled the [thing]
ῥηθὲν διὰ Ἠσαΐου τοῦ προφήτου
spoken through Isaiah the prophet
λέγοντος· **18** ἰδοὺ ὁ παῖς μου ὃν
saying: Behold[,] the servant of me whom
ἡρέτισα, ὁ ἀγαπητός μου ὃν εὐδόκησεν
I chose, the beloved of me [with] whom was well pleased
ἡ ψυχή μου· θήσω τὸ πνεῦμα μου ἐπ'
the soul of me; I will put the spirit of me on
αὐτόν, καὶ κρίσιν τοῖς ἔθνεσιν ἀπαγγελεῖ.
him, and judgment to the nations he will announce.
19 οὐκ ἐρίσει οὐδὲ κραυγάσει, οὐδὲ
He will not strive nor will shout, nor
ἀκούσει τις ἐν ταῖς πλατείαις τὴν
will hear anyone in the streets the
φωνὴν αὐτοῦ. **20** κάλαμον συντετριμμένον
voice of him. A reed *having been* bruised
οὐ κατεάξει καὶ λίνον τυφόμενον οὐ
he will not break and flax smoking not
σβέσει, ἕως ἂν ἐκβάλῃ εἰς νῖκος τὴν
he will quench, until he put forth to victory -
κρίσιν. **21** καὶ τῷ ὀνόματι αὐτοῦ ἔθνη
judgment. And in the name of him nations
ἐλπιοῦσιν.
will hope.

22 Then a blind and dumb demoniac was brought to him, and he healed him, so that the dumb man spoke and saw. 23And all the people were amazed, and said, "Can this be the Son of David?" 24But when the Pharisees heard it they said, "It is only by Be-el′zebul, the prince of demons, that this man casts out demons."
25Knowing their thoughts, he said to them, "Every kingdom divided against itself is laid waste, and no city or house divided against itself will stand; 26and if Satan casts out Satan, he is divided against himself; how then will his kingdom stand? 27And if I cast out demons by Be-el′zebul, by whom do your sons cast them out? Therefore they shall be your judges. 28But if it is by the Spirit of God that I cast out demons, then the kingdom of God has come upon you. 29Or how can one enter a strong man's house and plunder his goods, unless

22 Τότε   προσηνέχθη   αὐτῷ   δαιμονιζ-
    Then   was brought   to him   a demon-

όμενος   τυφλὸς   καὶ   κωφός·   καὶ   ἐθεράπευσεν
possessed man   blind   and   dumb;   and   he healed

αὐτόν,   ὥστε   τὸν   κωφὸν   λαλεῖν   καὶ
  him,   so as   the   dumb   to speak   and

βλέπειν.   23 καὶ   ἐξίσταντο   πάντες   οἱ
to seeᵇ.   And   were astonished   all   the

ὄχλοι   καὶ   ἔλεγον·   μήτι   οὗτός   ἐστιν   ὁ
crowds   and   said: not   This   is   the

υἱὸς   Δαυίδ;   24 οἱ   δὲ   Φαρισαῖοι   ἀκού-
son   of David?   But the   Pharisees   hear-

σαντες   εἶπον·   οὗτος   οὐκ   ἐκβάλλει   τὰ
ing   said: This man   does not expel   the

δαιμόνια   εἰ   μὴ   ἐν   τῷ   Βεεζεβοὺλ   ἄρχοντι
demons   except   by   Beelzebub   ruler

τῶν   δαιμονίων.   25 εἰδὼς   δὲ   τὰς   ἐνθυμήσεις
of the   demons.   But knowing   the   thoughts

αὐτῶν   εἶπεν   αὐτοῖς·   πᾶσα   βασιλεία
of them   he said   to them: Every   kingdom

μερισθεῖσα   καθ᾽   ἑαυτῆς   ἐρημοῦται,
divided   against   itself   is brought to desolation,

καὶ   πᾶσα   πόλις   ἢ   οἰκία   μερισθεῖσα   καθ᾽
and   every   city   or   house   divided   against

ἑαυτῆς   οὐ   σταθήσεται.   26 καὶ   εἰ
itself   will not stand.   And   if

ὁ   σατανᾶς   τὸν   σατανᾶν   ἐκβάλλει,   ἐφ᾽
–   Satan   –   ²Satan   ¹expels,   against

ἑαυτὸν   ἐμερίσθη·   πῶς   οὖν   σταθή-
himself   he was(is) divided;   how   therefore   will

σεται   ἡ   βασιλεία   αὐτοῦ;   27 καὶ   εἰ
stand   the   kingdom   of him?   And   if

ἐγὼ   ἐν   Βεεζεβοὺλ   ἐκβάλλω   τὰ   δαιμόνια,
I   by   Beelzebub   expel   the   demons,

οἱ   υἱοὶ   ὑμῶν   ἐν   τίνι   ἐκβάλλουσιν;
the   sons   of you   by   what   do they expel?

διὰ   τοῦτο   αὐτοὶ   κριταὶ   ἔσονται   ὑμῶν.
therefore   they   judges   shall be   of you.

28 εἰ   δὲ   ἐν   πνεύματι   θεοῦ   ἐγὼ
   But if   by [the]   Spirit   of God   I

ἐκβάλλω   τὰ   δαιμόνια,   ἄρα   ἔφθασεν
expel   the   demons,   then   came

ἐφ᾽   ὑμᾶς   ἡ   βασιλεία   τοῦ   θεοῦ.   29 ἢ
upon   you   the   kingdom   –   of God.   Or

πῶς   δύναταί   τις   εἰσελθεῖν   εἰς   τὴν
how   can   anyone   to enter   into   the

οἰκίαν   τοῦ   ἰσχυροῦ   καὶ   τὰ   σκεύη   αὐτοῦ
house   of the   strong man   and   the   vessels   of him

he first binds the strong man? Then indeed he may plunder his house. [30]He who is not with me is against me, and he who does not gather with me scatters. [31]Therefore I tell you, every sin and blasphemy will be forgiven men, but the blasphemy against the Spirit will not be forgiven. [32]And whoever says a word against the Son of man will be forgiven; but whoever speaks against the Holy Spirit will not be forgiven, either in this age or in the age to come.

33 "Either make the tree good, and its fruit good; or make the tree bad, and its fruit bad; for the tree is known by its fruit. [34]You brood of vipers! how can you speak good, when you are evil? For out of the abundance of the heart the mouth speaks. [35]The good man out of his good treasure brings forth good, and the evil man out of his evil treasure

ἁρπάσαι, ἐὰν μὴ πρῶτον δήσῃ τὸν
to seize,   if   not   first   he binds   the

ἰσχυρόν; καὶ τότε τὴν οἰκίαν αὐτοῦ
strong man?   and   then   the   house   of him

διαρπάσει. 30 ὁ μὴ ὢν μετ' ἐμοῦ
he will plunder.   The [one] not   being   with   me

κατ' ἐμοῦ ἐστιν, καὶ ὁ μὴ συνάγων μετ'
against me   is,   and the [one] not   gathering   with

ἐμοῦ σκορπίζει. 31 Διὰ τοῦτο λέγω
me   scatters.   31 Therefore   I tell

ὑμῖν, πᾶσα ἁμαρτία καὶ βλασφημία
you,   all   sin   and   blasphemy

ἀφεθήσεται τοῖς ἀνθρώποις, ἡ δὲ τοῦ
will be forgiven   — to men,   but the   of the

πνεύματος βλασφημία οὐκ ἀφεθήσεται.
Spirit   blasphemy   will not be forgiven.

32 καὶ ὃς ἐὰν εἴπῃ λόγον κατὰ τοῦ
And   whoever   speaks   a word   against   the

υἱοῦ τοῦ ἀνθρώπου, ἀφεθήσεται αὐτῷ·
Son   —   of man,   it will be forgiven   to him;

ὃς δ' ἂν εἴπῃ κατὰ τοῦ πνεύματος
but whoever   speaks   against   the   Spirit

τοῦ ἁγίου, οὐκ ἀφεθήσεται αὐτῷ
—   Holy,   it will not be forgiven   to him

οὔτε ἐν τούτῳ τῷ αἰῶνι οὔτε ἐν τῷ
neither in   this   —   age   nor   in the [one]

μέλλοντι. 33 Ἢ ποιήσατε τὸ δένδρον
coming.   Either   make   the   tree

καλὸν καὶ τὸν καρπὸν αὐτοῦ καλόν,
good   and the   fruit   of it   good,

ἢ ποιήσατε τὸ δένδρον σαπρὸν καὶ τὸν
or   make   the   tree   bad   and   the

καρπὸν αὐτοῦ σαπρόν· ἐκ γὰρ τοῦ
fruit   of it   bad;   for of(by)   the

καρποῦ τὸ δένδρον γινώσκεται. 34 γεννή-
fruit   the   tree   is known.   34 Off-

ματα ἐχιδνῶν, πῶς δύνασθε ἀγαθὰ λαλεῖν
spring   of vipers,   how   can ye   good things   to speak

πονηροὶ ὄντες; ἐκ γὰρ τοῦ περισ-
²evil   ¹being?   for out of   the   abund-

σεύματος τῆς καρδίας τὸ στόμα λαλεῖ.
ance   of the   heart   the   mouth   speaks.

35 ὁ ἀγαθὸς ἄνθρωπος ἐκ τοῦ ἀγαθοῦ
The   good   man   out of   the   good

θησαυροῦ ἐκβάλλει ἀγαθά, καὶ ὁ πονηρὸς
treasure   puts forth   good things, and   the   evil

ἄνθρωπος ἐκ τοῦ πονηροῦ θησαυροῦ
man   out of   the   evil   treasure

brings forth evil. ³⁶I tell you, on the day of judgment men will render account for every careless word they utter; ³⁷for by your words you will be justified, and by your words you will be condemned."

38 Then some of the scribes and Pharisees said to him, "Teacher, we wish to see a sign from you." ³⁹But he answered them, "An evil and adulterous generation seeks for a sign; but no sign shall be given to it except the sign of the prophet Jonah. ⁴⁰For as Jonah was three days and three nights in the belly of the whale, so will the Son of man be three days and three nights in the heart of the earth. ⁴¹The men of Nin'eveh will arise at the judgment with this generation and condemn it; for they repented at the preaching of Jonah, and behold, something greater than Jonah is here. ⁴²The queen of the South will arise at the judgment with this generation and condemn it;

ἐκβάλλει   πονηρά.   36 λέγω   δὲ
puts forth   evil things.   But I tell

ὑμῖν ὅτι πᾶν ῥῆμα ἀργὸν ὃ λαλήσουσιν
you that every word idle which will speak

οἱ ἄνθρωποι, ἀποδώσουσιν περὶ αὐτοῦ
-     men,   they will render concerning it

λόγον ἐν ἡμέρᾳ κρίσεως· 37 ἐκ γὰρ
account in [the] day of judgment;   for of(by)

τῶν λόγων σου δικαιωθήσῃ, καὶ ἐκ
the   words of thee thou wilt be justified, and of(by)

τῶν λόγων σου καταδικασθήσῃ.
the   words of thee thou wilt be condemned.

38 Τότε ἀπεκρίθησαν αὐτῷ τινες τῶν
Then   answered   him   some of the

γραμματέων καὶ Φαρισαίων λέγοντες·
scribes   and Pharisees   saying:

διδάσκαλε, θέλομεν ἀπὸ σοῦ σημεῖον ἰδεῖν.
Teacher,   we wish from thee a sign   to see.

39 ὁ δὲ ἀποκριθεὶς εἶπεν αὐτοῖς·
   But he answering   said   to them:

γενεὰ πονηρὰ καὶ μοιχαλὶς σημεῖον
generation An evil and adulterous a sign

ἐπιζητεῖ, καὶ σημεῖον οὐ δοθήσεται
seeks,   and a sign   shall not be given

αὐτῇ εἰ μὴ τὸ σημεῖον Ἰωνᾶ τοῦ
to it except the sign of Jonas the

προφήτου. 40 ὥσπερ γὰρ ἦν Ἰωνᾶς
prophet.   For as   was   Jonas

ἐν τῇ κοιλίᾳ τοῦ κήτους τρεῖς ἡμέρας
in the belly of the sea monster three days

καὶ τρεῖς νύκτας, οὕτως ἔσται ὁ υἱὸς
and three nights,   so   will be the Son

τοῦ ἀνθρώπου ἐν τῇ καρδίᾳ τῆς γῆς
-    of man   in the heart of the earth

τρεῖς ἡμέρας καὶ τρεῖς νύκτας. 41 ἄνδρες
three days   and three nights.   Men

Νινευῖται ἀναστήσονται ἐν τῇ κρίσει
Ninevites will stand up in the judgment

μετὰ τῆς γενεᾶς ταύτης καὶ κατα-
with   -   generation this and will

κρινοῦσιν αὐτήν· ὅτι μετενόησαν εἰς τὸ
condemn   it; because they repented at the

κήρυγμα Ἰωνᾶ, καὶ ἰδοὺ πλεῖον Ἰωνᾶ
proclamation of Jonas, and behold a greater thing [than] Jonas

ὧδε. 42 βασίλισσα νότου ἐγερθήσεται
[is] here.   [The] queen of [the] south will be raised

ἐν τῇ κρίσει μετὰ τῆς γενεᾶς ταύτης
in the judgment with   -   generation this

for she came from the ends of the earth to hear the wisdom of Solomon, and behold, something greater than Solomon is here.

43 "When the unclean spirit has gone out of a man, he passes through waterless places seeking rest, but he finds none. ⁴⁴Then he says, 'I will return to my house from which I came.' And when he comes he finds it empty, swept, and put in order. ⁴⁵Then he goes and brings with him seven other spirits more evil than himself, and they enter and dwell there; and the last state of that man becomes worse than the first. So shall it be also with this evil generation."

46 While he was still speaking to the people, behold, his mother and his brothers stood outside, asking to speak to him.ˣ ⁴⁸But he replied to the man who told him, "Who is my mother, and who are my brothers?"

ˣ Other ancient authorities insert verse 47: *Some one told him, "Your mother and your brothers are standing outside, asking to speak to you"*

καὶ   κατακρινεῖ   αὐτήν·   ὅτι   ἦλθεν   ἐκ
and   will condemn   it;   because   she came   out of

τῶν   περάτων   τῆς   γῆς   ἀκοῦσαι   τὴν   σοφίαν
the   limits   of the earth   to hear   the   wisdom

Σολομῶνος,   καὶ   ἰδοὺ   πλεῖον   Σολομῶνος
of Solomon,   and   behold   a greater thing [than]   Solomon

ὧδε.   43 Ὅταν   δὲ   τὸ   ἀκάθαρτον   πνεῦμα
[is] here.   Now when   the   unclean   spirit

ἐξέλθῃ   ἀπὸ   τοῦ   ἀνθρώπου,   διέρχεται   δι'
goes out   from   –   a man,   he goes   through

ἀνύδρων   τόπων   ζητοῦν   ἀνάπαυσιν,   καὶ
dry   places   seeking   rest,   and

οὐχ   εὑρίσκει.   44 τότε   λέγει·   εἰς   τὸν
finds not.   Then   he says: Into   the

οἶκόν   μου   ἐπιστρέψω   ὅθεν   ἐξῆλθον·
house   of me   I will return   whence   I came out;

καὶ   ἐλθὸν   εὑρίσκει   σχολάζοντα   [καὶ]
and   coming   he finds [it]   standing empty   and

σεσαρωμένον   καὶ   κεκοσμημένον.   45 τότε
having been swept   and   having been furnished.   Then

πορεύεται   καὶ   παραλαμβάνει   μεθ'   ἑαυτοῦ
he goes   and   takes   with   himself

ἑπτὰ   ἕτερα   πνεύματα   πονηρότερα   ἑαυτοῦ,
seven   other   spirits   more evil [than]   himself,

καὶ   εἰσελθόντα   κατοικεῖ   ἐκεῖ·   καὶ
and   entering   dwells   there;   and

γίνεται   τὰ   ἔσχατα   τοῦ   ἀνθρώπου   ἐκείνου
becomes   the   last things   –   man   of that

χείρονα   τῶν   πρώτων.   οὕτως   ἔσται
worse [than]   the   first.   Thus   it will be

καὶ   τῇ   γενεᾷ   ταύτῃ   τῇ   πονηρᾷ.
also   –   ²generation   ¹to this   –   ²evil.

46 Ἔτι   αὐτοῦ   λαλοῦντος   τοῖς   ὄχλοις,
Yet   him   speakingᵃ   to the   crowds,
=While he was still speaking

ἰδοὺ   ἡ   μήτηρ   καὶ   οἱ   ἀδελφοὶ   αὐτοῦ
behold   the   mother   and   the   brothers   of him

εἱστήκεισαν   ἔξω   ζητοῦντες   αὐτῷ   λαλῆσαι.
stood   outside   seeking   to him   to speak.

47 [εἶπεν   δέ   τις   αὐτῷ·   ἰδοὺ   ἡ   μήτηρ
And said   someone to him: Behold[,]   the   mother

σου   καὶ   οἱ   ἀδελφοί   σου   ἔξω   ἑστήκασιν
of thee   and   the   brothers   of thee   outside   are standing

ζητοῦντές   σοι   λαλῆσαι.]   48 ὁ   δὲ
seeking   to thee   to speak.]   And he

ἀποκριθεὶς   εἶπεν   τῷ   λέγοντι   αὐτῷ·   τίς
answering   said   to the [one] saying   to him: Who

ἐστιν   ἡ   μήτηρ   μου,   καὶ   τίνες   εἰσίν   οἱ
is   the   mother   of me,   and   who   are   the

⁴⁹And stretching out his hand toward his disciples, he said, "Here are my mother and my brothers! ⁵⁰For whoever does the will of my Father in heaven is my brother, and sister, and mother."

ἀδελφοί	μου;		**49** καὶ	ἐκτείνας	τὴν
brothers	of me?		And	stretching forth	the

χεῖρα	[αὐτοῦ]	ἐπὶ	τοὺς	μαθητὰς	αὐτοῦ
hand	of him	on	the	disciples	of him

εἶπεν·	ἰδοὺ	ἡ	μήτηρ	μου	καὶ	οἱ	ἀδελφοί
he said:	Behold[,]	the	mother	of me	and	the	brothers

μου.	**50** ὅστις	γὰρ	ἂν	ποιήσῃ	τὸ	θέλημα
of me.	For whoever		does	the	will

τοῦ	πατρός	μου	τοῦ	ἐν	οὐρανοῖς,	αὐτός
of the	Father	of me	–	in	heavens,	he

μου	ἀδελφὸς	καὶ	ἀδελφὴ	καὶ	μήτηρ	ἐστίν.
of me	brother	and	sister	and	mother	is.

CHAPTER 13

THAT same day Jesus went out of the house and sat beside the sea. ²And great crowds gathered about him, so that he got into a boat and sat there; and the whole crowd stood on the beach. ³And he told them many things in parables, saying: "A sower went out to sow. ⁴And as he sowed, some seeds fell along the path, and the birds came and devoured them. ⁵Other seeds fell on rocky ground, where they had not much soil, and immediately they sprang up, since they had no depth of soil, ⁶but when the sun rose they were scorched; and since they

13 Ἐν	τῇ	ἡμέρᾳ	ἐκείνῃ	ἐξελθὼν	ὁ
On	–	day	that	¹going out of	–

Ἰησοῦς	τῆς	οἰκίας	ἐκάθητο	παρὰ	τὴν
¹Jesus	of the	house	sat	beside	the

θάλασσαν·	**2** καὶ	συνήχθησαν	πρὸς	αὐτὸν
sea;	and	were assembled	to	him

ὄχλοι	πολλοί,	ὥστε	αὐτὸν	εἰς	πλοῖον
crowds	many,	so as	him	in	a ship

= so that embarking in a ship he sat,

ἐμβάντα	καθῆσθαι,	καὶ	πᾶς	ὁ	ὄχλος
embarking	to sit[b],	and	all	the	crowd

ἐπὶ	τὸν	αἰγιαλὸν	εἱστήκει.	**3** καὶ	ἐλάλησεν
on	the	beach	stood.	And	he spoke

αὐτοῖς	πολλὰ	ἐν	παραβολαῖς	λέγων·
to them	many things	in	parables	saying:

Ἰδοὺ	ἐξῆλθεν	ὁ	σπείρων	τοῦ	σπείρειν.
Behold	went out	the [one]	sowing	–	to sow[d].

4 καὶ	ἐν	τῷ	σπείρειν	αὐτὸν	ἃ	μὲν
And	in	the	to sow	him[e]	some indeed

= as he sowed

ἔπεσεν	παρὰ	τὴν	ὁδόν,	καὶ	ἐλθόντα	τὰ
fell	beside	the	way,	and	coming	the

πετεινὰ	κατέφαγεν	αὐτά.	**5** ἄλλα	δὲ
birds	devoured	them.	But others

ἔπεσεν	ἐπὶ	τὰ	πετρώδη	ὅπου	οὐκ
fell	on	the	rocky places	where	not

εἶχεν	γῆν	πολλήν,	καὶ	εὐθέως	ἐξανέτειλεν
it had	earth	much,	and	immediately	it sprang up

διὰ	τὸ	μὴ	ἔχειν	βάθος	γῆς·	**6** ἡλίου
on account of the	not	to have	depth	of earth;	[the] sun

= because it had not

δὲ	ἀνατείλαντος	ἐκαυματίσθη,	καὶ	διὰ
But	having risen[a]	it was scorched,	and	on account of

= when the sun rose   = because

had no root they with-
ered away. [7] Other seeds
fell upon thorns, and the
thorns grew up and
choked them. [8] Other
seeds fell on good soil
and brought forth grain,
some a hundredfold,
some sixty, some thirty.
[9] He who has ears,[y] let
him hear."

10 Then the disciples
came and said to him,
"Why do you speak to
them in parables?" [11]And
he answered them, "To
you it has been given to
know the secrets of the
kingdom of heaven, but
to them it has not been
given. [12] For to him who
has will more be given,
and he will have abun-
dance; but from him who
has not, even what he
has will be taken away.
[13] This is why I speak to
them in parables, be-
cause seeing they do not
see, and hearing they do
not hear, nor do they
understand. [14] With them
indeed is fulfilled the
prophecy of Isaiah which
says:
'You shall indeed hear
     but never under-
     stand,
and you shall indeed
     see but never
     perceive.
[15] For this people's heart
     has grown dull,
and their ears are
     heavy of hearing,

[y] Other ancient authorities add
here and in verse 43 to hear

τὸ μὴ ἔχειν ῥίζαν ἐξηράνθη.   7 ἄλλα δὲ
the not to have root it was dried up.   But others
it had not

ἔπεσεν ἐπὶ τὰς ἀκάνθας, καὶ ἀνέβησαν
fell on the thorns, and came up

αἱ ἄκανθαι καὶ ἀπέπνιξαν αὐτά.   8 ἄλλα δὲ
the thorns and choked them.   And others

ἔπεσεν ἐπὶ τὴν γῆν τὴν καλὴν καὶ
fell on the earth - good and

ἐδίδου καρπόν, ὃ μὲν ἑκατόν, ὃ δὲ
gave fruit, the one a hundred, the other

ἑξήκοντα, ὃ δὲ τριάκοντα.   9 ὁ ἔχων
sixty, the other thirty.   The [one] having

ὦτα ἀκουέτω.   10 Καὶ προσελθόντες οἱ
ears let him hear.   And approaching the

μαθηταὶ εἶπαν αὐτῷ· διὰ τί ἐν παρα-
disciples said to him: Why in par-

βολαῖς λαλεῖς αὐτοῖς;   11 ὁ δὲ
ables speakest thou to them?   And he

ἀποκριθεὶς εἶπεν· ὅτι ὑμῖν δέδοται
answering said: Because to you it has been given

γνῶναι τὰ μυστήρια τῆς βασιλείας τῶν
to know the mysteries of the kingdom of the

οὐρανῶν, ἐκείνοις δὲ οὐ δέδοται.   12 ὅστις
heavens, but to those it has not been given.   [he] who

γὰρ ἔχει, δοθήσεται αὐτῷ καὶ περισ-
For has, it will be given to him and he will

σευθήσεται· ὅστις δὲ οὐκ ἔχει, καὶ
have abundance; but [he] who has not, even

ὃ ἔχει ἀρθήσεται ἀπ’ αὐτοῦ.   13 διὰ
what he has will be taken from him.   There-

τοῦτο ἐν παραβολαῖς αὐτοῖς λαλῶ, ὅτι
fore in parables to them I speak, because

βλέποντες οὐ βλέπουσιν καὶ ἀκούοντες
seeing they see not and hearing

οὐκ ἀκούουσιν οὐδὲ συνιοῦσιν.   14 καὶ
they hear not neither understand.   And

ἀναπληροῦται αὐτοῖς ἡ προφητεία Ἠσαΐου
is fulfilled in them the prophecy of Isaiah

ἡ λέγουσα· ἀκοῇ ἀκούσετε καὶ οὐ μὴ
- saying: In hearing ye will hear and by no means

συνῆτε, καὶ βλέποντες βλέψετε
understand, and seeing ye will see

καὶ οὐ μὴ ἴδητε.   15 ἐπαχύνθη γὰρ
and by no means perceive.   For waxed gross

ἡ καρδία τοῦ λαοῦ τούτου, καὶ τοῖς
the heart - people of this, and with the

and their eyes they have closed, lest they should perceive with their eyes, and hear with their ears, and understand with their heart, and turn for me to heal them.'
¹⁶ But blessed are your eyes, for they see, and your ears, for they hear. ¹⁷ Truly, I say to you, many prophets and righteous men longed to see what you see, and did not see it, and to hear what you hear, and did not hear it.

18 "Hear then the parable of the sower. ¹⁹ When any one hears the word of the kingdom and does not understand it, the evil one comes and snatches away what is sown in his heart; this is what was sown along the path. ²⁰ As for what was sown on rocky ground, this is he who hears the word and immediately receives it with joy; ²¹ yet he has no root in himself, but endures for a while, and when tribulation or persecution arises on account of the word, immediately he falls away.^z

ὦσὶν βαρέως ἤκουσαν, καὶ τοὺς ὀφθαλμοὺς
ears heavily they heard, and the eyes

αὐτῶν ἐκάμμυσαν· μήποτε ἴδωσιν τοῖς
of them they closed; lest they see with the

ὀφθαλμοῖς καὶ τοῖς ὠσὶν ἀκούσωσιν
eyes and with the ears hear

καὶ τῇ καρδίᾳ συνῶσιν καὶ ἐπιστρέψωσιν,
and with the heart understand and turn back,

καὶ ἰάσομαι αὐτούς. 16 ὑμῶν δὲ μακάριοι
and I will heal them. But of you blessed

οἱ ὀφθαλμοὶ ὅτι βλέπουσιν, καὶ τὰ
the eyes because they see, and the

ὦτα [ὑμῶν] ὅτι ἀκούουσιν. 17 ἀμὴν
ears of you because they hear. truly

γὰρ λέγω ὑμῖν ὅτι πολλοὶ προφῆται καὶ
For I say to you that many prophets and

δίκαιοι ἐπεθύμησαν ἰδεῖν ἃ
righteous men desired to see [the things] which

βλέπετε καὶ οὐκ εἶδαν, καὶ ἀκοῦσαι
ye see and did not see, and to hear

ἃ ἀκούετε καὶ οὐκ ἤκουσαν.
[the things] which ye hear and did not hear.

18 Ὑμεῖς οὖν ἀκούσατε τὴν παραβολὴν
¹Ye ²therefore ¹hear the parable

τοῦ σπείραντος. 19 Παντὸς ἀκούοντος^a
of the sowing [one]. Everyone hearing^a
= When anyone hears

τὸν λόγον τῆς βασιλείας καὶ μὴ συνιέντος^a
the word of the kingdom and not understanding^a
= does not understand

ἔρχεται ὁ πονηρὸς καὶ ἁρπάζει τὸ
comes the evil one and seizes the [thing]

ἐσπαρμένον ἐν τῇ καρδίᾳ αὐτοῦ· οὗτός
having been sown in the heart of him; this

ἐστιν ὁ παρὰ τὴν ὁδὸν σπαρείς. 20 ὁ
is the [word] by the way sown. the [word]

δὲ ἐπὶ τὰ πετρώδη σπαρείς, οὗτός ἐστιν
And on the rocky places sown, this is

ὁ τὸν λόγον ἀκούων καὶ εὐθὺς μετὰ
the [one] ²the ³word ¹hearing and immediately with

χαρᾶς λαμβάνων αὐτόν· 21 οὐκ ἔχει δὲ
joy receiving it; but he has not

ῥίζαν ἐν ἑαυτῷ ἀλλὰ πρόσκαιρός ἐστιν,
root in himself but short-lived is,

γενομένης δὲ θλίψεως ἢ διωγμοῦ
and occurring tribulation or persecution^a
= when tribulation or persecution occurs

διὰ τὸν λόγον εὐθὺς σκανδαλίζεται.
on account of the word immediately he is offended.

^z Or *stumbles*

²²As for what was sown among thorns, this is he who hears the word, but the cares of the world and the delight in riches choke the word, and it proves unfruitful. ²³As for what was sown on good soil, this is he who hears the word and understands it; he indeed bears fruit, and yields, in one case a hundredfold, in another sixty, and in another thirty."

24 Another parable he put before them, saying, "The kingdom of heaven may be compared to a man who sowed good seed in his field; ²⁵but while men were sleeping, his enemy came and sowed weeds among the wheat, and went away. ²⁶So when the plants came up and bore grain, then the weeds appeared also. ²⁷And the servants of the householder came and said to him, 'Sir, did you not sow good seed in your field? How then has it weeds?' ²⁸He said to them, 'An enemy has

22 ὁ δὲ εἰς τὰς ἀκάνθας σπαρείς, οὗτός
But the [word] in the thorns sown, this

ἐστιν ὁ τὸν λόγον ἀκούων, καὶ ἡ
is the [one] ²the ³word ¹hearing, and the

μέριμνα τοῦ αἰῶνος καὶ ἡ ἀπάτη
anxiety of the age and the deceit

τοῦ πλούτου συμπνίγει τὸν λόγον, καὶ
– of riches chokes the word, and

ἄκαρπος γίνεται. **23** ὁ δὲ ἐπὶ τὴν
unfruitful it becomes. And the [word] on the

καλὴν γῆν σπαρείς, οὗτός ἐστιν ὁ
good earth sown, this is the [one]

τὸν λόγον ἀκούων καὶ συνιείς, ὃς
⁴the ⁵word ¹hearing ²and ³understanding, who

δὴ καρποφορεῖ καὶ ποιεῖ ὃ μὲν ἑκατόν,
indeed bears fruit and produces one indeed a hundred,

ὃ δὲ ἑξήκοντα, ὃ δὲ τριάκοντα.
the other sixty, the other thirty.

24 "Ἄλλην παραβολὴν παρέθηκεν αὐτοῖς
Another parable he set before them

λέγων· ὡμοιώθη ἡ βασιλεία τῶν
saying: was(is) likened The kingdom of the

οὐρανῶν ἀνθρώπῳ σπείραντι καλὸν σπέρμα
heavens to a man sowing good seed

ἐν τῷ ἀγρῷ αὐτοῦ. **25** ἐν δὲ τῷ
in the field of him. But in the
=while men slept

καθεύδειν τοὺς ἀνθρώπους ἦλθεν αὐτοῦ
to sleep – menᵉ came of him

ὁ ἐχθρὸς καὶ ἐπέσπειρεν ζιζάνια ἀνὰ μέσον
the enemy and oversowed tares in between

τοῦ σίτου καὶ ἀπῆλθεν. **26** ὅτε δὲ
the wheat and went away. But when

ἐβλάστησεν ὁ χόρτος καὶ καρπὸν
sprouted the grass and fruit

ἐποίησεν, τότε ἐφάνη καὶ τὰ ζιζάνια.
produced, then appeared also the tares.

27 προσελθόντες δὲ οἱ δοῦλοι τοῦ οἰκο-
So approaching the slaves of the house-

δεσπότου εἶπον αὐτῷ· κύριε, οὐχὶ καλὸν
master said to him: Lord, not good

σπέρμα ἔσπειρας ἐν τῷ σῷ ἀγρῷ;
seed sowedst thou in – thy field?

πόθεν οὖν ἔχει ζιζάνια; **28** ὁ δὲ ἔφη
whence then has it tares? And he said

αὐτοῖς· ἐχθρὸς ἄνθρωπος τοῦτο ἐποίησεν.
to them: An enemy man this did.

done this.' The servants said to him, 'Then do you want us to go and gather them?' [29] But he said, 'No; lest in gathering the weeds you root up the wheat along with them. [30] Let both grow together until the harvest; and at harvest time I will tell the reapers, Gather the weeds first and bind them in bundles to be burned, but gather the wheat into my barn.' ''

31 Another parable he put before them, saying, "The kingdom of heaven is like a grain of mustard seed which a man took and sowed in his field; [32] it is the smallest of all seeds, but when it has grown it is the greatest of shrubs and becomes a tree, so that the birds of the air come and make nests in its branches."

33 He told them another parable. "The kingdom of heaven is like leaven which a woman took and hid in three measures of meal, till it was all leavened."

οἱ	δὲ	δοῦλοι	αὐτῷ	λέγουσιν·		θέλεις
So the		slaves	to him	say:		Willest thou

οὖν	ἀπελθόντες	συλλέξωμεν	αὐτά;	29 ὁ
then	going away	we may collect	them?	he

δέ	φησιν·	οὔ,	μήποτε	συλλέγοντες	τὰ
But	says:	No,	lest	collecting	the

ζιζάνια	ἐκριζώσητε	ἅμα	αὐτοῖς	τὸν
tares	ye should root up	together with	them	the

σῖτον.	30 ἄφετε	συναυξάνεσθαι	ἀμφότερα
wheat.	Leave	to grow together	both

ἕως	τοῦ	θερισμοῦ·	καὶ	ἐν	καιρῷ	τοῦ
until	the	harvest;	and	in	time	of the

θερισμοῦ	ἐρῶ	τοῖς	θερισταῖς·	συλλέξατε
harvest	I will say	to the	reapers:	Collect ye

πρῶτον	τὰ	ζιζάνια	καὶ	δήσατε	αὐτὰ
first	the	tares	and	bind	them

εἰς	δέσμας	πρὸς	τὸ	κατακαῦσαι	αὐτά,
in	bundles	–	–	to burn	them,

τὸν	δὲ	σῖτον	συναγάγετε	εἰς	τὴν	ἀποθήκην
but the		wheat	gather ye	into	the	barn

μου.	31 Ἄλλην	παραβολὴν	παρέθηκεν
of me.	Another	parable	he set before

αὐτοῖς	λέγων·	ὁμοία	ἐστὶν	ἡ	βασιλεία
them	saying:	Like	is		the kingdom

τῶν	οὐρανῶν	κόκκῳ	σινάπεως,	ὃν
of the	heavens	to a grain	of mustard,	which

λαβὼν	ἄνθρωπος	ἔσπειρεν	ἐν	τῷ	ἀγρῷ
[1]taking	[1]a man	sowed	in	the	field

αὐτοῦ·	32 ὃ	μικρότερον	μέν	ἐστιν
of him;	which	less	indeed	is

πάντων	τῶν	σπερμάτων,	ὅταν	δὲ
[than] all	the	seeds,		but when

αὐξηθῇ,	μεῖζον	τῶν	λαχάνων	ἐστὶν
it grows,	greater [than] the		herbs	it is

καὶ	γίνεται	δένδρον,	ὥστε	ἐλθεῖν	τὰ
and	becomes	a tree,	so as	to come	the

πετεινὰ	τοῦ	οὐρανοῦ	καὶ	κατασκηνοῦν
birds	of the	heaven	and	dwell

ἐν	τοῖς	κλάδοις	αὐτοῦ.	33 Ἄλλην
in	the	branches	of it.	Another

παραβολὴν	ἐλάλησεν	αὐτοῖς·	ὁμοία
parable	he spoke	to them:	Like

ἐστὶν	ἡ	βασιλεία	τῶν	οὐρανῶν	ζύμη,
is	the	kingdom	of the	heavens	to leaven,

ἣν	λαβοῦσα	γυνὴ	ἐνέκρυψεν	εἰς	ἀλεύρου
which	[2]taking	[1]a woman	hid	in	[2]of meal

σάτα	τρία,	ἕως	οὗ	ἐζυμώθη	ὅλον.
[2]measures	[1]three,	until		was leavened [the] whole.

34 All this Jesus said to the crowds in parables; indeed he said nothing to them without a parable. [35] This was to fulfil what was spoken by the prophet:[a]

"I will open my mouth in parables,

I will utter what has been hidden since the foundation of the world."

36 Then he left the crowds and went into the house. And his disciples came to him, saying, "Explain to us the parable of the weeds of the field." [37] He answered, "He who sows the good seed is the Son of man; [38] the field is the world, and the good seed means the sons of the kingdom; the weeds are the sons of the evil one, [39] and the enemy who sowed them is the devil; the harvest is the close of the age, and the reapers are angels. [40] Just as the weeds are gathered and burned with fire, so will it be at the close of the age. [41] The Son of man will send his angels, and they will gather out of his kingdom

---

34 Ταῦτα πάντα ἐλάλησεν ὁ Ἰησοῦς ἐν
These things all spoke – Jesus in

παραβολαῖς τοῖς ὄχλοις, καὶ χωρὶς παραβολῆς
parables to the crowds, and without a parable

οὐδὲν ἐλάλει αὐτοῖς· 35 ὅπως πληρωθῇ
nothing he spoke to them; so that was fulfilled

τὸ ῥηθὲν διὰ τοῦ προφήτου λέγοντος·
the [thing] spoken through the prophet saying:

ἀνοίξω ἐν παραβολαῖς τὸ στόμα μου,
I will open in parables the mouth of me,

ἐρεύξομαι κεκρυμμένα ἀπὸ καταβολῆς.
I will utter things having been hidden from [the] foundation.

36 Τότε ἀφεὶς τοὺς ὄχλους ἦλθεν
Then sending away the crowds he came

εἰς τὴν οἰκίαν. Καὶ προσῆλθον αὐτῷ
into the house. And approached to him

οἱ μαθηταὶ αὐτοῦ λέγοντες· διασάφησον
the disciples of him saying: Explain thou

ἡμῖν τὴν παραβολὴν τῶν ζιζανίων τοῦ
to us the parable of the tares of the

ἀγροῦ. 37 ὁ δὲ ἀποκριθεὶς εἶπεν· ὁ
field. And he answering said: The [one]

σπείρων τὸ καλὸν σπέρμα ἐστὶν ὁ
sowing the good seed is the

υἱὸς τοῦ ἀνθρώπου· 38 ὁ δὲ ἀγρός
Son – of man; and the field

ἐστιν ὁ κόσμος· τὸ δὲ καλὸν σπέρμα,
is the world; and the good seed,

οὗτοί εἰσιν οἱ υἱοὶ τῆς βασιλείας· τὰ δὲ
these are the sons of the kingdom; and the

ζιζάνιά εἰσιν οἱ υἱοὶ τοῦ πονηροῦ, 39 ὁ
tares are the sons of the evil [one], the

δὲ ἐχθρὸς ὁ σπείρας αὐτά ἐστιν ὁ
and enemy the [one] sowing them is the

διάβολος· ὁ δὲ θερισμὸς συντέλεια
devil; and the harvest [the] completion

αἰῶνός ἐστιν, οἱ δὲ θερισταὶ ἄγγελοί
of [the] age is, and the reapers angels

εἰσιν. 40 ὥσπερ οὖν συλλέγεται τὰ
are. As therefore are collected the

ζιζάνια καὶ πυρὶ κατακαίεται, οὕτως
tares and with fire are consumed, thus

ἔσται ἐν τῇ συντελείᾳ τοῦ αἰῶνος·
it will be at the completion of the age;

41 ἀποστελεῖ ὁ υἱὸς τοῦ ἀνθρώπου
will send forth the Son – of man

---

[a] Other ancient authorities read the prophet Isaiah

τοὺς ἀγγέλους αὐτοῦ, καὶ συλλέξουσιν
the angels of him, and they will collect

all causes of sin and all evildoers, ⁴²and throw them into the furnace of fire; there men will weep and gnash their teeth. ⁴³Then the righteous will shine like the sun in the kingdom of their Father. He who has ears, let him hear.

44 "The kingdom of heaven is like treasure hidden in a field, which a man found and covered up; then in his joy he goes and sells all that he has and buys that field.

45 "Again, the kingdom of heaven is like a merchant in search of fine pearls, ⁴⁶who, on finding one pearl of great value, went and sold all that he had and bought it.

47 "Again, the kingdom of heaven is like a net which was thrown into the sea and gathered fish of every kind; ⁴⁸when it was full, men drew it ashore and sat down and sorted the good into vessels but threw away the bad. ⁴⁹So it will be at

ἐκ   τῆς   βασιλείας   αὐτοῦ   πάντα
out of   the   kingdom   of him   all

τὰ   σκάνδαλα   καὶ   τοὺς   ποιοῦντας
the things leading to sin   and   the [ones]   doing

τὴν   ἀνομίαν,   42 καὶ   βαλοῦσιν   αὐτοὺς   εἰς
-       lawlessness,   and   will cast   them   into

τὴν   κάμινον   τοῦ   πυρός·   ἐκεῖ   ἔσται   ὁ
the   furnace   -   of fire;   there   will be   the

κλαυθμὸς   καὶ   ὁ   βρυγμὸς   τῶν   ὀδόντων.
wailing   and   the   gnashing   of the   teeth.

43 τότε   οἱ   δίκαιοι   ἐκλάμψουσιν   ὡς   ὁ
Then   the   righteous   will shine forth   as   the

ἥλιος   ἐν   τῇ   βασιλείᾳ   τοῦ   πατρὸς
sun   in   the   kingdom   of the   Father

αὐτῶν.   ὁ   ἔχων   ὦτα   ἀκουέτω.
of them.   The [one] having ears   let him hear.

44 Ὁμοία   ἐστὶν   ἡ   βασιλεία   τῶν
Like   is   the   kingdom   of the

οὐρανῶν   θησαυρῷ   κεκρυμμένῳ   ἐν   τῷ
heavens   to treasure   having been hidden   in   the

ἀγρῷ,   ὃν   εὑρὼν   ἄνθρωπος   ἔκρυψεν,   καὶ
field,   which ²finding   ¹a man   hid,   and

ἀπὸ   τῆς   χαρᾶς   αὐτοῦ   ὑπάγει   καὶ   πωλεῖ
from   the   joy   of him   goes   and   sells

ὅσα   ἔχει   καὶ   ἀγοράζει   τὸν   ἀγρὸν
what things he has and   buys   -   field

ἐκεῖνον.   45 Πάλιν   ὁμοία   ἐστὶν   ἡ
that.   Again   like   is   the

βασιλεία   τῶν   οὐρανῶν   ἐμπόρῳ   ζητοῦντι
kingdom   of the   heavens   to a merchant   seeking

καλοὺς   μαργαρίτας·   46 εὑρὼν   δὲ   ἕνα   πολύτιμον
beautiful   pearls;   and finding   one   valuable

μαργαρίτην   ἀπελθὼν   πέπρακεν   πάντα
pearl   going away   sold   all things

ὅσα   εἶχεν   καὶ   ἠγόρασεν   αὐτόν.
what   he had   and   bought   it.

47 Πάλιν   ὁμοία   ἐστὶν   ἡ   βασιλεία   τῶν
Again   like   is   the   kingdom   of the

οὐρανῶν   σαγήνῃ   βληθείσῃ   εἰς   τὴν   θάλασσαν
heavens   to a net   cast   into   the   sea

καὶ   ἐκ   παντὸς   γένους   συναγαγούσῃ·
and   of   every   kind   gathering;

48 ἣν   ὅτε   ἐπληρώθη   ἀναβιβάσαντες   ἐπὶ
which   when   it was filled   bringing up   onto

τὸν   αἰγιαλὸν   καὶ   καθίσαντες   συνέλεξαν
the   shore   and   sitting   collected

τὰ   καλὰ   εἰς   ἄγγη,   τὰ   δὲ   σαπρὰ   ἔξω
the   good   into   vessels,   but the   bad   out

the close of the age. The angels will come out and separate the evil from the righteous, ⁵⁰ and throw them into the furnace of fire; there men will weep and gnash their teeth.

51 "Have you understood all this?" They said to him, "Yes." ⁵² And he said to them, "Therefore every scribe who has been trained for the kingdom of heaven is like a householder who brings out of his treasure what is new and what is old."

53 And when Jesus had finished these parables, he went away from there, ⁵⁴ and coming to his own country he taught them in their synagogue, so that they were astonished, and said, "Where did this man get this wisdom and these mighty works? ⁵⁵ Is not this the carpenter's son? Is not his mother called Mary? And are not his brothers James and Joseph and Simon and Judas? ⁵⁶ And are not all his sisters with us?

ἔβαλον.   **49** οὕτως ἔσται ἐν τῇ συντελείᾳ
cast.   Thus   it will be   at   the   completion

τοῦ αἰῶνος· ἐξελεύσονται οἱ ἄγγελοι καὶ
of the   age: will go forth   the   angels   and

ἀφοριοῦσιν τοὺς πονηροὺς ἐκ μέσου
will separate   the   evil men   from [the] midst

τῶν δικαίων,   **50** καὶ βαλοῦσιν αὐτοὺς
of the   righteous,   and   will cast   them

εἰς τὴν κάμινον τοῦ πυρός· ἐκεῖ
into   the   furnace   -   of fire;   there

ἔσται ὁ κλαυθμὸς καὶ ὁ βρυγμὸς τῶν
will be   the   wailing   and   the   gnashing   of the

ὀδόντων.   **51** Συνήκατε ταῦτα πάντα;
teeth.   Did ye understand   ²these things   ¹all?

λέγουσιν αὐτῷ· ναί.   **52** ὁ δὲ εἶπεν
They say   to him: Yes.   So he   said

αὐτοῖς· διὰ τοῦτο πᾶς γραμματεὺς
to them: Therefore   every   scribe

μαθητευθεὶς τῇ βασιλείᾳ τῶν οὐρανῶν
made a disciple   to the   kingdom   of the   heavens

ὅμοιός ἐστιν ἀνθρώπῳ οἰκοδεσπότῃ,
like   is   to a man   a housemaster,

ὅστις ἐκβάλλει ἐκ τοῦ θησαυροῦ
who   puts forth   out of   the   treasure

αὐτοῦ καινὰ καὶ παλαιά.
of him   new   and   old things.

53 Καὶ ἐγένετο ὅτε ἐτέλεσεν ὁ
And   it came to pass   when   ended   -

Ἰησοῦς τὰς παραβολὰς ταύτας, μετῆρεν
Jesus   parables   these,   he removed

ἐκεῖθεν.   **54** καὶ ἐλθὼν εἰς τὴν πατρίδα
thence.   And   coming into   the   native town

αὐτοῦ ἐδίδασκεν αὐτοὺς ἐν τῇ συνα-
of him   he taught   them   in   the   syna-

γωγῇ αὐτῶν, ὥστε ἐκπλήσσεσθαι αὐτοὺς
gogue   of them,   so as   to be astounded   them
             = so that they were astounded

καὶ λέγειν· πόθεν τούτῳ ἡ σοφία αὕτη
and   to sayᵇ: Whence   to this man   -   wisdom   this
and said:

καὶ αἱ δυνάμεις;   **55** οὐχ οὗτός ἐστιν
and   the   powerful deeds?   not   this man   is

ὁ τοῦ τέκτονος υἱός; οὐχ ἡ μήτηρ
the   of the   carpenter   son?   not   the   mother

αὐτοῦ λέγεται Μαριὰμ καὶ οἱ ἀδελφοὶ
of him   called   Mary   and   the   brothers

αὐτοῦ Ἰάκωβος καὶ Ἰωσὴφ καὶ Σίμων
of him   James   and   Joseph   and   Simon

καὶ Ἰούδας;   **56** καὶ αἱ ἀδελφαὶ αὐτοῦ
and   Judas?   and   the   sisters   of him

Where then did this man get all this?" [57]And they took offense at him. But Jesus said to them, "A prophet is not without honor except in his own country and in his own house." [58]And he did not do many mighty works there, because of their unbelief.

οὐχὶ	πᾶσαι	πρὸς	ἡμᾶς	εἰσιν;	πόθεν
not	all	with	us	are?	Whence

οὖν	τούτῳ	ταῦτα	πάντα;	57 καὶ
then	to this man	these things	all?	And

ἐσκανδαλίζοντο	ἐν	αὐτῷ.	ὁ δὲ	Ἰησοῦς
they were offended	in	him.	- But	Jesus

εἶπεν	αὐτοῖς·	οὐκ	ἔστιν	προφήτης
said	to them:	[2]not	[2]is	[1]A prophet

ἄτιμος	εἰ μὴ	ἐν	τῇ	πατρίδι	καὶ
unhonoured	except	in	the(his)	native town	and

ἐν	τῇ	οἰκίᾳ αὐτοῦ.	58 καὶ	οὐκ	ἐποίησεν	ἐκεῖ
in	the	house of him.	And	not	he did	there

δυνάμεις	πολλὰς	διὰ	τὴν	ἀπιστίαν	αὐτῶν.
powerful deeds	many	because of	the	unbelief	of them.

CHAPTER 14

A T that time Herod the tetrarch heard about the fame of Jesus; [2]and he said to his servants, "This is John the Baptist, he has been raised from the dead; that is why these powers are at work in him." [3]For Herod had seized John and bound him and put him in prison, for the sake of Hero'di-as, his brother Philip's wife;[b] [4]because John said to him, "It is not lawful for you to have her." [5]And though he wanted to put him to death, he feared the people, because they held him to be a prophet. [6]But when Herod's birthday came, the daughter of Hero'di-as danced before the company, and pleased Herod,

14 Ἐν	ἐκείνῳ	τῷ	καιρῷ	ἤκουσεν
At	that	-	time	heard

Ἡρῴδης	ὁ	τετραάρχης	τὴν	ἀκοὴν	Ἰησοῦ,
Herod	the	tetrarch	the	report	of Jesus,

2 καὶ	εἶπεν	τοῖς	παισὶν	αὐτοῦ·	οὗτός
and	said	to the	servants	of him:	This

ἐστιν	Ἰωάννης	ὁ	βαπτιστής·	αὐτὸς
is	John	the	Baptist;	he

ἠγέρθη	ἀπὸ	τῶν	νεκρῶν,	καὶ	διὰ	τοῦτο
was raised	from	the	dead,	and	therefore

αἱ	δυνάμεις	ἐνεργοῦσιν	ἐν	αὐτῷ.
the	powerful deeds	operate	in	him.

3 Ὁ	γὰρ	Ἡρῴδης	κρατήσας	τὸν	Ἰωάννην
-	For	Herod	seizing	-	John

ἔδησεν	καὶ	ἐν	φυλακῇ	ἀπέθετο	διὰ
bound	and	in	prison	put away	on account of

Ἡρῳδιάδα	τὴν	γυναῖκα	Φιλίππου	τοῦ
Herodias	the	wife	of Philip	the

ἀδελφοῦ	αὐτοῦ·	4 ἔλεγεν	γὰρ	ὁ	Ἰωάννης
brother	of him;	for said		-	John

αὐτῷ·	οὐκ	ἔξεστίν	σοι	ἔχειν	αὐτήν.
to him:	It is not lawful		for thee	to have	her.

5 καὶ	θέλων	αὐτὸν	ἀποκτεῖναι	ἐφοβήθη
And	wishing	him	to kill	he feared

τὸν	ὄχλον,	ὅτι	ὡς	προφήτην	αὐτὸν
the	crowd,	because	as	a prophet	him

εἶχον.	6 γενεσίοις	δὲ	γενομένοις	τοῦ
they had.	Now on the birthday		occurring	-

Ἡρῴδου	ὠρχήσατο	ἡ	θυγάτηρ	τῆς
of Herod	danced	the	daughter	of the

[b] Other ancient authorities read *his brother's wife*

Ἡρῳδιάδος	ἐν	τῷ	μέσῳ	καὶ	ἤρεσεν
of Herodias	in	the	midst	and	pleased

⁷so that he promised with an oath to give her whatever she might ask.
⁸Prompted by her mother, she said, "Give me the head of John the Baptist here on a platter."
⁹And the king was sorry; but because of his oaths and his guests he commanded it to be given;
¹⁰he sent and had John beheaded in the prison,
¹¹and his head was brought on a platter and given to the girl, and she brought it to her mother.
¹²And his disciples came and took the body and buried it; and they went and told Jesus.

13 Now when Jesus heard this, he withdrew from there in a boat to a lonely place apart. But when the crowds heard it, they followed him on foot from the towns. ¹⁴As he went ashore he saw a great throng; and he had compassion on them, and healed their sick. ¹⁵When it was evening, the disciples came to him and said, "This is a lonely place, and the day is now

τῷ Ἡρῴδῃ, 7 ὅθεν μεθ' ὅρκου ὡμολόγησεν
-    Herod,   whence with an oath he promised

αὐτῇ δοῦναι ὃ ἐὰν αἰτήσηται. 8 ἡ δὲ
²her ¹to give whatever she might ask.   So she

προβιβασθεῖσα ὑπὸ τῆς μητρὸς αὐτῆς·
being instructed by   the   mother of her:

δός μοι, φησίν, ὧδε ἐπὶ πίνακι τὴν
Give me, she says, here on a platter the

κεφαλὴν Ἰωάννου τοῦ βαπτιστοῦ. 9 καὶ
head   of John   the   Baptist.   And

λυπηθεὶς ὁ βασιλεὺς διὰ τοὺς
being grieved the king   on account of the

ὅρκους καὶ τοὺς συνανακειμένους
oaths   and the [ones] reclining at table with [him]

ἐκέλευσεν δοθῆναι, 10 καὶ πέμψας
he commanded to be given,   and   sending

ἀπεκεφάλισεν Ἰωάννην ἐν τῇ φυλακῇ.
beheaded   John   in the prison.

11 καὶ ἠνέχθη ἡ κεφαλὴ αὐτοῦ ἐπὶ
And was brought the head   of him on

πίνακι καὶ ἐδόθη τῷ κορασίῳ, καὶ
a platter and was given to the maid,   and

ἤνεγκεν τῇ μητρὶ αὐτῆς. 12 καὶ
she brought [it] to the mother of her.   And

προσελθόντες οἱ μαθηταὶ αὐτοῦ ἦραν τὸ
⁴approaching ¹the ²disciples ³of him took the

πτῶμα καὶ ἔθαψαν αὐτόν, καὶ ἐλθόντες
corpse and buried him,   and coming

ἀπήγγειλαν τῷ Ἰησοῦ. 13 Ἀκούσας δὲ
reported   -   to Jesus.   And ²hearing

ὁ Ἰησοῦς ἀνεχώρησεν ἐκεῖθεν ἐν
- ¹Jesus   departed   thence   in

πλοίῳ εἰς ἔρημον τόπον κατ' ἰδίαν·
a ship to a desert place   privately;

καὶ ἀκούσαντες οἱ ὄχλοι ἠκολούθησαν
and ³hearing ¹the ²crowds followed

αὐτῷ πεζῇ ἀπὸ τῶν πόλεων. 14 Καὶ
him afoot from the cities.   And

ἐξελθὼν εἶδεν πολὺν ὄχλον, καὶ
going forth he saw a much crowd, and

ἐσπλαγχνίσθη ἐπ' αὐτοῖς καὶ
was filled with tenderness over them and

ἐθεράπευσεν τοὺς ἀρρώστους αὐτῶν.
healed   the   sick   of them.

15 ὀψίας δὲ γενομένης προσῆλθον αὐτῷ
Now evening coming on⁸ approached to him
=when evening came on

οἱ μαθηταὶ λέγοντες· ἔρημός ἐστιν ὁ
the disciples saying: Desert   is   the

over; send the crowds away to go into the villages and buy food for themselves." [16]Jesus said, "They need not go away; you give them something to eat." [17]They said to him, "We have only five loaves here and two fish." [18]And he said, "Bring them here to me." [19]Then he ordered the crowds to sit down on the grass; and taking the five loaves and the two fish he looked up to heaven, and blessed, and broke and gave the loaves to the disciples, and the disciples gave them to the crowds. [20]And they all ate and were satisfied. And they took up twelve baskets full of the broken pieces left over. [21]And those who ate were about five thousand men, besides women and children.

22 Then he made the disciples get into the boat and go before him to the other side, while he dismissed the crowds. [23]And after he had dismissed the crowds, he went up into the hills by

τόπος καὶ ἡ ὥρα ἤδη παρῆλθεν·
place and the hour already passed;

ἀπόλυσον οὖν τοὺς ὄχλους, ἵνα ἀπελθόντες
dismiss therefore the crowds, that going away

εἰς τὰς κώμας ἀγοράσωσιν ἑαυτοῖς
into the villages they may buy for themselves

βρώματα. 16 ὁ δὲ Ἰησοῦς εἶπεν αὐτοῖς·
foods. – But Jesus said to them:

οὐ χρείαν ἔχουσιν ἀπελθεῖν· δότε
Not need they have to go away; give

αὐτοῖς ὑμεῖς φαγεῖν. 17 οἱ δὲ λέγουσιν
them ye to eat. But they say

αὐτῷ· οὐκ ἔχομεν ὧδε εἰ μὴ πέντε
to him: We have not here except five

ἄρτους καὶ δύο ἰχθύας. 18 ὁ δὲ εἶπεν·
loaves and two fishes. And he said:

φέρετέ μοι ὧδε αὐτούς. 19 καὶ κελεύσας
Bring to me here them. And having commanded

τοὺς ὄχλους ἀνακλιθῆναι ἐπὶ τοῦ χόρτου,
the crowds to recline on the grass,

λαβὼν τοὺς πέντε ἄρτους καὶ τοὺς δύο
taking the five loaves and the two

ἰχθύας, ἀναβλέψας εἰς τὸν οὐρανὸν
fishes, looking up to – heaven

εὐλόγησεν, καὶ κλάσας ἔδωκεν τοῖς
he blessed, and breaking gave to the

μαθηταῖς τοὺς ἄρτους, οἱ δὲ μαθηταὶ
disciples the loaves, and the disciples

τοῖς ὄχλοις. 20 καὶ ἔφαγον πάντες καὶ
to the crowds, And ate all and

ἐχορτάσθησαν· καὶ ἦραν τὸ περισσεῦον
were satisfied; and they took the excess

τῶν κλασμάτων, δώδεκα κοφίνους πλήρεις.
of the fragments, twelve baskets full.

21 οἱ δὲ ἐσθίοντες ἦσαν ἄνδρες ὡσεὶ
And the [ones] eating were men about

πεντακισχίλιοι χωρὶς γυναικῶν καὶ
five thousand apart from women and

παιδίων. 22 Καὶ [εὐθέως] ἠνάγκασεν
children. And immediately he constrained

τοὺς μαθητὰς ἐμβῆναι εἰς τὸ πλοῖον
the disciples to embark in the ship

καὶ προάγειν αὐτὸν εἰς τὸ πέραν,
and to go before him to the other side,

ἕως οὗ ἀπολύσῃ τοὺς ὄχλους. 23 Καὶ
until he should dismiss the crowds. And

ἀπολύσας τοὺς ὄχλους ἀνέβη εἰς τὸ
having dismissed the crowds he went up into the

himself to pray. When evening came, he was there alone, ²⁴but the boat by this time was many furlongs distant from the land,^c beaten by the waves; for the wind was against them. ²⁵And in the fourth watch of the night he came to them, walking on the sea. ²⁶But when the disciples saw him walking on the sea, they were terrified, saying, "It is a ghost!" And they cried out for fear. ²⁷But immediately he spoke to them, saying, "Take heart, it is I; have no fear."

28 And Peter answered him, "Lord, if it is you, bid me come to you on the water." ²⁹He said, "Come." So Peter got out of the boat and walked on the water and came to Jesus; ³⁰but when he saw the wind,^d he was afraid, and beginning to sink he cried out, "Lord, save me." ³¹Jesus immediately reached out his hand and caught him, saying to him, "O man of little

ὄρος κατ᾽ ἰδίαν προσεύξασθαι. ὀψίας
mountain privately   to pray.   evening
                                             = And when

δὲ γενομένης μόνος ἦν ἐκεῖ. 24 τὸ δὲ
And coming on   alone he was there.   But the
evening came on

πλοῖον ἤδη σταδίους πολλοὺς ἀπὸ τῆς
ship   now   furlongs   many   from   the

γῆς ἀπεῖχεν, βασανιζόμενον ὑπὸ τῶν
land   was away,   being distressed   by   the

κυμάτων, ἦν γὰρ ἐναντίος ὁ ἄνεμος.
waves,   ⁴was ¹for ⁵contrary ²the ³wind.

25 τετάρτῃ δὲ φυλακῇ τῆς νυκτὸς
    Now in [the] fourth watch   of the   night

ἦλθεν πρὸς αὐτοὺς περιπατῶν ἐπὶ τὴν
he came toward   them   walking   on   the

θάλασσαν. 26 οἱ δὲ μαθηταὶ ἰδόντες
sea.   And the   disciples   seeing

αὐτὸν ἐπὶ τῆς θαλάσσης περιπατοῦντα
him   on   the   sea   walking

ἐταράχθησαν λέγοντες ὅτι φάντασμά
were troubled   saying[,]   -   A phantasm

ἐστιν, καὶ ἀπὸ τοῦ φόβου ἔκραξαν.
it is,   and from   the   fear   they cried out.

27 εὐθὺς δὲ ἐλάλησεν [ὁ Ἰησοῦς]
    But immediately   spoke   -   Jesus

αὐτοῖς λέγων· θαρσεῖτε, ἐγώ εἰμι·
to them   saying: Be of good cheer, I   am;

μὴ φοβεῖσθε. 28 ἀποκριθεὶς δὲ αὐτῷ
do not fear.   And answering   him   -

Πέτρος εἶπεν· κύριε, εἰ σὺ εἶ, κέλευσόν
Peter   said: Lord, if thou art,   command

με ἐλθεῖν πρὸς σὲ ἐπὶ τὰ ὕδατα. 29 ὁ
me to come   to   thee on the waters.   he

δὲ εἶπεν· ἐλθέ. καὶ καταβὰς ἀπὸ τοῦ
And said: Come. And going down from   the

πλοίου Πέτρος περιπάτησεν ἐπὶ τὰ ὕδατα
ship   Peter   walked   on   the   waters

καὶ ἦλθεν πρὸς τὸν Ἰησοῦν. 30 βλέπων δὲ
and came toward   -   Jesus.   But seeing

τὸν ἄνεμον ἐφοβήθη, καὶ ἀρξάμενος
the   wind   he was afraid, and   beginning

καταποντίζεσθαι ἔκραξεν λέγων·
to sink   he cried out   saying:

κύριε, σῶσόν με. 31 εὐθέως δὲ ὁ
Lord, save   me.   And immediately   -

Ἰησοῦς ἐκτείνας τὴν χεῖρα ἐπελάβετο
Jesus stretching out the(his) hand   took hold

αὐτοῦ, καὶ λέγει αὐτῷ· ὀλιγόπιστε,
of him, and says to him: Little-faith,

faith, why did you doubt?" [32]And when they got into the boat, the wind ceased. [33]And those in the boat worshiped him, saying, "Truly you are the Son of God."

34 And when they had crossed over, they came to land at Gennes′aret. [35]And when the men of that place recognized him, they sent round to all that region and brought to him all that were sick, [36]and besought him that they might only touch the fringe of his garment; and as many as touched it were made well.

εἰς τί ἐδίστασας;   **32** καὶ ἀναβάντων
why   didst thou doubt?   And   going up
                                        = as they went up

αὐτῶν εἰς τὸ πλοῖον ἐκόπασεν ὁ ἄνεμος.
them[a]   into   the   ship   ceased   the   wind.

33 οἱ δὲ ἐν τῷ πλοίῳ προσεκύνησαν αὐτῷ
And the [ones] in the   ship   worshipped   him

λέγοντες· ἀληθῶς θεοῦ υἱὸς εἶ.   **34** Καὶ
saying: Truly   of God Son thou art.   And

διαπεράσαντες ἦλθον ἐπὶ τὴν γῆν εἰς
crossing over   they came   onto   the   land   to

Γεννησαρέτ.   **35** καὶ ἐπιγνόντες αὐτὸν
Gennesaret.   And   recognizing   him

οἱ ἄνδρες τοῦ τόπου ἐκείνου ἀπέστειλαν
the   men   -   place   of that   sent

εἰς ὅλην τὴν περίχωρον ἐκείνην, καὶ
into   all   -   neighbourhood   that,   and

προσήνεγκαν αὐτῷ πάντας τοὺς κακῶς
brought   to him   all   the [ones]   ill
                               = those who were ill,

ἔχοντας,   **36** καὶ παρεκάλουν αὐτὸν ἵνα
having,   and   besought   him   that

μόνον ἅψωνται τοῦ κρασπέδου τοῦ
only   they might touch   the   fringe   of the

ἱματίου αὐτοῦ· καὶ ὅσοι ἥψαντο διεσώθησαν.
garment of him; and as many as touched   were completely
                                            healed.

CHAPTER 15

THEN Pharisees and scribes came to Jesus from Jerusalem and said, [2]"Why do your disciples transgress the tradition of the elders? For they do not wash their hands when they eat." [3]He answered them, "And why do you transgress the commandment of God for the sake of your tradition? [4]For God commanded, 'Honor your father and your mother,' and, 'He who speaks evil of father or

15 Τότε προσέρχονται τῷ Ἰησοῦ
Then   approach   -   to Jesus

ἀπὸ Ἱεροσολύμων Φαρισαῖοι καὶ γραμματεῖς
from   Jerusalem   Pharisees   and   scribes

λέγοντες·   **2** διὰ τί οἱ μαθηταί σου
saying: Why   the   disciples   of thee

παραβαίνουσιν τὴν παράδοσιν τῶν
transgress   the   tradition   of the

πρεσβυτέρων; οὐ γὰρ νίπτονται τὰς χεῖρας
elders?   for not   they wash   the(ir)   hands

ὅταν ἄρτον ἐσθίωσιν.   **3** ὁ δὲ ἀπο-
whenever bread   they eat.   And he   answer-

κριθεὶς εἶπεν αὐτοῖς· διὰ τί καὶ ὑμεῖς
ing   said   to them: Why   indeed   ye

παραβαίνετε τὴν ἐντολὴν τοῦ θεοῦ
transgress   the   commandment   of God

διὰ τὴν παράδοσιν ὑμῶν;   **4** ὁ γὰρ
on account of the   tradition   of you?   -   For

θεὸς εἶπεν· τίμα τὸν πατέρα καὶ τὴν
God   said: Honour the   father   and   the

μητέρα, καί· ὁ κακολογῶν πατέρα
mother,   and: The [one] speaking evil of   father

mother, let him surely die.' ⁵ But you say, 'If any one tells his father or his mother, What you would have gained from me is given to God,ᵉ he need not honor his father.' ⁶ So, for the sake of your tradition, you have made void the wordᶠ of God. ⁷ You hypocrites! Well did Isaiah prophesy of you, when he said:

⁸ 'This people honors me with their lips, but their heart is far from me;
⁹ in vain do they worship me, teaching as doctrines the precepts of men.' "

10 And he called the people to him and said to them, "Hear and understand: ¹¹ not what goes into the mouth defiles a man, but what comes out of the mouth, this defiles a man." ¹² Then the disciples came and said to him, "Do you know that the Pharisees were offended when they heard this saying?" ¹³ He answered, "Every plant which my heavenly Father has not planted will be rooted up. ¹⁴ Let them alone; they are blind guides. And if a

ᵉ Or an offering
ᶠ Other ancient authorities read law

ἢ μητέρα θανάτῳ τελευτάτω. 5 ὑμεῖς δὲ
or mother by death let him die. But ye

λέγετε· ὃς ἂν εἴπῃ τῷ πατρὶ ἢ
say: Whoever says to the(his) father or

τῇ μητρί· δῶρον ὃ ἐὰν ἐξ ἐμοῦ
to the(his) mother: A gift whatever by me

ὠφελήθης, 6 οὐ μὴ τιμήσει τὸν
thou mightest be owed, by no means shall he honour the

πατέρα αὐτοῦ ἢ τὴν μητέρα αὐτοῦ·
father of him or the mother of him;

καὶ ἠκυρώσατε τὸν λόγον τοῦ θεοῦ
and ye annulled the word – of God

διὰ τὴν παράδοσιν ὑμῶν. 7 ὑποκρι-
on account of the tradition of you. Hypocrites,

ταί, καλῶς ἐπροφήτευσεν περὶ ὑμῶν
well prophesied concerning you

'Ησαΐας λέγων· 8 ὁ λαὸς οὗτος τοῖς
Isaiah saying: This people with the

χείλεσίν με τιμᾷ, ἡ δὲ καρδία αὐτῶν
lips me honours, but the heart of them

πόρρω ἀπέχει ἀπ' ἐμοῦ· 9 μάτην δὲ
far is away from me; and vainly

σέβονται με, διδάσκοντες διδασκαλίας
they worship me, teaching teachings

ἐντάλματα ἀνθρώπων. 10 Καὶ προσκαλε-
ordinances of men. And calling

σάμενος τὸν ὄχλον εἶπεν αὐτοῖς·
forward the crowd he said to them:

ἀκούετε καὶ συνίετε· 11 οὐ τὸ εἰσερχ-
Hear ye and understand: Not the [thing] enter-

όμενον εἰς τὸ στόμα κοινοῖ τὸν ἄνθρωπον,
ing into the mouth defiles the man,

ἀλλὰ τὸ ἐκπορευόμενον ἐκ τοῦ στόματος,
but the [thing] coming forth out of the mouth,

τοῦτο κοινοῖ τὸν ἄνθρωπον. 12 Τότε
this defiles the man. Then

προσελθόντες οἱ μαθηταὶ λέγουσιν αὐτῷ·
approaching the disciples say to him:

οἶδας ὅτι οἱ Φαρισαῖοι ἀκούσαντες τὸν
Dost thou know that the Pharisees hearing the

λόγον ἐσκανδαλίσθησαν; 13 ὁ δὲ ἀπο-
saying were offended? And he answer-

κριθεὶς εἶπεν· πᾶσα φυτεία ἣν οὐκ
ing said: Every plant which not

ἐφύτευσεν ὁ πατήρ μου ὁ οὐράνιος ἐκριζω-
planted the Father of me – heavenly shall be

θήσεται. 14 ἄφετε αὐτούς· τυφλοί εἰσιν
uprooted. Leave them; blind they are

blind man leads a blind man, both will fall into a pit." [15]But Peter said to him, "Explain the parable to us." [16]And he said, "Are you also still without understanding? [17]Do you not see that whatever goes into the mouth passes into the stomach, and so passes on?[9] [18]But what comes out of the mouth proceeds from the heart, and this defiles a man. [19]For out of the heart come evil thoughts, murder, adultery, fornication, theft, false witness, slander. [20]These are what defile a man; but to eat with unwashed hands does not defile a man."

21 And Jesus went away from there and withdrew to the district of Tyre and Sidon. [22]And behold, a Canaanite woman from that region came out and cried, "Have mercy on me, O Lord, Son of David; my daughter is severely possessed by a demon." [23]But he did not answer

---

ὁδηγοὶ   τυφλῶν·   τυφλὸς   δὲ   τυφλὸν
leaders   of blind;   [2]a blind man   [1]and   [2]a blind man

ἐὰν ὁδηγῇ,   ἀμφότεροι   εἰς βόθυνον πεσοῦνται.
[1]if   [4]leads,   both   into a ditch   will fall.

15 Ἀποκριθεὶς   δὲ   ὁ   Πέτρος εἶπεν αὐτῷ·
And answering   –   Peter   said   to him:

φράσον   ἡμῖν   τὴν   παραβολήν.   16 ὁ   δὲ
Explain   to us   the   parable.   So he

εἶπεν·   ἀκμὴν   καὶ   ὑμεῖς   ἀσύνετοί
said: Thus   also   ye   unintelligent

ἐστε;   17 οὐ   νοεῖτε   ὅτι   πᾶν   τὸ
are?   Do ye not understand   that   everything

εἰσπορευόμενον   εἰς   τὸ   στόμα   εἰς   τὴν
entering   into   the   mouth   into   the

κοιλίαν χωρεῖ   καὶ   εἰς   ἀφεδρῶνα   ἐκβάλλεται;
stomach   goes   and   into   a drain   is cast out?

18 τὰ   δὲ   ἐκπορευόμενα   ἐκ   τοῦ
but the things   coming forth   out of   the

στόματος   ἐκ   τῆς   καρδίας   ἐξέρχεται,
mouth   out of   the   heart   comes forth,

κἀκεῖνα   κοινοῖ   τὸν   ἄνθρωπον.   19 ἐκ
and those   defiles   the   man.   out of

γὰρ   τῆς   καρδίας   ἐξέρχονται   διαλογισμοὶ
For   the   heart   come forth   thoughts

πονηροί,   φόνοι,   μοιχεῖαι,   πορνεῖαι,   κλοπαί,
evil,   murders,   adulteries,   fornications,   thefts,

ψευδομαρτυρίαι,   βλασφημίαι.   20 ταῦτά
false witnessings,   blasphemies.   These things

ἐστιν   τὰ   κοινοῦντα   τὸν   ἄνθρωπον·
is(are)   the [ones]   defiling   the   man;

τὸ   δὲ   ἀνίπτοις   χερσὶν   φαγεῖν   οὐ
–   but   with unwashed   hands   to eat   not

κοινοῖ   τὸν   ἄνθρωπον.
defiles   the   man.

21 Καὶ   ἐξελθὼν   ἐκεῖθεν   ὁ   Ἰησοῦς
And   going forth   thence   –   Jesus

ἀνεχώρησεν   εἰς   τὰ   μέρη   Τύρου   καὶ
departed   into   the   parts   of Tyre   and

Σιδῶνος.   22 καὶ   ἰδοὺ   γυνὴ   Χαναναία
Sidon.   And   behold   woman   a Canaanite

ἀπὸ   τῶν   ὁρίων   ἐκείνων   ἐξελθοῦσα
from   –   borders   those   coming forth

ἔκραζεν   λέγουσα·   ἐλέησόν   με,   κύριε
cried out   saying: Pity   me,   Lord[,]

υἱὸς   Δαυίδ·   ἡ   θυγάτηρ   μου   κακῶς
son   of David;   the   daughter   of me   badly

δαιμονίζεται.   23 ὁ   δὲ   οὐκ   ἀπεκρίθη
is demon-possessed.   But he   answered not

---

[9] Or is evacuated

her a word. And his disciples came and begged him, saying, "Send her away, for she is crying after us." [24] He answered, "I was sent only to the lost sheep of the house of Israel." [25] But she came and knelt before him, saying, "Lord, help me." [26] And he answered, "It is not fair to take the children's bread and throw it to the dogs." [27] She said, "Yes, Lord, yet even the dogs eat the crumbs that fall from their master's table." [28] Then Jesus answered her, "O woman, great is your faith! Be it done for you as you desire." And her daughter was healed instantly.

29 And Jesus went on from there and passed along the Sea of Galilee. And he went up into the hills, and sat down there. [30] And great crowds came to him, bringing with them the lame, the maimed, the blind, the dumb, and many others, and they put them at his

αὐτῇ λόγον. καὶ προσελθόντες οἱ μαθηταὶ
her   a word.   And approaching   the disciples

αὐτοῦ ἠρώτων αὐτὸν λέγοντες· ἀπόλυσον
of him besought him   saying: Dismiss

αὐτήν, ὅτι κράζει ὄπισθεν ἡμῶν. 24 ὁ
her, because she is crying out behind   us.   he

δὲ ἀποκριθεὶς εἶπεν· οὐκ ἀπεστάλην
But answering   said: I was not sent

εἰ μὴ εἰς τὰ πρόβατα τὰ ἀπολωλότα
except   to   the   sheep   –   lost

οἴκου Ἰσραήλ. 25 ἡ δὲ ἐλθοῦσα
of [the] house of Israel.   But she   coming

προσεκύνει αὐτῷ λέγουσα· κύριε, βοήθει
worshipped   him   saying: Lord,   help

μοι. 26 ὁ δὲ ἀποκριθεὶς εἶπεν· οὐκ
me.   But he   answering   said: not

ἔστιν καλὸν λαβεῖν τὸν ἄρτον τῶν τέκνων
It is   good   to take   the   bread of the children

καὶ βαλεῖν τοῖς κυναρίοις. 27 ἡ δὲ
and to throw to the   dogs.   And she

εἶπεν· ναί, κύριε· καὶ γὰρ τὰ κυνάρια
said: Yes, Lord;   but even the   dogs

ἐσθίει ἀπὸ τῶν ψιχίων τῶν πιπτόντων
eats   from   the   crumbs   –   falling

ἀπὸ τῆς τραπέζης τῶν κυρίων αὐτῶν.
from the   table   of the masters   of them.

28 τότε ἀποκριθεὶς ὁ Ἰησοῦς εἶπεν αὐτῇ·
Then   answering   –   Jesus   said   to her:

ὦ γύναι, μεγάλη σου ἡ πίστις· γενηθήτω
O woman,   great of thee the faith;   let it be

σοι ὡς θέλεις. καὶ ἰάθη ἡ
to thee as thou desirest.   And was healed the

θυγάτηρ αὐτῆς ἀπὸ τῆς ὥρας ἐκείνης.
daughter of her from   –   hour   that.

29 Καὶ μεταβὰς ἐκεῖθεν ὁ Ἰησοῦς
And removing   thence   –   Jesus

ἦλθεν παρὰ τὴν θάλασσαν τῆς Γαλιλαίας,
came   by   the   sea   –   of Galilee,

καὶ ἀναβὰς εἰς τὸ ὄρος ἐκάθητο ἐκεῖ.
and going up into the mountain he sat   there.

30 καὶ προσῆλθον αὐτῷ ὄχλοι πολλοὶ ἔχοντες
And approached to him crowds   many   having

μεθ᾽ ἑαυτῶν χωλούς, κυλλούς, τυφλούς,
with themselves lame,   maimed,   blind,

κωφούς, καὶ ἑτέρους πολλούς, καὶ ἔρριψαν
dumb,   and others   many,   and   cast

αὐτοὺς παρὰ τοὺς πόδας αὐτοῦ· καὶ
them   at   the   feet   of him;   and

feet, and he healed them, [31]so that the throng wondered, when they saw the dumb speaking, the maimed whole, the lame walking, and the blind seeing; and they glorified the God of Israel.

32 Then Jesus called his disciples to him and said, "I have compassion on the crowd, because they have been with me now three days, and have nothing to eat; and I am unwilling to send them away hungry, lest they faint on the way." [33]And the disciples said to him, "Where are we to get bread enough in the desert to feed so great a crowd?" [34]And Jesus said to them, "How many loaves have you?" They said, "Seven, and a few small fish." [35]And commanding the crowd to sit down on the ground, [36]he took the seven loaves and the fish, and having given thanks he broke them and gave them to the disciples, and the disciples gave them to the crowds. [37]And they all ate and were satisfied; and they took up seven baskets full of the broken pieces left over. [38]Those who ate were four

ἐθεράπευσεν αὐτούς·
he healed   them;

31 ὥστε τὸν ὄχλον
so as the crowd
= so that the crowd marvelled

θαυμάσαι βλέποντας κωφοὺς λαλοῦντας,
to marvel[b] seeing   dumb men   speaking,

κυλλοὺς ὑγιεῖς καὶ χωλοὺς περιπατοῦντας
maimed whole and   lame   walking

καὶ τυφλοὺς βλέποντας· καὶ ἐδόξασαν
and blind   seeing;   and they glorified

τὸν θεὸν Ἰσραήλ.   **32** Ὁ δὲ Ἰησοῦς
the God of Israel.   – And   Jesus

προσκαλεσάμενος τοὺς μαθητὰς αὐτοῦ
calling forward   the   disciples of him

εἶπεν· σπλαγχνίζομαι ἐπὶ τὸν ὄχλον,
said: I am filled with tenderness over the crowd,

ὅτι ἤδη ἡμέραι τρεῖς προσμένουσίν
because now days   three   they remain

μοι καὶ οὐκ ἔχουσιν τί φάγωσιν·
with me and have not   anything they may eat;

καὶ ἀπολῦσαι αὐτοὺς νήστεις οὐ θέλω,
and to dismiss them   without food I am not willing,

μήποτε ἐκλυθῶσιν ἐν τῇ ὁδῷ.   **33** καὶ
lest they fail   in the way.   And

λέγουσιν αὐτῷ οἱ μαθηταί· πόθεν
say   to him the disciples: Whence

ἡμῖν ἐν ἐρημίᾳ ἄρτοι τοσοῦτοι ὥστε
to us in a desert loaves so many   so as

χορτάσαι ὄχλον τοσοῦτον; **34** καὶ λέγει
to satisfy a crowd so great?   And says

αὐτοῖς ὁ Ἰησοῦς· πόσους ἄρτους ἔχετε;
to them – Jesus: How many loaves have ye?

οἱ δὲ εἶπαν· ἑπτά, καὶ ὀλίγα ἰχθύδια.
And they said: Seven, and a few   fishes.

35 καὶ παραγγείλας τῷ ὄχλῳ ἀναπεσεῖν
And having enjoined the crowd   to recline

ἐπὶ τὴν γῆν **36** ἔλαβεν τοὺς ἑπτὰ
on the ground   he took the   seven

ἄρτους καὶ τοὺς ἰχθύας καὶ εὐχαριστήσας
loaves and the fishes   and giving thanks

ἔκλασεν καὶ ἐδίδου τοῖς μαθηταῖς, οἱ δὲ
he broke and gave   to the disciples,   and the

μαθηταὶ τοῖς ὄχλοις. **37** καὶ ἔφαγον πάντες
disciples to the crowds.   And   ate   all

καὶ ἐχορτάσθησαν, καὶ τὸ περισσεῦον τῶν
and were satisfied,   and the   excess   of the

κλασμάτων ἦραν, ἑπτὰ σπυρίδας πλήρεις.
fragments they took, seven   baskets   full.

38 οἱ δὲ ἐσθίοντες ἦσαν τετρακισχίλιοι
And the [ones] eating   were four thousand

thousand men, besides women and children. ³⁹And sending away the crowds, he got into the boat and went to the region of Mag'adan.

ἄνδρες   χωρὶς   γυναικῶν   καὶ   παιδίων.
men   apart from   women   and   children.
39 Καὶ   ἀπολύσας   τοὺς   ὄχλους   ἐνέβη   εἰς
And having dismissed   the   crowds he embarked   in
τὸ   πλοῖον,   καὶ   ἦλθεν   εἰς   τὰ   ὅρια   Μαγαδάν.
the   ship,   and   came   into   the   borders   of Magadan.

CHAPTER 16

AND the Pharisees and Sad'ducees came, and to test him they asked him to show them a sign from heaven. ²He answered them,ʰ "When it is evening, you say, 'It will be fair weather; for the sky is red.' ³And in the morning, 'It will be stormy today, for the sky is red and threatening.' You know how to interpret the appearance of the sky, but you cannot interpret the signs of the times. ⁴An evil and adulterous generation seeks for a sign, but no sign shall be given to it except the sign of Jonah." So he left them and departed.

5 When the disciples reached the other side, they had forgotten to bring any bread. ⁶Jesus said to them, "Take heed and beware of the leaven of the Pharisees and Sad'ducees." ⁷And they discussed it among themselves, saying, "We brought no bread." ⁸But Jesus, aware of this, said,

16 Καὶ   προσελθόντες   οἱ   Φαρισαῖοι   καὶ
And   approaching   the   Pharisees   and
Σαδδουκαῖοι   πειράζοντες   ἐπηρώτησαν   αὐτὸν
Sadducees   tempting   asked   him
σημεῖον   ἐκ   τοῦ   οὐρανοῦ   ἐπιδεῖξαι
a sign   out of   the   heaven   to show
αὐτοῖς.   2 ὁ   δὲ   ἀποκριθεὶς   εἶπεν   αὐτοῖς·
to them.   But he   answering   said   to them:
[ὀψίας   γενομένης   λέγετε·   εὐδία,
Evening   coming onᵃ   ye say: Fair weather,
=When evening comes on
πυρράζει   γὰρ   ὁ   οὐρανός·   3 καὶ   πρωΐ·
for is red   the   heaven(sky);   and in the morning:
σήμερον   χειμών,   πυρράζει   γὰρ   στυγνάζων
To-day   stormy weather,   for is red   being overcast
ὁ   οὐρανός.   τὸ   μὲν   πρόσωπον   τοῦ
the   heaven(sky).   The   -   face   of the
οὐρανοῦ   γινώσκετε   διακρίνειν,   τὰ   δὲ
heaven(sky)   ye know*   to discern,   but the
σημεῖα   τῶν   καιρῶν   οὐ   δύνασθε;]   4 γενεὰ
signs   of the   times   can ye not?   A generation
πονηρὰ   καὶ   μοιχαλὶς   σημεῖον   ἐπιζητεῖ,
evil   and   adulterous   a sign   seeks,
καὶ   σημεῖον   οὐ   δοθήσεται   αὐτῇ   εἰ   μὴ
and   a sign   shall not be given   to it   except
τὸ   σημεῖον   Ἰωνᾶ.   καὶ   καταλιπὼν   αὐτοὺς
the   sign   of Jonah. And   leaving   them
ἀπῆλθεν.   5 Καὶ   ἐλθόντες   οἱ   μαθηταὶ   εἰς
he went away.   And   coming   the   disciples   to
τὸ   πέραν   ἐπελάθοντο   ἄρτους   λαβεῖν.
the   other side   they forgot   loaves   to take.
ὁ   δὲ   Ἰησοῦς   εἶπεν   αὐτοῖς·   6 ὁρᾶτε   καὶ
-     And   Jesus   said   to them: Beware   and
προσέχετε   ἀπὸ   τῆς   ζύμης   τῶν   Φαρισαίων
take heed   from   the   leaven   of the   Pharisees
καὶ   Σαδδουκαίων.   7 οἱ   δὲ   διελογίζοντο
and   Sadducees.   But they   reasoned
ἐν   ἑαυτοῖς   λέγοντες   ὅτι   ἄρτους   οὐκ
among themselves   saying[:]   -   Loaves   not
ἐλάβομεν.   8 γνοὺς   δὲ   ὁ   Ἰησοῦς   εἶπεν·
we took.   But knowing   -   Jesus   said:

ʰ Other ancient authorities omit the following words to the end of verse 3

* See note on page xviii. Note the use in the next line of δύνασθε.

"O men of little faith, why do you discuss among yourselves the fact that you have no bread? 9 Do you not yet perceive? Do you not remember the five loaves of the five thousand, and how many baskets you gathered? 10 Or the seven loaves of the four thousand, and how many baskets you gathered? 11 How is it that you fail to perceive that I did not speak about bread? Beware of the leaven of the Pharisees and Sad'ducees." 12 Then they understood that he did not tell them to beware of the leaven of bread, but of the teaching of the Pharisees and Sad'ducees.

13 Now when Jesus came into the district of Caesare'a Philippi, he asked his disciples, "Who do men say that the Son of man is?" 14 And they said, "Some say John the Baptist, others say Eli'jah, and others Jeremiah or one of the prophets." 15 He said to them, "But who do you say that I am?" 16 Simon Peter replied, "You are the Christ, the Son of the living God." 17 And Jesus answered him, "Blessed

τί διαλογίζεσθε ἐν ἑαυτοῖς, ὀλιγόπιστοι,
Why reason ye among yourselves, little-faiths,
ὅτι ἄρτους οὐκ ἔχετε; 9 οὔπω νοεῖτε,
because loaves ye have not? Do ye not yet understand,
οὐδὲ μνημονεύετε τοὺς πέντε ἄρτους τῶν
neither remember ye the five loaves of the
πεντακισχιλίων καὶ πόσους κοφίνους
five thousand and how many baskets
ἐλάβετε; 10 οὐδὲ τοὺς ἑπτὰ ἄρτους τῶν
ye took? Neither the seven loaves of the
τετρακισχιλίων καὶ πόσας σπυρίδας
four thousand and how many baskets
ἐλάβετε; 11 πῶς οὐ νοεῖτε ὅτι οὐ
ye took? How do ye not understand that not
περὶ ἄρτων εἶπον ὑμῖν; προσέχετε δὲ ἀπὸ
concerning loaves I said to you? But take heed from
τῆς ζύμης τῶν Φαρισαίων καὶ Σαδ-
the leaven of the Pharisees and Sad-
δουκαίων. 12 τότε συνῆκαν ὅτι οὐκ
ducees. Then they understood that not
εἶπεν προσέχειν ἀπὸ τῆς ζύμης [τῶν
he said to take heed from the leaven of the
ἄρτων], ἀλλὰ ἀπὸ τῆς διδαχῆς τῶν
loaves, but from the teaching of the
Φαρισαίων καὶ Σαδδουκαίων.
Pharisees and Sadducees.

13 Ἐλθὼν δὲ ὁ Ἰησοῦς εἰς τὰ μέρη
And coming – Jesus into the parts
Καισαρείας τῆς Φιλίππου ἠρώτα τοὺς
of Cæsarea – of Philip he questioned the
μαθητὰς αὐτοῦ λέγων· τίνα λέγουσιν οἱ
disciples of him saying· Whom say –
ἄνθρωποι εἶναι τὸν υἱὸν τοῦ ἀνθρώπου;
men to be the Son – of man?
14 οἱ δὲ εἶπαν· οἱ μὲν Ἰωάννην τὸν
And they said: Some indeed John the
βαπτιστήν, ἄλλοι δὲ Ἠλίαν, ἕτεροι δὲ
Baptist, and others Elias, and others
Ἰερεμίαν ἢ ἕνα τῶν προφητῶν. 15 λέγει
Jeremias or one of the prophets. He says
αὐτοῖς· ὑμεῖς δὲ τίνα με λέγετε εἶναι;
to them: But ²ye ¹whom ⁴me ³say to be?
16 ἀποκριθεὶς δὲ Σίμων Πέτρος εἶπεν·
And answering Simon Peter said:
17 σὺ εἶ ὁ χριστὸς ὁ υἱὸς τοῦ θεοῦ
Thou art the Christ the Son – of God
τοῦ ζῶντος. ἀποκριθεὶς δὲ ὁ Ἰησοῦς
of the living. And answering – Jesus

are you, Simon Bar-Jona! For flesh and blood has not revealed this to you, but my Father who is in heaven. ¹⁸And I tell you, you are Peter, and on this rock I will build my church, and the powers of death shall not prevail against it. ¹⁹I will give you the keys of the kingdom of heaven, and whatever you bind on earth shall be bound in heaven, and whatever you loose on earth shall be loosed in heaven." ²⁰Then he strictly charged the disciples to tell no one that he was the Christ.

21 From that time Jesus began to show his disciples that he must go to Jerusalem and suffer many things from the elders and chief priests and scribes, and be killed, and on the third day be raised. ²²And Peter took him and began to rebuke him, saying, "God forbid, Lord! This shall never happen to you." ²³But he turned and said

εἶπεν αὐτῷ· μακάριος εἶ, Σίμων
said to him: Blessed art thou, Simon

Βαριωνά, ὅτι σὰρξ καὶ αἷμα οὐκ ἀπεκά-
Barjonas, because flesh and blood did not

λυψέν σοι ἀλλ' ὁ πατήρ μου ὁ ἐν
reveal to thee but the Father of me – in

τοῖς οὐρανοῖς. 18 κἀγὼ δέ σοι λέγω
the heavens. And I also to thee say[,]

ὅτι σὺ εἶ Πέτρος, καὶ ἐπὶ ταύτῃ τῇ
– Thou art Peter, and on this –

πέτρᾳ οἰκοδομήσω μου τὴν ἐκκλησίαν,
rock I will build of me the church,

καὶ πύλαι ᾅδου οὐ κατισχύσουσιν
and [the] gates of hades will not prevail against

αὐτῆς. 19 δώσω σοι τὰς κλεῖδας τῆς
it. I will give thee the keys of the

βασιλείας τῶν οὐρανῶν, καὶ ὃ ἐὰν
kingdom of the heavens, and whatever

δήσῃς ἐπὶ τῆς γῆς ἔσται δεδεμένον ἐν τοῖς
thou bindest on the earth shall be *having been* bound in the

οὐρανοῖς, καὶ ὃ ἐὰν λύσῃς ἐπὶ τῆς
heavens, and whatever thou loosest on the

γῆς ἔσται λελυμένον ἐν τοῖς οὐρανοῖς.
earth shall be *having been* loosed in the heavens.

20 τότε ἐπετίμησεν τοῖς μαθηταῖς ἵνα
Then he warned the disciples that

μηδενὶ εἴπωσιν ὅτι αὐτός ἐστιν ὁ
to no one they should tell that he is the

χριστός.
Christ.

21 Ἀπὸ τότε ἤρξατο Ἰησοῦς Χριστὸς
From then began Jesus Christ

δεικνύειν τοῖς μαθηταῖς αὐτοῦ ὅτι δεῖ
to show to the disciples of him that it behoves

αὐτὸν εἰς Ἱεροσόλυμα ἀπελθεῖν καὶ
him to Jerusalem to go and

πολλὰ παθεῖν ἀπὸ τῶν πρεσβυτέρων καὶ
many things to suffer from the elders and

ἀρχιερέων καὶ γραμματέων καὶ ἀποκτανθῆναι
chief priests and scribes and to be killed

καὶ τῇ τρίτῃ ἡμέρᾳ ἐγερθῆναι. 22 καὶ
and on the third day to be raised. And

προσλαβόμενος αὐτὸν ὁ Πέτρος ἤρξατο
taking him – Peter began

ἐπιτιμᾶν αὐτῷ λέγων· ἵλεώς σοι,
to rebuke him saying: Propitious to thee,
= May God help thee,

κύριε· οὐ μὴ ἔσται σοι τοῦτο. 23 ὁ δὲ
Lord: by no means shall be to thee this. But he

to Peter, "Get behind me, Satan! You are a hindrance to me; for you are not on the side of God, but of men."

24 Then Jesus told his disciples, "If any man would come after me, let him deny himself and take up his cross and follow me. 25 For whoever would save his life will lose it, and whoever loses his life for my sake will find it. 26 For what will it profit a man, if he gains the whole world and forfeits his life? Or what shall a man give in return for his life? 27 For the Son of man is to come with his angels in the glory of his Father, and then he will repay every man for what he has done. 28 Truly, I say to you, there are some standing here who will not taste death before they see the Son of man coming in his kingdom."

στραφεὶς εἶπεν τῷ Πέτρῳ· ὕπαγε ὀπίσω
turning said to Peter: Go behind

μου, σατανᾶ· σκάνδαλον εἶ ἐμοῦ,
me, Satan; an offence thou art of me,

ὅτι οὐ φρονεῖς τὰ τοῦ θεοῦ
because thou thinkest not the things – of God

ἀλλὰ τὰ τῶν ἀνθρώπων. 24 Τότε ὁ
but the things – of men. Then –

Ἰησοῦς εἶπεν τοῖς μαθηταῖς αὐτοῦ· εἴ
Jesus said to the disciples of him: If

τις θέλει ὀπίσω μου ἐλθεῖν, ἀπαρνησάσθω
anyone wishes after me to come, let him deny

ἑαυτὸν καὶ ἀράτω τὸν σταυρὸν αὐτοῦ,
himself and let him take the cross of him,

καὶ ἀκολουθείτω μοι. 25 ὃς γὰρ ἐὰν
and let him follow me. For whoever

θέλῃ τὴν ψυχὴν αὐτοῦ σῶσαι, ἀπολέσει
wishes the life of him to save, he will lose

αὐτήν· ὃς δ' ἂν ἀπολέσῃ τὴν ψυχὴν
it; and whoever loses the life

αὐτοῦ ἕνεκεν ἐμοῦ, εὑρήσει αὐτήν. 26 τί
of him for the sake of me, he will find it. what

γὰρ ὠφεληθήσεται ἄνθρωπος, ἐὰν τὸν
For will be benefited a man, if the

κόσμον ὅλον κερδήσῃ, τὴν δὲ ψυχὴν
world whole he should gain, but the soul

αὐτοῦ ζημιωθῇ; ἢ τί δώσει ἄνθρωπος
of him loses? or what will give a man

ἀντάλλαγμα τῆς ψυχῆς αὐτοῦ; 27 μέλλει
an exchange of the soul of him? is about

γὰρ ὁ υἱὸς τοῦ ἀνθρώπου ἔρχεσθαι ἐν τῇ
For the Son – of man to come in the

δόξῃ τοῦ πατρὸς αὐτοῦ μετὰ τῶν ἀγγέλων
glory of the Father of him with the angels

αὐτοῦ, καὶ τότε ἀποδώσει ἑκάστῳ
of him, and then he will reward to each man

κατὰ τὴν πρᾶξιν αὐτοῦ. 28 ἀμὴν λέγω
according to the conduct of him. Truly I say

ὑμῖν ὅτι εἰσίν τινες τῶν ὧδε ἑστώτων
to you[,] – There are some of the [ones] here standing

οἵτινες οὐ μὴ γεύσωνται θανάτου ἕως ἂν
who by no means may taste of death until

ἴδωσιν τὸν υἱὸν τοῦ ἀνθρώπου ἐρχόμενον
they see the Son – of man coming

ἐν τῇ βασιλείᾳ αὐτοῦ.
in the kingdom of him.

CHAPTER 17

AND after six days
Jesus took with him
Peter and James and
John his brother, and led
them up a high mountain
apart. ²And he was
transfigured before them,
and his face shone like
the sun, and his garments
became white as light.
³And behold, there
appeared to them Moses
and Eli'jah, talking with
him. ⁴And Peter said to
Jesus, "Lord, it is well
that we are here; if you
wish, I will make three
booths here, one for you
and one for Moses and
one for Eli'jah." ⁵He was
still speaking, when lo, a
bright cloud over-
shadowed them, and a
voice from the cloud
said, "This is my beloved
Son, with whom I am
well pleased; listen to
him." ⁶When the dis-
ciples heard this, they fell
on their faces, and were
filled with awe. ⁷But
Jesus came and touched
them, saying, "Rise, and
have no fear." ⁸And
when they lifted up their
eyes, they saw no one but
Jesus only.

17 Καὶ μεθ' ἡμέρας ἐξ παραλαμβάνει ὁ
And after days six takes -

'Ιησοῦς τὸν Πέτρον καὶ 'Ιάκωβον καὶ
Jesus - Peter and James and

'Ιωάννην τὸν ἀδελφὸν αὐτοῦ, καὶ ἀναφέρει
John the brother of him, and leads up

αὐτοὺς εἰς ὄρος ὑψηλὸν κατ' ἰδίαν. 2 καὶ
them to mountain a high privately. And

μετεμορφώθη ἔμπροσθεν αὐτῶν, καὶ
he was transfigured before them, and

ἔλαμψεν τὸ πρόσωπον αὐτοῦ ὡς ὁ ἥλιος,
shone the face of him as the sun,

τὰ δὲ ἱμάτια αὐτοῦ ἐγένετο λευκὰ ὡς
and the garments of him became white as

τὸ φῶς. 3 καὶ ἰδοὺ ὤφθη αὐτοῖς Μωϋσῆς
the light. And behold was seen by them Moses

καὶ 'Ηλίας συλλαλοῦντες μετ' αὐτοῦ.
and Elias conversing with him.

4 ἀποκριθεὶς δὲ ὁ Πέτρος εἶπεν τῷ
And answering - Peter said -

'Ιησοῦ· κύριε, καλόν ἐστιν ἡμᾶς ὧδε
to Jesus: Lord, good it is us here

εἶναι· εἰ θέλεις, ποιήσω ὧδε τρεῖς
to be; if thou willest, I will make here three

σκηνάς, σοὶ μίαν καὶ Μωϋσεῖ
tents, for thee one and for Moses

μίαν καὶ 'Ηλίᾳ μίαν. 5 ἔτι αὐτοῦ
one and for Elias one. Yet him
=While he was yet

λαλοῦντος, ἰδοὺ νεφέλη φωτεινὴ ἐπεσκίασεν
speakingᵃ, behold cloud a bright overshadowed
speaking,

αὐτούς, καὶ ἰδοὺ φωνὴ ἐκ τῆς νεφέλης
them, and behold a voice out of the cloud

λέγουσα· οὗτός ἐστιν ὁ υἱός μου ὁ
saying: This is the son of me the

ἀγαπητός, ἐν ᾧ εὐδόκησα· ἀκούετε
beloved, in whom I was well pleased; hear ye

αὐτοῦ. 6 καὶ ἀκούσαντες οἱ μαθηταὶ
him. And hearing the disciples

ἔπεσαν ἐπὶ πρόσωπον αὐτῶν καὶ
fell on [the] face[s] of them and

ἐφοβήθησαν σφόδρα. 7 καὶ προσῆλθεν ὁ
feared exceedingly. And approached -

'Ιησοῦς καὶ ἁψάμενος αὐτῶν εἶπεν·
Jesus and touching them said:

ἐγέρθητε καὶ μὴ φοβεῖσθε. 8 ἐπάραντες δὲ
Rise and do not fear. And lifting up

τοὺς ὀφθαλμοὺς αὐτῶν οὐδένα εἶδον εἰ
the eyes of them no one they saw ex-

9 And as they were coming down the mountain, Jesus commanded them, "Tell no one the vision, until the Son of man is raised from the dead." [10]And the disciples asked him, "Then why do the scribes say that first Eli'jah must come?" [11]He replied, "Eli'jah does come, and he is to restore all things; [12]but I tell you that Eli'jah has already come, and they did not know him, but did to him whatever they pleased. So also the Son of man will suffer at their hands." [13]Then the disciples understood that he was speaking to them of John the Baptist.

14 And when they came to the crowd, a man came up to him and kneeling before him said, [15]"Lord, have mercy on my son, for he is an epileptic and he suffers terribly; for often he falls into the fire, and often into the water. [16]And I brought him to your disciples, and they could not heal him." [17]And

μὴ αὐτὸν Ἰησοῦν μόνον.   9 Καὶ κατα-
cept himself Jesus only.   And com-
                                             = as
βαινόντων αὐτῶν ἐκ τοῦ ὄρους ἐνετείλατο
ing down   them   out of the mountain enjoined
they were coming down
αὐτοῖς ὁ Ἰησοῦς λέγων· μηδενὶ εἴπητε
them - Jesus saying: To no one tell
τὸ ὅραμα ἕως οὗ ὁ υἱὸς τοῦ ἀνθρώπου
the vision until the Son - of man
ἐκ νεκρῶν ἐγερθῇ.   10 Καὶ ἐπηρώτησαν
out of dead be raised.   And questioned
αὐτὸν οἱ μαθηταὶ λέγοντες· τί οὖν
him the disciples saying: Why then
οἱ γραμματεῖς λέγουσιν ὅτι Ἠλίαν δεῖ
the scribes say that [1]Elias [1]it behoves
ἐλθεῖν πρῶτον; 11 ὁ δὲ ἀποκριθεὶς εἶπεν·
to come first? And he answering said:
Ἠλίας μὲν ἔρχεται καὶ ἀποκαταστήσει
Elias indeed is coming and will restore
πάντα· 12 λέγω δὲ ὑμῖν ὅτι Ἠλίας
all things· but I tell you that Elias
ἤδη ἦλθεν, καὶ οὐκ ἐπέγνωσαν
already came, and they did not recognize
αὐτόν, ἀλλ' ἐποίησαν ἐν αὐτῷ ὅσα
him, but did by him whatever things
ἠθέλησαν· οὕτως καὶ ὁ υἱὸς τοῦ ἀνθρώπου
they wished; thus also the Son - of man
μέλλει πάσχειν ὑπ' αὐτῶν. 13 τότε
is about to suffer by them. Then
συνῆκαν οἱ μαθηταὶ ὅτι περὶ
understood the disciples that concerning
Ἰωάννου τοῦ βαπτιστοῦ εἶπεν αὐτοῖς.
John the Baptist he spoke to them.

14 Καὶ ἐλθόντων πρὸς τὸν ὄχλον προσ-
And [they] coming to the crowd ap-
ἦλθεν αὐτῷ ἄνθρωπος γονυπετῶν αὐτὸν
proached to him a man falling on knees to him
15 καὶ λέγων· κύριε, ἐλέησόν μου τὸν
and saying: Lord, pity of me the
υἱόν, ὅτι σεληνιάζεται καὶ κακῶς ἔχει·
son, because he is moonstruck and ill has;
                                             = is ill;
πολλάκις γὰρ πίπτει εἰς τὸ πῦρ καὶ
for often he falls into the fire and
πολλάκις εἰς τὸ ὕδωρ. 16 καὶ προσήνεγκα
often into the water. And I brought
αὐτὸν τοῖς μαθηταῖς σου, καὶ οὐκ
him to the disciples of thee, and not
ἠδυνήθησαν αὐτὸν θεραπεῦσαι. 17 ἀπο-
they were able him to heal.   an-

Jesus answered, "O faithless and perverse generation, how long am I to be with you? How long am I to bear with you? Bring him here to me." [18]And Jesus rebuked him, and the demon came out of him, and the boy was cured instantly. [19]Then the disciples came to Jesus privately and said, "Why could we not cast it out?" [20]He said to them, "Because of your little faith. For truly, I say to you, if you have faith as a grain of mustard seed, you will say to this mountain, 'Move hence to yonder place,' and it will move; and nothing will be impossible to you."[i]

22 As they were gathering[j] in Galilee, Jesus said to them, "The Son of man is to be delivered into the hands of men, [23]and they will kill him, and he will be raised on the third day." And they were greatly distressed.

24 When they came to Caper'na-um, the collectors of the half-shekel

κριθεὶς δὲ ὁ Ἰησοῦς εἶπεν· ὦ γενεὰ
swering And - Jesus said: O generation
ἄπιστος καὶ διεστραμμένη, ἕως πότε
unbelieving and *having been* perverted, until when
μεθ' ὑμῶν ἔσομαι; ἕως πότε
with you shall I be? until when
ἀνέξομαι ὑμῶν; φέρετέ μοι αὐτὸν
shall I endure you? bring to me him
ὧδε. 18 καὶ ἐπετίμησεν αὐτῷ ὁ Ἰησοῦς,
here. And rebuked it - Jesus,
καὶ ἐξῆλθεν ἀπ' αὐτοῦ τὸ δαιμόνιον,
and came out from him the demon,
καὶ ἐθεραπεύθη ὁ παῖς ἀπὸ τῆς ὥρας
and was healed the boy from - hour
ἐκείνης. 19 Τότε προσελθόντες οἱ μαθηταὶ
that. Then [2]approaching [1]the [2]disciples
τῷ Ἰησοῦ κατ' ἰδίαν εἶπον· διὰ
- to Jesus privately said: Why
τί ἡμεῖς οὐκ ἠδυνήθημεν ἐκβαλεῖν αὐτό;
we were not able to expel it?
20 ὁ δὲ λέγει αὐτοῖς· διὰ τὴν ὀλιγο-
And he says to them: Because of the little
πιστίαν ὑμῶν· ἀμὴν γὰρ λέγω ὑμῖν, ἐὰν
faith of you; for truly I say to you, if
ἔχητε πίστιν ὡς κόκκον σινάπεως,
ye have faith as a grain of mustard,
ἐρεῖτε τῷ ὄρει τούτῳ· μετάβα
ye will say - mountain to this: Remove
ἔνθεν ἐκεῖ, καὶ μεταβήσεται, καὶ οὐδὲν
hence there, and it will be removed, and nothing
ἀδυνατήσει ὑμῖν. ‡
will be impossible to you.

22 Συστρεφομένων δὲ αὐτῶν ἐν τῇ
And strolling them[a] in -
= as they were strolling
Γαλιλαίᾳ εἶπεν αὐτοῖς ὁ Ἰησοῦς· μέλλει
Galilee said to them - Jesus: is about
ὁ υἱὸς τοῦ ἀνθρώπου παραδίδοσθαι εἰς
The Son of man to be delivered into
χεῖρας ἀνθρώπων, 23 καὶ ἀποκτενοῦσιν
[the] hands of men, and they will kill
αὐτόν, καὶ τῇ τρίτῃ ἡμέρᾳ ἐγερθήσεται.
him, and on the third day he will be raised.
καὶ ἐλυπήθησαν σφόδρα.
And they were grieved exceedingly.

24 Ἐλθόντων δὲ αὐτῶν εἰς Καφαρναοὺμ
And coming them[a] to Capernaum
= when they came
προσῆλθον οἱ τὰ δίδραχμα λαμβάνοντες
approached the [ones] the didrachmæ receiving

[i] Other ancient authorities insert verse 21, "*But this kind never comes out except by prayer and fasting*"

[j] Other ancient authorities read *abode*

‡ Verse 21 omitted by Nestle; *cf.* R.V. marg., etc.

tax went up to Peter and said, "Does not your teacher pay the tax?" [25]He said, "Yes." And when he came home, Jesus spoke to him first, saying, "What do you think, Simon? From whom do kings of the earth take toll or tribute? From their sons or from others?" [26]And when he said, "From others," Jesus said to him, "Then the sons are free. [27]However, not to give offense to them, go to the sea and cast a hook, and take the first fish that comes up, and when you open its mouth you will find a shekel; take that and give it to them for me and for yourself."

τῷ   Πέτρῳ   καὶ   εἶπαν·   ὁ   διδάσκαλος
\-   Peter   and   said: The   teacher

ὑμῶν   οὐ   τελεῖ   δίδραχμα;   λέγει·   ναί.
of you   not   pays   drachmae?   He says: Yes.

25 καὶ   ἐλθόντα   εἰς   τὴν   οἰκίαν   προ-
     And   ⁴coming   ⁵into   ⁶the   ⁷house   ²pre-

ἔφθασεν   αὐτὸν   ὁ   Ἰησοῦς   λέγων·   τί   σοι
ceded   ³him   \-   ¹Jesus   saying: What to thee

δοκεῖ,   Σίμων;   οἱ   βασιλεῖς   τῆς   γῆς
seems it,   Simon?   the   kings   of the   earth

ἀπὸ   τίνων   λαμβάνουσιν   τέλη   ἢ   κῆνσον;
from   whom   do they take   toll   or   poll-tax?

ἀπὸ   τῶν   υἱῶν   αὐτῶν   ἢ   ἀπὸ   τῶν   ἀλλοτρίων;
from   the   sons   of them   or   from   \-   strangers?

26 εἰπόντος   δέ·   ἀπὸ   τῶν   ἀλλο-
     and [he] sayingᵃ: From   \-   strangers,
     = when he said:

τρίων,   ἔφη   αὐτῷ   ὁ   Ἰησοῦς·   ἄρα   γε
     said   to him   \-   Jesus: Then

ἐλεύθεροί   εἰσιν   οἱ   υἱοί.   **27** ἵνα   δὲ   μὴ
free   are   the   sons.   But lest

σκανδαλίσωμεν   αὐτούς,   πορευθεὶς   εἰς
we should offend   them,   going   to

θάλασσαν   βάλε   ἄγκιστρον   καὶ   τὸν
[the] sea   cast   a hook   and   the

ἀναβάντα   πρῶτον   ἰχθὺν   ἆρον,   καὶ   ἀνοίξας
²coming up   ³first   ¹fish   take,   and   opening

τὸ   στόμα   αὐτοῦ   εὑρήσεις   στατῆρα·
the   mouth   of it   thou wilt find   a stater;

ἐκεῖνον   λαβὼν   δὸς   αὐτοῖς   ἀντὶ   ἐμοῦ   καὶ
that   taking   give   them   for   me   and

σοῦ.
thee.

CHAPTER 18

A T that time the disciples came to Jesus, saying, "Who is the greatest in the kingdom of heaven?" [2]And calling to him a child, he put him in the midst of them, [3]and said, "Truly, I say to you, unless you turn and become like children, you will never enter the

18 Ἐν   ἐκείνῃ   τῇ   ὥρᾳ   προσῆλθον   οἱ
     In   that   \-   hour   approached   the

μαθηταὶ   τῷ   Ἰησοῦ   λέγοντες·   τίς   ἄρα
disciples   \-   to Jesus   saying: Who   then

μείζων   ἐστὶν   ἐν   τῇ   βασιλείᾳ   τῶν   οὐρανῶν;
greater   is   in   the   kingdom   of the   heavens?

2 καὶ   προσκαλεσάμενος   παιδίον   ἔστησεν
     And   calling forward   a child   he set

αὐτὸ   ἐν   μέσῳ   αὐτῶν   **3** καὶ   εἶπεν·   ἀμὴν
him   in [the] midst   of them   and   said: Truly

λέγω   ὑμῖν,   ἐὰν   μὴ   στραφῆτε   καὶ
I say   to you,   except   ye turn   and

γένησθε   ὡς   τὰ   παιδία,   οὐ   μὴ
become   as   \-   children,   by no means

kingdom of heaven.
⁴Whoever humbles himself like this child, he is the greatest in the kingdom of heaven.

5 "Whoever receives one such child in my name receives me; ⁶but whoever causes one of these little ones who believe in me to sin, it would be better for him to have a great millstone fastened round his neck and to be drowned in the depth of the sea.

7 "Woe to the world for temptations to sin! For it is necessary that temptations come, but woe to the man by whom the temptation comes! ⁸And if your hand or your foot causes you to sin, cut it off and throw it from you; it is better for you to enter life maimed or lame than with two hands or two feet to be thrown into the eternal fire. ⁹And if your eye causes you to sin, pluck it out and throw it from you; it is better for you to enter life with one eye than with two eyes to be thrown into the hell of fire.

εἰσέλθητε εἰς τὴν βασιλείαν τῶν
may ye enter into the kingdom of the

οὐρανῶν. 4 ὅστις οὖν ταπεινώσει ἑαυτὸν
heavens. ²[he] who ¹Therefore will humble himself

ὡς τὸ παιδίον τοῦτο, οὗτός ἐστιν ὁ
as – child this, this [one] is the

μείζων ἐν τῇ βασιλείᾳ τῶν οὐρανῶν.
greater in the kingdom of the heavens.

5 καὶ ὃς ἐὰν δέξηται ἓν παιδίον
And whoever receives one child

τοιοῦτο ἐπὶ τῷ ὀνόματί μου, ἐμὲ δέχεται·
such on(in) the name of me, me receives;

6 ὃς δ’ ἂν σκανδαλίσῃ ἕνα τῶν
and whoever offends one – of the

μικρῶν τούτων τῶν πιστευόντων εἰς ἐμέ,
little [ones] of these – believing in me,

συμφέρει αὐτῷ ἵνα κρεμασθῇ μύλος
it is expedient for him that be hanged an upper

ὀνικὸς περὶ τὸν τράχηλον αὐτοῦ καὶ
millstone round the neck of him and

καταποντισθῇ ἐν τῷ πελάγει τῆς θαλάσσης.
he be drowned in the depth of the sea.

7 Οὐαὶ τῷ κόσμῳ ἀπὸ τῶν σκανδάλων·
Woe to the world from – offences;

ἀνάγκη γὰρ ἐλθεῖν τὰ σκάνδαλα, πλὴν
for [it is] a necessity to come – offences, but

οὐαὶ τῷ ἀνθρώπῳ δι’ οὗ τὸ σκάνδαλον
woe to the man through whom the offence

ἔρχεται. 8 Εἰ δὲ ἡ χείρ σου ἢ ὁ
comes. Now if the hand of thee or the

πούς σου σκανδαλίζει σε, ἔκκοψον αὐτὸν
foot of thee offends thee, cut off it

καὶ βάλε ἀπὸ σοῦ· καλόν σοί ἐστιν
and cast from thee; good for thee it is

εἰσελθεῖν εἰς τὴν ζωὴν κυλλὸν ἢ χωλόν,
to enter into – life maimed or lame,

ἢ δύο χεῖρας ἢ δύο πόδας ἔχοντα βληθῆναι
than two hands or two feet having to be cast

εἰς τὸ πῦρ τὸ αἰώνιον. 9 καὶ εἰ ὁ
into the fire – eternal. And if the

ὀφθαλμός σου σκανδαλίζει σε, ἔξελε αὐτὸν
eye of thee offends thee, pluck out it

καὶ βάλε ἀπὸ σοῦ· καλόν σοί ἐστιν
and cast from thee; good for thee it is

μονόφθαλμον εἰς τὴν ζωὴν εἰσελθεῖν, ἢ
one-eyed into the life to enter, than

δύο ὀφθαλμοὺς ἔχοντα βληθῆναι εἰς
two eyes having to be cast into

10 "See that you do not despise one of these little ones; for I tell you that in heaven their angels always behold the face of my Father who is in heaven.[k] 12 What do you think? If a man has a hundred sheep, and one of them has gone astray, does he not leave the ninety-nine on the hills and go in search of the one that went astray? 13 And if he finds it, truly, I say to you, he rejoices over it more than over the ninety-nine that never went astray. 14 So it is not the will of my[l] Father who is in heaven that one of these little ones should perish.

15 "If your brother sins against you, go and tell him his fault, between you and him alone. If he listens to you, you have gained your brother. 16 But if he does not listen, take one or two others along with you, that every word may be confirmed by the evidence of two or three witnesses. 17 If he refuses to listen to them, tell it to the church; and if he

τὴν γέενναν τοῦ πυρός. **10** Ὁρᾶτε μὴ
the gehenna - of fire.   See [that] not

καταφρονήσητε ἑνὸς τῶν μικρῶν τούτων·
ye despise   one   -   little [ones]   of these;

λέγω γὰρ ὑμῖν ὅτι οἱ ἄγγελοι αὐτῶν
for I tell   you that the angels   of them

ἐν οὐρανοῖς διὰ παντὸς βλέπουσι τὸ
in heavens   always   see   the

πρόσωπον τοῦ πατρός μου τοῦ ἐν οὐρανοῖς.‡
face   of the Father of me - in heavens.

12 Τί ὑμῖν δοκεῖ; ἐὰν γένηταί τινι
What to you seems it? if there be to any
                                    =any man has

ἀνθρώπῳ ἑκατὸν πρόβατα καὶ πλανηθῇ
man[e]   a hundred sheep   and   wanders

ἐν ἐξ αὐτῶν, οὐχὶ ἀφήσει τὰ ἐνενήκοντα
one of them, will he not leave the   ninety-

ἐννέα ἐπὶ τὰ ὄρη καὶ πορευθεὶς ζητεῖ τὸ
nine on the mountains and   going   seeks the

πλανώμενον;   **13** καὶ   ἐὰν   γένηται
wandering [one]?   And   if   he happens

εὑρεῖν αὐτό, ἀμὴν λέγω ὑμῖν ὅτι
to find it,   truly I say to you that

χαίρει ἐπ' αὐτῷ μᾶλλον ἢ ἐπὶ τοῖς
he rejoices over it   more   than over the

ἐνενήκοντα ἐννέα τοῖς μὴ πεπλανημένοις.
ninety-nine   not having wandered.

14 οὕτως οὐκ ἔστιν θέλημα ἔμπροσθεν
So   it is not [the] will   before

τοῦ πατρὸς ὑμῶν τοῦ ἐν οὐρανοῖς ἵνα
the Father of you - in heavens   that

ἀπόληται ἓν τῶν μικρῶν τούτων.
should perish one - little [ones]   of these.

15 Ἐὰν δὲ ἁμαρτήσῃ ὁ ἀδελφός σου,
Now if   sins   the brother of thee,

ὕπαγε ἔλεγξον αὐτὸν μεταξὺ σοῦ καὶ
go   reprove   him   between thee and

αὐτοῦ μόνου. ἐάν σου ἀκούσῃ, ἐκέρδησας
him   alone. If thee he hears, thou gainedst

τὸν ἀδελφόν σου· **16** ἐὰν δὲ μὴ
the brother of thee;   but if   not

ἀκούσῃ, παράλαβε μετὰ σοῦ ἔτι ἕνα ἢ
he hears,   take   with thee more one or

δύο, ἵνα ἐπὶ στόματος δύο μαρτύρων
two, that on(by) [the] mouth of two witnesses

ἢ τριῶν σταθῇ πᾶν ῥῆμα· **17** ἐὰν δὲ
or three may be established every word;   but if

παρακούσῃ αὐτῶν, εἰπὸν τῇ ἐκκλησίᾳ·
he refuses to hear them,   tell to the church;

[k] Other ancient authorities add verse 11, For the Son of man came to save the lost
[l] Other ancient authorities read your

‡ Ver. 11 omitted by Nestle; cf. RSV note.

refuses to listen even to the church, let him be to you as a Gentile and a tax collector. ¹⁸Truly, I say to you, whatever you bind on earth shall be bound in heaven, and whatever you loose on earth shall be loosed in heaven. ¹⁹Again I say to you, if two of you agree on earth about anything they ask, it will be done for them by my Father in heaven. ²⁰For where two or three are gathered in my name, there am I in the midst of them."

21 Then Peter came up and said to him, "Lord, how often shall my brother sin against me, and I forgive him? As many as seven times?" ²²Jesus said to him, "I do not say to you seven times, but seventy times seven."ᵐ

23 "Therefore the kingdom of heaven may be compared to a king who wished to settle accounts with his servants. ²⁴When he began the reckoning, one was brought to him who

ᵐ Or *seventy-seven times*

ἐὰν δὲ καὶ τῆς ἐκκλησίας παρακούσῃ,
and if even the church he refuses to hear,

ἔστω σοι ὥσπερ ὁ ἐθνικὸς καὶ
let him be to thee as the gentile and

ὁ τελώνης. **18** Ἀμὴν λέγω ὑμῖν,
the tax-collector. Truly I say to you,

ὅσα ἐὰν δήσητε ἐπὶ τῆς γῆς ἔσται
whatever things ye bind on the earth shall be

δεδεμένα ἐν οὐρανῷ, καὶ ὅσα ἐὰν
having been bound in heaven, and whatever things

λύσητε ἐπὶ τῆς γῆς ἔσται λελυμένα
ye loose on the earth shall be having been loosed

ἐν οὐρανῷ. **19** Πάλιν [ἀμὴν] λέγω
in heaven. Again truly I say

ὑμῖν ὅτι ἐὰν δύο συμφωνήσωσιν ἐξ
to you that if two agree of

ὑμῶν ἐπὶ τῆς γῆς περὶ παντὸς πράγ-
you on the earth concerning every

ματος οὗ ἐὰν αἰτήσωνται, γενήσεται
thing whatever they ask, it shall be

αὐτοῖς παρὰ τοῦ πατρός μου τοῦ ἐν
to them from the Father of me – in

οὐρανοῖς. **20** οὗ γάρ εἰσιν δύο ἢ τρεῖς
heavens. For where are two or three

συνηγμένοι εἰς τὸ ἐμὸν ὄνομα, ἐκεῖ εἰμι
having been assembled in – my name, there I am

ἐν μέσῳ αὐτῶν.
in [the] midst of them.

21 Τότε προσελθὼν ὁ Πέτρος εἶπεν
Then approaching – Peter said

αὐτῷ· κύριε, ποσάκις ἁμαρτήσει εἰς
to him: Lord, how often will sin against

ἐμὲ ὁ ἀδελφός μου καὶ ἀφήσω αὐτῷ;
me the brother of me and I will forgive him?

ἕως ἑπτάκις; **22** λέγει αὐτῷ ὁ Ἰησοῦς·
until seven times? says to him – Jesus:

οὐ λέγω σοι ἕως ἑπτάκις, ἀλλὰ
I tell not to thee until seven times, but

ἕως ἑβδομηκοντάκις ἑπτά. **23** Διὰ τοῦτο
until seventy times seven. Therefore

ὡμοιώθη ἡ βασιλεία τῶν οὐρανῶν
was(is) likened the kingdom of the heavens

ἀνθρώπῳ βασιλεῖ, ὃς ἠθέλησεν συνᾶραι
to a man a king, who wished to take

λόγον μετὰ τῶν δούλων αὐτοῦ. **24** ἀρξα-
account with the slaves of him. And

μένου δὲ αὐτοῦ συναίρειν, προσήχθη
beginning him[a] to take, [b]was brought forward
= as he began

owed him ten thousand talents; [25] and as he could not pay, his lord ordered him to be sold, with his wife and children and all that he had, and payment to be made. [26] So the servant fell on his knees, imploring him, 'Lord, have patience with me, and I will pay you everything.' [27] And out of pity for him the lord of that servant released him and forgave him the debt. [28] But that same servant, as he went out, came upon one of his fellow servants who owed him a hundred denarii; and seizing him by the throat he said, 'Pay what you owe.' [29] So his fellow servant fell down and besought him, 'Have patience with me, and I will pay you.' [30] He refused and went and put him in prison till he should pay the debt. [31] When his fellow servants saw what had taken place, they were greatly distressed, and they went and reported to their lord all that had taken place. [32] Then his lord summoned him and said to

εἷς αὐτῷ ὀφειλέτης μυρίων ταλάντων.
[1]one [2]to him [2]debtor [3]of ten thousand [4]talents.

25 μὴ ἔχοντος δὲ αὐτοῦ ἀποδοῦναι, ἐκελευσεν
And not having him[a] to repay, commanded
=as he had not

αὐτὸν ὁ κύριος πραθῆναι καὶ τὴν
him the lord to be sold and the(his)

γυναῖκα καὶ τὰ τέκνα καὶ πάντα ὅσα
wife and – children and all things whatever

ἔχει, καὶ ἀποδοθῆναι. 26 πεσὼν οὖν ὁ
he has, and to be repaid. Falling therefore the

δοῦλος προσεκύνει αὐτῷ λέγων· μακρο-
slave did obeisance to him saying: Defer

θύμησον ἐπ᾽ ἐμοί, καὶ πάντα ἀποδώσω
anger over me, and all things I will repay

σοι. 27 σπλαγχνισθεὶς δὲ ὁ κύριος τοῦ
thee. And filled with tenderness the lord –

δούλου ἐκείνου ἀπέλυσεν αὐτόν, καὶ τὸ
slave of that released him, and the

δάνειον ἀφῆκεν αὐτῷ. 28 ἐξελθὼν δὲ
loan forgave him. But going out

ὁ δοῦλος ἐκεῖνος εὗρεν ἕνα τῶν
– slave that found one of the

συνδούλων αὐτοῦ, ὃς ὤφειλεν αὐτὸν ἑκατὸν
fellow-slaves of him, who owed him a hundred

δηνάρια, καὶ κρατήσας αὐτὸν ἔπνιγεν
denarii, and seizing him throttled

λέγων· ἀπόδος εἴ τι ὀφείλεις.
saying: Repay if something thou owest.

29 πεσὼν οὖν ὁ σύνδουλος αὐτοῦ παρε-
Falling therefore the fellow-slave of him be-

κάλει αὐτὸν λέγων· μακροθύμησον ἐπ᾽
sought him saying: Defer anger over

ἐμοί, καὶ ἀποδώσω σοι. 30 ὁ δὲ οὐκ
me, and I will repay thee. But he not

ἤθελεν, ἀλλὰ ἀπελθὼν ἔβαλεν αὐτὸν εἰς
wished, but going away threw him into

φυλακὴν ἕως ἀποδῷ τὸ ὀφειλόμενον.
prison until he should repay the thing owing.

31 ἰδόντες οὖν οἱ σύνδουλοι αὐτοῦ τὰ
Seeing therefore the fellow-slaves of him the things

γενόμενα ἐλυπήθησαν σφόδρα, καὶ
having taken place they were grieved exceedingly, and

ἐλθόντες διεσάφησαν τῷ κυρίῳ ἑαυτῶν
coming explained to the lord of them*selves*

πάντα τὰ γενόμενα. 32 τότε προσ-
all the things having taken place. Then [1]call-

καλεσάμενος αὐτὸν ὁ κύριος αὐτοῦ λέγει
ing [2]forward [3]him the lord of him says

him, 'You wicked ser-
vant! I forgave you all
that debt because you
besought me; ³³and
should not you have had
mercy on your fellow
servant, as I had mercy
on you?' ³⁴And in anger
his lord delivered him to
the jailers, till he should
pay all his debt. ³⁵So also
my heavenly Father will
do to every one of you,
if you do not forgive
your brother from your
heart.''

αὐτῷ·   δοῦλε   πονηρέ,   πᾶσαν   τὴν   ὀφειλὴν
to him: ²Slave   ¹wicked,   all   –   debt

ἐκείνην   ἀφῆκά   σοι,   ἐπεὶ   παρεκάλεσάς   με·
that   I forgave   thee,   since   thou besoughtest   me;

33 οὐκ   ἔδει   καὶ   σὲ   ἐλεῆσαι   τὸν
did it not behove   also   thee   to pity   the

σύνδουλόν   σου,   ὡς   κἀγὼ   σὲ   ἠλέησα;
fellow-slave   of thee,   as   I also   thee   pitied?

34 καὶ   ὀργισθεὶς   ὁ   κύριος   αὐτοῦ
And   being angry   the   lord   of him

παρέδωκεν   αὐτὸν   τοῖς   βασανισταῖς   ἕως   οὗ
delivered   him   to the   tormentors   until

ἀποδῷ   πᾶν   τὸ   ὀφειλόμενον   αὐτῷ.
he should repay   all   the thing   owing   to him.

35 Οὕτως   καὶ   ὁ   πατήρ   μου   ὁ   οὐράνιος
Thus   also   the   Father   of me   –   heavenly

ποιήσει   ὑμῖν,   ἐὰν   μὴ   ἀφῆτε   ἕκαστος
will do   to you,   unless   ye forgive   each one

τῷ   ἀδελφῷ   αὐτοῦ   ἀπὸ   τῶν   καρδιῶν
the   brother   of him   from   the   hearts

ὑμῶν.
of you.

CHAPTER 19

NOW when Jesus had
finished these say-
ings, he went away from
Galilee and entered the
region of Judea beyond
the Jordan; ²and large
crowds followed him, and
he healed them there.

3 And Pharisees came
up to him and tested him
by asking, "Is it lawful
to divorce one's wife for
any cause?" ⁴He
answered, "Have you not
read that he who made
them from the beginning
made them male and
female, ⁵and said, 'For

19 Καὶ   ἐγένετο   ὅτε   ἐτέλεσεν   ὁ
And   it came to pass   when   ended   –

Ἰησοῦς   τοὺς   λόγους   τούτους,   μετῆρεν
Jesus   –   words   these,   he removed

ἀπὸ   τῆς   Γαλιλαίας   καὶ   ἦλθεν   εἰς   τὰ
from   –   Galilee   and   came   into   the

ὅρια   τῆς   Ἰουδαίας   πέραν   τοῦ   Ἰορδάνου.
borders   –   of Judæa   across   the   Jordan.

2 καὶ   ἠκολούθησαν   αὐτῷ   ὄχλοι   πολλοί,
And   followed   him   crowds   many,

καὶ   ἐθεράπευσεν   αὐτοὺς   ἐκεῖ.
and   he healed   them   there.

3 Καὶ   προσῆλθον   αὐτῷ   Φαρισαῖοι
And   approached   to him   Pharisees

πειράζοντες   αὐτὸν   καὶ   λέγοντες·   εἰ   ἔξεστιν
tempting   him   and   saying: If   it is lawful

ἀπολῦσαι   τὴν   γυναῖκα   αὐτοῦ   κατὰ   πᾶσαν
to dismiss   the   wife   of him   for   every

αἰτίαν;   **4** ὁ   δὲ   ἀποκριθεὶς   εἶπεν·   οὐκ
cause?   And he   answering   said: not

ἀνέγνωτε   ὅτι   ὁ   κτίσας   ἀπ'
Did ye read   that   the [one]   creating   from

ἀρχῆς   ἄρσεν   καὶ   θῆλυ   ἐποίησεν   αὐτούς;
[the] beginning   male   and   female   made   them?

this reason a man shall leave his father and mother and be joined to his wife, and the two shall become one'? ⁶So they are no longer two but one. What therefore God has joined together, let no man put asunder.'' ⁷They said to him, "Why then did Moses command one to give a certificate of divorce, and to put her away?'' ⁸He said to them, "For your hardness of heart Moses allowed you to divorce your wives, but from the beginning it was not so. ⁹And I say to you: whoever divorces his wife, except for unchastity,ⁿ and marries another, commits adultery.''ᵒ

10 The disciples said to him, "If such is the case of a man with his wife, it is not expedient to marry.'' ¹¹But he said to them, "Not all men can receive this precept, but only those to whom it is given. ¹²For there are eunuchs who have been so from birth, and there are eunuchs who have been made eunuchs by men, and there are eunuchs who have made

ⁿ Other ancient authorities, after *unchastity*, read *makes her commit adultery*
ᵒ Other ancient authorities insert *and he who marries a divorced woman commits adultery*

5 καὶ εἶπεν· ἕνεκα τούτου καταλείψει
And he said: For the sake of this shall leave

ἄνθρωπος τὸν πατέρα καὶ τὴν μητέρα
a man the(his) father and the(his) mother

καὶ κολληθήσεται τῇ γυναικὶ αὐτοῦ,
and shall cleave to the wife of him,

καὶ ἔσονται οἱ δύο εἰς σάρκα μίαν·
and ²shall be ¹the ¹two ⁴in ⁵flesh ⁶one;

6 ὥστε οὐκέτι εἰσὶν δύο ἀλλὰ σὰρξ μία.
so as no longer are they two but flesh one.

ὃ οὖν ὁ θεὸς συνέζευξεν, ἄνθρωπος
What therefore – God yoked together, a man

μὴ χωριζέτω. 7 λέγουσιν αὐτῷ· τί οὖν
let not separate. They say to him: Why then

Μωϋσῆς ἐνετείλατο δοῦναι βιβλίον ἀπο-
¹Moses ¹did ²enjoin to give a document of

στασίου καὶ ἀπολῦσαι; 8 λέγει αὐτοῖς·
divorce and to dismiss? He says to them:

ὅτι Μωϋσῆς πρὸς τὴν σκληροκαρδίαν
– Moses in view of the obduracy

ὑμῶν ἐπέτρεψεν ὑμῖν ἀπολῦσαι τὰς
of you allowed you to dismiss the

γυναῖκας ὑμῶν· ἀπ' ἀρχῆς δὲ οὐ
wives of you; but from [the] beginning not

γέγονεν οὕτως. 9 λέγω δὲ ὑμῖν ὅτι
it has been so. But I say to you that

ὃς ἂν ἀπολύσῃ τὴν γυναῖκα αὐτοῦ
whoever dismisses the wife of him

μὴ ἐπὶ πορνείᾳ καὶ γαμήσῃ ἄλλην,
not of(for) fornication and marries another,

μοιχᾶται. 10 λέγουσιν αὐτῷ οἱ μαθηταί·
commits adultery. Say to him the disciples:

εἰ οὕτως ἐστὶν ἡ αἰτία τοῦ ἀνθρώπου
If so is the cause of the man

μετὰ τῆς γυναικός, οὐ συμφέρει γαμῆσαι.
with the wife, it is not expedient to marry.

11 ὁ δὲ εἶπεν αὐτοῖς· οὐ πάντες χωροῦσιν
And he said to them: Not all men grasp

τὸν λόγον τοῦτον, ἀλλ' οἷς δέδοται.
– saying this, but [those] to whom it has been given.

12 εἰσὶν γὰρ εὐνοῦχοι οἵτινες ἐκ κοιλίας
For there are eunuchs who from [the] womb

μητρὸς ἐγεννήθησαν οὕτως, καὶ εἰσὶν
of a mother were born so, and there are

εὐνοῦχοι οἵτινες εὐνουχίσθησαν ὑπὸ τῶν
eunuchs who were made eunuchs by –

ἀνθρώπων, καὶ εἰσὶν εὐνοῦχοι οἵτινες
men, and there are eunuchs who

themselves eunuchs for the sake of the kingdom of heaven. He who is able to receive this, let him receive it."

13 Then children were brought to him that he might lay his hands on them and pray. The disciples rebuked the people, [14]but Jesus said, "Let the children come to me, and do not hinder them; for to such belongs the kingdom of heaven." [15]And he laid his hands on them and went away.

16 And behold, one came up to him, saying, "Teacher, what good deed must I do, to have eternal life?" [17]And he said to him, "Why do you ask me about what is good? One there is who is good. If you would enter life, keep the commandments." [18]He said to him, "Which?" And Jesus said, "You shall not kill, You shall not commit adultery, You shall not steal, You shall not bear false witness, [19]Honor your father and mother, and, You shall love your neighbor as yourself." [20]The young man said to him, "All these I have observed; what do I still

εὐνούχισαν ἑαυτοὺς διὰ τὴν
made eunuchs   themselves   on account of   the
βασιλείαν τῶν οὐρανῶν. ὁ δυνάμενος
kingdom   of the   heavens. The [one]   being able
χωρεῖν χωρείτω.
to grasp [it]   let him grasp.

13 Τότε προσηνέχθησαν αὐτῷ παιδία,
Then   were brought   to him   children,
ἵνα τὰς χεῖρας ἐπιθῇ αὐτοῖς καὶ
that   the(his)   hands   he should put on   them   and
προσεύξηται· οἱ δὲ μαθηταὶ ἐπετίμησαν
pray;   but the   disciples   rebuked
αὐτοῖς. 14 ὁ δὲ Ἰησοῦς εἶπεν· ἄφετε
them.   - But   Jesus   said: Permit
τὰ παιδία καὶ μὴ κωλύετε αὐτὰ ἐλθεῖν
the   children   and   do not prevent   them   to come
πρός με· τῶν γὰρ τοιούτων ἐστὶν ἡ
unto   me;   -   for   of such   is   the
βασιλεία τῶν οὐρανῶν. 15 καὶ ἐπιθεὶς
kingdom   of the   heavens.   And   putting on
τὰς χεῖρας αὐτοῖς ἐπορεύθη ἐκεῖθεν.
the(his)   hands   on them   he went   thence.

16 Καὶ ἰδοὺ εἷς προσελθὼν αὐτῷ εἶπεν·
And   behold   one   approaching   to him   said:
διδάσκαλε, τί ἀγαθὸν ποιήσω ἵνα
Teacher,   what   good thing   may I do   that
σχῶ ζωὴν αἰώνιον; ὁ δὲ εἶπεν αὐτῷ·
I may have   life   eternal?   And he   said   to him:
17 τί με ἐρωτᾷς περὶ τοῦ ἀγαθοῦ;
Why   me questionest thou concerning   the   good?
εἷς ἐστιν ὁ ἀγαθός· εἰ δὲ θέλεις εἰς
one   is   the   good;   but if   thou wishest   into
τὴν ζωὴν εἰσελθεῖν, τήρει τὰς ἐντολάς.
-   life   to enter,   keep   the commandments.
18 λέγει αὐτῷ· ποίας; ὁ δὲ Ἰησοῦς
He says   to him: Which?   -   And   Jesus
ἔφη· τὸ οὐ φονεύσεις, οὐ μοιχεύσεις,
said: - Thou shalt not kill, Thou shalt not commit adultery,
οὐ κλέψεις, οὐ ψευδομαρτυρήσεις,
Thou shalt not steal,   Thou shalt not bear false witness,
19 τίμα τὸν πατέρα καὶ τὴν μητέρα,
Honour   the(thy)   father   and the(thy)   mother,
καὶ ἀγαπήσεις τὸν πλησίον σου ὡς
and   Thou shalt love   the   neighbour   of thee   as
σεαυτόν. 20 λέγει αὐτῷ ὁ νεανίσκος·
thyself.   Says   to him   the   young man:
ταῦτα πάντα ἐφύλαξα· τί ἔτι ὑστερῶ;
[3]These things   [1]all   I kept;   what   yet   do I lack?

lack?" ²¹Jesus said to him, "If you would be perfect, go, sell what you possess and give to the poor, and you will have treasure in heaven; and come, follow me."
²²When the young man heard this he went away sorrowful; for he had great possessions.

23 And Jesus said to his disciples, "Truly, I say to you, it will be hard for a rich man to enter the kingdom of heaven.
²⁴Again I tell you, it is easier for a camel to go through the eye of a needle than for a rich man to enter the kingdom of God." ²⁵When the disciples heard this they were greatly astonished, saying, "Who then can be saved?" ²⁶But Jesus looked at them and said to them, "With men this is impossible, but with God all things are possible." ²⁷Then Peter said in reply, "Lo, we have left everything and followed you. What then shall we have?" ²⁸Jesus said to them, "Truly, I say to you, in the new

21 ἔφη   αὐτῷ   ὁ Ἰησοῦς·   εἰ θέλεις τέλειος
   Said   to him   -   Jesus: If thou wishest perfect

εἶναι,   ὕπαγε   πώλησόν   σου   τὰ   ὑπάρχοντα
to be,   go   sell   of thee   the   belongings

καὶ   δὸς   πτωχοῖς,   καὶ   ἕξεις
and   give   to [the] poor,   and   thou shalt have

θησαυρὸν ἐν οὐρανοῖς, καὶ δεῦρο ἀκολούθει
treasure   in   heavens,   and   come   follow

μοι.   22 ἀκούσας   δὲ   ὁ   νεανίσκος   τὸν
me.   But hearing   the   young man   -

λόγον   [τοῦτον]   ἀπῆλθεν   λυπούμενος·
word   this   went away   grieving;

ἦν   γὰρ   ἔχων   κτήματα   πολλά.   23 Ὁ
for he was   having   possessions   many.

δὲ   Ἰησοῦς   εἶπεν   τοῖς   μαθηταῖς   αὐτοῦ·
So   Jesus   said   to the   disciples   of him:

ἀμὴν   λέγω   ὑμῖν   ὅτι   πλούσιος   δυσκόλως
Truly   I tell   you   that   a rich man   hardly

εἰσελεύσεται   εἰς   τὴν   βασιλείαν   τῶν
will enter   into   the   kingdom   of the

οὐρανῶν.   24 πάλιν   δὲ   λέγω   ὑμῖν,
heavens.   And again   I tell   you,

εὐκοπώτερόν ἐστιν κάμηλον διὰ τρήματος
easier   it is   a camel   through   [the] eye

ῥαφίδος   εἰσελθεῖν   ἢ   πλούσιον   εἰς   τὴν
of a needle   to enter   than   a rich man   into   the

βασιλείαν   τοῦ   θεοῦ.   25 ἀκούσαντες   δὲ
kingdom   -   of God.   And hearing

οἱ   μαθηταὶ   ἐξεπλήσσοντο   σφόδρα
the   disciples   were astounded   exceedingly

λέγοντες·   τίς   ἄρα   δύναται   σωθῆναι;
saying: Who   then   can   to be saved?

26 ἐμβλέψας   δὲ   ὁ   Ἰησοῦς   εἶπεν
And looking upon   -   Jesus   said

αὐτοῖς·   παρὰ   ἀνθρώποις   τοῦτο   ἀδύνατόν
to them: With   men   this   impossible

ἐστιν,   παρὰ   δὲ   θεῷ   πάντα   δυνατά.
is,   but with   God   all things   [are] possible.

27 Τότε ἀποκριθεὶς ὁ Πέτρος εἶπεν αὐτῷ·
Then   answering   -   Peter   said   to him:

ἰδοὺ   ἡμεῖς   ἀφήκαμεν   πάντα   καὶ
Behold   we   left   all things   and

ἠκολουθήσαμέν   σοι·   τί   ἄρα   ἔσται
followed   thee;   what   then   shall be
=shall we have?

ἡμῖν;   28 ὁ   δὲ   Ἰησοῦς   εἶπεν   αὐτοῖς·
to us?   - And   Jesus   said   to them;

ἀμὴν   λέγω   ὑμῖν   ὅτι   ὑμεῖς   οἱ   ἀκολουθή-
Truly   I tell   you   that   ye   the [ones]   having

world, when the Son of man shall sit on his glorious throne, you who have followed me will also sit on twelve thrones, judging the twelve tribes of Israel. 29And every one who has left houses or brothers or sisters or father or mother or children or lands, for my name's sake, will receive a hundredfold,ᵖ and inherit eternal life. 30But many that are first will be last, and the last first.

σαντές   μοι,   ἐν   τῇ   παλιγγενεσίᾳ,   ὅταν
followed   me,   in   the   regeneration,   when

καθίσῃ   ὁ   υἱὸς   τοῦ   ἀνθρώπου   ἐπὶ   θρόνου
sits   the   Son   –   of man   on [the] throne

δόξης   αὐτοῦ,   καθήσεσθε   καὶ   αὐτοὶ   ἐπὶ
of glory   of him,   ye will sit   also   [your]selves   on

δώδεκα   θρόνους   κρίνοντες   τὰς   δώδεκα
twelve   thrones   judging   the   twelve

φυλὰς   τοῦ   Ἰσραήλ.   29 καὶ   πᾶς   ὅστις
tribes   –   of Israel.   And   everyone   who

ἀφῆκεν   οἰκίας   ἢ   ἀδελφοὺς   ἢ   ἀδελφὰς   ἢ
left   houses   or   brothers   or   sisters   or

πατέρα   ἢ   μητέρα   ἢ   τέκνα   ἢ   ἀγροὺς
father   or   mother   or   children   or   fields

ἕνεκεν   τοῦ   ἐμοῦ   ὀνόματος,   πολλαπλα-
for the sake of   –   my   name,   mani-

σίονα   λήμψεται   καὶ   ζωὴν   αἰώνιον
fold   will receive   and   life   eternal

κληρονομήσει.   30 Πολλοὶ   δὲ   ἔσονται   πρῶτοι
will inherit.   But many   ˢwill be   ¹first

ἔσχατοι   καὶ   ἔσχατοι   πρῶτοι.
ˢlast   and   last   first.

CHAPTER 20

"FOR the kingdom of heaven is like a householder who went out early in the morning to hire laborers for his vineyard. 2After agreeing with the laborers for a denarius a day, he sent them into his vineyard. 3And going out about the third hour he saw others standing idle in the market place; 4and to them he said, 'You go into the vineyard too, and whatever is right I will give you.' So they went. 5Going out again

20 Ὁμοία   γάρ   ἐστιν   ἡ   βασιλεία   τῶν
For like   is   the   kingdom   of the

οὐρανῶν   ἀνθρώπῳ   οἰκοδεσπότῃ,   ὅστις
heavens   to a man   a housemaster,   who

ἐξῆλθεν   ἅμα   πρωὶ   μισθώσασθαι
went out   early in the morning   to hire

ἐργάτας   εἰς   τὸν   ἀμπελῶνα   αὐτοῦ.   2 συμ-
workmen   in   the   vineyard   of him.   And

φωνήσας   δὲ   μετὰ   τῶν   ἐργατῶν   ἐκ   δηναρίου
agreeing   with   the   workmen   out of(for)   a denarius

τὴν   ἡμέραν   ἀπέστειλεν   αὐτοὺς   εἰς   τὸν
the   day   he sent   them   into   the

ἀμπελῶνα   αὐτοῦ.   3 καὶ   ἐξελθὼν   περὶ
vineyard   of him.   And   going out   about

τρίτην   ὥραν   εἶδεν   ἄλλους   ἑστῶτας
[the] third   hour   he saw   others   standing

ἐν   τῇ   ἀγορᾷ   ἀργούς,   4 καὶ   ἐκείνοις
in   the   marketplace   idle,   and   to those

εἶπεν·   ὑπάγετε   καὶ   ὑμεῖς   εἰς   τὸν
said: Go   also   ye   into   the

ἀμπελῶνα,   καὶ   ὃ   ἐὰν   ᾖ   δίκαιον   δώσω
vineyard,   and   whatever may be   just   I will give

ὑμῖν.   οἱ   δὲ   ἀπῆλθον.   5 πάλιν   [δὲ]
you.   And they   went.   And again

ᵖ Other ancient authorities read manifold

about the sixth hour and the ninth hour, he did the same. ⁶And about the eleventh hour he went out and found others standing; and he said to them, 'Why do you stand here idle all day?' ⁷They said to him, 'Because no one has hired us.' He said to them, 'You go into the vineyard too.' ⁸And when evening came, the owner of the vineyard said to his steward, 'Call the laborers and pay them their wages, beginning with the last, up to the first.' ⁹And when those hired about the eleventh hour came, each of them received a denarius. ¹⁰Now when the first came, they thought they would receive more; but each of them also received a denarius. ¹¹And on receiving it they grumbled at the householder, ¹²saying, 'These last worked only one hour, and you have made them equal to us who have borne the burden of the day and the scorching heat.' ¹³But he replied to one of them, 'Friend, I am doing you no wrong; did you not agree with me for a denarius? ¹⁴Take what belongs to

Greek	English
ἐξελθὼν περὶ ἕκτην καὶ ἐνάτην ὥραν	going out about [the] sixth and [the] ninth hour
ἐποίησεν ὡσαύτως. 6 περὶ δὲ τὴν	he did similarly. And about the
ἐνδεκάτην ἐξελθὼν εὗρεν ἄλλους ἑστῶτας,	eleventh going out he found others standing,
καὶ λέγει αὐτοῖς· τί ὧδε ἑστήκατε	and says to them: Why here stand ye
ὅλην τὴν ἡμέραν ἀργοί; 7 λέγουσιν αὐτῷ·	all the day idle? They say to him:
ὅτι οὐδεὶς ἡμᾶς ἐμισθώσατο. λέγει αὐτοῖς·	Because no one us hired. He says to them:
ὑπάγετε καὶ ὑμεῖς εἰς τὸν ἀμπελῶνα.	Go also ye into the vineyard.
8 ὀψίας δὲ γενομένης λέγει ὁ κύριος	And evening having come = when evening had come says the lord
τοῦ ἀμπελῶνος τῷ ἐπιτρόπῳ αὐτοῦ·	of the vineyard to the steward of him:
κάλεσον τοὺς ἐργάτας καὶ ἀπόδος τὸν	Call the workmen and pay the
μισθόν, ἀρξάμενος ἀπὸ τῶν ἐσχάτων	wage, beginning from the last ones
ἕως τῶν πρώτων. 9 ἐλθόντες δὲ οἱ	until the first. And coming the [ones]
περὶ τὴν ἐνδεκάτην ὥραν ἔλαβον ἀνὰ	about the eleventh hour received each
δηνάριον. 10 καὶ ἐλθόντες οἱ πρῶτοι	a denarius. And coming the first
ἐνόμισαν ὅτι πλεῖον λήμψονται· καὶ	supposed that more they will receive; and
ἔλαβον τὸ ἀνὰ δηνάριον καὶ αὐτοί.	they received the each denarius also [them]selves.
11 λαβόντες δὲ ἐγόγγυζον κατὰ τοῦ	And receiving they grumbled against the
οἰκοδεσπότου λέγοντες· 12 οὗτοι οἱ ἔσχατοι	housemaster saying: These — last
μίαν ὥραν ἐποίησαν, καὶ ἴσους αὐτοὺς	one hour wrought, and equal them
ἡμῖν ἐποίησας τοῖς βαστάσασι τὸ	to us thou madest the [ones] having borne the
βάρος τῆς ἡμέρας καὶ τὸν καύσωνα.	burden of the day and the heat.
13 ὁ δὲ ἀποκριθεὶς ἑνὶ αὐτῶν εἶπεν·	But he answering one of them said:
ἑταῖρε, οὐκ ἀδικῶ σε· οὐχὶ	Comrade, I do not injure thee; not
δηναρίου συνεφώνησάς μοι; 14 ἆρον	of(for) a denarius thou didst agree with me? take

you, and go; I choose to give to this last as I give to you. ¹⁵Am I not allowed to do what I choose with what belongs to me? Or do you begrudge my generosity?�q ¹⁶So the last will be first, and the first last."

17 And as Jesus was going up to Jerusalem, he took the twelve disciples aside, and on the way he said to them, ¹⁸"Behold, we are going up to Jerusalem; and the Son of man will be delivered to the chief priests and scribes, and they will condemn him to death, ¹⁹and deliver him to the Gentiles to be mocked and scourged and crucified, and he will be raised on the third day."

20 Then the mother of the sons of Zeb'edee came up to him, with her sons, and kneeling before him she asked him for something. ²¹And he said to her, "What do you want?" She said to him, "Command that these two sons of mine may sit, one at your right hand and one at your left,

---

τὸ　σὸν　καὶ　ὕπαγε·　θέλω　δὲ
the thine and go; but I wish
= that which is thine

τούτῳ　τῷ　ἐσχάτῳ　δοῦναι　ὡς　καὶ
to this - last man to give as also

σοί·　15 οὐκ　ἔξεστίν　μοι　ὃ　θέλω
to thee; is it not lawful to me what I wish

ποιῆσαι　ἐν　τοῖς　ἐμοῖς;　ἢ　ὁ
to do among *the* my things? or the

ὀφθαλμός　σου　πονηρός　ἐστιν　ὅτι　ἐγὼ
eye of thee evil is because I

ἀγαθός　εἰμι;　16 Οὕτως　ἔσονται　οἱ　ἔσχατοι
good am? Thus will be the last [ones]

πρῶτοι　καὶ　οἱ　πρῶτοι　ἔσχατοι.
first and the first last.

17 Μέλλων　δὲ　ἀναβαίνειν　Ἰησοῦς　εἰς
And being about to go up Jesus to

Ἰεροσόλυμα　παρέλαβεν　τοὺς　δώδεκα　κατ'
Jerusalem he took the twelve private-

ἰδίαν,　καὶ　ἐν　τῇ　ὁδῷ　εἶπεν　αὐτοῖς·
ly, and in the way said to them:

18 ἰδοὺ　ἀναβαίνομεν　εἰς　Ἰεροσόλυμα,　καὶ
Behold we are going up to Jerusalem, and

ὁ　υἱὸς　τοῦ　ἀνθρώπου　παραδοθήσεται　τοῖς
the Son - of man will be delivered to the

ἀρχιερεῦσιν　καὶ　γραμματεῦσιν,　καὶ　κατα-
chief priests and scribes, and they will

κρινοῦσιν　αὐτὸν　εἰς　θάνατον,　19 καὶ
condemn him to death, and

παραδώσουσιν　αὐτὸν　τοῖς　ἔθνεσιν　εἰς
they will deliver him to the nations *for*

τὸ　ἐμπαῖξαι　καὶ　μαστιγῶσαι　καὶ
- to mock and to scourge and

σταυρῶσαι,　καὶ　τῇ　τρίτῃ　ἡμέρᾳ　ἐγερθή-
to crucify, and on the third day he will be

σεται.
raised.

20 Τότε　προσῆλθεν　αὐτῷ　ἡ　μήτηρ　τῶν
Then approached *to* him the mother of the

υἱῶν　Ζεβεδαίου　μετὰ　τῶν　υἱῶν　αὐτῆς
sons of Zebedee with the sons of her

προσκυνοῦσα　καὶ　αἰτοῦσά　τι　ἀπ'　αὐτοῦ.
doing obeisance and asking something from him.

21 ὁ　δὲ　εἶπεν　αὐτῇ·　τί　θέλεις;　λέγει
And he said to her: What wishest thou? She says

αὐτῷ·　εἰπὲ　ἵνα　καθίσωσιν　οὗτοι　οἱ
to him: Say that may sit these the

δύο　υἱοί　μου　εἷς　ἐκ　δεξιῶν　καὶ　εἷς
two sons of me one on [the] right and one

�q Or *is your eye evil because I am good?*

in your kingdom." [22] But Jesus answered, "You do not know what you are asking. Are you able to drink the cup that I am to drink?" They said to him, "We are able." [23] He said to them, "You will drink my cup, but to sit at my right hand and at my left is not mine to grant, but it is for those for whom it has been prepared by my Father." [24] And when the ten heard it, they were indignant at the two brothers. [25] But Jesus called them to him and said, "You know that the rulers of the Gentiles lord it over them, and their great men exercise authority over them. [26] It shall not be so among you; but whoever would be great among you must be your servant, [27] and whoever would be first among you must be your slave; [28] even as the Son of man came not to be served but to serve, and to give his life as a ransom for many."

29 And as they went out of Jericho, a great

ἐξ εὐωνύμων σου ἐν τῇ βασιλείᾳ
on [the] left   of thee   in   the   kingdom
σου. 22 ἀποκριθεὶς δὲ   ὁ Ἰησοῦς
of thee.   And answering   –   Jesus
εἶπεν· οὐκ οἴδατε τί αἰτεῖσθε.
said: Ye know not   what   ye ask.
δύνασθε πιεῖν τὸ ποτήριον ὃ ἐγὼ
Can ye to drink the   cup   which I
μέλλω πίνειν; λέγουσιν αὐτῷ· δυνάμεθα.
am about to drink?   They say   to him: We can.
23 λέγει αὐτοῖς· τὸ μὲν ποτήριόν μου
He says to them: Indeed the   cup   of me
πίεσθε, τὸ δὲ καθίσαι ἐκ δεξιῶν
ye shall drink, –   but   to sit   on [the] right
μου καὶ ἐξ εὐωνύμων οὐκ ἔστιν
of me   and on [the] left   is not
ἐμὸν τοῦτο δοῦναι, ἀλλ' οἷς ἡτοί-
mine   this   to give,   but to whom it has
μασται ὑπὸ τοῦ πατρός μου. 24 καὶ
been prepared by   the   Father   of me.   And
ἀκούσαντες οἱ δέκα ἠγανάκτησαν περὶ
hearing   the   ten   were incensed   about
τῶν δύο ἀδελφῶν. 25 ὁ δὲ Ἰησοῦς
the two   brothers.   –   So   Jesus
προσκαλεσάμενος αὐτοῖς εἶπεν· οἴδατε
calling forward   them   said: Ye know
ὅτι οἱ ἄρχοντες τῶν ἐθνῶν κατακυριεύουσιν
that the   rulers   of the nations   lord it over
αὐτῶν καὶ οἱ μεγάλοι κατεξουσιάζουσιν
them   and the   great ones   have authority over
αὐτῶν. 26 οὐχ οὕτως ἐστὶν ἐν ὑμῖν·
them.   Not   thus   is it among you;
ἀλλ' ὃς ἐὰν θέλῃ ἐν ὑμῖν μέγας γενέσθαι,
but   whoever wishes among you great   to become,
ἔσται ὑμῶν διάκονος, 27 καὶ ὃς ἂν
will be of you   servant,   and   whoever
θέλῃ ἐν ὑμῖν εἶναι πρῶτος, ἔσται ὑμῶν
wishes among you to be   first,   he shall be of you
δοῦλος· 28 ὥσπερ ὁ υἱὸς τοῦ ἀνθρώπου
slave;   as   the   Son   –   of man
οὐκ ἦλθεν διακονηθῆναι, ἀλλὰ διακο-
came not   to be served,   but   to
νῆσαι καὶ δοῦναι τὴν ψυχὴν αὐτοῦ
serve and to give   the   life   of him
λύτρον ἀντὶ πολλῶν.
a ransom instead of many.
29 Καὶ ἐκπορευομένων αὐτῶν ἀπὸ Ἰεριχὼ
And   going out   themᵃ from   Jericho
=as they were going out

crowd followed him.
³⁰And behold, two blind
men sitting by the road-
side, when they heard
that Jesus was passing by,
cried out,ʳ "Have mercy
on us, Son of David!"
³¹The crowd rebuked
them, telling them to be
silent; but they cried out
the more, "Lord, have
mercy on us, Son of
David!" ³²And Jesus
stopped and called them,
saying, "What do you
want me to do for you?"
³³They said to him,
"Lord, let our eyes be
opened." ³⁴And Jesus
in pity touched their
eyes, and immediately
they received their sight
and followed him.

ἠκολούθησεν αὐτῷ ὄχλος πολύς. 30 καὶ
followed   him   crowd a much.   And
ἰδοὺ δύο τυφλοὶ καθήμενοι παρὰ τὴν
behold two blind men   sitting   beside the
ὁδόν, ἀκούσαντες ὅτι Ἰησοῦς παράγει,
way,   hearing   that Jesus is passing by,
ἔκραξαν λέγοντες· κύριε, ἐλέησον ἡμᾶς,
cried out saying: Lord, pity   us,
υἱὸς Δαυίδ. 31 ὁ δὲ ὄχλος ἐπετίμησεν
son of David.   But the crowd   rebuked
αὐτοῖς ἵνα σιωπήσωσιν· οἱ δὲ μεῖζον
them   that they should be silent; but they more
ἔκραξαν λέγοντες· κύριε, ἐλέησον ἡμᾶς,
cried out saying: Lord, pity   us,
υἱὸς Δαυίδ. 32 καὶ στὰς ὁ Ἰησοῦς
son of David.   And standing -   Jesus
ἐφώνησεν αὐτοὺς καὶ εἶπεν· τί θέλετε
called   them   and said: What wish ye
ποιήσω ὑμῖν; 33 λέγουσιν αὐτῷ· κύριε,
I may do to you?   They say   to him: Lord,
ἵνα ἀνοιγῶσιν οἱ ὀφθαλμοὶ ἡμῶν.
that may be opened the   eyes   of us.
34 σπλαγχνισθεὶς δὲ ὁ Ἰησοῦς ἥψατο
And being filled with tenderness - Jesus touched
τῶν ὀμμάτων αὐτῶν, καὶ εὐθέως ἀνέβλεψαν
the   eyes   of them, and immediately they saw again
καὶ ἠκολούθησαν αὐτῷ.
and   followed   him.

CHAPTER 21

AND when they drew
near to Jerusalem
and came to Beth'phage,
to the Mount of Olives,
then Jesus sent two dis-
ciples, ²saying to them,
"Go into the village
opposite you, and im-
mediately you will find
an ass tied, and a colt
with her; untie them and
bring them to me. ³If any
one says anything to you,
you shall say, 'The Lord
has need of them,' and

21 Καὶ ὅτε ἤγγισαν εἰς Ἱεροσόλυμα
   And when they drew near to Jerusalem
καὶ ἦλθον εἰς Βηθφαγὴ εἰς τὸ ὄρος τῶν
and came to Bethphage to the mount of the
ἐλαιῶν, τότε Ἰησοῦς ἀπέστειλεν δύο
olives, then Jesus   sent   two
μαθητὰς 2 λέγων αὐτοῖς· πορεύεσθε εἰς
disciples   telling them: Go ye   into
τὴν κώμην τὴν κατέναντι ὑμῶν, καὶ εὐθὺς
the village -   opposite   you, and at once
εὑρήσετε ὄνον δεδεμένην καὶ πῶλον μετ'
ye will find an ass having been tied and a colt with
αὐτῆς· λύσαντες ἀγάγετέ μοι. 3 καὶ ἐάν
her/it; loosening bring   to me. And if
τις ὑμῖν εἴπῃ τι, ἐρεῖτε ὅτι ὁ
anyone to you says anything, ye shall say[,] - The
κύριος αὐτῶν χρείαν ἔχει· εὐθὺς δὲ
Lord   of them   need   has; and immediately

ʳ Other ancient authorities
insert Lord

he will send them im-
mediately." ⁴This took
place to fulfil what was
spoken by the prophet,
saying,
⁵"Tell the daughter of
    Zion,
  Behold, your king is
    coming to you,
  humble, and mounted
    on an ass,
  and on a colt, the foal
    of an ass."
⁶The disciples went and
did as Jesus had directed
them; ⁷they brought the
ass and the colt, and put
their garments on them,
and he sat thereon.
⁸Most of the crowd
spread their garments on
the road, and others cut
branches from the trees
and spread them on the
road. ⁹And the crowds
that went before him and
that followed him
shouted, "Hosanna to
the Son of David! Blessed
is he who comes in the
name of the Lord!
Hosanna in the highest!"
¹⁰And when he entered
Jerusalem, all the city
was stirred, saying, "Who
is this?" ¹¹And the
crowds said, "This is the
prophet Jesus from
Nazareth of Galilee."

12 And Jesus entered
the temple of God[a] and

ἀποστελεῖ αὐτούς. 4 Τοῦτο δὲ γέγονεν
he will send them.   Now this   has happened
ἵνα πληρωθῇ τὸ ῥηθὲν διὰ τοῦ
that might be fulfilled the thing spoken through the
προφήτου λέγοντος· 5 εἴπατε τῇ θυγατρὶ
prophet   saying·   Tell ye   the daughter
Σιών· ἰδοὺ ὁ βασιλεύς σου ἔρχεταί σοι
of Zion: Behold[,] the king of thee comes to thee
πραΰς καὶ ἐπιβεβηκὼς ἐπὶ ὄνον καὶ ἐπὶ
meek and having mounted on an ass and on
πῶλον υἱὸν ὑποζυγίου. 6 πορευθέντες δὲ
a colt son(foal) of an ass.   And going
οἱ μαθηταὶ καὶ ποιήσαντες καθὼς συνέταξεν
the disciples and   doing   as   directed
αὐτοῖς ὁ Ἰησοῦς 7 ἤγαγον τὴν ὄνον καὶ
them – Jesus   they brought the ass and
τὸν πῶλον, καὶ ἐπέθηκαν ἐπ' αὐτῶν
the colt, and put on   on   them
τὰ ἱμάτια, καὶ ἐπεκάθισεν ἐπάνω αὐτῶν.
the(ir) garments, and he sat on   on   them.
8 ὁ δὲ πλεῖστος ὄχλος ἔστρωσαν ἑαυτῶν
And the very large crowd strewed of themselves
τὰ ἱμάτια ἐν τῇ ὁδῷ, ἄλλοι δὲ ἔκοπτον
the garments in the way, and others cut
κλάδους ἀπὸ τῶν δένδρων καὶ ἐστρών-
branches from the   trees   and strewed
νυον ἐν τῇ ὁδῷ. 9 οἱ δὲ ὄχλοι οἱ
in the   way.   And the crowds the [ones]
προάγοντες αὐτὸν καὶ οἱ ἀκολουθοῦντες
going before him   and the [ones] following
ἔκραζον λέγοντες· ὡσαννὰ τῷ υἱῷ Δαυίδ·
cried out saying: Hosanna to the son of David;
εὐλογημένος ὁ ἐρχόμενος ἐν ὀνόματι
blessed   the [one] coming   in [the] name
κυρίου· ὡσαννὰ ἐν τοῖς ὑψίστοις. 10 καὶ
of [the] Lord; hosanna in the highest [places]. And
εἰσελθόντος αὐτοῦ εἰς Ἱεροσόλυμα ἐσείσθη
entering   him[a] into Jerusalem   was shaken
= as he entered
πᾶσα ἡ πόλις λέγουσα· τίς ἐστιν οὗτος;
all the city   saying: Who is   this?
11 οἱ δὲ ὄχλοι ἔλεγον· οὗτός ἐστιν ὁ
And the crowds said·   This   is   the
προφήτης Ἰησοῦς ὁ ἀπὸ Ναζαρὲθ τῆς
prophet Jesus the [one] from Nazareth   –
Γαλιλαίας.
of Galilee.
12 Καὶ εἰσῆλθεν Ἰησοῦς εἰς τὸ ἱερὸν
    And entered   Jesus into the temple

---

[a] Other ancient authorities
omit of God

drove out all who sold and bought in the temple, and he overturned the tables of the money-changers and the seats of those who sold pigeons. [13] He said to them, "It is written, 'My house shall be called a house of prayer'; but you make it a den of robbers."

14 And the blind and the lame came to him in the temple, and he healed them. [15] But when the chief priests and the scribes saw the wonderful things that he did, and the children crying out in the temple, "Hosanna to the Son of David!" they were indignant; [16] and they said to him, "Do you hear what these are saying?" And Jesus said to them, "Yes; have you never read,

'Out of the mouth of babes and sucklings thou hast brought perfect praise'?"

[17] And leaving them, he went out of the city to Bethany and lodged there.

18 In the morning, as he was returning to the city, he was hungry. [19] And seeing a fig tree by the wayside he went to it, and found nothing on it but leaves only. And he said to it, "May no fruit ever come from you

καὶ ἐξέβαλεν πάντας τοὺς πωλοῦντας καὶ
and cast out all the [ones] selling and
ἀγοράζοντας ἐν τῷ ἱερῷ, καὶ τὰς τραπέζας
buying in the temple, and the tables
τῶν κολλυβιστῶν κατέστρεψεν καὶ τὰς
of the money-changers he overturned and the
καθέδρας τῶν πωλούντων τὰς περιστεράς,
seats of the [ones] selling the doves,
13 καὶ λέγει αὐτοῖς· γέγραπται· ὁ οἶκός
and says to them: It has been written: The house
μου οἶκος προσευχῆς κληθήσεται, ὑμεῖς
of me a house of prayer shall be called, [2]ye
δὲ αὐτὸν ποιεῖτε σπήλαιον λῃστῶν. 14 Καὶ
[1]but [4]it [3]are making a den of robbers. And
προσῆλθον αὐτῷ τυφλοὶ καὶ χωλοὶ ἐν τῷ
approached to him blind and lame [ones] in the
ἱερῷ, καὶ ἐθεράπευσεν αὐτούς. 15 ἰδόντες
temple, and he healed them. [7]seeing
δὲ οἱ ἀρχιερεῖς καὶ οἱ γραμματεῖς τὰ
[1]But [2]the [3]chief priests [4]and [5]the [6]scribes the
θαυμάσια ἃ ἐποίησεν καὶ τοὺς παῖδας
marvels which he did and the children
τοὺς κράζοντας ἐν τῷ ἱερῷ καὶ λέγοντας·
- crying out in the temple and saying:
ὡσαννὰ τῷ υἱῷ Δαυίδ, ἠγανάκτησαν, 16 καὶ
Hosanna to the son of David, they were incensed, and
εἶπαν αὐτῷ· ἀκούεις τί οὗτοι λέγουσιν;
said to him: Hearest thou what these are saying?
ὁ δὲ Ἰησοῦς λέγει αὐτοῖς· ναί· οὐδέποτε
- And Jesus says to them: Yes; never
ἀνέγνωτε ὅτι ἐκ στόματος νηπίων καὶ
did ye read[,] - Out of [the] mouth of infants and
θηλαζόντων κατηρτίσω αἶνον; 17 Καὶ
sucking [ones] thou didst prepare praise? And
καταλιπὼν αὐτοὺς ἐξῆλθεν ἔξω τῆς
leaving them he went forth outside the
πόλεως εἰς Βηθανίαν, καὶ ηὐλίσθη ἐκεῖ.
city to Bethany, and lodged there.
18 Πρωὶ δὲ ἐπαναγαγὼν εἰς τὴν πόλιν
Now early going up to the city
ἐπείνασεν. 19 καὶ ἰδὼν συκῆν μίαν ἐπὶ τῆς
he hungered. And seeing fig-tree one on the
ὁδοῦ ἦλθεν ἐπ' αὐτήν, καὶ οὐδὲν εὗρεν
way he went up(to) it, and nothing found
ἐν αὐτῇ εἰ μὴ φύλλα μόνον, καὶ λέγει
in it except leaves only, and says
αὐτῇ· οὐ μηκέτι ἐκ σοῦ καρπὸς γένηται
to it: Never of thee fruit may be

again!" And the fig tree withered at once. ²⁰When the disciples saw it they marveled, saying, "How did the fig tree wither at once?" ²¹And Jesus answered them, "Truly, I say to you, if you have faith and never doubt, you will not only do what has been done to the fig tree, but even if you say to this mountain, 'Be taken up and cast into the sea,' it will be done. ²²And whatever you ask in prayer, you will receive, if you have faith."

23 And when he entered the temple, the chief priests and the elders of the people came up to him as he was teaching, and said, "By what authority are you doing these things, and who gave you this authority?" ²⁴Jesus answered them, "I also will ask you a question; and if you tell me the answer, then I also will tell you by what authority I do these things. ²⁵The baptism of John, whence was it? From heaven or from men?" And they argued with one another, "If we say, 'From heaven,' he will say to us, 'Why then did you not believe him?' ²⁶But if we

εἰς τὸν αἰῶνα. καὶ ἐξηράνθη παραχρῆμα
to the age. And was dried up instantly
ἡ συκῆ. 20 καὶ ἰδόντες οἱ μαθηταὶ
the fig-tree. And seeing the disciples
ἐθαύμασαν λέγοντες· πῶς παραχρῆμα
marvelled saying: How instantly
ἐξηράνθη ἡ συκῆ; 21 ἀποκριθεὶς δὲ ὁ
was withered the fig-tree? And answering –
Ἰησοῦς εἶπεν αὐτοῖς· ἀμὴν λέγω ὑμῖν,
Jesus said to them: Truly I say to you,
ἐὰν ἔχητε πίστιν καὶ μὴ διακριθῆτε,
If ye have faith and do not doubt,
οὐ μόνον τὸ τῆς συκῆς ποιήσετε, ἀλλὰ
not only the* of the fig-tree ye will do, but
κἂν τῷ ὄρει τούτῳ εἴπητε· ἄρθητι
also if – mountain to this ye say: Be thou taken
καὶ βλήθητι εἰς τὴν θάλασσαν, γενήσεται·
and cast into the sea, it shall be;
22 καὶ πάντα ὅσα ἂν αἰτήσητε ἐν τῇ
and all things whatever ye may ask in –
προσευχῇ πιστεύοντες λήμψεσθε.
prayer believing ye shall receive.
23 Καὶ ἐλθόντος αὐτοῦ εἰς τὸ ἱερὸν
And coming him* into the temple
=as he came
προσῆλθον αὐτῷ διδάσκοντι οἱ ἀρχιερεῖς
approached to him teaching* the chief priests
=while he taught
καὶ οἱ πρεσβύτεροι τοῦ λαοῦ λέγοντες·
and the elders of the people saying:
ἐν ποίᾳ ἐξουσίᾳ ταῦτα ποιεῖς; καὶ
By what authority these things doest thou? and
τίς σοι ἔδωκεν τὴν ἐξουσίαν ταύτην;
who thee gave – authority this?
24 ἀποκριθεὶς δὲ ὁ Ἰησοῦς εἶπεν αὐτοῖς·
And answering – Jesus said to them:
ἐρωτήσω ὑμᾶς κἀγὼ λόγον ἕνα, ὃν
will question you I also word one, which
ἐὰν εἴπητέ μοι, κἀγὼ ὑμῖν ἐρῶ ἐν ποίᾳ
if ye tell me, I also you will tell by what
ἐξουσίᾳ ταῦτα ποιῶ· 25 τὸ βάπτισμα
authority these things I do: The baptism
τὸ Ἰωάννου πόθεν ἦν; ἐξ οὐρανοῦ ἢ
– of John whence was it? from heaven or
ἐξ ἀνθρώπων; οἱ δὲ διελογίζοντο ἐν
from men? And they reasoned among
ἑαυτοῖς λέγοντες· ἐὰν εἴπωμεν· ἐξ οὐρανοῦ,
themselves saying: If we say: From heaven,
ἐρεῖ ἡμῖν· διὰ τί οὖν οὐκ ἐπιστεύσατε
he will say to us: Why then believed ye not

* Some such word as 'sign' must be supplied.

say, 'From men,' we are afraid of the multitude; for all hold that John was a prophet." ²⁷So they answered Jesus, "We do not know." And he said to them, "Neither will I tell you by what authority I do these things.

28 "What do you think? A man had two sons; and he went to the first and said, 'Son, go and work in the vineyard today.' ²⁹And he answered, 'I will not'; but afterward he repented and went. ³⁰And he went to the second and said the same; and he answered, 'I go, sir,' but did not go. ³¹Which of the two did the will of his father?" They said, "The first." Jesus said to them, "Truly, I say to you, the tax collectors and the harlots go into the kingdom of God before you. ³²For John came to you in the way of righteousness, and you did not believe him, but the tax collectors and the harlots believed him; and even when you saw it, you did not afterward repent and believe him.

33 "Hear another parable. There was a householder who planted a

αὐτῷ; 26 ἐὰν δὲ εἴπωμεν· ἐξ ἀνθρώπων,
him?   But if   we say: From   men,
φοβούμεθα τὸν ὄχλον· πάντες γὰρ ὡς
we fear   the   crowd·   for all   as
προφήτην ἔχουσιν τὸν Ἰωάννην. 27 καὶ
a prophet   have   -   John.   And
ἀποκριθέντες τῷ Ἰησοῦ εἶπαν· οὐκ
answering   -   Jesus   they said: We do
οἴδαμεν. ἔφη αὐτοῖς καὶ αὐτός· οὐδὲ
not know.   said   to them   also   He: Neither
ἐγὼ λέγω ὑμῖν ἐν ποίᾳ ἐξουσίᾳ ταῦτα
I   tell   you   by   what   authority   these things
ποιῶ. 28 Τί δὲ ὑμῖν δοκεῖ; ἄνθρωπος
I do.   But what   to you   seems it?   A man
εἶχεν τέκνα δύο· προσελθὼν τῷ πρώτῳ
had   children   two;   approaching   to the   first
εἶπεν· τέκνον, ὕπαγε σήμερον ἐργάζου ἐν
he said: Child,   go   to-day   work   in
τῷ ἀμπελῶνι. 29 ὁ δὲ ἀποκριθεὶς εἶπεν·
the   vineyard.   But he   answering   said:
ἐγὼ κύριε, καὶ οὐκ ἀπῆλθεν. 30 προσ—
I [go],   lord,   and   went not.   [go]
ελθὼν δὲ τῷ δευτέρῳ εἶπεν ὡσαύτως.
approaching   to the   second   he said   similarly.
ὁ δὲ ἀποκριθεὶς εἶπεν· οὐ θέλω, ὕστερον
And he   answering   said: I will not,   later
μεταμεληθεὶς ἀπῆλθεν. 31 τίς ἐκ τῶν δύο
repenting   he went.   Which of   the   two
ἐποίησεν τὸ θέλημα τοῦ πατρός; λέγουσιν·
did   the   will   of the   father?   They say:
ὁ ὕστερος. λέγει αὐτοῖς ὁ Ἰησοῦς· ἀμὴν
The latter.   Says   to them   -   Jesus: Truly
λέγω ὑμῖν ὅτι οἱ τελῶναι καὶ αἱ πόρναι
I tell   you[,]   -   The tax-collectors   and   the   harlots
προάγουσιν ὑμᾶς εἰς τὴν βασιλείαν τοῦ
are going before   you   into   the   kingdom   -
θεοῦ. 32 ἦλθεν γὰρ Ἰωάννης πρὸς ὑμᾶς
of God.   For came   John   to   you
ἐν ὁδῷ δικαιοσύνης, καὶ οὐκ ἐπιστεύσατε
in   a way   of righteousness,   and   ye believed not
αὐτῷ· οἱ δὲ τελῶναι καὶ αἱ πόρναι
him;   but the   tax-collectors   and   the   harlots
ἐπίστευσαν αὐτῷ· ὑμεῖς δὲ ἰδόντες οὐδὲ
believed   him;   but ye   seeing   not
μετεμελήθητε ὕστερον τοῦ πιστεῦσαι αὐτῷ.
repented   later   -   to believeᵈ   him.
=so as to believe
33 Ἄλλην παραβολὴν ἀκούσατε. Ἄνθρωπος
Another   parable   hear ye.   A man

vineyard, and set a hedge around it, and dug a wine press in it, and built a tower, and let it out to tenants, and went into another country. ³⁴When the season of fruit drew near, he sent his servants to the tenants, to get his fruit; ³⁵and the tenants took his servants and beat one, killed another, and stoned another. ³⁶Again he sent other servants, more than the first; and they did the same to them. ³⁷Afterward he sent his son to them, saying, 'They will respect my son.' ³⁸But when the tenants saw the son, they said to themselves, 'This is the heir; come, let us kill him and have his inheritance.' ³⁹And they took him and cast him out of the vineyard, and killed him. ⁴⁰When therefore the owner of the vineyard comes, what will he do to those tenants?" ⁴¹They said to him, "He will put those wretches to a miserable death, and let out the vineyard to other tenants who will

ἦν οἰκοδεσπότης ὅστις ἐφύτευσεν ἀμπελῶνα,
there was a housemaster who planted a vineyard,

καὶ φραγμὸν αὐτῷ περιέθηκεν καὶ ὤρυξεν
and ²a hedge ³it ¹put round and dug

ἐν αὐτῷ ληνὸν καὶ ᾠκοδόμησεν πύργον,
in it a winepress and built a tower,

καὶ ἐξέδοτο αὐτὸν γεωργοῖς, καὶ ἀπεδή-
and let it to husbandmen, and departed.

μησεν. 34 ὅτε δὲ ἤγγισεν ὁ καιρὸς τῶν
And when drew near the time of the

καρπῶν, ἀπέστειλεν τοὺς δούλους αὐτοῦ
fruits, he sent the slaves of him

πρὸς τοὺς γεωργοὺς λαβεῖν τοὺς καρποὺς
to the husbandmen to receive the fruits

αὐτοῦ. 35 καὶ λαβόντες οἱ γεωργοὶ
of it. And ²taking ¹the ²husbandmen

τοὺς δούλους αὐτοῦ ὃν μὲν ἔδειραν, ὃν
the slaves of him this one they flogged, that

δὲ ἀπέκτειναν, ὃν δὲ ἐλιθοβόλησαν. 36 πάλιν
one they killed, another they stoned. Again

ἀπέστειλεν ἄλλους δούλους πλείονας τῶν
he sent other slaves more [than] the

πρώτων, καὶ ἐποίησαν αὐτοῖς ὡσαύτως.
first [ones], and they did to them similarly.

37 ὕστερον δὲ ἀπέστειλεν πρὸς αὐτοὺς
But later he sent to them

τὸν υἱὸν αὐτοῦ λέγων· ἐντραπήσονται
the son of him saying: They will reverence

τὸν υἱόν μου. 38 οἱ δὲ γεωργοὶ ἰδόντες
the son of me. But the husbandmen seeing

τὸν υἱὸν εἶπον ἐν ἑαυτοῖς· οὗτός ἐστιν
the son said among themselves: This is

ὁ κληρονόμος· δεῦτε ἀποκτείνωμεν αὐτὸν
the heir; come[,] let us kill him

καὶ σχῶμεν τὴν κληρονομίαν αὐτοῦ·
and let us possess the inheritance of him;

39 καὶ λαβόντες αὐτὸν ἐξέβαλον ἔξω τοῦ
and taking ²him ¹they cast out outside the

ἀμπελῶνος καὶ ἀπέκτειναν. 40 ὅταν οὖν
vineyard and killed. When therefore

ἔλθῃ ὁ κύριος τοῦ ἀμπελῶνος, τί ποιήσει
comes the lord of the vineyard, what will he do

τοῖς γεωργοῖς ἐκείνοις; 41 λέγουσιν αὐτῷ·
-   husbandmen to those? They say to him:

κακοὺς κακῶς ἀπολέσει αὐτούς, καὶ τὸν
Bad men badly he will destroy them, and the

ἀμπελῶνα ἐκδώσεται ἄλλοις γεωργοῖς,
vineyard he will give out to other husbandmen,

give him the fruits in their seasons."

42 Jesus said to them, "Have you never read in the scriptures:

'The very stone which the builders rejected has become the head of the corner;

this was the Lord's doing,

and it is marvelous in our eyes'?

[43] Therefore I tell you, the kingdom of God will be taken away from you and given to a nation producing the fruits of it."[i]

45 When the chief priests and the Pharisees heard his parables, they perceived that he was speaking about them. [46] But when they tried to arrest him, they feared the multitudes, because they held him to be a prophet.

οἵτινες   ἀποδώσουσιν   αὐτῷ   τοὺς   καρπούς
who   will render   to him   the   fruits

ἐν τοῖς καιροῖς αὐτῶν. 42 λέγει αὐτοῖς ὁ
in   the   seasons   of them.   Says   to them   -

'Ιησοῦς·   οὐδέποτε   ἀνέγνωτε   ἐν   ταῖς
Jesus: Did ye never read   in   the

γραφαῖς·   λίθον   ὃν   ἀπεδοκίμασαν   οἱ
scriptures: A stone   which   rejected   the

οἰκοδομοῦντες,   οὗτος   ἐγενήθη   εἰς   κεφαλὴν
building [ones],   this   became   -   head

γωνίας·   παρὰ   κυρίου   ἐγένετο   αὕτη,   καὶ
of [the] corner; from [the] Lord   became   this,   and

ἔστιν   θαυμαστὴ   ἐν   ὀφθαλμοῖς   ἡμῶν;   43 διὰ
it is   marvellous   in   [the] eyes   of us?   There-

τοῦτο   λέγω   ὑμῖν   ὅτι   ἀρθήσεται   ἀφ'   ὑμῶν
fore   I tell   you[,]   -   will be taken   from   you

ἡ   βασιλεία   τοῦ   θεοῦ   καὶ   δοθήσεται
The   kingdom   -   of God   and   will be given

ἔθνει   ποιοῦντι   τοὺς   καρποὺς   αὐτῆς.
to a nation producing   the   fruits   of it.

44 [καὶ   ὁ   πεσὼν   ἐπὶ   τὸν   λίθον   τοῦτον
And the [one] falling   on   -   stone   this

συνθλασθήσεται·   ἐφ'   ὃν   δ'   ἂν   πέσῃ,
will be broken in pieces;   but on whomever   it falls,

λικμήσει   αὐτόν.] 45 Καὶ   ἀκούσαντες   οἱ
it will crush to powder him.   And   hearing   the

ἀρχιερεῖς   καὶ   οἱ   Φαρισαῖοι   τὰς   παραβολὰς
chief priests   and   the   Pharisees   the   parables

αὐτοῦ   ἔγνωσαν   ὅτι   περὶ   αὐτῶν   λέγει·
of him   they knew   that concerning   them   he tells;

46 καὶ   ζητοῦντες   αὐτὸν   κρατῆσαι   ἐφοβήθησαν
and   seeking   him   to seize   they feared

τοὺς   ὄχλους,   ἐπεὶ   εἰς   προφήτην   αὐτὸν   εἶχον.
the   crowds,   since   for   a prophet   him   they had.

CHAPTER 22

AND again Jesus spoke to them in parables, saying, [2] "The kingdom of heaven may be compared to a king who gave a marriage feast for his son, [3] and sent his servants to call those who were invited to the

---

22 Καὶ   ἀποκριθεὶς   ὁ   'Ιησοῦς   πάλιν
And   answering   -   Jesus   again

εἶπεν   ἐν   παραβολαῖς   αὐτοῖς   λέγων·
spoke   in   parables   to them   saying:

2 ὡμοιώθη   ἡ   βασιλεία   τῶν   οὐρανῶν
Was(is) likened   the   kingdom   of the   heavens

ἀνθρώπῳ   βασιλεῖ,   ὅστις   ἐποίησεν   γάμους
to a man   a king,   who   made   a wedding feast

τῷ   υἱῷ   αὐτοῦ. 3 καὶ   ἀπέστειλεν   τοὺς
for the son   of him.   And   he sent   the

δούλους   αὐτοῦ   καλέσαι   τοὺς   κεκλημένους
slaves   of him   to call   the [ones] having been invited

---

[i] Other ancient authorities add verse 44, "And he who falls on this stone will be broken to pieces; but when it falls on any one, it will crush him"

marriage feast; but they would not come. ⁴Again he sent other servants, saying, 'Tell those who are invited, Behold, I have made ready my dinner, my oxen and my fat calves are killed, and everything is ready; come to the marriage feast.' ⁵But they made light of it and went off, one to his farm, another to his business, ⁶while the rest seized his servants, treated them shamefully, and killed them. ⁷The king was angry, and he sent his troops and destroyed those murderers and burned their city. ⁸Then he said to his servants, 'The wedding is ready, but those invited were not worthy. ⁹Go therefore to the thoroughfares, and invite to the marriage feast as many as you find.' ¹⁰And those servants went out into the streets and gathered all whom they found, both bad and good; so the wedding hall was filled with guests.

11 "But when the king came in to look at the guests, he saw there a

---

εἰς τοὺς γάμους, καὶ οὐκ ἤθελον ἐλθεῖν.
to   the   feast,   and   they wished not   to come.

4 πάλιν ἀπέστειλεν ἄλλους δούλους λέγων·
Again   he sent   other   slaves   saying:

εἴπατε τοῖς κεκλημένοις· ἰδοὺ τὸ
Tell   the [ones] *having been* invited: Behold[,]   the

ἄριστόν μου ἡτοίμακα, οἱ ταῦροί μου
supper   of me   I have prepared,   the   oxen   of me

καὶ τὰ σιτιστὰ τεθυμένα, καὶ πάντα
and   the   fatted beasts having been killed, and   all things

ἕτοιμα· δεῦτε εἰς τοὺς γάμους. 5 οἱ δὲ
[are] ready;   come   to   the   feast.   But they

ἀμελήσαντες ἀπῆλθον, ὃς μὲν εἰς τὸν
not caring   went off,   one   to the(his)

ἴδιον ἀγρόν, ὃς δὲ ἐπὶ τὴν ἐμπορίαν
own   field,   another   on   the   trading

αὐτοῦ· 6 οἱ δὲ λοιποὶ κρατήσαντες
of him;   and the   rest   seizing

τοὺς δούλους αὐτοῦ ὕβρισαν καὶ ἀπέκτειναν.
the   slaves   of him   insulted   and   killed.

7 ὁ δὲ βασιλεὺς ὠργίσθη, καὶ πέμψας
So the   king   became angry,   and   sending

τὰ στρατεύματα αὐτοῦ ἀπώλεσεν τοὺς
the   armies   of him   destroyed   –

φονεῖς ἐκείνους καὶ τὴν πόλιν αὐτῶν
murderers   those   and   the   city   of them

ἐνέπρησεν. 8 τότε λέγει τοῖς δούλοις
burned.   Then   he says   to the   slaves

αὐτοῦ· ὁ μὲν γάμος ἕτοιμός ἐστιν, οἱ δὲ
of him: Indeed the   feast   ready   is,   but the [ones]

κεκλημένοι οὐκ ἦσαν ἄξιοι· 9 πορεύεσθε
having been invited   were not   worthy;   go ye

οὖν ἐπὶ τὰς διεξόδους τῶν ὁδῶν, καὶ
therefore onto   the   partings   of the   ways,   and

ὅσους ἐὰν εὕρητε καλέσατε εἰς τοὺς
as many as   ye find   call   to   the

γάμους. 10 καὶ ἐξελθόντες οἱ δοῦλοι
feast.   And   going forth   –   slaves

ἐκεῖνοι εἰς τὰς ὁδοὺς συνήγαγον πάντας
those   into   the   ways   assembled   all

οὓς εὗρον, πονηρούς τε καὶ ἀγαθούς·
whom they found,   both bad   and   good;

καὶ ἐπλήσθη ὁ νυμφὼν ἀνακειμένων.
and   was filled   the   wedding chamber of(with) reclining [ones].

11 εἰσελθὼν δὲ ὁ βασιλεὺς θεάσασθαι
But entering   the   king   to behold

τοὺς ἀνακειμένους εἶδεν ἐκεῖ
the   reclining [ones]   he saw   there

man who had no wedding garment; [12]and he said to him, 'Friend, how did you get in here without a wedding garment?' And he was speechless. [13]Then the king said to the attendants, 'Bind him hand and foot, and cast him into the outer darkness; there men will weep and gnash their teeth.' [14]For many are called, but few are chosen."

15 Then the Pharisees went and took counsel how to entangle him in his talk. [16]And they sent their disciples to him, along with the Hero'dians, saying, "Teacher, we know that you are true, and teach the way of God truthfully, and care for no man; for you do not regard the position of men. [17]Tell us, then, what you think. Is it lawful to pay taxes to Caesar, or not?" [18]But Jesus, aware of their malice, said, "Why put me to the test, you hypocrites? [19]Show me the money for the tax."

ἄνθρωπον οὐκ ἐνδεδυμένον ἔνδυμα γάμου·
a man   not having been dressed[in] a dress of wedding;

12 καὶ λέγει αὐτῷ· ἑταῖρε, πῶς
and he says to him: Comrade, how

εἰσῆλθες ὧδε μὴ ἔχων ἔνδυμα γάμου;
enteredst thou here not having a dress of wedding?

ὁ δὲ ἐφιμώθη. 13 τότε ὁ βασιλεὺς
And he was silenced.   Then   the   king

εἶπεν τοῖς διακόνοις· δήσαντες αὐτοῦ
said to the servants: Binding   of him

πόδας καὶ χεῖρας ἐκβάλετε αὐτὸν
feet and hands throw out   him

εἰς τὸ σκότος τὸ ἐξώτερον· ἐκεῖ ἔσται
into the darkness -   outer;   there will be

ὁ κλαυθμὸς καὶ ὁ βρυγμὸς τῶν
the wailing and the gnashing of the

ὀδόντων. 14 Πολλοὶ γάρ εἰσιν κλητοί,
teeth.   For many   are called,

ὀλίγοι δὲ ἐκλεκτοί.
but few   chosen.

15 Τότε πορευθέντες οἱ Φαρισαῖοι συμ-
Then going the Pharisees coun-

βούλιον ἔλαβον ὅπως αὐτὸν παγιδεύσωσιν
sel took so as him they might ensnare

ἐν λόγῳ. 16 καὶ ἀποστέλλουσιν αὐτῷ
in a word.   And they send to him

τοὺς μαθητὰς αὐτῶν μετὰ τῶν Ἡρω-
the disciples of them with the Hero-

διανῶν λέγοντας· διδάσκαλε, οἴδαμεν
dians saying: Teacher,   we know

ὅτι ἀληθὴς εἶ καὶ τὴν ὁδὸν τοῦ
that truthful thou art and the way -

θεοῦ ἐν ἀληθείᾳ διδάσκεις, καὶ οὐ
of God in truth thou teachest, and not

μέλει σοι περὶ οὐδενός, οὐ γὰρ
it concerns to thee about no one(anyone), [2]not [1]for

βλέπεις εἰς πρόσωπον ἀνθρώπων·
[2]thou lookest to face of men;

17 εἰπὸν οὖν ἡμῖν, τί σοι δοκεῖ;
tell therefore us, what to thee seems it?

ἔξεστιν δοῦναι κῆνσον Καίσαρι ἢ οὔ;
is it lawful to give tribute to Cæsar or no?

18 γνοὺς δὲ ὁ Ἰησοῦς τὴν πονηρίαν
But knowing - Jesus the wickedness

αὐτῶν εἶπεν· τί με πειράζετε, ὑποκριταί;
of them said: Why me tempt ye, hypocrites?

19 ἐπιδείξατέ μοι τὸ νόμισμα τοῦ κήνσου.
Show me the money of the tribute.

And they brought him a coin. ²⁰And Jesus said to them, "Whose likeness and inscription is this?" ²¹They said, "Caesar's." Then he said to them, "Render therefore to Caesar the things that are Caesar's, and to God the things that are God's." ²²When they heard it, they marveled; and they left him and went away.

23 The same day Sad′ducees came to him, who say that there is no resurrection; and they asked him a question, ²⁴saying, "Teacher, Moses said, 'If a man dies, having no children, his brother must marry the widow, and raise up children for his brother.' ²⁵Now there were seven brothers among us; the first married, and died, and having no children left his wife to his brother. ²⁶So too the second and third, down to the seventh. ²⁷After them all, the woman died. ²⁸In the resurrection, therefore, to which of the seven will she be wife? For they all had her."

29 But Jesus answered them, "You are wrong,

οἱ δὲ προσήνεγκαν αὐτῷ δηνάριον. **20** καὶ
And they brought to him a denarius. And
λέγει αὐτοῖς· τίνος ἡ εἰκὼν αὕτη
he says to them: Of whom image this
καὶ ἡ ἐπιγραφή; **21** λέγουσιν· Καίσαρος.
and - superscription? They say: Of Cæsar.
τότε λέγει αὐτοῖς· ἀπόδοτε οὖν τὰ
Then he says to them: Render then the things
Καίσαρος Καίσαρι καὶ τὰ τοῦ θεοῦ
of Cæsar to Cæsar and the things - of God
τῷ θεῷ. **22** καὶ ἀκούσαντες ἐθαύμασαν,
- to God. And hearing they marvelled,
καὶ ἀφέντες αὐτὸν ἀπῆλθαν.
and leaving him went away.

23 Ἐν ἐκείνῃ τῇ ἡμέρᾳ προσῆλθον
On that - day approached
αὐτῷ Σαδδουκαῖοι, λέγοντες μὴ εἶναι
to him Sadducees, saying not to be
ἀνάστασιν, καὶ ἐπηρώτησαν αὐτὸν
a resurrection, and questioned him
24 λέγοντες· διδάσκαλε, Μωϋσῆς εἶπεν·
saying: Teacher, Moses said:
ἐάν τις ἀποθάνῃ μὴ ἔχων τέκνα,
If any man dies not having children,
ἐπιγαμβρεύσει ὁ ἀδελφὸς αὐτοῦ τὴν
shall take to wife after the brother of him the
γυναῖκα αὐτοῦ καὶ ἀναστήσει σπέρμα
wife of him and shall raise up seed
τῷ ἀδελφῷ αὐτοῦ. **25** ἦσαν δὲ παρ'
to the brother of him. Now there were with
ἡμῖν ἑπτὰ ἀδελφοί· καὶ ὁ πρῶτος
us seven brothers; and the first
γήμας ἐτελεύτησεν, καὶ μὴ ἔχων
having married died, and not having
σπέρμα ἀφῆκεν τὴν γυναῖκα αὐτοῦ τῷ
seed left the wife of him to the
ἀδελφῷ αὐτοῦ· **26** ὁμοίως καὶ ὁ δεύτερος
brother of him; likewise also the second
καὶ ὁ τρίτος, ἕως τῶν ἑπτά. **27** ὕστερον
and the third, until the seven. last
δὲ πάντων ἀπέθανεν ἡ γυνή. **28** ἐν τῇ
And of all died the woman. In the
ἀναστάσει οὖν τίνος τῶν ἑπτὰ ἔσται
resurrection then of which of the seven will she be
γυνή; πάντες γὰρ ἔσχον αὐτήν. **29** ἀπο-
wife? for all had her. an-
κριθεὶς δὲ ὁ Ἰησοῦς εἶπεν αὐτοῖς·
swering And - Jesus said to them:

because you know neither the scriptures nor the power of God. [30]For in the resurrection they neither marry nor are given in marriage, but are like angels[u] in heaven. [31]And as for the resurrection of the dead, have you not read what was said to you by God, [32]'I am the God of Abraham, and the God of Isaac, and the God of Jacob'? He is not God of the dead, but of the living." [33]And when the crowd heard it, they were astonished at his teaching.

34 But when the Pharisees heard that he had silenced the Sad'-ducees, they came together, [35]And one of them, a lawyer, asked him a question, to test him. [36]"Teacher, which is the great commandment in the law?" [37]And he said to him, "You shall love the Lord your God with all your heart, and with all your soul, and with all your mind. [38]This is the great and first commandment. [39]And a second is like it, You shall love your neighbor as yourself. [40]On these two commandments depend all the law and the prophets."

[u] Other ancient authorities add of God

πλανᾶσθε μὴ εἰδότες τὰς γραφὰς μηδὲ
Ye err not knowing the scriptures nor

τὴν δύναμιν τοῦ θεοῦ. 30 ἐν γὰρ τῇ
the power — of God. For in the

ἀναστάσει οὔτε γαμοῦσιν οὔτε γαμίζονται,
resurrection neither they marry nor are given in marriage,

ἀλλ' ὡς ἄγγελοι ἐν τῷ οὐρανῷ εἰσιν.
but as angels in the heaven are.

31 περὶ δὲ τῆς ἀναστάσεως τῶν νεκρῶν
But concerning the resurrection of the dead

οὐκ ἀνέγνωτε τὸ ῥηθὲν ὑμῖν ὑπὸ
did ye not read the thing said to you by

τοῦ θεοῦ λέγοντος· 32 ἐγώ εἰμι ὁ θεὸς
— God saying: I am the God

Ἀβραὰμ καὶ ὁ θεὸς Ἰσαὰκ καὶ ὁ θεὸς
of Abraham and the God of Isaac and the God

Ἰακώβ; οὐκ ἔστιν [ὁ] θεὸς νεκρῶν
of Jacob? He is not the God of dead men

ἀλλὰ ζώντων. 33 καὶ ἀκούσαντες οἱ ὄχλοι
but of living [ones]. And hearing the crowds

ἐξεπλήσσοντο ἐπὶ τῇ διδαχῇ αὐτοῦ.
were astounded over(at) the teaching of him.

34 Οἱ δὲ Φαρισαῖοι ἀκούσαντες ὅτι
But the Pharisees hearing that

ἐφίμωσεν τοὺς Σαδδουκαίους, συνήχθησαν
he silenced the Sadducees, were assembled

ἐπὶ τὸ αὐτό, 35 καὶ ἐπηρώτησεν εἰς
together, and [5]questioned [1]one

ἐξ αὐτῶν νομικὸς πειράζων αὐτόν· 36 δι-
[2]of [3]them [4]a lawyer [6]tempting him: Teach-

δάσκαλε, ποία ἐντολὴ μεγάλη ἐν τῷ
er, what commandment [is] great in the

νόμῳ; 37 ὁ δὲ ἔφη αὐτῷ· ἀγαπήσεις
law? And he said to him: Thou shalt love

κύριον τὸν θεόν σου ἐν ὅλῃ τῇ καρδίᾳ
[the] Lord the God of thee with all the heart

σου καὶ ἐν ὅλῃ τῇ ψυχῇ σου καὶ ἐν
of thee and with all the soul of thee and with

ὅλῃ τῇ διανοίᾳ σου. 38 αὕτη ἐστὶν ἡ
all the understanding of thee. This is the

μεγάλη καὶ πρώτη ἐντολή. 39 δευτέρα
great and first commandment. [The] second

ὁμοία αὐτῇ· ἀγαπήσεις τὸν πλησίον σου
[is] like to it: Thou shalt love the neighbour of thee

ὡς σεαυτόν. 40 ἐν ταύταις ταῖς δυσὶν ἐντολαῖς
as thyself. In(on) these — two commandments

ὅλος ὁ νόμος κρέμαται καὶ οἱ προφῆται.
all the law hangs and the prophets.

41 Now while the Pharisees were gathered together, Jesus asked them a question, [42] saying, "What do you think of the Christ? Whose son is he?" They said to him, "The son of David." [43] He said to them, "How is it then that David, inspired by the Spirit,[v] calls him Lord, saying, [44] 'The Lord said to my Lord,

Sit at my right hand,
till I put thy enemies
under thy feet'?
[45] If David thus calls him Lord, how is he his son?" [46] And no one was able to answer him a word, nor from that day did any one dare to ask him any more questions.

41 Συνηγμένων δὲ τῶν Φαρισαίων
And having assembled the Pharisees[a]
= when the Pharisees were assembled
ἐπηρώτησεν αὐτοὺς ὁ Ἰησοῦς 42 λέγων· τι
questioned them – Jesus saying: What
ὑμῖν δοκεῖ περὶ τοῦ χριστοῦ; τίνος
to you seems it concerning the Christ? of whom
υἱός ἐστιν; λέγουσιν αὐτῷ· τοῦ Δαυίδ.
son is he? They say to him: – Of David.
43 λέγει αὐτοῖς· πῶς οὖν Δαυὶδ ἐν
He says to them: How then David in
πνεύματι καλεῖ αὐτὸν κύριον λέγων·
spirit calls him Lord saying:
44 εἶπεν κύριος τῷ κυρίῳ μου·
Said [the] LORD to the Lord of me:
κάθου ἐκ δεξιῶν μου ἕως ἂν θῶ τοὺς
Sit on [the] right of me until I put the
ἐχθρούς σου ὑποκάτω τῶν ποδῶν σου;
enemies of thee underneath the feet of thee?
45 εἰ οὖν Δαυὶδ καλεῖ αὐτὸν κύριον, πῶς
If then David calls him Lord, how
υἱὸς αὐτοῦ ἐστιν; 46 καὶ οὐδεὶς ἐδύνατο
son of him is he? And no one was able
ἀποκριθῆναι αὐτῷ λόγον οὐδὲ ἐτόλμησέν
to answer him a word nor dared
τις ἀπ᾽ ἐκείνης τῆς ἡμέρας ἐπερωτῆσαι
anyone from that – day to question
αὐτὸν οὐκέτι.
him no (any) more.

CHAPTER 23

THEN said Jesus to the crowds and to his disciples, [2] "The scribes and the Pharisees sit on Moses' seat; [3] so practice and observe whatever they tell you, but not what they do; for they preach, but do not practice. [4] They bind heavy burdens, hard to bear,[w] and lay them on men's shoulders; but

23 Τότε ὁ Ἰησοῦς ἐλάλησεν τοῖς ὄχλοις
Then – Jesus spoke to the crowds
καὶ τοῖς μαθηταῖς αὐτοῦ 2 λέγων· ἐπὶ
and to the disciples of him saying: On
τῆς Μωϋσέως καθέδρας ἐκάθισαν οἱ
the of Moses seat sat the
γραμματεῖς καὶ οἱ Φαρισαῖοι. 3 πάντα
scribes and the Pharisees. All things
οὖν ὅσα ἐὰν εἴπωσιν ὑμῖν ποιήσατε
therefore whatever they may tell you do ye
καὶ τηρεῖτε, κατὰ δὲ τὰ ἔργα αὐτῶν
and keep, but according to the works of them
μὴ ποιεῖτε· λέγουσιν γὰρ καὶ οὐ ποιοῦσιν.
do ye not; for they say and do not.
4 δεσμεύουσιν δὲ φορτία βαρέα καὶ
And they bind burdens heavy and
ἐπιτιθέασιν ἐπὶ τοὺς ὤμους τῶν ἀνθρώπων,
put on on the shoulders – of men,

---

[v] Or David in the Spirit

[w] Other ancient authorities omit hard to bear

they themselves will not move them with their finger. ⁵They do all their deeds to be seen by men; for they make their phylacteries broad and their fringes long, ⁶and they love the place of honor at feasts and the best seats in the synagogues, ⁷and salutations in the market places, and being called rabbi by men. ⁸But you are not to be called rabbi, for you have one teacher, and you are all brethren. ⁹And call no man your father on earth, for you have one Father, who is in heaven. ¹⁰Neither be called masters, for you have one master, the Christ. ¹¹He who is greatest among you shall be your servant; ¹²whoever exalts himself will be humbled, and whoever humbles himself will be exalted.

13 "But woe to you, scribes and Pharisees, hypocrites! because you shut the kingdom of heaven against men; for you neither enter yourselves, nor allow those

αὐτοὶ δὲ τῷ δακτύλῳ αὐτῶν οὐ
but they   with the   finger   of them   not

θέλουσιν κινῆσαι αὐτά. 5 πάντα δὲ
are willing to move   them.   But all

τὰ ἔργα αὐτῶν ποιοῦσιν πρὸς τὸ θεαθῆναι
the works of them they do for -   to be seen

τοῖς ἀνθρώποις· πλατύνουσιν γὰρ τὰ
  by men;   for they broaden   the

φυλακτήρια αὐτῶν καὶ μεγαλύνουσιν τὰ
phylacteries of them and   enlarge   the

κράσπεδα, 6 φιλοῦσιν δὲ τὴν πρωτο-
fringes,   and they like   the   chief

κλισίαν ἐν τοῖς δείπνοις καὶ τὰς πρωτο-
place   in the   suppers   and the   chief

καθεδρίας ἐν ταῖς συναγωγαῖς 7 καὶ τοὺς
seats   in the   synagogues .   and the

ἀσπασμοὺς ἐν ταῖς ἀγοραῖς καὶ
greetings in the   marketplaces and

καλεῖσθαι ὑπὸ τῶν ἀνθρώπων ῥαββί.
to be called by   -   men   rabbi.

8 ὑμεῖς δὲ μὴ κληθῆτε ῥαββί· εἷς γάρ
   But ye   be not called rabbi; for one

ἐστιν ὑμῶν ὁ διδάσκαλος, πάντες δὲ ὑμεῖς
is   of you the teacher,   and all   ye

ἀδελφοί ἐστε. 9 καὶ πατέρα μὴ καλέσητε
brothers are.   And father   call ye not

ὑμῶν ἐπὶ τῆς γῆς· εἷς γάρ ἐστιν
of you on the earth;   for one   is

ὑμῶν ὁ πατὴρ ὁ οὐράνιος. 10 μηδὲ
of you the Father - heavenly.   Neither

κληθῆτε καθηγηταί, ὅτι καθηγητὴς
be ye called   leaders,   because   leader

ὑμῶν ἐστιν εἷς ὁ Χριστός. 11 ὁ δὲ
of you is one the Christ.   And the

μείζων ὑμῶν ἔσται ὑμῶν διάκονος.
greater of you shall be of you   servant.

12 Ὅστις δὲ ὑψώσει ἑαυτὸν ταπεινωθήσεται,
  And [he] who will exalt himself shall be humbled,

καὶ ὅστις ταπεινώσει ἑαυτὸν ὑψωθήσεται.
and [he] who will humble   himself   shall be exalted.

13 Οὐαὶ δὲ ὑμῖν, γραμματεῖς καὶ Φαρισαῖοι
  But woe to you,   scribes   and Pharisees

ὑποκριταί, ὅτι κλείετε τὴν βασιλείαν
hypocrites, because ye shut the   kingdom

τῶν οὐρανῶν ἔμπροσθεν τῶν ἀνθρώπων
of the heavens   before   -   men;

ὑμεῖς γὰρ οὐκ εἰσέρχεσθε, οὐδὲ τοὺς
for ye   do not enter,   nor the [ones]

who would enter to go in.ˣ ¹⁵Woe to you, scribes and Pharisees, hypocrites! for you traverse sea and land to make a single proselyte, and when he becomes a proselyte, you make him twice as much a child of hell as yourselves.

16 "Woe to you, blind guides, who say, 'If any one swears by the temple, it is nothing; but if any one swears by the gold of the temple, he is bound by his oath.' ¹⁷You blind fools! For which is greater, the gold or the temple that has made the gold sacred? ¹⁸And you say, 'If any one swears by the altar, it is nothing; but if any one swears by the gift that is on the altar, he is bound by his oath.' ¹⁹You blind men! For which is greater, the gift or the altar that makes the gift sacred? ²⁰So he who swears by the altar, swears by it and by everything on it; ²¹and he who swears by the temple, swears by it and by him who dwells in it; ²²and he who swears by heaven, swears by the throne of God and by him who sits upon it.

23 "Woe to you, scribes and Pharisees, hypocrites! for you tithe

ˣ Other authorities add here (or after verse 12) verse 14, *Woe to you, scribes and Pharisees, hypocrites! for you devour widows' houses and for a pretense you make long prayers; therefore you will receive the greater condemnation*

εἰσερχομένους ἀφίετε εἰσελθεῖν.‡ 15 Οὐαὶ
entering do ye allow to enter. Woe

ὑμῖν, γραμματεῖς καὶ Φαρισαῖοι ὑποκριταί,
to you, scribes and Pharisees hypocrites,

ὅτι περιάγετε τὴν θάλασσαν καὶ τὴν
because ye go about the sea and the

ξηρὰν ποιῆσαι ἕνα προσήλυτον, καὶ ὅταν
dry [land] to make one proselyte, and when

γένηται, ποιεῖτε αὐτὸν υἱὸν γεέννης διπλό-
he becomes, ye make him a son of gehenna twofold

τερον ὑμῶν. 16 Οὐαὶ ὑμῖν, ὁδηγοὶ τυφλοὶ
more [than] you. Woe to you, leaders blind

οἱ λέγοντες· ὃς ἂν ὀμόσῃ ἐν τῷ ναῷ,
the [ones] saying: Whoever swears by the shrine,

οὐδέν ἐστιν· ὃς δ' ἂν ὀμόσῃ ἐν τῷ χρυσῷ
nothing it is; but whoever swears by the gold

τοῦ ναοῦ, ὀφείλει. 17 μωροὶ καὶ τυφλοί,
of the shrine, he owes. Fools and blind,

τίς γὰρ μείζων ἐστιν, ὁ χρυσὸς ἢ ὁ ναὸς
for which greater is, the gold or the shrine

ὁ ἁγιάσας τὸν χρυσόν; 18 καὶ· ὃς ἂν
— sanctifying the gold? And: whoever

ὀμόσῃ ἐν τῷ θυσιαστηρίῳ, οὐδέν ἐστιν·
swears by the altar, nothing it is;

ὃς δ' ἂν ὀμόσῃ ἐν τῷ δώρῳ τῷ ἐπάνω
but whoever swears by the gift — upon

αὐτοῦ, ὀφείλει. 19 τυφλοί, τί γὰρ μεῖζον,
it, he owes. Blind, for which [is] greater,

τὸ δῶρον ἢ τὸ θυσιαστήριον τὸ
the gift or the altar —

ἁγιάζον τὸ δῶρον; 20 ὁ οὖν ὀμόσας
sanctifying the gift? Therefore the [one] swearing

ἐν τῷ θυσιαστηρίῳ ὀμνύει ἐν αὐτῷ καὶ
by the altar swears by it and

ἐν πᾶσι τοῖς ἐπάνω αὐτοῦ· 21 καὶ ὁ
by all the things upon it; and the [one]

ὀμόσας ἐν τῷ ναῷ ὀμνύει ἐν αὐτῷ
swearing by the shrine swears by it

καὶ ἐν τῷ κατοικοῦντι αὐτόν· 22 καὶ
and by the [one] inhabiting it; and

ὁ ὀμόσας ἐν τῷ οὐρανῷ ὀμνύει ἐν τῷ
the [one] swearing by *the* heaven swears by the

θρόνῳ τοῦ θεοῦ καὶ ἐν τῷ καθημένῳ
throne of God and by the [one] sitting

ἐπάνω αὐτοῦ. 23 Οὐαὶ ὑμῖν, γραμματεῖς
upon it. Woe to you, scribes

καὶ Φαρισαῖοι ὑποκριταί, ὅτι ἀποδεκατοῦτε
and Pharisees hypocrites, because ye tithe

‡ Ver. 14 omitted by Nestle; cf. R.V. marg., etc.

MATTHEW 23   103

mint and dill and cum-
min, and have neglected
the weightier matters of
the law, justice and mercy
and faith; these you
ought to have done,
without neglecting the
others. ²⁴You blind
guides, straining out a
gnat and swallowing a
camel!

25 "Woe to you,
scribes and Pharisees,
hypocrites! for you
cleanse the outside of the
cup and of the plate, but
inside they are full of
extortion and rapacity.
²⁶You blind Pharisee!
first cleanse the inside of
the cup and of the plate,
that the outside also may
be clean.

27 "Woe to you,
scribes and Pharisees,
hypocrites! for you are
like whitewashed tombs,
which outwardly appear
beautiful, but within they
are full of dead men's
bones and all unclean-
ness. ²⁸So you also
outwardly appear right-
eous to men, but within
you are full of hypocrisy
and iniquity.

29 "Woe to you,
scribes and Pharisees,
hypocrites! for you build
the tombs of the
prophets and adorn the
monuments of the
righteous, ³⁰saying, 'If

τὸ ἡδύοσμον καὶ τὸ ἄνηθον καὶ τὸ
the mint and the dill and the
κύμινον, καὶ ἀφήκατε τὰ βαρύτερα
cummin, and ye [have] left the heavier things
τοῦ νόμου, τὴν κρίσιν καὶ τὸ ἔλεος
of the law, – judgment and – mercy
καὶ τὴν πίστιν· ταῦτα δὲ ἔδει ποιῆσαι
and – faith; but these things it behoved to do
κἀκεῖνα μὴ ἀφεῖναι. 24 ὁδηγοὶ τυφλοί,
and those not to leave. Leaders blind,
οἱ διϋλίζοντες τὸν κώνωπα, τὴν δὲ
the [ones] straining the gnat, but ²the
κάμηλον καταπίνοντες. 25 Οὐαὶ ὑμῖν,
²camel ¹swallowing. Woe to you,
γραμματεῖς καὶ Φαρισαῖοι ὑποκριταί, ὅτι
scribes and Pharisees hypocrites, because
καθαρίζετε τὸ ἔξωθεν τοῦ ποτηρίου καὶ
ye cleanse the outside of the cup and
τῆς παροψίδος, ἔσωθεν δὲ γέμουσιν ἐξ
the dish, but within they are full of
ἁρπαγῆς καὶ ἀκρασίας. 26 Φαρισαῖε τυφλέ,
robbery and intemperance. Pharisee blind,
καθάρισον πρῶτον τὸ ἐντὸς τοῦ ποτηρίου
cleanse thou first the inside of the cup
ἵνα γένηται καὶ τὸ ἐκτὸς αὐτοῦ καθαρόν.
that may be also the outside of it clean.
27 Οὐαὶ ὑμῖν, γραμματεῖς καὶ Φαρισαῖοι
Woe to you, scribes and Pharisees
ὑποκριταί, ὅτι παρομοιάζετε τάφοις κεκονια-
hypocrites, because ye resemble graves having been
μένοις, οἵτινες ἔξωθεν μὲν φαίνονται
whitewashed, who (which) outwardly indeed appear
ὡραῖοι, ἔσωθεν δὲ γέμουσιν ὀστέων
beautiful, but within they are full of bones
νεκρῶν καὶ πάσης ἀκαθαρσίας. 28 οὕτως
of dead men and of all uncleanness. Thus
καὶ ὑμεῖς ἔξωθεν μὲν φαίνεσθε τοῖς
also ye outwardly indeed appear –
ἀνθρώποις δίκαιοι, ἔσωθεν δέ ἐστε μεστοὶ
to men righteous, but within ye are full
ὑποκρίσεως καὶ ἀνομίας. 29 Οὐαὶ ὑμῖν,
of hypocrisy and of lawlessness. Woe to you
γραμματεῖς καὶ Φαρισαῖοι ὑποκριταί,
scribes and Pharisees hypocrites,
ὅτι οἰκοδομεῖτε τοὺς τάφους τῶν προφητῶν
because ye build the graves of the prophets
καὶ κοσμεῖτε τὰ μνημεῖα τῶν δικαίων,
and adorn the monuments of the righteous,

we had lived in the days of our fathers, we would not have taken part with them in shedding the blood of the prophets.' [31] Thus you witness against yourselves, that you are sons of those who murdered the prophets. [32] Fill up, then, the measure of your fathers. [33] You serpents, you brood of vipers, how are you to escape being sentenced to hell? [34] Therefore I send you prophets and wise men and scribes, some of whom you will kill and crucify, and some you will scourge in your synagogues and persecute from town to town, [35] that upon you may come all the righteous blood shed on earth, from the blood of innocent Abel to the blood of Zechari′ah the son of Barachi′ah, whom you murdered between the sanctuary and the altar. [36] Truly, I say to you, all this will come upon this generation.

37 "O Jerusalem, Jerusalem, killing the prophets and stoning those who are sent to you! How often would I have gathered your children together as a

30 καὶ λέγετε· εἰ ἤμεθα ἐν ταῖς ἡμέραις
and say: If we were in the days

τῶν πατέρων ἡμῶν, οὐκ ἂν ἤμεθα
of the fathers of us, we would not have been

αὐτῶν κοινωνοὶ ἐν τῷ αἵματι τῶν προ-
of them partakers in the blood of the pro-

φητῶν. 31 ὥστε μαρτυρεῖτε ἑαυτοῖς ὅτι
phets. So ye witness to [your]selves that

υἱοί ἐστε τῶν φονευσάντων τοὺς προφήτας.
sons ye are of the [ones] having killed the prophets.

32 καὶ ὑμεῖς πληρώσατε τὸ μέτρον τῶν
And ¹ye ¹fulfil the measure of the

πατέρων ὑμῶν. 33 ὄφεις, γεννήματα ἐχιδνῶν,
fathers of you. Serpents, offspring of vipers,

πῶς φύγητε ἀπὸ τῆς κρίσεως τῆς γεέννης;
how escape ye from the judgment - of gehenna?

34 διὰ τοῦτο ἰδοὺ ἐγὼ ἀποστέλλω πρὸς
Therefore behold I send to

ὑμᾶς προφήτας καὶ σοφοὺς καὶ γραμ-
you prophets and wise men and scribes;

ματεῖς· ἐξ αὐτῶν ἀποκτενεῖτε καὶ
of them ye will kill and

σταυρώσετε, καὶ ἐξ αὐτῶν μαστιγώσετε
will crucify, and of them ye will scourge

ἐν ταῖς συναγωγαῖς ὑμῶν καὶ διώξετε
in the synagogues of you and will persecute

ἀπὸ πόλεως εἰς πόλιν· 35 ὅπως ἔλθῃ
from city to city; so comes

ἐφ' ὑμᾶς πᾶν αἷμα δίκαιον ἐκχυννόμενον
on you all blood righteous being shed

ἐπὶ τῆς γῆς ἀπὸ τοῦ αἵματος Ἅβελ τοῦ
on the earth from the blood of Abel the

δικαίου ἕως τοῦ αἵματος Ζαχαρίου υἱοῦ
righteous until the blood of Zacharias son

Βαραχίου, ὃν ἐφονεύσατε μεταξὺ τοῦ ναοῦ
Barachias, whom ye murdered between the shrine

καὶ τοῦ θυσιαστηρίου. 36 ἀμὴν λέγω
and the altar. Truly I tell

ὑμῖν, ἥξει ταῦτα πάντα ἐπὶ τὴν
you, will come all these things on -

γενεὰν ταύτην. 37 Ἰερουσαλὴμ Ἰερουσαλήμ,
generation this. Jerusalem Jerusalem,

ἡ ἀποκτείνουσα τοὺς προφήτας καὶ
the [one] killing the prophets and

λιθοβολοῦσα τοὺς ἀπεσταλμένους πρὸς αὐτήν,
stoning the [ones] sent to her,

ποσάκις ἠθέλησα ἐπισυναγαγεῖν τὰ τέκνα
how often I wished to gather the children

hen gathers her brood under her wings, and you would not! [38]Behold, your house is forsaken and desolate.[ʸ] [39]For I tell you, you will not see me again, until you say, 'Blessed is he who comes in the name of the Lord.'"

σου,   ὃν   τρόπον   ὄρνις   ἐπισυνάγει   τὰ
of thee,   as   a bird   gathers   the
νοσσία [αὐτῆς] ὑπὸ   τὰς   πτέρυγας,   καὶ
young   of her   under   the(her)   wings,   and
οὐκ   ἠθελήσατε.   38 ἰδοὺ   ἀφίεται   ὑμῖν   ὁ
ye wished not.   Behold   is left   to you   the
οἶκος   ὑμῶν.   39 λέγω   γὰρ   ὑμῖν,   οὐ   μή
house   of you.   For I tell   you,   by no means
με   ἴδητε   ἀπ'   ἄρτι   ἕως   ἂν   εἴπητε·
me   ye see   from   now   until   ye say:
εὐλογημένος   ὁ   ἐρχόμενος   ἐν   ὀνόματι
Blessed   the [one]   coming   in   [the] name
κυρίου.
of [the] Lord.

CHAPTER 24

JESUS left the temple and was going away, when his disciples came to point out to him the buildings of the temple. [2]But he answered them, "You see all these, do you not? Truly, I say to you, there will not be left here one stone upon another, that will not be thrown down."

[3] As he sat on the Mount of Olives, the disciples came to him privately, saying, "Tell us, when will this be, and what will be the sign of your coming and of the close of the age?" [4]And Jesus answered them, "Take heed that no one leads you astray. [5]For many will come in my name, saying, 'I am the Christ,' and they will lead many astray. [6]And

24 Καὶ   ἐξελθὼν   ὁ   Ἰησοῦς   ἀπὸ   τοῦ
        And   going forth   -   Jesus   from   the
ἱεροῦ   ἐπορεύετο,   καὶ   προσῆλθον   οἱ   μαθηταὶ
temple   went,   and   ⁴approached   ¹the ²disciples
αὐτοῦ   ἐπιδεῖξαι   αὐτῷ   τὰς   οἰκοδομὰς
³of him   to show   him   the   buildings
τοῦ   ἱεροῦ.   2 ὁ   δὲ   ἀποκριθεὶς   εἶπεν
of the temple.   And he   answering   said
αὐτοῖς·   οὐ   βλέπετε   ταῦτα   πάντα;   ἀμὴν
to them: See ye not   all these things?   Truly
λέγω   ὑμῖν,   οὐ   μὴ   ἀφεθῇ   ὧδε   λίθος   ἐπὶ
I tell   you,   by no means will be left here   stone   on
λίθον   ὃς   οὐ   καταλυθήσεται.   3 Καθημένου
stone   which   shall not be overthrown.   sitting
δὲ   αὐτοῦ   ἐπὶ   τοῦ   ὄρους   τῶν   ἐλαιῶν
and   him[ᵃ]   on   the   mount   of the   olives
= And as he sat
προσῆλθον   αὐτῷ   οἱ   μαθηταὶ   κατ'   ἰδίαν
approached   to him the   disciples   privately
λέγοντες·   εἰπὲ   ἡμῖν,   πότε   ταῦτα   ἔσται,
saying: Tell   us,   when   these things   will be,
καὶ   τί   τὸ   σημεῖον   τῆς   σῆς   παρουσίας
and   what   the   sign   -   of thy   presence
καὶ   συντελείας   τοῦ   αἰῶνος;   4 καὶ   ἀπο-
and   of [the] completion of the   age?   And answer-
κριθεὶς   ὁ   Ἰησοῦς   εἶπεν   αὐτοῖς·   βλέπετε
ing   -   Jesus   said   to them: See ye
μή   τις   ὑμᾶς   πλανήσῃ.   5 πολλοὶ   γὰρ
not(lest) anyone ²you   ¹cause ³to err.   For many
ἐλεύσονται   ἐπὶ   τῷ   ὀνόματί   μου   λέγοντες·
will come   on(in)   the   name   of me   saying:
ἐγώ   εἰμι   ὁ   χριστός,   καὶ   πολλοὺς   πλανή-
I   am   the   Christ,   and   ²many   ¹will cause

[ʸ] Other ancient authorities omit and desolate

you will hear of wars and rumors of wars; see that you are not alarmed; for this must take place, but the end is not yet. [7] For nation will rise against nation, and kingdom against kingdom, and there will be famines and earthquakes in various places: [8] all this is but the beginning of the sufferings.

9 "Then they will deliver you up to tribulation, and put you to death; and you will be hated by all nations for my name's sake. [10] And then many will fall away,[z] and betray one another, and hate one another. [11] And many false prophets will arise and lead many astray. [12] And because wickedness is multiplied, most men's love will grow cold. [13] But he who endures to the end will be saved. [14] And this gospel of the kingdom will be preached throughout the whole world, as a testimony to all nations; and then the end will come.

15 "So when you see the desolating sacrilege spoken of by the prophet

σουσιν. 6 μελλήσετε δὲ ἀκούειν πολέ-
to err. But ye will be about to hear [of]

μους καὶ ἀκοὰς πολέμων· ὁρᾶτε μὴ
wars and rumours of wars; see not

θροεῖθε· δεῖ γὰρ γενέσθαι, ἀλλ'
ye are disturbed; for it behoves to happen, but

οὔπω ἐστὶν τὸ τέλος. 7 ἐγερθήσεται γὰρ
not yet is the end. For will be raised

ἔθνος ἐπὶ ἔθνος καὶ βασιλεία ἐπὶ βασιλείαν,
nation against nation and kingdom against kingdom,

καὶ ἔσονται λιμοὶ καὶ σεισμοὶ
and there will be famines and earthquakes

κατὰ τόπους· 8 πάντα δὲ ταῦτα ἀρχὴ
throughout places; but all these things [are] beginning

ὠδίνων. 9 τότε παραδώσουσιν ὑμᾶς
of birth-pangs. Then they will deliver you

εἰς θλῖψιν καὶ ἀποκτενοῦσιν ὑμᾶς,
to affliction and will kill you,

καὶ ἔσεσθε μισούμενοι ὑπὸ πάντων
and ye will be being hated by all

τῶν ἐθνῶν διὰ τὸ ὄνομά μου.
the nations because of the name of me.

10 καὶ τότε σκανδαλισθήσονται πολλοὶ καὶ
And then will be offended many and

ἀλλήλους παραδώσουσιν καὶ μισήσουσιν
one another will deliver and they will hate

ἀλλήλους· 11 καὶ πολλοὶ ψευδοπροφῆται
one another; and many false prophets

ἐγερθήσονται καὶ πλανήσουσιν πολλούς·
will be raised and will cause to err many;

12 καὶ διὰ τὸ πληθυνθῆναι τὴν
and because of – to be increased the

ἀνομίαν ψυγήσεται ἡ ἀγάπη τῶν
lawlessness will grow cold the love of the

πολλῶν. 13 ὁ δὲ ὑπομείνας εἰς τέλος,
many. But the [one] enduring to [the] end,

οὗτος σωθήσεται. 14 καὶ κηρυχθήσεται
this will be saved. And will be proclaimed

τοῦτο τὸ εὐαγγέλιον τῆς βασιλείας
this – gospel of the kingdom

ἐν ὅλῃ τῇ οἰκουμένῃ εἰς μαρτύριον
in all the inhabited earth for a testimony

πᾶσιν τοῖς ἔθνεσιν, καὶ τότε ἥξει τὸ
to all the nations, and then will come the

τέλος. 15 Ὅταν οὖν ἴδητε τὸ
end. When therefore ye see the

βδέλυγμα τῆς ἐρημώσεως τὸ ῥηθὲν διὰ
abomination – of desolation – spoken through

[z] Or stumble

Daniel, standing in the holy place (let the reader understand), ¹⁶then let those who are in Judea flee to the mountains; ¹⁷let him who is on the housetop not go down to take what is in his house; ¹⁸and let him who is in the field not turn back to take his mantle. ¹⁹And alas for those who are with child and for those who give suck in those days! ²⁰Pray that your flight may not be in winter or on a sabbath. ²¹For then there will be great tribulation, such as has not been from the beginning of the world until now, no, and never will be. ²²And if those days had not been shortened, no human being would be saved; but for the sake of the elect those days will be shortened. ²³Then if any one says to you, 'Lo, here is the Christ!' or 'There he is!' do not believe it. ²⁴For false Christs and false prophets will arise and show great signs and wonders, so as to lead astray, if possible, even the elect. ²⁵Lo, I have told you beforehand. ²⁶So, if they say to you,

Δανιὴλ   τοῦ   προφήτου   ἑστὸς   ἐν   τόπῳ
Daniel   the   prophet   stand   in   place

ἁγίῳ,   ὁ   ἀναγινώσκων   νοείτω,
holy,   the [one]   reading   let him understand,

16 τότε   οἱ   ἐν   τῇ   Ἰουδαίᾳ   φευγέτωσαν
then   the [ones] in - Judæa   let them flee

εἰς   τὰ   ὄρη,   17 ὁ   ἐπὶ   τοῦ   δώματος   μὴ
to   the mountains,   the [one] on   the   housetop   let him

καταβάτω   ἆραι   τὰ   ἐκ   τῆς   οἰκίας   αὐτοῦ,
not come down   to take   the things   out of   the   house   of him,

18 καὶ   ὁ   ἐν   τῷ   ἀγρῷ   μὴ   ἐπιστρεψάτω
and the [one]   in   the   field   let him not turn back

ὀπίσω   ἆραι   τὸ   ἱμάτιον   αὐτοῦ.   19 οὐαὶ
behind   to take   the   garment   of him.   woe

δὲ   ταῖς   ἐν   γαστρὶ   ἐχούσαις   καὶ   ταῖς
And to the women in   womb   having   and to the [ones]
= the pregnant women

θηλαζούσαις   ἐν   ἐκείναις   ταῖς   ἡμέραις.
giving suck   in   those - days.

20 προσεύχεσθε   δὲ   ἵνα   μὴ   γένηται   ἡ
And pray ye   lest   happen   the

φυγὴ   ὑμῶν   χειμῶνος   μηδὲ   σαββάτῳ·
flight   of you   of(in) winter   nor   on a sabbath;

21 ἔσται   γὰρ   τότε   θλῖψις   μεγάλη,   οἵα   οὐ
for will be   then   affliction   great,   such as not

γέγονεν   ἀπ'   ἀρχῆς   κόσμου   ἕως
has happened   from [the] beginning   of [the] world   until

τοῦ   νῦν   οὐδ'   οὐ   μὴ   γένηται.   22 καὶ
-   now   neither   by no means may happen.   And

εἰ   μὴ   ἐκολοβώθησαν   αἱ   ἡμέραι   ἐκεῖναι,
except   were cut short - days   those,

οὐκ   ἂν   ἐσώθη   πᾶσα   σάρξ·   διὰ   δὲ   τοὺς
not - was saved   all   flesh;   but on account of   the
= no flesh would be saved;

ἐκλεκτοὺς   κολοβωθήσονται   αἱ   ἡμέραι   ἐκεῖναι.
chosen   will be cut short - days   those.

23 τότε   ἐάν   τις   ὑμῖν   εἴπῃ·   ἰδοὺ   ὧδε
Then   if   anyone to you   says: Behold   here

ὁ   χριστός,   ἤ·   ὧδε,   μὴ   πιστεύσητε·
the   Christ,   or: Here,   do not believe;

24 ἐγερθήσονται   γὰρ   ψευδόχριστοι   καὶ
for will be raised   false Christs   and

ψευδοπροφῆται,   καὶ   δώσουσιν   σημεῖα   μεγάλα
false prophets,   and   they will give   signs   great

καὶ   τέρατα,   ὥστε   πλανῆσαι,   εἰ   δυνατόν,
and   marvels,   so as   to cause to err,   if   possible,

καὶ   τοὺς   ἐκλεκτούς.   25 ἰδοὺ   προείρηκα
even   the   chosen.   Behold   I have before told

ὑμῖν.   26 ἐὰν   οὖν   εἴπωσιν   ὑμῖν·   ἰδοὺ
you.   If therefore   they say   to you: Behold

'Lo, he is in the wilderness,' do not go out; if they say, 'Lo, he is in the inner rooms,' do not believe it. ²⁷ For as the lightning comes from the east and shines as far as the west, so will be the coming of the Son of man. ²⁸ Wherever the body is, there the eagles[a] will be gathered together.

29 "Immediately after the tribulation of those days the sun will be darkened, and the moon will not give its light, and the stars will fall from heaven, and the powers of the heavens will be shaken; ³⁰ then will appear the sign of the Son of man in heaven, and then all the tribes of the earth will mourn, and they will see the Son of man coming on the clouds of heaven with power and great glory; ³¹ and he will send out his angels with a loud trumpet call, and they will gather his elect from the four winds, from one end of heaven to the other.

32 "From the fig tree learn its lesson: as soon

ἐν τῇ ἐρήμῳ ἐστίν, μὴ ἐξέλθητε· ἰδοὺ
in the desert he is, go not ye forth; Behold

ἐν τοῖς ταμιείοις, μὴ πιστεύσητε·
in the private rooms, do not ye believe;

27 ὥσπερ γὰρ ἡ ἀστραπὴ ἐξέρχεται ἀπὸ
for as the lightning comes forth from

ἀνατολῶν καὶ φαίνεται ἕως δυσμῶν,
[the] east and shines unto [the] west,

οὕτως ἔσται ἡ παρουσία τοῦ υἱοῦ
so will be the presence of the Son

τοῦ ἀνθρώπου· 28 ὅπου ἐὰν ᾖ τὸ
- of man; wherever may be the

πτῶμα, ἐκεῖ συναχθήσονται οἱ ἀετοί.
carcase, there will be assembled the eagles.

29 Εὐθέως δὲ μετὰ τὴν θλῖψιν τῶν
And immediately after the affliction -

ἡμερῶν ἐκείνων ὁ ἥλιος σκοτισθήσεται,
days of those the sun will be darkened,

καὶ ἡ σελήνη οὐ δώσει τὸ φέγγος
and the moon will not give the light

αὐτῆς, καὶ οἱ ἀστέρες πεσοῦνται ἀπὸ τοῦ
of her, and the stars will fall from -

οὐρανοῦ, καὶ αἱ δυνάμεις τῶν οὐρανῶν
heaven, and the powers of the heavens

σαλευθήσονται. 30 καὶ τότε φανήσεται
will be shaken. And then will appear

τὸ σημεῖον τοῦ υἱοῦ τοῦ ἀνθρώπου ἐν
the sign of the Son - of man in

οὐρανῷ, καὶ τότε κόψονται πᾶσαι αἱ
heaven, and then will bewail all the

φυλαὶ τῆς γῆς καὶ ὄψονται τὸν υἱὸν
tribes of the land and they will see the Son

τοῦ ἀνθρώπου ἐρχόμενον ἐπὶ τῶν
- of man coming on the

νεφελῶν τοῦ οὐρανοῦ μετὰ δυνάμεως καὶ
clouds - of heaven with power and

δόξης πολλῆς· 31 καὶ ἀποστελεῖ τοὺς
glory much; and he will send the

ἀγγέλους αὐτοῦ μετὰ σάλπιγγος μεγάλης,
angels of him with trumpet a great,

καὶ ἐπισυνάξουσιν τοὺς ἐκλεκτοὺς αὐτοῦ
and they will assemble the chosen of him

ἐκ τῶν τεσσάρων ἀνέμων ἀπ' ἄκρων
out of the four winds from [the] extremities

οὐρανῶν ἕως [τῶν] ἄκρων αὐτῶν. 32 Ἀπὸ
of [the] heavens unto the extremities of them. from

δὲ τῆς συκῆς μάθετε τὴν παραβολήν·
Now the fig-tree learn ye the parable:

---

[a] Or vultures

as its branch becomes tender and puts forth its leaves, you know that summer is near. ³³ So also, when you see all these things, you know that he is near, at the very gates. ³⁴ Truly, I say to you, this generation will not pass away till all these things take place. ³⁵ Heaven and earth will pass away, but my words will not pass away.

36 "But of that day and hour no one knows, not even the angels of heaven, nor the Son,ᵇ but the Father only. ³⁷ As were the days of Noah, so will be the coming of the Son of man. ³⁸ For as in those days before the flood they were eating and drinking, marrying and giving in marriage, until the day when Noah entered the ark, ³⁹ and they did not know until the flood came and swept them all away, so will be the coming of the Son of man. ⁴⁰ Then two men will be in the field; one is taken and one is left. ⁴¹ Two women will be grinding at the mill; one

ᵇ Other ancient authorities omit *nor the Son*

ὅταν ἤδη ὁ κλάδος αὐτῆς γένηται ἁπαλὸς
When now the branch of it becomes tender
καὶ τὰ φύλλα ἐκφύῃ, γινώσκετε ὅτι
and the leaves it puts forth, ye know that
ἐγγὺς τὸ θέρος· 33 οὕτως καὶ ὑμεῖς
near [is] the summer; so also ye
ὅταν ἴδητε πάντα ταῦτα, γινώσκετε ὅτι
when ye see all these things, know that
ἐγγύς ἐστιν ἐπὶ θύραις. 34 ἀμὴν λέγω
near it is on(at) [the] doors. Truly I tell
ὑμῖν ὅτι οὐ μὴ παρέλθῃ ἡ γενεὰ
you that by no means passes away – generation
αὕτη ἕως ἂν πάντα ταῦτα γένηται.
this until all these things happens.
35 ὁ οὐρανὸς καὶ ἡ γῆ παρελεύσεται, οἱ
The heaven and the earth will pass away, ²the
δὲ λόγοι μου οὐ μὴ παρέλθωσιν. 36 Περὶ
¹but words of me by no means may pass away. concerning
δὲ τῆς ἡμέρας ἐκείνης καὶ ὥρας οὐδεὶς
But – day that and hour no one
οἶδεν, οὐδὲ οἱ ἄγγελοι τῶν οὐρανῶν
knows, neither the angels of the heavens
οὐδὲ ὁ υἱός, εἰ μὴ ὁ πατὴρ μόνος.
nor the Son, except the Father only.
37 ὥσπερ γὰρ αἱ ἡμέραι τοῦ Νῶε, οὕτως
For as the days – of Noah, so
ἔσται ἡ παρουσία τοῦ υἱοῦ τοῦ ἀνθρώπου.
will be the presence of the Son – of man.
38 ὡς γὰρ ἦσαν ἐν ταῖς ἡμέραις
For as they were in – days
[ἐκείναις] ταῖς πρὸ τοῦ κατακλυσμοῦ
those the [ones] before the flood
τρώγοντες καὶ πίνοντες, γαμοῦντες καὶ
eating and drinking, marrying and
γαμίζοντες, ἄχρι ἧς ἡμέρας εἰσῆλθεν
being given in marriage, until which day entered
Νῶε εἰς τὴν κιβωτόν, 39 καὶ οὐκ ἔγνωσαν
Noah into the ark, and knew not
ἕως ἦλθεν ὁ κατακλυσμὸς καὶ ἦρεν
until came the flood and took
ἅπαντας, οὕτως ἔσται καὶ ἡ παρουσία
all, so will be also the presence
τοῦ υἱοῦ τοῦ ἀνθρώπου. 40 τότε ἔσονται
of the Son – of man. Then will be
δύο ἐν τῷ ἀγρῷ, εἷς παραλαμβάνεται
two men in the field, one is taken
καὶ εἷς ἀφίεται· 41 δύο ἀλήθουσαι
and one is left; two women grinding

is taken and one is left.
⁴²Watch therefore, for you do not know on what day your Lord is coming. ⁴³But know this, that if the householder had known in what part of the night the thief was coming, he would have watched and would not have let his house be broken into. ⁴⁴Therefore you also must be ready; for the Son of man is coming at an hour you do not expect.

45 "Who then is the faithful and wise servant, whom his master has set over his household, to give them their food at the proper time? ⁴⁶Blessed is that servant whom his master when he comes will find so doing. ⁴⁷Truly, I say to you, he will set him over all his possessions. ⁴⁸But if that wicked servant says to himself, 'My master is delayed,' ⁴⁹and begins to beat his fellow servants, and eats and drinks with the drunken, ⁵⁰the master of that servant will come on a day when he does not expect him and at an hour he does not know, ⁵¹and

ἐν τῷ μύλῳ, μία παραλαμβάνεται καὶ
in(at) the mill, one is taken and

μία ἀφίεται. 42 γρηγορεῖτε οὖν, ὅτι
one is left. Watch ye therefore, because

οὐκ οἴδατε ποίᾳ ἡμέρᾳ ὁ κύριος
ye know not on what day the lord

ὑμῶν ἔρχεται. 43 Ἐκεῖνο δὲ γινώσκετε
of you is coming. And that know ye

ὅτι εἰ ᾔδει ὁ οἰκοδεσπότης ποίᾳ
that if knew the housemaster in what

φυλακῇ ὁ κλέπτης ἔρχεται, ἐγρηγόρησεν
watch the thief is coming, he would have

ἂν καὶ οὐκ ἂν εἴασεν διορυχθῆναι
watched and would not have allowed to be dug through

τὴν οἰκίαν αὐτοῦ. 44 διὰ τοῦτο καὶ
the house of him. Therefore also

ὑμεῖς γίνεσθε ἕτοιμοι, ὅτι ᾗ οὐ δοκεῖτε
ye be ready, because ¹in which ²ye think not

ὥρᾳ ὁ υἱὸς τοῦ ἀνθρώπου ἔρχεται. 45 Τίς
²hour the Son - of man comes. Who

ἄρα ἐστὶν ὁ πιστὸς δοῦλος καὶ φρόνιμος
then is the faithful slave and prudent

ὃν κατέστησεν ὁ κύριος ἐπὶ τῆς οἰκετείας
whom appointed the lord over the household

αὐτοῦ τοῦ δοῦναι αὐτοῖς τὴν τροφὴν ἐν
of him - to give[d] to them the food in

καιρῷ; 46 μακάριος ὁ δοῦλος ἐκεῖνος ὃν
season? blessed [is] - slave that whom

ἐλθὼν ὁ κύριος αὐτοῦ εὑρήσει οὕτως
coming the lord of him will find so

ποιοῦντα· 47 ἀμὴν λέγω ὑμῖν ὅτι ἐπὶ
doing; truly I tell you that over

πᾶσιν τοῖς ὑπάρχουσιν αὐτοῦ καταστήσει
all the goods of him he will appoint

αὐτόν. 48 ἐὰν δὲ εἴπῃ ὁ κακὸς δοῦλος
him. But if says - wicked slave

ἐκεῖνος ἐν τῇ καρδίᾳ αὐτοῦ· χρονίζει
that in the heart of him: Delays

μου ὁ κύριος, 49 καὶ ἄρξηται τύπτειν
of me the lord, and begins to strike

τοὺς συνδούλους αὐτοῦ, ἐσθίῃ δὲ καὶ
the fellow-slaves of him, and eats and

πίνῃ μετὰ τῶν μεθυόντων, 50 ἥξει ὁ
drinks with the [ones] being drunk, will come the

κύριος τοῦ δούλου ἐκείνου ἐν ἡμέρᾳ ᾗ
lord - slave of that on a day on which

οὐ προσδοκᾷ καὶ ἐν ὥρᾳ ᾗ οὐ
he does not expect and in an hour in which not

will punish[c] him, and
put him with the hypo-
crites; there men will
weep and gnash their
teeth.

γινώσκει, | **51** καὶ | διχοτομήσει | αὐτόν,
he knows, | and | will cut asunder | him,

καὶ τὸ | μέρος | αὐτοῦ | μετὰ | τῶν
and the | portion | of him | with | the

ὑποκριτῶν | θήσει· | ἐκεῖ | ἔσται | ὁ
hypocrites | will place; | there | will be | the

κλαυθμὸς | καὶ ὁ | βρυγμὸς | τῶν | ὀδόντων.
wailing | and the | gnashing | of the | teeth.

CHAPTER 25

"THEN the kingdom
of heaven shall be
compared to ten maidens
who took their lamps and
went to meet the bride-
groom.[d] ²Five of them
were foolish, and five
were wise. ³For when the
foolish took their lamps,
they took no oil with
them; ⁴but the wise took
flasks of oil with their
lamps. ⁵As the bride-
groom was delayed, they
all slumbered and slept.
⁶But at midnight there
was a cry, 'Behold, the
bridegroom! Come out
to meet him.' ⁷Then all
those maidens rose and
trimmed their lamps.
⁸And the foolish said to
the wise, 'Give us some
of your oil, for our
lamps are going out.'
⁹But the wise replied,

25 Τότε | ὁμοιωθήσεται | ἡ | βασιλεία
Then | shall be likened | the | kingdom

τῶν οὐρανῶν | δέκα | παρθένοις, | αἵτινες
of the heavens | to ten | virgins, | who

λαβοῦσαι τὰς | λαμπάδας | ἑαυτῶν | ἐξῆλθον
taking the | lamps | of them* | went forth

εἰς ὑπάντησιν | τοῦ νυμφίου. | **2** πέντε δὲ
to a meeting | of the bridegroom. | Now five

ἐξ αὐτῶν ἦσαν | μωραὶ | καὶ πέντε | φρόνιμοι.
of them were | foolish | and five | prudent.

3 αἱ γὰρ | μωραὶ | λαβοῦσαι | τὰς | λαμπάδας
For the foolish [ones] | taking | the | lamps

οὐκ ἔλαβον | μεθ᾽ | ἑαυτῶν | ἔλαιον.
did not take | with | them | oil.

4 αἱ δὲ | φρόνιμοι | ἔλαβον | ἔλαιον | ἐν
But the | prudent [ones] | took | oil | in

τοῖς ἀγγείοις | μετὰ τῶν | λαμπάδων | ἑαυτῶν.
the vessels | with the | lamps | of them.

5 χρονίζοντος | δὲ | τοῦ νυμφίου | ἐνύσταξαν
But delaying | the | bridegroom* | slumbered
=while the bridegroom delayed

πᾶσαι καὶ | ἐκάθευδον. | **6** μέσης | δὲ
all and | slept. | And of(in) [the] middle

νυκτὸς | κραυγὴ | γέγονεν· | ἰδοὺ ὁ
of [the] night | a cry | there has been: | Behold[,] the

νυμφίος, | ἐξέρχεσθε | εἰς | ἀπάντησιν. | **7** τότε
bridegroom, | go ye forth | to | a meeting. | Then

ἠγέρθησαν | πᾶσαι | αἱ | παρθένοι | ἐκεῖναι
were raised | all | - | virgins | those

καὶ | ἐκόσμησαν | τὰς | λαμπάδας | ἑαυτῶν.
and | trimmed | the | lamps | of them.

8 αἱ δὲ | μωραὶ | ταῖς | φρονίμοις | εἶπαν·
So the | foolish [ones] | to the | prudent | said:

δότε | ἡμῖν | ἐκ | τοῦ | ἐλαίου | ὑμῶν, | ὅτι
Give | us | of | the | oil | of you, | because

αἱ λαμπάδες | ἡμῶν | σβέννυνται. | **9** ἀπεκρί-
the lamps | of us | are being quenched. | But

[c] Or *cut him in pieces*

[d] Other ancient authorities add
and the bride

*Here, and in the three following occurrences, as elsewhere, the
strict meaning is emphatic or reflexive—'of themselves'; but this
cannot be insisted on.

'Perhaps there will not be enough for us and for you; go rather to the dealers and buy for yourselves.' [10]And while they went to buy, the bridegroom came, and those who were ready went in with him to the marriage feast; and the door was shut. [11]Afterward the other maidens came also, saying, 'Lord, lord, open to us.' [12]But he replied, 'Truly, I say to you, I do not know you.' [13]Watch therefore, for you know neither the day nor the hour.

14 "For it will be as when a man going on a journey called his servants and entrusted to them his property; [15]to one he gave five talents, to another two, to each according to his ability. Then he went away. [16]He who had received the five talents went at once and traded with them; and he made five talents more. [17]So also, he who had the two talents made two talents more. [18]But he who had received the

---

θησαν δὲ αἱ φρόνιμοι λέγουσαι· μήποτε
answered the prudent saying: Lest

οὐ μὴ ἀρκέσῃ ἡμῖν καὶ ὑμῖν·
by no means it suffices to us and to you;

πορεύεσθε μᾶλλον πρὸς τοὺς πωλοῦντας
go ye rather to the [ones] selling

καὶ ἀγοράσατε ἑαυταῖς. 10 ἀπερχομένων
and buy for [your]selves. And going
= as they

δὲ αὐτῶν ἀγοράσαι ἦλθεν ὁ νυμφίος,
away them[a] to buy came the bridegroom,
were going away

καὶ αἱ ἕτοιμοι εἰσῆλθον μετ' αὐτοῦ
and the ready [ones] went in with him

εἰς τοὺς γάμους, καὶ ἐκλείσθη ἡ
to the wedding festivities, and was shut the

θύρα. 11 ὕστερον δὲ ἔρχονται καὶ αἱ
door. Then later come also the

λοιπαὶ παρθένοι λέγουσαι· κύριε κύριε,
remaining virgins saying: Lord[,] Lord,

ἄνοιξον ἡμῖν. 12 ὁ δὲ ἀποκριθεὶς εἶπεν·
open to us. But he answering said:

ἀμὴν λέγω ὑμῖν, οὐκ οἶδα ὑμᾶς.
Truly I say to you, I know not you.

13 Γρηγορεῖτε οὖν, ὅτι οὐκ οἴδατε
Watch ye therefore, because ye know not

τὴν ἡμέραν οὐδὲ τὴν ὥραν. 14 Ὥσπερ
the day nor the hour. as

γὰρ ἄνθρωπος ἀποδημῶν ἐκάλεσεν
For a man going from home called

τοὺς ἰδίους δούλους καὶ παρέδωκεν αὐτοῖς
the(his) own slaves and delivered to them

τὰ ὑπάρχοντα αὐτοῦ, 15 καὶ ᾧ μὲν ἔδωκεν
the goods of him, and to one he gave

πέντε τάλαντα, ᾧ δὲ δύο, ᾧ δὲ
five talents, to another two, to another

ἕν, ἑκάστῳ κατὰ τὴν ἰδίαν δύναμιν,
one, to each according to the(his) own ability,

καὶ ἀπεδήμησεν. 16 εὐθέως πορευθεὶς
and went from home. Immediately going

ὁ τὰ πέντε τάλαντα λαβὼν ἠργάσατο
the [one] the five talents receiving traded

ἐν αὐτοῖς καὶ ἐκέρδησεν ἄλλα
in them and gained other

πέντε· 17 ὡσαύτως ὁ τὰ δύο ἐκέρδησεν
five; similarly the [one] the two gained
[receiving]

ἄλλα δύο. 18 ὁ δὲ τὸ ἓν λαβὼν
other two. But the [one] the one receiving

one talent, went and dug in the ground and hid his master's money. ¹⁹Now after a long time the master of those servants came and settled accounts with them. ²⁰And he who had received the five talents came forward, bringing five talents more, saying, 'Master, you delivered to me five talents; here I have made five talents more.' ²¹His master said to him, 'Well done, good and faithful servant; you have been faithful over a little, I will set you over much; enter into the joy of your master.' ²²And he also who had the two talents came forward, saying, 'Master, you delivered to me two talents; here I have made two talents more.' ²³His master said to him, 'Well done, good and faithful servant; you have been faithful over a little, I will set you over much; enter into the joy of your master.' ²⁴He also who had received the one talent came forward, saying, 'Master, I knew you to be a hard man,

ἀπελθὼν   ὤρυξεν   γῆν   καὶ   ἐκρυψεν
going away   dug   earth   and   hid
τὸ   ἀργύριον   τοῦ   κυρίου   αὐτοῦ.
the   silver   of the   lord   of him.
19 μετὰ   δὲ   πολὺν   χρόνον   ἔρχεται   ὁ
Then after   much   time   comes   the
κύριος   τῶν   δούλων   ἐκείνων   καὶ   συναίρει
lord   –   slaves   of those   and   takes
λόγον   μετ'   αὐτῶν.   20 καὶ   προσελθὼν
account   with   them.   And   approaching
ὁ   τὰ   πέντε   τάλαντα   λαβὼν   προσ-
the [one]   the   five   talents   receiving   brought
ἤνεγκεν   ἄλλα   πέντε   τάλαντα   λέγων·   κύριε,
          other   five   talents   saying: Lord,
πέντε   τάλαντά   μοι   παρέδωκας·   ἴδε   ἄλλα
five   talents   to me   thou deliveredst;   behold   other
πέντε   τάλαντα   ἐκέρδησα.   21 ἔφη   αὐτῷ
five   talents   I gained.   Said   to him
ὁ   κύριος   αὐτοῦ·   εὖ,   δοῦλε   ἀγαθὲ   καὶ
the   lord   of him: Well,   slave   good   and
πιστέ,   ἐπὶ   ὀλίγα   ἦς   πιστός,
faithful,   over   a few things   thou wast   faithful,
ἐπὶ   πολλῶν   σε   καταστήσω·   εἴσελθε
over   many   thee   I will set;   enter thou
εἰς   τὴν   χαρὰν   τοῦ   κυρίου   σου.   22 προσ-
into   the   joy   of the   lord   of thee.   Ap-
ελθὼν   καὶ   ὁ   τὰ   δύο   τάλαντα
proaching   also   the [one]   the   two   talents
          [having received]
εἶπεν·   κύριε,   δύο   τάλαντά   μοι
said: Lord,   two   talents   to me
παρέδωκας·   ἴδε   ἄλλα   δύο   τάλαντα
thou deliveredst;   behold   other   two   talents
ἐκέρδησα.   23 ἔφη   αὐτῷ   ὁ   κύριος   αὐτοῦ·
I gained.   Said   to him the   lord   of him:
εὖ,   δοῦλε   ἀγαθὲ   καὶ   πιστέ,   ἐπὶ
Well,   slave   good   and   faithful,   over
ὀλίγα   ἦς   πιστός,   ἐπὶ   πολλῶν
a few things   thou wast   faithful,   over   many
σε   καταστήσω·   εἴσελθε   εἰς   τὴν
thee   I will set;   enter thou   into   the
χαρὰν   τοῦ   κυρίου   σου.   24 προσ-
joy   of the   lord   of thee.   ap-
ελθὼν   δὲ   καὶ   ὁ   τὸ   ἓν   τάλαντον
proaching   And   also   the [one]   the   one   talent
εἰληφὼς   εἶπεν·   κύριε,   ἔγνων   σε
having received   said: Lord,   I knew   thee
ὅτι   σκληρὸς   εἶ   ἄνθρωπος,   θερίζων
that   ²a hard   ¹thou art   ³man,   reaping

reaping where you did not sow, and gathering where you did not winnow; ²⁵so I was afraid, and I went and hid your talent in the ground. Here you have what is yours.' ²⁶But his master answered him, 'You wicked and slothful servant! You knew that I reap where I have not sowed, and gather where I have not winnowed? ²⁷Then you ought to have invested my money with the bankers, and at my coming I should have received what was my own with interest. ²⁸So take the talent from him, and give it to him who has the ten talents. ²⁹For to every one who has will more be given, and he will have abundance; but from him who has not, even what he has will be taken away. ³⁰And cast the worthless servant into the outer darkness; there men will weep and gnash their teeth.'

31 "When the Son of man comes in his glory, and all the angels with him, then he will sit on his glorious throne. ³²Before him will be gathered all the nations,

ὅπου   οὐκ   ἔσπειρας,   καὶ   συνάγων
where   thou didst not sow,   and   gathering

ὅθεν   οὐ   διεσκόρπισας·   25 καὶ   φοβηθεὶς
whence   thou didst not scatter;   and   fearing

ἀπελθὼν   ἔκρυψα   τὸ   τάλαντόν   σου
going away   I hid   the   talent   of thee

ἐν   τῇ   γῇ·   ἴδε   ἔχεις   τὸ   σόν.
in   the   earth;   behold   thou hast   the   thine.

26 ἀποκριθεὶς   δὲ   ὁ   κύριος   αὐτοῦ   εἶπεν
And answering   the   lord   of him   said

αὐτῷ·   πονηρὲ   δοῦλε   καὶ   ὀκνηρέ,
to him: Evil   slave   and   slothful,

ᾔδεις   ὅτι   θερίζω   ὅπου   οὐκ   ἔσπειρα,
thou knewest that   I reap   where   I sowed not,

καὶ   συνάγω   ὅθεν   οὐ   διεσκόρπισα;
and   I gather   whence   I did not scatter?

27 ἔδει   σε   οὖν   βαλεῖν   τὰ   ἀργύριά
it behoved   thee   therefore   to put   the   silver pieces

μου   τοῖς   τραπεζίταις,   καὶ   ἐλθὼν   ἐγὼ
of me   to the   bankers,   and   coming   I

ἐκομισάμην   ἂν   τὸ   ἐμὸν   σὺν   τόκῳ.
would have received   the   mine   with   interest.

28 ἄρατε   οὖν   ἀπ᾽   αὐτοῦ   τὸ   τάλαντον
Take   therefore   from   him   the   talent

καὶ   δότε   τῷ   ἔχοντι   τὰ   δέκα   τάλαντα·
and   give to the [one]   having   the   ten   talents;

29 τῷ   γὰρ   ἔχοντι   παντὶ   δοθήσεται   καὶ
for to   ²having   ¹everyone   will be given   and

περισσευθήσεται·   τοῦ   δὲ   μὴ   ἔχοντος
he will have abundance;   but from the [one]   not   having

καὶ   ὃ   ἔχει   ἀρθήσεται   ἀπ᾽   αὐτοῦ.
even   what   he has   will be taken   from   him,

30 καὶ   τὸν   ἀχρεῖον   δοῦλον   ἐκβάλετε   εἰς
And   the   useless   slave   cast ye out   into

τὸ   σκότος   τὸ   ἐξώτερον·   ἐκεῖ   ἔσται   ὁ
the   darkness   -   outer;   there   will be the

κλαυθμὸς   καὶ   ὁ   βρυγμὸς   τῶν   ὀδόντων
wailing   and the   gnashing   of the   teeth.

31 Ὅταν   δὲ   ἔλθῃ   ὁ   υἱὸς   τοῦ   ἀνθρώπου
And when   comes   the Son   -   of man

ἐν   τῇ   δόξῃ   αὐτοῦ   καὶ   πάντες   οἱ   ἄγγελοι
in   the   glory   of him   and   all   the   angels

μετ᾽   αὐτοῦ,   τότε   καθίσει   ἐπὶ   θρόνου
with   him,   then   he will sit   on   a throne

δόξης   αὐτοῦ·   32 καὶ   συναχθήσονται
of glory   of him;   and   will be assembled

ἔμπροσθεν   αὐτοῦ   πάντα   τὰ   ἔθνη,   καὶ
before   him   all   the   nations,   and

and he will separate them one from another as a shepherd separates the sheep from the goats, ³³ and he will place the sheep at his right hand, but the goats at the left. ³⁴ Then the King will say to those at his right hand, 'Come, O blessed of my Father, inherit the kingdom prepared for you from the foundation of the world; ³⁵ for I was hungry and you gave me food, I was thirsty and you gave me drink, I was a stranger and you welcomed me, ³⁶ I was naked and you clothed me, I was sick and you visited me, I was in prison and you came to me.' ³⁷ Then the righteous will answer him, 'Lord, when did we see thee hungry and feed thee, or thirsty and give thee drink? ³⁸ And when did we see thee a stranger and welcome thee, or naked and clothe thee? ³⁹ And when did we see thee sick or in prison and visit thee?' ⁴⁰ And the King will answer them, 'Truly, I say to you, as you did it to one of the

ἀφορίσει αὐτοὺς ἀπ' ἀλλήλων, ὥσπερ
he will separate them from one another, as

ὁ ποιμὴν ἀφορίζει τὰ πρόβατα ἀπὸ
the shepherd separates the sheep from

τῶν ἐρίφων, 33 καὶ στήσει τὰ μὲν
the goats, and will set the –

πρόβατα ἐκ δεξιῶν αὐτοῦ, τὰ δὲ ἐρίφια
sheep on [the] right of him, but the goats

ἐξ εὐωνύμων. 34 τότε ἐρεῖ ὁ
on [the] left. Then will say the

βασιλεὺς τοῖς ἐκ δεξιῶν αὐτοῦ·
king to the [ones] on [the] right of him:

δεῦτε οἱ εὐλογημένοι τοῦ πατρός μου,
Come the [ones] blessed of the Father of me,

κληρονομήσατε τὴν ἡτοιμασμένην ὑμῖν
inherit ye the ³having been prepared ²for you

βασιλείαν ἀπὸ καταβολῆς κόσμου.
¹kingdom from [the] foundation of [the] world.

35 ἐπείνασα γὰρ καὶ ἐδώκατέ μοι
For I hungered and ye gave me

φαγεῖν, ἐδίψησα, καὶ ἐποτίσατέ με,
to eat, I thirsted and ye gave ²drink ¹me,

ξένος ἤμην καὶ συνηγάγετέ με,
a stranger I was and ye entertained me,

36 γυμνὸς καὶ περιεβάλετέ με, ἠσθένησα
naked and ye clothed me, I ailed

καὶ ἐπεσκέψασθέ με, ἐν φυλακῇ ἤμην
and ye visited me, in prison I was

καὶ ἤλθατε πρός με. 37 τότε ἀποκριθή-
and ye came to me. Then will

σονται αὐτῷ οἱ δίκαιοι λέγοντες· κύριε,
answer him the righteous saying: Lord,

πότε σε εἴδομεν πεινῶντα καὶ ἐθρέψαμεν,
when thee saw we hungering and fed,

ἢ διψῶντα καὶ ἐποτίσαμεν; 38 πότε δέ
or thirsting and gave drink? and when

σε εἴδομεν ξένον καὶ συνηγάγομεν,
thee saw we a stranger and entertained,

ἢ γυμνὸν καὶ περιεβάλομεν; 39 πότε δέ
or naked and clothed? and when

σε εἴδομεν ἀσθενοῦντα ἢ ἐν φυλακῇ καὶ
thee saw we ailing or in prison and

ἤλθομεν πρὸς σέ; 40 καὶ ἀποκριθεὶς ὁ
came to thee? And answering the

βασιλεὺς ἐρεῖ αὐτοῖς· ἀμὴν λέγω
king will say to them: Truly I tell

ὑμῖν, ἐφ' ὅσον ἐποιήσατε ἑνὶ τούτων
you, inasmuch as ye did to one of these

least of these my brethren, you did it to me.' ⁴¹Then he will say to those at his left hand, 'Depart from me, you cursed, into the eternal fire prepared for the devil and his angels; ⁴²for I was hungry and you gave me no food, I was thirsty and you gave me no drink, ⁴³I was a stranger and you did not welcome me, naked and you did not clothe me, sick and in prison and you did not visit me.' ⁴⁴Then they also will answer, 'Lord, when did we see thee hungry or thirsty or a stranger or naked or sick or in prison, and did not minister to thee?' ⁴⁵Then he will answer them, 'Truly, I say to you, as you did it not to one of the least of these, you did not to me.' ⁴⁶And they will go away into eternal punishment, but the righteous into eternal life.''

τῶν ἀδελφῶν μου τῶν ἐλαχίστων, ἐμοὶ
-    brothers   of me the   least,   to me

ἐποιήσατε. **41** τότε ἐρεῖ καὶ τοῖς ἐξ
ye did.   Then he will say also to the [ones] on

εὐωνύμων· πορεύεσθε ἀπ' ἐμοῦ κατ-
[the] left: Go   from   me having been

ηραμένοι εἰς τὸ πῦρ τὸ αἰώνιον
cursed [ones] into the fire -   eternal

τὸ ἡτοιμασμένον τῷ διαβόλῳ καὶ τοῖς
- having been prepared for the devil   and the

ἀγγέλοις αὐτοῦ. **42** ἐπείνασα γὰρ καὶ
angels   of him.   For I hungered   and

οὐκ ἐδώκατέ μοι φαγεῖν, ἐδίψησα
ye gave not   me   to eat,   I thirsted

καὶ οὐκ ἐποτίσατέ με, **43** ξένος
and   ye ¹gave ²not ⁴drink ³me,   a stranger

ἤμην καὶ οὐ συνηγάγετέ με, γυμνὸς
I was and ye entertained not me,   naked

καὶ οὐ περιεβάλετέ με, ἀσθενὴς καὶ ἐν
and ye clothed not me,   ill   and in

φυλακῇ καὶ οὐκ ἐπεσκέψασθέ με. **44** τότε
prison and ye visited not   me.   Then

ἀποκριθήσονται καὶ αὐτοὶ λέγοντες· κύριε,
will answer   also they   saying: Lord,

πότε σε εἴδομεν πεινῶντα ἢ διψῶντα ἢ
when thee saw we hungering or thirsting or

ξένον ἢ γυμνὸν ἢ ἀσθενῆ ἢ ἐν φυλακῇ
a stranger or naked or ill   or in prison

καὶ οὐ διηκονήσαμέν σοι; **45** τότε
and   did not minister   to thee?   Then

ἀποκριθήσεται αὐτοῖς λέγων· ἀμὴν λέγω
he will answer   them   saying: Truly I tell

ὑμῖν, ἐφ' ὅσον οὐκ ἐποιήσατε ἑνὶ
you, inasmuch as   ye did not   to one

τούτων τῶν ἐλαχίστων, οὐδὲ ἐμοὶ
of these -   least [ones],   neither to me

ἐποιήσατε. **46** καὶ ἀπελεύσονται οὗτοι εἰς
ye did.   And will go away   these into

κόλασιν αἰώνιον, οἱ δὲ δίκαιοι εἰς
punishment eternal,   but the righteous into

ζωὴν αἰώνιον.
life   eternal.

CHAPTER 26

WHEN Jesus had finished all these sayings, he said to his disciples, [2]"You know that after two days the Passover is coming, and the Son of man will be delivered up to be crucified."

3 Then the chief priests and the elders of the people gathered in the palace of the high priest, who was called Ca'iaphas, [4]and took counsel together in order to arrest Jesus by stealth and kill him. [5]But they said, "Not during the feast, lest there be a tumult among the people."

6 Now when Jesus was at Bethany in the house of Simon the leper, [7]a woman came up to him with an alabaster jar of very expensive ointment, and she poured it on his head, as he sat at table. [8]But when the disciples saw it, they were indignant, saying, "Why this waste? [9]For this ointment might have been sold for a large sum, and given to the poor." [10]But Jesus, aware of this, said to them, "Why do you trouble the woman? For she has done a beautiful

26 Καὶ   ἐγένετο   ὅτε   ἐτέλεσεν   ὁ
    And   it came to pass   when   ended   -

'Ιησοῦς   πάντας   τοὺς   λόγους   τούτους,
Jesus   all   -   words   these,

εἶπεν   τοῖς   μαθηταῖς   αὐτοῦ·   2 οἴδατε
he said   to the   disciples   of him: Ye know

ὅτι   μετὰ   δύο   ἡμέρας   τὸ   πάσχα   γίνεται,
that   after   two   days   the   passover   occurs,

καὶ   ὁ   υἱὸς   τοῦ   ἀνθρώπου   παραδίδοται   εἰς
and   the   Son   -   of man   is delivered   -

τὸ   σταυρωθῆναι.   3 Τότε   συνήχθησαν   οἱ
-    to be crucified.   Then   were assembled   the

ἀρχιερεῖς   καὶ   οἱ   πρεσβύτεροι   τοῦ   λαοῦ
chief priests   and   the   elders   of the   people

εἰς   τὴν   αὐλὴν   τοῦ   ἀρχιερέως   τοῦ
in   the   court   of the   high priest   -

λεγομένου   Καϊάφα,   4 καὶ   συνεβουλεύ-
named   Caiaphas,   and   con-

σαντο   ἵνα   τὸν   'Ιησοῦν   δόλῳ   κρατή-
sulted   that   -   Jesus   by guile   they might

σωσιν   καὶ   ἀποκτείνωσιν·   5 ἔλεγον   δέ·
seize   and   might kill;   but they said:

μὴ   ἐν   τῇ   ἑορτῇ,   ἵνα   μὴ   θόρυβος
Not   at   the   feast,   lest   a disturbance

γένηται   ἐν   τῷ   λαῷ.
occurs   among   the   people.

6 Τοῦ   δὲ   'Ιησοῦ   γενομένου   ἐν   Βηθανίᾳ
    -    And   Jesus   being[a]   in   Bethany
                        =when Jesus was

ἐν   οἰκίᾳ   Σίμωνος   τοῦ   λεπροῦ,
in [the]   house   of Simon   the   leper,

7 προσῆλθεν   αὐτῷ   γυνὴ   ἔχουσα   ἀλάβαστρον
approached   to him   a woman   having   an alabaster phial

μύρου   βαρυτίμου   καὶ   κατέχεεν   ἐπὶ
of ointment   very expensive   and   poured [it]   on

τῆς   κεφαλῆς   αὐτοῦ   ἀνακειμένου.   8 ἰδόντες
the   head   of him   reclining.   And see-

δὲ   οἱ   μαθηταὶ   ἠγανάκτησαν   λέγοντες·
ing   the   disciples   were angry   saying:

εἰς   τί   ἡ   ἀπώλεια   αὕτη;   9 ἐδύνατο   γὰρ
To   what   -   waste   this?   for could

τοῦτο   πραθῆναι   πολλοῦ   καὶ   δοθῆναι
this   to be sold   of(for) much   and   to be given

πτωχοῖς.   10 γνοὺς   δὲ   ὁ   'Ιησοῦς   εἶπεν
to poor.   And knowing   -   Jesus   said

αὐτοῖς·   τί   κόπους   παρέχετε   τῇ   γυναικί;
to them: Why   trouble ye   the   woman?

ἔργον   γὰρ   καλὸν   ἠργάσατο   εἰς   ἐμέ·
for work   a good   she wrought   to   me;

thing to me. ¹¹For you always have the poor with you, but you will not always have me. ¹²In pouring this ointment on my body she has done it to prepare me for burial. ¹³Truly, I say to you, wherever this gospel is preached in the whole world, what she has done will be told in memory of her."

14 Then one of the twelve, who was called Judas Iscariot, went to the chief priests ¹⁵and said, "What will you give me if I deliver him to you?" And they paid him thirty pieces of silver. ¹⁶And from that moment he sought an opportunity to betray him.

17 Now on the first day of Unleavened Bread the disciples came to Jesus, saying, "Where will you have us prepare for you to eat the passover?" ¹⁸He said, "Go into the city to such a one, and say to him, 'The Teacher says, My time is at hand; I will keep the passover at your house with my disciples.' " ¹⁹And the

11 πάντοτε γὰρ τοὺς πτωχοὺς ἔχετε μεθ'
for always   the   poor   ye have   with
ἑαυτῶν,   ἐμὲ   δὲ   οὐ   πάντοτε   ἔχετε·
yourselves,   but me   not   always   ye have;
12 βαλοῦσα γὰρ αὕτη τὸ μύρον τοῦτο
for ²putting   ¹this woman –   ⁴ointment   ⁵this
ἐπὶ τοῦ σώματός μου πρὸς τὸ ἐνταφιάσαι
on   the   body   of me   for   –   to bury
με ἐποίησεν. 13 ἀμὴν λέγω ὑμῖν, ὅπου
me   she did.   Truly   I tell   you,   wher-
ἐὰν κηρυχθῇ τὸ εὐαγγέλιον τοῦτο ἐν
ever   is proclaimed   –   gospel   this   in
ὅλῳ τῷ κόσμῳ, λαληθήσεται καὶ ὃ
all   the   world,   will be spoken   also what
ἐποίησεν αὕτη εἰς μνημόσυνον αὐτῆς.
did   this woman   for   a memorial   of her.
14 Τότε πορευθεὶς εἷς τῶν δώδεκα, ὁ
Then   going   one of the   twelve, the [one]
λεγόμενος Ἰούδας Ἰσκαριώτης, πρὸς
named   Judas   Iscariot,   to
τοὺς ἀρχιερεῖς 15 εἶπεν· τί θέλετε μοι
the   chief priests   he said: What are ye willing me
δοῦναι, κἀγὼ ὑμῖν παραδώσω αὐτόν;
to give,   and I   to you   will deliver   him?
οἱ δὲ ἔστησαν αὐτῷ τριάκοντα ἀργύρια.
And they   weighed   him   thirty   pieces of silver.
16 καὶ ἀπὸ τότε ἐζήτει εὐκαιρίαν ἵνα
And   from   then   he sought   opportunity   that
αὐτὸν παραδῷ.
him   he might deliver.
17 Τῇ δὲ πρώτῃ τῶν ἀζύμων
Now on the   first [day]   – of unleavened bread
προσῆλθον οἱ μαθηταὶ τῷ Ἰησοῦ
approached   the   disciples   –   to Jesus
λέγοντες· ποῦ θέλεις ἑτοιμάσωμέν
saying: Where   willest thou   we may prepare
σοι φαγεῖν τὸ πάσχα; 18 ὁ δὲ
for thee   to eat   the   passover?   So he
εἶπεν· ὑπάγετε εἰς τὴν πόλιν πρὸς
said: Go ye   into   the   city   to
τὸν δεῖνα καὶ εἴπατε αὐτῷ· ὁ
such a one   and   say   to him: The
διδάσκαλος λέγει· ὁ καιρός μου
teacher   says: The   time   of me
ἐγγύς ἐστιν· πρὸς σὲ ποιῶ τὸ πάσχα
near   is;   with   thee   I make   the   passover
μετὰ τῶν μαθητῶν μου. 19 καὶ ἐποίησαν
with   the   disciples   of me.   And   did

disciples did as Jesus had directed them, and they prepared the passover.

20 When it was evening, he sat at table with the twelve disciples;[e] [21]and as they were eating, he said, "Truly, I say to you, one of you will betray me." [22]And they were very sorrowful, and began to say to him one after another, "Is it I, Lord?" [23]He answered, "He who has dipped his hand in the dish with me will betray me. [24]The Son of man goes as it is written of him, but woe to that man by whom the Son of man is betrayed! It would have been better for that man if he had not been born." [25]Judas, who betrayed him, said, "Is it I, Master?"[f] He said to him, "You have said so."

26 Now as they were eating, Jesus took bread, and blessed, and broke it, and gave it to the disciples and said, "Take, eat; this is my body." [27]And he took a cup, and when he had given thanks

οἱ   μαθηταὶ   ὡς   συνέταξεν   αὐτοῖς   ὁ
the   disciples   as   enjoined   them

'Ιησοῦς,   καὶ   ἡτοίμασαν   τὸ   πάσχα.   20 'Οψίας
Jesus,   and   prepared   the   passover.   evening

δὲ   γενομένης   ἀνέκειτο   μετὰ   τῶν   δώδεκα
And   coming[a]   he reclined   with   the   twelve
      =when evening came

[μαθητῶν].   21 καὶ   ἐσθιόντων   αὐτῶν   εἶπεν·
disciples.   And   eating   them[a]   he said:
                           =as they were eating

ἀμὴν   λέγω   ὑμῖν   ὅτι   εἷς   ἐξ   ὑμῶν   παρα-
Truly   I tell   you   that   one   of   you   will

δώσει   με.   22 καὶ   λυπούμενοι   σφόδρα
betray   me.   And   grieving   exceedingly

ἤρξαντο   λέγειν   αὐτῷ   εἷς   ἕκαστος·
they began to say   to him   [a]one   [a]each:

μήτι   ἐγώ   εἰμι,   κύριε;   23 ὁ   δὲ   ἀποκριθεὶς
Not   I   am,   Lord?   And he   answering
=It is not I,

εἶπεν·   ὁ   ἐμβάψας   μετ'   ἐμοῦ   τὴν
said: The [one] dipping   with   me   the(his)

χεῖρα   ἐν   τῷ   τρυβλίῳ,   οὗτός   με   παρα-
hand   in   the   dish,   this man   me   will

δώσει.   24 ὁ   μὲν   υἱὸς   τοῦ   ἀνθρώπου
betray.   Indeed the   Son   -   of man

ὑπάγει   καθὼς   γέγραπται   περὶ   αὐτοῦ,
goes   as   it has been written concerning   him,

οὐαὶ   δὲ   τῷ   ἀνθρώπῳ   ἐκείνῳ   δι'
but woe   -   man   to that   through

οὗ   ὁ   υἱὸς   τοῦ   ἀνθρώπου   παραδίδοται·
whom the   Son   -   of man   is betrayed;

καλὸν   ἦν   αὐτῷ   εἰ   οὐκ   ἐγεννήθη
good   were it   for him   if   was not born

ὁ   ἄνθρωπος   ἐκεῖνος.   25 ἀποκριθεὶς   δὲ
-     man   that.   And answering

'Ιούδας   ὁ   παραδιδοὺς   αὐτὸν   εἶπεν·
Judas   the [one] betraying   him   said:

μήτι   ἐγώ   εἰμι,   ῥαββί;   λέγει   αὐτῷ·
Not   I   am,   rabbi?   He says   to him:
=It is not I,

σὺ   εἶπας.   26 'Εσθιόντων   δὲ   αὐτῶν
Thou   saidst.   And eating   them[a]
                         =as they were eating

λαβὼν   ὁ   'Ιησοῦς   ἄρτον   καὶ   εὐλογήσας
taking   -   Jesus   a loaf   and   blessing

ἔκλασεν   καὶ   δοὺς   τοῖς   μαθηταῖς   εἶπεν·
he broke   and   giving   to the   disciples   said:

λάβετε   φάγετε·   τοῦτό   ἐστιν   τὸ   σῶμά
Take ye[,] eat ye;   this   is   the   body

μου.   27 καὶ   λαβὼν   ποτήριον   καὶ   εὐχαρι-
of me.   And   taking   a cup   and   giving

[e] Other authorities omit disciples
[f] Or Rabbi

he gave it to them, saying, "Drink of it, all of you; [28] for this is my blood of the[g] covenant, which is poured out for many for the forgiveness of sins. [29] I tell you I shall not drink again of this fruit of the vine until that day when I drink it new with you in my Father's kingdom."

30 And when they had sung a hymn, they went out to the Mount[h] of Olives. [31] Then Jesus said to them, "You will all fall away because of me this night; for it is written, 'I will strike the shepherd, and the sheep of the flock will be scattered.' [32] But after I am raised up, I will go before you to Galilee." [33] Peter declared to him, "Though they all fall away because of you, I will never fall away." [34] Jesus said to him, "Truly, I say to you, this very night, before the cock crows, you will deny me three times." [35] Peter said to him, "Even if I must die with you, I will not

στήσας ἔδωκεν αὐτοῖς λέγων· πίετε ἐξ
thanks   he gave   to them   saying: Drink ye   of

αὐτοῦ πάντες·   28 τοῦτο γάρ ἐστιν τὸ
it   all;   for this   is   the

αἷμά μου τῆς διαθήκης τὸ περὶ πολλῶν
blood of me of the   covenant the [blood] concerning many

ἐκχυννόμενον εἰς ἄφεσιν ἁμαρτιῶν.   29 λέγω
being shed   for forgiveness of sins.   I tell

δὲ ὑμῖν, οὐ μὴ πίω ἀπ' ἄρτι ἐκ
And   you,   by no means will I drink from   now   of

τούτου τοῦ γενήματος τῆς ἀμπέλου ἕως
this   —   fruit   of the   vine   until

τῆς ἡμέρας ἐκείνης ὅταν αὐτὸ πίνω μεθ'
—   day   that   when it   I drink   with

ὑμῶν καινὸν ἐν τῇ βασιλείᾳ τοῦ πατρός
you   new   in   the   kingdom of the   Father

μου.
of me.

30 Καὶ ὑμνήσαντες ἐξῆλθον εἰς τὸ
And   having sung a hymn   they went forth   to   the

ὄρος τῶν ἐλαιῶν. 31 Τότε λέγει αὐτοῖς ὁ
mount of the   olives.   Then   says   to them –

Ἰησοῦς· πάντες ὑμεῖς σκανδαλισθήσεσθε
Jesus: All   ye   will be offended

ἐν ἐμοὶ ἐν τῇ νυκτὶ ταύτῃ· γέγραπται
in   me   to-night;   it has been written

γάρ· πατάξω τὸν ποιμένα, καὶ δια-
for: I will strike   the   shepherd,   and   will

σκορπισθήσονται τὰ πρόβατα τῆς ποίμνης·
be scattered   the   sheep   of the   flock;

32 μετὰ δὲ τὸ ἐγερθῆναί με προάξω
but after the   to be raised me[b] I will go before
    =I am raised

ὑμᾶς εἰς τὴν Γαλιλαίαν. 33 ἀποκριθεὶς
you   to –   Galilee.   answering

δὲ ὁ Πέτρος εἶπεν αὐτῷ· εἰ πάντες
And –   Peter   said   to him: If   all men

σκανδαλισθήσονται ἐν σοί, ἐγὼ οὐδέποτε
shall be offended   in   thee,   I   never

σκανδαλισθήσομαι. 34 ἔφη αὐτῷ ὁ Ἰησοῦς·
will be offended.   Said   to him –   Jesus:

ἀμὴν λέγω σοι ὅτι ἐν ταύτῃ τῇ νυκτὶ
Truly   I tell   thee   that   to-night

πρὶν ἀλέκτορα φωνῆσαι τρὶς ἀπαρνήσῃ
before   a cock   to crow[b] three times thou wilt deny

με. 35 λέγει αὐτῷ ὁ Πέτρος· κἂν
me.   Says   to him –   Peter: Even if

δέῃ με σὺν σοὶ ἀποθανεῖν, οὐ μή σε
it behoves me with   thee   to die,   by no means thee
=I must die with thee,

[g] Other ancient authorities insert new

deny you." And so said all the disciples.

36 Then Jesus went with them to a place called Gethsem'ane, and he said to his disciples, "Sit here, while I go yonder and pray." [37]And taking with him Peter and the two sons of Zeb'edee, he began to be sorrowful and troubled. [38]Then he said to them, "My soul is very sorrowful, even to death; remain here, and watch[h] with me." [39]And going a little farther he fell on his face and prayed, "My Father, if it be possible, let this cup pass from me; nevertheless, not as I will, but as thou wilt." [40]And he came to the disciples and found them sleeping; and he said to Peter, "So, could you not watch[h] with me one hour? [41]Watch[h] and pray that you may not enter into temptation; the spirit indeed is willing, but the flesh is weak." [42]Again, for the second time, he went away and prayed, "My Father, if

ἀπαρνήσομαι.   ὁμοίως   καὶ   πάντες   οἱ
I will deny.   Likewise   also   all   the

μαθηταὶ   εἶπαν.
disciples   said.

36 Τότε   ἔρχεται   μετ'   αὐτῶν   ὁ   Ἰησοῦς
Then   comes   with   them   –   Jesus

εἰς   χωρίον   λεγόμενον   Γεθσημανί,   καὶ   λέγει
to a piece of land   called   Gethsemane,   and   says

τοῖς   μαθηταῖς·   καθίσατε   αὐτοῦ   ἕως   οὗ
to the   disciples: Sit ye   here   until

ἀπελθὼν   ἐκεῖ   προσεύξωμαι.   37 καὶ   παρα-
going away   there   I may pray.   And   tak-

λαβὼν   τὸν   Πέτρον   καὶ   τοὺς   δύο   υἱοὺς
ing   –   Peter   and   the   two   sons

Ζεβεδαίου   ἤρξατο   λυπεῖσθαι   καὶ   ἀδημονεῖν.
of Zebedee   he began   to grieve   and to be distressed.

38 τότε   λέγει   αὐτοῖς·   περίλυπός   ἐστιν
Then   he says   to them: Deeply grieved   is

ἡ   ψυχή   μου   ἕως   θανάτου·   μείνατε
the   soul   of me   unto   death;   remain ye

ὧδε   καὶ   γρηγορεῖτε   μετ'   ἐμοῦ.   39 καὶ
here   and   watch ye   with   me.   And

προελθὼν   μικρὸν   ἔπεσεν   ἐπὶ   πρόσωπον
going forward   a little   he fell   on   [the] face

αὐτοῦ   προσευχόμενος   καὶ   λέγων·   πάτερ
of him   praying   and   saying: Father

μου,   εἰ   δυνατόν   ἐστιν,   παρελθάτω   ἀπ'
of me,   if   possible   it is,   let pass   from

ἐμοῦ   τὸ   ποτήριον   τοῦτο·   πλὴν   οὐχ
me   –   cup   this;   yet   not

ὡς   ἐγὼ   θέλω   ἀλλ'   ὡς   σύ.   40 καὶ
as   I   will   but   as   thou.   And

ἔρχεται   πρὸς   τοὺς   μαθητὰς   καὶ   εὑρίσκει
he comes   to   the   disciples   and   finds

αὐτοὺς   καθεύδοντας,   καὶ   λέγει   τῷ   Πέτρῳ·
them   sleeping,   and   says   –   to Peter:

οὕτως   οὐκ   ἰσχύσατε   μίαν   ὥραν
So   were ye not able   one   hour

γρηγορῆσαι   μετ'   ἐμοῦ;   41 γρηγορεῖτε   καὶ
to watch   with   me?   Watch ye   and

προσεύχεσθε,   ἵνα   μὴ   εἰσέλθητε   εἰς
pray,   lest   ye enter   into

πειρασμόν·   τὸ   μὲν   πνεῦμα   πρόθυμον,
temptation;   indeed the   spirit   [is] eager,

ἡ   δὲ   σὰρξ   ἀσθενής.   42 πάλιν   ἐκ
but the   flesh   weak.   Again

δευτέρου   ἀπελθὼν   προσηύξατο   λέγων·
second [time]   going away   he prayed   saying:

[h] Or keep awake

this cannot pass unless I drink it, thy will be done." [43]And again he came and found them sleeping, for their eyes were heavy. [44]So, leaving them again, he went away and prayed for the third time, saying the same words. [45]Then he came to the disciples and said to them, "Are you still sleeping and taking your rest? Behold, the hour is at hand, and the Son of man is betrayed into the hands of sinners. [46]Rise, let us be going; see, my betrayer is at hand."

47 While he was still speaking, Judas came, one of the twelve, and with him a great crowd with swords and clubs, from the chief priests and the elders of the people. [48]Now the betrayer had given them a sign, saying, "The one I shall kiss is the man; seize him." [49]And he came up to Jesus at once and said, "Hail Master!"[i] And he kissed him. [50]Jesus said to him, "Friend, why are you here?"[j] Then they

[i] Or Rabbi
[j] Or do that for which you have come

πάτερ μου, εἰ οὐ δύναται τοῦτο παρελθεῖν
Father of me, if cannot this to pass away

ἐὰν μὴ αὐτὸ πίω, γενηθήτω τὸ θέλημά
except it I drink, let be done the will

σου. 43 καὶ ἐλθὼν πάλιν εὗρεν αὐτοὺς
of thee. And coming again he found them

καθεύδοντας, ἦσαν γὰρ αὐτῶν οἱ ὀφθαλμοὶ
sleeping, for were of them the eyes

βεβαρημένοι. 44 καὶ ἀφεὶς αὐτοὺς πάλιν
having been burdened. And leaving them again

ἀπελθὼν προσηύξατο ἐκ τρίτου, τὸν
going away he prayed a third [time], the

αὐτὸν λόγον εἰπὼν πάλιν. 45 τότε ἔρχεται
same word saying again. Then he comes

πρὸς τοὺς μαθητὰς καὶ λέγει αὐτοῖς·
to the disciples and says to them:

καθεύδετε λοιπὸν καὶ ἀναπαύεσθε·
Sleep ye now and rest;

ἰδοὺ ἤγγικεν ἡ ὥρα καὶ ὁ υἱὸς τοῦ
behold has drawn near the hour and the Son –

ἀνθρώπου παραδίδοται εἰς χεῖρας
of man is betrayed into [the] hands

ἁμαρτωλῶν. 46 ἐγείρεσθε, ἄγωμεν· ἰδοὺ
of sinners. Rise ye, let us be going; behold

ἤγγικεν ὁ παραδιδούς με.
has drawn near the [one] betraying me.

47 Καὶ ἔτι αὐτοῦ λαλοῦντος, ἰδοὺ
And still him speaking,[a] behold
= while he was still speaking,

Ἰούδας εἷς τῶν δώδεκα ἦλθεν, καὶ μετ'
Judas one of the twelve came, and with

αὐτοῦ ὄχλος πολὺς μετὰ μαχαιρῶν καὶ
him crowd a much with swords and

ξύλων ἀπὸ τῶν ἀρχιερέων καὶ πρεσβυτέρων
clubs from the chief priests and elders

τοῦ λαοῦ. 48 ὁ δὲ παραδιδοὺς αὐτὸν ἔδωκεν
of the people. Now the [one] betraying him gave

αὐτοῖς σημεῖον λέγων· ὃν ἂν φιλήσω
them a sign saying: Whomever I may kiss

αὐτός ἐστιν· κρατήσατε αὐτόν. 49 καὶ
he it is; seize ye him. And

εὐθέως προσελθὼν τῷ Ἰησοῦ εἶπεν· χαῖρε,
immediately approaching – to Jesus he said: Hail,

ῥαββί, καὶ κατεφίλησεν αὐτόν. 50 ὁ
rabbi, and affectionately kissed him. –

δὲ Ἰησοῦς εἶπεν αὐτῷ· ἑταῖρε,
But Jesus said to him: Comrade, [do that]

ἐφ' ὃ πάρει. τότε προσελθόντες ἐπέβαλον
on what thou art here. Then approaching they laid on

came up and laid hands on Jesus and seized him. [51]And behold, one of those who were with Jesus stretched out his hand and drew his sword, and struck the slave of the high priest, and cut off his ear. [52]Then Jesus said to him, "Put your sword back into its place; for all who take the sword will perish by the sword. [53]Do you think that I cannot appeal to my Father, and he will at once send me more than twelve legions of angels? [54]But how then should the scriptures be fulfilled, that it must be so?" [55]At that hour Jesus said to the crowds, "Have you come out as against a robber, with swords and clubs to capture me? Day after day I sat in the temple teaching, and you did not seize me. [56]But all this has taken place, that the scriptures of the prophets might be fulfilled." Then all the disciples forsook him and fled.

57 Then those who had seized Jesus led him to Ca'iaphas the high

τὰς χεῖρας ἐπὶ τὸν Ἰησοῦν καὶ ἐκράτησαν
the(ir) hands on - Jesus and seized

αὐτόν. 51 καὶ ἰδοὺ εἷς τῶν μετὰ
him. And behold one of the [ones] with

Ἰησοῦ ἐκτείνας τὴν χεῖρα ἀπέσπασεν
Jesus stretching out the(his) hand drew

τὴν μάχαιραν αὐτοῦ, καὶ πατάξας τὸν
the sword of him, and striking the

δοῦλος τοῦ ἀρχιερέως ἀφεῖλεν αὐτοῦ τὸ
slave of the high priest cut off of him the

ὠτίον. 52 τότε λέγει αὐτῷ ὁ Ἰησοῦς·
ear. Then says to him - Jesus:

ἀπόστρεψον τὴν μάχαιράν σου εἰς τὸν
Put back the sword of thee into the

τόπον αὐτῆς· πάντες γὰρ οἱ λαβόντες
place of it; for all the [ones] taking

μάχαιραν ἐν μαχαίρῃ ἀπολοῦνται. 53 ἢ
a sword by a sword will perish. Or

δοκεῖς ὅτι οὐ δύναμαι παρακαλέσαι
thinkest thou that I cannot to ask

τὸν πατέρα μου, καὶ παραστήσει μοι
the Father of me, and he will provide me

ἄρτι πλείω δώδεκα λεγιώνας ἀγγέλων;
now more [than] twelve legions of angels?

54 πῶς οὖν πληρωθῶσιν αἱ γραφαὶ ὅτι
how then may be fulfilled the scriptures that

οὕτως δεῖ γενέσθαι; 55 Ἐν ἐκείνῃ τῇ ὥρᾳ
thus it must be? In that - hour

εἶπεν ὁ Ἰησοῦς τοῖς ὄχλοις· ὡς ἐπὶ
said - Jesus to the crowds: As against

λῃστὴν ἐξήλθατε μετὰ μαχαιρῶν καὶ
a robber came ye forth with swords and

ξύλων συλλαβεῖν με; καθ᾽ ἡμέραν ἐν
clubs to take me? daily in

τῷ ἱερῷ ἐκαθεζόμην διδάσκων, καὶ οὐκ
the temple I sat teaching, and not

ἐκρατήσατέ με. 56 τοῦτο δὲ ὅλον
ye seized me. But this all

γέγονεν ἵνα πληρωθῶσιν αἱ γραφαὶ
has come to pass that may be fulfilled the scriptures

τῶν προφητῶν. Τότε οἱ μαθηταὶ πάντες
of the prophets. Then the disciples all

ἀφέντες αὐτὸν ἔφυγον.
leaving him fled.

57 Οἱ δὲ κρατήσαντες τὸν Ἰησοῦν
But the [ones] having seized - Jesus

ἀπήγαγον πρὸς Καϊαφᾶν τὸν ἀρχιερέα,
led [him] away to Caiaphas the high priest,

priest, where the scribes and the elders had gathered. [58]But Peter followed him at a distance, as far as the courtyard of the high priest, and going inside he sat with the guards to see the end. [59]Now the chief priests and the whole council sought false testimony against Jesus that they might put him to death, [60]but they found none, though many false witnesses came forward. At last two came forward [61]and said, "This fellow said, 'I am able to destroy the temple of God, and to build it in three days.'" [62]And the high priest stood up and said, "Have you no answer to make? What is it that these men testify against you?" [63]But Jesus was silent. And the high priest said to him, "I adjure you by the living God, tell us if you are the Christ, the Son of God." [64]Jesus said to him, "You have said so. But I tell you, hereafter you will see the Son of man seated at the right hand of Power, and coming on the clouds of heaven." [65]Then the high

ὅπου   οἱ   γραμματεῖς   καὶ   οἱ   πρεσβύτεροι
where   the   scribes   and   the   elders
συνήχθησαν.   58 ὁ   δὲ   Πέτρος   ἠκολούθει
were assembled.   – And   Peter   followed
αὐτῷ   [ἀπὸ]   μακρόθεν   ἕως   τῆς   αὐλῆς
him   from   afar   up to   the   court
τοῦ   ἀρχιερέως,   καὶ   εἰσελθὼν   ἔσω   ἐκάθητο
of the   high priest,   and   entering   within   sat
μετὰ   τῶν   ὑπηρετῶν   ἰδεῖν   τὸ   τέλος.
with   the   attendants   to see   the   end.
59 Οἱ   δὲ   ἀρχιερεῖς   καὶ   τὸ   συνέδριον
   And the   chief priests   and   the   council
ὅλον   ἐζήτουν   ψευδομαρτυρίαν   κατὰ   τοῦ
whole   sought   false witness   against   –
Ἰησοῦ   ὅπως   αὐτὸν   θανατώσωσιν,   60 καὶ
Jesus   so as   him   they might put to death,   and
οὐχ   εὗρον   πολλῶν   προσελθόντων
did not find[,]   many   approaching
                        =when many false witnesses approached.
ψευδομαρτύρων.   ὕστερον   δὲ   προσελθόντες
false witnesses⁹.   But later   approaching
δύο   61 εἶπαν·   οὗτος   ἔφη·   δύναμαι   κατα-
two   said: This man   said: I can   to de-
λῦσαι   τὸν   ναὸν   τοῦ   θεοῦ   καὶ   διὰ   τριῶν
stroy   the   shrine   –   of God   and   through(after) three
ἡμερῶν   οἰκοδομῆσαι.   62 καὶ   ἀναστὰς
days   to build.   And   standing up
ὁ   ἀρχιερεὺς   εἶπεν   αὐτῷ·   οὐδὲν
the   high priest   said   to him: Nothing
ἀποκρίνῃ,   τί   οὗτοί   σου   κατα-
answerest thou,   what   these men   thee   give
μαρτυροῦσιν;   63 ὁ   δὲ   Ἰησοῦς   ἐσιώπα.
evidence against?   –   But   Jesus   remained silent.
καὶ   ὁ   ἀρχιερεὺς   εἶπεν   αὐτῷ·   ἐξορκίζω
And   the   high priest   said   to him: I adjure
σε   κατὰ   τοῦ   θεοῦ   τοῦ   ζῶντος   ἵνα   ἡμῖν
thee   by   –   God   the   living   that   us
εἴπῃς   εἰ   σὺ   εἶ   ὁ   χριστὸς   ὁ   υἱὸς   τοῦ
thou tell   if   thou   art   the   Christ   the   Son   –
θεοῦ.   64 λέγει   αὐτῷ   ὁ   Ἰησοῦς·   σὺ   εἶπας·
of God.   Says   to him   –   Jesus: Thou   saidst;
πλὴν   λέγω   ὑμῖν,   ἀπ'   ἄρτι   ὄψεσθε   τὸν
yet   I tell   you,   from   now   ye will see   the
υἱὸν   τοῦ   ἀνθρώπου   καθήμενον   ἐκ
Son   –   of man   sitting   on [the]
δεξιῶν   τῆς   δυνάμεως   καὶ   ἐρχόμενον
right [hand]   of the   power   and   coming
ἐπὶ   τῶν   νεφελῶν   τοῦ   οὐρανοῦ.   65 τότε
on   the   clouds   –   of heaven.   Then

priest tore his robes, and said, "He has uttered blasphemy. Why do we still need witnesses? You have now heard his blasphemy. ⁶⁶What is your judgment?" They answered, "He deserves death." ⁶⁷Then they spat in his face, and struck him; and some slapped him, ⁶⁸saying, "Prophesy to us, you Christ! Who is it that struck you?"

69 Now Peter was sitting outside in the courtyard. And a maid came up to him, and said, "You also were with Jesus the Galilean." ⁷⁰But he denied it before them all, saying, "I do not know what you mean." ⁷¹And when he went out to the porch, another maid saw him, and she said to the bystanders, "This man was with Jesus of Nazareth." ⁷²And again he denied it with an oath, "I do not know the man." ⁷³After a little while the bystanders came up and said to Peter, "Certainly you are also one of them, for your accent betrays you." ⁷⁴Then he began to invoke a curse on himself and to swear, "I do not

ὁ ἀρχιερεὺς διέρρηξεν τὰ ἱμάτια αὐτοῦ
the high priest rent the garments of him
λέγων· ἐβλασφήμησεν· τί ἔτι χρείαν ἔχομεν
saying: He blasphemed; what yet need have we
μαρτύρων; ἴδε νῦν ἠκούσατε τὴν βλασφη-
of witnesses? behold now ye heard the blas-
μίαν· 66 τί ὑμῖν δοκεῖ; οἱ δὲ ἀπο-
phemy; what to you seems it? And they answer-
κριθέντες εἶπαν· ἔνοχος θανάτου ἐστίν.
ing said: Liable of(to) death he is.
67 Τότε ἐνέπτυσαν εἰς τὸ πρόσωπον αὐτοῦ
Then they spat in the face of him
καὶ ἐκολάφισαν αὐτόν, οἱ δὲ
and violently maltreated him, and they
ἐρράπισαν 68 λέγοντες· προφήτευσον ἡμῖν,
slapped [him] saying: Prophesy to us,
χριστέ, τίς ἐστιν ὁ παίσας σε;
Christ, who is it the [one] having struck thee?
69 Ὁ δὲ Πέτρος ἐκάθητο ἔξω ἐν
- And Peter sat outside in
τῇ αὐλῇ· καὶ προσῆλθεν αὐτῷ μία
the court; and approached to him one
παιδίσκη λέγουσα· καὶ σὺ ἦσθα μετὰ
maidservant saying: Also thou wast with
Ἰησοῦ τοῦ Γαλιλαίου. 70 ὁ δὲ ἠρνήσατο
Jesus the Galilæan. But he denied
ἔμπροσθεν πάντων λέγων· οὐκ οἶδα
before all saying: I know not
τί λέγεις. 71 ἐξελθόντα δὲ εἰς τὸν
what thou sayest. And ⁴going out ⁵into ⁶the
πυλῶνα εἶδεν αὐτὸν ἄλλη καὶ λέγει
⁷porch ²saw ³him ¹another and says
τοῖς ἐκεῖ· οὗτος ἦν μετὰ Ἰησοῦ τοῦ
to the [ones] there: This man was with Jesus the
Ναζωραίου. 72 καὶ πάλιν ἠρνήσατο
Nazarene. And again he denied
μετὰ ὅρκου ὅτι οὐκ οἶδα τὸν ἄνθρωπον.
with an oath[,] - I know not the man.
73 μετὰ μικρὸν δὲ προσελθόντες οἱ
And after a little approaching the [ones]
ἑστῶτες εἶπον τῷ Πέτρῳ· ἀληθῶς καὶ
standing said - to Peter: Truly also
σὺ ἐξ αὐτῶν εἶ, καὶ γὰρ ἡ λαλιά σου
thou of them art, for indeed the speech of thee
δῆλόν σε ποιεῖ. 74 τότε ἤρξατο καταθε-
manifest thee makes. Then he began to
ματίζειν καὶ ὀμνύειν ὅτι οὐκ οἶδα τὸν
curse and to swear[,] - I know not the

know the man." And immediately the cock crowed. [75]And Peter remembered the saying of Jesus, "Before the cock crows, you will deny me three times." And he went out and wept bitterly.

ἄνθρωπον. καὶ εὐθὺς ἀλέκτωρ ἐφώνησεν
man.   And immediately a cock   crowed.

75 καὶ ἐμνήσθη ὁ Πέτρος τοῦ ῥήματος
And remembered – Peter the   word

Ἰησοῦ εἰρηκότος ὅτι πρὶν ἀλέκτορα
of Jesus having said[,] – Before   a cock

φωνῆσαι τρὶς ἀπαρνήσῃ με· καὶ
to crow[b] three times thou wilt deny me;   and

ἐξελθὼν ἔξω ἔκλαυσεν πικρῶς.
going forth outside he wept   bitterly.

CHAPTER 27

WHEN morning came, all the chief priests and the elders of the people took counsel against Jesus to put him to death; [2]and they bound him and led him away and delivered him to Pilate the governor.

3 When Judas, his betrayer, saw that he was condemned, he repented and brought back the thirty pieces of silver to the chief priests and the elders, [4]saying, "I have sinned in betraying innocent blood." They said, "What is that to us? See to it yourself." [5]And throwing down the pieces of silver in the temple, he departed; and he went and hanged himself. [6]But the chief priests, taking the pieces of silver, said, "It is not lawful to put them into the treasury, since they are blood money." [7]So they took counsel, and bought with

27 Πρωΐας δὲ γενομένης συμβούλιον
And early morning coming[a]   counsel
= when early morning came

ἔλαβον πάντες οἱ ἀρχιερεῖς καὶ οἱ
took all the chief priests and the

πρεσβύτεροι τοῦ λαοῦ κατὰ τοῦ
elders of the people against –

Ἰησοῦ ὥστε θανατῶσαι αὐτόν· **2** καὶ
Jesus so as to put to death him;   and

δήσαντες αὐτὸν ἀπήγαγον καὶ παρ-
having bound him they led away and de-

έδωκαν Πιλάτῳ τῷ ἡγεμόνι. **3** Τότε
livered to Pilate the governor.   Then

ἰδὼν Ἰούδας ὁ παραδοὺς αὐτὸν
[b]seeing [1]Judas [a]the [one] [2]having betrayed [4]him

ὅτι κατεκρίθη, μεταμεληθεὶς ἔστρεψεν τὰ
that he was condemned, repenting returned the

τριάκοντα ἀργύρια τοῖς ἀρχιερεῦσιν
thirty pieces of silver to the chief priests

καὶ πρεσβυτέροις **4** λέγων· ἥμαρτον
and elders   saying: I sinned

παραδοὺς αἷμα ἀθῶον. οἱ δὲ εἶπαν·
betraying blood innocent. But they said:

τί πρὸς ἡμᾶς; σὺ ὄψῃ. **5** καὶ ῥίψας
What to us? thou shalt see [to it]. And tossing

τὰ ἀργύρια εἰς τὸν ναὸν ἀν-
the pieces of silver into the shrine he

εχώρησεν, καὶ ἀπελθὼν ἀπήγξατο. **6** οἱ
departed, and going away hanged himself. the

δὲ ἀρχιερεῖς λαβόντες τὰ ἀργύρια εἶπαν·
But chief priests taking the pieces of silver said:

οὐκ ἔξεστιν βαλεῖν αὐτὰ εἰς τὸν
It is not lawful to put them into the

κορβανᾶν, ἐπεὶ τιμὴ αἵματός ἐστιν.
treasury, since price of blood it is.

7 συμβούλιον δὲ λαβόντες ἠγόρασαν ἐξ
So counsel   taking they bought of(with)

them the potter's field, to bury strangers in. 8 Therefore that field has been called the Field of Blood to this day. 9 Then was fulfilled what had been spoken by the prophet Jeremiah, saying, "And they took the thirty pieces of silver, the price of him on whom a price had been set by some of the sons of Israel, 10 and they gave them for the potter's field, as the Lord directed me."

11 Now Jesus stood before the governor; and the governor asked him, "Are you the King of the Jews?" Jesus said to him, "You have said so." 12 But when he was accused by the chief priests and elders, he made no answer. 13 Then Pilate said to him, "Do you not hear how many things they testify against you?" 14 But he gave him no answer, not even to a single charge; so that the governor wondered greatly.

15 Now at the feast the governor was accustomed to release for the crowd any one prisoner whom they wanted. 16 And they had then a notorious prisoner, called Barab'bas.[k] 17 So when

αὐτῶν τὸν ἀγρὸν τοῦ κεραμέως εἰς ταφὴν
them   the   field   of the   potter   for   burial
τοῖς ξένοις. 8 διὸ ἐκλήθη ὁ ἀγρὸς
for the strangers.   Wherefore was called - field
ἐκεῖνος ἀγρὸς αἵματος ἕως τῆς σήμερον.
that   Field   of blood   until - to-day.
9 τότε ἐπληρώθη τὸ ῥηθὲν διὰ
Then   was fulfilled   the[thing] spoken through
Ἰερεμίου τοῦ προφήτου λέγοντος· καὶ
Jeremiah   the   prophet   saying: And
ἔλαβον τὰ τριάκοντα ἀργύρια, τὴν
they took   the   thirty   pieces of silver,   the
τιμὴν τοῦ τετιμημένου ὃν ἐτιμήσαντο
price of the[one] having been priced whom they priced
ἀπὸ υἱῶν Ἰσραήλ, 10 καὶ ἔδωκαν
from[the] sons   of Israel,   and   gave
αὐτὰ εἰς τὸν ἀγρὸν τοῦ κεραμέως, καθὰ
them   for the   field   of the   potter,   as
συνέταξέν μοι κύριος. 11 Ὁ δὲ
directed   me   [the] Lord. - And
Ἰησοῦς ἐστάθη ἔμπροσθεν τοῦ ἡγεμόνος·
Jesus   stood   before   the   governor;
καὶ ἐπηρώτησεν αὐτὸν ὁ ἡγεμὼν λέγων·
and   questioned   him   the   governor   saying:
σὺ εἶ ὁ βασιλεὺς τῶν Ἰουδαίων; ὁ δὲ
Thou art the   king   of the   Jews? - And
Ἰησοῦς ἔφη· σὺ λέγεις. 12 καὶ ἐν
Jesus   said: Thou   sayest.   And   in
τῷ κατηγορεῖσθαι αὐτὸν ὑπὸ τῶν
the   to be accused   him[e]   by   the
  =as he was accused
ἀρχιερέων καὶ πρεσβυτέρων οὐδὲν
chief priests   and   elders   nothing
ἀπεκρίνατο. 13 τότε λέγει αὐτῷ ὁ Πιλᾶτος·
he answered.   Then   says to him - Pilate:
οὐκ ἀκούεις πόσα σου κατα-
Hearest thou not   what things [3]thee [1]they
μαρτυροῦσιν; 14 καὶ οὐκ ἀπεκρίθη αὐτῷ
[2]give evidence against?   And   he answered not   him
πρὸς οὐδὲ ἓν ῥῆμα, ὥστε θαυμάζειν
to   not   one   word,   so as   to marvel
  =so that the governor marvelled
τὸν ἡγεμόνα λίαν. 15 Κατὰ δὲ ἑορτὴν
the   governor[b] exceedingly.   Now at   a feast
εἰώθει ὁ ἡγεμὼν ἀπολύειν ἕνα τῷ ὄχλῳ
was accustomed the governor to release [3]one[1]to the [2]crowd
δέσμιον ὃν ἤθελον. 16 εἶχον δὲ τότε
[4]prisoner whom they wished.   And they had   then
δέσμιον ἐπίσημον λεγόμενον Βαραββᾶν
prisoner   a notable   named   Barabbas.

[k] Other ancient authorities read *Jesus Barabbas*

they had gathered, Pilate said to them, "Whom do you want me to release for you, Barab′bas[k] or Jesus who is called Christ?" [18] For he knew that it was out of envy that they had delivered him up. [19] Besides, while he was sitting on the judgment seat, his wife sent word to him, "Have nothing to do with that righteous man, for I have suffered much over him today in a dream." [20] Now the chief priests and the elders persuaded the people to ask for Barab′bas and destroy Jesus. [21] The governor again said to them, "Which of the two do you want me to release for you?" And they said, "Barab′bas." [22] Pilate said to them, "Then what shall I do with Jesus who is called Christ?" They all said, "Let him be crucified." [23] And he said, "Why, what evil has he done?" But they shouted all the more, "Let him be crucified."

24 So when Pilate saw that he was gaining nothing, but rather that a riot was beginning, he took water and washed his hands before the

---

17 συνηγμένων οὖν αὐτῶν εἶπεν αὐτοῖς
Therefore having assembled them[a] said to them
= when they were assembled

ὁ Πιλᾶτος· τίνα θέλετε ἀπολύσω
– Pilate: Whom do ye wish I may release

ὑμῖν, [τὸν] Βαραββᾶν ἢ Ἰησοῦν τὸν
to you, – Barabbas or Jesus –

λεγόμενον χριστόν; 18 ἤδει γὰρ ὅτι
called Christ? for he knew that

διὰ φθόνον παρέδωκαν αὐτόν. 19 Καθη-
because of envy they delivered him. sit-

μένου δὲ αὐτοῦ ἐπὶ τοῦ βήματος
ting Now him[a] on the tribunal
= Now as he sat

ἀπέστειλεν πρὸς αὐτὸν ἡ γυνὴ αὐτοῦ
sent to him the wife of him

λέγουσα· μηδὲν σοὶ καὶ τῷ δικαίῳ
saying: Nothing to thee and – just man

ἐκείνῳ· πολλὰ γὰρ ἔπαθον σήμερον κατ'
to that; for many things I suffered to-day by

ὄναρ δι' αὐτόν. 20 Οἱ δὲ ἀρχιερεῖς
a dream because of him. But the chief priests

καὶ οἱ πρεσβύτεροι ἔπεισαν τοὺς
and the elders persuaded the

ὄχλους ἵνα αἰτήσωνται τὸν Βαραββᾶν,
crowds that they should ask – Barabbas,

τὸν δὲ Ἰησοῦν ἀπολέσωσιν. 21 ἀπο-
– and Jesus should destroy. So

κριθεὶς δὲ ὁ ἡγεμὼν εἶπεν αὐτοῖς·
answering the governor said to them:

τίνα θέλετε ἀπὸ τῶν δύο ἀπολύσω
Which do ye wish from the two I may release

ὑμῖν; οἱ δὲ εἶπαν· τὸν Βαραββᾶν.
to you? And they said: – Barabbas.

22 λέγει αὐτοῖς ὁ Πιλᾶτος· τί οὖν
Says to them – Pilate: What then

ποιήσω Ἰησοῦν τὸν λεγόμενον χριστόν;
may I do [to] Jesus – called Christ?

λέγουσιν πάντες· σταυρωθήτω. 23 ὁ δὲ
They say all: Let him be crucified. But he

ἔφη· τί γὰρ κακὸν ἐποίησεν; οἱ δὲ
said: Why what evil did he? But they

περισσῶς ἔκραζον λέγοντες· σταυρω-
more cried out saying: Let him be

θήτω. 24 ἰδὼν δὲ ὁ Πιλᾶτος ὅτι οὐδὲν
crucified. And seeing – Pilate that nothing

ὠφελεῖ ἀλλὰ μᾶλλον θόρυβος γίνεται,
is gained but rather an uproar occurs,

λαβὼν ὕδωρ ἀπενίψατο τὰς χεῖρας
taking water he washed the(his) hands

---

[k] Other ancient authorities read Jesus Barabbas

crowd, saying, "I am innocent of this man's blood;[1] see to it yourselves." 25And all the people answered, "His blood be on us and on our children!" 26Then he released for them Barab'bas, and having scourged Jesus, delivered him to be crucified.

27 Then the soldiers of the governor took Jesus into the praetorium, and they gathered the whole battalion before him.28And they stripped him and put a scarlet robe upon him, 29and plaiting a crown of thorns they put it on his head, and put a reed in his right hand. And kneeling before him they mocked him, saying, "Hail, King of the Jews!" 30And they spat upon him, and took the reed and struck him on the head. 31And when they had mocked him, they stripped him of the robe, and put his own clothes on him, and led him away to crucify him.

32 As they were marching out, they came upon a man of Cyre'ne,

[1] Other authorities read *this righteous blood* or *this righteous man's blood*

κατέναντι   τοῦ   ὄχλου   λέγων·   ἀθῷός
in front of   the   crowd   saying: Innocent

εἰμι   ἀπὸ   τοῦ   αἵματος   τούτου·   ὑμεῖς
I am   from   the   blood   of this man;   ye

ὄψεσθε.   25 καὶ   ἀποκριθεὶς   πᾶς   ὁ   λαὸς
will see [to it].   And   answering   all   the   people

εἶπεν·   τὸ   αἷμα   αὐτοῦ   ἐφ᾽   ἡμᾶς   καὶ
said: The   blood   of him   on   us   and

ἐπὶ   τὰ   τέκνα   ἡμῶν.   26 τότε   ἀπέλυσεν
on   the   children   of us.   Then   he released

αὐτοῖς   τὸν   Βαραββᾶν,   τὸν   δὲ   Ἰησοῦν
to them   -   Barabbas,   -   but   Jesus

φραγελλώσας   παρέδωκεν   ἵνα   σταυρωθῇ.
having scourged   he delivered   that   he might be crucified.

27 Τότε   οἱ   στρατιῶται   τοῦ   ἡγεμόνος
Then   the   soldiers   of the   governor

παραλαβόντες   τὸν   Ἰησοῦν   εἰς   τὸ   πραιτώ-
having taken   -   Jesus   into   the   prae-

ριον   συνήγαγον   ἐπ᾽   αὐτὸν   ὅλην   τὴν
torium   assembled   against   him   all   the

σπεῖραν.   28 καὶ   ἐκδύσαντες   αὐτὸν   χλαμύδα
band.   And   stripping   him   cloak

κοκκίνην   περιέθηκαν   αὐτῷ,   29 καὶ
a purple   they placed round   him,   and

πλέξαντες   στέφανον   ἐξ   ἀκανθῶν   ἐπέθηκαν
having plaited   a crown   of   thorns   they placed [it] on

ἐπὶ   τῆς   κεφαλῆς   αὐτοῦ   καὶ   κάλαμον
on   the   head   of him   and   a reed

ἐν   τῇ   δεξιᾷ   αὐτοῦ,   καὶ   γονυπετή-
in   the   right [hand]   of him,   and   bowing

σαντες   ἔμπροσθεν   αὐτοῦ   ἐνέπαιξαν   αὐτῷ
the knee   in front of   him   mocked   at him

λέγοντες·   χαῖρε,   βασιλεῦ   τῶν   Ἰουδαίων,
saying: Hail,   king   of the   Jews,

30 καὶ   ἐμπτύσαντες   εἰς   αὐτὸν   ἔλαβον
and   spitting   at   him   took

τὸν   κάλαμον   καὶ   ἔτυπτον   εἰς   τὴν   κεφαλὴν
the   reed   and   struck   at   the   head

αὐτοῦ.   31 καὶ   ὅτε   ἐνέπαιξαν   αὐτῷ,
of him.   And   when   they mocked   at him,

ἐξέδυσαν   αὐτὸν   τὴν   χλαμύδα   καὶ   ἐνέδυσαν
they took off   him   the   cloak   and   put on

αὐτὸν   τὰ   ἱμάτια   αὐτοῦ,   καὶ   ἀπήγαγον
him   the   garments   of him,   and   led away

αὐτὸν   εἰς   τὸ   σταυρῶσαι.   32 Ἐξερχόμενοι
him   -   -   to crucify.   going forth

δὲ   εὗρον   ἄνθρωπον   Κυρηναῖον,   ὀνό-
And   they found   a man   a Cyrenian,   by

Simon by name; this man they compelled to carry his cross. ³³And when they came to a place called Gol'gotha (which means the place of a skull), ³⁴they offered him wine to drink, mingled with gall; but when he tasted it, he would not drink it. ³⁵And when they had crucified him, they divided his garments among them by casting lots; ³⁶then they sat down and kept watch over him there. ³⁷And over his head they put the charge against him, which read, "This is Jesus the King of the Jews." ³⁸Then two robbers were crucified with him, one on the right and one on the left. ³⁹And those who passed by derided him, wagging their heads ⁴⁰and saying, "You who would destroy the temple and build it in three days, save yourself! If you are the Son of God, come down from the cross." ⁴¹So also the chief priests, with the scribes and elders, mocked him, saying, ⁴²"He saved others; he cannot save himself. He

ματι	Σίμωνα·	τοῦτον	ἠγγάρευσαν	ἵνα
name	Simon;	this man	they impressed	that

ἄρη	τὸν	σταυρὸν	αὐτοῦ.	33 Καὶ
he should bear	the	cross	of him.	And

ἐλθόντες	εἰς	τόπον	λεγόμενον	Γολγοθά,
coming	to	a place	called	Golgotha,

ὅ	ἐστιν	κρανίου	τόπος	λεγόμενος,
which	is	³of a skull	²A place	¹called,

34 ἔδωκαν	αὐτῷ	πιεῖν	οἶνον	μετὰ
they gave	him	to drink	wine	with

χολῆς	μεμιγμένον·	καὶ	γευσάμενος	οὐκ
gall	having been mixed;	and	tasting	not

ἠθέλησεν	πιεῖν.	35 σταυρώσαντες	δὲ
he would	to drink.	And having crucified	

αὐτὸν	διεμερίσαντο	τὰ	ἱμάτια	αὐτοῦ
him	they divided	the	garments	of him

βάλλοντες	κλῆρον,	36 καὶ	καθήμενοι	ἐτήρουν
casting	a lot,	and	sitting	they guarded

αὐτὸν	ἐκεῖ.	37 καὶ	ἐπέθηκαν	ἐπάνω
him	there.	And	they placed on	above

τῆς	κεφαλῆς	αὐτοῦ	τὴν	αἰτίαν	αὐτοῦ
the	head	of him	the	charge	of him

γεγραμμένην·	ΟΥΤΟΣ	ΕΣΤΙΝ	ΙΗΣΟΥΣ
having been written:	THIS	IS	JESUS

Ο ΒΑΣΙΛΕΥΣ	ΤΩΝ	ΙΟΥΔΑΙΩΝ.	38 Τότε
THE KING	OF THE	JEWS.	Then

σταυροῦνται	σὺν	αὐτῷ	δύο	λησταί,
are crucified	with	him	two	robbers,

εἷς	ἐκ	δεξιῶν	καὶ	εἷς	ἐξ	εὐωνύμων.
one	on [the] right		and	one		on [the] left.

39 Οἱ	δὲ	παραπορευόμενοι	ἐβλασφήμουν
And the [ones]		passing by	blasphemed

αὐτὸν	κινοῦντες	τὰς	κεφαλὰς	αὐτῶν
him	wagging	the	heads	of them

40 καὶ	λέγοντες·	ὁ	καταλύων	τὸν	ναὸν
and	saying:	The [one]	destroying	the	shrine

καὶ	ἐν	τρισὶν	ἡμέραις	οἰκοδομῶν,
and	in	three	days	building [it],

σῶσον	σεαυτόν,	εἰ	υἱὸς	εἶ	τοῦ	θεοῦ,
save	thyself,	if	Son	thou art –		of God,

καὶ	κατάβηθι	ἀπὸ	τοῦ	σταυροῦ.	41 ὁμοίως
and	come down	from	the	cross.	Likewise

[καὶ]	οἱ	ἀρχιερεῖς	ἐμπαίζοντες	μετὰ
also	the	chief priests	mocking	with

τῶν	γραμματέων	καὶ	πρεσβυτέρων	ἔλεγον
the	scribes	and	elders	said:

42 ἄλλους	ἔσωσεν,	ἑαυτὸν	οὐ	δύναται
Others	he saved,	himself		he cannot

is the King of Israel; let him come down now from the cross, and we will believe in him. [43]He trusts in God; let God deliver him now, if he desires him; for he said, 'I am the Son of God.' " [44]And the robbers who were crucified with him also reviled him in the same way.

45 Now from the sixth hour there was darkness over all the land[m] until the ninth hour. [46]And about the ninth hour Jesus cried with a loud voice, "Eli, Eli, la'ma sabach-tha'-ni?" that is, "My God, my God, why hast thou forsaken me?" [47]And some of the bystanders hearing it said, "This man is calling Eli'jah." [48]And one of them at once ran and took a sponge, filled it with vinegar, and put it on a reed, and gave it to him to drink. [49]But the others said, "Wait, let us see whether Eli'jah will come to save him."[n] [50]And Jesus cried again with a loud voice and yielded up his spirit.

51 And behold, the curtain of the temple was torn in two, from top to bottom; and the earth

σῶσαι·   βασιλεὺς   Ἰσραήλ   ἐστιν,
to save;   King   of Israel   he is,

καταβάτω   νῦν   ἀπὸ   τοῦ   σταυροῦ   καὶ
let him come down now   from   the   cross   and

πιστεύσομεν   ἐπ'   αὐτόν.   43 πέποιθεν
we will believe   on   him.   He has trusted

ἐπὶ   τὸν   θεόν,   ῥυσάσθω   νῦν   εἰ   θέλει
on   -   God,   let him rescue   now   if   he wants

αὐτόν·   εἶπεν   γὰρ   ὅτι   θεοῦ   εἰμι   υἱός.
him;   for he said[,]   -   of God   I am   Son.

44 τὸ   δ'   αὐτὸ   καὶ   οἱ   λῃσταὶ   οἱ   συσταυρω-
And the   same   also   the robbers   -   crucified

θέντες   σὺν   αὐτῷ   ὠνείδιζον   αὐτόν.   45 Ἀπὸ
with   with him   reproached   him.   from

δὲ   ἕκτης   ὥρας   σκότος   ἐγένετο   ἐπὶ
Now [the] sixth   hour   darkness   occurred   over

πᾶσαν   τὴν   γῆν   ἕως   ὥρας   ἐνάτης.
all   the   land   until   hour   [the] ninth.

46 περὶ   δὲ   τὴν   ἐνάτην   ὥραν   ἀνεβόησεν   ὁ
And about   the   ninth   hour   cried out   -

Ἰησοῦς   φωνῇ   μεγάλῃ   λέγων·   ἠλὶ   ἠλὶ
Jesus   voice   with a great   saying: Eli   Eli

λεμὰ   σαβαχθάνι;   τοῦτ'   ἔστιν·   θεέ   μου
lema   sabachthani?   this   is: God of me[,]

θεέ   μου,   ἱνατί   με   ἐγκατέλιπες;   47 τινὲς
God   of me,   why   me   didst thou forsake?   some

δὲ   τῶν   ἐκεῖ   ἑστηκότων   ἀκούσαντες
And of the [ones] there   standing   hearing

ἔλεγον   ὅτι   Ἠλίαν   φωνεῖ   οὗτος.
said[,]   -   Elias   calls   this man.

48 καὶ   εὐθέως   δραμὼν   εἷς   ἐξ   αὐτῶν   καὶ
And immediately   running   one   of   them   and

λαβὼν   σπόγγον   πλήσας   τε   ὄξους   καὶ
taking   a sponge   and filling   of (with) vinegar   and

περιθεὶς   καλάμῳ   ἐπότιζεν   αὐτόν.
putting [it] round   a reed   gave to drink   him.

49 οἱ   δὲ   λοιποὶ   εἶπαν·   ἄφες   ἴδωμεν
But the   rest   said: Leave[,]   let us see

εἰ   ἔρχεται   Ἠλίας   σώσων   αὐτόν.   50 ὁ
if   comes   Elias   saving   him.   -

δὲ   Ἰησοῦς   πάλιν   κράξας   φωνῇ
And   Jesus   again   crying out   voice

μεγάλῃ   ἀφῆκεν   τὸ   πνεῦμα.   51 Καὶ
with a great   released   the (his)   spirit.   And

ἰδοὺ   τὸ   καταπέτασμα   τοῦ   ναοῦ   ἐσχίσθη
behold   the   veil   of the   shrine   was rent

[ἀπ']   ἄνωθεν   ἕως   κάτω   εἰς   δύο,   καὶ   ἡ
from   above   to   below   in two,   and the

---

[m] Or earth
[n] Other ancient authorities insert And another took a spear and pierced his side, and out came water and blood

shook, and the rocks
were split; [52] the tombs
also were opened, and
many bodies of the saints
who had fallen asleep
were raised, [53] and coming out of the tombs
after his resurrection they
went into the holy city
and appeared to many.
[54] When the centurion
and those who were with
him, keeping watch over
Jesus, saw the earth-
quake and what took
place, they were filled
with awe, and said,
"Truly this was the Son[nn]
of God!"

55 There were also
many women there, look-
ing on from afar, who
had followed Jesus from
Galilee, ministering to
him; [56] among whom
were Mary Mag'dalene,
and Mary the mother of
James and Joseph, and
the mother of the sons of
Zeb'edee.

57 When it was even-
ing, there came a rich
man from Arimathe'a,
named Joseph, who also
was a disciple of Jesus.
[58] He went to Pilate and
asked for the body of
Jesus. Then Pilate
ordered it to be given to
him. [59] And Joseph took

γῆ   ἐσείσθη,   καὶ   αἱ   πέτραι   ἐσχίσ-
earth   was shaken,   and   the   rocks   were
θησαν,   52 καὶ   τὰ   μνημεῖα   ἀνεῴχθησαν
rent,   and   the   tombs   were opened
καὶ   πολλὰ   σώματα   τῶν   κεκοιμημένων
and   many   bodies   of the   having fallen asleep
ἁγίων   ἠγέρθησαν·   53 καὶ   ἐξελθόντες
saints   were raised;   and   coming forth
ἐκ   τῶν   μνημείων   μετὰ   τὴν   ἔγερσιν
out of   the   tombs   after   the   rising
αὐτοῦ   εἰσῆλθον   εἰς   τὴν   ἁγίαν   πόλιν   καὶ
of him   entered   into   the   holy   city   and
ἐνεφανίσθησαν   πολλοῖς.   54 Ὁ   δὲ   ἑκατόν-
appeared   to many.   And the   centu-
ταρχος   καὶ   οἱ   μετ'   αὐτοῦ   τηροῦντες
rion   and the [ones] with   him   guarding
τὸν   Ἰησοῦν   ἰδόντες   τὸν   σεισμὸν   καὶ
-         Jesus   seeing   the   earthquake   and
τὰ   γινόμενα   ἐφοβήθησαν   σφόδρα,
the things   happening   feared   exceedingly,
λέγοντες·   ἀληθῶς   θεοῦ   υἱὸς   ἦν   οὗτος.
saying: Truly   [4]of God [3]Son [2]was [1]this man.
55 Ἦσαν   δὲ   ἐκεῖ   γυναῖκες   πολλαὶ
Now there were   there   women   many
ἀπὸ   μακρόθεν   θεωροῦσαι,   αἵτινες   ἠκολού-
from   afar   beholding,   who   followed
θησαν   τῷ   Ἰησοῦ   ἀπὸ   τῆς   Γαλιλαίας
-          -   Jesus   from   the   Galilee
διακονοῦσαι   αὐτῷ·   56 ἐν   αἷς   ἦν
ministering   to him;   among   whom   was
Μαρία   ἡ   Μαγδαληνή,   καὶ   Μαρία   ἡ
Mary   the   Magdalene,   and   Mary   the
τοῦ   Ἰακώβου   καὶ   Ἰωσὴφ   μήτηρ,   καὶ   ἡ
-       of James   and   of Joseph   mother,   and the
μήτηρ   τῶν   υἱῶν   Ζεβεδαίου.
mother   of the   sons   of Zebedee.
57 Ὀψίας   δὲ   γενομένης   ἦλθεν   ἄνθρωπος
Now evening   having come[a]   came   man
                    = when evening had come
πλούσιος   ἀπὸ   Ἀριμαθαίας,   τοὔνομα   Ἰωσήφ,
a rich   from   Arimathæa,   the name   Joseph,
ὃς   καὶ   αὐτὸς   ἐμαθητεύθη   τῷ   Ἰησοῦ·
who   also   himself   was discipled   -   to Jesus;
58 οὗτος   προσελθὼν   τῷ   Πιλάτῳ   ᾐτήσατο
this man   approaching   -   to Pilate   asked
τὸ   σῶμα   τοῦ   Ἰησοῦ.   τότε   ὁ   Πιλᾶτος
the   body   -   of Jesus.   Then   -   Pilate
ἐκέλευσεν   ἀποδοθῆναι.   59 καὶ   λαβὼν
commanded [it] to be given [him].   And   taking

[nn] Or a son

the body, and wrapped it in a clean linen shroud, [60] and laid it in his own new tomb, which he had hewn in the rock; and he rolled a great stone to the door of the tomb, and departed. [61] Mary Magdalene and the other Mary were there, sitting opposite the sepulchre.

62 Next day, that is, after the day of Preparation, the chief priests and the Pharisees gathered before Pilate [63] and said, "Sir, we remember how that impostor said, while he was still alive, 'After three days I will rise again.' [64] Therefore order the sepulchre to be made secure until the third day, lest his disciples go and steal him away, and tell the people, 'He has risen from the dead,' and the last fraud will be worse than the first." [65] Pilate said to them, "You have a guard[o] of soldiers; go, make it as secure as you can." [66] So they went and made the sepulchre secure by sealing the stone and setting a guard.

τὸ σῶμα ὁ Ἰωσὴφ ἐνετύλιξεν αὐτὸ [ἐν]
the body - Joseph wrapped it in

σινδόνι καθαρᾷ, 60 καὶ ἔθηκεν αὐτὸ ἐν
sheet a clean, and placed it in

τῷ καινῷ αὐτοῦ μνημείῳ ὃ ἐλατό-
the new of him tomb which he

μησεν ἐν τῇ πέτρᾳ, καὶ προσκυλίσας
hewed in the rock, and having rolled to

λίθον μέγαν τῇ θύρᾳ τοῦ μνημείου
stone a great to the door of the tomb

ἀπῆλθεν. 61 Ἦν δὲ ἐκεῖ Μαριὰμ
went away. And there was there Mary

ἡ Μαγδαληνὴ καὶ ἡ ἄλλη Μαρία,
the Magdalene and the other Mary,

καθήμεναι ἀπέναντι τοῦ τάφου. 62 Τῇ
sitting opposite the grave. on the

δὲ ἐπαύριον, ἥτις ἐστὶν μετὰ τὴν παρα-
And morrow, which is after the prepara-

σκευήν, συνήχθησαν οἱ ἀρχιερεῖς
tion, were assembled the chief priests

καὶ οἱ Φαρισαῖοι πρὸς Πιλᾶτον 63 λέ-
and the Pharisees to Pilate say-

γοντες· κύριε, ἐμνήσθημεν ὅτι ἐκεῖνος
ing: Sir, we remembered that that

ὁ πλάνος εἶπεν ἔτι ζῶν· μετὰ τρεῖς
- deceiver said yet living: After three

ἡμέρας ἐγείρομαι. 64 κέλευσον οὖν
days I am raised. Command therefore

ἀσφαλισθῆναι τὸν τάφον ἕως τῆς
to be made fast the grave until the

τρίτης ἡμέρας, μήποτε ἐλθόντες οἱ μαθηταὶ
third day, lest coming the disciples

κλέψωσιν αὐτὸν καὶ εἴπωσιν τῷ λαῷ·
may steal him and may say to the people:

ἠγέρθη ἀπὸ τῶν νεκρῶν, καὶ ἔσται
He was raised from the dead, and will be

ἡ ἐσχάτη πλάνη χείρων τῆς πρώτης.
the last deceit worse [than] the first.

65 ἔφη αὐτοῖς ὁ Πιλᾶτος· ἔχετε κου-
Said to them - Pilate: Ye have a

στωδίαν· ὑπάγετε ἀσφαλίσασθε ὡς οἴδατε.
guard; go ye make fast as ye know*.

66 οἱ δὲ πορευθέντες ἠσφαλίσαντο τὸν
And they going made fast the

τάφον σφραγίσαντες τὸν λίθον μετὰ τῆς
grave sealing the stone with the

κουστωδίας.
guard.

[o] Or *Take a guard*

* can. See note on page xviii.

CHAPTER 28

NOW after the
sabbath, toward the
dawn of the first day of
the week, Mary Mag'-
dalene and the other
Mary went to see the
sepulchre. [2]And behold,
there was a great earth-
quake; for an angel of
the Lord descended from
heaven and came and
rolled back the stone,
and sat upon it. [3]His
appearance was like
lightning, and his raiment
white as snow. [4]And for
fear of him the guards
trembled and became
like dead men. [5]But the
angel said to the women,
"Do not be afraid; for I
know that you seek Jesus
who was crucified. [6]He
is not here; for he has
risen, as he said. Come,
see the place where he[p]
lay. [7]Then go quickly and
tell his disciples that he
has risen from the dead,
and behold, he is going
before you to Galilee;
there you will see him.
Lo, I have told you."
[8]So they departed
quickly from the tomb
with fear and great joy,
and ran to tell his dis-
ciples. [9]And behold,

28 Ὀψὲ δὲ σαββάτων, τῇ ἐπιφωσκούσῃ
　　　But late　of [the] sabbaths, at the　　drawing on
εἰς μίαν σαββάτων, ἦλθεν Μαριὰμ ἡ
toward one of [the] sabbaths,　came　Mary　the
= the first day of the week,
Μαγδαληνὴ καὶ ἡ ἄλλη Μαρία θεωρῆσαι
Magdalene　and the other　Mary　to view
τὸν τάφον. **2** καὶ ἰδοὺ σεισμὸς ἐγένετο
the grave.　　And behold earthquake　occurred
μέγας· ἄγγελος γὰρ κυρίου καταβὰς
a great;　for an angel　of [the] Lord　descending
ἐξ οὐρανοῦ καὶ προσελθὼν ἀπεκύλισεν
out of heaven　and　approaching　rolled away
τὸν λίθον καὶ ἐκάθητο ἐπάνω αὐτοῦ.
the stone　and　sat　upon　it.
3 ἦν δὲ ἡ εἰδέα αὐτοῦ ὡς ἀστραπή,
　　And was the appearance of him as　lightning,
καὶ τὸ ἔνδυμα αὐτοῦ λευκὸν ὡς χιών.
and the　dress　of him　white as snow.
4 ἀπὸ δὲ τοῦ φόβου αὐτοῦ ἐσείσθησαν
　And from the　fear　of him were shaken
οἱ τηροῦντες καὶ ἐγενήθησαν ὡς
the [ones] guarding　and　they became　as
νεκροί. **5** ἀποκριθεὶς δὲ ὁ ἄγγελος
dead.　　And answering　the　angel
εἶπεν ταῖς γυναιξίν· μὴ φοβεῖσθε ὑμεῖς·
said to the　women;　Fear not　ye;
οἶδα γὰρ ὅτι Ἰησοῦν τὸν ἐσταυρω-
for I know　that Jesus the [one] having been
μένον ζητεῖτε· **6** οὐκ ἔστιν ὧδε·
crucified　ye seek;　he is not　here;
ἠγέρθη γὰρ καθὼς εἶπεν· δεῦτε ἴδετε τὸν
for he was raised as　he said;　come see ye the
τόπον ὅπου ἔκειτο. **7** καὶ ταχὺ πορευθεῖσαι
place where he lay.　And quickly　going
εἴπατε τοῖς μαθηταῖς αὐτοῦ ὅτι ἠγέρθη
tell　the　disciples　of him that he was raised
ἀπὸ τῶν νεκρῶν, καὶ ἰδοὺ προάγει ὑμᾶς
from the　dead,　and behold he goes before you
εἰς τὴν Γαλιλαίαν, ἐκεῖ αὐτὸν ὄψεσθε.
to　Galilee,　there him ye will see.
ἰδοὺ εἶπον ὑμῖν. **8** καὶ ἀπελθοῦσαι ταχὺ
Behold I told　you.　And going away quickly
ἀπὸ τοῦ μνημείου μετὰ φόβου καὶ χαρᾶς
from the　tomb　with fear and joy
μεγάλης ἔδραμον ἀπαγγεῖλαι τοῖς
great　they ran　to announce to the
μαθηταῖς αὐτοῦ. **9** καὶ ἰδοὺ Ἰησοῦς
disciples of him.　And behold Jesus

[p] Other ancient authorities
read the Lord

Jesus met them and said, "Hail!" And they came up and took hold of his feet and worshiped him. [10] Then Jesus said to them, "Do not be afraid; go and tell my brethren to go to Galilee, and there they will see me."

[11] While they were going, behold, some of the guard went into the city and told the chief priests all that had taken place. [12] And when they had assembled with the elders and taken counsel, they gave a sum of money to the soldiers [13] and said, "Tell people, 'His disciples came by night and stole him away while we were asleep.' [14] And if this comes to the governor's ears, we will satisfy him and keep you out of trouble." [15] So they took the money and did as they were directed; and this story has been spread among the Jews to this day.

[16] Now the eleven disciples went to Galilee, to the mountain to which Jesus had directed them. [17] And when they saw him

ὑπήντησεν αὐταῖς λέγων· χαίρετε. αἱ δὲ
met   them   saying: Hail.   And they
προσελθοῦσαι ἐκράτησαν αὐτοῦ τοὺς πόδας
approaching   held   of him   the   feet
καὶ προσεκύνησαν αὐτῷ. **10** τότε λέγει
and   worshipped   him.   Then   says
αὐταῖς ὁ Ἰησοῦς· μὴ φοβεῖσθε· ὑπάγετε
to them - Jesus: Fear ye not;   go ye
ἀπαγγείλατε τοῖς ἀδελφοῖς μου ἵνα
announce   to the brothers   of me that
ἀπέλθωσιν εἰς τὴν Γαλιλαίαν, κἀκεῖ
they may go away into -   Galilee,   and there
με ὄψονται. **11** Πορευομένων δὲ αὐτῶν[a]
me they will see.   And going   them
                                    =as they were going
ἰδού τινες τῆς κουστωδίας ἐλθόντες εἰς
behold some of the   guard   coming   into
τὴν πόλιν ἀπήγγειλαν τοῖς ἀρχιερεῦσιν
the   city   announced   to the   chief priests
ἅπαντα τὰ γενόμενα. **12** καὶ συν-
all the things having happened.   And   being
αχθέντες μετὰ τῶν πρεσβυτέρων συμβούλιόν[2]
assembled with   the   elders   counsel
τε λαβόντες[1] ἀργύρια ἱκανὰ ἔδωκαν τοῖς
and taking   silver   enough gave   to the
στρατιώταις, **13** λέγοντες· εἴπατε ὅτι οἱ
soldiers,   saying: Say ye   that the
μαθηταὶ αὐτοῦ νυκτὸς ἐλθόντες ἔκλεψαν
disciples of him of(by) night coming   stole
αὐτὸν ἡμῶν κοιμωμένων.[a] **14** καὶ ἐὰν
him   we   sleeping.   And   if
                  =while we slept.
ἀκουσθῇ τοῦτο ἐπὶ τοῦ ἡγεμόνος,
be heard   this   before the   governor,
ἡμεῖς πείσομεν καὶ ὑμᾶς ἀμερίμνους
we   will persuade and   you   free from anxiety
ποιήσομεν. **15** οἱ δὲ λαβόντες ἀργύρια
we will make.   And they   taking   silver
ἐποίησαν ὡς ἐδιδάχθησαν. Καὶ διεφη-
did   as   they were taught.   And was spread
μίσθη ὁ λόγος οὗτος παρὰ Ἰουδαίοις
about - saying   this   by   Jews
μέχρι τῆς σήμερον [ἡμέρας]. **16** Οἱ δὲ
until   the   to-day   So the
ἔνδεκα μαθηταὶ ἐπορεύθησαν εἰς τὴν
eleven   disciples   went   to   -
Γαλιλαίαν, εἰς τὸ ὄρος οὗ ἐτάξατο
Galilee,   to the mountain where appointed
αὐτοῖς ὁ Ἰησοῦς, **17** καὶ ἰδόντες αὐτὸν
them   - Jesus,   and   seeing   him

they worshiped him; but some doubted. [18]And Jesus came and said to them, "All authority in heaven and on earth has been given to me. [19]Go therefore and make disciples of all nations, baptizing them in the name of the Father and of the Son and of the Holy Spirit, [20]teaching them to observe all that I have commanded you; and lo, I am with you always, to the close of the age."

προσεκύνησαν,   οἱ δὲ   ἐδίστασαν.   **18** καὶ
they worshipped,   but some   doubted.   And

προσελθὼν   ὁ   Ἰησοῦς   ἐλάλησεν   αὐτοῖς
approaching   -   Jesus   talked   with them

λέγων·   ἐδόθη   μοι   πᾶσα   ἐξουσία   ἐν
saying: was given   to me   All   authority   in

οὐρανῷ καὶ ἐπὶ [τῆς] γῆς.   **19** πορευθέντες
heaven and on   the earth.   Going

οὖν μαθητεύσατε   πάντα   τὰ ἔθνη,   βαπτίζ-
therefore disciple ye   all   the nations,   baptiz-

οντες   αὐτοὺς   εἰς   τὸ   ὄνομα   τοῦ   πατρὸς
ing   them   in   the   name   of the   Father

καὶ   τοῦ   υἱοῦ   καὶ   τοῦ   ἁγίου   πνεύματος,
and   of the   Son   and   of the   Holy   Spirit,

20 διδάσκοντες   αὐτοὺς   τηρεῖν   πάντα
teaching   them   to observe   all things

ὅσα   ἐνετειλάμην   ὑμῖν·   καὶ   ἰδοὺ   ἐγὼ
whatever I gave command   to you;   and   behold   I

μεθ'   ὑμῶν   εἰμι   πάσας   τὰς   ἡμέρας   ἕως
with   you   am   all   the   days   until

τῆς   συντελείας   τοῦ   αἰῶνος.
the   completion   of the   age.

CHAPTER 1

THE beginning of the gospel of Jesus Christ, the Son of God.[a]

2 As it is written in Isaiah the prophet,[b]
"Behold, I send my messenger before thy face,
who shall prepare thy way;
[3]the voice of one crying in the wilderness:
Prepare the way of the Lord,
make his paths straight—"

[4]John the baptizer appeared[c] in the wilderness, preaching a baptism of repentance for the forgiveness of sins. [5]And there went out to him all the country of Judea, and all the people of Jerusalem; and they were baptized by him in the river Jordan, confessing their sins. [6]Now John was clothed with camel's hair, and had a leather girdle around his waist, and ate locusts and wild honey. [7]And he preached, saying, "After me comes he who is mightier than I, the thong of whose sandals I am not worthy to stoop down and untie. [8]I have baptized you with water; but he will baptize you with the Holy Spirit."

9 In those days Jesus came from Nazareth of

[a] Other ancient authorities omit the Son of God
[b] Other ancient authorities read in the prophets
[c] Other ancient authorities read John was baptizing

1 Ἀρχὴ τοῦ εὐαγγελίου Ἰησοῦ Χριστοῦ.
[The] beginning of the gospel of Jesus Christ.

2 Καθὼς .γέγραπται ἐν τῷ Ἡσαΐᾳ τῷ
As it has been written in   –   Isaiah the

προφήτῃ· ἰδοὺ ἀποστέλλω τὸν ἄγγελόν μου
prophet: Behold[,] I send the messenger of me

πρὸ προσώπου σου, ὃς κατασκευάσει τὴν ὁδόν
before [the] face of thee, who will prepare the way

σου· 3 φωνὴ βοῶντος ἐν τῇ ἐρήμῳ· ἑτοιμάσατε
of thee; a voice of [one] crying in the desert: Prepare ye

τὴν ὁδὸν κυρίου, εὐθείας ποιεῖτε τὰς τρίβους
the way of [the] Lord, straight make the paths

αὐτοῦ, 4 ἐγένετο Ἰωάννης ὁ βαπτίζων ἐν τῇ
of him, came John the [one] baptizing in the

ἐρήμῳ κηρύσσων βάπτισμα μετανοίας εἰς
desert proclaiming a baptism of repentance for

ἄφεσιν ἁμαρτιῶν. 5 καὶ ἐξεπορεύετο πρὸς
forgiveness of sins. And went out to

αὐτὸν πᾶσα ἡ Ἰουδαία χώρα καὶ οἱ Ἱεροσο-
him all the Judæan country and the Jerusa-

λυμῖται πάντες, καὶ ἐβαπτίζοντο ὑπ' αὐτοῦ
lemites all, and were baptized by him

ἐν τῷ Ἰορδάνῃ ποταμῷ ἐξομολογούμενοι τὰς
in the Jordan river confessing the

ἁμαρτίας αὐτῶν. 6 καὶ ἦν ὁ Ἰωάννης
sins of them. And was – John

ἐνδεδυμένος τρίχας καμήλου καὶ ζώνην
having been clothed [in] hairs of a camel and girdle

δερματίνην περὶ τὴν ὀσφὺν αὐτοῦ, καὶ ἔσθων
a leathern round the loin[s] of him, and eating

ἀκρίδας καὶ μέλι ἄγριον. 7 καὶ ἐκήρυσσεν
locusts and honey wild. And he proclaimed

λέγων· ἔρχεται ὁ ἰσχυρότερός μου ὀπίσω
saying: Comes the [one] stronger of me after
                        = than I

[μου], οὗ οὐκ εἰμὶ ἱκανὸς κύψας λῦσαι
me, of whom I am not competent stooping to loosen

τὸν ἱμάντα τῶν ὑποδημάτων αὐτοῦ. 8 ἐγὼ
the thong of the sandals of him. I

ἐβάπτισα ὑμᾶς ὕδατι, αὐτὸς δὲ βαπτίσει ὑμᾶς
baptized you in water, but he will baptize you

πνεύματι ἁγίῳ.
Spirit in [the] Holy.

9 Καὶ ἐγένετο ἐν ἐκείναις ταῖς ἡμέραις
And it came to pass in those – days

ἦλθεν Ἰησοῦς ἀπὸ Ναζαρὲθ τῆς Γαλιλαίας
came Jesus from Nazareth – of Galilee

Galilee and was baptized by John in the Jordan. [10]And when he came up out of the water, immediately he saw the heavens opened and the Spirit descending upon him like a dove; [11]and a voice came from heaven, "Thou art my beloved Son;[d] with thee I am well pleased."

12 The Spirit immediately drove him out into the wilderness. [13]And he was in the wilderness forty days, tempted by Satan; and he was with the wild beasts; and the angels ministered to him.

14 Now after John was arrested, Jesus came into Galilee, preaching the gospel of God, [15]and saying, "The time is fulfilled, and the kingdom of God is at hand; repent and believe in the gospel."

16 And passing along by the Sea of Galilee, he saw Simon and Andrew the brother of Simon casting a net in the sea; for they were fishermen. [17]And Jesus said to them, "Follow me and I will make you become fishers of men." [18]And immed-

καὶ   ἐβαπτίσθη   εἰς   τὸν   'Ιορδάνην   ὑπὸ
and   was baptized   in   the   Jordan   by
'Ιωάννου.   10 καὶ   εὐθὺς   ἀναβαίνων   ἐκ   τοῦ
John.   And immediately   going up   out of   the
ὕδατος   εἶδεν   σχιζομένους   τοὺς   οὐρανοὺς
water   he saw   being rent   the   heavens
καὶ   τὸ   πνεῦμα   ὡς   περιστερὰν   καταβαῖνον
and   the   Spirit   as   a dove   coming down
εἰς   αὐτόν·   11 καὶ   φωνὴ   [ἐγένετο]   ἐκ   τῶν
to   him;   and   a voice   there was   out of   the
οὐρανῶν·   σὺ   εἶ   ὁ   υἱός   μου   ὁ   ἀγαπητός,
heavens: Thou art   the   Son   of me   the   beloved,
ἐν   σοὶ   εὐδόκησα.   12 Καὶ   εὐθὺς   τὸ
in   thee   I was well pleased.   And   immediately   the
πνεῦμα   αὐτὸν   ἐκβάλλει   εἰς   τὴν   ἔρημον.
Spirit   him   thrusts forth   into   the   desert.
13 καὶ   ἦν   ἐν   τῇ   ἐρήμῳ   τεσσεράκοντα
And   he was   in   the   desert   forty
ἡμέρας   πειραζόμενος   ὑπὸ   τοῦ   σατανᾶ,   καὶ
days   being tempted   by   -   Satan,   and
ἦν   μετὰ   τῶν   θηρίων,   καὶ   οἱ   ἄγγελοι
was   with   the   wild beasts,   and   the   angels
διηκόνουν   αὐτῷ.
ministered   to him.

14 Καὶ   μετὰ   τὸ   παραδοθῆναι   τὸν   -
And   after   the   to be delivered   -
      = after John was delivered
'Ιωάννην   ἦλθεν   ὁ   'Ιησοῦς   εἰς   τὴν   Γαλιλαίαν
John[b]   came   -   Jesus   into   -   Galilee
κηρύσσων   τὸ   εὐαγγέλιον   τοῦ   θεοῦ   15 [καὶ
proclaiming   the   gospel   -   of God   and
λέγων],   ὅτι   πεπλήρωται   ὁ   καιρὸς   καὶ
saying,   -   Has been fulfilled   the   time   and
ἤγγικεν   ἡ   βασιλεία   τοῦ   θεοῦ·   μετανοεῖτε
has drawn near   the   kingdom   -   of God;   repent ye
καὶ   πιστεύετε   ἐν   τῷ   εὐαγγελίῳ.   16 Καὶ
and   believe   in   the   gospel.   And
παράγων   παρὰ   τὴν   θάλασσαν   τῆς   Γαλιλαίας
passing along   beside   the   sea   -   of Galilee
εἶδεν   Σίμωνα   καὶ   'Ανδρέαν   τὸν   ἀδελφὸν
he saw   Simon   and   Andrew   the   brother
Σίμωνος   ἀμφιβάλλοντας   ἐν   τῇ   θαλάσσῃ·
of Simon   casting [a net]   in   the   sea;
ἦσαν   γὰρ   ἁλεεῖς.   17 καὶ   εἶπεν   αὐτοῖς
for they were   fishers.   And   said   to them
ὁ   'Ιησοῦς·   δεῦτε   ὀπίσω   μου,   καὶ   ποιήσω
-   Jesus: Come   after   me,   and   I will make
ὑμᾶς   γενέσθαι   ἁλεεῖς   ἀνθρώπων.   18 καὶ
you   to become   fishers   of men.   And

[d] Or my Son, my (or the) Beloved

iately they left their nets and followed him. ¹⁹And going on a little farther, he saw James the son of Zeb'edee and John his brother, who were in their boat mending the nets. ²⁰And immediately he called them; and they left their father Zeb'edee in the boat with the hired servants, and followed him.

21 And they went into Caper'na-um; and immediately on the sabbath he entered the synagogue and taught. ²²And they were astonished at his teaching, for he taught them as one who had authority, and not as the scribes. ²³And immediately there was in their synagogue a man with an unclean spirit; ²⁴and he cried out, "What have you to do with us, Jesus of Nazareth? Have you come to destroy us? I know who you are, the Holy One of God." ²⁵But Jesus rebuked him, saying, "Be silent, and come out of him!" ²⁶And the unclean spirit, convulsing him and crying with a loud voice, came out of him. ²⁷And they were all amazed, so that

εὐθὺς ἀφέντες τὰ δίκτυα ἠκολούθησαν
immediately leaving the nets they followed
αὐτῷ. 19 Καὶ προβὰς ὀλίγον εἶδεν
him. And going forward a little he saw
Ἰάκωβον τὸν τοῦ Ζεβεδαίου καὶ Ἰωάννην
James the [son] of Zebedee and John
τὸν ἀδελφὸν αὐτοῦ καὶ αὐτοὺς ἐν τῷ
the brother of him even them in the
πλοίῳ καταρτίζοντας τὰ δίκτυα. 20 καὶ
ship mending the nets. And
εὐθὺς ἐκάλεσεν αὐτούς· καὶ ἀφέντες τὸν
immediately he called them; and leaving the
πατέρα αὐτῶν Ζεβεδαῖον ἐν τῷ πλοίῳ
father of them Zebedee in the ship
μετὰ τῶν μισθωτῶν ἀπῆλθον ὀπίσω αὐτοῦ.
with the hired servants they went after him.
21 Καὶ εἰσπορεύονται εἰς Καφαρναούμ·
And they enter into Capernaum;
καὶ εὐθὺς τοῖς σάββασιν εἰσελθὼν
and immediately on the sabbaths entering
εἰς τὴν συναγωγὴν ἐδίδασκεν. 22 καὶ
into the synagogue he taught. And
ἐξεπλήσσοντο ἐπὶ τῇ διδαχῇ αὐτοῦ· ἦν
they were astounded on(at) the teaching of him; ᵏhe was
γὰρ διδάσκων αὐτοὺς ὡς ἐξουσίαν ἔχων,
¹for teaching them as authority having,
καὶ οὐχ ὡς οἱ γραμματεῖς. 23 Καὶ εὐθὺς
and not as the scribes. And immediately
ἦν ἐν τῇ συναγωγῇ αὐτῶν ἄνθρωπος
there was in the synagogue of them a man
ἐν πνεύματι ἀκαθάρτῳ, καὶ ἀνέκραξεν
in spirit an unclean, and he cried out
24 λέγων· τί ἡμῖν καὶ σοί, Ἰησοῦ
saying: What to us and to thee, Jesus
Ναζαρηνέ; ἦλθες ἀπολέσαι ἡμᾶς; οἶδά
Nazarene? camest thou to destroy us? I know
σε τίς εἶ, ὁ ἅγιος τοῦ θεοῦ. 25 καὶ
thee who thou art, the holy [one] - of God. And
ἐπετίμησεν αὐτῷ ὁ Ἰησοῦς [λέγων]·
rebuked him - Jesus saying:
φιμώθητι καὶ ἔξελθε [ἐξ αὐτοῦ]. 26 καὶ
Be quiet and come out out of him. And
σπαράξαν αὐτὸν τὸ πνεῦμα τὸ ἀκάθαρτον
throwing him the spirit - unclean
καὶ φωνῆσαν φωνῇ μεγάλῃ ἐξῆλθεν ἐξ
and shouting voice with a great he came out out of
αὐτοῦ. 27 καὶ ἐθαμβήθησαν ἅπαντες, ὥστε
him. And were astounded all, so as
= so that

they questioned among themselves, saying, "What is this? A new teaching! With authority he commands even the unclean spirits, and they obey him." [28]And at once his fame spread everywhere throughout all the surrounding region of Galilee.

29 And immediately he[e] left the synagogue, and entered the house of Simon and Andrew, with James and John. [30]Now Simon's mother-in-law lay sick with a fever, and immediately they told him of her. [31]And he came and took her by the hand and lifted her up, and the fever left her; and she served them.

32 That evening, at sundown, they brought to him all who were sick or possessed with demons. [33]And the whole city was gathered together about the door. [34]And he healed many who were sick with various diseases, and cast out many demons; and he would not permit the demons to speak, because they knew him.

35 And in the morning, a great while before day, he rose and went out

συζητεῖν αὐτοὺς λέγοντας· τί ἐστιν τοῦτο;
to debate them[b] saying: What is this?
they debated

διδαχὴ καινὴ κατ' ἐξουσίαν· καὶ τοῖς
teaching a new by authority; and the

πνεύμασι τοῖς ἀκαθάρτοις ἐπιτάσσει, καὶ
spirits   – unclean he commands, and

ὑπακούουσιν αὐτῷ. 28 καὶ ἐξῆλθεν ἡ
they obey him.   And went forth the

ἀκοὴ αὐτοῦ εὐθὺς πανταχοῦ εἰς ὅλην
report of him immediately everywhere into all

τὴν περίχωρον τῆς Γαλιλαίας. 29 Καὶ
the neighbourhood – of Galilee.   And

εὐθὺς ἐκ τῆς συναγωγῆς ἐξελθόντες ἦλθον
immediately out of the synagogue going forth they came

εἰς τὴν οἰκίαν Σίμωνος καὶ Ἀνδρέου
into the house of Simon and Andrew

μετὰ Ἰακώβου καὶ Ἰωάννου. 30 ἡ δὲ
with James and John.   Now the

πενθερὰ Σίμωνος κατέκειτο πυρέσσουσα,
mother-in-law of Simon was laid [aside] fever-stricken,

καὶ εὐθὺς λέγουσιν αὐτῷ περὶ αὐτῆς.
and immediately they tell him about her.

31 καὶ προσελθὼν ἤγειρεν αὐτὴν κρατήσας
And approaching he raised her holding

τῆς χειρός· καὶ ἀφῆκεν αὐτὴν ὁ πυρετός,
the(her) hand; and left her the fever,

καὶ διηκόνει αὐτοῖς. 32 Ὀψίας δὲ γενο-
and she served them.   And evening com-
                            = when evening

μένης, ὅτε ἔδυσεν ὁ ἥλιος, ἔφερον πρὸς
ing,[a] when set the sun, they brought to
came,

αὐτὸν πάντας τοὺς κακῶς ἔχοντας καὶ
him all the [ones] ill having and
            = those who were ill

τοὺς δαιμονιζομένους· 33 καὶ ἦν ὅλη ἡ
the being demon-possessed; and was all the

πόλις ἐπισυνηγμένη πρὸς τὴν θύραν.
city having been assembled at the door.

34 καὶ ἐθεράπευσεν πολλοὺς κακῶς ἔχοντας
And he healed many ill having
                           = who were ill

ποικίλαις νόσοις, καὶ δαιμόνια πολλὰ
with various diseases, and demons many

ἐξέβαλεν, καὶ οὐκ ἤφιεν λαλεῖν τὰ δαιμόνια,
he expelled, and did not allow to speak the demons,

ὅτι ᾔδεισαν αὐτόν. 35 Καὶ πρωῒ ἔννυχα
because they knew him.   And [2]early [4]in the night

λίαν ἀναστὰς ἐξῆλθεν καὶ ἀπῆλθεν εἰς
[3]very [1]rising up he went out and went away to

[e] Other ancient authorities read they

to a lonely place, and there he prayed. And Simon and those who were with him followed him, [37]and they found him and said to him, "Every one is searching for you." [38]And he said to them, "Let us go on to the next towns, that I may preach there also; for that is why I came out." [39]And he went throughout all Galilee, preaching in their synagogues and casting out demons.

40 And a leper came to him beseeching him, and kneeling said to him, "If you will, you can make me clean." [41]Moved with pity, he stretched out his hand and touched him, and said to him, "I will; be clean." [42]And immediately the leprosy left him, and he was made clean. [43]And he sternly charged him, and sent him away at once, [44]and said to him, "See that you say nothing to any one; but go, show yourself to the priest, and offer for your cleansing what Moses commanded, for a proof to the people." [45]But he went out and began to talk freely about it, and to spread the news, so that

ἔρημον τόπον, κἀκεῖ προσηύχετο. 36 καὶ
a desert place, and there prayed. And

κατεδίωξεν αὐτὸν Σίμων καὶ οἱ μετ᾽
hunted down him Simon and the [ones] with

αὐτοῦ, καὶ εὗρον αὐτὸν καὶ λέγουσιν
him, and found him and say

αὐτῷ 37 ὅτι πάντες ζητοῦσίν σε. 38 καὶ
to him[,] – All are seeking thee. And

λέγει αὐτοῖς· ἄγωμεν ἀλλαχοῦ εἰς τὰς
he says to them: Let us go elsewhere into the

ἐχομένας κωμοπόλεις, ἵνα καὶ ἐκεῖ
neighbouring towns, that also there

κηρύξω· εἰς τοῦτο γὰρ ἐξῆλθον. 39 καὶ
I may proclaim; for for this [purpose] I came forth. And

ἦλθεν κηρύσσων εἰς τὰς συναγωγὰς αὐτῶν
he came proclaiming in the synagogues of them

εἰς ὅλην τὴν Γαλιλαίαν καὶ τὰ δαιμόνια
in all – Galilee and the demons

ἐκβάλλων.
expelling.

40 Καὶ ἔρχεται πρὸς αὐτὸν λεπρὸς
And comes to him a leper

παρακαλῶν αὐτὸν καὶ γονυπετῶν λέγων
beseeching him and falling on [his] knees saying

αὐτῷ ὅτι ἐὰν θέλῃς δύνασαί με καθαρίσαι.
to him[,] – If thou art willing thou art able me to cleanse.

41 καὶ σπλαγχνισθεὶς ἐκτείνας τὴν
And being filled with tenderness stretching forth the (his)

χεῖρα αὐτοῦ ἥψατο καὶ λέγει αὐτῷ· θέλω,
hand ¹him ¹he touched and says to him: I am willing,

καθαρίσθητι. 42 καὶ εὐθὺς ἀπῆλθεν ἀπ᾽
be thou cleansed. And immediately departed from

αὐτοῦ ἡ λέπρα, καὶ ἐκαθαρίσθη. 43 καὶ
him the leprosy, and he was cleansed. And

ἐμβριμησάμενος αὐτῷ εὐθὺς ἐξέβαλεν αὐτόν,
sternly admonishing him immediately he put out him,

44 καὶ λέγει αὐτῷ· ὅρα μηδενὶ μηδὲν
and says to him: See no one no(any)thing

εἴπῃς, ἀλλὰ ὕπαγε σεαυτὸν δεῖξον τῷ
thou tellest, but go thyself show to the

ἱερεῖ καὶ προσένεγκε περὶ τοῦ καθαρισμοῦ σου
priest and offer concerning the cleansing of thee

ἃ προσέταξεν Μωϋσῆς, εἰς μαρτύριον
[the things] which commanded Moses, for a testimony

αὐτοῖς. 45 ὁ δὲ ἐξελθὼν ἤρξατο κηρύσσειν
to them. But he going out began to proclaim

πολλὰ καὶ διαφημίζειν τὸν λόγον, ὥστε
many things and to spread about the matter, = so that

Jesus could no longer openly enter a town, but was out in the country; and people came to him from every quarter.

μηκέτι αὐτὸν δύνασθαι φανερῶς εἰς πόλιν
no longer him to be able[b] openly into a city
εἰσελθεῖν, ἀλλ' ἔξω ἐπ' ἐρήμοις τόποις
to enter, but outside on(in) desert places
ἦν· καὶ ἤρχοντο πρὸς αὐτὸν πάντοθεν.
he was; and they came to him from all directions.

CHAPTER 2

AND when he returned to Caper'na-um after some days, it was reported that he was at home. [2]And many were gathered together, so that there was no longer room for them, not even about the door; and he was preaching the word to them. [3]And they came, bringing to him a paralytic carried by four men. [4]And when they could not get near him because of the crowd, they removed the roof above him; and when they had made an opening, they let down the pallet on which the paralytic lay. [5]And when Jesus saw their faith, he said to the paralytic, "My son, your sins are forgiven." [6]Now some of the scribes were sitting there, questioning in their hearts, [7]"Why does this man speak thus? It is blasphemy! Who can forgive sins but God alone?" [8]And immediately Jesus, perceiving in his spirit that they thus questioned within themselves, said to them,

2 Καὶ εἰσελθὼν πάλιν εἰς Καφαρναοὺμ
And entering again into Capernaum
δι' ἡμερῶν ἠκούσθη ὅτι ἐν οἴκῳ ἐστίν.
through days it was heard that at home he is(was).
= after [some] days
2 καὶ συνήχθησαν πολλοί, ὥστε μηκέτι
And were assembled many, so as no longer
χωρεῖν μηδὲ τὰ πρὸς τὴν θύραν, καὶ
to have room not - at the door, and
ἐλάλει αὐτοῖς τὸν λόγον. 3 καὶ ἔρχονται
he spoke to them the word. And they come
φέροντες πρὸς αὐτὸν παραλυτικὸν αἰρόμενον
carrying to him a paralytic being borne
ὑπὸ τεσσάρων. 4 καὶ μὴ δυνάμενοι
by four [men]. And not being able
προσενέγκαι αὐτῷ διὰ τὸν ὄχλον
to bring to him because of the crowd
ἀπεστέγασαν τὴν στέγην ὅπου ἦν, καὶ
they unroofed the roof where he was, and
ἐξορύξαντες χαλῶσι τὸν κράβατον ὅπου ὁ
having opened up they lower the mattress where the
παραλυτικὸς κατέκειτο. 5 καὶ ἰδὼν ὁ
paralytic was lying. And seeing -
Ἰησοῦς τὴν πίστιν αὐτῶν λέγει τῷ
Jesus the faith of them he says to the
παραλυτικῷ· τέκνον, ἀφίενταί σου αἱ
paralytic: Child, are forgiven of thee the
ἁμαρτίαι. 6 ἦσαν δέ τινες τῶν γραμματέων
sins. Now there were some of the scribes
ἐκεῖ καθήμενοι καὶ διαλογιζόμενοι ἐν ταῖς
there sitting and reasoning in the
καρδίαις αὐτῶν· 7 τί οὗτος οὕτως λαλεῖ;
hearts of them: Why this [man] thus speaks?
βλασφημεῖ· τίς δύναται ἀφιέναι ἁμαρτίας
he blasphemes; who can to forgive sins
εἰ μὴ εἷς ὁ θεός; 8 καὶ εὐθὺς ἐπιγνοὺς
except one[,] - God? And immediately knowing
ὁ Ἰησοῦς τῷ πνεύματι αὐτοῦ ὅτι οὕτως
- Jesus in the spirit of him that thus
διαλογίζονται ἐν ἑαυτοῖς, λέγει αὐτοῖς·
they reason among themselves, he says to them:

"Why do you question thus in your hearts? 9 Which is easier, to say to the paralytic, 'Your sins are forgiven,' or to say, 'Rise, take up your pallet and walk'? 10 But that you may know that the Son of man has authority on earth to forgive sins"—he said to the paralytic—11 "I say to you, rise, take up your pallet and go home." 12 And he rose, and immediately took up the pallet and went out before them all; so that they were all amazed and glorified God, saying, "We never saw anything like this!"

13 He went out again beside the sea; and all the crowd gathered about him, and he taught them. 14 And as he passed on, he saw Levi the son of Alphaeus sitting at the tax office, and he said to him, "Follow me." And he rose and followed him.

15 And as he sat at table in his house, many tax collectors and sinners were sitting with Jesus

τί ταῦτα διαλογίζεσθε ἐν ταῖς καρδίαις
Why these things reason ye in the hearts
ὑμῶν; 9 τί ἐστιν εὐκοπώτερον, εἰπεῖν
of you? What is easier, to say
τῷ παραλυτικῷ· ἀφίενταί σου αἱ ἁμαρτίαι,
to the paralytic: are forgiven of thee the sins,
ἢ εἰπεῖν· ἔγειρε καὶ ἆρον τὸν κράβατόν
or to say: Rise and take the mattress
σου καὶ περιπάτει; 10 ἵνα δὲ εἰδῆτε
of thee and walk? But that ye may know
ὅτι ἐξουσίαν ἔχει ὁ υἱὸς τοῦ ἀνθρώπου
that authority has the Son - of man
ἀφιέναι ἁμαρτίας ἐπὶ τῆς γῆς,—λέγει τῷ
to forgive sins on the earth,—he says to the
παραλυτικῷ· 11 σοὶ λέγω, ἔγειρε ἆρον
paralytic: To thee I say, rise[,] take
τὸν κράβατόν σου καὶ ὕπαγε εἰς τὸν
the mattress of thee and go to the
οἶκόν σου. 12 καὶ ἠγέρθη καὶ εὐθὺς
house of thee. And he arose and immediately
ἄρας τὸν κράβατον ἐξῆλθεν ἔμπροσθεν
taking the mattress he went forth before
πάντων, ὥστε ἐξίστασθαι πάντας καὶ
all, so as to be astonished all and
= so that they were all astonished and glorified
δοξάζειν τὸν θεὸν λέγοντας ὅτι οὕτως
to glorify[b] - God saying[,] - Thus
οὐδέποτε εἴδαμεν.
never we saw.

13 Καὶ ἐξῆλθεν πάλιν παρὰ τὴν θάλασσαν·
And he went forth again by the sea;
καὶ πᾶς ὁ ὄχλος ἤρχετο πρὸς αὐτόν,
and all the crowd came to him,
καὶ ἐδίδασκεν αὐτούς. 14 Καὶ παράγων
and he taught them. And passing along
εἶδεν Λευὶν τὸν τοῦ Ἀλφαίου καθήμενον
he saw Levi the [son] - Alphæus sitting
ἐπὶ τὸ τελώνιον, καὶ λέγει αὐτῷ· ἀκολούθει
on(in or at)the custom house, and says to him: Follow
μοι. καὶ ἀναστὰς ἠκολούθησεν αὐτῷ.
me. And rising up he followed him.
15 Καὶ γίνεται κατακεῖσθαι αὐτὸν ἐν τῇ
And it comes to pass to recline him[b] in the
= he reclines
οἰκίᾳ αὐτοῦ, καὶ πολλοὶ τελῶναι καὶ
house of him, and many tax-collectors and
ἁμαρτωλοὶ συνανέκειντο τῷ Ἰησοῦ καὶ
sinners reclined with - Jesus and

and his disciples; for there were many who followed him. ¹⁶And the scribes of^f the Pharisees, when they saw that he was eating with sinners and tax collectors, said to his disciples, "Why does he eat^g with tax collectors and sinners?" ¹⁷And when Jesus heard it, he said to them, "Those who are well have no need of a physician, but those who are sick; I came not to call the righteous, but sinners."

18 Now John's disciples and the Pharisees were fasting; and people came and said to him, "Why do John's disciples and the disciples of the Pharisees fast, but your disciples do not fast?" ¹⁹And Jesus said to them, "Can the wedding guests fast while the bridegroom is with them? As long as they have the bridegroom with them, they cannot fast. ²⁰The days will come, when the bridegroom is taken away from them, and then they will fast in that day. ²¹No one sews a piece of unshrunk cloth on an old garment; if he does, the

---

τοῖς μαθηταῖς αὐτοῦ· ἦσαν γὰρ πολλοί,
the   disciples   of him; for there were many,

καὶ ἠκολούθουν αὐτῷ. 16 καὶ οἱ γραμματεῖς
and they followed him.   And the   scribes

τῶν Φαρισαίων ἰδόντες ὅτι ἐσθίει
of the Pharisees seeing that he eats(ate)

μετὰ τῶν ἁμαρτωλῶν καὶ τελωνῶν ἔλεγον
with   –   sinners and tax-collectors said

τοῖς μαθηταῖς αὐτοῦ· ὅτι μετὰ τῶν
to the disciples of him: – With –

τελωνῶν καὶ ἁμαρτωλῶν ἐσθίει; 17 καὶ
tax-collectors and sinners does he eat? And

ἀκούσας ὁ Ἰησοῦς λέγει αὐτοῖς [ὅτι] οὐ
hearing – Jesus says to them[,] – Not

χρείαν ἔχουσιν οἱ ἰσχύοντες ἰατροῦ ἀλλ'
need   have the [ones] being strong of a physician but

οἱ κακῶς ἔχοντες· οὐκ ἦλθον καλέσαι
the [ones] ill having; I came not to call
= those who are ill;

δικαίους ἀλλὰ ἁμαρτωλούς. 18 Καὶ ἦσαν
righteous men but sinners.   And ⁷were

οἱ μαθηταὶ Ἰωάννου καὶ οἱ Φαρισαῖοι
¹the ²disciples ³of John ⁴and ⁵the ⁶Pharisees

νηστεύοντες. καὶ ἔρχονται καὶ λέγουσιν
⁸fasting. And they come and say

αὐτῷ· διὰ τί οἱ μαθηταὶ Ἰωάννου καὶ
to him: Why the disciples of John and

οἱ μαθηταὶ τῶν Φαρισαίων νηστεύουσιν,
the disciples of the Pharisees fast,

οἱ δὲ σοὶ μαθηταὶ οὐ νηστεύουσιν; 19 καὶ
– but thy disciples do not fast? And

εἶπεν αὐτοῖς ὁ Ἰησοῦς· μὴ δύνανται οἱ
said to them – Jesus: not can the

υἱοὶ τοῦ νυμφῶνος, ἐν ᾧ ὁ νυμφίος
sons of the bridechamber, while† the bridegroom

μετ' αὐτῶν ἐστιν, νηστεύειν; ὅσον χρόνον
with them is, to fast? what time

ἔχουσιν τὸν νυμφίον μετ' αὐτῶν, οὐ
they have the bridegroom with them, not

δύνανται νηστεύειν. 20 ἐλεύσονται δὲ ἡμέραι
they can to fast. But will come days

ὅταν ἀπαρθῇ ἀπ' αὐτῶν ὁ νυμφίος, καὶ
when taken away from them the bridegroom, and

τότε νηστεύσουσιν ἐν ἐκείνῃ τῇ ἡμέρᾳ.
then they will fast in that – day.

21 Οὐδεὶς ἐπίβλημα ῥάκους ἀγνάφου ἐπιράπτει
No one a patch cloth of unfulled sews

ἐπὶ ἱμάτιον παλαιόν· εἰ δὲ μή, αἴρει
on garment an old; otherwise, ²takes

---

^f Other ancient authorities read *and*
^g Other ancient authorities add *and drink*

patch tears away from it, the new from the old, and a worse tear is made. ²²And no one puts new wine into old wineskins; if he does, the wine will burst the skins, and the wine is lost, and so are the skins; but new wine is for fresh skins."[h]

23 One sabbath he was going through the grainfields; and as they made their way his disciples began to pluck ears of grain. ²⁴And the Pharisees said to him, "Look, why are they doing what is not lawful on the sabbath?" ²⁵And he said to them, "Have you never read what David did, when he was in need and was hungry, he and those who were with him: ²⁶how he entered the house of God, when Abi'athar was high priest, and ate the bread of the Presence, which it is not lawful for any but the priests to eat, and also gave it to those who were with him?" ²⁷And he said to them, "The sabbath was made for man, not man for the sabbath; ²⁸so the Son of man is lord even of the sabbath."

τὸ πλήρωμα ἀπ' αὐτοῦ τὸ καινὸν τοῦ
⁴the ⁵fulness ⁶from ⁹itself ¹the ⁸new ⁷the
παλαιοῦ, καὶ χεῖρον σχίσμα γίνεται. 22 καὶ
⁸old, and a worse rent occurs. And
οὐδεὶς βάλλει οἶνον νέον εἰς ἀσκοὺς παλαιούς·
no one puts wine new into wineskins old;
εἰ δὲ μή, ῥήξει ὁ οἶνος τοὺς ἀσκούς,
otherwise, ³will burst ¹the ²wine the wineskins,
καὶ ὁ οἶνος ἀπόλλυται καὶ οἱ ἀσκοί.
and the wine perishes and the wineskins.
[ἀλλὰ οἶνον νέον εἰς ἀσκοὺς καινούς.]
But wine new into wineskins fresh.
23 Καὶ ἐγένετο αὐτὸν ἐν τοῖς σάββασιν
And it came to pass him on the sabbaths
= as he passed on the sabbath
παραπορεύεσθαι διὰ τῶν σπορίμων, καὶ
to pass[b] through the cornfields, and
οἱ μαθηταὶ αὐτοῦ ἤρξαντο ὁδὸν ποιεῖν
the disciples of him began way to make
τίλλοντες τοὺς στάχυας. 24 καὶ οἱ Φαρισαῖοι
plucking the ears of corn. And the Pharisees
ἔλεγον αὐτῷ· ἴδε τί ποιοῦσιν τοῖς σάββασιν
said to him: Behold[,] why do on the sabbaths
ὃ οὐκ ἔξεστιν; 25 καὶ λέγει αὐτοῖς·
what is not lawful? And he says to them:
οὐδέποτε ἀνέγνωτε τί ἐποίησεν Δαυίδ,
never read ye what did David,
ὅτε χρείαν ἔσχεν καὶ ἐπείνασεν αὐτὸς
when need he had and hungered he
καὶ οἱ μετ' αὐτοῦ; 26 [πῶς] εἰσῆλθεν
and the [ones] with him? how he entered
εἰς τὸν οἶκον τοῦ θεοῦ ἐπὶ 'Αβιαθὰρ
into the house – of God on(in the days of) Abiathar
ἀρχιερέως καὶ τοὺς ἄρτους τῆς προθέσεως
high priest and the loaves of the setting forth
ἔφαγεν, οὓς οὐκ ἔξεστιν φαγεῖν εἰ μὴ
ate, which it is not lawful to eat except
τοὺς ἱερεῖς, καὶ ἔδωκεν καὶ τοῖς σὺν
the priests, and gave also to the [ones] with
αὐτῷ οὖσιν; 27 καὶ ἔλεγεν αὐτοῖς·
him being? And he said to them:
τὸ σάββατον διὰ τὸν ἄνθρωπον ἐγένετο,
The sabbath on account of – man was,
καὶ οὐχ ὁ ἄνθρωπος διὰ τὸ σάββατον·
and not – man on account of the sabbath;
28 ὥστε κύριός ἐστιν ὁ υἱὸς τοῦ ἀνθρώπου
so as Lord is the Son – of man
καὶ τοῦ σαββάτου.
also of the sabbath.

[h] Other ancient authorities omit *but new wine is for fresh skins*

CHAPTER 3

AGAIN he entered the synagogue, and a man was there who had a withered hand. ²And they watched him, to see whether he would heal him on the sabbath, so that they might accuse him. ³And he said to the man who had the withered hand, "Come here." ⁴And he said to them, "Is it lawful on the sabbath to do good or to do harm, to save life or to kill?" But they were silent. ⁵And he looked around at them with anger, grieved at their hardness of heart, and said to the man, "Stretch out your hand." He stretched it out, and his hand was restored. ⁶The Pharisees went out, and immediately held counsel with the Hero'di-ans against him, how to destroy him.

7 Jesus withdrew with his disciples to the sea, and a great multitude from Galilee followed; also from Judea ⁸and Jerusalem and Idume'a and from beyond the Jordan and from about Tyre and Sidon a great multitude, hearing all

---

3 Καὶ εἰσῆλθεν πάλιν εἰς συναγωγήν.
And he entered again into a synagogue.

καὶ ἦν ἐκεῖ ἄνθρωπος ἐξηραμμένην ἔχων
And there was there a man ⁴having been withered ¹having

τὴν χεῖρα· **2** καὶ παρετήρουν αὐτὸν εἰ
²the ³hand; and they watched carefully him if

τοῖς σάββασιν θεραπεύσει αὐτόν, ἵνα
on the sabbaths he will heal him, that

κατηγορήσωσιν αὐτοῦ. **3** καὶ λέγει τῷ
they might accuse him. And he says to the

ἀνθρώπῳ τῷ τὴν χεῖρα ἔχοντι ξηράν·
man - the hand having dry:

ἔγειρε εἰς τὸ μέσον. **4** καὶ λέγει αὐτοῖς·
Rise into the midst. And he says to them:

ἔξεστιν τοῖς σάββασιν ἀγαθὸν ποιῆσαι
Lawful on the sabbaths good to do

ἢ κακοποιῆσαι, ψυχὴν σῶσαι ἢ ἀποκτεῖναι;
or to do evil, life to save or to kill ?

οἱ δὲ ἐσιώπων. **5** καὶ περιβλεψάμενος
But they were silent. And looking round

αὐτοὺς μετ' ὀργῆς, συλλυπούμενος ἐπὶ
[on] them with anger, being greatly grieved on(at)

τῇ πωρώσει τῆς καρδίας αὐτῶν, λέγει
the hardness of the heart of them, he says

τῷ ἀνθρώπῳ· ἔκτεινον τὴν χεῖρα. καὶ
to the man: Stretch forth the hand. And

ἐξέτεινεν, καὶ ἀπεκατεστάθη ἡ χεὶρ αὐτοῦ.
he stretched forth, and was restored the hand of him.

6 καὶ ἐξελθόντες οἱ Φαρισαῖοι εὐθὺς μετὰ
And going forth the Pharisees immediately with

τῶν Ἡρῳδιανῶν συμβούλιον ἐδίδουν κατ'
the Herodians counsel gave against

αὐτοῦ, ὅπως αὐτὸν ἀπολέσωσιν.
him, that him they might destroy.

7 Καὶ ὁ Ἰησοῦς μετὰ τῶν μαθητῶν
And - Jesus with the disciples

αὐτοῦ ἀνεχώρησεν πρὸς τὴν θάλασσαν·
of him departed to the sea;

καὶ πολὺ πλῆθος ἀπὸ τῆς Γαλιλαίας
and a much(great) multitude from - Galilee

ἠκολούθησεν· καὶ ἀπὸ τῆς Ἰουδαίας **8** καὶ
followed; and from - Judæa and

ἀπὸ Ἱεροσολύμων καὶ ἀπὸ τῆς Ἰδουμαίας
from Jerusalem and from - Idumæa

καὶ πέραν τοῦ Ἰορδάνου καὶ περὶ Τύρον
and beyond the Jordan and round Tyre

καὶ Σιδῶνα, πλῆθος πολύ, ἀκούοντες ὅσα
and Sidon, multitude a much(great), hearing what things

that he did, came to him. ⁹And he told his disciples to have a boat ready for him because of the crowd, lest they should crush him; ¹⁰so that all who had diseases pressed upon him to touch him ¹¹And whenever the unclean spirits beheld him, they fell down before him and cried out, "You are the Son of God." ¹²And he strictly ordered them not to make him known.

13 And he went up into the hills, and called to him those whom he desired; and they came to him. ¹⁴And he appointed twelve,ⁱ to be with him, and to be sent out to preach ¹⁵and have authority to cast out demons: ¹⁶Simon whom he surnamed Peter; ¹⁷James the son of Zeb'-edee and John the brother of James, whom he surnamed Bo-aner'ges, that is, sons of thunder; ¹⁸Andrew, and Philip, and Bartholomew, and Matthew, and Thomas, and James the son of Alphaeus, and Thaddaeus, and Simon the

ⁱ Other ancient authorities add *whom also he named apostles*

ποιεῖ, ἦλθον πρὸς αὐτόν. 9 καὶ εἶπεν
he does, came to him. And he told

τοῖς μαθηταῖς αὐτοῦ ἵνα πλοιάριον προσκαρτερῇ
the disciples of him that a boat should remain near

αὐτῷ διὰ τὸν ὄχλον, ἵνα μὴ θλίβωσιν
him because of the crowd, lest they should press upon

αὐτόν· 10 πολλοὺς γὰρ ἐθεράπευσεν, ὥστε
him; for many he healed, so as

ἐπιπίπτειν αὐτῷ ἵνα αὐτοῦ ἅψωνται
to fall upon him that him they might touch

ὅσοι εἶχον μάστιγας. 11 καὶ τὰ πνεύματα
as many as had plagues. And the spirits

τὰ ἀκάθαρτα, ὅταν αὐτὸν ἐθεώρουν, προσέπιπτον
- unclean, when him they saw, fell before

αὐτῷ καὶ ἔκραζον λέγοντα ὅτι σὺ εἶ ὁ
him and cried out saying[,] – Thou art the

υἱὸς τοῦ θεοῦ. 12 καὶ πολλὰ ἐπετίμα
Son – of God. And much he warned

αὐτοῖς ἵνα μὴ αὐτὸν φανερὸν ποιήσωσιν.
them that not him manifest they should make.

13 Καὶ ἀναβαίνει εἰς τὸ ὄρος, καὶ
And he goes up into the mountain, and

προσκαλεῖται οὓς ἤθελεν αὐτός, καὶ
calls to [him] [those] whom wished he, and

ἀπῆλθον πρὸς αὐτόν. 14 καὶ ἐποίησεν δώδεκα
they went to him. And he made twelve

ἵνα ὦσιν μετ' αὐτοῦ, καὶ ἵνα ἀποστέλλῃ
that they might be with him, and that he might send

αὐτοὺς κηρύσσειν 15 καὶ ἔχειν ἐξουσίαν
them to proclaim and to have authority

ἐκβάλλειν τὰ δαιμόνια· 16 καὶ ἐποίησεν
to expel the demons; and he made

τοὺς δώδεκα, καὶ ἐπέθηκεν ὄνομα τῷ
the twelve, and he added a name to

Σίμωνι Πέτρον· 17 καὶ Ἰάκωβον τὸν τοῦ
to Simon[,] Peter; and James the [son] –

Ζεβεδαίου καὶ Ἰωάννην τὸν ἀδελφὸν τοῦ
of Zebedee and John the brother –

Ἰακώβου, καὶ ἐπέθηκεν αὐτοῖς ὄνομα
of James, and he added to them a name[,]

Βοανηργές, ὃ ἐστιν υἱοὶ βροντῆς· 18 καὶ
Boanerges, which is sons of thunder; and

Ἀνδρέαν καὶ Φίλιππον καὶ Βαρθολομαῖον
Andrew and Philip and Bartholomew

καὶ Μαθθαῖον καὶ Θωμᾶν καὶ Ἰάκωβον
and Matthew and Thomas and James

τὸν τοῦ Ἀλφαίου καὶ Θαδδαῖον καὶ
the [son] – of Alphæus and Thaddæus and

Cananaean, ¹⁹and Judas Iscariot, who betrayed him.

Then he went home; ²⁰and the crowd came together again, so that they could not even eat. ²¹And when his friends heard it, they went out to seize him, for they said, "He is beside himself." ²²And the scribes who came down from Jerusalem said, "He is possessed by Be-el′zebul, and by the prince of demons he casts out the demons." ²³And he called them to him, and said to them in parables, "How can Satan cast out Satan? ²⁴If a kingdom is divided against itself, that kingdom cannot stand. ²⁵And if a house is divided against itself, that house will not be able to stand. ²⁶And if Satan has risen up against himself and is divided, he cannot stand, but is coming to an end. ²⁷But no one can enter a strong man's house and plunder his goods, unless he first binds the strong man; then indeed he may plunder his house.

28 "Truly, I say to you, all sins will be

Σίμωνα   τὸν   Καναναῖον   19 καὶ   Ἰούδαν
Simon   the   Cananæan   and   Judas

Ἰσκαριώθ,   ὃς   καὶ   παρέδωκεν   αὐτόν.
Iscariot,   who indeed   betrayed   him.

20 Καὶ   ἔρχεται   εἰς   οἶκον·   καὶ   συνέρχεται
And   he comes   into a house;   and   comes together

πάλιν   [ὁ]   ὄχλος,   ὥστε   μὴ   δύνασθαι
again   the   crowd,   so as   not   to be able
                                              = so that they were not able

αὐτοὺς   μηδὲ   ἄρτον   φαγεῖν.   21 καὶ   ἀκούσαντες
them[b]   not   bread   to eat.   And   hearing

οἱ   παρ'   αὐτοῦ   ἐξῆλθον   κρατῆσαι   αὐτόν·
the[ones] with   him   went forth   to seize   him;
= his relations

ἔλεγον   γὰρ   ὅτι   ἐξέστη.   22 καὶ   οἱ
for they said[,]   –   He is beside himself.   And   the

γραμματεῖς   οἱ   ἀπὸ   Ἱεροσολύμων   καταβάντες
scribes   –   from   Jerusalem   coming down

ἔλεγον   ὅτι   Βεεζεβοὺλ   ἔχει,   καὶ   ὅτι   ἐν
said[,]   –   Beelzebub   he has,   and[,]   –   By

τῷ   ἄρχοντι   τῶν   δαιμονίων   ἐκβάλλει   τὰ
the   ruler   of the   demons   he expels   the

δαιμόνια.   23 καὶ   προσκαλεσάμενος   αὐτοὺς
demons.   And   calling to [him]   them

ἐν   παραβολαῖς   ἔλεγεν   αὐτοῖς·   πῶς   δύναται
in   parables   he said   to them: How   can

σατανᾶς   σατανᾶν   ἐκβάλλειν;   24 καὶ   ἐὰν
Satan   ¹Satan   ¹to expel ?   and   if

βασιλεία   ἐφ'   ἑαυτὴν   μερισθῇ,   οὐ   δύναται
a kingdom   against   itself   be divided,   cannot

σταθῆναι   ἡ   βασιλεία   ἐκείνη·   25 καὶ   ἐὰν
stand   –   kingdom   that;   and   if

οἰκία   ἐφ'   ἑαυτὴν   μερισθῇ,   οὐ   δυνήσεται
a house   against   itself   be divided,   will not be able

ἡ   οἰκία   ἐκείνη   στῆναι.   26 καὶ   εἰ   ὁ
–   house   that   to stand.   And   if   –

σατανᾶς   ἀνέστη   ἐφ'   ἑαυτὸν   καὶ   ἐμερίσθη,
Satan   stood up   against   himself   and   was divided,

οὐ   δύναται   στῆναι   ἀλλὰ   τέλος   ἔχει.
he cannot   to stand   but   an end   has.

27 ἀλλ'   οὐ   δύναται   οὐδεὶς   εἰς   τὴν   οἰκίαν
But   cannot   no(any)one   into   the   house

τοῦ   ἰσχυροῦ   εἰσελθὼν   τὰ   σκεύη   αὐτοῦ
of the   strong man   entering   the   goods   of him

διαρπάσαι,   ἐὰν   μὴ   πρῶτον   τὸν   ἰσχυρὸν
to plunder,   unless   first   the   strong man

δήσῃ,   καὶ   τότε   τὴν   οἰκίαν   αὐτοῦ   διαρπάσει.
he bind,   and   then   the   house   of him   he will plunder.

28 Ἀμὴν   λέγω   ὑμῖν   ὅτι   πάντα   ἀφεθήσεται
Truly   I tell   you   that   all   will be forgiven

forgiven the sons of men, and whatever blasphemies they utter; [29]but whoever blasphemes against the Holy Spirit never has forgiveness, but is guilty of an eternal sin"—[30]for they had said, "He has an unclean spirit."

31 And his mother and his brothers came; and standing outside they sent to him and called him. [32]And a crowd was sitting about him; and they said to him, "Your mother and your brothers[j] are outside, asking for you." [33]And he replied, "Who are my mother and my brothers?" [34]And looking around on those who sat about him, he said, "Here are my mother and my brothers! [35]Whoever does the will of God is my brother, and sister, and mother."

τοῖς υἱοῖς τῶν ἀνθρώπων τὰ ἁμαρτήματα
to the   sons   –   of men   the   sins

καὶ αἱ βλασφημίαι, ὅσα ἐὰν βλασφημήσωσιν·
and the   blasphemies,   whatever   they may blaspheme;

29 ὃς δ' ἂν βλασφημήσῃ εἰς τὸ πνεῦμα
but whoever   blasphemes   against the   Spirit

τὸ ἅγιον, οὐκ ἔχει ἄφεσιν εἰς τὸν αἰῶνα,
–   Holy,   has not   forgiveness   unto   the   age,

ἀλλὰ ἔνοχός ἐστιν αἰωνίου ἁμαρτήματος.
but   liable   is   of an eternal   sin.

30 ὅτι ἔλεγον· πνεῦμα ἀκάθαρτον ἔχει.
Because   they said: spirit   an unclean   he has.

31 Καὶ ἔρχονται ἡ μήτηρ αὐτοῦ καὶ οἱ
And   come   the   mother   of him   and the

ἀδελφοὶ αὐτοῦ, καὶ ἔξω στήκοντες ἀπέστειλαν
brothers   of him,   and outside   standing   sent

πρὸς αὐτὸν καλοῦντες αὐτόν. 32 καὶ
to   him   calling   him.   And

ἐκάθητο περὶ αὐτὸν ὄχλος, καὶ λέγουσιν
sat   round   him   a crowd,   and   they say

αὐτῷ· ἰδοὺ ἡ μήτηρ σου καὶ οἱ ἀδελφοί
to him: Behold[,] the   mother   of thee   and the   brothers

σου καὶ αἱ ἀδελφαί σου ἔξω ζητοῦσίν σε.
of thee   and the   sisters   of thee   outside   seek   thee.

33 καὶ ἀποκριθεὶς αὐτοῖς λέγει· τίς ἐστιν
And   answering   them   he says: Who   is

ἡ μήτηρ μου καὶ οἱ ἀδελφοί; 34 καὶ
the   mother   of me   and the   brothers?   And

περιβλεψάμενος τοὺς περὶ αὐτὸν κύκλῳ
looking round   [at] the [ones] round   him   in a circle

καθημένους λέγει· ἴδε ἡ μήτηρ μου
sitting   he says: Behold[,] the   mother   of me

καὶ οἱ ἀδελφοί μου. 35 ὃς ἂν ποιήσῃ τὸ
and the   brothers   of me.   Whoever   does   the

θέλημα τοῦ θεοῦ, οὗτος ἀδελφός μου
will   –   of God,   this one   brother   of me

CHAPTER 4

καὶ ἀδελφὴ καὶ μήτηρ ἐστίν.
and   sister   and   mother   is.

AGAIN he began to teach beside the sea. And a very large crowd gathered about him, so that he got into a boat and sat in it on the sea;

4 Καὶ πάλιν ἤρξατο διδάσκειν παρὰ τὴν
And   again   he began   to teach   by   the

θάλασσαν· καὶ συνάγεται πρὸς αὐτὸν ὄχλος
sea;   and   is assembled   to   him   crowd

πλεῖστος, ὥστε αὐτὸν εἰς πλοῖον ἐμβάντα
a very large,   so as   him   in   a ship   embarking
= so that embarking in a ship he sat

[j] Other early authorities add and your sisters

καθῆσθαι ἐν τῇ θαλάσσῃ, καὶ πᾶς ὁ
to sit[b]   in   the   sea,   and   all   the

and the whole crowd was beside the sea on the land. ²And he taught them many things in parables, and in his teaching he said to them: ³"Listen! A sower went out to sow. ⁴And as he sowed, some seed fell along the path, and the birds came and devoured it. ⁵Other seed fell on rocky ground, where it had not much soil, and immediately it sprang up, since it had no depth of soil; ⁶and when the sun rose it was scorched, and since it had no root it withered away. ⁷Other seed fell among thorns and the thorns grew up and choked it, and it yielded no grain. ⁸And other seeds fell into good soil and brought forth grain, growing up and increasing and yielding thirtyfold and sixtyfold and a hundredfold." ⁹And he said, "He who has ears to hear, let him hear."

10 And when he was alone, those who were about him with the twelve asked him concerning the parables. ¹¹And he said to them, "To you has been given the secret of the kingdom

ὄχλος πρὸς τὴν θάλασσαν ἐπὶ τῆς γῆς
crowd toward the sea on the land
ἦσαν. 2 καὶ ἐδίδασκεν αὐτοὺς ἐν παραβολαῖς
were. And he taught them in parables
πολλά, καὶ ἔλεγεν αὐτοῖς ἐν τῇ διδαχῇ
many things, and said to them in the teaching
αὐτοῦ· 3 ἀκούετε. ἰδοὺ ἐξῆλθεν ὁ σπείρων
of him: Hear ye. Behold[,] went out the [one] sowing
σπεῖραι. 4 καὶ ἐγένετο ἐν τῷ σπείρειν
to sow. And it came to pass in the to sow⁰
= as he sowed
ὃ μὲν ἔπεσεν παρὰ τὴν ὁδόν, καὶ ἦλθεν
some fell by the way, and came
τὰ πετεινὰ καὶ κατέφαγεν αὐτό. 5 καὶ
the birds and devoured it. And
ἄλλο ἔπεσεν ἐπὶ τὸ πετρῶδες ὅπου οὐκ
other fell on the rocky place where not
εἶχεν γῆν πολλήν, καὶ εὐθὺς ἐξανέτειλεν
it had earth much, and immediately it sprang up
διὰ τὸ μὴ ἔχειν βάθος γῆς·
on account of the not to have depth of earth;
= because it had no depth of earth;
6 καὶ ὅτε ἀνέτειλεν ὁ ἥλιος ἐκαυματίσθη, καὶ
and when rose the sun it was scorched, and
διὰ τὸ μὴ ἔχειν ῥίζαν ἐξηράνθη. 7 καὶ
on account of the not to have root it was withered. And
= because it had no root
ἄλλο ἔπεσεν εἰς τὰς ἀκάνθας, καὶ ἀνέβησαν
other fell among the thorns, and came up
αἱ ἄκανθαι καὶ συνέπνιξαν αὐτό, καὶ
the thorns and choked it, and
καρπὸν οὐκ ἔδωκεν. 8 καὶ ἄλλα ἔπεσεν
fruit it gave not. And others fell
εἰς τὴν γῆν τὴν καλὴν καὶ ἐδίδου καρπὸν
into the earth – good and gave fruit
ἀναβαίνοντα καὶ αὐξανόμενα καὶ ἔφερεν
coming up and growing and bore
εἰς τριάκοντα καὶ ἐν ἑξήκοντα καὶ ἐν
in thirty and in sixty and in
ἑκατόν. 9 καὶ ἔλεγεν· ὃς ἔχει ὦτα
a hundred. And he said: Who has ears
ἀκούειν ἀκουέτω. 10 Καὶ ὅτε ἐγένετο
to hear let him hear. And when he was
κατὰ μόνας, ἠρώτων αὐτὸν οἱ περὶ
alone,† asked him the [ones] round
αὐτὸν σὺν τοῖς δώδεκα τὰς παραβολάς.
him with the twelve the parables.
11 καὶ ἔλεγεν αὐτοῖς· ὑμῖν τὸ μυστήριον
And he said to them: To you the mystery

of God, but for those outside everything is in parables; 12so that they may indeed see but not perceive, and may indeed hear but not understand; lest they should turn again, and be forgiven." 13And he said to them, "Do you not understand this parable? How then will you understand all the parables? 14The sower sows the word. 15And these are the ones along the path, where the word is sown; when they hear, Satan immediately comes and takes away the word which is sown in them. 16And these in like manner are the ones sown upon rocky ground, who, when they hear the word, immediately receive it with joy; 17and they have no root in themselves, but endure for a while; then, when tribulation or persecution arises on account of the word, immediately they fall away.[k] 18And others are the ones sown among thorns; they are those who hear the word, 19but the cares of the world, and the delight in riches, and the desire for other things, enter in and

δέδοται   τῆς βασιλείας τοῦ θεοῦ· ἐκείνοις δὲ
has been given of the kingdom   – of God; but to those

τοῖς   ἔξω   ἐν   παραβολαῖς   τὰ   πάντα
the [ones] outside in   parables   –   all things

γίνεται,   12 ἵνα   βλέποντες   βλέπωσιν   καὶ
is(are),   that   seeing   they may see and

μὴ   ἴδωσιν,   καὶ   ἀκούοντες   ἀκούωσιν   καὶ
not perceive, and   hearing   they may hear and

μὴ   συνιῶσιν,   μήποτε   ἐπιστρέψωσιν   καὶ
not   understand,   lest   they should turn   and

ἀφεθῇ   αὐτοῖς.   13 καὶ   λέγει   αὐτοῖς·
it should be forgiven them.   And   he says   to them:

οὐκ οἴδατε   τὴν παραβολὴν ταύτην, καὶ πῶς
Know ye not   –   parable   this,   and how

πάσας τὰς παραβολὰς γνώσεσθε;   14   ὁ
all   the   parables   will ye know?   The [one]

σπείρων τὸν λόγον σπείρει. 15 οὗτοι δέ εἰσιν
sowing ²the ³word ¹sows.   And these   are

οἱ   παρὰ   τὴν   ὁδόν,   ὅπου   σπείρεται ὁ
the [ones] by   the   way,   where   is sown   the

λόγος, καὶ   ὅταν ἀκούσωσιν, εὐθὺς ἔρχεται
word,   and   when   they hear,   immediately comes

ὁ σατανᾶς   καὶ   αἴρει   τὸν   λόγον   τὸν
– Satan   and   takes   the   word   –

ἐσπαρμένον εἰς αὐτούς. 16 καὶ οὗτοί εἰσιν
having been sown in them.   And   these   are

ὁμοίως   οἱ   ἐπὶ   τὰ   πετρώδη   σπειρόμενοι,
likewise the [ones] on   the   rocky places   being sown,

οἱ   ὅταν   ἀκούσωσιν   τὸν   λόγον   εὐθὺς
who when   they hear   the   word   immediately

μετὰ   χαρᾶς   λαμβάνουσιν   αὐτόν,   17 καὶ
with   joy   receive   it,   and

οὐκ   ἔχουσιν   ῥίζαν   ἐν   ἑαυτοῖς   ἀλλὰ
have not   root   in   themselves   but

πρόσκαιροί εἰσιν, εἶτα γενομένης θλίψεως
shortlived   are,   then happening   affliction
              = when affliction or persecution happens

ἢ   διωγμοῦ   διὰ   τὸν   λόγον   εὐθὺς
or persecution[a] on account of the   word immediately

σκανδαλίζονται. 18 καὶ ἄλλοι εἰσὶν οἱ   εἰς
they are offended.   And others are the [ones] among

τὰς ἀκάνθας σπειρόμενοι· οὗτοί εἰσιν   οἱ
the thorns   being sown;   these   are the [ones]

τὸν λόγον ἀκούσαντες, 19 καὶ αἱ μέριμναι
the word   hearing,   and the   cares

τοῦ   αἰῶνος   καὶ ἡ ἀπάτη τοῦ πλούτου
of the   age   and the deceitfulness – of riches

καὶ   αἱ   περὶ   τὰ   λοιπὰ   ἐπιθυμίαι
and ¹the ²about ⁴the ⁵other things ²desires

[k] Or *stumble*

choke the word, and it proves unfruitful. ²⁰ But those that were sown upon the good soil are the ones who hear the word and accept it and bear fruit, thirtyfold and sixtyfold and a hundredfold."

21 And he said to them, "Is a lamp brought in to be put under a bushel, or under a bed, and not on a stand? ²² For there is nothing hid, except to be made manifest; nor is anything secret, except to come to light. ²³ If any man has ears to hear, let him hear." ²⁴ And he said to them, "Take heed what you hear; the measure you give will be the measure you get, and still more will be given you. ²⁵ For to him who has will more be given; and from him who has not, even what he has will be taken away."

26 And he said, "The kingdom of God is as if a man should scatter seed upon the ground, ²⁷ and should sleep and rise night and day, and the seed should sprout and grow, he knows not how. ²⁸ The earth produces of itself, first the blade, then

---

εἰσπορευόμεναι συμπνίγουσιν τὸν λόγον, καὶ
coming in   choke   the   word,   and

ἄκαρπος γίνεται. **20** καὶ ἐκεῖνοί εἰσιν
unfruitful   it becomes.   And   those   are

οἱ ἐπὶ τὴν γῆν τὴν καλὴν σπαρέντες,
the [ones] on   the   earth   –   good   sown,

οἵτινες ἀκούουσιν τὸν λόγον καὶ παραδέχονται
who   hear   the   word   and   welcome [it]

καὶ καρποφοροῦσιν ἐν τριάκοντα καὶ ἐν
and   bear fruit   in   thirty   and   in

ἑξήκοντα καὶ ἐν ἑκατόν. **21** Καὶ ἔλεγεν
sixty   and   in   a hundred.   And   he said

αὐτοῖς ὅτι μήτι ἔρχεται ὁ λύχνος ἵνα
to them[,]   –   not   Comes   the   lamp   that

ὑπὸ τὸν μόδιον τεθῇ ἢ ὑπὸ τὴν
under   the   bushel   it may be placed   or   under   the

κλίνην; οὐχ ἵνα ἐπὶ τὴν λυχνίαν
couch?   not   that   on   the   lampstand

τεθῇ; **22** οὐ γάρ ἐστίν τι κρυπτόν,
it may be placed?   For there is not   anything   hidden,

ἐὰν μὴ ἵνα φανερωθῇ· οὐδὲ ἐγένετο
except   that it may be manifested;   nor   became

ἀπόκρυφον, ἀλλ' ἵνα ἔλθῃ εἰς φανερόν.
covered,   but   that it may come into [the] open.

23 εἴ τις ἔχει ὦτα ἀκούειν ἀκουέτω.
If   anyone   has   ears   to hear   let him hear.

24 Καὶ ἔλεγεν αὐτοῖς· βλέπετε τί
And   he said   to them: Take heed   what

ἀκούετε. ἐν ᾧ μέτρῳ μετρεῖτε
ye hear.   With   what   measure   ye measure

μετρηθήσεται ὑμῖν, καὶ προστεθήσεται ὑμῖν.
it will be measured   to you,   and   it will be added   to you.

25 ὃς γὰρ ἔχει, δοθήσεται αὐτῷ· καὶ ὃς
For [he] who   has,   it will be given   to him;   and   who

οὐκ ἔχει, καὶ ὃ ἔχει ἀρθήσεται ἀπ'
has not,   even   what he has   will be taken   from

αὐτοῦ. **26** Καὶ ἔλεγεν· οὕτως ἐστὶν ἡ
him.   And   he said: Thus   is   the

βασιλεία τοῦ θεοῦ, ὡς ἄνθρωπος βάλῃ
kingdom   –   of God,   as   a man   might cast

τὸν σπόρον ἐπὶ τῆς γῆς, **27** καὶ καθεύδῃ
the   seed   on   the   earth,   and   might sleep

καὶ ἐγείρηται νύκτα καὶ ἡμέραν, καὶ ὁ
and   rise   night   and   day,   and   the

σπόρος βλαστᾷ καὶ μηκύνηται ὡς οὐκ
seed   sprouts   and   lengthens   as   not

οἶδεν αὐτός. **28** αὐτομάτη ἡ γῆ καρποφορεῖ,
knows   he.   Of its own accord the earth   bears fruit,

the ear, then the full grain in the ear. ²⁹But when the grain is ripe, at once he puts in the sickle, because the harvest has come."

30 And he said, "With what can we compare the kingdom of God, or what parable shall we use for it? ³¹It is like a grain of mustard seed, which, when sown upon the ground, is the smallest of all the seeds on earth; ³²yet when it is sown it grows up and becomes the greatest of all shrubs, and puts forth large branches, so that the birds of the air can make nests in its shade."

33 With many such parables he spoke the word to them, as they were able to hear it; ³⁴he did not speak to them without a parable, but privately to his own disciples he explained everything.

35 On that day, when evening had come, he said to them, "Let us pass across to the other side." ³⁶And leaving the crowd, they took him with them, just as he was, in the boat. And other boats were with him. ³⁷And a great storm of wind

πρῶτον χόρτον, εἶτεν στάχυν, εἶτεν πλήρης
first   grass,   then an ear, then   full

σῖτος ἐν τῷ στάχυϊ. 29 ὅταν δὲ παραδοῖ
corn in the ear.   But when   permits

ὁ καρπός, εὐθὺς ἀποστέλλει τὸ δρέπανον,
the fruit, immediately he sends(puts) forth the sickle,

ὅτι παρέστηκεν ὁ θερισμός.   30 Καὶ ἔλεγεν·
because has come the harvest.   And   he said:

πῶς ὁμοιώσωμεν τὴν βασιλείαν τοῦ θεοῦ,
How   may we liken   the kingdom   – of God,

ἢ ἐν τίνι αὐτὴν παραβολῇ θῶμεν;   31 ὡς
or by ¹what ⁴it   ²parable ³may we place?   As

κόκκῳ σινάπεως, ὃς ὅταν σπαρῇ ἐπὶ τῆς
a grain of mustard, which when it is sown on the

γῆς, μικρότερον ὂν πάντων τῶν σπερμάτων
earth, smaller being [than] all the   seeds

τῶν ἐπὶ τῆς γῆς, 32 καὶ ὅταν σπαρῇ,
– on the earth,   and when it is sown,

ἀναβαίνει καὶ γίνεται μεῖζον πάντων τῶν
comes up and becomes greater [than] all the

λαχάνων, καὶ ποιεῖ κλάδους μεγάλους,
herbs,   and makes branches great,

ὥστε δύνασθαι ὑπὸ τὴν σκιὰν αὐτοῦ τὰ
so as to be able under the shade of it the
= so that the birds of heaven are able to dwell under its shade.

πετεινὰ τοῦ οὐρανοῦ κατασκηνοῦν. 33 Καὶ
birds   – of heaven to dwell.ᵇ   And

τοιαύταις παραβολαῖς πολλαῖς ἐλάλει αὐτοῖς
⁸such   ²parables ¹in many he spoke to them

τὸν λόγον, καθὼς ἠδύναντο ἀκούειν·
the word,   as   they were able to hear;

34 χωρὶς δὲ παραβολῆς οὐκ ἐλάλει αὐτοῖς,
and without a parable he spoke not to them,

κατ᾽ ἰδίαν δὲ τοῖς ἰδίοις μαθηταῖς ἐπέλυεν
but privately to the(his) own disciples he explained

πάντα.
all things.

35 Καὶ λέγει αὐτοῖς ἐν ἐκείνῃ τῇ
And he says to them on that   –

ἡμέρᾳ ὀψίας γενομένης· διέλθωμεν εἰς τὸ
day evening having comeª: Let us pass over to the
= when evening had come:

πέραν. 36 καὶ ἀφέντες τὸν ὄχλον
other side. And leaving the crowd

παραλαμβάνουσιν αὐτὸν ὡς ἦν ἐν τῷ
they take   him as he was in the

πλοίῳ, καὶ ἄλλα πλοῖα ἦν μετ᾽ αὐτοῦ.
ship,   and other ships were with him.

37 καὶ γίνεται λαῖλαψ μεγάλη ἀνέμου,
And occurs   storm a great of wind,

arose, and the waves beat into the boat, so that the boat was already filling. [38] But he was in the stern, asleep on the cushion; and they woke him and said to him, "Teacher, do you not care if we perish?" [39] And he awoke and rebuked the wind, and said to the sea, "Peace! Be still!" And the wind ceased, and there was a great calm. [40] He said to them, "Why are you afraid? Have you no faith?" [41] And they were filled with awe, and said to one another, "Who then is this, that even wind and sea obey him?"

καὶ τὰ κύματα ἐπέβαλλεν εἰς τὸ πλοῖον,
and the waves struck into the ship,
ὥστε ἤδη γεμίζεσθαι τὸ πλοῖον. [38] καὶ
so as now to be filled the ship.[b] And
αὐτὸς ἦν ἐν τῇ πρύμνῃ ἐπὶ τὸ
he was in the stern on the
προσκεφάλαιον καθεύδων. καὶ ἐγείρουσιν
pillow sleeping. And they rouse
αὐτὸν καὶ λέγουσιν αὐτῷ· διδάσκαλε, οὐ μέλει
him and say to him: Teacher, matters it not
σοι ὅτι ἀπολλύμεθα; [39] καὶ διεγερθεὶς
to thee that we are perishing? And being roused
ἐπετίμησεν τῷ ἀνέμῳ καὶ εἶπεν τῇ
he rebuked the wind and said to the
θαλάσσῃ· σιώπα, πεφίμωσο. καὶ ἐκόπασεν
sea: Be quiet, be muzzled. And dropped
ὁ ἄνεμος, καὶ ἐγένετο γαλήνη μεγάλη.
the wind, and there was calm a great.
[40] καὶ εἶπεν αὐτοῖς· τί δειλοί ἐστε
And he said to them: Why fearful are ye
οὕτως; πῶς οὐκ ἔχετε πίστιν; [41] καὶ
thus? how have ye not faith? And
ἐφοβήθησαν φόβον μέγαν, καὶ ἔλεγον πρὸς
they feared fear a great, and said to
ἀλλήλους· τίς ἄρα οὗτός ἐστιν, ὅτι καὶ
one another: Who then this man is, that both
ὁ ἄνεμος καὶ ἡ θάλασσα ὑπακούει αὐτῷ;
the wind and the sea obeys him?

CHAPTER 5

THEY came to the other side of the sea, to the country of the Ger'asenes. [1] [2] And when he had come out of the boat, there met him out of the tombs a man with an unclean spirit, [3] who lived among the tombs; and no one could bind him any more, even with a chain; [4] for he had often been bound with fetters and chains, but

[5] Καὶ ἦλθον εἰς τὸ πέραν τῆς θαλάσσης
And they came to the other side of the sea
εἰς τὴν χώραν τῶν Γερασηνῶν. [2] καὶ
into the country of the Gerasenes. And
ἐξελθόντος αὐτοῦ ἐκ τοῦ πλοίου, [εὐθὺς]
coming out him[a] out of the ship, immediately
= as he came out
ὑπήντησεν αὐτῷ ἐκ τῶν μνημείων ἄνθρωπος
met him out of the tombs a man
ἐν πνεύματι ἀκαθάρτῳ, [3] ὃς τὴν κατοίκησιν
in(with) spirit an unclean, who the(his) dwelling
εἶχεν ἐν τοῖς μνήμασιν, καὶ οὐδὲ ἁλύσει
had among the tombs, and not with a chain
= no one any more
οὐκέτι οὐδεὶς ἐδύνατο αὐτὸν δῆσαι, [4] διὰ
no longer no one was able him to bind, on account of
was able to bind him with a chain, = because
τὸ αὐτὸν πολλάκις πέδαις καὶ ἁλύσεσιν
the him often with fetters and chains
he had often been bound with fetters and chains, and . . .

[1] Other ancient authorities read *Gergesenes*, some *Gadarenes*

the chains he wrenched apart, and the fetters he broke in pieces; and no one had the strength to subdue him. [5] Night and day among the tombs and on the mountains he was always crying out, and bruising himself with stones. [6] And when he saw Jesus from afar, he ran and worshiped him; [7] and crying out with a loud voice, he said, "What have you to do with me, Jesus, Son of the Most High God? I adjure you by God, do not torment me." [8] For he had said to him, "Come out of the man, you unclean spirit!" [9] And Jesus asked him, "What is your name?" He replied, "My name is Legion; for we are many." [10] And he begged him eagerly not to send them out of the country. [11] Now a great herd of swine was feeding there on the hillside; [12] and they begged him, "Send us to the swine, let us enter them." [13] So he gave them leave. And the unclean spirits came out, and entered the swine; and the herd, numbering about two thousand, rushed down the steep

δεδέσθαι, καὶ διεσπάσθαι ὑπ' αὐτοῦ τὰς
to have been bound, and to be burst by him the

ἀλύσεις καὶ τὰς πέδας συντετρῖφθαι, καὶ
chains and the fetters to have been broken, and

οὐδεὶς ἴσχυεν αὐτὸν δαμάσαι· 5 καὶ
no one was able him to subdue; and

διὰ παντὸς νυκτὸς καὶ ἡμέρας ἐν τοῖς μνήμασιν
always of(by) night and day among the tombs

καὶ ἐν τοῖς ὄρεσιν ἦν κράζων καὶ
and in the mountains he was crying out and

κατακόπτων ἑαυτὸν λίθοις. 6 καὶ ἰδὼν
cutting himself with stones. And seeing

τὸν Ἰησοῦν ἀπὸ μακρόθεν ἔδραμεν καὶ
- Jesus from afar he ran and

προσεκύνησεν αὐτόν, 7 καὶ κράξας φωνῇ
worshipped him, and crying out with a voice

μεγάλῃ λέγει· τί ἐμοὶ καὶ σοί, Ἰησοῦ
great(loud) he says: What to me and to thee, Jesus

υἱὲ τοῦ θεοῦ τοῦ ὑψίστου; ὁρκίζω σε
Son - of God the most high? I adjure thee

τὸν θεόν, μή με βασανίσῃς. 8 ἔλεγεν
- by God, not me thou mayest torment. he said

γὰρ αὐτῷ· ἔξελθε τὸ πνεῦμα τὸ ἀκάθαρτον
For to him: Come out the spirit - unclean

ἐκ τοῦ ἀνθρώπου. 9 καὶ ἐπηρώτα αὐτόν·
out of the man. And he questioned him:

τί ὄνομά σοι; καὶ λέγει αὐτῷ· λεγιὼν
What name to thee?° And he says to him: Legion
= What name hast thou ? = My

ὄνομά μοι, ὅτι πολλοί ἐσμεν. 10 καὶ
name to me,° because many we are. And
name is Legion,

παρεκάλει αὐτὸν πολλὰ ἵνα μὴ αὐτὰ
he besought him much that not them

ἀποστείλῃ ἔξω τῆς χώρας. 11 ἦν δὲ
he would send outside the country. Now there was

ἐκεῖ πρὸς τῷ ὄρει ἀγέλη χοίρων μεγάλη
there near the mountain herd of pigs a great

βοσκομένη· 12 καὶ παρεκάλεσαν αὐτὸν
feeding; and they besought him

λέγοντες· πέμψον ἡμᾶς εἰς τοὺς χοίρους,
saying: Send us into the pigs,

ἵνα εἰς αὐτοὺς εἰσέλθωμεν. 13 καὶ ἐπέτρεψεν
that into them we may enter. And he allowed

αὐτοῖς. καὶ ἐξελθόντα τὰ πνεύματα τὰ
them. And coming out the spirits -

ἀκάθαρτα εἰσῆλθον εἰς τοὺς χοίρους, καὶ
unclean entered into the pigs, and

ὥρμησεν ἡ ἀγέλη κατὰ τοῦ κρημνοῦ εἰς
rushed the herd down the precipice into

bank into the sea, and were drowned in the sea.

14 The herdsmen fled, and told it in the city and in the country. And people came to see what it was that had happened. [15]And they came to Jesus, and saw the demoniac sitting there, clothed and in his right mind, the man who had had the legion; and they were afraid. [16]And those who had seen it told what had happened to the demoniac and to the swine. [17]And they began to beg Jesus to depart from their neighborhood. [18]And as he was getting into the boat, the man who had been possessed with demons begged him that he might be with him. [19]But he refused, and said to him, "Go home to your friends, and tell them how much the Lord has done for you, and how he has had mercy on you." [20]And he went away and began to proclaim in the Decap'olis how much Jesus had done for him; and all men marveled.

21 And when Jesus had crossed again in the boat to the other side, a great crowd gathered

τὴν θάλασσαν, ὡς δισχίλιοι, καὶ ἐπνίγοντο
the   sea,   about two thousand, and   were choked

ἐν τῇ θαλάσσῃ. 14 καὶ οἱ βόσκοντες
in   the   sea.   And the [ones] feeding

αὐτοὺς ἔφυγον καὶ ἀπήγγειλαν εἰς τὴν
them   fled   and   reported   in   the

πόλιν καὶ εἰς τοὺς ἀγρούς· καὶ ἦλθον
city   and in   the   fields;   and they came

ἰδεῖν τί ἐστιν τὸ γεγονός. 15 καὶ
to see what is the thing having happened.   And

ἔρχονται πρὸς τὸν Ἰησοῦν, καὶ θεωροῦσιν τὸν
they come to   -   Jesus,   and   see   the

δαιμονιζόμενον καθήμενον ἱματισμένον καὶ
demon-possessed man sitting having been clothed and

σωφρονοῦντα, τὸν ἐσχηκότα τὸν λεγιῶνα,
being in his senses, the man having had   the   legion,

καὶ ἐφοβήθησαν. 16 καὶ διηγήσαντο αὐτοῖς οἱ
and they were afraid.   And   related   to them the [ones]

ἰδόντες πῶς ἐγένετο τῷ δαιμονιζομένῳ
seeing   how it happened to the demon-possessed man

καὶ περὶ τῶν χοίρων. 17 καὶ ἤρξαντο
and about the   pigs.   And   they began

παρακαλεῖν αὐτὸν ἀπελθεῖν ἀπὸ τῶν ὁρίων
to beseech   him   to depart   from   the   territory

αὐτῶν. 18 καὶ ἐμβαίνοντος αὐτοῦ εἰς τὸ
of them.   And   embarking   him[a]   in   the
                  = as he embarked

πλοῖον παρεκάλει αὐτὸν ὁ δαιμονισθεὶς
ship   besought   him the [one] demon-possessed

ἵνα μετ᾽ αὐτοῦ ᾖ. 19 καὶ οὐκ ἀφῆκεν
that with him he might be.   And   he permitted not

αὐτόν, ἀλλὰ λέγει αὐτῷ· ὕπαγε εἰς τὸν
him,   but   says to him: Go   to the

οἶκόν σου πρὸς τοὺς σούς, καὶ ἀπάγγειλον
house of thee to   the   thine, and   report
                  = thy people,

αὐτοῖς ὅσα ὁ κύριός σοι πεποίηκεν καὶ
to them what things the Lord to thee has done   and

ἠλέησέν σε. 20 καὶ ἀπῆλθεν καὶ ἤρξατο
pitied thee.   And he departed and   began

κηρύσσειν ἐν τῇ Δεκαπόλει ὅσα ἐποίησεν
to proclaim in -   Decapolis what things did

αὐτῷ ὁ Ἰησοῦς, καὶ πάντες ἐθαύμαζον.
to him - Jesus,   and all men   marvelled.

21 Καὶ διαπεράσαντος τοῦ Ἰησοῦ ἐν τῷ
And   crossing over   -   Jesus[a] in the
         = when Jesus had crossed over

πλοίῳ πάλιν εἰς τὸ πέραν συνήχθη ὄχλος
ship   again to the other side was assembled crowd

about him; and he was
beside the sea. ²²Then
came one of the rulers of
the synagogue, Ja'irus by
name; and seeing him, he
fell at his feet, ²³and
besought him, saying,
"My little daughter is at
the point of death. Come
and lay your hands on
her, so that she may be
made well, and live."
²⁴And he went with him.
And a great crowd
followed him and
thronged about him.
²⁵And there was a woman
who had had a flow of
blood for twelve years,
²⁶and who had suffered
much under many physi-
cians, and had spent all
that she had, and was no
better but rather grew
worse. ²⁷She had heard
the reports about Jesus,
and came up behind him
in the crowd and touched
his garment. ²⁸For she
said, "If I touch even his
garments, I shall be made
well." ²⁹And immediately
the hemorrhage ceased;
and she felt in her body
that she was healed of
her disease. ³⁰And Jesus,
perceiving in himself that
power had gone forth
from him, immediately
turned about in the
crowd, and said, "Who
touched my garments?"
³¹And his disciples said

πολὺς ἐπ' αὐτόν, καὶ ἦν παρὰ τὴν θάλασσαν.
a much(great) to him, and he was by the sea.

22 Καὶ   ἔρχεται   εἷς   τῶν   ἀρχισυναγώγων,
And   comes   one of the   synagogue chiefs,

ὀνόματι   Ἰάϊρος,   καὶ   ἰδὼν   αὐτὸν   πίπτει
by name   Jairus,   and   seeing   him   falls

πρὸς τοὺς πόδας αὐτοῦ, **23** καὶ παρακαλεῖ
at   the   feet   of him,   and   beseeches

αὐτὸν πολλὰ λέγων ὅτι τὸ θυγάτριόν μου
him   much   saying[,] – The daughter of me

ἐσχάτως ἔχει, ἵνα ἐλθὼν ἐπιθῇς
is at the point of death,† that coming thou mayest lay on

τὰς χεῖρας αὐτῇ, ἵνα σωθῇ καὶ ζήσῃ.
the(thy) hands on her, that she may be healed and may live.

24 καὶ ἀπῆλθεν μετ' αὐτοῦ. καὶ ἠκολούθει αὐτῷ
And he went with him. And followed him

ὄχλος πολύς, καὶ συνέθλιβον αὐτόν. **25** Καὶ
crowd a much(great), and pressed upon him. And

γυνὴ οὖσα ἐν ῥύσει αἵματος δώδεκα
a woman being in a flow of blood twelve
= having

ἔτη, **26** καὶ πολλὰ παθοῦσα ὑπὸ πολλῶν
years, and many things suffering by many

ἰατρῶν καὶ δαπανήσασα τὰ παρ' αὐτῆς
physicians and having spent the with her

πάντα, καὶ μηδὲν ὠφεληθεῖσα ἀλλὰ μᾶλλον
all things, and nothing having been profited but rather

εἰς τὸ χεῖρον ἐλθοῦσα, **27** ἀκούσασα τὰ
to the worse having come, hearing the things

περὶ τοῦ Ἰησοῦ, ἐλθοῦσα ἐν τῷ ὄχλῳ
about – Jesus, coming in the crowd

ὄπισθεν ἥψατο τοῦ ἱματίου αὐτοῦ· **28** ἔλεγεν
behind touched the garment of him; she said[,]

γὰρ ὅτι ἐὰν ἅψωμαι κἂν τῶν ἱματίων
for – If I may touch even the garments

αὐτοῦ, σωθήσομαι. **29** καὶ εὐθὺς ἐξηράνθη
of him, I shall be healed. And immediately was dried up

ἡ πηγὴ τοῦ αἵματος αὐτῆς, καὶ ἔγνω
the fountain of the blood of her, and she knew

τῷ σώματι ὅτι ἴαται ἀπὸ τῆς
in the(her) body that she is(was) cured from the

μάστιγος. **30** καὶ εὐθὺς ὁ Ἰησοῦς ἐπιγνοὺς ἐν
plague. And immediately – Jesus knowing in

ἑαυτῷ τὴν ἐξ αὐτοῦ δύναμιν ἐξελθοῦσαν,
himself ¹the ⁴out of ⁵him ²power ³going forth,

ἐπιστραφεὶς ἐν τῷ ὄχλῳ ἔλεγεν· τίς μου ἥψατο τῶν
turning in the crowd said: Who of me touched the

ἱματίων; **31** καὶ ἔλεγον αὐτῷ οἱ μαθηταὶ
garments? And said to him the disciples

to him, "You see the
crowd pressing around
you, and yet you say,
'Who touched me?'"
32And he looked around
to see who had done it.
33But the woman, know-
ing what had been done
to her, came in fear and
trembling and fell down
before him, and told him
the whole truth. 34And
he said to her, "Daughter,
your faith has made you
well; go in peace, and be
healed of your disease."

35 While he was still
speaking, there came
from the ruler's house
some who said, "Your
daughter is dead. Why
trouble the Teacher any
further?"36But ignoring[m]
what they said, Jesus
said to the ruler of the
synagogue, "Do not fear,
only believe." 37And he
allowed no one to follow
him except Peter and
James and John the
brother of James.
38When they came to the
house of the ruler of the
synagogue, he saw a
tumult, and people weep-
ing and wailing loudly.
39And when he had
entered, he said to them,
"Why do you make a
tumult and weep? The
child is not dead but
sleeping." 40And they
laughed at him. But he
put them all outside, and

αὐτοῦ· βλέπεις τὸν ὄχλον συνθλίβοντά σε,
of him: Thou seest the crowd pressing upon thee,
καὶ λέγεις· τίς μου ἥψατο; 32 καὶ
and thou sayest: Who me touched? And
περιεβλέπετο ἰδεῖν τὴν τοῦτο ποιήσασαν.
he looked round to see the [one] this having done.
33 ἡ δὲ γυνὴ φοβηθεῖσα καὶ τρέμουσα,
And the woman fearing and trembling,
εἰδυῖα ὃ γέγονεν αὐτῇ, ἦλθεν καὶ προσέ-
knowing what has happened to her, came and fell
πεσεν αὐτῷ καὶ εἶπεν αὐτῷ πᾶσαν τὴν ἀλήθειαν.
before him and told him all the truth.
34 ὁ δὲ εἶπεν αὐτῇ· θυγάτηρ, ἡ πίστις
And he said to her: Daughter, the faith
σου σέσωκέν σε· ὕπαγε εἰς εἰρήνην, καὶ
of thee has healed thee; go in peace, and
ἴσθι ὑγιὴς ἀπὸ τῆς μάστιγός σου. 35 Ἔτι
be whole from the plague of thee. Still
= While
αὐτοῦ λαλοῦντος ἔρχονται ἀπὸ τοῦ
him speaking[a] they come from the
he was still speaking
ἀρχισυναγώγου λέγοντες ὅτι ἡ θυγάτηρ
synagogue chief saying[,] - The daughter
σου ἀπέθανεν· τί ἔτι σκύλλεις τὸν διδάσκαλον;
of thee died; why still troublest thou the teacher?
36 ὁ δὲ Ἰησοῦς παρακούσας τὸν λόγον
- But Jesus overhearing the word
λαλούμενον λέγει τῷ ἀρχισυναγώγῳ· μὴ
being spoken says to the synagogue chief: not
φοβοῦ, μόνον πίστευε. 37 καὶ οὐκ ἀφῆκεν
Fear, only believe. And he allowed not
οὐδένα μετ' αὐτοῦ συνακολουθῆσαι εἰ μὴ
no(any)one with him to accompany except
τὸν Πέτρον καὶ Ἰάκωβον καὶ Ἰωάννην
- Peter and James and John
τὸν ἀδελφὸν Ἰακώβου. 38 καὶ ἔρχονται
the brother of James. And they come
εἰς τὸν οἶκον τοῦ ἀρχισυναγώγου, καὶ
into the house of the synagogue chief, and
θεωρεῖ θόρυβον, καὶ κλαίοντας καὶ
he sees an uproar, and [men] weeping and
ἀλαλάζοντας πολλά, 39 καὶ εἰσελθὼν λέγει
crying aloud much, and entering he says
αὐτοῖς· τί θορυβεῖσθε καὶ κλαίετε; τὸ
to them: Why make ye an uproar and weep? the
παιδίον οὐκ ἀπέθανεν ἀλλὰ καθεύδει.
child did not die but sleeps.

m Or overhearing. Other
ancient authorities read hearing

40 καὶ κατεγέλων αὐτοῦ. αὐτὸς δὲ ἐκβαλὼν
And they ridiculed him. But he putting out

took the child's father and mother and those who were with him, and went in where the child was. [41] Taking her by the hand he said to her, "Tal'itha cu'mi"; which means, "Little girl, I say to thee, arise." [42] And immediately the girl got up and walked; for she was twelve years old. And immediately they were overcome with amazement. [43] And he strictly charged them that no one should know this, and told them to give her something to eat.

πάντας παραλαμβάνει τὸν πατέρα τοῦ
all   takes   the   father   of the
παιδίου καὶ τὴν μητέρα καὶ τοὺς μετ'
child   and   the   mother   and   the [ones] with
αὐτοῦ, καὶ εἰσπορεύεται ὅπου ἦν τὸ
him,   and   goes in   where   was   the
παιδίον. 41 καὶ κρατήσας τῆς χειρὸς
child.   And   taking hold   of the   hand
τοῦ παιδίου λέγει αὐτῇ· ταλιθὰ κούμ, ὅ
of the   child   he says   to her: Talitha   koum,   which
ἐστιν μεθερμηνευόμενον· τὸ κοράσιον, σοὶ
is   being interpreted: —   Maid,   to thee
λέγω, ἔγειρε. 42 καὶ εὐθὺς ἀνέστη τὸ
I say,   arise.   And immediately   rose up   the
κοράσιον καὶ περιεπάτει· ἦν γὰρ
maid   and   walked;   for she was
ἐτῶν δώδεκα. καὶ ἐξέστησαν εὐθὺς
[of the age]   twelve.   And they were astonished immediately
of years   =immediately they were exceedingly astonished.
ἐκστάσει μεγάλη. 43 καὶ διεστείλατο
astonishment   with a great.   And   he ordered
αὐτοῖς πολλὰ ἵνα μηδεὶς γνοῖ τοῦτο, καὶ
them   much   that   no one should know   this,   and
εἶπεν δοθῆναι αὐτῇ φαγεῖν.
told   to be given   to her   to eat.
=[them] to give her [something] to eat.

CHAPTER 6

HE went away from there and came to his own country; and his disciples followed him. [2] And on the sabbath he began to teach in the synagogue; and many who heard him were astonished, saying, "Where did this man get all this? What is the wisdom given to him? What mighty works are wrought by his hands! [3] Is not this the carpenter, the son of Mary and brother of James and

6 Καὶ ἐξῆλθεν ἐκεῖθεν, καὶ ἔρχεται εἰς
And   he went forth   thence,   and   comes   into
τὴν πατρίδα αὐτοῦ, καὶ ἀκολουθοῦσιν
the   native place   of him,   and   follow
αὐτῷ οἱ μαθηταὶ αὐτοῦ. 2 καὶ γενομένου
him   the   disciples   of him.   And   coming
    = when
σαββάτου ἤρξατο διδάσκειν ἐν τῇ συναγωγῇ·
a sabbath[a]   he began   to teach   in   the   synagogue;
a sabbath came
καὶ οἱ πολλοὶ ἀκούοντες ἐξεπλήσσοντο
and   the   many   hearing   were astonished
λέγοντες· πόθεν τούτῳ ταῦτα, καὶ τίς ἡ
saying: Whence to this man these things, and   what the
σοφία ἡ δοθεῖσα τούτῳ; καὶ αἱ δυνάμεις
wisdom   –   given   to this(him)? And the powerful deeds
τοιαῦται διὰ τῶν χειρῶν αὐτοῦ γινόμεναι;
such   through   the   hands   of him   coming about?
3 οὐχ οὗτός ἐστιν ὁ τέκτων, ὁ υἱὸς
[1]Not   [2]this man   [1]is   the   carpenter,   the   son
τῆς Μαρίας καὶ ἀδελφὸς Ἰακώβου καὶ
–   of Mary   and   brother   of James   and

Joses and Judas and Simon, and are not his sisters here with us?" And they took offense[n] at him. [4]And Jesus said to them, "A prophet is not without honor, except in his own country, and among his own kin, and in his own house." [5]And he could do no mighty work there, except that he laid his hands upon a few sick people and healed them. [6]And he marveled because of their unbelief.

And he went about among the villages teaching.

7 And he called to him the twelve, and began to send them out two by two, and gave them authority over the unclean spirits. [8]He charged them to take nothing for their journey except a staff; no bread, no bag, no money in their belts; [9]but to wear sandals and not put on two tunics. [10]And he said to them, "Where you enter a house, stay there until you leave the place. [11]And if any place will not receive you and they refuse to hear you, when

'Ιωσῆτος καὶ 'Ιούδα καὶ Σίμωνος; καὶ
Joses and Judas and Simon? and

οὐκ εἰσὶν αἱ ἀδελφαὶ αὐτοῦ ὧδε πρὸς
[2]not [1]are the sisters of him here with

ἡμᾶς; καὶ ἐσκανδαλίζοντο ἐν αὐτῷ. 4 καὶ
us? And they were offended in(at) him. And

ἔλεγεν αὐτοῖς ὁ 'Ιησοῦς ὅτι οὐκ ἔστιν
said to them - Jesus[,] - [3]not [2]is

προφήτης ἄτιμος εἰ μὴ ἐν τῇ πατρίδι
[1]A prophet unhonoured except in the native place

αὐτοῦ καὶ ἐν τοῖς συγγενεῦσιν αὐτοῦ
of him and among the relatives of him

καὶ ἐν τῇ οἰκίᾳ αὐτοῦ. 5 καὶ οὐκ
and in the house of him. And not

ἐδύνατο ἐκεῖ ποιῆσαι οὐδεμίαν δύναμιν,
he could there to do no(any) powerful deed,

εἰ μὴ ὀλίγοις ἀρρώστοις ἐπιθεὶς τὰς
except on a few sick [ones] laying on the(his)

χεῖρας ἐθεράπευσεν. 6 καὶ ἐθαύμασεν διὰ
hands he healed. And he marvelled because of

τὴν ἀπιστίαν αὐτῶν.
the unbelief of them.

Καὶ περιῆγεν τὰς κώμας κύκλῳ
And he went round the villages in circuit

διδάσκων. 7 Καὶ προσκαλεῖται τοὺς δώδεκα,
teaching. And he calls to [him] the twelve,

καὶ ἤρξατο αὐτοὺς ἀποστέλλειν δύο δύο,
and began them to send forth two [by] two,

καὶ ἐδίδου αὐτοῖς ἐξουσίαν τῶν πνευμάτων
and gave them authority the spirits

τῶν ἀκαθάρτων, 8 καὶ παρήγγειλεν αὐτοῖς
- of(over) unclean, and charged them

ἵνα μηδὲν αἴρωσιν εἰς ὁδὸν εἰ μὴ ῥάβδον
that nothing they should take in [the] way except a staff

μόνον, μὴ ἄρτον, μὴ πήραν, μὴ εἰς τὴν
only, not bread, not a wallet, not in the

ζώνην χαλκόν, 9 ἀλλὰ ὑποδεδεμένους σανδάλια,
girdle copper [money], but having had tied on sandals,

καὶ μὴ ἐνδύσησθε δύο χιτῶνας. 10 καὶ
and do not put on two tunics. And

ἔλεγεν αὐτοῖς· ὅπου ἐὰν εἰσέλθητε εἰς
he said to them: Wherever ye enter into

οἰκίαν, ἐκεῖ μένετε ἕως ἂν ἐξέλθητε
a house, there remain until ye go out

ἐκεῖθεν. 11 καὶ ὃς ἂν τόπος μὴ δέξηται
thence. And whatever place receives not

ὑμᾶς μηδὲ ἀκούσωσιν ὑμῶν, ἐκπορευόμενοι
you nor they hear you, going out

[n] Or stumbled

you leave, shake off the dust that is on your feet for a testimony against them." [12]So they went out and preached that men should repent. [13]And they cast out many demons, and anointed with oil many that were sick and healed them.

14 King Herod heard of it; for Jesus' name had become known. Some[o] said, "John the baptizer has been raised from the dead; that is why these powers are at work in him." [15]But others said, "It is Eli'jah." And others said, "It is a prophet, like one of the prophets of old." [16]But when Herod heard of it he said, "John, whom I beheaded, has been raised." [17]For Herod had sent and seized John, and bound him in prison for the sake of Hero'di-as, his brother Philip's wife; because he had married her. [18]For John said to Herod, "It is not lawful for you to have your brother's wife." [19]And Hero'di-as had a grudge against him, and wanted to kill him. But she could not, [20]for Herod feared John, knowing that he

ἐκεῖθεν ἐκτινάξατε τὸν χοῦν τὸν ὑποκάτω
thence   shake off   the   dust   -   under
τῶν ποδῶν ὑμῶν εἰς μαρτύριον αὐτοῖς.
the   feet of you for a testimony to them.
12 Καὶ ἐξελθόντες ἐκήρυξαν ἵνα μετανοῶσιν,
   And going forth they proclaimed that men should repent,
13 καὶ δαιμόνια πολλὰ ἐξέβαλλον, καὶ
   and   demons   many   they expelled,   and
ἤλειφον ἐλαίῳ πολλοὺς ἀρρώστους καὶ
anointed with oil   many   sick [ones]   and
ἐθεράπευον.
healed.

14 Καὶ ἤκουσεν ὁ βασιλεὺς Ἡρῴδης,
   And   heard   the   king   Herod,
φανερὸν γὰρ ἐγένετο τὸ ὄνομα αὐτοῦ, καὶ
for manifest   became the name of him, and
ἔλεγον ὅτι Ἰωάννης ὁ βαπτίζων ἐγήγερται
they said[,] -   John the baptizing [one] has been raised
ἐκ νεκρῶν, καὶ διὰ τοῦτο ἐνεργοῦσιν αἱ
from [the] dead, and therefore   operate   the
δυνάμεις ἐν αὐτῷ. 15 ἄλλοι δὲ ἔλεγον
powerful deeds in   him.   But others   said[,]
ὅτι Ἡλίας ἐστίν· ἄλλοι δὲ ἔλεγον ὅτι
 - Elias it/he is; and [yet] others said[,]   -
προφήτης ὡς εἷς τῶν προφητῶν. 16 ἀκούσας δὲ
A prophet as one of the prophets.   But hearing
ὁ Ἡρῴδης ἔλεγεν· ὃν ἐγὼ ἀπεκεφάλισα
- Herod   said: whom [2]I [4]beheaded
Ἰωάννην, οὗτος ἠγέρθη. 17 Αὐτὸς γὰρ ὁ
[1]John,   this was raised. For [2]himself -
Ἡρῴδης ἀποστείλας ἐκράτησεν τὸν Ἰωάννην
[1]Herod   sending   seized   -   John
καὶ ἔδησεν αὐτὸν ἐν φυλακῇ διὰ Ἡρῳδιάδα
and bound   him   in prison because of Herodias
τὴν γυναῖκα Φιλίππου τοῦ ἀδελφοῦ αὐτοῦ,
the   wife   of Philip   the   brother   of him,
ὅτι αὐτὴν ἐγάμησεν· 18 ἔλεγεν γὰρ ὁ
because her he married;   for said   -
Ἰωάννης τῷ Ἡρῴδῃ ὅτι οὐκ ἔξεστίν
John   - to Herod[,] -   It is not lawful
σοι ἔχειν τὴν γυναῖκα τοῦ ἀδελφοῦ σου.
for thee to have the   wife   of the brother of thee.
19 ἡ δὲ Ἡρῳδιὰς ἐνεῖχεν αὐτῷ καὶ
 - Now Herodias had a grudge against him   and
ἤθελεν αὐτὸν ἀποκτεῖναι, καὶ οὐκ ἠδύνατο·
wished [3]him [1]to kill,   and not   could not;
20 ὁ γὰρ Ἡρῴδης ἐφοβεῖτο τὸν Ἰωάννην,
 - for   Herod   feared   -   John,

[o] Other ancient authorities read he

was a righteous and holy man, and kept him safe. When he heard him, he was much perplexed; and yet he heard him gladly. ²¹But an opportunity came when Herod on his birthday gave a banquet for his courtiers and officers and the leading men of Galilee. ²²For when Hero'di-as' daughter came in and danced, she pleased Herod and his guests; and the king said to the girl, "Ask me for whatever you wish, and I will grant it." ²³And he vowed to her, "Whatever you ask me, I will give you, even half of my kingdom." ²⁴And she went out, and said to her mother, "What shall I ask?" And she said, "The head of John the baptizer." ²⁵And she came in immediately with haste to the king, and asked, saying, "I want you to give me at once the head of John the Baptist on a platter." ²⁶And the king was exceedingly sorry; but because of his oaths and his guests he did not want to break his word to her.

εἰδὼς αὐτὸν ἄνδρα δίκαιον καὶ ἅγιον, καὶ
knowing him a man just and holy, and

συνετήρει αὐτόν, καὶ ἀκούσας αὐτοῦ πολλὰ
kept safe him, and hearing him much = was

ἠπόρει, καὶ ἡδέως αὐτοῦ ἤκουεν. 21 καὶ
was in difficulties, and gladly him heard. And
in great difficulties,

γενομένης ἡμέρας εὐκαίρου ὅτε Ἡρῴδης
coming day a suitable when Herod
= when a suitable day came

τοῖς γενεσίοις αὐτοῦ δεῖπνον ἐποίησεν τοῖς
on the birthday festivities of him a supper made for the

μεγιστᾶσιν αὐτοῦ καὶ τοῖς χιλιάρχοις καὶ
courtiers of him and the chiliarchs and

τοῖς πρώτοις τῆς Γαλιλαίας, 22 καὶ
the chief men - of Galilee, and

εἰσελθούσης τῆς θυγατρὸς αὐτῆς τῆς
entering the daughter of herself -
= when the daughter of Herodias herself entered and danced,

Ἡρῳδιάδος καὶ ὀρχησαμένης, ἤρεσεν τῷ
of Herodias and dancing, she pleased -

Ἡρῴδῃ καὶ τοῖς συνανακειμένοις. ὁ δὲ
Herod and the [ones] reclining with [him]. And the

βασιλεὺς εἶπεν τῷ κορασίῳ· αἴτησόν με
king said to the girl: Ask me

ὃ ἐὰν θέλῃς, καὶ δώσω σοι· 23 καὶ
whatever thou wishest, and I will give thee; and

ὤμοσεν αὐτῇ ὅτι ὃ ἐὰν αἰτήσῃς δώσω
he swore to her[,] - Whatever thou askest I will give

σοι ἕως ἡμίσους τῆς βασιλείας μου.
thee up to half of the kingdom of me.

24 καὶ ἐξελθοῦσα εἶπεν τῇ μητρὶ αὐτῆς·
And going out she said to the mother of her:

τί αἰτήσωμαι; ἡ δὲ εἶπεν· τὴν κεφαλὴν
What may I ask? And she said: The head

Ἰωάννου τοῦ βαπτίζοντος. 25 καὶ
of John the [one] baptizing. And

εἰσελθοῦσα εὐθὺς μετὰ σπουδῆς πρὸς τὸν
entering immediately with haste to the

βασιλέα ᾐτήσατο λέγουσα· θέλω ἵνα ἐξαυτῆς
king she asked saying: I wish that at once

δῷς μοι ἐπὶ πίνακι τὴν κεφαλὴν Ἰωάννου
thou mayest give me on a dish the head of John

τοῦ βαπτιστοῦ. 26 καὶ περίλυπος γενόμενος
the Baptist. And deeply grieved becoming

ὁ βασιλεὺς διὰ τοὺς ὅρκους καὶ τοὺς
the king because of the oaths and the [ones]

ἀνακειμένους οὐκ ἠθέλησεν ἀθετῆσαι αὐτήν.
reclining did not wish to reject her.

²⁷And immediately the king sent a soldier of the guard and gave orders to bring his head. He went and beheaded him in the prison, ²⁸and brought his head on a platter, and gave it to the girl; and the girl gave it to her mother. ²⁹When his disciples heard of it, they came and took his body, and laid it in a tomb.

30 The apostles returned to Jesus, and told him all that they had done and taught. ³¹And he said to them, "Come away by yourselves to a lonely place, and rest a while." For many were coming and going, and they had no leisure even to eat. ³²And they went away in the boat to a lonely place by themselves. ³³Now many saw them going, and knew them, and they ran there on foot from all the towns, and got there ahead of them. ³⁴As he landed he saw a great throng, and he had compassion on them, because they were like sheep without a shepherd; and he began to teach them

27 καὶ εὐθὺς ἀποστείλας ὁ βασιλεὺς
And immediately ⁴sending ¹the ²king
σπεκουλάτορα ἐπέταξεν ἐνέγκαι τὴν κεφαλὴν
an executioner gave order to bring the head
αὐτοῦ. καὶ ἀπελθὼν ἀπεκεφάλισεν αὐτὸν
of him. And going he beheaded him
ἐν τῇ φυλακῇ, 28 καὶ ἤνεγκεν τὴν κεφαλὴν
in the prison, and brought the head
αὐτοῦ ἐπὶ πίνακι καὶ ἔδωκεν αὐτὴν τῷ
of him on a dish and gave it to the
κορασίῳ, καὶ τὸ κοράσιον ἔδωκεν αὐτὴν
girl, and the girl gave it
τῇ μητρὶ αὐτῆς. 29 καὶ ἀκούσαντες οἱ
to the mother of her. And hearing the
μαθηταὶ αὐτοῦ ἦλθαν καὶ ἦραν τὸ πτῶμα
disciples of him went and took the corpse
αὐτοῦ καὶ ἔθηκαν αὐτὸ ἐν μνημείῳ.
of him and put it in a tomb.

30 Καὶ συνάγονται οἱ ἀπόστολοι πρὸς
And assemble the apostles to
τὸν Ἰησοῦν, καὶ ἀπήγγειλαν αὐτῷ πάντα
- Jesus, and reported to him all things
ὅσα ἐποίησαν καὶ ὅσα ἐδίδαξαν. 31 καὶ
which they did and which they taught. And
λέγει αὐτοῖς· δεῦτε ὑμεῖς αὐτοὶ κατ'
he says to them: Come ye [your]selves privately to,
ἰδίαν εἰς ἔρημον τόπον καὶ ἀναπαύσασθε ὀλίγον.
a desert place and rest a little.
ἦσαν γὰρ οἱ ἐρχόμενοι καὶ οἱ
For ²were ³the [ones] ⁴coming ⁵and ⁶the [ones]
ὑπάγοντες πολλοί, καὶ οὐδὲ φαγεῖν
⁷going ¹many, and not to eat
εὐκαίρουν. 32 καὶ ἀπῆλθον ἐν τῷ πλοίῳ
they had opportunity. And they went away in the ship
εἰς ἔρημον τόπον κατ' ἰδίαν. 33 καὶ
to a desert place privately. And
εἶδον αὐτοὺς ὑπάγοντας καὶ ἐπέγνωσαν
²saw ³them ⁴going ⁵and ⁶knew
πολλοί, καὶ πεζῇ ἀπὸ πασῶν τῶν πόλεων
¹many, and on foot from all the cities
συνέδραμον ἐκεῖ καὶ προῆλθον αὐτούς.
ran together there and came before them.
34 Καὶ ἐξελθὼν εἶδεν πολὺν ὄχλον, καὶ
And going forth he saw a much(great) crowd, and
ἐσπλαγχνίσθη ἐπ' αὐτοὺς ὅτι ἦσαν ὡς
had compassion on them because they were as
πρόβατα μὴ ἔχοντα ποιμένα, καὶ ἤρξατο
sheep not having a shepherd, and he began

many things. ³⁵And when
it grew late, his disciples
came to him and said,
"This is a lonely place,
and the hour is now late;
³⁶send them away, to go
into the country and
villages round about and
buy themselves some-
thing to eat." ³⁷But he
answered them, "You
give them something to
eat." And they said to
him, "Shall we go and
buy two hundred denarii
worth of bread, and give
it to them to eat?"
³⁸And he said to them,
"How many loaves have
you? Go and see." And
when they had found out,
they said, "Five, and two
fish." ³⁹Then he commanded them all to sit
down by companies upon
the green grass. ⁴⁰So they
sat down in groups, by
hundreds and by fifties.
⁴¹And taking the five
loaves and the two fish he
looked up to heaven, and
blessed, and broke the
loaves, and gave them to
the disciples to set before
the people; and he
divided the two fish
among them all. ⁴²And

διδάσκειν αὐτοὺς πολλά. **35** Καὶ ἤδη ὥρας
to teach   them   many things.   And   now   an hour
                                                              = it being

πολλῆς γενομένης προσελθόντες αὐτῷ οἱ
much   coming[a]   approaching   to him   the
late

μαθηταὶ αὐτοῦ ἔλεγον ὅτι ἔρημός ἐστιν
disciples   of him   said[,]   –   Desert   is

ὁ τόπος καὶ ἤδη ὥρα πολλή· **36** ἀπόλυσον
the place   and now hour   a much;   dismiss
                                   = it is late;

αὐτούς, ἵνα ἀπελθόντες εἰς τοὺς κύκλῳ
them,   that   going away   to   the round about

ἀγροὺς καὶ κώμας ἀγοράσωσιν ἑαυτοῖς τί
fields   and villages they may buy for themselves what

φάγωσιν. **37** ὁ δὲ ἀποκριθεὶς εἶπεν αὐτοῖς·
they may eat.   But he   answering   said to them:

δότε αὐτοῖς ὑμεῖς φαγεῖν. καὶ λέγουσιν
Give   them   ye   to eat.   And   they say

αὐτῷ· ἀπελθόντες ἀγοράσωμεν δηναρίων
to him: Going away   may we buy   [2]of(for) [4]denarii

διακοσίων ἄρτους, καὶ δώσομεν αὐτοῖς
[3]two hundred [1]loaves,   and   shall we give   them

φαγεῖν; **38** ὁ δὲ λέγει αὐτοῖς· πόσους
to eat?   And he   says   to them: How many

ἔχετε ἄρτους; ὑπάγετε ἴδετε. καὶ γνόντες
have ye loaves?   Go   see.   And knowing

λέγουσιν· πέντε, καὶ δύο ἰχθύας. **39** καὶ
they say: Five,   and two fishes.   And

ἐπέταξεν αὐτοῖς ἀνακλιθῆναι πάντας συμπόσια
he instructed them   to recline   all   companies

συμπόσια ἐπὶ τῷ χλωρῷ χόρτῳ. **40** καὶ
companies   on the   green   grass.   And

ἀνέπεσαν πρασιαὶ πρασιαὶ κατὰ ἑκατὸν
they reclined   groups   groups   by   a hundred

καὶ κατὰ πεντήκοντα. **41** καὶ λαβὼν τοὺς
and by   fifty.   And taking   the

πέντε ἄρτους καὶ τοὺς δύο ἰχθύας,
five   loaves   and the   two   fishes,

ἀναβλέψας εἰς τὸν οὐρανὸν εὐλόγησεν καὶ
looking up   to   –   heaven   he blessed   and

κατέκλασεν τοὺς ἄρτους καὶ ἐδίδου τοῖς
broke   the   loaves   and   gave   to the

μαθηταῖς ἵνα παρατιθῶσιν αὐτοῖς, καὶ
disciples   that they might set before them,   and

τοὺς δύο ἰχθύας ἐμέρισεν πᾶσιν. **42** καὶ
the   two fishes he divided   to all.   And

they all ate and were
satisfied. ⁴³And they took
up twelve baskets full of
broken pieces and of the
fish. ⁴⁴And those who ate
the loaves were five
thousand men.

45 Immediately he
made his disciples get into
the boat and go before
him to the other side, to
Beth-sa'ida, while he dismissed the crowd. ⁴⁶And
after he had taken leave
of them, he went into the
hills to pray. ⁴⁷And when
evening came, the boat
was out on the sea, and
he was alone on the
land. ⁴⁸And he saw that
they were distressed in
rowing, for the wind was
against them. And about
the fourth watch of the
night he came to them,
walking on the sea. He
meant to pass by them,
⁴⁹but when they saw him
walking on the sea they
thought it was a ghost,
and cried out; ⁵⁰for they
all saw him, and were
terrified. But immed-
iately he spoke to them
and said, "Take heart, it
is I; have no fear."
⁵¹And he got into the
boat with them and the
wind ceased. And they
were utterly astounded,

ἔφαγον πάντες καὶ ἐχορτάσθησαν, **43** καὶ
they ate all and were satisfied, and

ἦραν κλάσματα δώδεκα κοφίνων πληρώματα
they took fragments twelve ²of baskets ¹fullnesses

καὶ ἀπὸ τῶν ἰχθύων **44** καὶ ἦσαν οἱ
and from the fishes. And were the

φαγόντες τοὺς ἄρτους πεντακισχίλιοι ἄνδρες.
[ones] eating the loaves five thousand males.

45 Καὶ εὐθὺς ἠνάγκασεν τοὺς μαθητὰς
And immediately he constrained the disciples

αὐτοῦ ἐμβῆναι εἰς τὸ πλοῖον καὶ προάγειν
of him to embark in the ship and to go before

εἰς τὸ πέραν πρὸς Βηθσαϊδάν, ἕως αὐτὸς
to the other side to Bethsaida, until he

ἀπολύει τὸν ὄχλον. **46** καὶ ἀποταξάμενος
dismisses the crowd. And having said farewell

αὐτοῖς ἀπῆλθεν εἰς τὸ ὄρος προσεύξασθαι.
to them he went away to the mountain to pray.

47 καὶ ὀψίας γενομένης ἦν τὸ πλοῖον ἐν
And evening coming onᵃ was the ship in
= when evening came on

μέσῳ τῆς θαλάσσης, καὶ αὐτὸς μόνος ἐπὶ
[the] midst of the sea, and he alone on

τῆς γῆς. **48** καὶ ἰδὼν αὐτοὺς βασανιζομένους
the land. And seeing them being distressed

ἐν τῷ ἐλαύνειν, ἦν γὰρ ὁ ἄνεμος ἐναντίος
in the to row, ⁴was ¹for ²the ³wind contrary
= rowing,

αὐτοῖς, περὶ τετάρτην φυλακὴν τῆς νυκτὸς
to them, about [the] fourth watch of the night

ἔρχεται πρὸς αὐτοὺς περιπατῶν ἐπὶ τῆς
he comes toward them walking on the

θαλάσσης· καὶ ἤθελεν παρελθεῖν αὐτούς.
sea; and wished to go by them.

49 οἱ δὲ ἰδόντες αὐτὸν ἐπὶ τῆς θαλάσσης
But they seeing him on the sea

περιπατοῦντα ἔδοξαν ὅτι φάντασμά ἐστιν,
walking thought that a phantasm it is(was),

καὶ ἀνέκραξαν· **50** πάντες γὰρ αὐτὸν εἶδαν
and cried out; for all him saw

καὶ ἐταράχθησαν. ὁ δὲ εὐθὺς ἐλάλησεν
and were troubled. But he immediately talked

μετ᾽ αὐτῶν, καὶ λέγει αὐτοῖς· θαρσεῖτε,
with them, and says to them: Be of good cheer,

ἐγώ εἰμι· μὴ φοβεῖσθε. **51** καὶ ἀνέβη
I am; be ye not afraid. And he went up

πρὸς αὐτοὺς εἰς τὸ πλοῖον, καὶ ἐκόπασεν
to them into the ship, and ceased

ὁ ἄνεμος· καὶ λίαν ἐκ περισσοῦ ἐν ἑαυτοῖς
the wind; and very much exceedingly in themselves

⁵²for they did not understand about the loaves, but their hearts were hardened.

53 And when they had crossed over, they came to land at Gennes'aret, and moored to the shore. ⁵⁴And when they got out of the boat, immediately the people recognized him, ⁵⁵and ran about the whole neighborhood and began to bring sick people on their pallets to any place where they heard he was. ⁵⁶And wherever he came, in villages, cities, or country, they laid the sick in the market places, and besought him that they might touch even the fringe of his garment; and as many as touched it were made well.

ἐξίσταντο·   52 οὐ γὰρ συνῆκαν ἐπὶ
they were astonished ; for they did not understand concerning

τοῖς ἄρτοις ἀλλ᾽ ἦν αὐτῶν ἡ καρδία
the loaves, but was of them the heart

πεπωρωμένη.   53 Καὶ διαπεράσαντες ἐπὶ
having been hardened. And crossing over ²onto

τὴν γῆν ἦλθον εἰς Γεννησαρὲτ καὶ
³the ⁴land ¹they came to Gennesaret and

προσωρμίσθησαν.   54 καὶ ἐξελθόντων αὐτῶν
anchored. And coming *out* them⁸
                                         = as they came

ἐκ τοῦ πλοίου εὐθὺς ἐπιγνόντες αὐτὸν
out of the ship immediately knowing him

55 περιέδραμον ὅλην τὴν χώραν ἐκείνην
they ran round all - country that

καὶ ἤρξαντο ἐπὶ τοῖς κραβάτοις τοὺς
and began on the pallets the [ones]
                                         = those

κακῶς ἔχοντας περιφέρειν, ὅπου ἤκουον
ill having to carry round, where they heard
who were ill

ὅτι ἐστίν.   56 καὶ ὅπου ἂν εἰσεπορεύετο
that he is(was). And wherever he entered

εἰς κώμας ἢ εἰς πόλεις ἢ εἰς ἀγρούς,
into villages or into cities or into country,

ἐν ταῖς ἀγοραῖς ἐτίθεσαν τοὺς ἀσθενοῦντας,
in the marketplaces they put the ailing [ones],

καὶ παρεκάλουν αὐτὸν ἵνα κἂν τοῦ
and besought him that if even the

κρασπέδου τοῦ ἱματίου αὐτοῦ ἅψωνται·
fringe of the garment of him they might touch;

καὶ ὅσοι ἂν ἥψαντο αὐτοῦ ἐσῴζοντο.
and as many as touched him were healed.

CHAPTER 7

NOW when the Phari-sees gathered together to him, with some of the scribes, who had come from Jerusalem, ²they saw that some of his disciples ate with hands defiled, that is, unwashed. ³(For the Pharisees, and all the Jews, do not eat unless they wash their hands,ᵖ

7 Καὶ συνάγονται πρὸς αὐτὸν οἱ Φαρισαῖοι
And assemble to him the Pharisees

καὶ τινες τῶν γραμματέων ἐλθόντες ἀπὸ
and some of the scribes coming from

Ἱεροσολύμων.   2 καὶ ἰδόντες τινὰς τῶν
Jerusalem. And seeing some of the

μαθητῶν αὐτοῦ ὅτι κοιναῖς χερσίν, τοῦτ᾽
disciples of him that with unclean hands, this

ἔστιν ἀνίπτοις, ἐσθίουσιν τοὺς ἄρτους,
is unwashed, they eat bread,

3 — οἱ γὰρ Φαρισαῖοι καὶ πάντες οἱ
— for the Pharisees and all the

Ἰουδαῖοι ἐὰν μὴ πυγμῇ νίψωνται τὰς
Jews unless with [the] fist they wash the
                                = ? carefully

ᵖ One Greek word is of un-certain meaning and is not translated observing the tradition of the elders; ⁴and when they come from the market place, they do not eat unless they purify⁹ themselves; and there are many other traditions which they observe, the washing of cups and pots and vessels of bronze.ʳ) ⁵And the Pharisees and the scribes asked him, "Why do your disciples not live according to the tradition of the elders, but eat with hands defiled?" ⁶And he said to them, "Well did Isaiah prophesy of you hypocrites, as it is written,

'This people honors me with their lips,
but their heart is far from me;
⁷in vain do they worship me,
teaching as doctrines the precepts of men.'

⁸You leave the commandment of God, and hold fast the tradition of men."

9 And he said to them, "You have a fine way of rejecting the commandment of God, in order to keep your tradition! ¹⁰For Moses said, 'Honor your father and your mother'; and, 'He who speaks evil of father or mother, let him surely die'; ¹¹but you say, 'If a man tells his father or his

χεῖρας οὐκ ἐσθίουσιν, κρατοῦντες τὴν
hands   eat not,   holding   the
παράδοσιν τῶν πρεσβυτέρων, 4 καὶ ἀπ᾽
tradition   of the   elders,   and   from
ἀγορᾶς ἐὰν μὴ ῥαντίσωνται οὐκ ἐσθίουσιν, καὶ
marketplaces unless they sprinkle   they eat not,   and
ἄλλα πολλά ἐστιν ἃ παρέλαβον κρατεῖν,
other things many there are which they received   to hold,
βαπτισμοὺς ποτηρίων καὶ ξεστῶν καὶ
washings   of cups   and   of utensils   and
χαλκίων, — 5 καὶ ἐπερωτῶσιν αὐτὸν οἱ
of bronze vessels, —   and   questioned   him   the
Φαρισαῖοι καὶ οἱ γραμματεῖς· διὰ τί
Pharisees   and   the   scribes: Why
οὐ περιπατοῦσιν οἱ μαθηταί σου κατὰ τὴν
walk not   the disciples of thee according to the
παράδοσιν τῶν πρεσβυτέρων, ἀλλὰ κοιναῖς
tradition   of the   elders,   but with unclean
χερσὶν ἐσθίουσιν τὸν ἄρτον; 6 ὁ δὲ εἶπεν
hands   eat   -   bread?   And he   said
αὐτοῖς· καλῶς ἐπροφήτευσεν Ἡσαΐας περὶ
to them: Well   prophesied   Esaias concerning
ὑμῶν τῶν ὑποκριτῶν, ὡς γέγραπται ὅτι
you   the   hypocrites,   as it has been written[:] -
οὗτος ὁ λαὸς τοῖς χείλεσίν με τιμᾷ,
This   -   people with the   lips   me honours,
ἡ δὲ καρδία αὐτῶν πόρρω ἀπέχει ἀπ᾽
but the   heart of them   ¹far   ¹is ²away from
ἐμοῦ· 7 μάτην δὲ σέβονταί με, διδάσκοντες
me;   and in vain they worship me,   teaching
διδασκαλίας ἐντάλματα ἀνθρώπων. 8 ἀφέντες
teachings [which are] commands   of men.   Leaving
τὴν ἐντολὴν τοῦ θεοῦ κρατεῖτε τὴν
the   commandment   -   of God   ye hold   the
παράδοσιν τῶν ἀνθρώπων. 9 καὶ ἔλεγεν
tradition   -   of men.   And   he said
αὐτοῖς· καλῶς ἀθετεῖτε τὴν ἐντολὴν τοῦ
to them: Well   ye set aside   the commandment -
θεοῦ, ἵνα τὴν παράδοσιν ὑμῶν τηρήσητε.
of God,   that the   tradition   of you   ye may keep.

10 Μωϋσῆς γὰρ εἶπεν· τίμα τὸν πατέρα σου
For Moses   said: Honour   the   father of thee
καὶ τὴν μητέρα σου, καὶ· ὁ κακολογῶν
and   the   mother   of thee, and: The [one] speaking evil of
πατέρα ἢ μητέρα θανάτῳ τελευτάτω. 11 ὑμεῖς
father or   mother   by death let him end(die).   ye
δὲ λέγετε· ἐὰν εἴπῃ ἄνθρωπος τῷ πατρὶ
But say: If   says   a man   to the(his) father

⁹ Other ancient authorities read *baptize*

ʳ Other ancient authorities add *and beds*

mother, What you would have gained from me is Corban' (that is, given to God)*—¹²then you no longer permit him to do anything for his father or mother, ¹³thus making void the word of God through your tradition which you hand on. And many such things you do."

14 And he called the people to him again, and said to them, "Hear me, all of you, and understand: ¹⁵there is nothing outside a man which by going into him can defile him; but the things which come out of a man are what defile him."ᵗ ¹⁷And when he had entered the house, and left the people, his disciples asked him about the parable. ¹⁸And he said to them, "Then are you also without understanding? Do you not see that whatever goes into a man from outside cannot defile him, ¹⁹since it enters, not his heart but his stomach, and so passes on?"ᵘ (Thus he declared all foods clean.) ²⁰And he said, "What comes out of a man is what defiles a man. ²¹For from within,

ἢ τῇ μητρί· κορβᾶν, ὅ ἐστιν δῶρον,
or to the mother: Korban,   which   is   a gift,

ὃ ἐὰν ἐξ ἐμοῦ ὠφεληθῇς, 12 οὐκέτι ἀφίετε
whatever by   me thou mightest profit,   no longer   ye allow

αὐτὸν οὐδὲν ποιῆσαι τῷ πατρὶ ἢ τῇ
him no(any)thing   to do   for the father   or   the

μητρί, 13 ἀκυροῦντες τὸν λόγον τοῦ θεοῦ
mother,   annulling   the   word   – of God

τῇ παραδόσει ὑμῶν ᾗ παρεδώκατε· καὶ
by the   tradition   of you   which ye received;   and

παρόμοια τοιαῦτα πολλὰ ποιεῖτε. 14 Καὶ
²similar things ²such   ¹many   ye do.   And

προσκαλεσάμενος πάλιν τὸν ὄχλον ἔλεγεν
calling to [him]   again   the   crowd   he said

αὐτοῖς· ἀκούσατέ μου πάντες καὶ σύνετε.
to them: Hear ye   me   all   and understand.

15 οὐδέν ἐστιν ἔξωθεν τοῦ ἀνθρώπου
Nothing   there is   from without   –   a man

εἰσπορευόμενον εἰς αὐτὸν ὃ δύναται κοινῶσαι
entering   into   him   which can   to defile

αὐτόν· ἀλλὰ τὰ ἐκ τοῦ ἀνθρώπου ἐκπο-
him;   but the things out of –   a man   coming

ρευόμενά ἐστιν τὰ κοινοῦντα τὸν ἄνθρωπον. ‡
forth   are the [ones] defiling   –   a man.

17 Καὶ ὅτε εἰσῆλθεν εἰς οἶκον ἀπὸ τοῦ
And   when he entered   into   a house   from   the

ὄχλου, ἐπηρώτων αὐτὸν οἱ μαθηταὶ αὐτοῦ
crowd,   questioned   him   the   disciples   of him

τὴν παραβολήν. 18 καὶ λέγει αὐτοῖς·
the   parable.   And   he says   to them:

οὕτως καὶ ὑμεῖς ἀσύνετοί ἐστε; οὐ
Thus   also   ye   undiscerning   are?   do ye not

νοεῖτε ὅτι πᾶν τὸ ἔξωθεν εἰσπορευόμενον
understand that   everything   from without   entering

εἰς τὸν ἄνθρωπον οὐ δύναται αὐτὸν
into   –   a man   cannot   him

κοινῶσαι, 19 ὅτι οὐκ εἰσπορεύεται αὐτοῦ
to defile,   because   it enters not   of him

εἰς τὴν καρδίαν ἀλλ' εἰς τὴν κοιλίαν,
into   the   heart   but   into   the   belly,

καὶ εἰς τὸν ἀφεδρῶνα ἐκπορεύεται, καθα-
and   into   the   drain   goes out,   purg-

ρίζων πάντα τὰ βρώματα; 20 ἔλεγεν δὲ
ing   all   –   foods?   And he said[,]

ὅτι τὸ ἐκ τοῦ ἀνθρώπου ἐκπορευόμενον,
–   The thing out of –   a man   coming forth,

ἐκεῖνο κοινοῖ τὸν ἄνθρωπον. 21 ἔσωθεν
that   defiles   –   a man.   from within

ˢ Or an *offering*
ᵗ Other ancient authorities add verse 16, "*If any man has ears to hear, let him hear*"
ᵘ Or is *evacuated*

‡ Verse 16 omitted by Nestle; *cf.* RSV footnote.

out of the heart of man, come evil thoughts, fornication, theft, murder, adultery, [22]coveting, wickedness, deceit, licentiousness, envy, slander, pride, foolishness. [23]All these evil things come from within, and they defile a man."

24 And from there he arose and went away to the region of Tyre and Sidon.[v] And he entered a house, and would not have any one know it; yet he could not be hid. [25]But immediately a woman, whose little daughter was possessed by an unclean spirit, heard of him, and came and fell down at his feet. [26]Now the woman was a Greek, a Syrophoeni'cian by birth. And she begged him to cast the demon out of her daughter. [27]And he said to her, "Let the children first be fed, for it is not right to take the children's bread and throw it to the dogs." [28]But she answered him, "Yes, Lord; yet even the dogs under the table eat the children's crumbs." [29]And he said to her, "For this saying you may

γὰρ ἐκ τῆς καρδίας τῶν ἀνθρώπων
For out of the   heart   -   of men
οἱ διαλογισμοὶ οἱ κακοὶ ἐκπορεύονται,
-   thoughts   -   evil   come forth,
πορνεῖαι, κλοπαί, φόνοι, 22 μοιχεῖαι,
fornications,   thefts,   murders,   adulteries,
πλεονεξίαι, πονηρίαι, δόλος, ἀσέλγεια, ὀφθαλμὸς
greedinesses,   iniquities,   deceit,   lewdness,   eye
πονηρός, βλασφημία, ὑπερηφανία, ἀφροσύνη·
an evil,   blasphemy,   arrogance,   foolishness;
23 πάντα ταῦτα τὰ πονηρὰ ἔσωθεν ἐκπορεύεται
all   these   - evil things from within   comes forth
καὶ κοινοῖ τὸν ἄνθρωπον.
and   defile   -   a man.

24 Ἐκεῖθεν δὲ ἀναστὰς ἀπῆλθεν εἰς τὰ ὅρια
And thence   rising up   he went away into the district
Τύρου. Καὶ εἰσελθὼν εἰς οἰκίαν οὐδένα ἤθελεν
of Tyre.   And   entering   into a house   no one he wished
γνῶναι, καὶ οὐκ ἠδυνάσθη λαθεῖν· 25 ἀλλ'
to know,   and   could not   to be hidden;   but
εὐθὺς ἀκούσασα γυνὴ περὶ αὐτοῦ, ἧς
immediately   [a]hearing [a]a woman   about   him,   of whom
                                                = whose
εἶχεν τὸ θυγάτριον αὐτῆς πνεῦμα ἀκάθαρτον,
had   the   daughter   of her   spirit   an unclean,
ἐλθοῦσα προσέπεσεν πρὸς τοὺς πόδας αὐτοῦ·
coming   fell   at   the   feet   of him;
26 ἡ δὲ γυνὴ ἦν Ἑλληνίς, Συροφοινίκισσα
and the   woman was   a Greek,   a Syrophenician
τῷ γένει· καὶ ἠρώτα αὐτὸν ἵνα τὸ
-   by race;   and   she asked   him   that   the
δαιμόνιον ἐκβάλῃ ἐκ τῆς θυγατρὸς αὐτῆς.
demon   he would expel out of   the   daughter   of her.
27 καὶ ἔλεγεν αὐτῇ· ἄφες πρῶτον
And   he said   to her: Permit   first
χορτασθῆναι τὰ τέκνα· οὐ γάρ ἐστιν καλὸν
to be satisfied   the   children;   for it is not   good
λαβεῖν τὸν ἄρτον τῶν τέκνων καὶ τοῖς
to take   the   bread   of the   children   and   to the
κυναρίοις βαλεῖν. 28 ἡ δὲ ἀπεκρίθη καὶ
dogs   to throw [it].   And she   answered   and
λέγει αὐτῷ· ναί, κύριε· καὶ τὰ κυνάρια
says   to him: Yes, Lord;   and yet   the   dogs
ὑποκάτω τῆς τραπέζης ἐσθίουσιν ἀπὸ τῶν
under   the   table   eat   from   the
ψιχίων τῶν παιδίων. 29 καὶ εἶπεν αὐτῇ·
crumbs   of the   children.   And   he said   to her:
διὰ τοῦτον τὸν λόγον ὕπαγε, ἐξελήλυθεν
Because of   this   -   word   go,   has gone forth

[v] Other ancient authorities omit *and Sidon*

go your way; the demon has left your daughter." ³⁰And she went home, and found the child lying in bed, and the demon gone.

31 Then he returned from the region of Tyre, and went through Sidon to the Sea of Galilee, through the region of the Decap'olis. ³²And they brought to him a man who was deaf and had an impediment in his speech; and they besought him to lay his hand upon him. ³³And taking him aside from the multitude privately, he put his fingers into his ears, and he spat and touched his tongue; ³⁴and looking up to heaven, he sighed, and said to him, "Eph'-phatha," that is, "Be opened." ³⁵And his ears were opened, his tongue was released, and he spoke plainly. ³⁶And he charged them to tell no one; but the more he charged them, the more zealously they proclaimed it. ³⁷And they were astonished beyond measure, saying, "He has done all things well; he even makes the deaf hear and the dumb speak."

ἐκ τῆς θυγατρός σου τὸ δαιμόνιον. 30 καὶ
out of the   daughter   of thee   the   demon.   And

ἀπελθοῦσα εἰς τὸν οἶκον αὐτῆς εὗρεν τὸ
going away   to   the   house   of her she found the

παιδίον βεβλημένον ἐπὶ τὴν κλίνην καὶ τὸ
child   having been laid   on   the   couch   and   the

δαιμόνιον ἐξεληλυθός. 31 Καὶ πάλιν ἐξελθὼν
demon   having gone forth.   And   again   going forth

ἐκ τῶν ὁρίων Τύρου ἦλθεν διὰ Σιδῶνος
out of the   district   of Tyre   he came through   Sidon

εἰς τὴν θάλασσαν τῆς Γαλιλαίας ἀνὰ
to   the   sea   -   of Galilee   in the

μέσον τῶν ὁρίων Δεκαπόλεως. 32 Καὶ
midst   of the   district   of Decapolis.   And

φέρουσιν αὐτῷ κωφὸν καὶ μογιλάλον, καὶ
they bring to him a man deaf and speaking with difficulty, and

παρακαλοῦσιν αὐτὸν ἵνα ἐπιθῇ αὐτῷ τὴν
they beseech   him   that he would put on on him the(his)

χεῖρα. 33 καὶ ἀπολαβόμενος αὐτὸν ἀπὸ
hand.   And   taking away   him   from

τοῦ ὄχλου κατ' ἰδίαν ἔβαλεν τοὺς δακτύλους
the   crowd   privately   he put   the   fingers

αὐτοῦ εἰς τὰ ὦτα αὐτοῦ καὶ πτύσας
of him   into   the   ears   of him   and   spitting

ἥψατο τῆς γλώσσης αὐτοῦ, 34 καὶ
he touched   the   tongue   of him,   and

ἀναβλέψας εἰς τὸν οὐρανὸν ἐστέναξεν,
looking up   to   -   heaven   he groaned,

καὶ λέγει αὐτῷ· ἐφφαθά, ὅ ἐστιν διανοίχθητι.
and   says   to him: Ephphatha, which is Be thou opened.

35 καὶ ἠνοίγησαν αὐτοῦ αἱ ἀκοαί, καὶ
And   were opened   of him   the   ears,   and

εὐθὺς ἐλύθη ὁ δεσμὸς τῆς γλώσσης αὐτοῦ,
immediately was loosened the bond of the tongue of him,

καὶ ἐλάλει ὀρθῶς. 36 καὶ διεστείλατο
and   he spoke   correctly.   And   he ordered

αὐτοῖς ἵνα μηδενὶ λέγωσιν· ὅσον δὲ
them   that   no one they should tell; but as much as

αὐτοῖς διεστέλλετο, αὐτοὶ μᾶλλον περισσότερον
them   he ordered,   they   more   exceedingly

ἐκήρυσσον. 37 καὶ ὑπερπερισσῶς ἐξεπλήσσοντο
proclaimed.   And most exceedingly they were astounded

λέγοντες· καλῶς πάντα πεποίηκεν, καὶ
saying: Well   all things   he has done,   both

τοὺς κωφοὺς ποιεῖ ἀκούειν καὶ ἀλάλους
the   deaf   he makes   to hear   and   dumb

λαλεῖν.
to speak.

CHAPTER 8

IN those days, when
again a great crowd
had gathered and they
had nothing to eat, he
called his disciples to him
and said to them, [2] "I
have compassion on the
crowd, because they have
been with me now three
days, and have nothing
to eat; [3] and if I send
them away hungry to
their homes, they will
faint on the way; and
some of them have come
a long way." [4] And his
disciples answered him,
"How can one feed
these men with bread
here in the desert?"
[5] And he asked them,
"How many loaves have
you?" They said,
"Seven." [6] And he com-
manded the crowd to sit
down on the ground;
and he took the seven
loaves, and having given
thanks he broke them
and gave them to his
disciples to set before the
people; and they set them
before the crowd. [7] And
they had a few small fish;
and having blessed them,
he commanded that these
also should be set before
them. [8] And they ate, and
were satisfied; and they
took up the broken pieces
left over, seven baskets
full. [9] And there were
about four thousand
people. [10] And he sent
them away; and immed-
iately he got into the
boat with his disciples,

8 Ἐν ἐκείναις ταῖς ἡμέραις πάλιν πολλοῦ
In   those   -   days   again a much(great)
                                      = there being

ὄχλου ὄντος καὶ μὴ ἐχόντων τί φάγωσιν,
crowd being[a] and not having[a] anything they might eat,
a great crowd

προσκαλεσάμενος τοὺς μαθητὰς λέγει αὐτοῖς·
calling to [him]   the   disciples he says to them:

2 σπλαγχνίζομαι ἐπὶ τὸν ὄχλον, ὅτι ἤδη
  I have compassion on the crowd, because now

ἡμέραι τρεῖς προσμένουσίν μοι καὶ οὐκ
days   three they remain with   me and not

ἔχουσιν τί φάγωσιν· 3 καὶ ἐὰν ἀπολύσω
they have anything they may eat; and if   I dismiss

αὐτοὺς νήστεις εἰς οἶκον αὐτῶν, ἐκλυθήσονται
them   fasting to house of them, they will faint

ἐν τῇ ὁδῷ· καί τινες αὐτῶν ἀπὸ μακρόθεν
in the way; and some of them from afar

εἰσίν. 4 καὶ ἀπεκρίθησαν αὐτῷ οἱ μαθηταὶ
are.   And answered   him the disciples

αὐτοῦ ὅτι πόθεν τούτους δυνήσεταί τις
of him[,] - [1]Whence [6]these people [2]will [4]be able [3]anyone

ὧδε χορτάσαι ἄρτων ἐπ᾽ ἐρημίας; 5 καὶ
[5]here [5]to satisfy [7]of(with) loaves [8]on(in) [10]a desert? And

ἠρώτα αὐτούς· πόσους ἔχετε ἄρτους;
he asked them: How many have ye   loaves?

οἱ δὲ εἶπαν· ἑπτά. 6 καὶ παραγγέλλει τῷ
And they said: Seven.   And he commands   the

ὄχλῳ ἀναπεσεῖν ἐπὶ τῆς γῆς· καὶ λαβὼν
crowd to recline on the ground; and taking

τοὺς ἑπτὰ ἄρτους εὐχαριστήσας ἔκλασεν
the seven loaves   giving thanks   he broke

καὶ ἐδίδου τοῖς μαθηταῖς αὐτοῦ ἵνα
and gave to the disciples of him that

παρατιθῶσιν, καὶ παρέθηκαν τῷ ὄχλῳ.
they might serve, and they served the crowd.

7 καὶ εἶχον ἰχθύδια ὀλίγα· καὶ εὐλογήσας
  And they had fishes   a few; and blessing

αὐτὰ εἶπεν καὶ ταῦτα παρατιθέναι. 8 καὶ
them he told also these to be served.   And

ἔφαγον καὶ ἐχορτάσθησαν, καὶ ἦραν
they ate and were satisfied, and took

περισσεύματα κλασμάτων, ἑπτὰ σπυρίδας.
excesses   of fragments, seven baskets.

9 ἦσαν δὲ ὡς τετρακισχίλιοι. καὶ ἀπέλυσεν
  Now they were about four thousand. And he dismissed

αὐτούς. 10 Καὶ εὐθὺς ἐμβὰς εἰς τὸ
them.   And immediately embarking in the

πλοῖον μετὰ τῶν μαθητῶν αὐτοῦ
ship   with the   disciples of him

and went to the district of Dalmanu'tha.[w]

11 The Pharisees came and began to argue with him, seeking from him a sign from heaven, to test him. [12]And he sighed deeply in his spirit, and said, "Why does this generation seek a sign? Truly, I say to you, no sign shall be given to this generation." [13]And he left them, and getting into the boat again he departed to the other side.

14 Now they had forgotten to bring bread; and they had only one loaf with them in the boat. [15]And he cautioned them, saying, "Take heed, beware of the leaven of the Pharisees and the leaven of Herod."[x] [16]And they discussed it with one another, saying, "We have no bread." [17]And being aware of it, Jesus said to them, "Why do you discuss the fact that you have no bread? Do you not yet perceive or understand? Are your hearts hardened? [18]Having eyes do you not see, and having ears do you not hear? And do you not remember? [19]When I broke the five loaves for the five thousand, how many baskets full of broken pieces did you take up?" They said to

[w] Other ancient authorities read *Magadan* or *Magdala*

[x] Other ancient authorities read *the Herodians*

ἦλθεν   εἰς   τὰ   μέρη   Δαλμανουθά.
he came   into   the   region   of Dalmanutha.

11 Καὶ   ἐξῆλθον   οἱ   Φαρισαῖοι   καὶ   ἤρξαντο
And   came forth   the   Pharisees   and   began

συζητεῖν   αὐτῷ,   ζητοῦντες   παρ'   αὐτοῦ
to debate   with him,   seeking   from   him

σημεῖον   ἀπὸ   τοῦ   οὐρανοῦ,   πειράζοντες
a sign   from   heaven,   tempting

αὐτόν.   12 καὶ   ἀναστενάξας   τῷ   πνεύματι
him.   And   groaning   in the   spirit

αὐτοῦ   λέγει·   τί   ἡ   γενεὰ   αὕτη   ζητεῖ
of him   he says: Why – [2]generation [3]this [1]does [4]seek

σημεῖον;   ἀμὴν   λέγω   ὑμῖν,   εἰ   δοθήσεται
a sign?   Truly   I tell   you,   if   will be given

τῇ   γενεᾷ   ταύτῃ   σημεῖον.   13 καὶ   ἀφεὶς
–   generation   to this   a sign.   And   leaving

αὐτοὺς   πάλιν   ἐμβὰς   ἀπῆλθεν   εἰς   τὸ
them   again   embarking   he went away   to   the

πέραν.   14 Καὶ   ἐπελάθοντο   λαβεῖν   ἄρτους,
other side.   And   they forgot   to take   loaves,

καὶ   εἰ   μὴ   ἕνα   ἄρτον   οὐκ   εἶχον   μεθ'
and   except   one   loaf   they had not   with

ἑαυτῶν   ἐν   τῷ   πλοίῳ.   15 καὶ   διεστέλλετο
them*selves*   in   the   ship.   And   he charged

αὐτοῖς   λέγων·   ὁρᾶτε,   βλέπετε   ἀπὸ   τῆς
them   saying :   See,   look ye   from   the
               =Beware of

ζύμης   τῶν   Φαρισαίων   καὶ   τῆς   ζύμης
leaven   of the   Pharisees   and   of the   leaven

Ἡρώδου.   16 καὶ   διελογίζοντο   πρὸς   ἀλλήλους
of Herod.   And   they reasoned   with   one another

ὅτι   ἄρτους   οὐκ   ἔχουσιν.   17 καὶ   γνοὺς
because   loaves   they have(had) not.   And   knowing

λέγει   αὐτοῖς·   τί   διαλογίζεσθε   ὅτι   ἄρτους
he says   to them: Why   reason ye   because   loaves

οὐκ   ἔχετε;   οὔπω   νοεῖτε   οὐδὲ   συνίετε;
ye have not ?   not yet   understand ye   nor   realize ?

πεπωρωμένην   ἔχετε   τὴν   καρδίαν   ὑμῶν;
having been hardened   have ye   the   heart   of you ?

18 ὀφθαλμοὺς   ἔχοντες   οὐ   βλέπετε,   καὶ
eyes   having   see ye not,   and

ὦτα   ἔχοντες   οὐκ   ἀκούετε;   καὶ
ears   having   hear ye not ?   and

οὐ   μνημονεύετε,   19 ὅτε   τοὺς   πέντε   ἄρτους
do ye not remember,   when   the   five   loaves

ἔκλασα   εἰς   τοὺς   πεντακισχιλίους,   πόσους
I broke   to   the   five thousand,   how many

κοφίνους   κλασμάτων   πλήρεις   ἤρατε;   λέγουσιν
baskets   of fragments   full   ye took ?   They say

him, "Twelve." ²⁰"And
the seven for the four
thousand, how many
baskets full of broken
pieces did you take up?"
And they said to him,
"Seven." ²¹And he said
to them, "Do you not
yet understand?"

22 And they came to
Beth-sa'ida. And some
people brought to him a
blind man, and begged
him to touch him. ²³And
he took the blind man by
the hand, and led him
out of the village; and
when he had spit on his
eyes and laid his hands
upon him, he asked him,
"Do you see anything?"
²⁴And he looked up and
said, "I see men; but
they look like trees,
walking." ²⁵Then again
he laid his hands upon
his eyes; and he looked
intently and was restored,
and saw everything
clearly. ²⁶And he sent
him away to his home,
saying, "Do not even
enter the village."

27 And Jesus went on
with his disciples, to the
villages of Caesare'a
Philippi; and on the way
he asked his disciples,
"Who do men say that I
am?" ²⁸And they told
him, "John the Baptist;

αὐτῷ·   δώδεκα.   20 ὅτε   τοὺς   ἑπτὰ   εἰς
to him: Twelve.   When   the   seven   to

τοὺς   τετρακισχιλίους,   πόσων   σπυρίδων
the   four thousand,   ²of how many   ³baskets

πληρώματα   κλασμάτων   ἤρατε;   καὶ   λέγουσιν·
¹fullnesses   ⁴of fragments   ye took ?   And   they say:

ἑπτά.   21 καὶ   ἔλεγεν   αὐτοῖς·   οὔπω   συνίετε;
Seven.   And   he said   to them: Not yet do ye realize?

22 Καὶ   ἔρχονται   εἰς   Βηθσαϊδάν.   Καὶ
And   they come   to   Bethsaida.   And

φέρουσιν   αὐτῷ   τυφλόν,   καὶ   παρακαλοῦσιν
they bring   to him   a blind man,   and   beseech

αὐτὸν   ἵνα   αὐτοῦ   ἅψηται.   23 καὶ   ἐπιλαβόμενος
him   that   him   he would touch.   And   laying hold of

τῆς   χειρὸς   τοῦ   τυφλοῦ   ἐξήνεγκεν   αὐτὸν
the   hand   of the   blind man   he led forth   him

ἔξω   τῆς   κώμης,   καὶ   πτύσας   εἰς   τὰ
outside   the   village,   and   spitting   in   the

ὄμματα   αὐτοῦ,   ἐπιθεὶς   τὰς   χεῖρας   αὐτῷ,
eyes   of him,   putting on   the   hands   on him,

ἐπηρώτα   αὐτόν·   εἴ   τι   βλέπεις;   24 καὶ
questioned   him: If   anything   thou seest ?   And

ἀναβλέψας   ἔλεγεν·   βλέπω   τοὺς   ἀνθρώπους,
looking up   he said :   I see   -   men,

ὅτι   ὡς   δένδρα   ὁρῶ   περιπατοῦντας.
that   as   trees   I behold   walking.

25 εἶτα   πάλιν   ἐπέθηκεν   τὰς   χεῖρας   ἐπὶ
Then   again   he put on   the   hands   on

τοὺς   ὀφθαλμοὺς   αὐτοῦ,   καὶ   διέβλεψεν   καὶ
the   eyes   of him,   and   he looked steadily   and

ἀπεκατέστη,   καὶ   ἐνέβλεπεν   τηλαυγῶς   ἅπαντα.
was restored,   and   saw   clearly   all things.

26 καὶ   ἀπέστειλεν   αὐτὸν   εἰς   οἶκον   αὐτοῦ
And   he sent   him   to   house   of him

λέγων·   μηδὲ   εἰς   τὴν   κώμην   εἰσέλθης.
saying: Not   into   the   village   thou mayest enter.

27 Καὶ   ἐξῆλθεν   ὁ   Ἰησοῦς   καὶ   οἱ   μαθηταὶ
And   went forth   -   Jesus   and   the   disciples

αὐτοῦ   εἰς   τὰς   κώμας   Καισαρείας   τῆς
of him   to   the   villages   of Cæsarea

Φιλίππου·   καὶ   ἐν   τῇ   ὁδῷ   ἐπηρώτα   τοὺς
of Philip;   and   in   the   way   he questioned   the

μαθητὰς   αὐτοῦ   λέγων   αὐτοῖς·   τίνα   με
disciples   of him   saying   to them: Whom   me

λέγουσιν   οἱ   ἄνθρωποι   εἶναι;   28 οἱ   δὲ
say   -   men   to be ?   And they

εἶπαν   αὐτῷ   λέγοντες   ὅτι   Ἰωάννην   τὸν
told   him   saying[,]   -   John   the

and others say, Eli'jah; and others one of the prophets." ²⁹And he asked them, "But who do you say that I am?" Peter answered him, "You are the Christ." ³⁰And he charged them to tell no one about him.

31 And he began to teach them that the Son of man must suffer many things, and be rejected by the elders and the chief priests and the scribes, and be killed, and after three days rise again. ³²And he said this plainly. And Peter took him, and began to rebuke him. ³³But turning and seeing his disciples, he rebuked Peter, and said, "Get behind me, Satan! For you are not on the side of God, but of men."

34 And he called to him the multitude with his disciples, and said to them, "If any man would come after me, let him deny himself and take up his cross and follow me. ³⁵For whoever would save his life will lose it; and whoever loses

βαπτιστήν, καὶ ἄλλοι Ἠλίαν, ἄλλοι δὲ
Baptist,　and　others　Elias,　but others[,]
ὅτι εἷς τῶν προφητῶν. 29 καὶ αὐτὸς
- one of the　prophets.　　And　he
ἐπηρώτα αὐτούς· ὑμεῖς δὲ τίνα με λέγετε
questioned　them:　But ye　whom me　say ye
εἶναι; ἀποκριθεὶς ὁ Πέτρος λέγει αὐτῷ·
to be?　Answering　-　Peter　says　to him:
σὺ εἶ ὁ χριστός. 30 καὶ ἐπετίμησεν
Thou art the　Christ.　　And　he warned
αὐτοῖς ἵνα μηδενὶ λέγωσιν περὶ αὐτοῦ.
them　that　no one they might tell about　him.
31 Καὶ ἤρξατο διδάσκειν αὐτοὺς ὅτι δεῖ
And he began　to teach　them　that it behoves
τὸν υἱὸν τοῦ ἀνθρώπου πολλὰ παθεῖν,
the　Son　-　of man　many things to suffer,
καὶ ἀποδοκιμασθῆναι ὑπὸ τῶν πρεσβυτέρων
and　to be rejected　by　the　elders
καὶ τῶν ἀρχιερέων καὶ τῶν γραμματέων
and the chief priests and the　scribes
καὶ ἀποκτανθῆναι καὶ μετὰ τρεῖς ἡμέρας
and　to be killed　and　after　three　days
ἀναστῆναι· 32 καὶ παρρησίᾳ τὸν λόγον
to rise again;　and　openly　the　word
ἐλάλει. καὶ προσλαβόμενος ὁ Πέτρος
he spoke.　And　²taking ⁴aside　-　¹Peter
αὐτὸν ἤρξατο ἐπιτιμᾶν αὐτῷ. 33 ὁ δὲ
³him　began　to rebuke　him.　　But he
ἐπιστραφεὶς καὶ ἰδὼν τοὺς μαθητὰς αὐτοῦ
turning round　and　seeing　the　disciples　of him
ἐπετίμησεν Πέτρῳ καὶ λέγει· ὕπαγε ὀπίσω
rebuked　Peter　and　says:　Go　behind
μου, σατανᾶ, ὅτι οὐ φρονεῖς τὰ τοῦ
me,　Satan, because thou mindest not the things　-
θεοῦ ἀλλὰ τὰ τῶν ἀνθρώπων. 34 Καὶ
of God　but the things　-　of men.　　And
προσκαλεσάμενος τὸν ὄχλον σὺν τοῖς μαθηταῖς
calling to [him]　the　crowd　with the　disciples
αὐτοῦ εἶπεν αὐτοῖς· εἴ τις θέλει ὀπίσω
of him　he said　to them:　If anyone wishes　after
μου ἐλθεῖν, ἀπαρνησάσθω ἑαυτὸν καὶ ἀράτω
me　to come,　let him deny　himself　and　take
τὸν σταυρὸν αὐτοῦ, καὶ ἀκολουθείτω μοι.
the　cross　of him,　and　let him follow　me.
35 ὃς γὰρ ἐὰν θέλῃ τὴν ψυχὴν αὐτοῦ σῶ-
For whoever　wishes　the　life　of him to
σαι, ἀπολέσει αὐτήν· ὃς δ᾽ ἂν ἀπολέσει
save,　will lose　it;　but whoever　will lose

his life for my sake and the gospel's will save it. ³⁶For what does it profit a man, to gain the whole world and forfeit his life? ³⁷For what can a man give in return for his life? ³⁸For whoever is ashamed of me and of my words in this adulterous and sinful generation, of him will the Son of man also be ashamed, when he comes in the glory of his Father with the holy angels."

τὴν ψυχὴν αὐτοῦ ἕνεκεν ἐμοῦ καὶ τοῦ
the   life   of him for the sake of me   and the
εὐαγγελίου, σώσει αὐτήν. 36 τί γὰρ ὠφελεῖ
gospel,   will save it.   For what profits
ἄνθρωπον κερδῆσαι τὸν κόσμον ὅλον καὶ
a man   to gain   the   world   whole and
ζημιωθῆναι τὴν ψυχὴν αὐτοῦ; 37 τί γὰρ
to be fined   the   soul   of him?   For what
δοῖ ἄνθρωπος ἀντάλλαγμα τῆς ψυχῆς αὐτοῦ;
might give a man   an exchange   of the soul   of him?
38 ὃς γὰρ ἐὰν ἐπαισχυνθῇ με καὶ
For whoever   is ashamed of   me   and
τοὺς ἐμοὺς λόγους ἐν τῇ γενεᾷ ταύτῃ
 -    my   words   in - generation this
τῇ μοιχαλίδι καὶ ἁμαρτωλῷ, καὶ ὁ
 - adulterous   and   sinful,   also the
υἱὸς τοῦ ἀνθρώπου ἐπαισχυνθήσεται αὐτόν,
Son   of   man   will be ashamed of   him,
ὅταν ἔλθῃ ἐν τῇ δόξῃ τοῦ πατρὸς
when he comes in the glory of the Father
αὐτοῦ μετὰ τῶν ἀγγέλων τῶν ἁγίων.
of him with   the   angels   -   holy.

CHAPTER 9

AND he said to them, "Truly, I say to you, there are some standing here who will not taste death before they see the kingdom of God come with power."

2 And after six days Jesus took with him Peter and James and John, and led them up a high mountain apart by themselves; and he was transfigured before them, ³and his garments became glistening, intensely white, as no fuller on earth could bleach them.

9 καὶ ἔλεγεν αὐτοῖς· ἀμὴν λέγω ὑμῖν
And he said   to them: Truly   I tell you
ὅτι εἰσίν τινες ὧδε τῶν ἑστηκότων
that there are some   here of the [ones] standing
οἵτινες οὐ μὴ γεύσωνται θανάτου ἕως ἂν
who   by no means may taste   of death until
ἴδωσιν τὴν βασιλείαν τοῦ θεοῦ ἐληλυθυῖαν
they see   the   kingdom   -   of God   having come
ἐν δυνάμει.
in power.

2 Καὶ μετὰ ἡμέρας ἓξ παραλαμβάνει
And after   days   six   takes
ὁ Ἰησοῦς τὸν Πέτρον καὶ τὸν Ἰάκωβον
- Jesus   -   Peter   and   -   James
καὶ Ἰωάννην, καὶ ἀναφέρει αὐτοὺς εἰς
and   John,   and leads up   them   into
ὄρος ὑψηλὸν κατ' ἰδίαν μόνους. καὶ
mountain a high   privately   alone.   And
μετεμορφώθη ἔμπροσθεν αὐτῶν, 3 καὶ τὰ
he was transfigured before   them,   and the
ἱμάτια αὐτοῦ ἐγένετο στίλβοντα λευκὰ λίαν,
garments of him became   gleaming   white exceedingly,
οἷα γναφεὺς ἐπὶ τῆς γῆς οὐ δύναται
such as fuller   on   the earth cannot

⁴And there appeared to them Eli'jah with Moses; and they were talking to Jesus. ⁵And Peter said to Jesus, "Master, it is well that we are here; let us make three booths, one for you and one for Moses and one for Eli'jah." ⁶For he did not know what to say, for they were exceedingly afraid. ⁷And a cloud overshadowed them, and a voice came out of the cloud, "This is my beloved Son;ᵛ listen to him." ⁸And suddenly looking around they no longer saw any one with them but Jesus only.

9 And as they were coming down the mountain, he charged them to tell no one what they had seen, until the Son of man should have risen from the dead. ¹⁰So they kept the matter to themselves, questioning what the rising from the dead meant. ¹¹And they asked him, "Why do the scribes say that first Eli'jah must come?" ¹²And he said to them, "Eli'jah does come first to restore all things; and how is it written of the Son of man, that he should suffer many

ᵛ Or *my Son, my* (or *the*) *Beloved*

οὕτως λευκᾶναι. 4 καὶ ὤφθη αὐτοῖς Ἡλίας
so   to whiten.   And appeared to them   Elias
σὺν Μωϋσεῖ, καὶ ἦσαν συλλαλοῦντες τῷ
with   Moses,   and they were   conversing with
Ἰησοῦ. 5 καὶ ἀποκριθεὶς ὁ Πέτρος λέγει
Jesus.   And   answering   -   Peter   says
τῷ Ἰησοῦ· ῥαββί, καλόν ἐστιν ἡμᾶς ὧδε
- to Jesus: Rabbi, good   it is   us   here
εἶναι, καὶ ποιήσωμεν τρεῖς σκηνάς, σοὶ
to be,   and   let us make   three   tents,   for thee
μίαν καὶ Μωϋσεῖ μίαν καὶ Ἡλίᾳ μίαν.
one   and for Moses   one   and   for Elias   one.
6 οὐ γὰρ ᾔδει τί ἀποκριθῇ· ἔκφοβοι γὰρ
For he knew not   what he answered; for exceedingly afraid
ἐγένοντο. 7 καὶ ἐγένετο νεφέλη ἐπισκιάζουσα
they became.   And there came a cloud   overshadowing
αὐτοῖς, καὶ ἐγένετο φωνὴ ἐκ τῆς νεφέλης·
them,   and there came   a voice out of the   cloud:
οὗτός ἐστιν ὁ υἱός μου ὁ ἀγαπητός,
This   is   the   Son   of me   *the*   beloved,
ἀκούετε αὐτοῦ. 8 καὶ ἐξάπινα περιβλεψάμενοι
hear ye   him.   And suddenly   looking round
οὐκέτι οὐδένα εἶδον εἰ μὴ τὸν Ἰησοῦν
no longer no(any)one they saw   except   -   Jesus
μόνον μεθ' ἑαυτῶν. 9 Καὶ καταβαινόντων
only   with themselves.   And   coming down
　　　　　　　　　　　　　　　　= as they came down
αὐτῶν ἐκ τοῦ ὄρους διεστείλατο αὐτοῖς
themᵃ out of   the   mountain   he ordered   them
ἵνα μηδενὶ ἃ εἶδον διηγήσωνται,
that to no one [the] things which they saw they should relate,
εἰ μὴ ὅταν ὁ υἱὸς τοῦ ἀνθρώπου ἐκ νεκρῶν
except when the Son - of man out of [the] dead
ἀναστῇ. 10 καὶ τὸν λόγον ἐκράτησαν πρὸς
should rise.   And the   word   they held   to
ἑαυτοὺς συζητοῦντες τί ἐστιν τὸ ἐκ
themselves   debating   what   is   the "out of
νεκρῶν ἀναστῆναι. 11 Καὶ ἐπηρώτων αὐτὸν
[the] dead   to rise."   And they questioned him
λέγοντες· ὅτι λέγουσιν οἱ γραμματεῖς ὅτι
saying: Why   say   the   scribes   that
Ἡλίαν δεῖ ἐλθεῖν πρῶτον; 12 ὁ δὲ ἔφη
Elias it behoves to come   first?   And he   said
αὐτοῖς· Ἡλίας μὲν ἐλθὼν πρῶτον
to them: Elias   indeed   coming   first
ἀποκαθιστάνει πάντα· καὶ πῶς γέγραπται
restores   all things;   and   how has it been written
ἐπὶ τὸν υἱὸν τοῦ ἀνθρώπου, ἵνα πολλὰ
on(concerning) the   Son   -   of man,   that many things

things and be treated with
contempt? [13] But I tell
you that Eli'jah has
come, and they did to
him whatever they
pleased, as it is written of
him."

14 And when they
came to the disciples,
they saw a great crowd
about them, and scribes
arguing with them. [15] And
immediately all the
crowd, when they saw
him, were greatly
amazed, and ran up to
him and greeted him.
[16] And he asked them,
"What are you discussing
with them?" [17] And one
of the crowd answered
him, "Teacher, I brought
my son to you, for he has
a dumb spirit; [18] and
wherever it seizes him, it
dashes him down; and
he foams and grinds his
teeth and becomes rigid;
and I asked your dis-
ciples to cast it out, and
they were not able."
[19] And he answered them,
"O faithless generation,
how long am I to be with
you? How long am I to
bear with you? Bring
him to me." [20] And they
brought the boy to him;
and when the spirit saw
him, immediately it con-
vulsed the boy, and he
fell on the ground and
rolled about, foaming at

πάθῃ   καὶ ἐξουδενηθῇ;   [13] ἀλλὰ λέγω ὑμῖν
he should suffer and be set at naught?   But   I tell you

ὅτι καὶ 'Ηλίας ἐλήλυθεν, καὶ ἐποίησαν
that indeed Elias   has come,   and   they did

αὐτῷ ὅσα ἤθελον, καθὼς γέγραπται
to him what they wished,   as   it has been written

ἐπ' αὐτόν.
on(concerning) him.

14 Καὶ ἐλθόντες πρὸς τοὺς μαθητὰς
And   coming   to   the   disciples

εἶδον ὄχλον πολὺν περὶ αὐτοὺς καὶ
they saw crowd a much(great) around   them   and

γραμματεῖς συζητοῦντας πρὸς αὐτούς.
scribes   debating   with   them.

15 καὶ εὐθὺς πᾶς ὁ ὄχλος ἰδόντες αὐτὸν
And immediately all the crowd seeing   him

ἐξεθαμβήθησαν, καὶ προστρέχοντες ἠσπάζοντο
were greatly astonished, and   running up to   greeted

αὐτόν. 16 καὶ ἐπηρώτησεν αὐτούς· τί
him.   And   he questioned   them: What

συνζητεῖτε πρὸς αὐτούς; 17 καὶ ἀπεκρίθη
are ye debating with   them ?   And   answered

αὐτῷ εἷς ἐκ τοῦ ὄχλου· διδάσκαλε,
him   one of   the   crowd: Teacher,

ἤνεγκα τὸν υἱόν μου πρὸς σέ, ἔχοντα
I brought the   son of me   to   thee, having

πνεῦμα ἄλαλον· 18 καὶ ὅπου ἐὰν αὐτὸν
spirit   a dumb;   and   wherever   him

καταλάβῃ, ῥήσσει αὐτόν, καὶ ἀφρίζει καὶ
it seizes,   it tears   him,   and he foams   and

τρίζει τοὺς ὀδόντας καὶ ξηραίνεται· καὶ
grinds the(his) teeth   and he wastes away;   and

εἶπα τοῖς μαθηταῖς σου ἵνα αὐτὸ
I told   the   disciples   of thee that   it

ἐκβάλωσιν, καὶ οὐκ ἴσχυσαν. 19 ὁ δὲ
they might expel, and   they were not able.   And he

ἀποκριθεὶς αὐτοῖς λέγει· ὦ γενεὰ ἄπιστος,
answering   them   says: O generation unbelieving,

ἕως πότε πρὸς ὑμᾶς ἔσομαι; ἕως πότε
until when with   you   shall I be ?   how long
= how long

ἀνέξομαι ὑμῶν; φέρετε αὐτὸν πρός με.
shall I endure you ?   bring   him   to   me.

20 καὶ ἤνεγκαν αὐτὸν πρὸς αὐτόν. καὶ
And   they brought   him   to   him.   And

ἰδὼν αὐτὸν τὸ πνεῦμα εὐθὺς συνεσπάραξεν
seeing   him   the   spirit   immediately violently threw

αὐτόν, καὶ πεσὼν ἐπὶ τῆς γῆς ἐκυλίετο
him,   and   falling   on   the   earth he wallowed

the mouth. ²¹And Jesus asked his father, "How long has he had this?" And he said, "From childhood. ²²And it has often cast him into the fire and into the water, to destroy him; but if you can do anything, have pity on us and help us." ²³And Jesus said to him, "If you can! All things are possible to him who believes." ²⁴Immediately the father of the child cried out² and said, "I believe; help my unbelief!" ²⁵And when Jesus saw that a crowd came running together, he rebuked the unclean spirit, saying to it, "You dumb and deaf spirit, I command you, come out of him, and never enter him again." ²⁶And after crying out and convulsing him terribly, it came out, and the boy was like a corpse; so that most of them said, "He is dead." ²⁷But Jesus took him by the hand and lifted him up, and he arose. ²⁸And when he had entered the house, his disciples asked him privately, "Why could we not cast it out?" ²⁹And he said to them, "This kind cannot be

ἀφρίζων. **21** καὶ ἐπηρώτησεν τὸν πατέρα
foaming.   And he questioned   the   father

αὐτοῦ· πόσος χρόνος ἐστὶν ὡς τοῦτο
of him: What   time   is it   while   this

γέγονεν αὐτῷ; ὁ δὲ εἶπεν· ἐκ παιδιόθεν·
has happened to him? And he said: From childhood;

22 καὶ πολλάκις καὶ εἰς πῦρ αὐτὸν
and   often   both into fire   him

ἔβαλεν καὶ εἰς ὕδατα ἵνα ἀπολέσῃ αὐτόν· ἀλλ'
it threw and into waters that it may destroy him;   but

εἴ τι δύνῃ, βοήθησον ἡμῖν σπλαγχνισθεὶς
if anything thou canst, help   us having compassion

ἐφ' ἡμᾶς. **23** ὁ δὲ Ἰησοῦς εἶπεν αὐτῷ· τὸ εἰ
on us.   - And Jesus   said   to him: The "if

δύνῃ, πάντα δυνατὰ τῷ πιστεύοντι.
thou canst," all things possible to the [one] believing.

24 εὐθὺς κράξας ὁ πατὴρ τοῦ παιδίου
Immediately crying out the father of the child

ἔλεγεν· πιστεύω· βοήθει μου τῇ ἀπιστίᾳ.
said: I believe; help thou of me the unbelief.

25 ἰδὼν δὲ ὁ Ἰησοῦς ὅτι ἐπισυντρέχει
And ²seeing - ¹Jesus that is(was) running together

ὄχλος, ἐπετίμησεν τῷ πνεύματι τῷ ἀκαθάρτῳ
a crowd, rebuked   the spirit   -   unclean

λέγων αὐτῷ· τὸ ἄλαλον καὶ κωφὸν
saying to it: the   Dumb   and deaf

πνεῦμα, ἐγὼ ἐπιτάσσω σοι, ἔξελθε ἐξ
spirit,   I   command thee, come forth out of

αὐτοῦ καὶ μηκέτι εἰσέλθῃς εἰς αὐτόν.
him and no more mayest thou enter into him.

26 καὶ κράξας καὶ πολλὰ σπαράξας
And crying out and   much convulsing [him]

ἐξῆλθεν· καὶ ἐγένετο ὡσεὶ νεκρός, ὥστε
it came out; and he was   as   dead,   so as

τοὺς πολλοὺς λέγειν ὅτι ἀπέθανεν. **27** ὁ
-     many   to say^b that he died.   -
          = many said

δὲ Ἰησοῦς κρατήσας τῆς χειρὸς αὐτοῦ
But Jesus taking hold of the   hand   of him

ἤγειρεν αὐτόν, καὶ ἀνέστη. **28** καὶ
raised   him,   and he stood up.   And

εἰσελθόντος αὐτοῦ εἰς οἶκον οἱ μαθηταὶ
entering   him^a into a house the disciples
=when he entered

αὐτοῦ κατ' ἰδίαν ἐπηρώτων αὐτόν· ὅτι
of him privately questioned him: Why

ἡμεῖς οὐκ ἠδυνήθημεν ἐκβαλεῖν αὐτό;
we   were not able   to expel   it?

² Other ancient authorities add *with tears*

29 καὶ εἶπεν αὐτοῖς· τοῦτο τὸ γένος ἐν
And he told them: This   -   kind   by

driven out by anything but prayer.""

30 They went on from there and passed through Galilee. And he would not have any one know it; ³¹for he was teaching his disciples, saying to them, "The Son of man will be delivered into the hands of men, and they will kill him; and when he is killed, after three days he will rise." ³²But they did not understand the saying, and they were afraid to ask him.

33 And they came to Caper'na-um; and when he was in the house he asked them, "What were you discussing on the way?" ³⁴But they were silent; for on the way they had discussed with one another who was the greatest. ³⁵And he sat down and called the twelve; and he said to them, "If any one would be first, he must be last of all and servant of all." ³⁶And he took a child, and put him in the midst of them; and taking him in his arms, he said to them, ³⁷"Whoever receives one such child in my name receives me; and whoever receives me, receives not me but him who sent me."

38 John said to him,

ᵃ Other ancient authorities add and fasting

οὐδενὶ δύναται ἐξελθεῖν εἰ μὴ ἐν προσευχῇ.
nothing can to come out except by prayer.

30 Κἀκεῖθεν ἐξελθόντες παρεπορεύοντο διὰ
And thence going forth they passed through

τῆς Γαλιλαίας, καὶ οὐκ ἤθελεν ἵνα
- Galilee, and he wished not that

τις γνοῖ· 31 ἐδίδασκεν γὰρ τοὺς μαθητὰς
anyone should know; for he was teaching the disciples

αὐτοῦ, καὶ ἔλεγεν αὐτοῖς ὅτι ὁ υἱὸς τοῦ
of him, and told them[,] - The Son -

ἀνθρώπου παραδίδοται εἰς χεῖρας ἀνθρώπων,
of man is betrayed into [the] hands of men,

καὶ ἀποκτενοῦσιν αὐτόν, καὶ ἀποκτανθεὶς
and they will kill him, and being killed

μετὰ τρεῖς ἡμέρας ἀναστήσεται. 32 οἱ
after three days he will rise up. they

δὲ ἠγνόουν τὸ ῥῆμα, καὶ ἐφοβοῦντο
But did not know the word, and feared

αὐτὸν ἐπερωτῆσαι.
him to question.

33 Καὶ ἦλθον εἰς Καφαρναούμ. Καὶ
And they came to Capernaum. And

ἐν τῇ οἰκίᾳ γενόμενος ἐπηρώτα αὐτούς·
in the house being he questioned them:

τί ἐν τῇ ὁδῷ διελογίζεσθε; 34 οἱ δὲ
What in the way were ye debating? And they

ἐσιώπων· πρὸς ἀλλήλους γὰρ διελέχθησαν
were silent; ¹with ²one another ¹for they debated

ἐν τῇ ὁδῷ τίς μείζων. 35 καὶ καθίσας
in the way who [was] greater. And sitting

ἐφώνησεν τοὺς δώδεκα καὶ λέγει αὐτοῖς·
he called the twelve and says to them:

εἴ τις θέλει πρῶτος εἶναι, ἔσται πάντων
If anyone wishes first to be, he shall be of all

ἔσχατος καὶ πάντων διάκονος. 36 καὶ
last and of all servant. And

λαβὼν παιδίον ἔστησεν αὐτὸ ἐν μέσῳ
taking a child he set it(him) in [the] midst

αὐτῶν, καὶ ἐναγκαλισάμενος αὐτὸ εἶπεν
of them, and folding in [his] arms it he said

αὐτοῖς· 37 ὃς ἂν ἓν τῶν τοιούτων παιδίων
to them: Whoever one - of such children

δέξηται ἐπὶ τῷ ὀνόματί μου, ἐμὲ δέχεται·
receives on(in) the name of me, me receives;

καὶ ὃς ἂν ἐμὲ δέχηται, οὐχ ἐμὲ δέχεται
and whoever me receives, not me receives

ἀλλὰ τὸν ἀποστείλαντά με. 38 Ἔφη αὐτῷ
but the [one] having sent me. Said to him

"Teacher, we saw a man casting out demons in your name,[b] and we forbade him, because he was not following us." [39] But Jesus said, "Do not forbid him; for no one who does a mighty work in my name will be able soon after to speak evil of me. [40] For he that is not against us is for us. [41] For truly, I say to you, whoever gives you a cup of water to drink because you bear the name of Christ, will by no means lose his reward.

[42] "Whoever causes one of these little ones who believe in me to sin, it would be better for him if a great millstone were hung round his neck and he were thrown into the sea. [43] And if your hand causes you to sin, cut it off; it is better for you to enter life maimed than with two hands to go to hell, to the unquenchable fire.[c] [45] And if your foot causes you to sin, cut it off; it is better for you to enter life lame than with two feet to be thrown into

ὁ   Ἰωάννης·   διδάσκαλε,   εἴδομέν   τινα   ἐν
John: Teacher,   we saw   someone   in

τῷ   ὀνόματί   σου   ἐκβάλλοντα   δαιμόνια,   ὃς
the   name   of thee   expelling   demons,   who

οὐκ   ἀκολουθεῖ   ἡμῖν,   καὶ   ἐκωλύομεν   αὐτόν,
does not follow   us,   and   we forbade   him,

ὅτι   οὐκ   ἠκολούθει   ἡμῖν.   **39** ὁ   δὲ   Ἰησοῦς
because he was not following   us.   – But   Jesus

εἶπεν·   μὴ   κωλύετε   αὐτόν·   οὐδεὶς   γὰρ
said: Do not forbid   him: for no one

ἐστιν   ὃς   ποιήσει   δύναμιν   ἐπὶ   τῷ   ὀνόματί
there is who   shall do   a mighty work   on(in) the   name

μου   καὶ   δυνήσεται   ταχὺ   κακολογῆσαί   με·
of me   and   will be able   quickly   to speak evil of   me;

40 ὃς   γὰρ   οὐκ   ἔστιν   καθ᾽   ἡμῶν,   ὑπὲρ
for who   is not   against   us,   for

ἡμῶν   ἐστιν.   **41** Ὃς   γὰρ   ἂν   ποτίσῃ
us   is.   For whoever   [1]gives [3]drink

ὑμᾶς   ποτήριον   ὕδατος   ἐν   ὀνόματι,   ὅτι
[2]you   a cup   of water   in   [the] name,   because

Χριστοῦ   ἐστε,   ἀμὴν   λέγω   ὑμῖν   ὅτι
of Christ   ye are,   truly   I tell   you   that

οὐ   μὴ   ἀπολέσῃ   τὸν   μισθὸν   αὐτοῦ.   **42** Καὶ
by no means he will lose   the   reward   of him.   And

ὃς   ἂν   σκανδαλίσῃ   ἕνα   τῶν   μικρῶν   τούτων
whoever   offends   one   – [3]little [ones] [1]of these

τῶν   πιστευόντων,   καλόν   ἐστιν   αὐτῷ   μᾶλλον
–   [3]believing,   good   is it   for him   rather

εἰ   περίκειται   μύλος   ὀνικὸς   περὶ   τὸν
if   be laid *round*   a [heavy] millstone   round   the

τράχηλον   αὐτοῦ   καὶ   βέβληται   εἰς   τὴν
neck   of him   and   he be thrown   into   the

θάλασσαν.   **43** Καὶ   ἐὰν   σκανδαλίσῃ   σε   ἡ
sea.   And   if   offends   thee the

χείρ   σου,   ἀπόκοψον   αὐτήν·   καλόν   ἐστίν
hand   of thee,   cut off   it;   good   is it

σε   κυλλὸν   εἰσελθεῖν   εἰς   τὴν   ζωήν,   ἢ   τὰς
thee maimed   to enter   into   –   life,   than the

δύο   χεῖρας   ἔχοντα   ἀπελθεῖν   εἰς   τὴν
two   hands   having   to go away   into   –

γέενναν,   εἰς   τὸ   πῦρ   τὸ   ἄσβεστον.‡   **45** καὶ
gehenna,   into the   fire   *the* unquenchable.   And

ἐὰν   ὁ   πούς   σου   σκανδαλίζῃ   σε,   ἀπόκοψον
if   the   foot   of thee   offends   thee,   cut off

αὐτόν·   καλόν   ἐστίν   σε   εἰσελθεῖν   εἰς   τὴν
it;   good   is it   thee   to enter   into   –

ζωὴν   χωλόν,   ἢ   τοὺς   δύο   πόδας   ἔχοντα
life   lame,   than the   two   feet   having

[b] Other ancient authorities add *who does not follow us*

[c] Verses 44 and 46 (which are identical with verse 48) are omitted by the best ancient authorities

‡ Verse 44 omitted by Nestle; *cf.* RSV footnote.

hell.[e] [47]And if your eye causes you to sin, pluck it out; it is better for you to enter the kingdom of God with one eye than with two eyes to be thrown into hell, [48]where their worm does not die, and the fire is not quenched. [49]For every one will be salted with fire.[d] [50]Salt is good; but if the salt has lost its saltness, how will you season it? Have salt in yourselves, and be at peace with one another."

βληθῆναι εἰς τὴν γέενναν.‡ [47] καὶ ἐὰν ὁ
to be cast   into - gehenna.   And if the

ὀφθαλμός σου σκανδαλίζῃ σε, ἔκβαλε αὐτόν·
eye   of thee   offends   thee, cast out   it;

καλόν σέ ἐστιν μονόφθαλμον εἰσελθεῖν εἰς
good thee is it   one-eyed   to enter   into

τὴν βασιλείαν τοῦ θεοῦ, ἢ δύο ὀφθαλμοὺς
the kingdom   - of God, than two   eyes

ἔχοντα βληθῆναι εἰς τὴν γέενναν, [48] ὅπου
having   to be cast into - gehenna,   where

ὁ σκώληξ αὐτῶν οὐ τελευτᾷ καὶ τὸ
the worm   of them   dies not   and the

πῦρ οὐ σβέννυται. [49] Πᾶς γὰρ πυρὶ
fire is not quenched.   For everyone with fire

ἁλισθήσεται. [50] καλὸν τὸ ἅλας· ἐὰν δὲ
shall be salted.   Good [is] - salt;   but if

τὸ ἅλας ἄναλον γένηται, ἐν τίνι αὐτὸ
- salt   saltless becomes, by what it

ἀρτύσετε; ἔχετε ἐν ἑαυτοῖς ἅλα καὶ
will ye season? Have in yourselves salt and

εἰρηνεύετε ἐν ἀλλήλοις.
be at peace among one another.

CHAPTER 10

AND he left there and went to the region of Judea and beyond the Jordan, and crowds gathered to him again; and again, as his custom was, he taught them.

2 And Pharisees came up and in order to test him asked, "Is it lawful for a man to divorce his wife?" [3]He answered them, "What did Moses command you?" [4]They said, "Moses allowed a man to write a certificate of divorce, and to put her away." [5]But Jesus said to them, "For your hardness of heart he

[10] Καὶ ἐκεῖθεν ἀναστὰς ἔρχεται εἰς τὰ
And thence   rising up   he comes into the

ὅρια τῆς Ἰουδαίας καὶ πέραν τοῦ
territory - of Judæa   and   beyond

Ἰορδάνου, καὶ συμπορεύονται πάλιν ὄχλοι
Jordan,   and   ³go with   ¹again ²crowds

πρὸς αὐτόν, καὶ ὡς εἰώθει πάλιν ἐδίδασκεν
⁴with   ⁵him, and as he was wont again   he taught

αὐτούς. 2 Καὶ προσελθόντες Φαρισαῖοι
them.   And   ²approaching   ¹Pharisees

ἐπηρώτων αὐτὸν εἰ ἔξεστιν ἀνδρὶ γυναῖκα
questioned   him if it is(was) lawful for a man a wife

ἀπολῦσαι, πειράζοντες αὐτόν. 3 ὁ δὲ
to dismiss,   testing   him.   And he

ἀποκριθεὶς εἶπεν αὐτοῖς· 4 τί ὑμῖν ἐνετείλατο
answering   said to them: What you   ordered

Μωϋσῆς; οἱ δὲ εἶπαν· ἐπέτρεψεν Μωϋσῆς
Moses?   And they said: permitted   Moses

βιβλίον ἀποστασίου γράψαι καὶ ἀπολῦσαι.
a roll   of divorce   to write and to dismiss.

5 ὁ δὲ Ἰησοῦς εἶπεν αὐτοῖς· πρὸς τὴν
- And Jesus   said to them: For the

σκληροκαρδίαν ὑμῶν ἔγραψεν ὑμῖν τὴν
hardheartedness of you he wrote to you   -

---

[e] Verses 44 and 46 (which are identical with verse 48) are omitted by the best ancient authorities

[d] Other ancient authorities add *and every sacrifice will be salted with salt*

‡ Verse 46 omitted by Nestle; cf. RSV footnote.

wrote you this command-ment. ⁶But from the beginning of creation, 'God made them male and female.' ⁷'For this reason a man shall leave his father and mother and be joined to his wife,ᵉ ⁸and the two shall become one.' So they are no longer two but one. ⁹What therefore God has joined together, let not man put asunder."

10 And in the house the disciples asked him again about this matter. ¹¹And he said to them, "Whoever divorces his wife and marries another, commits adultery against her; ¹²and if she divorces her husband and marries another, she commits adultery."

13 And they were bringing children to him, that he might touch them; and the disciples rebuked them. ¹⁴But when Jesus saw it he was indignant, and said to them, "Let the children come to me, do not hinder them; for to such belongs the kingdom of God. ¹⁵Truly, I say to you, whoever does not receive the kingdom of God like a child shall not enter it." ¹⁶And he took them in his arms and blessed them, laying his hands upon them.

ἐντολὴν ταύτην. 6 ἀπὸ δὲ ἀρχῆς κτίσεως
this commandment. But from [the] beginning of creation
ἄρσεν καὶ θῆλυ ἐποίησεν αὐτούς· 7 ἕνεκεν
male and female he made them; for the sake of
τούτου καταλείψει ἄνθρωπος τὸν πατέρα
this shall leave a man the father
αὐτοῦ καὶ τὴν μητέρα, 8 καὶ ἔσονται
of him and the mother, and shall be
οἱ δύο εἰς σάρκα μίαν· ὥστε οὐκέτι
the two – flesh one; so as no longer
εἰσὶν δύο ἀλλὰ μία σάρξ. 9 ὃ οὖν ὁ
are they two but one flesh. What then –
θεὸς συνέζευξεν, ἄνθρωπος μὴ χωριζέτω.
God yoked together, ²man ¹not ⁴let ⁴separate.
10 καὶ εἰς τὴν οἰκίαν πάλιν οἱ μαθηταὶ
And in the house again the disciples
περὶ τούτου ἐπηρώτων αὐτόν. 11 καὶ
about this questioned him. And
λέγει αὐτοῖς· ὃς ἂν ἀπολύσῃ τὴν γυναῖκα
he says to them: Whoever dismisses the wife
αὐτοῦ καὶ γαμήσῃ ἄλλην, μοιχᾶται ἐπ'
of him and marries another, commits adultery with
αὐτήν· 12 καὶ ἐὰν αὐτὴ ἀπολύσασα τὸν
her; and if she having dismissed the
ἄνδρα αὐτῆς γαμήσῃ ἄλλον, μοιχᾶται.
husband of her marries another, she commits adultery.
13 Καὶ προσέφερον αὐτῷ παιδία ἵνα
And they brought to him children that
αὐτῶν ἅψηται· οἱ δὲ μαθηταὶ ἐπετίμησαν
them he might touch; but the disciples rebuked
αὐτοῖς. 14 ἰδὼν δὲ ὁ Ἰησοῦς ἠγανάκτησεν
them. But ²seeing – ¹Jesus was angry
καὶ εἶπεν αὐτοῖς· ἄφετε τὰ παιδία
and said to them: Allow the children
ἔρχεσθαι πρός με, μὴ κωλύετε αὐτά·
to come to me, do not prevent them;
τῶν γὰρ τοιούτων ἐστὶν ἡ βασιλεία τοῦ
– for of such is the kingdom –
θεοῦ. 15 ἀμὴν λέγω ὑμῖν, ὃς ἂν
of God. Truly I tell you, whoever
μὴ δέξηται τὴν βασιλείαν τοῦ θεοῦ ὡς
receives not the kingdom – of God as
παιδίον, οὐ μὴ εἰσέλθῃ εἰς αὐτήν. 16 καὶ
a child, by no means may enter into it. And
ἐναγκαλισάμενος αὐτὰ κατευλόγει τιθεὶς τὰς
folding in [his] arms them he blesses putting the(his)
χεῖρας ἐπ' αὐτά.
hands on them.

ᵉ Other ancient authorities omit *and be joined to his wife*

17 And as he was setting out on his journey, a man ran up and knelt before him, and asked him, "Good Teacher, what must I do to inherit eternal life?" [18]And Jesus said to him, "Why do you call me good? No one is good but God alone. [19]You know the commandments: 'Do not kill, Do not commit adultery, Do not steal, Do not bear false witness, Do not defraud, Honor your father and mother.'" [20]And he said to him, "Teacher, all these I have observed from my youth." [21]And Jesus looking upon him loved him, and said to him, "You lack one thing; go, sell what you have, and give to the poor, and you will have treasure in heaven; and come, follow me." [22]At that saying his countenance fell, and he went away sorrowful; for he had great possessions.

23 And Jesus looked around and said to his disciples, "How hard it will be for those who have riches to enter the kingdom of God!" [24]And the disciples were amazed at his words. But Jesus said to them again,

17 Καὶ ἐκπορευομένου αὐτοῦ εἰς ὁδὸν
And   going forth   him[a]   into [the] way
  = as he went forth

προσδραμὼν εἷς καὶ γονυπετήσας αὐτὸν
running to   one   and   kneeling to   him

ἐπηρώτα αὐτόν· διδάσκαλε ἀγαθέ, τί ποιήσω
questioned   him: Teacher   good,   what may I do

ἵνα ζωὴν αἰώνιον κληρονομήσω; 18 ὁ δὲ
that   life   eternal   I may inherit?   18 — And

Ἰησοῦς εἶπεν αὐτῷ· τί με λέγεις ἀγαθόν;
Jesus   said   to him: Why me callest thou good?

οὐδεὶς ἀγαθὸς εἰ μὴ εἷς ὁ θεός. 19 τὰς ἐντολὰς
no one   good   except one — God.   19   The commandments

οἶδας· μὴ φονεύσῃς, μὴ μοιχεύσῃς,
thou knowest: Do not kill,   Do not commit adultery,

μὴ κλέψῃς, μὴ ψευδομαρτυρήσῃς, μὴ
Do not steal,   Do not bear false witness,   Do

ἀποστερήσῃς, τίμα τὸν πατέρα σου καὶ
not defraud,   Honour   the   father   of thee and

τὴν μητέρα. 20 ὁ δὲ ἔφη αὐτῷ· διδάσκαλε,
the   mother.   20 And he said   to him: Teacher,

ταῦτα πάντα ἐφυλαξάμην ἐκ νεότητός μου.
all these things   I observed   from   youth   of me.

21 ὁ δὲ Ἰησοῦς ἐμβλέψας αὐτῷ ἠγάπησεν
21 — But   Jesus   looking at   him   loved

αὐτὸν καὶ εἶπεν αὐτῷ· ἔν σε ὑστερεῖ·
him   and   said to him: One thing thee is wanting:

ὕπαγε, ὅσα ἔχεις πώλησον καὶ δὸς [τοῖς]
go,   what things thou hast   sell   and give to the

πτωχοῖς, καὶ ἕξεις θησαυρὸν ἐν οὐρανῷ,
poor,   and thou wilt have   treasure   in   heaven,

καὶ δεῦρο ἀκολούθει μοι. 22 ὁ δὲ στυγνάσας
and come   follow   me.   22 — But he   being sad

ἐπὶ τῷ λόγῳ ἀπῆλθεν λυπούμενος, ἦν
at   the   word   went away   grieving, [b]he was

γὰρ ἔχων κτήματα πολλά. 23 Καὶ
[1]for   having   possessions   many.   23 And

περιβλεψάμενος ὁ Ἰησοῦς λέγει τοῖς
looking round   — Jesus   says   to the

μαθηταῖς αὐτοῦ· πῶς δυσκόλως οἱ τὰ
disciples   of him: How   hardly the [ones] the

χρήματα ἔχοντες εἰς τὴν βασιλείαν τοῦ
riches   having   into   the   kingdom   —

θεοῦ εἰσελεύσονται. 24 οἱ δὲ μαθηταὶ
of God   shall enter.   24 And the   disciples

ἐθαμβοῦντο ἐπὶ τοῖς λόγοις αὐτοῦ. ὁ δὲ
were amazed   at   the   words   of him.   — And

Ἰησοῦς πάλιν ἀποκριθεὶς λέγει αὐτοῖς·
Jesus   again   answering   says   to them:

"Children, how hard it is[f] to enter the kingdom of God! [25]It is easier for a camel to go through the eye of a needle than for a rich man to enter the kingdom of God." [26]And they were exceedingly astonished, and said to him,[g] "Then who can be saved?" [27]Jesus looked at them and said, "With men it is impossible, but not with God; for all things are possible with God." [28]Peter began to say to him, "Lo, we have left everything and followed you." [29]Jesus said, "Truly, I say to you, there is no one who has left house or brothers or sisters or mother or father or children or lands, for my sake and for the gospel, [30]who will not receive a hundredfold now in this time, houses and brothers and sisters and mothers and children and lands, with persecutions, and in the age to come eternal life. [31]But many that are first will be last, and the last first."

32 And they were on the road, going up to

τέκνα, πῶς δύσκολόν ἐστιν εἰς τὴν
Children, how hard it is into the

βασιλείαν τοῦ θεοῦ εἰσελθεῖν· 25 εὐκοπώτερόν
kingdom – of God to enter; easier

ἐστιν κάμηλον διὰ τῆς τρυμαλιᾶς τῆς
it is a camel through the eye –

ῥαφίδος διελθεῖν ἢ πλούσιον εἰς τὴν
of a needle to go *through* than a rich man into the

βασιλείαν τοῦ θεοῦ εἰσελθεῖν. 26 οἱ δὲ
kingdom – of God to enter. But they

περισσῶς ἐξεπλήσσοντο λέγοντες πρὸς
exceedingly were astonished saying to

ἑαυτούς· καὶ τίς δύναται σωθῆναι;
themselves: And who can *to* be saved?

27 ἐμβλέψας αὐτοῖς ὁ Ἰησοῦς λέγει· παρὰ
Looking at them – Jesus says: With

ἀνθρώποις ἀδύνατον, ἀλλ' οὐ παρὰ θεῷ·
men [it is] impossible, but not with God;

πάντα γὰρ δυνατὰ παρὰ τῷ θεῷ. 28 Ἤρξατο
for all things [are] possible with – God. Began

λέγειν ὁ Πέτρος αὐτῷ· ἰδοὺ ἡμεῖς ἀφήκαμεν
to say – Peter to him: Behold [,] we left

πάντα καὶ ἠκολουθήκαμέν σοι. 29 ἔφη ὁ
all things and have followed thee. Said –

Ἰησοῦς· ἀμὴν λέγω ὑμῖν, οὐδείς ἐστιν
Jesus: Truly I tell you, no one there is

ὃς ἀφῆκεν οἰκίαν ἢ ἀδελφοὺς ἢ ἀδελφὰς
who left house or brothers or sisters

ἢ μητέρα ἢ πατέρα ἢ τέκνα ἢ ἀγροὺς
or mother or father or children or fields

ἕνεκεν ἐμοῦ καὶ ἕνεκεν τοῦ εὐαγγελίου,
for the sake of me and for the sake of the gospel,

30 ἐὰν μὴ λάβῃ ἑκατονταπλασίονα νῦν
but he receives a hundredfold now

ἐν τῷ καιρῷ τούτῳ οἰκίας καὶ ἀδελφοὺς
in – time this houses and brothers

καὶ ἀδελφὰς καὶ μητέρας καὶ τέκνα καὶ
and sisters and mothers and children and

ἀγροὺς μετὰ διωγμῶν, καὶ ἐν τῷ αἰῶνι
fields with persecutions, and in the age

τῷ ἐρχομένῳ ζωὴν αἰώνιον. 31 πολλοὶ δὲ
– coming life eternal. And [1]many

ἔσονται πρῶτοι ἔσχατοι καὶ οἱ ἔσχατοι
[3]will be [2]first [4]last and the last

πρῶτοι.
first.

32 Ἦσαν δὲ ἐν τῇ ὁδῷ ἀναβαίνοντες
Now they were in the way going up

---

[f] Other ancient authorities add *for those who trust in riches*

[g] Other ancient authorities read *to one another*

Jerusalem, and Jesus was walking ahead of them; and they were amazed, and those who followed were afraid. And taking the twelve again, he began to tell them what was to happen to him, ³³saying, "Behold, we are going up to Jerusalem; and the Son of man will be delivered to the chief priests and the scribes, and they will condemn him to death, and deliver him to the Gentiles; ³⁴and they will mock him, and spit upon him, and scourge him, and kill him; and after three days he will rise."

35 And James and John, the sons of Zeb'-edee, came forward to him, and said to him, "Teacher, we want you to do for us whatever we ask of you." ³⁶And he said to them, "What do you want me to do for you?" ³⁷And they said to him, "Grant us to sit, one at your right hand and one at your left, in your glory." ³⁸But Jesus said to them, "You do not know what you are asking. Are you able to drink the cup that I drink, or to be baptized with the baptism with

εἰς Ἰεροσόλυμα, καὶ ἦν προάγων αὐτοὺς
to   Jerusalem,   and was going before them

ὁ Ἰησοῦς, καὶ ἐθαμβοῦντο, οἱ δὲ
– Jesus,   and they were astonished, and the

ἀκολουθοῦντες ἐφοβοῦντο. καὶ παραλαβὼν
[ones] following   were afraid.   And   taking

πάλιν τοὺς δώδεκα ἤρξατο αὐτοῖς λέγειν
again   the   twelve he began them to tell

τὰ μέλλοντα αὐτῷ συμβαίνειν, 33 ὅτι ἰδοὺ
the things about to him to happen, – Behold

ἀναβαίνομεν εἰς Ἰεροσόλυμα, καὶ ὁ υἱὸς
we are going up to   Jerusalem,   and the Son

τοῦ ἀνθρώπου παραδοθήσεται τοῖς
 –   of man   will be betrayed to the

ἀρχιερεῦσιν καὶ τοῖς γραμματεῦσιν, καὶ
chief priests and to the   scribes,   and

κατακρινοῦσιν αὐτὸν θανάτῳ καὶ παραδώσουσιν
they will condemn him to death and will deliver

αὐτὸν τοῖς ἔθνεσιν 34 καὶ ἐμπαίξουσιν
him   to the nations   and they will mock

αὐτῷ καὶ ἐμπτύσουσιν αὐτῷ καὶ μαστι-
him and will spit at him and will

γώσουσιν αὐτὸν καὶ ἀποκτενοῦσιν, καὶ
scourge   him and   will kill,   and

μετὰ τρεῖς ἡμέρας ἀναστήσεται.
after three   days   he will rise again.

35 Καὶ προσπορεύονται αὐτῷ Ἰάκωβος
   And   approach   to him   James

καὶ Ἰωάννης οἱ [δύο] υἱοὶ Ζεβεδαίου
and John   the two   sons of Zebedee

λέγοντες αὐτῷ· διδάσκαλε, θέλομεν ἵνα ὃ ἐὰν
saying to him: Teacher, we wish that whatever

αἰτήσωμέν σε ποιήσῃς ἡμῖν. 36 ὁ
we may ask thee thou mayest do for us.   he

δὲ εἶπεν αὐτοῖς· τί θέλετέ με ποιήσω
And said to them: What wish ye me I may do

ὑμῖν; 37 οἱ δὲ εἶπαν αὐτῷ· δὸς ἡμῖν
for you? And they said to him: Give us

ἵνα εἷς σου ἐκ δεξιῶν καὶ εἷς ἐξ
that one of thee out of(on) [the] right and one on
                                        = on thy right

ἀριστερῶν καθίσωμεν ἐν τῇ δόξῃ σου.
[thy] left   we may sit in the glory of thee.

38 ὁ δὲ Ἰησοῦς εἶπεν αὐτοῖς· οὐκ οἴδατε
   – And Jesus said to them: Ye know not

τί αἰτεῖσθε. δύνασθε πιεῖν τὸ ποτήριον
what ye ask.   Can ye to drink the   cup

ὃ ἐγὼ πίνω, ἢ τὸ βάπτισμα ὃ ἐγὼ
which I drink, or the baptism which I

which I am baptized?"
39And they said to him,
"We are able." And
Jesus said to them, "The
cup that I drink you will
drink; and with the
baptism with which I am
baptized, you will be
baptized; **40**but to sit at
my right hand or at my
left is not mine to grant,
but it is for those for
whom it has been pre-
pared." **41**And when the
ten heard it, they began
to be indignant at James
and John. **42**And Jesus
called them to him and
said to them, "You know
that those who are sup-
posed to rule over the
Gentiles lord it over
them, and their great
men exercise authority
over them. **43**But it shall
not be so among you;
but whoever would be
great among you must
be your servant, **44**and
whoever would be first
among you must be slave
of all. **45**For the Son of
man also came not to be
served but to serve, and
to give his life as a
ransom for many."
  46 And they came to
Jericho; and as he was
leaving Jericho with his
disciples and a great
multitude, Bartimaeus, a

βαπτίζομαι   βαπτισθῆναι;   **39** οἱ δὲ   εἶπαν
am baptized   *to* be baptized [with]?   And they   said

αὐτῷ·   δυνάμεθα.   ὁ δὲ   'Ιησοῦς   εἶπεν
to him: We can.   - And   Jesus   said

αὐτοῖς· τὸ ποτήριον ὃ ἐγὼ πίνω πίεσθε,
to them: The   cup   which I drink shall ye drink,

καὶ   τὸ   βάπτισμα   ὃ   ἐγὼ   βαπτίζομαι
and   the   baptism   which   I am baptized [with]

βαπτισθήσεσθε· **40** τὸ δὲ καθίσαι ἐκ δεξιῶν
ye shall be baptized;   - but   to sit   on right

μου   ἢ   ἐξ   εὐωνύμων   οὐκ   ἔστιν   ἐμὸν
of me or   on   [my] left   is not   mine

δοῦναι,   ἀλλ'   οἷς   ἡτοίμασται.   **41** Καὶ
to give,   but   for whom it has been prepared.   And

ἀκούσαντες   οἱ   δέκα   ἤρξαντο   ἀγανακτεῖν
[3]hearing   [1]the   [2]ten   began   to be incensed

περὶ   'Ιακώβου   καὶ   'Ιωάννου.   **42** καὶ
about   James   and   John.   And

προσκαλεσάμενος   αὐτοὺς   ὁ   'Ιησοῦς   λέγει
[1]calling [3]to [4][him]   [2]them   -   Jesus   says

αὐτοῖς· οἴδατε ὅτι οἱ δοκοῦντες ἄρχειν
to them: Ye know that the [ones] thinking to rule

τῶν   ἐθνῶν   κατακυριεύουσιν   αὐτῶν   καὶ
the   nations   lord it over   them   and

οἱ μεγάλοι αὐτῶν κατεξουσιάζουσιν αὐτῶν.
the great [ones] of them exercise authority over   them.

43 οὐχ   οὕτως   δέ ἐστιν ἐν ὑμῖν· ἀλλ'
[2]not   [3]so   [1]But is it among you;   but

ὃς   ἂν   θέλῃ   μέγας   γενέσθαι   ἐν   ὑμῖν,
whoever   wishes   great   to become   among   you,

ἔσται   ὑμῶν   διάκονος,   **44** καὶ   ὃς   ἂν
shall be   of you   servant,   and   whoever

θέλῃ   ἐν   ὑμῖν   εἶναι   πρῶτος,   ἔσται   πάντων
wishes among you to be   first,   shall be of all

δοῦλος· **45** καὶ γὰρ ὁ υἱὸς τοῦ ἀνθρώπου
slave;   for even   the   Son   -   of man

οὐκ   ἦλθεν   διακονηθῆναι   ἀλλὰ   διακονῆσαι
did not come   to be served   but   to serve

καὶ δοῦναι τὴν ψυχὴν αὐτοῦ λύτρον   ἀντὶ
and to give   the   life   of him a ransom instead of

πολλῶν.
many.

46 Καὶ   ἔρχονται   εἰς   'Ιεριχώ.   Καὶ
And   they come   to   Jericho.   And

ἐκπορευομένου αὐτοῦ ἀπὸ 'Ιεριχὼ καὶ τῶν
going out   him[a]   from   Jericho   and   the
= as he was going out

μαθητῶν αὐτοῦ καὶ ὄχλου ἱκανοῦ ὁ υἱὸς
disciples[a] of him and crowd a considerable[a] the son

blind beggar, the son of Timae'us, was sitting by the roadside. [47]And when he heard that it was Jesus of Nazareth, he began to cry out and say, "Jesus, Son of David, have mercy on me!" [48]And many rebuked him, telling him to be silent; but he cried out all the more, "Son of David, have mercy on me!" [49]And Jesus stopped and said, "Call him." And they called the blind man, saying to him, "Take heart; rise, he is calling you." [50]And throwing off his mantle he sprang up and came to Jesus. [51]And Jesus said to him, "What do you want me to do for you?" And the blind man said to him, "Master, let me receive my sight." [52]And Jesus said to him, "Go your way; your faith has made you well." And immediately he received his sight and followed him on the way.

Τιμαίου   Βαρτιμαῖος,   τυφλὸς   προσαίτης,
of Timæus   Bartimæus,   a blind   beggar,

ἐκάθητο   παρὰ   τὴν   ὁδόν.   47 καὶ   ἀκούσας
sat   by   the   way.   And   hearing

ὅτι   Ἰησοῦς   ὁ   Ναζαρηνός   ἐστιν   ἤρξατο
that   Jesus   the   Nazarene   it is(was)   he began

κράζειν   καὶ   λέγειν·   υἱὲ   Δαυὶδ   Ἰησοῦ,
to cry out   and   to say: Son   of David   Jesus,

ἐλέησόν   με.   48 καὶ   ἐπετίμων   αὐτῷ   πολλοὶ
pity   me.   And   rebuked   him   many

ἵνα   σιωπήσῃ·   ὁ δὲ   πολλῷ   μᾶλλον   ἔκραζεν·
that   he should be quiet.   But he   much   more   cried out:

υἱὲ   Δαυίδ,   ἐλέησόν   με.   49 καὶ   στὰς
Son   of David,   pity   me.   And   standing

ὁ   Ἰησοῦς   εἶπεν·   φωνήσατε   αὐτόν.   καὶ
-    Jesus   said: Call   him.   And

φωνοῦσιν   τὸν   τυφλὸν   λέγοντες   αὐτῷ·
they call   the   blind man   saying   to him·

θάρσει,   ἔγειρε,   φωνεῖ   σε.   50 ὁ   δὲ
Be of good courage,   rise,   he calls   thee.   So he

ἀποβαλὼν   τὸ ἱμάτιον   αὐτοῦ   ἀναπηδήσας   ἦλθεν
throwing away   the garment   of him   leaping up   came

πρὸς   τὸν   Ἰησοῦν.   51 καὶ   ἀποκριθεὶς   αὐτῷ   ὁ
to   -   Jesus.   And   answering   him   -

Ἰησοῦς   εἶπεν·   τί   σοι   θέλεις   ποιήσω;
Jesus   said: What   for thee   wishest thou   I may do?

ὁ δὲ   τυφλὸς   εἶπεν   αὐτῷ·   ῥαββουνί,   ἵνα
And the   blind man   said   to him: Rabboni,   that

ἀναβλέψω.   52 καὶ   ὁ   Ἰησοῦς   εἶπεν   αὐτῷ·
I may see again.   And   -   Jesus   said   to him:

ὕπαγε,   ἡ   πίστις   σου   σέσωκέν   σε.   καὶ
Go,   the   faith   of thee   has healed   thee.   And

εὐθὺς   ἀνέβλεψεν,   καὶ   ἠκολούθει   αὐτῷ   ἐν
immediately   he saw again,   and   followed   him   in

τῇ   ὁδῷ.
the   way.

CHAPTER 11

AND when they drew near to Jerusalem, to Beth'phage and Bethany, at the Mount of Olives, he sent two of his disciples, [2]and said to them, "Go into the village opposite you, and

11 Καὶ   ὅτε   ἐγγίζουσιν   εἰς   Ἱεροσόλυμα
And   when   they draw near   to   Jerusalem

εἰς   Βηθφαγὴ   καὶ   Βηθανίαν   πρὸς   τὸ
to   Bethphage   and   Bethany   at   the

ὄρος   τῶν   ἐλαιῶν,   ἀποστέλλει   δύο   τῶν
mount   of the   olives,   he sends   two   of the

μαθητῶν   αὐτοῦ   2 καὶ   λέγει   αὐτοῖς·   ὑπάγετε
disciples   of him   and   tells   them: Go ye

εἰς   τὴν   κώμην   τὴν   κατέναντι   ὑμῶν,   καὶ
into   the   village   -   opposite   you,   and

immediately as you enter it you will find a colt tied, on which no one has ever sat; untie it and bring it. ³If any one says to you, 'Why are you doing this?' say, 'The Lord has need of it and will send it back here immediately.'" ⁴And they went away, and found a colt tied at the door out in the open street; and they untied it. ⁵And those who stood there said to them, "What are you doing, untying the colt?" ⁶And they told them what Jesus had said; and they let them go. ⁷And they brought the colt to Jesus, and threw their garments on it; and he sat upon it. ⁸And many spread their garments on the road, and others spread leafy branches which they had cut from the fields.⁹ And those who went before and those who followed cried out, "Hosanna! Blessed is he who comes in the name of the Lord! ¹⁰Blessed is the kingdom of our father David that is coming! Hosanna in the highest!"

11 And he entered Jerusalem, and went into the temple; and when he had looked round at

εὐθὺς   εἰσπορευόμενοι   εἰς   αὐτὴν   εὑρήσετε
immediately   entering   into   it   ye will find

πῶλον   δεδεμένον   ἐφ'   ὃν   οὐδεὶς   οὔπω
a colt   having been tied   on   which   ¹no one   ²not yet

ἀνθρώπων   ἐκάθισεν·   λύσατε   αὐτὸν   καὶ
²of men   ⁴sat;   loosen   it   and

φέρετε.   3 καὶ   ἐάν   τις   ὑμῖν   εἴπῃ·   τί
bring.   And   if   anyone   to you   says: Why

ποιεῖτε   τοῦτο;   εἴπατε·   ὁ   κύριος   αὐτοῦ
do ye   this?   say: The Lord   of it

χρείαν   ἔχει,   καὶ   εὐθὺς   αὐτὸν   ἀποστέλλει
need   has,   and   immediately   it   he sends

πάλιν   ὧδε.   4 καὶ   ἀπῆλθον   καὶ   εὗρον
again   here.   And   they went   and   found

πῶλον   δεδεμένον   πρὸς   θύραν   ἔξω   ἐπὶ
a colt   having been tied   at   a door   outside   on

τοῦ   ἀμφόδου,   καὶ   λύουσιν   αὐτόν.   5 καὶ
the   open street,   and   they loosen   it.   And

τινες   τῶν   ἐκεῖ   ἑστηκότων   ἔλεγον   αὐτοῖς·
some   of the [ones] there   standing   said   to them:

τί   ποιεῖτε   λύοντες   τὸν   πῶλον;   6 οἱ   δὲ
What do ye   loosening   the   colt?   And they

εἶπαν   αὐτοῖς   καθὼς   εἶπεν   ὁ   Ἰησοῦς·
said   to them   as   said   Jesus;

καὶ   ἀφῆκαν   αὐτούς.   7 καὶ   φέρουσιν   τὸν
and   they let go   them.   And   they bring   the

πῶλον   πρὸς   τὸν   Ἰησοῦν,   καὶ   ἐπιβάλλουσιν
colt   to   Jesus,   and   they throw on

αὐτῷ   τὰ   ἱμάτια   αὐτῶν,   καὶ   ἐκάθισεν
it   the   garments   of them,   and   he sat

ἐπ'   αὐτόν.   8 καὶ   πολλοὶ   τὰ   ἱμάτια   αὐτῶν
on   it.   And   many   the   garments   of them

ἔστρωσαν   εἰς   τὴν   ὁδόν,   ἄλλοι   δὲ   στιβάδας,
strewed   in   the   way,   and others   wisps of twigs,

κόψαντες   ἐκ   τῶν   ἀγρῶν.   9 καὶ   οἱ
cutting   out of   the   fields.   And the [ones]

προάγοντες   καὶ   οἱ   ἀκολουθοῦντες   ἔκραζον·
going before   and the [ones]   following   cried out:

ὡσαννά·   εὐλογημένος   ὁ   ἐρχόμενος   ἐν
Hosanna;   blessed   the [one]   coming   in

ὀνόματι   κυρίου·   10 εὐλογημένη   ἡ   ἐρχομένη
[the] name   of [the] Lord;   blessed   the   coming

βασιλεία   τοῦ   πατρὸς   ἡμῶν   Δαυίδ·   ὡσαννὰ
kingdom   of the   father   of us   David;   Hosanna

ἐν   τοῖς   ὑψίστοις.   11 Καὶ   εἰσῆλθεν   εἰς
in   the   highest [places].   And   he entered   into

Ἱεροσόλυμα   εἰς   τὸ   ἱερόν·   καὶ   περιβλεψάμενος
Jerusalem   into the temple;   and   looking round at

everything, as it was already late, he went out to Bethany with the twelve.

12 On the following day, when they came from Bethany, he was hungry. ¹³And seeing in the distance a fig tree in leaf, he went to see if he could find anything on it. When he came to it, he found nothing but leaves, for it was not the season for figs. ¹⁴And he said to it, "May no one ever eat fruit from you again." And his disciples heard it.

15 And they came to Jerusalem. And he entered the temple and began to drive out those who sold and those who bought in the temple, and he overturned the tables of the money-changers and the seats of those who sold pigeons; ¹⁶and he would not allow any one to carry anything through the temple. ¹⁷And he taught, and said to them, "Is it not written, 'My house shall be called a house of prayer for all the nations'? But you have made it a den of robbers." ¹⁸And the chief priests and the scribes heard it and sought a way to destroy him; for they

πάντα, ὀψὲ ἤδη οὔσης τῆς ὥρας, ἐξῆλθεν
all things, ⁵late ⁴now ³being ¹the ²hour,ᵃ he went forth
εἰς Βηθανίαν μετὰ τῶν δώδεκα.
to Bethany with the twelve.

12 Καὶ τῇ ἐπαύριον ἐξελθόντων αὐτῶν
And on the morrow going forth them ᵃ
= as they went forth
ἀπὸ Βηθανίας ἐπείνασεν. **13** καὶ ἰδὼν
from Bethany he hungered. And seeing
συκῆν ἀπὸ μακρόθεν ἔχουσαν φύλλα ἦλθεν
a fig-tree from afar having leaves he came
εἰ ἄρα τι εὑρήσει ἐν αὐτῇ, καὶ ἐλθὼν
if perhaps something he will find in it, and coming
ἐπ' αὐτὴν οὐδὲν εὗρεν εἰ μὴ φύλλα·
upon it nothing he found except leaves;
ὁ γὰρ καιρὸς οὐκ ἦν σύκων. **14** καὶ
for the time was not of figs. And
ἀποκριθεὶς εἶπεν αὐτῇ· μηκέτι εἰς τὸν
answering he said to it: No more to the
αἰῶνα ἐκ σοῦ μηδεὶς καρπὸν φάγοι.
age of thee no one fruit may eat.
= May no one eat fruit of thee for ever.
καὶ ἤκουον οἱ μαθηταὶ αὐτοῦ. **15** Καὶ
And ⁴heard ¹the ²disciples ³of him. And
ἔρχονται εἰς Ἱεροσόλυμα. Καὶ εἰσελθὼν
they come to Jerusalem. And entering
εἰς τὸ ἱερὸν ἤρξατο ἐκβάλλειν τοὺς
into the temple he began to cast out the [ones]
πωλοῦντας καὶ τοὺς ἀγοράζοντας ἐν τῷ
selling and the [ones] buying in the
ἱερῷ, καὶ τὰς τραπέζας τῶν κολλυβιστῶν
temple, and the tables of the moneychangers
καὶ τὰς καθέδρας τῶν πωλούντων τὰς
and the seats of the [ones] selling the
περιστερὰς κατέστρεψεν, **16** καὶ οὐκ ἤφιεν
doves he overturned, and did not permit
ἵνα τις διενέγκῃ σκεῦος διὰ τοῦ
that anyone should carry *through* a vessel through the
ἱεροῦ, **17** καὶ ἐδίδασκεν καὶ ἔλεγεν αὐτοῖς· οὐ
temple, and taught and said to them: Not
γέγραπται ὅτι ὁ οἶκός μου οἶκος προσευχῆς
has it been written that the house of me a house of prayer
κληθήσεται πᾶσιν τοῖς ἔθνεσιν; ὑμεῖς δὲ
shall be called for all the nations? but ye
πεποιήκατε αὐτὸν σπήλαιον λῃστῶν. **18** καὶ
have made it a den of robbers. And
ἤκουσαν οἱ ἀρχιερεῖς καὶ οἱ γραμματεῖς,
⁶heard ¹the ²chief priests ³and ⁴the ⁵scribes,
καὶ ἐζήτουν πῶς αὐτὸν ἀπολέσωσιν·
and they sought how him they might destroy;

feared him, because all the multitude was astonished at his teaching. [19]And when evening came they[h] went out of the city.

20 As they passed by in the morning, they saw the fig tree withered away to its roots. [21]And Peter remembered and said to him, "Master, look! The fig tree which you cursed has withered.' [22]And Jesus answered them, "Have faith in God. [23]Truly, I say to you, whoever says to this mountain, 'Be taken up and cast into the sea,' and does not doubt in his heart, but believes that what he says will come to pass, it will be done for him. [24]Therefore I tell you, whatever you ask in prayer, believe that you receive it, and you will. [25]And whenever you stand praying, forgive, if you have anything against any one; so that your Father also who is in heaven may forgive you your trespasses."[i]

27 And they came again to Jerusalem. And as he was walking in the temple, the chief priests and the scribes and the elders came to him,

ἐφοβοῦντο γὰρ αὐτόν, πᾶς γὰρ ὁ ὄχλος
for they feared   him,   for all   the   crowd
ἐξεπλήσσετο ἐπὶ τῇ διδαχῇ αὐτοῦ. 19 Καὶ
was astounded   at the   teaching of him.   And
ὅταν ὀψὲ ἐγένετο, ἐξεπορεύοντο ἔξω τῆς
when late it became, they went forth outside the
πόλεως. 20 Καὶ παραπορευόμενοι πρωῒ
city.   And   passing along   early
εἶδον τὴν συκῆν ἐξηραμμένην ἐκ ῥιζῶν.
they saw the fig-tree having been withered from [the] roots.
21 καὶ ἀναμνησθεὶς ὁ Πέτρος λέγει αὐτῷ·
And [2]remembering – [1]Peter   says   to him:
ῥαββί, ἴδε ἡ συκῆ ἣν κατηράσω
Rabbi, behold[,] the fig-tree which thou cursedst
ἐξήρανται. 22 καὶ ἀποκριθεὶς ὁ Ἰησοῦς λέγει
has been withered. And answering – Jesus says
αὐτοῖς· ἔχετε πίστιν θεοῦ. 23 ἀμὴν λέγω ὑμῖν
to them: Have [the] faith of God.   Truly I tell you
ὅτι ὃς ἂν εἴπῃ τῷ ὄρει τούτῳ· ἄρθητι
that whoever says – mountain to this: Be thou taken
καὶ βλήθητι εἰς τὴν θάλασσαν, καὶ μὴ
and be thou cast into the   sea,   and not
διακριθῇ ἐν τῇ καρδίᾳ αὐτοῦ ἀλλὰ πιστεύῃ
doubts in the   heart of him   but   believes
ὅτι ὃ λαλεῖ γίνεται, ἔσται αὐτῷ. 24 διὰ
that what he says happens, it will be to him.[c] There-
                                            = he will have it.
τοῦτο λέγω ὑμῖν, πάντα ὅσα προσεύχεσθε
fore I tell you, all things which ye pray
καὶ αἰτεῖσθε, πιστεύετε ὅτι ἐλάβετε, καὶ
and   ask,   believe   that ye received, and
ἔσται ὑμῖν. 25 καὶ ὅταν στήκετε
it will be to you.[c]   And   when   ye stand
                                      = ye will have it.
προσευχόμενοι, ἀφίετε εἴ τι ἔχετε κατά
praying,   forgive if anything ye have against
τινος, ἵνα καὶ ὁ πατὴρ ὑμῶν ὁ ἐν τοῖς
anyone, that also the Father of you – in the
οὐρανοῖς ἀφῇ ὑμῖν τὰ παραπτώματα ὑμῶν.‡
heavens may forgive you the   trespasses   of you.
27 Καὶ ἔρχονται πάλιν εἰς Ἰεροσόλυμα.
And   they come   again to   Jerusalem.
καὶ ἐν τῷ ἱερῷ περιπατοῦντος αὐτοῦ
And in the temple   walking   him[a]
                                    = as he walked
ἔρχονται πρὸς αὐτὸν οἱ ἀρχιερεῖς καὶ οἱ
come   to   him   the chief priests and the
γραμματεῖς καὶ οἱ πρεσβύτεροι, 28 καὶ
scribes   and the   elders,   and

[h] Other ancient authorities read he

[i] Other ancient authorities add verse 26, "But if you do not forgive, neither will your Father who is in heaven forgive your trespasses"

‡ Verse 26 omitted by Nestle; cf. RSV footnote.

28and they said to him, "By what authority are you doing these things, or who gave you this authority to do them?" 29Jesus said to them, "I will ask you a question; answer me, and I will tell you by what authority I do these things. 30Was the baptism of John from heaven or from men? Answer me." 31And they argued with one another, "If we say, 'From heaven,' he will say, 'Why then did you not believe him?' 32But shall we say, 'From men'?"—they were afraid of the people, for all held that John was a real prophet. 33So they answered Jesus, "We do not know." And Jesus said to them, "Neither will I tell you by what authority I do these things."

CHAPTER 12

AND he began to speak to them in parables. "A man planted a vineyard, and set a hedge around it, and dug a pit for the wine press, and built a tower, and let it out to tenants, and went into another country. 2When the time came, he sent a servant to the tenants, to get from them some of the fruit of the vineyard.

ἔλεγον αὐτῷ· ἐν ποίᾳ ἐξουσίᾳ ταῦτα
said to him: By what authority these things
ποιεῖς; ἢ τίς σοι ἔδωκεν τὴν ἐξουσίαν
doest thou? or who thee gave — authority
ταύτην ἵνα ταῦτα ποιῇς; 29 ὁ δὲ Ἰησοῦς
this that these things thou mayest do? - And Jesus
εἶπεν αὐτοῖς· ἐπερωτήσω ὑμᾶς ἕνα λόγον,
said to them: I will question you one word,
καὶ ἀποκρίθητέ μοι, καὶ ἐρῶ ὑμῖν ἐν
and answer ye me, and I will tell you by
ποίᾳ ἐξουσίᾳ ταῦτα ποιῶ. 30 τὸ βάπτισμα
what authority these things I do. The baptism
τὸ Ἰωάννου ἐξ οὐρανοῦ ἦν ἢ ἐξ ἀνθρώπων;
- of John of heaven was it or of men?
ἀποκρίθητέ μοι. 31 καὶ διελογίζοντο πρὸς
answer ye me. And they debated with
ἑαυτοὺς λέγοντες· ἐὰν εἴπωμεν· ἐξ οὐρανοῦ,
themselves saying: If we say: Of heaven,
ἐρεῖ· διὰ τί οὖν οὐκ ἐπιστεύσατε αὐτῷ;
he will say: Why then did ye not believe him?
32 ἀλλὰ εἴπωμεν· ἐξ ἀνθρώπων;—ἐφοβοῦντο
But may we say: Of men? — they feared
τὸν ὄχλον· ἅπαντες γὰρ εἶχον τὸν Ἰωάννην
the crowd; for all men held - John
ὄντως ὅτι προφήτης ἦν. 33 καὶ
²really ¹that ²a prophet ³he was. And
ἀποκριθέντες τῷ Ἰησοῦ λέγουσιν· οὐκ
answering - Jesus they say: not
οἴδαμεν. καὶ ὁ Ἰησοῦς λέγει αὐτοῖς·
We know. And - Jesus says to them:
οὐδὲ ἐγὼ λέγω ὑμῖν ἐν ποίᾳ ἐξουσίᾳ
Neither I tell you by what authority
ταῦτα ποιῶ. 12 Καὶ ἤρξατο αὐτοῖς ἐν
these things I do. And he began to them in
παραβολαῖς λαλεῖν. ἀμπελῶνα ἄνθρωπος
parables to speak. ²a vineyard ¹A man
ἐφύτευσεν, καὶ περιέθηκεν φραγμὸν καὶ ὤρυξεν
²planted, and put round [it] a hedge and dug
ὑπολήνιον καὶ ᾠκοδόμησεν πύργον, καὶ
a winepress and built a tower. and
ἐξέδοτο αὐτὸν γεωργοῖς, καὶ ἀπεδήμησεν.
let out it to husbandmen, and went away.
2 καὶ ἀπέστειλεν πρὸς τοὺς γεωργοὺς τῷ
And he sent to the husbandmen at the
καιρῷ δοῦλον, ἵνα παρὰ τῶν γεωργῶν
time a slave, that from the husbandmen
λάβῃ ἀπὸ τῶν καρπῶν τοῦ ἀμπελῶνος·
he might from(of) the fruits of the vineyard;
receive

³And they took him and beat him, and sent him away empty-handed. ⁴Again he sent to them another servant, and they wounded him in the head, and treated him shamefully. ⁵And he sent another, and him they killed; and so with many others, some they beat and some they killed. ⁶He had still one other, a beloved son; finally he sent him to them, saying, 'They will respect my son.' ⁷But those tenants said to one another, 'This is the heir; come, let us kill him, and the inheritance will be ours.' ⁸And they took him and killed him, and cast him out of the vineyard. ⁹What will the owner of the vineyard do? He will come and destroy the tenants, and give the vineyard to others. ¹⁰Have you not read this scripture:

'The very stone which the builders rejected

has become the head of the corner;

¹¹this was the Lord's doing,

and it is marvelous in our eyes'?"

12 And they tried to arrest him, but feared the multitude, for they perceived that he had told the parable against them;

---

3 καὶ λαβόντες αὐτὸν ἔδειραν καὶ ἀπέστειλαν
And taking him they beat and sent away

κενόν. 4 καὶ πάλιν ἀπέστειλεν πρὸς αὐτοὺς
empty. And again he sent to them

ἄλλον δοῦλον· κἀκεῖνον ἐκεφαλαίωσαν καὶ
another slave; and that one they wounded in the head and

ἠτίμασαν. 5 καὶ ἄλλον ἀπέστειλεν· κἀκεῖνον
insulted. And another he sent; and that one

ἀπέκτειναν, καὶ πολλοὺς ἄλλους, οὓς μὲν
they killed, and many others, ²some

δέροντες, οὓς δὲ ἀποκτέννοντες. 6 ἔτι ἕνα
¹beating, ²others ¹killing. Still one

εἶχεν, υἱὸν ἀγαπητόν· ἀπέστειλεν αὐτὸν
he had, a son beloved; he sent him

ἔσχατον πρὸς αὐτοὺς λέγων ὅτι ἐντραπήσονται
last to them saying[,] – They will reverence

τὸν υἱόν μου. 7 ἐκεῖνοι δὲ οἱ γεωργοὶ
the son of me. But those – husbandmen

πρὸς ἑαυτοὺς εἶπαν ὅτι οὗτός ἐστιν ὁ
to themselves said[,] – This is the

κληρονόμος· δεῦτε ἀποκτείνωμεν αὐτόν, καὶ
heir; come[,] let us kill him, and

ἡμῶν ἔσται ἡ κληρονομία. 8 καὶ λαβόντες
of us will be the inheritance. And taking

ἀπέκτειναν αὐτόν, καὶ ἐξέβαλον αὐτὸν
they killed him, and cast out him

ἔξω τοῦ ἀμπελῶνος. 9 τί ποιήσει ὁ
outside the vineyard. What will do the

κύριος τοῦ ἀμπελῶνος; ἐλεύσεται καὶ
lord of the vineyard? he will come and

ἀπολέσει τοὺς γεωργούς, καὶ δώσει τὸν
will destroy the husbandmen, and will give the

ἀμπελῶνα ἄλλοις. 10 οὐδὲ τὴν γραφὴν
vineyard to others. ²not – ⁴scripture

ταύτην ἀνέγνωτε· λίθον ὃν ἀπεδοκίμασαν
²this ¹Read ye: A stone which ³rejected

οἱ οἰκοδομοῦντες, οὗτος ἐγενήθη εἰς κεφαλὴν
¹the [ones] ²building, this became for head

γωνίας· 11 παρὰ κυρίου ἐγένετο αὕτη,
of corner; from [the] Lord was this,

καὶ ἔστιν θαυμαστὴ ἐν ὀφθαλμοῖς ἡμῶν;
and it is marvellous in eyes of us?

12 Καὶ ἐζήτουν αὐτὸν κρατῆσαι, καὶ
And they sought him to seize, and

ἐφοβήθησαν τὸν ὄχλον· ἔγνωσαν γὰρ
feared the crowd; for they knew

ὅτι πρὸς αὐτοὺς τὴν παραβολὴν
that to them the parable

so they left him and went away.

13 And they sent to him some of the Pharisees and some of the Herodians, to entrap him in his talk. ¹⁴And they came and said to him, "Teacher, we know that you are true, and care for no man; for you do not regard the position of men, but truly teach the way of God. Is it lawful to pay taxes to Caesar, or not? ¹⁵Should we pay them, or should we not?" But knowing their hypocrisy, he said to them, "Why put me to the test? Bring me a coin, and let me look at it." ¹⁶And they brought one. And he said to them, "Whose likeness and inscription is this?" They said to him, "Caesar's." ¹⁷Jesus said to them, "Render to Caesar the things that are Caesar's, and to God the things that are God's." And they were amazed at him.

18 And Sad'ducees came to him, who say that there is no resurrection; and they asked him a question, saying, ¹⁹"Teacher, Moses wrote for us that if a man's brother dies and leaves a wife, but leaves no child, the man must take the

---

εἶπεν. καὶ ἀφέντες αὐτὸν ἀπῆλθον.
he told. And leaving him they went away.

13 Καὶ ἀποστέλλουσιν πρὸς αὐτὸν τινας τῶν
And they send to him some of the

Φαρισαίων καὶ τῶν Ἡρωδιανῶν ἵνα αὐτὸν
Pharisees and of the Herodians that him

ἀγρεύσωσιν λόγῳ. 14 καὶ ἐλθόντες
they might catch in a word. And coming

λέγουσιν αὐτῷ· διδάσκαλε, οἴδαμεν ὅτι
they say to him: Teacher, we know that

ἀληθὴς εἶ καὶ οὐ μέλει σοι περὶ
true thou art and it matters not to thee about

οὐδενός· οὐ γὰρ βλέπεις εἰς πρόσωπον
no(any)one; for thou lookest not at [the] face

ἀνθρώπων, ἀλλ᾽ ἐπ᾽ ἀληθείας τὴν ὁδὸν
of men, but on(in) truth the way

τοῦ θεοῦ διδάσκεις· ἔξεστιν δοῦναι κῆνσον
– of God teachest; is it lawful to give tribute

Καίσαρι ἢ οὔ; δῶμεν ἢ μὴ δῶμεν;
to Caesar or no? may we give or may we not give?

15 ὁ δὲ εἰδὼς αὐτῶν τὴν ὑπόκρισιν εἶπεν
But he knowing of them the hypocrisy said

αὐτοῖς· τί με πειράζετε; φέρετέ μοι
to them: Why me tempt ye? bring me

δηνάριον ἵνα ἴδω. 16 οἱ δὲ ἤνεγκαν. καὶ
a denarius that I may see. And they brought. And

λέγει αὐτοῖς· τίνος ἡ εἰκὼν αὕτη καὶ ἡ
he says to them: Of whom – image this and –

ἐπιγραφή; οἱ δὲ εἶπαν αὐτῷ· Καίσαρος.
superscription? And they tell him: Of Caesar.

17 ὁ δὲ Ἰησοῦς εἶπεν αὐτοῖς· τὰ Καίσαρος
– So Jesus said to them: The things of Caesar

ἀπόδοτε Καίσαρι καὶ τὰ τοῦ θεοῦ τῷ
render to Caesar and the things – of God –

θεῷ. καὶ ἐξεθαύμαζον ἐπ᾽ αὐτῷ.
to God. And they marvelled at him.

18 Καὶ ἔρχονται Σαδδουκαῖοι πρὸς αὐτόν,
And come Sadducees to him,

οἵτινες λέγουσιν ἀνάστασιν μὴ εἶναι, καὶ
who say resurrection not to be, and
= that there is no resurrection,

ἐπηρώτων αὐτὸν λέγοντες· 19 διδάσκαλε,
questioned him saying: Teacher,

Μωϋσῆς ἔγραψεν ἡμῖν ὅτι ἐάν τινος
Moses wrote to us that if of anyone

ἀδελφὸς ἀποθάνῃ καὶ καταλίπῃ γυναῖκα
a brother should die and leave behind a wife

καὶ μὴ ἀφῇ τέκνον, ἵνα λάβῃ ὁ ἀδελφὸς
and leave not a child, – ⁴may take ¹the ²brother

wife, and raise up children for his brother. ²⁰There were seven brothers; the first took a wife, and when he died left no children; ²¹and the second took her, and died, leaving no children; and the third likewise; ²²and the seven left no children. Last of all the woman also died. ²³In the resurrection whose wife will she be? For the seven had her as wife."

24 Jesus said to them, "Is not this why you are wrong, that you know neither the scriptures nor the power of God? ²⁵For when they rise from the dead, they neither marry nor are given in marriage, but are like angels in heaven. ²⁶And as for the dead being raised, have you not read in the book of Moses, in the passage about the bush, how God said to him, 'I am the God of Abraham, and the God of Isaac, and the God of Jacob'? ²⁷He is not God of the dead, but of the living; you are quite wrong."

28 And one of the scribes came up and heard them disputing with one another, and

αὐτοῦ τὴν γυναῖκα καὶ ἐξαναστήσῃ σπέρμα
³of him   the   wife   and may raise up seed

τῷ ἀδελφῷ αὐτοῦ. 20 ἑπτὰ ἀδελφοὶ ἦσαν·
to the brother of him.   Seven brothers there were;

καὶ ὁ πρῶτος ἔλαβεν γυναῖκα, καὶ
and the first   took   a wife, and

ἀποθνῇσκων οὐκ ἀφῆκεν σπέρμα· 21 καὶ
dying   left not   seed·   and

ὁ δεύτερος ἔλαβεν αὐτήν, καὶ ἀπέθανεν μὴ
the second took   her, and   died   not

καταλιπὼν σπέρμα· καὶ ὁ τρίτος ὡσαύτως·
leaving behind seed; and the third   similarly;

22 καὶ οἱ ἑπτὰ οὐκ ἀφῆκαν σπέρμα.
and the seven   left not   seed.

ἔσχατον πάντων καὶ ἡ γυνὴ ἀπέθανεν.
Last   of all also the wife   died.

23 ἐν τῇ ἀναστάσει, ὅταν ἀναστῶσιν,
In   the resurrection, when they rise again,

τίνος αὐτῶν ἔσται γυνή; οἱ γὰρ ἑπτὰ
of which of them will she be wife? for the seven

ἔσχον αὐτὴν γυναῖκα. 24 ἔφη αὐτοῖς ὁ
had   her   [as] wife.   Said to them -

'Ἰησοῦς· οὐ διὰ τοῦτο πλανᾶσθε μὴ
Jesus: ³not ⁴therefore ¹Do ⁵ye ⁶err not

εἰδότες τὰς γραφὰς μηδὲ τὴν δύναμιν
knowing the scriptures nor the power

τοῦ θεοῦ; 25 ὅταν γὰρ ἐκ νεκρῶν
-    of God?   for when out of [the] dead

ἀναστῶσιν, οὔτε γαμοῦσιν οὔτε γαμίζονται,
they rise again, they neither marry nor are given in
                                          marriage,

ἀλλ' εἰσὶν ὡς ἄγγελοι ἐν τοῖς οὐρανοῖς.
but   are   as angels in the heavens.

26 περὶ δὲ τῶν νεκρῶν ὅτι ἐγείρονται,
But concerning the dead   that they are raised,

οὐκ ἀνέγνωτε ἐν τῇ βίβλῳ Μωϋσέως ἐπὶ
did ye not read in the roll of Moses   at

τοῦ βάτου πῶς εἶπεν αὐτῷ ὁ θεὸς λέγων·
the bush how said to him - God saying:

ἐγὼ ὁ θεὸς 'Ἀβραὰμ καὶ θεὸς 'Ἰσαὰκ
I [am] the God of Abraham and God of Isaac

καὶ θεὸς 'Ἰακώβ; 27 οὐκ ἔστιν θεὸς
and God of Jacob?   he is not   God

νεκρῶν ἀλλὰ ζώντων. πολὺ πλανᾶσθε.
of dead [persons] but of living [ones]. Much ye err.

28 Καὶ προσελθὼν εἷς τῶν γραμματέων,
And ⁴approaching ¹one ²of the ³scribes,

ἀκούσας αὐτῶν συζητούντων, εἰδὼς ὅτι
hearing them   debating,   knowing that

seeing that he answered them well, asked him, "Which commandment is the first of all?" [29]Jesus answered, "The first is, 'Hear, O Israel: The Lord our God, the Lord is one; [30]and you shall love the Lord your God with all your heart, and with all your soul, and with all your mind, and with all your strength.' [31]The second is this, 'You shall love your neighbor as yourself.' There is no other commandment greater than these." [32]And the scribe said to him, "You are right, Teacher; you have truly said that he is one, and there is no other but he; [33]and to love him with all the heart, and with all the understanding, and with all the strength, and to love one's neighbor as oneself, is much more than all whole burnt offerings and sacrifices." [34]And when Jesus saw that he answered wisely, he said to him, "You are not far from the kingdom of God." And after that no one dared to ask him any question.

35 And as Jesus taught

καλῶς ἀπεκρίθη αὐτοῖς, ἐπηρώτησεν αὐτόν·
well   he answered   them,   questioned   him:

ποία ἐστὶν ἐντολὴ πρώτη πάντων;
What   is [the] commandment   first   of all?

29 ἀπεκρίθη ὁ Ἰησοῦς ὅτι πρώτη ἐστίν·
Answered   —   Jesus[,]   —   [The] first   is:

ἄκουε, Ἰσραήλ, κύριος ὁ θεὸς ἡμῶν κύριος
Hear,   Israel,   Lord   the   God   of us   Lord
          = The Lord our God is one Lord,

εἷς ἐστιν, **30** καὶ ἀγαπήσεις κύριον τὸν
one   is,   and   thou shalt love   Lord   the

θεόν σου ἐξ ὅλης τῆς καρδίας σου καὶ
God   of thee from(with)   all   the   heart   of thee   and

ἐξ ὅλης τῆς ψυχῆς σου καὶ ἐξ ὅλης
with   all   the   soul   of thee   and   with   all

τῆς διανοίας σου καὶ ἐξ ὅλης τῆς ἰσχύος
the   mind   of thee   and   with   all   the   strength

σου. **31** δευτέρα αὕτη· ἀγαπήσεις τὸν
of thee.   [The] second [is]   this: Thou shalt love   the

πλησίον σου ὡς σεαυτόν. μείζων τούτων
neighbour   of thee   as   thyself.   Greater [than]   these

ἄλλη ἐντολὴ οὐκ ἔστιν. **32** καὶ εἶπεν
other   commandment   there is not.   And   said

αὐτῷ ὁ γραμματεύς· καλῶς, διδάσκαλε, ἐπ᾽
to him   the   scribe: Well,   teacher,   on(in)

ἀληθείας εἶπες ὅτι εἷς ἐστιν καὶ οὐκ
truth   thou sayest that   one   there is   and   not

ἔστιν ἄλλος πλὴν αὐτοῦ· **33** καὶ τὸ
there is   another   besides   him;   and   —

ἀγαπᾶν αὐτὸν ἐξ ὅλης τῆς καρδίας καὶ ἐξ
to love   him   with   all   the   heart   and with

ὅλης τῆς συνέσεως καὶ ἐξ ὅλης τῆς
all   the   understanding   and   with   all   the

ἰσχύος, καὶ τὸ ἀγαπᾶν τὸν πλησίον ὡς
strength,   and   —   to love   the(one's) neighbour   as

ἑαυτὸν περισσότερόν ἐστιν πάντων τῶν
himself   more   is [than]   all   the

ὁλοκαυτωμάτων καὶ θυσιῶν. **34** καὶ ὁ
burnt offerings   and   sacrifices.   And   —

Ἰησοῦς, ἰδὼν αὐτὸν ὅτι νουνεχῶς ἀπεκρίθη,
Jesus,   seeing   him   that   sensibly   he answered,

εἶπεν αὐτῷ· οὐ μακρὰν εἶ ἀπὸ τῆς
said   to him: Not   far   thou art   from   the

βασιλείας τοῦ θεοῦ. καὶ οὐδεὶς οὐκέτι
kingdom   —   of God.   And   no one   no(any) more

ἐτόλμα αὐτὸν ἐπερωτῆσαι.
dared   him   to question.

35 Καὶ ἀποκριθεὶς ὁ Ἰησοῦς ἔλεγεν
And   answering   —   Jesus   said

in the temple, he said, "How can the scribes say that the Christ is the son of David? [36]David himself, inspired by[j] the Holy Spirit, declared,

'The Lord said to my Lord,

Sit at my right hand, till I put thy enemies under thy feet.'

[37]David himself calls him Lord; so how is he his son?" And the great throng heard him gladly.

38 And in his teaching he said, "Beware of the scribes, who like to go about in long robes, and to have salutations in the market places [39]and the best seats in the synagogues and the places of honor at feasts,[40] who devour widows' houses and for a pretense make long prayers. They will receive the greater condemnation."

41 And he sat down opposite the treasury, and watched the multitude putting money into the treasury. Many rich people put in large sums. [42]And a poor widow came, and put in two copper coins, which make a penny. [43]And he called his disciples to him, and

διδάσκων ἐν τῷ ἱερῷ· πῶς λέγουσιν οἱ
teaching   in   the   temple: How   say   the

γραμματεῖς ὅτι ὁ χριστὸς υἱός Δαυὶδ
scribes   that the   Christ   son   of David

ἐστιν; 36 αὐτὸς Δαυὶδ εἶπεν ἐν τῷ πνεύματι
is?   himself David said   by   the   Spirit

τῷ ἁγίῳ· εἶπεν κύριος τῷ κυρίῳ μου·
-    Holy: said [the] LORD to the Lord of me:

κάθου ἐκ δεξιῶν μου ἕως ἂν θῶ τοὺς
Sit   at [the] right [hand] of me until   I put   the

ἐχθρούς σου ὑποκάτω τῶν ποδῶν σου.
enemies of thee under   the   feet   of thee.

37 αὐτὸς Δαυὶδ λέγει αὐτὸν κύριον, καὶ
    himself David says(calls) him   Lord,   and

πόθεν αὐτοῦ ἐστιν υἱός;
whence of him is he   son?

Καὶ ὁ πολὺς ὄχλος ἤκουεν αὐτοῦ
And the   much   crowd   heard   him

ἡδέως. 38 Καὶ ἐν τῇ διδαχῇ αὐτοῦ
gladly.   And   in   the   teaching   of him

ἔλεγεν· βλέπετε ἀπὸ τῶν γραμματέων
he said: Beware from(of) the   scribes

τῶν θελόντων ἐν στολαῖς περιπατεῖν καὶ
the [ones] wishing   in   robes   to walk about   and

ἀσπασμοὺς ἐν ταῖς ἀγοραῖς 39 καὶ
greetings   in   the   marketplaces   and

πρωτοκαθεδρίας ἐν ταῖς συναγωγαῖς καὶ
chief seats   in   the   synagogues   and

πρωτοκλισίας ἐν τοῖς δείπνοις· 40 οἱ
chief places   in   the   dinners;   the [ones]

κατέσθοντες τὰς οἰκίας τῶν χηρῶν καὶ
devouring   the   houses of the widows   and

προφάσει μακρὰ προσευχόμενοι, οὗτοι
under pretence long   praying,   these

λήμψονται περισσότερον κρίμα. 41 Καὶ
will receive   greater   condemnation.   And

καθίσας κατέναντι τοῦ γαζοφυλακείου ἐθεώρει
sitting   opposite the   treasury   he beheld

πῶς ὁ ὄχλος βάλλει χαλκὸν εἰς τὸ
how the   crowd   puts copper money into   the

γαζοφυλακεῖον· καὶ πολλοὶ πλούσιοι ἔβαλλον
treasury;   and   many   rich men   put

πολλά· 42 καὶ ἐλθοῦσα μία χήρα πτωχὴ
much;   and   coming one   widow   poor

ἔβαλεν λεπτὰ δύο, ὅ ἐστιν κοδράντης.
put   lepta   two,   which is   a quadrans.

43 καὶ προσκαλεσάμενος τοὺς μαθητὰς αὐτοῦ
    And   calling to [him]   the   disciples   of him

[j] Or himself, in

said to them, "Truly, I say to you, this poor widow has put in more than all those who are contributing to the treasury. [44] For they all contributed out of their abundance; but she out of her poverty has put in everything she had, her whole living."

εἶπεν αὐτοῖς· ἀμὴν λέγω ὑμῖν ὅτι
he said   to them: Truly   I tell   you   that
ἡ χήρα αὕτη ἡ πτωχὴ πλεῖον πάντων
- [3]widow [1]this - [2]poor [5]more [than] [4]all
ἔβαλεν τῶν βαλλόντων εἰς τὸ γαζοφυλακεῖον·
[6]put   the [ones] putting   into the   treasury;

[44] πάντες γὰρ ἐκ τοῦ περισσεύοντος αὐτοῖς
for all   out of the   abounding   to them[c]
                        = their abundance

ἔβαλον, αὕτη δὲ ἐκ τῆς ὑστερήσεως αὐτῆς
put,   but this woman out of the   want   of her
πάντα ὅσα εἶχεν ἔβαλεν, ὅλον τὸν βίον
[2]all things [3]how many [4]she had [1]put,   all   the   living
αὐτῆς.
of her.

CHAPTER 13

AND as he came out of the temple, one of his disciples said to him, "Look, Teacher, what wonderful stones and what wonderful buildings!" [2]And Jesus said to him, "Do you see these great buildings? There will not be left here one stone upon another, that will not be thrown down."

[3] And as he sat on the Mount of Olives opposite the temple, Peter and James and John and Andrew asked him privately, [4]"Tell us, when will this be, and what will be the sign when these things are all to be accomplished?" [5]And Jesus began to say to them, "Take heed that no one leads you astray. [6]Many will come in my name, saying, 'I

[13] Καὶ ἐκπορευομένου αὐτοῦ ἐκ τοῦ
And   going forth   him[a]   out of the
                = as he went forth
ἱεροῦ λέγει αὐτῷ εἷς τῶν μαθητῶν αὐτοῦ·
temple   says   to him   one of the   disciples   of him:
διδάσκαλε, ἴδε ποταποὶ λίθοι καὶ ποταπαὶ
Teacher,   behold[,] what great stones   and   what great
οἰκοδομαί. [2] καὶ ὁ Ἰησοῦς εἶπεν αὐτῷ·
buildings.   And - Jesus   said   to him:
βλέπεις ταύτας τὰς μεγάλας οἰκοδομάς;
Seest thou   these   -   great   buildings?
οὐ μὴ ἀφεθῇ λίθος ἐπὶ λίθον ὃς οὐ
by no means be left   stone   on   stone which by no
= there shall by no means be left stone on stone which will not
μὴ καταλυθῇ. [3] Καὶ καθημένου αὐτοῦ
means be overthrown.   And   sitting   him[a]
be overthrown.   = as he sat
εἰς τὸ ὄρος τῶν ἐλαιῶν κατέναντι τοῦ
in(on) the   mount of the   olives   opposite   the
ἱεροῦ, ἐπηρώτα αὐτὸν κατ' ἰδίαν Πέτρος
temple,   questioned   him   privately   Peter
καὶ Ἰάκωβος καὶ Ἰωάννης καὶ Ἀνδρέας·
and   James   and   John   and   Andrew:
[4] εἰπὸν ἡμῖν, πότε ταῦτα ἔσται, καὶ τί
Tell   us,   when   these things will be,   and what
τὸ σημεῖον ὅταν μέλλῃ ταῦτα συντελεῖσθαι
the   sign   when [3]are about [2]these things [4]to be completed
πάντα; [5] ὁ δὲ Ἰησοῦς ἤρξατο λέγειν
[1]all?   - And   Jesus   began   to say
αὐτοῖς· βλέπετε μή τις ὑμᾶς πλανήσῃ.
to them: See   lest anyone   you   lead astray.
[6] πολλοὶ ἐλεύσονται ἐπὶ τῷ ὀνόματί μου
Many   will come   on(in) the   name   of me

am he!' and they will lead many astray. ⁷And when you hear of wars and rumors of wars, do not be alarmed; this must take place, but the end is not yet. ⁸For nation will rise against nation, and kingdom against kingdom; there will be earthquakes in various places, there will be famines; this is but the beginning of the sufferings.

9 "But take heed to yourselves; for they will deliver you up to councils; and you will be beaten in synagogues; and you will stand before governors and kings for my sake, to bear testimony before them. ¹⁰And the gospel must first be preached to all nations. ¹¹And when they bring you to trial and deliver you up, do not be anxious beforehand what you are to say; but say whatever is given you in that hour, for it is not you who speak, but the Holy Spirit. ¹²And brother will deliver up brother to death, and the father his child, and children will rise against parents and have them put to death; ¹³and you will be hated by all for my name's sake. But he who endures to the end will be saved.

14 "But when you see the desolating sacrilege

λέγοντες ὅτι ἐγώ εἰμι, καὶ πολλοὺς
saying[,]   -   I   am,   and   many

πλανήσουσιν. 7 ὅταν δὲ ἀκούσητε πολέμους
they will lead astray.   But when   ye hear   [of] wars

καὶ ἀκοὰς πολέμων, μὴ θροεῖσθε· δεῖ
and   rumours   of wars,   be not disturbed;   it behoves

γενέσθαι, ἀλλ' οὔπω τὸ τέλος. 8 ἐγερθήσεται
to happen,   but   not yet   the   end.   will be raised

γὰρ ἔθνος ἐπ' ἔθνος καὶ βασιλεία ἐπὶ
For   nation   against   nation   and   kingdom against

βασιλείαν. ἔσονται σεισμοὶ κατὰ τόπους,
kingdom.   There will be earthquakes   in places,

ἔσονται λιμοί· ἀρχὴ ὠδίνων ταῦτα.
there will be famines;   beginning of birth-pangs   these things [are].

9 Βλέπετε δὲ ὑμεῖς ἑαυτούς· παραδώσουσιν
But see   ye   yourselves;   they will deliver

ὑμᾶς εἰς συνέδρια καὶ εἰς συναγωγὰς
you   to   councils   and   in   synagogues

δαρήσεσθε καὶ ἐπὶ ἡγεμόνων καὶ βασιλέων
ye will be beaten   and   before   rulers   and   kings

σταθήσεσθε ἔνεκεν ἐμοῦ, εἰς μαρτύριον
ye will stand   for the sake   of me,   for   a testimony

αὐτοῖς. 10 καὶ εἰς πάντα τὰ ἔθνη πρῶτον
to them.   And to   all   the   nations   first

δεῖ κηρυχθῆναι τὸ εὐαγγέλιον. 11 καὶ ὅταν
it behoves to be proclaimed the   gospel.   And when
= the gospel must be proclaimed.

ἄγωσιν ὑμᾶς παραδιδόντες, μὴ προμεριμνᾶτε
they lead   you   delivering,   be not anxious beforehand

τί λαλήσητε, ἀλλ' ὃ ἐὰν δοθῇ ὑμῖν ἐν
what ye speak,   but   whatever is given   you   in

ἐκείνῃ τῇ ὥρᾳ, τοῦτο λαλεῖτε· οὐ γὰρ
that   -   hour.   this   speak ye;   for not

ἐστε ὑμεῖς οἱ λαλοῦντες ἀλλὰ τὸ πνεῦμα
are   ye   the [ones] speaking   but   the   Spirit

τὸ ἅγιον. 12 καὶ παραδώσει ἀδελφὸς
-   Holy.   And   ²will deliver   ¹a brother

ἀδελφὸν εἰς θάνατον καὶ πατὴρ τέκνον, καὶ
a brother   to   death   and   a father   a child,   and

ἐπαναστήσονται τέκνα ἐπὶ γονεῖς καὶ
²will rise against   ¹children   against   parents   and

θανατώσουσιν αὐτούς· 13 καὶ ἔσεσθε
will put to death   them;   and   ye will be

μισούμενοι ὑπὸ πάντων διὰ τὸ ὄνομά
being hated   by   all men   on account of   the   name

μου· ὁ δὲ ὑπομείνας εἰς τέλος, οὗτος
of me;   but the [one]   enduring   to [the] end,   this

σωθήσεται. 14 Ὅταν δὲ ἴδητε τὸ βδέλυγμα
will be saved.   But when   ye see   the   abomination

set up where it ought not to be (let the reader understand), then let those who are in Judea flee to the mountains, [15] let him who is on the housetop not go down, nor enter his house, to take anything away; [16] and let him who is in the field not turn back to take his mantle. [17] And alas for those who are with child and for those who give suck in those days! [18] Pray that it may not happen in winter. [19] For in those days there will be such tribulation as has not been from the beginning of the creation which God created until now, and never will be. [20] And if the Lord had not shortened the days, no human being would be saved; but for the sake of the elect, whom he chose, he shortened the days. [21] And then if any one says to you, 'Look, here is the Christ!' or 'Look, there he is!' do not believe it. [22] False Christs and false prophets will arise and show signs and wonders, to lead astray, if possible, the elect. [23] But take heed; I have told you all things beforehand.

24 "But in those days,

τῆς ἐρημώσεως ἑστηκότα ὅπου οὐ δεῖ, ὁ
\- of desolation   stand   where he (it) behoves not, the
ἀναγινώσκων νοείτω, τότε οἱ ἐν τῇ
[one] reading let him understand, then the [ones] in   \-
'Ιουδαίᾳ φευγέτωσαν εἰς τὰ ὄρη, 15 ὁ ἐπὶ
Judæa   let them flee   to the mountains, the [one] on
τοῦ δώματος μὴ καταβάτω μηδὲ εἰσελθάτω
the   roof   let him not come down nor   let him enter
τι   ἆραι ἐκ τῆς οἰκίας αὐτοῦ, 16 καὶ   ὁ
anything to take out of the house   of him,   and the [one]
εἰς   τὸν ἀγρὸν μὴ ἐπιστρεψάτω εἰς τὰ
in   the   field   let him not return   to the things
ὀπίσω ἆραι τὸ ἱμάτιον αὐτοῦ. 17 οὐαὶ
behind   to take   the   garment   of him.   woe
δὲ ταῖς ἐν γαστρὶ ἐχούσαις καὶ ταῖς
But to the women   pregnant†   and   to the
θηλαζούσαις ἐν ἐκείναις ταῖς ἡμέραις.
[ones] giving suck in   those   \-   days.
18 προσεύχεσθε δὲ ἵνα μὴ γένηται χειμῶνος·
But pray ye   that it may not happen of(in) winter;
19 ἔσονται γὰρ αἱ ἡμέραι ἐκεῖναι θλῖψις, οἵα
for ²will be   \-   ³days   ¹those   ⁴affliction, of such
a kind
οὐ γέγονεν τοιαύτη ἀπ' ἀρχῆς κτίσεως
²has not happened   ¹as   from [the] beginning of [the] creation
ἣν ἔκτισεν ὁ θεὸς ἕως τοῦ νῦν καὶ οὐ
which created   \-   God   until   \-   now and by
μὴ γένηται. 20 καὶ εἰ μὴ ἐκολόβωσεν
no means may be.   And   unless   ²shortened
κύριος τὰς ἡμέρας, οὐκ ἂν ἐσώθη πᾶσα
¹[the] Lord the   days,   would not be saved   all
= no flesh would be saved;
σάρξ· ἀλλὰ διὰ τοὺς ἐκλεκτοὺς οὓς
flesh;   but on account of the   chosen   whom
ἐξελέξατο ἐκολόβωσεν τὰς ἡμέρας. 21 καὶ
he chose   he shortened   the   days.   And
τότε ἐάν τις ὑμῖν εἴπῃ· ἴδε ὧδε ὁ
then   if anyone ²you   ¹tells: Behold here [is] the
χριστός, ἴδε ἐκεῖ, μὴ πιστεύετε· 22 ἐγερθή-
Christ, behold there,   believe ye not;   ⁵will be
σονται δὲ ψευδόχριστοι καὶ ψευδοπροφῆται
raised   ¹and   ²false Christs   ³and   ⁴false prophets
καὶ ποιήσουσιν σημεῖα καὶ τέρατα πρὸς
and   they will do   signs   and   wonders   for
τὸ ἀποπλανᾶν, εἰ δυνατόν, τοὺς ἐκλεκτούς.
\-   to lead astray, if   possible,   the   chosen.
23 ὑμεῖς δὲ βλέπετε· προείρηκα ὑμῖν πάντα.
But ²ye   ¹see;   ¹I have told ⁴before ²you ³all things.
24 'Αλλὰ ἐν ἐκείναις ταῖς ἡμέραις μετὰ
But   in   those   \-   days   after

after that tribulation, the sun will be darkened, and the moon will not give its light, 25 and the stars will be falling from heaven, and the powers in the heavens will be shaken. 26 And then they will see the Son of man coming 'in clouds with great power and glory. 27 And then he will send out the angels, and gather his elect from the four winds, from the ends of the earth to the ends of heaven.

28 "From the fig tree learn its lesson: as soon as its branch becomes tender and puts forth its leaves, you know that summer is near. 29 So also, when you see these things taking place, you know that he is near, at the very gates. 30 Truly, I say to you, this generation will not pass away before all these things take place. 31 Heaven and earth will pass away, but my words will not pass away.

32 "But of that day or that hour no one knows, not even the angels in heaven, nor the Son, but only the Father. 33 Take heed, watch;*k* for you do not

τὴν θλῖψιν ἐκείνην ὁ ἥλιος σκοτισθήσεται,
\- affliction that the sun will be darkened,

καὶ ἡ σελήνη οὐ δώσει τὸ φέγγος αὐτῆς,
and the moon will not give the light of her,

25 καὶ οἱ ἀστέρες ἔσονται ἐκ τοῦ οὐρανοῦ
and the stars ¹will be ²out of ⁻ ⁴heaven

πίπτοντες, καὶ αἱ δυνάμεις αἱ ἐν τοῖς
³falling, and the powers ⁻ in the

οὐρανοῖς σαλευθήσονται. 26 καὶ τότε ὄψονται
heavens will be shaken. And then they will see

τὸν υἱὸν τοῦ ἀνθρώπου ἐρχόμενον ἐν
the Son ⁻ of man coming in

νεφέλαις μετὰ δυνάμεως πολλῆς καὶ δόξης.
clouds with power much and glory.

27 καὶ τότε ἀποστελεῖ τοὺς ἀγγέλους καὶ
And then he will send the angels and

ἐπισυνάξει τοὺς ἐκλεκτοὺς [αὐτοῦ] ἐκ τῶν
they will assemble the chosen of him out of the

τεσσάρων ἀνέμων ἀπ' ἄκρου γῆς ἕως
four winds from [the] extremity of earth to

ἄκρου οὐρανοῦ. 28 Ἀπὸ δὲ τῆς συκῆς
[the] extremity of heaven. Now from the fig-tree

μάθετε τὴν παραβολήν· ὅταν ἤδη ὁ
learn the parable; when now the

κλάδος αὐτῆς ἁπαλὸς γένηται καὶ ἐκφύῃ
branch of it tender becomes and puts forth

τὰ φύλλα, γινώσκετε ὅτι ἐγγὺς τὸ θέρος
the leaves, ye know that near the summer

ἐστίν· 29 οὕτως καὶ ὑμεῖς, ὅταν ἴδητε
is; so also ye, when ye see

ταῦτα γινόμενα, γινώσκετε ὅτι ἐγγύς ἐστιν
these things happening, know that near he/it is

ἐπὶ θύραις. 30 ἀμὴν λέγω ὑμῖν ὅτι οὐ
at [the] doors. Truly I tell you that by no

μὴ παρέλθῃ ἡ γενεὰ αὕτη μέχρις οὗ
means passes ⁻ generation this until

ταῦτα πάντα γένηται. 31 ὁ οὐρανὸς καὶ
these things all happen. The heaven and

ἡ γῆ παρελεύσονται, οἱ δὲ λόγοι μου
the earth will pass away, but the words of me

οὐ παρελεύσονται. 32 Περὶ δὲ τῆς ἡμέρας
will not pass away. But concerning ⁻ day

ἐκείνης ἢ τῆς ὥρας οὐδεὶς οἶδεν, οὐδὲ
that or ⁻ hour no one knows, not

οἱ ἄγγελοι ἐν οὐρανῷ οὐδὲ ὁ υἱός, εἰ
the angels in heaven neither the Son, ex-

μὴ ὁ πατήρ. 33 Βλέπετε, ἀγρυπνεῖτε·
cept the Father. Look, be wakeful;

k Other ancient authorities add *and pray*

know when the time will come. ³⁴It is like a man going on a journey, when he leaves home and puts his servants in charge, each with his work, and commands the door-keeper to be on the watch. ³⁵Watch therefore —for you do not know when the master of the house will come, in the evening, or at midnight, or at cockcrow, or in the morning—³⁶lest he come suddenly and find you asleep. ³⁷And what I say to you I say to all: Watch."

οὐκ οἴδατε γὰρ πότε ὁ καιρός ἐστιν.
for ye know not   when   the time   is.

34 ὡς ἄνθρωπος ἀπόδημος ἀφεὶς τὴν οἰκίαν
As   a man   away from home leaving the house

αὐτοῦ καὶ δοὺς τοῖς δούλοις αὐτοῦ τὴν
of him and giving to the slaves   of him   –

ἐξουσίαν, ἑκάστῳ τὸ ἔργον αὐτοῦ, καὶ
authority, to each   the work   of him, and

τῷ θυρωρῷ ἐνετείλατο ἵνα γρηγορῇ.
the doorkeeper he commanded that he should watch.

35 γρηγορεῖτε οὖν· οὐκ οἴδατε γὰρ πότε
Watch ye   therefore;   for ye know not   when

ὁ κύριος τῆς οἰκίας ἔρχεται, ἢ ὀψὲ ἢ
the lord of the house comes, either late or

μεσονύκτιον ἢ ἀλεκτοροφωνίας ἢ πρωΐ·
at midnight   or   at cock-crowing   or   early;

36 μὴ ἐλθὼν ἐξαίφνης εὕρῃ ὑμᾶς καθεύδ-
lest coming suddenly he find you   sleep-

οντας. **37** ὃ δὲ ὑμῖν λέγω, πᾶσιν λέγω,
ing.   And what to you I say,   to all   I say,

γρηγορεῖτε.
watch ye.

CHAPTER 14

IT was now two days before the Passover and the feast of Un-leavened Bread. And the chief priests and the scribes were seeking how to arrest him by stealth, and kill him; ²for they said, "Not during the feast, lest there be a tumult of the people."

3 And while he was at Bethany in the house of Simon the leper, as he sat at table, a woman came with an alabaster jar of ointment of pure nard, very costly, and she broke the jar and poured

14 ⁵Ἦν δὲ τὸ πάσχα καὶ τὰ ἄζυμα
Now it was   the Passover   and [the feast of] the
unleavened bread†

μετὰ δύο ἡμέρας. καὶ ἐζήτουν οἱ ἀρχιερεῖς
after   two   days.   And sought the chief priests

καὶ οἱ γραμματεῖς πῶς αὐτὸν ἐν δόλῳ
and the   scribes   how ¹him ³by ⁴guile

κρατήσαντες ἀποκτείνωσιν. **2** ἔλεγον γάρ·
¹seizing   they might kill.   For they said :

μὴ ἐν τῇ ἑορτῇ, μήποτε ἔσται θόρυβος
Not at the feast, lest there will be a disturbance

τοῦ λαοῦ.
of the people.

3 Καὶ ὄντος αὐτοῦ ἐν Βηθανίᾳ ἐν τῇ
And being himᵃ in Bethany in the
= when he was

οἰκίᾳ Σίμωνος τοῦ λεπροῦ, κατακειμένου
house of Simon the   leper,   reclining
= as he reclined

αὐτοῦ ἦλθεν γυνὴ ἔχουσα ἀλάβαστρον
himᵃ   came a woman having an alabaster phial

μύρου νάρδου πιστικῆς πολυτελοῦς·
of ointment ³nard   ¹of pure   ²costly;

συντρίψασα τὴν ἀλάβαστρον κατέχεεν αὐτοῦ
breaking   the   alabaster phial she poured over of him

it over his head. ⁴But there were some who said to themselves indignantly, "Why was the ointment thus wasted? ⁵For this ointment might have been sold for more than three hundred denarii, and given to the poor." And they reproached her. ⁶But Jesus said, "Let her alone; why do you trouble her? She has done a beautiful thing to me. ⁷For you always have the poor with you, and whenever you will, you can do good to them; but you will not always have me. ⁸She has done what she could; she has anointed my body beforehand for burying. ⁹And truly, I say to you, wherever the gospel is preached in the whole world, what she has done will be told in memory of her."

10 Then Judas Iscariot, who was one of the twelve, went to the chief priests in order to betray him to them. ¹¹And when they heard it they were glad, and promised to give him money. And he sought an opportunity to betray him.

12 And on the first day of Unleavened Bread, when they sacrificed the passover lamb, his disciples said to him,

τῆς κεφαλῆς. 4 ἦσαν δέ τινες ἀγανακτοῦντες
the   head.   Now there were some   being angry

πρὸς ἑαυτούς· εἰς τί ἡ ἀπώλεια αὕτη
with themselves: Why –   waste   this

τοῦ μύρου γέγονεν; 5 ἠδύνατο γὰρ τοῦτο
of the ointment has occurred?   for ²could   ¹this

τὸ μύρον πραθῆναι ἐπάνω δηναρίων
–   ²ointment to be sold [for] over denarii

τριακοσίων καὶ δοθῆναι τοῖς πτωχοῖς·
three hundred and to be given to the poor;

καὶ ἐνεβριμῶντο αὐτῇ. 6 ὁ δὲ Ἰησοῦς
and they were indignant with her.   – But   Jesus

εἶπεν· ἄφετε αὐτήν· τί αὐτῇ κόπους
said: Leave   her;   why ³to her ²troubles

παρέχετε; καλὸν ἔργον ἠργάσατο ἐν ἐμοί.
¹cause ye?   a good work she wrought in me.

7 πάντοτε γὰρ τοὺς πτωχοὺς ἔχετε μεθ'
For always   the   poor ye have with

ἑαυτῶν, καὶ ὅταν θέλητε δύνασθε αὐτοῖς
yourselves, and whenever ye wish ye can to them

εὖ ποιῆσαι, ἐμὲ δὲ οὐ πάντοτε ἔχετε.
well to do,   but me   not always   ye have.

8 ὃ ἔσχεν ἐποίησεν· προέλαβεν μυρίσαι τὸ
What she had she did; she was beforehand to anoint the

σῶμά μου εἰς τὸν ἐνταφιασμόν. 9 ἀμὴν
body of me for the   burial.   truly

δὲ λέγω ὑμῖν, ὅπου ἐὰν κηρυχθῇ τὸ
And I tell you, wherever is proclaimed the

εὐαγγέλιον εἰς ὅλον τὸν κόσμον, καὶ ὃ
gospel   in all the   world,   also what

ἐποίησεν αὕτη λαληθήσεται εἰς μνημόσυνον
did   this woman will be spoken for a memorial

αὐτῆς. 10 Καὶ Ἰούδας Ἰσκαριώθ, ὁ εἷς
of her.   And Judas Iscariot, the one

τῶν δώδεκα, ἀπῆλθεν πρὸς τοὺς ἀρχιερεῖς
of the twelve,   went   to   the chief priests

ἵνα αὐτὸν παραδοῖ αὐτοῖς. 11 οἱ δὲ
that him he might betray to them.   And they

ἀκούσαντες ἐχάρησαν καὶ ἐπηγγείλαντο αὐτῷ
hearing   rejoiced and promised   him

ἀργύριον δοῦναι. καὶ ἐζήτει πῶς αὐτὸν
silver   to give. And he sought how him

εὐκαίρως παραδοῖ.
opportunely he might betray.

12 Καὶ τῇ πρώτῃ ἡμέρᾳ τῶν ἀζύμων,
And on the first   day of unleavened bread,†

ὅτε τὸ πάσχα ἔθυον, λέγουσιν αὐτῷ οἱ
when the passover they sacrificed, say   to him the

"Where will you have us go and prepare for you to eat the passover?" [13]And he sent two of his disciples, and said to them, "Go into the city, and a man carrying a jar of water will meet you; follow him, [14]and wherever he enters, say to the householder, 'The Teacher says, Where is my guest room, where I am to eat the passover with my disciples?' [15]And he will show you a large upper room furnished and ready; there prepare for us." [16]And the disciples set out and went to the city, and found it as he had told them; and they prepared the passover.

17 And when it was evening he came with the twelve. [18]And as they were at table eating, Jesus said, "Truly, I say to you, one of you will betray me, one who is eating with me." [19]They began to be sorrowful, and to say to him one after another, "Is it I?" [20]He said to them, "It is one of the twelve, one who is dipping bread in the same dish with me. [21]For the Son of man goes as it is written of

μαθηταὶ   αὐτοῦ·   ποῦ   θέλεις   ἀπελθόντες
disciples   of him: Where   wishest thou ,   going

ἑτοιμάσωμεν   ἵνα   φάγῃς   τὸ   πάσχα;   13 καὶ
we may prepare   that   thou eatest   the   passover?   And

ἀποστέλλει   δύο   τῶν   μαθητῶν   αὐτοῦ   καὶ
he sends   two   of the   disciples   of him   and

λέγει   αὐτοῖς·   ὑπάγετε   εἰς   τὴν   πόλιν,   καὶ
tells   them: Go ye   into   the   city,   and

ἀπαντήσει   ὑμῖν   ἄνθρωπος   κεράμιον   ὕδατος
will meet   you   a man   a pitcher   of water

βαστάζων·   ἀκολουθήσατε   αὐτῷ,   14 καὶ   ὅπου
carrying;   follow   him,   14 and   wher-

ἐὰν   εἰσέλθῃ   εἴπατε   τῷ   οἰκοδεσπότῃ   ὅτι   ὁ
ever   he enters   tell   the   housemaster[,]   – The

διδάσκαλος   λέγει·   ποῦ   ἐστιν   τὸ   κατάλυμά
teacher   says: Where   is   the   guest room

μου,   ὅπου   τὸ   πάσχα   μετὰ   τῶν   μαθητῶν
of me,   where   the   passover   with   the   disciples

μου   φάγω;   15 καὶ   αὐτὸς   ὑμῖν   δείξει
of me   I may eat ?   And   he   you   will show

ἀνάγαιον   μέγα   ἐστρωμένον   ἕτοιμον·   καὶ
upper room   a large   having been spread   ready;   and

ἐκεῖ   ἑτοιμάσατε   ἡμῖν.   16 καὶ   ἐξῆλθον   οἱ
there   prepare ye   for us.   And   went forth   the

μαθηταὶ   καὶ   ἦλθον   εἰς   τὴν   πόλιν   καὶ
disciples   and   came   into   the   city   and

εὗρον   καθὼς   εἶπεν   αὐτοῖς,   καὶ   ἡτοίμασαν
found   as   he told   them,   and   they prepared

τὸ   πάσχα.   17 Καὶ   ὀψίας   γενομένης   ἔρχεται
the   passover.   And   evening   coming[a]   he comes
                                             = when evening came

μετὰ   τῶν   δώδεκα.   18 καὶ   ἀνακειμένων
with   the   twelve.   And   reclining
                                   = as they reclined and ate

αὐτῶν   καὶ   ἐσθιόντων   ὁ   Ἰησοῦς   εἶπεν·
them   and   eating[a]   the   Jesus   said:

ἀμὴν   λέγω   ὑμῖν   ὅτι   εἷς   ἐξ   ὑμῶν   παραδώσει
Truly   I tell   you   that   one   of   you   will betray

με,   ὁ   ἐσθίων   μετ'   ἐμοῦ.   19 ἤρξαντο
me, the [one]   eating   with   me.   They began

λυπεῖσθαι   καὶ   λέγειν   αὐτῷ   εἷς   κατὰ   εἷς·
to grieve   and   to say   to him   one   by   one:

μήτι   ἐγώ;   20 ὁ   δὲ   εἶπεν   αὐτοῖς·   εἷς   τῶν
Not   I ?   And he   said   to them: One   of the

δώδεκα,   ὁ   ἐμβαπτόμενος   μετ'   ἐμοῦ   εἰς
twelve, the [one]   dipping   with   me   in

τὸ   [ἓν]   τρύβλιον.   21 ὅτι   ὁ   μὲν   υἱὸς   τοῦ
the   one   dish.   Because indeed the   Son   –

ἀνθρώπου   ὑπάγει   καθὼς   γέγραπται   περὶ
of man   is going   as   it has been written concerning

him, but woe to that man by whom the Son of man is betrayed! It would have been better for that man if he had not been born."

22 And as they were eating, he took bread, and blessed, and broke it, and gave it to them, and said, "Take; this is my body." ²³And he took a cup, and when he had given thanks he gave it to them, and they all drank of it. ²⁴And he said to them, "This is my blood of the[l] covenant, which is poured out for many. ²⁵Truly, I say to you, I shall not drink again of the fruit of the vine until that day when I drink it new in the kingdom of God."

26 And when they had sung a hymn, they went out to the Mount of Olives. ²⁷And Jesus said to them, "You will all fall away; for it is written, 'I will strike the shepherd, and the sheep will be scattered.' ²⁸But after I am raised up, I will go before you to Galilee." ²⁹Peter said to him, "Even though they all fall away, I will not." ³⁰And Jesus said to him,

[l] Other ancient authorities insert *new*

αὐτοῦ· οὐαὶ δὲ τῷ ἀνθρώπῳ ἐκείνῳ δι'
him;   but woe   –   man   to that   through

οὗ ὁ υἱὸς τοῦ ἀνθρώπου παραδίδοται·
whom the Son   –   of man   is betrayed;

καλὸν αὐτῷ εἰ οὐκ ἐγεννήθη ὁ ἄνθρωπος
good   for him   if   was not born   –   man

ἐκεῖνος. 22 Καὶ ἐσθιόντων αὐτῶν λαβὼν
that.   And   eating   them[a]   taking
        = as they were eating

ἄρτον εὐλογήσας ἔκλασεν καὶ ἔδωκεν αὐτοῖς
a loaf   blessing   he broke   and   gave   to them

καὶ εἶπεν· λάβετε· τοῦτό ἐστιν τὸ σῶμά
and   said: Take ye;   this   is   the   body

μου. 23 καὶ λαβὼν ποτήριον εὐχαριστήσας
of me.   And   taking   a cup   giving thanks

ἔδωκεν αὐτοῖς, καὶ ἔπιον ἐξ αὐτοῦ πάντες.
he gave   to them,   and   drank   of   it   all.

24 καὶ εἶπεν αὐτοῖς· τοῦτό ἐστιν τὸ αἷμά
   And   he said   to them: This   is   the   blood

μου τῆς διαθήκης τὸ ἐκχυννόμενον ὑπὲρ
of me   of the   covenant   –   being shed   for

πολλῶν. 25 ἀμὴν λέγω ὑμῖν ὅτι οὐκέτι
many.   Truly   I tell   you[,]   –   No more

οὐ μὴ πίω ἐκ τοῦ γενήματος τῆς ἀμπέλου
by no(any) will I drink of the   fruit   of the   vine
means

ἕως τῆς ἡμέρας ἐκείνης ὅταν αὐτὸ πίνω
until   day   that   when   it   I drink

καινὸν ἐν τῇ βασιλείᾳ τοῦ θεοῦ.
new   in   the   kingdom   of God.

26 Καὶ ὑμνήσαντες ἐξῆλθον εἰς τὸ
   And   having sung a hymn   they went forth   to   the

ὄρος τῶν ἐλαιῶν. 27 Καὶ λέγει αὐτοῖς ὁ
mount of the   olives.   And   says   to them

Ἰησοῦς ὅτι πάντες σκανδαλισθήσεσθε, ὅτι
Jesus[,]   –   [2]All   [1]ye [2]will [4]be offended, because

γέγραπται· πατάξω τὸν ποιμένα, καὶ τὰ
it has been written: I will strike   the   shepherd,   and   the

πρόβατα διασκορπισθήσονται. 28 ἀλλὰ μετὰ
sheep   will be scattered.   But   after

τὸ ἐγερθῆναί με προάξω ὑμᾶς εἰς τὴν
the   to be raised   me[b] I will go before   you   to   –
= I am raised

Γαλιλαίαν. 29 ὁ δὲ Πέτρος ἔφη αὐτῷ·
Galilee.   –   And   Peter   said   to him·

εἰ καὶ πάντες σκανδαλισθήσονται, ἀλλ'
If   even   all men   shall be offended,   yet

οὐκ ἐγώ. 30 καὶ λέγει αὐτῷ ὁ Ἰησοῦς·
not   I.   And   says   to him   –   Jesus:

"Truly, I say to you, this very night, before the cock crows twice, you will deny me three times." [31]But he said vehemently, "If I must die with you, I will not deny you." And they all said the same.

32 And they went to a place which was called Gethsem'ane; and he said to his disciples, "Sit here, while I pray." [33]And he took with him Peter and James and John, and began to be greatly distressed and troubled. [34]And he said to them, "My soul is very sorrowful, even to death; remain here, and watch."[m] And going a little farther, he fell on the ground and prayed that, if it were possible, the hour might pass from him. [36]And he said, "Abba, Father, all things are possible to thee; remove this cup from me; yet not what I will, but what thou wilt." [37]And he came and found them sleeping, and he said to Peter, "Simon, are you asleep? Could you not watch[m] one hour? [38]Watch[m] and pray

ἀμὴν λέγω σοι ὅτι σὺ σήμερον ταύτῃ τῇ
Truly I tell thee[,] – Thou to-day in this –
νυκτὶ πρὶν ἢ δὶς ἀλέκτορα φωνῆσαι τρίς
night before twice a cock to sound[b] thrice
με ἀπαρνήσῃ. 31 ὁ δὲ ἐκπερισσῶς ἐλάλει·
me thou wilt deny. But he more exceedingly said:
ἐὰν δέῃ με συναποθανεῖν σοι, οὐ μή
If it should behove me to die with thee, by no means
= I must
σε ἀπαρνήσομαι. ὡσαύτως [δὲ] καὶ πάντες
thee will I deny. And similarly also all
ἔλεγον.
said.

32 Καὶ ἔρχονται εἰς χωρίον οὗ τὸ
And they come to a piece of land of which the
ὄνομα Γεθσημανί, καὶ λέγει τοῖς μαθηταῖς
name [was] Gethsemane, and he says to the disciples
αὐτοῦ· καθίσατε ὧδε ἕως προσεύξωμαι.
of him: Sit ye here while I pray.
33 καὶ παραλαμβάνει τὸν Πέτρον καὶ τὸν
And he takes – Peter and –
Ἰάκωβον καὶ τὸν Ἰωάννην μετ' αὐτοῦ,
James and – John with him,
καὶ ἤρξατο ἐκθαμβεῖσθαι καὶ ἀδημονεῖν,
and began to be greatly astonished and to be distressed,
34 καὶ λέγει αὐτοῖς· περίλυπός ἐστιν ἡ
and says to them: Deeply grieved is the
ψυχή μου ἕως θανάτου· μείνατε ὧδε καὶ
soul of me unto death; remain ye here and
γρηγορεῖτε. 35 καὶ προελθὼν μικρὸν ἔπιπτεν
watch. And going forward a little he fell
ἐπὶ τῆς γῆς, καὶ προσηύχετο ἵνα εἰ
on the ground, and prayed that if
δυνατόν ἐστιν παρέλθῃ ἀπ' αὐτοῦ ἡ ὥρα,
possible it is might pass away from him the hour,
36 καὶ ἔλεγεν· ἀββὰ ὁ πατήρ, πάντα
and said: Abba – Father, all things
δυνατά σοι· παρένεγκε τὸ ποτήριον τοῦτο
[are] possible to thee; remove – cup this
ἀπ' ἐμοῦ· ἀλλ' οὐ τί ἐγὼ θέλω ἀλλὰ
from me; but not what I wish but
τί σύ. 37 καὶ ἔρχεται καὶ εὑρίσκει
what thou. And he comes and finds
αὐτοὺς καθεύδοντας, καὶ λέγει τῷ Πέτρῳ·
them sleeping, and says – to Peter:
Σίμων, καθεύδεις; οὐκ ἴσχυσας μίαν ὥραν
Simon, sleepest thou? couldest thou not one hour
γρηγορῆσαι; 38 γρηγορεῖτε καὶ προσεύχεσθε,
to watch? Watch ye and pray,

[m] Or keep awake

that you may not enter into temptation; the spirit indeed is willing, but the flesh is weak."
³⁹And again he went away and prayed, saying the same words. ⁴⁰And again he came and found them sleeping, for their eyes were very heavy; and they did not know what to answer him. ⁴¹And he came the third time, and said to them, "Are you still sleeping and taking your rest? It is enough; the hour has come; the Son of man is betrayed into the hands of sinners. ⁴²Rise, let us be going; see, my betrayer is at hand."

43 And immediately, while he was still speaking, Judas came, one of the twelve, and with him a crowd with swords and clubs, from the chief priests and the scribes and the elders. ⁴⁴Now the betrayer had given them a sign, saying, "The one I shall kiss is the man; seize him and lead him away safely." ⁴⁵And when he came, he went up to him at once, and said, "Master!" And he kissed him. ⁴⁶And they laid hands on him and seized him. ⁴⁷But one of

ἵνα μὴ ἔλθητε εἰς πειρασμόν· τὸ μὲν
lest ye come into temptation; indeed the

πνεῦμα πρόθυμον, ἡ δὲ σὰρξ ἀσθενής.
spirit [is] eager, but the flesh weak.

39 καὶ πάλιν ἀπελθὼν προσηύξατο τὸν
And again going away he prayed ²the

αὐτὸν λόγον εἰπών. 40 καὶ πάλιν ἐλθὼν
³same ⁴word ¹saying. And again coming

εὗρεν αὐτοὺς καθεύδοντας, ἦσαν γὰρ αὐτῶν
he found them sleeping, for were of them

οἱ ὀφθαλμοὶ καταβαρυνόμενοι, καὶ οὐκ
the eyes becoming heavy, and not

ᾔδεισαν τί ἀποκριθῶσιν αὐτῷ. 41 καὶ
they knew what they might answer him. And

ἔρχεται τὸ τρίτον καὶ λέγει αὐτοῖς·
he comes the third [time] and says to them:

καθεύδετε τὸ λοιπὸν καὶ ἀναπαύεσθε·
Sleep ye now† and rest;

ἀπέχει· ἦλθεν ἡ ὥρα, ἰδοὺ παραδίδοται ὁ
it is enough; came the hour, behold is betrayed the

υἱὸς τοῦ ἀνθρώπου εἰς τὰς χεῖρας τῶν
Son - man into the hands -

ἁμαρτωλῶν. 42 ἐγείρεσθε, ἄγωμεν· ἰδοὺ ὁ
of sinners. Rise ye, let us go; behold the

παραδιδούς με ἤγγικεν. 43 Καὶ εὐθὺς ἔτι
[one] betraying me has drawn near. And immediately yet

αὐτοῦ λαλοῦντος παραγίνεται [ὁ] Ἰούδας
him speaking² arrives - Judas
= while he was still speaking

εἷς τῶν δώδεκα, καὶ μετ' αὐτοῦ ὄχλος
one of the twelve, and with him a crowd

μετὰ μαχαιρῶν καὶ ξύλων παρὰ τῶν
with swords and clubs from the

ἀρχιερέων καὶ τῶν γραμματέων καὶ τῶν
chief priests and the scribes and the

πρεσβυτέρων. 44 δεδώκει δὲ ὁ παραδιδοὺς
elders. ¹Now ⁵had given ²the [one] ³betraying

αὐτὸν σύσσημον αὐτοῖς λέγων· ὃν ἂν
⁴him ⁷a signal ⁶them saying: Whomever

φιλήσω αὐτός ἐστιν· κρατήσατε αὐτὸν καὶ
I may kiss he is; seize ye him and

ἀπάγετε ἀσφαλῶς. 45 καὶ ἐλθὼν εὐθὺς
lead away securely. And coming immediately

προσελθὼν αὐτῷ λέγει· ῥαββί, καὶ
approaching to him he says: Rabbi, and

κατεφίλησεν αὐτόν· 46 οἱ δὲ ἐπέβαλαν τὰς
fervently kissed him; and they ¹laid ⁴on ⁵the(their)

χεῖρας αὐτῷ καὶ ἐκράτησαν αὐτόν. 47 εἷς
²hands him and seized him. ⁶one

those who stood by drew his sword, and struck the slave of the high priest and cut off his ear. ⁴⁸And Jesus said to them, "Have you come out as against a robber, with swords and clubs to capture me? ⁴⁹Day after day I was with you in the temple teaching, and you did not seize me. But let the scriptures be fulfilled." ⁵⁰And they all forsook him, and fled.

51 And a young man followed him, with nothing but a linen cloth about his body; and they seized him, ⁵²but he left the linen cloth and ran away naked.

53 And they led Jesus to the high priest; and all the chief priests and the elders and the scribes were assembled. ⁵⁴And Peter had followed him at a distance, right into the courtyard of the high priest; and he was sitting with the guards, and warming himself at the fire. ⁵⁵Now the chief priests and the whole council sought testimony against Jesus to put him to death; but they found none. ⁵⁶For many bore false witness against him,

δέ τις τῶν παρεστηκότων σπασάμενος
¹But ¹ᵃa certain of the [ones] standing by   drawing

τὴν μάχαιραν ἔπαισεν τὸν δοῦλον τοῦ ἀρχιερέως
the   sword   struck   the slave of the high priest

καὶ ἀφεῖλεν αὐτοῦ τὸ ὠτάριον. 48 καὶ
and cut off of him the   ear.   And

ἀποκριθεὶς ὁ Ἰησοῦς εἶπεν αὐτοῖς· ὡς
answering   -   Jesus   said to them: As

ἐπὶ λῃστὴν ἐξήλθατε μετὰ μαχαιρῶν καὶ
against a robber came ye forth with   swords   and

ξύλων συλλαβεῖν με; 49 καθ' ἡμέραν ἤμην
clubs   to arrest   me ?   Daily   I was

πρὸς ὑμᾶς ἐν τῷ ἱερῷ διδάσκων, καὶ οὐκ
with   you in the temple teaching, and not

ἐκρατήσατέ με· ἀλλ' ἵνα πληρωθῶσιν αἱ
ye did seize me;   but that may be fulfilled the

γραφαί. 50 καὶ ἀφέντες αὐτὸν ἔφυγον
scriptures.   And leaving   him   they fled

πάντες. 51 Καὶ νεανίσκος τις συνηκολούθει
all.   And a certain young man   accompanied

αὐτῷ περιβεβλημένος σινδόνα ἐπὶ γυμνοῦ,
him   *having been* clothed [in] a nightgown over [his] naked
                                                        [body],

καὶ κρατοῦσιν αὐτόν· 52 ὁ δὲ καταλιπὼν
and they seize   him;   and he   leaving

τὴν σινδόνα γυμνὸς ἔφυγεν.
the nightgown naked   fled.

53 Καὶ ἀπήγαγον τὸν Ἰησοῦν πρὸς τὸν
    And they led away - Jesus   to   the

ἀρχιερέα, καὶ συνέρχονται πάντες οἱ
high priest, and come together   all   the

ἀρχιερεῖς καὶ οἱ πρεσβύτεροι καὶ οἱ
chief priests and the   elders   and the

γραμματεῖς. 54 καὶ ὁ Πέτρος ἀπὸ μακρόθεν
scribes.   And - Peter   from   afar

ἠκολούθησεν αὐτῷ ἕως ἔσω εἰς τὴν αὐλὴν
followed   him until within *in* the   court

τοῦ ἀρχιερέως, καὶ ἦν συγκαθήμενος μετὰ
of the high priest, and was   sitting *with*   with

τῶν ὑπηρετῶν καὶ θερμαινόμενος πρὸς τὸ
the   attendants and   warming himself   by   the

φῶς. 55 Οἱ δὲ ἀρχιερεῖς καὶ ὅλον τὸ
bright fire. Now the chief priests and   all   the

συνέδριον ἐζήτουν κατὰ τοῦ Ἰησοῦ
council   sought against   -   Jesus

μαρτυρίαν εἰς τὸ θανατῶσαι αὐτόν, καὶ
witness   for the to put to death him,   and
                      = so as

οὐχ ηὕρισκον· 56 πολλοὶ γὰρ ἐψευδομαρτύρουν
found not;   for many   falsely witnessed

and their witness did not agree. ⁵⁷And some stood up and bore false witness against him, saying, ⁵⁸"We heard him say, 'I will destroy this temple that is made with hands, and in three days I will build another, not made with hands.' " ⁵⁹Yet not even so did their testimony agree. ⁶⁰And the high priest stood up in the midst, and asked Jesus, "Have you no answer to make? What is it that these men testify against you?" ⁶¹But he was silent and made no answer. Again the high priest asked him, "Are you the Christ, the Son of the Blessed?" ⁶²And Jesus said, "I am; and you will see the Son of man sitting at the right hand of Power, and coming with the clouds of heaven." ⁶³And the high priest tore his mantle, and said, "Why do we still need witnesses? ⁶⁴You have heard his blasphemy. What is your decision?" And they all condemned him as deserving death. ⁶⁵And some began to spit on him, and to cover his face, and to strike

κατ’ αὐτοῦ, καὶ ἴσαι αἱ μαρτυρίαι οὐκ
against him, and ²identical ¹the ³testimonies ⁴not

ἦσαν. 57 καί τινες ἀναστάντες ἐψευδομαρτύρουν
³were. And some standing up falsely witnessed

κατ’ αὐτοῦ λέγοντες 58 ὅτι ἡμεῖς ἠκούσαμεν
against him saying[,] – We heard

αὐτοῦ λέγοντος ὅτι ἐγὼ καταλύσω τὸν
him saying[,] – I will overthrow –

ναὸν τοῦτον τὸν χειροποίητον καὶ διὰ
²shrine ¹this – ²handmade and through(after)

τριῶν ἡμερῶν ἄλλον ἀχειροποίητον οἰκο-
three days another not handmade I will

δομήσω. 59 καὶ οὐδὲ οὕτως ἴση ἦν ἡ
build. And not so identical was the

μαρτυρία αὐτῶν. 60 καὶ ἀναστὰς ὁ
witness of them. And standing up the

ἀρχιερεὺς εἰς μέσον ἐπηρώτησεν τὸν Ἰησοῦν
high priest in [the] midst questioned – Jesus

λέγων· οὐκ ἀποκρίνῃ οὐδὲν τί οὗτοί σου
saying: Answerest thou not no(any)thing what these men ²thee

καταμαρτυροῦσιν; 61 ὁ δὲ ἐσιώπα καὶ
¹testify against? But he was silent and

οὐκ ἀπεκρίνατο οὐδέν. πάλιν ὁ ἀρχιερεὺς
answered not no(any)thing. Again the high priest

ἐπηρώτα αὐτὸν καὶ λέγει αὐτῷ· σὺ εἶ ὁ
questioned him and says to him: Thou art the

χριστὸς ὁ υἱὸς τοῦ εὐλογητοῦ; 62 ὁ δὲ
Christ the Son of the Blessed [one]? – And

Ἰησοῦς εἶπεν· ἐγώ εἰμι, καὶ ὄψεσθε
Jesus said: I am, and ye will see

τὸν υἱὸν τοῦ ἀνθρώπου ἐκ δεξιῶν καθήμενον
the Son – of man ²at [the] right [hand] ¹sitting

τῆς δυνάμεως καὶ ἐρχόμενον μετὰ τῶν
of the Power and coming with the

νεφελῶν τοῦ οὐρανοῦ. 63 ὁ δὲ ἀρχιερεὺς
clouds – of heaven. And the high priest

διαρήξας τοὺς χιτῶνας αὐτοῦ λέγει· τί
rending the tunics of him says: What

ἔτι χρείαν ἔχομεν μαρτύρων; 64 ἠκούσατε
more need have we of witnesses? ye heard

τῆς βλασφημίας· τί ὑμῖν φαίνεται; οἱ δὲ
the blasphemy; what to you appears it? And they

πάντες κατέκριναν αὐτὸν ἔνοχον εἶναι
all condemned him liable to be

θανάτου. 65 Καὶ ἤρξαντό τινες ἐμπτύειν
of(to) death. And began some to spit at

αὐτῷ καὶ περικαλύπτειν αὐτοῦ τὸ πρόσωπον
him and to cover of him the face

him, saying to him, "Prophesy!" And the guards received him with blows.

66 And as Peter was below in the courtyard, one of the maids of the high priest came; [67] and seeing Peter warming himself, she looked at him, and said, "You also were with the Nazarene, Jesus." [68] But he denied it, saying, "I neither know nor understand what you mean." And he went out into the gateway.[n] [69] And the maid saw him, and began again to say to the bystanders, "This man is one of them." [70] But again he denied it. And after a little while again the bystanders said to Peter, "Certainly you are one of them; for you are a Galilean." [71] But he began to invoke a curse on himself and to swear, "I do not know this man of whom you speak." [72] And immediately the cock crowed a second time. And Peter remembered how Jesus had said to him, "Before the cock crows twice, you will deny me three times." And he broke down and wept.

καὶ κολαφίζειν αὐτὸν καὶ λέγειν αὐτῷ·
and to maltreat him and to say to him:

προφήτευσον, καὶ οἱ ὑπηρέται ῥαπίσμασιν
Prophesy, and the attendants with slaps

αὐτὸν ἔλαβον. 66 Καὶ ὄντος τοῦ Πέτρου
⁵him ¹took. And being – Peter[a]
= as Peter was

κάτω ἐν τῇ αὐλῇ ἔρχεται μία τῶν
below in the court comes one of the

παιδισκῶν τοῦ ἀρχιερέως, 67 καὶ ἰδοῦσα
maidservants of the high priest, and seeing

τὸν Πέτρον θερμαινόμενον ἐμβλέψασα αὐτῷ
– Peter warming himself looking at him

λέγει· καὶ σὺ μετὰ τοῦ Ναζαρηνοῦ ἦσθα
says: And ¹thou ³with ⁴the ⁵Nazarene ²wast

τοῦ Ἰησοῦ. 68 ὁ δὲ ἠρνήσατο λέγων· οὔτε
– ⁶Jesus. But he denied saying: ¹neither

οἶδα οὔτε ἐπίσταμαι σὺ τί λέγεις. καὶ
¹I ³know ²nor ⁵understand ⁷thou ⁶what ⁸sayest. And

ἐξῆλθεν ἔξω εἰς τὸ προαύλιον· 69 καὶ ἡ
he went forth outside into the forecourt; and the

παιδίσκη ἰδοῦσα αὐτὸν ἤρξατο πάλιν λέγειν
maidservant seeing him began again to say

τοῖς παρεστῶσιν ὅτι οὗτος ἐξ αὐτῶν ἐστιν.
to the [ones] standing by[,] – This man of them is.

70 ὁ δὲ πάλιν ἠρνεῖτο. καὶ μετὰ μικρὸν
But he again denied. And after a little

πάλιν οἱ παρεστῶτες ἔλεγον τῷ Πέτρῳ·
again the [ones] standing by said – to Peter:

ἀληθῶς ἐξ αὐτῶν εἶ· καὶ γὰρ Γαλιλαῖος
Truly of them thou art; ²indeed ¹for ⁴a Galilæan

εἶ. 71 ὁ δὲ ἤρξατο ἀναθεματίζειν καὶ
³thou art. And he began to curse and

ὀμνύναι ὅτι οὐκ οἶδα τὸν ἄνθρωπον
to swear[,] – I know not – man

τοῦτον ὃν λέγετε. 72 καὶ εὐθὺς ἐκ
this whom ye say. And immediately a

δευτέρου ἀλέκτωρ ἐφώνησεν. καὶ ἀνεμνήσθη
second time a cock crew. And remembered

ὁ Πέτρος τὸ ῥῆμα ὡς εἶπεν αὐτῷ ὁ
– Peter the word as said to him –

Ἰησοῦς ὅτι πρὶν ἀλέκτορα δὶς φωνῆσαι
Jesus[,] – Before a cock twice to crow[b]

τρίς με ἀπαρνήσῃ· καὶ ἐπιβαλὼν ἔκλαιεν.
thrice me thou wilt deny; and thinking thereon he wept.

---

[n] Or *fore-court*. Other ancient authorities add *and the cock crowed*

CHAPTER 15

AND as soon as it was morning the chief priests, with the elders and scribes, and the whole council held a consultation; and they bound Jesus and led him away and delivered him to Pilate. [2]And Pilate asked him, "Are you the King of the Jews?" And he answered him, "You have said so." [3]And the chief priests accused him of many things. [4]And Pilate again asked him, "Have you no answer to make? See how many charges they bring against you." [5]But Jesus made no further answer, so that Pilate wondered.

6 Now at the feast he used to release for them any one prisoner whom they asked. [7]And among the rebels in prison, who had committed murder in the insurrection, there was a man called Barab'bas. [8]And the crowd came up and began to ask Pilate to do as he was wont to do for them. [9]And he answered them, "Do you want me to release for you the King of the Jews?" [10]For he perceived that it was out of envy that the chief priests had delivered him up. [11]But the chief priests stirred up the crowd to have him release for them Barab'bas instead.

15 Καὶ εὐθὺς πρωῒ συμβούλιον ἑτοιμάσαντες
And immediately early   [a]a council   [1]preparing
οἱ ἀρχιερεῖς μετὰ τῶν πρεσβυτέρων καὶ
the chief priests   with   the   elders   and
γραμματέων καὶ ὅλον τὸ συνέδριον, δήσαντες
scribes   and   all   the   council,   having bound
τὸν Ἰησοῦν ἀπήνεγκαν καὶ παρέδωκαν
–   Jesus   led [him] away   and   delivered [him]
Πιλάτῳ. 2 καὶ ἐπηρώτησεν αὐτὸν ὁ
to Pilate.   And   questioned   him   –
Πιλᾶτος· σὺ εἶ ὁ βασιλεὺς τῶν Ἰουδαίων;
Pilate: Thou art   the   king   of the   Jews ?
ὁ δὲ ἀποκριθεὶς αὐτῷ λέγει· σὺ λέγεις.
And he   answering   him   says: Thou sayest.
3 καὶ κατηγόρουν αὐτοῦ οἱ ἀρχιερεῖς πολλά.
And   accused   him   the chief priests many things.
4 ὁ δὲ Πιλᾶτος πάλιν ἐπηρώτα αὐτόν [λέγων]·
– But   Pilate   again   questioned   him   saying:
οὐκ ἀποκρίνῃ οὐδέν; ἴδε πόσα
Answerest thou not   no(any)thing ?   Behold how many things
σου κατηγοροῦσιν. 5 ὁ δὲ Ἰησοῦς οὐκ-
thee   they accuse.   – But   Jesus   no(any)
ἔτι οὐδὲν ἀπεκρίθη, ὥστε θαυμάζειν
more   nothing   answered,   so as   to marvel
                  = so that Pilate marvelled.
τὸν Πιλᾶτον. 6 Κατὰ δὲ ἑορτὴν ἀπέλυεν
–   Pilate[b].   Now at   a feast   he released
αὐτοῖς ἕνα δέσμιον ὃν παρῃτοῦντο. 7 ἦν δὲ
to them one   prisoner whom they begged.   Now there was
ὁ λεγόμενος Βαραββᾶς μετὰ τῶν
the [one]   named   Barabbas   with   the
στασιαστῶν δεδεμένος, οἵτινες ἐν τῇ στάσει
rebels   having been bound, who[*]   in   the rebellion
φόνον πεποιήκεισαν. 8 καὶ ἀναβὰς ὁ ὄχλος
murder   had done.   And going up the crowd
ἤρξατο αἰτεῖσθαι καθὼς ἐποίει αὐτοῖς.
began   to ask   as   he used to do for them.
9 ὁ δὲ Πιλᾶτος ἀπεκρίθη αὐτοῖς λέγων·
– But   Pilate   answered   them   saying:
θέλετε ἀπολύσω ὑμῖν τὸν βασιλέα τῶν
Do ye wish I may release   to you   the   king   of the
Ἰουδαίων; 10 ἐγίνωσκεν γὰρ ὅτι διὰ φθόνον
Jews ?   For he knew   that on account of envy
παραδεδώκεισαν αὐτὸν οἱ ἀρχιερεῖς. 11 οἱ
had delivered   him   the   chief priests.   the
δὲ ἀρχιερεῖς ἀνέσεισαν τὸν ὄχλον ἵνα
But   chief priests   stirred up   the   crowd   that
μᾶλλον τὸν Βαραββᾶν ἀπολύσῃ αὐτοῖς.
rather   –   Barabbas   he should release   to them.

                * Note the plural.

¹²And Pilate again said to them, "Then what shall I do with the man whom you call the King of the Jews?" ¹³And they cried out again, "Crucify him." ¹⁴And Pilate said to them, "Why, what evil has he done?" But they shouted all the more, "Crucify him." ¹⁵So Pilate, wishing to satisfy the crowd, released for them Barab′bas; and having scourged Jesus, he delivered him to be crucified.

16 And the soldiers led him away inside the palace (that is, the praetorium); and they called together the whole battalion. ¹⁷And they clothed him in a purple cloak, and plaiting a crown of thorns they put it on him. ¹⁸And they began to salute him, "Hail, King of the Jews!" ¹⁹And they struck his head with a reed, and spat upon him, and they knelt down in homage to him. ²⁰And when they had mocked him, they stripped him of the purple cloak, and put his own clothes on him. And they led him out to crucify him.

21 And they compelled a passer-by, Simon of Cyre′ne, who was

12 ὁ δὲ Πιλᾶτος πάλιν ἀποκριθεὶς ἔλεγεν
   - So   Pilate   again   answering   said
αὐτοῖς· τί οὖν ποιήσω [ὃν] λέγετε τὸν
to them: What then may I do [to him] whom ye call the
βασιλέα τῶν Ἰουδαίων; 13 οἱ δὲ πάλιν
  king   of the   Jews?   And they   again
ἔκραξαν· σταύρωσον αὐτόν. 14 ὁ δὲ
cried out: Crucify   him.   - But
Πιλᾶτος ἔλεγεν αὐτοῖς· τί γὰρ ἐποίησεν
  Pilate   said   to them: Indeed what ²did he
κακόν; οἱ δὲ περισσῶς ἔκραξαν· σταύρωσον
¹evil?   and they   more   cried out: Crucify
αὐτόν. 15 ὁ δὲ Πιλᾶτος βουλόμενος τῷ
him.   - And   Pilate   resolving   the
ὄχλῳ τὸ ἱκανὸν ποιῆσαι ἀπέλυσεν αὐτοῖς
crowd   to satisfy†   released   to them
τὸν Βαραββᾶν, καὶ παρέδωκεν τὸν Ἰησοῦν
  - Barabbas,   and   delivered   - Jesus
φραγελλώσας ἵνα σταυρωθῇ.
having scourged [him] that he might be crucified.

16 Οἱ δὲ στρατιῶται ἀπήγαγον αὐτὸν
   Then the   soldiers   led away   him
ἔσω τῆς αὐλῆς, ὅ ἐστιν πραιτώριον, καὶ
inside the   court, which is   prætorium,   and
συγκαλοῦσιν ὅλην τὴν σπεῖραν. 17 καὶ
they call together   all   the   cohort.   And
ἐνδιδύσκουσιν αὐτὸν πορφύραν καὶ περιτιθέασιν
they put on   him a purple [robe] and   place round
αὐτῷ πλέξαντες ἀκάνθινον στέφανον· 18 καὶ
  him   plaiting   a thorny   crown;   and
ἤρξαντο ἀσπάζεσθαι αὐτόν· χαῖρε, βασιλεῦ
they began   to salute   him: Hail,   king
τῶν Ἰουδαίων· 19 καὶ ἔτυπτον αὐτοῦ τὴν
of the   Jews;   and   they struck of him the
κεφαλὴν καλάμῳ καὶ ἐνέπτυον αὐτῷ, καὶ
  head   with a reed   and   spat   at him,   and
τιθέντες τὰ γόνατα προσεκύνουν αὐτῷ.
placing(bending) the(their) knees   worshipped   him.

20 καὶ ὅτε ἐνέπαιξαν αὐτῷ, ἐξέδυσαν
    And   when   they mocked   him,   they took off
αὐτὸν τὴν πορφύραν καὶ ἐνέδυσαν αὐτὸν
  him   the   purple [robe]   and   put on   him
τὰ ἱμάτια αὐτοῦ. Καὶ ἐξάγουσιν αὐτὸν
the   garments   of him.   And   they lead forth   him
ἵνα σταυρώσωσιν αὐτόν. 21 καὶ ἀγγαρεύουσιν
that   they might crucify   him.   And   they impress
παράγοντά τινα Σίμωνα Κυρηναῖον ἐρχόμενον
passing by a certain Simon   a Cyrenian   coming

coming in from the
country, the father of
Alexander and Rufus, to
carry his cross. ²²And
they brought him to the
place called Gol'gotha
(which means the place
of a skull). ²³And they
offered him wine mingled
with myrrh; but he did
not take it. ²⁴And they
crucified him, and divided
his garments among
them, casting lots for
them, to decide what each
should take. ²⁵And it was
the third hour, when
they crucified him. ²⁶And
the inscription of the
charge against him read,
"The King of the Jews."
²⁷And with him they
crucified two robbers,
one on his right and one
on his left.º ²⁹And those
who passed by derided
him, wagging their heads,
and saying, "Aha! You
who would destroy the
temple and build it in
three days, ³⁰save your-
self, and come down
from the cross!" ³¹So
also the chief priests
mocked him to one
another with the scribes,
saying, "He saved others;
he cannot save himself.
³²Let the Christ, the
King of Israel, come
down now from the
cross, that we may see
and believe." Those who

ἀπ' ἀγροῦ, τὸν πατέρα Ἀλεξάνδρου καὶ
from [the] country, the   father   of Alexander and
Ῥούφου, ἵνα ἄρῃ τὸν σταυρὸν αὐτοῦ.
of Rufus,   that he might bear the   cross   of him.
22 καὶ φέρουσιν αὐτὸν ἐπὶ τὸν Γολγοθὰν
And   they bring   him   to the   Golgotha
τόπον, ὅ ἐστιν μεθερμηνευόμενος κρανίου
place, which is   being interpreted   of a skull
τόπος.   23 καὶ ἐδίδουν αὐτῷ ἐσμυρνισμένον
place.   And they gave   him   ¹having been spiced
                                          with myrrh
οἶνον· ὃς δὲ οὐκ ἔλαβεν.   24 καὶ σταυροῦσιν
¹wine; but who(he) received not.   And   they crucify
αὐτόν, καὶ διαμερίζονται τὰ ἱμάτια αὐτοῦ,
him, and   divide   the   garments of him,
βάλλοντες κλῆρον ἐπ' αὐτὰ τίς τί   ἄρῃ.
casting   a lot   on them ²one ¹what might take.
25 ἦν δὲ ὥρα τρίτη καὶ ἐσταύρωσαν
Now it was hour   third   and   they crucified
αὐτόν. 26 καὶ ἦν ἡ ἐπιγραφὴ τῆς αἰτίας
him.   And was the superscription of the accusation
αὐτοῦ ἐπιγεγραμμένη· Ο ΒΑΣΙΛΕΥΣ ΤΩΝ
of him having been written over: THE   KING   OF THE
ΙΟΥΔΑΙΩΝ. 27 Καὶ σὺν αὐτῷ σταυροῦσιν
JEWS.   And   with   him   they crucify
δύο ληστάς, ἕνα ἐκ δεξιῶν καὶ ἕνα ἐξ
two robbers, one on [the] right and   one   on
εὐωνύμων αὐτοῦ.‡ 29 Καὶ οἱ παραπορευόμενοι
[the] left of him.   And the [ones] passing by
ἐβλασφήμουν αὐτὸν κινοῦντες τὰς κεφαλὰς
blasphemed   him   wagging   the   heads
αὐτῶν καὶ λέγοντες· οὐὰ ὁ καταλύων
of them and   saying: Ah the [one] overthrowing
τὸν ναὸν καὶ οἰκοδομῶν [ἐν] τρισὶν
the shrine and building   in   three
ἡμέραις, 30 σῶσον σεαυτὸν καταβὰς ἀπὸ
days,   save   thyself coming down from
τοῦ σταυροῦ. 31 ὁμοίως καὶ οἱ ἀρχιερεῖς
the   cross.   Likewise also the   chief priests
ἐμπαίζοντες πρὸς ἀλλήλους μετὰ τῶν
mocking   to   one another with   the
γραμματέων ἔλεγον· ἄλλους ἔσωσεν, ἑαυτὸν
scribes   said: Others   he saved, himself
οὐ δύναται σῶσαι· 32 ὁ χριστὸς ὁ βασιλεὺς
he cannot to save: the Christ the king
Ἰσραὴλ καταβάτω νῦν ἀπὸ τοῦ σταυροῦ,
of Israel let come down now from   the   cross,
ἵνα ἴδωμεν καὶ πιστεύσωμεν. καὶ οἱ
that we may see and   believe.   And the

º Other ancient authorities
insert verse 28, And the
scripture was fulfilled which
says, "He was reckoned with
the transgressors."

‡ Verse 28 omitted by Nestle; cf. RSV footnote.

were crucified with him also reviled him.

33 And when the sixth hour had come, there was darkness over the whole land[p] until the ninth hour. [34] And at the ninth hour Jesus cried with a loud voice, "E'lo-i, E'lo-i, la'ma sabach-tha'ni?" which means, "My God, my God, why hast thou forsaken me?" [35] And some of the bystanders hearing it said, "Behold, he is calling Eli'jah." [36] And one ran and, filling a sponge full of vinegar, put it on a reed and gave it to him to drink, saying, "Wait, let us see whether Eli'jah will come to take him down." [37] And Jesus uttered a loud cry, and breathed his last. [38] And the curtain of the temple was torn in two, from top to bottom. [39] And when the centurion, who stood facing him, saw that he thus[q] breathed his last, he said, "Truly this man was the son[qq] of God!"

40 There were also women looking on from afar, among whom were Mary Mag'dalene, and Mary the mother of James the younger and of Joses, and Salo'me, [41] who, when he was in Galilee, followed him, and ministered to him;

συνεσταυρωμένοι σὺν αὐτῷ ὠνείδιζον αὐτόν.
[ones] crucified *with* with him reproached him.

33 Καὶ γενομένης ὥρας ἕκτης σκότος
And becoming hour sixth[a] darkness
= when it was the sixth hour

ἐγένετο ἐφ' ὅλην τὴν γῆν ἕως ὥρας
came over all the land until [the] hour

ἐνάτης. 34 καὶ τῇ ἐνάτῃ ὥρᾳ ἐβόησεν ὁ
ninth. And at the ninth hour cried –

Ἰησοῦς φωνῇ μεγάλῃ· ἐλωΐ ἐλωΐ λαμὰ
Jesus with a voice great(loud): Eloi[,] Eloi[,] lama

σαβαχθάνι; ὅ ἐστιν μεθερμηνευόμενον· ὁ
sabachthani? which is being interpreted: The

θεός μου ὁ θεός μου, εἰς τί ἐγκατέλιπές
God of me[,] the God of me, why didst thou forsake

με; 35 καί τινες τῶν παρεστηκότων
me? And some of the [ones] standing by

ἀκούσαντες ἔλεγον· ἴδε Ἠλίαν φωνεῖ.
hearing said: Behold Elias he calls.

36 δραμὼν δέ τις γεμίσας σπόγγον ὄξους
And running one having filled a sponge of(with) vinegar

περιθεὶς καλάμῳ ἐπότιζεν αὐτόν, λέγων·
placing it round a reed [1]gave [2]to drink [1]him, saying:

ἄφετε ἴδωμεν εἰ ἔρχεται Ἠλίας καθελεῖν
Leave[,] let us see if comes Elias [1]to take [3]down

αὐτόν. 37 ὁ δὲ Ἰησοῦς ἀφεὶς φωνὴν
[1]him. – But Jesus letting go voice

μεγάλην ἐξέπνευσεν. 38 Καὶ τὸ καταπέτασμα
a great(loud) expired. And the veil

τοῦ ναοῦ ἐσχίσθη εἰς δύο ἀπ' ἄνωθεν
of the shrine was rent in two from top

ἕως κάτω. 39 Ἰδὼν δὲ ὁ κεντυρίων ὁ
to bottom. And [6]seeing [1]the [2]centurion –

παρεστηκὼς ἐξ ἐναντίας αὐτοῦ ὅτι οὕτως
[3]standing by [4]opposite [5]him that thus

ἐξέπνευσεν, εἶπεν· ἀληθῶς οὗτος ὁ ἄνθρωπος
he expired, said: Truly this man

υἱὸς θεοῦ ἦν. 40 Ἦσαν δὲ καὶ γυναῖκες
son of God was. Now there were also women

ἀπὸ μακρόθεν θεωροῦσαι, ἐν αἷς καὶ
from afar beholding, among whom both

Μαρία ἡ Μαγδαληνὴ καὶ Μαρία ἡ
Mary the Magdalene and Mary [1]the

Ἰακώβου τοῦ μικροῦ καὶ Ἰωσῆτος μήτηρ
[2]of James [4]the [5]little [6]and [7]of Joses [3]mother

καὶ Σαλώμη, 41 αἳ ὅτε ἦν ἐν τῇ Γαλιλαίᾳ
and Salome, who when he was in – Galilee

ἠκολούθουν αὐτῷ καὶ διηκόνουν αὐτῷ, καὶ
followed him and served him, and

---

[p] Or earth
[q] Other ancient authorities insert cried out and
[qq] Or a son

and also many other women who came up with him to Jerusalem.

42 And when evening had come, since it was the day of Preparation, that is, the day before the sabbath, [43]Joseph of Arimathe'a, a respected member of the council, who was also himself looking for the kingdom of God, took courage and went to Pilate, and asked for the body of Jesus. [44]And Pilate wondered if it he were already dead; and summoning the centurion, he asked him whether he was already dead.[r] [45]And when he learned from the centurion that he was dead, he granted the body to Joseph. [46]And he bought a linen shroud, and taking him down, wrapped him in the linen shroud, and laid him in a tomb which had been hewn out of the rock; and he rolled a stone against the door of the tomb. [47]Mary Mag'-dalene and Mary the mother of Joses saw where he was laid.

CHAPTER 16

AND when the sabbath was past, Mary Mag'dalene, Mary the

[r] Other ancient authorities read whether he had been some time dead

---

ἄλλαι πολλαὶ αἱ συναναβᾶσαι αὐτῷ εἰς
others many – having come up with him to
Ἱεροσόλυμα.
Jerusalem.

42 Καὶ ἤδη ὀψίας γενομένης, ἐπεὶ ἦν
And now evening coming,[a] since it was
= when it was evening,
παρασκευή, ὅ ἐστιν προσάββατον, 43 ἐλθὼν
[the] preparation, which is the day before the sabbath, coming
Ἰωσὴφ ὁ ἀπὸ Ἀριμαθαίας, εὐσχήμων
Joseph the [one] from Arimathæa, an honourable
βουλευτής, ὃς καὶ αὐτὸς ἦν προσδεχόμενος
councillor, who also [him]self was expecting
τὴν βασιλείαν τοῦ θεοῦ, τολμήσας εἰσῆλθεν
the kingdom – of God, taking courage went in
πρὸς τὸν Πιλᾶτον καὶ ᾐτήσατο τὸ σῶμα
to – Pilate and asked the body
τοῦ Ἰησοῦ. 44 ὁ δὲ Πιλᾶτος ἐθαύμασεν
– of Jesus. – And Pilate marvelled
εἰ ἤδη τέθνηκεν, καὶ προσκαλεσάμενος τὸν
if already he has died, and calling to [him] the
κεντυρίωνα ἐπηρώτησεν αὐτὸν εἰ πάλαι
centurion questioned him if long ago
ἀπέθανεν· 45 καὶ γνοὺς ἀπὸ τοῦ κεντυρίωνος
he died; and knowing from the centurion
ἐδωρήσατο τὸ πτῶμα τῷ Ἰωσήφ. 46 καὶ
he granted the corpse – to Joseph. And
ἀγοράσας σινδόνα καθελὼν αὐτὸν ἐνείλησεν
having bought a piece of taking down him he wrapped
unused linen
τῇ σινδόνι καὶ κατέθηκεν αὐτὸν ἐν μνήματι
with the linen and deposited him in a tomb
ὃ ἦν λελατομημένον ἐκ πέτρας, καὶ
which was having been hewn out of rock, and
προσεκύλισεν λίθον ἐπὶ τὴν θύραν τοῦ
rolled a stone against the door of the
μνημείου. 47 ἡ δὲ Μαρία ἡ Μαγδαληνὴ
tomb. – And Mary the Magdalene
καὶ Μαρία ἡ Ἰωσῆτος ἐθεώρουν ποῦ
and Mary the [mother] of Joses beheld where
τέθειται.
he has been laid.

16 Καὶ διαγενομένου τοῦ σαββάτου [ἡ]
And passing the sabbath[a] –
= when the sabbath was past
Μαρία ἡ Μαγδαληνὴ καὶ Μαρία ἡ [τοῦ]
Mary the Magdalene and Mary the [mother] –

mother of James, and Salo'me bought spices, so that they might go and anoint him. ²And very early on the first day of the week they went to the tomb when the sun had risen. ³And they were saying to one another, "Who will roll away the stone for us from the door of the tomb?" ⁴And looking up, they saw that the stone was rolled back; for it was very large. ⁵And entering the tomb, they saw a young man sitting on the right side, dressed in a white robe; and they were amazed. ⁶And he said to them, "Do not be amazed; you seek Jesus of Nazareth, who was crucified. He has risen, he is not here; see the place where they laid him. ⁷But go, tell his disciples and Peter that he is going before you to Galilee; there you will see him, as he told you." ⁸And they went out and fled from the tomb; for trembling and astonishment had come upon them; and they said nothing to any one, for they were afraid.⁸

'Ιακώβου καὶ Σαλώμη ἠγόρασαν ἀρώματα
of James and Salome bought spices

ἵνα ἐλθοῦσαι ἀλείψωσιν αὐτόν. 2 καὶ λίαν
that coming they might anoint him. And very

πρωὶ [τῇ] μιᾷ τῶν σαββάτων ἔρχονται
early on the first day of the week† they come

ἐπὶ τὸ μνῆμα, ἀνατείλαντος τοῦ ἡλίου.
upon the tomb, rising the sun.ᵃ
                                        = as the sun rose.

3 καὶ ἔλεγον πρὸς ἑαυτάς· τίς ἀποκυλίσει
And they said to themselves: Who will roll away

ἡμῖν τὸν λίθον ἐκ τῆς θύρας τοῦ μνημείου;
for us the stone out of the door of the tomb?

4 καὶ ἀναβλέψασαι θεωροῦσιν ὅτι ἀνακεκύλισται
And looking up they behold that has been rolled back

ὁ λίθος· ἦν γὰρ μέγας σφόδρα. 5 καὶ
the stone; for it was great exceedingly. And

εἰσελθοῦσαι εἰς τὸ μνημεῖον εἶδον νεανίσκον
entering into the tomb they saw a young man

καθήμενον ἐν τοῖς δεξιοῖς περιβεβλημένον
sitting on the right having been clothed

στολὴν λευκήν, καὶ ἐξεθαμβήθησαν. 6 ὁ δὲ
robe [in] a white, and they were greatly astonished. But he

λέγει αὐταῖς· μὴ ἐκθαμβεῖσθε· Ἰησοῦν
says to them: Be not greatly astonished; Jesus

ζητεῖτε τὸν Ναζαρηνὸν τὸν ἐσταυρωμένον·
ye seek the Nazarene – having been crucified;

ἠγέρθη, οὐκ ἔστιν ὧδε· ἴδε ὁ τόπος
he was raised, he is not here; behold[.] the place

ὅπου ἔθηκαν αὐτόν. 7 ἀλλὰ ὑπάγετε εἴπατε
where they put him. But go ye tell

τοῖς μαθηταῖς αὐτοῦ καὶ τῷ Πέτρῳ ὅτι
the disciples of him and – Peter that

προάγει ὑμᾶς εἰς τὴν Γαλιλαίαν· ἐκεῖ
he goes before you to – Galilee; there

αὐτὸν ὄψεσθε, καθὼς εἶπεν ὑμῖν. 8 καὶ
him ye will see, as he told you. And

ἐξελθοῦσαι ἔφυγον ἀπὸ τοῦ μνημείου, εἶχεν
going forth they fled from the tomb, ᵇhad

γὰρ αὐτὰς τρόμος καὶ ἔκστασις· καὶ
¹for ⁵them ²trembling ³and ⁴bewilderment; and

οὐδενὶ οὐδὲν εἶπαν· ἐφοβοῦντο γάρ.
no one no(any)thing they told; for they were afraid.

⁸ Other texts and versions add as 16. 9–20 the following passage:

9 *Now when he rose early on the first day of the week, he appeared first to Mary Magdalene, from whom he had cast out seven demons.* ¹⁰ *She went*

9 Ἀναστὰς δὲ πρωὶ πρώτῃ σαββάτου
And rising early on the first day of the week†

ἐφάνη πρῶτον Μαρίᾳ τῇ Μαγδαληνῇ, παρ'
he appeared first to Mary the Magdalene, from

ἧς ἐκβεβλήκει ἑπτὰ δαιμόνια. 10 ἐκείνη
whom he had expelled seven demons. That [one]
                                           = She

πορευθεῖσα　ἀπήγγειλεν　τοῖς　μετ᾽　αὐτοῦ
going　　　　　reported　　to the [ones]　with　　him
　　　　　　　　　　　　　　　= those who had been with him

γενομένοις　πενθοῦσι καὶ κλαίουσιν　11 κἀκεῖνοι
having been　mourning　and　weeping;　　　and those

ἀκούσαντες　ὅτι　ζῇ　καὶ　ἐθεάθη　ὑπ᾽　αὐτῆς
hearing　　　that he lives　and　was seen　by　her

ἠπίστησαν.　12 Μετὰ　δὲ　ταῦτα　δυσὶν　ἐξ
disbelieved.　　And after　these things to two　of

αὐτῶν　περιπατοῦσιν　ἐφανερώθη　ἐν　ἑτέρᾳ
them　　　walking　　　he was manifested　in a different

μορφῇ　πορευομένοις　εἰς　ἀγρόν·　13 κἀκεῖνοι
form　　going　　　into [the] country;　　and those

ἀπελθόντες　ἀπήγγειλαν　τοῖς　λοιποῖς·　οὐδὲ
going　　　　reported　　　to the　　rest;　　neither

ἐκείνοις　ἐπίστευσαν.　14 Ὕστερον　[δὲ]
those　　they believed.　　　　　　And later

ἀνακειμένοις　αὐτοῖς　τοῖς　ἕνδεκα　ἐφανερώθη,
to the reclining　them　　the　　eleven　he was manifested,
= to the eleven as they reclined

καὶ　ὠνείδισεν　τὴν　ἀπιστίαν　αὐτῶν　καὶ
and　reproached　the　disbelief　　of them　and

σκληροκαρδίαν　ὅτι　τοῖς　θεασαμένοις　αὐτὸν
hardness of heart　because the [ones]　beholding　　him

ἐγηγερμένον　οὐκ　ἐπίστευσαν.　15 καὶ　εἶπεν
having been raised　they did not believe.　　And　he said

αὐτοῖς·　πορευθέντες　εἰς　τὸν　κόσμον　ἅπαντα
to them:　Going　　　into ²the　¹world　　¹all

κηρύξατε　τὸ　εὐαγγέλιον　πάσῃ　τῇ　κτίσει.
proclaim ye　the　gospel　　to all　the　creation.

16 ὁ　πιστεύσας καὶ βαπτισθεὶς σωθήσεται,
The [one] believing　and being baptized　will be saved,

ὁ　δὲ　ἀπιστήσας κατακριθήσεται.　17 σημεῖα
but the [one] disbelieving　will be condemned.　　²signs

δὲ　τοῖς　πιστεύσασιν ταῦτα παρακολουθήσει·
¹And　⁵the [ones]　⁶believing　³these　⁴will follow:

ἐν　τῷ　ὀνόματί　μου　δαιμόνια　ἐκβαλοῦσιν,
in　the　name　of me　demons　　they will expel,

γλώσσαις　λαλήσουσιν　καιναῖς,　18 ὄφεις
²tongues　　¹they will speak　²with new,　　serpents

ἀροῦσιν　κἂν　θανάσιμόν　τι　πίωσιν
they will take　and if　³deadly　²anything ¹they drink

οὐ μὴ αὐτοὺς βλάψῃ, ἐπὶ ἀρρώστους χεῖρας
by no means them　it will hurt,　on　sick [ones]　hands

ἐπιθήσουσιν καὶ καλῶς ἕξουσιν.　19 Ὁ　μὲν
they will place on　and　well　they will have.　¹The　⁴there-
= they will recover.

οὖν　κύριος　[Ἰησοῦς]　μετὰ　τὸ　λαλῆσαι
fore　¹Lord　³Jesus　　after　the　to speak
= speaking

---

and told those who had been with him, as they mourned and wept. ¹¹But when they heard that he was alive and had been seen by her, they would not believe it.

12 After this he appeared in another form to two of them, as they were walking into the country. ¹³And they went back and told the rest, but they did not believe them.

14 Afterward he appeared to the eleven themselves as they sat at table; and he upbraided them for their unbelief and hardness of heart, because they had not believed those who saw him after he had risen. ¹⁵And he said to them, "Go into all the world and preach the gospel to the whole creation. ¹⁶He who believes and is baptized will be saved; but he who does not believe will be condemned. ¹⁷And these signs will accompany those who believe: in my name they will cast out demons; they will speak in new tongues; ¹⁸they will pick up serpents, and if they drink any deadly thing, it will not hurt them; they will lay their hands on the sick; and they will recover."

19 So then the Lord Jesus, after he had spoken to them, was

αὐτοῖς ἀνελήμφθη εἰς τὸν οὐρανὸν καὶ
to them was taken up into –   heaven   and

ἐκάθισεν ἐκ δεξιῶν τοῦ θεοῦ. 20 ἐκεῖνοι
sat   at [the] right [hand] – of God.   those

δὲ ἐξελθόντες ἐκήρυξαν πανταχοῦ, τοῦ
But going forth proclaimed everywhere,   the

κυρίου συνεργοῦντος καὶ τὸν λόγον
Lord working with   and the word
= while the Lord worked with [them] and confirmed the word

βεβαιοῦντος διὰ τῶν ἐπακολουθούντων
confirming[a] through the   accompanying

σημείων.
signs.

taken up into heaven, and sat
down at the right hand of God.
²⁰And they went forth and
preached everywhere, while the
Lord worked with them and
confirmed the message by the
signs that attended it. Amen.
    Other ancient authorities
add after verse 8 the following:
But they reported briefly to
Peter and those with him all
that they had been told. And
after this, Jesus himself sent
out by means of them, from
east to west, the sacred and
imperishable proclamation of
eternal salvation.

CHAPTER 1

INASMUCH as many have undertaken to compile a narrative of the things which have been accomplished among us [2]just as they were delivered to us by those who from the beginning were eye witnesses and ministers of the word, [3]it seemed good to me also, having followed all things closely[a] for some time past, to write an orderly account for you, most excellent The·oph'i·lus, [4]that you may know the truth concerning the things of which you have been informed.

5 In the days of Herod, king of Judea, there was a priest named Zech·ari'ah, of the division of Abi'jah; and he had a wife of the daughters of Aaron, and her name was Elizabeth. [6]And they were both righteous before God, walking in all the commandments and ordinances of the Lord blameless. [7]But they had no child, because Elizabeth was barren, and both were advanced in years.

8 Now while he was serving as priest before God when his division

1 Ἐπειδήπερ πολλοὶ ἐπεχείρησαν ἀνατάξασθαι
Since   many   took in hand   to draw up

διήγησιν περὶ τῶν   πεπληροφορημένων
a narrative concerning [1]the   [2]having been fully carried out

ἐν ἡμῖν πραγμάτων, **2** καθὼς παρέδοσαν ἡμῖν
[4]among [3]us   [2]matters,   as   delivered to us

οἱ   ἀπ' ἀρχῆς αὐτόπται καὶ ὑπηρέται
the [ones] from [the] beginning eyewitnesses and attendants

γενόμενοι τοῦ λόγου, **3** ἔδοξε κἀμοὶ
becoming   of the Word, it seemed good to me also

παρηκολουθηκότι ἄνωθεν πᾶσιν ἀκριβῶς
having investigated from their source all things accurately

καθεξῆς σοι γράψαι, κράτιστε Θεόφιλε,
[3]in order [2]to thee [1]to write, most excellent Theophilus,

4 ἵνα   ἐπιγνῷς περὶ ὧν
that thou mightest know [4]concerning [5]which

κατηχήθης λόγων τὴν ἀσφάλειαν.
[6]thou wast instructed [3]of [the] things [1]the [2]reliability.

5 Ἐγένετο ἐν ταῖς ἡμέραις
There was   in   the   days

Ἡρῴδου βασιλέως τῆς Ἰουδαίας ἱερεύς
of Herod king - of Judæa [2]priest

τις ὀνόματι Ζαχαρίας ἐξ ἐφημερίας Ἀβιά,
[1]a certain by name Zacharias of [the] course of Abia,

καὶ γυνὴ αὐτῷ ἐκ τῶν θυγατέρων Ἀαρών,
and wife to him° of the daughters of Aaron,
= his wife

καὶ τὸ ὄνομα αὐτῆς Ἐλισάβετ. **6** ἦσαν δὲ
and the name of her Elisabeth. And they were

δίκαιοι ἀμφότεροι ἐναντίον τοῦ θεοῦ,
righteous both before - God,

πορευόμενοι ἐν πάσαις ταῖς ἐντολαῖς καὶ
going   in all   the commandments and

δικαιώμασιν τοῦ κυρίου ἄμεμπτοι. **7** καὶ
ordinances of the Lord blameless. And

οὐκ ἦν αὐτοῖς τέκνον, καθότι ἦν ἡ
there was not to them a child,° because [2]was - [3]
= they had no child,

Ἐλισάβετ στεῖρα, καὶ ἀμφότεροι προβεβηκότες
[1]Elisabeth barren, and both *having* advanced

ἐν ταῖς ἡμέραις αὐτῶν ἦσαν. **8** Ἐγένετο
in the days of them were. it came to pass

δὲ ἐν τῷ ἱερατεύειν αὐτὸν ἐν τῇ τάξει
Now in the to serve as priest him[be] in the order
= while he served as priest

[a] Or accurately

was on duty, ⁹according to the custom of the priesthood, it fell to him by lot to enter the temple of the Lord and burn incense. ¹⁰And the whole multitude of the people were praying outside at the hour of incense. ¹¹And there appeared to him an angel of the Lord standing on the right side of the altar of incense. ¹²And Zechari'-ah was troubled when he saw him, and fear fell upon him. ¹³But the angel said to him, "Do not be afraid, Zechari'ah, for your prayer is heard, and your wife Elizabeth will bear you a son, and you shall call his name John.

¹⁴And you will have joy and gladness, and many will rejoice at his birth;
¹⁵for he will be great before the Lord, and he shall drink no wine nor strong drink, and he will be filled with the Holy Spirit, even from his mother's womb.
¹⁶And he will turn many of the sons of Israel to the Lord their God,
¹⁷and he will go before him in the spirit and power of Eli'jah, to turn the hearts of the fathers to the children, and the disobedient to the wisdom of

τῆς ἐφημερίας αὐτοῦ ἔναντι τοῦ θεοῦ,
of the   course   of him   before   -   God,

9 κατὰ τὸ ἔθος τῆς ἱερατείας ἔλαχε τοῦ
according to the custom of the priesthood his lot was -

θυμιᾶσαι εἰσελθὼν εἰς τὸν ναὸν τοῦ κυρίου,
to burn incenseᵈ entering into the shrine of the Lord,

10 καὶ πᾶν τὸ πλῆθος ἦν τοῦ λαοῦ
and all ¹the ²multitude ³was ³of the ⁴people

προσευχόμενον ἔξω τῇ ὥρᾳ τοῦ θυμιάματος.
praying   outside at the hour - of incense.

11 ὤφθη δὲ αὐτῷ ἄγγελος κυρίου ἑστὼς
And there appeared to him an angel of [the] Lord standing

ἐκ δεξιῶν τοῦ θυσιαστηρίου τοῦ θυμιάματος.
on [the] right of the altar   of incense.

12 καὶ ἐταράχθη Ζαχαρίας ἰδών, καὶ φόβος
And was troubled Zacharias seeing, and fear

ἐπέπεσεν ἐπ' αὐτόν. **13** εἶπεν δὲ πρὸς
fell on upon him.   But said to

αὐτὸν ὁ ἄγγελος· μὴ φοβοῦ, Ζαχαρία,
him the angel: Fear not, Zacharias,

διότι εἰσηκούσθη ἡ δέησίς σου, καὶ ἡ
because was heard the request of thee, and the

γυνή σου Ἐλισάβετ γεννήσει υἱόν σοι,
wife of thee Elisabeth will bear a son to thee,

καὶ καλέσεις τὸ ὄνομα αὐτοῦ Ἰωάννην·
and thou shalt call the name of him John;

14 καὶ ἔσται χαρά σοι καὶ ἀγαλλίασις,
and there shall be joy to thee and gladness,ᵉ
=thou shalt have joy and gladness,

καὶ πολλοὶ ἐπὶ τῇ γενέσει αὐτοῦ χαρή-
and many over the birth of him will

σονται. **15** ἔσται γὰρ μέγας ἐνώπιον
rejoice.   For he will be great in the eyes of

κυρίου, καὶ οἶνον καὶ σίκερα οὐ μὴ
[the] Lord, and wine and strong drink by no means

πίῃ, καὶ πνεύματος ἁγίου πλησθήσεται
may he drink, and of(with) Spirit [the] Holy he will be filled

ἔτι ἐκ κοιλίας μητρὸς αὐτοῦ, **16** καὶ
even from [the] womb of [the] mother of him,   and

πολλοὺς τῶν υἱῶν Ἰσραὴλ ἐπιστρέψει ἐπὶ κύριον
many of the sons of Israel he will turn to [the] Lord

τὸν θεὸν αὐτῶν· **17** καὶ αὐτὸς προελεύσεται
the God of them;   and he will go before

ἐνώπιον αὐτοῦ ἐν πνεύματι καὶ δυνάμει
before him in [the] spirit and power

Ἠλίου, ἐπιστρέψαι καρδίας πατέρων ἐπὶ
of Elias, to turn [the] hearts of fathers to

τέκνα καὶ ἀπειθεῖς ἐν φρονήσει
children and disobedient [ones] to [the] understanding

the just,
to make ready for the Lord a people prepared."

¹⁸And Zechari'ah said to the angel, "How shall I know this? For I am an old man, and my wife is advanced in years."

¹⁹And the angel answered him, "I am Gabriel, who stand in the presence of God; and I was sent to speak to you, and to bring you this good news. ²⁰And behold, you will be silent and unable to speak until the day that these things come to pass, because you did not believe my words, which will be fulfilled in their time." ²¹And the people were waiting for Zechari'ah, and they wondered at his delay in the temple. ²²And when he came out, he could not speak to them, and they perceived that he had seen a vision in the temple; and he made signs to them and remained dumb. ²³And when his time of service was ended, he went to his home.

24 After these days his wife Elizabeth conceived, and for five months she hid herself,

---

δικαίων, ἑτοιμάσαι κυρίῳ λαὸν κατεσκευασ-
of [the] just, to prepare for [the] Lord a people   *having been*

μένον. 18 καὶ εἶπεν Ζαχαρίας πρὸς τὸν ἄγγελον·
prepared.   And said Zacharias to the angel:

κατὰ τί γνώσομαι τοῦτο; ἐγὼ γάρ εἰμι
By what shall I know this?   for I   am

πρεσβύτης καὶ ἡ γυνή μου προβεβηκυῖα
old   and the wife of me *having* advanced

ἐν ταῖς ἡμέραις αὐτῆς. 19 καὶ ἀποκριθεὶς
in the days of her.   And answering

ὁ ἄγγελος εἶπεν αὐτῷ· ἐγώ εἰμι Γαβριὴλ
the angel said to him: I am Gabriel

ὁ παρεστηκὼς ἐνώπιον τοῦ θεοῦ, καὶ
the [one] standing before - God, and

ἀπεστάλην λαλῆσαι πρὸς σὲ καὶ εὐαγ-
I was sent to speak to thee and to

γελίσασθαί σοι ταῦτα· 20 καὶ ἰδοὺ
announce to thee these things;   and behold

ἔσῃ σιωπῶν καὶ μὴ δυνάμενος λαλῆσαι
thou shalt be being silent and not being able to speak

ἄχρι ἧς ἡμέρας γένηται ταῦτα, ἀνθ' ὧν οὐκ
until which day happens these things, because not
             =the day when these things happen,

ἐπίστευσας τοῖς λόγοις μου, οἵτινες πληρω-
thou believedst the words of me, which will be

θήσονται εἰς τὸν καιρὸν αὐτῶν. 21 καὶ ἦν
fulfilled in the time of them.   And was

ὁ λαὸς προσδοκῶν τὸν Ζαχαρίαν, καὶ
the people expecting - Zacharias, and

ἐθαύμαζον ἐν τῷ χρονίζειν ἐν τῷ ναῷ
they marvelled in(at) the to delay in the shrine
          =when he delayed in the shrine.

αὐτόν. 22 ἐξελθὼν δὲ οὐκ ἐδύνατο λαλῆσαι
him.ᵇᵉ   And going out he was not able to speak

αὐτοῖς καὶ ἐπέγνωσαν ὅτι ὀπτασίαν ἑώρακεν
to them, and they knew that a vision he has(had) seen

ἐν τῷ ναῷ· καὶ αὐτὸς ἦν διανεύων
in the shrine; and he was beckoning

αὐτοῖς, καὶ διέμενεν κωφός. 23 καὶ
to them, and remained dumb.   And

ἐγένετο ὡς ἐπλήσθησαν αἱ ἡμέραι τῆς
it came to pass when were fulfilled the days of the

λειτουργίας αὐτοῦ, ἀπῆλθεν εἰς τὸν οἶκον
service of him, he went away to the house

αὐτοῦ. 24 Μετὰ δὲ ταύτας τὰς ἡμέρας
of him.   And after these - days

συνέλαβεν Ἐλισάβετ ἡ γυνὴ αὐτοῦ, καὶ
conceived Elisabeth the wife of him, and

περιέκρυβεν ἑαυτὴν μῆνας πέντε, λέγουσα
hid herself months five, saying[,]

saying, 25"Thus the Lord has done to me in the days when he looked on me, to take away my reproach among men."

26 In the sixth month the angel Gabriel was sent from God to a city of Galilee named Nazareth, 27to a virgin betrothed to a man whose name was Joseph, of the house of David; and the virgin's name was Mary. 28And he came to her and said, "Hail, O favored one, the Lord is with you!"[b] 29But she was greatly troubled at the saying, and considered in her mind what sort of greeting this might be. 30And the angel said to her, "Do not be afraid, Mary, for you have found favor with God. 31And behold, you will conceive in your womb and bear a son, and you shall call his name Jesus.

32He will be great, and will be called the Son of the Most High;

and the Lord God will give to him the throne of his father David,

33and he will reign over the house of Jacob for ever;

and of his kingdom there will be no end."

34And Mary said to the angel, "How can this be,

---

25 ὅτι οὕτως μοι πεποίηκεν κύριος ἐν
    Thus to me has done [the] Lord in
ἡμέραις αἷς ἐπεῖδεν ἀφελεῖν ὄνειδός
days in which he looked upon to take away reproach
μου ἐν ἀνθρώποις.
of me among men.

26 Ἐν δὲ τῷ μηνὶ τῷ ἕκτῳ ἀπεστάλη
   Now in the month – sixth was sent
ὁ ἄγγελος Γαβριὴλ ἀπὸ τοῦ θεοῦ εἰς
the angel Gabriel from – God to
πόλιν τῆς Γαλιλαίας ᾗ ὄνομα Ναζαρέθ,
a city – of Galilee to which name[e] Nazareth,
                   = the name of which [was]

27 πρὸς παρθένον ἐμνηστευμένην ἀνδρὶ ᾧ ὄνομα
to a virgin having been betrothed to a man to whom name[e]
Ἰωσήφ, ἐξ οἴκου Δαυίδ, καὶ τὸ ὄνομα
Joseph, of [the] house of David, and the name
τῆς παρθένου Μαριάμ. 28 καὶ εἰσελθὼν
of the virgin [was] Mary. And entering
πρὸς αὐτὴν εἶπεν· χαῖρε, κεχαριτωμένη, ὁ
to her he said: Hail, having been favoured [one], the
κύριος μετὰ σοῦ. 29 ἡ δὲ ἐπὶ τῷ λόγῳ
Lord [is] with thee. And she at the saying
διεταράχθη, καὶ διελογίζετο ποταπὸς εἴη
was greatly disturbed, and considered of what sort ²might be
ὁ ἀσπασμὸς οὗτος. 30 καὶ εἶπεν ὁ ἄγγελος
– ²greeting ¹this. And said the angel
αὐτῇ· μὴ φοβοῦ, Μαριάμ· εὗρες γὰρ
to her: Fear not, Mary: for thou didst find
χάριν παρὰ τῷ θεῷ. 31 καὶ ἰδοὺ συλλήμψῃ
favour with – God. And behold thou wilt conceive
ἐν γαστρὶ καὶ τέξῃ υἱόν, καὶ καλέσεις τὸ
in womb and bear a son, and thou shalt call the
ὄνομα αὐτοῦ Ἰησοῦν. 32 οὗτος ἔσται μέγας
name of him Jesus. This will be great
καὶ υἱὸς ὑψίστου κληθήσεται, καὶ δώσει
and Son of [the] Most High will be called, and will give
αὐτῷ κύριος ὁ θεὸς τὸν θρόνον Δαυίδ
him [the] Lord – God the throne of David
τοῦ πατρὸς αὐτοῦ, 33 καὶ βασιλεύσει ἐπὶ
the father of him, and he will reign over
τὸν οἶκον Ἰακὼβ εἰς τοὺς αἰῶνας, καὶ
the house of Jacob unto the ages, and
                    =for ever,
τῆς βασιλείας αὐτοῦ οὐκ ἔσται τέλος.
of the kingdom of him there will not be an end.

34 εἶπεν δὲ Μαριὰμ πρὸς τὸν ἄγγελον·
And said Mary to the angel:

---

[b] Other ancient authorities add "Blessed are you among women³"

since I have no husband?" ³⁵And the angel said to her,

"The Holy Spirit will come upon you, and the power of the Most High will overshadow you; therefore the child to be born^e will be called holy, the Son of God.

³⁶And behold, your kinswoman Elizabeth in her old age has also conceived a son; and this is the sixth month with her who was called barren. ³⁷For with God nothing will be impossible." ³⁸And Mary said, "Behold I am the handmaid of the Lord; let it be to me according to your word." And the angel departed from her.

39 In those days Mary arose and went with haste into the hill country, to a city of Judah, ⁴⁰and she entered the house of Zechari'ah and greeted Elizabeth. ⁴¹And when Elizabeth heard the greeting of Mary, the babe leaped in her womb; and Elizabeth was filled with the Holy Spirit ⁴²and she exclaimed with a loud cry, "Blessed are you among women, and blessed is the fruit of your womb! ⁴³And why is this granted me, that the mother of my Lord

---

πῶς ἔσται τοῦτο, ἐπεὶ ἄνδρα οὐ γινώσκω;
How will be this, since a man I know not?

35 καὶ ἀποκριθεὶς ὁ ἄγγελος εἶπεν αὐτῇ·
And answering the angel said to her:

πνεῦμα ἅγιον ἐπελεύσεται ἐπὶ σέ, καὶ
¹[The] ²Spirit ²Holy will come *upon* upon thee, and

δύναμις ὑψίστου ἐπισκιάσει σοι· διὸ
[the] power of [the] Most High will overshadow thee; wherefore

καὶ τὸ γεννώμενον ἅγιον κληθήσεται υἱὸς θεοῦ.
also the thing being born holy will be called[.] Son of God.

36 καὶ ἰδοὺ Ἐλισάβετ ἡ συγγενίς σου καὶ
And behold Elisabeth the relative of thee also

αὐτὴ συνείληφεν υἱὸν ἐν γήρει αὐτῆς, καὶ
she conceived a son in old age of her, and

οὗτος μὴν ἕκτος ἐστὶν αὐτῇ τῇ καλουμένῃ
this month sixth is with her the [one] *being* called

στείρᾳ· 37 ὅτι οὐκ ἀδυνατήσει παρὰ τοῦ
barren; because will not be impossible with –

θεοῦ πᾶν ῥῆμα. 38 εἶπεν δὲ Μαριάμ· ἰδοὺ ἡ
God every word. And said Mary: Behold[,] the

δούλη κυρίου· γένοιτό μοι κατὰ
handmaid of [the]Lord; may it be to me according to

τὸ ῥῆμά σου. καὶ ἀπῆλθεν ἀπ᾽ αὐτῆς
the word of thee. And went away from her

ὁ ἄγγελος. 39 Ἀναστᾶσα δὲ Μαριὰμ ἐν
the angel. And rising up Mary in

ταῖς ἡμέραις ταύταις ἐπορεύθη εἰς τὴν
– days these she went to the

ὀρεινὴν μετὰ σπουδῆς εἰς πόλιν Ἰούδα,
mountain country with haste to a city of Juda,

40 καὶ εἰσῆλθεν εἰς τὸν οἶκον Ζαχαρίου
and entered into the house of Zacharias

καὶ ἠσπάσατο τὴν Ἐλισάβετ. 41 καὶ
and greeted – Elisabeth. And

ἐγένετο ὡς ἤκουσεν τὸν ἀσπασμὸν τῆς
it came to pass when ²heard ³the ⁴greeting –

Μαρίας ἡ Ἐλισάβετ, ἐσκίρτησεν τὸ βρέφος
⁵of Mary, ¹Elisabeth, leaped the babe

ἐν τῇ κοιλίᾳ αὐτῆς, καὶ ἐπλήσθη πνεύματος
in the womb of her, and ²was filled ³of(with) ⁴Spirit

ἁγίου ἡ Ἐλισάβετ, 42 καὶ ἀνεφώνησεν
⁴[the] Holy – ¹Elisabeth, and she called out

κραυγῇ μεγάλῃ καὶ εἶπεν· εὐλογημένη
cry with a great and said : Blessed [art]

σὺ ἐν γυναιξίν, καὶ εὐλογημένος ὁ καρπὸς
thou among women, and blessed [is] the fruit

τῆς κοιλίας σου. 43 καὶ πόθεν μοι τοῦτο
of the womb of thee. And whence to me this

---

^e Other ancient authorities add *of you*

should come to me?
⁴⁴For behold, when the
voice of your greeting
came to my ears, the
babe in my womb leaped
for joy. ⁴⁵And blessed is
she who believed that
there would be*a fulfil-
ment of what was spoken
to her from the Lord."
⁴⁶And Mary said,
  "My soul magnifies
    the Lord,
  ⁴⁷and my spirit rejoices
    in God my Savior,
  ⁴⁸for he has regarded
    the low estate of
    his handmaiden.
  For behold, hence-
    forth all genera-
    tions will call me
    blessed;
  ⁴⁹for he who is mighty
    has done great
    things for me,
  and holy is his name.
  ⁵⁰And his mercy is on
    those who fear him
    from generation to
    generation.
  ⁵¹He has shown
    strength with his
    arm,
  he has scattered the
    proud in the imagi-
    nation of their
    hearts,
  ⁵²he has put down the
    mighty from their
    thrones,
  and exalted those of
    low degree;
  ⁵³he has filled the
    hungry with good
    things,
  and the rich he has
    sent empty away.
  ⁵⁴He has helped his
    servant Israel,
  in remembrance of
    his mercy,
  ⁵⁵as he spoke to our
    fathers,

*Or believed, for there will be

ἵνα ἔλθῃ ἡ μήτηρ τοῦ κυρίου μου πρὸς
that comes the mother of the Lord of me to
ἐμέ; 44 ἰδοὺ γὰρ ὡς ἐγένετο ἡ φωνὴ τοῦ
me? For behold when came the sound of the
ἀσπασμοῦ σου εἰς τὰ ὦτά μου, ἐσκίρτησεν
greeting of thee in the ears of me, leaped
ἐν ἀγαλλιάσει τὸ βρέφος ἐν τῇ κοιλίᾳ
in gladness the babe in the womb
μου. 45 καὶ μακαρία ἡ πιστεύσασα ὅτι
of me. And blessed the [one] believing because
ἔσται τελείωσις τοῖς λελαλημένοις αὐτῇ
there shall be a completion to the things having been to her
                                              spoken
παρὰ κυρίου. 46 Καὶ εἶπεν Μαριάμ·
from [the] Lord. And said Mary:
Μεγαλύνει ἡ ψυχή μου τὸν κύριον, 47 καὶ
Magnifies the soul of me the Lord, and
ἠγαλλίασεν τὸ πνεῦμά μου ἐπὶ τῷ θεῷ
exulted the spirit of me in – God
τῷ σωτῆρί μου· 48 ὅτι ἐπέβλεψεν ἐπὶ τὴν
the saviour of me; because he looked on upon the
ταπείνωσιν τῆς δούλης αὐτοῦ. ἰδοὺ γὰρ
humiliation of the handmaid of him. For behold
ἀπὸ τοῦ νῦν ⁴will ⁵deem ⁷blessed ⁶me ¹all ²the
from – now
γενεαί· 49 ὅτι ἐποίησέν μοι μεγάλα ὁ
³generations; because did to me great things the
δυνατός. καὶ ἅγιον τὸ ὄνομα αὐτοῦ,
Mighty [one]. And holy the name of him,
50 καὶ τὸ ἔλεος αὐτοῦ εἰς γενεὰς καὶ
and the mercy of him to generations and
γενεὰς τοῖς φοβουμένοις αὐτόν. 51 Ἐποίησεν
generations to the [ones] fearing him. He did
κράτος ἐν βραχίονι αὐτοῦ, διεσκόρπισεν
might with [the] arm of him, he scattered
ὑπερηφάνους διανοίᾳ καρδίας αὐτῶν·
haughty [ones] in [the] understanding of [the] heart of them;
52 καθεῖλεν δυνάστας ἀπὸ θρόνων καὶ ὕψω-
he pulled down potentates from thrones and exalt-
σεν ταπεινούς, 53 πεινῶντας ἐνέπλησεν
ed humble [ones], hungering [ones] he filled
ἀγαθῶν καὶ πλουτοῦντας ἐξαπέστειλεν
of(with) good things and rich [ones] he sent away
κενούς. 54 ἀντελάβετο Ἰσραὴλ παιδὸς αὐτοῦ,
empty. He succoured Israel servant of him,
μνησθῆναι ἐλέους, 55 καθὼς ἐλάλησεν
to remember mercy, as he spoke
πρὸς τοὺς πατέρας ἡμῶν, τῷ Ἀβραὰμ
to the fathers of us, – to Abraham

to Abraham and to his posterity for ever."

καὶ τῷ σπέρματι αὐτοῦ εἰς τὸν αἰῶνα.
and to the seed of him unto the age.
=for ever.

56And Mary remained with her about three months, and returned to her home.

56 Ἔμεινεν δὲ Μαριὰμ σὺν αὐτῇ ὡς
And remained Mary with her about
μῆνας τρεῖς, καὶ ὑπέστρεψεν εἰς τὸν
months three, and returned to the
οἶκον αὐτῆς.
house of her.

57 Now the time came for Elizabeth to be delivered, and she gave birth to a son. 58And her neighbors and kinsfolk heard that the Lord had shown great mercy to her, and they rejoiced with her. 59And on the eighth day they came to circumcise the child; and they would have named him Zechari'ah after his father, 60but his mother said, "Not so; he shall be called John." 61And they said to her, "None of your kindred is called by this name." 62And they made signs to his father, inquiring what he would have him called. 63And he asked for a writing tablet, and wrote, "His name is John." And they all marveled. 64And immediately his mouth was opened and his tongue loosed, and he spoke, blessing God. 65And fear came on all their neighbors. And all these things were talked about through all the hill

57 Τῇ δὲ Ἐλισάβετ ἐπλήσθη ὁ χρόνος
- Now 4to Elisabeth 3was fulfilled 1the 2time
τοῦ τεκεῖν αὐτήν, καὶ ἐγέννησεν υἱόν.
- to bear her,bd and she brought forth a son.
=that she should bear,

58 καὶ ἤκουσαν οἱ περίοικοι καὶ οἱ
And heard the neighbours and the
συγγενεῖς αὐτῆς ὅτι ἐμεγάλυνεν κύριος τὸ
relatives of her that magnified [the] Lord the
ἔλεος αὐτοῦ μετ᾽ αὐτῆς, καὶ συνέχαιρον
mercy of him with her, and they rejoiced with
αὐτῇ. 59 Καὶ ἐγένετο ἐν τῇ ἡμέρᾳ τῇ
her. And it came to pass on the day -
ὀγδόῃ ἦλθον περιτεμεῖν τὸ παιδίον, καὶ
eighth they came to circumcise the child, and
ἐκάλουν αὐτὸ ἐπὶ τῷ ὀνόματι τοῦ πατρὸς
were calling it(him) by the name of the father
αὐτοῦ Ζαχαρίαν. 60 καὶ ἀποκριθεῖσα ἡ
of him Zacharias. And answering the
μήτηρ αὐτοῦ εἶπεν· οὐχί, ἀλλὰ κληθήσεται
mother of him said : No, but he shall be called
Ἰωάννης. 61 καὶ εἶπαν πρὸς αὐτὴν ὅτι
John. And they said to her[,] -
οὐδείς ἐστιν ἐκ τῆς συγγενείας σου ὃς
No one there is of the kindred of thee who
καλεῖται τῷ ὀνόματι τούτῳ. 62 ἐνένευον
is called - name by this. they nodded
δὲ τῷ πατρὶ αὐτοῦ τὸ τί ἂν θέλοι
And to the father of him - what he might wish
καλεῖσθαι αὐτό. 63 καὶ αἰτήσας πινακίδιον
2to be called 1him. And asking for a tablet
ἔγραψεν λέγων· Ἰωάννης ἐστὶν ὄνομα
he wrote saying : John is name
αὐτοῦ. καὶ ἐθαύμασαν πάντες. 64 ἀνεῴχθη δὲ
of him. And they marvelled all. And was opened
τὸ στόμα αὐτοῦ παραχρῆμα καὶ ἡ
the mouth of him instantly and the
γλῶσσα αὐτοῦ, καὶ ἐλάλει εὐλογῶν τὸν
tongue of him, and he spoke blessing -
θεόν. 65 Καὶ ἐγένετο ἐπὶ πάντας φόβος
God. And 2came 3on 4all 1fear

country of Judea; ⁶⁶and all who heard them laid them up in their hearts, saying, "What then will this child be?" For the hand of the Lord was with him.

67 And his father Zechar'iah was filled with the Holy Spirit, and prophesied, saying,

⁶⁸"Blessed be the Lord God of Israel,

for he has visited and redeemed his people,

⁶⁹and has raised up a horn of salvation for us

in the house of his servant David.

⁷⁰as he spoke by the mouth of his holy prophets from of old,

⁷¹that we should be saved from our enemies,

and from the hand of all who hate us;

⁷²to perform the mercy promised to our fathers,

and to remember his holy covenant,

⁷³the oath which he swore to our father Abraham, ⁷⁴to grant us

that we, being delivered from the hand of our enemies,

might serve him without fear,

⁷⁵in holiness and righteousness before him all the days of our life.

⁷⁶And you, child, will be called the prophet of the Most High;

for you will go before

τοὺς περιοικοῦντας αὐτούς, καὶ ἐν ὅλῃ τῇ
the [ones] dwelling round them, and in all the

ὀρεινῇ τῆς Ἰουδαίας διελαλεῖτο πάντα
mountain country – of Judæa ⁴were talked over ¹all

τὰ ῥήματα ταῦτα, 66 καὶ ἔθεντο πάντες
– ²facts ³these, and ⁴put ¹all

οἱ ἀκούσαντες ἐν τῇ καρδίᾳ αὐτῶν,
²the [ones] ³hearing in the heart of them,

λέγοντες· τί ἄρα τὸ παιδίον τοῦτο ἔσται;
saying : What then – child this will be ?

καὶ γὰρ χεὶρ κυρίου ἦν μετ᾽ αὐτοῦ.
for indeed [the] hand of [the] Lord was with him.

67 Καὶ Ζαχαρίας ὁ πατὴρ αὐτοῦ ἐπλήσθη
And Zacharias the father of him was filled

πνεύματος ἁγίου καὶ ἐπροφήτευσεν λέγων·
of(with) Spirit [the] Holy and prophesied saying :

68 Εὐλογητὸς κύριος ὁ θεὸς τοῦ Ἰσραήλ,
Blessed [be] [the] Lord the God – of Israel,

ὅτι ἐπεσκέψατο καὶ ἐποίησεν λύτρωσιν τῷ
because he visited and wrought redemption for the

λαῷ αὐτοῦ, 69 καὶ ἤγειρεν κέρας σωτηρίας
people of him, and raised a horn of salvation

ἡμῖν ἐν οἴκῳ Δαυὶδ παιδὸς αὐτοῦ, 70 καθὼς
for us in [the] house of David servant of him, as

ἐλάλησεν διὰ στόματος τῶν ἁγίων ἀπ᾽
he spoke through [the] mouth of the ¹holy ᵃfrom

αἰῶνος προφητῶν αὐτοῦ, 71 σωτηρίαν ἐξ
⁵[the] age ²prophets ³of him, salvation out of

ἐχθρῶν ἡμῶν καὶ ἐκ χειρὸς πάντων τῶν
[the] enemies of us and out of [the] hand of all the [ones]

μισούντων ἡμᾶς, 72 ποιῆσαι ἔλεος μετὰ
hating us, to perform mercy with

τῶν πατέρων ἡμῶν καὶ μνησθῆναι διαθήκης
the fathers of us and to remember [the] covenant

ἁγίας αὐτοῦ, 73 ὅρκον ὃν ὤμοσεν πρὸς Ἀβραὰμ
holy of him, [the] oath which he swore to Abraham

τὸν πατέρα ἡμῶν, 74 τοῦ δοῦναι ἡμῖν
the father of us, – to give⁴ us

ἀφόβως ἐκ χειρὸς ἐχθρῶν ῥυσθέντας
⁶fearlessly ⁵out of ³[the] hand ⁴of [our] enemies ¹having been delivered

λατρεύειν αὐτῷ 75 ἐν ὁσιότητι καὶ δικαιοσύνῃ
⁶to serve him in holiness and righteousness

ἐνώπιον αὐτοῦ πάσαις ταῖς ἡμέραις ἡμῶν.
before him all the daysᵉ of us.

76 Καὶ σὺ δέ, παιδίον, προφήτης ὑψίστου
And thou also, child, a prophet of [the] Most High

κληθήσῃ· προπορεύσῃ γὰρ ἐνώπιον κυρίου
wilt be called; for thou wilt go before before [the] Lord

the Lord to prepare his ways,
77 to give knowledge of salvation to his people
in the forgiveness of their sins,
78 through the tender mercy of our God, when the day shall dawn upon[e] us from on high
79 to give light to those who sit in darkness and in the shadow of death, to guide our feet into the way of peace."
80 And the child grew and became strong in spirit, and he was in the wilderness till the day of his manifestation to Israel.

ἐτοιμάσαι ὁδοὺς αὐτοῦ, 77 τοῦ δοῦναι
to prepare [the] ways of him, - to give[d]
γνῶσιν σωτηρίας τῷ λαῷ αὐτοῦ ἐν
a knowledge of salvation to the people of him by
ἀφέσει ἁμαρτιῶν αὐτῶν, 78 διὰ σπλάγχνα·
forgiveness of sins of them, because of [the] bowels
ἐλέους θεοῦ ἡμῶν, ἐν οἷς ἐπισκέψεται
of mercy of God of us, whereby will visit
ἡμᾶς ἀνατολὴ ἐξ ὕψους, 79 ἐπιφᾶναι τοῖς
us a [sun]rising from [the] height, to appear [1]to the [ones]
ἐν σκότει καὶ σκιᾷ θανάτου καθημένοις,
[3]in [4]darkness [5]and [6]in a shadow [7]of death [2]sitting,
τοῦ κατευθῦναι τοὺς πόδας ἡμῶν εἰς ὁδὸν
- to guide[d] the feet of us into a way
εἰρήνης.
of peace.
80 Τὸ δὲ παιδίον ηὔξανεν καὶ ἐκραταιοῦτο
And the child grew and became strong
πνεύματι, καὶ ἦν ἐν ταῖς ἐρήμοις ἕως
in spirit, and was in the deserts until
ἡμέρας ἀναδείξεως αὐτοῦ πρὸς τὸν Ἰσραήλ.
[the] days of showing of him to - Israel.

CHAPTER 2

IN those days a decree went out from Caesar Augustus that all the world should be enrolled.
2 This was the first enrollment, when Quirin'ius was governor of Syria. 3 And all went to be enrolled, each to his own city. 4 And Joseph also went up from Galilee, from the city of Nazareth, to Judea, to the city of David, which is called Bethlehem, because he was of the house and lineage of David, 5 to be enrolled with Mary, his betrothed, who was with child. 6 And while

2 Ἐγένετο δὲ ἐν ταῖς ἡμέραις ἐκείναις
Now it came to pass in - days those
ἐξῆλθεν δόγμα παρὰ Καίσαρος Αὐγούστου
went out a decree from Cæsar Augustus
ἀπογράφεσθαι πᾶσαν τὴν οἰκουμένην. 2 αὕτη
to be enrolled all the inhabited earth. This
ἀπογραφὴ πρώτη ἐγένετο ἡγεμονεύοντος τῆς
[2]enrolment [1]first was governing -
= when Cyrenius governed Syria.
Συρίας Κυρηνίου. 3 καὶ ἐπορεύοντο πάντες
Syria Cyrenius.[a] And went all
ἀπογράφεσθαι, ἕκαστος εἰς τὴν ἑαυτοῦ
to be enrolled, each man to the of himself
πόλιν. 4 Ἀνέβη δὲ καὶ Ἰωσὴφ ἀπὸ τῆς
city. So went up also Joseph from -
Γαλιλαίας ἐκ πόλεως Ναζαρὲθ εἰς τὴν
Galilee out of a city Nazareth to -
Ἰουδαίαν εἰς πόλιν Δαυὶδ ἥτις καλεῖται Βηθλέεμ,
Judæa to a city of David which is called Bethlehem,
διὰ τὸ εἶναι αὐτὸν ἐξ οἴκου καὶ
because of the to be him[b] out of [the] house and
= because he was
πατριᾶς Δαυίδ, 5 ἀπογράψασθαι σὺν Μαριὰμ
family of David, to be enrolled with Mary
τῇ ἐμνηστευμένῃ αὐτῷ, οὔσῃ ἐγκύῳ.
the[one] having been betrothed to him, being pregnant.

[e] Or whereby the dayspring will visit. Other ancient authorities read since the dayspring has visited

they were there, the time came for her to be delivered. ⁷And she gave birth to her first-born son and wrapped him in swaddling cloths, and laid him in a manger, because there was no place for them in the inn.

8 And in that region there were shepherds out in the field, keeping watch over their flock by night. ⁹And an angel of the Lord appeared to them, and the glory of the Lord shone around them, and they were filled with fear. ¹⁰And the angel said to them, "Be not afraid; for behold, I bring you good news of a great joy which will come to all the people; ¹¹for to you is born this day in the city of David a Savior, who is Christ the Lord. ¹²And this will be a sign for you: you will find a babe wrapped in swaddling cloths and lying in a manger." ¹³And suddenly there was with the angel a multitude of the heavenly host praising God and saying, ¹⁴"Glory to God in the highest,

and on earth peace among men with whom he is pleased!"ᶠ

15 When the angels went away from them

ᶠ Other ancient authorities read *peace, goodwill among men*

6 Ἐγένετο δὲ ἐν τῷ εἶναι αὐτοὺς ἐκεῖ
And it came to pass in the to be themᵇᵉ there
= while they were

ἐπλήσθησαν αἱ ἡμέραι τοῦ τεκεῖν αὐτήν,
were fulfilled the days – to bear her,ᵇᵈ
=for her to bear,

7 καὶ ἔτεκεν τὸν υἱὸν αὐτῆς τὸν πρωτότοκον,
and she bore the son of her the firstborn,

καὶ ἐσπαργάνωσεν αὐτὸν καὶ ἀνέκλινεν
and she swathed him and laid

αὐτὸν ἐν φάτνῃ, διότι οὐκ ἦν αὐτοῖς
him in a manger, because there was not for them

τόπος ἐν τῷ καταλύματι. 8 Καὶ ποιμένες
place in the inn. And shepherds

ἦσαν ἐν τῇ χώρᾳ τῇ αὐτῇ ἀγραυλοῦντες
there were in the country – same living in the fields

καὶ φυλάσσοντες φυλακὰς τῆς νυκτὸς ἐπὶ
and keeping guard of(in) the night over

τὴν ποίμνην αὐτῶν. 9 καὶ ἄγγελος κυρίου
the flock of them. And an angel of [the] Lord

ἐπέστη αὐτοῖς καὶ δόξα κυρίου περιέλαμψεν
came upon them and [the] glory of[the]Lord shone around

αὐτούς, καὶ ἐφοβήθησαν φόβον μέγαν.
them, and they feared fear a great.
=exceedingly.

10 καὶ εἶπεν αὐτοῖς ὁ ἄγγελος· μὴ
And said to them the angel: not

φοβεῖσθε· ἰδοὺ γὰρ εὐαγγελίζομαι ὑμῖν
Fear ye; for behold I announce to you

χαρὰν μεγάλην, ἥτις ἔσται παντὶ τῷ λαῷ,
joy a great, which will be to all the people,

11 ὅτι ἐτέχθη ὑμῖν σήμερον σωτήρ, ὅς
because was born to you to-day a Saviour, who

ἐστιν χριστὸς κύριος, ἐν πόλει Δαυίδ.
is Christ [the] Lord, in a city of David.

12 καὶ τοῦτο ὑμῖν σημεῖον, εὑρήσετε βρέφος
And this to you a sign, ye will find a babe

ἐσπαργανωμένον καὶ κείμενον ἐν φάτνῃ.
having been swathed and lying in a manger.

13 καὶ ἐξαίφνης ἐγένετο σὺν τῷ ἀγγέλῳ
And suddenly there was with the angel

πλῆθος στρατιᾶς οὐρανίου αἰνούντων τὸν
a multitude army of a heavenly praising –

θεὸν καὶ λεγόντων· 14 δόξα ἐν ὑψίστοις
God and saying: Glory in highest [places]

θεῷ καὶ ἐπὶ γῆς εἰρήνη ἐν ἀνθρώποις
to God and on earth peace among men

εὐδοκίας. 15 Καὶ ἐγένετο ὡς ἀπῆλθον
of goodwill. And it came to pass when went away

into heaven, the shepherds said to one another, "Let us go over to Bethlehem and see this thing that has happened, which the Lord has made known to us." [16]And they went with haste, and found Mary and Joseph, and the babe lying in a manger. [17]And when they saw it they made known the saying which had been told them concerning this child; [18]and all who heard it wondered at what the shepherds told them. [19]But Mary kept all these things, pondering them in her heart. [20]And the shepherds returned, glorifying and praising God for all they had heard and seen, as it had been told them.

21 And at the end of eight days, when he was circumcised, he was called Jesus, the name given by the angel before he was conceived in the womb.

22 And when the time came for their purification according to the

ἀπ' αὐτῶν εἰς τὸν οὐρανὸν οἱ ἄγγελοι,
from them to – heaven the angels,

οἱ ποιμένες ἐλάλουν πρὸς ἀλλήλους·
the shepherds said to one another :

διέλθωμεν δὴ ἕως Βηθλέεμ καὶ ἴδωμεν
Let us go then unto Bethlehem and let us see

τὸ ῥῆμα τοῦτο τὸ γεγονὸς ὃ ὁ κύριος
– thing this – having happened which the Lord

ἐγνώρισεν ἡμῖν. 16 καὶ ἦλθαν σπεύσαντες,
made known to us. And they came hastening,

καὶ ἀνεῦραν τήν τε Μαριὰμ καὶ τὸν
and found – both Mary and –

Ἰωσὴφ καὶ τὸ βρέφος κείμενον ἐν τῇ
Joseph and the babe lying in the

φάτνῃ· 17 ἰδόντες δὲ ἐγνώρισαν περὶ τοῦ
manger; and seeing they made known concerning the

ῥήματος τοῦ λαληθέντος αὐτοῖς περὶ τοῦ
word – spoken to them concerning –

παιδίου τούτου. 18 καὶ πάντες οἱ ἀκούσαντες
child this. And all the [ones] hearing

ἐθαύμασαν περὶ τῶν λαληθέντων ὑπὸ τῶν
marvelled concerning the things spoken by the

ποιμένων πρὸς αὐτούς· 19 ἡ δὲ Μαρία
shepherds to them; – but Mary

πάντα συνετήρει τὰ ῥήματα ταῦτα συμβάλλουσα
[3]all [1]kept – [2]things [3]these pondering

ἐν τῇ καρδίᾳ αὐτῆς. 20 καὶ ὑπέστρεψαν
in the heart of her. And returned

οἱ ποιμένες δοξάζοντες καὶ αἰνοῦντες τὸν
the shepherds glorifying and praising –

θεὸν ἐπὶ πᾶσιν οἷς ἤκουσαν καὶ εἶδον
God at all things which they heard and saw

καθὼς ἐλαλήθη πρὸς αὐτούς.
as was spoken to them.

21 Καὶ ὅτε ἐπλήσθησαν ἡμέραι ὀκτὼ
And when were completed days eight

τοῦ περιτεμεῖν αὐτόν, καὶ ἐκλήθη τὸ
– to circumcise him[d], and was called the

ὄνομα αὐτοῦ Ἰησοῦς, τὸ κληθὲν ὑπὸ τοῦ
name of him Jesus, the [name] called by the

ἀγγέλου πρὸ τοῦ συλλημφθῆναι αὐτὸν ἐν
angel before the to be conceived him[b] in
=he was conceived

τῇ κοιλίᾳ.
the womb.

22 Καὶ ὅτε ἐπλήσθησαν αἱ ἡμέραι τοῦ
And when were completed the days of the

καθαρισμοῦ αὐτῶν κατὰ τὸν νόμον
cleansing of them according to the law

law of Moses, they brought him up to Jerusalem to present him to the Lord ²³(as it is written in the law of the Lord, "Every male that opens the womb shall be called holy to the Lord") ²⁴and to offer a sacrifice according to what is said in the law of the Lord, "a pair of turtledoves, or two young pigeons." ²⁵Now there was a man in Jerusalem, whose name was Simeon, and this man was righteous and devout, looking for the consolation of Israel, and the Holy Spirit was upon him. ²⁶And it had been revealed to him by the Holy Spirit that he should not see death before he had seen the Lord's Christ. ²⁷And inspired by the Spirit⁷ he came into the temple; and when the parents brought in the child Jesus, to do for him according to the custom of the law, ²⁸he took him up in his arms and blessed God and said, ²⁹"Lord, now lettest thou thy servant depart in peace, according to thy word; ³⁰for mine eyes have seen thy salvation

Μωϋσέως, ἀνήγαγον αὐτὸν εἰς Ἱεροσόλυμα
of Moses,   they took up   him   to   Jerusalem
παραστῆσαι τῷ κυρίῳ, 23 καθὼς γέγραπται
to present to the Lord,   as it has been written
ἐν νόμῳ κυρίου ὅτι πᾶν ἄρσεν διανοῖγον
in [the] law of the Lord[,] – Every male opening
μήτραν ἅγιον τῷ κυρίῳ κληθήσεται, 24 καὶ
a womb holy to the Lord shall be called,   and
τοῦ δοῦναι θυσίαν κατὰ τὸ εἰρημένον ἐν
– to give^d a sacrifice according to the thing said in
τῷ νόμῳ κυρίου, ζεῦγος τρυγόνων ἢ δύο
the law of [the] Lord, a pair of turtledoves or two
νοσσοὺς περιστερῶν. 25 Καὶ ἰδοὺ ἄνθρωπος
nestlings   of doves.   And behold[,] a man
ἦν ἐν Ἰερουσαλὴμ ᾧ ὄνομα Συμεών, καὶ
was in Jerusalem to whom name^e Simeon, and
= whose name was
ὁ ἄνθρωπος οὗτος δίκαιος καὶ εὐλαβής,
– man   this [was] just and devout,
προσδεχόμενος παράκλησιν τοῦ Ἰσραήλ, καὶ
expecting [the] consolation – of Israel, and
πνεῦμα ἦν ἅγιον ἐπ' αὐτόν· 26 καὶ ἦν
¹[the] ⁴Spirit ⁵was ³Holy upon him;   and it was
αὐτῷ κεχρηματισμένον ὑπὸ τοῦ πνεύματος
to him *having been* communicated by the Spirit
τοῦ ἁγίου μὴ ἰδεῖν θάνατον πρὶν ἢ ἂν
– Holy not to see death   before
ἤδη τὸν χριστὸν κυρίου. 27 καὶ ἦλθεν
he should see the Christ of [the] Lord. And he came
ἐν τῷ πνεύματι εἰς τὸ ἱερόν· καὶ ἐν τῷ
by the Spirit into the temple; and in the
= as the(his) parents brought in
εἰσαγαγεῖν τοὺς γονεῖς τὸ παιδίον Ἰησοῦν
to bring in the parents^be the child Jesus
τοῦ ποιῆσαι αὐτοὺς κατὰ τὸ εἰθισμένον
– to do   them^bd according to the custom
= for them to do
τοῦ νόμου περὶ αὐτοῦ, 28 καὶ αὐτὸς
of the · law concerning him,   *and*   he
ἐδέξατο αὐτὸ εἰς τὰς ἀγκάλας καὶ
received him   in the(his) arms   and
εὐλόγησεν τὸν θεὸν καὶ εἶπεν· 29 νῦν
blessed   –   God and said :   Now
ἀπολύεις τὸν δοῦλόν σου, δέσποτα, κατὰ
thou releasest the slave of thee, Master, according to
τὸ ῥῆμά σου ἐν εἰρήνῃ· 30 ὅτι εἶδον οἱ
the word of thee in peace; because saw the
ὀφθαλμοί μου τὸ σωτήριόν σου, 31 ὃ
eyes   of me the salvation of thee, which

⁷ Or *in the Spirit*

³¹which thou hast pre-
    pared in the
    presence of all
    peoples,
³²a light for revelation
    to the Gentiles,
    and for glory to thy
    people Israel."

33 And his father and
his mother marveled at
what was said about
him; ³⁴and Simeon
blessed them and said to
Mary his mother,
  "Behold, this child is
    set for the fall and
    rising of many in
    Israel,
  and for a sign that is
    spoken against
³⁵(and a sword will
    pierce through
    your own soul
    also),
  that thoughts out of
    many hearts may
    be revealed."

36 And there was a
prophetess, Anna, the
daughter of Phan'u-el, of
the tribe of Asher; she
was of a great age, having
lived with her husband
seven years from her
virginity, ³⁷and as a
widow till she was
eighty-four. She did not
depart from the temple,
worshiping with fasting
and prayer night and
day. ³⁸And coming up
at that very hour she
gave thanks to God, and
spoke of him to all who
were looking for the
redemption of Jerusalem.

ἡτοίμασας κατὰ πρόσωπον πάντων τῶν
thou didst prepare before [the] face of all the
λαῶν, 32 φῶς εἰς ἀποκάλυψιν ἐθνῶν καὶ
peoples, a light for a revelation of [the] nations and
δόξαν λαοῦ σου Ἰσραήλ. 33 καὶ ἦν
a glory of [the] people of thee Israel. And ⁷was(were)
ὁ πατὴρ αὐτοῦ καὶ ἡ μήτηρ θαυμάζοντες
¹the ²father ³of him ⁴and ⁵the ⁶mother ⁸marvelling
ἐπὶ τοῖς λαλουμένοις περὶ αὐτοῦ. 34 καὶ
at the things being said concerning him. And
εὐλόγησεν αὐτοὺς Συμεὼν καὶ εἶπεν πρὸς
blessed them Simeon and said to
Μαριὰμ τὴν μητέρα αὐτοῦ· ἰδοὺ οὗτος
Mary the mother of him : Behold[,] this
κεῖται εἰς πτῶσιν καὶ ἀνάστασιν πολλῶν
is set for fall and rising again of many
ἐν τῷ Ἰσραὴλ καὶ εἰς σημεῖον ἀντιλεγ-
in – Israel and for a sign spoken
όμενον — 35 καὶ σοῦ δὲ αὐτῆς τὴν ψυχὴν
against — and ⁶of thee ⁷also ⁶[thy]self ⁵the ⁴soul
διελεύσεται ῥομφαία—, ὅπως ἂν ἀποκαλυφθῶσιν
²will go through ¹a sword —, so as – may be revealed
ἐκ πολλῶν καρδιῶν διαλογισμοί. 36 Καὶ
of many hearts [the] thoughts. And
ἦν Ἄννα προφῆτις, θυγάτηρ Φανουήλ, ἐκ
there was Anna a prophetess, a daughter of Phanuel, of
φυλῆς Ἀσήρ· αὕτη προβεβηκυῖα ἐν ἡμέραις
[the] tribe of Asher; this having advanced in days
πολλαῖς, ζήσασα μετὰ ἀνδρὸς ἔτη ἑπτὰ
many, having lived with a husband years seven
ἀπὸ τῆς παρθενίας αὐτῆς, 37 καὶ αὐτὴ
from the virginity of her, and she [was]
χήρα ἕως ἐτῶν ὀγδοήκοντα τεσσάρων, ἣ
a widow until years eighty-four, who
οὐκ ἀφίστατο τοῦ ἱεροῦ νηστείαις καὶ
withdrew not from the temple with fastings and
δεήσεσιν λατρεύουσα νύκτα καὶ ἡμέραν.
petitionings serving night and day.
38 καὶ αὐτῇ τῇ ὥρᾳ ἐπιστᾶσα ἀνθωμολογεῖτο
And at the very hour* coming upon she gave thanks
τῷ θεῷ καὶ ἐλάλει περὶ αὐτοῦ πᾶσιν τοῖς
– to God and spoke about him to all the [ones]
προσδεχομένοις λύτρωσιν Ἰερουσαλήμ. 39 Καὶ
expecting redemption in Jerusalem. And

* Strictly, this construction should mean "the hour itself"; but
the context demands "the same hour". See 10. 7, 21; 12. 12;
13. 1, 31; 20. 19; 23. 12; 24. 13. "Luke seems to be the only
N.T. writer who affects the construction" (C. F. D. Moule). See
also Acts 16. 18; 22. 13. Of course there is not a great difference
between "the hour itself", "the very hour", and "the same hour".

39 And when they had performed everything according to the law of the Lord, they returned into Galilee, to their own city, Nazareth. 40And the child grew and became strong, filled with wisdom; and the favor of God was upon him.

41 Now his parents went to Jerusalem every year at the feast of the Passover. 42And when he was twelve years old, they went up according to custom; 43and when the feast was ended, as they were returning, the boy Jesus stayed behind in Jerusalem. His parents did not know it, 44but supposing him to be in the company they went a day's journey, and they sought him among their kinsfolk and acquaintances; 45and when they did not find him, they returned to Jerusalem, seeking him. 46After three days they found him in the temple, sitting among the teachers, listening to them and asking them questions; 47and all who heard him were amazed at his understanding and his answers. 48And when

ὡς ἐτέλεσαν πάντα τὰ κατὰ τὸν νόμον
when they finished all things – according to the law
κυρίου, ἐπέστρεψαν εἰς τὴν Γαλιλαίαν εἰς
of [the] Lord, they returned to – Galilee to
πόλιν ἑαυτῶν Ναζαρέθ.
a city of themselves Nazareth.

40 Τὸ δὲ παιδίον ηὔξανεν καὶ ἐκραταιοῦτο
And the child grew and became strong
πληρούμενον σοφίᾳ, καὶ χάρις θεοῦ ἦν ἐπ'
being filled with wisdom, and [the] grace of God was upon
αὐτό.
him.

41 Καὶ ἐπορεύοντο οἱ γονεῖς αὐτοῦ κατ'
And went the parents of him year
ἔτος εἰς Ἰερουσαλὴμ τῇ ἑορτῇ τοῦ πάσχα.
by year† to Jerusalem at the feast of the Passover.

42 Καὶ ὅτε ἐγένετο ἐτῶν δώδεκα, ἀναβαινόντων
And when he became of years twelve, going up
                                                    =as they went up
αὐτῶν κατὰ τὸ ἔθος τῆς ἑορτῆς, 43 καὶ
them[a] according to the custom of the feast, and
τελειωσάντων τὰς ἡμέρας, ἐν τῷ ὑποστρέφειν
fulfilling[a] the days, in the to return
                                                    =when they returned
αὐτοὺς ὑπέμεινεν Ἰησοῦς ὁ παῖς ἐν
them[be] 4remained 3Jesus 1the 2boy in
Ἰερουσαλήμ, καὶ οὐκ ἔγνωσαν οἱ γονεῖς
Jerusalem, and 4knew not 1the 2parents
αὐτοῦ. 44 νομίσαντες δὲ αὐτὸν εἶναι ἐν
3of him. But supposing him to be in
τῇ συνοδίᾳ ἦλθον ἡμέρας ὁδὸν καὶ ἀνεζήτουν
the company they went of a day a journey and sought
αὐτὸν ἐν τοῖς συγγενεῦσιν καὶ τοῖς
him among the(ir) relatives and the(ir)
γνωστοῖς, 45 καὶ μὴ εὑρόντες ὑπέστρεψαν
acquaintances, and not finding returned
εἰς Ἰερουσαλὴμ ἀναζητοῦντες αὐτόν. 46 καὶ
to Jerusalem seeking him. And
ἐγένετο μετὰ ἡμέρας τρεῖς εὗρον αὐτὸν
it came to pass after days three they found him
ἐν τῷ ἱερῷ καθεζόμενον ἐν μέσῳ τῶν
in the temple sitting in [the] midst of the
διδασκάλων καὶ ἀκούοντα αὐτῶν καὶ
teachers both hearing them and
ἐπερωτῶντα αὐτούς· 47 ἐξίσταντο δὲ πάντες
questioning them; and were astonished all
οἱ ἀκούοντες αὐτοῦ ἐπὶ τῇ συνέσει καὶ
the [ones] hearing him at the intelligence and
ταῖς ἀποκρίσεσιν αὐτοῦ. 48 καὶ ἰδόντες
the answers of him. And seeing

they saw him they were
astonished; and his
mother said to him,
"Son, why have you
treated us so? Behold,
your father and I have
been looking for you
anxiously." ⁴⁹And he said
to them, "How is it that
you sought me? Did you
not know that I must be
in my Father's house?"
⁵⁰And they did not
understand the saying
which he spoke to them.
⁵¹And he went down with
them and came to
Nazareth, and was obed-
ient to them; and his
mother kept all these
things in her heart.

52 And Jesus in-
creased in wisdom and
in stature,ʰ and in favor
with God and man.

αὐτὸν ἐξεπλάγησαν, καὶ εἶπεν πρὸς αὐτὸν
him   they were astounded, and   said   to   him
ἡ μήτηρ αὐτοῦ· τέκνον, τί ἐποίησας ἡμῖν
the mother of him :   Child, why didst thou   to us
οὕτως; ἰδοὺ ὁ πατήρ σου κἀγὼ ὀδυνώμενοι
thus?   behold[,] the father of thee and I greatly distressed
ζητοῦμέν σε.   49 καὶ εἶπεν πρὸς αὐτούς·
are seeking thee.   And he said   to   them :
τί ὅτι ἐζητεῖτέ με; οὐκ ᾔδειτε ὅτι ἐν
Why [is it] that ye sought   me? did ye not know   that   in
                                                        =I
τοῖς   τοῦ πατρός μου δεῖ εἶναί με;
the [affairs] of the Father   of me it behoves to be   me?
must be about my Father's business?
50 καὶ αὐτοὶ οὐ συνῆκαν τὸ ῥῆμα ὃ
     And   they   did not understand the   word which
ἐλάλησεν αὐτοῖς.   51 καὶ κατέβη μετ'
he spoke   to them.   And he went down with
αὐτῶν καὶ ἦλθεν εἰς Ναζαρέθ, καὶ ἦν
them   and   came   to   Nazareth,   and was
ὑποτασσόμενος αὐτοῖς.   καὶ ἡ μήτηρ
being subject   to them.   And   the mother
αὐτοῦ διετήρει πάντα τὰ ῥήματα ἐν τῇ
of him carefully kept all   the   matters   in   the
καρδίᾳ αὐτῆς.   52 Καὶ Ἰησοῦς προέκοπτεν
heart   of her.   And   Jesus   progressed
ἐν τῇ σοφίᾳ καὶ ἡλικίᾳ καὶ χάριτι παρὰ
in   -   wisdom and   age   and favour before
θεῷ καὶ ἀνθρώποις.
God   and   men.

CHAPTER 3

IN the fifteenth year of
the reign of Tibeʹri-us
Caesar, Pontius Pilate
being governor of Judea,
and Herod being tetrarch
of Galilee, and his
brother Philip tetrarch of
the region of Ituraeʹa and
Trachoniʹtis, and Lysaʹ-
ni-as tetrarch of Abileʹne,
²in the high-priesthood
of Annas and Caʹiaphas,

3 Ἐν ἔτει δὲ πεντεκαιδεκάτῳ τῆς
  Now in [the] year   fifteenth   of the
ἡγεμονίας Τιβερίου Καίσαρος, ἡγεμονεύοντος
government   of Tiberius Cæsar,   governing
                                       =while Pontius Pilate
Ποντίου Πιλάτου τῆς Ἰουδαίας, καὶ
Pontius   Pilateᵃ   -   of Judæa,   and
was governing
τετρααρχοῦντος τῆς Γαλιλαίας Ἡρώδου,
ruling as tetrarch   -   of Galilee   Herod,ᵃ
=while Herod was ruling as tetrarch of Galilee,
Φιλίππου δὲ τοῦ ἀδελφοῦ αὐτοῦ τετρα-
and Philip the   brother   of him   ruling
αρχοῦντος τῆς Ἰτουραίας καὶ Τραχωνίτιδος
as tetrarchᵃ ¹of the   ³of Ituræa ⁴and ⁵of Trachonitis
χώρας, καὶ Λυσανίου τῆς Ἀβιληνῆς
²country, and Lysanias   of Abilene
τετρααρχοῦντος,   2 ἐπὶ ἀρχιερέως Ἄννα
ruling as tetrarchᵃ,   in the time of [the] high priest Anna

the word of God came to John the son of Zechari'ah in the wilderness; [3] and he went into all the region about the Jordan, preaching a baptism of repentance for the forgiveness of sins. [4] As it is written in the book of the words of Isaiah the prophet,

"The voice of one crying in the wilderness:
Prepare the way of the Lord,
make his paths straight.
[5] Every valley shall be filled,
and every mountain and hill shall be brought low,
and the crooked shall be made straight,
and the rough ways shall be made smooth;
[6] and all flesh shall see the salvation of God."

7 He said therefore to the multitudes that came out to be baptized by him, "You brood of vipers! Who warned you to flee from the wrath to come? [8] Bear fruits that befit repentance, and do not begin to say to yourselves, 'We have Abraham as our father'; for I tell you, God is able from these stones to raise up children to Abraham. [9] Even now the ax is laid to the root of the trees; every tree therefore that does not bear good fruit

καὶ Καϊάφα, ἐγένετο ῥῆμα θεοῦ ἐπὶ Ἰωάννην
and Caiaphas, came a word of God to John
τὸν Ζαχαρίου υἱὸν ἐν τῇ ἐρήμῳ. 3 καὶ
the of Zacharias son in the desert. And
ἦλθεν εἰς πᾶσαν τὴν περίχωρον τοῦ
he came into all the neighbourhood of the
Ἰορδάνου κηρύσσων βάπτισμα μετανοίας
Jordan proclaiming a baptism of repentance
εἰς ἄφεσιν ἁμαρτιῶν, 4 ὡς γέγραπται ἐν
for forgiveness of sins, as it has been written in
βίβλῳ λόγων Ἡσαΐου τοῦ προφήτου·
[the] roll of [the] words of Esaias the prophet:
φωνὴ βοῶντος ἐν τῇ ἐρήμῳ· ἑτοιμάσατε
Voice of [one] crying in the desert: Prepare ye
τὴν ὁδὸν κυρίου, εὐθείας ποιεῖτε τὰς
the way of [the] Lord, straight make the
τρίβους αὐτοῦ· 5 πᾶσα φάραγξ πληρωθήσεται
paths of him; every valley shall be filled up
καὶ πᾶν ὄρος καὶ βουνὸς ταπεινωθήσεται,
and every mountain and hill shall be laid low,
καὶ ἔσται τὰ σκολιὰ εἰς εὐθείας καὶ αἱ
and shall be the crooked [places] into straight [ones] and the
τραχεῖαι εἰς ὁδοὺς λείας· 6 καὶ ὄψεται
rough [places] into ways smooth; and [2]shall see
πᾶσα σὰρξ τὸ σωτήριον τοῦ θεοῦ.
[1]all [2]flesh the salvation — of God.

7 Ἔλεγεν οὖν τοῖς ἐκπορευομένοις ὄχλοις
He said therefore to the [2]going out [1]crowds
βαπτισθῆναι ὑπ' αὐτοῦ· γεννήματα ἐχιδνῶν,
to be baptized by him: Offspring of vipers,
τίς ὑπέδειξεν ὑμῖν φυγεῖν ἀπὸ τῆς
who warned you to flee from the
μελλούσης ὀργῆς; 8 ποιήσατε οὖν καρποὺς
coming wrath? Produce therefore fruits
ἀξίους τῆς μετανοίας· καὶ μὴ ἄρξησθε
worthy of repentance; and do not begin
λέγειν ἐν ἑαυτοῖς· πατέρα ἔχομεν τὸν
to say among yourselves: Father we have —
Ἀβραάμ· λέγω γὰρ ὑμῖν ὅτι δύναται ὁ
Abraham; for I tell you that [2]can [1]
θεὸς ἐκ τῶν λίθων τούτων ἐγεῖραι τέκνα
[1]God out of — stones these to raise children
τῷ Ἀβραάμ. 9 ἤδη δὲ καὶ ἡ ἀξίνη πρὸς
— to Abraham. And [2]already [1]even the axe at
τὴν ῥίζαν τῶν δένδρων κεῖται· πᾶν οὖν
the root of the trees is laid; [2]every [1]therefore
δένδρον μὴ ποιοῦν καρπὸν καλὸν
tree not producing fruit good

is cut down and thrown into the fire."

10 And the multitudes asked him, "What then shall we do?" [11]And he answered them, "He who has two coats, let him share with him who has none; and he who has food, let him do likewise." [12]Tax collectors also came to be baptized, and said to him, "Teacher, what shall we do?" [13]And he said to them, "Collect no more than is appointed you." [14]Soldiers also asked him, "And we, what shall we do?" And he said to them, "Rob no one by violence or by false accusation, and be content with your wages."

15 As the people were in expectation, and all men questioned in their hearts concerning John, whether perhaps he were the Christ, [16]John answered them all, "I baptize you with water; but he who is mightier than I is coming, the thong of whose sandals I am not worthy to untie; he will baptize you with the Holy Spirit and with fire. [17]His winnowing fork is in his hand, to clear his threshing floor,

ἐκκόπτεται καὶ εἰς πῦρ βάλλεται. 10 Καὶ
is being cut down and into fire is being cast.   And
ἐπηρώτων αὐτὸν οἱ ὄχλοι λέγοντες· τί
asked   him   the crowds   saying :   What
οὖν ποιήσωμεν; 11 ἀποκριθεὶς δὲ ἔλεγεν
then   may we do?   And answering   he told
αὐτοῖς· ὁ ἔχων δύο χιτῶνας μεταδότω
them : The [one] having two   tunics   let him impart
τῷ μὴ ἔχοντι, καὶ ὁ ἔχων βρώματα
to the [one] not having,   and the [one] having   foods
ὁμοίως ποιείτω. 12 ἦλθον δὲ καὶ τελῶναι
likewise let him do.   And there came also tax-collectors
βαπτισθῆναι καὶ εἶπαν πρὸς αὐτόν·
to be baptized   and   they said   to   him :
διδάσκαλε, τί ποιήσωμεν; 13 ὁ δὲ εἶπεν
Teacher,   what   may we do?   And he   said
πρὸς αὐτούς· μηδὲν πλέον παρὰ τὸ
to   them :   Nothing   more   besides the [thing]
διατεταγμένον ὑμῖν πράσσετε. 14 ἐπηρώτων δὲ
having been commanded you   do ye.   And asked
αὐτὸν καὶ στρατευόμενοι λέγοντες· τί
him   also men serving in the army   saying :   What
ποιήσωμεν καὶ ἡμεῖς; καὶ εἶπεν αὐτοῖς·
may do   also   we?   And   he told   them :
μηδένα διασείσητε μηδὲ συκοφαντήσητε,
No one   intimidate   nor   accuse falsely,
καὶ ἀρκεῖσθε τοῖς ὀψωνίοις ὑμῶν.
and be satisfied   with the   pay   of you.
15 Προσδοκῶντος δὲ τοῦ λαοῦ καὶ
Now expecting   the   people[a] and
= while the people were expecting and all were debating
διαλογιζομένων πάντων ἐν ταῖς καρδίαις
debating   all[a]   in the   hearts
αὐτῶν περὶ τοῦ Ἰωάννου, μήποτε αὐτὸς
of them concerning -   John,   perhaps   he
εἴη ὁ χριστός, 16 ἀπεκρίνατο λέγων πᾶσιν
might be the Christ,   [2]answered [3]saying [4]to all
ὁ Ἰωάννης· ἐγὼ μὲν ὕδατι βαπτίζω ὑμᾶς·
-   [1]John :   I indeed with water baptize   you;
ἔρχεται δὲ ὁ ἰσχυρότερός μου, οὗ οὐκ
but there comes the [one] stronger   of me, of whom not
= than I,
εἰμὶ ἱκανὸς λῦσαι τὸν ἱμάντα τῶν ὑποδημά-
I am competent to loosen the   thong   of the   san-
των αὐτοῦ· αὐτὸς ὑμᾶς βαπτίσει ἐν
dals of him;   he   you   will baptize with
πνεύματι ἁγίῳ καὶ πυρί· 17 οὗ τὸ πτύον
Spirit   [the] Holy and fire;   of whom the   fan [is]
ἐν τῇ χειρὶ αὐτοῦ διακαθᾶραι τὴν ἅλωνα
in the hand of him thoroughly to cleanse the threshing-floor

and to gather the wheat into his granary, but the chaff he will burn with unquenchable fire."
18 So, with many other exhortations, he preached good news to the people. 19 But Herod the tetrarch, who had been reproved by him for Hero'di-as, his brother's wife, and for all the evil things that Herod had done, 20 added this to them all, that he shut up John in prison.

21 Now when all the people were baptized, and when Jesus also had been baptized and was praying, the heaven was opened, 22 and the Holy Spirit descended upon him in bodily form, as a dove, and a voice came from heaven, "Thou art my beloved Son;¹ with thee I am well pleased."ʲ

23 Jesus, when he began his ministry, was about thirty years of age, being the son (as was supposed) of Joseph, the son of Heli, 24 the son of Matthat, the son of Levi, the son of Melchi, the son of Jan'na-i, the son of Joseph, 25 the son of Mattathi'as, the son of Amos, the son of Nahum, the son of Esli, the son of Nag'ga-i, 26 the son of Ma'ath, the son of Mattathi'as, the son of Sem'e-in, the son of Josech, the son of Joda,

¹ Or my Son, my (or the) Beloved
ʲ Other ancient authorities read today I have begotten thee

αὐτοῦ   καὶ   συναγαγεῖν   τὸν   σῖτον   εἰς   τὴν
of him   and   to gather   the   wheat   into   the

ἀποθήκην   αὐτοῦ,   τὸ   δὲ   ἄχυρον   κατακαύσει
barn   of him,   but the   chaff   he will burn up

πυρὶ   ἀσβέστῳ.   18 Πολλὰ   μὲν   οὖν   καὶ
with fire unquenchable.   Many things   indeed   therefore   and

ἕτερα   παρακαλῶν   εὐηγγελίζετο   τὸν   λαόν·
different   exhorting   he evangelized   the   people;

19 ὁ   δὲ   Ἡρῴδης   ὁ   τετραάρχης,   ἐλεγχόμενος
- but   Herod   the   tetrarch,   being reproved

ὑπ'   αὐτοῦ   περὶ   Ἡρῳδιάδος   τῆς   γυναικὸς
by   him concerning   Herodias   the   wife

τοῦ   ἀδελφοῦ   αὐτοῦ   καὶ   περὶ   πάντων   ὧν
of the   brother   of him   and   concerning   ¹all   ²things   ⁴which

ἐποίησεν   πονηρῶν   ὁ   Ἡρῴδης,   20 προσέθηκεν
¹did   ²evil   -   ⁵Herod,   added

καὶ   τοῦτο   ἐπὶ   πᾶσιν,   κατέκλεισεν   τὸν
also   this   above   all,   he shut up

Ἰωάννην   ἐν   φυλακῇ.
John   in   prison.

21 Ἐγένετο   δὲ   ἐν   τῷ   βαπτισθῆναι   ἅπαντα
Now it came to pass in   the   to be baptized   all
                                =when all the people were baptized

τὸν   λαὸν   καὶ   Ἰησοῦ   βαπτισθέντος   καὶ
the   people*ᵇᵉ   and   Jesus   being baptized   and
                              =as Jesus had been baptized and was praying

προσευχομένου   ἀνεῳχθῆναι   τὸν   οὐρανὸν   22 καὶ
praying*   to be opened   the   heaven   and
          =the heaven was opened and the Holy Spirit came down

καταβῆναι   τὸ   πνεῦμα   τὸ   ἅγιον   σωματικῷ
to come down   the   Spirit   -   Holyᵇ   in a bodily

εἴδει   ὡς   περιστερὰν   ἐπ'   αὐτόν,   καὶ   φωνὴν
form   as   a dove   upon   him,   and   a voice

ἐξ   οὐρανοῦ   γενέσθαι·   σὺ   εἶ   ὁ   υἱός   μου
out of   heaven   to comeᵇ: Thou art   the   Son   of me

ὁ   ἀγαπητός,   ἐν   σοὶ   εὐδόκησα.   23 Καὶ
-   beloved,   in   thee   I was well pleased.   And

αὐτός   ἦν   Ἰησοῦς   ἀρχόμενος   ὡσεὶ   ἐτῶν
¹himself   ²was   ¹Jesus   ⁴beginning   about   years

τριάκοντα,   ὢν   υἱός,   ὡς   ἐνομίζετο,   Ἰωσήφ,
thirty,   being son,   as   was supposed,   of Joseph,

τοῦ   Ἡλὶ   24 τοῦ   Ματθὰτ   τοῦ   Λευὶ   τοῦ
-   of Eli   -   of Matthat   -   of Levi   -

Μελχὶ   τοῦ   Ἰανναὶ   τοῦ   Ἰωσὴφ   25 τοῦ
of Melchi   -   of Jannai   -   of Joseph   -

Ματταθίου   τοῦ   Ἀμὼς   τοῦ   Ναοὺμ   τοῦ
of Mattathias   -   of Amos   -   of Naum   -

Ἐσλὶ   τοῦ   Ναγγαὶ   26 τοῦ   Μάαθ   τοῦ
of Hesli   -   of Naggai   -   of Maath   -

[27] the son of Jo-an'an, the son of Rhesa, the son of Zerub'babel, the son of She-al'ti-el, the son of Neri, [28] the son of Melchi, the son of Addi, the son of Cosam, the son of Elma'dam, the son of Er, [29] the son of Joshua, the son of Elie'zer, the son of Jorim, the son of Matthat, the son of Levi, [30] the son of Simeon, the son of Judah, the son of Joseph, the son of Jonam, the son of Eli'akim, [31] the son of Me'le-a, the son of Menna, the son of Mat'-tatha, the son of Nathan, the son of David, [32] the son of Jesse, the son of Obed, the son of Bo'az, the son of Sala, the son of Nahshon, [33] the son of Ammin'adab, the son of Admin, the son of Arni, the son of Hezron, the son of Perez, the son of Judah, [34] the son of Jacob, the son of Isaac, the son of Abraham, the son of Terah, the son of Nahor, [35] the son of Serug, the son of Re'u, the son of Peleg, the son of Eber, the son of Shelah, [36] the son of Ca-i'nan, the son of Arpha'xad, the son of Shem, the son of Noah, the son of Lamech, [37] the son of Methuselah, the son of Enoch, the son of Jared, the son of Maha'lale-el, the son of Ca-i'nan, [38] the son of Enos, the son of Seth, the son of Adam, the son of God.

Ματταθίου	τοῦ	Σεμεῖν	τοῦ	Ἰωσὴχ	τοῦ
of Mattathias	–	of Semein	–	of Josech	–
Ἰωδὰ	27 τοῦ	Ἰωανὰν	τοῦ	Ῥησὰ	τοῦ
of Jodah	–	of Joanan	–	of Rhesa	–
Ζοροβαβὲλ	τοῦ	Σαλαθιὴλ	τοῦ	Νηρὶ	28 τοῦ
of Zorobabel	–	of Salathiel	–	of Neri	–
Μελχὶ	τοῦ	Ἀδδὶ	τοῦ	Κωσὰμ	τοῦ
of Melchi	–	of Addi	–	of Kosam	–
Ἐλμαδὰμ	τοῦ	Ἢρ	29 τοῦ	Ἰησοῦ	τοῦ
of Elmadam	–	of Er	–	of Jesus	–
Ἐλιέζερ	τοῦ	Ἰωρὶμ	τοῦ	Μαθθὰτ	τοῦ
of Eliezer	–	of Jorim	–	of Matthat	–
Λευὶ	30 τοῦ	Συμεὼν	τοῦ	Ἰούδα	τοῦ
of Levi	–	of Simeon	–	of Juda	–
Ἰωσὴφ	τοῦ	Ἰωνὰμ	τοῦ	Ἐλιακὶμ	31 τοῦ
of Joseph	–	of Jonam	–	of Eliakim	–
Μελεὰ	τοῦ	Μεννὰ	τοῦ	Ματταθὰ	τοῦ
of Melea	–	of Menna	–	of Mattatha	–
Ναθὰμ	τοῦ	Δαυὶδ	32 τοῦ	Ἰεσσαὶ	τοῦ
of Natham	–	of David	–	of Jesse	–
Ἰωβὴδ	τοῦ	Βόος	τοῦ	Σάλα	τοῦ Ναασσὼν
of Jobed	–	of Boos	–	of Sala	– of Naasson
33 τοῦ	Ἀμιναδὰβ	τοῦ	Ἀδμὶν	τοῦ	Ἀρνὶ
–	of Aminadab	–	of Admin	–	of Arni
τοῦ	Ἑσρὼμ	τοῦ	Φάρες	τοῦ	Ἰούδα
–	of Hesrom	–	of Phares	–	of Juda
34 τοῦ	Ἰακὼβ	τοῦ	Ἰσαὰκ	τοῦ	Ἀβραὰμ
–	of Jacob	–	of Isaac	–	of Abraham
τοῦ	Θάρα	τοῦ	Ναχὼρ	35 τοῦ	Σερούχ
–	of Thara	–	of Nachor	–	of Seruch
τοῦ	Ῥαγαὺ	τοῦ	Φάλεκ	τοῦ	Ἕβερ τοῦ
–	of Rhagau	–	of Phalek	–	of Eber –
Σάλα	36 τοῦ	Καϊνὰμ	τοῦ	Ἀρφαξὰδ	τοῦ
of Sala	–	of Cainam	–	of Arphaxad	–
Σὴμ	τοῦ Νῶε	τοῦ	Λάμεχ	37 τοῦ	Μαθουσάλα
of Sem	– of Noe	– of Lamech	–	of Mathusala
τοῦ	Ἑνὼχ	τοῦ	Ἰάρετ	τοῦ	Μαλελεὴλ
–	of Henoch	–	of Jaret	–	of Maleleel
τοῦ	Καϊνὰμ	38 τοῦ	Ἐνὼς	τοῦ	Σὴθ τοῦ
–	of Cainam	–	of Enos	–	of Seth –
Ἀδὰμ	τοῦ	θεοῦ.			
of Adam	–	of God.			

4 Ἰησοῦς	δὲ	πλήρης	πνεύματος	ἁγίου
And Jesus		full	of [the] [²]Spirit	[¹]Holy
ὑπέστρεψεν	ἀπὸ	τοῦ	Ἰορδάνου,	καὶ	ἤγετο
returned	from	the	Jordan,	and	was led

CHAPTER 4

AND Jesus, full of the Holy Spirit, returned from the Jordan, and was led by the Spirit ²for forty days in the wilderness, tempted by the devil. And he ate nothing in those days; and when they were ended, he was hungry. ³The devil said to him, "If you are the Son of God, command this stone to become bread." ⁴And Jesus answered him, "It is written, 'Man shall not live by bread alone.'" ⁵And the devil took him up, and showed him all the kingdoms of the world in a moment of time, ⁶and said to him, "To you I will give all this authority and their glory; for it has been delivered to me, and I give it to whom I will. ⁷If you, then, will worship me, it shall all be yours." ⁸And Jesus answered him, "It is written,

'You shall worship the Lord your God, and him only shall you serve.'"

⁹And he took him to Jerusalem, and set him on the pinnacle of the temple, and said to him, "If you are the Son of God, throw yourself down from here; ¹⁰for it is written,

'He will give his angels charge of you, to

ἐν τῷ πνεύματι ἐν τῇ ἐρήμῳ 2 ἡμέρας
by the Spirit in the desert days

τεσσεράκοντα πειραζόμενος ὑπὸ τοῦ διαβόλου.
forty being tempted by the devil.

Καὶ οὐκ ἔφαγεν οὐδὲν ἐν ταῖς ἡμέραις
And he ate not no(any)thing in - days

ἐκείναις, καὶ συντελεσθεισῶν αὐτῶν ἐπεί-
those, and being ended themᵃ he
=when they were ended

νασεν. 3 εἶπεν δὲ αὐτῷ ὁ διάβολος·
hungered. And said to him the devil:

εἰ υἱὸς εἶ τοῦ θεοῦ, εἰπὲ τῷ λίθῳ
If Son thou art - of God, tell the stone

τούτῳ ἵνα γένηται ἄρτος. 4 καὶ ἀπεκρίθη
this that it become a loaf. And made answer

πρὸς αὐτὸν ὁ Ἰησοῦς· γέγραπται ὅτι
to him - Jesus : It has been written[,] -

οὐκ ἐπ' ἄρτῳ μόνῳ ζήσεται ὁ ἄνθρωπος.
Not on bread only shall live - man.

5 Καὶ ἀναγαγὼν αὐτὸν ἔδειξεν αὐτῷ πάσας
And leading up him he showed him all

τὰς βασιλείας τῆς οἰκουμένης ἐν στιγμῇ
the kingdoms of the inhabited earth in a moment

χρόνου. 6 καὶ εἶπεν αὐτῷ ὁ διάβολος·
of time. And said to him the devil:

σοὶ δώσω τὴν ἐξουσίαν ταύτην ἅπασαν καὶ
To thee I will give - authority this all and

τὴν δόξαν αὐτῶν, ὅτι ἐμοὶ παραδέδοται
the glory of them, because to me it has been delivered

καὶ ᾧ ἐὰν θέλω δίδωμι αὐτήν· 7 σὺ οὖν
and to whomever I wish I give it; ⁸thou ¹therefore

ἐὰν προσκυνήσῃς ἐνώπιον ἐμοῦ, ἔσται σοῦ
²if worship before me, will be of thee

πᾶσα. 8 καὶ ἀποκριθεὶς ὁ Ἰησοῦς εἶπεν
all. And answering - Jesus said

αὐτῷ· γέγραπται· προσκυνήσεις κύριον τὸν
to him : It has been written: Thou shalt worship [the] Lord the

θεόν σου καὶ αὐτῷ μόνῳ λατρεύσεις.
God of thee and him only shalt thou serve.

9 Ἤγαγεν δὲ αὐτὸν εἰς Ἰερουσαλὴμ καὶ
And he led him to Jerusalem and

ἔστησεν ἐπὶ τὸ πτερύγιον τοῦ ἱεροῦ, καὶ
set on the gable of the temple, and

εἶπεν αὐτῷ· εἰ υἱὸς εἶ τοῦ θεοῦ, βάλε
said to him : If Son thou art - of God, throw

σεαυτὸν ἐντεῦθεν κάτω· 10 γέγραπται γὰρ ὅτι
thyself hence down; for it has been written[,] -

τοῖς ἀγγέλοις αὐτοῦ ἐντελεῖται περὶ
The angels of him he will command concerning

guard you,'
11 and
'On their hands they
will bear you up,
lest you strike your
foot against a
stone.' "
12 And Jesus answered
him, "It is said, 'You
shall not tempt the Lord
your God.' " 13 And when
the devil had ended every
temptation, he departed
from him until an
opportune time.
14 And Jesus returned
in the power of the
Spirit into Galilee, and a
report concerning him
went out through all the
surrounding country.
15 And he taught in their
synagogues, being glori-
fied by all.
16 And he came to
Nazareth, where he had
been brought up; and he
went to the synagogue,
as his custom was, on the
sabbath day. And he
stood up to read; 17 and
there was given to him
the book of the prophet
Isaiah. He opened the
book and found the
place where it was
written,
18 "The Spirit of the Lord
is upon me,
because he has
anointed me to
preach good news
to the poor.
He has sent me to
proclaim release to
the captives
and recovering of
sight to the blind,
to set at liberty those
who are oppressed,

σοῦ   τοῦ   διαφυλάξαι   σε,   11 καὶ ὅτι ἐπὶ
thee   –   to preserve[d]   thee,   and   –   on

χειρῶν   ἀροῦσίν   σε,   μήποτε   προσκόψῃς
[their] hands   they will bear   thee,   lest   thou dash

πρὸς   λίθον   τὸν   πόδα   σου.   12 καὶ
against   a stone   the   foot   of thee.   And

ἀποκριθεὶς   εἶπεν   αὐτῷ   ὁ   Ἰησοῦς   ὅτι
answering   said   to him   –   Jesus[,]   –

εἴρηται·   οὐκ   ἐκπειράσεις   κύριον   τὸν
It has been said :   Thou shalt not overtempt   [the] Lord   the

θεόν σου.   13 Καὶ   συντελέσας   πάντα   πειρασμὸν
God of thee.   And having finished   every   temptation

ὁ   διάβολος   ἀπέστη   ἀπ'   αὐτοῦ   ἄχρι   καιροῦ.
the   devil   went away   from   him   until   a season.

14 Καὶ   ὑπέστρεψεν   ὁ   Ἰησοῦς   ἐν   τῇ
And   returned   –   Jesus   in   the

δυνάμει   τοῦ   πνεύματος   εἰς   τὴν   Γαλιλαίαν·
power   of the   Spirit   to   –   Galilee;

καὶ   φήμη   ἐξῆλθεν   καθ'   ὅλης   τῆς   περιχώρου
and a rumour   went forth   throughout   all   the   neighbourhood

περὶ   αὐτοῦ.   15 καὶ   αὐτὸς   ἐδίδασκεν   ἐν
concerning   him.   And   he   taught   in

ταῖς   συναγωγαῖς   αὐτῶν,   δοξαζόμενος   ὑπὸ
the   synagogues   of them,   being glorified   by

πάντων.
all.

16 Καὶ   ἦλθεν   εἰς   Ναζαρά,   οὗ   ἦν
And   he came   to   Nazareth,   where   he was

τεθραμμένος,   καὶ   εἰσῆλθεν   κατὰ   τὸ   εἰωθὸς
having been   and   entered   accord-   the   custom
brought up,   ing to   = his custom

αὐτῷ   ἐν   τῇ   ἡμέρᾳ   τῶν   σαββάτων   εἰς   τὴν
to him[e]   on the   day   of the   sabbaths   into   the

συναγωγήν,   καὶ   ἀνέστη   ἀναγνῶναι.   17 καὶ
synagogue,   and   stood up   to read.   And

ἐπεδόθη   αὐτῷ   βιβλίον   τοῦ   προφήτου
was handed   to him   a roll   of the   prophet

Ἠσαΐου,   καὶ   ἀνοίξας   τὸ   βιβλίον   εὗρεν
Esaias,   and having opened   the   roll   he found

[τὸν]   τόπον   οὗ   ἦν   γεγραμμένον·   18 πνεῦμα
the   place   where it was   having been written :   [The] Spirit

κυρίου   ἐπ'   ἐμέ,   οὗ   εἵνεκεν   ἔχρισέν   με
of [the] Lord [is]   upon me,   wherefore   he anointed   me

εὐαγγελίσασθαι   πτωχοῖς,   ἀπέσταλκέν   με
to evangelize   [the] poor,   he has sent   me

κηρῦξαι   αἰχμαλώτοις   ἄφεσιν   καὶ   τυφλοῖς
to proclaim   to captives   release   and to blind [ones]

ἀνάβλεψιν,   ἀποστεῖλαι   τεθραυσμένους   ἐν
sight,   to send away   having been crushed [ones]   in

¹⁹to proclaim the acceptable year of the Lord."

²⁰And he closed the book, and gave it back to the attendant, and sat down; and the eyes of all in the synagogue were fixed on him. ²¹And he began to say to them, "Today this scripture has been fulfilled in your hearing." ²²And all spoke well of him, and wondered at the gracious words which proceeded out of his mouth; and they said, "Is not this Joseph's son?" ²³And he said to them, "Doubtless you will quote to me this proverb, 'Physician, heal yourself; what we have heard you did at Caper'-na-um, do here also in your own country.'" ²⁴And he said, "Truly, I say to you, no prophet is acceptable in his own country. ²⁵But in truth, I tell you, there were many widows in Israel in the days of Eli'jah, when the heaven was shut up three years and six months, when there came a great famine over all the land; ²⁶and Eli'jah was sent to none of them but only to Zar'ephath, in the land of Sidon, to a woman who was a widow. ²⁷And

ἀφέσει, **19** κηρῦξαι ἐνιαυτὸν κυρίου δεκτόν.
release,   to proclaim   a year   of [the] Lord acceptable.

20 καὶ πτύξας τὸ βιβλίον ἀποδοὺς τῷ
And having closed the roll returning [it] to the
ὑπηρέτῃ ἐκάθισεν· καὶ πάντων οἱ ὀφθαλμοὶ
attendant   he sat;   and   of all   the   eyes
ἐν τῇ συναγωγῇ ἦσαν ἀτενίζοντες αὐτῷ.
in   the synagogue were   gazing   at him.
21 ἤρξατο δὲ λέγειν πρὸς αὐτοὺς ὅτι –
And he began   to say   to   them[,]   –
σήμερον πεπλήρωται ἡ γραφὴ αὕτη ἐν
To-day   has been fulfilled – scripture this   in
τοῖς ὠσὶν ὑμῶν. **22** καὶ πάντες ἐμαρτύρουν
the   ears of you.   And   all   bore witness
αὐτῷ καὶ ἐθαύμαζον ἐπὶ τοῖς λόγοις τῆς
to him and   marvelled   at   the   words   –
χάριτος τοῖς ἐκπορευομένοις ἐκ τοῦ στόματος
of grace   –   proceeding   out of the   mouth
αὐτοῦ, καὶ ἔλεγον· οὐχὶ υἱός ἐστιν ᾽Ιωσὴφ
of him,   and they said: ²not   ¹son   ⁵of Joseph
οὗτος; **23** καὶ εἶπεν πρὸς αὐτούς· πάντως
³this man?   And   he said   to   them :   To be sure
ἐρεῖτέ μοι τὴν παραβολὴν ταύτην· ἰατρέ,
ye will say to me   the   parable   this :   Physician,
θεράπευσον σεαυτόν· ὅσα ἠκούσαμεν γεν-
heal   thyself;   what things   we heard   hap-
όμενα εἰς τὴν Καφαρναούμ, ποίησον καὶ
pening in   –   Capernaum,   do   also
ὧδε ἐν τῇ πατρίδι σου. **24** εἶπεν δέ·
here in   the   native place of thee.   And he said :
ἀμὴν λέγω ὑμῖν ὅτι οὐδεὶς προφήτης
Truly   I tell   you   that   no   prophet
δεκτός ἐστιν ἐν τῇ πατρίδι αὐτοῦ. **25** ἐπ᾽
acceptable is   in   the   native place of him.   ²on(in)
ἀληθείας δὲ λέγω ὑμῖν, πολλαὶ χῆραι ἦσαν
³truth   ¹But I tell   you,   many widows   were
ἐν ταῖς ἡμέραις ῾Ηλίου ἐν τῷ ᾽Ισραήλ,
in   the   days   of Elias   in   –   Israel,
ὅτε ἐκλείσθη ὁ οὐρανὸς ἐπὶ ἔτη τρία καὶ
when   was shut up the heaven   over years three   and
μῆνας ἕξ, ὡς ἐγένετο λιμὸς μέγας ἐπὶ
months six,   when   came   famine a great   over
πᾶσαν τὴν γῆν, **26** καὶ πρὸς οὐδεμίαν
all   the land,   and   to   not one
αὐτῶν ἐπέμφθη ῾Ηλίας εἰ μὴ εἰς Σάρεπτα
of them   was sent   Elias   except   to   Sarepta
τῆς Σιδωνίας πρὸς γυναῖκα χήραν. **27** καὶ
–   of Sidon   to   a woman a widow.   And

there were many lepers in Israel in the time of the prophet Eli'sha; and none of them was cleansed, but only Na'aman the Syrian." ²⁸When they heard this, all in the synagogue were filled with wrath. ²⁹And they rose up and put him out of the city, and led him to the brow of the hill on which their city was built, that they might throw him down headlong. ³⁰But passing through the midst of them he went away.

31 And he went down to Caper'na-um, a city of Galilee. And he was teaching them on the sabbath; ³²and they were astonished at his teaching, for his word was with authority. ³³And in the synagogue there was a man who had the spirit of an unclean demon; and he cried out with a loud voice, ³⁴"Ah!ᵏ What have you to do with us, Jesus of Nazareth? Have you come to destroy us? I know who you are, the Holy One of God." ³⁵But Jesus rebuked him, saying, "Be silent, and come out of him!" And when the demon had thrown him down in the midst, he came out of him, having done him no harm. ³⁶And they were all

ᵏ Or Let us alone

πολλοὶ λεπροὶ ἦσαν ἐν τῷ Ἰσραὴλ ἐπὶ
many lepers were in – Israel during
Ἐλισαίου τοῦ προφήτου, καὶ οὐδεὶς αὐτῶν
Elisæus the prophet, and not one of them
ἐκαθαρίσθη εἰ μὴ Ναιμὰν ὁ Σύρος.
was cleansed except Naaman the Syrian.
28 καὶ ἐπλήσθησαν πάντες θυμοῦ ἐν τῇ
And ²were filled ¹all of(with) anger in the
συναγωγῇ ἀκούοντες ταῦτα, 29 καὶ ἀναστάντες
synagogue hearing these things, and rising up
ἐξέβαλον αὐτὸν ἔξω τῆς πόλεως, καὶ
they cast out him outside the city, and
ἤγαγον αὐτὸν ἕως ὀφρύος τοῦ ὄρους ἐφ'
led him to a brow of the hill on
οὗ ἡ πόλις ᾠκοδόμητο αὐτῶν, ὥστε
which the city was built of them, so as
κατακρημνίσαι αὐτόν· 30 αὐτὸς δὲ διελθὼν
to throw down him; but he passing through
διὰ μέσου αὐτῶν ἐπορεύετο.
through [the] midst of them went.
31 Καὶ κατῆλθεν εἰς Καφαρναοὺμ πόλιν
And he went down to Capernaum a city
τῆς Γαλιλαίας. καὶ ἦν διδάσκων αὐτοὺς
of Galilee. And he was teaching them
ἐν τοῖς σάββασιν· 32 καὶ ἐξεπλήσσοντο
on the sabbaths; and they were astounded
ἐπὶ τῇ διδαχῇ αὐτοῦ, ὅτι ἐν ἐξουσίᾳ
at the teaching of him, because with authority
ἦν ὁ λόγος αὐτοῦ. 33 καὶ ἐν τῇ συναγωγῇ
was the word of him. And in the synagogue
ἦν ἄνθρωπος ἔχων πνεῦμα δαιμονίου
there was a man having a spirit ²demon
ἀκαθάρτου, καὶ ἀνέκραξεν φωνῇ μεγάλῃ·
¹of an unclean, and he shouted voice with a great :
34 ἔα, τί ἡμῖν καὶ σοί, Ἰησοῦ Ναζαρηνέ;
Ah, what to us and to thee, Jesus Nazarene?
ἦλθες ἀπολέσαι ἡμᾶς; οἶδά σε τίς εἶ,
Camest thou to destroy us? I know thee who thou art,
ὁ ἅγιος τοῦ θεοῦ. 35 καὶ ἐπετίμησεν αὐτῷ
the holy one of God. And rebuked him
ὁ Ἰησοῦς λέγων· φιμώθητι καὶ ἔξελθε
– Jesus saying : Be muzzled and come out
ἀπ' αὐτοῦ. καὶ ῥῖψαν αὐτὸν τὸ δαιμόνιον
from him. And ³throwing ⁴him ¹the ²demon
εἰς τὸ μέσον ἐξῆλθεν ἀπ' αὐτοῦ μηδὲν
in the midst came out from him nothing
βλάψαν αὐτόν. 36 καὶ ἐγένετο θάμβος
injuring him. And came astonishment

amazed and said to one another, "What is this word? For with authority and power he commands the unclean spirits, and they come out." [37]And reports of him went out into every place in the surrounding region.

38 And he arose and left the synagogue, and entered Simon's house. Now Simon's mother-in-law was ill with a high fever, and they besought him for her. [39]And he stood over her and rebuked the fever, and it left her; and immediately she rose and served them.

40 Now when the sun was setting, all those who had any that were sick with various diseases brought them to him; and he laid his hands on every one of them and healed them. [41]And demons also came out of many, crying, "You are the Son of God!" But he rebuked them, and would not allow them to speak, because they knew that he was the Christ.

42 And when it was day he departed and went into a lonely place. And the people sought

---

ἐπὶ πάντας, καὶ συνελάλουν πρὸς ἀλλήλους
on   all,   and they spoke   to   one another

λέγοντες· τίς ὁ λόγος οὗτος, ὅτι ἐν
saying : What [is] – word this, because with

ἐξουσίᾳ καὶ δυνάμει ἐπιτάσσει τοῖς
authority and power he commands the

ἀκαθάρτοις πνεύμασιν καὶ ἐξέρχονται; 37 καὶ
unclean   spirits   and they come out?   And

ἐξεπορεύετο ἦχος περὶ αὐτοῦ εἰς πάντα
went forth a rumour concerning him into every

τόπον τῆς περιχώρου.   38 Ἀναστὰς δὲ
place of the neighbourhood.   And rising up

ἀπὸ τῆς συναγωγῆς εἰσῆλθεν εἰς τὴν
from the synagogue   he entered into the

οἰκίαν Σίμωνος. πενθερὰ δὲ τοῦ Σίμωνος
house of Simon. And [the] mother-in-law – of Simon

ἦν συνεχομένη πυρετῷ μεγάλῳ, καὶ
was being seized fever   with a great,   and

ἠρώτησαν αὐτὸν περὶ αὐτῆς.   39 καὶ
they ask   him   about her.   And

ἐπιστὰς ἐπάνω αὐτῆς ἐπετίμησεν τῷ πυρετῷ,
standing   over her he rebuked the fever,

καὶ ἀφῆκεν αὐτήν· παραχρῆμα δὲ ἀναστᾶσα
and it left her;   and at once rising up

διηκόνει αὐτοῖς.   40 Δύνοντος δὲ τοῦ
she served them.   And setting   the
                                 = as the sun was setting

ἡλίου ἅπαντες ὅσοι εἶχον ἀσθενοῦντας
sun[a]   all   as many as had ailing [ones]

νόσοις ποικίλαις ἤγαγον αὐτοὺς πρὸς αὐτόν·
diseases with various brought them   to   him;

ὁ δὲ ἑνὶ ἑκάστῳ αὐτῶν τὰς χεῖρας
and he [5]one [6]on each [6]of them [2]the(his) [3]hands

ἐπιτιθεὶς ἐθεράπευεν αὐτούς. 41 ἐξήρχετο
[1]putting on healed   them.   came out

δὲ καὶ δαιμόνια ἀπὸ πολλῶν, κραυγάζοντα
And also demons from   many,   crying out

καὶ λέγοντα ὅτι σὺ εἶ ὁ υἱὸς τοῦ θεοῦ.
and saying[,] – Thou art the Son – of God.

καὶ ἐπιτιμῶν οὐκ εἴα αὐτὰ λαλεῖν, ὅτι
And rebuking he allowed not them to speak, because

ᾔδεισαν τὸν χριστὸν αὐτὸν εἶναι. 42 Γενομένης
they knew [3]the [4]Christ [1]him [2]to be.   coming
                                              = And when

δὲ ἡμέρας ἐξελθὼν ἐπορεύθη εἰς ἔρημον
And day[a] going forth he went   to a desert
day came

τόπον· καὶ οἱ ὄχλοι ἐπεζήτουν αὐτόν, καὶ
place; and the crowds sought   him,   and

him and came to him, and would have kept him from leaving them; 43 but he said to them, "I must preach the good news of the kingdom of God to the other cities also; for I was sent for this purpose." 44 And he was preaching in the synagogues of Judea.[1]

ἦλθον   ἕως   αὐτοῦ,   καὶ   κατεῖχον   αὐτὸν
came   up to   him,   and   detained   him
τοῦ   μὴ   πορεύεσθαι   ἀπ'   αὐτῶν.   43 ὁ δὲ
-   not   to go[d]   from   them.   And he
= so that he should not go
εἶπεν   πρὸς   αὐτοὺς   ὅτι   καὶ   ταῖς   ἑτέραις
said   to   them[,]   -   Also to the   other
πόλεσιν   εὐαγγελίσασθαί   με   δεῖ   τὴν
cities   [3]to preach   [2]me   [1]it behoves   the
βασιλείαν   τοῦ   θεοῦ,   ὅτι   ἐπὶ   τοῦτο   ἀπεστάλην.
kingdom   - of God, because on   this   I was sent.
44 καὶ   ἦν   κηρύσσων   εἰς   τὰς   συναγωγὰς
And   he was proclaiming   in   the   synagogues
τῆς   Ἰουδαίας.
-   of Judæa.

CHAPTER 5

WHILE the people pressed upon him to hear the word of God, he was standing by the lake of Gennes'aret. 2 And he saw two boats by the lake; but the fishermen had gone out of them and were washing their nets. 3 Getting into one of the boats, which was Simon's, he asked him to put out a little from the land. And he sat down and taught the people from the boat. 4 And when he had ceased speaking, he said to Simon, "Put out into the deep and let down your nets for a catch." 5 And Simon answered, "Master, we toiled all night and took nothing! But at your word I will let down the nets." 6 And

5 Ἐγένετο   δὲ   ἐν   τῷ   τὸν   ὄχλον   ἐπικεῖσθαι
Now it came to pass in   the   the   crowd   to press upon
= as the crowd pressed upon him and heard
αὐτῷ   καὶ   ἀκούειν   τὸν   λόγον   τοῦ   θεοῦ,
him   and   to hear[be]   the   word   - of God,
καὶ   αὐτὸς   ἦν   ἑστὼς   παρὰ   τὴν   λίμνην
and   he   was standing   by   the   lake
Γεννησαρέτ,   2 καὶ   εἶδεν   δύο   πλοιάρια
Gennesaret,   and   saw   two   boats
ἑστῶτα   παρὰ   τὴν   λίμνην·   οἱ   δὲ   ἁλεεῖς
standing   by   the   lake;   but the   fishermen
ἀπ'   αὐτῶν   ἀποβάντες   ἔπλυνον   τὰ   δίκτυα.
from   them   having gone away   were washing   the   nets.
3 ἐμβὰς   δὲ   εἰς   ἓν   τῶν   πλοίων,   ὃ   ἦν
And embarking in   one   of the   boats,   which was
Σίμωνος,   ἠρώτησεν   αὐτὸν   ἀπὸ   τῆς   γῆς
of Simon,   he asked   him   from   the   land
ἐπαναγαγεῖν   ὀλίγον·   καθίσας   δὲ   ἐκ   τοῦ
to put out   a little;   and sitting   [4]out of   [5]the
πλοίου   ἐδίδασκεν   τοὺς   ὄχλους.   4 ὡς   δὲ
[6]boat   [1]he taught   [3]the   [3]crowds.   And when
ἐπαύσατο   λαλῶν,   εἶπεν   πρὸς   τὸν   Σίμωνα·
he ceased   speaking,   he said   to   -   Simon:
ἐπανάγαγε   εἰς   τὸ   βάθος,   καὶ   χαλάσατε
Put out   into   the   deep,   and   let down
τὰ   δίκτυα   ὑμῶν   εἰς   ἄγραν.   5 καὶ
the   nets   of you   for   a draught.   And
ἀποκριθεὶς   Σίμων   εἶπεν·   ἐπιστάτα,   δι'
answering   Simon   said: Master,   through
ὅλης   νυκτὸς   κοπιάσαντες   οὐδὲν   ἐλάβομεν·
[the] whole   night   labouring   nothing   we took;
ἐπὶ   δὲ   τῷ   ῥήματί   σου   χαλάσω   τὰ   δίκτυα.
but at   the   word   of thee   I will let down   the   nets.

[1] Other ancient authorities read *Galilee*

when they had done this, they enclosed a great shoal of fish; and as their nets were breaking, [7]they beckoned to their partners in the other boat to come and help them. And they came and filled both the boats, so that they began to sink. [8]But when Simon Peter saw it, he fell down at Jesus' knees, saying, "Depart from me, for I am a sinful man, O Lord." [9]For he was astonished, and all that were with him, at the catch of fish which they had taken; [10]and so also were James and John, sons of Zeb'edee, who were partners with Simon. And Jesus said to Simon, "Do not be afraid; henceforth you will be catching men." [11]And when they had brought their boats to land, they left everything and followed him.

12 While he was in one of the cities, there came a man full of leprosy; and when he saw Jesus, he fell on his face and besought him, "Lord, if you will, you can make me clean."

6 καὶ τοῦτο ποιήσαντες συνέκλεισαν πλῆθος
And this doing they enclosed multitude

ἰχθύων πολύ· διερρήσσετο δὲ τὰ δίκτυα
of fishes a much; and were being torn the nets

αὐτῶν. 7 καὶ κατένευσαν τοῖς μετόχοις
of them. And they nodded to the(ir) partners

ἐν τῷ ἑτέρῳ πλοίῳ τοῦ ἐλθόντας
in the other boat - coming
                                      =that they should come

συλλαβέσθαι αὐτοῖς· καὶ ἦλθαν, καὶ ἔπλησαν
to help[d] them; and they came, and filled

ἀμφότερα τὰ πλοῖα ὥστε βυθίζεσθαι αὐτά.
both the boats so as to be sinking them.[b]
                                  =so that they were sinking

8 ἰδὼν δὲ Σίμων Πέτρος προσέπεσεν τοῖς
And seeing Simon Peter fell at the

γόνασιν Ἰησοῦ λέγων· ἔξελθε ἀπ' ἐμοῦ,
knees of Jesus saying: Depart from me,

ὅτι ἀνὴρ ἁμαρτωλός εἰμι, κύριε. 9 θάμβος
because man a sinful I am, Lord. astonishment

γὰρ περιέσχεν αὐτὸν καὶ πάντας τοὺς
For seized him and all the [ones]

σὺν αὐτῷ ἐπὶ τῇ ἄγρᾳ τῶν ἰχθύων ᾗ
with him at the draught of the fishes which

συνέλαβον, 10 ὁμοίως δὲ καὶ Ἰάκωβον καὶ
they took, and likewise both James and

Ἰωάννην υἱοὺς Ζεβεδαίου, οἳ ἦσαν κοινωνοὶ
John sons of Zebedee, who were sharers

τῷ Σίμωνι. καὶ εἶπεν πρὸς τὸν Σίμωνα
- with Simon. And said to - Simon

ὁ Ἰησοῦς· μὴ φοβοῦ· ἀπὸ τοῦ νῦν
- Jesus: Fear thou not; from - now

ἀνθρώπους ἔσῃ ζωγρῶν. 11 καὶ καταγαγόντες
men thou wilt be taking alive. And bringing down

τὰ πλοῖα ἐπὶ τὴν γῆν, ἀφέντες πάντα
the boats onto the land, leaving all things

ἠκολούθησαν αὐτῷ.
they followed him.

12 Καὶ ἐγένετο ἐν τῷ εἶναι αὐτὸν ἐν
And it came to pass in the to be him[be] in
                              =as he was

μιᾷ τῶν πόλεων καὶ ἰδοὺ ἀνὴρ πλήρης
one of the cities and behold[,] a man full

λέπρας· ἰδὼν δὲ τὸν Ἰησοῦν, πεσὼν ἐπὶ
of leprosy; and seeing — Jesus, falling on

πρόσωπον ἐδεήθη αὐτοῦ λέγων· κύριε,
[his] face he begged him saying: Lord,

ἐὰν θέλῃς, δύνασαί με καθαρίσαι. 13 καὶ
if thou willest, thou canst me to cleanse. And

¹³And he stretched out his hand, and touched him, saying, "I will; be clean." And immediately the leprosy left him. ¹⁴And he charged him to tell no one; but "go and show yourself to the priest, and make an offering for your cleansing, as Moses commanded, for a proof to the people." ¹⁵But so much the more the report went abroad concerning him; and great multitudes gathered to hear and to be healed of their infirmities. ¹⁶But he withdrew to the wilderness and prayed.

17 On one of those days, as he was teaching, there were Pharisees and teachers of the law sitting by, who had come from every village of Galilee and Judea and from Jerusalem; and the power of the Lord was with him to heal.ᵐ ¹⁸And behold, men were bringing on a bed a man who was paralyzed, and they sought to bring him in and lay him before Jesus; ¹⁹but finding no way to bring him in, because of the crowd, they went up on the roof and let him down with

ἐκτείνας τὴν χεῖρα ἥψατο αὐτοῦ λέγων·
stretching out the(his) hand he touched him saying:
θέλω, καθαρίσθητι· καὶ εὐθέως ἡ λέπρα
I am willing, be thou cleansed; and immediately the leprosy
ἀπῆλθεν ἀπ' αὐτοῦ. 14 καὶ αὐτὸς παρήγγειλεν
departed from him. And he charged
αὐτῷ μηδενὶ εἰπεῖν, ἀλλὰ ἀπελθὼν δεῖξον
him no one to tell, but going away show
σεαυτὸν τῷ ἱερεῖ, καὶ προσένεγκε περὶ
thyself to the priest, and offer concerning
τοῦ καθαρισμοῦ σου καθὼς προσέταξεν
the cleansing of thee as commanded
Μωϋσῆς, εἰς μαρτύριον αὐτοῖς. 15 διήρχετο
Moses, for a testimony to them. went
δὲ μᾶλλον ὁ λόγος περὶ αὐτοῦ, καὶ
But rather the word concerning him, and
συνήρχοντο ὄχλοι πολλοὶ ἀκούειν καὶ
²accompanied ²crowds ¹many to hear and
θεραπεύεσθαι ἀπὸ τῶν ἀσθενειῶν αὐτῶν·
to be healed from the infirmities of them;
16 αὐτὸς δὲ ἦν ὑποχωρῶν ἐν ταῖς ἐρήμοις
but he was withdrawing in the deserts
καὶ προσευχόμενος.
and praying.

17 Καὶ ἐγένετο ἐν μιᾷ τῶν ἡμερῶν καὶ
And it came to pass on one of the days and
αὐτὸς ἦν διδάσκων, καὶ ἦσαν καθήμενοι
he was teaching, and were sitting
Φαρισαῖοι καὶ νομοδιδάσκαλοι οἳ ἦσαν
Pharisees and law-teachers who were
ἐληλυθότες ἐκ πάσης κώμης τῆς Γαλιλαίας
having come out of every village – of Galilee
καὶ Ἰουδαίας καὶ Ἰερουσαλήμ· καὶ δύναμις
and Judæa and Jerusalem; and [the] power
κυρίου ἦν εἰς τὸ ἰᾶσθαι αὐτόν. 18 καὶ
of [the] Lord was ¹in – ³to cure ²him. And
ἰδοὺ ἄνδρες φέροντες ἐπὶ κλίνης ἄνθρωπον
behold[,] men bearing on a couch a man
ὃς ἦν παραλελυμένος, καὶ ἐζήτουν αὐτὸν
who was having been paralysed, and they sought ²him
εἰσενεγκεῖν καὶ θεῖναι [αὐτὸν] ἐνώπιον
¹to carry in and to lay him before
αὐτοῦ. 19 καὶ μὴ εὑρόντες ποίας εἰσ-
him. And not finding how† they
ἐνέγκωσιν αὐτὸν διὰ τὸν ὄχλον, ἀναβάντες
might carry in him because of the crowd, going up
ἐπὶ τὸ δῶμα διὰ τῶν κεράμων καθῆκαν
onto the roof through the tiles they let down

ᵐ Other ancient authorities read was present to heal them

his bed through the tiles into the midst before Jesus. ²⁰And when he saw their faith he said, "Man, your sins are forgiven you." ²¹And the scribes and the Pharisees began to question, saying, "Who is this that speaks blasphemies? Who can forgive sins but God only?" ²²When Jesus perceived their questionings, he answered them, "Why do you question in your hearts? ²³Which is easier, to say, 'Your sins are forgiven you,' or to say, 'Rise and walk'? ²⁴But that you may know that the Son of man has authority on earth to forgive sins"— he said to the man who was paralyzed—"I say to you, rise, take up your bed and go home." ²⁵And immediately he rose before them, and took up that on which he lay, and went home, glorifying God. ²⁶And amazement seized them all, and they glorified God and were filled with awe, saying, "We have seen strange things today."

27 After this he went out, and saw a tax

αὐτὸν σὺν τῷ κλινιδίῳ εἰς τὸ μέσον
him   with   the   couch   into   the   midst
ἔμπροσθεν τοῦ Ἰησοῦ. 20 καὶ ἰδὼν τὴν
in front of -   Jesus.   And seeing   the
πίστιν αὐτῶν εἶπεν· ἄνθρωπε, ἀφέωνταί
faith of them he said :   Man, have been forgiven
σοι αἱ ἁμαρτίαι σου. 21 καὶ ἤρξαντο
thee the sins   of thee.   And   began
διαλογίζεσθαι οἱ γραμματεῖς καὶ οἱ Φαρισαῖοι
to reason   the   scribes   and the Pharisees
λέγοντες· τίς ἐστιν οὗτος ὃς λαλεῖ
saying : Who is   this man who speaks
βλασφημίας; τίς δύναται ἁμαρτίας ἀφεῖναι
blasphemies? Who can   sins   to forgive
εἰ μὴ μόνος ὁ θεός; 22 ἐπιγνοὺς δὲ ὁ
except only - God?   But knowing   -
Ἰησοῦς τοὺς διαλογισμοὺς αὐτῶν, ἀποκριθεὶς
Jesus the   reasonings   of them, answering
εἶπεν πρὸς αὐτούς· τί διαλογίζεσθε ἐν
said   to   them : Why reason ye   in
ταῖς καρδίαις ὑμῶν; 23 τί ἐστιν εὐκοπώτερον,
the   hearts of you? What is   easier,
εἰπεῖν· ἀφέωνταί σοι αἱ ἁμαρτίαι σου, ἢ
to say : Have been forgiven thee the sins of thee, or
εἰπεῖν· ἔγειρε καὶ περιπάτει; 24 ἵνα δὲ
to say : Rise and walk ?   but that
εἰδῆτε ὅτι ὁ υἱὸς τοῦ ἀνθρώπου ἐξουσίαν
ye may know that the Son   -   of man   authority
ἔχει ἐπὶ τῆς γῆς ἀφιέναι ἁμαρτίας, —
has   on the earth to forgive sins,   —
εἶπεν τῷ παραλελυμένῳ· σοὶ λέγω, ἔγειρε
he said to the paralysed [one] : To thee I say, rise
καὶ ἄρας τὸ κλινίδιόν σου πορεύου εἰς
and taking the pallet   of thee go   to
τὸν οἶκόν σου. 25 καὶ παραχρῆμα ἀναστὰς
the house of thee. And   at once   rising up
ἐνώπιον αὐτῶν, ἄρας ἐφ' ὃ κατέκειτο,
before   them, taking [that] on which he was lying,
ἀπῆλθεν εἰς τὸν οἶκον αὐτοῦ δοξάζων τὸν
he went away to the house   of him glorifying -
θεόν. 26 καὶ ἔκστασις ἔλαβεν ἅπαντας, καὶ
God.   And bewilderment took   all,   and
ἐδόξαζον τὸν θεόν, καὶ ἐπλήσθησαν φόβου
they glorified - God, and were filled of(with) fear
λέγοντες ὅτι εἴδομεν παράδοξα σήμερον.
saying[,]   -   We saw wonderful things to-day.
27 Καὶ μετὰ ταῦτα ἐξῆλθεν, καὶ ἐθεάσατο
    And after these things he went forth, and   saw

collector, named Levi, sitting at the tax office; and he said to him, "Follow me." [28]And he left everything, and rose and followed him.

29 And Levi made him a great feast in his house; and there was a large company of tax collectors and others sitting at table with them. [30]And the Pharisees and their scribes murmured against his disciples, saying, "Why do you eat and drink with tax collectors and sinners?" [31]And Jesus answered them, "Those who are well have no need of a physician, but those who are sick; [32]I have not come to call the righteous, but sinners to repentance."

33 And they said to him, "The disciples of John fast often and offer prayers, and so do the disciples of the Pharisees, but yours eat and drink." [34]And Jesus said to them, "Can you make wedding guests fast while the bridegroom is with them. [35]The days will come, when the bridegroom is taken away from them, and then they will fast

τελώνην ὀνόματι Λευὶν καθήμενον ἐπὶ τὸ
a tax-collector by name   Levi   sitting   on(in) the
τελώνιον, καὶ εἶπεν αὐτῷ· ἀκολούθει μοι.
custom house,   and   said   to him: Follow   me.
28 καὶ καταλιπὼν πάντα ἀναστὰς ἠκολούθει
And   abandoning   all things   rising up   he followed
αὐτῷ.   29 Καὶ ἐποίησεν δοχὴν μεγάλην
him.   And   ²made   ⁴feast   ³a great
Λευὶς αὐτῷ ἐν τῇ οἰκίᾳ αὐτοῦ· καὶ ἦν
¹Levi   for him   in the   house   of him;   and there was
ὄχλος πολὺς τελωνῶν καὶ ἄλλων οἳ ἦσαν
crowd   a much of tax-collectors and   of others   who   were
μετ' αὐτῶν κατακείμενοι. 30 καὶ ἐγόγγυζον
²with   ³them   ¹reclining.   And   grumbled
οἱ Φαρισαῖοι καὶ οἱ γραμματεῖς αὐτῶν
the   Pharisees   and the   scribes   of them
πρὸς τοὺς μαθητὰς αὐτοῦ λέγοντες· διὰ
at   the   disciples   of him   saying: Why
τί μετὰ τῶν τελωνῶν καὶ ἁμαρτωλῶν
with   the   tax-collectors and   sinners
ἐσθίετε καὶ πίνετε; 31 καὶ ἀποκριθεὶς ὁ
eat ye   and   drink ye?   And   answering   –
Ἰησοῦς εἶπεν πρὸς αὐτούς· οὐ χρείαν
Jesus   said   to   them: not   need
ἔχουσιν οἱ ὑγιαίνοντες ἰατροῦ ἀλλὰ οἱ
have   the [ones]   being healthy   of a physician   but   the
=those who are ill;
κακῶς ἔχοντες· 32 οὐκ ἐλήλυθα καλέσαι
[ones] ill   having;   I have not come   to call
δικαίους ἀλλὰ ἁμαρτωλοὺς εἰς μετάνοιαν.
righteous persons   but   sinners   to   repentance.
33 Οἱ δὲ εἶπαν πρὸς αὐτόν· οἱ μαθηταὶ
And they   said   to   him: The   disciples
Ἰωάννου νηστεύουσιν πυκνὰ καὶ δεήσεις
of John   fast   often   and   prayers
ποιοῦνται, ὁμοίως καὶ οἱ τῶν Φαρισαίων,
make,   likewise   also   those of the   Pharisees,
οἱ δὲ σοὶ ἐσθίουσιν καὶ πίνουσιν. 34 ὁ
but those to thee°   eat   and   drink.   –
=but thine
δὲ Ἰησοῦς εἶπεν πρὸς αὐτούς· μὴ δύνασθε
And   Jesus   said   to   them: not   ¹Can ye
τοὺς υἱοὺς τοῦ νυμφῶνος, ἐν ᾧ ὁ νυμφίος
²the   ⁴sons   ⁵of the   ⁶bride-chamber,   ⁸while ⁹the ¹⁰bridegroom
μετ' αὐτῶν ἐστιν, ποιῆσαι νηστεῦσαι;
¹¹with   ¹²them   ¹³is,   ³to make   ⁷to fast?
35 ἐλεύσονται δὲ ἡμέραι, καὶ ὅταν ἀπαρθῇ
but will come   days,   and   when is taken away
ἀπ' αὐτῶν ὁ νυμφίος, τότε νηστεύσουσιν
from   them   the   bridegroom,   then   they will fast

in those days." ³⁶ He told them a parable also: "No one tears a piece from a new garment and puts it upon an old garment; if he does, he will tear the new, and the piece from the new will not match the old. ³⁷ And no one puts new wine into old wineskins; if he does, the new wine will burst the skins and it will be spilled, and the skins will be destroyed. ³⁸ But new wine must be put into fresh wineskins. ³⁹ And no one after drinking old wine desires new; for he says, 'The old is good.' "ⁿ

ἐν ἐκείναις ταῖς ἡμέραις. 36 Ἔλεγεν δὲ
in those - days. And he told

καὶ παραβολὴν πρὸς αὐτοὺς ὅτι οὐδεὶς
also a parable to them[:] — No one

ἐπίβλημα ἀπὸ ἱματίου καινοῦ σχίσας
²a patch ³from ⁵garment ⁴a new ¹tearing

ἐπιβάλλει ἐπὶ ἱμάτιον παλαιόν· εἰ δὲ μή γε,
⁶puts [it] ⁷on ⁹a garment ⁸an old; otherwise,

καὶ τὸ καινὸν σχίσει καὶ τῷ παλαιῷ
both the new will tear and ⁷with the ⁸old

οὐ συμφωνήσει τὸ ἐπίβλημα τὸ ἀπὸ τοῦ
⁶will not agree ¹the ²patch - ³from ⁴the

καινοῦ. 37 καὶ οὐδεὶς βάλλει οἶνον νέον
⁵new. And no one puts wine new

εἰς ἀσκοὺς παλαιούς· εἰ δὲ μή γε, ῥήξει
into wineskins old; otherwise, ⁴will burst

ὁ οἶνος ὁ νέος τοὺς ἀσκούς, καὶ αὐτὸς
¹the ³wine - ²new ⁵the ⁶wineskins, and it

ἐκχυθήσεται καὶ οἱ ἀσκοὶ ἀπολοῦνται.
will be poured out and the wineskins will perish.

38 ἀλλὰ οἶνον νέον εἰς ἀσκοὺς καινοὺς
But wine new into wineskins new

βλητέον. 39 καὶ οὐδεὶς πιὼν παλαιὸν
one must put. And no one having drunk old

θέλει νέον· λέγει γάρ· ὁ παλαιὸς χρηστός
desires new; for he says: The old good

ἐστιν.
is.

CHAPTER 6

ON a sabbath,° while he was going through the grainfields, his disciples plucked and ate some ears of grain, rubbing them in their hands. ² But some of the Pharisees said, "Why are you doing what is not lawful to do on the sabbath?" ³ And Jesus answered, "Have you not read what David did when he was hungry, he and those who were with him: ⁴ how he entered the

6 Ἐγένετο δὲ ἐν σαββάτῳ διαπορεύεσθαι
And it came to pass on a sabbath to go through
=he went through

αὐτὸν διὰ σπορίμων, καὶ ἔτιλλον οἱ
him through cornfields, and ⁴plucked ¹the

μαθηταὶ αὐτοῦ καὶ ἤσθιον τοὺς στάχυας
²disciples ³of him and ate the ears

ψώχοντες ταῖς χερσίν. 2 τινὲς δὲ τῶν
rubbing with the(ir) hands. And some of the

Φαρισαίων εἶπαν· τί ποιεῖτε ὃ οὐκ ἔξεστιν
Pharisees said: Why do ye what is not lawful

τοῖς σάββασιν; 3 καὶ ἀποκριθεὶς πρὸς
on the sabbaths? And replying to

αὐτοὺς εἶπεν ὁ Ἰησοῦς· οὐδὲ τοῦτο ἀνέγνωτε
them said - Jesus: ²not ³this ¹read ye

ὃ ἐποίησεν Δαυίδ, ὁπότε ἐπείνασεν αὐτὸς
which did David, when hungered he

καὶ οἱ μετ' αὐτοῦ ὄντες; 4 ὡς εἰσῆλθεν
and the [ones] with him being? how he entered

ⁿ Other ancient authorities read better
° Other ancient authorities read On the second first sabbath (on the second sabbath after the first)

house of God, and took and ate the bread of the Presence, which it is not lawful for any but the priests to eat, and also gave it to those with him?" [5]And he said to them, "The Son of man is lord of the sabbath."

6 On another sabbath, when he entered the synagogue and taught, a man was there whose right hand was withered. [7]And the scribes and the Pharisees watched him, to see whether he would heal on the sabbath, so that they might find an accusation against him. [8]But he knew their thoughts, and he said to the man who had the withered hand, "Come and stand here." And he rose and stood there. [9]And Jesus said to them, "I ask you, is it lawful on the sabbath to do good or to do harm, to save life or to destroy it?" [10]And he looked around on them all, and said to him, "Stretch out your hand." And he did so, and his hand was restored. [11]But they were filled with fury and discussed with one another what they might do to Jesus.

εἰς τὸν οἶκον τοῦ θεοῦ καὶ τοὺς ἄρτους
into the house - of God and the loaves
τῆς προθέσεως λαβὼν ἔφαγεν καὶ ἔδωκεν
of the setting forth taking he ate and gave
τοῖς μετ' αὐτοῦ, οὓς οὐκ ἔξεστιν φαγεῖν
to the [ones] with him, which it is not lawful to eat
εἰ μὴ μόνους τοὺς ἱερεῖς; 5 καὶ ἔλεγεν
except only the priests? And he said
αὐτοῖς· κύριός ἐστιν τοῦ σαββάτου ὁ
to them : Lord is of the sabbath the
υἱὸς τοῦ ἀνθρώπου. 6 Ἐγένετο δὲ ἐν
Son - of man. And it came to pass on
ἑτέρῳ σαββάτῳ εἰσελθεῖν αὐτὸν εἰς τὴν
another sabbath to enter him into the
                       =he entered into the synagogue and
συναγωγὴν καὶ διδάσκειν· καὶ ἦν ἄνθρωπος
synagogue and to teach[b]; and there was a man
      taught;
ἐκεῖ καὶ ἡ χεὶρ αὐτοῦ ἡ δεξιὰ ἦν ξηρά·
there and the [3]hand [6]of him - [1]right was withered.
7 παρετηροῦντο δὲ αὐτὸν οἱ γραμματεῖς
    and carefully watched him the scribes
καὶ οἱ Φαρισαῖοι εἰ ἐν τῷ σαββάτῳ
and the Pharisees if on the sabbath
θεραπεύει, ἵνα εὕρωσιν κατηγορεῖν αὐτοῦ.
he heals, that they might find to accuse him.
8 αὐτὸς δὲ ᾔδει τοὺς διαλογισμοὺς αὐτῶν,
But he knew the reasonings of them,
εἶπεν δὲ τῷ ἀνδρὶ τῷ ξηρὰν ἔχοντι τὴν
and said to the man - [2]withered [1]having [2]the
χεῖρα· ἔγειρε καὶ στῆθι εἰς τὸ μέσον·
[1]hand : Rise and stand in the midst;
καὶ ἀναστὰς ἔστη. 9 εἶπεν δὲ ὁ Ἰησοῦς
and rising up he stood. And said - Jesus
πρὸς αὐτούς· ἐπερωτῶ ὑμᾶς εἰ ἔξεστιν
to them: I ask you if it is lawful
τῷ σαββάτῳ ἀγαθοποιῆσαι ἢ κακοποιῆσαι,
on the sabbath to do good or to do evil,
ψυχὴν σῶσαι ἢ ἀπολέσαι; 10 καὶ περι-
life to save or to destroy? And looking
βλεψάμενος πάντας αὐτοὺς εἶπεν αὐτῷ·
round at all them he said to him :
ἔκτεινον τὴν χεῖρά σου. ὁ δὲ ἐποίησεν,
Stretch out the hand of thee. And he did,
καὶ ἀπεκατεστάθη ἡ χεὶρ αὐτοῦ. 11 αὐτοὶ
and was restored the hand of him. they
δὲ ἐπλήσθησαν ἀνοίας, καὶ διελάλουν πρὸς
But were filled of(with) madness, and talked to
ἀλλήλους τί ἂν ποιήσαιεν τῷ Ἰησοῦ.
one another what they might do - to Jesus.

12 In these days he went out into the hills to pray; and all night he continued in prayer to God. 13 And when it was day, he called his disciples, and chose from them twelve, whom he named apostles; 14 Simon, whom he named Peter, and Andrew his brother, and James and John, and Philip, and Bartholomew, 15 and Matthew, and Thomas, and James the son of Alphaeus, and Simon who was called the Zealot, 16 and Judas the son of James, and Judas Iscariot, who became a traitor.

17 And he came down with them and stood on a level place, with a great crowd of his disciples and a great multitude of people from all Judea and Jerusalem and the seacoast of Tyre and Sidon, who came to hear him and to be healed of their diseases; 18 and those who were troubled with unclean spirits were cured. 19 And all the crowd sought to touch him, for power came forth from him and healed them all.

20 And he lifted up

---

12 Ἐγένετο δὲ ἐν ταῖς ἡμέραις ταύταις
Now it came to pass in　–　days　these

ἐξελθεῖν αὐτὸν εἰς τὸ ὄρος προσεύξασθαι,
to go forth him[b] to the mountain to pray,
=he went forth

καὶ ἦν διανυκτερεύων ἐν τῇ προσευχῇ τοῦ
and was spending the whole in the prayer –
　　　　　night

θεοῦ. **13** καὶ ὅτε ἐγένετο ἡμέρα, προσεφώνησεν
of God. And when it became day, he called to [him]

τοὺς μαθητὰς αὐτοῦ, καὶ ἐκλεξάμενος ἀπ'
the disciples of him, and choosing from

αὐτῶν δώδεκα, οὓς καὶ ἀποστόλους ὠνόμασεν,
them twelve, whom also apostles he named,

14 Σίμωνα, ὃν καὶ ὠνόμασεν Πέτρον, καὶ
Simon, whom also he named Peter, and

Ἀνδρέαν τὸν ἀδελφὸν αὐτοῦ, καὶ Ἰάκωβον
Andrew the brother of him, and James

καὶ Ἰωάννην, καὶ Φίλιππον καὶ Βαρθο-
and John, and Philip and Bartho-

λομαῖον, **15** καὶ Μαθθαῖον καὶ Θωμᾶν,
lomew, and Matthew and Thomas,

[καὶ] Ἰάκωβον Ἀλφαίου καὶ Σίμωνα τὸν
and James [son] of Alphæus and Simon the [one]

καλούμενον ζηλωτήν, **16** καὶ Ἰούδαν Ἰακώβου,
being called a Zealot, and Judas of James,

καὶ Ἰούδαν Ἰσκαριώθ, ὃς ἐγένετο προδότης,
and Judas Iscariot, who became betrayer,

17 καὶ καταβὰς μετ' αὐτῶν ἔστη ἐπὶ
and coming down with them he stood on

τόπου πεδινοῦ, καὶ ὄχλος πολὺς μαθητῶν
place a level, and crowd a much of disciples

αὐτοῦ, καὶ πλῆθος πολὺ τοῦ λαοῦ ἀπὸ
of him, and multitude a much of the people from

πάσης τῆς Ἰουδαίας καὶ Ἱερουσαλὴμ καὶ
all – Judæa and Jerusalem and

τῆς παραλίου Τύρου καὶ Σιδῶνος, **18** οἳ
the coast country of Tyre and Sidon, who

ἦλθον ἀκοῦσαι αὐτοῦ καὶ ἰαθῆναι ἀπὸ
came to hear him and to be cured from

τῶν νόσων αὐτῶν, καὶ οἱ ἐνοχλούμενοι
the diseases of them, and the [ones] being tormented

ἀπὸ πνευμάτων ἀκαθάρτων ἐθεραπεύοντο.
from spirits unclean were healed.

19 καὶ πᾶς ὁ ὄχλος ἐζήτουν ἅπτεσθαι
And all the crowd sought to touch

αὐτοῦ, ὅτι δύναμις παρ' αὐτοῦ ἐξήρχετο
him, because power from him went forth

καὶ ἰᾶτο πάντας. **20** Καὶ αὐτὸς ἐπάρας
and cured all. And he lifting up

his eyes on his disciples, and said:

"Blessed are you poor, for yours is the kingdom of God.

21 "Blessed are you that hunger now, for you shall be satisfied.

"Blessed are you that weep now, for you shall laugh.

22 "Blessed are you when men hate you, and when they exclude you and revile you, and cast out your name as evil, on account of the Son of man! 23 Rejoice in that day, and leap for joy, for behold, your reward is great in heaven; for so their fathers did to the prophets.

24 "But woe to you that are rich, for you have received your consolation.

25 "Woe to you that are full now, for you shall hunger.

"Woe to you that laugh now, for you shall mourn and weep.

26 "Woe to you, when all men speak well of you, for so their fathers did to the false prophets.

27 "But I say to you that hear, Love your enemies, do good to those who hate you,

τοὺς ὀφθαλμοὺς αὐτοῦ εἰς τοὺς μαθητὰς
the eyes of him to the disciples
αὐτοῦ ἔλεγεν·
of him said:
Μακάριοι οἱ πτωχοί, ὅτι ὑμετέρα ἐστὶν
Blessed [are] the poor, because yours is
ἡ βασιλεία τοῦ θεοῦ. 21 μακάριοι οἱ
the kingdom – of God. Blessed [are] the [ones]
πεινῶντες νῦν, ὅτι χορτασθήσεσθε. μακάριοι
hungering now, because ye will be satisfied. Blessed [are]
οἱ κλαίοντες νῦν, ὅτι γελάσετε. 22 μακάριοί
the [ones] weeping now, because ye will laugh. Blessed
ἐστε ὅταν μισήσωσιν ὑμᾶς οἱ ἄνθρωποι,
are ye when ¹hate ²you ¹men,
καὶ ὅταν ἀφορίσωσιν ὑμᾶς καὶ ὀνειδίσωσιν
and when they separate you and reproach
καὶ ἐκβάλωσιν τὸ ὄνομα ὑμῶν ὡς πονηρὸν
and cast out the name of you as evil
ἕνεκα τοῦ υἱοῦ τοῦ ἀνθρώπου. 23 χάρητε
for the sake of the Son – of man. Rejoice
ἐν ἐκείνῃ τῇ ἡμέρᾳ καὶ σκιρτήσατε·
in that – day and leap for joy;
ἰδοὺ γὰρ ὁ μισθὸς ὑμῶν πολὺς ἐν τῷ
for behold[,] the reward of you much in –
οὐρανῷ· κατὰ τὰ αὐτὰ γὰρ ἐποίουν τοῖς
heaven; for according to the same things ⁴did ⁵to the
=in the same way
προφήταις οἱ πατέρες αὐτῶν.
⁶prophets ¹the ²fathers ³of them.
24 Πλὴν οὐαὶ ὑμῖν τοῖς πλουσίοις, ὅτι
But woe to you the rich [ones], because
ἀπέχετε τὴν παράκλησιν ὑμῶν. 25 οὐαὶ ὑμῖν,
ye have the consolation of you. Woe to you,
οἱ ἐμπεπλησμένοι νῦν, ὅτι πεινάσετε.
the [ones] having been filled up now, because ye will hunger.
οὐαί, οἱ γελῶντες νῦν, ὅτι πενθήσετε
Woe, the [ones] laughing now, because ye will mourn
καὶ κλαύσετε. 26 οὐαὶ ὅταν καλῶς ὑμᾶς
and lament. Woe when well [of] you
εἴπωσιν πάντες οἱ ἄνθρωποι· κατὰ τὰ
say all – men; for according to
=in the same way
αὐτὰ γὰρ ἐποίουν τοῖς ψευδοπροφήταις οἱ
the same things did to the false prophets the
πατέρες αὐτῶν. 27 Ἀλλὰ ὑμῖν λέγω
fathers of them. But you I tell
τοῖς ἀκούουσιν· ἀγαπᾶτε τοὺς ἐχθροὺς
the [ones] hearing: Love ye the enemies
ὑμῶν, καλῶς ποιεῖτε τοῖς μισοῦσιν ὑμᾶς,
of you, ¹well ¹do to the [ones] hating you,

28 bless those who curse you, pray for those who abuse you. 29 To him who strikes you on the cheek, offer the other also; and from him who takes away your cloak do not withhold your coat as well. 30 Give to every one who begs from you; and of him who takes away your goods do not ask them again. 31 And as you wish that men would do to you, do so to them.

32 "If you love those who love you, what credit is that to you? For even sinners love those who love them. 33 And if you do good to those who do good to you, what credit is that to you? For even sinners do the same. 34 And if you lend to those from whom you hope to receive, what credit is that to you? Even sinners lend to sinners, to receive as much again. 35 But love your enemies, and do good, and lend, expecting nothing in return;[q] and your reward will be great, and you will be sons of the Most High; for he is kind to the

28 εὐλογεῖτε τοὺς καταρωμένους ὑμᾶς,
   bless   the [ones]   cursing   you,
προσεύχεσθε περὶ τῶν ἐπηρεαζόντων ὑμᾶς.
   pray   about the [ones] insulting   you.

29 τῷ τύπτοντί σε ἐπὶ τὴν σιαγόνα
To the [one] striking thee on   the   cheek
πάρεχε καὶ τὴν ἄλλην, καὶ ἀπὸ τοῦ
turn   also the other,   and from the [one]
αἴροντός σου τὸ ἱμάτιον καὶ τὸν χιτῶνα
taking   of thee the garment also the   tunic
μὴ κωλύσῃς. 30 παντὶ αἰτοῦντί σε δίδου,
do not prevent.   To everyone asking thee give,
καὶ ἀπὸ τοῦ αἴροντος τὰ σὰ μὴ ἀπαίτει.
and from the [one] taking thy things do not ask back.

31 καὶ καθὼς θέλετε ἵνα ποιῶσιν ὑμῖν
   And as   ye wish that may do to you
οἱ ἄνθρωποι, ποιεῖτε αὐτοῖς ὁμοίως. 32 καὶ
   men,   do ye to them likewise.   And
εἰ ἀγαπᾶτε τοὺς ἀγαπῶντας ὑμᾶς, ποία
if ye love the [ones] loving   you,   what
ὑμῖν χάρις ἐστίν; καὶ γὰρ οἱ ἁμαρτωλοὶ
to you thanks is there?[c] for even -   sinners
=thanks have ye?
τοὺς ἀγαπῶντας αὐτοὺς ἀγαπῶσιν. 33 καὶ
²the [ones] ³loving ⁴them   ¹love.   even
γὰρ ἐὰν ἀγαθοποιῆτε τοὺς ἀγαθοποιοῦντας
For if ye do good to the [ones] doing good to
ὑμᾶς, ποία ὑμῖν χάρις ἐστίν; καὶ οἱ
you, what to you thanks is there?[c] even -
=thanks have ye?
ἁμαρτωλοὶ τὸ αὐτὸ ποιοῦσιν. 34 καὶ ἐὰν
sinners   the same thing do.   And if
δανείσητε παρ᾽ ὧν ἐλπίζετε λαβεῖν, ποία
ye lend   from whom ye hope to receive, what
ὑμῖν χάρις [ἐστίν]; καὶ ἁμαρτωλοὶ
to you thanks is there?[c]   even   sinners
=thanks have ye?
ἁμαρτωλοῖς δανείζουσιν ἵνα ἀπολάβωσιν τὰ
to sinners   lend   that they may receive back the
ἴσα. 35 πλὴν ἀγαπᾶτε τοὺς ἐχθροὺς ὑμῶν
equal things. But love ye   the enemies of you
καὶ ἀγαθοποιεῖτε καὶ δανείζετε μηδὲν
and   do good   and lend   nothing
ἀπελπίζοντες· καὶ ἔσται ὁ μισθὸς ὑμῶν
despairing;   and will be the reward of you
=despairing not at all;
πολύς, καὶ ἔσεσθε υἱοὶ ὑψίστου, ὅτι
much,   and ye will be sons of [the] Most High, because
αὐτὸς χρηστός ἐστιν ἐπὶ τοὺς ἀχαρίστους
he   kind   is   to the   unthankful

[q] Other ancient authorities read despairing of no man

ungrateful and the sel-
fish. [36] Be merciful, even
as your Father is merci-
ful.

37 "Judge not, and
you will not be judged;
condemn not, and you
will not be condemned;
forgive, and you will be
forgiven; [38] give, and it
will be given to you;
good measure, pressed
down, shaken together,
running over, will be put
into your lap. For the
measure you give will be
the measure you get
back."

39 He also told them
a parable: "Can a blind
man lead a blind man?
Will they not both fall
into a pit? [40] A disciple is
not above his teacher,
but every one when he is
fully taught will be like
his teacher. [41] Why do
you see the speck that is
in your brother's eye,
but do not notice the log
that is in your own eye?
[42] Or how can you say to
your brother, 'Brother,
let me take out the speck
that is in your eye,' when
you yourself do not see
the log that is in your
own eye? You hypocrite,
first take the log out of
your own eye, and then
you will see clearly to

καὶ   πονηρούς.   36 Γίνεσθε   οἰκτίρμονες,
and   evil.   Be ye   compassionate,

καθὼς   ὁ   πατὴρ   ὑμῶν   οἰκτίρμων   ἐστίν.
as   the   Father   of you   compassionate   is.

37 καὶ   μὴ   κρίνετε,   καὶ   οὐ   μὴ   κριθῆτε·   καὶ
And   do not judge,   and by no means ye may be   and
                                                              judged;

μὴ   καταδικάζετε,   καὶ   οὐ   μὴ   καταδικασθῆτε.
do not condemn,   and   by no means ye may be condemned.

ἀπολύετε,   καὶ   ἀπολυθήσεσθε·   38 δίδοτε,   καὶ
Forgive,   and   ye will be forgiven;   give,   and

δοθήσεται   ὑμῖν·   μέτρον   καλὸν   πεπιεσμένον
it will be given to you;   measure   good   having been pressed
                                                              down

σεσαλευμένον   ὑπερεκχυννόμενον   δώσουσιν   εἰς
having been shaken   running over   they will give   into

τὸν   κόλπον   ὑμῶν·   ᾧ   γὰρ   μέτρῳ   μετρεῖτε
the   bosom   of you;   for in what   measure   ye measure

ἀντιμετρηθήσεται   ὑμῖν.   39 Εἶπεν   δὲ   καὶ
it will be measured in return to you.   And he told   also

παραβολὴν   αὐτοῖς·   μήτι   δύναται   τυφλὸς
a parable   to them :   Not   can   a blind man

τυφλὸν   ὁδηγεῖν;   οὐχὶ   ἀμφότεροι   εἰς   βόθυνον
²a blind man   ¹guide?   not   both   into   a ditch

ἐμπεσοῦνται;   40 οὐκ   ἔστιν   μαθητὴς   ὑπὲρ
will fall in?   ³not   ²is   ¹A disciple   above

τὸν   διδάσκαλον·   κατηρτισμένος   δὲ   πᾶς
the   teacher;   ¹but   ⁴having been perfected   ³everyone

ἔσται   ὡς   ὁ   διδάσκαλος   αὐτοῦ.   41 Τί   δὲ
²will be as   the   teacher   of him.   And why

βλέπεις   τὸ   κάρφος   τὸ   ἐν   τῷ   ὀφθαλμῷ
seest thou   the   mote   –   in   the   eye

τοῦ   ἀδελφοῦ   σου,   τὴν   δὲ   δοκὸν   τὴν   ἐν
of the   brother   of thee,   but the   beam   –   in

τῷ   ἰδίῳ   ὀφθαλμῷ   οὐ   κατανοεῖς;   42 πῶς
thine own   eye   thou considerest not?   how

δύνασαι   λέγειν   τῷ   ἀδελφῷ   σου·   ἀδελφέ,
canst thou   to say   to the   brother   of thee :   Brother,

ἄφες   ἐκβάλω   τὸ   κάρφος   τὸ   ἐν   τῷ
allow   I may take out   the   mote   –   in   the
=allow me to take out

ὀφθαλμῷ   σου,   αὐτὸς   τὴν   ἐν   τῷ   ὀφθαλμῷ
eye   of thee,   ¹[thy]self   ⁴the   ⁶in   ⁷the   ⁸eye

σου   δοκὸν   οὐ   βλέπων;   ὑποκριτά,   ἔκβαλε
⁹of thee   ⁵beam   ²not   ³seeing?   hypocrite,   take out

πρῶτον   τὴν   δοκὸν   ἐκ   τοῦ   ὀφθαλμοῦ   σου,
first   the   beam   out of the   eye   of thee,

καὶ   τότε   διαβλέψεις   τὸ   κάρφος   τὸ   ἐν   τῷ
and   then   thou wilt see clearly   the   mote   –   in   the

take out the speck that is in your brother's eye.

43 "For no good tree bears bad fruit, nor again does a bad tree bear good fruit; [44]for each tree is known by its own fruit. For figs are not gathered from thorns, nor are grapes picked from a bramble bush. [45]The good man out of the good treasure of his heart produces good, and the evil man out of his evil treasure produces evil; for out of the abundance of the heart his mouth speaks.

46 "Why do you call me 'Lord, Lord,' and not do what I tell you? [47]Every one who comes to me and hears my words and does them, I will show you what he is like: [48]he is like a man building a house, who dug deep, and laid the foundation upon rock; and when a flood arose, the stream broke against that house, and could not shake it, because it had been well built.[r] [49]But he who hears and does not do them is like

ὀφθαλμῷ τοῦ ἀδελφοῦ σου ἐκβαλεῖν. 43 Οὐ
eye   of the   brother of thee to take out.   [2]no

γάρ ἐστιν δένδρον καλὸν ποιοῦν καρπὸν
[1]For [3]there is [5]tree [4]good producing fruit

σαπρόν, οὐδὲ πάλιν δένδρον σαπρὸν ποιοῦν
bad,   nor again tree   a bad   producing

καρπὸν καλόν. 44 ἕκαστον γὰρ δένδρον
fruit good.   For each   tree

ἐκ τοῦ ἰδίου καρποῦ γινώσκεται· οὐ γὰρ
by the(its) own fruit   is known;   for not

ἐξ ἀκανθῶν συλλέγουσιν σῦκα, οὐδὲ ἐκ
of thorns   do they gather figs,   nor   of

βάτου σταφυλὴν τρυγῶσιν. 45 ὁ ἀγαθὸς
a thorn bush a grape   do they pick.   The good

ἄνθρωπος ἐκ τοῦ ἀγαθοῦ θησαυροῦ τῆς
man   out of the   good   treasure of the(his)

καρδίας προφέρει τὸ ἀγαθόν, καὶ ὁ
heart   brings forth the   good,   and the
                        =that which is good,

πονηρὸς ἐκ τοῦ πονηροῦ προφέρει τὸ
evil man out of the   evil   brings forth the

πονηρόν· ἐκ γὰρ περισσεύματος καρδίας
evil;   for out of [the] abundance of [his] heart
=that which is evil;

λαλεῖ τὸ στόμα αὐτοῦ. 46 Τί δέ με καλεῖτε·
speaks the mouth of him.   And why me call ye :

κύριε κύριε, καὶ οὐ ποιεῖτε ἃ
Lord[,] Lord, and   do not [the things] which

λέγω; 47 Πᾶς ὁ ἐρχόμενος πρός με καὶ
I say? Everyone   coming   to me and

ἀκούων μου τῶν λόγων καὶ ποιῶν αὐτούς,
hearing of me the words and doing them,

ὑποδείξω ὑμῖν τίνι ἐστὶν ὅμοιος. 48 ὅμοιός
I will show you to whom he is like.   Like

ἐστιν ἀνθρώπῳ οἰκοδομοῦντι οἰκίαν, ὃς
he is   to a man   building   a house, who

ἔσκαψεν καὶ ἐβάθυνεν καὶ ἔθηκεν θεμέλιον
dug   and deepened and laid a foundation

ἐπὶ τὴν πέτραν· πλημμύρης δὲ γενομένης
on the rock;   and a flood   occurring[a]
                            =when a flood occurred

προσέρρηξεν ὁ ποταμὸς τῇ οἰκίᾳ ἐκείνῃ,
[2]dashed against [1]the [2]river - house that,

καὶ οὐκ ἴσχυσεν σαλεῦσαι αὐτὴν διὰ
and   was not able to shake it because of

τὸ καλῶς οἰκοδομῆσθαι αὐτήν. 49 ὁ δὲ
the well   to be built   it.[b]   But the
=because it was well built.   [one]

ἀκούσας καὶ μὴ ποιήσας ὅμοιός ἐστιν
hearing and not doing   [3]like [1]is

a man who built a house on the ground without a foundation; against which the stream broke, and immediately it fell, and the ruin of that house was great."

ἀνθρώπῳ   οἰκοδομήσαντι   οἰκίαν   ἐπὶ   τὴν
a man   having built   a house   on   the
γῆν   χωρὶς   θεμελίου,   ᾗ   προσέρρηξεν   ὁ
earth   without   a foundation,   ⁸which   ⁸dashed   ¹against   ⁸the
ποταμός,   καὶ   εὐθὺς   συνέπεσεν,   καὶ   ἐγένετο
⁵river,   and   immediately   it collapsed,   and   ⁸was
τὸ   ῥῆγμα   τῆς   οἰκίας   ἐκείνης   μέγα.
¹the   ²ruin   –   ⁴house   ⁵of that   ⁶great.

CHAPTER 7

AFTER he had ended all his sayings in the hearing of the people he entered Caper′na-um. ²Now a centurion had a slave who was dear[4] to him, who was sick and at the point of death. ³When he heard of Jesus, he sent to him elders of the Jews, asking him to come and heal his slave. ⁴And when they came to Jesus, they besought him earnestly, saying, "He is worthy to have you do this for him, ⁵for he loves our nation, and he built us our synagogue." ⁶And Jesus went with them. When he was not far from the house, the centurion sent friends to him, saying to him, "Lord, do not trouble yourself, for I am not worthy to have you come under my roof; ⁷therefore I did not presume to come to you. But say the

7 Ἐπειδὴ   ἐπλήρωσεν   πάντα   τὰ   ῥήματα
   When   he completed   all   the   words
αὐτοῦ   εἰς   τὰς   ἀκοὰς   τοῦ   λαοῦ,   εἰσῆλθεν
of him   in   the   ears   of the   people,   he entered
εἰς   Καφαρναούμ.   2 Ἑκατοντάρχου   δέ
into   Capernaum.   Now ⁵of ¹a ⁵centurion
τινος   δοῦλος   κακῶς   ἔχων   ἤμελλεν   τελευτᾶν,
⁴certain   ¹a slave   ⁸ill   ⁸having(being)   ¹²was about   ¹³to die,
ὃς   ἦν   αὐτῷ   ἔντιμος.   3 ἀκούσας   δὲ   περὶ
⁸who   ⁸was   ¹¹to him   ¹⁰dear.   And hearing   about
τοῦ   Ἰησοῦ   ἀπέστειλεν   πρὸς   αὐτὸν   πρε-
   Jesus   he sent   to   him   eld-
σβυτέρους   τῶν   Ἰουδαίων,   ἐρωτῶν   αὐτὸν
ers   of the   Jews,   asking   him
ὅπως   ἐλθὼν   διασώσῃ   τὸν   δοῦλον   αὐτοῦ.
that   coming   he might recover   the   slave   of him.
4 οἱ   δὲ   παραγενόμενοι   πρὸς   τὸν   Ἰησοῦν
   And they   coming   to   –   Jesus
παρεκάλουν   αὐτὸν   σπουδαίως,   λέγοντες   ὅτι   ἄξιός
besought   him   earnestly,   saying[,]   – Worthy
ἐστιν   ᾧ   παρέξῃ   τοῦτο·   5 ἀγαπᾷ   γὰρ
he is   for whom   thou shouldest grant   this;   for he loves
τὸ   ἔθνος   ἡμῶν   καὶ   τὴν   συναγωγὴν
the   nation   of us   and   the   synagogue
αὐτὸς   ᾠκοδόμησεν   ἡμῖν.   6 ὁ   δὲ   Ἰησοῦς
he   built   for us.   –   And   Jesus
ἐπορεύετο   σὺν   αὐτοῖς.   ἤδη   δὲ   αὐτοῦ   οὐ
went   with   them.   And yet   him   not
                                 =while he was yet
μακρὰν   ἀπέχοντος   ἀπὸ   τῆς   οἰκίας,   ἔπεμψεν
far   being away[a]   from   the   house,   sent
not far away
φίλους   ὁ   ἑκατοντάρχης   λέγων   αὐτῷ·   κύριε,
friends   the   centurion   saying   to him :   Lord,
μὴ   σκύλλου·   οὐ   γὰρ   ἱκανός   εἰμι   ἵνα   ὑπὸ
do not trouble;   for not   worthy   am I   that   under
τὴν   στέγην   μου   εἰσέλθῃς·   7 διὸ   οὐδὲ
the   roof   of me   thou shouldest enter;   wherefore   not
ἐμαυτὸν   ἠξίωσα   πρὸς   σὲ   ἐλθεῖν·   ἀλλὰ   εἰπὲ
myself   I accounted worthy   to   thee   to come;   but   say

[4] Or *valuable*

word, and let my servant be healed. [8]For I am a man set under authority, with soldiers under me: and I say to one, 'Go,' and he goes; and to another, 'Come,' and he comes; and to my slave, 'Do this,' and he does it." [9]When Jesus heard this he marveled at him, and turned and said to the multitude that followed him, "I tell you, not even in Israel have I found such faith." [10]And when those who had been sent returned to the house, they found the slave well.

11 Soon afterward[t] he went to a city called Na'in, and his disciples and a great crowd went with him. [12]As he drew near to the gate of the city, behold, a man who had died was being carried out, the only son of his mother, and she was a widow; and a large crowd from the city was with her. [13]And when the Lord saw her, he had compassion on her and said to her, "Do not weep." [14]And he came and touched the bier, and the bearers stood still. And he said, "Young man, I say to you, arise." [15]And the

[t] Other ancient authorities read Next day

λόγῳ, καὶ ἰαθήτω ὁ παῖς μου.   8 καὶ
in a word, and   let be cured the servant of me.   [a]also
γὰρ ἐγὼ ἄνθρωπός εἰμι ὑπὸ ἐξουσίαν
[1]For   [2]I   [3]a man   [4]am   [7]under   [8]authority
τασσόμενος, ἔχων ὑπ' ἐμαυτὸν στρατιώτας,
[9]being set,   having under myself   soldiers,
καὶ λέγω τούτῳ· πορεύθητι, καὶ πορεύεται,
and I tell this one :   Go,   and he goes,
καὶ ἄλλῳ· ἔρχου, καὶ ἔρχεται, καὶ τῷ
and another :   Come,   and he comes,   and the
δούλῳ μου· ποίησον τοῦτο, καὶ ποιεῖ.
slave   of me :   Do   this,   and he does.
9 ἀκούσας δὲ ταῦτα ὁ Ἰησοῦς ἐθαύμασεν
And hearing these [words] –   Jesus   marvelled at
αὐτόν, καὶ στραφεὶς τῷ ἀκολουθοῦντι αὐτῷ
him,   and   turning to the   [2]following   [3]him
ὄχλῳ εἶπεν· λέγω ὑμῖν, οὐδὲ ἐν τῷ
[1]crowd   said :   I tell   you,   not   in   –
Ἰσραὴλ τοσαύτην πίστιν εὗρον.   10 καὶ
Israel   such   faith I found.   And
ὑποστρέψαντες εἰς τὸν οἶκον οἱ πεμφθέντες
returning   to the   house   the [ones] sent
εὗρον τὸν δοῦλον ὑγιαίνοντα.   11 Καὶ
found   the   slave   well.   And
ἐγένετο ἐν τῷ ἑξῆς ἐπορεύθη εἰς πόλιν
it came to pass on the   next day   he went   into a city
καλουμένην Ναΐν, καὶ συνεπορεύοντο αὐτῷ
being called   Nain,   and   went with   him
οἱ μαθηταὶ αὐτοῦ καὶ ὄχλος πολύς.
the   disciples   of him   and   crowd   a much.
12 ὡς δὲ ἤγγισεν τῇ πύλῃ τῆς πόλεως, καὶ
And as he drew near to the gate   of the   city,   and
ἰδοὺ ἐξεκομίζετο τεθνηκὼς μονογενὴς
behold was being carried out   having died   an only born
[for burial]
υἱὸς τῇ μητρὶ αὐτοῦ, καὶ αὕτη ἦν χήρα,
son to the mother of him,   and   this   was a widow,
καὶ ὄχλος τῆς πόλεως ἱκανὸς ἦν σὺν
and   a [2]crowd   [3]of the   [4]city   [1]considerable was   with
αὐτῇ.   13 καὶ ἰδὼν αὐτὴν ὁ κύριος
her.   And   seeing   her   the   Lord
ἐσπλαγχνίσθη ἐπ' αὐτῇ καὶ εἶπεν αὐτῇ·
felt compassion   over   her   and   said   to her :
μὴ κλαῖε.   14 καὶ προσελθὼν ἥψατο τῆς
Do not weep.   And   approaching   he touched   the
σοροῦ, οἱ δὲ βαστάζοντες ἔστησαν, καὶ
bier,   and the [ones] bearing   stood,   and
εἶπεν· νεανίσκε, σοὶ λέγω, ἐγέρθητι.   15 καὶ
he said :   Young man, to thee I say,   Arise.   And

dead man sat up, and began to speak. And he gave him to his mother. ¹⁶Fear seized them all; and they glorified God, saying, "A great prophet has arisen among us!" and "God has visited his people!" ¹⁷And this report concerning him spread through the whole of Judea and all the surrounding country.

18 The disciples of John told him of all these things. ¹⁹And John, calling to him two of his disciples, sent them to the Lord, saying, "Are you he who is to come, or shall we look for another?" ²⁰And when the men had come to him, they said, "John the Baptist has sent us to you, saying, 'Are you he who is to come, or shall we look for another?'" ²¹In that hour he cured many of diseases and plagues and evil spirits, and on many that were blind he bestowed sight. ²²And he answered them, "Go and tell John what you have seen and heard: the blind receive their sight, the lame walk, lepers are cleansed, and the deaf hear, the dead

ἀνεκάθισεν ὁ νεκρὸς καὶ ἤρξατο λαλεῖν,
sat up   the dead man and   began   to speak,

καὶ ἔδωκεν αὐτὸν τῇ μητρὶ αὐτοῦ.
and he gave   him   to the mother   of him.

16 ἔλαβεν δὲ φόβος πάντας, καὶ ἐδόξαζον
And ²took ¹fear   ³all,   and they glorified

τὸν θεὸν λέγοντες ὅτι προφήτης μέγας
- God   saying[,]   -   prophet   A great

ἠγέρθη ἐν ἡμῖν, καὶ ὅτι ἐπεσκέψατο ὁ
was raised among us, and[,] -   ²visited   -

θεὸς τὸν λαὸν αὐτοῦ. 17 καὶ ἐξῆλθεν ὁ
¹God the people of him.   And went forth -

λόγος οὗτος ἐν ὅλῃ τῇ Ἰουδαίᾳ περὶ
word   this in all the Judæa ⁵concerning

αὐτοῦ καὶ πάσῃ τῇ περιχώρῳ.
⁶him ¹and ²all ³the ⁴neighbourhood.

18 Καὶ ἀπήγγειλαν Ἰωάννῃ οἱ μαθηταὶ
And reported   to John   the disciples

αὐτοῦ περὶ πάντων τούτων. καὶ
of him about   all   these things.   And

προσκαλεσάμενος δύο τινὰς τῶν μαθητῶν
calling to [him] ²two ¹a certain of the disciples

αὐτοῦ ὁ Ἰωάννης 19 ἔπεμψεν πρὸς τὸν
of him - John   sent   to   the

κύριον λέγων· σὺ εἶ ὁ ἐρχόμενος, ἢ ἄλλον
Lord saying: Thou art the coming [one], or another

προσδοκῶμεν; 20 παραγενόμενοι δὲ πρὸς
may we expect?   And coming   to

αὐτὸν οἱ ἄνδρες εἶπαν· Ἰωάννης ὁ βαπτιστὴς
him the men   said : John   the Baptist

ἀπέστειλεν ἡμᾶς πρὸς σὲ λέγων· σὺ εἶ ὁ
sent   us   to thee saying : Thou art the

ἐρχόμενος, ἢ ἄλλον προσδοκῶμεν; 21 ἐν
coming [one], or another may we expect?   In

ἐκείνῃ τῇ ὥρᾳ ἐθεράπευσεν πολλοὺς ἀπὸ
that - hour he healed   many from(of)

νόσων καὶ μαστίγων καὶ πνευμάτων πονηρῶν,
diseases and plagues   and   spirits   evil,

καὶ τυφλοῖς πολλοῖς ἐχαρίσατο βλέπειν.
and blind persons to many   he gave   to see.

22 καὶ ἀποκριθεὶς εἶπεν αὐτοῖς· πορευθέντες
And answering   he said to them :   Going

ἀπαγγείλατε Ἰωάννῃ ἃ εἴδετε καὶ
report   to John [the things] which ye saw and

ἠκούσατε· τυφλοὶ ἀναβλέπουσιν, χωλοὶ
heard: blind men see again,   lame men

περιπατοῦσιν, λεπροὶ καθαρίζονται, καὶ κωφοὶ
walk,   lepers are being cleansed, and deaf men

are raised up, the poor have good news preached to them. ²³And blessed is he who takes no offense at me."

24 When the messengers of John had gone, he began to speak to the crowds concerning John: "What did you go out into the wilderness to behold? A reed shaken by the wind? ²⁵What then did you go out to see? A man clothed in soft raiment? Behold, those who are gorgeously appareled and live in luxury are in kings' courts. ²⁶What then did you go out to see? A prophet? Yes, I tell you, and more than a prophet. ²⁷This is he of whom it is written,

'Behold, I send my messenger before thy face,
who shall prepare thy way before thee.'

²⁸I tell you, among those born of women none is greater than John; yet he who is least in the kingdom of God is greater than he." ²⁹(When they heard this all the people and the tax collectors justified God, having been baptized with the baptism of John; ³⁰but the Pharisees and the lawyers rejected the purpose of God for

ἀκούουσιν,   νεκροὶ   ἐγείρονται,   πτωχοὶ
hear,   dead men   are raised,   poor people
εὐαγγελίζονται· 23 καὶ μακάριός ἐστιν ὃς ἐὰν
are evangelized;   and blessed is whoever
μὴ σκανδαλισθῇ ἐν ἐμοί.   24 Ἀπελθόντων δὲ
is not offended in me.   And going away
                                        =as the
τῶν ἀγγέλων Ἰωάννου ἤρξατο λέγειν πρὸς
the messengers of Johnª he began to say   to
messengers of John went away
τοὺς ὄχλους περὶ Ἰωάννου· τί ἐξήλθατε
the   crowds concerning John : What went ye forth
εἰς τὴν ἔρημον θεάσασθαι; κάλαμον ὑπὸ
into the desert   to see?   a reed   by
ἀνέμου σαλευόμενον; 25 ἀλλὰ τί ἐξήλθατε
wind   being shaken?   But what went ye forth
ἰδεῖν; ἄνθρωπον ἐν μαλακοῖς ἱματίοις
to see? a man   in   soft   garments
ἠμφιεσμένον; ἰδοὺ οἱ ἐν ἱματισμῷ ἐνδόξῳ
having been behold[,] the ¹in ³raiment ²splendid
clothed?   [ones]
καὶ τρυφῇ ὑπάρχοντες ἐν τοῖς βασιλείοις
⁴and ⁶in luxury ⁵being   ⁸in – ⁷royal palaces
εἰσίν. 26 ἀλλὰ τί ἐξήλθατε ἰδεῖν; προφήτην;
⁷are.   But what went ye forth to see? a prophet?
ναὶ λέγω ὑμῖν, καὶ περισσότερον προφήτου.
yes I tell you, and   more [than]   a prophet.
27 οὗτός ἐστιν περὶ οὗ γέγραπται· ἰδοὺ
This is he concerning whom it has been written : Behold
ἀποστέλλω τὸν ἄγγελόν μου πρὸ προσώπου
I send   the messenger of me before [the] face
σου, ὃς κατασκευάσει τὴν ὁδόν σου
of thee, who will prepare   the   way of thee
ἔμπροσθέν σου. 28 λέγω ὑμῖν, μείζων
before   thee.   I tell you,   ⁶greater
ἐν γεννητοῖς γυναικῶν Ἰωάννου οὐδεὶς
¹among ²[those] born ³of women [⁷than] ⁴John ⁴no one
ἐστιν· ὁ δὲ μικρότερος ἐν τῇ βασιλείᾳ τοῦ
⁵is; but the   less   in the kingdom   –
θεοῦ μείζων αὐτοῦ ἐστιν. 29 καὶ πᾶς ὁ
of God greater [than] he   is.   And all the
λαὸς ἀκούσας καὶ οἱ τελῶναι ἐδικαίωσαν
people hearing and the tax-collectors justified
τὸν θεόν, βαπτισθέντες τὸ βάπτισμα
 –   God, being baptized [with] the   baptism
Ἰωάννου· 30 οἱ δὲ Φαρισαῖοι καὶ οἱ
of John;   but the Pharisees   and the
νομικοὶ τὴν βουλὴν τοῦ θεοῦ ἠθέτησαν εἰς
lawyers ⁴the ⁵counsel – ⁶of God   ¹rejected ²for

themselves, not having been baptized by him.)

31 "To what then shall I compare the men of this generation, and what are they like? [32]They are like children sitting in the market place and calling to one another,

'We piped to you, and you did not dance; we wailed, and you did not weep.

[33]For John the Baptist has come eating no bread and drinking no wine; and you say, 'He has a demon.' [34]The Son of man has come eating and drinking; and you say, 'Behold, a glutton and a drunkard, a friend of tax collectors and sinners!' [35]Yet wisdom is justified by all her children."

36 One of the Pharisees asked him to eat with him, and he went into the Pharisee's house, and sat at table. [37]And behold, a woman of the city, who was a sinner, when she learned that he was sitting at table in the Pharisee's house, brought an alabaster flask of ointment, [38]and standing behind him at his feet, weeping, she began to wet his feet with her tears, and wiped them with the hair of her head,

ἑαυτούς, μὴ βαπτισθέντες ὑπ' αὐτοῦ. 31 Τίνι
[3]themselves, not being baptized by him.   To what

οὖν ὁμοιώσω τοὺς ἀνθρώπους τῆς γενεᾶς
then may I liken the men – generation

ταύτης, καὶ τίνι εἰσὶν ὅμοιοι; 32 ὅμοιοί εἰσιν
of this, and to what are they like?   Like are they

παιδίοις τοῖς ἐν ἀγορᾷ καθημένοις καὶ
to children – in a marketplace sitting and

προσφωνοῦσιν ἀλλήλοις ἃ λέγει· ηὐλήσαμεν
calling to one another who says : We piped

ὑμῖν καὶ οὐκ ὠρχήσασθε· ἐθρηνήσαμεν καὶ
to you and ye did not dance; we mourned and

οὐκ ἐκλαύσατε. 33 ἐλήλυθεν γὰρ Ἰωάννης
ye did not weep. For has come John

ὁ βαπτιστὴς μὴ ἐσθίων ἄρτον μήτε πίνων
the Baptist not eating bread nor drinking

οἶνον, καὶ λέγετε· δαιμόνιον ἔχει.
wine, and ye say : A demon he has.

34 ἐλήλυθεν ὁ υἱὸς τοῦ ἀνθρώπου ἐσθίων
Has come the Son – of man eating

καὶ πίνων, καὶ λέγετε· ἰδοὺ ἄνθρωπος
and drinking, and ye say· Behold[,] a man

φάγος καὶ οἰνοπότης, φίλος τελωνῶν καὶ
a glutton and a winebibber, a friend of tax-collectors and

ἁμαρτωλῶν. 35 καὶ ἐδικαιώθη ἡ σοφία
of sinners. And was(is) justified – wisdom

ἀπὸ πάντων τῶν τέκνων αὐτῆς.
from(by) all the children of her.

36 Ἠρώτα δέ τις αὐτὸν τῶν Φαρισαίων
And [4]asked [1]a certain one [5]him [2]of the [3]Pharisees

ἵνα φάγῃ μετ' αὐτοῦ· καὶ εἰσελθὼν εἰς
that he would eat with him; and entering into

τὸν οἶκον τοῦ Φαρισαίου κατεκλίθη. 37 καὶ
the house of the Pharisee he reclined. And[,]

ἰδοὺ γυνὴ ἥτις ἦν ἐν τῇ πόλει ἁμαρτωλός,
behold[,] a woman who was in the city a sinner,

καὶ ἐπιγνοῦσα ὅτι κατάκειται ἐν τῇ
and knowing that he reclines in the

οἰκίᾳ τοῦ Φαρισαίου, κομίσασα ἀλάβαστρον
house of the Pharisee, bringing an alabaster box

μύρου 38 καὶ στᾶσα ὀπίσω παρὰ τοὺς
of ointment and standing behind at the

πόδας αὐτοῦ κλαίουσα, τοῖς δάκρυσιν
feet of him weeping, with the(her) tears

ἤρξατο βρέχειν τοὺς πόδας αὐτοῦ, καὶ
began to wet the feet of him, and

ταῖς θριξὶν τῆς κεφαλῆς αὐτῆς ἐξέμασσεν,
with the hairs of the head of her wiped off,

and kissed his feet, and anointed them with the ointment. ³⁹Now when the Pharisee who had invited him saw it, he said to himself, "If this man were a prophet, he would have known who and what sort of woman this is who is touching him, for she is a sinner." ⁴⁰And Jesus answering said to him, "Simon, I have something to say to you." And he answered, "What is it, Teacher?" ⁴¹"A certain creditor had two debtors; one owed five hundred denarii, and the other fifty. ⁴²When they could not pay, he forgave them both. Now which of them will love him more?" ⁴³Simon answered, "The one, I suppose, to whom he forgave more." And he said to him, "You have judged rightly." ⁴⁴Then turning toward the woman he said to Simon, "Do you see this woman? I entered your house, you gave me no water for my feet, but she has wet my feet with her tears and wiped them with her hair. ⁴⁵You gave me no kiss, but from the time I came in she has not ceased to kiss my

καὶ κατεφίλει τοὺς πόδας αὐτοῦ καὶ
and   fervently kissed   the   feet   of him   and

ἤλειφεν τῷ μύρῳ. 39 ἰδὼν δὲ ὁ Φαρισαῖος
anointed with the ointment.   But ⁵seeing ¹the   ²Pharisee

ὁ καλέσας αὐτὸν εἶπεν ἐν ἑαυτῷ λέγων·
- ³having invited ⁴him   spoke within himself   saying :

οὗτος εἰ ἦν [ὁ] προφήτης, ἐγίνωσκεν ἂν
This man if he was the   prophet,   would have known

τίς καὶ ποταπὴ ἡ γυνὴ ἥτις ἅπτεται
who   and   what sort   the   woman   who   is touching

αὐτοῦ, ὅτι ἁμαρτωλός ἐστιν.   40 καὶ
him,   because   a sinner   she is.   And

ἀποκριθεὶς ὁ Ἰησοῦς εἶπεν πρὸς αὐτόν·
answering   -   Jesus   said   to   him :

Σίμων, ἔχω σοί τι εἰπεῖν. ὁ δέ· διδάσκαλε,
Simon, I have to thee something to say. And he :   Teacher,

εἰπέ, φησίν.   41 δύο χρεοφειλέται ἦσαν
say,   says.   Two   debtors   were
=A certain creditor had two debtors;

δανειστῇ τινι· ὁ εἷς ὤφειλεν δηνάρια
creditor to a certain;ᶜ the one   owed   denarii

πεντακόσια, ὁ δὲ ἕτερος πεντήκοντα. 42 μὴ
five hundred,   and the   other   fifty.   Not
=As they had no[thing]

ἐχόντων αὐτῶν ἀποδοῦναι ἀμφοτέροις
having   themª   to repay   ²both

ἐχαρίσατο. τίς οὖν αὐτῶν πλεῖον ἀγαπήσει
¹he freely forgave. Who then of them more   will love

αὐτόν; 43 ἀποκριθεὶς Σίμων εἶπεν·
him?   Answering   Simon   said :

ὑπολαμβάνω ὅτι ᾧ τὸ πλεῖον ἐχαρίσατο.
I suppose[,]   - to whom the   more   he freely forgave.

ὁ δὲ εἶπεν αὐτῷ· ὀρθῶς ἔκρινας. 44 καὶ
And he   said   to him : Rightly thou didst judge.   And

στραφεὶς πρὸς τὴν γυναῖκα τῷ Σίμωνι
turning   to   the   woman   -   to Simon

ἔφη· βλέπεις ταύτην τὴν γυναῖκα; εἰσῆλθόν
he said : Seest thou   this   -   woman?   I entered

σου εἰς τὴν οἰκίαν, ὕδωρ μοι ἐπὶ πόδας
of thee into   the   house,   water to me on(for) [my] feet

οὐκ ἔδωκας· αὕτη δὲ τοῖς δάκρυσιν
thou gavest not;   but this woman with the(her)   tears

ἔβρεξέν μου τοὺς πόδας καὶ ταῖς θριξὶν
wet   of me the   feet   and with the   hairs

αὐτῆς ἐξέμαξεν. 45 φίλημά μοι οὐκ ἔδωκας·
of her   wiped off.   A kiss to me thou gavest not;

αὕτη δὲ ἀφ᾽ ἧς εἰσῆλθον οὐ διέλειπεν
but this woman from [the time] I entered   ceased not
which

feet. [46]You did not anoint my head with oil, but she has anointed my feet with ointment. [47]Therefore I tell you, her sins, which are many, are forgiven, for she loved much; but he who is forgiven little, loves little." [48]And he said to her, "Your sins are forgiven." [49]Then those who were at table with him began to say among themselves, "Who is this, who even forgives sins?" [50]And he said to the woman, "Your faith has saved you; go in peace."

καταφιλοῦσά μου τοὺς πόδας. **46** ἐλαίῳ
fervently kissing　of me　the　feet.　　　With oil
τὴν κεφαλήν μου οὐκ ἤλειψας· αὕτη δὲ
the　head　of me thou didst not anoint; but this woman
μύρῳ ἤλειψεν τοὺς πόδας μου. **47** οὗ
with ointment anointed　the　feet　of me.　Of which
　　　　　　　　　　　　　　　　　　　　=Wherefore
χάριν λέγω σοι, ἀφέωνται αἱ ἁμαρτίαι
for the sake of I tell thee, ⁵have been forgiven ¹the　　²sins
αὐτῆς αἱ πολλαί, ὅτι ἠγάπησεν πολύ·
⁴of her　²many,　because　she loved　much;
ᾧ δὲ ὀλίγον ἀφίεται, ὀλίγον ἀγαπᾷ.
but to whom little　is forgiven,　little　he loves.
48 εἶπεν δὲ αὐτῇ· ἀφέωνταί σου αἱ
And he said　to her : Have been forgiven of thee the
ἁμαρτίαι. **49** καὶ ἤρξαντο οἱ συνανακείμενοι
sins.　　　And began　the [ones] reclining with [him]
λέγειν ἐν ἑαυτοῖς· τίς οὗτός ἐστιν, ὃς καὶ
to say among themselves : Who　this　is,　who even
ἁμαρτίας ἀφίησιν; **50** εἶπεν δὲ πρὸς τὴν
sins　forgives?　But he said　to　the
γυναῖκα· ἡ πίστις σου σέσωκέν σε·
woman :　The　faith　of thee　has saved　thee;
πορεύου εἰς εἰρήνην.
go　in　peace.

CHAPTER 8

SOON afterward he went on through cities and villages, preaching and bringing the good news of the kingdom of God. And the twelve were with him, [2]and also some women who had been healed of evil spirits and infirmities: Mary, called Mag'dalene, from whom seven demons had gone out, [3]and Jo-an'na, the wife of Chu'za, Herod's steward, and Susanna, and many others, who provided for them[u] out of their means.

8 Καὶ ἐγένετο ἐν τῷ καθεξῆς καὶ αὐτός
And it came to pass　afterwards　and　he
διώδευεν κατὰ πόλιν καὶ κώμην κηρύσσων
journeyed through every† city　and　village　proclaiming
καὶ εὐαγγελιζόμενος τὴν βασιλείαν τοῦ
and　preaching　the　kingdom
θεοῦ, καὶ οἱ δώδεκα σὺν αὐτῷ, **2** καὶ
of God, and　the　twelve　with　him,　and
γυναῖκές τινες αἱ ἦσαν τεθεραπευμέναι ἀπὸ
women certain who were　having been healed from
πνευμάτων πονηρῶν καὶ ἀσθενειῶν, Μαρία
spirits　evil　and　infirmities,　Mary
ἡ καλουμένη Μαγδαληνή, ἀφ’ ἧς δαιμόνια
– being called　Magdalene,　from whom demons
ἑπτὰ ἐξεληλύθει, **3** καὶ Ἰωάννα γυνὴ Χουζᾶ
seven　had gone out,　and　Joanna wife of Chuza
ἐπιτρόπου Ἡρῴδου καὶ Σουσάννα καὶ
steward　of Herod and　Susanna　and
ἕτεραι πολλαί, αἵτινες διηκόνουν αὐτοῖς
others　many,　who　ministered　to them
ἐκ τῶν ὑπαρχόντων αὐταῖς.
out of the　possessions　to them.ᶜ

[u] Other ancient authorities read *him*

4 And when a great crowd came together and people from town after town came to him, he said in a parable: ⁵"A sower went out to sow his seed; and as he sowed, some fell along the path, and was trodden under foot, and the birds of the air devoured it. ⁶And some fell on the rock; and as it grew up, it withered away, because it had no moisture. ⁷And some fell among thorns; and the thorns grew with it and choked it. ⁸And some fell into good soil and grew, and yielded a hundredfold." As he said this, he called out, "He who has ears to hear, let him hear."

9 And when his disciples asked him what this parable meant, ¹⁰he said, "To you it has been given to know the secrets of the kingdom of God; but for others they are in parables, so that seeing they may not see, and hearing they may not understand. ¹¹Now the parable is this: The seed is the word of God. ¹²The ones

---

4 Συνιόντος δὲ ὄχλου πολλοῦ καὶ τῶν
And coming together crowd a much and the [ones]
=when a great crowd came together and people in each city

κατὰ πόλιν ἐπιπορευομένων πρὸς αὐτὸν
in each city† resorting° to him
resorted

εἶπεν διὰ παραβολῆς· 5 ἐξῆλθεν ὁ σπείρων
he said by a parable : Went forth the [one] sowing

τοῦ σπεῖραι τὸν σπόρον αὐτοῦ. καὶ ἐν τῷ
- to sowᵈ the seed of him. And in the

σπείρειν αὐτὸν ὃ μὲν ἔπεσεν παρὰ τὴν
to sow himᵇᵉ this fell by the
=as he sowed

ὁδὸν καὶ κατεπατήθη, καὶ τὰ πετεινὰ τοῦ
way and was trodden down, and the birds of the

οὐρανοῦ κατέφαγεν αὐτό. 6 καὶ ἕτερον
heaven(air) devoured it. And other [seed]

κατέπεσεν ἐπὶ τὴν πέτραν, καὶ φυὲν
fell on the rock, and grown

ἐξηράνθη διὰ τὸ μὴ ἔχειν ἰκμάδα.
it was withered because of the not to have moisture.
=because it had no moisture.

7 καὶ ἕτερον ἔπεσεν ἐν μέσῳ τῶν ἀκανθῶν, καὶ
And other fell in [the] of the thorns, and
midst

συμφυεῖσαι αἱ ἄκανθαι ἀπέπνιξαν αὐτό.
growing up with [it] the thorns choked it.

8 καὶ ἕτερον ἔπεσεν εἰς τὴν γῆν τὴν
And other fell in the soil -

ἀγαθὴν καὶ φυὲν ἐποίησεν καρπὸν
good and grown it produced fruit

ἑκατονταπλασίονα. ταῦτα λέγων ἐφώνει· ὁ
a hundredfold. These things saying he called: The [one]

ἔχων ὦτα ἀκούειν ἀκουέτω. 9 Ἐπηρώτων δὲ
having ears to hear let him hear. And questioned

αὐτὸν οἱ μαθηταὶ αὐτοῦ τίς αὕτη εἴη ἡ
him the disciples of him what ¹this ²might be -

παραβολή. 10 ὁ δὲ εἶπεν· ὑμῖν δέδοται
²parable. And he said : To you it has been given

γνῶναι τὰ μυστήρια τῆς βασιλείας τοῦ
to know the mysteries of the kingdom -

θεοῦ, τοῖς δὲ λοιποῖς ἐν παραβολαῖς, ἵνα
of God, but to the rest in parables, that

βλέποντες μὴ βλέπωσιν καὶ ἀκούοντες μὴ
seeing they may not see and hearing not

συνιῶσιν. 11 ἔστιν δὲ αὕτη ἡ παραβολή.
they may understand. ⁴is ¹Now ²this - ³parable.

ὁ σπόρος ἐστὶν ὁ λόγος τοῦ θεοῦ.
The seed is the word of God.

along the path are those who have heard; then the devil comes and takes away the word from their hearts, that they may not believe and be saved. 13And the ones on the rock are those who, when they hear the word, receive it with joy; but these have no root, they believe for a while and in time of temptation fall away. 14And as for what fell among the thorns, they are those who hear, but as they go on their way they are choked by the cares and riches and pleasures of life, and their fruit does not mature. 15And as for that in the good soil, they are those who, hearing the word, hold it fast in an honest and good heart, and bring forth fruit with patience.

16 "No one after lighting a lamp covers it with a vessel, or puts it under a bed, but puts it on a stand, that those who enter may see the light. 17For nothing is hid that shall not be made manifest, nor anything secret that shall not be known and come to light. 18Take heed then how you hear; for to him who has will more be given, and from him who

12 οἱ δὲ παρὰ τὴν ὁδόν εἰσιν οἱ ἀκούσαντες,
And the [ones] by the way are the [ones] hearing,

εἶτα ἔρχεται ὁ διάβολος καὶ αἴρει τὸν
then comes the devil and takes the

λόγον ἀπὸ τῆς καρδίας αὐτῶν, ἵνα μὴ
word from the heart of them, lest

πιστεύσαντες σωθῶσιν. 13 οἱ δὲ ἐπὶ τῆς
believing they may be saved. And the [ones] on the

πέτρας οἳ ὅταν ἀκούσωσιν μετὰ χαρᾶς
rock who when they hear with joy

δέχονται τὸν λόγον· καὶ οὗτοι ῥίζαν
receive the word; and these root

οὐκ ἔχουσιν, οἳ πρὸς καιρὸν πιστεύουσιν
have not, who for a time believe

καὶ ἐν καιρῷ πειρασμοῦ ἀφίστανται. 14 τὸ
and in time of trial withdraw. the [one]

δὲ εἰς τὰς ἀκάνθας πεσόν, οὗτοί εἰσιν
And in the thorns falling, these are

οἱ ἀκούσαντες, 1and 4by 5cares 6and
the [ones] hearing, ὑπὸ μεριμνῶν καὶ

πλούτου καὶ ἡδονῶν τοῦ βίου πορευόμενοι
7riches 8and 9pleasures – 10of life 2going

συμπνίγονται καὶ οὐ τελεσφοροῦσιν. 15 τὸ
3are choked and do not bear [fruit] to maturity. the [one]

δὲ ἐν τῇ καλῇ γῇ, οὗτοί εἰσιν οἵτινες ἐν
And in the good soil, these are [those] who in

καρδίᾳ καλῇ καὶ ἀγαθῇ ἀκούσαντες τὸν
heart a worthy and good hearing the

λόγον κατέχουσιν καὶ καρποφοροῦσιν ἐν
word hold fast and bear fruit in

ὑπομονῇ. 16 Οὐδεὶς δὲ λύχνον ἅψας
patience. Now no one a lamp having lit

καλύπτει αὐτὸν σκεύει ἢ ὑποκάτω κλίνης
hides it with a vessel or underneath a couch

τίθησιν, ἀλλ' ἐπὶ λυχνίας τίθησιν, ἵνα οἱ
puts, but on a lampstand puts, that the

εἰσπορευόμενοι βλέπωσιν τὸ φῶς. 17 οὐ
[ones] coming in may see the light. not

γάρ ἐστιν κρυπτὸν ὃ οὐ φανερὸν
For [anything] is hidden which 3not 4manifest

γενήσεται, οὐδὲ ἀπόκρυφον ὃ οὐ μὴ
1will 2become, nor secret which by no means

γνωσθῇ καὶ εἰς φανερὸν ἔλθῃ. 18 βλέπετε
will be known and to [be] manifest come. See

οὖν πῶς ἀκούετε· ὃς ἂν γὰρ ἔχῃ,
therefore how ye hear; for whoever has,

δοθήσεται αὐτῷ· καὶ ὃς ἂν μὴ ἔχῃ,
it will be given to him; and whoever has not,

has not, even what he thinks that he has will be taken away."

19 Then his mother and his brothers came to him, but they could not reach him for the crowd. 20 And he was told, "Your mother and your brothers are standing outside, desiring to see you." 21 But he said to them, "My mother and my brothers are those who hear the word of God and do it."

22 One day he got into a boat with his disciples, and he said to them, "Let us go across to the other side of the lake." So they set out, 23 and as they sailed he fell asleep. And a storm of wind came down on the lake, and they were filling with water, and were in danger. 24 And they went and woke him, saying, "Master, Master, we are perishing!" And he awoke and rebuked the wind and the raging waves; and they ceased, and there was a calm. 25 He said to them, "Where is your faith?" And they were afraid, and they marveled, saying to one another, "Who then is this, that he commands even wind and water, and they obey him?"

καὶ ὃ δοκεῖ ἔχειν ἀρθήσεται ἀπ' αὐτοῦ.
even what he seems to have   will be taken   from   him.

19 Παρεγένετο δὲ πρὸς αὐτὸν ἡ μήτηρ
      And came   to   him   the mother
καὶ οἱ ἀδελφοὶ αὐτοῦ, καὶ οὐκ ἠδύναντο
and the   brothers   of him,   and   were not able
συντυχεῖν αὐτῷ διὰ τὸν ὄχλον. 20 ἀπηγγέλη δὲ
to come up with him be- the crowd.   And it was reported
                     cause of
αὐτῷ· ἡ μήτηρ σου καὶ οἱ ἀδελφοί σου
to him : The mother of thee and the brothers of thee
ἑστήκασιν ἔξω ἰδεῖν θέλοντές σε. 21 ὁ δὲ
are standing outside ²to see ¹wishing thee.   But he
ἀποκριθεὶς εἶπεν πρὸς αὐτούς· μήτηρ μου
answering   said   to   them :   Mother of me
καὶ ἀδελφοί μου οὗτοί εἰσιν οἱ τὸν λόγον
and brothers of me ²these ¹are ³the [ones] ⁷the ⁴word
τοῦ θεοῦ ἀκούοντες καὶ ποιοῦντες.
- ⁵of God   ⁶hearing   ⁵and   ⁶doing.

22 Ἐγένετο δὲ ἐν μιᾷ τῶν ἡμερῶν καὶ
      And it came to pass on one   of the   days   and
αὐτὸς ἐνέβη εἰς πλοῖον καὶ οἱ μαθηταὶ
he   embarked in a boat   and the disciples
αὐτοῦ, καὶ εἶπεν πρὸς αὐτούς· διέλθωμεν
of him,   and he said to   them;   Let us go over
εἰς τὸ πέραν τῆς λίμνης· καὶ ἀνήχθησαν.
to the other side of the lake;   and they put to sea.
23 πλεόντων δὲ αὐτῶν ἀφύπνωσεν. καὶ
      And sailing   them*   he fell asleep.   And
                    =as they sailed
κατέβη λαῖλαψ ἀνέμου εἰς τὴν λίμνην, καὶ
came down a storm   of wind   to   the   lake,   and
συνεπληροῦντο καὶ ἐκινδύνευον. 24 προσ-
they were filling up and they were in danger.   ap-
ελθόντες δὲ διήγειραν αὐτὸν λέγοντες·
proaching   And they awoke   him   saying :
ἐπιστάτα ἐπιστάτα, ἀπολλύμεθα. ὁ δὲ
Master[,]   Master,   we are perishing.   But he
διεγερθεὶς ἐπετίμησεν τῷ ἀνέμῳ καὶ τῷ
being awakened rebuked   the   wind   and the
κλύδωνι τοῦ ὕδατος· καὶ ἐπαύσαντο, καὶ ἐγένετο
roughness of the water; and they ceased, and there was
γαλήνη. 25 εἶπεν δὲ αὐτοῖς· ποῦ ἡ πίστις ὑμῶν;
a calm.   Then he said to them : Where the faith   of you?
φοβηθέντες δὲ ἐθαύμασαν, λέγοντες πρὸς
      And fearing   they marvelled,   saying   to
ἀλλήλους· τίς ἄρα οὗτός ἐστιν, ὅτι καὶ
one another : Who then ¹this man ¹is,   that ²even
τοῖς ἀνέμοις ἐπιτάσσει καὶ τῷ ὕδατι, καὶ
³the ⁴winds   ¹he commands and the   water,   and

26 Then they arrived at the country of the Ger'asenes,[v] which is opposite Galilee. 27And as he stepped out on land, there met him a man from the city who had demons; for a long time he had worn no clothes, and he lived not in a house but among the tombs. 28When he saw Jesus, he cried out and fell down before him, and said with a loud voice, "What have you to do with me, Jesus, Son of the Most High God? I beseech you, do not torment me." 29For he had commanded the unclean spirit to come out of the man. (For many a time it had seized him; he was kept under guard, and bound with chains and fetters, but he broke the bonds and was driven by the demon into the desert.) 30Jesus then asked him, "What is your name?" And he said, "Legion"; for many demons had entered him. 31And they begged him not to command them to depart into the abyss. 32Now a large herd of swine was feeding there on the hillside; and they begged him to let them enter these. So he gave

[v] Other ancient authorities read *Gadarenes*, others *Gergesenes*

ὑπακούουσιν αὐτῷ; 26 Καὶ κατέπλευσαν εἰς
they obey   him?   And   they sailed down to

τὴν χώραν τῶν Γερασηνῶν, ἥτις ἐστὶν
the country of the Gerasenes,   which is

ἀντιπέρα τῆς Γαλιλαίας. 27 ἐξελθόντι δὲ
opposite   –   Galilee.   And going out
                                  =as he went out

αὐτῷ ἐπὶ τὴν γῆν ὑπήντησεν ἀνήρ τις
him[e] onto the   land   met [him]   man a certain

ἐκ τῆς πόλεως ἔχων δαιμόνια, καὶ χρόνῳ
out of the city having demons,   and ³time

ἱκανῷ οὐκ ἐνεδύσατο ἱμάτιον, καὶ ἐν οἰκίᾳ
¹for a con-   put not on   a garment, and in a house
siderable

οὐκ ἔμενεν ἀλλ' ἐν τοῖς μνήμασιν. 28 ἰδὼν
remained not but among the   tombs.   seeing

δὲ τὸν Ἰησοῦν ἀνακράξας προσέπεσεν αὐτῷ
And –   Jesus   crying out he fell prostrate before him

καὶ φωνῇ μεγάλῃ εἶπεν· τί ἐμοὶ καὶ σοί,
and voice in a great(loud) said : What to me and to thee,

Ἰησοῦ υἱὲ τοῦ θεοῦ τοῦ ὑψίστου; δέομαί
Jesus Son – of God –   most high?   I beg

σου, μή με βασανίσῃς. 29 παρήγγελλεν
of thee, do not me torment.   he charged

γὰρ τῷ πνεύματι τῷ ἀκαθάρτῳ ἐξελθεῖν
For the spirit   –   unclean   to come out

ἀπὸ τοῦ ἀνθρώπου. πολλοῖς γὰρ χρόνοις
from the man.   For many   times

συνηρπάκει αὐτόν, καὶ ἐδεσμεύετο ἁλύσεσιν
it had seized him,   and he was bound with chains

καὶ πέδαις φυλασσόμενος, καὶ διαρήσσων
and fetters   being guarded,   and tearing asunder

τὰ δεσμὰ ἠλαύνετο ἀπὸ τοῦ δαιμονίου εἰς
the bonds he was driven from(by) the demon   into

τὰς ἐρήμους. 30 ἐπηρώτησεν δὲ αὐτὸν ὁ
the deserts.   And questioned   him –

Ἰησοῦς· τί σοι ὄνομά ἐστιν; ὁ δὲ εἶπεν·
Jesus : What to thee name   is?[c] And he said :

λεγιών, ὅτι εἰσῆλθεν δαιμόνια πολλὰ εἰς
Legion, because ³entered ²demons   ¹many into

αὐτόν. 31 καὶ παρεκάλουν αὐτὸν ἵνα μὴ
him.   And they besought   him   that not

ἐπιτάξῃ αὐτοῖς εἰς τὴν ἄβυσσον ἀπελθεῖν.
he would order them into the abyss   to go away.

32 ἦν δὲ ἐκεῖ ἀγέλη χοίρων ἱκανῶν
Now there was there a herd   pigs   of many

βοσκομένη ἐν τῷ ὄρει· καὶ παρεκάλεσαν
feeding   in the mountain; and they besought

αὐτὸν ἵνα ἐπιτρέψῃ αὐτοῖς εἰς ἐκείνους
him   that he would allow them   into those

them leave. ³³Then the demons came out of the man and entered the swine, and the herd rushed down the steep bank into the lake and were drowned.

34 When the herdsmen saw what had happened, they fled, and told it in the city and in the country. ³⁵Then people went out to see what had happened, and they came to Jesus, and found the man from whom the demons had gone, sitting at the feet of Jesus, clothed and in his right mind; and they were afraid. ³⁶And those who had seen it told them how he who had been possessed with demons was healed. ³⁷Then all the people of the surrounding country of the Ger′asenes[v] asked him to depart from them; for they were seized with great fear; so he got into the boat and returned. ³⁸The man from whom the demons had gone begged that he might be with him; but he sent him away, saying, ³⁹"Return to your home, and declare how much God has done for you."

εἰσελθεῖν· καὶ ἐπέτρεψεν αὐτοῖς. 33 ἐξελθόντα
to enter;   and   he allowed   them.   ⁴coming out

δὲ τὰ δαιμόνια ἀπὸ τοῦ ἀνθρώπου εἰσῆλθον
¹So ²the ³demons   from   the   man   entered

εἰς τοὺς χοίρους, καὶ ὥρμησεν ἡ ἀγέλη
into   the   pigs,   and   rushed   the   herd

κατὰ τοῦ κρημνοῦ εἰς τὴν λίμνην καὶ
down   the   precipice   into   the   lake   and

ἀπεπνίγη. 34 ἰδόντες δὲ οἱ βόσκοντες
was choked.   And ²seeing   ¹the [ones] ²feeding

τὸ γεγονὸς ἔφυγον καὶ ἀπήγγειλαν εἰς
⁴the thing ⁵having   fled   and   reported   in
       happened
= what had happened

τὴν πόλιν καὶ εἰς τοὺς ἀγρούς. 35 ἐξῆλθον
the   city   and in the   farms.   they went out

δὲ ἰδεῖν τὸ γεγονός, καὶ ἦλθον πρὸς τὸν
And to see the thing having   and   came   to   –
       happened,
= what had happened,

Ἰησοῦν, καὶ εὗρον καθήμενον τὸν ἄνθρωπον
Jesus,   and   found   sitting   the   man

ἀφ᾽ οὗ τὰ δαιμόνια ἐξῆλθεν ἱματισμένον
from whom the   demons   went out *having been* clothed

καὶ σωφρονοῦντα παρὰ τοὺς πόδας τοῦ
and   being in his senses   by   the   feet   –

Ἰησοῦ, καὶ ἐφοβήθησαν. 36 ἀπήγγειλαν δὲ
of Jesus, and   they were afraid.   And ²reported

αὐτοῖς οἱ ἰδόντες πῶς ἐσώθη ὁ δαιμο-
⁴to them ¹the [ones] ²seeing   ⁵how ⁸was healed ⁶the ⁷demon-

νισθείς. 37 καὶ ἠρώτησεν αὐτὸν ἅπαν τὸ
possessed.   And   asked   him   all   the

πλῆθος τῆς περιχώρου τῶν Γερασηνῶν
multitude   of the   neighbourhood   of the   Gerasenes

ἀπελθεῖν ἀπ᾽ αὐτῶν, ὅτι φόβῳ μεγάλῳ
to go away   from   them,   because   fear   with a great

συνείχοντο· αὐτὸς δὲ ἐμβὰς εἰς πλοῖον
they were seized;   so he   embarking   in   a boat

ὑπέστρεψεν. 38 ἐδεῖτο δὲ αὐτοῦ ὁ ἀνὴρ
returned.   And begged   of him   the   man

ἀφ᾽ οὗ ἐξεληλύθει τὰ δαιμόνια εἶναι σὺν
from whom had gone out   the   demons   to be   with

αὐτῷ· ἀπέλυσεν δὲ αὐτὸν λέγων· 39 ὑπόστρεφε
him;   but he dismissed   him   saying :   Return

εἰς τὸν οἶκόν σου, καὶ διηγοῦ ὅσα σοι
to   the   house of thee,   and   relate   what ²to thee
                              things

ἐποίησεν ὁ θεός. καὶ ἀπῆλθεν καθ᾽ ὅλην
³did   – ¹God.   And he went away   throughout   all

And he went away, proclaiming throughout the whole city how much Jesus had done for him.

40 Now when Jesus returned, the crowd welcomed him, for they were all waiting for him. [41]And there came a man named Ja′irus, who was a ruler of the synagogue; and falling at Jesus' feet he besought him to come to his house, [42]for he had an only daughter, about twelve years of age, and she was dying.

As he went, the people pressed round him. [43]And a woman who had had a flow of blood for twelve years[w] and could not be healed by any one [44]came up behind him, and touched the fringe of his garment; and immediately her flow of blood ceased. [45]And Jesus said, "Who was it that touched me?" When all denied it, Peter[x] said, "Master, the multitudes surround you and press upon you!" [46]But Jesus said, "Some one touched me; for I perceive that power has gone forth from me."

τὴν πόλιν κηρύσσων ὅσα ἐποίησεν αὐτῷ
the city proclaiming what things [2]did [3]to him
ὁ Ἰησοῦς.
[1]Jesus.

40 Ἐν δὲ τῷ ὑποστρέφειν τὸν Ἰησοῦν
Now in the to return - Jesus[be]
=when Jesus returned
ἀπεδέξατο αὐτὸν ὁ ὄχλος· ἦσαν γὰρ
welcomed him the crowd; for they were
πάντες προσδοκῶντες αὐτόν. 41 καὶ ἰδοὺ
all expecting him. And behold
ἦλθεν ἀνὴρ ᾧ ὄνομα Ἰάϊρος, καὶ οὗτος
came a man to whom name Jairus,[c] and this man
ἄρχων τῆς συναγωγῆς ὑπῆρχεν· καὶ πεσὼν
a ruler of the synagogue was; and falling
παρὰ τοὺς πόδας Ἰησοῦ παρεκάλει αὐτὸν
at the feet of Jesus he besought him
εἰσελθεῖν εἰς τὸν οἶκον αὐτοῦ, 42 ὅτι
to enter into the house of him, because
θυγάτηρ μονογενὴς ἦν αὐτῷ ὡς ἐτῶν
daughter an only born was to him[c] about of years
=he had an only daughter
δώδεκα καὶ αὕτη ἀπέθνησκεν. Ἐν δὲ τῷ
twelve and this(she) was dying. Now in the
=as he went
ὑπάγειν αὐτὸν οἱ ὄχλοι συνέπνιγον αὐτόν.
to go him[be] the crowds pressed upon him.
43 καὶ γυνὴ οὖσα ἐν ῥύσει αἵματος ἀπὸ
And a woman being in a flow of blood from
=having
ἐτῶν δώδεκα, ἥτις οὐκ ἴσχυσεν ἀπ'
years twelve, who was not able from
οὐδενὸς θεραπευθῆναι, 44 προσελθοῦσα ὄπισθεν
no(any)one to be healed, approaching behind
ἥψατο τοῦ κρασπέδου τοῦ ἱματίου αὐτοῦ,
touched the fringe of the garment of him,
καὶ παραχρῆμα ἔστη ἡ ῥύσις τοῦ αἵματος
and at once stood the flow of the blood
αὐτῆς. 45 καὶ εἶπεν ὁ Ἰησοῦς· τίς ὁ
of her. And said - Jesus : Who the
ἁψάμενός μου; ἀρνουμένων δὲ πάντων[a]
[one] touching me? And denying all[a]
=when all denied
εἶπεν ὁ Πέτρος· ἐπιστάτα, οἱ ὄχλοι
said - Peter : Master, the crowds
συνέχουσίν σε καὶ ἀποθλίβουσιν. 46 ὁ δὲ
press upon thee and jostle. - But
Ἰησοῦς εἶπεν· ἥψατό μού τις· ἐγὼ γὰρ
Jesus said : Touched me someone; for I
ἔγνων δύναμιν ἐξεληλυθυῖαν ἀπ' ἐμοῦ.
knew power having gone forth from me.

[w] Other ancient authorities add and had spent all her living upon physicians
[x] Other ancient authorities add and those who were with him

⁴⁷And when the woman saw that she was not hidden, she came trembling, and falling down before him declared in the presence of all the people why she had touched him, and how she had been immediately healed. ⁴⁸And he said to her, "Daughter, your faith has made you well; go in peace."

49 While he was still speaking, a man from the ruler's house came and said, "Your daughter is dead; do not trouble the Teacher any more." ⁵⁰But Jesus on hearing this answered him, "Do not fear; only believe, and she shall be well." ⁵¹And when he came to the house, he permitted no one to enter with him, except Peter and John and James, and the father and mother of the child. ⁵²And all were weeping and bewailing her; but he said, "Do not weep; for she is not dead but sleeping." ⁵³And they laughed at him, knowing that she was dead. ⁵⁴But taking her by the hand he called, saying, "Child, arise." ⁵⁵And her spirit returned, and she got up at once; and he directed that something should be given her to eat. ⁵⁶And her parents were

47 ἰδοῦσα δὲ ἡ γυνὴ ὅτι οὐκ ἔλαθεν,
And ³seeing ¹the ²woman that she was not hidden,

τρέμουσα ἦλθεν καὶ προσπεσοῦσα αὐτῷ δι'
trembling came and prostrating before him ⁶for

ἣν αἰτίαν ἥψατο αὐτοῦ ἀπήγγειλεν ἐνώπιον
⁷what ⁸cause ⁹she touched ¹⁰him ¹declared ²before

παντὸς τοῦ λαοῦ, καὶ ὡς ἰάθη παραχρῆμα.
³all ⁴the ⁵people, and how she was cured at once.

48 ὁ δὲ εἶπεν αὐτῇ· θυγάτηρ, ἡ πίστις
And he said to her: Daughter, the faith

σου σέσωκέν σε· πορεύου εἰς εἰρήνην.
of thee has healed thee; go in peace.

49 Ἔτι αὐτοῦ λαλοῦντος ἔρχεταί τις παρὰ
Yet him speaking³ comes someone from
=While he was yet speaking

τοῦ ἀρχισυναγώγου λέγων ὅτι τέθνηκεν
the synagogue ruler saying[,] – Has died

ἡ θυγάτηρ σου· μηκέτι σκύλλε τὸν
the daughter of thee; no more trouble the

διδάσκαλον. 50 ὁ δὲ Ἰησοῦς ἀκούσας
teacher. – But Jesus hearing

ἀπεκρίθη αὐτῷ· μὴ φοβοῦ· μόνον πίστευσον,
answered him: Fear thou not; only believe,

καὶ σωθήσεται. 51 ἐλθὼν δὲ εἰς τὴν
and she will be healed. And coming into the

οἰκίαν οὐκ ἀφῆκεν εἰσελθεῖν τινα σὺν
house he allowed not to enter anyone with

αὐτῷ εἰ μὴ Πέτρον καὶ Ἰωάννην καὶ
him except Peter and John and

Ἰάκωβον καὶ τὸν πατέρα τῆς παιδὸς καὶ
James and the father of the maid and

τὴν μητέρα. 52 ἔκλαιον δὲ πάντες καὶ
the mother. And were weeping all and

ἐκόπτοντο αὐτήν. ὁ δὲ εἶπεν· μὴ κλαίετε·
bewailing her. But he said: Weep ye not;

οὐκ ἀπέθανεν ἀλλὰ καθεύδει. 53 καὶ
she did not die but sleeps. And

κατεγέλων αὐτοῦ, εἰδότες ὅτι ἀπέθανεν.
they ridiculed him, knowing that she died.

54 αὐτὸς δὲ κρατήσας τῆς χειρὸς αὐτῆς
But he holding the hand of her

ἐφώνησεν λέγων· ἡ παῖς, ἔγειρε. 55 καὶ
called saying: – Maid, arise. And

ἐπέστρεψεν τὸ πνεῦμα αὐτῆς, καὶ ἀνέστη
returned the spirit of her, and she rose up

παραχρῆμα, καὶ διέταξεν αὐτῇ δοθῆναι
at once, and he commanded ²to her ¹to be given

φαγεῖν. 56 καὶ ἐξέστησαν οἱ γονεῖς
to eat. And were amazed the parents

amazed; but he charged them to tell no one what had happened.

αὐτῆς·   ὁ δὲ   παρήγγειλεν   αὐτοῖς   μηδενὶ
of her;   but he   enjoined   them   [1]no one
εἰπεῖν   τὸ   γεγονός.
[1]to tell   the thing having happened.
         =what had happened.

CHAPTER 9

AND he called the twelve together and gave them power and authority over all demons and to cure diseases, [2]and he sent them out to preach the kingdom of God and to heal. [3]And he said to them, "Take nothing for your journey, no staff, nor bag, nor bread, nor money; and do not have two tunics. [4]And whatever house you enter, stay there, and from there depart. [5]And wherever they do not receive you, when you leave that town shake off the dust from your feet as a testimony against them." [6]And they departed and went through the villages, preaching the gospel and healing everywhere.

7 Now Herod the tetrarch heard of all that was done, and he was perplexed, because it was said by some that John had been raised from the dead, [8]by some that Eli′jah had appeared, and by others that one

9 Συγκαλεσάμενος δὲ τοὺς δώδεκα ἔδωκεν
And having called together   the   twelve   he gave
αὐτοῖς δύναμιν καὶ ἐξουσίαν ἐπὶ πάντα τὰ
them   power   and   authority   over   all   the
δαιμόνια   καὶ   νόσους   θεραπεύειν·   2 καὶ
demons   and   diseases   to heal;   and
ἀπέστειλεν αὐτοὺς κηρύσσειν τὴν βασιλείαν
sent   them   to proclaim   the   kingdom
τοῦ θεοῦ καὶ ἰᾶσθαι, 3 καὶ εἶπεν πρὸς
–   of God   and   to cure,   and   said   to
αὐτούς· μηδὲν αἴρετε εἰς τὴν ὁδόν, μήτε
them :   Nothing   take ye   for   the   way,   neither
ῥάβδον   μήτε   πήραν   μήτε   ἄρτον   μήτε
staff   nor   wallet   nor   bread   nor
ἀργύριον μήτε ἀνὰ δύο χιτῶνας ἔχειν.
silver   nor   each   two   tunics   to have.
4 καὶ εἰς ἣν ἂν οἰκίαν εἰσέλθητε, ἐκεῖ
And   into   whatever   house   ye may enter,   there
μένετε καὶ ἐκεῖθεν ἐξέρχεσθε.   5 καὶ
remain   and   thence   go forth.   And
ὅσοι ἂν μὴ δέχωνται ὑμᾶς, ἐξερχόμενοι
as many as   may not receive   you,   going forth
ἀπὸ τῆς πόλεως ἐκείνης τὸν κονιορτὸν
from   –   city   that   the   dust
ἀπὸ τῶν ποδῶν ὑμῶν ἀποτινάσσετε εἰς
from   the   feet   of you   shake off   for
μαρτύριον ἐπ' αὐτούς.   6 ἐξερχόμενοι δὲ
a testimony   against   them.   And going forth
διήρχοντο κατὰ τὰς κώμας εὐαγγελιζόμενοι
they went   throughout   the   villages   evangelizing
through
καὶ θεραπεύοντες πανταχοῦ.   7 Ἤκουσεν
and   healing   everywhere.   [8]heard
δὲ Ἡρῴδης ὁ τετραάρχης τὰ γινόμενα
[1]And [3]Herod [2]the [4]tetrarch   the things   happening
πάντα, καὶ διηπόρει διὰ τὸ λέγεσθαι
all,   and was in perplexity   because of the   to be said
=because it was said
ὑπό τινων ὅτι Ἰωάννης ἠγέρθη ἐκ νεκρῶν,
by   some   that   John   was raised from [the]   dead,
8 ὑπό τινων δὲ ὅτι Ἡλίας ἐφάνη, ἄλλων
and by some   that   Elias   appeared,   [3]others

of the old prophets had
risen. [9] Herod said, "John
I beheaded; but who is
this about whom I hear
such things?" And he
sought to see him.

10 On their return the
apostles told him what
they had done. And he
took them and withdrew
apart to a city called
Bethsa'ida. [11] When the
crowds learned it, they
followed him; and he
welcomed them and
spoke to them of the
kingdom of God, and
cured those who had
need of healing. [12] Now
the day began to wear
away; and the twelve
came and said to him,
"Send the crowd away,
to go into the villages
and country round about,
to lodge and get pro-
visions; for we are here
in a lonely place." [13] But
he said to them, "You
give them something to
eat." They said, "We
have no more than five
loaves and two fish—
unless we are to go and
buy food for all these
people." [14] For there were
about five thousand men.
And he said to his
disciples, "Make them

δὲ ὅτι προφήτης τις τῶν ἀρχαίων ἀνέστη.
but that prophet a certain of the ancients rose again.

9 εἶπεν δὲ [ὁ] Ἡρῴδης· Ἰωάννην ἐγὼ
But said – Herod : John I

ἀπεκεφάλισα· τίς δέ ἐστιν οὗτος περὶ οὗ
beheaded; but who is this about whom

ἀκούω τοιαῦτα; καὶ ἐζήτει ἰδεῖν αὐτόν.
I hear such things? And he sought to see him.

10 Καὶ ὑποστρέψαντες οἱ ἀπόστολοι
And having returned the apostles

διηγήσαντο αὐτῷ ὅσα ἐποίησαν. Καὶ
narrated to him what things they did. And

παραλαβὼν αὐτοὺς ὑπεχώρησεν κατ' ἰδίαν
taking them he departed privately

εἰς πόλιν καλουμένην Βηθσαϊδά. 11 οἱ δὲ
to a city being called Bethsaida. But the

ὄχλοι γνόντες ἠκολούθησαν αὐτῷ· καὶ
crowds knowing followed him; and

ἀποδεξάμενος αὐτοὺς ἐλάλει αὐτοῖς περὶ
welcoming them he spoke to them about

τῆς βασιλείας τοῦ θεοῦ, καὶ τοὺς χρείαν
the kingdom - of God, and the [ones] ²need

ἔχοντας θεραπείας ἰᾶτο. 12 Ἡ δὲ ἡμέρα
¹having of healing he cured. But the day

ἤρξατο κλίνειν· προσελθόντες δὲ οἱ δώδεκα
began to decline; and approaching the twelve

εἶπαν αὐτῷ· ἀπόλυσον τὸν ὄχλον, ἵνα
said to him : Dismiss the crowd, that

πορευθέντες εἰς τὰς κύκλῳ κώμας καὶ
going to ¹the ²around ³villages ³and

ἀγροὺς καταλύσωσιν καὶ εὕρωσιν ἐπισιτισμόν,
⁴farms they may lodge and may find provisions,

ὅτι ὧδε ἐν ἐρήμῳ τόπῳ ἐσμέν. 13 εἶπεν
because here in a desert place we are. he said

δὲ πρὸς αὐτούς· δότε αὐτοῖς φαγεῖν
And to them : ¹Give ³them ⁴to eat

ὑμεῖς. οἱ δὲ εἶπαν· οὐκ εἰσὶν ἡμῖν
²ye. But they said : There are not to us⁶
                                        =We have not

πλεῖον ἢ ἄρτοι πέντε καὶ ἰχθύες δύο, εἰ
more than loaves five and fishes two, un-

μήτι πορευθέντες ἡμεῖς ἀγοράσωμεν εἰς
less going we may buy for

πάντα τὸν λαὸν τοῦτον βρώματα. 14 ἦσαν
all - people this foods. there were

γὰρ ὡσεὶ ἄνδρες πεντακισχίλιοι. εἶπεν δὲ
For about men five thousand. And he said

πρὸς τοὺς μαθητὰς αὐτοῦ· κατακλίνατε
to the disciples of him : ¹Make ²to recline

sit down in companies, about fifty each." ¹⁵And they did so, and made them all sit down. ¹⁶And taking the five loaves and the two fish he looked up to heaven, and blessed and broke them, and gave them to the disciples to set before the crowd. ¹⁷And all ate and were satisfied. And they took up what was left over, twelve baskets of broken pieces.

18 Now it happened that as he was praying alone the disciples were with him; and he asked them, "Who do the people say that I am?" ¹⁹And they answered, "John the Baptist; but others say, Eli'jah; and others, that one of the old prophets has risen." ²⁰And he said to them, "But who do you say that I am?" And Peter answered, "The Christ of God." ²¹But he charged and commanded them to tell this to no one, ²²saying, "The Son of man must suffer many things, and be rejected by the elders and chief priests and scribes, and

---

αὐτοὺς κλισίας ὡσεὶ ἀνὰ πεντήκοντα
them [in] groups ¹about ²each ⁸fifty.

15 καὶ ἐποίησαν οὕτως καὶ κατέκλιναι
And they did so and made to recline

ἅπαντας. 16 λαβὼν δὲ τοὺς πέντε ἄρτους
all. And taking the five loaves

καὶ τοὺς δύο ἰχθύας, ἀναβλέψας εἰς τὸ
and the two fishes, looking up to –

οὐρανὸν εὐλόγησεν αὐτοὺς καὶ κατέκλασεν
heaven he blessed them and broke,

καὶ ἐδίδου τοῖς μαθηταῖς παραθεῖναι τᾳ
and gave to the disciples to set before the

ὄχλῳ. 17 καὶ ἔφαγον καὶ ἐχορτάσθησαν
crowd. And they ate and were satisfied

πάντες· καὶ ἤρθη τὸ περισσεῦσαν αὐτοῖς
all; and were taken the excess to them

κλασμάτων κόφινοι δώδεκα.
of fragments baskets twelve.

18 Καὶ ἐγένετο ἐν τῷ εἶναι αὐτὸι
And it came to pass in the to be him^{be}
=as he was

προσευχόμενον κατὰ μόνας συνῆσαν αὐτᾳ
praying alone were with him

οἱ μαθηταί, καὶ ἐπηρώτησεν αὐτοὺς λέγων
the disciples, and he questioned them saying :

τίνα με οἱ ὄχλοι λέγουσιν εἶναι; 19 οἱ δὲ
Whom me the crowds say to be? And they
=Whom do the crowds say that I am?

ἀποκριθέντες εἶπαν· Ἰωάννην τὸν βαπτιστήν
answering said : John the Baptist,

ἄλλοι δὲ Ἠλίαν, ἄλλοι δὲ ὅτι προφήτης
but others Elias, and others that prophet

τις τῶν ἀρχαίων ἀνέστη. 20 εἶπεν δὲ
a certain of the ancients rose again. And he said

αὐτοῖς· ὑμεῖς δὲ τίνα με λέγετε εἶναι
to them : But ye whom me say to be?
=whom say ye that I am?

Πέτρος δὲ ἀποκριθεὶς εἶπεν· τὸν χριστὸ
And Peter answering said: The Christ

τοῦ θεοῦ. 21 ὁ δὲ ἐπιτιμήσας αὐτοῖ
– of God. But he warning ²them

παρήγγειλεν μηδενὶ λέγειν τοῦτο, 22 εἰπὼ
¹charged ⁴no one ³to tell ⁵this, saying

ὅτι δεῖ τὸν υἱὸν τοῦ ἀνθρώπου πολλ
that it behoves the Son – of man many thing

παθεῖν καὶ ἀποδοκιμασθῆναι ἀπὸ τῶ
to suffer and to be rejected from(by) the

πρεσβυτέρων καὶ ἀρχιερέων καὶ γραμματέω
elders and chief priests and scribes

be killed, and on the third day be raised."

23 And he said to all, "If any man would come after me, let him deny himself and take up his cross daily and follow me. 24 For whoever would save his life will lose it; and whoever loses his life for my sake, he will save it. 25 For what does it profit a man if he gains the whole world and loses or forfeits himself? 26 For whoever is ashamed of me and of my words, of him will the Son of man be ashamed when he comes in his glory and the glory of the Father and of the holy angels. 27 But I tell you truly, there are some standing here who will not taste of death before they see the kingdom of God."

28 Now about eight days after these sayings he took with him Peter and John and James, and went up on the mountain to pray. 29 And as he was praying, the appearance of his countenance was

καὶ ἀποκτανθῆναι καὶ τῇ τρίτῃ ἡμέρᾳ
and   to be killed   and   on the third   day

ἐγερθῆναι. 23 Ἔλεγεν δὲ πρὸς πάντας·
to be raised.   And he said   to   all :

εἴ τις θέλει ὀπίσω μου ἔρχεσθαι, ἀρνησάσθω
If anyone wishes   after   me   to come,   let him deny

ἑαυτὸν καὶ ἀράτω τὸν σταυρὸν
himself   and   take   the   cross

αὐτοῦ καθ' ἡμέραν, καὶ ἀκολουθείτω μοι.
of him   daily,   and   let him follow   me.

24 ὃς γὰρ ἐὰν θέλῃ τὴν ψυχὴν αὐτοῦ
For whoever   wishes   the   life   of him

σῶσαι, ἀπολέσει αὐτήν· ὃς δ' ἂν ἀπολέσῃ
to save,   he will lose   it;   but whoever   loses

τὴν ψυχὴν αὐτοῦ ἕνεκεν ἐμοῦ, οὗτος
the   life   of him   for the sake of   me,   this [one]

σώσει αὐτήν. 25 τί γὰρ ὠφελεῖται
will save   it.   For what   is profited

ἄνθρωπος κερδήσας τὸν κόσμον ὅλον ἑαυτὸν
a man   gaining   the   world   whole   [3]himself

δὲ ἀπολέσας ἢ ζημιωθείς; 26 ὃς γὰρ ἂν
[1]but   [2]losing   or   suffering loss?   For whoever

ἐπαισχυνθῇ με καὶ τοὺς ἐμοὺς λόγους,
is ashamed of   me   and   -   my   words,

τοῦτον ὁ υἱὸς τοῦ ἀνθρώπου ἐπαι-
this [one]   the   Son   -   of man   will be

σχυνθήσεται, ὅταν ἔλθῃ ἐν τῇ δόξῃ
ashamed of,   when   he comes   in   the   glory

αὐτοῦ καὶ τοῦ πατρὸς καὶ τῶν ἁγίων
of him   and   of the   Father   and   of the   holy

ἀγγέλων. 27 λέγω δὲ ὑμῖν ἀληθῶς,
angels.   But I tell   you   truly,

εἰσίν τινες τῶν αὐτοῦ ἑστηκότων οἳ
there are some   of the [ones]   here   standing   who

οὐ μὴ γεύσωνται θανάτου ἕως ἂν ἴδωσιν
by no means   may taste   of death   until   they see

τὴν βασιλείαν τοῦ θεοῦ.
the   kingdom   -   of God.

28 Ἐγένετο δὲ μετὰ τοὺς λόγους τούτους
And it came to pass [4]after   -   [5]sayings   [6]these

ὡσεὶ ἡμέραι ὀκτώ, καὶ παραλαβὼν Πέτρον
[1]about   [3]days   [2]eight,   and   taking   Peter

καὶ Ἰωάννην καὶ Ἰάκωβον ἀνέβη εἰς τὸ
and   John   and   James   he went up   into   the

ὄρος προσεύξασθαι. 29 καὶ ἐγένετο ἐν τῷ
mountain   to pray.   And   [3]became   in   the
=[1]as [3]he [2]prayed

προσεύχεσθαι αὐτὸν τὸ εἶδος τοῦ προσώπου
to pray   him[be]   [4]the   [5]appearance [6]of the   [7]face

altered, and his raiment became dazzling white. [30]And behold, two men talked with him, Moses and Eli'jah, [31]who appeared in glory and spoke of his departure, which he was to accomplish at Jerusalem. [32]Now Peter and those who were with him were heavy with sleep but kept awake, and they saw his glory and the two men who stood with him. [33]And as the men were parting from him, Peter said to Jesus, "Master, it is well that we are here; let us make three booths, one for you and one for Moses and one for Eli'jah"—not knowing what he said. [34]As he said this, a cloud came and overshadowed them; and they were afraid as they entered the cloud. [35]And a voice came out of the cloud, saying, "This is my Son, my Chosen;[y] listen to him!" [36]And when the voice had spoken, Jesus was found alone. And they kept silence and told no one

αὐτοῦ ἕτερον καὶ ὁ ἱματισμὸς αὐτοῦ
[9]of him   [19]different and the   raiment   of him
λευκὸς ἐξαστράπτων.   30 καὶ ἰδοὺ ἄνδρες
[1]white   [1]gleaming.   And[,] behold[,] men
δύο συνελάλουν αὐτῷ, οἵτινες ἦσαν Μωϋσῆς
two conversed with him,   who   were   Moses
καὶ Ἠλίας,   31 οἳ ὀφθέντες ἐν δόξῃ ἔλεγον
and Elias,   who appearing in glory spoke of
τὴν ἔξοδον αὐτοῦ, ἣν ἤμελλεν πληροῦν
the exodus of him, which he was about to accomplish
ἐν Ἱερουσαλήμ.   32 ὁ δὲ Πέτρος καὶ οἱ
in Jerusalem.   - But Peter and the [ones]
σὺν αὐτῷ ἦσαν βεβαρημένοι ὕπνῳ· δια-
with him were having been burdened with sleep; [1]wak-
γρηγορήσαντες δὲ εἶδαν τὴν δόξαν αὐτοῦ
ing thoroughly   [1]but they saw the   glory   of him
καὶ τοὺς δύο ἄνδρας τοὺς συνεστῶτας
and the   two   men   -   standing with
αὐτῷ.   33 καὶ ἐγένετο ἐν τῷ διαχωρίζεσθαι
him.   And it came to pass in the   to part
                                        = when they parted
αὐτοὺς ἀπ᾽ αὐτοῦ εἶπεν ὁ Πέτρος πρὸς
them[be] from   him   said   - Peter   to
τὸν Ἰησοῦν· ἐπιστάτα, καλόν ἐστιν ἡμᾶς
  - Jesus :   Master,   good it is [for] us
ὧδε εἶναι, καὶ ποιήσωμεν σκηνὰς τρεῖς,
here to be,   and let us make   tents   three,
μίαν σοὶ καὶ μίαν Μωϋσεῖ καὶ μίαν
one for thee and one for Moses   and   one
Ἠλίᾳ, μὴ εἰδὼς ὃ λέγει.   34 ταῦτα δὲ
for Elias, not knowing what he says.   And these things
αὐτοῦ λέγοντος ἐγένετο νεφέλη καὶ
him   saying[a]   came   a cloud   and
= while he said these things
ἐπεσκίαζεν αὐτούς· ἐφοβήθησαν δὲ ἐν τῷ
overshadowed them;   and they feared   in the
                                        = as they entered
εἰσελθεῖν αὐτοὺς εἰς τὴν νεφέλην.   35 καὶ
to enter   them[be] into the   cloud.   And
φωνὴ ἐγένετο ἐκ τῆς νεφέλης λέγουσα·
a voice came   out of the   cloud   saying :
οὗτός ἐστιν ὁ υἱός μου ὁ ἐκλελεγμένος,
This   is   the Son of me - having been chosen,
αὐτοῦ ἀκούετε,   36 καὶ ἐν τῷ γενέσθαι
him   hear ye,   and in the   to become
                                    = when the voice came
τὴν φωνὴν εὑρέθη Ἰησοῦς μόνος.   καὶ
the   voice[be] was found Jesus   alone.   And

αὐτοὶ ἐσίγησαν καὶ οὐδενὶ ἀπήγγειλαν ἐν ἐκείναις
they   were silent and to no one reported   in those

in those days anything of what they had seen.

37 On the next day, when they had come down from the mountain, a great crowd met him. [38]And behold, a man from the crowd cried, "Teacher, I beg you to look upon my son, for he is my only child; [39]and behold, a spirit seizes him, and he suddenly cries out; it convulses him till he foams, and shatters him, and will hardly leave him. [40]And I begged your disciples to cast it out, but they could not." [41]Jesus answered, "O faithless and perverse generation, how long am I to be with you and bear with you? Bring your son here." [42]While he was coming, the demon tore him and convulsed him. But Jesus rebuked the unclean spirit, and healed the boy, and gave him back to his father. [43]And all were astonished at the majesty of God.

But while they were all marveling at everything

ταῖς ἡμέραις οὐδὲν ὧν ἐώρακαν.
— days no(any) of [the things] they have
thing which (had) seen.

37 Ἐγένετο δὲ τῇ ἑξῆς ἡμέρᾳ κατελ-
And it came to pass on the following day

θόντων αὐτῶν ἀπὸ τοῦ ὄρους συνήντησεν
down them[a] from the mountain met
=as they came down

αὐτῷ ὄχλος πολύς. 38 καὶ ἰδοὺ ἀνὴρ
him crowd a much. And[,] behold[,] a man

ἀπὸ τοῦ ὄχλου ἐβόησεν λέγων· διδάσκαλε,
from the crowd called aloud saying : Teacher,

δέομαί σου ἐπιβλέψαι ἐπὶ τὸν υἱόν μου,
I beg of thee to look at at the son of me,

ὅτι μονογενής μοί ἐστιν, 39 καὶ ἰδοὺ
because only born to me he is, and[,] behold[,]

πνεῦμα λαμβάνει αὐτόν, καὶ ἐξαίφνης
a spirit takes him, and suddenly

κράζει καὶ σπαράσσει αὐτὸν μετὰ ἀφροῦ,
cries out and throws him with foam,

καὶ μόλις ἀποχωρεῖ ἀπ' αὐτοῦ συντρῖβον
and scarcely departs from him bruising

αὐτόν· 40 καὶ ἐδεήθην τῶν μαθητῶν σου
him; and I begged of the disciples of thee

ἵνα ἐκβάλωσιν αὐτό, καὶ οὐκ ἠδυνήθησαν.
that they would expel it, and they were not able.

41 ἀποκριθεὶς δὲ ὁ Ἰησοῦς εἶπεν· ὦ
And answering — Jesus said : O

γενεὰ ἄπιστος καὶ διεστραμμένη, ἕως πότε
generation unbelieving and having been perverted, until when

ἔσομαι πρὸς ὑμᾶς καὶ ἀνέξομαι ὑμῶν;
shall I be with you and endure you?

προσάγαγε ὧδε τὸν υἱόν σου. 42 ἔτι
Bring here the son of thee. yet

δὲ προσερχομένου αὐτοῦ ἔρρηξεν αὐτὸν τὸ
But approaching him[a] tore him the
=But while he was yet approaching

δαιμόνιον καὶ συνεσπάραξεν· ἐπετίμησεν δὲ
demon and threw violently; but [2]rebuked

ὁ Ἰησοῦς τῷ πνεύματι τῷ ἀκαθάρτῳ, καὶ
— [1]Jesus [3]the [3]spirit — [4]unclean, and

ἰάσατο τὸν παῖδα καὶ ἀπέδωκεν αὐτὸν τῷ
cured the boy and restored him to the

πατρὶ αὐτοῦ. 43 ἐξεπλήσσοντο δὲ πάντες
father of him. And were astounded all

ἐπὶ τῇ μεγαλειότητι τοῦ θεοῦ.
at the majesty of God.

Πάντων δὲ θαυμαζόντων ἐπὶ πᾶσιν οἷς
And all marvelling[a] at all things which
=while all marvelled

he did, he said to his disciples, 44 "Let these words sink into your ears; for the Son of man is to be delivered into the hands of men." 45 But they did not understand this saying, and it was concealed from them, that they should not perceive it; and they were afraid to ask him about this saying.

46 And an argument arose among them as to which of them was the greatest. 47 But when Jesus perceived the thought of their hearts, he took a child and put him by his side, 48 and said to them, "Whoever receives this child in my name receives me, and whoever receives me receives him who sent me; for he who is least among you all is the one who is great."

49 John answered, "Master, we saw a man casting out demons in your name, and we forbade him, because he does not follow with us." 50 But Jesus said to him, "Do not forbid him; for he that is not against you is for you."

51 When the days drew near for him to be

ἐποίει εἶπεν πρὸς τοὺς μαθητὰς αὐτοῦ·
he did he said to the disciples of him :
44 θέσθε ὑμεῖς εἰς τὰ ὦτα ὑμῶν τοὺς
Lay ye in the ears of you –
λόγους τούτους· ὁ γὰρ υἱὸς τοῦ ἀνθρώπου
sayings these; for the Son – of man
μέλλει παραδίδοσθαι εἰς χεῖρας ἀνθρώπων.
is about to be betrayed into [the] hands of men.
45 οἱ δὲ ἠγνόουν τὸ ῥῆμα τοῦτο, καὶ ἦν
But they knew not – word this, and it was
παρακεκαλυμμένον ἀπ' αὐτῶν ἵνα μὴ
having been veiled from them lest
αἴσθωνται αὐτό, καὶ ἐφοβοῦντο ἐρωτῆσαι
they should perceive it, and they feared to ask
αὐτὸν περὶ τοῦ ῥήματος τούτου. 46 Εἰσῆλθεν
him about – word this. entered
δὲ διαλογισμὸς ἐν αὐτοῖς, τὸ τίς ἂν εἴη
And a debate among them, – who might be
= a debate arose
μείζων αὐτῶν. 47 ὁ δὲ Ἰησοῦς εἰδὼς τὸν
greater(est) of them. – And Jesus knowing the
διαλογισμὸν τῆς καρδίας αὐτῶν, ἐπιλαβόμενος
debate of the heart of them, taking
παιδίον ἔστησεν αὐτὸ παρ' ἑαυτῷ, 48 καὶ
a child stood it(him) beside himself, and
εἶπεν αὐτοῖς· ὃς ἐὰν δέξηται τοῦτο τὸ
said to them : Whoever receives this –
παιδίον ἐπὶ τῷ ὀνόματί μου, ἐμὲ δέχεται·
child on(in) the name of me, me receives;
καὶ ὃς ἂν ἐμὲ δέξηται, δέχεται τὸν
and whoever me receives, receives the [one]
ἀποστείλαντά με· ὁ γὰρ μικρότερος ἐν
having sent me; for [1]the [one] [2]lesser [4]among
πᾶσιν ὑμῖν ὑπάρχων, οὗτός ἐστιν μέγας.
[4]all [5]you [3]being, this [one] is great.
49 Ἀποκριθεὶς δὲ ὁ Ἰωάννης εἶπεν· ἐπιστάτα,
And answering – John said : Master,
εἴδομέν τινα ἐν τῷ ὀνόματί σου ἐκβάλλοντα
we saw someone in the name of thee expelling
δαιμόνια, καὶ ἐκωλύομεν αὐτόν, ὅτι
demons, and we prevented him, because
οὐκ ἀκολουθεῖ μεθ' ἡμῶν. 50 εἶπεν δὲ πρὸς
he does not follow with us. And said to
αὐτὸν Ἰησοῦς· μὴ κωλύετε· ὃς γὰρ οὐκ
him Jesus: Do not prevent; for [he] who not
ἔστιν καθ' ὑμῶν, ὑπὲρ ὑμῶν ἐστιν.
is against you, for you is.
51 Ἐγένετο δὲ ἐν τῷ συμπληροῦσθαι
And it came to pass in the to be fulfilled

received up, he set his face to go to Jerusalem. And he sent messengers ahead of him, [52]who went and entered a village of the Samaritans, to make ready for him; [53]but the people would not receive him, because his face was set toward Jerusalem. [54]And when his disciples James and John saw it, they said, "Lord, do you want us to bid fire come down from heaven and consume them?"[z] [55]But he turned and rebuked them.[a] [56]And they went on to another village.

[57] As they were going along the road, a man said to him, "I will follow you wherever you go." [58]And Jesus said to him, "Foxes have holes, and birds of the air have nests; but the Son of man has nowhere to lay his head." [59]To another he said, "Follow me." But he said, "Lord, let me first go and bury my father." [60]But he said to him, "Leave the dead to

τὰς ἡμέρας τῆς ἀναλήμψεως αὐτοῦ καὶ
the days of the assumption of him[be] and
=as the days of his assumption were fulfilled

αὐτὸς τὸ πρόσωπον ἐστήρισεν τοῦ
he the(his) face set −

πορεύεσθαι εἰς Ἰερουσαλήμ, 52 καὶ ἀπέστειλεν
to go[d] to Jerusalem, and sent

ἀγγέλους πρὸ προσώπου αὐτοῦ. καὶ
messengers before face of him. And

πορευθέντες εἰσῆλθον εἰς κώμην Σαμαριτῶν,
going they entered into a village of Samaritans,

ὥστε ἑτοιμάσαι αὐτῷ· 53 καὶ οὐκ ἐδέξαντο
so as to prepare for him; and they did not receive

αὐτόν, ὅτι τὸ πρόσωπον αὐτοῦ ἦν
him, because the face of him was

πορευόμενον εἰς Ἰερουσαλήμ. 54 ἰδόντες
going to Jerusalem. seeing

δὲ οἱ μαθηταὶ Ἰάκωβος καὶ Ἰωάννης
And [1]the [2]disciples [3]James [4]and [5]John

εἶπαν· κύριε, θέλεις εἴπωμεν πῦρ κατα-
[7]said: Lord, wilt thou we may tell fire to come

βῆναι ἀπὸ τοῦ οὐρανοῦ καὶ ἀναλῶσαι
down from − heaven and to destroy

αὐτούς; 55 στραφεὶς δὲ ἐπετίμησεν αὐτοῖς.
them? But turning he rebuked them.

56 καὶ ἐπορεύθησαν εἰς ἑτέραν κώμην.
And they went to another village.

57 Καὶ πορευομένων αὐτῶν ἐν τῇ ὁδῷ
And going them[a] in the way
=as they went

εἶπέν τις πρὸς αὐτόν· ἀκολουθήσω σοι
said one to him : I will follow thee

ὅπου ἐὰν ἀπέρχῃ. 58 καὶ εἶπεν αὐτῷ ὁ
wherever thou goest. And said to him −

Ἰησοῦς· αἱ ἀλώπεκες φωλεοὺς ἔχουσιν καὶ
Jesus: The foxes holes have and

τὰ πετεινὰ τοῦ οὐρανοῦ κατασκηνώσεις, ὁ
the birds − of heaven nests, [2]the

δὲ υἱὸς τοῦ ἀνθρώπου οὐκ ἔχει ποῦ τὴν
[1]but Son − of man has not where the(his)

κεφαλὴν κλίνῃ. 59 Εἶπεν δὲ πρὸς ἕτερον·
head he may lay. And he said to another :

ἀκολούθει μοι. ὁ δὲ εἶπεν· ἐπίτρεψόν μοι
Follow me. But he said : Allow me

πρῶτον ἀπελθόντι θάψαι τὸν πατέρα μου.
first going to bury the father of me.

60 εἶπεν δὲ αὐτῷ· ἄφες τοὺς νεκροὺς
But he said to him : Leave the dead

[z] Other ancient authorities add as Elijah did

[a] Other ancient authorities add and he said, "You do not know what manner of spirit you are of; for the Son of man came not to destroy men's lives but to save them"

bury their own dead; but as for you, go and proclaim the kingdom of God." ⁶¹Another said, "I will follow you, Lord; but let me first say farewell to those at my home." ⁶²Jesus said to him, "No one who puts his hand to the plow and looks back is fit for the kingdom of God."

θάψαι τοὺς ἑαυτῶν νεκρούς, σὺ δὲ ἀπελθὼν
to bury   the of themselves dead,   but thou   going
                                    =their own dead,
διάγγελλε τὴν βασιλείαν τοῦ θεοῦ.   61 Εἶπεν
announce   the   kingdom   – of God.   said
δὲ καὶ ἕτερος· ἀκολουθήσω σοι, κύριε·
And also another : I will follow thee,   Lord;
πρῶτον δὲ ἐπίτρεψόν μοι ἀποτάξασθαι τοῖς
but first   allow   me to say farewell to the [ones]
εἰς τὸν οἶκόν μου. 62 εἶπεν δὲ [πρὸς
in   the house of me.   But said   to
αὐτὸν] ὁ Ἰησοῦς· οὐδεὶς ἐπιβαλὼν τὴν
him]   Jesus: No one   putting on the(his)
χεῖρα ἐπ᾽ ἄροτρον καὶ βλέπων εἰς τὰ
hand   on   a plough   and   looking at the things
ὀπίσω εὔθετός ἐστιν τῇ βασιλείᾳ τοῦ θεοῦ.
behind   fit   is   for the   kingdom   – of God.

CHAPTER 10

AFTER this the Lord appointed seventy[b] others, and sent them on ahead of him, two by two, into every town and place where he himself was about to come. ²And he said to them, "The harvest is plentiful, but the laborers are few; pray therefore the LORD of the harvest to send out laborers into his harvest. ³Go your way; behold, I send you out as lambs in the midst of wolves. ⁴Carry no purse, no bag, no sandals; and salute no one on the road. ⁵Whatever house you enter, first say, 'Peace be to this house!' ⁶And if a son of peace is there, your peace shall rest upon him; but if not,

10 Μετὰ δὲ ταῦτα ἀνέδειξεν ὁ κύριος
Now after these things appointed the Lord
ἑτέρους ἑβδομήκοντα [δύο], καὶ ἀπέστειλεν
others   seventy-two,   and   sent
αὐτοὺς ἀνὰ δύο πρὸ προσώπου αὐτοῦ εἰς
them   two by two† before   face   of him   into
πᾶσαν πόλιν καὶ τόπον οὗ ἤμελλεν αὐτὸς
every   city   and place where ²was about ¹he
ἔρχεσθαι. 2 ἔλεγεν δὲ πρὸς αὐτούς· ὁ
to come.   And he said   to   them :   the
μὲν θερισμὸς πολύς, οἱ δὲ ἐργάται ὀλίγοι·
Indeed harvest   much,   but the workmen few;
δεήθητε οὖν τοῦ κυρίου τοῦ θερισμοῦ
beg ye therefore of the Lord   of the   harvest
ὅπως ἐργάτας ἐκβάλῃ εἰς τὸν θερισμὸν
that workmen he would thrust forth into the harvest
αὐτοῦ. 3 ὑπάγετε· ἰδοὺ ἀποστέλλω ὑμᾶς
of him.   Go ye;   behold   I send   you
ὡς ἄρνας ἐν μέσῳ λύκων. 4 μὴ βαστάζετε
as lambs in [the] midst of wolves.   Do not carry
βαλλάντιον, μὴ πήραν, μὴ ὑποδήματα· καὶ
a purse,   nor a wallet, nor sandals;   and
μηδένα κατὰ τὴν ὁδὸν ἀσπάσησθε. 5 εἰς
no one   by the   way   greet.   ²into
ἣν δ᾽ ἂν εἰσέλθητε οἰκίαν, πρῶτον λέγετε·
¹And ²whatever ⁵ye enter ⁴house,   first   say :
εἰρήνη τῷ οἴκῳ τούτῳ. 6 καὶ ἐὰν ἐκεῖ
Peace – house to this.   And if there
ᾖ υἱὸς εἰρήνης, ἐπαναπαήσεται ἐπ᾽ αὐτὸν
there is a son of peace,   shall rest   on it(?him)

b Other ancient authorities read seventy-two

it shall return to you.
⁷And remain in the same
house, eating and drink-
ing what they provide,
for the laborer deserves
his wages; do not go
from house to house.
⁸Whenever you enter a
town and they receive
you, eat what is set
before you; ⁹heal the
sick in it and say to them,
'The kingdom of God
has come near to you.'
¹⁰But whenever you enter
a town and they do not
receive you, go into its
streets and say, ¹¹'Even
the dust of your town
that clings to our feet,
we wipe off against you;
nevertheless know this,
that the kingdom of God
has come near.' ¹²I tell
you, it shall be more
tolerable on that day for
Sodom than for that
town.

13 "Woe to you,
Chora′zin! woe to you,
Beth-sa′ida! for if the
mighty works done in
you had been done in
Tyre and Sidon, they
would have repented long
ago, sitting in sackcloth
and ashes. ¹⁴But it shall

ἡ εἰρήνη ὑμῶν· εἰ δὲ μή γε, ἐφ' ὑμᾶς
the peace of you; otherwise, on you
ἀνακάμψει. 7 ἐν αὐτῇ δὲ τῇ οἰκίᾳ μένετε,
it shall return. ²in ⁴same ¹And ²the house* remain,
ἔσθοντες καὶ πίνοντες τὰ παρ' αὐτῶν·
eating and drinking the things with them;
ἄξιος γὰρ ὁ ἐργάτης τοῦ μισθοῦ αὐτοῦ.
for worthy [is] the workman of the pay of him.
μὴ μεταβαίνετε ἐξ οἰκίας εἰς οἰκίαν.
Do not remove from house to house.
8 καὶ εἰς ἣν ἂν πόλιν εἰσέρχησθε καὶ
And into whatever city ye enter and
δέχωνται ὑμᾶς, ἐσθίετε τὰ παρατιθέμενα
they receive you, eat the things being set before
ὑμῖν, 9 καὶ θεραπεύετε τοὺς ἐν αὐτῇ
you, and heal the ²in ²it
ἀσθενεῖς, καὶ λέγετε αὐτοῖς· ἤγγικεν ἐφ'
¹sick, and tell them : Has drawn near on(to)
ὑμᾶς ἡ βασιλεία τοῦ θεοῦ. 10 εἰς ἣν δ'
you the kingdom – of God. And into what-
ἂν πόλιν εἰσέλθητε καὶ μὴ δέχωνται ὑμᾶς,
ever city ye enter and they do not receive you,
ἐξελθόντες εἰς τὰς πλατείας αὐτῆς εἴπατε·
going forth into the streets of it say :
11 καὶ τὸν κονιορτὸν τὸν κολληθέντα ἡμῖν
Even the dust – adhering to us
=the dust of your city adhering to us, on our feet,
ἐκ τῆς πόλεως ὑμῶν εἰς τοὺς πόδας
of the city of you on the(our) feet
ἀπομασσόμεθα ὑμῖν· πλὴν τοῦτο γινώσκετε,
we shake off to you; nevertheless this know ye,
ὅτι ἤγγικεν ἡ βασιλεία τοῦ θεοῦ. 12 λέγω
that has drawn near the kingdom – of God. I tell
ὑμῖν ὅτι Σοδόμοις ἐν τῇ ἡμέρᾳ ἐκείνῃ
you that for Sodom in – day that
ἀνεκτότερον ἔσται ἢ τῇ πόλει ἐκείνῃ.
more endurable it will be than – city for that.
13 Οὐαί σοι, Χοραζίν, οὐαί σοι, Βηθσαϊδά·
Woe to thee, Chorazin, woe to thee, Bethsaida;
ὅτι εἰ ἐν Τύρῳ καὶ Σιδῶνι ἐγενήθησαν αἱ
because if in Tyre and Sidon happened the
δυνάμεις αἱ γενόμεναι ἐν ὑμῖν, πάλαι ἂν ἐν
powerful deeds – happening in you, long ago – in
σάκκῳ καὶ σποδῷ καθήμενοι μετενόησαν.
sackcloth and ashes sitting they would have repented.

* Luke here, and in 2. 38; 10. 21; 12. 12; 13. 31; 24. 13, as
well as in Acts 16. 18; 22. 13, ignores the strict idiomatic construction of αὐτός when in apposition. The words here should
mean "in the house itself" but obviously do mean "in the same
house". So elsewhere. See note on Luke 2. 38.

be more tolerable in the
judgment for Tyre and
Sidon than for you.
[15]And you, Caper'na-um,
will you be exalted to
heaven? You shall be
brought down to Hades.

16 "He who hears you
hears me, and he who
rejects you rejects me,
and he who rejects me
rejects him who sent
me."

17 The seventy[b] re-
turned with joy, saying,
"Lord, even the demons
are subject to us in your
name!" [18]And he said to
them, "I saw Satan fall
like lightning from
heaven. [19]Behold, I have
given you authority to
tread upon serpents and
scorpions, and over all
the power of the enemy;
and nothing shall hurt
you. [20]Nevertheless do
not rejoice in this, that
the spirits are subject to
you; but rejoice that
your names are written
in heaven."

21 In that same hour
he rejoiced in the Holy
Spirit and said, "I thank
thee, Father, Lord of
heaven and earth, that
thou hast hidden these
things from the wise and
understanding and re-
vealed them to babes;
yea, Father, for such was

[b]Other ancient authorities
read seventy-two

---

14 πλὴν   Τύρῳ   καὶ   Σιδῶνι   ἀνεκτότερον
Nevertheless for Tyre   and   Sidon   more endurable
ἔσται ἐν τῇ κρίσει ἢ ὑμῖν. 15 καὶ σύ,
it will be in the judgment than for you.   And thou,
Καφαρναούμ, μὴ ἕως οὐρανοῦ ὑψωθήσῃ;
Capernaum,   not to   heaven   wast thou lifted?
ἕως τοῦ ᾅδου καταβήσῃ. 16 Ὁ ἀκούων
to - hades thou shalt come down. The [one] hearing
ὑμῶν   ἐμοῦ   ἀκούει,   καὶ   ὁ   ἀθετῶν   ὑμᾶς
you   me   hears,   and the [one] rejecting   you
ἐμὲ ἀθετεῖ· ὁ δὲ ἐμὲ ἀθετῶν ἀθετεῖ τὸν
me   rejects; and the [one] me rejecting   rejects the [one]
ἀποστείλαντά με. 17 Ὑπέστρεψαν δὲ οἱ
having sent   me.   And returned   the
ἑβδομήκοντα [δύο] μετὰ χαρᾶς λέγοντες·
seventy-two   with   joy   saying :
κύριε, καὶ τὰ δαιμόνια ὑποτάσσεται ἡμῖν
Lord, even the demons   submits   to us
ἐν τῷ ὀνόματί σου. 18 εἶπεν δὲ αὐτοῖς·
in the name   of thee.   And he said to them :
ἐθεώρουν τὸν σατανᾶν ὡς ἀστραπὴν ἐκ
I beheld   -   Satan   as   lightning out of
τοῦ οὐρανοῦ πεσόντα. 19 ἰδοὺ δέδωκα
-   heaven   fall.   Behold I have given
ὑμῖν   τὴν   ἐξουσίαν   τοῦ   πατεῖν   ἐπάνω
you   the   authority   -   to tread[d]   on
ὄφεων καὶ σκορπίων, καὶ ἐπὶ πᾶσαν τὴν
serpents and scorpions, and on   all   the
δύναμιν τοῦ ἐχθροῦ, καὶ οὐδὲν ὑμᾶς οὐ μὴ
power   of the enemy, and nothing you by no(any)
                                              means
ἀδικήσει. 20 πλὴν ἐν τούτῳ μὴ χαίρετε
shall hurt.   Nevertheless in this   rejoice not
ὅτι τὰ πνεύματα ὑμῖν ὑποτάσσεται, χαίρετε
that the spirits to you   submits,   [2]rejoice
δὲ ὅτι τὰ ὀνόματα ὑμῶν ἐγγέγραπται ἐν
[1]but that the names of you have been enrolled in
τοῖς   οὐρανοῖς. 21 Ἐν   αὐτῇ   τῇ   ὥρᾳ
the   heavens.   In   [2]same [1]the hour
ἠγαλλιάσατο τῷ πνεύματι τῷ ἁγίῳ καὶ
he exulted in(?by) the Spirit   -   Holy and
εἶπεν· ἐξομολογοῦμαί σοι, πάτερ, κύριε
said: I praise   thee, Father, Lord
τοῦ οὐρανοῦ καὶ τῆς γῆς, ὅτι ἀπέκρυψας
- of heaven and - of earth, because thou didst hide
ταῦτα ἀπὸ σοφῶν καὶ συνετῶν, καὶ
these things from wise   and intelligent [ones], and
ἀπεκάλυψας αὐτὰ νηπίοις· ναί, ὁ πατήρ,
didst reveal   them to infants; yes - Father,

thy gracious will.[c] 22All things have been delivered to me by my Father; and no one knows who the Son is except the Father, or who the Father is except the Son and any one to whom the Son chooses to reveal him."

23 Then turning to the disciples he said privately, "Blessed are the eyes which see what you see! 24 For I tell you that many prophets and kings desired to see what you see, and did not see it, and to hear what you hear, and did not hear it."

25 And behold, a lawyer stood up to put him to the test, saying, "Teacher, what shall I do to inherit eternal life?" 26 He said to him, "What is written in the law? How do you read?" 27And he answered, "You shall love the Lord your God with all your heart, and with all your soul, and with all your strength, and with all your mind; and your neighbor as yourself." 28And he said to him, "You have answered right; do this, and you will live."

29 But he, desiring to justify himself, said to

[c] Or *so it was well-pleasing before thee*

ὅτι οὕτως εὐδοκία ἐγένετο ἔμπροσθέν σου.
because thus good pleasure it was before thee.

22 πάντα μοι παρεδόθη ὑπὸ τοῦ πατρός
All things to me were delivered by the Father

μου, καὶ οὐδεὶς γινώσκει τίς ἐστιν ὁ
of me, and no one knows who is the

υἱὸς εἰ μὴ ὁ πατήρ, καὶ τίς ἐστιν ὁ πατὴρ
Son except the Father, and who is the Father

εἰ μὴ ὁ υἱὸς καὶ ᾧ ἐὰν βούληται
except the Son and [he] to whomever wills

ὁ υἱὸς ἀποκαλύψαι. 23 Καὶ στραφεὶς
the Son to reveal [him]. And turning

πρὸς τοὺς μαθητὰς κατ᾽ ἰδίαν εἶπεν·
to the disciples privately he said:

μακάριοι οἱ ὀφθαλμοὶ οἱ βλέποντες ἃ
Blessed the eyes – seeing the things which

βλέπετε. 24 λέγω γὰρ ὑμῖν ὅτι πολλοὶ
ye see. For I tell you that many

προφῆται καὶ βασιλεῖς ἠθέλησαν ἰδεῖν ἃ
prophets and kings desired to see the things which

ὑμεῖς βλέπετε καὶ οὐκ εἶδαν, καὶ ἀκοῦσαι
ye see and did not see, and to hear

ἃ ἀκούετε καὶ οὐκ ἤκουσαν.
the things which ye hear and did not hear.

25 Καὶ ἰδοὺ νομικός τις ἀνέστη
And[,] behold[,] lawyer a certain stood up

ἐκπειράζων αὐτὸν λέγων· διδάσκαλε, τί
tempting him saying: Teacher, what

ποιήσας ζωὴν αἰώνιον κληρονομήσω; 26 ὁ
doing [5]life [4]eternal [2]I [1]may [3]inherit? he

δὲ εἶπεν πρὸς αὐτόν· ἐν τῷ νόμῳ τί
And said to him: In the law what

γέγραπται; πῶς ἀναγινώσκεις; 27 ὁ δὲ
has been written? how readest thou? And he

ἀποκριθεὶς εἶπεν· ἀγαπήσεις κύριον τὸν
answering said: Thou shalt love [the] Lord the

θεόν σου ἐξ ὅλης τῆς καρδίας σου καὶ
God of thee from all the heart of thee and

ἐν ὅλῃ τῇ ψυχῇ σου καὶ ἐν ὅλῃ τῇ
with all the soul of thee and with all the

ἰσχύϊ σου καὶ ἐν ὅλῃ τῇ διανοίᾳ σου,
strength of thee and with all the mind of thee,

καὶ τὸν πλησίον σου ὡς σεαυτόν. 28 εἶπεν
and the neighbour of thee as thyself. he said

δὲ αὐτῷ· ὀρθῶς ἀπεκρίθης· τοῦτο ποίει
And to him: Rightly thou didst answer; this do

καὶ ζήσῃ. 29 ὁ δὲ θέλων δικαιῶσαι ἑαυτὸν
and thou shalt live. But he wishing to justify himself

Jesus, "And who is my neighbor?" ³⁰Jesus replied, "A man was going down from Jerusalem to Jericho, and he fell among robbers, who stripped him and beat him, and departed, leaving him half-dead. ³¹Now by chance a priest was going down that road; and when he saw him he passed by on the other side. ³²So likewise a Levite, when he came to to the place and saw him, passed by on the other side. ³³But a Samaritan, as he journeyed, came to where he was; and when he saw him, he had compassion, ³⁴and went to him and bound up his wounds, pouring on oil and wine; then he set him on his own beast and brought him to an inn, and took care of him. ³⁵And the next day he took out two denarii and gave them to the innkeeper, saying, 'Take care of him; and whatever more you spend, I will repay you when I come back.' ³⁶Which of these three, do you think, proved neighbor to the man who fell among the robbers?" ³⁷He said, "The one who showed mercy on him." And Jesus said to him, "Go

εἶπεν πρὸς τὸν Ἰησοῦν· καὶ τίς ἐστίν
said   to -   Jesus :   And   who   is

μου πλησίον; 30 ὑπολαβὼν ὁ Ἰησοῦς
of me   neighbour?   Taking [him] up   -   Jesus

εἶπεν· ἄνθρωπός τις κατέβαινεν ἀπὸ
said :   A certain man   was going down   from

Ἰερουσαλὴμ εἰς Ἰεριχώ, καὶ λῃσταῖς
Jerusalem   to   Jericho,   and   ²robbers

περιέπεσεν, οἳ καὶ ἐκδύσαντες αὐτὸν καὶ
¹fell in with,   who both   stripping   him   and

πληγὰς ἐπιθέντες ἀπῆλθον ἀφέντες ἡμιθανῆ.
²blows   ¹laying ³on ⁴[him] went away leaving [him] half dead.

31 κατὰ συγκυρίαν δὲ ἱερεύς τις κατέβαινεν
   And by a coincidence   a certain priest was going down

ἐν τῇ ὁδῷ ἐκείνῃ, καὶ ἰδὼν αὐτὸν
in   -   way   that,   and   seeing   him

ἀντιπαρῆλθεν. 32 ὁμοίως δὲ καὶ Λευίτης
passed by opposite.   And likewise   also   a Levite

κατὰ τὸν τόπον ἐλθὼν καὶ ἰδὼν
upon   the   place   coming   and   seeing

ἀντιπαρῆλθεν. 33 Σαμαρίτης δέ τις ὁδεύων
passed by opposite.   And a certain Samaritan   journeying

ἦλθεν κατ' αὐτὸν καὶ ἰδὼν ἐσπλαγχνίσθη,
came   upon   him   and   seeing   was filled with pity,

34 καὶ προσελθὼν κατέδησεν τὰ τραύματα
   and   approaching   bound up   the   wounds

αὐτοῦ ἐπιχέων ἔλαιον καὶ οἶνον, ἐπιβιβάσας
of him   pouring on   oil   and   wine,   ³placing

δὲ αὐτὸν ἐπὶ τὸ ἴδιον κτῆνος ἤγαγεν
¹and   him   on the(his)   own   beast   brought

αὐτὸν εἰς πανδοχεῖον καὶ ἐπεμελήθη αὐτοῦ.
him   to   an inn   and   cared for   him.

35 καὶ ἐπὶ τὴν αὔριον ἐκβαλὼν δύο
   And   on   the   morrow   taking out   two

δηνάρια ἔδωκεν τῷ πανδοχεῖ καὶ εἶπεν·
denarii   he gave   to the   innkeeper   and   said:

ἐπιμελήθητι αὐτοῦ, καὶ ὅ τι ἂν προσδα-
Care thou for   him,   and   whatever thou spendest

πανήσῃς ἐγὼ ἐν τῷ ἐπανέρχεσθαί με
in addition   I   in   the   to return   me ᵇᵉ
                       =when I return

ἀποδώσω σοι. 36 τίς τούτων τῶν τριῶν πλησίον
will repay thee.   Who of these   -   three ⁴neighbour

δοκεῖ σοι γεγονέναι τοῦ ἐμπεσόντος
¹seems it ²to thee ³to have become of the [one] falling into

εἰς τοὺς λῃστάς; 37 ὁ δὲ εἶπεν· ὁ ποιήσας
among the   robbers?   And he said : The [one] doing

τὸ ἔλεος μετ' αὐτοῦ. εἶπεν δὲ αὐτῷ ὁ
the   mercy   with   him.   And said   to him

and do likewise."

38 Now as they went on their way, he entered a village; and a woman named Martha received him into her house. [39]And she had a sister called Mary, who sat at the Lord's feet and listened to his teaching. [40]But Martha was distracted with much serving; and she went to him and said, "Lord, do you not care that my sister has left me to serve alone? Tell her then to help me." [41]But the Lord answered her, "Martha, Martha, you are anxious and troubled about many things; [42]one thing is needful.[d] Mary has chosen the good portion, which shall not be taken away from her."

'Ιησοῦς·   πορεύου   καὶ   σὺ   ποίει   ὁμοίως.
Jesus: Go   and   thou   do   likewise.

38 'Εν   δὲ   τῷ   πορεύεσθαι   αὐτοὺς   αὐτὸς
And in   the   to go   them[be]   he
          =as they went

εἰσῆλθεν   εἰς   κώμην   τινά·   γυνὴ   δέ   τις
entered   into   a certain village;   and a certain woman

ὀνόματι   Μάρθα   ὑπεδέξατο   αὐτὸν   εἰς   τὴν
by name   Martha   received   him   into   the

οἰκίαν.   39 καὶ   τῇδε   ἦν   ἀδελφὴ   καλουμένη
house.   And to this   was   a sister[o]   being called
                                                  =she had a sister

Μαριάμ,   ἧ   καὶ   παρακαθεσθεῖσα   πρὸς   τοὺς
Mary,   who   also   sitting beside   at   the

πόδας   τοῦ   κυρίου   ἤκουεν   τὸν   λόγον   αὐτοῦ.
feet   of the   Lord   heard   the   word   of him.

40 ἡ   δὲ   Μάρθα   περιεσπᾶτο   περὶ   πολλὴν
—   But   Martha   was distracted   about   much

διακονίαν·   ἐπιστᾶσα   δὲ   εἶπεν·   κύριε,   οὐ
serving;   and coming upon [him]   she said :   Lord,   not

μέλει   σοι   ὅτι   ἡ   ἀδελφή   μου   μόνην   με
matters it to thee   that   the   sister   of me   [a]alone   [a]me

κατέλειπεν   διακονεῖν;   εἰπὸν   οὖν   αὐτῇ   ἵνα
[1]left   to serve?   tell   therefore   her   that

μοι   συναντιλάβηται.   41 ἀποκριθεὶς   δὲ   εἶπεν
[a]me   [1]she may help.   And answering   said

αὐτῇ   ὁ   κύριος·   Μάρθα   Μάρθα,   μεριμνᾷς
to her   the   Lord :   Martha[,]   Martha,   thou art anxious

καὶ   θορυβάζῃ   περὶ   πολλά,   42 ὀλίγων   δέ
and   disturbed   about   many things,   but of few things

ἐστιν   χρεία   ἤ   ἑνός·   Μαριὰμ   γὰρ   τὴν
there is   need   or   of one·   for Mary   the

ἀγαθὴν   μερίδα   ἐξελέξατο,   ἥτις   οὐκ
good   part   chose,   which   not

ἀφαιρεθήσεται   αὐτῆς.
shall be taken from   her.

CHAPTER 11

HE was praying in a certain place, and when he ceased, one of his disciples said to him, "Lord, teach us to pray, as John taught his dis-

[d] Other ancient authorities read *few things are needful, or only one*

11 Καὶ   ἐγένετο   ἐν   τῷ   εἶναι   αὐτὸν   ἐν
And it came to pass   in   the   to be   him[be]   in
                                      =when he was

τόπῳ   τινὶ   προσευχόμενον,   ὡς   ἐπαύσατο,
a certain place   praying,   as   he ceased,

εἶπέν   τις   τῶν   μαθητῶν   αὐτοῦ   πρὸς
said   a certain one   of the   disciples   of him   to

αὐτόν·   κύριε,   δίδαξον   ἡμᾶς   προσεύχεσθαι,
him :   Lord,   teach   us   to pray,

καθὼς   καὶ   'Ιωάννης   ἐδίδαξεν   τοὺς   μαθητὰς
even as   also   John   taught   the   disciples

ciples." ²And he said to them, "When you pray, say:

"Father, hallowed be thy name. Thy kingdom come. ³Give us each day our daily bread;ᵉ ⁴and forgive us our sins, for we ourselves forgive every one who is indebted to us; and lead us not into temptation."

5 And he said to them, "Which of you who has a friend will go to him at midnight and say to him, 'Friend, lend me three loaves; ⁶for a friend of mine has arrived on a journey, and I have nothing to set before him'; ⁷and he will answer from within, 'Do not bother me; the door is now shut, and my children are with me in bed; I cannot get up and give you anything'? ⁸I tell you, though he will not get up and give him anything because he is his friend, yet because of his importunity he will rise and give him whatever he needs. ⁹And I tell you, Ask, and it will be given you; seek, and you will find; knock, and it will be opened to you. ¹⁰For every one who asks receives, and he who

ᵉ Or *our bread for the morrow*

αὐτοῦ. 2 εἶπεν δὲ αὐτοῖς· ὅταν
of him.   And he said   to them :   When

προσεύχησθε, λέγετε· Πάτερ, ἁγιασθήτω τὸ
ye pray,   say :   Father,   let be hallowed the

ὄνομά σου· ἐλθάτω ἡ βασιλεία σου·
name of thee; let come the kingdom of thee;

3 τὸν ἄρτον ἡμῶν τὸν ἐπιούσιον δίδου
the bread of us — belonging to the morrow give

ἡμῖν τὸ καθ' ἡμέραν· 4 καὶ ἄφες ἡμῖν τὰς
us   each day†;   and forgive us the

ἁμαρτίας ἡμῶν, καὶ γὰρ αὐτοὶ ἀφίομεν
sins of us, for indeed [our]selves we forgive

παντὶ ὀφείλοντι ἡμῖν· καὶ μὴ εἰσενέγκῃς
everyone owing to us; and lead not

ἡμᾶς εἰς πειρασμόν. 5 Καὶ εἶπεν πρὸς
us into temptation.   And he said to

αὐτούς· τίς ἐξ ὑμῶν ἕξει φίλον, καὶ
them : Who of you shall have a friend, and

πορεύσεται πρὸς αὐτὸν μεσονυκτίου καὶ
will come to him at midnight and

εἴπῃ αὐτῷ· φίλε, χρῆσόν μοι τρεῖς ἄρτους,
say to him : Friend, lend me three loaves,

6 ἐπειδὴ φίλος μου παρεγένετο ἐξ ὁδοῦ
since a friend of me arrived off a journey

πρός με καὶ οὐκ ἔχω ὃ παραθήσω αὐτῷ·
to me and I have not what I may set before him;

7 κἀκεῖνος ἔσωθεν ἀποκριθεὶς εἴπῃ· μή
and that one within answering may say : Not

μοι κόπους πάρεχε· ἤδη ἡ θύρα κέκλεισται,
me troubles cause; now the door has been shut,

καὶ τὰ παιδία μου μετ' ἐμοῦ εἰς τὴν
and the children of me with me in the

κοίτην εἰσίν· οὐ δύναμαι ἀναστὰς δοῦναί
bed are; I cannot rising up to give

σοι. 8 λέγω ὑμῖν, εἰ καὶ οὐ δώσει
thee.   I tell you, if even he will not give

αὐτῷ ἀναστὰς διὰ τὸ εἶναι φίλον αὐτοῦ,
him rising up on account of the to be friend of him,
=because he is his friend,

διά γε τὴν ἀναίδειαν αὐτοῦ ἐγερθεὶς
yet on account of the importunity of him rising

δώσει αὐτῷ ὅσων χρῄζει. 9 Κἀγὼ ὑμῖν
he will give him as many as he needs.   And I ²you

λέγω, αἰτεῖτε, καὶ δοθήσεται ὑμῖν· ζητεῖτε,
¹tell, ask, and it will be given you; seek,

καὶ εὑρήσετε, κρούετε, καὶ ἀνοιγήσεται
and ye will find; knock, and it will be opened

ὑμῖν. 10 πᾶς γὰρ ὁ αἰτῶν λαμβάνει, καὶ
to you.   For everyone asking receives, and

seeks finds, and to him who knocks it will be opened. ¹¹What father among you, if his son asks forᶠ a fish, will instead of a fish give him a serpent; ¹²or if he asks for an egg, will give him a scorpion? ¹³If you then, who are evil, know how to give good gifts to your children, how much more will the heavenly Father give the Holy Spirit to those who ask him?"

14 Now he was casting out a demon that was dumb; when the demon had gone out, the dumb man spoke, and the people marveled. ¹⁵But some of them said, "He casts out demons by Be-el′zebul, the prince of demons"; ¹⁶while others, to test him, sought from him a sign from heaven. ¹⁷But he, knowing their thoughts, said to them, "Every kingdom divided against itself is laid waste, and house falls upon house. ¹⁸And if Satan also is divided against himself, how will his kingdom stand? For you say that I cast out demons by Be-el′zebul. ¹⁹And if I cast out

ὁ   ζητῶν   εὑρίσκει,   καὶ   τῷ   κρούοντι
the [one] seeking   finds,   and   to the [one]   knocking

ἀνοιγήσεται.   11 τίνα   δὲ   ἐξ   ὑμῶν   τὸν
it will be opened.   And ¹what   ᵃof   ⁵you   -

πατέρα   αἰτήσει   ὁ   υἱὸς   ἰχθύν,   μὴ
¹father ²[is there] ⁶[of whom]   ⁵will ask   ⁴the ⁸son   ¹ᵃa fish,   not

ἀντὶ   ἰχθύος   ὄφιν   αὐτῷ   ἐπιδώσει;   12 ἢ
instead of a fish   ³a serpent ²to him   ¹will hand?   or

καὶ αἰτήσει   ὠόν,   ἐπιδώσει   αὐτῷ   σκορπίον;
even he will ask   an egg,   will hand   to him   a scorpion?

13 εἰ οὖν ὑμεῖς πονηροὶ ὑπάρχοντες οἴδατε δόματα
If therefore ye   ²evil   ¹being   know   gifts

ἀγαθὰ   διδόναι   τοῖς   τέκνοις   ὑμῶν,   πόσῳ
good   to give   to the   children   of you,   how much

μᾶλλον   ὁ   πατὴρ   ὁ   ἐξ   οὐρανοῦ   δώσει
more   the   Father   -   of   heaven   will give

πνεῦμα   ἅγιον   τοῖς   αἰτοῦσιν   αὐτόν.
Spirit   [the] Holy   to the [ones]   asking   him.

14 Καὶ   ἦν   ἐκβάλλων   δαιμόνιον,   καὶ αὐτὸ
And he was   expelling   a demon,   and   it

ἦν   κωφόν·   ἐγένετο   δὲ   τοῦ   δαιμονίου
was   dumb;   and it came to pass   the   demon
                                    =as the demon went out

ἐξελθόντος   ἐλάλησεν   ὁ   κωφός·   καὶ
going outᵃ   spoke   the   dumb man;   and

ἐθαύμασαν   οἱ   ὄχλοι·   15 τινὲς   δὲ   ἐξ
marvelled   the   crowds;   but some   of

αὐτῶν   εἶπαν·   ἐν   Βεελζεβοὺλ   τῷ   ἄρχοντι
them   said :   By   Beelzebub   the   chief

τῶν   δαιμονίων   ἐκβάλλει   τὰ   δαιμόνια·
of the   demons   he expels   the   demons;

16 ἕτεροι   δὲ   πειράζοντες   σημεῖον   ἐξ   οὐρανοῦ
and others   tempting   a sign   out of heaven

ἐζήτουν   παρ'   αὐτοῦ.   17 αὐτὸς   δὲ   εἰδὼς
sought   from   him.   But he   knowing

αὐτῶν   τὰ   διανοήματα   εἶπεν   αὐτοῖς·   πᾶσα
of them   the   thoughts   said   to them :   Every

βασιλεία   ἐφ'   ἑαυτὴν   διαμερισθεῖσα   ἐρημοῦται,
kingdom   against   itself   divided   is made desolate,

καὶ   οἶκος   ἐπὶ   οἶκον   πίπτει.   18 εἰ   δὲ
and   a house   against   a house   falls.   And if

καὶ   ὁ   σατανᾶς   ἐφ'   ἑαυτὸν   διεμερίσθη,
also   -   Satan   against   himself   was divided,

πῶς   σταθήσεται   ἡ   βασιλεία   αὐτοῦ;   ὅτι
how   will stand   the   kingdom   of him?   because

λέγετε   ἐν   Βεελζεβοὺλ   ἐκβάλλειν   με   τὰ
ye say   by   Beelzebub   to expel   meᵇ   the
                          =[that] by Beelzebub I expel

δαιμόνια.   19 εἰ   δὲ   ἐγὼ...   ἐν   Βεελζεβοὺλ
demons.   But if   I   by   Beelzebub

demons by Be-el′zebul, by whom do your sons cast them out? Therefore they shall be your judges. [20] But if it is by the finger of God that I cast out demons, then the kingdom of God has come upon you. [21] When a strong man, fully armed, guards his own palace, his goods are in peace; [22] but when one stronger than he assails him and overcomes him, he takes away his armor in which he trusted, and divides his spoil. [23] He who is not with me is against me, and he who does not gather with me scatters.

24 "When the unclean spirit has gone out of a man, he passes through waterless places seeking rest; and finding none he says, 'I will return to my house from which I came.' [25] And when he comes he finds it swept and put in order. [26] Then he goes and brings seven other spirits more evil than himself, and they enter and dwell there; and the last state of that man becomes worse than the first."

27 As he said this, a woman in the crowd raised her voice and said

ἐκβάλλω τὰ δαιμόνια, οἱ υἱοὶ ὑμῶν ἐν
expel the demons, the sons of you by

τίνι ἐκβάλλουσιν; διὰ τοῦτο αὐτοὶ ὑμῶν
what do they expel? therefore they of you

κριταὶ ἔσονται. 20 εἰ δὲ ἐν δακτύλῳ
judges shall be. But if by [the] finger

θεοῦ [ἐγὼ] ἐκβάλλω τὰ δαιμόνια, ἄρα
of God I expel the demons, then

ἔφθασεν ἐφ' ὑμᾶς ἡ βασιλεία τοῦ θεοῦ.
came upon you the kingdom – of God.

21 ὅταν ὁ ἰσχυρὸς καθωπλισμένος φυλάσσῃ
When the strong man having been well armed guards

τὴν ἑαυτοῦ αὐλήν, ἐν εἰρήνῃ ἐστὶν τὰ
the of himself palace, in peace is(are) the

ὑπάρχοντα αὐτοῦ· 22 ἐπὰν δὲ ἰσχυρότερος
goods of him; but when a stronger

αὐτοῦ ἐπελθὼν νικήσῃ αὐτόν, τὴν πανοπλίαν
[than] him coming upon overcomes him, the armour

αὐτοῦ αἴρει, ἐφ' ᾗ ἐπεποίθει, καὶ τὰ
of him he takes, on which he had relied, and the

σκῦλα αὐτοῦ διαδίδωσιν. 23 Ὁ μὴ ὢν
arms of him distributes. The [one] not being

μετ' ἐμοῦ κατ' ἐμοῦ ἐστιν, καὶ ὁ μὴ
with me against me is, and the [one] not

συνάγων μετ' ἐμοῦ σκορπίζει. 24 Ὅταν
gathering with me scatters. When

τὸ ἀκάθαρτον πνεῦμα ἐξέλθῃ ἀπὸ τοῦ
the unclean spirit goes out from the

ἀνθρώπου, διέρχεται δι' ἀνύδρων τόπων
man, he goes through through dry places

ζητοῦν ἀνάπαυσιν, καὶ μὴ εὑρίσκον λέγει·
seeking rest, and not finding says:

ὑποστρέψω εἰς τὸν οἶκόν μου ὅθεν ἐξῆλθον·
I will return to the house of me whence I came out;

25 καὶ ἐλθὸν εὑρίσκει σεσαρωμένον καὶ
and coming he finds [it] having been swept and

κεκοσμημένον. 26 τότε πορεύεται καὶ
having been furnished. Then he goes and

παραλαμβάνει ἕτερα πνεύματα πονηρότερα
takes other spirits more wicked

ἑαυτοῦ ἑπτά, καὶ εἰσελθόντα κατοικεῖ
[than] himself seven, and entering he dwells

ἐκεῖ· καὶ γίνεται τὰ ἔσχατα τοῦ ἀνθρώπου
there; and becomes the last things – man

ἐκείνου χείρονα τῶν πρώτων. 27 Ἐγένετο
of that worse [than] the first. it came to pass

δὲ ἐν τῷ λέγειν αὐτὸν ταῦτα ἐπάρασά τις
And in the to say him[be] these things [s]lifting up [1]a certain
=as he said

to him, "Blessed is the
womb that bore you, and
the breasts that you
sucked!" ²⁸But he said,
"Blessed rather are those
who hear the word of
God and keep it!"

29 When the crowds
were increasing, he be-
gan to say, "This
generation is an evil
generation; it seeks a
sign, but no sign shall be
given to it except the
sign of Jonah. ³⁰For as
Jonah became a sign to
the men of Nin'eveh, so
will the Son of man be to
this generation. ³¹The
queen of the South will
arise at the judgment
with the men of this
generation and condemn
them; for she came from
the ends of the earth to
hear the wisdom of
Solomon, and behold,
something greater than
Solomon is here. ³²The
men of Nin'eveh will
arise at the judgment
with this generation and
condemn it; for they re-
pented at the preaching
of Jonah, and behold,
something greater than
Jonah is here.

33 "No one after
lighting a lamp puts it in
a cellar or under a
bushel, but on a stand,
that those who enter may
see the light. ³⁴Your eye

φωνὴν   γυνὴ ἐκ τοῦ ὄχλου εἶπεν αὐτῷ·
⁷[her] ⁸voice ²woman ⁵of ⁴the ⁶crowd said   to him :
μακαρία ἡ κοιλία ἡ βαστάσασά σε καὶ
Blessed the womb – having borne thee and
μαστοὶ   οὓς ἐθήλασας. 28 αὐτὸς δὲ εἶπεν·
[the] breasts which thou didst suck.   But he   said :
μενοῦν μακάριοι οἱ ἀκούοντες τὸν λόγον
Nay rather blessed the [ones] hearing   the   word
τοῦ θεοῦ καὶ φυλάσσοντες.
– of God and   keeping.

29 Τῶν δὲ ὄχλων ἐπαθροιζομένων ἤρξατο
   And the crowds   pressing upon²   he began
                     =as the crowds pressed upon [him]
λέγειν· ἡ γενεὰ αὕτη γενεὰ πονηρά ἐστιν·
to say : – ²generation ¹This ²generation ⁴an evil ⁵is;
σημεῖον ζητεῖ, καὶ σημεῖον οὐ δοθήσεται
a sign   it seeks, and   a sign   will not be given
αὐτῇ εἰ μὴ τὸ σημεῖον Ἰωνᾶ.   30 καθὼς
to it except the sign of Jonas.   even as
γὰρ ἐγένετο [ὁ] Ἰωνᾶς τοῖς Νινευίταις
For ²became   – ¹Jonas ⁴to the ⁵Ninevites
σημεῖον, οὕτως ἔσται καὶ ὁ υἱὸς τοῦ
³a sign,   so   will be also the Son   –
ἀνθρώπου τῇ γενεᾷ ταύτῃ. 31 βασίλισσα
of man   – generation to this.   [The] queen
νότου ἐγερθήσεται ἐν τῇ κρίσει μετὰ τῶν
of [the] south will be raised in the judgment with the
ἀνδρῶν τῆς γενεᾶς ταύτης καὶ κατακρινεῖ
men   – generation of this and will condemn
αὐτούς· ὅτι ἦλθεν ἐκ τῶν περάτων τῆς
them;   because she came from the extremities of the
γῆς ἀκοῦσαι τὴν σοφίαν Σολομῶνος, καὶ
earth to hear the wisdom of Solomon, and
ἰδοὺ πλεῖον Σολομῶνος ὧδε. 32 ἄνδρες
behold a greater [than] Solomon [is] here.   Men
Νινευῖται ἀναστήσονται ἐν τῇ κρίσει μετὰ
Ninevites   will rise up   in the judgment with
τῆς γενεᾶς ταύτης καὶ κατακρινοῦσιν αὐτήν·
 – generation this   and   will condemn   it;
ὅτι μετενόησαν εἰς τὸ κήρυγμα Ἰωνᾶ, καὶ
because they repented at the proclamation of Jonas, and
ἰδοὺ πλεῖον Ἰωνᾶ ὧδε. 33 Οὐδεὶς λύχνον
behold a greater [than] Jonas [is] here. No one ²a lamp
ἅψας εἰς κρύπτην τίθησιν οὐδὲ ὑπὸ τὸν
¹having lit ⁴in ⁵secret ³places [it] nor under the
μόδιον, ἀλλ' ἐπὶ τὴν λυχνίαν, ἵνα οἱ
bushel, but on the lampstand, that the
εἰσπορευόμενοι τὸ φέγγος βλέπωσιν. 34 ὁ
ones] entering   the light   may see.   The

is the lamp of your body; when your eye is sound, your whole body is full of light; but when it is not sound, your body is full of darkness. [35] Therefore be careful lest the light in you be darkness. [36] If then your whole body is full of light, having no part dark, it will be wholly bright, as when a lamp with its rays gives you light."

37 While he was speaking, a Pharisee asked him to dine with him; so he went in and sat at table. [38] The Pharisee was astonished to see that he did not first wash before dinner. [39] And the Lord said to him, "Now you Pharisees cleanse the outside of the cup and of the dish, but inside you are full of extortion and wickedness. [40] You fools! Did not he who made the outside make the inside also? [41] But give for alms those things which are within; and behold, everything is clean for you.

42 "But woe to you Pharisees! for you tithe mint and rue and every herb, and neglect justice

λύχνος τοῦ σώματός ἐστιν ὁ ὀφθαλμός σου.
lamp of the body is the eye of thee.

ὅταν ὁ ὀφθαλμός σου ἁπλοῦς ᾖ, καὶ
When the eye of thee single is, also

ὅλον τὸ σῶμά σου φωτεινόν ἐστιν· ἐπὰν
all the body of thee bright is; [2]when

δὲ πονηρὸς ᾖ, καὶ τὸ σῶμά σου σκοτεινόν.
[1]but evil it is, also the body of thee [is] dark.

35 σκόπει οὖν μὴ τὸ φῶς τὸ ἐν σοὶ
Watch therefore lest the light – in thee

σκότος ἐστίν. 36 εἰ οὖν τὸ σῶμά σου
darkness is. If therefore [1]the [2]body [4]of thee

ὅλον φωτεινόν, μὴ ἔχον μέρος τι σκοτεινόν,
[1]whole [is] bright, not having [2]part [1]any dark,

ἔσται φωτεινὸν ὅλον ὡς ὅταν ὁ λύχνος
[2]will be [3]bright [1]all as when the lamp

τῇ ἀστραπῇ φωτίζῃ σε.
with the(its) shining enlightens thee.

37 Ἐν δὲ τῷ λαλῆσαι ἐρωτᾷ αὐτὸν
Now in the to speak[e] asks him
= as [he] spoke

Φαρισαῖος ὅπως ἀριστήσῃ παρ' αὐτῷ
a Pharisee that he would dine with him;

εἰσελθὼν δὲ ἀνέπεσεν. 38 ὁ δὲ Φαρισαῖος
and entering he reclined. But the Pharisee

ἰδὼν ἐθαύμασεν ὅτι οὐ πρῶτον ἐβαπτίσθη
seeing marvelled that not first he washed

πρὸ τοῦ ἀρίστου. 39 εἶπεν δὲ ὁ κύριος
before the dinner. But said the Lord

πρὸς αὐτόν· νῦν ὑμεῖς οἱ Φαρισαῖοι τὸ
to him: Now ye – Pharisees the

ἔξωθεν τοῦ ποτηρίου καὶ τοῦ πίνακος
outside of the cup and of the dish

καθαρίζετε, τὸ δὲ ἔσωθεν ὑμῶν γέμει
cleanse, but the inside of you is full

ἁρπαγῆς καὶ πονηρίας. 40 ἄφρονες, οὐχ
of robbery and wickedness. Foolish men, not

ὁ ποιήσας τὸ ἔξωθεν καὶ τὸ ἔσωθεν
the [one] making the outside also the inside

ἐποίησεν; 41 πλὴν τὰ ἐνόντα δότε
made? Nevertheless the things being within give

ἐλεημοσύνην, καὶ ἰδοὺ πάντα καθαρὰ ὑμῖν
alms, and behold all things clean to you

ἐστιν. 42 ἀλλὰ οὐαὶ ὑμῖν τοῖς Φαρισαίοις,
is(are). But woe to you – Pharisees,

ὅτι ἀποδεκατοῦτε τὸ ἡδύοσμον καὶ τὸ
because ye tithe the mint and the

πήγανον καὶ πᾶν λάχανον, καὶ παρέρχεσθε
rue and every herb, and pass by

and the love of God; these you ought to have done, without neglecting the others. ⁴³Woe to you Pharisees! for you love the best seat in the synagogues and salutations in the market places. ⁴⁴Woe to you! for you are like graves which are not seen, and men walk over them without knowing it."

45 One of the lawyers answered him, "Teacher, in saying this you reproach us also." ⁴⁶And he said, "Woe to you lawyers also! for you load men with burdens hard to bear, and you yourselves do not touch the burdens with one of your fingers. ⁴⁷Woe to you! for you build the tombs of the prophets whom your fathers killed. ⁴⁸So you are witnesses and consent to the deeds of your fathers; for they killed them, and you build their tombs. ⁴⁹Therefore also the Wisdom of God said, 'I will send them prophets and apostles, some of whom they will kill and persecute,' ⁵⁰that the blood of all the prophets,

τὴν κρίσιν καὶ τὴν ἀγάπην τοῦ θεοῦ·
the judgment and the love – of God;
ταῦτα δὲ ἔδει ποιῆσαι κἀκεῖνα μὴ
but these things it behoved to do and those not
παρεῖναι. 43 οὐαὶ ὑμῖν τοῖς Φαρισαίοις,
to pass by. Woe to you – Pharisees,
ὅτι ἀγαπᾶτε τὴν πρωτοκαθεδρίαν ἐν ταῖς
because ye love the chief seat in the
συναγωγαῖς καὶ τοὺς ἀσπασμοὺς ἐν ταῖς
synagogues and the greetings in the
ἀγοραῖς. 44 οὐαὶ ὑμῖν, ὅτι ἐστὲ ὡς τὰ
marketplaces. Woe to you, because ye are as the
μνημεῖα τὰ ἄδηλα, καὶ οἱ ἄνθρωποι οἱ
tombs – unseen, and the men
περιπατοῦντες ἐπάνω οὐκ οἴδασιν.
walking over do not know.
45 Ἀποκριθεὶς δέ τις τῶν νομικῶν λέγει
And answering one of the lawyers says
αὐτῷ· διδάσκαλε, ταῦτα λέγων καὶ ἡμᾶς
to him : Teacher, these things saying also us
ὑβρίζεις. 46 ὁ δὲ εἶπεν· καὶ ὑμῖν τοῖς
thou insultest. And he said : Also to you –
νομικοῖς οὐαί, ὅτι φορτίζετε τοὺς ἀνθρώπους
lawyers woe, because ye burden – men
φορτία δυσβάστακτα, καὶ αὐτοὶ ἑνὶ τῶν
[with] burdens difficult to carry, and [your]selves with one of the
δακτύλων ὑμῶν οὐ προσψαύετε τοῖς φορτίοις.
fingers of you ye do not touch the burdens.
47 οὐαὶ ὑμῖν, ὅτι οἰκοδομεῖτε τὰ μνημεῖα
Woe to you, because ye build the tombs
τῶν προφητῶν, οἱ δὲ πατέρες ὑμῶν
of the prophets, and the fathers of you
ἀπέκτειναν αὐτούς. 48 ἄρα μάρτυρές ἐστε
killed them. Therefore witnesses ye are
καὶ συνευδοκεῖτε τοῖς ἔργοις τῶν πατέρων
and ye entirely approve the works of the fathers
ὑμῶν, ὅτι αὐτοὶ μὲν ἀπέκτειναν αὐτούς,
of you, because they on one hand killed them,
ὑμεῖς δὲ οἰκοδομεῖτε. 49 διὰ τοῦτο καὶ
ye on the other hand build. Therefore also
ἡ σοφία τοῦ θεοῦ εἶπεν· ἀποστελῶ εἰς
the Wisdom – of God said : I will send to
αὐτοὺς προφήτας καὶ ἀποστόλους, καὶ ἐξ
them prophets and apostles, and of
αὐτῶν ἀποκτενοῦσιν καὶ διώξουσιν, 50 ἵνα
them they will kill and persecute, that
ἐκζητηθῇ τὸ αἷμα πάντων τῶν προφητῶν
¹¹may be required ¹the ²blood ³of all ⁴the ⁵prophets

shed from the foundation of the world, may be required of this generation, [51]from the blood of Abel to the blood of Zechari'ah, who perished between the altar and the sanctuary. Yes, I tell you, it shall be required of this generation. [52]Woe to you lawyers! for you have taken away the key of knowledge; you did not enter yourselves, and you hindered those who were entering."

53 As he went away from there, the scribes and the Pharisees began to press him hard, and to provoke him to speak of many things, [54]lying in wait for him, to catch at something he might say.

τὸ ἐκκεχυμένον ἀπὸ καταβολῆς κόσμου
- 'having been shed 'from [the] 'foundation [10]of [the] world
ἀπὸ τῆς γενεᾶς ταύτης, 51 ἀπὸ αἵματος
[11]from - generation this,   from [the] blood
Ἀβελ ἕως αἵματος Ζαχαρίου τοῦ
of Abel   to   [the] blood   of Zacharias   -
ἀπολομένου μεταξὺ τοῦ θυσιαστηρίου καὶ
destroyed   between   the   altar   and
τοῦ οἴκου· ναὶ λέγω ὑμῖν, ἐκζητηθήσεται
the   house;   yes   I tell   you,   it will be required
ἀπὸ τῆς γενεᾶς ταύτης. 52 οὐαὶ ὑμῖν τοῖς
from -   generation   this.   Woe to you   -
νομικοῖς, ὅτι ἤρατε τὴν κλεῖδα τῆς
lawyers,   because   ye took   the   key   of
γνώσεως· αὐτοὶ οὐκ εἰσήλθατε καὶ τοὺς
of knowledge; [your]selves   ye did not enter   and   the
εἰσερχομένους ἐκωλύσατε. 53 Κἀκεῖθεν ἐξελ-
[ones] entering   ye prevented.   And thence going
                                  = as he went forth thence
θόντος αὐτοῦ ἤρξαντο οἱ γραμματεῖς καὶ
forth   him[a]   began   the   scribes   and
οἱ Φαρισαῖοι δεινῶς ἐνέχειν καὶ ἀποστοματίζειν
the Pharisees   [2]terribly   [1]to be [3]angry and   to [1]draw [3]out
αὐτὸν περὶ πλειόνων, 54 ἐνεδρεύοντες
[2]him   concerning   a great number of things,   lying in wait for
αὐτὸν θηρεῦσαί τι ἐκ τοῦ στόματος αὐτοῦ.
him   to catch something   out of the   mouth   of him.

CHAPTER 12

IN the meantime, when so many thousands of the multitude had gathered together that they trod upon one another, he began to say to his disciples first, "Beware of the leaven of the Pharisees, which is hypocrisy. [2]Nothing is covered up that will not be revealed, or hidden that will not be known. [3]Whatever you have said in the dark shall be heard in the light, and what you have whispered in

12 Ἐν οἷς ἐπισυναχθεισῶν τῶν μυριάδων
In which things being assembled   the   thousands
= Meanwhile as the thousands of the crowd were assembled,
τοῦ ὄχλου, ὥστε καταπατεῖν ἀλλήλους,
of the crowd,[a]   so as   to tread on   one another,
ἤρξατο λέγειν πρὸς τοὺς μαθητὰς αὐτοῦ
he began   to say   to   the   disciples   of him
πρῶτον· προσέχετε ἑαυτοῖς ἀπὸ τῆς ζύμης,
first :   Take heed to yourselves   from   the   leaven,
ἥτις ἐστὶν ὑπόκρισις, τῶν Φαρισαίων.
which   is   hypocrisy,   of the   Pharisees.
2 οὐδὲν δὲ συγκεκαλυμμένον ἐστὶν ὃ οὐκ
And [3]nothing   [2]having been   [1]there is which not
            completely covered
ἀποκαλυφθήσεται, καὶ κρυπτὸν ὃ οὐ γνωσθήσεται.
will be uncovered,   and   hidden which will not be known.
3 ἀνθ᾽ ὧν ὅσα ἐν τῇ σκοτίᾳ εἴπατε ἐν
Therefore   what things in   the   darkness   ye said   in
τῷ φωτὶ ἀκουσθήσεται, καὶ ὃ πρὸς τὸ
the   light   will be heard,   and   what   to   the

private rooms shall be proclaimed upon the housetops.

4 "I tell you, my friends, do not fear those who kill the body, and after that have no more that they can do. ⁵But I will warn you whom to fear: fear him who, after he has killed, has power to cast into hell; yes, I tell you, fear him! ⁶Are not five sparrows sold for two pennies? And not one of them is forgotten before God. ⁷Why, even the hairs of your head are all numbered. Fear not; you are of more value than many sparrows.

8 "And I tell you, every one who acknowledges me before men, the Son of man also will acknowledge before the angels of God; ⁹but he who denies me before men will be denied before the angels of God. ¹⁰And every one who speaks a word against the Son of man will be forgiven; but he who blasphemes against the Holy Spirit will not be forgiven. ¹¹And when they bring

οὓς ἐλαλήσατε ἐν τοῖς ταμείοις κηρυχθήσεται
ear   ye spoke   in   the private rooms   will be proclaimed
ἐπὶ τῶν δωμάτων. 4 Λέγω δὲ ὑμῖν τοῖς
on   the   roofs.   And I say   to you   the
φίλοις μου, μὴ φοβηθῆτε ἀπὸ τῶν
friends   of me,   do not be afraid   from(of)   the [ones]
ἀποκτεννόντων τὸ σῶμα καὶ μετὰ ταῦτα
killing   the   body   and   after   these things
μὴ ἐχόντων περισσότερόν τι ποιῆσαι.
not   having   anything more   to do.
5 ὑποδείξω δὲ ὑμῖν τίνα φοβηθῆτε·
But I will warn   you   whom   ye may fear:
φοβήθητε τὸν μετὰ τὸ ἀποκτεῖναι ἔχοντα
¹fear   ²the [one]   ⁴after   the   ⁴to kill(killing)   ⁵having
ἐξουσίαν ἐμβαλεῖν εἰς τὴν γέενναν. ναὶ
⁴authority   ⁷to cast in   into   –   gehenna.   Yes[,]
λέγω ὑμῖν, τοῦτον φοβήθητε. 6 οὐχὶ
I say   to you,   this one   fear ye.   Not
πέντε στρουθία πωλοῦνται ἀσσαρίων δύο;
five   sparrows   are sold   of(for) farthings   two?
καὶ ἓν ἐξ αὐτῶν οὐκ ἔστιν ἐπιλελησμένον
and one   of   them   is not   having been forgotten
ἐνώπιον τοῦ θεοῦ. 7 ἀλλὰ καὶ αἱ τρίχες
before   –   God.   But   even   the   hairs
τῆς κεφαλῆς ὑμῶν πᾶσαι ἠρίθμηνται.
of the   head   of you   all   have been numbered.
μὴ φοβεῖσθε· πολλῶν στρουθίων διαφέρετε.
Fear ye not;   from many   sparrows   ye differ.
8 λέγω δὲ ὑμῖν, πᾶς ὃς ἂν ὁμολογήσῃ
But I tell   you, everyone   whoever   confesses
ἐν ἐμοὶ ἔμπροσθεν τῶν ἀνθρώπων, καὶ ὁ
–   me   before   –   men,   also the
υἱὸς τοῦ ἀνθρώπου ὁμολογήσει ἐν αὐτῷ
Son   –   of man   will confess   –   him
ἔμπροσθεν τῶν ἀγγέλων τοῦ θεοῦ· 9 ὁ δὲ
before   the   angels   – of God;   and the
ἀρνησάμενός με ἐνώπιον τῶν ἀνθρώπων
[one] denying   me   before   –   men
ἀπαρνηθήσεται ἐνώπιον τῶν ἀγγέλων τοῦ
will be denied   before   the   angels   –
θεοῦ. 10 καὶ πᾶς ὃς ἐρεῖ λόγον εἰς τὸν
of God.   And everyone who shall say a word against the
υἱὸν τοῦ ἀνθρώπου, ἀφεθήσεται αὐτῷ· τῷ
Son   –   of man,   it will be forgiven him;   ²the [one]
δὲ εἰς τὸ ἅγιον πνεῦμα βλασφημήσαντι
¹but against   the   Holy   Spirit   blaspheming
οὐκ ἀφεθήσεται. 11 ὅταν δὲ εἰσφέρωσιν
will not be forgiven.   And when   they bring in

you before the syna-
gogues and the rulers
and the authorities, do
not be anxious how or
what you are to answer
or what you are to say;
[12]for the Holy Spirit will
teach you in that very
hour what you ought to
say."

13 One of the multi-
tude said to him,
"Teacher, bid my brother
divide the inheritance
with me." [14]But he said
to him, "Man, who
made me a judge or
divider over you?" [15]And
he said to them, "Take
heed, and beware of all
covetousness; for a man's
life does not consist in
the abundance of his
possessions." [16]And he
told them a parable,
saying, "The land of a
rich man brought forth
plentifully; [17]and he
thought to himself, 'What
shall I do, for I have
nowhere to store my
crops?' [18]And he said, 'I
will do this: I will pull
down my barns, and
build larger ones; and
there I will store all my
grain and my goods.
[19]And I will say to my
soul, Soul, you have
ample goods laid up for
many years; take your
ease, eat, drink, be
merry.' [20]But God said

ὑμᾶς ἐπὶ τὰς συναγωγὰς καὶ τὰς ἀρχὰς
you before – synagogues and – rulers
καὶ τὰς ἐξουσίας, μὴ μεριμνήσητε πῶς ἢ
and – authorities, do not be anxious how or
τί ἀπολογήσησθε ἢ τί εἴπητε· 12 τὸ γὰρ
what ye may answer or what ye may say; for the
ἅγιον πνεῦμα διδάξει ὑμᾶς ἐν αὐτῇ τῇ
Holy Spirit will teach you in ²same ¹the
ὥρᾳ ἃ δεῖ εἰπεῖν. 13 Εἶπεν δέ τις
hour what things it behoves [you] to say. And said someone
ἐκ τοῦ ὄχλου αὐτῷ· διδάσκαλε, εἰπὲ τῷ
out of the crowd to him : Teacher, tell the
ἀδελφῷ μου μερίσασθαι μετ᾽ ἐμοῦ τὴν
brother of me to divide with me the
κληρονομίαν. 14 ὁ δὲ εἶπεν αὐτῷ· ἄνθρωπε,
inheritance But he said to him : Man,
τίς με κατέστησεν κριτὴν ἢ μεριστὴν ἐφ᾽
who me appointed a judge or a divider over
ὑμᾶς; 15 εἶπεν δὲ πρὸς αὐτούς· ὁρᾶτε
you? And he said to them : Beware
καὶ φυλάσσεσθε ἀπὸ πάσης πλεονεξίας,
and guard from(against) all covetousness,
ὅτι οὐκ ἐν τῷ περισσεύειν τινὶ ἡ ζωὴ
because ⁶not ⁷in ⁷the ⁸to abound ⁹to anyone ¹the ¹life
αὐτοῦ ἐστιν ἐκ τῶν ὑπαρχόντων αὐτῷ.
²of him ⁴is ¹⁰of the things existing to him.°
                                    =¹¹his ¹²possessions.°
16 Εἶπεν δὲ παραβολὴν πρὸς αὐτοὺς λέγων·
  And he told a parable to them saying :
ἀνθρώπου τινὸς πλουσίου εὐφόρησεν ἡ
²of a certain ⁵man ⁴rich ⁶bore well ¹The
χώρα. 17 καὶ διελογίζετο ἐν ἑαυτῷ λέγων·
²land. And he reasoned in himself saying :
τί ποιήσω, ὅτι οὐκ ἔχω ποῦ συνάξω τοὺς
What may I do, because I have not where I may gather the
καρπούς μου; 18 καὶ εἶπεν· τοῦτο ποιήσω·
fruits of me? And he said : This will I do :
καθελῶ μου τὰς ἀποθήκας καὶ μείζονας
I will pull down of me the barns and larger ones
οἰκοδομήσω, καὶ συνάξω ἐκεῖ πάντα τὸν
I will build, and I will gather there all the
σῖτον καὶ τὰ ἀγαθά μου, 19 καὶ ἐρῶ τῇ
wheat and the goods of me, and I will say to the
ψυχῇ μου· ψυχή, ἔχεις πολλὰ ἀγαθὰ
soul of me : Soul, thou hast many goods
κείμενα εἰς ἔτη πολλά· ἀναπαύου, φάγε,
laid [up] for years many; take rest, eat,
πίε, εὐφραίνου. 20 εἶπεν δὲ αὐτῷ ὁ
drink, be glad. But said to him –

to him, 'Fool! This night your soul is required of you; and the things you have prepared, whose will they be?' ²¹ So is he who lays up treasure for himself, and is not rich toward God.''

22 And he said to his disciples, "Therefore I tell you, do not be anxious about your life, what you shall eat, nor about your body, what you shall put on. ²³ For life is more than food, and the body more than clothing. ²⁴ Consider the ravens: they neither sow nor reap, they have neither storehouse nor barn, and yet God feeds them. Of how much more value are you than the birds! ²⁵ And which of you by being anxious can add a cubit to his span of life?⁹ ²⁶ If then you are not able to do as small a thing as that, why are you anxious about the rest? ²⁷ Consider the lilies, how they grow; they neither toil nor spin;ʰ yet I tell you, even Solomon in all his glory was not arrayed like one of these. ²⁸ But if God so clothes the grass which is alive in the field today and tomorrow is thrown into the oven, how much more will he clothe you, O men of little faith? ²⁹ And do not

θεός· ἄφρων, ταύτῃ τῇ νυκτὶ τὴν ψυχήν
God : Foolish man, in this   night   the   soul

σου ἀπαιτοῦσιν ἀπὸ σοῦ·   ἃ   δὲ
of thee they demand   from   thee;   then [the] things which

ἡτοίμασας, τίνι ἔσται; 21 οὕτως ὁ
thou preparedst, to whom will they be?ᶜ   So the [one]
= whose will they be?

θησαυρίζων αὑτῷ καὶ μὴ εἰς θεὸν πλουτῶν.
treasuring to himself and not toward God being rich.

22 Εἶπεν δὲ πρὸς τοὺς μαθητὰς [αὐτοῦ]· διὰ τοῦτο
And he said to   the   disciples of him : Therefore

λέγω ὑμῖν· μὴ μεριμνᾶτε τῇ ψυχῇ τί
I tell you : Do not be anxious for the life what

φάγητε, μηδὲ τῷ σώματι [ὑμῶν] τί
ye may eat, nor for the body of you what

ἐνδύσησθε. 23 ἡ γὰρ ψυχὴ πλεῖόν ἐστιν
ye may put on.   For the life   more   is

τῆς τροφῆς καὶ τὸ σῶμα τοῦ ἐνδύματος.
[than] the food and the body [than] the clothing.

24 κατανοήσατε τοὺς κόρακας, ὅτι οὔτε
Consider ye   the   ravens, that neither

σπείρουσιν οὔτε θερίζουσιν, οἷς οὐκ ἔστινᶜ
they sow   nor   reap,   to which is not
= which have not

ταμεῖον οὐδὲ ἀποθήκη, καὶ ὁ θεὸς τρέφει
storehouse nor   barn, and - God feeds

αὐτούς· πόσῳ μᾶλλον ὑμεῖς διαφέρετε τῶν
them; by how much rather ye   differ from the

πετεινῶν. 25 τίς δὲ ἐξ ὑμῶν μεριμνῶν
birds.   And who of   you being anxious

δύναται ἐπὶ τὴν ἡλικίαν αὐτοῦ προσθεῖναι
can   on   the stature of him to add

πῆχυν; 26 εἰ οὖν οὐδὲ ἐλάχιστον δύνασθε,
a cubit?   If therefore not [the] least   ye can,

τί περὶ τῶν λοιπῶν μεριμνᾶτε; 27 κατα-
why concerning the other things are ye anxious?   Con-

νοήσατε τὰ κρίνα, πῶς οὔτε νήθει οὔτε
sider ye the lilies, how neither they spin nor

ὑφαίνει· λέγω δὲ ὑμῖν, οὐδὲ Σολομὼν ἐν
weave; but I tell you, not Solomon in

πάσῃ τῇ δόξῃ αὐτοῦ περιεβάλετο ὡς ἓν
all the glory of him was arrayed as one

τούτων. 28 εἰ δὲ ἐν ἀγρῷ τὸν χόρτον
of these.   ¹And ²if ⁹in ¹⁰a field ⁶the   ⁷grass

ὄντα σήμερον καὶ αὔριον εἰς κλίβανον
⁸being ¹¹to-day ¹²and ¹³tomorrow ¹⁵into ¹⁴an oven

βαλλόμενον ὁ θεὸς οὕτως ἀμφιάζει, πόσῳ
¹⁴being thrown - ³God ⁴so ⁵clothes, by how much

μᾶλλον ὑμᾶς, ὀλιγόπιστοι. 29 καὶ ὑμεῖς
rather you,   little-faiths.   And   ye

---

⁹ Or to his stature
ʰ Other ancient authorities read Consider the lilies; they neither spin nor weave

seek what you are to eat and what you are to drink, nor be of anxious mind. [30] For all the nations of the world seek these things; and your Father knows that you need them. [31] Instead, seek his[f] kingdom, and these things shall be yours as well.

32 "Fear not, little flock, for it is your Father's good pleasure to give you the kingdom. [33] Sell your possessions, and give alms; provide yourselves with purses that do not grow old, with a treasure in the heavens that does not fail, where no thief approaches and no moth destroys. [34] For where your treasure is, there will your heart be also.

35 "Let your loins be girded and your lamps burning, [36] and be like men who are waiting for their master to come home from the marriage feast, so that they may open to him at once when he comes and knocks. [37] Blessed are those servants whom the master finds awake when he comes; truly, I say to you, he will gird himself and have them sit at table, and he will come and serve them. [38] If he

μὴ ζητεῖτε τί φάγητε καὶ τί πίητε, καὶ
do not seek   what   ye may eat   and what ye may drink, and

μὴ μετεωρίζεσθε· 30 ταῦτα γὰρ πάντα τὰ
do not be in suspense;   for these things   all   the

ἔθνη τοῦ κόσμου ἐπιζητοῦσιν· ὑμῶν δὲ
nations of the   world   seek after;   but of you

ὁ πατὴρ οἶδεν ὅτι χρῄζετε τούτων·
the Father   knows   that   ye have need   of them;

31 πλὴν ζητεῖτε τὴν βασιλείαν αὐτοῦ, καὶ
    but   seek ye   the   kingdom   of him,   and

ταῦτα προστεθήσεται ὑμῖν. 32 Μὴ φοβοῦ,
these things will be added   to you.   Fear not,

τὸ μικρὸν ποίμνιον· ὅτι εὐδόκησεν ὁ
-   little   flock;   because was well pleased the

πατὴρ ὑμῶν δοῦναι ὑμῖν τὴν βασιλείαν.
Father of you   to give   you   the   kingdom.

33 Πωλήσατε τὰ ὑπάρχοντα ὑμῶν καὶ
   Sell   the   possessions   of you   and

δότε ἐλεημοσύνην· ποιήσατε ἑαυτοῖς βαλ-
give   alms;   make   for yourselves

λάντια μὴ παλαιούμενα, θησαυρὸν ἀνέκλειπτον
purses   not becoming old,   a treasure   unfailing

ἐν τοῖς οὐρανοῖς, ὅπου κλέπτης οὐκ
in   the   heavens,   where   a thief   not

ἐγγίζει οὐδὲ σὴς διαφθείρει· 34 ὅπου γάρ
comes near   nor   moth   corrupts;   for where

ἐστιν ὁ θησαυρὸς ὑμῶν, ἐκεῖ καὶ ἡ
is   the   treasure   of you,   there also the

καρδία ὑμῶν ἔσται. 35 Ἔστωσαν ὑμῶν αἱ
heart   of you   will be.   Let be   of you the

ὀσφύες περιεζωσμέναι καὶ οἱ λύχνοι
loins   having been girded   and   the   lamps

καιόμενοι· 36 καὶ ὑμεῖς ὅμοιοι ἀνθρώποις
burning;   and   ye   like   men

προσδεχομένοις τὸν κύριον ἑαυτῶν, πότε
awaiting   the   lord   of themselves,   when

ἀναλύσῃ ἐκ τῶν γάμων, ἵνα ἐλθόντος
he returns   from   the wedding festivities, that   coming[a]

καὶ κρούσαντος εὐθέως ἀνοίξωσιν αὐτῷ.
and   knocking[a]   immediately they may open   to him.

37 μακάριοι οἱ δοῦλοι ἐκεῖνοι, οὓς ἐλθὼν
   Blessed   -   slaves   those,   whom   coming

ὁ κύριος εὑρήσει γρηγοροῦντας· ἀμὴν λέγω
the lord   will find   watching;   truly   I tell

ὑμῖν ὅτι περιζώσεται καὶ ἀνακλινεῖ αὐτοὺς
you   that he will gird himself   and   [1]make [2]to recline [3]them

καὶ παρελθὼν διακονήσει αὐτοῖς. 38 κἂν
and   coming up to   will serve   them.   And if

comes in the second watch, or in the third, and finds them so, blessed are those servants! ³⁹But know this, that if the householder had known at what hour the thief was coming, he would have been awake and^j would not have left his house to be broken into. ⁴⁰You also must be ready; for the Son of man is coming at an hour you do not expect."

41 Peter said, "Lord, are you telling this parable for us or for all?" ⁴²And the Lord said, "Who then is the faithful and wise steward, whom his master will set over his household, to give them their portion of food at the proper time? ⁴³Blessed is that servant whom his master when he comes will find so doing. ⁴⁴Truly I tell you, he will set him over all his possessions. ⁴⁵But if that servant says to himself, 'My master is delayed in coming,' and begins to beat the menservants and the maidservants, and to eat and drink and get drunk, ⁴⁶the master of that servant will come on a day when he does not expect him and at an

ἐν τῇ δευτέρᾳ κἂν ἐν τῇ τρίτῃ φυλακῇ
in   the second and if in the third watch
ἔλθῃ καὶ εὕρῃ οὕτως, μακάριοί εἰσιν
he comes and finds so,   blessed   are
ἐκεῖνοι. 39 τοῦτο δὲ γινώσκετε, ὅτι εἰ
those [slaves]. But this   know ye,   that if
ᾔδει ὁ οἰκοδεσπότης ποίᾳ ὥρᾳ ὁ κλέπτης
knew the house-master in what hour the thief
ἔρχεται, οὐκ ἂν ἀφῆκεν διορυχθῆναι τὸν
comes, he would not have allowed to be dug through the
οἶκον αὐτοῦ. 40 καὶ ὑμεῖς γίνεσθε ἕτοιμοι,
house of him.   And ²ye   ¹be   prepared.
ὅτι ᾗ ὥρᾳ οὐ δοκεῖτε ὁ υἱὸς τοῦ
because in what hour ye think not   the Son   of
ἀνθρώπου ἔρχεται. 41 Εἶπεν δὲ ὁ Πέτρος·
of man   comes.   And said – Peter :
κύριε, πρὸς ἡμᾶς τὴν παραβολὴν ταύτην
Lord,   to   us   –   parable   this
λέγεις ἢ καὶ πρὸς πάντας; 42 καὶ εἶπεν
sayest thou or also to   all?   And said
ὁ κύριος· τίς ἄρα ἐστὶν ὁ πιστὸς
the Lord :   Who then   is   the faithful
οἰκονόμος ὁ φρόνιμος, ὃν καταστήσει ὁ
steward the prudent, whom will appoint the
κύριος ἐπὶ τῆς θεραπείας αὐτοῦ τοῦ
lord   over the household attendants of him   –
διδόναι ἐν καιρῷ [τὸ] σιτομέτριον;
to give^d in season the portion of food?
43 μακάριος ὁ δοῦλος ἐκεῖνος, ὃν ἐλθὼν
Blessed – slave   that, whom coming
ὁ κύριος αὐτοῦ εὑρήσει ποιοῦντα οὕτως.
the lord of him   will find doing   so.
44 ἀληθῶς λέγω ὑμῖν ὅτι ἐπὶ πᾶσιν τοῖς
Truly I tell you that over all the
ὑπάρχουσιν αὐτοῦ καταστήσει αὐτόν. 45 ἐὰν
possessions of him he will appoint him.   if
δὲ εἴπῃ ὁ δοῦλος ἐκεῖνος ἐν τῇ καρδίᾳ
But says – slave   that   in the heart
αὐτοῦ· χρονίζει ὁ κύριός μου ἔρχεσθαι,
of him :   Delays the lord of me   to come,
καὶ ἄρξηται τύπτειν τοὺς παῖδας καὶ τὰς
and begins to strike the menservants and the
παιδίσκας, ἐσθίειν τε καὶ πίνειν καὶ
maidservants, ²to eat ¹both and to drink and
μεθύσκεσθαι, 46 ἥξει ὁ κύριος τοῦ δούλου
to become drunk, will come the lord   – slave
ἐκείνου ἐν ἡμέρᾳ ᾗ οὐ προσδοκᾷ καὶ ἐν
of that   in a day in which he does not expect and in

---

^{j} Other ancient authorities omit *would have been awake and* hour he does not know, and will punish[k] him, and put him with the unfaithful. 47And that servant who knew his master's will, but did not make ready or act according to his will, shall receive a severe beating. 48But he who did not know, and did what deserved a beating, shall receive a light beating. Every one to whom much is given, of him will much be required; and of him to whom men commit much they will demand the more.

49 "I came to cast fire upon the earth; and would that it were already kindled! 50I have a baptism to be baptized with; and how I am constrained until it is accomplished! 51Do you think that I have come to give peace on earth? No, I tell you, but rather division; 52for henceforth in one house there will be five divided, three against two and two against three; 53they will be divided, father against son and son against father, mother against daughter and daughter against her mother, mother-in-law against her daughter-in-law and daughter-in-law against her mother-in-law."

54 He also said to the multitudes, "When you see a cloud rising in the

ὥρᾳ ᾗ οὐ γινώσκει, καὶ διχοτομήσει
an hour in which he knows not, and will cut asunder

αὐτόν, καὶ τὸ μέρος αὐτοῦ μετὰ τῶν
him, and the portion of him with the

ἀπίστων θήσει. 47 ἐκεῖνος δὲ ὁ δοῦλος
unbelievers will place. But that — slave

ὁ γνοὺς τὸ θέλημα τοῦ κυρίου αὐτοῦ
– having known the will of the lord of him

καὶ μὴ ἑτοιμάσας ἢ ποιήσας πρὸς τὸ θέλημα
and not having prepared or done according to the will

αὐτοῦ δαρήσεται πολλάς· 48 ὁ δὲ
of him will be beaten [with] many [stripes]; but the [one]

μὴ γνούς, ποιήσας δὲ ἄξια πληγῶν,
not having known, but having done things worthy of stripes,

δαρήσεται ὀλίγας. παντὶ δὲ ᾧ
will be beaten [with] few [stripes]. But to everyone to whom

ἐδόθη πολύ, πολὺ ζητηθήσεται παρ' αὐτοῦ, καὶ
was given much, much will be demanded from him, and

ᾧ παρέθεντο πολύ, περισσότερον αἰτήσουσιν
with whom was deposited much, more exceedingly they will ask

αὐτόν. 49 Πῦρ ἦλθον βαλεῖν ἐπὶ τὴν γῆν,
him. Fire I came to cast on the earth,

καὶ τί θέλω εἰ ἤδη ἀνήφθη. 50 βάπτισμα
and what will I if already it was kindled. aa baptism

δὲ ἔχω βαπτισθῆναι, καὶ πῶς συνέχομαι
1And 1I have to be baptized [with], and how am I pressed

ἕως ὅτου τελεσθῇ. 51 δοκεῖτε ὅτι εἰρήνην
until it is accomplished. Think ye that peace

παρεγενόμην δοῦναι ἐν τῇ γῇ; οὐχί, λέγω
I came to give in the earth? No, I tell

ὑμῖν, ἀλλ' ἢ διαμερισμόν. 52 ἔσονται γὰρ
you, but rather division. For there will be

ἀπὸ τοῦ νῦν πέντε ἐν ἑνὶ οἴκῳ διαμεμε-
from - now five in one house having been

ρισμένοι, τρεῖς ἐπὶ δυσὶν καὶ δύο ἐπὶ
divided, three against two and two against

τρισὶν 53 διαμερισθήσονται, πατὴρ ἐπὶ υἱῷ
three will be divided, father against son

καὶ υἱὸς ἐπὶ πατρί, μήτηρ ἐπὶ θυγατέρα
and son against father, mother against daughter

καὶ θυγάτηρ ἐπὶ τὴν μητέρα, πενθερὰ
and daughter against the mother, mother-in-law

ἐπὶ τὴν νύμφην αὐτῆς καὶ νύμφη ἐπὶ
against the daughter-in-law of her and daughter-in-law against

τὴν πενθεράν. 54 Ἔλεγεν δὲ καὶ τοῖς
the mother-in-law. And he said also to the

ὄχλοις· ὅταν ἴδητε νεφέλην ἀνατέλλουσαν
crowds: When ye see a cloud rising

[k] Or cut him in pieces

west, you say at once, 'A shower is coming'; and so it happens. ⁵⁵And when you see the south wind blowing, you say, 'There will be scorching heat'; and it happens. ⁵⁶You hypocrites! You know how to interpret the appearance of earth and sky; but why do you not know how to interpret the present time?

57 "And why do you not judge for yourselves what is right? ⁵⁸As you go with your accuser before the magistrate, make an effort to settle with him on the way, lest he drag you to the judge, and the judge hand you over to the officer, and the officer put you in prison. ⁵⁹I tell you, you will never get out till you have paid the very last copper."

ἐπὶ δυσμῶν, εὐθέως λέγετε ὅτι ὄμβρος
over [the] west, immediately ye say that a storm
ἔρχεται, καὶ γίνεται οὕτως· 55 καὶ ὅταν
is coming, and it becomes so; and when
νότον πνέοντα, λέγετε ὅτι καύσων ἔσται,
a south wind blowing, ye say that heat there will be,
καὶ γίνεται. 56 ὑποκριταί, τὸ πρόσωπον
and it becomes. Hypocrites, the face
τῆς γῆς καὶ τοῦ οὐρανοῦ οἴδατε δοκιμάζειν,
of the earth and of the heaven ye know* to discern,
τὸν καιρὸν δὲ τοῦτον πῶς οὐ δοκιμάζετε;
– ¹time ²but ³this how do ye not discern?
57 Τί δὲ καὶ ἀφ' ἑαυτῶν οὐ κρίνετε
And why even from yourselves do ye not judge
τὸ δίκαιον; 58 ὡς γὰρ ὑπάγεις μετὰ τοῦ
the righteous thing? For as thou goest with the
ἀντιδίκου σου ἐπ' ἄρχοντα, ἐν τῇ ὁδῷ
adversary of thee to a ruler, in the way
δὸς ἐργασίαν ἀπηλλάχθαι ἀπ' αὐτοῦ, μήποτε
give(take) pains to be rid from(of) him, lest
κατασύρῃ σε πρὸς τὸν κριτήν, καὶ ὁ
he drag thee to the judge, and the
κριτής σε παραδώσει τῷ πράκτορι, καὶ ὁ
judge thee will deliver to the usher, and the
πράκτωρ σε βαλεῖ εἰς φυλακήν. 59 λέγω
usher thee will cast into prison. I tell
σοι, οὐ μὴ ἐξέλθῃς ἐκεῖθεν ἕως
thee, by no means mayest thou come out thence until
καὶ τὸ ἔσχατον λεπτὸν ἀποδῷς.
even the last lepton thou payest.

CHAPTER 13

THERE were some present at that very time who told him of the Galileans whose blood Pilate had mingled with their sacrifices. ²And he answered them, "Do you think that these Galileans were worse sinners than all the other Galileans, because they suffered thus? ³I tell you, No; but unless you repent

13 Παρῆσαν δέ τινες ἐν αὐτῷ τῷ
And there were present some at ²same ¹the
καιρῷ ἀπαγγέλλοντες αὐτῷ περὶ τῶν
time reporting to him about the
Γαλιλαίων ὧν τὸ αἷμα Πιλᾶτος ἔμιξεν
Galilæans of whom the blood Pilate mixed
μετὰ τῶν θυσιῶν αὐτῶν. 2 καὶ ἀποκριθεὶς
with the sacrifices of them. And answering
εἶπεν αὐτοῖς· δοκεῖτε ὅτι οἱ Γαλιλαῖοι
he said to them : Think ye that – Galilæans
οὗτοι ἁμαρτωλοὶ παρὰ πάντας τοὺς Γαλι-
these sinners above all the Gali-
λαίους ἐγένοντο, ὅτι ταῦτα πεπόνθασιν;
læans were, because these things they have suffered?
3 οὐχί, λέγω ὑμῖν, ἀλλ' ἐὰν μὴ μετανοῆτε,
No, I tell you, but unless ye repent,

* can, as Mat. 16. 3. See note on page xviii.

you will all likewise perish. ⁴Or those eighteen upon whom the tower in Silo'am fell and killed them, do you think that they were worse offenders than all the others who dwelt in Jerusalem? ⁵I tell you, No; but unless you repent you will all likewise perish."

6 And he told this parable: "A man had a fig tree planted in his vineyard; and he came seeking fruit on it and found none. ⁷And he said to the vinedresser, 'Lo, these three years I have come seeking fruit on this fig tree, and I find none. Cut it down; why should it use up the ground?' ⁸And he answered him, 'Let it alone, sir, this year also, till I dig about it and put on manure. ⁹And if it bears fruit next year, well and good; but if not, you can cut it down.'"

10 Now he was teaching in one of the synagogues on the sabbath. ¹¹And there was a woman who had had a spirit of infirmity for eighteen years; she was bent over and could not

πάντες ὁμοίως ἀπολεῖσθε. 4 ἢ ἐκεῖνοι οἱ
all   likewise   ye will perish.   Or those -

δεκαοκτὼ ἐφ' οὓς ἔπεσεν ὁ πύργος ἐν
eighteen   on   whom   fell   the   tower   in

τῷ Σιλωὰμ καὶ ἀπέκτεινεν αὐτούς, δοκεῖτε
-   Siloam   and   killed   them,   think ye

ὅτι αὐτοὶ ὀφειλέται ἐγένοντο παρὰ πάντας
that   they   debtors   were   above   all

τοὺς ἀνθρώπους τοὺς κατοικοῦντας Ἰερου-
the   men   -   dwelling in   Jeru-

σαλήμ; 5 οὐχί, λέγω ὑμῖν, ἀλλ' ἐὰν μὴ
salem?   No,   I tell   you,   but   unless

μετανοήσητε, πάντες ὡσαύτως ἀπολεῖσθε.
ye repent,   all   similarly   ye will perish.

6 Ἔλεγεν δὲ ταύτην τὴν παραβολήν. συκῆν
And he told   this   -   parable.   ²A fig-tree

εἶχέν τις πεφυτευμένην ἐν τῷ ἀμπελῶνι
²had ¹a certain man *having been* planted in the   vineyard

αὐτοῦ, καὶ ἦλθεν ζητῶν καρπὸν ἐν αὐτῇ
of him,   and   came   seeking   fruit   in   it

καὶ οὐχ εὗρεν. 7 εἶπεν δὲ πρὸς τὸν
and   found not.   And he said   to   the

ἀμπελουργόν· ἰδοὺ τρία ἔτη ἀφ' οὗ
vinedresser :   Behold[,] three   years   [it is] since

ἔρχομαι ζητῶν καρπὸν ἐν τῇ συκῇ ταύτῃ
I come   seeking   fruit   in   -   fig-tree   this

καὶ οὐχ εὑρίσκω· ἔκκοψον αὐτήν· ἱνατί
and   find not;   cut down   it;   why

καὶ τὴν γῆν καταργεῖ; 8 ὁ δὲ ἀποκριθεὶς
even the ground it spoils?   But he   answering

λέγει αὐτῷ· κύριε, ἄφες αὐτὴν καὶ τοῦτο
says   to him : Lord,   leave   it   also   this

τὸ ἔτος, ἕως ὅτου σκάψω περὶ αὐτὴν καὶ
-   year,   until   I may dig   round   it   and

βάλω κόπρια, 9 κἂν μὲν ποιήσῃ καρπὸν
may throw dung,   and if indeed it makes   fruit

εἰς τὸ μέλλον· εἰ δὲ μή γε, ἐκκόψεις
in   the   future;   otherwise,   thou shalt cut down

αὐτήν.
it.

10 Ἦν δὲ διδάσκων ἐν μιᾷ τῶν συναγωγῶν
And he was   teaching   in one of the   synagogues

ἐν τοῖς σάββασιν. 11 καὶ ἰδοὺ γυνὴ
on   the   sabbaths.   And[,] behold[,] a woman

πνεῦμα ἔχουσα ἀσθενείας ἔτη δεκαοκτώ,
²a spirit ¹having   of infirmity   years   eighteen,

καὶ ἦν συγκύπτουσα καὶ μὴ δυναμένη
and was   bending double   and   not   being able

fully straighten herself. ¹²And when Jesus saw her, he called her and said to her, "Woman, you are freed from your infirmity." ¹³And he laid his hands upon her, and immediately she was made straight, and she praised God. ¹⁴But the ruler of the synagogue, indignant because Jesus had healed on the sabbath, said to the people, "There are six days on which work ought to be done; come on those days and be healed, and not on the sabbath day." ¹⁵Then the Lord answered him, "You hypocrites! Does not each of you on the sabbath untie his ox or his ass from the manger, and lead it away to water it? ¹⁶And ought not this woman, a daughter of Abraham whom Satan bound for eighteen years, be loosed from this bond on the sabbath day?" ¹⁷As he said this, all his adversaries were put to shame; and all the people rejoiced at all the glorious things that were done by him.

18 He said therefore, "What is the kingdom of God like? And to what shall I compare it? ¹⁹It

ἀνακῦψαι εἰς τὸ παντελές. **12** ἰδὼν δὲ
to become erect   entirely.†   And seeing

αὐτὴν ὁ 'Ιησοῦς προσεφώνησεν καὶ εἶπεν
her - Jesus   called to [him]   and   said

αὐτῇ· γύναι, ἀπολέλυσαι τῆς ἀσθενείας
to her : Woman, thou hast been loosed from the infirmity

σου, **13** καὶ ἐπέθηκεν αὐτῇ τὰς χεῖρας·
of thee,   and   he put on   her   the(his) hands;

καὶ παραχρῆμα ἀνωρθώθη, καὶ ἐδόξαζεν
and   at once   she was straightened, and   glorified

τὸν θεόν. **14** ἀποκριθεὶς δὲ ὁ ἀρχι-
-    God.   But answering   the   syn-

συνάγωγος, ἀγανακτῶν ὅτι τῷ σαββάτῳ
agogue ruler,   being angry   that ²on the ⁴sabbath

ἐθεράπευσεν ὁ 'Ιησοῦς, ἔλεγεν τῷ ὄχλῳ
³healed   - ¹Jesus,   said   to the crowd[,]

ὅτι ἐξ ἡμέραι εἰσὶν ἐν αἷς δεῖ ἐργάζεσθαι·
- six   days there are on which it behoves to work;

ἐν αὐταῖς οὖν ἐρχόμενοι θεραπεύεσθε καὶ
on them therefore coming be ye healed and

μὴ τῇ ἡμέρᾳ τοῦ σαββάτου. **15** ἀπεκρίθη δὲ
not on the day of the sabbath.   But answered

αὐτῷ ὁ κύριος καὶ εἶπεν· ὑποκριταί,
him the Lord and said : Hypocrites,

ἕκαστος ὑμῶν τῷ σαββάτῳ οὐ λύει τὸν
each one of you on the sabbath does he not loosen the

βοῦν αὐτοῦ ἢ τὸν ὄνον ἀπὸ τῆς φάτνης
ox of him or the ass from the manger

καὶ ἀπαγαγὼν ποτίζει; **16** ταύτην δὲ
and leading [it] away give drink?   And this woman

θυγατέρα 'Αβραὰμ οὖσαν, ἣν ἔδησεν ὁ
a daughter of Abraham being, whom bound -

σατανᾶς ἰδοὺ δέκα καὶ ὀκτὼ ἔτη, οὐκ ἔδει
Satan behold ten and eight years, behoved it not

λυθῆναι ἀπὸ τοῦ δεσμοῦ τούτου τῇ
to be loosened from - bond this on the

ἡμέρᾳ τοῦ σαββάτου; **17** καὶ ταῦτα λέγοντος
day of the sabbath?   And these things saying
=when he said these things

αὐτοῦ κατῃσχύνοντο πάντες οἱ ἀντικείμενοι
him² were put to shame all the [ones] opposing

αὐτῷ, καὶ πᾶς ὁ ὄχλος ἔχαιρεν ἐπὶ
him, and all the crowd rejoiced over

πᾶσιν τοῖς ἐνδόξοις τοῖς γινομένοις ὑπ'
all the glorious things - happening by

αὐτοῦ. **18** Ἔλεγεν οὖν· τίνι ὁμοία ἐστὶν ἡ
him.   He said therefore: To what like is the

βασιλεία τοῦ θεοῦ, καὶ τίνι ὁμοιώσω
kingdom - of God, and to what may I liken

is like a grain of mustard seed which a man took and sowed in his garden; and it grew and became a tree, and the birds of the air made nests in its branches."

20 And again he said, "To what shall I compare the kingdom of God? ²¹ It is like leaven which a woman took and hid in three measures of meal, till it was all leavened."

22 He went on his way through towns and villages, teaching, and journeying toward Jerusalem. ²³And some one said to him, "Lord, will those who are saved be few?" And he said to them, ²⁴ "Strive to enter by the narrow door; for many, I tell you, will seek to enter and will not be able. ²⁵When once the householder has risen up and shut the door, you will begin to stand outside and to knock at the door, saying, 'Lord, open to us.' He will answer you,'I do not know where you come from.' ²⁶Then you will begin to say, 'We ate and drank in your presence, and you taught in our streets.' ²⁷But he will say, 'I tell

αὐτήν; 19 ὁμοία ἐστὶν κόκκῳ σινάπεως, ὃν
it?   Like   it is   to a grain   of mustard, which
λαβὼν ἄνθρωπος ἔβαλεν εἰς κῆπον ἑαυτοῦ,
²taking   ¹a man   cast   into a garden of him*self*,
καὶ ηὔξησεν καὶ ἐγένετο εἰς δένδρον, καὶ
and   it grew   and   became   into   a tree,   and
τὰ πετεινὰ τοῦ οὐρανοῦ κατεσκήνωσεν
the   birds   of the   heaven(air)   lodged
ἐν τοῖς κλάδοις αὐτοῦ. 20 Καὶ πάλιν
in   the   branches   of it.   And   again
εἶπεν· τίνι ὁμοιώσω τὴν βασιλείαν τοῦ
he said : To what may I liken   the   kingdom   –
θεοῦ; 21 ὁμοία ἐστὶν ζύμῃ, ἣν λαβοῦσα
of God?   Like   it is   to leaven, which   ²taking
γυνὴ ἔκρυψεν εἰς ἀλεύρου σάτα τρία,
¹a woman   hid   in   of meal   measures   three,
ἕως οὗ ἐζυμώθη ὅλον.
until   was leavened all.

22 Καὶ διεπορεύετο κατὰ πόλεις καὶ
And he journeyed *through* throughout cities   and
κώμας διδάσκων καὶ πορείαν ποιούμενος
villages   teaching   and   journey   making
εἰς Ἱεροσόλυμα. 23 Εἶπεν δέ τις αὐτῷ·
to   Jerusalem.   And said   someone to him :
κύριε, εἰ ὀλίγοι οἱ σωζόμενοι; ὁ δὲ εἶπεν
Lord, if few the[ones] being saved? And he   said
πρὸς αὐτούς· 24 ἀγωνίζεσθε εἰσελθεῖν διὰ
to   them :   Struggle   to enter through
τῆς στενῆς θύρας, ὅτι πολλοί, λέγω ὑμῖν,
the   strait   door, because many,   I tell   you,
ζητήσουσιν εἰσελθεῖν καὶ οὐκ ἰσχύσουσιν.
will seek   to enter   and   will not be able.
25 ἀφ᾽ οὗ ἂν ἐγερθῇ ὁ οἰκοδεσπότης καὶ
From [the time] when is risen the   house-master   and
ἀποκλείσῃ τὴν θύραν, καὶ ἄρξησθε ἔξω
he shuts   the   door,   and   ye begin   outside
ἑστάναι καὶ κρούειν τὴν θύραν λέγοντες·
to stand   and   to knock   the   door   saying :
κύριε, ἄνοιξον ἡμῖν, καὶ ἀποκριθεὶς ἐρεῖ
Lord,   open   to us,   and   answering he will say
ὑμῖν· οὐκ οἶδα ὑμᾶς πόθεν ἐστέ. 26 τότε
to you : I know not   you   whence ye are.   Then
ἄρξεσθε λέγειν· ἐφάγομεν ἐνώπιόν σου καὶ
ye will begin to say :   We ate   before   thee   and
ἐπίομεν, καὶ ἐν ταῖς πλατείαις ἡμῶν
drank,   and   in   the   streets   of us
ἐδίδαξας· 27 καὶ ἐρεῖ λέγων ὑμῖν· οὐκ
thou didst teach;   and he will say telling   you :   not

you, I do not know where you come from; depart from me, all you workers of iniquity!' [28]There you will weep and gnash your teeth, when you see Abraham and Isaac and Jacob and all the prophets in the kingdom of God and you yourselves thrust out. [29]And men will come from east and west, and from north and south, and sit at table in the kingdom of God. [30]And behold, some are last who will be first, and some are first who will be last.''

31 At that very hour some Pharisees came, and said to him, "Get away from here, for Herod wants to kill you.'' [32]And he said to them, "Go and tell that fox, 'Behold, I cast out demons and perform cures today and tomorrow, and the third day I finish my course. [33]Nevertheless I must go on my way today and tomorrow and the day following; for it cannot be that a prophet should perish away from Jerusalem.' [34]O Jerusalem, Jerusalem, killing the prophets and stoning those who are sent to you! How often would I have gathered your

οἶδα πόθεν ἐστέ· ἀπόστητε ἀπ' ἐμοῦ
I know whence ye are; stand away from me

πάντες ἐργάται ἀδικίας. 28 ἐκεῖ ἔσται ὁ
all workers of unrighteousness. There will be the

κλαυθμὸς καὶ ὁ βρυγμὸς τῶν ὀδόντων,
weeping and the gnashing of the teeth,

ὅταν ὄψησθε Ἀβραὰμ καὶ Ἰσαὰκ καὶ
when ye see Abraham and Isaac and

Ἰακὼβ καὶ πάντας τοὺς προφήτας ἐν τῇ
Jacob and all the prophets in the

βασιλείᾳ τοῦ θεοῦ, ὑμᾶς δὲ ἐκβαλλομένους
kingdom - of God, but you being thrust *out*

ἔξω. 29 καὶ ἥξουσιν ἀπὸ ἀνατολῶν καὶ
outside. And they will come from east and

δυσμῶν καὶ ἀπὸ βορρᾶ καὶ νότου, καὶ
west and from north and south, and

ἀνακλιθήσονται ἐν τῇ βασιλείᾳ τοῦ θεοῦ.
will recline in the kingdom - of God.

30 καὶ ἰδοὺ εἰσὶν ἔσχατοι οἳ ἔσονται
And behold there are last [ones] who will be

πρῶτοι, καὶ εἰσὶν πρῶτοι οἳ ἔσονται
first, and there are first [ones] who will be

ἔσχατοι. 31 Ἐν αὐτῇ τῇ ὥρᾳ προσῆλθάν
last. In ²same ¹the hour approached

τινες Φαρισαῖοι λέγοντες αὐτῷ· ἔξελθε καὶ
some Pharisees saying to him : Depart and

πορεύου ἐντεῦθεν, ὅτι Ἡρώδης θέλει σε
go hence, because Herod wishes thee

ἀποκτεῖναι. 32 καὶ εἶπεν αὐτοῖς· πορευθέντες
to kill. And he said to them : Going

εἴπατε τῇ ἀλώπεκι ταύτῃ· ἰδοὺ ἐκβάλλω
tell - fox this : Behold I expel

δαιμόνια καὶ ἰάσεις ἀποτελῶ σήμερον καὶ
demons and ²cures ¹accomplish to-day and

αὔριον, καὶ τῇ τρίτῃ τελειοῦμαι. 33 πλὴν
to-morrow, and on the third [day] I am perfected. Nevertheless

δεῖ με σήμερον καὶ αὔριον καὶ τῇ ἐχομένῃ
it be- me to-day and to- and on the following
hoves   morrow   [day]

πορεύεσθαι, ὅτι οὐκ ἐνδέχεται προφήτην
to journey, because it is not possible a prophet

ἀπολέσθαι ἔξω Ἰερουσαλήμ. 34 Ἰερουσαλὴμ
to perish outside Jerusalem. Jerusalem[.]

Ἰερουσαλήμ, ἡ ἀποκτείνουσα τοὺς προφήτας
Jerusalem, the [one] killing the prophets

καὶ λιθοβολοῦσα τοὺς ἀπεσταλμένους πρὸς
and stoning the [ones] *having been* sent to

αὐτήν, ποσάκις ἠθέλησα ἐπισυνάξαι τὰ
her, how often I wished to gather the

children together as a
hen gathers her brood
under her wings, and
you would not! ³⁵Behold,
your house is forsaken.
And I tell you, you will
not see me until you
say, 'Blessed is he who
comes in the name of the
Lord!' "

τέκνα   σου   ὃν τρόπον ὄρνις τὴν ἑαυτῆς
children of thee   as †   a bird   the   of herself
νοσσιὰν   ὑπὸ   τὰς   πτέρυγας,   καὶ   οὐκ
brood   under   the(her)   wings,   and   not
ἠθελήσατε.   35 ἰδοὺ ἀφίεται ὑμῖν ὁ οἶκος
ye wished.   Behold is left   to you the house
ὑμῶν.   λέγω [δὲ] ὑμῖν, οὐ μὴ ἴδητέ με
of you.   And I tell   you,   by no means ye may see me
ἕως ἥξει ὅτε εἴπητε· εὐλογημένος ὁ
until shall come [the ye say :   Blessed   the
         time] when
ἐρχόμενος ἐν ὀνόματι κυρίου.
[one] coming   in [the] name of [the] Lord.

CHAPTER 14

ONE sabbath when
he went to dine at
the house of a ruler who
belonged to the Pharisees,
they were watching him.
²And behold, there was
a man before him who
had dropsy. ³And Jesus
spoke to the lawyers and
Pharisees, saying, "Is it
lawful to heal on the
sabbath, or not?" ⁴But
they were silent. Then he
took him and healed
him, and let him go.
⁵And he said to them,
"Which of you, having
an ass¹ or an ox that has
fallen into a well, will
not immediately pull him
out on a sabbath day?"
⁶And they could not
reply to this.

7 Now he told a
parable to those who
were invited, when he
marked how they chose
the places of honor, say-
ing to them, ⁸"When you
are invited by any one to

14 Καὶ ἐγένετο ἐν τῷ ἐλθεῖν αὐτὸν εἰς
    And it came to pass in the   to go   himᵇᵉ   into
                                        =as he went
οἶκόν τινος τῶν ἀρχόντων τῶν Φαρισαίων
a house of one of the   leaders   of the   Pharisees
σαββάτῳ φαγεῖν ἄρτον, καὶ αὐτοὶ ἦσαν
on a sabbath to eat   bread,   and   they   were
παρατηρούμενοι αὐτόν. 2 καὶ ἰδοὺ ἄνθρωπός
carefully watching   him.   And[,] behold[,] man
τις ἦν ὑδρωπικὸς ἔμπροσθεν αὐτοῦ. 3 καὶ
a certain was dropsical   before   him.   And
ἀποκριθεὶς ὁ Ἰησοῦς εἶπεν πρὸς τοὺς
answering   -   Jesus   spoke   to   the
νομικοὺς καὶ Φαρισαίους λέγων· ἔξεστιν
lawyers   and   Pharisees   saying : Is it lawful
τῷ σαββάτῳ θεραπεῦσαι ἢ οὔ; 4 οἱ δὲ
on the sabbath   to heal   or not? And they
ἡσύχασαν. καὶ ἐπιλαβόμενος ἰάσατο αὐτὸν
were silent.   And   taking   he cured   him
καὶ ἀπέλυσεν. 5 καὶ πρὸς αὐτοὺς εἶπεν·
and dismissed.   And   to   them   he said:
τίνος ὑμῶν υἱὸς ἢ βοῦς εἰς φρέαρ πεσεῖται,
Of whom of you a son or an ox into   a pit   shall fall,
καὶ οὐκ εὐθέως ἀνασπάσει αὐτὸν ἐν
and   not immediately he will pull up   it   on
ἡμέρᾳ τοῦ σαββάτου; 6 καὶ οὐκ ἴσχυσαν
a day   of the   sabbath?   And   they were not able
ἀνταποκριθῆναι πρὸς ταῦτα. 7 Ἔλεγεν δὲ
to reply   against these things.   And he said
πρὸς τοὺς κεκλημένους παραβολήν, ἐπέχων
to the [ones] having been invited   a parable,   noting
πῶς τὰς πρωτοκλισίας ἐξελέγοντο, λέγων
how ²the   ³chief seats   ¹they were choosing, saying
πρὸς αὐτούς· 8 ὅταν κληθῇς ὑπό τινος εἰς
to   them :   When thou art invited by   anyone to

¹ Other ancient authorities
read a son

a marriage feast, do not sit down in a place of honor, lest a more eminent man than you be invited by him; 9 and he who invited you both will come and say to you, 'Give place to this man,' and then you will begin with shame to take the lowest place. 10 But when you are invited, go and sit in the lowest place, so that when your host comes he may say to you, 'Friend, go up higher'; then you will be honored in the presence of all who sit at table with you. 11 For every one who exalts himself will be humbled, and he who humbles himself will be exalted."

12 He said also to the man who had invited him, "When you give a dinner or a banquet, do not invite your friends or your brothers or your kinsmen or rich neighbors, lest they also invite you in return, and you be repaid. 13 But when you give a feast, invite the poor, the maimed, the lame, the blind, 14 and you will be blessed, because they cannot repay you. You will be repaid at the resurrection of the just."

15 When one of those who sat at table with him heard this, he said to

γάμους, μὴ κατακλιθῇς εἰς τὴν πρωτοκλισίαν,
wedding festivities, do not recline in the chief seat,

μήποτε ἐντιμότερός σου ᾖ κεκλημένος ὑπ᾽
lest a more honour- thou be *having been* invited by
able [than]

αὐτοῦ, 9 καὶ ἐλθὼν ὁ σὲ καὶ αὐτὸν καλέσας
him, and coming ¹the [one] ³thee ⁴and ⁵him ²inviting

ἐρεῖ σοι· δὸς τούτῳ τόπον, καὶ τότε
will say to thee : Give this man place, and then

ἄρξῃ μετὰ αἰσχύνης τὸν ἔσχατον τόπον
thou wilt begin with shame the last place

κατέχειν. 10 ἀλλ᾽ ὅταν κληθῇς, πορευθεὶς
to take. But when thou art invited, going

ἀνάπεσε εἰς τὸν ἔσχατον τόπον, ἵνα ὅταν ἔλθῃ
recline in the last place, that when ⁴comes

ὁ κεκληκώς σε ἐρεῖ σοι· φίλε,
¹the [one] ²having invited ³thee he will say to thee : Friend,

προσανάβηθι ἀνώτερον· τότε ἔσται σοι δόξα
go up higher; then there will be to thee⁶ glory

ἐνώπιον πάντων τῶν συνανακειμένων σοι.
before all the [ones] reclining with thee.

11 ὅτι πᾶς ὁ ὑψῶν ἑαυτὸν ταπεινωθήσεται,
Because everyone exalting himself will be humbled,

καὶ ὁ ταπεινῶν ἑαυτὸν ὑψωθήσεται.
and the [one] humbling himself will be exalted.

12 Ἔλεγεν δὲ καὶ τῷ κεκληκότι αὐτόν·
And he said also to the [one] having invited him :

ὅταν ποιῇς ἄριστον ἢ δεῖπνον, μὴ φώνει
When thou makest a dinner or a supper, do not call

τοὺς φίλους σου μηδὲ τοὺς ἀδελφούς
the friends of thee nor the brothers

σου μηδὲ τοὺς συγγενεῖς σου μηδὲ
of thee nor the relatives of thee nor

γείτονας πλουσίους, μήποτε καὶ αὐτοὶ
neighbours rich, lest also they

ἀντικαλέσωσίν σε καὶ γένηται ἀνταπόδομά
¹invite ²in ⁴return ³thee and it becomes a recompence

σοι. 13 ἀλλ᾽ ὅταν δοχὴν ποιῇς, κάλει
to thee. But when a party thou makest, invite

πτωχούς, ἀναπήρους, χωλούς, τυφλούς·
poor [persons], maimed, lame, blind;

14 καὶ μακάριος ἔσῃ, ὅτι οὐκ ἔχουσιν
and blessed thou shalt be, because they have not

ἀνταποδοῦναί σοι· ἀνταποδοθήσεται γάρ σοι
to recompense thee; for it will be recompensed to thee

ἐν τῇ ἀναστάσει τῶν δικαίων. 15 Ἀκούσας
in the resurrection of the just. ¹hearing

δέ τις τῶν συνανακειμένων ταῦτα εἶπεν
¹And ⁴one ⁵of the [ones] ²reclining with ³these things said

him, "Blessed is he who shall eat bread in the kingdom of God!" [16] But he said to him, "A man once gave a great banquet, and invited many; [17] and at the time for the banquet he sent his servant to say to those who had been invited, 'Come; for all is now ready.' [18] But they all alike began to make excuses. The first said to him, 'I have bought a field, and I must go out and see it; I pray you, have me excused.' [19] And another said, 'I have bought five yoke of oxen, and I go to examine them; I pray you, have me excused.' [20] And another said, 'I have married a wife, and therefore I cannot come.' [21] So the servant came and reported this to his master. Then the householder in anger said to his servant, 'Go out quickly to the streets and lanes of the city, and bring in the poor and maimed and blind and lame.' [22] And the servant said, 'Sir, what you commanded has been done, and still there is room.' [23] And the master said to the servant, 'Go

αὐτῷ· μακάριος ὅστις φάγεται ἄρτον ἐν
to him : Blessed [is he] who shall eat bread in
τῇ βασιλείᾳ τοῦ θεοῦ. 16 ὁ δὲ εἶπεν
the kingdom – of God. And he said
αὐτῷ· ἄνθρωπός τις ἐποίει δεῖπνον μέγα,
to him : A certain man made supper a great,
καὶ ἐκάλεσεν πολλούς, 17 καὶ ἀπέστειλεν
and invited many, and sent
τὸν δοῦλον αὐτοῦ τῇ ὥρᾳ τοῦ δείπνου
the slave of him at the hour of the supper
εἰπεῖν τοῖς κεκλημένοις· ἔρχεσθε, ὅτι ἤδη
to say to the [ones] having been invited : Come, because ²now
ἑτοιμά ἐστιν. 18 καὶ ἤρξαντο ἀπὸ μιᾶς
¹prepared ¹it is. And they began from one [mind]
πάντες παραιτεῖσθαι. ὁ πρῶτος εἶπεν
all to beg off. The first said
αὐτῷ· ἀγρὸν ἠγόρασα, καὶ ἔχω ἀνάγκην
to him : ²A farm ¹I bought, and I am obliged†
ἐξελθὼν ἰδεῖν αὐτόν· ἐρωτῶ σε, ἔχε με
going out to see it; I ask thee, have me
παρητημένον. 19 καὶ ἕτερος εἶπεν· ζεύγη
begged off. And another said : ²Yoke
βοῶν ἠγόρασα πέντε, καὶ πορεύομαι
⁴of oxen ¹I bought ³five, and I am going
δοκιμάσαι αὐτά· ἐρωτῶ σε, ἔχε με
to prove them; I ask thee, have me
παρητημένον. 20 καὶ ἕτερος εἶπεν· γυναῖκα
begged off. And another said : ¹A wife
ἔγημα, καὶ διὰ τοῦτο οὐ δύναμαι ἐλθεῖν.
¹I married, and therefore I cannot to come.
21 καὶ παραγενόμενος ὁ δοῦλος ἀπήγγειλεν
And coming up the slave reported
τῷ κυρίῳ αὐτοῦ ταῦτα. τότε ὀργισθεὶς ὁ
to the lord of him these things. Then being angry the
οἰκοδεσπότης εἶπεν τῷ δούλῳ αὐτοῦ· ἔξελθε
house-master told the slave of him : Go out
ταχέως εἰς τὰς πλατείας καὶ ῥύμας τῆς
quickly into the streets and lanes of the
πόλεως, καὶ τοὺς πτωχοὺς καὶ ἀναπήρους
city, and the poor and maimed
καὶ τυφλοὺς καὶ χωλοὺς εἰσάγαγε ὧδε.
and blind and lame bring in here.
22 καὶ εἶπεν ὁ δοῦλος· κύριε, γέγονεν ὃ
And said the slave : Lord, has happened what
ἐπέταξας, καὶ ἔτι τόπος ἐστίν. 23 καὶ
thou didst command, and yet room there is. And
εἶπεν ὁ κύριος πρὸς τὸν δοῦλον· ἔξελθε εἰς
said the lord to the slave : Go out into

out to the highways and hedges, and compel people to come in, that my house may be filled. [24] For I tell you, none of those men who were invited shall taste my banquet.' "

25 Now great multitudes accompanied him; and he turned and said to them, [26] "If any one comes to me and does not hate his own father and mother and wife and children and brothers and sisters, yes, and even his own life, he cannot be my disciple. [27] Whoever does not bear his own cross and come after me, cannot be my disciple. [28] For which of you, desiring to build a tower, does not first sit down and count the cost, whether he has enough to complete it? [29] Otherwise, when he has laid a foundation, and is not able to finish, all who see it begin to mock him, [30] saying, 'This man began to build, and was not able to finish.' [31] Or what king, going to encounter another king in war, will not sit down

τὰς ὁδοὺς καὶ φραγμοὺς καὶ ἀνάγκασον
the ways and hedges and compel
εἰσελθεῖν, ἵνα γεμισθῇ μου ὁ οἶκος·
to come in, that may be filled of me the house;
24 λέγω γὰρ ὑμῖν ὅτι οὐδεὶς τῶν ἀνδρῶν
for I tell you that not one – men
ἐκείνων τῶν κεκλημένων γεύσεταί μου
of those – having been invited shall taste of me
τοῦ δείπνου.
the supper.

25 Συνεπορεύοντο δὲ αὐτῷ ὄχλοι πολλοί,
And came together to him crowds many,
καὶ στραφεὶς εἶπεν πρὸς αὐτούς· 26 εἴ τις
and turning he said to them: If anyone
ἔρχεται πρός με καὶ οὐ μισεῖ τὸν πατέρα
comes to me and hates not the father
αὐτοῦ καὶ τὴν μητέρα καὶ τὴν γυναῖκα
of him and the mother and the wife
καὶ τὰ τέκνα καὶ τοὺς ἀδελφοὺς καὶ τὰς
and the children and the brothers and the
ἀδελφάς, ἔτι τε καὶ τὴν ψυχὴν ἑαυτοῦ,
sisters, and besides also the life of himself,
οὐ δύναται εἶναί μου μαθητής. 27 ὅστις
he cannot to be of me a disciple. Who
οὐ βαστάζει τὸν σταυρὸν ἑαυτοῦ καὶ
bears not the cross of himself and
ἔρχεται ὀπίσω μου, οὐ δύναται εἶναί μου
comes after me, he cannot to be of me
μαθητής. 28 Τίς γὰρ ἐξ ὑμῶν θέλων
a disciple. For who of you wishing
πύργον οἰκοδομῆσαι οὐχὶ πρῶτον καθίσας
a tower to build not first sitting
ψηφίζει τὴν δαπάνην, εἰ ἔχει εἰς ἀπαρ-
counts the cost, if he has for com-
τισμόν; 29 ἵνα μή ποτε θέντος αὐτοῦ
pletion? Lest when laying him[a]
=he has laid
θεμέλιον καὶ μὴ ἰσχύοντος ἐκτελέσαι πάντες
a foundation and not being able[a] to finish all
οἱ θεωροῦντες ἄρξωνται αὐτῷ ἐμπαίζειν
the [ones] seeing begin him to mock
30 λέγοντες ὅτι οὗτος ὁ ἄνθρωπος ἤρξατο
saying[.] This – man began
οἰκοδομεῖν καὶ οὐκ ἴσχυσεν ἐκτελέσαι.
to build and was not able to finish.
31 Ἢ τίς βασιλεὺς πορευόμενος ἑτέρῳ βασιλεῖ
Or what king [1]going [2]another [3]king
συμβαλεῖν εἰς πόλεμον οὐχὶ καθίσας πρῶτον
[5]to attack [3]in [4]war not sitting first

first and take counsel whether he is able with ten thousand to meet him who comes against him with twenty thousand? ³²And if not, while the other is yet a great way off, he sends an embassy and asks terms of peace. ³³So therefore, whoever of you does not renounce all that he has cannot be my disciple.

34 "Salt is good; but if salt has lost its taste, how shall its saltness be restored? ³⁵It is fit neither for the land nor for the dunghill; men throw it away. He who has ears to hear, let him hear."

βουλεύσεται   εἰ   δυνατός   ἐστιν   ἐν   δέκα
will deliberate   if   able   he is   with   ten

χιλιάσιν   ὑπαντῆσαι   τῷ   μετὰ   εἴκοσι   χιλιάδων
thousands   to meet   ¹the [one]   ⁵with   ⁶twenty   ⁷thousands

ἐρχομένῳ   ἐπ᾽   αὐτόν;   32   εἰ   δὲ   μή   γε,   ἔτι
²coming   ³upon   ⁴him?   Otherwise,   yet
                                                                          =while

αὐτοῦ   πόρρω   ὄντος   πρεσβείαν   ἀποστείλας
him   afar   beingᵃ   a delegation   sending
he is yet at a distance

ἐρωτᾷ   τὰ   πρὸς   εἰρήνην.   33   οὕτως   οὖν
he asks the things for   peace.   So   therefore

πᾶς   ἐξ   ὑμῶν   ὃς   οὐκ   ἀποτάσσεται   πᾶσιν
everyone   of   you   who   does not say farewell   to all

τοῖς   ἑαυτοῦ   ὑπάρχουσιν   οὐ   δύναται   εἶναί
¹the   ²of himself   ³possessions   cannot   to be

μου   μαθητής.   34   Καλὸν   οὖν   τὸ   ἅλας·
of me   a disciple.   Good   therefore   the   salt;

ἐὰν   δὲ   καὶ   τὸ   ἅλας   μωρανθῇ,   ἐν   τίνι
but if   even   the   salt   becomes useless,   with   what

ἀρτυθήσεται;   35   οὔτε   εἰς   γῆν   οὔτε   εἰς
will it be seasoned?   neither   for   soil   nor   for

κοπρίαν   εὔθετόν   ἐστιν·   ἔξω   βάλλουσιν
manure   suitable   is it;   outside   they cast

αὐτό.   ὁ   ἔχων   ὦτα   ἀκούειν   ἀκουέτω.
it.   The [one] having   ears   to hear   let him hear.

CHAPTER 15

NOW the tax collectors and sinners were all drawing near to hear him. ²And the Pharisees and the scribes murmured, saying, "This man receives sinners and eats with them."

3 So he told them this parable: ⁴"What man of you, having a hundred sheep, if he has lost one of them, does not leave the ninety-nine in the wilderness, and go after the one which is lost, until he finds it? ⁵And

15   Ἦσαν   δὲ   αὐτῷ   ἐγγίζοντες   πάντες
Now there were   to him   drawing near   all

οἱ   τελῶναι   καὶ   οἱ   ἁμαρτωλοὶ   ἀκούειν
the tax-collectors   and   the   sinners   to hear

αὐτοῦ.   2   καὶ   διεγόγγυζον   οἵ   τε   Φαρισαῖοι
him.   And greatly murmured   both the   Pharisees

καὶ   οἱ   γραμματεῖς   λέγοντες   ὅτι   οὗτος
and   the   scribes   saying[,]   –   This man

ἁμαρτωλοὺς   προσδέχεται   καὶ   συνεσθίει   αὐ-
sinners   receives   and   eats with   them.

τοῖς.   3   εἶπεν   δὲ   πρὸς   αὐτοὺς   τὴν   παρα-
And he spoke   to   them   –   para-

βολὴν   ταύτην   λέγων·   4   τίς   ἄνθρωπος   ἐξ
ble   this   saying :   What   man   of

ὑμῶν   ἔχων   ἑκατὸν   πρόβατα   καὶ   ἀπολέσας
you   having a hundred   sheep   and   losing

ἐξ   αὐτῶν   ἓν   οὐ   καταλείπει   τὰ   ἐνενήκοντα
of   them   one   does not leave   the   ninety-

ἐννέα   ἐν   τῇ   ἐρήμῳ   καὶ   πορεύεται   ἐπὶ
nine   in the   desert   and   goes   after

τὸ   ἀπολωλὸς   ἕως   εὕρῃ   αὐτό;   5   καὶ
the [one] having been lost   until   he finds   it?   and

when he has found it, he lays it on his shoulders, rejoicing. ⁶And when he comes home, he calls together his friends and his neighbors, saying to them, 'Rejoice with me, for I have found my sheep which was lost.' ⁷Just so, I tell you, there will be more joy in heaven over one sinner who repents than over ninety-nine righteous persons who need no repentance.

8 "Or what woman, having ten silver coins, if she loses one coin, does not light a lamp and sweep the house and seek diligently until she finds it? ⁹And when she has found it, she calls together her friends and neighbors, saying, 'Rejoice with me, for I have found the coin which I had lost.' ¹⁰Just so, I tell you, there is joy before the angels of God over one sinner who repents.

11 And he said, "There was a man who had two sons; ¹²and the younger of them said to his father, 'Father, give me the share of property that falls to me.' And he divided his living between them. ¹³Not many days later, the younger son gathered all he had and took his journey into a far country, and there

εὑρὼν ἐπιτίθησιν ἐπὶ τοὺς ὤμους αὐτοῦ
finding places on [it] on the shoulders of him
χαίρων, 6 καὶ ἐλθὼν εἰς τὸν οἶκον
rejoicing, and coming into the house
συγκαλεῖ τοὺς φίλους καὶ τοὺς γείτονας,
he calls together the friends and the neighbours,
λέγων αὐτοῖς· συγχάρητέ μοι, ὅτι εὗρον
saying to them : Rejoice with me, because I found
τὸ πρόβατόν μου τὸ ἀπολωλός. 7 λέγω
the sheep of me – having been lost. I tell
ὑμῖν ὅτι οὕτως χαρὰ ἐν τῷ οὐρανῷ
you that thus joy in – heaven
ἔσται ἐπὶ ἑνὶ ἁμαρτωλῷ μετανοοῦντι ἢ
will be over one sinner repenting than
ἐπὶ ἐνενήκοντα ἐννέα δικαίοις οἵτινες οὐ
over ninety-nine just men who no
χρείαν ἔχουσιν μετανοίας. 8 Ἢ τίς γυνὴ
need have of repentance. Or what woman
δραχμὰς ἔχουσα δέκα, ἐὰν ἀπολέσῃ
¹drachmae ¹having ²ten, if she loses
δραχμὴν μίαν, οὐχὶ ἅπτει λύχνον καὶ
drachma one, does not light a lamp and
σαροῖ τὴν οἰκίαν καὶ ζητεῖ ἐπιμελῶς
sweep the house and seek carefully
ἕως οὗ εὕρῃ; 9 καὶ εὑροῦσα συγκαλεῖ
until she finds? and finding she calls together
τὰς φίλας καὶ γείτονας λέγουσα· συγχάρητέ
the friends and neighbours saying : Rejoice with
μοι, ὅτι εὗρον τὴν δραχμὴν ἣν ἀπώλεσα.
me, because I found the drachma which I lost.
10 οὕτως, λέγω ὑμῖν, γίνεται χαρὰ ἐνώπιον
So, I tell you, there is joy before
τῶν ἀγγέλων τοῦ θεοῦ ἐπὶ ἑνὶ ἁμαρτωλῷ
the angels – of God over one sinner
μετανοοῦντι. 11 Εἶπεν δέ· ἄνθρωπός τις
repenting. And he said: A certain man
εἶχεν δύο υἱούς. 12 καὶ εἶπεν ὁ νεώτερος
had two sons. And said the younger
αὐτῶν τῷ πατρί· πάτερ, δός μοι τὸ
of them to the father: Father, give me the
ἐπιβάλλον μέρος τῆς οὐσίας. ὁ δὲ διεῖλες
falling upon share of the property. And he divided
=share of the property falling to [me].
αὐτοῖς τὸν βίον. 13 καὶ μετ' οὐ πολλὰς
to them the living. And after not many
ἡμέρας συναγαγὼν πάντα ὁ νεώτερος υἱὸς
days having gathered all things the younger son
ἀπεδήμησεν εἰς χώραν μακράν, καὶ ἐκεῖ
departed to country a far, and there

he squandered his property in loose living. ¹⁴And when he had spent everything, a great famine arose in that country, and he began to be in want. ¹⁵So he went and joined himself to one of the citizens of that country, who sent him into his fields to feed swine. ¹⁶And he would gladly have fed on[m] the pods that the swine ate; and no one gave him anything. ¹⁷But when he came to himself he said, 'How many of my father's hired servants have bread enough and to spare, but I perish here with hunger! ¹⁸I will arise and go to my father, and I will say to him, "Father, I have sinned against heaven and before you; ¹⁹I am no longer worthy to be called your son; treat me as one of your hired servants."' ²⁰And he arose and came to his father. But while he was yet at a distance, his father saw him and had compassion, and ran and embraced him and kissed him. ²¹And the son said to him, 'Father, I have sinned against heaven

---

διεσκόρπισεν τὴν οὐσίαν αὐτοῦ ζῶν ἀσώτως.
scattered   the   property   of him   living   prodigally.

14 δαπανήσαντος δὲ αὐτοῦ πάντα ἐγένετο
But having spent   him[a]   all things   there came
= when he had spent

λιμὸς ἰσχυρὰ κατὰ τὴν χώραν ἐκείνην,
famine   a severe   throughout   country   that,

καὶ αὐτὸς ἤρξατο ὑστερεῖσθαι. 15 καὶ
and   he   began   to be in want.   And

πορευθεὶς ἐκολλήθη ἑνὶ τῶν πολιτῶν τῆς
going   he was joined   to one of the   citizens   -

χώρας ἐκείνης, καὶ ἔπεμψεν αὐτὸν εἰς
country   of that,   and   he sent   him   into

τοὺς ἀγροὺς αὐτοῦ βόσκειν χοίρους· 16 καὶ
the   fields   of him   to feed   pigs;   and

ἐπεθύμει γεμίσαι τὴν κοιλίαν αὐτοῦ ἐκ
he longed   to fill   the   stomach   of him   out of (with)

τῶν κερατίων ὧν ἤσθιον οἱ χοῖροι, καὶ
the   husks   which ¹ate ¹the ²pigs,   and

οὐδεὶς ἐδίδου αὐτῷ. 17 εἰς ἑαυτὸν δὲ
no one   gave   to him.   ³to ⁴himself ¹But

ἐλθὼν ἔφη· πόσοι μίσθιοι τοῦ πατρός μου
²coming he said: How many hired servants of the father of me

περισσεύονται ἄρτων, ἐγὼ δὲ λιμῷ ὧδε
abound   of loaves,   but I   with famine here
= have abundance of bread,

ἀπόλλυμαι. 18 ἀναστὰς πορεύσομαι πρὸς
am perishing.   Rising up   I will go   to

τὸν πατέρα μου καὶ ἐρῶ αὐτῷ· πάτερ,
the   father   of me   and I will say to him :   Father,

ἥμαρτον εἰς τὸν οὐρανὸν καὶ ἐνώπιόν σου,
I sinned against   -   heaven   and   before   thee,

19 οὐκέτι εἰμὶ ἄξιος κληθῆναι υἱός σου·
no longer   am I   worthy   to be called   a son   of thee;

ποίησόν με ὡς ἕνα τῶν μισθίων σου.
make   me   as   one   of the hired servants of thee.

20 καὶ ἀναστὰς ἦλθεν πρὸς τὸν πατέρα
And   rising up   he came   to   the   father

ἑαυτοῦ. ἔτι δὲ αὐτοῦ μακρὰν ἀπέχοντος
of him self.   But yet   him   afar   being away[a]
= while he was yet far away

εἶδεν αὐτὸν ὁ πατὴρ αὐτοῦ καὶ ἐσπλαγχνίσθη,
saw   him   the father   of him   and was moved with pity,

καὶ δραμὼν ἐπέπεσεν ἐπὶ τὸν τράχηλον
and   running   fell on   on   the   neck

αὐτοῦ καὶ κατεφίλησεν αὐτόν. 21 εἶπεν δὲ
of him   and   fervently kissed   him.   And said

ὁ υἱὸς αὐτῷ· πάτερ, ἥμαρτον εἰς τὸν
the   son   to him :   Father,   I sinned   against   -

---

[m] Other ancient authorities read *filled his belly with*

and before you; I am no longer worthy to be called your son.'[n] [22]But the father said to his servants, 'Bring quickly the best robe, and put it on him; and put a ring on his hand, and shoes on his feet; [23]and bring the fatted calf and kill it, and let us eat and make merry; [24]for this my son was dead, and is alive again; he was lost, and is found.' And they began to make merry.

[25] "Now his elder son was in the field; and as he came and drew near to the house, he heard music and dancing. [26]And he called one of the servants and asked what this meant. [27]And he said to him, 'Your brother has come, and your father has killed the fatted calf, because he has received him safe and sound.' [28]But he was angry and refused to go in. His father came out and entreated him, [29]but he answered his father, 'Lo, these many years I have served you, and I never disobeyed your command; yet you never gave me a kid, that I

[n] Other ancient authorities add treat me as one of your hired servants

οὐρανὸν καὶ ἐνώπιόν σου, οὐκέτι εἰμὶ
heaven and before thee, no longer am I
ἄξιος κληθῆναι υἱός σου. [22] εἶπεν δὲ
worthy to be called a son of thee.   But said
ὁ πατὴρ πρὸς τοὺς δούλους αὐτοῦ· ταχὺ
the father to the slaves of him : Quickly
ἐξενέγκατε στολὴν τὴν πρώτην καὶ ἐνδύσατε
bring ye out a robe the first and clothe
αὐτόν, καὶ δότε δακτύλιον εἰς τὴν χεῖρα
him, and give(put) a ring to the hand
αὐτοῦ καὶ ὑποδήματα εἰς τοὺς πόδας,
of him and sandals to the feet,
[23] καὶ φέρετε τὸν μόσχον τὸν σιτευτόν,
and bring the calf — fattened,
θύσατε, καὶ φαγόντες εὐφρανθῶμεν, [24] ὅτι
kill, and eating let us be merry, because
οὗτος ὁ υἱός μου νεκρὸς ἦν καὶ ἀνέζησεν,
this — son of me dead was and lived again,
ἦν ἀπολωλὼς καὶ εὑρέθη. καὶ ἤρξαντο
was having been lost and was found. And they began
εὐφραίνεσθαι. [25] ἦν δὲ ὁ υἱὸς αὐτοῦ
to be merry. But was the son of him
ὁ πρεσβύτερος ἐν ἀγρῷ· καὶ ὡς ἐρχόμενος
— older in a field; and as coming
ἤγγισεν τῇ οἰκίᾳ, ἤκουσεν συμφωνίας καὶ
he drew near to the house, he heard music and
χορῶν, [26] καὶ προσκαλεσάμενος ἕνα τῶν
dances, and calling to [him] one of the
παίδων ἐπυνθάνετο τί ἂν εἴη ταῦτα.
lads he inquired what might be these things.
[27] ὁ δὲ εἶπεν αὐτῷ ὅτι ὁ ἀδελφός σου
And he said to him[,] — The brother of thee
ἥκει, καὶ ἔθυσεν ὁ πατήρ σου τὸν μόσχον τὸν
has come, and [4]killed [1]the [3]father [3]of thee [5]the [7]calf —
σιτευτόν, ὅτι ὑγιαίνοντα αὐτὸν ἀπέλαβεν.
[6]fattened, because [8]being in health [3]him [1]he [2]received [4]back.
[28] ὠργίσθη δὲ καὶ οὐκ ἤθελεν εἰσελθεῖν·
But he was angry and did not wish to enter;
ὁ δὲ πατὴρ αὐτοῦ ἐξελθὼν παρεκάλει
so the father of him coming out besought
αὐτόν. [29] ὁ δὲ ἀποκριθεὶς εἶπεν τῷ
him. But he answering said to the
πατρί· ἰδοὺ τοσαῦτα ἔτη δουλεύω σοι καὶ
father : Behold[,] so many years I serve thee and
οὐδέποτε ἐντολήν σου παρῆλθον, καὶ ἐμοὶ
never a command of thee I transgressed, and to me
οὐδέποτε ἔδωκας ἔριφον ἵνα μετὰ τῶν
never thou gavest a goat that with the

might make merry with my friends. ³⁰But when this son of yours came, who has devoured your living with harlots, you killed for him the fatted calf!' ³¹And he said to him, 'Son, you are always with me, and all that is mine is yours. ³²It was fitting to make merry and be glad, for this your brother was dead, and is alive; and was lost, and is found.' ''

φίλων   μου   εὐφρανθῶ·   30 ὅτε   δὲ   ὁ   υἱός
friends of me I might be merry;   but when   –   ²son
σου   οὗτος   ὁ   καταφαγών   σου   τὸν   βίον
²of thee ¹this   –   having devoured of thee   the   living
μετὰ   πορνῶν   ἦλθεν,   ἔθυσας   αὐτῷ   τὸν
with   harlots   came,   thou killedst for him   the
σιτευτὸν   μόσχον.   31 ὁ   δὲ   εἶπεν   αὐτῷ·
fattened   calf.   And he   said   to him :
τέκνον,   σὺ   πάντοτε   μετ'   ἐμοῦ   εἶ,   καὶ
Child,   thou   always   with   me   art,   and
πάντα   τὰ   ἐμὰ   σά   ἐστιν·   32 εὐφρανθῆναι
¹all ³things   –   ²my   ⁴thine   ⁵is(are);   ⁵to be merry
δὲ   καὶ   χαρῆναι   ἔδει,   ὅτι   ὁ   ἀδελφός
¹And ⁴and   ⁵to rejoice   ²it be-   because   –   ²brother
                                      hoved [us],
σου   οὗτος   νεκρὸς   ἦν   καὶ   ἔζησεν,   καὶ   ἀπο-
²of thee ¹this   ⁵dead   ⁴was   and came to life,   and   having
λωλὼς   καὶ   εὑρέθη.
been lost   also   was found.

CHAPTER 16

HE also said to the disciples, ''There was a rich man who had a steward, and charges were brought to him that this man was wasting his goods. ²And he called him and said to him, 'What is this that I hear about you? Turn in the account of your stewardship, for you can no longer be steward.' ³And the steward said to himself, 'What shall I do, since my master is taking the stewardship away from me? I am not strong enough to dig, and I am ashamed to beg. ⁴I have decided what to do, so that people may receive me into their houses when I am put out of the stewardship.' ⁵So, summoning his master's debtors one by one, he

16 Ἔλεγεν   δὲ   καὶ   πρὸς   τοὺς   μαθητάς·
And he said   also   to   the   disciples :
ἄνθρωπός   τις   ἦν   πλούσιος   ὃς   εἶχεν
¹A certain ⁴man   ¹there was   ³rich   who   had
οἰκονόμον,   καὶ   οὗτος   διεβλήθη   αὐτῷ   ὡς
a steward,   and   this   was complained of   to him   as
διασκορπίζων   τὰ   ὑπάρχοντα   αὐτοῦ.   2 καὶ
wasting   the   possessions   of him.   And
φωνήσας   αὐτὸν   εἶπεν   αὐτῷ·   τί   τοῦτο
calling   him   he said   to him : What [is]   this
ἀκούω   περὶ   σοῦ;   ἀπόδος   τὸν   λόγον   τῆς
I hear   about   thee?   render   the   account   of the
οἰκονομίας   σου·   οὐ   γὰρ   δύνῃ   ἔτι   οἰκονομεῖν.
stewardship of thee;   for thou canst not longer   to be steward.
3 εἶπεν   δὲ   ἐν   ἑαυτῷ   ὁ   οἰκονόμος·   τί
And said   in   himself   the   steward :   What
ποιήσω,   ὅτι   ὁ   κύριός   μου   ἀφαιρεῖται   τὴν
may I do, because the   lord   of me   takes away   the
οἰκονομίαν   ἀπ'   ἐμοῦ;   σκάπτειν   οὐκ   ἰσχύω,
stewardship   from   me?   to dig   I am not able,
ἐπαιτεῖν   αἰσχύνομαι.   4 ἔγνων   τί   ποιήσω,
to beg   I am ashamed.   I knew(know) what   I may do,
ἵνα   ὅταν   μετασταθῶ   ἐκ   τῆς   οἰκονομίας
that   when   I am removed   out of   the   stewardship
δέξωνταί   με   εἰς   τοὺς   οἴκους   ἑαυτῶν.
they may receive me   into   the   houses   of themselves.
5 καὶ   προσκαλεσάμενος   ἕνα   ἕκαστον   τῶν
And   calling to [him]   ²one   ¹each   of the

said to the first, 'How much do you owe my master?' ⁶He said, 'A hundred measures of oil.' And he said to him, 'Take your bill, and sit down quickly and write fifty.' ⁷Then he said to another, 'And how much do you owe?' He said, 'A hundred measures of wheat.' He said to him, 'Take your bill, and write eighty.' ⁸The master commended the dishonest steward for his prudence; for the sons of this world are wiser in their own generation than the sons of light. ⁹And I tell you, make friends for yourselves by means of unrighteous mammon, so that when it fails they may receive you into the eternal habitations.

10 "He who is faithful in a very little is faithful also in much; and he who is dishonest in a very little is dishonest also in much. ¹¹If then you have not been faithful in the unrighteous mammon, who will entrust to you the true riches? ¹²And if you have not been faithful in that which is another's, who will give you that which is your own? ¹³No servant can serve two

χρεοφειλετῶν τοῦ κυρίου ἑαυτοῦ ἔλεγεν τῷ
debtors   of the   lord   of him*self* he said to the

πρώτῳ· πόσον ὀφείλεις τῷ κυρίῳ μου;
first :   How much owest thou to the lord   of me?

6 ὁ δὲ εἶπεν· ἑκατὸν βάτους ἐλαίου. ὁ δὲ
And he said : A hundred baths   of oil.   And he

εἶπεν αὐτῷ· δέξαι σου τὰ γράμματα καὶ
told   him :   Take of thee the   letters(bill)   and

καθίσας ταχέως γράψον πεντήκοντα. 7 ἔπειτα
sitting quickly   write   fifty.   Then

ἑτέρῳ εἶπεν· σὺ δὲ πόσον ὀφείλεις; ὁ δὲ
to another he said : ¹thou ²And ²how much ³owest? And he

εἶπεν· ἑκατὸν κόρους σίτου. λέγει αὐτῷ·
said : A hundred cors of wheat. He tells him :

δέξαι σου τὰ γράμματα καὶ γράψον
Take of thee the   bill   and   write

ὀγδοήκοντα. 8 καὶ ἐπήνεσεν ὁ κύριος τὸν
eighty.   And ²praised ¹the ³lord the

οἰκονόμον τῆς ἀδικίας ὅτι φρονίμως
steward   – of unrighteousness because prudently

ἐποίησεν· ὅτι οἱ υἱοὶ τοῦ αἰῶνος τούτου
he acted; because the sons   –   age   of this

φρονιμώτεροι ὑπὲρ τοὺς υἱοὺς τοῦ φωτὸς
more prudent than   the   sons   of the   light

εἰς τὴν γενεὰν τὴν ἑαυτῶν εἰσιν. 9 Καὶ
in the generation – of them*selves* are.   And

ἐγὼ ὑμῖν λέγω, ἑαυτοῖς ποιήσατε φίλους
I   ²you ¹tell, To yourselves make   friends

ἐκ τοῦ μαμωνᾶ τῆς ἀδικίας, ἵνα ὅταν
by   the   mammon   – of unrighteousness, that when

ἐκλίπῃ δέξωνται ὑμᾶς εἰς τὰς αἰωνίους
it fails they may receive you   into the   eternal

σκηνάς. 10 ὁ πιστὸς ἐν ἐλαχίστῳ καὶ ἐν
tabernacles. The man faithful in   least   also in

πολλῷ πιστός ἐστιν, καὶ ὁ ἐν ἐλαχίστῳ
much   faithful   is,   and the man in   least

ἄδικος καὶ ἐν πολλῷ ἄδικός ἐστιν. 11 εἰ
unrighteous also in   much   unrighteous is.   If

οὖν ἐν τῷ ἀδίκῳ μαμωνᾷ πιστοὶ οὐκ
therefore in the unrighteous mammon faithful   not

ἐγένεσθε, τὸ ἀληθινὸν τίς ὑμῖν πιστεύσει;
ye were,   the   true   who to you will entrust ?

12 καὶ εἰ ἐν τῷ ἀλλοτρίῳ πιστοὶ οὐκ
And if in the thing belonging to another faithful not

ἐγένεσθε, τὸ ἡμέτερον τίς δώσει ὑμῖν;
ye were,   the   ours   who will give you?
          =that which is ours

13 Οὐδεὶς οἰκέτης δύναται δυσὶ κυρίοις
No   household slave   can   two   lords

masters; for either he will hate the one and love the other, or he will be devoted to the one and despise the other. You cannot serve God and mammon."

14 The Pharisees, who were lovers of money, heard all this, and they scoffed at him. 15 But he said to them, "You are those who justify yourselves before men, but God knows your hearts; for what is exalted among men is an abomination in the sight of God.

16 "The law and the prophets were until John; since then the good news of the kingdom of God is preached, and every one enters it violently. 17 But it is easier for heaven and earth to pass away, than for one dot of the law to become void.

18 "Every one who divorces his wife and marries another commits adultery, and he who marries a woman divorced from her husband commits adultery.

19 "There was a rich man, who was clothed in purple and fine linen and who feasted sumptuously every day. 20 And at his gate lay a poor man named Laz'arus, full of

δουλεύειν· ἢ γὰρ τὸν ἕνα μισήσει καὶ τὸν
to serve; for either the one he will hate and the

ἕτερον ἀγαπήσει, ἢ ἑνὸς ἀνθέξεται καὶ
other he will love, or one he will hold fast to and

τοῦ ἑτέρου καταφρονήσει. οὐ δύνασθε
the other he will despise. Ye cannot

θεῷ δουλεύειν καὶ μαμωνᾷ. 14 Ἤκουον
God to serve and mammon. [6]heard

δὲ ταῦτα πάντα οἱ Φαρισαῖοι φιλάργυροι
[1]Now [8]these things [7]all [2]the [3]Pharisees [5]moneylovers

ὑπάρχοντες, καὶ ἐξεμυκτήριζον αὐτόν. 15 καὶ
[4]being, and they scoffed at him. And

εἶπεν αὐτοῖς· ὑμεῖς ἐστε οἱ δικαιοῦντες
he said to them : Ye are the [ones] justifying

ἑαυτοὺς ἐνώπιον τῶν ἀνθρώπων, ὁ δὲ
yourselves before - men, - but

θεὸς γινώσκει τὰς καρδίας ὑμῶν· ὅτι τὸ
God knows the hearts of you; because the thing

ἐν ἀνθρώποις ὑψηλὸν βδέλυγμα ἐνώπιον
[2]among [2]men [1]lofty [is] an abomination before

τοῦ θεοῦ. 16 Ὁ νόμος καὶ οἱ προφῆται
- God. The law and the prophets

μέχρι Ἰωάννου· ἀπὸ τότε ἡ βασιλεία τοῦ
[were] until John; from then the kingdom -

θεοῦ εὐαγγελίζεται καὶ πᾶς εἰς αὐτὴν
of God is being preached and everyone into it

βιάζεται. 17 εὐκοπώτερον δέ ἐστιν τὸν οὐρανὸν
is pressing. But easier it is the heaven

καὶ τὴν γῆν παρελθεῖν ἢ τοῦ νόμου μίαν
and the earth to pass away than of the law one

κεραίαν πεσεῖν. 18 Πᾶς ὁ ἀπολύων τὴν
little horn[*] to fall. Everyone dismissing the

γυναῖκα αὐτοῦ καὶ γαμῶν ἑτέραν μοιχεύει,
wife of him and marrying another commits adultery,

καὶ ὁ ἀπολελυμένην ἀπὸ
and [1]the [one] [3]a woman having been dismissed [4]from

ἀνδρὸς γαμῶν μοιχεύει. 19 Ἄνθρωπος δέ
[5]a husband [2]marrying [6]commits adultery. Now a certain

τις ἦν πλούσιος, καὶ ἐνεδιδύσκετο πορφύραν
man was rich, and used to put on a purple robe

καὶ βύσσον εὐφραινόμενος καθ᾽ ἡμέραν
and fine linen being merry every day†

λαμπρῶς. 20 πτωχὸς δέ τις ὀνόματι
splendidly. And a certain poor man by name

Λάζαρος ἐβέβλητο πρὸς τὸν πυλῶνα αὐτοῦ
Lazarus had been placed at the gate of him

* The little projection which distinguishes some Hebrew letters from those otherwise similar.

sores, ²¹who desired to be fed with what fell from the rich man's table; moreover the dogs came and licked his sores. ²²The poor man died and was carried by the angels to Abraham's bosom. The rich man also died and was buried; ²³and in Hades, being in torment, he lifted up his eyes, and saw Abraham far off and Laz′arus in his bosom. ²⁴And he called out, 'Father Abraham, have mercy upon me, and send Laz′arus to dip the end of his finger in water and cool my tongue; for I am in anguish in this flame.' ²⁵But Abraham said, 'Son, remember that you in your lifetime received your good things, and Laz′arus in like manner evil things; but now he is comforted here, and you are in anguish. ²⁶And besides all this, between us and you a great chasm has been fixed, in order that those who would pass from here to you may not be able, and none may cross from there to us.' ²⁷And he said, 'Then I beg you,

εἱλκωμένος **21** καὶ ἐπιθυμῶν χορτασθῆναι
being covered with sores and desiring to be satisfied

ἀπὸ τῶν πιπτόντων ἀπὸ τῆς τραπέζης
from the things falling from the table

τοῦ πλουσίου· ἀλλὰ καὶ οἱ κύνες ἐρχόμενοι
of the rich man; but even the dogs coming

ἐπέλειχον τὰ ἕλκη αὐτοῦ. **22** ἐγένετο δὲ
licked the sores of him. And it came to pass

ἀποθανεῖν τὸν πτωχὸν καὶ ἀπενεχθῆναι
to die the poor man and to be carried away
=that the poor man died and he was carried away

αὐτὸν ὑπὸ τῶν ἀγγέλων εἰς τὸν κόλπον
him by the angels into the bosom

'Αβραάμ· ἀπέθανεν δὲ καὶ ὁ πλούσιος καὶ
of Abraham; and died also the rich man and

ἐτάφη. **23** καὶ ἐν τῷ ᾅδῃ ἐπάρας τοὺς
was buried. And in – hades lifting up the

ὀφθαλμοὺς αὐτοῦ, ὑπάρχων ἐν βασάνοις,
eyes of him, being in torments,

ὁρᾷ 'Αβραὰμ ἀπὸ μακρόθεν καὶ Λάζαρον
he sees Abraham from afar and Lazarus

ἐν τοῖς κόλποις αὐτοῦ. **24** καὶ αὐτὸς
in the bosoms of him. And he

φωνήσας εἶπεν· πάτερ 'Αβραάμ, ἐλέησόν
calling said: Father Abraham, pity

με καὶ πέμψον Λάζαρον ἵνα βάψῃ τὸ
me and send Lazarus that he may dip the

ἄκρον τοῦ δακτύλου αὐτοῦ ὕδατος καὶ
tip of the finger of him of(in) water and

καταψύξῃ τὴν γλῶσσάν μου, ὅτι ὀδυνῶμαι
may cool the tongue of me, because I am suffering

ἐν τῇ φλογὶ ταύτῃ. **25** εἶπεν δὲ 'Αβραάμ·
in – flame this. But said Abraham:

τέκνον, μνήσθητι ὅτι ἀπέλαβες τὰ ἀγαθά
Child, remember that thou didst receive the good things

σου ἐν τῇ ζωῇ σου, καὶ Λάζαρος ὁμοίως
of thee in the life of thee, and Lazarus likewise

τὰ κακά· νῦν δὲ ὧδε παρακαλεῖται, σὺ δὲ
the bad; but now here he is comforted, but thou

ὀδυνᾶσαι. **26** καὶ ἐν πᾶσι τούτοις μεταξὺ
art suffering. And among all these things between

ἡμῶν καὶ ὑμῶν χάσμα μέγα ἐστήρικται,
us and you chasm a great has been firmly fixed,

ὅπως οἱ θέλοντες διαβῆναι ἔνθεν πρὸς
so that the [ones] wishing to pass hence to

ὑμᾶς μὴ δύνωνται, μηδὲ ἐκεῖθεν πρὸς
you cannot, neither thence to

ἡμᾶς διαπερῶσιν. **27** εἶπεν δέ· ἐρωτῶ
us may they cross over. And he said: I ask

father, to send him to my father's house, ²⁸ for I have five brothers, so that he may warn them, lest they also come into this place of torment.' ²⁹ But Abraham said, 'They have Moses and the prophets; let them hear them.' ³⁰ And he said, 'No, father Abraham; but if some one goes to them from the dead, they will repent.' ³¹ He said to them, 'If they do not hear Moses and the prophets, neither will they be convinced if some one should rise from the dead.' "

σε   οὖν,   πάτερ,   ἵνα   πέμψῃς   αὐτὸν   εἰς
thee therefore, father,   that thou mayest send him   to

τὸν   οἶκον   τοῦ   πατρός   μου·   28 ἔχω   γὰρ
the   house of the   father   of me;   for I have

πέντε   ἀδελφούς·   ὅπως   διαμαρτύρηται   αὐτοῖς,
five   brothers;   so that   he may witness   to them,

ἵνα   μὴ   καὶ   αὐτοὶ   ἔλθωσιν   εἰς   τὸν   τόπον
lest   also   they   come   to   –   place

τοῦτον   τῆς   βασάνου.   29 λέγει   δὲ   'Αβραάμ·
this   –   of torment.   But says   Abraham :

ἔχουσι   Μωϋσέα   καὶ   τοὺς   προφήτας·
They have   Moses   and   the   prophets;

ἀκουσάτωσαν   αὐτῶν.   30 ὁ   δὲ   εἶπεν·
let them hear   them.   But he   said :

οὐχί,   πάτερ   'Αβραάμ,   ἀλλ'   ἐάν   τις   ἀπὸ
No,   father   Abraham,   but   if   someone from

νεκρῶν   πορευθῇ   πρὸς   αὐτούς,   μετανοήσουσιν.
[the] dead   should go   to   them,   they will repent.

31 εἶπεν   δὲ   αὐτῷ·   εἰ   Μωϋσέως   καὶ   τῶν
But he said   to him :   If   Moses   and   the

προφητῶν   οὐκ   ἀκούουσιν,   οὐδὲ   ἐάν   τις
prophets   they do not hear,   neither   if   someone

ἐκ   νεκρῶν   ἀναστῇ   πεισθήσονται.
out of [the] dead   should rise again   will they be persuaded.

CHAPTER 17

AND he said to his disciples, "Temptations to sin are sure to come; but woe to him by whom they come! ² It would be better for him if a millstone were hung round his neck and he were cast into the sea, than that he should cause one of these little ones to sin. ³ Take heed to yourselves; if your brother sins, rebuke him, and if he repents, forgive him; ⁴ and if he sins against you seven times in the day, and turns to you seven times, and

17 Εἶπεν   δὲ   πρὸς   τοὺς   μαθητὰς   αὐτοῦ·
And he said   to   the   disciples   of him :

ἀνένδεκτόν   ἐστιν   τοῦ   τὰ   σκάνδαλα   μὴ   ἐλθεῖν,
Impossible   it is   –   the   offences   not to come,^d

οὐαὶ   δὲ   δι'   οὗ   ἔρχεται·   2 λυσιτελεῖ
but woe [to him] through whom they come;   it profits

αὐτῷ   εἰ   λίθος   μυλικὸς   περίκειται   περὶ
him   if   a millstone   is put round   round

τὸν   τράχηλον   αὐτοῦ   καὶ   ἔρριπται   εἰς   τὴν
the   neck   of him and he has been thrown into the

θάλασσαν,   ἢ   ἵνα   σκανδαλίσῃ   τῶν   μικρῶν
sea,   than that he should offend   –   ³little ones

τούτων   ἕνα.   3 προσέχετε   ἑαυτοῖς.   ἐὰν
²of these ¹one.   Take heed   to yourselves.   If

ἁμάρτῃ   ὁ   ἀδελφός   σου,   ἐπιτίμησον   αὐτῷ,
sins   the   brother   of thee,   rebuke   him,

καὶ   ἐὰν   μετανοήσῃ,   ἄφες   αὐτῷ.   4 καὶ
and   if   he repents,   forgive   him.   And

ἐὰν   ἑπτάκις   τῆς   ἡμέρας   ἁμαρτήσῃ   εἰς   σὲ
if   seven times of(in) the   day   he sins   against thee

καὶ   ἑπτάκις   ἐπιστρέψῃ   πρὸς   σὲ   λέγων·
and   seven times   turns   to   thee   saying :

says, 'I repent,' you must forgive him."

5 The apostles said to the Lord, "Increase our faith!" [6]And the Lord said, "If you had faith as a grain of mustard seed, you could say to this sycamine tree, 'Be rooted up, and be planted in the sea,' and it would obey you.

7 "Will any one of you, who has a servant plowing or keeping sheep, say to him when he has come in from the field, 'Come at once and sit down at table'? [8]Will he not rather say to him, 'Prepare supper for me, and gird yourself and serve me, till I eat and drink; and afterward you shall eat and drink'? [9]Does he thank the servant because he did what was commanded? [10]So you also, when you have done all that is commanded you, say, 'We are unworthy servants; we have only done what was our duty.' "

11 On the way to Jerusalem he was passing along between Samar′ia and Galilee. [12]And as he entered a village, he was met by ten lepers, who stood at a distance [13]and

μετανοῶ, ἀφήσεις αὐτῷ. 5 Καὶ εἶπαν οἱ
I repent, thou shalt forgive him.   And   said   the

ἀπόστολοι τῷ κυρίῳ· πρόσθες ἡμῖν πίστιν.
apostles   to the Lord :   Add   to us   faith.

6 εἶπεν δὲ ὁ κύριος· εἰ ἔχετε πίστιν ὡς
And said   the   Lord :   If ye have   faith   as

κόκκον σινάπεως, ἐλέγετε ἂν τῇ συκαμίνῳ
a grain   of mustard, ye would have said – sycamine-tree

ταύτῃ· ἐκριζώθητι καὶ φυτεύθητι ἐν τῇ
to this :   Be thou uprooted   and be thou planted in   the

θαλάσσῃ· καὶ ὑπήκουσεν ἂν ὑμῖν. 7 Τίς
sea;   and   it would have obeyed   you.   who

δὲ ἐξ ὑμῶν δοῦλον ἔχων ἀροτριῶντα ἢ
But of   you   [2]a slave [1]having   ploughing   or

ποιμαίνοντα, ὃς εἰσελθόντι ἐκ τοῦ ἀγροῦ
herding,   who on [his] coming in[e] out of the   farm

ἐρεῖ αὐτῷ· εὐθέως παρελθὼν ἀνάπεσε,
will say to him : Immediately   coming up   recline,

8 ἀλλ' οὐχὶ ἐρεῖ αὐτῷ· ἑτοίμασον τί
but   will not say   to him :   Prepare something

δειπνήσω, καὶ περιζωσάμενος διακόνει μοι
I may dine,   and   having girded thyself   serve   me

ἕως φάγω καὶ πίω, καὶ μετὰ ταῦτα
until   I eat   and   drink,   and   after these things

φάγεσαι καὶ πίεσαι σύ; 9 μὴ ἔχει χάριν
eat   and   drink   thou? Not he has thanks

τῷ δούλῳ ὅτι ἐποίησεν τὰ διαταχθέντα;
to the slave   because   he did   the things commanded?

10 οὕτως καὶ ὑμεῖς, ὅταν ποιήσητε πάντα
So   also ye,   when   ye do   all

τὰ διαταχθέντα ὑμῖν, λέγετε ὅτι – δοῦλοι
the things commanded   you,   say[,]   –   Slaves

ἀχρεῖοί ἐσμεν, ὃ ὠφείλομεν ποιῆσαι
unprofitable we are,   what   we ought   to do

πεποιήκαμεν.
we have done.

11 Καὶ ἐγένετο ἐν τῷ πορεύεσθαι εἰς
And it came to pass in   the   to go[e]   to
=as [he] went

Ἰερουσαλήμ, καὶ αὐτὸς διήρχετο διὰ μέσον
Jerusalem,   and   he   passed through [the]
through   midst

Σαμαρείας καὶ Γαλιλαίας. 12 καὶ εἰσερχομένου
of Samaria   and   Galilee.   And   entering
=as he entered

αὐτοῦ εἰς τινα κώμην ἀπήντησαν δέκα
him[a]   into a certain   village   met [him]   ten

λεπροὶ ἄνδρες, οἳ ἔστησαν πόρρωθεν, 13 καὶ
leprous   men,   who   stood   afar off,   and

lifted up their voices and said, "Jesus, Master, have mercy on us." ¹⁴When he saw them he said to them, "Go and show yourselves to the priests." And as they went they were cleansed. ¹⁵Then one of them, when he saw that he was healed, turned back, praising God with a loud voice; ¹⁶and he fell on his face at Jesus' feet, giving him thanks. Now he was a Samaritan. ¹⁷Then said Jesus, "Were not ten cleansed? Where are the nine? ¹⁸Was no one found to return and give praise to God except this foreigner?" ¹⁹And he said to him, "Rise and go your way; your faith has made you well."

20 Being asked by the Pharisees when the kingdom of God was coming, he answered them, "The kingdom of God is not coming with signs to be observed; ²¹nor will they say, 'Lo, here it is!' or 'There!' for behold, the kingdom of God is in the midst of you."⁰

22 And he said to the disciples, "The days are coming when you will desire to see one of the days of the Son of man,

αὐτοὶ ἦραν φωνὴν λέγοντες· Ἰησοῦ
they lifted voice saying : Jesus
ἐπιστάτα, ἐλέησον ἡμᾶς. 14 καὶ ἰδὼν εἶπεν
Master, pity us. And seeing he said
αὐτοῖς· πορευθέντες ἐπιδείξατε ἑαυτοὺς τοῖς
to them : Going show yourselves to the
ἱερεῦσιν. καὶ ἐγένετο ἐν τῷ ὑπάγειν
priests. And it came to pass in the to go
= as they went
αὐτοὺς ἐκαθαρίσθησαν. 15 εἷς δὲ ἐξ
them[be] they were cleansed. But one of
αὐτῶν, ἰδὼν ὅτι ἰάθη, ὑπέστρεψεν μετὰ
them, seeing that he was cured, returned with
φωνῆς μεγάλης δοξάζων τὸν θεόν, 16 καὶ
voice a great glorifying - God, and
ἔπεσεν ἐπὶ πρόσωπον παρὰ τοὺς πόδας
fell on [his] face at the feet
αὐτοῦ εὐχαριστῶν αὐτῷ· καὶ αὐτὸς ἦν
of him thanking him; and he was
Σαμαρίτης. 17 ἀποκριθεὶς δὲ ὁ Ἰησοῦς
a Samaritan. And answering - Jesus
εἶπεν· οὐχ οἱ δέκα ἐκαθαρίσθησαν; οἱ [δὲ]
said : Not the ten were cleansed? but the
ἐννέα ποῦ; 18 οὐχ εὑρέθησαν ὑποστρέψαντες
nine where? were there not found returning
δοῦναι δόξαν τῷ θεῷ εἰ μὴ ὁ ἀλλογενὴς
to give glory - to God only - stranger
οὗτος; 19 καὶ εἶπεν αὐτῷ· ἀναστὰς πορεύου·
this ? And he said to him : Rising up go;
ἡ πίστις σου σέσωκέν σε.
the faith of thee has healed thee.

20 Ἐπερωτηθεὶς δὲ ὑπὸ τῶν Φαρισαίων
And being questioned by the Pharisees
πότε ἔρχεται ἡ βασιλεία τοῦ θεοῦ,
when comes the kingdom - of God,
ἀπεκρίθη αὐτοῖς καὶ εἶπεν· οὐκ ἔρχεται
he answered them and said : Comes not
ἡ βασιλεία τοῦ θεοῦ μετὰ παρατηρήσεως,
the kingdom - of God with observation,
21 οὐδὲ ἐροῦσιν· ἰδοὺ ὧδε ἤ· ἐκεῖ· ἰδοὺ
nor will they say : Behold[,] here or: there; ²behold
γὰρ ἡ βασιλεία τοῦ θεοῦ ἐντὸς ὑμῶν
¹for the kingdom - of God within you
ἐστιν. 22 Εἶπεν δὲ πρὸς τοὺς μαθητάς·
is. And he said to the disciples :
ἐλεύσονται ἡμέραι ὅτε ἐπιθυμήσετε μίαν
Will come days when ye will long one
τῶν ἡμερῶν τοῦ υἱοῦ τοῦ ἀνθρώπου ἰδεῖν
of the days of the Son - of man to see

⁰ Or *within you*

and you will not see it.
23And they will say to
you, 'Lo, there!' or 'Lo,
here!' Do not go, do not
follow them. 24For as the
lightning flashes and
lights up the sky from
one side to the other, so
will the Son of man be in
his day.ᵖ 25But first he
must suffer many things
and be rejected by this
generation. 26As it was in
the days of Noah, so will
it be in the days of the
Son of man. 27They ate,
they drank, they married,
they were given in
marriage, until the day
when Noah entered the
ark, and the flood came
and destroyed them all.
28Likewise as it was in
the days of Lot—they
ate, they drank, they
bought, they sold, they
planted, they built, 29but
on the day when Lot
went out from Sodom
fire and brimstone rained
from heaven and de-
stroyed them all—30so
will it be on the day
when the Son of man is
revealed. 31On that day,
let him who is on the
housetop, with his goods
in the house, not come
down to take them away;
and likewise let him who
is in the field not turn

καὶ οὐκ ὄψεσθε. 23 καὶ ἐροῦσιν ὑμῖν·
and will not see.   And they will say to you :
ἰδοὺ ἐκεῖ, ἰδοὺ ὧδε· μὴ ἀπέλθητε μηδὲ
Behold there, behold here; do not go away   nor
διώξητε. 24 ὥσπερ γὰρ ἡ ἀστραπὴ
follow.   For as   the   lightning
ἀστράπτουσα ἐκ τῆς ὑπὸ τὸν οὐρανὸν
flashing   out of the [one part] under –   heaven
εἰς τὴν ὑπ' οὐρανὸν λάμπει, οὕτως ἔσται
to the [other part] under heaven shines, so   will be
ὁ υἱὸς τοῦ ἀνθρώπου ἐν τῇ ἡμέρᾳ αὐτοῦ.
the Son –   of man   in the day   of him.
25 πρῶτον δὲ δεῖ αὐτὸν πολλὰ παθεῖν καὶ
   But first it behoves him many things to suffer and
ἀποδοκιμασθῆναι ἀπὸ τῆς γενεᾶς ταύτης.
to be rejected   from –   generation this.
26 καὶ καθὼς ἐγένετο ἐν ταῖς ἡμέραις
   And as   it was   in the   days
Νῶε, οὕτως ἔσται καὶ ἐν ταῖς ἡμέραις
of Noah, so   it will be also in the   days
τοῦ υἱοῦ τοῦ ἀνθρώπου· 27 ἤσθιον, ἔπινον,
of the Son –   of man;   they were eating, drinking,
ἐγάμουν, ἐγαμίζοντο, ἄχρι ἧς ἡμέρας
marrying, giving in marriage, until which   day
                                        = the day when
εἰσῆλθεν Νῶε εἰς τὴν κιβωτόν, καὶ
entered   Noah into the   ark,   and
ἦλθεν ὁ κατακλυσμὸς καὶ ἀπώλεσεν πάντας.
came the   flood   and destroyed   all.
28 ὁμοίως καθὼς ἐγένετο ἐν ταῖς ἡμέραις
   Likewise as   it was   in the   days
Λώτ· ἤσθιον, ἔπινον, ἠγόραζον, ἐπώλουν,
of Lot; they were eating, drinking, buying,   selling,
ἐφύτευον, ᾠκοδόμουν· 29 ᾗ δὲ ἡμέρᾳ ἐξῆλθεν
planting, building;   but on which day went forth
Λὼτ ἀπὸ Σοδόμων, ἔβρεξεν πῦρ καὶ
Lot from Sodom,   it rained   fire and
θεῖον ἀπ' οὐρανοῦ καὶ ἀπώλεσεν πάντας.
brimstone from heaven and destroyed   all.
30 κατὰ τὰ αὐτὰ ἔσται ᾗ ἡμέρᾳ ὁ υἱὸς
According to the same things it will be in which day the Son
=In the same way   =on the day when
τοῦ ἀνθρώπου ἀποκαλύπτεται. 31 ἐν ἐκείνῃ
 –   of man   is revealed.   In   that
τῇ ἡμέρᾳ ὃς ἔσται ἐπὶ τοῦ δώματος καὶ
 –   day who will be on   the   roof   and
τὰ σκεύη αὐτοῦ ἐν τῇ οἰκίᾳ, μὴ καταβάτω
the goods of him in the house, let him not come down
ἆραι αὐτά, καὶ ὁ ἐν ἀγρῷ ὁμοίως μὴ
to take them, and the [one] in a field likewise   not

ᵖ Other ancient authorities
omit *in his day*

back. [32]Remember Lot's wife. [33]Whoever seeks to gain his life will lose it, but whoever loses his life will preserve it. [34]I tell you, in that night there will be two men in one bed; one will be taken and the other left. [35]There will be two women grinding together; one will be taken and the other left."[q] [37]And they said to him, "Where, Lord?" He said to them, "Where the body is, there the eagles[r] will be gathered together."

ἐπιστρεψάτω   εἰς   τὰ   ὀπίσω.   **32** μνημονεύετε
let him turn back   to   the things behind.   Remember

τῆς   γυναικὸς   Λώτ.   **33** ὃς   ἐὰν   ζητήσῃ
the   wife   of Lot.   Whoever   seeks

τὴν   ψυχὴν   αὐτοῦ   περιποιήσασθαι,   ἀπολέσει
the   life   of him   to preserve,   he will lose

αὐτήν,   καὶ   ὃς   ἂν   ἀπολέσει,   ζῳογονήσει
it,   and   whoever   will lose,   will preserve

αὐτήν.   **34** λέγω   ὑμῖν,   ταύτῃ   τῇ   νυκτὶ
it.   I tell   you,   in this   -   night

ἔσονται   δύο   ἐπὶ   κλίνης   μιᾶς,   ὁ   εἷς
there will be   two men   on   couch   one,   the   one

παραλημφθήσεται   καὶ   ὁ   ἕτερος   ἀφεθήσεται·
will be taken   and   the   other   will be left;

35 ἔσονται   δύο   ἀλήθουσαι   ἐπὶ   τὸ   αὐτό,   ἡ
there will be two women   grinding   together,†   the

μία   παραλημφθήσεται   ἡ   δὲ   ἑτέρα   ἀφεθήσεται.‡
one   will be taken   but   the   other   will be left.

37 καὶ   ἀποκριθέντες   λέγουσιν   αὐτῷ·   ποῦ,
And   answering   they say   to him :   Where,

κύριε;   ὁ   δὲ   εἶπεν   αὐτοῖς·   ὅπου   τὸ   σῶμα,
Lord?   And he   said   to them :   Where   the   body,

ἐκεῖ   καὶ   οἱ   ἀετοὶ   ἐπισυναχθήσονται.
there   also   the   eagles   will be gathered together.

CHAPTER 18

AND he told them a parable, to the effect that they ought always to pray and not lose heart. [2]He said, "In a certain city there was a judge who neither feared God nor regarded man; [3]and there was a widow in that city who kept coming to him and saying, 'Vindicate me against my adversary.' [4]For a while he refused; but afterward he said to himself, 'Though I neither fear God nor regard man, [5]yet because

18 Ἔλεγεν   δὲ   παραβολὴν   αὐτοῖς   πρὸς
And he told   ²a parable   ¹them   to
         =that

τὸ   δεῖν   πάντοτε   προσεύχεσθαι   αὐτοὺς   καὶ
the ¹to behove ³always   ⁴to pray   ²them   and
they must always pray and not faint,

μὴ   ἐγκακεῖν,   **2** λέγων·   κριτής   τις   ἦν   ἔν
not   to faint,   saying :   ²judge   ²a certain ¹There   ⁴in
         was

τινι   πόλει   τὸν   θεὸν   μὴ   φοβούμενος   καὶ
⁵a certain ⁶city   -   ³God   ¹not   ²fearing   and

ἄνθρωπον μὴ ἐντρεπόμενος.   **3** χήρα   δὲ   ἦν
³man   ¹not   ²regarding.   And ²a widow ¹there was

ἐν   τῇ   πόλει   ἐκείνῃ,   καὶ   ἤρχετο   πρὸς
in   -   city   that,   and   she came   to

αὐτὸν   λέγουσα·   ἐκδίκησόν   με   ἀπὸ   τοῦ
him   saying :   Vindicate   me   from   the

ἀντιδίκου   μου.   **4** καὶ   οὐκ   ἤθελεν   ἐπὶ
opponent   of me.   And   he would not   for

χρόνον·   μετὰ   ταῦτα   δὲ   εἶπεν   ἐν   ἑαυτῷ·
a time;   but after these things   he said   in   himself :

εἰ   καὶ   τὸν   θεὸν   οὐ   φοβοῦμαι   οὐδὲ   ἄνθρωπον
If indeed   -   God   I fear not   nor   man

---

[q] Other ancient authorities add verse 36, *"Two men will be in the field; one will be taken and the other left"*

[r] Or *vultures*

‡ Verse 36 omitted by Nestle; *cf.* RSV footnote.

this widow bothers me, I will vindicate her, or she will wear me out by her continual coming.' " [6]And the Lord said, "Hear what the unrighteous judge says. [7]And will not God vindicate his elect, who cry to him day and night? Will he delay long over them? [8]I tell you, he will vindicate them speedily. Nevertheless, when the Son of man comes, will he find faith on earth?"

[9] He also told this parable to some who trusted in themselves that they were righteous and despised others: [10]"Two men went up into the temple to pray, one a Pharisee and the other a tax collector. [11]The Pharisee stood and prayed thus with himself, 'God, I thank thee that I am not like other men, extortioners, unjust, adulters, or even like this tax collector. [12]I fast twice a week, I give tithes of all that I get.' [13]But the tax collector, standing far off, would not even lift up his eyes

ἐντρέπομαι, 5 διά γε τὸ παρέχειν
regard, at least because of – to cause
=because this widow causes me trouble

μοι κόπον τὴν χήραν ταύτην ἐκδικήσω αὐτήν,
me trouble – widow this[b] I will vindicate her,

ἵνα μὴ εἰς τέλος ἐρχομένη ὑπωπιάζῃ με.
lest in [the] end coming she exhausts me.

6 Εἶπεν δὲ ὁ κύριος· ἀκούσατε τί ὁ κριτὴς
And said the Lord: Hear ye what the judge

τῆς ἀδικίας λέγει· 7 ὁ δὲ θεὸς οὐ μὴ
– of unrighteousness says; – and God by no means

ποιήσῃ τὴν ἐκδίκησιν τῶν ἐκλεκτῶν
will he make the vindication of the chosen [ones]

αὐτοῦ τῶν βοώντων αὐτῷ ἡμέρας καὶ
of him – crying to him day and

νυκτός, καὶ μακροθυμεῖ ἐπ' αὐτοῖς; 8 λέγω
night, and be patient over them? I tell

ὑμῖν ὅτι ποιήσει τὴν ἐκδίκησιν αὐτῶν
you that he will make the vindication of them

ἐν τάχει. πλὴν ὁ υἱὸς τοῦ ἀνθρώπου ἐλθὼν
quickly. Nevertheless the Son – of man coming

ἆρα εὑρήσει τὴν πίστιν ἐπὶ τῆς γῆς;
then will he find the faith on the earth?

9 Εἶπεν δὲ καὶ πρός τινας τοὺς
And he said also to some the [ones]

πεποιθότας ἐφ' ἑαυτοῖς ὅτι εἰσὶν
relying on themselves that they are

δίκαιοι καὶ ἐξουθενοῦντας τοὺς λοιποὺς
righteous and despising the rest

τὴν παραβολὴν ταύτην. 10 Ἄνθρωποι δύο
– parable this. Men two

ἀνέβησαν εἰς τὸ ἱερὸν προσεύξασθαι, ὁ εἷς
went up to the temple to pray, the one

Φαρισαῖος καὶ ὁ ἕτερος τελώνης. 11 ὁ
a Pharisee and the other a tax-collector. The

Φαρισαῖος σταθεὶς ταῦτα πρὸς ἑαυτὸν
Pharisee standing these things to himself

προσηύχετο· ὁ θεός, εὐχαριστῶ σοι ὅτι
prayed: God, I thank thee that

οὐκ εἰμὶ ὥσπερ οἱ λοιποὶ τῶν ἀνθρώπων,
I am not as the rest – of men,

ἅρπαγες, ἄδικοι, μοιχοί, ἢ καὶ ὡς οὗτος
rapacious, unjust, adulterers, or even as this

ὁ τελώνης· 12 νηστεύω δὶς τοῦ σαββάτου,
– tax-collector; I fast twice of (in) the week,

ἀποδεκατεύω πάντα ὅσα κτῶμαι. 13 ὁ δὲ
I tithe all things how many I get. But the

τελώνης μακρόθεν ἑστὼς οὐκ ἤθελεν οὐδὲ
tax-collector far off standing would not not even

to heaven, but beat his breast, saying, 'God, be merciful to me a sinner!' 14I tell you, this man went down to his house justified rather than the other; for every one who exalts himself will be humbled, but he who humbles himself will be exalted."

15 Now they were bringing even infants to him that he might touch them; and when the disciples saw it, they rebuked them. 16But Jesus called them to him, saying, "Let the children come to me, and do not hinder them; for to such belongs the kingdom of God. 17Truly, I say to you, whoever does not receive the kingdom of God like a child shall not enter it."

18 And a ruler asked him, "Good Teacher, what shall I do to inherit eternal life?" 19And Jesus said to him, "Why do you call me good? No one is good but God alone. 20You know the commandments: 'Do not commit adultery, Do not kill, Do not steal, Do not bear false witness, Honor your father and mother.' " 21And he said,

τοὺς ὀφθαλμοὺς ἐπᾶραι εἰς τὸν οὐρανόν,
the(his) eyes to lift up to – heaven,
ἀλλ' ἔτυπτεν τὸ στῆθος αὐτοῦ λέγων· ὁ
but s:note the breast of him saying : –
θεός, ἱλάσθητί μοι τῷ ἁμαρτωλῷ. 14 λέγω
God, be propitious to me the sinner. I tell
ὑμῖν, κατέβη οὗτος δεδικαιωμένος εἰς τὸν
you, went down this man having been justified to the
οἶκον αὐτοῦ παρ' ἐκεῖνον· ὅτι πᾶς ὁ
house of him [rather] than that one; because everyone
ὑψῶν ἑαυτὸν ταπεινωθήσεται, ὁ δὲ ταπεινῶν
exalting himself will be humbled, and the [one] humbling
ἑαυτὸν ὑψωθήσεται.
himself will be exalted.

15 Προσέφερον δὲ αὐτῷ καὶ τὰ βρέφη
And they brought to him also the babes
ἵνα αὐτῶν ἅπτηται· ἰδόντες δὲ οἱ μαθηταὶ
that them he might touch; but s seeing 1the s disciples
ἐπετίμων αὐτοῖς. 16 ὁ δὲ Ἰησοῦς
rebuked them. – But Jesus
προσεκαλέσατο αὐτὰ λέγων· ἄφετε τὰ
called to [him] them* saying : Allow the
παιδία ἔρχεσθαι πρός με καὶ μὴ κωλύετε
children to come to me and do not prevent
αὐτά· τῶν γὰρ τοιούτων ἐστὶν ἡ βασιλεία
them; – for of such is the kingdom
τοῦ θεοῦ. 17 ἀμὴν λέγω ὑμῖν, ὃς ἂν
– of God. Truly I tell you, whoever
μὴ δέξηται τὴν βασιλείαν τοῦ θεοῦ ὡς
does not receive the kingdom – of God as
παιδίον, οὐ μὴ εἰσέλθῃ εἰς αὐτήν.
a child, by no means enters into it.

18 Καὶ ἐπηρώτησέν τις αὐτὸν ἄρχων
And s questioned 1a certain 4him 1ruler
λέγων· διδάσκαλε ἀγαθέ, τί ποιήσας ζωὴν
saying : Teacher good, what doing life
αἰώνιον κληρονομήσω; 19 εἶπεν δὲ αὐτῷ
eternal may I inherit? And said to him
ὁ Ἰησοῦς· τί με λέγεις ἀγαθόν; οὐδεὶς
– Jesus : Why me sayest thou good? no one
ἀγαθὸς εἰ μὴ εἷς [ὁ] θεός. 20 τὰς ἐντολὰς
[is] good except one[,] – God. The commandments
οἶδας· μὴ μοιχεύσῃς, μὴ φονεύσῃς,
thou knowest : Do not commit adultery, Do not kill,
μὴ κλέψῃς, μὴ ψευδομαρτυρήσῃς, τίμα
Do not steal, Do not bear false witness, Honour
τὸν πατέρα σου καὶ τὴν μητέρα. 21 ὁ δὲ
the father of thee and the mother. And he

* That is, "the babes" (τὰ βρέφη in ver. 15).

"All these I have ob-
served from my youth."
[22]And when Jesus heard
it, he said to him, "One
thing you still lack. Sell
all that you have and
distribute to the poor,
and you will have treasure
in heaven; and come,
follow me." [23]But when
he heard this he became
sad, for he was very
rich. [24]Jesus looking at
him said, "How hard it
is for those who have
riches to enter the king-
dom of God! [25]For it is
easier for a camel to go
through the eye of a
needle than for a rich
man to enter the king-
dom of God." [26]Those
who heard it said, "Then
who can be saved?"
[27]But he said, "What is
impossible with men is
possible with God."
[28]And Peter said, "Lo,
we have left our homes
and followed you." [29]And
he said to them, "Truly,
I say to you, there is no
man who has left house
or wife or brothers or
parents or children, for
the sake of the kingdom
of God, [30]who will not
receive manifold more in
this time, and in the age
to come eternal life."

εἶπεν· ταῦτα πάντα ἐφύλαξα ἐκ νεότητος.
said :   All these things   I kept   from   youth.
22 ἀκούσας δὲ ὁ Ἰησοῦς εἶπεν αὐτῷ· ἔτι
But hearing – Jesus said to him : Yet
ἕν σοι λείπει· πάντα ὅσα ἔχεις
one thing to thee is lacking· all things how many thou hast
πώλησον καὶ διάδος πτωχοῖς, καὶ ἔξεις
sell and distribute to poor people, and thou wilt have
θησαυρὸν ἐν [τοῖς] οὐρανοῖς, καὶ δεῦρο
treasure in – heavens, and come
ἀκολούθει μοι. 23 ὁ δὲ ἀκούσας ταῦτα
follow me.   But he hearing these things
περίλυπος ἐγενήθη, ἦν γὰρ πλούσιος σφόδρα.
very grieved became, for he was rich exceedingly.
24 ἰδὼν δὲ αὐτὸν ὁ Ἰησοῦς εἶπεν· πῶς
And seeing him – Jesus said : How
δυσκόλως οἱ τὰ χρήματα ἔχοντες εἰς τὴν
hardly [1]the [ones] – [2]property [3]having into the
βασιλείαν τοῦ θεοῦ εἰσπορεύονται· 25 εὐκο-
kingdom – of God go in; [2]easi-
πώτερον γάρ ἐστιν κάμηλον διὰ τρήματος
er [1]for it is [for] a camel through [the] eye
βελόνης εἰσελθεῖν ἢ πλούσιον εἰς τὴν
of a needle to enter than a rich man into the
βασιλείαν τοῦ θεοῦ εἰσελθεῖν. 26 εἶπαν
kingdom – of God to enter.   said
δὲ οἱ ἀκούσαντες· καὶ τίς δύναται
And the [ones] hearing : And who can
σωθῆναι; 27 ὁ δὲ εἶπεν· τὰ ἀδύνατα παρὰ
to be saved? And he said : The things impossible with
ἀνθρώποις δυνατὰ παρὰ τῷ θεῷ ἐστιν.
men possible with – God is(are).
28 Εἶπεν δὲ ὁ Πέτρος· ἰδοὺ ἡμεῖς ἀφέντες
And said – Peter : Behold[,] we leaving
τὰ ἴδια ἠκολουθήσαμέν σοι. 29 ὁ δὲ
our own things followed thee.   And he
εἶπεν αὐτοῖς· ἀμὴν λέγω ὑμῖν ὅτι οὐδείς
said to them : Truly I tell you that no one
ἐστιν ὃς ἀφῆκεν οἰκίαν ἢ γυναῖκα ἢ
there is who left house or wife or
ἀδελφοὺς ἢ γονεῖς ἢ τέκνα εἵνεκεν τῆς
brothers or parents or children for the sake of the
βασιλείας τοῦ θεοῦ, 30 ὃς οὐχὶ μὴ λάβῃ
kingdom – of God, who by no means receives
πολλαπλασίονα ἐν τῷ καιρῷ τούτῳ καὶ ἐν
many times over in – time this and in
τῷ αἰῶνι τῷ ἐρχομένῳ ζωὴν αἰώνιον.
the age – coming life eternal.

31 And taking the twelve, he said to them, "Behold, we are going up to Jerusalem, and everything that is written of the Son of man by the prophets will be accomplished. ³²For he will be delivered to the Gentiles, and will be mocked and shamefully treated and spit upon; ³³they will scourge him and kill him, and on the third day he will rise." ³⁴But they understood none of these things; this saying was hid from them, and they did not grasp what was said.

35 As he drew near to Jericho, a blind man was sitting by the roadside begging; ³⁶and hearing a multitude going by, he inquired what this meant. ³⁷They told him, "Jesus of Nazareth is passing by." ³⁸And he cried, "Jesus, Son of David, have mercy on me!" ³⁹And those who were in front rebuked him, telling him to be silent; but he cried out all the more, "Son of David, have mercy on me!" ⁴⁰And Jesus stopped, and commanded him to be brought to him; and when he came near, he

31 Παραλαβὼν δὲ τοὺς δώδεκα εἶπεν πρὸς
And taking   the   twelve   he said   to
αὐτούς· ἰδοὺ ἀναβαίνομεν εἰς Ἰερουσαλήμ,
them :   Behold we are going up   to   Jerusalem,
καὶ τελεσθήσεται πάντα τὰ γεγραμ-
and   will be accomplished all things   –   having been
μένα διὰ τῶν προφητῶν τῷ υἱῷ τοῦ
written through   the   prophets   to the Son   –
ἀνθρώπου· 32 παραδοθήσεται γὰρ τοῖς ἔθνεσιν
of man;   for he will be delivered to the nations
καὶ ἐμπαιχθήσεται καὶ ὑβρισθήσεται καὶ
and   will be mocked   and   will be insulted   and
ἐμπτυσθήσεται, 33 καὶ μαστιγώσαντες
will be spit at,   and   having scourged
ἀποκτενοῦσιν αὐτόν, καὶ τῇ ἡμέρᾳ τῇ
they will kill   him,   and on the   day   –
τρίτῃ ἀναστήσεται. 34 καὶ αὐτοὶ οὐδὲν
third   he will rise again.   And   they   none
τούτων συνῆκαν, καὶ ἦν τὸ ῥῆμα τοῦτο
of these things understood, and ²was – ²utterance ¹this
κεκρυμμένον ἀπ᾽ αὐτῶν, καὶ οὐκ ἐγίνωσκον
⁴having been hidden from   them,   and   they knew not
τὰ λεγόμενα.
the things being said.

35 Ἐγένετο δὲ ἐν τῷ ἐγγίζειν αὐτὸν εἰς
And it came to pass in the to draw near him⁽ᵇᵉ⁾ to
=as he drew near
Ἰεριχὼ τυφλός τις ἐκάθητο παρὰ τὴν ὁδὸν
Jericho a certain blind man sat   by   the   way
ἐπαιτῶν. 36 ἀκούσας δὲ ὄχλου διαπορευομένου
begging.   And hearing a crowd   passing through
ἐπυνθάνετο τί εἴη τοῦτο. 37 ἀπήγγειλαν
he inquired what ²might be ¹this.   And they re-
δὲ αὐτῷ ὅτι Ἰησοῦς ὁ Ναζωραῖος
ported to him[,]   –   Jesus   the   Nazarene
παρέρχεται. 38 καὶ ἐβόησεν λέγων· Ἰησοῦ
is passing by.   And   he cried   saying: Jesus
υἱὲ Δαυίδ, ἐλέησόν με. 39 καὶ οἱ
son   of David, pity   me.   And the [ones]
προάγοντες ἐπετίμων αὐτῷ ἵνα σιγήσῃ·
going before   rebuked   him   that he should be quiet;
αὐτὸς δὲ πολλῷ μᾶλλον ἔκραζεν· υἱὲ
but he   by much   more   cried out :   Son
Δαυίδ, ἐλέησόν με. 40 σταθεὶς δὲ ὁ
of David, pity   me.   And standing   –
Ἰησοῦς ἐκέλευσεν αὐτὸν ἀχθῆναι πρὸς
Jesus   commanded   him   to be brought   to
αὐτόν. ἐγγίσαντος δὲ αὐτοῦ ἐπηρώτησεν
him.   And drawing near   him⁽ᵃ⁾ he questioned
=as he drew near

asked him, [41]"What do you want me to do for you?" He said, "Lord, let me receive my sight." [42]And Jesus said to him, "Receive your sight; your faith has made you well." [43]And immediately he received his sight, and followed him, glorifying God; and all the people, when they saw it, gave praise to God.

αὐτόν· **41** τί σοι θέλεις ποιήσω; ὁ δὲ
him :   What for thee wishest thou I may do? And he
εἶπεν· κύριε, ἵνα ἀναβλέψω. **42** καὶ ὁ Ἰησοῦς
said : Lord, that I may see again.   And Jesus
εἶπεν αὐτῷ· ἀνάβλεψον· ἡ πίστις σου
said to him : See again; the faith of thee
σέσωκέν σε. **43** καὶ παραχρῆμα ἀνέβλεψεν,
has healed thee. And at once he saw again,
καὶ ἠκολούθει αὐτῷ δοξάζων τὸν θεόν.
and followed him glorifying — God.
καὶ πᾶς ὁ λαὸς ἰδὼν ἔδωκεν αἶνον τῷ
And all the people seeing gave praise —
θεῷ.
to God.

CHAPTER 19

HE entered Jericho and was passing through. [2]And there was a man named Zacchae′us; he was a chief tax collector, and rich. [3]And he sought to see who Jesus was, but could not, on account of the crowd, because he was small of stature. [4]So he ran on ahead and climbed up into a sycamore tree to see him, for he was to pass that way. [5]And when Jesus came to the place, he looked up and said to him, "Zacchae′us, make haste and come down; for I must stay at your house today." [6]So he made haste and came down, and received him joyfully. [7]And when they saw it they all murmured, "He has gone in to be the guest of a man who is a sinner."

19 Καὶ εἰσελθὼν διήρχετο τὴν Ἰεριχώ.
And having entered he passed through — Jericho.
2 Καὶ ἰδοὺ ἀνὴρ ὀνόματι καλούμενος
And behold[,] a man by name being called
Ζακχαῖος, καὶ αὐτὸς ἦν ἀρχιτελώνης, καὶ
Zacchæus, and he was a chief tax-collector, and
αὐτὸς πλούσιος· **3** καὶ ἐζήτει ἰδεῖν τὸν
he [was] rich; and he sought to see the
Ἰησοῦν τίς ἐστιν, καὶ οὐκ ἠδύνατο ἀπὸ
Jesus who he is(was), and was not able from
τοῦ ὄχλου, ὅτι τῇ ἡλικίᾳ μικρὸς ἦν.
the crowd, because — ²in stature ³little ¹he was.
4 καὶ προδραμὼν εἰς τὸ ἔμπροσθεν ἀνέβη
And having run forward to the front he went up
ἐπὶ συκομορέαν, ἵνα ἴδῃ αὐτόν, ὅτι
onto a sycamore-tree, that he might see him, because
ἐκείνης ἤμελλεν διέρχεσθαι. **5** καὶ ὡς
²that [way] ¹he was about ³to pass along. And as
ἦλθεν ἐπὶ τὸν τόπον, ἀναβλέψας ὁ Ἰησοῦς
he came upon the place, looking up — Jesus
εἶπεν πρὸς αὐτόν· Ζακχαῖε, σπεύσας
said to him : Zacchæus, making haste
κατάβηθι· σήμερον γὰρ ἐν τῷ οἴκῳ σου
come down; for to-day in the house of thee
δεῖ με μεῖναι. **6** καὶ σπεύσας κατέβη,
it behoves me to remain. And making haste he came down,
καὶ ὑπεδέξατο αὐτὸν χαίρων. **7** καὶ
and welcomed him rejoicing. And
ἰδόντες πάντες διεγόγγυζον λέγοντες ὅτι
seeing all murmured saying[,] —
παρὰ ἁμαρτωλῷ ἀνδρὶ εἰσῆλθεν καταλῦσαι.
With a sinful man he entered to lodge.

⁸And Zacchae'us stood and said to the Lord, "Behold, Lord, the half of my goods I give to the poor; and if I have defrauded any one of anything, I restore it fourfold." ⁹And Jesus said to him, "Today salvation has come to this house, since he also is a son of Abraham. ¹⁰For the Son of man came to seek and to save the lost."

11 As they heard these things, he proceeded to tell a parable, because he was near to Jerusalem, and because they supposed that the kingdom of God was to appear immediately. ¹²He said therefore, "A nobleman went into a far country to receive kingly power and then return. ¹³Calling ten of his servants, he gave them ten pounds, and said to them, 'Trade with these till I come.' ¹⁴But his citizens hated him and sent an embassy after him, saying, 'We do not want this man to reign over us.' ¹⁵When

8 σταθεὶς   δὲ   Ζακχαῖος   εἶπεν   πρὸς   τὸν
  And standing   Zacchæus   said   to   the

κύριον·   ἰδοὺ   τὰ   ἡμίση   μου   τῶν   ὑπαρχόντων,
Lord :   Behold[,]   the   half   of me   of the   possessions,

κύριε,   τοῖς   πτωχοῖς   δίδωμι,   καὶ   εἴ   τινός
Lord,   to the   poor   I give,   and   if   anyone

τι   ἐσυκοφάντησα,   ἀποδίδωμι   τετραπλοῦν.
anything   I accused falsely,   I restore   fourfold.

9 εἶπεν   δὲ   πρὸς   αὐτὸν   ὁ   Ἰησοῦς   ὅτι
  And said   to   him   -   Jesus[,]   that

σήμερον   σωτηρία   τῷ   οἴκῳ   τούτῳ   ἐγένετο,
To-day   salvation   -   house   to this   came,

καθότι   καὶ   αὐτὸς   υἱὸς   Ἀβραάμ   [ἐστιν]·
because   even   he   a son   of Abraham   is;

10 ἦλθεν   γὰρ   ὁ   υἱὸς   τοῦ   ἀνθρώπου   ζητῆσαι
   for came   the   Son   -   of man   to seek

καὶ   σῶσαι   τὸ   ἀπολωλός.
and   to save   the thing having been lost.

11 Ἀκουόντων   δὲ   αὐτῶν   ταῦτα   προσθεὶς
   And hearing   them*   these things   adding
                 =as they heard

εἶπεν   παραβολήν,   διὰ   τὸ   ἐγγὺς   εἶναι
he told   a parable,   because of the   near   to be
                        =because he was near to Jerusalem and they thought

Ἰερουσαλὴμ   αὐτὸν   καὶ   δοκεῖν   αὐτοὺς   ὅτι
Jerusalem   him   and   to think   them^b   that

παραχρῆμα   μέλλει   ἡ   βασιλεία   τοῦ   θεοῦ
at once   is(was) about the   kingdom   -   of God

ἀναφαίνεσθαι·   12 εἶπεν   οὖν·   ἄνθρωπός   τις
to appear;   he said therefore :   A certain man

εὐγενὴς   ἐπορεύθη   εἰς   χώραν   μακρὰν   λαβεῖν
well born   went   to   country   a far   to receive

ἑαυτῷ   βασιλείαν   καὶ   ὑποστρέψαι. 13 καλέσας
for himself   a kingdom   and   to return.   having called

δὲ   δέκα   δούλους   ἑαυτοῦ   ἔδωκεν   αὐτοῖς
And   ten   slaves   of himself   he gave   them

δέκα   μνᾶς,   καὶ   εἶπεν   πρὸς   αὐτούς·
ten   minas,   and   said   to   them :

πραγματεύσασθε   ἐν   ᾧ   ἔρχομαι. 14 οἱ   δὲ
Trade ye   while   I am coming.*   But the

πολῖται   αὐτοῦ   ἐμίσουν   αὐτόν,   καὶ   ἀπέστειλαν
citizens   of him   hated   him,   and   sent

πρεσβείαν   ὀπίσω   αὐτοῦ   λέγοντες·   οὐ   θέλομεν
a delegation   after   him   saying :   We do not wish

τοῦτον   βασιλεῦσαι   ἐφ’   ἡμᾶς.   15 καὶ
this man   to reign   over   us.   And

* That is, "again." The present of this verb often has a futurist significance; cf. John 14. 3.

he returned, having re-
ceived the kingly power,
he commanded these
servants, to whom he had
given the money, to be
called to him, that he
might know what they
had gained by trading.
¹⁶The first came before
him, saying, 'Lord, your
pound has made ten
pounds more.' ¹⁷And he
said to him, 'Well done,
good servant! Because
you have been faithful
in a very little, you shall
have authority over ten
cities.' ¹⁸And the second
came, saying, 'Lord,
your pound has made
five pounds.' ¹⁹And he
said to him, 'And you
are to be over five cities.'
²⁰Then another came,
saying, 'Lord, here is
your pound, which I
kept laid away in a
napkin; ²¹for I was
afraid of you, because
you are a severe man;
you take up what you
did not lay down, and
reap what you did not
sow.' ²²He said to him,
'I will condemn you out
of your own mouth, you
wicked servant! You
knew that I was a severe
man, taking up what I
did not lay down and
reaping what I did not
sow? ²³Why then did
you not put my money
into the bank, and at my
coming I should have
collected it with interest?'
²⁴And he said to those
who stood by, 'Take the

ἐγένετο   ἐν τῷ ἐπανελθεῖν αὐτὸν λαβόντα
it came to pass in the   to return   him^{be} having received
                                      =when he returned

τὴν βασιλείαν καὶ εἶπεν φωνηθῆναι αὐτῷ
the   kingdom   and he said   to be called   to him

τοὺς δούλους τούτους οἷς δεδώκει τὸ
  -   slaves   these   to whom he had given the

ἀργύριον,   ἵνα   γνοῖ   τίς   τί
money,   that he might know ²anyone ¹what

διεπραγματεύσατο. 16 παρεγένετο δὲ ὁ πρῶτος
gained by trading.   And came   the   first

λέγων· κύριε, ἡ μνᾶ σου δέκα προσηργάσατο
saying: Lord, the mina of thee ²ten   ¹gained

μνᾶς. 17 καὶ εἶπεν αὐτῷ· εὖ γε, ἀγαθὲ δοῦλε,
²minas.   And he said to him : Well,   good slave,

ὅτι ἐν ἐλαχίστῳ πιστὸς ἐγένου, ἴσθι
because in a least thing faithful thou wast, be thou

ἐξουσίαν ἔχων ἐπάνω δέκα πόλεων. 18 καὶ
²authority ¹having over   ten   cities.   And

ἦλθεν ὁ δεύτερος λέγων· ἡ μνᾶ σου,
came the second   saying: The mina of thee,

κύριε, ἐποίησεν πέντε μνᾶς. 19 εἶπεν δὲ
lord,   made   five minas.   And he said

καὶ τούτῳ· καὶ σὺ ἐπάνω γίνου πέντε
also to this one : And ²thou ³over   ¹be   five

πόλεων. 20 καὶ ὁ ἕτερος ἦλθεν λέγων·
cities.   And   the other   came   saying :

κύριε, ἰδοὺ ἡ μνᾶ σου, ἣν εἶχον
Lord, behold[,] the mina of thee, which I had

ἀποκειμένην ἐν σουδαρίῳ· 21 ἐφοβούμην γάρ
being put away in a napkin;   for I feared

σε, ὅτι ἄνθρωπος αὐστηρὸς εἶ, αἴρεις ὃ
thee, because man an exacting thou art, thou takest what

οὐκ ἔθηκας, καὶ θερίζεις ὃ οὐκ ἔσπειρας.
thou didst not lay, and thou reapest what thou didst not sow.

22 λέγει αὐτῷ· ἐκ τοῦ στόματός σου
He says   to him : Out of the   mouth   of thee

κρινῶ σε, πονηρὲ δοῦλε. ᾔδεις ὅτι ἐγὼ
I will judge thee, wicked slave. Knewest thou that I

ἄνθρωπος αὐστηρός εἰμι, αἴρων ὃ οὐκ
man   an exacting am,   taking what not

ἔθηκα, καὶ θερίζων ὃ οὐκ ἔσπειρα; 23 καὶ
I laid, and reaping what I sowed not?   And

διὰ τί οὐκ ἔδωκάς μου τὸ ἀργύριον ἐπὶ
why didst thou not give of me the   money   on

τράπεζαν; κἀγὼ ἐλθὼν σὺν τόκῳ ἂν
a table?*   And I coming   with interest

αὐτὸ ἔπραξα. 24 καὶ τοῖς παρεστῶσιν
it would have exacted. And to the [ones] standing by

* That is, a moneychanger's or banker's table.

pound from him, and
give it to him who has
the ten pounds.' ²⁵(And
they said to him, 'Lord,
he has ten pounds!') ²⁶'I
tell you, that to every
one who has will more
be given; but from him
who has not, even what
he has will be taken
away. ²⁷But as for these
enemies of mine, who
did not want me to reign
over them, bring them
here and slay them before
me.'"

28 And when he had
said this, he went on
ahead, going up to
Jerusalem. ²⁹When he
drew near to Beth'phage
and Bethany, at the
mount that is called
Olivet, he sent two of the
disciples, ³⁰saying, "Go
into the village opposite,
where on entering you
will find a colt tied, on
which no one has ever
yet sat; untie it and bring
it here. ³¹If any one asks
you, 'Why are you un-
tying it?' you shall say
this, 'The Lord has need
of it.'" ³²So those who
were sent went away and
found it as he had told
them. ³³And as they
were untying the colt, its
owners said to them,
"Why are you untying
the colt?" ³⁴And they

εἶπεν· ἄρατε ἀπ' αὐτοῦ τὴν μνᾶν καὶ
he said : Take from him the mina and
δότε τῷ τὰς δέκα μνᾶς ἔχοντι. 25 καὶ
give ¹to the [one] ²the ⁴ten ⁵minas ²having. And
εἶπαν αὐτῷ· κύριε, ἔχει δέκα μνᾶς.
they said to him : Lord, he has ten minas.
26 λέγω ὑμῖν ὅτι παντὶ τῷ ἔχοντι
I tell you that to everyone having
δοθήσεται, ἀπὸ δὲ τοῦ μὴ ἔχοντος καὶ
it will be given, and from the [one] not having even
ὃ ἔχει ἀρθήσεται. 27 πλὴν τοὺς ἐχθρούς
what he has will be taken. Nevertheless - enemies
μου τούτους τοὺς μὴ θελήσαντάς με
of me these the [ones] not wishing me
βασιλεῦσαι ἐπ' αὐτοὺς ἀγάγετε ὧδε καὶ
to reign over them bring ye here and
κατασφάξατε αὐτοὺς ἔμπροσθέν μου.
slay them before me.
28 Καὶ εἰπὼν ταῦτα ἐπορεύετο ἔμπροσθεν
And having said these things he went in front
ἀναβαίνων εἰς Ἱεροσόλυμα. 29 Καὶ ἐγένετο
going up to Jerusalem. And it came to pass
ὡς ἤγγισεν εἰς Βηθφαγὴ καὶ Βηθανίαν
as he drew near to Bethphage and Bethany
πρὸς τὸ ὄρος τὸ καλούμενον ἐλαιών,
toward the mount - being called of olives,
ἀπέστειλεν δύο τῶν μαθητῶν λέγων·
he sent two of the disciples saying :
30 ὑπάγετε εἰς τὴν κατέναντι κώμην, ἐν ᾗ
Go ye into the opposite village, in which
εἰσπορευόμενοι εὑρήσετε πῶλον δεδεμένον,
entering ye will find a colt having been tied,
ἐφ' ὃν οὐδεὶς πώποτε ἀνθρώπων ἐκάθισεν,
on which no one ever yet of men sat,
καὶ λύσαντες αὐτὸν ἀγάγετε. 31 καὶ ἐὰν
and loosening it bring. And if
τις ὑμᾶς ἐρωτᾷ· διὰ τί λύετε; οὕτως
anyone you asks : Why loosen ye? thus
ἐρεῖτε· ὅτι ὁ κύριος αὐτοῦ χρείαν ἔχει.
shall ye say : Because the Lord of it need has.
32 ἀπελθόντες δὲ οἱ ἀπεσταλμένοι εὗρον
And going the [ones] having been sent found
καθὼς εἶπεν αὐτοῖς. 33 λυόντων δὲ
as he told them. And loosening
                                        =as they were
αὐτῶν τὸν πῶλον εἶπαν οἱ κύριοι αὐτοῦ
themᵃ the colt said the owners of it
loosening
πρὸς αὐτούς· τί λύετε τὸν πῶλον; 34 οἱ
to them : Why loosen ye the colt? ¹they

said, "The Lord has need of it." ³⁵And they brought it to Jesus, and throwing their garments on the colt they set Jesus upon it. ³⁶And as he rode along, they spread their garments on the road. ³⁷As he was now drawing near, at the descent of the Mount of Olives, the whole multitude of the disciples began to rejoice and praise God with a loud voice for all the mighty works that they had seen, ³⁸saying, 'Blessed is the King who comes in the name of the Lord! Peace in heaven and glory in the highest!" ³⁹And some of the Pharisees in the multitude said to him, "Teacher, rebuke your disciples." ⁴⁰He answered, "I tell you, if these were silent, the very stones would cry out."

41 And when he drew near and saw the city he wept over it, ⁴²saying, "Would that even today you knew the things that make for peace! But now they are hid from your eyes. ⁴³For the days shall come upon you, when your enemies will

δὲ εἶπαν· ὅτι ὁ κύριος αὐτοῦ χρείαν ἔχει.
¹And said : Because the Lord of it need has.

35 καὶ ἤγαγον αὐτὸν πρὸς τὸν Ἰησοῦν,
And they led it to - Jesus,

καὶ ἐπιρίψαντες αὐτῶν τὰ ἱμάτια ἐπὶ τὸν
and throwing on of them the garments on the

πῶλον ἐπεβίβασαν τὸν Ἰησοῦν. 36 πορευ-
colt they put on [it] - Jesus. And

ομένου δὲ αὐτοῦ ὑπεστρώννυον τὰ ἱμάτια
going him* they strewed the garments
=as he went

ἑαυτῶν ἐν τῇ ὁδῷ. 37 ἐγγίζοντος δὲ
of themselves in the way. And drawing near
=as he drew near

αὐτοῦ ἤδη πρὸς τῇ καταβάσει τοῦ ὄρους
him* now to the descent of the mount

τῶν ἐλαιῶν ἤρξαντο ἅπαν τὸ πλῆθος τῶν
of the olives began all the multitude of the

μαθητῶν χαίροντες αἰνεῖν τὸν θεὸν φωνῇ
disciples rejoicing to praise - God voice

μεγάλῃ περὶ πασῶν ὧν εἶδον δυνάμεων,
with a about ¹all ³which ⁴they saw ⁵[the] powerful
great deeds,

38 λέγοντες· εὐλογημένος ὁ ἐρχόμενος, ὁ
saying : Blessed the coming [one], the

βασιλεὺς ἐν ὀνόματι κυρίου· ἐν οὐρανῷ
king in [the] name of [the] Lord; in heaven

εἰρήνη καὶ δόξα ἐν ὑψίστοις. 39 καί
peace and glory in highest places. And

τινες τῶν Φαρισαίων ἀπὸ τοῦ ὄχλου
some of the Pharisees from the crowd

εἶπαν πρὸς αὐτόν· διδάσκαλε, ἐπιτίμησον
said to him : Teacher, rebuke

τοῖς μαθηταῖς σου. 40 καὶ ἀποκριθεὶς
the disciples of thee. And answering

εἶπεν· λέγω ὑμῖν, ἐὰν οὗτοι σιωπήσουσιν,
he said : I tell you, if these shall(should) be silent,

οἱ λίθοι κράξουσιν. 41 Καὶ ὡς ἤγγισεν,
the stones will cry out. And as he drew near,

ἰδὼν τὴν πόλιν ἔκλαυσεν ἐπ᾽ αὐτήν,
seeing the city he wept over it,

42 λέγων ὅτι εἰ ἔγνως ἐν τῇ ἡμέρᾳ
saying[.] - If thou knewest in - day

ταύτῃ καὶ σὺ τὰ πρὸς εἰρήνην· νῦν δὲ
this even thou the things for peace; but now

ἐκρύβη ἀπὸ ὀφθαλμῶν σου. 43 ὅτι ἥξουσιν
they were hidden from eyes of thee. Because will come

ἡμέραι ἐπὶ σὲ καὶ παρεμβαλοῦσιν οἱ
days upon thee and ⁴will raise up ¹the

cast up a bank about you and surround you, and hem you in on every side, [44]and dash you to the ground, you and your children within you, and they will not leave one stone upon another in you; because you did not know the time of your visitation."

45 And he entered the temple and began to drive out those who sold, [46]saying to them, "It is written, 'My house shall be a house of prayer'; but you have made it a den of robbers."

47 And he was teaching daily in the temple. The chief priests and the scribes and the principal men of the people sought to destroy him; [48]but they did not find anything they could do, for all the people hung upon his words.

ἐχθροί σου χάρακά σοι καὶ περικυκλώσουσίν
[2]enemies [3]of thee [5]a rampart to thee and will surround

σε καὶ συνέξουσίν σε πάντοθεν, 44 καὶ
thee and will press thee on all sides, and

ἐδαφιοῦσίν σε καὶ τὰ τέκνα σου ἐν σοί,
dash to the ground thee and the children of thee in thee,

καὶ οὐκ ἀφήσουσιν λίθον ἐπὶ λίθον ἐν σοί,
and will not leave stone upon stone in thee,

ἀνθ᾽ ὧν οὐκ ἔγνως τὸν καιρὸν τῆς
because† thou knewest not the time of the

ἐπισκοπῆς σου. 45 Καὶ εἰσελθὼν εἰς τὸ
visitation of thee. And entering into the

ἱερὸν ἤρξατο ἐκβάλλειν τοὺς πωλοῦντας,
temple he began to expel the [ones] selling,

46 λέγων αὐτοῖς· γέγραπται· καὶ ἔσται ὁ
telling them : It has been written : And shall be the

οἶκός μου οἶκος προσευχῆς· ὑμεῖς δὲ
house of me a house of prayer; but ye

αὐτὸν ἐποιήσατε σπήλαιον λῃστῶν.
it made a den of robbers.

47 Καὶ ἦν διδάσκων τὸ καθ᾽ ἡμέραν ἐν
And he was teaching daily† in

τῷ ἱερῷ· οἱ δὲ ἀρχιερεῖς καὶ οἱ
the temple; but the chief priests and the

γραμματεῖς ἐζήτουν αὐτὸν ἀπολέσαι καὶ οἱ
scribes [5]sought [6]him [7]to destroy [1]and [2]the

πρῶτοι τοῦ λαοῦ, 48 καὶ οὐχ εὕρισκον
[3]chief men [4]of the [5]people, and did not find

τὸ τί ποιήσωσιν· ὁ λαὸς γὰρ ἅπας
– what they might do; [3]the [4]people [1]for [2]all

ἐξεκρέματο αὐτοῦ ἀκούων.
hung upon him hearing.

CHAPTER 20

ONE day, as he was teaching the people in the temple and preaching the gospel, the chief priests and the scribes with the elders came up [2]and said to him, "Tell us by what authority you do these things, or who it is that gave you this authority." [3]He

20 Καὶ ἐγένετο ἐν μιᾷ τῶν ἡμερῶν
And it came to pass on one of the days

διδάσκοντος αὐτοῦ τὸν λαὸν ἐν τῷ ἱερῷ
teaching him[a] the people in the temple
=as he was teaching

καὶ εὐαγγελιζομένου ἐπέστησαν οἱ ἀρχιερεῖς
and preaching good news[a] came upon [him] the chief priests

καὶ οἱ γραμματεῖς σὺν τοῖς πρεσβυτέροις,
and the scribes with the elders,

2 καὶ εἶπαν λέγοντες πρὸς αὐτόν· εἰπὸν
and spoke saying to him : Tell

ἡμῖν ἐν ποίᾳ ἐξουσίᾳ ταῦτα ποιεῖς, ἢ τίς
us by what authority these things thou doest, or who

ἐστιν ὁ δούς σοι τὴν ἐξουσίαν ταύτην;
is the [one] having given thee – authority this?

answered them, "I also will ask you a question; now tell me, ⁴Was the baptism of John from heaven or from men?" ⁵And they discussed it with one another, saying, "If we say, 'From heaven,' he will say, 'Why did you not believe him?' ⁶But if we say, 'From men,' all the people will stone us; for they are convinced that John was a prophet." ⁷So they answered that they did not know whence it was. ⁸And Jesus said to them, "Neither will I tell you by what authority I do these things."

9 And he began to tell the people this parable: "A man planted a vineyard, and let it out to tenants, and went into another country for a long while. ¹⁰When the time came, he sent a servant to the tenants, that they should give him some of the fruit of the vineyard; but the tenants beat him, and sent him away empty-handed. ¹¹And he sent another servant; him also they beat and treated shamefully, and sent him away empty-handed. ¹²And he sent yet a

3 ἀποκριθεὶς δὲ εἶπεν πρὸς αὐτούς·
And answering   he said   to   them:

ἐρωτήσω ὑμᾶς κἀγὼ λόγον, καὶ εἴπατέ
Will ask you I also a word, and tell ye

μοι· 4 τὸ βάπτισμα Ἰωάννου ἐξ οὐρανοῦ
me: The baptism of John from heaven

ἦν ἢ ἐξ ἀνθρώπων; 5 οἱ δὲ συνελογίσαντο
was it or from men? And they debated

πρὸς ἑαυτοὺς λέγοντες ὅτι ἐὰν εἴπωμεν·
with themselves saying[,] – If we say:

ἐξ οὐρανοῦ, ἐρεῖ· διὰ τί οὐκ ἐπιστεύσατε
From heaven, he will say: Why did ye not believe

αὐτῷ; 6 ἐὰν δὲ εἴπωμεν· ἐξ ἀνθρώπων, ὁ
him? And if we say: From men, the

λαὸς ἅπας καταλιθάσει ἡμᾶς· πεπεισμένος
people all will stone us; for having been per-

γάρ ἐστιν Ἰωάννην προφήτην εἶναι. 7 καὶ
suaded it is* John a prophet to be. And

ἀπεκρίθησαν μὴ εἰδέναι πόθεν. 8 καὶ ὁ
they answered not to know whence. And –

Ἰησοῦς εἶπεν αὐτοῖς· οὐδὲ ἐγὼ λέγω
Jesus said to them: Neither I tell

ὑμῖν ἐν ποίᾳ ἐξουσίᾳ ταῦτα ποιῶ. 9 Ἤρξατο
you by what authority these things I do. he began

δὲ πρὸς τὸν λαὸν λέγειν τὴν παραβολὴν
And to the people to tell – parable

ταύτην. ἄνθρωπος ἐφύτευσεν ἀμπελῶνα,
this. A man planted a vineyard,

καὶ ἐξέδοτο αὐτὸν γεωργοῖς, καὶ ἀπεδή-
and let out it to husbandmen, and went

μησεν χρόνους ἱκανούς. 10 καὶ καιρῷ
away periods for considerable. And in time
=a long time.

ἀπέστειλεν πρὸς τοὺς γεωργοὺς δοῦλον,
he sent to the husbandmen a slave,

ἵνα ἀπὸ τοῦ καρποῦ τοῦ ἀμπελῶνος
that from the fruit of the vineyard

δώσουσιν αὐτῷ· οἱ δὲ γεωργοὶ ἐξαπέστειλαν
they will give him; but the husbandmen ¹sent ²away out

αὐτὸν δείραντες κενόν. 11 καὶ προσέθετο
³him ¹beating ⁴empty. And he added

ἕτερον πέμψαι δοῦλον· οἱ δὲ κἀκεῖνον
³another ¹to send ²slave; but they that one also
=he sent another slave in addition;

δείραντες καὶ ἀτιμάσαντες ἐξαπέστειλαν
beating and insulting sent away out

κενόν. 12 καὶ προσέθετο τρίτον πέμψαι·
empty. And he added a third to send;

* That is, the people (a collective singular) have been (=are) persuaded.

third; this one they wounded and cast out. ¹³Then the owner of the vineyard said, 'What shall I do? I will send my beloved son; it may be they will respect him.' ¹⁴But when the tenants saw him, they said to themselves, 'This is the heir; let us kill him, that the inheritance may be ours.' ¹⁵And they cast him out of the vineyard and killed him. What then will the owner of the vineyard do to them? ¹⁶He will come and destroy those tenants, and give the vineyard to others." When they heard this, they said, "God forbid!" ¹⁷But he looked at them and said, "What then is this that is written:

'The very stone which the builders rejected

has become the head of the corner?'

¹⁸Every one who falls on that stone will be broken to pieces; but when it falls on any one it will crush him."

19 The scribes and the chief priests tried to lay hands on him at that very hour, but they feared the people; for they perceived that he had told this parable against them. ²⁰So they watched him, and sent

οἱ δὲ καὶ τοῦτον τραυματίσαντες ἐξέβαλον.
but they also this one wounding threw out.

13 εἶπεν δὲ ὁ κύριος τοῦ ἀμπελῶνος· τί
And said the owner of the vineyard : What

ποιήσω; πέμψω τὸν υἱόν μου τὸν ἀγαπητόν·
may I do? I will send the son of me – beloved;

ἴσως τοῦτον ἐντραπήσονται. 14 ἰδόντες δὲ
perhaps this one they will regard. But seeing

αὐτὸν οἱ γεωργοὶ διελογίζοντο πρὸς
him the husbandmen debated with

ἀλλήλους λέγοντες· οὗτός ἐστιν ὁ κληρονόμος·
one another saying : This is the heir;

ἀποκτείνωμεν αὐτόν, ἵνα ἡμῶν γένηται
let us kill him, that of us may become

ἡ κληρονομία. 15 καὶ ἐκβαλόντες αὐτὸν
the inheritance. And throwing out him

ἔξω τοῦ ἀμπελῶνος ἀπέκτειναν. τί οὖν
outside the vineyard they killed. What therefore

ποιήσει αὐτοῖς ὁ κύριος τοῦ ἀμπελῶνος;
will do to them the owner of the vineyard?

16 ἐλεύσεται καὶ ἀπολέσει τοὺς γεωργοὺς
he will come and will destroy – husbandmen

τούτους, καὶ δώσει τὸν ἀμπελῶνα ἄλλοις.
these, and will give the vineyard to others.

ἀκούσαντες δὲ εἶπαν· μὴ γένοιτο. 17 ὁ δὲ
And hearing they said : May it not be. And he

ἐμβλέψας αὐτοῖς εἶπεν· τί οὖν ἐστιν τὸ
looking at them said : What therefore is –

γεγραμμένον τοῦτο· λίθον ὃν ἀπεδοκίμασαν
having been written this : [The] stone which ²rejected

οἱ οἰκοδομοῦντες, οὗτος ἐγενήθη εἰς κεφαλὴν
¹the [ones] ²building, this came to be for [the] head

γωνίας; 18 πᾶς ὁ πεσὼν ἐπ' ἐκεῖνον τὸν
of [the] corner? Everyone falling on that –

λίθον συνθλασθήσεται· ἐφ' ὃν δ' ἂν πέσῃ,
stone will be broken to pieces; but on whomever it falls,

λικμήσει αὐτόν. 19 Καὶ ἐζήτησαν οἱ
it will crush to powder him. And sought the

γραμματεῖς καὶ οἱ ἀρχιερεῖς ἐπιβαλεῖν ἐπ'
scribes and the chief priests to lay on on

αὐτὸν τὰς χεῖρας ἐν αὐτῇ τῇ ὥρᾳ, καὶ
him the(ir) hands in ²same ¹the hour, and

ἐφοβήθησαν τὸν λαόν· ἔγνωσαν γὰρ ὅτι
feared the people; for they knew that

πρὸς αὐτοὺς εἶπεν τὴν παραβολὴν ταύτην.
at them he told – parable this.

20 Καὶ παρατηρήσαντες ἀπέστειλαν ἐγκαθέτους
And watching carefully they sent spies

spies, who pretended to be sincere, that they might take hold of what he said, so as to deliver him up to the authority and jurisdiction of the governor. ²¹They asked him, "Teacher, we know that you speak and teach rightly, and show no partiality, but truly teach the way of God. ²²Is it lawful for us to give tribute to Caesar, or not?" ²³But he perceived their craftiness, and said to them, ²⁴"Show me a coin. Whose likeness and inscription has it?" They said, "Caesar's." ²⁵He said to them, "Then render to Caesar the things that are Caesar's, and to God the things that are God's." ²⁶And they were not able in the presence of the people to catch him by what he said; but marveling at his answer they were silent.

27 There came to him some Sad'ducees, those who say that there is no resurrection, ²⁸and they asked him a question, saying, "Teacher, Moses wrote for us that if a man's brother dies, having a wife but no children, the man must

ὑποκρινομένους ἑαυτοὺς δικαίους εἶναι, ἵνα
pretending themselves righteous to be, that
ἐπιλάβωνται αὐτοῦ λόγου, ὥστε παραδοῦναι
they might seize of him a word, so as to deliver
αὐτὸν τῇ ἀρχῇ καὶ τῇ ἐξουσίᾳ τοῦ
him to the rule and to the authority of the
ἡγεμόνος. 21 καὶ ἐπηρώτησαν αὐτὸν
governor. And they questioned him
λέγοντες· διδάσκαλε, οἴδαμεν ὅτι ὀρθῶς
saying : Teacher, we know that ¹rightly
λέγεις καὶ διδάσκεις καὶ οὐ λαμβάνεις
¹thou speakest ²and ³teachest and receivest not
=regardest not persons,
πρόσωπον, ἀλλ᾽ ἐπ᾽ ἀληθείας τὴν ὁδὸν τοῦ
a face, but on [the basis of] truth the way –
θεοῦ διδάσκεις· 22 ἔξεστιν ἡμᾶς Καίσαρι
of God teachest; is it lawful for us to Cæsar
φόρον δοῦναι ἢ οὔ; 23 κατανοήσας δὲ
tribute to give or not? And perceiving
αὐτῶν τὴν πανουργίαν εἶπεν πρὸς αὐτούς·
of them the cleverness he said to them :
24 δείξατέ μοι δηνάριον· τίνος ἔχει εἰκόνα
Show me a denarius; of whom has it an image
καὶ ἐπιγραφήν; οἱ δὲ εἶπαν· Καίσαρος.
and superscription? And they said : Of Cæsar.
25 ὁ δὲ εἶπεν πρὸς αὐτούς· τοίνυν ἀπόδοτε
And he said to them : So render
τὰ Καίσαρος Καίσαρι καὶ τὰ τοῦ θεοῦ
the things of Cæsar to Cæsar and the things – of God
τῷ θεῷ. 26 καὶ οὐκ ἴσχυσαν ἐπιλαβέσθαι
– to God. And they were not able to seize
αὐτοῦ ῥήματος ἐναντίον τοῦ λαοῦ, καὶ
of him a word in the presence of the people, and
θαυμάσαντες ἐπὶ τῇ ἀποκρίσει αὐτοῦ
marvelling at the answer of him
ἐσίγησαν.
they were silent.

27 Προσελθόντες δέ τινες τῶν Σαδ-
And ⁴approaching ¹some ²of the ³Sad-
δουκαίων, οἱ ἀντιλέγοντες ἀνάστασιν μὴ
ducees, the [ones] saying in opposition* a resurrection not
εἶναι, ἐπηρώτησαν αὐτὸν 28 λέγοντες·
to be, they questioned him saying :
διδάσκαλε, Μωϋσῆς ἔγραψεν ἡμῖν, ἐάν
Teacher, Moses wrote to us, If
τινος ἀδελφὸς ἀποθάνῃ ἔχων γυναῖκα, καὶ
of anyone a brother dies having a wife, and
οὗτος ἄτεκνος ᾖ, ἵνα λάβῃ ὁ ἀδελφὸς
this man childless is, that ⁴should take ¹the ²brother

*That is, to the Pharisees and to the generally held opinion.

take the wife and raise up children for his brother. ²⁹Now there were seven brothers; the first took a wife, and died without children; ³⁰and the second ³¹and the third took her, and likewise all seven left no children and died. ³²Afterward the woman also died. ³³In the resurrection, therefore, whose wife will the woman be? For the seven had her as wife."

34 And Jesus said to them, "The sons of this age marry and are given in marriage; ³⁵but those who are accounted worthy to attain to that age and to the resurrection from the dead neither marry nor are given in marriage, ³⁶for they cannot die any more, because they are equal to angels and are sons of God, being sons of the resurrection. ³⁷But that the dead are raised, even Moses showed, in the passage about the bush, where he calls the Lord the God of Abraham and the God of Isaac and the God of Jacob. ³⁸Now he is not God of the dead, but of the living; for all live to him." ³⁹And some of the scribes answered, "Teacher, you have

αὐτοῦ τὴν γυναῖκα καὶ ἐξαναστήσῃ σπέρμα
³of him　⁵the　⁶wife　and　¹ raise up　seed

τῷ ἀδελφῷ αὐτοῦ. 29 ἑπτὰ οὖν ἀδελφοὶ
to the　brother　of him.　Seven therefore brothers

ἦσαν· καὶ ὁ πρῶτος λαβὼν γυναῖκα
there were; and　the　first　having taken　a wife

ἀπέθανεν ἄτεκνος· 30 καὶ ὁ δεύτερος 31 καὶ
died　childless;　and the　second　and

ὁ τρίτος ἔλαβεν αὐτήν, ὡσαύτως δὲ καὶ
the third　took　her,　and similarly　also

οἱ ἑπτὰ οὐ κατέλιπον τέκνα καὶ ἀπέθανον.
the seven　did not leave　children　and　died.

32 ὕστερον καὶ ἡ γυνὴ ἀπέθανεν. 33 ἡ
Lastly　also　the　woman　died.　The

γυνὴ οὖν ἐν τῇ ἀναστάσει τίνος αὐτῶν
woman therefore in　the　resurrection　of which of them

γίνεται γυνή; οἱ γὰρ ἑπτὰ ἔσχον αὐτὴν
becomes she wife?　for the　seven　had　her

γυναῖκα. 34 καὶ εἶπεν αὐτοῖς ὁ Ἰησοῦς·
[as] wife.　And　said　to them　–　Jesus :

οἱ υἱοὶ τοῦ αἰῶνος τούτου γαμοῦσιν καὶ
The sons　–　age　of this　marry　and

γαμίσκονται, 35 οἱ δὲ καταξιωθέντες τοῦ
are given in marriage,　but the [ones]　counted worthy　–

αἰῶνος ἐκείνου τυχεῖν καὶ τῆς ἀναστάσεως
³age　²of that　¹to obtain　and　of the　resurrection

τῆς ἐκ νεκρῶν οὔτε γαμοῦσιν οὔτε
–　out of [the] dead　neither　marry　nor

γαμίζονται· 36 οὐδὲ γὰρ ἀποθανεῖν ἔτι
are given in marriage;　for not even　to die　more

δύνανται, ἰσάγγελοι γάρ εἰσιν, καὶ υἱοὶ
can they,　for equal to angels　they are,　and　²sons

εἰσιν θεοῦ τῆς ἀναστάσεως υἱοὶ ὄντες.
¹they are ³of God ⁴of the　⁵resurrection　³sons　⁶being.

37 ὅτι δὲ ἐγείρονται οἱ νεκροί, καὶ
But that　are raised　the　dead,　even

Μωϋσῆς ἐμήνυσεν ἐπὶ τῆς βάτου, ὡς
Moses　pointed out　at　the　bush,　as

λέγει κύριον τὸν θεὸν Ἀβραὰμ καὶ θεὸν
he calls [the] Lord　the　God　of Abraham and　God

Ἰσαὰκ καὶ θεὸν Ἰακώβ· 38 θεὸς δὲ οὐκ
of Isaac　and　God　of Jacob;　but God　not

ἔστιν νεκρῶν ἀλλὰ ζώντων· πάντες γὰρ
he is　of dead persons but　of living;　for all

αὐτῷ ζῶσιν. 39 ἀποκριθέντες δέ τινες
to him　live.　And answering　some

τῶν γραμματέων εἶπαν· διδάσκαλε, καλῶς
of the　scribes　said :　Teacher,　well

spoken well." ⁴⁰ For they
no longer dared to ask
him any question.

εἶπας.   40 οὐκέτι γὰρ ἐτόλμων ἐπερωτᾶν
thou sayest.   For no more   dared they   *to* question

αὐτὸν οὐδέν.
him   no(any)thing.

41 But he said to them,
"How can they say that
the Christ is David's
son? ⁴² For David him-
self says in the Book of
Psalms,

'The Lord said to my
Lord,
Sit at my right hand,
⁴³ till I make thy enemies
a stool for thy
feet.'

⁴⁴ David thus calls him
Lord; so how is he his
son?"

41 Εἶπεν δὲ πρὸς αὐτούς· πῶς λέγουσιν
And he said   to   them :   How   say they

τὸν χριστὸν εἶναι Δαυὶδ υἱόν; 42 αὐτὸς
the   Christ   to be of David son?   himself

γὰρ Δαυὶδ λέγει ἐν βίβλῳ ψαλμῶν·
For   David   says   in [the] roll of psalms :

εἶπεν κύριος τῷ κυρίῳ μου· κάθου ἐκ
Said [the] LORD to the Lord of me : Sit thou   at

δεξιῶν μου 43 ἕως ἂν θῶ τοὺς ἐχθρούς σου
[the] right of me   until   I put   the   enemies of thee

ὑποπόδιον τῶν ποδῶν σου. 44 Δαυὶδ
a footstool   of the   feet   of thee.   David

οὖν αὐτὸν κύριον καλεῖ, καὶ πῶς αὐτοῦ
therefore him   Lord   calls,   and   how   of him

υἱός ἐστιν;
son   is he?

45 And in the hearing
of all the people he said
to his disciples, ⁴⁶ "Be-
ware of the scribes, who
like to go about in long
robes, and love saluta-
tions in the market places
and the best seats in the
synagogues and the
places of honor at feasts,
⁴⁷ who devour widows'
houses and for a pretense
make long prayers. They
will receive the greater
condemnation."

45 Ἀκούοντος δὲ παντὸς τοῦ λαοῦ εἶπεν
And hearing   all   the peopleᵃ he said
=as all the people heard

τοῖς μαθηταῖς· 46 προσέχετε ἀπὸ τῶν
to the disciples :   Beware   from(of) the

γραμματέων τῶν θελόντων περιπατεῖν ἐν
scribes   -   wishing   to walk about   in

στολαῖς καὶ φιλούντων ἀσπασμοὺς ἐν ταῖς
robes   and   liking   greetings   in   the

ἀγοραῖς καὶ πρωτοκαθεδρίας ἐν ταῖς
marketplaces and   chief seats   in   the

συναγωγαῖς καὶ πρωτοκλισίας ἐν τοῖς
synagogues   and   chief couches   in   the

δείπνοις, 47 οἳ κατεσθίουσιν τὰς οἰκίας
suppers,   who devour   the   houses

τῶν χηρῶν καὶ προφάσει μακρὰ προσεύχονται·
of the widows and under pretence long   pray;

οὗτοι λήμψονται περισσότερον κρίμα.
these   will receive   severer   judgment.

CHAPTER 21

HE looked up and saw
the rich putting
their gifts into the
treasury; ² and he saw a
poor widow put in two
copper coins. ³ And he

21 Ἀναβλέψας δὲ εἶδεν τοὺς βάλλοντας
And looking up   he saw ¹the   ²putting

εἰς τὸ γαζοφυλακεῖον τὰ δῶρα αὐτῶν
⁴into ⁵the ⁶treasury   ⁷the ⁸gifts ⁹of them

πλουσίους. 2 εἶδεν δέ τινα χήραν πενιχρὰν
³rich [ones].   And he saw a certain widow   poor

βάλλουσαν ἐκεῖ λεπτὰ δύο, 3 καὶ εἶπεν·
putting   there lepta   two,   and he said :

said, "Truly I tell you, this poor widow has put in more than all of them; ⁴for they all contributed out of their abundance, but she out of her poverty put in all the living that she had."

5 And as some spoke of the temple, how it was adorned with noble stones and offerings, he said, ⁶"As for these things which you see, the days will come when there shall not be left here one stone upon another that will not be thrown down." ⁷And they asked him, "Teacher, when will this be, and what will be the sign when this is about to take place?" ⁸And he said, "Take heed that you are not led astray; for many will come in my name, saying, 'I am he!' and, 'The time is at hand!' Do not go after them. ⁹And when you hear of wars and tumults, do not be terrified; for this must first take place, but the end will not be at once."

10 Then he said to them, "Nation will rise against nation, and kingdom against kingdom; ¹¹there will be great earthquakes, and in

ἀληθῶς λέγω ὑμῖν ὅτι ἡ χήρα αὕτη ἡ
Truly I tell you that – ²widow ¹this –

πτωχὴ πλεῖον πάντων ἔβαλεν· 4 πάντες
²poor more [than] all put; ²all

γὰρ οὗτοι ἐκ τοῦ περισσεύοντος αὐτοῖς
¹for these out of the abounding to them⁶
=their abundance

ἔβαλον εἰς τὰ δῶρα, αὕτη δὲ ἐκ τοῦ
put into the gifts, but this woman out of the

ὑστερήματος αὐτῆς πάντα τὸν βίον ὃν
want of her ²all ³the ⁴living ⁵which

εἶχεν ἔβαλεν.
⁶she had ¹put.

5 Καί τινων λεγόντων περὶ τοῦ ἱεροῦ, ὅτι
And some speaking³ about the temple, that
=as some spoke

λίθοις καλοῖς καὶ ἀναθήμασιν κεκόσμηται,
with stones beautiful and gifts it has(had)
been adorned,

εἶπεν· 6 ταῦτα ἃ θεωρεῖτε, ἐλεύσονται
he said: These things which ye behold, will come

ἡμέραι ἐν αἷς οὐκ ἀφεθήσεται λίθος ἐπὶ
days in which there will not be left stone on

λίθῳ ὃς οὐ καταλυθήσεται. 7 ἐπηρώτησαν δὲ
stone which will not be overthrown. And they questioned

αὐτὸν λέγοντες· διδάσκαλε, πότε οὖν
him saying: Teacher, when therefore

ταῦτα ἔσται; καὶ τί τὸ σημεῖον ὅταν
these things will be? And what [will be] the sign when

μέλλῃ ταῦτα γίνεσθαι; 8 ὁ δὲ εἶπεν·
²are about ¹these things ³to happen? And he said:

βλέπετε μὴ πλανηθῆτε· πολλοὶ γὰρ
Beware lest ye be led astray; for many

ἐλεύσονται ἐπὶ τῷ ὀνόματί μου λέγοντες·
will come on(in) the name of me saying:

ἐγώ εἰμι, καί· ὁ καιρὸς ἤγγικεν· μὴ
I am, and: The time has drawn near; not

πορευθῆτε ὀπίσω αὐτῶν. 9 ὅταν δὲ
go ye after them. And when

ἀκούσητε πολέμους καὶ ἀκαταστασίας, μὴ
ye hear [of] wars and commotions, not

πτοηθῆτε· δεῖ γὰρ ταῦτα γενέσθαι
be ye scared; for it behoves these things to happen

πρῶτον, ἀλλ' οὐκ εὐθέως τὸ τέλος. 10 Τότε
first, but not immediately the end. Then

ἔλεγεν αὐτοῖς· ἐγερθήσεται ἔθνος ἐπ' ἔθνος
he said to them: Will be raised nation against nation

καὶ βασιλεία ἐπὶ βασιλείαν, 11 σεισμοί τε
and kingdom against kingdom, and earthquakes

various places famines and pestilences; and there will be terrors and great signs from heaven. ¹²But before all this they will lay their hands on you and persecute you, delivering you up to the synagogues and prisons, and you will be brought before kings and governors for my name's sake. ¹³This will be a time for you to bear testimony. ¹⁴Settle it therefore in your minds, not to meditate beforehand how to answer; ¹⁵for I will give you a mouth and wisdom, which none of your adversaries will be able to withstand or contradict. ¹⁶You will be delivered up even by parents and brothers and kinsmen and friends, and some of you they will put to death; ¹⁷you will be hated by all for my name's sake. ¹⁸But not a hair of your head will perish. ¹⁹By your endurance you will gain your lives.

20 "But when you see Jerusalem surrounded by armies, then know that its desolation has come near. ²¹Then let those who are in Judea flee to the mountains, and let those who are inside the city depart, and let not

μεγάλοι καὶ κατὰ τόπους λοιμοὶ καὶ λιμοὶ
great   and from place to place† pestilences and famines

ἔσονται, φόβητρά τε καὶ ἀπ' οὐρανοῦ
there will be,   and terrors   and ²from ⁴heaven

σημεῖα μεγάλα ἔσται. 12 πρὸ δὲ τούτων
²signs ¹great there will be.   But before these things

πάντων ἐπιβαλοῦσιν ἐφ' ὑμᾶς τὰς χεῖρας
all   they will lay on   on you the   hands

αὐτῶν καὶ διώξουσιν, παραδιδόντες εἰς τὰς
of them and   will persecute, delivering   to the

συναγωγὰς καὶ φυλακάς, ἀπαγομένους ἐπὶ
synagogues and   prisons,   being led away on(before)

βασιλεῖς καὶ ἡγεμόνας ἕνεκεν τοῦ ὀνόματός
kings   and   governors for the sake of the   name

μου· 13 ἀποβήσεται ὑμῖν εἰς μαρτύριον.
of me;   it will turn out to you for   a testimony.

14 θέτε οὖν ἐν ταῖς καρδίαις ὑμῶν μὴ
Put therefore in the   hearts   of you not

προμελετᾶν ἀπολογηθῆναι· 15 ἐγὼ γὰρ
to practise beforehand to defend [yourselves];   for I

δώσω ὑμῖν στόμα καὶ σοφίαν, ᾗ οὐ
will give you a mouth and   wisdom, which not

δυνήσονται ἀντιστῆναι ἢ ἀντειπεῖν ἅπαντες οἱ
will be able to withstand or to contradict all   the

ἀντικείμενοι ὑμῖν. 16 παραδοθήσεσθε δὲ καὶ
[ones] opposing you.   And ye will be betrayed also

ὑπὸ γονέων καὶ ἀδελφῶν καὶ συγγενῶν
by parents   and   brothers   and   relatives

καὶ φίλων, καὶ θανατώσουσιν ἐξ ὑμῶν,
and friends,   and they will put to death [some] of you,

17 καὶ ἔσεσθε μισούμενοι ὑπὸ πάντων διὰ
and ye will be being hated   by   all men because of

τὸ ὄνομά μου. 18 καὶ θρὶξ ἐκ τῆς
the   name of me.   And a hair of   the

κεφαλῆς ὑμῶν οὐ μὴ ἀπόληται· 19 ἐν τῇ
head   of you by no means will perish;   in the

ὑπομονῇ ὑμῶν κτήσεσθε τὰς ψυχὰς ὑμῶν.
endurance of you ye will gain the   souls   of you.

20 Ὅταν δὲ ἴδητε κυκλουμένην ὑπὸ
But when ye see ²being surrounded ³by

στρατοπέδων Ἰερουσαλήμ, τότε γνῶτε ὅτι
⁴camps ¹Jerusalem,   then know ye that

ἤγγικεν ἡ ἐρήμωσις αὐτῆς. 21 τότε οἱ ἐν
has drawn near the desolation of it.   Then the [ones] in

τῇ Ἰουδαίᾳ φευγέτωσαν εἰς τὰ ὄρη, καὶ
the Judæa let them flee   to the mountains, and

οἱ ἐν μέσῳ αὐτῆς ἐκχωρείτωσαν, καὶ
the [ones] in [the] midst of it   let them depart out,   and

those who are out in the country enter it; [22]for these are days of vengeance, to fulfil all that is written. [23]Alas for those who are with child and for those who give suck in those days! For great distress shall be upon the earth and wrath upon this people; [24]they will fall by the edge of the sword, and be led captive among all nations; and Jerusalem will be trodden down by the Gentiles, until the times of the Gentiles are fulfilled.

25 "And there will be signs in sun and moon and stars, and upon the earth distress of nations in perplexity at the roaring of the sea and the waves, [26]men fainting with fear and with foreboding of what is coming on the world; for the powers of the heavens will be shaken. [27]And then they will see the Son of man coming in a cloud with power and great glory. [28]Now when these things begin to take place, look up and raise your heads, because your redemption is drawing near."

29 And he told them a parable: "Look at the fig tree, and all the trees; [30]as soon as they come out in leaf, you see for

οἱ ἐν ταῖς χώραις μὴ εἰσερχέσθωσαν εἰς
the [ones] in the districts let them not enter into
αὐτήν, 22 ὅτι ἡμέραι ἐκδικήσεως αὗταί
it, because days of vengeance these
εἰσιν τοῦ πλησθῆναι πάντα τὰ γεγραμμένα.
are – to be fulfilled[d] all the things having been written.
23 οὐαὶ ταῖς ἐν γαστρὶ ἐχούσαις καὶ ταῖς
Woe to the pregnant women† and to the
θηλαζούσαις ἐν ἐκείναις ταῖς ἡμέραις·
[ones] giving suck in those – days;
ἔσται γὰρ ἀνάγκη μεγάλη ἐπὶ τῆς γῆς
for there will be distress great on the land
καὶ ὀργὴ τῷ λαῷ τούτῳ, 24 καὶ πεσοῦνται
and wrath – people to this, and they will fall
στόματι μαχαίρης καὶ αἰχμαλωτισθή-
by [the] mouth(edge) of [the] sword and will be led
σονται εἰς τὰ ἔθνη πάντα, καὶ Ἰερουσαλὴμ
captive to the nations all, and Jerusalem
ἔσται πατουμένη ὑπὸ ἐθνῶν, ἄχρι οὗ
will be being trodden down by nations, until
πληρωθῶσιν καιροὶ ἐθνῶν. 25 Καὶ ἔσονται
are accomplished [the] times of [the] nations. And there will be
σημεῖα ἐν ἡλίῳ καὶ σελήνῃ καὶ ἄστροις,
signs in sun and moon and stars,
καὶ ἐπὶ τῆς γῆς συνοχὴ ἐθνῶν ἐν ἀπορίᾳ
and on the earth anxiety of nations in perplexity
ἤχους θαλάσσης καὶ σάλου, 26 ἀποψυχόντων
of [the] sound of [the] sea and surf, fainting
                                              =while men faint
ἀνθρώπων ἀπὸ φόβου καὶ προσδοκίας τῶν
men[a] from fear and expectation of the
ἐπερχομένων τῇ οἰκουμένῃ· αἱ γὰρ δυνάμεις
things coming on the inhabited earth; for the powers
τῶν οὐρανῶν σαλευθήσονται. 27 καὶ τότε
of the heavens will be shaken. And then
ὄψονται τὸν υἱὸν τοῦ ἀνθρώπου ἐρχόμενον
they will see the Son – of man coming
ἐν νεφέλῃ μετὰ δυνάμεως καὶ δόξης
in a cloud with power and glory
πολλῆς. 28 ἀρχομένων δὲ τούτων γίνεσθαι
much(great). And beginning these things[a] to happen
                                         =when these things begin
ἀνακύψατε καὶ ἐπάρατε τὰς κεφαλὰς ὑμῶν,
stand erect and lift up the heads of you,
διότι ἐγγίζει ἡ ἀπολύτρωσις ὑμῶν. 29 Καὶ
because draws near the redemption of you. And
εἶπεν παραβολὴν αὐτοῖς· ἴδετε τὴν συκῆν
he told a parable[1] them: Ye see the fig-tree
καὶ πάντα τὰ δένδρα· 30 ὅταν προβάλωσιν
and all the trees; when [a]they burst into leaf

yourselves and know that
the summer is already
near. [31] So also, when you
see these things taking
place, you know that the
kingdom of God is near.
[32] Truly, I say to you,
this generation will not
pass away till all has
taken place. [33] Heaven
and earth will pass away,
but my words will not
pass away.

34 "But take heed to
yourselves lest your
hearts be weighed down
with dissipation and
drunkenness and cares of
this life, and that day
come upon you suddenly
like a snare; [35] for it will
come upon all who dwell
upon the face of the
whole earth. [36] But watch
at all times, praying that
you may have strength
to escape all these things
that will take place, and
to stand before the Son
of man."

37 And every day he
was teaching in the
temple, but at night he
went out and lodged on
the mount called Olivet.
[38] And early in the morning all the people came
to him in the temple to
hear him.

ἤδη, βλέποντες ἀφ᾽ ἑαυτῶν γινώσκετε ὅτι
now, seeing from(of) yourselves ye know that
ἤδη ἐγγὺς τὸ θέρος ἐστίν· 31 οὕτως καὶ
now near the summer is; so also
ὑμεῖς, ὅταν ἴδητε ταῦτα γινόμενα,
ye, when ye see these things happening,
γινώσκετε ὅτι ἐγγύς ἐστιν ἡ βασιλεία
know that near is the kingdom
τοῦ θεοῦ. 32 ἀμὴν λέγω ὑμῖν ὅτι οὐ μὴ
– of God. Truly I tell you that by no means
παρέλθῃ ἡ γενεὰ αὕτη ἕως ἂν πάντα
will pass away – generation this until all things
γένηται. 33 ὁ οὐρανὸς καὶ ἡ γῆ παρ-
happens. The heaven and the earth will
ελεύσονται, οἱ δὲ λόγοι μου οὐ μὴ παρελεύ-
pass away, but the words of me by no means will pass
σονται. 34 Προσέχετε δὲ ἑαυτοῖς μήποτε
away. And take heed to yourselves lest
βαρηθῶσιν ὑμῶν αἱ καρδίαι ἐν κραιπάλῃ
become burdened of you the hearts with surfeiting
καὶ μέθῃ καὶ μερίμναις βιωτικαῖς, καὶ
and deep drinking and anxieties of life,† and
ἐπιστῇ ἐφ᾽ ὑμᾶς αἰφνίδιος ἡ ἡμέρα ἐκείνη
come on on you suddenly – day that
35 ὡς παγίς· ἐπεισελεύσεται γὰρ ἐπὶ πάντας
as a snare; for it will come in on on all
τοὺς καθημένους ἐπὶ πρόσωπον πάσης τῆς
the [ones] sitting on [the] face of all the
γῆς. 36 ἀγρυπνεῖτε δὲ ἐν παντὶ καιρῷ
earth. But be ye watchful at every time
δεόμενοι ἵνα κατισχύσητε ἐκφυγεῖν ταῦτα
begging that ye may be able to escape these things
πάντα τὰ μέλλοντα γίνεσθαι, καὶ σταθῆναι
all – being about to happen, and to stand
ἔμπροσθεν τοῦ υἱοῦ τοῦ ἀνθρώπου.
before the Son – of man.
37 Ἦν δὲ τὰς ἡμέρας ἐν τῷ ἱερῷ
Now he was [in] the days in the temple
διδάσκων, τὰς δὲ νύκτας ἐξερχόμενος
teaching, and [in] the nights going forth
ηὐλίζετο εἰς τὸ ὄρος τὸ καλούμενον
he lodged in the mountain – being called
ἐλαιῶν. 38 καὶ πᾶς ὁ λαὸς ὤρθριζεν
of olives. And all the people came in the morning
πρὸς αὐτὸν ἐν τῷ ἱερῷ ἀκούειν αὐτοῦ.
to him in the temple to hear him.

CHAPTER 22

NOW the feast of Unleavened Bread drew near, which is called the Passover. ²And the chief priests and the scribes were seeking how to put him to death; for they feared the people.

3 Then Satan entered into Judas called Iscariot, who was of the number of the twelve; ⁴he went away and conferred with the chief priests and captains how he might betray him to them. ⁵And they were glad, and engaged to give him money. ⁶So he agreed, and sought an opportunity to betray him to them in the absence of the multitude.

7 Then came the day of Unleavened Bread, on which the passover lamb had to be sacrificed. ⁸So Jesus sent Peter and John, saying, "Go and prepare the passover for us, that we may eat it." ⁹They said to him, "Where will you have us prepare it?" ¹⁰He said to them, "Behold, when you have entered the city, a man carrying a jar of water will meet you; follow him into the house which he enters, ¹¹and tell the householder, 'The Teacher says to you, Where is the guest room, where I am to eat the passover with

---

22 Ἤγγιζεν δὲ ἡ ἑορτὴ τῶν ἀζύμων ἡ
Now drew near   the   feast   of unleavened bread –

λεγομένη πάσχα. **2** καὶ ἐζήτουν οἱ ἀρχιερεῖς
being called Passover.   And   ⁶sought ¹the ²chief priests

καὶ οἱ γραμματεῖς τὸ πῶς ἀνέλωσιν
³and ⁴the   ⁵scribes   –   how they might destroy

αὐτόν· ἐφοβοῦντο γὰρ τὸν λαόν. **3** Εἰσῆλθεν δὲ
him;   for they feared   the   people.   And entered

σατανᾶς εἰς Ἰούδαν τὸν καλούμενον
Satan   into   Judas   –   being called

Ἰσκαριώτην, ὄντα ἐκ τοῦ ἀριθμοῦ τῶν
Iscariot,   being of   the   number   of the

δώδεκα· **4** καὶ ἀπελθὼν συνελάλησεν τοῖς
twelve;   and   going   he conversed with the

ἀρχιερεῦσιν καὶ στρατηγοῖς τὸ πῶς αὐτοῖς
chief priests   and   captains   –   how   to them

παραδῷ αὐτόν. **5** καὶ ἐχάρησαν, καὶ
he might betray him.   And   they rejoiced,   and

συνέθεντο αὐτῷ ἀργύριον δοῦναι. **6** καὶ
they agreed   ²him   ³money   ¹to give.   And

ἐξωμολόγησεν, καὶ ἐζήτει εὐκαιρίαν τοῦ
he fully consented,   and   sought   opportunity   –

παραδοῦναι αὐτὸν ἄτερ ὄχλου αὐτοῖς.
to betray[d]   him   apart from a crowd   to them.

7 Ἦλθεν δὲ ἡ ἡμέρα τῶν ἀζύμων, ᾗ
And came   the   day   of unleavened bread, on which

ἔδει θύεσθαι τὸ πάσχα· **8** καὶ ἀπέστειλεν
it behoved to kill   the passover [lamb];   and   he sent

Πέτρον καὶ Ἰωάννην εἰπών· πορευθέντες
Peter   and   John   saying :   Going

ἑτοιμάσατε ἡμῖν τὸ πάσχα, ἵνα φάγωμεν. **9** οἱ
prepare ye   for us the passover,   that we may eat.   they

δὲ εἶπαν αὐτῷ· ποῦ θέλεις ἑτοιμάσωμεν;
And said   to him : Where wishest thou [that] we may prepare?

10 ὁ δὲ εἶπεν αὐτοῖς· ἰδοὺ εἰσελθόντων
And he   told   them :   Behold[,]   entering
                                            =as ye enter

ὑμῶν εἰς τὴν πόλιν συναντήσει ὑμῖν
you[a]   into   the   city   will meet   you

ἄνθρωπος κεράμιον ὕδατος βαστάζων·
a man   a pitcher   of water   bearing;

ἀκολουθήσατε αὐτῷ εἰς τὴν οἰκίαν εἰς ἣν
follow   him   into   the   house   into which

εἰσπορεύεται· **11** καὶ ἐρεῖτε τῷ οἰκοδεσπότῃ
he enters;   and ye will say to the   house-master

τῆς οἰκίας· λέγει σοι ὁ διδάσκαλος·
of the   house :   Says   to thee the   teacher :

ποῦ ἐστιν τὸ κατάλυμα ὅπου τὸ πάσχα
Where   is   the   guest room   where   the   passover

my disciples?' [12]And he will show you a large upper room furnished; there make ready." [13]And they went, and found it as he had told them; and they prepared the passover.

14 And when the hour came, he sat at table, and the apostles with him. [15]And he said to them, "I have earnestly desired to eat this passover with you before I suffer; [16]for I tell you I shall not eat it[i] until it is fulfilled in the kingdom of God." [17]And he took a cup, and when he had given thanks he said, "Take this, and divide it among yourselves; [18]for I tell you that from now on I shall not drink of the fruit of the vine until the kingdom of God comes." [19]And he took bread, and when he had given thanks he broke it and gave it to them, saying, "This is my body.[j] [21]But

---

μετὰ τῶν μαθητῶν μου φαγω; 12 κἀκεῖνος
with   the   disciples   of me I may eat?   And that man

ὑμῖν δείξει ἀνάγαιον μέγα ἐστρωμένον·
you   will show   upper room   a large   having been spread;[*]

ἐκεῖ ἑτοιμάσατε. 13 ἀπελθόντες δὲ εὗρον
there   prepare ye.   And going   they found

καθὼς εἰρήκει αὐτοῖς, καὶ ἡτοίμασαν τὸ
as   he had told   them,   and   they prepared   the

πάσχα. 14 Καὶ ὅτε ἐγένετο ἡ ὥρα,
passover.   And, when   came   the   hour,

ἀνέπεσεν, καὶ οἱ ἀπόστολοι σὺν αὐτῷ.
he reclined,   and   the   apostles   with   him.

15 καὶ εἶπεν πρὸς αὐτούς· ἐπιθυμίᾳ
And   he said   to   them: With desire

ἐπεθύμησα τοῦτο τὸ πάσχα φαγεῖν μεθ'
I desired   this   —   passover   to eat   with

ὑμῶν πρὸ τοῦ με παθεῖν· 16 λέγω γὰρ
you   before   the   me   to suffer;[b]   for I tell
                =I suffer;

ὑμῖν ὅτι οὐκέτι οὐ μὴ φάγω αὐτὸ
you   that   no more by no(any) means I eat   it

ἕως ὅτου πληρωθῇ ἐν τῇ βασιλείᾳ τοῦ θεοῦ.
until   it is fulfilled   in   the   kingdom   — of God.

17 καὶ δεξάμενος ποτήριον εὐχαριστήσας
And   taking   a cup   having given thanks

εἶπεν· λάβετε τοῦτο καὶ διαμερίσατε εἰς
he said: Take   this   and   divide   among

ἑαυτούς· 18 λέγω γὰρ ὑμῖν, οὐ μὴ πίω
yourselves;   for I tell   you,   by no means I drink

ἀπὸ τοῦ νῦν ἀπὸ τοῦ γενήματος τῆς
from   —   now [on]   from   the   produce   of the

ἀμπέλου ἕως οὗ ἡ βασιλεία τοῦ θεοῦ
vine   until   the   kingdom   — of God

ἔλθῃ. 19 καὶ λαβὼν ἄρτον εὐχαριστήσας
comes.   And   taking   a loaf   having given thanks

ἔκλασεν καὶ ἔδωκεν αὐτοῖς λέγων· τοῦτό
he broke   and   gave   to them   saying: This

ἐστιν τὸ σῶμά μου [τὸ ὑπὲρ ὑμῶν
is   the   body   of me   —   for   you

διδόμενον· τοῦτο ποιεῖτε εἰς τὴν ἐμὴν
being given;   this   do ye   for   —   my

ἀνάμνησιν. 20 καὶ τὸ ποτήριον ὡσαύτως
memorial.   And   the   cup   similarly

μετὰ τὸ δειπνῆσαι, λέγων· τοῦτο τὸ
after   the   to sup,   saying: This   —

ποτήριον ἡ καινὴ διαθήκη ἐν τῷ αἵματί
cup [is]   the   new   covenant   in the   blood

---

[i] Other ancient authorities read never eat it again

[j] Other ancient authorities add which is given for you. Do this in remembrance of me. [20]And likewise the cup after supper, saying, "This cup which is poured out for you is the new covenant in my blood"

[*] That is, with carpets, and the dining couches supplied with cushions.

behold the hand of him who betrays me is with me on the table. [22]For the Son of man goes as it has been determined; but woe to that man by whom he is betrayed!" [23]And they began to question one another, which of them it was that would do this.

24 A dispute also arose among them, which of them was to be regarded as the greatest. [25]And he said to them, "The kings of the Gentiles exercise lordship over them; and those in authority over them are called benefactors. [26]But not so with you; rather let the greatest among you become as the youngest, and the leader as one who serves. [27]For which is the greater, one who sits at table, or one who serves? Is it not the one who sits at table? But I am among you as one who serves.

28 "You are those who have continued with me in my trials; [29]as my Father appointed a kingdom for me, so do I appoint for you [30]that you may eat and drink at my table in my kingdom, and sit on thrones

μου, τὸ ὑπὲρ ὑμῶν ἐκχυννόμενον.] 21 πλὴν
of me, - for you being shed. However

ἰδοὺ ἡ χεὶρ τοῦ παραδιδόντος με μετ᾽
behold[,] the hand of the [one] betraying me with

ἐμοῦ ἐπὶ τῆς τραπέζης. 22 ὅτι ὁ υἱὸς μὲν
me on the table. Because the Son indeed

τοῦ ἀνθρώπου κατὰ τὸ ὡρισμένον
of man according to the [thing] having been determined

πορεύεται, πλὴν οὐαὶ τῷ ἀνθρώπῳ ἐκείνῳ
goes, nevertheless woe - man to that

δι᾽ οὗ παραδίδοται. 23 καὶ αὐτοὶ ἤρξαντο
through whom he is betrayed. And they began

συζητεῖν πρὸς ἑαυτοὺς τὸ τίς ἄρα εἴη
to debate with themselves - who then it might be

ἐξ αὐτῶν ὁ τοῦτο μέλλων πράσσειν.
of them the [one] this being about to do.

24 Ἐγένετο δὲ καὶ φιλονεικία ἐν αὐτοῖς,
And there was also a rivalry among them,

τὸ τίς αὐτῶν δοκεῖ εἶναι μείζων. 25 ὁ δὲ
- who of them seems to be greater. So he

εἶπεν αὐτοῖς· οἱ βασιλεῖς τῶν ἐθνῶν
said to them: The kings of the nations

κυριεύουσιν αὐτῶν, καὶ οἱ ἐξουσιάζοντες
lord it over them, and the [ones] having authority over

αὐτῶν εὐεργέται καλοῦνται. 26 ὑμεῖς δὲ
them benefactors are called. But ye

οὐχ οὕτως, ἀλλ᾽ ὁ μείζων ἐν ὑμῖν
not so, but the greater among you

γινέσθω ὡς ὁ νεώτερος, καὶ ὁ ἡγούμενος
let him become as the younger, and the [one] governing

ὡς ὁ διακονῶν. 27 τίς γὰρ μείζων, ὁ
as the [one] serving. For who [is] greater, the

ἀνακείμενος ἢ ὁ διακονῶν; οὐχὶ ὁ
[one] reclining or the [one] serving? not the

ἀνακείμενος; ἐγὼ δὲ ἐν μέσῳ ὑμῶν εἰμι
[one] reclining? But I in [the] midst of you am

ὡς ὁ διακονῶν. 28 ὑμεῖς δέ ἐστε οἱ
as the [one] serving. But ye are the [ones]

διαμεμενηκότες μετ᾽ ἐμοῦ ἐν τοῖς πειρα-
having remained throughout with me in the tempta-

σμοῖς μου· 29 κἀγὼ διατίθεμαι ὑμῖν καθὼς
tions of me; and I appoint to you as

διέθετό μοι ὁ πατήρ μου βασιλείαν,
appointed to me the Father of me a kingdom,

30 ἵνα ἔσθητε καὶ πίνητε ἐπὶ τῆς τραπέζης
that ye may eat and drink at the table

μου ἐν τῇ βασιλείᾳ μου, καὶ καθήσεσθε
of me in the kingdom of me, and ye will sit

judging the twelve tribes of Israel.

31 "Simon, Simon, behold, Satan demanded to have you,[u] that he might sift you[u] like wheat, 32 but I have prayed for you that your faith may not fail; and when you have turned again, strengthen your brethren." 33 And he said to him, "Lord, I am ready to go with you to prison and to death." 34 He said, "I tell you, Peter, the cock will not crow this day, until you three times deny that you know me."

35 And he said to them, "When I sent you out with no purse or bag or sandals, did you lack anything?" They said, "Nothing." 36 He said to them, "But now, let him who has a purse take it, and likewise a bag. And let him who has no sword sell his mantle and buy one. 37 For I tell you that this scripture must be fulfilled in me, 'And he was reckoned with transgressors'; for what is written about me has its fulfilment." 38 And they said, "Look, Lord, here are two swords." And he said to them, "It is enough."

39 And he came out, and went, as was his

[u] The Greek word for *you* here is plural; in verse 32 it is singular

ἐπὶ θρόνων τὰς δώδεκα φυλὰς κρίνοντες
on thrones ²the ³twelve ⁴tribes ¹judging

τοῦ Ἰσραήλ. 31 Σίμων Σίμων, ἰδοὺ ὁ
of Israel. Simon[,] Simon, behold[,] -

σατανᾶς ἐξητήσατο ὑμᾶς τοῦ σινιάσαι ὡς
Satan begged earnestly for you - to sift[d] as

τὸν σῖτον· 32 ἐγὼ δὲ ἐδεήθην περὶ σοῦ
the wheat; but I requested concerning thee

ἵνα μὴ ἐκλίπῃ ἡ πίστις σου· καὶ σύ
that might not fail the faith of thee; and thou

ποτε ἐπιστρέψας στήρισον τοὺς ἀδελφούς
when having turned support the brothers

σου. 33 ὁ δὲ εἶπεν αὐτῷ· κύριε, μετὰ
of thee. And he said to him : Lord, with

σοῦ ἕτοιμός εἰμι καὶ εἰς φυλακὴν καὶ εἰς
thee prepared I am both to prison and to

θάνατον πορεύεσθαι. 34 ὁ δὲ εἶπεν· λέγω
death to go. But he said : I tell

σοι, Πέτρε, οὐ φωνήσει σήμερον ἀλέκτωρ
thee, Peter, will not sound to-day a cock

ἕως τρίς με ἀπαρνήσῃ μὴ εἰδέναι. 35 Καὶ
until thrice me thou wilt deny not to know. And

εἶπεν αὐτοῖς· ὅτε ἀπέστειλα ὑμᾶς ἄτερ
he said to them : When I sent you without

βαλλαντίου καὶ πήρας καὶ ὑποδημάτων, μή
a purse and a wallet and sandals, *not*

τινος ὑστερήσατε; οἱ δὲ εἶπαν· οὐθενός.
of anything were ye short? And they said : Of nothing.

36 εἶπεν δὲ αὐτοῖς· ἀλλὰ νῦν ὁ ἔχων
And he said to them : But now the [one] having

βαλλάντιον ἀράτω, ὁμοίως καὶ πήραν, καὶ
a purse let him take [it], likewise also a wallet, and

ὁ μὴ ἔχων πωλησάτω τὸ ἱμάτιον αὐτοῦ
the [one] not having let him sell the garment of him

καὶ ἀγορασάτω μάχαιραν. 37 λέγω γὰρ
and let him buy a sword. For I tell

ὑμῖν ὅτι τοῦτο τὸ γεγραμμένον δεῖ
you that this - having been written it behoves

τελεσθῆναι ἐν ἐμοί, τό· καὶ μετὰ ἀνόμων
to be finished in me, - And with lawless men

ἐλογίσθη· καὶ γὰρ τὸ περὶ ἐμοῦ τέλος
he was reckoned; for indeed the thing concerning me an end

ἔχει. 38 οἱ δὲ εἶπαν· κύριε, ἰδοὺ μάχαιραι
has. And they said : Lord, behold[,] swords

ὧδε δύο. ὁ δὲ εἶπεν αὐτοῖς· ἱκανόν ἐστιν.
here two. And he said to them : Enough it is.

39 Καὶ ἐξελθὼν ἐπορεύθη κατὰ τὸ ἔθος
And going forth he went according to the(his) habit

custom, to the Mount of Olives; and the disciples followed him. [40]And when he came to the place he said to them, "Pray that you may not enter into temptation." [41]And he withdrew from them about a stone's throw, and knelt down and prayed, [42]"Father, if thou art willing, remove this cup from me; nevertheless not my will, but thine, be done." [43]And there appeared to him an angel from heaven, strengthening him. [44]And being in an agony he prayed more earnestly; and his sweat became like great drops of blood falling down upon the ground.[v] [45]And when he rose from prayer, he came to the disciples and found them sleeping for sorrow, [46]and he said to them, "Why do you sleep? Rise and pray that you may not enter into temptation."

[47] While he was still speaking, there came a crowd, and the man called Judas, one of the twelve, was leading them. He drew near to Jesus to kiss him; [48]but Jesus said to him, "Judas, would you betray the Son of man with a kiss?" [49]And when those who

εἰς τὸ ὄρος τῶν ἐλαιῶν· ἠκολούθησαν δὲ
to the mountain of the olives; and [4]followed

αὐτῷ καὶ οἱ μαθηταί. 40 γενόμενος δὲ
[5]him [3]also [1]the [2]disciples. And coming

ἐπὶ τοῦ τόπου εἶπεν αὐτοῖς· προσεύχεσθε
upon the place he said to them : Pray ye

μὴ εἰσελθεῖν εἰς πειρασμόν. 41 καὶ αὐτὸς
not to enter into temptation. And he

ἀπεσπάσθη ἀπ' αὐτῶν ὡσεὶ λίθου βολὴν,
was withdrawn from them about of a stone a throw,

καὶ θεὶς τὰ γόνατα προσηύχετο 42 λέγων·
and placing the knees he prayed saying :

πάτερ, εἰ βούλει παρένεγκε τοῦτο τὸ
Father, if thou wilt take away this -

ποτήριον ἀπ' ἐμοῦ· πλὴν μὴ τὸ θέλημά
cup from me; nevertheless not the will

μου ἀλλὰ τὸ σὸν γινέσθω. 43 [ὤφθη δὲ
of me but - thine let be. And appeared

αὐτῷ ἄγγελος ἀπ' οὐρανοῦ ἐνισχύων αὐτόν.
to him an angel from heaven strengthening him.

44 καὶ γενόμενος ἐν ἀγωνίᾳ ἐκτενέστερον
And becoming in an agony more earnestly

προσηύχετο· καὶ ἐγένετο ὁ ἱδρὼς αὐτοῦ
he prayed; and became the sweat of him

ὡσεὶ θρόμβοι αἵματος καταβαίνοντες ἐπὶ
as drops of blood falling down onto

τὴν γῆν.] 45 καὶ ἀναστὰς ἀπὸ τῆς
the earth. And rising up from the

προσευχῆς, ἐλθὼν πρὸς τοὺς μαθητὰς
prayer, coming to the disciples

εὗρεν κοιμωμένους αὐτοὺς ἀπὸ τῆς λύπης,
he found [2]sleeping [1]them from the grief,

46 καὶ εἶπεν αὐτοῖς· τί καθεύδετε;
and said to them : Why sleep ye?

ἀναστάντες προσεύχεσθε, ἵνα μὴ εἰσέλθητε
rising up pray ye, lest ye enter

εἰς πειρασμόν. 47 Ἔτι αὐτοῦ λαλοῦντος
into temptation. Yet him speaking[a]
= While he was yet speaking

ἰδοὺ ὄχλος, καὶ ὁ λεγόμενος Ἰούδας εἷς
behold[,] a crowd, and the [one] being named Judas one

τῶν δώδεκα προήρχετο αὐτούς, καὶ ἤγγισεν
of the twelve came before them, and drew near

τῷ Ἰησοῦ φιλῆσαι αὐτόν. 48 Ἰησοῦς δὲ
- to Jesus to kiss him. But Jesus

εἶπεν αὐτῷ· Ἰούδα, φιλήματι τὸν υἱὸν
said to him : Judas, with a kiss the Son

τοῦ ἀνθρώπου παραδίδως; 49 ἰδόντες δὲ
- of man betrayest thou? And [4]seeing

[v] Other ancient authorities omit verses 43 and 44

were about him saw what would follow, they said, "Lord, shall we strike with the sword?" [50]And one of them struck the slave of the high priest and cut off his right ear. [51]But Jesus said, "No more of this!" And he touched his ear and healed him. [52]Then Jesus said to the chief priests and captains of the temple and elders, who had come out against him, "Have you come out as against a robber, with swords and clubs? [53]When I was with you day after day in the temple, you did not lay hands on me. But this is your hour, and the power of darkness."

54 Then they seized him and led him away, bringing him into the high priest's house. Peter followed at a distance; [55]and when they had kindled a fire in the middle of the courtyard and sat down together, Peter sat among them. [56]Then a maid, seeing him as he sat in the light and gazing at him, said, "This man also was with him." [57]But he denied it, saying, "Woman, I do not know

οἱ   περὶ αὐτὸν   τὸ   ἐσόμενον εἶπαν· κύριε,
[1]the [ones] [2]round [3]him the thing going to be said : Lord,

εἰ πατάξομεν ἐν μαχαίρῃ; 50 καὶ ἐπάταξεν
if we shall strike with   a sword?   And   [4]struck

εἶς   τις   ἐξ   αὐτῶν   τοῦ   ἀρχιερέως   τὸν
[1]a certain one [2]of [3]them [7]of the [5]high priest [6]the

δοῦλον καὶ   ἀφεῖλεν   τὸ   οὖς   αὐτοῦ   τὸ
[8]slave and   cut off [1]the [2]ear [4]of him −

δεξιόν.   51 ἀποκριθεὶς   δὲ   ὁ   Ἰησοῦς   εἶπεν·
[3]right.   And answering   −   Jesus   said :

ἐᾶτε   ἕως   τούτου·   καὶ   ἁψάμενος   τοῦ
Permit ye until   this;   and   touching   the

ὠτίου   ἰάσατο   αὐτόν.   52 Εἶπεν   δὲ   Ἰησοῦς
ear   he cured   him.   And said   Jesus

πρὸς   τοὺς   παραγενομένους   ἐπ'   αὐτὸν
to   [1]the   [2]coming   [11]upon   [11]him

ἀρχιερεῖς   καὶ   στρατηγοὺς   τοῦ   ἱεροῦ   καὶ
[1]chief priests [2]and [4]captains [5]of the [6]temple [7]and

πρεσβυτέρους·   ὡς   ἐπὶ   λῃστὴν   ἐξήλθατε
[8]elders :   As   against a robber   came ye out

μετὰ   μαχαιρῶν   καὶ   ξύλων;   53 καθ'   ἡμέραν
with   swords   and   clubs?   daily

ὄντος   μου   μεθ'   ὑμῶν   ἐν   τῷ   ἱερῷ   οὐκ
being me[a] with   you   in   the   temple   not
=while I was

ἐξετείνατε   τὰς   χεῖρας   ἐπ'   ἐμέ·   ἀλλ'   αὕτη
ye stretched out the(your) hands against me;   but   this

ἐστὶν   ὑμῶν   ἡ   ὥρα   καὶ   ἡ   ἐξουσία   τοῦ
is   of you   the   hour   and   the   authority   of the

σκότους.
darkness.

54 Συλλαβόντες   δὲ   αὐτὸν   ἤγαγον   καὶ
And having arrested   him   they led   and

εἰσήγαγον   εἰς   τὴν   οἰκίαν   τοῦ   ἀρχιερέως·
brought in   into   the   house   of the   high priest;

ὁ   δὲ   Πέτρος   ἠκολούθει   μακρόθεν.   55 περι-
− and   Peter   followed   afar off.   light-

αψάντων   δὲ   πῦρ   ἐν   μέσῳ   τῆς   αὐλῆς   καὶ
ing   And a fire in [the] centre of the   court   and
=when they had lit a fire . . . and had sat down together

συγκαθισάντων   ἐκάθητο   ὁ   Πέτρος   μέσος
sitting down together   sat   −   Peter   among

αὐτῶν.   56 ἰδοῦσα   δὲ   αὐτὸν   παιδίσκη   τις
them.   And [2]seeing   [3]him [1]a certain maidservant

καθήμενον   πρὸς   τὸ   φῶς   καὶ   ἀτενίσασα
sitting   near   the   light   and   gazing at

αὐτῷ   εἶπεν·   καὶ   οὗτος   σὺν   αὐτῷ   ἦν.   57 ὁ
him   said :   And this man with   him   was.   he

δὲ   ἠρνήσατο   λέγων·   οὐκ   οἶδα   αὐτόν,
But   denied   saying :   I know not   him,

him." ⁵⁸And a little later
some one else saw him
and said, "You also are
one of them." But Peter
said, "Man, I am not."
⁵⁹And after an interval
of about an hour still
another insisted, saying,
"Certainly this man also
was with him; for he is a
Galilean." ⁶⁰But Peter
said, "Man, I do not
know what you are say-
ing." And immediately,
while he was still
speaking, the cock
crowed. ⁶⁵And the Lord
turned and looked at
Peter. And Peter re-
membered the word of
the Lord, how he had
said to him, "Before the
cock crows today, you
will deny me three
times." ⁶²And he went
out and wept bitterly.

63 Now the men who
were holding Jesus
mocked him and beat
him; ⁶⁴they also blind-
folded him and asked
him, "Prophesy! Who is
it that struck you?"
⁶⁵And they spoke many
other words against him,
reviling him.

66 When day came,
the assembly of the elders
of the people gathered
together, both chief
priests and scribes; and
they led him away to their
council, and they said,
⁶⁷"If you are the Christ,

γύναι.   58 καὶ   μετὰ   βραχὺ   ἕτερος   ἰδὼν
woman.   And   after   a short while   another   seeing

αὐτὸν   ἔφη·   καὶ   σὺ   ἐξ   αὐτῶν   εἶ.   ὁ
him   said: And   thou   of   them   art.   -

δὲ   Πέτρος   ἔφη·   ἄνθρωπε,   οὐκ   εἰμί.
But   Peter   said: Man,   I am not.

59 καὶ   διαστάσης   ὡσεὶ   ὥρας   μιᾶς   ἄλλος
And   intervening   about   hour   oneᵃ   ²other man
      =when about an hour had intervened

τις   διϊσχυρίζετο   λέγων·   ἐπ᾽   ἀληθείας   καὶ
¹a cer-   emphatically   saying: Of a truth   also
tain   asserted

οὗτος   μετ᾽   αὐτοῦ   ἦν,   καὶ   γὰρ   Γαλιλαῖός
this man   with   him   was,   for indeed   a Galilæan

ἐστιν.   60 εἶπεν   δὲ   ὁ   Πέτρος·   ἄνθρωπε,
he is.   But said   -   Peter: Man,

οὐκ   οἶδα   ὃ   λέγεις.   καὶ   παραχρῆμα   ἔτι
I know not   what thou sayest.   And   at once   yet

λαλοῦντος   αὐτοῦ   ἐφώνησεν   ἀλέκτωρ.   61 καὶ
speaking   himᵃ   sounded   a cock.   And
=while he was yet speaking

στραφεὶς   ὁ   κύριος   ἐνέβλεψεν   τῷ   Πέτρῳ,
turning   the   Lord   looked at   -   Peter,

καὶ   ὑπεμνήσθη   ὁ   Πέτρος   τοῦ   λόγου   τοῦ
and   remembered   -   Peter   the   word of the

κυρίου,   ὡς   εἶπεν   αὐτῷ   ὅτι   πρὶν   ἀλέκτορα
Lord,   as   he told   him   that   before   a cock

φωνῆσαι   σήμερον   ἀπαρνήσῃ   με   τρίς.   62 καὶ
to soundᵇ   to-day   thou wilt deny   me   thrice.   And

ἐξελθὼν   ἔξω   ἔκλαυσεν   πικρῶς.   63 Καὶ   οἱ
going out   outside   he wept   bitterly.   And   the

ἄνδρες   οἱ   συνέχοντες   αὐτὸν   ἐνέπαιζον   αὐτῷ
men   -   having in charge   him*   mocked   him

δέροντες,   64 καὶ   περικαλύψαντες   αὐτὸν
beating,   and   covering over   him

ἐπηρώτων   λέγοντες·   προφήτευσον,   τίς   ἐστιν
questioned   saying: Prophesy,   who   is

ὁ   παίσας   σε;   65 καὶ   ἕτερα   πολλὰ
the [one]   playing   thee?   And   other things   many

βλασφημοῦντες   ἔλεγον   εἰς   αὐτόν.
blaspheming   they said   against   him.

66 Καὶ   ὡς   ἐγένετο   ἡμέρα,   συνήχθη   τὸ
And   when   came   day,   was assembled the

πρεσβυτέριον   τοῦ   λαοῦ,   ἀρχιερεῖς   τε   καὶ
body of elders   of the   people,   both chief priests   and

γραμματεῖς,   καὶ   ἀπήγαγον   αὐτὸν   εἰς   τὸ
scribes,   and   led away   him   to   the

συνέδριον   αὐτῶν,   67 λέγοντες·   εἰ   σὺ   εἶ   ὁ
council   of them,   saying: If   thou   art   the

* That is, Jesus (as some texts have it).

tell us." But he said to
them, "If I tell you, you
will not believe; [68]and if
I ask you, you will not
answer. [69]But from now
on the Son of man shall
be seated at the right
hand of the power of
God." [70]And they all
said, "Are you the Son
of God, then?" And he
said to them, "You say
that I am." [71]And they
said, "What further
testimony do we need?
We have heard it our-
selves from his own lips."

χριστός,   εἰπὸν   ἡμῖν.   εἶπεν   δὲ   αὐτοῖς·
Christ,   tell   us.   And he said   to them :

ἐὰν   ὑμῖν   εἴπω,   οὐ μὴ πιστεύσητε·   68 ἐὰν
If   you   I tell, by no means will ye believe;   [2]if

δὲ   ἐρωτήσω,   οὐ μὴ ἀποκριθῆτε.   69 ἀπὸ
[1]and I question, by no means will ye answer.   [3]from

τοῦ   νῦν   δὲ   ἔσται   ὁ   υἱὸς   τοῦ   ἀνθρώπου
-     [3]now [1]But [2]will be [4]the [5]Son   -   [6]of man

καθήμενος   ἐκ   δεξιῶν   τῆς   δυνάμεως   τοῦ
[8]sitting   at [the] right of the power   -

θεοῦ.   70 εἶπαν   δὲ   πάντες·   σὺ οὖν   εἶ ὁ
of God.   And they said all :   Thou therefore art the

υἱὸς   τοῦ   θεοῦ;   ὁ   δὲ   πρὸς   αὐτοὺς   ἔφη·
Son   -   of God? And he   to   them   said :

ὑμεῖς   λέγετε   ὅτι   ἐγώ   εἰμι.   71 οἱ   δὲ
Ye   say   that   I   am.   And they

εἶπαν·   τί   ἔτι   ἔχομεν   μαρτυρίας   χρείαν;
said :   Why yet have we of witness   need ?

αὐτοὶ   γὰρ   ἠκούσαμεν   ἀπὸ   τοῦ   στόματος
for [our]selves we heard   from   the   mouth

αὐτοῦ.
of him.

CHAPTER 23

THEN the whole
company of them
arose, and brought him
before Pilate. [2]And they
began to accuse him,
saying, "We found this
man perverting our
nation, and forbidding
us to give tribute to
Caesar, and saying that
he himself is Christ a
king." [3]And Pilate asked
him, "Are you the King
of the Jews?" And he
answered him, "You have
said so." [4]And Pilate said
to the chief priests and
the multitudes, "I find
no crime in this man."

23 Καὶ   ἀναστὰν   ἅπαν   τὸ   πλῆθος   αὐτῶν
And   rising up   all   the   multitude of them

ἤγαγον   αὐτὸν   ἐπὶ   τὸν   Πιλᾶτον.   2 ἤρξαντο
led   him   before -   Pilate.   they began

δὲ   κατηγορεῖν   αὐτοῦ   λέγοντες·   τοῦτον
And to accuse   him   saying :   This man

εὕραμεν   διαστρέφοντα   τὸ   ἔθνος   ἡμῶν   καὶ
we found perverting   the   nation of us   and

κωλύοντα   φόρους   Καίσαρι   διδόναι,   καὶ
forbidding tribute   to Cæsar   to give,   and

λέγοντα   ἑαυτὸν   χριστὸν   βασιλέα   εἶναι.
saying   himself   Christ   a king   to be.

3 ὁ   δὲ   Πιλᾶτος   ἠρώτησεν   αὐτὸν   λέγων·
-   And   Pilate   questioned   him   saying :

σὺ   εἶ   ὁ   βασιλεὺς   τῶν   Ἰουδαίων;   ὁ   δὲ
Thou art the king   of the   Jews?   And he

ἀποκριθεὶς   αὐτῷ   ἔφη·   σὺ   λέγεις.   4 ὁ   δὲ
answering   him   said : Thou sayest.   - And

Πιλᾶτος   εἶπεν   πρὸς   τοὺς   ἀρχιερεῖς   καὶ
Pilate   said   to   the   chief priests and

τοὺς   ὄχλους·   οὐδὲν   εὑρίσκω   αἴτιον   ἐν
the   crowds :   [2]No   [1]I find   [3]crime   in

⁵But they were urgent, saying, "He stirs up the people, teaching throughout all Judea, from Galilee even to this place."
6 When Pilate heard this, he asked whether the man was a Galilean. ⁷And when he learned that he belonged to Herod's jurisdiction, he sent him over to Herod, who was himself in Jerusalem at that time. ⁸When Herod saw Jesus, he was very glad, for he had long desired to see him, because he had heard about him, and he was hoping to see some sign done by him. ⁹So he questioned him at some length; but he made no answer. ¹⁰The chief priests and the scribes stood by, vehemently accusing him. ¹¹And Herod with his soldiers treated him with contempt and mocked him; then, arraying him in gorgeous apparel, he sent him back to Pilate. ¹²And Herod and Pilate became friends with each other that very day, for before this they had been at enmity with each other.
13 Pilate then called

τῷ ἀνθρώπῳ τούτῳ.
- man this.

5 οἱ δὲ ἐπίσχυον λέγοντες[.]
But they insisted saying[.]

ὅτι ἀνασείει τὸν λαόν, διδάσκων καθ'
- He excites the people, teaching throughout

ὅλης τῆς Ἰουδαίας, καὶ ἀρξάμενος ἀπὸ
all - Judæa, even beginning from

τῆς Γαλιλαίας ἕως ὧδε.
- Galilee to here.

6 Πιλᾶτος δὲ
And Pilate

ἀκούσας ἐπηρώτησεν εἰ ὁ ἄνθρωπος
hearing questioned if the man

Γαλιλαῖός ἐστιν, 7 καὶ ἐπιγνοὺς ὅτι ἐκ
a Galilæan is(was), and perceiving that of

τῆς ἐξουσίας Ἡρώδου ἐστίν, ἀνέπεμψεν
the authority of Herod he is(was), he sent up

αὐτὸν πρὸς Ἡρώδην, ὄντα καὶ αὐτὸν ἐν
him to Herod, being also him(he) in

Ἱεροσολύμοις ἐν ταύταις ταῖς ἡμέραις.
Jerusalem in these - days.

8 ὁ δὲ Ἡρώδης ἰδὼν τὸν Ἰησοῦν ἐχάρη
- And Herod seeing - Jesus rejoiced

λίαν· ἦν γὰρ ἐξ ἱκανῶν χρόνων θέλων
greatly; for he was of a long times wishing

ἰδεῖν αὐτὸν διὰ τὸ ἀκούειν περὶ αὐτοῦ,
to see him because of the to hear[b] about him,
=because he had heard

καὶ ἤλπιζέν τι σημεῖον ἰδεῖν ὑπ' αὐτοῦ
and he hoped some sign to see by him

γινόμενον. 9 ἐπηρώτα δὲ αὐτὸν ἐν λόγοις
brought about. And he questioned him in words

ἱκανοῖς· αὐτὸς δὲ οὐδὲν ἀπεκρίνατο αὐτῷ.
many; but he nothing answered him.

10 εἱστήκεισαν δὲ οἱ ἀρχιερεῖς καὶ οἱ
And stood the chief priests and the

γραμματεῖς εὐτόνως κατηγοροῦντες αὐτοῦ.
scribes vehemently accusing him.

11 ἐξουθενήσας δὲ αὐτὸν ὁ Ἡρώδης σὺν
And despising him - Herod with

τοῖς στρατεύμασιν αὐτοῦ καὶ ἐμπαίξας,
the soldiery of him and mocking,

περιβαλὼν ἐσθῆτα λαμπρὰν ἀνέπεμψεν αὐτὸν
throwing round clothing splendid sent back him

τῷ Πιλάτῳ. 12 ἐγένοντο δὲ φίλοι ὅ τε
- to Pilate. And became friends - both

Ἡρώδης καὶ ὁ Πιλᾶτος ἐν αὐτῇ τῇ
Herod and - Pilate on ²same ¹the

ἡμέρᾳ μετ' ἀλλήλων· προϋπῆρχον γὰρ ἐν
day with each other; for they were previously in

ἔχθρα ὄντες πρὸς αὐτούς. 13 Πιλᾶτος δὲ
enmity being with themselves. And Pilate

together the chief priests and the rulers and the people, [14]and said to them, "You brought me this man as one who was perverting the people; and after examining him before you, behold, I did not find this man guilty of any of your charges against him; [15]neither did Herod, for he sent him back to us. Behold, nothing deserving death has been done by him; [16]I will therefore chastise him and release him."[w]

18 But they all cried out together, "Away with this man, and release to us Barab′bas"—[19]a man who had been thrown into prison for an insurrection started in the city, and for murder. [20]Pilate addressed them once more, desiring to release Jesus; [21]but they shouted out, "Crucify, crucify him!" [22]A third time he said to them, "Why, what evil has he done? I have found in him no crime deserving death; I will therefore chastise him and release him." [23]But they were urgent, demanding with loud cries that he should be crucified. And their

συγκαλεσάμενος	τοὺς	ἀρχιερεῖς	καὶ	τοὺς
calling together	the	chief priests	and	the

ἄρχοντας	καὶ	τὸν	λαὸν	14 εἶπεν	πρὸς
leaders	and	the	people	said	to

αὐτούς·	προσηνέγκατέ	μοι	τὸν	ἄνθρωπον
them :	Ye brought	to me	–	man

τοῦτον	ὡς	ἀποστρέφοντα	τὸν	λαόν,	καὶ
this	as	perverting	the	people,	and

ἰδοὺ	ἐγὼ	ἐνώπιον	ὑμῶν	ἀνακρίνας	οὐθὲν
behold	I	³before	⁴you	¹examining	⁵nothing

εὗρον	ἐν	τῷ	ἀνθρώπῳ	τούτῳ	αἴτιον	ὧν
⁶found	⁷in	–	⁸man	⁹this	⁶crime	of the [things] which

κατηγορεῖτε	κατ'	αὐτοῦ.	15 ἀλλ'	οὐδὲ
ye bring accusation against		him.	And	neither

Ἡρῴδης·	ἀνέπεμψεν	γὰρ	αὐτὸν	πρὸς	ἡμᾶς·
Herod;	for he sent back		him	to	us;

καὶ	ἰδοὺ	οὐδὲν	ἄξιον	θανάτου	ἐστὶν
and	behold	nothing	worthy	of death	is

πεπραγμένον	αὐτῷ·	16 παιδεύσας	οὖν	αὐτὸν
having been done	by him;	chastising	therefore	him

ἀπολύσω.‡	18 ἀνέκραγον	δὲ	παμπληθεὶ
I will release.	But they shouted		with the whole multitude

λέγοντες·	αἶρε	τοῦτον,	ἀπόλυσον	δὲ	ἡμῖν
saying :	Take	this man,	and release		to us

τὸν	Βαραββᾶν·	19 ὅστις	ἦν	διὰ	στάσιν
–	Barabbas;	who	was	because of	²insurrection

τινὰ	γενομένην	ἐν	τῇ	πόλει	καὶ	φόνον
¹some	happening	in	the	city	and	murder

βληθεὶς	ἐν	τῇ	φυλακῇ.	20 πάλιν	δὲ
thrown	in	the	prison.	But again	

ὁ	Πιλᾶτος	προσεφώνησεν	αὐτοῖς,	θέλων
–	Pilate	called	to them,	wishing

ἀπολῦσαι	τὸν	Ἰησοῦν.	21 οἱ	δὲ	ἐπεφώνουν
to release	–	Jesus.	But they		shouted

λέγοντες·	σταύρου	σταύρου	αὐτόν.	22 ὁ	δὲ
saying :	Crucify[,]	crucify thou	him.	But he	

τρίτον	εἶπεν	πρὸς	αὐτούς·	τί	γὰρ	κακὸν
a third time	said	to	them :	But what		evil

ἐποίησεν	οὗτος;	οὐδὲν	αἴτιον	θανάτου
did	this man?	nothing	cause	of death

εὗρον	ἐν	αὐτῷ·	παιδεύσας	οὖν	αὐτὸν
I found	in	him;	chastising	therefore	him

ἀπολύσω.	23 οἱ	δὲ	ἐπέκειντο	φωναῖς
I will release.	But they		insisted	voices

μεγάλαις	αἰτούμενοι	αὐτὸν	σταυρωθῆναι,
with great	asking	him	to be crucified,

‡ Ver. 17 omitted by Nestle; *cf.* RSV footnote.

voices prevailed. ²⁴So Pilate gave sentence that their demand should be granted. ²⁵He released the man who had been thrown into prison for insurrection and murder, whom they asked for; but Jesus he delivered up to their will.

26 And as they led him away, they seized one Simon of Cyre′ne, who was coming in from the country, and laid on him the cross, to carry it behind Jesus. ²⁷And there followed him a great multitude of the people, and of women who bewailed and lamented him. ²⁸But Jesus turning to them said, "Daughters of Jerusalem, do not weep for me, but weep for yourselves and for your children. ²⁹For behold, the days are coming when they will say, 'Blessed are the barren, and the wombs that never bore, and the breasts that never gave suck!' ³⁰Then they will begin to say to the mountains, 'Fall on us'; and to the hills, 'Cover us.' ³¹For if they do this when the wood is green, what will happen when it is dry?''

32 Two others also,

καὶ κατίσχυον αἱ φωναὶ αὐτῶν. 24 καὶ
and prevailed the voices of them. And

Πιλᾶτος ἐπέκρινεν γενέσθαι τὸ αἴτημα
Pilate decided to be [carried out] the request

αὐτῶν· 25 ἀπέλυσεν δὲ τὸν διὰ στάσιν
of them; and he released the [one] because of insurrection

καὶ φόνον βεβλημένον εἰς φυλακήν, ὃν
and murder having been thrown into prison, whom

ἠτοῦντο, τὸν δὲ Ἰησοῦν παρέδωκεν τῷ
they asked, – but Jesus he delivered to the

θελήματι αὐτῶν.
will of them.

26 Καὶ ὡς ἀπήγαγον αὐτόν, ἐπιλαβόμενοι
And as they led away him, seizing

Σίμωνά τινα Κυρηναῖον ἐρχόμενον ἀπ'
Simon a certain Cyrenian coming from

ἀγροῦ ἐπέθηκαν αὐτῷ τὸν σταυρὸν φέρειν
[the] country they placed on him the cross to carry

ὄπισθεν τοῦ Ἰησοῦ. 27 Ἠκολούθει δὲ
behind – Jesus. And followed

αὐτῷ πολὺ πλῆθος τοῦ λαοῦ καὶ γυναικῶν
him a much multitude of the people and of women

αἳ ἐκόπτοντο καὶ ἐθρήνουν αὐτόν. 28 στρα-
who mourned and lamented him. turn

φεὶς δὲ πρὸς αὐτὰς Ἰησοῦς εἶπεν·
ing And to them Jesus said:

θυγατέρες Ἰερουσαλήμ, μὴ κλαίετε ἐπ'
Daughters of Jerusalem, do not weep over

ἐμέ· πλὴν ἐφ' ἑαυτὰς κλαίετε καὶ ἐπὶ
me; but over yourselves weep and over

τὰ τέκνα ὑμῶν, 29 ὅτι ἰδοὺ ἔρχονται
the children of you, because behold come

ἡμέραι ἐν αἷς ἐροῦσιν· μακάριαι αἱ
days in which they will say: Blessed the

στεῖραι, καὶ αἱ κοιλίαι αἱ οὐκ ἐγέννησαν,
barren, and the wombs which bare not,

καὶ μαστοὶ οἳ οὐκ ἔθρεψαν. 30 τότε
and breasts which gave not suck. Then

ἄρξονται λέγειν τοῖς ὄρεσιν· πέσατε ἐφ'
they will begin to say to the mountains: Fall on

ἡμᾶς, καὶ τοῖς βουνοῖς· καλύψατε ἡμᾶς·
us, and to the hills: Cover us;

31 ὅτι εἰ ἐν ὑγρῷ ξύλῳ ταῦτα ποιοῦσιν,
because if in ²full of sap ¹a tree these things they do,

ἐν τῷ ξηρῷ τί γένηται; 32 Ἤγοντο δὲ
in the dry what may happen? And were led

who were criminals, were
led away to be put to
death with him. ³³And
when they came to the
place which is called The
Skull, there they crucified
him, and the criminals,
one on the right and one
on the left. ³⁴And Jesus
said, "Father, forgive
them; for they know not
what they do."ˣ And
they cast lots to divide
his garments. ³⁵And the
people stood by, watch-
ing; but the rulers
scoffed at him, saying,
"He saved others; let
him save himself, if he is
the Christ of God, his
Chosen One!" ³⁶The
soldiers also mocked him,
coming up and offering
him vinegar, ³⁷and say-
ing, "If you are the King
of the Jews, save your-
self!" ³⁸There was also an
inscription over him,ʸ
"This is the King of the
Jews."

39 One of the crimi-
nals who were hanged
railed at him, saying,
"Are you not the Christ?
Save yourself and us!"
⁴⁰But the other rebuked
him, saying, "Do you
not fear God, since you
are under the same sen-
tence of condemnation?

καὶ   ἕτεροι   κακοῦργοι   δύο   σὺν   αὐτῷ
also   others*   criminals   two   with   him

ἀναιρεθῆναι.   33 Καὶ   ὅτε   ἦλθον   ἐπὶ   τὸν
to be killed.   And   when   they came   upon   the

τόπον   τὸν   καλούμενον   Κρανίον,   ἐκεῖ   ἐσταύ-
place   —   being called   Skull,   there   they

ρωσαν   αὐτὸν   καὶ   τοὺς   κακούργους,   ὃν μὲν
crucified   him   and   the   criminals,   one†

ἐκ   δεξιῶν   ὃν δὲ   ἐξ   ἀριστερῶν.   34 [ὁ δὲ
on [the] right   and one†   on [the] left.   – And

Ἰησοῦς   ἔλεγεν·   πάτερ,   ἄφες   αὐτοῖς·   οὐ
Jesus   said :   Father,   forgive   them;   ²not

γὰρ   οἴδασιν   τί   ποιοῦσιν.]   διαμεριζόμενοι
¹for   ³they know   what   they are doing.]   dividing

δὲ   τὰ   ἱμάτια   αὐτοῦ   ἔβαλον   κλῆρους.
And the   garments   of him   they cast   lots.

35 καὶ   εἱστήκει   ὁ λαὸς   θεωρῶν.   ἐξεμυκ-
And   stood   the people   beholding.   scoff-

τήριζον   δὲ   καὶ   οἱ   ἄρχοντες   λέγοντες·
ed   And   also   the   rulers   saying :

ἄλλους   ἔσωσεν,   σωσάτω   ἑαυτόν,   εἰ οὗτός
Others   he saved,   let him save   himself,   if this man

ἐστιν   ὁ   χριστὸς   τοῦ   θεοῦ   ὁ   ἐκλεκτός.
is   the   Christ   –   of God   the   chosen [one].

36 ἐνέπαιξαν   δὲ   αὐτῷ   καὶ   οἱ   στρατιῶται
And mocked   him   also   the   soldiers

προσερχόμενοι,   ὄξος   προσφέροντες   αὐτῷ
approaching,   vinegar   offering   to him

37 καὶ   λέγοντες·   εἰ   σὺ   εἶ   ὁ   βασιλεὺς
and   saying :   If   thou   art   the   king

τῶν   Ἰουδαίων,   σῶσον   σεαυτόν.   38 ἦν   δὲ
of the   Jews,   save   thyself.   And there was

καὶ   ἐπιγραφὴ   ἐπ'   αὐτῷ·   Ο   ΒΑΣΙΛΕΥΣ
also   a superscription   over   him :   THE   KING

ΤΩΝ   ΙΟΥΔΑΙΩΝ   ΟΥΤΟΣ.   39 Εἷς   δὲ
OF THE   JEWS   THIS.   And one

τῶν   κρεμασθέντων   κακούργων   ἐβλασφήμει
of the   hanged   criminals   blasphemed

αὐτόν·   οὐχὶ   σὺ   εἶ   ὁ   χριστός;   σῶσον
him :   Not   thou   art   the   Christ?   save

σεαυτὸν   καὶ   ἡμᾶς.   40 ἀποκριθεὶς   δὲ   ὁ
thyself   and   us.   But answering   the

ἕτερος   ἐπιτιμῶν   αὐτῷ   ἔφη·   οὐδὲ   φοβῇ   σὺ
other   rebuking   him   said :   Not   fearest thou

τὸν   θεόν,   ὅτι   ἐν   τῷ   αὐτῷ   κρίματι   εἶ;
–   God, because   in   the   same   judgment   thou art?

ˣ Other ancient authorities
omit the sentence And Jesus
. . . what they do
ʸ Other ancient authorities add
in letters of Greek and Latin
and Hebrew

* Luke uses ἕτεροι here with strict accuracy = "different."
Jesus was not himself a criminal. Note punctuation of A.V. Cf.
Acts 28. 1.

⁴¹And we indeed justly; for we are receiving the due reward of our deeds; but this man has done nothing wrong." ⁴²And he said, "Jesus, remember me when you come in your kingly power." ⁴³And he said to him, "Truly, I say to you, today you will be with me in Paradise."

44 It was now about the sixth hour, and there was darkness over the whole land² until the ninth hour, ⁴⁵while the sun's light failed;ᵃ and the curtain of the temple was torn in two. ⁴⁶Then Jesus, crying with a loud voice, said, "Father, into thy hands I commit my spirit!" And having said this he breathed his last. ⁴⁷Now when the centurion saw what had taken place, he praised God, and said, "Certainly this man was innocent!" ⁴⁸And all the multitudes who assembled to see the sight, when they saw what had taken place, returned home beating their breasts. ⁴⁹And all his acquaintances and the women who had followed him from Galilee stood at a distance and saw these things.

50 Now there was a man named Joseph from

---

41 καὶ ἡμεῖς μὲν δικαίως, ἄξια γὰρ ὧν
And we indeed justly, for things worthy of what

ἐπράξαμεν ἀπολαμβάνομεν· οὗτος δὲ οὐδὲν
we did we receive back; but this man nothing

ἄτοπον ἔπραξεν. **42** καὶ ἔλεγεν Ἰησοῦ,
amiss did. And he said : Jesus,

μνήσθητί μου ὅταν ἔλθῃς εἰς τὴν βασιλείαν
remember me when thou comest into the kingdom

σου. **43** καὶ εἶπεν αὐτῷ· ἀμήν σοι λέγω,
of thee. And he said to him. Truly thee I tell,

σήμερον μετ' ἐμοῦ ἔσῃ ἐν τῷ παραδείσῳ.
to-day with me thou wilt be in the paradise.

44 Καὶ ἦν ἤδη ὡσεὶ ὥρα ἕκτη καὶ
And it was now about hour sixth and

σκότος ἐγένετο ἐφ' ὅλην τὴν γῆν ἕως
darkness came over all the land until

ὥρας ἐνάτης **45** τοῦ ἡλίου ἐκλιπόντος·
hour ninth the sun failing;ᵃ
=as the sun failed;

ἐσχίσθη δὲ τὸ καταπέτασμα τοῦ ναοῦ
and was torn the veil of the shrine

μέσον. **46** καὶ φωνήσας φωνῇ μεγάλῃ ὁ
in the middle. And crying voice with a great -

Ἰησοῦς εἶπεν· πάτερ, εἰς χεῖράς σου
Jesus said : Father, into hands of thee

παρατίθεμαι τὸ πνεῦμά μου. τοῦτο δὲ
I commit the spirit of me. And this

εἰπὼν ἐξέπνευσεν. **47** ἰδὼν δὲ ὁ ἑκατον-
saying he expired. And ³seeing ¹the ²cen-

τάρχης τὸ γενόμενον ἐδόξαζεν τὸν θεὸν
turion the thing happening glorified - God

λέγων· ὄντως ὁ ἄνθρωπος οὗτος δίκαιος
saying : Really - man this righteous

ἦν. **48** καὶ πάντες οἱ συμπαραγενόμενοι
was. And all ¹the ²arriving together

ὄχλοι ἐπὶ τὴν θεωρίαν ταύτην, θεωρήσαντες τὰ
²crowds at - sight this, beholding the things

γενόμενα, τύπτοντες τὰ στήθη ὑπέστρεφον.
happening, smiting the(ir) breasts returned.

49 εἱστήκεισαν δὲ πάντες οἱ γνωστοὶ αὐτῷ
And ⁵stood ¹all ²the [ones] ³known ⁴to him

ἀπὸ μακρόθεν, καὶ γυναῖκες αἱ συνακο-
⁶afar off, and women the [ones] accom-

λουθοῦσαι αὐτῷ ἀπὸ τῆς Γαλιλαίας, ὁρῶσαι
panying him from the Galilee, seeing

ταῦτα.
these things.

50 Καὶ ἰδοὺ ἀνὴρ ὀνόματι Ἰωσὴφ
And behold[,] a man by name Joseph

---

² Or *earth*
ᵃ Or *the sun was eclipsed.* Other ancient authorities read *the sun was darkened*

the Jewish town of Arimathe′a. He was a member of the council, a good and righteous man, [51] who had not consented to their purpose and deed, and he was looking for the kingdom of God. [52] This man went to Pilate and asked for the body of Jesus. [53] Then he took it down and wrapped it in a linen shroud, and laid him in a rock-hewn tomb, where no one had ever yet been laid. [54] It was the day of Preparation, and the sabbath was beginning. [55] The women who had come with him from Galilee followed, and saw the tomb, and how his body was laid; [56] then they returned, and prepared spices and ointments.

On the sabbath they rested according to the commandment.

CHAPTER 24

BUT on the first day of the week, at early dawn, they went to the tomb, taking the spices which they had prepared. [2] And they found the stone rolled away from the tomb, [3] but when they went in they did not find the body.[b] [4] While they were perplexed about this, behold, two men

[b] Other ancient authorities add *of the Lord Jesus*

βουλευτὴς ὑπάρχων, ἀνὴρ ἀγαθὸς καὶ
a councillor being, a man good and

δίκαιος, — **51** οὗτος οὐκ ἦν συγκατατεθειμένος
righteous, — this man was not agreeing with

τῇ βουλῇ καὶ τῇ πράξει αὐτῶν, — ἀπὸ
the counsel and the action of them, — from

῾Αριμαθαίας πόλεως τῶν ᾽Ιουδαίων, ὃς
Arimathæa a city of the Jews, who

προσεδέχετο τὴν βασιλείαν τοῦ θεοῦ,
was awaiting the kingdom – of God,

52 οὗτος προσελθὼν τῷ Πιλάτῳ ᾐτήσατο
this man approaching – to Pilate asked

τὸ σῶμα τοῦ ᾽Ιησοῦ, **53** καὶ καθελὼν
the body – of Jesus, and taking down

ἐνετύλιξεν αὐτὸ σινδόνι, καὶ ἔθηκεν αὐτὸν
wrapped it in linen, and placed him

ἐν μνήματι λαξευτῷ, οὗ οὐκ ἦν οὐδεὶς
in tomb a hewn, where was not no(any)one

οὔπω κείμενος. **54** καὶ ἡμέρα ἦν παρασκευῆς,
not yet laid. And day it was of preparation,

καὶ σάββατον ἐπέφωσκεν. **55** Κατακολουθήσασαι
and a sabbath was coming on. [4]following after

δὲ αἱ γυναῖκες, αἵτινες ἦσαν συνεληλυθυῖαι
[1]And[2]the [3]women, who were [1]having come *with*

ἐκ τῆς Γαλιλαίας αὐτῷ, ἐθεάσαντο τὸ
[3]out of – [4]Galilee [2]with him, beheld the

μνημεῖον καὶ ὡς ἐτέθη τὸ σῶμα αὐτοῦ,
tomb and how was placed the body of him,

56 ὑποστρέψασαι δὲ ἡτοίμασαν ἀρώματα καὶ
and returning prepared spices and

μύρα.
ointment.

Καὶ τὸ μὲν σάββατον ἡσύχασαν κατὰ
And [on] the [2]indeed [1]sabbath they rested according to

τὴν ἐντολήν. **24** τῇ δὲ μιᾷ τῶν σαββάτων
the commandment. But on the one of the week

ὄρθρου βαθέως ἐπὶ τὸ μνῆμα ἦλθον φέρουσαι
while still very early† upon the tomb they came carrying

ἃ ἡτοίμασαν ἀρώματα. **2** εὗρον δὲ τὸν
[2]which [3]they prepared [1]spices. And they found the

λίθον ἀποκεκυλισμένον ἀπὸ τοῦ μνημείου,
stone *having been* rolled away from the tomb,

3 εἰσελθοῦσαι δὲ οὐχ εὗρον τὸ σῶμα
and entering they found not the body

τοῦ κυρίου ᾽Ιησοῦ. **4** καὶ ἐγένετο ἐν τῷ
of the Lord Jesus. And it was in the
=as they were perplexed

ἀπορεῖσθαι αὐτὰς περὶ τούτου καὶ ἰδοὺ
to be perplexed them[be] about this *and* behold[,]

stood by them in dazzling apparel; ⁶and as they were frightened and bowed their faces to the ground, the men said to them, "Why do you seek the living among the dead?ᶜ ⁶Remember how he told you, while he was still in Galilee, ⁷that the Son of man must be delivered into the hands of sinful men, and be crucified, and on the third day rise." ⁸And they remembered his words, ⁹and returning from the tomb they told all this to the eleven and to all the rest. ¹⁰Now it was Mary Mag'dalene and Jo-an'na and Mary the mother of James and the other women with them who told this to the apostles; ¹¹but these words seemed to them an idle tale, and they did not believe them.ᵈ

13 That very day two of them were going to a village named Emma'us, about seven milesᵈᵈ from Jerusalem, ¹⁴and talking

ἄνδρες δύο ἐπέστησαν αὐταῖς ἐν ἐσθῆτι
men   two   stood by   them   in   clothing
ἀστραπτούσῃ· 5 ἐμφόβων δὲ γενομένων
shining;   and terrified   becoming
              =as they became terrified and bent their faces
αὐτῶν καὶ κλινουσῶν τὰ πρόσωπα εἰς τὴν
them   and   bending   the(ir) faces*   to   the
γῆν, εἶπαν πρὸς αὐτάς· τί ζητεῖτε τὸν
earth, they said to   them : Why seek ye the
ζῶντα μετὰ τῶν νεκρῶν; 6 [οὐκ ἔστιν
living [one] with   the   dead [ones]?   He is not
ὧδε, ἀλλὰ ἠγέρθη.] μνήσθητε ὡς ἐλάλησεν
here, but   was raised.   Remember how he spoke
ὑμῖν ἔτι ὢν ἐν τῇ Γαλιλαίᾳ, 7 λέγων
to you yet being in -   Galilee,   saying[,]
τὸν υἱὸν τοῦ ἀνθρώπου ὅτι δεῖ παραδο-
The Son   -   of man   - it behoves to be de-
θῆναι εἰς χεῖρας ἀνθρώπων ἁμαρτωλῶν καὶ
livered into hands   men   of sinful   and
σταυρωθῆναι καὶ τῇ τρίτῃ ἡμέρᾳ ἀναστῆναι.
to be crucified and on the third   day   to rise again.
8 καὶ ἐμνήσθησαν τῶν ῥημάτων αὐτοῦ,
And   they remembered the   words   of him,
9 καὶ ὑποστρέψασαι ἀπὸ τοῦ μνημείου
and   returning   from   the   tomb
ἀπήγγειλαν ταῦτα πάντα τοῖς ἔνδεκα καὶ
reported   these things all   to the   eleven and
πᾶσιν τοῖς λοιποῖς.   10 ἦσαν δὲ ἡ
to all   the   rest.   Now they were the
Μαγδαληνὴ Μαρία καὶ Ἰωάννα καὶ Μαρία
Magdalene   Mary   and Joanna   and Mary
ἡ Ἰακώβου· καὶ αἱ λοιπαὶ* σὺν αὐταῖς*
the [mother] of James; and the rest   with them
ἔλεγον πρὸς τοὺς ἀποστόλους ταῦτα. 11 καὶ
told   to   the   apostles   these things. And
ἐφάνησαν ἐνώπιον αὐτῶν ὡσεὶ λῆρος
seemed   before   them   as   folly
τὰ ῥήματα ταῦτα, καὶ ἠπίστουν αὐταῖς.* ‡
-   words   these,   and they disbelieved them.
13 Καὶ ἰδοὺ δύο ἐξ αὐτῶν ἐν αὐτῇ τῇ
And behold[,] two   of   them   on   same the
ἡμέρᾳ ἦσαν πορευόμενοι εἰς κώμην ἀπέχουσαν
day   were   journeying   to a village being distant
σταδίους ἑξήκοντα ἀπὸ Ἰερουσαλήμ, ᾗ
furlongs   sixty   from   Jerusalem, to which
ὄνομα Ἐμμαοῦς, 14 καὶ αὐτοὶ ὡμίλουν
name   Emmaus,   and   they   talked

ᶜ Other ancient authorities add
He is not here, but has risen
ᵈ Other ancient authorities add
verse 12, But Peter rose and
ran to the tomb; stooping and
looking in, he saw the linen
cloths by themselves; and he
went home wondering at what
had happened
ᵈᵈ Sixty stadia; some ancient
authorities read a hundred and
sixty stadia

* Note the feminines.
‡ Verse 12 omitted by Nestle; cf. RSV footnote.

with each other about all these things that had happened. ¹⁵While they were talking and discussing together, Jesus himself drew near and went with them. ¹⁶But their eyes were kept from recognizing him. ¹⁷And he said to them, "What is this conversation which you are holding with each other as you walk?" And they stood still, looking sad. ¹⁸Then one of them, named Cle′opas, answered him, "Are you the only visitor to Jerusalem who does not know the things that have happened there in these days?" ¹⁹And he said to them, "What things?" And they said to him, "Concerning Jesus of Nazareth, who was a prophet mighty in deed and word before God and all the people, ²⁰and how our chief priests and rulers delivered him up to be condemned to death, and crucified him. ²¹But we had hoped that he was the one to redeem Israel. Yes, and besides all this, it is now the third day since this happened. ²²Moreover, some women of our company

πρὸς ἀλλήλους περὶ πάντων τῶν συμβεβηκότων
to each other about all - ¹having occurred

τούτων. 15 καὶ ἐγένετο ἐν τῷ ὁμιλεῖν
¹these things. And it came to pass in the to talk

αὐτοὺς καὶ συζητεῖν, καὶ αὐτὸς Ἰησοῦς
them and to discuss^be, and [him]self Jesus
=as they talked and discussed,

ἐγγίσας συνεπορεύετο αὐτοῖς· 16 οἱ δὲ
drawing near journeyed with them; but the¹

ὀφθαλμοὶ αὐτῶν ἐκρατοῦντο τοῦ μὴ
eyes of them were held - not

ἐπιγνῶναι αὐτόν. 17 εἶπεν δὲ πρὸς αὐτούς·
to recognize^d him. And he said to them:

τίνες οἱ λόγοι οὗτοι οὓς ἀντιβάλλετε
What words these which ye exchange

πρὸς ἀλλήλους περιπατοῦντες; καὶ ἐστάθησαν
with each other walking? And they stood

σκυθρωποί. 18 ἀποκριθεὶς δὲ εἷς ὀνόματι
sad-faced. And answering one by name

Κλεοπᾶς εἶπεν πρὸς αὐτόν· σὺ μόνος
Cleopas said to him: Thou only

παροικεῖς Ἰερουσαλὴμ καὶ οὐκ ἔγνως τὰ
a stranger in Jerusalem and knewest not the things

γενόμενα ἐν αὐτῇ ἐν ταῖς ἡμέραις ταύταις;
happening in it in - days these?

19 καὶ εἶπεν αὐτοῖς· ποῖα; οἱ δὲ εἶπαν
And he said to them: What things? And they said

αὐτῷ· τὰ περὶ Ἰησοῦ τοῦ Ναζαρηνοῦ, ὃς
to him: The things about Jesus the Nazarene, who

ἐγένετο ἀνὴρ προφήτης δυνατὸς ἐν ἔργῳ
was a man prophet powerful in work

καὶ λόγῳ ἐναντίον τοῦ θεοῦ καὶ παντὸς
and word before - God and all

τοῦ λαοῦ, 20 ὅπως τε παρέδωκαν αὐτὸν οἱ
the people, how both ⁷delivered ⁸him ¹the

ἀρχιερεῖς καὶ οἱ ἄρχοντες ἡμῶν εἰς
²chief priests ³and ⁴the ⁵rulers ⁶of us to

κρίμα θανάτου καὶ ἐσταύρωσαν αὐτόν.
[the] judgment of death and crucified him.

21 ἡμεῖς δὲ ἠλπίζομεν ὅτι αὐτός ἐστιν
But we were hoping that he it is(was)

ὁ μέλλων λυτροῦσθαι τὸν Ἰσραήλ· ἀλλά
the [one] being about to redeem - Israel; but

γε καὶ σὺν πᾶσιν τούτοις τρίτην ταύτην
- also with all these things third this
=this is the third day

ἡμέραν ἄγει ἀφ' οὗ ταῦτα ἐγένετο.
day it leads since these things happened.

22 ἀλλὰ καὶ γυναῖκές τινες ἐξ ἡμῶν
But also ²women ¹some of us

amazed us. They were at the tomb early in the morning 23and did not find his body; and they came back saying that they had even seen a vision of angels, who said that he was alive. 24Some of those who were with us went to the tomb, and found it just as the women had said; but him they did not see." 25And he said to them, "O foolish men, and slow of heart to believe all that the prophets have spoken! 26Was it not necessary that the Christ should suffer these things and enter into his glory?" 27And beginning with Moses and all the prophets, he interpreted to them in all the scriptures the things concerning himself.

28 So they drew near to the village to which they were going. He appeared to be going further, 29but they constrained him, saying, "Stay with us, for it is toward evening and the day is now far spent." So he went in to stay with them. 30When he was at table with them, he took the bread and blessed, and broke it, and gave

ἐξέστησαν ἡμᾶς, γενόμεναι ὀρθριναὶ ἐπὶ τὸ
astonished us, being early at the
μνημεῖον, 23 καὶ μὴ εὑροῦσαι τὸ σῶμα
tomb, and not finding the body
αὐτοῦ ἦλθον λέγουσαι καὶ ὀπτασίαν ἀγγέλων
of him came saying also a vision of angels
ἑωρακέναι, οἳ λέγουσιν αὐτὸν ζῆν. 24 καὶ
to have seen, who say him to live. And
=that he lives.
ἀπῆλθόν τινες τῶν σὺν ἡμῖν ἐπὶ τὸ
[5]went [1]some [2]of the [ones] [3]with [4]us to the
μνημεῖον, καὶ εὗρον οὕτως καθὼς καὶ αἱ
tomb, and found so as indeed the
γυναῖκες εἶπον, αὐτὸν δὲ οὐκ εἶδον.
women said, but him they saw not.
25 καὶ αὐτὸς εἶπεν πρὸς αὐτούς· ὦ
And he said to them: O
ἀνόητοι καὶ βραδεῖς τῇ καρδίᾳ τοῦ πιστεύειν
foolish [ones] and slow - in heart - to believe[d]
ἐπὶ πᾶσιν οἷς ἐλάλησαν οἱ προφῆται·
on(in) all things which spoke the prophets:
26 οὐχὶ ταῦτα ἔδει παθεῖν τὸν χριστὸν καὶ
[2]not [4]these things [1]behoved it [5]to suffer [2]the [4]Christ and
εἰσελθεῖν εἰς τὴν δόξαν αὐτοῦ; 27 καὶ
to enter into the glory of him? And
ἀρξάμενος ἀπὸ Μωϋσέως καὶ ἀπὸ πάντων
beginning from Moses and from all
τῶν προφητῶν διηρμήνευσεν αὐτοῖς ἐν
the prophets he explained to them in
πάσαις ταῖς γραφαῖς τὰ περὶ ἑαυτοῦ.
all the scriptures the things concerning himself.
28 Καὶ ἤγγισαν εἰς τὴν κώμην οὗ
And they drew near to the village whither
ἐπορεύοντο, καὶ αὐτὸς προσεποιήσατο
they were journeying, and he pretended
πορρώτερον πορεύεσθαι. 29 καὶ παρε-
farther to journey. And they
βιάσαντο αὐτὸν λέγοντες· μεῖνον μεθ᾽
urged him saying: Remain with
ἡμῶν, ὅτι πρὸς ἑσπέραν ἐστὶν καὶ κέκλικεν
us, because toward evening it is and has declined
ἤδη ἡ ἡμέρα. καὶ εἰσῆλθεν τοῦ μεῖναι
now the day. And he went in - to remain[d]
σὺν αὐτοῖς. 30 καὶ ἐγένετο ἐν τῷ
with them. And it came to pass in the
=as he reclined
κατακλιθῆναι αὐτὸν μετ᾽ αὐτῶν λαβὼν τὸν
to recline him[be] with them taking the
ἄρτον εὐλόγησεν καὶ κλάσας ἐπεδίδου
loaf he blessed and having broken he handed

it to them. ³¹And their eyes were opened and they recognized him; and he vanished out of their sight. ³²They said to each other, "Did not our hearts burn within us while he talked to us on the road, while he opened to us the scriptures?" ³³And they rose that same hour and returned to Jerusalem; and they found the eleven gathered together and those who were with them, ³⁴who said, "The Lord has risen indeed, and has appeared to Simon!" ³⁵Then they told what had happened on the road, and how he was known to them in the breaking of the bread.

36 As they were saying this, Jesus himself stood among them.ᵉ ³⁷But they were startled and frightened, and supposed that they saw a spirit. ³⁸And he said to them, "Why are you troubled, and why do questionings arise in your hearts? ³⁹See my hands and my feet, that it is I myself; handle me, and see; for a spirit has not flesh and bones as you see that I have."ᶠ ⁴¹And while they still disbelieved for joy, and wondered, he said to

αὐτοῖς·   31 αὐτῶν   δὲ   διηνοίχθησαν   οἱ
to them;   and of them   were opened up   the

ὀφθαλμοί,   καὶ   ἐπέγνωσαν   αὐτόν· καὶ   αὐτὸς
eyes,   and   they recognized   him;   and   he

ἄφαντος   ἐγένετο   ἀπ'   αὐτῶν.   32 καὶ
invisible   became   from   them.   And

εἶπαν   πρὸς   ἀλλήλους·   οὐχὶ   ἡ   καρδία
they said   to   each other: Not   the   heart

ἡμῶν   καιομένη   ἦν   ἐν   ἡμῖν,   ὡς   ἐλάλει
of us   burning   was   in   us,   as   he spoke

ἡμῖν   ἐν   τῇ   ὁδῷ,   ὡς   διήνοιγεν   ἡμῖν   τὰς
to us   in   the   way,   as   he opened up   to us   the

γραφάς;   33 Καὶ   ἀναστάντες   αὐτῇ   τῇ   ὥρᾳ
scriptures?   And   rising up   ²same   ¹in the   hour

ὑπέστρεψαν   εἰς   Ἰερουσαλήμ,   καὶ   εὗρον
they returned   to   Jerusalem,   and   found

ἠθροισμένους   τοὺς   ἔνδεκα   καὶ   τοὺς   σὺν
having been collected   the   eleven   and the [ones]   with

αὐτοῖς,   34 λέγοντας   ὅτι   ὄντως   ἠγέρθη   ὁ
them,   saying[,]   -   Really   was raised   the

κύριος   καὶ   ὤφθη   Σίμωνι.   35 καὶ   αὐτοὶ   ἐξηγοῦντο
Lord   and   appeared   to Simon.   And   they   related

τὰ   ἐν   τῇ   ὁδῷ   καὶ   ὡς   ἐγνώσθη
the things in   the   way   and   how   he was known

αὐτοῖς   ἐν   τῇ   κλάσει   τοῦ   ἄρτου.   36 Ταῦτα
by them   in   the   breaking   of the   loaf.   these things

δὲ   αὐτῶν   λαλούντων   αὐτὸς   ἔστη   ἐν
And   them   saying°   he   stood   in
=as they said these things

μέσῳ   αὐτῶν.   37 πτοηθέντες   δὲ   καὶ
[the] midst   of them.   But scared   and

ἔμφοβοι   γενόμενοι   ἐδόκουν   πνεῦμα   θεωρεῖν.
terrified   becoming   they thought   a spirit   to behold.

38 καὶ   εἶπεν   αὐτοῖς·   τί   τεταραγμένοι   ἐστέ,
And he said   to them :   Why   having been troubled   are ye,

καὶ   διὰ   τί   διαλογισμοὶ   ἀναβαίνουσιν   ἐν
and   why   thoughts   come up   in

τῇ   καρδίᾳ   ὑμῶν;   39 ἴδετε   τὰς   χεῖράς
the   heart   of you?   See   the   hands

μου   καὶ   τοὺς   πόδας   μου,   ὅτι   ἐγώ   εἰμι
of me   and   the   feet   of me,   that   I   am

αὐτός·   ψηλαφήσατέ   με   καὶ   ἴδετε,   ὅτι
[my]self;   feel   me   and   see,   because

πνεῦμα   σάρκα   καὶ   ὀστέα   οὐκ   ἔχει   καθὼς
a spirit   flesh   and   bones   has not   as

ἐμὲ   θεωρεῖτέ   ἔχοντα. ‡   41 ἔτι   δὲ   ἀπιστούντων
me   ye behold   having.   And yet   disbelieving
=while they yet disbelieved

αὐτῶν   ἀπὸ   τῆς   χαρᾶς   καὶ   θαυμαζόντων,
them°   from   the   joy   and   marvelling°,

ᵉ Other ancient authorities add *and said to them, "Peace to you!"*

ᶠ Other ancient authorities add verse 40, *And when he had said this, he showed them his hands and his feet*

‡ Verse 40 omitted by Nestle; *cf.* RSV footnote.

them, "Have you any-
thing here to eat?"
42 They gave him a piece
of broiled fish, 43 and he
took it and ate before
them.

44 Then he said to
them, "These are my
words which I spoke to
you, while I was still with
you, that everything
written about me in the
law of Moses and the
prophets and the psalms
must be fulfilled." 45 Then
he opened their minds to
understand the scrip-
tures, 46 and said to them,
"Thus it is written, that
the Christ should suffer
and on the third day rise
from the dead, 47 and
that repentance and for-
giveness of sins should
be preached in his name
to all nations,g beginning
from Jerusalem.48 You
are witnesses of these
things. 49 And behold, I
send the promise of my
Father upon you; but
stay in the city, until you
are clothed with power
from on high."

50 Then he led them
out as far as Bethany,
and lifting up his hands
he blessed them. 51 While
he blessed them, he
parted from them.h 52 And

εἶπεν αὐτοῖς· ἔχετέ τι βρώσιμον ἐνθάδε;
he said   to them :   Have ye any   food   here?

42 οἱ δὲ ἐπέδωκαν αὐτῷ ἰχθύος ὀπτοῦ
And they   handed   to him   ²fish ³of a broiled

μέρος· 43 καὶ λαβὼν ἐνώπιον αὐτῶν ἔφαγεν.
¹part;   and taking   before   them   he ate.

44 Εἶπεν δὲ πρὸς αὐτούς· οὗτοι οἱ λόγοι
And he said   to   them : These – words

μου οὓς ἐλάλησα πρὸς ὑμᾶς ἔτι ὢν σὺν
of me which I spoke   to   you yet being with

ὑμῖν, ὅτι δεῖ πληρωθῆναι πάντα τὰ
you,   that it behoves to be fulfilled all   the things

γεγραμμένα ἐν τῷ νόμῳ Μωϋσέως καὶ
having been written in   the   law   of Moses   and

τοῖς προφήταις καὶ ψαλμοῖς περὶ ἐμοῦ.
the   prophets   and   psalms   concerning me.

45 τότε διήνοιξεν αὐτῶν τὸν νοῦν τοῦ
Then he opened up of them the   mind   –

συνιέναι τὰς γραφάς· 46 καὶ εἶπεν αὐτοῖς
to understandd the scriptures;   and   said to them[,]

ὅτι οὕτως γέγραπται παθεῖν τὸν χριστὸν
– Thus it has been written ²to suffer ¹the ²Christ

καὶ ἀναστῆναι ἐκ νεκρῶν τῇ τρίτῃ ἡμέρᾳ,
and to rise again out of [the] dead on the third day,

47 καὶ κηρυχθῆναι ἐπὶ τῷ ὀνόματι αὐτοῦ
and to be proclaimed on(in) the   name   of him

μετάνοιαν εἰς ἄφεσιν ἁμαρτιῶν εἰς πάντα
repentance unto forgiveness of sins   to   all

τὰ ἔθνη, – ἀρξάμενοι ἀπὸ Ἱερουσαλήμ.
the nations, — beginning from   Jerusalem.

48 ὑμεῖς μάρτυρες τούτων. 49 καὶ ἰδοὺ
Ye [are] witnesses of these things.   And behold

ἐγὼ ἐξαποστέλλω τὴν ἐπαγγελίαν τοῦ
I   send forth   the   promise   of the

πατρός μου ἐφ᾽ ὑμᾶς· ὑμεῖς δὲ καθίσατε
Father of me on you; but ye   sit

ἐν τῇ πόλει ἕως οὗ ἐνδύσησθε ἐξ ὕψους
in the city   until ³ye are clothed[with]²out of ⁴height

δύναμιν.
¹power.

50 Ἐξήγαγεν δὲ αὐτοὺς ἕως πρὸς
And he led out   them   until   toward

Βηθανίαν, καὶ ἐπάρας τὰς χεῖρας αὐτοῦ
Bethany,   and lifting up the   hands   of him

εὐλόγησεν αὐτούς. 51 καὶ ἐγένετο ἐν τῷ
he blessed   them.   And it came to pass in the

εὐλογεῖν αὐτὸν αὐτοὺς διέστη ἀπ᾽ αὐτῶν.
to bless himbe them he withdrew from   them.
=while he blessed

---

g Or nations. Beginning from
Jerusalem you are witnesses
h Other ancient authorities add
and was carried up into
heaven

they[f] returned to Jerusalem with great joy, [53] and were continually in the temple blessing God.

52 καὶ αὐτοὶ ὑπέστρεψαν εἰς Ἰερουσαλὴμ
And they returned to Jerusalem
μετὰ χαρᾶς μεγάλης, **53** καὶ ἦσαν διὰ παντὸς
with joy great, and were continually
ἐν τῷ ἱερῷ εὐλογοῦντες τὸν θεόν.
in the temple blessing - God.

[f] Other ancient authorities add *worshipped him, and*

CHAPTER 1

IN the beginning was the Word, and the Word was with God, and the Word was God. [2] He was in the beginning with God; [3] all things were made through him, and without him was not anything made that was made. [4] In him was life,[a] and the life was the light of men. [5] The light shines in the darkness, and the darkness has not overcome it.

6 There was a man sent from God, whose name was John. [7] He came for testimony, to bear witness to the light, that all might believe through him. [8] He was not the light, but came to bear witness to the light.

9 The true light that enlightens every man was coming into the world. [10] He was in the world, and the world was made through him, yet the world knew him not. [11] He came to his own home, and his own people received him not. [12] But to all who received him, who believed in his name, he gave power to become children of God; [13] who

---

1 Ἐν ἀρχῇ ἦν ὁ λόγος, καὶ ὁ λόγος
In [the] beginning was the Word, and the Word
ἦν πρὸς τὸν θεόν, καὶ θεὸς ἦν ὁ λόγος.
was with – God, and God was the Word.*
2 οὗτος ἦν ἐν ἀρχῇ πρὸς τὸν θεόν.
This one was in [the] beginning with – God.
3 πάντα δι' αὐτοῦ ἐγένετο, καὶ χωρὶς
All things through him became, and without
αὐτοῦ ἐγένετο οὐδὲ ἓν ὃ γέγονεν. 4 ἐν
him became not one thing which has become. In
αὐτῷ ζωὴ ἦν, καὶ ἡ ζωὴ ἦν τὸ φῶς
him life was, and the life was the light
τῶν ἀνθρώπων· 5 καὶ τὸ φῶς ἐν τῇ
of men; and the light in the
σκοτίᾳ φαίνει, καὶ ἡ σκοτία αὐτὸ οὐ
darkness shines, and the darkness it not
κατέλαβεν. 6 Ἐγένετο ἄνθρωπος, ἀπεσταλμένος
overtook. There was a man, *having been* sent
παρὰ θεοῦ, ὄνομα αὐτῷ Ἰωάννης· 7 οὗτος
from God, name to him° John; this man
ἦλθεν εἰς μαρτυρίαν, ἵνα μαρτυρήσῃ περὶ
came for witness, that he might witness concerning
τοῦ φωτός, ἵνα πάντες πιστεύσωσιν δι'
the light, that all men might believe through
αὐτοῦ. 8 οὐκ ἦν ἐκεῖνος τὸ φῶς, ἀλλ' ἵνα
him. He was not that – light, but that
μαρτυρήσῃ περὶ τοῦ φωτός. 9 Ἦν τὸ φῶς
he might witness concerning the light. It was the light
τὸ ἀληθινόν, ὃ φωτίζει πάντα ἄνθρωπον,
– true, which enlightens every man,
ἐρχόμενον εἰς τὸν κόσμον. 10 ἐν τῷ
coming into the world. In the
κόσμῳ ἦν, καὶ ὁ κόσμος δι' αὐτοῦ
world he was, and the world through him
ἐγένετο, καὶ ὁ κόσμος αὐτὸν οὐκ ἔγνω.
became, and the world him knew not.
11 εἰς τὰ ἴδια ἦλθεν, καὶ οἱ ἴδιοι αὐτὸν
To his own things he came, and his own people him
οὐ παρέλαβον. 12 ὅσοι δὲ ἔλαβον αὐτόν,
received not. But as many as received him,
ἔδωκεν αὐτοῖς ἐξουσίαν τέκνα θεοῦ γεν-
he gave to them right children of God to be-

---

[a] Or *was not anything made.
That which has been made was
life in him*

* But note that the subject has the article and the predicate has it not; hence translate—" the Word was God."

were born, not of blood nor of the will of the flesh nor of the will of man, but of God.

14 And the Word became flesh and dwelt among us, full of grace and truth; we have beheld his glory, glory as of the only Son from the Father. [15] (John bore witness to him, and cried, "This was he of whom I said, 'He who comes after me ranks before me, for he was before me.' ") [16] And from his fulness have we all received, grace upon grace. [17] For the law was given through Moses; grace and truth came through Jesus Christ. [18] No one has ever seen God; the only Son,[b] who is in the bosom of the Father, he has made him known.

19 And this is the testimony of John, when the Jews sent priests and Levites from Jerusalem to ask him, "Who are you?" [20] He confessed, he did not deny, but confessed, "I am not the Christ." [21] And they

ἔσθαι, τοῖς πιστεύουσιν εἰς τὸ ὄνομα αὐτοῦ,
come,   to the [ones] believing in   the   name   of him,

13 οἳ οὐκ ἐξ αἱμάτων οὐδὲ ἐκ θελήματος
who not of bloods   nor   of [the] will

σαρκὸς οὐδὲ ἐκ θελήματος ἀνδρὸς ἀλλ᾽
of [the] flesh nor of [the] will of a man   but

ἐκ θεοῦ ἐγεννήθησαν. 14 Καὶ ὁ λόγος
of God   were born.   And the Word

σὰρξ ἐγένετο καὶ ἐσκήνωσεν ἐν ἡμῖν,
flesh became   and   tabernacled   among   us,

καὶ ἐθεασάμεθα τὴν δόξαν αὐτοῦ, δόξαν
and we beheld   the   glory   of him,   glory

ὡς μονογενοῦς παρὰ πατρός, πλήρης χάριτος
as of an only begotten from a father,   full   of grace

καὶ ἀληθείας. 15 Ἰωάννης μαρτυρεῖ περὶ
and of truth.   John   witnesses concerning

αὐτοῦ καὶ κέκραγεν λέγων· οὗτος ἦν ὃν
him and has cried out saying : This man was he whom

εἶπον· ὁ ὀπίσω μου ἐρχόμενος ἔμπροσθέν
I said : The [one] after me   coming   before

μου γέγονεν, ὅτι πρῶτός μου ἦν. 16 ὅτι
me has become, because first of me he was. Because

ἐκ τοῦ πληρώματος αὐτοῦ ἡμεῖς πάντες
of the   fulness   of him   we   all

ἐλάβομεν, καὶ χάριν ἀντὶ χάριτος· 17 ὅτι
received,   and grace instead of grace; because

ὁ νόμος διὰ Μωϋσέως ἐδόθη, ἡ χάρις καὶ
the law through Moses   was given, the grace and

ἡ ἀλήθεια διὰ Ἰησοῦ Χριστοῦ ἐγένετο.
the truth through Jesus   Christ   became.

18 Θεὸν οὐδεὶς ἑώρακεν πώποτε· μονογενὴς
God no man has seen   never; [the] only begotten

θεὸς ὁ ὢν εἰς τὸν κόλπον τοῦ πατρός,
God the [one] being in the bosom of the Father,

ἐκεῖνος ἐξηγήσατο.
that one declared [?him].

19 Καὶ αὕτη ἐστὶν ἡ μαρτυρία τοῦ
And this   is   the   witness   -

Ἰωάννου, ὅτε ἀπέστειλαν πρὸς αὐτὸν οἱ
of John,   when [3]sent   [4]to [5]him [1]the

Ἰουδαῖοι ἐξ Ἱεροσολύμων ἱερεῖς καὶ Λευίτας
[2]Jews [9]from [10]Jerusalem [6]priests [7]and [8]Levites

ἵνα ἐρωτήσωσιν αὐτόν· σὺ τίς εἶ; 20 καὶ
that they might ask him : Thou who art? And

ὡμολόγησεν καὶ οὐκ ἠρνήσατο, καὶ
he confessed   and   denied not,   and

ὡμολόγησεν ὅτι ἐγὼ οὐκ εἰμὶ ὁ χριστός.
he confessed[,] -   I   am not the Christ.

[b] Other ancient authorities read God

I.G.E.—13

asked him, "What then? Are you Eli'jah?" He said, "I am not." "Are you the prophet?" And he answered "No." ²²They said to him then, "Who are you? Let us have an answer for those who sent us. What do you say about yourself?" ²³He said, "I am the voice of one crying in the wilderness, 'Make straight the way of the Lord,' as the prophet Isaiah said."

24 Now they had been sent from the Pharisees. ²⁵They asked him, "Then why are you baptizing, if you are neither the Christ, nor Eli'jah, nor the prophet?" ²⁶John answered them, "I baptize with water; but among you stands one whom you do not know, ²⁷even he who comes after me, the thong of whose sandal I am not worthy to untie." ²⁸This took place in Bethany beyond the Jordan, where John was baptizing.

29 The next day he saw Jesus coming toward him, and said, "Behold, the Lamb of God, who takes away the sin of the world! ³⁰This is he of whom I said, 'After me comes a man who ranks before

21 καὶ ἠρώτησαν αὐτόν· τί οὖν; Ἠλίας εἶ
And they asked him: What then? Elias art

σύ; καὶ λέγει· οὐκ εἰμί. ὁ προφήτης εἶ σύ;
thou? And he says: I am not. The prophet art thou?

καὶ ἀπεκρίθη· οὔ. 22 εἶπαν οὖν αὐτῷ·
And he answered: No. They said therefore to him:

τίς εἶ; ἵνα ἀπόκρισιν δῶμεν τοῖς
Who art thou? that an answer we may give to the [ones]

πέμψασιν ἡμᾶς· τί λέγεις περὶ σεαυτοῦ;
having sent us; What sayest thou concerning thyself?

23 ἔφη· ἐγὼ φωνὴ βοῶντος ἐν τῇ ἐρήμῳ·
He said: I [am] a voice of [one] crying in the desert:

εὐθύνατε τὴν ὁδὸν κυρίου, καθὼς εἶπεν
Make straight the way of [the] Lord, as said

Ἠσαΐας ὁ προφήτης. 24 Καὶ ἀπεσταλμένοι
Esaias the prophet. And [the ones] having been sent

ἦσαν ἐκ τῶν Φαρισαίων. 25 καὶ ἠρώτησαν
were of the Pharisees. And they asked

αὐτὸν καὶ εἶπαν αὐτῷ· τι οὖν βαπτίζεις
him and said to him: Why then baptizest thou

εἰ σὺ οὐκ εἶ ὁ χριστὸς οὐδὲ Ἠλίας
if thou art not the Christ nor Elias

οὐδὲ ὁ προφήτης; 26 ἀπεκρίθη αὐτοῖς ὁ
nor the prophet? Answered them –

Ἰωάννης λέγων· ἐγὼ βαπτίζω ἐν ὕδατι·
John saying: I baptize in water;

μέσος ὑμῶν στήκει ὃν ὑμεῖς οὐκ οἴδατε,
among you stands [one] whom ye know not,

27 ὁ ὀπίσω μου ἐρχόμενος, οὗ οὐκ εἰμὶ
the [one] after me coming, of whom am not

ἐγὼ ἄξιος ἵνα λύσω αὐτοῦ τὸν ἱμάντα
I worthy that I should loosen of him the thong

τοῦ ὑποδήματος. 28 Ταῦτα ἐν Βηθανίᾳ
of the sandal. These things in Bethany

ἐγένετο πέραν τοῦ Ἰορδάνου, ὅπου ἦν ὁ
happened beyond the Jordan, where was –

Ἰωάννης βαπτίζων. 29 Τῇ ἐπαύριον βλέπει
John baptizing. On the morrow he sees

τὸν Ἰησοῦν ἐρχόμενον πρὸς αὐτόν, καὶ
– Jesus coming toward him, and

λέγει· ἴδε ὁ ἀμνὸς τοῦ θεοῦ ὁ αἴρων
says: Behold[,] the Lamb – of God – taking

τὴν ἁμαρτίαν τοῦ κόσμου. 30 οὗτός ἐστιν
the sin of the world. This is he

ὑπὲρ οὗ ἐγὼ εἶπον· ὀπίσω μου ἔρχεται
as to whom I said: After me comes

ἀνὴρ ὃς ἔμπροσθέν μου γέγονεν, ὅτι
a man who before me has become, because

me, for he was before me.' ³¹I myself did not know him; but for this I came baptizing with water, that he might be revealed to Israel." ³²And John bore witness, "I saw the Spirit descend as a dove from heaven, and it remained on him. ³³I myself did not know him; but he who sent me to baptize with water said to me, 'He on whom you see the Spirit descend and remain, this is he who baptizes with the Holy Spirit.' ³⁴And I have seen and have borne witness that this is the Son of God."

35 The next day again John was standing with two of his disciples; ³⁶and he looked at Jesus as he walked, and said, "Behold, the Lamb of God!" ³⁷The two disciples heard him say this, and they followed Jesus. ³⁸Jesus turned, and saw them following, and said to them, "What do you seek?" And they said to him, "Rabbi (which means Teacher), where are you staying?" ³⁹He said to them, "Come and see." They came and saw where he

πρῶτός μου ἦν. **31** κἀγὼ οὐκ ᾔδειν
first   of me he was.   And I   knew not

αὐτόν, ἀλλ' ἵνα φανερωθῇ τῷ Ἰσραήλ,
him, but   that he might be manifested – to Israel,

διὰ τοῦτο ἦλθον ἐγὼ ἐν ὕδατι βαπτίζων.
therefore came I   in water baptizing.

32 Καὶ ἐμαρτύρησεν Ἰωάννης λέγων ὅτι
And witnessed John saying[,] –

τεθέαμαι τὸ πνεῦμα καταβαῖνον ὡς
I have beheld the Spirit coming down as

περιστερὰν ἐξ οὐρανοῦ, καὶ ἔμεινεν ἐπ'
a dove out of heaven, and he remained on

αὐτόν. **33** κἀγὼ οὐκ ᾔδειν αὐτόν, ἀλλ'
him. And I knew not him, but

ὁ πέμψας με βαπτίζειν ἐν ὕδατι, ἐκεῖνός
the [one] having sent me to baptize in water, that [one]

μοι εἶπεν· ἐφ' ὃν ἂν ἴδῃς τὸ πνεῦμα
to me said: On whomever thou seest the Spirit

καταβαῖνον καὶ μένον ἐπ' αὐτόν, οὗτός
coming down and remaining on him, this

ἐστιν ὁ βαπτίζων ἐν πνεύματι ἁγίῳ.
is the [one] baptizing in Spirit Holy.

34 κἀγὼ ἑώρακα, καὶ μεμαρτύρηκα ὅτι
And I have seen, and have witnessed that

οὗτός ἐστιν ὁ υἱὸς τοῦ θεοῦ.
this [one] is the Son – of God.

35 Τῇ ἐπαύριον πάλιν εἱστήκει ὁ Ἰωάννης
On the morrow again stood – John

καὶ ἐκ τῶν μαθητῶν αὐτοῦ δύο, **36** καὶ
and of the disciples of him two, and

ἐμβλέψας τῷ Ἰησοῦ περιπατοῦντι λέγει·
looking at – Jesus walking he says:

ἴδε ὁ ἀμνὸς τοῦ θεοῦ. **37** καὶ ἤκουσαν
Behold[,] the Lamb – of God. And 'heard

οἱ δύο μαθηταὶ αὐτοῦ λαλοῦντος καὶ
'the ²two ³disciples ⁵him ⁴speaking and

ἠκολούθησαν τῷ Ἰησοῦ. **38** στραφεὶς δὲ
they followed – Jesus. And ²turning

ὁ Ἰησοῦς καὶ θεασάμενος αὐτοὺς ἀκολουθοῦντας
– ¹Jesus and beholding them following

λέγει αὐτοῖς· τί ζητεῖτε; οἱ δὲ εἶπαν
says to them : What seek ye? And they said

αὐτῷ· ῥαββί (ὃ λέγεται μεθερμηνευόμενον
to him : Rabbi (which is called being translated

διδάσκαλε), ποῦ μένεις; **39** λέγει αὐτοῖς·
Teacher), where remainest thou? He says to them :

ἔρχεσθε καὶ ὄψεσθε. ἦλθαν οὖν καὶ εἶδαν
Come and ye will see. They went therefore and saw

was staying; and they stayed with him that day, for it was about the tenth hour. [40] One of the two who heard John speak, and followed him, was Andrew, Simon Peter's brother. [41] He first found his brother Simon, and said to him, "We have found the Messiah" (which means Christ). [42] He brought him to Jesus. Jesus looked at him, and said, "So you are Simon the son of John? You shall be called Cephas" (which means Peter[c]).

[43] The next day Jesus decided to go to Galilee. And he found Philip and said to him, "Follow me." [44] Now Philip was from Beth-sa'ida, the city of Andrew and Peter. [45] Philip found Nathan'a-el, and said to him, "We have found him of whom Moses in the law and also the prophets wrote, Jesus of Nazareth, the son of Joseph." [46] Nathan'a-el said to him, "Can anything good come out of Nazareth?" Philip said to him, "Come and see." [47] Jesus saw Nathan'a-el

ποῦ μένει, καὶ παρ' αὐτῷ ἔμειναν τὴν
where he remains(ed), and with him remained –
ἡμέραν ἐκείνην· ὥρα ἦν ὡς δεκάτη.
day that; hour was about tenth.
40 Ἦν Ἀνδρέας ὁ ἀδελφὸς Σίμωνος Πέτρου
It was Andrew the brother of Simon Peter
εἷς ἐκ τῶν δύο τῶν ἀκουσάντων παρὰ
one of the two – hearing from
Ἰωάννου καὶ ἀκολουθησάντων αὐτῷ·
John and following him;
41 εὑρίσκει οὗτος πρῶτον τὸν ἀδελφὸν τὸν
[5]finds [1]this one [2]first [4]the(his) [6]brother
ἴδιον Σίμωνα καὶ λέγει αὐτῷ· εὑρήκαμεν
[5]own Simon and tells him : We have found
τὸν Μεσσίαν (ὅ ἐστιν μεθερμηνευόμενον
the Messiah (which is being translated
χριστός). 42 ἤγαγεν αὐτὸν πρὸς τὸν
Christ). He led him to –
Ἰησοῦν. ἐμβλέψας αὐτῷ ὁ Ἰησοῦς εἶπεν·
Jesus. Looking at him – Jesus said :
σὺ εἶ Σίμων ὁ υἱὸς Ἰωάννου, σὺ κληθήσῃ
Thou art Simon the son of John, thou shalt be called
Κηφᾶς (ὁ ἑρμηνεύεται Πέτρος). 43 Τῇ
Cephas (which is translated Peter). On the
ἐπαύριον ἠθέλησεν ἐξελθεῖν εἰς τὴν Γαλιλαίαν,
morrow he wished to go forth into – Galilee,
καὶ εὑρίσκει Φίλιππον. καὶ λέγει αὐτῷ ὁ
and finds Philip. And says to him –
Ἰησοῦς· ἀκολούθει μοι. 44 ἦν δὲ ὁ
Jesus : Follow me. Now was –
Φίλιππος ἀπὸ Βηθσαϊδά, ἐκ τῆς πόλεως
Philip from Bethsaida, of the city
Ἀνδρέου καὶ Πέτρου. 45 εὑρίσκει Φίλιππος
of Andrew and of Peter. [2]Finds [1]Philip
τὸν Ναθαναὴλ καὶ λέγει αὐτῷ· ὃν ἔγραψεν
– [3]Nathanael and tells him : [He] whom wrote
Μωϋσῆς ἐν τῷ νόμῳ καὶ οἱ προφῆται
Moses in the law and the prophets
εὑρήκαμεν, Ἰησοῦν υἱὸν τοῦ Ἰωσὴφ τὸν
we have found, Jesus son – of Joseph the
ἀπὸ Ναζαρέθ. 46 καὶ εἶπεν αὐτῷ
from Nazareth. And said to him
Ναθαναήλ· ἐκ Ναζαρὲθ δύναταί τι ἀγαθὸν
Nathanael : Out of Nazareth can anything good
εἶναι; λέγει αὐτῷ ὁ Φίλιππος· ἔρχου καὶ
to be? Says to him – Philip : Come and
ἴδε. 47 εἶδεν Ἰησοῦς τὸν Ναθαναὴλ
see. [2]Saw [1]Jesus – [3]Nathanael

[c] From the word for rock in Aramaic and Greek, respectively

coming to him, and said of him, "Behold, an Israelite indeed, in whom is no guile!" [48]Nathan'a-el said to him, "How do you know me?" Jesus answered him, "Before Philip called you, when you were under the fig tree, I saw you." [49]Nathan'a-el answered him, "Rabbi, you are the Son of God! You are the King of Israel!" [50]Jesus answered him, "Because I said to you, I saw you under the fig tree, do you believe? You shall see greater things than these." [51]And he said to him, "Truly, truly, I say to you, you will see heaven opened, and the angels of God ascending and descending upon the Son of man."

ἐρχόμενον πρὸς αὐτὸν καὶ λέγει περὶ
coming   toward   him   and   says concerning
αὐτοῦ· ἴδε ἀληθῶς Ἰσραηλίτης, ἐν ᾧ
him: Behold[,] truly   an Israelite, in whom
δόλος οὐκ ἔστιν. 48 λέγει αὐτῷ Ναθαναήλ·
guile is not.   Says to him Nathanael:
πόθεν με γινώσκεις; ἀπεκρίθη Ἰησοῦς καὶ
Whence me knowest thou? Answered Jesus   and
εἶπεν αὐτῷ· πρὸ τοῦ σε Φίλιππον φωνῆσαι
said to him: Before the thee   Philip   to call[b]
                              = Philip called thee
ὄντα ὑπὸ τὴν συκῆν εἶδόν σε. 49 ἀπεκρίθη
being under the fig-tree I saw thee.   Answered
αὐτῷ Ναθαναήλ· ῥαββί, σὺ εἶ ὁ υἱὸς τοῦ
him   Nathanael: Rabbi, thou art the Son
θεοῦ, σὺ βασιλεὺς εἶ τοῦ Ἰσραήλ.
of God, thou   king   art — of Israel.
50 ἀπεκρίθη Ἰησοῦς καὶ εἶπεν αὐτῷ·
     Answered   Jesus   and said to him:
ὅτι εἶπόν σοι ὅτι εἶδόν σε ὑποκάτω τῆς
Because I told thee that I saw thee underneath the
συκῆς, πιστεύεις; μείζω τούτων ὄψῃ.
fig-tree, believest thou? greater [than] these things thou shalt see.
51 καὶ λέγει αὐτῷ· ἀμὴν ἀμὴν λέγω
     And he says to him: Truly truly I tell
ὑμῖν, ὄψεσθε τὸν οὐρανὸν ἀνεῳγότα καὶ
you, ye shall see the   heaven having been opened and
τοὺς ἀγγέλους τοῦ θεοῦ ἀναβαίνοντας καὶ
the   angels   — of God going up   and
καταβαίνοντας ἐπὶ τὸν υἱὸν τοῦ ἀνθρώπου.
coming down   on the Son   — of man.

CHAPTER 2

ON the third day there was a marriage at Cana in Galilee, and the mother of Jesus was there; [2]Jesus also was invited to the marriage, with his disciples. [3]When the wine failed, the mother of Jesus said to him, "They have no wine." [4]And Jesus said to her, "O woman, what have you to do with me? My hour has not yet

2 Καὶ τῇ ἡμέρᾳ τῇ τρίτῃ γάμος ἐγένετο
   And on the day   — third a wedding there was
ἐν Κανὰ τῆς Γαλιλαίας, καὶ ἦν ἡ μήτηρ
in Cana — of Galilee,   and was the mother
τοῦ Ἰησοῦ ἐκεῖ· 2 ἐκλήθη δὲ καὶ ὁ
— of Jesus there;   and was invited both —
Ἰησοῦς καὶ οἱ μαθηταὶ αὐτοῦ εἰς τὸν
Jesus and the disciples of him   to the
γάμον. 3 καὶ ὑστερήσαντος οἴνου λέγει ἡ
wedding. And lacking   wine[a]   says the
                        = when wine was lacking
μήτηρ τοῦ Ἰησοῦ πρὸς αὐτόν· οἶνον
mother — of Jesus to   him: Wine
οὐκ ἔχουσιν. 4 καὶ λέγει αὐτῇ ὁ Ἰησοῦς·
they have not. And says to her — Jesus:
τί ἐμοὶ καὶ σοί, γύναι; οὔπω ἥκει ἡ
What to me and to thee, woman? not yet is come the

come." ⁵His mother said to the servants, "Do whatever he tells you." ⁶Now six stone jars were standing there, for the Jewish rites of purification, each holding twenty or thirty gallons. ⁷Jesus said to them, "Fill the jars with water." And they filled them up to the brim. ⁸He said to them, "Now draw some out, and take it to the steward of the feast." So they took it. ⁹When the steward of the feast tasted the water now become wine, and did not know where it came from (though the servants who had drawn the water knew), the steward of the feast called the bridegroom ¹⁰and said to him, "Every man serves the good wine first; and when men have drunk freely, then the poor wine; but you have kept the good wine until now." ¹¹This, the first of his signs, Jesus did at Cana in Galilee, and manifested his glory; and his disciples believed in him.

12 After this he went down to Caper′na-um, with his mother and his brothers and his disciples; and there they

ὥρα μου. 5 λέγει ἡ μήτηρ αὐτοῦ τοῖς
hour of me. Says the mother of him to the
διακόνοις· ὅ τι ἂν λέγῃ ὑμῖν, ποιήσατε.
servants: Whatever he tells you, do ye.
6 ἦσαν δὲ ἐκεῖ λίθιναι ὑδρίαι ἓξ κατὰ
Now there were there stone water-pots six according to
τὸν καθαρισμὸν τῶν Ἰουδαίων κείμεναι,
the purifying of the Jews lying.
χωροῦσαι ἀνὰ μετρητὰς δύο ἢ τρεῖς.
containing each† measures two or three.
7 λέγει αὐτοῖς ὁ Ἰησοῦς· γεμίσατε τὰς
Tells them - Jesus : Fill ye the
ὑδρίας ὕδατος. καὶ ἐγέμισαν αὐτὰς ἕως
water-pots of(with) water. And they filled them up to
ἄνω. 8 καὶ λέγει αὐτοῖς· ἀντλήσατε νῦν
[the] top. And he tells them : Draw now
καὶ φέρετε τῷ ἀρχιτρικλίνῳ. οἱ δὲ
and carry to the master of the feast. And they
ἤνεγκαν. 9 ὡς δὲ ἐγεύσατο ὁ ἀρχιτρίκλινος
carried. But when tasted the master of the feast
τὸ ὕδωρ οἶνον γεγενημένον, καὶ οὐκ ᾔδει
the water ²wine ¹having become, and did not know
πόθεν ἐστίν, οἱ δὲ διάκονοι ᾔδεισαν οἱ
whence it is(was), but the servants knew the [ones]
ἠντληκότες τὸ ὕδωρ, φωνεῖ τὸν νυμφίον
having drawn the water, ³calls ⁴the ⁵bridegroom
ὁ ἀρχιτρίκλινος 10 καὶ λέγει αὐτῷ· πᾶς
¹the ²master of the feast and says to him : Every
ἄνθρωπος πρῶτον τὸν καλὸν οἶνον τίθησιν,
man first the good wine sets forth,
καὶ ὅταν μεθυσθῶσιν τὸν ἐλάσσω· σὺ
and when they become drunk the worse· thou
τετήρηκας τὸν καλὸν οἶνον ἕως ἄρτι.
hast kept the good wine until now.
11 Ταύτην ἐποίησεν ἀρχὴν τῶν σημείων ὁ
¹This ³did ²beginning ³of the ⁴signs -
Ἰησοῦς ἐν Κανὰ τῆς Γαλιλαίας καὶ
Jesus in Cana - of Galilee and
ἐφανέρωσεν τὴν δόξαν αὐτοῦ, καὶ ἐπίστευσαν
manifested the glory of him, and believed
εἰς αὐτὸν οἱ μαθηταὶ αὐτοῦ.
in him the disciples of him.

12 Μετὰ τοῦτο κατέβη εἰς Καφαρναοὺμ
After this went down to Capernaum
αὐτὸς καὶ ἡ μήτηρ αὐτοῦ καὶ
he and the mother of him and
οἱ ἀδελφοὶ καὶ οἱ μαθηταὶ αὐτοῦ, καὶ
the brothers and the disciples of him, and

stayed for a few days.
13 The Passover of
the Jews was at hand,
and Jesus went up to
Jerusalem. [14] In the
temple he found those
who were selling oxen
and sheep and pigeons,
and the money-changers
at their business. [15] And
making a whip of cords,
he drove them all, with
the sheep and oxen, out
of the temple; and he
poured out the coins of
the money-changers and
overturned their tables.
[16] And he told those who
sold the pigeons, "Take
these things away; you
shall not make my
Father's house a house of
trade." [17] His disciples
remembered that it was
written, "Zeal for thy
house will consume me."
[18] The Jews then said to
him, "What sign have
you to show us for doing
this?" [19] Jesus answered
them, "Destroy this
temple, and in three days
I will raise it up." [20] The
Jews then said, "It has
taken forty-six years to
build this temple, and
will you raise it up in
three days?" [21] But he
spoke of the temple of

ἐκεῖ   ἔμειναν   οὐ   πολλὰς   ἡμέρας.
there remained not   many   days.

13 Καὶ ἐγγὺς ἦν τὸ πάσχα τῶν Ἰουδαίων,
And near   was the Passover of the Jews,
καὶ   ἀνέβη   εἰς   Ἱεροσόλυμα   ὁ   Ἰησοῦς.
and went up   to   Jerusalem   -   Jesus.
14 καὶ εὗρεν ἐν τῷ ἱερῷ τοὺς πωλοῦντας
And he found in the temple the [ones] selling
βόας καὶ πρόβατα καὶ περιστερὰς καὶ τοὺς
oxen and   sheep   and   doves   and the
κερματιστὰς   καθημένους,   15 καὶ   ποιήσας
coindealers   sitting,   and   having made
φραγέλλιον   ἐκ   σχοινίων   πάντας   ἐξέβαλεν
a lash   out of   ropes   ¹all   ¹he expelled
ἐκ τοῦ ἱεροῦ, τά τε πρόβατα καὶ τοὺς
out of the temple, both the   sheep   and the
βόας,   καὶ   τῶν   κολλυβιστῶν   ἐξέχεεν   τὰ
oxen,   and ⁴of the ⁵moneychangers ¹poured out ²the
κέρματα   καὶ   τὰς   τραπέζας   ἀνέτρεψεν,
³coins   ⁶and   ⁸the   ⁷tables   ⁷overturned,
16 καὶ τοῖς τὰς περιστερὰς πωλοῦσιν
and ²to the [ones] ⁴the   ⁵doves   ³selling
εἶπεν· ἄρατε ταῦτα ἐντεῦθεν, μὴ ποιεῖτε
¹said : Take these things hence,   do not make
τὸν οἶκον τοῦ πατρός μου οἶκον ἐμπορίου.
the house of the Father of me a house of merchandise.
17 ἐμνήσθησαν   οἱ   μαθηταὶ   αὐτοῦ   ὅτι
Remembered   the   disciples   of him   that
γεγραμμένον ἐστίν· ὁ ζῆλος τοῦ οἴκου
having been written it is : The zeal of the house
σου καταφάγεταί με. 18 ἀπεκρίθησαν οὖν
of thee will consume me.   Answered therefore
οἱ Ἰουδαῖοι καὶ εἶπαν αὐτῷ· τί σημεῖον
the Jews   and said to him: What   sign
δεικνύεις   ἡμῖν,   ὅτι   ταῦτα   ποιεῖς;
showest thou to us, because these things thou doest?
19 ἀπεκρίθη Ἰησοῦς καὶ εἶπεν αὐτοῖς· λύσατε τὸν
Answered   Jesus   and said to them: Destroy -
ναὸν τοῦτον, καὶ ἐν τρισὶν ἡμέραις ἐγερῶ αὐτόν.
shrine this,   and in three   days   I will raise it.
20 εἶπαν οὖν οἱ Ἰουδαῖοι· τεσσεράκοντα
Said   therefore the   Jews :   In forty
καὶ ἓξ ἔτεσιν οἰκοδομήθη ὁ ναὸς οὗτος,
and six years   was built   - shrine   this,
καὶ σὺ ἐν τρισὶν ἡμέραις ἐγερεῖς αὐτόν;
and thou in three   days   wilt raise   it?
21 ἐκεῖνος δὲ ἔλεγεν περὶ τοῦ ναοῦ τοῦ
But that [one]* spoke   about the shrine of the

---

* John repeatedly uses the demonstrative adjective ἐκεῖνος in
the sense of " he," referring to Christ.

his body. ²²When therefore he was raised from the dead, his disciples remembered that he had said this; and they believed the scripture and the word which Jesus had spoken.

23 Now when he was in Jerusalem at the Passover feast, many believed in his name when they saw the signs which he did; ²⁴but Jesus did not trust himself to them, ²⁵because he knew all men and needed no one to bear witness of man; for he himself knew what was in man.

CHAPTER 3

NOW there was a man of the Pharisees, named Nicode′mus, a ruler of the Jews. ²This man came to Jesus by night and said to him, "Rabbi, we know that you are a teacher come from God; for no one can do these signs that you do, unless God is with him." ³Jesus answered him, "Truly, truly, I say to you, unless one is born anew,^d he cannot see the kingdom of God." ⁴Nicode′mus said to him, "How can a man be born when he is

---

σώματος αὐτοῦ. 22 ὅτε οὖν ἠγέρθη ἐκ
body   of him.   When therefore he was raised from
νεκρῶν, ἐμνήσθησαν οἱ μαθηταὶ αὐτοῦ
[the] dead, remembered   the disciples   of him
ὅτι τοῦτο ἔλεγεν, καὶ ἐπίστευσαν τῇ
that this he said,   and they believed the
γραφῇ καὶ τῷ λόγῳ ὃν εἶπεν ὁ 'Ιησοῦς.
scripture and the word which said -   Jesus.
23 'Ως δὲ ἦν ἐν τοῖς 'Ιεροσολύμοις ἐν
   And when he was in -   Jerusalem   at
τῷ πάσχα ἐν τῇ ἑορτῇ, πολλοὶ ἐπίστευσαν
the Passover at the feast,   many believed
εἰς τὸ ὄνομα αὐτοῦ, θεωροῦντες αὐτοῦ τὰ
in the name of him, beholding of him the
σημεῖα ἃ ἐποίει· 24 αὐτὸς δὲ 'Ιησοῦς
signs which he was doing; ¹but ²[him]self, ²Jesus
οὐκ ἐπίστευεν αὐτὸν αὐτοῖς διὰ τὸ αὐτὸν
did not commit himself to them because of the him
                                    =because he knew
γινώσκειν πάντας, 25 καὶ ὅτι οὐ χρείαν εἶχεν
to know^b all men,   and because no need he had
ἵνα τις μαρτυρήσῃ περὶ τοῦ ἀνθρώπου·
that anyone should witness concerning -   man;
αὐτὸς γὰρ ἐγίνωσκεν τί ἦν ἐν τῷ ἀνθρώπῳ.
for he   knew   what was in -   man.
3 'Ην δὲ ἄνθρωπος ἐκ τῶν Φαρισαίων,
Now there was a man   of the Pharisees,
Νικόδημος ὄνομα αὐτῷ, ἄρχων τῶν
Nicodemus   name to him^c, a ruler of the
                   =his name,
'Ιουδαίων· 2 οὗτος ἦλθεν πρὸς αὐτὸν νυκτὸς
Jews;   this man came   to   him of(by) night
καὶ εἶπεν αὐτῷ· ῥαββί, οἴδαμεν ὅτι ἀπὸ
and said to him: Rabbi, we know that from
θεοῦ ἐλήλυθας διδάσκαλος· οὐδεὶς γὰρ
God thou hast come a teacher;   for no one
δύναται ταῦτα τὰ σημεῖα ποιεῖν ἃ σὺ
can   these - signs to do which thou
ποιεῖς, ἐὰν μὴ ᾖ ὁ θεὸς μετ' αὐτοῦ.
doest, except ²is - ¹God with him.
3 ἀπεκρίθη 'Ιησοῦς καὶ εἶπεν αὐτῷ· ἀμὴν
Answered Jesus   and said to him: Truly
ἀμὴν λέγω σοι, ἐὰν μή τις γεννηθῇ
truly I tell thee, except anyone is born
ἄνωθεν, οὐ δύναται ἰδεῖν τὴν βασιλείαν
from above, he cannot to see the kingdom
τοῦ θεοῦ. 4 λέγει πρὸς αὐτὸν ὁ Νικόδημος·
 - of God.   Says to him - Nicodemus :
πῶς δύναται ἄνθρωπος γεννηθῆναι γέρων ὤν;
How can   a man   to be born old being?

---

^d Or *from above*

old? Can he enter a
second time into his
mother's womb and be
born?" ⁵Jesus answered,
"Truly, truly, I say to
you, unless one is born
of water and the Spirit,
he cannot enter the
kingdom of God. ⁶That
which is born of the flesh
is flesh, and that which is
born of the Spirit is
spirit. ⁷Do not marvel
that I said to you, 'You
must be born anew.'ᵈ
⁸The wind e blows where
it wills, and you hear the
sound of it, but you do
not know whence it
comes or whither it goes;
so it is with every one
who is born of the
Spirit." ⁹Nicode'mus
said to him, "How can
this be?" ¹⁰Jesus answer-
ed him, "Are you a
teacher of Israel, and yet
you do not understand
this? ¹¹Truly, truly, I say
to you, we speak of what
we know, and bear wit-
ness to what we have
seen; but you do not
receive our testimony.
¹²If I have told you
earthly things and you
do not believe, how can
you believe if I tell you
heavenly things? ¹³No
one has ascended into

μὴ δύναται εἰς τὴν κοιλίαν τῆς μητρὸς
not can he into the womb of the mother
αὐτοῦ δεύτερον εἰσελθεῖν καὶ γεννηθῆναι;
of him secondly to enter and to be born?

5 ἀπεκρίθη Ἰησοῦς· ἀμὴν ἀμὴν λέγω σοι,
  Answered Jesus : Truly truly I tell thee,
ἐὰν μή τις γεννηθῇ ἐξ ὕδατος καὶ
except anyone is born of water and
πνεύματος, οὐ δύναται εἰσελθεῖν εἰς τὴν
spirit, he cannot to enter into the
βασιλείαν τοῦ θεοῦ. 6 τὸ γεγεννημένον ἐκ
kingdom – of God. The thing having been born of
τῆς σαρκὸς σάρξ ἐστιν, καὶ τὸ γεγεννημένον
the flesh flesh is, and the thing having been born
ἐκ τοῦ πνεύματος πνεῦμά ἐστιν. 7 μὴ
of the Spirit spirit is. not
θαυμάσῃς ὅτι εἶπόν σοι· δεῖ ὑμᾶς
Marvel because I told thee : It behoves you
γεννηθῆναι ἄνωθεν. 8 τὸ πνεῦμα ὅπου θέλει
to be born from above. The spirit(?wind) where it wishes
πνεῖ, καὶ τὴν φωνὴν αὐτοῦ ἀκούεις, ἀλλ'
blows, and the sound of it thou hearest, but
οὐκ οἶδας πόθεν ἔρχεται καὶ ποῦ ὑπάγει·
thou knowest not whence it comes and whither it goes;
οὕτως ἐστὶν πᾶς ὁ γεγεννημένος ἐκ τοῦ
so is everyone having been born of the
πνεύματος. 9 ἀπεκρίθη Νικόδημος καὶ
Spirit. Answered Nicodemus and
εἶπεν αὐτῷ· πῶς δύναται ταῦτα γενέσθαι;
said to him : How can these things to come about?

10 ἀπεκρίθη Ἰησοῦς καὶ εἶπεν αὐτῷ· σὺ
  Answered Jesus and said to him : Thou
εἶ ὁ διδάσκαλος τοῦ Ἰσραὴλ καὶ ταῦτα
art the teacher – of Israel and these things
οὐ γινώσκεις; 11 ἀμὴν ἀμὴν λέγω σοι ὅτι
knowest not? Truly truly I tell thee[,]
ὃ οἴδαμεν λαλοῦμεν καὶ ὃ ἑωράκαμεν
What we know we speak and what we have seen
μαρτυροῦμεν, καὶ τὴν μαρτυρίαν ἡμῶν
we witness, and the witness of us
οὐ λαμβάνετε. 12 εἰ τὰ ἐπίγεια εἶπον
ye receive not. If the earthly things I told
ὑμῖν καὶ οὐ πιστεύετε, πῶς ἐὰν εἴπω
you and ye believe not, how if I tell
ὑμῖν τὰ ἐπουράνια πιστεύσετε; 13 καὶ
you the heavenly things will ye believe? And
οὐδεὶς ἀναβέβηκεν εἰς τὸν οὐρανὸν εἰ μὴ
no man has gone up into – heaven except

ᵈ Or from above
ᵉ The same Greek word means
both wind and spirit

heaven but he who descended from heaven, the Son of man.[f] [14]And as Moses lifted up the serpent in the wilderness, so must the Son of man be lifted up, [15]that whoever believes in him may have eternal life."[g]

16 For God so loved the world that he gave his only Son, that whoever believes in him should not perish but have eternal life. [17]For God sent the Son into the world, not to condemn the world, but that the world might be saved through him. [18]He who believes in him is not condemned; he who does not believe is condemned already, because he has not believed in the name of the only Son of God. [19]And this is the judgment, that the light has come into the world, and men loved darkness rather than light, because their deeds were evil. [20]For every one who does evil hates the light, and does not come to the light, lest his deeds should be exposed. [21]But he who does what is true comes to the light, that it may be clearly

---

f Other ancient authorities add *who is in heaven*

g Some interpreters hold that the quotation continues through verse 21

ὁ   ἐκ τοῦ οὐρανοῦ   καταβάς,   ὁ υἱὸς
the[one] out of -   heaven   having come down, the Son

τοῦ ἀνθρώπου. 14 Καὶ καθὼς Μωϋσῆς ὕψωσεν
- of man.   And as   Moses   lifted up

τὸν ὄφιν ἐν τῇ ἐρήμῳ, οὕτως ὑψωθῆναι
the serpent in the desert,   so   to be lifted up

δεῖ   τὸν υἱὸν τοῦ ἀνθρώπου, 15 ἵνα πᾶς ὁ
it behoves the Son -   of man,   that everyone

πιστεύων ἐν αὐτῷ ἔχῃ ζωὴν αἰώνιον.
believing in him may have life   eternal.

16 οὕτως   γὰρ   ἠγάπησεν   ὁ θεὸς   τὸν
     For thus   ²loved   - ¹God   the

κόσμον, ὥστε   τὸν υἱὸν τὸν μονογενῆ
world,   so as   the Son   the only begotten

ἔδωκεν, ἵνα πᾶς ὁ πιστεύων εἰς αὐτὸν
he gave, that everyone believing in   him

μὴ ἀπόληται ἀλλ' ἔχῃ ζωὴν αἰώνιον.
may not perish   but may have life   eternal.

17 οὐ γὰρ ἀπέστειλεν ὁ θεὸς τὸν υἱὸν
    For ²not   ³sent   - ¹God the Son

εἰς τὸν κόσμον ἵνα κρίνῃ τὸν κόσμον,
into the world   that he might judge the world,

ἀλλ' ἵνα σωθῇ ὁ κόσμος δι' αὐτοῦ.
but   that ³might be saved ¹the ²world through him.

18 ὁ   πιστεύων εἰς αὐτὸν οὐ κρίνεται·
    The [one] believing in   him   is not judged;

ὁ μὴ πιστεύων ἤδη κέκριται, ὅτι
the[one]not believing already has been judged, because

μὴ πεπίστευκεν εἰς τὸ ὄνομα τοῦ μονογενοῦς
he has not believed in the name of the only begotten

υἱοῦ τοῦ θεοῦ.   19 αὕτη δέ ἐστιν ἡ
Son   - of God.   And this is   the

κρίσις, ὅτι τὸ φῶς ἐλήλυθεν εἰς τὸν
judgment, that the light has come   into the

κόσμον καὶ ἠγάπησαν οἱ ἄνθρωποι μᾶλλον
world   and   ²loved   - ¹men   ⁵rather

τὸ σκότος ἢ τὸ φῶς· ἦν γὰρ αὐτῶν
³the ⁴darkness ⁶than the light; for was(were) of them

πονηρὰ τὰ ἔργα. 20 πᾶς γὰρ ὁ φαῦλα
evil   the works.   For everyone evil things

πράσσων μισεῖ τὸ φῶς καὶ οὐκ ἔρχεται
doing   hates   the light and does not come

πρὸς τὸ φῶς, ἵνα μὴ ἐλεγχθῇ τὰ ἔργα
to   the light,   lest is(are) reproved the works

αὐτοῦ· 21 ὁ δὲ ποιῶν τὴν ἀλήθειαν ἔρχεται
of him; but the [one] doing the truth   comes

πρὸς τὸ φῶς, ἵνα φανερωθῇ αὐτοῦ τὰ
to   the light,   that may be manifested of him   the

seen that his deeds have
been wrought in God.

22 After this Jesus and
his disciples went into the
land of Judea; there he
remained with them and
baptized. [23]John also was
baptizing at Ae'non near
Salim, because there was
much water there; and
people came and were
baptized. [24]For John had
not yet been put in
prison.

25 Now a discussion
arose between John's
disciples and a Jew over
purifying. [26]And they
came to John, and said to
him, "Rabbi, he who
was with you beyond the
Jordan, to whom you
bore witness, here he is,
baptizing, and all are
going to him." [27]John
answered, "No one can
receive anything except
what is given him from
heaven. [28]You yourselves
bear me witness, that I
said, I am not the Christ,
but I have been sent
before him. [29]He who
has the bride is the
bridegroom; the friend
of the bridegroom, who
stands and hears him,
rejoices greatly at the
bridegroom's   voice;

ἔργα ὅτι ἐν θεῷ ἐστιν εἰργασμένα.
works   that   in   God   they are   *having been* wrought.

22 Μετὰ ταῦτα ἦλθεν ὁ Ἰησοῦς καὶ οἱ
After these things came – Jesus and the
μαθηταὶ αὐτοῦ εἰς τὴν Ἰουδαίαν γῆν, καὶ
disciples of him into *the* Judæan *land*, and
ἐκεῖ διέτριβεν μετ’ αὐτῶν καὶ ἐβάπτιζεν.
there continued   with   them   and   baptized.
23 ἦν δὲ καὶ Ἰωάννης βαπτίζων ἐν
And was   also   John   baptizing   in
Αἰνὼν ἐγγὺς τοῦ Σαλίμ, ὅτι ὕδατα
Ainon   near   –   Salim,   because   waters
πολλὰ ἦν ἐκεῖ, καὶ παρεγίνοντο καὶ
many was(were) there,   and   they came   and
ἐβαπτίζοντο· **24** οὔπω γὰρ ἦν βεβλημένος
were baptized;   for [3]not yet [2]was [4]*having been* cast
εἰς τὴν φυλακὴν Ἰωάννης. **25** Ἐγένετο
[5]into [6]the [7]prison [1]John.   There was
οὖν ζήτησις ἐκ τῶν μαθητῶν Ἰωάννου
therefore a questioning of   the   disciples   of John
μετὰ Ἰουδαίου περὶ καθαρισμοῦ. **26** καὶ
with   a Jew   about   purifying.   And
ἦλθον πρὸς τὸν Ἰωάννην καὶ εἶπαν αὐτῷ·
they came to   –   John   and   said   to him:
ῥαββί, ὃς ἦν μετὰ σοῦ πέραν τοῦ
Rabbi, [he] who was   with   thee   beyond   the
Ἰορδάνου, ᾧ σὺ μεμαρτύρηκας, ἴδε
Jordan,   to whom thou   hast borne witness, behold[,]
οὗτος βαπτίζει καὶ πάντες ἔρχονται πρὸς
this man baptizes   and   all men   are coming   to
αὐτόν. **27** ἀπεκρίθη Ἰωάννης καὶ εἶπεν·
him.   Answered   John   and   said:
οὐ δύναται ἄνθρωπος λαμβάνειν οὐδὲν ἐὰν μὴ
Cannot   a man   *to* receive no(any)thing unless
ᾖ δεδομένον αὐτῷ ἐκ τοῦ οὐρανοῦ.
it is *having been* given to him   out of   –   heaven.
28 αὐτοὶ ὑμεῖς μοι μαρτυρεῖτε ὅτι εἶπον·
[Your]selves ye   to me   bear witness   that   I said:
οὐκ εἰμὶ ἐγὼ ὁ χριστός, ἀλλ’ ὅτι
[3]not [4]am [1]I   the   Christ,   but   that
ἀπεσταλμένος εἰμὶ ἔμπροσθεν ἐκείνου. **29** ὁ
having been sent I am   before   that one.*   The [one]
ἔχων τὴν νύμφην νυμφίος ἐστίν· ὁ δὲ
having   the   bride   a bridegroom   is;   but the
φίλος τοῦ νυμφίου, ὁ ἑστηκὼς καὶ ἀκούων
friend of the bridegroom,   –   standing   and   hearing
αὐτοῦ, χαρᾷ χαίρει διὰ τὴν φωνὴν τοῦ
him,   with joy   rejoices because of the   voice   of the

* See note to 2. 21.

therefore this joy of mine is now full. [30]He must increase, but I must decrease."[h]

31 He who comes from above is above all; he who is of the earth belongs to the earth, and of the earth he speaks; he who comes from heaven is above all. [32]He bears witness to what he has seen and heard, yet no one receives his testimony; [33]he who receives his testimony sets his seal to this, that God is true. [34]For he whom God has sent utters the words of God, for it is not by measure that he gives the Spirit; [35]the Father loves the Son, and has given all things into his hand. [36]He who believes in the Son has eternal life; he who does not obey the Son shall not see life, but the wrath of God rests upon him.

νυμφίου. αὕτη οὖν ἡ χαρὰ ἡ ἐμὴ
bridegroom. [2]This   [1]therefore   the   [3]joy   –   [2]my
πεπλήρωται. 30 ἐκεῖνον δεῖ αὐξάνειν, ἐμὲ
has been fulfilled.   That one   it behoves   to increase,   [2]me
δὲ ἐλαττοῦσθαι. 31 Ὁ ἄνωθεν ἐρχόμενος
[1]but   to decrease.   The [one] from above   coming
ἐπάνω πάντων ἐστίν· ὁ ὢν ἐκ τῆς γῆς
over   all   is;   the [one] being   of   the   earth
ἐκ τῆς γῆς ἐστιν καὶ ἐκ τῆς γῆς λαλεῖ.
of   the   earth   is   and   of   the   earth   speaks.
ὁ ἐκ τοῦ οὐρανοῦ ἐρχόμενος ἐπάνω
The [one] of   –   heaven   coming   over
πάντων ἐστίν· 32 ὃ ἑώρακεν καὶ ἤκουσεν,
all   is;   what he has seen   and   heard,
τοῦτο μαρτυρεῖ, καὶ τὴν μαρτυρίαν αὐτοῦ
this   he witnesses [to],   and   the   witness   of him
οὐδεὶς λαμβάνει. 33 ὁ λαβὼν αὐτοῦ τὴν
no man   receives.   The [one] receiving of him   the
μαρτυρίαν ἐσφράγισεν ὅτι ὁ θεὸς ἀληθής
witness   sealed   that   –   God   true
ἐστιν. 34 ὃν γὰρ ἀπέστειλεν ὁ θεὸς τὰ
is.   For [he] whom   [2]sent   –   [1]God   the
ῥήματα τοῦ θεοῦ λαλεῖ· οὐ γὰρ ἐκ
words   –   of God   speaks;   for not   by
μέτρου δίδωσιν τὸ πνεῦμα. 35 ὁ πατὴρ
measure   he gives   the   Spirit.   The   Father
ἀγαπᾷ τὸν υἱόν, καὶ πάντα δέδωκεν ἐν
loves   the   Son,   and   all things   has given   in[to]
τῇ χειρὶ αὐτοῦ. 36 ὁ πιστεύων εἰς τὸν
the   hand   of him.   The [one] believing   in   the
υἱὸν ἔχει ζωὴν αἰώνιον· ὁ δὲ ἀπειθῶν
Son   has   life   eternal;   but the [one]   disobeying
τῷ υἱῷ οὐκ ὄψεται ζωήν, ἀλλ' ἡ ὀργὴ
the Son   will not see   life,   but   the   wrath
τοῦ θεοῦ μένει ἐπ' αὐτόν.
–   of God   remains   on   him.

CHAPTER 4

NOW when the Lord knew that the Pharisees had heard that Jesus was making and baptizing more disciples than John [2](although Jesus himself did not baptize, but only his disciples), [3]he left Judea

4 Ὡς οὖν ἔγνω ὁ κύριος ὅτι ἤκουσαν
[2]When [1]therefore [5]knew [3]the [4]Lord [6]that [8]heard
οἱ Φαρισαῖοι ὅτι Ἰησοῦς πλείονας μαθητὰς
[7]the [8]Pharisees   that   Jesus   more   disciples
ποιεῖ καὶ βαπτίζει ἢ Ἰωάννης, — 2 καίτοι γε
makes and   baptizes   than   John,   —   though
Ἰησοῦς αὐτὸς οὐκ ἐβάπτιζεν ἀλλ' οἱ
Jesus   [him]self   baptized not   but   the
μαθηταὶ αὐτοῦ, — 3 ἀφῆκεν τὴν Ἰουδαίαν
disciples   of him,   —   he left   –   Judæa

[h] Some interpreters hold that the quotation continues through verse 36

and departed again to Galilee. 4 He had to pass through Samar'ia. 5 So he came to a city of Samar'ia, called Sy'char, near the field that Jacob gave to his son Joseph. 6 Jacob's well was there, and so Jesus, wearied as he was with his journey, sat down beside the well. It was about the sixth hour.

7 There came a woman of Samar'ia to draw water. Jesus said to her, "Give me a drink." 8 For his disciples had gone away into the city to buy food. 9 The Samaritan woman said to him, "How is it that you, a Jew, ask a drink of me, a woman of Samar'ia?" For Jews have no dealings with Samaritans. 10 Jesus answered her, "If you knew the gift of God, and who it is that is saying to you, 'Give me a drink,' you would have asked him, and he would have given you living water." 11 The woman said to him, "Sir, you have nothing to draw with, and the well is deep; where do you get that living water? 12 Are you

καὶ ἀπῆλθεν πάλιν εἰς τὴν Γαλιλαίαν.
and went away again into - Galilee.

4 Ἔδει δὲ αὐτὸν διέρχεσθαι διὰ τῆς
And it behoved him to pass through through -

Σαμαρείας. 5 ἔρχεται οὖν εἰς πόλιν τῆς
Samaria. He comes therefore to a city -

Σαμαρείας λεγομένην Σύχαρ, πλησίον τοῦ
of Samaria being called Sychar, near the

χωρίου ὃ ἔδωκεν Ἰακὼβ [τῷ] Ἰωσὴφ
piece of land which 2gave 1Jacob - to Joseph

τῷ υἱῷ αὐτοῦ· 6 ἦν δὲ ἐκεῖ πηγὴ τοῦ
the son of him; and was there a fountain -

Ἰακώβ. ὁ οὖν Ἰησοῦς κεκοπιακὼς ἐκ
of Jacob. - Therefore Jesus having become wearied from

τῆς ὁδοιπορίας ἐκαθέζετο οὕτως ἐπὶ τῇ
the journey sat thus at the

πηγῇ· ὥρα ἦν ὡς ἕκτη. 7 ἔρχεται γυνὴ
fountain; [the] hour was about sixth. Comes a woman

ἐκ τῆς Σαμαρείας ἀντλῆσαι ὕδωρ. λέγει
of - Samaria to draw water. Says

αὐτῇ ὁ Ἰησοῦς· δός μοι πεῖν. 8 οἱ γὰρ
to her - Jesus : Give me to drink. For the

μαθηταὶ αὐτοῦ ἀπεληλύθεισαν εἰς τὴν
disciples of him had gone away into the

πόλιν, ἵνα τροφὰς ἀγοράσωσιν. 9 λέγει
city, that foods they might buy. Says

οὖν αὐτῷ ἡ γυνὴ ἡ Σαμαρῖτις· πῶς
therefore to him the woman - Samaritan : How

σὺ Ἰουδαῖος ὢν παρ᾽ ἐμοῦ πεῖν
thou 2a Jew 1being 5from 6me 4to drink

αἰτεῖς γυναικὸς Σαμαρίτιδος οὔσης;
3askest 9woman 8a Samaritan 7being?

[οὐ γὰρ συγχρῶνται Ἰουδαῖοι Σαμαρίταις.]
1For 4not 2associate 3Jews 5with Samaritans.

10 ἀπεκρίθη Ἰησοῦς καὶ εἶπεν αὐτῇ· εἰ ᾔδεις
Answered Jesus and said to her : If thou knewest

τὴν δωρεὰν τοῦ θεοῦ, καὶ τίς ἐστιν ὁ
the gift - of God, and who is the [one]

λέγων σοι· δός μοι πεῖν, σὺ ἂν ᾔτησας
saying to thee : Give me to drink, thou wouldest have asked

αὐτὸν καὶ ἔδωκεν ἄν σοι ὕδωρ ζῶν.
him and he would have given thee water living.

11 λέγει αὐτῷ· κύριε, οὔτε ἄντλημα ἔχεις
She says to him : Sir, no pail thou hast

καὶ τὸ φρέαρ ἐστὶν βαθύ· πόθεν οὖν
and the well is deep; whence then

ἔχεις τὸ ὕδωρ τὸ ζῶν; 12 μὴ σὺ μείζων
hast thou the water - living? not thou greater

greater than our father Jacob, who gave us the well, and drank from it himself, and his sons, and his cattle?" ¹³Jesus said to her, "Every one who drinks of this water will thirst again, ¹⁴but whoever drinks of the water that I shall give him will never thirst; the water that I shall give him will become in him a spring of water welling up to eternal life." ¹⁵The woman said to him, "Sir, give me this water, that I may not thirst, nor come here to draw."

16 Jesus said to her, "Go, call your husband, and come here." ¹⁷The woman answered him, "I have no husband." Jesus said to her, "You are right in saying, 'I have no husband'; ¹⁸for you have had five husbands, and he whom you now have is not your husband; this you said truly." ¹⁹The woman said to him, "Sir, I perceive that you are a prophet. ²⁰Our fathers worshiped on this mountain; and you say that in Jerusalem is the place where men ought to worship."

εἶ τοῦ πατρὸς ἡμῶν Ἰακώβ, ὃς ἔδωκεν
art [than] the father of us Jacob, who gave
ἡμῖν τὸ φρέαρ, καὶ αὐτὸς ἐξ αὐτοῦ
us the well, and [him]self of it
ἔπιεν καὶ οἱ υἱοὶ αὐτοῦ καὶ τὰ θρέμματα
drank and the sons of him and the cattle
αὐτοῦ; 13 ἀπεκρίθη Ἰησοῦς καὶ εἶπεν αὐτῇ·
of him? Answered Jesus and said to her:
πᾶς ὁ πίνων ἐκ τοῦ ὕδατος τούτου
Everyone drinking of – water this
διψήσει πάλιν· 14 ὃς δ' ἂν πίῃ ἐκ τοῦ
will thirst again; but whoever drinks of the
ὕδατος οὗ ἐγὼ δώσω αὐτῷ, οὐ μὴ
water which I will give him, by no means
διψήσει εἰς τὸν αἰῶνα, ἀλλὰ τὸ ὕδωρ ὃ
will thirst unto the age, but the water which
δώσω αὐτῷ γενήσεται ἐν αὐτῷ πηγὴ
I will give him will become in him a fountain
ὕδατος ἁλλομένου εἰς ζωὴν αἰώνιον. 15 λέγει
of water springing to life eternal. Says
πρὸς αὐτὸν ἡ γυνή· κύριε, δός μοι
to him the woman: Sir, give me
τοῦτο τὸ ὕδωρ, ἵνα μὴ διψῶ μηδὲ
this – water, that I thirst not nor
διέρχωμαι ἐνθάδε ἀντλεῖν. 16 λέγει αὐτῇ·
come through hither to draw. He says to her:
ὕπαγε φώνησον τὸν ἄνδρα σου καὶ ἐλθὲ
Go call the husband of thee and come
ἐνθάδε. 17 ἀπεκρίθη ἡ γυνὴ καὶ εἶπεν·
hither. Answered the woman and said:
οὐκ ἔχω ἄνδρα. λέγει αὐτῇ ὁ Ἰησοῦς·
I have not a husband. Says to her – Jesus:
καλῶς εἶπες ὅτι ἄνδρα οὐκ ἔχω· 18 πέντε
Well sayest thou[,] – A husband I have not; ⁵five
γὰρ ἄνδρας ἔσχες, καὶ νῦν ὃν ἔχεις
⁴for husbands thou hadst, and now [he] whom thou hast
οὐκ ἔστιν σου ἀνήρ· τοῦτο ἀληθὲς εἴρηκας.
is not of thee husband; this truly thou hast said.
19 λέγει αὐτῷ ἡ γυνή· κύριε, θεωρῶ
Says to him the woman: Sir, I perceive
ὅτι προφήτης εἶ σύ. 20 οἱ πατέρες
that a prophet art thou. The fathers
ἡμῶν ἐν τῷ ὄρει τούτῳ προσεκύνησαν·
of us in – mountain this worshipped;
καὶ ὑμεῖς λέγετε ὅτι ἐν Ἰεροσολύμοις
and ye say that in Jerusalem
ἐστὶν ὁ τόπος ὅπου προσκυνεῖν δεῖ.
is the place where to worship it behoves.

²¹Jesus said to her, "Woman, believe me, the hour is coming when neither on this mountain nor in Jerusalem will you worship the Father. ²²You worship what you do not know; we worship what we know, for salvation is from the Jews. ²³But the hour is coming, and now is, when the true worshipers will worship the Father in spirit and truth, for such the Father seeks to worship him. ²⁴God is spirit, and those who worship him must worship in spirit and truth." ²⁵The woman said to him, "I know that Messiah is coming (he who is called Christ); when he comes, he will show us all things." ²⁶Jesus said to her, "I who speak to you am he."

27 Just then his disciples came. They marveled that he was talking with a woman, but none said, "What do you wish?" or, "Why are you talking with her?" ²⁸So the woman left her water jar, and went away into the city, and said to the people,

21 λέγει αὐτῇ ὁ Ἰησοῦς· πίστευέ μοι,
Says to her – Jesus : Believe me,

γύναι, ὅτι ἔρχεται ὥρα ὅτε οὔτε ἐν
woman, that is coming an hour when neither in

τῷ ὄρει τούτῳ οὔτε ἐν Ἰεροσολύμοις
– mountain this nor in Jerusalem

προσκυνήσετε τῷ πατρί. 22 ὑμεῖς προσκυ-
will ye worship the Father. Ye wor-

νεῖτε ὃ οὐκ οἴδατε, ἡμεῖς προσκυνοῦμεν ὃ
ship what ye know not, we worship what

οἴδαμεν, ὅτι ἡ σωτηρία ἐκ τῶν Ἰουδαίων
we know, because – salvation of the Jews

ἐστίν· 23 ἀλλὰ ἔρχεται ὥρα καὶ νῦν
is; but is coming an hour and now

ἐστιν, ὅτε οἱ ἀληθινοὶ προσκυνηταὶ προσκυνή-
is, when the true worshippers will

σουσιν τῷ πατρὶ ἐν πνεύματι καὶ ἀληθείᾳ·
worship the Father in spirit and truth;

καὶ γὰρ ὁ πατὴρ τοιούτους ζητεῖ τοὺς
for indeed the Father ³such ¹seeks the [ones]

προσκυνοῦντας αὐτόν· 24 πνεῦμα ὁ θεός,*
worshipping him; God [is] spirit,*

καὶ τοὺς προσκυνοῦντας ἐν πνεύματι καὶ
and ²the [ones] ³worshipping ⁴in ⁵spirit ⁷and

ἀληθείᾳ δεῖ προσκυνεῖν. 25 λέγει αὐτῷ
⁸truth ¹it behoves ⁴to worship. Says to him

ἡ γυνή· οἶδα ὅτι Μεσσίας ἔρχεται, ὁ
the woman : I know that Messiah is coming, the [one]

λεγόμενος χριστός· ὅταν ἔλθῃ ἐκεῖνος,
being called Christ; when comes that one,

ἀναγγελεῖ ἡμῖν ἅπαντα. 26 λέγει αὐτῇ
he will announce to us all things. Says to her

ὁ Ἰησοῦς· ἐγώ εἰμι, ὁ λαλῶν σοι.
– Jesus : I am, the [one] speaking to thee.

27 Καὶ ἐπὶ τούτῳ ἦλθαν οἱ μαθηταὶ
And on this came the disciples

αὐτοῦ, καὶ ἐθαύμαζον ὅτι μετὰ γυναικὸς
of him, and marvelled that with a woman

ἐλάλει· οὐδεὶς μέντοι εἶπεν· τί ζητεῖς
he was speaking; no one however said : What seekest thou

ἢ τί λαλεῖς μετ' αὐτῆς; 28 ἀφῆκεν οὖν
or why speakest thou with her? ⁴Left ³therefore

τὴν ὑδρίαν αὐτῆς ἡ γυνὴ καὶ ἀπῆλθεν
⁵the ⁶waterpot ⁷of her ¹the ²woman and went away

εἰς τὴν πόλιν, καὶ λέγει τοῖς ἀνθρώποις·
into the city, and says to the men :

* See note on 1. 1.

²⁹"Come, see a man who told me all that I ever did. Can this be the Christ?" ³⁰They went out of the city and were coming to him.

31 Meanwhile the disciples besought him, saying, "Rabbi, eat." ³²But he said to them, "I have food to eat of which you do not know." ³³So the disciples said to one another, "Has any one brought him food?" ³⁴Jesus said to them, "My food is to do the will of him who sent me, and to accomplish his work. ³⁵Do you not say, 'There are yet four months, then comes the harvest'? I tell you, lift up your eyes, and see how the fields are already white for harvest. ³⁶He who reaps receives wages, and gathers fruit for eternal life, so that sower and reaper may rejoice together. ³⁷For here the saying holds true, 'One sows and another reaps.' ³⁸I sent you to reap that for which you did not labor; others have labored, and you have entered into their labor."

29 δεῦτε   ἴδετε   ἄνθρωπον   ὃς   εἶπέν   μοι
    Come   see   a man   who   told   me
πάντα   ἃ   ἐποίησα·   μήτι   οὗτός   ἐστιν   ὁ
all things which I did;   not   this   is   the
χριστός;   30 ἐξῆλθον   ἐκ   τῆς   πόλεως   καὶ
Christ?   They went forth out of the   city   and
ἤρχοντο   πρὸς   αὐτόν.   31 Ἐν   τῷ   μεταξὺ
came   to   him.   In   the   meantime
ἠρώτων   αὐτὸν   οἱ   μαθηταὶ   λέγοντες·   ῥαββί,
asked   him   the   disciples   saying :   Rabbi,
φάγε.   32 ὁ   δὲ   εἶπεν   αὐτοῖς·   ἐγὼ   βρῶσιν
eat.   But he   said   to them :   I   food
ἔχω   φαγεῖν   ἣν   ὑμεῖς   οὐκ   οἴδατε.   33 ἔλεγον
have   to eat   which   ye   do not know.   Said
οὖν   οἱ   μαθηταὶ   πρὸς   ἀλλήλους·   μή   τις
therefore the disciples   to   one another :   Not anyone
ἤνεγκεν   αὐτῷ   φαγεῖν;   34 λέγει   αὐτοῖς   ὁ
brought   him   to eat?   Says   to them   –
Ἰησοῦς·   ἐμὸν   βρῶμά   ἐστιν   ἵνα   ποιῶ   τὸ
Jesus :   My   food   is   that I may do the
θέλημα   τοῦ   πέμψαντός   με   καὶ   τελειώσω
will   of the [one] having sent   me   and   may finish
αὐτοῦ   τὸ   ἔργον.   35 οὐχ   ὑμεῖς   λέγετε   ὅτι
of him   the   work.   ²Not   ¹ye   ¹say   that
ἔτι   τετράμηνός   ἐστιν   καὶ   ὁ   θερισμὸς
yet   four months   it is   and   the   harvest
ἔρχεται;   ἰδοὺ   λέγω   ὑμῖν,   ἐπάρατε   τοὺς
comes?   Behold I tell   you,   lift up   the
ὀφθαλμοὺς   ὑμῶν   καὶ   θεάσασθε   τὰς   χώρας,
eyes   of you   and   behold   the   fields,
ὅτι   λευκαί   εἰσιν   πρὸς   θερισμόν.   ἤδη
because white   they are   to   harvest.   Already
36 ὁ   θερίζων   μισθὸν   λαμβάνει   καὶ   συνάγει
the [one] reaping   wages   receives   and   gathers
καρπὸν   εἰς   ζωὴν   αἰώνιον,   ἵνα   ὁ   σπείρων
fruit   to   life   eternal,   that the [one] ²sowing
ὁμοῦ   χαίρῃ   καὶ   ὁ   θερίζων.   37 ἐν   γὰρ
⁷together ⁶may rejoice ³and ⁴the [one] ⁵reaping.   For in
τούτῳ   ὁ   λόγος   ἐστὶν   ἀληθινὸς   ὅτι   ἄλλος
this   the   word   is   true   that another(one)
ἐστὶν   ὁ   σπείρων   καὶ   ἄλλος   ὁ   θερίζων.
is   the [one] sowing   and   another the [one] reaping.
38 ἐγὼ   ἀπέστειλα   ὑμᾶς   θερίζειν   ὃ   οὐχ
I   sent   you   to reap   what not
ὑμεῖς   κεκοπιάκατε·   ἄλλοι   κεκοπιάκασιν,   καὶ
ye   have laboured;   others   have laboured,   and
ὑμεῖς   εἰς   τὸν   κόπον   αὐ ῶν   εἰσεληλύθατε.
ye   into   the   labour   of them   have entered.

39 Many Samaritans from that city believed in him because of the woman's testimony, "He told me all that I ever did." [40]So when the Samaritans came to him, they asked him to stay with them; and he stayed there two days. [41]And many more believed because of his word. [42]They said to the woman, "It is no longer because of your words that we believe, for we have heard for ourselves, and we know that this is indeed the Savior of the world."

43 After the two days he departed to Galilee. [44]For Jesus himself testified that a prophet has no honor in his own country. [45]So when he came to Galilee, the Galileans welcomed him, having seen all that he had done in Jerusalem at the feast, for they too had gone to the feast.

46 So he came again to Cana in Galilee, where he had made the water wine. And at Caper′naum there was an official whose son was ill. [47]When

39 Ἐκ δὲ τῆς πόλεως ἐκείνης πολλοὶ
And out of – city that many

ἐπίστευσαν εἰς αὐτὸν τῶν Σαμαριτῶν διὰ
believed in him of the Samaritans because of

τὸν λόγον τῆς γυναικὸς μαρτυρούσης ὅτι
the word of the woman witnessing[,] –

εἶπέν μοι πάντα ἃ ἐποίησα. **40** ὡς
He told me all things which I did. When

οὖν ἦλθον πρὸς αὐτὸν οἱ Σαμαρῖται,
therefore came to him the Samaritans,

ἠρώτων αὐτὸν μεῖναι παρ᾽ αὐτοῖς· καὶ
they asked him to remain with them; and

ἔμεινεν ἐκεῖ δύο ἡμέρας. **41** καὶ πολλῷ
he remained there two days. And [2]more

πλείους ἐπίστευσαν διὰ τὸν λόγον αὐτοῦ,
[1]many believed because of the word of him,

42 τῇ τε γυναικὶ ἔλεγον ὅτι οὐκέτι διὰ
and to the woman they said[,] – No longer because of

τὴν σὴν λαλιὰν πιστεύομεν· αὐτοὶ γὰρ
– thy talk we believe; for [our]selves

ἀκηκόαμεν, καὶ οἴδαμεν ὅτι οὗτός ἐστιν
we have heard, and we know that this man is

ἀληθῶς ὁ σωτὴρ τοῦ κόσμου.
truly the Saviour of the world.

43 Μετὰ δὲ τὰς δύο ἡμέρας ἐξῆλθεν
And after the two days he went forth

ἐκεῖθεν εἰς τὴν Γαλιλαίαν. **44** αὐτὸς γὰρ
thence into – Galilee. For [2][him]self

Ἰησοῦς ἐμαρτύρησεν ὅτι προφήτης ἐν
[1]Jesus witnessed that a prophet in

τῇ ἰδίᾳ πατρίδι τιμὴν οὐκ ἔχει. **45** ὅτε
the(his) own native place honour has not. When

οὖν ἦλθεν εἰς τὴν Γαλιλαίαν, ἐδέξαντο
therefore he came into – Galilee, received

αὐτὸν οἱ Γαλιλαῖοι, πάντα ἑωρακότες
him the Galilæans, all things having seen

ὅσα ἐποίησεν ἐν Ἱεροσολύμοις ἐν τῇ
which he did in Jerusalem at the

ἑορτῇ· καὶ αὐτοὶ γὰρ ἦλθον εἰς τὴν
feast; [2]also [3]they [1]for went to the

ἑορτήν. **46** Ἦλθεν οὖν πάλιν εἰς τὴν
feast. He came therefore again to –

Κανὰ τῆς Γαλιλαίας, ὅπου ἐποίησεν τὸ
Cana – of Galilee, where he made the

ὕδωρ οἶνον. καὶ ἦν τις βασιλικὸς
water wine. And there was a certain courtier

οὗ ὁ υἱὸς ἠσθένει ἐν Καφαρναούμ· **47** οὗτος
of whom the son ailed in Capernaum; this man

he heard that Jesus had come from Judea to Galilee, he went and begged him to come down and heal his son, for he was at the point of death. [48]Jesus therefore said to him, "Unless you see signs and wonders you will not believe." [49]The official said to him, "Sir, come down before my child dies." [50]Jesus said to him, "Go; your son will live." The man believed the word that Jesus spoke to him and went his way. [51]As he was going down, his servants met him and told him that his son was living. [52]So he asked them the hour when he began to mend, and they said to him, "Yesterday at the seventh hour the fever left him." [53]The father knew that was the hour when Jesus had said to him, "Your son will live"; and he himself believed, and all his household. [54]This was now the second sign that Jesus did when he had come from Judea to Galilee.

ἀκούσας ὅτι ’Ιησοῦς ἥκει ἐκ τῆς ’Ιουδαίας
hearing that Jesus comes(came) out of - Judæa

εἰς τὴν Γαλιλαίαν, ἀπῆλθεν πρὸς αὐτὸν καὶ
into - Galilee, went to him and

ἠρώτα ἵνα καταβῇ καὶ ἰάσηται αὐτοῦ
asked that he would come down and would cure of him

τὸν υἱόν· ἤμελλεν γὰρ ἀποθνήσκειν. 48 εἶπεν
the son; for he was about to die. Said

οὖν ὁ ’Ιησοῦς πρὸς αὐτόν· ἐὰν μὴ σημεῖα
therefore - Jesus to him: Except signs

καὶ τέρατα ἴδητε, οὐ μὴ πιστεύσητε.
and prodigies ye see, by no means ye believe.

49 λέγει πρὸς αὐτὸν ὁ βασιλικός· κύριε,
Says to him the courtier: Sir,

κατάβηθι πρὶν ἀποθανεῖν τὸ παιδίον μου.
come down before to die the child[b] of me.

50 λέγει αὐτῷ ὁ ’Ιησοῦς· πορεύου, ὁ
Tells him - Jesus: Go, the

υἱός σου ζῇ. ²ἐπίστευσεν ὁ ⁴ἄνθρωπος τῷ
son of thee lives. ³Believed ¹the ²man ⁴the

λόγῳ ὃν εἶπεν αὐτῷ ὁ ’Ιησοῦς, καὶ
⁵word ⁶which ⁸said ⁹to him - ⁷Jesus, and

ἐπορεύετο. 51 ἤδη δὲ αὐτοῦ καταβαίνοντος
went. And already him going down[a]
=while he was going down

οἱ δοῦλοι ὑπήντησαν αὐτῷ λέγοντες ὅτι
the slaves met him saying that

ὁ παῖς αὐτοῦ ζῇ. 52 ἐπύθετο οὖν τὴν
the boy of him lives. He inquired therefore the

ὥραν παρ’ αὐτῶν ἐν ᾗ κομψότερον ἔσχεν·
hour from them in which better he had;
=he got better;

εἶπαν οὖν αὐτῷ ὅτι ἐχθὲς ὥραν ἑβδόμην
they said therefore to him[,] - Yesterday [at] hour seventh

ἀφῆκεν αὐτὸν ὁ πυρετός. 53 ἔγνω οὖν
left him the fever. Knew therefore

ὁ πατὴρ ὅτι ἐκείνῃ τῇ ὥρᾳ ἐν ᾗ εἶπεν
the father that in that - hour in which told

αὐτῷ ὁ ’Ιησοῦς· ὁ υἱός σου ζῇ· καὶ
him - Jesus: The son of thee lives; and

ἐπίστευσεν αὐτὸς καὶ ἡ οἰκία αὐτοῦ ὅλη.
believed he and the household of him whole.

54 Τοῦτο [δὲ] πάλιν δεύτερον σημεῖον
And this again a second sign

ἐποίησεν ὁ ’Ιησοῦς ἐλθὼν ἐκ τῆς ’Ιουδαίας
did - Jesus having come out of - Judæa

εἰς τὴν Γαλιλαίαν.
into - Galilee.

CHAPTER 5

AFTER this there was a feast of the Jews, and Jesus went up to Jerusalem.

2 Now there is in Jerusalem by the Sheep gate a pool, in Hebrew called Beth-za'tha,[f] which has five porticoes. ³In these lay a multitude of invalids, blind, lame, paralyzed.[j] ⁵One man was there, who had been ill for thirty-eight years. ⁶When Jesus saw him and knew that he had been lying there a long time, he said to him, "Do you want to be healed?" ⁷The sick man answered him, "Sir, I have no man to put me into the pool when the water is troubled, and while I am going another steps down before me." ⁸Jesus said to him, "Rise, take up your pallet, and walk." ⁹And at once the man was healed, and he took up his pallet and walked.

Now that day was the sabbath. ¹⁰So the Jews said to the man who was cured, "It is the sabbath, it is not lawful for you to carry your pallet." ¹¹But

[f] Other ancient authorities read Bethesda, others Bethsaida

[j] Other ancient authorities insert, wholly or in part, waiting for the moving of the water; [for an angel of the Lord went down at certain seasons into the pool, and troubled the water: whoever stepped in first after the troubling of the water was healed of whatever disease he had

---

5 Μετὰ ταῦτα ἦν ἑορτὴ τῶν Ἰουδαίων,
After these things there was a feast of the Jews,

καὶ ἀνέβη Ἰησοῦς εἰς Ἱεροσόλυμα. 2 ἔστιν
and went up Jesus to Jerusalem.   there is

δὲ ἐν τοῖς Ἱεροσολύμοις ἐπὶ τῇ προβατικῇ
Now in –   Jerusalem   at the   sheepgate

κολυμβήθρα, ἡ ἐπιλεγομένη Ἑβραϊστὶ
a pool, the [one] being called in Hebrew

Βηθζαθά, πέντε στοὰς ἔχουσα. 3 ἐν
Bethzatha, five porches having.   In

ταύταις κατέκειτο πλῆθος τῶν ἀσθενούντων,
these   lay   a multitude of the   ailing [ones],

τυφλῶν, χωλῶν, ξηρῶν. ‡ 5 ἦν δέ τις
blind,   lame,   withered.   And there was a

ἄνθρωπος ἐκεῖ τριάκοντα καὶ ὀκτὼ ἔτη
certain man there   thirty-eight   years

ἔχων ἐν τῇ ἀσθενείᾳ αὐτοῦ· 6 τοῦτον
having in the   ailment   of him;.   ³this man

ἰδὼν ὁ Ἰησοῦς κατακείμενον, καὶ γνοὺς
²seeing – ¹Jesus   ⁴lying,   and knowing

ὅτι πολὺν ἤδη χρόνον ἔχει, λέγει αὐτῷ·
that ³much ²already ⁴time ¹he has, says to him :

θέλεις ὑγιὴς γενέσθαι; 7 ἀπεκρίθη αὐτῷ
Wishest thou whole to become?   Answered   him

ὁ ἀσθενῶν· κύριε, ἄνθρωπον οὐκ ἔχω,
the ailing [one] : Sir,   a man   I have not,

ἵνα ὅταν ταραχθῇ τὸ ὕδωρ βάλῃ με εἰς
that when is troubled the water he may put me into

τὴν κολυμβήθραν· ἐν ᾧ δὲ ἔρχομαι ἐγώ,
the   pool;   but while am coming I,

ἄλλος πρὸ ἐμοῦ καταβαίνει. 8 λέγει αὐτῷ
another before me   goes down.   Says to him

ὁ Ἰησοῦς· ἔγειρε ἆρον τὸν κράβατόν
– Jesus :   Rise[.] take the   mattress

σου καὶ περιπάτει. 9 καὶ εὐθέως ἐγένετο
of thee and   walk.   And immediately became

ὑγιὴς ὁ ἄνθρωπος, καὶ ἦρεν τὸν κράβατον
whole the   man,   and took the   mattress

αὐτοῦ καὶ περιεπάτει. ⁷Ην δὲ σάββατον
of him and   walked.   And it was a sabbath

ἐν ἐκείνῃ τῇ ἡμέρᾳ. 10 ἔλεγον οὖν οἱ
on that   –   day.   Said therefore the

Ἰουδαῖοι τῷ τεθεραπευμένῳ· σάββατόν ἐστιν,
Jews   to the [one] having been healed : A sabbath   it is,

καὶ οὐκ ἔξεστίν σοι ἆραι τὸν κράβατον.
and it is not lawful for thee to take the   mattress.

‡ End of ver. 3 and ver. 4 omitted by Nestle; cf. RSV footnote.

he answered them, "The man who healed me said to me, 'Take up your pallet, and walk.'" [12] They asked him, "Who is the man who said to you, 'Take up your pallet, and walk'?" [13] Now the man who had been healed did not know who it was, for Jesus had withdrawn, as there was a crowd in the place. [14] Afterward, Jesus found him in the temple, and said to him, "See, you are well! Sin no more, that nothing worse befall you." [15] The man went away and told the Jews that it was Jesus who had healed him. [16] And this was why the Jews persecuted Jesus, because he did this on the sabbath. [17] But Jesus answered them, "My Father is working still, and I am working." [18] This was why the Jews sought all the more to kill him, because he not only broke the sabbath but also called God his Father, making himself equal with God.

[19] Jesus said to them, "Truly, truly, I say to you, the Son can do nothing of his own

11 ὃς   δὲ   ἀπεκρίθη   αὐτοῖς·   ὁ   ποιήσας
But who(he)   answered   them :   The [one]   making
με   ὑγιῆ,   ἐκεῖνός   μοι   εἶπεν·   ἆρον   τὸν
me   whole,   that one   me   told :   Take   the
κράβατόν   σου   καὶ   περιπάτει.   12 ἠρώτησαν
mattress   of thee   and   walk.   They asked
αὐτόν·   τίς   ἐστιν   ὁ   ἄνθρωπος   ὁ   εἰπών
him :   Who   is   the   man   –   telling
σοι·   ἆρον   καὶ   περιπάτει;   13 ὁ   δὲ   ἰαθεὶς
thee :   Take   and   walk?   But the [one]   cured
οὐκ   ᾔδει   τίς   ἐστιν·   ὁ   γὰρ   Ἰησοῦς
did not know   who   it is(was);   –   for   Jesus
ἐξένευσεν   ὄχλου   ὄντος   ἐν   τῷ   τόπῳ.
withdrew   a crowd   being   in   the   place.
              =as there was a crowd

14 μετὰ   ταῦτα   εὑρίσκει   αὐτὸν   ὁ   Ἰησοῦς
After   these things   finds   him   –   Jesus
ἐν   τῷ   ἱερῷ   καὶ   εἶπεν   αὐτῷ·   ἴδε   ὑγιὴς
in   the   temple   and   said   to him : Behold[,]   whole
γέγονας·   μηκέτι   ἁμάρτανε,   ἵνα   μὴ   χεῖρόν
thou hast become;   no longer   sin,   lest   [2]worse
σοί   τι   γένηται. 15 ἀπῆλθεν   ὁ   ἄνθρωπος
[4]to thee   [1]something   [3]happens.   Went away the   man
καὶ   εἶπεν   τοῖς   Ἰουδαίοις   ὅτι   Ἰησοῦς
and   told   the   Jews   that   Jesus
ἐστιν   ὁ   ποιήσας   αὐτὸν   ὑγιῆ. 16 καὶ   διὰ
it is(was)   the [one] having made   him   whole.   And there-
τοῦτο   ἐδίωκον   οἱ   Ἰουδαῖοι   τὸν   Ἰησοῦν,
fore   [3]persecuted   [1]the   [2]Jews   –   [4]Jesus,
ὅτι   ταῦτα   ἐποίει   ἐν   σαββάτῳ. 17 ὁ   δὲ
because   these things   he did   on   a sabbath.   But he
ἀπεκρίνατο   αὐτοῖς·   ὁ   πατήρ   μου   ἕως
answered   them :   The   Father   of me   until
ἄρτι   ἐργάζεται,   κἀγὼ   ἐργάζομαι· 18 διὰ
now   works,   and I   work;   because of
τοῦτο   οὖν   μᾶλλον   ἐζήτουν   αὐτὸν   οἱ
this   therefore   [4]the more   [3]sought   [5]him   [1]the
Ἰουδαῖοι   ἀποκτεῖναι,   ὅτι   οὐ   μόνον   ἔλυεν
[2]Jews   [6]to kill,   because not   only   he broke
τὸ   σάββατον,   ἀλλὰ   καὶ   πατέρα   ἴδιον
the   sabbath,   but   also   Father [his]   own
ἔλεγεν   τὸν   θεόν,   ἴσον   ἑαυτὸν   ποιῶν   τῷ
said   –   God [to be], equal   himself   making
θεῷ. 19 Ἀπεκρίνατο   οὖν   ὁ   Ἰησοῦς   καὶ
to God.   Answered   therefore   –   Jesus   and
ἔλεγεν   αὐτοῖς·   ἀμὴν   ἀμὴν   λέγω   ὑμῖν,
said   to them :   Truly   truly   I say   to you,
οὐ   δύναται   ὁ   υἱὸς   ποιεῖν   ἀφ'   ἑαυτοῦ
cannot   the   Son   to do   from   himself

accord, but only what he sees the Father doing; for whatever he does, that the Son does likewise. ²⁰For the Father loves the Son, and shows him all that he himself is doing; and greater works than these will he show him, that you may marvel. ²¹For as the Father raises the dead and gives them life, so also the Son gives life to whom he will. ²²The Father judges no one, but has given all judgment to the Son, ²³that all may honor the Son, even as they honor the Father. He who does not honor the Son does not honor the Father who sent him. ²⁴Truly, truly, I say to you, he who hears my word and believes him who sent me has eternal life; he does not come into judgment, but has passed from death to life.

²⁵"Truly, truly, I say to you, the hour is coming, and now is, when the dead will hear the voice of the Son of God, and those who hear will live. ²⁶For as the Father has life in himself, so he has granted the Son also to have life in himself,

οὐδέν, ἂν μή τι βλέπῃ τὸν πατέρα
no(any)thing, except what he sees the Father

ποιοῦντα· ἃ γὰρ ἂν ἐκεῖνος ποιῇ, ταῦτα
doing; for whatever things that one does, these

καὶ ὁ υἱὸς ὁμοίως ποιεῖ. 20 ὁ γὰρ
also the Son likewise does. For the

πατὴρ φιλεῖ τὸν υἱὸν καὶ πάντα δείκνυσιν
Father loves the Son and all things shows

αὐτῷ ἃ αὐτὸς ποιεῖ, καὶ μείζονα τούτων
him which he does, and ¹greater ³[than] ⁴these

δείξει αὐτῷ ἔργα, ἵνα ὑμεῖς θαυμάζητε.
⁵he will show ⁶him ²works, that ye may marvel.

21 ὥσπερ γὰρ ὁ πατὴρ ἐγείρει τοὺς
For as the Father raises the

νεκροὺς καὶ ζωοποιεῖ, οὕτως καὶ ὁ υἱὸς
dead and quickens, so also the Son

οὓς θέλει ζωοποιεῖ. 22 οὐδὲ γὰρ ὁ
whom he wills quickens. For not the

πατὴρ κρίνει οὐδένα, ἀλλὰ τὴν κρίσιν
Father judges no(any) one, but judgment

πᾶσαν δέδωκεν τῷ υἱῷ, 23 ἵνα πάντες
all he has given to the Son, that all men

τιμῶσι τὸν υἱὸν καθὼς τιμῶσι τὸν πατέρα.
may honour the Son as they honour the Father.

ὁ μὴ τιμῶν τὸν υἱὸν οὐ τιμᾷ τὸν πατέρα
The [one] not honouring the Son honours not the Father

τὸν πέμψαντα αὐτόν. 24 Ἀμὴν ἀμὴν
- having sent him. Truly truly

λέγω ὑμῖν ὅτι ὁ τὸν λόγον μου ἀκούων
I say to you[,] - The [one] the word of me hearing

καὶ πιστεύων τῷ πέμψαντί με ἔχει
and believing the [one] having sent me has

ζωὴν αἰώνιον, καὶ εἰς κρίσιν οὐκ ἔρχεται
life eternal, and into judgment comes not

ἀλλὰ μεταβέβηκεν ἐκ τοῦ θανάτου εἰς
but has passed over out of - death into

τὴν ζωήν. 25 ἀμὴν ἀμὴν λέγω ὑμῖν ὅτι
- life. Truly truly I say to you[,] -

ἔρχεται ὥρα καὶ νῦν ἐστιν ὅτε οἱ νεκροὶ
Comes an hour and now is when the dead

ἀκούσουσιν τῆς φωνῆς τοῦ υἱοῦ τοῦ
will hear the voice of the Son -

θεοῦ καὶ οἱ ἀκούσαντες ζήσουσιν. 26 ὥσπερ
of God and the [ones] hearing will live. as

γὰρ ὁ πατὴρ ἔχει ζωὴν ἐν ἑαυτῷ, οὕτως
For the Father has life in himself, so

καὶ τῷ υἱῷ ἔδωκεν ζωὴν ἔχειν ἐν ἑαυτῷ.
also to the Son he gave life to have in himself.

²⁷and has given him authority to execute judgment, because he is the Son of man. ²⁸Do not marvel at this; for the hour is coming when all who are in the tombs will hear his voice ²⁹and come forth, those who have done good, to the resurrection of life, and those who have done evil, to the resurrection of judgment.

30 "I can do nothing on my own authority; as I hear, I judge; and my judgment is just, because I seek not my own will but the will of him who sent me. ³¹If I bear witness to myself, my testimony is not true; ³²there is another who bears witness to me, and I know that the testimony which he bears to me is true. ³³You sent to John, and he has borne witness to the truth. ³⁴Not that the testimony which I receive is from man; but I say this that you may be saved. ³⁵He was a burning and shining lamp, and you were willing to rejoice for a while in his

27 καὶ ἐξουσίαν ἔδωκεν αὐτῷ κρίσιν ποιεῖν,
And　authority　he gave　him　judgment　to do,

ὅτι υἱὸς ἀνθρώπου ἐστίν. 28 μὴ θαυμάζετε
because son　of man*　he is.　　　Marvel not [at]

τοῦτο, ὅτι ἔρχεται ὥρα ἐν ᾗ πάντες οἱ
this, because comes　an hour in which all the [ones]

ἐν τοῖς μνημείοις ἀκούσουσιν τῆς φωνῆς
in　the　tombs　will hear　the　voice

αὐτοῦ 29 καὶ ἐκπορεύσονται οἱ τὰ ἀγαθὰ
of him　and　will come forth　the [ones] the good things

ποιήσαντες εἰς ἀνάστασιν ζωῆς, οἱ τὰ
having done　to　a resurrection of life, the [ones] the

φαῦλα πράξαντες εἰς ἀνάστασιν κρίσεως.
evil things having done　to　a resurrection of judgment.

30 Οὐ δύναμαι ἐγὼ ποιεῖν ἀπ' ἐμαυτοῦ
Cannot　I　to do　from　myself

οὐδέν· καθὼς ἀκούω κρίνω, καὶ ἡ κρίσις
no(any)thing; as　I hear　I judge, and – judgment

ἡ ἐμὴ δικαία ἐστίν, ὅτι οὐ ζητῶ τὸ
– my　just　is, because I seek not　–

θέλημα τὸ ἐμὸν ἀλλὰ τὸ θέλημα τοῦ
will　– my　but　the　will of the [one]

πέμψαντός με. 31 Ἐὰν ἐγὼ μαρτυρῶ
having sent　me.　If　I　witness

περὶ ἐμαυτοῦ, ἡ μαρτυρία μου οὐκ ἔστιν
concerning myself,　the　witness　of me　is not

ἀληθής· 32 ἄλλος ἐστιν ὁ μαρτυρῶν περὶ
true;　another there is the [one] witnessing concerning

ἐμοῦ, καὶ οἶδα ὅτι ἀληθής ἐστιν ἡ
me,　and I know that　true　is　the

μαρτυρία ἣν μαρτυρεῖ περὶ ἐμοῦ. 33 ὑμεῖς
witness　which he witnesses concerning me.　Ye

ἀπεστάλκατε πρὸς Ἰωάννην, καὶ μεμαρ-
have sent　to　John,　and　he has

τύρηκεν τῇ ἀληθείᾳ· 34 ἐγὼ δὲ οὐ παρὰ
witnessed to the　truth;　but I　not from

ἀνθρώπου τὴν μαρτυρίαν λαμβάνω, ἀλλὰ
man　the　witness　receive,　but

ταῦτα λέγω ἵνα ὑμεῖς σωθῆτε. 35 ἐκεῖνος
these things I say　that　ye　may be saved.　That man

ἦν ὁ λύχνος ὁ καιόμενος καὶ φαίνων,
was the　lamp　–　burning　and　shining,

ὑμεῖς δὲ ἠθελήσατε ἀγαλλιαθῆναι πρὸς
and ye　were willing　to exult　for

ὥραν ἐν τῷ φωτὶ αὐτοῦ. 36 Ἐγὼ δὲ
an hour in the　light　of him.　　But I

---

* Note the absence of the definite article here. See also Rev. 1. 13 and 14. 14.

light. ³⁶ But the testimony which I have is greater than that of John; for the works which the Father has granted me to accomplish, these very works which I am doing, bear me witness that the Father has sent me. ³⁷ And the Father who sent me has himself borne witness to me. His voice you have never heard, his form you have never seen; ³⁸ and you do not have his word abiding in you, for you do not believe him whom he has sent. ³⁹ You search the scriptures, because you think that in them you have eternal life; and it is they that bear witness to me; ⁴⁰ yet you refuse to come to me that you may have life. ⁴¹ I do not receive glory from men. ⁴² But I know that you have not the love of God within you. ⁴³ I have come in my Father's name, and you do not receive me; if another comes in his own name, him you will receive. ⁴⁴ How can you believe, who receive glory from one another and do not seek the glory that comes from the only God? ⁴⁵ Do not think that I shall accuse you

ἔχω τὴν μαρτυρίαν μείζω τοῦ Ἰωάννου·
have the witness greater [than] – of John;

τὰ γὰρ ἔργα ἃ δέδωκέν μοι ὁ πατὴρ ἵνα
for the works which has given me the Father that

τελειώσω αὐτά, αὐτὰ τὰ ἔργα ἃ ποιῶ,
I may finish them, ³[them]selves ¹the ²works which I do,

μαρτυρεῖ περὶ ἐμοῦ ὅτι ὁ πατήρ με
witnesses concerning me that the Father me

ἀπέσταλκεν. 37 καὶ ὁ πέμψας με πατήρ,
has sent. And ¹the ³having sent ⁴me ²Father,

ἐκεῖνος μεμαρτύρηκεν περὶ ἐμοῦ. οὔτε
that [one] has witnessed concerning me. Neither

φωνὴν αὐτοῦ πώποτε ἀκηκόατε οὔτε εἶδος
voice of him never ye have heard nor form

αὐτοῦ ἑωράκατε, 38 καὶ τὸν λόγον αὐτοῦ
of him ye have seen, and the word of him

οὐκ ἔχετε ἐν ὑμῖν μένοντα, ὅτι ὃν
ye have not in you remaining, because [he] whom

ἀπέστειλεν ἐκεῖνος, τούτῳ ὑμεῖς οὐ πιστεύετε.
²sent ¹that [one], this [one] ye do not believe.

39 ἐρευνᾶτε τὰς γραφάς, ὅτι ὑμεῖς δοκεῖτε
Ye search the scriptures, because ye think

ἐν αὐταῖς ζωὴν αἰώνιον ἔχειν· καὶ ἐκεῖναί
in them life eternal to have; and those

εἰσιν αἱ μαρτυροῦσαι περὶ ἐμοῦ· 40 καὶ
are the [ones] witnessing concerning me; and

οὐ θέλετε ἐλθεῖν πρός με ἵνα ζωὴν
ye wish not to come to me that life

ἔχητε. 41 Δόξαν παρὰ ἀνθρώπων οὐ
ye may have. Glory from men not

λαμβάνω, 42 ἀλλὰ ἔγνωκα ὑμᾶς ὅτι τὴν
I receive, but I have known you that the

ἀγάπην τοῦ θεοῦ οὐκ ἔχετε ἐν ἑαυτοῖς.
love – of God ye have not in yourselves.

43 ἐγὼ ἐλήλυθα ἐν τῷ ὀνόματι τοῦ πατρός
I have come in the name of the Father

μου, καὶ οὐ λαμβάνετέ με· ἐὰν ἄλλος
of me, and ye receive not me; if another

ἔλθῃ ἐν τῷ ὀνόματι τῷ ἰδίῳ, ἐκεῖνον
comes in – name the(his) own, that [one]

λήμψεσθε. 44 πῶς δύνασθε ὑμεῖς πιστεῦσαι,
ye will receive. How can ye to believe,

δόξαν παρὰ ἀλλήλων λαμβάνοντες, καὶ
glory from one another receiving, and

τὴν δόξαν τὴν παρὰ τοῦ μόνου θεοῦ
the glory – from the only God

οὐ ζητεῖτε; 45 μὴ δοκεῖτε ὅτι ἐγὼ κατηγορήσω
ye seek not? Do not think that I will accuse

to the Father; it is Moses who accuses you, on whom you set your hope. 46 If you believed Moses, you would believe me, for he wrote of me. 47 But if you do not believe his writings, how will you believe my words?"

ὑμῶν πρὸς τὸν πατέρα· ἐστιν ὁ κατηγορῶν
you to the Father; there is the [one] accusing
ὑμῶν Μωϋσῆς, εἰς ὃν ὑμεῖς ἠλπίκατε. 46 εἰ
you[,] Moses, in whom ye have hoped. if
γὰρ ἐπιστεύετε Μωϋσεῖ, ἐπιστεύετε ἂν
For ye believed Moses, ye would have believed
ἐμοί· περὶ γὰρ ἐμοῦ ἐκεῖνος ἔγραψεν.
me; for concerning me that [one] wrote.
47 εἰ δὲ τοῖς ἐκείνου γράμμασιν οὐ
But 3if 4the 6of that [one] 5letters 2not
πιστεύετε, πῶς τοῖς ἐμοῖς ῥήμασιν
2ye believe, how – my words
πιστεύσετε;
will ye believe?

CHAPTER 6

AFTER this Jesus went to the other side of the Sea of Galilee, which is the Sea of Tibe′ri-as. 2And a multitude followed him, because they saw the signs which he did on those who were diseased. 3Jesus went up into the hills, and there sat down with his disciples. 4Now the Passover, the feast of the Jews, was at hand. 5Lifting up his eyes, then, and seeing that a multitude was coming to him, Jesus said to Philip, "How are we to buy bread, so that these people may eat?" . This he said to test him, for he himself knew what he would do. 7Philip answered him, "Two hundred denarii would not buy enough bread for each of them to get a

6 Μετὰ ταῦτα ἀπῆλθεν ὁ Ἰησοῦς πέραν
After these things went away – Jesus across
τῆς θαλάσσης τῆς Γαλιλαίας τῆς Τιβεριάδος.
the sea – of Galilee[,] – of Tiberias.
2 ἠκολούθει δὲ αὐτῷ ὄχλος πολύς, ὅτι
And followed him crowd a much, because
ἑώρων τὰ σημεῖα ἃ ἐποίει ἐπὶ τῶν
they saw the signs which he did on the
ἀσθενούντων. 3 ἀνῆλθεν δὲ εἰς τὸ ὄρος
ailing [ones]. And went up to the mountain
Ἰησοῦς, καὶ ἐκεῖ ἐκάθητο μετὰ τῶν
Jesus, and there sat with the
μαθητῶν αὐτοῦ. 4 ἦν δὲ ἐγγὺς τὸ πάσχα,
disciples of him. And was near the Passover,
ἡ ἑορτὴ τῶν Ἰουδαίων. 5 ἐπάρας οὖν
the feast of the Jews. Lifting up therefore
τοὺς ὀφθαλμοὺς ὁ Ἰησοῦς καὶ θεασάμενος
the(his) eyes – Jesus and beholding
ὅτι πολὺς ὄχλος ἔρχεται πρὸς αὐτόν,
that a much crowd is(was) coming toward him,
λέγει πρὸς Φίλιππον· πόθεν ἀγοράσωμεν
he says to Philip: Whence may we buy
ἄρτους ἵνα φάγωσιν οὗτοι; 6 τοῦτο δὲ
loaves that may eat these? And this
ἔλεγεν πειράζων αὐτόν· αὐτὸς γὰρ ᾔδει
he said testing him; for he knew
τί ἔμελλεν ποιεῖν. 7 ἀπεκρίθη αὐτῷ ὁ
what he was about to do. Answered him –
Φίλιππος· διακοσίων δηναρίων ἄρτοι οὐκ
Philip : 3Of two hundred 2denarii 1loaves not
ἀρκοῦσιν αὐτοῖς, ἵνα ἕκαστος βραχύ τι
are enough for them, that each a little

little." ⁸One of his disciples, Andrew, Simon Peter's brother, said to him, ⁹"There is a lad here who has five barley loaves and two fish; but what are they among so many?" ¹⁰Jesus said, "Make the people sit down." Now there was much grass in the place; so the men sat down, in number about five thousand. ¹¹Jesus then took the loaves, and when he had given thanks, he distributed them to those who were seated; so also the fish, as much as they wanted. ¹²And when they had eaten their fill, he told his disciples, "Gather up the fragments left over, that nothing may be lost." ¹³So they gathered them up and filled twelve baskets with fragments from the five barley loaves, left by those who had eaten. ¹⁴When the people saw the sign which he had done, they said, "This is indeed the prophet who is to come into the world!"

15 Perceiving then that they were about to come and take him by force to make him king, Jesus

λάβῃ. 8 λέγει αὐτῷ εἷς ἐκ τῶν μαθητῶν
may take.   Says to him one of the   disciples

αὐτοῦ, Ἀνδρέας ὁ ἀδελφὸς Σίμωνος
of him, Andrew the   brother   of Simon

Πέτρου· 9 ἔστιν παιδάριον ὧδε ὃς ἔχει
Peter :   There is a lad   here who has

πέντε ἄρτους κριθίνους καὶ δύο ὀψάρια·
five   loaves   barley   and two fishes;

ἀλλὰ ταῦτα τί ἐστιν εἰς τοσούτους;
but ³these ¹what ²is(are) among so many?

10 εἶπεν ὁ Ἰησοῦς· ποιήσατε τοὺς ἀνθρώπους
Said – Jesus · Make   the   men*

ἀναπεσεῖν. ἦν δὲ χόρτος πολὺς ἐν τῷ
to recline. Now there was grass much   in the

τόπῳ. ἀνέπεσαν οὖν οἱ ἄνδρες τὸν ἀριθμὸν
place. Reclined therefore the men the number

ὡς πεντακισχίλιοι. 11 ἔλαβεν οὖν τοὺς
about five thousand.   Took therefore the

ἄρτους ὁ Ἰησοῦς καὶ εὐχαριστήσας
loaves – Jesus and having given thanks

διέδωκεν τοῖς ἀνακειμένοις, ὁμοίως καὶ
distributed to the [ones] lying down, likewise also

ἐκ τῶν ὀψαρίων ὅσον ἤθελον. 12 ὡς δὲ
of the fishes   as much as they wished. Now when

ἐνεπλήσθησαν, λέγει τοῖς μαθηταῖς αὐτοῦ·
they were filled, he tells the   disciples of him:

συναγάγετε τὰ περισσεύσαντα κλάσματα, ἵνα
Gather ye the   left over   fragments, that

μή τι ἀπόληται. 13 συνήγαγον οὖν, καὶ
not anything is lost.   They gathered therefore, and

ἐγέμισαν δώδεκα κοφίνους κλασμάτων ἐκ
filled twelve baskets of fragments of

τῶν πέντε ἄρτων τῶν κριθίνων ἃ ἐπερίσσευσαν
the five loaves – barley which were left over

τοῖς βεβρωκόσιν. 14 Οἱ οὖν ἄνθρωποι
to the [ones] having eaten.   Therefore the   men*

ἰδόντες ὃ ἐποίησεν σημεῖον ἔλεγον ὅτι
seeing ¹what ³he did ²sign   said[,]

οὗτός ἐστιν ἀληθῶς ὁ προφήτης ὁ
This is   truly   the prophet   –

ἐρχόμενος εἰς τὸν κόσμον. 15 Ἰησοῦς
coming into the world.   Jesus

οὖν γνοὺς ὅτι μέλλουσιν ἔρχεσθαι καὶ
therefore knowing that they are(were) about to come and

ἁρπάζειν αὐτὸν ἵνα ποιήσωσιν βασιλέα,
seize   him   that they might make a king,

---

* That is, people. Compare ἄνδρες in ver. 10.

withdrew again to the hills by himself.

16 When evening came, his disciples went down to the sea, [17]got into a boat, and started across the sea to Caper′na-um. It was now dark, and Jesus had not yet come to them. [18]The sea rose because a strong wind was blowing. [19]When they had rowed about three or four miles, they saw Jesus walking on the sea and drawing near to the boat. They were frightened, [20]but he said to them, "It is I; do not be afraid." [21]Then they were glad to take him into the boat, and immediately the boat was at the land to which they were going.

22 On the next day the people who remained on the other side of the sea saw that there had been only one boat there, and that Jesus had not entered the boat with his disciples, but that his disciples had gone away alone. [23]However, boats from Tibe′ri-as came near the place where they ate the bread after the Lord had

ἀνεχώρησεν πάλιν εἰς τὸ ὄρος αὐτὸς
departed   again   to   the mountain [him]self

μόνος. 16 Ὡς δὲ ὀψία ἐγένετο, κατέβησαν
alone.   And when evening came,   went down

οἱ μαθηταὶ αὐτοῦ ἐπὶ τὴν θάλασσαν,
the disciples of him   to   the   sea,

17 καὶ ἐμβάντες εἰς πλοῖον ἤρχοντο πέραν
and embarking in   a boat   came   across

τῆς θαλάσσης εἰς Καφαρναούμ. καὶ
the   sea   to   Capernaum.   And

σκοτία ἤδη ἐγεγόνει καὶ οὔπω ἐληλύθει
darkness now had come   and not yet had come

πρὸς αὐτούς ὁ Ἰησοῦς, 18 ἥ τε θάλασσα
to   them,   Jesus,   and the   sea

ἀνέμου μεγάλου πνέοντος⁽ᵃ⁾ διηγείρετο.
wind   a great   blowing[a]   was roused.
=as a great wind blew

19 ἐληλακότες οὖν ὡς σταδίους εἴκοσι
Having rowed therefore about furlongs   twenty-

πέντε ἢ τριάκοντα θεωροῦσιν τὸν Ἰησοῦν
five   or   thirty   they behold   –   Jesus

περιπατοῦντα ἐπὶ τῆς θαλάσσης καὶ ἐγγὺς
walking   on   the   sea   and near

τοῦ πλοίου γινόμενον, καὶ ἐφοβήθησαν.
the   boat   becoming,   and   they feared.

20 ὁ δὲ λέγει αὐτοῖς· ἐγώ εἰμι· μὴ
But he   says   to them :   I   am;   not

φοβεῖσθε. 21 ἤθελον οὖν λαβεῖν αὐτὸν εἰς
fear ye.   They wished therefore to take him   into

τὸ πλοῖον, καὶ εὐθέως ἐγένετο τὸ πλοῖον
the   boat,   and immediately was   the   boat

ἐπὶ τῆς γῆς εἰς ἣν ὑπῆγον.
at   the land to which they were going.

22 Τῇ ἐπαύριον ὁ ὄχλος ὁ ἑστηκὼς
On the morrow   the crowd   –   standing

πέραν τῆς θαλάσσης εἶδον ὅτι πλοιάριον
across   the   sea   saw   that   boat

ἄλλο οὐκ ἦν ἐκεῖ εἰ μὴ ἕν, καὶ ὅτι
other was not there except one, and that

οὐ συνεισῆλθεν τοῖς μαθηταῖς αὐτοῦ ὁ
[2]did not come in with [3]the [4]disciples [5]of him –

Ἰησοῦς εἰς τὸ πλοῖον ἀλλὰ μόνοι οἱ
[1]Jesus in   the   boat   but   alone   the

μαθηταὶ αὐτοῦ ἀπῆλθον· 23 ἄλλα ἦλθεν
disciples of him   went away;   [1]other   [3]came

πλοιάρια ἐκ Τιβεριάδος ἐγγὺς τοῦ τόπου
[2]boats from   Tiberias   near   the   place

ὅπου ἔφαγον τὸν ἄρτον εὐχαριστήσαντος
where they ate   the bread   having given thanks

given thanks. ²⁴So when the people saw that Jesus was not there, nor his disciples, they themselves got into the boats and went to Caper′na-um, seeking Jesus.

25 When they found him on the other side of the sea, they said to him, "Rabbi, when did you come here?" ²⁶Jesus answered them, "Truly, truly, I say to you, you seek me, not because you saw signs, but because you ate your fill of the loaves. ²⁷Do not labor for the food which perishes, but for the food which endures to eternal life, which the Son of man will give to you; for on him has God the Father set his seal." ²⁸Then they said to him, "What must we do, to be doing the works of God?" ²⁹Jesus answered them, "This is the work of God, that you believe in him whom he has sent." ³⁰So they said to him, "Then what sign do you do, that we may see, and believe you? What work do you perform? ³¹Our fathers ate the manna in the wilderness; as it is written, 'He gave them

τοῦ   κυρίου.   24 ὅτε   οὖν   εἶδεν   ὁ   ὄχλος
the   Lord.ᵃ   When therefore saw   the   crowd
=when the Lord had given thanks.

ὅτι   'Ιησοῦς   οὐκ   ἔστιν   ἐκεῖ   οὐδὲ   οἱ
that   Jesus   is(was) not   there   nor   the

μαθηταὶ   αὐτοῦ,   ἐνέβησαν   αὐτοὶ   εἰς   τὰ
disciples   of him,   embarked   they   in   the

πλοιάρια   καὶ   ἦλθον   εἰς   Καφαρναοὺμ
boats   and   came   to   Capernaum

ζητοῦντες   τὸν   'Ιησοῦν.   25 καὶ   εὑρόντες
seeking   -   Jesus.   And   finding

αὐτὸν   πέραν   τῆς   θαλάσσης   εἶπον   αὐτῷ·
him   across   the   sea   they said   to him :

ῥαββί,   πότε   ὧδε   γέγονας;   26 ἀπεκρίθη
Rabbi,   when   here   hast thou come?   Answered

αὐτοῖς   ὁ   'Ιησοῦς   καὶ   εἶπεν·   ἀμὴν   ἀμὴν
them   -   Jesus   and said: Truly   truly

λέγω   ὑμῖν,   ζητεῖτέ   με   οὐχ   ὅτι   εἴδετε
I say   to you,   ye seek   me   not because   ye saw

σημεῖα,   ἀλλ'   ὅτι   ἐφάγετε   ἐκ   τῶν   ἄρτων
signs,   but because   ye ate   of   the   loaves

καὶ   ἐχορτάσθητε.   27 ἐργάζεσθε   μὴ   τὴν
and   were satisfied.   Work   not [for] the

βρῶσιν   τὴν   ἀπολλυμένην,   ἀλλὰ   τὴν   βρῶσιν
food   -   perishing,   but [for] the   food

τὴν   μένουσαν   εἰς   ζωὴν   αἰώνιον,   ἣν   ὁ
-   remaining   to   life   eternal,   which   the

υἱὸς   τοῦ   ἀνθρώπου   ὑμῖν   δώσει· τοῦτον   γὰρ
Son   -   of man   you   will give;   for this [one]

ὁ   πατὴρ   ἐσφράγισεν   ὁ   θεός.   28 εἶπον
²the   ³Father   ⁴sealed   -   ¹God.   They said

οὖν   πρὸς   αὐτόν·   τί   ποιῶμεν   ἵνα   ἐργαζ-
therefore   to   him :   What   may we do   that   we may

ώμεθα   τὰ   ἔργα   τοῦ   θεοῦ;   29 ἀπεκρίθη
work   the   works   -   of God?   Answered

'Ιησοῦς   καὶ   εἶπεν   αὐτοῖς· τοῦτό   ἐστιν   τὸ
Jesus   and   said   to them ·   This   is   the

ἔργον   τοῦ   θεοῦ,   ἵνα   πιστεύητε   εἰς   ὃν
work   -   of God,   that   ye believe   in [him] whom

ἀπέστειλεν   ἐκεῖνος.   30 εἶπον   οὖν   αὐτῷ·
sent   that [one].   They said therefore   to him :

τί   οὖν   ποιεῖς   σὺ   σημεῖον,   ἵνα   ἴδωμεν
¹What   ²then   ³doest   ⁴thou   ⁵sign,   that   we may see

καὶ   πιστεύσωμέν   σοι;   τί   ἐργάζῃ;   31 οἱ
and   believe   thee?   what workest thou?   The

πατέρες   ἡμῶν   τὸ   μάννα   ἔφαγον   ἐν   τῇ
fathers   of us   the   manna   ate   in   the

ἐρήμῳ,   καθώς   ἐστιν   γεγραμμένον· ἄρτον
desert,   as   it is   *having been* written :   Bread

bread from heaven to eat.' " [32] Jesus then said to them, "Truly, truly, I say to you, it was not Moses who gave you the bread from heaven; my Father gives you the true bread from heaven. [33] For the bread of God is that which comes down from heaven, and gives life to the world." [34] They said to him, "Lord, give us this bread always."

[35] Jesus said to them, "I am the bread of life; he who comes to me shall not hunger, and he who believes in me shall never thirst. [36] But I said to you that you have seen me and yet do not believe. [37] All that the Father gives me will come to me; and him who comes to me I will not cast out. [38] For I have come down from heaven, not to do my own will, but the will of him who sent me; [39] and this is the will of him who sent me, that I should lose nothing of all that he has given me, but raise it up at the last day.

ἐκ τοῦ οὐρανοῦ ἔδωκεν αὐτοῖς φαγεῖν.
out of – heaven he gave them to eat.

32 Εἶπεν οὖν αὐτοῖς ὁ Ἰησοῦς· ἀμὴν
Said therefore to them – Jesus: Truly

ἀμὴν λέγω ὑμῖν, οὐ Μωϋσῆς δέδωκεν
truly I say to you, not Moses has given

ὑμῖν τὸν ἄρτον ἐκ τοῦ οὐρανοῦ, ἀλλ᾽ ὁ
you the bread out of – heaven, but the

πατήρ μου δίδωσιν ὑμῖν τὸν ἄρτον ἐκ
Father of me gives you ¹the ³bread ⁴out of

τοῦ οὐρανοῦ τὸν ἀληθινόν· 33 ὁ γὰρ ἄρτος
– ⁵heaven the ²true; for the bread

τοῦ θεοῦ ἐστιν ὁ καταβαίνων ἐκ τοῦ
– of God is the [one] coming down out of –

οὐρανοῦ καὶ ζωὴν διδοὺς τῷ κόσμῳ.
heaven and life giving to the world.

34 εἶπον οὖν πρὸς αὐτόν· κύριε, πάντοτε
They said therefore to him: Lord, always

δὸς ἡμῖν τὸν ἄρτον τοῦτον. 35 εἶπεν
give us – bread this. Said

αὐτοῖς ὁ Ἰησοῦς· ἐγώ εἰμι ὁ ἄρτος τῆς
to them – Jesus: I am the bread –

ζωῆς· ὁ ἐρχόμενος πρὸς ἐμὲ οὐ μὴ
of life; the [one] coming to me by no means

πεινάσῃ, καὶ ὁ πιστεύων εἰς ἐμὲ οὐ μὴ
hungers, and the [one] believing in me by no means

διψήσει πώποτε. 36 Ἀλλ᾽ εἶπον ὑμῖν ὅτι
will thirst never. But I told you that

καὶ ἑωράκατέ [με] καὶ οὐ πιστεύετε.
both ye have seen me and do not believe.

37 πᾶν ὃ δίδωσίν μοι ὁ πατὴρ πρὸς
All which gives to me the Father to

ἐμὲ ἥξει, καὶ τὸν ἐρχόμενον πρός με
me will come, and the [one] coming to me

οὐ μὴ ἐκβάλω ἔξω, 38 ὅτι καταβέβηκα
by no means I will cast out outside, because I have come down

ἀπὸ τοῦ οὐρανοῦ οὐχ ἵνα ποιῶ τὸ θέλημα
from – heaven not that I may do the ²will

τὸ ἐμὸν ἀλλὰ τὸ θέλημα τοῦ πέμψαντός
– ¹my but the will of the [one] having sent

με. 39 τοῦτο δέ ἐστιν τὸ θέλημα τοῦ
me. And this is the will of the [one]

πέμψαντός με, ἵνα πᾶν ὃ δέδωκέν μοι
having sent me, that all which he has given me

μὴ ἀπολέσω ἐξ αὐτοῦ, ἀλλὰ ἀναστήσω
I shall not lose of it, but shall raise up

αὐτὸ ἐν τῇ ἐσχάτῃ ἡμέρᾳ. 40 τοῦτο
it in the last day. this

⁴⁰For this is the will of my Father, that every one who sees the Son and believes in him should have eternal life; and I will raise him up at the last day."

41 The Jews then murmured at him, because he said, "I am the bread which came down from heaven." ⁴²They said, "Is not this Jesus, the son of Joseph, whose father and mother we know? How does he now say, 'I have come down from heaven'?" ⁴³Jesus answered them, "Do not murmur among yourselves. ⁴⁴No one can come to me unless the Father who sent me draws him; and I will raise him up at the last day. ⁴⁵It is written in the prophets, 'And they shall all be taught by God.' Every one who has heard and learned from the Father comes to me. ⁴⁶Not that any one has seen the Father except him who is from God; he has seen the Father. ⁴⁷Truly, truly, I say to you, he who believes has eternal life. ⁴⁸I am the bread of life. ⁴⁹Your

γάρ ἐστιν τὸ θέλημα τοῦ πατρός μου,
For   is   the   will   of the Father of me,

ἵνα πᾶς ὁ θεωρῶν τὸν υἱὸν καὶ πιστεύων
that everyone beholding the Son   and believing

εἰς αὐτὸν ἔχῃ ζωὴν αἰώνιον, καὶ ἀναστήσω
in   him may have life eternal,   and will raise up

αὐτὸν ἐγὼ ἐν τῇ ἐσχάτῃ ἡμέρᾳ. 41 Ἐγόγ-
him   I   in the   last   day.   Mur-

γυζον οὖν οἱ Ἰουδαῖοι περὶ αὐτοῦ ὅτι
mured therefore the Jews   about   him   because

εἶπεν· ἐγώ εἰμι ὁ ἄρτος ὁ καταβὰς ἐκ
he said: I   am   the bread – having come down out

τοῦ οὐρανοῦ, 42 καὶ ἔλεγον· οὐχ οὗτός
–   of heaven,   and they said: Not this man

ἐστιν Ἰησοῦς ὁ υἱὸς Ἰωσήφ, οὗ ἡμεῖς
is   Jesus   the son of Joseph, of whom   we

οἴδαμεν τὸν πατέρα καὶ τὴν μητέρα;
know   the   father   and   the   mother?

πῶς νῦν λέγει ὅτι ἐκ τοῦ οὐρανοῦ
how   now says he[,] – Out of –   heaven

καταβέβηκα; 43 ἀπεκρίθη Ἰησοῦς καὶ εἶπεν
I have come down? Answered   Jesus   and said

αὐτοῖς· μὴ γογγύζετε μετ' ἀλλήλων.
to them: Do not murmur   with   one another.

44 Οὐδεὶς δύναται ἐλθεῖν πρός με ἐὰν μὴ
No one   can   to come   to   me unless

ὁ πατὴρ ὁ πέμψας με ἑλκύσῃ αὐτόν,
the Father the [one] having sent me should draw him,

κἀγὼ ἀναστήσω αὐτὸν ἐν τῇ ἐσχάτῃ
and I will raise up   him   in the   last

ἡμέρᾳ. 45 ἔστιν γεγραμμένον ἐν τοῖς
day.   It is   having been written in   the

προφήταις· καὶ ἔσονται πάντες διδακτοὶ
prophets :   And they shall be all   taught

θεοῦ· πᾶς ὁ ἀκούσας παρὰ τοῦ πατρὸς
of God; everyone hearing   from   the   Father

καὶ μαθὼν ἔρχεται πρὸς ἐμέ. 46 οὐχ
and learning comes   to   me.   Not

ὅτι τὸν πατέρα ἑώρακέν τις, εἰ μὴ ὁ
that ²the ⁴Father ³has seen ¹anyone, except the [one]

ὢν παρὰ τοῦ θεοῦ, οὗτος ἑώρακεν τὸν
being from   –   God,   this [one] has seen   the

πατέρα. 47 ἀμὴν ἀμὴν λέγω ὑμῖν, ὁ
Father.   Truly   truly   I say   to you,   the

πιστεύων ἔχει ζωὴν αἰώνιον. 48 Ἐγώ
[one] believing has   life   eternal.   I

εἰμι ὁ ἄρτος τῆς ζωῆς. 49 οἱ πατέρες
am   the bread   –   of life.   The fathers

fathers ate the manna in the wilderness, and they died. [50]This is the bread which comes down from heaven, that a man may eat of it and not die. [51]I am the living bread which came down from heaven; if any one eats of this bread, he will live for ever; and the bread which I shall give for the life of the world is my flesh."

52 The Jews then disputed among themselves, saying, "How can this man give us his flesh to eat?" [53]So Jesus said to them, "Truly, truly, I say to you, unless you eat the flesh of the Son of man and drink his blood, you have no life in you; [54]he who eats my flesh and drinks my blood has eternal life, and I will raise him up at the last day. [55]For my flesh is food indeed, and my blood is drink indeed. [56]He who eats my flesh and drinks my blood abides in me, and I in him. [57]As the living Father sent me, and I live because of the Father, so

ὑμῶν ἔφαγον ἐν τῇ ἐρήμῳ τὸ μάννα καὶ
of you   ate   in the   desert   the manna and

ἀπέθανον· 50 οὗτός ἐστιν ὁ ἄρτος ὁ ἐκ
died ;   this   is   the bread – out of

τοῦ οὐρανοῦ καταβαίνων, ἵνα τις ἐξ
 –   heaven   coming down,   that anyone of

αὐτοῦ φάγῃ καὶ μὴ ἀποθάνῃ. 51 ἐγώ
 it   may eat and may not die.   I

εἰμι ὁ ἄρτος ὁ ζῶν ὁ ἐκ τοῦ οὐρανοῦ
am the bread – living the [one] out of – heaven

καταβάς· ἐάν τις φάγῃ ἐκ τούτου τοῦ
having come down; if anyone eats of this   the

ἄρτου, ζήσει εἰς τὸν αἰῶνα· καὶ ὁ ἄρτος
bread, he will live to the   age; [2]indeed [3]the [4]bread

δὲ ὃν ἐγὼ δώσω ἡ σάρξ μού ἐστιν
[1]and which I   will give the flesh of me   is

ὑπὲρ τῆς τοῦ κόσμου ζωῆς. 52 Ἐμάχοντο
for [1]the [3]of the [4]world [2]life.   Fought

οὖν πρὸς ἀλλήλους οἱ Ἰουδαῖοι λέγοντες·
therefore with one another the Jews   saying :

πῶς δύναται οὗτος ἡμῖν δοῦναι τὴν
How   can this man us to give the(his)

σάρκα φαγεῖν; 53 εἶπεν οὖν αὐτοῖς ὁ
flesh   to eat?   Said therefore to them –

Ἰησοῦς· ἀμὴν ἀμὴν λέγω ὑμῖν, ἐὰν μὴ
Jesus :   Truly truly I say to you,   unless

φάγητε τὴν σάρκα τοῦ υἱοῦ τοῦ ἀνθρώπου
ye eat   the flesh of the Son – of man

καὶ πίητε αὐτοῦ τὸ αἷμα, οὐκ ἔχετε
and drink of him   the blood, ye have not

ζωὴν ἐν ἑαυτοῖς. 54 ὁ τρώγων μου τὴν
life in yourselves.   The [one] eating of me the

σάρκα καὶ πίνων μου τὸ αἷμα ἔχει ζωὴν
flesh and drinking of me the blood has life

αἰώνιον, κἀγὼ ἀναστήσω αὐτὸν τῇ ἐσχάτῃ
eternal,   and I   will raise up him in the last

ἡμέρᾳ. 55 ἡ γὰρ σάρξ μου ἀληθής
day.   For the flesh of me [2]true

ἐστιν βρῶσις, καὶ τὸ αἷμά μου ἀληθής
[1]is   [2]food,   and the blood of me [2]true

ἐστιν πόσις. 56 ὁ τρώγων μου τὴν
[1]is   [2]drink.   The [one] eating of me the

σάρκα καὶ πίνων μου τὸ αἷμα ἐν ἐμοὶ
flesh and drinking of me the blood in   me

μένει κἀγὼ ἐν αὐτῷ. 57 καθὼς ἀπέστειλέν
remains and I in him.   As   sent

με ὁ ζῶν πατὴρ κἀγὼ ζῶ διὰ τὸν
me the living Father and I live because of the

he who eats me will live because of me. ⁵⁸This is the bread which came down from heaven, not such as the fathers ate and died; he who eats this bread will live for ever." ⁵⁹This he said in the synagogue, as he taught at Caper'na-um.

60 Many of his disciples, when they heard it, said, "This is a hard saying; who can listen to it?" ⁶¹But Jesus, knowing in himself that his disciples murmured at it, said to them, "Do you take offense at this? ⁶²Then what if you were to see the Son of man ascending where he was before? ⁶³It is the spirit that gives life, the flesh is of no avail; the words that I have spoken to you are spirit and life. ⁶⁴But there are some of you that do not believe." For Jesus knew from the first who those were that did not believe, and who it was that should betray him. ⁶⁵And he said, "This is why I told you that no one can come to me unless it is granted him by the Father."

πατέρα,   καὶ   ὁ   τρώγων   με   κἀκεῖνος
Father,   also   the [one]   eating   me   even that one

ζήσει   δι'   ἐμέ. 58 οὗτός   ἐστιν   ὁ   ἄρτος   ὁ
will live because of me.   This   is   the bread —

ἐξ   οὐρανοῦ   καταβάς,   οὐ   καθὼς   ἔφαγον
out of   heaven   having come down,   not   as   ate

οἱ   πατέρες   καὶ   ἀπέθανον·   ὁ   τρώγων
the   fathers   and   died;   the [one]   eating

τοῦτον   τὸν   ἄρτον   ζήσει   εἰς   τὸν   αἰῶνα.
this   —   bread   will live unto   the   age.

59 Ταῦτα   εἶπεν   ἐν   συναγωγῇ   διδάσκων   ἐν
These things   he said   in   a synagogue   teaching   in

Καφαρναούμ.   60 Πολλοὶ   οὖν   ἀκούσαντες
Capernaum.   ²Many   ¹therefore   ⁷hearing

ἐκ   τῶν   μαθητῶν   αὐτοῦ   εἶπαν·   σκληρός
³of   ⁴the   ⁵disciples   ⁶of him   said :   Hard

ἐστιν   ὁ   λόγος   οὗτος·   τίς   δύναται   αὐτοῦ
is   —   word   this;   who   can   it

ἀκούειν;   61 εἰδὼς   δὲ   ὁ   Ἰησοῦς   ἐν   ἑαυτῷ
to hear?   But knowing —   Jesus   in   himself

ὅτι   γογγύζουσιν   περὶ   τούτου   οἱ   μαθηταὶ
that   ⁴are murmuring   ⁵about   ⁶this   ¹the   ²disciples

αὐτοῦ,   εἶπεν   αὐτοῖς·   τοῦτο   ὑμᾶς   σκανδαλίζει;
³of him,   said   to them :   This   you   offends?

62 ἐὰν   οὖν   θεωρῆτε   τὸν   υἱὸν   τοῦ   ἀνθρώπου
If   then   ye behold   the   Son   —   of man

ἀναβαίνοντα   ὅπου   ἦν   τὸ   πρότερον; 63 τὸ
ascending   where   he was   at first? †   The

πνεῦμά   ἐστιν   τὸ   ζωοποιοῦν,   ἡ   σὰρξ   οὐκ
spirit   is   the [thing] quickening,   the   flesh   not

ὠφελεῖ   οὐδέν·   τὰ   ῥήματα   ἃ   ἐγὼ   λελάληκα
profits   no(any)thing;   the   words   which   I   have spoken

ὑμῖν   πνεῦμά   ἐστιν   καὶ   ζωή   ἐστιν. 64 ἀλλ'
to you   spirit   is(are)   and   life   is(are).   But

εἰσὶν   ἐξ   ὑμῶν   τινες   οἳ   οὐ   πιστεύουσιν.   ᾔδει
there are of   you   some   who   do not believe.   knew

γὰρ   ἐξ   ἀρχῆς   ὁ   Ἰησοῦς   τίνες   εἰσὶν
For   from [the] beginning —   Jesus   who are(were)

οἱ   μὴ   πιστεύοντες   καὶ   τίς   ἐστιν   ὁ
the [ones]   not believing   and   who   is(was)   the

παραδώσων   αὐτόν.   65 καὶ   ἔλεγεν·
[one] betraying   him.   And   he said :

διὰ   τοῦτο   εἴρηκα   ὑμῖν   ὅτι   οὐδεὶς   δύναται
Therefore   I have told   you   that   no one   can

ἐλθεῖν   πρός   με   ἐὰν   μὴ   ᾖ   δεδομένον
to come   to   me   unless   it is having been given

αὐτῷ   ἐκ   τοῦ   πατρός.
to him   of   the   Father.

66 After this many of his disciples drew back and no longer went about with him. 67Jesus said to the twelve, "Will you also go away?" 68Simon Peter answered him, "Lord, to whom shall we go? You have the words of eternal life; 69and we have believed, and have come to know, that you are the Holy One of God." 70Jesus answered them, "Did I not choose you, the twelve, and one of you is a devil?" 71He spoke of Judas the son of Simon Iscariot, for he, one of the twelve, was to betray him.

66 Ἐκ τούτου πολλοὶ τῶν μαθητῶν
From this many of the disciples
αὐτοῦ ἀπῆλθον εἰς τὰ ὀπίσω καὶ οὐκέτι
of him went away back† and no longer
μετ᾽ αὐτοῦ περιεπάτουν. 67 εἶπεν οὖν ὁ
with him walked. Said therefore –
Ἰησοῦς τοῖς δώδεκα· μὴ καὶ ὑμεῖς
Jesus to the twelve : Not also ye
θέλετε ὑπάγειν; 68 ἀπεκρίθη αὐτῷ Σίμων
wish to go? Answered him Simon
Πέτρος· κύριε, πρὸς τίνα ἀπελευσόμεθα;
Peter : Lord, to whom shall we go away?
ῥήματα ζωῆς αἰωνίου ἔχεις· 69 καὶ ἡμεῖς
words of life eternal thou hast; and we
πεπιστεύκαμεν καὶ ἐγνώκαμεν ὅτι σὺ εἶ
have believed and have known that thou art
ὁ ἅγιος τοῦ θεοῦ. 70 ἀπεκρίθη αὐτοῖς ὁ
the holy one – of God. Answered them –
Ἰησοῦς· οὐκ ἐγὼ ὑμᾶς τοὺς δώδεκα
Jesus : ³Not ²I ⁴you ⁵the ⁵twelve
ἐξελεξάμην; καὶ ἐξ ὑμῶν εἷς διάβολός
¹chose? and of you one a devil
ἐστιν. 71 ἔλεγεν δὲ τὸν Ἰούδαν Σίμωνος
is. Now he spoke [of] – Judas [son of] Simon
Ἰσκαριώτου· οὗτος γὰρ ἔμελλεν παραδιδόναι
Iscariot : for this one was about to betray
αὐτόν, εἷς ἐκ τῶν δώδεκα.
him, one of the twelve.

CHAPTER 7

AFTER this Jesus went about in Galilee; he would not go about in Judea, because the Jewsᵏ sought to kill him. 2Now the Jews' feast of Tabernacles was at hand. 3So his brothers said to him, "Leave here and go to Judea, that your disciples may see the works you are doing. 4For no man works in

7 Καὶ μετὰ ταῦτα περιεπάτει ὁ Ἰησοῦς
And after these things walked – Jesus
ἐν τῇ Γαλιλαίᾳ· οὐ γὰρ ἤθελεν ἐν τῇ
in – Galilee; for he did not wish in –
Ἰουδαίᾳ περιπατεῖν, ὅτι ἐζήτουν αὐτὸν οἱ
Judæa to walk, because ²were seeking ³him ¹the
Ἰουδαῖοι ἀποκτεῖναι. 2 ἦν δὲ ἐγγὺς ἡ
²Jews ⁴to kill. Now was near the
ἑορτὴ τῶν Ἰουδαίων ἡ σκηνοπηγία. 3 εἶπον
feast of the Jews the Tabernacles. Said
οὖν πρὸς αὐτὸν οἱ ἀδελφοὶ αὐτοῦ·
therefore to him the brothers of him :
μετάβηθι ἐντεῦθεν καὶ ὕπαγε εἰς τὴν Ἰουδαίαν,
Depart hence and go into – Judæa,
ἵνα καὶ οἱ μαθηταί σου θεωρήσουσιν τὰ
that also the disciples of thee will behold the
ἔργα σου ἃ ποιεῖς· 4 οὐδεὶς γάρ τι ἐν
works of thee which thou doest; for no one anything in

ᵏ Or Judeans

secret if he seeks to be known openly. If you do these things, show yourself to the world." [5]For even his brothers did not believe in him. [6]Jesus said to them, "My time has not yet come, but your time is always here. [7]The world cannot hate you, but it hates me because I testify of it that its works are evil. [8]Go to the feast yourselves; I am not[1] going up to this feast, for my time has not yet fully come." [9]So saying, he remained in Galilee.

10 But after his brothers had gone up to the feast, then he also went up, not publicly but in private. [11]The Jews were looking for him at the feast, and saying, "Where is he?" [12]And there was much muttering about him among the people. While some said, "He is a good man," others said, "No, he is leading the people astray." [13]Yet for fear of the Jews no one spoke openly of him.

κρυπτῷ ποιεῖ καὶ ζητεῖ αὐτὸς ἐν παρρησίᾳ
secret   does   and   seeks [him]self in [the] open

εἶναι. εἰ ταῦτα ποιεῖς, φανέρωσον σεαυτὸν
to be. If these things thou doest, manifest   thyself

τῷ κόσμῳ. 5 οὐδὲ γὰρ οἱ ἀδελφοὶ
to the world.   For not   the   brothers

αὐτοῦ ἐπίστευον εἰς αὐτόν. 6 λέγει οὖν
of him   believed   in   him.   Says therefore

αὐτοῖς ὁ Ἰησοῦς· ὁ καιρὸς ὁ ἐμὸς
to them   –   Jesus :   The ²time   –   ¹my

οὔπω πάρεστιν, ὁ δὲ καιρὸς ὁ ὑμέτερος
not yet is arrived, but the   ²time   –   ¹your

πάντοτέ ἐστιν ἕτοιμος. 7 οὐ δύναται ὁ
always   is   ready.   Cannot   the

κόσμος μισεῖν ὑμᾶς, ἐμὲ δὲ μισεῖ, ὅτι
world   to hate   you,   but me   it hates, because

ἐγὼ μαρτυρῶ περὶ αὐτοῦ ὅτι τὰ ἔργα
I witness   about   it   that the works

αὐτοῦ πονηρά ἐστιν. 8 ὑμεῖς ἀνάβητε εἰς
of it   evil   is(are).   ²Ye   ¹go ²up   to

τὴν ἑορτήν· ἐγὼ οὐκ ἀναβαίνω εἰς τὴν
the   feast;   I   am not going up   to   –

ἑορτὴν ταύτην, ὅτι ὁ ἐμὸς καιρὸς οὔπω
feast   this,   because the   my   time   not yet

πεπλήρωται. 9 ταῦτα δὲ εἰπὼν αὐτοῖς
has been fulfilled.   And these things saying   to them

ἔμεινεν ἐν τῇ Γαλιλαίᾳ. 10 Ὡς δὲ
he remained in   –   Galilee.   But when

ἀνέβησαν οἱ ἀδελφοὶ αὐτοῦ εἰς τὴν ἑορτήν,
went up   the   brothers of him to   the   feast,

τότε καὶ αὐτὸς ἀνέβη, οὐ φανερῶς ἀλλὰ
then   also   he   went up, not manifestly but

ὡς ἐν κρυπτῷ. 11 οἱ οὖν Ἰουδαῖοι
as   in   secret.   Therefore the   Jews

ἐζήτουν αὐτὸν ἐν τῇ ἑορτῇ καὶ ἔλεγον·
sought   him   at   the   feast   and   said :

ποῦ ἐστιν ἐκεῖνος; 12 καὶ γογγυσμὸς περὶ
Where is   that man?   And ²murmuring ⁴about

αὐτοῦ ἦν πολὺς ἐν τοῖς ὄχλοις· οἱ μὲν
⁵him ³there was ¹much in   the   crowds;   some

ἔλεγον ὅτι ἀγαθός ἐστιν· ἄλλοι [δὲ]
said[,]   –   A good man he is;   but others

ἔλεγον· οὔ, ἀλλὰ πλανᾷ τὸν ὄχλον.
said :   No,   but   he deceives the   crowd.

13 οὐδεὶς μέντοι παρρησίᾳ ἐλάλει περὶ
No one   however   openly   spoke   about

αὐτοῦ διὰ τὸν φόβον τῶν Ἰουδαίων.
him because of the   fear   of the   Jews.

---

[1] Other ancient authorities add yet

14 About the middle of the feast Jesus went up into the temple and taught. [15] The Jews marveled at it, saying, "How is it that this man has learning,[m] when he has never studied?" [16] So Jesus answered them, "My teaching is not mine, but his who sent me; [17] if any man's will is to do his will, he shall know whether the teaching is from God or whether I am speaking on my own authority. [18] He who speaks on his own authority seeks his own glory; but he who seeks the glory of him who sent him is true, and in him there is no falsehood. [19] Did not Moses give you the law? Yet none of you keeps the law. Why do you seek to kill me?" [20] The people answered, "You have a demon! Who is seeking to kill you?" [21] Jesus answered them, "I did one deed, and you all marvel at it. [22] Moses gave you circumcision (not that it is from Moses, but from the fathers), and you circumcise a man upon the sabbath. [23] If on the

14 "Ηδη δὲ τῆς ἑορτῆς μεσούσης ἀνέβη
But now the feast being in [its] middle[a] went up
= in the middle of the feast

'Ιησοῦς εἰς τὸ ἱερὸν καὶ ἐδίδασκεν.
Jesus to the temple and taught.

15 ἐθαύμαζον οὖν οἱ 'Ιουδαῖοι λέγοντες·
Marvelled therefore the Jews saying :

πῶς οὗτος γράμματα οἶδεν μὴ μεμαθηκώς;
How this man letters knows not having learned?

16 ἀπεκρίθη οὖν αὐτοῖς 'Ιησοῦς καὶ εἶπεν·
Answered therefore them Jesus and said :

ἡ ἐμὴ διδαχὴ οὐκ ἔστιν ἐμὴ ἀλλὰ τοῦ
The my teaching is not mine but of the

πέμψαντός με· 17 ἐάν τις θέλῃ τὸ θέλημα
[one] having sent me; if anyone wishes the will

αὐτοῦ ποιεῖν, γνώσεται περὶ τῆς διδαχῆς,
of him to do, he will know concerning the teaching,

πότερον ἐκ τοῦ θεοῦ ἐστιν ἢ ἐγὼ ἀπ'
whether of – God it is or I from

ἐμαυτοῦ λαλῶ. 18 ὁ ἀφ' ἑαυτοῦ λαλῶν
myself speak. The [one] from himself speaking

τὴν δόξαν τὴν ἰδίαν ζητεῖ· ὁ δὲ ζητῶν
his own glory seeks; but the [one] seeking

τὴν δόξαν τοῦ πέμψαντος αὐτόν, οὗτος
the glory of the [one] having sent him, this man

ἀληθής ἐστιν καὶ ἀδικία ἐν αὐτῷ οὐκ
true is and unrighteousness in him not

ἔστιν. 19 οὐ Μωϋσῆς ἔδωκεν ὑμῖν τὸν
is. Not Moses gave you the

νόμον; καὶ οὐδεὶς ἐξ ὑμῶν ποιεῖ τὸν
law? and no one of you does the

νόμον. τί με ζητεῖτε ἀποκτεῖναι;
law. Why me seek ye to kill?

20 ἀπεκρίθη ὁ ὄχλος· δαιμόνιον ἔχεις·
Answered the crowd : A demon thou hast;

τίς σε ζητεῖ ἀποκτεῖναι; 21 ἀπεκρίθη
who thee seeks to kill? Answered

'Ιησοῦς καὶ εἶπεν αὐτοῖς· ἓν ἔργον ἐποίησα
Jesus and said to them : One work I did

καὶ πάντες θαυμάζετε. 22 διὰ τοῦτο
and all ye marvel. Because of this

Μωϋσῆς δέδωκεν ὑμῖν τὴν περιτομήν, —
Moses has given you – circumcision, —

οὐχ ὅτι ἐκ τοῦ Μωϋσέως ἐστιν ἀλλ' ἐκ
not that of – Moses it is but of

τῶν πατέρων, — καὶ ἐν σαββάτῳ
the fathers, — and on a sabbath

περιτέμνετε ἄνθρωπον. 23 εἰ περιτομὴν
ye circumcise a man. If [a]circumcision

[m] Or this man knows his letters

sabbath a man receives circumcision, so that the law of Moses may not be broken, are you angry with me because on the sabbath I made a man's whole body well? ²⁴Do not judge by appearances, but judge with right judgment."

25 Some of the people of Jerusalem therefore said, "Is not this the man whom they seek to kill? ²⁶And here he is, speaking openly, and they say nothing to him! Can it be that the authorities really know that this is the Christ? ²⁷Yet we know where this man comes from; and when the Christ appears, no one will know where he comes from." ²⁸So Jesus proclaimed, as he taught in the temple, "You know me, and you know where I come from? But I have not come of my own accord; he who sent me is true, and him you do not know. ²⁹I know him, for I come from him, and he sent me." ³⁰So they sought to arrest him; but no one laid hands on him, because his hour had not yet come. ³¹Yet many of the people believed in him; they said, "When

λαμβάνει [ὁ] ἄνθρωπος ἐν σαββάτῳ ἵνα
²receives   ¹a man   on   a sabbath that

μὴ λυθῇ ὁ νόμος Μωϋσέως, ἐμοὶ χολᾶτε
is not broken the law of Moses, with me are ye angry

ὅτι ὅλον ἄνθρωπον ὑγιῆ ἐποίησα ἐν
because a whole man   healthy I made   on

σαββάτῳ; 24 μὴ κρίνετε κατ' ὄψιν, ἀλλὰ
a sabbath?   Judge not according to face, but

τὴν δικαίαν κρίσιν κρίνατε. 25 Ἔλεγον
 –   righteous judgment judge.   Said

οὖν τινες ἐκ τῶν Ἱεροσολυμιτῶν· οὐχ
therefore some of the   Jerusalemites·   ¹Not

οὗτός ἐστιν ὃν ζητοῦσιν ἀποκτεῖναι; 26 καὶ
²this man ¹is it whom they are seeking to kill?   and

ἴδε παρρησίᾳ λαλεῖ, καὶ οὐδὲν αὐτῷ
behold openly   he speaks, and nothing to him

λέγουσιν. μήποτε ἀληθῶς ἔγνωσαν οἱ
they say. Perhaps indeed   knew   the

ἄρχοντες ὅτι οὗτός ἐστιν ὁ χριστός; *
rulers   that this   is   the Christ? *

27 ἀλλὰ τοῦτον οἴδαμεν πόθεν ἐστίν· ὁ δὲ
 But this man we know whence he is; but ²the

χριστὸς ὅταν ἔρχηται, οὐδεὶς γινώσκει
³Christ ¹when comes,   no one knows

πόθεν ἐστίν. 28 ἔκραξεν οὖν ἐν τῷ ἱερῷ
whence he is. ³Cried out ²therefore ⁴in ⁵the ⁶temple

διδάσκων ὁ Ἰησοῦς καὶ λέγων· κἀμὲ
¹teaching – ¹Jesus ²and ⁸saying : Both me

οἴδατε καὶ οἴδατε πόθεν εἰμί· καὶ ἀπ'
ye know and ye know whence I am;   and from

ἐμαυτοῦ οὐκ ἐλήλυθα, ἀλλ' ἔστιν ἀληθινὸς
myself   I have not come, but he is   true

ὁ πέμψας με, ὃν ὑμεῖς οὐκ οἴδατε·
the [one] having sent me, whom ye   know not;

29 ἐγὼ οἶδα αὐτόν, ὅτι παρ' αὐτοῦ εἰμι
 I   know him, because ²from ³him ¹I am

κἀκεῖνός με ἀπέστειλεν. 30 Ἐζήτουν οὖν
⁴and that one ⁵me ⁵sent.   They sought therefore

αὐτὸν πιάσαι, καὶ οὐδεὶς ἐπέβαλεν ἐπ'
him   to arrest, and   no one   laid on   on

αὐτὸν τὴν χεῖρα, ὅτι οὔπω ἐληλύθει ἡ
him   the   hand, because not yet had come the

ὥρα αὐτοῦ. 31 Ἐκ τοῦ ὄχλου δὲ πολλοὶ
hour of him.   ²of ⁴the ⁵crowd ¹But ³many

ἐπίστευσαν εἰς αὐτόν, καὶ ἔλεγον· ὁ
believed   in him,   and   said : ²The

---

* As this question is introduced by μήποτε, a negative answer is expected; see page xiii, and note ver. 31 below.

the Christ appears, will he do more signs than this man has done?"

32 The Pharisees heard the crowd thus muttering about him, and the chief priests and Pharisees sent officers to arrest him. 33Jesus then said, "I shall be with you a little longer, and then I go to him who sent me; 34you will seek me and you will not find me; where I am you cannot come." 35The Jews said to one another, "Where does this man intend to go that we shall not find him? Does he intend to go to the Dispersion among the Greeks and teach the Greeks? 36What does he mean by saying, 'You will seek me and you will not find me,' and, 'Where I am you cannot come'?"

37 On the last day of the feast, the great day, Jesus stood up and proclaimed, "If any one thirst, let him come to me and drink. 38He who believes in me, asⁿ the scripture has said, 'Out of his heart shall flow rivers of living water.'"

χριστὸς ὅταν ἔλθῃ, μὴ πλείονα σημεῖα
³Christ ¹when ⁴comes, *not* more signs

ποιήσει ὧν οὗτος ἐποίησεν; 32 ἤκουσαν
will he do [than] which this man did? ³Heard

οἱ Φαρισαῖοι τοῦ ὄχλου γογγύζοντος περὶ
¹the ²Pharisees ⁴the ⁵crowd ⁶murmuring ⁸about

αὐτοῦ ταῦτα, καὶ ἀπέστειλαν οἱ ἀρχιερεῖς
⁹him ⁷these things, and ⁶sent ¹the ²chief priests

καὶ οἱ Φαρισαῖοι ὑπηρέτας ἵνα πιάσωσιν
³and ⁴the ⁵Pharisees ⁷attendants that they might arrest

αὐτόν. 33 εἶπεν οὖν ὁ Ἰησοῦς· ἔτι
him. Said therefore – Jesus: Yet

χρόνον μικρὸν μεθ' ὑμῶν εἰμι καὶ ὑπάγω
time a little with you I am and I go

πρὸς τὸν πέμψαντά με. 34 ζητήσετέ με
to the [one] having sent me. Ye will seek me

καὶ οὐχ εὑρήσετε, καὶ ὅπου εἰμὶ ἐγὼ
and will not find, and where am I

ὑμεῖς οὐ δύνασθε ἐλθεῖν. 35 εἶπον οὖν
ye cannot *to* come. Said therefore

οἱ Ἰουδαῖοι πρὸς ἑαυτούς· ποῦ οὗτος
the Jews to themselves: Where this man

μέλλει πορεύεσθαι, ὅτι ἡμεῖς οὐχ εὑρήσομεν
is about to go, that we will not find

αὐτόν; μὴ εἰς τὴν διασπορὰν τῶν Ἑλλήνων
him? *not* to the dispersion of the Greeks

μέλλει πορεύεσθαι καὶ διδάσκειν τοὺς
is he about to go and to teach the

Ἕλληνας; 36 τίς ἐστιν ὁ λόγος οὗτος
Greeks? What is – word this

ὃν εἶπεν· ζητήσετέ με καὶ οὐχ εὑρήσετε,
which he said: Ye will seek me and will not find,

καὶ ὅπου εἰμὶ ἐγὼ ὑμεῖς οὐ δύνασθε
and where am I ye cannot

ἐλθεῖν;
to come?

37 Ἐν δὲ τῇ ἐσχάτῃ ἡμέρᾳ τῇ μεγάλῃ
Now in the last day the great [day]

τῆς ἑορτῆς εἱστήκει ὁ Ἰησοῦς καὶ ἔκραξεν
of the feast stood – Jesus and cried out

λέγων· ἐάν τις διψᾷ, ἐρχέσθω πρός με
saying: If anyone thirsts, let him come to me

καὶ πινέτω. 38 ὁ πιστεύων εἰς ἐμέ,
and drink. The [one] believing in me,

καθὼς εἶπεν ἡ γραφή, ποταμοὶ ἐκ τῆς
as said the scripture, ¹rivers ⁵out of ⁶the

κοιλίας αὐτοῦ ῥεύσουσιν ὕδατος ζῶντος.
⁷belly ⁸of him ⁴will flow ³water ²of living.

ⁿ Or *let him come to me, and let him who believes in me drink.*
As

³⁹ Now this he said about the Spirit, which those who believed in him were to receive; for as yet the Spirit had not been given, because Jesus was not yet glorified.

40 When they heard these words, some of the people said, "This is really the prophet." ⁴¹ Others said, "This is the Christ." But some said, "Is the Christ to come from Galilee? ⁴² Has not the scripture said that the Christ is descended from David, and comes from Bethlehem, the village where David was?" ⁴³ So there was a division among the people over him. ⁴⁴ Some of them wanted to arrest him, but no one laid hands on him.

45 The officers then went back to the chief priests and Pharisees, who said to them, "Why did you not bring him?" ⁴⁶ The officers answered, "No man ever spoke like this man!" ⁴⁷ The Pharisees answered them, "Are you led astray, you also? ⁴⁸ Have any of the authorities or of the Pharisees believed in him? ⁴⁹ But this crowd,

---

39 τοῦτο δὲ εἶπεν περὶ τοῦ πνεύματος
But this   he said concerning the Spirit

οὗ ἔμελλον λαμβάνειν οἱ πιστεύσαντες
whom were about to receive the [ones] believing

εἰς αὐτόν· οὔπω γὰρ ἦν πνεῦμα, ὅτι
in him;   for not yet was [?the] Spirit, because

Ἰησοῦς οὐδέπω ἐδοξάσθη.   40 Ἐκ τοῦ
Jesus   not yet   was glorified.   [Some] of the

ὄχλου οὖν ἀκούσαντες τῶν λόγων τούτων
crowd therefore hearing   –   words these

ἔλεγον [ὅτι]· οὗτός ἐστιν ἀληθῶς ὁ
said – :   This man is   truly the

προφήτης· 41 ἄλλοι ἔλεγον· οὗτός ἐστιν ὁ
prophet; Others said· This man is the

χριστός· οἱ δὲ ἔλεγον· μὴ γὰρ ἐκ τῆς
Christ; But others† said : Not then out of –

Γαλιλαίας ὁ χριστὸς ἔρχεται; 42 οὐχ ἡ
Galilee the Christ   comes?   not the

γραφὴ εἶπεν ὅτι ἐκ τοῦ σπέρματος Δαυίδ,
scripture said that of the seed of David,

καὶ ἀπὸ Βηθλέεμ τῆς κώμης ὅπου ἦν
and from Bethlehem the village where was

Δαυίδ, ἔρχεται ὁ χριστός; 43 σχίσμα
David, comes the Christ?   A division

οὖν ἐγένετο ἐν τῷ ὄχλῳ δι' αὐτόν·
therefore became in the crowd because of him;

44 τινὲς δὲ ἤθελον ἐξ αὐτῶν πιάσαι αὐτόν,
and ¹some ²wished ²of ²them to arrest him,

ἀλλ' οὐδεὶς ἐπέβαλεν ἐπ' αὐτὸν τὰς χεῖρας.
but no one laid on on him the(his) hands.

45 Ἦλθον οὖν οἱ ὑπηρέται πρὸς τοὺς
Came therefore the attendants to the

ἀρχιερεῖς καὶ Φαρισαίους, καὶ εἶπον αὐτοῖς
chief priests and Pharisees, and ²said ³to them

ἐκεῖνοι· διὰ τί οὐκ ἠγάγετε αὐτόν;
¹those: Why did ye not bring him?

46 ἀπεκρίθησαν οἱ ὑπηρέται· οὐδέποτε
Answered   the attendants : Never

ἐλάλησεν οὕτως ἄνθρωπος, ὡς οὗτος λαλεῖ
spoke so   a man, as ¹this ²speaks

ὁ ἄνθρωπος. 47 ἀπεκρίθησαν οὖν αὐτοῖς
–   ²man.   Answered therefore them

οἱ Φαρισαῖοι· μὴ καὶ ὑμεῖς πεπλάνησθε;
the Pharisees· Not also ye have been deceived?

48 μή τις ἐκ τῶν ἀρχόντων ἐπίστευσεν
not anyone of the rulers believed

εἰς αὐτὸν ἢ ἐκ τῶν Φαρισαίων; 49 ἀλλὰ
in him or of the Pharisees?   But

who do not know the
law, are accursed."
⁵⁰Nicode′mus, who had
gone to him before, and
who was one of them,
said to them, ⁵¹"Does
our law judge a man with-
out first giving him a
hearing and learning
what he does?" ⁵²They
replied, "Are you from
Galilee too? Search and
you will see that no
prophet is to rise from
Galilee."⁰

⁰ Other ancient authorities add
7. 53–8. 11 either here or at the
end of this gospel or after
Luke 21. 38, with variations of
the text

8 ⁵³They went each to his own
house, ¹but Jesus went to
the Mount of Olives. ²Early in
the morning he came again to
the temple; all the people came
to him, and he sat down and
taught them. ³The scribes and
the Pharisees brought a woman
who had been caught in
adultery, and placing her in the
midst ⁴they said to him,
"Teacher, this woman has been
caught in the act of adultery.
⁵Now in the law Moses commanded us to stone such. What
do you say about her?" ⁶This
they said to test him, that they
might have some charge to

ὁ ὄχλος οὗτος ὁ μὴ γινώσκων τὸν
– crowd this – not knowing the
νόμον ἐπάρατοί εἰσιν. 50 λέγει Νικόδημος
law cursed are. Says Nicodemus
πρὸς αὐτούς, ὁ ἐλθὼν πρὸς αὐτὸν πρότερον,
to them, the [one] having come to him firstly,
εἷς ὢν ἐξ αὐτῶν· 51 μὴ ὁ νόμος ἡμῶν
²one ¹being of them : Not the law of us
κρίνει τὸν ἄνθρωπον ἐὰν μὴ ἀκούσῃ
judges the man unless it hears
πρῶτον παρ' αὐτοῦ καὶ γνῷ τί ποιεῖ;
first from him and knows what he does?
52 ἀπεκρίθησαν καὶ εἶπαν αὐτῷ· μὴ καὶ
They answered and said to him : Not also
σὺ ἐκ τῆς Γαλιλαίας εἶ; ἐρεύνησον καὶ
thou of – Galilee art? search and
ἴδε ὅτι ἐκ τῆς Γαλιλαίας προφήτης οὐκ
see that out of – Galilee a prophet not
ἐγείρεται.
is raised.

53 Καὶ ἐπορεύθησαν ἕκαστος εἰς τὸν οἶκον
And they went each one to the house
αὐτοῦ, 8 Ἰησοῦς δὲ ἐπορεύθη εἰς τὸ
of him, but Jesus went to the
Ὄρος τῶν Ἐλαιῶν. 2 Ὄρθρου δὲ πάλιν
Mount of the Olives. And at dawn again
παρεγένετο εἰς τὸ ἱερόν [, καὶ πᾶς ὁ
he arrived in the temple, and all the
λαὸς ἤρχετο πρὸς αὐτόν, καὶ καθίσας
people came to him, and sitting
ἐδίδασκεν αὐτούς]. 3 Ἄγουσιν δὲ οἱ
he taught them. And lead the
γραμματεῖς καὶ οἱ Φαρισαῖοι γυναῖκα ἐπὶ
scribes and the Pharisees a woman in
μοιχείᾳ κατειλημμένην, καὶ στήσαντες αὐτὴν
adultery having been caught, and standing her
ἐν μέσῳ 4 λέγουσιν αὐτῷ Διδάσκαλε,
in [the] midst they say to him[,] Teacher,
αὕτη ἡ γυνὴ κατείληπται ἐπ' αὐτοφώρῳ
this – woman has been caught in the act
μοιχευομένη· 5 ἐν δὲ τῷ νόμῳ [ἡμῖν]
committing adultery; now in the law to us⁰
Μωϋσῆς ἐνετείλατο τὰς τοιαύτας λιθάζειν·
Moses enjoined – ²such ¹to stone;
σὺ οὖν τί λέγεις; 6 [τοῦτο δὲ ἔλεγον
thou therefore what sayest thou? But this they said
πειράζοντες αὐτόν, ἵνα ἔχωσιν κατηγορεῖν
tempting him, that they might have to accuse

bring against him. Jesus bent down and wrote with his finger on the ground. ⁷And as they continued to ask him, he stood up and said to them, "Let him who is without sin among you be the first to throw a stone at her." ⁸And once more he bent down and wrote with his finger on the ground. ⁹But when they heard it, they went away, one by one, beginning with the eldest, and Jesus was left alone with the woman standing before him. ¹⁰Jesus looked up and said to her, "Woman, where are they? Has no one condemned you?" ¹¹She said, "No one, Lord." And Jesus said, "Neither do I condemn you; go, and do not sin again."

CHAPTER 8

¹² AGAIN Jesus spoke to them, saying, "I am the light of the world; he who follows me will not walk in darkness, but will have the light of life." ¹³The Pharisees then said to him, "You are bearing witness to yourself; your testimony is not true." ¹⁴Jesus answered, "Even if I do bear witness to myself, my testimony is true, for I know whence I have come and whither I am going, but you do

αὐτοῦ.]   ὁ   δὲ   Ἰησοῦς   κάτω   κύψας   τῷ
him.]   - But   Jesus   down stooping with the

δακτύλῳ   κατέγραφεν   εἰς   τὴν   γῆν.   7 ὡς   δὲ
finger   wrote   in   the   earth.   But as

ἐπέμενον   ἐρωτῶντες   [αὐτόν],   ἀνέκυψεν   καὶ
they remained questioning   him,   he stood erect   and

εἶπεν   [αὐτοῖς]   Ὁ   ἀναμάρτητος   ὑμῶν
said   to them[,]   The [one] sinless   of you

πρῶτος   ἐπ'   αὐτὴν   βαλέτω   λίθον.   8 καὶ
first   on   her   let him cast   a stone.   And

πάλιν   κατακύψας   ἔγραφεν   εἰς   τὴν   γῆν.
again   stooping down   he wrote   in   the   earth.

9 οἱ   δὲ   ἀκούσαντες   ἐξήρχοντο   εἷς   καθ'
And they   hearing   went out   one   by

εἷς   ἀρξάμενοι   ἀπὸ   τῶν   πρεσβυτέρων,   καὶ
one   beginning   from   the   older ones,   and

κατελείφθη   μόνος,   καὶ   ἡ   γυνὴ   ἐν   μέσῳ
he was left   alone,   and   the   woman   in [the] midst

οὖσα.   10 ἀνακύψας   δὲ   ὁ   Ἰησοῦς   εἶπεν
being.   And standing erect   -   Jesus   said

αὐτῇ   Γύναι,   ποῦ   εἰσιν;   οὐδείς   σε   κατέκρινεν;
to her[,] Woman, where are they? no one   thee condemned?

11 ἡ   δὲ   εἶπεν   Οὐδείς,   κύριε.   εἶπεν   δὲ
And she   said[,]   No one,   sir.   So said

ὁ   Ἰησοῦς   Οὐδὲ   ἐγώ   σε   κατακρίνω·
-   Jesus[,]   Neither   I   thee   condemn;

πορεύου,   ἀπὸ   τοῦ   νῦν   μηκέτι   ἁμάρτανε.
go,   from   -   now   no longer   sin.

12 Πάλιν   οὖν   αὐτοῖς   ἐλάλησεν   ὁ   Ἰησοῦς
Again therefore to them   spoke   -   Jesus

λέγων·   ἐγώ   εἰμι   τὸ   φῶς   τοῦ   κόσμου·
saying :   I   am   the   light   of the   world;

ὁ   ἀκολουθῶν   μοι   οὐ   μὴ   περιπατήσῃ   ἐν
the [one] following   me   by no means   will walk   in

τῇ   σκοτίᾳ,   ἀλλ'   ἕξει   τὸ   φῶς   τῆς   ζωῆς.
the darkness,   but   will have the   light   -   of life.

13 εἶπον   οὖν   αὐτῷ   οἱ   Φαρισαῖοι·   σὺ   περὶ
Said therefore to him   the   Pharisees;   Thou concerning

σεαυτοῦ   μαρτυρεῖς·   ἡ   μαρτυρία   σου   οὐκ
thyself   witnessest;   the   witness   of thee   not

ἔστιν   ἀληθής.   14 ἀπεκρίθη   Ἰησοῦς   καὶ
is   true.   Answered   Jesus   and

εἶπεν   αὐτοῖς·   κἂν   ἐγὼ   μαρτυρῶ   περὶ
said   to them :   Even if   I   witness   concerning

ἐμαυτοῦ,   ἀληθής   ἐστιν   ἡ   μαρτυρία   μου,
myself,   true   is   the   witness   of me,

ὅτι   οἶδα   πόθεν   ἦλθον   καὶ   ποῦ   ὑπάγω·
because I know whence   I came   and   where   I go;

not know whence I come
or whither I am going.
¹⁵ You judge according
to the flesh, I judge no
one. ¹⁶ Yet even if I do
judge, my judgment is
true, for it is not I alone
that judge, but I and he^p
who sent me. ¹⁷ In your
law it is written that the
testimony of two men is
true; ¹⁸ I bear witness to
myself, and the Father
who sent me bears wit-
ness to me." ¹⁹ They said
to him therefore, "Where
is your Father?" Jesus
answered, "You know
neither me nor my
Father; if you knew me,
you would know my
Father also." ²⁰ These
words he spoke in the
treasury, as he taught in
the temple; but no one
arrested him, because his
hour had not yet come.

21 Again he said to
them, "I go away, and
you will seek me and die
in your sin; where I am
going, you cannot come."
²² Then said the Jews,
"Will he kill himself,
since he says, 'Where I
am going, you cannot

ὑμεῖς δὲ οὐκ οἴδατε πόθεν ἔρχομαι ἢ
but ye   know not   whence   I come   or

ποῦ ὑπάγω. 15 ὑμεῖς κατὰ τὴν σάρκα
where I go.   Ye   according to the   flesh

κρίνετε, ἐγὼ οὐ κρίνω οὐδένα. 16 καὶ
judge,   I   judge not   no(any)one.   ²even

ἐὰν κρίνω δὲ ἐγώ, ἡ κρίσις ἡ ἐμὴ
³if ⁵judge ¹But ⁴I, the ²judgment – ¹my

ἀληθινή ἐστιν, ὅτι μόνος οὐκ εἰμί, ἀλλ'
true   is,   because alone   I am not,   but

ἐγὼ καὶ ὁ πέμψας με. 17 καὶ ἐν τῷ
I   and the [one] having sent me.   ²even ³in the

νόμῳ δὲ τῷ ὑμετέρῳ γέγραπται ὅτι δύο
⁵law ¹And –   ⁴your   it has been written that of two

ἀνθρώπων ἡ μαρτυρία ἀληθής ἐστιν.
men   the   witness   true   is.

18 ἐγώ εἰμι ὁ μαρτυρῶν περὶ ἐμαυτοῦ,
I   am the [one] witnessing concerning myself,

καὶ μαρτυρεῖ περὶ ἐμοῦ ὁ πέμψας με
and   witnesses concerning me   ¹the ³having sent ⁴me

πατήρ. 19 ἔλεγον οὖν αὐτῷ· ποῦ ἐστιν ὁ
²Father.   They said therefore to him : Where   is   the

πατήρ σου; ἀπεκρίθη Ἰησοῦς· οὔτε ἐμὲ
Father of thee? Answered Jesus :   Neither   me

οἴδατε οὔτε τὸν πατέρα μου· εἰ ἐμὲ
ye know   nor   the   Father   of me;   if   me

ᾔδειτε, καὶ τὸν πατέρα μου ἂν ᾔδειτε.
ye knew,   also   the   Father of me ye would have known.

20 Ταῦτα τὰ ῥήματα ἐλάλησεν ἐν τῷ
These   –   words   he spoke   in   the

γαζοφυλακείῳ διδάσκων ἐν τῷ ἱερῷ· καὶ
treasury   teaching   in   the   temple;   and

οὐδεὶς ἐπίασεν αὐτόν, ὅτι οὔπω ἐληλύθει
no one   seized   him,   because not yet   had come

ἡ ὥρα αὐτοῦ.
the hour   of him.

21 Εἶπεν οὖν πάλιν αὐτοῖς· ἐγὼ ὑπάγω
He said therefore again   to them :   I   go

καὶ ζητήσετέ με, καὶ ἐν τῇ ἁμαρτίᾳ
and   ye will seek   me,   and   in   the   sin

ὑμῶν ἀποθανεῖσθε· ὅπου ἐγὼ ὑπάγω ὑμεῖς
of you   ye will die;   where   I   go   ye

οὐ δύνασθε ἐλθεῖν. 22 ἔλεγον οὖν οἱ
cannot   to come.   Said therefore the

Ἰουδαῖοι· μήτι ἀποκτενεῖ ἑαυτόν, ὅτι
Jews :   Not   will he kill   himself,   because

λέγει· ὅπου ἐγὼ ὑπάγω ὑμεῖς οὐ δύνασθε
he says : Where   I   go   ye   cannot

^p Other ancient authorities
read *the Father*

come'?" ²³He said to them, "You are from below, I am from above; you are of this world, I am not of this world. ²⁴I told you that you would die in your sins, for you will die in your sins unless you believe that I am he." ²⁵They said to him, "Who are you?" Jesus said to them, "Even what I have told you from the beginning.⁴ ²⁶I have much to say about you and much to judge; but he who sent me is true, and I declare to the world what I have heard from him." ²⁷They did not understand that he spoke to them of the Father. ²⁸So Jesus said, "When you have lifted up the Son of man, then you will know that I am he, and that I do nothing on my own authority but speak thus as the Father taught me. ²⁹And he who sent me is with me; he has not left me alone, for I always do what is pleasing to him." ³⁰As he spoke thus, many believed in him.

31 Jesus then said to

⁴ Or Why do I talk to you at all?

ἐλθεῖν;   23 καὶ   ἔλεγεν   αὐτοῖς·   ὑμεῖς   ἐκ
to come?   And   he said   to them :   Ye   of

τῶν   κάτω   ἐστέ,   ἐγὼ   ἐκ   τῶν   ἄνω   εἰμί·
the things below   are,   I   of the things   above   am;

ὑμεῖς   ἐκ   τούτου   τοῦ   κόσμου   ἐστέ,   ἐγὼ
ye   of   this   —   world   are,   I

οὐκ   εἰμὶ   ἐκ   τοῦ   κόσμου   τούτου.   24 εἶπον
am not   of   —   world   this.   I said

οὖν   ὑμῖν   ὅτι   ἀποθανεῖσθε   ἐν   ταῖς   ἁμαρτίαις
therefore to you that   ye will die   in   the   sins

ὑμῶν·   ἐὰν   γὰρ   μὴ   πιστεύσητε   ὅτι   ἐγώ
of you ;   for if   ye believe not   that   I

εἰμι,   ἀποθανεῖσθε   ἐν   ταῖς   ἁμαρτίαις   ὑμῶν.
am,   ye will die   in   the   sins   of you.

25 ἔλεγον   οὖν   αὐτῷ·   σὺ   τίς   εἶ;   εἶπεν
They said   therefore to him :   ³Thou ¹who   ²art?   Said

αὐτοῖς   ὁ   Ἰησοῦς·   τὴν   ἀρχὴν   ὅ   τι   καὶ
to them   —   Jesus :   ⁵at all †   ¹Why   ²indeed

λαλῶ   ὑμῖν;   26 πολλὰ   ἔχω   περὶ   ὑμῶν
³speak I   ⁴to you?   Many things I have   about   you

λαλεῖν   καὶ   κρίνειν·   ἀλλ'   ὁ   πέμψας   με
to speak   and   to judge;   but the [one] having sent   me

ἀληθής   ἐστιν,   κἀγὼ   ἃ   ἤκουσα   παρ'
true   is,   and I   what   I heard   from

αὐτοῦ,   ταῦτα   λαλῶ   εἰς   τὸν   κόσμον.
him,   these things   I speak   in   the   world.

27 οὐκ   ἔγνωσαν   ὅτι   τὸν   πατέρα   αὐτοῖς
They did not know   that   ²the   ³Father   ⁴to them

ἔλεγεν.   28 εἶπεν   οὖν   ὁ   Ἰησοῦς·   ὅταν
¹he spoke [of].   Said therefore   —   Jesus :   When

ὑψώσητε   τὸν   υἱὸν   τοῦ   ἀνθρώπου,   τότε
ye lift up   the   Son   —   of man,   then

γνώσεσθε   ὅτι   ἐγώ   εἰμι,   καὶ   ἀπ'   ἐμαυτοῦ
ye will know   that   I   am,   and   from   myself

ποιῶ   οὐδέν,   ἀλλὰ   καθὼς   ἐδίδαξέν   με   ὁ
I do   nothing,   but   as   taught   me   the

πατήρ,   ταῦτα   λαλῶ.   29 καὶ   ὁ   πέμψας
Father,   these things   I speak.   And   the [one] having sent

με   μετ'   ἐμοῦ   ἐστιν·   οὐκ   ἀφῆκέν   με
me   with   me   is;   he did not leave   me

μόνον,   ὅτι   ἐγὼ   τὰ   ἀρεστὰ   αὐτῷ   ποιῶ
alone,   because   I   the things pleasing   to him   do

πάντοτε.
always.

30 Ταῦτα   αὐτοῦ   λαλοῦντος   πολλοὶ   ἐπίσ-
These things   him   saying⁸   many   be-
=As he said these things

τευσαν   εἰς   αὐτόν.   31 ἔλεγεν   οὖν   ὁ   Ἰησοῦς
lieved   in   him.   Said therefore   —   Jesus

the Jews who had believed in him, "If you continue in my word, you are truly my disciples, [32] and you will know the truth, and the truth will make you free." [33] They answered him, "We are descendants of Abraham, and have never been in bondage to any one. How is it that you say, 'You will be made free'?"

[34] Jesus answered them, "Truly, truly, I say to you, every one who commits sin is a slave to sin. [35] The slave does not continue in the house for ever; the son continues for ever. [36] So if the Son makes you free, you will be free indeed. [37] I know that you are descendants of Abraham; yet you seek to kill me, because my word finds no place in you. [38] I speak of what I have seen with my Father, and you do what you have heard from your father."

[39] They answered him, "Abraham is our father." Jesus said to them, "If you were Abraham's children, you would do what Abraham did, [40] but now you seek to kill me, a man who has told you the truth which

πρὸς τοὺς πεπιστευκότας αὐτῷ Ἰουδαίους·
to ¹the ²having believed ⁴him ³Jews :

ἐὰν ὑμεῖς μείνητε ἐν τῷ λόγῳ τῷ ἐμῷ,
If ye continue in the ²word - ¹my,

ἀληθῶς μαθηταί μού ἐστε, 32 καὶ γνώσεσθε
truly disciples of me ye are, and ye will know

τὴν ἀλήθειαν, καὶ ἡ ἀλήθεια ἐλευθερώσει
the truth, and the truth will free

ὑμᾶς. 33 ἀπεκρίθησαν πρὸς αὐτόν· σπέρμα
you. They answered to him : Seed

Ἀβραάμ ἐσμεν, καὶ οὐδενὶ δεδουλεύκαμεν
of Abraham we are, and to no one have we been enslaved

πώποτε· πῶς σὺ λέγεις ὅτι ἐλεύθεροι
never; how thou sayest that free

γενήσεσθε; 34 ἀπεκρίθη αὐτοῖς ὁ Ἰησοῦς·
ye will become? Answered them - Jesus :

ἀμὴν ἀμὴν λέγω ὑμῖν ὅτι πᾶς ὁ ποιῶν
Truly truly I tell you that everyone doing

τὴν ἁμαρτίαν δοῦλός ἐστιν τῆς ἁμαρτίας.
- sin a slave is - of sin.

35 ὁ δὲ δοῦλος οὐ μένει ἐν τῇ οἰκίᾳ
But the slave does not remain in the house

εἰς τὸν αἰῶνα· ὁ υἱὸς μένει εἰς τὸν
unto the age; the son remains unto the

αἰῶνα. 36 ἐὰν οὖν ὁ υἱὸς ὑμᾶς ἐλευθερώσῃ,
age. If therefore the Son you frees,

ὄντως ἐλεύθεροι ἔσεσθε. 37 Οἶδα ὅτι
really free ye will be. I know that

σπέρμα Ἀβραάμ ἐστε· ἀλλὰ ζητεῖτέ με
seed of Abraham ye are; but ye seek me

ἀποκτεῖναι, ὅτι ὁ λόγος ὁ ἐμὸς οὐ χωρεῖ
to kill, because the ²word - ¹my finds no room

ἐν ὑμῖν. 38 ἃ ἐγὼ ἑώρακα παρὰ τῷ
in you. What I have seen with the

πατρὶ λαλῶ· καὶ ὑμεῖς οὖν ἃ ἠκού-
Father I speak; and ye therefore what ye

σατε παρὰ τοῦ πατρὸς ποιεῖτε. 39 ἀπεκρί-
heard from the father ye do. They

θησαν καὶ εἶπαν αὐτῷ· ὁ πατὴρ ἡμῶν Ἀβραάμ
answered and said to him: The father of us Abraham

ἐστιν. λέγει αὐτοῖς ὁ Ἰησοῦς· εἰ τέκνα
is. Says to them - Jesus : If children

τοῦ Ἀβραάμ ἐστε, τὰ ἔργα τοῦ Ἀβραὰμ
- of Abraham ye are, the works - of Abraham

ποιεῖτε· 40 νῦν δὲ ζητεῖτέ με ἀποκτεῖναι,
ye do; but now ye seek me to kill,

ἄνθρωπον ὃς τὴν ἀλήθειαν ὑμῖν λελάληκα,
a man who the truth to you has spoken,

I heard from God; this is not what Abraham did. ⁴¹You do what your father did." They said to him, "We were not born of fornication; we have one Father, even God." ⁴²Jesus said to them, "If God were your Father, you would love me, for I proceeded and came forth from God; I came not of my own accord, but he sent me. ⁴³Why do you not understand what I say? It is because you cannot bear to hear my word. ⁴⁴You are of your father the devil, and your will is to do your father's desires. He was a murderer from the beginning, and has nothing to do with the truth, because there is no truth in him. When he lies, he speaks according to his own nature, for he is a liar and the father of lies. ⁴⁵But, because I tell the truth, you do not believe me. ⁴⁶Which of you convicts me of sin? If I tell the truth, why do you not believe me? ⁴⁷He who is of God hears the words of God; the reason why you do not

ἦν ἤκουσα παρὰ τοῦ θεοῦ· τοῦτο Ἀβραὰμ
which I heard from – God; this Abraham

οὐκ ἐποίησεν. 41 ὑμεῖς ποιεῖτε τὰ ἔργα
did not. Ye do the works

τοῦ πατρὸς ὑμῶν. εἶπαν αὐτῷ· ἡμεῖς ἐκ
of the father of you. They said to him : We of

πορνείας οὐκ ἐγεννήθημεν, ἕνα πατέρα
fornication were not born, one father

ἔχομεν τὸν θεόν. 42 εἶπεν αὐτοῖς ὁ
we have[,] – God. Said to them –

Ἰησοῦς· εἰ ὁ θεὸς πατὴρ ὑμῶν ἦν,
Jesus : If – God father of you was,

ἠγαπᾶτε ἂν ἐμέ· ἐγὼ γὰρ ἐκ τοῦ θεοῦ
ye would have loved me; for I of – God

ἐξῆλθον καὶ ἥκω· οὐδὲ γὰρ ἀπ’ ἐμαυτοῦ
came forth and have come; for not from myself

ἐλήλυθα, ἀλλ’ ἐκεῖνός με ἀπέστειλεν. 43 διὰ τί
I have come, but that one me sent. Why

τὴν λαλιὰν τὴν ἐμὴν οὐ γινώσκετε;
the ²speech – ¹my know ye not?

ὅτι οὐ δύνασθε ἀκούειν τὸν λόγον τὸν
because ye cannot to hear the ²word –

ἐμόν. 44 ὑμεῖς ἐκ τοῦ πατρὸς τοῦ
¹my. Ye of the father of the

διαβόλου ἐστὲ καὶ τὰς ἐπιθυμίας τοῦ
devil are and the desires of the

πατρὸς ὑμῶν θέλετε ποιεῖν. ἐκεῖνος
father of you ye wish to do. That one

ἀνθρωποκτόνος ἦν ἀπ’ ἀρχῆς, καὶ ἐν
a murderer was from [the] beginning, and in

τῇ ἀληθείᾳ οὐκ ἔστηκεν, ὅτι οὐκ ἔστιν
the truth stood not, because not is

ἀλήθεια ἐν αὐτῷ. ὅταν λαλῇ τὸ ψεῦδος,
truth in him. When he speaks the lie,

ἐκ τῶν ἰδίων λαλεῖ, ὅτι ψεύστης ἐστὶν
out of his own things he speaks, because a liar he is

καὶ ὁ πατὴρ αὐτοῦ. 45 ἐγὼ δὲ ὅτι τὴν
and the father of it. But ³I ¹because ⁴the

ἀλήθειαν λέγω, οὐ πιστεύετέ μοι. 46 τίς
⁵truth ²say, ye do not believe me. Who

ἐξ ὑμῶν ἐλέγχει με περὶ ἁμαρτίας; εἰ
of you reproves me concerning sin? If

ἀλήθειαν λέγω, διὰ τί ὑμεῖς οὐ πιστεύετέ
truth I say, why ²ye ¹do not believe

μοι; 47 ὁ ὢν ἐκ τοῦ θεοῦ τὰ ῥήματα
me? The [one] being of – God the words

τοῦ θεοῦ ἀκούει· διὰ τοῦτο ὑμεῖς οὐκ
– of God hears; therefore ye not

hear them is that you are not of God."

48 The Jews answered him, "Are we not right in saying that you are a Samaritan and have a demon?" [49]Jesus answered, "I have not a demon; but I honor my Father, and you dishonor me. [50]Yet I do not seek my own glory; there is One who seeks it and he will be the judge. [51]Truly, truly, I say to you, if any one keeps my word, he will never see death." [52]The Jews said to him, "Now we know that you have a demon. Abraham died, as did the prophets; and you say, 'If any one keeps my word, he will never taste death.' [53]Are you greater than our father Abraham, who died? And the prophets died! Who do you claim to be?" [54]Jesus answered, "If I glorify myself, my glory is nothing; it is my Father who glorifies me, of whom you say that he is your God. [55]But you have not known him; I know him. If I said, I do not know him, I

ἀκούετε, ὅτι ἐκ τοῦ θεοῦ οὐκ ἐστέ.
hear,　because of　–　God　ye are not.

48 Ἀπεκρίθησαν οἱ Ἰουδαῖοι καὶ εἶπαν
Answered　the　Jews　and　said

αὐτῷ· οὐ καλῶς λέγομεν ἡμεῖς ὅτι
to him :　[3]Not　[4]well　[1]say　[2]we　[5]that

Σαμαρίτης εἶ σὺ καὶ δαιμόνιον ἔχεις;
[7]a Samaritan　[7]art　[6]thou　[8]and　[11]a demon　[10]hast?

49 ἀπεκρίθη Ἰησοῦς· ἐγὼ δαιμόνιον οὐκ
Answered　Jesus :　I　a demon　not

ἔχω, ἀλλὰ τιμῶ τὸν πατέρα μου, καὶ
have,　but I honour the　Father　of me,　and

ὑμεῖς ἀτιμάζετέ με. 50 ἐγὼ δὲ οὐ ζητῶ
ye　dishonour me.　But I　seek not

τὴν δόξαν μου· ἔστιν ὁ ζητῶν καὶ
the　glory　of me;　there is the [one]　seeking and

κρίνων. 51 ἀμὴν ἀμὴν λέγω ὑμῖν, ἐάν
judging.　Truly　truly　I tell　you,　if

τις τὸν ἐμὸν λόγον τηρήσῃ, θάνατον
anyone　–　my　word　keeps,　death

οὐ μὴ θεωρήσῃ εἰς τὸν αἰῶνα. 52 εἶπαν
by no means will he behold unto the　age.　Said

αὐτῷ οἱ Ἰουδαῖοι· νῦν ἐγνώκαμεν ὅτι
to him　the　Jews :　Now　we have known　that

δαιμόνιον ἔχεις. Ἀβραὰμ ἀπέθανεν καὶ οἱ
a demon　thou hast.　Abraham　died　and the

προφῆται, καὶ σὺ λέγεις· ἐάν τις τὸν
prophets,　and　thou sayest :　If　anyone　the

λόγον μου τηρήσῃ, οὐ μὴ γεύσηται
word　of me　keeps,　by no means　will he taste

θανάτου εἰς τὸν αἰῶνα. 53 μὴ σὺ μείζων
of death　unto the　age.　Not thou greater

εἶ τοῦ πατρὸς ἡμῶν Ἀβραάμ, ὅστις
art [than] the　father　of us　Abraham,　who

ἀπέθανεν; καὶ οἱ προφῆται ἀπέθανον· τίνα
died?　and the　prophets　died;.　whom

σεαυτὸν ποιεῖς; 54 ἀπεκρίθη Ἰησοῦς· ἐὰν
thyself　makest thou?　Answered　Jesus :　If

ἐγὼ δοξάσω ἐμαυτόν, ἡ δόξα μου οὐδέν
I　glorify　myself,　the glory of me　nothing

ἐστιν· ἔστιν ὁ πατήρ μου ὁ δοξάζων με,
is;　[4]is　[1]the [2]Father　[3]of me the [one] glorifying　me,

ὃν ὑμεῖς λέγετε ὅτι θεὸς ἡμῶν ἐστιν,
whom ye　say[,]　–　God　of us　he is,

55 καὶ οὐκ ἐγνώκατε αὐτόν, ἐγὼ δὲ
and　ye have not known　him,　but I

οἶδα αὐτόν. κἂν εἴπω ὅτι οὐκ οἶδα
know　him.　Even if I say　that　I know not

should be a liar like you; but I do know him and I keep his word. ⁵⁶ Your father Abraham rejoiced that he was to see my day; he saw it and was glad." ⁵⁷ The Jews then said to him, "You are not yet fifty years old, and have you seen Abraham?"ʳ ⁵⁸ Jesus said to him, "Truly, truly, I say to you, before Abraham was, I am." ⁵⁹ So they took up stones to throw at him; but Jesus hid himself, and went out of the temple.

αὐτόν, ἔσομαι ὅμοιος ὑμῖν ψεύστης· ἀλλὰ
him,   I shall be   like   you   a liar;   but

οἶδα αὐτὸν καὶ τὸν λόγον αὐτοῦ τηρῶ.
I know   him   and   the   word   of him   I keep.

56 'Αβραὰμ ὁ πατὴρ ὑμῶν ἠγαλλιάσατο
Abraham   the   father   of you   was glad

ἵνα ἴδῃ τὴν ἡμέραν τὴν ἐμήν, καὶ εἶδεν
that he should see *the*   ²day   –   ¹my,   and   he saw

καὶ ἐχάρη.   **57** εἶπαν οὖν οἱ 'Ιουδαῖοι
and   rejoiced.   Said therefore the   Jews

πρὸς αὐτόν· πεντήκοντα ἔτη οὔπω ἔχεις
to   him :   Fifty   years not yet thou hast

καὶ 'Αβραὰμ ἑώρακας;   **58** εἶπεν αὐτοῖς
and   Abraham   hast thou seen?   Said   to them

'Ιησοῦς· ἀμὴν ἀμὴν λέγω ὑμῖν, πρὶν
Jesus: Truly   truly   I tell   you,   before

'Αβραὰμ γενέσθαι ἐγὼ εἰμί.   **59** ἦραν
Abraham   to becomeᵇ   I   am.   They took
        =became

οὖν λίθους ἵνα βάλωσιν ἐπ' αὐτόν·
therefore stones that they might cast on   him;

'Ιησοῦς δὲ ἐκρύβη καὶ ἐξῆλθεν ἐκ τοῦ
but Jesus   was hidden and   went forth out of the

ἱεροῦ.
temple.

CHAPTER 9

AS he passed by, he saw a man blind from his birth. ²And his disciples asked him, "Rabbi, who sinned, this man or his parents, that he was born blind?" ³Jesus answered, "It was not that this man sinned, or his parents, but that the works of God might be made manifest in him. ⁴We must work the works of him who sent me, while it is day; night comes, when no one can work. ⁵As long as I am in the world, I am the light of the world."

9 Καὶ παράγων εἶδεν ἄνθρωπον τυφλὸν
And   passing along   he saw   a man   blind

ἐκ γενετῆς.   **2** καὶ ἠρώτησαν αὐτὸν οἱ
from birth.   And   asked   him   the

μαθηταὶ αὐτοῦ λέγοντες· ῥαββί, τίς ἥμαρτεν,
disciples   of him   saying :   Rabbi, who   sinned,

οὗτος ἢ οἱ γονεῖς αὐτοῦ, ἵνα τυφλὸς
this man or   the   parents   of him,   that   blind

γεννηθῇ;   **3** ἀπεκρίθη 'Ιησοῦς· οὔτε οὗτος
he was born?   Answered   Jesus :   Neither this man

ἥμαρτεν οὔτε οἱ γονεῖς αὐτοῦ, ἀλλ' ἵνα
sinned   nor   the   parents   of him,   but   that

φανερωθῇ τὰ ἔργα τοῦ θεοῦ ἐν αὐτῷ.
might be manifested the   works   –   of God   in   him.

4 ἡμᾶς δεῖ ἐργάζεσθαι τὰ ἔργα τοῦ
Us   it behoves   to work   the   works   of the

πέμψαντός με ἕως ἡμέρα ἐστίν· ἔρχεται
[one] having sent me   while   day   it is;   comes

νὺξ ὅτε οὐδεὶς δύναται ἐργάζεσθαι.   **5** ὅταν
night when no one   can   *to* work.   When

ἐν τῷ κόσμῳ ὦ, φῶς εἰμι τοῦ κόσμου.
in   the   world I am, light I am of the   world.

ʳ Other ancient authorities read *has Abraham seen you?*

⁶As he said this, he spat on the ground and made clay of the spittle and anointed the man's eyes with the clay, ⁷saying to him, "Go, wash in the pool of Silo′am" (which means Sent). So he went and washed and came back seeing. ⁸The neighbors and those who had seen him before as a beggar, said, "Is not this the man who used to sit and beg?" ⁹Some said, "It is he"; others said, "No, but he is like him." He said, "I am the man." ¹⁰They said to him, "Then how were your eyes opened?" ¹¹He answered, "The man called Jesus made clay and anointed my eyes and said to me, 'Go to Silo′am and wash'; so I went and washed and received my sight." ¹²They said to him, "Where is he?" He said, "I do not know."

13 They brought to the Pharisees the man who had formerly been blind. ¹⁴Now it was a sabbath day when Jesus made the clay and opened

---

6 ταῦτα εἰπὼν ἔπτυσεν χαμαὶ καὶ ἐποίησεν
These things having said he spat on the ground and made

πηλὸν ἐκ τοῦ πτύσματος, καὶ ἐπέθηκεν
clay out of the spittle, and ¹put on

αὐτοῦ τὸν πηλὸν ἐπὶ τοὺς ὀφθαλμούς,
⁷of him ²the ³clay ⁴on ⁵the ⁶eyes,

7 καὶ εἶπεν αὐτῷ· ὕπαγε νίψαι εἰς τὴν
and said to him : Go wash in the

κολυμβήθραν τοῦ Σιλωάμ (ὃ ἑρμηνεύεται
pool — of Siloam (which is translated

ἀπεσταλμένος). ἀπῆλθεν οὖν καὶ ἐνίψατο,
having been sent). He went therefore and washed,

καὶ ἦλθεν βλέπων. **8** Οἱ οὖν γείτονες
and came seeing. Therefore the neighbours

καὶ οἱ θεωροῦντες αὐτὸν τὸ πρότερον, †
and the [ones] beholding him formerly,

ὅτι προσαίτης ἦν, ἔλεγον· οὐχ ¹this man
that a beggar he was, said : ¹Not ³this man

ἔστιν ὁ καθήμενος καὶ προσαιτῶν; **9** ἄλλοι
¹is the [one] sitting and begging? Some

ἔλεγον ὅτι οὗτός ἐστιν· ἄλλοι ἔλεγον·
said[,] — This is he; others said :

οὐχί, ἀλλὰ ὅμοιος αὐτῷ ἐστιν. ἐκεῖνος
No, but like to him he is. That [one]

ἔλεγεν ὅτι ἐγώ εἰμι. **10** ἔλεγον οὖν
said[,] — I am. They said therefore

αὐτῷ· πῶς [οὖν] ἠνεῴχθησάν σου οἱ
to him : How then were opened of thee the

ὀφθαλμοί; **11** ἀπεκρίθη ἐκεῖνος· ὁ ἄνθρωπος
eyes? Answered that [one] : The man

ὁ λεγόμενος Ἰησοῦς πηλὸν ἐποίησεν καὶ
— being named Jesus clay made and

ἐπέχρισέν μου τοὺς ὀφθαλμοὺς καὶ εἶπέν
anointed of me the eyes and told

μοι ὅτι ὕπαγε εἰς τὸν Σιλωὰμ καὶ
me[,] — Go to — Siloam and

νίψαι· ἀπελθὼν οὖν καὶ νιψάμενος ἀνέβλεψα.
wash; going therefore and washing I saw.

12 καὶ εἶπαν αὐτῷ· ποῦ ἐστιν ἐκεῖνος;
And they said to him : Where is that [one]?

λέγει· οὐκ οἶδα. **13** Ἄγουσιν αὐτὸν
He says: I do not know. They lead him

πρὸς τοὺς Φαρισαίους, τόν ποτε τυφλόν.
to the Pharisees, the at one time blind.

14 ἦν δὲ σάββατον ἐν ᾗ ἡμέρᾳ τὸν
Now it was a sabbath on which day ²the

πηλὸν ἐποίησεν ὁ Ἰησοῦς καὶ ἀνέῳξεν
⁴clay ¹made — ¹Jesus and opened

his eyes. [15] The Pharisees again asked him how he had received his sight. And he said to them, "He put clay on my eyes, and I washed, and I see." [16] Some of the Pharisees said, "This man is not from God, for he does not keep the sabbath." But others said, "How can a man who is a sinner do such signs?" There was a division among them. [17] So they again said to the blind man, "What do you say about him, since he has opened your eyes?" He said, "He is a prophet."

[18] The Jews did not believe that he had been blind and had received his sight, until they called the parents of the man who had received his sight, [19] and asked them, "Is this your son, who you say was born blind? How then does he now see?" [20] His parents answered, "We know that this is our son, and that he was born blind; [21] but how he now sees we do not know, nor do we know who opened his

αὐτοῦ τοὺς ὀφθαλμούς. **15** πάλιν οὖν
of him   the   eyes.   Again   therefore

ἠρώτων αὐτὸν καὶ οἱ Φαρισαῖοι πῶς
⁴asked ¹him ²also ³the ⁵Pharisees how

ἀνέβλεψεν. ὁ δὲ εἶπεν αὐτοῖς· πηλὸν
he saw.   And he said to them: Clay

ἐπέθηκέν μου ἐπὶ τοὺς ὀφθαλμούς, καὶ
he put on ⁴of me ¹on ²the ³eyes,   and

ἐνιψάμην, καὶ βλέπω. **16** ἔλεγον οὖν ἐκ
I washed,   and I see.   Said therefore of

τῶν Φαρισαίων τινές· οὐκ ἔστιν οὗτος
the   Pharisees   some: ⁴not ³is   ¹This

παρὰ θεοῦ ὁ ἄνθρωπος, ὅτι τὸ σάββατον
⁵from ⁶God –   ²man, because the   sabbath

οὐ τηρεῖ. ἄλλοι [δὲ] ἔλεγον· πῶς δύναται
he keeps not. But others said: How can

ἄνθρωπος ἁμαρτωλὸς τοιαῦτα σημεῖα ποιεῖν;
man   a sinful   such   signs   to do?

καὶ σχίσμα ἦν ἐν αὐτοῖς. **17** λέγουσιν
And a division there was among them.   They say

οὖν τῷ τυφλῷ πάλιν· τί σὺ λέγεις
therefore to the blind man again : What thou sayest

περὶ αὐτοῦ, ὅτι ἠνέῳξέν σου τοὺς
about him,   because he opened of thee the

ὀφθαλμούς; ὁ δὲ εἶπεν ὅτι προφήτης ἐστίν.
eyes?   And he said[,] – A prophet   he is.

18 οὐκ ἐπίστευσαν οὖν οἱ Ἰουδαῖοι περὶ
Did not believe therefore the Jews   about

αὐτοῦ ὅτι ἦν τυφλὸς καὶ ἀνέβλεψεν,
him   that he was blind   and   saw,

ἕως ὅτου ἐφώνησαν τοὺς γονεῖς αὐτοῦ
until   they called   the   parents of him

τοῦ ἀναβλέψαντος **19** καὶ ἠρώτησαν αὐτοὺς
of the [one] having seen   and   asked   them

λέγοντες· οὗτός ἐστιν ὁ υἱὸς ὑμῶν, ὃν
saying: This   is   the son of you, whom

ὑμεῖς λέγετε ὅτι τυφλὸς ἐγεννήθη; πῶς
ye   say   that   blind   he was born?   how

οὖν βλέπει ἄρτι; **20** ἀπεκρίθησαν οὖν οἱ
then sees he now?   Answered   therefore the

γονεῖς αὐτοῦ καὶ εἶπαν· οἴδαμεν ὅτι
parents of him and   said : We know   that

οὗτός ἐστιν ὁ υἱὸς ἡμῶν καὶ ὅτι τυφλὸς
this   is   the son of us   and that blind

ἐγεννήθη· **21** πῶς δὲ νῦν βλέπει οὐκ
he was born;   but how now he sees   not

οἴδαμεν, ἢ τίς ἤνοιξεν αὐτοῦ τοὺς ὀφθαλμοὺς
we know, or who opened of him the   eyes

eyes. Ask him; he is of age, he will speak for himself." ²²His parents said this because they feared the Jews, for the Jews had already agreed that if any one should confess him to be Christ, he was to be put out of the synagogue. ²³Therefore his parents said, "He is of age, ask him."

24 So for the second time they called the man who had been blind, and said to him, "Give God the praise; we know that this man is a sinner." ²⁵He answered, "Whether he is a sinner, I do not know; one thing I know, that though I was blind, now I see." ²⁶They said to him, "What did he do to you? How did he open your eyes?" ²⁷He answered them, "I have told you already, and you would not listen. Why do you want to hear it again? Do you too want to become his disciples?" ²⁸And they reviled him, saying, "You are his disciple, but we are disciples of Moses. ²⁹We know that God has spoken to Moses, but as for this man, we do not know where he comes from." ³⁰The man an-

---

ἡμεῖς οὐκ οἴδαμεν· αὐτὸν ἐρωτήσατε,
we   know not;   him   ask ye,

ἡλικίαν ἔχει, αὐτὸς περὶ ἑαυτοῦ λαλήσει.
age   he has, he   about himself   will speak.

22 ταῦτα εἶπαν οἱ γονεῖς αὐτοῦ ὅτι ἐφο-
These things said   the parents of him because they

βοῦντο τοὺς Ἰουδαίους· ἤδη γὰρ συνετέθειντο
feared   the   Jews;   for already   had agreed

οἱ Ἰουδαῖοι ἵνα ἐάν τις αὐτὸν ὁμολογήσῃ
the Jews   that if anyone him should acknowledge

χριστόν,   ἀποσυνάγωγος   γένηται.
[to be] Christ, put away from [the] synagogue he would be.

23 διὰ τοῦτο οἱ γονεῖς αὐτοῦ εἶπαν ὅτι
Therefore   the   parents of him said[,]

ἡλικίαν ἔχει, αὐτὸν ἐπερωτήσατε. **24** Ἐφώνησαν
Age   he has, him   question ye.   They called

οὖν τὸν ἄνθρωπον ἐκ δευτέρου ὃς ἦν
therefore the man   a second time   who was

τυφλός, καὶ εἶπαν αὐτῷ· δὸς δόξαν τῷ
blind,   and said to him : Give glory   –

θεῷ· ἡμεῖς οἴδαμεν ὅτι οὗτος ὁ ἄνθρωπος
to God; we   know   that this   –   man

ἁμαρτωλός ἐστιν. **25** ἀπεκρίθη οὖν ἐκεῖνος·
sinful   is.   Answered therefore the [one]:

εἰ ἁμαρτωλός ἐστιν οὐκ οἶδα· ἓν οἶδα,
If   sinful   he is I know not; one thing I know,

ὅτι τυφλὸς ὢν ἄρτι βλέπω. **26** εἶπαν
that blind being now I see.   They said

οὖν αὐτῷ· τί ἐποίησέν σοι; πῶς ἤνοιξέν
therefore to him : What did he to thee? how opened he

σου τοὺς ὀφθαλμούς; **27** ἀπεκρίθη αὐτοῖς·
of thee the   eyes?   He answered   them :

εἶπον ὑμῖν ἤδη καὶ οὐκ ἠκούσατε· τί
I told you already and ye heard not;   why

πάλιν θέλετε ἀκούειν; μὴ καὶ ὑμεῖς
again wish ye to hear?   not also   ye

θέλετε αὐτοῦ μαθηταὶ γενέσθαι; **28** καὶ
wish   of him disciples to become?   And

ἐλοιδόρησαν αὐτὸν καὶ εἶπαν· σὺ μαθητὴς
they reviled   him   and said : Thou a disciple

εἶ ἐκείνου, ἡμεῖς δὲ τοῦ Μωϋσέως ἐσμὲν
art of that man, but we   – of Moses   are

μαθηταί· **29** ἡμεῖς οἴδαμεν ὅτι Μωϋσεῖ
disciples;   we   know   that by Moses

λελάληκεν ὁ θεός, τοῦτον δὲ οὐκ οἴδαμεν
has spoken   – God, but this man we know not

πόθεν ἐστίν. **30** ἀπεκρίθη ὁ ἄνθρωπος
whence he is.   Answered   the   man

swered, "Why, this is a marvel! You do not know where he comes from, and yet he opened my eyes. [31] We know that God does not listen to sinners, but if any one is a worshiper of God and does his will, God listens to him. [32] Never since the world began has it been heard that any one opened the eyes of a man born blind. [33] If this man were not from God, he could do nothing." [34] They answered him, "You were born in utter sin, and would you teach us?" And they cast him out.

35 Jesus heard that they had cast him out, and having found him he said, "Do you believe in the Son of man?" [36] He answered, "And who is he, sir, that I may believe in him?" [37] Jesus said to him, "You have seen him, and it is he who speaks to you." [38] He said, "Lord, I believe"; and he worshipped him. [39] Jesus said, "For judgment I came into this world, that those who do not see may see, and that those who see may become blind."

καὶ εἶπεν αὐτοῖς· ἐν τούτῳ γὰρ τὸ
and said to them: In this then the

θαυμαστόν ἐστιν, ὅτι ὑμεῖς οὐκ οἴδατε
marvellous thing is, that ye do not know

πόθεν ἐστίν, καὶ ἤνοιξέν μου τοὺς
whence he is, and he opened of me the

ὀφθαλμούς. 31 οἴδαμεν ὅτι ὁ θεὸς
eyes. We know that — God

ἁμαρτωλῶν οὐκ ἀκούει, ἀλλ' ἐάν τις
sinful men does not hear, ↩ but if anyone

θεοσεβὴς ᾖ καὶ τὸ θέλημα αὐτοῦ ποιῇ,
godfearing is and the will of him does,

τούτου ἀκούει. 32 ἐκ τοῦ αἰῶνος οὐκ
this man he hears. From the age not

ἠκούσθη ὅτι ἠνέῳξέν τις ὀφθαλμοὺς τυφλοῦ
it was heard that ²opened ¹anyone eyes of a blind man

γεγεννημένου· 33 εἰ μὴ ἦν οὗτος παρὰ
having been born; if ²not ¹was ¹this man from

θεοῦ, οὐκ ἠδύνατο ποιεῖν οὐδέν. 34 ἀπεκρίθησαν
God, he could not *to* do no(any)thing. They answered

καὶ εἶπαν αὐτῷ· ἐν ἁμαρτίαις σὺ ἐγεννήθης
and said to him: In sins thou wast born

ὅλος, καὶ σὺ διδάσκεις ἡμᾶς; καὶ ἐξέβαλον
wholly, and thou teachest us? and they cast *out*

αὐτὸν ἔξω. 35 Ἤκουσεν Ἰησοῦς ὅτι
him outside. Heard Jesus that

ἐξέβαλον αὐτὸν ἔξω, καὶ εὑρὼν αὐτὸν
they cast *out* him outside, and finding him

εἶπεν· σὺ πιστεύεις εἰς τὸν υἱὸν τοῦ
said: Thou believest in the Son —

ἀνθρώπου; 36 ἀπεκρίθη ἐκεῖνος καὶ εἶπεν·
of man? Answered that [one] and said:

καὶ τίς ἐστιν, κύριε, ἵνα πιστεύσω εἰς
And who is he, sir, that I may believe in

αὐτόν; 37 εἶπεν αὐτῷ ὁ Ἰησοῦς· καὶ
him? Said to him — Jesus: Both

ἑώρακας αὐτὸν καὶ ὁ λαλῶν μετὰ σοῦ
thou hast seen him and the [one] speaking with thee

ἐκεῖνός ἐστιν. 38 ὁ δὲ ἔφη· πιστεύω, κύριε·
that [one] is. And he said: I believe, sir;

καὶ προσεκύνησεν αὐτῷ. 39 καὶ εἶπεν ὁ
and he worshipped him. And said —

Ἰησοῦς· εἰς κρίμα ἐγὼ εἰς τὸν κόσμον
Jesus: For judgment I into — world

τοῦτον ἦλθον, ἵνα οἱ μὴ βλέποντες
this came, that the [ones] not seeing

βλέπωσιν καὶ οἱ βλέποντες τυφλοὶ γένωνται.
may see and the [ones] seeing blind may become.

⁴⁰Some of the Pharisees near him heard this, and they said to him, "Are we also blind?" ⁴¹Jesus said to them, "If you were blind, you would have no guilt; but now that you say, 'We see,' your guilt remains.

40 Ἤκουσαν ἐκ τῶν Φαρισαίων ταῦτα
heard ¹[Some] ²of ³the ⁴Pharisees ⁵these things
οἱ μετ' αὐτοῦ ὄντες, καὶ εἶπαν αὐτῷ·
– ⁶with ⁷him ⁸being, and they said to him :
μὴ καὶ ἡμεῖς τυφλοί ἐσμεν; **41** εἶπεν
Not also we blind are? Said
αὐτοῖς ὁ Ἰησοῦς· εἰ τυφλοὶ ἦτε, οὐκ
to them – Jesus : If blind ye were, not
ἂν εἴχετε ἁμαρτίαν· νῦν δὲ λέγετε ὅτι
ye would have had sin; but now ye say[,]
βλέπομεν· ἡ ἁμαρτία ὑμῶν μένει.
We see; the sin of you remains.

CHAPTER 10

"TRULY, truly, I say to you, he who does not enter the sheepfold by the door but climbs in by another way, that man is a thief and a robber; ²but he who enters by the door is the shepherd of the sheep. ³To him the gatekeeper opens; the sheep hear his voice, and he calls his own sheep by name and leads them out. ⁴When he has brought out all his own, he goes before them, and the sheep follow him, for they know his voice. ⁵A stranger they will not follow, but they will flee from him, for they do not know the voice of strangers." ⁶This figure Jesus used with them, but they did not under-

10 Ἀμὴν ἀμὴν λέγω ὑμῖν, ὁ μὴ
Truly truly I say to you, the [one] not
εἰσερχόμενος διὰ τῆς θύρας εἰς τὴν
entering through the door into the
αὐλὴν τῶν προβάτων ἀλλὰ ἀναβαίνων
fold of the sheep but going up
ἀλλαχόθεν, ἐκεῖνος κλέπτης ἐστὶν καὶ
by another way, that [one] a thief is and
λῃστής· **2** ὁ δὲ εἰσερχόμενος διὰ τῆς
a robber; but the [one] entering through the
θύρας ποιμήν ἐστιν τῶν προβάτων. **3** τούτῳ
door shepherd is of the sheep. To this [one]
ὁ θυρωρὸς ἀνοίγει, καὶ τὰ πρόβατα τῆς
the doorkeeper opens, and the sheep the
φωνῆς αὐτοῦ ἀκούει, καὶ τὰ ἴδια πρόβατα
voice of him hears, and the(his) own sheep
φωνεῖ κατ' ὄνομα καὶ ἐξάγει αὐτά.
he calls by name and leads out them.
4 ὅταν τὰ ἴδια πάντα ἐκβάλῃ, ἔμπροσθεν
When the(his) own all he puts forth, in front of
αὐτῶν πορεύεται, καὶ τὰ πρόβατα αὐτῷ
them he goes, and the sheep him
ἀκολουθεῖ, ὅτι οἴδασιν τὴν φωνὴν αὐτοῦ·
follows, because they know the voice of him;
5 ἀλλοτρίῳ δὲ οὐ μὴ ἀκολουθήσουσιν,
but a stranger by no means will they follow,
ἀλλὰ φεύξονται ἀπ' αὐτοῦ, ὅτι οὐκ
but will flee from him, because not
οἴδασιν τῶν ἀλλοτρίων τὴν φωνήν.
they know of the strangers the voice.
6 Ταύτην τὴν παροιμίαν εἶπεν αὐτοῖς ὁ
This – allegory told them –
Ἰησοῦς· ἐκεῖνοι δὲ οὐκ ἔγνωσαν τίνα
Jesus; but those men knew not what things

stand what he was saying to them.

7 So Jesus again said to them, "Truly, truly, I say to you, I am the door of the sheep. 8 All who came before me are thieves and robbers; but the sheep did not heed them. 9 I am the door; if any one enters by me, he will be saved, and will go in and out and find pasture. 10 The thief comes only to steal and kill and destroy; I came that they may have life, and have it abundantly. 11 I am the good shepherd. The good shepherd lays down his life for the sheep. 12 He who is a hireling and not a shepherd, whose own the sheep are not, sees the wolf coming and leaves the sheep and flees; and the wolf snatches them and scatters them. 13 He flees because he is a hireling and cares nothing for the sheep. 14 I am the good shepherd; I know my own and my own know me, 15 as the Father knows me and I know the Father; and I lay down my life for the

ἦν   ἃ ἐλάλει αὐτοῖς. 7 Εἶπεν οὖν πάλιν
they were which he spoke to them.   Said therefore again

ὁ Ἰησοῦς· ἀμὴν ἀμὴν λέγω ὑμῖν ὅτι
_   Jesus: Truly   truly   I say   to you   that

ἐγώ εἰμι ἡ θύρα τῶν προβάτων. 8 πάντες
I   am the door   of the   sheep.   All

ὅσοι ἦλθον πρὸ ἐμοῦ κλέπται εἰσὶν καὶ
who   came before   me   thieves   are   and

λησταί· ἀλλ' οὐκ ἤκουσαν αὐτῶν τὰ
robbers;   but   did not hear   them   the

πρόβατα. 9 ἐγώ εἰμι ἡ θύρα· δι' ἐμοῦ
sheep.   I   am the   door; through   me

ἐάν τις εἰσέλθῃ, σωθήσεται, καὶ εἰσελεύ-
if   anyone   enters,   he will be saved, and   will go

σεται καὶ ἐξελεύσεται καὶ νομὴν εὑρήσει.
in   and   *will* go out   and   pasture   *will* find.

10 ὁ κλέπτης οὐκ ἔρχεται εἰ μὴ ἵνα
The   thief   comes not   except   that

κλέψῃ καὶ θύσῃ καὶ ἀπολέσῃ· ἐγὼ ἦλθον
he may steal and   kill   and   destroy;   I   came

ἵνα ζωὴν ἔχωσιν καὶ περισσὸν ἔχωσιν.
that   life   they may have and   abundantly   *they* may have.

11 Ἐγώ εἰμι ὁ ποιμὴν ὁ καλός. ὁ
I   am the shepherd - good.   The

ποιμὴν ὁ καλὸς τὴν ψυχὴν αὐτοῦ τίθησιν
shepherd - good   the   life   of him   lays down

ὑπὲρ τῶν προβάτων· 12 ὁ μισθωτὸς καὶ
for   the   sheep;   the   hireling   and

οὐκ ὢν ποιμήν, οὗ οὐκ ἔστιν τὰ πρόβατα
not being a shepherd, of whom is(are) not   the   sheep

ἴδια, θεωρεῖ τὸν λύκον ἐρχόμενον καὶ
[his] own, beholds   the   wolf   coming   and

ἀφίησιν τὰ πρόβατα καὶ φεύγει, — καὶ
leaves   the   sheep   and   flees,   —   and

ὁ λύκος ἁρπάζει αὐτὰ καὶ σκορπίζει· —
the wolf   seizes   them   and   scatters;   —

13 ὅτι μισθωτός ἐστιν καὶ οὐ μέλει
because   a hireling   he is   and   it matters not

αὐτῷ περὶ τῶν προβάτων. 14 ἐγώ εἰμι
to him   about   the   sheep.   I   am

ὁ ποιμὴν ὁ καλός, καὶ γινώσκω τὰ
the shepherd - good,   and   I know   –

ἐμὰ καὶ γινώσκουσί με τὰ ἐμά, 15 καθὼς
mine and   ²know   ³me – ¹mine,   as

γινώσκει με ὁ πατὴρ κἀγὼ γινώσκω τὸν
³knows   ⁴me ¹the ²Father   and I   know   the

πατέρα, καὶ τὴν ψυχήν μου τίθημι ὑπὲρ
Father,   and   the   life   of me I lay down   for

sheep. ¹⁶And I have other sheep, that are not of this fold; I must bring them also, and they will heed my voice. So there shall be one flock, one shepherd. ¹⁷For this reason the Father loves me, because I lay down my life, that I may take it again. ¹⁸No one takes it from me, but I lay it down of my own accord. I have power to lay it down, and I have power to take it again; this charge I have received from my Father."

19 There was again a division among the Jews because of these words. ²⁰Many of them said, "He has a demon, and he is mad; why listen to him?" ²¹Others said, "These are not the sayings of one who has a demon. Can a demon open the eyes of the blind?"

22 It was the feast of the Dedication at Jerusalem; ²³it was winter, and Jesus was walking in the temple, in the portico of Solomon. ²⁴So the Jews gathered round him and said to him, "How long will you keep us in suspense? If you are the

τῶν προβάτων. **16** καὶ ἄλλα πρόβατα
the sheep. And other sheep
ἔχω ἃ οὐκ ἔστιν ἐκ τῆς αὐλῆς ταύτης·
I have which is(are) not of — fold this;
κἀκεῖνα δεῖ με ἀγαγεῖν, καὶ τῆς φωνῆς
those also it behoves me to bring, and the voice
μου ἀκούσουσιν, καὶ γενήσεται μία ποίμνη,
of me they will hear, and there will become one flock,
εἷς ποιμήν. **17** διὰ τοῦτό με ὁ πατὴρ
one shepherd. Therefore me the Father
ἀγαπᾷ ὅτι ἐγὼ τίθημι τὴν ψυχήν μου,
loves because I lay down the life of me,
ἵνα πάλιν λάβω αὐτήν. **18** οὐδεὶς ἦρεν
that again I may take it. No one took
αὐτὴν ἀπ᾽ ἐμοῦ, ἀλλ᾽ ἐγὼ τίθημι αὐτὴν
it from me, but I lay down it
ἀπ᾽ ἐμαυτοῦ. ἐξουσίαν ἔχω θεῖναι αὐτήν,
from myself. Authority I have to lay down it,
καὶ ἐξουσίαν ἔχω πάλιν λαβεῖν αὐτήν·
and authority I have again to take it;
ταύτην τὴν ἐντολὴν ἔλαβον παρὰ τοῦ
this — commandment I received from the
πατρός μου. **19** Σχίσμα πάλιν ἐγένετο ἐν
Father of me. A division again there was among
τοῖς Ἰουδαίοις διὰ τοὺς λόγους τούτους.
the Jews because of — words these.
20 ἔλεγον δὲ πολλοὶ ἐξ αὐτῶν· δαιμόνιον
And said many of them: A demon
ἔχει καὶ μαίνεται· τί αὐτοῦ ἀκούετε;
he has and raves; why him hear ye?
21 ἄλλοι ἔλεγον· ταῦτα τὰ ῥήματα οὐκ
Others said: These — words not
ἔστιν δαιμονιζομένου· μὴ δαιμόνιον δύναται
is(are) of one demon-possessed; not a demon can
τυφλῶν ὀφθαλμοὺς ἀνοῖξαι;
of blind men eyes to open?
22 Ἐγένετο τότε τὰ ἐγκαίνια ἐν τοῖς
There was then the Dedication in —
Ἱεροσολύμοις· χειμὼν ἦν· **23** καὶ περιεπάτει
Jerusalem; winter it was; and walked
ὁ Ἰησοῦς ἐν τῷ ἱερῷ ἐν τῇ στοᾷ τοῦ
— Jesus in the temple in the porch —
Σολομῶνος. **24** ἐκύκλωσαν οὖν αὐτὸν οἱ
of Solomon. Surrounded therefore him the
Ἰουδαῖοι καὶ ἔλεγον αὐτῷ· ἕως πότε
Jews and said to him: Until when
τὴν ψυχὴν ἡμῶν αἴρεις; εἰ σὺ εἶ
the life(soul) of us holdest thou * ? if thou art

* That is, in suspense.

Christ, tell us plainly."
²⁵Jesus answered them,
"I told you, and you do
not believe. The works
that I do in my Father's
name, they bear witness
to me; ²⁶but you do not
believe, because you do
not belong to my sheep.
²⁷My sheep hear my
voice, and I know them,
and they follow me;
²⁸and I give them eternal
life, and they shall never
perish, and no one shall
snatch them out of my
hand. ²⁹My Father, who
has given them to me,ᵗ
is greater than all, and
no one is able to snatch
them out of the Father's
hand. ³⁰I and the Father
are one."

31 The Jews took up
stones again to stone
him. ³²Jesus answered
them, "I have shown you
many good works from
the Father; for which of
these do you stone me?"
³³The Jews answered him,
"We stone you for no
good work but for blas-
phemy; because you,
being a man, make your-
self God." ³⁴Jesus an-

ὁ χριστός, εἰπὸν ἡμῖν παρρησίᾳ.   25 ἀπεκρίθη
the Christ,   tell us plainly.   Answered

αὐτοῖς   ὁ   'Ιησοῦς· εἶπον ὑμῖν,   καὶ
them   -   Jesus :   I told   you,   and

οὐ πιστεύετε· τὰ ἔργα ἃ ἐγὼ ποιῶ ἐν τῷ
ye do not believe; the works which I do   in the

ὀνόματι τοῦ πατρός μου, ταῦτα μαρτυρεῖ
name   of the Father of me, these witnesses

περὶ ἐμοῦ· 26 ἀλλὰ ὑμεῖς οὐ πιστεύετε,
concerning me; but   ye   do not believe,

ὅτι οὐκ ἐστὲ ἐκ τῶν προβάτων τῶν
because ye are not of the ²sheep   -

ἐμῶν. 27 τὰ πρόβατα τὰ ἐμὰ τῆς φωνῆς
¹my.   the   sheep   the My   the voice

μου ἀκούουσιν, κἀγὼ γινώσκω αὐτά, καὶ
of me   hear,   and I   know   them, and

ἀκολουθοῦσίν μοι, 28 κἀγὼ δίδωμι αὐτοῖς
they follow   me,   and I   give   to them

ζωὴν αἰώνιον, καὶ οὐ μὴ ἀπόλωνται εἰς
life   eternal, and by no means they perish unto

τὸν αἰῶνα, καὶ οὐχ ἁρπάσει τις αὐτὰ
the   age,   and ²shall not seize ¹anyone them

ἐκ τῆς χειρός μου. 29 ὁ πατήρ μου ὁ
out of the hand of me.   The Father of me who

δέδωκέν μοι πάντων μεῖζόν ἐστιν, καὶ
has given to me [than] all greater   is,   and

οὐδεὶς δύναται ἁρπάζειν ἐκ τῆς χειρὸς
no one   can   to seize out of the hand

τοῦ πατρός. 30 ἐγὼ καὶ ὁ πατὴρ ἕν
of the Father.   I   and the Father one

ἐσμεν. 31 'Εβάστασαν πάλιν λίθους οἱ
we are.   Lifted   again stones the

'Ιουδαῖοι ἵνα λιθάσωσιν αὐτόν. 32 ἀπ-
Jews   that they might stone him.   An-

εκρίθη αὐτοῖς ὁ 'Ιησοῦς· πολλὰ ἔργα
swered them   - Jesus :   Many ²works

ἔδειξα ὑμῖν καλὰ ἐκ τοῦ πατρός· διὰ
¹I showed ⁴you ¹good of the Father; because of

ποῖον αὐτῶν ἔργον ἐμὲ λιθάζετε;
which ²of them ¹work   ⁴me   ³stone ye?

33 ἀπεκρίθησαν αὐτῷ οἱ 'Ιουδαῖοι· περὶ
Answered   him   the Jews : Concerning

καλοῦ ἔργου οὐ λιθάζομέν σε ἀλλὰ περὶ
a good work we do not stone thee but concerning

βλασφημίας, καὶ ὅτι σὺ ἄνθρωπος ὢν
blasphemy,   and because thou a man being

ποιεῖς σεαυτὸν θεόν. 34 ἀπεκρίθη αὐτοῖς
makest thyself God.   Answered   them

ᵗ Other ancient authorities
read *What my Father has
given to me*

swered them, "Is it not written in your law, 'I said, you are gods'? [35] If he called them gods to whom the word of God came (and scripture cannot be broken), [36] do you say of him whom the Father consecrated and sent into the world, 'You are blaspheming,' because I said, 'I am the Son of God'? [37] If I am not doing the works of my Father, then do not believe me; [38] but if I do them, even though you do not believe me, believe the works, that you may know and understand that the Father is in me and I am in the Father." [39] Again they tried to arrest him, but he escaped from their hands.

[40] He went away again across the Jordan to the place where John at first baptized, and there he remained. [41] And many came to him; and they said, "John did no sign, but everything that John said about this man was true." [42] And many believed in him there.

ὁ Ἰησοῦς· οὐκ ἔστιν γεγραμμένον ἐν τῷ
Jesus : Is it not *having been* written in the
νόμῳ ὑμῶν ὅτι ἐγὼ εἶπα· θεοί ἐστε;
law of you[,] – I said : Gods ye are?
35 εἰ ἐκείνους εἶπεν θεοὺς πρὸς οὓς ὁ
¹if ³those ²he called ⁴gods with whom the
λόγος τοῦ θεοῦ ἐγένετο, καὶ οὐ δύναται
word – of God was, and cannot
λυθῆναι ἡ γραφή, 36 ὃν ὁ πατὴρ
to be broken the scripture, ³[him] whom ⁴the ⁵Father
ἡγίασεν καὶ ἀπέστειλεν εἰς τὸν κόσμον
⁶sanctified ⁷and ⁸sent ⁹into ¹⁰the ¹¹world
ὑμεῖς λέγετε ὅτι βλασφημεῖς, ὅτι εἶπον·
¹ye ²tell[,] – Thou blasphemest, because I said :
υἱὸς τοῦ θεοῦ εἰμι; 37 εἰ οὐ ποιῶ τὰ ἔργα
Son – of God I am? If I do not the works
τοῦ πατρός μου, μὴ πιστεύετέ μοι· 38 εἰ δὲ
of the Father of me, do not believe me; but if
ποιῶ, κἂν ἐμοὶ μὴ πιστεύητε, τοῖς ἔργοις
I do, even if me ye do not believe, the works
πιστεύετε, ἵνα γνῶτε καὶ γινώσκητε
believe, that ye may know* and continue to know*
ὅτι ἐν ἐμοὶ ὁ πατὴρ κἀγὼ ἐν τῷ πατρί.
that in me the Father [is] and I in the Father.
39 Ἐζήτουν οὖν αὐτὸν πάλιν πιάσαι· καὶ
They sought therefore him again to arrest; and
ἐξῆλθεν ἐκ τῆς χειρὸς αὐτῶν.
he went forth out of the hand of them.

40 Καὶ ἀπῆλθεν πάλιν πέραν τοῦ
And he went away again across the
Ἰορδάνου εἰς τὸν τόπον ὅπου ἦν Ἰωάννης
Jordan to the place where was John
τὸ πρῶτον βαπτίζων, καὶ ἔμενεν ἐκεῖ.
at first baptizing, and remained there.

41 καὶ πολλοὶ ἦλθον πρὸς αὐτὸν καὶ
And many came to him and
ἔλεγον ὅτι Ἰωάννης μὲν σημεῖον ἐποίησεν
said[,] – John indeed sign did
οὐδέν, πάντα δὲ ὅσα εἶπεν Ἰωάννης περὶ
none, but all things how many said John about
τούτου ἀληθῆ ἦν. 42 καὶ πολλοὶ ἐπίστευσαν
this man true was(were). And many believed
εἰς αὐτὸν ἐκεῖ.
in him there.

CHAPTER 11

NOW a certain man was ill, Laz′arus of

11 Ἦν δέ τις ἀσθενῶν, Λάζαρος ἀπὸ
Now there was a certain [man] ailing, Lazarus from

* Different tenses (aorist and present) of the same verb.

Bethany, the village of
Mary and her sister
Martha. ²It was Mary
who anointed the Lord
with ointment and wiped
his feet with her hair,
whose brother Laz′arus
was ill. ³So the sisters
sent to him, saying,
"Lord, he whom you
love is ill." ⁴But when
Jesus heard it he said,
"This illness is not unto
death; it is for the glory
of God, so that the Son
of God may be glorified
by means of it."

5 Now Jesus loved
Martha and her sister
and Laz′arus. ⁶So when
he heard that he was ill,
he stayed two days longer
in the place where he
was. ⁷Then after this he
said to the disciples,
"Let us go into Judea
again." ⁸The disciples
said to him, "Rabbi, the
Jews were but now seek-
ing to stone you, and you
are going there again?"
⁹Jesus answered, "Are
there not twelve hours in
the day? If any one walks
in the day, he does not
stumble, because he sees
the light of this world.
¹⁰But if any one walks in
the night, he stumbles,

Βηθανίας,   ἐκ   τῆς   κώμης   Μαρίας   καὶ
Bethany,   of   the   village   of Mary   and

Μάρθας   τῆς   ἀδελφῆς   αὐτῆς.   2 ἦν   δὲ
Martha   the   sister   of her.   And it was

Μαριὰμ   ἡ   ἀλείψασα   τὸν   κύριον   μύρῳ
Mary   the [one] anointing   the   Lord   with ointment

καὶ   ἐκμάξασα   τοὺς   πόδας   αὐτοῦ   ταῖς
and   wiping off   the   feet   of him   with the

θριξὶν   αὐτῆς,   ἧς   ὁ   ἀδελφὸς   Λάζαρος
hairs   of her,   of whom the   brother   Lazarus

ἠσθένει.   3 ἀπέστειλαν   οὖν   αἱ   ἀδελφαὶ
ailed.   Sent   therefore the   sisters

πρὸς   αὐτὸν   λέγουσαι·   κύριε,   ἴδε   ὃν
to   him   saying :   Lord,   behold[,] [he] whom

φιλεῖς   ἀσθενεῖ.   4 ἀκούσας   δὲ   ὁ   Ἰησοῦς
thou lovest   ails.   And hearing   -   Jesus

εἶπεν·   αὕτη   ἡ   ἀσθένεια   οὐκ   ἔστιν   πρὸς
said: This   -   ailment   is not   to

θάνατον   ἀλλ'   ὑπὲρ   τῆς   δόξης   τοῦ   θεοῦ,
death   but   for   the   glory   -   of God,

ἵνα   δοξασθῇ   ὁ   υἱὸς   τοῦ   θεοῦ   δι'   αὐτῆς.
that may be glorified the   Son   -   of God through   it.

5 ἠγάπα   δὲ   ὁ   Ἰησοῦς   τὴν   Μάρθαν   καὶ
Now ²loved   -   ¹Jesus   -   Martha   and

τὴν   ἀδελφὴν   αὐτῆς   καὶ   τὸν   Λάζαρον.
the   sister   of her   and   -   Lazarus.

6 ὡς   οὖν   ἤκουσεν   ὅτι   ἀσθενεῖ,   τότε   μὲν
When therefore he heard   that   he ails(ed),   then   -

ἔμεινεν   ἐν   ᾧ   ἦν   τόπῳ   δύο   ἡμέρας·
he remained ¹in ²which ⁴he was ³place   two   days;

7 ἔπειτα   μετὰ   τοῦτο   λέγει   τοῖς   μαθηταῖς·
then   after   this   he says   to the   disciples :

ἄγωμεν   εἰς   τὴν   Ἰουδαίαν   πάλιν.   8 λέγουσιν
Let us go into   -   Judæa   again.   Say

αὐτῷ   οἱ   μαθηταί·   ῥαββί,   νῦν   ἐζήτουν
to him   the   disciples :   Rabbi,   ⁴now ²were ³seeking

σε   λιθάσαι   οἱ   Ἰουδαῖοι,   καὶ   πάλιν   ὑπάγεις
⁷thee ⁶to stone ¹the   ²Jews,   and   again   goest thou

ἐκεῖ;   9 ἀπεκρίθη   Ἰησοῦς·   οὐχὶ   δώδεκα
there?   Answered   Jesus :   Not   twelve

ὧραί   εἰσιν   τῆς   ἡμέρας;   ἐάν   τις   περιπατῇ
hours   are there of the   day?   if   anyone   walks

ἐν   τῇ   ἡμέρᾳ,   οὐ   προσκόπτει,   ὅτι   τὸ   φῶς
in   the   day,   he does not stumble, because the   light

τοῦ   κόσμου   τούτου   βλέπει·   10 ἐὰν   δέ
 -    world   of this   he sees;   but if

τις   περιπατῇ   ἐν   τῇ   νυκτί,   προσκόπτει,
anyone walks   in   the   night,   he stumbles,

because the light is not in him." ¹¹Thus he spoke, and then he said to them, "Our friend Laz'arus has fallen asleep, but I go to awake him out of sleep." ¹²The disciples said to him, "Lord, if he has fallen alseep, he will recover." ¹³Now Jesus had spoken of his death, but they thought that he meant taking rest in sleep. ¹⁴Then Jesus told them plainly, "Laz'arus is dead; ¹⁵and for your sake I am glad that I was not there, so that you may believe. But let us go to him." ¹⁶Thomas, called the Twin, said to his fellow disciples, "Let us also go, that we may die with him."

¹⁷Now when Jesus came, he found that Laz'arus had already been in the tomb four days. ¹⁸Bethany was near Jerusalem, about two miles off, ¹⁹and many of the Jews had come to Martha and Mary to console them concerning their brother. ²⁰When Martha heard that Jesus was coming, she went and met him, while Mary sat in the house. ²¹Martha

ὅτι τὸ φῶς οὐκ ἔστιν ἐν αὐτῷ. 11 ταῦτα
because the light is not in him. These things

εἶπεν, καὶ μετὰ τοῦτο λέγει αὐτοῖς·
he said, and after this he says to them :

Λάζαρος ὁ φίλος ἡμῶν κεκοίμηται· ἀλλὰ
Lazarus the friend of us has fallen asleep; but

πορεύομαι ἵνα ἐξυπνίσω αὐτόν. 12 εἶπαν
I am going that I may awaken him. Said

οὖν οἱ μαθηταὶ αὐτῷ· κύριε, εἰ κεκοίμηται,
there- the disciples to him: Lord, if he has fallen asleep,
fore

σωθήσεται. 13 εἰρήκει δὲ ὁ Ἰησοῦς περὶ
he will be healed. Now had spoken – Jesus concerning

τοῦ θανάτου αὐτοῦ· ἐκεῖνοι δὲ ἔδοξαν ὅτι
the death of him; but those men thought that

περὶ τῆς κοιμήσεως τοῦ ὕπνου λέγει.
concerning the sleep – of slumber he says.

14 τότε οὖν εἶπεν αὐτοῖς ὁ Ἰησοῦς
Then therefore told them – Jesus

παρρησίᾳ· Λάζαρος ἀπέθανεν, 15 καὶ χαίρω
plainly : Lazarus died, and I rejoice

δι᾽ ὑμᾶς, ἵνα πιστεύσητε, ὅτι οὐκ ἤμην
because of you, that ye may believe, that I was not

ἐκεῖ· ἀλλὰ ἄγωμεν πρὸς αὐτόν. 16 εἶπεν
there; but let us go to him. Said

οὖν Θωμᾶς ὁ λεγόμενος Δίδυμος τοῖς
therefore Thomas – being called Twin to the(his)

συμμαθηταῖς· ἄγωμεν καὶ ἡμεῖς ἵνα
fellow-disciples : Let go also we(us) that

ἀποθάνωμεν μετ᾽ αὐτοῦ. 17 Ἐλθὼν οὖν
we may die with him. Coming therefore

ὁ Ἰησοῦς εὗρεν αὐτὸν τέσσαρας ἤδη
– Jesus found him ⁵four ¹already

ἡμέρας ἔχοντα ἐν τῷ μνημείῳ. 18 ἦν δὲ
⁵days having(being) in the tomb. Now was

Βηθανία ἐγγὺς τῶν Ἱεροσολύμων ὡς ἀπὸ
Bethany near – Jerusalem about ³away

σταδίων δεκαπέντε. 19 πολλοὶ δὲ ἐκ τῶν
²furlongs ¹fifteen. And many of the

Ἰουδαίων ἐληλύθεισαν πρὸς τὴν Μάρθαν
Jews had come to – Martha

καὶ Μαριάμ, ἵνα παραμυθήσωνται αὐτὰς
and Mary, that they might console them

περὶ τοῦ ἀδελφοῦ. 20 ἡ οὖν Μάρθα ὡς
concerning the(ir) brother. – Therefore Martha when

ἤκουσεν ὅτι Ἰησοῦς ἔρχεται, ὑπήντησεν
she heard that Jesus is(was) coming, met

αὐτῷ· Μαριὰμ δὲ ἐν τῷ οἴκῳ ἐκαθέζετο.
him; but Mary in the house sat.

said to Jesus, "Lord, if you had been here, my brother would not have died. ²²And even now I know that whatever you ask from God, God will give you." ²³Jesus said to her, "Your brother will rise again." ²⁴Martha said to him, "I know that he will rise again in the resurrection at the last day." ²⁵Jesus said to her, "I am the resurrection and the life;ᵘ he who believes in me, though he die, yet shall he live, ²⁶and whoever lives and believes in me shall never die. Do you believe this?" ²⁷She said to him, "Yes, Lord; I believe that you are the Christ, the Son of God, he who is coming into the world."

28 When she had said this, she went and called her sister Mary, saying quietly, "The Teacher is here and is calling for you." ²⁹And when she heard it, she rose quickly and went to him. ³⁰Now Jesus had not yet come to the village, but was still in the place where Martha had met him. ³¹When the Jews who were with her in the

21 εἶπεν οὖν ἡ Μάρθα πρὸς Ἰησοῦν·
Said therefore – Martha to Jesus :

κύριε, εἰ ἦς ὧδε, οὐκ ἂν ἀπέθανεν ὁ
Lord, if thou wast here, would not have died the

ἀδελφός μου. 22 καὶ νῦν οἶδα ὅτι ὅσα ἂν
brother of me. And now I know that whatever things

αἰτήσῃ τὸν θεὸν δώσει σοι ὁ θεός.
thou askest – God ³will give ²thee – ¹God.

23 λέγει αὐτῇ ὁ Ἰησοῦς· ἀναστήσεται ὁ
Says to her – Jesus : Will rise again the

ἀδελφός σου. 24 λέγει αὐτῷ ἡ Μάρθα·
brother of thee. Says to him – Martha :

οἶδα ὅτι ἀναστήσεται ἐν τῇ ἀναστάσει
I know that he will rise again in the resurrection

ἐν τῇ ἐσχάτῃ ἡμέρᾳ. 25 εἶπεν αὐτῇ ὁ
in the last day. Said to her –

Ἰησοῦς· ἐγώ εἰμι ἡ ἀνάστασις καὶ ἡ
Jesus : I am the resurrection and the

ζωή· ὁ πιστεύων εἰς ἐμὲ κἂν ἀποθάνῃ
life; the [one] believing in me even if he should die

ζήσεται, 26 καὶ πᾶς ὁ ζῶν καὶ πιστεύων
will live, and everyone living and believing

εἰς ἐμὲ οὐ μὴ ἀποθάνῃ εἰς τὸν αἰῶνα·
in me by no means dies unto the age :

πιστεύεις τοῦτο; 27 λέγει αὐτῷ· ναί, κύριε,
believest thou this? She says to him : Yes, Lord;

ἐγὼ πεπίστευκα ὅτι σὺ εἶ ὁ χριστὸς ὁ
I have believed that thou art the Christ the

υἱὸς τοῦ θεοῦ ὁ εἰς τὸν κόσμον ἐρχόμενος.
Son – of God ¹the ²into ⁴the ⁵world ³[one] coming.

28 καὶ τοῦτο εἰποῦσα ἀπῆλθεν καὶ ἐφώνησεν
And this saying she went away and called

Μαριὰμ τὴν ἀδελφὴν αὐτῆς λάθρα εἰποῦσα·
Mary the sister of her secretly saying :

ὁ διδάσκαλος πάρεστιν καὶ φωνεῖ σε.
The Teacher is here and calls thee.

29 ἐκείνη δὲ ὡς ἤκουσεν, ἐγείρεται ταχὺ
And that [one] when she heard, rose quickly

καὶ ἤρχετο πρὸς αὐτόν· 30 οὔπω δὲ
and came to him; now not yet

ἐληλύθει ὁ Ἰησοῦς εἰς τὴν κώμην, ἀλλ'
had come – Jesus into the village, but

ἦν ἔτι ἐν τῷ τόπῳ ὅπου ὑπήντησεν
was still in the place where met

αὐτῷ ἡ Μάρθα. 31 οἱ οὖν Ἰουδαῖοι
him – Martha. Therefore the Jews

οἱ ὄντες μετ' αὐτῆς ἐν τῇ οἰκίᾳ καὶ
the [ones] being with her in the house and

house, consoling her, saw Mary rise quickly and go out, they followed her, supposing that she was going to the tomb to weep there. [32] Then Mary, when she came where Jesus was and saw him, fell at his feet, saying to him, "Lord, if you had been here, my brother would not have died." [33] When Jesus saw her weeping, and the Jews who came with her also weeping, he was deeply moved in spirit and troubled; [34] and he said, "Where have you laid him?" They said to him, "Lord, come and see." [35] Jesus wept. [36] So the Jews said, "See how he loved him!" [37] But some of them said, "Could not he who opened the eyes of the blind man have kept this man from dying?"

38 Then Jesus, deeply moved again, came to the tomb; it was a cave, and a stone lay upon it. [39] Jesus said, "Take away the stone." Martha, the sister of the dead man,

παραμυθούμενοι αὐτήν, ἰδόντες τὴν Μαριὰμ
consoling　　her,　seeing　－　Mary

ὅτι ταχέως ἀνέστη καὶ ἐξῆλθεν,
that　quickly　she rose up　and　went out,

ἠκολούθησαν αὐτῇ, δόξαντες ὅτι ὑπάγει
followed　　her,　thinking[,]　－ She is going

εἰς τὸ μνημεῖον ἵνα κλαύσῃ ἐκεῖ.　32 ἡ
to　the　tomb　that she may weep　there.　－

οὖν Μαριὰμ ὡς ἦλθεν ὅπου ἦν Ἰησοῦς,
Therefore Mary　when she came　where　was　Jesus,

ἰδοῦσα αὐτὸν ἔπεσεν αὐτοῦ πρὸς τοὺς
seeing　him　fell　of him　at　the

πόδας, λέγουσα αὐτῷ· κύριε, εἰ ἦς ὧδε,
feet,　saying　to him : Lord,　if thou wast here,

οὐκ ἄν μου ἀπέθανεν ὁ ἀδελφός.
⁴would not　²of me　⁵have died　¹the　⁶brother.

33 Ἰησοῦς οὖν ὡς εἶδεν αὐτὴν κλαίουσαν
Jesus therefore when he saw　her　weeping

καὶ τοὺς συνελθόντας αὐτῇ Ἰουδαίους
and　¹the　²coming with　⁴her　³Jews

κλαίοντας, ἐνεβριμήσατο τῷ πνεύματι καὶ
weeping,　groaned　in the(his) spirit　and

ἐτάραξεν ἑαυτόν, 34 καὶ εἶπεν· ποῦ
troubled　himself,　and　said :　Where

τεθείκατε αὐτόν; λέγουσιν αὐτῷ· κύριε,
have ye put　him?　They say　to him : Lord,

ἔρχου καὶ ἴδε. 35 ἐδάκρυσεν ὁ Ἰησοῦς.
come　and　see.　Shed tears　－　Jesus.

36 ἔλεγον οὖν οἱ Ἰουδαῖοι· ἴδε πῶς
Said　therefore the　Jews :　See　how

ἐφίλει αὐτόν. 37 τινὲς δὲ ἐξ αὐτῶν
he loved　him.　But some　of　them

εἶπαν· οὐκ ἐδύνατο οὗτος ὁ ἀνοίξας
said :　Could not　this man　the [one] opening

τοὺς ὀφθαλμοὺς τοῦ τυφλοῦ ποιῆσαι ἵνα
the　eyes　of the blind man　to cause　that

καὶ οὗτος μὴ ἀποθάνῃ; 38 Ἰησοῦς οὖν
even this man　should not die ?　Jesus therefore

πάλιν ἐμβριμώμενος ἐν ἑαυτῷ ἔρχεται
again　groaning　in　himself　comes

εἰς τὸ μνημεῖον· ἦν δὲ σπήλαιον, καὶ
to　the　tomb;　now it was　a cave,　and

λίθος ἐπέκειτο ἐπ' αὐτῷ. 39 λέγει ὁ
a stone　was lying on　on　it.　Says　－

Ἰησοῦς· ἄρατε τὸν λίθον. λέγει αὐτῷ
Jesus :　Lift ye　the　stone.　Says　to him

ἡ ἀδελφὴ τοῦ τετελευτηκότος Μάρθα·
the　sister　of the [one]　having died　Martha :

said to him, "Lord, by this time there will be an odor, for he has been dead four days." ⁴⁰Jesus said to her, "Did I not tell you that if you would believe you would see the glory of God?" ⁴¹So they took away the stone. And Jesus lifted up his eyes and said, "Father, I thank thee that thou hast heard me. ⁴²I knew that thou hearest me always, but I have said this on account of the people standing by, that they may believe that thou didst send me." ⁴³When he had said this, he cried with a loud voice, "Laz'arus, come out." ⁴⁴The dead man came out, his hands and feet bound with bandages, and his face wrapped with a cloth. Jesus said to them, "Unbind him, and let him go."

45 Many of the Jews therefore, who had come with Mary and had seen what he did, believed in him; ⁴⁶but some of them went to the Pharisees and told them what Jesus had done. ⁴⁷So the chief priests and the Pharisees gathered the council, and said, "What are we to do? For this man performs many signs. ⁴⁸If

κύριε, ἤδη ὄζει· τεταρταῖος γάρ ἐστιν.
Lord, now he smells; for fourth [day] it is.
40 λέγει αὐτῇ ὁ Ἰησοῦς· οὐκ εἶπόν
Says to her – Jesus: Not I told
σοι ὅτι ἐὰν πιστεύσῃς ὄψῃ τὴν δόξαν
thee that if thou believest thou wilt see the glory
τοῦ θεοῦ; 41 ἦραν οὖν τὸν λίθον. ὁ
of God? They lifted therefore the stone. –
δὲ Ἰησοῦς ἦρεν τοὺς ὀφθαλμοὺς ἄνω
And Jesus lifted the(his) eyes up
καὶ εἶπεν· πάτερ, εὐχαριστῶ σοι ὅτι
and said: Father, I thank thee that
ἤκουσάς μου. 42 ἐγὼ δὲ ᾔδειν ὅτι
thou didst hear me. And I knew that
πάντοτέ μου ἀκούεις· ἀλλὰ διὰ τὸν
always me thou hearest; but because of the
ὄχλον τὸν περιεστῶτα εἶπον, ἵνα
crowd – standing round I said, that
πιστεύσωσιν ὅτι σύ με ἀπέστειλας.
they may believe that thou me didst send.
43 καὶ ταῦτα εἰπὼν φωνῇ μεγάλῃ
And these things saying voice with a great
ἐκραύγασεν· Λάζαρε, δεῦρο ἔξω. 44 ἐξῆλθεν
he cried out: Lazarus, come out. Came out
ὁ τεθνηκὼς δεδεμένος τοὺς πόδας καὶ
the [one] having died having been bound the feet and
τὰς χεῖρας κειρίαις, καὶ ἡ ὄψις αὐτοῦ
the hands with bandages, and the face of him
σουδαρίῳ περιεδέδετο. λέγει αὐτοῖς ὁ
with a napkin had been bound round. Says to them –
Ἰησοῦς· λύσατε αὐτὸν καὶ ἄφετε αὐτὸν ὑπάγειν.
Jesus: Loosen him and let him to go.
45 Πολλοὶ οὖν ἐκ τῶν Ἰουδαίων, οἱ
Many therefore of the Jews, the [ones]
ἐλθόντες πρὸς τὴν Μαριὰμ καὶ θεασάμενοι
having come to – Mary and having beheld
ὃ ἐποίησεν, ἐπίστευσαν εἰς αὐτόν· 46 τινὲς δὲ
what he did, believed in him; but some
ἐξ αὐτῶν ἀπῆλθον πρὸς τοὺς Φαρισαίους
of them went away to the Pharisees
καὶ εἶπαν αὐτοῖς ἃ ἐποίησεν Ἰησοῦς.
and told them what things did Jesus.
47 συνήγαγον οὖν οἱ ἀρχιερεῖς καὶ οἱ
Assembled therefore the chief priests and the
Φαρισαῖοι συνέδριον, καὶ ἔλεγον· τί
Pharisees a council, and said: What
ποιοῦμεν, ὅτι οὗτος ὁ ἄνθρωπος πολλὰ
are we doing, because this – man ¹many

we let him go on thus, ποιεῖ σημεῖα; 48 ἐὰν ἀφῶμεν αὐτὸν οὕτως,
every one will believe in ¹does   ²signs?   If   we leave   him   thus,
him, and the Romans πάντες   πιστεύσουσιν   εἰς   αὐτόν,   καὶ
will come and destroy all men   will believe   in   him,   and
both our holy place and ἐλεύσονται οἱ 'Ρωμαῖοι καὶ ἀροῦσιν ἡμῶν
our nation." ⁴⁹But one will come   the   Romans   and   will take   of us
of them, Ca′iaphas, who καὶ   τὸν   τόπον   καὶ   τὸ   ἔθνος.   49 εἰς
was high priest that year, both   the   place   and   the   nation.   ²one
said to them, "You δέ   τις   ἐξ   αὐτῶν   Καϊαφᾶς,   ἀρχιερεὺς
know nothing at all; ¹But ²a certain of   them[,]   Caiaphas,   high priest
⁵⁰you do not understand ὢν   τοῦ   ἐνιαυτοῦ   ἐκείνου,   εἶπεν   αὐτοῖς·
that it is expedient for being   -   year   of that,   said   to them :
you that one man should ὑμεῖς   οὐκ   οἴδατε   οὐδέν,   50 οὐδὲ λογίζεσθε
die for the people, and Ye   know not   no(any)thing,   nor   reckon
that the whole nation ὅτι   συμφέρει   ὑμῖν   ἵνα   εἷς   ἄνθρωπος
should not perish." ⁵¹He that   it is expedient   for us   that   one   man
did not say this of his ἀποθάνῃ   ὑπὲρ   τοῦ   λαοῦ   καὶ   μὴ   ὅλον
own accord, but being should die   for   the   people   and   not   all
high priest that year he τὸ   ἔθνος   ἀπόληται.   51 τοῦτο   δὲ   ἀφ'
prophesied that Jesus the   nation   perish.   But this   from
should die for the nation, ἑαυτοῦ   οὐκ   εἶπεν,   ἀλλὰ   ἀρχιερεὺς   ὢν
⁵²and not for the nation himself   he said not,   but   high priest   being
only, but to gather into τοῦ   ἐνιαυτοῦ   ἐκείνου   ἐπροφήτευσεν   ὅτι
one the children of God   -   year   of that   he prophesied   that
who are scattered abroad. ἔμελλεν 'Ιησοῦς   ἀποθνῄσκειν   ὑπὲρ   τοῦ
⁵³So from that day on was about   Jesus   to die   for   the
they took counsel how ἔθνους,   52 καὶ   οὐχ   ὑπὲρ   τοῦ   ἔθνους
to put him to death. nation,   and   not   for   the   nation
54 Jesus therefore no μόνον,   ἀλλ'   ἵνα   καὶ   τὰ   τέκνα   τοῦ   θεοῦ
longer went about only,   but   that   also   the   children   -   of God
openly among the Jews, τὰ   διεσκορπισμένα   συναγάγῃ   εἰς   ἕν.
but went from there to   -   having been scattered   he might gather   into   one.
the country near the 53 ἀπ'   ἐκείνης   οὖν   τῆς   ἡμέρας   ἐβουλεύσαντο
wilderness, to a town From   ¹that   ³therefore -   ²day   they took counsel
called E′phraim; and ἵνα   ἀποκτείνωσιν   αὐτόν.   54 'Ο   οὖν
there he stayed with the that   they might kill   him.   -   Therefore
disciples. 'Ιησοῦς   οὐκέτι   παρρησίᾳ   περιεπάτει   ἐν
55 Now the Passover Jesus   no longer   openly   walked   among
of the Jews was at hand, τοῖς   'Ιουδαίοις,   ἀλλὰ   ἀπῆλθεν   ἐκεῖθεν   εἰς
the   Jews,   but   went away   thence   into
τὴν   χώραν   ἐγγὺς   τῆς   ἐρήμου,   εἰς   'Εφράϊμ
the   country   near   the   desert,   to   ²Ephraim
λεγομένην   πόλιν,   κἀκεῖ   ἔμεινεν   μετὰ   τῶν
¹being called   ¹a city,   and there   remained   with   the
μαθητῶν.
disciples.

55 ῏Ην   δὲ   ἐγγὺς   τὸ   πάσχα   τῶν
Now was   near   the   Passover   of the

and many went up from
the country to Jerusalem
before the Passover, to
purify themselves.
⁵⁶They were looking for
Jesus and saying to one
another as they stood in
the temple, "What do
you think? That he will
not come to the feast?"
⁵⁷Now the chief priests
and the Pharisees had
given orders that if any
one knew where he was,
he should let them know,
so that they might arrest
him.

CHAPTER 12

SIX days before the
Passover, Jesus came
to Bethany, where Laz′-
arus was, whom Jesus
had raised from the
dead. ²There they made
him a supper; Martha
served, and Laz′arus was
one of those at table with
him. ³Mary took a
pound of costly ointment
of pure nard and
anointed the feet of
Jesus and wiped his feet
with her hair; and the
house was filled with the
fragrance of the oint-
ment. ⁴But Judas Is-
cariot, one of his dis-
ciples (he who was to
betray him), said, ⁵"Why
was this ointment not
sold for three hundred
denarii and given to the

Ἰουδαίων,   καὶ   ἀνέβησαν   πολλοὶ   εἰς
Jews,   and   went up   many   to

Ἱεροσόλυμα   ἐκ   τῆς   χώρας   πρὸ   τοῦ
Jerusalem   out of the   country   before the

πάσχα,   ἵνα   ἁγνίσωσιν   ἑαυτούς.
Passover,   that   they might purify   themselves.

56 ἐζήτουν   οὖν   τὸν   Ἰησοῦν   καὶ   ἔλεγον
They sought   therefore   -   Jesus   and   said

μετ'   ἀλλήλων   ἐν   τῷ   ἱερῷ   ἑστηκότες·
with   one another in   the   temple   standing :

τί   δοκεῖ   ὑμῖν;   ὅτι   οὐ   μὴ   ἔλθῃ   εἰς
What seems it to you? that by no means he comes to

τὴν   ἑορτήν;   57 δεδώκεισαν   δὲ   οἱ   ἀρχιερεῖς
the   feast?   Now had given   the   chief priests

καὶ   οἱ   Φαρισαῖοι   ἐντολὰς   ἵνα   ἐάν   τις
and   the   Pharisees   commands that   if anyone

γνῷ   ποῦ   ἐστιν   μηνύσῃ,   ὅπως   πιάσωσιν
knew where he is (was) he should inform, so as they might
                                                    arrest

αὐτόν. 12 Ὁ   οὖν   Ἰησοῦς   πρὸ   ἓξ   ἡμερῶν
him.   - Therefore Jesus   ²before ¹six ³days

τοῦ   πάσχα   ἦλθεν   εἰς   Βηθανίαν,   ὅπου
the   Passover came   to   Bethany,   where

ἦν   Λάζαρος,   ὃν   ἤγειρεν   ἐκ   νεκρῶν
was Lazarus,   whom ²raised   ²out of [the] ⁴dead

Ἰησοῦς. 2 ἐποίησαν   οὖν   αὐτῷ   δεῖπνον   ἐκεῖ,
¹Jesus.   They made   therefore for him a supper   there,

καὶ   ἡ   Μάρθα   διηκόνει,   ὁ   δὲ   Λάζαρος   εἷς
and   - Martha   served,   - but Lazarus   one

ἦν   ἐκ   τῶν   ἀνακειμένων   σὺν   αὐτῷ· 3 ἡ
was of the [ones] reclining   with   him;

οὖν   Μαριὰμ   λαβοῦσα   λίτραν   μύρου
therefore Mary   taking   a pound   ²ointment

νάρδου   πιστικῆς   πολυτίμου   ἤλειψεν   τοὺς
¹of spikenard ¹of pure ²costly   anointed   the

πόδας   τοῦ   Ἰησοῦ   καὶ   ἐξέμαξεν   ταῖς
feet   - of Jesus   and   wiped off   with the

θριξὶν   αὐτῆς   τοὺς   πόδας   αὐτοῦ·   ἡ   δὲ
hairs   of her   the   feet   of him; and the

οἰκία   ἐπληρώθη   ἐκ   τῆς   ὀσμῆς   τοῦ
house   was filled of(with) the   odour   of the

μύρου. 4 λέγει   δὲ   Ἰούδας   ὁ   Ἰσκαριώτης
ointment.   And says   Judas   the   Iscariot

εἷς   τῶν   μαθητῶν   αὐτοῦ,   ὁ   μέλλων
one   of the   disciples   of him, the [one] being about

αὐτὸν   παραδιδόναι· 5 διὰ   τί   τοῦτο   τὸ
him   to betray :   Why   this   -

μύρον   οὐκ   ἐπράθη   τριακοσίων   δηναρίων
ointment not   was sold of(for) three hundred denarii

poor?" ⁶This he said, not that he cared for the poor but because he was a thief, and as he had the money box he used to take what was put into it. ⁷Jesus said, "Let her alone, let her keep it for the day of my burial. ⁸The poor you always have with you, but you do not always have me."

9 When the great crowd of the Jews learned that he was there, they came, not only on account of Jesus but also to see Laz′arus, whom he had raised from the dead. ¹⁰So the chief priests planned to put Laz′arus also to death, ¹¹because on account of him many of the Jews were going away and believing in Jesus.

12 The next day a great crowd who had come to the feast heard that Jesus was coming to Jerusalem. ¹³So they took branches of palm trees and went out to meet him, crying, "Hosanna! Blessed is he who comes in the name of the Lord,

καὶ ἐδόθη πτωχοῖς; 6 εἶπεν δὲ τοῦτο
and given to [the] poor? But he said this
οὐχ ὅτι περὶ τῶν πτωχῶν ἔμελεν αὐτῷ,
not because about the poor it mattered to him,
ἀλλ' ὅτι κλέπτης ἦν καὶ τὸ γλωσσόκομον
but because a thief he was and ⁵the ⁶bag
ἔχων τὰ βαλλόμενα ἐβάσταζεν. *
¹having ⁵the things ⁶being put [in] ⁴carried. *
7 εἶπεν οὖν ὁ Ἰησοῦς· ἄφες αὐτήν,
Said therefore – Jesus: Leave her,
ἵνα εἰς τὴν ἡμέραν τοῦ ἐνταφιασμοῦ
that to the day of the burial
μου τηρήσῃ αὐτό· 8 τοὺς πτωχοὺς γὰρ
of me she may keep it; ²the ²poor ¹for
πάντοτε ἔχετε μεθ' ἑαυτῶν, ἐμὲ δὲ
always ye have with yourselves, but me
οὐ πάντοτε ἔχετε. 9 Ἔγνω οὖν ὁ ὄχλος
not always ye have. Knew therefore the crowd
πολὺς ἐκ τῶν Ἰουδαίων ὅτι ἐκεῖ ἐστιν,
great of the Jews that there he is(was),
καὶ ἦλθον οὐ διὰ τὸν Ἰησοῦν μόνον,
and they came not because of – Jesus only,
ἀλλ' ἵνα καὶ τὸν Λάζαρον ἴδωσιν ὃν
but that also – Lazarus they might see whom
ἤγειρεν ἐκ νεκρῶν. 10 ἐβουλεύσαντο δὲ
he raised out of [the] dead. But took counsel
οἱ ἀρχιερεῖς ἵνα καὶ τὸν Λάζαρον
the chief priests that also – Lazarus
ἀποκτείνωσιν, 11 ὅτι πολλοὶ δι' αὐτὸν
they might kill, because ¹many ⁴because of ⁵him
ὑπῆγον τῶν Ἰουδαίων καὶ ἐπίστευον εἰς
⁴went ²of the ³Jews and believed in
τὸν Ἰησοῦς.
– Jesus.

12 Τῇ ἐπαύριον ὁ ὄχλος πολὺς ὁ
On the morrow the crowd much –
ἐλθὼν εἰς τὴν ἑορτήν, ἀκούσαντες ὅτι
coming to the feast, hearing that
ἔρχεται Ἰησοῦς εἰς Ἱεροσόλυμα, 13 ἔλαβον
is(was) coming Jesus to Jerusalem, took
τὰ βαῖα τῶν φοινίκων καὶ ἐξῆλθον εἰς
the branches of the palm-trees and went out to
ὑπάντησιν αὐτῷ, καὶ ἐκραύγαζον· ὡσαννά,
a meeting with him, and cried out : Hosanna,
εὐλογημένος ὁ ἐρχόμενος ἐν ὀνόματι
being blessed the [one] coming in [the] name

* This may mean " stole "; cf. our euphemism for " steal "—to " lift " a thing.

even the King of Israel!"
[14]And Jesus found a young ass and sat upon it; as it is written,
[15]"Fear not, daughter of Zion;
   behold thy king is coming,
   sitting on an ass's colt!"
[16]His disciples did not understand this at first; but when Jesus was glorified, then they remembered that this had been written of him and had been done to him. [17]The crowd that had been with him when he called Laz'arus out of the tomb and raised him from the dead bore witness. [18]The reason why the crowd went to meet him was that they heard he had done this sign. [19]The Pharisees then said to one another, "You see that you can do nothing; look, the world has gone after him."

20 Now among those who went up to worship at the feast were some Greeks. [21]So these came to Philip, who was from Beth-sa'ida in Galilee, and said to him, "Sir, we wish to see Jesus." [22]Philip went and told

κυρίου,   καὶ   ὁ   βασιλεὺς   τοῦ   Ἰσραήλ.
of [the] Lord, even the   king   –   of Israel.

14 εὑρὼν   δὲ   ὁ   Ἰησοῦς   ὀνάριον   ἐκάθισεν
And [2]having found –   [1]Jesus   a young ass   sat

ἐπ᾽   αὐτό,   καθώς   ἐστιν   γεγραμμένον·
on   it,   as   it is   *having been* written :

15 μὴ φοβοῦ,   θυγάτηρ   Σιών·   ἰδοὺ ὁ
Fear not,   daughter   of Sion : behold[,] the

βασιλεύς   σου   ἔρχεται,   καθήμενος   ἐπὶ
king   of thee   comes,   sitting   on

πῶλον   ὄνου.   16 ταῦτα   οὐκ   ἔγνωσαν
a foal   of an ass.   These things   knew not

αὐτοῦ οἱ μαθηταὶ   τὸ   πρῶτον,   ἀλλ᾽ ὅτε
of him the disciples   at first,   but   when

ἐδοξάσθη   Ἰησοῦς,   τότε   ἐμνήσθησαν   ὅτι
was glorified   Jesus,   then   they remembered that

ταῦτα   ἦν ἐπ᾽   αὐτῷ   γεγραμμένα   καὶ
these things were on   him   *having been* written and

ταῦτα   ἐποίησαν   αὐτῷ.   17 ἐμαρτύρει   οὖν
these things they did   to him.   Witnessed therefore

ὁ ὄχλος ὁ ὢν μετ᾽   αὐτοῦ   ὅτε   τὸν
the crowd – being with   him   when   –

Λάζαρον   ἐφώνησεν   ἐκ   τοῦ   μνημείου   καὶ
Lazarus   he called   out of the   tomb   and

ἤγειρεν   αὐτὸν   ἐκ   νεκρῶν.   18 διὰ τοῦτο
raised   him   out of [the] dead.   Therefore

καὶ   ὑπήντησεν   αὐτῷ   ὁ   ὄχλος,   ὅτι
also   met   him   the   crowd,   because

ἤκουσαν   τοῦτο   αὐτὸν   πεποιηκέναι   τὸ
[1]they heard [4]this   [3]him   [2]to have done[b]   –

σημεῖον.   19 οἱ   οὖν   Φαρισαῖοι   εἶπαν
[5]sign.   Therefore the   Pharisees   said

πρὸς ἑαυτούς·   θεωρεῖτε   ὅτι   οὐκ   ὠφελεῖτε
to themselves· Behold ye   that   ye profit not

οὐδέν·   ἴδε ὁ κόσμος   ὀπίσω αὐτοῦ ἀπῆλθεν.
no(any)thing; see[,] the world   after   him   went(is gone).

20 Ἦσαν   δὲ   Ἕλληνές   τινες   ἐκ   τῶν
Now there were   [2]Greeks   [1]some   of   the

ἀναβαινόντων   ἵνα   προσκυνήσωσιν   ἐν   τῇ
[ones] going up   that   they might worship   at   the

ἑορτῇ·   21 οὗτοι   οὖν   προσῆλθον   Φιλίππῳ
feast;   these   therefore   approached   *to* Philip

τῷ   ἀπὸ Βηθσαϊδὰ   τῆς   Γαλιλαίας.   καὶ
the [one] from Bethsaida   of Galilee,   and

ἠρώτων   αὐτὸν   λέγοντες·   κύριε,   θέλομεν
asked   him   saying :   Sir,   we wish

τὸν Ἰησοῦν ἰδεῖν.   22 ἔρχεται ὁ   Φίλιππος
–   Jesus   to see.   Comes   –   Philip

Andrew; Andrew went with Philip and they told Jesus. ²³And Jesus answered them, "The hour has come for the Son of man to be glorified. ²⁴Truly, truly, I say to you, unless a grain of wheat falls into the earth and dies, it remains alone; but if it dies, it bears much fruit. ²⁵He who loves his life loses it, and he who hates his life in this world will keep it for eternal life. ²⁶If any one serves me, he must follow me; and where I am, there shall my servant be also; if any one serves me, the Father will honor him.

²⁷ "Now is my soul troubled. And what shall I say? 'Father, save me from this hour'? No, for this purpose I have come to this hour. ²⁸Father, glorify thy name." Then a voice came from heaven, "I have glorified it, and I will glorify it again." ²⁹The crowd standing by heard it and said that it had thundered. Others said, "An angel had spoken to

καὶ λέγει τῷ Ἀνδρέᾳ· ἔρχεται Ἀνδρέας
and tells – Andrew; comes Andrew

καὶ Φίλιππος καὶ λέγουσιν τῷ Ἰησοῦ.
and Philip and tell – Jesus.

23 ὁ δὲ Ἰησοῦς ἀποκρίνεται αὐτοῖς λέγων·
– And Jesus answers them saying:

ἐλήλυθεν ἡ ὥρα ἵνα δοξασθῇ ὁ υἱὸς τοῦ
Has come the hour that is glorified the Son –

ἀνθρώπου. 24 ἀμὴν ἀμὴν λέγω ὑμῖν,
of man. Truly truly I say to you,

ἐὰν μὴ ὁ κόκκος τοῦ σίτου πεσὼν εἰς
unless the grain – of wheat falling into

τὴν γῆν ἀποθάνῃ, αὐτὸς μόνος μένει·
the ground dies, it alone remains;

ἐὰν δὲ ἀποθάνῃ, πολὺν καρπὸν φέρει.
but if it dies, much fruit it bears.

25 ὁ φιλῶν τὴν ψυχὴν αὐτοῦ ἀπολλύει
The [one] loving the life of him loses

αὐτήν, καὶ ὁ μισῶν τὴν ψυχὴν αὐτοῦ
it, and the [one] hating the life of him

ἐν τῷ κόσμῳ τούτῳ εἰς ζωὴν αἰώνιον
in – world this unto life eternal

φυλάξει αὐτήν. 26 ἐὰν ἐμοί τις διακονῇ,
will keep it. If me anyone serves,

ἐμοὶ ἀκολουθείτω, καὶ ὅπου εἰμὶ ἐγώ,
me let him follow, and where am I,

ἐκεῖ καὶ ὁ διάκονος ὁ ἐμὸς ἔσται·
there also the ¹servant – ¹my will be;

ἐάν τις ἐμοὶ διακονῇ, τιμήσει αὐτὸν
if anyone me serves, will honour him

ὁ πατήρ. 27 νῦν ἡ ψυχή μου τετάρακται,
the Father. Now the soul of me has been troubled,

καὶ τί εἴπω; πάτερ, σῶσόν με ἐκ
and what may I say? Father, save me out of

τῆς ὥρας ταύτης. ἀλλὰ διὰ τοῦτο ἦλθον
– hour this. But therefore I came

εἰς τὴν ὥραν ταύτην. 28 πάτερ, δόξασόν
to – hour this. Father, glorify

σου τὸ ὄνομα. ἦλθεν οὖν φωνὴ ἐκ
of thee the name. Came therefore a voice out of

τοῦ οὐρανοῦ· καὶ ἐδόξασα καὶ πάλιν
– heaven: Both I glorified and again

δοξάσω. 29 ὁ οὖν ὄχλος ὁ ἑστὼς καὶ
I will glorify. Therefore the crowd – standing and

ἀκούσας ἔλεγεν βροντὴν γεγονέναι· ἄλλοι
hearing said thunder to have happened; others

ἔλεγον· ἄγγελος αὐτῷ λελάληκεν.
said : An angel to him has spoken.

him." ³⁰Jesus answered, "This voice has come for your sake, not for mine. ³¹Now is the judgment of this world, now shall the ruler of this world be cast out; ³²and I, when I am lifted up from the earth, will draw all men to myself." ³³He said this to show by what death he was to die. ³⁴The crowd answered him, "We have heard from the law that the Christ remains for ever. How can you say that the Son of man must be lifted up? Who is this Son of man?" ³⁵Jesus said to them, "The light is with you for a little longer. Walk while you have the light, lest the darkness overtake you; he who walks in the darkness does not know where he goes. ³⁶While you have the light, believe in the light, that you may become sons of light."

When Jesus had said this, he departed and hid himself from them. ³⁷Though he had done so many signs before them, yet they did not

---

30 ἀπεκρίθη Ἰησοῦς καὶ εἶπεν· οὐ δι᾽ ἐμὲ
Answered Jesus and said: Not because of me

ἡ φωνὴ αὕτη γέγονεν ἀλλὰ δι᾽ ὑμᾶς.
the voice this has happened but because of you.

31 νῦν κρίσις ἐστὶν τοῦ κόσμου τούτου·
Now judgment is - world of this;

νῦν ὁ ἄρχων τοῦ κόσμου τούτου
now the ruler - world of this

ἐκβληθήσεται ἔξω· **32** κἀγὼ ἐὰν ὑψωθῶ
shall be cast *out* outside; and I if I am lifted up

ἐκ τῆς γῆς, πάντας ἑλκύσω πρὸς
out of the earth, all men will draw to

ἐμαυτόν. **33** τοῦτο δὲ ἔλεγεν σημαίνων
myself. And this he said signifying

ποίῳ θανάτῳ ἤμελλεν ἀποθνῄσκειν.
by what kind of death he was about to die.

34 ἀπεκρίθη οὖν αὐτῷ ὁ ὄχλος· ἡμεῖς
Answered therefore him the crowd: We

ἠκούσαμεν ἐκ τοῦ νόμου ὅτι ὁ χριστὸς
heard out of the law that the Christ

μένει εἰς τὸν αἰῶνα, καὶ πῶς λέγεις
remains unto the age, and how sayest

σὺ ὅτι δεῖ ὑψωθῆναι τὸν υἱὸν τοῦ
thou that it behoves to be lifted up the Son -

ἀνθρώπου; τίς ἐστιν οὗτος ὁ υἱὸς τοῦ
of man? who is this - Son -

ἀνθρώπου; **35** εἶπεν οὖν αὐτοῖς ὁ Ἰησοῦς·
of man? Said therefore to them - Jesus:

ἔτι μικρὸν χρόνον τὸ φῶς ἐν ὑμῖν
Yet a little time the light among you

ἐστιν. περιπατεῖτε ὡς τὸ φῶς ἔχετε,
is. Walk while the light ye have,

ἵνα μὴ σκοτία ὑμᾶς καταλάβῃ· καὶ
lest darkness you overtakes; and

ὁ περιπατῶν ἐν τῇ σκοτίᾳ οὐκ οἶδεν
the [one] walking in the darkness knows not

ποῦ ὑπάγει. **36** ὡς τὸ φῶς ἔχετε,
where he is going. While the light ye have,

πιστεύετε εἰς τὸ φῶς, ἵνα υἱοὶ φωτὸς
believe in the light, that sons of light

γένησθε.
ye may become.

Ταῦτα ἐλάλησεν Ἰησοῦς, καὶ ἀπελθὼν
These things spoke Jesus, and going away

ἐκρύβη ἀπ᾽ αὐτῶν. **37** Τοσαῦτα δὲ αὐτοῦ
was hidden from them. But so many him

σημεῖα πεποιηκότος ἔμπροσθεν αὐτῶν οὐκ
signs having doneᵃ before them not
=But while he did so many signs

believe in him; ³⁸ it was that the word spoken by the prophet Isaiah might be fulfilled:

"Lord, who has believed our report,
and to whom has the arm of the Lord been revealed?"

³⁹ Therefore they could not believe. For Isaiah again said,

⁴⁰ "He has blinded their eyes and hardened their heart,
lest they should see with their eyes and perceive with their heart,
and turn for me to heal them."

⁴¹ Isaiah said this because he saw his glory and spoke of him.
⁴² Nevertheless many even of the authorities believed in him, but for fear of the Pharisees they did not confess it, lest they should be put out of the synagogue: ⁴³ for they loved the praise of men more than the praise of God.

44 And Jesus cried out and said, "He who believes in me, believes not in me but in him who sent me. ⁴⁵ And he who sees me sees him who sent me. ⁴⁶ I have come as light into the world, that whoever believes in me

ἐπίστευον   εἰς   αὐτόν,   38 ἵνα   ὁ   λόγος
they believed   in   him,   that   the   word

'Ησαΐου   τοῦ   προφήτου   πληρωθῇ   ὃν
of Esaias   the   prophet   might be fulfilled   which

εἶπεν·   κύριε,   τίς   ἐπίστευσεν   τῇ   ἀκοῇ
he said :   Lord,   who   believed   the   report

ἡμῶν;   καὶ   ὁ   βραχίων   κυρίου   τίνι
of us?   and   the   arm   of [the] Lord   to whom

ἀπεκαλύφθη;   39 διὰ   τοῦτο   οὐκ   ἠδύναντο
was it revealed?   Therefore   they could not

πιστεύειν,   ὅτι   πάλιν   εἶπεν   'Ησαΐας·
to believe,   because   again   said   Esaias :

40 τετύφλωκεν   αὐτῶν   τοὺς   ὀφθαλμοὺς   καὶ
He has blinded   of them   the   eyes   and

ἐπώρωσεν   αὐτῶν   τὴν   καρδίαν,   ἵνα
hardened   of them   the   heart,   that

μὴ   ἴδωσιν   τοῖς   ὀφθαλμοῖς   καὶ   νοήσωσιν
they might not see   with the   eyes   and   understand

τῇ   καρδίᾳ   καὶ   στραφῶσιν,   καὶ   ἰάσομαι
with the heart   and   might turn,   and   I will cure

αὐτούς.   41 ταῦτα   εἶπεν   'Ησαΐας   ὅτι
them.   These things   said   Esaias   because

εἶδεν   τὴν   δόξαν   αὐτοῦ,   καὶ   ἐλάλησεν
he saw   the   glory   of him,   and   spoke

περὶ   αὐτοῦ.   42 ὅμως   μέντοι   καὶ   ἐκ
about   him.   Nevertheless   however   even   of

τῶν   ἀρχόντων   πολλοὶ   ἐπίστευσαν   εἰς   αὐτόν,
the   rulers   many   believed   in   him,

ἀλλὰ   διὰ   τοὺς   Φαρισαίους   οὐχ   ὡμολόγουν,
but   because of the   Pharisees   did not confess,

ἵνα   μὴ   ἀποσυνάγωγοι   γένωνται·
lest   put out of [the] synagogue   they should become;

43 ἠγάπησαν   γὰρ   τὴν   δόξαν   τῶν   ἀνθρώπων
for they loved   the   glory   –   of men

μᾶλλον   ἤπερ   τὴν   δόξαν   τοῦ   θεοῦ.
more   than   the   glory   –   of God.

44 'Ιησοῦς   δὲ   ἔκραξεν   καὶ   εἶπεν·   ὁ
But Jesus   cried out   and   said :   The

πιστεύων   εἰς   ἐμὲ   οὐ   πιστεύει   εἰς   ἐμὲ
[one] believing   in   me   believes not   in   me

ἀλλὰ   εἰς   τὸν   πέμψαντά   με,   45 καὶ   ὁ
but   in   the [one] having sent   me,   and the

θεωρῶν   ἐμὲ   θεωρεῖ   τὸν   πέμψαντά   με.
[one] beholding me   beholds   the [one] having sent   me.

46 ἐγὼ   φῶς   εἰς   τὸν   κόσμον   ἐλήλυθα,
I   a light   into   the   world   have come,

ἵνα   πᾶς   ὁ   πιστεύων   εἰς   ἐμὲ   ἐν   τῇ
that   everyone   believing   in   me   in   the

may not remain in darkness. [47] If any one hears my sayings and does not keep them, I do not judge him; for I did not come to judge the world but to save the world. [48] He who rejects me and does not receive my sayings has a judge; the word that I have spoken will be his judge on the last day. [49] For I have not spoken on my own authority; the Father who sent me has himself given me commandment what to say and what to speak. [50] And I know that his commandment is eternal life. What I say, therefore, I say as the Father has bidden me."

σκοτίᾳ μὴ μείνῃ.   **47** καὶ ἐάν τίς μου
darkness may not remain.   And if anyone of me
ἀκούσῃ   τῶν ῥημάτων καὶ μὴ φυλάξῃ,
hears   the   words   and   keeps not,
ἐγὼ οὐ κρίνω   αὐτόν· οὐ γὰρ ἦλθον
I   do not judge him;   for I came not
ἵνα κρίνω τὸν κόσμον, ἀλλ' ἵνα σώσω
that I might judge the   world,   but that I might save
τὸν κόσμον. **48** ὁ   ἀθετῶν ἐμὲ καὶ μὴ
the world.   The [one] rejecting me   and not
λαμβάνων   τὰ   ῥήματά μου ἔχει τὸν
receiving   the   words   of me has   the
κρίνοντα αὐτόν· ὁ λόγος ὃν ἐλάλησα,
[one] judging him; the word which I spoke,
ἐκεῖνος κρινεῖ αὐτὸν ἐν τῇ ἐσχάτῃ ἡμέρᾳ.
that   will judge him   in the   last   day.
49 ὅτι ἐγὼ ἐξ ἐμαυτοῦ οὐκ ἐλάλησα,
Because I   of   myself   did not speak,
ἀλλ' ὁ πέμψας με πατὴρ αὐτός μοι
but   the [1]having sent [4]me [2]Father [5]he [7]me
ἐντολὴν δέδωκεν τί εἴπω καὶ τί
[3]commandment [6]has given what I may say and what
λαλήσω. **50** καὶ οἶδα ὅτι ἡ ἐντολὴ
I may speak.   And I know that the commandment
αὐτοῦ ζωὴ αἰώνιός ἐστιν. ἃ οὖν ἐγὼ
of him life eternal   is.   What things therefore I
λαλῶ, καθὼς εἴρηκέν μοι ὁ πατήρ,
speak,   as   has said to me the Father,
οὕτως λαλῶ.
so   I speak.

CHAPTER 13

NOW before the feast of the Passover, when Jesus knew that his hour had come to depart out of this world to the Father, having loved his own who were in the world, he loved them to the end. [2] And during supper, when the devil had already put it into the heart of Judas Iscariot, Simon's son, to

13 Πρὸ δὲ τῆς ἑορτῆς τοῦ πάσχα
Now before the   feast   of the Passover
εἰδὼς ὁ Ἰησοῦς ὅτι ἦλθεν αὐτοῦ ἡ
[2]knowing - [1]Jesus that   came of him the
ὥρα ἵνα μεταβῇ ἐκ τοῦ κόσμου τούτου
hour that he should remove out of world   this
πρὸς τὸν πατέρα, ἀγαπήσας τοὺς ἰδίους
to   the Father,   loving   the(his) own
τοὺς ἐν τῷ κόσμῳ, εἰς τέλος ἠγάπησεν
those in the world, to [the] end he loved
αὐτούς. **2** καὶ δείπνου γινομένου, τοῦ
them.   And supper taking place,[a] the
=during supper,
διαβόλου ἤδη βεβληκότος εἰς τὴν καρδίαν
devil   now having put[a]   into the   heart
=as the devil had now put
ἵνα παραδοῖ αὐτὸν Ἰούδας Σίμωνος
that [4]should betray [5]him [1]Judas [2][son] of Simon

betray him, ³Jesus, knowing that the Father had given all things into his hands, and that he had come from God and was going to God, ⁴rose from supper, laid aside his garments, and girded himself with a towel. ⁵Then he poured water into a basin, and began to wash the disciples' feet, and to wipe them with the towel with which he was girded. ⁶He came to Simon Peter; and Peter said to him, "Lord, do you wash my feet?" ⁷Jesus answered him, "What I am doing you do not know now, but afterward you will understand." ⁸Peter said to him, "You shall never wash my feet." Jesus answered him, "If I do not wash you, you have no part in me." ⁹Simon Peter said to him, "Lord, not my feet only but also my hands and my head!" ¹⁰Jesus said to him, "He who has bathed does not need to wash, except for his feet,ᵛ but he is clean all over; and you are clean, but not all of you."

Ἰσκαριώτης,	3 εἰδὼς	ὅτι	πάντα	ἔδωκεν
³Iscariot,	knowing*	that	all things	gave

αὐτῷ ὁ πατὴρ εἰς τὰς χεῖρας, καὶ
him the Father into the(his) hands, and

ὅτι ἀπὸ θεοῦ ἐξῆλθεν καὶ πρὸς τὸν
that from God he came forth and to -

θεὸν ὑπάγει, 4 ἐγείρεται ἐκ τοῦ δείπνου
God goes, he rises out of(from) the supper

καὶ τίθησιν τὰ ἱμάτια, καὶ λαβὼν
and places [aside] the(his) garments, and taking

λέντιον διέζωσεν ἑαυτόν· 5 εἶτα βάλλει
a towel he girded himself; then he puts

ὕδωρ εἰς τὸν νιπτῆρα, καὶ ἤρξατο νίπτειν
water into the basin, and began to wash

τοὺς πόδας τῶν μαθητῶν καὶ ἐκμάσσειν
the feet of the disciples and to wipe off

τῷ λεντίῳ ᾧ ἦν διεζωσμένος.
with the towel with which he was *having been* girded.

6 ἔρχεται οὖν πρὸς Σίμωνα Πέτρον·
He comes therefore to Simon Peter;

λέγει αὐτῷ· κύριε, σύ μου νίπτεις τοὺς
he says to him: Lord, thou of me washest the

πόδας; 7 ἀπεκρίθη Ἰησοῦς καὶ εἶπεν αὐτῷ·
feet? Answered Jesus and said to him :

ὃ ἐγὼ ποιῶ σὺ οὐκ οἶδας ἄρτι,
What I am doing thou knowest not yet,

γνώσῃ δὲ μετὰ ταῦτα. 8 λέγει αὐτῷ
but thou wilt know after these things. Says to him

Πέτρος· οὐ μὴ νίψῃς μου τοὺς πόδας
Peter : By no means shalt thou wash of me the feet

εἰς τὸν αἰῶνα. ἀπεκρίθη Ἰησοῦς αὐτῷ·
unto the age. ³Answered ¹Jesus ²him :

ἐὰν μὴ νίψω σε, οὐκ ἔχεις μέρος μετ'
Unless I wash thee, thou hast no part with

ἐμοῦ. 9 λέγει αὐτῷ Σίμων Πέτρος·
me. Says to him Simon Peter :

κύριε, μὴ τοὺς πόδας μου μόνον ἀλλὰ
Lord, not the feet of me only but

καὶ τὰς χεῖρας καὶ τὴν κεφαλήν. 10 λέγει
also the hands and the head. Says

αὐτῷ Ἰησοῦς· ὁ λελουμένος οὐκ ἔχει
to him Jesus : The [one] having been bathed has not

χρείαν [εἰ μὴ τοὺς πόδας] νίψασθαι,
need except the feet to wash,

ἀλλ' ἔστιν καθαρὸς ὅλος· καὶ ὑμεῖς
but is clean wholly; and ye

καθαροί ἐστε, ἀλλ' οὐχὶ πάντες. 11 ᾔδει
clean are, but not all. he knew

ᵛ Other ancient authorities omit *except for his feet*

* Repeated from ver. 1; the subject is therefore again "Jesus".

¹¹For he knew who was to betray him; that was why he said, "You are not all clean."

12 When he had washed their feet, and taken his garments, and resumed his place, he said to them, "Do you know what I have done to you? ¹³You call me Teacher and Lord; and you are right, for so I am. ¹⁴If I then, your Lord and Teacher, have washed your feet, you also ought to wash one another's feet. ¹⁵For I have given you an example, that you also should do as I have done to you. ¹⁶Truly, truly, I say to you, a servant is not greater than his master; nor is he who is sent greater than he who sent him. ¹⁷If you know these things, blessed are you if you do them. ¹⁸I am not speaking of you all; I know whom I have chosen; it is that the scripture may be fulfilled, 'He who ate my bread has lifted his heel against me.' ¹⁹I tell you this now, before it takes place, that when it does take place you may believe that I am he. ²⁰Truly, truly, I say to you, he

γὰρ τὸν παραδιδόντα αὐτόν· διὰ τοῦτο
For   the [one] betraying   him;   therefore
εἶπεν ὅτι οὐχὶ πάντες καθαροί ἐστε.
he said[,] –   Not   all   clean   ye are.
12 Ὅτε οὖν ἔνιψεν τοὺς πόδας αὐτῶν
When therefore he washed the   feet   of them
καὶ ἔλαβεν τὰ ἱμάτια αὐτοῦ καὶ ἀνέπεσεν
and took   the garments of him and   reclined
πάλιν, εἶπεν αὐτοῖς· γινώσκετε τί πε-
again, he said to them :   Do ye know   what I
ποίηκα ὑμῖν; 13 ὑμεῖς φωνεῖτέ με· ὁ
have done to you? Ye   call   me : The
διδάσκαλος καὶ ὁ κύριος, καὶ καλῶς
Teacher   and the Lord,   and   well
λέγετε· εἰμὶ γάρ. 14 εἰ οὖν ἐγὼ ἔνιψα
ye say;   for I am. If therefore I   washed
ὑμῶν τοὺς πόδας ὁ κύριος καὶ ὁ
of you the   feet   the Lord and the
διδάσκαλος, καὶ ὑμεῖς ὀφείλετε ἀλλήλων
Teacher,   also   ye   ought of one another
νίπτειν τοὺς πόδας· 15 ὑπόδειγμα γὰρ
to wash the   feet;   for an example
ἔδωκα ὑμῖν ἵνα καθὼς ἐγὼ ἐποίησα
I gave you that   as   I   did
ὑμῖν καὶ ὑμεῖς ποιῆτε. 16 ἀμὴν ἀμὴν
to you also   ye   may do.   Truly   truly
λέγω ὑμῖν, οὐκ ἔστιν δοῦλος μείζων
I tell you,   is not   a slave greater [than]
τοῦ κυρίου αὐτοῦ, οὐδὲ ἀπόστολος μείζων
the lord of him, nor a sent one greater [than]
τοῦ πέμψαντος αὐτόν. 17 εἰ ταῦτα
the [one] sending   him.   If   these things
οἴδατε, μακάριοί ἐστε ἐὰν ποιῆτε αὐτά.
ye know, blessed are ye if ye do them.
18 Οὐ περὶ πάντων ὑμῶν λέγω· ἐγὼ
Not concerning ²all   ¹you I speak;   I
οἶδα τίνας ἐξελεξάμην· ἀλλ' ἵνα ἡ
know whom   I chose;   but   that the
γραφὴ πληρωθῇ· ὁ τρώγων μου τὸν
scripture may be fulfilled : The [one] eating of me the
ἄρτον ἐπῆρεν ἐπ' ἐμὲ τὴν πτέρναν αὐτοῦ.
bread lifted up against me the   heel   of him.
19 ἀπ' ἄρτι λέγω ὑμῖν πρὸ τοῦ γενέσθαι,
From now I tell you before the to happen,
                                        =it happens,
ἵνα πιστεύητε ὅταν γένηται ὅτι ἐγώ
that ye may believe when it happens that I
εἰμι. 20 ἀμὴν ἀμὴν λέγω ὑμῖν, ὁ
am.   Truly   truly I say to you, the

who receives any one
whom I send receives me;
and he who receives me
receives him who sent
me."

21 When Jesus had
thus spoken, he was
troubled in spirit, and
testified, "Truly, truly, I
say to you, one of you
will betray me." [22]The
disciples looked at one
another, uncertain of
whom he spoke. [23]One
of his disciples, whom
Jesus loved, was lying
close to the breast of
Jesus; [24]so Simon Peter
beckoned to him and
said, "Tell us who it is of
whom he speaks." [25]So
lying thus, close to the
breast of Jesus, he said
to him, "Lord, who is
it?" [26]Jesus answered,
"It is he to whom I shall
give this morsel when I
have dipped it." So when
he had dipped the morsel,
he gave it to Judas, the
son of Simon Iscariot.
[27]Then after the morsel,
Satan entered into him.
Jesus said to him, "What
you are going to do, do
quickly." [28]Now no one
at the table knew why he
said this to him. [29]Some
thought that, because

λαμβάνων ἄν τινα πέμψω ἐμὲ λαμβάνει,
[one] receiving whomever I may send me receives,
ὁ δὲ ἐμὲ λαμβάνων λαμβάνει τὸν
and the [one] me receiving receives the [one]
πέμψαντά με. 21 ταῦτα εἰπὼν Ἰησοῦς
having sent me. These things saying Jesus
ἐταράχθη τῷ πνεύματι καὶ ἐμαρτύρησεν
was troubled in the(his) spirit and witnessed
καὶ εἶπεν· ἀμὴν ἀμὴν λέγω ὑμῖν ὅτι
and said: Truly truly I tell you that
εἷς ἐξ ὑμῶν παραδώσει με. 22 ἔβλεπον
one of you will betray me. Looked
εἰς ἀλλήλους οἱ μαθηταὶ ἀπορούμενοι περὶ
at one another the disciples being perplexed about
τίνος λέγει. 23 ἦν ἀνακείμενος εἷς ἐκ
whom he speaks. Was reclining one of
τῶν μαθητῶν αὐτοῦ ἐν τῷ κόλπῳ τοῦ
the disciples of him in the bosom -
Ἰησοῦ, ὃν ἠγάπα ὁ Ἰησοῦς· 24 νεύει
of Jesus, whom ¹loved - ¹Jesus; nods
οὖν τούτῳ Σίμων Πέτρος καὶ λέγει
therefore to this one Simon Peter and says
αὐτῷ· εἰπὲ τίς ἐστιν περὶ οὗ λέγει.
to him : Say who it is about whom he speaks.
25 ἀναπεσὼν ἐκεῖνος οὕτως ἐπὶ τὸ
Falling back that one thus on the
στῆθος τοῦ Ἰησοῦ λέγει αὐτῷ· κύριε,
breast - of Jesus he says to him : Lord,
τίς ἐστιν; 26 ἀποκρίνεται οὖν ὁ Ἰησοῦς·
who is it? Answers therefore - Jesus :
ἐκεῖνός ἐστιν ᾧ ἐγὼ βάψω τὸ ψωμίον
That one it is to whom I shall dip the morsel
καὶ δώσω αὐτῷ. βάψας οὖν [τὸ]
and shall give him. Dipping therefore the
ψωμίον λαμβάνει καὶ δίδωσιν Ἰούδᾳ
morsel he takes and gives to Judas
Σίμωνος Ἰσκαριώτου. 27 καὶ μετὰ τὸ
[son] of Simon Iscariot. And after the
ψωμίον τότε εἰσῆλθεν εἰς ἐκεῖνον ὁ
morsel then entered into that one -
σατανᾶς. λέγει οὖν αὐτῷ Ἰησοῦς· ὃ
Satan. Says therefore to him Jesus : What
ποιεῖς ποίησον τάχιον. 28 τοῦτο [δὲ]
thou doest do quickly. But this
οὐδεὶς ἔγνω τῶν ἀνακειμένων πρὸς τί
no one knew of the [ones] reclining for what
εἶπεν αὐτῷ· 29 τινὲς γὰρ ἐδόκουν, ἐπεὶ
he told him; for some thought, since

Judas had the money box, Jesus was telling him, "Buy what we need for the feast"; or, that he should give something to the poor. [30] So, after receiving the morsel, he immediately went out; and it was night.

[31] When he had gone out, Jesus said, "Now is the Son of man glorified, and in him God is glorified; [32] if God is glorified in him, God will also glorify him in himself, and glorify him at once. [33] Little children, yet a little while I am with you. You will seek me; and as I said to the Jews so now I say to you, 'Where I am going you cannot come.' [34] A new commandment I give to you, that you love one another; even as I have loved you, that you also love one another. [35] By this all men will know that you are my disciples, if you have love for one another."

[36] Simon Peter said to him, "Lord, where are you going?" Jesus answered, "Where I am going you cannot follow me now; but you shall follow afterward."

τὸ γλωσσόκομον εἶχεν Ἰούδας, ὅτι λέγει
'the   'bag   'had   'Judas,   that   tells
αὐτῷ Ἰησοῦς· ἀγόρασον ὧν χρείαν
him   Jesus :   Buy [the] things of which   need
ἔχομεν εἰς τὴν ἑορτήν, ἢ τοῖς πτωχοῖς
we have   for   the   feast,   or   to the   poor
ἵνα τι δῷ. 30 λαβὼν οὖν τὸ
that something he should give.   Having taken therefore   the
ψωμίον ἐκεῖνος ἐξῆλθεν εὐθύς· ἦν δὲ
morsel   that one   went out   immediately;   and it was
νύξ.
night.

31 Ὅτε οὖν ἐξῆλθεν, λέγει Ἰησοῦς·
When therefore he went out,   says   Jesus :
νῦν ἐδοξάσθη ὁ υἱὸς τοῦ ἀνθρώπου,
Now was(is) glorified   the   Son   -   of man,
καὶ ὁ θεὸς ἐδοξάσθη ἐν αὐτῷ. 32 εἰ
and   -   God   was(is) glorified   in   him;   if
ὁ θεὸς ἐδοξάσθη ἐν αὐτῷ, καὶ ὁ θεὸς
-   God   was(is) glorified   in   him,   both   -   God
δοξάσει αὐτὸν ἐν αὐτῷ, καὶ εὐθὺς
will glorify   him   in   him,   and immediately
δοξάσει αὐτόν. 33 τεκνία, ἔτι μικρὸν
will glorify   him.   Children,   yet a little while
μεθ' ὑμῶν εἰμι· ζητήσετέ με, καὶ καθὼς
with   you   I am;   ye will seek   me,   and   as
εἶπον τοῖς Ἰουδαίοις ὅτι ὅπου ἐγὼ
I said   to the   Jews   that   where   I
ὑπάγω ὑμεῖς οὐ δύνασθε ἐλθεῖν, καὶ
go   ye   cannot   to come,   also
ὑμῖν λέγω ἄρτι. 34 Ἐντολὴν καινὴν
to you   I say   now.   commandment A new
δίδωμι ὑμῖν, ἵνα ἀγαπᾶτε ἀλλήλους,
I give   you,   that   ye love   one another,
καθὼς ἠγάπησα ὑμᾶς ἵνα καὶ ὑμεῖς
as   I loved   you   that   also   ye
ἀγαπᾶτε ἀλλήλους. 35 ἐν τούτῳ γνώσονται
love   one another.   By   this   will know
πάντες ὅτι ἐμοὶ μαθηταί ἐστε, ἐὰν
all men   that   to me   disciples   ye are,   if
ἀγάπην ἔχητε ἐν ἀλλήλοις. 36 Λέγει
love   ye have   among   one another.   Says
αὐτῷ Σίμων Πέτρος· κύριε, ποῦ ὑπάγεις;
to him   Simon   Peter :   Lord,   where   goest thou?
ἀπεκρίθη Ἰησοῦς· ὅπου ὑπάγω οὐ δύνασαί
Answered   Jesus :   Where   I go   thou canst not
μοι νῦν ἀκολουθῆσαι, ἀκολουθήσεις δὲ
me   now   to follow,   but thou wilt follow

37 Peter said to him, "Lord, why cannot I follow you now? I will lay down my life for you." 38 Jesus answered, "Will you lay down your life for me? Truly, truly, I say to you, the cock will not crow, till you have denied me three times.

CHAPTER 14

"LET not your hearts be troubled; believe[w] in God, believe also in me. 2 In my Father's house are many rooms; if it were not so, would I have told you that I go to prepare a place for you? 3 And when I go and prepare a place for you, I will come again and will take you to myself, that where I am you may be also. 4 And you know the way where I am going."[x] 5 Thomas said to him, "Lord, we do not know where you are going; how can we know the way?" 6 Jesus said to him, "I am the way, and the truth, and the life; no one comes to the Father, but by me. 7 If you had known me, you would have known my Father also; henceforth you know him and have seen him."

8 Philip said to him,

w Or you believe
x Other ancient authorities read where I am going you know, and the way you know

ὕστερον. 37 λέγει αὐτῷ [ὁ] Πέτρος·
later. Says to him – Peter :
κύριε, διὰ τί οὐ δύναμαί σοι ἀκολουθῆσαι
Lord, why can I not thee to follow
ἄρτι; τὴν ψυχήν μου ὑπὲρ σοῦ θήσω.
yet? the life of me for thee I will lay down.
38 ἀποκρίνεται Ἰησοῦς· τὴν ψυχήν σου
Answers Jesus : The life of thee
ὑπὲρ ἐμοῦ θήσεις; ἀμὴν ἀμὴν λέγω
for me wilt thou lay down? truly truly I tell
σοι, οὐ μὴ ἀλέκτωρ φωνήσῃ ἕως οὗ
thee, by no means a cock crows until
ἀρνήσῃ με τρίς. 14 Μὴ ταρασσέσθω
thou deniest me thrice. Let not be troubled
ὑμῶν ἡ καρδία· πιστεύετε εἰς τὸν θεόν, καὶ
of you the heart; believe in – God, also
εἰς ἐμὲ πιστεύετε. 2 ἐν τῇ οἰκίᾳ τοῦ
in me believe. In the house of the
πατρός μου μοναὶ πολλαί εἰσιν· εἰ δὲ μή,
Father of me abodes many there are; otherwise,
εἶπον ἂν ὑμῖν· ὅτι πορεύομαι ἑτοιμάσαι
I would have told you; because I go to prepare
τόπον ὑμῖν· 3 καὶ ἐὰν πορευθῶ καὶ
a place for you; and if I go and
ἑτοιμάσω τόπον ὑμῖν, πάλιν ἔρχομαι καὶ
prepare a place for you, again I come and
παραλήμψομαι ὑμᾶς πρὸς ἐμαυτόν, ἵνα
will receive you to myself, that
ὅπου εἰμὶ ἐγὼ καὶ ὑμεῖς ἦτε. 4 Καὶ
where am I also ye may be. And
ὅπου ἐγὼ ὑπάγω οἴδατε τὴν ὁδόν.
where I go ye know the way.
5 λέγει αὐτῷ Θωμᾶς· κύριε, οὐκ οἴδαμεν
Says to him Thomas : Lord, we know not
ποῦ ὑπάγεις· πῶς οἴδαμεν τὴν ὁδόν;
where thou goest; how do we know the way?
6 λέγει αὐτῷ Ἰησοῦς· ἐγώ εἰμι ἡ ὁδὸς
Says to him Jesus : I am the way
καὶ ἡ ἀλήθεια καὶ ἡ ζωή· οὐδεὶς ἔρχεται
and the truth and the life; no one comes
πρὸς τὸν πατέρα εἰ μὴ δι' ἐμοῦ. 7 εἰ
to the Father except through me. If
ἐγνώκειτέ με, καὶ τὸν πατέρα μου
ye had known me, also the Father of me
ἂν ᾔδειτε. ἀπ' ἄρτι γινώσκετε αὐτὸν
ye would have known. From now ye know him
καὶ ἑωράκατε. 8 Λέγει αὐτῷ Φίλιππος·
and have seen. Says to him Philip:

"Lord, show us the Father, and we shall be satisfied." ⁹Jesus said to him, "Have I been with you so long, and yet you do not know me, Philip? He who has seen me has seen the Father; how can you say, 'Show us the Father'? ¹⁰Do you not believe that I am in the Father and the Father in me? The words that I say to you I do not speak on my own authority; but the Father who dwells in me does his works. ¹¹Believe me that I am in the Father and the Father in me; or else believe me for the sake of the works themselves.

12 "Truly, truly, I say to you, he who believes in me will also do the works that I do; and greater works than these will he do, because I go to the Father. ¹³Whatever you ask in my name, I will do it, that the Father may be glorified in the Son; ¹⁴if you ask⁰ anything in my name, I will do it.

15 "If you love me, you will keep my commandments. ¹⁶And I will pray the Father, and he will give you another Counselor, to be with

⁰ Other ancient authorities add *me*

κύριε,   δεῖξον   ἡμῖν   τὸν   πατέρα,   καὶ
Lord,   show   us   the   Father,   and

ἀρκεῖ   ἡμῖν.   9 λέγει   αὐτῷ   ὁ   Ἰησοῦς·
it suffices for us.   Says   to him   –   Jesus:

τοσοῦτον   χρόνον   μεθ'   ὑμῶν   εἰμι   καὶ
So long   time   with   you   I am   and

οὐκ   ἔγνωκάς   με,   Φίλιππε;   ὁ   ἑωρακὼς
thou hast not known me,   Philip?   The [one] having seen

ἐμὲ   ἑώρακεν   τὸν   πατέρα·   πῶς   σὺ   λέγεις·
me   has seen   the   Father;   how   thou sayest:

δεῖξον   ἡμῖν   τὸν   πατέρα;   10 οὐ   πιστεύεις
Show   us   the   Father?   believest thou not

ὅτι   ἐγὼ   ἐν   τῷ   πατρὶ   καὶ   ὁ   πατὴρ
that   I   in   the   Father   and   the   Father

ἐν   ἐμοί   ἐστιν;   τὰ   ῥήματα   ἃ   ἐγὼ   λέγω
in   me   is?   the   words which   I   say

ὑμῖν   ἀπ'   ἐμαυτοῦ   οὐ   λαλῶ·   ὁ   δὲ   πατὴρ
to you from   myself   I speak not;   but the Father

ἐν   ἐμοὶ   μένων   ποιεῖ   τὰ   ἔργα   αὐτοῦ.
in   me   remaining   does   the   works   of him.

11 πιστεύετέ   μοι   ὅτι   ἐγὼ   ἐν   τῷ   πατρὶ
   Believe ye   me   that   I   in   the   Father

καὶ   ὁ   πατὴρ   ἐν   ἐμοί·   εἰ   δὲ   μή,   διὰ
and   the Father   in   me; otherwise, because of

τὰ   ἔργα   αὐτὰ   πιστεύετε.   12 ἀμὴν   ἀμὴν
the   works [them]selves believe ye.   Truly   truly

λέγω   ὑμῖν,   ὁ   πιστεύων   εἰς   ἐμὲ   τὰ
I tell   you, the [one] believing   in   me   the

ἔργα   ἃ   ἐγὼ   ποιῶ   κἀκεῖνος   ποιήσει,
works which   I   do   that one also   will do,

καὶ   μείζονα   τούτων   ποιήσει,   ὅτι   ἐγὼ
and   greater [than] these he will do, because   I

πρὸς   τὸν   πατέρα   πορεύομαι·   13 καὶ   ὅ τι
to   the   Father   am going;   and   what-

ἂν   αἰτήσητε   ἐν   τῷ   ὀνόματί   μου,   τοῦτο
ever ye ask   in   the   name   of me,   this

ποιήσω,   ἵνα   δοξασθῇ   ὁ   πατὴρ   ἐν   τῷ
I will do, that may be glorified the Father   in   the

υἱῷ.   14 ἐάν   τι   αἰτήσητέ   με   ἐν   τῷ
Son.   If   anything ye ask   me   in   the

ὀνόματί   μου,   ἐγὼ   ποιήσω.   15 Ἐὰν
name   of me,   I   will do.   If

ἀγαπᾶτέ   με,   τὰς   ἐντολὰς   τὰς   ἐμὰς
ye love   me,   the ³commandments –   ¹my

τηρήσετε.   16 κἀγὼ   ἐρωτήσω   τὸν   πατέρα
ye will keep.   And I   will request   the   Father

καὶ   ἄλλον   παράκλητον   δώσει   ὑμῖν,   ἵνα
and another   Comforter   he will give you,   that

you for ever, [17] even the Spirit of truth, whom the world cannot receive, because it neither sees him nor knows him; you know him, for he dwells with you, and will be in you.

18 "I will not leave you desolate; I will come to you. [19] Yet a little while, and the world will see me no more, but you will see me; because I live, you will live also. [20] In that day you will know that I am in my Father, and you in me, and I in you. [21] He who has my commandments and keeps them, he it is who loves me; and he who loves me will be loved by my Father, and I will love him and manifest myself to him." [22] Judas (not Iscariot) said to him, "Lord, how is it that you will manifest yourself to us, and not to the world?" [23] Jesus answered him, "If a man loves me, he will keep my word, and my Father will love him, and we will come to him

ᾗ μεθ' ὑμῶν εἰς τὸν αἰῶνα, 17 τὸ
he may be with　you　unto the　age,　　the
πνεῦμα τῆς ἀληθείας, ὃ ὁ κόσμος
Spirit　－　of truth, which* the　world
οὐ δύναται λαβεῖν, ὅτι οὐ θεωρεῖ αὐτὸ
cannot　to receive, because　it beholds not　it*
οὐδὲ γινώσκει· ὑμεῖς γινώσκετε αὐτό,
nor　knows;　ye　know　it,*
ὅτι παρ' ὑμῖν μένει καὶ ἐν ὑμῖν ἔσται.
because with　you he remains and　in　you　will be.
18 Οὐκ ἀφήσω ὑμᾶς ὀρφανούς, ἔρχομαι
I will not leave　you　orphans,　I am coming
πρὸς ὑμᾶς. 19 ἔτι μικρὸν καὶ ὁ κόσμος
to you.　Yet a little　and the　world
με οὐκέτι θεωρεῖ, ὑμεῖς δὲ θεωρεῖτέ
me　no longer　beholds,　but ye　behold
με, ὅτι ἐγὼ ζῶ καὶ ὑμεῖς ζήσετε.
me,　because　I　live　also　ye　will live.
20 ἐν ἐκείνῃ τῇ ἡμέρᾳ γνώσεσθε ὑμεῖς
In　that　－　day　will know　ye
ὅτι ἐγὼ ἐν τῷ πατρί μου καὶ ὑμεῖς
that　I　in　the　Father of me and　ye
ἐν ἐμοὶ κἀγὼ ἐν ὑμῖν. 21 Ὁ ἔχων
in　me　and I　in　you.　The [one] having
τὰς ἐντολάς μου καὶ τηρῶν αὐτάς,
the　commandments of me　and　keeping　them,
ἐκεῖνός ἐστιν ὁ ἀγαπῶν με· ὁ δὲ ἀγαπῶν
that　is the [one] loving me;　and the [one] loving
με ἀγαπηθήσεται ὑπὸ τοῦ πατρός μου,
me　will be loved　by　the　Father　of me,
κἀγὼ ἀγαπήσω αὐτὸν καὶ ἐμφανίσω αὐτῷ
and I　will love　him　and　will manifest　to him
ἐμαυτόν. 22 λέγει αὐτῷ Ἰούδας, οὐχ
myself.　Says　to him　Judas,　not
ὁ Ἰσκαριώτης· κύριε, καὶ τί γέγονεν
the　Iscariot :　Lord,　and　what has happened
ὅτι ἡμῖν μέλλεις ἐμφανίζειν σεαυτὸν καὶ
that　to us thou art about to manifest　thyself　and
οὐχὶ τῷ κόσμῳ; 23 ἀπεκρίθη Ἰησοῦς
not　to the　world?　Answered　Jesus
καὶ εἶπεν αὐτῷ· ἐάν τις ἀγαπᾷ με,
and　said　to him :　If　anyone　loves　me,
τὸν λόγον μου τηρήσει, καὶ ὁ πατήρ
the　word　of me he will keep,　and　the　Father
μου ἀγαπήσει αὐτόν, καὶ πρὸς αὐτὸν
of me　will love　him,　and　to　him

---

* The gender of these pronouns agrees, of course, with the antecedent πνεῦμα (neuter); and this has been kept though the personal Spirit of God is meant. Elsewhere, masculine pronouns are in fact used.

and make our home with | ἐλευσόμεθα | καὶ | μονὴν | παρ' | αὐτῷ
 | we will come | and | abode | with | him

him. 24 He who does not | ποιησόμεθα. | 24 ὁ | μὴ | ἀγαπῶν | με τοὺς
love me does not keep | we will make. | The [one] not | loving | me the

my words; and the word | λόγους | μου | οὐ | τηρεῖ· | καὶ ὁ | λόγος | ὃν
which you hear is not | words | of me | keeps not; | and the | word | which

mine but the Father's | ἀκούετε | οὐκ | ἔστιν | ἐμὸς | ἀλλὰ | τοῦ
who sent me. | ye hear | is not | mine | but | ¹of the

25 "These things I | πέμψαντός | με | πατρός. | 25 Ταῦτα | λελάληκα
have spoken to you, | ³having sent | ⁴me | ²Father. | These things I have spoken

while I am still with you. | ὑμῖν | παρ' | ὑμῖν | μένων· | 26 ὁ δὲ | παρά-
26 But the Counselor, the | to you with | you | remaining; | but the Com-

Holy Spirit, whom the | κλητος, | τὸ | πνεῦμα | τὸ ἅγιον | ὃ | πέμψει | ὁ
Father will send in my | forter, | the | Spirit | — Holy | which will send | the

name, he will teach you | πατὴρ | ἐν τῷ | ὀνόματί | μου, | ἐκεῖνος | ὑμᾶς
all things, and bring to | Father | in the | name | of me, | that one | you

your remembrance all | διδάξει | πάντα | καὶ | ὑπομνήσει | ὑμᾶς | πάντα
that I have said to you. | will teach | all things | and | remind | you [of] | all things

27 Peace I leave with you; | ἃ | εἶπον | ὑμῖν | ἐγώ. | 27 Εἰρήνην | ἀφίημι
my peace I give to you; | which | ²told | ³you | ¹I. | Peace | I leave

not as the world gives do | ὑμῖν, | εἰρήνην | τὴν | ἐμὴν | δίδωμι | ὑμῖν·
I give to you. Let not | to you, | ²peace | — | ¹my | I give | you;

your hearts be troubled, | οὐ | καθὼς ὁ | κόσμος | δίδωσιν | ἐγὼ | δίδωμι
neither let them be | not | as the | world | gives | I | give

afraid. 28 You heard me | ὑμῖν. | μὴ | ταρασσέσθω | ὑμῶν ἡ | καρδία
say to you, 'I go away, | you. | Let not be troubled | of you the | heart

and I will come to you.' | μηδὲ | δειλιάτω. | 28 ἠκούσατε | ὅτι | ἐγὼ
If you loved me, you | nor | let it be fearful. | Ye heard | that | I

would have rejoiced, be- | εἶπον | ὑμῖν· | ὑπάγω | καὶ | ἔρχομαι | πρὸς
cause I go to the Father; | told | you : | I go | and | come | to

for the Father is greater | ὑμᾶς. | εἰ | ἠγαπᾶτέ | με, | ἐχάρητε | ἂν | ὅτι
than I. 29 And now I have | you. | If | ye loved | me, ye would have rejoiced that

told you before it takes | πορεύομαι | πρὸς | τὸν | πατέρα, | ὅτι ὁ | πατὴρ
place, so that when it | I am going | to | the | Father, | because the | Father

does take place, you may | μείζων | μού | ἐστιν. | 29 καὶ | νῦν | εἴρηκα
believe. 30 I will no longer | greater [than] me(I) | is. | And | now I have told

talk much with you, for | ὑμῖν | πρὶν | γενέσθαι, | ἵνα | ὅταν | γένηται
the ruler of this world is | you | before | to happen, | that | when | it happens
 | | | = it happens,

coming. He has no power | πιστεύσητε. | 30 οὐκέτι | πολλὰ | λαλήσω | μεθ'
over me; 31 but I do as the | ye may believe. | No longer | many things I will speak | with

Father has commanded | ὑμῶν, | ἔρχεται | γὰρ ὁ | τοῦ | κόσμου | ἄρχων·
 | you, | for ⁵is coming | ¹the ³of the | ⁴world | ²ruler;

 | καὶ | ἐν | ἐμοὶ | οὐκ | ἔχει | οὐδέν, | 31 ἀλλ'
 | and | in | me | he has not | no(any)thing, | but

 | ἵνα | γνῷ ὁ | κόσμος | ὅτι | ἀγαπῶ | τὸν
 | that | may know the | world | that | I love | the

 | πατέρα, | καὶ | καθὼς | ἐνετείλατό | μοι ὁ
 | Father, | and | as | commanded | me the

me, so that the world may / πατήρ, οὕτως ποιῶ. / Ἐγείρεσθε, ἄγωμεν / know that I love the / Father, so I do. / Rise, let us go / Father. Rise, let us go / ἐντεῦθεν. / hence. / hence.

CHAPTER 15

15 Ἐγώ εἰμι ἡ ἄμπελος ἡ ἀληθινή,
I   am   the   vine –   true,

"I am the true vine, / καὶ ὁ πατήρ μου ὁ γεωργός ἐστιν.
and my Father is the / and the Father of me the husbandman is.
vine-dresser. ²Every
branch of mine that / 2 πᾶν κλῆμα ἐν ἐμοὶ μὴ φέρον καρπόν,
bears no fruit, he takes / Every branch in me not bearing fruit,
away, and every branch / αἴρει αὐτό, καὶ πᾶν τὸ καρπὸν φέρον,
that does bear fruit he / he takes it, and every [branch] the fruit bearing,
prunes, that it may bear / καθαίρει αὐτὸ ἵνα καρπὸν πλείονα φέρῃ.
more fruit. ³You are / he prunes it that fruit more it may bear.
already made clean by / 3 ἤδη ὑμεῖς καθαροί ἐστε διὰ τὸν λόγον
the word which I have / Now ye clean are because of the word
spoken to you. ⁴Abide in / ὃν λελάληκα ὑμῖν· 4 μείνατε ἐν ἐμοί,
me, and I in you. As the / which I have spoken to you; remain in me,
branch cannot bear fruit / κἀγὼ ἐν ὑμῖν. καθὼς τὸ κλῆμα
by itself, unless it abides / and I in you. As the branch
in the vine, neither can / οὐ δύναται καρπὸν φέρειν ἀφ᾽ ἑαυτοῦ ἐὰν μὴ
you, unless you abide in / cannot fruit to bear from itself unless
me. ⁵I am the vine, you / μένῃ ἐν τῇ ἀμπέλῳ, οὕτως οὐδὲ ὑμεῖς
are the branches. He who / it remains in the vine, so not ye
abides in me, and I in / ἐὰν μὴ ἐν ἐμοὶ μένητε. 5 ἐγώ εἰμι
him, he it is that bears / unless in me ye remain. I am
much fruit, for apart / ἡ ἄμπελος, ὑμεῖς τὰ κλήματα. ὁ μένων
from me you can do / the vine, ye the branches. The [one] remaining
nothing. ⁶If a man does / ἐν ἐμοὶ κἀγὼ ἐν αὐτῷ, οὗτος φέρει
not abide in me, he is / in me and I in him, this one bears
cast forth as a branch / καρπὸν πολύν, ὅτι χωρὶς ἐμοῦ οὐ δύνασθε
and withers; and the / fruit much, because apart from me ye cannot
branches are gathered, / ποιεῖν οὐδέν. 6 ἐὰν μή τις μένῃ ἐν
thrown into the fire and / to do no(any)thing. Unless anyone remains in
burned. ⁷If you abide in / ἐμοί, ἐβλήθη ἔξω ὡς τὸ κλῆμα καὶ
me, and my words abide / me, he was(is) cast outside as the branch and
in you, ask whatever you / ἐξηράνθη, καὶ συνάγουσιν αὐτὰ καὶ εἰς
will, and it shall be done / was(is) dried, and they gather them and into
for you. ⁸By this my / τὸ πῦρ βάλλουσιν, καὶ καίεται. 7 ἐὰν
the fire they cast, and they are burned. If
μείνητε ἐν ἐμοὶ καὶ τὰ ῥήματά μου
ye remain in me and the words of me
ἐν ὑμῖν μείνῃ, ὃ ἐὰν θέλητε αἰτήσασθε,
in you remains, whatever ye wish ask,
καὶ γενήσεται ὑμῖν. 8 ἐν τούτῳ ἐδοξάσθη
and it shall happen to you. By this was glorified

Father is glorified, that you bear much fruit, and so prove to be my disciples. ⁹As the Father has loved me, so have I loved you; abide in my love. ¹⁰If you keep my commandments, you will abide in my love, just as I have kept my Father's commandments and abide in his love. ¹¹These things I have spoken to you, that my joy may be in you, and that your joy may be full.

12 "This is my commandment, that you love one another as I have loved you. ¹³Greater love has no man than this, that a man lay down his life for his friends. ¹⁴You are my friends if you do what I command you. ¹⁵No longer do I call you servants, for the servant does not know what his master is doing; but I have called you friends, for all that I have heard from my Father I have made known to you. ¹⁶You did not choose me, but I chose you and appointed you that you should go and bear fruit and that your fruit should abide; so that

ὁ πατήρ μου, ἵνα καρπὸν πολὺν φέρητε
the Father of me, that fruit much ye bear
καὶ γενήσεσθε ἐμοὶ μαθηταί. 9 καθὼς
and ye will be to me° disciples. As
ἠγάπησέν με ὁ πατήρ, κἀγὼ ὑμᾶς
loved me the Father, I also you
ἠγάπησα· μείνατε ἐν τῇ ἀγάπῃ τῇ ἐμῇ.
loved; remain ye in the ¹love – ¹my.
10 ἐὰν τὰς ἐντολάς μου τηρήσητε, μενεῖτε
If the commandments of me ye keep, ye will remain
ἐν τῇ ἀγάπῃ μου, καθὼς ἐγὼ τοῦ πατρός
in the love of me, as I of the Father
μου τὰς ἐντολὰς τετήρηκα καὶ μένω
of me the commandments have kept and remain
αὐτοῦ ἐν τῇ ἀγάπῃ. 11 Ταῦτα λελάληκα
of him in the love. These things I have spoken
ὑμῖν ἵνα ἡ χαρὰ ἡ ἐμὴ ἐν ὑμῖν ᾖ
to you that the ²joy – ¹my in you may be
καὶ ἡ χαρὰ ὑμῶν πληρωθῇ. 12 αὕτη
and the joy of you may be filled. This
ἐστὶν ἡ ἐντολὴ ἡ ἐμή, ἵνα ἀγαπᾶτε
is the ²commandment – ¹my, that ye love
ἀλλήλους καθὼς ἠγάπησα ὑμᾶς. 13 μείζονα
one another as I loved you. ¹Greater
ταύτης ἀγάπην οὐδεὶς ἔχει, ἵνα τις
[²than] ⁴this ²love no one has, that anyone
τὴν ψυχὴν αὐτοῦ θῇ ὑπὲρ τῶν φίλων
the life of him should lay down for the friends
αὐτοῦ. 14 ὑμεῖς φίλοι μού ἐστε, ἐὰν
of him. Ye friends of me are, if
ποιῆτε ὃ ἐγὼ ἐντέλλομαι ὑμῖν. 15 οὐκέτι
ye do what I command you. No longer
λέγω ὑμᾶς δούλους, ὅτι ὁ δοῦλος οὐκ οἶδεν
I call you slaves, because the slave knows not
τί ποιεῖ αὐτοῦ ὁ κύριος· ὑμᾶς δὲ
what does of him the lord; but you
εἴρηκα φίλους, ὅτι πάντα ἃ ἤκουσα
I have called friends, because all things which I heard
παρὰ τοῦ πατρός μου ἐγνώρισα ὑμῖν.
from the Father of me I made known to you.
16 οὐχ ὑμεῖς με ἐξελέξασθε, ἀλλ' ἐγὼ
Not ye me chose, but I
ἐξελεξάμην ὑμᾶς, καὶ ἔθηκα ὑμᾶς ἵνα
chose you, and appointed you that
ὑμεῖς ὑπάγητε καὶ καρπὸν φέρητε καὶ
ye should go and fruit should bear and
ὁ καρπὸς ὑμῶν μένῃ, ἵνα ὅ τι ἂν
the fruit of you should remain, that whatever

whatever you ask the
Father in my name, he
may give it to you.
¹⁷This I command you,
to love one another.

18 "If the world hates
you, know that it has
hated me before it hated
you. ¹⁹If you were of the
world, the world would
love its own; but be-
cause you are not of the
world, but I chose you
out of the world, there-
fore the world hates you.
²⁰Remember the word
that I said to you, 'A
servant is not greater
than his master.' If they
persecuted me, they will
persecute you; if they
kept my word, they will
keep yours also. ²¹But all
this they will do to you
on my account, because
they do not know him
who sent me. ²²If I had
not come and spoken to
them, they would not
have sin; but now they
have no excuse for their
sin. ²³He who hates me
hates my Father also.
²⁴If I had not done
among them the works
which no one else did,
they would not have sin;
but now they have seen
and hated both me and
my Father. ²⁵It is to ful-

αἰτήσητε   τὸν   πατέρα   ἐν   τῷ   ὀνόματί
ye may ask   the   Father   in   the   name

μου   δῷ   ὑμῖν.   17 ταῦτα   ἐντέλλομαι ὑμῖν,
of me he may give you.   These things   I command   you,

ἵνα   ἀγαπᾶτε   ἀλλήλους.   18 Εἰ   ὁ   κόσμος
that   ye love   one another.   If   the   world

ὑμᾶς   μισεῖ,   γινώσκετε   ὅτι   ἐμὲ   πρῶτον
you   hates,   ye know   that   me   before

ὑμῶν μεμίσηκεν.   19 εἰ   ἐκ   τοῦ   κόσμου   ἦτε,
you it has hated.   If   of   the   world   ye were,

ὁ   κόσμος   ἂν   τὸ   ἴδιον   ἐφίλει·   ὅτι   δὲ
the   world   ¹would ²the(its) ⁴own   ³have loved; but because

ἐκ   τοῦ   κόσμου   οὐκ   ἐστέ,   ἀλλ'   ἐγὼ
of   the   world   ye are not,   but   I

ἐξελεξάμην ὑμᾶς   ἐκ   τοῦ   κόσμου,   διὰ τοῦτο
chose   you   out of the   world,   therefore

μισεῖ   ὑμᾶς   ὁ   κόσμος.   20 μνημονεύετε
hates   you   the   world.   Remember ye

τοῦ   λόγου   οὗ   ἐγὼ   εἶπον   ὑμῖν·   οὐκ
the   word   which   I   said   to you :   Not

ἔστιν   δοῦλος   μείζων   τοῦ   κυρίου   αὐτοῦ.
is   a slave   greater [than] the   lord   of him.

εἰ   ἐμὲ   ἐδίωξαν,   καὶ   ὑμᾶς   διώξουσιν·
If   me   they persecuted,   also   you   they will persecute:

εἰ   τὸν   λόγον   μου   ἐτήρησαν,   καὶ   τὸν
if   the   word   of me   they kept,   also   the

ὑμέτερον τηρήσουσιν.   21 ἀλλὰ   ταῦτα   πάντα
yours   they will keep.   But   these things   all

ποιήσουσιν   εἰς   ὑμᾶς   διὰ   τὸ   ὄνομά   μου,
they will do   to   you because of the   name   of me,

ὅτι   οὐκ   οἴδασιν   τὸν   πέμψαντά   με.
because   they know not   the [one]   having sent   me.

22 εἰ μὴ   ἦλθον καὶ   ἐλάλησα   αὐτοῖς,   ἁμαρτίαν
Unless I came and   spoke   to them,   sin

οὐκ   εἴχοσαν·   νῦν   δὲ   πρόφασιν   οὐκ   ἔχουσιν
they had not had;   but now   cloak   they have not

περὶ   τῆς   ἁμαρτίας   αὐτῶν.   23 ὁ   ἐμὲ
concerning   the   sin   of them.   The [one]   me

μισῶν   καὶ   τὸν   πατέρα   μου   μισεῖ.   24 εἰ
hating   also   the   Father   of me   hates.   If

τὰ   ἔργα   μὴ   ἐποίησα   ἐν   αὐτοῖς   ἃ   οὐδεὶς
the   works   I did not   among   them   which no man

ἄλλος   ἐποίησεν,   ἁμαρτίαν   οὐκ   εἴχοσαν·
other   did,   sin   they had not had;

νῦν   δὲ   καὶ   ἑωράκασιν   καὶ   μεμισήκασιν
but now   both   they have seen   and   have hated

καὶ   ἐμὲ   καὶ   τὸν   πατέρα   μου.   25 ἀλλ'
both   me   and   the   Father   of me.   But

fil the word that is written in their law, 'They hated me without a cause.' ²⁶ But when the Counselor comes, whom I shall send to you from the Father, even the Spirit of truth, who proceeds from the Father, he will bear witness to me; ²⁷ and you also are witnesses, because you have been with me from the beginning.

ἵνα   πληρωθῇ   ὁ   λόγος   ὁ   ἐν   τῷ   νόμῳ
that may be fulfilled the   word   –   in   the   law
αὐτῶν   γεγραμμένος   ὅτι   ἐμίσησάν   με
of them   having been written[,]   –   They hated   me
δωρεάν.   26 Ὅταν   ἔλθῃ   ὁ   παράκλητος
freely.   When   comes   the   Comforter
ὃν   ἐγὼ   πέμψω   ὑμῖν   παρὰ   τοῦ   πατρός,
whom I   will send to you from   the   Father,
τὸ   πνεῦμα   τῆς   ἀληθείας   ὃ   παρὰ   τοῦ
the   Spirit   –   of truth   which from   the
πατρὸς   ἐκπορεύεται,   ἐκεῖνος   μαρτυρήσει
Father   proceeds,   that one   will witness
περὶ   ἐμοῦ·   27 καὶ   ὑμεῖς   δὲ   μαρτυρεῖτε,
concerning me;   ²also   ²ye   ¹and   witness,
ὅτι   ἀπ'   ἀρχῆς   μετ'   ἐμοῦ   ἐστε.
because from [the] beginning with   me   ye are.

CHAPTER 16

"I have said all this to keep you from falling away. ²They will put you out of the synagogues; indeed, the hour is coming when whoever kills you will think he is offering service to God. ³And they will do this because they have not known the Father, nor me. ⁴But I have said these things to you, that when their hour comes you may remember that I told you of them.

"I did not say these things to you from the beginning, because I was with you. ⁵But now I am going to him who sent me; yet none of you asks me, 'Where are you going?' ⁶But because I have said these things to you, sorrow has filled your hearts. ⁷Nevertheless I tell you the truth:

16 Ταῦτα   λελάληκα   ὑμῖν   ἵνα   μὴ
These things I have spoken to you   that   not
σκανδαλισθῆτε.   2 ἀποσυναγώγους   ποιή-
ye be offended.   Put away from [the] synagogue they
σουσιν   ὑμᾶς·   ἀλλ'   ἔρχεται   ὥρα   ἵνα   πᾶς   ὁ
will make you;   but   comes an hour that everyone
ἀποκτείνας   ὑμᾶς   δόξῃ   λατρείαν   προσφέρειν
killing   you   thinks   service   to offer
τῷ   θεῷ.   3 καὶ   ταῦτα   ποιήσουσιν   ὅτι
–   to God.   And these things they will do because
οὐκ   ἔγνωσαν   τὸν   πατέρα   οὐδὲ   ἐμέ.
they knew not   the   Father   nor   me.
4 ἀλλὰ   ταῦτα   λελάληκα   ὑμῖν   ἵνα   ὅταν
But   these things I have spoken to you   that   when
ἔλθῃ   ἡ   ὥρα   αὐτῶν   μνημονεύητε   αὐτῶν,
comes the   hour of them ye may remember   them,
ὅτι   ἐγὼ   εἶπον   ὑμῖν.   Ταῦτα   δὲ   ὑμῖν
that   I   told   you.   And these things to you
ἐξ   ἀρχῆς   οὐκ   εἶπον,   ὅτι   μεθ'   ὑμῶν
from [the] beginning I said not,   because with   you
ἤμην.   5 νῦν   δὲ   ὑπάγω   πρὸς   τὸν   πέμψαντά
I was.   But now I am going to the [one] having sent
με,   καὶ   οὐδεὶς   ἐξ   ὑμῶν   ἐρωτᾷ   με·
me,   and   not one   of   you   asks   me:
ποῦ   ὑπάγεις;   6 ἀλλ'   ὅτι   ταῦτα   λελάληκα
Where goest thou?   but because these things I have spoken
ὑμῖν,   ἡ   λύπη   πεπλήρωκεν   ὑμῶν   τὴν
to you,   the   grief   has filled   of you   the
καρδίαν.   7 ἀλλ'   ἐγὼ   τὴν   ἀλήθειαν   λέγω
heart.   But   I   the   truth   tell

it is to your advantage that I go away, for if I do not go away, the Counselor will not come to you; but if I go, I will send him to you. ⁸And when he comes, he will convince the world of sin and of righteousness and of judgment: ⁹of sin, because they do not believe in me; ¹⁰of righteousness, because I go to the Father, and you will see me no more; ¹¹of judgment, because the ruler of this world is judged.

12 "I have yet many things to say to you, but you cannot bear them now. ¹³When the Spirit of truth comes, he will guide you into all the truth; for he will not speak on his own authority, but whatever he hears he will speak, and he will declare to you the things that are to come. ¹⁴He will glorify me, for he will take what is mine and declare it to you. ¹⁵All that the Father has is mine; therefore I said that he will take what is mine and declare it to you.

16 "A little while, and you will see me no more; again a little while, and you will see me." ¹⁷Some

ὑμῖν,   συμφέρει   ὑμῖν   ἵνα   ἐγὼ   ἀπέλθω.
you,   it is expedient   for you   that   I   should go away.
ἐὰν   γὰρ   μὴ   ἀπέλθω,   ὁ   παράκλητος
For if   I go not away,   the   Comforter
οὐ   μὴ   ἔλθῃ   πρὸς   ὑμᾶς·   ἐὰν   δὲ   πορευθῶ,
by no means   comes   to   you;   but if   I go,
πέμψω   αὐτὸν   πρὸς   ὑμᾶς.   8 καὶ   ἐλθὼν
I will send   him   to   you.   And   coming
ἐκεῖνος   ἐλέγξει   τὸν   κόσμον   περὶ   ἁμαρτίας
that one   will reprove the   world   concerning   sin
καὶ   περὶ   δικαιοσύνης   καὶ   περὶ   κρίσεως·
and concerning righteousness   and concerning judgment;
9 περὶ   ἁμαρτίας   μέν,   ὅτι   οὐ   πιστεύουσιν
concerning   sin,   –   because   they believe not
εἰς   ἐμέ·   10 περὶ   δικαιοσύνης   δέ,   ὅτι
in   me;   concerning   righteousness   –   because
πρὸς   τὸν   πατέρα   ὑπάγω   καὶ   οὐκέτι
to   the   Father   I am going   and   no longer
θεωρεῖτέ   με·   11 περὶ   δὲ   κρίσεως,   ὅτι
ye behold   me;   concerning   –   judgment, because
ὁ   ἄρχων   τοῦ   κόσμου   τούτου   κέκριται.
the   ruler   –   world   of this   has been judged.
12 "Ἔτι   πολλὰ   ἔχω   ὑμῖν   λέγειν,   ἀλλ'
   Yet   many things I have   you   to tell,   but
οὐ   δύνασθε   βαστάζειν   ἄρτι·   13 ὅταν   δὲ
ye cannot   to bear   now;   but when
ἔλθῃ   ἐκεῖνος,   τὸ   πνεῦμα   τῆς   ἀληθείας,
comes   that one,   the   Spirit   –   of truth,
ὁδηγήσει   ὑμᾶς   εἰς   τὴν   ἀλήθειαν   πᾶσαν·
he will guide   you   into   the   truth   all;
οὐ   γὰρ   λαλήσει   ἀφ'   ἑαυτοῦ,   ἀλλ'   ὅσα
for not   will he speak   from   himself,   but what things
ἀκούει   λαλήσει,   καὶ   τὰ   ἐρχόμενα
he hears   he will speak,   and   the   coming things
ἀναγγελεῖ   ὑμῖν.   14 ἐκεῖνος   ἐμὲ   δοξάσει,
he will announce   to you.   That one   me   will glorify,
ὅτι   ἐκ   τοῦ   ἐμοῦ   λήμψεται   καὶ   ἀναγγελεῖ
because of   the   of me* he will receive   and will announce
ὑμῖν.   15 πάντα   ὅσα   ἔχει   ὁ   πατὴρ   ἐμά
to you.   All things which   has   the   Father   mine
ἐστιν·   διὰ   τοῦτο   εἶπον   ὅτι   ἐκ   τοῦ   ἐμοῦ
is(are);   therefore   I said   that   of   the   of me*
λαμβάνει   καὶ   ἀναγγελεῖ   ὑμῖν.   16 Μικρὸν
he receives   and   will announce   to you.   A little while
καὶ   οὐκέτι   θεωρεῖτέ   με,   καὶ   πάλιν
and   no longer   ye behold   me,   and   again
μικρὸν   καὶ   ὄψεσθέ   με.   17 εἶπαν   οὖν
a little while   and   ye will see   me.   Said   therefore

* Understand "that which is mine".

of his disciples said to one another, "What is this that he says to us, 'A little while, and you will not see me, and again a little while, and you will see me'; and, 'because I go to the Father'?" 18 They said, "What does he mean by 'a little while'? We do not know what he means." 19 Jesus knew that they wanted to ask him; so he said to them, "Is this what you are asking yourselves, what I meant by saying, 'A little while, and you will not see me, and again a little while, and you will see me'? 20 Truly, truly, I say to you, you will weep and lament, but the world will rejoice; you will be sorrowful, but your sorrow will turn into joy. 21 When a woman is in travail she has sorrow, because her hour has come; but when she is delivered of the child, she no longer remembers the anguish, for joy that a child is born into the world. 22 So you have sorrow now, but I will see you again and your hearts will rejoice, and no one will take your joy from you. 23 In that day you will ask nothing

ἐκ τῶν μαθητῶν αὐτοῦ πρὸς ἀλλήλους·
[some] of the disciples of him to one another :
τί ἐστιν τοῦτο ὃ λέγει ἡμῖν· μικρὸν
What is this which he tells us : A little while
καὶ οὐ θεωρεῖτέ με, καὶ πάλιν μικρὸν
and ye behold not me, and again a little while
καὶ ὄψεσθέ με; καί· ὅτι ὑπάγω
and ye will see me? and : Because I am going
πρὸς τὸν πατέρα; 18 ἔλεγον οὖν· τοῦτο
to the Father? They said therefore : ᵃThis
τί ἐστιν ὃ λέγει τὸ μικρόν; οὐκ οἴδαμεν
¹what ²is which he says[,] the "little while"? We do not know
τί λαλεῖ. 19 ἔγνω Ἰησοῦς ὅτι ἤθελον
what he speaks. Knew Jesus that they wished
αὐτὸν ἐρωτᾶν, καὶ εἶπεν αὐτοῖς· περὶ
him to question, and said to them : Concerning
τούτου ζητεῖτε μετ' ἀλλήλων ὅτι εἶπον·
this seek ye with one another because I said :
μικρὸν καὶ οὐ θεωρεῖτέ με, καὶ πάλιν
A little while and ye behold not me, and again
μικρὸν καὶ ὄψεσθέ με; 20 ἀμὴν ἀμὴν
a little while and ye will see me? Truly truly
λέγω ὑμῖν ὅτι κλαύσετε καὶ θρηνήσετε
I tell you that will weep and will lament
ὑμεῖς, ὁ δὲ κόσμος χαρήσεται· ὑμεῖς
ye, and the world will rejoice; ye
λυπηθήσεσθε, ἀλλ' ἡ λύπη ὑμῶν εἰς
will be grieved, but the grief of you into
χαρὰν γενήσεται. 21 ἡ γυνὴ ὅταν τίκτῃ
joy will become. The woman when she gives birth
λύπην ἔχει, ὅτι ἦλθεν ἡ ὥρα αὐτῆς·
grief has, because came the hour of her;
ὅταν δὲ γεννήσῃ τὸ παιδίον, οὐκέτι
but when she brings forth the child, no longer
μνημονεύει τῆς θλίψεως διὰ τὴν χαρὰν
she remembers the distress because of the joy
ὅτι ἐγεννήθη ἄνθρωπος εἰς τὸν κόσμον.
that was born a man into the world.
22 καὶ ὑμεῖς οὖν νῦν μὲν λύπην ἔχετε·
And ye therefore now indeed grief have;
πάλιν δὲ ὄψομαι ὑμᾶς, καὶ χαρήσεται
but again I will see you, and ⁴will rejoice
ὑμῶν ἡ καρδία, καὶ τὴν χαρὰν ὑμῶν
²of you ¹the ³heart, and the joy of you
οὐδεὶς αἴρει ἀφ' ὑμῶν. 23 καὶ ἐν ἐκείνῃ τῇ
no one takes from you. And in that —
ἡμέρᾳ ἐμὲ οὐκ ἐρωτήσετε οὐδέν.
day me ye will not question no(any)thing.

of me. Truly, truly, I say to you, if you ask anything of the Father, he will give it to you in my name. ²⁴ Hitherto you have asked nothing in my name; ask, and you will receive, that your joy may be full.

25 "I have said this to you in figures; the hour is coming when I shall no longer speak to you in figures but tell you plainly of the Father. ²⁶ In that day you will ask in my name; and I do not say to you I shall pray the Father for you; ²⁷ for the Father himself loves you, because you have loved me and have believed that I came from the Father. ²⁸ I came from the Father and have come into the world; again, I am leaving the world and going to the Father."

29 His disciples said, "Ah, now you are speaking plainly, not in any figure! ³⁰ Now we know that you know all things, and need none to question you; by this we believe that you came from God." ³¹ Jesus answered them, "Do you now believe? ³² The hour

ἀμὴν ἀμὴν λέγω ὑμῖν, ἄν τι αἰτήσητε
Truly   truly   I tell   you,   whatever   ye ask
τὸν πατέρα δώσει ὑμῖν ἐν τῷ ὀνόματί
the Father he will give you   in the   name
μου. 24 ἕως ἄρτι οὐκ ᾐτήσατε οὐδὲν
of me.   Until now ye asked not no(any)thing
ἐν τῷ ὀνόματί μου· αἰτεῖτε, καὶ λήμψεσθε,
in the   name   of me; ask, and ye will receive,
ἵνα ἡ χαρὰ ὑμῶν ἦ πεπληρωμένη.
that the joy of you may be *having been* filled.
25 Ταῦτα ἐν παροιμίαις λελάληκα ὑμῖν·
These things in allegories I have spoken to you;
ἔρχεται ὥρα ὅτε οὐκέτι ἐν παροιμίαις
comes an hour when no longer in allegories
λαλήσω ὑμῖν, ἀλλὰ παρρησίᾳ περὶ τοῦ
I will speak to you, but plainly concerning the
πατρὸς ἀπαγγελῶ ὑμῖν. 26 ἐν ἐκείνῃ τῇ
Father will declare to you.   In that
ἡμέρᾳ ἐν τῷ ὀνόματί μου αἰτήσεσθε,
day   in the   name of me ye will ask,
καὶ οὐ λέγω ὑμῖν ὅτι ἐγὼ ἐρωτήσω
and I tell not you that I   will request
τὸν πατέρα περὶ ὑμῶν· 27 αὐτὸς γὰρ
the Father concerning you;   for [him]self
ὁ πατὴρ φιλεῖ ὑμᾶς, ὅτι ὑμεῖς ἐμὲ
the Father loves you, because ye   me
πεφιλήκατε καὶ πεπιστεύκατε ὅτι ἐγὼ
have loved and have believed that I
παρὰ τοῦ θεοῦ ἐξῆλθον. 28 ἐξῆλθον
from - God came forth.   I came forth
ἐκ τοῦ πατρὸς καὶ ἐλήλυθα εἰς τὸν
out of the Father and have come into the
κόσμον· πάλιν ἀφίημι τὸν κόσμον καὶ
world; again I leave the world and
πορεύομαι πρὸς τὸν πατέρα. 29 Λέγουσιν
go   to   the Father.   Say
οἱ μαθηταὶ αὐτοῦ· ἴδε νῦν ἐν παρρησίᾳ
the disciples of him: Behold[,] now in plainness
λαλεῖς, καὶ παροιμίαν οὐδεμίαν λέγεις.
thou speakest, and ¹allegory ¹no thou sayest.
30 νῦν οἴδαμεν ὅτι οἶδας πάντα καὶ
Now we know that thou knowest all things and
οὐ χρείαν ἔχεις ἵνα τίς σε ἐρωτᾷ· ἐν
no   need hast that anyone thee should question; by
τούτῳ πιστεύομεν ὅτι ἀπὸ θεοῦ ἐξῆλθες.
this   we believe that from God thou camest forth.
31 ἀπεκρίθη αὐτοῖς Ἰησοῦς· ἄρτι πιστεύετε;
Answered   them   Jesus : Now   believe ye?

is coming, indeed it has come, when you will be scattered, every man to his home, and will leave me alone; yet I am not alone, for the Father is with me. ³³I have said this to you, that in me you may have peace. In the world you have tribulation; but be of good cheer, I have overcome the world."

32 ἰδοὺ ἔρχεται ὥρα καὶ ἐλήλυθεν ἵνα
behold[,] comes an hour and has come that
σκορπισθῆτε ἕκαστος εἰς τὰ ἴδια κἀμὲ
ye are scattered each one to the(his) own and me
μόνον ἀφῆτε· καὶ οὐκ εἰμὶ μόνος, ὅτι
alone ye leave; and I am not alone, because
ὁ πατὴρ μετ' ἐμοῦ ἐστιν. 33 ταῦτα
the Father with me is. These things
λελάληκα ὑμῖν ἵνα ἐν ἐμοὶ εἰρήνην
I have spoken to you that in me peace
ἔχητε. ἐν τῷ κόσμῳ θλῖψιν ἔχετε·
ye may have. In the world distress ye have;
ἀλλὰ θαρσεῖτε, ἐγὼ νενίκηκα τὸν κόσμον.
but cheer ye up, I have overcome the world.

CHAPTER 17

WHEN Jesus had spoken these words, he lifted up his eyes to heaven and said, "Father, the hour has come; glorify thy Son that the Son may glorify thee, ²since thou hast given him power over all flesh, to give eternal life to all whom thou hast given him. ³And this is eternal life, that they know thee the only true God, and Jesus Christ whom thou hast sent. ⁴I glorified thee on earth, having accomplished the work which thou gavest me to do; ⁵and now, Father, glorify thou me in thy own presence with the glory which I had with thee before the world was made.

6 "I have manifested thy name to the men whom thou gavest me

17 Ταῦτα ἐλάλησεν Ἰησοῦς, καὶ ἐπάρας
These things spoke Jesus, and lifting up
τοὺς ὀφθαλμοὺς αὐτοῦ εἰς τὸν οὐρανὸν
the eyes of him to — heaven
εἶπεν· πάτερ, ἐλήλυθεν ἡ ὥρα· δόξασόν
said: Father, has come the hour; glorify
σου τὸν υἱόν, ἵνα ὁ υἱὸς δοξάσῃ σέ,
of thee the Son, that the Son may glorify thee,
2 καθὼς ἔδωκας αὐτῷ ἐξουσίαν πάσης
as thou gavest him authority of(over) all
σαρκός, ἵνα πᾶν ὃ δέδωκας αὐτῷ δώσῃ
flesh, that all which thou hast given him he may give
αὐτοῖς ζωὴν αἰώνιον. 3 αὕτη δέ ἐστιν
to them life eternal. And this is
ἡ αἰώνιος ζωή, ἵνα γινώσκωσιν σὲ τὸν
— eternal life, that they may know thee the
μόνον ἀληθινὸν θεὸν καὶ ὃν ἀπέστειλας
only true God and [he] whom thou didst send
Ἰησοῦν Χριστόν. 4 ἐγώ σε ἐδόξασα
Jesus Christ. I thee glorified
ἐπὶ τῆς γῆς, τὸ ἔργον τελειώσας ὃ
on the earth, the work finishing which
δέδωκάς μοι ἵνα ποιήσω· 5 καὶ νῦν
thou hast given to me that I should do; and now
δόξασόν με σύ, πάτερ, παρὰ σεαυτῷ
glorify me thou, Father, with thyself
τῇ δόξῃ ᾗ εἶχον πρὸ τοῦ τὸν κόσμον
with the glory which I had before the the world
= before the world was
εἶναι παρὰ σοί. 6 Ἐφανέρωσά σου τὸ
to beᵇ with thee. I manifested of thee the
ὄνομα τοῖς ἀνθρώποις οὓς ἔδωκάς μοι
name to the men whom thou gavest to me

out of the world; thine they were, and thou gavest them to me, and they have kept thy word. ⁷Now they know that everything that thou hast given me is from thee; ⁸for I have given them the words which thou gavest me, and they have received them and know in truth that I came from thee; and they have believed that thou didst send me. ⁹I am praying for them; I am not praying for the world but for those whom thou hast given me, for they are thine; ¹⁰all mine are thine, and thine are mine, and I am glorified in them. ¹¹And now I am no more in the world, but they are in the world, and I am coming to thee. Holy Father, keep them in thy name, which thou hast given me, that they may be one, even as we are one. ¹²While I was with them, I kept them in thy name, which thou hast given me; I have guarded them, and none of them is lost but the son of perdition, that the scripture might be fulfilled. ¹³But now I am coming to thee; and these things I speak in the world, that they may

ἐκ τοῦ κόσμου. σοὶ ἦσαν κἀμοὶ αὐτοὺς
out of the   world.   To thee[e] they were and to me   them
=Thine

ἔδωκας, καὶ τὸν λόγον σου τετήρηκαν.
thou gavest, and   the   word   of thee   they have kept.

7 νῦν ἔγνωκαν ὅτι πάντα ὅσα δέδωκάς
Now they have known that all things as many as thou hast given

μοι παρὰ σοῦ εἰσιν· 8 ὅτι τὰ ῥήματα
to me from   thee   are;   because   the   words

ἃ ἔδωκάς μοι δέδωκα αὐτοῖς, καὶ αὐτοὶ
which thou gavest to me I have given to them,   and   they

ἔλαβον, καὶ ἔγνωσαν ἀληθῶς ὅτι παρὰ
received,   and   knew   truly   that from

σοῦ ἐξῆλθον, καὶ ἐπίστευσαν ὅτι σύ
thee I came forth,   and   they believed   that   thou

με ἀπέστειλας. 9 ἐγὼ περὶ αὐτῶν ἐρωτῶ·
me   didst send.   I concerning them make request:

οὐ περὶ τοῦ κόσμου ἐρωτῶ, ἀλλὰ περὶ
not concerning the   world do I make request, but concerning

ὧν δέδωκάς μοι, ὅτι σοί εἰσιν,
[those] whom thou hast given to me, because to thee[e] they are,
=thine

10 καὶ τὰ ἐμὰ πάντα σά ἐστιν καὶ
and   ²the ³my things ¹all   ⁵thine ⁴is(are)   and

τὰ σὰ ἐμά, καὶ δεδόξασμαι ἐν αὐτοῖς.
the thy things mine,   and I have been glorified in   them.

11 καὶ οὐκέτι εἰμὶ ἐν τῷ κόσμῳ, καὶ
And   no longer   am I   in   the   world,   and

αὐτοὶ ἐν τῷ κόσμῳ εἰσίν, κἀγὼ πρὸς
they   in   the   world   are,   and I   to

σὲ ἔρχομαι. πάτερ ἅγιε, τήρησον αὐτοὺς
thee come.   Father   holy,   keep   them

ἐν τῷ ὀνόματί σου ᾧ δέδωκάς μοι,
in   the   name   of thee which   thou hast given to me,

ἵνα ὦσιν ἓν καθὼς ἡμεῖς. 12 ὅτε ἤμην
that they may be one   as   we.   When I was

μετ' αὐτῶν, ἐγὼ ἐτήρουν αὐτοὺς ἐν
with   them,   I   kept   them   in

τῷ ὀνόματί σου ᾧ δέδωκάς μοι, καὶ
the   name   of thee which thou hast given to me, and

ἐφύλαξα, καὶ οὐδεὶς ἐξ αὐτῶν ἀπώλετο
I guarded,   and   not one   of   them   perished

εἰ μὴ ὁ υἱὸς τῆς ἀπωλείας, ἵνα ἡ
except   the   son   -   perdition,   that   the

γραφὴ πληρωθῇ. 13 νῦν δὲ πρὸς σὲ
scripture might be fulfilled.   But now   to   thee

ἔρχομαι, καὶ ταῦτα λαλῶ ἐν τῷ κόσμῳ
I come,   and these things I speak in   the   world

ἵνα ἔχωσιν τὴν χαρὰν τὴν ἐμὴν
that   they may have   the   ²joy   -   ¹my

have my joy fulfilled in themselves. ¹⁴I have given them thy word; and the world has hated them because they are not of the world, even as I am not of the world. ¹⁵I do not pray that thou shouldst take them out of the world, but that thou shouldst keep them from the evil one.ᶻ ¹⁶They are not of the world, even as I am not of the world. ¹⁷Sanctify them in the truth; thy word is truth. ¹⁸As thou didst send me into the world, so I have sent them into the world. ¹⁹And for their sake I consecrate myself, that they also may be consecrated in truth.

20 "I do not pray for these only, but also for those who believe in me through their word, ²¹that they may all be one; even as thou, Father, art in me, and I in thee, that they also may be in us, so that the world may believe that thou hast sent me. ²²The glory which thou hast given me I have given to them, that they may be one even as we are one, ²³I in them and thou in me, that they may become perfectly one, so

---

πεπληρωμένην ἐν ἑαυτοῖς. 14 ἐγὼ δέδωκα
having been fulfilled in themselves.   I have given

αὐτοῖς τὸν λόγον σου, καὶ ὁ κόσμος
to them the   word of thee, and the world

ἐμίσησεν αὐτούς, ὅτι οὐκ εἰσὶν ἐκ τοῦ
hated   them,   because they are not of the

κόσμου καθὼς ἐγὼ οὐκ εἰμὶ ἐκ τοῦ
world   as   I   am not of the

κόσμου. 15 οὐκ ἐρωτῶ ἵνα ἄρῃς αὐτοὺς
world.   I do not request that thou shouldest take them

ἐκ τοῦ κόσμου, ἀλλ' ἵνα τηρήσῃς αὐτοὺς
out of the world, but that thou shouldest keep them

ἐκ τοῦ πονηροῦ. 16 ἐκ τοῦ κόσμου
out of the evil [?one].   Of the world

οὐκ εἰσὶν καθὼς ἐγὼ οὐκ εἰμὶ ἐκ τοῦ
they are not as   I   am not of the

κόσμου. 17 ἁγίασον αὐτοὺς ἐν τῇ
world.   Sanctify them in(?by) the

ἀληθείᾳ· ὁ λόγος ὁ σὸς ἀλήθειά ἐστιν.
truth; *the* ²word – ¹thy truth is.

18 καθὼς ἐμὲ ἀπέστειλας εἰς τὸν κόσμον,
As   me thou didst send into the world,

κἀγὼ ἀπέστειλα αὐτοὺς εἰς τὸν κόσμον·
I also sent   them into the world;

19 καὶ ὑπὲρ αὐτῶν [ἐγὼ] ἁγιάζω ἐμαυτόν,
and on behalf of them I   sanctify myself,

ἵνα ὦσιν καὶ αὐτοὶ ἡγιασμένοι ἐν ἀληθείᾳ.
that ²may be ³also ¹they *having been* sanctified in truth.

20 Οὐ περὶ τούτων δὲ ἐρωτῶ μόνον,
²Not ³concerning ⁴these ¹but I make request only,

ἀλλὰ καὶ περὶ τῶν πιστευόντων διὰ
but also concerning the [ones] believing through

τοῦ λόγου αὐτῶν εἰς ἐμέ, 21 ἵνα πάντες
the word of them in me,   that all

ἓν ὦσιν, καθὼς σύ, πατήρ, ἐν ἐμοὶ
one may be, as thou, Father, in me

κἀγὼ ἐν σοί, ἵνα καὶ αὐτοὶ ἐν ἡμῖν
and I in thee, that also they in us

ὦσιν, ἵνα ὁ κόσμος πιστεύῃ ὅτι σύ
may be, that the world may believe that thou

με ἀπέστειλας. 22 κἀγὼ τὴν δόξαν ἣν
me didst send.   And I the glory which

δέδωκάς μοι δέδωκα αὐτοῖς, ἵνα ὦσιν
thou hast given to me have given to them, that they may be

ἓν καθὼς ἡμεῖς ἕν· 23 ἐγὼ ἐν αὐτοῖς
one as we [are] one;   I   in them

καὶ σὺ ἐν ἐμοί, ἵνα ὦσιν τετελειωμένοι
and thou in me, that they may be *having been* perfected

ᶻ Or *from evil*

that the world may know that thou hast sent me and hast loved them even as thou hast loved me. ²⁴Father, I desire that they also, whom thou hast given to me, may be with me where I am, to behold my glory which thou hast given me in thy love for me before the foundation of the world. ²⁵O righteous Father, the world has not known thee, but I have known thee; and these know that thou hast sent me. ²⁶I made known to them thy name, and I will make it known, that the love with which thou hast loved me may be in them, and I in them."

εἰς   ἕν,   ἵνα   γινώσκῃ   ὁ   κόσμος   ὅτι   σύ
in   one,   that may know   the   world   that thou
με   ἀπέστειλας   καὶ   ἠγάπησας   αὐτοὺς
me   didst send   and   didst love   them
καθὼς   ἐμὲ   ἠγάπησας.   24 Πατήρ,   ὁ
as   me   thou didst love.   Father,   what
δέδωκάς   μοι,   θέλω   ἵνα   ὅπου   εἰμὶ   ἐγὼ
thou hast given to me,   I wish   that   where   am   I
κἀκεῖνοι   ὦσιν   μετ᾽   ἐμοῦ,   ἵνα   θεωρῶσιν
those also   may be   with   me,   that they may behold
τὴν   δόξαν   τὴν   ἐμήν,   ἣν   δέδωκάς   μοι
the   ²glory –   ¹my,   which thou hast given to me
ὅτι   ἠγάπησάς   με   πρὸ   καταβολῆς   κόσμου.
because thou didst love me before [the] foundation of [the] world.
25 πατὴρ   δίκαιε,   καὶ   ὁ   κόσμος   σε
Father   righteous, indeed the   world   thee
οὐκ   ἔγνω,   ἐγὼ   δέ   σε   ἔγνων,   καὶ   οὗτοι
knew not,   but I   thee knew,   and   these
ἔγνωσαν   ὅτι   σύ   με   ἀπέστειλας·   26 καὶ
knew   that   thou me   didst send;   and
ἐγνώρισα   αὐτοῖς   τὸ   ὄνομά   σου   καὶ
I made known to them   the   name   of thee and
γνωρίσω,   ἵνα   ἡ   ἀγάπη   ἣν   ἠγάπησάς
will make known,   that the   love [with] which thou lovedst
με   ἐν   αὐτοῖς   ᾖ   κἀγὼ   ἐν   αὐτοῖς.
me   in   them   may be   and I   in   them.

CHAPTER 18

WHEN Jesus had spoken these words, he went forth with his disciples across the Kidron valley, where there was a garden, which he and his disciples entered. ²Now Judas, who betrayed him, also knew the place; for Jesus often met there with his disciples. ³So Judas, procuring a band of soldiers and some officers from the chief priests and the Pharisees, went there with lanterns

18 Ταῦτα   εἰπὼν   Ἰησοῦς   ἐξῆλθεν   σὺν
These things having said Jesus   went forth   with
τοῖς   μαθηταῖς   αὐτοῦ   πέραν   τοῦ   χειμάρρου
the   disciples   of him   across   the   torrent
τοῦ   Κεδρών,   ὅπου   ἦν   κῆπος,   εἰς   ὃν
–   Kedron,   where there was a garden,   into which
εἰσῆλθεν   αὐτὸς   καὶ   οἱ   μαθηταὶ   αὐτοῦ.
entered   he   and   the   disciples   of him.
2 ᾔδει   δὲ   καὶ   Ἰούδας   ὁ   παραδιδοὺς
¹Now ⁷knew   ⁸also   ²Judas   ⁴the [one]   ⁵betraying
αὐτὸν   τὸν   τόπον,   ὅτι   πολλάκις   συνήχθη
⁶him   ³the   ⁹place, because often   assembled
Ἰησοῦς   ἐκεῖ   μετὰ   τῶν   μαθητῶν   αὐτου.
Jesus   there   with   the   disciples   of him.
3 ὁ   οὖν   Ἰούδας   λαβὼν   τὴν   σπεῖραν
–   Therefore Judas   taking   the   band
καὶ   ἐκ   τῶν   ἀρχιερέων   καὶ   [ἐκ]   τῶν
and   ²from   ³the   ⁴chief priests   ⁵and   ⁶from   ⁷the
Φαρισαίων   ὑπηρέτας   ἔρχεται   ἐκεῖ   μετὰ
⁸Pharisees   ¹attendants   comes   there   with

and torches and weapons. [4]Then Jesus, knowing all that was to befall him, came forward and said to them, "Whom do you seek?" [5]They answered him, "Jesus of Nazareth." Jesus said to them, "I am he." Judas, who betrayed him, was standing with them. [6]When he said to them, "I am he," they drew back and fell to the ground. [7]Again he asked them, "Whom do you seek?" And they said, "Jesus of Nazareth." [8]Jesus answered, "I told you that I am he; so, if you seek me, let these men go." [9]This was to fulfil the word which he had spoken, "Of those whom thou gavest me I lost not one." [10]Then Simon Peter, having a sword, drew it and struck the high priest's slave and cut off his right ear. The slave's name was Malchus. [11]Jesus said to Peter, "Put your sword into its sheath; shall I not drink the cup which the Father has given me?"

[12] So the band of

φανῶν καὶ λαμπάδων καὶ ὅπλων. **4** Ἰησοῦς
lanterns   and   lamps   and   weapons.   Jesus

οὖν   εἰδὼς   πάντα   τὰ   ἐρχόμενα   ἐπ᾽   αὐτὸν
therefore knowing   all   the things coming on   him

ἐξῆλθεν   καὶ   λέγει   αὐτοῖς·   τίνα   ζητεῖτε;
went forth   and   says   to them: Whom   seek ye?

5 ἀπεκρίθησαν   αὐτῷ·   Ἰησοῦν   τὸν
They answered   him: Jesus   the

Ναζωραῖον.   λέγει   αὐτοῖς·   ἐγώ   εἰμι.
Nazarene.   He tells   them: I   am.

εἱστήκει   δὲ   καὶ   Ἰούδας   ὁ   παραδιδοὺς
Now stood   also   Judas   the [one] betraying

αὐτὸν   μετ᾽   αὐτῶν.   **6** ὡς   οὖν   εἶπεν
him   with   them.   When therefore   he told

αὐτοῖς·   ἐγώ   εἰμι,   ἀπῆλθαν   εἰς   τὰ   ὀπίσω
them: I   am,   they went away   back †

καὶ   ἔπεσαν   χαμαί.   **7** πάλιν   οὖν
and   fell   on the ground.   Again therefore

ἐπηρώτησεν   αὐτούς·   τίνα   ζητεῖτε;   οἱ   δὲ
he questioned   them: Whom   seek ye?   And they

εἶπαν·   Ἰησοῦν   τὸν   Ναζωραῖον.   **8** ἀπεκρίθη
said: Jesus   the   Nazarene.   Answered

Ἰησοῦς·   εἶπον   ὑμῖν   ὅτι   ἐγώ   εἰμι·   εἰ
Jesus: I told   you   that   I   am;   if

οὖν   ἐμὲ   ζητεῖτε,   ἄφετε   τούτους   ὑπάγειν·
therefore me   ye seek,   allow   these   to go;

9 ἵνα   πληρωθῇ   ὁ   λόγος   ὃν   εἶπεν,   ὅτι
that might be fulfilled   the   word   which   he said,   –

οὓς   δέδωκάς   μοι,   οὐκ   ἀπώλεσα   ἐξ
[Those] whom thou hast given to me,   I lost not   of

αὐτῶν   οὐδένα.   **10** Σίμων   οὖν   Πέτρος
them   no(any)one.   ¹Simon   ³therefore   ²Peter

ἔχων   μάχαιραν   εἵλκυσεν   αὐτὴν   καὶ   ἔπαισεν
having   a sword   drew   it   and   smote

τὸν   τοῦ   ἀρχιερέως   δοῦλον   καὶ   ἀπέκοψεν
¹the   ³of the   ⁴high priest   ²slave   and   cut off

αὐτοῦ   τὸ   ὠτάριον   τὸ   δεξιόν·   ἦν   δὲ
of him   the   ²ear   –   ¹right;   and was

ὄνομα   τῷ   δούλῳ   Μάλχος.   **11** εἶπεν   οὖν
name   to the   slave⁶   Malchus.   Said therefore

ὁ   Ἰησοῦς   τῷ   Πέτρῳ·   βάλε   τὴν   μάχαιραν
–   Jesus   –   to Peter: Put   the   sword

εἰς   τὴν   θήκην·   τὸ   ποτήριον   ὃ   δέδωκέν
into   the   sheath;   the   cup   which   has given

μοι   ὁ   πατήρ,   οὐ   μὴ   πίω   αὐτό;
to me   the   Father,   by no means   shall I drink   it?

12 Ἡ   οὖν   σπεῖρα   καὶ   ὁ   χιλίαρχος
    Therefore the   band   and   the   chiliarch

soldiers and their captain and the officers of the Jews seized Jesus and bound him. [13] First they led him to Annas; for he was the father-in-law of Ca'iaphas, who was high priest that year. [14] It was Ca'iaphas who had given counsel to the Jews that it was expedient that one man should die for the people.

15 Simon Peter followed Jesus, and so did another disciple. As this disciple was known to the high priest, he entered the court of the high priest along with Jesus, [16] while Peter stood outside at the door. So the other disciple, who was known to the high priest, went out and spoke to the maid who kept the door, and brought Peter in. [17] The maid who kept the door said to Peter, "Are not you also one of this man's disciples?" He said, "I am not." [18] Now the servants and officers had made a charcoal fire, because it was cold, and they were standing and warming themselves; Peter also was with them, standing and warming himself.

19 The high priest then questioned Jesus

καὶ οἱ ὑπηρέται τῶν Ἰουδαίων συνέλαβον
and the attendants of the Jews took

τὸν Ἰησοῦν καὶ ἔδησαν αὐτόν, 13 καὶ
- Jesus and bound him, 13 and

ἤγαγον πρὸς Ἄνναν πρῶτον· ἦν γὰρ
led to Annas first; for he was

πενθερὸς τοῦ Καϊαφᾶ, ὃς ἦν ἀρχιερεὺς
father-in-law of Caiaphas, who was high priest

τοῦ ἐνιαυτοῦ ἐκείνου· 14 ἦν δὲ Καϊαφᾶς
- year of that; now it was Caiaphas

ὁ συμβουλεύσας τοῖς Ἰουδαίοις ὅτι
the [one] having advised the Jews that

συμφέρει ἕνα ἄνθρωπον ἀποθανεῖν ὑπὲρ
it is(was) expedient one man to die on behalf of

τοῦ λαοῦ. 15 Ἠκολούθει δὲ τῷ Ἰησοῦ
the people. And followed - Jesus

Σίμων Πέτρος καὶ ἄλλος μαθητής. ὁ δὲ
Simon Peter and another disciple. - And

μαθητὴς ἐκεῖνος ἦν γνωστὸς τῷ ἀρχιερεῖ,
disciple that was known to the high priest,

καὶ συνεισῆλθεν τῷ Ἰησοῦ εἰς τὴν αὐλὴν
and entered with - Jesus into the court

τοῦ ἀρχιερέως, 16 ὁ δὲ Πέτρος εἱστήκει
of the high priest, - but Peter stood

πρὸς τῇ θύρᾳ ἔξω. ἐξῆλθεν οὖν ὁ
at the door outside. Went out therefore the

μαθητὴς ὁ ἄλλος ὁ γνωστὸς τοῦ ἀρχιερέως
²disciple - ¹other - known of(to) the high priest

καὶ εἶπεν τῇ θυρωρῷ, καὶ εἰσήγαγεν
and told the portress, and brought in

τὸν Πέτρον. 17 λέγει οὖν τῷ Πέτρῳ ἡ
- Peter. Says therefore - to Peter the

παιδίσκη ἡ θυρωρός· μὴ καὶ σὺ ἐκ
maidservant the portress : Not also thou of

τῶν μαθητῶν εἶ τοῦ ἀνθρώπου τούτου;
the disciples art - man of this?

λέγει ἐκεῖνος· οὐκ εἰμί. 18 εἱστήκεισαν δὲ
Says that one : I am not. And stood

οἱ δοῦλοι καὶ οἱ ὑπηρέται ἀνθρακιὰν
the slaves and the attendants a fire

πεποιηκότες, ὅτι ψῦχος ἦν, καὶ
having made, because cold it was, and

ἐθερμαίνοντο· ἦν δὲ καὶ ὁ Πέτρος μετ᾽
were warming themselves; and was also - Peter with

αὐτῶν ἑστὼς καὶ θερμαινόμενος. 19 Ὁ
them standing and warming himself. - ¹The

οὖν ἀρχιερεὺς ἠρώτησεν τὸν Ἰησοῦν
²therefore ³high priest questioned - Jesus

about his disciples and
his teaching. ²⁰Jesus an-
swered him, "I have
spoken openly to the
world; I have always
taught in synagogues and
in the temple, where all
Jews come together; I
have said nothing
secretly. ²¹Why do you
ask me? Ask those who
have heard me, what I
said to them; they know
what I said." ²²When he
had said this, one of the
officers standing by
struck Jesus with his
hand, saying, "Is that
how you answer the high
priest?" ²³Jesus an-
swered him, "If I have
spoken wrongly, bear
witness to the wrong; but
if I have spoken rightly,
why do you strike me?"
²⁴Annas then sent him
bound to Ca'iaphas the
high priest.

25 Now Simon Peter
was standing and warm-
ing himself. They said to
him, "Are not you also
one of his disciples?" He
denied it and said, "I am
not." ²⁶One of the serv-
ants of the high priest,
a kinsman of the man
whose ear Peter had cut
off, asked, "Did I not
see you in the garden with
him?" ²⁷Peter again de-

περὶ   τῶν   μαθητῶν   αὐτοῦ   καὶ   περὶ   τῆς
about   the   disciples   of him   and   about   the

διδαχῆς   αὐτοῦ.   20 ἀπεκρίθη   αὐτῷ   Ἰησοῦς·
teaching   of him.   Answered   him   Jesus:

ἐγὼ   παρρησίᾳ   λελάληκα   τῷ   κόσμῳ·   ἐγὼ
I   with plainness   have spoken   to the   world;   I

πάντοτε   ἐδίδαξα   ἐν   συναγωγῇ   καὶ   ἐν
always   taught   in   a synagogue   and   in

τῷ   ἱερῷ,   ὅπου   πάντες   οἱ   Ἰουδαῖοι
the   temple,   where   all   the   Jews

συνέρχονται,   καὶ   ἐν   κρυπτῷ   ἐλάλησα
come together,   and   in   secret   I spoke

οὐδέν.   21 τί   με   ἐρωτᾷς;   ἐρώτησον
nothing.   Why   me   questionest thou?   question

τοὺς   ἀκηκοότας   τί   ἐλάλησα   αὐτοῖς·   ἴδε
the [ones] having heard   what   I spoke   to them;   behold[,]

οὗτοι   οἴδασιν   ἃ   εἶπον   ἐγώ.   22 ταῦτα
these   know   what things said   I.   These things

δὲ   αὐτοῦ   εἰπόντος   εἷς   παρεστηκὼς   τῶν
and   him   saying²   one   standing by   of the
=And as he said this

ὑπηρετῶν   ἔδωκεν   ῥάπισμα   τῷ   Ἰησοῦ
attendants   gave   a blow   -   to Jesus

εἰπών·   οὕτως   ἀποκρίνῃ   τῷ   ἀρχιερεῖ;
saying: Thus   answerest thou   the   high priest?

23 ἀπεκρίθη   αὐτῷ   Ἰησοῦς·   εἰ   κακῶς
Answered   him   Jesus: If   ill

ἐλάλησα,   μαρτύρησον   περὶ   τοῦ   κακοῦ·
I spoke,   witness   concerning   the   evil;

εἰ   δὲ   καλῶς,   τί   με   δέρεις;   24 ἀπέστειλεν
but if   well,   why   me beatest thou?   ²Sent

οὖν   αὐτὸν   ὁ   Ἄννας   δεδεμένον   πρὸς
³therefore   ⁴him   -   ¹Annas   having been bound   to

Καϊάφαν   τὸν   ἀρχιερέα.   25 Ἦν   δὲ   Σίμων
Caiaphas   the   high priest.   Now was   Simon

Πέτρος   ἑστὼς   καὶ   θερμαινόμενος.   εἶπον
Peter   standing   and   warming himself.   They said

οὖν   αὐτῷ·   μὴ   καὶ   σὺ   ἐκ   τῶν   μαθητῶν
therefore to him: Not   also   thou   of   the   disciples

αὐτοῦ   εἶ;   ἠρνήσατο   ἐκεῖνος   καὶ   εἶπεν·
of him   art?   Denied   that one   and   said:

οὐκ   εἰμί.   26 λέγει   εἷς   ἐκ   τῶν   δούλων   τοῦ
I am not.   Says   one   of   the   slaves   of the

ἀρχιερέως,   συγγενὴς   ὢν   οὗ   ἀπέκοψεν
high priest,   ³a relative   ¹being   ²[of him] of whom   ⁵cut off

Πέτρος   τὸ   ὠτίον·   οὐκ   ἐγώ   σε   εἶδον
⁴Peter   ⁶the   ⁷ear: ²Not   ¹I   ⁴thee   ¹saw

ἐν   τῷ   κήπῳ   μετ᾽   αὐτοῦ;   27 πάλιν   οὖν
in   the   garden   with   him?   Again   therefore

nied it; and at once the cock crowed.

28 Then they led Jesus from the house of Ca'iaphas to the praetorium. It was early. They themselves did not enter the praetorium, so that they might not be defiled, but might eat the passover. ²⁹ So Pilate went out to them and said, "What accusation do you bring against this man?" ³⁰ They answered him, "If this man were not an evildoer, we would not have handed him over." ³¹ Pilate said to them, "Take him yourselves and judge him by your own law." The Jews said to him, "It is not lawful for us to put any man to death." ³² This was to fulfil the word which Jesus had spoken to show by what death he was to die.

33 Pilate entered the praetorium again and called Jesus, and said to him, "Are you the King of the Jews?" ³⁴ Jesus answered, "Do you say this of your own accord, or did others say it to you about me?" ³⁵ Pilate answered, "Am I a Jew?"

ἠρνήσατο Πέτρος, καὶ εὐθέως ἀλέκτωρ
denied   Peter,   and immediately a cock
ἐφώνησεν.
sounded(crew).

28 Ἄγουσιν οὖν τὸν Ἰησοῦν ἀπὸ τοῦ
They lead therefore – Jesus   from   –
Καϊάφα εἰς τὸ πραιτώριον· ἦν δὲ πρωΐ·
Caiaphas to the praetorium; and it was early;
καὶ αὐτοὶ οὐκ εἰσῆλθον εἰς τὸ πραιτώριον,
and they entered not into the praetorium,
ἵνα μὴ μιανθῶσιν ἀλλὰ φάγωσιν τὸ
lest they should be defiled but might eat the
πάσχα. 29 ἐξῆλθεν οὖν ὁ Πιλᾶτος ἔξω
passover.   Went forth therefore – Pilate outside
πρὸς αὐτοὺς καὶ φησίν· τίνα κατηγορίαν
to   them and says : What accusation
φέρετε τοῦ ἀνθρώπου τούτου; 30 ἀπεκρίθησαν
bring ye –   man   of this?   They answered
καὶ εἶπαν αὐτῷ· εἰ μὴ ἦν
and said to him : Unless   was
οὗτος κακὸν ποιῶν, οὐκ ἄν σοι
this man evil doing, ¹would ²not ⁷to thee
παρεδώκαμεν αὐτόν. 31 εἶπεν οὖν αὐτοῖς
¹we ⁴have ⁵delivered ⁶him. Said therefore to them
ὁ Πιλᾶτος· λάβετε αὐτὸν ὑμεῖς, καὶ
– Pilate : Take him ye, and
κατὰ τὸν νόμον ὑμῶν κρίνατε αὐτόν.
according to the law of you judge ye him.
εἶπον αὐτῷ οἱ Ἰουδαῖοι· ἡμῖν οὐκ ἔξεστιν
Said to him the Jews : For us it is not lawful
ἀποκτεῖναι οὐδένα· 32 ἵνα ὁ λόγος τοῦ
to kill no(any)one; that the word –
Ἰησοῦ πληρωθῇ ὃν εἶπεν σημαίνων ποίῳ
of Jesus might be fulfilled which he said signifying by what
θανάτῳ ἤμελλεν ἀποθνήσκειν. 33 Εἰσῆλθεν
death he was about to die.   Entered
οὖν πάλιν εἰς τὸ πραιτώριον ὁ Πιλᾶτος
therefore again into the praetorium – Pilate
καὶ ἐφώνησεν τὸν Ἰησοῦν καὶ εἶπεν
and called – Jesus and said
αὐτῷ· σὺ εἶ ὁ βασιλεὺς τῶν Ἰουδαίων;
to him : Thou art the king of the Jews?
34 ἀπεκρίθη Ἰησοῦς· ἀφ' ἑαυτοῦ σὺ τοῦτο
Answered Jesus : From [thy]self ²thou ³this
λέγεις, ἢ ἄλλοι εἶπόν σοι περὶ ἐμοῦ;
¹sayest, or others told thee about me?
35 ἀπεκρίθη ὁ Πιλᾶτος· μήτι ἐγὼ
Answered – Pilate : not I

Your own nation and the chief priests have handed you over to me; what have you done?" ³⁶Jesus answered, "My kingship is not of this world; if my kingship were of this world, my servants would fight, that I might not be handed over to the Jews; but my kingship is not from the world." ³⁷Pilate said to him, "So you are a king?" Jesus answered, "You say that I am a king. For this I was born, and for this I have come into the world, to bear witness to the truth. Every one who is of the truth hears my voice." ³⁸Pilate said to him, "What is truth?"

After he had said this, he went out to the Jews again, and told them, "I find no crime in him. ³⁹But you have a custom that I should release one man for you at the Passover; will you have me release for you the King of the Jews?" ⁴⁰They cried out again, "Not this man, but Barab′bas!" Now Barab′bas was a robber.

'Ιουδαῖός   εἰμι;   τὸ   ἔθνος   τὸ   σὸν   καὶ
a Jew   am?   the   ¹nation   –   ¹thy   and

οἱ   ἀρχιερεῖς   παρέδωκάν   σε   ἐμοί·   τί
the   chief priests delivered   thee   to me;   what

ἐποίησας;   36 ἀπεκρίθη   'Ιησοῦς·   ἡ   βασιλεία
didst thou?   Answered   Jesus :   The ²kingdom

ἡ   ἐμὴ   οὐκ   ἔστιν   ἐκ   τοῦ   κόσμου   τούτου·
–   ¹my   is not   of   –   world   this;

εἰ   ἐκ   τοῦ   κόσμου   τούτου   ἦν   ἡ   βασιλεία
if   of   –   world   this   was   the   ²kingdom

ἡ   ἐμή,   οἱ   ὑπηρέται   ἂν   οἱ   ἐμοὶ   ἠγωνίζοντο,
–   ¹my,   the ²attendants ³would   –   ¹my ⁴have struggled,

ἵνα   μὴ   παραδοθῶ   τοῖς   'Ιουδαίοις·   νῦν
that   I should not be delivered   to the   Jews;   ²now

δὲ   ἡ   βασιλεία   ἡ   ἐμὴ   οὐκ   ἔστιν   ἐντεῦθεν.
¹but the   ²kingdom   –   ¹my   is not   hence.

37 εἶπεν   οὖν   αὐτῷ   ὁ   Πιλᾶτος·   οὐκοῦν
   Said   therefore to him –   Pilate :   Not really

βασιλεὺς   εἶ   σύ;   ἀπεκρίθη   [ὁ]   'Ιησοῦς·
a king   art thou?   Answered   –   Jesus :

σὺ   λέγεις   ὅτι   βασιλεύς   εἰμι.   ἐγὼ   εἰς
Thou sayest   that   a king   I am.   I   for

τοῦτο   γεγέννημαι   καὶ   εἰς   τοῦτο   ἐλήλυθα
this   have been born   and   for   this   I have come

εἰς   τὸν   κόσμον,   ἵνα   μαρτυρήσω   τῇ
into   the   world,   that   I might witness   to the

ἀληθείᾳ·   πᾶς   ὁ   ὢν   ἐκ   τῆς   ἀληθείας
truth;   everyone   being   of   the   truth

ἀκούει   μου   τῆς   φωνῆς.   38 λέγει   αὐτῷ
hears   of me   the   voice.   Says   to him

ὁ   Πιλᾶτος·   τί   ἐστιν   ἀλήθεια;   Καὶ
–   Pilate :   What   is   truth?   And

τοῦτο   εἰπὼν   πάλιν   ἐξῆλθεν   πρὸς   τοὺς
this   having said   again   he went forth   to   the

'Ιουδαίους,   καὶ   λέγει   αὐτοῖς·   ἐγὼ   οὐδεμίαν
Jews,   and   tells   them :   ¹I   ²no

εὑρίσκω   ἐν   αὐτῷ   αἰτίαν.   39 ἔστιν   δὲ
⁵find   ⁵in   ⁶him   ⁴crime.   But there is

συνήθεια   ὑμῖν   ἵνα   ἕνα   ἀπολύσω   ὑμῖν
a custom   to youᵉ   that   one   I should release to you

ἐν   τῷ   πάσχα·   βούλεσθε   οὖν   ἀπολύσω
at   the   Passover;   will ye   therefore [that] I release

ὑμῖν   τὸν   βασιλέα   τῶν   'Ιουδαίων;   40 ἐκραύ-
to you the   king   of the   Jews?   They cried

γασαν   οὖν   πάλιν   λέγοντες·   μὴ   τοῦτον,
out   therefore   again   saying :   Not   this man,

ἀλλὰ   τὸν   Βαραββᾶν.   ἦν   δὲ   ὁ   Βαραββᾶς
but   –   Barabbas   ¹But ³was   –   ²Barabbas

CHAPTER 19

THEN Pilate took Jesus and scourged him. ²And the soldiers plaited a crown of thorns, and put it on his head, and arrayed him in a purple robe; ³they came up to him, saying, "Hail, King of the Jews!" and struck him with their hands. ⁴Pilate went out again, and said to them, "Behold, I am bringing him out to you, that you may know that I find no crime in him." ⁵So Jesus came out, wearing the crown of thorns and the purple robe. Pilate said to them, "Here is the man!" ⁶When the chief priests and the officers saw him, they cried out, "Crucify him, crucify him!" Pilate said to them, "Take him yourselves and crucify him, for I find no crime in him." ⁷The Jews answered him, "We have a law, and by that law he ought to die, because he has made himself the Son of God." ⁸When Pilate heard these words, he was the more afraid; ⁹he entered the

ληστής.   19 Τότε οὖν ἔλαβεν ὁ Πιλᾶτος
⁴a robber.   Then therefore ⁵took - ¹Pilate
τὸν Ἰησοῦν καὶ ἐμαστίγωσεν. 2 καὶ οἱ
- ³Jesus and scourged [him].   And the
στρατιῶται πλέξαντες στέφανον ἐξ ἀκανθῶν
soldiers having plaited a wreath out of thorns
ἐπέθηκαν αὐτοῦ τῇ κεφαλῇ, καὶ ἱμάτιον
put [it] on of him the head, and ⁴garment
πορφυροῦν περιέβαλον αὐτόν, 3 καὶ ἤρχοντο
²a purple ¹threw round ³him, and came
πρὸς αὐτὸν καὶ ἔλεγον· χαῖρε ὁ βασιλεὺς
to him and said: Hail[,] - king
τῶν Ἰουδαίων· καὶ ἐδίδοσαν αὐτῷ
of the Jews; and they gave him
ῥαπίσματα. 4 Καὶ ἐξῆλθεν πάλιν ἔξω
blows.   And went forth again outside
ὁ Πιλᾶτος καὶ λέγει αὐτοῖς· ἴδε ἄγω
- Pilate and says to them: Behold ¹I bring
ὑμῖν αὐτὸν ἔξω, ἵνα γνῶτε ὅτι οὐδεμίαν
⁴to you ³him ⁵out, that ye may know that no
αἰτίαν εὑρίσκω ἐν αὐτῷ. 5 ἐξῆλθεν
crime I find in him.   Came forth
οὖν ὁ Ἰησοῦς ἔξω, φορῶν τὸν ἀκάνθινον
therefore - Jesus outside, wearing the thorny
στέφανον καὶ τὸ πορφυροῦν ἱμάτιον. καὶ
wreath and the purple garment. And
λέγει αὐτοῖς· ἰδοὺ ὁ ἄνθρωπος. 6 ὅτε
he says to them: Behold[,] the man.   When
οὖν εἶδον αὐτὸν οἱ ἀρχιερεῖς καὶ οἱ
therefore saw him the chief priests and the
ὑπηρέται, ἐκραύγασαν λέγοντες· σταύρωσον
attendants, they shouted saying : Crucify[,]
σταύρωσον. λέγει αὐτοῖς ὁ Πιλᾶτος·
crucify.   Says to them - Pilate :
λάβετε αὐτὸν ὑμεῖς καὶ σταυρώσατε·
¹Take ³him ²ye and crucify;
ἐγὼ γὰρ οὐχ εὑρίσκω ἐν αὐτῷ αἰτίαν.
for I find not in him crime.
7 ἀπεκρίθησαν αὐτῷ οἱ Ἰουδαῖοι· ἡμεῖς
Answered him the Jews : We
νόμον ἔχομεν, καὶ κατὰ τὸν νόμον
a law have, and according to the law
ὀφείλει ἀποθανεῖν, ὅτι υἱὸν θεοῦ ἑαυτὸν
he ought to die, because Son of God himself
ἐποίησεν. 8 Ὅτε οὖν ἤκουσεν ὁ Πιλᾶτος
he made.   When therefore heard - Pilate
τοῦτον τὸν λόγον, μᾶλλον ἐφοβήθη, 9 καὶ
this - word, more he was afraid, and

praetorium again and said to Jesus, "Where are you from?" But Jesus gave no answer. [10] Pilate therefore said to him, "You will not speak to me? Do you not know that I have power to release you, and power to crucify you?" [11] Jesus answered him, "You would have no power over me unless it had been given you from above; therefore he who delivered me to you has the greater sin."

[12] Upon this Pilate sought to release him, but the Jews cried out, "If you release this man, you are not Caesar's friend; every one who makes himself a king sets himself against Caesar." [13] When Pilate heard these words, he brought Jesus out and sat down on the judgment seat at a place called The Pavement, and in Hebrew, Gab'batha. [14] Now it was the day of Preparation of the Passover; it was about the sixth hour. He said to the Jews, "Here is your King!" [15] They cried out, "Away with him, away with him, crucify him!" Pilate said to them, "Shall I crucify your King?" The chief

εἰσῆλθεν   εἰς   τὸ   πραιτώριον   πάλιν   καὶ
entered   into   the   praetorium   again   and

λέγει   τῷ   'Ιησοῦ·   πόθεν   εἶ   σύ;   ὁ   δὲ
says   –   to Jesus :   Whence   art   thou?   –   But

'Ιησοῦς   ἀπόκρισιν   οὐκ   ἔδωκεν   αὐτῷ.
Jesus   answer   did not give   him.

10 λέγει   οὖν   αὐτῷ   ὁ   Πιλᾶτος·   ἐμοὶ
Says   therefore   to him   –   Pilate :   To me

οὐ   λαλεῖς;   οὐκ   οἶδας   ὅτι   ἐξουσίαν   ἔχω
speakest thou not?   knowest thou not   that   authority   I have

ἀπολῦσαί   σε   καὶ   ἐξουσίαν   ἔχω   σταυρῶσαί
to release   thee   and   authority   I have   to crucify

σε;   **11** ἀπεκρίθη   'Ιησοῦς·   οὐκ   εἶχες
thee?   Answered   Jesus :   Thou hadst not

ἐξουσίαν   κατ'   ἐμοῦ   οὐδεμίαν   εἰ   μὴ   ἦν
²authority   ³against   ⁴me   ¹no(any)   unless   it was

δεδομένον   σοι   ἄνωθεν·   διὰ   τοῦτο   ὁ
having been given   thee   from above;   therefore   the [one]

παραδούς   μέ   σοι   μείζονα   ἁμαρτίαν   ἔχει.
having delivered   me   to thee   a greater   sin   has.

12 ἐκ   τούτου   ὁ   Πιλᾶτος   ἐζήτει   ἀπολῦσαι
From   this   –   Pilate   sought   to release

αὐτόν·   οἱ   δὲ   'Ιουδαῖοι   ἐκραύγασαν   λέγοντες·
him;   but the   Jews   shouted   saying :

ἐὰν   τοῦτον   ἀπολύσῃς,   οὐκ   εἶ   φίλος   τοῦ
If   this man   thou releasest,   thou art not   a friend   –

Καίσαρος·   πᾶς   ὁ   βασιλέα   ἑαυτὸν   ποιῶν
of Cæsar;   everyone   a king   himself   making

ἀντιλέγει   τῷ   Καίσαρι.   **13** Ὁ   οὖν   Πιλᾶτος
speaks against   –   Cæsar.   –   Therefore   Pilate

ἀκούσας   τῶν   λόγων   τούτων   ἤγαγεν   ἔξω
hearing   –   words   these   brought   outside

τὸν   'Ιησοῦν,   καὶ   ἐκάθισεν   ἐπὶ   βήματος
–   Jesus,   and   sat   on   a tribunal

εἰς   τόπον   λεγόμενον   Λιθόστρωτον,   'Εβραϊστὶ   δὲ
in a place   being called   Pavement,   but in Hebrew

Γαββαθά.   **14** ἦν   δὲ   παρασκευὴ   τοῦ
Gabbatha.   Now it was   preparation   of the

πάσχα,   ὥρα   ἦν   ὡς   ἕκτη·   καὶ   λέγει
Passover,   hour   it was about   sixth;   and   he says

τοῖς   'Ιουδαίοις·   ἴδε   ὁ   βασιλεὺς   ὑμῶν.
to the   Jews;   Behold[,] the   king   of you.

15 ἐκραύγασαν   οὖν   ἐκεῖνοι·   ἆρον   ἆρον,
Shouted   therefore   those :   Take[,]   take,

σταύρωσον   αὐτόν.   λέγει   αὐτοῖς   ὁ   Πιλᾶτος·
crucify   him.   Says   to them   –   Pilate :

τὸν   βασιλέα   ὑμῶν   σταυρώσω;   ἀπεκρίθησαν
/The   king   of you   shall I crucify?   Answered

priests answered, "We have no king but Caesar." [16] Then he handed him over to them to be crucified.

17 So they took Jesus, and he went out, bearing his own cross, to the place called the place of a skull, which is called in Hebrew Gol'gotha. [18] There they crucified him, and with him two others, one on either side, and Jesus between them. [19] Pilate also wrote a title and put it on the cross; it read, "Jesus of Nazareth, the King of the Jews." [20] Many of the Jews read this title, for the place where Jesus was crucified was near the city; and it was written in Hebrew, in Latin, and in Greek. [21] The chief priests of the Jews then said to Pilate, "Do not write, 'The King of the Jews,' but, 'This man said, I am King of the Jews.'" [22] Pilate answered, "What I have written I have written."

23 When the soldiers had crucified Jesus they

οἱ   ἀρχιερεῖς·   οὐκ   ἔχομεν   βασιλέα   εἰ
the   chief priests :   We have not   a king   ex-

μὴ   Καίσαρα.   16 τότε   οὖν   παρέδωκεν
cept   Caesar.   Then therefore   he delivered

αὐτὸν   αὐτοῖς   ἵνα   σταυρωθῇ.
him   to them   that   he should be crucified.

Παρέλαβον   οὖν   τὸν   Ἰησοῦν·   17 καὶ
They took   therefore   –   Jesus ;   and

βαστάζων   ἑαυτῷ   τὸν   σταυρὸν   ἐξῆλθεν
carrying   ²to himself °   ²the   ²cross   he went forth

εἰς   τὸν   λεγόμενον   κρανίου   τόπον,   ὃ
to   ¹the   ²being called   ⁴of a skull   ²place,   which

λέγεται   Ἑβραϊστὶ   Γολγοθά,   18 ὅπου   αὐτὸν
is called   in Hebrew   Golgotha,   where   him

ἐσταύρωσαν,   καὶ   μετ'   αὐτοῦ   ἄλλους   δύο
they crucified,   and   with   him   others   two

ἐντεῦθεν   καὶ   ἐντεῦθεν,   μέσον   δὲ   τὸν
on this side and on that, †   and in the middle   –

Ἰησοῦν.   19 ἔγραψεν   δὲ   καὶ   τίτλον   ὁ
Jesus.   And wrote   also   a title   –

Πιλᾶτος   καὶ   ἔθηκεν   ἐπὶ   τοῦ   σταυροῦ·
Pilate   and   put [it]   on   the   cross ;

ἦν   δὲ   γεγραμμένον·   ΙΗΣΟΥΣ   Ο
and it was   having been written :   JESUS   THE

ΝΑΖΩΡΑΙΟΣ   Ο   ΒΑΣΙΛΕΥΣ   ΤΩΝ
NAZARENE   THE   KING   OF THE

ΙΟΥΔΑΙΩΝ.   20 τοῦτον   οὖν   τὸν   τίτλον
JEWS.   ¹This   ²therefore   –   ²title

πολλοὶ   ἀνέγνωσαν   τῶν   Ἰουδαίων,   ὅτι
¹many   ²read   ²of the   ²Jews,   because

ἐγγὺς   ἦν   ὁ   τόπος   τῆς   πόλεως   ὅπου
²near   ⁶was   ¹the   ²place   ²the   ²city   ²where

ἐσταυρώθη   ὁ   Ἰησοῦς·   καὶ   ἦν   γεγραμμένον
²was crucified   –   ²Jesus ;   and it was   having been written

Ἑβραϊστί,   Ῥωμαϊστί,   Ἑλληνιστί.   21 ἔλεγον
in Hebrew,   in Latin,   in Greek.   Said

οὖν   τῷ   Πιλάτῳ   οἱ   ἀρχιερεῖς   τῶν   Ἰουδαίων·
therefore –   to Pilate   the   chief priests of the   Jews :

μὴ   γράφε·   ὁ   βασιλεὺς   τῶν   Ἰουδαίων,
Write not :   The   king   of the   Jews,

ἀλλ'   ὅτι   ἐκεῖνος   εἶπεν·   βασιλεύς   εἰμι
but   that   that man   said :   King   I am

τῶν   Ἰουδαίων.   22 ἀπεκρίθη   ὁ   Πιλᾶτος·
of the   Jews.   Answered   –   Pilate :

ὃ   γέγραφα,   γέγραφα.   23 Οἱ   οὖν
What   I have written,   I have written.   Therefore the

στρατιῶται,   ὅτε   ἐσταύρωσαν   τὸν   Ἰησοῦν,
soldiers,   when   they crucified   –   Jesus,

took his garments and made four parts, one for each soldier; also his tunic. But the tunic was without seam, woven from top to bottom; ²⁴so they said to one another, "Let us not tear it, but cast lots for it to see whose it shall be." This was to fulfil the

"They parted my garments among them, and for my clothing they cast lots."

25 So the soldiers did this. But standing by the cross of Jesus were his mother, and his mother's sister, Mary the wife of Clopas, and Mary Mag'dalene. ²⁶When Jesus saw his mother, and the disciple whom he loved standing near, he said to his mother, "Woman, behold, your son!" ²⁷Then he said to the disciple, "Behold, your mother!" And from that hour the disciple took her to his own home.

28 After this Jesus, knowing that all was now finished, said (to fulfil the scripture), "I thirst." ²⁹A bowl full of vinegar stood there; so they put a sponge full of the vinegar on hyssop and

ἔλαβον τὰ ἱμάτια αὐτοῦ καὶ ἐποίησαν
took the garments of him and made
τέσσερα μέρη, ἑκάστῳ στρατιώτῃ μέρος,
four parts, to each soldier a part,
καὶ τὸν χιτῶνα. ἦν δὲ ὁ χιτὼν ἄρραφος,
and the tunic. Now was the tunic seamless,
ἐκ τῶν ἄνωθεν ὑφαντὸς δι' ὅλου. 24 εἶπαν
from the top woven throughout. They said
οὖν πρὸς ἀλλήλους· μὴ σχίσωμεν αὐτόν,
therefore to one another : Let us not tear it,
ἀλλὰ λάχωμεν περὶ αὐτοῦ τίνος ἔσται·
but let us cast lots about it of whom it shall be;
ἵνα ἡ γραφὴ πληρωθῇ· διεμερίσαντο τὰ
that the scripture might be fulfilled : They parted the
ἱμάτιά μου ἑαυτοῖς καὶ ἐπὶ τὸν ἱματισμόν
garments of me to themselves and over the raiment
μου ἔβαλον κλῆρον. Οἱ μὲν οὖν στρατιῶται
of me they cast a lot. *The –**therefore ⁴soldiers
ταῦτα ἐποίησαν. 25 εἱστήκεισαν δὲ παρὰ
¹these things did. ²there stood ¹But by
τῷ σταυρῷ τοῦ Ἰησοῦ ἡ μήτηρ αὐτοῦ
the cross – of Jesus the mother of him
καὶ ἡ ἀδελφὴ τῆς μητρὸς αὐτοῦ, Μαρία
and the sister of the mother of him, Mary
ἡ τοῦ Κλωπᾶ καὶ Μαρία ἡ Μαγδαληνή.
the [?wife] – of Clopas and Mary the Magdalene.
26 Ἰησοῦς οὖν ἰδὼν τὴν μητέρα καὶ
Jesus therefore seeing the(his) mother and
τὸν μαθητὴν παρεστῶτα ὃν ἠγάπα, λέγει
the disciple standing by whom he loved, says
τῇ μητρί· γύναι, ἴδε ὁ υἱός σου.
to the(his) mother : Woman, behold[,] the son of thee.
27 εἶτα λέγει τῷ μαθητῇ· ἴδε ἡ μήτηρ
Then he says to the disciple : Behold[,] the mother
σου. καὶ ἀπ' ἐκείνης τῆς ὥρας ἔλαβεν
of thee. And from that – hour took
ὁ μαθητὴς αὐτὴν εἰς τὰ ἴδια. 28 Μετὰ
the disciple her to his own [home]. † After
τοῦτο εἰδὼς ὁ Ἰησοῦς ὅτι ἤδη πάντα
this knowing – Jesus that now all things
τετέλεσται, ἵνα τελειωθῇ ἡ γραφή, λέγει·
have been finished, that might be fulfilled the scripture, says:
διψῶ. 29 σκεῦος ἔκειτο ὄξους μεστόν·
I thirst. A vessel was set of vinegar full;
σπόγγον οὖν μεστὸν τοῦ ὄξους ὑσσώπῳ
³a sponge therefore ⁴full ⁵of the ⁶vinegar ⁸a hyssop §

---

* μέν is scarcely translatable. But note the δέ in ver. 25 : John contrasts two groups—the soldiers and the women.

§ It has been suggested that ὑσσώπῳ is a graphic error for ὑσσῷ (pilum), pike; but cf. Mat. 27. 48.

held it to his mouth.
³⁰When Jesus had re-
ceived the vinegar, he
said, "It is finished";
and he bowed his head
and gave up his spirit.
  31 Since it was the
day of Preparation, in
order to prevent the
bodies from remaining
on the cross on the sab-
bath (for that sabbath
was a high day), the
Jews asked Pilate that
their legs might be
broken, and that they
might be taken away.
³²So the soldiers came
and broke the legs of the
first, and of the other
who had been crucified
with him; ³³but when
they came to Jesus and
saw that he was already
dead, they did not break
his legs. ³⁴But one of the
soldiers pierced his side
with a spear, and at once
there came out blood and
water. ³⁵He who saw it
has borne witness—his
testimony is true, and he
knows that he tells the
truth—that you also may
believe. ³⁶For these
things took place that
the scripture might be
fulfilled, "Not a bone of
him shall be broken."
³⁷And again another
scripture says, "They
shall look on him whom

περιθέντες προσήνεγκαν αὐτοῦ τῷ · στόματι.
²putting ⁷round they brought [it] to   of him   the   mouth.
30 ὅτε οὖν ἔλαβεν τὸ ὄξος [ὁ] Ἰησοῦς
When therefore took   the   vinegar   -   Jesus
εἶπεν· τετέλεσται, καὶ κλίνας τὴν κεφαλὴν
he said : It has been finished, and inclining the(his) head
παρέδωκεν τὸ πνεῦμα.
delivered up the(his) spirit.

  31 Οἱ οὖν Ἰουδαῖοι, ἐπεὶ παρασκευὴ
      The ²therefore ¹Jews,   since   preparation
ἦν, ἵνα μὴ μείνῃ ἐπὶ τοῦ σταυροῦ τὰ
it was, that might not remain on   the   cross   the
σώματα ἐν τῷ σαββάτῳ, ἦν γὰρ μεγάλη
bodies   on   the sabbath,   for was   great
ἡ ἡμέρα ἐκείνου τοῦ σαββάτου, ἠρώτησαν
the day   of that   -   sabbath,   they asked
τὸν Πιλᾶτον ἵνα κατεαγῶσιν αὐτῶν τὰ
   -   Pilate   that might be broken of them the
σκέλη καὶ ἀρθῶσιν. 32 ἦλθον οὖν οἱ
legs and they might be taken.   Came therefore the
στρατιῶται, καὶ τοῦ μὲν πρώτου κατέαξαν
soldiers,   and of the -*   first   broke
τὰ σκέλη καὶ τοῦ ἄλλου τοῦ
the legs   and   of the   other   -
συσταυρωθέντος αὐτῷ· 33 ἐπὶ δὲ τὸν
crucified with   him;   ³on ¹but   -
Ἰησοῦν ἐλθόντες, ὡς εἶδον ἤδη αὐτὸν
⁴Jesus ²coming,   when they saw already him
τεθνηκότα, οὐ κατέαξαν αὐτοῦ τὰ σκέλη,
to have died, they did not break of him   the legs,
34 ἀλλ' εἰς τῶν στρατιωτῶν λόγχῃ αὐτοῦ
but   one of the   soldiers   with a lance of him
τὴν πλευρὰν ἔνυξεν, καὶ ἐξῆλθεν εὐθὺς αἷμα
the   side   pricked, and there came imme-   blood
                                           diately
καὶ ὕδωρ. 35 καὶ ὁ ἑωρακὼς μεμαρτύρηκεν,
and water. And the [one] having seen has witnessed,
καὶ ἀληθινὴ αὐτοῦ ἐστιν ἡ μαρτυρία,
and   true   of him   is   the   witness,
καὶ ἐκεῖνος οἶδεν ὅτι ἀληθῆ λέγει, ἵνα
and that one knows that · truly he says, that
καὶ ὑμεῖς πιστεύητε. 36 ἐγένετο γὰρ
also   ye   may believe.   For happened
ταῦτα ἵνα ἡ γραφὴ πληρωθῇ· ὀστοῦν
these things that the scripture might be fulfilled : A bone
οὐ συντριβήσεται αὐτοῦ. 37 καὶ πάλιν
shall not be broken   of him.   And again
ἑτέρα γραφὴ λέγει· ὄψονται εἰς ὃν
another scripture says : They shall look at [him] whom

---

* See note on 19. 24. Here see ver. 33—two actions contrasted.

they have pierced."
38 After this Joseph
of Arimathe′a, who was
a disciple of Jesus, but
secretly, for fear of the
Jews, asked Pilate that
he might take away the
body of Jesus, and Pilate
gave him leave. So he
came and took away his
body. 39 Nicode′mus also,
who had at first come to
him by night, came
bringing a mixture of
myrrh and aloes, about a
hundred pounds' weight.
40 They took the body of
Jesus, and bound it in
linen cloths with the
spices, as is the burial
custom of the Jews.
41 Now in the place where
he was crucified there
was a garden, and in the
garden a new tomb where
no one had ever been
laid. 42 So because of the
Jewish day of Prepara-
tion, as the tomb was
close at hand, they laid
Jesus there.

ἐξεκέντησαν.   38 Μετὰ δὲ ταῦτα ἠρώτησεν
they pierced.   Now after these things   14asked
τὸν   Πιλᾶτον   Ἰωσὴφ   ἀπὸ   Ἀριμαθαίας,
     15Pilate   1Joseph   2from   3Arimathæa,
ὢν   μαθητὴς   [τοῦ]   Ἰησοῦ   κεκρυμμένος
4being 5a disciple   -   6of Jesus 8having been hidden
δὲ   διὰ   τὸν   φόβον   τῶν   Ἰουδαίων,   ἵνα
7but 9because 10the 11fear 12of the   13Jews,   that
        of
ἄρῃ   τὸ   σῶμα   τοῦ   Ἰησοῦ·   καὶ
he might take the   body   of   Jesus;   and
ἐπέτρεψεν ὁ Πιλᾶτος.   ἦλθεν οὖν καὶ ἦρεν
allowed   -   Pilate.   He came there- and took
                                    fore
τὸ σῶμα αὐτοῦ.   39 ἦλθεν δὲ καὶ Νικόδημος,
the body of him.   And came also Nicodemus,
ὁ   ἐλθὼν   πρὸς αὐτὸν νυκτὸς τὸ πρῶτον,
the [one] having come to   him of(by) night   at first,†
φέρων   μίγμα   σμύρνης   καὶ   ἀλόης   ὡς
bearing a mixture of myrrh   and   aloes   about
λίτρας   ἑκατόν.   40 ἔλαβον   οὖν   τὸ   σῶμα
pounds   a hundred.   They took there-   the   body
                                  fore
τοῦ   Ἰησοῦ   καὶ   ἔδησαν   αὐτὸ   ὀθονίοις
 -    of Jesus   and   bound   it   in sheets
μετὰ   τῶν   ἀρωμάτων,   καθὼς   ἔθος   ἐστὶν
with   the   spices,   as   custom   is
τοῖς   Ἰουδαίοις   ἐνταφιάζειν.   41 ἦν   δὲ
with the Jews   to bury.   Now there was
ἐν   τῷ   τόπῳ   ὅπου   ἐσταυρώθη   κῆπος,
in   the   place   where   he was crucified a garden,
καὶ   ἐν   τῷ   κήπῳ   μνημεῖον   καινόν,   ἐν
and   in   the   garden   tomb   a new,   in
ᾧ   οὐδέπω οὐδεὶς ἦν τεθειμένος·   42 ἐκεῖ
which never yet no(any) was having been put;   there
                        one
οὖν   διὰ   τὴν   παρασκευὴν   τῶν   Ἰουδαίων,
therefore because of the   preparation   of the   Jews,
ὅτι   ἐγγὺς   ἦν   τὸ   μνημεῖον,   ἔθηκαν   τὸν
because near   was the   tomb,   they put   -
Ἰησοῦν.
Jesus.

CHAPTER 20

N OW on the first day
of the week Mary
Mag′dalene came to the
tomb early, while it was
still dark, and saw that

20 Τῇ   δὲ   μιᾷ   τῶν σαββάτων Μαρία
   Now on the one(first) [day] of the   week   Mary
ἡ   Μαγδαληνὴ   ἔρχεται   πρωὶ   σκοτίας   ἔτι
the Magdalene   comes   early   darkness   yet
                                   =while it was yet dark
οὔσης   εἰς   τὸ   μνημεῖον,   καὶ   βλέπει   τὸν
being*   to   the   tomb,   and   sees   the

the stone had been taken away from the tomb. ²So she ran, and went to Simon Peter and the other disciple, the one whom Jesus loved, and said to them, "They have taken the Lord out of the tomb, and we do not know where they have laid him." ³Peter then came out with the other disciple, and they went toward the tomb. ⁴They both ran, but the other disciple outran Peter and reached the tomb first; ⁵and stooping to look in, he saw the linen cloths lying there, but he did not go in. ⁶Then Simon Peter came, following him, and went into the tomb; he saw the linen cloths lying, ⁷and the napkin, which had been on his head, not lying with the linen cloths but rolled up in a place by itself. ⁸Then the other disciple, who reached the tomb first, also went in, and he saw and believed; ⁹for as yet they did not know the scripture, that he must rise from the dead. ¹⁰Then the disciples went back to their homes.

λίθον   ἠρμένον   ἐκ   τοῦ   μνημείου.
stone   having been taken   out of   the   tomb.

2 τρέχει   οὖν   καὶ   ἔρχεται   πρὸς   Σίμωνα
She runs   therefore and   comes   to   Simon

Πέτρον   καὶ   πρὸς   τὸν   ἄλλον   μαθητὴν   ὃν
Peter   and   to   the   other   disciple   whom

ἐφίλει   ὁ   Ἰησοῦς,   καὶ   λέγει   αὐτοῖς·   ἦραν
²loved —   ¹Jesus,   and   says   to them :   They took

τὸν κύριον ἐκ τοῦ μνημείου, καὶ οὐκ οἴδαμεν
the   Lord out of   the   tomb,   and   we do not know

ποῦ   ἔθηκαν   αὐτόν.   3 Ἐξῆλθεν   οὖν   ὁ
where   they put   him.   Went forth   therefore –

Πέτρος   καὶ   ὁ   ἄλλος   μαθητής,   καὶ   ἤρχοντο
Peter   and   the   other   disciple,   and   came

εἰς   τὸ   μνημεῖον.   4 ἔτρεχον   δὲ   οἱ   δύο
to   the   tomb.   And ran   the   two

ὁμοῦ·   καὶ   ὁ   ἄλλος   μαθητὴς   προέδραμεν
together;   and   the   other   disciple   ran before

τάχιον   τοῦ   Πέτρου   καὶ   ἦλθεν   πρῶτος
more quickly [than] –   Peter   and   came   first

εἰς   τὸ   μνημεῖον,   5 καὶ   παρακύψας   βλέπει
to   the   tomb,   and   stooping   sees

κείμενα   τὰ   ὀθόνια,   οὐ   μέντοι   εἰσῆλθεν.
lying   the   sheets,   not   however   he entered.

6 ἔρχεται   οὖν   καὶ   Σίμων   Πέτρος   ἀκο-
Comes   therefore also   Simon   Peter   follow-

λουθῶν   αὐτῷ,   καὶ   εἰσῆλθεν   εἰς   τὸ
ing   him,   and   entered   into the

μνημεῖον·   καὶ   θεωρεῖ   τὰ   ὀθόνια   κείμενα,
tomb;   and   he beholds   the   sheets   lying,

7 καὶ   τὸ   σουδάριον,   ὃ   ἦν   ἐπὶ   τῆς
and   the   kerchief,   which was   on   the

κεφαλῆς   αὐτοῦ,   οὐ   μετὰ   τῶν   ὀθονίων
head   of him,   not   with   the   sheets

κείμενον   ἀλλὰ   χωρὶς   ἐντετυλιγμένον   εἰς
lying   but   apart   having been wrapped up   in

ἕνα   τόπον.   8 τότε   οὖν   εἰσῆλθεν   καὶ
one   place.   Then   therefore   entered   also

ὁ   ἄλλος   μαθητὴς   ὁ   ἐλθὼν   πρῶτος   εἰς
the   other   disciple   –   having come   first   to

τὸ   μνημεῖον,   καὶ   εἶδεν   καὶ   ἐπίστευσεν·
the   tomb,   and   he saw   and   believed;

9 οὐδέπω   γὰρ   ᾔδεισαν   τὴν   γραφήν,   ὅτι
for not yet   they knew   the   scripture,   that

δεῖ   αὐτὸν   ἐκ   νεκρῶν   ἀναστῆναι.
it behoves   him   from [the]   dead   to rise again.

10 ἀπῆλθον   οὖν   πάλιν   πρὸς   αὐτοὺς   οἱ
Went away   therefore   again   to   themselves*   the

* That is, to their own home; cf. 19. 27.

11 But Mary stood weeping outside the tomb, and as she wept she stooped to look into the tomb; ¹²and she saw two angels in white, sitting where the body of Jesus had lain, one at the head and one at the feet. ¹³They said to her, "Woman, why are you weeping?" She said to them, "Because they have taken away my Lord, and I do not know where they have laid him." ¹⁴Saying this, she turned round and saw Jesus standing, but she did not know that it was Jesus. ¹⁵Jesus said to her, "Woman, why are you weeping? Whom do you seek?" Supposing him to be the gardener, she said to him, "Sir, if you have carried him away, tell me where you have laid him, and I will take him away." ¹⁶Jesus said to her, "Mary." She turned and said to him in Hebrew, "Rab-bo'ni!" (which means Teacher). ¹⁷Jesus said to her, "Do not hold me, for I have not yet ascended to the Father; but go to my brethren and say to them, I am ascending to my Father and your Father,

μαθηταί. 11 Μαρία δὲ εἱστήκει πρὸς
disciples.   But Mary   stood   at

τῷ μνημείῳ ἔξω κλαίουσα. ὡς οὖν
the tomb   outside weeping. As therefore

ἔκλαιεν, παρέκυψεν εἰς τὸ μνημεῖον,
she was weeping, she stooped into the tomb,

12 καὶ θεωρεῖ δύο ἀγγέλους ἐν λευκοῖς
and beholds two   angels   in white

καθεζομένους, ἕνα πρὸς τῇ κεφαλῇ καὶ
sitting,   one at the head and

ἕνα πρὸς τοῖς ποσίν, ὅπου ἔκειτο τὸ
one at the feet, where lay the

σῶμα τοῦ Ἰησοῦ. 13 καὶ λέγουσιν αὐτῇ
body - of Jesus. And say to her

ἐκεῖνοι· γύναι, τί κλαίεις; λέγει αὐτοῖς
those: Woman, why weepest thou? She says to them[,]

ὅτι ἦραν τὸν κύριόν μου, καὶ οὐκ οἶδα
- They took the Lord of me, and I know not

ποῦ ἔθηκαν αὐτόν. 14 ταῦτα εἰποῦσα
where they put him. These things saying

ἐστράφη εἰς τὰ ὀπίσω, καὶ θεωρεῖ τὸν
she turned back,† and beholds -

Ἰησοῦν ἑστῶτα, καὶ οὐκ ᾔδει ὅτι Ἰησοῦς
Jesus standing, and knew not that Jesus

ἐστιν. 15 λέγει αὐτῇ Ἰησοῦς· γύναι,
it is(was). Says to her Jesus: Woman,

τί κλαίεις; τίνα ζητεῖς; ἐκείνη δοκοῦσα
why weepest thou? whom seekest thou? That one thinking

ὅτι ὁ κηπουρός ἐστιν, λέγει αὐτῷ· κύριε,
that the gardener is(was), says to him: Sir,

εἰ σὺ ἐβάστασας αὐτόν, εἰπέ μοι ποῦ
if thou didst carry him, tell me where

ἔθηκας αὐτόν, κἀγὼ αὐτὸν ἀρῶ. 16 λέγει
thou didst put him, and I him will take. Says

αὐτῇ Ἰησοῦς· Μαριάμ. στραφεῖσα ἐκείνη
to her Jesus: Mary. Turning that one

λέγει αὐτῷ Ἑβραϊστί· ῥαββουνί (ὃ λέγεται
says to him in Hebrew: Rabboni (which is said

διδάσκαλε). 17 λέγει αὐτῇ Ἰησοῦς· μή
Teacher). Says to her Jesus: Not

μου ἅπτου, οὔπω γὰρ ἀναβέβηκα πρὸς
me touch, for not yet have I ascended to

τὸν πατέρα· πορεύου δὲ πρὸς τοὺς
the Father; but go thou to the

ἀδελφούς μου καὶ εἰπέ αὐτοῖς· ἀναβαίνω
brothers of me and tell them: I ascend

πρὸς τὸν πατέρα μου καὶ πατέρα ὑμῶν
to the Father of me and Father of you

to my God and your God." [18] Mary Magdalene went and said to the disciples, "I have seen the Lord"; and she told them that he had said these things to her.

19 On the evening of that day, the first day of the week, the doors being shut where the disciples were, for fear of the Jews, Jesus came and stood among them and said to them, "Peace be with you." [20] When he had said this, he showed them his hands and his side. Then the disciples were glad when they saw the Lord. [21] Jesus said to them again, "Peace be with you. As the Father has sent me, even so I send you." [22] And when he had said this, he breathed on them, and said to them, "Receive the Holy Spirit. [23] If you forgive the sins of any, they are forgiven; if you retain the sins of any, they are retained."

24 Now Thomas, one of the twelve, called the Twin, was not with them when Jesus came. [25] So the other disciples told him, "We have seen the

καὶ   θεόν   μου   καὶ   θεὸν   ὑμῶν.   18 ἔρχεται
and   God   of me   and   God   of you.   Comes

Μαριὰμ   ἡ   Μαγδαληνὴ   ἀγγέλλουσα   τοῖς
Mary   the   Magdalene   announcing   to the

μαθηταῖς   ὅτι   ἑώρακα   τὸν   κύριον,   καὶ
disciples[,]   –   I have seen   the   Lord,   and

ταῦτα   εἶπεν   αὐτῇ.
these things   he said   to her.

19 Οὔσης   οὖν   ὀψίας   τῇ   ἡμέρᾳ   ἐκείνῃ
Being   therefore   early evening[a]   –   day   on that
=Therefore when it was early evening

τῇ   μιᾷ   σαββάτων,   καὶ   τῶν   θυρῶν
the   one(first)   of the week,   and   the   doors

κεκλεισμένων   ὅπου   ἦσαν   οἱ   μαθηταὶ   διὰ
having been shut[a]   where   were   the   disciples   because of

τὸν   φόβον   τῶν   Ἰουδαίων,   ἦλθεν   ὁ   Ἰησοῦς
the   fear   of the   Jews,   came   –   Jesus

καὶ   ἔστη   εἰς   τὸ   μέσον,   καὶ   λέγει   αὐτοῖς·
and   stood   in   the   midst,   and   says   to them :

εἰρήνη   ὑμῖν.   20 καὶ   τοῦτο   εἰπὼν   ἔδειξεν
Peace   to you.   And   this   saying   he showed

καὶ   τὰς   χεῖρας   καὶ   τὴν   πλευρὰν   αὐτοῖς.
both   the(his)   hands   and   the(his)   side   to them.

ἐχάρησαν   οὖν   οἱ   μαθηταὶ   ἰδόντες   τὸν
Rejoiced   therefore   the   disciples   seeing   the

κύριον.   21 εἶπεν   οὖν   αὐτοῖς   [ὁ   Ἰησοῦς]
Lord.   Said   therefore   to them   –   Jesus

πάλιν·   εἰρήνη   ὑμῖν·   καθὼς   ἀπέσταλκέν
again :   Peace   to you;   as   has sent

με   ὁ   πατήρ,   κἀγὼ   πέμπω   ὑμᾶς.   22 καὶ
me   the   Father,   I also   send   you.   And

τοῦτο   εἰπὼν   ἐνεφύσησεν   καὶ   λέγει   αὐτοῖς·
this   saying   he breathed in   and   says   to them :

λάβετε   πνεῦμα   ἅγιον.   23 ἄν   τινων
Receive ye   Spirit   Holy.   Of whomever

ἀφῆτε   τὰς   ἁμαρτίας,   ἀφέωνται   αὐτοῖς·
ye forgive   the   sins,   they have been   to them;
                              forgiven

ἄν   τινων   κρατῆτε,   κεκράτηνται.
of whomever   ye hold,   they have been held.

24 Θωμᾶς   δὲ   εἷς   ἐκ   τῶν   δώδεκα,
But Thomas   one   of   the   twelve,

ὁ   λεγόμενος   Δίδυμος,   οὐκ   ἦν   μετ᾽   αὐτῶν
–   being called   Twin,   was not   with   them

ὅτε   ἦλθεν   Ἰησοῦς.   25 ἔλεγον   οὖν   αὐτῷ
when   came   Jesus.   Said   therefore   to him

οἱ   ἄλλοι   μαθηταί·   ἑωράκαμεν   τὸν   κύριον.
the   other   disciples :   We have seen   the   Lord.

Lord." But he said to them, "Unless I see in his hands the print of the nails, and place my finger in the mark of the nails, and place my hand in his side, I will not believe."

26 Eight days later, his disciples were again in the house, and Thomas was with them. The doors were shut, but Jesus came and stood among them, and said, "Peace be with you." ²⁷ Then he said to Thomas, "Put your finger here, and see my hands; and put out your hand, and place it in my side; do not be faithless, but believing." ²⁸ Thomas answered him, "My Lord and my God!" ²⁹ Jesus said to him, "Have you believed because you have seen me? Blessed are those who have not seen and yet believe."

30 Now Jesus did many others signs in the presence of the disciples, which are not written in this book; ³¹ but these are written that you may believe that Jesus is the

ὁ δὲ εἶπεν αὐτοῖς· ἐὰν μὴ ἴδω ἐν
But he said to them: Unless I see in

ταῖς χερσὶν αὐτοῦ τὸν τύπον τῶν ἥλων
the hands of him the mark of the nails

καὶ βάλω τὸν δάκτυλόν μου εἰς τὸν
and put the finger of me into the

τόπον τῶν ἥλων καὶ βάλω μου τὴν
place of the nails and put of me the

χεῖρα εἰς τὴν πλευρὰν αὐτοῦ, οὐ μὴ
hand into the side of him, by no means

πιστεύσω. 26 Καὶ μεθ' ἡμέρας ὀκτὼ
will I believe. And after days eight

πάλιν ἦσαν ἔσω οἱ μαθηταὶ αὐτοῦ, καὶ
again were within the disciples of him, and

Θωμᾶς μετ' αὐτῶν. ἔρχεται ὁ Ἰησοῦς
Thomas with them. Comes - Jesus

τῶν θυρῶν κεκλεισμένων, καὶ ἔστη εἰς
the doors having been shut*, and stood in

τὸ μέσον καὶ εἶπεν· εἰρήνη ὑμῖν. 27 εἶτα
the midst and said: Peace to you. Then

λέγει τῷ Θωμᾷ· φέρε τὸν δάκτυλόν
he says - to Thomas: Bring the finger

σου ὧδε καὶ ἴδε τὰς χεῖράς μου, καὶ
of thee here and see the hands of me, and

φέρε τὴν χεῖρά σου καὶ βάλε εἰς τὴν
bring the hand of thee and put into the

πλευράν μου, καὶ μὴ γίνου ἄπιστος
side of me, and be not faithless

ἀλλὰ πιστός. 28 ἀπεκρίθη Θωμᾶς καὶ
but faithful. Answered Thomas and

εἶπεν αὐτῷ· ὁ κύριός μου καὶ ὁ θεός
said to him: The Lord of me and the God

μου. 29 λέγει αὐτῷ ὁ Ἰησοῦς· ὅτι
of me. Says to him - Jesus: Because

ἑώρακάς με, πεπίστευκας; μακάριοι οἱ
thou hast seen me, hast thou believed? blessed the [ones]

μὴ ἰδόντες καὶ πιστεύσαντες.
not seeing and§ believing.

30 Πολλὰ μὲν οὖν καὶ ἄλλα σημεῖα
Many -* therefore and other signs

ἐποίησεν ὁ Ἰησοῦς ἐνώπιον τῶν μαθητῶν,
did - Jesus before the disciples,

ἃ οὐκ ἔστιν γεγραμμένα ἐν τῷ βιβλίῳ
which is(are) not having been written in - roll

τούτῳ· 31 ταῦτα δὲ γέγραπται ἵνα
this; but these* has(ve) been written that

πιστεύητε ὅτι Ἰησοῦς ἐστιν ὁ χριστὸς ὁ
ye may believe that Jesus is the Christ the

* See note on 19. 24 and 32.

§ καὶ sometimes = and yet; see 5. 40; 8. 55; 9. 30; 16. 32; 17. 11.

Christ, the Son of God, | υἱὸς τοῦ θεοῦ, καὶ ἵνα πιστεύοντες ζωὴν
and that believing you | Son - of God, and that believing life
may have life in his | ἔχητε ἐν τῷ ὀνόματι αὐτοῦ.
name. | ye may have in the name of him.

CHAPTER 21

AFTER this Jesus revealed himself again to the disciples by the Sea of Tibe′ri-as; and he revealed himself in this way. [2]Simon Peter, Thomas called the Twin, Nathan′a-el of Cana in Galilee, the sons of Zeb′edee, and two others of his disciples were together. [3]Simon Peter said to them, "I am going fishing." They said to him, "We will go with you." They went out and got into the boat; but that night they caught nothing.

[4] Just as day was breaking, Jesus stood on the beach; yet the disciples did not know it was Jesus. [5]Jesus said to them, "Children, have you any fish?" They answered him, "No." [6]He said to them, "Cast the net on the right side of the boat, and you will find some." So they cast it, and now they were not able to haul it in, for the quantity of fish. [7]That disciple

21 Μετὰ ταῦτα ἐφανέρωσεν ἑαυτὸν πάλιν
After these things manifested himself again
ʼΙησοῦς τοῖς μαθηταῖς ἐπὶ τῆς θαλάσσης
Jesus to the disciples on the sea
τῆς Τιβεριάδος· ἐφανέρωσεν δὲ οὕτως.
- of Tiberias; and he manifested [himself] thus.
2 ἦσαν ὁμοῦ Σίμων Πέτρος καὶ Θωμᾶς
There were together Simon Peter and Thomas
ὁ λεγόμενος Δίδυμος καὶ Ναθαναὴλ ὁ
- being called Twin and Nathanael -
ἀπὸ Κανὰ τῆς Γαλιλαίας καὶ οἱ τοῦ
from Cana of Galilee and the [sons] -
Ζεβεδαίου καὶ ἄλλοι ἐκ τῶν μαθητῶν
of Zebedee and others of the disciples
αὐτοῦ δύο. **3** λέγει αὐτοῖς Σίμων Πέτρος·
of him two. Says to them Simon Peter :
ὑπάγω ἁλιεύειν. λέγουσιν αὐτῷ· ἐρχόμεθα
I am going to fish. They say to him : Are coming
καὶ ἡμεῖς σὺν σοί. ἐξῆλθον καὶ ἐνέβησαν
also we with thee. They went forth and embarked
εἰς τὸ πλοῖον, καὶ ἐν ἐκείνῃ τῇ νυκτὶ
in the boat, and in that - night
ἐπίασαν οὐδέν. **4** πρωΐας δὲ ἤδη γινομένης⁴
they caught nothing. Early morning but now becoming⁴
= But when it became early morning
ἔστη ʼΙησοῦς εἰς τὸν αἰγιαλόν· οὐ μέντοι
stood Jesus in(on) the shore; not however
ᾔδεισαν οἱ μαθηταὶ ὅτι ʼΙησοῦς ἐστιν.
knew the disciples that Jesus it is(was).
5 λέγει οὖν αὐτοῖς ʼΙησοῦς· παιδία, μή
Says therefore to them Jesus : Children, not
τι προσφάγιον ἔχετε; ἀπεκρίθησαν αὐτῷ·
any fish have ye? They answered him :
οὔ. **6** ὁ δὲ εἶπεν αὐτοῖς· βάλετε εἰς τὰ
No. So he said to them : Cast in the
δεξιὰ μέρη τοῦ πλοίου τὸ δίκτυον, καὶ
right parts of the boat the net, and
εὑρήσετε. ἔβαλον οὖν, καὶ οὐκέτι αὐτὸ
ye will find. They cast therefore, and ¹no longer ⁴it
ἑλκύσαι ἴσχυον ἀπὸ τοῦ πλήθους τῶν
²to drag ²were they able from the multitude of the
ἰχθύων. **7** λέγει οὖν ὁ μαθητὴς ἐκεῖνος
fishes. Says therefore - disciple that

whom Jesus loved said to Peter, "It is the Lord!" When Simon Peter heard that it was the Lord, he put on his clothes, for he was stripped for work, and sprang into the sea. ⁸But the other disciples came in the boat, dragging the net full of fish, for they were not far from the land, but about a hundred yards off.

9 When they got out on land, they saw a charcoal fire there, with fish lying on it, and bread. ¹⁰Jesus said to them, "Bring some of the fish that you have just caught." ¹¹So Simon Peter went aboard and hauled the net ashore, full of large fish, a hundred and fifty-three of them; and although there were so many, the net was not torn. ¹²Jesus said to them, "Come and have breakfast." Now none of the disciples dared ask him, "Who are you?" They knew it was the Lord. ¹³Jesus came and took the bread and gave it to them, and so with the fish. ¹⁴This was now the third time that Jesus was revealed to the disciples after he was raised from the dead.

ὃν ἠγάπα ὁ Ἰησοῦς τῷ Πέτρῳ· ὁ κύριός
whom ²loved – ¹Jesus – to Peter: The Lord

ἐστιν. Σίμων οὖν Πέτρος, ἀκούσας ὅτι
it is. ²Simon ¹therefore ²Peter, hearing that

ὁ κύριός ἐστιν, τὸν ἐπενδύτην διεζώσατο,
the Lord it is(was), ²[with]the ²coat ¹girded himself,

ἦν γὰρ γυμνός, καὶ ἔβαλεν ἑαυτὸν εἰς
for he was naked, and threw himself into

τὴν θάλασσαν· 8 οἱ δὲ ἄλλοι μαθηταὶ
the sea; but the other disciples

τῷ πλοιαρίῳ ἦλθον, οὐ γὰρ ἦσαν μακρὰν
in the little boat came, for not they were far

ἀπὸ τῆς γῆς ἀλλὰ ὡς ἀπὸ πηχῶν
from the land but about from cubits

διακοσίων, σύροντες τὸ δίκτυον τῶν ἰχθύων.
two hundred dragging the net of the fishes.

9 ὡς οὖν ἀπέβησαν εἰς τὴν γῆν, βλέπουσιν
When therefore they disembarked onto the land, they see

ἀνθρακιὰν κειμένην καὶ ὀψάριον ἐπικείμενον
a coal fire lying and a fish lying on

καὶ ἄρτον. 10 λέγει αὐτοῖς ὁ Ἰησοῦς·
and bread. Says to them – Jesus:

ἐνέγκατε ἀπὸ τῶν ὀψαρίων ὧν ἐπιάσατε
Bring from the fishes which ye caught

νῦν. 11 ἀνέβη Σίμων Πέτρος καὶ εἵλκυσεν
now. Went up Simon Peter and dragged

τὸ δίκτυον εἰς τὴν γῆν μεστὸν ἰχθύων
the net to the land full fishes

μεγάλων ἑκατὸν πεντήκοντα τριῶν· καὶ
of great a hundred fifty three; and

τοσούτων ὄντων οὐκ ἐσχίσθη τὸ δίκτυον.
so many being was not torn the net.

12 λέγει αὐτοῖς ὁ Ἰησοῦς· δεῦτε ἀριστήσατε.
Says to them – Jesus: Come breakfast ye.

οὐδεὶς ἐτόλμα τῶν μαθητῶν ἐξετάσαι
No one dared of the disciples to question

αὐτόν· σὺ τίς εἶ; εἰδότες ὅτι ὁ κύριός
him: Thou who art? knowing that the Lord

ἐστιν. 13 ἔρχεται Ἰησοῦς καὶ λαμβάνει
it is(was). Comes Jesus and takes

τὸν ἄρτον καὶ δίδωσιν αὐτοῖς, καὶ τὸ
the bread and gives to them, and the

ὀψάριον ὁμοίως. 14 τοῦτο ἤδη τρίτον
fish likewise. This [was] now [the] third [time] [that]

ἐφανερώθη Ἰησοῦς τοῖς μαθηταῖς ἐγερθεὶς
²was manifested ¹Jesus to the disciples raised

ἐκ νεκρῶν.
from [the] dead.

15 When they had finished breakfast, Jesus said to Simon Peter, "Simon, son of John, do you love me more than these?" He said to him, "Yes, Lord; you know that I love you." He said to him, "Feed my lambs." [16]A second time he said to him, "Simon, son of John, do you love me?" He said to him, "Yes, Lord; you know that I love you." He said to him, "Tend my sheep." [17]He said to him the third time, "Simon, son of John, do you love me?" Peter was grieved because he said to him the third time, "Do you love me?" And he said to him, "Lord, you know everything; you know that I love you." Jesus said to him, "Feed my sheep. [18]Truly, truly, I say to you, when you were young, you girded yourself and walked where you would; but when you are old, you will stretch out your hands, and another will gird you and carry you where you do not wish to go." [19](This he said to show by what death he was to glorify God.) And after this he said to him, "Follow me."

20 Peter turned and saw following them the disciple whom Jesus loved, who had lain close

15 Ὅτε οὖν ἠρίστησαν, λέγει τῷ
When therefore they breakfasted, says –

Σίμωνι Πέτρῳ ὁ Ἰησοῦς· Σίμων Ἰωάννου,
to Simon Peter – Jesus : Simon [son] of John,

ἀγαπᾷς με πλέον τούτων; λέγει αὐτῷ·
lovest thou me more [than] these? He says to him :

ναί, κύριε, σὺ οἶδας ὅτι φιλῶ σε. λέγει
Yes, Lord, thou knowest that I love thee. He says

αὐτῷ· βόσκε τὰ ἀρνία μου. 16 λέγει
to him : Feed the lambs of me. He says

αὐτῷ πάλιν δεύτερον· Σίμων Ἰωάννου,
to him again secondly: Simon [son] of John,

ἀγαπᾷς με; λέγει αὐτῷ· ναί, κύριε,
lovest thou me? He says to him : Yes, Lord,

σὺ οἶδας ὅτι φιλῶ σε. λέγει αὐτῷ·
thou knowest that I love thee. He says to him:

ποίμαινε τὰ προβάτιά μου. 17 λέγει
Shepherd the little sheep of me. He says

αὐτῷ τὸ τρίτον· Σίμων Ἰωάννου, φιλεῖς
to him the third [time]: Simon [son] of John, lovest thou

με; ἐλυπήθη ὁ Πέτρος ὅτι εἶπεν αὐτῷ
me? Was grieved – Peter that he said to him

τὸ τρίτον· φιλεῖς με; καὶ εἶπεν αὐτῷ·
the third [time]: Lovest thou me? and said to him :

κύριε, πάντα σὺ οἶδας, σὺ γινώσκεις
Lord, all things thou knowest, thou knowest

ὅτι φιλῶ σε· λέγει αὐτῷ Ἰησοῦς· βόσκε
that I love thee; says to him Jesus : Feed

τὰ προβάτιά μου. 18 ἀμὴν ἀμὴν λέγω
the little sheep of me. Truly truly I tell

σοι, ὅτε ἦς νεώτερος, ἐζώννυες σεαυτὸν
thee, when thou wast younger, thou girdedst thyself

καὶ περιεπάτεις ὅπου ἤθελες· ὅταν δὲ
and walkedst where thou wishedst; but when

γηράσῃς, ἐκτενεῖς τὰς χεῖράς σου, καὶ
thou growest thou wilt the hands of thee, and
old, stretch out

ἄλλος ζώσει σε καὶ οἴσει ὅπου οὐ θέλεις.
another will gird thee and will carry where thou wishest not.

19 τοῦτο δὲ εἶπεν σημαίνων ποίῳ θανάτῳ
And this he said signifying by what death

δοξάσει τὸν θεόν. καὶ τοῦτο εἰπὼν λέγει
he will glorify – God. And this saying he tells

αὐτῷ· ἀκολούθει μοι. 20 ἐπιστραφεὶς ὁ
him : Follow me. Turning –

Πέτρος βλέπει τὸν μαθητὴν ὃν ἠγάπα ὁ
Peter sees the disciple whom [1]loved –

Ἰησοῦς ἀκολουθοῦντα, ὃς καὶ ἀνέπεσεν
[1]Jesus following, who also leaned

to his breast at the supper and had said, "Lord, who is it that is going to betray you?" ²¹When Peter saw him, he said to Jesus, "Lord, what about this man?" ²²Jesus said to him, "If it is my will that he remain until I come, what is that to you? Follow me!" ²³The saying spread abroad among the brethren that this disciple was not to die; yet Jesus did not say to him that he was not to die, but, "If it is my will that he remain until I come, what is that to you?"

24 This is the disciple who is bearing witness to these things, and who has written these things; and we know that his testimony is true.

25 But there are also many other things which Jesus did, were every one of them to be written, I suppose that the world itself could not contain the books that would be written.

ἐν τῷ δείπνῳ · ἐπὶ τὸ στῆθος αὐτοῦ καὶ
at the supper on the breast of him and

εἶπεν · κύριε, τίς ἐστιν ὁ παραδιδούς σε;
said: Lord, who is the[one] betraying thee?

21 τοῦτον οὖν ἰδὼν ὁ Πέτρος λέγει τῷ
⁴This one ²therefore ³seeing – ¹Peter says –

᾽Ιησοῦ · κύριε, οὗτος δὲ τί; 22 λέγει
to Jesus: Lord, and this one what? Says

αὐτῷ ὁ ᾽Ιησοῦς · ἐὰν αὐτὸν θέλω μένειν
to him – Jesus: If him I wish to remain

ἕως ἔρχομαι, τί πρὸς σέ; σύ μοι
until I come, what to thee? ²thou ³me

ἀκολούθει. 23 ἐξῆλθεν οὖν οὗτος ὁ λόγος
¹follow. Went forth therefore this – word

εἰς τοὺς ἀδελφοὺς ὅτι ὁ μαθητὴς ἐκεῖνος
to the brothers that – disciple that

οὐκ ἀποθνῄσκει · οὐκ εἶπεν δὲ αὐτῷ ὁ
does not die; but said not to him –

᾽Ιησοῦς ὅτι οὐκ ἀποθνῄσκει, ἀλλ᾽ · ἐὰν
Jesus that he does not die, but: If

αὐτὸν θέλω μένειν ἕως ἔρχομαι, τί πρὸς
him I wish to remain until I come, what to

σέ;
thee?

24 Οὗτός ἐστιν ὁ μαθητὴς ὁ μαρτυρῶν
This is the disciple – witnessing

περὶ τούτων καὶ ὁ γράψας ταῦτα,
concerning these and – having these
things written things,

καὶ οἴδαμεν ὅτι ἀληθὴς αὐτοῦ ἡ μαρτυρία
and we know that true of him the witness

ἐστίν. 25 ῎Εστιν δὲ καὶ ἄλλα πολλὰ ἃ
is. And there are also other many which
things

ἐποίησεν ὁ ᾽Ιησοῦς, ἅτινα ἐὰν γράφηται
did – Jesus, which if they were written

καθ᾽ ἕν, οὐδ᾽ αὐτὸν οἶμαι τὸν κόσμον
singly,† ⁵not ⁴[it]self ¹I think ²the ³world

χωρήσειν τὰ γραφόμενα βιβλία.
⁶to contain ⁷the ⁸being written ⁹rolls.

CHAPTER 1

IN the first book, O The-oph'ilus, I have dealt with all that Jesus began to do and teach, [2]until the day when he was taken up, after he had given commandment through the Holy Spirit to the apostles whom he had chosen. [3]To them he presented himself alive after his passion by many proofs, appearing to them during forty days, and speaking of the kingdom of God. [4]And while staying[a] with them he charged them not to depart from Jerusalem, but to wait for the promise of the Father, which, he said, "you heard from me,[5] for John baptized with water, but before many days you shall be baptized with the Holy Spirit."

6 So when they had come together, they asked him, "Lord, will you at this time restore the kingdom to Israel?" [7]He said to them, "It is not for you to know times or seasons which the Father has fixed by his own authority. [8]But you shall receive power

1 Τὸν   μὲν   πρῶτον   λόγον   ἐποιησάμην
The   –   first   account   I made

περὶ   πάντων,   ὦ   Θεόφιλε,   ὧν   ἤρξατο
concerning all things,   O   Theophilus,   which   began

ὁ   Ἰησοῦς   ποιεῖν   τε   καὶ   διδάσκειν,
–   Jesus   both to do   and   to teach,

2 ἄχρι   ἧς   ἡμέρας   ἐντειλάμενος   τοῖς
until   which   day   [1]having given injunctions [2]to the
=the day on which

ἀποστόλοις   διὰ   πνεύματος   ἁγίου   οὓς
[2]apostles   [3]through   [5]Spirit   [4]Holy   [6]whom

ἐξελέξατο   ἀνελήμφθη·   3 οἷς   καὶ   παρέστησεν
[6]he chose   [1]he was taken up;   to whom also   he presented

ἑαυτὸν   ζῶντα   μετὰ   τὸ   παθεῖν   αὐτὸν   ἐν
himself   living   after   the   to suffer   him[b]   by
=he suffered

πολλοῖς   τεκμηρίοις,   δι'   ἡμερῶν   τεσσεράκοντα
many   infallible proofs, through   days   forty

ὀπτανόμενος   αὐτοῖς   καὶ   λέγων   τὰ   περὶ
being seen   by them   and   speaking the things concerning

τῆς   βασιλείας   τοῦ   θεοῦ·   4 καὶ   συναλιζόμενος
the   kingdom   of God;   and   meeting with [them]

παρήγγειλεν   αὐτοῖς   ἀπὸ   Ἱεροσολύμων   μὴ
he charged   them   from   Jerusalem   not

χωρίζεσθαι,   ἀλλὰ   περιμένειν   τὴν   ἐπαγγελίαν
to depart,   but   to await   the   promise

τοῦ   πατρὸς   ἣν   ἠκούσατέ   μου·   5 ὅτι
of the   Father   which   ye heard   of me :   because

Ἰωάννης   μὲν   ἐβάπτισεν   ὕδατι,   ὑμεῖς   δὲ
John   indeed   baptized   in water,   but ye

ἐν   πνεύματι   βαπτισθήσεσθε   ἁγίῳ   οὐ   μετὰ
in   [1]Spirit   [3]will be baptized   [1]Holy   not   after

πολλὰς   ταύτας   ἡμέρας.   6 Οἱ   μὲν   οὖν
many   these   days.   [2]the [ones]   [1]So then

συνελθόντες   ἠρώτων   αὐτὸν   λέγοντες·   κύριε,
[2]coming together questioned   him   saying :   Lord,

εἰ   ἐν   τῷ   χρόνῳ   τούτῳ   ἀποκαθιστάνεις
if   at   the   this time   restorest thou

τὴν   βασιλείαν   τῷ   Ἰσραήλ;   7 εἶπεν   πρὸς
the   kingdom   –   to Israel?   He said   to

αὐτούς·   οὐχ   ὑμῶν   ἐστιν   γνῶναι   χρόνους
them :   Not   of you   it is   to know   times

ἢ   καιροὺς   οὓς   ὁ   πατὴρ   ἔθετο   ἐν   τῇ
or   seasons   which   the   Father   placed   in the(his)

ἰδίᾳ   ἐξουσίᾳ,   8 ἀλλὰ   λήμψεσθε   δύναμιν
own   authority,   but   ye will receive   power

[a] Or eating

when the Holy Spirit has come upon you; and you shall be my witnesses in Jerusalem and in all Judea and Samar'ia and to the end of the earth." ⁹And when he had said this, as they were looking on, he was lifted up, and a cloud took him out of their sight. ¹⁰And while they were gazing into heaven as he went, behold, two men stood by them in white robes, ¹¹and said, "Men of Galilee, why do you stand looking into heaven? This Jesus, who was taken up from you into heaven, will come in the same way as you saw him go into heaven."

12 Then they returned to Jerusalem from the mount called Olivet, which is near Jerusalem, a sabbath day's journey away; ¹³and when they had entered, they went up to the upper room, where they were staying, Peter and John and James and Andrew, Philip and Thomas, Bartholomew and Matthew, James the son of Alphaeus and Simon the Zealot and Judas the

ἐπελθόντος τοῦ ἁγίου πνεύματος ἐφ᾽ ὑμᾶς,
coming *upon* the Holy Spirit[a] upon you,
=when the Holy Spirit comes

καὶ ἔσεσθέ μου μάρτυρες ἔν τε Ἰερουσαλὴμ
and ye will be of me witnesses both in Jerusalem

καὶ ἐν πάσῃ τῇ Ἰουδαίᾳ καὶ Σαμαρείᾳ
and in all — Judæa and Samaria

καὶ ἕως ἐσχάτου τῆς γῆς. 9 καὶ ταῦτα
and unto [the] extremity of the earth. And these things

εἰπὼν βλεπόντων αὐτῶν ἐπήρθη, καὶ
saying looking them[a] he was taken up, and
=as they looked

νεφέλη ὑπέλαβεν αὐτὸν ἀπὸ τῶν ὀφθαλμῶν
a cloud received him from the eyes

αὐτῶν. 10 καὶ ὡς ἀτενίζοντες ἦσαν εἰς
of them. And as gazing they were to

τὸν οὐρανὸν πορευομένου αὐτοῦ, καὶ ἰδοὺ
— heaven going him,[a] — behold[,]
=as he went,

ἄνδρες δύο παρειστήκεισαν αὐτοῖς ἐν ἐσθήσεσι
men two stood by them in garments

λευκαῖς, 11 οἳ καὶ εἶπαν· ἄνδρες Γαλιλαῖοι,
white, who also said: *Men* Galilæans,

τί ἑστήκατε βλέποντες εἰς τὸν οὐρανόν;
why stand ye looking to — heaven?

οὗτος ὁ Ἰησοῦς ὁ ἀναλημφθεὶς
This — Jesus the [one] having been taken up

ἀφ᾽ ὑμῶν εἰς τὸν οὐρανὸν οὕτως ἐλεύσεται
from you to — heaven thus will come

ὃν τρόπον ἐθεάσασθε αὐτὸν πορευόμενον
in the way† ye beheld him going

εἰς τὸν οὐρανόν. 12 Τότε ὑπέστρεψαν
to — heaven. Then they returned

εἰς Ἰερουσαλὴμ ἀπὸ ὄρους τοῦ καλου-
to Jerusalem from [the] mount the [one] *being*

μένου ἐλαιῶνος, ὅ ἐστιν ἐγγὺς Ἰερουσαλὴμ
called of [the] olive grove, which is near Jerusalem

σαββάτου ἔχον ὁδόν. 13 καὶ ὅτε εἰσῆλθον,
of a sabbath having a way. And when they entered,
=a sabbath's journey off.

εἰς τὸ ὑπερῷον ἀνέβησαν οὗ ἦσαν
into the upper room they went up where they were

καταμένοντες, ὅ τε Πέτρος καὶ Ἰωάννης
waiting, — both Peter and John

καὶ Ἰάκωβος καὶ Ἀνδρέας, Φίλιππος καὶ
and James and Andrew, Philip and

Θωμᾶς, Βαρθολομαῖος καὶ Μαθθαῖος,
Thomas, Bartholomew and Matthew,

Ἰάκωβος Ἀλφαίου καὶ Σίμων ὁ ζηλωτὴς
James [son] of Alphæus and Simon the zealot

son of James. [14]All these
with one accord devoted
themselves to prayer, to-
gether with the women
and Mary the mother of
Jesus, and with his
brothers.

15 In those days Peter
stood up among the
brethren (the company
of persons was in all
about a hundred and
twenty), and said,
[16]"Brethren, the scripture
had to be fulfilled, which
the Holy Spirit spoke
beforehand by the mouth
of David, concerning
Judas who was guide to
those who arrested Jesus.
[17]For he was numbered
among us, and was
allotted his share in this
ministry. [18](Now this
man bought a field with
the reward of his wicked-
ness; and falling head-
long[b] he burst open in
the middle and all his
bowels gushed out. [19]And
it became known to all
the inhabitants of Jerusalem, so that the field was
called in their language
Akel'dama, that is, Field
of Blood.) [20]For it is
written in the book of
Psalms,
'Let his habitation be-
　　come desolate,

[b] Or swelling up

καὶ Ἰούδας Ἰακώβου.
and Judas [brother] of James.

14 οὗτοι πάντες
These all

ἦσαν προσκαρτεροῦντες ὁμοθυμαδὸν τῇ
were continuing steadfastly with one mind -

προσευχῇ σὺν γυναιξὶν καὶ Μαριὰμ
in prayer with [the] women and Mary the

μητρὶ [τοῦ] Ἰησοῦ καὶ σὺν τοῖς ἀδελφοῖς
mother - of Jesus and with the brothers

αὐτοῦ.
of him.

15 Καὶ ἐν ταῖς ἡμέραις ταύταις ἀναστὰς
And in these days standing up

Πέτρος ἐν μέσῳ τῶν ἀδελφῶν εἶπεν·
Peter in [the] midst of the brothers said:

ἦν τε ὄχλος ὀνομάτων ἐπὶ τὸ αὐτὸ
[b]was [1]and [2][the] [3]crowd [4]of names [5]together

ὡσεὶ ἑκατὸν εἴκοσι· **16** ἄνδρες ἀδελφοί,
about a hundred twenty: Men brothers,

ἔδει πληρωθῆναι τὴν γραφὴν ἣν
it behoved to be fulfilled the scripture which

προεῖπεν τὸ πνεῦμα τὸ ἅγιον διὰ στόματος
spoke before the Spirit - Holy through [the] mouth

Δαυὶδ περὶ Ἰούδα τοῦ γενομένου ὁδηγοῦ
of David concerning Judas the [one] having become guide

τοῖς συλλαβοῦσιν Ἰησοῦν, **17** ὅτι κατ-
to the [ones] taking Jesus, because having

ηριθμημένος ἦν ἐν ἡμῖν καὶ ἔλαχεν τὸν
been numbered he was among us and obtained the

κλῆρον τῆς διακονίας ταύτης. **18** οὗτος μὲν οὖν
portion of this ministry. This one therefore

ἐκτήσατο χωρίον ἐκ μισθοῦ τῆς
bought a field out of [the] reward -

ἀδικίας, καὶ πρηνὴς γενόμενος ἐλάκησεν
of unrighteousness, and swollen up having become he burst asunder

μέσος, καὶ ἐξεχύθη πάντα τὰ σπλάγχνα
in the middle, and were poured out all the bowels

αὐτοῦ· **19** καὶ γνωστὸν ἐγένετο πᾶσι τοῖς
of him; and known it became to all the

κατοικοῦσιν Ἰερουσαλήμ, ὥστε κληθῆναι
[ones] inhabiting Jerusalem, so as to be called

τὸ χωρίον ἐκεῖνο τῇ ἰδίᾳ διαλέκτῳ αὐτῶν
that field in their own language

Ἀκελδαμάχ, τοῦτ' ἔστιν χωρίον
Aceldamach, this is Field

αἵματος. **20** γέγραπται γὰρ ἐν βίβλῳ
of blood. For it has been written in [the] roll

ψαλμῶν· γενηθήτω ἡ ἔπαυλις αὐτοῦ ἔρημος
of Psalms: Let become the estate of him deserted

and let there be no one to live in it';
and
'His office let another take.'

²¹ So one of the men who have accompanied us during all the time that the Lord Jesus went in and out among us, ²² beginning from the baptism of John until the day when he was taken up from us—one of these men must become with us a witness to his resurrection." ²³ And they put forward two, Joseph called Barsabbas, who was surnamed Justus, and Matthi'as. ²⁴ And they prayed and said, "Lord, who knowest the hearts of all men, show which one of these two thou hast chosen ²⁵ to take the place in this ministry and apostleship from which Judas turned aside, to go to his own place." ²⁶ And they cast lots for them, and the lot fell on Matthi'as; and he was enrolled with the eleven apostles.

καὶ μὴ ἔστω ὁ κατοικῶν ἐν αὐτῇ, καὶ·
and   let not be   the [one] dwelling   in   it,   and :

τὴν ἐπισκοπὴν αὐτοῦ λαβέτω ἔτερος.
The   office   of him   let take   another.

21 δεῖ οὖν τῶν συνελθόντων ἡμῖν ἀνδρῶν
It behoves* therefore ¹of the ²accompanying ⁴us ⁵men

ἐν παντὶ χρόνῳ ᾧ εἰσῆλθεν καὶ
in   all   [the] time   in which   went in   and

ἐξῆλθεν ἐφ' ἡμᾶς ὁ κύριος Ἰησοῦς,
went out   among   us   the   Lord   Jesus,

22 ἀρξάμενος ἀπὸ τοῦ βαπτίσματος
beginning   from   the   baptism

Ἰωάννου ἕως τῆς ἡμέρας ἧς ἀνελήμφθη
of John   until   the   day   when   he was taken up

ἀφ' ἡμῶν, μάρτυρα τῆς ἀναστάσεως
from   us,   ⁴a witness*   ⁷of the   ⁸resurrection

αὐτοῦ σὺν ἡμῖν γενέσθαι ἕνα τούτων.
⁹of him   ⁵with   ⁶us   ³to become   ¹one*   ²of these.

23 Καὶ ἔστησαν δύο, Ἰωσὴφ τὸν καλού-
And   they set   two,   Joseph   the [one] being

μενον Βαρσαββᾶν, ὃς ἐπεκλήθη Ἰοῦστος,
called   Barsabbas,   who   was surnamed   Justus,

καὶ Μαθθίαν. 24 καὶ προσευξάμενοι εἶπαν·
and   Matthias.   And   praying   they said :

σὺ κύριε καρδιογνῶστα πάντων, ἀνάδειξον
Thou Lord   Heart-knower   of all men,   show

ὃν ἐξελέξω ἐκ τούτων τῶν δύο ἕνα
whom thou didst choose of   these   –   two   one

25 λαβεῖν τὸν τόπον τῆς διακονίας ταύτης
to take   the   place   of this ministry

καὶ ἀποστολῆς, ἀφ' ἧς παρέβη Ἰούδας
and   apostleship,   from which   fell   Judas

πορευθῆναι εἰς τὸν τόπον τὸν ἴδιον.
to go   to   the(his)   place   –   own.

26 καὶ ἔδωκαν κλήρους αὐτοῖς, καὶ ἔπεσεν
And   they gave   lots   for them,   and   fell

ὁ κλῆρος ἐπὶ Μαθθίαν, καὶ συγκατεψηφίσθη
the   lot   on   Matthias,   and   he was reckoned along with

μετὰ τῶν ἕνδεκα ἀποστόλων.
with   the   eleven   apostles.

CHAPTER 2

WHEN the day of Pentecost had come they were all together in one place.

2 Καὶ ἐν τῷ συμπληροῦσθαι τὴν ἡμέραν
And   in   the   to be completed   the   day
= when the day of Pentecost was completed

τῆς πεντηκοστῆς ἦσαν πάντες ὁμοῦ ἐπὶ
–   of Pentecost^e   they were   all   together   to-

---

* The object (according to the Greek construction) of the verb δεῖ is ἕνα, with μάρτυρα as its complement after γενέσθαι.

²And suddenly a sound came from heaven like the rush of a mighty wind, and it filled all the house where they were sitting. ³And there appeared to them tongues as of fire, distributed and resting on each one of them. ⁴And they were all filled with the Holy Spirit and began to speak in other tongues, as the Spirit gave them utterance.

5 Now there were dwelling in Jerusalem Jews, devout men from every nation under heaven. ⁶And at this sound the multitude came together, and they were bewildered, because each one heard them speaking in his own language. ⁷And they were amazed and wondered, saying, "Are not all these who are speaking Galileans? ⁸And how is it that we hear, each of us in his own native language? ⁹Par'thians and Medes and E'lamites and residents of Mesopota'mia, Judea and Cappado'cia, Pontus and Asia, ¹⁰Phryg'ia and Pamphyl'ia, Egypt and the

τὸ αὐτό· 2 καὶ ἐγένετο ἄφνω ἐκ τοῦ
gether;† and there was suddenly out of –

οὐρανοῦ ἦχος ὥσπερ φερομένης πνοῆς
heaven a sound as ⁵being borne ¹of ²a ⁴wind

βιαίας καὶ ἐπλήρωσεν ὅλον τὸν οἶκον
³violent and it filled all the house

οὗ ἦσαν καθήμενοι, 3 καὶ ὤφθησαν αὐτοῖς
where they were sitting, and there appeared to them

διαμεριζόμεναι γλῶσσαι ὡσεὶ πυρός, καὶ
being distributed tongues as of fire, and

ἐκάθισεν ἐφ' ἕνα ἕκαστον αὐτῶν, 4 καὶ
it sat on ²one ¹each of them, and

ἐπλήσθησαν πάντες πνεύματος ἁγίου, καὶ
they were filled all of(with) Spirit Holy, and

ἤρξαντο λαλεῖν ἑτέραις γλώσσαις καθὼς
began to speak in other tongues as

τὸ πνεῦμα ἐδίδου ἀποφθέγγεσθαι αὐτοῖς.
the Spirit gave ²to speak out ¹them.

5 Ἦσαν δὲ εἰς Ἰερουσαλὴμ κατοικοῦντες
Now there were in Jerusalem dwelling

Ἰουδαῖοι, ἄνδρες εὐλαβεῖς ἀπὸ παντὸς ἔθνους
Jews, men devout from every nation

τῶν ὑπὸ τὸν οὐρανόν· 6 γενομένης
of the [ones] under – heaven; happening

δὲ τῆς φωνῆς ταύτης συνῆλθεν τὸ πλῆθος
and this sound came together the multitude
= when this sound happened

καὶ συνεχύθη, ὅτι ἤκουον εἰς ἕκαστος
and were confounded, because they heard ²one ³each

τῇ ἰδίᾳ διαλέκτῳ λαλούντων αὐτῶν.
⁵in his own language ¹speaking ⁴them.

7 ἐξίσταντο δὲ καὶ ἐθαύμαζον λέγοντες·
And they were amazed and marvelled saying:

οὐχὶ ἰδοὺ πάντες οὗτοί εἰσιν οἱ λαλοῦντες
³not ¹behold ⁴all ⁵these ²are ⁶the [ones] ⁷speaking

Γαλιλαῖοι; 8 καὶ πῶς ἡμεῖς ἀκούομεν
⁸Galilæans? and how ²we ¹hear

ἕκαστος τῇ ἰδίᾳ διαλέκτῳ ἡμῶν ἐν ᾗ
³each ⁵in his own language ⁴of us in which

ἐγεννήθημεν, 9 Πάρθοι καὶ Μῆδοι καὶ
we were born, Parthians and Medes and

Ἐλαμῖται, καὶ οἱ κατοικοῦντες τὴν
Elamites, and the [ones] inhabiting –

Μεσοποταμίαν, Ἰουδαίαν τε καὶ Καππα-
Mesopotamia, both Judæa and Cappa-

δοκίαν, Πόντον καὶ τὴν Ἀσίαν, 10 Φρυγίαν
docia, Pontus and Asia, Phrygia

τε καὶ Παμφυλίαν, Αἴγυπτον καὶ τὰ
both and Pamphylia, Egypt and the

parts of Libya belonging to Cyre'ne, and visitors from Rome, both Jews and proselytes, [11]Cretans and Arabians, we hear them telling in our own tongues the mighty works of God." [12]And all were amazed and perplexed, saying to one another, "What does this mean?" [13]But others mocking said, "They are filled with new wine."

14 But Peter, standing with the eleven, lifted up his voice and addressed them, "Men of Judea and all who dwell in Jerusalem, let this be known to you, and give ear to my words. [15]For these men are not drunk, as you suppose, since it is only the third hour of the day; [16]but this is what was spoken by the prophet Joel:

[17]'And in the last days it shall be, God declares,

that I will pour out my Spirit upon all flesh,

and your sons and your daughters shall prophesy,

and your young men shall see visions,

μέρη   τῆς   Λιβύης   τῆς   κατὰ   Κυρήνην,
regions   –   of Libya   –   over against   Cyrene,

καὶ   οἱ   ἐπιδημοῦντες   'Ρωμαῖοι,   11   'Ιουδαῖοί
and   the   temporarily residing   Romans,   [1]Jews

τε   καὶ   προσήλυτοι,   Κρῆτες   καὶ   "Αραβες,
[1]both and   proselytes,   Cretans   and   Arabians,

ἀκούομεν   λαλούντων   αὐτῶν   ταῖς   ἡμετέραις
we hear   [2]speaking   [1]them   in the   our

γλώσσαις   τὰ   μεγαλεῖα   τοῦ   θεοῦ;
tongues   the   great deeds   –   of God?

12   ἐξίσταντο   δὲ   πάντες   καὶ   διηποροῦντο,
And were amazed   all   and   were troubled,

ἄλλος   πρὸς   ἄλλον   λέγοντες·   τί   θέλει
other   to   other   saying :   What   wishes

τοῦτο   εἶναι;   13   ἕτεροι   δὲ   διαχλευάζοντες
this   to be?   But others   mocking

ἔλεγον   ὅτι   γλεύκους   μεμεστωμένοι   εἰσίν.
said[,]   –   Of(with) sweet wine   having been filled   they are.

14   Σταθεὶς   δὲ   ὁ   Πέτρος   σὺν   τοῖς   ἕνδεκα
But standing   –   Peter   with   the   eleven

ἐπῆρεν   τὴν   φωνὴν   αὐτοῦ   καὶ   ἀπεφθέγξατο
lifted up   the   voice   of him   and   spoke out

αὐτοῖς·
to them :

"Ανδρες   'Ιουδαῖοι   καὶ   οἱ   κατοικοῦντες
Men   Jews   and   the [ones]   inhabiting

'Ιερουσαλὴμ   πάντες,   τοῦτο   ὑμῖν   γνωστὸν
Jerusalem   all,   this   to you   known

ἔστω,   καὶ   ἐνωτίσασθε   τὰ   ῥήματά   μου.
let be,   and   give ear to   the   words   of me.

15   οὐ   γὰρ   ὡς   ὑμεῖς   ὑπολαμβάνετε   οὗτοι
For not   as   ye   imagine   these men

μεθύουσιν,   ἔστιν   γὰρ   ὥρα   τρίτη   τῆς
are drunk,   for it is   hour   third   of the

ἡμέρας,   16   ἀλλὰ   τοῦτό   ἐστιν   τὸ   εἰρημένον
day,   but   this   is the thing   having been
spoken

διὰ   τοῦ   προφήτου   'Ιωήλ·   17   καὶ   ἔσται
through the   prophet   Joel :   And it shall be

ἐν   ταῖς   ἐσχάταις   ἡμέραις,   λέγει   ὁ   θεός,
in   the   last   days,   says   –   God,

ἐκχεῶ   ἀπὸ   τοῦ   πνεύματός   μου   ἐπὶ
I will pour out from   the   Spirit   of me   on

πᾶσαν   σάρκα,   καὶ   προφητεύσουσιν   οἱ   υἱοὶ
all   flesh,   and   will prophesy   the   sons

ὑμῶν   καὶ   αἱ   θυγατέρες   ὑμῶν,   καὶ   οἱ
of you   and   the   daughters   of you,   and   the

νεανίσκοι   ὑμῶν   ὁράσεις   ὄψονται,   καὶ   οἱ
young men   of you   visions   will see,   and   the

and your old men shall dream dreams;

[18] yea, and on my menservants and my maidservants in those days I will pour out my Spirit; and they shall prophesy.

[19] And I will show wonders in the heaven above and signs on the earth beneath, blood, and fire, and vapor of smoke;

[20] the sun shall be turned into darkness and the moon into blood, before the day of the Lord comes, the great and manifest day.

[21] And it shall be that whoever calls on the name of the Lord shall be saved.'

22 "Men of Israel, hear these words: Jesus of Nazareth, a man attested to you by God with mighty works and wonders and signs which God did through him in your midst, as you yourselves know—[23] this Jesus, delivered up according to the definite plan and foreknowledge of God, you crucified and killed by the hands of lawless men. [24] But God raised him up, having loosed the pangs of death, because it was not possible for him to be held by it. [25] For David says concerning

πρεσβύτεροι ὑμῶν ἐνυπνίοις ἐνυπνιασθήσονται·
old men   of you   dreams   will dream;

18 καὶ γε ἐπὶ τοὺς δούλους μου καὶ ἐπὶ
and — on the male slaves of me and on

τὰς δούλας μου ἐν ταῖς ἡμέραις ἐκείναις
the female slaves of me in those days

ἐκχεῶ ἀπὸ τοῦ πνεύματός μου, καὶ
I will pour out from the Spirit of me, and

προφητεύσουσιν. 19 καὶ δώσω τέρατα ἐν
they will prophesy. And I will give wonders in

τῷ οὐρανῷ ἄνω καὶ σημεῖα ἐπὶ τῆς
the heaven above and signs on the

γῆς κάτω, αἷμα καὶ πῦρ καὶ ἀτμίδα
earth below, blood and fire and vapour

καπνοῦ. 20 ὁ ἥλιος μεταστραφήσεται εἰς
of smoke. The sun will be turned into

σκότος καὶ ἡ σελήνη εἰς αἷμα, πρὶν
darkness and the moon into blood, before

ἐλθεῖν ἡμέραν κυρίου τὴν μεγάλην καὶ
[7]to come(comes) [5]day [6]of [the] Lord [1]the [2]great [3]and

ἐπιφανῆ. 21 καὶ ἔσται πᾶς ὃς ἐὰν
[4]notable.[b] And it will be everyone whoever

ἐπικαλέσηται τὸ ὄνομα κυρίου σωθήσεται.
invokes the name of [the] Lord will be saved.

22 Ἄνδρες Ἰσραηλῖται, ἀκούσατε τοὺς
Men Israelites, hear ye the

λόγους τούτους· Ἰησοῦν τὸν Ναζωραῖον,
words these: Jesus the Nazarene,

ἄνδρα ἀποδεδειγμένον ἀπὸ τοῦ θεοῦ εἰς
a man having been approved from — God among

ὑμᾶς δυνάμεσι καὶ τέρασι καὶ σημείοις,
you by powerful deeds and wonders and signs,

οἷς ἐποίησεν δι' αὐτοῦ ὁ θεὸς ἐν μέσῳ
which did through him — God in [the] midst

ὑμῶν, καθὼς αὐτοὶ οἴδατε, 23 τοῦτον
of you, as [your]selves ye know, this man

τῇ ὡρισμένῃ βουλῇ καὶ προγνώσει τοῦ
[2]by the [3]having been fixed [4]counsel [5]and [6]foreknowledge —

θεοῦ ἔκδοτον διὰ χειρὸς ἀνόμων
[1]of God [1]given up [9]through [10][the] hand [11]of lawless men

προσπήξαντες ἀνείλατε, 24 ὃν ὁ θεὸς
[8]fastening* [12]ye killed, whom — God

ἀνέστησεν λύσας τὰς ὠδῖνας τοῦ θανάτου,
raised up loosening the pangs — of death,

καθότι οὐκ ἦν δυνατὸν κρατεῖσθαι αὐτὸν
because it was not possible [2]to be held [1]him

ὑπ' αὐτοῦ. 25 Δαυὶδ γὰρ λέγει εἰς
by it. For David says [as] to

* That is, to a tree; see ch. 5. 30.

him,
'I saw the Lord always
before me,
for he is at my right
hand that I may not
be shaken;
²⁶therefore my heart
was glad, and my
tongue rejoiced;
moreover my flesh will
dwell in hope.
²⁷For thou wilt not
abandon my soul
to Hades,
nor let thy Holy One
see corruption.
²⁸Thou hast made
known to me the
ways of life;
thou wilt make me
full of gladness with
thy presence.'
29 "Brethren, I may
say to you confidently of
the patriarch David that
he both died and was
buried, and his tomb is
with us to this day.
³⁰Being therefore a
prophet, and knowing
that God had sworn with
an oath to him that he
would set one of his
descendants upon his
throne, ³¹he foresaw and
spoke of the resurrection
of the Christ, that he
was not abandoned to
Hades, nor did his flesh
see corruption. ³²This
Jesus God raised up, and
of that we all are wit-
nesses. ³³Being therefore

αὐτόν· προορώμην τὸν κύριον ἐνώπιον
him :   I foresaw   the   Lord   before

μου διὰ παντός, ὅτι ἐκ δεξιῶν μού
me   always,   because on right of me

ἐστιν, ἵνα μὴ σαλευθῶ. 26 διὰ τοῦτο
he is,   lest I be moved.   Therefore

ηὐφράνθη μου ἡ καρδία καὶ ἠγαλλιάσατο
was glad of me the   heart   and   exulted

ἡ γλῶσσά μου, ἔτι δὲ καὶ ἡ σάρξ
the tongue of me, and now also the flesh

μου κατασκηνώσει ἐπ' ἐλπίδι, 27 ὅτι οὐκ
of me   will dwell   on(in) hope,   because not

ἐγκαταλείψεις τὴν ψυχήν μου εἰς ἄδην
thou wilt abandon the   soul of me in   hades

οὐδὲ δώσεις τὸν ὅσιόν σου ἰδεῖν
nor wilt thou give the holy one of thee to see

διαφθοράν. 28 ἐγνώρισάς μοι ὁδοὺς ζωῆς,
corruption.   Thou madest known to me ways of life,

πληρώσεις με εὐφροσύνης μετὰ τοῦ προσώ-
thou wilt fill me of(with) gladness with the pres-

που σου. 29 Ἄνδρες ἀδελφοί, ἐξὸν εἰπεῖν
ence of thee. Men   brothers, it is permitted to speak

μετὰ παρρησίας πρὸς ὑμᾶς περὶ τοῦ
with   plainness   to   you   concerning the

πατριάρχου Δαυίδ, ὅτι καὶ ἐτελεύτησεν
patriarch   David, that both   he died

καὶ ἐτάφη, καὶ τὸ μνῆμα αὐτοῦ ἔστιν
and was buried, and the   tomb   of him   is

ἐν ἡμῖν ἄχρι τῆς ἡμέρας ταύτης.
among us until the   this day.

30 προφήτης οὖν ὑπάρχων καὶ εἰδὼς ὅτι
A prophet therefore being   and knowing that

ὅρκῳ ὤμοσεν αὐτῷ ὁ θεὸς ἐκ καρποῦ
with an oath swore to him – God of [the] fruit

τῆς ὀσφύος αὐτοῦ καθίσαι ἐπὶ τὸν θρόνον
of the loin[s] of him to sit on the throne

αὐτοῦ, 31 προϊδὼν ἐλάλησεν περὶ τῆς
of him,   foreseeing he spoke concerning the

ἀναστάσεως τοῦ Χριστοῦ, ὅτι οὔτε
resurrection   of the Christ,   that   neither

ἐγκατελείφθη εἰς ἄδην οὔτε ἡ σάρξ
he was abandoned in hades nor the flesh

αὐτοῦ εἶδεν διαφθοράν. 32 τοῦτον τὸν
of him saw   corruption.   This   –

Ἰησοῦν ἀνέστησεν ὁ θεός, οὗ πάντες
Jesus ¹raised up – ¹God, of which all

ἡμεῖς ἐσμεν μάρτυρες· 33 τῇ δεξιᾷ οὖν
we   are witnesses;   to the right [hand] therefore

exalted at the right hand of God, and having received from the Father the promise of the Holy Spirit, he has poured out this which you see and hear. ³⁴ For David did not ascend into the heavens; but he himself says,

'The Lord said to my Lord, Sit at my right hand,

³⁵ till I make thy enemies a stool for thy feet.'

³⁶ Let all the house of Israel therefore know assuredly that God has made him both Lord and Christ, this Jesus whom you crucified."

37 Now when they heard this they were cut to the heart, and said to Peter and the rest of the apostles, "Brethren, what shall we do?"

³⁸ And Peter said to them, "Repent, and be baptized every one of you in the name of Jesus Christ for the forgiveness of your sins; and you shall receive the gift of the Holy Spirit. ³⁹ For the promise is to you and to your children and to all that are far off, every one whom the Lord our God calls to him." ⁴⁰ And he testified with many other words

τοῦ θεοῦ ὑψωθεὶς τήν τε ἐπαγγελίαν
- of God having been exalted ⁴the ¹and ⁷promise

τοῦ πνεύματος τοῦ ἁγίου λαβὼν παρὰ
⁵of the ¹⁰Spirit ⁹Holy ²receiving ⁸from

τοῦ πατρὸς ἐξέχεεν τοῦτο ὃ ὑμεῖς καὶ
⁴the ⁶Father he poured out this which ye both

βλέπετε καὶ ἀκούετε. 34 οὐ γὰρ Δαυὶδ
see and hear. For not David

ἀνέβη εἰς τοὺς οὐρανούς, λέγει δὲ αὐτός·
ascended to the heavens, but says he:

εἶπεν κύριος τῷ κυρίῳ μου· κάθου ἐκ
Said [the] LORD to the Lord of me: Sit at

δεξιῶν μου, 35 ἕως ἂν θῶ τοὺς ἐχθρούς
right of me, until I put the enemies

σου ὑποπόδιον τῶν ποδῶν σου. 36 ἀσφαλῶς
of thee a footstool of the feet of thee. Assuredly

οὖν γινωσκέτω πᾶς οἶκος Ἰσραὴλ ὅτι
therefore ¹let ²know ³all ³[the] ⁴house ⁵of Israel that

καὶ κύριον αὐτὸν καὶ χριστὸν ἐποίησεν
⁴both ⁵Lord ⁶him ⁶and ⁷Christ ⁸made

ὁ θεος, τοῦτον τὸν Ἰησοῦν ὃν ὑμεῖς
- ¹God, this - Jesus whom ye

ἐσταυρώσατε. 37 Ἀκούσαντες δὲ κατενύγ-
crucified. And hearing they were

ησαν τὴν καρδίαν, εἶπόν τε πρὸς τὸν
stung [in] the heart, and said to -

Πέτρον καὶ τοὺς λοιποὺς ἀποστόλους·
Peter and the remaining apostles:

τί ποιήσωμεν, ἄνδρες ἀδελφοί; 38 Πέτρος
What may we do, men brothers? Peter

δὲ πρὸς αὐτούς· μετανοήσατε, καὶ
And to them: Repent ye, and

βαπτισθήτω ἕκαστος ὑμῶν ἐπὶ τῷ ὀνόματι
let be baptized each of you on the name

Ἰησοῦ Χριστοῦ εἰς ἄφεσιν τῶν
of Jesus Christ [with a view] to forgiveness of the

ἁμαρτιῶν ὑμῶν, καὶ λήμψεσθε τὴν δωρεὰν
sins of you, and ye will receive the gift

τοῦ ἁγίου πνεύματος. 39 ὑμῖν γάρ ἐστιν
of the Holy Spirit. For to you is

ἡ ἐπαγγελία καὶ τοῖς τέκνοις ὑμῶν καὶ
the promise and to the children of you and

πᾶσιν τοῖς εἰς μακράν, ὅσους ἂν
to all the [ones] far away, as many as

προσκαλέσηται κύριος ὁ θεὸς ἡμῶν.
may call to [him] [the] Lord the God of us.

40 ἑτέροις τε λόγοις πλείοσιν διεμαρτύρατο,
And with other words many he solemnly witnessed,

and exhorted them, saying, "Save yourselves from this crooked generation." ⁴¹So those who received his word were baptized, and there were added that day about three thousand souls. ⁴²And they devoted themselves to the apostles' teaching and fellowship, to the breaking of bread and the prayers.

43 And fear came upon every soul; and many wonders and signs were done through the apostles. ⁴⁴And all who believed were together and had all things in common; ⁴⁵and they sold their possessions and goods and distributed them to all, as any had need. ⁴⁶And day by day, attending the temple together and breaking bread in their homes, they partook of food with glad and generous hearts, ⁴⁷praising God and having favor with all the people. And the Lord added to their number day by day those who were being saved.

καὶ παρεκάλει αὐτοὺς λέγων· σώθητε
and exhorted them saying : Be ye saved

ἀπὸ τῆς γενεᾶς τῆς σκολιᾶς ταύτης. 41 οἱ
from – ³generation – ²perverse ¹this. The [ones]

μὲν οὖν ἀποδεξάμενοι τὸν λόγον αὐτοῦ
– therefore welcoming the word of him

ἐβαπτίσθησαν, καὶ προσετέθησαν ἐν
were baptized, and there were added in

τῇ ἡμέρᾳ ἐκείνῃ ψυχαὶ ὡσεὶ τρισχίλιαι·
that day souls about three thousand;

42 ἦσαν δὲ προσκαρτεροῦντες τῇ διδαχῇ
and they were continuing steadfastly in the teaching

τῶν ἀποστόλων καὶ τῇ κοινωνίᾳ, τῇ
of the apostles and in the fellowship, in the

κλάσει τοῦ ἄρτου καὶ ταῖς προσευχαῖς.
breaking of the loaf and in the prayers.

43 Ἐγίνετο δὲ πάσῃ ψυχῇ φόβος· πολλὰ δὲ
And came to every soul fear; and many

τέρατα καὶ σημεῖα διὰ τῶν ἀποστόλων
wonders and signs through the apostles

ἐγίνετο. 44 πάντες δὲ οἱ πιστεύσαντες
happened. And all the believing [ones]

ἐπὶ τὸ αὐτὸ εἶχον ἅπαντα κοινά, 45 καὶ
together had all things common, and

τὰ κτήματα καὶ τὰς ὑπάρξεις ἐπίπρασκον
the properties and the possessions they sold

καὶ διεμέριζον αὐτὰ πᾶσιν, καθότι ἄν
and distributed them to all, according as

τις χρείαν εἶχεν. 46 καθ' ἡμέραν τε
anyone need had. And from day to day†

προσκαρτεροῦντες ὁμοθυμαδὸν ἐν τῷ ἱερῷ,
continuing steadfastly with one mind in the temple,

κλῶντές τε κατ' οἶκον ἄρτον, μετε-
and ¹breaking ³from house to house† ²bread, they

λάμβανον τροφῆς ἐν ἀγαλλιάσει καὶ
shared food in gladness and

ἀφελότητι καρδίας, 47 αἰνοῦντες τὸν θεὸν
simplicity of heart, praising – God

καὶ ἔχοντες χάριν πρὸς ὅλον τὸν λαόν.
and having favour with all the people.

ὁ δὲ κύριος προσετίθει τοὺς σῳζομένους
And the Lord added the [ones] being saved

καθ' ἡμέραν ἐπὶ τὸ αὐτό.
from day to day† together.†

CHAPTER 3

NOW Peter and John were going up to the temple at the hour of prayer, the ninth hour. [2]And a man lame from birth was being carried, whom they laid daily at that gate of the temple which is called Beautiful to ask alms of those who entered the temple. [3]Seeing Peter and John about to go into the temple, he asked for alms. [4]And Peter directed his gaze at him, with John, and said, "Look at us." [5]And he fixed his attention upon them, expecting to receive something from them. [6]But Peter said, "I have no silver and gold, but I give you what I have; in the name of Jesus Christ of Nazareth, walk." [7]And he took him by the right hand and raised him up; and immediately his feet and ankles were made strong. [8]And leaping up he stood and walked and entered the temple with them, walking and leaping and praising God. [9]And all the people saw

---

3 Πέτρος δὲ καὶ Ἰωάννης ἀνέβαινον
  Now Peter   and   John   were going up

εἰς τὸ ἱερὸν ἐπὶ τὴν ὥραν τῆς προσευχῆς
to the temple at   the   hour of the   prayer

τὴν ἐνάτην. 2 καί τις ἀνὴρ χωλὸς ἐκ
the ninth.   And a certain man [2]lame [3]from

κοιλίας μητρὸς αὐτοῦ ὑπάρχων ἐβαστάζετο,
[4][the] [5]of [the] [6]of him [1]being   was being
 womb mother   carried,

ὃν ἐτίθουν καθ' ἡμέραν πρὸς τὴν θύραν
whom they used from day to day† at the   door
  to put

τοῦ ἱεροῦ τὴν λεγομένην ὡραίαν τοῦ
of the temple   -   being called Beautiful -

αἰτεῖν ἐλεημοσύνην παρὰ τῶν εἰσπορευομέ-
to ask[d]   alms   from the [ones]   enter-

νων εἰς τὸ ἱερόν· 3 ὃς ἰδὼν Πέτρον καὶ
ing into the temple;   who seeing Peter   and

Ἰωάννην μέλλοντας εἰσιέναι εἰς τὸ ἱερὸν
John   being about to go in into the   temple

ἠρώτα ἐλεημοσύνην λαβεῖν. 4 ἀτενίσας δὲ
asked   alms   to receive.   And [2]gazing

Πέτρος εἰς αὐτὸν σὺν τῷ Ἰωάννῃ εἶπεν·
[1]Peter at him   with -   John   said:

βλέψον εἰς ἡμᾶς. 5 ὁ δὲ ἐπεῖχεν αὐτοῖς
Look at us.   And he paid heed to them

προσδοκῶν τι παρ' αὐτῶν λαβεῖν. 6 εἶπεν
expecting something from them to receive. said

δὲ Πέτρος· ἀργύριον καὶ χρυσίον οὐχ
And Peter: Silver   and   gold   not

ὑπάρχει μοι· ὃ δὲ ἔχω, τοῦτό σοι δίδωμι·
is   to me[e]; but what I have, this to thee I give;
=I have not;

ἐν τῷ ὀνόματι Ἰησοῦ Χριστοῦ τοῦ
in the   name   of Jesus Christ   the

Ναζωραίου περιπάτει. 7 καὶ πιάσας αὐτὸν τῆς
Nazarene   walk.   And seizing him of(by)

δεξιᾶς χειρὸς ἤγειρεν αὐτόν· παραχρῆμα
the right hand he raised him;   [2]at once

δὲ ἐστερεώθησαν αἱ βάσεις αὐτοῦ καὶ τὰ
[1]and were made firm the feet of him and the

σφυδρά, 8 καὶ ἐξαλλόμενος ἔστη, καὶ
ankle-bones, and leaping up he stood, and

περιεπάτει, καὶ εἰσῆλθεν σὺν αὐτοῖς εἰς
walked,   and entered with them into

τὸ ἱερὸν περιπατῶν καὶ ἁλλόμενος καὶ
the temple walking and leaping   and

αἰνῶν τὸν θεόν. 9 καὶ εἶδεν πᾶς ὁ
praising -   God.   And [4]saw [1]all [2]the

him walking and praising God, [10]and recognized him as the one who sat for alms at the Beautiful Gate of the temple; and they were filled with wonder and amazement at what had happened to him.

[11] While he clung to Peter and John, all the people ran together to them in the portico called Solomon's, astounded. [12]And when Peter saw it he addressed the people, "Men of Israel, why do you wonder at this, or why do you stare at us, as though by our own power or piety we had made him walk? [13]The God of Abraham and of Isaac and of Jacob, the God of our fathers, glorified his servant[c] Jesus, whom you delivered up and denied in the presence of Pilate, when he had decided to release him. [14]But you denied the Holy and Righteous One, and asked for a murderer to be granted to you, [15]and killed the Author of life, whom God raised from the dead. To this we are

---

λαὸς αὐτὸν περιπατοῦντα καὶ αἰνοῦντα
[a]people him walking and praising

τὸν θεόν· 10 ἐπεγίνωσκον δὲ αὐτόν, ὅτι
- God; and they recognized him, that

οὗτος ἦν ὁ πρὸς τὴν ἐλεημοσύνην
this was the [one] for - alms

καθήμενος ἐπὶ τῇ ὡραίᾳ πύλῃ τοῦ ἱεροῦ,
sitting at the Beautiful gate of the temple,

καὶ ἐπλήσθησαν θάμβους καὶ ἐκστάσεως
and they were filled of(with) and bewilderment
                    amazement

ἐπὶ τῷ συμβεβηκότι αὐτῷ. 11 Κρατοῦντος δὲ
at the thing having happened to him.   And holding
                                               =as he held

αὐτοῦ τὸν Πέτρον καὶ τὸν Ἰωάννην
him[a] - Peter and - John

συνέδραμεν πᾶς ὁ λαὸς πρὸς αὐτοὺς
ran together all the people to them

ἐπὶ τῇ στοᾷ τῇ καλουμένῃ Σολομῶντος
at the porch - being called of Solomon

ἔκθαμβοι. 12 ἰδὼν δὲ ὁ Πέτρος ἀπεκρίνατο
greatly amazed. And [a]seeing - [1]Peter answered

πρὸς τὸν λαόν· ἄνδρες Ἰσραηλῖται, τί
to the people : Men Israelites, why

θαυμάζετε ἐπὶ τούτῳ, ἢ ἡμῖν τί ἀτενίζετε
marvel ye at this man, or at us why gaze ye

ὡς ἰδίᾳ δυνάμει ἢ εὐσεβείᾳ πεποιηκόσιν
as by [our] own power or piety having made

τοῦ περιπατεῖν αὐτόν; 13 ὁ θεὸς Ἀβραὰμ
- to walk[d] him? The God of Abraham

καὶ Ἰσαὰκ καὶ Ἰακώβ, ὁ θεὸς τῶν
and Isaac and Jacob, the God of the

πατέρων ἡμῶν, ἐδόξασεν τὸν παῖδα αὐτοῦ
fathers of us, glorified the servant of him

Ἰησοῦν, ὃν ὑμεῖς μὲν παρεδώκατε καὶ
Jesus, whom ye - delivered and

ἠρνήσασθε κατὰ πρόσωπον Πιλάτου,
denied in [the] presence of Pilate,

κρίναντος ἐκείνου ἀπολύειν· 14 ὑμεῖς δὲ
having decided that one[a] to release [him]; but ye
=when he had decided

τὸν ἅγιον καὶ δίκαιον ἠρνήσασθε, καὶ
the holy and just one denied, and

ᾐτήσασθε ἄνδρα φονέα χαρισθῆναι ὑμῖν,
asked a man a murderer to be granted you,

15 τὸν δὲ ἀρχηγὸν τῆς ζωῆς ἀπεκτείνατε,
and the Author of life ye killed,

ὃν ὁ θεὸς ἤγειρεν ἐκ νεκρῶν, οὗ ἡμεῖς
whom - God raised from [the] dead, of which we

---

[c] Or child

witnesses. [16]And his name, by faith in his name, has made this man strong whom you see and know; and the faith which is through Jesus has given the man this perfect health in the presence of you all.

17 "And now, brethren, I know that you acted in ignorance, as did also your rulers. [18]But what God foretold by the mouth of all the prophets, that his Christ should suffer, he thus fulfilled. [19]Repent therefore, and turn again, that your sins may be blotted out, that times of refreshing may come from the presence of the Lord, [20]and that he may send the Christ appointed for you, Jesus, [21]whom heaven must receive until the time for establishing all that God spoke by the mouth of his holy prophets from of old. [22]Moses said, 'The Lord God will raise up for you a prophet from your brethren as he raised me up. You shall listen to

μάρτυρές ἐσμεν. 16 καὶ ἐπὶ τῇ πίστει
witnesses   are.   And on the   faith

τοῦ ὀνόματος αὐτοῦ τοῦτον, ὃν θεωρεῖτε
of(in) the name* of him [5]this man, [6]whom [7]ye behold

καὶ οἴδατε, ἐστερέωσεν τὸ ὄνομα αὐτοῦ,
[8]and [9]know, [4]made firm [1]the [2]name [3]of him,

καὶ ἡ πίστις ἡ δι’ αὐτοῦ ἔδωκεν αὐτῷ
and the faith — through him gave him

τὴν ὁλοκληρίαν ταύτην ἀπέναντι πάντων
this soundness before all

ὑμῶν. 17 καὶ νῦν, ἀδελφοί, οἶδα ὅτι
you.   And now, brothers, I know that

κατὰ ἄγνοιαν ἐπράξατε, ὥσπερ καὶ οἱ
by way of ignorance ye acted, as also the

ἄρχοντες ὑμῶν· 18 ὁ δὲ θεὸς ἃ
rulers of you;   — but God the things
                                          which

προκατήγγειλεν διὰ στόματος πάντων
he foreannounced through [the] mouth of all

τῶν προφητῶν, παθεῖν τὸν χριστὸν αὐτοῦ,
the prophets, to suffer the Christ of him[b],
                          =that his Christ was to suffer,

ἐπλήρωσεν οὕτως. 19 μετανοήσατε οὖν
fulfilled thus.   Repent ye therefore

καὶ ἐπιστρέψατε πρὸς τὸ ἐξαλειφθῆναι
and turn for the to be wiped away
                    =that your sins may be wiped away,

ὑμῶν τὰς ἁμαρτίας, 20 ὅπως ἂν ἔλθωσιν
of you the sins,   so as may come

καιροὶ ἀναψύξεως ἀπὸ προσώπου τοῦ
times of refreshing from [the] presence of the

κυρίου καὶ ἀποστείλῃ τὸν προκεχειρισμένον
Lord and he may send [1]the [2]having been foreappointed

ὑμῖν χριστὸν Ἰησοῦν, 21 ὃν δεῖ οὐρανὸν
[4]for you [3]Christ [5]Jesus, whom it behoves heaven

μὲν δέξασθαι ἄχρι χρόνων ἀποκαταστάσεως
— to receive until [the] times of restitution

πάντων ὧν ἐλάλησεν ὁ θεὸς διὰ στόματος
of all things which [2]spoke — [1]God [3]through [4][the] mouth

τῶν ἁγίων ἀπ’ αἰῶνος αὐτοῦ προφητῶν.
[5]of the [6]holy [8]from [10][the] age [6]of him [7]prophets.

22 Μωϋσῆς μὲν εἶπεν ὅτι προφήτην ὑμῖν
Moses indeed said[,] — [4]A prophet [5]for you

ἀναστήσει κύριος ὁ θεὸς ἐκ τῶν ἀδελφῶν
[3]will raise up [1](the) Lord — [2]God of the brothers

ὑμῶν ὡς ἐμέ· αὐτοῦ ἀκούσεσθε κατὰ
of you as me; him shall ye hear according to

---

* Objective genitive; cf. "the fear of God"=the fear which has God for its object; and see Gal. 2. 20, etc.

him in whatever he tells you. ²³And it shall be that every soul that does not listen to that prophet shall be destroyed from the people.' ²⁴And all the prophets who have spoken, from Samuel and those who came afterward, also proclaimed these days. ²⁵You are the sons of the prophets and of the covenant which God gave to your fathers, saying to Abraham, 'And in your posterity shall all the families of the earth be blessed.' ²⁶God, having raised up his servant,[c] sent him to you first, to bless you in turning every one of you from your wickedness."

πάντα	ὅσα	ἂν	λαλήσῃ	πρὸς	ὑμᾶς.
all things	whatever		he may speak	to	you.

23 ἔσται δὲ πᾶσα ψυχὴ ἥτις ἐὰν μὴ ἀκούσῃ
And it shall be every soul whoever hears not

τοῦ προφήτου ἐκείνου ἐξολεθρευθήσεται
that prophet will be utterly destroyed

ἐκ τοῦ λαοῦ. 24 καὶ πάντες δὲ οἱ
out of the people. ²also ³all ¹And the

προφῆται ἀπὸ Σαμουὴλ καὶ τῶν καθεξῆς
prophets from Samuel and the [ones] in order

ὅσοι ἐλάλησαν καὶ κατήγγειλαν τὰς ἡμέρας
as many as spoke also announced – days

ταύτας. 25 ὑμεῖς ἐστε οἱ υἱοὶ τῶν
these. Ye are the sons of the

προφητῶν καὶ τῆς διαθήκης ἧς ὁ θεὸς
prophets and of the covenant which – God

διέθετο πρὸς τοὺς πατέρας ὑμῶν, λέγων
made with the fathers of us, saying

πρὸς Ἀβραάμ· καὶ ἐν τῷ σπέρματί
to Abraham: And in the seed

σου ἐνευλογηθήσονται πᾶσαι αἱ πατριαὶ
of thee shall be blessed all the families

τῆς γῆς. 26 ὑμῖν πρῶτον ἀναστήσας ὁ
of the earth. To you first ²having raised up –

θεὸς τὸν παῖδα αὐτοῦ ἀπέστειλεν αὐτὸν
¹God the servant of him sent him

εὐλογοῦντα ὑμᾶς ἐν τῷ ἀποστρέφειν
blessing you in the to turn away
= in turning away

ἕκαστον ἀπὸ τῶν πονηριῶν ὑμῶν.
each one from the iniquities of you.

CHAPTER 4

AND as they were speaking to the people, the priests and the captain of the temple and the Sadducees came upon them, ²annoyed because they were teaching the people and proclaiming in Jesus the resurrection from the dead. ³And they arrested them and put them in custody until the morrow, for it was already evening. ⁴But many of

4 Λαλούντων δὲ αὐτῶν πρὸς τὸν λαόν,
And speaking them[a] to the people,
= while they were speaking

ἐπέστησαν αὐτοῖς οἱ ἱερεῖς καὶ ὁ στρατηγὸς
came upon them the priests and the commandant

τοῦ ἱεροῦ καὶ οἱ Σαδδουκαῖοι, 2 διαπονούμενοι
of the temple and the Sadducees, being greatly troubled

διὰ τὸ διδάσκειν αὐτοὺς τὸν λαὸν καὶ
because of the to teach them[b] the people and
= because they taught . . . announced

καταγγέλλειν ἐν τῷ Ἰησοῦ τὴν ἀνάστασιν
to announce[b] by – Jesus the resurrection

τὴν ἐκ νεκρῶν, 3 καὶ ἐπέβαλον αὐτοῖς
– from [the] dead, and laid on them

τὰς χεῖρας καὶ ἔθεντο εἰς τήρησιν εἰς
the(ir) hands and put in guard till

τὴν αὔριον· ἦν γὰρ ἑσπέρα ἤδη. 4 πολλοὶ
the morrow; for it was evening now. many

[c] Or child

those who heard the word believed; and the number of the men came to about five thousand.

5 On the morrow their rulers and elders and scribes were gathered together in Jerusalem, [6] with Annas the high priest and Ca'iaphas and John and Alexander, and all who were of the high-priestly family. [7] And when they had set them in the midst, they inquired, "By what power or by what name did you do this?" [8] Then Peter, filled with the Holy Spirit, said to them, "Rulers of the people and elders, [9] if we are being examined today concerning a good deed done to a cripple, by what means this man has been healed, [10] be it known to you all, and to all the people of Israel, that by the name of Jesus Christ of Nazareth, whom you crucified, whom God raised from the dead, by him this man is standing before you well. [11] This is the stone which was rejected by you builders, but which

δὲ τῶν ἀκουσάντων τὸν λόγον ἐπίστευσαν,
But of the [ones] hearing the word believed,

καὶ ἐγενήθη ἀριθμὸς τῶν ἀνδρῶν ὡς
and became [the] number of the men about

χιλιάδες πέντε.
thousands five.

5 Ἐγένετο δὲ ἐπὶ τὴν αὔριον
Now it came to pass on the morrow

συναχθῆναι αὐτῶν τοὺς ἄρχοντας καὶ τοὺς
to be assembled of them the rulers and the

πρεσβυτέρους καὶ τοὺς γραμματεῖς ἐν
elders and the scribes in

Ἰερουσαλήμ, 6 καὶ Ἄννας ὁ ἀρχιερεὺς
Jerusalem, and Annas* the high priest

καὶ Καϊάφας καὶ Ἰωάννης καὶ Ἀλέξανδρος
and Caiaphas and John and Alexander

καὶ ὅσοι ἦσαν ἐκ γένους ἀρχιερατικοῦ,
and as many as were of [the] race high-priestly,

7 καὶ στήσαντες αὐτοὺς ἐν τῷ μέσῳ
and having stood them in the midst

ἐπυνθάνοντο· ἐν ποίᾳ δυνάμει ἢ ἐν ποίῳ
inquired: By what power or in what

ὀνόματι ἐποιήσατε τοῦτο ὑμεῖς; 8 τότε
name did this ye? Then

Πέτρος πλησθεὶς πνεύματος ἁγίου εἶπεν
Peter filled of(with) [the] Spirit Holy said

πρὸς αὐτούς· ἄρχοντες τοῦ λαοῦ καὶ
to them: Rulers of the people and

πρεσβύτεροι, 9 εἰ ἡμεῖς σήμερον ἀνα-
elders, if we to-day are be-

κρινόμεθα ἐπὶ εὐεργεσίᾳ ἀνθρώπου ἀσθενοῦς,
ing examined on a good deed man of an infirm,
=[done to] an infirm man,

ἐν τίνι οὗτος σέσωσται, 10 γνωστὸν ἔστω
by what this man has been healed, known let it be

πᾶσιν ὑμῖν καὶ παντὶ τῷ λαῷ Ἰσραήλ,
to all you and to all the people of Israel,

ὅτι ἐν τῷ ὀνόματι Ἰησοῦ Χριστοῦ τοῦ
that in the name of Jesus Christ the

Ναζωραίου, ὃν ὑμεῖς ἐσταυρώσατε, ὃν ὁ
Nazarene, whom ye crucified, whom –

θεὸς ἤγειρεν ἐκ νεκρῶν, ἐν τούτῳ οὗτος
God raised from [the] dead, in this [name] this man

παρέστηκεν ἐνώπιον ὑμῶν ὑγιής. 11 οὗτός
stands before you whole. This

ἐστιν ὁ λίθος ὁ ἐξουθενηθεὶς ὑφ' ὑμῶν
is the stone – despised by you

---

* The rough breathing in the Greek is ignored in the trans-literation of some familiar proper names.

has become the head of the corner. [12]And there is salvation in no one else, for there is no other name under heaven given among men by which we must be saved."

[13] Now when they saw the boldness of Peter and John, and perceived that they were uneducated, common men, they wondered; and they recognized that they had been with Jesus. [14]But seeing the man that had been healed standing beside them, they had nothing to say in opposition. [15]But when they had commanded them to go aside out of the council, they conferred with one another, [16]saying, "What shall we do with these men? For that a notable sign has been performed through them is manifest to all the inhabitants of Jerusalem, and we cannot deny it. [17]But in order that it may spread no further among the people, let us warn them to speak no more to any one in this name." [18]So they called them and charged them not to speak or teach at all in the name of Jesus. [19]But

---

τῶν οἰκοδόμων, ὁ γενόμενος εἰς κεφαλὴν
the [ones] building, the [one] become _to_ head

γωνίας. 12 καὶ οὐκ ἔστιν ἐν ἄλλῳ οὐδενὶ
of [the] corner. And there is not ¹in ³other ²no(any)

ἡ σωτηρία· οὐδὲ γὰρ ὄνομά ἐστιν ἕτερον
the salvation: for neither ²name ¹is there ²other

ὑπὸ τὸν οὐρανὸν τὸ δεδομένον ἐν
under – heaven the – having been given among

ἀνθρώποις ἐν ᾧ δεῖ σωθῆναι ἡμᾶς.
men by which it behoves ²to be saved ¹us.

13 Θεωροῦντες δὲ τὴν τοῦ Πέτρου
And beholding the – of Peter

παρρησίαν καὶ Ἰωάννου, καὶ καταλαβόμενοι
boldness and of John, and perceiving

ὅτι ἄνθρωποι ἀγράμματοί εἰσιν καὶ
that men unlettered they are(were) and

ἰδιῶται, ἐθαύμαζον, ἐπεγίνωσκόν τε αὐτοὺς
laymen, they marvelled, and recognized them

ὅτι σὺν τῷ Ἰησοῦ ἦσαν, 14 τόν τε
that with – Jesus they were(had been), ²the ¹and

ἄνθρωπον βλέποντες σὺν αὐτοῖς ἑστῶτα τὸν
⁴man ⁵seeing ⁷with ⁸them ⁶standing

τεθεραπευμένον, οὐδὲν εἶχον ἀντειπεῖν.
⁵having been healed, nothing they had to say against.

15 κελεύσαντες δὲ αὐτοὺς ἔξω τοῦ συνεδρίου
So having commanded them outside the council

ἀπελθεῖν, συνέβαλλον πρὸς ἀλλήλους
to go, they discussed _with_ with one another

16 λέγοντες· τί ποιήσωμεν τοῖς ἀνθρώποις
saying : What may we do men

τούτοις; ὅτι μὲν γὰρ γνωστὸν σημεῖον
to these? for that indeed a notable sign

γέγονεν δι' αὐτῶν, πᾶσιν τοῖς κατοικοῦσιν
has happened through them, to all the [ones] inhabiting

Ἰερουσαλὴμ φανερόν, καὶ οὐ δυνάμεθα
Jerusalem [is] manifest, and we cannot

ἀρνεῖσθαι· 17 ἀλλ' ἵνα μὴ ἐπὶ πλεῖον
to deny [it]; but ¹lest ³more†

διανεμηθῇ εἰς τὸν λαόν, ἀπειλησώμεθα
²it is spread abroad ⁴to the people, let us threaten

αὐτοῖς μηκέτι λαλεῖν ἐπὶ τῷ ὀνόματι
them no longer to speak on – name

τούτῳ μηδενὶ ἀνθρώπων. 18 καὶ καλέσαντες
this to no(any)one of men. And calling

αὐτοὺς παρήγγειλαν καθόλου μὴ φθέγγεσθαι
them they charged at all not to utter

μηδὲ διδάσκειν ἐπὶ τῷ ὀνόματι τοῦ
nor to teach on the name –

Peter and John answered them, "Whether it is right in the sight of God to listen to you rather than to God, you must judge; [20] for we cannot but speak of what we have seen and heard." [21] And when they had further threatened them, they let them go, finding no way to punish them, because of the people; for all men praised God for what had happened. [22] For the man on whom this sign of healing was performed was more than forty years old.

23 When they were released they went to their friends and reported what the chief priests and the elders had said to them. [24] And when they heard it, they lifted their voices together to God and said, "Sovereign Lord, who didst make the heaven and the earth and the sea and everything in them, [25] who by the mouth of our father David, thy servant,[c] didst say by the Holy Spirit,

'Why did the Gentiles rage,
    and the peoples imagine vain
    things?

Ἰησοῦ.   **19** ὁ   δὲ   Πέτρος   καὶ   Ἰωάννης
of Jesus.   –   But   Peter   and   John
ἀποκριθέντες   εἶπον   πρὸς   αὐτούς·   εἰ
answering   said   to   them :   If
δίκαιόν   ἐστιν   ἐνώπιον   τοῦ   θεοῦ,   ὑμῶν
right   it is   before   –   God,   you
ἀκούειν   μᾶλλον   ἢ   τοῦ   θεοῦ,   κρίνατε·
to hear   rather   than   –   God,   decide ye;
20 οὐ   δυνάμεθα   γὰρ   ἡμεῖς   ἃ   εἴδαμεν
for cannot   we   [the] things which   we saw
καὶ   ἠκούσαμεν   μὴ   λαλεῖν.   **21** οἱ   δὲ
and   heard   not   *to* speak.   And they
προσαπειλησάμενοι   ἀπέλυσαν   αὐτούς, μηδὲν
having added threats   released   them,   nothing
εὑρίσκοντες   τὸ   πῶς   κολάσωνται   αὐτούς,
finding   –   how   they might punish   them,
διὰ   τὸν   λαόν,   ὅτι   πάντες   ἐδόξαζον τὸν
because of the   people,   because   all men   glorified
θεὸν   ἐπὶ   τῷ   γεγονότι·   **22** ἐτῶν   γὰρ
God   on   the thing having happened;   for of years
ἦν   πλειόνων   τεσσεράκοντα   ὁ   ἄνθρωπος
was   more [than]   forty   the   man
ἐφ᾽   ὃν   γεγόνει   τὸ σημεῖον   τοῦτο   τῆς
on   whom   had happened   this sign   of the
ἰάσεως.   **23** Ἀπολυθέντες   δὲ   ἦλθον   πρὸς
of cure.   And being released   they went   to
τοὺς   ἰδίους   καὶ   ἀπήγγειλαν   ὅσα   πρὸς
the(ir) own [people]   and   reported   what things   to
αὐτοὺς   οἱ   ἀρχιερεῖς   καὶ   οἱ   πρεσβύτεροι
them   the   chief priests   and   the   elders
εἶπαν.   **24** οἱ   δὲ   ἀκούσαντες   ὁμοθυμαδὸν
said.   And they   having heard   with one mind
ἦραν   φωνὴν   πρὸς   τὸν   θεὸν   καὶ   εἶπαν·
lifted   voice   to   –   God   and   said :
δέσποτα,   σὺ   ὁ   ποιήσας   τὸν   οὐρανὸν καὶ
Master,   thou the [one] having made   the   heaven   and
τὴν   γῆν   καὶ   τὴν   θάλασσαν   καὶ   πάντα
the   earth   and   the   sea   and   all things
τὰ   ἐν   αὐτοῖς,   **25** ὁ   τοῦ   πατρὸς   ἡμῶν
–   in   them,   ¹the   ⁸the   ⁹father   ¹⁰of us
[one]
διὰ   πνεύματος   ἁγίου   στόματος   Δαυὶδ
³through   ⁵[the] Spirit   ⁴Holy   ⁶[by] mouth   ⁷of David
παιδός   σου   εἰπών·   ἱνατί   ἐφρύαξαν   ἔθνη
¹¹servant   ¹²of thee   ²saying :*   Why   raged   nations
καὶ   λαοὶ   ἐμελέτησαν   κενά;   **26** παρέστησαν
and   peoples   devised   vain things?   came

---

* It is recognized that there is a primitive error in the text in the first half of ver. 25; it is impossible to construe it as it stands. See ch. 1. 16.

[c] Or *child*

26 The kings of the earth set themselves in array, and the rulers were gathered together, against the Lord and against his Anointed'[d]—

27 for truly in this city there were gathered together against thy holy servant[e] Jesus, whom thou didst anoint, both Herod and Pontius Pilate, with the Gentiles and the peoples of Israel, 28 to do whatever thy hand and thy plan had predestined to take place. 29 And now, Lord, look upon their threats, and grant to thy servants to speak thy word with all boldness, 30 while thou stretchest out thy hand to heal, and signs and wonders are performed through the name of thy holy servant[e] Jesus." 31 And when they had prayed, the place in which they were gathered together was shaken; and they were all filled with the Holy Spirit and spoke the word of God with boldness.

32 Now the company of those who believed were of one heart and soul, and no one said that any of the things which he possessed was his own, but they had everything in common.

οἱ βασιλεῖς τῆς γῆς καὶ οἱ ἄρχοντες
the kings of the earth and the rulers
συνήχθησαν ἐπὶ τὸ αὐτὸ κατὰ τοῦ κυρίου
assembled together against the Lord
καὶ κατὰ τοῦ χριστοῦ αὐτοῦ.
and against the Christ of him.

27 συνήχθησαν γὰρ ἐπ' ἀληθείας ἐν τῇ
For assembled in truth in –
πόλει ταύτῃ ἐπὶ τὸν ἅγιον παῖδά σου
city this against the holy servant of thee
Ἰησοῦν, ὃν ἔχρισας, Ἡρώδης τε καὶ
Jesus, whom thou didst anoint, both Herod and
Πόντιος Πιλᾶτος σὺν ἔθνεσιν καὶ λαοῖς
Pontius Pilate with nations and peoples
Ἰσραήλ, 28 ποιῆσαι ὅσα ἡ χείρ σου καὶ
of Israel, to do what the hand of thee and
things
ἡ βουλὴ προώρισεν γενέσθαι. 29 καὶ τὰ
the counsel foreordained to happen. And –
νῦν, κύριε, ἔπιδε ἐπὶ τὰς ἀπειλὰς αὐτῶν,
now, Lord, look on on the threatenings of them,
καὶ δὸς τοῖς δούλοις σου μετὰ παρρησίας
and give to the slaves of thee with ²boldness
πάσης λαλεῖν τὸν λόγον σου, 30 ἐν τῷ
¹all to speak the word of thee, by the
τὴν χεῖρα ἐκτείνειν σε εἰς ἴασιν καὶ
the hand to stretch forth thee[b] for cure and
=by stretching forth thy hand
σημεῖα καὶ τέρατα γίνεσθαι διὰ τοῦ
signs and wonders to happen through the
ὀνόματος τοῦ ἁγίου παιδός σου Ἰησοῦ.
name of the holy servant of thee Jesus.

31 καὶ δεηθέντων αὐτῶν ἐσαλεύθη ὁ τόπος
And requesting them[a] was shaken the place
=as they were making request
ἐν ᾧ ἦσαν συνηγμένοι, καὶ ἐπλήσθησαν
in which they were having been and they were filled
assembled,
ἅπαντες τοῦ ἁγίου πνεύματος, καὶ ἐλάλουν
all of(with) the Holy Spirit, and spoke
τὸν λόγον τοῦ θεοῦ μετὰ παρρησίας.
the word – of God with boldness.

32 Τοῦ δὲ πλήθους τῶν πιστευσάντων
¹Now ⁶of ⁷the ⁸multitude ⁹of the [ones] ¹⁰having believed
ἦν καρδία καὶ ψυχὴ μία, καὶ οὐδὲ
¹¹was ²[the] ³heart ⁴and ⁵soul ¹²one, and ¹not
εἷς τι τῶν ὑπαρχόντων αὐτῷ ἔλεγεν
²one ⁴any- ⁵of the ⁶possessions [belonging] ³said
thing ᵗᵒ ʰⁱᵐᵉ
ἴδιον εἶναι, ἀλλ' ἦν αὐτοῖς πάντα κοινά.
³[his] own ⁸to be, but were to them[c] all things common.

[d] Or Christ

[e] Or child

[33]And with great power the apostles gave their testimony to the resurrection of the Lord Jesus, and great grace was upon them all. [34]There was not a needy person among them, for as many as were possessors of lands or houses sold them, and brought the proceeds of what was sold [35]and laid it at the apostles' feet; and distribution was made to each as any had need. [36]Thus Joseph who was surnamed by the apostles Barnabas (which means, Son of encouragement), a Levite, a native of Cyprus, [37]sold a field which belonged to him, and brought the money and laid it at the apostles' feet.

33 καὶ   δυνάμει   μεγάλῃ   ἀπεδίδουν   τὸ
And   [1]with [2]power   [2]great   [6]gave   [7]the

μαρτύριον   οἱ   ἀπόστολοι   τοῦ   κυρίου   Ἰησοῦ
[8]testimony [4]the [6]apostles [11]of the [12]Lord [13]Jesus

τῆς   ἀναστάσεως,   χάρις   τε   μεγάλη   ἦν
[9]of the [10]resurrection,   and [2]grace [1]great was

ἐπὶ   πάντας   αὐτούς.   34 οὐδὲ   γὰρ   ἐνδεής
upon all   them.   [1]For [2]neither [3]needy

τις   ἦν   ἐν   αὐτοῖς·   ὅσοι   γὰρ   κτήτορες
[4]anyone [3]was among them; for as many as owners

χωρίων   ἢ   οἰκιῶν   ὑπῆρχον,   πωλοῦντες
of lands or of houses were,   selling

ἔφερον   τὰς   τιμὰς   τῶν   πιπρασκομένων
brought   the prices of the things being sold

35 καὶ   ἐτίθουν   παρὰ   τοὺς   πόδας   τῶν
and   placed   at   the   feet   of the

ἀποστόλων·   διεδίδοτο   δὲ   ἑκάστῳ   καθότι   ἄν
apostles;   and it was distributed to each   according as

τις   χρείαν   εἶχεν.   36 Ἰωσὴφ   δὲ   ὁ
anyone need   had.   And Joseph   the [one]

ἐπικληθεὶς   Βαρναβᾶς   ἀπὸ   τῶν   ἀποστόλων,
surnamed   Barnabas   from(by) the   apostles,

ὅ   ἐστιν   μεθερμηνευόμενον   υἱὸς   παρακλήσεως,
which is   being translated   Son   of consolation,

Λευίτης,   Κύπριος   τῷ   γένει,   37 ὑπάρχοντος
a Levite, a Cypriote   -   by race,   being

αὐτῷ   ἀγροῦ,   πωλήσας   ἤνεγκεν   τὸ   χρῆμα
to him[e] a field,[a] having sold [it] brought   the proceeds
=as he had a field,

καὶ   ἔθηκεν   πρὸς   τοὺς   πόδας   τῶν   ἀποστόλων.
and placed   at   the   feet of the apostles.

CHAPTER 5

BUT a man named Anani'as with his wife Sapphi'ra sold a piece of property, [2]and with his wife's knowledge he kept back some of the proceeds, and brought only a part and laid it at the apostles' feet. [3]But Peter said, "Anani'as, why has Satan filled your heart to lie to

5 Ἀνὴρ   δέ   τις   Ἁνανίας   ὀνόματι   σὺν
And a certain man   Ananias[*] by name   with

Σαπφίρῃ   τῇ   γυναικὶ   αὐτοῦ   ἐπώλησεν
Sapphira   the   wife   of him   sold

κτῆμα,   2 καὶ   ἐνοσφίσατο   ἀπὸ   τῆς   τιμῆς,
a property, and appropriated from   the price,

συνειδυίης   καὶ   τῆς   γυναικός,   καὶ   ἐνέγκας
aware of [it] also the(his) wife,[a]   and   bringing
=his wife also being aware of it,

μέρος   τι   παρὰ   τοὺς   πόδας   τῶν   ἀποστόλων
a certain part at   the   feet of the apostles

ἔθηκεν.   3 εἶπεν   δὲ   ὁ   Πέτρος·   Ἁνανία,
placed [it]. But said   -   Peter: Ananias,

διὰ   τί   ἐπλήρωσεν   ὁ   σατανᾶς   τὴν   καρδίαν
why   filled   Satan   the   heart

* See note to 4. 6.

the Holy Spirit and to keep back part of the proceeds of the land? ⁴While it remained unsold, did it not remain your own? And after it was sold, was it not at your disposal? How is it that you have contrived this deed in your heart? You have not lied to men but to God." ⁵When Anani'as heard these words, he fell down and died. And great fear came upon all who heard of it. ⁶The young men rose and wrapped him up and carried him out and buried him.

7 After an interval of about three hours his wife came in, not knowing what had happened. ⁸And Peter said to her, "Tell me whether you sold the land for so much." And she said, "Yes, for so much." ⁹But Peter said to her, "How is it that you have agreed together to tempt the Spirit of the Lord? Hark, the feet of those that have buried your husband are at the door, and they will carry you out." ¹⁰Immediately she fell down at his feet and died. When the young men came in they found her dead, and they carried

σου,	ψεύσασθαί	σε	τὸ	πνεῦμα	τὸ	ἅγιον
of thee,	to deceive =that thou shouldest deceive	theeᵇ	the	Spirit	–	Holy

καὶ	νοσφίσασθαι	ἀπὸ	τῆς	τιμῆς	τοῦ
and	to appropriate	from	the	price	of the

χωρίου;	4 οὐχὶ	μένον	σοὶ	ἔμενεν	καὶ
land?	Not	remaining	to thee	it remained	and

πραθὲν	ἐν	τῇ	σῇ	ἐξουσίᾳ	ὑπῆρχεν;	τί	ὅτι
sold	in	–	thy	authority	it was?	Why

ἔθου	ἐν	τῇ	καρδίᾳ	σου	τὸ	πρᾶγμα
was put	in	the	heart	of thee	–	action

τοῦτο;	οὐκ	ἐψεύσω	ἀνθρώποις	ἀλλὰ
this?	thou didst not lie	to men	but

τῷ	θεῷ.	5 ἀκούων	δὲ	ὁ	'Ανανίας
–	to God.	And hearing	–	Ananias

τοὺς	λόγους	τούτους	πεσὼν	ἐξέψυξεν·	καὶ
these words			falling	expired;	and

ἐγένετο	φόβος	μέγας	ἐπὶ	πάντας	τοὺς
came	fear	great	on	all	the [ones]

ἀκούοντας.	6 ἀναστάντες	δὲ	οἱ	νεώτεροι
hearing.	And rising up		the	young men

συνέστειλαν	αὐτὸν	καὶ	ἐξενέγκαντες	ἔθαψαν.
wrapped	him	and	carrying out	buried [him].

7 Ἐγένετο	δὲ	ὡς	ὡρῶν	τριῶν	διάστημα
¹And there was	²of	about	⁵hours	⁴three	³an interval

καὶ	ἡ	γυνὴ	αὐτοῦ	μὴ	εἰδυῖα	τὸ	γεγονὸς
and	the	wife	of him	not	knowing	the thing having happened

εἰσῆλθεν.	8 ἀπεκρίθη	δὲ	πρὸς	αὐτὴν
entered.	And answered		to	her

Πέτρος·	εἰπέ	μοι,	εἰ	τοσούτου	τὸ	χωρίον
Peter:	Tell	me,	if	of(for) so much	the	land

ἀπέδοσθε;	ἡ	δὲ	εἶπεν·	ναί,	τοσούτου.
ye sold?	And she		said:	Yes,	of(for) so much.

9 ὁ	δὲ	Πέτρος	πρὸς	αὐτήν·	τί	ὅτι
–	And	Peter	to	her:		Why

συνεφωνήθη	ὑμῖν	πειράσαι	τὸ	πνεῦμα
was it agreed	with you	to tempt	the	Spirit

κυρίου;	ἰδοὺ	οἱ	πόδες	τῶν	θαψάντων	τὸν
of [the] Lord?	behold[,] the		feet	of the	[ones] having	the buried

ἄνδρα	σου	ἐπὶ	τῇ	θύρᾳ	καὶ	ἐξοίσουσίν
husband	of thee	at	the	door	and	they will carry out

σε.	10 ἔπεσεν	δὲ	παραχρῆμα	πρὸς	τοὺς
thee.	And she fell		at once	at	the

πόδας	αὐτοῦ	καὶ	ἐξέψυξεν·	εἰσελθόντες	δὲ
feet	of him	and	expired;	and entering	

οἱ	νεανίσκοι	εὗρον	αὐτὴν	νεκράν,	καὶ
the	young men	found	her	dead,	and

her out and buried her
beside her husband.
[11]And great fear came
upon the whole church,
and upon all who heard
of these things.

12 Now many signs
and wonders were done
among the people by the
hands of the apostles.
And they were all to-
gether in Solomon's
Portico. [13]None of the
rest dared join them, but
the people held them in
high honor. [14]And more
than ever believers were
added to the Lord, multi-
tudes both of men and
women, [15]so that they
even carried out the sick
into the streets, and laid
them as beds and pallets,
that as Peter came by at
least his shadow might
fall on some of them.
[16]The people also gath-
ered from the towns
around Jerusalem, bring-
ing the sick and those
afflicted with unclean
spirits, and they were all
healed.

17 But the high priest
rose up and all who were
with him, that is, the
party of the Sad'ducees,
and filled with jealousy
[18]they arrested the

ἐξενέγκαντες   ἔθαψαν   πρὸς   τὸν   ἄνδρα
carrying out   buried [her] beside   the   husband

αὐτῆς.   11 Καὶ   ἐγένετο   φόβος   μέγας
of her.   And   came   fear   great

ἐφ᾽   ὅλην   τὴν   ἐκκλησίαν   καὶ   ἐπὶ   πάντας
on   all   the   church   and   on   all

τοὺς   ἀκούοντας   ταῦτα.
the [ones] hearing   these things.

12 Διὰ   δὲ   τῶν   χειρῶν   τῶν   ἀποστόλων
And through the   hands   of the   apostles

ἐγίνετο   σημεῖα   καὶ   τέρατα   πολλὰ   ἐν
[1]happened [2]signs [3]and [4]wonders [1]many among

τῷ   λαῷ·   καὶ   ἦσαν   ὁμοθυμαδὸν   πάντες
the people; and   were   with one mind   all

ἐν   τῇ   στοᾷ   Σολομῶντος·   13 τῶν   δὲ
in the   porch   of Solomon;   and of the

λοιπῶν   οὐδεὶς   ἐτόλμα   κολλᾶσθαι   αὐτοῖς,
rest   no one   dared   to be joined   to them,

ἀλλ᾽   ἐμεγάλυνεν   αὐτοὺς   ὁ   λαός·   14 μᾶλλον
but   magnified   them   the people;   [2]more

δὲ   προσετίθεντο   πιστεύοντες   τῷ   κυρίῳ,
[1]and were added   believing [ones] to the Lord,

πλήθη   ἀνδρῶν   τε   καὶ   γυναικῶν·   15 ὥστε
multitudes both of men   and   of women;   so as

καὶ   εἰς   τὰς   πλατείας   ἐκφέρειν   τοὺς
even into   the   streets   to bring out   the
                                            =they brought out

ἀσθενεῖς   καὶ   τιθέναι   ἐπὶ   κλιναρίων   καὶ
ailing   and   to place   on   pallets   and

κραβάτων,   ἵνα ἐρχομένου   Πέτρου   κἂν   ἡ   σκιὰ
mattresses,   that [3]coming [4]of Peter [1]if even [2]the [3]shadow

ἐπισκιάσῃ   τινὶ   αὐτῶν.   16 συνήρχετο   δὲ
might overshadow some one of them.   And came together

καὶ   τὸ   πλῆθος   τῶν   πέριξ   πόλεων
also   the multitude of the [2]round about [1]cities

Ἰερουσαλήμ,   φέροντες   ἀσθενεῖς   καὶ
Jerusalem,   carrying   ailing [ones] and

ὀχλουμένους   ὑπὸ   πνευμάτων   ἀκαθάρτων,
being tormented   by   spirits   unclean,

οἵτινες   ἐθεραπεύοντο   ἅπαντες.
who   were healed   all.

17 Ἀναστὰς   δὲ   ὁ   ἀρχιερεὺς   καὶ   πάντες
And rising up   the   high priest   and   all

οἱ   σὺν   αὐτῷ,   ἡ   οὖσα   αἵρεσις   τῶν
the[ones] with   him,   the existing   sect   of the

Σαδδουκαίων,   ἐπλήσθησαν   ζήλου   18 καὶ
Sadducees,   were filled   of(with) jealousy and

ἐπέβαλον   τὰς   χεῖρας   ἐπὶ   τοὺς   ἀποστόλους
laid on   the(ir) hands   on   the   apostles

apostles and put them in the common prison. ¹⁹But at night an angel of the Lord opened the prison doors and brought them out and said, ²⁰"Go and stand in the temple and speak to the people all the words of this Life." ²¹And when they heard this, they entered the temple at daybreak and taught.

Now the high priest came and those who were with him and called together the council and all the senate of Israel, and sent to the prison to have them brought. ²²But when the officers came, they did not find them in the prison, and they returned and reported, ²³"We found the prison securely locked and the sentries standing at the doors, but when we opened it we found no one inside." ²⁴Now when the captain of the temple and the chief priests heard these words, they were much perplexed about them, wondering what this would come to. ²⁵And some one came and told them, "The men whom you put in prison are standing in the temple

καὶ   ἔθεντο   αὐτοὺς   ἐν   τηρήσει   δημοσίᾳ.
and   put   them   in   custody   publicly.

19 Ἄγγελος   δὲ   κυρίου   διὰ   νυκτὸς
But an angel   of [the] Lord   through(during) [the] night

ἤνοιξε   τὰς   θύρας   τῆς   φυλακῆς   ἐξαγαγών   τε
opened   the   doors   of the   prison   and leading out

αὐτοὺς   εἶπεν·   20 πορεύεσθε   καὶ   σταθέντες
them   said :   Go ye   and   standing

λαλεῖτε   ἐν   τῷ   ἱερῷ   τῷ   λαῷ   πάντα
speak   in   the   temple   to the people   all

τὰ   ῥήματα   τῆς   ζωῆς   ταύτης.
the   words   of this life.

21 ἀκούσαντες   δὲ   εἰσῆλθον   ὑπὸ   τὸν   ὄρθρον
And having heard   they entered   about   the   dawn

εἰς   τὸ   ἱερὸν   καὶ   ἐδίδασκον.   Παραγενόμενος   δὲ
into   the   temple   and   taught.   And having come

ὁ   ἀρχιερεὺς   καὶ   οἱ   σὺν   αὐτῷ
the   high priest   and   the [ones]   with   him

συνεκάλεσαν   τὸ   συνέδριον   καὶ   πᾶσαν   τὴν
called together   the   council   and   all   the

γερουσίαν   τῶν   υἱῶν   Ἰσραήλ,   καὶ   ἀπέστειλαν
senate   of the sons   of Israel,   and   sent

εἰς   τὸ   δεσμωτήριον   ἀχθῆναι   αὐτούς.ᵇ
to the   jail   to be brought   them.ᵇ

22 οἱ   δὲ   παραγενόμενοι   ὑπηρέται   οὐχ   εὗρον
¹But ²the   ⁴having come   ³attendants   found not

αὐτοὺς   ἐν   τῇ   φυλακῇ·   ἀναστρέψαντες   δὲ
them   in   the   prison;   and having returned

ἀπήγγειλαν   23 λέγοντες   ὅτι   τὸ   δεσμωτήριον
they reported   saying[,]   –   The   jail

εὕρομεν   κεκλεισμένον   ἐν   πάσῃ   ἀσφαλείᾳ
we found   having been shut   in   all   security

καὶ   τοὺς   φύλακας   ἑστῶτας   ἐπὶ   τῶν
and   the   guards   standing   at   the

θυρῶν,   ἀνοίξαντες   δὲ   ἔσω   οὐδένα   εὕρομεν.
doors,   but having opened   ³inside   ²no one   ¹we found.

24 ὡς   δὲ   ἤκουσαν   τοὺς   λόγους   τούτους
And as   ⁹heard   ¹⁰these ¹¹words

ὅ   τε   στρατηγὸς   τοῦ   ἱεροῦ   καὶ   οἱ   ἀρχιερεῖς,
¹the ¹both ²commandant ⁴of the ⁵temple ⁶and ⁷the ⁸chief priests,

διηπόρουν   περὶ   αὐτῶν   τί   ἂν   γένοιτο
they were in doubt   about   them   what   ²might become

τοῦτο.   25 παραγενόμενος   δέ   τις   ἀπήγγειλεν
¹this thing.   And having come   someone   reported

αὐτοῖς   ὅτι   ἰδοὺ   οἱ   ἄνδρες,   οὓς
to them[,]   –   Behold[,]   the   men,   whom

ἔθεσθε   ἐν   τῇ   φυλακῇ,   εἰσὶν   ἐν   τῷ   ἱερῷ
ye put   in   the   prison,   are   in   the   temple

and teaching the people."
²⁶ Then the captain with
the officers went and
brought them, but with-
out violence, for they
were afraid of being
stoned by the people.

27 And when they had
brought them, they set
them before the council.
And the high priest
questioned them, ²⁸ say-
ing, "We strictly charged
you not to teach in this
name, yet here you have
filled Jerusalem with
your teaching and you
intend to bring this man's
blood upon us." ²⁹ But
Peter and the apostles
answered, "We must
obey God rather than
men. ³⁰ The God of our
fathers raised Jesus whom
you killed by hanging
him on a tree. ³¹ God
exalted him at his right
hand as Leader and
Savior, to give repen-
tance to Israel and for-
giveness of sins. ³² And
we are witnesses to these
things, and so is the
Holy Spirit whom God
has given to those who
obey him."

33 When they heard

ἑστῶτες	καὶ	διδάσκοντες	τὸν λαόν.
standing	and	teaching	the people.

26 Τότε ἀπελθὼν ὁ στρατηγὸς σὺν τοῖς
Then going the commandant with the

ὑπηρέταις ἦγεν αὐτούς, οὐ μετὰ βίας,
attendants brought them, not with force,

ἐφοβοῦντο γὰρ τὸν λαόν, μὴ λιθασθῶσιν·
for they feared the people, lest they should be stoned;

27 ἀγαγόντες δὲ αὐτοὺς ἔστησαν ἐν τῷ
and bringing them they stood in the

συνεδρίῳ. καὶ ἐπηρώτησεν αὐτοὺς ὁ
council. And questioned them the

ἀρχιερεὺς 28 λέγων· παραγγελίᾳ παρηγ-
high priest saying : With charge we
=We strictly

γείλαμεν ὑμῖν μὴ διδάσκειν ἐπὶ
charged you not to teach on(in)

τῷ ὀνόματι τούτῳ, καὶ ἰδοὺ πεπληρώκατε
this name, and behold ye have filled

τὴν Ἰερουσαλὴμ τῆς διδαχῆς ὑμῶν, καὶ
- Jerusalem of(with) the teaching of you, and

βούλεσθε ἐπαγαγεῖν ἐφ' ἡμᾶς τὸ αἷμα
intend to bring on on us the blood

τοῦ ἀνθρώπου τούτου. 29 ἀποκριθεὶς δὲ
of this man. And answering

Πέτρος καὶ οἱ ἀπόστολοι εἶπαν· ¹πειθαρχεῖν
Peter and the apostles said : ¹to obey

δεῖ θεῷ μᾶλλον ἢ ἀνθρώποις. 30 ὁ
¹It behoves God rather than men. The

θεὸς τῶν πατέρων ἡμῶν ἤγειρεν Ἰησοῦν,
God of the fathers of us raised Jesus,

ὃν ὑμεῖς διεχειρίσασθε κρεμάσαντες ἐπὶ
whom ye killed hanging on

ξύλου· 31 τοῦτον ὁ θεὸς ἀρχηγὸν καὶ
a tree; this man - God a Ruler and

σωτῆρα ὕψωσεν τῇ δεξιᾷ αὐτοῦ τοῦ
a Saviour exalted to the right [hand] of him -

δοῦναι μετάνοιαν τῷ Ἰσραὴλ καὶ ἄφεσιν
to giveᵈ repentance - to Israel and forgiveness

ἁμαρτιῶν. 32 καὶ ἡμεῖς ἐσμεν μάρτυρες
of sins. And we are witnesses

τῶν ῥημάτων τούτων, καὶ τὸ πνεῦμα
of these words(things), and the Spirit

τὸ ἅγιον ὃ ἔδωκεν ὁ θεὸς τοῖς
- Holy which ²gave - ¹God to the

πειθαρχοῦσιν αὐτῷ. 33 οἱ δὲ ἀκούσαντες
[ones] obeying him. And the [ones] hearing

this they were enraged and wanted to kill them. [34]But a Pharisee in the council named Gama'liel, a teacher of the law, held in honor by all the people, stood up and ordered the men to be put outside for a while. [35]And he said to them, "Men of Israel, take care what you do with these men. [36]For before these days Theu'das arose, giving himself out to be somebody, and a number of men, about four hundred, joined him; but he was slain and all who followed him were dispersed and came to nothing. [37]After him Judas the Galilean arose in the days of the census and drew away some of the people after him; he also perished, and all who followed him were scattered. [38]So in the present case I tell you, keep away from these men and let them alone; for if this plan or this undertaking is of men, it will fail; [39]but if it is of God, you will not be able to overthrow them. You

διεπρίοντο   καὶ   ἐβούλοντο   ἀνελεῖν   αὐτούς.
were cut*   and   intended   to kill   them.

34 Ἀναστὰς   δέ   τις   ἐν   τῷ   συνεδρίῳ
¹But ⁴standing up ²a certain ⁵in   ⁶the   ⁷council

Φαρισαῖος   ὀνόματι   Γαμαλιήλ,   νομοδιδάσκαλος
³Pharisee   by name   Gamaliel,   a teacher of the law

τίμιος   παντὶ   τῷ   λαῷ,   ἐκέλευσεν   ἔξω
honoured   by all   the   people,   commanded   ⁴outside

βραχὺ   τοὺς   ἀνθρώπους   ποιῆσαι,   **35** εἶπέν
⁵a little ³the   ²men   ¹to make(put),   ²said

τε   πρὸς   αὐτούς·   ἄνδρες   Ἰσραηλῖται,
¹and   to   them :   Men   Israelites,

προσέχετε   ἑαυτοῖς   ἐπὶ   τοῖς   ἀνθρώποις   τούτοις
take heed   to yourselves   ⁴on(to)   ⁵these ⁶men

τί   μέλλετε   πράσσειν.   **36** πρὸ   γὰρ
¹what   ²ye intend   ³to do.   For before

τούτων   τῶν   ἡμερῶν   ἀνέστη   Θευδᾶς,   λέγων
these   -   days   stood up   Theudas,   saying

εἶναί   τινα   ἑαυτόν,   ᾧ   προσεκλίθη   ἀνδρῶν
to be   someone   himself,   ¹to whom   ⁴were attached   ²of men

ἀριθμὸς   ὡς   τετρακοσίων·   ὃς   ἀνῃρέθη,   καὶ
²a number   ⁴about   ⁵four hundreds;   who   was killed,   and

πάντες   ὅσοι   ἐπείθοντο   αὐτῷ   διελύθησαν
all   as many as   obeyed   him   were dispersed

καὶ   ἐγένοντο   εἰς   οὐδέν.   **37** μετὰ   τοῦτον
and   came   to   nothing.   After   this

ἀνέστη   Ἰούδας   ὁ   Γαλιλαῖος   ἐν   ταῖς
stood up   Judas   the   Galilæan   in   the

ἡμέραις   τῆς   ἀπογραφῆς   καὶ   ἀπέστησεν
days   of the   enrolment   and   drew away

λαὸν   ὀπίσω   αὐτοῦ·   κἀκεῖνος   ἀπώλετο,
people   after   him;   and that man   perished,

καὶ   πάντες   ὅσοι   ἐπείθοντο   αὐτῷ
and   all   as many as   obeyed   him

διεσκορπίσθησαν.   **38** καὶ   τὰ   νῦν   λέγω
were scattered.   And   -   now   I say

ὑμῖν,   ἀπόστητε   ἀπὸ   τῶν   ἀνθρώπων   τούτων
to you,   stand away   from   these men

καὶ   ἄφετε   αὐτούς·   ὅτι   ἐὰν   ᾖ   ἐξ   ἀνθρώπων
and   leave   them;   because   if   be   of   men

ἡ   βουλὴ   αὕτη   ἢ   τὸ   ἔργον   τοῦτο,
this   counsel   this   or   this work,

καταλυθήσεται·   **39** εἰ   δὲ   ἐκ   θεοῦ   ἐστιν,
it will be destroyed;   but if   of   God   it is,

οὐ   δυνήσεσθε   καταλῦσαι   αὐτούς,   μήποτε
ye will not be able   to destroy   them,   lest

* That is, to the heart; cf. 7. 54.

might even be found opposing God!"

40 So they took his advice, and when they had called in the apostles, they beat them and charged them not to speak in the name of Jesus, and let them go. ⁴¹Then they left the presence of the council, rejoicing that they were counted worthy to suffer dishonor for the name. ⁴²And every day in the temple and at home they did not cease teaching and preaching Jesus as the Christ.

καὶ   θεομάχοι   εὑρεθῆτε.   ἐπείσθησαν   δὲ
even fighters against God ye be found.   And they obeyed

αὐτῷ,   40 καὶ   προσκαλεσάμενοι   τοὺς
him,   and   having called to [them]   the

ἀποστόλους   δείραντες   παρήγγειλαν   μὴ
apostles   beating   charged   not

λαλεῖν ἐπὶ   τῷ   ὀνόματι   τοῦ   Ἰησοῦ καὶ
to speak on(in) the   name   –   of Jesus and

ἀπέλυσαν.   41 Οἱ   μὲν   οὖν   ἐπορεύοντο
released [them].   They   –   therefore   went

χαίροντες   ἀπὸ   προσώπου   τοῦ   συνεδρίου,
rejoicing from [the] presence   of the   council,

ὅτι   κατηξιώθησαν   ὑπὲρ τοῦ ὀνόματος
because they were deemed worthy on behalf of the   name

ἀτιμασθῆναι·   42 πᾶσάν τε   ἡμέραν ἐν   τῷ
to be dishonoured;   and every   day   in   the

ἱερῷ   καὶ   κατ'   οἶκον   οὐκ   ἐπαύοντο
temple and from house to house† they ceased not

διδάσκοντες   καὶ   εὐαγγελιζόμενοι   τὸν   χριστὸν
teaching   and   preaching   the   Christ

Ἰησοῦν.
Jesus.

CHAPTER 6

NOW in these days when the disciples were increasing in number, the Hellenists murmured against the Hebrews because their widows were neglected in the daily distribution. ²And the twelve summoned the body of the disciples and said, "It is not right that we should give up preaching the word of God to serve tables. ³Therefore, brethren, pick out from among you seven men of good repute, full of the Spirit and of wisdom, whom we may appoint to this

6 Ἐν   δὲ   ταῖς   ἡμέραις   ταύταις
  Now in   these days

πληθυνόντων   τῶν   μαθητῶν   ἐγένετο
being multiplied   the   disciplesª   there was
=as the disciples were multiplied

γογγυσμὸς   τῶν   Ἑλληνιστῶν   πρὸς   τοὺς
a murmuring   of the   Hellenists   against   the

Ἑβραίους,   ὅτι   παρεθεωροῦντο   ἐν   τῇ
Hebrews,   because   ⁴were overlooked   ⁵in ⁶the

διακονίᾳ   τῇ   καθημερινῇ   αἱ   χῆραι   αὐτῶν.
⁸service   –   ⁷daily   ¹the ²widows ³of them.

2 προσκαλεσάμενοι   δὲ   οἱ   δώδεκα   τὸ
¹having called to [them]   ¹And   ²the   ²twelve   τὸ

πλῆθος   τῶν   μαθητῶν   εἶπαν·   οὐκ   ἀρεστόν
multitude of the   disciples   said :   not   pleasing

ἐστιν   ἡμᾶς   καταλείψαντας   τὸν   λόγον   τοῦ
It is   us   leaving   the   word   –

θεοῦ   διακονεῖν   τραπέζαις.   3 ἐπισκέψασθε
of God   to serve   tables.   look ye out

δέ, ἀδελφοί, ἄνδρας ἐξ ὑμῶν μαρτυρουμένους
But, brothers, ²men ³of ⁴you ⁵being witnessed to

ἑπτὰ   πλήρεις   πνεύματος   καὶ   σοφίας,   οὓς
¹seven [seven] of Spirit   and   of wisdom, whom

καταστήσομεν   ἐπὶ   τῆς   χρείας   ταύτης·
we will appoint   over   this office;

duty. ⁴But we will devote ourselves to prayer and to the ministry of the word." ⁵And what they said pleased the whole multitude, and they chose Stephen, a man full of faith and of the Holy Spirit, and Philip, and Proch'orus, and Nica'nor, and Timon, and Par'menas, and Nicola'us, a proselyte of Antioch. ⁶These they set before the apostles, and they prayed and laid their hands upon them.

7 And the word of God increased; and the number of the disciples multiplied greatly in Jerusalem, and a great many of the priests were obedient to the faith.

8 And Stephen, full of grace and power, did great wonders and signs among the people. ⁹Then some of those who belonged to the synagogue of the Freedmen (as it was called), and of the Cyre'nians, and of the Alexandrians, and of those from Cili'cia and Asia, arose and disputed with Stephen. ¹⁰But they could not withstand the wisdom and the Spirit with which he spoke. ¹¹Then they secretly instigated men, who said, "We have heard him

---

4 ἡμεῖς δὲ τῇ προσευχῇ καὶ τῇ διακονίᾳ
but we to the prayer and to the service

τοῦ λόγου προσκαρτερήσομεν. 5 καὶ ἤρεσεν
of the word will keep. And ³pleased

ὁ λόγος ἐνώπιον παντὸς τοῦ πλήθους,
¹the ²word before all the multitude,

καὶ ἐξελέξαντο Στέφανον, ἄνδρα πλήρη
and they chose Stephen, a man full

πίστεως καὶ πνεύματος ἁγίου, καὶ Φίλιππον
of faith and Spirit of Holy, and Philip

καὶ Πρόχορον καὶ Νικάνορα καὶ Τίμωνα
and Prochorus and Nicanor and Timon

καὶ Παρμενᾶν καὶ Νικόλαον προσήλυτον
and Parmenas and Nicolaus a proselyte

Ἀντιοχέα, 6 οὓς ἔστησαν ἐνώπιον τῶν
of Antioch, whom they set before the

ἀποστόλων, καὶ προσευξάμενοι ἐπέθηκαν
apostles, and having prayed they placed on

αὐτοῖς τὰς χεῖρας.
them the(ir) hands.

7 Καὶ ὁ λόγος τοῦ θεοῦ ηὔξανεν, καὶ
And the word – of God grew, and

ἐπληθύνετο ὁ ἀριθμὸς τῶν μαθητῶν ἐν
was multiplied the number of the disciples in

Ἰερουσαλὴμ σφόδρα, πολύς τε ὄχλος τῶν
Jerusalem greatly, and a much(great) crowd of the

ἱερέων ὑπήκουον τῇ πίστει.
priests obeyed the faith.

8 Στέφανος δὲ πλήρης χάριτος καὶ
And Stephen full of grace and

δυνάμεως ἐποίει τέρατα καὶ σημεῖα μεγάλα
of power did wonders and signs great

ἐν τῷ λαῷ. 9 ἀνέστησαν δέ τινες τῶν
among the people. But rose up some of the
[ones]

ἐκ τῆς συναγωγῆς τῆς λεγομένης
of the synagogue – being called

Λιβερτίνων καὶ Κυρηναίων καὶ Ἀλεξ-
of Freedmen and of Cyrenians and of

ανδρέων καὶ τῶν ἀπὸ Κιλικίας καὶ
Alexandrians and of the [ones] from Cilicia and

Ἀσίας συζητοῦντες τῷ Στεφάνῳ, 10 καὶ
Asia discussing with Stephen, and

οὐκ ἴσχυον ἀντιστῆναι τῇ σοφίᾳ καὶ
were not able to withstand the wisdom and

τῷ πνεύματι ᾧ ἐλάλει. 11 τότε ὑπέβαλον
the spirit with which he spoke. Then they suborned

ἄνδρας λέγοντας ὅτι ἀκηκόαμεν αὐτοῦ
men saying[,] – We have heard him

speak blasphemous words against Moses and God." [12]And they stirred up the people and the elders and the scribes, and they came upon him and seized him and brought him before the council, [13]and set up false witnesses who said, "This man never ceases to speak words against this holy place and the law; [14]for we have heard him say that this Jesus of Nazareth will destroy this place, and will change the customs which Moses delivered to us." [15]And gazing at him, all who sat in the council saw that his face was like the face of an angel.

λαλοῦντος ῥήματα βλάσφημα εἰς Μωϋσῆν
speaking words blasphemous against Moses
καὶ τὸν θεόν· 12 συνεκίνησάν τε τὸν
and - God; and they stirred up the
λαὸν καὶ τοὺς πρεσβυτέρους καὶ τοὺς
people and the elders and the
γραμματεῖς, καὶ ἐπιστάντες συνήρπασαν
scribes, and coming on they seized
αὐτὸν καὶ ἤγαγον εἰς τὸ συνέδριον,
him and led to the council,
13 ἔστησάν τε μάρτυρας ψευδεῖς λέγοντας·
and stood witnesses false saying :
ὁ ἄνθρωπος οὗτος οὐ παύεται λαλῶν
This man ceases not speaking
ῥήματα κατὰ τοῦ τόπου τοῦ ἁγίου [τούτου]
words against - ³place - ²holy ¹this
καὶ τοῦ νόμου· 14 ἀκηκόαμεν γὰρ αὐτοῦ
and the law; for we have heard him
λέγοντος ὅτι Ἰησοῦς ὁ Ναζωραῖος οὗτος
saying that ²Jesus ³the ⁴Nazarene ¹this
καταλύσει τὸν τόπον τοῦτον καὶ ἀλλάξει
will destroy this place and will change
τὰ ἔθη ἃ παρέδωκεν ἡμῖν Μωϋσῆς.
the customs which delivered to us Moses.
15 καὶ ἀτενίσαντες εἰς αὐτὸν πάντες οἱ
And gazing at him all the
καθεζόμενοι ἐν τῷ συνεδρίῳ εἶδον τὸ
[ones] sitting in the council saw the
πρόσωπον αὐτοῦ ὡσεὶ πρόσωπον ἀγγέλου.
face of him as a face of an angel.

CHAPTER 7

AND the high priest said, "Is this so?" [2]And Stephen said:

"Brethren and fathers, hear me. The God of glory appeared to our father Abraham, when he was in Mesopota'mia, before he lived in Haran, [3]and said to him, 'Depart from your land and from your kindred and go into

7 Εἶπεν δὲ ὁ ἀρχιερεύς· εἰ ταῦτα
And said the high priest : If these things
οὕτως ἔχει; 2 ὁ δὲ ἔφη·
thus have(are)? And he said:
Ἄνδρες ἀδελφοὶ καὶ πατέρες, ἀκούσατε.
Men brothers and fathers, hear ye.
Ὁ θεὸς τῆς δόξης ὤφθη τῷ πατρὶ
The God - of glory appeared to the father
ἡμῶν Ἀβραὰμ ὄντι ἐν τῇ Μεσοποταμίᾳ
of us Abraham being in - Mesopotamia
πρὶν ἢ κατοικῆσαι αὐτὸν ἐν Χαρράν,
before to dwell himᵇ in Charran,
=he dwelt
3 καὶ εἶπεν πρὸς αὐτόν· ἔξελθε ἐκ τῆς
and said to him : Go forth out of the
γῆς σου καὶ τῆς συγγενείας σου, καὶ
land of thee and the kindred of thee, and

the land which I will show you.' **4** Then he departed from the land of the Chalde'ans, and lived in Haran. And after his father died, God removed him from there into this land in which you are now living; **5** yet he gave him no inheritance in it, not even a foot's length, but promised to give it to him in possession and to his posterity after him, though he had no child. **6** And God spoke to this effect, that his posterity would be aliens in a land belonging to others, who would enslave them and ill-treat them four hundred years. **7** 'But I will judge the nation which they serve,' said God, 'and after that they shall come out and worship me in this place.' **8** And he gave him the covenant of circumcision. And so Abraham became the father of Isaac, and circumcised him on the eighth day; and Isaac became the father of Jacob, and Jacob of the twelve patriarchs.

9 "And the patriarchs, jealous of Joseph, sold

δεῦρο εἰς τὴν γῆν ἣν ἄν σοι δείξω.
come into the land whichever to thee I may show.

4 τότε ἐξελθὼν ἐκ γῆς Χαλδαίων
Then going forth out of [the] land of [the] Chaldæans

κατῴκησεν ἐν Χαρράν. κἀκεῖθεν μετὰ
he dwelt in Charran. And thence after

τὸ ἀποθανεῖν τὸν πατέρα αὐτοῦ μετῴκισεν
the to die the father of him[b] [God] removed
=his father died

αὐτὸν εἰς τὴν γῆν ταύτην εἰς ἣν ὑμεῖς
him into this land in which ye

νῦν κατοικεῖτε, **5** καὶ οὐκ ἔδωκεν αὐτῷ
now dwell, and gave not to him

κληρονομίαν ἐν αὐτῇ οὐδὲ βῆμα ποδός,
an inheritance in it nor a foot's space,

καὶ ἐπηγγείλατο δοῦναι αὐτῷ εἰς
and promised to give him for

κατάσχεσιν αὐτὴν καὶ τῷ σπέρματι αὐτοῦ
a possession it and to the seed of him

μετ' αὐτόν, οὐκ ὄντος αὐτῷ τέκνου.[a]
after him, not being to him[e] a child.[a]
=while he had no child.

6 ἐλάλησεν δὲ οὕτως ὁ θεός, ὅτι ἔσται
And spoke thus - God, that will be

τὸ σπέρμα αὐτοῦ πάροικον ἐν γῇ ἀλλοτρίᾳ,
the seed of him a sojourner in a land belonging to others,

καὶ δουλώσουσιν αὐτὸ καὶ κακώσουσιν
and they will enslave it and will ill-treat

ἔτη τετρακόσια· **7** καὶ τὸ ἔθνος ᾧ ἐὰν
years four hundred; and the nation whichever

δουλεύσουσιν κρινῶ ἐγώ, ὁ θεὸς εἶπεν,
they will serve will judge I, - God said,

καὶ μετὰ ταῦτα ἐξελεύσονται καὶ
and after these things they will come forth and

λατρεύσουσίν μοι ἐν τῷ τόπῳ τούτῳ.
will worship me in this place.

8 καὶ ἔδωκεν αὐτῷ διαθήκην περιτομῆς·
And he gave him a covenant of circumcision;

καὶ οὕτως ἐγέννησεν τὸν Ἰσαὰκ καὶ
and thus he begat - Isaac and

περιέτεμεν αὐτὸν τῇ ἡμέρᾳ τῇ ὀγδόῃ,
circumcised him on the day - eighth,

καὶ Ἰσαὰκ τὸν Ἰακώβ, καὶ Ἰακὼβ
and Isaac [begat] - Jacob, and Jacob [begat]

τοὺς δώδεκα πατριάρχας. **9** Καὶ οἱ
the twelve patriarchs. And the

πατριάρχαι ζηλώσαντες τὸν Ἰωσὴφ
patriarchs becoming jealous - [a]Joseph

him into Egypt; but God was with him, ¹⁰and rescued him out of all his afflictions, and gave him favor and wisdom before Pharaoh, king of Egypt, who made him governor over Egypt and over all his household. ¹¹Now there came a famine throughout all Egypt and Canaan, and great affliction, and our fathers could find no food. ¹²But when Jacob heard that there was grain in Egypt, he sent forth our fathers the first time. ¹³And at the second visit Joseph made himself known to his brothers, and Joseph's family became known to Pharaoh. ¹⁴And Joseph sent and called to him Jacob his father and all his kindred, seventy-five souls; ¹⁵and Jacob went down into Egypt. And he died, himself and our fathers, ¹⁶and they were carried back to Shechem and laid in the tomb that Abraham had bought for a sum of silver from the sons of Hamor in Shechem.

17 "But as the time of

ἀπέδοντο   εἰς   Αἴγυπτον·   καὶ   ἦν   ὁ   θεὸς
¹sold   into   Egypt;   and   was   –   God

μετ'   αὐτοῦ,   10 καὶ   ἐξείλατο   αὐτὸν   ἐκ
with   him,   and   rescued   him   out of

πασῶν   τῶν   θλίψεων   αὐτοῦ,   καὶ   ἔδωκεν
all   the   afflictions   of him,   and   gave

αὐτῷ   χάριν   καὶ   σοφίαν   ἐναντίον   Φαραὼ
him   favour   and   wisdom   before   Pharaoh

βασιλέως   Αἰγύπτου,   καὶ   κατέστησεν   αὐτὸν
king   of Egypt,   and   he appointed   him

ἡγούμενον   ἐπ'   Αἴγυπτον   καὶ   ὅλον   τὸν
governor   over   Egypt   and   all   the

οἶκον   αὐτοῦ.   11 ἦλθεν   δὲ   λιμὸς   ἐφ'
household   of him.   But came   a famine   over

ὅλην   τὴν   Αἴγυπτον   καὶ   Χανάαν   καὶ
all   –   Egypt   and   Canaan   and

θλῖψις   μεγάλη,   καὶ   οὐχ   ηὕρισκον
affliction   great,   and   found not

χορτάσματα   οἱ   πατέρες   ἡμῶν.   12 ἀκούσας
sustenance   the   fathers   of us.   ²having heard

δὲ   'Ιακὼβ   ὄντα   σιτία   εἰς   Αἴγυπτον
¹But   ³Jacob   ⁵being   ⁴corn   in   Egypt

ἐξαπέστειλεν   τοὺς   πατέρας   ἡμῶν   πρῶτον·
sent forth   the   fathers   of us   first;

13 καὶ   ἐν   τῷ   δευτέρῳ   ἐγνωρίσθη   'Ιωσὴφ
and   at   the   second [time]   was made known   Joseph

τοῖς   ἀδελφοῖς   αὐτοῦ,   καὶ   φανερὸν   ἐγένετο   τῷ
to the   brothers   of him,   and   ⁵manifest   ⁴became

Φαραὼ   τὸ   γένος   'Ιωσήφ.   14 ἀποστείλας   δὲ
⁶to Pharaoh   ¹the   ²race   ³of Joseph.   And sending

'Ιωσὴφ   μετεκαλέσατο   'Ιακὼβ   τὸν   πατέρα
Joseph   called   Jacob   the   father

αὐτοῦ   καὶ   πᾶσαν   τὴν   συγγένειαν   ἐν
of him   and   all   the(his)   kindred   in

ψυχαῖς   ἑβδομήκοντα   πέντε.   15 καὶ   κατέβη
souls   seventy-five.   And went down

'Ιακὼβ   εἰς   Αἴγυπτον,   καὶ   ἐτελεύτησεν
Jacob   to   Egypt,   and   died

αὐτὸς   καὶ   οἱ   πατέρες   ἡμῶν,   16 καὶ
he   and   the   fathers   of us,   and

μετετέθησαν   εἰς   Συχὲμ   καὶ   ἐτέθησαν   ἐν
were transferred   to   Sychem   and   were put   in

τῷ   μνήματι   ᾧ   ὠνήσατο   'Αβραὰμ   τιμῆς
the   tomb   which   ²bought   ¹Abraham   of(for) a price

ἀργυρίου   παρὰ   τῶν   υἱῶν   'Εμμὼρ   ἐν
of silver   from   the   sons   of Emmor   in

Συχέμ.   17 Καθὼς   δὲ   ἤγγιζεν   ὁ   χρόνος
Sychem.   And as   drew near   the   time

the promise drew near, which God had granted to Abraham, the people grew and multiplied in Egypt [18]till there arose over Egypt another king who had not known Joseph. [19]He dealt craftily with our race and forced our fathers to expose their infants, that they might not be kept alive. [20]At this time Moses was born, and was beautiful before God. And he was brought up for three months in his father's house; [21]and when he was exposed, Pharaoh's daughter adopted him and brought him up as her own son. [22]And Moses was instructed in all the wisdom of the Egyptians, and he was mighty in his words and deeds.

23 "When he was forty years old, it came into his heart to visit his brethren, the sons of Israel. [24]And seeing one of them being wronged, he defended the oppressed man and avenged him by striking the Egyptian. [25]He supposed that his brethren understood that God was

τῆς ἐπαγγελίας ἧς ὡμολόγησεν ὁ θεὸς
of the promise which [2]declared – [1]God

τῷ 'Αβραάμ, ηὔξησεν ὁ λαὸς καὶ
to Abraham, [3]grew [1]the [2]people and

ἐπληθύνθη ἐν Αἰγύπτῳ, 18 ἄχρι οὗ ἀνέστη
were multiplied in Egypt, until [2]rose up

βασιλεὺς ἕτερος ἐπ' Αἴγυπτον, ὃς οὐκ ᾔδει
[2]king [1]another over Egypt, who did not know

τὸν 'Ιωσήφ. 19 οὗτος κατασοφισάμενος
– Joseph. This man dealing craftily with

τὸ γένος ἡμῶν ἐκάκωσεν τοὺς πατέρας
the race of us ill-treated the fathers

τοῦ ποιεῖν τὰ βρέφη ἔκθετα αὐτῶν
to make[d] [1]the [2]babes [4]exposed [3]of them

εἰς τὸ μὴ ζωογονεῖσθαι. 20 'Εν ᾧ
to the not to be preserved alive. At which
=so that they should not be . . .

καιρῷ ἐγεννήθη Μωϋσῆς, καὶ ἦν ἀστεῖος
time was born Moses, and was fair

τῷ θεῷ· ὃς ἀνετράφη μῆνας τρεῖς ἐν
to God; who was reared months three in

τῷ οἴκῳ τοῦ πατρός· 21 ἐκτεθέντος δὲ
the house of the(his) father; being exposed and
=and when he was exposed

αὐτοῦ ἀνείλατο αὐτὸν ἡ θυγάτηρ Φαραὼ
him[a] took up him the daughter of Pharaoh

καὶ ἀνεθρέψατο αὐτὸν ἑαυτῇ εἰς υἱόν.
and reared him to herself for a son.
=as her own son.

22 καὶ ἐπαιδεύθη Μωϋσῆς πάσῃ σοφίᾳ
And was trained Moses in all [the] wisdom

Αἰγυπτίων, ἦν δὲ δυνατὸς ἐν λόγοις
of [the] Egyptians, and was powerful in words

καὶ ἔργοις αὐτοῦ. 23 'Ως δὲ ἐπληροῦτο
and works of him. But when [3]was fulfilled

αὐτῷ τεσσερακονταετὴς χρόνος, ἀνέβη ἐπὶ
[4]to him [2]of forty years [1]a time, it came up upon

τὴν καρδίαν αὐτοῦ ἐπισκέψασθαι τοὺς
the heart of him to visit the

ἀδελφοὺς αὐτοῦ τοὺς υἱοὺς 'Ισραήλ. 24 καὶ
brothers of him the sons of Israel. And

ἰδών τινα ἀδικούμενον ἠμύνατο, καὶ
seeing one being injured he defended [him], and

ἐποίησεν ἐκδίκησιν τῷ καταπονουμένῳ
he wrought vengeance for the [one] getting the worse

πατάξας τὸν Αἰγύπτιον. 25 ἐνόμιζεν δὲ
striking the Egyptian. Now he supposed

συνιέναι τοὺς ἀδελφοὺς ὅτι ὁ θεὸς διὰ
to understand the(his) brothers[b] that – God through
=that his brothers would understand

giving them deliverance by his hand, but they did not understand. ²⁶And on the following day he appeared to them as they were quarreling and would have reconciled them, saying, 'Men, you are brethren, why do you wrong each other?' ²⁷But the man who was wronging his neighbor thrust him aside, saying, 'Who made you a ruler and a judge over us? ²⁸Do you want to kill me as you killed the Egyptian yesterday?' ²⁹At this retort Moses fled, and became an exile in the land of Mid'ian, where he became the father of two sons.

30 "Now when forty years had passed, an angel appeared to him in the wilderness of Mount Sinai, in a flame of fire in a bush. ³¹When Moses saw it he wondered at the sight; and as he drew near to look, the voice of the Lord came, ³²'I am the God of your fathers, the God of Abraham and of Isaac and of Jacob.' And Moses trembled and did not dare to look. ³³And the Lord said to him, 'Take off the shoes from your feet, for the

χειρὸς	αὐτοῦ	δίδωσιν	σωτηρίαν	αὐτοῖς·
hand	of him	would give	salvation	to them;

οἱ δὲ οὐ συνῆκαν. 26 τῇ τε ἐπιούσῃ
but they understood not. And on the coming

ἡμέρᾳ ὤφθη αὐτοῖς μαχομένοις, καὶ
day he appeared to them fighting, and

συνήλλασσεν αὐτοὺς εἰς εἰρήνην εἰπών·
attempted to reconcile them in peace saying :

ἄνδρες, ἀδελφοί ἐστε· ἱνατί ἀδικεῖτε
Men, brothers ye are; why injure ye

ἀλλήλους; 27 ὁ δὲ ἀδικῶν τὸν πλησίον
each other? But the [one] injuring the(his) neighbour

ἀπώσατο αὐτὸν εἰπών· τίς σε κατέστησεν
thrust away him saying: Who thee appointed

ἄρχοντα καὶ δικαστὴν ἐφ᾽ ἡμῶν; 28 μὴ
a ruler and a judge over us? not

ἀνελεῖν με σὺ θέλεις ὃν τρόπον ἀνεῖλες
to kill me thou wishest in the same way as† thou killedst

ἐχθὲς τὸν Αἰγύπτιον; 29 ἔφυγεν δὲ
yesterday the Egyptian? So fled

Μωϋσῆς ἐν τῷ λόγῳ τούτῳ, καὶ ἐγένετο
Moses at this word, and became

πάροικος ἐν γῇ Μαδιάμ, οὗ ἐγέννησεν
a sojourner in [the] land Midian, where he begat

υἱοὺς δύο. 30 Καὶ πληρωθέντων ἐτῶν
sons two. And being fulfilled years
=when forty years were fulfilled

τεσσεράκοντα ὤφθη αὐτῷ ἐν τῇ ἐρήμῳ
forty[a] appeared to him in the desert

τοῦ ὄρους Σινὰ ἄγγελος ἐν φλογὶ πυρὸς
of the mount Sinai an angel in a flame of fire

βάτου. 31 ὁ δὲ Μωϋσῆς ἰδὼν ἐθαύμαζεν
of a thorn bush. - And Moses seeing marvelled at

τὸ ὅραμα· προσερχομένου δὲ αὐτοῦ κατα-
the vision; and approaching him[a] to take
=as he approached

νοῆσαι ἐγένετο φωνὴ κυρίου· 32 ἐγὼ ὁ
notice there was a voice of [the] Lord : I the

θεὸς τῶν πατέρων σου, ὁ θεὸς Ἀβραὰμ
God of the fathers of thee, the God of Abraham

καὶ Ἰσαὰκ καὶ Ἰακώβ. ἔντρομος δὲ
and of Isaac and of Jacob. But trembling

γενόμενος Μωϋσῆς οὐκ ἐτόλμα κατανοῆσαι.
becoming Moses dared not to take notice.

33 εἶπεν δὲ αὐτῷ ὁ κύριος· λῦσον τὸ
And said to him the Lord : Loosen the

ὑπόδημα τῶν ποδῶν σου· ὁ γὰρ τόπος
sandal of the feet of thee; for the place

place where you are standing is holy ground. ³⁴I have surely seen the ill-treatment of my people that are in Egypt and heard their groaning, and I have come down to deliver them. And now come, I will send you to Egypt.'

35 "This Moses whom they refused, saying, 'Who made you a ruler and a judge?' God sent as both ruler and deliverer by the hand of the angel that appeared to him in the bush. ³⁶He led them out, having performed wonders and signs in Egypt and at the Red Sea, and in the wilderness for forty years. ³⁷This is the Moses who said to the Israelites, 'God will raise up for you a prophet from your brethren as he raised me up.' ³⁸This is he who was in the congregation in the wilderness with the angel who spoke to him at Mount Sinai, and with our fathers; and he received living oracles to give to us. ³⁹Our fathers refused to obey him, but thrust him aside, and in their hearts they turned to Egypt, ⁴⁰saying to

ἐφ' ᾧ ἕστηκας γῆ ἁγία ἐστίν. 34 ἰδὼν
on which thou standest ground holy is. Seeing

εἶδον τὴν κάκωσιν τοῦ λαοῦ μου τοῦ
I saw the ill-treatment of the people of me –

ἐν Αἰγύπτῳ, καὶ τοῦ στεναγμοῦ αὐτοῦ
in Egypt, and the groan of it

ἤκουσα, καὶ κατέβην ἐξελέσθαι αὐτούς·
I heard, and I came down to rescue them;

καὶ νῦν δεῦρο ἀποστείλω σε εἰς Αἴγυπτον.
and now come I will send thee to Egypt.

35 Τοῦτον τὸν Μωϋσῆν, ὃν ἠρνήσαντο
This – Moses, whom they denied

εἰπόντες· τίς σε κατέστησεν ἄρχοντα καὶ
saying: Who thee appointed a ruler and

δικαστήν; τοῦτον ὁ θεὸς καὶ ἄρχοντα
a judge? this man – God both a ruler

καὶ λυτρωτὴν ἀπέσταλκεν σὺν χειρὶ
and a redeemer has sent with [the] hand

ἀγγέλου τοῦ ὀφθέντος αὐτῷ ἐν τῇ βάτῳ.
of [the] angel – appearing to him in the bush.

36 οὗτος ἐξήγαγεν αὐτοὺς ποιήσας τέρατα
This man led forth them doing wonders

καὶ σημεῖα ἐν γῇ Αἰγύπτῳ καὶ ἐν
and signs in [the] land Egypt and in

ἐρυθρᾷ θαλάσσῃ καὶ ἐν τῇ ἐρήμῳ ἔτη
[the] Red Sea and in the desert years

τεσσεράκοντα. 37 οὗτός ἐστιν ὁ Μωϋσῆς
forty. This is the Moses

ὁ εἴπας τοῖς υἱοῖς Ἰσραήλ· προφήτην
– saying to the sons of Israel: A prophet

ὑμῖν ἀναστήσει ὁ θεὸς ἐκ τῶν ἀδελφῶν
for you will raise up – God of the brothers

ὑμῶν ὡς ἐμέ. 38 οὗτός ἐστιν ὁ γενόμενος
of you as me. This is the [one] having been

ἐν τῇ ἐκκλησίᾳ ἐν τῇ ἐρήμῳ μετὰ τοῦ
in the church in the desert with the

ἀγγέλου τοῦ λαλοῦντος αὐτῷ ἐν τῷ
angel – speaking to him in the

ὄρει Σινὰ καὶ τῶν πατέρων ἡμῶν, ὃς
mount Sinai and [with] the fathers of us, who

ἐδέξατο λόγια ζῶντα δοῦναι ὑμῖν, 39 ᾧ
received oracles living to give to you, ¹to whom

οὐκ ἠθέλησαν ὑπήκοοι γενέσθαι οἱ πατέρες
²wished ⁶not ⁵obedient ⁷to become ³the ⁴fathers

ἡμῶν, ἀλλὰ ἀπώσαντο καὶ ἐστράφησαν
⁴of us, but thrust away and turned

ἐν ταῖς καρδίαις αὐτῶν εἰς Αἴγυπτον,
in the hearts of them to Egypt,

Aaron, 'Make for us gods to go before us; as for this Moses who led us out from the land of Egypt, we do not know what has become of him.' ⁴¹And they made a calf in those days, and offered a sacrifice to the idol and rejoiced in the works of their hands. ⁴²But God turned and gave them over to worship the host of heaven, as it is written in the book of the prophets:

'Did you offer me slain beasts and sacrifices, forty years in the wilderness, O house of Israel?
⁴³And you took up the tent of Moloch, and the star of the god Rephan, the figures which you made to worship; and I will remove you beyond Babylon.'

44 "Our fathers had the tent of witness in the wilderness, even as he who spoke to Moses directed him to make it, according to the pattern that he had seen. ⁴⁵Our fathers in turn brought it in with Joshua when they dispossessed the nations which God thrust

40 εἰπόντες τῷ Ἀαρών· ποίησον ἡμῖ
saying – to Aaron: Make for us

θεοὺς οἳ προπορεύσονται ἡμῶν· ὁ γὰρ
gods which will go before us; – for

Μωϋσῆς οὗτος, ὃς ἐξήγαγεν ἡμᾶς ἐκ
this Moses, who led forth us out of

γῆς Αἰγύπτου, οὐκ οἴδαμεν τί ἐγένετο
[the] land Egypt, we know not what happened

αὐτῷ. 41 καὶ ἐμοσχοποίησαν ἐν
to him. And they made [a model of] a calf in

ταῖς ἡμέραις ἐκείναις καὶ ἀνήγαγον θυσίαν τῷ
those days and brought up a sacrifice to the

εἰδώλῳ, καὶ εὐφραίνοντο ἐν τοῖς ἔργοις
idol, and made merry in the works

τῶν χειρῶν αὐτῶν. 42 ἔστρεψεν δὲ ὁ
of the hands of them. And ²turned ¹God

θεὸς καὶ παρέδωκεν αὐτοὺς λατρεύειν
and delivered them to worship

τῇ στρατιᾷ τοῦ οὐρανοῦ, καθὼς γέγραπται
the host of heaven, as it has been written

ἐν βίβλῳ τῶν προφητῶν· μὴ σφάγια
in [the] roll of the prophets: Not victims

καὶ θυσίας προσηνέγκατέ μοι ἔτη
and sacrifices ye offered to me years

τεσσεράκοντα ἐν τῇ ἐρήμῳ, οἶκος Ἰσραήλ,
forty in the desert, [O] house of Israel,

43 καὶ ἀνελάβετε τὴν σκηνὴν τοῦ Μόλοχ
and ye took up the tent – of Moloch

καὶ τὸ ἄστρον τοῦ θεοῦ Ῥομφά, τοὺς
and the star of the god Rompha, the

τύπους οὓς ἐποιήσατε προσκυνεῖν αὐτοῖς;
models which ye made to worship them?

καὶ μετοικιῶ ὑμᾶς ἐπέκεινα Βαβυλῶνος.
and I will deport you beyond Babylon.

44 Ἡ σκηνὴ τοῦ μαρτυρίου ἦν τοῖς
The tent – of witness was to the
=Our fathers had the tent of witness

πατράσιν ἡμῶν ἐν τῇ ἐρήμῳ, καθὼς
fathers of usᵉ in the desert, as

διετάξατο ὁ λαλῶν τῷ Μωϋσῇ ποιῆσαι
commanded the [one] speaking – to Moses to make

αὐτὴν κατὰ τὸν τύπον ὃν ἑωράκει·
it according to the model which he had seen,

45 ἣν καὶ εἰσήγαγον διαδεξάμενοι οἱ
which also ⁵brought in ⁴having received ¹the

πατέρες ἡμῶν μετὰ Ἰησοῦ ἐν τῇ κατα-
²fathers ³of us with Jesus in the pos-

σχέσει τῶν ἐθνῶν, ὧν ἐξῶσεν ὁ θεὸς
session of the nations, whom put out – God

out before our fathers. So it was until the days of David, [46] who found favor in the sight of God and asked leave to find a habitation for the God of Jacob. [47] But it was Solomon who built a house for him. [48] Yet the Most High does not dwell in houses made with hands; as the prophet says,

[49] 'Heaven is my throne, and earth my footstool.

What house will you build for me, says the Lord,

or what is the place of my rest?

[50] Did not my hand make all these things?'

[51] "You stiff-necked people, uncircumcised in heart and ears, you always resist the Holy Spirit. As your fathers did, so do you. [52] Which of the prophets did not your fathers persecute? And they killed those who announced beforehand the coming of the Righteous One, whom you have now betrayed and murdered, [53] you who received the law as delivered by angels and did not keep it."

54 Now when they heard these things they were enraged, and they ground their teeth against him. [55] But he, full of the

ἀπὸ προσώπου τῶν πατέρων ἡμῶν, ἕως
from [the] face of the fathers of us, until

τῶν ἡμερῶν Δαυίδ· 46 ὃς εὗρεν χάριν
the days of David; who found favour

ἐνώπιον τοῦ θεοῦ καὶ ᾐτήσατο εὑρεῖν
before — God and asked to find

σκήνωμα τῷ οἴκῳ Ἰακώβ. 47 Σολομὼν δὲ
a tent for the house of Jacob. But Solomon

οἰκοδόμησεν αὐτῷ οἶκον. 48 ἀλλ'
built for him a house. But

οὐχ ὁ ὕψιστος ἐν χειροποιήτοις κατοικεῖ·
[4]not [1]the [2]Most High [5]in [6][places] made by hand [3]dwells;

καθὼς ὁ προφήτης λέγει· 49 ὁ οὐρανός
as the prophet says : The heaven

μοι θρόνος, ἡ δὲ γῆ ὑποπόδιον τῶν
to me a throne, and the earth a footstool of the

ποδῶν μου· ποῖον οἶκον οἰκοδομήσετέ μοι,
feet of me; what house will ye build for me,

λέγει κύριος, ἢ τίς τόπος τῆς καταπαύσεώς
says [the] Lord, or what place of the rest

μου; 50 οὐχὶ ἡ χείρ μου ἐποίησεν ταῦτα
of me? not the hand of me made these things

πάντα; 51 Σκληροτράχηλοι καὶ ἀπερίτμητοι
all? Hard-necked and uncircumcised

καρδίαις καὶ τοῖς ὠσίν, ὑμεῖς ἀεὶ τῷ
in hearts and — ears, ye always the

πνεύματι τῷ ἁγίῳ ἀντιπίπτετε, ὡς οἱ
Spirit — Holy oppose, as the

πατέρες ὑμῶν καὶ ὑμεῖς. 52 τίνα τῶν
fathers of you also ye. Which of the

προφητῶν οὐκ ἐδίωξαν οἱ πατέρες ὑμῶν;
prophets persecuted not the fathers of you?

καὶ ἀπέκτειναν τοὺς προκαταγγείλαντας
and they killed the [ones] announcing beforehand

περὶ τῆς ἐλεύσεως τοῦ δικαίου, οὗ
concerning the coming of the righteous one, of whom

νῦν ὑμεῖς προδόται καὶ φονεῖς ἐγένεσθε,
now ye betrayers and murderers became,

53 οἵτινες ἐλάβετε τὸν νόμον εἰς διαταγὰς
who received the law in(by) dispositions

ἀγγέλων, καὶ οὐκ ἐφυλάξατε.
of angels, and did not keep [it].

54 Ἀκούοντες δὲ ταῦτα διεπρίοντο ταῖς
And hearing these things they were cut to the

καρδίαις αὐτῶν καὶ ἔβρυχον τοὺς ὀδόντας
hearts of them and gnashed the teeth

ἐπ' αὐτόν. 55 ὑπάρχων δὲ πλήρης
at him. But being full

Holy Spirit, gazed into heaven and saw the glory of God, and Jesus standing at the right hand of God; [56]and he said, "Behold, I see the heavens opened, and the Son of man standing at the right hand of God." [57]But they cried out with a loud voice, and stopped their ears and rushed together upon him. [58]Then they cast him out of the city and stoned him; and the witnesses laid down their garments at the feet of a young man named Saul. [59]And as they were stoning Stephen, he prayed, "Lord Jesus, receive my spirit." [60]And he knelt down and cried with a loud voice, "Lord, do not hold this sin against them." And when he had said this, he fell asleep.

CHAPTER 8

AND Saul was consenting to his death.

And on that day a great persecution arose against the church in Jerusalem; and they were all scattered throughout the region of Judea and Samar ia, except the apostles. [2]Devout men buried Stephen, and

---

πνεύματος ἁγίου ἀτενίσας εἰς τὸν οὐρανὸν
of [the] Spirit Holy gazing into – heaven

εἶδεν δόξαν θεοῦ καὶ Ἰησοῦν ἑστῶτα ἐκ
he saw [the] glory of God and Jesus standing at

δεξιῶν τοῦ θεοῦ, 56 καὶ εἶπεν· ἰδοὺ
[the] right [hand] – of God, and said: Behold

θεωρῶ τοὺς οὐρανοὺς διηνοιγμένους καὶ
I see the heavens *having been* opened up and

τὸν υἱὸν τοῦ ἀνθρώπου ἐκ δεξιῶν ἑστῶτα
the Son – of man at [the] right [hand] standing

τοῦ θεοῦ. 57 κράξαντες δὲ φωνῇ μεγάλῃ
– of God. And crying out voice with a great

συνέσχον τὰ ὦτα αὐτῶν, καὶ ὥρμησαν
they closed the ears of them, and rushed

ὁμοθυμαδὸν ἐπ’ αὐτόν, 58 καὶ ἐκβαλόντες
with one mind on him, and casting *out*

ἔξω τῆς πόλεως ἐλιθοβόλουν. καὶ οἱ
outside the city they stoned [him]. And the

μάρτυρες ἀπέθεντο τὰ ἱμάτια αὐτῶν παρὰ
witnesses put off the garments of them at

τοὺς πόδας νεανίου καλουμένου Σαύλου.
the feet of a young man *being* called Saul.

59 καὶ ἐλιθοβόλουν τὸν Στέφανον, ἐπικαλ-
And they stoned – Stephen, invok-

ούμενον καὶ λέγοντα· κύριε Ἰησοῦ, δέξαι
ing [God] and saying: Lord Jesus, receive

τὸ πνεῦμά μου. 60 θεὶς δὲ τὰ γόνατα
the spirit of me. And placing the knees
= kneeling down

ἔκραξεν φωνῇ μεγάλῃ· κύριε, μὴ στήσῃς
he cried voice with a great: Lord, place not

αὐτοῖς ταύτην τὴν ἁμαρτίαν. καὶ τοῦτο
to them this – sin. And [2]this

εἰπὼν ἐκοιμήθη. 8 Σαῦλος δὲ ἦν συνευδοκῶν
[1]saying he fell asleep. And Saul was consenting

τῇ ἀναιρέσει αὐτοῦ.
to the killing of him.

Ἐγένετο δὲ ἐν ἐκείνῃ τῇ ἡμέρᾳ
And there was in that – day

διωγμὸς μέγας ἐπὶ τὴν ἐκκλησίαν τὴν
persecution a great on(against) the church

ἐν Ἱεροσολύμοις· πάντες [δὲ] διεσπάρησαν
in Jerusalem; and all were scattered

κατὰ τὰς χώρας τῆς Ἰουδαίας καὶ
throughout the countries – of Judæa and

Σαμαρείας πλὴν τῶν ἀποστόλων.
Samaria except the apostles.

2 συνεκόμισαν δὲ τὸν Στέφανον ἄνδρες
And [3]recovered – [4]Stephen [2]men

made great lamentation over him. ³But Saul laid waste the church, and entering house after house, he dragged off men and women and committed them to prison.

4 Now those who were scattered went about preaching the word. ⁵Philip went down to a city of Samar′ia, and proclaimed to them the Christ. ⁶And the multitudes with one accord gave heed to what was said by Philip, when they heard him and saw the signs which he did. ⁷For unclean spirits came out of many who were possessed, crying with a loud voice; and many who were paralyzed or lame were healed. ⁸So there was much joy in that city.

9 But there was a man named Simon who had previously practiced magic in the city and amazed the nation of Samar′ia, saying that he himself was somebody great. ¹⁰They all gave heed to him, from the least to the greatest, saying, "This man is that power of God which is

εὐλαβεῖς καὶ ἐποίησαν κοπετὸν μέγαν
¹devout   and   made   lamentation   great

ἐπ' αὐτῷ. 3 Σαῦλος δὲ ἐλυμαίνετο τὴν
over him.   But Saul   ravaged   the

ἐκκλησίαν κατὰ τοὺς οἴκους εἰσπορευόμενος,
church   house by house†   entering,

σύρων τε ἄνδρας καὶ γυναῖκας παρεδίδου
dragging both   men   and   women   delivered

εἰς φυλακήν.
to   prison.

4 Οἱ μὲν οὖν διασπαρέντες διῆλθον
The [ones] –* therefore being scattered passed through

εὐαγγελιζόμενοι τὸν λόγον. 5 Φίλιππος δὲ
preaching   the   word.   But Philip

κατελθὼν εἰς τὴν πόλιν τῆς
going down   to   the   city   –

Σαμαρείας ἐκήρυσσεν αὐτοῖς τὸν Χριστόν.
of Samaria   proclaimed   to them   the   Christ.

6 προσεῖχον δὲ οἱ ὄχλοι τοῖς
    And gave heed   the   crowds to the things

λεγομένοις ὑπὸ τοῦ Φιλίππου ὁμοθυμαδὸν
being said   by   –   Philip   with one mind

ἐν τῷ ἀκούειν αὐτοὺς καὶ βλέπειν τὰ
in the   to hear   them   and   to see ᵇᵉ   the
=as they heard and saw

σημεῖα ἃ ἐποίει. 7 πολλοὶ γὰρ τῶν
signs   which he was doing.   For many   of the

ἐχόντων πνεύματα ἀκάθαρτα βοῶντα φωνῇ
[ones] having   spirits   unclean   crying   ²voice

μεγάλῃ ἐξήρχοντο· πολλοὶ δὲ παραλελυμένοι
¹with a great   came out;   and many   having been paralysed

καὶ χωλοὶ ἐθεραπεύθησαν· 8 ἐγένετο δὲ
and   lame   were healed;   and there was

πολλὴ χαρὰ ἐν τῇ πόλει ἐκείνῃ. 9 Ἀνὴρ δέ τις
much   joy in   that city.   And a certain man

ὀνόματι Σίμων προϋπῆρχεν ἐν τῇ
by name   Simon   was previously   in   the

πόλει μαγεύων καὶ ἐξιστάνων τὸ
city   practising sorcery   and   astonishing   the

ἔθνος τῆς Σαμαρείας, λέγων εἶναί τινα
nation   –   of Samaria,   saying   ²to be ³someone

ἑαυτὸν μέγαν, 10 ᾧ προσεῖχον πάντες
¹himself   ⁴great,   to whom   gave heed   all

ἀπὸ μικροῦ ἕως μεγάλου λέγοντες· οὗτός
from   small   to   great   saying :   This man

ἐστιν ἡ δύναμις τοῦ θεοῦ ἡ καλουμένη
is   the   power   –   of God   –   being called

* See note on John 19. 24.

called Great." ¹¹And they
gave heed to him, be-
cause for a long time he
had amazed them with
his magic. ¹²But when
they believed Philip as he
preached good news
about the kingdom of
God and the name of
Jesus Christ, they were
baptized, both men and
women. ¹³Even Simon
himself believed, and
after being baptized he
continued with Philip.
And seeing signs and
great miracles performed,
he was amazed.

14 Now when the
apostles at Jerusalem
heard that Samar′ia had
received the word of
God, they sent to them
Peter and John, ¹⁵who
came down and prayed
for them that they might
receive the Holy Spirit;
¹⁶for it had not yet
fallen on any of them,
but they had only been
baptized in the name of
the Lord Jesus. ¹⁷Then
they laid their hands on
them and they received
the Holy Spirit. ¹⁸Now
when Simon saw that the
Spirit was given through
the laying on of the
apostles' hands, he
offered them money,

μεγάλη. 11 προσεῖχον δὲ αὐτῷ διὰ τὸ
great.   And they gave heed to him   because of the

ἱκανῷ   χρόνῳ ταῖς μαγείαις ἐξεστακέναι
for a considerable time by the sorceries to have astonished
=because for a considerable time he had astonished them by his
sorceries.

αὐτούς. 12 ὅτε δὲ ἐπίστευσαν τῷ Φιλίππῳ
them.   But when they believed   –   Philip

εὐαγγελιζομένῳ περὶ τῆς βασιλείας τοῦ
preaching   about   the   kingdom

θεοῦ καὶ τοῦ ὀνόματος Ἰησοῦ Χριστοῦ,
of God and the   name   of Jesus   Christ,

ἐβαπτίζοντο   ἄνδρες τε καὶ γυναῖκες.
they were baptized   both men   and   women.

13 ὁ δὲ Σίμων καὶ αὐτὸς ἐπίστευσεν,
    –   And Simon   also [him]self   believed,

καὶ βαπτισθεὶς ἦν προσκαρτερῶν τῷ
and having been baptized was   attaching himself   –

Φιλίππῳ, θεωρῶν τε σημεῖα καὶ δυνάμεις
to Philip,   and beholding signs   and powerful deeds

μεγάλας γινομένας ἐξίστατο. 14 Ἀκούσαντες
great   happening he was amazed.   ᵃhearing

δὲ οἱ ἐν Ἱεροσολύμοις ἀπόστολοι ὅτι
¹And ²the ⁴in   ⁵Jerusalem   ³apostles   that

δέδεκται ἡ Σαμάρεια τὸν λόγον τοῦ
²has received –   ¹Samaria   the   word   of God,

θεοῦ, ἀπέστειλαν πρὸς αὐτοὺς Πέτρον
of God,   they sent   to   them   Peter

καὶ Ἰωάννην, 15 οἵτινες καταβάντες
and   John,   who   going down

προσηύξαντο περὶ αὐτῶν ὅπως λάβωσιν
prayed   concerning them   so as they might receive

πνεῦμα ἅγιον· 16 οὐδέπω γὰρ ἦν ἐπ'
Spirit Holy;   for ²not yet ¹he was ⁴on

οὐδενὶ αὐτῶν ἐπιπεπτωκός, μόνον δὲ
⁵no(any)one ⁶of them ³having fallen on,   but only

βεβαπτισμένοι ὑπῆρχον εἰς τὸ ὄνομα τοῦ
having been baptized   they were   in   the name of the

κυρίου Ἰησοῦ. 17 τότε ἐπετίθεσαν τὰς
Lord   Jesus.   Then   they laid on   the(ir)

χεῖρας ἐπ' αὐτούς, καὶ ἐλάμβανον πνεῦμα
hands   on them,   and   they received   ²Spirit

ἅγιον. 18 ἰδὼν δὲ ὁ Σίμων ὅτι διὰ
¹Holy.   And ²seeing –   ¹Simon   that through

τῆς ἐπιθέσεως τῶν χειρῶν τῶν ἀποστόλων
the laying on   of the hands of the apostles

δίδοται τὸ πνεῦμα, προσήνεγκεν αὐτοῖς
is(was) given the   Spirit,   he offered   them

¹⁹saying, "Give me also this power, that any one on whom I lay my hands may receive the Holy Spirit." ²⁰But Peter said to him, "Your silver perish with you, because you thought you could obtain the gift of God with money! ²¹You have neither part nor lot in this matter, for your heart is not right before God. ²²Repent therefore of this wickedness of yours, and pray to the Lord that, if possible, the intent of your heart may be forgiven you. ²³For I see that you are in the gall of bitterness and in the bond of iniquity." ²⁴And Simon answered, "Pray for me to the Lord, that nothing of what you have said may come upon me."

25 Now when they had testified and spoken the word of the Lord, they returned to Jerusalem, preaching the gospel to many villages of the Samaritans.

26 But an angel of the Lord said to Philip, "Rise and go toward the

χρήματα λέγων· **19** δότε κἀμοὶ τὴν
money   saying :   Give me also   –

ἐξουσίαν ταύτην ἵνα ᾧ ἐὰν ἐπιθῶ τὰς
authority this   that whomever I lay on the(my)

χεῖρας λαμβάνῃ πνεῦμα ἅγιον. **20** Πέτρος δὲ
hands he may receive Spirit Holy.   But Peter

εἶπεν πρὸς αὐτόν· τὸ ἀργύριόν σου
said   to   him :   The   silver   of thee

σὺν σοὶ εἴη εἰς ἀπώλειαν, ὅτι τὴν δωρεὰν
with thee may it be into perdition, because the gift

τοῦ θεοῦ ἐνόμισας διὰ χρημάτων κτᾶσθαι.
– of God thou didst suppose through money   to get.

21 οὐκ ἔστιν σοι μερὶς οὐδὲ κλῆρος
     There is not to thee° part   nor   lot
     =Thou hast no

ἐν τῷ λόγῳ τούτῳ· ἡ γὰρ καρδία σου
in   this matter;   for the heart of thee

οὐκ ἔστιν εὐθεῖα ἔναντι τοῦ θεοῦ.
is not   right   before   –   God.

22 μετανόησον οὖν ἀπὸ τῆς κακίας σου
     Repent thou therefore from – ²wickedness ³of thee

ταύτης, καὶ δεήθητι τοῦ κυρίου εἰ ἄρα
¹this,   and petition   the Lord if perhaps

ἀφεθήσεταί σοι ἡ ἐπίνοια τῆς καρδίας
will be forgiven thee the thought   of the   heart

σου· **23** εἰς γὰρ χολὴν πικρίας καὶ
of thee;   for in   gall of bitterness and

σύνδεσμον ἀδικίας ὁρῶ σε ὄντα.
bond   of unrighteousness I see thee being.

24 ἀποκριθεὶς δὲ ὁ Σίμων εἶπεν· δεήθητε
     And answering – Simon said :   Petition

ὑμεῖς ὑπὲρ ἐμοῦ πρὸς τὸν κύριον, ὅπως
ye   for   me   to   the Lord,   so as

μηδὲν ἐπέλθῃ ἐπ᾽ ἐμὲ ὧν εἰρήκατε.
¹not one ⁴may come on ²on ⁶me ⁵of the ⁷ye have
                         things which spoken.

25 Οἱ μὲν οὖν διαμαρτυράμενοι καὶ λαλή-
     They – therefore having solemnly witnessed and having

σαντες τὸν λόγον τοῦ κυρίου ὑπέστρεφον
spoken the word of the Lord   returned

εἰς Ἱεροσόλυμα, πολλάς τε κώμας τῶν
to   Jerusalem,   and ²many   ²villages ⁴of the

Σαμαριτῶν εὐηγγελίζοντο.
³Samaritans ¹evangelized.

26 Ἄγγελος δὲ κυρίου ἐλάλησεν πρὸς
     But an angel of [the] Lord spoke   to

Φίλιππον λέγων· ἀνάστηθι καὶ πορεύου
Philip   saying : Rise up   and   go

south[e] to the road that goes down from Jerusalem to Gaza." This is a desert road. [27] And he rose and went. And behold, an Ethiopian, a eunuch, a minister of Canda'ce the queen of the Ethiopians, in charge of all her treasure, had come to Jerusalem to worship [28] and was returning; seated in his chariot, he was reading the prophet Isaiah. [29] And the Spirit said to Philip, "Go up and join this chariot." [30] So Philip ran to him, and heard him reading Isaiah the prophet, and asked, "Do you understand what you are reading?" [31] And he said, "How can I, unless some one guides me?" And he invited Philip to come up and sit with him. [32] Now the passage of the scripture which he was reading was this:

"As a sheep led to the slaughter
or a lamb before its shearer is dumb,
so he opens not his mouth.

[33] In his humiliation justice was denied him.

κατὰ   μεσημβρίαν   ἐπὶ   τὴν   ὁδὸν   τὴν
along   south   on   the   way

καταβαίνουσαν   ἀπὸ   Ἰερουσαλὴμ   εἰς   Γάζαν·
going down   from   Jerusalem   to   Gaza;

αὕτη   ἐστὶν   ἔρημος.   27 καὶ   ἀναστὰς
this   is   desert.   And   rising up

ἐπορεύθη.   καὶ   ἰδοὺ   ἀνὴρ   Αἰθίοψ   εὐνοῦχος
he went.   And behold[,]   a man   Ethiopian   a eunuch

δυνάστης   Κανδάκης   βασιλίσσης   Αἰθιόπων,
a courtier   of Candace   queen   of [the] Ethiopians,

ὃς   ἦν   ἐπὶ   πάσης   τῆς   γάζης   αὐτῆς,
who   was   over   all   the   treasure   of her,

[ὃς]   ἐληλύθει   προσκυνήσων   εἰς   Ἰερουσαλήμ,
who   had come   worshipping   in   Jerusalem,

28 ἦν   δὲ   ὑποστρέφων   καὶ   καθήμενος   ἐπὶ
and was   returning   and   sitting   on

τοῦ   ἅρματος   αὐτοῦ   καὶ   ἀνεγίνωσκεν   τὸν
the   chariot   of him   and   was reading   the

προφήτην   Ἠσαΐαν.   29 εἶπεν   δὲ   τὸ   πνεῦμα
prophet   Esaias.   And said   the   Spirit

τῷ   Φιλίππῳ·   πρόσελθε   καὶ   κολλήθητι
-    to Philip: Approach   and   keep company with

τῷ   ἅρματι   τούτῳ.   30 προσδραμὼν   δὲ
this chariot.   And running up

ὁ   Φίλιππος   ἤκουσεν   αὐτοῦ   ἀναγινώσκοντος
-    Philip   heard   him   reading

Ἠσαΐαν   τὸν   προφήτην,   καὶ   εἶπεν·   ἆρά   γε
Esaias   the   prophet,   and   said :   Then

γινώσκεις   ἃ   ἀναγινώσκεις;   31 ὁ   δὲ
knowest thou   what things   thou art reading?   And he

εἶπεν·   πῶς   γὰρ   ἂν   δυναίμην   ἐὰν   μή
said :   How   indeed   should I be able   unless

τις   ὁδηγήσει   με;   παρεκάλεσέν   τε   τὸν
someone   shall guide   me?   And he besought   -

Φίλιππον   ἀναβάντα   καθίσαι   σὺν   αὐτῷ.
Philip   coming up   to sit   with   him.

32 ἡ   δὲ   περιοχὴ   τῆς   γραφῆς   ἦν   ἀνεγίνω-
Now the   passage   of the scripture   which   he was

σκεν   ἦν   αὕτη·   ὡς   πρόβατον   ἐπὶ   σφαγὴν
reading   was   this: As   a sheep   to   slaughter

ἤχθη,   καὶ   ὡς   ἀμνὸς   ἐναντίον   τοῦ   κείροντος
he was led,   and as   a lamb   before   the [one]   shearing

αὐτὸν   ἄφωνος,   οὕτως   οὐκ   ἀνοίγει   τὸ
it   [is] dumb,   so   he opens not   the

στόμα   αὐτοῦ.   33 Ἐν   τῇ   ταπεινώσει
mouth   of him.   In   the   humiliation

ἡ   κρίσις   αὐτοῦ   ἤρθη·   τὴν   γενεὰν   αὐτοῦ
the judgment   of him   was taken away;   the generation of him

---

[e] Or *at noon*

Who can describe his
generation?
For his life is taken
up from the earth."
³⁴And the eunuch said to
Philip, "About whom,
pray, does the prophet
say this, about himself
or about some one else?"
³⁵Then Philip opened his
mouth, and beginning
with this scripture he
told him the good news
of Jesus. ³⁶And as they
went along the road they
came to some water, and
the eunuch said, "See,
here is water! What is to
prevent my being bap-
tized?"ᶠ ³⁸And he com-
manded the chariot to
stop, and they both went
down into the water,
Philip and the eunuch,
and he baptized him.
³⁹And when they came
up out of the water, the
Spirit of the Lord caught
up Philip; and the eunuch
saw him no more, and
went on his way rejoicing.
⁴⁰But Philip was found
at Azo'tus, and passing
on he preached the gospel
to all the towns till he
came to Caesare'a.

τίς διηγήσεται; ὅτι αἴρεται ἀπὸ τῆς
who will relate? because is taken from the

γῆς ἡ ζωὴ αὐτοῦ. 34 ἀποκριθεὶς δὲ ὁ
earth the life of him.   And answering the

εὐνοῦχος τῷ Φιλίππῳ εἶπεν· δέομαί σου,
eunuch   –   to Philip said: I ask thee,

περὶ τίνος ὁ προφήτης λέγει τοῦτο;
about whom the prophet says this?

περὶ ἑαυτοῦ ἢ περὶ ἑτέρου τινός;
about himself or about other someone?

35 ἀνοίξας δὲ ὁ Φίλιππος τὸ στόμα
And opening   –   Philip the mouth

αὐτοῦ καὶ ἀρξάμενος ἀπὸ τῆς γραφῆς ταύτης
of him and beginning from this scripture

εὐηγγελίσατο αὐτῷ τὸν Ἰησοῦν.
preached to him – Jesus.

36 ὡς δὲ ἐπορεύοντο κατὰ τὴν ὁδόν,
And as they were going along the way,

ἦλθον ἐπί τι ὕδωρ, καί φησιν ὁ εὐνοῦχος·
they came upon certain water, and says the eunuch·

ἰδοὺ ὕδωρ· τί κωλύει με βαπτισθῆναι;‡
Behold[,] water; what prevents me to be baptized?

38 καὶ ἐκέλευσεν στῆναι τὸ ἅρμα, καὶ
And he commanded to stand the chariot, and

κατέβησαν ἀμφότεροι εἰς τὸ ὕδωρ, ὅ
went down both into the water, –

τε Φίλιππος καὶ ὁ εὐνοῦχος, καὶ ἐβάπτισεν
both Philip and the eunuch, and he baptized

αὐτόν. 39 ὅτε δὲ ἀνέβησαν ἐκ τοῦ ὕδατος,
him.   And when they came up out of the water,

πνεῦμα κυρίου ἥρπασεν τὸν Φίλιππον,
[the] Spirit of [the] Lord seized – Philip,

καὶ οὐκ εἶδεν αὐτὸν οὐκέτι ὁ εὐνοῦχος,
and saw not him no(any) more the eunuch,

ἐπορεύετο γὰρ τὴν ὁδὸν αὐτοῦ χαίρων.
for he went the way of him rejoicing.

40 Φίλιππος δὲ εὑρέθη εἰς Ἄζωτον, καὶ
But Philip was found in Azotus, and

διερχόμενος εὐηγγελίζετο τὰς πόλεις πάσας
passing through he evangelized the cities all

ἕως τοῦ ἐλθεῖν αὐτὸνᵇ εἰς Καισάρειαν.
until the to come himᵇ to Caesarea.
= he came

ᶠ Other ancient authorities add
all or most of verse 37, *And
Philip said, "If you believe with
all your heart, you may." And
he replied, "I believe that Jesus
Christ is the Son of God."*

‡ Verse 37 omitted by Nestle; *cf.* RSV footnote.

CHAPTER 9

BUT Saul, still breath-
ing threats and
murder against the dis-
ciples of the Lord, went
to the high priest [2]and
asked him for letters to
the synagogues at
Damascus, so that if he
found any belonging to
the Way, men or women,
he might bring them
bound to Jerusalem.
[3]Now as he journeyed he
approached Damascus,
and suddenly a light
from heaven flashed
about him. [4]And he fell
to the ground and heard
a voice saying to him,
"Saul, Saul, why do you
persecute me?" [5]And he
said, "Who are you,
Lord?" And he said, "I
am Jesus, whom thou
are persecuting; [6]but rise
and enter the city, and
you will be told what
you are to do." [7]The
men who were traveling
with him stood speech-
less, hearing the voice
but seeing no one. [8]Saul
arose from the ground;
and when his eyes were
opened, he could see
nothing; so they led him
by the hand and brought
him into Damascus.
[9]And for three days he

9 Ὁ δὲ Σαῦλος ἔτι ἐμπνέων ἀπειλῆς
   –   But   Saul   still breathing threatening
καὶ φόνου εἰς τοὺς μαθητὰς τοῦ κυρίου,
and murder against the   disciples of the Lord,
προσελθὼν τῷ ἀρχιερεῖ 2 ᾐτήσατο παρ'
approaching to the high priest   asked   from
αὐτοῦ ἐπιστολὰς εἰς Δαμασκὸν πρὸς τὰς
 him   letters   to   Damascus   for   the
συναγωγάς, ὅπως ἐάν τινας εὕρῃ τῆς
 synagogues,   so as   if [2]any [1]he found [4]of the
ὁδοῦ ὄντας, ἄνδρας τε καὶ γυναῖκας, δεδεμένους
[5]way [3]being,   both men   and   women, [3]having been bound
ἀγάγῃ   εἰς   Ἰερουσαλήμ.   3 Ἐν
[1]he might bring [them] to   Jerusalem.   in
δὲ τῷ πορεύεσθαι ἐγένετο αὐτὸν ἐγγίζειν
Now the   to go[e]   it came to pass him to draw near[b]
                    =as he went   =he drew near
τῇ Δαμασκῷ, ἐξαίφνης τε αὐτὸν περιήστ-
 –   to Damascus,   and suddenly   [5]him   [4]shone
ραψεν φῶς ἐκ τοῦ οὐρανοῦ, 4 καὶ πεσὼν
round [1]a light [2]out of –   [3]heaven,   and   falling
ἐπὶ τὴν γῆν ἤκουσεν φωνὴν λέγουσαν
on   the   earth   he heard   a voice   saying
αὐτῷ· Σαοὺλ Σαούλ, τί με διώκεις;
to him :   Saul[,]   Saul,   why me persecutest thou?
5 εἶπεν δέ· τίς εἶ, κύριε; ὁ δὲ ἐγώ
And he said :   Who art thou, Lord? And he [said] : I
εἰμι Ἰησοῦς ὃν σὺ διώκεις· 6 ἀλλὰ
am   Jesus whom thou persecutest;   but
ἀνάστηθι καὶ εἴσελθε εἰς τὴν πόλιν,
rise thou up, and   enter   into   the   city,
καὶ λαληθήσεταί σοι ὅ τί σε δεῖ ποιεῖν.
and   it shall be told thee   what thee it behoves to do.
7 οἱ δὲ ἄνδρες οἱ συνοδεύοντες αὐτῷ
Now the   men   – journeying with   him
εἱστήκεισαν ἐνεοί, ἀκούοντες μὲν τῆς
stood   speechless, hearing   indeed the
φωνῆς, μηδένα δὲ θεωροῦντες. 8 ἠγέρθη δὲ
sound, but no man   beholding.   And was raised
Σαῦλος ἀπὸ τῆς γῆς, ἀνεῳγμένων δὲ
Saul   from the   ground, and having been opened
                              =when his eyes were opened
τῶν ὀφθαλμῶν αὐτοῦ οὐδὲν ἔβλεπεν·
the   eyes   of him[a] nothing   he saw;
χειραγωγοῦντες δὲ αὐτὸν εἰσήγαγον εἰς
and leading by the hand   him   they brought in into
Δαμασκόν. 9 καὶ ἦν ἡμέρας τρεῖς μὴ
Damascus.   And he was days   three   not

was without sight, and neither ate nor drank.

10 Now there was a disciple at Damascus named Anani′as. The Lord said to him in a vision, "Anani′as." And he said, "Here I am, Lord." ¹¹And the Lord said to him, "Rise and go to the street called Straight, and inquire in the house of Judas for a man of Tarsus named Saul; for behold, he is praying, ¹²and he has seen a man named Anani′as come in and lay his hands on him so that he might regain his sight." ¹³But Anani′as answered, "Lord, I have heard from many about this man, how much evil he has done to thy saints at Jerusalem; ¹⁴and here he has authority from the chief priests to bind all who call upon thy name." ¹⁵But the Lord said to him, "Go, for he is a chosen instrument of mine to carry my name before the Gentiles and kings and the sons of Israel; ¹⁶for I will show him how much he must suffer for the sake of my name." ¹⁷So Anani′as departed and entered the

βλέπων, καὶ οὐκ ἔφαγεν οὐδὲ ἔπιεν.
seeing, and ate not nor drank.

10 ᾿Ην δέ τις μαθητὴς ἐν Δαμασκῷ
Now there was a certain disciple in Damascus

ὀνόματι ᾿Ανανίας, καὶ εἶπεν πρὸς αὐτὸν
by name Ananias, and said to him

ἐν ὁράματι ὁ κύριος· ᾿Ανανία. ὁ δὲ
in a vision the Lord: Ananias. And he

εἶπεν· ἰδοὺ ἐγώ, κύριε. 11 ὁ δὲ κύριος
said: Behold[,] I, Lord. And the Lord

πρὸς αὐτόν· ἀναστὰς πορεύθητι ἐπὶ τὴν
[said] to him: Rising up go thou to the

ῥύμην τὴν καλουμένην εὐθεῖαν καὶ ζήτησον
street – being called Straight and seek

ἐν οἰκίᾳ ᾿Ιούδα Σαῦλον ὀνόματι Ταρσέα·
in [the] house of Judas ²Saul ³by name ¹a Tarsian;

ἰδοὺ γὰρ προσεύχεται, 12 καὶ εἶδεν ἄνδρα
for behold he is praying, and saw ²a man

[ἐν ὁράματι] ᾿Ανανίαν ὀνόματι εἰσελθόντα
¹in ²a vision Ananias by name coming in

καὶ ἐπιθέντα αὐτῷ χεῖρας, ὅπως ἀναβλέψῃ.
and putting on him hands, so as he may see again.

13 ἀπεκρίθη δὲ ᾿Ανανίας· κύριε, ἤκουσα
And answered Ananias: Lord, I heard

ἀπὸ πολλῶν περὶ τοῦ ἀνδρὸς τούτου,
from many about this man,

ὅσα κακὰ τοῖς ἁγίοις σου ἐποίησεν
how many evil things to the saints of thee he did

ἐν ᾿Ιερουσαλήμ· 14 καὶ ὧδε ἔχει ἐξουσίαν
in Jerusalem; and here he has authority

παρὰ τῶν ἀρχιερέων δῆσαι πάντας τοὺς
from the chief priests to bind all the

ἐπικαλουμένους τὸ ὄνομά σου. 15 εἶπεν
[ones] invoking the name of thee. said

δὲ πρὸς αὐτὸν ὁ κύριος· πορεύου, ὅτι
But to him the Lord: Go thou, because

σκεῦος ἐκλογῆς ἐστίν μοι οὗτος τοῦ
³a vessel ⁴of choice ²is ⁵to me ¹this man –

βαστάσαι τὸ ὄνομά μου ἐνώπιον [τῶν]
to bearᵈ the name of me ²before ³the

ἐθνῶν τε καὶ βασιλέων υἱῶν τε ᾿Ισραήλ·
⁴nations ¹both ⁵and ⁶kings ⁸sons ⁷and ⁹of Israel;

16 ἐγὼ γὰρ ὑποδείξω αὐτῷ ὅσα δεῖ
for I will show him how many things it behoves

αὐτὸν ὑπὲρ τοῦ ὀνόματός μου παθεῖν.
him on behalf of the name of me to suffer.

17 ᾿Απῆλθεν δὲ ᾿Ανανίας καὶ εἰσῆλθεν
And went away Ananias and entered

house. And laying his hands on him he said, "Brother Saul, the Lord Jesus, who appeared to you on the road by which you came, has sent me that you may regain your sight and be filled with the Holy Spirit." ¹⁸And immediately something like scales fell from his eyes and he regained his sight. Then he rose and was baptized, ¹⁹and took food and was strengthened.

For several days he was with the disciples at Damascus. ²⁰And in the synagogues immediately he proclaimed Jesus, saying, "He is the Son of God." ²¹And all who heard him were amazed, and said, "Is not this the man who made havoc in Jerusalem of those who called on this name? And he has come here for this purpose, to bring them bound before the chief priests." ²²But Saul increased all the more in strength, and confounded the Jews who lived in Damascus by proving that Jesus was the Christ.

23 When many days had passed, the Jews plotted to kill him, ²⁴but their plot became known

εἰς τὴν οἰκίαν, καὶ ἐπιθεὶς ἐπ᾽ αὐτὸν
into the house, and putting on on him
τὰς χεῖρας εἶπεν· Σαοὺλ ἀδελφέ, ὁ
the(his) hands said: Saul brother, the
κύριος ἀπέσταλκέν με, Ἰησοῦς ὁ ὀφθείς σοι
Lord has sent me, Jesus the [one] appear- to
ing thee
ἐν τῇ ὁδῷ ᾗ ἤρχου, ὅπως ἀναβλέψῃς
in the way which thou camest, so as thou mayest see again
καὶ πλησθῇς πνεύματος ἁγίου. 18 καὶ
and be filled of(with) Spirit Holy. And
εὐθέως ἀπέπεσαν αὐτοῦ ἀπὸ τῶν ὀφθαλμῶν
immediately fell away of him from the eyes
ὡς λεπίδες, ἀνέβλεψέν τε, καὶ ἀναστὰς
as scales, and he saw again, and rising up
ἐβαπτίσθη, 19 καὶ λαβὼν τροφὴν ἐνίσχυσεν.
was baptized, and taking food was strengthened.
Ἐγένετο δὲ μετὰ τῶν ἐν Δαμασκῷ
Now he was with the in Damascus
μαθητῶν ἡμέρας τινάς, 20 καὶ εὐθέως
disciples days some, and immediately
ἐν ταῖς συναγωγαῖς ἐκήρυσσεν τὸν Ἰησοῦν,
in the synagogues he proclaimed - Jesus,
ὅτι οὗτός ἐστιν ὁ υἱὸς τοῦ θεοῦ.
that this one is the Son of God.
21 ἐξίσταντο δὲ πάντες οἱ ἀκούοντες καὶ
And were amazed all the [ones] hearing and
ἔλεγον· οὐχ οὗτός ἐστιν ὁ πορθήσας
said: Not this man is the [one] having destroyed
εἰς Ἰερουσαλὴμ τοὺς ἐπικαλουμένους
in Jerusalem the [ones] invoking
τὸ ὄνομα τοῦτο, καὶ ὧδε εἰς τοῦτο ἐληλύθει,
this name, and here for this he had come,
ἵνα δεδεμένους αὐτοὺς ἀγάγῃ ἐπὶ τοὺς
that having been bound them he might bring before the
ἀρχιερεῖς; 22 Σαῦλος δὲ μᾶλλον ἐνε-
chief priests? But Saul more was filled
δυναμοῦτο καὶ συνέχυννεν Ἰουδαίους τοὺς κατ-
with power and confounded Jews the [ones]
οἰκοῦντας ἐν Δαμασκῷ, συμβιβάζων ὅτι οὗτός
dwelling in Damascus, proving that this one
ἐστιν ὁ χριστός. 23 Ὡς δὲ ἐπληροῦντο
is the Christ. And when were fulfilled
ἡμέραι ἱκαναί, 24 συνεβουλεύσαντο
days considerable(many), consulted together
οἱ Ἰουδαῖοι ἀνελεῖν αὐτόν· ἐγνώσθη δὲ
the Jews to kill him; but was known
τῷ Σαύλῳ ἡ ἐπιβουλὴ αὐτῶν. παρετη-
- to Saul the plot of them. And they

to Saul. They were watching the gates day and night, to kill him; 25 but his disciples took him by night and let him down over the wall, lowering him in a basket.

26 And when he had come to Jerusalem he attempted to join the disciples; and they were all afraid of him, for they did not believe that he was a disciple. 27 But Barnabas took him, and brought him to the apostles, and declared to them how on the road he had seen the Lord, who spoke to him, and how at Damascus he had preached boldly in the name of Jesus. 28 So he went in and out among them at Jerusalem, 29 preaching boldly in the name of the Lord. And he spoke and disputed against the Hellenists; but they were seeking to kill him. 30 And when the brethren knew it, they brought him down to Caesare'a, and sent him off to Tarsus.

31 So the church throughout all Judea and Galilee and Samar'ia had peace and was built up;

ροῦντο δὲ καὶ τὰς πύλας ἡμέρας τε καὶ
carefully watched also the gates both by day and
νυκτὸς ὅπως αὐτὸν ἀνέλωσιν· 25 λαβόντες δὲ
by night so as him they might but ⁴taking
destroy;
οἱ μαθηταὶ αὐτοῦ νυκτὸς διὰ τοῦ
¹the ²disciples ³of him by night through the
τείχους καθῆκαν αὐτὸν χαλάσαντες ἐν
wall let down him lowering in
σπυρίδι. 26 Παραγενόμενος δὲ εἰς
a basket. And arriving at
Ἰερουσαλὴμ ἐπείραζεν κολλᾶσθαι τοῖς
Jerusalem he tried to be joined to the
μαθηταῖς· καὶ πάντες ἐφοβοῦντο αὐτόν,
disciples; and all feared him,
μὴ πιστεύοντες ὅτι ἐστὶν μαθητής.
not believing that he is(was) a disciple.
27 Βαρναβᾶς δὲ ἐπιλαβόμενος αὐτὸν ἤγαγεν
But Barnabas taking hold of him led
πρὸς τοὺς ἀποστόλους, καὶ διηγήσατο
to the apostles, and narrated
αὐτοῖς πῶς ἐν τῇ ὁδῷ εἶδεν τὸν κύριον
to them how in the way he saw the Lord
καὶ ὅτι ἐλάλησεν αὐτῷ, καὶ πῶς ἐν
and that he spoke to him, and how in
Δαμασκῷ ἐπαρρησιάσατο ἐν τῷ ὀνόματι
Damascus he spoke boldly in the name
Ἰησοῦ. 28 καὶ ἦν μετ' αὐτῶν εἰσπορευόμενος
of Jesus. And he was with them going in
καὶ ἐκπορευόμενος εἰς Ἰερουσαλήμ,
and going out in Jerusalem,
παρρησιαζόμενος ἐν τῷ ὀνόματι τοῦ
speaking boldly in the name of the
κυρίου, 29 ἐλάλει τε καὶ συνεζήτει πρὸς
Lord, ²spoke ¹both ³and ⁴discussed with
τοὺς Ἑλληνιστάς· οἱ δὲ ἐπεχείρουν ἀνελεῖν
the Hellenists; and they attempted to kill
αὐτόν. 30 ἐπιγνόντες δὲ οἱ ἀδελφοὶ
him. But ³knowing ¹the ²brothers
κατήγαγον αὐτὸν εἰς Καισάρειαν καὶ
brought down him to Cæsarea and
ἐξαπέστειλαν αὐτὸν εἰς Ταρσόν.
sent forth him to Tarsus.
31 Ἡ μὲν οὖν ἐκκλησία καθ' ὅλης
²The – ¹therefore ³church throughout all
τῆς Ἰουδαίας καὶ Γαλιλαίας καὶ Σαμαρείας
– Judæa and Galilee and Samaria
εἶχεν εἰρήνην οἰκοδομουμένη καὶ πορευομένη
had peace being built and going

and walking in the fear of the Lord and in the comfort of the Holy Spirit it was multiplied.

32 Now as Peter went here and there among them all, he came down also to the saints that lived at Lydda. ³³There he found a man named Aene′as, who had been bedridden for eight years and was paralyzed. ³⁴And Peter said to him, "Aene′as, Jesus Christ heals you; rise and make your bed." And immediately he rose. ³⁵And all the residents of Lydda and Sharon saw him, and they turned to the Lord.

36 Now there was at Joppa a disciple named Tabitha, which means Dorcas or Gazelle. She was full of good works and acts of charity. ³⁷In those days she fell sick and died; and when they had washed her, they laid her in an upper room. ³⁸Since Lydda was near Joppa, the disciples, hearing that Peter was there, sent two men to him entreating him, "Please come to us without delay." ³⁹So Peter rose and

τῷ φόβῳ τοῦ κυρίου, καὶ τῇ παρακλήσει
in the fear of the Lord, and in the comfort
τοῦ ἁγίου πνεύματος ἐπληθύνετο.
of the Holy Spirit was multiplied.

32 Ἐγένετο δὲ Πέτρον διερχόμενον διὰ
Now it came to pass Peter passing through through
πάντων κατελθεῖν καὶ πρὸς τοὺς ἁγίους
all [quarters] to come down[b] also to the saints
τοὺς κατοικοῦντας Λύδδα. 33 εὗρεν δὲ
- inhabiting Lydda. And he found
ἐκεῖ ἄνθρωπόν τινα ὀνόματι Αἰνέαν ἐξ
there a certain man by name Aeneas of
ἐτῶν ὀκτὼ κατακείμενον ἐπὶ κραβάτου,
years eight lying on a mattress,
ὃς ἦν παραλελυμένος. 34 καὶ εἶπεν αὐτῷ
who was having been paralysed. And said to him
ὁ Πέτρος· Αἰνέα, ἰαταί σε Ἰησοῦς Χριστός·
- Peter: Aeneas, cures thee Jesus Christ;
ἀνάστηθι καὶ στρῶσον σεαυτῷ. καὶ
rise up and gird thyself. And
εὐθέως ἀνέστη. 35 καὶ εἶδαν αὐτὸν
immediately he rose up. And saw him
πάντες οἱ κατοικοῦντες Λύδδα καὶ τὸν
all the [ones] inhabiting Lydda and -
Σαρῶνα, οἵτινες ἐπέστρεψαν ἐπὶ τὸν κύριον.
Saron, who turned to the Lord.
Ἐν Ἰόππῃ δέ τις ἦν μαθήτρια ὀνόματι
²in ³Joppa ¹Now ⁴a certain ⁵was ⁶disciple by name
Ταβιθά, 36 ἣ διερμηνευομένη λέγεται
Tabitha, who being translated is called
Δορκάς· αὕτη ἦν πλήρης ἔργων ἀγαθῶν
Dorcas; this woman was full works of good
καὶ ἐλεημοσυνῶν ὧν ἐποίει. 37 ἐγένετο δὲ
and of alms which she did. And it happened
ἐν ταῖς ἡμέραις ἐκείναις ἀσθενήσασαν
in those days ailing
αὐτὴν ἀποθανεῖν· λούσαντες δὲ ἔθηκαν
she to die[b]; and having washed they put [her]
=being ill she died;
ἐν ὑπερῴῳ. 38 ἐγγὺς δὲ οὔσης Λύδδας
in an upper room. Now ³near ²being ¹Lydda⁴
τῇ Ἰόππῃ οἱ μαθηταὶ ἀκούσαντες ὅτι
- to Joppa the disciples having heard that
Πέτρος ἐστὶν ἐν αὐτῇ ἀπέστειλαν δύο
Peter is(was) in it sent two
ἄνδρας πρὸς αὐτὸν παρακαλοῦντες· μὴ
men to him beseeching: ²not
ὀκνήσῃς διελθεῖν ἕως ἡμῶν. 39 ἀναστὰς δὲ
¹hesitate to come to us. And rising up

went with them. And when he had come, they took him to the upper room. All the widows stood beside him weeping, and showing coats and garments which Dorcas made while she was with them. 40 But Peter put them all outside and knelt down and prayed; then turning to the body he said, "Tabitha, rise." And she opened her eyes, and when she saw Peter she sat up. 41 And he gave her his hand and lifted her up. Then calling the saints and widows he presented her alive. 42 And it became known throughout all Joppa, and many believed in the Lord. 43 And he stayed in Joppa for many days with one Simon, a tanner.

Πέτρος συνῆλθεν αὐτοῖς· ὃν παραγενόμενον
Peter   went with them; whom arriving

ἀνήγαγον εἰς τὸ ὑπερῷον, καὶ παρέστησαν
they led up into the upper room, and stood by

αὐτῷ πᾶσαι αἱ χῆραι κλαίουσαι καὶ
him   all   the widows weeping   and

ἐπιδεικνύμεναι χιτῶνας καὶ ἱμάτια, ὅσα
showing   tunics   and garments, which

ἐποίει μετ᾽ αὐτῶν οὖσα ἡ Δορκάς.
¹made ⁴with ⁵them ³being - ¹Dorcas.

40 ἐκβαλὼν δὲ ἔξω πάντας ὁ Πέτρος
And ²putting out ⁴outside ³all - ¹Peter

καὶ θεὶς τὰ γόνατα προσηύξατο, καὶ
and placing the knees he prayed, and
        =kneeling down

ἐπιστρέψας πρὸς τὸ σῶμα εἶπεν· Ταβιθά,
turning   to   the body said: Tabitha,

ἀνάστηθι. ἡ δὲ ἤνοιξεν τοὺς ὀφθαλμοὺς
rise up.   And she opened the   eyes

αὐτῆς, καὶ ἰδοῦσα τὸν Πέτρον ἀνεκάθισεν.
of her, and seeing - Peter   sat up.

41 δοὺς δὲ αὐτῇ χεῖρα ἀνέστησεν αὐτήν·
And giving her a hand he raised up her;

φωνήσας δὲ τοὺς ἁγίους καὶ τὰς χήρας
and calling the saints and the widows

παρέστησεν αὐτὴν ζῶσαν. 42 γνωστὸν δὲ
he presented her   living.   And known

ἐγένετο καθ᾽ ὅλης τῆς Ἰόππης, καὶ
it became throughout all - Joppa, and

ἐπίστευσαν πολλοὶ ἐπὶ τὸν κύριον.
believed   many   on   the   Lord.

43 Ἐγένετο δὲ ἡμέρας ἱκανὰς μεῖναι ἐν
And it came to pass days several to remain in
                              =he remained many days

Ἰόππῃ παρά τινι Σίμωνι βυρσεῖ.
Joppa with one Simon   a tanner.

CHAPTER 10

AT Caesare'a there was a man named Cornelius, a centurion of what was known as the Italian Cohort, ²a devout man who feared God with all his household, gave alms liberally

10 Ἀνὴρ δέ τις ἐν Καισαρείᾳ ὀνόματι
Now a certain man in Cæsarea   by name

Κορνήλιος, ἑκατοντάρχης ἐκ σπείρης τῆς
Cornelius,   a centurion   of a cohort   -

καλουμένης Ἰταλικῆς, 2 εὐσεβὴς καὶ
being called   Italian,   devout   and

φοβούμενος τὸν θεὸν σὺν παντὶ τῷ οἴκῳ
fearing   - God with all   the household

αὐτοῦ, ποιῶν ἐλεημοσύνας πολλὰς τῷ
of him, doing   alms   many   to the

to the people, and prayed constantly to God. ³About the ninth hour of the day he saw clearly in a vision an angel of God coming in and saying to him, "Cornelius." ⁴And he stared at him in terror, and said, "What is it, Lord?" And he said to him, "Your prayers and your alms have ascended as a memorial before God. ⁵And now send men to Joppa, and bring one Simon who is called Peter; ⁶he is lodging with Simon, a tanner, whose house is by the seaside." ⁷When the angel who spoke to him had departed, he called two of his servants and a devout soldier from among those that waited on him, ⁸and having related everything to them, he sent them to Joppa.

9 The next day, as they were on their journey and coming near the city, Peter went up on the housetop to pray, about the sixth hour. ¹⁰And he became hungry and desired something to eat; but while they

λαῷ καὶ δεόμενος τοῦ θεοῦ διὰ παντός,
people and petitioning – God continually,

3 εἶδεν ἐν ὁράματι φανερῶς, ὡσεὶ περὶ
saw in a vision clearly, as it were around

ὥραν ἐνάτην τῆς ἡμέρας, ἄγγελον τοῦ
hour ninth of the day, an angel

θεοῦ εἰσελθόντα πρὸς αὐτὸν καὶ εἰπόντα
of God entering to him and saying

αὐτῷ· Κορνήλιε. 4 ὁ δὲ ἀτενίσας αὐτῷ
to him: Cornelius. And he gazing at him

καὶ ἔμφοβος γενόμενος εἶπεν· τί ἐστιν,
and terrified becoming said: What is it,

κύριε; εἶπεν δὲ αὐτῷ· αἱ προσευχαί
lord? And he said to him: The prayers

σου καὶ αἱ ἐλεημοσύναι σου ἀνέβησαν
of thee and the alms of thee went up

εἰς μνημόσυνον ἔμπροσθεν τοῦ θεοῦ. 5 καὶ
for a memorial before – God. And

νῦν πέμψον ἄνδρας εἰς Ἰόππην καὶ
now send men to Joppa and

μετάπεμψαι Σίμωνά τινα ὃς ἐπικαλεῖται
[summon ²Simon ¹one who is surnamed

Πέτρος· 6 οὗτος ξενίζεται παρά τινι
Peter; this man is lodged with one

Σίμωνι βυρσεῖ, ᾧ ἐστιν οἰκία παρὰ
Simon a tanner, to whom is a houseᶜ by
=who has a house

θάλασσαν. 7 ὡς δὲ ἀπῆλθεν ὁ ἄγγελος ὁ
[the] sea. And as went away the angel

λαλῶν αὐτῷ, φωνήσας δύο τῶν οἰκετῶν
speaking to him, calling two of the household slaves

καὶ στρατιώτην εὐσεβῆ τῶν προσκαρτερούν-
and soldier a devout of the [ones] waiting

των αὐτῷ, 8 καὶ ἐξηγησάμενος ἅπαντα
on him, and explaining all things

αὐτοῖς ἀπέστειλεν αὐτοὺς εἰς τὴν Ἰόππην.
to them sent them to – Joppa.

9 Τῇ δὲ ἐπαύριον ὁδοιπορούντων ἐκείνων
And on the morrow journeying those

καὶ τῇ πόλει ἐγγιζόντων ἀνέβη Πέτρος
and to the city drawing nearᵃ went up Peter
=as they journeyed and drew near to the city

ἐπὶ τὸ δῶμα προσεύξασθαι περὶ ὥραν
onto the roof to pray about hour

ἕκτην. 10 ἐγένετο δὲ πρόσπεινος καὶ
sixth. And he became hungry and

ἤθελεν γεύσασθαι· παρασκευαζόντων δὲ
wished to taste(eat); and preparing
=while they prepared

were preparing it, he fell into a trance [11] and saw the heaven opened, and something descending, like a great sheet, let down by four corners upon the earth. [12] In it were all kinds of animals and reptiles and birds of the air. [13] And there came a voice to him, "Rise, Peter; kill and eat." [14] But Peter said, "No, Lord; for I have never eaten anything that is common or unclean." [15] And the voice came to him again a second time, "What God has cleansed, you must not call common." [16] This happened three times, and the thing was taken up at once to heaven.

17 Now while Peter was inwardly perplexed as to what the vision which he had seen might mean, behold, the men that were sent by Cornelius, having made inquiry for Simon's house, stood before the gate [18] and called out to ask whether Simon who was called Peter was lodging there. [19] And while Peter was pondering the vision, the Spirit said to him, "Behold, three men are looking for you. [20] Rise

αὐτῶν ἐγένετο ἐπ᾽ αὐτὸν ἔκστασις, 11 καὶ
them[a] there came on   him   an ecstasy,   and

θεωρεῖ τὸν οὐρανὸν ἀνεῳγμένον καὶ
he beholds the heaven   having been opened   and

καταβαῖνον σκεῦός τι ὡς ὀθόνην μεγάλην,
coming down a certain vessel like sheet   a great,

τέσσαρσιν ἀρχαῖς καθιέμενον ἐπὶ τῆς γῆς,
by four   corners being let down onto the earth,

12 ἐν ᾧ ὑπῆρχεν πάντα τὰ τετράποδα
in which were   all   the   quadrupeds

καὶ ἑρπετὰ τῆς γῆς καὶ πετεινὰ τοῦ
and reptiles of the earth and birds   of the

οὐρανοῦ. 13 καὶ ἐγένετο φωνὴ πρὸς
heaven(air).   And there came a voice   to

αὐτόν· ἀναστάς, Πέτρε, θῦσον καὶ φάγε.
him : Rise up,   Peter,   slay   and   eat.

14 ὁ δὲ Πέτρος εἶπεν· μηδαμῶς, κύριε,
  – But Peter   said :   Not at all,   Lord,

ὅτι οὐδέποτε ἔφαγον πᾶν κοινὸν καὶ
because never did I eat every(any)thing common and

ἀκάθαρτον. 15 καὶ φωνὴ πάλιν ἐκ δευτέρου
unclean.   And a voice again a second [time]

πρὸς αὐτόν· ἃ ὁ θεὸς ἐκαθάρισεν σὺ
[came] to him : What things – God cleansed [3]thou

μὴ κοίνου. 16 τοῦτο δὲ ἐγένετο ἐπὶ
[2]not [1]treat [4]as [5]unclean. And this   occurred   on

τρίς, καὶ εὐθὺς ἀνελήμφθη τὸ σκεῦος
three [occasions], and immediately was taken up the vessel

εἰς τὸν οὐρανόν. 17 Ὡς δὲ ἐν ἑαυτῷ
into – heaven.   Now as   in himself

διηπόρει ὁ Πέτρος τί ἂν εἴη τὸ ὅραμα
was doubting – Peter   what might be the   vision

ὃ εἶδεν, ἰδοὺ οἱ ἄνδρες οἱ ἀπεσταλμένοι
which he saw, behold[,] the men – having been sent

ὑπὸ τοῦ Κορνηλίου διερωτήσαντες τὴν
by   – Cornelius   asking for   the

οἰκίαν τοῦ Σίμωνος ἐπέστησαν ἐπὶ τὸν
house – of Simon   stood at   at the

πυλῶνα, 18 καὶ · φωνήσαντες ἐπυνθάνοντο
porch,   and   calling   inquired

εἰ Σίμων ὁ ἐπικαλούμενος Πέτρος ἐνθάδε
if Simon – being surnamed   Peter   here

ξενίζεται. 19 Τοῦ δὲ Πέτρου διενθυμουμένου
is lodged.   – And Peter   pondering[a]
                              =while Peter pondered

περὶ τοῦ ὁράματος εἶπεν τὸ πνεῦμα·
about the vision   [3]said [1]the [2]Spirit :

ἰδοὺ ἄνδρες δύο ζητοῦντές σε· 20 ἀλλὰ
Behold[,] men two seeking   thee;   but

and go down, and accompany them without hesitation; for I have sent them." 21And Peter went down to the men and said, "I am the one you are looking for; what is the reason for your coming?" 22And they said, "Cornelius, a centurion, an upright and God-fearing man, who is well spoken of by the whole Jewish nation, was directed by a holy angel to send for you to come to his house, and to hear what you have to say." 23So he called them in to be his guests.

The next day he rose and went off with them, and some of the brethren from Joppa accompanied him. 24And on the following day they entered Caesarea. Cornelius was expecting them and had called together his kinsmen and close friends. 25When Peter entered, Cornelius met him and fell down at his feet and worshiped him. 26But Peter lifted him up, saying, "Stand up; I too am a man." 27And as he

ἀναστὰς κατάβηθι, καὶ πορεύου σὺν αὐτοῖς
rising up go down, and go with them
μηδὲν διακρινόμενος, ὅτι ἐγὼ ἀπέσταλκα
nothing doubting, because I have sent
αὐτούς. 21 καταβὰς δὲ Πέτρος πρὸς
them. And going down Peter to
τοὺς ἄνδρας εἶπεν· ἰδοὺ ἐγώ εἰμι ὃν
the men said: Behold[,] I am [he] whom
ζητεῖτε· τίς ἡ αἰτία δι᾿ ἣν πάρεστε;
ye seek; what [is] the cause for which ye are here?
22 οἱ δὲ εἶπαν· Κορνήλιος ἑκατοντάρχης,
And they said: Cornelius a centurion,
ἀνὴρ δίκαιος καὶ φοβούμενος τὸν θεόν,
a man just and fearing – God,
μαρτυρούμενός τε ὑπὸ ὅλου τοῦ ἔθνους
and being witnessed by all the nation
τῶν Ἰουδαίων, ἐχρηματίσθη ὑπὸ ἀγγέλου
of the Jews, was warned by angel
ἁγίου μεταπέμψασθαί σε εἰς τὸν οἶκον
a holy to summon thee to the house
αὐτοῦ καὶ ἀκοῦσαι ῥήματα παρὰ σοῦ.
of him and to hear words from thee.
23 εἰσκαλεσάμενος οὖν αὐτοὺς ἐξένισεν.
Calling in therefore them he lodged.
Τῇ δὲ ἐπαύριον ἀναστὰς ἐξῆλθεν σὺν
And on the morrow rising up he went forth with
αὐτοῖς, καί τινες τῶν ἀδελφῶν τῶν
them, and some of the brothers –
ἀπὸ Ἰόππης συνῆλθον αὐτῷ. 24 τῇ δὲ
from Joppa accompanied him. And on the
ἐπαύριον εἰσῆλθεν εἰς τὴν Καισάρειαν·
morrow he entered into – Cæsarea;
ὁ δὲ Κορνήλιος ἦν προσδοκῶν αὐτούς,
– and Cornelius was awaiting them,
συγκαλεσάμενος τοὺς συγγενεῖς αὐτοῦ καὶ
having called together the relatives of him and
τοὺς ἀναγκαίους φίλους. 25 Ὡς δὲ
the intimate friends. Now when
ἐγένετο τοῦ εἰσελθεῖν τὸν Πέτρον,
it came to pass the to enter – Peter,[b]
= Now it came to pass when Peter entered,
συναντήσας αὐτῷ ὁ Κορνήλιος πεσὼν
[2]meeting [3]him – [1]Cornelius falling
ἐπὶ τοὺς πόδας προσεκύνησεν. 26 ὁ δὲ
at the(his) feet worshipped. – But
Πέτρος ἤγειρεν αὐτὸν λέγων· ἀνάστηθι·
Peter raised him saying: Stand up;
καὶ ἐγὼ αὐτὸς ἄνθρωπός εἰμι. 27 καὶ
also I [my]self a man am. And

talked with him, he went in and found many persons gathered; ²⁸and he said to them, "You yourselves know how unlawful it is for a Jew to associate with or to visit any one of another nation; but God has shown me that I should not call any man common or unclean. ²⁹So when I was sent for, I came without objection. I ask then why you sent for me."

30 And Cornelius said, "Four days ago, about this hour, I was keeping the ninth hour of prayer in my house; and behold, a man stood before me in bright apparel, ³¹saying, 'Cornelius, your prayer has been heard and your alms have been remembered before God. ³²Send therefore to Joppa and ask for Simon who is called Peter; he is lodging in the house of Simon, a tanner, by the seaside.' ³³So I sent to you at once, and you have been kind enough to come. Now therefore we are all here present in the sight of God, to hear all that you have been commanded by the Lord."

34 And Peter opened

συνομιλῶν   αὐτῷ   εἰσῆλθεν,   καὶ   εὑρίσκει
talking with   him   he entered,   and   finds

συνεληλυθότας   πολλούς,   28 ἔφη   τε   πρὸς
having come together   many,   and said   to

αὐτούς· ὑμεῖς   ἐπίστασθε   ὡς   ἀθέμιτόν ἐστιν
them: Ye   understand   how   unlawful   it is

ἀνδρὶ   Ἰουδαίῳ   κολλᾶσθαι ἢ   προσέρχεσθαι
for a man   a Jew   to adhere   or   to approach

ἀλλοφύλῳ· κἀμοὶ ὁ θεὸς   ἔδειξεν μηδένα
a foreigner;   and to me - God   showed ²not any

κοινὸν ἢ   ἀκάθαρτον   λέγειν   ἄνθρωπον·
¹common ⁵or   ⁶unclean   ¹to call   ³man;

29 διὸ   καὶ   ἀναντιρρήτως   ἦλθον   μετα-
wherefore indeed ³unquestioningly ²I came ¹being

πεμφθείς.   πυνθάνομαι οὖν,   τίνι   λόγῳ
summoned.   I inquire   therefore,   for what   reason

μετεπέμψασθέ   με;   30 καὶ ὁ   Κορνήλιος
ye summoned   me?   And - Cornelius

ἔφη· ἀπὸ τετάρτης ἡμέρας μέχρι ταύτης τῆς
said: From   fourth   day   until   this -
=Four days ago

ὥρας   ἤμην   τὴν   ἐνάτην   προσευχόμενος
hour   I was   [at] the   ninth   praying

ἐν τῷ   οἴκῳ   μου, καὶ ἰδοὺ ἀνὴρ ἔστη
in   the   house   of me,   and behold[,] a man   stood

ἐνώπιόν   μου ἐν ἐσθῆτι λαμπρᾷ, 31 καὶ
before   me   in   clothing   bright,   and

φησίν·   Κορνήλιε,   εἰσηκούσθη   σου ἡ
says: Cornelius,   was heard   of thee   the

προσευχὴ καὶ αἱ ἐλεημοσύναι σου ἐμνήσθησαν
prayer   and the   alms   of thee were remembered

ἐνώπιον   τοῦ   θεοῦ.   32 πέμψον   οὖν   εἰς
before - God.   Send thou   therefore   to

Ἰόππην   καὶ   μετακάλεσαι   Σίμωνα ὃς ἐπι-
Joppa   and   send for   Simon   who   is

καλεῖται   Πέτρος· οὗτος ξενίζεται ἐν οἰκίᾳ
surnamed   Peter;   this man   is lodged in [the] house

Σίμωνος βυρσέως παρὰ θάλασσαν. 33 ἐξαυτῆς
of Simon   a tanner , by   [the] sea.   At once

οὖν   ἔπεμψα   πρὸς σέ, σύ τε   καλῶς
therefore   I sent   to   thee,   and thou   well

ἐποίησας   παραγενόμενος.   νῦν οὖν   πάντες
didst   arriving.   Now therefore   all

ἡμεῖς ἐνώπιον τοῦ θεοῦ πάρεσμεν ἀκοῦσαι
we   before - God   are present   to hear

πάντα   τὰ   προστεταγμένα   σοι ὑπὸ   τοῦ
all   the things having been commanded   thee   by   the

κυρίου.   34 Ἀνοίξας δὲ Πέτρος τὸ στόμα
Lord.   And opening   Peter   the(his)   mouth

his mouth and said: "Truly I perceive that God shows no partiality, [35] but in every nation any one who fears him and does what is right is acceptable to him. [36] You know the word which he sent to Israel, preaching good news of peace by Jesus Christ (he is Lord of all), [37] the word which was proclaimed throughout all Judea, beginning from Galilee after the baptism which John preached: [38] how God anointed Jesus of Nazareth with the Holy Spirit and with power; how he went about doing good and healing all that were oppressed by the devil, for God was with him. [39] And we are witnesses to all that he did both in the country of the Jews and in Jerusalem. They put him to death by hanging him on a tree; [40] but God raised him on the third day and made him manifest; [41] not to all the people but to us who were chosen by God as witnesses, who ate and drank with him after he

εἶπεν· ἐπ' ἀληθείας καταλαμβάνομαι ὅτι
said: On(in) truth I perceive that

οὐκ ἔστιν προσωπολήμπτης ὁ θεός, 35 ἀλλ'
³not ²is ⁴a respecter of persons – ¹God, but

ἐν παντὶ ἔθνει ὁ φοβούμενος αὐτὸν καὶ
in every nation the [one] fearing him and

ἐργαζόμενος δικαιοσύνην δεκτὸς αὐτῷ ἐστιν·
working righteousness acceptable to him is;

36 τὸν λόγον ὃν ἀπέστειλεν τοῖς υἱοῖς
the word which he sent to the sons

'Ισραὴλ εὐαγγελιζόμενος εἰρήνην διὰ 'Ιησοῦ
of Israel preaching peace through Jesus

Χριστοῦ· οὗτός ἐστιν πάντων κύριος.
Christ: this one is of all Lord.

37 ὑμεῖς οἴδατε τὸ γενόμενον ῥῆμα καθ'
Ye know the having become thing throughout
=that which took place

ὅλης τῆς 'Ιουδαίας, ἀρξάμενος ἀπὸ τῆς
all – Judæa, beginning from –

Γαλιλαίας μετὰ τὸ βάπτισμα ὃ ἐκήρυξεν
Galilee after the baptism which ²proclaimed

'Ιωάννης, 38 'Ιησοῦν τὸν ἀπὸ Ναζαρέθ,
¹John, Jesus the one from Nazareth,

ὡς ἔχρισεν αὐτὸν ὁ θεὸς πνεύματι ἁγίῳ
how anointed him – God with Spirit Holy

καὶ δυνάμει, ὃς διῆλθεν εὐεργετῶν καὶ
and power, who went about doing good and

ἰώμενος πάντας τοὺς καταδυναστευομένους
curing all the [ones] being oppressed

ὑπὸ τοῦ διαβόλου, ὅτι ὁ θεὸς ἦν μετ'
by the devil, because – God was with

αὐτοῦ· 39 καὶ ἡμεῖς μάρτυρες πάντων
him; and we [are] witnesses of all things

ὧν ἐποίησεν ἔν τε τῇ χώρᾳ τῶν 'Ιουδαίων
which he did both in the country of the Jews

καὶ 'Ιερουσαλήμ· ὃν καὶ ἀνεῖλαν
and Jerusalem; whom indeed they killed

κρεμάσαντες ἐπὶ ξύλου. 40 τοῦτον ὁ
hanging on a tree. This one –

θεὸς ἤγειρεν ἐν τῇ τρίτῃ ἡμέρᾳ καὶ
God raised on the third day and

ἔδωκεν αὐτὸν ἐμφανῆ γενέσθαι, 41 οὐ
gave him visible to become, not

παντὶ τῷ λαῷ, ἀλλὰ μάρτυσιν τοῖς
to all the people, but to witnesses the

προκεχειροτονημένοις ὑπὸ τοῦ θεοῦ, ἡμῖν,
having been previously appointed by – God, to us,

οἴτινες συνεφάγομεν καὶ συνεπίομεν αὐτῷ
who ate with and drank with him

rose from the dead. ⁴²And he commanded us to preach to the people, and to testify that he is the one ordained by God to be judge of the living and the dead. ⁴³To him all the prophets bear witness that every one who believes in him receives forgiveness of sins through his name."

44 While Peter was still saying this, the Holy Spirit fell on all who heard the word. ⁴⁵And the believers from among the circumcised who came with Peter were amazed, because the gift of the Holy Spirit had been poured out even on the Gentiles. ⁴⁶For they heard them speaking in tongues and extolling God. Then Peter declared, ⁴⁷"Can any one forbid water for baptizing these people who have received the Holy Spirit just as we have?" ⁴⁸And he commanded them to be baptized in the name of Jesus Christ. Then they asked him to remain for some days.

μετὰ τὸ ἀναστῆναι αὐτὸν ἐκ νεκρῶν·
after the to rise again him[b] out of [the] dead;
= he rose again

42 καὶ παρήγγειλεν ἡμῖν κηρῦξαι τῷ λαῷ
and he commanded us to proclaim to the people

καὶ διαμαρτύρασθαι ὅτι οὗτός ἐστιν ὁ
and solemnly to witness that this man is the [one]

ὡρισμένος ὑπὸ τοῦ θεοῦ κριτὴς ζώντων
having been by - God judge of living
designated

καὶ νεκρῶν. 43 τούτῳ πάντες οἱ προφῆται
and of dead. To this man all the prophets

μαρτυροῦσιν, ἄφεσιν ἁμαρτιῶν λαβεῖν διὰ
witness, ⁶forgiveness ⁷of sins ⁵to receive ⁸through

τοῦ ὀνόματος αὐτοῦ πάντα τὸν πιστεύοντα
⁹the ¹⁰name ¹¹of him ¹everyone ²believing

εἰς αὐτόν. 44 Ἔτι λαλοῦντος τοῦ Πέτρου
³in ⁴him. Yet speaking - Peter[a]
= While Peter was still speaking

τὰ ῥήματα ταῦτα ἐπέπεσεν τὸ πνεῦμα
these words ⁴fell on ¹the ²Spirit

τὸ ἅγιον ἐπὶ πάντας τοὺς ἀκούοντας
- ³Holy on all the [ones] hearing

τὸν λόγον. 45 καὶ ἐξέστησαν οἱ ἐκ
the discourse. And ⁵were amazed ¹the ²of [the]

περιτομῆς πιστοὶ ὅσοι συνῆλθαν τῷ Πέτρῳ,
⁴circumcision ³faithful as many as accompanied - Peter,

ὅτι καὶ ἐπὶ τὰ ἔθνη ἡ δωρεὰ τοῦ ἁγίου
because also on the nations the gift of the Holy

πνεύματος ἐκκέχυται· 46 ἤκουον γὰρ
Spirit has been poured out; for they heard

αὐτῶν λαλούντων γλώσσαις καὶ μεγαλυνόν-
them speaking in tongues and magnify-

των τὸν θεόν. τότε ἀπεκρίθη Πέτρος·
ing - God. Then answered Peter:

47 μήτι τὸ ὕδωρ δύναται κωλῦσαί τις
Not ⁴the ⁵water ³can ²to forbid ¹anyone

τοῦ μὴ βαπτισθῆναι τούτους, οἵτινες τὸ
- ⁷not ⁶to be baptized[d] ⁶these, who the

πνεῦμα τὸ ἅγιον ἔλαβον ὡς καὶ ἡμεῖς;
Spirit - Holy received as also we?

48 προσέταξεν δὲ αὐτοὺς ἐν τῷ ὀνόματι
And he commanded them in the name

Ἰησοῦ Χριστοῦ βαπτισθῆναι. τότε ἠρώτησαν
of Jesus Christ to be baptized. Then they asked

αὐτὸν ἐπιμεῖναι ἡμέρας τινάς.
him to remain days some.

CHAPTER 11

NOW the apostles and the brethren who were in Judea heard that the Gentiles also had received the word of God. ²So when Peter went up to Jerusalem, the circumcision party criticized him, ³saying, "Why did you go to uncircumcised men and eat with them?" ⁴But Peter began and explained to them in order: ⁵"I was in the city of Joppa praying; and in a trance I saw a vision, something descending, like a great sheet, let down from heaven by four corners; and it came down to me. ⁶Looking at it closely I observed animals and beasts of prey and reptiles and birds of the air. ⁷And I heard a voice saying to me, 'Rise, Peter; kill and eat.' ⁸But I said, 'No, Lord; for nothing common or unclean has ever entered my mouth.' ⁹But the voice answered a second time from heaven, 'What God has cleansed you must not call common.' ¹⁰This happened three times,

11 ʺΗκουσαν δὲ οἱ ἀπόστολοι καὶ οἱ
Now heard   the   apostles   and   the
ἀδελφοὶ οἱ ὄντες κατὰ τὴν Ἰουδαίαν
brothers –   being throughout –   Judæa
ὅτι καὶ τὰ ἔθνη ἐδέξαντο τὸν λόγον
that also the nations received   the   word
τοῦ θεοῦ. 2 ʺΟτε δὲ ἀνέβη Πέτρος εἰς
– of God.   And when went up Peter to
Ἰερουσαλήμ, διεκρίνοντο πρὸς αὐτὸν οἱ
Jerusalem,   disputed   with   him the [ones]
ἐκ περιτομῆς 3 λέγοντες ὅτι εἰσῆλθες
of [the] circumcision   saying[.]   –   Thou enteredst
πρὸς ἄνδρας ἀκροβυστίαν ἔχοντας καὶ
to   men   uncircumcision   having   and
συνέφαγες αὐτοῖς. 4 ἀρξάμενος δὲ Πέτρος
didst eat with them.   And beginning   Peter
ἐξετίθετο αὐτοῖς καθεξῆς λέγων· 5 ἐγὼ
explained   to them in order   saying: I
ἤμην ἐν πόλει Ἰόππῃ προσευχόμενος, καὶ
was in [the] city Joppa   praying,   and
εἶδον ἐν ἐκστάσει ὅραμα, καταβαῖνον
I saw in an ecstasy a vision,   coming down
σκεῦός τι ὡς ὀθόνην μεγάλην τέσσαρσιν
a certain vessel as sheet   a great   by four
ἀρχαῖς καθιεμένην ἐκ τοῦ οὐρανοῦ, καὶ
corners having been let down out of –   heaven,   and
ἦλθεν ἄχρι ἐμοῦ· 6 εἰς ἣν ἀτενίσας
it came up to me;   into which   gazing
κατενόουν, καὶ εἶδον τὰ τετράποδα τῆς
I perceived, and I saw the quadrupeds of the
γῆς καὶ τὰ θηρία καὶ τὰ ἑρπετὰ καὶ τὰ
earth and the wild beasts and the reptiles and the
πετεινὰ τοῦ οὐρανοῦ. 7 ἤκουσα δὲ καὶ
birds   of the heaven(air).   And I heard   also
φωνῆς λεγούσης μοι· ἀναστάς, Πέτρε,
a voice saying   to me: Rise up,   Peter,
θῦσον καὶ φάγε. 8 εἶπον δέ· μηδαμῶς,
slay   and eat.   And I said : Not at all,
κύριε, ὅτι κοινὸν ἢ ἀκάθαρτον οὐδέποτε
Lord, because a common or unclean thing   never
εἰσῆλθεν εἰς τὸ στόμα μου. 9 ἀπεκρίθη δὲ
entered   into the mouth of me.   And answered
ἐκ δευτέρου φωνὴ ἐκ τοῦ οὐρανοῦ·
a second [time] a voice out of –   heaven:
ἃ ὁ θεὸς ἐκαθάρισεν σὺ μὴ κοίνου.
What – God cleansed   thou regard not common.
things
10 τοῦτο δὲ ἐγένετο ἐπὶ τρίς, καὶ
And this   happened on three [occasions], and

and all was drawn up again into heaven. ¹¹At that very moment three men arrived at the house in which we were, sent to me from Caesare′a. ¹²And the Spirit told me to go with them, making no distinction. These six brethren also accompanied me, and we entered the man's house. ¹³And he told us how he had seen the angel standing in his house and saying, 'Send to Joppa and bring Simon called Peter; ¹⁴he will declare to you a message by which you will be saved, you and all your household.' ¹⁵As I began to speak, the Holy Spirit fell on them just as on us at the beginning. ¹⁶And I remembered the word of the Lord, how he said, 'John baptized with water, but you shall be baptized with the Holy Spirit.' ¹⁷If then God gave the same gift to them as he gave to us when we believed in the Lord Jesus Christ, who was I that I could withstand God?" ¹⁸When they heard this they were

ἀνεσπάσθη   πάλιν   ἅπαντα   εἰς   τὸν   οὐρανόν.
was pulled up   again   all things   to   —   ʰeaven.

11 καὶ   ἰδοὺ   ἐξαυτῆς   τρεῖς   ἄνδρες   ἐπέστησαν
And behold   at once   three   men   stood at

ἐπὶ   τὴν   οἰκίαν   ἐν   ᾗ   ἦμεν,   ἀπεσταλμένοι
at   the   house   in which   I was,   having been sent

ἀπὸ   Καισαρείας   πρός   με.   **12** εἶπεν   δὲ
from   Cæsarea   to   me.   And ²told

τὸ   πνεῦμά   μοι   συνελθεῖν   αὐτοῖς   μηδὲν
¹the   ²Spirit   ⁴me   to go with   them   nothing

διακρίναντα.   ἦλθον   δὲ   σὺν   ἐμοὶ   καὶ
doubting.   And came   with   me   also

οἱ   ἓξ   ἀδελφοὶ   οὗτοι,   καὶ   εἰσήλθομεν   εἰς
—   six   brothers   these,   and   we entered   into

τὸν   οἶκον   τοῦ   ἀνδρός.   **13** ἀπήγγειλεν   δὲ
the   house   of the   man.   And he reported

ἡμῖν   πῶς   εἶδεν   τὸν   ἄγγελον   ἐν   τῷ
to us   how   he saw   the   angel   in   the

οἴκῳ   αὐτοῦ   σταθέντα   καὶ   εἰπόντα·
house   of him   standing   and   saying:

ἀπόστειλον   εἰς   Ἰόππην   καὶ   μετάπεμψαι
Send   to   Joppa   and   summon

Σίμωνα   τὸν   ἐπικαλούμενον   Πέτρον,   **14** ὃς
Simon   the   —being surnamed   Peter,   who

λαλήσει   ῥήματα   πρὸς   σὲ   ἐν   οἷς   σωθήσῃ
will speak   words   to   thee   by   which   mayest be saved

σὺ   καὶ   πᾶς   ὁ   οἶκός   σου.   **15** ἐν   δὲ
thou   and   all   the   household   of thee.   And in

τῷ   ἄρξασθαί   με   λαλεῖν   ἐπέπεσεν   τὸ
the   to begin   me^{be}   to speak   ⁴fell on   ¹the
=as I began

πνεῦμα   τὸ   ἅγιον   ἐπ᾽   αὐτοὺς   ὥσπερ   καὶ
²Spirit   —   ³Holy   on   them   as   also

ἐφ᾽   ἡμᾶς   ἐν   ἀρχῇ.   **16** ἐμνήσθην   δὲ   τοῦ
on   us   at [the] beginning.   And I remembered   the

ῥήματος   τοῦ   κυρίου,   ὡς   ἔλεγεν·   Ἰωάννης
word   of the   Lord,   how   he said: John

μὲν   ἐβάπτισεν   ὕδατι,   ὑμεῖς   δὲ   βαπτισθήσεσθε
indeed   baptized   with water,   but ye   will be baptized

ἐν   πνεύματι   ἁγίῳ.   **17** εἰ   οὖν   τὴν   ἴσην
in   Spirit   Holy.   If   therefore   ⁴the   ⁵equal

δωρεὰν   ἔδωκεν   αὐτοῖς   ὁ   θεὸς   ὡς   καὶ
⁶gift   ³gave   ³them   —   ¹God   as   also

ἡμῖν,   πιστεύσασιν   ἐπὶ   τὸν   κύριον   Ἰησοῦν
to us,   having believed   on   the   Lord   Jesus

Χριστόν,   ἐγὼ   τίς   ἤμην   δυνατὸς   κωλῦσαι
Christ,   ²I   ¹who   ¹was   [to be] able   to hinder

τὸν   θεόν;   **18** ἀκούσαντες   δὲ   ταῦτα   ἡσύχασαν,
—   God?   And hearing   these things   they kept silence

silenced. And they glorified God, saying, "Then to the Gentiles also God has granted repentance unto life."

19 Now those who were scattered because of the persecution that arose over Stephen traveled as far as Phoeni'cia and Cyprus and Antioch, speaking the word to none except Jews. [20]But there were some of them, men of Cyprus and Cyre'ne, who on coming to Antioch spoke to the Greeks[9] also, preaching the Lord Jesus. [21]And the hand of the Lord was with them, and a great number that believed turned to the Lord. [22]News of this came to the ears of the church in Jerusalem, and they sent Barnabas to Antioch. [23]When he came and saw the grace of God, he was glad; and he exhorted them all to remain faithful to the Lord with steadfast purpose; [24]for he was a good man, full of the Holy Spirit and of faith. And a large company was added to the Lord. [25]So

[9] Other ancient authorities read Hellenists

καὶ ἐδόξασαν τὸν θεὸν λέγοντες· ἄρα καὶ
and glorified – God saying : Then also

τοῖς ἔθνεσιν ὁ θεὸς τὴν μετάνοιαν εἰς
to the nations – God – repentance to

ζωὴν ἔδωκεν.
life gave.

19 Οἱ μὲν οὖν διασπαρέντες ἀπὸ τῆς
The [ones] – therefore being scattered from the

θλίψεως τῆς γενομένης ἐπὶ Στεφάνῳ
affliction – occurring over Stephen

διῆλθον ἕως Φοινίκης καὶ Κύπρου καὶ
passed through to Phœnicia and Cyprus and

Ἀντιοχείας, μηδενὶ λαλοῦντες τὸν λόγον
Antioch, to no one speaking the word

εἰ μὴ μόνον Ἰουδαίοις. 20 Ἦσαν δέ
except only to Jews. But [4]were

τινες ἐξ αὐτῶν ἄνδρες Κύπριοι καὶ
[1]some [2]of [3]them men Cypriotes and

Κυρηναῖοι, οἵτινες ἐλθόντες εἰς Ἀντιόχειαν
Cyrenians, who coming to Antioch

ἐλάλουν καὶ πρὸς τοὺς Ἕλληνας,
spoke also to the Greeks,

εὐαγγελιζόμενοι τὸν κύριον Ἰησοῦν. 21 καὶ ἦν
preaching the Lord Jesus. And was

χεὶρ κυρίου μετ᾽ αὐτῶν, πολύς τε
[the] hand of [the] Lord with them, and a much(great)

ἀριθμὸς ὁ πιστεύσας ἐπέστρεψεν ἐπὶ τὸν
number – believing turned to the

κύριον. 22 Ἠκούσθη δὲ ὁ λόγος εἰς
Lord. And was heard the account in

τὰ ὦτα τῆς ἐκκλησίας τῆς οὔσης ἐν
the ears of the church – being in

Ἰερουσαλὴμ περὶ αὐτῶν, καὶ ἐξαπέστειλαν
Jerusalem about them, and they sent out

Βαρναβᾶν ἕως Ἀντιοχείας· 23 ὃς παραγεν-
Barnabas to Antioch; who arriv-

όμενος καὶ ἰδὼν τὴν χάριν τὴν τοῦ
ing and seeing the grace the of

θεοῦ ἐχάρη, καὶ παρεκάλει πάντας τῇ
of God rejoiced, and exhorted all –

προθέσει τῆς καρδίας προσμένειν τῷ
with purpose – of heart to remain with the

κυρίῳ, 24 ὅτι ἦν ἀνὴρ ἀγαθὸς καὶ
Lord, because he was man a good and

πλήρης πνεύματος ἁγίου καὶ πίστεως.
full of [the] Spirit Holy and of faith.

καὶ προσετέθη ὄχλος ἱκανὸς τῷ κυρίῳ.
And was added a crowd considerable to the Lord.

Barnabas went to Tarsus to look for Saul; [26]and when he had found him, he brought him to Antioch. For a whole year they met with the church, and taught a large company of people; and in Antioch the disciples were for the first time called Christians.

27 Now in these days prophets came down from Jerusalem to Antioch. [28]And one of them named Ag'abus stood up and foretold by the Spirit that there would be a great famine over all the world; and this took place in the days of Claudius. [29]And the disciples determined, every one according to his ability, to send relief to the brethren who lived in Judea; [30]and they did so, sending it to the elders by the hand of Barnabas and Saul.

25 ἐξῆλθεν δὲ εἰς Ταρσὸν ἀναζητῆσαι
And he went forth to Tarsus to seek
Σαῦλον, 26 καὶ εὑρὼν ἤγαγεν εἰς 'Αντιόχειαν.
Saul, and finding brought to Antioch.
ἐγένετο δὲ αὐτοῖς καὶ ἐνιαυτὸν ὅλον
And it happened to them also year a whole
συναχθῆναι ἐν τῇ ἐκκλησίᾳ καὶ διδάξαι
to be assembled in the church and to teach
ὄχλον ἱκανόν, χρηματίσαι τε πρώτως ἐν
a crowd considerable, and to call firstly in
'Αντιοχείᾳ τοὺς μαθητὰς Χριστιανούς.
Antioch the disciples Christians.

27 'Εν ταύταις δὲ ταῖς ἡμέραις κατῆλθον
And in these - days came down
ἀπὸ 'Ιεροσολύμων προφῆται εἰς 'Αντιόχειαν·
from Jerusalem prophets to Antioch;
28 ἀναστὰς δὲ εἷς ἐξ αὐτῶν ὀνόματι
and rising up one of them by name
"Αγαβος ἐσήμαινεν διὰ τοῦ πνεύματος
Agabus signified through the Spirit
λιμὸν μεγάλην μέλλειν ἔσεσθαι ἐφ' ὅλην τὴν
famine a great to be about to be over all the
οἰκουμένην· ἥτις ἐγένετο ἐπὶ Κλαυδίου.
inhabited earth; which happened in the time of Claudius.
29 τῶν δὲ μαθητῶν καθὼς εὐπορεῖτό
So [3]of the [4]disciples [1]as [6]was prosperous
τις, ὥρισαν ἕκαστος αὐτῶν εἰς διακονίαν
[2]anyone, they determined each of them for ministration
πέμψαι τοῖς κατοικοῦσιν ἐν τῇ 'Ιουδαίᾳ
to send [1]to the [3]dwelling [4]in - [5]Judæa
ἀδελφοῖς· 30 ὃ καὶ ἐποίησαν ἀποστείλαντες
[2]brothers; which indeed they did sending
πρὸς τοὺς πρεσβυτέρους διὰ χειρὸς
to the elders through [the] hand
Βαρναβᾶ καὶ Σαύλου.
of Barnabas and of Saul.

CHAPTER 12

ABOUT that time Herod the king laid violent hands upon some who belonged to the church. [2]He killed James the brother of John with the sword; [3]and when he saw that it pleased the

12 Κατ' ἐκεῖνον δὲ τὸν καιρὸν ἐπέβαλεν
Now at that - time laid on
'Ηρῴδης ὁ βασιλεὺς τὰς χεῖρας κακῶσαί
Herod the king the(his) hands to ill-treat
τινας τῶν ἀπὸ τῆς ἐκκλησίας. 2 ἀνεῖλεν δὲ
some of the [ones] from the church. And he killed
'Ιάκωβον τὸν ἀδελφὸν 'Ιωάννου μαχαίρῃ.
James the brother of John with a sword.
3 ἰδὼν δὲ ὅτι ἀρεστόν ἐστιν τοῖς 'Ιουδαίοις
And seeing that pleasing it is(was) to the Jews

Jews, he proceeded to arrest Peter also. This was during the days of Unleavened Bread. ⁴And when he had seized him, he put him in prison, and delivered him to four squads of soldiers to guard him, intending after the Passover to bring him out to the people. ⁵So Peter was kept in prison; but earnest prayer for him was made to God by the church.

6 The very night when Herod was about to bring him out, Peter was sleeping between two soldiers, bound with two chains, and sentries before the door were guarding the prison; ⁷and behold, an angel of the Lord appeared, and a light shone in the cell; and he struck Peter on the side and woke him, saying, "Get up quickly." And the chains fell off his hands. ⁸And the angel said to him, "Dress yourself and put on your sandals." And he did so. And he said to him, "Wrap your mantle around you and follow me." ⁹And he went out

προσέθετο συλλαβεῖν καὶ Πέτρον, ἦσαν δὲ
he added   to arrest   also   Peter,   and they were

ἡμέραι τῶν ἀζύμων, 4 ὃν καὶ πιάσας
days   of unleavened bread,   whom also   seizing

ἔθετο εἰς φυλακήν, παραδοὺς τέσσαρσιν
he put in   prison,   delivering   to four

τετραδίοις στρατιωτῶν φυλάσσειν αὐτόν,
quaternions   of soldiers   to guard   him,

βουλόμενος μετὰ τὸ πάσχα ἀναγαγεῖν
intending   after   the Passover   to bring up

αὐτὸν τῷ λαῷ. 5 ὁ μὲν οὖν Πέτρος
him   to the people.   -   -* therefore Peter

ἐτηρεῖτο ἐν τῇ φυλακῇ· προσευχὴ δὲ ἦν
was kept   in   the   prison;   but prayer   was

ἐκτενῶς γινομένη ὑπὸ τῆς ἐκκλησίας πρὸς
earnestly being made   by   the   church   to

τὸν θεὸν περὶ αὐτοῦ. 6 Ὅτε δὲ ἤμελλεν
-    God concerning him.   And when ¹was about

προαγαγεῖν αὐτὸν ὁ Ἡρῴδης, τῇ νυκτὶ
²to bring forward ⁴him   -   ¹Herod,   the ²night

ἐκείνῃ ἦν ὁ Πέτρος κοιμώμενος μεταξὺ
¹in that   was -   Peter   sleeping   between

δύο στρατιωτῶν δεδεμένος ἁλύσεσιν δυσίν,
two   soldiers   having been bound with chains   two,

φύλακές τε πρὸ τῆς θύρας ἐτήρουν τὴν
and guards   before   the   door   were keeping the

φυλακήν. 7 καὶ ἰδοὺ ἄγγελος κυρίου
prison.   And   behold[,]   an angel   of [the] Lord

ἐπέστη, καὶ φῶς ἔλαμψεν ἐν τῷ οἰκήματι·
came upon, and a light   shone   in   the   building;

πατάξας δὲ τὴν πλευρὰν τοῦ Πέτρου
and striking   the   side   -   of Peter

ἤγειρεν αὐτὸν λέγων· ἀνάστα ἐν τάχει.
he raised   him   saying: Rise up   in   haste.

καὶ ἐξέπεσαν αὐτοῦ αἱ ἁλύσεις ἐκ τῶν
And   fell off   of him   the chains   off the(his)

χειρῶν. 8 εἶπεν δὲ ὁ ἄγγελος πρὸς
hands.   And said   the   angel   to

αὐτόν· ζῶσαι καὶ ὑπόδησαι τὰ σανδάλιά
him: Gird thyself and   put on   the   sandals

σου. ἐποίησεν δὲ οὕτως. καὶ λέγει
of thee.   And he did   so.   And   he tells

αὐτῷ· περιβαλοῦ τὸ ἱμάτιόν σου καὶ
him: Cast round   the   garment   of thee and

ἀκολούθει μοι. 9 καὶ ἐξελθὼν ἠκολούθει,
follow   me.   And going forth   he followed,

---

* μέν and δέ are in contrast : " on one hand . . ."—" on the other . . ."

and followed him; he did not know that what was done by the angel was real, but thought he was seeing a vision. ¹⁰When they had passed the first and the second guard, they came to the iron gate leading into the city. It opened to them of its own accord, and they went out and passed on through one street; and immediately the angel left him. ¹¹And Peter came to himself, and said, "Now I am sure that the Lord has sent his angel and rescued me from the hand of Herod and from all that the Jewish people were expecting."

12 When he realized this, he went to the house of Mary, the mother of John whose other name was Mark, where many were gathered together and were praying. ¹³And when he knocked at the door of the gateway, a maid named Rhoda came to answer. ¹⁴Recognizing Peter's voice, in her joy she did not open the gate but ran in and told that Peter was standing at the gate. ¹⁵They said to her, "You are mad." But she insisted that it

καὶ   οὐκ   ἤδει   ὅτι   ἀληθές ἐστιν   τὸ
and   knew not   that   ²true   ²is(was) ¹the thing
γινόμενον   διὰ   τοῦ   ἀγγέλου,   ἐδόκει   δὲ
happening   through   the   angel,   but he thought
ὅραμα   βλέπειν.   10 διελθόντες   δὲ   πρώτην
a vision   to see.   And going through [the] first
φυλακὴν   καὶ   δευτέραν   ἦλθαν   ἐπὶ   τὴν
prison   and   [the] second   they came   on   the
πύλην   τὴν   σιδηρᾶν   τὴν   φέρουσαν   εἰς   τὴν
gate   –   iron   –   leading   to   the
πόλιν,   ἥτις   αὐτομάτη   ἠνοίγη   αὐτοῖς,   καὶ
city,   which   of itself   was opened   to them,   and
ἐξελθόντες   προῆλθον   ῥύμην   μίαν,   καὶ
going out   they went forward   street   one,   and
εὐθέως   ἀπέστη   ὁ   ἄγγελος   ἀπ'   αὐτοῦ.
immediately   departed   the   angel   from   him.
11 καὶ   ὁ   Πέτρος   ἐν   ἑαυτῷ   γενόμενος
And   –   Peter   in   himself   having become
εἶπεν·   νῦν   οἶδα   ἀληθῶς   ὅτι   ἐξαπέστειλεν
said: Now   I know   truly   that   sent forth
ὁ   κύριος   τὸν   ἄγγελον   αὐτοῦ   καὶ   ἐξείλατό
the   Lord   the   angel   of him   and   delivered
με   ἐκ   χειρὸς   Ἡρῴδου   καὶ   πάσης   τῆς
me   out of [the] hand   of Herod   and   of all   the
προσδοκίας   τοῦ   λαοῦ   τῶν   Ἰουδαίων.
expectation   of the   people   of the   Jews.
12 συνιδών   τε   ἦλθεν   ἐπὶ   τὴν   οἰκίαν   τῆς
And realizing   he came   on   the   house   –
Μαρίας   τῆς   μητρὸς   Ἰωάννου   τοῦ
of Mary   the   mother   of John   –
ἐπικαλουμένου   Μάρκου,   οὗ   ἦσαν   ἱκανοὶ
being surnamed   Mark,   where   were   many
συνηθροισμένοι   καὶ   προσευχόμενοι.   13 κρού-
having been assembled   and   praying.   And
σαντος   δὲ   αὐτοῦ   τὴν   θύραν   τοῦ   πυλῶνος
knocking   him[a]   the   door   of the   porch
=as he knocked
προσῆλθεν   παιδίσκη   ὑπακοῦσαι   ὀνόματι
approached   a maidservant   to listen   by name
Ῥόδη,   14 καὶ   ἐπιγνοῦσα   τὴν   φωνὴν   τοῦ
Rhoda,   and   recognizing   the   voice   –
Πέτρου   ἀπὸ   τῆς   χαρᾶς   οὐκ   ἤνοιξεν   τὸν
of Peter   from   –   joy   she did not open   the
πυλῶνα,   εἰσδραμοῦσα   δὲ   ἀπήγγειλεν   ἑστάναι
porch,   but running in   announced   ²to stand
τὸν   Πέτρον   πρὸ   τοῦ   πυλῶνος.   15 οἱ   δὲ
–   ¹Peter   before   the   porch.   But they
πρὸς   αὐτὴν   εἶπαν·   μαίνῃ.   ἡ   δὲ   διϊσχυρίζετο
to   her   said: Thou ravest. But she emphatically asserted

was so. They said, "It is his angel!" 16 But Peter continued knocking; and when they opened, they saw him and were amazed. 17 But motioning to them with his hand to be silent, he described to them how the Lord had brought him out of the prison. And he said, "Tell this to James and to the brethren." Then he departed and went to another place.

18 Now when day came, there was no small stir among the soldiers over what had become of Peter. 19 And when Herod had sought for him and could not find him, he examined the sentries and ordered that they should be put to death. Then he went down from Judea to Caesare'a, and remained there.

20 Now Herod was angry with the people of Tyre and Sidon; and they came to him in a body, and having persuaded Blastus, the king's chamberlain, they asked for peace, because their country depended on the king's country for food. 21 On an appointed day Herod put on his royal robes, took his seat upon the throne, and made an oration to them. 22 And

οὕτως   ἔχειν.   οἱ   δὲ   ἔλεγον·   ὁ   ἄγγελός
so   to have(be).   So they   said: The   angel
ἐστιν   αὐτοῦ.   16 ὁ   δὲ   Πέτρος   ἐπέμενεν
it is   of him.   — But   Peter   continued
κρούων·   ἀνοίξαντες   δὲ   εἶδαν   αὐτὸν   καὶ
knocking;   and having opened   they saw   him   and
ἐξέστησαν.   17 κατασείσας   δὲ   αὐτοῖς   τῇ
were amazed.   And beckoning   to them with the
χειρὶ   σιγᾶν   διηγήσατο   αὐτοῖς   πῶς   ὁ
hand   to be quiet   he related   to them   how   the
κύριος   αὐτὸν   ἐξήγαγεν   ἐκ   τῆς   φυλακῆς,
Lord   him   led out   out of   the   prison,
εἶπέν   τε·   ἀπαγγείλατε   Ἰακώβῳ   καὶ   τοῖς
and said: Report   to James   and   to the
ἀδελφοῖς   ταῦτα.   καὶ   ἐξελθὼν   ἐπορεύθη   εἰς
brothers   these things.   And   going out   he went   to
ἕτερον   τόπον.   18 Γενομένης   δὲ   ἡμέρας   ἦν
another   place.   And becoming   day*   there was
=when it became day
τάραχος   οὐκ   ὀλίγος   ἐν   τοῖς   στρατιώταις,
disturbance   not   a little   among   the   soldiers,
τί   ἄρα   ὁ   Πέτρος   ἐγένετο.   19 Ἡρῴδης   δὲ
what then   —   [of] Peter   became.   And Herod
ἐπιζητήσας   αὐτὸν   καὶ   μὴ   εὑρών,
searching for   him   and   not   finding,
ἀνακρίνας   τοὺς   φύλακας   ἐκέλευσεν   ἀπ-
examining   the   guards   commanded   to
αχθῆναι,   καὶ   κατελθὼν   ἀπὸ   τῆς   Ἰουδαίας
be led away,*   and   going down   from   —   Judæa
εἰς   Καισάρειαν   διέτριβεν.   20 Ἦν   δὲ
to   Cæsarea   stayed.   Now he was
θυμομαχῶν   Τυρίοις   καὶ   Σιδωνίοις·
being furiously angry with   Tyrians   and   Sidonians;
ὁμοθυμαδὸν   δὲ   παρῆσαν   πρὸς   αὐτόν,   καὶ
and with one mind   they came   to   him,   and
πείσαντες   Βλάστον   τὸν   ἐπὶ   τοῦ   κοιτῶνος
having persuaded   Blastus   the one   over   the   bedchamber
τοῦ   βασιλέως   ἠτοῦντο   εἰρήνην,   διὰ   τὸ
of the   king   they asked   peace,   because the
τρέφεσθαι   αὐτῶν   τὴν   χώραν   ἀπὸ   τῆς
to be fed   of them   the   countryᵇ   from   the
=their country was fed
βασιλικῆς.   21 τακτῇ   δὲ   ἡμέρᾳ   ὁ   Ἡρῴδης
royal.   And on an appointed   day   —   Herod
ἐνδυσάμενος   ἐσθῆτα   βασιλικὴν   καθίσας   ἐπὶ
having been arrayed with   clothing   regal   sitting   on
τοῦ   βήματος   ἐδημηγόρει   πρὸς   αὐτούς·
the   tribunal   made a public speech   to   them;

* That is, to execution.

the people shouted, "The voice of a god, and not of man!" [23]Immediately an angel of the Lord smote him, because he did not give God the glory; and he was eaten by worms and died.

24 But the word of God grew and multiplied.

25 And Barnabas and Saul returned from[h] Jerusalem when they had fulfilled their mission, bringing with them John whose other name was Mark.

22 ὁ   δὲ   δῆμος   ἐπεφώνει·   θεοῦ   φωνὴ
and the   mob   cried out :   Of a god   a voice
καὶ   οὐκ   ἀνθρώπου.   23 παραχρῆμα   δὲ
and   not   of a man.   And at once
ἐπάταξεν   αὐτὸν   ἄγγελος   κυρίου   ἀνθ᾽   ὧν
smote   him   an angel   of [the] Lord   because
οὐκ   ἔδωκεν   τὴν   δόξαν   τῷ   θεῷ,   καὶ
he gave not   the   glory   -   to God,   and
γενόμενος   σκωληκόβρωτος   ἐξέψυξεν.
becoming   eaten by worms   he expired.

24 Ὁ   δὲ   λόγος   τοῦ   κυρίου   ηὔξανεν
But the   word   of the   Lord   grew
καὶ   ἐπληθύνετο.   25 Βαρναβᾶς   δὲ   καὶ
and   increased.   And Barnabas   and
Σαῦλος   ὑπέστρεψαν   ἐξ   Ἰερουσαλήμ,
Saul   returned   out of   Jerusalem,
πληρώσαντες   τὴν   διακονίαν,   συμπαρα-
having completed   the   ministration,   taking
λαβόντες   Ἰωάννην   τὸν   ἐπικληθέντα   Μᾶρκον.
with [them]   John   -   surnamed   Mark.

CHAPTER 13

NOW in the church at Antioch there were prophets and teachers, Barnabas, Symeon who was called Niger, Lucius of Cyre'ne, Man'a-en a member of the court of Herod the tetrarch, and Saul. [2]While they were worshiping the Lord and fasting, the Holy Spirit said, "Set apart for me Barnabas and Saul for the work to which I have called them." [3]Then after fasting and praying they laid their hands on them and sent them off.

4 So, being sent out

13 Ἦσαν   δὲ   ἐν   Ἀντιοχείᾳ   κατὰ   τὴν
Now there were   in   Antioch   among   the
οὖσαν   ἐκκλησίαν   προφῆται   καὶ   διδάσκαλοι
existing   church   prophets   and   teachers
ὅ   τε   Βαρναβᾶς   καὶ   Συμεὼν   ὁ   καλούμενος
- both   Barnabas   and   Simeon   ὁ   being called
Νίγερ,   καὶ   Λούκιος   ὁ   Κυρηναῖος,   Μαναήν   τε
Niger,   and   Lucius   the   Cyrenian,   and Manaen
Ἡρώδου   τοῦ   τετραάρχου   σύντροφος
[2]of Herod   [3]the   [4]tetrarch   [1]foster brother
καὶ   Σαῦλος.   2 Λειτουργούντων   δὲ   αὐτῶν
and   Saul.   And ministering   -   them[a]
                                                    = as they ministered
τῷ   κυρίῳ   καὶ   νηστευόντων   εἶπεν   τὸ
to the Lord   and   fasting[a]   said   the
πνεῦμα   τὸ   ἅγιον·   ἀφορίσατε   δή   μοι
Spirit   -   Holy: [2]Separate ye   [1]so then   [3]to me
τὸν   Βαρναβᾶν   καὶ   Σαῦλον   εἰς   τὸ   ἔργον
-     Barnabas   and   Saul   for   the   work
ὃ   προσκέκλημαι   αὐτούς·   3 τότε   νηστεύ-
[to] which   I have called   them;   then   having
σαντες   καὶ   προσευξάμενοι   καὶ   ἐπιθέντες
fasted   and   having prayed   and   [1]laying [on
τὰς   χεῖρας   αὐτοῖς   ἀπέλυσαν.
[2]the(ir)   [3]hands   [4]them   they dismissed [them].

4 Αὐτοὶ   μὲν   οὖν   ἐκπεμφθέντες   ὑπὸ   τοῦ
They   -   therefore   sent out   by   the

[h] Other ancient authorities read to

by the Holy Spirit, they went down to Seleu'cia; and from there they sailed to Cyprus. ⁵When they arrived at Sal'amis, they proclaimed the word of God in the synagogues of the Jews. And they had John to assist them. ⁶When they had gone through the whole island as far as Paphos, they came upon a certain magician, a Jewish false prophet, named Bar-Jesus. ⁷He was with the proconsul, Sergius Paulus, a man of intelligence, who summoned Barnabas and Saul and sought to hear the word of God. ⁸But El'ymas the magician (for that is the meaning of his name) withstood them, seeking to turn away the proconsul from the faith. ⁹But Saul, who is also called Paul, filled with the Holy Spirit, looked intently at him ¹⁰and said, "You son of the devil, you enemy of all righteousness, full of all deceit and villainy, will you not stop making crooked the straight paths of the Lord? ¹¹And now, behold, the hand of the Lord is upon you, and you shall be blind and unable to see the sun for a time." Immediately

ἁγίου πνεύματος κατῆλθον εἰς Σελεύκειαν,
Holy   Spirit   went down   to   Seleucia,

ἐκεῖθέν τε ἀπέπλευσαν εἰς Κύπρον, 5 καὶ
and thence   sailed away   to   Cyprus,   and

γενόμενοι ἐν Σαλαμῖνι κατήγγελλον τὸν
being   in   Salamis   they announced   the

λόγον τοῦ θεοῦ ἐν ταῖς συναγωγαῖς τῶν
word   –   of God in   the   synagogues   of the

Ἰουδαίων· εἶχον δὲ καὶ Ἰωάννην ὑπηρέτην.
Jews;   and they had also   John [as]   attendant.

6 Διελθόντες δὲ ὅλην τὴν νῆσον ἄχρι
And passing through all the island unto

Πάφου εὗρον ἄνδρα τινὰ μάγον ψευδο-
Paphos they found a certain man a sorcerer a ²false

προφήτην Ἰουδαῖον, ᾧ ὄνομα Βαριησοῦς,
²prophet ¹Jewish, to whom name^c   Barjesus,
                              =whose name was

7 ὃς ἦν σὺν τῷ ἀνθυπάτῳ Σεργίῳ
who was with the   proconsul   Sergius

Παύλῳ, ἀνδρὶ συνετῷ. οὗτος προσ-
Paulus,   man an intelligent. This man calling

καλεσάμενος Βαρναβᾶν καὶ Σαῦλον ἐπεζήτησεν
to [him]   Barnabas   and   Saul   sought

ἀκοῦσαι τὸν λόγον τοῦ θεοῦ· 8 ἀντίστατο δὲ
to hear the word   of God;   but opposed

αὐτοῖς Ἐλύμας ὁ μάγος, οὕτως γὰρ
them   Elymas the sorcerer,   for so

μεθερμηνεύεται τὸ ὄνομα αὐτοῦ, ζητῶν
is translated   the   name   of him,   seeking

διαστρέψαι τὸν ἀνθύπατον ἀπὸ τῆς
to divert   the   proconsul   from the

πίστεως. 9 Σαῦλος δέ, ὁ καὶ Παῦλος,
faith.   But Saul, the [one] also   Paul,

πλησθεὶς πνεύματος ἁγίου ἀτενίσας εἰς
filled   of(with) Spirit Holy   gazing   at

αὐτὸν εἶπεν· 10 ὦ πλήρης παντὸς δόλου
him   said: O   full   of all   deceit

καὶ πάσης ῥᾳδιουργίας, υἱὲ διαβόλου,
and of all   fraud,   son of [the] devil,

ἐχθρὲ πάσης δικαιοσύνης, οὐ παύσῃ
enemy of all righteousness, wilt thou not cease

διαστρέφων τὰς ὁδοὺς τοῦ κυρίου τὰς
perverting   the   ways   of the Lord   –

εὐθείας; 11 καὶ νῦν ἰδοὺ χεὶρ κυρίου
right?   And now behold[,] [the] hand of [the] Lord

ἐπὶ σέ, καὶ ἔσῃ τυφλὸς μὴ βλέπων
[is] on thee, and thou wilt be blind not seeing

τὸν ἥλιον ἄχρι καιροῦ. παραχρῆμα δὲ
the sun until [such] a time.   And at once

mist and darkness fell upon him and he went about seeking people to lead him by the hand. 12Then the proconsul believed, when he saw what had occurred, for he was astonished at the teaching of the Lord.

13 Now Paul and his company set sail from Paphos, and came to Perga in Pamphyl'ia. And John left them and returned to Jerusalem; 14but they passed on from Perga and came to Antioch of Pisid'ia. And on the sabbath day they went into the synagogue and sat down. 15After the reading of the law and the prophets, the rulers of the synagogue sent to them, saying, "Brethren, if you have any word of exhortation for the people, say it." 16So Paul stood up, and motioning with his hand said:

"Men of Israel, and you that fear God, listen. 17The God of this people Israel chose our fathers and made the people great during their stay in the land of Egypt, and

---

ἔπεσεν ἐπ᾿ αὐτὸν ἀχλὺς καὶ σκότος, καὶ
fell   on   him   a mist   and   darkness,   and

περιάγων ἐζήτει χειραγωγούς.   12 τότε
going about   he sought   leaders by the hand.   Then

ἰδὼν ὁ ἀνθύπατος τὸ γεγονὸς
³seeing   ¹the   ²proconsul   the thing having occurred

ἐπίστευσεν, ἐκπλησσόμενος ἐπὶ τῇ διδαχῇ
believed,   being astounded   at   the   teaching

τοῦ κυρίου.
of the   Lord.

13 Ἀναχθέντες δὲ ἀπὸ τῆς Πάφου οἱ
And setting sail   from   —   Paphos   the ones

περὶ Παῦλον ἦλθον εἰς Πέργην τῆς
around(with) Paul   came   to   Perga   —

Παμφυλίας· Ἰωάννης δὲ ἀποχωρήσας ἀπ᾿
of Pamphylia;   and John   departing   from

αὐτῶν ὑπέστρεψεν εἰς Ἰεροσόλυμα.
them   returned   to   Jerusalem.

14 Αὐτοὶ δὲ διελθόντες ἀπὸ τῆς Πέργης
And they   going through   from   —   Perga

παρεγένοντο εἰς Ἀντιόχειαν τὴν Πισιδίαν,
arrived   in   Antioch   the   Pisidian,

καὶ ἐλθόντες εἰς τὴν συναγωγὴν τῇ
and   going   into   the   synagogue   on the

ἡμέρᾳ τῶν σαββάτων ἐκάθισαν. 15 μετὰ δὲ
day   of the   sabbaths   sat down.   And after

τὴν ἀνάγνωσιν τοῦ νόμου καὶ τῶν
the   reading   of the   law   and   of the

προφητῶν ἀπέστειλαν οἱ ἀρχισυνάγωγοι
prophets   sent   the   synagogue rulers

πρὸς αὐτοὺς λέγοντες· ἄνδρες ἀδελφοί,
to   them   saying: Men   brothers,

εἴ τίς ἐστιν ἐν ὑμῖν λόγος παρακλήσεως
¹if   ⁵any   ²there is   ³among   ⁴you   ⁶word   of exhortation

πρὸς τὸν λαόν, λέγετε. 16 ἀναστὰς δὲ
to   the   people,   say ye.   And ʼrising up

Παῦλος καὶ κατασείσας τῇ χειρὶ εἶπεν·
²Paul   ¹and   ³beckoning   ⁴with the(his) ⁵hand   said:

ἄνδρες Ἰσραηλῖται καὶ οἱ φοβούμενοι τὸν
Men   Israelites   and   the [ones] fearing   —

θεόν, ἀκούσατε. 17 ὁ θεὸς τοῦ λαοῦ
God,   hear ye.   The   God   —   people

τούτου Ἰσραὴλ ἐξελέξατο τοὺς πατέρας
of this   Israel   chose   the   fathers

ἡμῶν, καὶ τὸν λαὸν ὕψωσεν ἐν τῇ
of us,   and   ²the   ³people   ¹exalted   in   the

παροικίᾳ ἐν γῇ Αἰγύπτου, καὶ μετὰ
sojourn   in [the] land   of Egypt,   and   with

with uplifted arm he led them out of it. [18]And for about forty years he bore with[f] them in the wilderness. [19]And when he had destroyed seven nations in the land of Canaan, he gave them their land as an inheritance, for about four hundred and fifty years. [20]And after that he gave them judges until Samuel the prophet. [21]Then they asked for a king; and God gave them Saul the son of Kish, a man of the tribe of Benjamin, for forty years. [22]And when he had removed him, he raised up David to be their king; of whom he testified and said, 'I have found in David the son of Jesse a man after my heart, who will do all my will.' [23]Of this man's posterity God has brought to Israel a Savior, Jesus, as he promised. [24]Before his coming John had preached a baptism of repentance to all the people of Israel. [25]And as John was finishing his course, he said, 'What do you suppose that I am? I am not he. No, but after me one is coming,

βραχίονος ὑψηλοῦ ἐξήγαγεν αὐτοὺς ἐξ
arm   a high   he led forth   them   out of

αὐτῆς, 18 καὶ ὡς τεσσερακονταέτη χρόνον
it,   and about   forty years   time

ἐτροποφόρησεν αὐτοὺς ἐν τῇ ἐρήμῳ, 19 καὶ
endured   them   in the   desert,   and

καθελὼν ἔθνη ἑπτὰ ἐν γῇ Χανάαν
having destroyed   nations   seven   in [the] land   Canaan

κατεκληρονόμησεν τὴν γῆν αὐτῶν 20 ὡς
gave as an inheritance   the   land   of them   about

ἔτεσιν τετρακοσίοις καὶ πεντήκοντα. καὶ
years   four hundreds   and   fifty.   And

μετὰ ταῦτα ἔδωκεν κριτὰς ἕως Σαμουὴλ
after   these things   he gave   judges   until   Samuel

προφήτου. 21 κἀκεῖθεν ᾐτήσαντο βασιλέα,
a prophet.   And thence   they asked   a king,

καὶ ἔδωκεν αὐτοῖς ὁ θεὸς τὸν Σαοὺλ
and   gave   them   -   God   -   Saul

υἱὸν Κίς, ἄνδρα ἐκ φυλῆς Βενιαμίν,
son   of Cis,   a man   of [the] tribe   of Benjamin,

ἔτη τεσσεράκοντα· 22 καὶ μεταστήσας
years   forty;   and   removing

αὐτὸν ἤγειρεν τὸν Δαυὶδ αὐτοῖς εἰς
him   he raised   -   David   to them   for

βασιλέα, ᾧ καὶ εἶπεν μαρτυρήσας·
a king,   to whom   also   he said   giving witness:

εὗρον Δαυὶδ τὸν τοῦ Ἰεσσαί, ἄνδρα
I found   David   the [son] -   of Jesse,   a man

κατὰ τὴν καρδίαν μου, ὃς ποιήσει πάντα
according to the   heart   of me,   who   will do   all

τὰ θελήματά μου. 23 τούτου ὁ θεὸς
the   wishes   of me.   [4]Of this man -   [1]God

ἀπὸ τοῦ σπέρματος κατ' ἐπαγγελίαν
[1]from   [2]the   [3]seed   according to   promise

ἤγαγεν τῷ Ἰσραὴλ σωτῆρα Ἰησοῦν,
brought   -   to Israel   a Saviour   Jesus,

24 προκηρύξαντος Ἰωάννου πρὸ προσώπου
previously proclaiming   John[a]   before   face
= when John had previously proclaimed

τῆς εἰσόδου αὐτοῦ βάπτισμα μετανοίας
of the   entrance   of him   a baptism   of repentance

παντὶ τῷ λαῷ Ἰσραήλ. 25 ὡς δὲ
to all   the   people   of Israel.   Now as

ἐπλήρου Ἰωάννης τὸν δρόμον, ἔλεγεν·
completed   John   the(his)   course,   he said:

τί ἐμὲ ὑπονοεῖτε εἶναι; οὐκ εἰμὶ ἐγώ·
What   me   suppose ye   to be?   [3]Not   [2]am   [1]I;

ἀλλ' ἰδοὺ ἔρχεται μετ' ἐμὲ οὗ οὐκ εἰμὶ
but   behold   he comes   after   me   of whom   I am not

---

[f] Other ancient authorities read *cared for* (Deut. 1. 31)

he sandals of whose feet am not worthy to untie.'
26 "Brethren, sons of the family of Abraham, and those among you that fear God, to us has been sent the message of this salvation. ²⁷For those who live in Jerusalem and their rulers, because they did not recognize him nor understand the utterances of the prophets which are read every sabbath, fulfilled these by condemning him. ⁸Though they could charge him with nothing deserving death, yet they asked Pilate to have him killed. ²⁹And when they had fulfilled all that was written of him, they took him down from the tree, and laid him in a tomb. ⁰But God raised him from the dead; ³¹and for many days he appeared to those who came up with him from Galilee to Jerusalem, who are now his witnesses to the people. ³²And we bring you the good news that what God promised to the fathers, ³³this he has fulfilled to us their children by raising Jesus; as also it is written in the second psalm,

'Thou art my Son, today I have begotten thee.'

ἄξιος τὸ ὑπόδημα τῶν ποδῶ λῦσαι.
worthy the sandal of the feet to loosen.

26 "Ανδρες ἀδελφοί, υἱοὶ γένους ᾿Αβραὰμ
Men brothers, sons of [the] race of Abraham

καὶ οἱ ἐν ὑμῖν φοβούμενοι τὸν θεόν,
and the [ones] among you fearing – God,

ἡμῖν ὁ λόγος τῆς σωτηρίας ταύτης
to us the word of this salvation

ἐξαπεστάλη. 27 οἱ γὰρ κατοικοῦντες ἐν
was sent forth. For the [ones] dwelling in

᾿Ιερουσαλὴμ καὶ οἱ ἄρχοντες αὐτῶν τοῦτον
Jerusalem and the rulers of them ²this man

ἀγνοήσαντες καὶ τὰς φωνὰς τῶν προφητῶν τὰς
¹not knowing and the voices of the prophets –

κατὰ πᾶν σάββατον ἀναγινωσκομένας
²throughout(on) ³every ⁴sabbath ¹being read

κρίναντες ἐπλήρωσαν, 28 καὶ μηδεμίαν
judging they fulfilled, and no

αἰτίαν θανάτου εὑρόντες ᾐτήσαντο Πιλᾶτον
cause of death finding they asked Pilate

ἀναιρεθῆναι αὐτόν· 29 ὡς δὲ ἐτέλεσαν πάντα
to be destroyed him; and when they finished all

τὰ περὶ αὐτοῦ γεγραμμένα, καθελόντες
the things concerning him having been written, taking down

ἀπὸ τοῦ ξύλου ἔθηκαν εἰς μνημεῖον.
from the tree they laid in a tomb.

30 ὁ δὲ θεὸς ἤγειρεν αὐτὸν ἐκ νεκρῶν·
– But God raised him out of [the] dead;

31 ὃς ὤφθη ἐπὶ ἡμέρας πλείους τοῖς
who appeared over days many to the [ones]

συναναβᾶσιν αὐτῷ ἀπὸ τῆς Γαλιλαίας εἰς
having come up with him from – Galilee to

᾿Ιερουσαλήμ, οἵτινες [νῦν] εἰσιν μάρτυρες
Jerusalem, who now are witnesses

αὐτοῦ πρὸς τὸν λαόν. 32 καὶ ἡμεῖς
of him to the people. And we

ὑμᾶς εὐαγγελιζόμεθα τὴν πρὸς τοὺς
[to] you preach ²the ⁴to ⁵the

πατέρας ἐπαγγελίαν γενομένην, 33 ὅτι
⁶fathers ²promise ³having come, that

ταύτην ὁ θεὸς ἐκπεπλήρωκεν τοῖς τέκνοις
this [promise] – God has fulfilled ²to the ³children

ἡμῖν ἀναστήσας ᾿Ιησοῦν, ὡς καὶ ἐν τῷ
¹to us raising up Jesus, as also in the

ψαλμῷ γέγραπται τῷ δευτέρῳ· υἱός μου
²psalm ³it has been written – ¹second : Son of me

εἶ σύ, ἐγὼ σήμερον γεγέννηκά σε. 34 ὅτι δὲ
art thou, I to-day have begotten thee. And that

³⁴And as for the fact that
he raised him from the
dead, no more to return
to corruption, he spoke
in this way,
'I will give you the
holy and sure bless-
ings of David.'
³⁵Therefore he says also
in another psalm,
' Thou wilt not let thy
Holy One see
corruption.'
³⁶For David, after he had
served the counsel of
God in his own genera-
tion, fell asleep, and was
laid with his fathers, and
saw corruption; ³⁷but he
whom God raised up saw
no corruption. ³⁸Let it
be known to you there-
fore, brethren, that
through this man for-
giveness of sins is
proclaimed to you, ³⁹and
by him every one that
believes is freed from
everything from which
you could not be freed by
the law of Moses.
⁴⁰Beware, therefore, lest
there come upon you
what is said in the
prophets:
⁴¹'Behold, you scoffers,
and wonder and
perish;
for I do a deed in your
days,
a deed you will never
believe, if one de-
clares it to you.' "
42 As they went out,
the people begged that
these things might be
told them the next

ἀνέστησεν   αὐτὸν   ἐκ   νεκρῶν   μηκέτ
he raised up   him   out of   [the] dead   no mor

μέλλοντα   ὑποστρέφειν   εἰς   διαφθοράν,   οὕτω
being about   to return   to   corruption,   thus

εἴρηκεν   ὅτι   δώσω   ὑμῖν   τὰ   ὅσια   Δαυὶδ   τε
he has said[,] – I will give you the ^aholy things ^aof David the

πιστά.   35   διότι   καὶ   ἐν   ἑτέρῳ   λέγει
¹faithful.   Wherefore also   in another [psalm] he says

οὐ   δώσεις   τὸν   ὅσιόν   σου   ἰδεῖν   διαφθοράν
Thou wilt not give the holy one of thee to see corruption.

36   Δαυὶδ   μὲν   γὰρ   ἰδίᾳ   γενεᾷ   ὑπηρετήσα
For David indeed [his] own generation having served

τῇ   τοῦ   θεοῦ   βουλῇ   ἐκοιμήθη   καὶ   προσετέθη
by the – of God counsel fell asleep and was added

πρὸς   τοὺς   πατέρας   αὐτοῦ   καὶ   εἶδε
to   the   fathers   of him   and   saw

διαφθοράν·   37   ὃν   δὲ   ὁ   θεὸς   ἤγειρεν
corruption;   but [he] whom – God raised,

οὐκ   εἶδεν   διαφθοράν.   38   γνωστὸν   οὖ
did not see   corruption.   Known therefor

ἔστω   ὑμῖν,   ἄνδρες   ἀδελφοί,   ὅτι   διὰ
let it be to you, men brothers, that throug'

τούτου   ὑμῖν   ἄφεσις   ἁμαρτιῶν   καταγγέλ
this man to you forgiveness of sins is an

λεται,   καὶ   ἀπὸ   πάντων   ὧν   οὐκ   ἠδυνήθητ
nounced, and from all things from which ye could not

ἐν   νόμῳ   Μωϋσέως   δικαιωθῆναι,   39   ἐ
by [the] law of Moses to be justified, b

τούτῳ   πᾶς   ὁ   πιστεύων   δικαιοῦται.   40   βλέπετε
this man everyone believing is justified.   Look ye

οὖν   μὴ   ἐπέλθῃ   τὸ   εἰρημένον
therefore lest come on [you] the thing having been sai

ἐν   τοῖς   προφήταις·   41   ἴδετε,   οἱ   κατα-
in   the   prophets: See,   the   des

φρονηταί,   καὶ   θαυμάσατε   καὶ   ἀφανίσθητε
pisers,   and   marvel ye   and   perish,

ὅτι   ἔργον   ἐργάζομαι   ἐγὼ   ἐν   ταῖς   ἡμέραις
because a work work I in the days

ὑμῶν,   ἔργον   ὃ   οὐ   μὴ   πιστεύσητε   ἐάν
of you, a work which by no means ye believe if

τις   ἐκδιηγῆται   ὑμῖν.   42   Ἐξιόντων   δὲ
anyone declares to you.   And going out
=as they went ou

αὐτῶν   παρεκάλουν   εἰς   τὸ   μεταξὺ   σάββατο
themⁿ   they besought in the intervening sabbath(wee

λαληθῆναι   αὐτοῖς   τὰ   ῥήματα   ταῦτα.
to be spoken   to them   these words.

sabbath. [43]And when the meeting of the synagogue broke up, many Jews and devout converts to Judaism followed Paul and Barnabas, who spoke to them and urged them to continue in the grace of God.

44 The next sabbath almost the whole city gathered together to hear the word of God. [45]But when the Jews saw the multitudes, they were filled with jealousy, and contradicted what was spoken by Paul, and reviled him. [46]And Paul and Barnabas spoke out boldly, saying, "It was necessary that the word of God should be spoken first to you. Since you thrust it from you, and judge yourselves unworthy of eternal life, behold, we turn to the Gentiles. [47]For so the Lord has commanded us, saying,

'I have set you to be a light for the Gentiles,
that you may bring salvation to the uttermost parts of the earth.'"

48 And when the Gentiles heard this, they were glad and glorified the word of God; and as many as were ordained to eternal life believed. [49]And the word of the Lord spread throughout all the region. [50]But the Jews incited the devout women of high standing

43 λυθείσης δὲ τῆς συναγωγῆς ἠκολούθησαν
And being broken up the assembly[a] [5]followed
= when the assembly was broken up
πολλοὶ τῶν Ἰουδαίων καὶ τῶν σεβομένων
[1]many [2]of the [3]Jews [4]and [5]of the [6]worshipping
προσηλύτων τῷ Παύλῳ καὶ τῷ Βαρναβᾷ,
[7]proselytes [8]Paul and — Barnabas,
οἵτινες προσλαλοῦντες αὐτοῖς ἔπειθον αὐτοὺς
who speaking to them persuaded them
προσμένειν τῇ χάριτι τοῦ θεοῦ. 44 Τῷ δὲ
to continue in the grace — of God. And on the
ἐρχομένῳ σαββάτῳ σχεδὸν πᾶσα ἡ
coming sabbath almost all the
πόλις συνήχθη ἀκοῦσαι τὸν λόγον τοῦ
city was assembled to hear the word —
θεοῦ. 45 ἰδόντες δὲ οἱ Ἰουδαῖοι τοὺς
of God. But [3]seeing [2]the [1]Jews the
ὄχλους ἐπλήσθησαν ζήλου, καὶ ἀντέλεγον
crowds were filled of(with) jealousy, and contradicted
τοῖς ὑπὸ Παύλου λαλουμένοις βλασφημοῦντες.
the things by Paul being spoken blaspheming.
46 παρρησιασάμενοί τε ὁ Παῦλος καὶ ὁ
And speaking boldly — Paul and —
Βαρναβᾶς εἶπαν· ὑμῖν ἦν ἀναγκαῖον πρῶτον
Barnabas said: To you it was necessary firstly
λαληθῆναι τὸν λόγον τοῦ θεοῦ· ἐπειδὴ
to be spoken the word of God; since
ἀπωθεῖσθε αὐτὸν καὶ οὐκ ἀξίους κρίνετε
ye put away it and not worthy judge
ἑαυτοὺς τῆς αἰωνίου ζωῆς, ἰδοὺ στρεφόμεθα
yourselves of the eternal life, behold we turn
εἰς τὰ ἔθνη. 47 οὕτως γὰρ ἐντέταλται
to the nations. For thus has commanded
ἡμῖν ὁ κύριος· τέθεικά σε εἰς φῶς
us the Lord: I have set thee for a light
ἐθνῶν τοῦ εἶναί σε εἰς σωτηρίαν ἕως
of nations — to be thee[b] for salvation to
ἐσχάτου τῆς γῆς. 48 ἀκούοντα δὲ τὰ ἔθνη
[the] end of the earth. And [3]hearing [1]the [2]nations
ἔχαιρον καὶ ἐδόξαζον τὸν λόγον τοῦ κυρίου, καὶ
rejoiced and glorified the word of the Lord, and
ἐπίστευσαν ὅσοι ἦσαν τεταγμένοι εἰς
[7]believed [1]as many as [2]were [3]having been disposed [4]to
ζωὴν αἰώνιον· 49 διεφέρετο δὲ ὁ λόγος τοῦ
[6]life [5]eternal; and was carried through the word of the
κυρίου δι᾽ ὅλης τῆς χώρας. 50 οἱ δὲ
Lord through all the country. But the
Ἰουδαῖοι παρώτρυναν τὰς σεβομένας γυναῖκας
Jews urged on the [1]worshipping [2]women

and the leading men of the city, and stirred up persecution against Paul and Barnabas, and drove them out of their district. [51] But they shook off the dust from their feet against them, and went to Ico'nium. [52] And the disciples were filled with joy and with the Holy Spirit.

τὰς   εὐσχήμονας   καὶ   τοὺς   πρώτους   τῆς
-         ¹honourable   and   the   chief men   of the
πόλεως,   καὶ   ἐπήγειραν   διωγμὸν   ἐπὶ   τὸν
city,   and   raised up   persecution   against   -
Παῦλον   καὶ   Βαρναβᾶν,   καὶ   ἐξέβαλον   αὐτοὺς
Paul   and   Barnabas,   and   expelled   them
ἀπὸ   τῶν   ὁρίων   αὐτῶν.   51   οἱ   δὲ   ἐκτιναξάμενοι
from   the   borders   of them.   But they   shaking off
τὸν   κονιορτὸν   τῶν   ποδῶν   ἐπ᾽   αὐτοὺς   ἦλθον
the   dust   of the(ir)   feet   on   them   came
εἰς   Ἰκόνιον,   52   οἵ   τε   μαθηταὶ   ἐπλη-
to   Iconium,   and the   disciples   were
ροῦντο   χαρᾶς   καὶ   πνεύματος   ἁγίου.
filled   of(with) joy   and   of(with) Spirit   Holy.

CHAPTER 14

NOW at Ico'nium they entered together into the Jewish synagogue, and so spoke that a great company believed, both of Jews and of Greeks. [2] But the unbelieving Jews stirred up the Gentiles and poisoned their minds against the brethren. [3] So they remained for a long time, speaking boldly for the Lord, who bore witness to the word of his grace, granting signs and wonders to be done by their hands. [4] But the people of the city were divided; some sided with the Jews, and some with the apostles. [5] When an attempt was made by both Gentiles and Jews, with their rulers, to

14   Ἐγένετο   δὲ   ἐν   Ἰκονίῳ   κατὰ   τὸ   αὐτὸ
Now it happened   in   Iconium   ²together†
εἰσελθεῖν   αὐτοὺς   εἰς   τὴν   συναγωγὴν
¹to enter   them^b   into   the   synagogue
=they entered
τῶν   Ἰουδαίων   καὶ   λαλῆσαι   οὕτως   ὥστε
of the   Jews   and   to speak^b   so   as
πιστεῦσαι   Ἰουδαίων   τε   καὶ   Ἑλλήνων
to believe   both of Jews   and   of Greeks
πολὺ   πλῆθος.   2   οἱ   δὲ   ἀπειθήσαντες
a much(great) multitude.   But the   disobeying
Ἰουδαῖοι   ἐπήγειραν   καὶ   ἐκάκωσαν   τὰς
Jews   excited   and   embittered   the
ψυχὰς   τῶν   ἐθνῶν   κατὰ   τῶν   ἀδελφῶν.
minds   of the   nations   against   the   brothers.
3   ἱκανὸν   μὲν   οὖν   χρόνον   διέτριψαν
A considerable   -   ²therefore   ¹time   they continued
παρρησιαζόμενοι   ἐπὶ   τῷ   κυρίῳ   τῷ   μαρ-
speaking boldly   on   the   Lord   -   wit-
τυροῦντι   ἐπὶ   τῷ   λόγῳ   τῆς   χάριτος   αὐτοῦ,
nessing   to   the   word   of the   grace   of him,
διδόντι   σημεῖα   καὶ   τέρατα   γίνεσθαι   διὰ
giving   signs   and   wonders   to happen   through
τῶν   χειρῶν   αὐτῶν.   4   ἐσχίσθη   δὲ   τὸ
the   hands   of them.   But was divided   -   the
πλῆθος   τῆς   πόλεως,   καὶ   οἱ   μὲν   ἦσαν
multitude   of the   city,   and   some   were
σὺν   τοῖς   Ἰουδαίοις,   οἱ   δὲ   σὺν   τοῖς
with   the   Jews,   but others   with   the
ἀποστόλοις.   5   ὡς   δὲ   ἐγένετο   ὁρμὴ   τῶν
apostles.   And when   there was   a rush   ²of the
ἐθνῶν   τε   καὶ   Ἰουδαίων   σὺν   τοῖς   ἄρχουσιν
³nations   ¹both   ⁴and   of Jews   with   the   rulers

molest them and to stone them, [6]they learned of it and fled to Lystra and Derbe, cities of Lycao'nia, and to the surrounding country; [7]and there they preached the gospel.

8 Now at Lystra there was a man sitting, who could not use his feet; he was a cripple from birth, who had never walked. [9]He listened to Paul speaking; and Paul, looking intently at him and seeing that he had faith to be made well, [10]said in a loud voice, "Stand upright on your feet." And he sprang up and walked. [11]And when the crowds saw what Paul had done, they lifted up their voices, saying in Lycao'nian, "The gods have come down to us in the likeness of men!" [12]Barnabas they called Zeus, and Paul, because he was the chief speaker, they called Hermes. [13]And the priest of Zeus, whose temple was in front of the city, brought oxen and garlands to the gates and wanted to offer sacrifice with the people. [14]But when the apostles Barnabas and Paul heard of it, they tore their garments and rushed out

αὐτῶν   ὑβρίσαι   καὶ   λιθοβολῆσαι   αὐτούς,
of them   to insult   and   to stone   them,

6 συνιδόντες   κατέφυγον   εἰς   τὰς   πόλεις
perceiving   they escaped   to   the   cities

τῆς   Λυκαονίας   Λύστραν   καὶ   Δέρβην   καὶ
-    of Lycaonia   Lystra   and   Derbe   and

τὴν   περίχωρον·   7 κἀκεῖ   εὐαγγελιζόμενοι
the   neighbourhood;   and there   evangelizing

ἦσαν.   8 Καὶ   τις   ἀνὴρ   ἀδύνατος   ἐν
they were.   And   a certain   man   impotent   in

Λύστροις   τοῖς   ποσὶν   ἐκάθητο,   χωλὸς   ἐκ
Lystra   in the   feet   sat,   lame   from

κοιλίας   μητρὸς   αὐτοῦ   ὃς   οὐδέποτε
[the] womb   of [the] mother   of him   who   never

περιεπάτησεν.   9 οὗτος   ἤκουεν   τοῦ   Παύλου
walked.   This man   heard   -   Paul

λαλοῦντος·   ὃς   ἀτενίσας   αὐτῷ   καὶ   ἰδὼν
speaking;   who   gazing   at him   and   seeing

ὅτι   ἔχει   πίστιν   τοῦ   σωθῆναι,   10 εἶπεν
that he has(had)   faith   -   to be healed,[d]   said

μεγάλῃ   φωνῇ·   ἀνάστηθι   ἐπὶ   τοὺς   πόδας
with a   voice: Stand up   on   the   feet
great(loud)

σου   ὀρθός.   καὶ   ἥλατο   καὶ   περιεπάτει.
of thee   erect.   And   he leaped up and   walked.

11 οἵ   τε   ὄχλοι   ἰδόντες   ὃ   ἐποίησεν   Παῦλος
And the   crowds   seeing   what   did   Paul

ἐπῆραν   τὴν   φωνὴν   αὐτῶν   Λυκαονιστὶ
lifted up   the   voice   of them   in Lycaonian

λέγοντες·   οἱ   θεοὶ   ὁμοιωθέντες   ἀνθρώποις
saying: The   gods   made like   men

κατέβησαν   πρὸς   ἡμᾶς,   12 ἐκάλουν   τε   τὸν
came down   to   us,   and they called   -

Βαρναβᾶν   Δία,   τὸν   δὲ   Παῦλον   Ἑρμῆν,
Barnabas   Zeus,   -   and   Paul   Hermes,

ἐπειδὴ   αὐτὸς   ἦν   ἡγούμενος   τοῦ   λόγου.
since   he   was the   leader   of the discourse.

13 ὅ   τε   ἱερεὺς   τοῦ   Διὸς   τοῦ   ὄντος   πρὸ
And the   priest   -   of Zeus   -   being   before

τῆς   πόλεως,   ταύρους   καὶ   στέμματα   ἐπὶ
the   city,   bulls   and   garlands   to

τοὺς   πυλῶνας   ἐνέγκας,   σὺν   τοῖς   ὄχλοις
the   gates   bringing,   with   the   crowds

ἤθελεν   θύειν.   14 ἀκούσαντες   δὲ   οἱ
wished   to sacrifice.   But [6]hearing   [1]the

ἀπόστολοι   Βαρναβᾶς   καὶ   Παῦλος,   διαρ-
[2]apostles   [3]Barnabas   [4]and   [5]Paul,   rend-

ρήξαντες   τὰ   ἱμάτια   ἑαυτῶν   ἐξεπήδησαν   εἰς
ing   the   garments of themselves   rushed out   into

among the multitude, crying, [15] "Men, why are you doing this? We also are men, of like nature with you, and bring you good news, that you should turn from these vain things to a living God who made the heaven and the earth and the sea and all that is in them. [16] In past generations he allowed all the nations to walk in their own ways; [17] yet he did not leave himself without witness, for he did good and gave you from heaven rains and fruitful seasons, satisfying your hearts with food and gladness." [18] With these words they scarcely restrained the people from offering sacrifice to them.

[19] But Jews came there from Antioch and Ico'nium; and having persuaded the people, they stoned Paul and dragged him out of the city, supposing that he was dead. [20] But when the disciples gathered about him, he rose up and entered the city; and on the next day he went on with Barnabas to Derbe. [21] When they had preached the gospel to

τὸν ὄχλον, κράζοντες **15** καὶ λέγοντες·
the crowd, crying out and saying:

ἄνδρες, τί ταῦτα ποιεῖτε; καὶ ἡμεῖς
Men, why these things do ye? [2]also [1]we

ὁμοιοπαθεῖς ἐσμεν ὑμῖν ἄνθρωποι, εὐαγ-
[6]of like nature [3]are [5]to you [4]men, preach-

γελιζόμενοι ὑμᾶς ἀπὸ τούτων τῶν ματαίων
ing [to] you from these – vanities

ἐπιστρέφειν ἐπὶ θεὸν ζῶντα, ὃς ἐποίησεν
to turn to God a living, who made

τὸν οὐρανὸν καὶ τὴν γῆν καὶ τὴν
the heaven and the earth and the

θάλασσαν καὶ πάντα τὰ ἐν αὐτοῖς· **16** ὃς
sea and all the things in them; who

ἐν ταῖς παρῳχημέναις γενεαῖς εἴασεν πάντα
in the having passed generations allowed all

τὰ ἔθνη πορεύεσθαι ταῖς ὁδοῖς αὐτῶν·
the nations to go in the ways of them;

17 καίτοι οὐκ ἀμάρτυρον αὐτὸν ἀφῆκεν
and yet [2]not [4]unwitnessed [3]himself [1]left

ἀγαθουργῶν, οὐρανόθεν ὑμῖν ὑετοὺς διδοὺς
doing good, [4]from heaven [5]us [2]rain [1]giving

καὶ καιροὺς καρποφόρους, ἐμπιπλῶν τροφῆς
and times fruit-bearing, filling of(with) food

καὶ εὐφροσύνης τὰς καρδίας ὑμῶν. **18** καὶ
and of(with) gladness the hearts of us. And

ταῦτα λέγοντες μόλις κατέπαυσαν τοὺς
these things saying scarcely they restrained the

ὄχλους τοῦ μὴ θύειν αὐτοῖς. **19** Ἐπῆλθαν
crowds – not to sacrifice[d] to them. [6]came upon
[the scene]

δὲ ἀπὸ Ἀντιοχείας καὶ Ἰκονίου Ἰουδαῖοι,
And [2]from [3]Antioch [4]and [5]Iconium [1]Jews,

καὶ πείσαντες τοὺς ὄχλους καὶ λιθάσαντες
and persuading the crowds and stoning

τὸν Παῦλον ἔσυρον ἔξω τῆς πόλεως,
– Paul dragged outside the city,

νομίζοντες αὐτὸν τεθνηκέναι. **20** κυκλω-
supposing him to have died. But sur-

σάντων δὲ τῶν μαθητῶν αὐτὸν ἀναστὰς
rounding the disciples[a] him rising up
=as the disciples surrounded

εἰσῆλθεν εἰς τὴν πόλιν. Καὶ τῇ ἐπαύριον
he entered into the city. And on the morrow

ἐξῆλθεν σὺν τῷ Βαρναβᾷ εἰς Δέρβην.
he went forth with – Barnabas to Derbe.

21 εὐαγγελιζόμενοί τε τὴν πόλιν ἐκείνην
And evangelizing that city

that city and had made many disciples, they returned to Lystra and to Ico′nium and to Antioch, ²²strengthening the souls of the disciples, exhorting them to continue in the faith, and saying that through many tribulations we must enter the kingdom of God. ²³And when they had appointed elders for them in every church, with prayer and fasting, they committed them to the Lord in whom they believed.

24 Then they passed through Pisid′ia, and came to Pamphyl′ia. ²⁵And when they had spoken the word in Perga, they went down to Attali′a; ²⁶and from there they sailed to Antioch, where they had been commended to the grace of God for the work which they had fulfilled. ²⁷And when they arrived, they gathered the church together and declared all that God had done with them, and how he had opened a door of faith to the Gentiles. ²⁸And they remained no little time with the disciples.

καὶ μαθητεύσαντες ἱκανοὺς ὑπέστρεψαν εἰς
and having made disciples many they returned to
τὴν Λύστραν καὶ εἰς Ἰκόνιον καὶ [εἰς]
— Lystra and to Iconium and to
Ἀντιόχειαν, 22 ἐπιστηρίζοντες τὰς ψυχὰς
Antioch, confirming the minds
τῶν μαθητῶν, παρακαλοῦντες ἐμμένειν τῇ
of the disciples, exhorting to continue in the
πίστει, καὶ ὅτι διὰ πολλῶν θλίψεων
faith, and that through many afflictions
δεῖ ἡμᾶς εἰσελθεῖν εἰς τὴν βασιλείαν τοῦ
it behoves us to enter into the kingdom —
θεοῦ. 23 χειροτονήσαντες δὲ αὐτοῖς κατ'
of God. And having appointed for them in
ἐκκλησίαν πρεσβυτέρους, προσευξάμενοι
every church elders, praying
μετὰ νηστειῶν παρέθεντο αὐτοὺς τῷ κυρίῳ
with fastings they committed them to the Lord
εἰς ὃν πεπιστεύκεισαν. 24 καὶ διελθόντες
in whom they had believed. And passing through
τὴν Πισιδίαν ἦλθον εἰς τὴν Παμφυλίαν,
— Pisidia they came to — Pamphylia,
25 καὶ λαλήσαντες εἰς τὴν Πέργην τὸν
and speaking in — Perga the
λόγον κατέβησαν εἰς Ἀττάλειαν, κἀκεῖθεν
word they came down to Attalia, and thence
ἀπέπλευσαν εἰς Ἀντιόχειαν, 26 ὅθεν ἦσαν
sailed away to Antioch, whence they were
παραδεδομένοι τῇ χάριτι τοῦ θεοῦ εἰς
having been commended to the grace — of God for
τὸ ἔργον ὃ ἐπλήρωσαν. 27 Παραγεν-
the work which they accomplished. And having
όμενοι δὲ καὶ συναγαγόντες τὴν ἐκκλησίαν,
arrived and assembling the church,
ἀνήγγελλον ὅσα ἐποίησεν ὁ θεὸς μετ'
they reported what things did — God with
αὐτῶν, καὶ ὅτι ἤνοιξεν τοῖς ἔθνεσιν
them, and that he opened to the nations
θύραν πίστεως. 28 διέτριβον δὲ χρόνον
a door of faith. And they continued time
οὐκ ὀλίγον σὺν τοῖς μαθηταῖς.
not a little with the disciples.

CHAPTER 15

BUT some men came down from Judea and were teaching the

15 Καί τινες κατελθόντες ἀπὸ τῆς
And some going down from —
Ἰουδαίας ἐδίδασκον τοὺς ἀδελφοὺς ὅτι
Judæa taught the brothers[,] —

brethren, "Unless you are circumcised according to the custom of Moses, you cannot be saved." ²And when Paul and Barnabas had no small dissension and debate with them, Paul and Barnabas and some of the others were appointed to go up to Jerusalem to the apostles and the elders about this question. ³So, being sent on their way by the church, they passed through both Phoeni'cia and Samar'ia, reporting the conversion of the Gentiles, and they gave great joy to all the brethren. ⁴When they came to Jerusalem, they were welcomed by the church and the apostles and the elders, and they declared all that God had done with them. ⁵But some believers who belonged to the party of the Pharisees rose up, and said, "It is necessary to circumcise them, and to charge them to keep the law of Moses."

6 The apostles and the elders were gathered together to consider this

ἐὰν μὴ περιτμηθῆτε τῷ ἔθει τῷ Μωϋσέως,
Unless   ye are circumcised by the custom   –   of Moses,

οὐ δύνασθε σωθῆναι.   2 γενομένης δὲ
ye cannot   to be saved.   And taking place

στάσεως καὶ ζητήσεως οὐκ ὀλίγης τῷ
discord   and   questioning   not   a little[a]
=when there took place not a little . . .

Παύλῳ καὶ τῷ Βαρναβᾷ πρὸς αὐτούς,
by Paul   and   –   Barnabas   with   them,

ἔταξαν ἀναβαίνειν Παῦλον καὶ Βαρναβᾶν
they assigned to go up   Paul   and   Barnabas

καί τινας ἄλλους ἐξ αὐτῶν πρὸς τοὺς
and   some   others   of   them   to   the

ἀποστόλους καὶ πρεσβυτέρους εἰς Ἰερουσαλὴμ
apostles   and   elders   in   Jerusalem

περὶ τοῦ ζητήματος τούτου. 3 Οἱ μὲν
about   this question.   They   –

οὖν προπεμφθέντες ὑπὸ τῆς ἐκκλησίας
therefore being set forward   by   the   church

διήρχοντο τήν τε Φοινίκην καὶ Σαμάρειαν
passed through – both Phœnicia and Samaria

ἐκδιηγούμενοι τὴν ἐπιστροφὴν τῶν ἐθνῶν,
telling in detail   the   conversion   of the   nations,

καὶ ἐποίουν χαρὰν μεγάλην πᾶσιν τοῖς
and   caused   joy   great   to all   the

ἀδελφοῖς. 4 παραγενόμενοι δὲ εἰς Ἰεροσόλυμα
brothers.   And having arrived   in   Jerusalem

παρεδέχθησαν ἀπὸ τῆς ἐκκλησίας καὶ τῶν
they were welcomed from   the   church   and   the

ἀποστόλων καὶ τῶν πρεσβυτερων, ἀνήγ-
apostles   and   the   elders,   and

γειλάν τε ὅσα ὁ θεὸς ἐποίησεν μετ'
reported   what things – God   did   with

αὐτῶν. 5 Ἐξανέστησαν δέ τινες τῶν
them.   But stood forth   some of the [ones]

ἀπὸ τῆς αἱρέσεως τῶν Φαρισαίων
from   the   sect   of the   Pharisees

πεπιστευκότες, λέγοντες ὅτι δεῖ περιτέμνειν
having believed,   saying[,]   –   It be- to circumcise
                                    hoves

αὐτοὺς παραγγέλλειν τε τηρεῖν τὸν νόμον
them   and to charge   to keep   the   law

Μωϋσέως.
of Moses.

6 Συνήχθησάν τε οἱ ἀπόστολοι καὶ οἱ
And were assembled   the   apostles   and the

πρεσβύτεροι ἰδεῖν περὶ τοῦ λόγου τούτου.
elders   to see   about   this matter.

matter. ⁷And after there had been much debate, Peter rose and said to them, "Brethren, you know that in the early days God made choice among you, that by my mouth the Gentiles should hear the word of the gospel and believe. ⁸And God who knows the heart bore witness to them, giving them the Holy Spirit just as he did to us; ⁹and he made no distinction between us and them, but cleansed their hearts by faith. ¹⁰Now therefore why do you make trial of God by putting a yoke upon the neck of the disciples which neither our fathers nor we have been able to bear? ¹¹But we believe that we shall be saved through the grace of the Lord Jesus, just as they will."

12 And all the assembly kept silence; and they listened to Barnabas and Paul as they related what signs and wonders God had done through them among the Gentiles. ¹³After they finished speaking, James replied, "Brethren, listen to me. ¹⁴Symeon has related

---

7 Πολλῆς δὲ ζητήσεως γενομένης ἀναστὰς
And much questioning having taken place[a] rising up
= When much questioning had . . .

Πέτρος εἶπεν πρὸς αὐτούς· ἄνδρες ἀδελφοί,
Peter said to them: Men brothers,

ὑμεῖς ἐπίστασθε ὅτι ἀφ᾽ ἡμερῶν ἀρχαίων
ye understand that from days olden

ἐν ὑμῖν ἐξελέξατο ὁ θεὸς διὰ τοῦ στόματός
²among ¹you ²chose - ¹God through the mouth

μου ἀκοῦσαι τὰ ἔθνη τὸν λόγον τοῦ
of me ³to hear ¹the ²nations the word of the

εὐαγγελίου καὶ πιστεῦσαι. 8 καὶ ὁ
gospel and to believe. And ²the

καρδιογνώστης θεὸς ἐμαρτύρησεν αὐτοῖς
³Heart-knower ¹God witnessed to them

δοὺς τὸ πνεῦμα τὸ ἅγιον καθὼς καὶ
giving the Spirit - Holy as also

ἡμῖν, 9 καὶ οὐθὲν διέκρινεν μεταξὺ ἡμῶν
to us, and nothing distinguished between ²us

τε καὶ αὐτῶν, τῇ πίστει καθαρίσας τὰς
¹both and them, - by faith cleansing the

καρδίας αὐτῶν. 10 νῦν οὖν τί πειράζετε
hearts of them. Now therefore why test ye

τὸν θεόν, ἐπιθεῖναι ζυγὸν ἐπὶ τὸν
- God, to put on a yoke on the

τράχηλον τῶν μαθητῶν, ὃν οὔτε οἱ
neck of the disciples, which neither the

πατέρες ἡμῶν οὔτε ἡμεῖς ἰσχύσαμεν
fathers of us nor we were able

βαστάσαι; 11 ἀλλὰ διὰ τῆς χάριτος τοῦ
to bear? but through the grace of the

κυρίου Ἰησοῦ πιστεύομεν σωθῆναι καθ᾽
Lord Jesus we believe to be saved in

ὃν τρόπον κἀκεῖνοι. 12 Ἐσίγησεν δὲ
the same way as† those also. And was silent

πᾶν τὸ πλῆθος, καὶ ἤκουον Βαρναβᾶ
all the multitude, and heard Barnabas

καὶ Παύλου ἐξηγουμένων ὅσα ἐποίησεν
and Paul relating ¹what ⁶did

ὁ θεὸς σημεῖα καὶ τέρατα ἐν τοῖς
- ⁵God ²signs ³and ⁴wonders among

ἔθνεσιν δι᾽ αὐτῶν. 13 Μετὰ δὲ τὸ σιγῆσαι
nations through them. And after the to keep silence
= they kept silence

αὐτοὺς ἀπεκρίθη Ἰάκωβος λέγων· 14 ἄνδρες
them[b] answered James saying: Men

ἀδελφοί, ἀκούσατέ μου. Συμεὼν ἐξηγήσατο
brothers, hear ye me. Simeon declared

how God first visited the Gentiles, to take out of them a people for his name. [15]And with this the words of the prophets agree, as it is written,

[16]'After this I will return, and I will rebuild the dwelling of David, which has fallen; I will rebuild its ruins, and I will set it up,

[17]that the rest of men may seek the Lord, and all the Gentiles who are called by my name,

[18]says the Lord, who has made these things known from of old.'

[19]Therefore my judgment is that we should not trouble those of the Gentiles who turn to God, [20]but should write to them to abstain from the pollutions of idols and from unchastity and from what is strangled[j] and from blood. [21]For from early generations Moses had has in every city those who preach him, for he is read every sabbath in the synagogues."

22 Then it seemed good to the apostles and the elders, with the whole church, to choose men

[j] Other early authorities omit *and from what is strangled*

καθὼς πρῶτον ὁ θεὸς ἐπεσκέψατο λαβεῖν ἐξ
even as firstly – God visited to take out of

ἐθνῶν λαὸν τῷ ὀνόματι αὐτοῦ. 15 καὶ
[the] nations a people for the name of him. And

τούτῳ συμφωνοῦσιν οἱ λόγοι τῶν προφητῶν,
to this agree the words of the prophets,

καθὼς γέγραπται· 16 μετὰ ταῦτα
even as it has been written: After these things

ἀναστρέψω καὶ ἀνοικοδομήσω τὴν σκηνὴν
I will return and I will rebuild the tent

Δαυὶδ τὴν πεπτωκυῖαν, καὶ τὰ κατεστραμ-
of David – having fallen, and the having been things

μένα αὐτῆς ἀνοικοδομήσω καὶ ἀνορθώσω
overturned of it I will rebuild and I will rear again
=its ruins

αὐτήν, 17 ὅπως ἂν ἐκζητήσωσιν οἱ
it, so as – [4]may seek [1]the

κατάλοιποι τῶν ἀνθρώπων τὸν κύριον,
[2]rest – [3]of men [5]the [6]Lord,

καὶ πάντα τὰ ἔθνη ἐφ' οὓς ἐπικέκληται
even all the nations on whom has been invoked

τὸ ὄνομά μου ἐπ' αὐτούς, λέγει κύριος
the name of me *on* *them,* says [the] Lord

ποιῶν ταῦτα 18 γνωστὰ ἀπ' αἰῶνος.
doing these things known from [the] age.

19 διὸ ἐγὼ κρίνω μὴ παρενοχλεῖν τοῖς
Wherefore I decide not to trouble the [ones]

ἀπὸ τῶν ἐθνῶν ἐπιστρέφουσιν ἐπὶ τὸν
from the nations turning to –

θεόν, 20 ἀλλὰ ἐπιστεῖλαι αὐτοῖς τοῦ
God, but to write word to them –

ἀπέχεσθαι τῶν ἀλισγημάτων τῶν εἰδώλων
to abstain from[d] the pollutions – of idols

καὶ τῆς πορνείας καὶ πνικτοῦ καὶ τοῦ
and the fornication and a thing strangled and –

αἵματος. 21 Μωϋσῆς γὰρ ἐκ γενεῶν
blood. For [1]Moses [2]from [4]generations

ἀρχαίων κατὰ πόλιν τοὺς κηρύσσοντας
[3]ancient [6]in every city [7]the [ones] [8]proclaiming

αὐτὸν ἔχει ἐν ταῖς συναγωγαῖς κατὰ
[9]him [5]has [11]in [12]the [13]synagogues [14]on

πᾶν σάββατον ἀναγινωσκόμενος. 22 Τότε
[15]every [16]sabbath [10]being read. Then

ἔδοξε τοῖς ἀποστόλοις καὶ τοῖς πρεσ-
it seemed [good] to the apostles and to the el-

βυτέροις σὺν ὅλῃ τῇ ἐκκλησίᾳ ἐκλεξαμένους
ders with all the church chosen

from among them and
send them to Antioch
with Paul and Barnabas.
They sent Judas called
Barsabbas, and Silas,
leading men among the
brethren, [23] with the
following letter: "The
brethren, both the
apostles and the elders,
to the brethren who are
of the Gentiles in Antioch
and Syria and Cili'cia,
greeting. [24] Since we have
heard that some persons
from us have troubled
you with words, un-
settling your minds,
although we gave them
no instructions, [25] it has
seemed good to us in
assembly to choose men
and send them to you
with our beloved Barna-
bas and Paul, [26] men who
have risked their lives
for the sake of our Lord
Jesus Christ. [27] We have
therefore sent Judas and
Silas, who themselves
will tell you the same
things by word of mouth.
[28] For it has seemed good
to the Holy Spirit and
to us to lay upon you no
greater burden than these
necessary things: [29] that
you abstain from what
has been sacrificed to
idols and from blood and

ἄνδρας   ἐξ   αὐτῶν   πέμψαι   εἰς   'Αντιόχειαν
men   of   them   to send   to   Antioch

σὺν   τῷ   Παύλῳ   καὶ   Βαρναβᾷ,   'Ιούδαν
with   -   Paul   and   Barnabas,   Judas

τὸν   καλούμενον   Βαρσαββᾶν   καὶ   Σιλᾶν,
-       being called Barsabbas   and   Silas,

ἄνδρας   ἡγουμένους   ἐν   τοῖς   ἀδελφοῖς,
men   leading   among the   brothers,

23 γράψαντες   διὰ   χειρὸς   αὐτῶν·   Οἱ
   writing   through [the] hand of them: The

ἀπόστολοι   καὶ   οἱ   πρεσβύτεροι   ἀδελφοὶ
apostles   and   the   elder   brothers

τοῖς   κατὰ   τὴν   'Αντιόχειαν   καὶ   Συρίαν
¹to the ⁸throughout -   ⁶Antioch   ⁷and   ⁸Syria

καὶ   Κιλικίαν   ἀδελφοῖς   τοῖς   ἐξ   ἐθνῶν
⁹and   ¹⁰Cilicia   ²brothers   -   ⁸of [the] ⁴nations

χαίρειν.   24 'Επειδὴ   ἠκούσαμεν   ὅτι   τινὲς
¹¹greeting.   Since   we heard   that   some

ἐξ   ἡμῶν   ἐτάραξαν   ὑμᾶς   λόγοις   ἀνασκευάζ-
of   us   troubled   you   with words unsettl-

οντες   τὰς   ψυχὰς   ὑμῶν,   οἷς   οὐ   διεστειλάμεθα,
ing   the   minds   of you,   to   whom we did not give
                                                 commission,

25 ἔδοξεν   ἡμῖν   γενομένοις   ὁμοθυμαδόν,
   it seemed [good] to us   becoming   of one mind,

ἐκλεξαμένους   ἄνδρας   πέμψαι   πρὸς   ὑμᾶς
chosen   men   to send   to   you

σὺν   τοῖς   ἀγαπητοῖς   ἡμῶν   Βαρναβᾷ   καὶ
with   the   beloved   of us   Barnabas   and

Παύλῳ,   26 ἀνθρώποις   παραδεδωκόσι   τὰς
Paul,   men   having given up   the

ψυχὰς   αὐτῶν   ὑπὲρ   τοῦ   ὀνόματος   τοῦ
lives   of them   on behalf of the   name   of the

κυρίου   ἡμῶν   'Ιησοῦ   Χριστοῦ.   27 ἀπεστάλ-
Lord   of us   Jesus   Christ.   We have

καμεν   οὖν   'Ιούδαν   καὶ   Σιλᾶν,   καὶ   αὐτοὺς
sent   therefore Judas   and   Silas,   and   they

διὰ   λόγου   ἀπαγγέλλοντας   τὰ   αὐτά.
through speech   announcing   the   same
(by)   things.

28 ἔδοξεν   γὰρ   τῷ   πνεύματι   τῷ   ἁγίῳ
   For it seemed [good] to the Spirit   -   Holy

καὶ   ἡμῖν   μηδὲν   πλέον   ἐπιτίθεσθαι   ὑμῖν
and   to us   ³nothing ⁵more   ¹to be put on   ²you

βάρος   πλὴν   τούτων   τῶν   ἐπάναγκες,
⁴burden   than   these   -   necessary things,

29 ἀπέχεσθαι   εἰδωλοθύτων   καὶ   αἵματος   καὶ
   to abstain from idol sacrifices   and   blood   and

from what is strangled[j] and from unchastity. If you keep yourselves from these, you will do well. Farewell."

πνικτῶν καὶ πορνείας· ἐξ ὧν διατηροῦντες
things and fornication; from which keeping
strangled

ἑαυτοὺς εὖ πράξετε. "Ἔρρωσθε.
yourselves well ye will do. Farewell.

30 So when they were sent off, they went down to Antioch; and having gathered the congregation together, they delivered the letter. [31]And when they read it, they rejoiced at the exhortation. [32]And Judas and Silas, who were themselves prophets, exhorted the brethren with many words and strengthened them. [33]And after they had spent some time, they were sent off in peace by the brethren to those who had sent them.[k] [35]But Paul and Barnabas remained in Antioch, teaching and preaching the word of the Lord, with many others also.

30 Οἱ μὲν οὖν ἀπολυθέντες κατῆλθον εἰς
They - therefore being dismissed went down to

Ἀντιόχειαν, καὶ συναγαγόντες τὸ πλῆθος
Antioch, and assembling the multitude

ἐπέδωκαν τὴν ἐπιστολήν. 31 ἀναγνόντες δὲ
handed in the letter. And having read

ἐχάρησαν ἐπὶ τῇ παρακλήσει. 32 Ἰούδας τε
they rejoiced at the exhortation. And Judas

καὶ Σιλᾶς, καὶ αὐτοὶ προφῆται ὄντες,
and Silas, also [them]selves prophets being,

διὰ λόγου πολλοῦ παρεκάλεσαν τοὺς
through speech much exhorted the
(by)

ἀδελφοὺς καὶ ἐπεστήριξαν· 33 ποιήσαντες δὲ
brothers and confirmed; and having continued

χρόνον ἀπελύθησαν μετ᾽ εἰρήνης ἀπὸ
a time they were dismissed with peace from

τῶν ἀδελφῶν πρὸς τοὺς ἀποστείλαντας
the brothers to the [ones] having sent

αὐτούς. ‡ 35 Παῦλος δὲ καὶ Βαρναβᾶς
them. But Paul and Barnabas

διέτριβον ἐν Ἀντιοχείᾳ, διδάσκοντες καὶ
stayed in Antioch, teaching and

36 And after some days Paul said to Barnabas, "Come, let us return and visit the brethren in every city where we proclaimed the word of the Lord, and see how they are." [37]And Barnabas wanted to take with them John called Mark. [38]But Paul thought best not to take with them one who had withdrawn from

εὐαγγελιζόμενοι μετὰ καὶ ἑτέρων πολλῶν
preaching [1]with [4]also [3]others [2]many

τὸν λόγον τοῦ κυρίου.
the word of the Lord.

36 Μετὰ δέ τινας ἡμέρας εἶπεν πρὸς
· Now after some days [2]said [3]to

Βαρναβᾶν Παῦλος· ἐπιστρέψαντες δὴ
[4]Barnabas [1]Paul: Returning then

ἐπισκεψώμεθα τοὺς ἀδελφοὺς κατὰ πόλιν
let us visit the brothers throughout [2]city

πᾶσαν ἐν αἷς κατηγγείλαμεν τὸν λόγον
[1]every in which we announced the word

τοῦ κυρίου, πῶς ἔχουσιν. 37 Βαρναβᾶς
of the Lord, how they have(are). Barnabas

δὲ ἐβούλετο συμπαραλαβεῖν καὶ τὸν
And wished to take with [them] also -

Ἰωάννην τὸν καλούμενον Μᾶρκον· 38 Παῦλος
John - being called Mark; [2]Paul

[j] Other early authorities omit and from what is strangled

[k] Other ancient authorities insert verse 34, But it seemed good to Silas to remain there

δὲ ἠξίου, τὸν ἀποστάντα ἀπ᾽ αὐτῶν
[1]but [3]thought fit, - [7]withdrawing [8]from [9]them

‡ Verse 34 omitted by Nestle; cf. R.V. marg.

them in Pamphyl′ia, and had not gone with them to the work. ³⁹And there arose a sharp contention, so that they separated from each other; Barnabas took Mark with him and sailed away to Cyprus, ⁴⁰but Paul chose Silas and departed, being commended by the brethren to the grace of the Lord. ⁴¹And he went through Syria and Cili′cia, strengthening the churches.

ἀπὸ Παμφυλίας καὶ μὴ συνελθόντα αὐτοῖς
¹⁰from ¹¹Pamphylia ¹²and ¹³not ¹⁴going with ¹⁵them

εἰς τὸ ἔργον, μὴ συμπαραλαμβάνειν τοῦτον.
¹⁶to ¹⁷the ¹⁸work, ⁴not ⁵to take with [them] ⁶this one.

39 ἐγένετο δὲ παροξυσμός, ὥστε ἀποχωρισ-
And there was   sharp feeling,   so as   to separ-

θῆναι αὐτοὺς ἀπ᾽ ἀλλήλων, τόν τε
ate   them   from   each other,   –   and

Βαρναβᾶν παραλαβόντα τὸν Μᾶρκον
Barnabas   taking   –   Mark

ἐκπλεῦσαι εἰς Κύπρον. 40 Παῦλος δὲ
to sail away   to   Cyprus.   But Paul

ἐπιλεξάμενος Σιλᾶν ἐξῆλθεν, παραδοθεὶς
having chosen   Silas   went forth,   being commended

τῇ χάριτι τοῦ κυρίου ὑπὸ τῶν
to the   grace   of the   Lord   by   the

ἀδελφῶν· 41 διήρχετο δὲ τὴν Συρίαν
brothers;   and he went through   –   the   Syria

καὶ Κιλικίαν ἐπιστηρίζων τὰς ἐκκλησίας.
and   Cilicia   confirming   the   churches.

CHAPTER 16

AND he came also to Derbe and to Lystra. A disciple was there, named Timothy, the son of a Jewish woman who was a believer; but his father was a Greek. ²He was well spoken of by the brethren at Lystra and Ico′nium. ³Paul wanted Timothy to accompany him; and he took him and circumcised him because of the Jews that were in those places, for they all knew that his father was a Greek. ⁴As they went on their way through the cities, they delivered to them for observance the

16 Κατήντησεν δὲ καὶ εἰς Δέρβην καὶ
And he came down   also   to   Derbe   and

εἰς Λύστραν. καὶ ἰδοὺ μαθητής τις ἦν
to   Lystra.   And behold[,]   a certain disciple   was

ἐκεῖ ὀνόματι Τιμόθεος, υἱὸς γυναικὸς
there   by name   Timothy,   son   ²woman

Ἰουδαίας πιστῆς πατρὸς δὲ Ἕλληνος,
¹Jewish ³of a faithful ⁶but ⁵father ⁴of a Greek,

2 ὃς ἐμαρτυρεῖτο ὑπὸ τῶν ἐν Λύστροις
who   was witnessed to   by   ¹the   ²in   ³Lystra

καὶ Ἰκονίῳ ἀδελφῶν. 3 τοῦτον ἠθέλησεν
⁴and ⁵Iconium ³brothers.   ³This one   ²wished

ὁ Παῦλος σὺν αὐτῷ ἐξελθεῖν, καὶ λαβὼν
–   ¹Paul   with   him   to go forth,   and   taking

περιέτεμεν αὐτὸν διὰ τοὺς Ἰουδαίους τοὺς
circumcised   him   on account   the   Jews   –
of

ὄντας ἐν τοῖς τόποις ἐκείνοις· ἤδεισαν
being   in   those places;   ²they knew

γὰρ ἅπαντες ὅτι Ἕλλην ὁ πατὴρ αὐτοῦ
¹for   all   that   a Greek   the   father   of him

ὑπῆρχεν. 4 Ὡς δὲ διεπορεύοντο τὰς
was.   Now as   they went through   the

πόλεις, παρεδίδοσαν αὐτοῖς φυλάσσειν τὰ
cities,   they delivered   to them*   to keep   the

---

* Note the gender: πόλις is feminine.

decisions which had been reached by the apostles and elders who were at Jerusalem. ⁵So the churches were strengthened in the faith, and they increased in numbers daily.

6 And they went through the region of Phry′gia and Galatia, having been forbidden by the Holy Spirit to speak the word in Asia. ⁷And when they had come opposite My′sia, they attempted to go into Bithyn′ia, but the Spirit of Jesus did not allow them; ⁸so, passing by My′sia, they went down to Tro′as. ⁹And a vision appeared to Paul in the night: a man of Macedo′nia was standing beseeching him and saying, "Come over to Macedo′nia and help us." ¹⁰And when he had seen the vision, immediately we sought to go into Macedo′nia, concluding that God had called us to preach the gospel to them.

11 Setting sail therefore from Tro′as, we made a direct voyage to Sam′othrace, and the following day to Ne-ap′olis, ¹²and from there to

δόγματα τὰ κεκριμένα ὑπὸ τῶν ἀποστόλων
decrees – having been by the apostles
decided [on]

καὶ πρεσβυτέρων τῶν ἐν Ἱεροσολύμοις.
and elders – in Jerusalem.

5 Αἱ μὲν οὖν ἐκκλησίαι ἐστερεοῦντο
²The – ¹therefore ³churches were strengthened

τῇ πίστει καὶ ἐπερίσσευον τῷ ἀριθμῷ
in the faith and increased – in number

καθ᾽ ἡμέραν.
daily.

6 Διῆλθον δὲ τὴν Φρυγίαν καὶ Γαλατικὴν
And they went through the Phrygian and Galatian

χώραν, κωλυθέντες ὑπὸ τοῦ ἁγίου
country, being prevented by the Holy

πνεύματος λαλῆσαι τὸν λόγον ἐν τῇ
Spirit to speak the word in –
=from speaking

Ἀσίᾳ· 7 ἐλθόντες δὲ κατὰ τὴν Μυσίαν
Asia; but coming against – Mysia

ἐπείραζον εἰς τὴν Βιθυνίαν πορευθῆναι,
they attempted into – Bithynia to go,

καὶ οὐκ εἴασεν αὐτοὺς τὸ πνεῦμα Ἰησοῦ·
and ⁴not ⁵allowed ⁶them ¹the ²Spirit ³of Jesus;

8 παρελθόντες δὲ τὴν Μυσίαν κατέβησαν
so passing by – Mysia they came down

εἰς Τρῳάδα. 9 καὶ ὅραμα διὰ νυκτὸς
to Troas. And a vision through [the]
(during) night

τῷ Παύλῳ ὤφθη, ἀνὴρ Μακεδών τις
– to Paul appeared, a man Macedonian certain

ἦν ἑστὼς καὶ παρακαλῶν αὐτὸν καὶ
was standing and beseeching him and

λέγων· διαβὰς εἰς Μακεδονίαν βοήθησον
saying· Crossing into Macedonia help

ἡμῖν. 10 ὡς δὲ τὸ ὅραμα εἶδεν, εὐθέως
us. So when the vision he saw, immediately

ἐζητήσαμεν ἐξελθεῖν εἰς Μακεδονίαν,
we sought to go forth to Macedonia,

συμβιβάζοντες ὅτι προσκέκληται ἡμᾶς ὁ
concluding that ¹has(had) called ²us –

θεὸς εὐαγγελίσασθαι αὐτούς.
¹God to evangelize them.

11 Ἀναχθέντες δὲ ἀπὸ Τρῳάδος εὐθυδρο-
And setting sail from Troas we ran a

μήσαμεν εἰς Σαμοθράκην, τῇ δὲ ἐπιούσῃ
straight course to Samothracia, and on the next day

εἰς Νέαν πόλιν, 12 κἀκεῖθεν εἰς Φιλίππους,
to Neapolis, and thence to Philippi,

Philippi, which is the leading city of the district[jj] of Macedo'nia, and a Roman colony. We remained in this city some days; ¹³and on the sabbath day we went outside the gate to the riverside, where we supposed there was a place of prayer; and we sat down and spoke to the women who had come together. ¹⁴One who heard us was a woman named Lydia, from the city of Thyati'ra, a seller of purple goods, who was a worshiper of God. The Lord opened her heart to give heed to what was said by Paul. ¹⁵And when she was baptized, with her household, she besought us, saying, "If you have judged me to be faithful to the Lord, come to my house and stay." And she prevailed upon us.

16 As we were going to the place of prayer, we were met by a slave girl who had a spirit of divination and brought her owners much gain by soothsaying. ¹⁷She followed Paul and us, crying, "These men are servants of the Most High God, who proclaim

[jj] The Greek text is uncertain

ἥτις ἐστὶν πρώτη τῆς μερίδος Μακεδονίας
which is ¹[the] ²first ⁴of the ⁵part ⁶of Macedonia

πόλις, κολωνία. Ἦμεν δὲ ἐν ταύτῃ τῇ
³city, a colony. And we were in this -

πόλει διατρίβοντες ἡμέρας τινάς. 13 τῇ τε
city staying days some. And on the

ἡμέρᾳ τῶν σαββάτων ἐξήλθομεν ἔξω τῆς
day of the sabbaths we went forth outside the

πύλης παρὰ ποταμὸν οὗ ἐνομίζομεν
gate by a river where we supposed

προσευχὴν εἶναι, καὶ καθίσαντες ἐλαλοῦμεν
a place of prayer to be, and sitting we spoke

ταῖς συνελθούσαις γυναιξίν. 14 καὶ τις
to the ²coming together ¹women. And a certain

γυνὴ ὀνόματι Λυδία, πορφυρόπωλις
woman by name Lydia, a dealer in purple-dyed [garments]

πόλεως Θυατίρων, σεβομένη τὸν θεόν,
of [the] city of Thyatira, worshipping - God,

ἤκουεν, ἧς ὁ κύριος διήνοιξεν τὴν καρδίαν
heard, of whom the Lord opened up the heart

προσέχειν τοῖς λαλουμένοις ὑπὸ Παύλου.
to take heed to the things being spoken by Paul.

15 ὡς δὲ ἐβαπτίσθη καὶ ὁ οἶκος αὐτῆς,
And when she was baptized and the household of her,

παρεκάλεσεν λέγουσα· εἰ κεκρίκατέ με
she besought saying: If ye have decided me

πιστὴν τῷ κυρίῳ εἶναι, εἰσελθόντες εἰς
faithful to the Lord to be, entering into

τὸν οἶκόν μου μένετε· καὶ παρεβιάσατο
the house of me remain; and she urged

ἡμᾶς. 16 Ἐγένετο δὲ πορευομένων ἡμῶν
us. And it happened going = as we went us

εἰς τὴν προσευχήν, παιδίσκην τινὰ ἔχουσαν
to the place of prayer, a certain maid having

πνεῦμα πύθωνα ὑπαντῆσαι ἡμῖν, ἥτις
a spirit of a python to meet us, who

ἐργασίαν πολλὴν παρεῖχεν τοῖς κυρίοις
²gain ¹much ¹brought to the masters

αὐτῆς μαντευομένη. 17 αὕτη κατακολουθοῦσα
of her practising soothsaying. This one following after

τῷ Παύλῳ καὶ ἡμῖν ἔκραζεν λέγουσα·
- Paul and us cried out saying:

οὗτοι οἱ ἄνθρωποι δοῦλοι τοῦ θεοῦ τοῦ
These - men slaves of the God -

ὑψίστου εἰσίν, οἵτινες καταγγέλλουσιν ὑμῖν
most high are, who announce to you

to you the way of | ὁδὸν σωτηρίας. | 18 τοῦτο δὲ ἐποίει ἐπὶ
salvation." ¹⁸And this she | a way of salvation. | And this she did over
did for many days. But | πολλὰς ἡμέρας. διαπονηθεὶς· δὲ Παῦλος
Paul was annoyed, and | many days. But becoming greatly troubled Paul
turned and said to the | καὶ ἐπιστρέψας τῷ πνεύματι εἶπεν· παραγ-
spirit, "I charge you in | and turning ²to the ³spirit ¹he said: I
the name of Jesus Christ | γέλλω σοι ἐν ὀνόματι Ἰησοῦ Χριστοῦ
to come out of her." | charge thee in [the] name of Jesus Christ
And it came out that | ἐξελθεῖν ἀπ᾽ αὐτῆς· καὶ ἐξῆλθεν αὐτῇ
very hour. | to come out from her; and it came out in the

19 But when her | τῇ ὥρα. 19 Ἰδόντες δὲ οἱ κύριοι αὐτῆς
owners saw that their | same hour.* And ⁴seeing ¹the ²masters ³of her
hope of gain was gone, | ὅτι ἐξῆλθεν ἡ ἐλπὶς τῆς ἐργασίας αὐτῶν,
they seized Paul and Silas | ⁵that ¹¹went out ⁶the ⁷hope ⁸of the ⁹gain ¹⁰of them,
and dragged them into | ἐπιλαβόμενοι τὸν Παῦλον καὶ τὸν Σιλᾶν
the market place before | having seized – Paul and – Silas
the rulers; ²⁰and when | εἵλκυσαν εἰς τὴν ἀγορὰν ἐπὶ τοὺς ἄρχοντας,
they had brought them | dragged to the marketplace before the rulers,
to the magistrates they | 20 καὶ προσαγαγόντες αὐτοὺς τοῖς στρατηγοῖς
said, "These men are | and ¹bringing ³to ²them the prætors
Jews and they are | εἶπαν· οὗτοι οἱ ἄνθρωποι ἐκταράσσουσιν
disturbing our city. | said: These – men are greatly troubling
²¹They advocate customs | ἡμῶν τὴν πόλιν, Ἰουδαῖοι ὑπάρχοντες,
which it is not lawful for | of us the city, ²Jews ¹being,
us Romans to accept or | 21 καὶ καταγγέλλουσιν ἔθη ἃ οὐκ ἔξεστιν
practice." ²²The crowd | and they announce customs which it is not lawful
joined in attacking them; | ἡμῖν παραδέχεσθαι οὐδὲ ποιεῖν Ῥωμαίοις
and the magistrates tore | for us to receive nor to do ²Romans
the garments off them | οὖσιν. 22 καὶ συνεπέστη ὁ ὄχλος κατ᾽
and gave orders to beat | ¹being. And rose up together the crowd against
them with rods. ²³And | αὐτῶν, καὶ οἱ στρατηγοὶ περιρήξαντες
when they had inflicted | them, and the prætors tearing off
many blows upon them, | αὐτῶν τὰ ἱμάτια ἐκέλευον ῥαβδίζειν,
they threw them into | of them the garments commanded to flog,
prison, charging the | 23 πολλὰς δὲ ἐπιθέντες αὐτοῖς πληγὰς
jailer to keep them safely. | and ³many ¹laying on ²them ²stripes
²⁴Having received this | ἔβαλον εἰς φυλακήν, παραγγείλαντες τῷ
charge, he put them into | threw into prison, charging the
the inner prison and | δεσμοφύλακι ἀσφαλῶς τηρεῖν αὐτούς· 24 ὃς
fastened their feet in the | jailer securely to keep them; who
stocks. | παραγγελίαν τοιαύτην λαβὼν ἔβαλεν αὐτοὺς
 | ²a charge ²such ¹having received threw them
25 But about mid- | εἰς τὴν ἐσωτέραν φυλακὴν καὶ τοὺς
night Paul and Silas were | into the inner prison and ²the
 | πόδας ἠσφαλίσατο αὐτῶν εἰς τὸ ξύλον.
 | ²feet ¹secured ⁴of them in the stocks.
 | 25 Κατὰ δὲ τὸ μεσονύκτιον Παῦλος καὶ
 | And about – midnight Paul and

* See Luke 2. 38.

praying and singing hymns to God, and the prisoners were listening to them, ²⁶ and suddenly there was a great earthquake, so that the foundations of the prison were shaken; and immediately all the doors were opened and every one's fetters were unfastened. ²⁷ When the jailer woke and saw that the prison doors were open, he drew his sword and was about to kill himself, supposing that the prisoners had escaped. ²⁸ But Paul cried with a loud voice, "Do not harm yourself, for we are all here." ²⁹ And he called for lights and rushed in, and trembling with fear he fell down before Paul and Silas, ³⁰ and brought them out and said, "Men, what must I do to be saved?" ³¹ And they said, "Believe in the Lord Jesus, and you will be saved, you and your household." ³² And they spoke the word of the Lord to him and to all that were in his house. ³³ And he took them the same hour of the night, and washed

Σιλᾶς   προσευχόμενοι   ὕμνουν   τὸν   θεόν,
Silas   praying   ¹praised ²in a hymn -   ³God,

ἐπηκροῶντο δὲ αὐτῶν οἱ δέσμιοι· 26 ἄφνω δὲ
and ³listened to ⁴them ¹the ²prisoners;   and suddenly

σεισμὸς   ἐγένετο   μέγας,   ὥστε   σαλευ-
²earthquake ¹there was   ³a great,   so as   to be

θῆναι   τὰ   θεμέλια   τοῦ   δεσμωτηρίου·
shaken   the   foundations   of the   jail;

ἠνεῴχθησαν δὲ παραχρῆμα αἱ θύραι πᾶσαι,
and ⁵were opened ¹at once ³the ⁴doors ²all,

καὶ πάντων τὰ δεσμὰ ἀνέθη. 27 ἔξυπνος δὲ
and ³of all   ¹the ²bonds were   And ⁴awake
                           loosened.

γενόμενος   ὁ   δεσμοφύλαξ   καὶ   ἰδὼν
²having become ¹the   ³jailer   and   seeing

ἀνεῳγμένας   τὰς   θύρας   τῆς   φυλακῆς,
having been opened   the   doors   of the   prison,

σπασάμενος τὴν μάχαιραν ἤμελλεν ἑαυτὸν
having drawn   the   sword   was about himself

ἀναιρεῖν,   νομίζων   ἐκπεφευγέναι   τοὺς
to kill,   supposing   to have escaped   the

δεσμίους. 28 ἐφώνησεν δὲ Παῦλος μεγάλῃ
prisoners.   But called   Paul   with a
                                        great(loud)

φωνῇ λέγων· μηδὲν πράξῃς σεαυτῷ κακόν,
voice saying: ¹Nothing   ³do   ⁴thyself   ²harm,

ἅπαντες γάρ ἐσμεν ἐνθάδε. 29 αἰτήσας
for ²all   ¹we are   ³here.   asking

δὲ φῶτα εἰσεπήδησεν, καὶ ἔντρομος
And lights he rushed in,   and   trembling

γενόμενος προσέπεσεν τῷ Παύλῳ καὶ
becoming   he fell before   -   Paul   and

Σιλᾷ, 30 καὶ προαγαγὼν αὐτοὺς ἔξω ἔφη·
Silas,   and ¹leading ³forward ⁴them   outside said :

κύριοι, τί με δεῖ ποιεῖν ἵνα σωθῶ;
Sirs,   what ²me ¹behoves it to do that   I may
                                        be saved?

31 οἱ δὲ εἶπαν· πίστευσον ἐπὶ τὸν κύριον
And they   said: Believe   on   the   Lord

Ἰησοῦν, καὶ σωθήσῃ σὺ καὶ ὁ οἶκός
Jesus,   and shalt be saved thou and the household

σου. 32 καὶ ἐλάλησαν αὐτῷ τὸν λόγον
of thee.   And they spoke   to him   the   word

τοῦ θεοῦ σὺν πᾶσιν τοῖς ἐν τῇ οἰκίᾳ
 - of God with   all   the [ones] in   the   house

αὐτοῦ. 33 καὶ παραλαβὼν αὐτοὺς ἐν
of him.   And   taking   them   in

ἐκείνῃ τῇ ὥρᾳ τῆς νυκτὸς ἔλουσεν ἀπὸ
that   -   hour of the night   he washed   from

their wounds, and he was baptized at once, with all his family. [34] Then he brought them up into his house, and set food before them; and he rejoiced with all his household that he had believed in God.

35 But when it was day, the magistrates sent the police, saying, "Let those men go." [36] And the jailer reported the words to Paul, saying, "The magistrates have sent to let you go; now therefore come out and go in peace." [37] But Paul said to them, "They have beaten us publicly, uncondemned, men who are Roman citizens, and have thrown us into prison; and do they now cast us out secretly? No! let them come themselves and take us out." [38] The police reported these words to the magistrates, and they were afraid when they heard that they were Roman citizens; [39] so they came and apologized to them. And they took them out and asked them to leave the city. [40] So they went out of the

---

τῶν πληγῶν, καὶ ἐβαπτίσθη αὐτὸς καὶ
the stripes, and was baptized he and

οἱ αὐτοῦ ἅπαντες παραχρῆμα, **34** ἀναγαγών
the of him all at once, [2]bringing up
=all his

τε αὐτοὺς εἰς τὸν οἶκον παρέθηκεν
[1]and them to the house he set
before [them]

τράπεζαν, καὶ ἠγαλλιάσατο πανοικεὶ πεπι-
a table, and exulted with all the having
household

στευκὼς τῷ θεῷ. **35** Ἡμέρας δὲ γενομένης
believed - God. And day coming[a]
=when day came

ἀπέστειλαν οἱ στρατηγοὶ τοὺς ῥαβδούχους
[2]sent [1]the [2]prætors the tipstaffs

λέγοντες· ἀπόλυσον τοὺς ἀνθρώπους
saying: Release - men

ἐκείνους. **36** ἀπήγγειλεν δὲ ὁ δεσμοφύλαξ
those. And announced the jailer

τοὺς λόγους τούτους πρὸς τὸν Παῦλον,
these words to - Paul,

ὅτι ἀπέσταλκαν οἱ στρατηγοὶ ἵνα ἀπολυθῆτε.
- [2]have sent [1]The [2]prætors that ye may be
released.

νῦν οὖν ἐξελθόντες πορεύεσθε ἐν εἰρήνῃ.
Now therefore going forth proceed in peace.

37 ὁ δὲ Παῦλος ἔφη πρὸς αὐτούς·
- But Paul said to them:

δείραντες ἡμᾶς δημοσίᾳ ἀκατακρίτους,
Having beaten us publicly uncondemned,

ἀνθρώπους Ῥωμαίους ὑπάρχοντας, ἔβαλαν
men [2]Romans [1]being, they threw [us]

εἰς φυλακήν· καὶ νῦν λάθρα ἡμᾶς ἐκβάλ-
into prison; and now secretly us they

λουσιν; οὐ γάρ, ἀλλὰ ἐλθόντες αὐτοὶ
expel? No indeed, but coming [them]selves

ἡμᾶς ἐξαγαγέτωσαν. **38** ἀπήγγειλαν δὲ τοῖς
us let them bring out. And [3]reported [4]to the

στρατηγοῖς οἱ ῥαβδοῦχοι τὰ ῥήματα ταῦτα.
[2]prætors [1]the [2]tipstaffs these words.

ἐφοβήθησαν δὲ ἀκούσαντες ὅτι Ῥωμαῖοι
And they were afraid hearing that Romans

εἰσιν, **39** καὶ ἐλθόντες παρεκάλεσαν
they are(were), and coming besought

αὐτούς, καὶ ἐξαγαγόντες ἠρώτων ἀπελθεῖν
them, and bringing out asked to go away

ἀπὸ τῆς πόλεως. **40** ἐξελθόντες δὲ ἀπὸ
from the city. And going out from

prison, and visited Lydia; and when they had seen the brethren, they exhorted them and departed.

τῆς φυλακῆς εἰσῆλθον πρὸς τὴν Λυδίαν,
the prison they entered to [the] - Lydia,
house of]

καὶ ἰδόντες παρεκάλεσαν τοὺς ἀδελφοὺς
and seeing they exhorted the brothers

καὶ ἐξῆλθαν.
and went forth.

CHAPTER 17

NOW when they had passed through Amphip'olis and Apollo'-nia, they came to Thessaloni'ca, where there was a synagogue of the Jews. ²And Paul went in, as was his custom, and for three weeks he argued with them from the scriptures, ³explaining and proving that it was necessary for the Christ to suffer and to rise from the dead, and saying, "This Jesus, whom I proclaim to you, is the Christ." ⁴And some of them were persuaded, and joined Paul and Silas; as did a great many of the devout Greeks and not a few of the leading women. ⁵But the Jews were jealous, and taking some wicked fellows of the rabble, they gathered a crowd, set the city in an uproar, and attacked the house of Jason, seeking to bring them out to the people. ⁶And when they

17 Διοδεύσαντες δὲ τὴν Ἀμφίπολιν καὶ
And travelling through - Amphipolis and

τὴν Ἀπολλωνίαν ἦλθον εἰς Θεσσαλονίκην,
- Apollonia they came to Thessalonica,

ὅπου ἦν συναγωγὴ τῶν Ἰουδαίων. **2** κατὰ
where was a synagogue of the Jews. according to

δὲ τὸ εἰωθὸς τῷ Παύλῳ εἰσῆλθεν πρὸς
And the custom - with Paul⁰ he entered to

αὐτούς, καὶ ἐπὶ σάββατα τρία διελέξατο
them, and on sabbaths three lectured

αὐτοῖς ἀπὸ τῶν γραφῶν, **3** διανοίγων
to them from the scriptures, opening up

καὶ παρατιθέμενος ὅτι τὸν χριστὸν ἔδει
and setting before [them] that ¹the ²Christ ¹it behoved

παθεῖν καὶ ἀναστῆναι ἐκ νεκρῶν, καὶ
to suffer and to rise again out of [the] dead, and

ὅτι οὗτός ἐστιν ὁ χριστός, ὁ Ἰησοῦς,
that this is(was) the Christ, - Jesus,

ὃν ἐγὼ καταγγέλλω ὑμῖν. **4** καί τινες
whom I announce to you. And some

ἐξ αὐτῶν ἐπείσθησαν καὶ προσεκληρώθησαν
of them were persuaded and threw in their lot

τῷ Παύλῳ καὶ τῷ Σιλᾷ, τῶν τε
- with Paul and - Silas, both of the

σεβομένων Ἑλλήνων πλῆθος πολύ, γυναικῶν τε
worshipping Greeks ²multitude ¹a much and of ²women
(great),

τῶν πρώτων οὐκ ὀλίγαι. **5** Ζηλώσαντες δὲ
¹the ²chief not a few. But becoming jealous

οἱ Ἰουδαῖοι καὶ προσλαβόμενοι τῶν
the Jews and taking aside of the

ἀγοραίων ἄνδρας τινὰς πονηροὺς καὶ
loungers in the men some wicked and
marketplace

ὀχλοποιήσαντες ἐθορύβουν τὴν πόλιν, καὶ
having gathered a disturbed the city, and
crowd

ἐπιστάντες τῇ οἰκίᾳ Ἰάσονος ἐζήτουν
coming on the house of Jason sought

αὐτοὺς προαγαγεῖν εἰς τὸν δῆμον· **6** μὴ
them to bring forward to the mob; ¹not

could not find them, they dragged Jason and some of the brethren before the city authorities, crying, "These men who have turned the world upside down have come here also, [7]and Jason has received them; and they are all acting against the decrees of Caesar, saying that there is another king, Jesus." [8]And the people and the city authorities were disturbed when they heard this. [9]And when they had taken security from Jason and the rest, they let them go.

10 The brethren immediately sent Paul and Silas away by night to Beroe'a; and when they arrived they went into the Jewish synagogue. [11]Now these Jews were more noble than those in Thessaloni'ca, for they received the word with all eagerness, examining the scriptures daily to see if these things were so. [12]Many of them therefore believed, with not a few Greek women of high standing as well as men. [13]But when the Jews of Thessaloni'ca learned

εὑρόντες δὲ αὐτοὺς ἔσυρον Ἰάσονα καί
²finding ¹but them they dragged Jason and

τινας ἀδελφοὺς ἐπὶ τοὺς πολιτάρχας,
some brothers to the politarchs,

βοῶντες ὅτι οἱ τὴν οἰκουμένην ἀναστατώ-
crying[,] – ²the ⁴the ⁵inhabited ³having turned
[ones] earth

σαντες οὗτοι καὶ ἐνθάδε πάρεισιν, 7 οὓς
upside ¹these also here have arrived, whom
down men

ὑποδέδεκται Ἰάσων· καὶ οὗτοι πάντες
²has received ¹Jason; and these all

ἀπέναντι τῶν δογμάτων Καίσαρος
²contrary to ³the ⁴decrees ⁵of Cæsar

πράσσουσιν, βασιλέα ἕτερον λέγοντες εἶναι
¹act, ⁴king ³another ¹saying ²to be

Ἰησοῦν. 8 ἐτάραξαν δὲ τὸν ὄχλον καὶ
⁵Jesus. And they troubled the crowd and

τοὺς πολιτάρχας ἀκούοντας ταῦτα, 9 καὶ
the politarchs hearing these things, and

λαβόντες τὸ ἱκανὸν παρὰ τοῦ Ἰάσονος
taking the surety from – Jason

καὶ τῶν λοιπῶν ἀπέλυσαν αὐτούς. 10 Οἱ δὲ
and the rest released them. And the

ἀδελφοὶ εὐθέως διὰ νυκτὸς ἐξεπεμψαν
brothers immediately through [the] night sent forth
(during)

τόν τε Παῦλον καὶ τὸν Σιλᾶν εἰς Βέροιαν,
– both Paul and – Silas to Berœa,

οἵτινες παραγενόμενοι εἰς τὴν συναγωγὴν
who having arrived ²into ³the synagogue

τῶν Ἰουδαίων ἀπῄεσαν· 11 οὗτοι δὲ ἦσαν
⁴of the ⁵Jews ¹went; and these were

εὐγενέστεροι τῶν ἐν Θεσσαλονίκῃ, οἵτινες
more noble [than] the [ones] in Thessalonica, who

ἐδέξαντο τὸν λόγον μετὰ πάσης προθυμίας,
received the word with all eagerness,

[τὸ] καθ᾽ ἡμέραν ἀνακρίνοντες τὰς γραφὰς
– daily examining the scriptures

εἰ ἔχοι ταῦτα οὕτως. 12 πολλοὶ μὲν
if ²have(are) ¹these things ³so. Many

οὖν ἐξ αὐτῶν ἐπίστευσαν, καὶ τῶν
therefore of them believed, and of the

Ἑλληνίδων γυναικῶν τῶν εὐσχημόνων καὶ
²Greek ³women – ¹honourable and

ἀνδρῶν οὐκ ὀλίγοι. 13 Ὡς δὲ ἔγνωσαν
of men not a few. But when ⁵knew

οἱ ἀπὸ τῆς Θεσσαλονίκης Ἰουδαῖοι ὅτι
¹the ²from – ⁴Thessalonica ³Jews that

that the word of God was proclaimed by Paul at Beroe′a also, they came there too, stirring up and inciting the crowds. ¹⁴Then the brethren immediately sent Paul off on his way to the sea, but Silas and Timothy remained there. ¹⁵Those who conducted Paul brought him as far as Athens; and receiving a command for Silas and Timothy to come to him as soon as possible, they departed.

16 Now while Paul was waiting for them at Athens, his spirit was provoked within him as he saw that the city was full of idols. ¹⁷So he argued in the synagogue with the Jews and the devout persons, and in the market place every day with those who chanced to be there. ¹⁸Some also of the Epicurean and Stoic philosophers met him. And some said, "What would this babbler say?" Others said, "He seems to be a preacher of foreign divinities"—because he preached Jesus

καὶ ἐν τῇ Βεροίᾳ κατηγγέλη ὑπὸ τοῦ
also in - Berœa was announced by -

Παύλου ὁ λόγος τοῦ θεοῦ, ἦλθον κἀκεῖ
Paul the word - of God, they came there also

σαλεύοντες καὶ ταράσσοντες τοὺς ὄχλους.
shaking and troubling the crowds.

14 εὐθέως δὲ τότε τὸν Παῦλον ἐξαπέστειλαν
So immediately then - ⁴Paul ³sent away

οἱ ἀδελφοὶ πορεύεσθαι ἕως ἐπὶ τὴν
¹the ²brothers to go as far as to the

θάλασσαν· ὑπέμεινάν τε ὅ τε Σιλᾶς καὶ
sea; ¹but ²remained - ²both ³Silas ⁴and

ὁ Τιμόθεος ἐκεῖ. 15 οἱ δὲ καθιστάνοντες
- ⁵Timothy ⁷there. And the [ones] conducting

τὸν Παῦλον ἤγαγον ἕως Ἀθηνῶν, καὶ
- Paul brought [him] as far as Athens, and

λαβόντες ἐντολὴν πρὸς τὸν Σιλᾶν καὶ τὸν
receiving a command to - Silas and -

Τιμόθεον ἵνα ὡς τάχιστα ἔλθωσιν πρὸς
Timothy that as quickly they should to
[as possible] come

αὐτὸν ἐξῄεσαν.
him they departed.

16 Ἐν δὲ ταῖς Ἀθήναις ἐκδεχομένου
And in - Athens awaiting
=while Paul awaited them,

αὐτοὺς τοῦ Παύλου, παρωξύνετο τὸ πνεῦμα
them - Paul,ᵃ ⁴was provoked ¹the ²spirit

αὐτοῦ ἐν αὐτῷ θεωροῦντος κατείδωλον
³of him in him beholding ⁴full of images

οὖσαν τὴν πόλιν. 17 διελέγετο μὲν οὖν
³being ¹the ²city. He addressed -* therefore

ἐν τῇ συναγωγῇ τοῖς Ἰουδαίοις καὶ
in the synagogue the Jews and

τοῖς σεβομένοις καὶ ἐν τῇ ἀγορᾷ κατὰ
the [ones] worshipping and in the marketplace

πᾶσαν ἡμέραν πρὸς τοὺς παρατυγχάνοντας.
every day to the [ones] chancing to be [there].

18 τινὲς δὲ καὶ τῶν Ἐπικουρείων καὶ
But some also of the Epicurean and

Στωϊκῶν φιλοσόφων συνέβαλλον αὐτῷ, καί
Stoic philosophers fell in with him, and

τινες ἔλεγον· τί ἂν θέλοι ὁ σπερμολόγος
some said: What may wish - ²ignorant plagiarist

οὗτος λέγειν; οἱ δέ· ξένων δαιμονίων
¹this to say? And others [said]: Of foreign demons

δοκεῖ καταγγελεὺς εἶναι· ὅτι τὸν Ἰησοῦν
he seems an announcer to be; because - Jesus

* See note on ch. 12. 5.

and the resurrection. [19]And they took hold of him and brought him to the Are-op′agus, saying, "May we know what this new teaching is which you present? [20]For you bring some strange things to our ears; we wish to know therefore what these things mean." [21]Now all the Athenians and the foreigners who lived there spent their time in nothing except telling or hearing something new.

[22]So Paul, standing in the middle of the Are-op′agus, said: "Men of Athens, I perceive that in every way you are very religious. [23]For as I passed along, and observed the objects of your worship, I found also an altar with this inscription, 'To an unknown god.' What therefore you worship as unknown, this I proclaim to you. [24]The God who made the world and everything in it, being Lord of heaven and earth, does not live in shrines made by man, [25]nor is he served by human hands, as though he needed anything, since he himself gives to all men life and breath and everything. [26]And he made from one every

καὶ τὴν ἀνάστασιν εὐηγγελίζετο. 19 ἐπιλα-
and the resurrection he preached. taking

βόμενοι δὲ αὐτοῦ ἐπὶ τὸν Ἄρειον πάγον
hold And of him to the Areopagus

ἤγαγον, λέγοντες· δυνάμεθα γνῶναι τίς
they led [him], saying: Can we to know what

ἡ καινὴ αὕτη ἡ ὑπὸ σοῦ λαλουμένη
¹this ²new – ⁵by ⁶thee ⁴being spoken

διδαχή; 20 ξενίζοντα γάρ τινα εἰσφέρεις
³teaching [is]? for ²startling things ¹some thou bringest in

εἰς τὰς ἀκοὰς ἡμῶν· βουλόμεθα οὖν
to the ears of us; we are minded therefore

γνῶναι τίνα θέλει ταῦτα εἶναι. 21 Ἀθηναῖοι
to know what wishes these things to be. ²Athenians

δὲ πάντες καὶ οἱ ἐπιδημοῦντες ξένοι εἰς
Now ¹all ³and ⁴the ⁶dwelling ⁵strangers ⁸for

οὐδὲν ἕτερον ηὐκαίρουν ἢ λέγειν τι ἢ
⁹nothing ¹⁰different ⁷have leisure either to say something or

ἀκούειν τι καινότερον. 22 Σταθεὶς δὲ
to hear something newer. And standing

Παῦλος ἐν μέσῳ τοῦ Ἀρείου πάγου
⁵Paul ¹in ²[the] midst ³of the ⁴Areopagus

ἔφη· ἄνδρες Ἀθηναῖοι, κατὰ πάντα ὡς
said: Men Athenians, in everything how

δεισιδαιμονεστέρους ὑμᾶς θεωρῶ. 23 διερχόμενος
very religious ²you ¹I behold. passing along

γὰρ καὶ ἀναθεωρῶν τὰ σεβάσματα ὑμῶν
For and looking up at the objects of worship of you

εὗρον καὶ βωμὸν ἐν ᾧ ἐπεγέγραπτο·
I found also an altar in which had been inscribed:

ΑΓΝΩΣΤΩ ΘΕΩ. ὃ οὖν ἀγνοοῦντες
TO AN UNKNOWN GOD. What therefore being ignorant

εὐσεβεῖτε, τοῦτο ἐγὼ καταγγέλλω ὑμῖν.
ye reverence, this I announce to you.

24 ὁ θεὸς ὁ ποιήσας τὸν κόσμον καὶ
The God the [one] having made the world and

πάντα τὰ ἐν αὐτῷ, οὗτος οὐρανοῦ καὶ
all the things in it, this one ³of heaven ⁴and

γῆς ὑπάρχων κύριος οὐκ ἐν χειροποιήτοις
⁵of earth ¹being ²lord ¹not ³in ⁴hand-made

ναοῖς κατοικεῖ, 25 οὐδὲ ὑπὸ χειρῶν
⁵shrines ¹dwells, nor ²by ¹hands

ἀνθρωπίνων θεραπεύεται προσδεόμενός
³human ¹is served having need

τινος, αὐτὸς διδοὺς πᾶσι ζωὴν καὶ πνοὴν
of anything, he giving to all life and breath

καὶ τὰ πάντα· 26 ἐποίησέν τε ἐξ ἑνὸς
and – all things; and he made of one

nation of men to live on all the face of the earth, having determined allotted periods and the boundaries of their habitation, [27]that they should seek God, in the hope that they might feel after him and find him. Yet he is not far from each one of us, [28]for 'In him we live and move and have our being'; as even some of your poets have said, 'For we are indeed his offspring.' [29]Being then God's offspring, we ought not to think that the Deity is like gold, or silver, or stone, a representation by the art and imagination of man. [30]The times of ignorance God overlooked, but now he commands all men everywhere to repent, [31]because he has fixed a day on which he will judge the world in righteousness by a man whom he has appointed, and of this he has given assurance to all men by raising him from the dead."

32 Now when they heard of the resurrection of the dead, some mocked; but others said, "We will hear you again

---

πᾶν ἔθνος ἀνθρώπων κατοικεῖν ἐπὶ παντὸς
every nation of men to dwell on all

προσώπου τῆς γῆς, ὁρίσας προστεταγμένους
[the] face of the earth, fixing having been appointed

καιροὺς καὶ τὰς ὁροθεσίας τῆς κατοικίας
seasons and the boundaries of the dwelling

αὐτῶν, 27 ζητεῖν τὸν θεόν, εἰ ἄρα γε
of them, to seek God, if perchance

ψηλαφήσειαν αὐτὸν καὶ εὕροιεν, καὶ γε
they might feel after him and might find, though

οὐ μακρὰν ἀπὸ ἑνὸς ἑκάστου ἡμῶν
[2]not [3]far [4]from [5]one [6]each [7]of us

ὑπάρχοντα. 28 ἐν αὐτῷ γὰρ ζῶμεν καὶ
[1]being. [2]in [3]him [1]For we live and

κινούμεθα καὶ ἐσμέν, ὡς καί τινες τῶν
move and are, as indeed some of the

καθ' ὑμᾶς ποιητῶν εἰρήκασιν· τοῦ γὰρ
[2]among [3]you [4]poets have said: [5]of him [1]For

καὶ γένος ἐσμέν. 29 γένος οὖν ὑπάρχοντες
[2]also [3]offspring [4]we are. Offspring therefore being

τοῦ θεοῦ οὐκ ὀφείλομεν νομίζειν, χρυσῷ
- of God we ought not to suppose, [5]to gold

ἢ ἀργύρῳ ἢ λίθῳ, χαράγματι τέχνης
[6]or [7]to silver [8]or [9]to stone, [10]to an [11]of art
                              engraved work

καὶ ἐνθυμήσεως ἀνθρώπου, τὸ θεῖον εἶναι
[12]and [13]of meditation [14]of man, [1]the [2]divine [3]to be
                                 nature

ὅμοιον. 30 τοὺς μὲν οὖν χρόνους τῆς
[4]like. [5]The [1]so [2]then [3]times

ἀγνοίας ὑπεριδὼν ὁ θεὸς τὰ νῦν
[3]of ignorance [4]having overlooked - [2]God the now

ἀπαγγέλλει τοῖς ἀνθρώποις πάντας πανταχοῦ
declares to men all men everywhere

μετανοεῖν, 31 καθότι ἔστησεν ἡμέραν ἐν
to repent, because he set a day in

ᾗ μέλλει κρίνειν τὴν οἰκουμένην ἐν
which he is about to judge the inhabited earth in

δικαιοσύνῃ, ἐν ἀνδρὶ ᾧ ὥρισεν, πίστιν
righteousness, by a man whom he desig- [2]a
                                nated, guarantee

παρασχὼν πᾶσιν ἀναστήσας αὐτὸν ἐκ
[1]offering to all having raised up him out of

νεκρῶν. 32 ἀκούσαντες δὲ ἀνάστασιν
[the] dead. And hearing [of] a resurrection

νεκρῶν, οἱ μὲν ἐχλεύαζον, οἱ δὲ εἶπαν·
of dead some scoffed, others said:
persons,

ἀκουσόμεθά σου περὶ τούτου καὶ πάλιν.
We will hear thee concerning this also again.

about this." ³³So Paul went out from among them. ³⁴But some men joined him and believed, among them Dionys'ius the Are-op'agite and a woman named Dam'aris and others with them.

33 οὕτως   ὁ   Παῦλος   ἐξῆλθεν   ἐκ   μέσου
Thus   -   Paul   went forth from [the] midst
αὐτῶν.   34 τινὲς   δὲ   ἄνδρες   κολληθέντες
of them.   some   men   adhering
αὐτῷ   ἐπίστευσαν,   ἐν   οἷς   καὶ   Διονύσιος
to him   believed,   among whom both   Dionysius
ὁ   Ἀρεοπαγίτης   καὶ   γυνὴ   ὀνόματι   Δαμαρὶς
the Areopagite   and a woman by name   Damaris
καὶ   ἕτεροι   σὺν   αὐτοῖς.
and   others   with   them.

CHAPTER 18

AFTER this he left Athens and went to Corinth. ²And he found a Jew named Aquila, a native of Pontus, lately come from Italy with his wife Priscilla, because Claudius had commanded all the Jews to leave Rome. And he went to see them; ³and because he was of the same trade he stayed with them, and they worked, for by trade they were tentmakers. ⁴And he argued in the synagogue every sabbath, and persuaded Jews and Greeks.

5 When Silas and Timothy arrived from Macedo'nia, Paul was occupied with preaching, testifying to the Jews that the Christ was Jesus. ⁶And when they opposed

18 Μετὰ   ταῦτα   χωρισθεὶς   ἐκ   τῶν
After   these things departing   out of -
Ἀθηνῶν   ἦλθεν   εἰς   Κόρινθον.   2 καὶ
Athens   he came   to   Corinth.   And
εὑρών   τινα   Ἰουδαῖον   ὀνόματι   Ἀκύλαν,
finding a certain Jew   by name   Aquila,
Ποντικὸν   τῷ   γένει,   προσφάτως   ἐληλυθότα
belonging to -   by race,   recently   having come
Pontus
ἀπὸ   τῆς   Ἰταλίας,   καὶ   Πρίσκιλλαν   γυναῖκα
from   -   Italy,   and   Priscilla   wife
αὐτοῦ,   διὰ   τὸ   διατετάχέναι   Κλαύδιον
of him, because of the to have commanded Claudius[b]
=because Claudius had commanded
χωρίζεσθαι   πάντας   τοὺς   Ἰουδαίους   ἀπὸ
to depart   all   the   Jews   from
τῆς   Ῥώμης,   προσῆλθεν   αὐτοῖς,   3 καὶ
-    Rome,   he came to   them,   and
διὰ   τὸ   ὁμότεχνον   εἶναι   ἔμενεν   παρ᾽
because of the of the same trade to be[b] he remained with
=because [he] was of the same trade
αὐτοῖς,   καὶ   ἠργάζοντο·   ἦσαν   γὰρ   σκηνοποιοὶ
them,   and   they wrought; for they were tentmakers
τῇ   τέχνῃ.   4 διελέγετο   δὲ   ἐν   τῇ   συναγωγῇ
-   by trade.   And he lectured - in   the   synagogue
κατὰ   πᾶν   σάββατον,   ἔπειθέν   τε   Ἰουδαίους
on   every   sabbath,   he persuaded both   Jews
καὶ   Ἕλληνας.   5 Ὡς   δὲ   κατῆλθον   ἀπὸ
and   Greeks.   And when   came down   from
τῆς   Μακεδονίας   ὅ   τε   Σιλᾶς   καὶ   ὁ
-   Macedonia   both   Silas   and
Τιμόθεος,   συνείχετο   τῷ   λόγῳ   ὁ   Παῦλος,
Timothy,   was pressed by the word   -   Paul,
διαμαρτυρόμενος   τοῖς   Ἰουδαίοις   εἶναι   τὸν
solemnly witnessing to the   Jews   to be   the
=that Jesus was the Christ.
χριστὸν   Ἰησοῦν.   6 ἀντιτασσομένων   δὲ   αὐτῶν
Christ   Jesus.   But resisting   them
=when they resisted and blasphemed

and reviled him, he shook out his garments and said to them, "Your blood be upon your heads! I am innocent. From now on I will go to the Gentiles." [7]And he left there and went to the house of a man named Titius[l] Justus, a worshiper of God; his house was next door to the synagogue. [8]Crispus, the ruler of the synagogue, believed in the Lord, together with all his household; and many of the Corinthians hearing Paul believed and were baptized. [9]And the Lord said to Paul one night in a vision, "Do not be afraid, but speak and do not be silent; [10]for I am with you, and no man shall attack you to harm you; for I have many people in this city." [11]And he stayed a year and six months, teaching the word of God among them.

12 But when Gallio was proconsul of Acha′ia, the Jews made a united attack upon Paul and brought him before the tribunal, [13]saying, "This

καὶ βλασφημούντων ἐκτιναξάμενος τὰ ἱμάτια
and   blaspheming[a]   shaking off the(his) garments

εἶπεν πρὸς αὐτούς· τὸ αἷμα ὑμῶν ἐπὶ
he said   to   them: The blood of you   on

τὴν κεφαλὴν ὑμῶν· καθαρὸς ἐγὼ ἀπὸ
the   head   of you;   clean   I   from

τοῦ νῦν εἰς τὰ ἔθνη πορεύσομαι. 7 καὶ
–   now   to   the nations   will go.   And

μεταβὰς ἐκεῖθεν ἦλθεν εἰς οἰκίαν τινὸς
removing   thence   he went into [the] house   of one

ὀνόματι Τιτίου Ἰούστου σεβομένου τὸν
by name   Titius   Justus   worshipping

θεόν, οὗ ἡ οἰκία ἦν συνομοροῦσα τῇ
God, of whom the   house   was   being next door to the

συναγωγῇ. 8 Κρίσπος δὲ ὁ ἀρχισυνάγωγος
synagogue.   Now Crispus   the   synagogue ruler

ἐπίστευσεν τῷ κυρίῳ σὺν ὅλῳ τῷ οἴκῳ
believed   the Lord   with all   the household

αὐτοῦ, καὶ πολλοὶ τῶν Κορινθίων ἀκούοντες
of him,   and   many of the   Corinthians   hearing

ἐπίστευον καὶ ἐβαπτίζοντο. 9 Εἶπεν δὲ
believed   and   were baptized.   And said

ὁ κύριος ἐν νυκτὶ δι' ὁράματος τῷ
the Lord   in [the] night through a vision   –

Παύλῳ· μὴ φοβοῦ, ἀλλὰ λάλει καὶ
to Paul: Do not fear,   but   speak   and

μὴ σιωπήσῃς, 10 διότι ἐγώ εἰμι μετὰ σοῦ
keep not silence,   because   I   am   with thee

καὶ οὐδεὶς ἐπιθήσεταί σοι τοῦ κακῶσαί
and   no one   shall set on   thee   –   to illtreat[d]

σε, διότι λαός ἐστί μοι πολὺς ἐν
thee, because   people   is   to me   much[e]   in
= I have a great people

τῇ πόλει ταύτῃ. 11 Ἐκάθισεν δὲ ἐνιαυτὸν
this city.   And he sat   a year

καὶ μῆνας ἓξ διδάσκων ἐν αὐτοῖς τὸν
and   months   six   teaching   among them   the

λόγον τοῦ θεοῦ. 12 Γαλλίωνος δὲ
word   –   of God.   And Gallio
= when Gallio

ἀνθυπάτου ὄντος τῆς Ἀχαΐας κατεπέστησαν
proconsul   being[a]   –   of Achaia   [4]set on
was proconsul

ὁμοθυμαδὸν οἱ Ἰουδαῖοι τῷ Παύλῳ καὶ
[3]with one mind   [1]the   [2]Jews   –   Paul   and

ἤγαγον αὐτὸν ἐπὶ τὸ βῆμα, 13 λέγοντες
brought   him   to   the tribunal,   saying[,]

[l] Other early authorities read Titus

ὅτι παρὰ τὸν νόμον ἀναπείθει οὗτος
–   [6][differently] from [7]the   [8]law   [5]urges   [1]This man

man is persuading men to worship God contrary to the law." [14]But when Paul was about to open his mouth, Gallio said to the Jews, "If it were a matter of wrongdoing or vicious crime, I should have reason to bear with you, O Jews; [15]but since it is a matter of questions about words and names and your own law, see to it yourselves; I refuse to be a judge of these things." [16]And he drove them from the tribunal. [17]And they all seized Sos'thenes, the ruler of the synagogue, and beat him in front of the tribunal. But Gallio paid no attention to this.

18 After this Paul stayed many days longer, and then took leave of the brethren and sailed for Syria, and with him Priscilla and Aquila. At Cen'chre-ae he cut his hair, for he had a vow. [19]And they came to Ephesus, and he left them there; but he himself went into the synagogue and argued with the Jews. [20]When they asked him to stay for a longer period, he declined; [21]but on taking

τοὺς ἀνθρώπους σέβεσθαι τὸν θεόν.
- ¹men ⁴to worship - ⁵God.

14 μέλλοντος δὲ τοῦ Παύλου ἀνοίγειν τὸ
And being about - Paulª to open the(his)
=when Paul was about

στόμα εἶπεν ὁ Γαλλίων πρὸς τοὺς
mouth said - Gallio to the

'Ιουδαίους· εἰ μὲν ἦν ἀδίκημά τι
Jews: If indeed it was crime some

ἢ ῥᾳδιούργημα πονηρόν, ὦ 'Ιουδαῖοι,
or villainy evil, O Jews,

κατὰ λόγον ἂν ἀνεσχόμην ὑμῶν· 15 εἰ δὲ ζητή-
- rightly I would endure you; but if ques-

ματά ἐστιν περὶ λόγου καὶ ὀνομάτων καὶ
tions it is concerning a word and names and

νόμου τοῦ καθ' ὑμᾶς, ὄψεσθε αὐτοί·
law the according to you, ye will see [your]selves;
=your law,

κριτὴς ἐγὼ τούτων οὐ βούλομαι εἶναι.
a judge ¹I ³of these things ²do not intend ²to be.

16 καὶ ἀπήλασεν αὐτοὺς ἀπὸ τοῦ βήματος.
And he drove away them from the tribunal.

17 ἐπιλαβόμενοι δὲ πάντες Σωσθένην τὸν
But ²seizing ¹all Sosthenes the

ἀρχισυνάγωγον ἔτυπτον ἔμπροσθεν τοῦ
synagogue ruler they struck [him] in front of the

βήματος· καὶ οὐδὲν τούτων τῷ Γαλλίωνι
tribunal; and not one of these things - ²to Gallio

ἔμελεν. 18 Ὁ δὲ Παῦλος ἔτι προσμείνας
¹mattered. - But Paul yet having remained

ἡμέρας ἱκανάς, τοῖς ἀδελφοῖς ἀποταξάμενος
days many, to the brothers bidding farewell

ἐξέπλει εἰς τὴν Συρίαν, καὶ σὺν αὐτῷ
he sailed away to - Syria, and with him

Πρίσκιλλα καὶ 'Ακύλας, κειράμενος ἐν
Priscilla and Aquila, having shorn in

Κεγχρεαῖς τὴν κεφαλήν· εἶχεν γὰρ εὐχήν.
Cenchrea the(his) head; for he had a vow.

19 κατήντησαν δὲ εἰς "Εφεσον, κἀκείνους
And they came down to Ephesus, and those

κατέλιπεν αὐτοῦ, αὐτὸς δὲ εἰσελθὼν εἰς
he left there, but he entering into

τὴν συναγωγὴν διελέξατο τοῖς 'Ιουδαίοις.
the synagogue lectured to the Jews.

20 ἐρωτώντων δὲ αὐτῶνª ἐπὶ πλείονα
And asking themª over a more(longer)
=as they asked

χρόνον μεῖναι οὐκ ἐπένευσεν, 21 ἀλλὰ
time to remain he consented not, but

leave of them he said, "I will return to you if God wills," and he set sail from Ephesus. ²² When he had landed at Caesare'a, he went up and greeted the church, and then went down to Antioch. ²³ After spending some time there he departed and went from place to place through the region of Galatia and Phryg'ia, strengthening all the disciples.

24 Now a Jew named Apol'los, a native of Alexandria, came to Ephesus. He was an eloquent man, well versed in the scriptures. ²⁵ He had been instructed in the way of the Lord; and being fervent in spirit, he spoke and taught accurately the things concerning Jesus, though he knew only the baptism of John. ²⁶ He began to speak boldly in the synagogue; but when Priscilla and Aquila heard him, they took him and expounded to him the way of God more accurately. ²⁷ And when he wished to cross to Acha'ia, the brethren encouraged him, and wrote to the disciples to receive him. When he

ἀποταξάμενος καὶ εἰπών· πάλιν ἀνακάμψω
bidding farewell   and   saying :   Again   I will return

πρὸς ὑμᾶς τοῦ θεοῦ θέλοντος, ἀνήχθη
to   you   -   God   willing,ᵃ   he set sail
    =if God wills,

ἀπὸ τῆς Ἐφέσου, 22 καὶ κατελθὼν εἰς
from   -   Ephesus,   and   coming down to

Καισάρειαν, ἀναβὰς καὶ ἀσπασάμενος τὴν
Cæsarea,   going up   and   greeting   the

ἐκκλησίαν, κατέβη εἰς Ἀντιόχειαν, 23 καὶ
church,   he went down to   Antioch,   and

ποιήσας χρόνον τινὰ ἐξῆλθεν, διερχόμενος
having spent   time   some   he went forth, passing through

καθεξῆς τὴν Γαλατικὴν χώραν καὶ Φρυγίαν,
in order   the   Galatian   country and   Phrygia,

στηρίζων πάντας τοὺς μαθητάς.
confirming   all   the   disciples.

24 Ἰουδαῖος δέ τις Ἀπολλῶς ὀνόματι,
And a certain Jew   Apollos   by name,

Ἀλεξανδρεὺς τῷ γένει, ἀνὴρ λόγιος,
an Alexandrian   -   by race,   a man   eloquent,

κατήντησεν εἰς Ἔφεσον, δυνατὸς ὢν ἐν
came   to   Ephesus,   powerful   being   in

ταῖς γραφαῖς. 25 οὗτος ἦν κατηχημένος
the   scriptures.   This man   was orally instructed [in]

τὴν ὁδὸν τοῦ κυρίου, καὶ ζέων τῷ
the   way   of the   Lord,   and   burning   -

πνεύματι ἐλάλει καὶ ἐδίδασκεν ἀκριβῶς
in spirit   he spoke   and   taught   accurately

τὰ περὶ τοῦ Ἰησοῦ, ἐπιστάμενος
the things concerning   -   Jesus,   understanding

μόνον τὸ βάπτισμα Ἰωάννου· 26 οὗτός τε
only   the   baptism   of John;   and this man

ἤρξατο παρρησιάζεσθαι ἐν τῇ συναγωγῇ.
began   to speak boldly   in   the   synagogue.

ἀκούσαντες δὲ αὐτοῦ Πρίσκιλλα καὶ
And hearing   him   Priscilla   and

Ἀκύλας προσελάβοντο αὐτὸν καὶ ἀκριβέστε-
Aquila   took   him   and more accurate-

ρον αὐτῷ ἐξέθεντο τὴν ὁδὸν τοῦ θεοῦ.
ly   to him   explained   the   way   of God.

27 βουλομένου δὲ αὐτοῦ διελθεῖν εἰς τὴν
And intending   him ᵃ   to go through into   -
    =when he intended

Ἀχαΐαν, προτρεψάμενοι οἱ ἀδελφοὶ ἔγραψαν
Achaia,   being encouraged   the   brothers   wrote

τοῖς μαθηταῖς ἀποδέξασθαι αὐτόν· ὃς
to the   disciples   to welcome   him;   who

arrived, he greatly helped those who through grace had believed, [28]for he powerfully confuted the Jews in public, showing by the scriptures that the Christ was Jesus.

παραγενόμενος συνεβάλετο πολὺ τοῖς
arriving   contributed   much   to the [ones]
πεπιστευκόσιν διὰ τῆς χάριτος· 28 εὐτόνως
having believed   through   grace;   [2]vehemently
γὰρ τοῖς 'Ιουδαίοις διακατηλέγχετο δημοσίᾳ
[1]for [4]the [5]Jews   [3]he confuted   publicly
ἐπιδεικνὺς διὰ τῶν γραφῶν εἶναι τὸν
proving   through   the   scriptures [2]to be [3]the
χριστὸν 'Ιησοῦν.
[4]Christ   [1]Jesus.

CHAPTER 19

WHILE Apol'los was at Corinth, Paul passed through the upper country and came to Ephesus. There he found some disciples. [2]And he said to them, "Did you receive the Holy Spirit when you believed?" And they said, "No, we have never even heard that there is a Holy Spirit." [3]And he said, "Into what then were you baptized?" They said, "Into John's baptism." [4]And Paul said, "John baptized with the baptism of repentance, telling the people to believe in the one who was to come after him, that is, Jesus." [5]On hearing this, they were baptized in the name of the Lord Jesus. [6]And when Paul had laid his hands upon them, the Holy Spirit came on them; and they spoke with tongues and prophesied. [7]There were about twelve of them in all.

19 'Εγένετο δὲ ἐν τῷ τὸν 'Απολλῶ
Now it came to pass in the –   Apollo
                              =while Apollos was
εἶναι ἐν Κορίνθῳ Παῦλον διελθόντα τὰ
to be[be] in Corinth   Paul   having passed through the
ἀνωτερικὰ μέρη ἐλθεῖν εἰς "Εφεσον καὶ
higher   parts to come[b] to Ephesus   and
εὑρεῖν τινας μαθητάς, 2 εἶπέν τε πρὸς
to find[b] some disciples,   and said to   to
αὐτούς· εἰ πνεῦμα ἅγιον ἐλάβετε πιστεύσαν-
them: If Spirit Holy ye received believ-
τες; οἱ δὲ πρὸς αὐτόν· ἀλλ' οὐδ' εἰ
ing? And they [said] to him: But [1]not [2]if
πνεῦμα ἅγιον ἔστιν ἠκούσαμεν. 3 εἶπέν τε·
[6]Spirit [5]Holy [4]there is [1]we heard.   And he said:
εἰς τί οὖν ἐβαπτίσθητε; οἱ δὲ εἶπαν·
To what therefore were ye baptized? And they said:
εἰς τὸ 'Ιωάννου βάπτισμα. 4 εἶπεν δὲ
To the   of John   baptism.   And said
Παῦλος· 'Ιωάννης ἐβάπτισεν βάπτισμα μετα-
Paul: John   baptized [with] a baptism of repent-
νοίας, τῷ λαῷ λέγων εἰς τὸν ἐρχόμενον
ance, [2]to the [3]people [1]saying [6]in [7]the [one] [8]coming
μετ' αὐτὸν ἵνα πιστεύσωσιν, τοῦτ' ἔστιν
[9]after [10]him [4]that [5]they should believe, this   is
εἰς τὸν 'Ιησοῦν. 5 ἀκούσαντες δὲ ἐβαπτίσ-
in –   Jesus.   And hearing   they were
θησαν εἰς τὸ ὄνομα τοῦ κυρίου 'Ιησοῦ.
baptized in the name of the Lord   Jesus.
6 καὶ ἐπιθέντος αὐτοῖς τοῦ Παύλου χεῖρας
And laying on   them   –   Paul   hands[a]
                    =as Paul laid [his] hands on them
ἦλθε τὸ πνεῦμα τὸ ἅγιον ἐπ' αὐτούς,
came the Spirit –   Holy   on them,
ἐλάλουν τε γλώσσαις καὶ ἐπροφήτευον.
and they spoke in tongues and   prophesied.
7 ἦσαν δὲ οἱ πάντες ἄνδρες ὡσεὶ δώδεκα.
And [4]were [2]the [1]all   [3]men   about   twelve.

8 And he entered the synagogue and for three months spoke boldly, arguing and pleading about the kingdom of God; ⁹but when some were stubborn and disbelieved, speaking evil of the Way before the congregation, he withdrew from them, taking the disciples with him, and argued daily in the hall of Tyran'nus.ᵐ ¹⁰This continued for two years, so that all the residents of Asia heard the word of the Lord, both Jews and Greeks.

11 And God did extraordinary miracles by the hands of Paul, ¹²so that handkerchiefs or aprons were carried away from his body to the sick, and diseases left them and the evil spirits came out of them. ¹³Then some of the itinerant Jewish exorcists undertook to pronounce the name of the Lord Jesus over those who had evil spirits, saying, "I adjure you by

8 Εἰσελθὼν δὲ εἰς τὴν συναγωγὴν
And entering into the synagogue

ἐπαρρησιάζετο ἐπὶ μῆνας τρεῖς διαλεγόμενος
he spoke boldly over months three lecturing

καὶ πείθων περὶ τῆς βασιλείας τοῦ θεοῦ.
and persuading concerning the kingdom – of God.

9 ὡς δέ τινες ἐσκληρύνοντο καὶ ἠπείθουν
But as some were hardened and disobeyed

κακολογοῦντες τὴν ὁδὸν ἐνώπιον τοῦ
speaking ill [of] the way before the

πλήθους, ἀποστὰς ἀπ' αὐτῶν ἀφώρισεν
multitude, withdrawing from them he separated

τοὺς μαθητάς, καθ' ἡμέραν διαλεγόμενος
the disciples, daily lecturing

ἐν τῇ σχολῇ Τυράννου. 10 τοῦτο δὲ
in the school of Tyrannus. And this

ἐγένετο ἐπὶ ἔτη δύο, ὥστε πάντας τοὺς
happened over years two, so as all the
=so that all who inhabited

κατοικοῦντας τὴν Ἀσίαν ἀκοῦσαι τὸν
[ones] inhabiting – Asia to hearᵇ the
Asia heard

λόγον τοῦ κυρίου, Ἰουδαίους τε καὶ
word of the Lord, ¹Jews ¹both and

Ἕλληνας. 11 Δυνάμεις τε οὐ τὰς τυχούσας
Greeks. And powerful deeds not the ordinary

ὁ θεὸς ἐποίει διὰ τῶν χειρῶν Παύλου,
– God did through the hands of Paul,

12 ὥστε καὶ ἐπὶ τοὺς ἀσθενοῦντας
so as even onto the [ones] ailing
=so that there were even brought away from his skin hand-

ἀποφέρεσθαι ἀπὸ τοῦ χρωτὸς αὐτοῦ
to be brought away from the skin of him
kerchiefs or aprons onto those who ailed and the diseases were rid

σουδάρια ἢ σιμικίνθια καὶ ἀπαλλάσσεσθαι
handkerchiefs or aprons and to be rid
from them, and the evil spirits went out

ἀπ' αὐτῶν τὰς νόσους, τά τε πνεύματα
from them the diseases, and the spirits

τὰ πονηρὰ ἐκπορεύεσθαι. 13 Ἐπεχείρησαν δέ
evil to go out. But ⁷attempted

τινες καὶ τῶν περιερχομένων Ἰουδαίων
¹some ²also ³of the ⁴strolling ⁵Jews

ἐξορκιστῶν ὀνομάζειν ἐπὶ τοὺς ἔχοντας
⁶exorcists to name over the [ones] having

τὰ πνεύματα τὰ πονηρὰ τὸ ὄνομα τοῦ
the spirits – evil the name of the

κυρίου Ἰησοῦ λέγοντες· ὁρκίζω ὑμᾶς τὸν
Lord Jesus saying: I exorcise you [by] –

ᵐ Other ancient authorities add, from the fifth hour to the tenth the Jesus whom Paul preaches." [14] Seven sons of a Jewish high priest named Sceva were doing this. [15] But the evil spirit answered them, "Jesus I know, and Paul I know; but who are you?" [16] And the man in whom the evil spirit was leaped in them, mastered all of them, and overpowered them, so that they fled out of that house naked and wounded. [17] And this became known to all residents of Ephesus, both Jews and Greeks; and fear fell upon them all; and the name of the Lord Jesus was extolled. [18] Many also of those who were now believers came, confessing and divulging their practices. [19] And a number of those who practiced magic arts brought their books together and burned them in the sight of all; and they counted the value of them and found it came to fifty thousand pieces of silver. [20] So the word of the Lord grew and prevailed mightily.

Ἰησοῦν ὃν Παῦλος κηρύσσει. **14** ἦσαν δέ
Jesus   whom Paul   proclaims.   And there were

τινος Σκευᾶ Ἰουδαίου ἀρχιερέως ἑπτὰ
²of one   ⁴Sceva   ⁵a Jewish   ⁶chief priest   ¹seven

υἱοὶ τοῦτο ποιοῦντες. **15** ἀποκριθὲν δὲ
²sons ⁸this ⁷doing.   And answering

τὸ πνεῦμα τὸ πονηρὸν εἶπεν αὐτοῖς·
the spirit   -   evil   said   to them:

τὸν [μὲν] Ἰησοῦν γινώσκω καὶ τὸν
-   ²indeed   ¹Jesus   I know   and   -

Παῦλον ἐπίσταμαι· ὑμεῖς δὲ τίνες ἐστέ;
Paul   I understand;   but ye   who   are?

16 καὶ ἐφαλόμενος ὁ ἄνθρωπος ἐπ' αὐτούς,
And   ⁹leaping on   ¹the   ²man   ¹⁰on   ¹¹them,

ἐν ᾧ ἦν τὸ πνεῦμα τὸ πονηρόν,
³in ⁴whom ⁵was ⁶the ⁷spirit - ⁷evil,

κατακυριεύσας ἀμφοτέρων ἴσχυσεν κατ'
overmastering   both   was strong   against

αὐτῶν, ὥστε γυμνοὺς καὶ τετραυματισμένους
them,   so as   naked   and   *having been* wounded

ἐκφυγεῖν ἐκ τοῦ οἴκου ἐκείνου. **17** τοῦτο
to escape   out of   that house.   this

δὲ ἐγένετο γνωστὸν πᾶσιν Ἰουδαίοις τε
And   became   known   to all   ²Jews   ¹both

καὶ Ἕλλησιν τοῖς κατοικοῦσιν τὴν Ἔφεσον,
and   Greeks   -   inhabiting   -   Ephesus,

καὶ ἐπέπεσεν φόβος ἐπὶ πάντας αὐτούς,
and   ²fell on   ¹fear   ³on   ⁵all   ⁴them,

καὶ ἐμεγαλύνετο τὸ ὄνομα τοῦ κυρίου
and   was magnified   the   name   of the   Lord

Ἰησοῦ· **18** πολλοί τε τῶν πεπιστευκότων
Jesus;   and many   of the [ones]   having believed

ἤρχοντο ἐξομολογούμενοι καὶ ἀναγγέλλοντες
came   confessing   and   telling

τὰς πράξεις αὐτῶν. **19** ἱκανοὶ δὲ τῶν τὰ
the   doings   of them.   And a consider-   of the   the
                         able number   [ones]

περίεργα πραξάντων συνενέγκαντες τὰς βίβλους
curious things   doing   bringing together   the   rolls

κατέκαιον ἐνώπιον πάντων· καὶ συνεψήφισαν
burnt   before   all;   and   they reckoned up

τὰς τιμὰς αὐτῶν καὶ εὗρον ἀργυρίου μυριάδας
the   prices   of them   and   found   [pieces]   ²thousand
                              ³of silver

πέντε. **20** Οὕτως κατὰ κράτος τοῦ κυρίου
¹five.   Thus   by   might   ²of the   ⁴Lord

ὁ λόγος ηὔξανεν καὶ ἴσχυεν.
¹the ²word   increased   and   was strong.

21 Now after these events Paul resolved in the Spirit to pass through Macedo'nia and Acha'ia and go to Jerusalem, saying, "After I have been there, I must also see Rome." ²²And having sent into Macedo'nia two of his helpers, Timothy and Eras'tus, he himself stayed in Asia for a while.

23 About that time there arose no little stir concerning the Way. ²⁴For a man named Deme'trius, a silversmith, who made silver shrines of Ar'temis, brought no little business to the craftsmen. ²⁵These he gathered together, with the workmen of like occupation, and said, "Men, you know that from this business we have our wealth. ²⁶And you see and hear that not only at Ephesus but almost throughout all Asia this Paul has persuaded and turned away a considerable company of people, saying that gods made with hands are not gods. ²⁷And there is danger not only that

---

21 Ὡς δὲ ἐπληρώθη ταῦτα, ἔθετο ὁ
And when were fulfilled these things, purposed -

Παῦλος ἐν τῷ πνεύματι διελθὼν τὴν
Paul in the(his) spirit passing through -

Μακεδονίαν καὶ Ἀχαΐαν πορεύεσθαι εἰς
Macedonia and Achaia to go to

Ἱεροσόλυμα, εἰπὼν ὅτι μετὰ τὸ γενέσθαι
Jerusalem, saying[,] - After the to become
=After I am

με ἐκεῖ δεῖ με καὶ Ῥώμην ἰδεῖν.
meᵇ there it behoves me ²also ¹Rome ¹to see.

22 ἀποστείλας δὲ εἰς Μακεδονίαν δύο
And sending into Macedonia two

τῶν διακονούντων αὐτῷ, Τιμόθεον καὶ
of the [ones] ministering to him, Timothy and

Ἔραστον, αὐτὸς ἐπέσχεν χρόνον εἰς τὴν
Erastus, he delayed a time in -

Ἀσίαν. 23 Ἐγένετο δὲ κατὰ τὸν καιρὸν
Asia. Now there was about - time

ἐκεῖνον τάραχος οὐκ ὀλίγος περὶ τῆς
that ²trouble ¹no ³little concerning the

ὁδοῦ. 24 Δημήτριος γάρ τις ὀνόματι,
way. For ²Demetrius ¹one by name,

ἀργυροκόπος, ποιῶν ναοὺς ἀργυροῦς
a silversmith, making shrines silver

Ἀρτέμιδος παρείχετο τοῖς τεχνίταις οὐκ
of Artemis provided the artisans no

ὀλίγην ἐργασίαν, 25 οὓς συναθροίσας καὶ
little trade, ²whom ¹assembling also

τοὺς περὶ τὰ τοιαῦτα ἐργάτας εἶπεν·
¹the ²about(in) ³such things ⁴workmen said:

ἄνδρες, ἐπίστασθε ὅτι ἐκ ταύτης τῆς
Men, ye understand that from this -

ἐργασίας ἡ εὐπορία ἡμῖν ἐστιν, 26 καὶ
trade the gain to us is,⁶ and
=we have [our] gain,

θεωρεῖτε καὶ ἀκούετε ὅτι οὐ μόνον
ye behold and hear that ⁷not ⁸only

Ἐφέσου ἀλλὰ σχεδὸν πάσης τῆς Ἀσίας
⁹of Ephesus ¹⁰but ¹¹almost ¹²of all - ¹³Asia

ὁ Παῦλος οὗτος πείσας μετέστησεν ἱκανὸν
- ²Paul ¹this ³having ⁴perverted ⁵a considerable
persuaded

ὄχλον, λέγων ὅτι οὐκ εἰσὶν θεοὶ οἱ διὰ
⁶crowd, saying that they are not gods ¹the ²through
[ones]

χειρῶν γινόμενοι. 27 οὐ μόνον δὲ τοῦτο
³hands ²coming into being. ²not ³only ¹Now ⁴this

this trade of ours may come into disrepute but also that the temple of the great goddess Ar'temis may count for nothing, and that she may even be deposed from her magnificence, she whom all Asia and the world worship."

28 When they heard this they were enraged, and cried out, "Great is Ar'temis of the Ephesians!" 29 So the city was filled with the confusion; and they rushed together into the theater, dragging with them Ga'ius and Aristar'chus, Macedo'nians who were Paul's companions in travel. 30 Paul wished to go in among the crowd, but the disciples would not let him; 31 some of the A'si-archs also, who were friends of his, sent to him and begged him not to venture into the theater. 32 Now some cried one thing, some another; for the assembly was in confusion, and most of them did not know why they had come together. 33 Some of the crowd prompted Alexander, whom the Jews had put forward. And Alexander motioned with his hand, wishing to

κινδυνεύει ἡμῖν τὸ μέρος εἰς ἀπελεγμὸν
⁴is in danger　to us　the　²share°　⁸into　⁹disrepute
　　　　　　　　　=⁵our share

ἐλθεῖν, ἀλλὰ καὶ τὸ τῆς μεγάλης θεᾶς
⁷to come,　but　also　¹the　²of the　⁴great　⁵goddess

'Αρτέμιδος ἱερὸν εἰς οὐθὲν λογισθῆναι,
⁴Artemis　⁶temple　⁸for(as)　⁹nothing　⁷to be reckoned,

μέλλειν τε καὶ καθαιρεῖσθαι τῆς μεγα-
²to be about ¹and　²also　⁴to be diminished　the　great-

λειότητος αὐτῆς, ἣν ὅλη ἡ 'Ασία καὶ
ness　　　of her,　whom　all　–　Asia　and

ἡ οἰκουμένη σέβεται. 28 ἀκούσαντες δὲ
the inhabited earth　worships.　　And hearing

καὶ γενόμενοι πλήρεις θυμοῦ ἔκραζον
and　becoming　full　of anger　they cried out

λέγοντες· μεγάλη ἡ "Αρτεμις 'Εφεσίων.
saying:　　Great [is]　–　Artemis of[the] Ephesians.

29 καὶ ἐπλήσθη ἡ πόλις τῆς συγχύσεως,
And　was filled　the　city　of(with)　the　confusion,

ὥρμησάν τε ὁμοθυμαδὸν εἰς τὸ θέατρον,
and they rushed　with one mind　into　the　theatre,

συναρπάσαντες Γάϊον καὶ 'Αρίσταρχον
keeping a firm grip on　Gaius　and　Aristarchus[,]

Μακεδόνας, συνεκδήμους Παύλου. 30 Παύλου
Macedonians,　travelling companions of Paul.　Paul

δὲ βουλομένου εἰσελθεῖν εἰς τὸν δῆμον
And　intendingᵃ　to enter　into　the　mob
=as Paul intended

οὐκ εἴων αὐτὸν οἱ μαθηταί· 31 τινὲς
²not　³allowed　⁴him　¹the　⁵disciples;　some

δὲ καὶ τῶν 'Ασιαρχῶν, ὄντες αὐτῷ
and　also　of the　Asiarchs,　being　to him

φίλοι, πέμψαντες πρὸς αὐτὸν παρεκάλουν
friends,　sending　to　him　besought

μὴ δοῦναι ἑαυτὸν εἰς τὸ θέατρον. 32 ἄλλοι
not　to give　himself　in　the　theatre.　Others

μὲν οὖν ἄλλο τι ἔκραζον· ἦν γὰρ
indeed therefore ²different ³something cried out;　for ¹was

ἡ ἐκκλησία συγκεχυμένη, καὶ οἱ πλείους
¹the　²assembly　having been confounded, and the　majority

οὐκ ᾔδεισαν τίνος ἕνεκα συνεληλύθεισαν.
knew not　　²of what ¹on account　they had come
　　　　　　　　　　　　　　　　together.

33 ἐκ δὲ τοῦ ὄχλου συνεβίβασαν 'Αλέξανδρον,
But [some] of the　crowd　instructed　Alexander,

προβαλόντων αὐτὸν τῶν 'Ιουδαίων· ὁ δὲ
putting forward　him　the　Jewsᵃ;　–　and
=as the Jews put him forward;

'Αλέξανδρος κατασείσας τὴν χεῖρα ἤθελεν
Alexander　waving　the(his) hand　wished

make a defense to the people. [34] But when they recognized that he was a Jew, for about two hours they all with one voice cried out, "Great is Ar'temis of the Ephesians!" [35] And when the town clerk had quieted the crowd, he said, "Men of Ephesus, what man is there who does not know that the city of the Ephesians is temple keeper of the great Ar'temis, and of the sacred stone that fell from the sky?[n] [36] Seeing then that these things cannot be contradicted, you ought to be quiet and do nothing rash. [37] For you have brought these men here who are neither sacrilegious nor blasphemers of our goddess. [38] If therefore Deme'trius and the craftsmen with him have a complaint against any one, the courts are open, and there are proconsuls; let them bring charges against one another. [39] But if you seek anything further,[o] it shall be settled in the regular assembly. [40] For we are in danger of being charged with rioting to-day, there being no cause that we can give to justify this commotion."

[n] The meaning of the Greek is uncertain

[o] Other ancient authorities read about other matters

ἀπολογεῖσθαι τῷ δήμῳ.
to defend himself to the mob.

34 ἐπιγνόντες δὲ
But knowing

ὅτι Ἰουδαῖός ἐστιν, φωνὴ ἐγένετο μία
that a Jew he is(was), [2]voice [1]there was [2]one

ἐκ πάντων, ὡς ἐπὶ ὥρας δύο κράζοντες·
from all, about over hours two crying out:

μεγάλη ἡ Ἄρτεμις Ἐφεσίων.
Great [is] - Artemis of [the] Ephesians.

35 κατα-
[4]having

στείλας δὲ ὁ γραμματεὺς τὸν ὄχλον
quietened [1]And [2]the [3]town clerk the crowd

φησίν· ἄνδρες Ἐφέσιοι, τίς γάρ ἐστιν
says: Men Ephesians, who indeed is there

ἀνθρώπων ὃς οὐ γινώσκει τὴν Ἐφεσίων
of men who does not know [1]the [2]of [the] Ephesians

πόλιν νεωκόρον οὖσαν τῆς μεγάλης
[2]city [3]temple warden [4]being of the great

Ἀρτέμιδος καὶ τοῦ διοπετοῦς;
Artemis and of the fallen from [image] the sky?

36 ἀναντιρ-
undeni-

ρήτων οὖν ὄντων τούτων δέον ἐστὶν
able therefore being these things[a] necessary it is
=as these things are undeniable

ὑμᾶς κατεσταλμένους ὑπάρχειν καὶ μηδὲν
you [2]having been quietened [1]to be and [2]nothing

προπετὲς πράσσειν.
[3]rash [1]to do.

37 ἠγάγετε γὰρ τοὺς
For ye brought -

ἄνδρας τούτους οὔτε ἱεροσύλους οὔτε
men these neither temple robbers nor

βλασφημοῦντας τὴν θεὸν ἡμῶν.
blaspheming the goddess of you.

38 εἰ
If

μὲν οὖν Δημήτριος καὶ οἱ σὺν αὐτῷ
indeed therefore Demetrius and [1]the [2]with [4]him

τεχνῖται ἔχουσι πρός τινα λόγον, ἀγοραῖοι
[3]artisans have against anyone an account, assizes

ἄγονται καὶ ἀνθύπατοί εἰσιν, ἐγκαλείτωσαν
are and proconsuls there are, let them bring a
being(held) charge against

ἀλλήλοις.
one another.

39 εἰ δέ τι περαιτέρω ἐπιζητεῖτε,
But if [2]anything [3]further [1]ye seek,

ἐν τῇ ἐννόμῳ ἐκκλησίᾳ ἐπιλυθήσεται.
in the lawful assembly it will be settled.

40 καὶ γὰρ κινδυνεύομεν ἐγκαλεῖσθαι
For indeed we are in danger to be charged with

στάσεως περὶ τῆς σήμερον, μηδενὸς
insurrection concerning to-day, nothing

αἰτίου ὑπάρχοντος, περὶ οὗ οὐ δυνησόμεθα
cause being[a], concerning which we shall not be able
=there being no cause,

ἀποδοῦναι λόγον περὶ τῆς συστροφῆς
to give account concerning - [2]crowding together

⁴¹And when he had said this, he dismissed the assembly.

ταύτης. **41** καὶ ταῦτα εἰπὼν ἀπέλυσεν τὴν
¹this.   And these things saying   he dismissed the
ἐκκλησίαν.
assembly.

CHAPTER 20

20 Μετὰ δὲ τὸ παύσασθαι τὸν θόρυβον
     And after the to cease   the uproarᵇ
     =after the uproar ceased

AFTER the uproar ceased, Paul sent for the disciples and having exhorted them took leave of them and departed for Macedo'nia. ²When he had gone through these parts and had given them much encouragement, he came to Greece. ³There he spent three months, and when a plot was made against him by the Jews as he was about to set sail for Syria, he determined to return through Macedo'nia. ⁴Sop'ater of Beroe'a, the son of Pyrrhus, accompanied him; and of the Thessalo'nians, Aristar'-chus and Secun'dus; and Ga'ius of Derbe, and Timothy; and the Asians, Tych'icus and Troph'-imus. ⁵These went on and were waiting for us at Tro'as, ⁶but we sailed away from Philippi after the days of Unleavened Bread, and in five days we came to them at Tro'as, where we stayed for seven days.

7 On the first day of

μεταπεμψάμενος ὁ Παῦλος τοὺς μαθητὰς
⁴summoning   ¹Paul   ⁵the   ⁶disciples
καὶ παρακαλέσας, ἀσπασάμενος ἐξῆλθεν
²and ⁶exhorting,   taking leave   he went forth
πορεύεσθαι εἰς Μακεδονίαν. **2** διελθὼν δὲ
to go   to   Macedonia.   And having gone through
τὰ μέρη ἐκεῖνα καὶ παρακαλέσας αὐτοὺς
those parts   and   having exhorted   them
λόγῳ πολλῷ ἦλθεν εἰς τὴν Ἑλλάδα,
¹with ²speech ³much he came into -   Greece,
3 ποιήσας τε μῆνας τρεῖς, γενομένης
    and spending   months three,   there being
ἐπιβουλῆς αὐτῷ ὑπὸ τῶν Ἰουδαίων
a plotᵃ   [against] him   by   the   Jews
μέλλοντι ἀνάγεσθαι εἰς τὴν Συρίαν, ἐγένετο
being about to set sail to(for) - Syria,   he was
=as he was about
γνώμης τοῦ ὑποστρέφειν διὰ Μακεδονίας.
of a mind - to returnᵈ   through Macedonia.
4 συνείπετο δὲ αὐτῷ Σώπατρος Πύρρου
    And there accompanied him Sopater [son] of Pyrrhus
Βεροιαῖος, Θεσσαλονικέων δὲ Ἀρίσταρχος
a Berœan,   and of Thessalonians   Aristarchus
καὶ Σέκουνδος, καὶ Γάϊος Δερβαῖος καὶ
and Secundus,   and Gaius   a Derbæan   and
Τιμόθεος, Ἀσιανοὶ δὲ Τύχικος καὶ
Timothy,   and Asians   Tychicus   and
Τρόφιμος. **5** οὗτοι δὲ προελθόντες ἔμενον
Trophimus.   And these men going forward   awaited
ἡμᾶς ἐν Τρῳάδι· **6** ἡμεῖς δὲ ἐξεπλεύσαμεν
us   in Troas;   and we   sailed away
μετὰ τὰς ἡμέρας τῶν ἀζύμων ἀπὸ
after the   days   - of unleavened bread from
Φιλίππων, καὶ ἤλθομεν πρὸς αὐτοὺς εἰς
Philippi,   and   came   to   them   in
τὴν Τρῳάδα ἄχρι ἡμερῶν πέντε, ὅπου
-   Troas   until   days   five,   where
διετρίψαμεν ἡμέρας ἑπτά. **7** Ἐν δὲ τῇ
we stayed   days   seven.   And on the

the week, when we were gathered together to break bread, Paul talked with them, intending to depart on the morrow; and he prolonged his speech until midnight. [8] There were many lights in the upper chamber where we were gathered. [9] And a young man named Eu'tychus was sitting in the window. He sank into a deep sleep as Paul talked still longer; and being overcome by sleep, he fell down from the third story and was taken up dead. [10] But Paul went down and bent over him, and embracing him said, "Do not be alarmed, for his life is in him." [11] And when Paul had gone up and had broken bread and eaten, he conversed with them a long while, until daybreak, and so departed. [12] And they took the lad away alive, and were not a little comforted.

13 But going ahead to the ship, we set sail for Assos, intending to take

μιᾷ   τῶν   σαββάτων   συνηγμένων   ἡμῶν
one(first) of the   sabbaths(week)   having been   us[a]
[day]   assembled
                              =as we were assembled

κλάσαι   ἄρτον   ὁ Παῦλος   διελέγετο   αὐτοῖς,
to break   bread   –   Paul   lectured   to them,

μέλλων   ἐξιέναι   τῇ ἐπαύριον,   παρέτεινέν τε
being about to depart   on the   morrow,   and continued

τὸν   λόγον   μέχρι   μεσονυκτίου.   8 ἦσαν   δὲ
the   speech   until   midnight.   Now there were

λαμπάδες   ἱκαναὶ   ἐν   τῷ   ὑπερῴῳ   οὗ
lamps   a considerable   in   the   upper room   where
           number of

ἦμεν   συνηγμένοι.   9 καθεζόμενος   δέ   τις
we were having been assembled.   And sitting   a certain

νεανίας   ὀνόματι   Εὔτυχος   ἐπὶ   τῆς   θυρίδος,
young man   by name   Eutychus   on   the   window sill,

καταφερόμενος   ὕπνῳ   βαθεῖ,   διαλεγομένου
being overborne   sleep   by a deep,   lecturing

τοῦ   Παύλου   ἐπὶ   πλεῖον,   κατενεχθεὶς   ἀπὸ
–   Paul[a]   for a longer time,   having been   from
=while Paul lectured   overborne

τοῦ   ὕπνου   ἔπεσεν   ἀπὸ   τοῦ   τριστέγου
the   sleep   he fell   from   the   third floor[*]

κάτω   καὶ   ἤρθη   νεκρός.   10 καταβὰς   δὲ
down   and was taken up   dead.   But going down

ὁ Παῦλος   ἐπέπεσεν   αὐτῷ   καὶ   συμπεριλαβὼν
– Paul   fell on   him   and   closely embracing
                                        [him]

εἶπεν·   μὴ   θορυβεῖσθε·   ἡ γὰρ   ψυχὴ   αὐτοῦ
said: Be ye not terrified;   for the   life   of him

ἐν   αὐτῷ   ἐστιν.   11 ἀναβὰς   δὲ καὶ   κλάσας
in   him   is.   And going up   and   breaking

τὸν   ἄρτον   καὶ   γευσάμενος,   ἐφ’   ἱκανόν τε
the   bread   and   tasting,   and over a considerable
                                              [time]

ὁμιλήσας   ἄχρι   αὐγῆς,   οὕτως   ἐξῆλθεν.
conversing   until   light [of day],   thus   he went forth.

12 ἤγαγον   δὲ   τὸν   παῖδα   ζῶντα,   καὶ
And they brought   the   lad   living,   and

παρεκλήθησαν   οὐ   μετρίως.   13 Ἡμεῖς   δὲ
were comforted   not   moderately.   And we

προελθόντες   ἐπὶ   τὸ   πλοῖον   ἀνήχθημεν
going before   onto   the   ship   set sail

ἐπὶ   τὴν   Ἄσσον,   ἐκεῖθεν   μέλλοντες   ἀνα-
to(for)   Assos,   thence   intending   to

* Souter remarks that it is uncertain whether the ground floor was counted or not in the enunciation; "if so, we should have to translate 'the second floor'."

Paul aboard there; for so he had arranged, intending himself to go by land. ¹⁴And when he met us at Assos, we took him on board and came to Mityle'ne. ¹⁵And sailing from there we came the following day opposite Chi os; the next day we touched at Samos; and ᵖ the day after that we came to Mile tus. ¹⁶For Paul had decided to sail past Ephesus, so that he might not have to spend time in Asia; for he was hastening to be at Jerusalem, if possible, on the day of Pentecost.

17 And from Mile'tus he sent to Ephesus and called to him the elders of the church. ¹⁸And when they came to him, he said to them:

"You yourselves know how I lived among you all the time from the first day that I set foot in Asia, ¹⁹serving the Lord with all humility and with tears and with trials which befell me through the plots of the Jews; ²⁰how I did not shrink from declaring to you anything that was profitable, and teaching

λαμβάνειν τὸν Παῦλον· οὕτως γὰρ
take up – Paul; for thus

διατεταγμένος ἦν, μέλλων αὐτὸς πεζεύειν.
having been arranged it was, ²intending ¹he to go afoot.

14 ὡς δὲ συνέβαλλεν ἡμῖν εἰς τὴν Ἄσσον,
Now when he met with us in – Assos,

ἀναλαβόντες αὐτὸν ἤλθομεν εἰς Μιτυλήνην·
taking up him we came to Mitylene;

15 κἀκεῖθεν ἀποπλεύσαντες τῇ ἐπιούσῃ
and thence sailing away on the next [day]

κατηντήσαμεν ἄντικρυς Χίου, τῇ δὲ ἑτέρᾳ
we arrived off Chios, and on the other(next)

παρεβάλομεν εἰς Σάμον, τῇ δὲ ἐχομένῃ
we crossed over to Samos, and on the next

ἤλθομεν εἰς Μίλητον. 16 κεκρίκει γὰρ ὁ
we came to Miletus. For had decided –

Παῦλος παραπλεῦσαι τὴν Ἔφεσον, ὅπως
Paul to sail past – Ephesus, so as

μὴ γένηται αὐτῷ χρονοτριβῆσαι ἐν τῇ
not be to him to spend time in –
=so that he should not . . .

Ἀσίᾳ· ἔσπευδεν γάρ, εἰ δυνατὸν εἴη
Asia; for he hasted, if possible it might be

αὐτῷ, τὴν ἡμέραν τῆς πεντηκοστῆς
to him, the day – of Pentecost

γενέσθαι εἰς Ἱεροσόλυμα.
to be in Jerusalem.

17 Ἀπὸ δὲ τῆς Μιλήτου πέμψας εἰς
And from – Miletus sending to

Ἔφεσον μετεκαλέσατο τοὺς πρεσβυτέρους
Ephesus he summoned the elders

τῆς ἐκκλησίας. 18 ὡς δὲ παρεγένοντο
of the church. And when they came

πρὸς αὐτόν, εἶπεν αὐτοῖς· ὑμεῖς ἐπίστασθε,
to him, he said to them: Ye understand,

ἀπὸ πρώτης ἡμέρας ἀφ᾽ ἧς ἐπέβην εἰς
from [the] first day from which I set foot on in

τὴν Ἀσίαν, πῶς μεθ᾽ ὑμῶν τὸν πάντα
– Asia, how with you the whole

χρόνον ἐγενόμην, 19 δουλεύων τῷ κυρίῳ
time I was, serving the Lord

μετὰ πάσης ταπεινοφροσύνης καὶ δακρύων
with all humility and tears

καὶ πειρασμῶν τῶν συμβάντων μοι ἐν
and trials – happening to me by

ταῖς ἐπιβουλαῖς τῶν Ἰουδαίων, 20 ὡς
the plots of the Jews, as

οὐδὲν ὑπεστειλάμην τῶν συμφερόντων τοῦ
²nothing ¹I kept back of the things beneficial –

ᵖ Other ancient authorities add after remaining at Trogyllium you in public and from house to house, 21 testifying both to Jews and to Greeks of repentance to God and of faith in our Lord Jesus Christ. 22 And now, behold, I am going to Jerusalem, bound in the Spirit, not knowing what shall befall me there; 23 except that the Holy Spirit testifies to me in every city that imprisonment and afflictions await me. 24 But I do not account my life of any value nor as precious to myself, if only I may accomplish my course and the ministry which I received from the Lord Jesus, to testify to the gospel of the grace of God. 25 And now, behold, I know that all you among whom I have gone about preaching the kingdom will see my face no more. 26 Therefore I testify to you this day that I am innocent of the blood of all of you, 27 for I did not shrink from declaring to you the whole counsel of God. 28 Take heed to yourselves and to all the flock, in which the Holy

μὴ ἀναγγεῖλαι ὑμῖν καὶ διδάξαι ὑμᾶς
not to declare^d to you and to teach^d you
δημοσίᾳ καὶ κατ' οἴκους, 21 διαμαρτυρόμενος
publicly and from house to house,† solemnly witnessing
Ἰουδαίοις τε καὶ Ἕλλησιν τὴν εἰς θεὸν
²to Jews ¹both and to Greeks – toward God
μετάνοιαν καὶ πίστιν εἰς τὸν κύριον
repentance and faith toward(?in) the Lord
ἡμῶν Ἰησοῦν. 22 καὶ νῦν ἰδοὺ δεδεμένος
of us Jesus. And now behold having been bound
ἐγὼ τῷ πνεύματι πορεύομαι εἰς Ἱερου-
I by the Spirit am going to Jeru-
σαλήμ, τὰ ἐν αὐτῇ συναντήσοντα ἐμοὶ
salem, ³the things ⁴in ⁵it ⁴going to meet ⁵me
μὴ εἰδώς, 23 πλὴν ὅτι τὸ πνεῦμα τὸ
¹not ²knowing, except that the Spirit –
ἅγιον κατὰ πόλιν διαμαρτύρεταί μοι λέγον
Holy in every city† solemnly witnesses to me saying
ὅτι δεσμὰ καὶ θλίψεις με μένουσιν.
that bonds and afflictions me await.
24 ἀλλ' οὐδενὸς λόγου ποιοῦμαι τὴν ψυχὴν
But ⁴of nothing ⁵account ¹I make ²the(my) ³life
τιμίαν ἐμαυτῷ ὡς τελειώσω τὸν δρόμον
precious to myself so as I may finish the course
μου καὶ τὴν διακονίαν ἣν ἔλαβον παρὰ
of me and the ministry which I received from
τοῦ κυρίου Ἰησοῦ, διαμαρτύρασθαι τὸ
the Lord Jesus, to witness solemnly the
εὐαγγέλιον τῆς χάριτος τοῦ θεοῦ. 25 καὶ
gospel of the grace – of God. And
νῦν ἰδοὺ ἐγὼ οἶδα ὅτι οὐκέτι ὄψεσθε
now behold I know that ⁴no more ³will see
τὸ πρόσωπόν μου ὑμεῖς πάντες ἐν οἷς
¹the ²face ⁴of me ¹ye ³all among whom
διῆλθον κηρύσσων τὴν βασιλείαν. 26 διότι
I went about proclaiming the kingdom. Wherefore
μαρτύρομαι ὑμῖν ἐν τῇ σήμερον ἡμέρᾳ
I witness to you on this day
ὅτι καθαρός εἰμι ἀπὸ τοῦ αἵματος πάντων·
that clean I am from the blood of all men;
27 οὐ γὰρ ὑπεστειλάμην τοῦ μὴ ἀναγγεῖλαι
for I kept not back – not to declare^d
πᾶσαν τὴν βουλὴν τοῦ θεοῦ ὑμῖν.
all the counsel – of God to you.
28 προσέχετε ἑαυτοῖς καὶ παντὶ τῷ
Take heed to yourselves and to all the
ποιμνίῳ, ἐν ᾧ ὑμᾶς τὸ πνεῦμα τὸ
flock, in which ⁵you ¹the ²Spirit –

Spirit has made you guardians, to feed the church of the Lord*q* which he obtained with his own blood.*r* ²⁹I know that after my departure fierce wolves will come in among you, not sparing the flock; ³⁰and from among your own selves will arise men speaking perverse things, to draw away the disciples after them. ³¹Therefore be alert, remembering that for three years I did not cease night or day to admonish every one with tears. ³²And now I commend you to God and to the word of his grace, which is able to build you up and to give you the inheritance among all those who are sanctified. ³³I coveted no one's silver or gold or apparel. ³⁴You yourselves know that these hands ministered to my necessities, and to those who were with me. ³⁵In all things I have shown you that by so toiling one must help the weak, remembering the words of the Lord Jesus, how he said, 'It is more blessed

ἅγιον   ἔθετο   ἐπισκόπους,   ποιμαίνειν   τὴν
²Holy   ⁴placed   overseers,   to shepherd   the

ἐκκλησίαν   τοῦ   θεοῦ,   ἣν   περιεποιήσατο
church   –   of God,   which   he acquired

διὰ   τοῦ   αἵματος   τοῦ   ἰδίου.   29 ἐγὼ
through the   blood   of the(his)   own.*   I

οἶδα   ὅτι   εἰσελεύσονται   μετὰ   τὴν   ἄφιξίν
know   that   ⁷will come in   ¹after   ²the   ³departure

μου   λύκοι   βαρεῖς   εἰς   ὑμᾶς   μὴ   φειδόμενοι
⁴of me   ⁵wolves   ⁶grievous   ⁸into   you   not   sparing

τοῦ   ποιμνίου,   30 καὶ   ἐξ   ὑμῶν   αὐτῶν
the   flock,   and   of   you   [your]selves

ἀναστήσονται   ἄνδρες   λαλοῦντες   διεστραμμένα
will rise up   men   speaking   *having been perverted things*

τοῦ   ἀποσπᾶν   τοὺς   μαθητὰς   ὀπίσω   ἑαυτῶν.
–   to drag away*d*   the   disciples   after   themselves.

31 διὸ   γρηγορεῖτε,   μνημονεύοντες   ὅτι
Wherefore   watch ye,   remembering   that

τριετίαν   νύκτα   καὶ   ἡμέραν   οὐκ   ἐπαυσάμην
for three years   night   and   day   I ceased not

μετὰ   δακρύων   νουθετῶν   ἕνα   ἕκαστον.
with   tears   admonishing   ²one   ¹each.

32 καὶ   τὰ   νῦν   παρατίθεμαι   ὑμᾶς   τῷ
And   –   now   I commend   you   to the

κυρίῳ   καὶ   τῷ   λόγῳ   τῆς   χάριτος   αὐτοῦ
Lord   and   to the   word   of the   grace   of him

τῷ   δυναμένῳ   οἰκοδομῆσαι   καὶ   δοῦναι   τὴν
–   being able   to build   and   to give   the

κληρονομίαν   ἐν   τοῖς   ἡγιασμένοις   πᾶσιν.
inheritance   among ²the [ones]   ³having been sanctified   ¹all.

33 ἀργυρίου   ἢ   χρυσίου   ἢ   ἱματισμοῦ   οὐδενὸς
Silver   or   gold   or   raiment   of no one

ἐπεθύμησα·   34 αὐτοὶ   γινώσκετε   ὅτι   ταῖς
I coveted;   [your]selves   ye know   that   ⁴to the

χρείαις   μου   καὶ   τοῖς   οὖσιν   μετ᾽   ἐμοῦ
⁵needs   ⁶of me   ⁷and   ⁸to the [ones]⁹being   ¹⁰with   ¹¹me

ὑπηρέτησαν   αἱ   χεῖρες   αὗται.   35 πάντα
²ministered   ¹these   ²hands.   All things

ὑπέδειξα   ὑμῖν,   ὅτι   οὕτως   κοπιῶντας   δεῖ
I showed   you,   that   thus   labouring   it be-hoves

ἀντιλαμβάνεσθαι   τῶν   ἀσθενούντων,   μνημονεύειν
to succour   the   ailing [ones],   ²to remember

τε   τῶν   λόγων   τοῦ   κυρίου   Ἰησοῦ,   ὅτι
¹and   the   words   of the   Lord   Jesus,   that

αὐτὸς   εἶπεν·   μακάριόν   ἐστιν   μᾶλλον   διδόναι
he   said: Blessed   it is   rather   to give

q Other ancient authorities read *of God*

r Or *with the blood of his Own*

* This = his own blood *or* the blood of his own [?Son].

to give than to receive.' "

36 And when he had spoken thus, he knelt down and prayed with them all. [37]And they all wept and embraced Paul and kissed him, [38]sorrowing most of all because of the word he had spoken, that they should see his face no more. And they brought him to the ship.

ἢ   λαμβάνειν.   36 καὶ   ταῦτα   εἰπών,
than   to receive.   And   [2]these things [1]having said,

θεὶς   τὰ   γόνατα   αὐτοῦ   σὺν   πᾶσιν   αὐτοῖς
placing the   knees   of him   with   [2]all   [1]them
= kneeling down

προσηύξατο.   37 ἱκανὸς   δὲ   κλαυθμὸς   ἐγένετο
he prayed.   And [2]considerable   [3]weeping   [1]there was

πάντων,   καὶ   ἐπιπεσόντες   ἐπὶ   τὸν   τράχηλον
of all,   and   falling on   on   the   neck

τοῦ   Παύλου   κατεφίλουν   αὐτόν,   38 ὀδυνώ-
of Paul   they kissed fervently   him,   suffer-

μενοι   μάλιστα   ἐπὶ   τῷ   λόγῳ   ᾧ   εἰρήκει,
ing   most   over   the   word   which he had said,

ὅτι   οὐκέτι   μέλλουσιν   τὸ   πρόσωπον   αὐτοῦ
that   no more   they are(were)   the   face   of him

θεωρεῖν.   προέπεμπον   δὲ   αὐτὸν   εἰς   τὸ
to behold.   And they escorted   him   to   the

πλοῖον.
ship.

CHAPTER 21

AND when we had parted from them and set sail, we came by a straight course to Cos, and the next day to Rhodes, and from there to Pat'ara.[8] [2]And having found a ship crossing to Phoeni'cia, we went aboard, and set sail. [3]When we had come in sight of Cyprus, leaving it on the left we sailed to Syria, and landed at Tyre; for there the ship was to unload its cargo. [4]And having sought out the disciples, we stayed there for seven days. Through the Spirit they told Paul not to go on to Jerusalem. [5]And when our days there were

21 Ὡς   δὲ   ἐγένετο   ἀναχθῆναι   ἡμᾶς
Now when   it came to pass   to set sail   we

ἀποσπασθέντας   ἀπ'   αὐτῶν,   εὐθυδρομήσαντες
having been withdrawn from   them,   taking a straight course

ἤλθομεν   εἰς   τὴν   Κῶ,   τῇ   δὲ   ἑξῆς   εἰς
we came   to   -   Cos,   and on the next [day]   to

τὴν   Ῥόδον   κἀκεῖθεν   εἰς   Πάταρα·   2 καὶ
-    Rhodes   and thence   to   Patara;   and

εὑρόντες   πλοῖον   διαπερῶν   εἰς   Φοινίκην,
having found   a ship   crossing over   to   Phœnice,

ἐπιβάντες   ἀνήχθημεν.   3 ἀναφάναντες   δὲ
embarking   we set sail.   And sighting

τὴν   Κύπρον   καὶ   καταλιπόντες   αὐτὴν
-    Cyprus   and   leaving   it

εὐώνυμον   ἐπλέομεν   εἰς   Συρίαν,   καὶ   κατήλ-
on the left   we sailed   to   Syria,   and   came

θομεν   εἰς   Τύρον·   ἐκεῖσε   γὰρ   τὸ   πλοῖον
down   to   Tyre;   for there   the   ship

ἦν   ἀποφορτιζόμενον   τὸν   γόμον.   4 ἀνευρ-
was   unloading   the   cargo.   find-

όντες   δὲ   τοὺς   μαθητὰς   ἐπεμείναμεν   αὐτοῦ
ing   And   the   disciples   we remained   there

ἡμέρας   ἑπτά·   οἵτινες   τῷ   Παύλῳ   ἔλεγον
days   seven;   who   -   [2]Paul   [1]told

διὰ   τοῦ   πνεύματος   μὴ   ἐπιβαίνειν   εἰς
through the   Spirit   not   to go up   to

Ἱεροσόλυμα.   5 ὅτε   δὲ   ἐγένετο   ἐξαρτίσαι
Jerusalem.   But when   it came to pass   to accomplish
= we accomplished

[8] Other ancient authorities add and Myra

ended, we departed and went on our journey; and they all, with wives and children, brought us on our way till we were outside the city; and kneeling down on the beach we prayed and bade one another farewell. ⁶Then we went on board the ship, and they returned home.

7 When we had finished the voyage from Tyre, we arrived at Ptolema'is; and we greeted the brethren and stayed with them for one day. ⁸On the morrow we departed and came to Caesare'a; and we entered the house of Philip the evangelist, who was one of the seven, and stayed with him. ⁹And he had four unmarried daughters, who prophesied. ¹⁰While we were staying for some days, a prophet named Ag'abus came down from Judea. ¹¹And coming to us he took Paul's girdle and bound his own feet and hands, and said, "Thus says the Holy Spirit, 'So shall the Jews at Jerusalem bind the man who owns this girdle and

ἡμᾶς τὰς ἡμέρας, ἐξελθόντες ἐπορευόμεθα
us[b] the days, going forth we journeyed

προπεμπόντων ἡμᾶς πάντων σὺν γυναιξὶ
²escorting ³us ¹all[a] with women

καὶ τέκνοις ἕως ἔξω τῆς πόλεως, καὶ
and children as far as outside the city, and

θέντες τὰ γόνατα ἐπὶ τὸν αἰγιαλὸν
placing the knees on the shore
=kneeling

προσευξάμενοι 6 ἀπησπασάμεθα ἀλλήλους,
praying we gave parting greetings to one another,

καὶ ἐνέβημεν εἰς τὸ πλοῖον, ἐκεῖνοι δὲ
and embarked in the ship, and those

ὑπέστρεψαν εἰς τὰ ἴδια. 7 Ἡμεῖς δὲ
returned to ¹the(ir) ³things ²own. But we
=home.

τὸν πλοῦν διανύσαντες ἀπὸ Τύρου κατηντή-
²the ³voyage ¹finishing from Tyre ar-

σαμεν εἰς Πτολεμαΐδα, καὶ ἀσπασάμενοι
rived at Ptolemais, and greeting

τοὺς ἀδελφοὺς ἐμείναμεν ἡμέραν μίαν
the brothers we remained day one

παρ' αὐτοῖς. 8 τῇ δὲ ἐπαύριον ἐξελθόντες
with them. And on the morrow going forth

ἤλθομεν εἰς Καισάρειαν, καὶ εἰσελθόντες
we came to Cæsarea, and entering

εἰς τὸν οἶκον Φιλίππου τοῦ εὐαγγελιστοῦ
into the house of Philip the evangelist

ὄντος ἐκ τῶν ἑπτά, ἐμείναμεν παρ'
being of the seven, we remained with

αὐτῷ. 9 τούτῳ δὲ ἦσαν θυγατέρες
him. Now to this man were daughters
=this man had four daughters

τέσσαρες παρθένοι προφητεύουσαι. 10 Ἐπιμεν-
four[c] virgins prophesying. remain-

όντων δὲ ἡμέρας πλείους κατῆλθέν τις
ing[a] And days more(many) ⁵came down ¹a certain

ἀπὸ τῆς Ἰουδαίας προφήτης ὀνόματι
⁶from — ⁷Judæa ²prophet ³by name

Ἄγαβος, 11 καὶ ἐλθὼν πρὸς ἡμᾶς καὶ
⁴Agabus, and coming to us and

ἄρας τὴν ζώνην τοῦ Παύλου, δήσας
taking the girdle — of Paul, having bound

ἑαυτοῦ τοὺς πόδας καὶ τὰς χεῖρας εἶπεν·
of himself the feet and the hands said:

τάδε λέγει τὸ πνεῦμα τὸ ἅγιον· τὸν
These things says the Spirit — Holy: ⁷The

ἄνδρα οὗ ἐστιν ἡ ζώνη αὕτη οὕτως
⁸man ⁹of whom ¹⁰is ¹¹this ¹²girdle ¹thus

deliver him into the hands of the Gentiles.' " [12]When we heard this, we and the people there begged him not to go up to Jerusalem. [13]Then Paul answered, "What are you doing, weeping and breaking my heart? For I am ready not only to be imprisoned but even to die at Jerusalem for the name of the Lord Jesus." [14]And when he would not be persuaded, we ceased and said, "The will of the Lord be done."

15 After these days we made ready and went up to Jerusalem. [16]And some of the disciples from Caesare′a went with us, bringing us to the house of Mnason of Cyprus, an early disciple, with whom we should lodge.

17 When we had come to Jerusalem, the brethren received us gladly. [18]On the following day Paul went in with us to James; and all the elders were present. [19]After greeting them, he related

---

δήσουσιν ἐν Ἰερουσαλὴμ οἱ Ἰουδαῖοι καὶ
will bind ⁵in   ⁴Jerusalem   ²the   ³Jews   and

παραδώσουσιν εἰς χεῖρας ἐθνῶν.   12 ὡς
will deliver   into [the] hands of [the] nations.   when

δὲ ἠκούσαμεν ταῦτα, παρεκαλοῦμεν ἡμεῖς
And we heard these things, ⁶besought   ¹we

τε καὶ οἱ ἐντόπιοι τοῦ μὴ ἀναβαίνειν
¹both ³and ⁴the ⁵residents – ⁸not ⁹to go up⁴

αὐτὸν εἰς Ἰερουσαλήμ.   13 τότε ἀπεκρίθη
⁷him to Jerusalem.   Then answered

ὁ Παῦλος τί ποιεῖτε κλαίοντες καὶ
- Paul: What are ye doing weeping and

συνθρύπτοντές μου τὴν καρδίαν; ἐγὼ γὰρ
weakening   of me the heart?   For I

οὐ μόνον δεθῆναι ἀλλὰ καὶ ἀποθανεῖν
not only to be bound but also to die

εἰς Ἰερουσαλὴμ ἑτοίμως ἔχω ὑπὲρ τοῦ
in Jerusalem   readily have on behalf of the
                      =am ready

ὀνόματος τοῦ κυρίου Ἰησοῦ.   14 μὴ
name   of the Lord   Jesus.   Not

πειθομένου δὲ αὐτοῦ ἡσυχάσαμεν εἰπόντες·
being persuaded and him³ we kept silence having said:
= And when he was not persuaded

τοῦ κυρίου τὸ θέλημα γινέσθω.
⁴Of the ⁵Lord ²the ³will ¹let ⁶be [done].

15 Μετὰ δὲ τὰς ἡμέρας ταύτας
And after   these days

ἐπισκευασάμενοι ἀνεβαίνομεν εἰς Ἱεροσόλυμα·
having made ready we went up to Jerusalem;

16 συνῆλθον δὲ καὶ τῶν μαθητῶν ἀπὸ
and went with also [some] of the disciples from

Καισαρείας σὺν ἡμῖν, ἄγοντες παρ' ᾧ
Cæsarea with us, bringing [one] with whom

ξενισθῶμεν Μνάσωνί τινι Κυπρίῳ,
we might be lodged Mnason a certain Cypriote,

ἀρχαίῳ μαθητῇ. 17 Γενομένων δὲ ἡμῶν εἰς
an ancient disciple.   And being   us³ in
(early)   = when we were

Ἱεροσόλυμα ἀσμένως ἀπεδέξαντο ἡμᾶς οἱ
Jerusalem ⁵joyfully ⁴received   ⁴us ¹the

ἀδελφοί. 18 τῇ δὲ ἐπιούσῃ εἰσῄει ὁ
²brothers.   And on the next day went in –

Παῦλος σὺν ἡμῖν πρὸς Ἰάκωβον, πάντες
Paul with us to James, ³all

τε παρεγένοντο οἱ πρεσβύτεροι. 19 καὶ
¹and ⁵came ²the ⁴elders.   And

ἀσπασάμενος αὐτοὺς ἐξηγεῖτο καθ' ἓν
having greeted them he related according to one
                          =singly

one by one the things that God had done among the Gentiles through his ministry. ²⁰And when they heard it, they glorified God. And they said to him, "You see, brother, how many thousands there are among the Jews of those who have believed; they are all zealous for the law, ²¹and they have been told about you that you teach all the Jews who are among the Gentiles to forsake Moses, telling them not to circumcise their children or observe the customs. ²²What then is to be done? They will certainly hear that you have come. ²³Do therefore what we tell you. We have four men who are under a vow; ²⁴take these men and purify yourself along with them and pay their expenses, so that they may shave their heads. Thus all will know that there is nothing in what they have been told about you but that you yourself live in observance of the law. ²⁵But as for the Gentiles who have believed, we have sent a letter with our judgment that they should abstain from what has been sacrificed to idols and from blood and from what is strangled[1] and from unchastity." ²⁶Then Paul

---

[1] Other early authorities omit *and from what is strangled*

ἕκαστον ὧν ἐποίησεν ὁ θεὸς ἐν τοῖς
each of [the things] which did - God among the

ἔθνεσιν διὰ τῆς διακονίας αὐτοῦ. 20 οἱ
nations through the ministry of him. they

δὲ ἀκούσαντες ἐδόξαζον τὸν θεόν, εἶπάν τε
And hearing glorified - God, and said

αὐτῷ· θεωρεῖς, ἀδελφέ, πόσαι μυριάδες
to him: Thou beholdest, brother, how many *ten* thousands

εἰσὶν ἐν τοῖς Ἰουδαίοις τῶν πεπιστευκότων,
there are among the Jews - having believed,

καὶ πάντες ζηλωταὶ τοῦ νόμου ὑπάρχουσιν·
and all zealots of the law are;

21 κατηχήθησαν δὲ περὶ σοῦ ὅτι ἀποστα-
and they were informed about thee that ⁸apo-

σίαν διδάσκεις ἀπὸ Μωϋσέως τοὺς κατὰ
stasy ¹thou teachest ⁹from ¹⁰Moses ²the ⁵throughout

τὰ ἔθνη πάντας Ἰουδαίους, λέγων μὴ
⁶the ⁷nations ³all ⁴Jews, ¹telling ²not

περιτέμνειν αὐτοὺς τὰ τέκνα μηδὲ τοῖς
⁴to circumcise ²them the children nor in the

ἔθεσιν περιπατεῖν. 22 τί οὖν ἐστιν;
customs to walk. What therefore is it?

πάντως ἀκούσονται ὅτι ἐλήλυθας. 23 τοῦτο
At all events they will hear that thou hast come. This

οὖν ποίησον ὅ σοι λέγομεν· εἰσὶν ἡμῖν
therefore do thou which thee we tell: There are to us*
= We have

ἄνδρες τέσσαρες εὐχὴν ἔχοντες ἐφ᾽ ἑαυτῶν·
men four a vow having on themselves;

24 τούτους παραλαβὼν ἁγνίσθητι σὺν αὐτοῖς,
these taking be thou purified with them,

καὶ δαπάνησον ἐπ᾽ αὐτοῖς ἵνα ξυρήσονται
and spend on them that they will shave

τὴν κεφαλήν, καὶ γνώσονται πάντες ὅτι
the head, and will know all men that

ὧν κατήχηνται περὶ σοῦ οὐδέν
²[of the things] ⁴they have been ³about ⁶thee ²nothing
of which informed

ἔστιν, ἀλλὰ στοιχεῖς καὶ αὐτὸς φυλάσσων τὸν
¹there is, but thou walkest also [thy]self keeping the

νόμον. 25 περὶ δὲ τῶν πεπιστευκότων
law. And concerning ¹the ²having believed

ἐθνῶν ἡμεῖς ἐπεστείλαμεν κρίναντες φυλάσ-
³nations we joined in writing ¹judging ³to keep

σεσθαι αὐτοὺς τό τε εἰδωλόθυτον καὶ
themselves ²them ⁴[from] ³the ⁵both idol sacrifice and

αἷμα καὶ πνικτὸν καὶ πορνείαν. 26 τότε
blood and a thing strangled and fornication. Then

took the men, and the next day he purified himself with them and went into the temple, to give notice when the days of purification would be fulfilled and the offering presented for every one of them.

27 When the seven days were almost completed, the Jews from Asia, who had seen him in the temple, stirred up all the crowd, and laid hands on him, 28 crying out, "Men of Israel, help! This is the man who is teaching men everywhere against the people and the law and this place; moreover he also brought Greeks into the temple, and he has defiled this holy place." 29 For they had previously seen Troph imus the Ephesian with him in the city, and they supposed that Paul had brought him into the temple. 30 Then all the city was aroused, and the people ran together; they seized Paul and dragged him out of the temple, and at once the gates were shut. 31 And as they

ὁ Παῦλος παραλαβὼν τοὺς ἄνδρας τῇ
- Paul taking the men on the
ἐχομένῃ ἡμέρᾳ σὺν αὐτοῖς ἁγνισθεὶς εἰσῄει
next day with them having been purified went in
εἰς τὸ ἱερόν, διαγγέλλων τὴν ἐκπλήρωσιν
to the temple, announcing the completion
τῶν ἡμερῶν τοῦ ἁγνισμοῦ, ἕως οὗ
of the days of the purification, until
προσηνέχθη ὑπὲρ ἑνὸς ἑκάστου αὐτῶν ἡ
should be offered on behalf of ²one ¹each of them the
προσφορά.
offering.

27 Ὡς δὲ ἔμελλον αἱ ἑπτὰ ἡμέραι
Now when were about the seven days
συντελεῖσθαι, οἱ ἀπὸ τῆς Ἀσίας Ἰουδαῖοι
to be fulfilled, ¹the ³from - ⁴Asia ²Jews
θεασάμενοι αὐτὸν ἐν τῷ ἱερῷ συνέχεον
seeing him in the temple stirred up
πάντα τὸν ὄχλον, καὶ ἐπέβαλαν ἐπ'
all the crowd, and laid on on
αὐτὸν τὰς χεῖρας, 28 κράζοντες· ἄνδρες
him the(ir) hands, crying out: Men
Ἰσραηλῖται, βοηθεῖτε· οὗτός ἐστιν ὁ
Israelites, help: this is the
ἄνθρωπος ὁ κατὰ τοῦ λαοῦ καὶ τοῦ
man ¹the [one] ⁵against ⁶the ⁷people ⁸and ⁹the
νόμου καὶ τοῦ τόπου τούτου πάντας
¹⁰law ¹¹and ¹²this ¹³place ³all men
πανταχῇ διδάσκων, ἔτι τε καὶ Ἕλληνας
⁴everywhere ²teaching, and even also Greeks
εἰσήγαγεν εἰς τὸ ἱερὸν καὶ κεκοίνωκεν
brought in into the temple and has profaned
τὸν ἅγιον τόπον τοῦτον. 29 ἦσαν γὰρ
- ²holy ³place ¹this. For they were
προεωρακότες Τρόφιμον τὸν Ἐφέσιον ἐν
having previously seen Trophimus the Ephesian in
τῇ πόλει σὺν αὐτῷ, ὃν ἐνόμιζον ὅτι
the city with him, whom they supposed that
εἰς τὸ ἱερὸν εἰσήγαγεν ὁ Παῦλος. 30 ἐκινήθη
³into ⁴the ⁵temple ²brought in - ¹Paul. ⁵was moved
τε ἡ πόλις ὅλη καὶ ἐγένετο συνδρομὴ
¹And ²the ⁴city ³whole and there was a running together
τοῦ λαοῦ, καὶ ἐπιλαβόμενοι τοῦ Παύλου
of the people, and laying hold - of Paul
εἷλκον αὐτὸν ἔξω τοῦ ἱεροῦ, καὶ εὐθέως
they dragged him outside the temple, and immediately
ἐκλείσθησαν αἱ θύραι. 31 Ζητούντων τε
were shut the doors. And [while they were] seeking²

were trying to kill him, word came to the tribune of the cohort that all Jerusalem was in confusion. [32] He at once took soldiers and centurions, and ran down to them; and when they saw the tribune and the soldiers, they stopped beating Paul. [33] Then the tribune came up and arrested him, and ordered him to be bound with two chains. He inquired who he was and what he had done. [34] Some in the crowd shouted one thing, some another; and as he could not learn the facts because of the uproar, he ordered him to be brought into the barracks. [35] And when he came to the steps, he was actually carried by the soldiers because of the violence of the crowd; [36] for the mob of the people followed, crying, "Away with him!"

[37] As Paul was about to be brought into the barracks, he said to the tribune, "May I say something to you?" And he said, "Do you know

αὐτὸν   ἀποκτεῖναι   ἀνέβη   φάσις   τῷ
²him   ¹to kill   ⁴came up   ³information   to the

χιλιάρχῳ   τῆς   σπείρης   ὅτι   ὅλη   συγχύν-
chiliarch   of the   cohort   that   ¹all   ²is(was) in

νεται   Ἰερουσαλήμ·   32   ὃς   ἐξαυτῆς   παρα-
confusion   ³Jerusalem;   who   at once   tak-

λαβὼν   στρατιώτας   καὶ   ἑκατοντάρχας
ing   soldiers   and   centurions

κατέδραμεν   ἐπ᾽   αὐτούς·   οἱ   δὲ   ἰδόντες
ran down   on   them;   and they   seeing

τὸν   χιλίαρχον   καὶ   τοὺς   στρατιώτας
the   chiliarch   and   the   soldiers

ἐπαύσαντο   τύπτοντες   τὸν   Παῦλον.   33   τότε
ceased   beating   -   Paul.   Then

ἐγγίσας   ὁ   χιλίαρχος   ἐπελάβετο   αὐτοῦ
drawing near   the   chiliarch   laid hold   of him

καὶ   ἐκέλευσεν   δεθῆναι   ἁλύσεσι   δυσί,   καὶ
and   commanded   to be bound   chains   with two,   and

ἐπυνθάνετο   τίς   εἴη   καὶ   τί   ἐστιν   πεποιηκώς.
inquired   who   might be   and   what   he is   having done.

34   ἄλλοι   δὲ   ἄλλο   τι   ἐπεφώνουν   ἐν   τῷ
And   ¹others   ²different   ⁵some-   ⁴called out   ²among   ³the
                                    thing

ὄχλῳ·   μὴ   δυναμένου   δὲ   αὐτοῦ   γνῶναι
⁴crowd;   and not being able   himᵃ   to know
          =as he was not able

τὸ   ἀσφαλὲς   διὰ   τὸν   θόρυβον,   ἐκέλευσεν
the   certain thing   because of the   uproar,   he commanded

ἄγεσθαι   αὐτὸν   εἰς   τὴν   παρεμβολήν.   35   ὅτε
to be brought   him   into   the   fort.   when

δὲ   ἐγένετο   ἐπὶ   τοὺς   ἀναβαθμούς,   συνέβη
And   he was   on   the   steps,   it happened

βαστάζεσθαι   αὐτὸν   ὑπὸ   τῶν   στρατιωτῶν
to be carried   himᵇ   by   the   soldiers
=he was carried

διὰ   τὴν   βίαν   τοῦ   ὄχλου·   36   ἠκολούθει
because of the   violence   of the   crowd;   ⁶followed

γὰρ   τὸ   πλῆθος   τοῦ   λαοῦ   κράζοντες·
¹for   ²the   ³multitude   ⁴of the   ⁵people   crying out:

αἶρε   αὐτόν.   37   Μέλλων   τε   εἰσάγεσθαι
Take away   him.   And being about   to be brought in

εἰς   τὴν   παρεμβολὴν   ὁ   Παῦλος   λέγει   τῷ
into   the   fort   -   Paul   says   to the

χιλιάρχῳ·   εἰ   ἔξεστίν   μοι   εἰπεῖν   τι   πρὸς
chiliarch: If   it is lawful   for me   to say   something   to

σέ;   ὁ   δὲ   ἔφη·   Ἑλληνιστὶ   γινώσκεις;
thee?   And he   said: in Greek   Knowest thou
                                          [to speak]?*

* See note on page xviii.

Greek? [38]Are you not the
Egyptian, then, who re-
cently stirred up a revolt
and led the four thousand
men of the Assassins out
into the wilderness?"
[39]Paul replied, "I am a
Jew, from Tarsus in
Cili'cia, a citizen of no
mean city; I beg you,
let me speak to the
people." [40]And when he
had given him leave,
Paul, standing on the
steps, motioned with his
hand to the people; and
when there was a great
hush, he spoke to them
in the Hebrew language,
saying:

38 οὐκ   ἄρα   σὺ   εἶ   ὁ   Αἰγύπτιος   ὁ   πρὸ
   [2]Not [4]then [3]thou [1]art the   Egyptian   the [one] before
τούτων   τῶν   ἡμερῶν   ἀναστατώσας   καὶ
these'   -   days   unsettling   and
ἐξαγαγὼν   εἰς   τὴν   ἔρημον   τοὺς   τετρα-
leading out   into   the   desert   the   four
κισχιλίους   ἄνδρας   τῶν   σικαρίων;   39 εἶπεν
thousand   men   of the   Sicarii?   said
δὲ   ὁ   Παῦλος·   ἐγὼ   ἄνθρωπος   μέν   εἰμι
And -   Paul: I   a man   indeed   am
'Ιουδαῖος,   Ταρσεύς,   τῆς   Κιλικίας   οὐκ
a Jew,   a Tarsian,   -   of Cilicia   not
ἀσήμου   πόλεως   πολίτης·   δέομαι   δέ   σου,
of a mean   city   a citizen;   and I beg   of thee,
ἐπίτρεψόν   μοι   λαλῆσαι   πρὸς   τὸν   λαόν.
permit   me   to speak   to   the   people.
40 ἐπιτρέψαντος   δὲ   αὐτοῦ   ὁ   Παῦλος   ἑστὼς
And permitting   him[a]   -   Paul   standing
                  =when he gave permission
ἐπὶ   τῶν   ἀναβαθμῶν   κατέσεισεν   τῇ   χειρὶ
on   the   steps   beckoned   with the(his) hand
τῷ   λαῷ·   πολλῆς   δὲ   σιγῆς   γενομένης
to the people;   and much   silence   becoming[a]
                 =when there was great silence
προσεφώνησεν   τῇ   'Εβραΐδι   διαλέκτῳ   λέγων·
he addressed   in the   Hebrew   language   saying:

CHAPTER 22

"BRETHREN   and
fathers, hear the
defense which I now
make before you."
2 And when they
heard that he addressed
them in the Hebrew
language, they were the
more quiet. And he said:
3 "I am a Jew, born
at Tarsus in Cili'cia, but
brought up in this city
at the feet of Gama'li-el,
educated according to
the strict manner of the
law of our fathers, being
zealous for God as you

22 "Ανδρες   ἀδελφοὶ   καὶ   πατέρες,   ἀκούσατέ
   Men   brothers   and   fathers,   hear ye
μου   τῆς   πρὸς   ὑμᾶς   νυνὶ   ἀπολογίας.
[3]of me [1]the   [2]to   [4]you   [5]now   [2]defence.
— 2 ἀκούσαντες   δὲ   ὅτι   τῇ   'Εβραΐδι
    (And hearing   that   in the   Hebrew
διαλέκτῳ   προσεφώνει   αὐτοῖς   μᾶλλον
language   he addressed   them   more
παρέσχον   ἡσυχίαν.   καὶ   φησίν·   3 ἐγώ   εἰμι
they showed   quietness.   And   he says:)   I   am
ἀνὴρ   'Ιουδαῖος,   γεγεννημένος   ἐν   Ταρσῷ
a man   a Jew,   having been born   in   Tarsus
τῆς   Κιλικίας,   ἀνατεθραμμένος   δὲ   ἐν   τῇ
of Cilicia,   and having been brought up   in   -
πόλει   ταύτῃ,   παρὰ   τοὺς   πόδας   Γαμαλιὴλ
city   this,   at   the   feet   of Gamaliel
πεπαιδευμένος   κατὰ   ἀκρίβειαν   τοῦ   πατρῴου
having been trained   according   exactness   of the   ancestral
                              to [the]
νόμου,   ζηλωτὴς   ὑπάρχων   τοῦ   θεοῦ   καθὼς
law   a zealot   being   -   of God   even as

all are this day. [4]I persecuted this Way to the death, binding and delivering to prison both men and women, [5]as the high priest and the whole council of elders bear me witness. From them I received letters to the brethren, and I journeyed to Damascus to take those also who were there and bring them in bonds to Jerusalem to be punished.

6 "As I made my journey and drew near to Damascus, about noon a great light from heaven suddenly shone about me. [7]And I fell to the ground and heard a voice saying to me, 'Saul, Saul, why do you persecute me?' [8]And I answered, 'Who are you, Lord?' And he said to me, 'I am Jesus of Nazareth whom you are persecuting.' [9]Now those who were with me saw the light but did not hear the voice of the one who was speaking to me. [10]And I said, 'What shall I do, Lord?' And the Lord said to me, 'Rise, and go into Damascus, and there you will be told all that is appointed for you to do.' [11]And when I could not see because of

πάντες ὑμεῖς ἐστε σήμερον· **4** ὃς ταύτην
all ye are to-day; who this

τὴν ὁδὸν ἐδίωξα ἄχρι θανάτου, δεσμεύων
- way persecuted as far as to death, binding

καὶ παραδιδοὺς εἰς φυλακὰς ἄνδρας τε
and delivering to prisons both men

καὶ γυναῖκας. **5** ὡς καὶ ὁ ἀρχιερεὺς
and women. As even the high priest

μαρτυρεῖ μοι καὶ πᾶν τὸ πρεσβυτέριον·
witnesses to me and all the senate;

παρ' ὧν καὶ ἐπιστολὰς δεξάμενος πρὸς
from whom also letters having received to

τοὺς ἀδελφοὺς εἰς Δαμασκὸν ἐπορευόμην,
the brothers in Damascus I journeyed,

ἄξων καὶ τοὺς ἐκεῖσε ὄντας δεδεμένους
leading also the [ones] [2]there [1]being *having been* bound

εἰς Ἰερουσαλὴμ ἵνα τιμωρηθῶσιν.
to Jerusalem that they might be punished.

6 Ἐγένετο δέ μοι πορευομένῳ καὶ ἐγγίζοντι
Now it happened to me journeying and drawing near

τῇ Δαμασκῷ περὶ μεσημβρίαν ἐξαίφνης ἐκ
- to Damascus about midday suddenly out of

τοῦ οὐρανοῦ περιαστράψαι φῶς ἱκανὸν
- heaven [4]to shine *round* [1]a [3]light [2]considerable

περὶ ἐμέ, **7** ἔπεσά τε εἰς τὸ ἔδαφος
round me, and I fell to the ground

καὶ ἤκουσα φωνῆς λεγούσης μοι· Σαοὺλ
and heard a voice saying to me: Saul[,]

Σαούλ, τί με διώκεις; **8** ἐγὼ δὲ ἀπεκρίθην·
Saul, why me persecutest thou? And I answered:

τίς εἶ, κύριε; εἶπέν τε πρὸς ἐμέ· ἐγώ
Who art thou, Lord? And he said to me: I

εἰμι Ἰησοῦς ὁ Ναζωραῖος, ὃν σὺ διώκεις.
am Jesus the Nazarene, whom thou persecutest.

9 οἱ δὲ σὺν ἐμοὶ ὄντες τὸ μὲν φῶς
Now [1]the [ones] [3]with [4]me [2]being [7]the [6]indeed [5]light

ἐθεάσαντο, τὴν δὲ φωνὴν οὐκ ἤκουσαν
[8]beheld, but the voice they heard not

τοῦ λαλοῦντός μοι. **10** εἶπον δέ· τί
of the [one] speaking to me. And I said: What

ποιήσω, κύριε; ὁ δὲ κύριος εἶπεν πρός
may I do, Lord? And the Lord said to

με· ἀναστὰς πορεύου εἰς Δαμασκόν, κἀκεῖ σοι
me: Rising up go into Damascus, and there to thee

λαληθήσεται περὶ πάντων ὧν τέτακταί
it will be told concerning all things which has(ve) been arranged

σοι ποιῆσαι. **11** ὡς δὲ οὐκ ἐνέβλεπον
for thee to do. And as I saw not

the brightness of that light, I was led by the hand by those who were with me, and came into Damascus.

12 "And one Anani'as, a devout man according to the law, well spoken of by all the Jews who lived there, [13]came to me, and standing by me said to me, 'Brother Saul, receive your sight.' And in that very hour I received my sight and saw him. [14]And he said, 'The God of our fathers appointed you to know his will, to see the Just One and to hear a voice from his mouth; [15]for you will be a witness for him to all men of what you have seen and heard. [16]And now why do you wait? Rise and be baptized, and wash away your sins, calling on his name.'

17 "When I had returned to Jerusalem and was praying in the temple, I fell into a trance [18]and saw him saying to me, 'Make haste and get quickly out of Jerusalem, because they will not accept your testimony about me.' [19]And I said, 'Lord, they

ἀπὸ τῆς δόξης τοῦ φωτὸς ἐκείνου,
from the glory of that light,

χειραγωγούμενος · ὑπὸ τῶν συνόντων μοι
being led by the hand by the [ones] being with me

ἦλθον εἰς Δαμασκόν. 12 Ἀνανίας δέ τις,
I went into Damascus.   And a certain Ananias,

ἀνὴρ εὐλαβὴς κατὰ τὸν νόμον, μαρτυρού-
a man devout according to the law, being witnessed

μενος ὑπὸ πάντων τῶν κατοικούντων
[to] by all ¹the ³dwelling ⁴[there]

Ἰουδαίων, 13 ἐλθὼν πρὸς ἐμὲ καὶ ἐπιστὰς
²Jews,   coming to me and standing by

εἶπέν μοι· Σαοὺλ ἀδελφέ, ἀνάβλεψον.
said to me: Saul brother, look up.

κἀγὼ αὐτῇ τῇ ὥρᾳ ἀνέβλεψα εἰς αὐτόν.
And I in that hour* looked up at him.

14 ὁ δὲ εἶπεν· ὁ θεὸς τῶν πατέρων
And he said: The God of the fathers

ἡμῶν προεχειρίσατό σε γνῶναι τὸ θέλημα
of us previously appointed thee to know the will

αὐτοῦ καὶ ἰδεῖν τὸν δίκαιον καὶ ἀκοῦσαι
of him and to see the Just One and to hear

φωνὴν ἐκ τοῦ στόματος αὐτοῦ, 15 ὅτι
a voice out of the mouth of him, because

ἔσῃ μάρτυς αὐτῷ πρὸς πάντας ἀνθρώπους
thou wilt be a witness to himᵉ to all men

ὧν ἑώρακας καὶ ἤκουσας. 16 καὶ νῦν
of things which thou hast seen and didst hear.   And now

τί μέλλεις; ἀναστὰς βάπτισαι καὶ ἀπόλου-
what intendest thou? Rising up be baptized and wash

σαι τὰς ἁμαρτίας σου, ἐπικαλεσάμενος τὸ
away the sins of thee, invoking the

ὄνομα αὐτοῦ. 17 Ἐγένετο δέ μοι ὑποστρέ-
name of him.   And it happened to me having

ψαντι εἰς Ἰερουσαλὴμ καὶ προσευχομένου
returned to Jerusalem and praying
                                    =as I was praying

μου ἐν τῷ ἱερῷ γενέσθαι με ἐν ἐκστάσει,
meᵃ in the temple to become meᵇ in an ecstasy,
                                    =I became

18 καὶ ἰδεῖν αὐτὸν λέγοντά μοι· σπεῦσον
and to seeᵇ him saying to me; Haste
=I saw

καὶ ἔξελθε ἐν τάχει ἐξ Ἰερουσαλήμ,
and go forth quickly out of Jerusalem,

διότι οὐ παραδέξονταί σου μαρτυρίαν
because they will not receive of thee witness

περὶ ἐμοῦ. 19 κἀγὼ εἶπον· κύριε, αὐτοὶ
concerning me.   And I said: Lord, they

* See Luke 2. 38.

themselves know that in
every synagogue I im-
prisoned and beat those
who believed in thee.
²⁰And when the blood of
Stephen thy witness was
shed, I also was standing
by and approving, and
keeping the garments of
those who killed him.'
²¹And he said to me,
'Depart; for I will send
you far away to the
Gentiles.' "

22 Up to this word
they listened to ·him;
then they lifted up their
voices and said, "Away
with such a fellow from
the earth! For he ought
not to live." ²³And as
they cried out and waved
their garments and threw
dust into the air, ²⁴the
tribune commanded him
to be brought into the
barracks, and ordered
him to be examined by
scourging, to find out
why they shouted thus
against him. ²⁵But when
they had tied him up with
the thongs, Paul said to
the centurion who was
standing by, "Is it lawful
for you to scourge a man
who is a Roman citizen,
and uncondemned?"
²⁶When the centurion
heard that, he went to
the tribune and said to

ἐπίστανται ὅτι ἐγὼ ἤμην φυλακίζων καὶ
understand that I was imprisoning and

δέρων κατὰ τὰς συναγωγὰς τοὺς πιστεύον-
beating throughout the synagogues the [ones] believ-

τας ἐπὶ σέ· 20 καὶ ὅτε ἐξεχύννετο τὸ αἷμα
ing on thee; and when was being shed the blood

Στεφάνου τοῦ μάρτυρός σου, καὶ αὐτὸς
of Stephen the witness of thee, even [my]self

ἤμην ἐφεστὼς καὶ συνευδοκῶν καὶ
I was standing by and consenting and

φυλάσσων τὰ ἱμάτια τῶν ἀναιρούντων
keeping the garments of the [ones] killing

αὐτόν. 21 καὶ εἶπεν πρός με· πορεύου,
him. And he said to me: Go,

ὅτι ἐγὼ εἰς ἔθνη μακρὰν ἐξαποστελῶ σε.
because I to nations afar will send forth thee.

22 Ἤκουον δὲ αὐτοῦ ἄχρι τούτου τοῦ
And they heard him as far as to this —

λόγου, καὶ ἐπῆραν τὴν φωνὴν αὐτῶν
word, and lifted up the voice of them

λέγοντες· αἶρε ἀπὸ τῆς γῆς τὸν τοιοῦτον·
saying: Take from the earth such a man;

οὐ γὰρ καθῆκεν αὐτὸν ζῆν. 23 κραυγαζόν-
for not it is fitting him to live. And shout-

των τε αὐτῶν καὶ ῥιπτούντων τὰ ἱμάτια
ing them and tearing[a] the(ir) garments
=as they shouted and tore . . .

καὶ κονιορτὸν βαλλόντων εἰς τὸν ἀέρα,
and ²dust ¹throwing[a] in the air,
=threw dust

24 ἐκέλευσεν ὁ χιλίαρχος εἰσάγεσθαι αὐτὸν
commanded the chiliarch to be brought in him

εἰς τὴν παρεμβολήν, εἴπας μάστιξιν
into the fort, bidding ³with scourges

ἀνετάζεσθαι αὐτόν, ἵνα ἐπιγνῷ δι' ἣν
²to be examined ¹him, that he might fully know for what

αἰτίαν οὕτως ἐπεφώνουν αὐτῷ. 25 ὡς δὲ
crime thus they were calling against him. But as

προέτειναν αὐτὸν τοῖς ἱμᾶσιν, εἶπεν πρὸς
they stretched him with the thongs, ²said ³to
forward

τὸν ἑστῶτα ἑκατόνταρχον ὁ Παῦλος· εἰ
⁴the ⁵standing [by] ⁵centurion — ¹Paul: ¹If

ἄνθρωπον Ῥωμαῖον καὶ ἀκατάκριτον ἔξεστιν
a man ³a Roman ⁶and ⁷uncondemned ²it is lawful

ὑμῖν μαστίζειν; 26 ἀκούσας δὲ ὁ ἑκατον-
⁵for you ⁴to scourge? And ³hearing ¹the ²cen-

τάρχης προσελθὼν τῷ χιλιάρχῳ ἀπήγγειλεν
turion approaching to the chiliarch reported

him, "What are you about to do? For this man is a Roman citizen." [27] So the tribune came and said to him, "Tell me, are you a Roman citizen?" And he said, "Yes." [28] The tribune answered, "I bought this citizenship for a large sum." Paul said, "But I was born a citizen." [29] So those who were about to examine him withdrew from him instantly; and the tribune also was afraid, for he realized that Paul was a Roman citizen and that he had bound him.

[30] But on the morrow, desiring to know the real reason why the Jews accused him, he unbound him, and commanded the chief priests and all the council to meet, and he brought Paul down and set him before them.

CHAPTER 23

AND Paul, looking intently at the council, said, "Brethren, I have lived before God in all good conscience up to this day." [2] And the high priest Anani'as commanded those who stood by him to strike him on the mouth. [3] Then Paul

λέγων· τί μέλλεις ποιεῖν; ὁ γὰρ ἄνθρωπος
saying: What art thou about to do? – for ²man

οὗτος Ῥωμαῖός ἐστιν. 27 προσελθὼν δὲ
¹this ⁴a Roman ³is. And approaching

ὁ χιλίαρχος εἶπεν αὐτῷ· λέγε μοι, σὺ
the chiliarch said to him: Tell me, thou

Ῥωμαῖος εἶ; ὁ δὲ ἔφη· ναί. 28 ἀπεκρίθη
a Roman art? And he said: Yes. answered

δὲ ὁ χιλίαρχος· ἐγὼ πολλοῦ κεφαλαίου
And the chiliarch: ¹I ⁵sum [of money] much(great)

τὴν πολιτείαν ταύτην ἐκτησάμην. ὁ δὲ
³this ⁴citizenship ²acquired. – So

Παῦλος ἔφη· ἐγὼ δὲ καὶ γεγέννημαι.
Paul said: But I indeed have been born.

29 εὐθέως οὖν ἀπέστησαν ἀπ' αὐτοῦ οἱ
Immediately therefore ⁵stood away ⁶from ⁷him ¹the [ones]

μέλλοντες αὐτὸν ἀνετάζειν· καὶ ὁ χιλίαρχος
²being about ⁴him ³to examine; ⁴also ²the ³chiliarch

δὲ ἐφοβήθη ἐπιγνοὺς ὅτι Ῥωμαῖός ἐστιν
¹and feared fully knowing that a Roman he is(was)

καὶ ὅτι αὐτὸν ἦν δεδεκώς.
and that ³him ¹he was ²having bound.

30 Τῇ δὲ ἐπαύριον βουλόμενος γνῶναι τὸ
And on the morrow being minded to know the

ἀσφαλές, τὸ τί κατηγορεῖται ὑπὸ τῶν
certain thing, – why he was accused by the

Ἰουδαίων, ἔλυσεν αὐτόν, καὶ ἐκέλευσεν
Jews, he released him, and commanded

συνελθεῖν τοὺς ἀρχιερεῖς καὶ πᾶν τὸ
to come together the chief priests and all the

συνέδριον, καὶ καταγαγὼν τὸν Παῦλον
council, and having brought down Paul

ἔστησεν εἰς αὐτούς. 23 ἀτενίσας δὲ
set [him] among them. And ²gazing

ὁ Παῦλος τῷ συνεδρίῳ εἶπεν· ἄνδρες
– ¹Paul at the council said: Men

ἀδελφοί, ἐγὼ πάσῃ συνειδήσει ἀγαθῇ
brothers, I in all conscience good

πεπολίτευμαι τῷ θεῷ ἄχρι ταύτης τῆς
have lived – to God until this –

ἡμέρας. 2 ὁ δὲ ἀρχιερεὺς Ἁνανίας
day. And the high priest Ananias

ἐπέταξεν τοῖς παρεστῶσιν αὐτῷ τύπτειν
gave order to the [ones] standing by him to strike

αὐτοῦ τὸ στόμα. 3 τότε ὁ Παῦλος πρὸς
of him the mouth. Then – Paul to

said to him, "God shall strike you, you white-washed wall! Are you sitting to judge me according to the law, and yet contrary to the law you order me to be struck?" ⁴Those who stood by said, "Would you revile God's high priest?" ⁵And Paul said, "I did not know, brethren, that he was the high priest; for it is written, 'You shall not speak evil of a ruler of your people.'"

6 But when Paul perceived that one part were Sad'ducees and the other Pharisees, he cried out in the council, "Brethren, I am a Pharisee, a son of Pharisees; with respect to the hope and the resurrection of the dead I am on trial." ⁷And when he had said this, a dissension arose between the Pharisees and the Sad'ducees; and the assembly was divided. ⁸For the Sad'ducees say that there is no resurrection, nor angel, nor spirit; but the Pharisees acknowledge them all. ⁹Then a great clamor arose; and some of the scribes of the Pharisees' party stood up and contended, "We find nothing wrong in this man. What if a spirit or an angel

αὐτὸν εἶπεν· τύπτειν σε μέλλει ὁ θεός,
him   said: ³To strike ⁴thee ²is about – ¹God,

τοῖχε κεκονιαμένε· καὶ σὺ κάθη κρίνων
wall having been whitened; and thou sittest judging

με κατὰ τὸν νόμον, καὶ παρανομῶν
me according to the law, and contravening law

κελεύεις με τύπτεσθαι; 4 οἱ δὲ παρεστῶτες
commandest me to be struck? And the [ones] standing by

εἶπαν· τὸν ἀρχιερέα τοῦ θεοῦ λοιδορεῖς;
said: The high priest – of God revilest thou?

5 ἔφη τε ὁ Παῦλος· οὐκ ᾔδειν, ἀδελφοί,
And said – Paul: I did not know, brothers,

ὅτι ἐστὶν ἀρχιερεύς· γέγραπται γὰρ ὅτι
that he is high priest; for it has been written[,] –

ἄρχοντα τοῦ λαοῦ σου οὐκ ἐρεῖς κακῶς.
A ruler of the people of thee thou shalt not speak evilly.

6 γνοὺς δὲ ὁ Παῦλος ὅτι τὸ ἓν μέρος
And knowing – Paul that the one part

ἐστὶν Σαδδουκαίων τὸ δὲ ἕτερον Φαρισαίων
is(was) of Sadducees but the other of Pharisees

ἔκραζεν ἐν τῷ συνεδρίῳ· ἄνδρες ἀδελφοί,
cried out in the council: Men brothers,

ἐγὼ Φαρισαῖός εἰμι, υἱὸς Φαρισαίων· περὶ
I a Pharisee am, a son of Pharisees; concerning

ἐλπίδος καὶ ἀναστάσεως νεκρῶν κρίνομαι.
hope and resurrection of dead ones I am being judged.

7 τοῦτο δὲ αὐτοῦ λαλοῦντος ἐγένετο
And this him saying^a there was
=as he said this

στάσις τῶν Φαρισαίων καὶ Σαδδουκαίων,
a discord of the Pharisees and Sadducees,

καὶ ἐσχίσθη τὸ πλῆθος. 8 Σαδδουκαῖοι
and was divided the multitude. Sadducees

γὰρ λέγουσιν μὴ εἶναι ἀνάστασιν μήτε
For say not to be a resurrection nor

ἄγγελον μήτε πνεῦμα, Φαρισαῖοι δὲ
angel nor spirit, but Pharisees

ὁμολογοῦσιν τὰ ἀμφότερα. 9 ἐγένετο δὲ
confess – both. And there was

κραυγὴ μεγάλη, καὶ ἀναστάντες τινὲς
cry a great, and rising up some

τῶν γραμματέων τοῦ μέρους τῶν Φαρισαίων
of the scribes of the part of the Pharisees

διεμάχοντο λέγοντες· οὐδὲν κακὸν εὑρίσκομεν
strove saying: Nothing evil we find

ἐν τῷ ἀνθρώπῳ τούτῳ· εἰ δὲ πνεῦμα
in the this man; and if ¹a spirit

spoke to him?" [10]And when the dissension became violent, the tribune, afraid that Paul would be torn in pieces by them, commanded the soldiers to go down and take him by force from among them and bring him into the barracks.

11 The following night the Lord stood by him and said, "Take courage, for as you have testified about me at Jerusalem, so you must bear witness also at Rome."

12 When it was day, the Jews made a plot and bound themselves by an oath neither to eat nor drink till they had killed Paul. [13]There were more than forty who made this conspiracy. [14]And they went to the chief priests and elders, and said, "We have strictly bound ourselves by an oath to taste no food till we have killed Paul. [15]You therefore, along with the council, give notice now to the tribune to bring him down to you, as though you were going to determine his case more exactly. And we are

ἐλάλησεν   αὐτῷ   ἢ   ἄγγελος —. 10 Πολλῆς δὲ
⁴spoke   ⁵to him ²or   ³an angel —.   And much

γινομένης   στάσεως   φοβηθεὶς   ὁ   χιλίαρχος
arising   discord³   ³fearing   ¹the ²chiliarch
=when much³ discord arose

μὴ   διασπασθῇ   ὁ   Παῦλος   ὑπ'   αὐτῶν,
⁴lest   ⁶should be   -   ⁵Paul   by   them,
        torn asunder

ἐκέλευσεν   τὸ   στράτευμα   καταβὰν   ἁρπάσαι
commanded   the   soldiery   coming down   to seize

αὐτὸν   ἐκ   μέσου   αὐτῶν   ἄγειν   τε   εἰς
him   out of [the] midst   of them   and to bring [him] into

τὴν   παρεμβολήν.   11 Τῇ   δὲ   ἐπιούσῃ
the   fort.   And in the   following

νυκτὶ   ἐπιστὰς   αὐτῷ   ὁ   κύριος   εἶπεν·
night   ²coming on   ⁴to him   ¹the ²Lord   said:

θάρσει·   ὡς   γὰρ   διεμαρτύρω   τὰ   περὶ
Be of good   for as   thou didst   the concerning
courage;   solemnly witness   things

ἐμοῦ   εἰς   Ἰερουσαλήμ,   οὕτω   σε   δεῖ   καὶ
me   in   Jerusalem,   so   thee it behoves also

εἰς   Ῥώμην   μαρτυρῆσαι.   12 Γενομένης   δὲ
in   Rome   to witness.   And becoming

ἡμέρας   ποιήσαντες   συστροφὴν   οἱ   Ἰουδαῖοι
day³   ³making   ⁴a conspiracy   ¹the   ²Jews
=when it became day

ἀνεθεμάτισαν   ἑαυτούς,   λέγοντες   μήτε   φαγεῖν
cursed   themselves,   saying   neither   to eat

μήτε   πεῖν   ἕως   οὗ   ἀποκτείνωσιν   τὸν
nor   to drink   until   they should kill   -

Παῦλον.   13 ἦσαν   δὲ   πλείους   τεσσεράκοντα
Paul.   And there were   more [than]   forty

οἱ   ταύτην   τὴν   συνωμοσίαν   ποιησάμενοι·
the [ones]   this   -   plot   making;

14 οἵτινες   προσελθόντες   τοῖς   ἀρχιερεῦσιν
who   approaching   to the   chief priests

καὶ   τοῖς   πρεσβυτέροις   εἶπαν·   ἀναθέματι
and   to the   elders   said: With a curse

ἀνεθεματίσαμεν   ἑαυτοὺς   μηδενὸς   γεύσασθαι
we cursed   ourselves   of nothing   to taste

ἕως   οὗ   ἀποκτείνωμεν   τὸν   Παῦλον.   15 νῦν
until   we may kill   -   Paul.   Now

οὖν   ὑμεῖς   ἐμφανίσατε   τῷ   χιλιάρχῳ   σὺν
therefore ²ye   ¹inform   the   chiliarch   with

τῷ   συνεδρίῳ   ὅπως   καταγάγῃ   αὐτὸι   εἰς
the   council   so as   he may bring down   him   to

ὑμᾶς   ὡς   μέλλοντας   διαγινώσκειν   ἀκριβέστε-
you   as   intending   to ascertain exactly   more accurate-

ρον   τὰ   περὶ   αὐτοῦ·   ἡμεῖς   δὲ   πρὸ   τοῦ
ly the things concerning him;   and we   before   -

ready to kill him before he comes near."

16 Now the son of Paul's sister heard of their ambush; so he went and entered the barracks and told Paul. [17]And Paul called one of the centurions and said, "Bring this young man to the tribune; for he has something to tell him." [18]So he took him and brought him to the tribune and said, "Paul the prisoner called me and asked me to bring this young man to you, as he has something to say to you." [19]The tribune took him by the hand, and going aside asked him privately, "What is it that you have to tell me?" [20]And he said, "The Jews have agreed to ask you to bring Paul down to the council tomorrow, as though they were going to inquire somewhat more closely about him. [21]But do not yield to them; for more than forty of their men lie in ambush for him, having bound themselves by an oath neither to eat

ἐγγίσαι αὐτὸν ἔτοιμοί ἐσμεν τοῦ ἀνελεῖν
to draw near him[b] ready are – to kill[d]
= he draws near

αὐτόν. 16 Ἀκούσας δὲ ὁ υἱὸς τῆς ἀδελφῆς
him. And [6]hearing [1]the [2]son [3]of the [4]sister

Παύλου τὴν ἐνέδραν, παραγενόμενος καὶ
[5]of Paul the treachery, coming and

εἰσελθὼν εἰς τὴν παρεμβολὴν ἀπήγγειλεν
entering into the fort reported

τῷ Παύλῳ. 17 προσκαλεσάμενος δὲ ὁ
– to Paul. And [2]calling to [him] –

Παῦλος ἕνα τῶν ἑκατονταρχῶν ἔφη· τὸν
[1]Paul one of the centurions said: the

νεανίαν τοῦτον ἄπαγε πρὸς τὸν χιλίαρχον,
[3]youth [2]this [1]Bring up to the chiliarch,

ἔχει γὰρ ἀπαγγεῖλαί τι αὐτῷ. 18 ὁ
for [1]he has [3]to report [2]something [4]to him. He

μὲν οὖν παραλαβὼν αὐτὸν ἤγαγεν πρὸς
– therefore taking [2]him [1]brought to

τὸν χιλίαρχον καὶ φησίν· ὁ δέσμιος
the chiliarch and says: The prisoner

Παῦλος προσκαλεσάμενός με ἠρώτησεν
Paul calling to [him] me asked

τοῦτον τὸν νεανίσκον ἀγαγεῖν πρὸς σέ,
[2]this – [3]young man [1]to bring to thee,

ἔχοντά τι λαλῆσαί σοι. 19 ἐπιλαβόμενος
having something to tell thee. [2]laying hold

δὲ τῆς χειρὸς αὐτοῦ ὁ χιλίαρχος καὶ
And [4]of the [3]hand [5]of him [1]the [1]chiliarch and

ἀναχωρήσας κατ᾿ ἰδίαν ἐπυνθάνετο· τί
retiring [2]privately [1]inquired: What

ἐστιν ὃ ἔχεις ἀπαγγεῖλαί μοι; 20 εἶπεν
is it which thou hast to report to me? he said[,]

δὲ ὅτι οἱ Ἰουδαῖοι συνέθεντο τοῦ ἐρωτῆσαί
And – The Jews agreed – to ask[d]

σε ὅπως αὔριον τὸν Παῦλον καταγάγῃς
thee so as to-morrow – [2]Paul [1]thou shouldest
bring down

εἰς τὸ συνέδριον ὡς μέλλον τι ἀκριβέστερον
to the council as intending some- more accurately
thing

πυνθάνεσθαι περὶ αὐτοῦ. 21 σὺ οὖν μὴ
to inquire concerning him. Thou therefore not

πεισθῇς αὐτοῖς· ἐνεδρεύουσιν γὰρ αὐτὸν
be persuaded by them; for there lie in wait for him

ἐξ αὐτῶν ἄνδρες πλείους τεσσεράκοντα,
of them [4]men [1]more [2][than] [3]forty,

οἵτινες ἀνεθεμάτισαν ἑαυτοὺς μήτε φαγεῖν
who cursed themselves neither to eat

nor drink till they have killed him; and now they are ready, waiting for the promise from you." 22 So the tribune dismissed the young man, charging him, "Tell no one that you have informed me of this."

23 Then he called two of the centurions and said, "At the third hour of the night get ready two hundred soldiers with seventy horsemen and two hundred spearmen to go as far as Caesare'a. 24 Also provide mounts for Paul to ride, and bring him safely to Felix the governor." 25 And he wrote a letter to this effect:

26 "Claudius Lys'ias to his Excellency the governor Felix, greeting. 27 This man was seized by the Jews, and was about to be killed by them, when I came upon them with the soldiers and rescued him, having learned that he was a Roman citizen. 28 And desiring to know the charge on which they accused him, I brought him down to their council. 29 I found that he was accused about questions of their law,

μήτε πεῖν ἕως οὗ ἀνέλωσιν αὐτόν, καὶ νῦν
nor to drink until they kill him, and now

εἰσιν ἕτοιμοι προσδεχόμενοι τὴν ἀπὸ σοῦ
they are ¹ready awaiting ¹the ²from ⁴thee

ἐπαγγελίαν. 22 ὁ μὲν οὖν χιλίαρχος
²promise. the – Therefore chiliarch

ἀπέλυσε τὸν νεανίσκον, παραγγείλας μηδενὶ
dismissed the young man, charging [him] to no one

ἐκλαλῆσαι ὅτι ταῦτα ἐνεφάνισας πρὸς ἐμέ.
to divulge that these things thou reportedst to me.

23 Καὶ προσκαλεσάμενός τινας δύο τῶν
And calling to [him] a certain two of the

ἑκατονταρχῶν εἶπεν· ἑτοιμάσατε στρατιώτας
centurions he said: Prepare ye soldiers

διακοσίους ὅπως πορευθῶσιν ἕως Καισαρείας,
two hundred so as they may go as far as Cæsarea,

καὶ ἱππεῖς ἑβδομήκοντα καὶ δεξιολάβους
and horsemen seventy and spearmen

διακοσίους, ἀπὸ τρίτης ὥρας τῆς νυκτός,
two hundred, from third hour of the night,

24 κτήνη τε παραστῆσαι, ἵνα ἐπιβιβάσαντες
and beasts to stand by, that putting on

τὸν Παῦλον διασώσωσι πρὸς Φήλικα τὸν
– Paul they may bring to Felix the
[him] safely

ἡγεμόνα, 25 γράψας ἐπιστολὴν ἔχουσαν
governor, writing a letter having

τὸν τύπον τοῦτον· 26 Κλαύδιος Λυσίας τῷ
this pattern: Claudius Lysias to the

κρατίστῳ ἡγεμόνι Φήλικι χαίρειν. 27 Τὸν
most excellent governor Felix greeting. –

ἄνδρα τοῦτον συλλημφθέντα ὑπὸ τῶν
man This having been arrested by the

Ἰουδαίων καὶ μέλλοντα ἀναιρεῖσθαι ὑπ'
Jews and being about to be killed by

αὐτῶν ἐπιστὰς σὺν τῷ στρατεύματι
them coming on with the soldiery
[the scene]

ἐξειλάμην, μαθὼν ὅτι Ῥωμαῖός ἐστιν·
I rescued, having learned that a Roman he is;

28 βουλόμενός τε ἐπιγνῶναι τὴν αἰτίαν
and being minded to know fully the cause

δι' ἣν ἐνεκάλουν αὐτῷ, κατήγαγον εἰς
on ac- which they were him, I brought to
count of accusing [him] down

τὸ συνέδριον αὐτῶν· 29 ὃν εὗρον ἐγκαλούμενον
the council of them; whom I found being accused

περὶ ζητημάτων τοῦ νόμου αὐτῶν, μηδὲν
about questions of the law of them, ³nothing

but charged with nothing
deserving death or im-
prisonment. ³⁰And when
it was disclosed to me
that there would be a
plot against the man, I
sent him to you at once,
ordering his accusers also
to state before you what
they have against him."

31 So the soldiers,
according to their in-
structions, took Paul and
brought him by night to
Antip′atris. ³²And on the
morrow they returned to
the barracks, leaving the
horsemen to go on with
him. ³³When they came
to Caesare′a and de-
livered the letter to the
governor, they presented
Paul also before him.
³⁴On reading the letter,
he asked to what
province he belonged.
When he learned that he
was from Cili′cia ³⁵he
said, "I will hear you
when your accusers
arrive." And he com-
manded him to be
guarded in Herod's
praetorium.

δὲ   ἄξιον   θανάτου   ἢ   δεσμῶν   ἔχοντα
¹but   ⁵worthy   ⁶of death   ⁷or   ⁸of bonds   ³having

ἔγκλημα.   30 μηνυθείσης   δὲ   μοι   ἐπιβουλῆς
⁴charge.   And being revealed   to me   a plot⁸
                =when it was revealed to me that there was a plot

εἰς   τὸν   ἄνδρα   ἔσεσθαι,   ἐξαυτῆς   ἔπεμψα
against the   man   to be,   at once   I sent

πρὸς   σέ,   παραγγείλας   καὶ   τοῖς   κατηγόροις
to   thee,   commanding   also   the   accusers

λέγειν   πρὸς   αὐτὸν   ἐπὶ   σοῦ.   31 Οἱ   μὲν
to say   to   him   before   thee.   the   –

οὖν   στρατιῶται   κατὰ   τὸ   διατεταγμένον
Therefore   soldiers   according   the   having been
                to   thing   appointed

αὐτοῖς   ἀναλαβόντες   τὸν   Παῦλον   ἤγαγον
them   taking up   –   Paul   brought

διὰ   νυκτὸς   εἰς   τὴν   Ἀντιπατρίδα·   32 τῇ   δὲ
through [the] night   to   –   Antipatris;   and on the
(during)

ἐπαύριον   ἐάσαντες   τοὺς   ἱππεῖς   ἀπέρχεσθαι
morrow   allowing   the   horsemen   to depart

σὺν   αὐτῷ,   ὑπέστρεψαν   εἰς   τὴν   παρεμβολήν·
with   him,   they returned   to   the   fort;

33 οἵτινες   εἰσελθόντες   εἰς   τὴν   Καισάρειαν
who   entering   into   –   Caesarea

καὶ   ἀναδόντες   τὴν   ἐπιστολὴν   τῷ   ἡγεμόνι,
and   handing over   the   letter   to the   governor,

παρέστησαν   καὶ   τὸν   Παῦλον   αὐτῷ.
presented   also   –   Paul   to him.

34 ἀναγνοὺς   δὲ   καὶ   ἐπερωτήσας   ἐκ   ποίας
And having read   and   asking   of   what

ἐπαρχείας   ἐστίν,   καὶ   πυθόμενος   ὅτι   ἀπὸ
province   he is(was),   and   learning[,]   –   From

Κιλικίας,   35 διακούσομαί   σου,   ἔφη,   ὅταν
Cilicia,   I will hear   thee,   he said,   when

καὶ   οἱ   κατήγοροί   σου   παραγένωνται·
also   the   accusers   of thee   arrive;

κελεύσας   ἐν   τῷ   πραιτωρίῳ   τοῦ   Ἡρώδου
commanding   in   the   prætorium   –   of Herod
                =that he be kept in Herod's prætorium.

φυλάσσεσθαι   αὐτόν.
to be kept   him.

CHAPTER 24

AND after five days
the high priest
Anani′as came down with
some elders and a spokes-
man, one Tertul′lus.

24 Μετὰ   δὲ   πέντε   ἡμέρας   κατέβη   ὁ
And after   five   days   came down   the

ἀρχιερεὺς   Ἀνανίας   μετὰ   πρεσβυτέρων   τινῶν
high priest   Ananias   with   elders   some

καὶ   ῥήτορος   Τερτύλλου   τινός,   οἵτινες
and   an orator   Tertullus   one,   who

They laid before the governor their case against Paul; [2]and when he was called, Tertul'lus began to accuse him, saying:

"Since through you we enjoy much peace, and since by your provision, most excellent Felix, reforms are introduced on behalf of this nation, [3]in every way and everywhere we accept this with all gratitude. [4]But, to detain you no further, I beg you in your kindness to hear us briefly. [5]For we have found this man a pestilent fellow, an agitator among all the Jews throughout the world, and a ringleader of the sect of the Nazarenes. [6]He even tried to profane the temple, but we seized him.ᵘ [8]By examining him yourself you will be able to learn from him about everything of which we accuse him."

9 The Jews also joined in the charge, affirming that all this was so.

10 And when the governor had motioned to him to speak, Paul replied:

"Realizing that for many years you have been judge over this

ᵘ Other ancient authorities add *and we would have judged him according to our law.* [7]*But the chief captain Lysias came and with great violence took him out of our hands,* [8]*commanding his accusers to come before you.*

ἐνεφάνισαν τῷ ἡγεμόνι κατὰ τοῦ Παύλου.
informed　the　governor　against　-　Paul.

2 κληθέντος δὲ [αὐτοῦ] ἤρξατο κατηγορεῖν
And being called　himᵃ　　²began　³to accuse
=when he was called

ὁ Τέρτυλλος λέγων· πολλῆς εἰρήνης
-　¹Tertullus　saying:　Much　peace

τυγχάνοντες διὰ σοῦ καὶ διορθωμάτων
obtaining　through thee　and　reforms

γινομένων τῷ ἔθνει τούτῳ διὰ τῆς σῆς
coming　to this nation　through　-　thy

προνοίας, 3 πάντη τε καὶ πανταχοῦ
forethought,　both in everything　and　everywhere

ἀποδεχόμεθα, κράτιστε Φῆλιξ, μετὰ πάσης
we welcome,　most excellent Felix,　with　all

εὐχαριστίας. 4 ἵνα δὲ μὴ ἐπὶ πλεῖόν
thankfulness.　But that　³not　⁴more

σε ἐγκόπτω, παρακαλῶ ἀκοῦσαί σε ἡμῶν
²thee　¹I hinder,　I beseech　²to hear　¹thee　us

συντόμως τῇ σῇ ἐπιεικείᾳ. 5 εὑρόντες γὰρ
briefly　-　in thy forbearance.　For having found

τὸν ἄνδρα τοῦτον λοιμὸν καὶ κινοῦντα
this man　pestilent　and　moving

στάσεις πᾶσιν τοῖς Ἰουδαίοις τοῖς κατὰ
seditions [among] all　the　Jews　-　throughout

τὴν οἰκουμένην πρωτοστάτην τε τῆς τῶν
the　inhabited [earth]　and a ringleader　of the　²of the

Ναζωραίων αἱρέσεως, 6 ὃς καὶ τὸ ἱερὸν
³Nazarenes　¹sect,　who also　³the　⁴temple

ἐπείρασεν βεβηλῶσαι, ὃν καὶ ἐκρατήσαμεν,
¹attempted　²to profane,　whom also　we laid hold of,‡

8 παρ' οὗ δυνήσῃ αὐτὸς ἀνακρίνας
from whom thou wilt be able [thy]self　²having examined

περὶ πάντων τούτων ἐπιγνῶναι ὧν ἡμεῖς
³concerning　⁴all　⁵these things　¹to know fully of which　we

κατηγοροῦμεν αὐτοῦ. 9 συνεπέθεντο δὲ
accuse　him.　And ⁴joined in

καὶ οἱ Ἰουδαῖοι ˙ φάσκοντες ταῦτα οὕτως
²also　¹the　³Jews　alleging　these things　thus

ἔχειν. 10 Ἀπεκρίθη τε ὁ Παῦλος,
to have(be).　And answered　-　Paul,

νεύσαντος αὐτῷ τοῦ ἡγεμόνος λέγειν· ἐκ
³having　⁴to him　¹the　²governorᵃ　to speak:　⁴of
beckoned　　　　　　　　　　　　　　　　　　　(for)

πολλῶν ἐτῶν ὄντα σε κριτὴν τῷ ἔθνει τούτῳ
⁵many　⁶years　³being　²thee　⁷a judge　⁸to ⁹this ¹⁰nation
　　　　　　　(to be)

‡ Verse 7 omitted by Nestle; *cf.* RSV footnote.

nation, I cheerfully make
my defense. ¹¹As you
may ascertain, it is not
more than twelve days
since I went up to wor-
ship at Jerusalem; ¹²and
they did not find me
disputing with any one
or stirring up a crowd,
either in the temple or in
the synagogues, or in the
city. ¹³Neither can they
prove to you what they
now bring up against me.
¹⁴But this I admit to
you, that according to
the Way, which they call
a sect, I worship the God
of our fathers, believing
everything laid down by
the law or written in the
prophets, ¹⁵having a hope
in God which these
themselves accept, that
there will be a resur-
rection of both the just
and the unjust. ¹⁶So I
always take pains to have
a clear conscience to-
ward God and toward
men. ¹⁷Now after some
years I came to bring to
my nation alms and
offerings. ¹⁸As I was

ἐπιστάμενος   εὐθύμως   τὰ   περὶ
¹understanding   ¹²cheerfully ¹³[as to] ¹⁴the things ¹⁵concerning

ἐμαυτοῦ   ἀπολογοῦμαι,   11 δυναμένου   σου
¹⁶myself   ¹¹I defend myself,   being able   thee ª
                                      = as thou art able

ἐπιγνῶναι ὅτι οὐ πλείους εἰσίν μοι ἡμέραι
to know fully that ³not ⁴more ¹there ²to ⁵[than] ⁷days
                                       are   me

δώδεκα   ἀφ'   ἧς   ἀνέβην   προσκυνήσων   εἰς
⁶twelve from which I went up worshipping   in
         = since

Ἰερουσαλήμ.   12 καὶ οὔτε ἐν τῷ ἱερῷ
Jerusalem.   And neither in the temple

εὑρόν με πρός τινα διαλεγόμενον ἢ
they found me ²with ³anyone ¹discoursing or

ἐπίστασιν   ποιοῦντα   ὄχλου, οὔτε ἐν ταῖς
²collection ¹making   of a crowd, neither in the

συναγωγαῖς οὔτε κατὰ τὴν πόλιν, 13 οὐδὲ
synagogues nor throughout the city,   nor

παραστῆσαι δύνανταί σοι περὶ ὧν νυνὶ
²to prove ¹are they able to thee con- [the] things now
                                   cerning of which

κατηγοροῦσίν μου.   14 ὁμολογῶ δὲ τοῦτο
they accuse   me.   But I confess this

σοι, ὅτι κατὰ τὴν ὁδὸν ἣν λέγουσιν
to thee, that according to the way which they say(call)

αἵρεσιν οὕτως λατρεύω τῷ πατρῴῳ θεῷ,
a sect   thus   I worship the ancestral God,

πιστεύων πᾶσι τοῖς κατὰ τὸν νόμον καὶ
believing   all   the according the law   and
                  things to

τοῖς ἐν τοῖς προφήταις γεγραμμένοις,
the things in the prophets   having been written,

15 ἐλπίδα ἔχων εἰς τὸν θεόν, ἣν καὶ
    hope   having toward -   God, which ²also

αὐτοὶ · οὗτοι προσδέχονται, ἀνάστασιν μέλ-
²[them]selves ¹these expect,   a resurrection to be

λειν ἔσεσθαι δικαίων τε καὶ ἀδίκων.
about   to be   both of just and   of unjust.

16 ἐν τούτῳ καὶ αὐτὸς ἀσκῶ ἀπρόσκοπον
    By this also ²[my]self ¹I exercise ⁴a blameless

συνείδησιν ἔχειν πρὸς τὸν θεὸν καὶ τοὺς
⁵conscience ³to have toward - God and -

ἀνθρώπους διὰ παντός.   17 δι' ἐτῶν δὲ
men   always.   And after years

πλειόνων ἐλεημοσύνας ποιήσων εἰς τὸ
many   ²alms   ¹making(bringing) ³to ⁴the

ἔθνος μου παρεγενόμην καὶ προσφοράς,
³nation ⁶of me ³I arrived   ⁷and ⁸offerings,

doing this, they found me purified in the temple, without any crowd or tumult. But some Jews from Asia—[19] they ought to be here before you and to make an accusation, if they have anything against me. [20] Or else let these men themselves say what wrongdoing they found when I stood before the council, [21] except this one thing which I cried out while standing among them, 'With respect to the resurrection of the dead I am on trial before you this day.'"

22 But Felix, having a rather accurate knowledge of the Way, put them off, saying, "When Lys'ias the tribune comes down, I will decide your case." [23] Then he gave orders to the centurion that he should be kept in custody but should have some liberty, and that none of his friends should be prevented from attending to his needs.

24 After some days Felix came with his wife Drusil'la, who was a Jewess; and he sent for Paul and heard him speak upon faith in Christ Jesus. [25] And as he argued

18 ἐν αἷς εὗρόν με ἡγνισμένον ἐν τῷ
among which they found me *having been* purified in the

ἱερῷ, οὐ μετὰ ὄχλου οὐδὲ μετὰ θορύβου,
temple, not with a crowd nor with uproar,

19 τινὲς δὲ ἀπὸ τῆς Ἀσίας Ἰουδαῖοι,
but some ³from – ²Asia ¹Jews,

οὓς ἔδει ἐπὶ σοῦ παρεῖναι καὶ κατηγορεῖν
whom it be- before thee to be present and to accuse
hoved

εἴ τι ἔχοιεν πρὸς ἐμέ. 20 ἢ αὐτοὶ
if anything they have against me. Or ³[them]selves

οὗτοι εἰπάτωσαν τί εὗρον ἀδίκημα στάντος
²these ¹let ⁴say ³what ⁵they found ⁶misdeed standing

μου ἐπὶ τοῦ συνεδρίου, 21 ἢ περὶ μιᾶς
me⁸ before the council, unless concerning ²one
=while I stood

ταύτης φωνῆς ἧς ἐκέκραξα ἐν αὐτοῖς
¹this voice which I have cried out ²among ³them

ἑστὼς ὅτι περὶ ἀναστάσεως νεκρῶν ἐγὼ
¹standing[.] – Concerning a resurrection of dead persons I

κρίνομαι σήμερον ἐφ᾽ ὑμῶν. 22 Ἀνεβάλετο
am being judged to-day before you. ²postponed

δὲ αὐτοὺς ὁ Φῆλιξ, ἀκριβέστερον εἰδὼς
And ³them – ¹Felix, more exactly knowing

τὰ περὶ τῆς ὁδοῦ, εἴπας· ὅταν Λυσίας ὁ
the con- the way, saying: When Lysias the
things cerning

χιλίαρχος καταβῇ, διαγνώσομαι τὰ καθ᾽
chiliarch comes down, I will determine the things as to

ὑμᾶς· 23 διαταξάμενος τῷ ἑκατοντάρχῃ
you; commanding the centurion

τηρεῖσθαι αὐτὸν ἔχειν τε ἄνεσιν καὶ
to keep him and to have indulgence and

μηδένα κωλύειν τῶν ἰδίων αὐτοῦ ὑπηρετεῖν
²no one ¹to forbid of his own [people] to attend

αὐτῷ. 24 Μετὰ δὲ ἡμέρας τινὰς παραγενό-
him. And after days some ²arriv-

μενος ὁ Φῆλιξ σὺν Δρουσίλλῃ τῇ ἰδίᾳ
ing – ¹Felix with Drusilla the(his) own

γυναικὶ οὔσῃ Ἰουδαίᾳ μετεπέμψατο τὸν
wife being a Jewess he sent for –

Παῦλον, καὶ ἤκουσεν αὐτοῦ περὶ τῆς
Paul, and heard him about ¹the(the?his)

εἰς Χριστὸν Ἰησοῦν πίστεως. 25 διαλεγομέ-
³in ⁴Christ ⁵Jesus ²faith. discours-
=And as he discoursed

νου δὲ αὐτοῦ περὶ δικαιοσύνης καὶ
ing And him⁸ concerning righteousness and

about justice and self-control and future judgment, Felix was alarmed and said, "Go away for the present; when I have an opportunity I will summon you." [26]At the same time he hoped that money would be given him by Paul. So he sent for him often and conversed with him. [27]But when two years had elapsed, Felix was succeeded by Porcius Festus; and desiring to do the Jews a favor, Felix left Paul in prison.

ἐγκρατείας   καὶ   τοῦ   κρίματος   τοῦ   μέλλοντος
self-control   and   the   ²judgment   –   ¹coming

ἔμφοβος   γενόμενος   ὁ   Φῆλιξ   ἀπεκρίθη·
afraid   becoming   –   Felix   answered:

τὸ   νῦν   ἔχον   πορεύου,   καιρὸν   δὲ   μεταλαβὼν
For the present†   go thou,   but ²time   ¹taking ³later

μετακαλέσομαί   σε·   26 ἅμα   καὶ   ἐλπίζων
I will send for   thee;   at the also   hoping
                        same time

ὅτι   χρήματα   δοθήσεται   αὐτῷ   ὑπὸ   τοῦ
that   money   will be given   him   by   –

Παύλου·   διὸ   καὶ   πυκνότερον   αὐτὸν
Paul: wherefore   also   more frequently   him

μεταπεμπόμενος   ὡμίλει   αὐτῷ. 27 Διετίας   δὲ
sending for   he conversed   him.   And two years
                with

πληρωθείσης   ἔλαβεν   διάδοχον   ὁ   Φῆλιξ
being completed²   ²received   ³a successor   –   ¹Felix

Πόρκιον   Φῆστον·   θέλων   τε   χάριτα   κατα-
Porcius   Festus;   and wishing   a favour   to

θέσθαι   τοῖς   Ἰουδαίοις   ὁ   Φῆλιξ   κατέλιπε
show   to the   Jews   –   Felix   left

τὸν   Παῦλον   δεδεμένον.
–   Paul   *having been* bound.

CHAPTER 25

NOW when Festus had come into his province, after three days he went up to Jerusalem from Caesare′a. [2]And the chief priests and the principal men of the Jews informed him against Paul; and they urged him, [3]asking as a favor to have the man sent to Jerusalem, planning an ambush to kill him on the way. [4]Festus replied that Paul was being kept at Caesare′a, and that he himself intended to go there shortly. [5]"So," said he, "let the men of

25 Φῆστος   οὖν   ἐπιβὰς   τῇ   ἐπαρχείῳ
Festus   therefore   having entered   the   province

μετὰ   τρεῖς   ἡμέρας   ἀνέβη   εἰς   Ἰεροσόλυμα
after   three   days   went up   to   Jerusalem

ἀπὸ   Καισαρείας,   2 ἐνεφάνισάν   τε   αὐτῷ
from   Cæsarea,   and ³informed   ⁰him

οἱ   ἀρχιερεῖς   καὶ   οἱ   πρῶτοι   τῶν   Ἰουδαίων
¹the   ²chief priests   ³and   ⁴the   ⁵chiefs   ⁶of the   ⁷Jews

κατὰ   τοῦ   Παύλου,   καὶ   παρεκάλουν   αὐτὸν
against   –   Paul,   and   they besought   him

3 αἰτούμενοι   χάριν   κατ᾽   αὐτοῦ,   ὅπως   μετα-
asking   a favour against   him,   so as   he might

πέμψηται   αὐτὸν   εἰς   Ἰερουσαλήμ,   ἐνέδραν
summon   him   to   Jerusalem,   a plot

ποιοῦντες   ἀνελεῖν   αὐτὸν   κατὰ   τὴν   ὁδόν.
making   to kill   him   by   the   way.

4 ὁ   μὲν   οὖν   Φῆστος   ἀπεκρίθη   τηρεῖσθαι
–   –   Therefore   Festus   answered   ²to be kept

τὸν   Παῦλον   εἰς   Καισάρειαν,   ἑαυτὸν   δὲ
–   ¹Paul   in   Cæsarea,   and ²himself

μέλλειν   ἐν   τάχει   ἐκπορεύεσθαι· 5 οἱ   οὖν
¹to intend   shortly   to go forth;   ²the ¹therefore

authority among you go
down with me, and if
there is anything wrong
about the man, let them
accuse him."

6 When he had stayed
among them not more
than eight or ten days,
he went down to
Caesare'a; and the next
day he took his seat on
the tribunal and ordered
Paul to be brought. 7 And
when he had come, the
Jews who had gone
down from Jerusalem
stood against him, bring-
ing against him many
serious charges which
they could not prove.
8 Paul said in his defense,
"Neither against the law
of the Jews, nor against
the temple, nor against
Caesar have I offended
at all." 9 But Festus,
wishing to do the Jews a
favor, said to Paul, "Do
you wish to go up to
Jerusalem, and there be
tried on these charges
before me?" 10 But Paul
said, "I am standing
before Caesar's tribunal,
where I ought to be tried;
to the Jews I have done
no wrong, as you know
very well. 11 If then I am
a wrongdoer, and have
committed anything for
which I deserve to die, I
do not seek to escape

ἐν   ὑμῖν,   φησίν,   δυνατοὶ   συγκαταβάντες,
'among 'you,   'he says,   ²able men   going down with [me],
εἴ   τί   ἐστιν   ἐν   τῷ   ἀνδρὶ   ἄτοπον,
if anything there is   in   the   man   amiss,
κατηγορείτωσαν   αὐτοῦ.   6 Διατρίψας   δὲ   ἐν
let them accuse   him.   And having stayed among
αὐτοῖς   ἡμέρας   οὐ   πλείους   ὀκτὼ   ἢ   δέκα,
them   days   not   more [than]   eight   or   ten,
καταβὰς   εἰς   Καισάρειαν,   τῇ   ἐπαύριον
going down   to   Cæsarea,   on the   morrow
καθίσας   ἐπὶ   τοῦ   βήματος   ἐκέλευσεν   τὸν
sitting   on   the   tribunal   he commanded   –
Παῦλον   ἀχθῆναι.   7   παραγενομένου   δὲ
Paul   to be brought.   And arriving
=when he arrived
αὐτοῦ   περιέστησαν   αὐτὸν   οἱ   ἀπὸ   Ἱεροσο-
him²   ⁶stood round   ³him   ¹the   ⁴from   ⁵Jeru-
λύμων   καταβεβηκότες   Ἰουδαῖοι,   πολλὰ   καὶ
salem   ⁵having come down   ²Jews,   many   and
βαρέα   αἰτιώματα   καταφέροντες,   ἃ   οὐκ
heavy   charges   bringing against [him],   which   not
ἴσχυον   ἀποδεῖξαι,   8 τοῦ   Παύλου   ἀπολογου-
they were able to prove,   –   Paul   defending him-
μένου   ὅτι   οὔτε   εἰς   τὸν   νόμον   τῶν
self[.]²   –   Neither   against   the   law   of the
=while Paul defended himself,
Ἰουδαίων   οὔτε   εἰς   τὸ   ἱερὸν   οὔτε   εἰς
Jews   nor   against   the   temple   nor   against
Καισάρά   τι   ἥμαρτον.   9 ὁ   Φῆστος   δὲ,
Cæsar   anything   I sinned.   –   But Festus,
θέλων   τοῖς   Ἰουδαίοις   χάριν   καταθέσθαι,
wishing   the   Jews   a favour   to show,
ἀποκριθεὶς   τῷ   Παύλῳ   εἶπεν·   θέλεις   εἰς
answering   the   Paul   said: Dost thou wish ²to
Ἱεροσόλυμα   ἀναβὰς   ἐκεῖ   περὶ   τούτων
³Jerusalem   ¹going up   ⁴there   ⁵concerning   ⁶these things
κριθῆναι   ἐπ'   ἐμοῦ;   10 εἶπεν   δὲ   ὁ   Παῦλος·
⁵to be judged   ⁶before   ⁷me?   And said –   Paul:
ἑστὼς   ἐπὶ   τοῦ   βήματος   Καίσαρός   εἰμι,
Standing   before   the   tribunal   of Cæsar   I am,
οὗ   με   δεῖ   κρίνεσθαι.   Ἰουδαίους   οὐδὲν
where   me   it behoves to be judged.   Jews   nothing
ἠδίκηκα,   ὡς   καὶ   σὺ   κάλλιον   ἐπιγινώσκεις.
I have wronged,   as   indeed thou   very well   knowest.
11 εἰ   μὲν   οὖν   ἀδικῶ   καὶ   ἄξιον   θανάτου
If   –   therefore   I do wrong and   worthy   of death
πέπραχά   τι,   οὐ   παραιτοῦμαι   τὸ   ἀποθανεῖν·
I have done anything,   I do not refuse   the   to die;

death; but if there is nothing in their charges against me, no one can give me up to them. I appeal to Caesar." [12] Then Festus, when he had conferred with his council, answered, "You have appealed to Caesar; to Caesar you shall go."

13 Now when some days had passed, Agrippa the king and Berni'ce arrived at Caesare'a to welcome Festus. [14] And as they stayed there many days, Festus laid Paul's case before the king, saying, "There is a man left prisoner by Felix; [15] and when I was at Jerusalem, the chief priests and the elders of the Jews gave information about him, asking for sentence against him. [16] I answered them that it was not the custom of the Romans to give up any one before the accused met the accusers face to face, and had opportunity to make his defense concerning the charge laid against him. [17] When therefore they came together here, I made no delay, but on the next

εἰ	δὲ	οὐδέν	ἐστιν	ὧν οὗτοι	κατηγοροῦσίν
but if		not one	there is	of [the these things] which	these accuse

μου,	οὐδείς	με δύναται	αὐτοῖς	χαρίσασθαι·
me,	no one	[2]me [1]can	[4]to them	[3]to grant;

Καίσαρα	ἐπικαλοῦμαι.	12 τότε	ὁ Φῆστος
[2]Cæsar	[1]I appeal to.	Then	– Festus

συλλαλήσας	μετὰ	τοῦ συμβουλίου	ἀπεκρίθη·
having talked with	with	the council	answered:

Καίσαρα	ἐπικέκλησαι,	ἐπὶ Καίσαρα	πορεύσῃ.
[2]Cæsar	[1]thou hast appealed to,	before Cæsar	thou shalt go.

13 ‘Ημερῶν   δὲ   διαγενομένων   τινῶν
        And days   passing   some[a]
            =when some days had passed

'Αγρίππας	ὁ βασιλεὺς	καὶ	Βερνίκη
Agrippa	the king	and	Bernice

κατήντησαν	εἰς Καισάρειαν	ἀσπασάμενοι
arrived	at Cæsarea	greeting

τὸν	Φῆστον.	14 ὡς δὲ	πλείους	ἡμέρας
–	Festus.	And as	more	days

διέτριβον	ἐκεῖ,	ὁ Φῆστος	τῷ βασιλεῖ
they stayed	there,	– Festus	[2]to the [3]king

ἀνέθετο	τὰ κατὰ	τὸν Παῦλον	λέγων·
[1]set forth	the matters regarding	– Paul	saying:

ἀνήρ	τίς ἐστιν	καταλελειμμένος	ὑπὸ
A certain man	there is	having been left behind	by

Φήλικος	δέσμιος,	15 περὶ οὗ	γενομένου
Felix	prisoner,	about whom	being
			=when I was

μου εἰς	'Ιεροσόλυμα	ἐνεφάνισαν	οἱ ἀρχιερεῖς
me[a] in	Jerusalem	[3]informed	[1]the [2]chief priests

καὶ	οἱ	πρεσβύτεροι τῶν	'Ιουδαίων,
[3]and	[4]the	[5]elders	[6]of the	[7]Jews,

αἰτούμενοι	κατ' αὐτοῦ	καταδίκην·	16 πρὸς
asking	against him	sentence;	to

οὓς	ἀπεκρίθην ὅτι	οὐκ ἔστιν	ἔθος 'Ρωμαίοις
whom	I answered that	it is not	a custom with Romans

χαρίζεσθαί	τινα	ἄνθρωπον	πρὶν ἢ	ὁ
to grant	any	man	before	the

κατηγορούμενος	κατὰ πρόσωπον	ἔχοι τοὺς
[one] being accused	face to face†	should have the

κατηγόρους	τόπον τε	ἀπολογίας	λάβοι
accusers	[3]place* [1]and	[4]of defence	[2]receive

περὶ τοῦ	ἐγκλήματος.	17 συνελθόντων
concerning the	charge.	Coming together[a]

οὖν ἐνθάδε	ἀναβολὴν	μηδεμίαν	ποιησάμενος
therefore thither	[3]delay	[2]no	[1]making

* That is, opportunity.

day took my seat on the tribunal and ordered the man to be brought in. [18]When the accusers stood up, they brought no charge in his case of such evils as I supposed; [19]but they had certain points of dispute with him about their own superstition and about one Jesus, who was dead, but whom Paul asserted to be alive. [20]Being at a loss how to investigate these questions, I asked whether he wished to go to Jerusalem and be tried there regarding them. [21]But when Paul had appealed to be kept in custody for the decision of the emperor, I commanded him to be held until I could send him to Caesar." [22]And Agrippa said to Festus, "I should like to hear the man myself." "Tomorrow," said he, "you shall hear him."

23 So on the morrow Agrippa and Berni'ce came with great pomp, and they entered the audience hall with the military tribunes and the prominent men of the city. Then by command of Festus Paul was brought in. [24]And Festus said, "King Agrippa and

τῇ ἑξῆς καθίσας ἐπὶ τοῦ βήματος ἐκέλευσα
on the next [day] sitting on the tribunal I commanded

ἀχθῆναι τὸν ἄνδρα· 18 περὶ οὗ σταθέντες
to be brought the man; concerning whom standing

οἱ κατήγοροι οὐδεμίαν αἰτίαν ἔφερον ὧν
the accusers ²no ³charge ¹brought ⁴of ⁶things ⁷which

ἐγὼ ὑπενόουν πονηρῶν, 19 ζητήματα δέ
⁵I ⁹suspected ⁵evil, but ²questions

τινα περὶ τῆς ἰδίας δεισιδαιμονίας εἶχον
³certain ⁴about ⁵the(ir) own ⁸religion ¹they had

πρὸς αὐτὸν καὶ περὶ τινος Ἰησοῦ
with him and about one Jesus

τεθνηκότος, ὃν ἔφασκεν ὁ Παῦλος ζῆν.
having died, whom ²asserted - ¹Paul to live.

20 ἀπορούμενος δὲ ἐγὼ τὴν περὶ τούτων
And ²being perplexed at ¹I ³the ⁵about ⁶these things

ζήτησιν ἔλεγον εἰ βούλοιτο πορεύεσθαι εἰς
⁴debate said if he wished to go to

Ἱεροσόλυμα κἀκεῖ κρίνεσθαι περὶ τούτων.
Jerusalem and there to be judged about these things.

21 τοῦ δὲ Παύλου ἐπικαλεσαμένου τηρηθῆναι
- But Paul having appealedᵃ to be kept
= when Paul appealed

αὐτὸν εἰς τὴν τοῦ Σεβαστοῦ διάγνωσιν,
him to the - ²of Augustus ¹decision,

ἐκέλευσα τηρεῖσθαι αὐτὸν ἕως οὗ ἀναπέμψω
I commanded to be kept him until I may send up

αὐτὸν πρὸς Καίσαρα. 22 Ἀγρίππας δὲ
him to Caesar. And Agrippa

πρὸς τὸν Φῆστον· ἐβουλόμην καὶ αὐτὸς
[said] to - Festus: I was minded also [my]self

τοῦ ἀνθρώπου ἀκοῦσαι. αὔριον, φησίν,
the man to hear. Tomorrow, he says,

ἀκούσῃ αὐτοῦ. 23 Τῇ οὖν ἐπαύριον
thou shalt hear him. ²On the ¹therefore ³morrow

ἐλθόντος τοῦ Ἀγρίππα καὶ τῆς Βερνίκης
coming - Agrippa and - Berniceᵃ
= when Agrippa and Bernice came

μετὰ πολλῆς φαντασίας καὶ εἰσελθόντων
with much display and enteringᵃ

εἰς τὸ ἀκροατήριον σύν τε χιλιάρχοις
into the place of audience with both chiliarchs

καὶ ἀνδράσιν τοῖς κατ᾽ ἐξοχὴν τῆς πόλεως,
and ²men ¹the ²chief † of the city,

καὶ κελεύσαντος τοῦ Φήστου ἤχθη ὁ
and having commanded - Festusᵃ ¹was brought -
= when Festus commanded

Παῦλος. 24 καί φησιν ὁ Φῆστος· Ἀγρίππα
¹Paul. And says - Festus: Agrippa

all who are present with us, you see this man about whom the whole Jewish people petitioned me, both at Jerusalem and here, shouting that he ought not to live any longer. 25 But I found that he had done nothing deserving death; and as he himself appealed to the emperor, I decided to send him. 26 But I have nothing definite to write to my lord about him. Therefore I have brought him before you, and, especially before you, King Agrippa, that, after we have examined him, I may have something to write. 27 For it seems to me unreasonable, in sending a prisoner, not to indicate the charges against him."

βασιλεῦ καὶ πάντες οἱ συμπαρόντες ἡμῖν
king   and   all   the *present together with   ²us

ἄνδρες, θεωρεῖτε τοῦτον περὶ οὗ ἅπαν τὸ
¹men,   ye behold   this man   about whom   all   the

πλῆθος τῶν Ἰουδαίων ἐνέτυχόν μοι ἔν τε
multitude of the Jews   petitioned   me   ²in ¹both

Ἱεροσολύμοις καὶ ἐνθάδε, βοῶντες μὴ
Jerusalem   and   here,   crying   not

δεῖν αὐτὸν ζῆν μηκέτι. 25 ἐγὼ δὲ κατε-
ought him to live no longer.   But I   dis-
=that he ought not to live any longer.

λαβόμην μηδὲν ἄξιον αὐτὸν θανάτου
covered   ³nothing ⁴worthy   ¹him   ⁵of death

πεπραχέναι, αὐτοῦ δὲ τούτου ἐπικαλεσαμένου
²to have done,   but [him]self this man   appealing to³
=when he himself appealed to

τὸν Σεβαστὸν ἔκρινα πέμπειν. 26 περὶ
—   Augustus   I decided to send.   Concerning

οὗ ἀσφαλές τι γράψαι τῷ κυρίῳ οὐκ
whom ⁴certain ³anything ⁵to write ⁶to the ⁷lord ²not

ἔχω· διὸ προήγαγον αὐτὸν ἐφ᾽ ὑμῶν καὶ
¹I have; where- I brought him before you   and
    fore   forth

μάλιστα ἐπὶ σοῦ, βασιλεῦ Ἀγρίππα, ὅπως
most of all before thee,   king   Agrippa,   so as
                           =when

τῆς ἀνακρίσεως γενομένης σχῶ τί γράψω·
the   examination   being³   I may what I may
there has been an examination   have   write;

27 ἄλογον γάρ μοι δοκεῖ πέμποντα δέσμιον
for ²unreasonable ³to me ¹it seems sending   a prisoner

μὴ καὶ τας κατ᾽ αὐτοῦ αἰτίας σημᾶναι.
not also ²the ⁴against ³him ²charges ¹to signify.

CHAPTER 26

AGRIPPA said to Paul, "You have permission to speak for yourself." Then Paul stretched out his hand and made his defense:
2 "I think myself fortunate that it is before you, King Agrippa, I am to make my defense today against all the accusations of the Jews, 3 because you are especially familiar with

26 Ἀγρίππας δὲ πρὸς τὸν Παῦλον ἔφη·
And Agrippa   to   —   Paul   said:

ἐπιτρέπεταί σοι ὑπὲρ σεαυτοῦ λέγειν.
It is permitted to thee on behalf of thyself to speak.

τότε ὁ Παῦλος ἐκτείνας τὴν χεῖρα
Then —   Paul   stretching out the(his) hand

ἀπελογεῖτο· 2 Περὶ πάντων ὧν ἐγκαλοῦμαι
defended himself: Concerning all things of which I am being
                                      accused

ὑπὸ Ἰουδαίων, βασιλεῦ Ἀγρίππα, ἥγημαι
by   Jews,   king   Agrippa,   I consider

ἐμαυτὸν μακάριον ἐπὶ σοῦ μέλλων σήμερον
myself   happy   ³before ⁴thee ¹being about   ⁵to-day

ἀπολογεῖσθαι, 3 μάλιστα γνώστην ὄντα σε
²to defend myself,   most of all   ²an expert ²being ¹thee

all customs and controversies of the Jews; therefore I beg you to listen to me patiently.

4 "My manner of life from my youth, spent from the beginning among my own nation and at Jerusalem, is known by all the Jews. [5] They have known for a long time, if they are willing to testify, that according to the strictest party of our religion I have lived as a Pharisee. [6] And now I stand here on trial for hope in the promise made by God to our fathers, [7] to which our twelve tribes hope to attain, as they earnestly worship night and day. And for this hope I am accused by Jews, O king! [8] Why is it thought incredible by any of you that God raises the dead?

9 "I myself was convinced that I ought to do many things in opposing the name of Jesus of Nazareth. [10] And I did so in Jerusalem; I not only shut up many of the saints in prison, by authority from the chief priests, but when they were put to death I cast

πάντων   τῶν   κατὰ   Ἰουδαίους   ἐθῶν   τε
[5]of all   [4]the   [3]among   [6]Jews   [7]customs [2]both

καὶ   ζητημάτων·   διὸ   δέομαι   μακροθύμως
[10]and   [11]questions;   wherefore   I beg   patiently

ἀκοῦσαί   μου.   4 Τὴν   μὲν   οὖν   βίωσίν
to hear   me.   [2]the   [1]So   [2]then   [4]manner of life

μου   ἐκ   νεότητος   τὴν   ἀπ᾽   ἀρχῆς   γενομένην
of me   from   youth   –   [2]from [4]beginning [1]having been
[3][the]

ἐν   τῷ   ἔθνει   μου   ἔν   τε   Ἰεροσολύμοις
in   the   nation   of me   [2]in   [1]and   Jerusalem

ἴσασι   πάντες   Ἰουδαῖοι,   5 προγινώσκοντές
know   all   Jews,   previously knowing

με   ἄνωθεν,   ἐὰν   θέλωσι   μαρτυρεῖν,   ὅτι
me   from the first,   if   they are willing   to testify,   that

κατὰ   τὴν   ἀκριβεστάτην ·   αἵρεσιν   τῆς
according to the   most exact   sect   –

ἡμετέρας   θρησκείας   ἔζησα   Φαρισαῖος.   6 καὶ
of our   religion   I lived   a Pharisee.   And

νῦν   ἐπ᾽   ἐλπίδι   τῆς   εἰς   τοὺς   πατέρας
now   on(in)   hope   of the   [2]to   [4]the   [3]fathers

ἡμῶν   ἐπαγγελίας   γενομένης   ὑπὸ   τοῦ   θεοῦ
[2]of us   [1]promise   [3]having been [made]   [5]by   –   [4]God

ἕστηκα   κρινόμενος,   7 εἰς   ἣν   τὸ   δωδεκά-
I stand   being judged,   to   which   the   twelve

φυλον   ἡμῶν   ἐν   ἐκτενείᾳ   νύκτα   καὶ
tribes   of us   with   earnestness   night   and

ἡμέραν   λατρεῦον   ἐλπίζει   καταντῆσαι·   περὶ
day   worshipping   hopes   to arrive;   concerning

ἧς   ἐλπίδος   ἐγκαλοῦμαι   ὑπὸ   Ἰουδαίων,
which   hope   I am accused   by   Jews,

βασιλεῦ.   8 τί   ἄπιστον   κρίνεται   παρ᾽
[O] king.   Why   incredible   is it judged   by

ὑμῖν   εἰ   ὁ   θεὸς   νεκροὺς   ἐγείρει;   9 ἐγὼ
you   if   –   God   [2]dead persons   [1]raises?   [3]I

μὲν   οὖν   ἔδοξα   ἐμαυτῷ   πρὸς   τὸ   ὄνομα
[1]indeed [2]then   [4]thought   [5]to myself   [6]to   [11]the   [11]name

Ἰησοῦ   τοῦ   Ναζωραίου   δεῖν   πολλὰ   ἐναντία
[13]of Jesus   [14]the   [15]Nazarene   [6]ought   [8]many   [9]contrary
things

πρᾶξαι·   10 ὃ   καὶ   ἐποίησα   ἐν   Ἰεροσολύμοις,
[7]to do;   which indeed   I did   in   Jerusalem,

καὶ   πολλούς   τε   τῶν   ἁγίων   ἐγὼ   ἐν
and   many   –   of the   saints   [1]I   [2]in

φυλακαῖς   κατέκλεισα   τὴν   παρὰ   τῶν
[2]prisons   [3]shut up   [4]the   [5]from   [6]the

ἀρχιερέων   ἐξουσίαν   λαβών,   ἀναιρουμένων   τε
[10]chief priests   [7]authority   [8]having received,   being killed   and
= and when they were killed

my vote against them. [11]And I punished them often in all the synagogues and tried to make them blaspheme; and in raging fury against them, I persecuted them even to foreign cities.

12 "Thus I journeyed to Damascus with the authority and commission of the chief priests. [13]At midday, O king, I saw on the way a light from heaven, brighter than the sun, shining round me and those who journeyed with me. [14]And when we had all fallen to the ground, I heard a voice saying to me in the Hebrew language, 'Saul, Saul, why do you persecute me? It hurts you to kick against the goads.' [15]And I said, 'Who are you, Lord?' And the Lord said, 'I am Jesus whom you are persecuting. [16]But rise and stand upon your feet; for I have appeared to you for this purpose, to appoint you to serve and bear witness to the things in which you have seen me and to those in which I will appear to you, [17]delivering you from the people and from the Gentiles—to whom I send you [18]to open their eyes, that they may turn from darkness

αὐτῶν   κατήνεγκα   ψῆφον,   11 καὶ   κατὰ
them[a]   I cast   a vote,   and throughout

πάσας   τὰς   συναγωγὰς   πολλάκις   τιμωρῶν
all   the   synagogues   often   punishing

αὐτοὺς   ἠνάγκαζον   βλασφημεῖν,   περισσῶς   τε
them   I compelled [them]   to blaspheme,   and excessively

ἐμμαινόμενος   αὐτοῖς   ἐδίωκον   ἕως   καὶ   εἰς
raging against   them   I persecuted   as far as   even   to

τὰς   ἔξω   πόλεις.   12 Ἐν   οἷς   πορευόμενος
the   outside   cities.   In   which   journeying

εἰς   τὴν   Δαμασκὸν   μετ᾽   ἐξουσίας   καὶ
to   –   Damascon   with   authority   and

ἐπιτροπῆς   τῆς   τῶν   ἀρχιερέων,   13 ἡμέρας
power to decide   –   of the   chief priests,   at [2]day

μέσης   κατὰ   τὴν   ὁδὸν   εἶδον,   βασιλεῦ,
[1]mid   along   the   way   I saw,   [O] king,

οὐρανόθεν   ὑπὲρ   τὴν   λαμπρότητα   τοῦ   ἡλίου
[1]from heaven   [3]above   [4]the   [5]brightness   [6]of the   [7]sun

περιλάμψαν   με   φῶς   καὶ   τοὺς   σὺν   ἐμοὶ
[8]shining round   [9]me   [1]a light   [10]and   [11]the [ones]   [13]with   [14]me

πορευομένους·   14 πάντων   τε   καταπεσόντων
[12]journeying;   and all   having fallen down
   =when we had all fallen

ἡμῶν   εἰς   τὴν   γῆν   ἤκουσα   φωνὴν   λέγουσαν
us[a]   to   the   earth   I heard   a voice   saying

πρός   με   τῇ   Ἑβραΐδι   διαλέκτῳ·   Σαούλ
to   me   in the   Hebrew   language: Saul[,]

Σαούλ,   τί   με   διώκεις;   σκληρόν   σοι
Saul,   why   me   persecutest thou?   hard   for thee

πρὸς   κέντρα   λακτίζειν.   15 ἐγὼ   δὲ   εἶπα·
against   goads   to kick.   And I   said:

τίς   εἶ,   κύριε;   ὁ   δὲ   κύριος   εἶπεν·   ἐγώ
Who art thou, Lord?   And the   Lord   said: I

εἰμι   Ἰησοῦς   ὃν   σὺ   διώκεις.   16 ἀλλὰ
am   Jesus   whom   thou   persecutest.   But

ἀνάστηθι   καὶ   στῆθι   ἐπὶ   τοὺς   πόδας   σου·
rise thou up   and   stand   on   the   feet   of thee;

εἰς   τοῦτο   γὰρ   ὤφθην   σοι,   προχειρίσασθαί
[2]for   [3]this [purpose]   [1]for   I appeared   to thee,   to appoint

σε   ὑπηρέτην   καὶ   μάρτυρα   ὧν   τε
thee   an attendant   and   a witness   [2]of the things   [1]both
       which

εἰδές   με   ὧν   τε   ὀφθήσομαί   σοι,
[3]thou sawest   [4]me   [6]of the things   [5]and   I will appear   to thee,
       which

17 ἐξαιρούμενός   σε   ἐκ   τοῦ   λαοῦ   καὶ   ἐκ
delivering   thee   from the   people   and from

τῶν   ἐθνῶν,   εἰς   οὓς   ἐγὼ   ἀποστέλλω   σε,
the   nations,   to   whom   I   send   thee,

18 ἀνοῖξαι   ὀφθαλμοὺς   αὐτῶν,   τοῦ   ἐπιστρέψαι
to open   eyes   of them,   –   to turn[b]

to light and from the power of Satan to God, that they may receive forgiveness of sins and a place among those who are sanctified by faith in me.'

19 "Wherefore, O King Agrippa, I was not disobedient to the heavenly vision, 20 but declared first to those at Damascus, then at Jerusalem and throughout all the country of Judea, and also to the Gentiles, that they should repent and turn to God and perform deeds worthy of their repentance. 21 For this reason the Jews seized me in the temple and tried to kill me. 22 To this day I have had the help that comes from God, and so I stand here testifying both to small and great, saying nothing but what the prophets and Moses said would come to pass: 23 that the Christ must suffer, and that, by being the first to rise from the dead, he would proclaim light both to the people and to the Gentiles."

24 And as he thus made his defense, Festus

ἀπὸ σκότους εἰς φῶς καὶ τῆς ἐξουσίας
from darkness to light and [from] the authority

τοῦ σατανᾶ ἐπὶ τὸν θεόν, τοῦ λαβεῖν
- of Satan to - God, - to receive
                                        =that they may receive

αὐτοὺς ἄφεσιν ἁμαρτιῶν καὶ κλῆρον ἐν
them[bd] forgiveness of sins and a lot among

τοῖς ἡγιασμένοις πίστει τῇ εἰς ἐμέ.
the [ones] having been sanctified by faith - in me.

19 Ὅθεν, βασιλεῦ Ἀγρίππα, οὐκ ἐγενόμην
Whence, king Agrippa, I was not

ἀπειθὴς τῇ οὐρανίῳ ὀπτασίᾳ, 20 ἀλλὰ
disobedient to the heavenly vision, but

τοῖς ἐν Δαμασκῷ πρῶτόν τε καὶ
to the [ones] in Damascus firstly and also

Ἱεροσολύμοις, πᾶσάν τε τὴν χώραν τῆς
[in] Jerusalem, and all the country -

Ἰουδαίας καὶ τοῖς ἔθνεσιν ἀπήγγελλον
of Judæa and to the nations I announced

μετανοεῖν καὶ ἐπιστρέφειν ἐπὶ τὸν θεόν,
to repent and to turn to - God,

ἄξια τῆς μετανοίας ἔργα πράσσοντας.
²worthy ⁴of the ⁵repentance ³works ¹doing.

21 ἕνεκα τούτων με Ἰουδαῖοι συλλαβόμενοι
On these things ³me ¹Jews ²having seized
account of

ἐν τῷ ἱερῷ ἐπειρῶντο διαχειρίσασθαι.
in the temple tried to kill [me].

22 ἐπικουρίας οὖν τυχὼν τῆς ἀπὸ τοῦ
Succour therefore having - from -
obtained

θεοῦ ἄχρι τῆς ἡμέρας ταύτης ἔστηκα
God until this day I stand

μαρτυρόμενος μικρῷ τε καὶ μεγάλῳ, οὐδὲν
witnessing ²to small ¹both and to great, ¹nothing

ἐκτὸς λέγων ὧν τε οἱ προφῆται
³apart ¹saying ⁴the things ⁵both ⁶the ⁷prophets
from which

ἐλάλησαν μελλόντων γίνεσθαι καὶ Μωϋσῆς,
¹⁰said ¹¹being about ¹²to happen ⁸and ⁹Moses,

23 εἰ παθητὸς ὁ χριστός, εἰ πρῶτος
if subject to suffering the Christ, if first

ἐξ ἀναστάσεως νεκρῶν φῶς μέλλει
by a resurrection of dead ²a light ¹he is
persons about

καταγγέλλειν τῷ τε λαῷ καὶ τοῖς ἔθνεσιν.
²to announce ⁵to the ⁴both people and to the nations.

24 Ταῦτα δὲ αὐτοῦ ἀπολογουμένου ὁ Φῆστος
And these things him defending himself[a] - Festus
=as he defended himself with these things

said with a loud voice, "Paul, you are mad; your great learning is turning you mad." [25] But Paul said, "I am not mad, most excellent Festus, but I am speaking the sober truth. [26] For the king knows about these things, and to him I speak freely; for I am persuaded that none of these things has escaped his notice, for this was not done in a corner. [27] King Agrippa, do you believe the prophets? I know that you believe." [28] And Agrippa said to Paul, "In a short time you think to make me a Christian!" [29] And Paul said, "Whether short or long, I would to God that not only you but also all who hear me this day might become such as I am—except for these chains."

30 Then the king rose, and the governor and Berni'ce and those who were sitting with them; [31] and when they had withdrawn, they said to one another, "This man is doing nothing to deserve death or imprisonment." [32] And

μεγάλῃ τῇ φωνῇ φησιν· μαίνῃ, Παῦλε·
great with the(his) voice says: Thou ravest, Paul:

τὰ πολλά σε γράμματα εἰς μανίαν
the many thee letters to madness

περιτρέπει. 25 ὁ δὲ Παῦλος· οὐ μαίνομαι,
turn[s]. – But Paul: I do not rave,

φησίν, κράτιστε Φῆστε, ἀλλὰ ἀληθείας
he says, most excellent Festus, but of truth

καὶ σωφροσύνης ῥήματα ἀποφθέγγομαι.
and of good sense words I speak forth.

26 ἐπίσταται γὰρ περὶ τούτων ὁ βασιλεύς,
For understands about these things the king,

πρὸς ὃν καὶ παρρησιαζόμενος λαλῶ·
to whom indeed being bold of speech I speak;

λανθάνειν γὰρ αὐτὸν τούτων οὐ πείθομαι
for to be hidden [from] him of these things not I am persuaded

οὐθέν· οὐ γάρ ἐστιν ἐν γωνίᾳ πεπραγμένον
nothing; for not is in a corner having been done

τοῦτο. 27 πιστεύεις, βασιλεῦ Ἀγρίππα,
this. Believest thou, king Agrippa,

τοῖς προφήταις; οἶδα ὅτι πιστεύεις. 28 ὁ
the prophets? I know that thou believest. –

δὲ Ἀγρίππας πρὸς τὸν Παῦλον· ἐν
And Agrippa [said] to – Paul: In

ὀλίγῳ με πείθεις Χριστιανὸν ποιῆσαι.
a little me thou persuadest a Christian to make(act).

29 ὁ δὲ Παῦλος· εὐξαίμην ἂν τῷ θεῷ
– And Paul [said]: I would pray – God

καὶ ἐν ὀλίγῳ καὶ ἐν μεγάλῳ οὐ μόνον
both in a little and in great not only

σὲ ἀλλὰ καὶ πάντας τοὺς ἀκούοντάς
thee but also all the [ones] hearing

μου σήμερον γενέσθαι τοιούτους ὁποῖος
me to-day to become such of what kind

καὶ ἐγώ εἰμι, παρεκτὸς τῶν δεσμῶν
indeed I am, except – bonds

τούτων. 30 Ἀνέστη τε ὁ βασιλεὺς καὶ
these. Rose up both the king and

ὁ ἡγεμὼν ἥ τε Βερνίκη καὶ οἱ συγ-
the governor – and Bernice and the [ones] sit-

καθήμενοι αὐτοῖς, 31 καὶ ἀναχωρήσαντες
ting with them, and having left

ἐλάλουν πρὸς ἀλλήλους λέγοντες ὅτι οὐδὲν
spoke to one another saying [.] nothing

θανάτου ἢ δεσμῶν ἄξιον πράσσει ὁ
of death or of bonds worthy does the

ἄνθρωπος οὗτος. 32 Ἀγρίππας δὲ τῷ
man This. And Agrippa –

Agrippa said to Festus, "This man could have been set free if he had not appealed to Caesar."

Φήστῳ   ἔφη·   ἀπολελύσθαι   ἐδύνατο
to Festus   said: [3]to have been released   [1]was able(could)

ὁ ἄνθρωπος οὗτος εἰ μὴ ἐπεκέκλητο Καίσαρα.
[1]This man   if   he had not appealed to   Cæsar.

CHAPTER 27

AND when it was decided that we should sail for Italy, they delivered Paul and some other prisoners to a centurion of the Augustan Cohort, named Julius. [2]And embarking in a ship of Adramyt'tium, which was about to sail to the ports along the coast of Asia, we put to sea, accompanied by Aristar'chus, a Macedo'nian from Thessaloni'ca. [3]The next day we put in at Sidon; and Julius treated Paul kindly, and gave him leave to go to his friends and be cared for. [4]And putting to sea from there we sailed under the lee of Cyprus, because the winds were against us. [5]And when we had sailed across the sea which is off Cili'cia and Pamphyl'ia, we came to Myra in Ly'cia. [6]There the centurion found a ship of Alexandria sailing for Italy, and put us on board. [7]We sailed slowly for a number of days, and

27 Ὡς δὲ ἐκρίθη τοῦ ἀποπλεῖν ἡμᾶς
And when it was decided - to sail us[b]
=that we should sail

εἰς τὴν Ἰταλίαν, παρεδίδουν τόν τε
to   Italy,   they delivered   τόν   both

Παῦλον καί τινας ἑτέρους δεσμώτας
Paul   and   some   other   prisoners

ἑκατοντάρχῃ ὀνόματι Ἰουλίῳ σπείρης
to a centurion   by name   Julius   of a cohort

Σεβαστῆς. 2 ἐπιβάντες δὲ πλοίῳ Ἀδρα-
Augustan.   And embarking in   a ship belonging to

μυττηνῷ μέλλοντι πλεῖν εἰς τοὺς κατὰ
Adramyttium being about to sail [1]for [3]the [4]along [the coast of]

τὴν Ἀσίαν τόπους ἀνήχθημεν, ὄντος σὺν
- [5]Asia [2]places   we set sail,   being with

ἡμῖν Ἀριστάρχου Μακεδόνος Θεσσαλονικέως·
us   Aristarchus   a Macedonian[a]   of Thessalonica;

3 τῇ τε ἑτέρα κατήχθημεν εἰς Σιδῶνα,
and on the   next [day] we were brought   at   Sidon,
to land

φιλανθρώπως τε ὁ Ἰούλιος τῷ Παύλῳ
and [3]kindly   - [1]Julius   [5]Paul

χρησάμενος ἐπέτρεψεν πρὸς τοὺς φίλους
[2]treating [him]   [4]allowed   [7]to   [8]the   [9]friends

πορευθέντι ἐπιμελείας τυχεῖν. 4 κἀκεῖθεν
[6]going   [11]attention [10]to obtain.   And thence

ἀναχθέντες ὑπεπλεύσαμεν τὴν Κύπρον διὰ
putting to sea   we sailed close to   -   Cyprus because of

τὸ τοὺς ἀνέμους εἶναι ἐναντίους, 5 τό τε
-   the   winds   to be(being) contrary,   and [3]the

πέλαγος τὸ κατὰ τὴν Κιλικίαν καὶ
[2]sea   - [4]against   -   [5]Cilicia   [6]and

Παμφυλίαν διαπλεύσαντες κατήλθαμεν εἰς
[7]Pamphylia [1]sailing over we came down   to

Μύρα τῆς Λυκίας. 6 Κἀκεῖ εὑρὼν ὁ
Myra   - of Lycia.   And there [3]having found [1]the

ἑκατοντάρχης πλοῖον Ἀλεξανδρῖνον πλέον
[2]centurion   ship   an Alexandrian   sailing

εἰς τὴν Ἰταλίαν ἐνεβίβασεν ἡμᾶς εἰς
to   -   Italy   he embarked   us   in

αὐτό. 7 ἐν ἱκαναῖς δὲ ἡμέραις βραδυπλο-
it.   And in a number of   days   sailing

arrived with difficulty off Cni′dus, and as the wind did not allow us to go on, we sailed under the lee of Crete off Salmo′ne. [8]Coasting along it with difficulty, we came to a place called Fair Havens, near which was the city of Lase′a.

9 As much time had been lost, and the voyage was already dangerous because the fast had already gone by, Paul advised them, [10]saying, "Sirs, I perceive that the voyage will be with injury and much loss, not only of the cargo and the ship, but also of our lives." [11]But the centurion paid more attention to the captain and to the owner of the ship than to what Paul said. [12]And because the harbor was not suitable to winter in, the majority advised to put to sea from there, on the chance that somehow they could reach Phoenix, a harbor of Crete, looking northeast

οὖντες καὶ μόλις γενόμενοι κατὰ τὴν
slowly and hardly coming against –
Κνίδον, μὴ προσεῶντος ἡμᾶς τοῦ ἀνέμου,[a]
Cnidus, not allowing us the wind,
= as the wind did not allow us,

ὑπεπλεύσαμεν τὴν Κρήτην κατὰ Σαλμώνην,
we sailed close to – Crete against Salmone,

8 μόλις τε παραλεγόμενοι αὐτὴν ἤλθομεν
and hardly sailing along it we came

εἰς τόπον τινὰ καλούμενον Καλοὺς λιμένας,
to place a certain being called Fair Havens,

ᾧ ἐγγὺς ἦν πόλις Λασαία. 9 Ἱκανοῦ δὲ
[2]to which [1]near was a city Lasæa. And much
= when

χρόνου διαγενομένου καὶ ὄντος ἤδη
time having passed[a] and being now
much time had passed = as the voyage

ἐπισφαλοῦς τοῦ πλοὸς διὰ τὸ καὶ τὴν
dangerous the voyage[a] on account of – also the
was now dangerous = because also the fast had now

νηστείαν ἤδη παρεληλυθέναι, παρήνει ὁ
fast now to have gone by, [2]advised –
gone by,

Παῦλος 10 λέγων αὐτοῖς· ἄνδρες, θεωρῶ
[1]Paul saying to them: Men, I see

ὅτι μετὰ ὕβρεως καὶ πολλῆς ζημίας οὐ
that with injury and much loss not

μόνον τοῦ φορτίου καὶ τοῦ πλοίου ἀλλὰ
only of the cargo and of the ship but

καὶ τῶν ψυχῶν ἡμῶν μέλλειν ἔσεσθαι
also of the lives of us [3]to be about [4]to be
= will be

τὸν πλοῦν. 11 ὁ δὲ ἑκατοντάρχης τῷ
[1]the [2]voyage. But the centurion [2]the

κυβερνήτῃ καὶ τῷ ναυκλήρῳ μᾶλλον
[3]steersman [4]and [5]the [6]shipmaster [7]rather

ἐπείθετο ἢ τοῖς ὑπὸ Παύλου λεγομένοις.
[1]was persuaded by [8]than [9]the [11]by [12]Paul [10]things said.

12 ἀνευθέτου δὲ τοῦ λιμένος ὑπάρχοντος
But unsuitable the port being[a]
= as the port was unsuitable

πρὸς παραχειμασίαν οἱ πλείονες ἔθεντο
for wintering the majority placed
= decided

βουλὴν ἀναχθῆναι ἐκεῖθεν, εἴ πως δύναιντο
counsel to set sail thence, if some- they might
how be able

καταντήσαντες εἰς Φοίνικα παραχειμάσαι,
having arrived at Phœnix to pass the winter,

λιμένα τῆς Κρήτης βλέποντα κατὰ λίβα
a port – of Crete looking toward southwest

and southeast,[v] and winter there.

13 And when the south wind blew gently, supposing that they had obtained their purpose, they weighed anchor and sailed along Crete, close inshore. [14]But soon a tempestuous wind, called the northeaster, struck down from the land; [15]and when the ship was caught and could not face the wind, we gave way to it and were driven. [16]And running under the lee of a small island called Cauda,[w] we managed with difficulty to secure the boat; [17]after hoisting it up, they took measures to undergird the ship; then, fearing that they should run on the Syr'tis, they lowered the gear, and so were driven. [18]As we were violently storm-tossed, they began next day to throw the cargo overboard; [19]and the third day they cast out with their own hands the tackle of the ship. [20]And when neither sun nor stars appeared for many a day, and no small tempest lay on us, all hope of our being saved was at last abandoned.

καὶ   κατὰ   χῶρον.
and   toward   north-west.

13 Ὑποπνεύσαντος   δὲ
And blowing gently
=when a south wind

νότου   δόξαντες τῆς προθέσεως κεκρατηκέναι,
a south wind[a] thinking ²the(ir) ³purpose ¹to have obtained,
blew gently

ἄραντες   ἆσσον   παρελέγοντο   τὴν   Κρήτην.
raising   ²close in- ¹they coasted by   –   ²Crete.
[anchor]   shore

14 μετ'   οὐ   πολὺ   δὲ   ἔβαλεν   κατ'   αὐτῆς
And after not much   there beat down   it

ἄνεμος   τυφωνικὸς   ὁ   καλούμενος   εὐρακύλων·
wind   a tempestuous   –   being called   Euraquilo;

15 συναρπασθέντος   δὲ   τοῦ   πλοίου   καὶ   μὴ
and ³being seized   ¹the   ²ship[a]   and   not

δυναμένου   ἀντοφθαλμεῖν   τῷ   ἀνέμῳ   ἐπιδόντες
being able[a]   to beat up against   the   wind   giving way

ἐφερόμεθα.   16 νησίον   δέ   τι   ὑποδραμόντες
we were borne.   And ²islet   ²a certain   ¹running under
the lee of

καλούμενον   Κλαῦδα   ἰσχύσαμεν   μόλις
being called   Clauda   we were able   hardly

περικρατεῖς   γενέσθαι   τῆς   σκάφης,   17 ἣν
control   to get   of the   boat,   which

ἄραντες   βοηθείαις   ἐχρῶντο,   ὑποζωννύντες
taking   ²helps   ¹they used,   undergirding

τὸ   πλοῖον·   φοβούμενοί   τε   μὴ   εἰς   τὴν
the   ship;   and fearing   lest   into   –

Σύρτιν   ἐκπέσωσιν,   χαλάσαντες   τὸ   σκεῦος,
Syrtis   they might fall off,*   lowering   the   tackle,

οὕτως   ἐφέροντο.   18 σφοδρῶς   δὲ   χειμαζ-
thus   they were borne.   But exceedingly   being in
=as we were exceedingly in . . .

ομένων   ἡμῶν   τῇ   ἑξῆς   ἐκβολὴν   ἐποιοῦντο,
the grip   us[a]   on the next   a jettisoning   they made,
of a storm   [day]

19 καὶ   τῇ   τρίτῃ   αὐτόχειρες   τὴν   σκευὴν
and   on the   third   with their   the   tackle
[day]   own hands

τοῦ   πλοίου   ἔρριψαν.   20 μήτε   δὲ   ἡλίου
of the   ship   they threw [out].   And neither   sun
=when neither . . .

μήτε   ἄστρων   ἐπιφαινόντων   ἐπὶ   πλείονας
nor   stars   appearing[a]   over   many
appeared

ἡμέρας,   χειμῶνός   τε   οὐκ   ὀλίγου   ἐπικειμένου,
days,   and stormy weather   no   little   pressing hard,[a]

λοιπὸν   περιῃρεῖτο   ἐλπὶς   πᾶσα   τοῦ   σώζεσθαι
now   was taken away   ²hope   ¹all   –   to be saved
=that we might

---

[v] Or *southwest and northwest*
[w] Other ancient authorities read *Clauda*

* This is the classical Greek word for a ship being driven out of her course on to shoals, rocks, etc. (Page). See also vers 26 and 29.

21 As they had been long without food, Paul then came forward among them and said, "Men, you should have listened to me, and should not have set sail from Crete and incurred this injury and loss. ²²I now bid you take heart; for there will be no loss of life among you, but only of the ship. ²³For this very night there stood by me an angel of the God to whom I belong and whom I worship, ²⁴and he said, 'Do not be afraid, Paul; you must stand before Caesar; and lo, God has granted you all those who sail with you.' ²⁵So take heart, men, for I have faith in God that it will be exactly as I have been told. ²⁶But we shall have to run on some island."

27 When the fourteenth night had come, as we were drifting across the sea of A'dria, about midnight the sailors suspected that they were nearing land. ²⁸So they sounded and found twenty fathoms; a little farther on they

ἡμᾶς.
us.ᵇᵈ
be saved.

21 Πολλῆς τε ἀσιτίας ὑπαρχούσης
And much   abstinence   beingᵃ
= when there was long abstinence

τότε σταθεὶς ὁ Παῦλος ἐν μέσῳ αὐτῶν εἶπεν·
then ¹standing – ¹Paul   in [the] midst of them   said:

ἔδει   μέν,   ὦ   ἄνδρες,   πειθαρχήσαντάς
It behoved – O men, obeying
[you],

μοι   μὴ   ἀνάγεσθαι   ἀπὸ   τῆς   Κρήτης
me not to set sail from – Crete

κερδῆσαί τε   τὴν   ὕβριν   ταύτην   καὶ   τὴν
and to come by – injury this and –

ζημίαν.   **22** καὶ   τὰ   νῦν   παραινῶ   ὑμᾶς
loss.   And – now I advise you

εὐθυμεῖν·   ἀποβολὴ   γὰρ   ψυχῆς   οὐδεμία
to be of good for ³throwing away ⁴of life ²no
cheer;

ἔσται   ἐξ   ὑμῶν   πλὴν   τοῦ   πλοίου.
¹there will be of you but of the ship.

23 παρέστη   γάρ   μοι   ταύτῃ   τῇ   νυκτὶ
For there stood by me in this – night

τοῦ   θεοῦ   οὗ   εἰμι,   ᾧ   καὶ   λατρεύω,
– ²of God ³of whom ¹I am, ⁵whom ⁶also ⁷I serve,

ἄγγελος   **24** λέγων·   μὴ   φοβοῦ,   Παῦλε·
¹an angel saying: Fear not, Paul;

Καίσαρί   σε   δεῖ   παραστῆναι,   καὶ   ἰδοὺ
⁴Caesar ²thee ¹it behoves ³to stand before, and behold

κεχάρισταί   σοι   ὁ   θεὸς   πάντας   τοὺς
²has given ³thee – ¹God all the [ones]

πλέοντας   μετὰ   σοῦ.   **25** διὸ   εὐθυμεῖτε,
sailing with thee. Wherefore be ye of
good cheer,

ἄνδρες·   πιστεύω   γὰρ   τῷ   θεῷ   ὅτι   οὕτως
men; for I believe – God that thus

ἔσται   καθ'   ὃν   τρόπον   λελάληταί   μοι.
it will be in the way in which† it has been spoken to me.

26 εἰς   νῆσον   δέ   τινα   δεῖ   ἡμᾶς   ἐκπεσεῖν.
⁵Onto ⁷island ¹but ⁶a ²it ³us ⁴to fall off.
certain behoves

27 Ὡς   δὲ   τεσσαρεσκαιδεκάτη   νὺξ   ἐγένετο
Now when [the] fourteenth night came

διαφερομένων   ἡμῶν   ἐν   τῷ   Ἀδρίᾳ,   κατὰ
being carried about usᵃ in the Adria, about
= while we were being carried about

μέσον   τῆς   νυκτὸς   ὑπενόουν   οἱ   ναῦται
[the] middle of the night ³supposed ¹the ²sailors

προσάγειν   τινὰ   αὐτοῖς   χώραν.   **28** καὶ
⁴to approach ⁵some ⁶to them ⁷country. And

βολίσαντες   εὗρον   ὀργυιὰς   εἴκοσι, βραχὺ   δὲ
sounding they found fathoms twenty, and ¹a little

sounded again and found fifteen fathoms. ²⁹And fearing that we might run on the rocks, they let out four anchors from the stern, and prayed for day to come. ³⁰And as the sailors were seeking to escape from the ship, and had lowered the boat into the sea, under pretense of laying out anchors from the bow, ³¹Paul said to the centurion and the soldiers, "Unless these men stay in the ship, you cannot be saved." ³²Then the soldiers cut away the ropes of the boat, and let it go.

33 As day was about to dawn, Paul urged them all to take some food, saying, "Today is the fourteenth day that you have continued in suspense and without food, having taken nothing. ³⁴Therefore I urge you to take some food; it will give you strength, since not a hair is to perish from the head of any of you." ³⁵And when he had said this, he took

διαστήσαντες   καὶ   πάλιν   βολίσαντες   εὗρον
¹having moved   also   again   sounding   they found

ὀργυιὰς   δεκαπέντε·   29 φοβούμενοί   τε   μὴ
fathoms   fifteen;   and fearing   lest

που   κατὰ   τραχεῖς   τόπους   ἐκπέσωμεν,
²somewhere ³against   ⁴rough   ⁵places   ¹we might fall off,

ἐκ   πρύμνης   ῥίψαντες   ἀγκύρας   τέσσαρας
out of [the] stern   throwing   anchors   four

ηὔχοντο   ἡμέραν   γενέσθαι.   30 Τῶν   δὲ
they prayed   day   to become.   And the

ναυτῶν   ζητούντων   φυγεῖν   ἐκ   τοῦ   πλοίου
sailors   seekingª   to flee   out of the   ship
=when the sailors sought

καὶ   χαλασάντων   τὴν   σκάφην   εἰς   τὴν
and   loweringª   the   boat   into   the
=lowered

θάλασσαν   προφάσει   ὡς   ἐκ   πρώρης   ἀγκύρας
sea   under pretence   as   ⁴out of ⁵[the] prow   ³anchors

μελλόντων   ἐκτείνειν,   31 εἶπεν   ὁ   Παῦλος
¹intending   ²to cast out,   said   –   Paul

τῷ   ἑκατοντάρχῃ   καὶ   τοῖς   στρατιώταις·
to the   centurion   and   to the   soldiers:

ἐὰν   μὴ   οὗτοι   μείνωσιν   ἐν   τῷ   πλοίῳ,
Unless   these   remain   in   the   ship,

ὑμεῖς   σωθῆναι   οὐ   δύνασθε.   32 τότε
ye   ²to be saved   ¹cannot.   Then

ἀπέκοψαν   οἱ   στρατιῶται   τὰ   σχοινία   τῆς
cut away   the   soldiers   the   ropes   of the

σκάφης   καὶ   εἴασαν   αὐτὴν   ἐκπεσεῖν.
boat   and   let   it   to fall off.

33 Ἄχρι   δὲ   οὗ   ἡμέρα   ἤμελλεν   γίνεσθαι,
And until   day   was about   to come,

παρεκάλει   ὁ   Παῦλος   ἅπαντας   μεταλαβεῖν
besought   –   Paul   all   to partake

τροφῆς   λέγων·   τεσσαρεσκαιδεκάτην   σήμερον
of food   saying: ²[the] fourteenth   ¹To-day [is]

ἡμέραν   προσδοκῶντες   ἄσιτοι   διατελεῖτε,
³day   ⁵waiting   ⁶without food   ⁴ye continued,

μηθὲν   προσλαβόμενοι.   34 διὸ   παρακαλῶ
nothing   taking.   Wherefore   I beseech

ὑμᾶς   μεταλαβεῖν   τροφῆς·   τοῦτο   γὰρ   πρὸς
you   to partake   of food;   for this   to

τῆς   ὑμετέρας   σωτηρίας   ὑπάρχει·   οὐδενὸς
–   your   salvation   is;   ²of no one

γὰρ   ὑμῶν   θρὶξ   ἀπὸ   τῆς   κεφαλῆς   ἀπολεῖται.
¹for   of you   a hair   from the   head   shall perish.

35 εἰπὼς   δὲ   ταῦτα   καὶ   λαβὼν   ἄρτον
And saying   these things   and   taking   bread

bread, and giving thanks to God in the presence of all he broke it and began to eat. ³⁶ Then they all were encouraged and ate some food themselves. ³⁷ (We were in all two hundred and seventy-six[z] persons in the ship.) ³⁸ And when they had eaten enough, they lightened the ship, throwing out the wheat into the sea.

39 Now when it was day, they did not recognize the land, but they noticed a bay with a beach, on which they planned if possible to bring the ship ashore. ⁴⁰ So they cast off the anchors and left them in the sea, at the same time loosening the ropes that tied the rudders; then hoisting the foresail to the wind they made for the beach. ⁴¹ But striking a shoal they ran the vessel aground; the bow stuck and remained immovable, and the stern was broken up by the surf. ⁴² The soldiers' plan was to kill the prisoners, lest any should swim away and escape; ⁴³ but the centurion, wishing to save Paul, kept them from carrying out their

εὐχαρίστησεν τῷ θεῷ ἐνώπιον πάντων
he gave thanks   to God   before   all

καὶ κλάσας ἤρξατο ἐσθίειν. 36 εὔθυμοι δὲ
and breaking began   to eat.   And ⁴in good spirits

γενόμενοι πάντες καὶ αὐτοὶ προσελάβοντο
³becoming ¹all ²also they   took

τροφῆς. 37 ἤμεθα δὲ αἱ πᾶσαι ψυχαὶ
food.   Now we were ²the ¹all   souls

ἐν τῷ πλοίῳ διακόσιαι ἑβδομήκοντα ἕξ.
in the   ship   two hundreds [and] seventy   six.

38 κορεσθέντες δὲ τροφῆς ἐκούφιζον τὸ
And having been satisfied of(with) food they lightened the

πλοῖον ἐκβαλλόμενοι τὸν σῖτον εἰς τὴν
ship   ⁴throwing out the   wheat   into the

θάλασσαν. 39 Ὅτε δὲ ἡμέρα ἐγένετο,
sea.   And when   day   came,

τὴν γῆν οὐκ ἐπεγίνωσκον, κόλπον δέ
⁴the ³land ¹they did not recognize,   but ²bay

τινα κατενόουν ἔχοντα αἰγιαλόν, εἰς ὃν
²a certain ¹they noticed   having   a shore,   into which

ἐβουλεύοντο εἰ δύναιντο ἐξῶσαι τὸ πλοῖον.
they were minded if they were able to drive the   ship.

40 καὶ τὰς ἀγκύρας περιελόντες εἴων
And ²the ³anchors ¹having cast off they left [them]

εἰς τὴν θάλασσαν, ἅμα ἀνέντες τὰς
in the   sea,   at the same time loosening   the

ζευκτηρίας τῶν πηδαλίων, καὶ ἐπάραντες
fastenings of the   rudders,   and   raising

τὸν ἀρτέμωνα τῇ πνεούσῃ κατεῖχον εἰς
the   foresail   to the   breeze they held [the ship] to

τὸν αἰγιαλόν. 41 περιπεσόντες δὲ εἰς
the   shore.   And coming upon   to

τόπον διθάλασσον ἐπέκειλαν τὴν ναῦν,
a place between two seas they drove   the   vessel,

καὶ ἡ μὲν πρῷρα ἐρείσασα ἔμεινεν
and ²the ¹while   prow   having run aground remained

ἀσάλευτος, ἡ δὲ πρύμνα ἐλύετο ὑπὸ
immovable, ²the ¹yet   stern   was broken   by

τῆς βίας. 42 Τῶν δὲ στρατιωτῶν βουλὴ
the   force.*   Now ²of the ³soldiers ¹[the] mind

ἐγένετο ἵνα τοὺς δεσμώτας ἀποκτείνωσιν,
was   that ²the   ³prisoners ¹they should kill,

μή τις ἐκκολυμβήσας διαφύγῃ· 43 ὁ δὲ
lest anyone   swimming out   should escape;   but the

ἑκατοντάρχης βουλόμενος διασῶσαι τὸν
centurion   being minded   to save   the

Παῦλον ἐκώλυσεν αὐτοὺς τοῦ βουλήματος,
Paul   forbade   them   the(ir)   intention,

---

[z] Other ancient authorities read *seventy-six* or *about seventy-six*

* That is, of the waves, as indeed some MSS have.

purpose. He ordered those who could swim to throw themselves overboard first and make for the land, ⁴⁴ and the rest on planks or on pieces of the ship. And so it was that all escaped to land.

ἐκέλευσέν τε τοὺς δυναμένους κολυμβᾶν
and commanded the [ones] being able to swim

ἀπορίψαντας πρώτους ἐπὶ τὴν γῆν
casting [themselves] first onto the land
overboard

ἐξιέναι, 44 καὶ τοὺς λοιποὺς οὓς μὲν ἐπὶ
to go out, and the rest some on

σανίσιν, οὓς δὲ ἐπί τινων τῶν ἀπὸ τοῦ
planks, others on some of the things from the

πλοίου. καὶ οὕτως ἐγένετο πάντας
ship. And thus it came to pass all

διασωθῆναι ἐπὶ τὴν γῆν.
to be saved on the land.

CHAPTER 28

AFTER we had escaped, we then learned that the island was called Malta. ²And the natives showed us unusual kindness, for they kindled a fire and welcomed us all, because it had begun to rain and was cold. ³Paul had gathered a bundle of sticks and put them on the fire, when a viper came out because of the heat and fastened on his hand. ⁴When the natives saw the creature hanging from his hand, they said to one another, "No doubt this man is a murderer. Though he has escaped from the sea, justice has not allowed him to live." ⁵He, however, shook off the creature into the fire and

28 Καὶ διασωθέντες τότε ἐπέγνωμεν ὅτι
And having been saved then we found out that

Μελίτη ἡ νῆσος καλεῖται. 2 οἵ τε
Melita the island is(was) called. And the

βάρβαροι παρεῖχον οὐ τὴν τυχοῦσαν
foreigners ¹showed ³not ⁴the ⁵ordinary

φιλανθρωπίαν ἡμῖν· ἅψαντες γὰρ πυρὰν
kindness ²us; for having lit a fire

προσελάβοντο πάντας ἡμᾶς διὰ τὸν ὑετὸν
they welcomed ²all ¹us because of the rain

τὸν ἐφεστῶτα καὶ διὰ τὸ ψῦχος. 3 συστρέ-
coming on and because of the cold. col-

ψαντος δὲ τοῦ Παύλου φρυγάνων τι
lecting And Paulᵃ ²of sticks ¹a
=when Paul collected

πλῆθος καὶ ἐπιθέντος ἐπὶ τὴν πυράν,
²quantity and putting onᵃ on the fire,
=put them

ἔχιδνα ἀπὸ τῆς θέρμης ἐξελθοῦσα καθῆψεν
a snake from the heat coming out fastened on

τῆς χειρὸς αὐτοῦ. 4 ὡς δὲ εἶδον οἱ
the hand of him. And when ³saw ¹the

βάρβαροι κρεμάμενον τὸ θηρίον ἐκ τῆς
²foreigners ⁶hanging ⁴the ⁵beast from the

χειρὸς αὐτοῦ, πρὸς ἀλλήλους ἔλεγον·
hand of him, to one another they said:

πάντως φονεύς ἐστιν ὁ ἄνθρωπος οὗτος,
To be sure ⁴a murderer ³is ¹this man,

ὃν διασωθέντα ἐκ τῆς θαλάσσης ἡ δίκη
whom having been out of the sea - justice
saved

ζῆν οὐκ εἴασεν. 5 ὁ μὲν οὖν ἀποτινάξας
²to live ¹did not allow. He - then shaking off

τὸ θηρίον εἰς τὸ πῦρ ἔπαθεν οὐδὲν
the beast into the fire suffered no

suffered no harm. ⁶They waited, expecting him to swell up or suddenly fall down dead; but when they had waited a long time and saw no misfortune come to him, they changed their minds and said that he was a god.

7 Now in the neighborhood of that place were lands belonging to the chief man of the island, named Publius, who received us and entertained us hospitably for three days. ⁸It happened that the father of Publius lay sick with fever and dysentery; and Paul visited him and prayed, and putting his hands on him healed him. ⁹And when this had taken place, the rest of the people on the island who had diseases also came and were cured. ¹⁰They presented many gifts to us;[y] and when we sailed, they put on board whatever we needed.

11 After three months we set sail in a ship which had wintered in the island, a ship of Alexandria, with the Twin Brothers as figurehead. ¹²Putting in at Syracuse, we stayed there for three

---

κακόν· **6** οἱ δὲ προσεδόκων αὐτὸν μέλλειν
harm; but they expected him to be about

πίμπρασθαι ἢ καταπίπτειν ἄφνω νεκρόν.
to swell or to fall down suddenly dead.

ἐπὶ πολὺ δὲ αὐτῶν προσδοκώντων καὶ
But over much [time] they expecting and
= while they expected and beheld

θεωρούντων μηδὲν ἄτοπον εἰς αὐτὸν
beholding[a] nothing amiss ²to ³him

γινόμενον, μεταβαλόμενοι ἔλεγον αὐτὸν εἶναι
¹happening, changing their minds they said him to be

θεόν. **7** Ἐν δὲ τοῖς περὶ τὸν τόπον
a god. Now in the [parts] about — place

ἐκεῖνον ὑπῆρχεν χωρία τῷ πρώτῳ τῆς
that were lands to the chief man[c] of the
= the chief man . . . had lands

νήσου ὀνόματι Ποπλίῳ, ὃς ἀναδεξάμενος
island by name Publius, who welcoming

ἡμᾶς ἡμέρας τρεῖς φιλοφρόνως ἐξένισεν.
us ⁴days ³three friendlily ¹lodged [us].

8 ἐγένετο δὲ τὸν πατέρα τοῦ Ποπλίου
Now it happened the father of Publius

πυρετοῖς καὶ δυσεντερίῳ συνεχόμενον
²feverish attacks ⁴and ⁵dysentery ²suffering from

κατακεῖσθαι, πρὸς ὃν ὁ Παῦλος εἰσελθὼν
¹to be lying down, to whom — Paul entering

καὶ προσευξάμενος, ἐπιθεὶς τὰς χεῖρας
and praying, ¹putting ⁴on ²the(his) ³hands

αὐτῷ ἰάσατο αὐτόν. **9** τούτου δὲ γενομένου
⁵him cured him. And this happening[a]
= when this happened

καὶ οἱ λοιποὶ οἱ ἐν τῇ νήσῳ ἔχοντες
²also ¹the ²rest — in the island having

ἀσθενείας προσήρχοντο καὶ ἐθεραπεύοντο,
ailments came up and were healed,

10 οἳ καὶ πολλαῖς τιμαῖς ἐτίμησαν ἡμᾶς
who also with many honours honoured us

καὶ ἀναγομένοις ἐπέθεντο τὰ πρὸς τὰς
and on our putting to sea placed on [us] the things for the(our)

χρείας.
needs.

11 Μετὰ δὲ τρεῖς μῆνας ἀνήχθημεν ἐν
And after three months we embarked in

πλοίῳ παρακεχειμακότι ἐν τῇ νήσῳ,
a ship having passed the winter in the island,

Ἀλεξανδρίνῳ, παρασήμῳ Διοσκούροις. **12** καὶ
an Alexandrian, with a sign Dioscuri. And

καταχθέντες εἰς Συρακούσας ἐπεμείναμεν
being brought to land to(at) Syracuse we remained

days. ¹³And from there we made a circuit and arrived at Rhe′gium; and after one day a south wind sprang up, and on the second day we came to Pute′oli. ¹⁴There we found brethren, and were invited to stay with them for seven days. And so we came to Rome. ¹⁵And the brethren there, when they heard of us, came as far as the Forum of Ap′pius and Three Taverns to meet us. On seeing them Paul thanked God and took courage. ¹⁶And when we came into Rome, Paul was allowed to stay by himself, with the soldier that guarded him.

17 After three days he called together the local leaders of the Jews; and when they had gathered, he said to them, "Brethren, though I had done nothing against the people or the customs of our fathers, yet I was delivered prisoner from Jerusalem into the hands of the Romans. ¹⁸When they had examined me, they wished to set me at

ἡμέρας   τρεῖς,   13 ὅθεν   περιελθόντες   κατην-
days   three,   whence   tacking   we ar-
τήσαμεν   εἰς   ʽΡήγιον.   καὶ   μετὰ   μίαν
rived   at   Rhegium.   And   after   one
ἡμέραν   ἐπιγενομένου   νότου   δευτεραῖοι
day   coming on   a south wind[a]   on the
            =as a south wind came on   second day
ἤλθομεν   εἰς   Ποτιόλους,   14 οὗ   εὑρόντες
we came   to   Puteoli,   where having found
ἀδελφοὺς   παρεκλήθημεν   παρ'   αὐτοῖς   ἐπιμεῖναι
brothers   we were besought   with   them   to remain
ἡμέρας   ἑπτά·   καὶ   οὕτως   εἰς   τὴν   ʽΡώμην
days   seven;   and   thus   to   –   Rome
ἤλθαμεν.   15 κἀκεῖθεν   οἱ   ἀδελφοὶ   ἀκούσαντες
we went.   And thence   the   brothers   having heard
τὰ   περὶ   ἡμῶν   ἦλθαν   εἰς   ἀπάντησιν   ἡμῖν
the   con-   us   came   to   a meeting   with us
things cerning
ἄχρι   ʼΑππίου   φόρου   καὶ   Τριῶν   ταβερνῶν,
as far as   Appii   Forum   and   Three   Taverns,
οὓς   ἰδὼν   ὁ   Παῦλος   εὐχαριστήσας   τῷ
whom   seeing   –   Paul   thanking   –
θεῷ   ἔλαβε   θάρσος.   16 ʽΟτε   δὲ   εἰσήλθομεν
God   he took   courage.   And when   we entered
εἰς   ʽΡώμην,   ἐπετράπη   τῷ   Παύλῳ   μένειν
into   Rome,   he* permitted   –   Paul   to remain
καθ'   ἑαυτὸν   σὺν   τῷ   φυλάσσοντι   αὐτὸν
by   himself   with   ¹the   ²guarding   ⁴him
στρατιώτῃ.
²soldier.

17 ʼΕγένετο   δὲ   μετὰ   ἡμέρας   τρεῖς
And it came to pass   after   days   three
συγκαλέσασθαι   αὐτὸν   τοὺς   ὄντας   τῶν
to call together   him[b]   the [ones]   being   of the
=he called together
ʼΙουδαίων   πρώτους·   συνελθόντων   δὲ   αὐτῶν
Jews   first(chief);   and coming together   them[a]
                                        =and when they came together
ἔλεγεν   πρὸς   αὐτούς·   ἐγώ,   ἄνδρες   ἀδελφοί,
he said   to   them: I,   men   brothers,
οὐδὲν   ἐναντίον   ποιήσας   τῷ   λαῷ   ἢ   τοῖς
²nothing   ³contrary   ¹having done   to the   people   or   to the
ἔθεσι   τοῖς   πατρῴοις,   δέσμιος   ἐξ   ʼΙεροσο-
customs   –   ancestral,   a prisoner   from   Jeru-
λύμων   παρεδόθην   εἰς   τὰς   χεῖρας   τῶν
salem   I was delivered   into   the   hands   of the
ʽΡωμαίων,   18 οἵτινες   ἀνακρίναντές   με   ἐβούλοντο
Romans,   who   having examined   me   were minded

* That is, the officer to whom Paul was handed over by the centurion Julius.

liberty, because there was no reason for the death penalty in my case. [19] But when the Jews objected, I was compelled to appeal to Caesar—though I had no charge to bring against my nation. [20] For this reason therefore I have asked to see you and speak with you, since it is because of the hope of Israel that I am bound with this chain." [21] And they said to him, "We have received no letters from Judea about you, and none of the brethren coming here has reported or spoken any evil about you. [22] But we desire to hear from you what your views are; for with regard to this sect we know that everywhere it is spoken against."

[23] When they had appointed a day for him, they came to him at his lodging in great numbers. And he expounded the matter to them from morning till evening, testifying to the kingdom of God and trying to convince them about Jesus both from the law of Moses and from the prophets. [24] And some were convinced by what he said, while others disbelieved. [25] So, as they

ἀπολῦσαι   διὰ   τὸ   μηδεμίαν   αἰτίαν   θανάτου
to release   on account   -   no   cause   of death
     of

ὑπάρχειν   ἐν   ἐμοί·   19 ἀντιλεγόντων   δὲ
to be   in   me;   but speaking against [this]
     = when the Jews spoke

τῶν   Ἰουδαίων[a]   ἠναγκάσθην   ἐπικαλέσασθαι
the   Jews[a]   I was compelled   to appeal to
against this

Καίσαρα,   οὐχ   ὡς   τοῦ   ἔθνους   μου   ἔχων
Cæsar,   not   as   [4]the   [5]nation   [6]of me   [1]having

τι   κατηγορεῖν.   20 διὰ   ταύτην   οὖν   τὴν
[2]anything   [3]to accuse.   [1]On account of   [2]this   [4]therefore   -

αἰτίαν   παρεκάλεσα   ὑμᾶς   ἰδεῖν   καὶ   προσ-
[3]cause   I called   you   to see   and   to

λαλῆσαι·   εἵνεκεν   γὰρ   τῆς   ἐλπίδος   τοῦ
speak to;   for for the sake of   the   hope   -

Ἰσραὴλ   τὴν   ἅλυσιν   ταύτην   περίκειμαι.
of Israel   [3]this [4]chain   [1]I have round [me].

21 οἱ   δὲ   πρὸς   αὐτὸν   εἶπαν·   ἡμεῖς   οὔτε
And they   to   him   said: We   neither

γράμματα   περὶ   σοῦ   ἐδεξάμεθα   ἀπὸ   τῆς
[2]letters   [3]about   [4]thee   [1]received   from   -

Ἰουδαίας,   οὔτε   παραγενόμενός   τις   τῶν
Judæa,   nor   arriving   anyone   of the

ἀδελφῶν   ἀπήγγειλεν   ἢ   ἐλάλησέν   τι   περὶ
brothers   told   or   spoke   anything   [2]about

σοῦ   πονηρόν.   22 ἀξιοῦμεν   δὲ   παρὰ   σοῦ
[3]thee   [1]evil.   But we think fit   from   thee

ἀκοῦσαι   ἃ   φρονεῖς·   περὶ   μὲν   γὰρ   τῆς
to hear   what   thou   [2]concerning   [2]indeed   [1]for   -
     things   thinkest;

αἱρέσεως   ταύτης   γνωστὸν   ἡμῖν   ἐστιν   ὅτι
[5]sect   [4]this   [7]known   [8]to us   [6]it is   that

πανταχοῦ   ἀντιλέγεται.   23 Ταξάμενοι   δὲ
everywhere   it is spoken against.   And arranging

αὐτῷ   ἡμέραν   ἦλθον   πρὸς   αὐτὸν   εἰς   τὴν
with him   a day   [2]came   [3]to   [4]him   [5]in   the(his)

ξενίαν   πλείονες,   οἷς   ἐξετίθετο   διαμαρτυρ-
[7]lodging   [1]more,   to whom he set forth   solemnly

όμενος   τὴν   βασιλείαν   τοῦ   θεοῦ,   πείθων
witnessing   the   kingdom   -   of God,   [2]persuading

τε   αὐτοὺς   περὶ   τοῦ   Ἰησοῦ   ἀπό   τε   τοῦ
[1]and   them   concerning   -   Jesus   from   both   the

νόμου   Μωϋσέως   καὶ   τῶν   προφητῶν,   ἀπὸ
law   of Moses   and   the   prophets,   from

πρωῒ   ἕως   ἑσπέρας.   24 καὶ   οἱ   μὲν
morning   until   evening.   And   some

ἐπείθοντο   τοῖς   λεγομένοις,   25 οἱ   δὲ
were persuaded   by the things   being said,   others

disagreed among themselves, they departed, after Paul had made one statement: "The Holy Spirit was right in saying to your fathers through Isaiah the prophet:

26 'Go to this people, and say,

You shall indeed hear but never understand,

and you shall indeed see but never perceive.

27 For this people's heart has grown dull,

and their ears are heavy of hearing,

and their eyes they have closed;

lest they should perceive with their eyes,

and hear with their ears,

and understand with their heart,

and turn for me to heal them.'

28 Let it be known to you then that this salvation of God has been sent to the Gentiles; they will listen."[z]

30 And he lived there two whole years at his own expense,[a] and welcomed all who came to him, 31 preaching the kingdom of God and teaching about the Lord Jesus Christ quite openly and unhindered.

ἠπίστουν· ἀσύμφωνοι δὲ ὄντες πρὸς ἀλλή-
disbelieved;   and ²disagreed   ¹being   with   one an-

λους ἀπελύοντο, εἰπόντος τοῦ Παύλου
other   they were dismissed,   having said   –   Paul[a]
                                  =after Paul had said

ῥῆμα ἕν, ὅτι καλῶς τὸ πνεῦμα τὸ ἅγιον
word one,   –   Well   the   Spirit   –   Holy

ἐλάλησεν διὰ Ἠσαΐου τοῦ προφήτου πρὸς
spoke   through   Esaias   the   prophet   to

τοὺς πατέρας ὑμῶν 26 λέγων· πορεύθητι
the   fathers   of you   saying: Go thou

πρὸς τὸν λαὸν τοῦτον καὶ εἰπόν· ἀκοῇ
to   this people   and   say: In hearing

ἀκούσετε καὶ οὐ μὴ συνῆτε, καὶ βλέποντες
ye will hear   and by no means understand, and   looking

βλέψετε καὶ οὐ μὴ ἴδητε· 27 ²ἐπαχύνθη
ye will look   and   by no means   see;   ²was thickened

γὰρ ἡ καρδία τοῦ λαοῦ τούτου, καὶ
¹for   the   heart   of this people,   and

τοῖς ὠσὶν βαρέως ἤκουσαν, καὶ τοὺς
with the(ir) ears   heavily   they heard,   and   the

ὀφθαλμοὺς αὐτῶν ἐκάμμυσαν· μήποτε ἴδωσιν
eyes   of them   they closed;   lest at any time they see

τοῖς ὀφθαλμοῖς καὶ τοῖς ὠσὶν ἀκούσωσιν
with the   eyes   and   with the ears   hear

καὶ τῇ καρδίᾳ συνῶσιν καὶ ἐπιστρέψωσιν,
and with the   heart   understand   and   turn,

καὶ ἰάσομαι αὐτούς. 28 γνωστὸν οὖν
and   I shall cure   them.   Known   therefore

ἔστω ὑμῖν ὅτι τοῖς ἔθνεσιν ἀπεστάλη
let it be   to you   that   to the   nations   was sent

τοῦτο τὸ σωτήριον τοῦ θεοῦ· αὐτοὶ καὶ
this   –   salvation   –   of God;   and they

ἀκούσονται.‡
will hear.

30 Ἐνέμεινεν δὲ διετίαν ὅλην ἐν ἰδίῳ
And he remained   a whole two years   in [his] own

μισθώματι, καὶ ἀπεδέχετο πάντας τοὺς
hired apartment,   and   welcomed   all   the

εἰσπορευομένους πρὸς αὐτόν, 31 κηρύσσων
[ones] coming in   to   him,   proclaiming

τὴν βασιλείαν τοῦ θεοῦ καὶ διδάσκων
the   kingdom   –   of God   and   teaching

τὰ περὶ τοῦ κυρίου Ἰησοῦ Χριστοῦ
the things   concerning   the   Lord   Jesus   Christ

μετὰ πάσης παρρησίας ἀκωλύτως.
with   all   boldness   unhinderedly.

‡ Verse 29 omitted by Nestle; cf. RSV footnote.

---

[z] Other ancient authorities add verse 29, *And when he had said these words, the Jews departed, holding much dispute among themselves.*

[a] Or *in his own hired dwelling*

CHAPTER 1

PAUL, a servant of Jesus Christ, called to be an apostle, set apart for the gospel of God [2] which he promised beforehand through his prophets in the holy scriptures, [3] the gospel concerning his Son, who was descended from David according to the flesh [4] and designated Son of God in power according to the Spirit of holiness by his resurrection from the dead, Jesus Christ our Lord, [5] through whom we have received grace and apostleship to bring about the obedience of faith for the sake of his name among all the nations, [6] including yourselves who are called to belong to Jesus Christ;

[7] To all God's beloved in Rome, who are called to be saints:

Grace to you and peace from God our Father and the Lord Jesus Christ.

[8] First, I thank my God through Jesus Christ for all of you, because your faith is proclaimed in all the world. [9] For God is my witness, whom I serve with my spirit in

1 Παῦλος δοῦλος Χριστοῦ Ἰησοῦ, κλητὸς
Paul   a slave   of Christ   Jesus,   called

ἀπόστολος   ἀφωρισμένος   εἰς   εὐαγγέλιον
an apostle   *having been* separated   to   [the] gospel

θεοῦ, **2** ὃ   προεπηγγείλατο   διὰ   τῶν
of God,   which   he promised beforehand   through   the

προφητῶν αὐτοῦ ἐν γραφαῖς ἁγίαις **3** περὶ
prophets   of him   in   writings   holy   concerning

τοῦ   υἱοῦ   αὐτοῦ   τοῦ   γενομένου   ἐκ
the   Son   of him   –   come   of

σπέρματος   Δαυὶδ   κατὰ   σάρκα,   **4** τοῦ
[the] seed   of David   according to   [the] flesh,   –

ὁρισθέντος   υἱοῦ   θεοῦ   ἐν   δυνάμει
designated   Son   of God   in   power

κατὰ   πνεῦμα ἁγιωσύνης ἐξ ἀναστάσεως
according to [the] Spirit   of holiness   by   a resurrection

νεκρῶν,   Ἰησοῦ Χριστοῦ τοῦ κυρίου ἡμῶν,
of dead persons, Jesus   Christ   the   Lord   of us,

5 δι'   οὗ   ἐλάβομεν χάριν καὶ ἀποστολὴν
through whom we received   grace   and   apostleship

εἰς   ὑπακοὴν   πίστεως   ἐν   πᾶσιν   τοῖς
for   obedience   of faith   among   all   the

ἔθνεσιν   ὑπὲρ   τοῦ   ὀνόματος   αὐτοῦ, **6** ἐν
nations   on behalf of   the   name   of him,   among

οἷς ἐστε καὶ ὑμεῖς κλητοὶ Ἰησοῦ Χριστοῦ,
whom are   also   ye   called   of Jesus   Christ,

7 πᾶσιν   τοῖς   οὖσιν   ἐν   Ῥώμῃ   ἀγαπητοῖς
to all   the [ones]   being   in   Rome   beloved

θεοῦ,   κλητοῖς   ἁγίοις·   χάρις   ὑμῖν   καὶ
of God,   called   holy·   Grace   to you   and

εἰρήνη   ἀπὸ θεοῦ πατρὸς ἡμῶν καὶ κυρίου
peace   from   God [the] Father   of us   and   Lord

Ἰησοῦ   Χριστοῦ.
Jesus   Christ.

8 Πρῶτον   μὲν   εὐχαριστῶ   τῷ   θεῷ   μου
Firstly   –   I thank   the   God   of me

διὰ   Ἰησοῦ   Χριστοῦ   περὶ   πάντων   ὑμῶν,
through Jesus   Christ   concerning   all   you,

ὅτι   ἡ   πίστις   ὑμῶν   καταγγέλλεται   ἐν
because the   faith   of you   is being announced   in

ὅλῳ   τῷ   κόσμῳ.   **9** μάρτυς   γάρ   μού
all   the   world.   For witness   of me

ἐστιν ὁ θεός, ᾧ λατρεύω ἐν τῷ πνεύματί
is   –   God, whom   I serve   in   the   spirit

the gospel of his Son, that without ceasing I mention you always in my prayers, ¹⁰asking that somehow by God's will I may now at last succeed in coming to you. ¹¹For I long to see you, that I may impart to you some spiritual gift to strengthen you, ¹²that is, that we may be mutually encouraged by each other's faith, both yours and mine. ¹³I want you to know, brethren, that I have often intended to come to you (but thus far have been prevented), in order that I may reap some harvest among you as well as among the rest of the Gentiles. ¹⁴I am under obligation both to Greeks and to barbarians, both to the wise and to the foolish: ¹⁵so I am eager to preach the gospel to you also who are in Rome.

16 For I am not ashamed of the gospel: it is the power of God for salvation to every one who has faith, to the Jew first and also to the Greek. ¹⁷For in it the righteousness of God is revealed through faith for faith; as it is written,

μου ἐν τῷ εὐαγγελίῳ τοῦ υἱοῦ αὐτοῦ,
of me in the gospel of the Son of him,

ὡς ἀδιαλείπτως μνείαν ὑμῶν ποιοῦμαι
how unceasingly mention of you I make

10 πάντοτε ἐπὶ τῶν προσευχῶν μου,
always on(in) the prayers of me,

δεόμενος εἴ πως ἤδη ποτὲ εὐοδω-
requesting if somehow now at some time I shall have

θήσομαι ἐν τῷ θελήματι τοῦ θεοῦ ἐλθεῖν
a happy journey in the will – of God to come

πρὸς ὑμᾶς. 11 ἐπιποθῶ γὰρ ἰδεῖν ὑμᾶς,
unto you. For I long to see you,

ἵνα τι μεταδῶ χάρισμα ὑμῖν πνευματικὸν
that ²some ¹I may impart ⁴gift ⁵to you ³spiritual

εἰς τὸ στηριχθῆναι ὑμᾶς, 12 τοῦτο δέ
for the to be established you,ᵇ and this
=that ye may be established,

ἐστιν συμπαρακληθῆναι ἐν ὑμῖν διὰ τῆς
is to be encouraged *with* among you through ¹the

ἐν ἀλλήλοις πίστεως ὑμῶν τε καὶ ἐμοῦ.
³in ⁴one another ²faith ⁶of you ⁵both ⁷and ⁸of me.

13 οὐ θέλω δὲ ὑμᾶς ἀγνοεῖν, ἀδελφοί,
²not ¹I wish ¹But you to be ignorant, brothers,

ὅτι πολλάκις προεθέμην ἐλθεῖν πρὸς ὑμᾶς,
that often ¹I purposed to come unto you,

καὶ ἐκωλύθην ἄχρι τοῦ δεῦρο, ἵνα τινὰ
and was hindered until the present, that some

καρπὸν σχῶ καὶ ἐν ὑμῖν καθὼς καὶ
fruit I may have also among you as indeed

ἐν τοῖς λοιποῖς ἔθνεσιν. 14 Ἕλλησίν
among the remaining nations. ²to Greeks

τε καὶ βαρβάροις, σοφοῖς τε καὶ ἀνοήτοις
¹Both ³and ⁴to foreigners, ⁵to wise men ⁶both ⁷and ⁸to foolish

ὀφειλέτης εἰμί· 15 οὕτως τὸ κατ' ἐμὲ
¹⁰a debtor ⁹I am; so as far as in me lies†

πρόθυμον καὶ ὑμῖν τοῖς ἐν Ῥώμη
[I am] eager ²also ³to you *the* [ones] ⁴in ⁵Rome

εὐαγγελίσασθαι. 16 οὐ γὰρ ἐπαισχύνομαι
¹to preach. For I am not ashamed of

τὸ εὐαγγέλιον· δύναμις γὰρ θεοῦ ἐστιν
the gospel; ²power ¹for of God it is

εἰς σωτηρίαν παντὶ τῷ πιστεύοντι, Ἰουδαίῳ
to salvation to everyone believing, ²to Jew

τε πρῶτον καὶ Ἕλληνι. 17 δικαιοσύνη
¹both firstly and to Greek. a righteousness

γὰρ θεοῦ ἐν αὐτῷ ἀποκαλύπτεται ἐκ
For of God in it is revealed from

πίστεως εἰς πίστιν, καθὼς γέγραπται·
faith to faith, as it has been written:

"He who through faith is righteous shall live."[a]

18 For the wrath of God is revealed from heaven against all ungodliness and wickedness of men who by their wickedness suppress the truth. [19] For what can be known about God is plain to them, because God has shown it to them. [20] Ever since the creation of the world his invisible nature, namely, his eternal power and deity, has been clearly perceived in the things that have been made. So they are without excuse; [21] for although they knew God they did not honor him as God or give thanks to him, but they became futile in their thinking and their senseless minds were darkened. [22] Claiming to be wise, they became fools, [23] and exchanged the glory of the immortal God for images resembling mortal man or birds or animals or reptiles.

24 Therefore God gave them up in the lusts of their hearts to impurity, to the dishonoring of their bodies among themselves, [25] because they exchanged the truth about God for a lie and

---

ὁ δὲ δίκαιος ἐκ πίστεως ζήσεται.
Now the   just man   by   faith   will live.

18 Ἀποκαλύπτεται γὰρ ὀργὴ θεοῦ ἀπ'
For [4]is revealed   [1][the] [2]wrath [3]of God from

οὐρανοῦ ἐπὶ πᾶσαν ἀσέβειαν καὶ ἀδικίαν
heaven against all   impiety   and unrighteousness

ἀνθρώπων τῶν τὴν ἀλήθειαν ἐν ἀδικίᾳ
of men   –   [2]the   [3]truth   [4]in [5]unrighteousness

κατεχόντων, 19 διότι τὸ γνωστὸν τοῦ θεοῦ
[1]holding fast,   because the thing known   – of God

φανερόν ἐστιν ἐν αὐτοῖς· ὁ θεὸς γὰρ αὐτοῖς
manifest   is among them;   – for God   to them

ἐφανέρωσεν. 20 τὰ γὰρ ἀόρατα αὐτοῦ
manifested [it].   For the   invisible things   of him

ἀπὸ κτίσεως κόσμου τοῖς ποιήμασιν
[2]from [3][the] [4]creation [5]of [the] world [7]by the [8]things made

νοούμενα καθορᾶται, ἥ τε
[6]being understood [1]is(are) clearly seen,   [10]the   [9]both

ἀΐδιος αὐτοῦ δύναμις καὶ θειότης, εἰς
[11]everlasting [12]of him [13]power   [13]and   [14]divinity, for

τὸ εἶναι αὐτοὺς ἀναπολογήτους, 21 διότι
the   to be   them[b]   without excuse,   because
=so that they are

γνόντες τὸν θεὸν οὐχ ὡς θεὸν ἐδόξασαν
knowing   – God [2]not [3]as [4]God [1]they glorified [him]

ἢ ηὐχαρίστησαν, ἀλλὰ ἐματαιώθησαν ἐν
[5]or   [6]thanked [him],   but   became vain   in

τοῖς διαλογισμοῖς αὐτῶν, καὶ ἐσκοτίσθη
the   reasonings   of them, and [6]was darkened

ἡ ἀσύνετος αὐτῶν καρδία. 22 φάσκοντες
[1]the [2]undiscerning [4]of them [3]heart.   Asserting

εἶναι σοφοὶ ἐμωράνθησαν, 23 καὶ ἤλλαξαν
to be   wise   they became foolish,   and   changed

τὴν δόξαν τοῦ ἀφθάρτου θεοῦ ἐν ὁμοιώματι
the   glory of the incorruptible God in[to]   a likeness

εἰκόνος φθαρτοῦ ἀνθρώπου καὶ πετεινῶν
of an image of corruptible   man   and   birds

καὶ τετραπόδων καὶ ἑρπετῶν· 24 διὸ
and   quadrupeds   and   reptiles;   wherefore

παρέδωκεν αὐτοὺς ὁ θεὸς ἐν ταῖς
[2]gave up   [3]them   – [1]God   in   the

ἐπιθυμίαις τῶν καρδιῶν αὐτῶν εἰς ἀκαθαρ-
desires   of the   hearts   of them   to   unclean-

σίαν τοῦ ἀτιμάζεσθαι τὰ σώματα αὐτῶν
ness   – to be dishonoured[d] the   bodies   of them

ἐν αὐτοῖς. 25 Οἵτινες μετήλλαξαν τὴν
among them[selves].   Who   changed   the

ἀλήθειαν τοῦ θεοῦ ἐν τῷ ψεύδει, καὶ
truth   – of God in[to] the   lie,   and

---

[a] Or The righteous shall live by faith

worshiped and served the creature rather than the Creator, who is blessed for ever! Amen.
26 For this reason God gave them up to dishonorable passions. Their women exchanged natural relations for unnatural, [27] and the men likewise gave up natural relations with women and were consumed with passion for one another, men committing shameless acts with men and receiving in their own persons the due penalty for their error.
28 And since they did not see fit to acknowledge God, God gave them up to a base mind and to improper conduct. [29] They were filled with all all manner of wickedness, evil, covetousness, malice. Full of envy, murder, strife, deceit, malignity, they are gossips, [30] slanderers, haters of God, insolent, haughty, boastful, inventors of evil, disobedient to parents, [31] foolish, faithless, heartless, ruthless. [32] Though they know

ἐσεβάσθησαν καὶ ἐλάτρευσαν τῇ κτίσει
worshipped and served the creature
παρὰ τὸν κτίσαντα, ὅς ἐστιν εὐλογητὸς
rather the [one] having created, who is blessed
than
εἰς τοὺς αἰῶνας· ἀμήν. 26 διὰ τοῦτο
unto the ages: Amen. Therefore
παρέδωκεν αὐτοὺς ὁ θεὸς εἰς πάθη
²gave up ³them – ¹God to passions
ἀτιμίας· αἵ τε γὰρ θήλειαι αὐτῶν
of dishonour; ³the ²even ¹for females of them
μετήλλαξαν τὴν φυσικὴν χρῆσιν εἰς τὴν
changed the natural use to the [use]
παρὰ φύσιν, 27 ὁμοίως τε καὶ οἱ ἄρσενες
against nature, ²likewise ¹and also the males
ἀφέντες τὴν φυσικὴν χρῆσιν τῆς θηλείας
leaving the natural use of the female
ἐξεκαύθησαν ἐν τῇ ὀρέξει αὐτῶν εἰς
burned in the desire of them toward
ἀλλήλους, ἄρσενες ἐν ἄρσεσιν τὴν
one another, males among males ²the
ἀσχημοσύνην κατεργαζόμενοι καὶ τὴν
³unseemliness ¹working and ⁴the
ἀντιμισθίαν ἣν ἔδει τῆς πλάνης αὐτῶν
⁵requital ⁹which¹⁰behoved ⁶of the ⁷error ⁸of them
ἐν ἑαυτοῖς ἀπολαμβάνοντες. 28 Καὶ
²in ³themselves ¹receiving back. And
καθὼς οὐκ ἐδοκίμασαν τὸν θεὸν ἔχειν
as they thought not fit – God to have
ἐν ἐπιγνώσει, παρέδωκεν αὐτοὺς ὁ θεὸς
in knowledge, ²gave up ³them – ¹God
εἰς ἀδόκιμον νοῦν, ποιεῖν τὰ μὴ καθήκοντα,
to a reprobate mind, to do the not *being* proper,
things
29 πεπληρωμένους πάσῃ ἀδικίᾳ πονηρίᾳ
having been filled with all unrighteousness wickedness
πλεονεξίᾳ κακίᾳ, μεστοὺς φθόνου φόνου
covetousness evil, full of envy *of* murder
ἔριδος δόλου κακοηθείας, ψιθυριστάς,*
of strife *of* guile *of* malignity, whisperers,*
30 καταλάλους, θεοστυγεῖς, ὑβριστάς, ὑπερ-
railers, God-haters, insolent, arro-
ηφάνους, ἀλαζόνας, ἐφευρετὰς κακῶν,
gant, boasters, inventors of evil things,
γονεῦσιν ἀπειθεῖς, 31 ἀσυνέτους, ἀσυνθέτους,
to parents disobedient, undiscerning, faithless,
ἀστόργους, ἀνελεήμονας· 32 οἵτινες τὸ
without unmerciful; who ²the
natural affection,

* " In a bad sense " (Abbott-Smith).

God's decree that those who do such things deserve to die, they not only do them but approve those who practice them.

δικαίωμα τοῦ θεοῦ ἐπιγνόντες, ὅτι οἱ
[3]ordinance – [4]of God [1]knowing, that the

τὰ τοιαῦτα πράσσοντες ἄξιοι θανάτου
the [2]such things [1][ones] practising worthy of death

εἰσίν, οὐ μόνον αὐτὰ ποιοῦσιν, ἀλλὰ
are, not only them do, but

καὶ συνευδοκοῦσιν τοῖς πράσσουσιν.
also consent to the [ones] practising.

CHAPTER 2

THEREFORE you have no excuse, O man, whoever you are, when you judge another; for in passing judgment upon him you condemn yourself, because you, the judge, are doing the very same things. [2]We know that the judgment of God rightly falls upon those who do such things. [3]Do you suppose, O man, that when you judge those who do such things and yet do them yourself, you will escape the judgment of God? [4]Or do you presume upon the riches of his kindness and forbearance and patience? Do you not know that God's kindness is meant to lead you to repentance? [5]But by your hard and impenitent heart you are storing up wrath for yourself on the day of wrath when God's righteous judgment will be revealed. [6]For he will render to every man according to his works:

2 Διὸ ἀναπολόγητος εἶ, ὦ ἄνθρωπε
Wherefore inexcusable thou art, O man

πᾶς ὁ κρίνων· ἐν ᾧ γὰρ κρίνεις τὸν
everyone judging; [2]in [3]what [1]for thou judgest the

ἕτερον, σεαυτὸν κατακρίνεις· τὰ γὰρ αὐτὰ
other, thyself thou condemnest; for the same things

πράσσεις ὁ κρίνων. 2 οἴδαμεν δὲ ὅτι τὸ
thou the judging. But we know that the
practisest [one]

κρίμα τοῦ θεοῦ ἐστιν κατὰ ἀλήθειαν ἐπὶ
judg- – of is accord- truth on
ment God

τοὺς τὰ τοιαῦτα πράσσοντας. 3 λογίζῃ
the the [2]such things [1][ones] practising. reckonest thou

δὲ τοῦτο, ὦ ἄνθρωπε ὁ κρίνων τοὺς
And this, O man the judging the
[one] [ones]

τὰ τοιαῦτα πράσσοντας καὶ ποιῶν αὐτά,
the such things practising and doing them,

ὅτι σὺ ἐκφεύξῃ τὸ κρίμα τοῦ θεοῦ;
that thou wilt escape the judgment – of God?

4 ἢ τοῦ πλούτου τῆς χρηστότητος αὐτοῦ
or the riches of the kindness of him

καὶ τῆς ἀνοχῆς καὶ τῆς μακροθυμίας
and the forbearance and the longsuffering

καταφρονεῖς, ἀγνοῶν ὅτι τὸ χρηστὸν τοῦ
despisest thou, not knowing that the kindness –

θεοῦ εἰς μετάνοιάν σε ἄγει; 5 κατὰ δὲ
of God to repentance thee leads? but according to

τὴν σκληρότητά σου καὶ ἀμετανόητον
the hardness of thee and impenitent

καρδίαν θησαυρίζεις σεαυτῷ ὀργὴν ἐν
heart treasurest for thyself wrath in

ἡμέρᾳ ὀργῆς καὶ ἀποκαλύψεως δικαιοκρισίας
a day of wrath and of revelation of a righteous
judgment

τοῦ θεοῦ, 6 ὃς ἀποδώσει ἑκάστῳ κατὰ τὰ
– of God, who will requite to each man accord- the
ing to

[7] to those who by
patience in well-doing
seek for glory and honor
and immortality, he will
give eternal life; [8] but for
those who are factious
and do not obey the
truth, but obey wicked-
ness, there will be wrath
and fury. [9] There will be
tribulation and distress
for every human being
who does evil, the Jew
first and also the Greek,
[10] but glory and honor
and peace for every one
who does good, the Jew
first and also the Greek.
[11] For God shows no
partiality.

12 All who have
sinned without the law
will also perish without
the law, and all who have
sinned under the law will
be judged by the law.
[13] For it is not the
hearers of the law who
are righteous before God,
but the doers of the law
who will be justified.
[14] When Gentiles who
have not the law do by
nature what the law
requires, they are a law
to themselves, even
though they do not have
the law. [15] They show
that what the law requires
is written on their hearts,
while their conscience
also bears witness and

ἔργα αὐτοῦ· 7 τοῖς μὲν καθ' ὑπομονὴν
works of him : to the [ones] one hand [2]by [3]endurance

ἔργου ἀγαθοῦ δόξαν καὶ τιμὴν καὶ
[5]work [4]of(in) good [6]glory [7]and [8]honour [9]and

ἀφθαρσίαν ζητοῦσιν ζωὴν αἰώνιον·
[10]incorruption [1]seeking [12]life [11]eternal;

8 τοῖς δὲ ἐξ ἐριθείας καὶ ἀπειθοῦσι τῇ
to the [ones] of self-seeking and disobeying the
on the other

ἀληθείᾳ πειθομένοις δὲ τῇ ἀδικίᾳ, ὀργὴ
truth [2]obeying [1]but – unrighteousness, wrath

καὶ θυμός. 9 θλῖψις καὶ στενοχωρία ἐπὶ
and anger. Affliction and anguish on

πᾶσαν ψυχὴν ἀνθρώπου τοῦ κατεργαζομένου
every soul of man – working

τὸ κακόν, Ἰουδαίου τε πρῶτον καὶ
the evil, both of Jew firstly and

Ἕλληνος· 10 δόξα δὲ καὶ τιμὴ καὶ
of Greek; but glory and honour and

εἰρήνη παντὶ τῷ ἐργαζομένῳ τὸ ἀγαθόν,
peace to everyone working the good,

Ἰουδαίῳ τε πρῶτον καὶ Ἕλληνι. 11 οὐ
both to Jew firstly and to Greek. not

γάρ ἐστιν προσωπολημψία παρὰ τῷ θεῷ.
For is respect of persons with – God.

12 Ὅσοι γὰρ ἀνόμως ἥμαρτον, ἀνόμως
For as many as without law sinned, without law

καὶ ἀπολοῦνται· καὶ ὅσοι ἐν νόμῳ
also will perish; and as in law
                            many as (under)

ἥμαρτον, διὰ νόμου κριθήσονται· 13 οὐ
sinned, through law will be judged; [2]not

γὰρ οἱ ἀκροαταὶ νόμου δίκαιοι παρὰ
[1]for the hearers of law [are] just with

[τῷ] θεῷ, ἀλλ' οἱ ποιηταὶ νόμου
– God, but the doers of law

δικαιωθήσονται. 14 ὅταν γὰρ ἔθνη τὰ
will be justified. For whenever nations τὰ

μὴ νόμον ἔχοντα φύσει τὰ τοῦ νόμου
[1]not [3]law [2]having by nature the things of the law

ποιῶσιν, οὗτοι νόμον μὴ ἔχοντες ἑαυτοῖς
do, these [3]law [1]not [2]having to themselves

εἰσιν νόμος· 15 οἵτινες ἐνδείκνυνται τὸ
are a law; who show the

ἔργον τοῦ νόμου γραπτὸν ἐν ταῖς καρδίαις
work of the law written in the hearts

αὐτῶν, συμμαρτυρούσης αὐτῶν τῆς συνει-
of them, witnessing with of them the con-
= while their conscience witnesses with and their

their conflicting thoughts accuse or perhaps excuse them [16] on that day when, according to my gospel, God judges the secrets of men by Christ Jesus.

17 But if you call yourself a Jew and rely upon the law and boast of your relation to God [18] and know his will and approve what is excellent, because you are instructed in the law, [19] and if you are sure that you are a guide to the blind, a light to those who are in darkness, [20] a corrector of the foolish, a teacher of children, having in the law the embodiment of knowledge and truth—[21] you then who teach others, will you not teach yourself? While you preach against stealing, do you steal? [22] You who say that one must not commit adultery, do you commit adultery? You who abhor idols, do you rob temples? [23] You who boast in the law, do you dishonor God by breaking the law? [24] For, as it is written, "The name of God is blasphemed among the Gentiles because of you."

25 Circumcision indeed is of value if you

δήσεως καὶ μεταξὺ ἀλλήλων τῶν λογισμῶν
science and between one another the thoughts

κατηγορούντων ἢ καὶ ἀπολογουμένων, 16 ἐν
accusing or even excusing,[a] in

ᾗ ἡμέρᾳ κρίνει ὁ θεὸς τὰ κρυπτὰ τῶν
what day judges – God the hidden things –

ἀνθρώπων κατὰ τὸ εὐαγγέλιόν μου διὰ
of men according to the gospel of me through

Χριστοῦ Ἰησοῦ. 17 Εἰ δὲ σὺ Ἰουδαῖος
Christ Jesus. But if thou [a] Jew

ἐπονομάζῃ καὶ ἐπαναπαύῃ νόμῳ καὶ
[1] art named and restest on law and

καυχᾶσαι ἐν θεῷ 18 καὶ γινώσκεις τὸ
boastest in God and knowest the

θέλημα καὶ δοκιμάζεις τὰ διαφέροντα
will and approvest the things excelling

κατηχούμενος ἐκ τοῦ νόμου, 19 πέποιθάς τε
being instructed out of the law, and having persuaded

σεαυτὸν ὁδηγὸν εἶναι τυφλῶν, φῶς
thyself a guide to be of blind a light
[persons],

τῶν ἐν σκότει, 20 παιδευτὴν ἀφρόνων,
of the in darkness, an instructor of foolish
[ones] [persons],

διδάσκαλον νηπίων, ἔχοντα τὴν μόρφωσιν
a teacher of infants, having the form

τῆς γνώσεως καὶ τῆς ἀληθείας ἐν τῷ
– of knowledge and of the truth in the

νόμῳ· 21 ὁ οὖν διδάσκων ἕτερον σεαυτὸν
law: the there- teaching another thyself
[one] fore

οὐ διδάσκεις; ὁ κηρύσσων μὴ κλέπτειν
teachest thou not? the [one] proclaiming not to steal

κλέπτεις; 22 ὁ λέγων μὴ μοιχεύειν
stealest thou? the [one] saying not to commit adultery

μοιχεύεις; ὁ βδελυσσόμενος τὰ εἴδωλα
dost thou commit the detesting the idols
adultery? [one]

ἱεροσυλεῖς; 23 ὃς ἐν νόμῳ καυχᾶσαι, διὰ
dost thou rob who in law boastest, through
temples?

τῆς παραβάσεως τοῦ νόμου τὸν θεὸν
– transgression of the law – [2]God

ἀτιμάζεις; 24 τὸ γὰρ ὄνομα τοῦ θεοῦ
[1]dishonourest thou? for the name – of God

δι’ ὑμᾶς βλασφημεῖται ἐν τοῖς ἔθνεσιν,
because you is blasphemed among the nations,
of

καθὼς γέγραπται. 25 περιτομὴ μὲν γὰρ
as it has been written. circumcision indeed For

obey the law; but if you break the law, your circumcision becomes uncircumcision. 26 So, if a man who is uncircumcised keeps the precepts of the law, will not his uncircumcision be regarded as circumcision? 27 Then those who are physically uncircumcised but keep the law will condemn you who have the written code and circumcision but break the law. 28 For he is not a real Jew who is one outwardly, nor is true circumcision something external and physical. 29 He is a Jew who is one inwardly, and real circumcision is a matter of the heart, spiritual and not literal. His praise is not from men but from God.

ὠφελεῖ ἐὰν νόμον πράσσῃς· ἐὰν δὲ
profits if law thou practisest; but if

παραβάτης νόμου ᾖς, ἡ περιτομή σου
a transgressor of law thou art, the circumcision of thee

ἀκροβυστία γέγονεν. 26 ἐὰν οὖν ἡ ἀκρο-
uncircumcision has become. If therefore the uncir-

βυστία τὰ δικαιώματα τοῦ νόμου φυλάσσῃ,
cumcision the ordinances of the law keeps,

οὐχ ἡ ἀκροβυστία αὐτοῦ εἰς περιτομὴν
not the uncircumcision of him for circumcision

λογισθήσεται; 27 καὶ κρινεῖ ἡ ἐκ φύσεως
will be reckoned? and ⁸will judge ¹the ³by ⁴nature

ἀκροβυστία τὸν νόμον τελοῦσα σὲ τὸν
²uncircumcision ⁶the ⁷law ⁵keeping ⁹thee ¹⁰the

διὰ γράμματος καὶ περιτομῆς παραβάτην
¹³through ¹⁴letter ¹⁵and ¹⁶circumcision ¹¹transgressor

νόμου. 28 οὐ γὰρ ὁ ἐν τῷ φανερῷ
¹²of law. For ²not ³the ⁵in ⁶the ⁷open

Ἰουδαῖός ἐστιν, οὐδὲ ἡ ἐν τῷ φανερῷ
⁴Jew ¹he is, nor ¹the ³in ⁴the ⁵open

ἐν σαρκὶ περιτομή· 29 ἀλλ' ὁ ἐν τῷ
⁶in ⁷flesh ²circumcision; but ¹the ³in ⁴the

κρυπτῷ Ἰουδαῖος, καὶ περιτομὴ καρδίας
⁵secret ²Jew [is], and circumcision [is] of heart

ἐν πνεύματι οὐ γράμματι, οὗ ὁ ἔπαινος
in spirit not letter, of the praise [is]
　　　　　　　　　　　　　　　　　whom

οὐκ ἐξ ἀνθρώπων ἀλλ' ἐκ τοῦ θεοῦ.
not from men but from - God.

CHAPTER 3

THEN what advantage has the Jew? Or what is the value of circumcision? 2 Much in every way. To begin with, the Jews are entrusted with the oracles of God. 3 What if some were unfaithful? Does their faithlessness nullify the faithfulness of God? 4 By no means! Let God be true though every man be false, as it is written,

"That thou mayest be justified in thy words,

3 Τί οὖν τὸ περισσὸν τοῦ Ἰουδαίου,
What therefore the advantage of the Jew,

ἢ τίς ἡ ὠφέλεια τῆς περιτομῆς; 2 πολὺ
or what the profit - of circumcision? Much

κατὰ πάντα τρόπον. πρῶτον μὲν [γὰρ]
by every way. ³Firstly ²indeed ¹for

ὅτι ἐπιστεύθησαν τὰ λόγια τοῦ θεοῦ.
because they were the oracles - of God.
　　　　　　　entrusted [with]

3 τί γάρ; εἰ ἠπίστησάν τινες, μὴ ἡ
For what? If ²disbelieved ¹some, not the

ἀπιστία αὐτῶν τὴν πίστιν τοῦ θεοῦ
unbelief of them the faith - of God

καταργήσει; 4 μὴ γένοιτο· γινέσθω δὲ
will destroy? May it not be; but let be

ὁ θεὸς ἀληθής, πᾶς δὲ ἄνθρωπος ψεύστης,
- God true, and every man a liar,

καθάπερ γέγραπται· ὅπως ἂν δικαιωθῇς
as it has been So as - thou mayest
　written: be justified

and prevail when thou art judged."
[5]But if our wickedness serves to show the justice of God, what shall we say? That God is unjust to inflict wrath on us? (I speak in a human way.) [6]By no means! For then how could God judge the world? [7]But if through my falsehood God's truthfulness abounds to his glory, why am I still being condemned as a sinner? [8]And why not do evil that good may come?—as some people slanderously charge us with saying. Their condemnation is just.

9 What then? Are we Jews any better off?[b] No, not at all; for I have already charged that all men, both Jews and Greeks, are under the power of sin, [10]as it is written:
"None is righteous, no, not one;
[11]no one understands, no one seeks for God.
[12]All have turned aside, together they have gone wrong;
no one does good, not even one."
[13]"Their throat is an open grave,

ἐν τοῖς λόγοις σου καὶ νικήσεις ἐν
in   the   sayings   of thee   and   wilt overcome   in

τῷ κρίνεσθαί σε. 5 εἰ δὲ ἡ ἀδικία
the   to be judged   thee.[be]   Now if   the   unright-
=when thou art judged.   eousness

ἡμῶν θεοῦ δικαιοσύνην συνίστησιν, τί
of us   [3]of God   [2]a righteousness   [1]commends,   what

ἐροῦμεν; μὴ ἄδικος ὁ θεὸς ὁ ἐπιφέρων
shall we say?   not   unrighteous   –   God   the [one] inflicting

τὴν ὀργήν; κατὰ ἄνθρωπον λέγω. 6 μὴ
–   wrath? according to   man   I say.   not

γένοιτο· ἐπεὶ πῶς κρινεῖ ὁ θεὸς τὸν
May it be;   otherwise   how   will judge   –   God   the

κόσμον; 7 εἰ δὲ ἡ ἀλήθεια τοῦ θεοῦ
world?   But if   the   truth   –   of God

ἐν τῷ ἐμῷ ψεύσματι ἐπερίσσευσεν εἰς
by   –   my   lie   abounded   to

τὴν δόξαν αὐτοῦ, τί ἔτι κἀγὼ ὡς
the   glory   of him,   why   still   I also   as

ἁμαρτωλὸς κρίνομαι; 8 καὶ μὴ καθὼς
a sinner   am judged?   and   not   as

βλασφημούμεθα καὶ καθώς φασίν τινες
we are blasphemed   and   as   [2]say   [1]some

ἡμᾶς λέγειν ὅτι ποιήσωμεν τὰ κακὰ
us   to say[,]   –   Let us do   –   evil things
=that we say,

ἵνα ἔλθῃ τὰ ἀγαθά; ὧν τὸ κρίμα
that may come   –   good things? of whom   the   judgment

ἔνδικόν ἐστιν. 9 Τί οὖν; προεχόμεθα;
just   is.   What therefore?   Do we excel?

οὐ πάντως· προῃτιασάμεθα γὰρ Ἰουδαίους
not   at all;   for we previously accused   [2]Jews

τε καὶ Ἕλληνας πάντας ὑφ' ἁμαρτίαν
[1]both and   Greeks   all   under   sin

εἶναι, 10 καθὼς γέγραπται ὅτι οὐκ ἔστιν
to be,   as   it has been written[,]   –   There is not

δίκαιος οὐδὲ εἷς, οὐκ ἔστιν ὁ
a righteous man   not   one,   there is not   the [one]

συνίων, 11 οὐκ ἔστιν ὁ ἐκζητῶν τὸν θεόν·
under-   there is not   the   seeking   –   God;
standing,   [one]

12 πάντες ἐξέκλιναν, ἅμα ἠχρεώθησαν·
all   turned away,   together became unprofitable;

οὐκ ἔστιν ὁ ποιῶν χρηστότητα, οὐκ
there is not   the [one] doing   kindness,   not

ἔστιν ἕως ἑνός. 13 τάφος ἀνεῳγμένος
there is   so much as   one.   A grave   *having been* opened

[b] Or *at any disadvantage?*

they use their tongues
to deceive."
"The venom of asps is
under their lips."
14 "Their mouth is full of
curses and bitter-
ness."
15 "Their feet are swift to
shed blood,
16 in their paths are
ruin and misery,
17 and the way of peace
they do not know."
18 "There is no fear of
God before their
eyes."
19 Now we know that
whatever the law says it
speaks to those who are
under the law, so that
every mouth may be
stopped, and the whole
world may be held
accountable to God.
20 For no human being
will be justified in his
sight by works of the
law, since through the law
comes knowledge of sin.
21 But now the
righteousness of God has
been manifested apart
from law, although the
law and the prophets
bear witness to it, 22 the
righteousness of God
through faith in Jesus
Christ for all who be-
lieve. For there is no
distinction; 23 since all
have sinned and fall
short of the glory of God,
24 they are justified by
his grace as a gift,
through the redemption
which is in Christ Jesus,

ὁ   λάρυγξ   αὐτῶν,   ταῖς   γλώσσαις   αὐτῶν
the   throat   of them,   with the   tongues   of them

ἐδολιοῦσαν,   ἰὸς   ἀσπίδων   ὑπὸ   τὰ   χείλη
they acted   poison   of asps   under   the   lips
deceitfully,

αὐτῶν·   14   ὧν   τὸ   στόμα   ἀρᾶς   καὶ   πικρίας
of them;   of whom the   mouth   [2]of cursing   [3]and   [4]bitterness

γέμει·   15   ὀξεῖς   οἱ   πόδες   αὐτῶν   ἐκχέαι
[1]is full;   swift   the   feet   of them   to shed

αἷμα,   16   σύντριμμα   καὶ   ταλαιπωρία   ἐν
blood,   ruin   and   misery   in

ταῖς   ὁδοῖς   αὐτῶν,   17   καὶ   ὁδὸν   εἰρήνης
the   ways   of them,   and   a way   of peace

οὐκ   ἔγνωσαν.   18   οὐκ   ἔστιν   φόβος   θεοῦ
they knew not.   There is not   fear   of God

ἀπέναντι   τῶν   ὀφθαλμῶν   αὐτῶν.   19   οἴδαμεν
before   the   eyes   of them.   we know

δὲ   ὅτι   ὅσα   ὁ   νόμος   λέγει   τοῖς   ἐν   τῷ
But   that   whatever the   law   says   to the   in   the
    things   [ones]

νόμῳ   λαλεῖ,   ἵνα   πᾶν   στόμα   φραγῇ   καὶ
law   it speaks, in order that every   mouth   may be stopped and

ὑπόδικος   γένηται   πᾶς   ὁ   κόσμος   τῷ
[5]under   [4]may become   [1]all   [2]the   [3]world   –
judgment

θεῷ·   20   διότι   ἐξ   ἔργων   νόμου   οὐ
to God;   because   by   works   of law   not

δικαιωθήσεται   πᾶσα   σὰρξ   ἐνώπιον   αὐτοῦ·
will be justified   all   flesh*   before   him;

διὰ   γὰρ   νόμου   ἐπίγνωσις   ἁμαρτίας.
for through   law [is]   full knowledge   of sin.

21   Νυνὶ   δὲ   χωρὶς   νόμου   δικαιοσύνη
But now   without   law   a righteousness

θεοῦ   πεφανέρωται,   μαρτυρουμένη   ὑπὸ   τοῦ
of God has been manifested,   being witnessed   by   the

νόμου   καὶ   τῶν   προφητῶν,   22   δικαιοσύνη
law   and   the   prophets,   [2]a righteousness

δὲ   θεοῦ   διὰ   πίστεως   [Ἰησοῦ]   Χριστοῦ,
[1]and   of God   through   faith   of(in) Jesus   Christ,

εἰς   πάντας   τοὺς   πιστεύοντας·   οὐ   γάρ
to   all   the [ones]   believing;   for not

ἐστιν   διαστολή·   23   πάντες   γὰρ   ἥμαρτον
there is   difference;   for all   sinned

καὶ   ὑστεροῦνται   τῆς   δόξης   τοῦ   θεοῦ,
and   come short   of the   glory   –   of God,

24   δικαιούμενοι   δωρεὰν   τῇ   αὐτοῦ   χάριτι
being justified   freely   by the   of him   grace

διὰ   τῆς   ἀπολυτρώσεως   τῆς   ἐν   Χριστῷ
through the   redemption   –   in   Christ

* That is, no flesh will be justified . . .

²⁵whom God put forward as an expiation by his blood, to be received by faith. This was to show God's righteousness, because in his divine forbearance he had passed over former sins; ²⁶it was to prove at the present time that he himself is righteous and that he justifies him who has faith in Jesus.

27 Then what becomes of our boasting? It is excluded. On what principle? On the principle of works? No, but on the principle of faith. ²⁸For we hold that a man is justified by faith apart from works of law. ²⁹Or is God the God of Jews only? Is he not the God of Gentiles also? Yes, of Gentiles also, ³⁰since God is one; and he will justify the circumcised on the ground of their faith and the uncircumcised through their faith. ³¹Do we then overthrow the law by this faith? By no means! On the contrary, we uphold the law.

CHAPTER 4

WHAT then shall we say about[e] Abraham, our forefather according to the flesh? ²For if Abraham was justified by works, he has something to boast about, but not before God. ³For what does the

---

[e] Other ancient authorities read *was gained by*

Ἰησοῦ· 25 ὃν προέθετο ὁ θεὸς ἱλαστήριον
Jesus;   whom set forth – God a propitiation
διὰ πίστεως ἐν τῷ αὐτοῦ αἵματι, εἰς
through faith by the of him blood, for
ἔνδειξιν τῆς δικαιοσύνης αὐτοῦ διὰ τὴν
a showing of the righteousness of him because of the
                                        forth
πάρεσιν τῶν προγεγονότων ἁμαρτημάτων
passing by of the ²having previously ¹sins
                    occurred
26 ἐν τῇ ἀνοχῇ τοῦ θεοῦ, πρὸς τὴν
in the forbearance – of God, for the
ἔνδειξιν τῆς δικαιοσύνης αὐτοῦ ἐν τῷ
showing of the righteousness of him in the
forth
νῦν καιρῷ, εἰς τὸ εἶναι αὐτὸν δίκαιον
present time, for the to be him[b] just
                        =that he should be
καὶ δικαιοῦντα τὸν ἐκ πίστεως Ἰησοῦ.
and justifying the [one] of faith of(in) Jesus.
27 Ποῦ οὖν ἡ καύχησις; ἐξεκλείσθη. διὰ
Where there- the boasting? It was shut out. Through
     fore
ποίου νόμου; τῶν ἔργων; οὐχί, ἀλλὰ
what law? – of works? no, but
διὰ νόμου πίστεως. 28 λογιζόμεθα γὰρ
through a law of faith.   For we reckon
δικαιοῦσθαι πίστει ἄνθρωπον χωρὶς ἔργων
¹to be justified ³by faith ¹a man without works
νόμου. 29 ἢ Ἰουδαίων ὁ θεὸς μόνον;
of law. Or of Jews [is he] the God only?
οὐχὶ καὶ ἐθνῶν; ναὶ καὶ ἐθνῶν, 30 εἴπερ
not also of nations? Yes[,] also of nations, since [there is]
εἷς ὁ θεὸς ὃς δικαιώσει περιτομὴν ἐκ
one – God who will justify circumcision by
πίστεως καὶ ἀκροβυστίαν διὰ τῆς πίστεως.
faith and uncircumcision through the faith.
31 νόμον οὖν καταργοῦμεν διὰ τῆς
²Law ³therefore ¹do we destroy through the
πίστεως; μὴ γένοιτο, ἀλλὰ νόμον ἱστάνομεν.
faith? May it not be, but ²law ¹we establish.

4 Τί οὖν ἐροῦμεν εὑρηκέναι Ἀβραὰμ
What therefore shall we say to have found Abraham
τὸν προπάτορα ἡμῶν κατὰ σάρκα; 2 εἰ
the forefather of us according to flesh? if
γὰρ Ἀβραὰμ ἐξ ἔργων ἐδικαιώθη, ἔχει
For Abraham by works was justified, he has
καύχημα· ἀλλ᾽ οὐ πρὸς θεόν. 3 τί γὰρ
a boast; but not with God. For what

scripture say? "Abraham believed God, and it was reckoned to him as righteousness." ⁴Now to one who works, his wages are not reckoned as a gift but as his due. ⁵And to one who does not work but trusts him who justifies the ungodly, his faith is reckoned as righteousness. ⁶So also David pronounces a blessing upon the man to whom God reckons righteousness apart from works:

⁷"Blessed are those whose iniquities are forgiven, and whose sins are covered;

⁸blessed is the man against whom the Lord will not reckon his sin."

9 Is this blessing pronounced only upon the circumcised, or also upon the uncircumcised? We say that faith was reckoned to Abraham as righteousness. ¹⁰How then was it reckoned to him? Was it before or after he had been circumcised? It was not after, but before he was circumcised. ¹¹He received circumcision as a sign or seal of the righteousness which he had by faith while he was still uncircumcised. The purpose was to make him the father of all

---

ἡ γραφὴ λέγει; ἐπίστευσεν δὲ Ἀβραὰμ
the scripture says? And ²believed ¹Abraham

τῷ θεῷ, καὶ ἐλογίσθη αὐτῷ εἰς
- God, and it was reckoned to him for

δικαιοσύνην. 4 τῷ δὲ ἐργαζομένῳ ὁ
righteousness. Now to the [one] working the

μισθὸς οὐ λογίζεται κατὰ χάριν ἀλλὰ
reward is not reckoned according to grace but

κατὰ ὀφείλημα· 5 τῷ δὲ μὴ ἐργαζομένῳ,
according to debt; but to the [one] not working,

πιστεύοντι δὲ ἐπὶ τὸν δικαιοῦντα τὸν
but believing on the [one] justifying the

ἀσεβῆ, λογίζεται ἡ πίστις αὐτοῦ εἰς
impious man, is reckoned the faith of him for

δικαιοσύνην, 6 καθάπερ καὶ Δαυὶδ λέγει
righteousness, even as also David says

τὸν μακαρισμὸν τοῦ ἀνθρώπου ᾧ ὁ
the blessedness of the man to whom -

θεὸς λογίζεται δικαιοσύνην χωρὶς ἔργων·
God reckons righteousness without works:

7 μακάριοι ὧν ἀφέθησαν αἱ ἀνομίαι
Blessed [are they] of whom were forgiven the lawlessnesses

καὶ ὧν ἐπεκαλύφθησαν αἱ ἁμαρτίαι·
and of whom were covered over the sins;

8 μακάριος ἀνὴρ οὗ οὐ μὴ λογίσηται
blessed [is] a man of whom by no means ²may reckon

κύριος ἁμαρτίαν 9 ὁ μακαρισμὸς οὖν
¹[the] Lord sin. - ²blessedness ³then

οὗτος ἐπὶ τὴν περιτομὴν ἢ καὶ ἐπὶ
¹This on the circumcision or also on

τὴν ἀκροβυστίαν; λέγομεν γάρ· ⁸ἐλογίσθη
the uncircumcision? for we say : ²was reckoned

τῷ Ἀβραὰμ ἡ πίστις εἰς δικαιοσύνην.
- ⁴to Abraham ¹The(his) ²faith for righteousness.

10 πῶς οὖν ἐλογίσθη; ἐν περιτομῇ ὄντι
How then was it reckoned? in circumcision being

ἢ ἐν ἀκροβυστίᾳ; οὐκ ἐν περιτομῇ ἀλλ᾽
or in uncircumcision? not in circumcision but

ἐν ἀκροβυστίᾳ· 11 καὶ σημεῖον ἔλαβεν
in uncircumcision; and ²a sign ¹he received

περιτομῆς σφραγῖδα τῆς δικαιοσύνης τῆς
of circumcision a seal of the righteousness of the

πίστεως τῆς ἐν τῇ ἀκροβυστίᾳ, εἰς
faith - [while] in - uncircumcision, for
=so

τὸ εἶναι αὐτὸν πατέρα πάντων τῶν
the to be him[b] a father of all the
that he should be

who believe without being circumcised and who thus have righteousness reckoned to them, and likewise the father of the circumcised who are not merely circumcised but also follow the example of the faith which our father Abraham had before he was circumcised.

13 The promise to Abraham and his descendants, that they should inherit the world, did not come through the law but through the righteousness of faith. If it is the adherents of the law who are to be the heirs, faith is null and the promise is void. For the law bring wrath, but where there is no law there is no transgression.

16 That is why it depends on faith, in order that the promise may rest on grace and be guaranteed to all his descendants—not only to the adherents of the law but also to those who share the faith of Abraham, for he is the father of us all, as it is written, "I have made you the father of many nations" —in the presence of the God in whom he believed, who gives life to

πιστευόντων δι' ἀκροβυστίας, εἰς τό
[ones] believing through uncircumcision, for the
=that right-

λογισθῆναι αὐτοῖς [τὴν] δικαιοσύνην, 12 καὶ
to be reckoned to them – righteousness,[b] and
eousness should be reckoned to them,

πατέρα περιτομῆς τοῖς οὐκ ἐκ περιτομῆς
a father of circumcision to the not of circumcision
[ones]

μόνον ἀλλὰ καὶ τοῖς στοιχοῦσιν τοῖς
only but also to the [ones] walking in the

ἴχνεσιν τῆς ἐν ἀκροβυστίᾳ πίστεως τοῦ
steps [1]of the [7]in [8]uncircumcision [2]faith [3]of the

πατρὸς ἡμῶν Ἀβραάμ. 13 Οὐ γὰρ διὰ
[4]father [5]of us [6]Abraham. For not through

νόμου ἡ ἐπαγγελία τῷ Ἀβραὰμ ἢ τῷ
law the promise – to Abraham or to the

σπέρματι αὐτοῦ, τὸ κληρονόμον αὐτὸν
seed of him, the heir him
=that he should be heir

εἶναι κόσμου, ἀλλὰ διὰ δικαιοσύνης πίστεως.
to be[b] of [the] world, but through a righteousness of faith.

14 εἰ γὰρ οἱ ἐκ νόμου κληρονόμοι,
For if [1]the [3][are] [4]of [5]law [2]heirs,

κεκένωται ἡ πίστις καὶ κατήργηται
[3]has been emptied – [1]faith and [2]has been destroyed

ἡ ἐπαγγελία· 15 ὁ γὰρ νόμος ὀργὴν
[1]the [2]promise; for the law [2]wrath

κατεργάζεται· οὗ δὲ οὐκ ἔστιν νόμος,
[1]works; and where there is not law,

οὐδὲ παράβασις. 16 Διὰ τοῦτο ἐκ πίστεως,
neither [is there] Therefore [it is] of faith,
transgression.

ἵνα κατὰ χάριν, εἰς τὸ εἶναι βεβαίαν
in [it may be] grace, for the to be firm
order according =so that the promise shall be firm
that to

τὴν ἐπαγγελίαν παντὶ τῷ σπέρματι, οὐ
the promise[b] to all the seed, not

τῷ ἐκ τοῦ νόμου μόνον ἀλλὰ καὶ τῷ
to the of the law only but also to the
[seed] [seed]

ἐκ πίστεως Ἀβραάμ, ὅς ἐστιν πατὴρ
of [the] faith of Abraham, who is father

πάντων ἡμῶν, 17 καθὼς γέγραπται ὅτι
of all us, as it has been written[,] –

πατέρα πολλῶν ἐθνῶν τέθεικά σε,
A father of many nations I have appointed thee,

κατέναντι οὗ ἐπίστευσεν θεοῦ τοῦ ζωο-
before [2]whom [3]he believed [1]God the [one] quick-

the dead and calls into existence the things that do not exist. [18] In hope he believed against hope, that he should become the father of many nations; as he had been told, "So shall your descendants be." [19] He did not weaken in faith when he considered his own body, which was as good as dead because he was about a hundred years old, or when he considered the barrenness of Sarah's womb. [20] No distrust made him waver concerning the promise of God, but he grew strong in his faith as he gave glory to God, [21] fully convinced that God was able to do what he had promised. [22] That is why his faith was "reckoned to him as righteousness." [23] But the words, "it was reckoned to him," were written not for his sake alone, [24] but for ours also. It will be reckoned to us who believe in him that raised from the dead Jesus our Lord, [25] who was put to death for our trespasses and raised for our justification.

ποιοῦντος   τοὺς   νεκροὺς   καὶ   καλοῦντος
ening   the   dead [ones]   and   calling

τὰ   μὴ   ὄντα   ὡς   ὄντα·   18 ὃς   παρ'   ἐλπίδα
the   not   being   as   being;   who beyond   hope
things

ἐπ'   ἐλπίδι   ἐπίστευσεν,   εἰς   τὸ   γενέσθαι
on   hope   believed,   for   the   to become
                                    =so that he should become

αὐτὸν   πατέρα   πολλῶν   ἐθνῶν   κατὰ   τὸ
him[b]   a father   of many   nations   accord-   the
                                    ing to   thing

εἰρημένον·   οὕτως   ἔσται   τὸ   σπέρμα   σου·
having been said :   So   shall be   the   seed   of thee;

19 καὶ   μὴ   ἀσθενήσας   τῇ   πίστει   κατενόησεν
and   not   weakening   —   in faith   he considered

τὸ   ἑαυτοῦ   σῶμα   νενεκρωμένον,   ἑκατονταέτης
[1]the   [3]of himself   [2]body   to have died,   a hundred years

που   ὑπάρχων,   καὶ   τὴν   νέκρωσιν   τῆς
about   being,   and   the   death   of the

μήτρας   Σάρρας·   20 εἰς   δὲ   τὴν   ἐπαγγελίαν
womb   of Sarah;   but [2]against [3]the   [4]promise

τοῦ   θεοῦ   οὐ   διεκρίθη   τῇ   ἀπιστίᾳ,   ἀλλὰ
—   [5]of God   [1]he did not decide   —   [6]by unbelief,   but

ἐνεδυναμώθη   τῇ   πίστει,   δοὺς   δόξαν   τῷ
was empowered   —   by faith,   giving   glory   —

θεῷ   21 καὶ   πληροφορηθεὶς   ὅτι   ὁ   ἐπήγγελται
to God   and   being fully   that what   he has
                  persuaded   promised

δυνατός   ἐστιν   καὶ   ποιῆσαι.   22 διὸ   [καὶ]
able   he is   also   to do.   Wherefore   also

ἐλογίσθη   αὐτῷ   εἰς   δικαιοσύνην.   23 Οὐκ
it was   to him   for   righteousness.   not
reckoned

ἐγράφη   δὲ   δι'   αὐτὸν   μόνον   ὅτι   ἐλογίσθη
it was   Now because   him   only   that   it was
written   of   reckoned

αὐτῷ,   24 ἀλλὰ   καὶ   δι'   ἡμᾶς,   οἷς   μέλλει
to him,   but   also because   us,   to whom   it is
                  of   about

λογίζεσθαι,   τοῖς   πιστεύουσιν   ἐπὶ   τὸν
to be reckoned,   to the [ones] believing   on   the [one]

ἐγείραντα   Ἰησοῦν   τὸν   κύριον   ἡμῶν   ἐκ
having raised   Jesus   the   Lord   of us   out of

νεκρῶν,   25 ὃς   παρεδόθη   διὰ   τὰ   παραπ-
[the] dead,   who was delivered because of the   of-

τώματα   ἡμῶν   καὶ   ἠγέρθη   διὰ   τὴν
fences   of us   and   was raised because of   the

δικαίωσιν   ἡμῶν.
justification   of us.

CHAPTER 5

THEREFORE, since we are justified by faith, we[d] have peace with God through our Lord Jesus Christ. [2]Through him we have obtained access[e] to this grace in which we stand, and we[f] rejoice in our hope of sharing the glory of God. [3]More than that, we[f] rejoice in our sufferings, knowing that suffering produces endurance, [4]and endurance produces character, and character produces hope, [5]and hope does not disappoint us, because God's love has been poured into our hearts through the Holy Spirit which has been given to us.

6 While we were yet helpless, at the right time Christ died for the ungodly. [7]Why, one will hardly die for a righteous man—though perhaps for a good man one will dare even to die. [8]But God shows his love for us in that while we were yet sinners Christ died for us. [9]Since, therefore, we are now justified by his blood,

5 Δικαιωθέντες οὖν ἐκ πίστεως εἰρήνην
Having been justified therefore by   faith   peace

ἔχομεν πρὸς τὸν θεὸν διὰ τοῦ κυρίου
we have   with   -   God   through the   Lord

ἡμῶν Ἰησοῦ Χριστοῦ, 2 δι' οὗ καὶ τὴν
of us Jesus   Christ,   through whom also   the

προσαγωγὴν ἐσχήκαμεν [τῇ πίστει] εἰς
access   we have had   -   by faith   into

τὴν χάριν ταύτην ἐν ᾗ ἑστήκαμεν, καὶ
this grace   in which   we stand,   and

καυχώμεθα ἐπ' ἐλπίδι τῆς δόξης τοῦ
boast   on   hope   of the glory   -

θεοῦ. 3 οὐ μόνον δέ, ἀλλὰ καὶ καυχώμεθα
of God.   And not only [so], but   also   we boast

ἐν ταῖς θλίψεσιν, εἰδότες ὅτι ἡ θλῖψις
in   -   afflictions, knowing that - affliction

ὑπομονὴν κατεργάζεται, 4 ἡ δὲ ὑπομονὴ
patience   works,   - and   patience

δοκιμήν, ἡ δὲ δοκιμὴ ἐλπίδα· 5 ἡ δὲ
proof,   - and   proof   hope;   - and

ἐλπὶς οὐ καταισχύνει, ὅτι ἡ ἀγάπη
hope   does not put to shame, because the   love

τοῦ θεοῦ ἐκκέχυται ἐν ταῖς καρδίαις
- of God has been poured out in   the   hearts

ἡμῶν διὰ πνεύματος ἁγίου τοῦ δοθέντος
of us through Spirit   Holy   -   given

ἡμῖν· 6 εἴ γε Χριστὸς ὄντων ἡμῶν
to us;   indeed [7]Christ [2]being [1]us
                                    = when we were weak

ἀσθενῶν ἔτι κατὰ καιρὸν ὑπὲρ ἀσεβῶν
[4]weak[a] [3]yet [5]accord- [6]time [9]on [10]impious
                   ing to   behalf of ones

ἀπέθανεν. 7 μόλις γὰρ ὑπὲρ δικαίου
[8]died.   For hardly   on behalf of a just man

τις ἀποθανεῖται· ὑπὲρ γὰρ τοῦ ἀγαθοῦ
anyone   will die;   for on behalf of the good man

τάχα τις καὶ τολμᾷ ἀποθανεῖν· 8 συνίστησιν
perhaps some- even dares   to die;   [2]commends
        one

δὲ τὴν ἑαυτοῦ ἀγάπην εἰς ἡμᾶς ὁ θεὸς
but [3]the [5]of himself [4]love [6]to [7]us - [1]God

ὅτι ἔτι ἁμαρτωλῶν ὄντων ἡμῶν Χριστὸς
that yet   sinners   being   us[a]   Christ
        = while we were yet sinners

ὑπὲρ ἡμῶν ἀπέθανεν. 9 πολλῷ οὖν μᾶλλον
on be-   us   died.   By much there- rather
half of   fore

δικαιωθέντες νῦν ἐν τῷ αἵματι αὐτοῦ
having been justified now by the blood   of him

[d] Other ancient authorities read let us
[e] Other ancient authorities add by faith
[f] Or let us

much more shall we be saved by him from the wrath of God. ¹⁰For if while we were enemies we were reconciled to God by the death of his Son, much more, now that we are reconciled, shall we be saved by his life. ¹¹Not only so, but we also rejoice in God through our Lord Jesus Christ, through whom we have now received our reconciliation.

12 Therefore as sin came into the world through one man and death through sin, and so death spread to all men because all men sinned— ¹³sin indeed was in the world before the law was given, but sin is not counted where there is no law. ¹⁴Yet death reigned from Adam to Moses, even over those whose sins were not like the transgression of Adam, who was a type of the one who was to come.

15 But the free gift is not like the trespass. For if many died through one man's trespass, much more have the grace of God and the free gift in the grace of that one man

σωθησόμεθα δι' αὐτοῦ ἀπὸ τῆς ὀργῆς.
we shall be saved through him from the wrath.

10 εἰ γὰρ ἐχθροὶ ὄντες κατηλλάγημεν
For if enemies being we were reconciled

τῷ θεῷ διὰ τοῦ θανάτου τοῦ υἱοῦ αὐτοῦ,
- to God through the death of the Son of him,

πολλῷ μᾶλλον καταλλαγέντες σωθησόμεθα
by much rather having been reconciled we shall be saved

ἐν τῇ ζωῇ αὐτοῦ· 11 οὐ μόνον δὲ, ἀλλὰ
by the life of him; and not only [so], but

καὶ καυχώμενοι ἐν τῷ θεῷ διὰ τοῦ
also boasting in - God through the

κυρίου ἡμῶν Ἰησοῦ [Χριστοῦ], δι' οὗ
Lord of us Jesus Christ, through whom

νῦν τὴν καταλλαγὴν ἐλάβομεν.
now the reconciliation we received.

12 Διὰ τοῦτο ὥσπερ δι' ἑνὸς ἀνθρώπου
Therefore as through one man

ἡ ἁμαρτία εἰς τὸν κόσμον εἰσῆλθεν,
- sin into the world entered,

καὶ διὰ τῆς ἁμαρτίας ὁ θάνατος, καὶ
and through - sin - death, ²also

οὕτως εἰς πάντας ἀνθρώπους ὁ θάνατος
¹so to all men - death

διῆλθεν, ἐφ' ᾧ πάντες ἥμαρτον· 13 ἄχρι
passed, inasmuch as all sinned; until

γὰρ νόμου ἁμαρτία ἦν ἐν κόσμῳ, ἁμαρτία
for law sin was in [the] world, sin

δὲ οὐκ ἐλλογεῖται μὴ ὄντος νόμου·
but is not reckoned not being lawª;
=when there is no law;

14 ἀλλὰ ἐβασίλευσεν ὁ θάνατος ἀπὸ Ἀδὰμ
but ²reigned - ¹death from Adam

μέχρι Μωϋσέως καὶ ἐπὶ τοὺς μὴ
until Moses even over the [ones] not

ἁμαρτήσαντας ἐπὶ τῷ ὁμοιώματι τῆς
sinning on the likeness of the

παραβάσεως Ἀδάμ, ὅς ἐστιν τύπος τοῦ
transgression of Adam, who is a type of the

μέλλοντος. 15 Ἀλλ' οὐχ ὡς τὸ παράπτωμα,
[one] coming. But not as the offence,

οὕτως [καὶ] τὸ χάρισμα· εἰ γὰρ τῷ
so also the free gift; for if ¹by the

τοῦ ἑνὸς παραπτώματι οἱ πολλοὶ
²of the ⁴one [man] ³offence the many

ἀπέθανον, πολλῷ μᾶλλον ἡ χάρις τοῦ θεοῦ
died, by much rather the grace - of God

καὶ ἡ δωρεὰ ἐν χάριτι τῇ τοῦ ἑνὸς
and the gift in grace - of the one

Jesus Christ abounded for many. ¹⁶And the free gift is not like the effect of that one man's sin. For the judgment following one trespass brought condemnation, but the free gift following many trespasses brings justification. ¹⁷If, because of ˊone man's trespass, death reigned through that one man, much more will those who receive the abundance of grace and the free gift of righteousness reign in life through the one man Jesus Christ.

18 Then as one man's trespass led to condemnation for all men, so one man's act of righteousness leads to acquittal and life for all men. ¹⁹For as by one man's disobedience many were made sinners, so by one man's obedience many will be made righteous. ²⁰Law came in, to increase the trespass; but where sin increased, grace abounded all the more, ²¹so that, as sin reigned in death,

ἀνθρώπου Ἰησοῦ Χριστοῦ εἰς τοὺς πολλοὺς
man   Jesus   Christ   to the   many

ἐπερίσσευσεν. 16 καὶ οὐχ ὡς δι᾽ ἑνὸς
abounded.   And not as through one
                                          [man]

ἁμαρτήσαντος τὸ δώρημα· τὸ μὲν γὰρ
sinning   the gift;   ²the ²on one hand ¹for

κρίμα ἐξ ἑνὸς εἰς κατάκριμα, τὸ δὲ
judgment [is] of one to condemna-   on the other
               [offence]   tion,   the

χάρισμα ἐκ πολλῶν παραπτωμάτων εἰς
free gift [is] of many   offences   to

δικαίωμα. 17 εἰ γὰρ τῷ τοῦ ἑνὸς
justification.   For if ¹by the ²of the ⁴one [man]

παραπτώματι ὁ θάνατος ἐβασίλευσεν διὰ
²offence   -   death   reigned   through

τοῦ ἑνὸς, πολλῷ μᾶλλον οἱ τὴν περισσείαν
the one   by much rather ¹the ³the ⁴abundance
[man],   [ones]

τῆς χάριτος καὶ τῆς δωρεᾶς τῆς
⁵of the ⁶grace ⁷and ⁸of the ⁹gift -

δικαιοσύνης λαμβάνοντες ἐν ζωῇ βασιλεύ-
¹⁰of righteousness ¹receiving ¹²in ¹³life ¹¹will

σουσιν διὰ τοῦ ἑνὸς Ἰησοῦ Χριστοῦ.
reign   through the one [man] Jesus   Christ.

18 Ἄρα οὖν ὡς δι᾽ ἑνὸς παραπτώματος
So therefore as through one   offence

εἰς πάντας ἀνθρώπους εἰς κατάκριμα,
to all   men   to condemnation,

οὕτως καὶ δι᾽ ἑνὸς δικαιώματος εἰς
so   also through one righteous act to

πάντας ἀνθρώπους εἰς δικαίωσιν ζωῆς·
all   men   to justification of life;

19 ὥσπερ γὰρ διὰ τῆς παρακοῆς τοῦ
for as   through the disobedience of the

ἑνὸς ἀνθρώπου ἁμαρτωλοὶ κατεστάθησαν
one   man   ⁴sinners   ³were constituted

οἱ πολλοί, οὕτως καὶ διὰ τῆς ὑπακοῆς
¹the ²many, so   also through the obedience

τοῦ ἑνὸς δίκαιοι κατασταθήσονται οἱ
of the one [man] ⁴righteous ³will be constituted ¹the

πολλοί. 20 νόμος δὲ παρεισῆλθεν ἵνα
²many.   But law   entered   in order
                                   that

πλεονάσῃ τὸ παράπτωμα· οὗ δὲ ἐπλεόνασεν
might abound the offence;   but where abounded

ἡ ἁμαρτία, ὑπερεπερίσσευσεν ἡ χάρις,
- sin,   more abounded   - grace,

21 ἵνα ὥσπερ ἐβασίλευσεν ἡ ἁμαρτία ἐν
in order that as reigned   - sin   by

grace also might reign through righteousness to eternal life through Jesus Christ our Lord.

τῷ θανάτῳ, οὕτως καὶ ἡ χάρις βασιλεύσῃ
death,   so   also – grace   might reign

διὰ   δικαιοσύνης   εἰς   ζωὴν   αἰώνιον   διὰ
through righteousness to   life   eternal   through

Ἰησοῦ   Χριστοῦ   τοῦ   κυρίου   ἡμῶν.
Jesus   Christ   the   Lord   of us.

CHAPTER 6

WHAT shall we say then? Are we to continue in sin that grace may abound? [2]By no means! How can we who died to sin still live in it? [3]Do you not know that all of us who have been baptized into Christ Jesus were baptized into his death? [4]We were buried therefore with him by baptism into death, so that as Christ was raised from the dead by the glory of the Father, we too might walk in newness of life.

5 For if we have been united with him in a death like his, we shall certainly be united with him in a resurrection like his. [6]We know that our old self was crucified with him so that the sinful body might be destroyed, and we might no longer be enslaved to sin. [7]For he who has died is freed from sin. [8]But if we have died with Christ,

6 Τί   οὖν   ἐροῦμεν;   ἐπιμένωμεν   τῇ
What therefore shall we say? May we continue

ἁμαρτίᾳ,   ἵνα   ἡ   χάρις   πλεονάσῃ;   2 μὴ
in sin, in order that – grace may abound?   not

γένοιτο.   οἵτινες   ἀπεθάνομεν   τῇ   ἁμαρτίᾳ,
May it be. Who   we died   –   to sin,

πῶς   ἔτι   ζήσομεν   ἐν   αὐτῇ;   3 ἢ   ἀγνοεῖτε
how yet shall we live in it? or are ye ignorant

ὅτι   ὅσοι   ἐβαπτίσθημεν   εἰς   Χριστὸν
that as many as we were baptized into Christ

Ἰησοῦν,   εἰς   τὸν   θάνατον   αὐτοῦ   ἐβαπτίσ-
Jesus, into the   death   of him   we were

θημεν;   4 συνετάφημεν   οὖν   αὐτῷ   διὰ   τοῦ
baptized?   [2]We were   [1]there him through –
              buried with fore

βαπτίσματος   εἰς   τὸν   θάνατον,   ἵνα   ὥσπερ
baptism   into –   death,   in order as
                                       that

ἠγέρθη   Χριστὸς   ἐκ   νεκρῶν   διὰ   τῆς
was raised Christ   from [the] dead through –

δόξης   τοῦ   πατρός,   οὕτως   καὶ   ἡμεῖς   ἐν
glory of the Father,   so   also   we   in

καινότητι   ζωῆς   περιπατήσωμεν.   5 εἰ   γὰρ
newness of life   might walk.   For if

σύμφυτοι   γεγόναμεν   τῷ   ὁμοιώματι   τοῦ
united with we have become in the likeness of the

θανάτου   αὐτοῦ,   ἀλλὰ   καὶ   τῆς   ἀναστάσεως
death of him, but(so) also of the(his) resurrection

ἐσόμεθα·   6 τοῦτο   γινώσκοντες,   ὅτι   ὁ
we shall be;   this   knowing,   that the

παλαιὸς   ἡμῶν   ἄνθρωπος   συνεσταυρώθη,   ἵνα
[1]old   [2]of us   [3]man   was crucified in or-
                                     with [him], der that

καταργηθῇ   τὸ   σῶμα   τῆς   ἁμαρτίας,   τοῦ
might be   the body   –   of sin,   –
destroyed

μηκέτι   δουλεύειν   ἡμᾶς   τῇ   ἁμαρτίᾳ·   7 ὁ
no longer to serve   us[bd] –   sin;   [2]the
=that we should no longer serve   (one)

γὰρ   ἀποθανὼν   δεδικαίωται   ἀπὸ   τῆς
[1]for having died   has been justified from –

ἁμαρτίας.   8 εἰ   δὲ   ἀπεθάνομεν   σὺν   Χριστῷ,
sin.   But if   we died   with   Christ

we believe that we shall also live with him. [9]For we know that Christ being raised from the dead will never die again; death no longer has dominion over him. [10]The death he died to sin, once for all, but the life he lives he lives to God. [11]So you also must consider yourselves dead to sin and alive to God in Christ Jesus.

[12] Let not sin therefore reign in your mortal bodies, to make you obey their passions. [13]Do not yield your members to sin as instruments of wickedness, but yield yourselves to God as men who have been brought from death to life, and your members to God as instruments of righteousness. [14]For sin will have no dominion over you, since you are not under law but under grace.

15 What then? Are we to sin because we are not under law but under grace? By no means! [16]Do you not know that if you yield yourselves to any one as obedient slaves, you are slaves of the one whom you obey, either of sin, which leads to death, or of obedience,

πιστεύομεν ὅτι καὶ συζήσομεν αὐτῷ,
we believe that also we shall live with him,

9 εἰδότες ὅτι Χριστὸς ἐγερθεὶς ἐκ νεκρῶν
knowing that Christ having from [the] dead
been raised

οὐκέτι ἀποθνῄσκει, θάνατος αὐτοῦ οὐκέτι
no more dies, death [3]of him [1]no more

κυριεύει. 10 ὃ γὰρ ἀπέθανεν, τῇ ἁμαρτίᾳ
[2]lords it over. For in that† he died, − to sin

ἀπέθανεν ἐφάπαξ· ὃ δὲ ζῇ, ζῇ τῷ θεῷ.
he died once; but in that† he he − to
lives, lives God.

11 οὕτως καὶ ὑμεῖς λογίζεσθε ἑαυτοὺς
So also [2]ye [1]reckon yourselves

εἶναι νεκροὺς μὲν τῇ ἁμαρτίᾳ ζῶντας
to be dead indeed − to sin [2]living

δὲ τῷ θεῷ ἐν Χριστῷ Ἰησοῦ. 12 μὴ
[1]but − to God in Christ Jesus. [3]not

οὖν βασιλευέτω ἡ ἁμαρτία ἐν τῷ θνητῷ
[1]There- [2]let [5]reign − [4]sin [6]in [7]the [8]mortal
fore

ὑμῶν σώματι εἰς τὸ ὑπακούειν ταῖς
[10]of you [9]body for the to obey the
= to obey its lusts,

ἐπιθυμίαις αὐτοῦ, 13 μηδὲ παριστάνετε τὰ
lusts of it, neither present ye the

μέλη ὑμῶν ὅπλα ἀδικίας τῇ ἁμαρτίᾳ,
members of you weapons of unright- − to sin,
eousness

ἀλλὰ παραστήσατε ἑαυτοὺς τῷ θεῷ ὡσεὶ
but present ye yourselves − to God as

ἐκ νεκρῶν ζῶντας καὶ τὰ μέλη ὑμῶν
from [the] dead living and the members of you

ὅπλα δικαιοσύνης τῷ θεῷ, 14 ἁμαρτία
weapons of righteousness to God, [2]sin

γὰρ ὑμῶν οὐ κυριεύσει· οὐ γάρ ἐστε
[1]for [4]of you [3]shall not lord it over; for ye are not

ὑπὸ νόμον ἀλλὰ ὑπὸ χάριν. 15 Τί οὖν;
under law but under grace. What therefore?

ἁμαρτήσωμεν, ὅτι οὐκ ἐσμὲν ὑπὸ νόμον
may we sin, because we are not under law

ἀλλὰ ὑπὸ χάριν; μὴ γένοιτο. 16 οὐκ
but under grace? May it not be. not

οἴδατε ὅτι ᾧ παριστάνετε ἑαυτοὺς δούλους
Know ye that to ye present yourselves slaves
whom

εἰς ὑπακοήν, δοῦλοί ἐστε ᾧ ὑπακούετε,
for obedience, slaves ye are whom ye obey,

ἤτοι ἁμαρτίας εἰς θάνατον ἢ ὑπακοῆς
whether of sin to death or of obedience

which leads to righteousness? [17]But thanks be to God, that you who were once slaves of sin have become obedient from the heart to the standard of teaching to which you were committed, [18]and, having been set free from sin, have become slaves of righteousness. [19]I am speaking in human terms, because of your natural limitations. For just as you once yielded your members to impurity and to greater and greater iniquity, so now yield your members to righteousness for sanctification.

20 When you were slaves of sin, you were free in regard to righteousness. [21]But then what return did you get from the things of which you are now ashamed? The end of those things is death. [22]But now that you have been set free from sin and have become slaves of God, the return you get is sanctification and its end, eternal life. [23]For the wages of sin is death, but the free gift of God is eternal life in Christ Jesus our Lord.

εἰς δικαιοσύνην, 17 χάρις δὲ τῷ θεῷ
to righteousness? But thanks – to God

ὅτι ἦτε δοῦλοι τῆς ἁμαρτίας, ὑπηκούσατε
that ye were slaves – of sin, [2]ye obeyed

δὲ ἐκ καρδίας εἰς ὃν παρεδόθητε τύπον
[1]but out of [the] heart [3]to [4]which [5]ye were delivered [1]a form

διδαχῆς, 18 ἐλευθερωθέντες δὲ ἀπὸ τῆς
[2]of teaching, and having been freed from –

ἁμαρτίας ἐδουλώθητε τῇ δικαιοσύνῃ.
sin ye were enslaved – to righteousness.

19 ἀνθρώπινον λέγω διὰ τὴν ἀσθένειαν
Humanly I say because of the weakness

τῆς σαρκὸς ὑμῶν. ὥσπερ γὰρ παρεστήσατε
of the flesh of you. For as ye presented

τὰ μέλη ὑμῶν δοῦλα τῇ ἀκαθαρσίᾳ καὶ
the members of you slaves – to uncleanness and

τῇ ἀνομίᾳ εἰς τὴν ἀνομίαν, οὕτως νῦν
– to iniquity unto – iniquity, so now

παραστήσατε τὰ μέλη ὑμῶν δοῦλα τῇ
present ye the members of you slaves –

δικαιοσύνῃ εἰς ἁγιασμόν. 20 ὅτε γὰρ
to righteousness unto sanctification. For when

δοῦλοι ἦτε τῆς ἁμαρτίας, ἐλεύθεροι ἦτε
slaves ye were – of sin, free ye were

τῇ δικαιοσύνῃ. 21 τίνα οὖν καρπὸν εἴχετε
– to righteousness. What [2]therefore [1]fruit had ye

τότε; ἐφ᾽ οἷς νῦν ἐπαισχύνεσθε· τὸ γὰρ
then? Over which now ye are ashamed; for the
things

τέλος ἐκείνων θάνατος. 22 νυνὶ δὲ ἐλευ-
end of those things [is] death. But now having

θερωθέντες ἀπὸ τῆς ἁμαρτίας δουλωθέντες
been freed from – sin [2]having been enslaved

δὲ τῷ θεῷ, ἔχετε τὸν καρπὸν ὑμῶν εἰς
[1]and – to God, ye have the fruit of you to

ἁγιασμόν, τὸ δὲ τέλος ζωὴν αἰώνιον.
sanctification, and the end life eternal.

23 τὰ γὰρ ὀψώνια τῆς ἁμαρτίας θάνατος,
For the wages of sin [is] death,

τὸ δὲ χάρισμα τοῦ θεοῦ ζωὴ αἰώνιος
but the free gift – of God life eternal

ἐν Χριστῷ Ἰησοῦ τῷ κυρίῳ ἡμῶν.
in Christ Jesus the Lord of us.

CHAPTER 7

DO you not know, brethren—for I am speaking to those who know the law—that the law is binding on a person only during his life? ²Thus a married woman is bound by law to her husband as long as he lives; but if her husband dies she is discharged from the law concerning the husband. ³Accordingly, she will be called an adulteress if she lives with another man while her husband is alive. But if her husband dies she is free from that law, and if she marries another man she is not an adulteress.

4 Likewise, my brethren, you have died to the law through the body of Christ, so that you may belong to another, to him who has been raised from the dead in order that we may bear fruit for God. ⁵While we were living in the flesh, our sinful passions, aroused by the law, were at work in our members to bear fruit for death. ⁶But now we are discharged from the law, dead to that which held us captive, so that we serve not under the old

7 ῾Η ἀγνοεῖτε, ἀδελφοί, γινώσκουσιν γὰρ
Or are ye ignorant, brothers, for to [ones] knowing

νόμον λαλῶ, ὅτι ὁ νόμος κυριεύει τοῦ
law I speak, that the law lords it over the

ἀνθρώπου ἐφ' ὅσον χρόνον ζῇ; 2 ἡ γὰρ
man over such time [as] he lives? For the

ὕπανδρος γυνὴ τῷ ζῶντι ἀνδρὶ δέδεται
²married ¹woman to the living husband has been bound

νόμῳ· ἐὰν δὲ ἀποθάνῃ ὁ ἀνήρ, κατήργηται
by law; but if dies the husband, she has been discharged

ἀπὸ τοῦ νόμου τοῦ ἀνδρός. 3 ἄρα οὖν
from the law of the husband. Therefore

ζῶντος τοῦ ἀνδρὸς μοιχαλὶς χρηματίσει
living the husbandᵃ an adulteress she will be called
= while the husband lives

ἐὰν γένηται ἀνδρὶ ἑτέρῳ· ἐὰν δὲ ἀποθάνῃ
if she ²husband ¹to a but if dies
becomes different;

ὁ ἀνήρ, ἐλευθέρα ἐστὶν ἀπὸ τοῦ νόμου,
the husband, free she is from the law,

τοῦ μὴ εἶναι αὐτὴν μοιχαλίδα γενομένην
- not to be herᵈ an adulteress having become
= so that she is not

ἀνδρὶ ἑτέρῳ. 4 ὥστε, ἀδελφοί μου, καὶ
²husband ¹to a So, brothers of me, also
different.

ὑμεῖς ἐθανατώθητε τῷ νόμῳ διὰ τοῦ
ye were put to death to the law through the

σώματος τοῦ Χριστοῦ, εἰς τὸ γενέσθαι
body - of Christ, for the to become
= that ye might belong

ὑμᾶς ἑτέρῳ, τῷ ἐκ νεκρῶν ἐγερθέντι,
youᵇ to a to the from dead having been
different, [one] [the] raised,

ἵνα καρποφορήσωμεν τῷ θεῷ. 5 ὅτε
in order we may bear fruit - to God. when
that

γὰρ ἦμεν ἐν τῇ σαρκί, τὰ παθήματα
For we were in the flesh, the passions

τῶν ἁμαρτιῶν τὰ διὰ τοῦ νόμου ἐνηργεῖτο
- of sins - through the law operated

ἐν τοῖς μέλεσιν ἡμῶν εἰς τὸ καρποφορῆσαι
in the members of us for the to bear fruit

τῷ θανάτῳ· 6 νυνὶ δὲ κατηργήθημεν ἀπὸ
- to death; but now we were discharged from

τοῦ νόμου, ἀποθανόντες ἐν ᾧ κατειχόμεθα,
the law, having died [to that] in which we were held fast,

ὥστε δουλεύειν [ἡμᾶς] ἐν καινότητι
so as to serve usᵇ in newness

written code but in the new life of the Spirit.

7 What then shall we say? That the law is sin? By no means! Yet, if it had not been for the law, I should not have known sin. I should not have known what it is to covet if the law had not said, "You shall not covet." ⁸But sin, finding opportunity in the commandment, wrought in me all kinds of covetousness. Apart from the law sin lies dead. ⁹I was once alive apart from the law, but when the commandment came, sin revived and I died; ¹⁰the very commandment which promised life proved to be death to me. ¹¹For sin, finding opportunity in the commandment, deceived me and by it killed me. ¹²So the law is holy, and the commandment is holy and just and good.

13 Did that which is good, then, bring death to me? By no means! It was sin, working death in me through what is good, in order that sin might be shown to be sin, and through the commandment might become sinful beyond

πνεύματος καὶ οὐ παλαιότητι γράμματος.
of spirit and not [in] oldness of letter.

7 Τί οὖν ἐροῦμεν; ὁ νόμος ἁμαρτία;
What therefore shall we say? the law sin?

μὴ γένοιτο· ἀλλὰ τὴν ἁμαρτίαν οὐκ
May it not be; yet – sin not

ἔγνων εἰ μὴ διὰ νόμου· τήν τε γὰρ
I knew except through law; – ²also ¹for

ἐπιθυμίαν οὐκ ᾔδειν εἰ μὴ ὁ νόμος
lust I knew not except the law

ἔλεγεν· οὐκ ἐπιθυμήσεις· 8 ἀφορμὴν δὲ
said : Thou shalt not lust; but ²occasion

λαβοῦσα ἡ ἁμαρτία διὰ τῆς ἐντολῆς
¹taking – ¹sin through the commandment

κατειργάσατο ἐν ἐμοὶ πᾶσαν ἐπιθυμίαν·
wrought in me every lust;

χωρὶς γὰρ νόμου ἁμαρτία νεκρά. 9 ἐγὼ
for without law sin [is] dead. I

δὲ ἔζων χωρὶς νόμου ποτέ· ἐλθούσης δὲ
And was living without law then; but coming
=when the

τῆς ἐντολῆς ἡ ἁμαρτία ἀνέζησεν, 10 ἐγὼ
the commandment² – sin revived, ¹I
commandment came

δὲ ἀπέθανον, καὶ εὑρέθη μοι ἡ ἐντολὴ
¹and died, and ⁴was ²to me ¹the ³command-
found ment

ἡ εἰς ζωήν, αὕτη εἰς θάνατον· 11 ἡ γὰρ
– ²for ⁴life, ⁵this to death; – for

ἁμαρτία ἀφορμὴν λαβοῦσα διὰ τῆς
sin ²occasion ¹taking through the

ἐντολῆς ἐξηπάτησέν με καὶ δι' αὐτῆς
commandment deceived me and through it

ἀπέκτεινεν. 12 ὥστε ὁ μὲν νόμος ἅγιος,
killed [me]. So the – law [is] holy,

καὶ ἡ ἐντολὴ ἁγία καὶ δικαία καὶ ἀγαθή.
and the command- holy and just and good.
ment

13 Τὸ οὖν ἀγαθὸν ἐμοὶ ἐγένετο θάνατος;
²The ¹therefore good to me became death?

μὴ γένοιτο· ἀλλὰ ἡ ἁμαρτία, ἵνα φανῇ
May it not be; yet – sin, in or- it might
der that appear

ἁμαρτία, διὰ τοῦ ἀγαθοῦ μοι κατεργα-
sin, through the good ³to me ¹work-

ζομένη θάνατον, ἵνα γένηται καθ' ὑπερβολὴν
ing ²death, in or- ⁵might ⁶excessively†
der that become

ἁμαρτωλὸς ἡ ἁμαρτία διὰ τῆς ἐντολῆς.
⁷sinful – ¹sin ²through ³the ⁴command-
ment.

measure. ¹⁴ We know that the law is spiritual; but I am carnal, sold under sin. ¹⁵ I do not understand my own actions. For I do not do what I want, but I do the very thing I hate. ¹⁶ Now if I do what I do not want, I agree that the law is good. ¹⁷ So then it is no longer I that do it, but sin which dwells within me. ¹⁸ For I know that nothing good dwells within me, that is, in my flesh. I can will what is right, but I cannot do it. ¹⁹ For I do not do the good I want, but the evil I do not want is what I do. ²⁰ Now if I do what I do not want, it is no longer I that do it, but sin which dwells within me.

21 So I find it to be a law that when I want to do right, evil lies close at hand. ²² For I delight in the law of God, in my inmost self, ²³ but I see in my members another law at war with the law of my mind and making

14 οἴδαμεν γὰρ ὅτι ὁ νόμος πνευματικός
For we know that the law spiritual

ἐστιν· ἐγὼ δὲ σάρκινός εἰμι, πεπραμένος
is; but I fleshy am, *having been sold*

ὑπὸ τὴν ἁμαρτίαν. **15** ὃ γὰρ κατεργάζομαι
under - sin. For what I work

οὐ γινώσκω· οὐ γὰρ ὃ θέλω τοῦτο
I know not; for not what I wish this

πράσσω, ἀλλ' ὃ μισῶ τοῦτο ποιῶ. **16** εἰ
I practise, but what I hate this I do. if

δὲ ὃ οὐ θέλω τοῦτο ποιῶ, σύμφημι
But what I wish not this I do, I agree with

τῷ νόμῳ ὅτι καλός. **17** νυνὶ δὲ οὐκέτι
the law that [it is] good. But now no longer

ἐγὼ κατεργάζομαι αὐτὸ ἀλλὰ ἡ ἐνοικοῦσα
I work it but ¹the ²indwelling

ἐν ἐμοὶ ἁμαρτία. **18** οἶδα γὰρ ὅτι οὐκ
⁴in ⁵me ²sin. For I know that not

οἰκεῖ ἐν ἐμοί, τοῦτ' ἔστιν ἐν τῇ σαρκί
dwells in me, this is in the flesh

μου, ἀγαθόν· τὸ γὰρ θέλειν παράκειται
of me, [that which is] - for to wish is present

μοι, τὸ δὲ κατεργάζεσθαι τὸ καλὸν
good; to me, - but ²to work ¹the ²good

οὔ. **19** οὐ γὰρ ὃ θέλω ποιῶ ἀγαθόν,
²not; for not what ²I wish ¹I do ²good,

ἀλλὰ ὃ οὐ θέλω κακὸν τοῦτο πράσσω.
but what ²I wish not ¹evil this I practise.

20 εἰ δὲ ὃ οὐ θέλω ἐγὼ τοῦτο ποιῶ,
But if what ²wish not ¹I this I do,

οὐκέτι ἐγὼ κατεργάζομαι αὐτὸ ἀλλὰ ἡ
no longer I work it but ¹the

οἰκοῦσα ἐν ἐμοὶ ἁμαρτία. **21** εὑρίσκω
²dwelling ⁴in ⁵me ²sin. I find

ἄρα τὸν νόμον τῷ θέλοντι ἐμοὶ ποιεῖν
then the law ²the [one] ²wishing ²to me to do

τὸ καλόν, ὅτι ἐμοὶ τὸ κακὸν παράκειται·
the good, that to me the evil is present;

22 συνήδομαι γὰρ τῷ νόμῳ τοῦ θεοῦ κατὰ
for I delight in the law - of God according to

τὸν ἔσω ἄνθρωπον, **23** βλέπω δὲ ἕτερον
the inner man, but I see a different

νόμον ἐν τοῖς μέλεσίν μου ἀντιστρατευόμενον
law in the members of me warring against

τῷ νόμῳ τοῦ νοός μου καὶ αἰχμαλωτίζοντά
the law of the mind of me and taking captive

me captive to the law of sin which dwells in my members. **24**Wretched man that I am! Who will deliver me from this body of death? **25**Thanks be to God through Jesus Christ our Lord! So then, I of myself serve the law of God with my mind, but with my flesh I serve the law of sin.

CHAPTER 8

THERE is therefore now no condemnation for those who are in Christ Jesus. **2**For the law of the Spirit of life in Christ Jesus has set me free from the law of sin and death. **3**For God has done what the law, weakened by the flesh, could not do: sending his own Son in the likeness of sinful flesh and for sin,[g] he condemned sin in the flesh, **4**in order that the just requirement of the law might be fulfilled in us, who walk not according to the flesh but according to the Spirit. **5**For those who live according to the flesh set their minds on the things of the flesh, but those who live according to the

με   ἐν   τῷ   νόμῳ   τῆς   ἁμαρτίας   τῷ   ὄντι
me   by   the   law   –   of sin   the [one] being

ἐν   τοῖς   μέλεσίν   μου.   24 Ταλαίπωρος
in   the   members   of me.   ¹Wretched

ἐγὼ   ἄνθρωπος·   τίς   με   ῥύσεται   ἐκ   τοῦ
³I   ²man;   who   me   will deliver from   the

σώματος   τοῦ   θανάτου   τούτου;   25 χάρις
body   of this death?   Thanks

τῷ   θεῷ   διὰ   Ἰησοῦ   Χριστοῦ   τοῦ   κυρίου
–   to God through Jesus   Christ   the   Lord

ἡμῶν.   Ἄρα   οὖν   αὐτὸς   ἐγὼ   τῷ   μὲν
of us.   So then ²[my]self ¹I   ⁴with ³on one
                                            the hand

νοῒ   δουλεύω   νόμῳ   θεοῦ,   τῇ   δὲ   σαρκὶ
⁵mind   serve   [the] law   of God,   on the other   flesh
                                                with the

νόμῳ   ἁμαρτίας.   8 οὐδὲν   ἄρα   νῦν   κατάκριμα
[the] law   of sin.   ⁴No   ¹then   ³now   ⁵condemnation
                                                    ²[there is]

τοῖς   ἐν   Χριστῷ   Ἰησοῦ.   2 ὁ γὰρ   νόμος   τοῦ
to the   in   Christ   Jesus.   For the   law   of the
[ones]

πνεύματος   τῆς   ζωῆς   ἐν   Χριστῷ   Ἰησοῦ
spirit   – of life   in   Christ   Jesus

ἠλευθέρωσέν   σε   ἀπὸ   τοῦ   νόμου   τῆς
freed   thee   from   the   law   –

ἁμαρτίας   καὶ   τοῦ   θανάτου.   3 τὸ   γὰρ
of sin   and   –   of death.   For the

ἀδύνατον   τοῦ   νόμου,   ἐν   ᾧ   ἠσθένει   διὰ
impossible   of the   law,   in   which   it was   through
thing   weak

τῆς   σαρκός,   ὁ   θεὸς   τὸν   ἑαυτοῦ   υἱὸν
the   flesh,   –   ¹God   ³the   ⁵of himself   ⁴Son

πέμψας   ἐν   ὁμοιώματι   σαρκὸς   ἁμαρτίας
²sending   in   likeness   of flesh   of sin

καὶ   περὶ   ἁμαρτίας   κατέκρινεν   τὴν   ἁμαρτίαν
and concerning   sin   condemned   –   sin

ἐν   τῇ   σαρκί,   4 ἵνα   τὸ   δικαίωμα   τοῦ
in   the   flesh,   in order   the   ordinance   of the
                    that

νόμου   πληρωθῇ   ἐν   ἡμῖν   τοῖς   μὴ   κατὰ
law   may be   in   us   the   not   accord-
        fulfilled   [ones]   ing to

σάρκα   περιπατοῦσιν   ἀλλὰ   κατὰ   πνεῦμα.
flesh   walking   but according to   spirit.

5 οἱ   γὰρ   κατὰ   σάρκα   ὄντες   τὰ   τῆς
For the [ones] accord-   flesh   being   the   of the
        ing to   things

σαρκὸς   φρονοῦσιν,   οἱ   δὲ   κατὰ   πνεῦμα
flesh   mind,   but the   accord-   spirit
            [ones]   ing to

---

[g] Or and as a sin offering

Spirit set their minds on the things of the Spirit. [6]To set the mind on the flesh is death, but to set the mind on the Spirit is life and peace. [7]For the mind that is set on the flesh is hostile to God; it does not submit to God's law, indeed it cannot; [8]and those who are in the flesh cannot please God.

[9]But you are not in the flesh, you are in the Spirit, if the Spirit of God really dwells in you. Any one who does not have the Spirit of Christ does not belong to him. [10]But if Christ is in you, although your bodies are dead because of sin, your spirits are alive because of righteousness. [11]If the Spirit of him who raised Jesus from the dead dwells in you, he who raised Christ Jesus from the dead will give life to your mortal bodies also through his Spirit which dwells in you.

[12]So then, brethren, we are debtors, not to the flesh, to live according to the flesh—[13]for if you live according to the flesh you will die, but if by the

τὰ τοῦ πνεύματος. **6** τὸ γὰρ φρόνημα
the of the Spirit. For the mind
things

τῆς σαρκὸς θάνατος, τὸ δὲ φρόνημα
of the flesh [is] death, but the mind

τοῦ πνεύματος ζωὴ καὶ εἰρήνη. **7** διότι
of the Spirit life and peace. Wherefore

τὸ φρόνημα τῆς σαρκὸς ἔχθρα εἰς θεόν·
the mind of the flesh [is] enmity against God;

τῷ γὰρ νόμῳ τοῦ θεοῦ οὐχ ὑποτάσσεται,
for to the law — of God it is not subject,

οὐδὲ γὰρ δύναται· **8** οἱ δὲ ἐν σαρκὶ
neither indeed can it; and the [ones] [2]in [3]flesh

ὄντες θεῷ ἀρέσαι οὐ δύνανται. **9** ὑμεῖς
[1]being [6]God [7]to please [4]cannot. ye

δὲ οὐκ ἐστὲ ἐν σαρκὶ ἀλλὰ ἐν πνεύματι,
But are not in flesh but in Spirit,

εἴπερ πνεῦμα θεοῦ οἰκεῖ ἐν ὑμῖν. εἰ
since [the] Spirit of God dwells in you. if

δέ τις πνεῦμα Χριστοῦ οὐκ ἔχει, οὗτος
But anyone [the] Spirit of Christ has not, this one

οὐκ ἔστιν αὐτοῦ. **10** εἰ δὲ Χριστὸς
is not of him. But if Christ

ἐν ὑμῖν, τὸ μὲν σῶμα νεκρὸν διὰ
[is] in you, [2]the [1]on one [2]body [is] dead because
      hand   of

ἁμαρτίαν, τὸ δὲ πνεῦμα ζωὴ διὰ
sin, [2]the [1]on the [2]spirit [is] because
    other   life of

δικαιοσύνην. **11** εἰ δὲ τὸ πνεῦμα τοῦ
righteousness. But if the Spirit of the
         [one]

ἐγείραντος τὸν Ἰησοῦν ἐκ νεκρῶν οἰκεῖ ἐν
having raised — Jesus from [the] dead dwells in

ὑμῖν, ὁ ἐγείρας ἐκ νεκρῶν Χριστὸν
you, the having from [the] dead Christ
  [one] raised

Ἰησοῦν ζωοποιήσει καὶ τὰ θνητὰ σώματα
Jesus will quicken also the mortal bodies

ὑμῶν διὰ τοῦ ἐνοικοῦντος αὐτοῦ πνεύματος
of you through the [3]indwelling [2]of him [1]Spirit

ἐν ὑμῖν.
[4]in [5]you.

12 Ἄρα οὖν, ἀδελφοί, ὀφειλέται ἐσμέν,
So then, brothers, debtors we are,

οὐ τῇ σαρκὶ τοῦ κατὰ σάρκα ζῆν. **13** εἰ
not to the flesh — accord- flesh to live[d] if
      ing to

γὰρ κατὰ σάρκα ζῆτε, μέλλετε ἀποθνήσκειν·
For accord- flesh ye live, ye are to die:
  ing to   about

Spirit you put to death the deeds of the body you will live. [14] For all who are led by the Spirit of God are sons of God. [15] For you did not receive the spirit of slavery to fall back into fear, but you have received the spirit of sonship. When we cry, "Abba! Father!" [16] it is the Spirit himself bearing witness with our spirit that we are children of God, [17] and if children, then heirs, heirs of God and fellow heirs with Christ, provided we suffer with him in order that we may also be glorified with him.

[18] I consider that the sufferings of this present time are not worth comparing with the glory that is to be revealed to us. [19] For the creation waits with eager longing for the revealing of the sons of God; [20] for the creation was subjected to futility, not of its own will but by the will of him who subjected it in hope; [21] because the creation itself will be set free from its bondage to decay and obtain the glorious liberty of the children of God. [22] We know that the whole creation has been groaning in travail

εἰ δὲ πνεύματι τὰς πράξεις τοῦ σώματος
but if by [the] Spirit the practices of the body

θανατοῦτε, ζήσεσθε. 14 ὅσοι γὰρ πνεύματι
ye put to death, ye will live. For as many as by [the] Spirit

θεοῦ ἄγονται, οὗτοι υἱοί εἰσιν θεοῦ.
of God are led, these sons are of God.

15 οὐ γὰρ ἐλάβετε πνεῦμα δουλείας πάλιν
For ye received not a spirit of slavery again

εἰς φόβον, ἀλλὰ ἐλάβετε πνεῦμα υἱοθεσίας,
for fear, but ye received a spirit of adoption,

ἐν ᾧ κράζομεν· ἀββὰ ὁ πατήρ. 16 αὐτὸ
by which we cry : Abba - Father. [3]it(him)self

τὸ πνεῦμα συμμαρτυρεῖ τῷ πνεύματι ἡμῶν
[1]The [2]Spirit witnesses with the spirit of us

ὅτι ἐσμὲν τέκνα θεοῦ. 17 εἰ δὲ τέκνα,
that we are children of God. And if children,

καὶ κληρονόμοι· κληρονόμοι μὲν θεοῦ,
also heirs; heirs on one hand of God,

συγκληρονόμοι δὲ Χριστοῦ, εἴπερ συμπάσ-
joint heirs on the of Christ, since we suffer
other

χομεν ἵνα καὶ συνδοξασθῶμεν. 18 Λογίζομαι
with[him] in or- also we may be glorified I reckon
der that with [him].

γὰρ ὅτι οὐκ ἄξια τὰ παθήματα τοῦ
For that [6][are] [7]not [8]worthy [1]the [2]sufferings [3]of the

νῦν καιροῦ πρὸς τὴν μέλλουσαν δόξαν
[4]now [5]time [to with the coming glory
(present) be compared]

ἀποκαλυφθῆναι εἰς ἡμᾶς. 19 ἡ γὰρ
to be revealed to us. For the

ἀποκαραδοκία τῆς κτίσεως τὴν ἀποκάλυψιν
anxious watching of the creation [2]the [3]revelation

τῶν υἱῶν τοῦ θεοῦ ἀπεκδέχεται. 20 τῇ
[4]of the [5]sons - [6]of God [1]is eagerly expecting. -

γὰρ ματαιότητι ἡ κτίσις ὑπετάγη, οὐχ
For to vanity the creation was subjected, not

ἑκοῦσα, ἀλλὰ διὰ τὸν ὑποτάξαντα, ἐφ'
willing[ly], but because of the [one] subjecting, in

ἐλπίδι 21 διότι καὶ αὐτὴ ἡ κτίσις
hope because even itself the creation

ἐλευθερωθήσεται ἀπὸ τῆς δουλείας τῆς
will be freed from the slavery -

φθορᾶς εἰς τὴν ἐλευθερίαν τῆς δόξης
of corruption to the freedom of the glory

τῶν τέκνων τοῦ θεοῦ. 22 οἴδαμεν γὰρ
of the children - of God. For we know

ὅτι πᾶσα ἡ κτίσις συστενάζει καὶ
that all the creation groans together and

together until now; ²³and not only the creation, but we ourselves, who have the first fruits of the Spirit, groan inwardly as we wait for adoption as sons, the redemption of our bodies. ²⁴For in this hope we were saved. Now hope that is seen is not hope. For who hopes for what he sees? ²⁵But if we hope for what we do not see, we wait for it with patience.

26 Likewise the Spirit helps us in our weakness; for we do not know how to pray as we ought, but the Spirit himself intercedes for us with sighs too deep for words. ²⁷And he who searches the hearts of men knows what is the mind of the Spirit, because[h] the Spirit intercedes for the saints according to the will of God.

28 We know that in everything God works for good[i] with those who love him, who are called according to his purpose. ²⁹For those whom he foreknew he also predestined to be conformed to the image of his Son, in order that he might be the first-born among many brethren. ³⁰And those whom he predestined he also called;

---

[h] Or that
[i] Other ancient authorities read in everything he works for good, or everything works for good

---

συνωδίνει ἄχρι τοῦ νῦν· 23 οὐ μόνον δέ,
travails together until – now; and not only [so],

ἀλλὰ καὶ αὐτοὶ τὴν ἀπαρχὴν τοῦ πνεύματος
but also [our]selves ²the ³firstfruit ⁴of the ¹Spirit

ἔχοντες [ἡμεῖς] καὶ αὐτοὶ ἐν ἑαυτοῖς
¹having we also [our]selves in ourselves

στενάζομεν υἱοθεσίαν ἀπεκδεχόμενοι, τὴν
groan adoption eagerly expecting, the

ἀπολύτρωσιν τοῦ σώματος ἡμῶν. 24 τῇ
redemption of the body of us.

γὰρ ἐλπίδι ἐσώθημεν· ἐλπὶς δὲ βλεπομένη
For by hope we were saved; but hope being seen

οὐκ ἔστιν ἐλπίς· ὃ γὰρ βλέπει τις,
is not hope; for what sees anyone,

τί καὶ ἐλπίζει; 25 εἰ δὲ ὃ οὐ βλέπομεν
why also he hopes? but if what we do not see

ἐλπίζομεν, δι' ὑπομονῆς ἀπεκδεχόμεθα.
we hope [for], through patience we eagerly expect.

26 ὡσαύτως δὲ καὶ τὸ πνεῦμα συναντιλαμ-
And similarly also the Spirit takes

βάνεται τῇ ἀσθενείᾳ ἡμῶν· τὸ γὰρ τί
share in the weakness of us; – for what

προσευξώμεθα καθὸ δεῖ οὐκ οἴδαμεν, ἀλλὰ
we may pray as it behoves we know not, but

αὐτὸ τὸ πνεῦμα ὑπερεντυγχάνει στεναγμοῖς
it(him)self the Spirit supplicates on [our] behalf with groanings

ἀλαλήτοις· 27 ὁ δὲ ἐρευνῶν τὰς καρδίας
unutterable; and the [one] searching the hearts

οἶδεν τί τὸ φρόνημα τοῦ πνεύματος,
knows what [is] the mind of the Spirit,

ὅτι κατὰ θεὸν ἐντυγχάνει ὑπὲρ ἁγίων.
be- according God he supplicates on behalf saints.
cause to

28 οἴδαμεν δὲ ὅτι τοῖς ἀγαπῶσιν τὸν
And we know that to the [ones] loving –

θεὸν πάντα συνεργεῖ [ὁ θεὸς] εἰς ἀγαθόν,
God ³all things ²works together – ¹God for good.

τοῖς κατὰ πρόθεσιν κλητοῖς οὖσιν. 29 ὅτι
to the ²accord- ⁴purpose ³called ¹being. Because
[ones] ing to

οὓς προέγνω, καὶ προώρισεν συμμόρφους
whom he foreknew, also he foreordained conformed to

τῆς εἰκόνος τοῦ υἱοῦ αὐτοῦ, εἰς τὸ
of the image of the Son of him, for the
=that he should be

εἶναι αὐτὸν πρωτότοκον ἐν πολλοῖς
to be him[b] firstborn among many

ἀδελφοῖς· 30 οὓς δὲ προώρισεν, τούτους
brothers; but whom he foreordained, these

and those whom he called he also justified; and those whom he justified he also glorified. 31 What then shall we say to this? If God is for us, who is against us? 32 He who did not spare his own Son but gave him up for us all, will he not also give us all things with him? 33 Who shall bring any charge against God's elect? It is God who justifies; 34 who is to condemn? Is it Christ Jesus, who died, yes, who was raised from the dead, who is at the right hand of God, who indeed intercedes for us?[ʲ] 35 Who shall separate us from the love of Christ? Shall tribulation, or distress, or persecution, or famine, or nakedness, or peril, or sword? 36 As it is written,

"For thy sake we are being killed all the day long;
we are regarded as sheep to be slaughtered."

37 No, in all these things we are more than conquerors through him who loved us. 38 For I am sure that neither death, nor life, nor angels, nor principalities, nor things present, nor things to come, nor powers, 39 nor height, nor depth, nor

καὶ ἐκάλεσεν· καὶ οὓς ἐκάλεσεν, τούτους
also   he called;   and whom   he called,   these
καὶ ἐδικαίωσεν· οὓς δὲ ἐδικαίωσεν, τούτους
also   he justified;   but whom   he justified,   these
καὶ ἐδόξασεν. 31 Τί οὖν ἐροῦμεν πρὸς
also   he glorified.   What therefore shall we say   to
ταῦτα; εἰ ὁ θεὸς ὑπὲρ ἡμῶν, τίς καθ'
these things? If   –   God on behalf of   us,   who against
ἡμῶν; ὅς γε τοῦ ἰδίου υἱοῦ οὐκ ἐφείσατο,
us?   Who indeed the (his) own   Son   spared not,
32 ἀλλὰ ὑπὲρ ἡμῶν πάντων παρέδωκεν
but   on behalf of   us   all   delivered
αὐτόν, πῶς οὐχὶ καὶ σὺν αὐτῷ τὰ πάντα
him,   how   not   also   with   him   – all things
ἡμῖν χαρίσεται; 33 τίς ἐγκαλέσει κατὰ
to us   will he   Who   will bring a   against
      freely give?   charge against
ἐκλεκτῶν θεοῦ; θεὸς ὁ δικαιῶν· 34 τίς
chosen ones   of God?   God [is] the [one] justifying;   who
ὁ κατακρινῶν; Χριστὸς Ἰησοῦς ὁ ἀποθανών,
the condemning?   Christ   Jesus [is] the   having died,
[one]   [one]
μᾶλλον δὲ ἐγερθείς, ὅς ἐστιν ἐν δεξιᾷ
but rather   having   who   is   at [the] right
      been raised,   [hand]
τοῦ θεοῦ, ὃς καὶ ἐντυγχάνει ὑπὲρ ἡμῶν.
– of God,   who also supplicates on behalf of   us.
35· τίς ἡμᾶς χωρίσει ἀπὸ τῆς ἀγάπης
Who   us   will separate   from   the   love
τοῦ Χριστοῦ; θλῖψις ἢ στενοχωρία ἢ
– of Christ?   affliction   or   distress   or
διωγμὸς ἢ λιμὸς ἢ γυμνότης ἢ κίνδυνος
persecution or famine or   nakedness   or   peril
ἢ μάχαιρα; 36 καθὼς γέγραπται ὅτι ἕνεκεν
or   sword?   As   it has been   –   For the
                written[,]   sake
σοῦ θανατούμεθα ὅλην τὴν ἡμέραν,
of thee we are being put to death all   the   day,
ἐλογίσθημεν ὡς πρόβατα σφαγῆς. 37 ἀλλ'
we were reckoned as   sheep of (for) slaughter.   But
ἐν τούτοις πᾶσιν ὑπερνικῶμεν διὰ τοῦ
in these things   all   we overconquer through the
ἀγαπήσαντος ἡμᾶς. 38 πέπεισμαι γὰρ
[one] having loved   us.   For I have been persuaded
ὅτι οὔτε θάνατος οὔτε ζωὴ οὔτε ἄγγελοι
that   not   death   nor   life   nor   angels
οὔτε ἀρχαὶ οὔτε ἐνεστῶτα οὔτε μέλλοντα
nor   rulers   nor   things present   nor   things coming
οὔτε δυνάμεις 39 οὔτε ὕψωμα οὔτε βάθος
nor   powers   nor   height   nor   depth

ʲ Or It is Christ Jesus . . . for us

anything else in all creation, will be able to separate us from the love of God in Christ Jesus our Lord.

οὔτε τις κτίσις ἑτέρα δυνήσεται ἡμᾶς
nor   any   creature   other   will be able   us

χωρίσαι ἀπὸ τῆς ἀγάπης τοῦ θεοῦ τῆς
to separate   from   the   love   –   of God   –

ἐν Χριστῷ Ἰησοῦ τῷ κυρίῳ ἡμῶν.
in   Christ   Jesus   the   Lord   of us.

CHAPTER 9

I am speaking the truth in Christ, I am not lying; my conscience bears me witness in the Holy Spirit, [2] that I have great sorrow and unceasing anguish in my heart. [3] For I could wish that I myself were accursed and cut off from Christ for the sake of my brethren, my kinsmen by race. [4] They are Israelites, and to them belong the sonship, the glory, the covenants, the giving of the law, the worship, and the promises; [5] to them belong the patriarchs, and of their race, according to the flesh, is the Christ. God who is over all be blessed for ever.[k] Amen.

6 But it is not as though the word of God had failed. For not all who are descended from Israel belong to Israel, [7] and not all are children of Abraham because they are his descendants; but "Through Isaac shall your descendants be named." [8] This means that it is not the children

9 Ἀλήθειαν λέγω ἐν Χριστῷ, οὐ
Truth   I say   in   Christ,   not

ψεύδομαι, συμμαρτυρούσης μοι τῆς
I lie,   witnessing with   me   the

συνειδήσεώς μου ἐν πνεύματι ἁγίῳ, 2 ὅτι
conscience[a]   of me   in   [the] Spirit   Holy,   that

λύπη μοί ἐστιν μεγάλη καὶ ἀδιάλειπτος
grief   to me   is   great   and   incessant
= I have great grief and . . .

ὀδύνη τῇ καρδίᾳ μου. 3 ηὐχόμην γὰρ
pain[c]   in the   heart   of me.   For I was praying

ἀνάθεμα εἶναι αὐτὸς ἐγὼ ἀπὸ τοῦ Χριστοῦ
[a] a curse   [b] to be   [b] [my]self   [1] I   from   –   Christ

ὑπὲρ τῶν ἀδελφῶν μου τῶν συγγενῶν
on behalf of the   brothers   of me   the   kinsmen

μου κατὰ σάρκα, 4 οἵτινές εἰσιν Ἰσραη-
of me according to flesh,   who   are   Israel-

λῖται, ὧν ἡ υἱοθεσία καὶ ἡ δόξα καὶ
ites,   of whom   the   adoption   and   the   glory   and

αἱ διαθῆκαι καὶ ἡ νομοθεσία καὶ ἡ
the   covenants   and   the giving of [the] law   and   the

λατρεία καὶ αἱ ἐπαγγελίαι, 5 ὧν οἱ
service   and   the   promises,   of whom the

πατέρες, καὶ ἐξ ὧν ὁ Χριστὸς τὸ κατὰ
fathers,   and   from whom   the   Christ   –   according to

σάρκα· ὁ ὢν ἐπὶ πάντων θεὸς εὐλογητὸς
flesh;   the [one] being over   all   God   blessed

εἰς τοὺς αἰῶνας, ἀμήν. 6 Οὐχ οἷον δὲ
unto   the   ages,   amen.   Not of course

ὅτι ἐκπέπτωκεν ὁ λόγος τοῦ θεοῦ. οὐ
that   has failed   the   word   –   of God.   not

γὰρ πάντες οἱ ἐξ Ἰσραήλ, οὗτοι Ἰσραήλ·
For   all the [ones] of   Israel,   these [are of] Israel;

7 οὐδ' ὅτι εἰσὶν σπέρμα Ἀβραάμ, πάντες
neither because they are   seed   Abraham,   of [are they] all

τέκνα, ἀλλ'· ἐν Ἰσαὰκ κληθήσεταί σοι
children,   but: In   Isaac   will be called   to thee

σπέρμα. 8 τοῦτ' ἔστιν, οὐ τὰ τέκνα τῆς
seed.[e]   This   is,   not   the   children of the
= thy seed.

---

[k] Or Christ, who is God over all, blessed for ever

of the flesh who are the children of God, but the children of the promise are reckoned as descendants. [9]For this is what the promise said, "About this time I will return and Sarah shall have a son." [10]And not only so, but also when Rebecca had conceived children by one man, our forefather Isaac, [11]though they were not yet born and had done nothing either good or bad, in order that God's purpose of election might continue, not because of works but because of his call, [12]she was told, "The elder will serve the younger." [13]As it is written, "Jacob I loved, but Esau I hated."

14 What shall we say then? Is there injustice on God's part? By no means! [15]For he says to Moses, "I will have mercy on whom I have mercy, and I will have compassion on whom I have compassiion." [16]So it depends not upon man's will or exertion, but upon God's mercy. [17]For the scripture says to Pharaoh, "I have raised you up for the very purpose of showing

σαρκὸς ταῦτα τέκνα τοῦ θεοῦ, ἀλλὰ
flesh   these children of   God,   but

τὰ τέκνα τῆς ἐπαγγελίας λογίζεται εἰς
the children of the promise is(are) reckoned for

σπέρμα. 9 ἐπαγγελίας γὰρ ὁ λόγος οὗτος·
a seed.   For [5]of promise [3]the [4]word [1]this [2][is]:

κατὰ τὸν καιρὸν τοῦτον ἐλεύσομαι καὶ
According to   this time   I will come   and

ἔσται τῇ Σάρρα υἱός. 10 οὐ μόνον δέ,
will be - to Sara a son.[c]   And not only [so],
=Sarah will have a son.

ἀλλὰ καὶ 'Ρεβέκκα ἐξ ἑνὸς κοίτην ἔχουσα,
but also Rebecca [2]from [3]one   [1]conceiving,†

'Ισαὰκ τοῦ πατρὸς ἡμῶν· 11 μήπω γὰρ
Isaac the father of us;   for not yet

γεννηθέντων μηδὲ πραξάντων τι ἀγαθὸν
being born[a] nor practising[a] anything good

ἢ φαῦλον, ἵνα ἡ κατ' ἐκλογὴν πρόθεσις
or bad, in order [1]the [4]accord- [5]choice [2]purpose
           that   ing to

τοῦ θεοῦ μένῃ, 12 οὐκ ἐξ ἔργων ἀλλ'
  - [3]of God might not of works but
         remain,

ἐκ τοῦ καλοῦντος, ἐρρέθη αὐτῇ ὅτι ὁ
of the [one] calling,   it was said to her[,] - The

μείζων δουλεύσει τῷ ἐλάσσονι· 13 καθάπερ
greater will serve the lesser·   even as

γέγραπται· τὸν 'Ιακὼβ ἠγάπησα, τὸν δὲ
it has been - Jacob I loved,   - but
written:

'Ησαῦ ἐμίσησα.
Esau   I hated.

14 Τί οὖν ἐροῦμεν; μὴ ἀδικία παρὰ
What therefore shall we say? not unrighteousness with

τῷ θεῷ; μὴ γένοιτο. 15 τῷ Μωϋσεῖ
 - God? May it not be.   - [2]to Moses

γὰρ λέγει· ἐλεήσω ὃν ἂν ἐλεῶ, καὶ
[1]For he says: I will whomever I have and
          have mercy on   mercy,

οἰκτιρήσω ὃν ἂν οἰκτίρω. 16 ἄρα οὖν
I will pity whomever I pity.   So therefore
                                    [it is]

οὐ τοῦ θέλοντος οὐδὲ τοῦ τρέχοντος,
not of the [one] wishing nor of the [one] running,

ἀλλὰ τοῦ ἐλεῶντος θεοῦ. 17 λέγει γὰρ
but of the [one] having mercy God.   For says

ἡ γραφὴ τῷ Φαραὼ ὅτι εἰς αὐτὸ τοῦτο
the scripture - to Pharaoh[,] - For this very thing

ἐξήγειρά σε, ὅπως ἐνδείξωμαι ἐν σοὶ
I raised up thee, so as I may show forth in thee

my power in you, so that my name may be proclaimed in all the earth." [18]So then he has mercy upon whomever he wills, and he hardens the heart of whomever he wills.

19 You will say to me then, "Why does he still find fault? For who can resist his will?" [20]But who are you, a man, to answer back to God? Will what is molded say to its molder, "Why have you made me thus?" [21]Has the potter no right over the clay, to make out of the same lump one vessel for beauty and another for menial use? [22]What if God, desiring to show his wrath and to make known his power, has endured with much patience the vessels of wrath made for destruction, [23]in order to make known the riches of his glory for the vessels of mercy, which he has prepared beforehand for glory, [24]even us whom he has called, not from the Jews only but also from the Gentiles? [25]As indeed he says in Hose′a,

"Those who were not my people
I will call 'my people,'
and her who was not beloved
I will call 'my beloved.' "
[26]"And in the very place

τὴν δύναμίν μου, καὶ ὅπως διαγγελῇ τὸ
the   power   of me,   and   so as   might be pub- the
                                      lished abroad

ὄνομά μου ἐν πάσῃ τῇ γῇ. 18 ἄρα οὖν
name   of me   in   all   the   earth.   So therefore

ὃν θέλει ἐλεεῖ, ὃν δὲ θέλει σκληρύνει.
whom he   he has   but whom he wishes   he hardens.
         wishes   mercy,

19 Ἐρεῖς μοι οὖν· τί ἔτι μέμφεται;
Thou wilt say to me therefore: Why   still   finds he fault?

τῷ γὰρ βουλήματι αὐτοῦ τίς ἀνθέστηκεν;
for ²the   ⁴counsel   ⁵of him   ¹who   ³resisted?

20 ὦ ἄνθρωπε, μενοῦν γε σὺ τίς εἶ ὁ
O   man,   nay rather   ³thou ¹who ²art the

ἀνταποκρινόμενος τῷ θεῷ; μὴ ἐρεῖ τὸ
[one] replying against   –   God?   not ³Will say ¹the

πλάσμα τῷ πλάσαντι· τί με ἐποίησας
²thing   to the   having formed: Why   ²me   ¹madest
formed   [one]   thou

οὕτως; 21 ἢ οὐκ ἔχει ἐξουσίαν ὁ κεραμεὺς
thus?   or   has not   ²authority ¹the   ²potter

τοῦ πηλοῦ ἐκ τοῦ αὐτοῦ φυράματος
of the   clay   out of   the   same   lump

ποιῆσαι ὃ μὲν εἰς τιμὴν σκεῦος, ὃ δὲ
to make   ¹this   ²to ⁴honour   ²vessel,   that

εἰς ἀτιμίαν; 22 εἰ δὲ θέλων ὁ θεὸς
to   dishonour?   But if   wishing   –   God

ἐνδείξασθαι τὴν ὀργὴν καὶ γνωρίσαι τὸ
to show forth   the(his) wrath   and to make known   the

δυνατὸν αὐτοῦ ἤνεγκεν ἐν πολλῇ μακρο-
ability   of him   bore   in   much   long-

θυμίᾳ σκεύη ὀργῆς κατηρτισμένα εἰς
suffering vessels   of wrath   having been fitted   for

ἀπώλειαν, 23 καὶ ἵνα γνωρίσῃ τὸν πλοῦτον
destruction,   and in or- he might   the   riches
               der that make known

τῆς δόξης αὐτοῦ ἐπὶ σκεύη ἐλέους, ἃ
of the glory   of him   on   vessels   of mercy, which

προητοίμασεν εἰς δόξαν, 24 οὓς καὶ
he previously prepared for   glory,   whom   also

ἐκάλεσεν ἡμᾶς οὐ μόνον ἐξ Ἰουδαίων
he called[,]   us   not   only of   Jews

ἀλλὰ καὶ ἐξ ἐθνῶν; 25 ὡς καὶ ἐν τῷ
but   also   of   nations?   As   also   in   –

Ὡσηὲ λέγει· καλέσω τὸν οὐ λαόν μου
Osee   he says: I will call   the   ²not ¹people of me

λαόν μου καὶ τὴν οὐκ ἠγαπημένην
a people of me   and   the   not   having been loved

ἠγαπημένην· 26 καὶ ἔσται ἐν τῷ τόπῳ
having been loved;   and   it shall be   in   the   place

where it was said to them, 'You are not my people,' they will be called 'sons of the living God.' "

27 And Isaiah cries out concerning Israel: "Though the number of the sons of Israel be as the sand of the sea, only a remnant of them will be saved; [28] for the Lord will execute his sentence upon the earth with vigor and dispatch."
[29] And as Isaiah predicted,

"If the Lord of hosts had not left us children,
we would have fared like Sodom and been made like Gomor'rah."

30 What shall we say, then? That Gentiles who did not pursue righteousness have attained it, that is, righteousness through faith; [31] but that Israel who pursued the righteousness which is based on law did not succeed in fulfilling that law. [32] Why? Because they did not pursue it through faith, but as if it were based on works. They have stumbled over the stumbling-stone, [33] as it is written,

"Behold I am laying in Zion a stone that will make men stumble,
a rock that will make them fall;
and he who believes in him will not be put to shame."

οὖ ἐρρέθη [αὐτοῖς]· οὐ λαός μου ὑμεῖς,
where it was said to them: not a people of me   ye [are],
ἐκεῖ κληθήσονται υἱοὶ θεοῦ ζῶντος.
there   they will be called   sons   [2]God   [1]of a living.

27 Ἡσαΐας δὲ κράζει ὑπὲρ τοῦ Ἰσραήλ·
   But Esaias   cries   on behalf of –   Israel:
ἐὰν ᾖ ὁ ἀριθμὸς τῶν υἱῶν Ἰσραὴλ
If   be   the   number   of the   sons   of Israel
ὡς ἡ ἄμμος τῆς θαλάσσης, τὸ ὑπόλειμμα
as   the   sand   of the   sea,   the   remnant
σωθήσεται· 28 λόγον γὰρ συντελῶν καὶ
will be saved;   for [6]an account   [1]accomplishing   [2]and
συντέμνων ποιήσει κύριος ἐπὶ τῆς γῆς.
[3]cutting short   [5]will make   [4][the] Lord   on   the   earth.

29 καὶ καθὼς προείρηκεν Ἡσαΐας· εἰ μὴ
   And   as   [2]has previously said   [1]Esaias: Except
κύριος σαβαὼθ ἐγκατέλιπεν ἡμῖν σπέρμα,
[the] Lord of hosts   left   to us   a seed,
ὡς Σόδομα ἂν ἐγενήθημεν καὶ ὡς Γόμορρα
as   Sodom   we would have become   and   as   Gomorra
ἂν ὡμοιώθημεν.
we would have been likened.

30 Τί οὖν ἐροῦμεν; ὅτι ἔθνη τὰ μὴ
   What therefore shall we say?   that   nations –   not
διώκοντα δικαιοσύνην κατέλαβεν δικαιοσύνην,
pursuing   righteousness   apprehended   righteousness,
δικαιοσύνην δὲ τὴν ἐκ πίστεως· 31 Ἰσραὴλ
but a righteousness –   of   faith;   [2]Israel
δὲ διώκων νόμον δικαιοσύνης εἰς νόμον
[1]but   pursuing   a law   of righteousness   [2]to(at)   [3]a law
οὐκ ἔφθασεν. 32 διὰ τί; ὅτι οὐκ ἐκ
[1]did not arrive.   Why?   Because   not   of
πίστεως ἀλλ' ὡς ἐξ ἔργων· προσέκοψαν
faith   but   as   of   works;   they stumbled
τῷ λίθῳ τοῦ προσκόμματος, 33 καθὼς
at the   stone –   of stumbling,   as
γέγραπται· ἰδοὺ τίθημι ἐν Σιὼν λίθον
it has been   Behold   I place   in   Sion   a stone
written:
προσκόμματος καὶ πέτραν σκανδάλου, καὶ
of stumbling   and   a rock   of offence,   and
ὁ πιστεύων ἐπ' αὐτῷ οὐ καταισχυνθήσεται.
the [one] believing   on   him   will not be put to shame.

CHAPTER 10

BRETHREN, my heart's desire and prayer to God for them is that they may be saved. ²I bear them witness that they have a zeal for God, but it is not enlightened. ³For, being ignorant of the righteousness that comes from God, and seeking to establish their own, they did not submit to God's righteousness. ⁴For Christ is the end of the law, that every one who has faith may be justified.

5 Moses writes that the man who practices the righteousness which is based on the law shall live by it. ⁶But the righteousness based on faith says, Do not say in your heart, "Who will ascend into heaven?" (that is, to bring Christ down) ⁷or "Who will descend into the abyss?" (that is, to bring Christ up from the dead). ⁸But what does it say? The word is near you, on your lips and in your heart (that is, the word of faith which we preach); ⁹because, if you confess with your lips that Jesus is Lord and believe in your heart that God raised him from the

10 Ἀδελφοί, ἡ μὲν εὐδοκία τῆς ἐμῆς
Brothers, the – good pleasure – of my
καρδίας καὶ ἡ δέησις πρὸς τὸν θεὸν
heart and the request to – God
ὑπὲρ αὐτῶν εἰς σωτηρίαν. 2 μαρτυρῶ
on behalf of them [is] for salvation. I witness
γὰρ αὐτοῖς ὅτι ζῆλον θεοῦ ἔχουσιν, ἀλλ᾽
For to them that a zeal of God they have, but
οὐ κατ᾽ ἐπίγνωσιν· 3 ἀγνοοῦντες γὰρ τὴν
not according to knowledge; for not knowing the
τοῦ θεοῦ δικαιοσύνην, καὶ τὴν ἰδίαν
– ²of God ¹righteousness, and the(ir) own
ζητοῦντες στῆσαι, τῇ δικαιοσύνῃ τοῦ θεοῦ
seeking to establish, to the righteousness ¹ – of God
οὐχ ὑπετάγησαν. 4 τέλος γὰρ νόμου
they did not submit. For end of law
Χριστὸς εἰς δικαιοσύνην παντὶ τῷ
Christ [is] for righteousness to everyone
πιστεύοντι. 5 Μωϋσῆς γὰρ γράφει ὅτι
believing. For Moses writes[.] –
τὴν δικαιοσύνην τὴν ἐκ νόμου ὁ ποιήσας
⁴the ⁵righteousness – ⁶of ⁷law ¹The ³doing
ἄνθρωπος ζήσεται ἐν αὐτῇ. 6 ἡ δὲ
²man will live by it. But the
ἐκ πίστεως δικαιοσύνη οὕτως λέγει· μὴ
²of ³faith ¹righteousness thus says: not
εἴπῃς ἐν τῇ καρδίᾳ σου· τίς ἀναβήσεται
Say in the heart of thee: Who will ascend
εἰς τὸν οὐρανόν; τοῦτ᾽ ἔστιν Χριστὸν
into heaven? this is Christ
καταγαγεῖν· 7 ἤ· τίς καταβήσεται εἰς
to bring down; or: Who will descend into
τὴν ἄβυσσον; τοῦτ᾽ ἔστιν Χριστὸν ἐκ
the abyss? this is Christ from
νεκρῶν ἀναγαγεῖν. 8 ἀλλὰ τί λέγει;
[the] dead to bring up. But what says it?
ἐγγύς σου τὸ ῥῆμά ἐστιν, ἐν τῷ στόματί
Near thee the word is, in the mouth
σου καὶ ἐν τῇ καρδίᾳ σου· τοῦτ᾽ ἔστιν
of thee and in the heart of thee; this is
τὸ ῥῆμα τῆς πίστεως ὃ κηρύσσομεν.
the word – of faith which we proclaim.
9 ὅτι ἐὰν ὁμολογήσῃς ἐν τῷ στόματί
Because if thou confessest with the mouth
σου κύριον Ἰησοῦν, καὶ πιστεύσῃς ἐν
of thee Lord Jesus, and believest in
τῇ καρδίᾳ σου ὅτι ὁ θεὸς αὐτὸν ἤγειρεν
the heart of thee that – God him raised

dead, you will be saved.
¹⁰ For man believes with
his heart and so is
justified, and he con-
fesses with his lips and so
is saved. ¹¹ The scripture
says, "No one who be-
lieves in him will be put
to shame." ¹² For there is
no distinction between
Jew and Greek; the
same Lord is Lord of all
and bestows his riches
upon all who call upon
him. ¹³ For, "every one
who calls upon the name
of the Lord will be
saved."

14 But how are men to
call upon him in whom
they have not believed?
And how are they to
believe in him of whom
they have never heard?
And how are they to hear
without a preacher?
¹⁵ And how can men
preach unless they are
sent? As it is written,
"How beautiful are the
feet of those who preach
good news!" ¹⁶ But they
have not all heeded the
gospel; for Isaiah says,
"Lord, who has be-
lieved what he has heard
from us?" ¹⁷ So faith
comes from what is
heard, and what is heard
comes by the preaching of
Christ.

18 But I ask, have
they not heard? Indeed
they have; for

"Their voice has gone
     out to all the
     earth,

ἐκ νεκρῶν, σωθήσῃ·   **10** καρδίᾳ γὰρ
from [the] dead, thou wilt be saved;   for with heart

πιστεύεται εἰς δικαιοσύνην, στόματι δὲ
[one] believes to righteousness, and with mouth

ὁμολογεῖται εἰς σωτηρίαν.   **11** λέγει γὰρ
[one] confesses to salvation.   For says

ἡ γραφή· πᾶς ὁ πιστεύων ἐπ' αὐτῷ
the scripture: Everyone believing on him

οὐ καταισχυνθήσεται.   **12** οὐ γάρ ἐστιν
will not be put to shame.   For there is no

διαστολὴ Ἰουδαίου τε καὶ Ἕλληνος. ὁ
difference ²of Jew ¹both ³and ⁴of Greek.* the

γὰρ αὐτὸς κύριος πάντων, πλουτῶν εἰς
For same Lord of all, is rich to

πάντας τοὺς ἐπικαλουμένους αὐτόν·   **13** πᾶς
all the [ones] calling on him;   ²everyone

γὰρ ὃς ἂν ἐπικαλέσηται τὸ ὄνομα κυρίου
¹for whoever calls on the name of [the] Lord

σωθήσεται.   **14** Πῶς οὖν ἐπικαλέσωνται εἰς
will be saved.   How therefore may they call on in [one]

ὃν οὐκ ἐπίστευσαν; πῶς δὲ πιστεύσωσιν
whom they believed not? And how may they believe

οὗ οὐκ ἤκουσαν; πῶς δὲ ἀκούσωσιν
of whom they heard not? And how may they hear

χωρὶς κηρύσσοντος;   **15** πῶς δὲ κηρύξωσιν
without [one] heralding? And how may they herald

ἐὰν μὴ ἀποσταλῶσιν; καθάπερ γέγραπται·
if they are not sent? As it has been written:

ὡς ὡραῖοι οἱ πόδες τῶν εὐαγγελιζομένων
How beautiful the feet of the [ones] announcing good

ἀγαθά.   **16** ἀλλ' οὐ πάντες ὑπήκουσαν τῷ
good things. But not all obeyed the

εὐαγγελίῳ. Ἠσαΐας γὰρ λέγει· κύριε,
gospel. For Esaias says: Lord,

τίς ἐπίστευσεν τῇ ἀκοῇ ἡμῶν;   **17** ἄρα
who believed the hearing of us?   Then

ἡ πίστις ἐξ ἀκοῆς, ἡ δὲ ἀκοὴ διὰ
– faith [is] from hearing, and the hearing through

ῥήματος Χριστοῦ.   **18** ἀλλὰ λέγω, μὴ
a word of Christ. But I say, not

οὐκ ἤκουσαν; μενοῦν γε· εἰς πᾶσαν
did they not hear? Nay rather: To all

τὴν γῆν ἐξῆλθεν ὁ φθόγγος αὐτῶν,
the earth went out the utterance of them,

---

* That is, between these two classes.

and their words to the ends of the world."
[19]Again I ask, did Israel not understand? First Moses says,
"I will make you jealous of those who are not a nation;
with a foolish nation I will make you angry."
[20]Then Isaiah is so bold as to say,
"I have been found by those who did not seek me;
I have shown myself to those who did not ask for me."
[21]But of Israel he says, "All day long I have held out my hands to a disobedient and contrary people."

καὶ   εἰς   τὰ   πέρατα   τῆς   οἰκουμένης   τὰ
and   to   the   ends   of the   inhabited earth   the
ῥήματα   αὐτῶν.   19 ἀλλὰ   λέγω,   μὴ   Ἰσραὴλ
words   of them.   But   I say,   not   Israel
οὐκ   ἔγνω;   πρῶτος   Μωϋσῆς   λέγει·   ἐγὼ
did not know?   First   Moses   says :   I
παραζηλώσω   ὑμᾶς   ἐπ᾽   οὐκ   ἔθνει,   ἐπ᾽
will provoke to jealousy   you   on(by)   not   a nation,   on(by)
ἔθνει   ἀσυνέτῳ   παροργιῶ   ὑμᾶς.   20 Ἠσαΐας
a nation   unintelligent   I will anger   you.   Esaias
δὲ   ἀποτολμᾷ   καὶ   λέγει·   εὑρέθην   τοῖς
But   is quite bold   and   says :   I was found   by the [ones]
ἐμὲ   μὴ   ζητοῦσιν,   ἐμφανὴς   ἐγενόμην   τοῖς
[2]me   [1]not   [2]seeking,   manifest   I became   to the [ones]
ἐμὲ   μὴ   ἐπερωτῶσιν.   21 πρὸς   δὲ   τὸν
[2]me   [1]not   [2]inquiring [for].   But to   the
Ἰσραὴλ   λέγει·   ὅλην   τὴν   ἡμέραν   ἐξεπέτασα
Israel   he says: All   the   day   I stretched out
τὰς   χεῖράς   μου   πρὸς   λαὸν   ἀπειθοῦντα
the   hands   of me   to   a people   disobeying
καὶ   ἀντιλέγοντα.
and   contradicting.

CHAPTER 11

I ask, then, has God rejected his people? By no means! I myself am an Israelite, a descendant of Abraham, a member of the tribe of Benjamin. [2]God has not rejected his people whom he foreknew. Do you not know what the scripture says of Eli′jah, how he pleads with God against Israel? [3]"Lord, they have killed thy prophets, they have demolished thy altars, and I alone am left, and they seek my life." [4]But what is God's reply to him?

11 Λέγω   οὖν,   μὴ   ἀπώσατο   ὁ   θεὸς
I say,   therefore,   [2]did not   put away   -   [1]God
τὸν   λαὸν   αὐτοῦ;   μὴ   γένοιτο·   καὶ   γὰρ
the   people   of him?   May it not be;   for even
ἐγὼ   Ἰσραηλίτης   εἰμί,   ἐκ   σπέρματος
I   an Israelite   am,   of   [the] seed
Ἀβραάμ,   φυλῆς   Βενιαμίν.   2 οὐκ   ἀπώσατο
of Abraham,   of [the] tribe   of Benjamin.   did not   put away
ὁ   θεὸς   τὸν   λαὸν   αὐτοῦ   ὃν   προέγνω.
-   God   the   people   of him   whom   he foreknew.
ἢ   οὐκ   οἴδατε   ἐν   Ἠλίᾳ   τί   λέγει   ἡ
Or   know ye not   in   Elias   what   says   the
γραφή,   ὡς   ἐντυγχάνει   τῷ   θεῷ   κατὰ   τοῦ
scripture,   how   he supplicates   -   God   against   -
Ἰσραήλ;   3 κύριε,   τοὺς   προφήτας   σου
Israel?   Lord,   the   prophets   of thee
ἀπέκτειναν,   τὰ   θυσιαστήριά   σου   κατέσκαψαν,
they killed,   the   altars   of thee   they dug down,
κἀγὼ   ὑπελείφθην   μόνος   καὶ   ζητοῦσιν   τὴν
and I   was left behind   alone   and   they seek   the
ψυχήν   μου.   4 ἀλλὰ   τί   λέγει   αὐτῷ   ὁ
life   of me.   But   what   says   to him   the

"I have kept for myself seven thousand men who have not bowed the knee to Ba'al." [5] So too at the present time there is a remnant, chosen by grace. [6] But if it is by grace, it is no longer on the basis of works; otherwise grace would no longer be grace.

7 What then? Israel failed to obtain what it sought. The elect obtained it, but the rest were hardened, [8] as it is written,

"God gave them a spirit of stupor, eyes that should not see and ears that should not hear, down to this very day."

[9] And David says,

"Let their feast become a snare and a trap, a pitfall and a retribution for them;
[10] let their eyes be darkened so that they cannot see, and bend their backs for ever."

11 So I ask, have they stumbled so as to fall? By no means! But through their trespass salvation has come to the Gentiles, so as to make Israel jealous. [12] Now if their trespass means riches for the world, and if their failure means

χρηματισμός; κατέλιπον ἐμαυτῷ ἑπτακισ-
[divine] response? I reserved to myself seven

χιλίους ἄνδρας, οἵτινες οὐκ ἔκαμψαν γόνυ
thousands men, who bowed not knee

τῇ Βάαλ. 5 οὕτως οὖν καὶ ἐν τῷ νῦν
– to Baal. So therefore also in the present

καιρῷ λεῖμμα κατ᾿ ἐκλογὴν χάριτος
time a remnant according to a choice of grace

γέγονεν· 6 εἰ δὲ χάριτι, οὐκέτι ἐξ ἔργων,
has become; and if by grace, no more of works,

ἐπεὶ ἡ χάρις οὐκέτι γίνεται χάρις. 7 Τί
since – grace no more becomes grace. What

οὖν; ὃ ἐπιζητεῖ Ἰσραήλ, τοῦτο οὐκ
there- What ²seeks after ¹Israel, this not
fore?

ἐπέτυχεν, ἡ δὲ ἐκλογὴ ἐπέτυχεν· οἱ δὲ
he obtained, but the choice obtained [it]; and the

λοιποὶ ἐπωρώθησαν, 8 καθάπερ γέγραπται·
rest were hardened, as it has been written:

ἔδωκεν αὐτοῖς ὁ θεὸς πνεῦμα κατανύξεως,
Gave to them – God a spirit of torpor,

ὀφθαλμοὺς τοῦ μὴ βλέπειν καὶ ὦτα
eyes – not to see ᵈ and ears

τοῦ μὴ ἀκούειν, ἕως τῆς σήμερον ἡμέρας.
– not to hear,ᵈ until the present† day.

9 καὶ Δαυὶδ λέγει· γενηθήτω ἡ τράπεζα
And David says: Let become the table

αὐτῶν εἰς παγίδα καὶ εἰς θήραν καὶ
of them for a snare and for a net and

εἰς σκάνδαλον καὶ εἰς ἀνταπόδομα αὐτοῖς,
for an offence and for a recompence to them,

10 σκοτισθήτωσαν οἱ ὀφθαλμοὶ αὐτῶν τοῦ
let be darkened the eyes of them –

μὴ βλέπειν, καὶ τὸν νῶτον αὐτῶν διὰ
not to see,ᵈ and the back of them al-

παντὸς σύγκαμψον.
ways bending.

11 Λέγω οὖν, μὴ ἔπταισαν ἵνα πέσωσιν;
I say therefore, did they not in order they might
stumble that fall?

μὴ γένοιτο· ἀλλὰ τῷ αὐτῶν παραπτώματι
May it not be; but by the ²of them ¹trespass

ἡ σωτηρία τοῖς ἔθνεσιν, εἰς τὸ παραζηλῶσαι
– salvation to the nations, for the to provoke to
[came] jealousy

αὐτούς. 12 εἰ δὲ τὸ παράπτωμα αὐτῶν
them. But if the trespass of them

πλοῦτος κόσμου καὶ τὸ ἥττημα αὐτῶν
[is] [the] of [the] and the defect of them
riches world

riches for the Gentiles, how much more will their full inclusion mean! 13 Now I am speaking to you Gentiles. Inasmuch then as I am an apostle to the Gentiles, I magnify my ministry [14] in order to make my fellow Jews jealous, and thus save some of them. [15] For if their rejection means the reconciliation of the world, what will their acceptance mean but life from the dead? [16] If the dough offered as first fruits is holy, so is the whole lump; and if the root is holy, so are the branches.

17 But if some of the branches were broken off, and you, a wild olive shoot, were grafted in their place to share the richness[1] of the olive tree, [18] do not boast over the branches. If you do boast, remember it is not you that support the root, but the root that supports you. [19] You will say, "Branches were broken off so that I might be grafted in." [20] That is true. They were broken off because of their unbelief, but you stand fast only through faith. So do not become proud, but stand in awe. [21] For if God did not spare the natural branches, neither will he spare you. [22] Note

πλοῦτος ἐθνῶν, πόσῳ μᾶλλον τὸ πλήρωμα
[is] [the] of [the] by how more the fulness
riches nations, much

αὐτῶν. 13 Ὑμῖν δὲ λέγω τοῖς ἔθνεσιν.
of them. But to you [3]I say[,] [1]the [2]nations.

ἐφ' ὅσον μὲν οὖν εἰμι ἐγὼ ἐθνῶν ἀπόστο-
Forasmuch in- there- [2]am [1]I [6]of [3]an apos-
as deed fore nations

λος, τὴν διακονίαν μου δοξάζω, 14 εἴ πως
tle, the ministry of me I glorify, if somehow

παραζηλώσω μου τὴν σάρκα καὶ σώσω
I may provoke to of me the flesh and may save
jealousy

τινὰς ἐξ αὐτῶν. 15 εἰ γὰρ ἡ ἀποβολὴ
some of them. For if the casting away

αὐτῶν καταλλαγὴ κόσμου, τίς ἡ πρόσλημψις
of them [is] [the] of [the] what the reception
reconciliation world,

εἰ μὴ ζωὴ ἐκ νεκρῶν; 16 εἰ δὲ ἡ
if not life from [the] dead? And if the

ἀπαρχὴ ἁγία, καὶ τὸ φύραμα· καὶ εἰ
firstfruit [is] holy, also the lump; and if

ἡ ῥίζα ἁγία, καὶ οἱ κλάδοι. 17 Εἰ δέ
the root [is] holy, also the branches. But if

τινες τῶν κλάδων ἐξεκλάσθησαν, σὺ δὲ
some of the branches were broken off, and thou

ἀγριέλαιος ὢν ἐνεκεντρίσθης ἐν αὐτοῖς
[2]a wild olive [1]being wast grafted in among them

καὶ συγκοινωνὸς τῆς ῥίζης τῆς πιότητος
and [2]a partaker [3]of the [4]root* [5]of the [6]fatness

τῆς ἐλαίας ἐγένου, 18 μὴ κατακαυχῶ
[7]of the [8]olive-tree [1]didst become, boast not against

τῶν κλάδων· εἰ δὲ κατακαυχᾶσαι, οὐ
of the branches; but if thou boastest, not

σὺ τὴν ῥίζαν βαστάζεις ἀλλὰ ἡ ῥίζα σέ.
thou the root bearest but the root thee.

19 ἐρεῖς οὖν· ἐξεκλάσθησαν κλάδοι ἵνα
Thou wilt therefore: [2]Were broken off [1]branches in order
say that

ἐγὼ ἐγκεντρισθῶ. 20 καλῶς· τῇ ἀπιστίᾳ
I might be grafted in. Well: - for unbelief

ἐξεκλάσθησαν, σὺ δὲ τῇ πίστει ἕστηκας.
they were broken off, and thou - by faith standest.

μὴ ὑψηλὰ φρόνει, ἀλλὰ φοβοῦ· 21 εἰ
[2]Not [3]high things [1]mind, but fear; [4]if

γὰρ ὁ θεὸς τῶν κατὰ φύσιν κλάδων
[1]for - [3]God [5]the [7]according to [6]nature [5]branches

οὐκ ἐφείσατο, οὐδὲ σοῦ φείσεται. 22 ἴδε
[6]spared not, neither thee will he spare. See

---

[1] Other ancient authorities read rich root

* Some MSS insert καί (and) here; as it is, the two nouns in the genitive must be in apposition; cf. Col. 1. 18, 2. 2; John 8. 44.

then the kindness and the severity of God; severity toward those who have fallen, but God's kindness to you, provided you continue in his kindness; otherwise you too will be cut off. [23]And even the others, if they do not persist in their unbelief, will be grafted in, for God has the power to graft them in again. [24]For if you have been cut from what is by nature a wild olive tree, and grafted, contrary to nature, into a cultivated olive tree, how much more will these natural branches be grafted back into their own olive tree.

[25]Lest you be wise in your own conceits, I want you to understand this mystery, brethren: a hardening has come upon part of Israel, until the full number of the Gentiles come in, [26]and so all Israel will be saved; as it is written,

"The Deliverer will come from Zion,
he will banish ungodliness from Jacob";
[27]"and this will be my covenant with them
when I take away their sins."

[28]As regards the gospel they are enemies of God,

οὖν χρηστότητα καὶ ἀποτομίαν θεοῦ· ἐπὶ
therefore [the] kindness and [the] severity of God: [2]on
μὲν τοὺς πεσόντας ἀποτομία, ἐπὶ δὲ
[1]on one, the having fallen severity, [2]on [3]on the
hand [ones] other
σὲ χρηστότης θεοῦ, ἐὰν ἐπιμένῃς τῇ
thee [the] kindness of God, if thou continuest in the
(his)
χρηστότητι, ἐπεὶ καὶ σὺ ἐκκοπήσῃ.
kindness, since also thou wilt be cut off.
23 κἀκεῖνοι δέ, ἐὰν μὴ ἐπιμένωσιν τῇ
And those also, if they continue not -
ἀπιστίᾳ, ἐγκεντρισθήσονται· δυνατὸς γάρ
in unbelief, will be grafted in; for [2]able
ἐστιν ὁ θεὸς πάλιν ἐγκεντρίσαι αὐτούς.
[2]is - [1]God [2]again [1]to graft [3]in [5]them.
24 εἰ γὰρ σὺ ἐκ τῆς κατὰ φύσιν ἐξεκόπης
For if thou [2]out [3]the [4]according [6]nature [1]wast cut
of to out
ἀγριελαίου καὶ παρὰ φύσιν ἐνεκεντρίσθης
[4]wild olive and against nature wast grafted in
εἰς καλλιέλαιον, πόσῳ μᾶλλον οὗτοι οἱ
into a cultivated by how more these the
olive, much [ones]
κατὰ φύσιν ἐγκεντρισθήσονται τῇ ἰδίᾳ
according to nature will be grafted in the(ir) own
ἐλαίᾳ. 25 Οὐ γὰρ θέλω ὑμᾶς ἀγνοεῖν,
olive-tree. For I wish not you to be ignorant,
ἀδελφοί, τὸ μυστήριον τοῦτο, ἵνα μὴ
brothers, [of] this mystery, lest
ἦτε ἐν ἑαυτοῖς φρόνιμοι, ὅτι πώρωσις
ye be in yourselves wise, that hardness
ἀπὸ μέρους τῷ Ἰσραὴλ γέγονεν ἄχρι οὗ
from(in) part - to Israel has happened until
τὸ πλήρωμα τῶν ἐθνῶν εἰσέλθῃ, 26 καὶ
the fulness of the nations comes in, and
οὕτως πᾶς Ἰσραὴλ σωθήσεται, καθὼς
so all Israel will be saved, as
γέγραπται· ἥξει ἐκ Σιὼν ὁ ῥυόμενος,
it has been [1]will [4]out [2]Sion [1]The [2]delivering,
written: come of [one]
ἀποστρέψει ἀσεβείας ἀπὸ Ἰακώβ. 27 καὶ
he will turn away impiety from Jacob. And
αὕτη αὐτοῖς ἡ παρ᾽ ἐμοῦ διαθήκη, ὅταν
this [is] [5]with them [1]the [3]from [4]me [2]covenant, when
ἀφέλωμαι τὰς ἁμαρτίας αὐτῶν. 28 κατὰ
I take away the sins of them. [3]According to
μὲν τὸ εὐαγγέλιον ἐχθροὶ δι᾽ ὑμᾶς,
[1]on one the gospel enemies because you,
hand of

for your sake; but as regards election they are beloved for the sake of their forefathers. [29]For the gifts and the call of God are irrevocable. [30]Just as you were once disobedient to God but now have received mercy because of their disobedience,[31] so they have now been disobedient in order that by the mercy shown to you they also may[m] receive mercy. [32]For God has consigned all men to disobedience, that he may have mercy upon all.

33 O the depth of the riches and wisdom and knowledge of God! How unsearchable are his judgments and how inscrutable his ways!
[34]"For who has known the mind of the Lord,
    or who has been his counselor?"
[35]"Or who has given a gift to him
    that he might be repaid?"
[36]For from him and through him and to him are all things. To him be glory for ever. Amen.

CHAPTER 12

I appeal to you therefore, brethren, by the mercies of God, to present your bodies as a living sacrifice, holy and

[m] Other ancient authorities add now

κατὰ   δὲ   τὴν   ἐκλογὴν   ἀγαπητοὶ   διὰ
[2]accord- [1]on the the   choice   beloved   because
ing to   other   of
τοὺς   πατέρας·   29 ἀμεταμέλητα   γὰρ   τὰ
the   fathers;   for unrepented   the
χαρίσματα   καὶ   ἡ   κλῆσις   τοῦ   θεοῦ.
free gifts   and   the   calling   –   of God.
30 ὥσπερ   γὰρ   ὑμεῖς   ποτε   ἠπειθήσατε
        For as   ye   then   disobeyed
τῷ   θεῷ,   νῦν   δὲ   ἠλεήθητε   τῇ   τούτων
–   God,   but now   ye obtained mercy [1]by the [3]of these
ἀπειθείᾳ,   31 οὕτως   καὶ   οὗτοι   νῦν   ἠπείθησαν
[2]disobedience,   so   also   these   now   disobeyed
τῷ   ὑμετέρῳ   ἐλέει   ἵνα   καὶ   αὐτοὶ   νῦν
        [2]by your   [3]mercy   [1]in order also   they   now
                                        that
ἐλεηθῶσιν.   32 συνέκλεισεν   γὰρ   ὁ   θεὸς
may obtain mercy.   For [2]shut up   –   [1]God
τοὺς   πάντας   εἰς   ἀπείθειαν   ἵνα   τοὺς
    all   in   disobedience in order that   –
πάντας   ἐλεήσῃ.
to all   he may show mercy.
33 Ὦ   βάθος   πλούτου   καὶ   σοφίας   καὶ
O   [the] depth of [the] riches and of [the] wisdom and
γνώσεως   θεοῦ·   ὡς   ἀνεξερεύνητα   τὰ   κρίματα
of [the]   of God; how   inscrutable   the   judgments
knowledge
αὐτοῦ   καὶ   ἀνεξιχνίαστοι   αἱ   ὁδοὶ   αὐτοῦ.
of him   and   unsearchable   the   ways   of him.
34 τίς   γὰρ   ἔγνω   νοῦν   κυρίου;   ἢ   τίς
    For who   knew [the] mind of [the] Lord? or   who
σύμβουλος   αὐτοῦ   ἐγένετο;   35 ἢ   τίς
counsellor   of him   became?   or   who
προέδωκεν   αὐτῷ,   καὶ   ἀνταποδοθήσεται
previously gave to him,   and   it will be repaid
αὐτῷ;   36 ὅτι   ἐξ   αὐτοῦ   καὶ   δι᾽   αὐτοῦ
to him?   Because of   him   and through him
καὶ   εἰς   αὐτὸν   τὰ   πάντα·   αὐτῷ   ἡ   δόξα
and   to   him   –   all things;   to him   the glory
εἰς   τοὺς   αἰῶνας·   ἀμήν.
unto   the   ages: Amen.

12 Παρακαλῶ   οὖν   ὑμᾶς,   ἀδελφοί,   διὰ
    I beseech   therefore you,   brothers, through
τῶν   οἰκτιρμῶν   τοῦ   θεοῦ,   παραστῆσαι   τὰ
the   compassions   –   of God,   to present   the
σώματα   ὑμῶν   θυσίαν   ζῶσαν   ἁγίαν   τῷ
bodies   of you   sacrifice   a living   holy   –

acceptable to God, which is your spiritual worship. [2]Do not be conformed to this world but be transformed by the renewal of your mind, that you may prove what is the will of God, what is good and acceptable and perfect.[n]

3 For by the grace given to me I bid every one among you not to think of himself more highly than he ought to think, but to think with sober judgment, each according to the measure of faith which God has assigned him. [4]For as in one body we have many members, and all the members do not have the same function, [5]so we, though many, are one body in Christ, and individually members one of another. [6]Having gifts that differ according to the grace given to us, let us use them: if prophecy, in proportion to our faith; [7]if service, in our serving; he who teaches, in his teaching; [8]he who exhorts, in his exhortation; he who contributes, in liberality; he who gives aid, with

θεῷ   εὐάρεστον,   τὴν   λογικὴν   λατρείαν
[3]to God [1]well-pleasing,   the   reasonable   service
ὑμῶν· 2 καὶ μὴ συσχηματίζεσθε τῷ αἰῶνι
of you;   and   be ye not conformed   the   age
τούτῳ, ἀλλὰ μεταμορφοῦσθε τῇ ἀνακαινώσει
to this,   but   be ye transformed   by the   renewing
τοῦ νοός, εἰς τὸ δοκιμάζειν ὑμᾶς τί τὸ
of the mind,   for   the   to prove   you[b]   what the
                      =so that ye may prove
θέλημα τοῦ θεοῦ, τὸ ἀγαθὸν καὶ εὐάρεστον
will   –   of God, the   good   and   well-pleasing
καὶ τέλειον.
and   perfect.

3 Λέγω γὰρ διὰ τῆς χάριτος τῆς
   For I say   through   the   grace   –
δοθείσης μοι παντὶ τῷ ὄντι ἐν ὑμῖν,
given   to me to everyone   being   among you,
μὴ ὑπερφρονεῖν παρ' ὃ δεῖ φρονεῖν,
not   to have high   beyond what it   to think,
       thoughts   behoves
ἀλλὰ φρονεῖν εἰς τὸ σωφρονεῖν, ἑκάστῳ
but   to think   to   the to be sober-minded, [4]to each
ὡς ὁ θεὸς ἐμέρισεν μέτρον πίστεως.
[1]as – [2]God   [3]divided   a measure   of faith.

4 καθάπερ γὰρ ἐν ἑνὶ σώματι πολλὰ
   For as   in one   body   many
μέλη ἔχομεν, τὰ δὲ μέλη πάντα οὐ τὴν
members we have,   but [the] [3]members [1]all   [5]not [6]the
αὐτὴν ἔχει πρᾶξιν, 5 οὕτως οἱ πολλοὶ
[7]same   [4]has(ve) [2]action,   so   the   many
ἓν σῶμά ἐσμεν ἐν Χριστῷ, τὸ δὲ καθ'
one body   we are   in   Christ,   –   and each
εἰς ἀλλήλων μέλη. 6 ἔχοντες δὲ χαρίσματα
one   [2]of one [1]members.   And having   gifts
           another
κατὰ τὴν χάριν τὴν δοθεῖσαν ἡμῖν διάφορα,
[2]accord- [3]the [4]grace   –   [5]given   [6]to us   [1]differing.
ing to
εἴτε προφητείαν, κατὰ τὴν ἀναλογίαν τῆς
whether prophecy,   according to the   proportion   of the
πίστεως· 7 εἴτε διακονίαν, ἐν τῇ διακονίᾳ·
faith;   or   ministry,   in   the   ministry;
εἴτε ὁ διδάσκων, ἐν τῇ διδασκαλίᾳ·
or the [one] teaching,   in   the   teaching;
8 εἴτε ὁ παρακαλῶν, ἐν τῇ παρακλήσει·
  or the [one] exhorting,   in   the   exhortation;
ὁ μεταδιδοὺς ἐν ἁπλότητι, ὁ προϊστάμενος
the [one] sharing   in   simplicity,   the [one] taking the lead

[n] Or what is the good and acceptable and perfect will of God

zeal; he who does acts of mercy, with cheerfulness.

9 Let love be genuine; hate what is evil, hold fast to what is good; [10]love one another with brotherly affection; outdo one another in showing honor. [11]Never flag in zeal, be aglow with the Spirit, serve the Lord. [12]Rejoice in your hope, be patient in tribulation, be constant in prayer. [13]Contribute to the needs of the saints, practice hospitality.

14 Bless those who persecute you; bless and do not curse them. [15]Rejoice with those who rejoice, weep with those who weep. [16]Live in harmony with one another; do not be haughty, but associate with the lowly;[o] never be conceited. [17]Repay no one evil for evil, but take thought for what is noble in the sight of all. [18]If possible, so far as it depends upon you, live peaceably with all. [19]Beloved, never avenge yourselves, but leave it to the wrath of God; for it is written, "Vengeance is mine, I will repay,

[o] Or *give yourselves to humble tasks*

ἐν σπουδῇ, ὁ ἐλεῶν ἐν ἱλαρότητι.   **9** ἡ
in diligence, the showing in cheerfulness.   –
        [one] mercy

ἀγάπη ἀνυπόκριτος.   ἀποστυγοῦντες τὸ
[Let] love [be] unassumed.   Shrinking from the

πονηρόν, κολλώμενοι τῷ ἀγαθῷ·   **10** τῇ
evil, cleaving to the good;   –

φιλαδελφίᾳ εἰς ἀλλήλους φιλόστοργοι, τῇ
in brotherly love to one another loving warmly, –

τιμῇ ἀλλήλους προηγούμενοι, **11** τῇ σπουδῇ
in one another preferring, – in zeal
honour

μὴ ὀκνηροί, τῷ πνεύματι ζέοντες, τῷ
not slothful, – in spirit burning, the

κυρίῳ δουλεύοντες, **12** τῇ ἐλπίδι χαίροντες,
Lord serving, – in hope rejoicing,

τῇ θλίψει ὑπομένοντες, τῇ προσευχῇ
– in affliction showing endurance, – in prayer

προσκαρτεροῦντες, **13** ταῖς χρείαις τῶν
steadfastly continuing, to the needs of the

ἁγίων κοινωνοῦντες, τὴν φιλοξενίαν
saints imparting, – hospitality

διώκοντες. **14** εὐλογεῖτε τοὺς διώκοντας,
pursuing. Bless ye the [ones] persecuting,

εὐλογεῖτε καὶ μὴ καταρᾶσθε. **15** χαίρειν
bless and do not curse. To rejoice

μετὰ χαιρόντων, κλαίειν μετὰ κλαιόντων.
with rejoicing [ones], to weep with weeping [ones].

16 τὸ αὐτὸ εἰς ἀλλήλους φρονοῦντες· μὴ
The same thing toward one another minding; not

τὰ ὑψηλὰ φρονοῦντες ἀλλὰ τοῖς ταπεινοῖς
[2]the [3]high things [1]minding but to the humble

συναπαγόμενοι. μὴ γίνεσθε φρόνιμοι παρ'
condescending. Become not wise with

ἑαυτοῖς. **17** μηδενὶ κακὸν ἀντὶ κακοῦ
yourselves. To no one evil instead of evil

ἀποδιδόντες· προνοούμενοι καλὰ ἐνώπιον
returning; providing for good things before

πάντων ἀνθρώπων· **18** εἰ δυνατόν, τὸ ἐξ
all men; if possible, as far as it

ὑμῶν, μετὰ πάντων ἀνθρώπων εἰρηνεύοντες·
rests with with all men seeking peace;
you,†

19 μὴ ἑαυτοὺς ἐκδικοῦντες, ἀγαπητοί, ἀλλὰ
not [2]yourselves [1]avenging, beloved, but

δότε τόπον τῇ ὀργῇ· γέγραπται γάρ·
give place – to wrath; for it has been written:

ἐμοὶ ἐκδίκησις, ἐγὼ ἀνταποδώσω, λέγει
To me vengeance,[o] I will repay, says
=Vengeance is mine,

says the Lord." ²⁰No, "if your enemy is hungry, feed him; if he is thirsty, give him drink; for by so doing you will heap burning coals upon his head." ²¹Do not be overcome by evil, but overcome evil with good.

CHAPTER 13

LET every person be subject to the governing authorities. For there is no authority except from God, and those that exist have been instituted by God. ²Therefore he who resists the authorities resists what God has appointed, and those who resist will incur judgment. ³For rulers are not a terror to good conduct, but to bad. Would you have no fear of him who is in authority? Then do what is good, and you will receive his approval, ⁴for he is God's servant for your good. But if you do wrong, be afraid, for he does not bear the sword in vain; he is the servant of God to execute his wrath on the wrongdoer. ⁵Therefore one must be subject, not only to avoid God's wrath but also for the sake of conscience.

κύριος. **20** ἀλλὰ ἐὰν πεινᾷ ὁ ἐχθρός
[the] Lord. But if hungers the enemy

σου, ψώμιζε αὐτόν· ἐὰν διψᾷ, πότιζε
of thee, feed him; if he thirsts, give ²drink

αὐτόν· τοῦτο γὰρ ποιῶν ἄνθρακας πυρὸς
¹him; for this doing coals of fire

σωρεύσεις ἐπὶ τὴν κεφαλὴν αὐτοῦ. **21** μὴ
thou wilt heap on the head of him. not

νικῶ ὑπὸ τοῦ κακοῦ, ἀλλὰ νίκα
Be conquered by the evil, but conquer

ἐν τῷ ἀγαθῷ τὸ κακόν. **13** Πᾶσα
³by ⁴the ⁵good ¹the ²evil. ¹Every

ψυχὴ ἐξουσίαις ὑπερεχούσαις ὑποτασσέσθω.
²soul ⁷authorities ⁶to superior ³let ⁴be ⁵subject.

οὐ γὰρ ἔστιν ἐξουσία εἰ μὴ
For there is no authority except

ὑπὸ θεοῦ, αἱ δὲ οὖσαι ὑπὸ θεοῦ
by God, and the existing [ones] by God

τεταγμέναι εἰσίν. **2** ὥστε ὁ ἀντιτασσόμενος
having been are. So the [one] resisting
ordained

τῇ ἐξουσίᾳ τῇ τοῦ θεοῦ διαταγῇ ἀνθέστη-
the authority ¹the – ⁴of God ³ordinance ¹has op-

κεν· οἱ δὲ ἀνθεστηκότες ἑαυτοῖς κρίμα
posed; and the [ones] having opposed to themselves judgment

λήμψονται. **3** οἱ γὰρ ἄρχοντες οὐκ εἰσὶν
will receive. For the rulers are not

φόβος τῷ ἀγαθῷ ἔργῳ ἀλλὰ τῷ κακῷ.
a fear to the good work but to the evil.

θέλεις δὲ μὴ φοβεῖσθαι τὴν ἐξουσίαν;
And wishest thou not to fear the authority?

τὸ ἀγαθὸν ποίει, καὶ ἕξεις ἔπαινον ἐξ
²the ³good ¹do, and thou wilt praise from
have

αὐτῆς· **4** θεοῦ γὰρ διάκονός ἐστιν σοὶ
it; for of God a minister he is to thee

εἰς τὸ ἀγαθόν. ἐὰν δὲ τὸ κακὸν ποιῇς,
for the good. But if the evil thou doest,

φοβοῦ· οὐ γὰρ εἰκῆ τὴν μάχαιραν φορεῖ·
fear; for not in vain the sword he bears;

θεοῦ γὰρ διάκονός ἐστιν ἔκδικος εἰς
for of God a minister he is an avenger for

ὀργὴν τῷ τὸ κακὸν πράσσοντι. **5** διὸ
wrath to the [one] ²the ³evil ¹practising. Wherefore

ἀνάγκη ὑποτάσσεσθαι, οὐ μόνον διὰ τὴν
it is necessary to be subject, not only because of –

ὀργὴν ἀλλὰ καὶ διὰ τὴν συνείδησιν.
wrath but also because of – conscience.

6 For the same reason you also pay taxes, for the authorities are ministers of God, attending to this very thing. 7 Pay all of them their dues, taxes to whom taxes are due, revenue to whom revenue is due, respect to whom respect is due, honor to whom honor is due.

8 Owe no one anything, except to love one another; for he who loves his neighbor has fulfilled the law. 9 The commandments, "You shall not commit adultery, You shall not kill, You shall not steal, You shall not covet," and any other commandment, are summed up in this sentence, "You shall love your neighbor as yourself." 10 Love does no wrong to a neighbor; therefore love is the fulfilling of the law.

11 Besides this you know what hour it is, how it is full time now for you to wake from sleep. For salvation is nearer to us now than when we first believed; 12 the night is far gone, the day is at hand. Let us then cast off the works of darkness and put on-the

6 διὰ τοῦτο γὰρ καὶ φόρους τελεῖτε·
For therefore also taxes pay ye;

λειτουργοὶ γὰρ θεοῦ εἰσιν εἰς αὐτὸ τοῦτο
for ministers of God they are for this very thing

προσκαρτεροῦντες. 7 ἀπόδοτε πᾶσιν τὰς
attending constantly. Render to all men the

ὀφειλάς, τῷ τὸν φόρον τὸν φόρον,
dues, to the [one] the tax the tax,*

τῷ τὸ τέλος τὸ τέλος, τῷ τὸν φόβον
to the the tribute the tribute, to the the fear
[one]　　　　　　　　　　　　　[one]

τὸν φόβον, τῷ τὴν τιμὴν τὴν τιμήν.
the fear, to the [one] the honour the honour.

8 Μηδενὶ μηδὲν ὀφείλετε, εἰ μὴ τὸ
To no one no(any)thing owe ye, except –

ἀλλήλους ἀγαπᾶν· ὁ γὰρ ἀγαπῶν τὸν
one another to love; for the [one] loving the

ἕτερον νόμον πεπλήρωκεν. 9 τὸ γὰρ
other law has fulfilled. – For

οὐ μοιχεύσεις, οὐ φονεύσεις, οὐ κλέψεις,
Thou shalt not Thou shalt not kill, Thou shalt not
commit adultery, steal,

οὐκ ἐπιθυμήσεις, καὶ εἴ τις ἑτέρα ἐντολή,
Thou shalt not covet, and if any other command-
[there is] ment,

ἐν τῷ λόγῳ τούτῳ ἀνακεφαλαιοῦται, [ἐν
²in ³this ⁴word ¹it is summed up, in

τῷ]· ἀγαπήσεις τὸν πλησίον σου ὡς
– : Thou shalt love the neighbour of thee as

σεαυτόν. 10 ἡ ἀγάπη τῷ πλησίον κακὸν
thyself. – Love ³to the ⁴neighbour ²evil
(one's)

οὐκ ἐργάζεται· πλήρωμα οὖν νόμου ἡ
¹works not; ³[is] ⁴fulfilment ¹therefore ²of law the

ἀγάπη. 11 Καὶ τοῦτο εἰδότες τὸν καιρόν,
²love. And this[,] knowing the time,

ὅτι ὥρα ἤδη ὑμᾶς ἐξ ὕπνου ἐγερθῆναι·
that hour now you out of sleep to be raised;ᵇ
= it is now an hour for you to be raised out of sleep;

νῦν γὰρ ἐγγύτερον ἡμῶν ἡ σωτηρία
for now nearer [is] of us the salvation

ἢ ὅτε ἐπιστεύσαμεν. 12 ἡ νὺξ προέκοψεν,
than when we believed. The night advanced,

ἡ δὲ ἡμέρα ἤγγικεν. ἀποθώμεθα οὖν
and the day has drawn near. Let us cast off therefore

τὰ ἔργα τοῦ σκότους, ἐνδυσώμεθα δὲ
the works of the darkness, and let us put on

* The phrase between the commas is elliptical; understand— to the [one demanding] the tax [render] the tax. So of the following phrases.

armor of light; [13]let us conduct ourselves becomingly as in the day, not in reveling and drunkenness, not in debauchery and licentiousness, not in quarreling and jealousy. [14]But put on the Lord Jesus Christ, and make no provision for the flesh, to gratify its desires.

τὰ   ὅπλα   τοῦ   φωτός.   **13** ὡς   ἐν   ἡμέρᾳ
the   weapons of the   light.   As in [the] day

εὐσχημόνως   περιπατήσωμεν,   μὴ   κώμοις   καὶ
becomingly   let us walk,   not in revellings and

μέθαις,   μὴ   κοίταις   καὶ   ἀσελγείαις,   μὴ
in drunken   not   in beds*   and   excesses,   not
bouts,

ἔριδι   καὶ   ζήλῳ·   **14** ἀλλὰ   ἐνδύσασθε   τὸν
in strife   and   in jealousy;   but   put ye on   the

κύριον   Ἰησοῦν   Χριστόν,   καὶ   τῆς   σαρκὸς
Lord   Jesus   Christ,   and   of the   flesh

πρόνοιαν   μὴ   ποιεῖσθε   εἰς   ἐπιθυμίας.
forethought   make not   for [its]   lusts.

CHAPTER 14

AS for the man who is weak in faith, welcome him, but not for disputes over opinions. [2]One believes he may eat anything, while the weak man eats only vegetables. [3]Let not him who eats despise him who abstains, and let not him who abstains pass judgment on him who eats; for God has welcomed him. [4]Who are you to pass judgment on the servant of another? It is before his own master that he stands or falls. And he will be upheld, for the Master is able to make him stand.

[5]One man esteems one day as better than another, while another man esteems all days alike. Let every one be fully convinced in his own mind. [6]He who observes the day, observes

14 Τὸν   δὲ   ἀσθενοῦντα   τῇ   πίστει
Now the [one]   being weak   in the   faith

προσλαμβάνεσθε,   μὴ   εἰς   διακρίσεις   διαλογισ-
receive ye,   not to   judgments   of

μῶν.   **2** ὃς   μὲν   πιστεύει   φαγεῖν   πάντα,
thoughts.   One indeed   believes   to eat   all things,
man†

ὁ   δὲ   ἀσθενῶν   λάχανα   ἐσθίει.   **3** ὁ   ἐσθίων
but the   being weak   herbs   eats.   [3]The   [4]eating
[one]   [one]

τὸν   μὴ   ἐσθίοντα   μὴ   ἐξουθενείτω,   ὁ   δὲ
[4]the   [7]not   [8]eating   [9]not   [1]let [5]despise,   and [3]the
[one]

μὴ   ἐσθίων   τὸν   ἐσθίοντα   μὴ   κρινέτω,
[4]not   [5]eating   [7]the [one]   [8]eating   [9]not   [1]let [6]judge,

ὁ   θεὸς   γὰρ   αὐτὸν   προσελάβετο.   **4** σὺ
for God   him   received.   [4]Thou

τίς   εἶ   ὁ   κρίνων   ἀλλότριον   οἰκέτην;   τῷ
[1]who   [3]art [4]the   [5]judging   [7]belonging to   [6]a household   to
[one]   another   servant? the(his)

ἰδίῳ   κυρίῳ   στήκει   ἢ   πίπτει·   σταθήσεται
own   lord   he stands   or   falls;   [3]he will stand

δέ,   δυνατεῖ   γὰρ   ὁ   κύριος   στῆσαι   αὐτόν.
[1]but,   for is able   the   Lord   to stand   him.

5 ὃς   μὲν   [γὰρ]   κρίνει   ἡμέραν   παρ᾽
one man†   indeed   judges   a day   above

ἡμέραν,   ὃς   δὲ   κρίνει   πᾶσαν   ἡμέραν·
a day,   another†   judges   every   day;

ἕκαστος   ἐν   τῷ   ἰδίῳ   νοΐ   πληροφορείσθω.
each man   in the(his)   own   mind   let him be fully
persuaded.

6 ὁ   φρονῶν   τὴν   ἡμέραν   κυρίῳ   φρονεῖ.
The   minding   the   day   to [the]   he minds
[one]   Lord   [it].

* That is, illicit sexual intercourse.

I.G.E.—22

it in honor of the Lord
He also who eats, eats
in honor of the Lord,
since he gives thanks to
God; while he who
abstains, abstains in
honor of the Lord and
gives thanks to God.
⁷None of us lives to
himself, and none of us
dies to himself. ⁸If we
live, we live to the Lord,
and if we die, we die to
the Lord; so then,
whether we live or
whether we die, we are
the Lord's. ⁹For to this
end Christ died and lived
again, that he might be
Lord both of the dead
and of the living.

10 Why do you pass
judgment on your
brother? Or you, why do
you despise your
brother? For we shall all
stand before the judg-
ment seat of God; ¹¹for
it is written,

"As I live, says the
Lord, every knee
shall bow to me,
and every tongue
shall give praise^p
to God."

¹²So each of us shall give
account of himself to
God.

13 Then let us no
more pass judgment on
one another, but rather
decide never to put
a stumbling-block or
hindrance in the way of
a brother. ¹⁴I know and
am persuaded in the
Lord Jesus that nothing
is unclean in itself; but

^p Or confess

καὶ ὁ ἐσθίων κυρίῳ ἐσθίει, εὐχαριστεῖ γὰρ
And the eating   to [the]   he eats,   for he gives thanks
[one]   Lord

τῷ θεῷ· καὶ ὁ μὴ ἐσθίων κυρίῳ
-   to God; and the [one] not eating to [the] Lord

οὐκ ἐσθίει, καὶ εὐχαριστεῖ τῷ θεῷ.
he eats not,   and   gives thanks   -   to God.

7 οὐδεὶς γὰρ ἡμῶν ἑαυτῷ ζῇ, καὶ οὐδεὶς
For no one   of us   to himself lives, and   no one

ἑαυτῷ ἀποθνῄσκει· 8 ἐάν τε γὰρ ζῶμεν,
to himself   dies;   for whether   we live,

τῷ κυρίῳ ζῶμεν, ἐάν τε ἀποθνῄσκωμεν,
to the Lord   we live,   or if   we die,

τῷ κυρίῳ ἀποθνῄσκομεν. ἐάν τε οὖν
to the Lord   we die.   Whether therefore

ζῶμεν ἐάν τε ἀποθνῄσκωμεν, τοῦ κυρίου
we live   or if   we die,   of the   Lord

ἐσμέν. 9 εἰς τοῦτο γὰρ Χριστὸς ἀπέθανεν
we are. for   this   For   Christ   died

καὶ ἔζησεν, ἵνα καὶ νεκρῶν καὶ ζώντων
and lived [again], in order both of dead and of living
that   [ones]

κυριεύσῃ. 10 σὺ δὲ τί κρίνεις τὸν ἀδελφόν
he might be Lord. ³thou And ¹why ²judgest   the   brother

σου; ἢ καὶ σὺ τί ἐξουθενεῖς τὸν ἀδελφόν
of thee? or ²indeed ⁴thou ¹why ³despisest the   brother

σου; πάντες γὰρ παραστησόμεθα τῷ
of thee?   for all   we shall stand before   the

βήματι τοῦ θεοῦ. 11 γέγραπται γάρ·
tribunal   - of God.   For it has been written:

ζῶ ἐγώ, λέγει κύριος, ὅτι ἐμοὶ κάμψει
Live I,   says [the] Lord, that to me will bend

πᾶν γόνυ, καὶ πᾶσα γλῶσσα ἐξομολογήσεται
every knee, and every tongue   will confess

τῷ θεῷ. 12 ἄρα [οὖν] ἕκαστος ἡμῶν
- to God.   So therefore   each one   of us

περὶ ἑαυτοῦ λόγον δώσει [τῷ θεῷ].
concerning himself account will give   - to God.

13 Μηκέτι οὖν ἀλλήλους κρίνωμεν· ἀλλὰ
No longer therefore one another   let us judge;   but

τοῦτο κρίνατε μᾶλλον, τὸ μὴ τιθέναι
this   judge ye   rather,   -   not to put

πρόσκομμα τῷ ἀδελφῷ ἢ σκάνδαλον.
a stumbling-block to the   brother   or   an offence.

14 οἶδα καὶ πέπεισμαι ἐν κυρίῳ Ἰησοῦ
I know and   have been   by [the] Lord Jesus
persuaded

ὅτι οὐδὲν κοινὸν δι' ἑαυτοῦ· εἰ μὴ
that nothing [is] common through itself;   except

it is unclean for any one who thinks it unclean. ¹⁵ If your brother is being injured by what you eat, you are no longer walking in love. Do not let what you eat cause the ruin of one for whom Christ died. ¹⁶ So do not let what is good to you be spoken of as evil. ¹⁷ For the kingdom of God does not mean food and drink but righteousness and peace and joy in the Holy Spirit; ¹⁸ he who thus serves Christ is acceptable to God and approved by men. ¹⁹ Let us then pursue what makes for peace and for mutual upbuilding. ²⁰ Do not, for the sake of food, destroy the work of God. Everything is indeed clean, but it is wrong for any one to make others fall by what he eats; ²¹ it is right not to eat meat or drink wine or do anything that makes your brother stumble.⁹ ²² The faith that you have, keep between yourself and God; happy is he who has no reason to judge himself for what he approves. ²³ But he

τῷ   λογιζομένῳ   τι   κοινὸν   εἶναι,   ἐκείνῳ
to the   reckoning   anything common   to be,   to that man
[one]   [it is]

κοινόν.   15 εἰ   γὰρ   διὰ   βρῶμα   ὁ   ἀδελφός
common.   For if   because   food   the   brother
                                         of

σου   λυπεῖται,   οὐκέτι   κατὰ   ἀγάπην
of thee   is grieved,   no longer   according to   love

περιπατεῖς.   μὴ   τῷ   βρώματί   σου   ἐκεῖνον
thou walkest.   ⁵Not ³by the   ⁴food   ⁵of thee   ⁶that man

ἀπόλλυε,   ὑπὲρ   οὗ   Χριστὸς   ἀπέθανεν.
¹destroy,   on behalf of whom   Christ   died.

16 μὴ   βλασφημείσθω   οὖν   ὑμῶν   τὸ   ἀγαθόν.
Let not be blasphemed   therefore of you   the   good.

17 οὐ   γάρ   ἐστιν   ἡ   βασιλεία   τοῦ   θεοῦ
For not   is   the   kingdom   -   of God

βρῶσις   καὶ   πόσις,   ἀλλὰ   δικαιοσύνη   καὶ
eating   and   drinking,   but   righteousness   and

εἰρήνη   καὶ   χαρὰ   ἐν   πνεύματι   ἁγίῳ·
peace   and   joy   in   [the] Spirit   Holy;

18 ὁ   γὰρ   ἐν   τούτῳ   δουλεύων   τῷ   Χριστῷ
for the [one]   in   this   serving   -   Christ

εὐάρεστος   τῷ   θεῷ   καὶ   δόκιμος   τοῖς
[is] well-pleasing   -   to God   and   approved   -

ἀνθρώποις.   19 ἄρα   οὖν   τὰ   τῆς   εἰρήνης
by men.   So there-   the   -   of peace
                     fore   things

διώκωμεν   καὶ   τὰ   τῆς   οἰκοδομῆς   τῆς
let us pursue   and the things   -   of building [up]   -

εἰς   ἀλλήλους.   20 μὴ   ἕνεκεν   βρώματος
for   one another.   Not for the sake of   food

κατάλυε   τὸ   ἔργον   τοῦ   θεοῦ.   πάντα
undo thou   the   work   -   of God.   All things

μὲν   καθαρά,   ἀλλὰ   κακὸν   τῷ   ἀνθρώπῳ
indeed [are] clean,   but   evil   to the   man

τῷ   διὰ   προσκόμματος   ἐσθίοντι.   21 καλὸν
-   ²through   ³a stumbling-block   ¹eating.   Good [it is]

τὸ   μὴ   φαγεῖν   κρέα   μηδὲ   πιεῖν   οἶνον
-   not   to eat   flesh   nor   to drink   wine

μηδὲ   ἐν   ᾧ   ὁ   ἀδελφός   σου   προσκόπτει.
nor   by which   the   brother   of thee   stumbles.
[anything]

22 σὺ   πίστιν   ἣν   ἔχεις   κατὰ   σεαυτὸν
³Thou   ⁵faith   ²which   ⁴hast   ⁶by   ⁷thyself

ἔχε   ἐνώπιον   τοῦ   θεοῦ.   μακάριος   ὁ
⁵have   before   -   God.   Blessed   the
                                         [one]

μὴ   κρίνων   ἑαυτὸν   ἐν   ᾧ   δοκιμάζει·
not   judging   himself   in   what   he approves;

who has doubts is con-
demned, if he eats,
because he does not act
from faith; for whatever
does not proceed from
faith is sin.[r]

CHAPTER 15

WE who are strong
ought to bear with
the failings of the weak,
and not to please our-
selves; [2]let each of us
please his neighbor for
his good, to edify him.
[3]For Christ did not
please himself; but, as it
is written, "The re-
proaches of those who
reproached thee fell on
me." [4]For whatever was
written in former days
was written for our in-
struction, that by
steadfastness and by the
encouragement of the
scriptures we might have
hope. [5]May the God of
steadfastness and en-
couragement grant you
to live in such harmony
with one another, in
accord with Christ Jesus,
[6]that together you may
with one voice glorify the
God and Father of our
Lord Jesus Christ.

[7] Welcome one
another, therefore, as
Christ has welcomed you,

23 ὁ δὲ διακρινόμενος ἐὰν φάγῃ κατα-
but the [one]   doubting   if   he eats   has been
κέκριται, ὅτι οὐκ ἐκ πίστεως· πᾶν
condemned, because not of faith; [2]all
δὲ ὃ οὐκ ἐκ πίστεως ἁμαρτία ἐστίν.
[1]and which [is] not of faith sin is.

15 Ὀφείλομεν δὲ ἡμεῖς οἱ δυνατοὶ τὰ
[6]Ought   [1]so   [2]we   [3]the   [4]strong   [7]the
ἀσθενήματα τῶν ἀδυνάτων βαστάζειν, καὶ
[8]weaknesses   [9]of the   [10]not strong   [5]to bear,   and
μὴ ἑαυτοῖς ἀρέσκειν. 2 ἕκαστος ἡμῶν
not [our]selves to please. Each one of us
τῷ πλησίον ἀρεσκέτω εἰς τὸ ἀγαθὸν
the(his) neighbour let him please for - good
πρὸς οἰκοδομήν· 3 καὶ γὰρ ὁ Χριστὸς
to building [up];   for even   -   Christ
οὐχ ἑαυτῷ ἤρεσεν· ἀλλὰ καθὼς γέ-
[2]not [3]himself [1]pleased; but as it has
γραπται· οἱ ὀνειδισμοὶ τῶν ὀνειδιζόντων
been written: The reproaches of the [ones] reproaching
σε ἐπέπεσαν ἐπ' ἐμέ. 4 ὅσα γὰρ
thee fell on   on me. For whatever things
προεγράφη, εἰς τὴν ἡμετέραν διδασκαλίαν
were previously for   our   teaching
written,
ἐγράφη, ἵνα διὰ τῆς ὑπομονῆς καὶ
were in order through   -   patience and
written, that
διὰ τῆς παρακλήσεως τῶν γραφῶν τὴν
through the comfort of the writings -
ἐλπίδα ἔχωμεν. 5 ὁ δὲ θεὸς τῆς ὑπομονῆς
hope we may have. And the God - of patience
καὶ τῆς παρακλήσεως δῴη ὑμῖν τὸ
and   -   of comfort give to you [2]the
αὐτὸ φρονεῖν ἐν ἀλλήλοις κατὰ Χριστὸν
[3]same   [1]to mind among one another according to Christ
thing
Ἰησοῦν, 6 ἵνα ὁμοθυμαδὸν ἐν ἑνὶ στόματι
Jesus,   in order with one accord with one mouth
that
δοξάζητε τὸν θεὸν καὶ πατέρα τοῦ
ye may glorify the God and Father of the
κυρίου ἡμῶν Ἰησοῦ Χριστοῦ.
Lord of us Jesus Christ.
7 Διὸ προσλαμβάνεσθε ἀλλήλους, καθὼς
Wherefore receive ye one another, as
καὶ ὁ Χριστὸς προσελάβετο ἡμᾶς εἰς
also   -   Christ received us to

[r] Other authorities, some ancient, insert here Ch. 16. 25-27

for the glory of God.
⁸For I tell you that Christ became a servant to the circumcised to show God's truthfulness, in order to confirm the promises given to the patriarchs, ⁹and in order that the Gentiles might glorify God for his mercy. As it is written,
"Therefore I will praise thee among the Gentiles,
and sing to thy name";
¹⁰and again it is said,
"Rejoice, O Gentiles, with his people";
¹¹and again,
"Praise the Lord, all Gentiles,
and let all the peoples praise him";
¹²and further Isaiah says,
"The root of Jesse shall come,
he who rises to rule the Gentiles;
in him shall the Gentiles hope."
¹³May the God of hope fill you with all joy and peace in believing, so that by the power of the Holy Spirit you may abound in hope.
14 I myself am satisfied about you, my brethren, that you yourselves are full of goodness, filled with all knowledge, and able to

δόξαν τοῦ θεοῦ.   8 λέγω γὰρ Χριστὸν
[the] glory – of God.   For I say   Christ

διάκονον   γεγενῆσθαι   περιτομῆς   ὑπὲρ
a minister   to have become   of [the]   on be-
                              circumcision   half of

ἀληθείας   θεοῦ,   εἰς   τὸ   βεβαιῶσαι   τὰς
[the] truth of God,   –   –   to confirm   the

ἐπαγγελίας   τῶν   πατέρων,   9 τὰ   δὲ   ἔθνη
promises   of the   fathers,   and ¹the   ²nations

ὑπὲρ   ἐλέους   δοξάσαι   τὸν   θεόν,   καθὼς
⁵on be- ⁶mercy   ³to glorify –   ⁴God,   as
half of

γέγραπται·   διὰ   τοῦτο   ἐξομολογήσομαί   σοι
it has been written: Therefore   I will confess   to thee

ἐν   ἔθνεσιν   καὶ   τῷ   ὀνόματί   σου   ψαλῶ.
among nations and   to the   name   of thee I will sing
                                                 praise.

10 καὶ   πάλιν   λέγει·   εὐφράνθητε,   ἔθνη,
And   again   he says: Be glad,   nations,

μετὰ   τοῦ   λαοῦ   αὐτοῦ.   11 καὶ   πάλιν·
with   the   people   of him.   And   again:

αἰνεῖτε,   πάντα   τὰ   ἔθνη,   τὸν   κύριον,
Praise,   all   the   nations,   the   Lord,

καὶ   ἐπαινεσάτωσαν   αὐτὸν   πάντες   οἱ   λαοί.
and   let praise   him   all   the peoples.

12 καὶ   πάλιν   Ἠσαΐας   λέγει·   ἔσται
And   again   Esaias   says: There
                                         shall be

ἡ   ῥίζα   τοῦ   Ἰεσσαί,   καὶ   ὁ   ἀνιστάμενος
the root   of Jesse,   and the [one] rising up

ἄρχειν   ἐθνῶν·   ἐπ᾽   αὐτῷ   ἔθνη   ἐλπιοῦσιν.
to rule   nations;   on   him   nations   will hope.

13 Ὁ   δὲ   θεὸς   τῆς   ἐλπίδος   πληρῶσαι
Now the   God   –   of hope   fill

ὑμᾶς   πάσης   χαρᾶς   καὶ   εἰρήνης   ἐν   τῷ
you   of(with) all   joy   and   peace   in   –

πιστεύειν,   εἰς   τὸ   περισσεύειν   ὑμᾶς   ἐν
to believe   for   –   to abound   youᵇ   in
(believing),

τῇ   ἐλπίδι   ἐν   δυνάμει   πνεύματος   ἁγίου.
–   hope   by   [the] power   of [the] Spirit   Holy.

14 Πέπεισμαι   δέ,   ἀδελφοί   μου,   καὶ
But I have been persuaded, brothers of me, even

αὐτὸς   ἐγὼ   περὶ   ὑμῶν,   ὅτι   καὶ   αὐτοί
³[my]self ¹I concerning you, that also [your]-
                                                 selves

μεστοί   ἐστε   ἀγαθωσύνης,   πεπληρωμένοι
full   ye are   of goodness,   having been filled

πάσης   τῆς   γνώσεως,   δυνάμενοι   καὶ
of(with) all – knowledge, being able also

instruct one another.
15 But on some points I
have written to you very
boldly by way of re-
minder, because of the
grace given me by God
16 to be a minister of
Christ Jesus to the
Gentiles in the priestly
service of the gospel of
God, so that the offering
of the Gentiles may be
acceptable, sanctified by
the Holy Spirit. 17 In
Christ Jesus, then, I have
reason to be proud of my
work for God. 18 For I
will not venture to speak
of anything except what
Christ has wrought
through me to win
obedience from the
Gentiles, by word and
deed, 19 by the power of
signs and wonders, by
the power of the Holy
Spirit, so that from
Jerusalem and as far
round as Illyr′icum I
have fully preached the
gospel of Christ, 20 thus
making it my ambition to
preach the gospel, not
where Christ has already
been named, lest I build
on another man's
foundation, 21 but as it is
written,

"They shall see who
have never been
told of him,

ἀλλήλους   νουθετεῖν.   15 τολμηροτέρως   δὲ
one another   to admonish.   And more daringly

ἔγραψα ὑμῖν ἀπὸ μέρους, ὡς ἐπαναμιμνή-
I wrote   to you   in   part,   as   remind-

σκων ὑμᾶς διὰ τὴν χάριν τὴν δοθεῖσάν
ing   you   by   the   grace –   given

μοι ἀπὸ τοῦ θεοῦ 16 εἰς τὸ εἶναί με
to me from – God   for the   to be   me[b]
                                =that I should be

λειτουργὸν Χριστοῦ Ἰησοῦ εἰς τὰ ἔθνη,
a minister   of Christ   Jesus   to   the nations,

ἱερουργοῦντα τὸ εὐαγγέλιον τοῦ θεοῦ,
sacrificing   the   gospel   –   of God,

ἵνα γένηται ἡ προσφορὰ τῶν ἐθνῶν
in order ⁵may be ¹the   ²offering   ³of the ⁴nations
that

εὐπρόσδεκτος, ἡγιασμένη ἐν πνεύματι
acceptable,   having been sanctified by   [the] Spirit

ἁγίῳ. 17 ἔχω οὖν τὴν καύχησιν ἐν
Holy.   I have therefore the   boasting   in

Χριστῷ Ἰησοῦ τὰ πρὸς τὸν θεόν· 18 οὐ
Christ   Jesus the things with* –   God;   ⁴not

γὰρ τολμήσω τι λαλεῖν ὧν οὐ
¹for   ²I ³will ⁴dare   ⁵any-   ⁶to speak   of [the] ²not
                        thing   things which

κατειργάσατο Χριστὸς δι' ἐμοῦ εἰς ὑπακοὴν
³did ⁴work ⁵out   ¹Christ through me   for   obedience

ἐθνῶν, λόγῳ καὶ ἔργῳ, 19 ἐν δυνάμει
of [the]   in word   and   work,   by   power
nations,

σημείων καὶ τεράτων, ἐν δυνάμει πνεύματος·
of signs   and   wonders,   by   power   of [the] Spirit;

ὥστε με ἀπὸ Ἰερουσαλὴμ καὶ κύκλῳ
so as   me   from   Jerusalem   and   around
=I should fulfil the gospel . . . from . . . Illyricum.

μέχρι τοῦ Ἰλλυρικοῦ πεπληρωκέναι τὸ
unto   –   Illyricum   to have fulfilled[b]   the

εὐαγγέλιον τοῦ Χριστοῦ. 20 οὕτως δὲ
gospel   –   of Christ.   And so

φιλοτιμούμενον εὐαγγελίζεσθαι οὐχ ὅπου
eagerly striving   to evangelize   not   where

ὠνομάσθη Χριστός, ἵνα μὴ ἐπ' ἀλλότριον
²was named   ¹Christ,   in order not   on   ⁵belonging to
                    that   another

θεμέλιον οἰκοδομῶ, 21 ἀλλὰ καθὼς
¹a foundation   I should build,   but   as

γέγραπται· ὄψονται οἷς οὐκ ἀνηγγέλη
it has been   They shall see to whom   it was not announced
written:

* That is, the things that have to do with . . .

and they shall understand who have never heard of him."

22 This is the reason why I have so often been hindered from coming to you. 23 But now, since I no longer have any room for work in these regions, and since I have longed for many years to come to you, 24 I hope to see you in passing as I go to Spain, and to be sped on my journey there by you, once I have enjoyed your company for a little. 25 At present, however, I am going to Jerusalem with aid for the saints. 26 For Macedo'nia and Acha'ia have been pleased to make some contribution for the poor among the saints at Jerusalem; 27 they were pleased to do it, and indeed they are in debt to them, for if the Gentiles have come to share in their spiritual blessings, they ought also to be of service to them in material blessings. 28 When therefore I have completed this, and have delivered to them what has been raised, I shall go on by way of you to Spain; 29 and I know that when I come to you I shall come in the fulness of the blessing* of Christ.

30 I appeal to you,

περὶ   αὐτοῦ,   καὶ   οἳ   οὐκ   ἀκηκόασιν
concerning   him,   and [those] who   have not heard

συνήσουσιν.   22 διὸ   καὶ   ἐνεκοπτόμην   τὰ
will understand.   Wherefore   also   I was hindered   –

πολλὰ   τοῦ   ἐλθεῖν   πρὸς   ὑμᾶς·   23 νυνὶ
many(much) –   to come^d   to   you;   ²now

δὲ   μηκέτι   τόπον   ἔχων   ἐν   τοῖς   κλίμασι
¹but no longer   ³place   ¹having in – ²regions

τούτοις,   ἐπιποθίαν   δὲ   ἔχων   τοῦ   ἐλθεῖν
¹these,   and ²a desire   ¹having   –   to come^d

πρὸς   ὑμᾶς   ἀπὸ   ἱκανῶν   ἐτῶν,   24 ὡς   ἂν
to   you   from   several   years,   whenever

πορεύωμαι   εἰς   τὴν   Σπανίαν·   ἐλπίζω   γὰρ
I journey   to   –   Spain;   for I hope

διαπορευόμενος   θεάσασθαι   ὑμᾶς   καὶ   ὑφ'
journeying through   to behold   you   and   by

ὑμῶν   προπεμφθῆναι   ἐκεῖ,   ἐὰν   ὑμῶν   πρῶτον
you   to be set forward   there,   if of(with) you   firstly

ἀπὸ   μέρους   ἐμπλησθῶ,   25 —   νυνὶ   δὲ
in   part   I may be filled,   —   but now

πορεύομαι   εἰς   Ἰερουσαλὴμ   διακονῶν   τοῖς
I am going   to   Jerusalem   ministering   to the

ἁγίοις.   26 ηὐδόκησαν   γὰρ   Μακεδονία   καὶ
saints.   For thought it good   Macedonia   and

Ἀχαΐα   κοινωνίαν   τινὰ   ποιήσασθαι   εἰς
Achaia   ²contribution   ²some   ¹to make   for

τοὺς   πτωχοὺς   τῶν   ἁγίων   τῶν   ἐν   Ἰερου-
the   poor   of the saints   –   in   Jeru-

σαλήμ.   27 ηὐδόκησαν   γάρ,   καὶ   ὀφειλέται
salem.   For they thought it good,   and   debtors

εἰσὶν   αὐτῶν·   εἰ   γὰρ   τοῖς   πνευματικοῖς
they are   of them;   for if   in the   spiritual things

αὐτῶν   ἐκοινώνησαν   τὰ   ἔθνη,   ὀφείλουσιν
of them   ³shared   ¹the   ²nations,   they ought

καὶ   ἐν   τοῖς   σαρκικοῖς   λειτουργῆσαι   αὐτοῖς.
also   in   the   fleshly things   to minister   to them.

28 τοῦτο   οὖν   ἐπιτελέσας,   καὶ   σφραγισάμενος
This   therefore   having   and   having sealed
completed,

αὐτοῖς   τὸν   καρπὸν   τοῦτον,   29 ἀπελεύσομαι
to them   this fruit,   I will go away

δι'   ὑμῶν   εἰς   Σπανίαν·   οἶδα   δὲ   ὅτι
through you   to   Spain;   and I know   that

ἐρχόμενος   πρὸς   ὑμᾶς   ἐν   πληρώματι
coming   to   you   in [the]   fulness

εὐλογίας   Χριστοῦ   ἐλεύσομαι.   30 Παρακαλῶ
of [the]   of Christ   I will come.   I beseech
blessing

* Other ancient authorities insert *of the gospel*

brethren, by our Lord Jesus Christ and by the love of the Spirit, to strive together with me in your prayers to God on my behalf, [31] that I may be delivered from the unbelievers in Judea, and that my service for Jerusalem may be acceptable to the saints, [32] so that by God's will I may come to you with joy and be refreshed in your company. [33] The God of peace be with you all. Amen.

δὲ   ὑμᾶς,   [ἀδελφοί],   διὰ   τοῦ   κυρίου
Now   you,   brothers,   through   the   Lord
ἡμῶν   Ἰησοῦ   Χριστοῦ   καὶ   διὰ   τῆς   ἀγάπης
of us   Jesus   Christ   and through the   love
τοῦ   πνεύματος,   συναγωνίσασθαί   μοι   ἐν
of the   Spirit,   to strive with   me   in
ταῖς   προσευχαῖς   ὑπὲρ   ἐμοῦ   πρὸς   τὸν
the   prayers   on behalf of   me   to   -
θεόν,   31 ἵνα   ῥυσθῶ   ἀπὸ   τῶν   ἀπειθούντων
God,   in order   I may be   from   the   disobeying
    that   delivered   [ones]
ἐν   τῇ   Ἰουδαίᾳ   καὶ   ἡ   διακονία   μου
in   -   Judæa   and   the   ministry   of me
ἡ   εἰς   Ἰερουσαλὴμ   εὐπρόσδεκτος   τοῖς
-    to   Jerusalem   [2]acceptable   [3]to the
ἁγίοις   γένηται,   32 ἵνα   ἐν   χαρᾷ   ἐλθὼν
[4]saints   [1]may be,   in order that   in   joy   coming
πρὸς   ὑμᾶς   διὰ   θελήματος   θεοῦ   συνανα-
to   you   through   [the] will   of God   I may
παύσωμαι   ὑμῖν.   33 ὁ   δὲ   θεὸς   τῆς
rest with   you.   And the   God   -
εἰρήνης   μετὰ   πάντων   ὑμῶν·   ἀμήν.
of peace   [be] with   all   you: Amen.

CHAPTER 16

I commend to you our sister Phoebe, a deaconess of the church at Cen'chre-ae, [2] that you may receive her in the Lord as befits the saints, and help her in whatever she may require from you, for she has been a helper of many and of myself as well.

3 Greet Prisca and Aquila, my fellow workers in Christ Jesus, [4] who risked their necks for my life, to whom not only I

16 Συνίστημι   δὲ   ὑμῖν   Φοίβην   τὴν
Now I commend   to you   Phœbe   the
ἀδελφὴν   ἡμῶν,   οὖσαν   [καὶ]   διάκονον   τῆς
sister   of us,   being   also   a minister   of the
ἐκκλησίας   τῆς   ἐν   Κεγχρεαῖς,   2 ἵνα
church   -   in   Cenchrea,   in order that
αὐτὴν   προσδέξησθε   ἐν   κυρίῳ   ἀξίως   τῶν
[2]her   [1]ye may receive   in   [the] Lord   worthily   of the
ἁγίων,   καὶ   παραστῆτε   αὐτῇ   ἐν   ᾧ   ἂν
saints,   and   may stand by   her   in   [1]whatever
ὑμῶν   χρῄζῃ   πράγματι·   καὶ   γὰρ   αὐτὴ
[4]of you   [3]she may   [2]thing;   for indeed   she
    have need
προστάτις   πολλῶν   ἐγενήθη   καὶ   ἐμοῦ   αὐτοῦ.
a protectress   of many   became   and   of myself.
3 Ἀσπάσασθε   Πρίσκαν   καὶ   Ἀκύλαν   τοὺς
Greet ye   Prisca   and   Aquila   the
συνεργούς   μου   ἐν   Χριστῷ   Ἰησοῦ,   4 οἵτινες
fellow-workers of me   in   Christ   Jesus,   who
ὑπὲρ   τῆς   ψυχῆς   μου   τὸν   ἑαυτῶν   τράχηλον
on be-   the   life   of me   [2]the   [4]of   [3]neck
half of   themselves
ὑπέθηκαν,   οἷς   οὐκ   ἐγὼ   μόνος   εὐχαριστῶ
[1]risked,   to whom   not   I   only   give thanks

but also all the churches of the Gentiles give thanks; ⁵greet also the church in their house. Greet my beloved Epae′netus, who was the first convert in Asia for Christ. ⁶Greet Mary, who has worked hard among you. ⁷Greet Andron′icus and Ju′nias, my kinsmen and my fellow prisoners; they are men of note among the apostles, and they were in Christ before me. ⁸Greet Amplia′tus, my beloved in the Lord. ⁹Greet Urba′nus, our fellow worker in Christ, and my beloved Stachys. ¹⁰Greet Apel′les, who is approved in Christ. Greet those who belong to the family of Aristob′ulus. ¹¹Greet my kinsman Herodion. Greet those in the Lord who belong to the family of Narcis′sus. ¹²Greet those workers in the Lord, Tryphae′na and Trypho′sa. Greet the beloved Persis, who has worked hard in the Lord. ¹³Greet Rufus, eminent in the Lord, also his mother and mine. ¹⁴Greet Asyn′critus, Phlegon, Hermes, Pat′robas, Her-

ἀλλὰ καὶ πᾶσαι αἱ ἐκκλησίαι τῶν ἐθνῶν,
but also all   the churches of the nations,

5 καὶ τὴν κατ' οἶκον αὐτῶν ἐκκλησίαν.
and ¹the ³in ⁴house ⁵of them ²church.

ἀσπάσασθε Ἐπαίνετον τὸν ἀγαπητόν μου,
Greet   Epænetus   the beloved   of me,

ὅς ἐστιν ἀπαρχὴ τῆς Ἀσίας εἰς Χριστόν.
who is firstfruit – of Asia for Christ.

6 ἀσπάσασθε Μαρίαν, ἥτις πολλὰ ἐκοπίασεν
Greet   Mary,   who many things laboured
                                     (much)

εἰς ὑμᾶς. 7 ἀσπάσασθε Ἀνδρόνικον καὶ
for you.   Greet   Andronicus   and

Ἰουνιᾶν τοὺς συγγενεῖς μου καὶ συναιχμα-
Junius   the   kinsmen   of me and   fellow-

λώτους μου, οἵτινές εἰσιν ἐπίσημοι ἐν
captives of me, who are   notable among

τοῖς ἀποστόλοις, οἳ καὶ πρὸ ἐμοῦ γέγοναν
the   apostles, who indeed before me have been

ἐν Χριστῷ. 8 ἀσπάσασθε Ἀμπλιᾶτον τὸν
in Christ.   Greet   Ampliatus   the

ἀγαπητόν μου ἐν κυρίῳ. 9 ἀσπάσασθε
beloved   of me in [the] Lord.   Greet

Οὐρβανὸν τὸν συνεργὸν ἡμῶν ἐν Χριστῷ
Urbanus   the fellow-worker of us in Christ

καὶ Στάχυν τὸν ἀγαπητόν μου. 10 ἀσπά-
and Stachys the beloved   of me.   Greet

ασθε Ἀπελλῆν τὸν δόκιμον ἐν Χριστῷ.
Apelles   the approved in Christ.

ἀσπάσασθε τοὺς ἐκ τῶν Ἀριστοβούλου.
Greet   the [ones] of the [family] of Aristobulus.

11 ἀσπάσασθε Ἡρωδίωνα τὸν συγγενῆ μου.
Greet   Herodion   the kinsman of me.

ἀσπάσασθε τοὺς ἐκ τῶν Ναρκίσσου τοὺς
Greet   the [ones] of the [family] of Narcissus –

ὄντας ἐν κυρίῳ. 12 ἀσπάσασθε Τρύφαιναν
being in [the] Lord.   Greet   Tryphæna

καὶ Τρυφῶσαν τὰς κοπιώσας ἐν κυρίῳ.
and Tryphosa the [ones] labouring in [the] Lord.

ἀσπάσασθε Περσίδα τὴν ἀγαπητήν, ἥτις
Greet   Persis   the beloved,   who

πολλὰ ἐκοπίασεν ἐν κυρίῳ. 13 ἀσπάσασθε
many things laboured in [the] Lord.   Greet
(much)

Ῥοῦφον τὸν ἐκλεκτὸν ἐν κυρίῳ καὶ
Rufus   the chosen   in [the] Lord and

τὴν μητέρα αὐτοῦ καὶ ἐμοῦ. 14 ἀσπάσασθε
the mother of him and of me.   Greet

Ἀσύγκριτον, Φλέγοντα, Ἑρμῆν, Πατροβᾶν,
Asyncritus, Phlegon,   Hermes, Patrobas,

mas, and the brethren who are with them. [15] Greet Philol'ogus, Julia, Nereus and his sister, and Olym'pas, and all the saints who are with them. [16] Greet one another with a holy kiss. All the churches of Christ greet you.

17 I appeal to you, brethren, to take note of those who create dissensions and difficulties, in opposition to the doctrine which you have been taught; avoid them. [18] For such persons do not serve our Lord Christ, but their own appetites, and by fair and flattering words they deceive the hearts of the simple-minded. [19] For while your obedience is known to all, so that I rejoice over you, I would have you wise as to what is good and guileless as to what is evil; [20] then the God of peace will soon crush Satan under your feet. The grace of our Lord Jesus Christ be with you.[1]

Ἑρμᾶν,	καὶ	τοὺς	σὺν αὐτοῖς	ἀδελφούς.
Hermas,	and	the	[4]with [5]them	[1]brothers.

15 ἀσπάσασθε   Φιλόλογον   καὶ   Ἰουλίαν,
    Greet   Philologus   and   Julia,

Νηρέα   καὶ   τὴν   ἀδελφὴν   αὐτοῦ,   καὶ
Nereus   and   the   sister   of him,   and

Ὀλυμπᾶν,   καὶ   τοὺς   σὺν αὐτοῖς   πάντας
Olympas,   and   [2]the   [4]with [5]them   [1]all

ἁγίους.   16 ἀσπάσασθε   ἀλλήλους   ἐν   φιλήματι
[3]saints.   Greet   one another   with   kiss

ἁγίῳ.   ἀσπάζονται   ὑμᾶς   αἱ   ἐκκλησίαι
a holy.   [5]greet   [4]you   [2]the   [3]churches

πᾶσαι   τοῦ   Χριστοῦ.
[1]All   –   [6]of Christ.

17 Παρακαλῶ   δὲ   ὑμᾶς,   ἀδελφοί,   σκοπεῖν
   Now I beseech   you,   brothers,   to watch

τοὺς   τὰς   διχοστασίας   καὶ   τὰ   σκάνδαλα
[1]the   [3]the   [4]divisions   [5]and   [6]the   [7]offences
[ones]

παρὰ   τὴν   διδαχὴν   ἣν   ὑμεῖς   ἐμάθετε
[8]beside   [9]the   [10]teaching   [11]which   [12]ye   [13]learned

ποιοῦντας,   καὶ   ἐκκλίνετε   ἀπ᾽ αὐτῶν·   18 οἱ
[1]making,   and   turn away   from   them;

γὰρ   τοιοῦτοι   τῷ   κυρίῳ   ἡμῶν   Χριστῷ
for   such men   [3]the   [4]Lord   [5]of us   [2]Christ

οὐ   δουλεύουσιν   ἀλλὰ   τῇ   ἑαυτῶν   κοιλίᾳ,
[1]serve not   but   the   of themselves   belly,

καὶ   διὰ   τῆς   χρηστολογίας   καὶ   εὐλογίας
and   through   –   fair speech   and   flattering
                                         speech

ἐξαπατῶσιν   τὰς   καρδίας   τῶν   ἀκάκων.
deceive   the   hearts   of the   guileless.

19 ἡ   γὰρ   ὑμῶν   ὑπακοὴ   εἰς   πάντας
[1]the   [2]For   [3]of you   [4]obedience   [5]to   [7]all men

ἀφίκετο·   ἐφ᾽   ὑμῖν   οὖν   χαίρω,   θέλω
[6]came;   over   you   therefore   I rejoice,   [1]I wish

δὲ   ὑμᾶς   σοφοὺς   εἶναι   εἰς   τὸ   ἀγαθόν,
[1]and   you   wise   to be   to   the   good,

ἀκεραίους   δὲ   εἰς   τὸ   κακόν.   20 ὁ   δὲ
but simple   to   the   evil.   And the

θεὸς   τῆς   εἰρήνης   συντρίψει   τὸν   σατανᾶν
God   –   of peace   will crush   –   Satan

ὑπὸ   τοὺς   πόδας   ὑμῶν   ἐν   τάχει.
under   the   feet   of you   soon.

Ἡ   χάρις   τοῦ   κυρίου   ἡμῶν   Ἰησοῦ
The   grace   of the   Lord   of us   Jesus [be]

μεθ᾽   ὑμῶν.
with   you.

---

[1] Other ancient authorities omit this sentence

21 Timothy, my fellow worker, greets you; so do Lucius and Jason and Sosip′ater, my kinsmen.

22 I Tertius, the writer of this letter, greet you in the Lord.

23 Ga′ius, who is host to me and to the whole church, greets you. Eras′tus, the city treasurer, and our brother Quartus, greet you.[u]

25 Now to him who is able to strengthen you according to my gospel and the preaching of Jesus Christ, according to the revelation of the mystery which was kept secret for long ages 26 but is now disclosed and through the prophetic writings is made known to all nations, according to the command of the eternal God, to bring about the obedience of faith—27 to the only wise God be glory for evermore through Jesus Christ! Amen.

21 Ἀσπάζεται ὑμᾶς Τιμόθεος ὁ συνεργός
[5]greets   [6]you   [1]Timothy   [1]the   [3]fellow-worker

μου, καὶ Λούκιος καὶ Ἰάσων καὶ
[4]of me,   and   Lucius   and   Jason   and

Σωσίπατρος οἱ συγγενεῖς μου. 22 ἀσπάζ-
Sosipater   the   kinsmen   of me.   [2]greet

ομαι ὑμᾶς ἐγὼ Τέρτιος ὁ γράψας τὴν
[3]you   [1]I   [2]Tertius   [3]the [one]   [4]writing   [5]the

ἐπιστολὴν ἐν κυρίῳ. 23 ἀσπάζεται ὑμᾶς
[6]epistle   in   [the] Lord.   [9]greets   [10]you

Γάϊος ὁ ξένος μου καὶ ὅλης τῆς
[1]Gaius   [2]the   [3]host   [4]of me   [5]and   [6]of all   [7]the

ἐκκλησίας. ἀσπάζεται ὑμᾶς Ἔραστος ὁ
[8]church.   [6]greets   [7]you   [1]Erastus   [2]the

οἰκονόμος τῆς πόλεως καὶ Κούαρτος ὁ
[3]treasurer   [4]of the   [5]city   and   Quartus   the

ἀδελφός. ‡
brother.

25 Τῷ δὲ δυναμένῳ ὑμᾶς στηρίξαι κατὰ
Now to the   being able   [2]you   [1]to establish   accord-
[one]   ing to

τὸ εὐαγγέλιόν μου καὶ τὸ κήρυγμα
the   gospel   of me   and   the   proclamation

Ἰησοῦ Χριστοῦ, κατὰ ἀποκάλυψιν μυστηρίου
of Jesus   Christ,   according [the] revelation   of [the]
to   mystery

χρόνοις αἰωνίοις σεσιγημένου, 26 φανερω-
[2]in times   [3]eternal   [1]having been kept silent,   [2]mani-

θέντος δὲ νῦν διά τε γραφῶν προφητικῶν
fested   [1]but   now   and through   writings   prophetic

κατ' ἐπιταγὴν τοῦ αἰωνίου θεοῦ εἰς
accord-   [the]   of the   eternal   God   [2]for
ing to   command

ὑπακοὴν πίστεως εἰς πάντα τὰ ἔθνη
[7]obedience   [8]of faith   [3]to   [3]all   [4]the   [5]nations

γνωρισθέντος, 27 μόνῳ σοφῷ θεῷ, διὰ
[1]made known,   [2]only   [3]wise   [1]to God, through

Ἰησοῦ Χριστοῦ, ᾧ ἡ δόξα εἰς τοὺς
Jesus   Christ,   to whom the   glory   unto   the
(him)[c]

αἰῶνας τῶν αἰώνων· ἀμήν.
ages   of the   ages: Amen.

---

[u] Other ancient authorities insert verse 24, *The grace of our Lord Jesus Christ be with you all. Amen.*

‡ Verse 24 omitted by Nestle; *cf.* RSV footnote.

CHAPTER 1

PAUL, called by the will of God to be an apostle of Christ Jesus, and our brother Sos'thenes,

2 To the church of God which is at Corinth, to those sanctified in Christ Jesus, called to be saints together with all those who in every place call on the name of our Lord Jesus Christ, both their Lord and ours:

3 Grace to you and peace from God our Father and the Lord Jesus Christ.

4 I give thanks to God[a] always for you because of the grace of God which was given you in Christ Jesus, [5]that in every way you were enriched in him with all speech and all knowledge—[6]even as the testimony to Christ was confirmed among you—[7]so that you are not lacking in any spiritual gift, as you wait for the revealing of our Lord Jesus Christ; [8]who will sustain you to the end, guiltless in the day of our Lord Jesus Christ. [9]God is faithful, by whom you were called

---

1 Παῦλος κλητὸς ἀπόστολος Χριστοῦ
Paul a called apostle of Christ
Ἰησοῦ διὰ θελήματος θεοῦ καὶ Σωσθένης
Jesus through [the] will of God and Sosthenes
ὁ ἀδελφὸς 2 τῇ ἐκκλησίᾳ τοῦ θεοῦ
the(?his) brother to the church – of God
τῇ οὔσῃ ἐν Κορίνθῳ, ἡγιασμένοις ἐν
– existing in Corinth, to [ones] in
having been sanctified
Χριστῷ Ἰησοῦ, κλητοῖς ἁγίοις, σὺν πᾶσιν
Christ Jesus, called saints, with all
τοῖς ἐπικαλουμένοις τὸ ὄνομα τοῦ κυρίου
the [ones] calling on the name of the Lord
ἡμῶν Ἰησοῦ Χριστοῦ ἐν παντὶ τόπῳ,
of us Jesus Christ in every place,
αὐτῶν καὶ ἡμῶν· 3 χάρις ὑμῖν καὶ
of them and of us: Grace to you and
εἰρήνη ἀπὸ θεοῦ πατρὸς ἡμῶν καὶ κυρίου
peace from God Father of us and Lord
Ἰησοῦ Χριστοῦ.
Jesus Christ.

4 Εὐχαριστῶ τῷ θεῷ πάντοτε περὶ
I gave thanks – to God always concerning
ὑμῶν ἐπὶ τῇ χάριτι τοῦ θεοῦ τῇ δοθείσῃ
you on the grace of God the – given
ὑμῖν ἐν Χριστῷ Ἰησοῦ, 5 ὅτι ἐν παντὶ
to you in Christ Jesus, because in everything
ἐπλουτίσθητε ἐν αὐτῷ, ἐν παντὶ λόγῳ
ye were enriched in him, in all speech
καὶ πάσῃ γνώσει, 6 καθὼς τὸ μαρτύριον
and all knowledge, as the testimony
τοῦ Χριστοῦ ἐβεβαιώθη ἐν ὑμῖν, 7 ὥστε
– of Christ was confirmed in you, so as
ὑμᾶς μὴ ὑστερεῖσθαι ἐν μηδενὶ χαρίσματι,
you not to be wanting[b] in no(any) gift,
ἀπεκδεχομένους τὴν ἀποκάλυψιν τοῦ κυρίου
awaiting the revelation of the Lord
ἡμῶν Ἰησοῦ Χριστοῦ· 8 ὃς καὶ βεβαιώσει
of us Jesus Christ; who also will confirm
ὑμᾶς ἕως τέλους ἀνεγκλήτους ἐν τῇ
you till [the] end blameless in the
ἡμέρᾳ τοῦ κυρίου ἡμῶν Ἰησοῦ [Χριστοῦ].
day of the Lord of us Jesus Christ.
9 πιστὸς ὁ θεός, δι' οὗ ἐκλήθητε εἰς
Faithful [is] – God, through whom ye were called to

---

[a] Other ancient authorities read *my God*

into the fellowship of his Son, Jesus Christ our Lord.

10 I appeal to you, brethren, by the name of our Lord Jesus Christ, that all of you agree that there be no dissensions among you, but that you be united in the same mind and the same judgment. [11] For it has been reported to me by Chlo'e's people that there is quarreling among you, my brethren. [12] What I mean is that each one of you says, "I belong to Paul," or "I belong to Apol'los," or "I belong to Cephas," or "I belong to Christ." [13] Is Christ divided? Was Paul crucified for you? Or were you baptized in the name of Paul? [14] I am thankful[b] that I baptized none of you except Crispus and Ga'ius; [15] lest any one should say that you were baptized in my name. [16] (I did baptize also the household of Steph'anas. Beyond that, I do not know whether I baptized any one else.) [17] For Christ did not send me to baptize but to preach the gospel, and not with eloquent

κοινωνίαν τοῦ υἱοῦ αὐτοῦ Ἰησοῦ Χριστοῦ
[the] fellowship of the Son of him Jesus Christ
τοῦ κυρίου ἡμῶν.
the Lord of us.

10 Παρακαλῶ δὲ ὑμᾶς, ἀδελφοί, διὰ
Now I beseech you, brothers, through
τοῦ ὀνόματος τοῦ κυρίου ἡμῶν Ἰησοῦ
the name of the Lord of us Jesus
Χριστοῦ, ἵνα τὸ αὐτὸ λέγητε πάντες,
Christ, in order the same ye say all,
that thing
καὶ μὴ ᾖ ἐν ὑμῖν σχίσματα, ἦτε δὲ
and not be among you divisions, but ye may be
κατηρτισμένοι ἐν τῷ αὐτῷ νοῒ καὶ
having been joined in the same mind and
together
ἐν τῇ αὐτῇ γνώμῃ. 11 ἐδηλώθη γάρ μοι
in the same opinion. For it was shown to me
περὶ ὑμῶν, ἀδελφοί μου, ὑπὸ τῶν
concerning you, brothers of me, by the [ones]
Χλόης, ὅτι ἔριδες ἐν ὑμῖν εἰσιν. 12 λέγω
of Chloe, that strifes among you there are. I say
δὲ τοῦτο, ὅτι ἕκαστος ὑμῶν λέγει· ἐγὼ
Now this, because each of you says: I
μέν εἰμι Παύλου, ἐγὼ δὲ Ἀπολλῶ,
indeed am of Paul, but I of Apollos,
ἐγὼ δὲ Κηφᾶ, ἐγὼ δὲ Χριστοῦ.
but I of Cephas, but I of Christ.
13 μεμέρισται ὁ Χριστός; μὴ Παῦλος
Has been divided - Christ? Not Paul
ἐσταυρώθη ὑπὲρ ὑμῶν, ἢ εἰς τὸ ὄνομα
was crucified on behalf of you, or in the name
Παύλου ἐβαπτίσθητε; 14 εὐχαριστῶ ὅτι
of Paul were ye baptized? I give thanks that
οὐδένα ὑμῶν ἐβάπτισα εἰ μὴ Κρίσπον
not one of you I baptized except Crispus
καὶ Γάιον· 15 ἵνα μή τις εἴπῃ ὅτι
and Gaius; lest anyone should say that
εἰς τὸ ἐμὸν ὄνομα ἐβαπτίσθητε. 16 ἐβάπτισα δὲ
in - my name ye were baptized. But I baptized
καὶ τὸν Στεφανᾶ οἶκον· λοιπὸν οὐκ οἶδα
also the of Stephanas household; for the rest I know not
εἴ τινα ἄλλον ἐβάπτισα. 17 οὐ
if any other I baptized. [1]not
γὰρ ἀπέστειλέν με Χριστὸς βαπτίζειν
[1]For [2]sent [4]me [3]Christ to baptize
ἀλλὰ εὐαγγελίζεσθαι, οὐκ ἐν σοφίᾳ λόγου,
but to evangelize, not in wisdom of speech,

[b] Other ancient authorities read I thank God

wisdom, lest the cross of
Christ be emptied of its
power.
18 For the word of the
cross is folly to those who
are perishing, but to us
who are being saved it is
the power of God. 19 For
it is written,

"I will destroy the
    wisdom of the
    wise,
and the cleverness of
    the clever I will
    thwart."

20 Where is the wise man?
Where is the scribe?
Where is the debater of
this age? Has not God
made foolish the wisdom
of the world? 21 For
since, in the wisdom of
God, the world did not
know God through wis-
dom, it pleased God
through the folly of what
we preach to save those
who believe. 22 For Jews
demand signs and Greeks
seek wisdom, 23 but we
preach Christ crucified, a
stumbling-block to Jews
and folly to Gentiles,
24 but to those who are
called, both Jews and
Greeks, Christ the power
of God and the wisdom
of God. 25 For the fool-
ishness of God is wiser
than men, and the weak-
ness of God is stronger
than men.

ἵνα μὴ κενωθῇ ὁ σταυρὸς τοῦ Χριστοῦ.
lest ⁴be made vain ¹the ²cross - ³of Christ.

18 Ὁ λόγος γὰρ ὁ τοῦ σταυροῦ τοῖς
For the word - of the cross ²to the
                                                    [ones]

μὲν ἀπολλυμένοις μωρία ἐστίν, τοῖς
¹on one ²perishing ⁵folly ⁴is, ¹to the
hand   [ones]

δὲ σῳζομένοις ἡμῖν δύναμις θεοῦ ἐστιν.
¹on the ⁴being saved ²to us ⁵[the] ⁷power ⁶of God ⁵it is.
other

19 γέγραπται γάρ· ἀπολῶ τὴν σοφίαν
For it has been written: I will destroy the wisdom

τῶν σοφῶν, καὶ τὴν σύνεσιν τῶν συνετῶν
of the wise ones, and the understanding of the prudent

ἀθετήσω. 20 ποῦ σοφός; ποῦ γραμματεύς;
I will set Where [is the] where [is the] scribe?
aside.   wise man?

ποῦ συζητητὴς τοῦ αἰῶνος τούτου; οὐχὶ
where disputant of this age? ³Not
[is the]

ἐμώρανεν ὁ θεὸς τὴν σοφίαν τοῦ κόσμου;
¹made ²foolish - ³God ⁴the ⁵wisdom ⁶of the ⁷world?

21 ἐπειδὴ γὰρ ἐν τῇ σοφίᾳ τοῦ θεοῦ
for since in the wisdom - of God

οὐκ ἔγνω ὁ κόσμος διὰ τῆς σοφίας
⁶knew ⁷not ¹the ²world ³through ⁴the(its) ⁵wisdom

τὸν θεόν, εὐδόκησεν ὁ θεὸς διὰ τῆς
- ⁶God, ²thought well - ¹God through the

μωρίας τοῦ κηρύγματος σῶσαι τοὺς
folly of the proclamation to save the

πιστεύοντας. 22 ἐπειδὴ καὶ Ἰουδαῖοι σημεῖα
[ones] believing. Seeing that both Jews ²signs

αἰτοῦσιν καὶ Ἕλληνες σοφίαν ζητοῦσιν,
¹ask and Greeks ⁴wisdom ³seek,

23 ἡμεῖς δὲ κηρύσσομεν Χριστὸν ἐσταυρωμένον,
²we ¹yet proclaim Christ having been crucified,

Ἰουδαίοις μὲν σκάνδαλον, ἔθνεσιν δὲ
to Jews on one hand an offence, to nations on the
                                                    other

μωρίαν, 24 αὐτοῖς δὲ τοῖς κλητοῖς,
folly, but to them the called ones,

Ἰουδαίοις τε καὶ Ἕλλησιν, Χριστὸν θεοῦ
²to Jews ¹both and to Greeks, Christ of God

δύναμιν καὶ θεοῦ σοφίαν. 25 ὅτι τὸ
power and of God wisdom. Because the

μωρὸν τοῦ θεοῦ σοφώτερον τῶν ἀνθρώπων
foolish - of God wiser [than] - men
thing

ἐστίν, καὶ τὸ ἀσθενὲς τοῦ θεοῦ ἰσχυρότερον
is, and the weak thing - of God stronger [than]

26 For consider your call, brethren; not many of you were wise according to worldly standards, not many were powerful, not many were of noble birth; [27] but God chose what is foolish in the world to shame the wise, God chose what is weak in the world to shame the strong, [28] God chose what is low and despised in the world, even things that are not, to bring to nothing things that are, [29] so that no human being might boast in the presence of God. [30] He is the source of your life in Christ Jesus, whom God made our wisdom, our righteousness and sanctification and redemption; [31] therefore, as it is written, "Let him who boasts, boast of the Lord."

CHAPTER 2

WHEN I came to you, brethren, I did not come proclaiming to you the testimony[e] of God in lofty words or wisdom. [2] For I decided to know nothing among

[e] Other ancient authorities read *mystery* (or *secret*)

τῶν ἀνθρώπων. 26 Βλέπετε γὰρ τὴν
- men.   For ye see   the

κλῆσιν ὑμῶν, ἀδελφοί, ὅτι οὐ πολλοὶ
calling of you, brothers, that not many

σοφοὶ κατὰ σάρκα, οὐ πολλοὶ δυνατοί,
wise men according flesh, not many powerful,
          to

οὐ πολλοὶ εὐγενεῖς· 27 ἀλλὰ τὰ μωρὰ
not many well born;   but the foolish
                                        things

τοῦ κόσμου ἐξελέξατο ὁ θεὸς ἵνα καται-
of the world ²chose - ¹God in order he might
                                    that

σχύνῃ τοὺς σοφούς, καὶ τὰ ἀσθενῆ τοῦ
shame the wise men, and the weak things of the

κόσμου ἐξελέξατο ὁ θεὸς ἵνα καταισχύνῃ
world ²chose - ¹God in order he might shame
                                    that

τὰ ἰσχυρά, 28 καὶ τὰ ἀγενῆ τοῦ κόσμου
the strong things, and the base things of the world

καὶ τὰ ἐξουθενημένα ἐξελέξατο ὁ θεός,
and the things being despised ²chose - ¹God,

τὰ μὴ ὄντα, ἵνα τὰ ὄντα καταργήσῃ,
the not being, in order ²the ³being ¹he might
things   that things abolish,

29 ὅπως μὴ καυχήσηται πᾶσα σὰρξ
so as not might boast all flesh*

ἐνώπιον τοῦ θεοῦ. 30 ἐξ αὐτοῦ δὲ ὑμεῖς
before - God.   And of him ye

ἐστε ἐν Χριστῷ Ἰησοῦ, ὃς ἐγενήθη
are in Christ Jesus, who became

σοφία ἡμῖν ἀπὸ θεοῦ, δικαιοσύνη τε
wisdom to us from God, ²righteousness ¹both

καὶ ἁγιασμὸς καὶ ἀπολύτρωσις, 31 ἵνα καθὼς
and sanctification and redemption, in order that as

γέγραπται· ὁ καυχώμενος ἐν κυρίῳ καυχάσθω.
it has been The [one] boasting ²in ³[the] ¹let him boast.
written: Lord

2 Κἀγὼ ἐλθὼν πρὸς ὑμᾶς, ἀδελφοί,
And I coming to you, brothers,

ἦλθον οὐ καθ’ ὑπεροχὴν λόγου ἢ σοφίας
came not accord- excellence of speech or of wisdom
            ing to

καταγγέλλων ὑμῖν τὸ μαρτύριον τοῦ θεοῦ.
announcing to you the testimony - of God.

2 οὐ γὰρ ἔκρινά τι εἰδέναι ἐν ὑμῖν
For I decided not anything to know among you

* That is, so that no flesh might boast. *Cf.* Mat. 24. 22.

you except Jesus Christ and him crucified. [3]And I was with you in weakness and in much fear and trembling; [4]and my speech and my message were not in plausible words of wisdom, but in demonstration of the Spirit and power, [5]that your faith might not rest in the wisdom of men but in the power of God.

6 Yet among the mature we do impart wisdom, although it is not a wisdom of this age or of the rulers of this age, who are doomed to pass away. [7]But we impart a secret and hidden wisdom of God, which God decreed before the ages for our glorification. [8]None of the rulers of this age understood this; for if they had, they would not have crucified the Lord of glory. [9]But, as it is written,

"What no eye has seen, nor ear heard, nor the heart of man conceived,
what God has prepared for those who love him,"
[10]God has revealed to us

εἰ μὴ Ἰησοῦν Χριστὸν καὶ τοῦτον
except   Jesus   Christ   and   this one

ἐσταυρωμένον. 3 κἀγὼ ἐν ἀσθενείᾳ καὶ
having been crucified.   And I   in   weakness   and

ἐν φόβῳ καὶ ἐν τρόμῳ πολλῷ ἐγενόμην
in fear   and in trembling much   was

πρὸς ὑμᾶς, 4 καὶ ὁ λόγος μου καὶ τὸ
with   you,   and the speech of me and the

κήρυγμά μου οὐκ ἐν πειθοῖς σοφίας
proclamation of me not in [1]persuasive [2]of wisdom

λόγοις, ἀλλ' ἐν ἀποδείξει πνεύματος καὶ
[2]words,   but in demonstration of spirit and

δυνάμεως, 5 ἵνα ἡ πίστις ὑμῶν μὴ ᾖ
of power, in order that the faith of you may not be

ἐν σοφίᾳ ἀνθρώπων ἀλλ' ἐν δυνάμει
in [the] wisdom of men   but   in [the] power

θεοῦ.
of God.

6 Σοφίαν δὲ λαλοῦμεν ἐν τοῖς τελείοις,
    But [2]wisdom [1]we speak among the perfect ones,

σοφίαν δὲ οὐ τοῦ αἰῶνος τούτου οὐδὲ
yet wisdom not of this age   neither

τῶν ἀρχόντων τοῦ αἰῶνος τούτου τῶν
of the leaders   of this age   of the [ones]

καταργουμένων· 7 ἀλλὰ λαλοῦμεν θεοῦ
being brought to naught;   but   we speak [2]of God

σοφίαν ἐν μυστηρίῳ, τὴν ἀποκεκρυμμένην,
[1]a wisdom in mystery,   –   having been hidden,

ἣν προώρισεν ὁ θεὸς πρὸ τῶν αἰώνων
which [2]foreordained – [1]God before the ages

εἰς δόξαν ἡμῶν· 8 ἣν οὐδεὶς τῶν ἀρχόντων
for glory of us;   which not one of the leaders

τοῦ αἰῶνος τούτου ἔγνωκεν· εἰ γὰρ
of this age   has known;   for if

ἔγνωσαν, οὐκ ἂν τὸν κύριον τῆς δόξης
they knew,   not – the Lord – of glory

ἐσταύρωσαν· 9 ἀλλὰ καθὼς γέγραπται·   ἃ
they would have but as   it has been written: Things
crucified;[*]   which

ὀφθαλμὸς οὐκ εἶδεν καὶ οὖς οὐκ ἤκουσεν
eye   saw not and ear   heard not

καὶ ἐπὶ καρδίαν ἀνθρώπου οὐκ ἀνέβη,
and on heart   of man   came not up,

ὅσα ἡτοίμασεν ὁ θεὸς τοῖς ἀγαπῶσιν
how many [2]prepared – [1]God for the [ones] loving

αὐτόν. 10 ἡμῖν γὰρ ἀπεκάλυψεν ὁ θεὸς
him.   [1]For [4]to us   [3]revealed – [2]God

* This rendering is demanded by the preceding ἄν.

through the Spirit. For the Spirit searches everything, even the depths of God. [11] For what person knows a man's thoughts except the spirit of the man which is in him? So also no one comprehends the thoughts of God except the Spirit of God. [12] Now we have received not the spirit of the world, but the Spirit which is from God, that we might understand the gifts bestowed on us by God. [13] And we impart this in words not taught by human wisdom but taught by the Spirit, interpreting spiritual truths to those who possess the Spirit.[d]

14 The unspiritual[e] man does not receive the gifts of the Spirit of God, for they are folly to him, and he is not able to understand them because they are spiritually discerned. [15] The spiritual man judges all things, but is himself to be judged by no one. [16] "For who has known the mind of the Lord so as to instruct him?" But we have the mind of Christ.

διὰ τοῦ πνεύματος· τὸ γὰρ πνεῦμα πάντα
through the Spirit; for the Spirit all things
ἐρευνᾷ, καὶ τὰ βάθη τοῦ θεοῦ. 11 τίς
searches, even the deep things – of God. [2]who
γὰρ οἶδεν ἀνθρώπων τὰ τοῦ ἀνθρώπου
[1]For [4]knows [2]of men the things – of a man
εἰ μὴ τὸ πνεῦμα τοῦ ἀνθρώπου τὸ
except the spirit – of a man –
ἐν αὐτῷ; οὕτως καὶ τὰ τοῦ θεοῦ οὐδεὶς
in him? so also the things – of God no one
ἔγνωκεν εἰ μὴ τὸ πνεῦμα τοῦ θεοῦ.
has known except the Spirit – of God.
12 ἡμεῖς δὲ οὐ τὸ πνεῦμα τοῦ κόσμου
And we not the spirit of the world
ἐλάβομεν ἀλλὰ τὸ πνεῦμα τὸ ἐκ τοῦ θεοῦ,
received but the Spirit – from – God,
ἵνα εἰδῶμεν τὰ ὑπὸ τοῦ θεοῦ
in order we may the things by – God
that know
χαρισθέντα ἡμῖν· 13 ἃ καὶ λαλοῦμεν οὐκ
freely given to us; which things also we speak not
ἐν διδακτοῖς ἀνθρωπίνης σοφίας λόγοις,
in [2]taught [3]of human [4]wisdom [1]words,
ἀλλ' ἐν διδακτοῖς πνεύματος, πνευματικοῖς
but in [words] taught of [the] Spirit, [3]with spiritual things
πνευματικὰ συγκρίνοντες. 14 ψυχικὸς δὲ
[2]spiritual things [1]comparing. But a natural
ἄνθρωπος οὐ δέχεται τὰ τοῦ πνεύματος
man receives not the things of the Spirit
τοῦ θεοῦ· μωρία γὰρ αὐτῷ ἐστιν, καὶ
– of God; for folly to him they are, and
οὐ δύναται γνῶναι, ὅτι πνευματικῶς
he cannot to know, because [2]spiritually
ἀνακρίνεται. 15 ὁ δὲ πνευματικὸς ἀνακρίνει
[1]they are [2]discerned. But the spiritual man [2]discerns
μὲν πάντα, αὐτὸς δὲ ὑπ' οὐδενὸς
[1]on one all things, [3]he [1]on the [4]by [5]no one
hand other
ἀνακρίνεται. 16 τίς γὰρ ἔγνω νοῦν
[2]is discerned. For who knew [the] mind
κυρίου, ὃς συμβιβάσει αὐτόν; ἡμεῖς δὲ
of [the] who will instruct him? But we
Lord,
νοῦν Χριστοῦ ἔχομεν.
[the] mind of Christ have.

---

[d] Or interpreting spiritual truths in spiritual language; or comparing spiritual things with spiritual

[e] Or natural

CHAPTER 3

BUT I, brethren, could not address you as spiritual men, but as men of the flesh, as babes in Christ. ²I fed you with milk, not solid food; for you were not ready for it; and even yet you are not ready, ³for you are still of the flesh. For while there is jealousy and strife among you, are you not of the flesh, and behaving like ordinary men? ⁴For when one says, "I belong to Paul," and another, "I belong to Apol'los," are you not merely men?

5 What then is Apol'los? What is Paul? Servants through whom you believed, as the Lord assigned to each. ⁶I planted, Apol'los watered, but God gave the growth. ⁷So neither he who plants nor he who waters is anything, but only God who gives the growth. ⁸He who plants and he who waters are equal, and each shall receive his wages according to his labor. ⁹For we are fellow workers for God; you are God's field, God's building.

10 According to the commission of God given

3 Κἀγώ, ἀδελφοί, οὐκ ἠδυνήθην λαλῆσαι
And I,   brothers,   was not able   to speak

ὑμῖν ὡς πνευματικοῖς ἀλλ' ὡς σαρκίνοις,
to you as to spiritual men but as to fleshy,

ὡς νηπίοις ἐν Χριστῷ.   2 γάλα ὑμᾶς
as to infants in Christ.   ²Milk ²you

ἐπότισα, οὐ βρῶμα· οὔπω γὰρ ἐδύνασθε.
¹I gave not food; for ye were not then able.
⁴to drink,

ἀλλ' οὐδὲ [ἔτι] νῦν δύνασθε, 3 ἔτι γὰρ
But neither yet now are ye able,   for still

σαρκικοί ἐστε. ὅπου γὰρ ἐν ὑμῖν ζῆλος
fleshly ye are. For whereas among you [there is]
                                            jealousy

καὶ ἔρις, οὐχὶ σαρκικοί ἐστε καὶ κατὰ
and strife, ²not ²fleshly ¹are ye ⁴and ⁶accord-
                                            ing to

ἄνθρωπον περιπατεῖτε; 4 ὅταν γὰρ λέγῃ
⁷man   ⁵walk?   For whenever says

τις· ἐγὼ μέν εἰμι Παύλου, ἕτερος δέ·
anyone: I – am of Paul, and another:

ἐγὼ Ἀπολλῶ, οὐκ ἄνθρωποί ἐστε; 5 Τί
I of Apollos, ²not ³men ¹are ye? What

οὖν ἐστιν Ἀπολλῶς; τί δέ ἐστιν Παῦλος;
there- is Apollos? and what is Paul?
fore

διάκονοι δι' ὧν ἐπιστεύσατε, καὶ ἑκάστῳ
Ministers through whom ye believed, even ²to each one

ὡς ὁ κύριος ἔδωκεν. 6 ἐγὼ ἐφύτευσα,
¹as the Lord gave.   I planted,

Ἀπολλῶς ἐπότισεν, ἀλλὰ ὁ θεὸς ηὔξανεν·
Apollos watered, but – God made to
                                            grow;

7 ὥστε οὔτε ὁ φυτεύων ἐστίν τι οὔτε
so as neither the [one] planting is anything nor

ὁ ποτίζων, ἀλλ' ὁ αὐξάνων θεός. 8 ὁ
the [one] watering, but ²the ¹making to ¹God. ²The
                                            grow [one]

φυτεύων δὲ καὶ ὁ ποτίζων ἕν εἰσιν,
²planting ¹so and the [one] watering one* are,

ἕκαστος δὲ τὸν ἴδιον μισθὸν λήμψεται
and each one the(his) own reward will receive

κατὰ τὸν ἴδιον κόπον. 9 θεοῦ γάρ ἐσμεν
accord- his own labour. For of God we are
ing to

συνεργοί· θεοῦ γεώργιον, θεοῦ οἰκοδομή
fellow-workers; ²of God ³a tillage, ⁵of God ⁴a building

ἐστε. 10 Κατὰ τὴν χάριν τοῦ θεοῦ τὴν
¹ye are. According to the grace – of God –

---

* Notice the neuter gender, though "thing" cannot very well be expressed; cf. John 10. 30.

to me, like a skilled master builder I laid a foundation, and another man is building upon it. Let each man take care how he builds upon it. [11]For no other foundation can any one lay than that which is laid, which is Jesus Christ. [12]Now if any one builds on the foundation with gold, silver, precious stones, wood, hay, stubble—[13]each man's work will become manifest; for the Day will disclose it, because it will be revealed with fire, and the fire will test what sort of work each one has done. [14]If the work which any man has built on the foundation survives, he will receive a reward. [15]If any man's work is burned up, he will suffer loss, though he himself will be saved, but only as through fire.

16 Do you not know that you are God's temple and that God's Spirit dwells in you? [17]If any one destroys God's temple, God will destroy him. For God's temple is holy, and that temple you are.

18 Let no one deceive himself. If any one among you thinks that he is wise in this age, let him become a fool that he may become wise.

δοθεῖσάν μοι ὡς σοφὸς ἀρχιτέκτων
given to me as a wise master builder

θεμέλιον ἔθηκα, ἄλλος δὲ ἐποικοδομεῖ.
a foundation I laid, but another builds on [it].

ἕκαστος δὲ βλεπέτω πῶς ἐποικοδομεῖ.
But each one let him look how he builds on [it].

11 θεμέλιον γὰρ ἄλλον οὐδεὶς δύναται θεῖναι
For foundation other no one is able to lay

παρὰ τὸν κείμενον, ὅς ἐστιν Ἰησοῦς
beside the [one] being laid, who is Jesus

Χριστός. 12 εἰ δέ τις ἐποικοδομεῖ ἐπὶ
Christ. Now if anyone builds on on

τὸν θεμέλιον χρυσίον, ἀργύριον, λίθους
the foundation gold, silver, stones

τιμίους, ξύλα, χόρτον, καλάμην, 13 ἑκάστου
precious, woods, hay, stubble, of each one

τὸ ἔργον φανερὸν γενήσεται· ἡ γὰρ ἡμέρα
the work manifest will become; for the day

δηλώσει, ὅτι ἐν πυρὶ ἀποκαλύπτεται,
will declare because by fire it is revealed,
[it],

καὶ ἑκάστου τὸ ἔργον ὁποῖόν ἐστιν
and [2]of each one [1]the [3]work [5]of what sort [4]it is

τὸ πῦρ αὐτὸ δοκιμάσει. 14 εἴ τινος
[2]the [5]fire [3]it [4]will prove. If of anyone

τὸ ἔργον μενεῖ ὃ ἐποικοδόμησεν, μισθὸν
the work remains which he built on, a reward

λήμψεται· 15 εἴ τινος τὸ ἔργον κατακαής-
he will receive; if of anyone the work will be con-

εται, ζημιωθήσεται, αὐτὸς δὲ σωθήσεται,
sumed, he will suffer loss, but he will be saved,

οὕτως δὲ ὡς διὰ πυρός. 16 Οὐκ οἴδατε
yet so as through fire. Know ye not

ὅτι ναὸς θεοῦ ἐστε καὶ τὸ πνεῦμα τοῦ
that a shrine of God ye are and the Spirit –

θεοῦ ἐν ὑμῖν οἰκεῖ; 17 εἴ τις τὸν ναὸν
of God in you dwells? If anyone the shrine

τοῦ θεοῦ φθείρει, φθερεῖ τοῦτον ὁ θεός·
– of God defiles, [2]will defile [3]this man – [1]God;

ὁ γὰρ ναὸς τοῦ θεοῦ ἅγιός ἐστιν, οἵτινές
for the shrine – of God holy is, who(which)

ἐστε ὑμεῖς.
are ye.

18 Μηδεὶς ἑαυτὸν ἐξαπατάτω· εἴ τις
No one himself let deceive; if anyone

δοκεῖ σοφὸς εἶναι ἐν ὑμῖν ἐν τῷ αἰῶνι
thinks wise to be among you in – age

τούτῳ, μωρὸς γενέσθω, ἵνα γένηται
this, foolish let him in order he may
become, that become

19 For the wisdom of this world is folly with God. For it is written, "He catches the wise in their craftiness," 20 and again, "The Lord knows that the thoughts of the wise are futile." 21 So let no one boast of men. For all things are yours, 22 whether Paul or Apollos or Cephas or the world or life or death or the present or the future, all are yours; 23 and you are Christ's; and Christ is God's.

σοφός.
wise.

19 ἡ γὰρ σοφία τοῦ κόσμοι
For the wisdom – world

τούτου μωρία παρὰ τῷ θεῷ ἐστιν.
of this folly with – God is.

γέγραπται γάρ· ὁ δρασσόμενος τοὺς σοφοὺς
For it has been written: The [one] grasping the wise

ἐν τῇ πανουργίᾳ αὐτῶν· 20 καὶ πάλιν :
in the craftiness of them; and again :

κύριος γινώσκει τοὺς διαλογισμοὺς τῶν
[The] Lord knows the reasonings of the

σοφῶν, ὅτι εἰσὶν μάταιοι. 21 ὥστε μηδεὶς
wise, that they are vain. So as no one

καυχάσθω ἐν ἀνθρώποις· πάντα γὰρ ὑμῶν
let boast in men; for all things of you

ἐστιν, 22 εἴτε Παῦλος εἴτε Ἀπολλῶς
is(are), whether Paul or Apollos

εἴτε Κηφᾶς, εἴτε κόσμος εἴτε ζωὴ εἴτε
or Cephas, or [the] world or life or

θάνατος, εἴτε ἐνεστῶτα εἴτε μέλλοντα,
death, or things present or things coming,

πάντα ὑμῶν, 23 ὑμεῖς δὲ Χριστοῦ, Χριστὸς δὲ
all things of you, and ye of Christ, and Christ

CHAPTER 4

THIS is how one should regard us, as servants of Christ and stewards of the mysteries of God. 2 Moreover it is required of stewards that they be found trustworthy. 3 But with me it is a very small thing that I should be judged by you or by any human court. I do not even judge myself. 4 I am not aware of anything against myself, but I am not thereby acquitted. It is the Lord who judges me. 5 Therefore do not pronounce judgment before the time, before the Lord comes, who will

θεοῦ. 4 Οὕτως ἡμᾶς λογιζέσθω ἄνθρωπος ὡς
of God. So 4us 1let 3reckon 2a man as

ὑπηρέτας Χριστοῦ καὶ οἰκονόμους μυστηρίων
attendants of Christ and stewards of mysteries

θεοῦ. 2 ὧδε λοιπὸν ζητεῖται ἐν τοῖς
of God. Here for the rest it is sought among

οἰκονόμοις ἵνα πιστός τις εὑρεθῇ. 3 ἐμοὶ
stewards in order 2faithful 1anyone 3be found. to me
that

δὲ εἰς ἐλάχιστόν ἐστιν ἵνα ὑφ' ὑμῶν
And for a very little thing it is in order that by you

ἀνακριθῶ ἢ ὑπὸ ἀνθρωπίνης ἡμέρας· ἀλλ'
I am judged or by a human day;* but

οὐδὲ ἐμαυτὸν ἀνακρίνω· 4 οὐδὲν γὰρ
not myself I judge; for nothing

ἐμαυτῷ σύνοιδα, ἀλλ' οὐκ ἐν τούτῳ
against myself I know, but not by this

δεδικαίωμαι· ὁ δὲ ἀνακρίνων με κύριός
have I been but the [one] judging me [the] Lord
justified;

ἐστιν. 5 ὥστε μὴ πρὸ καιροῦ τι κρίνετε,
is. So as not before time anything judge ye,

ἕως ἂν ἔλθῃ ὁ κύριος, ὃς καὶ φωτίσει
until comes the Lord, who both will shed light on

* ? of judgment.

bring to light the things now hidden in darkness and will disclose the purposes of the heart. Then every man will receive his commendation from God.

6 I have applied all this to myself and Apol'los for your benefit, brethren, that you may learn by us to live according to scripture, that none of you may be puffed up in favor of one against another. [7]For who sees anything different in you? What have you that you did not receive? If then you received it, why do you boast as if it were not a gift?

8 Already you are filled! Already you have become rich! Without us you have become kings! And would that you did reign, so that we might share the rule with you! [9]For I think that God has exhibited us apostles as last of all, like men sentenced to death; because we have become a spectacle to the world, to angels and to men. [10]We are fools for Christ's sake, but you are wise in Christ. We are weak, but you are strong. You are held in honor, but we in disrepute. [11]To the present hour we hunger and thirst, we are ill-clad and buffeted and homeless,

τὰ κρυπτὰ τοῦ σκότους καὶ φανερώσει
the hidden things of the   darkness   and   will manifest

τὰς βουλὰς τῶν καρδιῶν· καὶ τότε ὁ
the   counsels   of the   hearts;   and   then   the

ἔπαινος γενήσεται ἑκάστῳ ἀπὸ τοῦ θεοῦ.
praise   will be   to each one°   from   -   God.

6 Ταῦτα δέ, ἀδελφοί, μετεσχημάτισα εἰς
Now these things,   brothers,   I adapted   to

ἐμαυτὸν καὶ Ἀπολλῶν δι' ὑμᾶς, ἵνα
myself   and   Apollos   because   you,   in order
                                 of of   that

ἐν ἡμῖν μάθητε τὸ μὴ ὑπὲρ ἃ
among us   ye may learn   - not [to think] above what
                                                        things

γέγραπται, ἵνα μὴ εἷς ὑπὲρ τοῦ ἑνὸς
has(ve) been written, lest   ²one ²on behalf of ⁴the   ⁵one

φυσιοῦσθε κατὰ τοῦ ἑτέρου. 7 τίς γάρ σε
¹ye are puffed up against   the   other.   For who thee

διακρίνει; τί δὲ ἔχεις ὃ οὐκ ἔλαβες;
distinguishes?   and what hast thou which thou didst not receive?

εἰ δὲ καὶ ἔλαβες, τί καυχᾶσαι ὡς μὴ
and if   indeed   thou didst   why boastest thou   as   not
                                                            receive,

λαβών; 8 ἤδη κεκορεσμένοι ἐστέ· ἤδη
receiving?   Now   having been glutted   ye are;   now

ἐπλουτήσατε· χωρὶς ἡμῶν ἐβασιλεύσατε· καὶ
ye became rich;   without   us   ye reigned;   and

ὄφελόν γε ἐβασιλεύσατε, ἵνα
¹an advantage   ²really ¹[it is]   [that] ye reigned,   in order that

καὶ ἡμεῖς ὑμῖν συμβασιλεύσωμεν. 9 δοκῶ
also   we   ²you   ¹might reign with.   I think

γάρ, ὁ θεὸς ἡμᾶς τοὺς ἀποστόλους
For,   -   God   us   the   apostles

ἐσχάτους ἀπέδειξεν ὡς ἐπιθανατίους, ὅτι
last   showed forth   as   doomed to death,   because

θέατρον ἐγενήθημεν τῷ κόσμῳ καὶ ἀγγέλοις
a spectacle   we became   to the world   both   to angels

καὶ ἀνθρώποις. 10 ἡμεῖς μωροὶ διὰ
and   to men.   We [are]   fools   because of

Χριστόν, ὑμεῖς δὲ φρόνιμοι ἐν Χριστῷ·
Christ,   but ye [are]   prudent   in   Christ;

ἡμεῖς ἀσθενεῖς, ὑμεῖς δὲ ἰσχυροί· ὑμεῖς
we [are]   weak,   but ye [are]   strong;   ye [are]

ἔνδοξοι, ἡμεῖς δὲ ἄτιμοι. 11 ἄχρι τῆς
held in honour,   but we [are]   unhonoured.   Until   the

ἄρτι ὥρας καὶ πεινῶμεν καὶ διψῶμεν
present   hour   ³both   ¹we ²hunger   and   thirst

καὶ γυμνιτεύομεν καὶ κολαφιζόμεθα καὶ
and   are naked   and   are buffeted   and

¹²and we labor, working with our own hands. When reviled, we bless; when persecuted, we endure; ¹³when slandered, we try to conciliate; we have become, and are now, as the refuse of the world, the offscouring of all things.

14 I do not write this to make you ashamed, but to admonish you as my beloved children. ¹⁵For though you have countless guides in Christ, you do not have many fathers. For I became your father in Christ Jesus through the gospel. ¹⁶I urge you, then, be imitators of me. ¹⁷Therefore I sent[f] to you Timothy, my beloved and faithful child in the Lord, to remind you of my ways in Christ, as I teach them everywhere in every church. ¹⁸Some are arrogant, as though I were not coming to you. ¹⁹But I will come to you soon, if the Lord wills, and I will find out not the talk of these arrogant people but their power. ²⁰For the king-

[f] Or am sending

ἀστατοῦμεν   12 καὶ   κοπιῶμεν   ἐργαζόμενοι
are unsettled   and   labour   working

ταῖς   ἰδίαις   χερσίν·   λοιδορούμενοι   εὐλο-
with the(our) own   hands;   being reviled   we

γοῦμεν,   διωκόμενοι   ἀνεχόμεθα,   13 δυσφημού-
bless,   being persecuted   we endure,   being de-

μενοι   παρακαλοῦμεν·   ὡς   περικαθάρματα   τοῦ
famed   we beseech;   as   refuse   of the

κόσμου   ἐγενήθημεν,   ²πάντων   περίψημα   ἕως
world   we became,   ²of all things   ¹offscouring   until

ἄρτι.
now.

14 Οὐκ   ἐντρέπων   ὑμᾶς   γράφω   ταῦτα,
Not   shaming   you   I write   these things,

ἀλλ'   ὡς   τέκνα   μου   ἀγαπητὰ   νουθετῶν.
but   as   children   of me   beloved   admonishing.

15 ἐὰν   γὰρ   μυρίους   παιδαγωγοὺς   ἔχητε
For if   ten thousand   trainers   ye have

ἐν   Χριστῷ,   ἀλλ'   οὐ   πολλοὺς   πατέρας·
in   Christ,   yet   not   many   fathers;

ἐν γὰρ   Χριστῷ   Ἰησοῦ   διὰ   τοῦ   εὐαγγελίου
for in   Christ   Jesus   through the   gospel

ἐγὼ   ὑμᾶς   ἐγέννησα.   16 παρακαλῶ   οὖν
I   ¹you   ¹begat.   I beseech   therefore

ὑμᾶς,   μιμηταί   μου   γίνεσθε.   17 Διὰ   τοῦτο
you,   imitators   of me   become ye.   Because of this

αὐτὸ   ἔπεμψα   ὑμῖν   Τιμόθεον,   ὃς   ἐστίν
very thing   I sent   to you   Timothy,   who   is

μου   τέκνον   ἀγαπητὸν   καὶ   πιστὸν   ἐν
of me   a child   beloved   and   faithful   in

κυρίῳ,   ὃς   ὑμᾶς   ἀναμνήσει   τὰς   ὁδούς
[the] Lord,   who   ²you   ¹will remind [of] the   ways

μου   τὰς   ἐν   Χριστῷ   [Ἰησοῦ],   καθὼς
of me   —   in   Christ   Jesus,   as

πανταχοῦ   ἐν   πάσῃ   ἐκκλησίᾳ   διδάσκω.
everywhere   in   every   church   I teach.

18 ὡς   μὴ   ἐρχομένου   δέ   μου   πρὸς   ὑμᾶς
When not   coming   now   meˢ   to   you
=Now when I did not come

ἐφυσιώθησάν   τινες·   19 ἐλεύσομαι   δὲ   ταχέως
²were puffed up   ¹some;   but I will come   shortly

πρὸς   ὑμᾶς,   ἐὰν   ὁ   κύριος   θελήσῃ,   καὶ
to   you,   if   the   Lord   wills,   and

γνώσομαι   οὐ   τὸν   λόγον   τῶν   πεφυσιωμένων
I will know   not   the   speech   of the   having been
[ones]   puffed up

ἀλλὰ   τὴν   δύναμιν·   20 οὐ   γὰρ   ἐν   λόγῳ
but   the   power;   for ⁴[is]   ²not   ⁶in   ¹speech

dom of God does not consist in talk but in power. 21 What do you wish? Shall I come to you with a rod, or with love in a spirit of gentleness?

ἡ βασιλεία τοῦ θεοῦ, ἀλλ' ἐν δυνάμει.
the kingdom – of God, but in power.

21 τί θέλετε; ἐν ῥάβδῳ ἔλθω πρὸς ὑμᾶς,
What will ye? with a rod I come to you,

ἢ ἐν ἀγάπῃ πνεύματί τε πραΰτητος;
or in love and a spirit of meekness?

CHAPTER 5

IT is actually reported that there is immorality among you, and of a kind that is not found even among pagans; for a man is living with his father's wife. ²And you are arrogant! Ought you not rather to mourn? Let him who has done this be removed from among you.

3 For though absent in body I am present in spirit, and as if present, I have already pronounced judgment ⁴in the name of the Lord Jesus on the man who has done such a thing. When you are assembled, and my spirit is present, with the power of our Lord Jesus, ⁵you are to deliver this man to Satan for the destruction of the flesh, that his spirit may be saved in the day of the Lord Jesus.ᵍ

6 Your boasting is not good. Do you not know that a little leaven leavens the whole lump? ⁷Cleanse out the old leaven that you may be a new lump, as you

5 Ὅλως ἀκούεται ἐν ὑμῖν πορνεία,
Actually is heard among you fornication,

καὶ τοιαύτη πορνεία ἥτις οὐδὲ ἐν τοῖς
and such fornication which [is] not among the

ἔθνεσιν, ὥστε γυναῖκά τινα τοῦ πατρὸς
nations, so as ²wife ¹one ⁴of the ⁵father

ἔχειν. 2 καὶ ὑμεῖς πεφυσιωμένοι ἐστέ,
³to have.ᵇ And ye having been puffed up are,

καὶ οὐχὶ μᾶλλον ἐπενθήσατε, ἵνα ἀρθῇ
and not rather mourned, in order ⁵might be
                                  that removed

ἐκ μέσου ὑμῶν ὁ τὸ ἔργον τοῦτο πράξας;
⁶from ⁵midst ⁹of you ¹the ³this ²deed ⁸having done?
⁷[the]   [one]

3 ἐγὼ μὲν γάρ, ἀπὼν τῷ σώματι,
For I indeed, being absent in the body,

παρὼν δὲ τῷ πνεύματι, ἤδη κέκρικα
but being present in the spirit, already have judged

ὡς παρὼν τὸν οὕτως τοῦτο κατεργα-
as being present ¹the [one] ²thus 'this thing ³having

σάμενον 4 ἐν τῷ ὀνόματι τοῦ κυρίου
wrought in the name of the Lord

Ἰησοῦ συναχθέντων ὑμῶν καὶ τοῦ ἐμοῦ
Jesus being assembled you and – my
         =when you are assembled...

πνεύματος σὺν τῇ δυνάμει τοῦ κυρίου
spiritᵃ with the power of the Lord

ἡμῶν Ἰησοῦ 5 παραδοῦναι τὸν τοιοῦτον
of us Jesus to deliver such a person

τῷ σατανᾷ εἰς ὄλεθρον τῆς σαρκός,
– to Satan for destruction of the flesh,

ἵνα τὸ πνεῦμα σωθῇ ἐν τῇ ἡμέρᾳ τοῦ
in order the spirit may be in the day of the
that   saved

κυρίου. 6 Οὐ καλὸν τὸ καύχημα ὑμῶν.
Lord. Not good [is] the boast of you.

οὐκ οἴδατε ὅτι μικρὰ ζύμη ὅλον τὸ
Know ye not that a little leaven all the

φύραμα ζυμοῖ; 7 ἐκκαθάρατε τὴν παλαιὰν
lump leavens? Purge out the old

ζύμην, ἵνα ἦτε νέον φύραμα, καθώς
leaven, in order ye a new lump, as
        that may be

ᵍ Other ancient authorities omit Jesus

really are unleavened. For Christ, our paschal lamb, has been sacrificed. [8] Let us, therefore, celebrate the festival, not with the old leaven, the leaven of malice and evil, but with the unleavened bread of sincerity and truth.

[9] I wrote to you in my letter not to associate with immoral men; [10] not at all meaning the immoral of this world, or the greedy and robbers, or idolaters, since then you would need to go out of the world. [11] But rather I wrote[h] to you not to associate with any one who bears the name of brother if he is guilty of immorality or greed, or is an idolater, reviler, drunkard, or robber—not even to eat with such a one. [12] For what have I to do with judging outsiders? Is it not those inside the church whom you are to judge? [13] God judges those outside. "Drive out the wicked person from among you."

CHAPTER 6

WHEN one of you has a grievance against a brother, does he dare go to law before the unrighteous instead of the saints? [2] Do you not know that the saints will judge the world?

[h] Or now I write

ἐστε ἄζυμοι. καὶ γὰρ τὸ πάσχα ἡμῶν
ye are unleavened. For indeed the passover of us

ἐτύθη Χριστός. 8 ὥστε ἑορτάζωμεν μὴ
was Christ. So as let us keep feast not
sacrificed[,]

ἐν ζύμῃ παλαιᾷ μηδὲ ἐν ζύμῃ κακίας
with leaven old nor with leaven of malice

καὶ πονηρίας, ἀλλ᾽ ἐν ἀζύμοις εἰλικρινείας
and of evil, but with unleavened of sincerity
[loaves]

καὶ ἀληθείας. 9 Ἔγραψα ὑμῖν ἐν τῇ
and of truth. I wrote to you in the

ἐπιστολῇ μὴ συναναμίγνυσθαι πόρνοις,
epistle not to associate with
intimately with fornicators,

10 οὐ πάντως τοῖς πόρνοις τοῦ κόσμου
not altogether with the fornicators - world

τούτου ἢ τοῖς πλεονέκταις καὶ ἅρπαξιν
of this or with the covetous and rapacious

ἢ εἰδωλολάτραις, ἐπεὶ ὠφείλετε ἄρα ἐκ
or idolaters, since ye ought then out of

τοῦ κόσμου ἐξελθεῖν. 11 νῦν δὲ ἔγραψα
the world to go out. But now I wrote

ὑμῖν μὴ συναναμίγνυσθαι ἐάν τις ἀδελφὸς
to you not to associate intimately with if anyone a brother

ὀνομαζόμενος ἢ πόρνος ἢ πλεονέκτης ἢ
being named is a fornicator or a covetous man or

εἰδωλολάτρης ἢ λοίδορος ἢ μέθυσος ἢ
an idolater or a railer or a drunkard or

ἅρπαξ, τῷ τοιούτῳ μηδὲ συνεσθίειν. 12 τί
a rapa- with such a man not to eat with. what
cious man,

γάρ μοι τοὺς ἔξω κρίνειν; οὐχὶ τοὺς
For [is it] to me [2]the ones [3]without [1]to judge? [1]Not [4]the ones

ἔσω ὑμεῖς κρίνετε; 13 τοὺς δὲ ἔξω
[5]within [2]ye [1]judge? But the ones without

ὁ θεὸς κρινεῖ. ἐξάρατε τὸν πονηρὸν ἐξ
- God will judge. Remove the evil man out of

ὑμῶν αὐτῶν.
yourselves.

6 Τολμᾷ τις ὑμῶν πρᾶγμα ἔχων πρὸς
Dares anyone of you [2]a matter [1]having against

τὸν ἕτερον κρίνεσθαι ἐπὶ τῶν ἀδίκων,
the(an) other to be judged before the unjust,

καὶ οὐχὶ ἐπὶ τῶν ἁγίων; 2 ἢ οὐκ οἴδατε
and not before the saints? or know ye not

ὅτι οἱ ἅγιοι τὸν κόσμον κρινοῦσιν; καὶ
that the saints the world will judge? and

And if the world is to be judged by you, are you incompetent to try trivial cases? ³Do you not know that we are to judge angels? How much more, matters pertaining to this life! ⁴If then you have such cases, why do you lay them before those who are least esteemed by the church? ⁵I say this to your shame. Can it be that there is no man among you wise enough to decide between members of the brotherhood, ⁶but brother goes to law against brother, and that before unbelievers?

7 To have lawsuits at all with one another is defeat for you. Why not rather suffer wrong? Why not rather be defrauded? ⁸But you yourselves wrong and defraud, and that even your own brethren.

9 Do you not know that the unrighteous will not inherit the kingdom of God? Do not be deceived; neither the immoral, nor idolaters, nor adulterers, nor homosexuals,ᶠ ¹⁰nor thieves, nor the greedy, nor drunkards, nor revilers, nor robbers will inherit the kingdom of God. ¹¹And such were

---

εἰ ἐν ὑμῖν κρίνεται ὁ κόσμος, ἀνάξιοί
if ⁴by ⁵you ²is judged ¹the ³world, ¹unworthy

ἐστε κριτηρίων ἐλαχίστων; 3 οὐκ οἴδατε
¹are ye ⁴judgments? ²of very little? Know ye not

ὅτι ἀγγέλους κρινοῦμεν, μήτι γε βιωτικά;
that angels we will judge, not to speak of things of this life?

4 βιωτικὰ μὲν οὖν κριτήρια ἐὰν ἔχητε,
⁶Of this life ⁴indeed ²therefore ⁵judgments ¹if ³ye have,

τοὺς ἐξουθενημένους ἐν τῇ ἐκκλησίᾳ,
the ones being despised in the church,

τούτους καθίζετε; 5 πρὸς ἐντροπὴν ὑμῖν
these sit ye? For shame to you

λέγω. οὕτως οὐκ ἔνι ἐν ὑμῖν οὐδεὶς
I say. Thus there is no room among you [for] no one

σοφός, ὃς δυνήσεται διακρῖναι ἀνὰ μέσον
wise man, who will be able to discern in your midst

τοῦ ἀδελφοῦ αὐτοῦ; 6 ἀλλὰ ἀδελφὸς μετὰ
the brother of him? But brother with

ἀδελφοῦ κρίνεται, καὶ τοῦτο ἐπὶ ἀπίστων;
brother is judged, and this before unbelievers?

7 ἤδη μὲν οὖν ὅλως ἥττημα ὑμῖν ἐστιν
Now indeed there-fore ²altogether ³a failure ⁴with you ¹there is

ὅτι κρίματα ἔχετε μεθ' ἑαυτῶν. διὰ τί
²that ¹lawsuits ⁵ye have with yourselves. Why

οὐχὶ μᾶλλον ἀδικεῖσθε; διὰ τί οὐχὶ
not rather be wronged? Why not

μᾶλλον ἀποστερεῖσθε; 8 ἀλλὰ ὑμεῖς ἀδικεῖτε
rather be deprived? But ye do wrong

καὶ ἀποστερεῖτε, καὶ τοῦτο ἀδελφούς.
and deprive, and this brothers.

9 ἢ οὐκ οἴδατε ὅτι ἄδικοι θεοῦ βασιλείαν
Or know ye not that unrighteous ²of God ¹[the]
men kingdom

οὐ κληρονομήσουσιν; μὴ πλανᾶσθε· οὔτε
¹will not inherit? Be not led astray; not

πόρνοι οὔτε εἰδωλολάτραι οὔτε μοιχοὶ
fornicators nor idolaters nor adulterers

οὔτε μαλακοὶ οὔτε ἀρσενοκοῖται 10 οὔτε
nor voluptuous nor sodomites nor
persons

κλέπται οὔτε πλεονέκται, οὐ μέθυσοι,
thieves nor covetous persons, not drunkards,

οὐ λοίδοροι, οὐχ ἅρπαγες βασιλείαν θεοῦ
not revilers, not rapacious ²[the] kingdom ³of
persons God

κληρονομήσουσιν. 11 καὶ ταῦτά τινες ἦτε·
¹will inherit. And these ²some ¹ye
things [of you] were;

ᶠ Two Greek words are rendered by this expression

some of you. But you were washed, you were sanctified, you were justified in the name of the Lord Jesus Christ and in the Spirit of our God. 12 "All things are lawful for me," but not all things are helpful. "All things are lawful for me," but I will not be enslaved by anything. ¹³ "Food is meant for the stomach and the stomach for food"—and God will destroy both one and the other. The body is not meant for immorality, but for the Lord, and the Lord for the body. ¹⁴ And God raised the Lord and will also raise us up by his power. ¹⁵ Do you not know that your bodies are members of Christ? Shall I therefore take the members of Christ and make them members of a prostitute? Never! ¹⁶ Do you not know that he who joins himself to a prostitute becomes one body with her? For, as it is written, "The two shall become one." ¹⁷ But he who is united to the Lord becomes one spirit with him. ¹⁸ Shun immorality. Every other sin which a man commits is outside the body; but the immoral man sins against

ἀλλὰ ἀπελούσασθε, ἀλλὰ ἡγιάσθητε, ἀλλὰ
but   ye were washed, but ye were sanctified, but

ἐδικαιώθητε ἐν τῷ ὀνόματι τοῦ κυρίου
ye were justified in   the   name   of the Lord

Ἰησοῦ Χριστοῦ καὶ ἐν τῷ πνεύματι
Jesus   Christ   and by the   Spirit

τοῦ θεοῦ ἡμῶν.
of the God of us.

12 Πάντα μοι ἔξεστιν, ἀλλ' οὐ πάντα
All things to me [are] lawful, but   not all things

συμφέρει.   πάντα μοι ἔξεστιν, ἀλλ' οὐκ
expedient. All things to me [are] lawful, but   not

ἐγὼ ἐξουσιασθήσομαι ὑπό τινος. 13 τὰ
I   will be ruled   by anyone.

βρώματα τῇ κοιλίᾳ, καὶ ἡ κοιλία τοῖς
Foods   for the belly, and the belly

βρώμασιν· ὁ δὲ θεὸς καὶ ταύτην καὶ
for foods; – but God both this and

ταῦτα καταργήσει. τὸ δὲ σῶμα οὐ τῇ
these will destroy. But the body [is] not –

πορνείᾳ ἀλλὰ τῷ κυρίῳ, καὶ ὁ κύριος
for fornication but for the Lord, and the Lord

τῷ σώματι· 14 ὁ δὲ θεὸς καὶ τὸν κύριον
for the body; – and God both the Lord

ἤγειρεν καὶ ἡμᾶς ἐξεγερεῖ διὰ τῆς
raised   and us will raise up through the

δυνάμεως αὐτοῦ. 15 οὐκ οἴδατε ὅτι τὰ
power   of him. Know ye not that

σώματα ὑμῶν μέλη Χριστοῦ ἐστιν; ἄρας
bodies of you members of Christ (is)are? Taking

οὖν τὰ μέλη τοῦ Χριστοῦ ποιήσω πόρνης
there- the members – of Christ shall I make ³of a
fore   [them]   harlot

μέλη; μὴ γένοιτο. 16 ἢ οὐκ οἴδατε ὅτι
¹members? May it not be. Or know ye not that

ὁ κολλώμενος τῇ πόρνῃ ἐν σῶμά ἐστιν;
the being joined – to a harlot one body is?
[one]

ἔσονται γάρ, φησίν, οἱ δύο εἰς σάρκα
For ⁴will be, ³he says, ¹the ²two ⁵into ⁷flesh

μίαν. 17 ὁ δὲ κολλώμενος τῷ κυρίῳ
⁶one.   But the [one] being joined to the Lord

ἐν πνεῦμά ἐστιν. 18 φεύγετε τὴν πορνείαν.
one spirit is.   Flee ye –   fornication.

πᾶν ἁμάρτημα ὃ ἐὰν ποιήσῃ ἄνθρωπος
Every sin   whichever ²may do ¹a man

ἐκτὸς τοῦ σώματός ἐστιν· ὁ δὲ πορνεύων
outside the body   is;   but the committing
[one]   fornication

his own body. ¹⁹Do you not know that your body is a temple of the Holy Spirit within you, which you have from God? You are not your own; ²⁰you were bought with a price. So glorify God in your body.

εἰς τὸ ἴδιον σῶμα ἁμαρτάνει. 19
against the(his) own body sins. Or

οὐκ οἴδατε ὅτι τὸ σῶμα ὑμῶν ναὸς
know ye not that the body of you ²a shrine

τοῦ ἐν ὑμῖν ἁγίου πνεύματός ἐστιν,
³of the ⁴in ⁷you ⁴Holy ⁵Spirit ¹is,

οὗ ἔχετε ἀπὸ θεοῦ, καὶ οὐκ ἐστὲ ἑαυτῶν;
which ye have from God, and ye are not of yourselves?

20 ἠγοράσθητε γὰρ τιμῆς· δοξάσατε δὴ
For ye were bought of(with) a price; glorify ye then

τὸν θεὸν ἐν τῷ σώματι ὑμῶν.
- God in the body of you.

CHAPTER 7

NOW concerning the matters about which you wrote. It is well for a man not to touch a woman. ²But because of the temptation to immorality, each man should have his own wife and each woman her own husband. ³The husband should give to his wife her conjugal rights, and likewise the wife to her husband. ⁴For the wife does not rule over her own body, but the husband does; likewise the husband does not rule over his own body, but the wife does. ⁵Do not refuse one another except perhaps by agreement for a season, that you may devote yourselves to prayer; but then come together again, lest Satan tempt you through lack of self-control. ⁶I say this by way of concession,

7 Περὶ δὲ ὧν ἐγράψατε, καλὸν ἀνθρώπῳ
Now about things ye wrote, [it is] good for a man
of which

γυναικὸς μὴ ἅπτεσθαι· 2 διὰ δὲ τὰς
²a woman* ¹not ³to touch; but because of the

πορνείας ἕκαστος τὴν ἑαυτοῦ γυναῖκα
fornications each man ¹the ²of himself ²wife

ἐχέτω, καὶ ἑκάστη τὸν ἴδιον ἄνδρα
¹let him have, and each woman the(her) own husband

ἐχέτω. 3 τῇ γυναικὶ ὁ ἀνὴρ τὴν ὀφειλὴν
let her have. To the wife ²the ³husband ⁴the ⁵debt

ἀποδιδότω, ὁμοίως δὲ καὶ ἡ γυνὴ τῷ
¹let him pay, and likewise also the wife to the

ἀνδρί. 4 ἡ γυνὴ τοῦ ἰδίου σώματος
husband. The wife of the(her) own body

οὐκ ἐξουσιάζει ἀλλὰ ὁ ἀνήρ· ὁμοίως
has not authority but the husband; ¹likewise

δὲ καὶ ὁ ἀνὴρ τοῦ ἰδίου σώματος οὐκ
²and also the husband of the(his) own body not

ἐξουσιάζει ἀλλὰ ἡ γυνή. 5 μὴ ἀποστερεῖτε
has authority but the wife. Deprive not ye

ἀλλήλους, εἰ μήτι ἂν ἐκ συμφώνου πρὸς
each other, unless by agreement for

καιρὸν ἵνα σχολάσητε τῇ προσευχῇ καὶ
a time in order ye may have - for prayer and
that leisure

πάλιν ἐπὶ τὸ αὐτὸ ἦτε, ἵνα μὴ πειράζῃ
²again ²together ¹ye may be, lest ²tempt

ὑμᾶς ὁ σατανᾶς διὰ τὴν ἀκρασίαν [ὑμῶν].
²you - ¹Satan because the want of of you.
of self-control

6 τοῦτο δὲ λέγω κατὰ συγγνώμην, οὐ
Now this I say by allowance, not

---

* As the same Greek word γυνή means "wife" or "(?married) woman" it is not always easy to differentiate in translating. So also the one Greek word ἀνήρ means "man" or "husband"

not of command. [7]I wish that all were as I myself am. But each has his own special gift from God, one of one kind and one of another.

8 To the unmarried and the widows I say that it is well for them to remain single as I do. [9]But if they cannot exercise self-control, they should marry. For it is better to marry than to be aflame with passion.

10 To the married I give charge, not I but the Lord, that the wife should not separate from her husband [11](but if she does, let her remain single or else be reconciled to her husband)— and that the husband should not divorce his wife.

12 To the rest I say, not the Lord, that if any brother has a wife who is an unbeliever, and she consents to live with him, he should not divorce her. [13]If any woman has a husband who is an unbeliever, and he consents to live with her, she should not divorce him. [14]For the unbelieving husband is consecrated through his wife, and the unbelieving wife is consecrated through her husband. Otherwise, your children would be unclean, but as it is they are

κατ’   ἐπιταγήν.   **7** θέλω   δὲ   πάντας
by   command.   And I wish   all

ἀνθρώπους   εἶναι   ὡς   καὶ   ἐμαυτόν·   ἀλλὰ
men   to be   as   even   myself;   but

ἕκαστος   ἴδιον   ἔχει   χάρισμα   ἐκ   θεοῦ,
each man   [3][his] own   [1]has   gift   of   God,

ὁ   μὲν   οὕτως,   ὁ   δὲ   οὕτως.
one   thus,   another   thus.

8 Λέγω   δὲ   τοῖς   ἀγάμοις   καὶ   ταῖς   χήραις,
Now I say   to the unmarried men and   to the   widows,

καλὸν   αὐτοῖς   ἐὰν   μείνωσιν   ὡς   κἀγώ·   **9** εἰ   δὲ
[it is] good for them   if   they remain   as   I also;   but if

οὐκ   ἐγκρατεύονται,   γαμησάτωσαν·   κρεῖττον
they do not exercise self-control, let them marry;   better

γάρ   ἐστιν   γαμεῖν   ἢ   πυροῦσθαι.   **10** τοῖς
for   it is   to marry   than   to burn.   to the [ones]

δὲ   γεγαμηκόσιν   παραγγέλλω,   οὐκ   ἐγὼ
But   having married   I enjoin,   not   I

ἀλλὰ   ὁ   κύριος,   γυναῖκα   ἀπὸ   ἀνδρὸς   μὴ
but   the   Lord,   a woman   from [her] husband not

χωρισθῆναι,   **11** — ἐὰν   δὲ   καὶ   χωρισθῇ,
to be separated,[b]   but if   indeed   she is separated,

μενέτω   ἄγαμος   ἢ   τῷ   ἀνδρὶ   καταλλαγήτω,
let her   unmarried   or   to   husband   be reconciled,
remain   the(her)

— καὶ   ἄνδρα   γυναῖκα   μὴ   ἀφιέναι.   **12** Τοῖς
and a husband   [his] wife   not   to leave.[b]   to the

δὲ   λοιποῖς   λέγω   ἐγώ,   οὐχ   ὁ   κύριος·
And   rest   say   I,   not   the   Lord:

εἴ   τις   ἀδελφὸς   γυναῖκα   ἔχει   ἄπιστον,   καὶ
If   any   brother   [3]a wife   [1]has   unbelieving,   and

αὕτη   συνευδοκεῖ   οἰκεῖν   μετ’   αὐτοῦ,   μὴ
this one   consents   to dwell   with   him,   not

ἀφιέτω   αὐτήν·   **13** καὶ   γυνὴ   ἥτις   ἔχει
let him leave   her;   and   a woman   who   has

ἄνδρα   ἄπιστον,   καὶ   οὗτος   συνευδοκεῖ   οἰκεῖν
a husband unbelieving,   and   this one   consents   to dwell

μετ’   αὐτῆς,   μὴ   ἀφιέτω   τὸν   ἄνδρα.
with   her,   let her not leave   the(her)   husband.

14 ἡγίασται   γὰρ   ὁ   ἀνὴρ   ὁ   ἄπιστος   ἐν
For [4]has been sanctified [1]the [3]husband – [2]unbelieving by

τῇ   γυναικί,   καὶ   ἡγίασται   ἡ   γυνὴ   ἡ
the   wife,   and   [4]has been   [1]the   [3]wife   –
           sanctified

ἄπιστος   ἐν   τῷ   ἀδελφῷ·   ἐπεὶ   ἄρα   τὰ
[2]unbelieving by   the   brother;   since   then   the

τέκνα   ὑμῶν   ἀκάθαρτά   ἐστιν,   νῦν   δὲ
children   of you   [3]unclean   [1]is(are).   but now

holy. [15]But if the unbelieving partner desires to separate, let it be so; in such a case the brother or sister is not bound. For God has called us[j] to peace. [16]Wife, how do you know whether you will save your husband? Husband, how do you know whether you will save your wife?

[17]Only, let every one lead the life which the Lord has assigned to him, and in which God has called him. This is my rule in all the churches. [18]Was any one at the time of his call already circumcised? Let him not seek to remove the marks of circumcision. Was any one at the time of his call uncircumcised? Let him not seek circumcision. [19]For neither circumcision counts for anything nor uncircumcision, but keeping the commandments of God. [20]Every one should remain in the state in which he was called. [21]Were you a slave when called? Never mind. But if you can gain your freedom, avail yourself of the opportunity[jj]. [22]For he who was called in the Lord as a slave is a freedman of the Lord. Likewise he who was free when called is a slave of Christ. [23]You were bought with a price; do

ἁγιά ἐστιν.
[1]holy   [1]they are.

15 εἰ δὲ ὁ ἄπιστος χωρίζ-
But if   the   unbelieving   separates one

εται, χωριζέσθω· οὐ δεδούλωται ὁ
him/herself,   let him/her be   [6]has not been enslaved   [1]the
separated;

ἀδελφὸς ἢ ἡ ἀδελφὴ ἐν τοῖς τοιούτοις·
[2]brother   [3]or   [4]the   [5]sister   in   such matters;

ἐν δὲ εἰρήνη κέκληκεν ὑμᾶς ὁ θεός.
but [4]in   [5]peace   [3]has called   [2]you   -   [1]God.

16 τί γὰρ οἶδας, γύναι, εἰ τὸν ἄνδρα
For what knowest thou, wife, if the(thy) husband

σώσεις; ἢ τί οἶδας, ἄνερ, εἰ τὴν
thou wilt save? or what knowest husband, if the(thy) thou,

γυναῖκα σώσεις; **17** Εἰ μὴ ἑκάστῳ ὡς
wife   thou wilt save?   Only   [1]to each ,   [1]as

μεμέρικεν ὁ κύριος, ἕκαστον ὡς κέκληκεν
[4]has divided   [3]the   [2]Lord,   [4]each   [1]as   [3]has called

ὁ θεός, οὕτως περιπατείτω. καὶ οὕτως
-   [2]God,   so   let him walk.   And   so

ἐν ταῖς ἐκκλησίαις πάσαις διατάσσομαι.
[2]in   [4]the   [5]churches   [3]all   [1]I command.

18 περιτετμημένος τις ἐκλήθη; μὴ
[6]Having been circumcised   [2]anyone   [1]was [3]called?   not

ἐπισπάσθω· ἐν ἀκροβυστίᾳ κέκληταί τις;
let him be un-   in   uncircumcision   has been anyone?
circumcised;   called

μὴ περιτεμνέσθω. **19** ἡ περιτομὴ οὐδέν
let him not be circumcised.   -   Circumcision   nothing

ἐστιν, καὶ ἡ ἀκροβυστία οὐδέν ἐστιν,
is,   and   -   uncircumcision   nothing   is,

ἀλλὰ τήρησις ἐντολῶν θεοῦ. **20** ἕκαστος
but   [the]   of command-   of   Each one
keeping   ments   God.

ἐν τῇ κλήσει ᾗ ἐκλήθη, ἐν ταύτῃ
in   the   calling in which he was called, in   this

μενέτω. **21** δοῦλος ἐκλήθης; μή σοι
let him remain.   A slave   wast thou called? not to thee

μελέτω· ἀλλ' εἰ καὶ δύνασαι ἐλεύθερος
let it matter;   but   if   indeed thou art able   [2]free

γενέσθαι, μᾶλλον χρῆσαι. **22** ὁ γὰρ ἐν
[1]to become,   [2]rather   [1]use [it].   For [1]the [one]   [4]in

κυρίῳ κληθεὶς δοῦλος ἀπελεύθερος κυρίου
[5][the]   [2]called   [3]a slave   [7]a freed man   [6]of [the]
Lord   Lord

ἐστίν· ὁμοίως ὁ ἐλεύθερος κληθεὶς δοῦλός
[4]is;   likewise   [1]the   [3]a free man   [2]called   [5]a slave
[one]

ἐστιν Χριστοῦ. **23** τιμῆς ἠγοράσθητε· μὴ
[4]is   [5]of Christ.   Of(with) a price ye were bought;   not

[j] Other ancient authorities read *you*

[jj] Or *make use of your present condition instead.*

not become slaves of men. ²⁴ So, brethren, in whatever state each was called, there let him remain with God.

25 Now concerning the unmarried, I have no command of the Lord, but I give my opinion as one who by the Lord's mercy is trustworthy. ²⁶ I think that in view of the impending^k distress it is well for a person to remain as he is. ²⁷ Are you bound to a wife? Do not seek to be free. Are you free from a wife? Do not seek marriage. ²⁸ But if you marry, you do not sin, and if a girl marries she does not sin. Yet those who marry will have worldly troubles, and I would spare you that. ²⁹ I mean, brethren, the appointed time has grown very short; from now on, let those who have wives live as though they had none, ³⁰ and those who mourn as though they were not mourning, and those who rejoice as though they were not rejoicing, and those who buy as though they had no goods, ³¹ and those who deal with the world as though they

γίνεσθε δοῦλοι ἀνθρώπων. 24 ἕκαστος ἐν
become ye slaves of men.   Each one in

ᾧ ἐκλήθη, ἀδελφοί, ἐν τούτῳ μενέτω
what he was brothers, in this let him
[state] called,   remain

παρὰ θεῷ.
with God.

25 Περὶ δὲ τῶν παρθένων ἐπιταγὴν
   Now about the virgins a command

κυρίου οὐκ ἔχω, γνώμην δὲ δίδωμι ὡς
of [the] Lord I have not, but an opinion I give as

ἠλεημένος ὑπὸ κυρίου πιστὸς εἶναι.
having had mercy by [the] Lord faithful to be.

26 Νομίζω οὖν τοῦτο καλὸν ὑπάρχειν
   I suppose therefore this good to be

διὰ τὴν ἐνεστῶσαν ἀνάγκην, ὅτι καλὸν
because the present necessity, that [it is] good
of

ἀνθρώπῳ τὸ οὕτως εἶναι. 27 δέδεσαι
for a man - so to be.   Hast thou
                              been bound

γυναικί; μὴ ζήτει λύσιν· λέλυσαι ἀπὸ
to a woman? do not seek release; hast thou been from
                               released

γυναικός; μὴ ζήτει γυναῖκα. 28 ἐὰν
a woman? do not seek a woman.   if

δὲ καὶ γαμήσῃς, οὐχ ἥμαρτες, καὶ ἐὰν
But indeed thou marriest, thou sinnedst not, and if

γήμῃ ἡ παρθένος, οὐχ ἥμαρτεν· θλῖψιν
²marries ¹the ²virgin, she sinned not; ³affliction

δὲ τῇ σαρκὶ ἕξουσιν οἱ τοιοῦτοι, ἐγὼ
but ⁴in the ⁵flesh ²will have - ¹such, ²I

δὲ ὑμῶν φείδομαι. 29 Τοῦτο δέ φημι,
¹and ²you ³am sparing.   But this I say,

ἀδελφοί, ὁ καιρὸς συνεσταλμένος ἐστίν·
brothers, the time *having been* shortened is;

τὸ λοιπὸν ἵνα καὶ οἱ ἔχοντες γυναῖκας
for the rest in order both the [ones] having wives
            that

ὡς μὴ ἔχοντες ὦσιν, 30 καὶ οἱ κλαίοντες
as not having may be, and the [ones] weeping

ὡς μὴ κλαίοντες, καὶ οἱ χαίροντες ὡς
as not weeping, and the [ones] rejoicing as

μὴ χαίροντες, καὶ οἱ ἀγοράζοντες ὡς
not rejoicing, and the [ones] buying as

μὴ κατέχοντες, 31 καὶ οἱ χρώμενοι τὸν
not holding, and the [ones] using the

κόσμον ὡς μὴ καταχρώμενοι· παράγει
world as not abusing [it]; ⁴is passing
                                       away

^{k} Or *present*

had no dealings with it. For the form of this world is passing away.

32 I want you to be free from anxieties. The unmarried man is anxious about the affairs of the Lord, how to please the Lord; 33 but the married man is anxious about worldly affairs, how to please his wife, 34 and his interests are divided. And the unmarried woman or girl is anxious about the affairs of the Lord, how to be holy in body and spirit; but the married woman is anxious about worldly affairs, how to please her husband. 35 I say this for your own benefit, not to lay any restraint upon you, but to promote good order and to secure your undivided devotion to the Lord.

36 If any one thinks that he is not behaving properly toward his betrothed, if his passions are strong, and it has to be, let him do as he wishes: let them marry— it is no sin. 37 But whoever is firmly established in his heart, being under no necessity but having his desire under control, and has determined this

γὰρ τὸ σχῆμα τοῦ κόσμου τούτου.
for ¹the ²fashion ³of this world.

32 Θέλω δὲ ὑμᾶς ἀμερίμνους εἶναι. ὁ
But I wish you without care to be. The

ἄγαμος μεριμνᾷ τὰ τοῦ κυρίου, 33 πῶς
unmarried cares for the of the Lord, how
man things

ἀρέσῃ τῷ κυρίῳ· ὁ δὲ γαμήσας μεριμνᾷ
he may the Lord; but the having married cares for
please [one]

τὰ τοῦ κόσμου, πῶς ἀρέσῃ τῇ γυναικί,
the of the world, how he may the(his) wife,
things please

34 καὶ μεμέρισται. καὶ ἡ γυνὴ ἡ ἄγαμος
and has been divided. And the ²woman – ¹unmarried

καὶ ἡ παρθένος μεριμνᾷ τὰ τοῦ κυρίου,
and the virgin cares for the things of the Lord,

ἵνα ᾖ ἁγία καὶ τῷ σώματι καὶ τῷ
in she holy both in the body and in
order may the
that be

πνεύματι· ἡ δὲ γαμήσασα μεριμνᾷ τὰ
spirit; but the [one] having married cares for the
things

τοῦ κόσμου, πῶς ἀρέσῃ τῷ ἀνδρί.
of the world, how she may please the(her) husband.

35 τοῦτο δὲ πρὸς τὸ ὑμῶν αὐτῶν σύμφορον
And ²this ³for ⁴the ⁵of yourselves ⁶advantage

λέγω, οὐχ ἵνα βρόχον ὑμῖν ἐπιβάλω,
¹I say, not in order ²a restraint ³you ¹I may put on,
that

ἀλλὰ πρὸς τὸ εὔσχημον καὶ εὐπάρεδρον
but for the thing comely and waiting on

τῷ κυρίῳ ἀπερισπάστως. 36 Εἰ δέ τις
the Lord undistractedly. But if anyone

ἀσχημονεῖν ἐπὶ τὴν παρθένον αὐτοῦ
²to behave ³toward ⁴the ⁵virgin ⁶of him
dishonourably

νομίζει, ἐὰν ᾖ ὑπέρακμος, καὶ οὕτως
¹thinks, if he/she is past the bloom and so
of youth,

ὀφείλει γίνεσθαι, ὃ θέλει ποιείτω· οὐχ
ought to be, what he wishes let him do; not

ἁμαρτάνει· γαμείτωσαν. 37 ὃς δὲ ἕστηκεν
he sins; let them marry. But [he] who stands

ἐν τῇ καρδίᾳ αὐτοῦ ἑδραῖος, μὴ
in the heart of him firm, not

ἔχων ἀνάγκην, ἐξουσίαν δὲ ἔχει περὶ
having necessity, but authority has concerning

τοῦ ἰδίου θελήματος, καὶ τοῦτο κέκρικεν
the(his) own will, and this has decided

in his heart, to keep her as his betrothed, he will do well. ³⁸ So that he who marries his betrothed does well; and he who refrains from marriage will do better.

39 A wife is bound to her husband as long as he lives. If the husband dies, she is free to be married to whom she wishes, only in the Lord. ⁴⁰ But in my judgment she is happier if she remains as she is. And I think that I have the Spirit of God.

ἐν τῇ ἰδίᾳ καρδίᾳ, τηρεῖν τὴν ἑαυτοῦ
in the(his) own   heart,   to keep   the   of himself
παρθένον, καλῶς ποιήσει.   38 ὥστε καὶ
virgin,   ²well   ¹he will do.   So as   both
ὁ γαμίζων τὴν ἑαυτοῦ παρθένον καλῶς
the marrying   the   of himself   virgin   ²well
[one]
ποιεῖ, καὶ ὁ μὴ γαμίζων κρεῖσσον ποιήσει.
¹does,   and   the not marrying   ²better   ¹will do.
[one]
39 Γυνὴ δέδεται ἐφ' ὅσον χρόνον ζῇ
A wife   has been bound   for   so long a time as   lives
ὁ ἀνὴρ αὐτῆς· ἐὰν δὲ κοιμηθῇ ὁ ἀνήρ,
the husband   of her;   but if   sleeps   the husband,
ἐλευθέρα ἐστὶν ᾧ θέλει γαμηθῆναι, μόνον
²free   ¹she is   ⁴to   ⁵she   ³to be married,   only
whom wishes
ἐν κυρίῳ.   40 μακαριωτέρα δέ ἐστιν
in [the] Lord.   But happier   she is
ἐὰν οὕτως μείνῃ, κατὰ τὴν ἐμὴν γνώμην·
if   so   she   according – my   opinion;
remains, to
δοκῶ δὲ κἀγὼ πνεῦμα θεοῦ ἔχειν.
and I think   I also   [the] Spirit   of God   to have.

CHAPTER 8

NOW concerning food offered to idols: we know that "all of us possess knowledge." "Knowledge" puffs up, but love builds up. ²If any one imagines that he knows something, he does not yet know as he ought to know. ³But if one loves God, one is known by him.

4 Hence, as to the eating of food offered to idols, we know that "an idol has no real existence," and that "there is no God but one." ⁵For although there may be so-called gods in heaven or on earth—as indeed there are many "gods"

8 Περὶ δὲ τῶν εἰδωλοθύτων, οἴδαμεν
Now about   the   idolatrous sacrifices,   we know
ὅτι πάντες γνῶσιν ἔχομεν. ἡ γνῶσις
that   ³all   ⁴knowledge   ¹we ²have. – Knowledge
φυσιοῖ, ἡ δὲ ἀγάπη οἰκοδομεῖ· εἴ τις
puffs up, – but   love   builds up;   if anyone
δοκεῖ ἐγνωκέναι τι, 2 οὔπω ἔγνω καθὼς
thinks   to have known anything,   not yet   he knew   as
δεῖ γνῶναι· 3 εἰ δέ τις ἀγαπᾷ τὸν
it be-   to know;   but if   anyone   loves   –
hoves [him]
θεόν, οὗτος ἔγνωσται ὑπ' αὐτοῦ. 4 Περὶ
God,   this one   has been known   by   him.   About
τῆς βρώσεως οὖν τῶν εἰδωλοθύτων
the   eating   therefore – of idolatrous sacrifices
οἴδαμεν ὅτι οὐδὲν εἴδωλον ἐν κόσμῳ,
we know   that [there is]no   idol   in [the] world,
καὶ ὅτι οὐδεὶς θεὸς εἰ μὴ εἷς. 5 καὶ
and   that [there is] no   God   except   one.   even
γὰρ εἴπερ εἰσὶν λεγόμενοι θεοὶ εἴτε ἐν
For   if   there are   being called   gods   either   in
οὐρανῷ εἴτε ἐπὶ γῆς, ὥσπερ εἰσὶν θεοὶ
heaven   or   on earth,   even as   there are   gods

and many "lords"—⁶yet
for us there is one God,
the Father, from whom
are all things and for
whom we exist, and one
Lord, Jesus Christ,
through whom are all
things and through whom
we exist.

7 However, not all
possess this knowledge.
But some, through being
hitherto accustomed to
idols, eat food as really
offered to an idol; and
their conscience, being
weak, is defiled. ⁸Food
will not commend us to
God. We are no worse
off if we do not eat, and
no better off if we do.
⁹Only take care lest this
liberty of yours some-
how become a stumbling-
block to the weak. ¹⁰For
if any one sees you, a
man of knowledge, at
table in an idol's temple,
might he not be en-
couraged, if his con-
science is weak, to eat
food offered to idols?
¹¹And so by your know-
ledge this weak man is
destroyed, the brother
for whom Christ died.
¹²Thus, sinning against
your brethren and
wounding their con-
science when it is weak,
you sin against Christ.
¹³Therefore, if food is a
cause of my brother's
falling, I will never eat

πολλοὶ καὶ κύριοι πολλοί, 6 ἀλλ' ἡμῖν
many and lords many,   yet   to us

εἰς θεὸς ὁ πατήρ, ἐξ οὗ τὰ πάντα καὶ
[there God the Father, of whom – [are] all and
is] one   things

ἡμεῖς εἰς αὐτόν, καὶ εἰς κύριος Ἰησοῦς
we in him,   and one Lord   Jesus

Χριστός, δι' οὗ τὰ πάντα καὶ ἡμεῖς
Christ, through whom –   [are] all and   we

δι' αὐτοῦ. 7 Ἀλλ' οὐκ ἐν πᾶσιν ἡ
through him.   But [there is] not in all men the
                                          (this)

γνῶσις· τινὲς δὲ τῇ συνηθείᾳ ἕως ἄρτι
knowledge; and some by the habit until now

τοῦ εἰδώλου ὡς εἰδωλόθυτον ἐσθίουσιν,
³of the ²idol ⁴as ⁵an idolatrous sacrifice ¹eat,

καὶ ἡ συνείδησις αὐτῶν ἀσθενὴς οὖσα
and the conscience of them ²weak ¹being

μολύνεται. 8 βρῶμα δὲ ἡμᾶς οὐ παραστήσει
is defiled.   But food ²us ¹will not commend

τῷ θεῷ· οὔτε ἐὰν μὴ φάγωμεν ὑστερούμεθα,
– to God; neither if we eat not are we behind,

οὔτε ἐὰν φάγωμεν περισσεύομεν. 9 βλέπετε
nor if we eat do we excel. look ye

δὲ μή πως ἡ ἐξουσία ὑμῶν αὕτη
But lest somehow the ²authority ³of you ¹this

πρόσκομμα γένηται τοῖς ἀσθενέσιν. 10 ἐὰν
a stumbling-block becomes to the weak ones. if

γάρ τις ἴδῃ σὲ τὸν ἔχοντα γνῶσιν ἐν
For anyone sees thee the [one] having knowledge ²in

εἰδωλείῳ κατακείμενον, οὐχὶ ἡ συνείδησις
³an idol's temple ¹sitting, ²not ³the ⁴conscience

αὐτοῦ ἀσθενοῦς ὄντος οἰκοδομηθήσεται εἰς
⁵of him ⁷weak ⁶[he]being⁸ ¹will ⁹be emboldened

τὸ τὰ εἰδωλόθυτα ἐσθίειν; 11 ἀπόλλυται
– ¹⁰the ¹¹idolatrous sacrifices ⁹to eat? ¹is destroyed

γὰρ ὁ ἀσθενῶν ἐν τῇ σῇ γνώσει, ὁ
For ¹the [one] ²being weak by – thy knowledge, the

ἀδελφὸς δι' ὃν Χριστὸς ἀπέθανεν. 12 οὕτως
brother because of whom Christ died. so

δὲ ἁμαρτάνοντες εἰς τοὺς ἀδελφοὺς καὶ
And sinning against the brothers and

τύπτοντες αὐτῶν τὴν συνείδησιν ἀσθενοῦσαν
wounding of them the conscience being weak

εἰς Χριστὸν ἁμαρτάνετε. 13 διόπερ εἰ
³against ²Christ ¹ye sin. Wherefore if

βρῶμα σκανδαλίζει τὸν ἀδελφόν μου, οὐ
food offends the brother of me, by no

meat, lest I cause my brother to fall.

μὴ φάγω κρέα εἰς τὸν αἰῶνα, ἵνα μὴ
means I eat flesh unto the age, lest

τὸν ἀδελφόν μου σκανδαλίσω.
²the ³brother ⁴of me ¹I offend.

CHAPTER 9

AM I not free? Am I not an apostle? Have I not seen Jesus our Lord? Are not you my workmanship in the Lord? ²If to others I am not an apostle, at least I am to you; for you are the seal of my apostleship in the Lord.

3 This is my defense to those who would examine me. ⁴Do we not have the right to our food and drink? ⁵Do we not have the right to be accompanied by a wife,¹ as the other apostles and the brothers of the Lord and Cephas? ⁶Or is it only Barnabas and I who have no right to refrain from working for a living? ⁷Who serves as a soldier at his own expense? Who plants a vineyard without eating any of its fruit? Who tends a flock without getting some of the milk?

8 Do I say this on human authority? Does not the law say the same? ⁹For it is written in the law of Moses, "You shall not muzzle

9 Οὐκ εἰμὶ ἐλεύθερος; οὐκ εἰμὶ ἀπόστολος;
Am I not free? am I not an apostle?

οὐχὶ Ἰησοῦν τὸν κύριον ἡμῶν ἑόρακα;
not Jesus the Lord of us I have seen?

οὐ τὸ ἔργον μου ὑμεῖς ἐστε ἐν κυρίῳ;
not the work of me ye are in [the] Lord?

2 εἰ ἄλλοις οὐκ εἰμὶ ἀπόστολος, ἀλλά
If to others I am not an apostle, yet

γε ὑμῖν εἰμι· ἡ γὰρ σφραγίς μου τῆς
indeed to you I am; for the seal ²of me ¹of the

ἀποστολῆς ὑμεῖς ἐστε ἐν κυρίῳ. 3 Ἡ
³apostleship ye are in [the] Lord. -

ἐμὴ ἀπολογία τοῖς ἐμὲ ἀνακρίνουσίν ἐστιν
My defence to the ²me ¹examining is
[ones]

αὕτη. 4 μὴ οὐκ ἔχομεν ἐξουσίαν φαγεῖν
this. not Have we not authority to eat

καὶ πεῖν; 5 μὴ οὐκ ἔχομεν ἐξουσίαν
and to drink? not have we not authority

ἀδελφὴν γυναῖκα περιάγειν, ὡς καὶ οἱ
a sister a wife to lead about, as also the

λοιποὶ ἀπόστολοι καὶ οἱ ἀδελφοὶ τοῦ
remaining apostles and the brothers of the

κυρίου καὶ Κηφᾶς; 6 ἢ μόνος ἐγὼ καὶ
Lord and Cephas? or only I and

Βαρναβᾶς οὐκ ἔχομεν ἐξουσίαν μὴ
Barnabas have we not authority not

ἐργάζεσθαι; 7 Τίς στρατεύεται ἰδίοις
to work? Who soldiers at [his] own

ὀψωνίοις ποτέ; τίς φυτεύει ἀμπελῶνα καὶ
wages at any time? who plants a vineyard and

τὸν καρπὸν αὐτοῦ οὐκ ἐσθίει; ἢ τίς
the fruit of it eats not? or who

ποιμαίνει ποίμνην καὶ ἐκ τοῦ γάλακτος
shepherds a flock and of the milk

τῆς ποίμνης οὐκ ἐσθίει; 8 μὴ κατὰ
of the flock eats not? Not according to

ἄνθρωπον ταῦτα λαλῶ, ἢ καὶ ὁ νόμος
man these things I speak, or also the law

ταῦτα οὐ λέγει; 9 ἐν γὰρ τῷ Μωϋσέως
these things says not? for in the of Moses

νόμῳ γέγραπται· οὐ κημώσεις βοῦν
law it has been written: Thou shalt not muzzle an ox

¹ Greek a sister as wife

an ox when it is treading out the grain." Is it for oxen that God is concerned? [10] Does he not speak entirely for our sake? It was written for our sake, because the plowman should plow in hope and the thresher thresh in hope of a share in the crop. [11] If we have sown spiritual good among you, is it too much if we reap your material benefits? [12] If others share this rightful claim upon you, do not we still more?

Nevertheless, we have not made use of this right, but we endure anything rather than put an obstacle in the way of the gospel of Christ. [13] Do you not know that those who are employed in the temple service get their food from the temple, and those who serve at the altar share in the sacrificial offerings? [14] In the same way, the Lord commanded that those who proclaim the gospel should get their living by the gospel.

15 But I have made no use of any of these rights, nor am I writing this to secure any such provision. For I would rather die than have any one deprive me of my ground for boasting. [16] For if I preach the gospel, that gives me no

---

ἀλοῶντα.   μὴ   τῶν   βοῶν   μέλει   τῷ   θεῷ;
threshing.   *not* –   of oxen   matters it   –   to God?

10 ἢ   δι'   ἡμᾶς   πάντως   λέγει;   δι'   ἡμᾶς
or because of us   altogether   he says? because of   us

γὰρ   ἐγράφη,   ὅτι   ὀφείλει   ἐπ'   ἐλπίδι
for   it was written, because   *ought   *on(in)   *hope

ὁ   ἀροτριῶν   ἀροτριᾶν,   καὶ   ὁ   ἀλοῶν   ἐπ'
¹the   ²ploughing   ⁴to plough,   and   the   threshing   on(in)
[one]   [one]

ἐλπίδι   τοῦ   μετέχειν.   11 εἰ   ἡμεῖς   ὑμῖν
hope   of the   to partake.   If   we   to you
=of partaking.

τὰ   πνευματικὰ   ἐσπείραμεν,   μέγα   εἰ   ἡμεῖς
–   spiritual things   sowed, [is it]   a great thing if   we

ὑμῶν   τὰ   σαρκικὰ   θερίσομεν;   12 εἰ   ἄλλοι
of you   –   fleshly things   shall reap?   If   others

τῆς   ὑμῶν   ἐξουσίας   μετέχουσιν,   οὐ
³of the   ⁴of you   ²authority   ¹have a share of,   not

μᾶλλον   ἡμεῖς;   ἀλλ'   οὐκ   ἐχρησάμεθα
rather   we?   But   we did not use

τῇ   ἐξουσίᾳ   ταύτῃ,   ἀλλὰ   πάντα   στέγομεν
this authority,   but   ⁴all things   ¹we put up with

ἵνα   μή   τινα   ἐγκοπὴν   δῶμεν   τῷ   εὐαγγελίῳ
lest   ²anyone   ²an obstacle   ¹we should to the   gospel
give

τοῦ   Χριστοῦ.   13 Οὐκ   οἴδατε   ὅτι   οἱ
–   of Christ.   Know ye not   that   the
[ones]

τὰ   ἱερὰ   ἐργαζόμενοι   τὰ   ἐκ   τοῦ   ἱεροῦ
–²sacred things   ¹working [at]   ⁴the things   ⁵of   ⁶the   ⁷temple

ἐσθίουσιν,   οἱ   τῷ   θυσιαστηρίῳ   παρεδρεύοντες
³eat,   the   ²the   ³altar   ¹attending [on]
[ones]

τῷ   θυσιαστηρίῳ   συμμερίζονται;   14 οὕτως
²the   ²altar   ¹partake with?   So

καὶ   ὁ   κύριος   διέταξεν   τοῖς   τὸ   εὐαγγέλιον
also   the   Lord   ordained   the [ones] ²the   ²gospel

καταγγέλλουσιν   ἐκ   τοῦ   εὐαγγελίου   ζῆν.
¹announcing   ⁵of   ⁴the   ³gospel   ⁴to live.

15 ἐγὼ   δὲ   οὐ   κέχρημαι   οὐδενὶ   τούτων.
But I   have not used   *not* one   of these
things.

Οὐκ   ἔγραψα   δὲ   ταῦτα   ἵνα   οὕτως   γένηται
And I did not write   these   in order   so   it might be
things

ἐν   ἐμοί·   καλὸν   γάρ   μοι   μᾶλλον   ἀποθανεῖν
in   me;   for good [it is] to me   rather   to die

ἢ   —   τὸ   καύχημά   μου   οὐδεὶς   κενώσει.
than   —   the   boast   of me   no man   shall empty.

16 ἐὰν   γὰρ   εὐαγγελίζωμαι,   οὐκ   ἔστιν
For if   I preach good news,   there is not
=I have no boast;

ground for boasting. For necessity is laid upon me. Woe to me if I do not preach the gospel! [17] For if I do this of my own will, I have a reward; but if not of my own will, I am entrusted with a commission. [18] What then is my reward? Just this: that in my preaching I may make the gospel free of charge, not making full use of my right in the gospel.

19 For though I am free from all men, I have made myself a slave to all, that I might win the more. [20] To the Jews I became as a Jew, in order to win Jews; to those under the law I became as one under the law—though not being myself under the law— that I might win those under the law. [21] To those outside the law I became as one outside the law— not being without law toward God but under the law of Christ—that I might win those outside the law. [22] To the weak I became weak, that I might win the weak. I have become all things to all men, that I might by all means save some. [23] I do it all for the sake of the gospel, that I may share in its blessings.

μοι καύχημα· ἀνάγκη γάρ μοι ἐπίκειται·
to me   boast;°   for necessity   ²me   ¹is laid on;

οὐαὶ γάρ μοί ἐστιν ἐὰν μὴ εὐαγγελίσωμαι.
for woe   ²to me   ¹is   if   I do not preach good tidings.

17 εἰ γὰρ ἑκὼν τοῦτο πράσσω, μισθὸν
    For if   willingly   ²this   ¹I do,   ²a reward

ἔχω· εἰ δὲ ἄκων, οἰκονομίαν πεπίστευμαι.
¹I have;   but if   unwillingly,   ²a stewardship   ¹I have been
                                     entrusted [with].

18 τίς οὖν μού ἐστιν ὁ μισθός; ἵνα
   What therefore   ⁴of me   ¹is   ²the   ³reward?   in order
                                        that

εὐαγγελιζόμενος ἀδάπανον θήσω τὸ
preaching good tidings   ⁴without charge   ¹I may place   ³the

εὐαγγέλιον, εἰς τὸ μὴ καταχρήσασθαι
²good tidings,   so as†   not   to use to the full

τῇ ἐξουσίᾳ μου ἐν τῷ εὐαγγελίῳ.
the   authority   of me   in   the   good tidings.

19 Ἐλεύθερος γὰρ ὢν ἐκ πάντων πᾶσιν
     For ²free   ¹being   of   all men   ³to all men

ἐμαυτὸν ἐδούλωσα, ἵνα τοὺς πλείονας
²myself   ¹I enslaved,   in order that   the   more

κερδήσω· 20 καὶ ἐγενόμην τοῖς Ἰουδαίοις
I might gain;   and   I became   to the   Jews

ὡς Ἰουδαῖος, ἵνα Ἰουδαίους κερδήσω·
as   a Jew,   in order that   Jews   I might gain;

τοῖς ὑπὸ νόμον ὡς ὑπὸ νόμον, μὴ ὢν
to the   under   law   as   under   law,   not being
ones

αὐτὸς ὑπὸ νόμον, ἵνα τοὺς ὑπὸ νόμον
[my]self   under   law,   in order   the   under   law
                      that   ones

κερδήσω· 21 τοῖς ἀνόμοις ὡς ἄνομος,
I might gain;   to the ones   without law   as   without law,

μὴ ὢν ἄνομος θεοῦ ἀλλ' ἔννομος Χριστοῦ,
not being   without   of God   but   under   of Christ,
      [the] law   [the] law

ἵνα κερδάνω τοὺς ἀνόμους· 22 ἐγενόμην
in order   I may gain   the ones   without law;   I became
that

τοῖς ἀσθενέσιν ἀσθενής, ἵνα τοὺς ἀσθενεῖς
²to the   ³weak   ¹weak,   in order   the   weak
                      that

κερδήσω· τοῖς πᾶσιν γέγονα πάντα, ἵνα
I might gain;   –   to all men   I have   all   in order
                    become   things,   that

πάντως τινὰς σώσω. 23 πάντα δὲ ποιῶ
in any case   ²some   ¹I might save.   But all things   I do

διὰ τὸ εὐαγγέλιον, ἵνα συγκοινωνὸς αὐτοῦ
because the   good tidings,   in order   ²a joint partaker   ³of it
of   that

24 Do you not know that in a race all the runners compete, but only one receives the prize? So run that you may obtain it. [25] Every athlete exercises self-control in all things. They do it to receive a perishable wreath, but we an imperishable. [26] Well, I do not run aimlessly, I do not box as one beating the air; [27] but I pommel my body and subdue it, lest after preaching to others I myself should be disqualified.

γένωμαι.   24 Οὐκ οἴδατε ὅτι οἱ ἐν
[1]I may become.   Know ye not   that the [ones] [2]in

σταδίῳ τρέχοντες πάντες μὲν τρέχουσιν,
[2]a racecourse [1]running   all   indeed   run,

εἷς δὲ λαμβάνει τὸ βραβεῖον; οὕτως
but one   receives   the   prize?   So

τρέχετε ἵνα καταλάβητε. 25 πᾶς δὲ ὁ
run   in order that ye may obtain.   And everyone

ἀγωνιζόμενος πάντα ἐγκρατεύεται, ἐκεῖνοι
struggling   [in] all things exercises self-control,   those

μὲν οὖν ἵνα φθαρτὸν στέφανον λάβωσιν,
indeed there- in order [2]a corruptible [3]crown [1]they may
fore   that   receive,

ἡμεῖς δὲ ἄφθαρτον. 26 ἐγὼ τοίνυν οὕτως
but we   an incorruptible.   I accordingly   so

τρέχω ὡς οὐκ ἀδήλως, οὕτως πυκτεύω
run   as   not   unclearly,   so   I box

ὡς οὐκ ἀέρα δέρων· 27 ἀλλὰ ὑπωπιάζω
as   not   [2]air   [1]beating;   but   I treat severely

μου τὸ σῶμα καὶ δουλαγωγῶ, μή πως
of me the   body   and lead [it] as a slave, lest

ἄλλοις κηρύξας αὐτὸς ἀδόκιμος γένωμαι.
to others having pro- [2][my]self [5]disapproved [1]I [3]may
claimed   [4]become.

CHAPTER 10

I want you to know, brethren, that our fathers were all under the cloud, and all passed through the sea, [2]and all were baptized into Moses in the cloud and in the sea, [3]and all ate the same supernatural food [4]and all drank the same supernatural drink. For they drank from the supernatural Rock which followed them, and the Rock was Christ. [5]Nevertheless with most of them God was not pleased; for they were overthrown in the wilderness.

10 Οὐ θέλω γὰρ ὑμᾶς ἀγνοεῖν, ἀδελφοί,
For I wish not   you   to be ignorant, brothers,

ὅτι οἱ πατέρες ἡμῶν πάντες ὑπὸ τὴν
that the   fathers   of us   all   under the

νεφέλην ἦσαν καὶ πάντες διὰ τῆς θαλάσσης
cloud   were and   all   through the   sea

διῆλθον, 2 καὶ πάντες εἰς τὸν Μωϋσῆν
passed through, and   all   [1]to - [2]Moses

ἐβαπτίσαντο ἐν τῇ νεφέλῃ καὶ ἐν τῇ
[1]were baptized in   the   cloud   and in   the

θαλάσσῃ, 3 καὶ πάντες τὸ αὐτὸ πνευματικὸν
sea,   and   all   [1]the [2]same [4]spiritual

βρῶμα ἔφαγον, 4 καὶ πάντες τὸ αὐτὸ
[5]food   [3]ate,   and   all   [2]the [3]same

πνευματικὸν ἔπιον πόμα· ἔπινον γὰρ ἐκ
[4]spiritual [1]drank [2]drink; for they drank of

πνευματικῆς ἀκολουθούσης πέτρας, ἡ πέτρα
a spiritual [2]following [1]rock, [2]the [3]rock

δὲ ἦν ὁ Χριστός. 5 Ἀλλ' οὐκ ἐν τοῖς
[1]and was the Christ. But [1]not [2]in(with) [3]the

πλείοσιν αὐτῶν εὐδόκησεν ὁ θεός·
[2]majority [4]of them [5]was [5]well [5]pleased - [6]God;

κατεστρώθησαν γὰρ ἐν τῇ ἐρήμῳ.
for they were scattered   in   the   desert.

6 Now these things are warnings for us, not to desire evil as they did. [7] Do not be idolaters as some of them were; as it is written, "The people sat down to eat and drink and rose up to dance." [8] We must not indulge in immorality as some of them did and twenty-three thousand fell in a single day. [9] We must not put the Lord[m] to the test, as some of them did and were destroyed by serpents; [10] nor grumble, as some of them did and were destroyed by the Destroyer. [11] Now these things happened to them as a warning, but they were written down for our instruction, upon whom the end of the ages has come. [12] Therefore let any one who thinks that he stands take heed lest he fall. [13] No temptation has overtaken you that is not common to man. God is faithful, and he will not let you be tempted beyond your strength, but with the temptation will also provide the way of escape, that you may be able to endure it.

6 ταῦτα δὲ τύποι ἡμῶν ἐγενήθησαν, εἰς
Now these things　types　of us　were,　for

τὸ μὴ εἶναι ἡμᾶς ἐπιθυμητὰς κακῶν,
the　not　to be　us[b]　longers after　evil things,
=so that we should not be . . .

καθὼς κἀκεῖνοι ἐπεθύμησαν. 7 μηδὲ
as　those indeed　longed.　　　　Neither

εἰδωλολάτραι γίνεσθε, καθώς τινες αὐτῶν·
idolaters　be ye,　　as　some　of them;

ὥσπερ γέγραπται· ἐκάθισεν ὁ λαὸς φαγεῖν
as　it has been written:　Sat　the people　to eat

καὶ πεῖν, καὶ ἀνέστησαν παίζειν. 8 μηδὲ
and to drink, and　stood up　to play.　Neither

πορνεύωμεν, καθώς τινες αὐτῶν ἐπόρνευσαν
let us commit　as　some　of them　committed
fornication,　　　　　　　　　　　fornication

καὶ ἔπεσαν μιᾷ ἡμέρᾳ εἴκοσι τρεῖς
and　fell　in one　day　twenty-three

χιλιάδες. 9 μηδὲ ἐκπειράζωμεν τὸν κύριον,
thousands.　Neither　let us overtempt　the　Lord,

καθώς τινες αὐτῶν ἐπείρασαν καὶ ὑπὸ
as　some　of them　tempted　and　by

τῶν ὄφεων ἀπώλλυντο. 10 μηδὲ γογγύζετε,
the　serpents　were destroyed.　Neither　murmur ye,

καθάπερ τινὲς αὐτῶν ἐγόγγυσαν, καὶ
even as　some　of them　murmured,　and

ἀπώλοντο ὑπὸ τοῦ ὀλεθρευτοῦ. 11 ταῦτα δὲ
were destroyed　by　the　destroyer.　Now these things

τυπικῶς συνέβαινεν ἐκείνοις, ἐγράφη δὲ
[2]typically　[1]happened　[2]to those men,　and was(were)
　　　　　　　　　　　　　　　　written

πρὸς νουθεσίαν ἡμῶν, εἰς οὓς τὰ
for　admonition　of us,　to　whom　the

τέλη τῶν αἰώνων κατήντηκεν. 12 Ὥστε
ends　of the　ages　has(ve) arrived.　So as

ὁ δοκῶν ἑστάναι βλεπέτω μὴ πέσῃ.
the thinking　to stand　let him look　lest　he falls.
[one]

13 πειρασμὸς ὑμᾶς οὐκ εἴληφεν εἰ μὴ
Temptation　you　has not taken　except

ἀνθρώπινος· πιστὸς δὲ ὁ θεός, ὃς οὐκ
[what is] human;　but faithful [is]　–　God,　who　not

ἐάσει ὑμᾶς πειρασθῆναι ὑπὲρ ὃ δύνασθε,
will allow　you　to be tempted　beyond what　you are able
　　　　　　　　　　　　　　　　　　[to bear],

ἀλλὰ ποιήσει σὺν τῷ πειρασμῷ καὶ τὴν
but　will make　with　the　temptation　also　the

ἔκβασιν τοῦ δύνασθαι ὑπενεγκεῖν.
way out　–　to be able　to endure.[d]
=so that ye may be able . . .

[m] Other ancient authorities read *Christ*

14 Therefore, my be-loved, shun the worship of idols. ¹⁵I speak as to sensible men; judge for yourselves what I say. ¹⁶The cup of blessing which we bless, is it not a participation in the blood of Christ? The bread which we break, is it not a participation in the body of Christ? ¹⁷Be-cause there is one bread, we who are many are one body, for we all partake of the same loaf. ¹⁸Consider the practice of Israel; are not those who eat the sacrifices partners in the altar? ¹⁹What do I imply then? That food offered to idols is anything, or that an idol is anything? ²⁰No, I imply that what pagans sacrifice they offer to demons and not to God. I do not want you to be partners with demons. ²¹You cannot drink the cup of the Lord and the cup of demons. You cannot partake of the table of the Lord and the table of demons. ²²Shall we provoke the Lord to jealousy? Are we stronger than he?

23 "All things are lawful," but not all things are helpful. "All things are lawful," but not all things build up.

14 Διόπερ, ἀγαπητοί μου, φεύγετε ἀπὸ
Wherefore, beloved of me, flee ye from
τῆς εἰδωλολατρίας. 15 ὡς φρονίμοις λέγω·
- idolatry. ²As ²to prudent men ¹I say;
κρίνατε ὑμεῖς ὃ φημι. 16 Τὸ ποτήριον
judge ye what I say. The cup
τῆς εὐλογίας ὃ εὐλογοῦμεν, οὐχὶ κοινωνία
- of blessing which we bless, ²not ³a communion
ἐστὶν τοῦ αἵματος τοῦ Χριστοῦ; τὸν
¹is it of the blood - of Christ? the
ἄρτον ὃν κλῶμεν, οὐχὶ κοινωνία τοῦ
bread which we break, ²not ³a communion ⁴of the
σώματος τοῦ Χριστοῦ ἐστιν; 17 ὅτι εἷς
⁵body - ⁶of Christ ¹is it? Because ⁴one
ἄρτος, ἓν σῶμα οἱ πολλοί ἐσμεν· οἱ γὰρ
⁵bread, ⁶one ⁷body ³the ²many ¹we are; - for
πάντες ἐκ τοῦ ἑνὸς ἄρτου μετέχομεν.
all of the one bread we partake.
18 βλέπετε τὸν Ἰσραὴλ κατὰ σάρκα·
See ye - Israel according to [the] flesh;
οὐχ οἱ ἐσθίοντες τὰς θυσίας κοινωνοὶ
²not ³the [ones] ⁴eating ⁵the ⁶sacrifices ⁷sharers
τοῦ θυσιαστηρίου εἰσίν; 19 τί οὖν φημι;
⁸of the ⁹altar ¹are? What there- do I say?
fore
ὅτι εἰδωλόθυτόν τί ἐστιν; ἢ ὅτι εἴδωλόν
that an idolatrous ²anything ¹is? or that an idol
sacrifice
τί ἐστιν; 20 ἀλλ' ὅτι ἃ θύουσιν,
²anything ¹is? but that [the] things they
which sacrifice,
δαιμονίοις καὶ οὐ θεῷ θύουσιν· οὐ θέλω
to demons and not to God they sacrifice; ²not ¹I wish
δὲ ὑμᾶς κοινωνοὺς τῶν δαιμονίων γίνεσθαι.
¹and you sharers of the demons to become.
21 οὐ δύνασθε ποτήριον κυρίου πίνειν
Ye cannot ²a cup ³of [the] Lord ¹to drink
καὶ ποτήριον δαιμονίων· οὐ δύνασθε
and a cup of demons; ye cannot
τραπέζης κυρίου μετέχειν καὶ τραπέζης
²of a table ³of [the] Lord ¹to partake and of a table
δαιμονίων. 22 ἢ παραζηλοῦμεν τὸν κύριον;
of demons. Or do we make jealous the Lord?
μὴ ἰσχυρότεροι αὐτοῦ ἐσμεν;
Not ²stronger [than] ³he ¹are we?

23 Πάντα ἔξεστιν, ἀλλ' οὐ πάντα
All things [are] lawful, but not all things
συμφέρει· πάντα ἔξεστιν, ἀλλ' οὐ πάντα
[are] expedient; all things lawful, but not all things
[are]

²⁴ Let no one seek his own good, but the good of his neighbor. ²⁵ Eat whatever is sold in the meat market without raising any question on the ground of conscience. ²⁶ For "the earth is the Lord's, and everything in it." ²⁷ If one of the unbelievers invites you to dinner and you are disposed to go, eat whatever is set before you without raising any question on the ground of conscience. ²⁸ (But if some one says to you, "This has been offered in sacrifice," then out of consideration for the man who informed you, and for conscience' sake—²⁹ I mean his conscience, not yours—do not eat it.) For why should my liberty be determined by another man's scruples? ³⁰ If I partake with thankfulness, why am I denounced because of that for which I give thanks?

31 So, whether you eat or drink, or whatever you do, do all to the glory of God. ³² Give no offense to Jews or to Greeks or to the church of God, ³³ just as I try to please all men in everything I do, not seeking my own advantage, but that of many, that they may be saved.

οἰκοδομεῖ.   24 μηδεὶς τὸ ἑαυτοῦ ζητείτω
edifies(fy).   No one the thing of himself let him seek

ἀλλὰ τὸ τοῦ ἑτέρου.   25 Πᾶν τὸ ἐν
but the thing of the other.   Everything ²in

μακέλλῳ πωλούμενον ἐσθίετε μηδὲν
²a meat market ¹being sold   eat ye   ²nothing

ἀνακρίνοντες διὰ τὴν συνείδησιν· 26 τοῦ
¹examining because of - conscience;   ²of the

κυρίου γὰρ ἡ γῆ καὶ τὸ πλήρωμα
³Lord ¹for   the   earth   and   the   fulness

αὐτῆς. 27 εἴ τις καλεῖ ὑμᾶς τῶν ἀπίστων
of it.   If anyone invites   you   of the unbelievers

καὶ θέλετε πορεύεσθαι, πᾶν τὸ παρατι-
and   ye wish   to go,   ²everything ³being set

θέμενον ὑμῖν ἐσθίετε μηδὲν ἀνακρίνοντες
before   ⁴you   ¹eat   ¹nothing   ⁵examining

διὰ τὴν συνείδησιν. 28 ἐὰν δέ τις ὑμῖν
because - conscience.   But if   anyone ²to you
of

εἴπῃ· τοῦτο ἱερόθυτόν ἐστιν, μὴ ἐσθίετε
¹says: This   ²slain in sacrifice   ¹is,   do not eat

δι᾽ ἐκεῖνον τὸν μηνύσαντα καὶ τὴν
because that   the   pointing out   and   -
of   man   [one]

συνείδησιν· 29 συνείδησιν δὲ λέγω οὐχὶ
conscience: ²conscience ¹but   ²I say   not

τὴν ἑαυτοῦ ἀλλὰ τὴν τοῦ ἑτέρου. ἱνατί
the one of himself   but   the one of the other.*   why

γὰρ ἡ ἐλευθερία μου κρίνεται ὑπὸ ἄλλης
For   the   freedom   of me   is judged   by ³of another

συνειδήσεως; 30 εἰ ἐγὼ χάριτι μετέχω,
¹conscience?   If   I   by grace   partake,

τί βλασφημοῦμαι ὑπὲρ οὗ ἐγὼ εὐχαριστῶ;
why   am I evil   because what   I   give thanks
    spoken of   of   [for]?

31 Εἴτε οὖν ἐσθίετε εἴτε πίνετε εἴτε
Whether therefore ye eat   or   ye drink   or

τι ποιεῖτε, πάντα εἰς δόξαν θεοῦ ποιεῖτε.
what ye do,   all things to [the] glory of God   do ye.
[ever]

32 ἀπρόσκοποι καὶ Ἰουδαίοις γίνεσθε καὶ
²Without offence ³both   ⁴to Jews   ¹be ye   ⁵and

Ἕλλησιν καὶ τῇ ἐκκλησίᾳ τοῦ θεοῦ,
⁶to Greeks   and   to the   church   -   of God,

33 καθὼς κἀγὼ πάντα πᾶσιν ἀρέσκω,
as   I also [in] all things   all men   please,

μὴ ζητῶν τὸ ἐμαυτοῦ σύμφορον ἀλλὰ
not   seeking   the   of myself   advantage   but

* That is, not the conscience of the person invited, to whom the apostle's words are addressed, but the conscience of the person "pointing out."

CHAPTER 11

BE imitators of me, as I am of Christ.

2 I commend you because you remember me in everything and maintain the traditions even as I have delivered them to you. ³But I want you to understand that the head of every man is Christ, the head of a woman is her husband, and the head of Christ is God. ⁴Any man who prays or prophesies with his head covered dishonors his head, ⁵but any woman who prays or prophesies with her head unveiled dishonors her head—it is the same as if her head were shaven. ⁶For if a woman will not veil herself, then she should cut off her hair; but if it is disgraceful for a woman to be shorn or shaven, let her wear a veil. ⁷For a man ought not to cover his head, since he is the image and glory of God; but woman is the glory of man. ⁸(For man was not made from woman, but woman from man. ⁹Neither was man created

τὸ τῶν πολλῶν, ἵνα σωθῶσιν. **11** μιμηταί
the of the many, in order they may   Imitators
(that)   that be saved.

μου γίνεσθε, καθὼς κἀγὼ Χριστοῦ.
of me   be ye,   as   I also [am] of Christ.

2 Ἐπαινῶ δὲ ὑμᾶς ὅτι πάντα μου
   But I praise   you   because ²all things ³of me

μέμνησθε καὶ καθὼς παρέδωκα ὑμῖν τὰς
¹ye have   and   ⁴as   ⁵I delivered   ⁶to you   ²the
remembered

παραδόσεις κατέχετε. **3** Θέλω δὲ ὑμᾶς
³traditions   ¹ye hold fast.   But I wish   you

εἰδέναι ὅτι παντὸς ἀνδρὸς ἡ κεφαλὴ ὁ
to know   that   ⁵of every   ⁶man   ³the   ⁴head   –

Χριστός ἐστιν, κεφαλὴ δὲ γυναικὸς ὁ
¹Christ   ²is,   and [the] head   of a woman   the

ἀνήρ, κεφαλὴ δὲ τοῦ Χριστοῦ ὁ θεός.
man,   and [the] head   –   of Christ   –   God.

4 πᾶς ἀνὴρ προσευχόμενος ἢ προφητεύων
   Every   man   praying   or   prophesying

κατὰ κεφαλῆς ἔχων καταισχύνει τὴν
³down over ⁴[his] head   ¹having   shames   the
           ²[anything]

κεφαλὴν αὐτοῦ. **5** πᾶσα δὲ γυνὴ προσ–
head   of him.   But every   woman   pray–

ευχομένη ἢ προφητεύουσα ἀκατακαλύπτῳ
ing   or   prophesying   ³unveiled

τῇ κεφαλῇ καταισχύνει τὴν κεφαλὴν αὐτῆς·
¹with   ²head   shames   the   head   of her;
the(her)

ἓν γάρ ἐστιν καὶ τὸ αὐτὸ τῇ ἐξυρημένῃ.
for ²one   ¹it is   and the   same with the   having been
           thing   woman   shaved.

6 εἰ γὰρ οὐ κατακαλύπτεται γυνή, καὶ
   For if   ²is not veiled   ¹a woman,   also

κειράσθω· εἰ δὲ αἰσχρὸν γυναικὶ τὸ
let her be shorn;   but if   shameful   for a woman   –

κείρασθαι ἢ ξυρᾶσθαι, κατακαλυπτέσθω.
to be shorn   or   to be shaved,   let her be veiled.

7 ἀνὴρ μὲν γὰρ οὐκ ὀφείλει κατα–
   For a man indeed   ought not   to be

καλύπτεσθαι τὴν κεφαλήν, εἰκὼν καὶ δόξα
veiled   the   head,ᵇ   ²[the] image ³and   ⁴glory

θεοῦ ὑπάρχων· ἡ γυνὴ δὲ δόξα ἀνδρός
⁵of God   ¹being;   but the woman   ²[the] glory ³of a man

ἐστιν. **8** οὐ γάρ ἐστιν ἀνὴρ ἐκ γυναικός,
¹is.   For ²not   ²is   ¹man of   woman,

ἀλλὰ γυνὴ ἐξ ἀνδρός· **9** καὶ γὰρ οὐκ
but   woman   of   man;   for indeed   ³not

for woman, but woman for man.) ¹⁰That is why a woman ought to have a veil[n] on her head, because of the angels. ¹¹(Nevertheless, in the Lord woman is not independent of man nor man of woman; ¹²for as woman was made from man, so man is now born of woman. And all things are from God.) ¹³Judge for yourselves; is it proper for a woman to pray to God with her head uncovered? ¹⁴Does not nature itself teach you that for a man to wear long hair is degrading to him, ¹⁵but if a woman has long hair, it is her pride? For her hair is given to her for a covering. ¹⁶If any one is disposed to be contentious, we recognize no other practice, nor do the churches of God.

17 But in the following instructions I do not commend you, because when you come together it is not for the better but for the worse. ¹⁸For, in the first place, when you assemble as a church, I hear that there are divisions among you;

ἐκτίσθη	ἀνὴρ	διὰ	τὴν	γυναῖκα, ἀλλὰ
²was ⁴created	¹man	because of	the	woman, but

γυνὴ	διὰ	τὸν	ἄνδρα.
woman	because of	the	man.

10 διὰ τοῦτο
Therefore

ὀφείλει	ἡ γυνὴ	ἐξουσίαν	ἔχειν	ἐπὶ τῆς
ought	the woman	authority	to have	on the

κεφαλῆς	διὰ	τοὺς	ἀγγέλους.
head	because of	the	angels.

11 πλὴν
Nevertheless

οὔτε	γυνὴ	χωρὶς	ἀνδρὸς οὔτε	ἀνὴρ χωρὶς
neither	woman	without	man nor	man without

γυναικὸς	ἐν	κυρίῳ·	**12** ὥσπερ	γὰρ ἡ
woman	in	[the] Lord;	for as	the

γυνὴ	ἐκ	τοῦ ἀνδρός,	οὕτως	καὶ ὁ ἀνὴρ
woman	of	the man,	so	also the man

διὰ	τῆς	γυναικός·	τὰ δὲ	πάντα ἐκ τοῦ
through	the	woman;	– but	all things of –

θεοῦ.	**13** Ἐν ὑμῖν αὐτοῖς κρίνατε· πρέπον
God.	Among you [your]selves judge: ²fitting

ἐστὶν	γυναῖκα	ἀκατακάλυπτον τῷ θεῷ
¹is it	²[for] ⁴a woman	³unveiled – ⁶to God

προσεύχεσθαι;	**14** οὐδὲ	ἡ	φύσις αὐτὴ
⁵to pray?	Not	–	nature [her]self

διδάσκει	ὑμᾶς	ὅτι	ἀνὴρ μὲν	ἐὰν κομᾷ,
teaches	you	that	a man indeed	if he wears his hair long,

ἀτιμία	αὐτῷ	ἐστιν,	**15** γυνὴ	δὲ ἐὰν
²a dishonour	³to him	¹it is,	but a woman	if

κομᾷ,	δόξα αὐτῇ	ἐστιν;	ὅτι ἡ κόμη
she wears	²a glory ³to her	¹it is?	because the long hair

her hair long,			
ἀντὶ	περιβολαίου	δέδοται	αὐτῇ.
instead of	a veil	has been given	to her.

16 Εἰ
if

δέ	τις	δοκεῖ	φιλόνεικος εἶναι,	ἡμεῖς
But	anyone	thinks	²contentious ¹to be,	we

τοιαύτην	συνήθειαν	οὐκ	ἔχομεν,	οὐδὲ αἱ
²such	³a custom	¹have not,		neither the

ἐκκλησίαι	τοῦ	θεοῦ.
churches	–	of God.

17 Τοῦτο	δὲ	παραγγέλλων	οὐκ	ἐπαινῶ
But this		charging	I do not praise

ὅτι	οὐκ	εἰς	τὸ	κρεῖσσον ἀλλὰ	εἰς τὸ
because not		for	the	better but	for the

ἧσσον	συνέρχεσθε.	**18** πρῶτον μὲν γὰρ
worse	ye come together.	For firstly indeed

συνερχομένων	ὑμῶν	ἐν	ἐκκλησίᾳ	ἀκούω
coming together	you[a]	in	church	I hear
=when ye come together				

σχίσματα	ἐν	ὑμῖν	ὑπάρχειν,	καὶ μέρος
divisions	among	you	to be,	and ²part

[n] Greek *authority* (the veil being a symbol of this)

and I partly believe it, [19]for there must be factions among you in order that those who are genuine among you may be recognized. [20]When you meet together, it is not the Lord's supper that you eat. [21]For in eating, each one goes ahead with his own meal, and one is hungry and another is drunk. [22]What! Do you not have houses to eat and drink in? Or do you despise the church of God and humiliate those who have nothing? What shall I say to you? Shall I commend you in this? No, I will not.

23 For I received from the Lord what I also delivered to you, that the Lord Jesus on the night when he was betrayed took bread, [24]and when he had given thanks, he broke it, and said, "This is my body which is for[o] you. Do this in remembrance of me." [25]In the same way also the cup, after supper, saying, "This cup is the new covenant in my blood. Do this, as often

τι πιστεύω.   19 δεῖ γὰρ καὶ αἱρέσεις
[s]some I believe.   For it behoves indeed   sects

ἐν ὑμῖν εἶναι, ἵνα [καὶ] οἱ δόκιμοι
among you to be, in order also   the   approved
             that   ones

φανεροὶ γένωνται ἐν ὑμῖν.   20 Συν-
manifest may become among you.   Coming

ερχομένων οὖν ὑμῶν ἐπὶ τὸ αὐτὸ οὐκ
together   therefore you[a]   together   not
=When therefore ye come

ἔστιν κυριακὸν δεῖπνον φαγεῖν· 21 ἕκαστος
it is of the Lord[*] a supper to eat;   [s]each one

γὰρ τὸ ἴδιον δεῖπνον προλαμβάνει ἐν
[s]for the(his) own   supper   takes before   in

τῷ φαγεῖν, καὶ ὃς μὲν πεινᾷ, ὃς δὲ
- to eat(eating), and one†   hungers,   another†

μεθύει.   22 μὴ γὰρ οἰκίας οὐκ ἔχετε
is drunken.   Not indeed [s]houses [1]have ye not

εἰς τὸ ἐσθίειν καὶ πίνειν; ἢ τῆς ἐκκλησίας
-    to eat and to drink? or the   church

τοῦ θεοῦ καταφρονεῖτε, καὶ καταισχύνετε
- of God despise ye,   and   shame

τοὺς μὴ ἔχοντας; τί εἴπω ὑμῖν; ἐπαινέσω
the not having? What may I say to you? shall I praise
[ones]

ὑμᾶς; ἐν τούτῳ οὐκ ἐπαινῶ.   23 Ἐγὼ
you?   In   this   I praise not.   I

γὰρ παρέλαβον ἀπὸ τοῦ κυρίου, ὃ καὶ
For   received   from the Lord, what also

παρέδωκα ὑμῖν, ὅτι ὁ κύριος Ἰησοῦς
I delivered to you, that the Lord   Jesus

ἐν τῇ νυκτὶ ᾗ παρεδίδοτο ἔλαβεν ἄρτον
in the night in which he was   took   bread
                 betrayed

24 καὶ εὐχαριστήσας ἔκλασεν καὶ εἶπεν·
     and having given thanks broke and said:

τοῦτό μού ἐστιν τὸ σῶμα τὸ ὑπὲρ
This of me is   the body   -   on be-
                             half of

ὑμῶν· τοῦτο ποιεῖτε εἰς τὴν ἐμὴν
you;   this   do ye   for   -   my

ἀνάμνησιν.   25 ὡσαύτως καὶ τὸ ποτήριον
remembrance.   Similarly also the cup

μετὰ τὸ δειπνῆσαι, λέγων· τοῦτο τὸ
after the to sup,   saying: This   -

ποτήριον ἡ καινὴ διαθήκη ἐστὶν ἐν τῷ
cup   [s]the [s]new [4]covenant [1]is   in   -

ἐμῷ αἵματι· τοῦτο ποιεῖτε, ὁσάκις ἐὰν
my   blood;   this   do ye,   as often as

[o] Other ancient authorities read *broken for*

[*] Note that κυριακός is an adjective, for which no exact English equivalent is available. Only other occurrence in N.T., Rev. 1. 10.

as you drink it, in remembrance of me." ²⁶For as often as you eat this bread and drink the cup, you proclaim the Lord's death until he comes.

27 Whoever, therefore, eats the bread or drinks the cup of the Lord in an unworthy manner will be guilty of profaning the body and blood of the Lord. ²⁸Let a man examine himself, and so eat of the bread and drink of the cup. ²⁹For any one who eats and drinks without discerning the body eats and drinks judgment upon himself. ³⁰That is why many of you are weak and ill, and some have died. ³¹But if we judged ourselves truly, we should not be judged. ³²But when we are judged by the Lord, we are chastened[p] so that we may not be condemned along with the world.

33 So then, my brethren, when you come together to eat, wait for one another—³⁴if any one is hungry, let him eat at home—lest you come together to be condemned. About the other things I will give directions when I come.

πίνητε, εἰς τὴν ἐμὴν ἀνάμνησιν. 26 ὁσάκις
ye drink, for - my remembrance. as often

γὰρ ἐὰν ἐσθίητε τὸν ἄρτον τοῦτον καὶ
For as ye eat   this bread   and

τὸ ποτήριον πίνητε, τὸν θάνατον τοῦ
²the ²cup ¹drink, the death of the

κυρίου καταγγέλλετε, ἄχρι οὗ ἔλθη.
Lord ye declare,   until he comes.

27 Ὥστε ὃς ἂν ἐσθίῃ τὸν ἄρτον ἢ
So as whoever eats the bread or

πίνῃ τὸ ποτήριον τοῦ κυρίου ἀναξίως,
drinks the cup of the Lord unworthily,

ἔνοχος ἔσται τοῦ σώματος καὶ τοῦ
guilty will be of the body and of the

αἵματος τοῦ κυρίου. 28 δοκιμαζέτω δὲ
blood of the Lord. But ¹let ²prove

ἄνθρωπος ἑαυτόν, καὶ οὕτως ἐκ τοῦ
²a man ⁴himself, and so of the

ἄρτου ἐσθιέτω καὶ ἐκ τοῦ ποτηρίου
bread let him eat and of the cup

πινέτω· 29 ὁ γὰρ ἐσθίων καὶ πίνων
let him drink; for the [one] eating and drinking

κρίμα ἑαυτῷ ἐσθίει καὶ πίνει μὴ διακρίνων
⁴judgment ⁵to ¹eats ²and ³drinks not discerning
       himself

τὸ σῶμα. 30 διὰ τοῦτο ἐν ὑμῖν πολλοὶ
the body. Therefore among you many

ἀσθενεῖς καὶ ἄρρωστοι καὶ κοιμῶνται
[are] weak and feeble and ²sleep

ἱκανοί. 31 εἰ δὲ ἑαυτοὺς διεκρίνομεν,
¹a number. But if ourselves we discerned,

οὐκ ἂν ἐκρινόμεθα· 32 κρινόμενοι δὲ ὑπὸ
we should not be judged; but being judged by

τοῦ κυρίου παιδευόμεθα, ἵνα μὴ σὺν
the Lord we are chastened, lest with

τῷ κόσμῳ κατακριθῶμεν. 33 Ὥστε,
the world we are condemned. So as,

ἀδελφοί μου, συνερχόμενοι εἰς τὸ φαγεῖν
brothers of me, coming together for the to eat

ἀλλήλους ἐκδέχεσθε. 34 εἴ τις πεινᾷ,
one another await ye. If anyone hungers,

ἐν οἴκῳ ἐσθιέτω, ἵνα μὴ εἰς κρίμα
at home let him eat, lest to judgment

συνέρχησθε. τὰ δὲ λοιπὰ ὡς ἂν ἔλθω
ye come together. And the remaining matters whenever I come

διατάξομαι.
I will arrange.

[p] Or when we are judged we are being chastened by the Lord

CHAPTER 12

NOW concerning spiritual gifts, brethren, I do not want you to be uninformed. [2] You know that when you were heathen, you were led astray to dumb idols, however you may have been moved. [3] Therefore I want you to understand that no one speaking by the Spirit of God ever says "Jesus be cursed!" and no one can say "Jesus is Lord" except by the Holy Spirit.

[4] Now there are varieties of gifts, but the same Spirit; [5] and there are varieties of service, but the same Lord; [6] and there are varieties of working, but it is the same God who inspires them all in every one. [7] To each is given the manifestation of the Spirit for the common good. [8] To one is given through the Spirit the utterance of wisdom, and to another the utterance of knowledge according to the same Spirit, [9] to another faith by the same Spirit, to another gifts of healing by the one Spirit, [10] to another the working of miracles, to another prophecy, to another the ability to distinguish between spirits, to another various kinds of tongues,

12 Περὶ δὲ τῶν πνευματικῶν, ἀδελφοί,
Now about   the   spiritual matters,   brothers,

οὐ θέλω ὑμᾶς ἀγνοεῖν. 2 Οἴδατε ὅτι
I do not wish you to be ignorant.   Ye know   that

ὅτε ἔθνη ἦτε πρὸς τὰ εἴδωλα τὰ ἄφωνα
when [1]nations [2]ye were [4]to [5]the [7]idols – [6]voiceless

ὡς ἂν ἤγεσθε ἀπαγόμενοι. 3 διὸ γνωρίζω
[8]however [3]ye were led [9][ye were]   Where- I make
                    [10]being led away.[*]   fore   known

ὑμῖν ὅτι οὐδεὶς ἐν πνεύματι θεοῦ λαλῶν
to you that no one [2]by [3][the] Spirit [4]of God [5]speaking

λέγει· ΑΝΑΘΕΜΑ ΙΗΣΟΥΣ, καὶ οὐδεὶς
says: A CURSE [IS] JESUS,   and no one

δύναται εἰπεῖν· ΚΥΡΙΟΣ ΙΗΣΟΥΣ, εἰ μὴ
can   to say: LORD   JESUS,   except

ἐν πνεύματι ἁγίῳ.
by [the] [2]Spirit [1]Holy.

4 Διαιρέσεις δὲ χαρισμάτων εἰσίν, τὸ δὲ αὐτὸ
Now differences of gifts   there are, but the same

πνεῦμα· 5 καὶ διαιρέσεις διακονιῶν εἰσίν, καὶ
Spirit;   and differences of ministries there are, and

ὁ αὐτὸς κύριος· 6 καὶ διαιρέσεις ἐνεργημάτων
the same Lord;   and differences of operations

εἰσίν, ὁ δὲ αὐτὸς θεὸς ὁ ἐνεργῶν τὰ
there are, but the same God – operating –

πάντα ἐν πᾶσιν. 7 ἑκάστῳ δὲ δίδοται
all things in   all.   But to each one is given

ἡ φανέρωσις τοῦ πνεύματος πρὸς τὸ
the manifestation of the Spirit to the

συμφέρον. 8 ᾧ μὲν γὰρ διὰ τοῦ πνεύματος
profiting.   For to one through the Spirit

δίδοται λόγος σοφίας, ἄλλῳ δὲ λόγος
is given a word of wisdom, and to another a word

γνώσεως κατὰ τὸ αὐτὸ πνεῦμα, 9 ἑτέρῳ
of   accord- the same Spirit,   to
knowledge ing to   another

πίστις ἐν τῷ αὐτῷ πνεύματι, ἄλλῳ δὲ
faith by the same Spirit,   and to another

χαρίσματα ἰαμάτων ἐν τῷ ἑνὶ πνεύματι,
gifts   of cures by the one Spirit,

10 ἄλλῳ δὲ ἐνεργήματα δυνάμεων, ἄλλῳ
and to another operations of powers, to another

[δὲ] προφητεία, ἄλλῳ δὲ διακρίσεις πνευ-
and prophecy, and to another discernings of

μάτων, ἑτέρῳ γένη γλωσσῶν, ἄλλῳ δὲ
spirits, to another kinds of tongues, and to another

---

* It is thought that there is a scribal error in this verse; see commentaries on the Greek text. We have been guided by G. G. Findlay, *The Expositor's Greek Testament*.

to another the interpretation of tongues. [11]All these are inspired by one and the same Spirit, who apportions to each one individually as he wills.

12 For just as the body is one and has many members, and all the members of the body, though many, are one body, so it is with Christ. [13]For by one Spirit we were all baptized into one body—Jews or Greeks, slaves or free—and all were made to drink of one Spirit.

14 For the body does not consist of one member but of many. [15]If the foot should say, "Because I am not a hand, I do not belong to the body," that would not make it any less a part of the body. [16]And if the ear should say, "Because I am not an eye, I do not belong to the body," that would not make it any less a part of the body. [17]If the whole body were an eye, where would be the hearing? If the whole body were an ear, where would be the sense of smell? [18]But as it is, God arranged the organs in the body, each one of them, as he chose. [19]If all were a single organ, where would the body be? [20]As it is, there are

ἑρμηνεία γλωσσῶν· 11 πάντα δὲ ταῦτα
interpretation of tongues: and [3]all [9]these things
ἐνεργεῖ τὸ ἓν καὶ τὸ αὐτὸ πνεῦμα,
[7]operates [1]the [2]one [3]and [4]the [5]same [6]Spirit,
διαιροῦν ἰδίᾳ ἑκάστῳ καθὼς βούλεται.
distributing [2]separately† [1]to each one   as   he purposes.

12 Καθάπερ γὰρ τὸ σῶμα ἕν ἐστιν
   For as   the body [4]one [1]is
καὶ μέλη πολλὰ ἔχει, πάντα δὲ τὰ
and [3]members [4]many [1]has,   but all   the
μέλη τοῦ σώματος πολλὰ ὄντα ἕν ἐστιν
members of the body   [2]many [1]being [4]one [3]is(are)
σῶμα, οὕτως καὶ ὁ Χριστός· 13 καὶ γὰρ
body, so also the Christ;   for indeed
ἐν ἑνὶ πνεύματι ἡμεῖς πάντες εἰς ἓν
[1]by [one] [5]Spirit [1]we   [2]all   [3]into [4]one
σῶμα ἐβαπτίσθημεν, εἴτε Ἰουδαῖοι εἴτε
[5]body   [2]were baptized, whether Jews   or
Ἕλληνες, εἴτε δοῦλοι εἴτε ἐλεύθεροι, καὶ
Greeks, whether slaves or   free,   and
πάντες ἓν πνεῦμα ἐποτίσθημεν. 14 καὶ
all   one Spirit we were given to drink.   indeed
γὰρ τὸ σῶμα οὐκ ἔστιν ἓν μέλος ἀλλὰ
For the body   is not   one member but
πολλά. 15 ἐὰν εἴπῃ ὁ πούς· ὅτι οὐκ
many.   If [2]says [1]the [foot: Because not
εἰμὶ χείρ, οὐκ εἰμὶ ἐκ τοῦ σώματος,
I am a hand, I am not   of the body,
οὐ παρὰ τοῦτο οὐκ ἔστιν ἐκ τοῦ σώματος.
not for   this   it is not of the body.
16 καὶ ἐὰν εἴπῃ τὸ οὖς· ὅτι οὐκ εἰμὶ
And if says the ear: Because I am not
ὀφθαλμός, οὐκ εἰμὶ ἐκ τοῦ σώματος,
an eye,   I am not of the body,
οὐ παρὰ τοῦτο οὐκ ἔστιν ἐκ τοῦ σώματος.
not for   this   it is not of the body.
17 εἰ ὅλον τὸ σῶμα ὀφθαλμός, ποῦ
If all the body [was] an eye, where
ἡ ἀκοή; εἰ ὅλον ἀκοή, ποῦ ἡ ὄσφρησις;
[would be] if all hearing, where the smelling?
the hearing?
18 νῦν δὲ ὁ θεὸς ἔθετο τὰ μέλη, ἓν
But now - God   set   the members, [2]one
ἕκαστον αὐτῶν ἐν τῷ σώματι καθὼς
[1]each of them in the body   as
ἠθέλησεν. 19 εἰ δὲ ἦν τὰ πάντα ἓν
he wished.   And if [2]was - [1]all   one
μέλος, ποῦ τὸ σῶμα; 20 νῦν δὲ πολλὰ
member, where the body?   But now many

many parts, yet one body. [21] The eye cannot say to the hand, "I have no need of you," nor again the head to the feet, "I have no need of you." [22] On the contrary, the parts of the body which seem to be weaker are indispensable, [23] and those parts of the body which we think less honorable we invest with the greater honor, and our unpresentable parts are treated with greater modesty, [24] which our more presentable parts do not require. But God has so adjusted the body, giving the greater honor to the inferior part, [25] that there may be no discord in the body, but that the members may have the same care for one another. [26] If one member suffers, all suffer together; if one member is honored, all rejoice together.

[27] Now you are the body of Christ and individually members of it. [28] And God has appointed in the church first apostles, second prophets, third teachers, then workers of miracles, then healers, helpers,

μὲν μέλη, ἓν δὲ σῶμα. 21 οὐ δύναται
²indeed ¹members, but one body. ⁵cannot

δὲ ὁ ὀφθαλμὸς εἰπεῖν τῇ χειρί· χρείαν
And ¹the ²eye to say to the hand: Need

σου οὐκ ἔχω, ἢ πάλιν ἡ κεφαλὴ τοῖς
of thee I have not, or again the head to the

ποσίν· χρείαν ὑμῶν οὐκ ἔχω· 22 ἀλλὰ
feet: Need of you I have not; but

πολλῷ μᾶλλον τὰ δοκοῦντα μέλη τοῦ
by much more ¹the ²seeming ⁵members ³of the

σώματος ἀσθενέστερα ὑπάρχειν ἀναγκαῖά ἐστιν,
⁴body ⁷weaker ⁶to be ⁹necessary ⁸is(are),

23 καὶ ἃ δοκοῦμεν ἀτιμότερα εἶναι
and ¹[members] ⁵we think ⁷less honourable ⁶to be
⁴which

τοῦ σώματος, τούτοις τιμὴν περισσοτέραν
²of the ³body, to these honour more abundant

περιτίθεμεν, καὶ τὰ ἀσχήμονα ἡμῶν
we put round, and the uncomely [members] of us

εὐσχημοσύνην περισσοτέραν ἔχει, 24 τὰ δὲ
²comeliness ³more abundant ¹has(ve), but th⁻

εὐσχήμονα ἡμῶν οὐ χρείαν ἔχει. ἀλλὰ ὁ
comely [members] of us ²no ¹need ¹has(ve). But -

θεὸς συνεκέρασεν τὸ σῶμα, τῷ ὑστερουμένῳ
God blended together the body, ⁴to the [member] ⁵lacking

περισσοτέραν δοὺς τιμήν, 25 ἵνα μὴ ᾖ
²more abundant ¹giving ³honour, lest there be

σχίσμα ἐν τῷ σώματι, ἀλλὰ τὸ αὐτὸ
division in the body, but ⁴the ⁵same

ὑπὲρ ἀλλήλων μεριμνῶσιν τὰ μέλη.
²on be- ⁷one ²should care ¹the ⁸members.
half of another

26 καὶ εἴτε πάσχει ἓν μέλος, συμπάσχει
And whether ³suffers ¹one ²member, ⁴suffers with[it]

πάντα τὰ μέλη· εἴτε δοξάζεται μέλος,
⁴all ⁵the ⁶members; or ²is glorified ¹a member,

συγχαίρει πάντα τὰ μέλη. 27 ὑμεῖς
⁶rejoices with [it] ³all ⁴the ⁵members. ye

δέ ἐστε σῶμα Χριστοῦ καὶ μέλη ἐκ
And are a body of Christ and members in

μέρους. 28 Καὶ οὓς μὲν ἔθετο ὁ θεὸς
part. And ²some† ²placed - ¹God

ἐν τῇ ἐκκλησίᾳ πρῶτον ἀποστόλους, δεύτε-
in the church firstly apostles, second-

ρον προφήτας, τρίτον διδασκάλους, ἔπειτα
ly prophets, thirdly teachers, then

δυνάμεις, ἔπειτα χαρίσματα ἰαμάτων,
powers, then gifts of cures,

administrators, speakers in various kinds of tongues. [29]Are all apostles? Are all prophets? Are all teachers? Do all work miracles? [30]Do all possess gifts of healing? Do all speak with tongues? Do all interpret? [31]But earnestly desire the higher gifts.

And I will show you a still more excellent way.

CHAPTER 13

IF I speak in the tongues of men and of angels, but have not love, I am a noisy gong or a clanging cymbal. [2]And if I have prophetic powers, and understand all mysteries and all knowledge, and if I have all faith, so as to remove mountains, but have not love, I am nothing. [3]If I give away all I have, and if I deliver my body to be burned,[q] but have not love, I gain nothing.

[4] Love is patient and kind; love is not jealous or boastful; [5]it is not arrogant or rude. Love does not insist on its own way; it is not irritable or resentful; [6]it does not rejoice at wrong, but

[q] Other ancient authorities read *body that I may glory*

ἀντιλήμψεις,   κυβερνήσεις,   γένη   γλωσσῶν,
helps,   governings,   kinds   of tongues.

29 μὴ   πάντες   ἀπόστολοι;   μὴ   πάντες
   Not   all [are]   apostles?   not   all

προφῆται;   μὴ   πάντες   διδάσκαλοι;   μὴ
prophets;   not   all   teachers?   not

πάντες   δυνάμεις;   30 μὴ   πάντες   χαρίσματα
all   powers?   not   all   ²gifts

ἔχουσιν   ἰαμάτων;   μὴ   πάντες   γλώσσαις
¹have   of cures?   not   all   ²with tongues

λαλοῦσιν;   μὴ   πάντες   διερμηνεύουσιν;
¹speak?   not   all   interpret?

31 ζηλοῦτε   δὲ   τὰ   χαρίσματα   τὰ   μείζονα.
   but desire ye eagerly the   ²gifts   -   ¹greater.

Καὶ   ἔτι   καθ'   ὑπερβολὴν   ὁδὸν   ὑμῖν
And   yet   ⁴according to   ³excellence   ²a way   ³to you

δείκνυμι. 13 Ἐὰν   ταῖς   γλώσσαις   τῶν   ἀνθρώπων
¹I show.   If   in the   tongues   -   of men

λαλῶ   καὶ   τῶν   ἀγγέλων,   ἀγάπην   δὲ
I speak   and   -   of angels,   but love

μὴ   ἔχω,   γέγονα   χαλκὸς   ἠχῶν   ἢ
I have not,   I have become   ²brass   ¹sounding   or

κύμβαλον   ἀλαλάζον.   2 καὶ   ἐὰν   ἔχω
cymbal   a tinkling.   And   if   I have

προφητείαν   καὶ   εἰδῶ   τὰ   μυστήρια   πάντα
prophecy   and   know   ²the   ¹mysteries   ¹all

καὶ   πᾶσαν   τὴν   γνῶσιν,   κἂν   ἔχω   πᾶσαν
and   all   -   knowledge,   and if   I have   all

τὴν   πίστιν   ὥστε   ὄρη   μεθιστάναι,   ἀγάπην
-    faith   so as   mountains   to remove,   ²love

δὲ   μὴ   ἔχω,   οὐθέν   εἰμι.   3 κἂν   ψωμίσω
¹but   I have not,   nothing   I am.   And if   I dole out

πάντα   τὰ   ὑπάρχοντά   μου,   καὶ   ἐὰν   παραδῶ
all   the   goods   of me,   and   if   I deliver

τὸ   σῶμά   μου   ἵνα   καυθήσομαι,   ἀγάπην
the   body   of me in order   I shall be   ²love
                  that   burned,

δὲ   μὴ   ἔχω,   οὐδὲν   ὠφελοῦμαι.   4 Ἡ
¹but   I have not,   nothing   I am profited.   -

ἀγάπη   μακροθυμεῖ,   χρηστεύεται   ἡ   ἀγάπη,
Love   suffers long,   is kind   -   love,

οὐ   ζηλοῖ,   ἡ   ἀγάπη   οὐ   περπερεύεται,
is not jealous,   -   love   does not vaunt itself,

οὐ   φυσιοῦται,   5 οὐκ   ἀσχημονεῖ,   οὐ   ζητεῖ
is not puffed up,   does not act unbecomingly,   does not seek

τὰ   ἑαυτῆς,   οὐ   παροξύνεται,   οὐ   λογίζεται
the   of   is not provoked,   does not reckon
things her(it)self,

τὸ   κακόν,   6 οὐ   χαίρει   ἐπὶ   τῇ   ἀδικίᾳ,
the   evil,   rejoices not   over   the   wrong,

rejoices in the right. ⁷Love bears all things, believes all things, hopes all things, endures all things.

8 Love never ends; as for prophecies, they will pass away; as for tongues, they will cease; as for knowledge, it will pass away. ⁹For our knowledge is imperfect and our prophecy is imperfect; ¹⁰but when the perfect comes, the imperfect will pass away. ¹¹When I was a child, I spoke like a child, I thought like a child, I reasoned like a child; when I became a man, I gave up childish ways. ¹²For now we see in a mirror dimly, but then face to face. Now I know in part; then I shall understand fully, even as I have been fully understood. ¹³So faith, hope, love abide, these three; but the greatest of these is love.

συγχαίρει δὲ τῇ ἀληθείᾳ· 7 πάντα στέγει,
but rejoices with   the   truth;   all things   covers,
πάντα πιστεύει, πάντα ἐλπίζει, πάντα
all things   believes,   all things   hopes,   all things
ὑπομένει. 8 Ἡ ἀγάπη οὐδέποτε πίπτει·
endures.   –   Love   never   falls;
εἴτε δὲ προφητεῖαι, καταργηθήσονται· εἴτε
but whether   prophecies,   they will be abolished;   or
γλῶσσαι, παύσονται· εἴτε γνῶσις, κατ-
tongues,   they will cease;   or   knowledge,   it will
αργηθήσεται. 9 ἐκ μέρους γὰρ γινώσκομεν
be abolished.   For in part   we know
καὶ ἐκ μέρους προφητεύομεν· 10 ὅταν
and   in   part   we prophesy;   ¹when
δὲ ἔλθῃ τὸ τέλειον, τὸ ἐκ μέρους
¹but ²comes ³the ⁴perfect thing, the thing in   part
καταργηθήσεται. 11 ὅτε ἤμην νήπιος,
will be abolished.   When   I was   an infant,
ἐλάλουν ὡς νήπιος, ἐφρόνουν ὡς νήπιος,
I spoke   as   an infant,   I thought   as   an infant,
ἐλογιζόμην ὡς νήπιος· ὅτε γέγονα ἀνήρ,
I reckoned   as   an infant;   when I have become a man,
κατήργηκα τὰ τοῦ νηπίου. 12 βλέπομεν
I have   the of the   infant.   we see
abolished things
γὰρ ἄρτι δι᾽ ἐσόπτρου ἐν αἰνίγματι,
For   yet   through   a mirror   in   a riddle,
τότε δὲ πρόσωπον πρὸς πρόσωπον· ἄρτι
but then   face   to   face;   yet
γινώσκω ἐκ μέρους, τότε δὲ ἐπιγνώσομαι
I know   in   part,   but then   I shall fully know
καθὼς καὶ ἐπεγνώσθην. 13 νυνὶ δὲ μένει
as   also   I was fully known.   But now   remains
πίστις, ἐλπίς, ἀγάπη, τὰ τρία ταῦτα·
faith,   hope,   love,   these three;
μείζων δὲ τούτων ἡ ἀγάπη.
and [the] greater   of these [is] –   love.

CHAPTER 14

MAKE love your aim, and earnestly desire the spiritual gifts, especially that you may prophesy. ²For one who speaks in a tongue speaks not to men but to God; for no one understands him, but he utters mysteries in the Spirit.

14 Διώκετε τὴν ἀγάπην, ζηλοῦτε δὲ
Pursue ye   –   love,   but desire eagerly
τὰ πνευματικά, μᾶλλον δὲ ἵνα προφητεύητε.
the spiritual [gifts],   and rather   in order ye may prophesy.
that
2 ὁ γὰρ λαλῶν γλώσσῃ οὐκ ἀνθρώποις
For the [one] speaking in a tongue   ²not   ¹ to men
λαλεῖ ἀλλὰ θεῷ· οὐδεὶς γὰρ ἀκούει,
¹speaks   but   to God;   for no one   hears,
πνεύματι δὲ λαλεῖ μυστήρια· 3 ὁ δὲ
but in spirit   he speaks   mysteries;   but the [one]

³On the other hand, he who prophesies speaks to men for their upbuilding and encouragement and consolation. ⁴He who speaks in a tongue edifies himself, but he who prophesies edifies the church. ⁵Now I want you all to speak in tongues, but even more to prophesy. He who prophesies is greater than he who speaks in tongues unless some one interprets, so that the church may be edified.

6 Now, brethren, if I come to you speaking in tongues, how shall I benefit you unless I bring you some revelation or knowledge or prophecy or teaching? ⁷If even lifeless instruments, such as the flute or the harp, do not give distinct notes, how will any one know what is played? ⁸And if the bugle gives an indistinct sound, who will get ready for battle? ⁹So with yourselves; if you in a tongue utter speech that is not intelligible, how will any one know what is said? For you will be speaking into the air. ¹⁰There are doubtless many different languages in the world,

---

προφητεύων ἀνθρώποις λαλεῖ οἰκοδομὴν καὶ
prophesying   to men   speaks edification and

παράκλησιν καὶ παραμυθίαν. 4 ὁ λαλῶν
encouragement and consolation. The [one] speaking

γλώσσῃ ἑαυτὸν οἰκοδομεῖ· ὁ δὲ προφητεύων
in a tongue himself   edifies; but the [one] prophesying

ἐκκλησίαν οἰκοδομεῖ. 5 θέλω δὲ πάντας
a church   edifies.   Now I wish   all

ὑμᾶς λαλεῖν γλώσσαις, μᾶλλον δὲ ἵνα
you to speak in tongues, but rather in order that

προφητεύητε· μείζων δὲ ὁ προφητεύων ἢ
ye may prophesy; and greater the [one] prophesying than

ὁ λαλῶν γλώσσαις, ἐκτὸς εἰ μὴ διερμηνεύῃ,
the speaking in tongues, except unless he interprets, [one]

ἵνα ἡ ἐκκλησία οἰκοδομὴν λάβῃ. 6 νῦν δέ,
in or- the church edification may receive. But now, der that

ἀδελφοί, ἐὰν ἔλθω πρὸς ὑμᾶς γλώσσαις
brothers, if I come to you in tongues

λαλῶν, τί ὑμᾶς ὠφελήσω, ἐὰν μὴ ὑμῖν
speaking, what ²you ¹shall I profit, except ²to you

λαλήσω ἢ ἐν ἀποκαλύψει ἢ ἐν γνώσει
¹I speak either in a revelation or in knowledge

ἢ ἐν προφητείᾳ ἢ διδαχῇ; 7 ὅμως τὰ
or in prophecy or in teaching? Yet -

ἄψυχα φωνὴν διδόντα, εἴτε αὐλὸς εἴτε
lifeless things ²a sound ¹giving, whether pipe or

κιθάρα, ἐὰν διαστολὴν τοῖς φθόγγοις μὴ
harp, if ²a distinction ⁴in the ⁵sounds ³not

δῷ, πῶς γνωσθήσεται τὸ αὐλούμενον ἢ
¹they how will it be known the being piped or give,   thing

τὸ κιθαριζόμενον; 8 καὶ γὰρ ἐὰν ἄδηλον
the being harped? For indeed if ²an thing   uncertain

σάλπιγξ φωνὴν δῷ, τίς παρασκευάσεται
¹a trumpet ⁴sound ³gives, who will prepare himself

εἰς πόλεμον; 9 οὕτως καὶ ὑμεῖς διὰ
for war?   so also ¹ye ⁶through

τῆς γλώσσης ἐὰν μὴ εὔσημον λόγον·
⁷the ⁸tongue ¹unless ⁴a clear ⁵word

δῶτε, πῶς γνωσθήσεται τὸ λαλούμενον;
²give, how will it be known the thing being said?

ἔσεσθε γὰρ εἰς ἀέρα λαλοῦντες. 10 τοσαῦτα
for ¹ye will be ³into ⁴air ²speaking. ²So many

εἰ τύχοι γένη φωνῶν εἰσιν ἐν κόσμῳ,
³it may be† ⁴kinds ⁵of sounds ¹there are in [the] world,

and none is without meaning; ¹¹but if I do not know the meaning of the language, I shall be a foreigner to the speaker and the speaker a foreigner to me. ¹²So with yourselves; since you are eager for manifestations of the Spirit, strive to excel in building up the church.

13 Therefore, he who speaks in a tongue should pray for the power to interpret. ¹⁴For if I pray in a tongue, my spirit prays but my mind is unfruitful. ¹⁵What am I to do? I will pray with the spirit and I will pray with the mind also; I will sing with the spirit and I will sing with the mind also. ¹⁶Otherwise, if you blessʳ with the spirit, how can any one in the position of an outsiderˢ say the "Amen" to your thanksgiving when he does not know what you are saying? ¹⁷For you may give thanks well enough, but the other man is not edified. ¹⁸I thank God that I speak in tongues more than you all; ¹⁹nevertheless, in church I would rather speak five words with my mind, in order to instruct others, than ten thousand

καὶ οὐδὲν ἄφωνον· 11 ἐὰν οὖν μὴ εἰδῶ
and not one [is] voiceless;   if   therefore I know not
τὴν   δύναμιν   τῆς   φωνῆς,   ἔσομαι   τῷ
the   power   of the   sound,   I shall be   to the
λαλοῦντι βάρβαρος καὶ ὁ λαλῶν ἐν ἐμοὶ
[one] speaking a foreigner and the speaking in(to) me
                                                    [one]
βάρβαρος.   12 οὕτως   καὶ   ὑμεῖς,   ἐπεὶ
a foreigner.   So   also   ye,   since
ζηλωταί   ἐστε   πνευμάτων,   πρὸς   τὴν
zealots   ye are   of spirit[ual thing]s,   ²to   ³the
οἰκοδομὴν τῆς ἐκκλησίας ζητεῖτε ἵνα περισ-
⁴edification ⁵of the ⁶church   ¹seek ye in order ye may
                                                    that
σεύητε.   13 Διὸ ὁ λαλῶν γλώσσῃ προσευχ-
abound.   Wherefore the speaking in a tongue   let him
                        [one]
ἔσθω ἵνα διερμηνεύῃ. 14 ἐὰν γὰρ προσεύχωμαι
pray in order he may   For if   I pray
        that   interpret.
γλώσσῃ,   τὸ   πνεῦμά   μου   προσεύχεται,
in a tongue, the   spirit   of me   prays,
ὁ δὲ νοῦς μου ἄκαρπός ἐστιν. 15 τί
but the mind of me unfruitful is.   What
οὖν   ἐστιν;   προσεύξομαι   τῷ   πνεύματι,
therefore is it?   I will pray   with the   spirit,
προσεύξομαι δὲ καὶ τῷ νοΐ· ψαλῶ τῷ
²I will pray ¹and ³also with the mind; I will with
                        the   sing the
πνεύματι, ψαλῶ δὲ καὶ τῷ νοΐ. 16 ἐπεὶ
spirit, ²I will sing ¹and ³also with the mind. Otherwise
ἐὰν εὐλογῇς [ἐν] πνεύματι, ὁ ἀναπληρῶν
if thou blessest in spirit, the [one] occupying
τὸν τόπον τοῦ ἰδιώτου πῶς ἐρεῖ τὸ
the place of the uninstructed how will he say the
ἀμὴν ἐπὶ τῇ σῇ εὐχαριστίᾳ; ἐπειδὴ τί
"amen" at   thy giving thanks? Since what
λέγεις οὐκ οἶδεν· 17 σὺ μὲν γὰρ καλῶς
thou sayest he knows not; ²thou ³indeed ¹for ⁵well
εὐχαριστεῖς, ἀλλ᾽ ὁ ἕτερος οὐκ οἰκοδομεῖται.
⁴givest thanks, but the other   is not edified.
18 εὐχαριστῶ τῷ θεῷ, πάντων ὑμῶν μᾶλ-
I give thanks to God, ²all ⁴you ³more
λον γλώσσαις λαλῶ· 19 ἀλλὰ ἐν ἐκκλησίᾳ
than ²in tongues ¹I speak; but in a church
θέλω πέντε λόγους τῷ νοΐ μου λαλῆσαι,
¹I wish ²five ⁴words ⁵with the ⁶mind ⁷of me ³to speak,
ἵνα καὶ ἄλλους κατηχήσω, ἢ μυρίους
in or- also others I may instruct, than ten
der that   thousands

ʳ That is, give thanks to God
ˢ Or him that is without gifts

words in a tongue.

20 Brethren, do not be children in your thinking; be babes in evil, but in thinking be mature. [21] In the law it is written, "By men of strange tongues and by the lips of foreigners will I speak to this people, and even then they will not listen to me, says the Lord." [22] Thus, tongues are a sign not for believers but for unbelievers, while prophecy is not for unbelievers but for believers. [23] If, therefore, the whole church assembles and all speak in tongues, and outsiders or unbelievers enter, will they not say that you are mad? [24] But if all prophesy, and an unbeliever or outsider enters, he is convicted by all, he is called to account by all, [25] the secrets of his heart are disclosed; and so, falling on his face, he will worship God and declare that God is really among you.

26 What then, brethren? When you come together, each one has a hymn, a lesson, a revelation, a tongue, or an interpretation. Let all

λόγους ἐν γλώσσῃ.   20 Ἀδελφοί, μὴ
words   in   a tongue.   Brothers,   [1]not

παιδία γίνεσθε ταῖς φρεσίν, ἀλλὰ τῇ
[2]children   [1]be ye in the(your) minds, but   –

κακίᾳ νηπιάζετε, ταῖς δὲ φρεσὶν τέλειοι
in malice be ye infantlike, and in the(your) minds mature

γίνεσθε.   21 ἐν τῷ νόμῳ γέγραπται ὅτι
be ye.   In the law it has been written that

ἐν ἑτερογλώσσοις καὶ ἐν χείλεσιν ἑτέρων
in   other tongues and in lips   of others

λαλήσω τῷ λαῷ τούτῳ, καὶ οὐδ' οὕτως
I will speak to this people,   and not   so

εἰσακούσονταί μου, λέγει κύριος.   22 ὥστε
will they hear me, says [the] Lord.   So as

αἱ γλῶσσαι εἰς σημεῖόν εἰσιν οὐ τοῖς
[the] tongues [2]for [a sign [1]are not to the

πιστεύουσιν ἀλλὰ τοῖς ἀπίστοις, ἡ δὲ
[ones] believing but to the unbelievers, and the

προφητεία οὐ τοῖς ἀπίστοις ἀλλὰ τοῖς
prophecy [is] not to the unbelievers but to the

πιστεύουσιν.   23 Ἐὰν οὖν συνέλθῃ ἡ
[ones] believing.   If therefore [4]comes [1]the
                                        together

ἐκκλησία ὅλη ἐπὶ τὸ αὐτὸ καὶ πάντες
[2]church [3]whole together and all

λαλῶσιν γλώσσαις, εἰσέλθωσιν δὲ ἰδιῶται
speak in tongues,   and [4]enter [1]uninstructed

ἢ ἄπιστοι, οὐκ ἐροῦσιν ὅτι μαίνεσθε;
[2]or [3]unbelievers, will they not say that ye rave?

24 ἐὰν δὲ πάντες προφητεύωσιν, εἰσέλθῃ δέ
but if all prophesy,   and [2]enters

τις ἄπιστος ἢ ἰδιώτης, ἐλέγχεται ὑπὸ
[some [1]unbeliever [2]or [3]uninstructed, he is convicted by

πάντων, ἀνακρίνεται ὑπὸ πάντων, 25 τὰ
all,   he is judged by all,   the

κρυπτὰ τῆς καρδίας αὐτοῦ φανερὰ γίνεται,
hidden of the heart of him [2]manifest [1]becomes,
things

καὶ οὕτως πεσὼν ἐπὶ πρόσωπον προσκυνή-
and so falling on [his] face   he will wor-

σει τῷ θεῷ, ἀπαγγέλλων ὅτι ὄντως
ship – God,   declaring that really

ὁ θεὸς ἐν ὑμῖν ἐστιν.   26 Τί οὖν ἐστιν,
– God [2]among [3]you [1]is.   What therefore is it,

ἀδελφοί; ὅταν συνέρχησθε, ἕκαστος ψαλμὸν
brothers? whenever ye come together, each one a psalm

ἔχει, διδαχὴν ἔχει, ἀποκάλυψιν ἔχει, γλῶσ-
has, a teaching he has, a revelation he has, a

σαν ἔχει, ἑρμηνείαν ἔχει· πάντα πρὸς
tongue he has, an interpretation he has; [3]all things [4]for

things be done for edification. [27] If any speak in a tongue, let there be only two or at most three, and each in turn; and let one interpret. [28] But if there is no one to interpret, let each of them keep silence in church and speak to himself and to God. [29] Let two or three prophets speak, and let the others weigh what is said. [30] If a revelation is made to another sitting by, let the first be silent. [31] For you can all prophesy one by one, so that all may learn and all be encouraged; [32] and the spirits of prophets are subject to prophets. [33] For God is not a God of confusion but of peace.

As in all the churches of the saints, [34] the women should keep silence in the churches. For they are not permitted to speak, but should be subordinate, as even the law says. [35] If there is anything they desire to know, let them ask their husbands at home. For it is shameful for a woman to speak in church. [36] What! Did the word of God originate with you, or are you the only ones it has reached?

[37] If any one thinks that he is a prophet, or spiritual, he should

---

οἰκοδομὴν γινέσθω. 27 εἴτε γλώσσῃ τις
edification ¹let ⁵be.   If in a tongue anyone

λαλεῖ, κατὰ δύο ἢ τὸ πλεῖστον τρεῖς,
speaks, by two or the most three,

καὶ ἀνὰ μέρος, 28 καὶ εἰς διερμηνευέτω·
and in turn,† and ²one ¹let ³interpret;

ἐὰν δὲ μὴ ᾖ διερμηνευτής, σιγάτω ἐν
but if there is not an interpreter, let him be silent in

ἐκκλησίᾳ, ἑαυτῷ δὲ λαλείτω καὶ τῷ
church, and to himself let him speak and

θεῷ. 29 προφῆται δὲ δύο ἢ τρεῖς λαλεί-
to God. And prophets two or three let them

τωσαν, καὶ οἱ ἄλλοι διακρινέτωσαν·
speak, and the others let discern;

30 ἐὰν δὲ ἄλλῳ ἀποκαλυφθῇ καθημένῳ, ὁ
but if ¹to another ²[something] ²sitting, the
                                    is revealed

πρῶτος σιγάτω. 31 δύνασθε γὰρ καθ᾽
first let be silent. For ye can ³sin-

ἕνα πάντες προφητεύειν, ἵνα πάντες
gly† ¹all ²to prophesy, in order that all

μανθάνωσιν καὶ πάντες παρακαλῶνται.
may learn and all may be encouraged.

32 καὶ πνεύματα προφητῶν προφήταις
And [the] spirits of prophets to prophets

ὑποτάσσεται· 33 οὐ γάρ ἐστιν ἀκαταστασίας
is(are) subject; for ²not ³is ⁴of tumult

ὁ θεὸς ἀλλὰ εἰρήνης. Ὡς ἐν πάσαις
¹God but of peace. As in all

ταῖς ἐκκλησίαις τῶν ἁγίων, 34 αἱ γυναῖκες
the churches of the saints, ²the ²women

ἐν ταῖς ἐκκλησίαις σιγάτωσαν· οὐ γὰρ
²in ⁴the ³churches ¹let ⁴be silent; ²not ¹for

ἐπιτρέπεται αὐταῖς λαλεῖν, ἀλλὰ ὑποτασ-
²it is ²permitted to them to speak, but let them

σέσθωσαν, καθὼς καὶ ὁ νόμος λέγει.
be subject, as also the law says.

35 εἰ δέ τι μαθεῖν θέλουσιν, ἐν οἴκῳ
But if ²anything ³to learn ¹they wish, ²at home

τοὺς ἰδίους ἄνδρας ἐπερωτάτωσαν· αἰσχρὸν
³the(ir) ³own ⁴husbands ¹let them question; ²a shame

γάρ ἐστιν γυναικὶ λαλεῖν ἐν ἐκκλησίᾳ.
¹for ²it is for a woman to speak in a church.

36 ἢ ἀφ᾽ ὑμῶν ὁ λόγος τοῦ θεοῦ ἐξῆλθεν,
Or from you ²the ³word - ⁴of God ¹went forth,

ἢ εἰς ὑμᾶς μόνους κατήντησεν; 37 Εἴ
or to you only did it reach? If

τις δοκεῖ προφήτης εἶναι ἢ πνευματικός,
any- thinks ²a prophet ¹to be or a spiritual man,
one

acknowledge that what I am writing to you is a command of the Lord. [38] If any one does not recognize this, he is not recognized. [39] So, my brethren, earnestly desire to prophesy, and do not forbid speaking in tongues; [40] but all things should be done decently and in order.

ἐπιγινωσκέτω   ἃ   γράφω   ὑμῖν   ὅτι
let him clearly [the] things I write   to you   that
know   which

κυρίου   ἐστὶν   ἐντολή·   38 εἰ   δέ   τις
of [the] Lord they are a commandment;   but if   anyone

ἀγνοεῖ,   ἀγνοεῖται.   39 Ὥστε,   ἀδελφοί
is ignorant, let him be ignorant.   So as,   brothers

μου,   ζηλοῦτε   τὸ   προφητεύειν,   καὶ   τὸ
of me,   be ye eager   –   to prophesy,   and   –

λαλεῖν   μὴ   κωλύετε   γλώσσαις·   40 πάντα
²to speak ¹forbid not   in tongues;   ²all things

δὲ   εὐσχημόνως   καὶ   κατὰ   τάξιν   γινέσθω.
and ⁴becomingly   ⁵and ⁶according to ⁷order ¹let ³be done.

CHAPTER 15

N OW I would remind you, brethren, in what terms I preached to you the gospel, which you received, in which you stand, [2] by which you are saved, if you hold it fast—unless you believed in vain.

3 For I delivered to you as of first importance what I also received, that Christ died for our sins in accordance with the scriptures, [4] that he was buried, that he was raised on the third day in accordance with the scriptures, [5] and that he appeared to Cephas, then to the twelve. [6] Then he appeared to more than five hundred brethren at one time, most of whom are still alive, though some have fallen asleep. [7] Then he appeared to James, then to all the apostles. [8] Last of all, as

15 Γνωρίζω   δὲ   ὑμῖν,   ἀδελφοί,   τὸ
Now I make known   to you,   brothers,   the

εὐαγγέλιον   ὃ   εὐηγγελισάμην   ὑμῖν,   ὃ   καὶ
good tidings   which   I preached   to you, which also

παρελάβετε,   ἐν   ᾧ   καὶ   ἑστήκατε,   2 δι᾽
ye received,   in which also   ye stand,   through

οὗ   καὶ   σῴζεσθε,   τίνι   λόγῳ   εὐηγγελισάμην
which also ye are saved, ³to what ⁴word   ¹I preached

ὑμῖν   εἰ   κατέχετε,   ἐκτὸς   εἰ   μὴ   εἰκῇ
²to you ¹if ³ye hold fast, except unless in vain

ἐπιστεύσατε.   3 παρέδωκα   γὰρ   ὑμῖν   ἐν
ye believed.   For I delivered   to you among

πρώτοις,   ὃ   καὶ   παρέλαβον,   ὅτι   Χριστὸς
[the] first what also   I received,   that   Christ
things,

ἀπέθανεν   ὑπὲρ   τῶν   ἁμαρτιῶν   ἡμῶν   κατὰ
died   on be-   the   sins   of us accord-
half of   ing to

τὰς   γραφάς,   4 καὶ   ὅτι   ἐτάφη,   καὶ   ὅτι
the   scriptures,   and   that he was buried, and   that

ἐγήγερται   τῇ   ἡμέρᾳ   τῇ   τρίτῃ   κατὰ
he has   on the   ²day   –   ¹third   accord-
been raised   ing to

τὰς   γραφάς,   5 καὶ   ὅτι   ὤφθη   Κηφᾷ,
the   scriptures,   and   that he was seen by Cephas,

εἶτα   τοῖς   δώδεκα·   6 ἔπειτα   ὤφθη   ἐπάνω
then   by the   twelve;   afterward he was seen ²over

πεντακοσίοις   ἀδελφοῖς   ἐφάπαξ,   ἐξ   ὧν   οἱ
¹by ³five hundreds brothers at one time, of whom the

πλείονες   μένουσιν   ἕως   ἄρτι,   τινὲς   δὲ
majority   remain   until   now,   though some

ἐκοιμήθησαν·   7 ἔπειτα   ὤφθη   Ἰακώβῳ,   εἶτα
fell asleep·   afterward he was seen by James,   then

τοῖς   ἀποστόλοις   πᾶσιν·   8 ἔσχατον   δὲ
by the   apostles   all;   and lastly

<table>
<tr><td>

to one untimely born, he appeared also to me. ⁹For I am the least of the apostles, unfit to be called an apostle, because I persecuted the church of God. ¹⁰But by the grace of God I am what I am, and his grace toward me was not in vain. On the contrary, I worked harder than any of them, though it was not I, but the grace of God which is with me. ¹¹Whether then it was I or they, so we preach and so you believed.

12 Now if Christ is preached as raised from the dead, how can some of you say that there is no resurrection of the dead? ¹³But if there is no resurrection of the dead, then Christ has not been raised; ¹⁴if Christ has not been raised, then our preaching is in vain and your faith is in vain. ¹⁵We are even found to be misrepresenting God, because we testified of God that he raised Christ, whom he did not raise if it is true that the dead are not raised. ¹⁶For if the dead are not raised, then Christ has not been raised. ¹⁷If Christ has not been raised, your faith is

</td><td>

πάντων   ὡσπερεὶ   τῷ·   ἐκτρώματι   ὤφθη
of all   even as if   to the(an) abortion he was seen

κἀμοί.   9 Ἐγὼ   γάρ   εἰμι   ὁ   ἐλάχιστος
by me also.   For I   am   the   least

τῶν   ἀποστόλων,   ὃς   οὐκ   εἰμὶ   ἱκανὸς
of the apostles, who   am not   sufficient

καλεῖσθαι   ἀπόστολος,   διότι   ἐδίωξα   τὴν
to be called an apostle,   because I persecuted the

ἐκκλησίαν   τοῦ   θεοῦ·   10 χάριτι   δὲ   θεοῦ
church   -   of God;   but by [the] grace of God

εἰμι   ὅ   εἰμι,   καὶ   ἡ   χάρις   αὐτοῦ   ἡ   εἰς
I am what I am,   and the grace of him -   to

ἐμὲ   οὐ   κενὴ   ἐγενήθη,   ἀλλὰ   περισσότερον
me   not empty   was,   but   ²more abundantly
                                          [than]

αὐτῶν   πάντων   ἐκοπίασα,   οὐκ   ἐγὼ   δὲ
³them   ⁴all   ¹I laboured,   ²not   ³I   ¹yet

ἀλλὰ   ἡ   χάρις   τοῦ   θεοῦ   σὺν   ἐμοί.   11 εἴτε
but the grace   - of God with me.   Whether

οὖν   ἐγὼ   εἴτε   ἐκεῖνοι,   οὕτως   κηρύσσομεν
therefore I   or   those,   so   we proclaim

καὶ   οὕτως   ἐπιστεύσατε.
and   so   ye believed.

12 Εἰ   δὲ   Χριστὸς   κηρύσσεται   ὅτι   ἐκ
But if   Christ   is proclaimed that from

νεκρῶν   ἐγήγερται,   πῶς   λέγουσιν   ἐν   ὑμῖν
[the] dead he has been raised, how   say   ²among ³you

τινες   ὅτι   ἀνάστασις   νεκρῶν   οὐκ   ἔστιν;
¹some   that a resurrection of dead persons there is not?

13 εἰ   δὲ   ἀνάστασις   νεκρῶν   οὐκ   ἔστιν,
Now if   a resurrection of dead persons there is not,

οὐδὲ   Χριστὸς   ἐγήγερται·   14 εἰ   δὲ   Χριστὸς
neither Christ   has been raised;   and if   Christ

οὐκ   ἐγήγερται,   κενὸν   ἄρα   τὸ   κήρυγμα
has not been raised, empty   then the proclamation

ἡμῶν,   κενὴ   καὶ   ἡ   πίστις   ὑμῶν·   15 εὑρισκ-
of us, empty also the faith   of you;   ¹we are

όμεθα   δὲ   καὶ   ψευδομάρτυρες   τοῦ   θεοῦ,
found   ¹and also   false witnesses   -   of God,

ὅτι   ἐμαρτυρήσαμεν   κατὰ   τοῦ   θεοῦ   ὅτι
because we witnessed   as to   -   God that

ἤγειρεν   τὸν   Χριστόν,   ὃν   οὐκ   ἤγειρεν
he raised   -   Christ,   whom   he raised not

εἴπερ   ἄρα   νεκροὶ   οὐκ   ἐγείρονται.   16 εἰ
if   then dead persons are not raised.   if

γὰρ   νεκροὶ   οὐκ   ἐγείρονται,   οὐδὲ   Χριστὸς
For dead persons are not raised,   neither Christ

ἐγήγερται·   17 εἰ   δὲ   Χριστὸς   οὐκ   ἐγήγερται,
has been raised; and if   Christ   has not been raised,

</td></tr>
</table>

futile and you are still in your sins. ¹⁸Then those also who have fallen asleep in Christ have perished. ¹⁹If for this life only we have hoped in Christ, we are of all men most to be pitied.

20 But in fact Christ has been raised from the dead, the first fruits of those who have fallen asleep. ²¹For as by a man came death, by a man has come also the resurrection of the dead. ²²For as in Adam all die, so also in Christ shall all be made alive. ²³But each in his own order: Christ the first fruits, then at his coming those who belong to Christ. ²⁴Then comes the end, when he delivers the kingdom to God the Father after destroying every rule and every authority and power. ²⁵For he must reign until he has put all his enemies under his feet. ²⁶The last enemy to be destroyed is death. ²⁷"For God has put all things in subjection under his feet." But when it says, "All things are put in subjection under him," it is

ματαία ἡ πίστις ὑμῶν [ἐστιν], ἔτι ἐστὲ
ᵇuseless ¹the ²faith ³of you ⁴is, ⁵still ¹ye are

ἐν ταῖς ἁμαρτίαις ὑμῶν. 18 ἄρα καὶ οἱ
in the sins of you. Then also the [ones]

κοιμηθέντες ἐν Χριστῷ ἀπώλοντο. 19 εἰ
having fallen asleep in Christ perished. If

ἐν τῇ ζωῇ ταύτῃ ἐν Χριστῷ ἠλπικότες
in this life ²in ⁴Christ ³having hoped

ἐσμὲν μόνον, ἐλεεινότεροι πάντων ἀνθρώπων
¹we are ⁵only, more pitiful [than] all men

ἐσμέν. 20 Νυνὶ δὲ Χριστὸς ἐγήγερται
we are. But now Christ has been raised

ἐκ νεκρῶν, ἀπαρχὴ τῶν κεκοιμημένων.
from [the] dead, firstfruit of the [ones] having fallen asleep.

21 ἐπειδὴ γὰρ δι' ἀνθρώπου θάνατος, καὶ
For since through a man death [came], also

δι' ἀνθρώπου ἀνάστασις νεκρῶν. 22 ὥσπερ
through a man a resurrection of dead persons as
[came].

γὰρ ἐν τῷ Ἀδὰμ πάντες ἀποθνήσκουσιν,
For in - Adam all die,

οὕτως καὶ ἐν τῷ Χριστῷ πάντες ζωοποιη-
so also in - Christ all will be

θήσονται. 23 Ἕκαστος δὲ ἐν τῷ ἰδίῳ
made alive. But each one in the(his) own

τάγματι· ἀπαρχὴ Χριστός, ἔπειτα οἱ τοῦ
order: [the] Christ, afterward the -
firstfruit [ones]

Χριστοῦ ἐν τῇ παρουσίᾳ αὐτοῦ, 24 εἶτα
of Christ in the presence of him, then

τὸ τέλος, ὅταν παραδιδοῖ τὴν βασιλείαν
the end, whenever he delivers the kingdom

τῷ θεῷ καὶ πατρί, ὅταν καταργήσῃ
- to God even [the] Father, whenever he abolishes

πᾶσαν ἀρχὴν καὶ πᾶσαν ἐξουσίαν καὶ
all rule and all authority and

δύναμιν. 25 δεῖ γὰρ αὐτὸν βασιλεύειν
power. For it behoves him to reign

ἄχρι οὗ θῇ πάντας τοὺς ἐχθροὺς ὑπὸ
until he puts all the(his) enemies under

τοὺς πόδας αὐτοῦ. 26 ἔσχατος ἐχθρὸς
the feet of him. [The] last enemy

καταργεῖται ὁ θάνατος· πάντα γὰρ ὑπέταξεν
is abolished - death; for all things he subjected

ὑπὸ τοὺς πόδας αὐτοῦ. 27 ὅταν δὲ
under the feet of him. But whenever

εἴπῃ ὅτι πάντα ὑποτέτακται, δῆλον ὅτι
he says that all things have been subjected, [it is] clear that

plain that he is excepted who put all things under him. [28] When all things are subjected to him, then the Son himself will also be subjected to him who put all things under him, that God may be everything to every one.

29 Otherwise, what do people mean by being baptized on behalf of the dead? If the dead are not raised at all, why are people baptized on their behalf? [30] Why am I in peril every hour? [31] I protest, brethren, by my pride in you which I have in Christ Jesus our Lord, I die every day! [32] What do I gain if, humanly speaking, I fought with beasts at Ephesus? If the dead are not raised, "Let us eat and drink, for to-morrow we die." [33] Do not be deceived: "Bad company ruins good morals." [34] Come to your right mind, and sin no more. For some have no knowledge of God. I say this to your shame.

35 But some one will ask, "How are the dead raised? With what kind of body do they come?" [36] You foolish man! What you sow does not come to life unless it dies.

ἐκτὸς τοῦ ὑποτάξαντος αὐτῷ τὰ πάντα.
[it is] the having to him - all
apart from [one] subjected things.

28 ὅταν δὲ ὑποταγῇ αὐτῷ τὰ πάντα,
But whenever is(are) subjected to him - all things,

τότε καὶ αὐτὸς ὁ υἱὸς ὑποταγήσεται
then also [him]self the Son will be subjected

τῷ ὑποτάξαντι αὐτῷ τὰ πάντα, ἵνα
to the having to him - all in order
[one] subjected things, that

ᾖ ὁ θεὸς πάντα ἐν πᾶσιν. 29 Ἐπεὶ
may - God all in all. Other-
be things wise

τί ποιήσουσιν οἱ βαπτιζόμενοι ὑπὲρ τῶν
what will they do the [ones] being baptized on behalf of the

νεκρῶν; εἰ ὅλως νεκροὶ οὐκ ἐγείρονται,
dead? if actually dead persons are not raised,

τί καὶ βαπτίζονται ὑπὲρ αὐτῶν; 30 τί
why indeed are they baptized on behalf of them? why

καὶ ἡμεῖς κινδυνεύομεν πᾶσαν ὥραν;
also we are in danger every hour?

31 καθ' ἡμέραν ἀποθνῄσκω, νὴ τὴν
Daily I die, by -

ὑμετέραν καύχησιν, ἀδελφοί, ἣν ἔχω ἐν
your boasting, brothers, which I have in

Χριστῷ Ἰησοῦ τῷ κυρίῳ ἡμῶν. 32 εἰ
Christ Jesus the Lord of us. If

κατὰ ἄνθρωπον ἐθηριομάχησα ἐν Ἐφέσῳ,
according man I fought with wild in Ephesus,
to beasts

τί μοι τὸ ὄφελος; εἰ νεκροὶ οὐκ ἐγείρονται,
what to me the profit? If dead persons are not raised,
= what profit have I?

φάγωμεν καὶ πίωμεν, αὔριον γὰρ ἀποθνῄ-
let us eat and let us drink, for to-morrow we

σκομεν. 33 μὴ πλανᾶσθε· φθείρουσιν ἤθη
die. Be ye not led astray: Corrupt customs

χρηστὰ ὁμιλίαι κακαί. 34 ἐκνήψατε δικαίως
good associations bad. Become ye sober righteously

καὶ μὴ ἁμαρτάνετε· ἀγνωσίαν γὰρ θεοῦ
and do not sin; for ignorance of God

τινες ἔχουσιν· πρὸς ἐντροπὴν ὑμῖν λαλῶ.
some have: for shame to you I speak.

35 Ἀλλὰ ἐρεῖ τις· πῶς ἐγείρονται οἱ
But will say someone: How are raised the

νεκροί; ποίῳ δὲ σώματι ἔρχονται; 36 ἄφρων,
dead? and with what body do they Foolish
sort [of] come? man,

σὺ ὃ σπείρεις, οὐ ζωοποιεῖται ἐὰν μὴ
thou what sowest, is not made alive unless

[37] And what you sow is not the body which is to be, but a bare kernel, perhaps of wheat or of some other grain. [38] But God gives it a body as he has chosen, and to each kind of seed its own body. [39] For not all flesh is alike, but there is one kind for men, another for animals, another for birds, and another for fish. [40] There are celestial bodies and there are terrestrial bodies; but the glory of the celestial is one, and the glory of the terrestrial is another. [41] There is one glory of the sun, and another glory of the moon, and another glory of the stars; for star differs from star in glory.

42 So is it with the resurrection of the dead. What is sown is perishable, what is raised is imperishable. [43] It is sown in dishonor, it is raised in glory. It is sown in weakness, it is raised in power. [44] It is sown a physical body, it is raised a spiritual body. If there is a physical body, there is also a spiritual body. [45] Thus it is written, "The first man Adam became a living being"; the last

ἀποθάνῃ‚ 37 καὶ ὃ σπείρεις, οὐ τὸ σῶμα
it dies;   and what thou sowest, not the body

τὸ γενησόμενον σπείρεις, ἀλλὰ γυμνὸν
– going to become thou sowest, but a naked

κόκκον εἰ τύχοι σίτου ἤ τινος τῶν
grain it may be† of wheat or some one of the

λοιπῶν· 38 ὁ δὲ θεὸς δίδωσιν αὐτῷ
rest; – but God gives to it

σῶμα καθὼς ἠθέλησεν, καὶ ἑκάστῳ τῶν
a body as he wished, and to each of the

σπερμάτων ἴδιον σῶμα. 39 οὐ πᾶσα
seeds [its] own body. [is] not [1]All

σὰρξ ἡ αὐτὴ σάρξ, ἀλλὰ ἄλλη μὲν
[1]flesh the same flesh, but other(one) indeed

ἀνθρώπων, ἄλλη δὲ σὰρξ κτηνῶν, ἄλλη δὲ
of men, and another flesh of animals, and another

σὰρξ πτηνῶν, ἄλλη δὲ ἰχθύων. 40 καὶ
flesh of birds, and another of fishes. And [there

σώματα ἐπουράνια, καὶ σώματα ἐπίγεια·
are] bodies heavenly, and bodies earthly;

ἀλλὰ ἑτέρα μὲν ἡ τῶν ἐπουρανίων δόξα,
but [7]other [5][is] [1]the [8]of the [4]heavenly [2]glory,
    (one) [6]indeed   [bodies]

ἑτέρα δὲ ἡ τῶν ἐπιγείων. 41 ἄλλη
and other the [glory] of the earthly [bodies]. Other(one)

δόξα ἡλίου, καὶ ἄλλη δόξα σελήνης,
glory of [the] sun, and another glory of [the] moon,

καὶ ἄλλη δόξα ἀστέρων· ἀστὴρ γὰρ
and another glory of [the] stars; for star

ἀστέρος διαφέρει ἐν δόξῃ. 42 οὕτως καὶ
from star differs in glory. So also

ἡ ἀνάστασις τῶν νεκρῶν. σπείρεται ἐν
the resurrection of the dead. It is sown in

φθορᾷ, ἐγείρεται ἐν ἀφθαρσίᾳ· 43 σπείρεται
corruption, it is raised in incorruption; it is sown

ἐν ἀτιμίᾳ, ἐγείρεται ἐν δόξῃ· σπείρεται
in dishonour, it is raised in glory; it is sown

ἐν ἀσθενείᾳ, ἐγείρεται ἐν δυνάμει· 44 σπείρ-
in weakness, it is raised in power; it is

εται σῶμα ψυχικόν, ἐγείρεται σῶμα
sown body a natural, it is raised body

πνευματικόν. Εἰ ἔστιν σῶμα ψυχικόν,
a spiritual. If there is body a natural,

ἔστιν καὶ πνευματικόν. 45 οὕτως καὶ
there is also a spiritual [body]. So also

γέγραπται· ἐγένετο ὁ πρῶτος ἄνθρωπος
it has been written: [5]became [1]The [2]first [3]man

Ἀδὰμ εἰς ψυχὴν ζῶσαν· ὁ ἔσχατος
[4]Adam – soul a living; the last

Adam became a life-giving spirit. [46]But it is not the spiritual which is first but the physical, and then the spiritual. [47]The first man was from the earth, a man of dust; the second man is from heaven. [48]As was the man of dust, so are those who are of the dust; and as is the man of heaven, so are those who are of heaven. [49]Just as we have borne the image of the man of dust, we shall[u] also bear the image of the man of heaven. [50]I tell you this, brethren: flesh and blood cannot inherit the kingdom of God, nor does the perishable inherit the imperishable.

[51]Lo! I tell you a mystery. We shall not all sleep, but we shall all be changed, [52]in a moment, in the twinkling of an eye, at the last trumpet. For the trumpet will sound, and the dead will be raised imperishable, and we shall be changed. [53]For this perishable nature must put on the imperishable, and this mortal nature must put on immortality. [54]When the perishable puts on the imperishable, and the mortal puts on immortality, then shall come to pass the saying that is written:

"Death is swallowed

Ἀδὰμ εἰς πνεῦμα ζωοποιοῦν. **46** ἀλλ'
Adam   –   spirit   a life-giving.   But

οὐ πρῶτον τὸ πνευματικὸν ἀλλὰ τὸ
not   firstly   the   spiritual [body]   but   the

ψυχικόν, ἔπειτα τὸ πνευματικόν. **47** ὁ
natural,   afterward   the   spiritual.   The

πρῶτος ἄνθρωπος ἐκ γῆς χοϊκός, ὁ
first   man   [was] out of earth   earthy,   the

δεύτερος ἄνθρωπος ἐξ οὐρανοῦ. **48** οἷος ὁ
second   man [is]   out of heaven.   Such   the

χοϊκός, τοιοῦτοι καὶ οἱ χοϊκοί, καὶ οἷος
earthy man,   such   also   the earthy ones, and   such

ὁ ἐπουράνιος, τοιοῦτοι καὶ οἱ ἐπουράνιοι·
the heavenly man,   such   also   the   heavenly ones;

49 καὶ καθὼς ἐφορέσαμεν τὴν εἰκόνα τοῦ
and   as   we bore   the   image   of the

χοϊκοῦ, φορέσομεν καὶ τὴν εἰκόνα τοῦ
earthy man, we shall bear   also   the   image   of the

ἐπουρανίου. **50** Τοῦτο δέ φημι, ἀδελφοί,
heavenly man.   And this   I say,   brothers,

ὅτι σὰρξ καὶ αἷμα βασιλείαν θεοῦ κληρο-
that   flesh   and   blood [3][the] kingdom [4]of God   [2]to

νομῆσαι οὐ δύναται, οὐδὲ ἡ φθορὰ τὴν
inherit   [1]cannot,   neither   –   [1]corruption   –

ἀφθαρσίαν κληρονομεῖ. **51** ἰδοὺ μυστήριον
[3]incorruption   [2]inherits.   Behold[,]   a mystery

ὑμῖν λέγω· πάντες οὐ κοιμηθησόμεθα,
to you   I tell: all   We shall not fall asleep,

πάντες δὲ ἀλλαγησόμεθα, **52** ἐν ἀτόμῳ,
but all   we shall be changed,   in   a moment,

ἐν ῥιπῇ ὀφθαλμοῦ, ἐν τῇ ἐσχάτῃ σάλπιγγι·
in a glance   of an eye,   at   the   last   trumpet;

σαλπίσει γάρ, καὶ οἱ νεκροὶ ἐγερθήσονται
for a trumpet will   and   the   dead   will be raised
sound,

ἄφθαρτοι, καὶ ἡμεῖς ἀλλαγησόμεθα. **53** Δεῖ
incorruptible,   and   we   shall be changed.   it behoves

γὰρ τὸ φθαρτὸν τοῦτο ἐνδύσασθαι
For   –   corruptible   this   to put on

ἀφθαρσίαν καὶ τὸ θνητὸν τοῦτο ἐνδύσασθαι
incorruption   and   –   mortal   this   to put on

ἀθανασίαν. **54** ὅταν δὲ τὸ φθαρτὸν τοῦτο
immortality.   And when*ever*   this [that is] corruptible

ἐνδύσηται ἀφθαρσίαν καὶ τὸ θνητὸν τοῦτο
shall put on   incorruption   and   this [that is] mortal

ἐνδύσηται ἀθανασίαν, τότε γενήσεται ὁ
shall put on   immortality,   then   will be   the

λόγος ὁ γεγραμμένος· κατεπόθη ὁ θάνατος
word   –   having been   [3]was   –   [1]Death
written: swallowed up

---

[u] Other ancient authorities read *let us*

up in victory."

⁵⁵ "O death, where is thy victory? O death, where is thy sting?"

⁵⁶ The sting of death is sin, and the power of sin is the law. ⁵⁷ But thanks be to God, who gives us the victory through our Lord Jesus Christ.

58 Therefore, my beloved brethren, be steadfast, immovable, always abounding in the work of the Lord, knowing that in the Lord your labor is not in vain.

εἰς νῖκος.   55 ποῦ σου, θάνατε, τὸ νῖκος;
in victory.   Where of thee, [O] death, the victory?

ποῦ σου, θάνατε, τὸ κέντρον; 56 τὸ δὲ
where of thee, [O] death,   the sting?   Now the

κέντρον τοῦ θανάτου ἡ ἁμαρτία, ἡ δὲ
sting   -   of death   -   [is] sin,   and the

δύναμις τῆς ἁμαρτίας ὁ νόμος· 57 τῷ
power   -   of sin   [is] the law;   -

δὲ θεῷ χάρις τῷ διδόντι ἡμῖν τὸ νῖκος
but to God thanks the [one] giving to us   the victory

διὰ τοῦ κυρίου ἡμῶν Ἰησοῦ Χριστοῦ.
through the Lord   of us   Jesus   Christ.

58 Ὥστε, ἀδελφοί μου ἀγαπητοί, ἑδραῖοι
So as,   brothers of me beloved,   firm

γίνεσθε, ἀμετακίνητοι, περισσεύοντες ἐν τῷ
be ye,   unmovable,   abounding   in the

ἔργῳ τοῦ κυρίου πάντοτε, εἰδότες ὅτι
work of the Lord   always,   knowing   that

ὁ κόπος ὑμῶν οὐκ ἔστιν κενὸς ἐν κυρίῳ.
the labour of you   is not   empty in [the] Lord.

CHAPTER 16

NOW concerning the contribution for the saints: as I directed the churches of Galatia, so you also are to do. ² On the first day of every week, each of you is to put something aside and store it up, as he may prosper, so that contributions need not be made when I come. ³ And when I arrive, I will send those whom you accredit by letter to carry your gift to Jerusalem. ⁴ If it seems advisable that I should go also, they will accompany me.

5 I will visit you after passing through Mace-

16 Περὶ δὲ τῆς λογείας τῆς εἰς τοὺς
Now about   the collection   -   for the

ἁγίους, ὥσπερ διέταξα ταῖς ἐκκλησίαις
saints,   as   I charged   the churches

τῆς Γαλατίας, οὕτως καὶ ὑμεῖς ποιήσατε.
- of Galatia,   so   also   ²ye   ¹do.

2 κατὰ μίαν σαββάτου ἕκαστος ὑμῶν
Every   one   of a week   each   of you
=On the first day of every week

παρ' ἑαυτῷ τιθέτω θησαυρίζων ὅ τι ἐὰν
by himself let him put storing up   whatever

εὐοδῶται, ἵνα μὴ ὅταν ἔλθω τότε λογεῖαι
he is prospered, lest whenever I come then ²collections

γίνωνται. 3 ὅταν δὲ παραγένωμαι, οὓς
¹there are.   And whenever   I arrive,   whom-

ἐὰν δοκιμάσητε, δι' ἐπιστολῶν τούτους
ever   ye approve,   through   epistles   these

πέμψω ἀπενεγκεῖν τὴν χάριν ὑμῶν εἰς
I will send   to carry   the grace(gift) of you   to

Ἱερουσαλήμ· 4 ἐὰν δὲ ἄξιον ᾖ τοῦ κἀμὲ
Jerusalem;   and if   ²fitting ¹it is - me also

πορεύεσθαι, σὺν ἐμοὶ πορεύσονται.
to go,ᵈ   with   me   they shall go.

5 Ἐλεύσομαι δὲ πρὸς ὑμᾶς ὅταν Μακε-
And I will come   to   you   whenever ²Mace-

do'nia, for I intend to pass through Macedo'nia, [6]and perhaps I will stay with you or even spend the winter, so that you may speed me on my journey, wherever I go. [7]For I do not want to see you now just in passing; I hope to spend some time with you, if the Lord permits. [8]But I will stay in Ephesus until Pentecost, [9]for a wide door for effective work has opened to me, and there are many adversaries.

[10]When Timothy comes, see that you put him at ease among you, for he is doing the work of the Lord, as I am. [11]So let no one despise him. Speed him on his way in peace, that he may return to me; for I am expecting him with the brethren.

[12]As for our brother Apol'los, I strongly urged him to visit you with the other brethren, but it was not at all his will[v] to come now. He will come when he has opportunity.

[13]Be watchful, stand

δονίαν διέλθω·　Μακεδονίαν γὰρ διέρχομαι,
donia　[1]I pass　for [2]Macedonia　[1]I am passing
　　through;　　　　　　　through,[*]

6 πρὸς　ὑμᾶς　δὲ　τυχὸν　καταμενῶ　ἢ
[2]with　[3]you　[1]and　[2]possibly　[3]I will remain　[4]or
καὶ παραχειμάσω, ἵνα ὑμεῖς με προπέμ-
[5]even [6]spend the winter, in order [2]ye [1]me　may set
　　　　　　　　　　　that
ψητε οὗ ἐὰν πορεύωμαι.　**7** οὐ θέλω γὰρ
forward wherever　I may go.　For I do not wish
ὑμᾶς ἄρτι ἐν παρόδῳ ἰδεῖν· ἐλπίζω γὰρ
[2]you [3]yet [4]in [5]passage [1]to see; for I am hoping
χρόνον τινὰ ἐπιμεῖναι πρὸς ὑμᾶς, ἐὰν
[3]time [2]some [1]to remain　with　you,　if
ὁ κύριος ἐπιτρέψῃ.　　**8** ἐπιμενῶ δὲ ἐν
the Lord　permits.　　But I will remain in
Ἐφέσῳ ἕως τῆς πεντηκοστῆς·　**9** θύρα
Ephesus until　－　　Pentecost;　　[5]door
γάρ μοι ἀνέῳγεν μεγάλη καὶ ἐνεργής,
[1]for [7]to me [6]opened [2]a great [3]and [4]effective,
καὶ ἀντικείμενοι πολλοί.　　**10** Ἐὰν δὲ
and [2]opposing [1]many.　　　　Now if
　　　　　　　　　　[there are]
ἔλθῃ Τιμόθεος, βλέπετε ἵνα ἀφόβως
[2]comes [1]Timothy,　see in order that fearlessly
γένηται πρὸς ὑμᾶς· τὸ γὰρ ἔργον κυρίου
he is　with　you;　for the　work of [the] Lord
ἐργάζεται ὡς κἀγώ·　**11** μή τις οὖν αὐτὸν
he works　as　I also;　[2]not [3]any- [4]there- [2]him
　　　　　　　　　　　　one fore
ἐξουθενήσῃ.　προπέμψατε δὲ αὐτὸν ἐν
[1]despise.　　But set ye forward　him in
εἰρήνῃ, ἵνα ἔλθῃ πρός με· ἐκδέχομαι γὰρ
peace, in order he may to me; for I am awaiting
　　　　that come
αὐτὸν μετὰ τῶν ἀδελφῶν.　**12** Περὶ δὲ
him with the brothers.　　　Now about
Ἀπολλῶ τοῦ ἀδελφοῦ, πολλὰ παρεκάλεσα
[2]Apollos the [1]brother,　[2]much　　[1]I besought
αὐτὸν ἵνα ἔλθῃ πρὸς ὑμᾶς μετὰ τῶν
[2]him in order he would to　you　with the
　　　that　come
ἀδελφῶν· καὶ πάντως οὐκ ἦν θέλημα
brothers;　and altogether it was not [his] will
ἵνα νῦν ἔλθῃ, ἐλεύσεται δὲ ὅταν εὐκαιρήσῃ.
in [2]now [1]he but he will come whenever he has
order should　　　　　　　　opportunity.
that come,
13 Γρηγορεῖτε, στήκετε ἐν τῇ πίστει,
Watch ye,　　stand　in　the　faith,

---

[v] Or God's will for him

[*] " Futuristic present "; cf. John 14. 3 and ch. 15. 32.

firm in your faith, be courageous, be strong. [14]Let all that you do be done in love.

15 Now, brethren, you know that the household of Steph'anas were the first converts in Acha'ia, and they have devoted themselves to the service of the saints; [16]I urge you to be subject to such men and to every fellow worker and laborer. [17]I rejoice at the coming of Steph'anas and Fortuna'tus and Acha'icus, because they have made up for your absence; [18]for they refreshed my spirit as well as yours. Give recognition to such men.

19 The churches of Asia send greetings. Aquila and Prisca, together with the church in their house, send you hearty greetings in the Lord. [20]All the brethren send greetings. Greet one another with a holy kiss.

21 I, Paul, write this greeting with my own hand. [22]If any one has no love for the Lord, let him be accursed. Our Lord, come! [23]The grace of the Lord Jesus be with you. [24]My love be with you all in Christ Jesus. Amen.

ἀνδρίζεσθε, κραταιοῦσθε.   14 πάντα ὑμῶν
play the man,   be strong.   [1]All things [2]of you
ἐν ἀγάπῃ γινέσθω.
[4]in [5]love   [1]let be.

15 Παρακαλῶ δὲ ὑμᾶς, ἀδελφοί· οἴδατε
  Now I beseech   you,   brothers: Know ye
τὴν οἰκίαν Στεφανᾶ, ὅτι ἐστὶν ἀπαρχὴ
the   household of Stephanas, that   it is   firstfruit
τῆς Ἀχαΐας καὶ εἰς διακονίαν τοῖς
 –   of Achaia   and   to   ministry   to the
ἁγίοις ἔταξαν ἑαυτούς· 16 ἵνα καὶ ὑμεῖς
saints   they   themselves;   in order also   ye
     appointed   that
ὑποτάσσησθε τοῖς τοιούτοις καὶ παντὶ τῷ
may submit   –   to such ones   and   to everyone
συνεργοῦντι καὶ κοπιῶντι. 17 χαίρω δὲ
working with [?me] and   labouring.   Now I rejoice
ἐπὶ τῇ παρουσίᾳ Στεφανᾶ καὶ Φορτουνάτου
at   the   presence   of Stephanas and   of Fortunatus
καὶ Ἀχαϊκοῦ, ὅτι τὸ ὑμέτερον ὑστέρημα
and   of Achaicus, that   –   [2]your   [1]lack
οὗτοι ἀνεπλήρωσαν· 18 ἀνέπαυσαν γὰρ τὸ
[1]these   [2]supplied;   for they refreshed   –
ἐμὸν πνεῦμα καὶ τὸ ὑμῶν. ἐπιγινώσκετε
my   spirit   and   – of you(yours).   Recognize ye
οὖν τοὺς τοιούτους.
therefore –   such ones.

19 Ἀσπάζονται ὑμᾶς αἱ ἐκκλησίαι τῆς
   [4]Greet   [5]you [1]the   [2]churches   –
Ἀσίας. ἀσπάζεται ὑμᾶς ἐν κυρίῳ πολλὰ
[3]of Asia.   [4]Greets   [5]you [7]in [8][the] Lord [6]much
Ἀκύλας καὶ Πρίσκα σὺν τῇ κατ᾽ οἶκον
[1]Aquila   [2]and [3]Prisca [9]with [10]the [11]in [the] house
αὐτῶν ἐκκλησίᾳ. 20 ἀσπάζονται ὑμᾶς οἱ
[12]of them [11]church.   [4]Greet   [5]you   [1]the
ἀδελφοὶ πάντες. Ἀσπάσασθε ἀλλήλους ἐν
[2]brothers   [1]all.   Greet ye   one another   with
φιλήματι ἁγίῳ. 21 Ὁ ἀσπασμὸς τῇ
kiss   a holy.   [1]The   [2]greeting   –
ἐμῇ χειρὶ Παύλου. 22 εἴ τις οὐ φιλεῖ
[3]with my [4]hand [2]of Paul.   If anyone   loves not
τὸν κύριον, ἤτω ἀνάθεμα. μαρὰνα θά.
the   Lord,   let him be   a curse.   Marana   tha.

23 ἡ χάρις τοῦ κυρίου Ἰησοῦ μεθ᾽ ὑμῶν.
The grace of the Lord   Jesus [be] with   you.

24 ἡ ἀγάπη μου μετὰ πάντων ὑμῶν ἐν
The   love   of me [be] with   [2]all   [1]you   in
Χριστῷ Ἰησοῦ.
Christ   Jesus.

CHAPTER 1

PAUL, an apostle of Christ Jesus by the will of God, and Timothy our brother.

To the church of God which is at Corinth, with all the saints who are in the whole of Acha'ia:

2 Grace to you and peace from God our Father and the Lord Jesus Christ.

3 Blessed be the God and Father of our Lord Jesus Christ, the Father of mercies and God of all comfort, 4 who comforts us in all our affliction, so that we may be able to comfort those who are in any affliction, with the comfort with which we ourselves are comforted by God. 5 For as we share abundantly in Christ's sufferings, so through Christ we share abundantly in comfort too.[a] 6 If we are afflicted, it is for your comfort and salvation; and if we are comforted, it is for your comfort, which you experience when you patiently endure the

1 Παῦλος ἀπόστολος Χριστοῦ Ἰησοῦ
Paul   an apostle   of Christ   Jesus
διὰ θελήματος θεοῦ καὶ Τιμόθεος ὁ
through [the] will of God and Timothy the
ἀδελφὸς τῇ ἐκκλησίᾳ τοῦ θεοῦ τῇ οὔσῃ
brother to the church   – of God – being
ἐν Κορίνθῳ σὺν τοῖς ἁγίοις πᾶσιν τοῖς
in Corinth with ²the ³saints ¹all
οὖσιν ἐν ὅλῃ τῇ Ἀχαΐᾳ· 2 χάρις ὑμῖν καὶ
being in all – Achaia: Grace to you and
εἰρήνη ἀπὸ θεοῦ πατρὸς ἡμῶν καὶ κυρίου
peace from God [the] Father of us and [the] Lord
Ἰησοῦ Χριστοῦ.
Jesus   Christ.

3 Εὐλογητὸς ὁ θεὸς καὶ πατὴρ .τοῦ
Blessed [be] the God and Father of the
κυρίου ἡμῶν Ἰησοῦ Χριστοῦ, ὁ πατὴρ
Lord of us Jesus Christ, the Father
τῶν οἰκτιρμῶν καὶ θεὸς πάσης παρακλή-
– of compassions and God of all com-
εως, 4 ὁ παρακαλῶν ἡμᾶς ἐπὶ πάσῃ
fort, the [one] comforting us on(in) all
τῇ θλίψει ἡμῶν, εἰς τὸ δύνασθαι ἡμᾶς
the affliction of us, [with a – to be able us[b]
view] to =our being able
παρακαλεῖν τοὺς ἐν πάσῃ θλίψει διὰ
to comfort the ones in every affliction through
τῆς παρακλήσεως ἧς παρακαλούμεθα αὐτοὶ
the comfort of(with) we are comforted [our-]
which selves
ὑπὸ τοῦ θεοῦ. 5 ὅτι καθὼς περισσεύει τὰ
by – God. Because as abounds the
παθήματα τοῦ Χριστοῦ εἰς ἡμᾶς, οὕτως
sufferings – of Christ in us, so
διὰ τοῦ Χριστοῦ περισσεύει καὶ ἡ παρά-
through – Christ abounds also the com-
κλησις ἡμῶν. 6 εἴτε δὲ θλιβόμεθα, ὑπὲρ
fort of us. Now whether we are on be-
afflicted, half of
τῆς ὑμῶν παρακλήσεως καὶ σωτηρίας· εἴτε
the ⁴of you ¹comfort ²and ³salvation: or
παρακαλούμεθα, ὑπὲρ τῆς ὑμῶν παρακλή-
we are comforted, on behalf of the ²of you ¹com-
σεως τῆς ἐνεργουμένης ἐν ὑπομονῇ τῶν
fort – operating in endurance of the

[a] Or, For as the suffering of Christ abound for us, so also our comfort abounds through Christ.

same sufferings that we suffer. [7] Our hope for you is unshaken; for we know that as you share in our sufferings, you will also share in our comfort.

[8] For we do not want you to be ignorant, brethren, of the affliction we experienced in Asia; for we were so utterly, unbearably crushed that we despaired of life itself. [9] Why, we felt that we had received the sentence of death; but that was to make us rely not on ourselves but on God who raises the dead; [10] he delivered us from so deadly a peril, and he will deliver us; on him we have set our hope that he will deliver us again. [11] You also must help us by prayer, so that many will give thanks on our behalf for the blessing granted us in answer to many prayers.

[12] For our boast is this, the testimony of our conscience that we have

αὐτῶν παθημάτων ὧν καὶ ἡμεῖς πάσχομεν,
same   sufferings   which also   we   suffer,

[7] καὶ ἡ ἐλπὶς ἡμῶν βεβαία ὑπὲρ ὑμῶν
and the hope   of us [is] firm on behalf of   you

εἰδότες ὅτι ὡς κοινωνοί ἐστε τῶν παθημά-
knowing that as partakers ye are of the   suffer-

των, οὕτως καὶ τῆς παρακλήσεως. [8] Οὐ
ings,   so   also of the   comfort.   not

γὰρ θέλομεν ὑμᾶς ἀγνοεῖν, ἀδελφοί, ὑπὲρ
For   we wish   you   to be ignorant, brothers,   as to

τῆς θλίψεως ἡμῶν τῆς γενομένης ἐν
the   affliction   of us   -   having been   in

τῇ Ἀσίᾳ, ὅτι καθ' ὑπερβολὴν ὑπὲρ
-   Asia,   that   excessively†   beyond

δύναμιν ἐβαρήθημεν, ὥστε ἐξαπορηθῆναι
power   we were burdened,   so as   to despair
                            =so that we despaired even

ἡμᾶς καὶ τοῦ ζῆν· [9] ἀλλὰ αὐτοὶ ἐν
us[b] even   -   to live;   but [our]selves   in
of life;

ἑαυτοῖς τὸ ἀπόκριμα τοῦ θανάτου ἐσχήκα-
ourselves the   sentence   -   of death   we have

μεν, ἵνα μὴ πεποιθότες ὦμεν ἐφ' ἑαυτοῖς
had, in order [2]not   [3]having   [1]we   on   ourselves
     that   trusted   might be

ἀλλ' ἐπὶ τῷ θεῷ τῷ ἐγείροντι τοὺς
but   on   -   God the [one]   raising   the

νεκρούς· [10] ὃς ἐκ τηλικούτου θανάτου
dead;   who out of   so great   a death

ἐρρύσατο ἡμᾶς καὶ ῥύσεται, εἰς ὃν
delivered   us   and   will deliver, in whom

ἠλπίκαμεν [ὅτι] καὶ ἔτι ῥύσεται, [11] συν-
we have hoped that   indeed   yet he will deliver,   co-

υπουργούντων καὶ ὑμῶν ὑπὲρ ἡμῶν τῇ
operating   also   you[a] on behalf of   us   -
=while ye also coöperate

δεήσει, ἵνα ἐκ πολλῶν προσώπων τὸ
in petition, in order [4]by   [5]many   [6]persons   [7][for]
      that   the

εἰς ἡμᾶς χάρισμα διὰ πολλῶν εὐχαριστηθῇ
[10]to [11]us   [8]gift [12]through [13]many   [1]thanks may
                                    be given

ὑπὲρ ἡμῶν.
[2]on behalf of   [3]us.

[12] Ἡ γὰρ καύχησις ἡμῶν αὕτη ἐστίν,
For the   boasting   of us   [2]this   [1]is,

τὸ μαρτύριον τῆς συνειδήσεως ἡμῶν, ὅτι
the testimony of the   conscience   of us, because

ἐν ἁγιότητι καὶ εἰλικρινείᾳ τοῦ θεοῦ,
in sanctity   and   sincerity   -   of God,

behaved in the world, and still more toward you, with holiness and godly sincerity, not by earthly wisdom but by the grace of God. ¹³For we write you nothing but what you can read and understand; I hope you will understand fully, ¹⁴as you have understood in part, that you can be proud of us as we can be of you, on the day of the Lord Jesus.

15 Because I was sure of this, I wanted to come to you first, so that you might have a double pleasure;[b] ¹⁶I wanted to visit you on my way to Macedo′nia, and to come back to you from Macedo′nia and have you send me on my way to Judea. ¹⁷Was I vacillating when I wanted to do this? Do I make my plans like a worldly man, ready to say Yes and No at once? ¹⁸As surely as God is faithful, our word to you has not been Yes and No. ¹⁹For the Son of God, Jesus Christ, whom we preached among you,

---

οὐκ ἐν σοφίᾳ σαρκικῇ ἀλλ' ἐν χάριτι
not in wisdom fleshly but in [the] grace

θεοῦ, ἀνεστράφημεν ἐν τῷ κόσμῳ, περισ-
of God, we behaved in the world, ²more

σοτέρως δὲ πρὸς ὑμᾶς. 13 οὐ γὰρ ἄλλα
³especially ¹and with you. ³Not ¹for ⁴other
things

γράφομεν ὑμῖν ἀλλ' ἢ ἃ ἀναγινώσκετε
¹we write to you other than what ye read

ἢ καὶ ἐπιγινώσκετε, ἐλπίζω δὲ ὅτι
or even perceive, and I hope that

ἕως τέλους ἐπιγνώσεσθε, 14 καθὼς καὶ
to [the] end ye will perceive, as also

ἐπέγνωτε ἡμᾶς ἀπὸ μέρους, ὅτι καύχημα
ye perceived us from(in) part, because ²boast

ὑμῶν ἐσμεν καθάπερ καὶ ὑμεῖς ἡμῶν
³of you ¹we are even as also ye of us

ἐν τῇ ἡμέρᾳ τοῦ κυρίου ἡμῶν Ἰησοῦ.
in the day of the Lord of us Jesus.

15 Καὶ ταύτῃ τῇ πεποιθήσει ἐβουλόμην
And in this — persuasion I determined

πρότερον πρὸς ὑμᾶς ἐλθεῖν ἵνα δευτέραν
formerly to you to come in order a second
that

χάριν σχῆτε, 16 καὶ δι' ὑμῶν διελθεῖν
grace ye might have, and through you to pass through

εἰς Μακεδονίαν, καὶ πάλιν ἀπὸ Μακεδονίας
into Macedonia, and again from Macedonia

ἐλθεῖν πρὸς ὑμᾶς καὶ ὑφ' ὑμῶν
to come to you and by you

προπεμφθῆναι εἰς τὴν Ἰουδαίαν. 17 τοῦτο
to be set forward to — Judæa. This

οὖν βουλόμενος μήτι ἄρα τῇ ἐλαφρίᾳ
therefore determining not ²then — ²fickleness

ἐχρησάμην; ἢ ἃ βουλεύομαι κατὰ σάρκα
¹did I use? or [the] I determine according [the]
things which to flesh

βουλεύομαι, ἵνα ᾖ παρ' ἐμοὶ τὸ ναὶ
do I determine, in order there with me the Yes
that may be

ναὶ καὶ τὸ οὒ οὔ; 18 πιστὸς δὲ ὁ
yes and the No no? But faithful [is] —

θεὸς ὅτι ὁ λόγος ἡμῶν ὁ πρὸς ὑμᾶς
God that the word of us — to you

οὐκ ἔστιν ναὶ καὶ οὔ. 19 ὁ τοῦ θεοῦ
is not yes and no. ³the — ⁴of God

γὰρ υἱὸς Χριστὸς Ἰησοῦς ὁ ἐν ὑμῖν
¹For ²Son Christ Jesus ¹the ³among ⁴you
[one]

Silva'nus and Timothy and I, was not Yes and No; but in him it is always Yes. ²⁰ For all the promises of God find their Yes in him. That is why we utter the Amen through him, to the glory of God. ²¹ But it is God who establishes us with you in Christ, and has commissioned us; ²² he has put his seal upon us and given us his Spirit in our hearts as a guarantee.

23 But I call God to witness against me—it was to spare you that I refrained from coming to Corinth. ²⁴ Not that we lord it over your faith; we work with you for your joy, for you stand firm in your faith.

CHAPTER 2

FOR I made up my mind not to make you another painful visit. ² For if I cause you pain, who is there to make me glad but the one whom I have pained? ³ And I wrote as I did, so that when I came I might not be pained by those who should have made me rejoice, for I felt sure of all of you, that my joy would be the joy of you

δι' ἡμῶν κηρυχθείς, δι' ἐμοῦ καὶ Σιλουανοῦ
⁴through ⁶us ⁵proclaimed, through me and Silvanus

καὶ Τιμοθέου, οὐκ ἐγένετο ναὶ καὶ οὔ,
and Timothy, was not yes and no,

ἀλλὰ ναὶ ἐν αὐτῷ γέγονεν. 20 ὅσαι γὰρ
but ²Yes ³in ⁴him ¹has been. For as many

ἐπαγγελίαι θεοῦ, ἐν αὐτῷ τὸ ναί· διὸ
[as are] of God, in him [is] the Yes; where-
promises   fore

καὶ δι' αὐτοῦ τὸ ἀμὴν τῷ θεῷ πρὸς
also through him the Amen — ¹to God ¹unto

δόξαν δι' ἡμῶν. 21 ὁ δὲ βεβαιῶν ἡμᾶς
²glory through us. But the [one] making firm us

σὺν ὑμῖν εἰς Χριστὸν καὶ χρίσας ἡμᾶς
with you in Christ and having anointed us [is]

θεός, 22 ὁ καὶ σφραγισάμενος ἡμᾶς καὶ
God, the [one] both having sealed us and

δοὺς τὸν ἀρραβῶνα τοῦ πνεύματος ἐν
having the earnest of the Spirit in
given

ταῖς καρδίαις ἡμῶν.
the hearts of us.

23 Ἐγὼ δὲ μάρτυρα τὸν θεὸν ἐπικαλοῦμαι
Now ⁴I ⁷[as] witness - ⁶God ⁵invoke

ἐπὶ τὴν ἐμὴν ψυχήν, ὅτι φειδόμενος
¹on - ²my ³life, that sparing

ὑμῶν οὐκέτι ἦλθον εἰς Κόρινθον. 24 οὐχ ὅτι
you ²no more ¹I came to Corinth. Not that

κυριεύομεν ὑμῶν τῆς πίστεως, ἀλλὰ συνεργοί
we rule over ³of you ¹the ²faith, but ²fellow-
                                              workers

ἐσμεν τῆς χαρᾶς ὑμῶν· τῇ γὰρ πίστει
¹we are of the joy of you; - for by faith

ἐστήκατε. 2 ἔκρινα δὲ ἐμαυτῷ τοῦτο, τὸ μὴ
ye stand. But I decided in myself this, - not

πάλιν ἐν λύπῃ πρὸς ὑμᾶς ἐλθεῖν. 2 εἰ
again ⁴in ⁵grief ³to ²you ¹to come. if

γὰρ ἐγὼ λυπῶ ὑμᾶς, καὶ τίς ὁ εὐφραίνων
For I grieve you, then who the making glad
                                           [one]

με εἰ μὴ ὁ λυπούμενος ἐξ ἐμοῦ; 3 καὶ
me except the [one] being grieved by me? And

ἔγραψα τοῦτο αὐτὸ ἵνα μὴ ἐλθὼν λύπην
I wrote this very thing lest coming grief

σχῶ ἀφ' ὧν ἔδει με χαίρειν, πεποιθὼς
I should from [those] it me to rejoice, having
have whom behoved confidence

ἐπὶ πάντας ὑμᾶς ὅτι ἡ ἐμὴ χαρὰ πάντων
in ²all ¹you that - my joy ²all

all. ⁴For I wrote you out of much affliction and anguish of heart and with many tears, not to cause you pain but to let you know the abundant love that I have for you.

5 But if any one has caused pain, he has caused it not to me, but in some measure—not to put it too severely—to you all. ⁶For such a one this punishment by the majority is enough; ⁷so you should rather turn to forgive and comfort him, or he may be overwhelmed by excessive sorrow. ⁸So I beg you to reaffirm your love for him. ⁹For this is why I wrote, that I might test you and know whether you are obedient in everything. ¹⁰Any one whom you forgive, I also forgive. What I have forgiven, if I have forgiven anything, has been for your sake in the presence of Christ, ¹¹to keep Satan from gaining the advantage over us; for we are not ignorant of his designs.

12 When I came to Tro′as to preach the gospel of Christ, a door was opened for me in the Lord; ¹³but my mind

ὑμῶν ἐστιν. 4 ἐκ γὰρ πολλῆς θλίψεως
²of you ¹is.   For out of   much   affliction

καὶ συνοχῆς καρδίας ἔγραψα ὑμῖν διὰ
and anxiety of heart I wrote to you through

πολλῶν δακρύων, οὐχ ἵνα λυπηθῆτε, ἀλλὰ
many   tears,   not in order ye should be but
                      that grieved,

τὴν ἀγάπην ἵνα γνῶτε ἣν ἔχω περισ-
²the ⁴love ¹in order ²ye should ⁵which I have more
             that know

σοτέρως εἰς ὑμᾶς. 5 Εἰ δέ τις λελύπηκεν,
abundantly to   you.   But if anyone has grieved,

οὐκ ἐμὲ λελύπηκεν, ἀλλὰ ἀπὸ μέρους,
not   me he has grieved, but from(in) part,

ἵνα μὴ ἐπιβαρῶ, πάντας ὑμᾶς. 6 ἱκανὸν
lest I am burdensome, ²all ¹you.   Enough

τῷ τοιούτῳ ἡ ἐπιτιμία αὕτη ἡ ὑπὸ
for such a one this punishment - by

τῶν πλειόνων, 7 ὥστε τοὐναντίον μᾶλλον
the majority,   so as on the contrary rather

ὑμᾶς χαρίσασθαι καὶ παρακαλέσαι, μή πως
you   to forgive   and to comfort,ᵇ   lest
=ye should rather forgive and comfort,

τῇ περισσοτέρᾳ λύπῃ καταποθῇ ὁ τοιοῦτος.
³by ⁴more abundant ⁵grief ²should be ¹such a one.
the   swallowed up

8 διὸ παρακαλῶ ὑμᾶς κυρῶσαι εἰς αὐτὸν
Wherefore I beseech you   to confirm to him

ἀγάπην· 9 εἰς τοῦτο γὰρ καὶ ἔγραψα,
[your] love; ²to ³this [end] ¹for indeed I wrote,

ἵνα γνῶ τὴν δοκιμὴν ὑμῶν, εἰ εἰς πάντα
in or- I might the proof   of you, if in all things
der that know

ὑπήκοοι ἐστε. 10 ᾧ δέ τι χαρίζεσθε,
obedient ye are.   Now to whom anything ye forgive,

κἀγώ· καὶ γὰρ ἐγὼ ὃ κεχάρισμαι, εἴ
I also;   for indeed ²I ¹what ²have forgiven, if

τι κεχάρισμαι, δι’ ὑμᾶς ἐν προσώπῳ
²any-   ¹I have [it is] on you   in [the] person
thing forgiven, account of

Χριστοῦ, 11 ἵνα μὴ πλεονεκτηθῶμεν ὑπὸ
of Christ,   lest we are taken advantage of by

τοῦ σατανᾶ· οὐ γὰρ αὐτοῦ τὰ νοήματα
-   Satan;   for ²not ⁴of him ³the ⁶designs

ἀγνοοῦμεν. 12 Ἐλθὼν δὲ εἰς τὴν Τρῳάδα εἰς
¹we ²are ⁴ignorant [of]. But coming to - Troas in

τὸ εὐαγγέλιον τοῦ Χριστοῦ, καὶ θύρας
the gospel   -   of Christ, and a door

μοι ἀνεῳγμένης ἐν κυρίῳ, 13 οὐκ ἔσχηκα
to me having been by [the] Lord,   I have had no
     openedᵃ

could not rest because I did not find my brother Titus there. So I took leave of them and went on to Macedo′nia.

14 But thanks be to God, who in Christ always leads us in triumph, and through us spreads the fragrance of the knowledge of him everywhere. [15]For we are the aroma of Christ to God among those who are being saved and among those who are perishing, [16]to one a fragrance from death to death, to the other a fragrance from life to life. Who is sufficient for these things? [17]For we are not, like so many, peddlers of God's word; but as men of sincerity, as commissioned by God, in the sight of God we speak in Christ.

ἄνεσιν τῷ πνεύματί μου τῷ μὴ εὑρεῖν
rest   to the   spirit   of me in the not   to find
                                          = when I did not find ...
με Τίτον τὸν ἀδελφόν μου, ἀλλὰ ἀποτα-
me[be] Titus the brother of me, but   saying
ξάμενος αὐτοῖς ἐξῆλθον εἰς Μακεδονίαν.
farewell to them I went forth into Macedonia.
14 Τῷ δὲ θεῷ χάρις τῷ πάντοτε
    -   But [2]to God [1]thanks the [one] always
θριαμβεύοντι ἡμᾶς ἐν τῷ Χριστῷ καὶ
leading in triumph us in - Christ and
τὴν ὀσμὴν τῆς γνώσεως αὐτοῦ φανεροῦντι
[4]the [5]odour [6]of the [7]knowledge [8]of him [1]manifesting
δι᾽ ἡμῶν ἐν παντὶ τόπῳ· 15 ὅτι Χριστοῦ
[2]through [3]us in every place; because of Christ
εὐωδία ἐσμὲν τῷ θεῷ ἐν τοῖς σωζομένοις
a sweet we are - to God in the [ones] being saved
smell
καὶ ἐν τοῖς ἀπολλυμένοις, 16 οἷς μέν
and in the [ones] perishing,   to the [latter]†
ὀσμὴ ἐκ θανάτου εἰς θάνατον, οἷς δὲ
an odour out of death unto death, to the [former]†
ὀσμὴ ἐκ ζωῆς εἰς ζωήν. καὶ πρὸς
an odour out of life unto life. And for
ταῦτα τίς ἱκανός; 17 οὐ γάρ ἐσμεν
these things who [is] competent? For we are not
ὡς οἱ πολλοὶ καπηλεύοντες τὸν λόγον
as the many   hawking   the word
τοῦ θεοῦ, ἀλλ᾽ ὡς ἐξ εἰλικρινείας, ἀλλ᾽
- of God, but as of sincerity, but
ὡς ἐκ θεοῦ κατέναντι θεοῦ ἐν Χριστῷ
as of God before God in Christ
λαλοῦμεν.
we speak.

CHAPTER 3

ARE we beginning to commend ourselves again? Or do we need, as some do, letters of recommendation to you, or from you? [2]You yourselves are our letter of recommendation, written on your[c] hearts, to be known and read by all men; [3]and you show that you are a letter

[c] Other ancient authorities read our

3 Ἀρχόμεθα πάλιν ἑαυτοὺς συνιστάνειν;
  Do we begin again ourselves to commend?
ἢ μὴ χρῄζομεν ὥς τινες συστατικῶν
or not need we as some commendatory
ἐπιστολῶν πρὸς ὑμᾶς ἢ ἐξ ὑμῶν; 2 ἡ
epistles to you or from you? The
ἐπιστολὴ ἡμῶν ὑμεῖς ἐστε, ἐγγεγραμμένη
epistle of us ye are, having been inscribed
ἐν ταῖς καρδίαις ἡμῶν, γινωσκομένη καὶ
in the hearts of us, being known and
ἀναγινωσκομένη ὑπὸ πάντων ἀνθρώπων,
being read by all men,
3 φανερούμενοι ὅτι ἐστὲ ἐπιστολὴ Χριστοῦ
being manifested that ye are an epistle of Christ

from Christ delivered by us, written not with ink but with the Spirit of the living God, not on tablets of stone but on tablets of human hearts. 4 Such is the confidence that we have through Christ toward God. [5] Not that we are sufficient of ourselves to claim anything as coming from us; our sufficiency is from God, [6] who has qualified us to be ministers of a new covenant, not in a written code but in the Spirit; for the written code kills, but the Spirit gives life.

7 Now if the dispensation of death, carved in letters on stone, came with such splendor that the Israelites could not look at Moses' face because of its brightness, fading as this was, [8] will not the dispensation of the Spirit be attended with greater splendor? [9] For if there was splendor in the dispensation of condemnation, the dispensation of righteousness must far exceed it in splendor. [10] Indeed, in this case, what once had splendor has come to have no splendor at all, because of the splen-

διακονηθεῖσα ὑφ' ἡμῶν, ἐγγεγραμμένη οὐ
ministered   by   us,   *having been* inscribed   not
μέλανι ἀλλὰ πνεύματι θεοῦ ζῶντος, οὐκ
by ink   but   by [the] Spirit   of [2]God   [1]a living,   not
ἐν πλαξὶν λιθίναις ἀλλ' ἐν πλαξὶν καρδίαις
in   [2]tablets   [1]stony   but   in   tablets   [which are]
σαρκίναις.
[2]hearts
[1]fleshy.

4 Πεποίθησιν δὲ τοιαύτην ἔχομεν διὰ
  [2]confidence   [1]And   [3]such   we have through
τοῦ Χριστοῦ πρὸς τὸν θεόν.   5 οὐχ
  -   Christ   toward   -   God.   Not
ὅτι ἀφ' ἑαυτῶν ἱκανοί ἐσμεν λογίσασθαί
that   [3]from   [4]ourselves [2]competent   [1]we are   to reckon
τι ὡς ἐξ ἑαυτῶν, ἀλλ' ἡ ἱκανότης
any-thing   as   of   ourselves,   but   the   competence
ἡμῶν ἐκ τοῦ θεοῦ, 6 ὃς καὶ ἱκάνωσεν
of us [is]   of   -   God,   who also made competent
ἡμᾶς διακόνους καινῆς διαθήκης, οὐ
us   [as] ministers   of a new   covenant,   not
γράμματος ἀλλὰ πνεύματος· τὸ γὰρ γράμμα
of letter   but   of spirit;   for the   letter
ἀποκτείνει, τὸ δὲ πνεῦμα ζωοποιεῖ. 7 Εἰ
kills,   but the   spirit   makes alive.   if
δὲ ἡ διακονία τοῦ θανάτου ἐν γράμμασιν
Now the   ministry   -   of death   in   letters
ἐντετυπωμένη λίθοις ἐγενήθη ἐν δόξῃ,
having been engraved in stones   was   in   glory,
ὥστε μὴ δύνασθαι ἀτενίσαι τοὺς υἱοὺς
so as   not   to be able   to gaze   the   sons
=so that the sons of Israel were not able to gaze
Ἰσραὴλ εἰς τὸ πρόσωπον Μωϋσέως διὰ
of Israel[b]   at   the   face   of Moses on account of
τὴν δόξαν τοῦ προσώπου αὐτοῦ τὴν
the   glory   of the   face   of him   -
καταργουμένην, 8 πῶς οὐχὶ μᾶλλον ἡ
being done away,   how   [2]not   [3]rather   [4]the
διακονία τοῦ πνεύματος ἔσται ἐν δόξῃ;
[5]ministry   [6]of the   [7]Spirit   [1]will [8]be   in   glory?
9 εἰ γὰρ ἡ διακονία τῆς κατακρίσεως
For if   the   ministry   -   of condemnation
δόξα, πολλῷ μᾶλλον περισσεύει ἡ διακονία
[was]   by much   rather   [4]abounds   [1]the   [2]ministry
glory,
τῆς δικαιοσύνης δόξῃ. 10 καὶ γὰρ οὐ
-   [3]of righteousness   in glory.   For indeed   [2]not
δεδόξασται τὸ δεδοξασμένον ἐν τούτῳ
[4]has been   [1]the   [2]having been   in   this
glorified   [thing]   glorified

dor that surpasses it.
¹¹For if what faded
away came with splendor,
what is permanent must
have much more splen-
dor.
12 Since we have such
a hope, we are very bold,
¹³not like Moses, who
put a veil over his face
so that the Israelites
might not see the end of
the fading splendor. ¹⁴But
their minds were hard-
ened; for to this day,
when they read the old
covenant, that same veil
remains unlifted, because
only through Christ is it
taken away. ¹⁵Yes, to
this day whenever Moses
is read a veil lies over
their minds; ¹⁶but when
a man turns to the Lord
the veil is removed.
¹⁷Now the Lord is the
Spirit, and where the
Spirit of the Lord is,
there is freedom. ¹⁸And
we all, with unveiled face,
beholding[d] the glory of
the Lord, are being
changed into his likeness
from one degree of glory
to another; for this
comes from the Lord
who is the Spirit.

τῷ μέρει εἵνεκεν τῆς ὑπερβαλλούσης δόξης.
respect for the / the / excelling / glory.
sake of

11 εἰ γὰρ τὸ καταργούμενον διὰ δόξης,
For if / the / being done away / [was] / glory,
[thing] / through

πολλῷ μᾶλλον τὸ μένον ἐν δόξῃ.
by much / more / the [thing] remaining / [is] in / glory.

12 Ἔχοντες οὖν τοιαύτην ἐλπίδα πολλῇ
Having / therefore / such / hope / ²much

παρρησίᾳ χρώμεθα, 13 καὶ οὐ καθάπερ
³boldness / ¹we use, / and / not / as

Μωϋσῆς ἐτίθει κάλυμμα ἐπὶ τὸ πρόσωπον
Moses / put / a veil / on / the / face

αὐτοῦ, πρὸς τὸ μὴ ἀτενίσαι τοὺς υἱοὺς
of him, / for / the / ⁴not / ⁵to gaze / ¹the / ²sons

Ἰσραὴλ εἰς τὸ τέλος τοῦ καταργουμένου.
³of israel[b] / at / the / end / of the [thing] being done away.

14 ἀλλὰ ἐπωρώθη τὰ νοήματα αὐτῶν.
But / were hardened / the / thoughts / of them.

ἄχρι γὰρ τῆς σήμερον ἡμέρας τὸ αὐτὸ
For until / the / present / day / the / same

κάλυμμα ἐπὶ τῇ ἀναγνώσει τῆς παλαιᾶς
veil / ²on(at) / ³the / ⁴reading / ⁵of the / ⁶old

διαθήκης μένει, μὴ ἀνακαλυπτόμενον ὅτι
⁷covenant / ¹remains, / not / being unveiled* / that

ἐν Χριστῷ καταργεῖται. 15 ἀλλ᾽ ἕως
in / Christ / it is being done away. / But / until

σήμερον ἡνίκα ἂν ἀναγινώσκηται Μωϋσῆς
to-day / whenever / ²is being read / ¹Moses

κάλυμμα ἐπὶ τὴν καρδίαν αὐτῶν κεῖται·
a veil / ²on / ³the / ⁴heart / ⁵of them / ¹lies;

16 ἡνίκα δὲ ἐὰν ἐπιστρέψῃ πρὸς κύριον,
but whenever / it§ turns / to / [the] Lord,

περιαιρεῖται τὸ κάλυμμα. 17 ὁ δὲ κύριος
²is taken away / ¹the / ²veil. / Now the / Lord

τὸ πνεῦμά ἐστιν· οὗ δὲ τὸ πνεῦμα
²the / ³Spirit / ¹is; / and where / the / Spirit

κυρίου, ἐλευθερία. 18 ἡμεῖς δὲ πάντες
of [the] / [there is] freedom. / But we / all
Lord [is],

ἀνακεκαλυμμένῳ προσώπῳ τὴν δόξαν
¹having been unveiled / ⁴with face / ²the / ³glory

κυρίου κατοπτριζόμενοι τὴν αὐτὴν εἰκόνα
⁴of [the] / ¹beholding in / ⁶the / ⁷same / ⁸image
Lord / a mirror

μεταμορφούμεθα ἀπὸ δόξης εἰς δόξαν,
⁵are being changed [into] / from / glory / to / glory,

καθάπερ ἀπὸ κυρίου πνεύματος.
even as / from [the] Lord / Spirit.

---

[d] Or reflecting

* That is, revealed (Conybeare and Howson). § ? their heart.

CHAPTER 4

THEREFORE, having this ministry by the mercy of God, we do not lose heart. ²We have renounced disgraceful, underhanded ways; we refuse to practice cunning or to tamper with God's word, but by the open statement of the truth we would commend ourselves to every man's conscience in the sight of God. ³And even if our gospel is veiled, it is veiled only to those who are perishing. ⁴In their case the god of this world has blinded the minds of the unbelievers, to keep them from seeing the light of the gospel of the glory of Christ, who is the likeness of God. ⁵For what we preach is not ourselves, but Jesus Christ as Lord, with ourselves as your servants for Jesus' sake. ⁶For it is the God who said, "Let light shine out of darkness," who has shone in our hearts to give the light of the knowledge of the glory of God in the face of Christ.

7 But we have this treasure in earthen vessels, to show that the

---

4 Διὰ τοῦτο, ἔχοντες τὴν διακονίαν
Therefore, having - ministry

ταύτην, καθὼς ἠλεήθημεν, οὐκ ἐγκακοῦμεν,
this, as we obtained mercy, we faint not,

2 ἀλλὰ ἀπειπάμεθα τὰ κρυπτὰ τῆς αἰσχύνης,
but we have renounced the hidden things - of shame,

μὴ περιπατοῦντες ἐν πανουργίᾳ μηδὲ
not walking in craftiness nor

δολοῦντες τὸν λόγον τοῦ θεοῦ, ἀλλὰ
adulterating the word - of God, but

τῇ φανερώσει τῆς ἀληθείας συνιστάνοντες
by the manifestation of the truth commending

ἑαυτοὺς πρὸς πᾶσαν συνείδησιν ἀνθρώπων
ourselves to every conscience of men

ἐνώπιον τοῦ θεοῦ. 3 εἰ δὲ καὶ ἔστιν
before - God. But if indeed ⁴is

κεκαλυμμένον τὸ εὐαγγέλιον ἡμῶν, ἐν
⁵having been hidden ¹the ²gospel ³of us, in

τοῖς ἀπολλυμένοις ἐστὶν κεκαλυμμένον, 4 ἐν
the [ones] perishing it is having been hidden, in

οἷς ὁ θεὸς τοῦ αἰῶνος τούτου ἐτύφλωσεν
whom the god of this age blinded

τὰ νοήματα τῶν ἀπίστων εἰς τὸ μὴ
the thoughts of the unbelieving [with a the not
[ones] view] to
=so that the enlightenment . . . should not shine forth,

αὐγάσαι τὸν φωτισμὸν τοῦ εὐαγγελίου
to shine forth the enlightenment of the gospel

τῆς δόξης τοῦ Χριστοῦ, ὅς ἐστιν εἰκὼν
of the glory - of Christ, who is [the] image

τοῦ θεοῦ. 5 οὐ γὰρ ἑαυτοὺς κηρύσσομεν
- of God. For ²not ³ourselves ¹we proclaim

ἀλλὰ Χριστὸν Ἰησοῦν κύριον, ἑαυτοὺς δὲ
but Christ Jesus [as] Lord, and ourselves

δούλους ὑμῶν διὰ Ἰησοῦν. 6 ὅτι ὁ
slaves of you on account of Jesus. Because -

θεὸς ὁ εἰπών· ἐκ σκότους φῶς λάμψει,
God the [one] saying: Out of darkness light shall shine,

ὃς ἔλαμψεν ἐν ταῖς καρδίαις ἡμῶν πρὸς
[is] [he] shone in the hearts of us for
who

φωτισμὸν τῆς γνώσεως τῆς δόξης τοῦ
enlightenment of the knowledge of the glory -

θεοῦ ἐν προσώπῳ Χριστοῦ.
of God in [the] face of Christ.

7 Ἔχομεν δὲ τὸν θησαυρὸν τοῦτον ἐν
And we have this treasure in

ὀστρακίνοις σκεύεσιν, ἵνα ἡ ὑπερβολὴ
earthenware vessels, in order that the excellence

transcendent power belongs to God and not to us. [8]We are afflicted in every way, but not crushed; perplexed, but not driven to despair; [9]persecuted, but not forsaken; struck down, but not destroyed; [10]always carrying in the body the death of Jesus, so that the life of Jesus may also be manifested in our bodies. [11]For while we live we are always being given up to death for Jesus' sake, so that the life of Jesus may be manifested in our mortal flesh. [12]So death is at work in us, but life in you.

13 Since we have the same spirit of faith as he had who wrote, "I believed, and so I spoke," we too believe, and so we speak, [14]knowing that he who raised the Lord Jesus will raise us also with Jesus and bring us with you into his presence. [15]For it is all for your sake, so that as grace extends to more

τῆς δυνάμεως ᾖ τοῦ θεοῦ καὶ μὴ ἐξ
of the power may be – of God and not of

ἡμῶν· 8 ἐν παντὶ θλιβόμενοι ἀλλ' οὐ
us; in every [way] being afflicted but not

στενοχωρούμενοι, ἀπορούμενοι ἀλλ' οὐκ
being restrained, being in difficulties but not

ἐξαπορούμενοι, 9 διωκόμενοι ἀλλ' οὐκ
despairing, being persecuted but not

ἐγκαταλειπόμενοι, καταβαλλόμενοι ἀλλ' οὐκ
being deserted, being cast down but not

ἀπολλύμενοι, 10 πάντοτε τὴν νέκρωσιν τοῦ
perishing, always ⁵the ⁶dying –

'Ιησοῦ ἐν τῷ σώματι περιφέροντες, ἵνα
⁷of Jesus ²in ³the ⁴body ¹bearing about, in order that

καὶ ἡ ζωὴ τοῦ 'Ιησοῦ ἐν τῷ σώματι
also the life – of Jesus in the body

ἡμῶν φανερωθῇ. 11 ἀεὶ γὰρ ἡμεῖς οἱ
of us might be manifested. For always we the

ζῶντες εἰς θάνατον παραδιδόμεθα διὰ
[ones] living to death are being on ac-
delivered count of

'Ιησοῦν, ἵνα καὶ ἡ ζωὴ τοῦ 'Ιησοῦ
Jesus, in order that also the life – of Jesus

φανερωθῇ ἐν τῇ θνητῇ σαρκὶ ἡμῶν.
might be in the mortal flesh of us.
manifested

12 ὥστε ὁ θάνατος ἐν ἡμῖν ἐνεργεῖται,
So as – death in us operates,

ἡ δὲ ζωὴ ἐν ὑμῖν. 13 ἔχοντες δὲ τὸ
– but life in you. And having the

αὐτὸ πνεῦμα τῆς πίστεως, κατὰ τὸ
same spirit – of faith, according to the thing

γεγραμμένον· ἐπίστευσα, διὸ ἐλάλησα, καὶ
having been written: I believed, therefore I spoke, both

ἡμεῖς πιστεύομεν, διὸ καὶ λαλοῦμεν, 14 εἰδότες
we believe, and therefore we speak, knowing

ὅτι ὁ ἐγείρας τὸν κύριον 'Ιησοῦν καὶ
that the having the Lord Jesus ²also
[one] raised

ἡμᾶς σὺν 'Ιησοῦ ἐγερεῖ καὶ παραστήσει
³us ⁴with ⁵Jesus ¹will raise and will present [us]

σὺν ὑμῖν. 15 τὰ γὰρ πάντα δι' ὑμᾶς,
with you. – For all things [are] on ac- you,
count of

ἵνα ἡ χάρις πλεονάσασα διὰ τῶν πλειόνων
in or- – grace increased through the majority
der that

and more people it may increase thanksgiving, to the glory of God.

16 So we do not lose heart. Though our outer nature is wasting away, our inner nature is being renewed every day. [17] For this slight momentary affliction is preparing for us an eternal weight of glory beyond all comparison, [18] because we look not to the things that are seen but to the things that are unseen; for the things that are seen are transient, but the things that are unseen are eternal.

τὴν εὐχαριστίαν περισσεύσῃ εἰς τὴν δόξαν
²the   ³thanksgiving ¹may cause to abound to   the   glory

τοῦ θεοῦ. 16 Διὸ οὐκ ἐγκακοῦμεν, ἀλλ᾽
– of God.   Wherefore   we faint not,   but

εἰ καὶ ὁ ἔξω ἡμῶν ἄνθρωπος διαφθείρεται,
if indeed the outward ²of us ¹man   is being disabled,

ἀλλ᾽ ὁ ἔσω ἡμῶν ἀνακαινοῦται ἡμέρᾳ
yet the inward [man] of us is being renewed   day

καὶ ἡμέρᾳ. 17 τὸ γὰρ παραυτίκα ἐλαφρὸν
and (by) day.   For the   present   lightness

τῆς θλίψεως καθ᾽ ὑπερβολὴν εἰς ὑπερβολὴν
of the affliction ²excessively   ⁴to   ³excess

αἰώνιον βάρος δόξης κατεργάζεται ἡμῖν,
⁶an eternal ⁷weight ⁸of glory ¹works   ⁵for us,

18 μὴ σκοπούντων ἡμῶν τὰ βλεπόμενα
   not   considering   us³ the things being seen
= while we do not consider

ἀλλὰ τὰ μὴ βλεπόμενα· τὰ γὰρ βλεπόμενα
but   the not being seen; for the things being seen
         things

πρόσκαιρα, τὰ δὲ μὴ βλεπόμενα αἰώνια.
[are] temporary, but the things not   being seen [are] eternal.

CHAPTER 5

FOR we know that if the earthly tent we live in is destroyed, we have a building from God, a house not made with hands, eternal in the heavens. [2] Here indeed we groan, and long to put on our heavenly dwelling, [3] so that by putting it on we may not be found naked. [4] For while we are still in this tent, we sigh with anxiety; not that we would be unclothed, but that we would be further clothed, so that what is mortal may be swallowed up by life. [5] He who has

5 Οἴδαμεν γὰρ ὅτι ἐὰν ἡ ἐπίγειος
  For we know   that   if the earthly

ἡμῶν οἰκία τοῦ σκήνους καταλυθῇ,
⁴of us ¹house ²of the ³tabernacle is destroyed,

οἰκοδομὴν ἐκ θεοῦ ἔχομεν, οἰκίαν ἀχειρο-
a building   of God we have, a house not made

ποίητον αἰώνιον ἐν τοῖς οὐρανοῖς. 2 καὶ
by hands eternal in the heavens.   indeed

γὰρ ἐν τούτῳ στενάζομεν, τὸ οἰκητήριον
For in this⁵   we groan, ³the ⁴dwelling-place

ἡμῶν τὸ ἐξ οὐρανοῦ ἐπενδύσασθαι ἐπιπο-
⁵of us – ⁶out of ⁷heaven   ⁸to put on   ¹greatly

θοῦντες, 3 εἴ γε καὶ ἐνδυσάμενοι οὐ
desiring,   if indeed   being clothed   not

γυμνοὶ εὑρεθησόμεθα. 4 καὶ γὰρ οἱ
naked   we shall be found.   For indeed ²the
                                         [ones]

ὄντες ἐν τῷ σκήνει στενάζομεν βαρούμενοι,
³being ⁴in ⁵the ⁶tabernacle ¹we groan being burdened,

ἐφ᾽ ᾧ οὐ θέλομεν ἐκδύσασθαι ἀλλ᾽
inasmuch as we do not wish   to put off   but

ἐπενδύσασθαι, ἵνα καταποθῇ τὸ θνητὸν
to put on,   in order ²may be ¹the ²mortal
              that   swallowed up

ὑπὸ τῆς ζωῆς. 5 ὁ δὲ κατεργασάμενος
by the life.   Now the [one] having wrought

* Neuter, going back to σκῆνος in the preceding verse.

prepared us for this very thing is God, who has given us the Spirit as a guarantee.

6 So we are always of good courage; we know that while we are at home in the body we are away from the Lord, [7] for we walk by faith, not by sight. [8] We are of good courage, and we would rather be away from the body and at home with the Lord. [9] So whether we are at home or away, we make it our aim to please him. [10] For we must all appear before the judgment seat of Christ, so that each one may receive good or evil, according to what he has done in the body.

11 Therefore, knowing the fear of the Lord, we persuade men; but what we are is known to God, and I hope it is known also to your conscience. [12] We are not commending ourselves to you again but giving you cause to be proud of us, so that you may be able

ἡμᾶς εἰς αὐτὸ τοῦτο θεός, ὁ δοὺς
us for this very thing [is] the having God, [one] given

ἡμῖν τὸν ἀρραβῶνα τοῦ πνεύματος. 6 Θαρ-
to us the earnest of the Spirit. Being

ροῦντες οὖν πάντοτε καὶ εἰδότες ὅτι
of good therefore always and knowing that
cheer

ἐνδημοῦντες ἐν τῷ σώματι ἐκδημοῦμεν
being at home in the body we are away
from home

ἀπὸ τοῦ κυρίου· 7 διὰ πίστεως γὰρ
from the Lord; [3]through [2]faith [1]for

περιπατοῦμεν, οὐ διὰ εἴδους· 8 θαρροῦμεν
we walk, not through appearance; we are of
good cheer

δὲ καὶ εὐδοκοῦμεν μᾶλλον ἐκδημῆσαι ἐκ
then and think it good rather to go away out
from home of

τοῦ σώματος καὶ ἐνδημῆσαι πρὸς τὸν
the body and to come home to the

κύριον. 9 διὸ καὶ φιλοτιμούμεθα, εἴτε
Lord. Wherefore also we are ambitious, whether

ἐνδημοῦντες εἴτε ἐκδημοῦντες, εὐάρεστοι
being at home or being away from home, wellpleasing

αὐτῷ εἶναι. 10 τοὺς γὰρ πάντας ἡμᾶς
to him to be. For [3]all [2]us

φανερωθῆναι δεῖ ἔμπροσθεν τοῦ βήματος
[4]to be manifested [1]it behoves before the tribunal

τοῦ Χριστοῦ, ἵνα κομίσηται ἕκαστος τὰ
- of Christ, in order [2]may receive [1]each one the
that things

διὰ τοῦ σώματος πρὸς ἃ ἔπραξεν, εἴτε
through the body accord- what he either
ing to things practised,

ἀγαθὸν εἴτε φαῦλον.
good or worthless.

11 Εἰδότες οὖν τὸν φόβον τοῦ κυρίου
Knowing therefore the fear of the Lord

ἀνθρώπους πείθομεν, θεῷ δὲ πεφανερώμεθα·
[2]men [1]we persuade, and to God we have been made
manifest;

ἐλπίζω δὲ καὶ ἐν ταῖς συνειδήσεσιν
and I hope also in the consciences

ὑμῶν πεφανερῶσθαι. 12 οὐ πάλιν ἑαυτοὺς
of you to have been made Not again [2]ourselves
manifest.

συνιστάνομεν ὑμῖν, ἀλλὰ ἀφορμὴν διδόντες
[1]we commend to you, but [2]an occasion [1]giving

ὑμῖν καυχήματος ὑπὲρ ἡμῶν, ἵνα ἔχητε
[2]to you of a boast on be- us, in order ye may
half of that have [it]

to answer those who pride themselves on a man's position and not on his heart. [13]For if we are beside ourselves, it is for God; if we are in our right mind, it is for you. [14]For the love of Christ controls us, because we are convinced that one has died for all; therefore all have died. [15]And he died for all, that those who live might live no longer for themselves but for him who for their sake died and was raised.

16 From now on, therefore, we regard no one from a human point of view; even though we once regarded Christ from a human point of view, we regard him thus no longer. [17]Therefore, if any one is in Christ, he is a new creation;[e] the old has passed away, behold, the new has come. [18]All this is from God, who through Christ reconciled us to himself and gave us the ministry of reconciliation; [19]that is, God was in Christ reconciling[f] the world to himself, not counting their trespasses against them, and entrusting to us the message of reconciliation. [20]So we are ambassadors for Christ,

πρὸς τοὺς ἐν προσώπῳ καυχωμένους καὶ
in refer- the   ²in   ³face   ¹boasting   and
ence to   [ones]

μὴ ἐν καρδίᾳ.   13 εἴτε γὰρ ἐξέστημεν,
not in   heart.   For whether we are mad,

θεῷ· εἴτε σωφρονοῦμεν. ὑμῖν.   14 ἡ γὰρ
[it is] or   we are in our senses, [it is]   For the
to God;   for you.

ἀγάπη τοῦ Χριστοῦ συνέχει ἡμᾶς, κρίναντας
love   -   of Christ constrains us,   judging

τοῦτο, ὅτι εἷς ὑπὲρ πάντων ἀπέθανεν·
this,   that one on behalf of all men   died;

ἄρα οἱ πάντες ἀπέθανον· 15 καὶ ὑπὲρ
then the   all   died;   and ²on be-
                                          half of

πάντων ἀπέθανεν ἵνα οἱ ζῶντες μηκέτι
³all   ¹he died in order the living no more
                          that [ones]

ἑαυτοῖς ζῶσιν ἀλλὰ τῷ ὑπὲρ αὐτῶν
to themselves may live but to the on behalf them
                                [one]

ἀποθανόντι καὶ ἐγερθέντι. 16 Ὥστε ἡμεῖς
having died   and having been raised. So as   ²we

ἀπὸ τοῦ νῦν οὐδένα οἴδαμεν κατὰ σάρκα·
¹from -   ²now ³no man ⁴know according to flesh;

εἰ καὶ ἐγνώκαμεν κατὰ σάρκα Χριστόν,
if indeed ¹we have known ²according to ³flesh   ²Christ,

ἀλλὰ νῦν οὐκέτι γινώσκομεν.   17 ὥστε
yet   now no more we know [him].   So as

εἴ τις ἐν Χριστῷ, καινὴ κτίσις· τὰ
if anyone [is] in Christ, [he is] a new creation; the

ἀρχαῖα παρῆλθεν, ἰδοὺ γέγονεν καινά.
old things passed away, behold they have become new.

18 τὰ δὲ πάντα ἐκ τοῦ θεοῦ τοῦ καταλ-
   - And all things [are] of - God the [one] having

λάξαντος ἡμᾶς ἑαυτῷ διὰ Χριστοῦ καὶ
reconciled   us   to himself through Christ   and

δόντος ἡμῖν τὴν διακονίαν τῆς καταλλαγῆς,
having given to us the   ministry   -   of reconciliation.

19 ὡς ὅτι θεὸς ἦν ἐν Χριστῷ κόσμον
   as that God was in Christ ²[the] world

καταλλάσσων ἑαυτῷ, μὴ λογιζόμενος αὐτοῖς
¹reconciling   to himself, not   reckoning   to them

τὰ παραπτώματα αὐτῶν, καὶ θέμενος
the   trespasses   of them, and   placing

ἐν ἡμῖν τὸν λόγον τῆς καταλλαγῆς.
in   us   the   word   -   of reconciliation.

20 Ὑπὲρ Χριστοῦ οὖν πρεσβεύομεν ὡς
On behalf of Christ therefore we are ambassadors as

---

[e] Or *creature*
[f] Or *in Christ God was reconciling*

God making his appeal through us. We beseech you on behalf of Christ, be reconciled to God. [21] For our sake he made him to be sin who knew no sin, so that in him we might become the righteousness of God.

τοῦ θεοῦ παρακαλοῦντος δι' ἡμῶν· δεόμεθα
- God beseeching[a] through us; we beg
ὑπὲρ Χριστοῦ, καταλλάγητε τῷ θεῷ.
on behalf of Christ, Be ye reconciled – to God.
21 τὸν μὴ γνόντα ἁμαρτίαν ὑπὲρ ἡμῶν
[a]The [one] [3]not [4]knowing [5]sin [7]on behalf of [8]us
ἁμαρτίαν ἐποίησεν, ἵνα ἡμεῖς γενώμεθα
[5]sin [1]he made, in order that we might become
δικαιοσύνη θεοῦ ἐν αὐτῷ.
[the] righteousness of God in him.

CHAPTER 6

WORKING together with him, then, we entreat you not to accept the grace of God in vain. [2] For he says,

"At the acceptable time I have listened to you,
and helped you on the day of salvation."

Behold, now is the acceptable time; behold, now is the day of salvation. [3] We put no obstacle in any one's way, so that no fault may be found with our ministry, [4] but as servants of God we commend ourselves in every way: through great endurance, in afflictions, hardships, calamities, [5] beatings, imprisonments, tumults, labors, watching, hunger; [6] by purity, knowledge, forbearance, kindness, the Holy Spirit, genuine love, [7] truthful speech, and the power of God; with the weapons of righteousness for the right hand and for the left; [8] in honor and dis-

6 Συνεργοῦντες δὲ καὶ παρακαλοῦμεν μὴ
And working together also we beseech [2]not
εἰς κενὸν τὴν χάριν τοῦ θεοῦ δέξασθαι
[1]to no purpose [4]the [5]grace – [6]of God [3]to receive
ὑμᾶς· 2 λέγει γάρ· καιρῷ δεκτῷ ἐπήκουσά
[1]you; for he says: In a time acceptable I heard
σου καὶ ἐν ἡμέρᾳ σωτηρίας ἐβοήθησά
thee and in a day of salvation I helped
σοι· ἰδοὺ νῦν καιρὸς εὐπρόσδεκτος, ἰδοὺ
thee; behold now a time acceptable, behold
νῦν ἡμέρα σωτηρίας· 3 — μηδεμίαν ἐν
now a day of salvation; [2]no [4]in
μηδενὶ διδόντες προσκοπήν, ἵνα μὴ
[2]no(any)thing [1]giving [3]cause of stumbling, lest
μωμηθῇ ἡ διακονία, 4 ἀλλ' ἐν παντὶ
[2]be blamed [1]the [2]ministry, but in everything
συνιστάνοντες ἑαυτοὺς ὡς θεοῦ διάκονοι,
commending ourselves as [2]of God [1]ministers,
ἐν ὑπομονῇ πολλῇ, ἐν θλίψεσιν, ἐν
in [2]endurance [1]much, in afflictions, in
ἀνάγκαις, ἐν στενοχωρίαις, ἐν πληγαῖς,
necessities, in straits, in stripes,
5 ἐν φυλακαῖς, ἐν ἀκαταστασίαις, ἐν κόποις,
in prisons, in commotions, in labours,
ἐν ἀγρυπνίαις, ἐν νηστείαις, 6 ἐν ἁγνότητι,
in watchings, in fastings, in purity,
ἐν γνώσει, ἐν μακροθυμίᾳ, ἐν χρηστότητι,
in knowledge, in long-suffering, in kindness,
ἐν πνεύματι ἁγίῳ, ἐν ἀγάπῃ ἀνυποκρίτῳ,
in spirit a holy, in love unfeigned,
7 ἐν λόγῳ ἀληθείας, ἐν δυνάμει θεοῦ·
in a word of truth, in power of God;
διὰ τῶν ὅπλων τῆς δικαιοσύνης τῶν
through the weapons – of righteousness of the
δεξιῶν καὶ ἀριστερῶν, 8 διὰ δόξης καὶ
right [hand] and of left, through glory and

honor, in ill repute and good repute. We are treated as impostors, and yet are true; [9] as unknown, and yet well known; as dying, and behold we live; as punished, and yet not killed; [10] as sorrowful, yet always rejoicing; as poor, yet making many rich; as having nothing, and yet possessing everything.

11 Our mouth is open to you, Corinthians; our heart is wide. [12] You are not restricted by us, but you are restricted in your own affections. [13] In return—I speak as to children—widen your hearts also.

14 Do not be mismated with unbelievers. For what partnership have righteousness and iniquity? Or what fellowship has light with darkness? [15] What accord has Christ with Be'lial? Or what has a believer in common with an unbeliever? [16] What agreement has the temple of God with idols? For we are the temple of the living God; as God said, "I will live in them and move among

---

ἀτιμίας,   διὰ   δυσφημίας   καὶ   εὐφημίας·
dishonour,   through   ill report   and   good report;

ὡς   πλάνοι   καὶ   ἀληθεῖς,   9   ὡς   ἀγνοούμενοι
as   deceivers   and*   true men,   as   being unknown

καὶ   ἐπιγινωσκόμενοι,   ὡς   ἀποθνῄσκοντες   καὶ
and*   being well known,   as   dying   and

ἰδοὺ   ζῶμεν,   ὡς   παιδευόμενοι   καὶ   μὴ
behold   we live,   as   being chastened   and   not

θανατούμενοι,   10 ὡς   λυπούμενοι   ἀεὶ   δὲ
being put to death,   as   being grieved   [2]always [1]but

χαίροντες,   ὡς   πτωχοὶ   πολλοὺς   δὲ   πλουτίζ-
rejoicing,   as   poor   [2]many   [1]but   [1]en-

οντες,   ὡς   μηδὲν   ἔχοντες   καὶ   πάντα
riching,   as   [2]nothing   [1]having   [3]and*   [4]all things

κατέχοντες.
[4]possessing.

11 Τὸ   στόμα   ἡμῶν   ἀνέῳγεν   πρὸς   ὑμᾶς,
The   mouth   of us   has opened   to   you,

Κορίνθιοι,   ἡ   καρδία   ἡμῶν   πεπλάτυνται·
Corinthians,   the   heart   of us   has been enlarged;

12 οὐ   στενοχωρεῖσθε   ἐν   ἡμῖν,   στενοχωρεῖσθε
ye are not restrained   in   us,   [2]ye are restrained

δὲ   ἐν   τοῖς   σπλάγχνοις   ὑμῶν·   13 τὴν   δὲ
[1]but   in   the   bowels   of you;   but [for] the

αὐτὴν   ἀντιμισθίαν,   ὡς   τέκνοις   λέγω,
same   recompence,   as   to children   I say,

πλατύνθητε   καὶ   ὑμεῖς.
be enlarged   also   ye.

14 Μὴ   γίνεσθε   ἑτεροζυγοῦντες   ἀπίστοις·
Do not ye become   unequally yoked [with] unbelievers;

τίς   γὰρ   μετοχὴ   δικαιοσύνῃ   καὶ   ἀνομίᾳ,
for what   share   righteousness[c]   and   lawlessness,[c]
          = have righteousness and lawlessness,

ἢ   τίς   κοινωνία   φωτὶ   πρὸς   σκότος;   15 τίς
or   what   fellowship   light[c]   with   darkness?   what
        = has light

δὲ   συμφώνησις   Χριστοῦ   πρὸς   Βελίαρ,
and   agreement   of Christ   with   Beliar,

ἢ   τίς   μερὶς   πιστῷ   μετὰ   ἀπίστου;   16 τίς
or   what   part   a believer[c]   with   an unbeliever?   what
        = has a believer

δὲ   συγκατάθεσις   ναῷ   θεοῦ   μετὰ   εἰδώλων;
and   union   a shrine[c] of God   with   idols?
       = has a shrine

ἡμεῖς   γὰρ   ναὸς   θεοῦ   ἐσμεν   ζῶντος·
For [1]we   [3]a shrine   [5]God   [2]are   [4]of a living;

καθὼς   εἶπεν   ὁ   θεὸς   ὅτι   ἐνοικήσω   ἐν
as   said   -   God[,]   -   I will dwell among

---

* Evidently = and yet, as in some other places; *cf.* John 20. 29.

them,
and I will be their God,
and they shall be my people.

αὐτοῖς καὶ ἐμπεριπατήσω, καὶ ἔσομαι
them   and   *I* will walk among [them],   and   I will be
αὐτῶν θεός, καὶ αὐτοὶ ἔσονταί μου λαός.
of them   God,   and   they   shall be   of me a people.

17 Therefore come out from them,
and be separate from them, says the Lord,
and touch nothing unclean;
then I will welcome you,

17 διὸ ἐξέλθατε ἐκ μέσου αὐτῶν καὶ
Wherefore   come ye out   from [the] midst   of them   and
ἀφορίσθητε, λέγει κύριος, καὶ ἀκαθάρτου
be ye separated,   says   [the] Lord,   and   an unclean thing
μὴ ἅπτεσθε· 18 κἀγὼ εἰσδέξομαι ὑμᾶς, καὶ
do not touch;   and I   will welcome in   you,   and

18 and I will be a father to you,
and you shall be my sons and daughters,
says the Lord Almighty."

ἔσομαι ὑμῖν εἰς πατέρα, καὶ ὑμεῖς ἔσεσθέ
I will be to you   for   a father,   and   ye   shall be
μοι εἰς υἱοὺς καὶ θυγατέρας, λέγει κύριος
to me   for   sons   and   daughters,   says   [the] Lord
παντοκράτωρ. 7 ταύτας οὖν ἔχοντες τὰς ἐπ-
[the] Almighty.   [3]These [2]therefore [1]having   –   [4]pro-

CHAPTER 7

SINCE we have these promises, beloved, let us cleanse ourselves from every defilement of body and spirit, and make holiness perfect in the fear of God.

αγγελίας, ἀγαπητοί, καθαρίσωμεν ἑαυτοὺς ἀπὸ
mises,   beloved,   let us cleanse   ourselves   from
παντὸς μολυσμοῦ σαρκὸς καὶ πνεύματος,
all   pollution   of flesh   and   of spirit,
ἐπιτελοῦντες ἁγιωσύνην ἐν φόβῳ θεοῦ.
perfecting   holiness   in [the] fear   of God.

2 Open your hearts to us; we have wronged no one, we have corrupted no one, we have taken advantage of no one. [3] I do not say this to condemn you, for I said before that you are in our hearts, to die together and to live together. [4] I have great confidence in you; I have great pride in you; I am filled with comfort. With all our affliction, I am overjoyed.

2 Χωρήσατε ἡμᾶς· οὐδένα ἠδικήσαμεν,
Make room for   us;   no one   we wronged,
οὐδένα ἐφθείραμεν, οὐδένα ἐπλεονεκτήσαμεν.
no one   we injured,   no one   we defrauded.
3 πρὸς κατάκρισιν οὐ λέγω· προείρηκα
For   condemnation   I say not;   [1]I have previously said
γὰρ ὅτι ἐν ταῖς καρδίαις ἡμῶν ἐστε
[1]for   that in   the   hearts   of us   ye are
εἰς τὸ συναποθανεῖν καὶ συζῆν. πολλή
for   –   to die with [you]   and to live with [you].   Much
μοι παρρησία πρὸς ὑμᾶς, πολλή μοι
to me°   boldness   toward   you,   much   to me°
=I have much   =I have much
καύχησις ὑπὲρ ὑμῶν· πεπλήρωμαι τῇ
boasting   on behalf of   you;   I have been filled   –
παρακλήσει, ὑπερπερισσεύομαι τῇ χαρᾷ ἐπὶ
with comfort,   I overflow   –   with joy on(in)
πάσῃ τῇ θλίψει ἡμῶν. 5 Καὶ γὰρ
all   the   affliction   of us.   For indeed

5 For even when we came into Macedo′nia, our bodies had no rest but we were afflicted at every turn—fighting without and fear within.

ἐλθόντων ἡμῶν εἰς Μακεδονίαν οὐδεμίαν
coming   us[a]   into   Macedonia   [5]no
=when we came
ἔσχηκεν ἄνεσιν ἡ σὰρξ ἡμῶν, ἀλλ' ἐν
[4]has had   [6]rest   [1]the   [2]flesh [3]of us,   but   in
παντὶ θλιβόμενοι· ἔξωθεν μάχαι, ἔσωθεν
every way   being afflicted;   without [were] fightings,   within

⁶But God, who comforts the downcast, comforted us by the coming of Titus, ⁷and not only by his coming but also by the comfort with which he was comforted in you, as he told us of your longing, your mourning, your zeal for me, so that I rejoiced still more. ⁸For even if I made you sorry with my letter, I do not regret it (though I did regret it), for I see that that letter grieved you, though only for a while. ⁹As it is, I rejoice, not because you were grieved, but because you were grieved into repenting; for you felt a godly grief, so that you suffered no loss through us. ¹⁰For godly grief produces a repentance that leads to salvation and brings no regret, but worldly grief produces death. ¹¹For see what earnestness this godly grief has produced in you, what eagerness to clear yourselves, what indignation, what alarm, what longing, what zeal, what punishment! At every point you have proved yourselves guiltless in the matter. ¹²So

φόβοι. 6 ἀλλ' ὁ παρακαλῶν τοὺς ταπεινοὺς
[were] fears. But ²the [one] ³comforting ⁴the ⁵humble

παρεκάλεσεν ἡμᾶς ὁ θεὸς ἐν τῇ παρουσίᾳ
⁶comforted ⁷us – ¹God by the presence

Τίτου· 7 οὐ μόνον δὲ ἐν τῇ παρουσίᾳ
of Titus; and not only by the presence

αὐτοῦ, ἀλλὰ καὶ ἐν τῇ παρακλήσει ᾗ
of him, but also by the comfort with which

παρεκλήθη ἐφ' ὑμῖν, ἀναγγέλλων ἡμῖν
he was comforted over you, reporting to us

τὴν ὑμῶν ἐπιπόθησιν, τὸν ὑμῶν ὀδυρμόν,
¹the ³of you ²eager longing, ¹the ³of you ²mourning,

τὸν ὑμῶν ζῆλον ὑπὲρ ἐμοῦ, ὥστε με
¹the ³of you ²zeal on behalf of me, so as me

μᾶλλον χαρῆναι. 8 Ὅτι εἰ καὶ ἐλύπησα
more to rejoice.ᵇ Because if indeed I grieved
=so that I rejoiced more.

ὑμᾶς ἐν τῇ ἐπιστολῇ, οὐ μεταμέλομαι·
you by the epistle, I do not regret;

εἰ καὶ μετεμελόμην, βλέπω ὅτι ἡ ἐπιστολὴ
if indeed I regretted, I see that – epistle

ἐκείνη εἰ καὶ πρὸς ὥραν ἐλύπησεν ὑμᾶς,
that if indeed for an hour it grieved you,

9 νῦν χαίρω, οὐχ ὅτι ἐλυπήθητε, ἀλλ'
now I rejoice, not that ye were grieved, but

ὅτι ἐλυπήθητε εἰς μετάνοιαν· ἐλυπήθητε
that ye were grieved to repentance; ²ye were grieved

γὰρ κατὰ θεόν, ἵνα ἐν μηδενὶ ζημιωθῆτε
¹for according God, in order in nothing ye might suffer
to that loss

ἐξ ἡμῶν. 10 ἡ γὰρ κατὰ θεὸν λύπη
by us. For ¹the ³according to ⁴God ²grief

μετάνοιαν εἰς σωτηρίαν ἀμεταμέλητον
⁷repentance ⁸to ⁵salvation ⁶unregrettable

ἐργάζεται· ἡ δὲ τοῦ κόσμου λύπη θάνατον
⁹works; but ¹the ³of the ⁴world ²grief ⁶death

κατεργάζεται. 11 ἰδοὺ γὰρ αὐτὸ τοῦτο
⁵works out. For behold this very thing[.]

τὸ κατὰ θεὸν λυπηθῆναι πόσην κατειργά-
– ²according to ³God ¹to be grieved[.] ¹what ²it worked

σατο ὑμῖν σπουδήν, ἀλλὰ ἀπολογίαν, ἀλλὰ
out ⁴in you ²earnestness, but [what] defence, but

ἀγανάκτησιν, ἀλλὰ φόβον, ἀλλὰ ἐπιπόθησιν,
vexation, but fear, but eager desire,

ἀλλὰ ζῆλον, ἀλλὰ ἐκδίκησιν. ἐν παντὶ
but zeal, but vengeance. In everything

συνεστήσατε ἑαυτοὺς ἁγνοὺς εἶναι τῷ
ye commended yourselves pure to be in the

although I wrote to you, it was not on account of the one who did the wrong, nor on account of the one who suffered the wrong, but in order that your zeal for us might be revealed to you in the sight of God. [13] Therefore we are comforted.

And besides our own comfort we rejoiced still more at the joy of Titus, because his mind has been set at rest by you all. [14] For if I have expressed to him some pride in you, I was not put to shame; but just as everything we said to you was true, so our boasting before Titus has proved true. [15] And his heart goes out all the more to you, as he remembers the obedience of you all, and the fear and trembling with which you received him. [16] I rejoice, because I have perfect confidence in you.

πράγματι.   **12** ἄρα   εἰ   καὶ   ἔγραψα   ὑμῖν,
affair.   **Then   if   indeed   I wrote   to you,**

οὐχ   ἔνεκεν   τοῦ   ἀδικήσαντος   οὐδὲ   ἔνεκεν
not   for the   the [one]   having done   nor   for the
    sake of   wrong   sake of

τοῦ   ἀδικηθέντος,   ἀλλ'   ἔνεκεν   τοῦ   φανερω-
the   having been   but   for the   -   to be mani-
[one]   wronged,   sake of

θῆναι   τὴν   σπουδὴν   ὑμῶν   τὴν   ὑπὲρ   ἡμῶν
fested   the   earnestness[bd]   of you   -   on behalf of   us

πρὸς   ὑμᾶς   ἐνώπιον   τοῦ   θεοῦ.   **13** διὰ
toward   you   before   -   God.   There-

τοῦτο   παρακεκλήμεθα.   Ἐπὶ   δὲ   τῇ
fore   we have been comforted.   But as to   the

παρακλήσει   ἡμῶν   περισσοτέρως   μᾶλλον
comfort   of us   abundantly   more

ἐχάρημεν   ἐπὶ   τῇ   χαρᾷ   Τίτου,   ὅτι   ἀναπέ-
we rejoiced   over   the   joy   of Titus,   because   has been

παυται   τὸ   πνεῦμα   αὐτοῦ   ἀπὸ   πάντων
rested   the   spirit   of him   from(by)   all

ὑμῶν·   **14** ὅτι   εἴ   τι   αὐτῷ   ὑπὲρ   ὑμῶν
you;   because   if   [2]anything   [3]to him   [4]on behalf of   [5]you

κεκαύχημαι,   οὐ   κατῃσχύνθην,   ἀλλ'   ὡς
[1]I have boasted,   I was not ashamed,   but   as

πάντα   ἐν   ἀληθείᾳ   ἐλαλήσαμεν   ὑμῖν,   οὕτως
[2]all things   [3]in   [4]truth   [1]we spoke   [5]to you,   so

καὶ   ἡ   καύχησις   ἡμῶν   ἐπὶ   Τίτου   ἀλήθεια
also   the   boasting   of us   over   Titus   [2]truth

ἐγενήθη.   **15** καὶ   τὰ   σπλάγχνα   αὐτοῦ
[1]became.   And   the   bowels   of him

περισσοτέρως   εἰς   ὑμᾶς   ἐστιν   ἀναμιμνησκομέ-
[2]abundantly   [3]toward   [4]you   [1]is(are)   [he]   remember-

νου   τὴν   πάντων   ὑμῶν   ὑπακοήν,   ὡς   μετὰ
ing[a]   [1]the   [3]of all   [4]you   [2]obedience,   as   with

φόβου   καὶ   τρόμου   ἐδέξασθε   αὐτόν.
fear   and   trembling   ye received   him.

16 χαίρω   ὅτι   ἐν   παντὶ   θαρρῶ   ἐν   ὑμῖν.
I rejoice   that   in everything   I am confident in   you.

CHAPTER 8

WE want you to know, brethren, about the grace of God which has been shown in the churches of Macedo'-nia, [2] for in a severe test of affliction, their abundance of joy and their extreme poverty

8 Γνωρίζομεν   δὲ   ὑμῖν,   ἀδελφοί,   τὴν
Now we make known   to you,   brothers,   the

χάριν   τοῦ   θεοῦ   τὴν   δεδομένην   ἐν   ταῖς
grace   -   of God   -   *having been* given   among   the

ἐκκλησίαις   τῆς   Μακεδονίας,   **2** ὅτι   ἐν   πολλῇ
churches   -   of Macedonia,   that   in   much

δοκιμῇ   θλίψεως   ἡ   περισσεία   τῆς   χαρᾶς
proving   of affliction   the   abundance   of the   joy

αὐτῶν   καὶ   ἡ   κατὰ   βάθους   πτωχεία
of them   and   [1]the   [3]according to   [4]depth   [2]poverty
                    = their extreme poverty

have overflowed in a wealth of liberality on their part. ³For they gave according to their means, as I can testify, and beyond their means, of their own free will, ⁴begging us earnestly for the favor of taking part in the relief of the saints —⁵and this, not as we expected, but first they gave themselves to the Lord and to us by the will of God. ⁶Accordingly we have urged Titus that as he had already made a beginning, he should also complete among you this gracious work. ⁷Now as you excel in everything— in faith, in utterance, in knowledge, in all earnestness, and in your love for us—see that you excel in this gracious work also.

8 I say this not as a command, but to prove by the earnestness of others that your love also is genuine. ⁹For you know the grace of our Lord Jesus Christ, that though he was rich, yet for your sake he became poor, so that by his poverty you might become rich. ¹⁰And in this matter I give my advice:

αὐτῶν	ἐπερίσσευσεν	εἰς	τὸ	πλοῦτος τῆς
of them	abounded	to	the	riches of the

ἁπλότητος	αὐτῶν·	3 ὅτι κατὰ	δύναμιν,
liberality	of them;	that according to	[their] power,

μαρτυρῶ,	καὶ	παρὰ δύναμιν,	αὐθαίρετοι·
I witness,	and	beyond [their] power,	of their own accord

4 μετὰ	πολλῆς	παρακλήσεως δεόμενοι	ἡμῶν
with	much	beseeching requesting	of us

τὴν χάριν	καὶ	τὴν κοινωνίαν τῆς	διακονίας
the grace	and	the fellowship of the	ministry

τῆς	εἰς	τοὺς ἁγίους,	5 καὶ οὐ	καθὼς
–	to	the saints,	and not	as

ἠλπίσαμεν,	ἀλλὰ	ἑαυτοὺς ἔδωκαν	πρῶτον
we hoped,	but	themselves gave	firstly

τῷ κυρίῳ	καὶ	ἡμῖν διὰ θελήματος	θεοῦ,
to the Lord	and	to us through [the] will	of God,

6 εἰς	τὸ	παρακαλέσαι ἡμᾶς	Τίτον,	ἵνα
for	–	to beseech us[b]	Titus,	in order that

=that we should beseech

καθὼς	προενήρξατο	οὕτως	καὶ	ἐπιτελέσῃ
as	previously he began	so	also	he should complete

εἰς ὑμᾶς	καὶ	τὴν χάριν ταύτην.	7 ἀλλ᾽
in you	also	this grace.	But

ὥσπερ	ἐν παντὶ περισσεύετε,	πίστει	καὶ
as	in everything ye abound,	in faith	and

λόγῳ	καὶ γνώσει	καὶ πάσῃ	σπουδῇ
in word	and in knowledge	and in all	diligence

κὰὶ	τῇ ἐξ ἡμῶν	ἐν ὑμῖν	ἀγάπῃ,	ἵνα
and	– ²from ³us	⁴in(to) ⁵you	¹in love,	[see] that

καὶ	ἐν ταύτῃ	τῇ χάριτι	περισσεύητε.
⁵also	²in ³this	– ⁴grace	¹ye may abound.

8 Οὐ	κατ᾽ ἐπιταγὴν	λέγω,	ἀλλὰ διὰ
¹Not	²by way of ⁴command	¹I say,*	but through

τῆς ἑτέρων	σπουδῆς	καὶ τὸ	τῆς ὑμετέρας
¹the	⁵of others ²diligence	also ¹the	– ⁶of your

ἀγάπης	γνήσιον δοκιμάζων·	9 γινώσκετε
⁵love	²reality ³proving;	²ye know

γὰρ τὴν	χάριν τοῦ κυρίου	ἡμῶν Ἰησοῦ
¹for the	grace of the Lord	of us Jesus

[Χριστοῦ],	ὅτι δι᾽ ὑμᾶς	ἐπτώχευσεν
Christ,	that on account of you	³he impoverished [himself]

πλούσιος ὤν,	ἵνα ὑμεῖς τῇ ἐκείνου	πτωχείᾳ
²rich ¹being,	in order that ye ¹by ⁵of that	²poverty
	der that	the one

πλουτήσητε.	10 καὶ γνώμην	ἐν τούτῳ
might become rich.	And ⁴an opinion	¹in ²this

---

* That is, Paul is not issuing a command. *Cf.* I. Cor. 7. 6.

it is best for you now to complete what a year ago you began not only to do but to desire, ¹¹ so that your readiness in desiring it may be matched by your completing it out of what you have. ¹² For if the readiness is there, it is acceptable according to what a man has, not according to what he has not. ¹³ I do not mean that others should be eased and you burdened, ¹⁴ but that as a matter of equality your abundance at the present time should supply their want, · so that their abundance may supply your want, that there may be equality. ¹⁵ As it is written, "He who gathered much had nothing over, and he who gathered little had no lack."

16 But thanks be to God who puts the same earnest care for you into the heart of Titus. ¹⁷ For he not only accepted our appeal, but being himself very earnest he is going to you of his own accord. ¹⁸ With him we are sending the brother

δίδωμι· τοῦτο γὰρ ὑμῖν συμφέρει, οἵτινες
¹I give: for this   ²for you ¹is expedient,   who

οὐ μόνον τὸ ποιῆσαι ἀλλὰ καὶ τὸ θέλειν
not only the   to do   but also the   to will

προενήρξασθε ἀπὸ πέρυσι· 11 νυνὶ δὲ καὶ
previously ye began from last year;   but now also
            = a year ago;

τὸ ποιῆσαι ἐπιτελέσατε, ὅπως καθάπερ ἡ
²the ²to do ¹complete ye, so as   as   the

προθυμία τοῦ θέλειν, οὕτως καὶ τὸ
eagerness of the to will,   so   also   the

ἐπιτελέσαι ἐκ τοῦ ἔχειν. 12 εἰ γὰρ ἡ
to complete out of the to have.   For if the
                        = what ye have.

προθυμία πρόκειται, καθὸ ἐὰν ἔχῃ
eagerness is already there, according to whatever one has

εὐπρόσδεκτος, οὐ καθὸ οὐκ ἔχει. 13 οὐ
it is acceptable, not according [what] one not
                        to   has not.

γὰρ ἵνα ἄλλοις ἄνεσις, ὑμῖν θλῖψις,
For in order to others relief,   to you distress,
    that [there may be]

ἀλλ' ἐξ ἰσότητος 14 ἐν τῷ νῦν καιρῷ
but by equality   at the present time

τὸ ὑμῶν περίσσευμα εἰς τὸ ἐκείνων
the ²of you ¹abundance [may be] for the ²of those

ὑστέρημα, ἵνα καὶ τὸ ἐκείνων περίσσευμα
¹lack, in order also the ²of those ¹abundance
        that

γένηται εἰς τὸ ὑμῶν ὑστέρημα, ὅπως
may be for the ²of you ¹lack,   so as

γένηται ἰσότης, 15 καθὼς γέγραπται· ὁ
there may be equality, as   it has been He
                        written:

τὸ πολὺ οὐκ ἐπλεόνασεν, καὶ ὁ τὸ
the much   did not abound,   and he the

ὀλίγον οὐκ ἠλαττόνησεν. 16 Χάρις δὲ
little   had not less.   But thanks [be]

τῷ θεῷ τῷ διδόντι τὴν αὐτὴν σπουδὴν
- to God - giving the same diligence

ὑπὲρ ὑμῶν ἐν τῇ καρδίᾳ Τίτου, 17 ὅτι
on be- you in the heart of Titus, because
half of

τὴν μὲν παράκλησιν ἐδέξατο, σπουδαιότερος
²the ¹indeed ⁴beseeching ³he received, ³more diligent

δὲ ὑπάρχων αὐθαίρετος ἐξῆλθεν πρὸς ὑμᾶς.
¹and ²being of his own he went to you.
            accord   forth

18 συνεπέμψαμεν δὲ μετ' αὐτοῦ τὸν
And we sent with   with   him   the

who is famous among all the churches for his preaching of the gospel; [19]and not only that, but he has been appointed by the churches to travel with us in this gracious work which we are carrying on, for the glory of the Lord and to show our good will. [20]We intend that no one should blame us about this liberal gift which we are administering, [21]for we aim at what is honorable not only in the Lord's sight but also in the sight of men. [22]And with them we are sending our brother whom we have often tested and found earnest in many matters, but who is now more earnest than ever because of his great confidence in you. [23]As for Titus, he is my partner and fellow worker in your service; and as for our brethren, they are messengers of the churches, the glory of Christ. [24]So give proof, before the churches, of your love and of our boasting about you to these men.

ἀδελφὸν	οὗ	ὁ	ἔπαινος	ἐν	τῷ	εὐαγγελίῳ
brother	of whom	the	praise	in	the	gospel

διὰ πασῶν τῶν ἐκκλησιῶν, 19 οὐ μόνον δὲ
[is] all the churches, and not only [this]
through[out]

ἀλλὰ καὶ χειροτονηθεὶς ὑπὸ τῶν ἐκκλησιῶν
but also ³having been elected ⁴by ⁵the ⁶churches

συνέκδημος ἡμῶν ἐν τῇ χάριτι ταύτῃ
¹a travelling ²of us in this grace
companion

τῇ διακονουμένῃ ὑφ' ἡμῶν πρὸς τὴν
- being ministered by us to ¹the

αὐτοῦ τοῦ κυρίου δόξαν καὶ προθυμίαν
⁵[him]self ²of the ⁴Lord ³glory and eagerness

ἡμῶν, 20 στελλόμενοι τοῦτο, μή τις ἡμᾶς
of us, avoiding this, lest anyone ²us

μωμήσηται ἐν τῇ ἁδρότητι ταύτῃ τῇ
¹should blame in this bounty -

διακονουμένῃ ὑφ' ἡμῶν· 21 προνοοῦμεν γὰρ
being ministered by us; for we provide

καλὰ οὐ μόνον ἐνώπιον κυρίου ἀλλὰ καὶ
good not only before [the] Lord but also
things

ἐνώπιον ἀνθρώπων. 22 συνεπέμψαμεν δὲ
before men. And we sent with

αὐτοῖς τὸν ἀδελφὸν ἡμῶν, ὃν ἐδοκιμάσαμεν
them the brother of us, whom ¹we proved

ἐν πολλοῖς πολλάκις σπουδαῖον ὄντα, νυνὶ
⁵in ⁶many things ⁴many times ³diligent ²being, ¹now

δὲ πολὺ σπουδαιότερον πεποιθήσει πολλῇ
¹and much more diligent ¹in ²confidence ²much

τῇ εἰς ὑμᾶς. 23 εἴτε ὑπὲρ Τίτου, κοινωνὸς
- toward you. Whether as to Titus, ³partner

ἐμὸς καὶ εἰς ὑμᾶς συνεργός· εἴτε ἀδελφοὶ
¹my ²and ⁵for ⁶you ⁴fellow-worker; or brothers

ἡμῶν, ἀπόστολοι ἐκκλησιῶν, δόξα Χριστοῦ.
of us, apostles of churches, [the] of Christ.
glory

24 τὴν οὖν ἔνδειξιν τῆς ἀγάπης ὑμῶν
⁷The ¹therefore ⁸demon- ⁹of the ¹⁰love ¹¹of you
stration

καὶ ἡμῶν καυχήσεως ὑπὲρ ὑμῶν εἰς
¹²and ¹⁴of us ¹³boasting ¹⁵on behalf of ¹⁶you ¹⁷to

αὐτοὺς ἐνδεικνύμενοι εἰς πρόσωπον τῶν
¹⁸them ²showing forth ³in ⁴[the] presence ⁵of the

ἐκκλησιῶν.
⁶churches.

CHAPTER 9

NOW it is superfluous for me to write to you about the offering for the saints, [2]for I know your readiness, of which I boast about you to the people of Macedo'nia, saying that Acha'ia has been ready since last year; and your zeal has stirred up most of them. [3]But I am sending the brethren so that our boasting about you may not prove vain in this case, so that you may be ready, as I said you would be; [4]lest if some Macedo'nians come with me and find that you are not ready, we be humiliated—to say nothing of you—for being so confident. [5]So I thought it necessary to urge the brethren to go on to you before me, and arrange in advance for this gift you have promised, so that it may be ready not as an exaction but as a willing gift.

[6] The point is this: he who sows sparingly will also reap sparingly, and he who sows bountifully will also reap bountifully. [7]Each one must do

---

9 Περὶ μὲν γὰρ τῆς διακονίας τῆς
Concerning indeed for the ministry –

εἰς τοὺς ἁγίους περισσόν μοί ἐστιν τὸ
to the saints superfluous for me it is –

γράφειν ὑμῖν· 2 οἶδα γὰρ τὴν προθυμίαν
to write to you; for I know the eagerness

ὑμῶν ἣν ὑπὲρ ὑμῶν καυχῶμαι Μακε-
of you which on behalf of you I boast to Mace-

δόσιν ὅτι Ἀχαΐα παρεσκεύασται ἀπὸ
donians that Achaia has made preparations from

πέρυσι, καὶ τὸ ὑμῶν ζῆλος ἠρέθισεν
last year, and the of you zeal stirred up
=a year ago,

τοὺς πλείονας. 3 ἔπεμψα δὲ τοὺς ἀδελφούς,
the greater number. And I sent the brothers,

ἵνα μὴ τὸ καύχημα ἡμῶν τὸ ὑπὲρ
lest the boast of us – on behalf

ὑμῶν κενωθῇ ἐν τῷ μέρει τούτῳ, ἵνα
of you should be in this respect, in order
emptied that

καθὼς ἔλεγον παρεσκευασμένοι ἦτε, 4 μή
as I said having been prepared ye were,

πως ἐὰν ἔλθωσιν σὺν ἐμοὶ Μακεδόνες
lest if come with me Macedonians

καὶ εὕρωσιν ὑμᾶς ἀπαρασκευάστους
and find you unprepared

καταισχυνθῶμεν ἡμεῖς, ἵνα μὴ λέγωμεν
should be shamed we, in order we say not
that

ὑμεῖς, ἐν τῇ ὑποστάσει ταύτῃ. 5 ἀναγκαῖον
ye, in this confidence. Necessary

οὖν ἡγησάμην παρακαλέσαι τοὺς ἀδελφοὺς
there- I thought [it] to beseech the brothers
fore

ἵνα προέλθωσιν εἰς ὑμᾶς καὶ προκαταρτί-
in order they go to you and arrange before-
that forward

σωσιν τὴν προεπηγγελμένην εὐλογίαν ὑμῶν,
hand the having been promised blessing of you,

ταύτην ἑτοίμην εἶναι οὕτως ὡς εὐλογίαν
this ready to be thus as a blessing

καὶ μὴ ὡς πλεονεξίαν. 6 Τοῦτο δέ,
and not as greediness. And this,

ὁ σπείρων φειδομένως φειδομένως καὶ
the [one] sowing sparingly sparingly also

θερίσει, καὶ ὁ σπείρων ἐπ' εὐλογίαις ἐπ'
will reap, and the [one] sowing on(for) blessings on(for)

εὐλογίαις καὶ θερίσει. 7 ἕκαστος καθὼς
blessings also will reap. Each one as

as he has made up his mind, not reluctantly or under compulsion, for God loves a cheerful giver. [8]And God is able to provide you with every blessing in abundance, so that you may always have enough of everything and may provide in abundance for every good work. [9]As it is written,

"He scatters abroad, he gives to the poor; his righteousness[g] endures for ever."

[10]He who supplies seed to the sower and bread for food will supply and multiply your resources and increase the harvest of your righteousness.[g] [11]You will be enriched in every way for great generosity, which through us will produce thanksgiving to God; [12]for the rendering of this service not only supplies the wants of the saints but also overflows in many thanksgivings to God. [13]Under the test of this service, you[h] will glorify God by your obedience in acknowledging the gospel of Christ, and by the generosity of your contribution for them and for all others; [14]while they long for you and pray

προῄρηται τῇ καρδίᾳ, μὴ ἐκ λύπης ἢ
he chose in the(his) heart,   not of grief or

ἐξ ἀνάγκης· ἱλαρὸν γὰρ δότην ἀγαπᾷ ὁ
of necessity; for ²a cheerful ⁴giver ¹loves –

θεός.   8 δυνατεῖ δὲ ὁ θεὸς πᾶσαν χάριν
¹God.   And ²is able – ¹God ⁴all ⁵grace

περισσεῦσαι εἰς ὑμᾶς, ἵνα ἐν παντὶ
³to cause to abound toward you, in order that ⁵in ⁶everything

πάντοτε πᾶσαν αὐτάρκειαν ἔχοντες περισ-
¹always ²all ³self-sufficiency ⁴having ye may

σεύητε εἰς πᾶν ἔργον ἀγαθόν, 9 καθὼς
abound to every work good,   as

γέγραπται· ἐσκόρπισεν, ἔδωκεν τοῖς πένησιν,
it has been written: He scattered, he gave to the poor,

ἡ δικαιοσύνη αὐτοῦ μένει εἰς τὸν αἰῶνα.
the righteousness of him remains unto the age.

10 ὁ δὲ ἐπιχορηγῶν σπέρμα τῷ σπείροντι
Now the [one] providing seed for the [one] sowing

καὶ ἄρτον εἰς βρῶσιν χορηγήσει καὶ
¹both ²bread ⁴for ³food ¹will supply and

πληθυνεῖ τὸν σπόρον ὑμῶν καὶ αὐξήσει
will multiply the seed of you and will increase

τὰ γενήματα τῆς δικαιοσύνης ὑμῶν· 11 ἐν
the fruits of the righteousness of you;   in

παντὶ πλουτιζόμενοι εἰς πᾶσαν ἁπλότητα,
everything being enriched to all liberality,

ἥτις κατεργάζεται δι' ἡμῶν εὐχαριστίαν
which works out through us thanksgiving

τῷ θεῷ· 12 ὅτι ἡ διακονία τῆς λειτουργίας
– to God; because the ministry – service

ταύτης οὐ μόνον ἐστὶν προσαναπληροῦσα
of this not only is making up

τὰ ὑστερήματα τῶν ἁγίων, ἀλλὰ καὶ
the things lacking of the saints, but [is] also

περισσεύουσα διὰ πολλῶν εὐχαριστιῶν τῷ
abounding through many thanksgivings

θεῷ. 13 διὰ τῆς δοκιμῆς τῆς διακονίας
to God; through the proof – ministry

ταύτης δοξάζοντες τὸν θεὸν ἐπὶ τῇ
of this glorifying God on the

ὑποταγῇ τῆς ὁμολογίας ὑμῶν εἰς τὸ
submission of the confession of you to the

εὐαγγέλιον τοῦ Χριστοῦ καὶ ἁπλότητι
gospel – of Christ and [on the] liberality

τῆς κοινωνίας εἰς αὐτοὺς καὶ εἰς πάντας,
of the fellowship toward them and toward all men,

14 καὶ αὐτῶν δεήσει ὑπὲρ ὑμῶν ἐπιποθούν-
and ¹them ⁴with ⁵on be- ⁶you ²longing
      request half of

[g] Or benevolence
[h] Or they

for you, because of the surpassing grace of God in you. [15] Thanks be to God for his inexpressible gift!

τῶν ὑμᾶς διὰ τὴν ὑπερβάλλουσαν χάριν
after⁸ ⁸you on account the   excelling   grace
             of

τοῦ θεοῦ ἐφ᾽ ὑμῖν.   15 Χάρις τῷ θεῷ
– of God upon you.   Thanks – to God

ἐπὶ τῇ ἀνεκδιηγήτῳ αὐτοῦ δωρεᾷ.
for the indescribable of him gift.

CHAPTER 10

I, Paul, myself entreat you, by the meekness and gentleness of Christ —I who am humble when face to face with you, but bold to you when I am away!—[2] I beg of you that when I am present I may not have to show boldness with such confidence as I count on showing against some who suspect us of acting in worldly fashion. [3] For though we live in the world we are not carrying on a worldly war, [4] for the weapons of our warfare are not worldly but have divine power to destroy strongholds. [5] We destroy arguments and every proud obstacle to the knowledge of God, and take every thought captive to obey Christ, [6] being ready to punish every disobedience, when your obedience is complete.

[7] Look at what is before your eyes. If any one is confident that he is Christ's, let him re-

10 Αὐτὸς δὲ ἐγὼ Παῦλος παρακαλῶ
[my]self Now I   Paul   beseech

ὑμᾶς διὰ τῆς πραΰτητος καὶ ἐπιεικείας
you through the meekness and forbearance

τοῦ Χριστοῦ, ὃς κατὰ πρόσωπον μὲν
– of Christ, who according to face   indeed

ταπεινὸς ἐν ὑμῖν, ἀπὼν δὲ θαρρῶ εἰς
[am] humble among you, but being absent am bold toward

ὑμᾶς· 2 δέομαι δὲ τὸ μὴ παρὼν θαρρῆσαι
you: now I request – not being present to be bold

τῇ πεποιθήσει ᾗ λογίζομαι τολμῆσαι ἐπί
in the confidence which I reckon to be daring toward

τινας τοὺς λογιζομένους ἡμᾶς ὡς κατὰ
some the [ones] reckoning us   as ⁸according to

σάρκα περιπατοῦντας. 3 Ἐν σαρκὶ γὰρ
⁸flesh ¹walking.   in flesh For

περιπατοῦντες οὐ κατὰ σάρκα στρατευόμεθα,
walking not accord- flesh   we war,
         ing to

4 τὰ γὰρ ὅπλα τῆς στρατείας ἡμῶν
for the weapons of the warfare of us [are]

οὐ σαρκικὰ ἀλλὰ δυνατὰ τῷ θεῷ πρὸς
not fleshly but powerful – to God to

καθαίρεσιν ὀχυρωμάτων, λογισμοὺς καθαιροῦν-
overthrow of strongholds, ⁸reasonings ¹overthrow-

τες 5 καὶ πᾶν ὕψωμα ἐπαιρόμενον κατὰ
ing and every high thing rising up against

τῆς γνώσεως τοῦ θεοῦ, καὶ αἰχμαλωτίζοντες
the knowledge – of God, and taking captive

πᾶν νόημα εἰς τὴν ὑπακοὴν τοῦ Χριστοῦ,
every design to the obedience – of Christ,

6 καὶ ἐν ἑτοίμῳ ἔχοντες ἐκδικῆσαι πᾶσαν
and in readiness having to avenge all
     = being ready

παρακοήν, ὅταν πληρωθῇ ὑμῶν ἡ ὑπακοή.
disobedience, whenever ⁴is fulfilled ⁸of you ¹the ²obedience.

7 Τὰ κατὰ πρόσωπον βλέπετε. εἴ τις
²The ⁸according ⁴face   ¹ye look [at]. If any-
things to (appearance)   one

πέποιθεν ἑαυτῷ Χριστοῦ εἶναι, τοῦτο
has persuaded himself ²of Christ ¹to be, this

mind himself that as he is Christ's, so are we. [8]For even if I boast a little too much of our authority, which the Lord gave for building you up and not for destroying you, I shall not be put to shame. [9]I would not seem to be frightening you with letters. [10]For they say, "His letters are weighty and strong, but his bodily presence is weak, and his speech of no account." [11]Let such people understand that what we say by letter when absent, we do when present. [12]Not that we venture to class or compare ourselves with some of those who commend themselves. But when they measure themselves by one another, and compare themselves with one another, they are without understanding.

[13]But we will not boast beyond limit, but will keep to the limits God has apportioned us, to reach even to you. [14]For we are not overextending ourselves, as though we did not reach you; we were the first to come all the way to you

λογιζέσθω   πάλιν   ἐφ’   ἑαυτοῦ,   ὅτι   καθὼς
let him reckon   again   as to   himself,   that   as

αὐτὸς   Χριστοῦ,   οὕτως   καὶ   ἡμεῖς.   8 ἐάν
he [is]   of Christ,   so   also [are]   we.   [9]if

τε   γὰρ   περισσότερόν   τι   καυχήσωμαι   περὶ
[2]even   [1]For   [3]more abundantly   [5]some-   [4]I should boast concern-
                                        what   ing

τῆς   ἐξουσίας   ἡμῶν,   ἧς   ἔδωκεν   ὁ   κύριος
the   authority   of us,   which   [2]gave   [1]the   [3]Lord

εἰς   οἰκοδομὴν   καὶ   οὐκ   εἰς   καθαίρεσιν
for   edification   and   not   for   overthrow

ὑμῶν,   οὐκ   αἰσχυνθήσομαι,   9 ἵνα   μὴ   δόξω
of you,   I shall not be shamed,   in order that I may not seem

ὡσὰν   ἐκφοβεῖν   ὑμᾶς   διὰ   τῶν   ἐπιστολῶν.
as though to frighten   you   through the   epistles.

10 ὅτι   αἱ   ἐπιστολαὶ   μέν,   φησίν,   βαρεῖαι
Because the(his)   epistles   indeed,   he says,   [are] weighty

καὶ   ἰσχυραί,   ἡ   δὲ   παρουσία   τοῦ   σώματος
and   strong,   but the   presence   of the(his) body [is]

ἀσθενὴς   καὶ   ὁ   λόγος   ἐξουθενημένος.
weak   and   the(his)   speech   being despised.

11 τοῦτο   λογιζέσθω   ὁ   τοιοῦτος,   ὅτι   οἷοί
This   let reckon   such a one,   that such as

ἐσμεν   τῷ   λόγῳ   δι’   ἐπιστολῶν   ἀπόντες,
we are   –   in word   through   epistles   being absent,

τοιοῦτοι   καὶ   παρόντες   τῷ   ἔργῳ.   12 Οὐ
such   also   being present –   in work.   [2]not

γὰρ   τολμῶμεν   ἐγκρῖναι   ἢ   συγκρῖναι
[1]For   [3]we dare   to class with   or   to compare

ἑαυτούς   τισιν   τῶν   ἑαυτοὺς   συνιστανόντων·
ourselves   with some   of the   [2]themselves   [1]commending;
                                [ones]

ἀλλὰ   αὐτοὶ   ἐν   ἑαυτοῖς   ἑαυτοὺς   μετροῦντες
but   they   [3]among   [4]them-   [2]them-   [1]measuring
                                selves   selves

καὶ   συγκρίνοντες   ἑαυτοὺς   ἑαυτοῖς   οὐ
and   comparing   themselves   with themselves   not

συνιᾶσιν.   13 ἡμεῖς   δὲ   οὐκ   εἰς   τὰ   ἄμετρα
do understand.   But we   [2]not   [1]immeasurably†

καυχησόμεθα,   ἀλλὰ   κατὰ   τὸ   μέτρον   τοῦ
[1]will [2]boast,   but according to the   measure   of the

κανόνος   οὗ   ἐμέρισεν   ἡμῖν   ὁ   θεὸς   μέτρου,
rule   which   [2]divided   [3]to us   –   [1]God of(in) measure,

ἐφικέσθαι   ἄχρι   καὶ   ὑμῶν.   14 οὐ   γὰρ
to reach   as far as   even   you.   For not

ὡς   μὴ   ἐφικνούμενοι   εἰς   ὑμᾶς   ὑπερεκτείνομεν
as not   reaching   to   you   do we overstretch

ἑαυτούς,   ἄχρι   γὰρ   καὶ   ὑμῶν   ἐφθάσαμεν
ourselves,   for as far as   even   you   we came

with the gospel of Christ.
15 We do not boast be-
yond limit, in other men's
labors; but our hope is
that as your faith in-
creases, our field among
you may be greatly
enlarged, 16 so that we
may preach the gospel
in lands beyond you,
without boasting of work
already done in another's
field. 17 "Let him who
boasts, boast of the
Lord." 18 For it is not the
man who commends
himself that is accepted,
but the man whom the
Lord commends.

ἐν   τῷ   εὐαγγελίῳ   τοῦ   Χριστοῦ,   15 οὐκ
in   the   gospel   -   of Christ,   not

εἰς   τὰ   ἄμετρα   καυχώμενοι   ἐν   ἀλλοτρίοις
immeasurably†   boasting   in   others'†

κόποις,   ἐλπίδα   δὲ   ἔχοντες   αὐξανομένης
labours,   but ²hope   ¹having   growing
=as your faith grows

τῆς   πίστεως   ὑμῶν   ἐν   ὑμῖν   μεγαλυνθῆναι
the   faith   of youᵃ   ²among   ³you   ¹to be magnified

κατὰ   τὸν   κανόνα   ἡμῶν   εἰς   περισσείαν,
according the   rule   of us   in   abundance,
to

16 εἰς   τὰ   ὑπερέκεινα   ὑμῶν   εὐαγγελίσασθαι,
in   the [parts] beyond   you   to preach good tidings,

οὐκ   ἐν   ἀλλοτρίῳ   κανόνι   εἰς   τὰ   ἕτοιμα
not   ²in   ³another's†   ⁴rule   ⁵in   - ⁶things ready

καυχήσασθαι.   17 Ὁ   δὲ   καυχώμενος   ἐν
¹to boast.   But the [one]   boasting   ²in

κυρίῳ   καυχάσθω·   18 οὐ   γὰρ   ὁ   ἑαυτὸν
³[the] Lord   ¹let him boast;   for not   the [one]   himself

συνιστάνων,   ἐκεῖνός   ἐστιν   δόκιμος,   ἀλλὰ
commending,   that one   is   approved,   but

ὃν   ὁ   κύριος   συνίστησιν.
whom the   Lord   commends.

CHAPTER 11

I wish you would bear
with me in a little
foolishness. Do bear with
me! 2 I feel a divine
jealousy for you, for I
betrothed you to Christ
to present you as a
pure bride to her one
husband. 3 But I am
afraid that as the serpent
deceived Eve by his
cunning, your thoughts
will be led astray from a
sincere and pure
devotion to Christ. 4 For
if some one comes and
preaches another Jesus
than the one we
preached, or if you re-
ceive a different spirit

11 Ὄφελον   ἀνείχεσθέ   μου   μικρόν   τι
I would that   ye endured   me   a little [bit]

ἀφροσύνης·   ἀλλὰ   καὶ   ἀνέχεσθέ   μου.
of foolishness;   but   indeed   ye do endure   me.

2 ζηλῶ   γὰρ   ὑμᾶς   θεοῦ   ζήλῳ,   ἡρμοσάμην
For I am jealous [of]   you   ²of God   ¹with a   ²I betrothed
jealousy,

γὰρ   ὑμᾶς   ἑνὶ   ἀνδρὶ   παρθένον   ἁγνὴν
¹for   you   to one   husband   ²virgin   ³a pure

παραστῆσαι   τῷ   Χριστῷ·   3 φοβοῦμαι   δὲ
¹to present   -   to Christ;   and I fear

μή   πως,   ὡς   ὁ   ὄφις   ἐξηπάτησεν   Εὔαν
lest somehow,   as   the   serpent   deceived   Eve

ἐν   τῇ   πανουργίᾳ   αὐτοῦ,   φθαρῇ   τὰ   νοήματα
by the   cleverness   of him,   ⁴should ¹the   ²thoughts
be seduced

ὑμῶν   ἀπὸ   τῆς   ἁπλότητος   [καὶ   τῆς
³of you   from   the   simplicity   and   the

ἁγνότητος]   τῆς   εἰς   Χριστόν.   4 εἰ   μὲν
purity]   -   in   Christ.   ²if ³indeed

γὰρ   ὁ   ἐρχόμενος   ἄλλον   Ἰησοῦν   κηρύσσει
¹For the [one]   coming   ²another   ³Jesus   ¹proclaims

ὃν   οὐκ   ἐκηρύξαμεν,   ἢ   πνεῦμα   ἕτερον
whom   we did not proclaim,   or   ³spirit   ²a different

from the one you received, or if you accept a different gospel from the one you accepted, you submit to it readily enough. [5]I think that I am not in the least inferior to these superlative apostles. [6]Even if I am unskilled in speaking, I am not in knowledge; in every way we have made this plain to you in all things.

[7]Did I commit a sin in abasing myself so that you might be exalted, because I preached God's gospel without cost to you? [8]I robbed other churches by accepting support from them in order to serve you. [9]And when I was with you and was in want, I did not burden any one, for my needs were supplied by the brethren who came from Macedo′nia. So I refrained and will refrain from burdening you in any way. [10]As the truth of Christ is in me, this boast of mine shall not be silenced in the regions of Acha′ia. [11]And why? Because I do not love you? God knows I do!

[12]And what I do I will continue to do, in order to undermine the claim of those who would like to claim that in their

λαμβάνετε ὃ οὐκ ἐλάβετε, ἢ εὐαγγέλιον
[1]ye receive　which　ye did not receive,　or　[2]gospel

ἕτερον ὃ οὐκ ἐδέξασθε, καλῶς ἀνέχεσθε.
[1]a different which ye did not receive,　[2][him] [3]well　[1]ye endure.

5 λογίζομαι γὰρ μηδὲν ὑστερηκέναι τῶν
For I reckon　nothing　to have come behind of the

ὑπερλίαν ἀποστόλων. 6 εἰ δὲ καὶ ἰδιώτης
super-　apostles.　But if　indeed　unskilled
　　　　　　　　　　　　　　　　　　　[I am]

τῷ λόγῳ, ἀλλ᾽ οὐ τῇ γνώσει, ἀλλ᾽ ἐν
- in speech,　yet　not　- in knowledge,　but　in

παντὶ φανερώσαντες ἐν πᾶσιν εἰς ὑμᾶς.
every　having manifested　in　all things　to　you.
[way]　[ourselves]

7 Ἢ ἁμαρτίαν ἐποίησα ἐμαυτὸν ταπεινῶν
Or　[2]sin　[1]did I commit　[4]myself　[3]humbling

ἵνα ὑμεῖς ὑψωθῆτε, ὅτι δωρεὰν τὸ τοῦ
in order ye　might be　because [5]freely [1]the　-
that　　　　　exalted,

θεοῦ εὐαγγέλιον εὐηγγελισάμην ὑμῖν;
[4]of God　[3]gospel　[1]I preached good tidings　to you?

8 ἄλλας ἐκκλησίας ἐσύλησα λαβὼν ὀψώνιον
Other　churches　I robbed　taking　wages

πρὸς τὴν ὑμῶν διακονίαν, 9 καὶ παρὼν
for　[1]the　[3]of you　[2]ministry,　and being present

πρὸς ὑμᾶς καὶ ὑστερηθεὶς οὐ κατενάρκησα
with　you　and　lacking　I was not an encumbrance

οὐθενός· τὸ γὰρ ὑστέρημά μου προσανε-
of no man;　for the　lack　of me　[6]made

πλήρωσαν οἱ ἀδελφοὶ ἐλθόντες ἀπὸ Μακε-
up　[1]the　[2]brothers　[4]coming　[5]from　[3]Mace-

δονίας· καὶ ἐν παντὶ ἀβαρῆ ἐμαυτὸν
donia;　and　in every [way] [3]unburdensome [2]myself

ὑμῖν ἐτήρησα καὶ τηρήσω. 10 ἔστιν
[4]to you　[1]I kept　and　I will keep.　[2]is

ἀλήθεια Χριστοῦ ἐν ἐμοί, ὅτι ἡ καύχησις
[1][The] truth [2]of Christ　in　me,　that　-　boasting

αὕτη οὐ φραγήσεται εἰς ἐμὲ ἐν τοῖς
this　shall not be stopped　in　me　in　the

κλίμασιν τῆς Ἀχαΐας. 11 διὰ τί; ὅτι
regions　-　of Achaia.　　Why?　because

οὐκ ἀγαπῶ ὑμᾶς; ὁ θεὸς οἶδεν. 12 Ὃ
I love not　you?　-　God knows.　　　what

δὲ ποιῶ, καὶ ποιήσω, ἵνα ἐκκόψω τὴν
But　I do,　also　I will do,　in order I may cut　the
　　　　　　　　　　　　　　that　off

ἀφορμὴν τῶν θελόντων ἀφορμήν, ἵνα ἐν
occasion　of the　desiring　an occasion,　in or- where-
　　　　　[ones]　　　　　　　　　der that

boasted mission they work on the same terms as we do. [13] For such men are false apostles, deceitful workmen, disguising themselves as apostles of Christ. [14] And no wonder, for even Satan disguises himself as an angel of light. [15] So it is not strange if his servants also disguise themselves as servants of righteousness. Their end will correspond to their deeds.

16 I repeat, let no one think me foolish; but even if you do, accept me as a fool, so that I too may boast a little. [17] (What I am saying I say not with the Lord's authority but as a fool, in this boastful confidence; [18] since many boast of worldly things, I too will boast.) [19] For you gladly bear with fools, being wise yourselves! [20] For you bear it if a man makes slaves of you, or preys upon you, or takes advantage of you, or puts on airs, or strikes you in the face. [21] To my shame, I must say, we were too weak for that!

But whatever any one dares to boast of—I am speaking as a fool—I also

ᾧ καυχῶνται εὑρεθῶσιν καθὼς καὶ ἡμεῖς.
in they boast they may be found as also we.

13 οἱ γὰρ τοιοῦτοι ψευδαπόστολοι, ἐργάται
- For such [are] false apostles, [2]workmen

δόλιοι, μετασχηματιζόμενοι εἰς ἀποστόλους
[1]deceitful, transforming themselves into apostles

Χριστοῦ. 14 καὶ οὐ θαῦμα· αὐτὸς γὰρ
of Christ. And no wonder; [3][him]self [1]for

ὁ σατανᾶς μετασχηματίζεται εἰς ἄγγελον
- [2]Satan transforms himself into an angel

φωτός. 15 οὐ μέγα οὖν εἰ καὶ οἱ
of light. No great thing therefore if also the

διάκονοι αὐτοῦ μετασχηματίζονται ὡς
ministers of him transform themselves as

διάκονοι δικαιοσύνης· ὧν τὸ τέλος ἔσται
ministers of righteousness; of whom the end will be

κατὰ τὰ ἔργα αὐτῶν.
according to the works of them.

16 Πάλιν λέγω, μή τίς με δόξῃ ἄφρονα
Again I say, [3]not [2]anyone [4]me [1]think [5]foolish

εἶναι· εἰ δὲ μή γε, κἂν ὡς ἄφρονα
[6]to be; otherwise, even if as foolish

δέξασθέ με, ἵνα κἀγὼ μικρόν τι καυχήσ-
receive ye me, in order I also a little [bit] may
that

ωμαι. 17 ὃ λαλῶ, οὐ κατὰ κύριον λαλῶ,
boast. What I speak, not according to [the] Lord I speak,
to

ἀλλ' ὡς ἐν ἀφροσύνῃ, ἐν ταύτῃ τῇ
but as in folly, in this the

ὑποστάσει τῆς καυχήσεως. 18 ἐπεὶ πολλοὶ
confidence - of boasting. Since many

καυχῶνται κατὰ [τὴν] σάρκα, κἀγὼ
boast according to the flesh, I also

καυχήσομαι. 19 ἡδέως γὰρ ἀνέχεσθε τῶν
will boast. For gladly ye endure -

ἀφρόνων φρόνιμοι ὄντες· 20 ἀνέχεσθε γὰρ
fools [2]prudent [1]being; for ye endure

εἴ τις ὑμᾶς καταδουλοῖ, εἴ τις κατεσθίει,
if anyone [2]you [1]enslaves, if anyone devours [you],

εἴ τις λαμβάνει, εἴ τις ἐπαίρεται, εἰ
if anyone receives [you],* if anyone lifts himself up, if

τις εἰς πρόσωπον ὑμᾶς δέρει. 21 κατὰ
anyone [3]in [4][the] face [2]you [1]beats(hits). According to

ἀτιμίαν λέγω, ὡς ὅτι ἡμεῖς ἠσθενήκαμεν·
dishonour I say, as that we have been weak;

ἐν ᾧ δ' ἄν τις τολμᾷ, ἐν ἀφροσύνῃ
but in whatever [respect] anyone dares, in folly

* ? takes [you in].

dare to boast of that.
²²Are they Hebrews? So
am I. Are they Israelites?
So am I. Are they de-
scendants of Abraham?
So am I. ²³Are they
servants of Christ? I am
a better one—I am talk-
ing like a madman—
with far greater labors,
far more imprisonments,
with countless beatings,
and often near death.
²⁴Five times I have re-
ceived at the hands of the
Jews the forty lashes less
one. ²⁵Three times I have
been beaten with rods;
once I was stoned. Three
times I have been ship-
wrecked; a night and a
day I have been adrift
at sea; ²⁶on frequent
journeys, in danger from
rivers, danger from
robbers, danger from my
own people, danger from
Gentiles, danger in the
city, danger in the
wilderness, danger at sea,
danger from false
brethren; ²⁷in toil and
hardship, through many
a sleepless night, in
hunger and thirst, often
without food, in cold
and exposure. ²⁸And,
apart from other things,
there is the daily pressure
upon me of my anxiety
for all the churches.
²⁹Who is weak, and I am
not weak? Who is made
to fall, and I am not
indignant?
30 If I must boast, I
will boast of the things
that show my weakness.

λέγω, τολμῶ κἀγώ. 22 Ἑβραῖοί εἰσιν;
I say, ³dare ¹I ²also. Hebrews are they?

κἀγώ. Ἰσραηλῖταί εἰσιν; κἀγώ. σπέρμα
I also. Israelites are they? I also. Seed

Ἀβραάμ εἰσιν; κἀγώ. 23 διάκονοι Χριστοῦ
of Abraham are they? I also. Ministers of Christ

εἰσιν; παραφρονῶν λαλῶ, ὑπὲρ ἐγώ· ἐν
are they? being out of I speak, ²beyond ¹I: in
    my mind   (more)

κόποις περισσοτέρως, ἐν φυλακαῖς περισ-
labours more abundantly, in prisons more

σοτέρως, ἐν πληγαῖς ὑπερβαλλόντως, ἐν
abundantly, in stripes excessively, in

θανάτοις πολλάκις. 24 ὑπὸ Ἰουδαίων
deaths many times. By Jews

πεντάκις τεσσεράκοντα παρὰ μίαν ἔλαβον,
five times forty [stripes] less one I received,

25 τρὶς ἐρραβδίσθην, ἅπαξ ἐλιθάσθην, τρὶς
thrice I was beaten with rods, once I was stoned, thrice

ἐναυάγησα, 26 νυχθήμερον ἐν τῷ βυθῷ
I was shipwrecked, a night and a day in the deep

πεποίηκα· ὁδοιπορίαις πολλάκις, κινδύνοις
I have done(been); in travels many times, in perils

ποταμῶν, κινδύνοις λῃστῶν, κινδύνοις ἐκ
of rivers, in perils of robbers, in perils of

γένους, κινδύνοις ἐξ ἐθνῶν, κινδύνοις ἐν
[my] kind, in perils of nations, in perils in

πόλει, κινδύνοις ἐν ἐρημίᾳ, κινδύνοις ἐν
a city, in perils in a desert, in perils in(at)

θαλάσσῃ, κινδύνοις ἐν ψευδαδέλφοις, 27 κόπῳ
sea, in perils among false brothers, in labour

καὶ μόχθῳ, ἐν ἀγρυπνίαις πολλάκις, ἐν
and hardship, in watchings many times, in

λιμῷ καὶ δίψει, ἐν νηστείαις πολλάκις,
famine and thirst, in fastings many times,

ἐν ψύχει καὶ γυμνότητι· 28 χωρὶς τῶν
in cold and nakedness; apart from the things

παρεκτὸς ἡ ἐπίστασίς μοι ἡ καθ' ἡμέραν,
without[,] the conspiring me - daily,
    against

ἡ μέριμνα πασῶν τῶν ἐκκλησιῶν. 29 τίς
the care of all the churches. Who

ἀσθενεῖ, καὶ οὐκ ἀσθενῶ; τίς σκανδαλίζεται,
is weak, and I am not weak? who is offended,

καὶ οὐκ ἐγὼ πυροῦμαι; 30 εἰ καυχᾶσθαι
and ²not ¹I ¹burn? If to boast

δεῖ, τὰ τῆς ἀσθενείας μου καυχήσομαι.
it be- the of the weakness of me I will boast.
hoves things
[me],

[31] The God and Father of the Lord Jesus, he who is blessed for ever, knows that I do not lie. [32] At Damascus, the governor under King Ar'etas guarded the city of Damascus in order to seize me, [33] but I was let down in a basket through a window in the wall, and escaped his hands.

31 ὁ θεὸς καὶ πατὴρ τοῦ κυρίου Ἰησοῦ
The God and Father of the Lord Jesus
οἶδεν, ὁ ὢν εὐλογητὸς εἰς τοὺς αἰῶνας,
knows, the being blessed unto the ages,
    [one]
ὅτι οὐ ψεύδομαι. 32 ἐν Δαμασκῷ ὁ
that I am not lying.   In Damascus the
ἐθνάρχης Ἀρέτα τοῦ βασιλέως ἐφρούρει
ethnarch of Aretas of the king guarded
τὴν πόλιν Δαμασκηνῶν πιάσαι με, 33 καὶ
the city of [the] Damascenes to seize me, and
διὰ θυρίδος ἐν σαργάνῃ ἐχαλάσθην διὰ
through a window in a basket I was lowered through
τοῦ τείχους καὶ ἐξέφυγον τὰς χεῖρας αὐτοῦ.
the wall and escaped the hands of him.

CHAPTER 12

I must boast; there is nothing to be gained by it, but I will go on to visions and revelations of the Lord. [2] I know a man in Christ who fourteen years ago was caught up to the third heaven—whether in the body or out of the body I do not know, God knows. [3] And I know that this man was caught up into Paradise—whether in the body or out of the body I do not know, God knows— [4] and he heard things that cannot be told, which man may not utter. [5] On behalf of this man I will boast, but on my own behalf I will not boast, except of my weaknesses. [6] Though if I wish to boast, I shall not be a fool, for I shall

12 Καυχᾶσθαι δεῖ, οὐ συμφέρον μέν,
To boast it behoves not expedient indeed,
            [me],
ἐλεύσομαι δὲ εἰς ὀπτασίας καὶ ἀποκαλύψεις
so I will come to visions and revelations
κυρίου. 2 οἶδα ἄνθρωπον ἐν Χριστῷ
of [the] Lord. I know a man in Christ
πρὸ ἐτῶν δεκατεσσάρων, — εἴτε ἐν
before years fourteen, (whether in
σώματι οὐκ οἶδα, εἴτε ἐκτὸς τοῦ σώματος
[the] body I know not, or outside the body
οὐκ οἶδα, ὁ θεὸς οἶδεν, — ἁρπαγέντα
I know not, - God knows,) [2]caught
τὸν τοιοῦτον ἕως τρίτου οὐρανοῦ. 3 καὶ
- [1]such a one to [the] third heaven. And
οἶδα τὸν τοιοῦτον ἄνθρωπον — εἴτε
I know - such a man (whether
ἐν σώματι εἴτε χωρὶς τοῦ σώματος
in [the] body or apart from the body
[οὐκ οἶδα], ὁ θεὸς οἶδεν, — 4 ὅτι
I know not, - God knows,) that
ἡρπάγη εἰς τὸν παράδεισον καὶ ἤκουσεν
he was caught into the paradise and heard
ἄρρητα ῥήματα, ἃ οὐκ ἐξὸν ἀνθρώπῳ
unspeakable words, which it is not for a man
                permissible
λαλῆσαι. 5 ὑπὲρ τοῦ τοιούτου καυχήσομαι,
to speak. On behalf of - such a one I will boast,
ὑπὲρ δὲ ἐμαυτοῦ οὐ καυχήσομαι εἰ
but on behalf of myself I will not boast ex-
μὴ ἐν ταῖς ἀσθενείαις. 6 ἐὰν γὰρ θελήσω
cept in the(my) weaknesses. For if I shall wish
καυχήσασθαι, οὐκ ἔσομαι ἄφρων, ἀλήθειαν
to boast, I shall not be foolish, [2]truth

be speaking the truth. But I refrain from it, so that no one may think more of me than he sees in me or hears from me. ⁷And to keep me from being too elated by the abundance of revelations, a thorn was given me in the flesh, a messenger of Satan, to harass me, to keep me from being too elated. ⁸Three times I besought the Lord about this, that it should leave me; ⁹but he said to me, "My grace is sufficient for you, for my power is made perfect in weakness." I will all the more gladly boast of my weaknesses, that the power of Christ may rest upon me. ¹⁰For the sake of Christ, then, I am content with weaknesses, insults, hardships, persecutions, and calamities; for when I am weak, then I am strong.

11 I have been a fool! You forced me to it, for I ought to have been commended by you. For I am not at all inferior to these superlative apostles, even though I am nothing. ¹²The signs of a true apostle were performed among you in all patience, with signs and wonders and mighty works. ¹³For in what were

γὰρ ἐρῶ· φείδομαι δέ, μή τις εἰς ἐμὲ
¹for ²I will speak;   but I spare,   lest anyone to   me
λογίσηται ὑπὲρ ὃ βλέπει με ἢ ἀκούει
reckons   beyond what he sees   me   or   hears
ἐξ ἐμοῦ   7 καὶ τῇ ὑπερβολῇ τῶν ἀποκα-
of   me   and by the   excess   of the   revela-
λύψεων.   διὸ ἵνα μὴ ὑπεραίρωμαι,   ἐδόθη
tions.   Where-   lest   I should be   there was
fore   exceedingly uplifted,   given
μοι σκόλοψ τῇ σαρκί, ἄγγελος σατανᾶ,
to me   a thorn   in the flesh,   a messenger   of Satan,
ἵνα με κολαφίζῃ,   ἵνα μὴ ὑπεραίρωμαι.
in order ²me ¹he might buffet,   lest   I should be
that   exceedingly uplifted.
8 ὑπὲρ τούτου τρὶς τὸν κύριον παρεκάλεσα,
As to   this   thrice the   Lord   I besought,
ἵνα ἀποστῇ ἀπ' ἐμοῦ.   9 καὶ εἴρηκέν
in or- it might from   me.   And he has said
der that depart
μοι· ἀρκεῖ σοι ἡ χάρις μου· ἡ γὰρ
to me: ⁴Suffices ²thee ¹the ³grace ⁵of me; for the(my)
δύναμις ἐν ἀσθενείᾳ τελεῖται. Ἥδιστα
power   in   weakness   is perfected.   Most gladly
οὖν μᾶλλον καυχήσομαι ἐν ταῖς ἀσθενείαις,
therefore rather   I will boast   in the(my) weaknesses,
ἵνα ἐπισκηνώσῃ ἐπ' ἐμὲ ἡ δύναμις τοῦ
in order ⁴might   over   ⁶me ¹the ²power   –
that   overshadow
Χριστοῦ.   10 διὸ εὐδοκῶ ἐν ἀσθενείαις,
³of Christ.   Wherefore I am well   in   weaknesses,
pleased
ἐν ὕβρεσιν, ἐν ἀνάγκαις, ἐν διωγμοῖς
in   insults,   in   necessities,   in persecutions
καὶ στενοχωρίαις, ὑπὲρ Χριστοῦ· ὅταν
and   difficulties,   on behalf of   Christ; ¹whenever
γὰρ ἀσθενῶ, τότε δυνατός εἰμι.
²for I am weak,   then   ²powerful ¹I am.

11 Γέγονα ἄφρων· ὑμεῖς με ἠναγκάσατε.
I have become foolish;   ye   me   compelled.
ἐγὼ γὰρ ὤφειλον ὑφ' ὑμῶν συνίστασθαι.
For I   ought   by   you   to be commended.
οὐδὲν γὰρ ὑστέρησα τῶν ὑπερλίαν
For nothing   I lacked   of the   super-
ἀποστόλων, εἰ καὶ οὐδέν εἰμι.   12 τὰ
apostles,   ²if ¹even ³nothing ⁴I am.   ⁶The
μὲν σημεῖα τοῦ ἀποστόλου κατειργάσθη
¹indeed signs   of the   apostle   were wrought
ἐν ὑμῖν ἐν πάσῃ ὑπομονῇ, σημείοις τε
among you in   all   endurance,   ²by signs ¹both
καὶ τέρασιν καὶ δυνάμεσιν.   13 τί γὰρ
and   by wonders   and by powerful deeds.   For what

you less favored than the rest of the churches, except that I myself did not burden you? Forgive me this wrong!

14 Here for the third time I am ready to come to you. And I will not be a burden, for I seek not what is yours but you; for children ought not to lay up for their parents, but parents for their children. ¹⁵I will most gladly spend and be spent for your souls. If I love you the more, am I to be loved the less? ¹⁶But granting that I myself did not burden you, I was crafty, you say, and got the better of you by guile. ¹⁷Did I take advantage of you through any of those whom I sent to you? ¹⁸I urged Titus to go, and sent the brother with him. Did Titus take advantage of you? Did we not act in the same spirit? Did we not take the same steps?

19 Have you been thinking all along that we have been defending ourselves before you? It is in the sight of God that we have been speaking in Christ, and all for your upbuilding, be-

ἐστιν   ὃ   ἡσσώθητε   ὑπὲρ   τὰς   λοιπὰς
is it   which   ye were less   than   the   remaining
ἐκκλησίας,   εἰ   μὴ   ὅτι   αὐτὸς   ἐγὼ   οὐ
churches,   except   that   ⁵[my]self   ¹I   ⁵not
κατενάρκησα   ὑμῶν;   χαρίσασθέ   μοι   τὴν
³encumbered   ⁴of you?   Forgive ye   me   –
ἀδικίαν   ταύτην.   14 Ἰδοὺ   τρίτον   τοῦτο
wrong   this.   Behold   ⁵[the]   ¹this
                                                        third [time]   [is]
ἑτοίμως   ἔχω   ἐλθεῖν   πρὸς   ὑμᾶς,   καὶ
I am ready†   to come   to   you,   and
οὐ   καταναρκήσω·   οὐ   γὰρ   ζητῶ   τὰ   ὑμῶν
I will not encumber [you];   ³not   ¹for   ²I seek   the   of
                                                                        things   you
ἀλλὰ   ὑμᾶς.   οὐ   γὰρ   ὀφείλει   τὰ   τέκνα
but   you.   For ⁴not   ³ought   ¹the   ²children
τοῖς   γονεῦσιν   θησαυρίζειν,   ἀλλὰ   οἱ   γονεῖς
for the   parents   to lay up treasure,   but   the   parents
τοῖς   τέκνοις.   15 ἐγὼ   δὲ   ἥδιστα   δαπανήσω
for the   children.   But I   most gladly   will spend
καὶ   ἐκδαπανηθήσομαι   ὑπὲρ   τῶν   ψυχῶν
and   will be spent out   on behalf of   the   souls
ὑμῶν.   εἰ   περισσοτέρως   ὑμᾶς   ἀγαπῶ,
of you.   If   more abundantly   ²you   ¹I love,
ἧσσον   ἀγαπῶμαι;   16 Ἔστω   δέ,   ἐγὼ   οὐ
[the] less   am I loved?   But let it be,   I   not
κατεβάρησα   ὑμᾶς·   ἀλλὰ   ὑπάρχων   πανοῦργος
burdened   you;   but   being   crafty
δόλῳ   ὑμᾶς   ἔλαβον.   17 μή   τινα   ὧν
³with guile   ²you   ¹I took.   Not   anyone   of
                                                                                    whom
ἀπέσταλκα   πρὸς   ὑμᾶς,   18 δι'   αὐτοῦ
I have sent   to   you,   through   him
ἐπλεονέκτησα   ὑμᾶς;   παρεκάλεσα   Τίτον   καὶ
did I defraud   you?   I besought   Titus   and
συναπέστειλα   τὸν   ἀδελφόν·   μήτι   ἐπλεο-
sent with [him]   the   brother;   not   ²de-
νέκτησεν   ὑμᾶς   Τίτος;   οὐ   τῷ   αὐτῷ
frauded   ³you   ¹Titus?   ²not   ⁵by the   ⁴same
πνεύματι   περιεπατήσαμεν;   οὐ   τοῖς   αὐτοῖς
¹spirit   ¹walked we?   not   in the   same
ἴχνεσιν;
steps?

19 Πάλαι   δοκεῖτε   ὅτι   ὑμῖν   ἀπολογούμεθα.
Already   ye think   that   to you   we are making a
                                                                        defence.
κατέναντι   θεοῦ   ἐν   Χριστῷ   λαλοῦμεν·   τὰ
Before   God   in   Christ   we speak;   –
δὲ   πάντα,   ἀγαπητοί,   ὑπὲρ   τῆς   ὑμῶν
but   all things,   beloved,   [are] on behalf of   ¹the   ²of you

loved. ²⁰ For I fear that perhaps I may come and find you not what I wish, and that you may find me not what you wish; that perhaps there may be quarreling, jealousy, anger, selfishness, slander, gossip, conceit, and disorder. ²¹ I fear that when I come again my God may humble me before you, and I may have to mourn over many of those who sinned before and have not repented of the impurity, immorality, and licentiousness which they have practiced.

CHAPTER 13

THIS is the third time I am coming to you. Any charge must be sustained by the evidence of two or three witnesses. ²I warned those who sinned before and all the others, and I warn them now while absent, as I did when present on my second visit, that if I come again I will not spare them—³since you desire proof that Christ is speaking in me. He is not weak in dealing with you, but is powerful in you. ⁴For he was crucified in weakness, but lives by the power of God. For we are weak in him, but in dealing with you we shall live

---

οἰκοδομῆς. **20** φοβοῦμαι γὰρ μή πως ἐλθὼν
²edification.   For I fear   lest   coming

οὐχ οἵους θέλω εὕρω ὑμᾶς, κἀγὼ εὑρεθῶ
²not ⁴such as ⁵I wish ¹I may find ³you,   and I   am found

ὑμῖν οἷον οὐ θέλετε, μή πως ἔρις,
by you such as   ye wish not,   lest   strife,

ζῆλος, θυμοί, ἐριθεῖαι, καταλαλιαί, ψιθυρισ-
jealousy, angers, rivalries, detractions,   whisper-

μοί, φυσιώσεις, ἀκαταστασίαι· **21** μὴ πάλιν
ings, puffings up,   disturbances;   lest again

ἐλθόντος μου ταπεινώσῃ με ὁ θεός μου
coming   meᵃ ⁴may humble ⁵me ¹the ²God ³of me
=when I come

πρὸς ὑμᾶς, καὶ πενθήσω πολλοὺς τῶν
with   you,   and I shall mourn   many   of the
                                          [ones]

προημαρτηκότων καὶ μὴ μετανοησάντων
having previously sinned and not   repenting

ἐπὶ τῇ ἀκαθαρσίᾳ καὶ πορνείᾳ καὶ
over the uncleanness and fornication and

ἀσελγείᾳ ᾗ ἔπραξαν. **13** Τρίτον τοῦτο
lewdness which they practised. ²[The] third ¹this
                                       [time]   [is]

ἔρχομαι πρὸς ὑμᾶς· ἐπὶ στόματος
I am coming   to   you;   at [the] mouth

δύο μαρτύρων καὶ τριῶν σταθήσεται
of two witnesses and of three shall be established

πᾶν ῥῆμα. **2** προείρηκα καὶ προλέγω,
every word.   I have previously and   I say
                         said   beforehand,

ὡς παρὼν τὸ δεύτερον καὶ ἀπὼν
as being present the second [time] and being absent

νῦν, τοῖς προημαρτηκόσιν καὶ τοῖς
now, to the [ones] having previously sinned and ¹to ³the

λοιποῖς πᾶσιν, ὅτι ἐὰν ἔλθω εἰς τὸ
⁴remaining ²all,   that if I come in the
[ones]

πάλιν οὐ φείσομαι, **3** ἐπεὶ δοκιμὴν ζητεῖτε
again I will not spare,   since ²a proof ¹ye seek

τοῦ ἐν ἐμοὶ λαλοῦντος Χριστοῦ, ὃς εἰς
  – ⁵in ⁶me ⁴speaking ³of Christ, who toward

ὑμᾶς οὐκ ἀσθενεῖ ἀλλὰ δυνατεῖ ἐν ὑμῖν.
you   is not weak but   is powerful in you.

4 καὶ γὰρ ἐσταυρώθη ἐξ ἀσθενείας, ἀλλὰ
For indeed he was crucified out of weakness,   but

ζῇ ἐκ δυνάμεως θεοῦ. καὶ γὰρ ἡμεῖς
he lives by [the] power of God. For indeed   we

ἀσθενοῦμεν ἐν αὐτῷ, ἀλλὰ ζήσομεν σὺν
are weak   in   him,   but   we shall live with

with him by the power of God.

5 Examine yourselves, to see whether you are holding to your faith. Test yourselves. Do you not realize that Jesus Christ is in you?—unless indeed you fail to meet the test! [6] I hope you will find out that we have not failed. [7] But we pray God that you may not do wrong—not that we may appear to have met the test, but that you may do what is right, though we may seem to have failed. [8] For we cannot do anything against the truth, but only for the truth. [9] For we are glad when we are weak and you are strong. What we pray for is your improvement. [10] I write this while I am away from you, in order that when I come I may not have to be severe in my use of the authority which the Lord has given me for building up and not for tearing down.

11 Finally, brethren, farewell. Mend your ways, heed my appeal, agree with one another, live in peace, and the God of love and peace will be with you. [12] Greet one

αὐτῷ ἐκ δυνάμεως θεοῦ εἰς ὑμᾶς.
him by [the] power of God toward you.

5 Ἑαυτοὺς πειράζετε εἰ ἐστὲ ἐν τῇ
[3]Yourselves [1]test if ye are in the

πίστει, ἑαυτοὺς δοκιμάζετε· ἢ οὐκ
faith, [2]yourselves [1]prove; or not

ἐπιγινώσκετε ἑαυτοὺς ὅτι Ἰησοῦς Χριστὸς
perceive ye yourselves that Jesus Christ [is]

ἐν ὑμῖν, εἰ μήτι ἀδόκιμοί ἐστε. 6 ἐλπίζω
in you, unless [2]counterfeits [1]ye are. I hope

δὲ ὅτι γνώσεσθε ὅτι ἡμεῖς οὐκ ἐσμὲν
But that ye will know that we are not

ἀδόκιμοι. 7 εὐχόμεθα δὲ πρὸς τὸν θεὸν
counterfeits. Now we pray to – God

μὴ ποιῆσαι ὑμᾶς κακὸν μηδέν, οὐχ
not to do you evil none, not
=that ye do no ...

ἵνα ἡμεῖς δόκιμοι φανῶμεν, ἀλλ᾽ ἵνα
in order we [2]approved [1]may appear, but in order
that that

ὑμεῖς τὸ καλὸν ποιῆτε, ἡμεῖς δὲ ὡς
ye [2]the [2]good [1]may do, and we [2]as

ἀδόκιμοι ὦμεν. 8 οὐ γὰρ δυνάμεθά
[2]counterfeits [1]may be. For we cannot [do]

τι κατὰ τῆς ἀληθείας, ἀλλὰ ὑπὲρ τῆς
any- against the truth, but on behalf of the
thing

ἀληθείας. 9 χαίρομεν γὰρ ὅταν ἡμεῖς
truth. For we rejoice whenever we

ἀσθενῶμεν, ὑμεῖς δὲ δυνατοὶ ἦτε· τοῦτο
are weak, and ye powerful are; this

καὶ εὐχόμεθα, τὴν ὑμῶν κατάρτισιν. 10 Διὰ
also we pray, the [2]of you [1]restoration. There-

τοῦτο ταῦτα ἀπὼν γράφω, ἵνα παρὼν
fore [2]these things [2]being [1]I write, in order being
absent that present

μὴ ἀποτόμως χρήσωμαι κατὰ τὴν ἐξουσίαν
[2]not [3]sharply [1]I may deal according to the authority

ἣν ὁ κύριος ἔδωκέν μοι εἰς οἰκοδομὴν
which the Lord gave me for edification

καὶ οὐκ εἰς καθαίρεσιν.
and not for overthrow.

11 Λοιπόν, ἀδελφοί, χαίρετε, καταρτίζεσθε,
For the rest,† brothers, rejoice, restore yourselves,

παρακαλεῖσθε, τὸ αὐτὸ φρονεῖτε, εἰρηνεύετε,
admonish yourselves, the same thing think, be at peace,

καὶ ὁ θεὸς τῆς ἀγάπης καὶ εἰρήνης
and the God – of love and of peace

ἔσται μεθ᾽ ὑμῶν. 12 Ἀσπάσασθε ἀλλήλους
will be with you. Greet ye one another

another with a holy kiss. *ἐν ἁγίῳ φιλήματι.* *᾽Ασπάζονται ὑμᾶς οἱ*
¹³All the saints greet   with a holy   kiss.   ⁴greet   ⁷you   ⁸the
you.
    14 The grace of the   *ἅγιοι   πάντες.*
Lord Jesus Christ and   ³saints   ¹All.
the love of God and the
fellowship of[ᶦ] the Holy 13 *῾Η   χάρις   τοῦ   κυρίου   ᾽Ιησοῦ   Χριστοῦ*
Spirit be with you all.   The   grace   of the   Lord   Jesus   Christ

                           καὶ   ἡ   ἀγάπη   τοῦ   θεοῦ   καὶ   ἡ   κοινωνία
                           and   the   love   –   of God   and   the   fellowship

                           τοῦ   ἁγίου   πνεύματος   μετὰ   πάντων   ὑμῶν.
                           of the   Holy   Spirit   [be] with   ³all   ¹you.

GALATIANS 1   *ΠΡΟΣ ΓΑΛΑΤΑΣ*
                           To Galatians

CHAPTER 1   1 *Παῦλος   ἀπόστολος,   οὐκ   ἀπ᾽   ἀνθρώπων*
                           Paul   an apostle,   not   from   men
PAUL an apostle—
   not from men nor   *οὐδὲ   δι᾽   ἀνθρώπου   ἀλλὰ   διὰ   ᾽Ιησοῦ*
through   man,   but   nor   through   man   but   through   Jesus
through Jesus Christ and
God the Father, who   *Χριστοῦ   καὶ   θεοῦ   πατρὸς   τοῦ   ἐγείραντος*
raised   him from the   Christ   and   God [the] Father the [one] having raised
dead—²and all the breth-
ren who are with me,   *αὐτὸν   ἐκ   νεκρῶν,   2 καὶ   οἱ   σὺν   ἐμοὶ*
   To the churches of   him   out of [the] dead, and   ²the ⁴with ⁵me
Galatia:
   3 Grace to you and   *πάντες   ἀδελφοί,   ταῖς   ἐκκλησίαις   τῆς*
peace from God the   ¹all   ³brothers,   to the   churches   –
Father and our Lord
Jesus Christ, ⁴who gave *Γαλατίας·   3 χάρις   ὑμῖν   καὶ   εἰρήνη   ἀπὸ*
himself for our sins to   of Galatia: Grace   to you   and   peace   from
deliver us from the
present evil age, accord- *θεοῦ   πατρὸς   ἡμῶν   καὶ   κυρίου   ᾽Ιησοῦ*
ing to the will of our God   God   Father   of us   and   Lord   Jesus
and Father; ⁵to whom
be the glory for ever and *Χριστοῦ,   4 τοῦ   δόντος   ἑαυτὸν   ὑπὲρ   τῶν*
ever. Amen.   Christ,   the [one] having given himself on behalf of the

                           ἁμαρτιῶν   ἡμῶν,   ὅπως   ἐξέληται   ἡμᾶς   ἐκ
                           sins   of us,   so as   he might deliver us   out of

                           τοῦ   αἰῶνος   τοῦ   ἐνεστῶτος   πονηροῦ   κατὰ
                           the   ²age   –   ¹present   ²evil   according to

                           τὸ   θέλημα   τοῦ   θεοῦ   καὶ   πατρὸς   ἡμῶν,
                           the   will   of the   God   and   Father   of us,

                           5 *ᾧ   ἡ   δόξα   εἰς   τοὺς   αἰῶνας   τῶν*
                           to whom the glory   unto   the   ages   of the
                           [be]

                           αἰώνων·   ἀμήν.
                           ages: Amen.

ᶦ Or *and participation in*

6 I am astonished that you are so quickly deserting him who called you in the grace of Christ and turning to a different gospel—⁷not that there is another gospel, but there are some who trouble you and want to pervert the gospel of Christ. ⁸But even if we, or an angel from heaven, should preach to you a gospel contrary to that which we preached to you, let him be accursed. ⁹As we have said before, so now I say again, If any one is preaching to you a gospel contrary to that which you received, let him be accursed.

10 Am I now seeking the favor of men, or of God? Or am I trying to please men? If I were still pleasing men, I should not be a servant of Christ.

11 For I would have you know, brethren, that the gospel which was preached by me is not man's gospel. ¹²For I did not receive it from man, nor was I taught it, but it came through a revelation of Jesus Christ. ¹³For you have heard of my former life in Judaism, how I persecuted the church of

6 Θαυμάζω ὅτι οὕτως ταχέως μετατίθεσθε
I wonder   that   thus   quickly ye are removing

ἀπὸ τοῦ καλέσαντος ὑμᾶς ἐν χάριτι
from the [one] having called you by [the] grace

Χριστοῦ εἰς ἕτερον εὐαγγέλιον, 7 ὃ οὐκ
of Christ to another gospel, which not

ἔστιν ἄλλο· εἰ μή τινές εἰσιν οἱ ταράσ-
is another; only ²some ¹there are – troubl-

σοντες ὑμᾶς καὶ θέλοντες μεταστρέψαι
ing you and wishing to pervert

τὸ εὐαγγέλιον τοῦ Χριστοῦ. 8 ἀλλὰ
the gospel – of Christ. But

καὶ ἐὰν ἡμεῖς ἢ ἄγγελος ἐξ οὐρανοῦ
even if we or an angel out of heaven

εὐαγγελίσηται [ὑμῖν] παρ' ὃ εὐηγγελισάμεθα
should preach to you beside what we preached
a gospel

ὑμῖν, ἀνάθεμα ἔστω. 9 ὡς προειρήκαμεν,
to you, ²a curse ¹let him be. As we have previously said,

καὶ ἄρτι πάλιν λέγω, εἴ τις ὑμᾶς εὐαγ-
also now again I say, if anyone ²you ¹preaches

γελίζεται παρ' ὃ παρελάβετε, ἀνάθεμα
¹a gospel beside what ye received, ²a curse

ἔστω.
¹let him be.

10 Ἄρτι γὰρ ἀνθρώπους πείθω ἢ τὸν
For now men do I persuade or –

θεόν; ἢ ζητῶ ἀνθρώποις ἀρέσκειν; εἰ
God? or do I seek men to please? If

ἔτι ἀνθρώποις ἤρεσκον, Χριστοῦ δοῦλος
still men I pleased, ²of Christ ³a slave

οὐκ ἂν ἤμην. 11 γνωρίζω γὰρ ὑμῖν,
¹I would not have been. For I make known to you,

ἀδελφοί, τὸ εὐαγγέλιον τὸ εὐαγγελισθὲν
brothers, the gospel – preached

ὑπ' ἐμοῦ ὅτι οὐκ ἔστιν κατὰ ἄνθρωπον
by me that it is not according to man;

12 οὐδὲ γὰρ ἐγὼ παρὰ ἀνθρώπου παρέλαβον
for ²not ¹I ⁵from ³man ⁴received

αὐτὸ οὔτε ἐδιδάχθην, ἀλλὰ δι' ἀποκαλύψεως
³it nor was I taught but through a revelation
[by man],

Ἰησοῦ Χριστοῦ. 13 Ἠκούσατε γὰρ τὴν
of Jesus Christ. For ye heard –

ἐμὴν ἀναστροφήν ποτε ἐν τῷ Ἰουδαϊσμῷ,
my conduct then in – Judaism,

ὅτι καθ' ὑπερβολὴν ἐδίωκον τὴν ἐκκλησίαν
that excessively† I persecuted the church

God violently and tried to destroy it; [14]and I advanced in Judaism beyond many of my own age among my people, so extremely zealous was I for the traditions of my fathers. [15]But when he who had set me apart before I was born, and had called me through his grace, [16]was pleased to reveal his Son to me, in order that I might preach him among the Gentiles, I did not confer with flesh and blood, [17]nor did I go up to Jerusalem to those who were apostles before me, but I went away into Arabia; and again I returned to Damascus.

[18] Then after three years I went up to Jerusalem to visit Cephas, and remained with him fifteen days. [19]But I saw none of the other apostles except James the Lord's brother. [20](In what I am writing to you, before God, I do not lie!) [21]Then I went into the regions of Syria and Cili'cia. [22]And I was still not known by sight to the churches of Christ

τοῦ θεοῦ καὶ ἐπόρθουν αὐτήν, **14** καὶ
of God and wasted it, and

προέκοπτον ἐν τῷ Ἰουδαϊσμῷ ὑπὲρ πολλοὺς
progressed in - Judaism beyond many

συνηλικιώτας ἐν τῷ γένει μου, περισ-
contemporaries in the race of me, [2]abun-

σοτέρως ζηλωτὴς ὑπάρχων τῶν πατρικῶν
dantly [3]a zealot [1]being [4]of the [5]ancestral

μου παραδόσεων. **15** Ὅτε δὲ εὐδόκησεν
[6]of me [5]traditions. But when [14]was pleased

ὁ ἀφορίσας με ἐκ κοιλίας μητρός μου
[1]the [2]having [3]me [4]from [5][the] womb [6]of mother [7]of me
[one] separated

καὶ καλέσας διὰ τῆς χάριτος αὐτοῦ
[8]and [9]having called [10]through [11]the [13]grace [12]of him

16 ἀποκαλύψαι τὸν υἱὸν αὐτοῦ ἐν ἐμοί,
to reveal the Son of him in me,

ἵνα εὐαγγελίζωμαι αὐτὸν ἐν τοῖς ἔθνεσιν,
in order I might preach him among the nations,
that

εὐθέως οὐ προσανεθέμην σαρκὶ καὶ αἵματι,
immediately I conferred not with flesh and blood,

17 οὐδὲ ἀνῆλθον εἰς Ἱεροσόλυμα πρὸς
neither did I go up to Jerusalem to

τοὺς πρὸ ἐμοῦ ἀποστόλους, ἀλλὰ ἀπῆλθον
[1]the [3]before [4]me [2]apostles, but I went away

εἰς Ἀραβίαν, καὶ πάλιν ὑπέστρεψα εἰς
into Arabia, and again returned to

Δαμασκόν. **18** Ἔπειτα μετὰ τρία ἔτη
Damascus. Then after three years

ἀνῆλθον εἰς Ἱεροσόλυμα ἱστορῆσαι Κηφᾶν,
I went up to Jerusalem to visit Cephas,

καὶ ἐπέμεινα πρὸς αὐτὸν ἡμέρας δεκαπέντε·
and remained with him days fifteen;

19 ἕτερον δὲ τῶν ἀποστόλων οὐκ εἶδον,
but other of the apostles I saw not,

εἰ μὴ Ἰάκωβον τὸν ἀδελφὸν τοῦ κυρίου.
except James the brother of the Lord.

20 ἃ δὲ γράφω ὑμῖν, ἰδοὺ ἐνώπιον τοῦ
Now what I write to you, behold before -
things

θεοῦ ὅτι οὐ ψεύδομαι. **21** ἔπειτα ἦλθον
God - I lie not. Then I went

εἰς τὰ κλίματα τῆς Συρίας καὶ τῆς
into the regions - of Syria and -

Κιλικίας. **22** ἤμην δὲ ἀγνοούμενος τῷ
of Cilicia. And I was being unknown -

προσώπῳ ταῖς ἐκκλησίαις τῆς Ἰουδαίας
by face to the churches - of Judæa

in Judea; [23] they only heard it said, "He who once persecuted us is now preaching the faith he once tried to destroy." [24] And they glorified God because of me.

ταῖς   ἐν   Χριστῷ.   23 μόνον   δὲ   ἀκούοντες
-       in   Christ.   But only   hearing

ἦσαν   ὅτι   ὁ   διώκων   ἡμᾶς   ποτε   νῦν
they were that the [one] [2]persecuting [3]us   [1]then   now

εὐαγγελίζεται   τὴν   πίστιν   ἥν   ποτε   ἐπόρθει,
preaches   the   faith   which then   he was
                                                   destroying,

24 καὶ   ἐδόξαζον   ἐν   ἐμοὶ   τὸν   θεόν.
   and   they glorified [2]in   [3]me   -   [1]God.

CHAPTER 2

THEN after fourteen years I went up again to Jerusalem with Barnabas, taking Titus along with me. [2] I went up by revelation; and I laid before them (but privately before those who were of repute) the gospel which I preach among the Gentiles, lest somehow I should be running or had run in vain. [3] But even Titus, who was with me, was not compelled to be circumcised, though he was a Greek. [4] But because of false brethren secretly brought in, who slipped in to spy out our freedom which we have in Christ Jesus, that they might bring us into bondage—[5] to them we did not yield submission even for a moment, that the truth of the gospel might be preserved for you. [6] And from those who were reputed to be something (what they were makes no difference to me; God shows no partiality)—those, I say, who were of repute added nothing to me;

2 Ἔπειτα   διὰ   δεκατεσσάρων   ἐτῶν   πάλιν
  Then   through   fourteen   years   again

ἀνέβην   εἰς   Ἱεροσόλυμα   μετὰ   Βαρναβᾶ,
I went up to   Jerusalem   with   Barnabas,

συμπαραλαβὼν   καὶ   Τίτον·   2 ἀνέβην   δὲ
taking with [me]   also   Titus;   and I went up

κατὰ   ἀποκάλυψιν·   καὶ   ἀνεθέμην   αὐτοῖς
according to a revelation;   and   I put before   them

τὸ   εὐαγγέλιον   ὃ   κηρύσσω   ἐν   τοῖς   ἔθνεσιν,
the   gospel   which   I proclaim   among the   nations,

κατ'   ἰδίαν   δὲ   τοῖς   δοκοῦσιν,   μή   πως
[2]privately   [1]but to the [ones]   seeming,[*]   lest

εἰς   κενὸν   τρέχω   ἢ   ἔδραμον.   3 ἀλλ'
in   vain   I run   or   I ran.   But

οὐδὲ   Τίτος   ὁ   σὺν   ἐμοί,   Ἕλλην   ὤν,
not   Titus   the [one] with   me,   a Greek   being,

ἠναγκάσθη   περιτμηθῆναι·   4 διὰ   δὲ   τοὺς
was compelled   to be circumcised;   but on account of [1]the

παρεισάκτους   ψευδαδέλφους,   οἵτινες   παρεισ-
[2]brought in secretly   [2]false brothers,   who   stole

ἦλθον   κατασκοπῆσαι   τὴν   ἐλευθερίαν   ἡμῶν
in   to spy on   the   freedom   of us

ἣν   ἔχομεν   ἐν   Χριστῷ   Ἰησοῦ,   ἵνα   ἡμᾶς
which we have in   Christ   Jesus,   in order that [2]us

καταδουλώσουσιν·   5 οἷς   οὐδὲ   πρὸς   ὥραν
[1]they will(might) enslave;   to whom not   for   an hour

εἴξαμεν   τῇ   ὑποταγῇ,   ἵνα   ἡ   ἀλήθεια
yielded we   -   in subjection, in order that the   truth

τοῦ   εὐαγγελίου   διαμείνῃ   πρὸς   ὑμᾶς.   6 ἀπὸ
of the   gospel   might continue with   you.   from

δὲ   τῶν   δοκούντων   εἶναί   τι,   —   ὁποῖοί
But the [ones]   seeming   to be something, (of what kind

ποτε   ἦσαν   οὐδέν   μοι   διαφέρει·   πρόσωπον
[2]then [1]they were [4]nothing [5]to me   [3]matters: [6][the] face

[ὁ]   θεὸς   ἀνθρώπου   οὐ   λαμβάνει   —   ἐμοὶ
  -    [6]God   [5]of a man   [7]receives not,)   [8]to me

γὰρ   οἱ   δοκοῦντες   οὐδὲν   προσανέθεντο,
[1]for the [ones] seeming[*]   nothing   added,

---

* Cf. the full expressions in vers. 6 (earlier) and 9.

7 but on the contrary, when they saw that I had been entrusted with the gospel to the uncircumcised, just as Peter had been entrusted with the gospel to the circumcised 8 (for he who worked through Peter for the mission to the circumcised worked through me also for the Gentiles), 9 and when they perceived the grace that was given to me, James and Cephas and John, who were reputed to be pillars, gave to me and Barnabas the right hand of fellowship, that we should go to the Gentiles and they to the circumcised; 10 only they would have us remember the poor, which very thing I was eager to do.

11 But when Cephas came to Antioch I opposed him to his face, because he stood condemned. 12 For before certain men came from James, he ate with the Gentiles; but when they came he drew back and separated himself, fearing the circumcision party. 13 And with him the rest of the Jews acted insincerely, so that even Barnabas was carried away by their insincerity. 14 But when I saw that they were not straightforward about the truth of the gospel, I said to

---

7 ἀλλὰ τοὐναντίον ἰδόντες ὅτι πεπίστευμαι
but on the contrary seeing that I have been
entrusted [with]

τὸ εὐαγγέλιον τῆς ἀκροβυστίας καθὼς
the gospel of the uncircumcision as

Πέτρος τῆς περιτομῆς, 8 ὁ γὰρ ἐνεργήσας
Peter [that] of the circumcision, for the [one] operating

Πέτρῳ εἰς ἀποστολὴν τῆς περιτομῆς
in Peter to an apostleship of the circumcision

ἐνήργησεν καὶ ἐμοὶ εἰς τὰ ἔθνη, 9 καὶ
operated also in me to the nations, and

γνόντες τὴν χάριν τὴν δοθεῖσάν μοι,
knowing the grace - given to me,

Ἰάκωβος καὶ Κηφᾶς καὶ Ἰωάννης, οἱ
James and Cephas and John, the

δοκοῦντες στῦλοι εἶναι, δεξιὰς ἔδωκαν
[ones] seeming ²pillars ¹to be, ⁴right [hands] ¹gave

ἐμοὶ καὶ Βαρναβᾷ κοινωνίας, ἵνα ἡμεῖς
²to me ³and ⁴to Barnabas ⁵of fellowship, in order we
that [should

εἰς τὰ ἔθνη, αὐτοὶ δὲ εἰς τὴν περιτομήν·
go] to the nations, but they to the circumcision;

10 μόνον τῶν πτωχῶν ἵνα μνημονεύωμεν,
only ²the ⁴poor in order ¹that ³we might remember,

ὃ καὶ ἐσπούδασα αὐτὸ τοῦτο ποιῆσαι.
which indeed ²I was eager ¹this very thing to do.

11 Ὅτε δὲ ἦλθεν Κηφᾶς εἰς Ἀντιόχειαν,
But when ²came ¹Cephas to Antioch,

κατὰ πρόσωπον αὐτῷ ἀντέστην, ὅτι
against [his] face to him I opposed, because

κατεγνωσμένος ἦν. 12 πρὸ τοῦ γὰρ
²having been condemned ¹he was. Before the for
= For before some came . . .

ἐλθεῖν τινας ἀπὸ Ἰακώβου μετὰ τῶν
to come someᵇ from James ²with ³the

ἐθνῶν συνήσθιεν· ὅτε δὲ ἦλθον, ὑπέστελλεν
⁴nations ¹he ate with; but when they came, he withdrew

καὶ ἀφώριζεν ἑαυτόν, φοβούμενος τοὺς
and separated himself, fearing the [ones]

ἐκ περιτομῆς· 13 καὶ συνυπεκρίθησαν αὐτῷ
of [the] circumcision; and dissembled along with him

[καὶ] οἱ λοιποὶ Ἰουδαῖοι, ὥστε καὶ
also the remaining Jews, so as even

Βαρναβᾶς συναπήχθη αὐτῶν τῇ ὑποκρίσει.
Barnabas was led away with ³of them ¹the ²dissembling.

14 ἀλλ' ὅτε εἶδον ὅτι οὐκ ὀρθοποδοῦσιν
But when I saw that they walk[ed] not straight

πρὸς τὴν ἀλήθειαν τοῦ εὐαγγελίου, εἶπον
with the truth of the gospel, I said

Cephas before them all, "If you, though a Jew, live like a Gentile and not like a Jew, how can you compel the Gentiles to live like Jews?" [15] We ourselves, who are Jews by birth and not Gentile sinners, [16] yet who know that a man is not justified[a] by works of the law but through faith in Jesus Christ, even we have believed in Christ Jesus, in order to be justified by faith in Christ, and not by works of the law, because by works of the law shall no one be justified. [17] But if, in our endeavor to be justified in Christ, we ourselves were found to be sinners, is Christ then an agent of sin? Certainly not! [18] But if I build up again those things which I tore down, then I prove myself a transgressor. [19] For I through the law died to the law, that I might live to God. [20] I have been crucified with Christ; it is no longer I who live, but Christ who lives in me; and the life I now live in the flesh I live by faith in the Son of God, who loved me and gave himself for me.

τῷ   Κηφᾷ   ἔμπροσθεν   πάντων·   εἰ   σὺ
\-   to Cephas   in front of   all: If   thou

Ἰουδαῖος   ὑπάρχων   ἐθνικῶς   καὶ   οὐκ
[2]a Jew   [1]being   as a Gentile   and   not

Ἰουδαϊκῶς   ζῇς,   πῶς   τὰ   ἔθνη   ἀναγκάζεις
as a Jew   livest,   how   [2]the [3]nations [1]compellest thou

ἰουδαΐζειν;   15 Ἡμεῖς   φύσει   Ἰουδαῖοι   καὶ
to judaize?   We   by nature   Jews   and

οὐκ   ἐξ   ἐθνῶν   ἁμαρτωλοί,   16 εἰδότες   δὲ
not   [3]of   [2]nations   [1]sinners,   and knowing

ὅτι   οὐ   δικαιοῦται   ἄνθρωπος   ἐξ   ἔργων
that   [2]is not justified   [1]a man   by   works

νόμου   ἐὰν   μὴ   διὰ   πίστεως   Χριστοῦ
of law   except(but)   through   faith   of(in) Christ

Ἰησοῦ,   καὶ   ἡμεῖς   εἰς   Χριστὸν   Ἰησοῦν
Jesus,*   even   we   [2]in   [3]Christ   [4]Jesus

ἐπιστεύσαμεν,   ἵνα   δικαιωθῶμεν   ἐκ   πίστεως
[1]believed,   in order that   we might be   by   faith
       justified

Χριστοῦ   καὶ   οὐκ   ἐξ   ἔργων   νόμου,   ὅτι
of(in) Christ*   and   not   by   works   of law, because

ἐξ   ἔργων   νόμου   οὐ   δικαιωθήσεται   πᾶσα
by   works   of law   not   will be justified   all
       =no flesh will be justified.

σάρξ.   17 εἰ   δὲ   ζητοῦντες   δικαιωθῆναι
flesh.   But if   seeking   to be justified

ἐν   Χριστῷ   εὑρέθημεν   καὶ   αὐτοὶ   ἁμαρτωλοί,
in   Christ   we were found   also   [our]selves   sinners,

ἆρα   Χριστὸς   ἁμαρτίας   διάκονος;   μὴ
then   [is] Christ   [2]of sin   [1]a minister?   not

γένοιτο.   18 εἰ   γὰρ   ἃ   κατέλυσα   ταῦτα
May it be.   For if   what things I destroyed these things

πάλιν   οἰκοδομῶ,   παραβάτην   ἐμαυτὸν   συνισ-
again   I build,   [2]a transgressor   [3]myself   [1]I con-

τάνω.   19 ἐγὼ   γὰρ   διὰ   νόμου   νόμῳ
stitute.   For I   through   law   [2]to law

ἀπέθανον   ἵνα   θεῷ   ζήσω.   20 Χριστῷ   συνεσ-
[1]died   in order to God I might live.   With Christ   I have
       that

ταύρωμαι·   ζῶ   δὲ   οὐκέτι   ἐγώ,   ζῇ   δὲ
been co-crucified;   and [3]live   [2]no more   [1]I,   but [2]lives

ἐν   ἐμοὶ   Χριστός·   ὃ   δὲ   νῦν   ζῶ   ἐν   σαρκί,
[3]in   [4]me   [1]Christ;   and what now I live   in [the] flesh,

ἐν   πίστει   ζῶ   τῇ   τοῦ   υἱοῦ   τοῦ   θεοῦ
[3]by   [2]faith   [1]I live   \- of(in) the Son   \- of God

τοῦ   ἀγαπήσαντός   με   καὶ   παραδόντος   ἑαυτὸν
\-   loving   me   and   giving up   himself

---

[a] Or reckoned righteous; and so elsewhere

* Objective genitive, as is shown by the intervening sentence see also 3. 22, 26). Cf. " fear of God".

²¹I do not nullify the grace of God; for if justification[b] were through the law, then Christ died to no purpose.

ὑπέρ ἐμοῦ. 21 Οὐκ ἀθετῶ τὴν χάριν
on behalf of me.   I do not set aside the   grace

τοῦ θεοῦ· εἰ γὰρ διὰ νόμου δικαιοσύνη,
–   of God; for if through law   righteousness
                                              [comes],

ἄρα Χριστὸς δωρεὰν ἀπέθανεν.
then Christ   without cause   died.

CHAPTER 3

O foolish Galatians! Who has bewitched you, before whose eyes Jesus Christ was publicly portrayed as crucified? ²Let me ask you only this: Did you receive the Spirit by works of the law, or by hearing with faith? ³Are you so foolish? Having begun with the Spirit, are you now ending with the flesh? ⁴Did you experience so many things in vain?—if it really is in vain. ⁵Does he who supplies the Spirit to you and works miracles among you do so by works of the law, or by hearing with faith?

6 Thus Abraham "believed God, and it was reckoned to him as righteousness." ⁷So you see that it is men of faith who are the sons of Abraham. ⁸And the scripture, foreseeing that God would justify the Gentiles by faith, preached the gospel beforehand to Abraham, saying, "In you shall all the nations be blessed." ⁹So then, those who are men of faith are blessed

3 ¹Ὦ ἀνόητοι Γαλάται, τίς ὑμᾶς
   O   foolish Galatians, who you

ἐβάσκανεν, οἷς κατ᾽ ὀφθαλμοὺς Ἰησοῦς
bewitched, to before   eyes   Jesus
            whom [the]

Χριστὸς προεγράφη ἐσταυρωμένος; 2 τοῦτο
Christ   was portrayed having been crucified?   This

μόνον θέλω μαθεῖν ἀφ᾽ ὑμῶν, ἐξ ἔργων
only I wish to learn from   you, by works

νόμου τὸ πνεῦμα ἐλάβετε ἢ ἐξ ἀκοῆς
of law the Spirit received ye or by hearing

πίστεως; 3 οὕτως ἀνόητοί ἐστε; ἐναρξάμενοι
of faith? thus   foolish are ye? having begun

πνεύματι νῦν σαρκὶ ἐπιτελεῖσθε; 4 τοσαῦτα
in [the] Spirit now in [the] flesh are ye being so many things
                              perfected?

ἐπάθετε εἰκῇ; 5 εἴ γε καὶ εἰκῇ. ὁ
suffered ye in vain?   if indeed   in vain. The [one]

οὖν ἐπιχορηγῶν ὑμῖν τὸ πνεῦμα καὶ
therefore supplying to you the Spirit   and

ἐνεργῶν δυνάμεις ἐν ὑμῖν ἐξ ἔργων
working powerful deeds among you [is it] by works

νόμου ἢ ἐξ ἀκοῆς πίστεως; 6 Καθὼς
of law or by hearing of faith?   As

Ἀβραὰμ ἐπίστευσεν τῷ θεῷ, καὶ ἐλογίσθη
Abraham believed   –   God, and it was reckoned

αὐτῷ εἰς δικαιοσύνην. 7 γινώσκετε ἄρα
to him for righteousness.   Know ye   then

ὅτι οἱ ἐκ πίστεως, οὗτοι υἱοί εἰσιν
that the [ones] of   faith,   ¹these ²sons ²are

Ἀβραάμ. 8 προϊδοῦσα δὲ ἡ γραφὴ ὅτι
⁴of Abraham. And ³foreseeing ¹the ²scripture ⁴that

ἐκ πίστεως δικαιοῖ τὰ ἔθνη ὁ θεός,
⁹by ¹⁰faith ⁷would justify ⁷the ⁸nations – ⁶God,

προευηγγελίσατο τῷ Ἀβραὰμ ὅτι ἐνευλογη-
preached good tidings – to Abraham that   ⁶will be
before

θήσονται ἐν σοὶ πάντα τὰ ἔθνη. 9 ὥστε
blessed ¹in ²thee ³all ⁴the ⁵nations.   So as

οἱ ἐκ πίστεως εὐλογοῦνται σὺν τῷ πιστῷ
the [ones] of faith   are blessed with the believing

[b] Or righteousness

with Abraham who had faith.

10 For all who rely on works of the law are under a curse; for it is written, "Cursed be every one who does not abide by all things written in the book of the law, and do them." 11 Now it is evident that no man is justified before God by the law; for "He who through faith is righteous shall live";c 12 but the law does not rest on faith, for "He who does them shall live by them." 13 Christ redeemed us from the curse of the law, having become a curse for us—for it is written, "Cursed be every one who hangs on a tree"—14 that in Christ Jesus the blessing of Abraham might come upon the Gentiles, that we might receive the promise of the Spirit through faith.

15 To give a human example, brethren: no man annuls even a man's willd or adds to it, once it has been ratified. 16 Now the promises were made to Abraham and to his offspring. It does not say, "And to offsprings," referring to many; but, referring to one, "And to your offspring," which is Christ. 17 This is what I mean:

c Or *the righteous shall live by faith*

d Or *covenant* (as in verse 17)

'Αβραάμ.   10 ῞Οσοι   γὰρ   ἐξ   ἔργων   νόμου
Abraham.   For as many as   ²of   ³works   ⁴of law

εἰσίν,   ὑπὸ   κατάραν   εἰσίν·   γέγραπται   γὰρ
¹are,   ⁶under   ⁷a curse   ⁵are;   for it has been written[,]

ὅτι   ἐπικατάρατος   πᾶς   ὃς   οὐκ   ἐμμένει
—   Accursed   everyone who   continues not

πᾶσιν   τοῖς   γεγραμμένοις   ἐν   τῷ   βιβλίῳ
in all   the things having been written   in   the   roll

τοῦ   νόμου   τοῦ   ποιῆσαι   αὐτά.   11 ὅτι
of the   law   —   to dod   them.   that

δὲ   ἐν   νόμῳ   οὐδεὶς   δικαιοῦται   παρὰ   τῷ
Now by   law   no man   is justified   before   —

θεῷ   δῆλον,   ὅτι   ὁ   δίκαιος   ἐκ   πίστεως
God   [is] clear,   because the   just man   by   faith

ζήσεται·   12 ὁ   δὲ   νόμος   οὐκ   ἔστιν   ἐκ
will live;   and the   law   is not   of

πίστεως,   ἀλλ'   ὁ   ποιήσας   αὐτὰ   ζήσεται
faith,   but   the [one] doing   them   will live

ἐν   αὐτοῖς.   13 Χριστὸς   ἡμᾶς   ἐξηγόρασεν
by   them.   Christ   ²us   ¹redeemed

ἐκ   τῆς   κατάρας   τοῦ   νόμου   γενόμενος
out of   the   curse   of the   law   becoming

ὑπὲρ   ἡμῶν   κατάρα,   ὅτι   γέγραπται·
²on behalf of   ³us   ¹a curse,   because   it has been written:

ἐπικατάρατος   πᾶς   ὁ   κρεμάμενος   ἐπὶ
Accursed   everyone   hanging   on

ξύλου,   14 ἵνα   εἰς   τὰ   ἔθνη   ἡ   εὐλογία
a tree,   in order that   ⁵to   ⁶the   ⁷nations   ¹the   ²blessing

τοῦ   'Αβραὰμ   γένηται   ἐν   'Ιησοῦ   Χριστῷ,
—   ³of Abraham   ⁴might be   in   Jesus   Christ,

ἵνα   τὴν   ἐπαγγελίαν   τοῦ   πνεύματος   λάβωμεν
in order   ²the   ³promise   ⁴of the   ⁵Spirit   ¹we might that receive

διὰ   τῆς   πίστεως.   15 'Αδελφοί,   κατὰ
through *the*   faith.   Brothers,   according to

ἄνθρωπον   λέγω.   ὅμως   ἀνθρώπου   κεκυρω-
man   I say.   Nevertheless   ⁶of man   ¹having been

μένην   διαθήκην   οὐδεὶς   ἀθετεῖ   ἢ   ἐπιδια-
ratified   ⁵a covenant   ¹no one   ²sets aside   ³or   ⁴makes

τάσσεται.   16 τῷ   δὲ   'Αβραὰμ   ἐρρέθησαν
additions [to].   —   Now   to Abraham   were said

αἱ   ἐπαγγελίαι   καὶ   τῷ   σπέρματι   αὐτοῦ.
the   promises   and   to the   seed   of him.

οὐ   λέγει·   καὶ   τοῖς   σπέρμασιν,   ὡς   ἐπὶ
It says not: And   to the   seeds,   as concerning

πολλῶν,   ἀλλ'   ὡς   ἐφ'   ἑνός·   καὶ   τῷ
many,   but   as concerning one: And   to the

σπέρματί   σου,   ὅς   ἐστιν   Χριστός.   17 τοῦτο   δὲ
seed   of thee,   who   is   Christ.   And this

the law, which came four hundred and thirty years afterward, does not annul a covenant previously ratified by God, so as to make the promise void. ¹⁸ For if the inheritance is by the law, it is no longer by promise; but God gave it to Abraham by a promise.

19 Why then the law? It was added because of transgressions, till the offspring should come to whom the promise had been made; and it was ordained by angels through an intermediary. ²⁰ Now an intermediary implies more than one; but God is one.

21 Is the law then against the promises of God? Certainly not; for if a law had been given which could make alive, then righteousness would indeed be by the law. ²² But the scripture consigned all things to sin, that what was promised to faith in Jesus Christ might be given to those who believe.

23 Now before faith came, we were confined under the law, kept under restraint until faith should be revealed. ²⁴ So that the law was our custodian until Christ

λέγω·   διαθήκην   προκεκυρωμένην   ὑπὸ
I say: ¹⁰A covenant   ¹¹having been previously ratified   ¹²by

τοῦ   θεοῦ   ὁ μετὰ   τετρακόσια   καὶ   τριάκοντα
–   ¹³God ¹the   ⁴after   ⁵four hundred   ⁶and   ⁷thirty

ἔτη   γεγονὼς   νόμος   οὐκ   ἀκυροῖ,   εἰς   τὸ
⁸years ⁹having come   ²law   ⁹does not annul,   so as† into being

καταργῆσαι   τὴν   ἐπαγγελίαν.   18 εἰ   γὰρ
to abolish   the   promise.   18 For if

ἐκ   νόμου   ἡ   κληρονομία,   οὐκέτι   ἐξ
⁴of   ⁵law   ¹the   ²inheritance ³[is],   no more [is it] of

ἐπαγγελίας·   τῷ   δὲ   Ἀβραὰμ   δι᾽   ἐπαγγελίας
promise;   – but   ⁴to Abraham ⁵through   ⁶promise

κεχάρισται   ὁ   θεός.   19 Τί   οὖν   ὁ   νόμος;
²has given ³[it]   –   ¹God.   Why therefore the   law?

τῶν   παραβάσεων   χάριν   προσετέθη,   ἄχρις
³the   ⁴transgressions ²by reason of ¹it was added,   until

ἂν   ἔλθῃ   τὸ   σπέρμα   ᾧ   ἐπήγγελται,
³should come   ¹the   ²seed   to whom   it has been promised,

διαταγεὶς   δι᾽   ἀγγέλων,   ἐν   χειρὶ   μεσίτου.
being ordained through   angels,   by [the]   hand of a mediator.

20 ὁ   δὲ   μεσίτης   ἑνὸς   οὐκ   ἔστιν,   ὁ
20 Now the   mediator   ²of one   ¹is not,   –

δὲ   θεὸς   εἷς   ἐστιν.   21 ὁ   οὖν   νόμος   κατὰ
but God   ²one   ¹is.   [Is] the ²therefore ¹law   against

τῶν   ἐπαγγελιῶν   [τοῦ   θεοῦ];   μὴ   γένοιτο.
the   promises   –   of God?   May it not be.

εἰ   γὰρ   ἐδόθη   νόμος   ὁ   δυνάμενος   ζωοποι-
For if   ²was given ¹a law   –   being able   to make

ῆσαι,   ὄντως   ἐκ   νόμου   ἂν   ἦν   ἡ   δικαιοσύνη·
alive,   really   ³by   ⁴law   ²would   –   ¹righteousness; have been

22 ἀλλὰ   συνέκλεισεν   ἡ   γραφὴ   τὰ   πάντα
22 but   ²shut up   ¹the   ²scripture   all mankind†

ὑπὸ   ἁμαρτίαν   ἵνα   ἡ   ἐπαγγελία   ἐκ   πίστεως
under   sin   in or- the   promise   by   faith der that

Ἰησοῦ   Χριστοῦ   δοθῇ   τοῖς   πιστεύουσιν.
of(in) Jesus   Christ   might be given to the [ones]   believing.

23 Πρὸ   τοῦ   δὲ   ἐλθεῖν   τὴν   πίστιν   ὑπὸ
23 before   *the*   But   to come   *the*   faithᵇ   under
= But before faith came

νόμον   ἐφρουρούμεθα   συγκλειόμενοι   εἰς   τὴν
law   we were guarded   being shut up   to   the

μέλλουσαν   πίστιν   ἀποκαλυφθῆναι.   24 ὥστε
²being about   ¹faith   to be revealed.   24 So as

ὁ   νόμος   παιδαγωγὸς   ἡμῶν   γέγονεν   εἰς
the   law   ²a trainer   ²of us   ¹has become [up] to

came, that we might be justified by faith. ²⁵But now that faith has come, we are no longer under a custodian; ²⁶for in Christ Jesus you are all sons of God, through faith. ²⁷For as many of you as were baptized into Christ have put on Christ. ²⁸There is neither Jew not Greek, there is neither slave nor free, there is neither male nor female; for you are all one in Christ Jesus. ²⁹And if you are Christ's, then you are Abraham's offspring, heirs according to promise.

CHAPTER 4

I mean that the heir, as long as he is a child, is no better than a slave, though he is the owner of all the estate; ²but he is under guardians and trustees until the date set by the father. ³So with us; when we were children, we were slaves to the elemental spirits of the universe. ⁴But when the time had fully come, God sent forth his Son, born of woman, born under the law, ⁵to redeem those who were under the law, so that we might receive adoption as sons. ⁶And because you are sons,

Χριστόν, ἵνα ἐκ πίστεως δικαιωθῶμεν·
Christ, in order that by faith we might be justified;
25 ἐλθούσης δὲ τῆς πίστεως οὐκέτι ὑπὸ
but ³having come ¹the ²faith ⁴no more ⁵under
παιδαγωγόν ἐσμεν. 26 Πάντες γὰρ υἱοὶ
⁷a trainer ⁶we are. For all sons
θεοῦ ἐστε διὰ τῆς πίστεως ἐν Χριστῷ
of God ye are through the faith in Christ
Ἰησοῦ· 27 ὅσοι γὰρ εἰς Χριστὸν ἐβαπτίσ-
Jesus; for as many as ²into ³Christ ¹ye were
θητε, Χριστὸν ἐνεδύσασθε. 28 οὐκ ἔνι
baptized, ¹Christ ¹ye put on. There cannot be
Ἰουδαῖος οὐδὲ Ἕλλην, οὐκ ἔνι δοῦλος
Jew nor Greek, there cannot be slave
οὐδὲ ἐλεύθερος, οὐκ ἔνι ἄρσεν καὶ θῆλυ·
nor freeman, there cannot be male and female;
πάντες γὰρ ὑμεῖς εἷς ἐστε ἐν Χριστῷ
for ²all ¹ye ¹one ²are in Christ
Ἰησοῦ. 29 εἰ δὲ ὑμεῖς Χριστοῦ, ἄρα
Jesus. But if ye [are] of Christ, then
τοῦ Ἀβραὰμ σπέρμα ἐστέ, κατ' ἐπαγγελίαν
- ³of Abraham ²a seed ¹are ye, according to promise
κληρονόμοι. 4 Λέγω δέ, ἐφ' ὅσον χρόνον ὁ
heirs. But I say, over so long a time as the
κληρονόμος νήπιός ἐστιν, οὐδὲν διαφέρει
heir ²an infant ¹is, ³nothing ¹he differs
²[from]
δούλου κύριος πάντων ὤν, 2 ἀλλὰ ὑπὸ
⁴a slave ⁶lord ⁷of all ⁵being, but ³under
ἐπιτρόπους ἐστὶν καὶ οἰκονόμους ἄχρι τῆς
²guardians ¹is and stewards until the
προθεσμίας τοῦ πατρός. 3 οὕτως καὶ
term previously of the father. So also
appointed
ἡμεῖς, ὅτε ἦμεν νήπιοι, ὑπὸ τὰ στοιχεῖα
we, when we were infants, under the elements
τοῦ κόσμου ἤμεθα δεδουλωμένοι· 4 ὅτε
of the world we were having been enslaved; when
δὲ ἦλθεν τὸ πλήρωμα τοῦ χρόνου,
but came the fulness of the time,
ἐξαπέστειλεν ὁ θεὸς τὸν υἱὸν αὐτοῦ,
sent forth - God the Son of him,
γενόμενον ἐκ γυναικός, γενόμενον ὑπὸ
becoming of a woman, becoming under
νόμον, 5 ἵνα τοὺς ὑπὸ νόμον ἐξαγοράσῃ,
law, in order that ²the ones ³under ⁴law ¹he might redeem,
ἵνα τὴν υἱοθεσίαν ἀπολάβωμεν. 6 Ὅτι δέ
in order ²the ³adoption of sons ¹we might receive. And because
that

God has sent the Spirit of his Son into our hearts, crying, "Abba! Father!" [7]So through God you are no longer a slave but a son, and if a son then an heir.

8 Formerly, when you did not know God, you were in bondage to beings that by nature are no gods; [9]but now that you have come to know God, or rather to be known by God, how can you turn back again to the weak and beggarly elemental spirits, whose slaves you want to be once more? [10]You observe days, and months, and seasons, and years! [11]I am afraid I have labored over you in vain.

12 Brethren, I beseech you, become as I am, for I also have become as you are. You did me no wrong; [13]you know it was because of a bodily ailment that I preached the gospel to you at first; [14]and though my condition was a trial to you, you did not scorn or despise me, but received me as an angel of God, as Christ Jesus. [15]What has become of the satisfaction you felt? For I bear you witness that, if possible, you would have plucked out your

ἐστε   υἱοί,   ἐξαπέστειλεν   ὁ   θεὸς   τὸ
ye are   sons,   [3]sent forth   -   [1]God   the
πνεῦμα   τοῦ   υἱοῦ   αὐτοῦ   εἰς   τὰς   καρδίας
Spirit   of the   Son   of him   into   the   hearts
ἡμῶν,   κρᾶζον·   ἀββὰ   ὁ   πατήρ.   7 ὥστε
of us,   crying: Abba   -   Father.   So as
οὐκέτι   εἶ   δοῦλος   ἀλλὰ   υἱός·   εἰ   δὲ   υἱός,
no more art thou a slave   but   a son;   and if   a son,
καὶ   κληρονόμος   διὰ   θεοῦ.
also   an heir   through   God.

8 Ἀλλὰ   τότε   μὲν   οὐκ   εἰδότες   θεὸν
But   then   indeed   not   knowing   God
ἐδουλεύσατε   τοῖς   φύσει   μὴ   οὖσιν   θεοῖς·
ye served as slaves   [1]the   [3]by nature   [4]not   [5]being   [2]gods;
9 νῦν   δὲ   γνόντες   θεόν,   μᾶλλον   δὲ
but now   knowing   God,   but rather
γνωσθέντες   ὑπὸ   θεοῦ,   πῶς   ἐπιστρέφετε
being known   by   God,   how   turn ye
πάλιν   ἐπὶ   τὰ   ἀσθενῆ   καὶ   πτωχὰ   στοιχεῖα,
again   to the   weak   and   poor   elements,
οἷς   πάλιν   ἄνωθεν   δουλεῦσαι   θέλετε;
to which again   [3]anew   [2]to serve   [1]ye wish?
10 ἡμέρας   παρατηρεῖσθε   καὶ   μῆνας   καὶ
[2]days   [1]Ye observe   and   months   and
καιροὺς   καὶ   ἐνιαυτούς.   11 φοβοῦμαι   ὑμᾶς
seasons   and   years.   I fear [for]   you
μή   πως   εἰκῇ   κεκοπίακα   εἰς   ὑμᾶς.
lest   in vain   I have laboured among   you.

12 Γίνεσθε   ὡς   ἐγώ,   ὅτι   κἀγὼ   ὡς
Be ye   as   I [am],   because   I also [am]   as
ὑμεῖς,   ἀδελφοί,   δέομαι   ὑμῶν.   οὐδέν   με
ye [are],   brothers,   I beg   of you.   Nothing   me
ἠδικήσατε·   13 οἴδατε   δὲ   ὅτι   δι'   ἀσθένειαν
ye wronged;   and ye know   that on account of   weakness
τῆς   σαρκὸς   εὐηγγελισάμην   ὑμῖν   τὸ
of the   flesh   I preached good tidings   to you   -
πρότερον,   14 καὶ   τὸν   πειρασμὸν   ὑμῶν
formerly,   and   the   trial   of you
ἐν   τῇ   σαρκί   μου   οὐκ   ἐξουθενήσατε   οὐδὲ
in   the   flesh   of me   ye despised not   nor
ἐξεπτύσατε,   ἀλλὰ   ὡς   ἄγγελον   θεοῦ   ἐδέξασθέ
disdained ye,   but   as   a messenger of God   ye received
με,   ὡς   Χριστὸν   Ἰησοῦν.   15 ποῦ   οὖν
me,   as   Christ   Jesus.   Where therefore
ὁ   μακαρισμὸς   ὑμῶν;   μαρτυρῶ   γὰρ   ὑμῖν
the   felicitation   of you?*   for I witness   to you
ὅτι   εἰ   δυνατὸν   τοὺς   ὀφθαλμοὺς   ὑμῶν
that   if   possible   [3]the   [2]eyes   [4]of you

* That is, "your felicitation [of me]".

eyes and given them to me. ¹⁶ Have I then become your enemy by telling you the truth?ᵉ ¹⁷They make much of you, but for no good purpose; they want to shut you out, that you may make much of them. ¹⁸For a good purpose it is always good to be made much of, and not only when I am present with you. ¹⁹My little children, with whom I am again in travail until Christ be formed in you! ²⁰I could wish to be present with you now and to change my tone, for I am perplexed about you.

21 Tell me, you who desire to be under law, do you not hear the law? ²²For it is written that Abraham had two sons, one by a slave and one by a free woman. ²³But the son of the slave was born according to the flesh, the son of the free woman through promise. ²⁴Now this is an allegory: these women are two covenants. One is from Mount Sinai, bearing children for slavery; she is Hagar. ²⁵Now Hagar is Mount Sinai in Arabia;ᶠ she corresponds to the present Jerusalem, for she is in slavery with

---

ἐξορύξαντες ἐδώκατέ μοι. **16** ὥστε ἐχθρὸς
¹gouging out ye gave [them] to me. So that ²an enemy

ὑμῶν γέγονα ἀληθεύων ὑμῖν; **17** ζηλοῦσιν
³of you ¹have I become speaking truth to you? They are zealous of

ὑμᾶς οὐ καλῶς, ἀλλὰ ἐκκλεῖσαι ὑμᾶς
you not well, but ²to exclude ³you

θέλουσιν, **18** ἵνα αὐτοὺς ζηλοῦτε. καλὸν δὲ
¹wish, in order them ye may be But [it is] good
that zealous of.

ζηλοῦσθαι ἐν καλῷ πάντοτε, καὶ μὴ
to be zealous in a good thing always, and not

μόνον ἐν τῷ παρεῖναί με πρὸς ὑμᾶς,
only in the to be present mebe with you,
=when I am present

19 τέκνα μου, οὓς πάλιν ὠδίνω μέχρις οὗ
children of me,[for] whom again I travail until
in birth

μορφωθῇ Χριστὸς ἐν ὑμῖν· **20** ἤθελον δὲ
²is formed ¹Christ in you; and I wished

παρεῖναι πρὸς ὑμᾶς ἄρτι καὶ ἀλλάξαι
to be present with you just now and to change

τὴν φωνήν μου, ὅτι ἀποροῦμαι ἐν ὑμῖν.
the voice of me, because I am perplexed in(about) you.

21 Λέγετέ μοι, οἱ ὑπὸ νόμον θέλοντες
Tell me, the [ones] ³under ⁴law ¹wishing

εἶναι, τὸν νόμον οὐκ ἀκούετε; **22** γέγραπται
²to be, ²the ³law ¹hear ye not? ²it has been written

γὰρ ὅτι Ἀβραὰμ δύο υἱοὺς ἔσχεν, ἕνα
¹for that Abraham two sons had, one

ἐκ τῆς παιδίσκης καὶ ἕνα ἐκ τῆς ἐλευ-
of the maidservant and one of the free

θέρας. **23** ἀλλ' ὁ [μὲν] ἐκ τῆς παιδίσκης
woman. But the [one] indeed of the maidservant

κατὰ σάρκα γεγέννηται, ὁ δὲ ἐκ τῆς
according to flesh has been born, and the [one] of the

ἐλευθέρας διὰ τῆς ἐπαγγελίας. **24** ἅτινά
free woman through the promise. Which things

ἐστιν ἀλληγορούμενα· αὗται γάρ εἰσιν
is(are) being allegorized; for these are

δύο διαθῆκαι, μία μὲν ἀπὸ ὄρους Σινά,
two covenants, one indeed from mount Sina,

εἰς δουλείαν γεννῶσα, ἥτις ἐστὶν Ἀγάρ.
to slavery bringing forth, which is Hagar.

25 τὸ δὲ Ἀγὰρ Σινὰ ὄρος ἐστὶν ἐν
⁶The ²now ³Hagar ⁴Sina ⁵mount ³is in

τῇ Ἀραβίᾳ· συστοιχεῖ δὲ τῇ νῦν
- Arabia; and corresponds to the now

Ἰερουσαλήμ, δουλεύει γὰρ μετὰ τῶν
Jerusalem, for she serves as a slave with the

ᵉ Or by dealing truly with you
ᶠ Other ancient authorities read For Sinai is a mountain in Arabia

her children. [26] But the Jerusalem above is free, and she is our mother. [27] For it is written,

"Rejoice, O barren one that dost not bear; break forth and shout, thou who art not in travail; for the desolate hath more children than she who hath a husband."

[28] Now we,[g] brethren, like Isaac, are children of promise. [29] But as at that time he who was born according to the flesh persecuted him who was born according to the Spirit, so it is now. [30] But what does the scripture say? "Cast out the slave and her son; for the son of the slave shall not inherit with the son of the free woman." [31] So, brethren, we are not children of the slave but of the free woman.

τέκνων αὐτῆς. **26** ἡ δὲ ἄνω Ἰερουσαλὴμ
children   of her.   But the   above   Jerusalem

ἐλευθέρα ἐστίν, ἥτις ἐστὶν μήτηρ ἡμῶν·
free   is,   who   is   mother   of us;

27 γέγραπται γάρ· εὐφράνθητι, στείρα ἡ
for it has been written: Be thou glad,   barren[,]   the
                                                      [one]

οὐ τίκτουσα, ῥῆξον καὶ βόησον, ἡ οὐκ
not   bearing,   break forth and   shout,   the [one] not

ὠδίνουσα· ὅτι πολλὰ τὰ τέκνα τῆς ἐρήμου
travailing;   because many [are] the children of the   desolate

μᾶλλον ἢ τῆς ἐχούσης τὸν ἄνδρα. **28** ὑμεῖς
rather   than of the   having   the   husband.   ye
            [one]

δέ, ἀδελφοί, κατὰ Ἰσαὰκ ἐπαγγελίας τέκνα
But,   brothers, [4]according to [5]Isaac [3]of promise [2]children

ἐστέ. **29** ἀλλ᾽ ὥσπερ τότε ὁ κατὰ σάρκα
[1]are.   But   even as   then the [one] according to flesh

γεννηθεὶς ἐδίωκεν τὸν κατὰ πνεῦμα, οὕτως
born   persecuted the [one] according   spirit,   so
                              [born]   to

καὶ νῦν. **30** ἀλλὰ τί λέγει ἡ γραφή;
also now.   But what says the   scripture?

ἔκβαλε τὴν παιδίσκην καὶ τὸν υἱὸν αὐτῆς·
Cast out   the   maidservant   and   the   son   of her;

οὐ γὰρ μὴ κληρονομήσει ὁ υἱὸς τῆς
for by no means [5]shall inherit [1]the [2]son [3]of the

παιδίσκης μετὰ τοῦ υἱοῦ τῆς ἐλευθέρας.
[4]maidservant   with   the   son of the   free woman.

31 διό, ἀδελφοί, οὐκ ἐσμὲν παιδίσκης
Wherefore,   brothers,   we are not [2]of a maidservant

τέκνα ἀλλὰ τῆς ἐλευθέρας.
[1]children   but   of the   free woman.

CHAPTER 5

FOR freedom Christ has set us free; stand fast therefore, and do not submit again to a yoke of slavery.

2 Now I, Paul, say to you that if you receive circumcision, Christ will be of no advantage to you. [3] I testify again to every man who receives circumcision that he is

5 Τῇ ἐλευθερίᾳ ἡμᾶς Χριστὸς ἠλευθέρωσεν·
For the   freedom [2]us [1]Christ [2]freed;

στήκετε οὖν καὶ μὴ πάλιν ζυγῷ δουλείας
stand firm therefore and   not   again with a yoke of slavery

ἐνέχεσθε.
be entangled.

2 Ἴδε ἐγὼ Παῦλος λέγω ὑμῖν ὅτι
Behold[,]   I   Paul   tell   you   that

ἐὰν περιτέμνησθε Χριστὸς ὑμᾶς οὐδὲν
if   ye are circumcised   Christ [2]you [2]nothing

ὠφελήσει. **3** μαρτύρομαι δὲ πάλιν παντὶ
[1]will profit.   And I testify   again   to every

ἀνθρώπῳ περιτεμνομένῳ ὅτι ὀφειλέτης ἐστὶν
man   being circumcised   that [2]a debtor [1]he is

bound to keep the whole law. ⁴You are severed from Christ, you who would be justified by the law; you have fallen away from grace. ⁵For through the Spirit, by faith, we wait for the hope of righteousness. ⁶For in Christ Jesus neither circumcision nor uncircumcision is of any avail, but faith working through love. ⁷You were running well; who hindered you from obeying the truth? ⁸This persuasion is not from him who called you. ⁹A little leaven leavens the whole lump. ¹⁰I have confidence in the Lord that you will take no other view than mine; and he who is troubling you will bear his judgment, whoever he is. ¹¹But if I, brethren, still preach circumcision, why am I still persecuted? In that case the stumbling-block of the cross has been removed. ¹²I wish those who unsettle you would mutilate themselves!

13 For you were called to freedom, brethren; only do not use your freedom as an opportunity for the flesh, but through love be servants of one another. ¹⁴For the whole law is fulfilled in one word, "You shall love your neighbor as

ὅλον   τὸν   νόμον   ποιῆσαι.   4 κατηργήθητε
⁴all   ⁵the   ⁶law   ³to do.   Ye were discharged

ἀπὸ   Χριστοῦ   οἵτινες   ἐν   νόμῳ   δικαιοῦσθε,
from   Christ   who   by   law   are justified,

τῆς   χάριτος   ἐξεπέσατε.   5 ἡμεῖς   γὰρ
the   ²grace   ¹ye fell from.   For we

πνεύματι   ἐκ   πίστεως   ἐλπίδα   δικαιοσύνης
in spirit   by   faith   [the] hope of righteousness

ἀπεκδεχόμεθα.   6 ἐν   γὰρ   Χριστῷ   Ἰησοῦ
eagerly expect.   For in   Christ   Jesus

οὔτε   περιτομή   τι   ἰσχύει   οὔτε   ἀκροβυστία,
neither circumcision ²anything ¹avails   nor   uncircumcision,

ἀλλὰ   πίστις   δι'   ἀγάπης   ἐνεργουμένη.
but   faith   ²through ¹love   ³operating.

7 Ἐτρέχετε   καλῶς·   τίς   ὑμᾶς   ἐνέκοψεν
Ye were running well: who   ²you   ¹hindered

ἀληθείᾳ   μὴ   πείθεσθαι;   8 ἡ   πεισμονὴ   οὐκ
⁵by truth   ³not   ⁴to be persuaded? the(this) persuasion not

ἐκ   τοῦ   καλοῦντος   ὑμᾶς.   9 μικρὰ   ζύμη
of   the [one] calling   you.   A little   leaven

ὅλον   τὸ   φύραμα   ζυμοῖ.   10 ἐγὼ   πέποιθα
all   the   lump   leavens.   I   trust

εἰς   ὑμᾶς   ἐν   κυρίῳ   ὅτι   οὐδὲν   ἄλλο   φρο-
as to† you   in   [the] Lord that   ²nothing   ³other   ¹ye

νήσετε·   ὁ   δὲ   ταράσσων   ὑμᾶς   βαστάσει
will think;   but the [one] troubling   you   shall bear

τὸ   κρίμα,   ὅστις   ἐὰν   ᾖ.   11 Ἐγὼ   δέ,
the   judgment, whoever   he may be.   ¹But ⁴I,

ἀδελφοί,   εἰ   περιτομὴν   ἔτι   κηρύσσω,   τί
²brothers,   ³if   ⁷circumcision   ⁵still   ⁶proclaim,   why

ἔτι   διώκομαι;   ἄρα   κατήργηται   τὸ
still am I being persecuted? then   has been annulled   the

σκάνδαλον   τοῦ   σταυροῦ.   12 Ὄφελον   καὶ
offence   of the   cross.   I would that indeed

ἀποκόψονται   οἱ   ἀναστατοῦντες   ὑμᾶς.
⁴will(might) cut ¹the [ones] ²unsettling   ³you.
themselves off

13 Ὑμεῖς   γὰρ   ἐπ'   ἐλευθερίᾳ   ἐκλήθητε,
For ye   for   freedom   were called,

ἀδελφοί·   μόνον   μὴ   τὴν   ἐλευθερίαν   εἰς
brothers;   only [use] not   the   freedom   for

ἀφορμὴν   τῇ   σαρκί,   ἀλλὰ   διὰ   τῆς   ἀγάπης
advantage   to the   flesh,   but   through –   love

δουλεύετε   ἀλλήλοις.   14 ὁ   γὰρ   πᾶς   νόμος
serve ye as slaves one another.   For the   whole   law

ἐν   ἑνὶ   λόγῳ   πεπλήρωται,   ἐν   τῷ·   ἀγα-
in   one   word   has been summed up, in the [word]: Thou

πήσεις   τὸν   πλησίον   σου   ὡς   σεαυτόν.
shalt love the   neighbour   of thee   as   thyself.

yourself." [15] But if you bite and devour one another take heed that you are not consumed by one another.

16 But I say, walk by the Spirit, and do not gratify the desires of the flesh. [17] For the desires of the flesh are against the Spirit, and the desires of the Spirit are against the flesh; for these are opposed to each other, to prevent you from doing what you would. [18] But if you are led by the Spirit you are not under the law. [19] Now the works of the flesh are plain: immorality, impurity, licentiousness, [20] idolatry, sorcery, enmity, strife, jealousy, anger, selfishness, dissension, party spirit, [21] envy,[h] drunkenness, carousing, and the like. I warn you, as I warned you before, that those who do such things shall not inherit the kingdom of God. [22] But the fruit of the Spirit is love, joy, peace, patience, kindness, goodness, faithfulness, [23] gentleness, self-control; against such there is no law. [24] And those who belong to Christ Jesus have crucified the flesh with its passions and desires.

25 If we live by the Spirit, let us also walk by the Spirit. [26] Let us

---

15 εἰ δὲ ἀλλήλους δάκνετε καὶ κατεσθίετε,
But if   'one another 'ye bite 'and 'ye devour,
βλέπετε μὴ ὑπ' ἀλλήλων ἀναλωθῆτε.
see   lest by   one another ye are destroyed.
16 Λέγω δέ, πνεύματι περιπατεῖτε καὶ
Now I say, in spirit walk ye and
ἐπιθυμίαν σαρκὸς οὐ μὴ τελέσητε. 17 ἡ
[the] lust of [the] flesh by no means ye will perform. the
γὰρ σὰρξ ἐπιθυμεῖ κατὰ τοῦ πνεύματος,
For flesh lusts against the spirit,
τὸ δὲ πνεῦμα κατὰ τῆς σαρκός, ταῦτα
and the spirit against the flesh, 'these
γὰρ ἀλλήλοις ἀντίκειται, ἵνα μὴ ἃ ἐὰν
'for 'each other 'opposes, lest whatever things
θέλητε ταῦτα ποιῆτε. 18 εἰ δὲ πνεύματι
ye wish these ye do. But if by [the] Spirit
ἄγεσθε, οὐκ ἐστὲ ὑπὸ νόμον. 19 φανερὰ δέ
ye are led, ye are not under law. Now 'manifest
ἐστιν τὰ ἔργα τῆς σαρκός, ἅτινά ἐστιν
'is(are) 'the 'works 'of the 'flesh, which is(are)
πορνεία, ἀκαθαρσία, ἀσέλγεια, 20 εἰδωλο-
fornication, uncleanness, lewdness, idola-
λατρία, φαρμακεία, ἔχθραι, ἔρις, ζῆλος,
try, sorcery, enmities, strife, jealousy,
θυμοί, ἐριθεῖαι, διχοστασίαι, αἱρέσεις,
angers, rivalries, divisions, sects,
21 φθόνοι, μέθαι, κῶμοι, καὶ τὰ ὅμοια
envyings, drunken- revellings, and - like
nesses, things
τούτοις, ἃ προλέγω ὑμῖν καθὼς προεῖπον,
to these, which I tell 'beforehand 'you as I previously
said,
ὅτι οἱ τὰ τοιαῦτα πράσσοντες βασιλείαν
that the [ones] - 'such things 'practising '[the] kingdom
θεοῦ οὐ κληρονομήσουσιν. 22 ὁ δὲ καρπὸς
'of God 'will not inherit. But the fruit
τοῦ πνεύματός ἐστιν ἀγάπη, χαρά, εἰρήνη,
of the Spirit is love, joy, peace,
μακροθυμία, χρηστότης, ἀγαθωσύνη, πίστις,
longsuffering, kindness, goodness, faithfulness,
23 πραΰτης, ἐγκράτεια· κατὰ τῶν τοιούτων
meekness, self-control; against - such things
οὐκ ἔστιν νόμος. 24 οἱ δὲ τοῦ Χριστοῦ
there is no law. Now the ones - of Christ
Ἰησοῦ τὴν σάρκα ἐσταύρωσαν σὺν τοῖς
Jesus 'the 'flesh 'crucified with the(its)
παθήμασιν καὶ ταῖς ἐπιθυμίαις. 25 Εἰ
passions and the(its) lusts. If
ζῶμεν πνεύματι, πνεύματι καὶ στοιχῶμεν.
we live in [the] Spirit, in [the] Spirit also let us walk.

---

[h] Other ancient authorities add *murder*

have no self-conceit, no provoking of one another, no envy of one another.

26 μὴ γινώμεθα κενόδοξοι, ἀλλήλους
Let us not become vainglorious, one another
προκαλούμενοι, ἀλλήλοις φθονοῦντες.
provoking, one another envying.

CHAPTER 6

BRETHREN, if a man is overtaken in any trespass, you who are spiritual should restore him in a spirit of gentleness. Look to yourself, lest you too be tempted. [2]Bear one another's burdens, and so fulfil the law of Christ. [3]For if any one thinks he is something, when he is nothing, he deceives himself. [4]But let each one test his own work, and then his reason to boast will be in himself alone and not in his neighbor. [5]For each man will have to bear his own load.

6 Let him who is taught the word share all good things with him who teaches.

7 Do not be deceived; God is not mocked, for whatever a man sows, that he will also reap. [8]For he who sows to his own flesh will from the flesh reap corruption; but he who sows to the Spirit will from the Spirit reap eternal life. [9]And let us not grow weary in well-doing, for

6 Ἀδελφοί, ἐὰν καὶ προλημφθῇ ἄνθρω-
Brothers, if indeed [2]is overtaken [1]a
πος ἔν τινι παραπτώματι, ὑμεῖς οἱ
man in some trespass, ye the
πνευματικοὶ καταρτίζετε τὸν τοιοῦτον ἐν
spiritual [ones] restore – such a one in
πνεύματι πραΰτητος, σκοπῶν σεαυτόν, μὴ
a spirit of meekness, considering thyself, lest
καὶ σὺ πειρασθῇς. 2 Ἀλλήλων τὰ βάρη
also thou art tempted. Of one another the loads
βαστάζετε, καὶ οὕτως ἀναπληρώσετε τὸν
bear ye, and so ye will fulfil the
νόμον τοῦ Χριστοῦ. 3 εἰ γὰρ δοκεῖ
law – of Christ. For if [2]thinks
τις εἶναί τι μηδὲν ὤν, φρεναπατᾷ ἑαυτόν.
[1]anyone [2]to be [4]some- [4]no- [5]being, he deceives himself.
thing thing

4 τὸ δὲ ἔργον ἑαυτοῦ δοκιμαζέτω ἕκαστος,
But the work of himself [1]let [2]prove [2]each man,
καὶ τότε εἰς ἑαυτὸν μόνον τὸ καύχημα
and then in himself alone the boast
ἕξει καὶ οὐκ εἰς τὸν ἕτερον· 5 ἕκαστος
he will and not in the other man; [2]each man
have
γὰρ τὸ ἴδιον φορτίον βαστάσει. 6 Κοινωνείτω δὲ
[1]for the(his) own burden will bear. And [2]let him share
ὁ κατηχούμενος τὸν λόγον τῷ κατη-
[1]the [2]being instructed [in] [3]the [4]word [6]with the [one] in-
[one]
χοῦντι ἐν πᾶσιν ἀγαθοῖς. 7 Μὴ πλανᾶσθε,
structing in all good things. Be ye not led astray,
θεὸς οὐ μυκτηρίζεται. ὃ γὰρ ἐὰν σπείρῃ
God is not mocked. For whatever [1]may sow
ἄνθρωπος, τοῦτο καὶ θερίσει· 8 ὅτι ὁ
[1]a man, this also he will reap; because the
σπείρων εἰς τὴν σάρκα ἑαυτοῦ ἐκ τῆς
[one] sowing to the flesh of himself of the
σαρκὸς θερίσει φθοράν, ὁ δὲ σπείρων
flesh will reap corruption, but the [one] sowing
εἰς τὸ πνεῦμα ἐκ τοῦ πνεύματος θερίσει
to the spirit of the Spirit will reap
ζωὴν αἰώνιον. 9 τὸ δὲ καλὸν ποιοῦντες
life eternal. And [2]the [2]good [1]doing
μὴ ἐγκακῶμεν· καιρῷ γὰρ ἰδίῳ
let us not lose heart; for in its own time

in due season we shall reap, if we do not lose heart. ¹⁰So then, as we have opportunity, let us do good to all men, and especially to those who are of the household of faith.

11 See with what large letters I am writing to you with my own hand. ¹²It is those who want to make a good showing in the flesh that would compel you to be circumcised, and only in order that they may not be persecuted for the cross of Christ. ¹³For even those who receive circumcision do not themselves keep the law, but they desire to have you circumcised that they may glory in your flesh. ¹⁴But far be it from me to glory except in the cross of our Lord Jesus Christ, by which[i] the world has been crucified to me, and I to the world. ¹⁵For neither circumcision counts for anything, nor uncircumcision, but a new creation. ¹⁶Peace and mercy be upon all who walk by this rule, upon the Israel of God.

17 Henceforth let no man trouble me; for I bear on my body the marks of Jesus.

θερίσομεν   μὴ   ἐκλυόμενοι.   10 Ἄρα   οὖν
we shall reap   not   failing.   Then therefore

ὡς   καιρὸν   ἔχομεν,   ἐργαζώμεθα   τὸ   ἀγαθὸν
as   ¹time   we have,   let us do   the   good

πρὸς   πάντας,   μάλιστα   δὲ   πρὸς   τοὺς
to   all men,   and most of all   to   the

οἰκείους   τῆς   πίστεως.
members   of the   faith.
the family

11 Ἴδετε   πηλίκοις   ὑμῖν   γράμμασιν
Ye see   in how large   ²to you   ¹letters

ἔγραψα   τῇ   ἐμῇ   χειρί.   12 Ὅσοι   θέλουσιν
¹I wrote   –   with my hand.   As many as   wish

εὐπροσωπῆσαι   ἐν   σαρκί,   οὗτοι   ἀναγκάζουσιν
to look well   in [the] flesh,   these   compel

ὑμᾶς   περιτέμνεσθαι,   μόνον   ἵνα   τῷ
you   to be circumcised,   only   in order that   ²for the

σταυρῷ   τοῦ   Χριστοῦ   ['Ιησοῦ]   μὴ
⁴cross   –   ⁵of Christ   ⁶Jesus   ¹not

διώκωνται.   13 οὐδὲ   γὰρ   οἱ   περιτεμνόμενοι
³they are persecuted.   For ¹not   ¹the [ones]   ²being circumcised

αὐτοὶ   νόμον   φυλάσσουσιν,   ἀλλὰ   θέλουσιν
⁵themselves   ⁶law   ⁴keep,   but   they wish

ὑμᾶς   περιτέμνεσθαι   ἵνα   ἐν   τῇ   ὑμετέρᾳ
you   to be circumcised   in order that   ²in   –   ³your

σαρκὶ   καυχήσωνται.   14 ἐμοὶ   δὲ   μὴ   γένοιτο
¹flesh   ¹they may boast.   But to me   may it not be

καυχᾶσθαι   εἰ   μὴ   ἐν   τῷ   σταυρῷ   τοῦ
to boast   except   in   the   cross   of the

κυρίου   ἡμῶν   'Ιησοῦ   Χριστοῦ,   δι'   οὗ
Lord   of us   Jesus   Christ,   through whom

ἐμοὶ   κόσμος   ἐσταύρωται   κἀγὼ   κόσμῳ.
to me   [the] world   has been crucified   and I   to [the] world.

15 οὔτε   γὰρ   περιτομή   τί   ἐστιν   οὔτε
For neither   circumcision   ²anything   ¹is   nor

ἀκροβυστία,   ἀλλὰ   καινὴ   κτίσις.   16 καὶ
uncircumcision,   but   a new   creation.   And

ὅσοι   τῷ   κανόνι   τούτῳ   στοιχήσουσιν,
as many as   by this rule   will walk,

εἰρήνη   ἐπ'   αὐτοὺς   καὶ   ἔλεος,   καὶ   ἐπὶ   τὸν
peace   on   them   and   mercy,   and   on   the

'Ισραὴλ   τοῦ   θεοῦ.
Israel   –   of God.

17 Τοῦ   λοιποῦ   κόπους   μοι   μηδεὶς
For the rest   ³troubles   ⁴me   ²no one

παρεχέτω·   ἐγὼ   γὰρ   τὰ   στίγματα   τοῦ
¹let ⁵cause;   for ¹I   ²the   ⁴brands   –

'Ιησοῦ   ἐν   τῷ   σώματί   μου   βαστάζω.
⁵of Jesus   ⁶in   ⁷the   ⁸body   ⁹of me   ²bear.

---

[i] Or through whom

18 The grace of our Lord Jesus Christ be with your spirit, brethren. Amen.

18 Ἡ χάρις τοῦ κυρίου ἡμῶν Ἰησοῦ
The grace of the Lord of us Jesus
Χριστοῦ μετὰ τοῦ πνεύματος ὑμῶν.
Christ with the spirit of you,
ἀδελφοί· ἀμήν.
brothers : Amen.

EPHESIANS 1

ΠΡΟΣ ΕΦΕΣΙΟΥΣ
To Ephesians

CHAPTER 1

PAUL, an apostle of Christ Jesus by the will of God,
To the saints who are also faithful[a] in Christ Jesus:
2 Grace to you and peace from God our Father and the Lord Jesus Christ.
3 Blessed be the God and Father of our Lord Jesus Christ, who has blessed us in Christ with every spiritual blessing in the heavenly places, [4] even as he chose us in him before the foundation of the world, that we should be holy and blameless before him. [5] He destined us in love[b] to be his sons through Jesus Christ, according to the purpose of his will, [6] to the praise of his

1 Παῦλος ἀπόστολος Χριστοῦ Ἰησοῦ διὰ
Paul an apostle of Christ Jesus through
θελήματος θεοῦ τοῖς ἁγίοις τοῖς οὖσιν
[the] will of God to the saints – being
[ἐν Ἐφέσῳ] καὶ πιστοῖς ἐν Χριστῷ
in Ephesus and faithful in Christ
Ἰησοῦ· 2 χάρις ὑμῖν καὶ εἰρήνη ἀπὸ
Jesus: Grace to you and peace from
θεοῦ πατρὸς ἡμῶν καὶ κυρίου Ἰησοῦ
God Father of us and Lord Jesus
Χριστοῦ.
Christ.

3 Εὐλογητὸς ὁ θεὸς καὶ πατὴρ τοῦ
Blessed the God and Father of the
κυρίου ἡμῶν Ἰησοῦ Χριστοῦ, ὁ εὐλογήσας
Lord of us Jesus Christ, the having
[one] blessed
ἡμᾶς ἐν πάσῃ εὐλογίᾳ πνευματικῇ ἐν
us with every blessing spiritual in
τοῖς ἐπουρανίοις ἐν Χριστῷ, 4 καθὼς
the heavenlies in Christ, as
ἐξελέξατο ἡμᾶς ἐν αὐτῷ πρὸ καταβολῆς
he chose us in him before [the] foundation
κόσμου, εἶναι ἡμᾶς ἁγίους καὶ ἀμώμους
of [the] world, to be us holy and unblemished[b]
= that we should be . . .
κατενώπιον αὐτοῦ, ἐν ἀγάπῃ 5 προορίσας
before him, in love predestinating
ἡμᾶς εἰς υἱοθεσίαν διὰ Ἰησοῦ Χριστοῦ
us to adoption of sons through Jesus Christ
εἰς αὐτόν, κατὰ τὴν εὐδοκίαν τοῦ
to him[self], according to the good pleasure of the
θελήματος αὐτοῦ, 6 εἰς ἔπαινον δόξης
will of him, to [the] praise of [the] glory

[a] Other ancient authorities read who are at Ephesus and faithful
[b] Or before him in love, having destined us

glorious grace which he freely bestowed on us in the Beloved. [7] In him we have redemption through his blood, the forgiveness of our trespasses, according to the riches of his grace [8] which he lavished upon us. [9] For he has made known to us in all wisdom and insight the mystery of his will, according to his purpose which he set forth in Christ [10] as a plan for the fulness of time, to unite all things in him, things in heaven and things on earth.

[11] In him, according to the purpose of him who accomplishes all things according to the counsel of his will, [12] we who first hoped in Christ have been destined and appointed to live for the praise of his glory. [13] In him you also, who have heard the word of truth, the gospel of your salvation, and have believed in him, were sealed with the promised Holy

τῆς χάριτος αὐτοῦ, ἧς ἐχαρίτωσεν ἡμᾶς
of the grace of him, of(with) he favoured us
which

ἐν τῷ ἠγαπημένῳ, 7 ἐν ᾧ ἔχομεν τὴν
in the [one] *having been* loved, in whom we have the

ἀπολύτρωσιν διὰ τοῦ αἵματος αὐτοῦ, τὴν
redemption through the blood of him, the

ἄφεσιν τῶν παραπτωμάτων, κατὰ τὸ
forgiveness – of trespasses, according to the

πλοῦτος τῆς χάριτος αὐτοῦ, 8 ἧς ἐπερίσ-
riches of the grace of him, which he made to

σευσεν εἰς ἡμᾶς ἐν πάσῃ σοφίᾳ καὶ
abound to us in all wisdom and

φρονήσει 9 γνωρίσας ἡμῖν τὸ μυστήριον
intelligence making known to us the mystery

τοῦ θελήματος αὐτοῦ, κατὰ τὴν εὐδοκίαν
of the will of him, according to the good pleasure

αὐτοῦ, ἣν προέθετο ἐν αὐτῷ 10 εἰς
of him, which he purposed in him[self] for

οἰκονομίαν τοῦ πληρώματος τῶν καιρῶν,
a stewardship of the fulness of the times,

ἀνακεφαλαιώσασθαι τὰ πάντα ἐν τῷ
to head up – all things in –

Χριστῷ, τὰ ἐπὶ τοῖς οὐρανοῖς καὶ τὰ
Christ, the things on(in) *the* heavens and the
things

ἐπὶ τῆς γῆς· ἐν αὐτῷ, 11 ἐν ᾧ καὶ
on the earth; in him, in whom also

ἐκληρώθημεν προορισθέντες κατὰ πρόθεσιν
we were chosen as being predestinated according to [the] purpose
[his] inheritance

τοῦ τὰ πάντα ἐνεργοῦντος κατὰ τὴν
of the – [2]all things [1]operating according to the
[one]

βουλὴν τοῦ θελήματος αὐτοῦ, 12 εἰς τὸ
counsel of the will of him, for *the*

εἶναι ἡμᾶς εἰς ἔπαινον δόξης αὐτοῦ
to be us[b] to [the] praise of [the] glory of him
=that we should be

τοὺς προηλπικότας ἐν τῷ Χριστῷ· 13 ἐν
the having previously in – Christ; in
[ones] hoped

ᾧ καὶ ὑμεῖς, ἀκούσαντες τὸν λόγον
whom also ye, hearing the word

τῆς ἀληθείας, τὸ εὐαγγέλιον τῆς σωτηρίας
– of truth, the gospel of the salvation

ὑμῶν, ἐν ᾧ καὶ πιστεύσαντες ἐσφραγίσθητε
of you, in whom also believing ye were sealed

τῷ πνεύματι τῆς ἐπαγγελίας τῷ ἁγίῳ,
with [1]the [3]Spirit – [4]of promise – [2]holy,

Spirit, [14]which is the guarantee of our inheritance until we acquire possession of it, to the praise of his glory.

15 For this reason, because I have heard of your faith in the Lord Jesus and your love[e] toward all the saints, [16]I do not cease to give thanks for you, remembering you in my prayers, [17]that the God of our Lord Jesus Christ, the Father of glory, may give you a spirit of wisdom and of revelation in the knowledge of him, [18]having the eyes of your hearts enlightened, that you may know what is the hope to which he has called you, what are the riches of his glorious inheritance in the saints, [19]and what is the immeasurable greatness of his power in us who believe, according to the working of his great might [20]which he accomplished in Christ when he raised him from the dead and made him sit at his right hand in the heavenly places, [21]far above all rule and authority and power and dominion, and above

14 ὅς ἐστιν ἀρραβὼν τῆς κληρονομίας
who is an earnest of the inheritance
ἡμῶν, εἰς ἀπολύτρωσιν τῆς περιποιήσεως,
of us, till [the] redemption of the possession.
εἰς ἔπαινον τῆς δόξης αὐτοῦ.
to [the] praise of the glory of him.

15 Διὰ τοῦτο κἀγώ, ἀκούσας τὴν καθ᾽
Therefore I also, hearing the [a]among
ὑμᾶς πίστιν ἐν τῷ κυρίῳ Ἰησοῦ καὶ
[a]you [1]faith in the Lord Jesus and
τὴν ἀγάπην τὴν εἰς πάντας τοὺς ἁγίους,
the love to all the saints,
16 οὐ παύομαι εὐχαριστῶν ὑπὲρ ὑμῶν
do not cease giving thanks on behalf of you
μνείαν ποιούμενος ἐπὶ τῶν προσευχῶν
mention making on(in) the prayers
μου, 17 ἵνα ὁ θεὸς τοῦ κυρίου ἡμῶν
of me, in order that the God of the Lord of us
Ἰησοῦ Χριστοῦ, ὁ πατὴρ τῆς δόξης,
Jesus Christ, the Father - of glory,
δώῃ ὑμῖν πνεῦμα σοφίας καὶ ἀποκαλύψεως
may give to you a spirit of wisdom and of revelation
ἐν ἐπιγνώσει αὐτοῦ, 18 πεφωτισμένους τοὺς
in a full knowledge of him, having been enlightened the
ὀφθαλμοὺς τῆς καρδίας [ὑμῶν,] εἰς τὸ
eyes of the heart of you, for the
εἰδέναι ὑμᾶς τίς ἐστιν ἡ ἐλπὶς τῆς
to know you[b] what is the hope of the
=that ye should know
κλήσεως αὐτοῦ, τίς ὁ πλοῦτος τῆς δόξης
calling of him, what the riches of the glory
τῆς κληρονομίας αὐτοῦ ἐν τοῖς ἁγίοις,
of the inheritance of him in the saints,
19 καὶ τί τὸ ὑπερβάλλον μέγεθος τῆς
and what the excelling greatness of the
δυνάμεως αὐτοῦ εἰς ἡμᾶς τοὺς πιστεύοντας
power of him toward us the [ones] believing
κατὰ τὴν ἐνέργειαν τοῦ κράτους τῆς
according to the operation of the might of the
ἰσχύος αὐτοῦ, 20 ἣν ἐνήργηκεν ἐν τῷ
strength of him, which he has operated in -
Χριστῷ ἐγείρας αὐτὸν ἐκ νεκρῶν, καὶ
Christ raising him from [the] dead, and
καθίσας ἐν δεξιᾷ αὐτοῦ ἐν τοῖς ἐπου-
seating [him] at [the] right [hand] of him in the heaven-
ρανίοις 21 ὑπεράνω πάσης ἀρχῆς καὶ
lies far above all rule and
ἐξουσίας καὶ δυνάμεως καὶ κυριότητος
authority and power and lordship

[e] Other ancient authorities omit *your love*

every name that is named, not only in this age but also in that which is to come; [22]and he has put all things under his feet and has made him the head over all things for the church, [23]which is his body, the fulness of him who fills all in all.

καὶ παντὸς ὀνόματος ὀνομαζομένου οὐ
and every name being named not

μόνον ἐν τῷ αἰῶνι τούτῳ ἀλλὰ καὶ
only in this age but also

ἐν τῷ μέλλοντι· 22 καὶ πάντα ὑπέταξεν
in the coming; and all things subjected

ὑπὸ τοὺς πόδας αὐτοῦ, καὶ αὐτὸν ἔδωκεν
under the feet of him, and [2]him [1]gave

κεφαλὴν ὑπὲρ πάντα τῇ ἐκκλησίᾳ, 23 ἥτις
[to be] head over all things to the church, which

ἐστὶν τὸ σῶμα αὐτοῦ, τὸ πλήρωμα
is the body of him, the fulness

τοῦ τὰ πάντα ἐν πᾶσιν πληρουμένου.
of the – [2]all things [3]with [4]all things [1]filling.
[one]

CHAPTER 2

AND you he made alive, when you were dead through the trespasses and sins [2]in which you once walked, following the course of this world, following the prince of the power of the air, the spirit that is now at work in the sons of disobedience. [3]Among these we all once lived in the passions of our flesh, following the desires of body and mind, and so we were by nature children of wrath, like the rest of mankind. [4]But God, who is rich in mercy, out of the great love with which he loved us, [5]even when we were dead through our trespasses, made us alive together with Christ (by grace you have been

2 Καὶ ὑμᾶς ὄντας νεκροὺς τοῖς παραπτώ-
And you being dead in the tres-

μασιν καὶ ταῖς ἁμαρτίαις ὑμῶν, 2 ἐν
passes and in the sins of you, in

αἷς ποτε περιεπατήσατε κατὰ τὸν αἰῶνα
which then ye walked according to the age

τοῦ κόσμου τούτου, κατὰ τὸν ἄρχοντα
of this world, according to the ruler

τῆς ἐξουσίας τοῦ ἀέρος, τοῦ πνεύματος
of the authority of the air, of the spirit

τοῦ νῦν ἐνεργοῦντος ἐν τοῖς υἱοῖς τῆς
– now operating in the sons –

ἀπειθείας· 3 ἐν οἷς καὶ ἡμεῖς πάντες
of disobedience; among whom also we all

ἀνεστράφημέν ποτε ἐν ταῖς ἐπιθυμίαις
conducted ourselves then in the lusts

τῆς σαρκὸς ἡμῶν, ποιοῦντες τὰ θελήματα
of the flesh of us, doing the wishes

τῆς σαρκὸς καὶ τῶν διανοιῶν, καὶ
of the flesh and of the understandings, and

ἤμεθα τέκνα φύσει ὀργῆς ὡς καὶ οἱ
were [2]children [1]by nature of wrath as also the

λοιποί· 4 ὁ δὲ θεὸς πλούσιος ὢν ἐν
rest; – but God [2]rich [1]being in

ἐλέει, διὰ τὴν πολλὴν ἀγάπην αὐτοῦ
mercy, because of the much love of his

ἣν ἠγάπησεν ἡμᾶς, 5 καὶ ὄντας ἡμᾶς
[with] he loved us, even being us
which   =when we were

νεκροὺς τοῖς παραπτώμασιν συνεζωοποίησεν
dead – in trespasses quickened [us] with

τῷ Χριστῷ, — χάριτί ἐστε σεσωσμένοι,
– Christ, (by grace ye are having been saved,)

saved), [6] and raised us up with him, and made us sit with him in the heavenly places in Christ Jesus, [7] that in the coming ages he might show the immeasurable riches of his grace in kindness toward us in Christ Jesus. [8] For by grace you have been saved through faith; and this is not your own doing, it is the gift of God—[9] not because of works, lest any man should boast. [10] For we are his workmanship, created in Christ Jesus for good works, which God prepared beforehand, that we should walk in them.

[11] Therefore remember that at one time you Gentiles in the flesh, called the uncircumcision by what is called the circumcision, which is made in the flesh by hands—[12] remember that you were at that time separated from Christ, alienated from the commonwealth of Israel, and strangers to the covenants of promise, having no hope and without God in the world. [13] But now in Christ Jesus you who once were far off have been brought near in the blood of Christ. [14] For

— 6 καὶ συνήγειρεν καὶ συνεκάθισεν ἐν
and raised [us] with and seated [us] with in

τοῖς ἐπουρανίοις ἐν Χριστῷ Ἰησοῦ, 7 ἵνα
the heavenlies in Christ Jesus, in order that

ἐνδείξηται ἐν τοῖς αἰῶσιν τοῖς ἐπερχομένοις
he might show in the ages – coming on
forth

τὸ ὑπερβάλλον πλοῦτος τῆς χάριτος αὐτοῦ
the excelling riches of the grace of him

ἐν χρηστότητι ἐφ᾽ ἡμᾶς ἐν Χριστῷ
in kindness toward us in Christ

Ἰησοῦ. 8 τῇ γὰρ χάριτί ἐστε σεσωσμένοι
Jesus. – For by grace ye are *having been* saved

διὰ πίστεως· καὶ τοῦτο οὐκ ἐξ ὑμῶν,
through faith; and this not of you,

θεοῦ τὸ δῶρον· 9 οὐκ ἐξ ἔργων, ἵνα μή
of [is] the gift; not of works, lest
God

τις καυχήσηται. 10 αὐτοῦ γάρ ἐσμεν
anyone should boast. For of him we are

ποίημα, κτισθέντες ἐν Χριστῷ Ἰησοῦ
a product, created in Christ Jesus

ἐπὶ ἔργοις ἀγαθοῖς, οἷς προητοίμασεν
unto works good, which [1]previously prepared

ὁ θεὸς ἵνα ἐν αὐτοῖς περιπατήσωμεν.
– [1]God in order that in them we might walk.

11 Διὸ μνημονεύετε ὅτι ποτὲ ὑμεῖς τὰ
Wherefore remember ye that when ye the

ἔθνη ἐν σαρκί, οἱ λεγόμενοι ἀκροβυστία
nations in [the] flesh, the [ones] *being* called uncircumcision

ὑπὸ τῆς λεγομένης περιτομῆς ἐν σαρκὶ
by the *being* called circumcision in [the] flesh

χειροποιήτου, 12 ὅτι ἦτε τῷ καιρῷ ἐκείνῳ
made by hand, that ye were at that time

χωρὶς Χριστοῦ, ἀπηλλοτριωμένοι τῆς
without Christ, having been alienated from the

πολιτείας τοῦ Ἰσραὴλ καὶ ξένοι τῶν
commonwealth – of Israel and strangers of(from)
the

διαθηκῶν τῆς ἐπαγγελίας, ἐλπίδα μὴ
covenants – of promise, hope not

ἔχοντες καὶ ἄθεοι ἐν τῷ κόσμῳ. 13 νυνὶ
having and godless in the world. now

δὲ ἐν Χριστῷ Ἰησοῦ ὑμεῖς οἵ ποτε
But in Christ Jesus ye the [ones] then

ὄντες μακρὰν ἐγενήθητε ἐγγὺς ἐν τῷ
being afar became near by the

αἵματι τοῦ Χριστοῦ. 14 Αὐτὸς γάρ
blood – of Christ. For he

he is our peace, who has made us both one, and has broken down the dividing wall of hostility, [15] by abolishing in his flesh the law of commandments and ordinances, that he might create in himself one new man in place of the two, so making peace, [16] and might reconcile us both to God in one body through the cross, thereby bringing the hostility to an end. [17] And he came and preached peace to you who were far off and peace to those who were near; [18] for through him we both have access in one Spirit to the Father. [19] So then you are no longer strangers and sojourners, but you are fellow citizens with the saints and members of the household of God, [20] built upon the foundation of the apostles and prophets, Christ Jesus himself being the chief cornerstone, [21] in whom the whole structure is joined together and grows into a holy temple in the Lord; [22] in whom you also are built into it for a dwelling place of God in the Spirit.

ἐστιν ἡ εἰρήνη ἡμῶν, ὁ ποιήσας τὰ
is the peace of us, the [one] having made –

ἀμφότερα ἓν καὶ τὸ μεσότοιχον τοῦ
both one and ¹the ³middle wall –

φραγμοῦ λύσας, τὴν ἔχθραν, ἐν τῇ σαρκὶ
⁴of partition ¹having the enmity, ²in ³the ⁴flesh
broken,

αὐτοῦ 15 τὸν νόμον τῶν ἐντολῶν ἐν
⁵of him ⁶the ⁷law ⁸of the ⁹commandments ¹⁰in

δόγμασιν καταργήσας, ἵνα τοὺς δύο κτίσῃ
¹¹decrees ¹having abolished, in order ⁴the ⁵two ³he might
that create

ἐν αὐτῷ εἰς ἕνα καινὸν ἄνθρωπον ποιῶν
⁶in ⁷him[self] ⁸into ⁹one ¹⁰new ¹¹man ¹making

εἰρήνην, 16 καὶ ἀποκαταλλάξῃ τοὺς
²peace, and might reconcile the

ἀμφοτέρους ἐν ἑνὶ σώματι τῷ θεῷ διὰ
both in one body – to God through

τοῦ σταυροῦ, ἀποκτείνας τὴν ἔχθραν ἐν
the cross, killing the enmity in

αὐτῷ· 17 καὶ ἐλθὼν εὐηγγελίσατο εἰρήνην
him[self]; and coming preached peace

ὑμῖν τοῖς μακρὰν καὶ εἰρήνην τοῖς ἐγγύς·
to you the ones afar and peace to the ones near;

18 ὅτι δι' αὐτοῦ ἔχομεν τὴν προσαγωγὴν
because through him ¹we ²have ⁴access

οἱ ἀμφότεροι ἐν ἑνὶ πνεύματι πρὸς τὸν
– ³both by one Spirit unto the

πατέρα. 19 ἄρα οὖν οὐκέτι ἐστὲ ξένοι
Father. Then therefore no more are ye strangers

καὶ πάροικοι, ἀλλὰ ἐστὲ συμπολῖται τῶν
and sojourners, but ye are fellow-citizens of the

ἁγίων καὶ οἰκεῖοι τοῦ θεοῦ, 20 ἐποικοδομη-
saints and members of – of God, having been
the family

θέντες ἐπὶ τῷ θεμελίῳ τῶν ἀποστόλων
built on on the foundation of the apostles

καὶ προφητῶν, ὄντος ἀκρογωνιαίου αὐτοῦ
and prophets, ⁴being ⁵cornerstone ³[him]self

Χριστοῦ Ἰησοῦ, 21 ἐν ᾧ πᾶσα οἰκοδομὴ
¹Christ ²Jesus,ᵃ in whom all [the] building

συναρμολογουμένη αὔξει εἰς ναὸν ἅγιον
being fitted together grows into shrine a holy

ἐν κυρίῳ, 22 ἐν ᾧ καὶ ὑμεῖς συνοικοδομεῖσθε
in [the] Lord, in whom also ye are being built together

εἰς κατοικητήριον τοῦ θεοῦ ἐν πνεύματι.
into a dwelling-place – of God in spirit.

CHAPTER 3

FOR this reason I, Paul, a prisoner for Christ Jesus on behalf of you Gentiles—²assuming that you have heard of the stewardship of God's grace that was given to me for you, ³how the mystery was made known to me by revelation, as I have written briefly. ⁴When you read this you can perceive my insight into the mystery of Christ, ⁵which was not made known to the sons of men in other generations as it has now been revealed to his holy apostles and prophets by the Spirit; ⁶that is, how the Gentiles are fellow heirs, members of the same body, and partakers of the promise in Christ Jesus through the gospel.

7 Of this gospel I was made a minister according to the gift of God's grace which was given me by the working of his power. ⁸To me, though I am the very least of all the saints, this grace was given, to preach to the Gentiles the unsearchable riches of Christ, ⁹and to make all men see what is the plan of the mystery hidden for

3 Τούτου χάριν ἐγὼ Παῦλος ὁ δέσμιος
²of this   ¹By reason of   I   Paul   the   prisoner

τοῦ   Χριστοῦ   ᾽Ιησοῦ   ὑπὲρ   ὑμῶν   τῶν
— of Christ   Jesus on behalf of you   the

ἐθνῶν   2 —   εἴ γε   ἠκούσατε   τὴν   οἰκονομίαν
nations   — if indeed ye heard   the   stewardship

τῆς   χάριτος   τοῦ   θεοῦ   τῆς   δοθείσης   μοι
of the   grace   —   of God   —   given   to me

εἰς   ὑμᾶς,   3 ὅτι   κατὰ   ἀποκάλυψιν   ἐγνωρίσθη
for   you,   that by way of revelation   was made known

μοι   τὸ   μυστήριον,   καθὼς   προέγραψα   ἐν
to me the   mystery,   as   I previously wrote in

ὀλίγῳ,   4 πρὸς   ὃ   δύνασθε   ἀναγινώσκοντες
brief,   as to   which ²ye can   ¹reading

νοῆσαι   τὴν   σύνεσίν   μου   ἐν   τῷ   μυστηρίῳ
to realize the   understanding of me in   the   mystery

τοῦ   Χριστοῦ,   5 ὃ   ἑτέραις   γενεαῖς   οὐκ
— of Christ,   which in other generations not

ἐγνωρίσθη   τοῖς   υἱοῖς   τῶν   ἀνθρώπων   ὡς
was made known to the sons   —   of men   as

νῦν   ἀπεκαλύφθη   τοῖς   ἁγίοις   ἀποστόλοις
now   it was revealed   to the   holy   apostles

αὐτοῦ   καὶ   προφήταις   ἐν   πνεύματι,   6 εἶναι
of him   and   prophets   in   spirit,   ²to be

τὰ   ἔθνη   συγκληρονόμα   καὶ   σύσσωμα   καὶ
¹the ²nations   joint-heirs   and   a joint-body and

συμμέτοχα   τῆς   ἐπαγγελίας   ἐν   Χριστῷ
joint-sharers   of the   promise   in   Christ

᾽Ιησοῦ   διὰ   τοῦ   εὐαγγελίου,   7 οὗ   ἐγενήθην
Jesus through the   gospel,   of which I became

διάκονος   κατὰ   τὴν   δωρεὰν   τῆς   χάριτος
a minister according to the   gift   of the   grace

τοῦ   θεοῦ   τῆς   δοθείσης   μοι   κατὰ   τὴν
—   of God   —   given   to me according to the

ἐνέργειαν   τῆς   δυνάμεως   αὐτοῦ.   8 ἐμοὶ
operation   of the   power   of him.   To me

τῷ   ἐλαχιστοτέρῳ   πάντων   ἁγίων   ἐδόθη
the   leaster*   of all   saints   was given

ἡ   χάρις   αὕτη,   τοῖς   ἔθνεσιν   εὐαγγελίσασθαι
this grace,   to the   nations   to preach

τὸ   ἀνεξιχνίαστον   πλοῦτος   τοῦ   Χριστον,
the   unsearchable   riches   — of Christ,

9 καὶ   φωτίσαι   τίς   ἡ   οἰκονομία   τοῦ
and   to bring to light what [is] the   stewardship   of the

μυστηρίου   τοῦ   ἀποκεκρυμμένου   ἀπὸ   τῶν
mystery   —   having been hidden   from   the

* This is quite literal!—the apostle coins a word.

ages in[d] God who created all things; [10] that through the church the manifold wisdom of God might now be made known to the principalities and powers in the heavenly places. [11] This was according to the eternal purpose which he has realized in Christ Jesus our Lord, [12] in whom we have boldness and confidence of access through our faith in him. [13] So I ask you not to[e] lose heart over what I am suffering for you, which is your glory.

[14] For this reason I bow my knees before the Father, [15] from whom every family in heaven and on earth is named, [16] that according to the riches of his glory he may grant you to be strengthened with might through his Spirit in the inner man, [17] and that Christ may dwell in your hearts through faith; that you, being rooted and grounded in love, [18] may have power to comprehend with all the saints what is the breadth and

αἰώνων ἐν τῷ θεῷ τῷ τὰ πάντα κτίσαντι,
ages in - God [1]the [one] - [2]all things [3]having created,

10 ἵνα γνωρισθῇ νῦν ταῖς ἀρχαῖς καὶ
in order that might be made known now to the rulers and

ταῖς ἐξουσίαις ἐν τοῖς ἐπουρανίοις διὰ
to the authorities in the heavenlies through

τῆς ἐκκλησίας ἡ πολυποίκιλος σοφία τοῦ
the church the manifold wisdom -

θεοῦ, 11 κατὰ πρόθεσιν τῶν αἰώνων ἣν
of God, according to [the] purpose of the ages which

ἐποίησεν ἐν τῷ Χριστῷ Ἰησοῦ τῷ κυρίῳ
he made in - Christ Jesus the Lord

ἡμῶν, 12 ἐν ᾧ ἔχομεν τὴν παρρησίαν
of us, in whom we have - boldness

καὶ προσαγωγὴν ἐν πεποιθήσει διὰ τῆς
and access in confidence through the

πίστεως αὐτοῦ. 13 διὸ αἰτοῦμαι μὴ
faith of(in) him.* Wherefore I ask [you] not

ἐγκακεῖν ἐν ταῖς θλίψεσίν μου ὑπὲρ
to faint in the afflictions of me on behalf

ὑμῶν, ἥτις ἐστὶν δόξα ὑμῶν. 14 Τούτου
of you, which is glory of you. [3]of this

χάριν κάμπτω τὰ γόνατά μου πρὸς
[1]By reason of I bend the knees of me unto

τὸν πατέρα, 15 ἐξ οὗ πᾶσα πατριὰ
the Father, of whom every fatherhood

ἐν οὐρανοῖς καὶ ἐπὶ γῆς ὀνομάζεται,
in heavens and on earth is named,

16 ἵνα δῷ ὑμῖν κατὰ τὸ πλοῦτος τῆς
in order he may you according to the riches of the
that give

δόξης αὐτοῦ δυνάμει κραταιωθῆναι διὰ
glory of him by power to become mighty through

τοῦ πνεύματος αὐτοῦ εἰς τὸν ἔσω ἄνθρω-
the Spirit of him in the inward man,

πον, 17 κατοικῆσαι τὸν Χριστὸν[b] διὰ τῆς
to dwell - Christ through -
=that Christ may dwell

πίστεως ἐν ταῖς καρδίαις ὑμῶν, ἐν
faith in the hearts of you, in

ἀγάπῃ ἐρριζωμένοι καὶ τεθεμελιωμένοι,
love having been rooted and having been founded,

18 ἵνα ἐξισχύσητε καταλαβέσθαι σὺν πᾶσιν
in order ye may have strength to apprehend with all
that

τοῖς ἁγίοις τί τὸ πλάτος καὶ μῆκος
the saints what [is] the breadth and length

---

[d] Or by

[e] Or I ask that I may not

* See Gal. 2. 16.

length and height and depth, [19] and to know the love of Christ which surpasses knowledge, that you may be filled with all the fulness of God.

20 Now to him who by the power at work within us is able to do far more abundantly than all that we ask or think, [21] to him be glory in the church and in Christ Jesus to all generations, for ever and ever. Amen.

καὶ ὕψος καὶ βάθος, 19 γνῶναί τε τὴν
and height and depth,   and to know [the]

ὑπερβάλλουσαν τῆς γνώσεως ἀγάπην τοῦ
[4]excelling   -   [3]knowledge [2]love

Χριστοῦ, ἵνα πληρωθῆτε εἰς πᾶν τὸ
[1]of Christ, in order that ye may be filled to all the

πλήρωμα τοῦ θεοῦ.
fulness   - of God.

20 Τῷ δὲ δυναμένῳ ὑπὲρ πάντα ποιῆσαι
Now to the [one] being able beyond all things to do

ὑπερεκπερισσοῦ ὧν αἰτούμεθα ἢ νοοῦμεν
superabundantly of which we ask or we think

κατὰ τὴν δύναμιν τὴν ἐνεργουμένην ἐν
according to the   power   -   operating   in

ἡμῖν, 21 αὐτῷ ἡ δόξα ἐν τῇ ἐκκλησίᾳ
us,   to him [be] the glory in the church

καὶ ἐν Χριστῷ Ἰησοῦ εἰς πάσας τὰς
and in Christ Jesus unto all the

γενεὰς τοῦ αἰῶνος τῶν αἰώνων· ἀμήν.
generations of the age   of the ages: Amen.

CHAPTER 4

I therefore, a prisoner for the Lord, beg you to lead a life worthy of the calling to which you have been called, [2] with all lowliness and meekness, with patience, forbearing one another in love, [3] eager to maintain the unity of the Spirit in the bond of peace. [4] There is one body and one Spirit, just as you were called to the one hope that belongs to your call, [5] one Lord, one faith, one baptism, [6] one God and Father of us all, who is above all and through all and in all. [7] But grace was given to each of us according to the measure

4 Παρακαλῶ οὖν ὑμᾶς ἐγὼ ὁ δέσμιος
[7]beseech [therefore] [8]you [1]I [5]the [2]prisoner

ἐν κυρίῳ ἀξίως περιπατῆσαι τῆς κλήσεως
[4]in [5][the] Lord [10]worthily [9]to walk of the calling

ἧς ἐκλήθητε, 2 μετὰ πάσης ταπεινοφροσύνης
of(with) ye were   with all   humility
which called,

καὶ πραΰτητος, μετὰ μακροθυμίας,
and meekness,   with longsuffering,

ἀνεχόμενοι ἀλλήλων ἐν ἀγάπῃ, 3 σπου-
forbearing one another in love,   being

δάζοντες τηρεῖν τὴν ἑνότητα τοῦ πνεύματος
eager   to keep the unity of the Spirit

ἐν τῷ συνδέσμῳ τῆς εἰρήνης· ἓν σῶμα
in the bond   - of peace; [there is] one body

καὶ ἓν πνεῦμα, 4 καθὼς καὶ ἐκλήθητε
and one Spirit,   as   also ye were called

ἐν μιᾷ ἐλπίδι τῆς κλήσεως ὑμῶν· 5 εἷς
in one hope of the calling of you;   one

κύριος, μία πίστις, ἓν βάπτισμα· 6 εἷς
Lord, one faith, one baptism;   one

θεὸς καὶ πατὴρ πάντων, ὁ ἐπὶ πάντων
God and Father of all, the [one] over all

καὶ διὰ πάντων καὶ ἐν πᾶσιν. 7 Ἑνὶ
and through all and in all.   [2]to [4]one

δὲ ἑκάστῳ ἡμῶν ἐδόθη ἡ χάρις κατὰ
[1]But [3]each of us was given - grace according to

of Christ's gift. [8]Therefore it is said,

"When he ascended on high he led a host of captives, and he gave gifts to men."

[9](In saying, "He ascended," what does it mean but that he had also descended into the lower parts of the earth? [10]He who descended is he who also ascended far above all the heavens, that he might fill all things.) [11]And his gifts were that some should be apostles, some prophets, some evangelists, some pastors and teachers, [12]for the equipment of the saints, for the work of ministry, for building up the body of Christ, [13]until we all attain to the unity of the faith and of the knowledge of the Son of God, to mature manhood, to the measure of the stature of the fulness of Christ; [14]so that we may no longer be children, tossed to and fro and carried about with every wind of doctrine, by the cunning of men, by their craftiness in deceitful wiles. [15]Rather, speaking the truth in love, we are to grow up in every way into him who is the head,

τὸ   μέτρον   τῆς   δωρεᾶς   τοῦ   Χριστοῦ.
the   measure   of the   gift   -   of Christ.

8 διὸ   λέγει·   ἀναβὰς   εἰς   ὕψος   ᾐχμαλώτευσεν
Where-   he says: Having   to   height   he led captive
fore   ascended

αἰχμαλωσίαν,   ἔδωκεν   δόματα   τοῖς   ἀνθρώποις.
captivity,   he gave   gifts   -   to men.

9 τὸ   δὲ   ἀνέβη   τί   ἐστιν   εἰ   μὴ   ὅτι   καὶ
Now the   "he   what   is it   except   that   also
ascended"

κατέβη   εἰς   τὰ   κατώτερα   μέρη   τῆς   γῆς;
he descended into   the   lower   parts   of the earth?

10 ὁ   καταβὰς   αὐτός   ἐστιν   καὶ   ὁ   ἀναβὰς
The   descending   himself   is   also the   ascending
[one]   [one]

ὑπεράνω   πάντων   τῶν   οὐρανῶν,   ἵνα
far above   all   the   heavens,   in order that

πληρώσῃ   τὰ   πάντα.   11 καὶ   αὐτὸς   ἔδωκεν
he might fill   -   all things.   And   he   gave

τοὺς   μὲν   ἀποστόλους,   τοὺς   δὲ   προφήτας,
some†   apostles,   some†   prophets,

τοὺς   δὲ   εὐαγγελιστάς,   τοὺς   δὲ   ποιμένας
some†   evangelists,   some†   shepherds

καὶ   διδασκάλους,   12 πρὸς   τὸν   καταρτισμὸν
and   teachers,   for   the   perfecting

τῶν   ἁγίων   εἰς   ἔργον   διακονίας,   εἰς
of the   saints   to [the] work   of ministry,   to

οἰκοδομὴν   τοῦ   σώματος   τοῦ   Χριστοῦ,
building   of the   body   -   of Christ,

13 μέχρι   καταντήσωμεν   οἱ   πάντες   εἰς
until   [1]we [2]arrive   -   [2]all   at

τὴν   ἑνότητα   τῆς   πίστεως   καὶ   τῆς   ἐπιγνώ-
the   unity   of the   faith   and   of the   full know-

σεως   τοῦ   υἱοῦ   τοῦ   θεοῦ,   εἰς   ἄνδρα   τέλειον,
ledge   of the Son   -   of God,   at   [2]man [1]a complete,

εἰς   μέτρον   ἡλικίας   τοῦ   πληρώματος   τοῦ
at [the] measure   of [the]   of the   fulness   -
stature

Χριστοῦ,   14 ἵνα   μηκέτι   ὦμεν   νήπιοι,
of Christ,   in order that   no more   we may be   infants,

κλυδωνιζόμενοι   καὶ   περιφερόμενοι   παντὶ   ἀνέμῳ
being blown   and being carried round   by every   wind

τῆς   διδασκαλίας   ἐν   τῇ   κυβείᾳ   τῶν   ἀνθρώ-
-   of teaching   in   the   sleight   -   of

πων,   ἐν   πανουργίᾳ   πρὸς   τὴν   μεθοδείαν
men,   in   cleverness   unto   the   craftiness

τῆς   πλάνης,   15 ἀληθεύοντες   δὲ   ἐν   ἀγάπῃ
-   of error,   but speaking truth   in   love

αὐξήσωμεν   εἰς   αὐτὸν   τὰ   πάντα,   ὅς   ἐστιν
we may grow   into   him   in all respects,†   who   is

into Christ, [16] from whom the whole body, joined and knit together by every joint with which it is supplied, when each part is working properly, makes bodily growth and upbuilds itself in love.

[17] Now this I affirm and testify in the Lord, that you must no longer live as the Gentiles do, in the futility of their minds; [18] they are darkened in their understanding, alienated from the life of God because of the ignorance that is in them, due to their hardness of heart; [19] they have become callous and have given themselves up to licentiousness, greedy to practice every kind of uncleanness. [20] You did not so learn Christ!—[21] assuming that you have heard about him and were taught in him, as the truth is in Jesus. [22] Put off your old nature which belongs to your former manner of life and is corrupt through deceitful lusts, [23] and be renewed in the

ἡ κεφαλή, Χριστός, **16** ἐξ οὗ πᾶν τὸ
the head, Christ, of whom all the

σῶμα συναρμολογούμενον καὶ συμβιβαζόμενον
body being fitted together and *being* brought together

διὰ πάσης ἀφῆς τῆς ἐπιχορηγίας κατ'
through every band - of supply according to

ἐνέργειαν ἐν μέτρῳ ἑνὸς ἑκάστου μέρους
[the] operation in measure of [2]one [1]each part

τὴν αὔξησιν τοῦ σώματος ποιεῖται εἰς
[2]the [3]growth [4]of the [5]body [1]makes for

οἰκοδομὴν ἑαυτοῦ ἐν ἀγάπῃ.
building of itself in love.

17 Τοῦτο οὖν λέγω καὶ μαρτύρομαι ἐν
This therefore I say and witness in

κυρίῳ, μηκέτι ὑμᾶς περιπατεῖν καθὼς
[the] Lord, no more you to walk as

καὶ τὰ ἔθνη περιπατεῖ ἐν ματαιότητι
also the nations walks in vanity

τοῦ νοὸς αὐτῶν, **18** ἐσκοτωμένοι τῇ
of the mind of them, [1]having been darkened [2]in the (their)

διανοίᾳ ὄντες, ἀπηλλοτριωμένοι τῆς ζωῆς
[4]intellect [1]being, having been alienated [from] the life

τοῦ θεοῦ, διὰ τὴν ἄγνοιαν τὴν οὖσαν
- of God, through the ignorance - being

ἐν αὐτοῖς, διὰ τὴν πώρωσιν τῆς καρδίας
in them, on account of the hardness of the heart

αὐτῶν, **19** οἵτινες ἀπηλγηκότες ἑαυτοὺς
of them, who having ceased to care [2]themselves

παρέδωκαν τῇ ἀσελγείᾳ εἰς ἐργασίαν
[1]gave up - to lewdness for work

ἀκαθαρσίας πάσης ἐν πλεονεξίᾳ. **20** ὑμεῖς
[2]uncleanness [1]of all in greediness. ye

δὲ οὐχ οὕτως ἐμάθετε τὸν Χριστόν,
But not so learned - Christ,

21 εἴ γε αὐτὸν ἠκούσατε καὶ ἐν αὐτῷ
if indeed [2]him [1]ye heard and [2]by [1]him

ἐδιδάχθητε καθώς ἐστιν ἀλήθεια ἐν τῷ
[1]were taught as [2]is [1]truth in -

Ἰησοῦ, **22** ἀποθέσθαι ὑμᾶς κατὰ τὴν
Jesus, to put off you[b] as regards the(your)
=that ye put off

προτέραν ἀναστροφὴν τὸν παλαιὸν ἄνθρωπον
former conduct the old man

τὸν φθειρόμενον κατὰ τὰς ἐπιθυμίας τῆς
- being corrupted according to the lusts -

ἀπάτης, **23** ἀνανεοῦσθαι δὲ τῷ πνεύματι
of deceit, and to be renewed in the spirit

spirit of your minds, ²⁴and put on the new nature, created after the likeness of God in true righteousness and holiness.

25 Therefore, putting away falsehood, let every one speak the truth with his neighbor, for we are members one of another. ²⁶Be angry but do not sin; do not let the sun go down on your anger, ²⁷and give no opportunity to the devil. ²⁸Let the thief no longer steal, but rather let him labor, doing honest work with his hands, so that he may be able to give to those in need. ²⁹Let no evil talk come out of your mouths, but only such as is good for edifying, as fits the occasion, that it may impart grace to those who hear. ³⁰And do not grieve the Holy Spirit of God, in whom you were sealed for the day of redemption. ³¹Let all bitterness and wrath and anger and clamor and slander be put away from you, with all malice, ³²and be kind to one another, tenderhearted,

τοῦ   νοὸς   ὑμῶν   24 καὶ   ἐνδύσασθαι   τὸν
of the   mind   of you   and   to put on   the

καινὸν   ἄνθρωπον   τὸν   κατὰ   θεὸν   κτισθέντα
new   man   –   ²according to   ³God   ¹created

ἐν   δικαιοσύνῃ   καὶ   ὁσιότητι   τῆς   ἀληθείας.
in   righteousness   and   holiness   –   of truth.

25 Διὸ   ἀποθέμενοι   τὸ   ψεῦδος   λαλεῖτε
Wherefore   putting off   the   lie   speak ye

ἀλήθειαν   ἕκαστος   μετὰ   τοῦ   πλησίον   αὐτοῦ,
truth   each man   with   the   neighbour   of him,

ὅτι   ἐσμὲν   ἀλλήλων   μέλη.   26 ὀργίζεσθε
because we are   of one another   members.   Be ye wrathful

καὶ   μὴ   ἁμαρτάνετε·   ὁ   ἥλιος   μὴ
and   do not sin;   ²the   ⁴sun   ³not

ἐπιδυέτω   ἐπὶ   παροργισμῷ   ὑμῶν,   27 μηδὲ
¹let ⁵set on   on   provocation   of you,   nor

δίδοτε   τόπον   τῷ   διαβόλῳ.   28 ὁ   κλέπτων
give ye   place   to the   devil.   The [one] stealing

μηκέτι   κλεπτέτω,   μᾶλλον   δὲ   κοπιάτω
no more   let him steal,   but rather   let him labour

ἐργαζόμενος   ταῖς   ἰδίαις   χερσὶν   τὸ   ἀγαθόν,
working   with the(his) own   hands   the   good thing,

ἵνα   ἔχῃ   μεταδιδόναι   τῷ   χρείαν   ἔχοντι.
in order he may   to share [with]   the [one]   ²need   ¹having
that   have

29 πᾶς   λόγος   σαπρὸς   ἐκ   τοῦ   στόματος
Every   ²word   ¹corrupt   out of   the   mouth

ὑμῶν   μὴ   ἐκπορευέσθω,   ἀλλὰ   εἴ   τις
of you   let not proceed*,   but   if   any

ἀγαθὸς   πρὸς   οἰκοδομὴν   τῆς   χρείας,   ἵνα
[is] good   to   improvement   of the   need,   in order
that

δῷ   χάριν   τοῖς   ἀκούουσιν.   30 καὶ   μὴ   λυπεῖτε
it may   grace   to the [ones] hearing.   And   do not grieve
give

τὸ   πνεῦμα   τὸ   ἅγιον   τοῦ   θεοῦ,   ἐν   ᾧ
the   Spirit   -   Holy   -   of God,   by whom

ἐσφραγίσθητε   εἰς   ἡμέραν   ἀπολυτρώσεως.
ye were sealed   for   a day   of redemption.

31 πᾶσα   πικρία   καὶ   θυμὸς   καὶ
All   bitterness   and   anger   and

ὀργὴ   καὶ   κραυγὴ   καὶ   βλασφημία   ἀρθήτω
wrath   and   clamour   and   blasphemy   let it be
removed

ἀφ'   ὑμῶν   σὺν   πάσῃ   κακίᾳ.   32 γίνεσθε
from   you   with   all   evil.   be ye

δὲ   εἰς   ἀλλήλους   χρηστοί,   εὔσπλαγχνοι,
And   to   one another   kind,   tenderhearted,

* That is, " let no corrupt word proceed . . . "

forgiving one another, as God in Christ forgave you.

χαριζόμενοι ἑαυτοῖς καθὼς καὶ ὁ θεὸς
forgiving   yourselves   as   also - God

ἐν Χριστῷ ἐχαρίσατο ὑμῖν. 5 Γίνεσθε
in Christ   forgave   you.   Be ye

CHAPTER 5

THEREFORE be imitators of God, as beloved children. ²And walk in love, as Christ loved us and gave himself up for us, a fragrant offering and sacrifice to God.

οὖν μιμηταὶ τοῦ θεοῦ, ὡς τέκνα
therefore imitators - of God, as children

ἀγαπητά, 2 καὶ περιπατεῖτε ἐν ἀγάπῃ,
beloved,   and walk ye   in   love,

καθὼς καὶ ὁ Χριστὸς ἠγάπησεν ὑμᾶς
as also - Christ   loved   you

καὶ παρέδωκεν ἑαυτὸν ὑπὲρ ἡμῶν
and gave up   himself on behalf of us

3 But immorality and all impurity or covetousness must not even be named among you, as is fitting among saints. ⁴Let there be no filthiness, nor silly talk, nor levity, which are not fitting; but instead let there be thanksgiving. ⁵Be sure of this, that no immoral or impure man, or one who is covetous (that is, an idolator), has any inheritance in the kingdom of Christ and of God. ⁶Let no one deceive you with empty words, for it is because of these things that the wrath of God comes upon the sons of disobedience. ⁷Therefore do not associate with them, ⁸for once you were darkness, but now you are light in the Lord; walk as children of light ⁹(for the fruit of light is found in all that is good and right and true), ¹⁰and try to learn what is

προσφορὰν καὶ θυσίαν τῷ θεῷ εἰς ὀσμὴν
an offering and a sacrifice - to God for an odour

εὐωδίας. 3 Πορνεία δὲ καὶ ἀκαθαρσία
of sweet smell. But fornication and ³uncleanness

πᾶσα ἢ πλεονεξία μηδὲ ὀνομαζέσθω ἐν
¹all or greediness not let it be named among

ὑμῖν, καθὼς πρέπει ἁγίοις, 4 καὶ αἰσχρότης
you, as is fitting for saints, and baseness

καὶ μωρολογία ἢ εὐτραπελία, ἃ οὐκ
and foolish talking or raillery, which things not

ἀνῆκεν, ἀλλὰ μᾶλλον εὐχαριστία. 5 τοῦτο
are becoming, but rather thanksgiving. this

γὰρ ἴστε γινώσκοντες, ὅτι πᾶς πόρνος
For ye be knowing,   that every fornicator

ἢ ἀκάθαρτος ἢ πλεονέκτης, ὅ ἐστιν
or unclean man or greedy, who is

εἰδωλολάτρης, οὐκ ἔχει κληρονομίαν ἐν τῇ
an idolater, not has   inheritance   in the

βασιλείᾳ τοῦ Χριστοῦ καὶ θεοῦ. 6 Μηδεὶς
kingdom - of Christ and of God. ³No man

ὑμᾶς ἀπατάτω κενοῖς λόγοις· διὰ ταῦτα
⁴you ¹let ²deceive with empty words; because these
                                              of things

γὰρ ἔρχεται ἡ ὀργὴ τοῦ θεοῦ ἐπὶ τοὺς
for is coming the wrath - of God on the

υἱοὺς τῆς ἀπειθείας. 7 μὴ οὖν γίνεσθε
sons - of disobedience. Not therefore be ye

συμμέτοχοι αὐτῶν· 8 ἦτε γάρ ποτε σκότος,
partakers of them; for ye were then darkness,

νῦν δὲ φῶς ἐν κυρίῳ· ὡς τέκνα φωτὸς
but now light in [the] Lord; as children of light

περιπατεῖτε, 9 — ὁ γὰρ καρπὸς τοῦ
walk ye,   (for the fruit of the

φωτὸς ἐν πάσῃ ἀγαθωσύνῃ καὶ δικαιοσύνῃ
light [is] in all goodness and righteousness

καὶ ἀληθείᾳ, — 10 δοκιμάζοντες τί ἐστιν
and truth,)   proving what is

pleasing to the Lord.
[11] Take no part in the
unfruitful works of
darkness, but instead
expose them. [12] For it is
a shame even to speak
of the things that they
do in secret; [13] but when
anything is exposed by
the light it becomes
visible, for anything that
becomes visible is light.
[14] Therefore it is said,

"Awake, O sleeper,
  and arise from the
  dead,
and Christ shall give
  you light."

15 Look carefully then
how you walk, not as
unwise men but as wise,
[16] making the most of the
time, because the days
are evil. [17] Therefore do
not be foolish, but understand what the will of the
Lord is. [18] And do not get
drunk with wine, for
that is debauchery; but
be filled with the Spirit,
[19] addressing one another
in psalms and hymns and
spiritual songs, singing
and making melody to
the Lord with all your
heart, [20] always and for
everything giving thanks
in the name of our Lord
Jesus Christ to God the
Father.

21 Be subject to one
another out of reverence
for Christ. [22] Wives, be
subject to your husbands,

εὐάρεστον τῷ κυρίῳ,
well-pleasing   to the   Lord,

11 καὶ μὴ συγκοι-
and   do not have fellow-

νωνεῖτε τοῖς ἔργοις τοῖς ἀκάρποις τοῦ
ship with   the   ²works   -   ¹unfruitful   -

σκότους, μᾶλλον δὲ καὶ ἐλέγχετε, 12 τὰ
of darkness,   but rather   even   reprove [them],   ⁵the

γὰρ κρυφῇ γινόμενα ὑπ' αὐτῶν αἰσχρόν
for   ⁶hidden things ⁷being done   ⁸by   ⁹them   ²shameful

ἐστιν καὶ λέγειν· 13 τὰ δὲ πάντα ἐλεγχόμενα
¹it is   ³even ⁴to speak [of];   -   but all things being reproved

ὑπὸ τοῦ φωτὸς φανεροῦται· 14 πᾶν γὰρ
by   the   light   is(are) manifested;   for everything

τὸ φανερούμενον φῶς ἐστιν. διὸ λέγει·
-   being manifested   ²light   ¹is.   Wherefore he says:

ἔγειρε, ὁ καθεύδων, καὶ ἀνάστα ἐκ τῶν
Rise,   the   sleeping [one],   and   stand up   out of   the

νεκρῶν, καὶ ἐπιφαύσει σοι ὁ Χριστός.
dead [ones],   and   will shine on   thee   -   Christ.

15 Βλέπετε οὖν ἀκριβῶς πῶς περιπατεῖτε,
See ye   therefore carefully   how   ye walk,

μὴ ὡς ἄσοφοι ἀλλ' ὡς σοφοί, 16 ἐξαγοραζ-
not   as   unwise   but   as   wise,   redeem-

όμενοι τὸν καιρόν, ὅτι αἱ ἡμέραι πονηραί
ing   the   time,   because the   days   evil

εἰσιν. 17 διὰ τοῦτο μὴ γίνεσθε ἄφρονες,
are.   Therefore   be ye not   foolish,

ἀλλὰ συνίετε τί τὸ θέλημα τοῦ κυρίου.
but   understand what the   will   of the   Lord [is].

18 καὶ μὴ μεθύσκεσθε οἴνῳ, ἐν ᾧ ἐστιν
And   be ye not drunk   with wine,   in which   is

ἀσωτία, ἀλλὰ πληροῦσθε ἐν πνεύματι,
wantonness,   but   be filled   by   [the] Spirit,

19 λαλοῦντες ἑαυτοῖς ψαλμοῖς καὶ ὕμνοις
speaking   to yourselves   in psalms   and   hymns

καὶ ᾠδαῖς πνευματικαῖς, ᾄδοντες καὶ
and   songs   spiritual,   singing   and

ψάλλοντες τῇ καρδίᾳ ὑμῶν τῷ κυρίῳ,
psalming   with the   heart   of you   to the   Lord,

20 εὐχαριστοῦντες πάντοτε ὑπὲρ πάντων
giving thanks   always   for   all things

ἐν ὀνόματι τοῦ κυρίου ἡμῶν Ἰησοῦ
in   [the] name   of the   Lord   of us   Jesus

Χριστοῦ τῷ θεῷ καὶ πατρί, 21 ὑποτασ-
Christ   -   to God   even   [the] Father,   being

σόμενοι ἀλλήλοις ἐν φόβῳ Χριστοῦ. 22 Αἱ
subject   to one another in   [the] fear   of Christ.   The

γυναῖκες τοῖς ἰδίοις ἀνδράσιν ὡς τῷ
wives   to the(ir)   own   husbands   as   to the

as to the Lord. ²³For the husband is the head of the wife as Christ is the head of the church, his body, and is himself its Savior. ²⁴As the church is subject to Christ, so let wives also be subject in everything to their husbands. ²⁵Husbands, love your wives, as Christ loved the church and gave himself up for her, ²⁶that he might sanctify her, having cleansed her by the washing of water with the word, ²⁷that he might present the church to himself in splendor, without spot or wrinkle or any such thing, that she might be holy and without blemish. ²⁸Even so husbands should love their wives as their own bodies. He who loves his wife loves himself. ²⁹For no man ever hates his own flesh, but nourishes and cherishes it, as Christ does the church, ³⁰because we are members of his body. ³¹"For this reason a man shall leave his father and mother and

κυρίῳ,   23 ὅτι   ἀνήρ   ἐστιν   κεφαλὴ   τῆς
Lord,   because   a man   is   head   of the

γυναικὸς   ὡς   καὶ   ὁ   Χριστὸς   κεφαλὴ
woman   as   also   –   Christ [is]   head

τῆς   ἐκκλησίας,   αὐτὸς   σωτὴρ   τοῦ   σώματος.
of the   church,   [him]self   Saviour   of the   body.

24 ἀλλὰ   ὡς   ἡ   ἐκκλησία   ὑποτάσσεται   τῷ
But   as   the   church   is subject   to

Χριστῷ,   οὕτως   καὶ   αἱ   γυναῖκες   τοῖς
Christ,   so   also   the   wives   to the(ir)

ἀνδράσιν   ἐν   παντί.   25 Οἱ   ἄνδρες,   ἀγαπᾶτε
husbands   in   everything.   The husbands,   love ye

τὰς   γυναῖκας,   καθὼς   καὶ   ὁ   Χριστὸς
the(your)   wives,   as   also   –   Christ

ἠγάπησεν   τὴν   ἐκκλησίαν   καὶ   ἑαυτὸν
loved   the   church   and   himself

παρέδωκεν   ὑπὲρ   αὐτῆς,   26 ἵνα   αὐτὴν
gave up   on behalf of   it,   in order that   it

ἁγιάσῃ   καθαρίσας   τῷ   λουτρῷ   τοῦ
he might sanctify   cleansing   by the   washing   of the

ὕδατος   ἐν   ῥήματι,   27 ἵνα   παραστήσῃ   αὐτὸς
water   by   word,   in order ²might present   ¹he
                              that

ἑαυτῷ   ἔνδοξον   τὴν   ἐκκλησίαν,   μὴ   ἔχουσαν
⁵to himself   ⁶glorious   ³the   ⁴church,   not   having

σπίλον   ἢ   ῥυτίδα   ἤ   τι   τῶν   τοιούτων,
spot   or   wrinkle   or   any   of the   such things,

ἀλλ'   ἵνα   ᾖ   ἁγία   καὶ   ἄμωμος.   28 οὕτως
but   in order   it   might   holy   and   unblemished.   So
        that   be

ὀφείλουσιν   [καὶ]   οἱ   ἄνδρες   ἀγαπᾶν   τὰς
ought   also   the   husbands   to love   the

ἑαυτῶν   γυναῖκας   ὡς   τὰ   ἑαυτῶν   σώματα.
of themselves   wives   as   the   of themselves   bodies.

ὁ   ἀγαπῶν   τὴν   ἑαυτοῦ   γυναῖκα   ἑαυτὸν
The [one] loving   the   of himself   wife   himself

ἀγαπᾷ·   29 οὐδεὶς   γάρ   ποτε   τὴν   ἑαυτοῦ
loves;   for no man   ever   the   of himself

σάρκα   ἐμίσησεν,   ἀλλὰ   ἐκτρέφει   καὶ   θάλπει
flesh   hated,   but   nourishes   and   cherishes

αὐτήν,   καθὼς   καὶ   ὁ   Χριστὸς   τὴν   ἐκ-
it,   as   also   –   Christ   the

κλησίαν,   30 ὅτι   μέλη   ἐσμὲν   τοῦ   σώματος
church,   because   members   we are   of the   body

αὐτοῦ.   31 ἀντὶ   τούτου   καταλείψει   ἄνθρωπος
of him.   For   this   ²shall leave   ¹a man

[τὸν]   πατέρα   καὶ   [τὴν]   μητέρα   καὶ
the(his)   father   and   the(his)   mother   and

be joined to his wife, and the two shall become one." ³²This is a great mystery, and I take it to mean Christ and the church; ³³however, let each one of you love his wife as himself, and let the wife see that she respects her husband.

προσκολληθήσεται πρὸς τὴν γυναῖκα αὐτοῦ,
shall cleave   to   the   wife   of him,

καὶ ἔσονται οἱ δύο εἰς σάρκα μίαν.
and   ³shall be ¹the ²two ⁴for ⁵flesh ⁶one.

32 τὸ μυστήριον τοῦτο μέγα ἐστίν, ἐγὼ
This mystery   great   is,   ²I

δὲ λέγω εἰς Χριστὸν καὶ [εἰς] τὴν
¹but say as to Christ   and as to   the

ἐκκλησίαν. 33 πλὴν καὶ ὑμεῖς οἱ
church.   Nevertheless also   ye   the

καθ' ἕνα ἕκαστος τὴν ἑαυτοῦ γυναῖκα
one by one†   each   ¹the ²of himself ³wife

οὕτως ἀγαπάτω ὡς ἑαυτόν, ἡ δὲ
so   let him love   as himself,   and the

CHAPTER 6

γυνὴ ἵνα φοβῆται τὸν ἄνδρα. 6 Τὰ
wife in order that she fears the(her) husband. The

CHILDREN, obey your parents in the Lord, for this is right. ²"Honor your father and mother" (this is the first commandment with a promise), ³"that it may be well with you and that you may live long on the earth." ⁴Fathers, do not provoke your children to anger, but bring them up in the discipline and instruction of the Lord.

τέκνα, ὑπακούετε τοῖς γονεῦσιν ὑμῶν
children,   obey ye   the   parents   of you

ἐν κυρίῳ· τοῦτο γάρ ἐστιν δίκαιον.
in [the] Lord; for this   is   right.

2 τίμα τὸν πατέρα σου καὶ τὴν μητέρα,
Honour   the   father   of thee and the   mother,

ἥτις ἐστὶν ἐντολὴ πρώτη ἐν ἐπαγγελίᾳ,
which   is   ²commandment ¹[the] ³first with   a promise,

3 ἵνα εὖ σοι γένηται καὶ ἔσῃ μακρο-
in order well with thee it may be   and thou may-   long-
that   est be

χρόνιος ἐπὶ τῆς γῆς. 4 Καὶ οἱ πατέρες,
timed(lived) on   the   earth.   And the   fathers,

5 Slaves, be obedient to those who are your earthly masters, with fear and trembling, in singleness of heart, as to Christ; ⁶not in the way of eye-service, as men-pleasers, but as servants of Christ, doing the will of God from the heart, ⁷rendering service with a good will as to the Lord and not to men, ⁸knowing that whatever good

μὴ παροργίζετε τὰ τέκνα ὑμῶν, ἀλλὰ
do not ye provoke to wrath the children of you,   but

ἐκτρέφετε αὐτὰ ἐν παιδείᾳ καὶ νουθεσίᾳ
nurture   them in [the] discipline and   admonition

κυρίου. 5 Οἱ δοῦλοι, ὑπακούετε τοῖς
of [the] Lord. The   slaves,   obey ye   ¹the(your)

κατὰ σάρκα κυρίοις μετὰ φόβου καὶ
²according to ⁴flesh ³lords   with   fear   and

τρόμου ἐν ἁπλότητι τῆς καρδίας ὑμῶν
trembling in singleness   of the   heart   of you

ὡς τῷ Χριστῷ, 6 μὴ κατ' ὀφθαλμοδουλίαν
as -   to Christ,   not by way of   eye-service

ὡς ἀνθρωπάρεσκοι, ἀλλ' ὡς δοῦλοι Χριστοῦ
as   men-pleasers,   but   as slaves of Christ

ποιοῦντες τὸ θέλημα τοῦ θεοῦ ἐκ ψυχῆς,
doing   the   will   -   of God from [the] soul,

7 μετ' εὐνοίας δουλεύοντες ὡς τῷ κυρίῳ
with goodwill serving as slaves   as to the Lord

καὶ οὐκ ἀνθρώποις, 8 εἰδότες ὅτι ἕκαστος
and not   to men,   knowing that each man

any one does, he will receive the same again from the Lord, whether he is a slave or free. [9] Masters, do the same to them, and forbear threatening, knowing that he who is both their Master and yours is in heaven, and that there is no partiality with him.

10 Finally, be strong in the Lord and in the strength of his might. [11] Put on the whole armor of God, that you may be able to stand against the wiles of the devil. [12] For we are not contending against flesh and blood, but against the principalities, against the powers, against the world rulers of this present darkness, against the spiritual hosts of wickedness in the heavenly places. [13] Therefore take the whole armor of God, that you may be able to withstand in the evil day, and having done all, to stand. [14] Stand therefore, having girded your loins with truth, and having put on the breastplate of righteousness, [15] and having

ἐάν τι ποιήσῃ ἀγαθόν, τοῦτο κομίσεται
whatever [1]he does [1]good thing,   this   he will get

παρὰ κυρίου, εἴτε δοῦλος εἴτε ἐλεύθερος.
from [the] Lord, whether a slave   or   a freeman.

9 Καὶ οἱ κύριοι, τὰ αὐτὰ ποιεῖτε πρὸς
And the lords,   the same things do ye   toward

αὐτούς, ἀνιέντες τὴν ἀπειλήν, εἰδότες ὅτι
them,   forbearing *the* threatening, knowing   that

καὶ αὐτῶν καὶ ὑμῶν ὁ κύριός ἐστιν
both of them and   of you the Lord   is

ἐν οὐρανοῖς, καὶ προσωπολημψία οὐκ
in   heavens, and   respect of persons   not

ἔστιν παρ' αὐτῷ.
is   with   him.

10 Τοῦ λοιποῦ, ἐνδυναμοῦσθε ἐν κυρίῳ
For the rest,†   be ye empowered   in [the] Lord

καὶ ἐν τῷ κράτει τῆς ἰσχύος αὐτοῦ.
and   in   the   might   of the strength   of him.

11 ἐνδύσασθε τὴν πανοπλίαν τοῦ θεοῦ
Put ye on   the   whole armour   -   of God

πρὸς τὸ δύνασθαι ὑμᾶς στῆναι πρὸς
for   the   to be able   you[b]   to stand   against
=so that ye are able . . .

τὰς μεθοδείας τοῦ διαβόλου· 12 ὅτι οὐκ
the   craftinesses of the   devil;   because not

ἔστιν ἡμῖν ἡ πάλη πρὸς αἷμα καὶ σάρκα,
is   to us the conflict[c] against blood and   flesh,
=our conflict is not

ἀλλὰ πρὸς τὰς ἀρχάς, πρὸς τὰς ἐξουσίας,
but   against   the   rulers,   against   the   authorities,

πρὸς τοὺς κοσμοκράτορας τοῦ σκότους
against   the   world rulers   -   darkness

τούτου, πρὸς τὰ πνευματικὰ τῆς πονηρίας
of this, against   the   spiritual [hosts]   -   of evil

ἐν τοῖς ἐπουρανίοις. 13 διὰ τοῦτο
in   the   heavenlies.   Therefore

ἀναλάβετε τὴν πανοπλίαν τοῦ θεοῦ, ἵνα
take ye up   the   whole armour   -   of God, in order
                                         that

δυνηθῆτε ἀντιστῆναι ἐν τῇ ἡμέρᾳ τῇ
ye may be able   to resist   in   the   day   the

πονηρᾷ καὶ ἅπαντα κατεργασάμενοι στῆναι.
evil   and   all things   having wrought   to stand.

14 στῆτε οὖν περιζωσάμενοι τὴν ὀσφὺν
Stand ye therefore   girding round   the   loin[s]

ὑμῶν ἐν ἀληθείᾳ, καὶ ἐνδυσάμενοι τὸν
of you with   truth,   and   putting on   the

θώρακα τῆς δικαιοσύνης, 15 καὶ ὑπο-
breastplate   -   of righteousness,   and   shoe-

shod your feet with the equipment of the gospel of peace; [16]above all taking the shield of faith, with which you can quench all the flaming darts of the evil one. [17]And take the helmet of salvation, and the sword of the Spirit, which is the word of God. [18]Pray at all times in the Spirit, with all prayer and supplication. To that end keep alert with all perseverance, making supplication for all the saints, [19]and also for me, that utterance may be given me in opening my mouth boldly to proclaim the mystery of the gospel, [20]for which I am an ambassador in chains; that I may declare it boldly, as I ought to speak.

[21]Now that you also may know how I am and what I am doing, Tych'icus the beloved brother and faithful minister in the Lord will tell you everything. [22]I have sent him to you for

δησάμενοι τοὺς πόδας ἐν ἑτοιμασίᾳ τοῦ
ing   the   feet with readiness of the

εὐαγγελίου τῆς εἰρήνης, 16 ἐν πᾶσιν
gospel   -   of peace,   in   all

ἀναλαβόντες τὸν θυρεὸν τῆς πίστεως, ἐν
taking up   the shield   -   of faith, by

ᾧ δυνήσεσθε πάντα τὰ βέλη τοῦ πονηροῦ
which ye will be able ³all ³the ⁴darts ⁵of the ⁶evil one

τὰ πεπυρωμένα σβέσαι· 17 καὶ τὴν
-   ⁵having been equipped ¹to quench;   and   the
    with fire

περικεφαλαίαν τοῦ σωτηρίου δέξασθε, καὶ
helmet   -   of salvation take ye,   and

τὴν μάχαιραν τοῦ πνεύματος, ὅ ἐστιν
the   sword   of the Spirit,   which* is

ῥῆμα θεοῦ, 18 διὰ πάσης προσευχῆς καὶ
[the] word of God, by means of all   prayer   and

δεήσεως, προσευχόμενοι ἐν παντὶ καιρῷ
petition,   praying   at every time

ἐν πνεύματι, καὶ εἰς αὐτὸ ἀγρυπνοῦντες
in spirit,   and ²to ³it   ¹watching

ἐν πάσῃ προσκαρτερήσει καὶ δεήσει περὶ
in all   perseverance   and petition con-
                                        cerning

πάντων τῶν ἁγίων, 19 καὶ ὑπὲρ ἐμοῦ,
all   the   saints,   and on behalf of me,

ἵνα μοι δοθῇ λόγος ἐν ἀνοίξει τοῦ
in order to me may be given speech in opening of the
that

στόματός μου, ἐν παρρησίᾳ γνωρίσαι τὸ
mouth   of me, in boldness to make known the

μυστήριον τοῦ εὐαγγελίου, 20 ὑπὲρ οὗ
mystery   of the gospel,   on behalf of which

πρεσβεύω ἐν ἁλύσει, ἵνα ἐν αὐτῷ παρ-
I am an   in a chain, in order in it   I may
ambassador   that

ρησιάσωμαι ὡς δεῖ με λαλῆσαι.
speak boldly as it behoves me to speak.

21 Ἵνα δὲ εἰδῆτε καὶ ὑμεῖς τὰ κατ'
Now in order that ²may know ³also ¹ye the things about

ἐμέ, τί πράσσω, πάντα γνωρίσει ὑμῖν
me, what I am doing, all things ¹⁰will make ¹¹to you
                                  known

Τύχικος ὁ ἀγαπητὸς ἀδελφὸς καὶ πιστὸς
¹Tychicus ²the ³beloved   ⁴brother ⁵and ⁶faithful

διάκονος ἐν κυρίῳ, 22 ὃν ἔπεμψα πρὸς
⁷minister ⁸in ⁹[the] Lord, whom I sent   to

---

* Neuter, agreeing with πνεῦμα, not feminine to agree with μάχαιρα.

this very purpose, that you may know how we are, and that he may encourage your hearts.

23 Peace be to the brethren, and love with faith, from God the Father and the Lord Jesus Christ. 24 Grace be with all who love our Lord Jesus Christ with love undying.

ὑμᾶς εἰς αὐτὸ τοῦτο, ἵνα γνῶτε τὰ
you for this very thing, in order ye may the
that know things
περὶ ἡμῶν καὶ παρακαλέσῃ τὰς καρδίας
concerning us and may comfort the hearts
ὑμῶν.
of you.

23 Εἰρήνη τοῖς ἀδελφοῖς καὶ ἀγάπη
Peace to the brothers and love
μετὰ πίστεως ἀπὸ θεοῦ πατρὸς καὶ
with faith from God [the] Father and
κυρίου Ἰησοῦ Χριστοῦ. 24 ἡ χάρις μετὰ
[the] Lord Jesus Christ. – Grace [be] with
πάντων τῶν ἀγαπώντων τὸν κύριον ἡμῶν
all the [ones] loving the Lord of us
Ἰησοῦν Χριστὸν ἐν ἀφθαρσίᾳ.
Jesus Christ in incorruptibility.

PHILIPPIANS 1   ΠΡΟΣ ΦΙΛΙΠΠΗΣΙΟΥΣ
To Philippians

CHAPTER 1

PAUL and Timothy, servants of Christ Jesus,

To all the saints in Christ Jesus who are at Philippi, with the bishops[a] and deacons:

2 Grace to you and peace from God our Father and the Lord Jesus Christ.

3 I thank my God in all my remembrance of you, 4 always in every prayer of mine for you all making my prayer with joy, 5 thankful for your partnership in the gospel

1 Παῦλος καὶ Τιμόθεος δοῦλοι Χριστοῦ
Paul and Timothy slaves of Christ
Ἰησοῦ πᾶσιν τοῖς ἁγίοις ἐν Χριστῷ
Jesus to all the saints in Christ
Ἰησοῦ τοῖς οὖσιν ἐν Φιλίπποις σὺν
Jesus – being in Philippi with
ἐπισκόποις καὶ διακόνοις· 2 χάρις ὑμῖν
bishops and ministers: Grace to you
καὶ εἰρήνη ἀπὸ θεοῦ πατρὸς ἡμῶν καὶ
and peace from God Father of us and
κυρίου Ἰησοῦ Χριστοῦ.
[the] Lord Jesus Christ.

3 Εὐχαριστῶ τῷ θεῷ μου ἐπὶ πάσῃ
I thank the God of me at all
τῇ μνείᾳ ὑμῶν, 4 πάντοτε ἐν πάσῃ
the remembrance of you, always in every
δεήσει μου ὑπὲρ πάντων ὑμῶν μετὰ
petition of me on behalf of all you with
χαρᾶς τὴν δέησιν ποιούμενος, 5 ἐπὶ τῇ
joy the petition making, over the
κοινωνίᾳ ὑμῶν εἰς τὸ εὐαγγέλιον ἀπὸ
fellowship of you in the gospel from

[a] Or overseers

from the first day until now. ⁶And I am sure that he who began a good work in you will bring it to completion at the day of Jesus Christ. ⁷It is right for me to feel thus about you all, because I hold you in my heart, for you are all partakers with me of grace, both in my imprisonment and in the defense and confirmation of the gospel. ⁸For God is my witness, how I yearn for you all with the affection of Christ Jesus. ⁹And it is my prayer that your love may abound more and more, with knowledge and all discernment, ¹⁰so that you may approve what is excellent, and may be pure and blameless for the day of Christ, ¹¹filled with the fruits of righteousness which come through Jesus Christ, to the glory and praise of God.

12 I want you to know, brethren, that what has happened to me has really served to

τῆς πρώτης ἡμέρας ἄχρι τοῦ νῦν,
the first day until the now,

6 πεποιθὼς αὐτὸ τοῦτο, ὅτι ὁ ἐναρξάμενος
being confident [of] this very thing, that the [one] having begun

ἐν ὑμῖν ἔργον ἀγαθὸν ἐπιτελέσει ἄχρι
in you work a good will complete [it] until

ἡμέρας Χριστοῦ Ἰησοῦ· 7 καθώς ἐστιν
[the] day of Christ Jesus; as it is

δίκαιον ἐμοὶ τοῦτο φρονεῖν ὑπὲρ πάντων
right for me this to think on behalf of all

ὑμῶν, διὰ τὸ ἔχειν με ἐν τῇ καρδίᾳ
you, because of the to have me⁰ in the heart
= because I have you in the(my) heart,

ὑμᾶς, ἔν τε τοῖς δεσμοῖς μου καὶ ἐν
you, both in the bonds of me and in

τῇ ἀπολογίᾳ καὶ βεβαιώσει τοῦ εὐαγγελίου
the defence and confirmation of the gospel

συγκοινωνούς μου τῆς χάριτος πάντας
⁴partakers ⁷of me ⁵of the ⁶grace ²all

ὑμᾶς ὄντας. 8 μάρτυς γάρ μου ὁ θεός,
¹you ³being. ⁴witness ¹For ⁵of me – ²God ³[is],

ὡς ἐπιποθῶ πάντας ὑμᾶς ἐν σπλάγχνοις
how I long after all you in [the] bowels

Χριστοῦ Ἰησοῦ. 9 Καὶ τοῦτο προσεύχομαι,
of Christ Jesus. And this I pray,

ἵνα ἡ ἀγάπη ὑμῶν ἔτι μᾶλλον καὶ
in order the love of you yet more and
that

μᾶλλον περισσεύῃ ἐν ἐπιγνώσει καὶ πάσῃ
more may abound in full knowledge and all

αἰσθήσει, 10 εἰς τὸ δοκιμάζειν ὑμᾶς τὰ
perception, for the to prove you⁰ the
= that ye may prove things

διαφέροντα, ἵνα ἦτε εἰλικρινεῖς καὶ
differing, in order ye may sincere and
that be

ἀπρόσκοποι εἰς ἡμέραν Χριστοῦ, 11 πεπληρω-
unoffending in [the] day of Christ, having been

μένοι καρπὸν δικαιοσύνης τὸν διὰ Ἰησοῦ
filled [with] [the] fruit of righteousness – through Jesus

Χριστοῦ, εἰς δόξαν καὶ ἔπαινον θεοῦ.
Christ, to [the] glory and praise of God.

12 Γινώσκειν δὲ ὑμᾶς βούλομαι, ἀδελφοί,
Now ³to know ²you ¹I wish, brothers,

ὅτι τὰ κατ᾽ ἐμὲ μᾶλλον εἰς προκοπὴν
that the about me* ²rather ³to ⁴[the] advance
things
= my affairs

* Cf. ver. 27; ch. 2. 19, 20, 23; Eph. 6. 21, 22; Col. 4. 7, 8.

advance the gospel, [13]so that it has become known throughout the whole praetorian guard and to all the rest that my imprisonment is for Christ; [14]and most of the brethren have been made confident in the Lord because of my imprisonment, and are much more bold to speak the word of God without fear.

15 Some indeed preach Christ from envy and rivalry, but others from good will. [16]The latter do it out of love, knowing that I am put here for the defense of the gospel; [17]the former proclaim Christ out of partisanship, not sincerely but thinking to afflict me in my imprisonment. [18]What then? Only that in every way, whether in pretense or in truth, Christ is proclaimed; and in that I rejoice.

19 Yes, and I shall rejoice. For I know that through your prayers and the help of the Spirit of Jesus Christ this will turn out for my deliverance, [20]as it is my eager expectation and hope that I shall not be at all ashamed, but that with full courage now as always Christ will be

τοῦ εὐαγγελίου ἐλήλυθεν, 13 ὥστε τοὺς
⁵of the ⁶gospel ¹has(ve) come, so as the

δεσμούς μου φανεροὺς ἐν Χριστῷ γενέσθαι
bonds of me ²manifest ³in ⁴Christ ¹to become

ἐν ὅλῳ τῷ πραιτωρίῳ καὶ τοῖς λοιποῖς
in all the prætorium and to ²the ³rest

πᾶσιν, 14 καὶ τοὺς πλείονας τῶν ἀδελφῶν
¹all, and the majority of the brothers

ἐν κυρίῳ πεποιθότας τοῖς δεσμοῖς μου
in [the] Lord being confident in the bonds of me

περισσοτέρως τολμᾶν ἀφόβως τὸν λόγον
²more exceedingly ¹to dare ³fearlessly ⁵the ⁶word

τοῦ θεοῦ λαλεῖν. 15 τινὲς μὲν καὶ διὰ
- ⁷of God ⁴to speak. Some indeed even because of

φθόνον καὶ ἔριν, τινὲς δὲ καὶ δι’ εὐδοκίαν
envy and strife, but some also because good-of will

τὸν Χριστὸν κηρύσσουσιν· 16 οἱ μὲν ἐξ
- Christ proclaim; these† from

ἀγάπης, εἰδότες ὅτι εἰς ἀπολογίαν τοῦ
love, knowing that for defence of the

εὐαγγελίου κεῖμαι, 17 οἱ δὲ ἐξ ἐριθείας
gospel I am set, those† from rivalry

τὸν Χριστὸν καταγγέλλουσιν, οὐχ ἁγνῶς,
- ²Christ ¹announce, not purely,

οἰόμενοι θλῖψιν ἐγείρειν τοῖς δεσμοῖς μου.
thinking ²affliction ¹to raise to the bonds of me.

18 Τί γάρ; πλὴν ὅτι παντὶ τρόπῳ,
What then? nevertheless that in every way,

εἴτε προφάσει εἴτε ἀληθείᾳ, Χριστὸς
whether in pretence or in truth, Christ

καταγγέλλεται, καὶ ἐν τούτῳ χαίρω· ἀλλὰ
is announced, and in this I rejoice; yet

καὶ χαρήσομαι· 19 οἶδα γὰρ ὅτι τοῦτό
also I will rejoice; for I know that this

μοι ἀποβήσεται εἰς σωτηρίαν διὰ τῆς
to me will result in salvation through the

ὑμῶν δεήσεως καὶ ἐπιχορηγίας τοῦ
²of you ¹petition and supply of the

πνεύματος Ἰησοῦ Χριστοῦ, 20 κατὰ τὴν
spirit of Jesus Christ, according to the

ἀποκαραδοκίαν καὶ ἐλπίδα μου ὅτι ἐν
eager expectation and hope of me that in

οὐδενὶ αἰσχυνθήσομαι, ἀλλ’ ἐν πάσῃ παρ-
nothing I shall be shamed, but with all bold-

ρησίᾳ ὡς πάντοτε καὶ νῦν μεγαλυνθήσεται
ness as always also now shall be magnified

honored in my body, whether by life or by death. ²¹ For to me to live is Christ, and to die is gain. ²² If it is to be life in the flesh, that means fruitful labor for me. Yet which I shall choose I cannot tell. ²³ I am hard pressed between the two. My desire is to depart and be with Christ, for that is far better. ²⁴ But to remain in the flesh is more necessary on your account. ²⁵ Convinced of this, I know that I shall remain and continue with you all, for your progress and joy in the faith, ²⁶ so that in me you may have ample cause to glory in Christ Jesus, because of my coming to you again.

27 Only let your manner of life be worthy of the gospel of Christ, so that whether I come and see you or am absent, I may hear of you that you stand firm in one spirit, with one mind striving side by side for the faith of the gospel, ²⁸ and not frightened in

Χριστὸς ἐν τῷ σώματί μου, εἴτε διὰ
Christ in the body of me, whether through

ζωῆς εἴτε διὰ θανάτου. 21 ἐμοὶ γὰρ
life or through death. For to me

τὸ ζῆν Χριστὸς καὶ τὸ ἀποθανεῖν κέρδος.
– to live [is] Christ and – to die [is] gain.

22 εἰ δὲ τὸ ζῆν ἐν σαρκί, τοῦτό μοι
But if – to live in [the] flesh, this to me

καρπὸς ἔργου, καὶ τί αἱρήσομαι οὐ
[is] fruit of [?my] work, and what I shall choose not

γνωρίζω. 23 συνέχομαι δὲ ἐκ τῶν δύο,
I perceive. But I am constrained by the two,

τὴν ἐπιθυμίαν ἔχων εἰς τὸ ἀναλῦσαι καὶ
²the ³desire ¹having for the to depart and

σὺν Χριστῷ εἶναι, πολλῷ γὰρ μᾶλλον
²with ³Christ ¹to be, for by much [this is] rather

κρεῖσσον· 24 τὸ δὲ ἐπιμένειν τῇ σαρκὶ
better; – but to remain in the flesh [is]

ἀναγκαιότερον δι᾽ ὑμᾶς. 25 καὶ τοῦτο
more necessary on account of you. And this

πεποιθὼς οἶδα, ὅτι μενῶ καὶ παραμενῶ
being I know, that I shall and continue
confident remain

πᾶσιν ὑμῖν εἰς τὴν ὑμῶν προκοπὴν καὶ
with all you for the ⁶of you ¹advance ²and

χαρὰν τῆς πίστεως, 26 ἵνα τὸ καύχημα
³joy ⁴of the ⁵faith, in order the boast
that

ὑμῶν περισσεύῃ ἐν Χριστῷ Ἰησοῦ ἐν
of you may abound in Christ Jesus in

ἐμοὶ διὰ τῆς ἐμῆς παρουσίας πάλιν
me through – my presence again

πρὸς ὑμᾶς.
with you.

27 Μόνον ἀξίως τοῦ εὐαγγελίου τοῦ
Only ²worthily ³of the ⁴gospel –

Χριστοῦ πολιτεύεσθε, ἵνα εἴτε ἐλθὼν καὶ
⁵of Christ ¹conduct in order whether coming and
yourselves, that

ἰδὼν ὑμᾶς εἴτε ἀπὼν ἀκούω τὰ περὶ
seeing you or being I hear the con-
absent things cerning

ὑμῶν, ὅτι στήκετε ἐν ἑνὶ πνεύματι,
you, that ye stand in one spirit,

μιᾷ ψυχῇ συναθλοῦντες τῇ πίστει τοῦ
with one soul striving together in the faith of the

εὐαγγελίου, 28 καὶ μὴ πτυρόμενοι ἐν
gospel, and not being terrified in

anything by your opponents. This is a clear omen to them of their destruction, but of your salvation, and that from God. [29] For it has been granted to you that for the sake of Christ you should not only believe in him but also suffer for his sake, [30] engaged in the same conflict which you saw and now hear to be mine.

CHAPTER 2

SO if there is any encouragement in Christ, any incentive of love, any participation in the Spirit, any affection and sympathy, [2] complete my joy by being of the same mind, having the same love, being in full accord and of one mind. [3] Do nothing from selfishness or conceit, but in humility count others better than yourselves. [4] Let each of you look not only to his own interests, but also to the interests of others. [5] Have this mind among yourselves, which you have in Christ Jesus, [6] who, though he was in the form of God, did not count equality with God a thing to be grasped, [7] but emptied himself,

μηδενὶ ὑπὸ τῶν ἀντικειμένων, ἥτις ἐστὶν
no(any) by the [ones] opposing, which is
thing

αὐτοῖς ἔνδειξις ἀπωλείας, ὑμῶν δὲ
to them a proof of destruction, but of you

σωτηρίας, καὶ τοῦτο ἀπὸ θεοῦ· 29 ὅτι
of salvation, and this from God; because

ὑμῖν ἐχαρίσθη τὸ ὑπὲρ Χριστοῦ, οὐ
to you it was given – on behalf of Christ, not

μόνον τὸ εἰς αὐτὸν πιστεύειν ἀλλὰ καὶ
only – in him to believe but also

τὸ ὑπὲρ αὐτοῦ πάσχειν, 30 τὸν αὐτὸν
– on behalf of him to suffer, the same

ἀγῶνα ἔχοντες οἷον εἴδετε ἐν ἐμοὶ
struggle having which ye saw in me

καὶ νῦν ἀκούετε ἐν ἐμοί. 2 Εἴ τις
and now hear in me. [2]If [there [3]any
is]

οὖν παράκλησις ἐν Χριστῷ, εἴ τι
[1]therefore comfort in Christ, if any

παραμύθιον ἀγάπης, εἴ τις κοινωνία
consolation of love, if any fellowship

πνεύματος, εἴ τις σπλάγχνα καὶ οἰκτιρμοί,
of spirit, if any compassions and pities,

2 πληρώσατέ μου τὴν χαρὰν ἵνα τὸ
fulfil ye of me the joy in order that the

αὐτὸ φρονῆτε, τὴν αὐτὴν ἀγάπην ἔχοντες,
same thing ye think, the same love having,

σύμψυχοι, τὸ ἓν φρονοῦντες, 3 μηδὲν κατ'
one in soul, the one thinking, [doing] by
thing

ἐριθείαν μηδὲ κατὰ κενοδοξίαν, ἀλλὰ τῇ
rivalry nor by way of vainglory, but

ταπεινοφροσύνῃ ἀλλήλους ἡγούμενοι ὑπερ-
in humility [3]one another [1]deeming sur-

έχοντας ἑαυτῶν, 4 μὴ τὰ ἑαυτῶν ἕκαστοι
passing themselves, not [3]the [4]of them- [1]each ones
things selves

σκοποῦντες, ἀλλὰ καὶ τὰ ἑτέρων ἕκαστοι.
[2]looking at, but [2]also [3]the [1]each ones.
[of
things others

5 τοῦτο φρονεῖτε ἐν ὑμῖν ὃ καὶ ἐν
This think ye among you which also [was] in

Χριστῷ Ἰησοῦ, 6 ὃς ἐν μορφῇ θεοῦ
Christ Jesus, who in [the] form of God

ὑπάρχων οὐχ ἁρπαγμὸν ἡγήσατο τὸ εἶναι
subsisting [2]not [2]robbery [1]deemed [it] the to be

ἴσα θεῷ, 7 ἀλλὰ ἑαυτὸν ἐκένωσεν μορφὴν
equal with God, but himself emptied [2][the] form
things

taking the form of a servant, being born in the likeness of men. [8]And being found in human form he humbled himself and became obedient unto death, even death on a cross. [9]Therefore God has highly exalted him and bestowed on him the name which is above every name, [10]that at the name of Jesus every knee should bow, in heaven and on earth and under the earth, [11]and every tongue confess that Jesus Christ is Lord, to the glory of God the Father.

[12] Therefore, my beloved, as you have always obeyed, so now, not only as in my presence but much more in my absence, work out your own salvation with fear and trembling; [13]for God is at work in you, both to will and to work for his good pleasure.

[14] Do all things without grumbling or questioning, [15]that you may be blameless and innocent, children of God without blemish in the midst of a crooked and perverse generation, among whom you shine as lights in the world,

δούλου λαβών, ἐν ὁμοιώματι ἀνθρώπων
²of a slave ¹taking, ²in ¹likeness ⁴of men

γενόμενος· καὶ σχήματι εὑρεθεὶς ὡς
¹becoming; and ²in fashion ¹being found as

ἄνθρωπος 8 ἐταπείνωσεν ἑαυτὸν γενόμενος
a man he humbled himself becoming

ὑπήκοος μέχρι θανάτου, θανάτου δὲ σταυροῦ.
obedient until death, and death of a cross.

9 διὸ καὶ ὁ θεὸς αὐτὸν ὑπερύψωσεν
Wherefore also – God ²him ¹highly exalted

καὶ ἐχαρίσατο αὐτῷ τὸ ὄνομα τὸ ὑπὲρ
and gave to him the name – above

πᾶν ὄνομα, 10 ἵνα ἐν τῷ ὀνόματι Ἰησοῦ
every name, in order that in the name of Jesus

πᾶν γόνυ κάμψῃ ἐπουρανίων καὶ ἐπιγείων
every knee should of heavenly and earthly
bend [beings] [beings]

καὶ καταχθονίων, 11 καὶ πᾶσα γλῶσσα
and [beings] under the earth, and every tongue

ἐξομολογήσηται ὅτι κύριος Ἰησοῦς
should acknowledge that ²Lord ¹Jesus

Χριστὸς εἰς δόξαν θεοῦ πατρός.
²Christ [is] to [the] glory of God [the] Father.

12 Ὥστε, ἀγαπητοί μου, καθὼς πάντοτε
So as, beloved of me, as always

ὑπηκούσατε, μὴ ὡς ἐν τῇ παρουσίᾳ
ye obeyed, not as in the presence

μου μόνον ἀλλὰ νῦν πολλῷ μᾶλλον ἐν
of me only but now by more rather in

τῇ ἀπουσίᾳ μου, μετὰ φόβου καὶ τρόμου
the absence of me, with fear and trembling

τὴν ἑαυτῶν σωτηρίαν κατεργάζεσθε· 13 θεὸς
¹the ²of yourselves ³salvation work out; ¹God

γάρ ἐστιν ὁ ἐνεργῶν ἐν ὑμῖν καὶ τὸ
²for is the [one] operating in you both the

θέλειν καὶ τὸ ἐνεργεῖν ὑπὲρ τῆς εὐδοκίας.
to will and the to operate on behalf of the(his) goodwill.

14 πάντα ποιεῖτε χωρὶς γογγυσμῶν καὶ
All things do ye without murmurings and

διαλογισμῶν, 15 ἵνα γένησθε ἄμεμπτοι καὶ
disputings, in order that ye may be blameless and

ἀκέραιοι, τέκνα θεοῦ ἄμωμα μέσον
harmless, children of God faultless in the
midst of

γενεᾶς σκολιᾶς καὶ διεστραμμένης, ἐν
a generation crooked and having been perverted, among

οἷς φαίνεσθε ὡς φωστῆρες ἐν κόσμῳ,
whom ye shine as luminaries in [the] world,

[16] holding fast the word of life, so that in the day of Christ I may be proud that I did not run in vain or labor in vain. [17] Even if I am to be poured as a libation upon the sacrificial offering of your faith, I am glad and rejoice with you all. [18] Likewise you also should be glad and rejoice with me.

19 I hope in the Lord Jesus to send Timothy to you soon, so that I may be cheered by news of you. [20] I have no one like him, who will be genuinely anxious for your welfare. [21] They all look after their own interests, not those of Jesus Christ. [22] But Timothy's worth you know, how as a son with a father he has served with me in the gospel. [23] I hope therefore to send him just as soon as I see how it will go with me; [24] and I trust in the Lord that shortly I myself shall come also.

25 I have thought it necessary to send to you Epaphroditus my brother and fellow worker and fellow soldier, and your messenger and minister to

16 λόγον ζωῆς ἐπέχοντες, εἰς καύχημα
    a word of life holding up, for a boast
ἐμοὶ εἰς ἡμέραν Χριστοῦ, ὅτι οὐκ εἰς
to me[e] in [the] day of Christ, that not in
κενὸν ἔδραμον οὐδὲ εἰς κενὸν ἐκοπίασα.
vain I ran nor in vain laboured.

17 Ἀλλὰ εἰ καὶ σπένδομαι ἐπὶ τῇ θυσίᾳ
    But if indeed I am poured out on the sacrifice
καὶ λειτουργίᾳ τῆς πίστεως ὑμῶν, χαίρω
and service of the faith of you, I rejoice
καὶ συγχαίρω πᾶσιν ὑμῖν· 18 τὸ δὲ αὐτὸ
and rejoice with [3]all [1]you; and the same
καὶ ὑμεῖς χαίρετε καὶ συγχαίρετέ μοι.
also ye rejoice and rejoice with me.

19 Ἐλπίζω δὲ ἐν κυρίῳ Ἰησοῦ Τιμόθεον
    But I hope in [the] Lord Jesus [2]Timothy
ταχέως πέμψαι ὑμῖν, ἵνα κἀγὼ εὐψυχῶ
[4]shortly [1]to send [3]to you, in order I also may be of
                   that   good cheer
γνοὺς τὰ περὶ ὑμῶν. 20 οὐδένα γὰρ
knowing the con- you. For no one
        things cerning
ἔχω ἰσόψυχον, ὅστις γνησίως τὰ περὶ
I have likeminded, who genuinely [2]the [3]con-
                       things cerning
ὑμῶν μεριμνήσει· 21 οἱ πάντες γὰρ τὰ
[4]you [1]will care for; the for all [3]the
                                things
ἑαυτῶν ζητοῦσιν, οὐ τὰ Χριστοῦ Ἰησοῦ.
[1]of them- [1]seek, not the of Christ Jesus.
selves
22 τὴν δὲ δοκιμὴν αὐτοῦ γινώσκετε, ὅτι
    But the character of him ye know, that
ὡς πατρὶ τέκνον σὺν ἐμοὶ ἐδούλευσεν
as [3]a father [1]a child[2][serves] [5]with [6]me [4]he served
εἰς τὸ εὐαγγέλιον. 23 τοῦτον μὲν οὖν
in the gospel. This one – therefore
ἐλπίζω πέμψαι ὡς ἂν ἀφίδω τὰ περὶ
I hope to send [3]whenever [1]I see [4]the [5]con-
                         things cerning
ἐμὲ ἐξαυτῆς· 24 πέποιθα δὲ ἐν κυρίῳ
[6]me [1]immediately; but I trust in [the] Lord
ὅτι καὶ αὐτὸς ταχέως ἐλεύσομαι. 25 Ἀναγ-
that [2]also [3][my]self [1]shortly I will come. [1]neces-
καῖον δὲ ἡγησάμην Ἐπαφρόδιτον τὸν
sary But [1]I deemed [it] [2]Epaphroditus [3]the
ἀδελφὸν καὶ συνεργὸν καὶ συστρατιώτην
[8]brother [9]and [10]fellow-worker [11]and [12]fellow-soldier
μου, ὑμῶν δὲ ἀπόστολον καὶ λειτουργὸν
[13]of me, [14]and [4]of you [15]apostle [17]and [18]minister

my need, ²⁶for he has
been longing for you all,
and has been distressed
because you heard that
he was ill. ²⁷Indeed he
was ill, near to death.
But God had mercy on
him, and not only on him
but on me also, lest I
should have sorrow upon
sorrow. ²⁸I am the more
eager to send him, there-
fore, that you may rejoice
at seeing him again, and
that I may be less
anxious. ²⁹So receive
him in the Lord with all
joy; and honor such
men, ³⁰for he nearly
died for the work of
Christ, risking his life
to complete your service
to me.

τῆς   χρείας   μου,   πέμψαι   πρὸς   ὑμᾶς,
¹⁹of the ²⁰need ²¹of me, ²to send ⁴to   ⁵you,

26 ἐπειδὴ   ἐπιποθῶν   ἦν   πάντας   ὑμᾶς,   καὶ
since   ²longing after ¹he was ⁴all   ³you,   and

ἀδημονῶν,   διότι   ἠκούσατε   ὅτι   ἠσθένησεν.
[was] being because   ye heard   that   he ailed.
troubled,

27 καὶ   γὰρ   ἠσθένησεν   παραπλήσιον   θανάτῳ·
For indeed   he ailed   coming near   to death;

ἀλλὰ   ὁ   θεὸς   ἠλέησεν   αὐτόν,   οὐκ   αὐτὸν
but –   God had mercy on   him,   ²not   ³him

δὲ   μόνον   ἀλλὰ   καὶ   ἐμέ,   ἵνα   μὴ   λύπην
¹and   only   but   also   me,   lest   grief

ἐπὶ   λύπην   σχῶ.   28 σπουδαιοτέρως   οὖν
on   grief I should have.   More eagerly   therefore

ἔπεμψα   αὐτόν,   ἵνα   ἰδόντες   αὐτὸν   πάλιν
I sent   him, in order that seeing   him   again

χαρῆτε   κἀγὼ   ἀλυπότερος   ὦ.   29 προσδέχεσθε
ye may   and ¹I   ³less grieved ²may be.   Receive ye
rejoice

οὖν   αὐτὸν   ἐν   κυρίῳ   μετὰ   πάσης   χαρᾶς,
therefore him   in [the] Lord   with   all   joy,

καὶ   τοὺς   τοιούτους   ἐντίμους   ἔχετε,   30 ὅτι
and –   ²such ones   ³honoured ¹hold ye,   because

διὰ   τὸ   ἔργον   Χριστοῦ   μέχρι   θανάτου
on ac- the   work   of Christ   ²as far as   ³death
count of

ἤγγισεν   παραβολευσάμενος   τῇ   ψυχῇ,   ἵνα
¹he drew   exposing   the(his)   life,   in or-
near   der that

ἀναπληρώσῃ   τὸ   ὑμῶν   ὑστέρημα   τῆς   πρός
he might fill up   ¹the   ²of you   ³lack   –   ⁴toward

με   λειτουργίας.
⁵me   ⁶of service.

CHAPTER 3

FINALLY, my breth-
ren, rejoice in the
Lord. To write the same
things to you is not
irksome to me, and is
safe for you.
2 Look out for the
dogs, look out for the
evil-workers, look out
for those who mutilate

3 Τὸ   λοιπόν,   ἀδελφοί   μου,   χαίρετε   ἐν
For the rest,   brothers   of me,   rejoice ye   in

κυρίῳ.   τὰ   αὐτὰ   γράφειν   ὑμῖν   ἐμοὶ   μὲν
[the] Lord. ³The ²same things ¹to write to you for me indeed

οὐκ   ὀκνηρόν,   ὑμῖν   δὲ   ἀσφαλές.
[is] not irksome,   but for you   safe.

2 Βλέπετε   τοὺς   κύνας,   βλέπετε   τοὺς
Look [to]   the   dogs,   look [to]   the

κακοὺς   ἐργάτας,   βλέπετε   τὴν   κατατομήν.*
evil   workmen,   look [to]   the   concision.*

* The apostle uses a " studiously contemptuous paronomasia "
(Ellicott). He does not use περιτομή, the proper word for " circumcision ", " as this, though now abrogated in Christ, had still
its spiritual aspects."

the flesh. ³For we are the true circumcision, who worship God in spirit,[b] and glory in Christ Jesus, and put no confidence in the flesh. ⁴Though I myself have reason for confidence in the flesh also. If any other man thinks he has reason for confidence in the flesh, I have more: ⁵circumcised on the eighth day, of the people of Israel, of the tribe of Benjamin, a Hebrew born of Hebrews; as to the law a Pharisee, ⁶as to zeal a persecutor of the church, as to righteousness under the law blameless. ⁷But whatever gain I had, I counted as loss for the sake of Christ. ⁸Indeed I count everything as loss because of the surpassing worth of knowing Christ Jesus my Lord. For his sake I have suffered the loss of all things, and count them as refuse, in order that I may gain Christ ⁹and be found in him, not having a righteousness of my own, based on law, but that which is through faith in Christ, the righteousness from God that depends

3 ἡμεῖς γάρ ἐσμεν ἡ περιτομή, οἱ
For we are the circumcision, the [ones]

πνεύματι θεοῦ λατρεύοντες καὶ καυχώμενοι
²by [the] Spirit ³of God ¹worshipping and boasting

ἐν Χριστῷ Ἰησοῦ καὶ οὐκ ἐν σαρκὶ
in Christ Jesus and ²not ³in [the] ⁴flesh

πεποιθότες, 4 καίπερ ἐγὼ ἔχων πεποίθησιν
¹trusting, even though I having trust

καὶ ἐν σαρκί. Εἴ τις δοκεῖ ἄλλος
also in [the] flesh. If any ²thinks ¹other man

πεποιθέναι ἐν σαρκί, ἐγὼ μᾶλλον·
to trust in [the] flesh, I more:

5 περιτομῇ ὀκταήμερος, ἐκ γένους Ἰσραήλ,
in circumcision eighth day, of [the] race of Israel,

φυλῆς Βενιαμίν, Ἑβραῖος ἐξ Ἑβραίων,
[the] tribe of Benjamin, a Hebrew of Hebrew [parents],

κατὰ νόμον Φαρισαῖος, 6 κατὰ ζῆλος
according [the] law a Pharisee, by way of zeal
to

διώκων τὴν ἐκκλησίαν, κατὰ δικαιοσύνην
persecuting the church, according [the]
to righteousness

τὴν ἐν νόμῳ γενόμενος ἄμεμπτος. 7 ἀλλὰ
– in [the] law being blameless. But

ἅτινα ἦν μοι κέρδη, ταῦτα ἥγημαι διὰ
what were to me gain, these I have ²on ac-
things deemed count of

τὸν Χριστὸν ζημίαν. 8 ἀλλὰ μενοῦν γε
³- ³Christ ¹loss. But nay rather

καὶ ἡγοῦμαι πάντα ζημίαν εἶναι διὰ
²also ¹I deem ³all things ⁵loss ⁴to be on account of

τὸ ὑπερέχον τῆς γνώσεως Χριστοῦ Ἰησοῦ
the excellency of the knowledge of Christ Jesus

τοῦ κυρίου μου, δι' ὃν τὰ πάντα
the Lord of me, on ac- whom – all things
count of

ἐζημιώθην, καὶ ἡγοῦμαι σκύβαλα ἵνα
I suffered loss, and deem [them] refuse in order
that

Χριστὸν κερδήσω 9 καὶ εὑρεθῶ ἐν αὐτῷ,
Christ I might gain and be found in him,

μὴ ἔχων ἐμὴν δικαιοσύνην τὴν ἐκ νόμου,
not having my righteousness the [one] of law,

ἀλλὰ τὴν διὰ πίστεως Χριστοῦ, τὴν
but the [one] through faith of(in) Christ,* ¹the

ἐκ θεοῦ δικαιοσύνην ἐπὶ τῇ πίστει,
³of ⁴God ²righteousness [based] on – faith,

[b] Other ancient authorities read *worship by the Spirit of God*

* See Gal. 2. 20.

on faith; ¹⁰that I may know him and the power of his resurrection, and may share his sufferings, becoming like him in his death, ¹¹that if possible I may attain the resurrection from the dead.

12 Not that I have already obtained this or am already perfect; but I press on to make it my own, because Christ Jesus has made me his own. ¹³Brethren, I do not consider that I have made it my own; but one thing I do, forgetting what lies behind and straining forward to what lies ahead, ¹⁴I press on toward the goal for the prize of the upward call of God in Christ Jesus. ¹⁵Let those of us who are mature be thus minded; and if in anything you are otherwise minded, God will reveal that also to you. ¹⁶Only let us hold true to what we have attained.

17 Brethren, join in imitating me, and mark those who so live as you have an example in us. ¹⁸For many, of whom I have often told you and now tell you even with tears, live as enemies of the cross of Christ.

---

10 τοῦ γνῶναι αὐτὸν καὶ τὴν δύναμιν
　　 - to know[d] him and the power

τῆς ἀναστάσεως αὐτοῦ καὶ κοινωνίαν
of the resurrection of him and [the] fellowship

παθημάτων αὐτοῦ, συμμορφιζόμενος τῷ
of sufferings of him, being conformed to the

θανάτῳ αὐτοῦ, 11 εἴ πως καταντήσω εἰς
death of him, if [some]how I may attain to to

τὴν ἐξανάστασιν τὴν ἐκ νεκρῶν. 12 Οὐχ
the out-resurrection - from [the] dead. Not

ὅτι ἤδη ἔλαβον ἢ ἤδη τετελείωμαι,
that already I received or already have been perfected,

διώκω δὲ εἰ καὶ καταλάβω, ἐφ' ᾧ
but I follow if indeed I may lay hold, inasmuch as

καὶ κατελήμφθην ὑπὸ Χριστοῦ Ἰησοῦ.
also I was laid hold of by Christ Jesus.

13 ἀδελφοί, ἐγὼ ἐμαυτὸν οὔπω λογίζομαι
Brothers, ²I ⁴myself ¹not yet ³reckon

κατειληφέναι· ἕν δέ, τὰ μὲν ὀπίσω
to have but one thing ²the ²on one ⁴behind

laid hold; [I do], things hand

ἐπιλανθανόμενος τοῖς δὲ ἔμπροσθεν ἐπεκ-
¹forgetting ³the ¹on the ⁴before ²stretching

τεινόμενος, 14 κατὰ σκοπὸν διώκω εἰς
forward to, according to a mark I follow for

τὸ βραβεῖον τῆς ἄνω κλήσεως τοῦ θεοῦ
the prize of the above calling - of God

ἐν Χριστῷ Ἰησοῦ. 15 Ὅσοι οὖν τέλειοι,
in Christ Jesus. ²As many ¹there- [are]
　　　　　　　　　　　　as fore perfect,

τοῦτο φρονῶμεν· καὶ εἴ τι ἑτέρως
²this ¹let us think; and if anything otherwise

φρονεῖτε, καὶ τοῦτο ὁ θεὸς ὑμῖν ἀποκα-
ye think, even this - God to you will

λύψει· 16 πλὴν εἰς ὃ ἐφθάσαμεν, τῷ
reveal; nevertheless to what we arrived, by the

αὐτῷ στοιχεῖν. 17 Συμμιμηταί μου
same to walk. Fellow-imitators of me

γίνεσθε, ἀδελφοί, καὶ σκοπεῖτε τοὺς οὕτω
be ye, brothers, and mark the [ones] thus

περιπατοῦντας καθὼς ἔχετε τύπον ἡμᾶς.
walking as ye have ²an example ¹us.

18 πολλοὶ γὰρ περιπατοῦσιν οὓς πολλάκις
For many walk [of] whom often

ἔλεγον ὑμῖν, νῦν δὲ καὶ κλαίων λέγω,
I said to you, and now also weeping I say,

τοὺς ἐχθροὺς τοῦ σταυροῦ τοῦ Χριστοῦ,
the enemies of the cross - of Christ,

[19] Their end is destruction, their god is the belly, and they glory in their shame, with minds set on earthly things. [20] But our commonwealth is in heaven, and from it we await a Savior, the Lord Jesus Christ, [21] who will change our lowly body to be like his glorious body, by the power which enables him even to subject all things to himself.

19 ὧν τὸ τέλος ἀπώλεια, ὧν ὁ θεὸς
of whom the end [is] destruction, of whom the god [is]

ἡ κοιλία καὶ ἡ δόξα ἐν τῇ αἰσχύνῃ
the belly and the glory in the shame

αὐτῶν, οἱ τὰ ἐπίγεια φρονοῦντες. 20 ἡμῶν
of them, the the earthly things thinking. of us
  [ones]

γὰρ τὸ πολίτευμα ἐν οὐρανοῖς ὑπάρχει,
For the citizenship in heavens is,

ἐξ οὗ καὶ σωτῆρα ἀπεκδεχόμεθα κύριον
from where also ²a Saviour ¹we await Lord

Ἰησοῦν Χριστόν, 21 ὃς μετασχηματίσει τὸ
Jesus Christ, who will change the

σῶμα τῆς ταπεινώσεως ἡμῶν σύμμορφον
body of the humiliation of us [making it] conformed

τῷ σώματι τῆς δόξης αὐτοῦ, κατὰ τὴν
to the body of the glory of him, according to the

ἐνέργειαν τοῦ δύνασθαι αὐτὸν καὶ ὑποτάξαι
operation of the to be able him[b] even to subject
= of his ability

CHAPTER 4

THEREFORE, my brethren, whom I love and long for, my joy and crown, stand firm thus in the Lord, my beloved.

2 I entreat Eu-o′dia and I entreat Syn′tyche to agree in the Lord. ³And I ask you also, true yokefellow, help these women, for they have labored side by side with me in the gospel together with Clement and the rest of my fellow workers, whose names are in the book of life.

4 Rejoice in the Lord always; again I will say, Rejoice. ⁵Let all men know your forbearance. The Lord is at hand. ⁶Have no anxiety about anything, but in everything by prayer and

αὐτῷ τὰ πάντα. 4 Ὥστε, ἀδελφοί μου
to him[self] – all things. So as, brothers of me

ἀγαπητοὶ καὶ ἐπιπόθητοι, χαρὰ καὶ
beloved and longed for, joy and

στέφανός μου, οὕτως στήκετε ἐν κυρίῳ, ἀγαπητοί.
crown of me, so stand in [the] Lord, beloved.

2 Εὐοδίαν παρακαλῶ καὶ Συντύχην
²Euodia ¹I beseech ²Syntyche

παρακαλῶ τὸ αὐτὸ φρονεῖν ἐν κυρίῳ.
¹I beseech ⁴the ²same thing ³to think in [the] Lord.

3 ναὶ ἐρωτῶ καὶ σέ, γνήσιε σύζυγε,
Yes[,] I ask also thee, genuine yoke-fellow,

συλλαμβάνου αὐταῖς, αἵτινες ἐν τῷ εὐαγ-
help them, who ²in ⁴the ⁵gos-

γελίῳ συνήθλησάν μοι μετὰ καὶ Κλήμεντος
pel ¹struggled with ²me with both Clement

καὶ τῶν λοιπῶν συνεργῶν μου, ὧν
and the remaining fellow-workers of me, of whom

τὰ ὀνόματα ἐν βίβλῳ ζωῆς. 4 Χαίρετε
the names [are] in [the] book of life. Rejoice ye

ἐν κυρίῳ πάντοτε· πάλιν ἐρῶ, χαίρετε.
in [the] Lord always; again I will say, rejoice.

5 τὸ ἐπιεικὲς ὑμῶν γνωσθήτω πᾶσιν
The forbearance of you let it be known to all

ἀνθρώποις. ὁ κύριος ἐγγύς. 6 μηδὲν
men. The Lord [is] near. ²Nothing

μεριμνᾶτε, ἀλλ᾽ ἐν παντὶ τῇ προσευχῇ
¹be ye anxious but in everything – by prayer
about,

supplication with thanks-giving let your requests be made known to God. 7And the peace of God, which passes all understanding, will keep your hearts and your minds in Christ Jesus.

8 Finally, brethren, whatever is true, whatever is honorable, whatever is just, whatever is pure, whatever is lovely, whatever is gracious, if there is any excellence, if there is anything worthy of praise, think about these things. 9What you have learned and received and heard and seen in me, do; and the God of peace will be with you.

10 I rejoice in the Lord greatly that now at length you have revived your concern for me; you were indeed concerned for me, but you had no opportunity. 11Not that I complain of want; for I have learned, in whatever state I am, to be content. 12I know how to be abased, and I know how to abound; in any and all circumstances I have learned the secret of facing plenty and hunger,

---

καὶ   τῇ   δεήσει   μετὰ   εὐχαριστίας   τὰ
and   -   by petition   with   thanksgivings   the

αἰτήματα   ὑμῶν   γνωριζέσθω   πρὸς   τὸν
requests   of you   let be made known   to   -

θεόν.   7 καὶ   ἡ   εἰρήνη   τοῦ   θεοῦ   ἡ
God.   And   the   peace   -   of God   -

ὑπερέχουσα   πάντα   νοῦν   φρουρήσει   τὰς
surpassing   all   understanding   will guard   the

καρδίας   ὑμῶν   καὶ   τὰ   νοήματα   ὑμῶν
hearts   of you   and   the   thoughts   of you

ἐν   Χριστῷ   Ἰησοῦ.   8 Τὸ   λοιπόν,   ἀδελφοί,
in   Christ   Jesus.   For the rest,   brothers,

ὅσα   ἐστὶν   ἀληθῆ,   ὅσα   σεμνά,   ὅσα   δίκαια,
whatever are   true,   whatever grave,   whatever just,
things   things   things

ὅσα   ἁγνά,   ὅσα   προσφιλῆ,   ὅσα   εὔφημα,
whatever pure,   whatever   lovable,   whatever well-spoken
things   things   things   of,

εἴ   τις   ἀρετὴ   καὶ   εἴ   τις   ἔπαινος,   9 ταῦτα
if   any   virtue   and   if   any   praise,   these things

λογίζεσθε·   ἃ   καὶ   ἐμάθετε   καὶ   παρελάβετε
consider ye;   which ²both   ¹ye ³learned   and   ye received
                              things

καὶ   ἠκούσατε   καὶ   εἴδετε   ἐν   ἐμοί,   ταῦτα
and   ye heard   and   ye saw   in   me,   these

πράσσετε·   καὶ   ὁ   θεὸς   τῆς   εἰρήνης   ἔσται
practise;   and   the God   -   of peace   will be

μεθ᾽   ὑμῶν.
with   you.

10 Ἐχάρην   δὲ   ἐν   κυρίῳ   μεγάλως   ὅτι
Now I rejoiced   in   [the] Lord   greatly   that

ἤδη   ποτὲ   ἀνεθάλετε   τὸ   ὑπὲρ   ἐμοῦ   φρονεῖν·
al-   at one   ye revived   the   on behalf   me   to think;
ready   time   of
=now at length   =your thought for me;

ἐφ᾽   ᾧ   καὶ   ἐφρονεῖτε,   ἠκαιρεῖσθε   δέ.
as to   which   indeed   ye thought,   but ye had no opportunity.

11 οὐχ   ὅτι   καθ᾽   ὑστέρησιν   λέγω·   ἐγὼ
Not   that   ²by way of   ³lack   ¹I say;   ²I

γὰρ   ἔμαθον   ἐν   οἷς   εἰμι   αὐτάρκης   εἶναι.
¹for   learned   in   what   I am   ²self-   ¹to be.
                            conditions   sufficient

12 οἶδα   καὶ   ταπεινοῦσθαι,   οἶδα   καὶ   περισ-
I know   both   to be humbled,   and I know   to

σεύειν·   ἐν   παντὶ   καὶ   ἐν   πᾶσιν   μεμύημαι,
abound;   in everything   and   in   all things   I have been
                                                    initiated,

καὶ   χορτάζεσθαι   καὶ   πεινᾶν,   καὶ   περισ-
both   to be filled   and   to hunger,   both   to

abundance and want. ¹³I
can do all things in him
who strengthens me.

14 Yet it was kind of
you to share my trouble.
¹⁵And you Philippians
yourselves know that in
the beginning of the
gospel, when I left
Macedo′nia, no church
entered into partnership
with me in giving and
receiving except you
only; ¹⁶for even in
Thessaloni′ca you sent
me help^c once and again.
¹⁷Not that I seek the
gift; but I seek the fruit
which increases to your
credit. ¹⁸I have received
full payment, and more;
I am filled, having re-
ceived from Epaphrodi′-
tus the gifts you sent, a
fragrant offering, a
sacrifice acceptable and
pleasing to God. ¹⁹And
my God will supply every
need of yours according
to his riches in glory in
Christ Jesus. ²⁰To our
God and Father be
glory for ever and ever.
Amen.

21 Greet every saint
in Christ Jesus. The
brethren who are with
me greet you. ²²All the

σεύειν   καὶ   ὑστερεῖσθαι.   13 πάντα   ἰσχύω
abound   and   to lack.   ¹All things ¹I can do

ἐν τῷ ἐνδυναμοῦντί με.   14 πλὴν   καλῶς
in the [one] empowering   me.   Nevertheless ²well

ἐποιήσατε συγκοινωνήσαντές μου τῇ θλίψει.
¹ye did   having partnership in ²of me ¹the ³affliction.

15 οἴδατε   δὲ   καὶ ὑμεῖς,   Φιλιππήσιοι,   ὅτι
And ²know   ³also ¹ye,   Philippians,   that

ἐν ἀρχῇ τοῦ εὐαγγελίου, ὅτε ἐξῆλθον
in [the] of the gospel,   when I went out
beginning

ἀπὸ Μακεδονίας, οὐδεμία μοι ἐκκλησία
from Macedonia, not one ²me ¹church

ἐκοινώνησεν εἰς λόγον δόσεως καὶ λήμψεως
²shared with in matter of giving and receiving

εἰ μὴ ὑμεῖς μόνοι, 16 ὅτι καὶ ἐν
except ye only,   because indeed in

Θεσσαλονίκῃ καὶ ἅπαξ καὶ δὶς εἰς τὴν
Thessalonica both once and twice to the
=to my need

χρείαν μοι ἐπέμψατε.   17 οὐχ ὅτι ἐπιζητῶ
need to me^c ye sent.   Not that I seek

τὸ δόμα, ἀλλὰ ἐπιζητῶ τὸν καρπὸν
the gift,   but I seek the fruit

τὸν πλεονάζοντα εἰς λόγον ὑμῶν. 18 ἀπέχω
– increasing to account of you.   I have

δὲ πάντα καὶ περισσεύω· πεπλήρωμαι
But all things and abound;   I have been filled

δεξάμενος παρὰ Ἐπαφροδίτου τὰ παρ’
receiving from Epaphroditus the things from

ὑμῶν, ὀσμὴν εὐωδίας, θυσίαν δεκτήν,
you,   an odour of sweet smell, a sacrifice acceptable,

εὐάρεστον τῷ θεῷ. 19 ὁ δὲ θεός μου
well-pleasing – to God.   And the God of me

πληρώσει πᾶσαν χρείαν ὑμῶν κατὰ τὸ
will fill every need of you according to the

πλοῦτος αὐτοῦ ἐν δόξῃ ἐν Χριστῷ Ἰησοῦ.
riches of him in glory in Christ Jesus.

20 τῷ δὲ θεῷ καὶ πατρὶ ἡμῶν ἡ δόξα
to the Now God and Father of us [be] the glory

εἰς τοὺς αἰῶνας τῶν αἰώνων· ἀμήν.
unto the ages of the ages: Amen.

21 Ἀσπάσασθε πάντα ἅγιον ἐν Χριστῷ
Greet ye every saint in Christ

Ἰησοῦ. ἀσπάζονται ὑμᾶς οἱ σὺν ἐμοὶ
Jesus.   ³greet ⁴you ¹The ²with ⁴me

ἀδελφοί. 22 ἀσπάζονται ὑμᾶς πάντες οἱ
³brothers.   ⁴greet ⁵you ¹All ²the

^c Other ancient authorities
read *money for my needs*

saints greet you, especially those of Caesar's household.

23 The grace of the Lord Jesus Christ be with your spirit.

ἅγιοι, μάλιστα δὲ οἱ ἐκ τῆς Καίσαρος
³saints,   but most of all the ones of ¹the   ²of Cæsar

οἰκίας.
²household.

23 Ἡ χάρις τοῦ κυρίου Ἰησοῦ Χριστοῦ
   The grace of the Lord   Jesus   Christ

μετὰ τοῦ πνεύματος ὑμῶν.
[be] with the   spirit   of you.

COLOSSIANS 1

ΠΡΟΣ ΚΟΛΟΣΣΑΕΙΣ
To Colossians

CHAPTER 1

PAUL, an apostle of Christ Jesus by the will of God, and Timothy our brother,

2 To the saints and faithful brethren in Christ at Colos'sae:

Grace to you and peace from God our Father.

3 We always thank God, the Father of our Lord Jesus Christ, when we pray for you, [4] because we have heard of your faith in Christ Jesus and of the love which you have for all the saints, [5] because of the hope laid up for you in heaven. Of this you have heard before in the word of the truth, the gospel [6] which has come to you, as indeed in the whole world it is bearing fruit and growing—so

1 Παῦλος ἀπόστολος Χριστοῦ Ἰησοῦ διὰ
  Paul   an apostle of Christ Jesus through

θελήματος θεοῦ καὶ Τιμόθεος ὁ ἀδελφὸς
[the] will of God and Timothy the brother

2 τοῖς ἐν Κολοσσαῖς ἁγίοις καὶ πιστοῖς
  to the in Colosse   saints and faithful

ἀδελφοῖς ἐν Χριστῷ· χάρις ὑμῖν καὶ
brothers in Christ: Grace to you and

εἰρήνη ἀπὸ θεοῦ πατρὸς ἡμῶν.
peace from God Father of us.

3 Εὐχαριστοῦμεν τῷ θεῷ πατρὶ τοῦ
  We give thanks   – to God Father of the

κυρίου ἡμῶν Ἰησοῦ [Χριστοῦ] πάντοτε
Lord   of us Jesus   Christ   always

περὶ ὑμῶν προσευχόμενοι, 4 ἀκούσαντες
²concerning ³you ¹praying,   having heard

τὴν πίστιν ὑμῶν ἐν Χριστῷ Ἰησοῦ
the faith of you in Christ   Jesus

καὶ τὴν ἀγάπην ἣν ἔχετε εἰς πάντας
and the   love which ye have toward all

τοὺς ἁγίους 5 διὰ τὴν ἐλπίδα τὴν
the   saints   because of the hope   –

ἀποκειμένην ὑμῖν ἐν τοῖς οὐρανοῖς, ἣν
being laid up for you in the heavens, which

προηκούσατε ἐν τῷ λόγῳ τῆς ἀληθείας
ye previously in the word of the truth
heard

τοῦ εὐαγγελίου 6 τοῦ παρόντος εἰς ὑμᾶς,
of the gospel   –   coming   to you,

καθὼς καὶ ἐν παντὶ τῷ κόσμῳ ἐστὶν
as   also in all the world it is

καρποφορούμενον καὶ αὐξανόμενον καθὼς
bearing fruit   and   growing   as

among yourselves, from the day you heard and understood the grace of God in truth, [7]as you learned it from Ep'aphras our beloved fellow servant. He is a faithful minister of Christ on our[a] behalf [8]and has made known to us your love in the Spirit.

9 And so, from the day we heard of it, we have not ceased to pray for you, asking that you may be filled with the knowledge of his will in all spiritual wisdom and understanding, [10]to lead a life worthy of the Lord, fully pleasing to him, bearing fruit in every good work and increasing in the knowledge of God. [11]May you be strengthened with all power, according to his glorious might, for all endurance and patience with joy, [12]giving thanks to the Father, who has qualified us[b] to share in the inheritance of the saints in light. [13]He has delivered us from the dominion of darkness

καὶ ἐν ὑμῖν, ἀφ' ἧς ἡμέρας ἠκούσατε
also in you, from which day ye heard
                = the day on which

καὶ ἐπέγνωτε τὴν χάριν τοῦ θεοῦ ἐν
and fully knew the grace – of God in

ἀληθείᾳ· 7 καθὼς ἐμάθετε ἀπὸ 'Επαφρᾶ
truth; as ye learned from Epaphras

τοῦ ἀγαπητοῦ συνδούλου ἡμῶν, ὅς ἐστιν
the beloved fellow-slave of us, who is

πιστὸς ὑπὲρ ὑμῶν διάκονος τοῦ Χριστοῦ,
[1]a [4]on behalf [5]you [3]minister – [2]of Christ,
faithful of

8 ὁ καὶ δηλώσας ἡμῖν τὴν ὑμῶν ἀγάπην
the also having shown to us [1]the [2]of you [3]love
[one]

ἐν πνεύματι.
in spirit.

9 Διὰ τοῦτο καὶ ἡμεῖς, ἀφ' ἧς ἡμέρας
Therefore also we, from which day
                = the day on which

ἠκούσαμεν, οὐ παυόμεθα ὑπὲρ ὑμῶν
we heard, do not cease on behalf of you

προσευχόμενοι καὶ αἰτούμενοι ἵνα πληρω-
praying and asking in order ye may be
                                  that

θῆτε τὴν ἐπίγνωσιν τοῦ θελήματος αὐτοῦ
filled the full knowledge of the will of him
[with]

ἐν πάσῃ σοφίᾳ καὶ συνέσει πνευματικῇ,
in all wisdom and understanding spiritual,

10 περιπατῆσαι ἀξίως τοῦ κυρίου εἰς
to walk worthily of the Lord to

πᾶσαν ἀρεσκείαν, ἐν παντὶ ἔργῳ ἀγαθῷ
all pleasing, in every work good

καρποφοροῦντες καὶ αὐξανόμενοι τῇ
bearing fruit and growing in the

ἐπιγνώσει τοῦ θεοῦ, 11 ἐν πάσῃ δυνάμει
full knowledge – of God, with all power

δυναμούμενοι κατὰ τὸ κράτος τῆς δόξης
being empowered according to the might of the glory

αὐτοῦ εἰς πᾶσαν ὑπομονὴν καὶ μακρο-
of him to all endurance and long-

θυμίαν, μετὰ χαρᾶς 12 εὐχαριστοῦντες τῷ
suffering, with joy giving thanks to the

πατρὶ τῷ ἱκανώσαντι ὑμᾶς εἰς τὴν μερίδα
Father – having made [2]fit [1]you for the part

τοῦ κλήρου τῶν ἁγίων ἐν τῷ φωτί·
of the lot of the saints in the light;

13 ὃς ἐρρύσατο ἡμᾶς ἐκ τῆς ἐξουσίας
who delivered us out of the authority

[a] Other ancient authorities read *your*

[b] Other ancient authorities read *you*

Left column (translation)	Interlinear

and transferred us to the kingdom of his beloved Son, ¹⁴in whom we have redemption, the forgiveness of sins.

15 He is the image of the invisible God, the first-born of all creation; ¹⁶for in him all things were created, in heaven and on earth, visible and invisible, whether thrones or dominions or principalities or authorities— all things were created through him and for him. ¹⁷He is before all things, and in him all things hold together. ¹⁸He is the head of the body, the church; he is the beginning, the first-born from the dead, that in everything he might be preëminent. ¹⁹For in him all the fulness of God was pleased to dwell, ²⁰and through him to reconcile to himself all things, whether on earth or in heaven, making peace by the blood of his cross.

21 And you, who once were estranged and

τοῦ σκότους καὶ μετέστησεν εἰς τὴν
of *the* darkness and transferred into the

βασιλείαν τοῦ υἱοῦ τῆς ἀγάπης αὐτοῦ,
kingdom of the Son of the love of him,

14 ἐν ᾧ ἔχομεν τὴν ἀπολύτρωσιν, τὴν
in whom we have *the* redemption, the

ἄφεσιν τῶν ἁμαρτιῶν· **15** ὅς ἐστιν εἰκὼν
forgiveness of the sins; who is an image
(our)

τοῦ θεοῦ τοῦ ἀοράτου, πρωτότοκος πάσης
of the God – invisible, firstborn of all

κτίσεως, **16** ὅτι ἐν αὐτῷ ἐκτίσθη τὰ
creation, because in him were created –

πάντα ἐν τοῖς οὐρανοῖς καὶ ἐπὶ τῆς
all things in *the* heavens and on the

γῆς, τὰ ὁρατὰ καὶ τὰ ἀόρατα, εἴτε
earth, the visible and the invisible, whether

θρόνοι εἴτε κυριότητες εἴτε ἀρχαὶ εἴτε
thrones or lordships or rulers or

ἐξουσίαι· τὰ πάντα δι' αὐτοῦ καὶ εἰς
authorities; – all things through him and for

αὐτὸν ἔκτισται· **17** καὶ αὐτός ἐστιν πρὸ
him have been created; and he is before

πάντων καὶ τὰ πάντα ἐν αὐτῷ συνέστηκεν,
all things and – all things in him consisted,

18 καὶ αὐτός ἐστιν ἡ κεφαλὴ τοῦ σώματος,
and he is the head of the body,

τῆς ἐκκλησίας· ὅς ἐστιν ἀρχή, πρωτότοκος
of the church; who is [the] firstborn
beginning,

ἐκ τῶν νεκρῶν, ἵνα γένηται ἐν πᾶσιν
from the dead, in order 'may be ²in ³all
that things

αὐτὸς πρωτεύων, **19** ὅτι ἐν αὐτῷ εὐδόκησεν
¹he ²holding the because in him ⁴was well
first place, pleased

πᾶν τὸ πλήρωμα κατοικῆσαι **20** καὶ δι'
¹all ²the ³fulness to dwell and through

αὐτοῦ ἀποκαταλλάξαι τὰ πάντα εἰς αὐτόν,
him to reconcile – all things to him[?self],

εἰρηνοποιήσας διὰ τοῦ αἵματος τοῦ σταυροῦ
making peace through the blood of the cross

αὐτοῦ, δι' αὐτοῦ εἴτε τὰ ἐπὶ τῆς γῆς
of him, through him whether the on the earth
things

εἴτε τὰ ἐν τοῖς οὐρανοῖς. **21** Καὶ ὑμᾶς
or the things in *the* heavens. And you

ποτε ὄντας ἀπηλλοτριωμένους καὶ ἐχθροὺς
then being *having been* alienated and enemies

hostile in mind, doing evil deeds, [22]he has now reconciled in his body of flesh by his death, in order to present you holy and blameless and irreproachable before him, [23]provided that you continue in the faith, stable and steadfast, not shifting from the hope of the gospel which you heard, which has been preached to every creature under heaven, and of which I, Paul, became a minister.

24 Now I rejoice in my sufferings for your sake, and in my flesh I complete what is lacking in Christ's afflictions for the sake of his body, that is, the church, [25]of which I became a minister according to the divine office which was given to me for you, to make the word of God fully known, [26]the mystery hidden for ages and generations[c] but now made manifest to his saints. [27]To them God chose to make known how great among the Gentiles are the riches of

τῇ   διανοίᾳ   ἐν   τοῖς   ἔργοις   τοῖς   πονηροῖς,
in the   mind   by the(your) works   -   evil,

22 νυνὶ   δὲ   ἀποκατήλλαξεν   ἐν   τῷ   σώματι
but now   he reconciled   in   the   body

τῆς   σαρκὸς   αὐτοῦ   διὰ   τοῦ   θανάτου,
of the   flesh   of him   through the(his) death,

παραστῆσαι   ὑμᾶς   ἁγίους   καὶ   ἀμώμους
to present   you   holy   and   blameless

καὶ   ἀνεγκλήτους   κατενώπιον   αὐτοῦ,   23 εἴ
and   irreproachable   before   him,   if

γε   ἐπιμένετε   τῇ   πίστει   τεθεμελιωμένοι
indeed ye continue in the faith   having been founded

καὶ   ἑδραῖοι   καὶ   μὴ   μετακινούμενοι   ἀπὸ
and   steadfast and not   being moved away   from

τῆς   ἐλπίδος   τοῦ   εὐαγγελίου   οὗ   ἠκούσατε,
the   hope   of the   gospel   which ye heard,

τοῦ   κηρυχθέντος   ἐν   πάσῃ   κτίσει   τῇ
-       proclaimed   in   all   creation   -

ὑπὸ   τὸν   οὐρανόν,   οὗ   ἐγενόμην   ἐγὼ
under the   heaven,   of which ²became   ¹I

Παῦλος   διάκονος.
¹Paul   a minister.

24 Νῦν   χαίρω   ἐν   τοῖς   παθήμασιν   ὑπὲρ
Now   I rejoice in the(my)   sufferings   on be-
                                              half of

ὑμῶν,   καὶ   ἀνταναπληρῶ   τὰ   ὑστερήματα
you,   and   fill up   the   things lacking

τῶν   θλίψεων   τοῦ   Χριστοῦ   ἐν   τῇ   σαρκί
of the afflictions   -   of Christ   in the   flesh

μου   ὑπὲρ   τοῦ   σώματος   αὐτοῦ,   ὅ   ἐστιν
of me on behalf of the   body   of him, which is

ἡ   ἐκκλησία,   25 ἧς   ἐγενόμην   ἐγὼ   διάκονος
the   church,   of which became   I   a minister

κατὰ   τὴν   οἰκονομίαν   τοῦ   θεοῦ   τὴν
accord- the   stewardship   -   of God   -
ing to

δοθεῖσάν   μοι   εἰς   ὑμᾶς   πληρῶσαι   τὸν
given   to me   for   you   to fulfil   the

λόγον   τοῦ   θεοῦ,   26 τὸ   μυστήριον   τὸ
word   -   of God,   the   mystery   -

ἀποκεκρυμμένον   ἀπὸ   τῶν   αἰώνων   καὶ
having been hidden   from   the   ages   and

ἀπὸ   τῶν   γενεῶν   —   νῦν   δὲ   ἐφανερώθη
from the   generations —   but now   was manifested

τοῖς   ἁγίοις   αὐτοῦ,   27 οἷς   ἠθέλησεν   ὁ
to the   saints   of him,   to whom ²wished   -

θεὸς   γνωρίσαι   τί   τὸ   πλοῦτος   τῆς   δόξης
¹God to make known what [is] the   riches   of the glory

[c] Or from angels and men

the glory of this mystery, which is Christ in you, the hope of glory. [28] Him we proclaim, warning every man and teaching every man in all wisdom, that we may present every man mature in Christ. [29] For this I toil, striving with all the energy which he mightily inspires within me.

τοῦ   μυστηρίου   τούτου   ἐν   τοῖς   ἔθνεσιν,
-          mystery   of this   among   the   nations,

ὅς   ἐστιν   Χριστὸς   ἐν   ὑμῖν,   ἡ   ἐλπὶς   τῆς
who   is   Christ   in   you,   the   hope   of the

δόξης·   28   ὃν   ἡμεῖς   καταγγέλλομεν   νου-
glory;   whom   we   announce   warn-

θετοῦντες   πάντα   ἄνθρωπον   καὶ   διδάσκοντες
ing   every   man   and   teaching

πάντα   ἄνθρωπον   ἐν   πάσῃ   σοφίᾳ,
every   man   in   all   wisdom,

ἵνα   παραστήσωμεν   πάντα   ἄνθρωπον
in or-   we may present   every   man
der that

τέλειον   ἐν   Χριστῷ·   29   εἰς   ὃ   καὶ   κοπιῶ
mature   in   Christ;   for which also   I labour

ἀγωνιζόμενος   κατὰ   τὴν   ἐνέργειαν   αὐτοῦ
struggling   accord-   the   operation   of him
                    ing to

τὴν   ἐνεργουμένην   ἐν   ἐμοὶ   ἐν   δυνάμει.
-        operating   in   me   in   power.

CHAPTER 2

FOR I want you to know how greatly I strive for you, and for those at La-odice′a, and for all who have not seen my face, [2] that their hearts may be encouraged as they are knit together in love, to have all the riches of assured understanding and the knowledge of God's mystery, of Christ, [3] in whom are hid all the treasures of wisdom and knowledge. [4] I say this in order that no one may delude you with beguiling speech. [5] For though I am absent in body, yet I am with you in spirit, rejoicing to see your good

2   Θέλω   γὰρ   ὑμᾶς   εἰδέναι   ἡλίκον   ἀγῶνα
For I wish   you   to know   how great   a struggle

ἔχω   ὑπὲρ   ὑμῶν   καὶ   τῶν   ἐν   Λαοδικείᾳ
I have on behalf of   you   and the [ones] in   Laodicea

καὶ   ὅσοι   οὐχ   ἑόρακαν   τὸ   πρόσωπόν   μου
and as many as   have not seen   the   face   of me

ἐν   σαρκί,   2   ἵνα   παρακληθῶσιν   αἱ   καρδίαι
in   flesh,   in order   [4]may be   [1]the   [2]hearts
                 that   comforted

αὐτῶν,   συμβιβασθέντες   ἐν   ἀγάπῃ   καὶ   εἰς
[3]of them,   being joined together   in   love   and   for

πᾶν   πλοῦτος   τῆς   πληροφορίας   τῆς
all   riches   of the   full assurance   -

συνέσεως,   εἰς   ἐπίγνωσιν   τοῦ   μυστηρίου
of under-   for   full knowledge   of the   mystery
standing,

τοῦ   θεοῦ,   Χριστοῦ,   3   ἐν   ᾧ   εἰσιν   πάντες
-   of God,   of Christ,   in whom   [3]all

οἱ   θησαυροὶ   τῆς   σοφίας   καὶ   γνώσεως
[4]the   [5]treasures   -   [6]of wisdom   [7]and   [8]of knowledge

ἀπόκρυφοι.   4   Τοῦτο   λέγω   ἵνα   μηδεὶς
[2]hidden.   This   I say   in order   no one
                              that

ὑμᾶς   παραλογίζηται   ἐν   πιθανολογίᾳ.   5   εἰ
[2]you   [1]may beguile   with   persuasive speech.   if

γὰρ   καὶ   τῇ   σαρκὶ   ἄπειμι,   ἀλλὰ   τῷ
For   indeed   in the   flesh   I am absent,   yet   in the

πνεύματι   σὺν   ὑμῖν   εἰμι,   χαίρων   καὶ
spirit   [2]with   [3]you   [1]I am,   rejoicing   and

order and the firmness of your faith in Christ.

6 As therefore you received Christ Jesus the Lord, so live in him, [7]rooted and built up in him and established in the faith, just as you were taught, abounding in thanksgiving.

8 See to it that no one makes a prey of you by philosophy and empty deceit, according to human tradition, according to the elemental spirits of the universe, and not according to Christ. [9]For in him the whole fulness of deity dwells bodily, [10]and you have come to fulness of life in him, who is the head of all rule and authority. [11]In him also you were circumcised with a circumcision made without hands, by putting off the body of flesh in the circumcision of Christ; [12]and you were buried with him in baptism, in which you were also raised with him through faith in the working of God, who raised him from the dead. [13]And you, who

βλέπων ὑμῶν τὴν τάξιν καὶ τὸ στερέωμα
seeing ²of you ¹the ²order and the firmness

τῆς εἰς Χριστὸν πίστεως ὑμῶν.
of the ³in ⁴Christ ¹faith ²of you.

6 Ὡς οὖν παρελάβετε τὸν Χριστὸν
As therefore ye received – Christ

Ἰησοῦν τὸν κύριον, ἐν αὐτῷ περιπατεῖτε,
Jesus the Lord, in him walk ye,

7 ἐρριζωμένοι καὶ ἐποικοδομούμενοι ἐν αὐτῷ
having been rooted and being built up in him

καὶ βεβαιούμενοι τῇ πίστει καθὼς ἐδιδάχ-
and being confirmed in the faith as ye were

θητε, περισσεύοντες ἐν εὐχαριστίᾳ.
taught, abounding in thanksgiving.

8 Βλέπετε μή τις ὑμᾶς ἔσται ὁ συλαγωγῶν
Look ye lest ²anyone ⁴you ¹there – ²robbing
shall be

διὰ τῆς φιλοσοφίας καὶ κενῆς ἀπάτης
through – philosophy and empty deceit

κατὰ τὴν παράδοσιν τῶν ἀνθρώπων, κατὰ
according the tradition – of men, according
to to

τὰ στοιχεῖα τοῦ κόσμου καὶ οὐ κατὰ
the elements of the world and not according
to

Χριστόν· 9 ὅτι ἐν αὐτῷ κατοικεῖ πᾶν
Christ; because in him dwells all

τὸ πλήρωμα τῆς θεότητος σωματικῶς,
the fulness of the Godhead bodily,

10 καὶ ἐστὲ ἐν αὐτῷ πεπληρωμένοι, ὅς
and ye are in him having been filled, who

ἐστιν ἡ κεφαλὴ πάσης ἀρχῆς καὶ ἐξουσίας,
is the head of all rule and authority,

11 ἐν ᾧ καὶ περιετμήθητε περιτομῇ
in whom also ye were with a
circumcised circumcision

ἀχειροποιήτῳ ἐν τῇ ἀπεκδύσει τοῦ σώματος
not handwrought by the putting off of the body

τῆς σαρκός, ἐν τῇ περιτομῇ τοῦ Χριστοῦ,
of the flesh, by the circumcision – of Christ,

12 συνταφέντες αὐτῷ ἐν τῷ βαπτίσματι,
co-buried with him in the baptism,

ἐν ᾧ καὶ συνηγέρθητε διὰ τῆς πίστεως
in whom also ye were co-raised through the faith

τῆς ἐνεργείας τοῦ θεοῦ τοῦ ἐγείραντος
of(in)the operation – of God – raising

αὐτὸν ἐκ νεκρῶν· 13 καὶ ὑμᾶς νεκροὺς
him from [the] dead; and you dead

were dead in trespasses and the uncircumcision of your flesh, God made alive together with him, having forgiven us all our trespasses, [14]having canceled the bond which stood against us with its legal demands; this he set aside, nailing it to the cross. [15] He disarmed the principalities and powers and made a public example of them, triumphing over them in him.[d]

16 Therefore let no one pass judgment on you in questions of food and drink or with regard to a festival or a new moon or a sabbath. [17]These are only a shadow of what is to come; but the substance belongs to Christ. [18]Let no one disqualify you, insisting on self-abasement and worship of angels, taking his stand on visions, puffed up without reason by his sensuous mind, [19]and not holding fast to the Head, from whom the whole body, nourished and knit together through its joints and ligaments, grows with a growth that is from God.

ὄντας τοῖς παραπτώμασιν καὶ τῇ ἀκρο-
being in the trespasses and in the uncir-

βυστίᾳ τῆς σαρκὸς ὑμῶν, συνεζωοποίησεν
cumcision of the flesh of you, he co-quickened

ὑμᾶς σὺν αὐτῷ, χαρισάμενος ἡμῖν πάντα
you with him, forgiving us all

τὰ παραπτώματα· 14 ἐξαλείψας τὸ καθ᾽
the trespasses; wiping out [1]the [2]against

ἡμῶν χειρόγραφον τοῖς δόγμασιν ὃ ἦν
[1]us [2]handwriting – in ordinances which was

ὑπεναντίον ἡμῖν, καὶ αὐτὸ ἦρκεν ἐκ
contrary to us, and [2]it [1]has taken out of

τοῦ μέσου, προσηλώσας αὐτὸ τῷ σταυρῷ·
the midst(way), nailing it to the cross;

15 ἀπεκδυσάμενος τὰς ἀρχὰς καὶ τὰς
putting off the rulers and the

ἐξουσίας ἐδειγμάτισεν ἐν παρρησίᾳ,
authorities he exposed [them] with openness,

θριαμβεύσας αὐτοὺς ἐν αὐτῷ.
triumphing [over] them in it.

16 Μὴ οὖν τις ὑμᾶς κρινέτω ἐν βρώσει
[1]Not [3]there-[4]any-[2]you [1]let [5]judge in eating
fore one

καὶ ἐν πόσει ἢ ἐν μέρει ἑορτῆς ἢ
and in drinking or in respect of a feast or

νεομηνίας ἢ σαββάτων, 17 ἅ ἐστιν σκιὰ
of a new moon or of sabbaths, which is(are) a
things shadow

τῶν μελλόντων, τὸ δὲ σῶμα τοῦ Χριστοῦ.
of things coming, but the body [is] – of Christ.

18 μηδεὶς ὑμᾶς καταβραβευέτω θέλων ἐν
[1]No one [4]you [1]let [2]give judgment wishing in
against [to do so]

ταπεινοφροσύνῃ καὶ θρησκείᾳ τῶν ἀγγέλων,
humility* and worship of the angels,

ἃ ἑόρακεν ἐμβατεύων, εἰκῇ φυσιούμενος
[3]things [2]he has [1]intruding into, in vain being puffed up
which seen

ὑπὸ τοῦ νοὸς τῆς σαρκὸς αὐτοῦ, 19 καὶ
by the mind of the flesh of him, and

οὐ κρατῶν τὴν κεφαλήν, ἐξ οὗ πᾶν
not holding the head, from whom all

τὸ σῶμα διὰ τῶν ἁφῶν καὶ συνδέσμων
the body [4]by means [5]the [6]joints [7]and [8]bands
of (its)

ἐπιχορηγούμενον καὶ συμβιβαζόμενον αὔξει
[1]being supplied [2]and [3]being joined together will grow

τὴν αὔξησιν τοῦ θεοῦ.
[with] the growth of God.

---

[d] Or in it (that is, the cross)

* Ellicott supplies " false ". Cf. ver. 22.

20 If with Christ you died to the elemental spirits of the universe, why do you live as if you still belonged to the world? Why do you submit to regulations, ²¹"Do not handle, Do not taste, Do not touch" ²²(referring to things which all perish as they are used), according to human precepts and doctrines? ²³These have indeed an appearance of wisdom in promoting rigor of devotion and self-abasement and severity to the body, but they are of no value in checking the indulgence of the flesh.ᵉ

CHAPTER 3

IF then you have been raised with Christ, seek the things that are above, where Christ is, seated at the right hand of God. ²Set your minds on things that are above, not on things that are on earth. ³For you have died, and your life is hid with Christ in God. ⁴When Christ who is our life appears, then you also will appear with him in glory.

5 Put to death therefore what is earthly in you: immorality, impurity, passion, evil desire, and covetousness, which is idolatry. ⁶On account of these the

20 Εἰ ἀπεθάνετε σὺν Χριστῷ ἀπὸ τῶν στοι-
    If   ye died   with Christ from the ele-
χείων τοῦ κόσμου, τί ὡς ζῶντες ἐν κόσμῳ
ments of the world, why as living in [the] world
δογματίζεσθε· 21 μὴ ἅψῃ μηδὲ γεύσῃ μηδὲ
are ye subject to   Do not touch nor taste nor
[its] decrees:
θίγῃς,   22 ἅ   ἐστιν πάντα εἰς φθορὰν
handle,   which is(are)   all   for corruption
           things
τῇ ἀποχρήσει, κατὰ τὰ ἐντάλματα καὶ
in the   using, according to the injunctions and
διδασκαλίας τῶν ἀνθρώπων; 23 ἅτινά ἐστιν
teachings   –   of men?   ¹which ²is(are)
                              things
λόγον μὲν ἔχοντα σοφίας ἐν ἐθελοθρησκίᾳ
³a repute ²indeed ⁴having of wisdom in self-imposed
                                        worship
καὶ ταπεινοφροσύνῃ καὶ ἀφειδίᾳ σώματος, οὐκ
and humility   and severity of [the] body, not
ἐν τιμῇ τινι πρὸς πλησμονὴν τῆς σαρκός.
in ¹honour ¹any for satisfaction of the flesh.

3 Εἰ οὖν συνηγέρθητε τῷ Χριστῷ, τὰ
  If therefore ye were co-raised – with Christ, the
                                                things
ἄνω ζητεῖτε, οὗ ὁ Χριστός ἐστιν ἐν
above seek, where – Christ ¹is ²at
δεξιᾷ τοῦ θεοῦ καθήμενος· 2 τὰ ἄνω
⁴[the] right – ⁵of God ²sitting;   the above
[hand]   things
φρονεῖτε, μὴ τὰ ἐπὶ τῆς γῆς. 3 ἀπεθάνετε
mind ye, not the on the earth.   ye died
           things
γάρ, καὶ ἡ ζωὴ ὑμῶν κέκρυπται σὺν
For, and the life of you has been hidden with
τῷ Χριστῷ ἐν τῷ θεῷ· 4 ὅταν ὁ Χριστὸς
 – Christ in – God; whenever – Christ
φανερωθῇ, ἡ ζωὴ ἡμῶν, τότε καὶ ὑμεῖς
is manifested, the life of us, then also ye
σὺν αὐτῷ φανερωθήσεσθε ἐν δόξῃ.
with him will be manifested in glory.

5 Νεκρώσατε οὖν τὰ μέλη τὰ ἐπὶ
  Put ye to death therefore the members – on
                            (your)
τῆς γῆς, πορνείαν, ἀκαθαρσίαν, πάθος,
the earth, fornication, uncleanness, passion,
ἐπιθυμίαν κακήν, καὶ τὴν πλεονεξίαν ἥτις
desire   bad, and the – covetousness which
ἐστιν εἰδωλολατρία, 6 δι' ἃ ἔρχεται ἡ
is   idolatry,   because which is coming the
                           of things

_____
ᵉ Or are of no value, serving
only to indulge the flesh

wrath of God is coming.ᶠ
⁷In these you once walked, when you lived in them. ⁸But now put them all away; anger, wrath, malice, slander, and foul talk from your mouth. ⁹Do not lie to one another, seeing that you have put off the old nature with its practices ¹⁰and have put on the new nature, which is being renewed in knowledge after the image of its creator. ¹¹Here there cannot be Greek and Jew, circumcised and uncircumcised, barbarian, Scyth′ian, slave, free man, but Christ is all, and in all.

12 Put on then, as God's chosen ones, holy and beloved, compassion, kindness, lowliness, meekness, and patience, ¹³forbearing one another and, if one has a complaint against another, forgiving each other; as the Lord has forgiven you, so you also must forgive. ¹⁴And above all these put on love, which binds everything together in perfect harmony. ¹⁵And let the peace of Christ rule in your

ὀργὴ   τοῦ   θεοῦ·   7 ἐν   οἷς   καὶ   ὑμεῖς
wrath   -   of God;   in   which   indeed   ye

περιεπατήσατέ   ποτε,   ὅτε   ἐζῆτε   ἐν   τούτοις·
walked   then,   when   ye lived   in   these things;

8 νυνὶ   δὲ   ἀπόθεσθε   καὶ   ὑμεῖς   τὰ   πάντα,
but now   ¹put ²away   ⁴also   ³ye   -   all things,

ὀργήν,   θυμόν,   κακίαν,   βλασφημίαν,   αἰσχρο-
wrath,   anger,   malice,   blasphemy,   a-

λογίαν   ἐκ   τοῦ   στόματος   ὑμῶν·   9 μὴ
buse   out of   the   mouth   of you;   not

ψεύδεσθε   εἰς   ἀλλήλους,   ἀπεκδυσάμενοι   τὸν
lie ye   to   one another,   having put off   the

παλαιὸν   ἄνθρωπον   σὺν   ταῖς   πράξεσιν
old   man   with   the   practices

αὐτοῦ,   10 καὶ   ἐνδυσάμενοι   τὸν   νέον   τὸν
of him,   and   having put on   the   new man   -

ἀνακαινούμενον   εἰς   ἐπίγνωσιν   κατ'   εἰκόνα
being renewed   in   full knowledge   according   [the]
                                      to   image

τοῦ   κτίσαντος   αὐτόν,   11 ὅπου   οὐκ   ἔνι
of the [one] creating   him,   where   ⁴have no place

"Ελλην   καὶ   'Ιουδαῖος,   περιτομὴ   καὶ
¹Greek   ²and   ³Jew,   circumcision   and

ἀκροβυστία,   βάρβαρος,   Σκύθης,   δοῦλος,
uncircumcision,   barbarian,   Scythian,   slave,

ἐλεύθερος,   ἀλλὰ   πάντα   καὶ   ἐν   πᾶσιν
freeman,   but   ³all things   ⁴and   ⁵in   ⁶all

Χριστός.   12 'Ενδύσασθε   οὖν,   ὡς   ἐκλεκτοὶ
¹Christ ²[is].   Put ye on   therefore,   as   chosen ones

τοῦ   θεοῦ   ἅγιοι   καὶ   ἠγαπημένοι,   σπλάγχνα
-   of God   holy   and   having been loved,   bowels

οἰκτιρμοῦ,   χρηστότητα,   ταπεινοφροσύνην,
of compassion,   kindness,   humility,

πραΰτητα,   μακροθυμίαν,   13 ἀνεχόμενοι   ἀλ-
meekness,   long-suffering,   forbearing   one

λήλων   καὶ   χαριζόμενοι   ἑαυτοῖς,   ἐάν   τις
another   and   forgiving   yourselves,   if anyone

πρός   τινα   ἔχῃ   μομφήν·   καθὼς   καὶ   ὁ
²against ⁴anyone   ¹has   ²a complaint;   as   indeed the

κύριος   ἐχαρίσατο   ὑμῖν   οὕτως   καὶ   ὑμεῖς·
Lord   forgave   you   so   also   ye;

14 ἐπὶ   πᾶσιν   δὲ   τούτοις   τὴν   ἀγάπην,
²over   ³all   ¹and   these things   -   love,

ὅ   ἐστιν   σύνδεσμος   τῆς   τελειότητος.   15 καὶ
which is   [the] bond   -   of completeness.   And

ἡ   εἰρήνη   τοῦ   Χριστοῦ   βραβευέτω   ἐν   ταῖς
²the   ³peace   -   ⁴of Christ   ¹let ⁵rule   in   the

ᶠ Other ancient authorities add *upon the sons of disobedience* hearts, to which indeed you were called in the one body. And be thankful. ¹⁶Let the word of Christ dwell in you richly, as you teach and admonish one another in all wisdom, and as you sing psalms and hymns and spiritual songs with thankfulness in your hearts to God. ¹⁷And whatever you do, in word or deed, do everything in the name of the Lord Jesus, giving thanks to God the Father through him.

18 Wives, be subject to your husbands, as is fitting in the Lord. ¹⁹Husbands, love your wives, and do not be harsh with them. ²⁰Children, obey your parents in everything, for this pleases the Lord. ²¹Fathers, do not provoke your children, lest they become discouraged. ²²Slaves, obey in everything those who are your earthly masters, not with eyeservice, as menpleasers, but in singleness of heart, fearing the Lord. ²³Whatever

καρδίαις ὑμῶν, εἰς ἣν καὶ ἐκλήθητε
hearts   of you,   to   which indeed ye were called

ἐν ἑνὶ σώματι· καὶ εὐχάριστοι γίνεσθε.
in one body;   and   thankful   be ye.

16 ὁ λόγος τοῦ Χριστοῦ ἐνοικείτω ἐν
²The ³word – ⁴of Christ ¹let ⁵indwell in

ὑμῖν πλουσίως, ἐν πάσῃ σοφίᾳ διδάσκοντες
you   richly,   in   all   wisdom   teaching

καὶ νουθετοῦντες ἑαυτούς, ψαλμοῖς ὕμνοις
and admonishing yourselves, in psalms[,] hymns[,]

ᾠδαῖς πνευματικαῖς ἐν τῇ χάριτι ᾄδοντες
[and] ²songs ¹spiritual   with – grace   singing

ἐν ταῖς καρδίαις ὑμῶν τῷ θεῷ· 17 καὶ
in the hearts of you – to God;   and

πᾶν ὅ τι ἐὰν ποιῆτε ἐν λόγῳ ἢ ἐν
every whatever   ye do   in word or in
thing

ἔργῳ, πάντα ἐν ὀνόματι κυρίου Ἰησοῦ,
work, all things [do] in [the] name of [the] Lord Jesus,

εὐχαριστοῦντες τῷ θεῷ πατρὶ δι᾽ αὐτοῦ.
giving thanks – to God [the] through him.
Father

18 Αἱ γυναῖκες, ὑποτάσσεσθε τοῖς
The   wives,   be ye subject to the(your)

ἀνδράσιν, ὡς ἀνῆκεν ἐν κυρίῳ. 19 Οἱ
husbands,   as is befitting in [the] Lord.   The

ἄνδρες, ἀγαπᾶτε τὰς γυναῖκας καὶ μὴ
husbands, love ye the(your) wives   and not

πικραίνεσθε πρὸς αὐτάς. 20 Τὰ τέκνα,
be bitter toward them.   The children,

ὑπακούετε τοῖς γονεῦσιν κατὰ πάντα,
obey ye   the(your) parents   in all respects,

τοῦτο γὰρ εὐάρεστόν ἐστιν ἐν κυρίῳ.
for this   well-pleasing   is   in [the] Lord.

21 Οἱ πατέρες, μὴ ἐρεθίζετε τὰ τέκνα
The   fathers,   do not ye provoke the children

ὑμῶν, ἵνα μὴ ἀθυμῶσιν. 22 Οἱ δοῦλοι,
of you,   lest they be disheartened. The slaves,

ὑπακούετε κατὰ πάντα τοῖς κατὰ σάρκα
obey ye   in all respects ¹the ²accord- ⁴[the]
                         (your) ing to flesh

κυρίοις, μὴ ἐν ὀφθαλμοδουλίαις ὡς
²lords,   not with   eyeservice   as

ἀνθρωπάρεσκοι, ἀλλ᾽ ἐν ἁπλότητι καρδίας
men-pleasers,   but in   singleness of heart

φοβούμενοι τὸν κύριον. 23 ὃ ἐὰν ποιῆτε,
fearing   the Lord.   Whatever ye do,

your task, work heartily, as serving the Lord and not men, [24] knowing that from the Lord you will receive the inheritance as your reward; you are serving the Lord Christ. [25] For the wrongdoer will be paid back for the wrong he has done, and there is no partiality.

ἐκ ψυχῆς ἐργάζεσθε ὡς τῷ κυρίῳ καὶ
from [the] soul   work ye   as   to the   Lord   and

οὐκ ἀνθρώποις, 24 εἰδότες ὅτι ἀπὸ κυρίου
not   to men,   knowing   that   from [the] Lord

ἀπολήμψεσθε τὴν ἀνταπόδοσιν τῆς κλη-
ye will receive   the   reward   of the   in-

ρονομίας. τῷ κυρίῳ Χριστῷ δουλεύετε·
heritance.   The   Lord   Christ   ye serve;

25 ὁ γὰρ ἀδικῶν κομίσεται ὃ ἠδίκησεν,
for the [one]   doing wrong   will receive   what he did wrong,

καὶ οὐκ ἔστιν προσωπολημψία. 4 Οἱ κύριοι,
and   there is no   respect of persons.   The lords,

CHAPTER 4

MASTERS, treat your slaves justly and fairly, knowing that you also have a Master in heaven.

2 Continue steadfastly in prayer, being watchful in it with thanksgiving; [3] and pray for us also, that God may open to us a door for the word, to declare the mystery of Christ, on account of which I am in prison, [4] that I may make it clear, as I ought to speak.

5 Conduct yourselves wisely toward outsiders, making the most of the time. [6] Let your speech always be gracious, seasoned with salt, so that you may know how you ought to answer every one.

7 Tych'icus will tell you all about my affairs;

τὸ δίκαιον καὶ τὴν ἰσότητα τοῖς δούλοις
³the ²just thing ⁴and ⁵the ⁶equality ⁷to the(your) ⁸slaves

παρέχεσθε, εἰδότες ὅτι καὶ ὑμεῖς ἔχετε
¹supply ye,   knowing   that   also   ye   have

κύριον ἐν οὐρανῷ.
a Lord   in   heaven.

2 Τῇ προσευχῇ προσκαρτερεῖτε, γρηγο-
In the   prayer   continue ye,   watch-

ροῦντες ἐν αὐτῇ ἐν εὐχαριστίᾳ, 3 προσευ-
ing   in   it   with   thanksgiving,   pray-

χόμενοι ἅμα καὶ περὶ ἡμῶν, ἵνα ὁ
ing   together   also   concerning   us,   in order   –
    that

θεὸς ἀνοίξῃ ἡμῖν θύραν τοῦ λόγου,
God   may open   to us   a door   of the   word,

λαλῆσαι τὸ μυστήριον τοῦ Χριστοῦ, δι'
to speak   the   mystery   –   of   because
       Christ,   of

ὃ καὶ δέδεμαι, 4 ἵνα φανερώσω αὐτὸ
which indeed I have been   in order   I may manifest   it
   bound,   that

ὡς δεῖ με λαλῆσαι. 5 Ἐν σοφίᾳ
as   it behoves   me   to speak.   In   wisdom

περιπατεῖτε πρὸς τοὺς ἔξω, ⁵τὸν καιρὸν
walk ye   toward the ones outside,   ⁴the   ³time

ἐξαγοραζόμενοι. 6 ὁ λόγος ὑμῶν πάντοτε
¹redeeming.   The speech   of you   always
     [let it be]

ἐν χάριτι, ἅλατι ἠρτυμένος, εἰδέναι πῶς
in   grace,   with salt   having been   to know   how
     seasoned,

δεῖ ὑμᾶς ἑνὶ ἑκάστῳ ἀποκρίνεσθαι.
it be-   you   ³one   ²each   ¹to answer.
hoves

7 Τὰ κατ' ἐμὲ πάντα γνωρίσει ὑμῖν Τύχικος
²The ³about ⁴me ¹all   ⁶will make ⁷to you   ⁵Tychicus
things   known

he is a beloved brother and faithful minister and fellow servant in the Lord. [8]I have sent him to you for this very purpose, that you may know how we are and that he may encourage your hearts, [9]and with him Ones'imus, the faithful and beloved brother, who is one of yourselves. They will tell you of everything that has taken place here.

10 Aristar'chus my fellow prisoner greets you, and Mark the cousin of Barnabas (concerning whom you have received instructions—if he comes to you, receive him), [11]and Jesus who is called Justus. These are the only men of the circumcision among my fellow workers for the kingdom of God, and they have been a comfort to me. [12]Ep'aphras, who is one of yourselves, a servant of Christ Jesus, greets you, always remembering you earnestly in his prayers, that you may stand mature and fully assured in all the will of God. [13]For I bear him witness that he has worked hard for you and for those in La-odice'a and in

ὁ ἀγαπητὸς ἀδελφὸς καὶ πιστὸς διάκονος
the beloved brother and faithful minister

καὶ σύνδουλος ἐν κυρίῳ, 8 ὃν ἔπεμψα
and fellow-slave in [the] Lord, whom I sent

πρὸς ὑμᾶς εἰς αὐτὸ τοῦτο, ἵνα γνῶτε
to you for this very thing, in order ye might
that know

τὰ περὶ ἡμῶν καὶ παρακαλέσῃ τὰς
the concern- us and he might comfort the
things ing

καρδίας ὑμῶν, 9 σὺν Ὀνησίμῳ τῷ πιστῷ
hearts of you, with Onesimus the faithful

καὶ ἀγαπητῷ ἀδελφῷ, ὅς ἐστιν ἐξ ὑμῶν·
and beloved brother, who is of you;

πάντα ὑμῖν γνωρίσουσιν τὰ ὧδε.
[1]all [5]to you [4]they will [2]the [3]here.
make known things

10 Ἀσπάζεται ὑμᾶς Ἀρίσταρχος ὁ
[2]greets [3]you [1]Aristarchus [4]the

συναιχμάλωτός μου, καὶ Μάρκος ὁ ἀνεψιὸς
[5]fellow-captive [6]of me, and Mark the cousin

Βαρναβᾶ, (περὶ οὗ ἐλάβετε ἐντολάς, ἐὰν
of Barnabas, (concerning whom ye received commandments, if

ἔλθῃ πρὸς ὑμᾶς, δέξασθε αὐτόν,) 11 καὶ
he comes to you, receive ye him,) and

Ἰησοῦς ὁ λεγόμενος Ἰοῦστος, οἱ ὄντες
Jesus the [one] being named Justus, the [ones] being

ἐκ περιτομῆς οὗτοι μόνοι συνεργοὶ εἰς
of [the] circumcision these only fellow-workers for

τὴν βασιλείαν τοῦ θεοῦ, οἵτινες ἐγενή-
the kingdom — of God, who be-

θησάν μοι παρηγορία. 12 ἀσπάζεται ὑμᾶς
came to me a comfort. [2]greets [3]you

Ἐπαφρᾶς ὁ ἐξ ὑμῶν, δοῦλος Χριστοῦ
[1]Epaphras the [one] of you, a slave of Christ

Ἰησοῦ, πάντοτε ἀγωνιζόμενος ὑπὲρ ὑμῶν
Jesus, always struggling on behalf of you

ἐν ταῖς προσευχαῖς, ἵνα σταθῆτε τέλειοι
in the prayers, in order ye may complete
that stand

καὶ πεπληροφορημένοι ἐν παντὶ θελήματι
and having been fully assured in all [the] will

τοῦ Θεοῦ. 13 μαρτυρῶ γὰρ αὐτῷ ὅτι
— of God. For I bear witness to him that

ἔχει πολὺν πόνον ὑπὲρ ὑμῶν καὶ τῶν
he has much distress on behalf of you and the ones

ἐν Λαοδικείᾳ καὶ τῶν ἐν Ἱεραπόλει.
in Laodicea and the ones in Hierapolis.

Hi-erap′olis. ¹⁴Luke the beloved physician and Demas greet you. ¹⁵Give my greetings to the brethren at La-odice′a, and to Nympha and the church in her house. ¹⁶And when this letter has been read among you, have it read also in the church of the La-odice′ans; and see that you read also the letter from La-odice′a. ¹⁷And say to Archip′pus, "See that you fulfil the ministry which you have received in the Lord."

18 I, Paul, write this greeting with my own hand. Remember my fetters. Grace be with you.

14 ἀσπάζεται ὑμᾶς Λουκᾶς ὁ ἰατρὸς ὁ
⁷greets   ⁸you   ¹Luke   ⁹the   ⁶physician –

ἀγαπητὸς καὶ Δημᾶς.   15 Ἀσπάσασθε
²beloved   ⁵and   ⁹Demas.   Greet ye

τοὺς ἐν Λαοδικείᾳ ἀδελφοὺς καὶ Νύμφαν
¹the ²in ⁴Laodicea ³brothers and Nymphas

καὶ τὴν κατ᾽ οἶκον αὐτῆς ἐκκλησίαν.
and ¹the ³at ⁴[the] house ⁵of her ²church.

16 καὶ ὅταν ἀναγνωσθῇ παρ᾽ ὑμῖν ἡ
And whenever is read before you the(this)

ἐπιστολή, ποιήσατε ἵνα καὶ ἐν τῇ
epistle,   cause   in order that ⁴also   ³in   ⁴the

Λαοδικέων ἐκκλησίᾳ ἀναγνωσθῇ, καὶ τὴν
⁶of [the] ¹church ²it is read, and ⁵the
Laodiceans [one]

ἐκ Λαοδικείας ἵνα καὶ ὑμεῖς ἀναγνῶτε.
⁶of ⁷Laodicea ¹in order ²also ³ye ⁴read.
that

17 καὶ εἴπατε Ἀρχίππῳ· βλέπε τὴν
And tell   Archippus : Look [to] the

διακονίαν ἣν παρέλαβες ἐν κυρίῳ, ἵνα
ministry which thou receivedst in [the] Lord, in order that

αὐτὴν πληροῖς.
²it ¹thou mayest fulfil.

18 Ὁ ἀσπασμὸς τῇ ἐμῇ χειρὶ Παύλου.
The greeting – by my my hand[,] of Paul.

μνημονεύετέ μου τῶν δεσμῶν. ἡ χάρις
Remember ye of me the bonds. – Grace [be]

μεθ᾽ ὑμῶν.
with you.

I.
THESSALONIANS
1

CHAPTER 1

PAUL, Silva′nus, and Timothy,

To the church of the Thessalo′nians in God the Father and the Lord Jesus Christ:

Grace to you and peace.

2 We give thanks to God always for you all,

ΠΡΟΣ ΘΕΣΣΑΛΟΝΙΚΕΙΣ Α
To Thessalonians 1

1 Παῦλος καὶ Σιλουανὸς καὶ Τιμόθεος
Paul and Silvanus and Timothy

τῇ ἐκκλησίᾳ Θεσσαλονικέων ἐν θεῷ πατρὶ
to the church of [the] Thessalonians in God [the] Father

καὶ κυρίῳ Ἰησοῦ Χριστῷ· χάρις ὑμῖν
and [the] Lord Jesus Christ: Grace [be] to you

καὶ εἰρήνη.
and peace.

2 Εὐχαριστοῦμεν τῷ θεῷ πάντοτε περὶ
We give thanks – to God always concerning

constantly mentioning you in our prayers, [3] remembering before our God and Father your work of faith and labor of love and steadfastness of hope in our Lord Jesus Christ. [4] For we know, brethren beloved by God, that he has chosen you; [5] for our gospel came to you not only in word, but also in power and in the Holy Spirit and with full conviction. You know what kind of men we proved to be among you for your sake. [6] And you became imitators of us and of the Lord, for you received the word in much affliction, with joy inspired by the Holy Spirit; [7] so that you became an example to all the believers in Macedo'nia and in Acha'ia. [8] For not only has the word of the Lord sounded forth from you in Macedo'nia and Acha'ia, but your faith in God has gone forth everywhere, so that we need not say anything. [9] For they them-

πάντων ὑμῶν, μνείαν ποιούμενοι ἐπὶ τῶν
[2]all [1]you, mention making on(in) the

προσευχῶν ἡμῶν, ἀδιαλείπτως 3 μνημο-
prayers of us, unceasingly remember-

νεύοντες ὑμῶν τοῦ ἔργου τῆς πίστεως
ing of you the work – of faith

καὶ τοῦ κόπου τῆς ἀγάπης καὶ τῆς
and the labour – of love and the

ὑπομονῆς τῆς ἐλπίδος τοῦ κυρίου ἡμῶν
endurance – of hope of(in) the Lord of us

Ἰησοῦ Χριστοῦ ἔμπροσθεν τοῦ θεοῦ καὶ
Jesus Christ before the God and

πατρὸς ἡμῶν, 4 εἰδότες, ἀδελφοὶ ἠγαπημένοι
Father of us, knowing, brothers having been loved

ὑπὸ [τοῦ] θεοῦ, τὴν ἐκλογὴν ὑμῶν,
by – God, the choice of you,

5 ὅτι τὸ εὐαγγέλιον ἡμῶν οὐκ ἐγενήθη
because the gospel of us became not

εἰς ὑμᾶς ἐν λόγῳ μόνον, ἀλλὰ καὶ ἐν
to you in word only, but also in

δυνάμει καὶ ἐν πνεύματι ἁγίῳ καὶ
power and in Spirit Holy and

πληροφορίᾳ πολλῇ, καθὼς οἴδατε οἷοι
[2]assurance [1]much, as ye know what sort

ἐγενήθημεν ἐν ὑμῖν δι' ὑμᾶς. 6 καὶ
we were among you because of you. And

ὑμεῖς μιμηταὶ ἡμῶν ἐγενήθητε καὶ τοῦ
[1]ye [2]imitators [4]of us [3]became and of the

κυρίου, δεξάμενοι τὸν λόγον ἐν θλίψει
Lord, welcoming the word in [3]affliction

πολλῇ μετὰ χαρᾶς πνεύματος ἁγίου, 7 ὥστε
[1]much with joy of [2]Spirit [1][the] Holy, so as

γενέσθαι ὑμᾶς τύπον πᾶσιν τοῖς πιστεύουσιν
to become you[b] a pattern to all the [ones] believing
– so that ye became

ἐν τῇ Μακεδονίᾳ καὶ ἐν τῇ Ἀχαίᾳ.
in – Macedonia and in – Achaia.

8 ἀφ' ὑμῶν γὰρ ἐξήχηται ὁ λόγος τοῦ
[2]from [3]you [1]For sounded the word of the

κυρίου οὐ μόνον ἐν τῇ Μακεδονίᾳ καὶ
Lord not only in – Macedonia and

Ἀχαίᾳ, ἀλλ' ἐν παντὶ τόπῳ ἡ πίστις
Achaia, but in every place the faith

ὑμῶν ἡ πρὸς τὸν θεὸν ἐξελήλυθεν, ὥστε
of you – toward – God has gone out, so as

μὴ χρείαν ἔχειν ἡμᾶς λαλεῖν τι· 9 αὐτοὶ
not need to have us[b] to speak anything; [3][them]-
– so that we have no need selves

selves report concerning us what a welcome we had among you, and how you turned to God from idols, to serve a living and true God, ¹⁰and to wait for his Son from heaven, whom he raised from the dead, Jesus who delivers us from the wrath to come.

γὰρ περὶ ἡμῶν ἀπαγγέλλουσιν ὁποίαν
¹for ⁴concerning ⁵us ³they relate what sort of

εἴσοδον ἔσχομεν πρὸς ὑμᾶς, καὶ πῶς
entrance we had to you, and how

ἐπεστρέψατε πρὸς τὸν θεὸν ἀπὸ τῶν
ye turned to – God from the

εἰδώλων δουλεύειν θεῷ ζῶντι καὶ ἀληθινῷ,
idols to serve a God living and true,

10 καὶ ἀναμένειν τὸν υἱὸν αὐτοῦ ἐκ
and to await the Son of him from

τῶν οὐρανῶν, ὃν ἤγειρεν ἐκ τῶν νεκρῶν,
the heavens, whom he raised from the dead,

Ἰησοῦν τὸν ῥυόμενον ἡμᾶς ἐκ τῆς ὀργῆς
Jesus the [one] delivering us from the wrath

τῆς ἐρχομένης.
– coming.

CHAPTER 2

FOR you yourselves know, brethren, that our visit to you was not in vain; ²but though we had already suffered and been shamefully treated at Philippi, as you know, we had courage in our God to declare to you the gospel of God in the face of great opposition. ³For our appeal does not spring from error or uncleanness, nor is it made with guile; ⁴but just as we have been approved by God to be entrusted with the gospel, so we speak, not to please men, but to please God who tests our hearts. ⁵For we never used either words of flattery, as you know, or a cloak

2 Αὐτοὶ γὰρ οἴδατε, ἀδελφοί, τὴν
For [your]selves ye know, brothers, the

εἴσοδον ἡμῶν τὴν πρὸς ὑμᾶς, ὅτι οὐ
entrance of us – to you, that not

κενὴ γέγονεν, 2 ἀλλὰ προπαθόντες καὶ
in vain it has been, but having previously and
suffered

ὑβρισθέντες καθὼς οἴδατε ἐν Φιλίπποις
having been as ye know in Philippi
insulted

ἐπαρρησιασάμεθα ἐν τῷ θεῷ ἡμῶν λαλῆσαι
we were bold in the God of us to speak

πρὸς ὑμᾶς τὸ εὐαγγέλιον τοῦ θεοῦ ἐν
to you the gospel – of God in

πολλῷ ἀγῶνι. 3 ἡ γὰρ παράκλησις
much struggle. For the exhortation

ἡμῶν οὐκ ἐκ πλάνης οὐδὲ ἐξ ἀκαθαρσίας
of us not of error nor of uncleanness

οὐδὲ ἐν δόλῳ, 4 ἀλλὰ καθὼς δεδοκιμάσμεθα
nor in guile, but as we have been
approved

ὑπὸ τοῦ θεοῦ πιστευθῆναι τὸ εὐαγγέλιον
by – God to be entrusted [with] the gospel

οὕτως λαλοῦμεν, οὐχ ὡς ἀνθρώποις ἀρέ-
so we speak, not as ¹men ¹pleas-

σκοντες, ἀλλὰ θεῷ τῷ δοκιμάζοντι τὰς
ing, but God the [one] proving the

καρδίας ἡμῶν. 5 οὔτε γὰρ ποτε ἐν
hearts of us. For neither then with

λόγῳ κολακείας ἐγενήθημεν, καθὼς οἴδατε,
word of flattery were we, as ye know,

for greed, as God is witness; [6]nor did we seek glory from men, whether from you or from others, though we might have made demands as apostles of Christ. [7]But we were gentle[a] among you, like a nurse taking care of her children. [8]So, being affectionately desirous of you, we were ready to share with you not only the gospel of God but also our own selves, because you had become very dear to us.

9 For you remember our labor and toil, brethren; we worked night and day, that we might not burden any of you, while we preached to you the gospel of God. [10]You are witnesses, and God also, how holy and righteous and blameless was our behavior to you believers; [11]for you know how, like a father with his children, we exhorted each one of you and encouraged you and charged you [12]to lead a life worthy of God, who

οὔτε	ἐν	προφάσει	πλεονεξίας,	θεὸς	μάρτυς,
nor	with	pretext	of covetousness,	God [is]	witness,

6 οὔτε	ζητοῦντες	ἐξ	ἀνθρώπων	δόξαν,
nor	seeking	from	men	glory,

οὔτε	ἀφ'	ὑμῶν	οὔτε	ἀπ'	ἄλλων,	7 δυνάμε-
neither	from	you	nor	from	others,	being

νοι	ἐν	βάρει	εἶναι	ὡς	Χριστοῦ	ἀπόστολοι·
able	[1]with	[2]weight*	[1]to be	as	[2]of Christ	[1]apostles;

ἀλλὰ	ἐγενήθημεν	ἤπιοι	ἐν	[the] μέσῳ	ὑμῶν,
but	we were	gentle	in [the]	midst	of you,

ὡς	ἐὰν	τροφὸς	θάλπῃ	τὰ	ἑαυτῆς	τέκνα·
as	if	a nurse	should cherish	[1]the	[2]of herself	[3]children;

8 οὕτως	ὁμειρόμενοι	ὑμῶν	ηὐδοκοῦμεν
so	longing for	you	we were well pleased

μεταδοῦναι	ὑμῖν	οὐ	μόνον	τὸ	εὐαγγέλιον
to impart	to you	not	only	the	gospel

τοῦ	θεοῦ	ἀλλὰ	καὶ	τὰς	ἑαυτῶν	ψυχάς,
–	of God	but	also	[1]the	[2]of ourselves	[3]souls,

διότι	ἀγαπητοὶ	ἡμῖν	ἐγενήθητε.	9 μνημο-
because	[2]beloved	[3]to us	[1]ye became.	ye re-

νεύετε	γάρ,	ἀδελφοί,	τὸν	κόπον	ἡμῶν
member	For,	brothers,	the	labour	of us

καὶ	τὸν	μόχθον·	νυκτὸς	καὶ	ἡμέρας
and	the	toil;	night	and	day

ἐργαζόμενοι	πρὸς	τὸ	μὴ	ἐπιβαρῆσαί	τινα
working	for	the	not	to put a burden on	any-one

ὑμῶν	ἐκηρύξαμεν	εἰς	ὑμᾶς	τὸ	εὐαγγέλιον
of you	we proclaimed	to	you	the	gospel

τοῦ	θεοῦ.	10 ὑμεῖς	μάρτυρες	καὶ	ὁ
–	of God.	Ye [are]	witnesses	and	–

θεός,	ὡς	ὁσίως	καὶ	δικαίως	καὶ	ἀμέμπτως
God,	how	holily	and	righteously	and	blamelessly

ὑμῖν	τοῖς	πιστεύουσιν	ἐγενήθημεν,	11 καθά-
[1]to you	[2]the [ones]	[3]believing	[1]we were,	even

περ	οἴδατε	ὡς	ἕνα	ἕκαστον	ὑμῶν	ὡς
as	ye know	how	[2]one	[1]each	of you	as

πατὴρ	τέκνα	ἑαυτοῦ	παρακαλοῦντες	ὑμᾶς
a father	children	of himself	exhorting	you

καὶ	παραμυθούμενοι	12 καὶ	μαρτυρόμενοι	εἰς
and	consoling	and	witnessing	for

τὸ	περιπατεῖν	ὑμᾶς	ἀξίως	τοῦ	θεοῦ
the	to walk	you[b]	worthily	–	of God
	=that ye should walk				

[a] Other ancient authorities read *babes*

* ? dignity, authority.

calls you into his own kingdom and glory.

13 And we also thank God constantly for this, that when you received the word of God which you heard from us, you accepted it not as the word of men but as what it really is, the word of God, which is at work in you believers. [14] For you, brethren, became imitators of the churches of God in Christ Jesus which are in Judea; for you suffered the same things from your own countrymen as they did from the Jews, [15] who killed both the Lord Jesus and the prophets, and drove us out, and displease God and oppose all men [16] by hindering us from speaking to the Gentiles that they may be saved—so as always to fill up the measure of their sins. But God's wrath has come upon them at last![b]

17 But since we were bereft of you, brethren,

τοῦ   καλοῦντος   ὑμᾶς   εἰς   τὴν   ἑαυτοῦ
the [one] calling   you   to   [1]the   [5]of himself

βασιλείαν   καὶ   δόξαν.
[2]kingdom   [3]and   [4]glory.

13 Καὶ   διὰ   τοῦτο   καὶ   ἡμεῖς   εὐχαρισ-
   And   therefore   also   we   give

τοῦμεν   τῷ   θεῷ   ἀδιαλείπτως,   ὅτι   παρα-
thanks   –   to God   unceasingly,   that   having

λαβόντες   λόγον   ἀκοῆς   παρ'   ἡμῶν   τοῦ
received   [1][the] word [2]of hearing [4]from   [5]us   –

θεοῦ   ἐδέξασθε   οὐ   λόγον   ἀνθρώπων   ἀλλὰ
[3]of God ye welcomed not   [as] a   of men   but
                             [it] word

καθὼς   ἀληθῶς   ἐστιν   λόγον   θεοῦ,   ὃς
as   truly   it is   a word   of God, which

καὶ   ἐνεργεῖται   ἐν   ὑμῖν   τοῖς   πιστεύουσιν.
also   operates   in   you   the [ones] believing.

14 ὑμεῖς   γὰρ   μιμηταὶ   ἐγενήθητε,   ἀδελφοί,
   For ye   [2]imitators   [1]became,   brothers,

τῶν   ἐκκλησιῶν   τοῦ   θεοῦ   τῶν   οὐσῶν   ἐν
of the   churches   –   of God   –   being   in

τῇ   Ἰουδαίᾳ   ἐν   Χριστῷ   Ἰησοῦ,   ὅτι   τὰ
–   Judæa   in   Christ   Jesus,   because [4]the

αὐτὰ   ἐπάθετε   καὶ   ὑμεῖς   ὑπὸ   τῶν   ἰδίων
[5]same   [3]suffered   [2]also   [1]ye   by   the(your) own
things

συμφυλετῶν,   καθὼς   καὶ   αὐτοὶ   ὑπὸ   τῶν
fellow-tribesmen,   as   also   they   by   the

Ἰουδαίων,   15 τῶν   καὶ   τὸν   κύριον
Jews,   the [ones] [1]both   [3]the   [4]Lord

ἀποκτεινάντων   Ἰησοῦν   καὶ   τοὺς   προφήτας,
[2]killing   [3]Jesus   and   the   prophets,

καὶ   ἡμᾶς   ἐκδιωξάντων,   καὶ   θεῷ   μὴ
and   [2]us   [1]chasing [2]out,   and   [3]God   [1]not

ἀρεσκόντων,   καὶ   πᾶσιν   ἀνθρώποις   ἐναντίων,
[3]pleasing,   and   to all   men   contrary,

16 κωλυόντων   ἡμᾶς   τοῖς   ἔθνεσιν   λαλῆσαι
   hindering   us   [2]to the   [3]nations   [1]to speak
                                              =from speaking . . .

ἵνα   σωθῶσιν,   εἰς   τὸ   ἀναπληρῶσαι   αὐτῶν
in order they may   for   the   to fill up   [5]of them
that   be saved,

τὰς   ἁμαρτίας   πάντοτε.   ἔφθασεν   δὲ   ἐπ'
[1]the   [2]sins   always.   [3]came   But   [4]on

αὐτοὺς   ἡ   ὀργὴ   εἰς   τέλος.
[5]them   [1]the   [2]wrath   to [the] end.

17 Ἡμεῖς   δέ,   ἀδελφοί,   ἀπορφανισθέντες
   But we   brothers,   being bereaved

[b] Or *completely*, or *for ever*

for a short time, in person not in heart, we endeavored the more eagerly and with great desire to see you face to face; [18] because we wanted to come to you— I, Paul, again and again —but Satan hindered us. [19] For what is our hope or joy or crown of boasting before our Lord Jesus at his coming? Is it not you? [20] For you are our glory and joy.

ἀφ'	ὑμῶν	πρὸς	καιρὸν	ὥρας	προσώπῳ
from	you	for	time	of an hour	in face
					(presence)

οὐ	καρδίᾳ,	περισσοτέρως	ἐσπουδάσαμεν	τὸ
not	in heart,	more abundantly	were eager	[the

πρόσωπον	ὑμῶν	ἰδεῖν	ἐν	πολλῇ	ἐπιθυμίᾳ.
[face	[of you	[to see	with	much	desire.

18 διότι	ἠθελήσαμεν	ἐλθεῖν	πρὸς	ὑμᾶς,
Wherefore	we wished	to come	to	you,

ἐγὼ	μὲν	Παῦλος	καὶ	ἅπαξ	καὶ	δίς,
I	[indeed	[Paul	both	once	and	twice
						(again),

καὶ	ἐνέκοψεν	ἡμᾶς	ὁ	σατανᾶς.	**19** τίς
and	[hindered	[us	-	[Satan.	what

γὰρ	ἡμῶν	ἐλπὶς	ἢ	χαρὰ	ἢ	στέφανος
For [is]	of us	[hope	or	joy	or	crown

καυχήσεως	—	ἢ	οὐχὶ	καὶ	ὑμεῖς	—
of boasting	—	—	not even	ye	—

ἔμπροσθεν	τοῦ	κυρίου	ἡμῶν	Ἰησοῦ
before	the	Lord	of us	Jesus

ἐν	τῇ	αὐτοῦ	παρουσίᾳ;	**20** ὑμεῖς	γάρ
in(at)	the	[of him	[presence?	for ye

ἐστε	ἡ	δόξα	ἡμῶν	καὶ	ἡ	χαρά.
are	[the	[glory	[of us	[and	[the	[joy.

CHAPTER 3

THEREFORE when we could bear it no longer, we were willing to be left behind at Athens alone, [2] and we sent Timothy, our brother and God's servant in the gospel of Christ, to establish you in your faith and to exhort you, [3] that no one be moved by these afflictions. You yourselves know that this is to be our lot. [4] For when we were with you, we told you beforehand that we were to suffer affliction; just as it has come to pass, and as you know.

3 Διὸ	μηκέτι	στέγοντες	ηὐδοκήσαμεν
Wherefore	no longer	bearing up	we were well pleased

καταλειφθῆναι	ἐν	Ἀθήναις	μόνοι,	**2** καὶ
to be left	in	Athens	alone,	and

ἐπέμψαμεν	Τιμόθεον,	τὸν	ἀδελφὸν	ἡμῶν
we sent	Timothy,	the	brother	of us

καὶ	συνεργὸν	τοῦ	θεοῦ	ἐν	τῷ	εὐαγγελίῳ
and	fellow-worker	-	of God	in	the	gospel

τοῦ	Χριστοῦ,	εἰς	τὸ	στηρίξαι	ὑμᾶς	καὶ
-	of Christ,	for	the	to establish	you	and

παρακαλέσαι	ὑπὲρ	τῆς	πίστεως	ὑμῶν	**3** τὸ
to exhort	on behalf of the	faith	of you	-

μηδένα	σαίνεσθαι	ἐν	ταῖς	θλίψεσιν	ταύταις.
no one	to be drawn	by	these	afflictions.
	asideᵇ

αὐτοὶ	γὰρ	οἴδατε	ὅτι	εἰς	τοῦτο	κείμεθα·
For [your]selves	ye know	that	to	this	we are
						appointed;

4 καὶ	γὰρ	ὅτε	πρὸς	ὑμᾶς	ἦμεν,
	for even	when	with	you	we were,

προελέγομεν	ὑμῖν	ὅτι	μέλλομεν	θλίβεσθαι,
we said before	to you	that	we are about	to be afflicted,

καθὼς	καὶ	ἐγένετο	καὶ	οἴδατε.	**5** διὰ
as	indeed	it happened	and	ye know.	There-

⁵For this reason, when I could bear it no longer, I sent that I might know your faith, for fear that somehow the tempter had tempted you and that our labor would be in vain.

6 But now that Timothy has come to us from you, and has brought us the good news of your faith and love and reported that you always remember us kindly and long to see us, as we long to see you— ⁷for this reason, brethren, in all our distress and affliction we have been comforted about you through your faith; ⁸for now we live, if you stand fast in the Lord.

⁹For what thanksgiving can we render to God for you, for all the joy which we feel for your sake before our God, ¹⁰praying earnestly night and day that we may see you face to face and supply what is lacking in your faith?

11 Now may our God and Father himself, and our Lord Jesus, direct our way to you; ¹²and

Greek	English
τοῦτο κἀγὼ μηκέτι στέγων ἔπεμψα εἰς	fore I also no longer bearing up sent for
τὸ γνῶναι τὴν πίστιν ὑμῶν, μή πως	the to know the faith of you, lest [some]how
ἐπείρασεν ὑμᾶς ὁ πειράζων καὶ εἰς	³tempted ⁴you ¹the [one] ²tempting and in =the tempter
κενὸν γένηται ὁ κόπος ἡμῶν. 6 Ἄρτι	vain became the labour of us. now
δὲ ἐλθόντος Τιμοθέου πρὸς ἡμᾶς ἀφ'	But coming Timothy³ to us from =when Timothy came
ὑμῶν καὶ εὐαγγελισαμένου ἡμῖν τὴν πίστιν	you and announcing good news³ to us [of] the faith
καὶ τὴν ἀγάπην ὑμῶν, καὶ ὅτι ἔχετε	and the love of you, and that ye have
μνείαν ἡμῶν ἀγαθὴν πάντοτε, ἐπιποθοῦντες	¹remem- ²of us ¹good always, longing brance
ἡμᾶς ἰδεῖν καθάπερ καὶ ἡμεῖς ὑμᾶς,	²us ¹to see even as also we you,
7 διὰ τοῦτο παρεκλήθημεν, ἀδελφοί, ἐφ'	therefore we were comforted, brothers, over
ὑμῖν ἐπὶ πάσῃ τῇ ἀνάγκῃ καὶ θλίψει	you on all the distress and affliction
ἡμῶν διὰ τῆς ὑμῶν πίστεως, 8 ὅτι	of us through the ²of you ¹faith, because
νῦν ζῶμεν ἐὰν ὑμεῖς στήκετε ἐν [τῷ] κυρίῳ.	now we live if ye stand in [the] Lord.
9 τίνα γὰρ εὐχαριστίαν δυνάμεθα τῷ θεῷ	For what thanks are we able - to God
ἀνταποδοῦναι περὶ ὑμῶν ἐπὶ πάσῃ τῇ	to return concerning you over all the
χαρᾷ ᾗ χαίρομεν δι' ὑμᾶς ἔμπροσθεν	joy [with] we rejoice because you before which of
τοῦ θεοῦ ἡμῶν, 10 νυκτὸς καὶ ἡμέρας	the God of us, night and day
ὑπερεκπερισσοῦ δεόμενοι εἰς τὸ ἰδεῖν ὑμῶν	exceedingly petitioning for the to see of you
τὸ πρόσωπον καὶ καταρτίσαι τὰ ὑστερήματα	the face and to adjust the shortcomings
τῆς πίστεως ὑμῶν; 11 Αὐτὸς δὲ ὁ θεὸς	of the faith of you? Now [him]self the God
καὶ πατὴρ ἡμῶν καὶ ὁ κύριος ἡμῶν	and Father of us and the Lord of us
Ἰησοῦς κατευθύναι τὴν ὁδὸν ἡμῶν πρὸς	Jesus may he direct the way of us to

may the Lord make you increase and abound in love to one another and to all men, as we do to you, [13]so that he may establish your hearts unblamable in holiness before our God and Father, at the coming of our Lord Jesus with all his saints.

ὑμᾶς· 12 ὑμᾶς δὲ ὁ κύριος πλεονάσαι
you;   and [4]you   [1]the [2]Lord [3]make [5]to abound

καὶ περισσεῦσαι τῇ ἀγάπῃ εἰς ἀλλήλους
and   to exceed   -   in love to   one another

καὶ εἰς πάντας, καθάπερ καὶ ἡμεῖς
and to all men,   even as   also   we

εἰς ὑμᾶς, 13 εἰς τὸ στηρίξαι ὑμῶν τὰς
to   you,   for the to establish of you the

καρδίας ἀμέμπτους ἐν ἁγιωσύνῃ ἔμπροσθεν
hearts   blameless   in   holiness   before

τοῦ θεοῦ καὶ πατρὸς ἡμῶν ἐν τῇ παρουσίᾳ
the God and Father of us in(at) the   presence

τοῦ κυρίου ἡμῶν Ἰησοῦ μετὰ πάντων
of the Lord of us Jesus with   all

τῶν ἁγίων αὐτοῦ.
the saints   of him.

CHAPTER 4

FINALLY, brethren, we beseech and exhort you in the Lord Jesus, that as you learned from us how you ought to live and to please God, just as you are doing, you do so more and more. [2]For you know what instructions we gave you through the Lord Jesus. [3]For this is the will of God, your sanctification: that you abstain from immorality; [4]that each one of you know how to take a wife for himself in holiness and honor, [5]not in the passion of lust like heathen who do not know God; [6]that no man transgress, and

4 Λοιπὸν οὖν, ἀδελφοί, ἐρωτῶμεν ὑμᾶς
For the rest therefore, brothers,   we ask   you

καὶ παρακαλοῦμεν ἐν κυρίῳ Ἰησοῦ, ἵνα
and   we beseech   in [the] Lord Jesus, in order
                                              that

καθὼς παρελάβετε παρ' ἡμῶν τὸ πῶς
as   ye received   from   us   the how

δεῖ ὑμᾶς περιπατεῖν καὶ ἀρέσκειν θεῷ,
it you   to walk   and to please God,
behoves

καθὼς καὶ περιπατεῖτε, ἵνα περισσεύητε
as   indeed ye do walk, in order that ye abound

μᾶλλον. 2 οἴδατε γὰρ τίνας παραγγελίας
more.   For ye know what   injunctions

ἐδώκαμεν ὑμῖν διὰ τοῦ κυρίου Ἰησοῦ.
we gave   you through the   Lord   Jesus.

3 Τοῦτο γάρ ἐστιν θέλημα τοῦ θεοῦ,
For this   is   [the] will   of God,

ὁ ἁγιασμὸς ὑμῶν, ἀπέχεσθαι ὑμᾶς ἀπὸ
the sanctification of you,   to abstain   you[b] from

τῆς πορνείας, 4 εἰδέναι ἕκαστον ὑμῶν
-    fornication,   [3]to know* [1]each one[b] [2]of you

τὸ ἑαυτοῦ σκεῦος κτᾶσθαι ἐν ἁγιασμῷ
[5]the [7]of himself [6]vessel [4]to possess in sanctification

καὶ τιμῇ, 5 μὴ ἐν πάθει ἐπιθυμίας
and honour,   not in passion   of lust

καθάπερ καὶ τὰ ἔθνη τὰ μὴ εἰδότα
even as   indeed the nations the not knowing

τὸν θεόν, 6 τὸ μὴ ὑπερβαίνειν καὶ
-   God,   -   not to go beyond   and

* That is, " to be able "; see note on page xviii.

wrong his brother in this matter,[c] because the Lord is an avenger in all these things, as we solemnly forewarned you. [7]For God has not called us for uncleanness, but in holiness. [8]Therefore whoever disregards this, disregards not man but God, who gives his Holy Spirit to you.

9 But concerning love of the brethren you have no need to have any one write to you, for you yourselves have been taught by God to love one another; [10]and indeed you do love all the brethren throughout Macedo′nia. But we exhort you, brethren, to do so more and more, [11]to aspire to live quietly, to mind your own affairs, and to work with your hands, as we charged you; [12]so that you may command the respect of outsiders, and be dependent on nobody.

13 But we would not have you ignorant,

πλεονεκτεῖν	ἐν τῷ	πράγματι τὸν	ἀδελφὸν
to defraud	in the	matter the	brother

αὐτοῦ,   διότι   ἔκδικος   κύριος   περὶ   πάντων
of him,   be-   [2][the]   [1][the] Lord   con-   all
          cause   avenger   cerning

τούτων,   καθὼς   καὶ   προείπαμεν   ὑμῖν   καὶ
these,   as   in-   we previously   you   and
          deed   told

διεμαρτυράμεθα.   7 οὐ   γὰρ   ἐκάλεσεν   ἡμᾶς
solemnly witnessed.   For [4]not   [2]called   [3]us

ὁ θεὸς   ἐπὶ   ἀκαθαρσίᾳ   ἀλλ᾽   ἐν   ἁγιασμῷ.
- [1]God   to   uncleanness   but   in   sanctification.

8 τοιγαροῦν   ὁ   ἀθετῶν   οὐκ   ἄνθρωπον
Wherefore   the [one] rejecting   [2]not   [3]man

ἀθετεῖ   ἀλλὰ   τὸν   θεὸν   τὸν   καὶ   διδόντα
[1]rejects   but   -   God   the   in-   giving
                                    [one]   deed

τὸ   πνεῦμα   αὐτοῦ   τὸ   ἅγιον   εἰς   ὑμᾶς.
the   [2]Spirit   [3]of him   -   [1]Holy   to   you.

9 Περὶ   δὲ   τῆς   φιλαδελφίας   οὐ   χρείαν
Now concerning   -   brotherly love   not   need

ἔχετε   γράφειν   ὑμῖν·   αὐτοὶ   γὰρ   ὑμεῖς
ye have   to write   to you;   for [2][your]selves   [1]ye
[for me]

θεοδίδακτοί   ἐστε   εἰς   τὸ   ἀγαπᾶν   ἀλλήλους·
[4]taught by God   [3]are   for   the   to love   one another;

10 καὶ   γὰρ   ποιεῖτε   αὐτὸ   εἰς   πάντας
for indeed   ye do   it   toward   all

τοὺς   ἀδελφοὺς   [τοὺς]   ἐν   ὅλῃ   τῇ   Μακεδο-
the   brothers   -   in   all   -   Macedo-

νίᾳ.   Παρακαλοῦμεν   δὲ   ὑμᾶς,   ἀδελφοί,
nia.   But we exhort   you,   brothers,

περισσεύειν   μᾶλλον,   11 καὶ   φιλοτιμεῖσθαι
to abound   more,   and   to strive eagerly

ἡσυχάζειν   καὶ   πράσσειν   τὰ   ἴδια   καὶ
to be quiet   and   to practise   the   own   and
                            (your)   things

ἐργάζεσθαι   ταῖς   χερσὶν   ὑμῶν,   καθὼς   ὑμῖν
to work   with the   hands   of you,   as   [2]you

παρηγγείλαμεν,   12 ἵνα   περιπατῆτε   εὐσχη-
[1]we enjoined,   in or-   ye may walk   becom-
                    der that

μόνως   πρὸς   τοὺς   ἔξω   καὶ   μηδενὸς
ingly   toward   the [ones] outside   and   [3]of nothing

χρείαν   ἔχητε.
[2]need   [1]ye may have.

13 Οὐ   θέλομεν   δὲ   ὑμᾶς   ἀγνοεῖν,   ἀδελφοί,
Now we do not wish   you   to be   brothers,
                            ignorant,

[c] Or defraud his brother in business

brethren, concerning those who are asleep, that you may not grieve as others do who have no hope. ¹⁴For since we believe that Jesus died and rose again, even so, through Jesus, God will bring with him those who have fallen asleep. ¹⁵For this we declare to you by the word of the Lord, that we who are alive, who are left until the coming of the Lord, shall not precede those who have fallen asleep. ¹⁶For the Lord himself will descend from heaven with a cry of command, with the archangel's call, and with the sound of the trumpet of God. And the dead in Christ will rise first; ¹⁷then we who are alive, who are left, shall be caught up together with them in the clouds to meet the Lord in the air; and so we shall always be with the Lord. ¹⁸Therefore comfort one another with these words.

περὶ τῶν κοιμωμένων, ἵνα μὴ λυπῆσθε
con-   the   sleeping,   lest   ye grieve
cerning [ones]

καθὼς καὶ οἱ λοιποὶ οἱ μὴ ἔχοντες
as   indeed the rest   –   not having

ἐλπίδα. 14 εἰ γὰρ πιστεύομεν ὅτι Ἰησοῦς
hope.   For if we believe that Jesus

ἀπέθανεν καὶ ἀνέστη, οὕτως καὶ ὁ θεὸς
died   and rose again, so   also – ²God

τοὺς κοιμηθέντας διὰ τοῦ Ἰησοῦ ἄξει
¹the ²having slept ³through – ⁴Jesus will
[ones]   bring

σὺν αὐτῷ. 15 Τοῦτο γὰρ ὑμῖν λέγομεν
with him.   For this to you we say

ἐν λόγῳ κυρίου, ὅτι ἡμεῖς οἱ ζῶντες
by a word of [the] that we   the living
         Lord,   [ones]

οἱ περιλειπόμενοι εἰς τὴν παρουσίαν τοῦ
–   remaining   to the presence of the

κυρίου οὐ μὴ φθάσωμεν τοὺς κοιμηθέντας·
Lord by no may precede the having slept;
      means   [ones]

16 ὅτι αὐτὸς ὁ κύριος ἐν κελεύσματι,
  be- ³[him]- ¹the ²Lord with a word of
  cause self   command,

ἐν φωνῇ ἀρχαγγέλου καὶ ἐν σάλπιγγι
with a voice of an archangel and with a trumpet

θεοῦ, καταβήσεται ἀπ' οὐρανοῦ, καὶ οἱ
of God, will descend from heaven,   and the

νεκροὶ ἐν Χριστῷ ἀναστήσονται πρῶτον,
dead   in Christ   will rise again   firstly,

17 ἔπειτα ἡμεῖς οἱ ζῶντες οἱ περιλειπόμενοι
  then   we   the living –   remaining
             [ones]

ἅμα σὺν αὐτοῖς ἁρπαγησόμεθα ἐν νεφέλαις
to- with them   shall be seized in clouds
gether

εἰς ἀπάντησιν τοῦ κυρίου εἰς ἀέρα·
to a meeting of the Lord   in   air;

καὶ οὕτως πάντοτε σὺν κυρίῳ ἐσόμεθα.
and so   always with [the] Lord we shall be.

18 Ὥστε παρακαλεῖτε ἀλλήλους ἐν τοῖς λόγοις
  Therefore comfort ye   one   with – words
                      another

τούτοις.
these.

CHAPTER 5

BUT as to the times and the seasons, brethren, you have no need to have anything written to you. ² For you yourselves know well that the day of the Lord will come like a thief in the night. ³ When people say, "There is peace and security," then sudden destruction will come upon them as travail comes upon a woman with child, and there will be no escape. ⁴ But you are not in darkness, brethren, for that day to surprise you like a thief. ⁵ For you are all sons of light and sons of the day; we are not of the night or of darkness. ⁶ So then let us not sleep, as others do, but let us keep awake and be sober. ⁷ For those who sleep sleep at night, and those who get drunk are drunk at night. ⁸ But, since we belong to the day, let us be sober, and put on the breastplate of faith and love, and for a helmet the hope of salvation. ⁹ For God has not destined us for wrath, but to obtain salvation through our Lord Jesus Christ, ¹⁰ who died for us so that whether we wake or

5 Περὶ δὲ τῶν χρόνων καὶ τῶν καιρῶν,
But concerning the times and the seasons,
ἀδελφοί, οὐ χρείαν ἔχετε ὑμῖν γράφεσθαι·
brothers, ²not ¹need ¹ye have ²to you ⁴to be written;
2 αὐτοὶ γὰρ ἀκριβῶς οἴδατε ὅτι ἡμέρα
for ²[your]selves ²accurately ¹ye know that [the] day
κυρίου ὡς κλέπτης ἐν νυκτὶ οὕτως
of [the] Lord as a thief at night so
ἔρχεται. 3 ὅταν λέγωσιν· εἰρήνη καὶ
it comes. Whenever they say : Peace and
ἀσφάλεια, τότε αἰφνίδιος αὐτοῖς ἐφίσταται
safety, then ¹sudden ⁴them ²comes on
ὄλεθρος ὥσπερ ἡ ὠδὶν τῇ ἐν γαστρὶ
³destruction as the birth pang to the pregnant
ἐχούσῃ, καὶ οὐ μὴ ἐκφύγωσιν. 4 ὑμεῖς
woman,† and by no may they ye
means escape.
δέ, ἀδελφοί, οὐκ ἐστὲ ἐν σκότει, ἵνα
But, brothers, are not in dark- in or-
ness, der that
ἡ ἡμέρα ὑμᾶς ὡς κλέπτης καταλάβῃ·
the day you as a thief should overtake;
5 πάντες γὰρ ὑμεῖς υἱοὶ φωτός ἐστε
for all ye ²sons ³of light ¹are
καὶ υἱοὶ ἡμέρας. Οὐκ ἐσμὲν νυκτὸς
and sons of [the] day. We are not of [the]
night
οὐδὲ σκότους· 6 ἄρα οὖν μὴ καθεύδωμεν
nor of darkness; therefore let us not sleep
ὡς οἱ λοιποί, ἀλλὰ γρηγορῶμεν καὶ
as the rest, but let us watch and
νήφωμεν. 7 οἱ γὰρ καθεύδοντες νυκτὸς
be sober. For the [ones] sleeping by night
καθεύδουσιν, καὶ οἱ μεθυσκόμενοι νυκτὸς
sleep, and the [ones] being drunk by night
μεθύουσιν· 8 ἡμεῖς δὲ ἡμέρας ὄντες
are drunk; but we of [the] day being
νήφωμεν, ἐνδυσάμενοι θώρακα πίστεως καὶ
let us be sober, putting on a breastplate of faith and
ἀγάπης καὶ περικεφαλαίαν ἐλπίδα σωτηρίας·
of love and a helmet hope of salvation;
9 ὅτι οὐκ ἔθετο ἡμᾶς ὁ θεὸς εἰς ὀργὴν
because ²did not appoint ³us – ¹God to wrath
ἀλλὰ εἰς περιποίησιν σωτηρίας διὰ τοῦ
but to obtainment of salvation through the
κυρίου ἡμῶν Ἰησοῦ Χριστοῦ, 10 τοῦ
Lord of us Jesus Christ, the
ἀποθανόντος περὶ ἡμῶν, ἵνα εἴτε γρηγορ-
[one] having died concern- us, in or- whether we
ing der that

sleep we might live with him. [11]Therefore encourage one another and build one another up, just as you are doing.

12 But we beseech you, brethren, to respect those who labor among you and are over you in the Lord and admonish you, [13]and to esteem them very highly in love because of their work. Be at peace among yourselves. [14]And we exhort you, brethren, admonish the idle, encourage the fainthearted, help the weak, be patient with them all. [15]See that none of you repays evil for evil, but always seek to do good to one another and to all. [16]Rejoice always, [17]pray constantly, [18]give thanks in all circumstances; for this is the will of God in Christ Jesus for you. [19]Do not quench the Spirit, [20]do not despise prophesying, [21]but test everything; hold fast what is good, [22]abstain from every form of evil.

ὦμεν　εἴτε　καθεύδωμεν　ἅμα　σὺν　αὐτῷ
watch　or　we sleep　[2]together　[1]with　[4]him

ζήσωμεν.　11 Διὸ　παρακαλεῖτε　ἀλλήλους
[1]we may live.　There-fore　comfort ye　one another

καὶ　οἰκοδομεῖτε　εἷς　τὸν　ἕνα,　καθὼς　καὶ
and　edify ye　one　the one(other),　as　indeed

ποιεῖτε.
ye do.

12 Ἐρωτῶμεν　δὲ　ὑμᾶς,　ἀδελφοί,　εἰδέναι
Now we ask　　　you,　brothers,　to know

τοὺς　κοπιῶντας　ἐν　ὑμῖν　καὶ　προϊσταμένους
the [ones]　labouring　among　you　and　taking the lead

ὑμῶν　ἐν　κυρίῳ　καὶ　νουθετοῦντας　ὑμᾶς,
of you　in　[the] Lord　and　admonishing　you,

13 καὶ　ἡγεῖσθαι　αὐτοὺς　ὑπερεκπερισσῶς
and　consider　them　most exceedingly

ἐν　ἀγάπῃ　διὰ　τὸ　ἔργον　αὐτῶν.　εἰρηνεύετε
in　love　be-cause of　the　work　of them.　Be at peace

ἐν　ἑαυτοῖς.　14 Παρακαλοῦμεν　δὲ　ὑμᾶς,
among yourselves.　　　And we exhort　　　you,

ἀδελφοί,　νουθετεῖτε　τοὺς　ἀτάκτους,　παρα-
brothers,　admonish　the　idle,　con-

μυθεῖσθε　τοὺς　ὀλιγοψύχους,　ἀντέχεσθε　τῶν
sole　the　faint-hearted,　hold on to　the [ones]

ἀσθενῶν,　μακροθυμεῖτε　πρὸς　πάντας.
being weak,　be longsuffering　with　all men.

15 ὁρᾶτε　μή　τις　κακὸν　ἀντὶ　κακοῦ　τινι
See　lest　anyone　[2]evil　[4]instead of　[3]evil　[1]to anyone

ἀποδῷ,　ἀλλὰ　πάντοτε　τὸ　ἀγαθὸν　διώκετε
[1]returns,　but　always　[3]the　[2]good　[1]follow ye

εἰς　ἀλλήλους　καὶ　εἰς　πάντας.　16 Πάντοτε
in re-gard to　one another　and　in re-gard to　all men.　Always

χαίρετε,　17 ἀδιαλείπτως　προσεύχεσθε,　18 ἐν
rejoice ye,　unceasingly　pray,　in

παντὶ　εὐχαριστεῖτε·　τοῦτο　γὰρ　θέλημα
everything　give thanks;　for this [is]　[the] will

θεοῦ　ἐν　Χριστῷ　Ἰησοῦ　εἰς　ὑμᾶς.　19 τὸ
of God　in　Christ　Jesus in regard to　you.　The

πνεῦμα　μὴ　σβέννυτε,　20 προφητείας　μὴ
Spirit　do not quench,　prophecies　not

ἐξουθενεῖτε·　21 πάντα　δὲ　δοκιμάζετε,　τὸ
despise;　and [2]all things　[1]prove,　the

καλὸν　κατέχετε·　22 ἀπὸ　παντὸς　εἴδους
good　hold fast;　from　every　form

23 May the God of peace himself sanctify you wholly; and may your spirit and soul and body be kept sound and blameless at the coming of our Lord Jesus Christ.
24 He who calls you is faithful, and he will do it.
25 Brethren, pray for us.
26 Greet all the brethren with a holy kiss.
27 I adjure you by the Lord that this letter be read to all the brethren.
28 The grace of our Lord Jesus Christ be with you.

πονηροῦ ἀπέχεσθε.
of evil   abstain.

23 Αὐτὸς δὲ ὁ θεὸς
And [him]self ¹the ¹God
τῆς εἰρήνης ἁγιάσαι ὑμᾶς ὁλοτελεῖς, καὶ
–   ³of peace may he sanctify you   complete,   and
ὁλόκληρον ὑμῶν τὸ πνεῦμα καὶ ἡ ψυχὴ
entire   of you the   spirit   and the soul
καὶ τὸ σῶμα ἀμέμπτως ἐν τῇ παρουσίᾳ
and the   body   blamelessly in(at) the   presence
τοῦ κυρίου ἡμῶν Ἰησοῦ Χριστοῦ τηρηθείη.
of the Lord   of us   Jesus   Christ   may be kept.

24 πιστὸς ὁ καλῶν ὑμᾶς, ὃς καὶ ποιήσει.
Faithful [is] the [one] calling you, who indeed will do [it].

25 Ἀδελφοί, προσεύχεσθε [καὶ] περὶ
Brothers,   pray ye   also concerning
ἡμῶν.
us.

26 Ἀσπάσασθε τοὺς ἀδελφοὺς πάντας
Greet ye   the   ³brothers   ¹all
ἐν φιλήματι ἁγίῳ. 27 Ἐνορκίζω ὑμᾶς τὸν
with kiss   a holy.   I adjure   you [by] the
κύριον ἀναγνωσθῆναι τὴν ἐπιστολὴν πᾶσιν
Lord   ²to be read   ¹the(this)   ²epistle   to all
τοῖς ἀδελφοῖς.
the   brothers.

28 Ἡ χάρις τοῦ κυρίου ἡμῶν Ἰησοῦ
The grace of the Lord   of us   Jesus
Χριστοῦ μεθ᾽ ὑμῶν.
Christ [be] with   you.

II. THESSALONIANS 1
CHAPTER 1

PAUL, Silva'nus, and Timothy.
To the church of the Thessalo'nians in God our Father and the Lord Jesus Christ:
2 Grace to you and peace from God the Father and the Lord Jesus Christ.
3 We are bound to give thanks to God

ΠΡΟΣ ΘΕΣΣΑΛΟΝΙΚΕΙΣ Β
To Thessalonians 2

1 Παῦλος καὶ Σιλουανὸς καὶ Τιμόθεος
Paul   and   Silvanus   and   Timothy
τῇ ἐκκλησίᾳ Θεσσαλονικέων ἐν θεῷ πατρὶ
to the church of [the] Thessalonians in God Father
ἡμῶν καὶ κυρίῳ Ἰησοῦ Χριστῷ· 2 χάρις
of us and [the] Lord Jesus   Christ: Grace [be]
ὑμῖν καὶ εἰρήνη ἀπὸ θεοῦ πατρὸς καὶ
to you and   peace   from God [the] Father and
κυρίου Ἰησοῦ Χριστοῦ.
[the] Lord Jesus   Christ.

3 Εὐχαριστεῖν ὀφείλομεν τῷ θεῷ πάντοτε
To give thanks   we ought   –   to God   always

always for you, brethren, as is fitting, because your faith is growing abundantly, and the love of every one of you for one another is increasing. [4]Therefore we ourselves boast of you in the churches of God for your steadfastness and faith in all your persecutions and in the afflictions which you are enduring.

5 This is evidence of the righteous judgment of God, that you may be made worthy of the kingdom of God, for which you are suffering —[6]since indeed God deems it just to repay with affliction those who afflict you, [7]and to grant rest with us to you who are afflicted, when the Lord Jesus is revealed from heaven with his mighty angels in flaming fire, [8]inflicting vengeance upon those who do not know God and upon those who do not obey the gospel of our Lord Jesus. [9]They shall suffer the punishment of eternal destruction and

περὶ ὑμῶν, ἀδελφοί, καθὼς ἄξιόν ἐστιν,
con- you, brothers, as [2]meet [1]it is,
cerning

ὅτι ὑπεραυξάνει ἡ πίστις ὑμῶν καὶ
because [4]grows [1]the [2]faith [3]of you and
       exceedingly

πλεονάζει ἡ ἀγάπη ἑνὸς ἑκάστου πάντων
[3]increases [1]the [2]love [5]one [6]of each [4]all

ὑμῶν εἰς ἀλλήλους, 4 ὥστε αὐτοὺς ἡμᾶς
[5]of you [7]to [6]one another,   so as [our]selves us
               =so that we ourselves boast

ἐν ὑμῖν ἐγκαυχᾶσθαι ἐν ταῖς ἐκκλησίαις
in you   to boast[b]   in the churches
in you

τοῦ θεοῦ ὑπὲρ τῆς ὑπομονῆς ὑμῶν καὶ
– of God for the [1]endurance [2]of you [3]and

πίστεως ἐν πᾶσιν τοῖς διωγμοῖς ὑμῶν
[1]faith in all the persecutions of you

καὶ ταῖς θλίψεσιν αἷς ἀνέχεσθε, 5 ἔνδειγμα
and the afflictions which ye endure, a plain token

τῆς δικαίας κρίσεως τοῦ θεοῦ, εἰς τὸ
of the just judgment – of God, for the

καταξιωθῆναι ὑμᾶς τῆς βασιλείας τοῦ
to be accounted you[b] of the kingdom –
worthy
=so that ye may be accounted worthy

θεοῦ, ὑπὲρ ἧς καὶ πάσχετε, 6 εἴπερ
of God, on behalf which indeed ye suffer, since
       of

δίκαιον παρὰ θεῷ ἀνταποδοῦναι τοῖς
[it is] a just with God to repay [2]to the
thing   [ones]

θλίβουσιν ὑμᾶς θλῖψιν 7 καὶ ὑμῖν τοῖς
[3]afflicting [4]you [1]affliction and [4]to you [5]the
                            [ones]

θλιβομένοις ἄνεσιν μεθ' ἡμῶν, ἐν τῇ
[6]being afflicted [1]rest [2]with [3]us, at the

ἀποκαλύψει τοῦ κυρίου Ἰησοῦ ἀπ'
revelation of the Lord Jesus from

οὐρανοῦ μετ' ἀγγέλων δυνάμεως αὐτοῦ
heaven with angels of power of him

8 ἐν πυρὶ φλογός, διδόντος ἐκδίκησιν τοῖς
in fire of flame, giving full vengeance to the
                                  [ones]

μὴ εἰδόσιν θεὸν καὶ τοῖς μὴ ὑπακούουσιν
not knowing God and to the not obeying
                       [ones]

τῷ εὐαγγελίῳ τοῦ κυρίου ἡμῶν Ἰησοῦ,
the gospel of the Lord of us Jesus,

9 οἵτινες δίκην τίσουσιν ὄλεθρον αἰώνιον
who [2][the] penalty [1]will pay [4]destruction [3]eternal

exclusion from the
presence of the Lord
and from the glory of his
might, [10] when he comes
on that day to be
glorified in his saints,
and to be marveled at in
all who have believed,
because our testimony to
you was believed. [11] To
this end we always pray
for you, that our God
may make you worthy of
his call, and may fulfil
every good resolve and
work of faith by his
power, [12] so that the
name of our Lord Jesus
may be glorified in you,
and you in him, accord-
ing to the grace of our
God and the Lord Jesus
Christ.

ἀπὸ   προσώπου   τοῦ   κυρίου   καὶ   ἀπὸ
from   [the] face   of the   Lord   and   from

τῆς   δόξης   τῆς   ἰσχύος   αὐτοῦ,   10 ὅταν
the   glory   of the   strength   of him,   whenever

ἔλθῃ   ἐνδοξασθῆναι   ἐν   τοῖς   ἁγίοις   αὐτοῦ
he comes   to be glorified   in   the   saints   of him

καὶ   θαυμασθῆναι   ἐν   πᾶσιν   τοῖς   πιστεύσασιν,
and   to be admired   in   all   the [ones] having believed,

ὅτι   ἐπιστεύθη   τὸ   μαρτύριον   ἡμῶν   ἐφ᾽
be-   ⁶was believed   ¹the   ²testimony   ³of us   ⁴to
cause

ὑμᾶς,   ἐν   τῇ   ἡμέρᾳ   ἐκείνῃ.   11 Εἰς   ὃ
⁵you,   in   the   that day.   For which

καὶ   προσευχόμεθα   πάντοτε   περὶ   ὑμῶν,
indeed   we pray   always   concerning   you,

ἵνα   ὑμᾶς   ἀξιώσῃ   τῆς   κλήσεως   ὁ   θεὸς
in or- ⁵you   ⁴may ⁶deem   ⁸of the   ⁹calling   ¹the   ²God
der that   ⁷worthy

ἡμῶν   καὶ   πληρώσῃ   πᾶσαν   εὐδοκίαν
³of us   and   may fulfil   every   good pleasure

ἀγαθωσύνης   καὶ   ἔργον   πίστεως   ἐν   δυνάμει,
of goodness   and   work   of faith   in   power,

12 ὅπως   ἐνδοξασθῇ   τὸ   ὄνομα   τοῦ   κυρίου
so as   ⁷may be glorified   ¹the   ²name   ³of the   ⁴Lord

ἡμῶν   Ἰησοῦ   ἐν   ὑμῖν,   καὶ   ὑμεῖς   ἐν
⁵of us   ⁶Jesus   in   you,   and   ye   in

αὐτῷ,   κατὰ   τὴν   χάριν   τοῦ   θεοῦ   ἡμῶν
him,   according to the   grace   of the   ¹God   ⁴of us

καὶ   κυρίου   Ἰησοῦ   Χριστοῦ.
²and   ³Lord   Jesus   Christ.

CHAPTER 2

NOW concerning the
coming of our Lord
Jesus Christ and our
assembling to meet him,
we beg you, brethren,
[2] not to be quickly
shaken in mind or
excited, either by spirit
or by word, or by letter
purporting to be from
us, to the effect that the
day of the Lord has

2 Ἐρωτῶμεν   δὲ   ὑμᾶς,   ἀδελφοί,   ὑπὲρ
Now we request   you,   brothers,   by

τῆς   παρουσίας   τοῦ   κυρίου   [ἡμῶν]   Ἰησοῦ
the   presence   of the   Lord   of us   Jesus

Χριστοῦ   καὶ   ἡμῶν   ἐπισυναγωγῆς   ἐπ᾽   αὐτόν,
Christ   and   ²of us   ¹gathering together   to   him,

2 εἰς   τὸ   μὴ   ταχέως   σαλευθῆναι   ὑμᾶς
-    -   not   quickly   to be shaken   youᵇ

ἀπὸ   τοῦ   νοὸς   μηδὲ   θροεῖσθαι,   μήτε
from   the(your) mind   nor   to be disturbed,   neither

διὰ   πνεύματος   μήτε   διὰ   λόγου   μήτε
through   a spirit   nor   through   speech   nor

δι᾽   ἐπιστολῆς   ὡς   δι᾽   ἡμῶν,   ὡς   ὅτι
through an epistle   as   through   us,   as   that

ἐνέστηκεν   ἡ   ἡμέρα   τοῦ   κυρίου.   3 μὴ
⁵is come   ¹the   ²day   ³of the   ⁴Lord.   Not

come. ³Let no one deceive you in any way; for that day will not come, unless the rebellion comes first, and the man of lawlessness[a] is revealed, the son of perdition, ⁴who opposes and exalts himself against every so-called god or object of worship, so that he takes his seat in the temple of God, proclaiming himself to be God. ⁵Do you not remember that when I was still with you I told you this? ⁶And you know what is restraining him now so that he may be revealed in his time. ⁷For the mystery of lawlessness is already at work; only he who now restrains it will do so until he is out of the way. ⁸And then the lawless one will be revealed, and the Lord Jesus will slay him with the breath of his mouth and destroy him by his appearing and his coming. ⁹The coming of the lawless one by the activity of Satan will be with all power and with pretended signs and wonders, ¹⁰and with all wicked deception for those who are to perish, because they refused to

---

τις   ὑμᾶς   ἐξαπατήσῃ   κατὰ   μηδένα   τρόπον·
anyone ²you   ¹may deceive   by(in)   no(any)   way;

ὅτι   ἐὰν   μὴ   ἔλθῃ   ἡ   ἀποστασία   πρῶτον
because   unless   ²comes   ¹the   ²apostasy   ⁴firstly

καὶ   ἀποκαλυφθῇ   ὁ   ἄνθρωπος   τῆς   ἀνομίας,
and   ⁴is revealed   ¹the   ²man   –   ³of lawlessness,

ὁ   υἱὸς   τῆς   ἀπωλείας,   4 ὁ   ἀντικείμενος
the   son   –   of perdition,   the [one] setting against

καὶ   ὑπεραιρόμενος   ἐπὶ   πάντα   λεγόμενον
and   exalting himself   over   everything   being called

θεὸν   ἢ   σέβασμα,   ὥστε   αὐτὸν   εἰς   τὸν
God   or   object of worship,   so as   him   in   the

ναὸν   τοῦ   θεοῦ   καθίσαι,   ἀποδεικνύντα   ἑαυ-
shrine   –   of God   to sit,[b]   showing   him-

τὸν   ὅτι   ἐστὶν   θεός.   5 Οὐ   μνημονεύετε
self   that   he is   a god.   Do ye not remember

ὅτι   ἔτι   ὢν   πρὸς   ὑμᾶς   ταῦτα   ἔλεγον
that   yet   being   with   you   ²these things   ¹I used to tell

ὑμῖν;   6 καὶ   νῦν   τὸ   κατέχον   οἴδατε,
²you?   and   now   the [thing]   restraining   ye know,

εἰς   τὸ   ἀποκαλυφθῆναι   αὐτὸν   ἐν   τῷ
for   the   ²to be revealed   ¹him[b]   in   the

αὐτοῦ   καιρῷ.   7 τὸ   γὰρ   μυστήριον   ἤδη
²of him   ¹time.   For the   mystery   ²already

ἐνεργεῖται   τῆς   ἀνομίας·   μόνον   ὁ   κατέχων
³operates   –   ¹of lawlessness;   only   the restraining [there is] [one]

ἄρτι   ἕως   ἐκ   μέσου   γένηται.   8 καὶ   τότε
just now   until   ²out of ²[the] midst   ¹it comes.   And   then

ἀποκαλυφθήσεται   ὁ   ἄνομος,   ὃν   ὁ   κύριος
will be revealed   the   lawless one,   whom   the   Lord

[Ἰησοῦς]   ἀνελεῖ   τῷ   πνεύματι   τοῦ   στό-
Jesus   will destroy   by the   spirit   of the   mouth

ματος   αὐτοῦ   καὶ   καταργήσει   τῇ   ἐπιφανείᾳ
  of him   and   bring to nothing by the   outshining

τῆς   παρουσίας   αὐτοῦ,   9 οὗ   ἐστιν   ἡ
of the   presence   of him,   of whom   ²is   ¹the

παρουσία   κατ᾽   ἐνέργειαν   τοῦ   σατανᾶ   ἐν
²presence   according to [the]   operation   –   of Satan   with

πάσῃ   δυνάμει   καὶ   σημείοις   καὶ   τέρασιν
all   power   and   signs   and   wonders

ψεύδους   10 καὶ   ἐν   πάσῃ   ἀπάτῃ   ἀδικίας
of a lie   and   with   all   deceit   of unrighteousness

τοῖς   ἀπολλυμένοις,   ἀνθ᾽   ὧν   τὴν   ἀγάπην
in the [ones] perishing,   because   the   love

---

[a] Other ancient authorities read *sin*

love the truth and so be
saved. ¹¹Therefore God
sends upon them a strong
delusion, to make them
believe what is false,
¹²so that all may be
condemned who did not
believe the truth but had
pleasure in unrighteous-
ness.

13 But we are bound
to give thanks to God
always for you, brethren
beloved by the Lord,
because God chose you
from the beginning[b] to be
saved, through sancti-
fication by the Spirit[e] and
belief in the truth. ¹⁴To
this he called you
through our gospel, so
that you may obtain the
glory of our Lord Jesus
Christ. ¹⁵So then, breth-
ren, stand firm and hold
to the traditions which
you were taught by us,
either by word of mouth
or by letter.

16 Now may our
Lord Jesus Christ him-
self, and God our
Father, who loved us and
gave us eternal comfort
and good hope through
grace, ¹⁷comfort your
hearts and establish them
in every good work and
word.

τῆς ἀληθείας οὐκ ἐδέξαντο εἰς τὸ σωθῆναι
of the   truth   they received not for the ²to be saved

αὐτούς. 11 καὶ διὰ τοῦτο πέμπει αὐτοῖς
¹them.[b]   And   therefore ²sends ³to them

ὁ θεὸς ἐνέργειαν πλάνης εἰς τὸ πιστεῦσαι
- ¹God an operation of error for the ²to believe

αὐτοὺς τῷ ψεύδει, 12 ἵνα κριθῶσιν πάντες
¹them[b]   the lie,   in or- ¹⁰may be ¹all
                         der that judged

οἱ μὴ πιστεύσαντες τῇ ἀληθείᾳ ἀλλὰ
²the ³not ⁴having believed ⁵the ⁶truth ⁷but
[ones]

εὐδοκήσαντες τῇ ἀδικίᾳ.
⁸having had pleasure - ⁹in unrighteousness.

13 Ἡμεῖς δὲ ὀφείλομεν εὐχαριστεῖν τῷ
    But we   ought   to thank   -

θεῷ πάντοτε περὶ ὑμῶν, ἀδελφοὶ ἠγαπη-
God always concerning you, brothers having been

μένοι ὑπὸ κυρίου, ὅτι εἵλατο ὑμᾶς ὁ
loved by [the] Lord, because ²chose ³you -

θεὸς ἀπαρχὴν εἰς σωτηρίαν ἐν ἁγιασμῷ
¹God firstfruit to salvation by sanctification

πνεύματος καὶ πίστει ἀληθείας, 14 εἰς
of spirit   and   faith of(in) [the] truth, to

ὃ καὶ ἐκάλεσεν ὑμᾶς διὰ τοῦ εὐαγγελίου
which also he called you through the gospel

ἡμῶν, εἰς περιποίησιν δόξης τοῦ κυρίου
of us, to obtainment of [the] glory of the Lord

ἡμῶν Ἰησοῦ Χριστοῦ. 15 Ἄρα οὖν,
of us Jesus Christ.   So   then,

ἀδελφοί, στήκετε, καὶ κρατεῖτε τὰς
brothers, stand,   and   hold   the

παραδόσεις ἃς ἐδιδάχθητε εἴτε διὰ λόγου
traditions which ye were taught either through speech

εἴτε δι᾽ ἐπιστολῆς ἡμῶν. 16 Αὐτὸς δὲ
or through an epistle of us.   And ⁶[him]self

ὁ κύριος ἡμῶν Ἰησοῦς Χριστὸς καὶ
¹the ²Lord ³of us ⁴Jesus ⁵Christ and

ὁ θεὸς ὁ πατὴρ ἡμῶν, ὁ ἀγαπήσας
the God the Father of us, the [one] having loved

ἡμᾶς καὶ δοὺς παράκλησιν αἰωνίαν καὶ
us   and having given ²comfort ¹eternal ³and

ἐλπίδα ἀγαθὴν ἐν χάριτι, 17 παρακαλέσαι
⁵hope ⁴a good by grace,   may he comfort

ὑμῶν τὰς καρδίας καὶ στηρίξαι ἐν παντὶ
of you the hearts and may he in every
                           confirm

[b] Other ancient authorities
read as the first converts
[e] Or of spirit

ἔργῳ καὶ λόγῳ ἀγαθῷ.
²work ³and ⁴word ¹good.

CHAPTER 3

FINALLY, brethren, pray for us, that the word of the Lord may speed on and triumph, as it did among you, [2]and that we may be delivered from wicked and evil men; for not all have faith. [3]But the Lord is faithful; he will strengthen you and guard you from evil.[d] [4]And we have confidence in the Lord about you, that you are doing and will do the things which we command. [5]May the Lord direct your hearts to the love of God and to the steadfastness of Christ.

[6]Now we command you, brethren, in the name of our Lord Jesus Christ, that you keep away from any brother who is living in idleness and not in accord with the tradition that you received from us. [7]For you yourselves know how you ought to imitate us; we were not idle when we were with you, [8]we did not eat any one's bread without paying, but with toil and labor we worked night and day, that we

---

3 Τὸ   λοιπὸν   προσεύχεσθε,   ἀδελφοί,   περὶ
For the rest   pray ye,   brothers,   concerning

ἡμῶν,   ἵνα   ὁ   λόγος   τοῦ   κυρίου   τρέχῃ
us,   in order that   the   word   of the   Lord   may run

καὶ   δοξάζηται   καθὼς   καὶ   πρὸς   ὑμᾶς,
and   be glorified   as   indeed   with   you,

2 καὶ   ἵνα   ῥυσθῶμεν   ἀπὸ   τῶν   ἀτόπων
and   in order that   we may be delivered   from   -   perverse

καὶ   πονηρῶν   ἀνθρώπων·   οὐ   γὰρ   πάντων
and   evil   men·   for [is] not   [4]of all men

ἡ   πίστις.   **3** Πιστὸς   δέ   ἐστιν   ὁ   κύριος,
[1]the   [3]faith.   But faithful   is   the   Lord,

ὃς   στηρίξει   ὑμᾶς   καὶ   φυλάξει   ἀπὸ   τοῦ
who will confirm   you   and   will guard   from   the

πονηροῦ.   **4** πεποίθαμεν   δὲ   ἐν   κυρίῳ
evil [?one].   And we are persuaded   in   [the] Lord

ἐφ᾽   ὑμᾶς,   ὅτι   ἃ   παραγγέλλομεν   [καὶ]
as to   you,   that what   we charge   both

ποιεῖτε   καὶ   ποιήσετε.   **5** Ὁ   δὲ   κύριος
ye do   and   will do.   And [1]the   [2]Lord

κατευθύναι   ὑμῶν   τὰς   καρδίας   εἰς   τὴν
[1]may [3]direct   [7]of you   [6]the   [5]hearts   into   the

ἀγάπην   τοῦ   θεοῦ   καὶ   εἰς   τὴν   ὑπομονὴν
love   -   of God   and   into   the   patience

τοῦ   Χριστοῦ.
-   of Christ.

6 Παραγγέλλομεν   δὲ   ὑμῖν,   ἀδελφοί,   ἐν
Now we charge   you,   brothers,   in

ὀνόματι   τοῦ   κυρίου   Ἰησοῦ   Χριστοῦ,
[the] name   of the   Lord   Jesus   Christ,

στέλλεσθαι   ὑμᾶς   ἀπὸ   παντὸς   ἀδελφοῦ
to draw back   you   from   every   brother

ἀτάκτως   περιπατοῦντος   καὶ   μὴ   κατὰ   τὴν
[2]idly   [1]walking   and   not   according to   the

παράδοσιν   ἣν   παρελάβετε   παρ᾽   ἡμῶν.
tradition   which   ye received   from   us.

7 αὐτοὶ   γὰρ   οἴδατε   πῶς   δεῖ   μιμεῖσθαι
For [your]selves   ye know   how   it behoves   to imitate

ἡμᾶς,   ὅτι   οὐκ   ἠτακτήσαμεν   ἐν   ὑμῖν,
us,   because   we were not idle   among   you,

8 οὐδὲ   δωρεὰν   ἄρτον   ἐφάγομεν   παρά   τινος,
nor   [3][as] a gift   [2]bread   [1]ate   [5]from   [4]anyone,

ἀλλ᾽   ἐν   κόπῳ   καὶ   μόχθῳ   νυκτὸς   καὶ
but   by   labour   and   struggle   by night   and

---

[d] Or the evil one

might not burden any of you. [9]It was not because we have not that right, but to give you in our conduct an example to imitate. [10]For even when we were with you, we gave you this command: If any one will not work, let him not eat. [11]For we hear that some of you are living in idleness, mere busybodies, not doing any work. [12]Now such persons we command and exhort in the Lord Jesus Christ to do their work in quietness and to earn their own living. [13]Brethren, do not be weary in well-doing.

14 If any one refuses to obey what we say in this letter, note that man, and have nothing to do with him, that he may be ashamed. [15]Do not look on him as an enemy, but warn him as a brother.

16 Now may the Lord of peace himself give you peace at all times in all ways. The Lord be with you all.

ἡμέρας ἐργαζόμενοι πρὸς τὸ μὴ ἐπιβαρῆσαί
by day   working   for   the not to emburden
τινα ὑμῶν· 9 οὐχ ὅτι οὐκ ἔχομεν
anyone of you;   not that   we have not
ἐξουσίαν, ἀλλ' ἵνα ἑαυτοὺς τύπον δῶμεν
authority,   but in or- ²our-   ²an   ¹we might
              der that selves   example give
ὑμῖν εἰς τὸ μιμεῖσθαι ἡμᾶς.   10 καὶ
to you for the to imitate   us.   even
γὰρ ὅτε ἦμεν πρὸς ὑμᾶς, τοῦτο παρηγ-
For when we were with you,   this   we
γέλλομεν ὑμῖν, ὅτι εἴ τις οὐ θέλει
charged   you, that if anyone does not wish
ἐργάζεσθαι, μηδὲ ἐσθιέτω.   11 ἀκούομεν
to work,   neither let him eat.   we hear [of]
γάρ τινας περιπατοῦντας ἐν ὑμῖν ἀτάκτως,
For some   walking   among you   idly,
μηδὲν ἐργαζομένους ἀλλὰ περιεργαζομένους·
nothing working   but   working round;
12 τοῖς δὲ τοιούτοις παραγγέλλομεν καὶ
      and to such   we charge   and
παρακαλοῦμεν ἐν κυρίῳ Ἰησοῦ Χριστῷ
exhort   in [the] Lord Jesus Christ
ἵνα μετὰ ἡσυχίας ἐργαζόμενοι τὸν
in or- ²with ³quietness   ¹working   ⁵the
der that
ἑαυτῶν ἄρτον ἐσθίωσιν.   13 Ὑμεῖς δέ,
⁷of them- ⁶bread ⁴they may eat.   And ye,
selves
ἀδελφοί,   μὴ ἐγκακήσητε καλοποιοῦντες
brothers,   do not lose heart   doing good.
14 εἰ δέ τις οὐχ ὑπακούει τῷ λόγῳ
     And if anyone obeys not   the   word
ἡμῶν διὰ τῆς ἐπιστολῆς, τοῦτον σημειοῦσθε,
of us through the   epistle,   this man   mark,
μὴ συναναμίγνυσθαι αὐτῷ, ἵνα ἐντραπῇ·
not to mix with*   him, in or- he may be put
                               der that to shame;
15 καὶ μὴ ὡς ἐχθρὸν ἡγεῖσθε, ἀλλὰ
    and yet not as an enemy deem ye [him],   but
·ουθετεῖτε ὡς ἀδελφόν.   16 Αὐτὸς δὲ
admonish   as a brother.   And ⁴[him]self
ὁ κύριος τῆς εἰρήνης δῴη ὑμῖν τὴν
¹the ²Lord -   ³of peace may he to you the
                            give   (?his)
εἰρήνην διὰ παντὸς ἐν παντὶ τρόπῳ.
peace   always   in every   way.
ὁ κύριος μετὰ πάντων ὑμῶν.
The Lord [be] with   ²all   ¹you.

* Imperatival infinitive, as elsewhere (Phil. 3. 16, etc.).

17 I, Paul, write this greeting with my own hand. This is the mark in every letter of mine; it is the way I write. [18] The grace of our Lord Jesus Christ be with you all.

17 Ὁ ἀσπασμὸς τῇ ἐμῇ χειρὶ Παύλου,
The greeting – by my hand[,] of Paul,
ὅ ἐστιν σημεῖον ἐν πάσῃ ἐπιστολῇ·
which is a sign in every epistle:
οὕτως γράφω. 18 ἡ χάρις τοῦ κυρίου
thus I write. The grace of the Lord
ἡμῶν Ἰησοῦ Χριστοῦ μετὰ πάντων ὑμῶν.
of us Jesus Christ [be] with [2]all [1]you.

I. TIMOTHY
1

ΠΡΟΣ ΤΙΜΟΘΕΟΝ Α
To Timothy 1

CHAPTER 1

PAUL, an apostle of Christ Jesus by command of God our Savior and of Christ Jesus our hope,

2 To Timothy, my true child in the faith:
Grace, mercy, and peace from God the Father and Christ Jesus our Lord.

3 As I urged you when I was going to Macedo'-nia, remain at Ephesus that you may charge certain persons not to teach any different doctrine, [4]nor to occupy themselves with myths and endless genealogies which promote speculations rather than the divine training[a] that is in faith; [5]whereas the aim of our charge is love that issues from a pure heart and a good conscience and sincere faith.

1 Παῦλος ἀπόστολος Χριστοῦ Ἰησοῦ κατ'
Paul an apostle of Christ Jesus accord-ing to
ἐπιταγὴν θεοῦ σωτῆρος ἡμῶν καὶ Χριστοῦ
a command of God Saviour of us and of Christ
Ἰησοῦ τῆς ἐλπίδος ἡμῶν 2 Τιμοθέῳ
Jesus the hope of us to Timothy
γνησίῳ τέκνῳ ἐν πίστει· χάρις, ἔλεος,
a true child in [the] faith: Grace, mercy,
εἰρήνη ἀπὸ θεοῦ πατρὸς καὶ Χριστοῦ
peace from God [the] Father and Christ
Ἰησοῦ τοῦ κυρίου ἡμῶν.
Jesus the Lord of us.

3 Καθὼς παρεκάλεσά σε προσμεῖναι ἐν
As I besought thee to remain in
Ἐφέσῳ, πορευόμενος εἰς Μακεδονίαν, ἵνα
Ephesus, [I] going into Macedonia, in or-der that
παραγγείλῃς τισὶν μὴ ἑτεροδιδασκαλεῖν
thou mightest certain not to teach differently
charge persons

4 μηδὲ προσέχειν μύθοις καὶ γενεαλογίαις
nor to pay attention to tales and to [2]genealogies
ἀπεράντοις, αἵτινες ἐκζητήσεις παρέχουσιν
[1]unending, which [2]questionings [1]provide
μᾶλλον ἢ οἰκονομίαν θεοῦ τὴν ἐν πίστει·
rather than a stewardship of God – in faith:
5 τὸ δὲ τέλος τῆς παραγγελίας ἐστὶν
now the end of the charge is
ἀγάπη ἐκ καθαρᾶς καρδίας καὶ συνειδήσεως
love out of a clean heart and conscience
ἀγαθῆς καὶ πίστεως ἀνυποκρίτου, 6 ὧν
a good and faith unfeigned, from which things

[a] Or stewardship, or order

⁶Certain persons by swerving from these have wandered away into vain discussion, ⁷desiring to be teachers of the law, without understanding either what they are saying or the things about which they make assertions.

8 Now we know that the law is good, if any one uses it lawfully, ⁹understanding this, that the law is not laid down for the just but for the lawless and disobedient, for the ungodly and sinners, for the unholy and profane, for murderers of fathers and murderers of mothers, for manslayers, ¹⁰immoral persons, sodomites, kidnapers, liars, perjurers, and whatever else is contrary to sound doctrine, ¹¹in accordance with the glorious gospel of the blessed God with which I have been entrusted.

12 I thank him who has given me strength for this, Christ Jesus our Lord, because he judged me faithful by appointing me to his service, ¹³though I formerly blasphemed and persecuted and insulted him; but I received mercy because I had acted ignorantly in unbelief, ¹⁴and the grace of our Lord overflowed for me with the faith and love that are in Christ Jesus. ¹⁵The saying is sure and

τινες ἀστοχήσαντες ἐξετράπησαν εἰς
some missing aim turned aside to
ματαιολογίαν, 7 θέλοντες εἶναι νομοδιδάσ-
vain talking, wishing to be law-
καλοι, μὴ νοοῦντες μήτε ἃ λέγουσιν
teachers, not understanding either what things they say
μήτε περὶ τίνων διαβεβαιοῦνται. 8 οἴδαμεν
nor concerning what things they emphatically assert. we know
δὲ ὅτι καλὸς ὁ νόμος, ἐάν τις αὐτῷ
Now that ³[is] ⁴good ¹the ²law, if anyone ⁵it
νομίμως χρῆται, 9 εἰδὼς τοῦτο, ὅτι
¹lawfully ¹uses, knowing this, that
δικαίῳ νόμος οὐ κεῖται, ἀνόμοις δὲ
³for a just ¹law ²is not laid down, but for lawless men
man
καὶ ἀνυποτάκτοις, ἀσεβέσι καὶ ἁμαρτωλοῖς,
and for unruly, for impious and for sinners,
ἀνοσίοις καὶ βεβήλοις, πατρολῴαις καὶ
for unholy and for profane, for parricides and
μητρολῴαις, ἀνδροφόνοις, 10 πόρνοις, ἀρ-
for matricides, for menkillers, for fornicators, for
σενοκοίταις, ἀνδραποδισταῖς, ψεύσταις, ἐπιόρ-
paederasts, for menstealers, for liars, for per-
κοις, καὶ εἴ τι ἕτερον τῇ ὑγιαινούσῃ
jurers, and if any other thing ²to the ³being healthful
διδασκαλίᾳ ἀντίκειται, 11 κατὰ τὸ εὐαγ-
⁴teaching ¹opposes, according to the gos-
γέλιον τῆς δόξης τοῦ μακαρίου θεοῦ,
pel of the glory of the blessed God,
ὃ ἐπιστεύθην ἐγώ. 12 Χάριν ἔχω τῷ
which ²was entrusted ¹I. Thanks I have to the
[with]
ἐνδυναμώσαντί με Χριστῷ Ἰησοῦ τῷ κυρίῳ
[one] empowering me Christ Jesus the Lord
ἡμῶν, ὅτι πιστόν με ἡγήσατο θέμενος
of us, because ²faithful ²me ¹he deemed putting [me]
εἰς διακονίαν, 13 τὸ πρότερον ὄντα
into [the] ministry, formerly being
βλάσφημον καὶ διώκτην καὶ ὑβριστήν·
a blasphemer and a persecutor and insolent;
ἀλλὰ ἠλεήθην, ὅτι ἀγνοῶν ἐποίησα ἐν
but I obtained mercy, because being ignorant I acted in
ἀπιστίᾳ, 14 ὑπερεπλεόνασεν δὲ ἡ χάρις
unbelief, and superabounded the grace
τοῦ κυρίου ἡμῶν μετὰ πίστεως καὶ
of the Lord of us with faith and
ἀγάπης τῆς ἐν Χριστῷ Ἰησοῦ. 15 πιστὸς
love – in Christ Jesus. Faithful [is]

worthy of full accept-ance, that Christ Jesus came into the world to save sinners. And I am the foremost of sinners; [16] but I received mercy for this reason, that in me, as the foremost, Jesus Christ might display his perfect patience for an example to those who were to believe in him for eternal life. [17] To the King of ages, immortal, invisible, the only God, be honor and glory for ever and ever. Amen.

18 This charge I commit to you, Timothy, my son, in accordance with the prophetic utterances which pointed to you, that inspired by them you may wage the good warfare, [19] holding faith and a good conscience. By rejecting conscience, certain persons have made shipwreck of their faith, [20] among them Hymenae'us and Alexander, whom I have delivered to Satan that they may learn not to blaspheme.

ὁ λόγος καὶ πάσης ἀποδοχῆς ἄξιος,
the word and ²of all ³acceptance ¹worthy,

ὅτι Χριστὸς Ἰησοῦς ἦλθεν εἰς τὸν κόσμον
that Christ Jesus came into the world

ἁμαρτωλοὺς σῶσαι· ὧν πρῶτός εἰμι ἐγώ·
sinners to save; of whom first(chief) am I;

16 ἀλλὰ διὰ τοῦτο ἠλεήθην, ἵνα ἐν
but because of this I obtained in or- in
mercy, der that

ἐμοὶ πρώτῳ ἐνδείξηται Ἰησοῦς Χριστὸς
me first might show forth Jesus Christ

τὴν ἅπασαν μακροθυμίαν, πρὸς ὑποτύπωσιν
- all longsuffering, for a pattern

τῶν μελλόντων πιστεύειν ἐπ' αὐτῷ εἰς
of the [ones] coming to believe on him to

ζωὴν αἰώνιον. 17 Τῷ δὲ βασιλεῖ τῶν
life eternal. Now to the King of the

αἰώνων, ἀφθάρτῳ ἀοράτῳ μόνῳ θεῷ, τιμὴ
ages, incorruptible invisible only God, [be]
honour

καὶ δόξα εἰς τοὺς αἰῶνας τῶν αἰώνων·
and glory unto the ages of the ages:

ἀμήν. 18 Ταύτην τὴν παραγγελίαν παρα-
Amen. This - charge I com-

τίθεμαί σοι, τέκνον Τιμόθεε, κατὰ τὰς
mit to thee, child Timothy, according to the

προαγούσας ἐπὶ σὲ προφητείας, ἵνα
preceding ²respecting ³thee ¹prophecies, in order
that

στρατεύῃ ἐν αὐταῖς τὴν καλὴν στρατείαν,
thou by them the good warfare,
mightest war

19 ἔχων πίστιν καὶ ἀγαθὴν συνείδησιν,
having faith and a good conscience,

ἥν τινες ἀπωσάμενοι περὶ τὴν πίστιν
which some thrusting away ²concerning ³the ⁴faith

ἐναυάγησαν· 20 ὧν ἐστιν Ὑμέναιος καὶ
¹made ship- of whom is Hymenæus and
wreck;

Ἀλέξανδρος, οὓς παρέδωκα τῷ σατανᾷ,
Alexander, whom I delivered - to Satan,

ἵνα παιδευθῶσιν μὴ βλασφημεῖν.
in or- they may be taught not to blaspheme.
der that

CHAPTER 2

FIRST of all, then, I urge that supplications, prayers, interces-

2 Παρακαλῶ οὖν πρῶτον πάντων
I exhort therefore first/y of all

ποιεῖσθαι δεήσεις, προσευχάς, ἐντεύξεις,
to be made petitions, prayers, intercessions,

sions, and thanksgivings be made for all men, [2] for kings and all who are in high positions, that we may lead a quiet and peaceable life, godly and respectful in every way. [3] This is good, and it is acceptable in the sight of God our Savior, [4] who desires all men to be saved and to come to the knowledge of the truth. [5] For there is one God, and there is one mediator between God and men, the man Christ Jesus, [6] who gave himself as a ransom for all, the testimony to which was borne at the proper time. [7] For this I was appointed a preacher and apostle (I am telling the truth, I am not lying), a teacher of the Gentiles in faith and truth.

8 I desire then that in every place the men should pray, lifting holy hands without anger or quarreling; [9] also that women should adorn themselves modestly and sensibly in seemly apparel, not with braided hair or gold or pearls or costly attire [10] but by good deeds, as befits women who profess

εὐχαριστίας, ὑπὲρ πάντων ἀνθρώπων,
thanksgivings, on behalf of all men,

2 ὑπὲρ βασιλέων καὶ πάντων τῶν ἐν
on behalf of kings and all the [ones] [2] in

ὑπεροχῇ ὄντων, ἵνα ἤρεμον καὶ ἡσύχιον
[3] eminence [1] being, in or- [2] a tranquil [3] and [4] quiet
der that

βίον διάγωμεν ἐν πάσῃ εὐσεβείᾳ καὶ
[5] life [1] we may lead in all piety and

σεμνότητι. 3 τοῦτο καλὸν καὶ ἀπόδεκτον
gravity. This [is] good and acceptable

ἐνώπιον τοῦ σωτῆρος ἡμῶν θεοῦ, 4 ὅς
before the Saviour of us God, who

πάντας ἀνθρώπους θέλει σωθῆναι καὶ εἰς
[2] all [3] men [1] wishes to be saved and [3] to

ἐπίγνωσιν ἀληθείας ἐλθεῖν. 5 εἷς γὰρ
[3] a full [4] of truth [1] to come. For [2] one
knowledge

θεός, εἷς καὶ μεσίτης θεοῦ καὶ ἀνθρώπων,
[1] [there one also mediator of God and of men,
is] [3] God,

ἄνθρωπος Χριστὸς Ἰησοῦς, 6 ὁ δοὺς
a man Christ Jesus, the [one] having
given

ἑαυτὸν ἀντίλυτρον ὑπὲρ πάντων, τὸ
himself a ransom on behalf of all, the

μαρτύριον καιροῖς ἰδίοις· 7 εἰς ὃ ἐτέθην
testimony in its own times; for which [2] was
appointed

ἐγὼ κῆρυξ καὶ ἀπόστολος, ἀλήθειαν λέγω,
[1] I a herald and an apostle, [truth [1] I say,

οὐ ψεύδομαι, διδάσκαλος ἐθνῶν ἐν πίστει
I do not lie, a teacher of nations in faith

καὶ ἀληθείᾳ. 8 Βούλομαι οὖν προσεύχεσθαι
and truth. I desire therefore [3] to pray

τοὺς ἄνδρας ἐν παντὶ τόπῳ ἐπαίροντας
[1] the [2] men in every place lifting up

ὁσίους χεῖρας χωρὶς ὀργῆς καὶ διαλογισμοῦ.
holy hands without wrath and doubting.

9 Ὡσαύτως γυναῖκας ἐν καταστολῇ κοσμίῳ,
Similarly women in clothing orderly,

μετὰ αἰδοῦς καὶ σωφροσύνης κοσμεῖν
[3] with [4] modesty [5] and [6] sobriety [1] to adorn

ἑαυτάς, μὴ ἐν πλέγμασιν καὶ χρυσίῳ
[2] themselves, not with plaiting and gold

ἢ μαργαρίταις ἢ ἱματισμῷ πολυτελεῖ,
or pearls or raiment costly,

10 ἀλλ' ὃ πρέπει γυναιξὶν ἐπαγγελλομέναις
but what suits women professing

religion. ¹¹Let a woman learn in silence with all submissiveness. ¹²I permit no woman to teach or to have authority over men; she is to keep silent. ¹³For Adam was formed first, then Eve; ¹⁴and Adam was not deceived, but the woman was deceived and became a transgressor. ¹⁵Yet woman will be saved through bearing children,[b] if she continues in faith and love and holiness, with modesty.

θεοσέβειαν,   δι'   ἔργων   ἀγαθῶν.   **11** γυνὴ
reverence,   by   ²works   ¹good.   A woman
 means of

ἐν   ἡσυχίᾳ   μανθανέτω   ἐν   πάσῃ   ὑποταγῇ·
in   silence   let learn   in   all   subjection;

12 διδάσκειν   δὲ   γυναικὶ   οὐκ   ἐπιτρέπω,
 but ³to teach   ²a woman   ¹I do not permit,

οὐδὲ   αὐθεντεῖν   ἀνδρός,   ἀλλ'   εἶναι   ἐν
nor   to exercise   of(over) a man,   but   to be   in
 authority

ἡσυχίᾳ.   **13** Ἀδὰμ   γὰρ   πρῶτος   ἐπλάσθη,
silence.   For Adam   first   was formed,

εἶτα   Εὕα.   **14** καὶ   Ἀδὰμ   οὐκ   ἠπατήθη,
then   Eve.   And   Adam   was not deceived,

ἡ   δὲ   γυνὴ   ἐξαπατηθεῖσα   ἐν   παραβάσει
but the   woman   being deceived   ²in   ³transgression

γέγονεν·   **15** σωθήσεται   δὲ   διὰ   τῆς
¹has become;   but she will be saved   through the(her)

τεκνογονίας,   ἐὰν   μείνωσιν   ἐν   πίστει   καὶ
childbearing,   if   they remain   in   faith   and

ἀγάπῃ   καὶ   ἁγιασμῷ   μετὰ   σωφροσύνης.
love   and   sanctification   with   sobriety.

CHAPTER 3

THE saying is sure: If any one aspires to the office of bishop, he desires a noble task. ²Now a bishop must be above reproach, the husband of one wife, temperate, sensible, dignified hospitable, an apt teacher, ³no drunkard, not violent but gentle, not quarrelsome, and no lover of money. ⁴He must manage his own household well, keeping his children submissive and respectful in every way; ⁵for if a man does not know how to manage his own household, how can he care for God's church? ⁶He

3 Πιστὸς   ὁ   λόγος·   εἴ   τις   ἐπισκοπῆς
Faithful [is]   the   word: If   anyone   ²oversight

ὀρέγεται,   καλοῦ   ἔργου   ἐπιθυμεῖ.   **2** δεῖ
¹aspires to,   ²a good   ³work   ¹he desires.   It behoves

οὖν   τὸν   ἐπίσκοπον   ἀνεπίλημπτον   εἶναι,
there-   the   bishop   without reproach   to be,
fore

μιᾶς   γυναικὸς   ἄνδρα,   νηφάλιον,   σώφρονα,
of one   wife   husband,   temperate,   sensible,

κόσμιον,   φιλόξενον,   διδακτικόν,   **3** μὴ
orderly,   hospitable,   apt at teaching,   not

πάροινον,   μὴ   πλήκτην,   ἀλλὰ   ἐπιεικῆ,
an excessive   not   a striker,   but   forbearing,
drinker,

ἄμαχον,   ἀφιλάργυρον,   **4** τοῦ   ἰδίου   οἴκου
uncontentious,   not avaricious,   ³the(his)   ⁴own   ⁵household

καλῶς   προϊστάμενον,   τέκνα   ἔχοντα   ἐν
²well   ¹ruling,   children   having   in

ὑποταγῇ   μετὰ   πάσης   σεμνότητος,   **5** (εἰ
subjection   with   all   gravity,   ²(if

δέ   τις   τοῦ   ἰδίου   οἴκου   προστῆναι   οὐκ
¹but ³anyone   ⁷the(his)   ⁵own   ⁶household   ⁴to rule   ¹not*

οἶδεν,   πῶς   ἐκκλησίας   θεοῦ   ἐπιμελήσεται;)
⁴knows,   how   ²a church   ³of God   ¹will he care for ?)

---

[b] Or by the birth of the child

* That is, "cannot"; see note on page xviii.

must not be a recent
convert, or he may be
puffed up with conceit
and fall into the con-
demnation of the devil;[d]
[7] moreover he must be
well thought of by out-
siders, or he may fall into
reproach and the snare
of the devil.[d]

[8] Deacons   likewise
must be serious, not
double-tongued,   not
addicted to much wine,
not greedy for gain;
[9] they must hold the
mystery of the faith with
a clear conscience. [10] And
let them also be tested
first; then if they prove
themselves blameless let
them serve as deacons.
[11] The women likewise
must be serious, no
slanderers, but temp-
erate, faithful in all
things. [12] Let deacons be
the husband of one wife,
and let them manage their
children and their house-
holds well; [13] for those
who serve well as deacons
gain a good standing for
themselves and also great
confidence in the faith
which is in Christ Jesus.

[14] I hope to come to
you soon, but I am
writing these instructions
to you so that, [15] if I am
delayed, you may know
how one ought to behave
in the household of God,
which is the church of
the living God, the pillar

6 μὴ   νεόφυτον,   ἵνα   μὴ   τυφωθεὶς   εἰς
not a neophyte(recent lest   being puffed up [2]into
          convert),

κρίμα   ἐμπέσῃ   τοῦ   διαβόλου.   7 δεῖ   δὲ
[3]judgment [1]he fall in of the   devil.   And it behoves

καὶ   μαρτυρίαν   καλὴν   ἔχειν   ἀπὸ   τῶν
also   [3]witness   [2]a good   [1]to have from the [ones]

ἔξωθεν,   7 ἵνα   μὴ   εἰς   ὀνειδισμὸν   ἐμπέσῃ
outside,   lest   [2]into [3]reproach   [1]he fall in

καὶ   παγίδα   τοῦ   διαβόλου.   8 Διακόνους
and   a snare   of the   devil.   [It behoves] deacons

ὡσαύτως   σεμνούς,   μὴ   διλόγους,   μὴ   οἴνῳ
similarly [to be] grave,   not double-tongued, not   [2]wine

πολλῷ   προσέχοντας,   μὴ   αἰσχροκερδεῖς,
[3]to much   [1]being addicted,   not   fond of base gain,

9 ἔχοντας   τὸ   μυστήριον   τῆς   πίστεως   ἐν
having   the   mystery   of the   faith   with

καθαρᾷ   συνειδήσει.   10 καὶ   οὗτοι   δὲ
a clean   conscience.   [4]Also   [5]these   [1]and

δοκιμαζέσθωσαν   πρῶτον,   εἶτα   διακονείτωσαν
[2]let [3]be proved   firstly,   then   let them minister

ἀνέγκλητοι   ὄντες.   11 γυναῖκας   ὡσαύτως
[2]irreproachable   [1]being.   [It behoves][*] wives   similarly

σεμνάς,   μὴ   διαβόλους,   νηφαλίους,   πιστὰς
[to be] grave, not   slanderers,   sober,   faithful

ἐν   πᾶσιν.   12 διάκονοι   ἔστωσαν   μιᾶς
in   all things.   [2]Deacons   [1]let [3]be   [4]of one

γυναικὸς   ἄνδρες,   τέκνων   καλῶς   προϊστάμενοι
[5]wife   [4]husbands,   [6]children   [7]well   [8]ruling

καὶ   τῶν   ἰδίων   οἴκων.   13 οἱ   γὰρ   καλῶς
[2]and   [3]the(ir)   [4]own   [5]households.   For the [ones]   [2]well

διακονήσαντες   βαθμὸν   ἑαυτοῖς   καλὸν
[1]having ministered   [6]position   [4]for themselves   [5]a good

περιποιοῦνται   καὶ   πολλὴν   παρρησίαν   ἐν
[3]acquire   and   much   boldness   in

πίστει   τῇ   ἐν   Χριστῷ   Ἰησοῦ.   14 Ταῦτά
faith   the [one] in   Christ   Jesus.   These things

σοι   γράφω   ἐλπίζων   ἐλθεῖν   πρός   σὲ
to thee   I write   hoping   to come   to   thee

τάχιον·   15 ἐὰν   δὲ   βραδύνω,   ἵνα   εἰδῇς
shortly;   but if   I delay,   in order   thou
                                              that   mayest
                                                      know

πῶς   δεῖ   ἐν   οἴκῳ   θεοῦ   ἀναστρέφεσθαι,
how   it behoves in   [the]   of God   to behave,
                        household

ἥτις   ἐστὶν   ἐκκλησία   θεοῦ   ζῶντος,   στῦλος
which   is   [the] church   [2]God   [1]of [the] living,   pillar

---

[d] Or slanderer   [*] See verses 7 and 8.

and bulwark of the truth.
[16] Great indeed, we confess, is the mystery of our religion:

He[e] was manifested in the flesh,
vindicated[f] in the Spirit,
seen by angels,
preached among the nations,
believed on in the world,
taken up in glory.

καὶ   ἑδραίωμα   τῆς   ἀληθείας.   16 καὶ
and   bulwark   of the   truth.   And
ὁμολογουμένως   μέγα   ἐστὶν   τὸ   τῆς   εὐσεβείας
confessedly   great   is   the   –   [2]of piety
μυστήριον·   ὃς   ἐφανερώθη   ἐν   σαρκί,
[1]mystery: Who   was manifested   in   flesh,
ἐδικαιώθη   ἐν   πνεύματι,   ὤφθη   ἀγγέλοις,
was justified   in   spirit,   was seen   by angels,
ἐκηρύχθη   ἐν   ἔθνεσιν,   ἐπιστεύθη   ἐν   κόσμῳ,
was pro-   among nations,   was believed   in [the] world,
claimed
ἀνελήμφθη   ἐν   δόξῃ.
was taken up   in   glory.

CHAPTER 4

NOW the Spirit expressly says that in later times some will depart from the faith by giving heed to deceitful spirits and doctrines of demons, [2]through the pretensions of liars whose consciences are seared, [3]who forbid marriage and enjoin abstinence from foods which God created to be received with thanksgiving by those who believe and know the truth. [4]For everything created by God is good, and nothing is to be rejected if it is received with thanksgiving; [5]for then it is consecrated by the word of God and prayer.

6 If you put these instructions before the brethren, you will be a good minister of Christ Jesus, nourished on the words of the faith and of

4 Τὸ   δὲ   πνεῦμα   ῥητῶς   λέγει   ὅτι
Now the   Spirit   [2]in words†   [1]says   that
ἐν   ὑστέροις   καιροῖς   ἀποστήσονταί   τινες
in   later   times   [2]will depart from   [1]some
τῆς   πίστεως,   προσέχοντες   πνεύμασιν
the   faith,   attending to   [2]spirits
πλάνοις   καὶ   διδασκαλίαις   δαιμονίων,   2 ἐν
[1]misleading and   teachings   of demons,   [2]in
ὑποκρίσει   ψευδολόγων,   κεκαυστηριασμένων
[3]hypocrisy   [1]of men who speak lies,   having been branded on
τὴν   ἰδίαν   συνείδησιν,   3 κωλυόντων   γαμεῖν,
the(ir) own   conscience,   forbidding   to marry,
ἀπέχεσθαι   βρωμάτων,   ἃ   ὁ   θεὸς   ἔκτισεν
[bidding] to   foods,   which   –   God   created
abstain from
εἰς   μετάλημψιν   μετὰ   εὐχαριστίας   τοῖς
for   partaking   with   thanksgiving   by the
πιστοῖς   καὶ   ἐπεγνωκόσι   τὴν   ἀλήθειαν.
believers   and [those] having fully   the   truth.
known
4 ὅτι   πᾶν   κτίσμα   θεοῦ   καλόν,   καὶ
Because   every   creature   of God [is]   good,   and
οὐδὲν   ἀπόβλητον   μετὰ   εὐχαριστίας   λαμβαν-
nothing   to be put away   [2]with   [3]thanksgiving   [1]being
[is]
όμενον·   5 ἁγιάζεται   γὰρ   διὰ   λόγου   θεοῦ
received;   for it is being sanctified   through   a word   of God
καὶ   ἐντεύξεως.   6 Ταῦτα   ὑποτιθέμενος
and   petition.   [2]These things   [1]suggesting
τοῖς   ἀδελφοῖς   καλὸς   ἔσῃ   διάκονος   Χριστοῦ
[3]to the   [4]brothers   [5]a good   [6]thou   [7]minister   of Christ
wilt be
Ἰησοῦ,   ἐντρεφόμενος   τοῖς   λόγοις   τῆς
Jesus,   being nourished   by the   words   of the

[e] Greek Who; other ancient authorities read God; others, Which

[f] Or justified

the good doctrine which you have followed. [7] Have nothing to do with godless and silly myths. Train yourself in godliness; [8] for while bodily training is of some value, godliness is of value in every way, as it holds promise for the present life and also for the life to come. [9] The saying is sure and worthy of full acceptance. [10] For to this end we toil and strive,[f] because we have our hope set on the living God, who is the Savior of all men, especially of those who believe.

11 Command and teach these things. [12] Let no one despise your youth, but set the believers an example in speech and conduct, in love, in faith, in purity. [13] Till I come, attend to the public reading of scripture, to preaching, to teaching. [14] Do not neglect the gift you have, which was given you by prophetic utterance when the elders laid their hands upon you.

πίστεως καὶ τῆς καλῆς διδασκαλίας ᾗ
faith   and   of the   good   teaching   which

παρηκολούθηκας· 7 τοὺς δὲ βεβήλους καὶ
thou hast followed;   but the   profane   and

γραώδεις μύθους παραιτοῦ. γύμναζε δὲ
old-womanish tales   refuse.   And exercise

σεαυτὸν πρὸς εὐσέβειαν. 8 ἡ γὰρ σωματικὴ
thyself   to   piety.   – For   bodily

γυμνασία πρὸς ὀλίγον ἐστὶν ὠφέλιμος·
exercise   ²for   ⁴a little ¹is   ²profitable;

ἡ δὲ εὐσέβεια πρὸς πάντα ὠφέλιμός
– but   piety   ²for ⁴all things ²profitable

ἐστιν, ἐπαγγελίαν ἔχουσα ζωῆς τῆς νῦν
¹is,   promise   having ⁴life ¹of the ²now
                                     (present)

καὶ τῆς μελλούσης. 9 πιστὸς ὁ λόγος
and of the coming.   Faithful [is] the word

καὶ πάσης ἀποδοχῆς ἄξιος· 10 εἰς τοῦτο
and ³of all ²acceptance ¹worthy;   ²to   ³this

γὰρ κοπιῶμεν καὶ ἀγωνιζόμεθα, ὅτι
¹for   we labour   and   struggle,   because

ἠλπίκαμεν ἐπὶ θεῷ ζῶντι, ὅς ἐστιν
we have set   on ²God ¹a living, who   is
[our] hope

σωτὴρ πάντων ἀνθρώπων, μάλιστα πιστῶν.
[the]   of all   men,   especially of believers.
Saviour

11 Παράγγελλε ταῦτα καὶ δίδασκε.
Charge thou these things and   teach.

12 μηδείς σου τῆς νεότητος καταφρονείτω,
¹No one ⁵of thee ²the   ⁴youth   ¹let despise,

ἀλλὰ τύπος γίνου τῶν πιστῶν ἐν λόγῳ,
but   ²a pattern ¹become of the believers in   speech,
         thou

ἐν ἀναστροφῇ, ἐν ἀγάπῃ, ἐν πίστει,
in   behaviour,   in   love,   in   faith,

ἐν ἁγνείᾳ. 13 ἕως ἔρχομαι πρόσεχε
in purity.   Until   I come   attend

τῇ ἀναγνώσει, τῇ παρακλήσει, τῇ διδασ-
to the reading,* to the exhortation, to the teach-

καλίᾳ. 14 μὴ ἀμέλει τοῦ ἐν σοὶ
ing.   Do not be neglectful ¹of the ²in ⁴thee

χαρίσματος, ὃ ἐδόθη σοι διὰ προφητείας
²gift,   which was to thee by   prophecy
                         given   means of

μετὰ ἐπιθέσεως τῶν χειρῶν τοῦ πρε-
with   laying on of the hands   of the body

---

[f] Other ancient authorities read *suffer reproach*

* That is, the reading aloud in public worship of the Scriptures (as nearly always in the N.T.).

¹⁵Practice these duties, devote yourself to them, so that all may see your progress. ¹⁶Take heed to yourself and to your teaching; hold to that, for by so doing you will save both yourself and your hearers.

σβυτερίου. 15 ταῦτα μελέτα, ἐν τούτοις
of elders. ¹These things ¹attend to, ²in ³these things

ἴσθι, ἵνα σου ἡ προκοπὴ φανερὰ ᾖ
¹be in order of thee the advance clear may be
thou, that

πᾶσιν. 16 ἔπεχε σεαυτῷ καὶ τῇ διδασκαλίᾳ,
to all men. Take heed to thyself and to the teaching,

ἐπίμενε αὐτοῖς· τοῦτο γὰρ ποιῶν καὶ
continue in them; for this doing both

σεαυτὸν σώσεις καὶ τοὺς ἀκούοντάς σου.
thyself thou wilt save and the [ones] hearing thee.

CHAPTER 5

DO not rebuke an older man but exhort him as you would a father; treat younger men like brothers, ²older women like mothers, younger women like sisters, in all purity.

3 Honor widows who are real widows. ⁴If a widow has children or grandchildren, let them first learn their religious duty to their own family and make some return to their parents; for this is acceptable in the sight of God. ⁵She who is a real widow, and is left all alone, has set her hope on God and continues in supplications and prayers night and day; ⁶whereas she who is self-indulgent is dead even while she lives. ⁷Command this, so that they may be without reproach. ⁸If any one does not provide for his relatives, and especially

5 Πρεσβυτέρῳ μὴ ἐπιπλήξῃς, ἀλλὰ
An older man do not rebuke, but

παρακάλει ὡς πατέρα, νεωτέρους ὡς
exhort as a father, younger men as

ἀδελφούς, 2 πρεσβυτέρας ὡς μητέρας,
brothers, older women as mothers,

νεωτέρας ὡς ἀδελφὰς ἐν πάσῃ ἁγνείᾳ.
younger women as sisters with all purity.

3 Χήρας τίμα τὰς ὄντως χήρας. 4 εἰ δέ
³Widows ¹honour ²the ⁴really ⁵widows. But if

τις χήρα τέκνα ἢ ἔκγονα ἔχει, μαν-
any widow ²children ³or ⁴grandchildren ¹has, let

θανέτωσαν πρῶτον τὸν ἴδιον οἶκον εὐσεβεῖν
them learn firstly ²the(ir) ³own ⁴household ¹to show piety to

καὶ ἀμοιβὰς ἀποδιδόναι τοῖς προγόνοις·
and ²requitals ¹to return to the(ir) forebears;

τοῦτο γὰρ ἐστιν ἀπόδεκτον ἐνώπιον τοῦ
for this is acceptable before

θεοῦ. 5 ἡ δὲ ὄντως χήρα καὶ μεμονωμένη
God. But the really widow and having been left alone

ἤλπικεν ἐπὶ θεὸν καὶ προσμένει ταῖς
has set on God and continues in the
[her] hope

δεήσεσιν καὶ ταῖς προσευχαῖς νυκτὸς καὶ
petitions and the prayers night and

ἡμέρας· 6 ἡ δὲ σπαταλῶσα ζῶσα τέθνηκεν.
day; but the living wantonly ²living ¹has died.
[one]

7 καὶ ταῦτα παράγγελλε, ἵνα ἀνεπίλημπτοι
And these charge thou, in order ²without reproach
things that

ὦσιν. 8 εἰ δέ τις τῶν ἰδίων καὶ μάλιστα
¹they But if anyone ²the(his) ³own ⁴and ⁵especially
may be. [people]

for his own family, he has disowned the faith and is worse than an unbeliever. 9 Let a widow be enrolled if she is not less than sixty years of age, having been the wife of one husband; 10 and she must be well attested for her good deeds, as one who has brought up children, shown hospitality, washed the feet of the saints, relieved the afflicted, and devoted herself to doing good in every way. 11 But refuse to enrol younger widows; for when they grow wanton against Christ they desire to marry, 12 and so they incur condemnation for having violated their first pledge. 13 Besides that, they learn to be idlers, gadding about from house to house, and not only idlers but gossips and busybodies, saying what they should not. 14 So I would have younger widows marry, bear children, rule their households, and give the enemy no occasion to revile us. 15 For some have already strayed after Satan. 16 If any believing woman[i] has relatives who are widows, let her assist them; let the church not be burdened,

οἰκείων   οὐ   προνοεῖ,   τὴν πίστιν   ἤρνηται
[his] ¹provides not [for], ²the ³faith   ¹he has
⁴family   denied

καὶ   ἔστιν   ἀπίστου   χείρων.   9 χήρα
and is   ²an unbeliever ¹worse [than].   A widow

καταλεγέσθω   μὴ   ἔλαττον   ἐτῶν   ἐξήκοντα
let be enrolled ²not ³less [than] ²of years   ⁴sixty

γεγονυῖα,   ἑνὸς   ἀνδρὸς   γυνή,   10 ἐν   ἔργοις
¹having   of one   man   wife,   ²by   ¹works
become,

καλοῖς   μαρτυρουμένη,   εἰ   ἐτεκνοτρόφησεν,
²good   ¹being witnessed,   if she brought up children,

εἰ   ἐξενοδόχησεν,   εἰ   ἁγίων   πόδας   ἔνιψεν,
if   she entertained if ³of saints ²feet ¹she
strangers,   washed,

εἰ   θλιβομένοις   ἐπήρκεσεν,   εἰ   παντὶ   ἔργῳ
if ²being afflicted ¹she relieved, if ²every ⁴work
   [ones],

ἀγαθῷ   ἐπηκολούθησεν.   11 νεωτέρας   δὲ
²good   ¹she followed after.   ¹younger   But

χήρας   παραιτοῦ·   ὅταν   γὰρ   καταστρηνιάσωσιν
widows   refuse;   for whenever they grow wanton against

τοῦ   Χριστοῦ,   γαμεῖν   θέλουσιν,   12 ἔχουσαι
-    Christ,   ²to marry ¹they wish,   having

κρίμα   ὅτι   τὴν   πρώτην   πίστιν   ἠθέτησαν·
judgment because ²the(ir) ³first   ⁴faith ¹they set aside;

13 ἅμα   δὲ   καὶ   ἀργαὶ   μανθάνουσιν
and at the same time also ²idle ¹they learn [to be]

περιερχόμεναι   τὰς   οἰκίας,   οὐ   μόνον   δὲ
going round   the   houses,   ²not ³only ¹and

ἀργαὶ   ἀλλὰ   καὶ   φλύαροι   καὶ   περίεργοι,
idle   but   also   gossips   and   busybodies,

λαλοῦσαι   τὰ   μὴ   δέοντα.   14 βούλομαι
speaking the things not proper.   I will

οὖν   νεωτέρας   γαμεῖν,   τεκνογονεῖν,
there- younger women to marry,   to bear children,
fore

οἰκοδεσποτεῖν,   μηδεμίαν   ἀφορμὴν   διδόναι
to be mistress of   ²no   ³occasion   ¹to give
a house,

τῷ   ἀντικειμένῳ   λοιδορίας   χάριν·   15 ἤδη
to the [one] opposing ²reproach ¹on account of; ²already

γὰρ   τινες   ἐξετράπησαν   ὀπίσω   τοῦ   σατανᾶ.
¹for   some   turned aside   behind   -   Satan.

16 εἴ   τις   πιστὴ   ἔχει   χήρας,   ἐπαρκείτω
If   any believing has   widows,   let her relieve
woman

αὐταῖς,   καὶ   μὴ   βαρείσθω   ἡ   ἐκκλησία,
them,   and   not let be burdened the   church,

---

[i] Other ancient authorities read man or woman; others, simply man

so that it may assist those who are real widows.

17 Let the elders who rule well be considered worthy of double honor, especially those who labor in preaching and teaching; [18]for the scripture says, "You shall not muzzle an ox when it is treading out the grain," and, "The laborer deserves his wages." [19]Never admit any charge against an elder except on the evidence of two or three witnesses. [20]As for those who persist in sin, rebuke them in the presence of all, so that the rest may stand in fear. [21]In the presence of God and of Christ Jesus and of the elect angels I charge you to keep these rules without favor, doing nothing from partiality. [22]Do not be hasty in the laying on of hands, nor participate in another man's sins; keep yourself pure.

23 No longer drink only water, but use a little wine for the sake of your stomach and your frequent ailments.

24 The sins of some men are conspicuous, pointing to judgment, but the sins of others appear later. [25]So also

ἵνα   ταῖς   ὄντως   χήραις   ἐπαρκέσῃ.   **17** Οἱ
in or- [a]the   [b]real*ly*   [4]widows   [1]it may relieve.   [2]The
der that

καλῶς   προεστῶτες   πρεσβύτεροι   διπλῆς
[5]well   [6]ruling   [3]elders   [9]of double

τιμῆς   ἀξιούσθωσαν,   μάλιστα   οἱ   κοπιῶντες
[10]honour   [1]let [8]be [7]deemed   especially   the   labouring
[8]worthy,   [ones]

ἐν   λόγῳ   καὶ   διδασκαλίᾳ.   **18** λέγει   γὰρ
in   speech   and   teaching.   For says

ἡ   γραφή·   βοῦν   ἀλοῶντα   οὐ   φιμώσεις,
the scripture: An ox   threshing   thou shalt not muzzle,

καὶ·   ἄξιος   ὁ   ἐργάτης   τοῦ   μισθοῦ   αὐτοῦ.
and: Worthy [is]   the   workman   of the   pay   of him.

19 κατὰ   πρεσβυτέρου   κατηγορίαν   μὴ   παρα-
Against   an elder   accusation   do not re-

δέχου,   ἐκτὸς   εἰ   μὴ   ἐπὶ   δύο   ἢ   τριῶν
ceive,   except   unless   on [the   two   or   three
word of]

μαρτύρων.   **20** Τοὺς   ἁμαρτάνοντας   ἐνώπιον
witnesses.   The [ones]   sinning   [2]before

πάντων   ἔλεγχε,   ἵνα   καὶ   οἱ   λοιποὶ   φόβον
[3]all   [1]reprove   in   [2]also   [1]the   [2]rest   [5]fear
thou,   order that

ἔχωσιν.   **21** Διαμαρτύρομαι   ἐνώπιον   τοῦ
[4]may have.   I solemnly witness   before   –

θεοῦ   καὶ   Χριστοῦ   Ἰησοῦ   καὶ   τῶν
God   and   Christ   Jesus   and   the

ἐκλεκτῶν   ἀγγέλων   ἵνα   ταῦτα   φυλάξῃς
chosen   angels   *in order*   these things   thou guard
that

χωρὶς   προκρίματος,   μηδὲν   ποιῶν   κατὰ
without   prejudgment,   [2]nothing   [1]doing   by way of

πρόσκλισιν.   **22** χεῖρας   ταχέως   μηδενὶ
inclination.   [2]Hands   [3]quickly   [1]no man

ἐπιτίθει,   μηδὲ   κοινώνει   ἁμαρτίαις   ἀλ-
[1]lay [2]on,   nor   share   [2]sins   [1]in

λοτρίαις·   σεαυτὸν   ἁγνὸν   τήρει.   **23** Μηκέτι
others'†:   [2]thyself   [3]pure   [1]keep.   No longer

ὑδροπότει,   ἀλλὰ   οἴνῳ   ὀλίγῳ   χρῶ   διὰ
drink water,   but   [3]wine   [2]a little   [1]use   on account of

τὸν   στόμαχον   καὶ   τὰς   πυκνάς   σου
the(thy)   stomach   and   the   frequent   [2]of thee

ἀσθενείας.   **24** Τινῶν   ἀνθρώπων   αἱ   ἁμαρτίαι
[1]weaknesses.   [3]of some   [4]men   [1]The   [2]sins

πρόδηλοί   εἰσιν   προάγουσαι   εἰς   κρίσιν,
[5]clear   [5]are   going before   to   judgment,
beforehand

τισὶν   δὲ   καὶ   ἐπακολουθοῦσιν·   **25** ὡσαύτως
but some   indeed   they follow on;   similarly

good deeds are conspicuous; and even when they are not, they cannot remain hidden.

καὶ τὰ ἔργα τὰ καλὰ πρόδηλα, καὶ
also the ²works – ¹good [are] clear and
beforehand,

τὰ ἄλλως ἔχοντα κρυβῆναι οὐ δύνανται.
the ²otherwise ¹having ⁴to be hidden ³cannot.
[ones] (being)

CHAPTER 6

6 Ὅσοι εἰσὶν ὑπὸ ζυγὸν δοῦλοι, τοὺς
As many as are under a yoke slaves, ¹the(ir)
[being]

LET all who are under the yoke of slavery regard their masters as worthy of all honor, so that the name of God and the teaching may not be defamed. ²Those who have believing masters must not be disrespectful on the ground that they are brethren; rather they must serve all the better since those who benefit by their service are believers and beloved.

ἰδίους δεσπότας πάσης τιμῆς ἀξίους ἡγείς-
³own ⁴masters ⁵of all ⁷honour ⁶worthy ¹let them

θωσαν, ἵνα μὴ τὸ ὄνομα τοῦ θεοῦ καὶ
deem, lest the name – of God and

ἡ διδασκαλία βλασφημῆται. 2 οἱ δὲ
the teaching be blasphemed. And ¹the [ones]

πιστοὺς ἔχοντες δεσπότας μὴ καταφρο-
³believing ²having ⁴masters not let them

νείτωσαν, ὅτι ἀδελφοί εἰσιν, ἀλλὰ μᾶλλον
despise [them], because brothers they are, but rather

δουλευέτωσαν, ὅτι πιστοί εἰσιν καὶ
let them serve as slaves, because ⁶believing ⁵are ⁷and

ἀγαπητοὶ οἱ τῆς εὐεργεσίας ἀντιλαμ-
⁸beloved ¹the [ones] ³of the ⁴good service ²receiving in

βανόμενοι.
return.

Teach and urge these duties. ³If any one teaches otherwise and does not agree with the sound words of our Lord Jesus Christ and the teaching which accords with godliness, ⁴he is puffed up with conceit, he knows nothing; he has a morbid craving for controversy and for disputes about words, which produce envy, dissension, slander, base suspicions, ⁵and wrangling among men who are depraved in mind and bereft of the truth, imagining that godliness is a means of

Ταῦτα δίδασκε καὶ παρακάλει. 3 εἴ
These things teach thou and exhort. If

τις ἑτεροδιδασκαλεῖ καὶ μὴ προσέρχεται
anyone teaches differently and consents not

ὑγιαίνουσιν λόγοις τοῖς τοῦ κυρίου ἡμῶν
to being healthy words the of the Lord of us
[words]

Ἰησοῦ Χριστοῦ, καὶ τῇ κατ' εὐσέβειαν
Jesus Christ, and ¹to the ²according to ⁴piety

διδασκαλίᾳ, 4 τετύφωται, μηδὲν ἐπιστά-
²teaching, he has been puffed up, ²nothing ¹under-

μενος, ἀλλὰ νοσῶν περὶ ζητήσεις καὶ
standing, but being diseased about questionings and

λογομαχίας, ἐξ ὧν γίνεται φθόνος, ἔρις,
battles of words, out of which comes envy, strife,

βλασφημίαι, ὑπόνοιαι πονηραί, 5 διαπαρα-
blasphemies, ²suspicions ²evil, perpetual

τριβαὶ διεφθαρμένων ἀνθρώπων τὸν νοῦν
wranglings ²having been corrupted ¹of men the mind
=of men with corrupted mind

καὶ ἀπεστερημένων τῆς ἀληθείας, νομιζ-
and having been deprived of the truth, sup-

όντων πορισμὸν εἶναι τὴν εὐσέβειαν.*
posing ³gain ²to be the ¹piety.*

* For order of words see note on John 1. 1.

gain. ⁶There is great gain in godliness with contentment; ⁷for we brought nothing into the world, and*j* we cannot take anything out of the world; ⁸but if we have food and clothing, with these we shall be content. ⁹But those who desire to be rich fall into temptation, into a snare, into many senseless and hurtful desires that plunge men into ruin and destruction. ¹⁰For the love of money is the root of all evils; it is through this craving that some have wandered away from the faith and pierced their hearts with many pangs.

11 But as for you, man of God, shun all this; aim at righteousness, godliness, faith, love, steadfastness, gentleness. ¹²Fight the good fight of the faith; take hold of the eternal life to which you were called when you made the good confession in the presence of many witnesses. ¹³In the presence of God who gives life to all things, and of Christ Jesus who in his testimony before

---

6 ἔστιν   δὲ   πορισμὸς   μέγας   ἡ   εὐσέβεια
But ⁴is   ⁵gain   ⁶great   the   ¹piety

μετὰ   αὐταρκείας·   7 οὐδὲν   γὰρ   εἰσηνέγκαμεν
²with ³self-sufficiency;²   for nothing we have brought *in*

εἰς   τὸν   κόσμον,   ὅτι   οὐδὲ   ἐξενεγκεῖν
into   the   world,   because neither ²to carry out

τι   δυνάμεθα·   8 ἔχοντες   δὲ   διατροφὰς   καὶ
³any- ¹can we;   but having   foods   and
thing

σκεπάσματα,   τούτοις   ἀρκεσθησόμεθα.   9 οἱ
clothings, with these things we will be satisfied.   the

δὲ   βουλόμενοι   πλουτεῖν   ἐμπίπτουσιν   εἰς
But [ones] resolving   to be rich   fall *in*   into

πειρασμὸν   καὶ   παγίδα   καὶ   ἐπιθυμίας   πολλὰς
temptation   and   a snare   and   ²lusts   ¹many

ἀνοήτους   καὶ   βλαβεράς,   αἵτινες   βυθίζουσιν
²foolish   ¹and   ³injurious,   which   ²cause ³to sink

τοὺς   ἀνθρώπους   εἰς   ὄλεθρον   καὶ   ἀπώλειαν.
-       ¹men   into   ruin   and   destruction.

10 ῥίζα   γὰρ   πάντων   τῶν   κακῶν   ἐστιν
For ⁴a root   ⁵of all   -   ⁶evils   ³is

ἡ   φιλαργυρία,   ἧς   τινες   ὀρεγόμενοι
¹the ²love of money,² of which some   hankering after

ἀπεπλανήθησαν   ἀπὸ   τῆς   πίστεως   καὶ
wandered away   from   the   faith   and

ἑαυτοὺς   περιέπειραν   ὀδύναις   πολλαῖς.   11 Σὺ
themselves   pierced round   ²pains   ¹by many.   thou

δέ,   ὦ   ἄνθρωπε   θεοῦ,   ταῦτα   φεῦγε·   ²δίωκε
But, O   man   of God, these things flee;   ²pursue

δὲ   δικαιοσύνην,   εὐσέβειαν,   πίστιν,   ἀγάπην,
¹and righteousness,   piety,   faith,   love,

ὑπομονήν,   πραϋπαθίαν.   12 ἀγωνίζου   τὸν
endurance,   meekness.   Struggle   the

καλὸν   ἀγῶνα   τῆς   πίστεως,   ἐπιλαβοῦ   τῆς
good   struggle of the   faith,   lay hold on   *the*

αἰωνίου   ζωῆς,   εἰς   ἣν   ἐκλήθης   καὶ   ὡμολό-
eternal   life,   to which thou wast   and   didst con-
called

γησας   τὴν   καλὴν   ὁμολογίαν   ἐνώπιον
fess   the   good   confession   before

πολλῶν   μαρτύρων.   13 παραγγέλλω   ἐνώπιον
many   witnesses.   I charge   before

τοῦ   θεοῦ   τοῦ   ζωογονοῦντος   τὰ   πάντα
-     God   the [one]   quickening   -   all things

καὶ   Χριστοῦ   Ἰησοῦ   τοῦ   μαρτυρήσαντος
and   Christ   Jesus   the [one] having witnessed

---

j Other ancient authorities insert *it is certain that*

* For order of words see note on John 1. 1.

Pontius Pilate made the good confession, [14] I charge you to keep the commandment unstained and free from reproach until the appearing of our Lord Jesus Christ; [15] and this will be made manifest at the proper time by the blessed and only Sovereign, the King of kings and Lord of lords, [16] who alone has immortality and dwells in unapproachable light, whom no man has ever seen or can see. To him be honor and eternal dominion. Amen.

[17] As for the rich in this world, charge them not to be haughty, nor to set their hopes on uncertain riches but on God who richly furnishes us with everything to enjoy. [18] They are to do good, to be rich in good deeds, liberal and generous, [19] thus laying up for themselves a good foundation for the future, so that they may take hold of the life which is life indeed.

[20] O Timothy, guard what has been entrusted to you. Avoid the godless

ἐπὶ Ποντίου Πιλάτου τὴν καλὴν ὁμολογίαν,
in the Pontius Pilate the good confession.
time of

14 τηρῆσαί σε τὴν ἐντολὴν ἄσπιλον
   [2]to keep [1]thee* the(this) commandment unspotted

ἀνεπίλημπτον μέχρι τῆς ἐπιφανείας τοῦ
without reproach until the appearance of the

κυρίου ἡμῶν Ἰησοῦ Χριστοῦ, 15 ἣν
Lord of us Jesus Christ,   which§

καιροῖς ἰδίοις δείξει ὁ μακάριος καὶ
[2]in its/his own times [1]will show [1]the [2]blessed [3]and

μόνος δυνάστης, ὁ βασιλεὺς τῶν βασιλευ-
[4]only [5]Potentate, the King of the [ones] reign-

όντων καὶ κύριος τῶν κυριευόντων, 16 ὁ
ing and Lord of the [ones] ruling,   the

μόνος ἔχων ἀθανασίαν, φῶς οἰκῶν
only [one] having immortality, [2]light [1]inhabiting

ἀπρόσιτον, ὃν εἶδεν οὐδεὶς ἀνθρώπων οὐδὲ
unapproach- whom [2]saw [1]no one [2]of men nor
able,

ἰδεῖν δύναται· ᾧ τιμὴ καὶ κράτος αἰώνιον·
[2]to see [1]can; to [be] and might eternal:
        whom honour

ἀμήν. 17 Τοῖς πλουσίοις ἐν τῷ νῦν
Amen.   [2]the [3]rich [4]in [5]the [6]now
                                (present)

αἰῶνι παράγγελλε μὴ ὑψηλοφρονεῖν, μηδὲ
[7]age [1]Charge thou not to be highminded, nor

ἠλπικέναι ἐπὶ πλούτου ἀδηλότητι, ἀλλ'
to have set on [2]of riches [1][the] uncertainty, but
[their] hope

ἐπὶ θεῷ τῷ παρέχοντι ἡμῖν πάντα
on God the [one] offering to us all things

πλουσίως εἰς ἀπόλαυσιν, 18 ἀγαθοεργεῖν,
richly for enjoyment,   to work good,

πλουτεῖν ἐν ἔργοις καλοῖς, εὐμεταδότους
to be rich in [2]works [1]good, [2]ready to impart

εἶναι, κοινωνικούς, 19 ἀποθησαυρίζοντας
[1]to be, generous,   treasuring away

ἑαυτοῖς θεμέλιον καλὸν εἰς τὸ μέλλον,
for   [2]foundation [1]a good for the future,
themselves

ἵνα ἐπιλάβωνται τῆς ὄντως ζωῆς. 20 Ὦ
in or- they may lay the real*ly* life.   O
der that hold on

Τιμόθεε, τὴν παραθήκην φύλαξον, ἐκτρεπ-
Timothy, [2]the [3]deposit [1]guard, turning

---

* " thee " is the direct object of the verb " charge " in ver. 13: " I charge . . . thee to keep . . ."

§ The antecedent to this relative pronoun is " appearance ", not " Jesus Christ ".

chatter and contra-dictions of what is falsely called knowledge, [21] for by professing it some have missed the mark as regards the faith.

Grace be with you.

ὅμενος   τὰς   βεβήλους   κενοφωνίας   καὶ
aside from   the   profane   empty utterances   and

ἀντιθέσεις   τῆς   ψευδωνύμου   γνώσεως,   21 ἣν
opposing   of the   falsely named   knowledge,   which
tenets

τινες   ἐπαγγελλόμενοι   περὶ   τὴν   πίστιν
some   promising   concerning the   faith

ἠστόχησαν.
missed aim.

Ἡ   χάρις   μεθ᾿   ὑμῶν.
– Grace [be] with   you.

II. TIMOTHY 1

ΠΡΟΣ ΤΙΜΟΘΕΟΝ Β
To Timothy 2

CHAPTER 1

PAUL, an apostle of Christ Jesus by the will of God according to the promise of the life which is in Christ Jesus,

2 To Timothy, my beloved child:

Grace, mercy, and peace from God the Father and Christ Jesus our Lord.

3 I thank God whom I serve with a clear conscience, as did my fathers, when I remember you constantly in my prayers. [4] As I remember your tears, I long night and day to see you, that I may be filled with joy. [5] I am reminded of your sincere faith, a faith that

1 Παῦλος   ἀπόστολος   Χριστοῦ   Ἰησοῦ   διὰ
Paul   an apostle   of Christ   Jesus through

θελήματος   θεοῦ   κατ᾿   ἐπαγγελίαν   ζωῆς
[the] will   of God   by way of   a promise   of life

τῆς   ἐν   Χριστῷ   Ἰησοῦ   2 Τιμοθέῳ   ἀγαπητῷ
– in   Christ   Jesus   to Timothy   beloved

τέκνῳ·   χάρις,   ἔλεος,   εἰρήνη   ἀπὸ   θεοῦ
child: Grace,   mercy,   peace   from   God

πατρὸς   καὶ   Χριστοῦ   Ἰησοῦ   τοῦ   κυρίου
[our] Father and   Christ   Jesus   the   Lord

ἡμῶν.
of us.

3 Χάριν   ἔχω   τῷ   θεῷ,   ᾧ   λατρεύω
Thanks   I have   –   to God, whom   I worship

ἀπὸ   προγόνων   ἐν   καθαρᾷ   συνειδήσει,   ὡς
from [my] forebears in   a clean   conscience,   as

ἀδιάλειπτον   ἔχω   τὴν   περὶ   σοῦ   μνείαν
unceasingly   I have   [1]the [3]concerning [4]thee [2]remem-
                                                    brance

ἐν   ταῖς   δεήσεσίν   μου   νυκτὸς   καὶ   ἡμέρας,
in   the   petitions   of me   night   and   day,

4 ἐπιποθῶν   σε   ἰδεῖν,   μεμνημένος   σου
longing   [2]thee   [1]to see,   having been   [3]of thee
                                            reminded

τῶν   δακρύων,   ἵνα   χαρᾶς   πληρωθῶ,
[1]of the   [2]tears,   in order of(with) joy I may be filled,
                      that

5 ὑπόμνησιν   λαβὼν   τῆς   ἐν   σοὶ   ἀνυποκρίτου
[2]recollection   [1]taking   [5]of the [6]in [7]thee   [4]unfeigned

dwelt first in your grandmother Lo'is and your mother Eunice and now, I am sure, dwells in you. [6]Hence I remind you to rekindle the gift of God that is within you through the laying on of my hands; [7]for God did not give us a spirit of timidity but a spirit of power and love and self-control.

8 Do not be ashamed then of testifying to our Lord, nor of me his prisoner, but take your share of suffering for the gospel in the power of God, [9]who saved us and called us with a holy calling, not in virtue of our works but in virtue of his own purpose and the grace which he gave us in Christ Jesus ages ago, [10]and now has manifested through the appearing of our Savior Christ Jesus, who abolished death and brought life and immortality to light through the gospel. [11]For this gospel I was appointed a preacher and apostle

πίστεως, ἥτις ἐνώκησεν πρῶτον ἐν τῇ
'faith, which indwelt firstly in the

μάμμῃ σου Λωῒδι καὶ τῇ μητρί σου
grand- of thee Lois and [in] the mother of thee
mother

Εὐνίκῃ, πέπεισμαι δὲ ὅτι καὶ ἐν σοί.
Eunice, and I have been that [it dwells] in thee.
persuaded also

6 Δι' ἣν αἰτίαν ἀναμιμνήσκω σε ἀνα-
For which cause I remind thee to fan

ζωπυρεῖν τὸ χάρισμα τοῦ θεοῦ, ὅ ἐστιν
the flame [of] the gift – of God, which is

ἐν σοὶ διὰ τῆς ἐπιθέσεως τῶν χειρῶν
in thee through the laying on of the hands

μου. 7 οὐ γὰρ ἔδωκεν ἡμῖν ὁ θεὸς
of me. 'not For 'gave ; 'to us – 'God

πνεῦμα δειλίας, ἀλλὰ δυνάμεως καὶ ἀγάπης
a spirit of cowardice, but of power and of love

καὶ σωφρονισμοῦ. 8 μὴ οὖν ἐπαισχυνθῇς
and of self-control. 'not 'Therefore 'be 'thou
ashamed [of]

τὸ μαρτύριον τοῦ κυρίου ἡμῶν μηδὲ
the testimony of the Lord of us nor

ἐμὲ τὸν δέσμιον αὐτοῦ, ἀλλὰ συγ-
[of] me the prisoner of him, but suffer

κακοπάθησον τῷ εὐαγγελίῳ κατὰ δύναμιν
ill with the gospel according to [the] power

θεοῦ, 9 τοῦ σώσαντος ἡμᾶς καὶ καλέσαντος
of God, of the having saved us and having called
[one]

κλήσει ἁγίᾳ, οὐ κατὰ τὰ ἔργα ἡμῶν
'calling 'with a holy, not according to the works of us

ἀλλὰ κατὰ ἰδίαν πρόθεσιν καὶ χάριν,
but according to [his] own purpose and grace,

τὴν δοθεῖσαν ἡμῖν ἐν Χριστῷ Ἰησοῦ
– given to us in Christ Jesus

πρὸ χρόνων αἰωνίων, 10 φανερωθεῖσαν δὲ
before times eternal, but manifested

νῦν διὰ τῆς ἐπιφανείας τοῦ σωτῆρος
now through the appearance of the Saviour

ἡμῶν Χριστοῦ Ἰησοῦ, καταργήσαντος μὲν
of us Christ Jesus, 'abrogating 'on one
hand

τὸν θάνατον φωτίσαντος δὲ ζωὴν καὶ
– death 'bringing to 'on the life and
light other

ἀφθαρσίαν διὰ τοῦ εὐαγγελίου, 11 εἰς ὃ
incorruption through the gospel, for which

ἐτέθην ἐγὼ κῆρυξ καὶ ἀπόστολος καὶ
'was 'I a herald and an apostle and
appointed

and teacher, [12]and therefore I suffer as I do. But I am not ashamed, for I know whom I have believed, and I am sure that he is able to guard until that Day what has been entrusted to me.[a] [13]Follow the pattern of the sound words which you have heard from me, in the faith and love which are in Christ Jesus; [14]guard the truth that has been entrusted to you by the Holy Spirit who dwells within us.

15 You are aware that all who are in Asia turned away from me, and among them Phy'gelus and Hermog'-enes. [16]May the Lord grant mercy to the household of Onesiph'-orus, for he often refreshed me; he was not ashamed of my chains, [17]but when he arrived in Rome he searched for me eagerly and found me—[18]may the Lord grant him to find mercy from the Lord on that Day—and you well know all the service he rendered at Ephesus.

CHAPTER 2

YOU then, my son, be strong in the grace that is in Christ

[a] Or what I have entrusted to him

διδάσκαλος· 12 δι' ἣν αἰτίαν καὶ ταῦτα
a teacher; for which cause also these things

πάσχω, ἀλλ' οὐκ ἐπαισχύνομαι, οἶδα γὰρ
I suffer, but I am not ashamed, for I know

ᾧ πεπίστευκα, καὶ πέπεισμαι ὅτι δυνατός
whom I have and I have been that [2]able
believed, persuaded

ἐστιν τὴν παραθήκην μου φυλάξαι εἰς
[1]he is [4]the [5]deposit [6]of me [3]to guard to

ἐκείνην τὴν ἡμέραν. 13 ὑποτύπωσιν ἔχε
that - day. [2]a pattern [1]Have
thou

ὑγιαινόντων λόγων ὧν παρ' ἐμοῦ ἤκουσας
of being healthy words which [2]from [3]me [1]thou
heardest

ἐν πίστει καὶ ἀγάπῃ τῇ ἐν Χριστῷ
in faith and love - in Christ

Ἰησοῦ· 14 τὴν καλὴν παραθήκην φύλαξον
Jesus; the good deposit guard

διὰ πνεύματος ἁγίου τοῦ ἐνοικοῦντος ἐν
through Spirit [the] Holy - indwelling in

ἡμῖν. 15 Οἶδας τοῦτο, ὅτι ἀπεστράφησάν
us. Thou knowest this, that turned away from

με πάντες οἱ ἐν τῇ Ἀσίᾳ, ὧν ἐστιν
me all the ones in - Asia, of whom is

Φύγελος καὶ Ἑρμογένης. 16 δῴη ἔλεος
Phygelus and Hermogenes. [1]May [4]give [5]mercy

ὁ κύριος τῷ Ὀνησιφόρου οἴκῳ, ὅτι
[2]the [3]Lord [6]to the [9]of Onesiphorus [7]house- because
hold,

πολλάκις με ἀνέψυξεν καὶ τὴν ἅλυσίν
often me he refreshed and the chain

μου οὐκ ἐπαισχύνθη, 17 ἀλλὰ γενόμενος
of me was not ashamed [of], but coming to be

ἐν Ῥώμῃ σπουδαίως ἐζήτησέν με καὶ
in Rome [2]diligently [1]he [3]sought [4]me [4]and

εὗρεν· — 18 δῴη αὐτῷ ὁ κύριος εὑρεῖν
[5]found; ([1]May [4]give [5]to him [2]the [3]Lord to find

ἔλεος παρὰ κυρίου ἐν ἐκείνῃ τῇ ἡμέρᾳ·
mercy from [the] Lord in that the day;)

— καὶ ὅσα ἐν Ἐφέσῳ διηκόνησεν,
and what things in Ephesus he served,

βέλτιον σὺ γινώσκεις.
very well thou knowest.

2 Σὺ οὖν, τέκνον μου, ἐνδυναμοῦ ἐν
Thou therefore, child of me, be empowered by

τῇ χάριτι τῇ ἐν Χριστῷ Ἰησοῦ, 2 καὶ
the grace - in Christ Jesus, and

Jesus, ²and what you have heard from me before many witnesses entrust to faithful men who will be able to teach others also. ³Take your share of suffering as a good soldier of Christ Jesus. ⁴No soldier on service gets entangled in civilian pursuits, since his aim is to satisfy the one who enlisted him. ⁵An athlete is not crowned unless he competes according to the rules. ⁶It is the hard-working farmer who ought to have the first share of the crops. ⁷Think over what I say, for the Lord will grant you understanding in everything.

8 Remember Jesus Christ, risen from the dead, descended from David, as preached in my gospel, ⁹the gospel for which I am suffering and wearing fetters like a criminal. But the word of God is not fettered. ¹⁰Therefore I endure everything for the sake of the elect, that they also may obtain the salvation which in Christ Jesus goes with eternal glory. ¹¹The saying is sure:

ἃ   ἤκουσας   παρ'   ἐμοῦ   διὰ   πολλῶν
what   thou   from   me   through many
things heardest

μαρτύρων,   ταῦτα   παράθου   πιστοῖς   ἀνθρώ-
witnesses,   these   commit   to faithful men,

ποις,   οἵτινες   ἱκανοὶ   ἔσονται   καὶ   ἑτέρους
who   ²competent ¹will be ²also ⁴others

διδάξαι.   3 Συγκακοπάθησον   ὡς   καλὸς
²to teach.   Suffer ill with*   as   a good

στρατιώτης   Χριστοῦ   Ἰησοῦ.   4 οὐδεὶς
soldier   of Christ   Jesus.   No one

στρατευόμενος   ἐμπλέκεται   ταῖς   τοῦ   βίου
soldiering   is involved   ¹with the -   ²of life

πραγματείαις,   ἵνα   τῷ   στρατολογήσαντι
²affairs,   in order   ²the   ³having enlisted
that   [one]   [him]

ἀρέσῃ.   5 ἐὰν   δὲ   καὶ   ἀθλῇ   τις,   οὐ
¹he may   And if   also   ²wrestles ¹any-   not
please.   one,

στεφανοῦται   ἐὰν   μὴ   νομίμως   ἀθλήσῃ.
he is crowned   unless   ²lawfully   ¹he wrestles.

6 τὸν   κοπιῶντα   γεωργὸν   δεῖ   πρῶτον   τῶν
²the   ³labouring ⁴husbandman ¹It be-   ⁶firstly ⁷of the
hoves

καρπῶν   μεταλαμβάνειν.   7 νόει   ὃ   λέγω·
⁵fruits   ⁵to partake.   Consider what I say;

δώσει   γὰρ   σοι   ὁ   κύριος   σύνεσιν   ἐν
for ²will give ⁴thee ¹the ²Lord   understanding in

πᾶσιν.   8 μνημόνευε   Ἰησοῦν   Χριστὸν
all things.   Remember   Jesus   Christ

ἐγηγερμένον   ἐκ   νεκρῶν,   ἐκ   σπέρματος
having been raised from [the] dead, of [the] seed

Δαυίδ,   κατὰ   τὸ   εὐαγγέλιόν   μου·   9 ἐν
of David, according to the   gospel   of me;   in

ᾧ   κακοπαθῶ   μέχρι   δεσμῶν   ὡς   κακοῦργος,
which I suffer ill unto   bonds   as   an evildoer,

ἀλλὰ   ὁ   λόγος   τοῦ   θεοῦ   οὐ   δέδεται.
but   the   word   -   of God has not been bound.

10 διὰ   τοῦτο   πάντα   ὑπομένω   διὰ   τοὺς
Therefore   all things   I endure   on ac-   the
count of

ἐκλεκτούς,   ἵνα   καὶ   αὐτοὶ   σωτηρίας   τύχωσιν
chosen ones,   in or- ²also ¹they ⁴salvation ³may obtain
der that

τῆς   ἐν   Χριστῷ   Ἰησοῦ   μετὰ   δόξης
-    in   Christ   Jesus   with   glory

αἰωνίου.   11 πιστὸς   ὁ   λόγος·   εἰ   γὰρ
eternal.   Faithful [is] the   word: for if

* See 1. 8.

If we have died with him, we shall also live with him; [12] if we endure, we shall also reign with him; if we deny him, he also will deny us; [13] if we are faithless, he remains faithful— for he cannot deny himself.

14 Remind them of this, and charge them before the Lord[b] to avoid disputing about words, which does no good, but only ruins the hearers. [15] Do your best to present yourself to God as one approved, a workman who has no need to be ashamed, rightly handling the word of truth. [16] Avoid such godless chatter, for it will lead people into more and more ungodliness, [17] and their talk will eat its way like gangrene. Among them are Hymenaeus and Phile′tus, [18] who have swerved from the truth by holding that the resurrection is past already. They are upsetting the faith of some. [19] But God's firm foundation stands, bearing this seal: "The Lord knows those who are his," and "Let every one who names the name of the Lord depart from iniquity."

συναπεθάνομεν,   καὶ   συζήσομεν·   12 εἰ
we died with [him],   also   we shall live with [him];   if

ὑπομένομεν,   καὶ   συμβασιλεύσομεν·   εἰ
we endure,   also   we shall reign with [him];   if

ἀρνησόμεθα,   κἀκεῖνος   ἀρνήσεται   ἡμᾶς·   13 εἰ
we shall deny,   that one also   will deny   us;   if

ἀπιστοῦμεν,   ἐκεῖνος   πιστὸς   μένει,   ἀρνή-
we disbelieve,   that one   ¹faithful   ¹remains,   ²to

σασθαι   γὰρ   ἑαυτὸν   οὐ   δύναται.   14 Ταῦτα
deny   ¹for   ⁴himself   ³he cannot.   These things

ὑπομίμνησκε,   διαμαρτυρόμενος   ἐνώπιον   τοῦ
remind thou   solemnly witnessing   before   -
[them] [of],

θεοῦ   μὴ   λογομαχεῖν,   ἐπ'   οὐδὲν   χρήσιμον,
God   not to fight with words,   ²for   ³nothing   ¹useful,

ἐπὶ   καταστροφῇ   τῶν   ἀκουόντων.   15 σπού-
for   overthrowing   of the [ones] hearing.   ¹Be

δασον   σεαυτὸν   δόκιμον   παραστῆσαι   τῷ
eager   ³thyself   ⁴approved   ⁵to present

θεῷ,   ἐργάτην   ἀνεπαίσχυντον,   ὀρθοτομοῦντα
to God,   a workman   unashamed,   cutting straight

τὸν   λόγον   τῆς   ἀληθείας.   16 τὰς   δὲ
the   word   -   of truth.   -   But

βεβήλους   κενοφωνίας   περιΐστασο·   ἐπὶ   πλεῖον
profane   empty   shun;   ³to   ⁴more
    utterances

γὰρ   προκόψουσιν   ἀσεβείας,   17 καὶ   ὁ   λόγος
¹for   ²they will advance   of impiety,   and the   word

αὐτῶν   ὡς   γάγγραινα   νομὴν   ἕξει·   ὧν
of them   as   a canker   feeding   will have;   of
    whom

ἐστιν   Ὑμέναιος   καὶ   Φίλητος,   18 οἵτινες
is(are)   Hymenæus   and   Philetus,   who

περὶ   τὴν   ἀλήθειαν   ἠστόχησαν,   λέγοντες
con-   the   truth   missed aim,   saying
cerning

ἀνάστασιν   ἤδη   γεγονέναι,   καὶ   ἀνατρέπουσιν
[the]   already   to have   and   overturn
resurrection   become,

τήν   τινων   πίστιν.   19 ὁ   μέντοι   στερεὸς
the   ²of some   ¹faith.   ²the ¹However   firm

θεμέλιος   τοῦ   θεοῦ   ἕστηκεν,   ἔχων   τὴν
foundation   -   of God   stands,   having   -

σφραγῖδα   ταύτην·   ἔγνω   κύριος   τοὺς   ὄντας
seal   this: ²knew   ¹[The]   the   being
    Lord   [ones]

αὐτοῦ,   καὶ·   ἀποστήτω   ἀπὸ   ἀδικίας   πᾶς
of him,   and: Let stand away   from   iniquity   every-

ὁ   ὀνομάζων   τὸ   ὄνομα   κυρίου.   20 ἐν
one   naming   the   name   of [the] Lord.   ²in

[b] Other ancient authorities read God

20 In a great house there are not only vessels of gold and silver but also of wood and earthenware, and some for noble use, some for ignoble. ²¹ If any one purifies himself from what is ignoble, then he will be a vessel for noble use, consecrated and useful to the master of the house, ready for any good work. ²² So shun youthful passions and aim at righteousness, faith, love, and peace, along with those who call upon the Lord from a pure heart. ²³ Have nothing to do with stupid, senseless controversies; you know that they breed quarrels. ²⁴ And the Lord's servant must not be quarrelsome but kindly to every one, an apt teacher, forbearing, ²⁵ correcting his opponents with gentleness. God may perhaps grant that they will repent and come to know the truth, ²⁶ and they may escape from the snare of the devil, after being captured by him to do his will.ᶜ

μεγάλη	δὲ	οἰκίᾳ	οὐκ	ἔστιν	μόνον	σκεύη
²a great	¹Now	⁴house	there is(are)	not	only	vessels

χρυσᾶ	καὶ	ἀργυρᾶ,	ἀλλὰ	καὶ	ξύλινα
golden	and	silvern,	but	also	wooden

καὶ	ὀστράκινα,	καὶ	ἃ	μὲν	εἰς	τιμὴν	ἃ	δὲ
and	earthen,	and	some		to	honour		others

εἰς	ἀτιμίαν·	21 ἐὰν	οὖν	τις	ἐκκαθάρῃ
to	dishonour;	if	therefore	anyone	cleanses

ἑαυτὸν	ἀπὸ	τούτων,	ἔσται	σκεῦος	εἰς
himself	from	these [latter],	he will be	a vessel	to

τιμήν,	ἡγιασμένον,	εὔχρηστον	τῷ	δεσπότῃ,
honour,	having been sanctified;	suitable	for the	master,

εἰς	πᾶν	ἔργον	ἀγαθὸν	ἡτοιμασμένον.
to	every	work	good	having been prepared.

22 τὰς	δὲ	νεωτερικὰς	ἐπιθυμίας	φεῦγε,
Now the		²youthful	³lusts	¹flee,

δίωκε	δὲ	δικαιοσύνην,	πίστιν,	ἀγάπην,
but pursue		righteousness,	faith,	love,

εἰρήνην	μετὰ	τῶν	ἐπικαλουμένων	τὸν
peace	with	the [ones]	calling on	the

κύριον	ἐκ	καθαρᾶς	καρδίας.	23 τὰς	δὲ
Lord	out of	a clean	heart.	– But	

μωρὰς	καὶ	ἀπαιδεύτους	ζητήσεις	παραιτοῦ,
foolish	and	uninstructed	questionings	refuse,

εἰδὼς	ὅτι	γεννῶσιν	μάχας·	24 δοῦλον	δὲ
knowing	that	they beget	fights;	and ²a slave	

κυρίου	οὐ	δεῖ	μάχεσθαι	ἀλλὰ	ἤπιον
³of [the] Lord	¹it behoves not		to fight	but	gentle

εἶναι	πρὸς	πάντας,	διδακτικόν,	ἀνεξίκακον,
to be	toward	all men,	apt to teach,	forbearing,

25 ἐν	πραΰτητι	παιδεύοντα	τοὺς	ἀντιδιατι-
in	meekness	instructing	the [ones]	oppos-

θεμένους,	μήποτε	δώῃ	αὐτοῖς	ὁ	θεὸς
ing,	[if] perhaps	²may give	³them	–	¹God

μετάνοιαν	εἰς	ἐπίγνωσιν	ἀληθείας,	26 καὶ
repentance	for	a full knowledge	of truth,	and

ἀνανήψωσιν	ἐκ	τῆς	τοῦ	διαβόλου	παγίδος,
they may return to soberness	out of	¹the	³of the	⁴devil	²snare,

ἐζωγρημένοι	ὑπ᾽	αὐτοῦ	εἰς	τὸ	ἐκείνου	θέλημα.
having been caught	by	him[,]	to	¹the	³of that one*	²will.

ᶜ Or *by him, to do his* (that is, God's) *will*

* That is, of God (the remoter antecedent).

CHAPTER 3

BUT understand this, that in the last days there will come times of stress. ²For men will be lovers of self, lovers of money, proud, arrogant, abusive, disobedient to their parents, ungrateful, unholy, ³inhuman, implacable, slanderers, profligates, fierce, haters of good, ⁴treacherous, reckless, swollen with conceit, lovers of pleasure rather than lovers of God, ⁵holding the form of religion but denying the power of it. Avoid such people. ⁶For among them are those who make their way into households and capture weak women, burdened with sins and swayed by various impulses, ⁷who will listen to anybody and can never arrive at a knowledge of the truth. ⁸As Jannes and Jambres opposed Moses, so these men also oppose the truth, men of corrupt mind and counterfeit faith; ⁹but they will not get very far, for their

3 Τοῦτο   δὲ   γίνωσκε,   ὅτι   ἐν   ἐσχάταις
   And this   know thou,   that   in   [the] last

ἡμέραις   ἐνστήσονται   καιροὶ   χαλεποί·
days   ⁸will be at hand   ²times   ¹grievous·

2 ἔσονται   γὰρ   οἱ   ἄνθρωποι   φίλαυτοι,
   for ²will be   -   ¹men   self-lovers,

φιλάργυροι,   ἀλαζόνες,   ὑπερήφανοι,   βλάσφημοι,
money-lovers,   boasters,   arrogant,   blasphemers,

γονεῦσιν   ἀπειθεῖς,   ἀχάριστοι,   ἀνόσιοι,
²to parents   ¹disobedient,   unthankful,   unholy,

3 ἄστοργοι,   ἄσπονδοι,   διάβολοι,   ἀκρατεῖς,
   without natural   implacable,   slanderers,   incontinent,
   affection,

ἀνήμεροι,   ἀφιλάγαθοι,   4 προδόται,   προπετεῖς,
untamed,   haters of good   betrayers,   reckless,
            [things/men],

τετυφωμένοι,   φιλήδονοι   μᾶλλον   ἢ   φιλόθεοι,
having been   pleasure-lovers   rather   than   God-lovers,
puffed up,

5 ἔχοντες   μόρφωσιν   εὐσεβείας   τὴν   δὲ
   having   a form   of piety   but the

δύναμιν   αὐτῆς   ἠρνημένοι·   καὶ   τούτους
power   of it   having denied: and   ⁸these

ἀποτρέπου.   6 ἐκ   τούτων   γάρ   εἰσιν   οἱ
⁸turn away ¹from.   ⁸of   ²these   ¹For   are   the

ἐνδύνοντες   εἰς   τὰς   οἰκίας   καὶ   αἰχμαλωτίζ-
[ones] creeping into   -   houses   and   captur-

οντες   γυναικάρια   σεσωρευμένα   ἁμαρτίαις,
ing   silly women   *having been* heaped*   with sins,

ἀγόμενα   ἐπιθυμίαις   ποικίλαις,   7 πάντοτε
being led*   lusts   by various,   always

μανθάνοντα   καὶ   μηδέποτε   εἰς   ἐπίγνωσιν
learning*   and   never   ⁸to   ⁴a full knowledge

ἀληθείας   ἐλθεῖν   δυνάμενα.   8 ὃν   τρόπον
⁵of truth   ²to come   ¹being able.*   by what way

δὲ   Ἰάννης   καὶ   Ἰαμβρῆς   ἀντέστησαν
Now   Jannes   and   Jambres   opposed

Μωϋσεῖ,   οὕτως   καὶ   οὗτοι   ἀνθίστανται   τῇ
Moses,   so   also   these   oppose   the

ἀληθείᾳ,   ἄνθρωποι   κατεφθαρμένοι   τὸν   νοῦν,
truth,   men   having been corrupted   the   mind,
                        =with corrupted mind,

ἀδόκιμοι   περὶ   τὴν   πίστιν.   9 ἀλλ'   οὐ
reprobate   as to   the   faith.   But   not

προκόψουσιν   ἐπὶ   πλεῖον·   ἡ   γὰρ   ἄνοια
they will advance   to   more;   for the   folly
                   =farther;

---

* Agreeing with "silly women" (neut. pl.).

folly will be plain to all,
as was that of those two
men.

10 Now you have
observed my teaching,
my conduct, my aim in
life, my faith, my
patience, my love, my
steadfastness, [11] my persecutions, my sufferings,
what befell me at
Antioch, at Ico'nium,
and at Lystra, what
persecutions I endured;
yet from them all the
Lord rescued me.
[12] Indeed all who desire
to live a godly life in
Christ Jesus will be
persecuted, [13] while evil
men and impostors will
go on from bad to worse,
deceivers and deceived.
[14] But as for you, con-
tinue in what you have
learned and have firmly
believed, knowing from
whom you learned it
[15] and how from child-
hood you have been
acquainted with the
sacred writings which are
able to instruct you for
salvation through faith
in Christ Jesus. [16] All
scripture is inspired by
God and[d] profitable for
teaching, for reproof,
for correction, and for
training in righteousness,
[17] that the man of God
may be complete,

[d] Or *Every scripture inspired by
God*

αὐτῶν ἔκδηλος ἔσται πᾶσιν, ὡς καὶ
of them very clear will be to all men, as also
ἡ ἐκείνων ἐγένετο. 10 Σὺ δὲ παρηκολού-
the of those became. But thou hast closely
θησάς μου τῇ διδασκαλίᾳ, τῇ ἀγωγῇ,
followed of me the teaching, the conduct,
τῇ προθέσει, τῇ πίστει, τῇ μακροθυμίᾳ,
the purpose, the faith, the longsuffering,
τῇ ἀγάπῃ, τῇ ὑπομονῇ, 11 τοῖς διωγμοῖς,
the love, the endurance, the persecutions,
τοῖς παθήμασιν, οἷά μοι ἐγένετο ἐν
the sufferings, which [2]to me [1]happened in
Ἀντιοχείᾳ, ἐν Ἰκονίῳ, ἐν Λύστροις· οἵους
Antioch, in Iconium, in Lystra: what
διωγμοὺς ὑπήνεγκα, καὶ ἐκ πάντων με
persecutions I bore, and out of all [6]me
ἐρρύσατο ὁ κύριος. 12 καὶ πάντες δὲ
[3]delivered [1]the [2]Lord. [2]indeed [3]all [1]And
οἱ θέλοντες ζῆν εὐσεβῶς ἐν Χριστῷ
[the ones] wishing to live piously in Christ
Ἰησοῦ διωχθήσονται. 13 πονηροὶ δὲ ἄν-
Jesus will be persecuted. But evil men
θρωποι καὶ γόητες προκόψουσιν ἐπὶ τὸ
and impostors will advance to the
χεῖρον, πλανῶντες καὶ πλανώμενοι. 14 σὺ
worse, deceiving and being deceived. [2]thou
δὲ μένε ἐν οἷς ἔμαθες καὶ ἐπιστώθης,
But [1]continue in what thou didst and wast assured of,
things learn
εἰδὼς παρὰ τίνων ἔμαθες, 15 καὶ ὅτι
knowing from whom* thou didst learn, and that
ἀπὸ βρέφους ἱερὰ γράμματα οἶδας, τὰ
from a babe [2]sacred [3]letters [1]thou know- the
est, [ones]
δυνάμενά σε σοφίσαι εἰς σωτηρίαν διὰ
being able thee to make wise to salvation through
πίστεως τῆς ἐν Χριστῷ Ἰησοῦ. 16 πᾶσα
faith – in Christ Jesus. Every
γραφὴ θεόπνευστος καὶ ὠφέλιμος πρὸς
scripture [is] God-breathed and profitable for
διδασκαλίαν, πρὸς ἐλεγμόν, πρὸς ἐπανόρ-
teaching, for reproof, for cor-
θωσιν, πρὸς παιδείαν τὴν ἐν δικαιοσύνῃ,
rection, for instruction – in righteousness,
17 ἵνα ἄρτιος ᾖ ὁ τοῦ θεοῦ ἄνθρωπος,
in order [5]fitted [4]may [1]the – [3]of God [2]man,
that be

* Plural.

equipped for every good work.

πρὸς πᾶν ἔργον ἀγαθὸν ἐξηρτισμένος.
for every work good *having been* furnished.

CHAPTER 4

I charge you in the presence of God and of Christ Jesus who is to judge the living and the dead, and by his appearing and his kingdom: [2]preach the word, be urgent in season and out of season, convince, rebuke, and exhort, be unfailing in patience and in teaching. [3]For the time is coming when people will not endure sound teaching, but having itching ears they will accumulate for themselves teachers to suit their own likings, [4]and will turn away from listening to the truth and wander into myths. [5]As for you, always be steady, endure suffering, do the work of an evangelist, fulfil your ministry.

6 For I am already on the point of being sacrificed; the time of my departure has come. [7]I have fought the good fight, I have finished the race, I have kept the faith. [8]Henceforth there is laid up for me the crown of righteousness, which the Lord, the righteous judge, will

4 Διαμαρτύρομαι ἐνώπιον τοῦ θεοῦ καὶ
I solemnly witness before - God and

Χριστοῦ Ἰησοῦ, τοῦ μέλλοντος κρίνειν
Christ Jesus, the [one] being about to judge

ζῶντας καὶ νεκρούς, καὶ τὴν ἐπιφάνειαν
living [ones] and dead, both [by] the appearance

αὐτοῦ καὶ τὴν βασιλείαν αὐτοῦ· 2 κήρυξον
of him and [by] the kingdom of him: proclaim

τὸν λόγον, ἐπίστηθι εὐκαίρως ἀκαίρως,
the word, be attentive seasonably[,] unseasonably,

ἔλεγξον, ἐπιτίμησον, παρακάλεσον, ἐν πάσῃ
reprove, admonish, exhort, with all

μακροθυμίᾳ καὶ διδαχῇ. 3 ἔσται γὰρ
longsuffering and teaching. For there will be

καιρὸς ὅτε τῆς ὑγιαινούσης διδασκαλίας
a time when [2]the [2]*being* healthy [4]teaching

οὐκ ἀνέξονται, ἀλλὰ κατὰ τὰς ἰδίας
[1]they will not bear with, but according to the(ir) own

ἐπιθυμίας ἑαυτοῖς ἐπισωρεύσουσιν διδασ-
lusts [3]to themselves [1]they will heap up [2]teach-

κάλους κνηθόμενοι τὴν ἀκοήν, 4 καὶ ἀπὸ
ers tickling the ear, and [2]from

μὲν τῆς ἀληθείας τὴν ἀκοὴν ἀποστρέψουσιν,
[1]on [4]the [5]truth [3]the [1]ear [2]will turn away,
one hand

ἐπὶ δὲ τοὺς μύθους ἐκτραπήσονται. 5 σὺ
[2]to [1]on the *the* [4]tales [3]will be turned aside. [2]thou
other

δὲ νῆφε ἐν πᾶσιν, κακοπάθησον, ἔργον
But [1]be in all things, suffer evil, [2][the] work
sober

ποίησον εὐαγγελιστοῦ, τὴν διακονίαν σου
[1]do of an evangelist, [2]the [3]ministry [4]of thee

πληροφόρησον. 6 Ἐγὼ γὰρ ἤδη σπένδομαι,
[1]fulfil. For I already am being
poured out,

καὶ ὁ καιρὸς τῆς ἀναλύσεώς μου ἐφέστη-
and the time of the departure of me has

κεν. 7 τὸν καλὸν ἀγῶνα ἠγώνισμαι,
arrived. The good struggle I have struggled,

τὸν δρόμον τετέλεκα, τὴν πίστιν τετήρηκα·
the course I have finished, the faith I have kept:

8 λοιπὸν ἀπόκειταί μοι ὁ τῆς δικαιοσύνης
for the rest there is laid up for me [1]the - [2]of righteousness

στέφανος, ὃν ἀποδώσει μοι ὁ κύριος
[2]crown, which [6]will render [7]to me [1]the [5]Lord

ἐν ἐκείνῃ τῇ ἡμέρᾳ, ὁ δίκαιος κριτής,
[8]in [9]that - [10]day, [3]the [4]righteous [5]judge,

award to me on that Day, and not only to me but also to all who have loved his appearing.

9 Do your best to come to me soon. ¹⁰For Demas, in love with this present world, has deserted me and gone to Thessaloni′ca; Crescens has gone to Galatia,ᵉ Titus to Dalmatia. ¹¹Luke alone is with me. Get Mark and bring him with you; for he is very useful in serving me. ¹²Tych′icus I have sent to Ephesus. ¹³When you come, bring the cloak that I left with Carpus at Tro′as, also the books, and above all the parchments. ¹⁴Alexander the coppersmith did me great harm; the Lord will requite him for his deeds. ¹⁵Beware of him yourself, for he strongly opposed our message. ¹⁶At my first defense no one took my part; all deserted me. May it not be charged against them! ¹⁷But the Lord stood by me and gave me strength to proclaim the word fully, that all the Gentiles might hear it. So I was

οὐ μόνον δὲ ἐμοὶ ἀλλὰ καὶ πᾶσι τοῖς
¹not ²only ¹and to me but also to all the [ones]
ἠγαπηκόσι τὴν ἐπιφάνειαν αὐτοῦ.
having loved the appearance of him.

9 Σπούδασον ἐλθεῖν πρός με ταχέως·
Hasten to come to me shortly;

10 Δημᾶς γάρ με ἐγκατέλιπεν ἀγαπήσας
²Demas ¹For ⁴me ³forsook loving
τὸν νῦν αἰῶνα, καὶ ἐπορεύθη εἰς Θεσσαλο-
the now age, and went to Thessalo-
(present)
νίκην, Κρήσκης εἰς Γαλατίαν, Τίτος εἰς
nica, Crescens to Galatia, Titus to
Δαλματίαν· 11 Λουκᾶς ἐστιν μόνος μετ'
Dalmatia; Luke is alone with
ἐμοῦ. Μάρκον ἀναλαβὼν ἄγε μετὰ σεαυτοῦ·
me. Mark taking bring with thyself;
ἔστιν γάρ μοι εὔχρηστος εἰς διακονίαν.
²he is ¹for ⁴to me ³useful for ministry.

12 Τύχικον δὲ ἀπέστειλα εἰς Ἔφεσον.
And Tychicus I sent to Ephesus.

13 τὸν φαιλόνην, ὃν ἀπέλιπον ἐν Τρωάδι
The cloak, which I left in Troas
παρὰ Κάρπῳ, ἐρχόμενος φέρε, καὶ τὰ
with Carpus, coming bring thou, and the
βιβλία, μάλιστα τὰς μεμβράνας. 14 Ἀλέξ-
scrolls, especially the parchments. Alex-
ανδρος ὁ χαλκεὺς πολλά μοι κακὰ
ander the coppersmith ²many ¹to me ⁴evils
ἐνεδείξατο· ἀποδώσει αὐτῷ ὁ κύριος κατὰ
¹showed; ²will render ⁴to him ¹the ³Lord according to
τὰ ἔργα αὐτοῦ· 15 ὃν καὶ σὺ φυλάσσου·
the works of him; whom also ²thou ¹guard
³[against];
λίαν γὰρ ἀντέστη τοῖς ἡμετέροις λόγοις.
for greatly he opposed - our words.

16 Ἐν τῇ πρώτῃ μου ἀπολογίᾳ οὐδείς
At the first ²of me ¹defence no one
μοι παρεγένετο, ἀλλὰ πάντες με ἐγκατέ-
²me ¹was beside, but all men ⁴me ³for-
λιπον· μὴ αὐτοῖς λογισθείη· 17 ὁ δὲ
sook; not to them may it be reckoned; but the
κύριός μοι παρέστη καὶ ἐνεδυνάμωσέν με,
Lord ²me ¹stood with and empowered me,
ἵνα δι' ἐμοῦ τὸ κήρυγμα πληροφορηθῇ
in or- through me the proclamation might be
der that accomplished
καὶ ἀκούσωσιν πάντα τὰ ἔθνη, καὶ
and ⁴might hear ¹all ²the ³nations, and

ᵉ Other ancient authorities read Gaul

rescued from the lion's mouth. [18] The Lord will rescue me from every evil and save me for his heavenly kingdom. To him be the glory for ever and ever. Amen.

[19] Greet Prisca and Aquila, and the household of Onesiph'orus. [20] Eras'tus remained at Corinth; Troph'imus I left ill at Mile'tus. [21] Do your best to come before winter. Eubu'lus sends greetings to you, as do Pudens and Linus and Claudia and all the brethren.

[22] The Lord be with your spirit. Grace be with you.

ἐρρύσθην	ἐκ	στόματος	λέοντος.		[18] ῥύσεταί
I was delivered	out of	[the] mouth	of [the] lion.		[5]will deliver

με	ὁ	κύριος	ἀπὸ	παντὸς	ἔργου	πονηροῦ
[4]me	[1]The	[2]Lord	from	every	work	wicked

καὶ	σώσει	εἰς	τὴν	βασιλείαν	αὐτοῦ	τὴν
and	will save	to	the	[3]kingdom	[2]of him	

ἐπουράνιον·	ᾧ	ἡ	δόξα	εἰς	τοὺς	αἰῶνας
[1]heavenly:	to [be] whom the		glory	unto	the	ages

τῶν	αἰώνων,	ἀμήν.
of the	ages,	Amen.

[19] Ἄσπασαι	Πρίσκαν	καὶ	Ἀκύλαν	καὶ
Greet	Prisca	and	Aquila	and

τὸν	Ὀνησιφόρου	οἶκον.	[20] Ἔραστος
the	[2]of Onesiphorus	[1]household.	Erastus

ἔμεινεν	ἐν	Κορίνθῳ,	Τρόφιμον	δὲ	ἀπέλιπον
remained	in	Corinth,	but Trophimus		I left

ἐν	Μιλήτῳ	ἀσθενοῦντα.	[21] Σπούδασον
in	Miletus	ailing.	Hasten

πρὸ	χειμῶνος	ἐλθεῖν.	Ἀσπάζεταί	σε
before	winter	to come.	Greets	thee

Εὔβουλος	καὶ	Πούδης	καὶ	Λίνος	καὶ
Eubulus	and	Pudens	and	Linus	and

Κλαυδία	καὶ	οἱ	ἀδελφοὶ	πάντες.
Claudia	and	[2]the	[3]brothers	[1]all.

[22] Ὁ	κύριος	μετὰ	τοῦ	πνεύματός	σου.
The	Lord	[be] with	the	spirit	of thee.

ἡ	χάρις	μεθ᾽	ὑμῶν.
Grace	[be] with	you.	

TITUS 1

CHAPTER 1

PAUL, a servant of God and an apostle of Jesus Christ, to further the faith of God's elect and their knowledge of the truth which accords with godliness, [2] in hope of eternal life which God,

ΠΡΟΣ ΤΙΤΟΝ
To Titus

[1] Παῦλος	δοῦλος	θεοῦ,	ἀπόστολος	δὲ
Paul	a slave	of God,	and an apostle	

Ἰησοῦ	Χριστοῦ	κατὰ	πίστιν	ἐκλεκτῶν
of Jesus	Christ	according to	[the] faith	of chosen ones

θεοῦ	καὶ	ἐπίγνωσιν	ἀληθείας	τῆς	κατ᾽
of God	and	full knowledge	of [the] truth	-	according to

εὐσέβειαν	[2] ἐπ᾽	ἐλπίδι	ζωῆς	αἰωνίον,
piety	on(in)	hope	life	of eternal,

ἣν	ἐπηγγείλατο	ὁ	ἀψευδὴς	θεὸς	πρὸ
which	[4]promised	[1]the	[2]unlying	[3]God	before

who never lies, promised ages ago [3]and at the proper time manifested in his word through the preaching with which I have been entrusted by command of God our Savior;

4 To Titus, my true child in a common faith: Grace and peace from God the Father and Christ Jesus our Savior.

5 This is why I left you in Crete, that you might amend what was defective, and appoint elders in every town as I directed you, [6]if any man is blameless, the husband of one wife, and his children are believers and not open to the charge of being profligate or insubordinate. [7]For a bishop, as God's steward, must be blameless; he must not be arrogant or quick-tempered or a drunkard or violent or greedy for gain, [8]but hospitable, a lover of goodness, master of himself, upright, holy, and self-controlled; [9]he must hold firm to the sure word as taught, so that he may be able to give instruction in sound doctrine and also to confute those who contradict it. [10]For there

χρόνων	αἰωνίων,	3 ἐφανέρωσεν	δὲ	καιροῖς
times	eternal,	but [3]manifested		[3]times

ἰδίοις	τὸν	λόγον	αὐτοῦ	ἐν	κηρύγματι
[1]in [its] own	the	word	of him	in	a proclamation

ὃ	ἐπιστεύθην	ἐγὼ	κατ'	ἐπιταγὴν	τοῦ
which [2]was entrusted [with]		[1]I	according to	[the] command	of the

σωτῆρος	ἡμῶν	θεοῦ,	4 Τίτῳ	γνησίῳ	τέκνῳ
Saviour	of us	God,	to Titus	a true	child

κατὰ	κοινὴν	πίστιν·	χάρις	καὶ	εἰρήνη
according to	a common	faith:	Grace	and	peace

ἀπὸ	θεοῦ	πατρὸς	καὶ	Χριστοῦ	Ἰησοῦ
from	God	[the] Father	and	Christ	Jesus

τοῦ	σωτῆρος	ἡμῶν.
the	Saviour	of us.

5 Τούτου	χάριν	ἀπέλιπόν	σε	ἐν	Κρήτῃ,
For this reason†		I left	thee	in	Crete,

ἵνα	τὰ	λείποντα	ἐπιδιορθώσῃ,	καὶ
in order that	the things	wanting	thou shouldest set in order,	and

καταστήσῃς	κατὰ	πόλιν	πρεσβυτέρους,	ὡς	ἐγώ
shouldest appoint	in each	city	elders,	as	I

σοι	διεταξάμην,	6 εἴ	τίς	ἐστιν	ἀνέγκλητος,
[2]thee	[1]charged,	if	anyone	is	unreprovable,

μιᾶς	γυναικὸς	ἀνήρ,	τέκνα	ἔχων	πιστά,
[2]of one	[3]wife	[1]husband,	[3]children	[1]having	[2]believing,

μὴ	ἐν	κατηγορίᾳ	ἀσωτίας	ἢ	ἀνυπότακτα.
not	in	accusation	of profligacy	or	unruly.*

7 δεῖ	γὰρ	τὸν	ἐπίσκοπον	ἀνέγκλητον	εἶναι
For it behoves		the	bishop	[2]unreprovable	[1]to be

ὡς	θεοῦ	οἰκονόμον,	μὴ	αὐθάδη,	μὴ
as	of God	a steward,	not	self-pleasing,	not

ὀργίλον,	μὴ	πάροινον,	μὴ	πλήκτην,	μὴ
passionate,	not	given to wine,	not	a striker,	not

αἰσχροκερδῆ,	8 ἀλλὰ	φιλόξενον,	φιλάγαθον,
greedy of base gain,	but	hospitable,	a lover of good [men/things],

σώφρονα,	δίκαιον,	ὅσιον,	ἐγκρατῆ,	9 ἀντεχ-
sensible,	just,	holy,	self-controlled,	holding

όμενον	τοῦ	κατὰ	τὴν	διδαχὴν	πιστοῦ
to	[1]the	[4]according to	[5]the	[3]teaching	[2]faithful

λόγου,	ἵνα	δυνατὸς	ᾖ	καὶ	παρακαλεῖν
[2]word,	in order that	[3]able	[1]he may be	both	to exhort

ἐν	τῇ	διδασκαλίᾳ	τῇ	ὑγιαινούσῃ	καὶ
by	the	[2]teaching	-	[1]being healthy	and

τοὺς	ἀντιλέγοντας	ἐλέγχειν.	10 Εἰσὶν	γὰρ
[3]the [ones]	[2]contradicting	[1]to convince.	For there are

* In agreement with " children " (neut. pl.).

are many insubordinate men, empty talkers and deceivers, especially the circumcision party; [11] they must be silenced, since they are upsetting whole families by teaching for base gain what they have no right to teach. [12] One of themselves, a prophet of their own, said, "Cretans are always liars, evil beasts, lazy gluttons." [13] This testimony is true. Therefore rebuke them sharply, that they may be sound in the faith, [14] instead of giving heed to Jewish myths or to commands of men who reject the truth. [15] To the pure all things are pure, but to the corrupt and unbelieving nothing is pure; their very minds and consciences are corrupted. [16] They profess to know God, but they deny him by their deeds; they are detestable, disobedient, unfit for any good deed. [2] Bid the older

πολλοὶ ἀνυπότακτοι, ματαιολόγοι καὶ
many unruly men, vain talkers and

φρεναπάται, μάλιστα οἱ ἐκ τῆς περιτομῆς,
deceivers, specially the ones of the circumcision,

11 οὓς δεῖ ἐπιστομίζειν, οἵτινες ὅλους
whom it to stop the who [2]whole
behoves mouth,

οἴκους ἀνατρέπουσιν διδάσκοντες ἃ μὴ
[3]households [1]overturn teaching things [4]not
which

δεῖ αἰσχροῦ κέρδους χάριν. 12 εἶπέν
[1]it be- [4]base [3]gain [2]for the [1]Said
hoves sake of.

τις ἐξ αὐτῶν ἴδιος αὐτῶν προφήτης·
[1]a cer- [2]of [3]them [4]an own [5]of them [6]prophet:
tain one

Κρῆτες ἀεὶ ψεῦσται, κακὰ θηρία, γαστέρες
Cretans always liars, evil beasts, [2]gluttons
[are]

ἀργαί. 13 ἡ μαρτυρία αὕτη ἐστὶν ἀληθής.
[1]idle. This witness is true.

δι' ἣν αἰτίαν ἔλεγχε αὐτοὺς ἀποτόμως,
For which cause reprove them severely,

ἵνα ὑγιαίνωσιν ἐν τῇ πίστει, 14 μὴ
in or- they may in the faith, not
der that be healthy

προσέχοντες Ἰουδαϊκοῖς μύθοις καὶ
giving heed to Jewish tales and

ἐντολαῖς ἀνθρώπων ἀποστρεφομένων τὴν
commandments of men perverting the

ἀλήθειαν. 15 πάντα καθαρὰ τοῖς καθαροῖς·
truth. All things [are] clean to the clean;

τοῖς δὲ μεμιαμμένοις καὶ ἀπίστοις οὐδὲν
but to having been and unfaithful nothing
the [ones] defiled

καθαρόν, ἀλλὰ μεμίανται αὐτῶν καὶ ὁ
[is] clean, but [2]has(ve) been defiled [1]of them [2]both [3]the

νοῦς καὶ ἡ συνείδησις. 16 θεὸν ὁμολο-
[3]mind [4]and [5]the [6]conscience. [2]God [1]they pro-

γοῦσιν εἰδέναι, τοῖς δὲ ἔργοις ἀρνοῦνται,
fess [2]to know, but by the(ir) works they deny [him],

βδελυκτοὶ ὄντες καὶ ἀπειθεῖς καὶ πρὸς
[2]abominable [1]being and disobedient and to

πᾶν ἔργον ἀγαθὸν ἀδόκιμοι.
every [2]work [1]good reprobate.

CHAPTER 2

BUT as for you, teach what befits sound doctrine. [2] Bid the older

2 Σὺ δὲ λάλει ἃ πρέπει τῇ ὑγιαινούσῃ
But [2]thou [1]speak things becomes the being
which healthy

διδασκαλίᾳ. 2 Πρεσβύτας νηφαλίους εἶναι,
teaching. Aged men [2]sober [1]to be,

men be temperate, serious, sensible, sound in faith, in love, and in steadfastness. ³Bid the older women likewise to be reverent in behavior, not to be slanderers or slaves to drink; they are to teach what is good, ⁴and so train the young women to love their husbands and children, ⁵to be sensible, chaste, domestic, kind, and submissive to their husbands, that the word of God may not be discredited. ⁶Likewise urge the younger men to control themselves. ⁷Show yourself in all respects a model of good deeds, and in your teaching show integrity, gravity, ⁸and sound speech that cannot be censured, so that an opponent may be put to shame, having nothing evil to say of us. ⁹Bid slaves to be submissive to their masters and to give satisfaction in every respect; they are not to be refractory, ¹⁰nor to pilfer, but to show entire and true fidelity, so that in everything they may adorn the doctrine of God our Savior.

¹¹ For the grace of God has appeared for the salvation of all men,

σεμνούς, σώφρονας, ὑγιαίνοντας τῇ πίστει,
grave, sensible, being healthy in the faith,

τῇ ἀγάπῃ, τῇ ὑπομονῇ· 3 πρεσβύτιδας
– in love, – in endurance; aged women

ὡσαύτως ἐν καταστήματι ἱεροπρεπεῖς, μὴ
similarly in demeanour reverent, not

διαβόλους, μηδὲ οἴνῳ πολλῷ δεδουλωμένας,
slanderers, nor ²wine ⁵by much ¹having been
enslaved,

καλοδιδασκάλους, 4 ἵνα σωφρονίζωσιν τὰς
teachers of what is good, in or- they may train the
der that

νέας φιλάνδρους εἶναι, φιλοτέκνους,
young ²lovers of ¹to be, child-lovers,
women [their] husbands

5 σώφρονας, ἁγνάς, οἰκουργούς, ἀγαθάς,
sensible, pure, home-workers, good,

ὑποτασσομένας τοῖς ἰδίοις ἀνδράσιν,
being subject to the(ir) own husbands,

ἵνα μὴ ὁ λόγος τοῦ θεοῦ βλασφημῆται.
lest the word – of God be blasphemed.

6 Τοὺς νεωτέρους ὡσαύτως παρακάλει
The younger men similarly exhort

σωφρονεῖν 7 περὶ πάντα, σεαυτὸν παρ-
to be sensible about all things, ²thyself ¹show-

εχόμενος τύπον καλῶν ἔργων, ἐν τῇ
ing a pattern of good works, in the

διδασκαλίᾳ ἀφθορίαν, σεμνότητα, 8 λόγον
teaching uncorruptness, gravity, ²speech

ὑγιῆ ἀκατάγνωστον, ἵνα ὁ ἐξ ἐναντίας
¹healthy ²irreprehensible, in or- the of contrary
der that man [the] [side]

ἐντραπῇ μηδὲν ἔχων λέγειν περὶ ἡμῶν
may be put ²nothing ¹having ⁴to say ³about ⁵us
to shame

φαῦλον. 9 Δούλους ἰδίοις δεσπόταις
³bad. Slaves to [their] own masters

ὑποτάσσεσθαι ἐν πᾶσιν, εὐαρέστους εἶναι,
to be subject in all things, well-pleasing to be,

μὴ ἀντιλέγοντας, 10 μὴ νοσφιζομένους, ἀλλὰ
not contradicting, not peculating, but

πᾶσαν πίστιν ἐνδεικνυμένους ἀγαθήν, ἵνα
²all ⁴faith ¹showing ³good, in order that

τὴν διδασκαλίαν τὴν τοῦ σωτῆρος ἡμῶν
²the ³teaching – ⁴of the ⁵Saviour ⁶of us

θεοῦ κοσμῶσιν ἐν πᾶσιν. 11 Ἐπεφάνη
⁷God ¹they may adorn in all things. ⁵appeared

γὰρ ἡ χάρις τοῦ θεοῦ σωτήριος πᾶσιν
For ¹the ²grace – ³of God ⁴saving to all

¹²training us to renounce irreligion and worldly passions, and to live sober, upright, and godly lives in this world, ¹³awaiting our blessed hope, the appearing of the glory of our great God and Savior*a* Jesus Christ, ¹⁴who gave himself for us to redeem us from all iniquity and to purify for himself a people of his own who are zealous for good deeds.

15 Declare these things; exhort and reprove with all authority. Let no one disregard you.

CHAPTER 3

REMIND them to be submissive to rulers and authorities, to be obedient, to be ready for any honest work, ²to speak evil of no one, to avoid quarreling, to be gentle, and to show perfect courtesy toward all men. ³For we ourselves were once foolish, disobedient, led astray, slaves to various passions and pleasures, passing our days in malice and envy, hated by men and hating one another; ⁴but when the goodness and loving kindness of God our Savior appeared, ⁵he

a Or *of the great God and our Savior*

ἀνθρώποις, 12 παιδεύουσα ἡμᾶς, ἵνα
men,   instructing   us,   in order
                                      that

ἀρνησάμενοι τὴν ἀσέβειαν καὶ τὰς κοσμικὰς
denying   -   impiety   and   -   worldly

ἐπιθυμίας σωφρόνως καὶ δικαίως καὶ
lusts   ²sensibly ³and ⁴righteously ⁵and

εὐσεβῶς ζήσωμεν ἐν τῷ νῦν αἰῶνι,
⁶piously ¹we might live in the now(present) age,

13 προσδεχόμενοι τὴν μακαρίαν ἐλπίδα καὶ
   expecting   the   blessed   hope   and

ἐπιφάνειαν τῆς δόξης τοῦ μεγάλου θεοῦ
appearance of the glory of the great God

καὶ σωτῆρος ἡμῶν Χριστοῦ Ἰησοῦ, 14 ὃς
and Saviour of us   Christ Jesus,   who

ἔδωκεν ἑαυτὸν ὑπὲρ ἡμῶν ἵνα λυτρώσηται
gave   himself on behalf us in or- he might
                         of   der that ransom

ἡμᾶς ἀπὸ πάσης ἀνομίας καὶ καθαρίσῃ
us   from all iniquity and might cleanse

ἑαυτῷ λαὸν περιούσιον, ζηλωτὴν καλῶν ἔργων.
for a people [his] own   zealous of good works.
himself possession,

15 Ταῦτα λάλει καὶ παρακάλει καὶ ἔλεγχε
These things speak thou and   exhort   and reprove

μετὰ πάσης ἐπιταγῆς· μηδείς σου περιφρονείτω.
with all command; ²no one ⁴of thee ¹let ³despise.

3 Ὑπομίμνῃσκε αὐτοὺς ἀρχαῖς ἐξουσίαις
  Remind thou them ²to rulers ³[and] ⁴authorities

ὑποτάσσεσθαι, πειθαρχεῖν, πρὸς πᾶν ἔργον
¹to be subject, to be obedient, ²to ⁴every ⁵work

ἀγαθὸν ἑτοίμους εἶναι, 2 μηδένα βλασ-
³good ⁶ready ¹to be,   no one to

φημεῖν, ἀμάχους εἶναι, ἐπιεικεῖς, πᾶσαν
rail at, uncontentious to be, forbearing, ²all

ἐνδεικνυμένους πρᾳύτητα πρὸς πάντας
¹showing forth meekness   to   all

ἀνθρώπους. 3 Ἦμεν γάρ ποτε καὶ ἡμεῖς
men.   For ³were ⁴then ²also ¹we

ἀνόητοι, ἀπειθεῖς, πλανώμενοι, δουλεύοντες
senseless, disobedient, being deceived, serving [as slaves]

ἐπιθυμίαις καὶ ἡδοναῖς ποικίλαις, ἐν κακίᾳ
¹lusts   ³and ⁴pleasures ¹various, ²in ²evil

καὶ φθόνῳ διάγοντες, στυγητοί, μισοῦντες
⁴and ⁵envy ¹living, hateful, hating

ἀλλήλους. 4 ὅτε δὲ ἡ χρηστότης καὶ
one another. But when the kindness and

ἡ φιλανθρωπία ἐπεφάνη τοῦ σωτῆρος ἡμῶν
the love to man ²appeared ¹of the ²Saviour ³of us

saved us, not because of
deeds done by us in
righteousness, but in
virtue of his own mercy,
by the washing of
regeneration and renewal
in the Holy Spirit, ⁶which
he poured out upon us
richly through Jesus
Christ our Savior, ⁷so
that we might be justified
by his grace and become
heirs in hope of eternal
life. ⁸The saying is sure.

I desire you to insist
on these things, so that
those who have believed
in God may be careful
to apply themselves to
good deeds;ᵇ these are
excellent and profitable
to men. ⁹But avoid stupid
controversies, genealo-
gies, dissensions, and
quarrels over the law,
for they are unprofitable
and futile. ¹⁰As for a man
who is factious, after
admonishing him once
or twice, have nothing
more to do with him,
¹¹knowing that such a
person is perverted and
sinful; he is self-
condemned.

12 When I send
Artemas or Tych'icus to
you, do your best to

θεοῦ,   5 οὐκ ἐξ ἔργων τῶν ἐν δικαιοσύνῃ
'God,   not by works   – ¹in ¹righteousness

ἃ   ἐποιήσαμεν ἡμεῖς, ἀλλὰ κατὰ τὸ
¹which   ³did   ²we,   but according to the

αὐτοῦ ἔλεος ἔσωσεν ἡμᾶς διὰ λουτροῦ
of him mercy he saved   us through [the] washing

παλιγγενεσίας καὶ ἀνακαινώσεως πνεύματος
of regeneration and   renewal   ¹Spirit

ἁγίου, 6 οὗ ἐξέχεεν ἐφ' ἡμᾶς πλουσίως
¹of [the] which he shed   on   us   richly
Holy,

διὰ Ἰησοῦ Χριστοῦ τοῦ σωτῆρος ἡμῶν,
through Jesus Christ   the   Saviour   of us,

7 ἵνα   δικαιωθέντες τῇ   ἐκείνου χάριτι
in or-   being justified ¹by the ²of that one ¹grace
der that

κληρονόμοι γενηθῶμεν κατ' ἐλπίδα ζωῆς
heirs   we might accord- a hope of life
           become   ing to

αἰωνίου. 8 Πιστὸς ὁ λόγος, καὶ περὶ
eternal.   Faithful [is] the word,   and as to

τούτων βούλομαί σε διαβεβαιοῦσθαι, ἵνα
these   I wish   thee   to affirm   in or-
things   confidently, der that

φροντίζωσιν καλῶν ἔργων προΐστασθαι οἱ
⁴may take   ⁶of good ⁷works ⁵to maintain ¹the
thought   [ones]

πεπιστευκότες θεῷ.   ταῦτά ἐστιν καλὰ
³having believed ²God.   These things is(are) good

καὶ ὠφέλιμα τοῖς ἀνθρώποις· 9 μωρὰς
and profitable   –   to men;   ²foolish

δὲ ζητήσεις καὶ γενεαλογίας καὶ ἔριν
¹but questionings and genealogies and strife

καὶ μάχας νομικὰς περιΐστασο· εἰσὶν γὰρ
and ²fights ¹legal   shun thou;   for they are

ἀνωφελεῖς καὶ μάταιοι. 10 αἱρετικὸν
unprofitable and   vain.   A factious

ἄνθρωπον μετὰ μίαν καὶ δευτέραν
man   after   one   and   a second

νουθεσίαν παραιτοῦ, 11 εἰδὼς ὅτι ἐξέστραπ-
admonition   avoid,   knowing that ²has been per-

ται ὁ τοιοῦτος καὶ ἁμαρτάνει ὢν αὐτο-
verted ¹such a man and   sins   being self-

κατάκριτος.
condemned.

12 Ὅταν πέμψω Ἀρτεμᾶν πρὸς σὲ
Whenever I send   Artemas   to   thee

ἢ Τύχικον, σπούδασον ἐλθεῖν πρός με
or Tychicus,   hasten   to come   to   me

come to me at Nicop'-
olis, for I have decided
to spend the winter there.
[13] Do your best to speed
Zenas the lawyer and
Apol'los on their way;
see that they lack noth-
ing. [14] And let our people
learn to apply themselves
to good deeds,[c] so as to
help cases of urgent
need, and not to be
unfruitful.

[15] All who are with
me send greetings to you.
Greet those who love
us in the faith.

Grace be with you all.

εἰς Νικόπολιν· ἐκεῖ γὰρ κέκρικα παραχειμά-
in Nicopolis; for there I have decided to spend [the]
σαι. 13 Ζηνᾶν τὸν νομικὸν καὶ Ἀπολλῶν
winter. Zenas the lawyer and Apollos
σπουδαίως πρόπεμψον, ἵνα μηδὲν αὐτοῖς
urgently send forward, in or- nothing to them
der that
λείπῃ. 14 μανθανέτωσαν δὲ καὶ οἱ ἡμέτεροι
may be lacking. And [1]let [4]learn [3]also – [2]our [people]
καλῶν ἔργων προΐστασθαι εἰς τὰς ἀναγ-
[6]of good [7]works [5]to maintain for – neces-
καίας χρείας, ἵνα μὴ ὦσιν ἄκαρποι.
sary wants, lest they be unfruitful.
15 Ἀσπάζονταί σε οἱ μετ᾽ ἐμοῦ πάντες.
[2]greet [3]thee [7]the [3]with [4]me [1]All.
[ones]
ἄσπασαι τοὺς φιλοῦντας ἡμᾶς ἐν πίστει.
Greet thou the [ones] loving us in [the] faith.
Ἡ χάρις μετὰ πάντων ὑμῶν.
– Grace [be] with [2]all [1]you.

PHILEMON

ΠΡΟΣ ΦΙΛΗΜΟΝΑ
To Philemon

PAUL, a prisoner for
Christ Jesus, and
Timothy our brother,
To Phile'mon our be-
loved fellow worker [2]and
Ap'phia our sister and
Archip'pus our fellow
soldier, and the church
in your house:
[3] Grace to you and
peace from God our
Father and the Lord
Jesus Christ.
[4] I thank my God
always when I remember
you in my prayers,
[5]because I hear of your
love and of the faith

1 Παῦλος δέσμιος Χριστοῦ Ἰησοῦ καὶ
Paul a prisoner of Christ Jesus and
Τιμόθεος ὁ ἀδελφὸς Φιλήμονι τῷ ἀγαπητῷ
Timothy the brother to Philemon the beloved
καὶ συνεργῷ ἡμῶν 2 καὶ Ἀπφίᾳ τῇ
and a fellow-worker of us and to Apphia the
ἀδελφῇ καὶ Ἀρχίππῳ τῷ συστρατιώτῃ
sister and to Archippus the fellow-soldier
ἡμῶν καὶ τῇ κατ᾽ οἶκόν σου ἐκκλησίᾳ·
of us and [1]to the [3]at [4]house [5]of thee [2]church:
3 χάρις ὑμῖν καὶ εἰρήνη ἀπὸ θεοῦ πατρὸς
Grace to you and peace from God Father
ἡμῶν καὶ κυρίου Ἰησοῦ Χριστοῦ.
of us and Lord Jesus Christ.
4 Εὐχαριστῶ τῷ θεῷ μου πάντοτε μνείαν
I give thanks to the God of me always [2]mention
σου ποιούμενος ἐπὶ τῶν προσευχῶν μου,
[3]of thee [1]making at the prayers of me,
5 ἀκούων σου τὴν ἀγάπην καὶ τὴν
hearing of thee the love and the

[c] Or enter honorable occupa-
tions

which you have toward the Lord Jesus and all the saints, ⁶and I pray that the sharing of your faith may promote the knowledge of all the good that is ours in Christ. ⁷For I have derived much joy and comfort from your love, my brother, because the hearts of the saints have been refreshed through you.

8 Accordingly, though I am bold enough in Christ to command you to do what is required, ⁹yet for love's sake I prefer to appeal to you— I, Paul, an ambassador*ᵃ* and now a prisoner also for Christ Jesus—¹⁰I appeal to you for my child, Ones'imus, whose father I have become in my imprisonment. ¹¹(Formerly he was useless to you, but now he is indeed useful*ᵇ* to you and to me.) ¹²I am sending him back to you, sending my very heart. ¹³I would have been glad to keep him with me, in order that he might serve me on your behalf during my imprisonment for the gospel; ¹⁴but I preferred to do nothing

ᵃ Or *an old man*
ᵇ The name Onesimus means *useful* or (compare verse 20) *beneficial*

πίστιν ἣν ἔχεις πρὸς τὸν κύριον Ἰησοῦν
faith which thou hast toward the Lord Jesus

καὶ εἰς πάντας τοὺς ἁγίους, 6 ὅπως
and to all the saints, so as

ἡ κοινωνία τῆς πίστεώς σου ἐνεργὴς
the fellowship of the faith of thee ²operative

γένηται ἐν ἐπιγνώσει παντὸς ἀγαθοῦ τοῦ
¹may in a full of every good thing –
become knowledge

ἐν ἡμῖν εἰς Χριστόν. 7 χαρὰν γὰρ
in us for Christ. ⁴joy ¹For

πολλὴν ἔσχον καὶ παράκλησιν ἐπὶ τῇ
³much ²I had and consolation over the

ἀγάπῃ σου, ὅτι τὰ σπλάγχνα τῶν ἁγίων
love of because the bowels of the saints
thee,

ἀναπέπαυται διὰ σοῦ, ἀδελφέ. 8 Διό,
has(ve) been through thee, brother. Wherefore,
refreshed

πολλὴν ἐν Χριστῷ παρρησίαν ἔχων ἐπιτάσ-
²much ⁴in ⁵Christ ³boldness ¹having to

σειν σοι τὸ ἀνῆκον, 9 διὰ τὴν ἀγάπην
charge thee the befitting, because – love
thing of

μᾶλλον παρακαλῶ· τοιοῦτος ὢν ὡς Παῦλος
rather I beseech; such a one being as Paul

πρεσβύτης, νυνὶ δὲ καὶ δέσμιος Χριστοῦ
an old man, and now also a prisoner of Christ

Ἰησοῦ, 10 παρακαλῶ σε περὶ τοῦ ἐμοῦ
Jesus, I beseech thee con- – my
cerning

τέκνου, ὃν ἐγέννησα ἐν τοῖς δεσμοῖς,
child, whom I begat in the(my) bonds,

Ὀνήσιμον, 11 τόν ποτέ σοι ἄχρηστον
Onesimus, the [one] then ²to thee ¹useless
(formerly)

νυνὶ δὲ καὶ σοὶ καὶ ἐμοὶ εὔχρηστον,
but now ²both ³to thee ⁴and ⁵to me ¹useful,

12 ὃν ἀνέπεμψά σοι, αὐτόν, τοῦτ' ἔστιν
whom I sent back to thee, him, this is

τὰ ἐμὰ σπλάγχνα· 13 ὃν ἐγὼ ἐβουλόμην
– my bowels; whom I resolved

πρὸς ἐμαυτὸν κατέχειν, ἵνα ὑπὲρ σοῦ
with myself to retain, in order on thee
that behalf of

μοι διακονῇ ἐν τοῖς δεσμοῖς τοῦ εὐαγ-
to me he might in the bonds of the gos-
minister

γελίου, 14 χωρὶς δὲ τῆς σῆς γνώμης
pel, but without – thy opinion

without your consent in order that your goodness might not be by compulsion but of your own free will.

15 Perhaps this is why he was parted from you for a while, that you might have him back for ever, [16]no longer as a slave but more than a slave, as a beloved brother, especially to me but how much more to you, both in the flesh and in the Lord. [17]So if you consider me your partner, receive him as you would receive me. [18]If he has wronged you at all, or owes you anything, charge that to my account. [19]I, Paul, write this with my own hand, I will repay it—to say nothing of your owing me even your own self. [20]Yes, brother, I want some benefit from you in the Lord. Refresh my heart in Christ.

21 Confident of your obedience, I write to you, knowing that you will do even more than I say. [22]At the same time, prepare a guest room for me, for I am hoping through your prayers to be granted to you.

23 Ep'aphras, my

οὐδὲν ἠθέλησα ποιῆσαι, ἵνα μὴ ὡς κατὰ
'nothing ¹I was ²to do, in order that not ⁸as ⁶by way
          willing   of

ἀνάγκην τὸ ἀγαθόν σου ᾖ ἀλλὰ κατὰ
⁷necessity ¹the ²good ³of ⁴might but by way
                        thee be   of

ἑκούσιον. 15 τάχα γὰρ διὰ τοῦτο ἐχωρίσθη
[being]   For perhaps therefore he departed
voluntary.

πρὸς ὥραν, ἵνα αἰώνιον αὐτὸν ἀπέχῃς,
for an hour, in order ³eternally ²him ¹thou mightest
              that   receive,

16 οὐκέτι ὡς δοῦλον ἀλλὰ ὑπὲρ δοῦλον,
no longer as a slave but beyond a slave,

ἀδελφὸν ἀγαπητόν, μάλιστα ἐμοί, πόσῳ
a brother beloved, specially to me, ²by how
                                        much

δὲ μᾶλλον σοὶ καὶ ἐν σαρκὶ καὶ ἐν
¹and more to thee both in [the] flesh and in

κυρίῳ. 17 εἰ οὖν με ἔχεις κοινωνόν,
[the] Lord. If therefore me thou hast [as] a partner,

προσλαβοῦ αὐτὸν ὡς ἐμέ. 18 εἰ δέ
receive him as me. And if

τι ἠδίκησέν σε ἢ ὀφείλει, τοῦτο ἐμοὶ
any- he wronged thee or owes, ²this ¹to me
thing

ἐλλόγα· 19 ἐγὼ Παῦλος ἔγραψα τῇ ἐμῇ
¹reckon: I Paul wrote – with my

χειρί, ἐγὼ ἀποτίσω· ἵνα μὴ λέγω σοι
hand, I will repay; lest I say to thee

ὅτι καὶ σεαυτόν μοι προσοφείλεις. 20 ναί,
that indeed ³thyself ²to me ¹thou owest besides. Yes,

ἀδελφέ, ἐγώ σου ὀναίμην ἐν κυρίῳ·
brother, ⁴I ⁵of thee ¹may ²have ⁶help in [the] Lord;

ἀνάπαυσόν μου τὰ σπλάγχνα ἐν Χριστῷ.
refresh of me the bowels in Christ.

21 Πεποιθὼς τῇ ὑπακοῇ σου ἔγραψά
Having trusted to the obedience of thee I wrote

σοι, εἰδὼς ὅτι καὶ ὑπὲρ ἃ λέγω ποιήσεις.
to knowing that indeed beyond what I say thou wilt
thee,   things   do.

22 ἅμα δὲ καὶ ἑτοίμαζέ μοι ξενίαν·
And at the also prepare for me lodging;
same time

ἐλπίζω γὰρ ὅτι διὰ τῶν προσευχῶν
for I hope that through the prayers

ὑμῶν χαρισθήσομαι ὑμῖν.
of you I shall be given to you.

23 Ἀσπάζεταί σε Ἐπαφρᾶς ὁ συναιχμά-
⁸greets ⁹thee ¹Epaphras ²the ³fellow-

fellow prisoner in Christ
Jesus, sends greetings to
you, 24 and so do Mark,
Aristar'chus, Demas, and
Luke, my fellow workers.
25 The grace of the
Lord Jesus Christ be
with your spirit.

λωτός μου ἐν Χριστῷ Ἰησοῦ, 24 Μᾶρκος,
captive 'of me 'in 'Christ 'Jesus, [also] Mark,

Ἀρίσταρχος, Δημᾶς, Λουκᾶς, οἱ συνεργοί
Aristarchus, Demas, Luke, the fellow-
workers

μου.
of me.

25 Ἡ χάρις τοῦ κυρίου Ἰησοῦ Χριστοῦ
The grace of the Lord Jesus Christ

μετὰ τοῦ πνεύματος ὑμῶν.
[be] with the spirit of you.

HEBREWS 1

ΠΡΟΣ ΕΒΡΑΙΟΥΣ
To Hebrews

CHAPTER 1

IN many and various
ways God spoke of
old to our fathers by the
prophets; 2 but in these
last days he has spoken
to us by a Son, whom he
appointed the heir of
all things, through whom
also he created the world.
3 He reflects the glory of
God and bears the very
stamp of his nature,
upholding the universe
by his word of power.
When he had made
purification for sins, he
sat down at the right
hand of the Majesty on
high, 4 having become as
much superior to angels
as the name he has
obtained is more excellent
than theirs.

1 Πολυμερῶς καὶ πολυτρόπως πάλαι ὁ
'In many 'and 'in many ways 'of old -
portions

θεὸς λαλήσας τοῖς πατράσιν ἐν τοῖς
'God 'having spoken 'to the 'fathers by the

προφήταις 2 ἐπ' ἐσχάτου τῶν ἡμερῶν
prophets in [the] last - days

τούτων ἐλάλησεν ἡμῖν ἐν υἱῷ, ὃν ἔθηκεν
of these spoke to us in a Son, whom he appointed

κληρονόμον πάντων, δι' οὗ καὶ ἐποίησεν
heir of all through whom indeed he made
things,

τοὺς αἰῶνας· 3 ὃς ὢν ἀπαύγασμα τῆς
the ages; who being [the] radiance of the
(his)

δόξης καὶ χαρακτὴρ τῆς ὑποστάσεως αὐτοῦ,
glory and [the] of the reality of him,
representation

φέρων τε τὰ πάντα τῷ ῥήματι τῆς
and bearing - all things by the word of the

δυνάμεως αὐτοῦ, καθαρισμὸν τῶν ἁμαρτιῶν
power of him, 'cleansing - 'of sins

ποιησάμενος ἐκάθισεν ἐν δεξιᾷ τῆς
'having made sat on [the] right [hand] of the

μεγαλωσύνης ἐν ὑψηλοῖς, 4 τοσούτῳ
greatness in high places, 'by so much

κρείττων γενόμενος τῶν ἀγγέλων ὅσῳ
'better 'becoming '[than] the angels as

διαφορώτερον παρ' αὐτοὺς κεκληρονόμηκεν
'a more excellent 'than 'them 'he has inherited

5 For to what angel did God ever say,
"Thou art my Son, today I have begotten thee"?
Or again,
"I will be to him a father,
and he shall be to me a son"?
⁶And again, when he brings the first-born into the world, he says,
"Let all God's angels worship him."
⁷Of the angels he says,
"Who makes his angels winds,
and his servants flames of fire."
⁸But of the Son he says,
"Thy throne, O God,ᵃ is for ever and ever,
the righteous scepter is the scepter of thyᵇ kingdom.
⁹Thou hast loved righteousness and hated lawlessness;
therefore God, thy God, has anointed thee
with the oil of gladness beyond thy comrades."
¹⁰And,
"Thou, Lord, didst found the earth in the beginning,
and the heavens are the work of thy hands;
¹¹they will perish, but thou remainest;
they will all grow old like a garment,
¹²like a mantle thou wilt roll them up,

ᵃ Or *God is thy throne*
ᵇ Other ancient authorities read *his*

ὄνομα. 5 Τίνι γὰρ εἶπέν ποτε τῶν
ⁿname.   For to which ³said he ⁴ever ¹of the
ἀγγέλων· υἱός μου εἶ σύ, ἐγὼ σήμερον
²angels: Son of me art thou, I to-day
γεγέννηκά σε; καὶ πάλιν· ἐγὼ ἔσομαι
have begotten thee? and again: I will be
αὐτῷ εἰς πατέρα, καὶ αὐτὸς ἔσται μοι
to him for a father, and he shall be to me
εἰς υἱόν; 6 ὅταν δὲ πάλιν εἰσαγάγῃ
for a son? and whenever again he brings *in*
τὸν πρωτότοκον εἰς τὴν οἰκουμένην, λέγει·
the firstborn into the inhabited [earth], he says:
καὶ προσκυνησάτωσαν αὐτῷ πάντες ἄγγελοι
And let worship him all angels
θεοῦ. 7 καὶ πρὸς μὲν τοὺς ἀγγέλους
of God. And with re-gard to the angels
λέγει· ὁ ποιῶν τοὺς ἀγγέλους αὐτοῦ
he says: The making the angels of him
[one]
πνεύματα, καὶ τοὺς λειτουργοὺς αὐτοῦ
spirits, and the ministers of him
πυρὸς φλόγα, 8 πρὸς δὲ τὸν υἱόν· ὁ
²of fire ¹a flame; but with regard to the Son: The
θρόνος σου ὁ θεὸς εἰς τὸν αἰῶνα τοῦ
throne of thee[,] – God[,]ᵃ[is] unto the age of the
αἰῶνος, καὶ ἡ ῥάβδος τῆς εὐθύτητος
age, and the rod – of uprightness [is]
ῥάβδος τῆς βασιλείας αὐτοῦ. 9 ἠγάπησας
[the] rod of the kingdom of him. Thou lovedst
δικαιοσύνην καὶ ἐμίσησας ἀνομίαν· διὰ
righteousness and hatedst lawlessness; there-
τοῦτο ἔχρισέν σε, ὁ θεός, ὁ θεός σου
fore ⁴anointed ⁵thee, – ⁶God,ᵃ ¹the ²God ³of thee
ἔλαιον ἀγαλλιάσεως παρὰ τοὺς μετόχους
[with] oil of gladness above the partners
σου. 10 καὶ· σὺ κατ' ἀρχάς, κύριε,
of thee. And: Thou at [the] beginnings, Lord,
τὴν γῆν ἐθεμελίωσας, καὶ ἔργα τῶν
²the ³earth ¹didst found, and ⁵works ⁴of the
χειρῶν σού εἰσιν οἱ οὐρανοί· 11 αὐτοὶ
⁶hands ⁷of thee ⁸are ¹the ²heavens; they
ἀπολοῦνται, σὺ δὲ διαμένεις· καὶ πάντες
will perish, but thou remainest; and all
ὡς ἱμάτιον παλαιωθήσονται, 12 καὶ ὡσεὶ
as a garment will become old, and as
περιβόλαιον ἑλίξεις αὐτούς, ὡς ἱμάτιον
a mantle thou wilt roll up them, as a garment

* Articular vocative; see ver. 10.

and they will be
changed.[c]
But thou art the
same,
and thy years will
never end."
13 But to what angel has
he ever said,
"Sit at my right hand,
till I make thy
enemies
a stool for thy feet"?
14 Are they not all
ministering spirits ˙ sent
forth to serve, for the
sake of those who are to
obtain salvation?

CHAPTER 2

THEREFORE we
must pay the closer
attention to what we
have heard, lest we drift
away from it. 2 For if the
message declared by
angels was valid and
every transgression or
disobedience received a
just retribution, 3 how
shall we escape if we
neglect such a great
salvation? It was de-
clared at first by the
Lord, and it was attested
to us by those who heard
him, 4 while God also
bore witness by signs
and wonders and various
miracles and by gifts of
the Holy Spirit distri-
buted according to his
own will.

5 For it was not to
angels that God sub-
jected the world to come,

καὶ   ἀλλαγήσονται·   σὺ   δὲ   ὁ   αὐτὸς   εἶ
also   they will be changed;   but thou   the   same   art

καὶ   τὰ   ἔτη   σου   οὐκ   ἐκλείψουσιν.   13 πρὸς
and   the   years   of thee   will not fail.   [2]to

τίνα   δὲ   τῶν   ἀγγέλων   εἴρηκέν   ποτε·
[3]which   [1]But   of the   angels   has he said   at any time:

κάθου   ἐκ   δεξιῶν   μου   ἕως   ἂν   θῶ   τοὺς
Sit   at   [the] right   of me   until   I put   the

ἐχθρούς   σου   ὑποπόδιον   τῶν   ποδῶν   σου;
enemies   of thee   a footstool   of the   feet   of thee?

14 οὐχὶ   πάντες   εἰσὶν   λειτουργικὰ   πνεύματα
[2]not   [3]all   [1]are they   [4]ministering   [5]spirits

εἰς   διακονίαν   ἀποστελλόμενα   διὰ   τοὺς
[7]for   [8]service   [6]being sent forth   because of   [ones]

μέλλοντας   κληρονομεῖν   σωτηρίαν;   2 Διὰ
being about   to inherit   salvation?   There-

τοῦτο   δεῖ   περισσοτέρως   προσέχειν   ἡμᾶς
fore   [1]it behoves   [4]more abundantly   [3]to give heed   [2]us

τοῖς   ἀκουσθεῖσιν,   μήποτε   παραρυῶμεν.
to the   things heard,   lest   we drift away.

2 εἰ   γὰρ   ὁ   δι'   ἀγγέλων   λαληθεὶς   λόγος
For if   [1]the   [4]through   [5]angels   [3]spoken   [2]word

ἐγένετο   βέβαιος,   καὶ   πᾶσα   παράβασις
was   firm,   and   every   transgression

καὶ   παρακοὴ   ἔλαβεν   ἔνδικον   μισθαποδοσίαν,
and   disobedience   received   a just   recompence,

3 πῶς   ἡμεῖς   ἐκφευξόμεθα   τηλικαύτης
how   [1]we   [2]shall escape   [3]so great

ἀμελήσαντες   σωτηρίας;   ἥτις   ἀρχὴν   λαβοῦσα
[4]neglecting   [5]a salvation?   which   [3]a beginning   [1]having received

λαλεῖσθαι   διὰ   τοῦ   κυρίου,   ὑπὸ   τῶν
to be spoken   through   the   Lord,   by   the

ἀκουσάντων   εἰς   ἡμᾶς   ἐβεβαιώθη,   4 συνεπι-
[ones] hearing   to   us   was confirmed,   [2]bearing

μαρτυροῦντος   τοῦ   θεοῦ   σημείοις   τε   καὶ
witness with   -   [1]God[a]   [4]by signs   [3]both   and

τέρασιν   καὶ   ποικίλαις   δυνάμεσιν   καὶ
by wonders   and   by various   powerful deeds   and

πνεύματος   ἁγίου   μερισμοῖς   κατὰ   τὴν   αὐτοῦ
[2]Spirit   [1]of [the]   [1]by distribu-   according   the   [2]of him
               Holy   tions   to

θέλησιν.
[1]will.

5 Οὐ   γὰρ   ἀγγέλοις   ὑπέταξεν   τὴν
For not   to angels   subjected he   the

οἰκουμένην   τὴν   μέλλουσαν,   περὶ   ἧς
[2]inhabited [earth]   -   [1]coming,   about   which

---

[c] Other ancient authorities add
like a garment

of which we are speak-
ing. [6] It has been testified
somewhere,

"What is man that
thou art mindful of
him,
or the son of man,
that thou carest for
him?
[7] Thou didst make him
for a little while
lower than the
angels,
thou hast crowned
him with glory and
honor,[d]
[8] putting everything in
subjection under
his feet."
Now in putting every-
thing in subjection to
him, he left nothing
outside his control. As it
is, we do not yet see
everything in subjection
to him. [9] But we see
Jesus, who for a little
while was made lower
than the angels, crowned
with glory and honor
because of the suffering
of death, so that by the
grace of God he might
taste death for every one.

10 For it was fitting
that he, for whom and
by whom all things exist,
in bringing many sons
to glory, should make
the pioneer of their
salvation perfect through
suffering. [11] For he who
sanctifies and those who
are sanctified have all
one origin. That is why
he is not ashamed to call

λαλοῦμεν.
we speak.

6 διεμαρτύρατο   δέ   πού   τις
But [2]solemnly witnessed   [3]some-   [1]one
where

λέγων·   τί   ἐστιν   ἄνθρωπος   ὅτι   μιμνῄσκῃ
saying: What   is   man   that   thou
rememberest

αὐτοῦ;   ἢ   υἱὸς   ἀνθρώπου   ὅτι   ἐπισκέπτῃ
him?   or   a son   of man   that   thou observest

αὐτόν;   7 ἠλάττωσας   αὐτὸν   βραχύ   τι   παρ'
him?   Thou madest [3]less [1]him   [2]a little   than

ἀγγέλους,   δόξῃ   καὶ   τιμῇ   ἐστεφάνωσας
angels,   with glory and   with honour   thou crownedst

αὐτόν,   8 πάντα   ὑπέταξας   ὑποκάτω   τῶν
him,   all things thou subjectedst   underneath   the

ποδῶν   αὐτοῦ.   ἐν   τῷ   γὰρ   ὑποτάξαι
feet   of him.   [1]in   the   For   [2]to subject[ing]

[αὐτῷ]   τὰ   πάντα   οὐδὲν   ἀφῆκεν   αὐτῷ
[4]to him   –   [3]all things [6]nothing [5]he left [8]to him

ἀνυπότακτον.   Νῦν   δὲ   οὔπω   ὁρῶμεν
[7]unsubjected.   But now   not yet   we see

αὐτῷ   τὰ   πάντα   ὑποτεταγμένα·   9 τὸν   δὲ
[3]to him   –   [1]all things [2]having been   [3]the   [1]but
subjected;   [one]

βραχύ   τι   παρ'   ἀγγέλους   ἠλαττωμένον
[5]a little   [4]than   [7]angels   [6]having been
made less

βλέπομεν   Ἰησοῦν   διὰ   τὸ   πάθημα   τοῦ
[2]we see   [8]Jesus   because of the   suffering   –

θανάτου   δόξῃ   καὶ   τιμῇ   ἐστεφανωμένον,
of death   with glory and   with honour   having been
crowned,

ὅπως   χάριτι   θεοῦ   ὑπὲρ   παντὸς   γεύσηται
so as   by [the] of God [3]on   [2]every man [1]he might
grace   behalf of   taste

θανάτου.   10 ἔπρεπεν   γὰρ   αὐτῷ,   δι'
of [2]death.   For it was fitting   for him, because
of

ὃν   τὰ   πάντα   καὶ   δι'   οὗ   τὰ   πάντα,
whom –   all things   and through whom –   all things,

πολλοὺς   υἱοὺς   εἰς   δόξαν   ἀγαγόντα   τὸν
[10]many   [11]sons   [12]to   [13]glory   [9]leading   [4]the

ἀρχηγὸν   τῆς   σωτηρίας   αὐτῶν   διὰ
[5]author   [6]of the [7]salvation   [8]of them [2]through

παθημάτων   τελειῶσαι.   11 ὅ   τε   γὰρ
[3]sufferings   [1]to perfect.   [3]the [one] [2]both [1]For

ἀγιάζων   καὶ   οἱ   ἀγιαζόμενοι   ἐξ   ἑνὸς
sanctifying and the [ones] being sanctified [are] [2]of   [1]one

πάντες·   δι'   ἣν   αἰτίαν   οὐκ   ἐπαισχύνεται
[1]all;   for   which   cause   he is not ashamed

[d] Other ancient authorities
insert *and didst set him over the
works of thy hands*

them brethren, [12]saying,
"I will proclaim thy
name to my
brethren,
in the midst of the
congregation I will
praise thee."
[13]And again,
"I will put my trust in
him."
And again,
"Here am I, and the
children God has
given me."
14 Since therefore the
children share in flesh
and blood, he himself
likewise partook of the
same nature, that through
death he might destroy
him who has the power of
death, that is, the devil,
[15]and deliver all those
who through fear of
death were subject to
lifelong bondage. [16]For
surely it is not with
angels that he is con-
cerned but with the
descendants of Abraham.
[17]Therefore he had to be
made like his brethren
in every respect, so that
he might become a
merciful and faithful high
priest in the service of
God, to make expiation
for the sins of the
people. [18]For because he
himself has suffered and
been tempted, he is able
to help those who are
tempted.

ἀδελφοὺς αὐτοὺς καλεῖν, 12 λέγων· ἀπαγ-
³brothers ²them ¹to call, saying: I will

γελῶ τὸ ὄνομά σου τοῖς ἀδελφοῖς μου,
announce the name of thee to the brothers of me,

ἐν μέσῳ ἐκκλησίας ὑμνήσω σε· 13 καὶ
in [the] midst of [the] church I will hymn thee; and

πάλιν· ἐγὼ ἔσομαι πεποιθὼς ἐπ' αὐτῷ·
again: I will be having trusted on(in) him;

καὶ πάλιν· ἰδοὺ ἐγὼ καὶ τὰ παιδία
and again: Behold[,] I and the children

ἅ / μοι ἔδωκεν ὁ θεός. 14 Ἐπεὶ οὖν
whom ²to me ²gave – ¹God. Since therefore

τὰ παιδία κεκοινώνηκεν αἵματος καὶ
the children has(ve) partaken of blood and

σαρκός, καὶ αὐτὸς παραπλησίως μετέσχεν
of flesh, ²also ³[him]self ⁴in like manner ¹he shared

τῶν αὐτῶν, ἵνα διὰ τοῦ θανάτου
the same things, in order through the(?his) death
                        that

καταργήσῃ τὸν τὸ κράτος ἔχοντα τοῦ
he might destroy ¹the [one] ²the ⁴might ³having –

θανάτου, τοῦτ' ἔστιν τὸν διάβολον, 15 καὶ
of death, this is the devil, and

ἀπαλλάξῃ τούτους, ὅσοι φόβῳ θανάτου
release these, as many as by fear of death

διὰ παντὸς τοῦ ζῆν ἔνοχοι ἦσαν δουλείας.
through all the(ir) to ²involved ¹were slavery.
                   [time] live in

16 οὐ γὰρ δήπου ἀγγέλων ἐπιλαμβάνεται,
⁴not ¹For ²of course ³of angels ⁵he takes hold,

ἀλλὰ σπέρματος Ἀβραὰμ ἐπιλαμβάνεται.
but of [the] seed of Abraham he takes hold.

17 ὅθεν ὤφειλεν κατὰ πάντα τοῖς ἀδελφοῖς
Whence he owed by all means† ²to the ³brothers
        (ought)   (his)

ὁμοιωθῆναι, ἵνα ἐλεήμων γένηται καὶ
¹to become like, in order ²a merciful ¹he might become and
              that

πιστὸς ἀρχιερεὺς τὰ πρὸς τὸν θεόν,
faithful high priest [in] the in regard – God,
                     things to

εἰς τὸ ἱλάσκεσθαι τὰς ἁμαρτίας τοῦ
for the to make propitia- the sins of the
         tion for

λαοῦ. 18 ἐν ᾧ γὰρ πέπονθεν αὐτὸς
people. ²in ³what ¹For ⁵has suffered ⁴he
            [way]

πειρασθείς, δύναται τοῖς πειραζομένοις
being tempted, he is able ²the [ones] ³being tempted

βοηθῆσαι.
¹to help.

CHAPTER 3

THEREFORE, holy brethren, who share in a heavenly call, consider Jesus, the apostle and high priest of our confession. [2] He was faithful to him who appointed him, just as Moses also was faithful in[e] God's house. [3] Yet Jesus has been counted worthy of as much more glory than Moses as the builder of a house has more honor than the house. [4] (For every house is built by some one, but the builder of all things is God.) [5] Now Moses was faithful in all God's house as a servant, to testify to the things that were to be spoken later, [6] but Christ was faithful over God's house as a son. And we are his house if we hold fast our confidence and pride in our hope[f].

[7] Therefore, as the Holy Spirit says,

"Today, when you hear his voice,
[8] do not harden your hearts as in the rebellion,
on the day of testing in the wilderness,
[9] where your fathers

---

3 Ὅθεν,   ἀδελφοὶ   ἅγιοι,   κλήσεως
Whence,   brothers   holy,   [3]calling
ἐπουρανίου   μέτοχοι,   κατανοήσατε   τὸν
[2]of a heavenly   [1]sharers,   consider   the
ἀπόστολον   καὶ   ἀρχιερέα   τῆς   ὁμολογίας
apostle   and   high priest   of the   confession
ἡμῶν   Ἰησοῦν,   2 πιστὸν   ὄντα   τῷ   ποιήσαντι
of us[,]   Jesus,   faithful   being to the   [one] making
αὐτόν,   ὡς   καὶ   Μωϋσῆς   ἐν   [ὅλῳ]   τῷ
him,   as   also   Moses   in   [all]   the
οἴκῳ   αὐτοῦ.   3 πλείονος   γὰρ   οὗτος   δόξης
household of him.   For [3]of more   [1]this one   [4]glory
παρὰ   Μωϋσῆν   ἠξίωται   καθ᾽   ὅσον   πλείονα
[2]than   [5]Moses   [2]has been   by so much as   [5]more
                                         counted worthy
τιμὴν   ἔχει   τοῦ   οἴκου   ὁ   κατασκευάσας
[6]honour   [3]has   [8]the   [9]house   [1]the   [2]having prepared
              [7][than]   [one]
αὐτόν.   4 πᾶς   γὰρ   οἶκος   κατασκευάζεται
[3]it.   For every   house   is prepared
ὑπό   τινος,   ὁ   δὲ   πάντα   κατασκευάσας
by   someone, but [1]the [one] [2]all things   [3]having prepared
θεός.   5 καὶ   Μωϋσῆς   μὲν   πιστὸς   ἐν
[is] God.   And   Moses   on one hand faithful   in
                                                    [was]
ὅλῳ   τῷ   οἴκῳ   αὐτοῦ   ὡς   θεράπων   εἰς
all   the   household of him   as   a servant   for
μαρτύριον   τῶν   λαληθησομένων,   6 Χριστὸς
a testimony of the things   being spoken   Christ
                              [in the future],
δὲ   ὡς   υἱὸς   ἐπὶ   τὸν   οἶκον   αὐτοῦ·   οὗ
on the as   a Son   over   the   household of him;   of
other   whom
οἶκός   ἐσμεν   ἡμεῖς,   ἐὰν   τὴν   παρρησίαν
a household are   we,   if   [2]the   [3]confidence
καὶ   τὸ   καύχημα   τῆς   ἐλπίδος   [μέχρι
[4]and   [5]the   [6]boast   [7]of the   [8]hope   [10]until
τέλους   βεβαίαν]   κατάσχωμεν.   7 Διό,
[11][the] end   [9]firm   [1]we hold fast.   Wherefore,
καθὼς   λέγει   τὸ   πνεῦμα   τὸ   ἅγιον·   σήμερον
as   says   the   Spirit   -   Holy: To-day
ἐὰν   τῆς   φωνῆς   αὐτοῦ   ἀκούσητε,   8 μὴ
if   the   voice   of him   ye hear,   not
σκληρύνητε   τὰς   καρδίας   ὑμῶν   ὡς   ἐν
harden ye   the   hearts   of you   as   in
τῷ   παραπικρασμῷ   κατὰ   τὴν   ἡμέραν   τοῦ
the   provocation   in   the   day   of the
πειρασμοῦ   ἐν   τῇ   ἐρήμῳ,   9 οὗ   ἐπείρασαν
temptation   in   the   desert,   when   [4]tempted

---

[e] Other ancient authorities insert all

[f] Other ancient authorities insert firm to the end

put me to the test and saw my works for forty years.
[10] Therefore I was provoked with that generation,
and said, 'They always go astray in their hearts;
they have not known my ways.'
[11] As I swore in my wrath,
'They shall never enter my rest.' "
[12] Take care, brethren, lest there be in any of you an evil, unbelieving heart, leading you to fall away from the living God. [13] But exhort one another every day, as long as it is called "today," that none of you may be hardened by the deceitfulness of sin. [14] For we share in Christ, if only we hold our first confidence firm to the end, [15] while it is said,
"Today, when you hear his voice
do not harden your hearts as in the rebellion."
[16] Who were they that heard and yet were rebellious? Was it not all those who left Egypt under the leadership of Moses? [17] And with whom was he provoked

οἱ πατέρες ὑμῶν ἐν δοκιμασίᾳ καὶ εἶδον
[1]the   [2]fathers   [3]of you   in   proving   and   saw

τὰ   ἔργα   μου   τεσσεράκοντα   ἔτη· 10 διὸ
the   works   of me   forty   years; wherefore

προσώχθισα   τῇ   γενεᾷ   ταύτῃ   καὶ   εἶπον·
I was angry   with this generation   and   I said:

ἀεὶ   πλανῶνται   τῇ   καρδίᾳ·   αὐτοὶ   δὲ
Always   they err   in the   heart;   and they

οὐκ   ἔγνωσαν   τὰς   ὁδούς   μου,   11 ὡς
knew not   the   ways   of me,   as

ὤμοσα   ἐν   τῇ   ὀργῇ   μου·   εἰ   εἰσελεύσονται
I swore   in   the   wrath   of me: If   they shall enter

εἰς   τὴν   κατάπαυσίν   μου.   12 Βλέπετε,
into   the   rest   of me.   Look ye,

ἀδελφοί,   μήποτε   ἔσται   ἔν   τινι   ὑμῶν
brothers,   lest   there shall be in   anyone   of you

καρδία   πονηρὰ   ἀπιστίας   ἐν   τῷ   ἀποστῆναι
[1]heart   [2]an evil   of unbelief   in   the   [1]to depart[ing]

ἀπὸ   θεοῦ   ζῶντος,   13 ἀλλὰ   παρακαλεῖτε
from   God   a living,   but   exhort

ἑαυτοὺς   καθ'   ἑκάστην   ἡμέραν,   ἄχρις   οὗ
yourselves   -   each   day,   while

τὸ   σήμερον   καλεῖται,   ἵνα   μὴ   σκληρυνθῇ
the   to-day   it is being called,   lest   [4]be hardened

τις   ἐξ   ὑμῶν   ἀπάτῃ   τῆς   ἁμαρτίας·   14 μέτ-
[1]any- [2]of [3]you   by [the]   of sin;   [5]shar-
one   deceit

οχοι   γὰρ   τοῦ   Χριστοῦ   γεγόναμεν,   ἐάνπερ
ers   [1]for   [6]of   [5]Christ   [2]we have   if indeed
the   become,

τὴν   ἀρχὴν   τῆς   ὑποστάσεως   μέχρι   τέλους
[3]the   [6]beginning   [4]of the   [5]assurance   [7]until   [8][the] end

βεβαίαν   κατάσχωμεν.   15 ἐν   τῷ   λέγεσθαι·
[6]firm   [1]we hold fast.   In   the   to be said[6]:
                              = While it is said:

σήμερον   ἐὰν   τῆς   φωνῆς   αὐτοῦ   ἀκούσητε,
To-day   if   the   voice   of him   ye hear,

μὴ   σκληρύνητε   τὰς   καρδίας   ὑμῶν   ὡς
do not harden   the   hearts   of you   as

ἐν   τῷ   παραπικρασμῷ.   16 τίνες   γὰρ
in   the   provocation.   For some

ἀκούσαντες   παρεπίκραναν;   ἀλλ'   οὐ   πάντες
hearing   provoked;   yet   not   all

οἱ   ἐξελθόντες   ἐξ   Αἰγύπτου   διὰ
the [ones] coming out   out of   Egypt   through

Μωϋσέως;   17 τίσιν   δὲ   προσώχθισεν   τεσ-
Moses ?   but with whom   was he angry   for-

forty years? Was it not with those who sinned, whose bodies fell in the wilderness? ¹⁸And to whom did he swear that they should never enter his rest, but to those who were disobedient? ¹⁹So we see that they were unable to enter because of unbelief.

CHAPTER 4

THEREFORE, while the promise of entering his rest remains, let us fear lest any of you be judged to have failed to reach it. ²For good news came to us just as to them; but the message which they heard did not benefit them, because it did not meet with faith in the hearers.^g ³For we who have believed enter that rest, as he has said,

"As I swore in my wrath,
They shall never enter my rest,'"

although his works were finished from the foundation of the world. ⁴For he has somewhere spoken of the seventh day in this way, "And God rested on the seventh day from all his works." ⁵And again in this place he said,

"They shall never enter my rest."

^g Other manuscripts read *they were not united in faith with the hearers*

σεράκοντα ἔτη; οὐχὶ τοῖς ἁμαρτήσασιν,
ty years? [was it] with the [ones] sinning,
            not

ὧν τὰ κῶλα ἔπεσεν ἐν τῇ ἐρήμῳ;
of the corpses fell in the desert?
whom

18 τίσιν δὲ ὤμοσεν μὴ εἰσελεύσεσθαι εἰς
and to whom swore he not to enter into

τὴν κατάπαυσιν αὐτοῦ εἰ μὴ τοῖς
the rest of him except to the

ἀπειθήσασιν; **19** καὶ βλέπομεν ὅτι οὐκ
[ones] disobeying? and we see that not

ἠδυνήθησαν εἰσελθεῖν δι' ἀπιστίαν.
they were able to enter because of disbelief.

4 Φοβηθῶμεν οὖν μήποτε καταλειπομένης
Let us fear therefore lest ²being left

ἐπαγγελίας εἰσελθεῖν εἰς τὴν κατάπαυσιν
¹a promise^a to enter into the rest

αὐτοῦ δοκῇ τις ἐξ ὑμῶν ὑστερηκέναι.
of him ⁴seems ¹anyone ²of ³you to have come short.

2 καὶ γάρ ἐσμεν εὐηγγελισμένοι καθάπερ
For indeed we are having had good news even as
                   preached [to us]

κἀκεῖνοι· ἀλλ' οὐκ ὠφέλησεν ὁ λόγος
those also; but ⁴did not profit ¹the ²word

τῆς ἀκοῆς ἐκείνους μὴ συγκεκερασμένος
³of hearing those not having been mixed
                      together

τῇ πίστει τοῖς ἀκούσασιν. **3** Εἰσερχόμεθα
- with faith in the [ones] hearing. we enter

γὰρ εἰς [τὴν] κατάπαυσιν οἱ πιστεύσαντες,
For into the rest the [ones] believing,

καθὼς εἴρηκεν· ὡς ὤμοσα ἐν τῇ ὀργῇ
as he has said: As I swore in the wrath

μου· εἰ εἰσελεύσονται εἰς τὴν κατάπαυσίν
of me: If they shall enter into the rest

μου, καίτοι τῶν ἔργων ἀπὸ καταβολῆς
of me, though the works ²from ³[the] foundation

κόσμου γενηθέντων. **4** εἴρηκεν γάρ που
⁴of [the] ¹having come into For he has said some-
world being.^a where

περὶ τῆς ἑβδόμης οὕτως· καὶ κατέπαυσεν
con- the seventh [day] thus: And ²rested
cerning

ὁ θεὸς ἐν τῇ ἡμέρᾳ τῇ ἑβδόμῃ ἀπὸ
- ¹God in the ²day the ¹seventh from

πάντων τῶν ἔργων αὐτοῦ· **5** καὶ ἐν
all the works of him; and in

τούτῳ πάλιν· εἰ εἰσελεύσονται εἰς τὴν
this [place] again: If they shall enter into the

6 Since therefore it remains for some to enter it, and those who formerly received the good news failed to enter because of disobedience, 7 again he sets a certain day, "Today," saying through David so long afterward, in the words already quoted,

"Today, when you hear his voice,
do not harden your hearts."

8 For if Joshua had given them rest, God would not speak later of another day. 9 So then, there remains a sabbath rest for the people of God; 10 for whoever enters God's rest also ceases from his labors as God did from his.

11 Let us therefore strive to enter that rest, that no one fall by the same sort of disobedience. 12 For the word of God is living and active, sharper than any two-edged sword, piercing to the division of soul and spirit, of joints and

κατάπαυσίν μου. 6 ἐπεὶ οὖν ἀπολείπεται
rest   of me.   Since therefore it remains

τινὰς εἰσελθεῖν εἰς αὐτήν, καὶ οἱ πρότερον
[for] to enter into it, and the formerly
some   [ones]

εὐαγγελισθέντες οὐκ εἰσῆλθον δι' ἀπείθειαν,
having good news did not enter because disobedience,
preached [to them]   of

7 πάλιν τινὰ ὁρίζει ἡμέραν, σήμερον, ἐν
again ²a certain ¹he de- day,   to-day,   ²in
              fines

Δαυὶδ λέγων μετὰ τοσοῦτον χρόνον, καθὼς
²David ¹saying after such   a time,   as

προείρηται· σήμερον ἐὰν τῆς φωνῆς αὐτοῦ
he has   To-day if the voice of him
previously said:

ἀκούσητε, μὴ σκληρύνητε τὰς καρδίας
ye hear,   do not harden the   hearts

ὑμῶν. 8 εἰ γὰρ αὐτοὺς Ἰησοῦς κατέπαυσεν,
of you. For if ³them ¹Jesus(Joshua) ²rested,

οὐκ ἂν περὶ ἄλλης ἐλάλει μετὰ ταῦτα
³not - ⁵concerning ⁶another ¹he ²would ⁸after ⁹these
                              ⁴have spoken   things

ἡμέρας. 9 ἄρα ἀπολείπεται σαββατισμὸς
⁷day.   Then ²remains   ¹a sabbath rest

τῷ λαῷ τοῦ θεοῦ. 10 ὁ γὰρ εἰσελθὼν
to the people - of God. For the [one] having
                                         entered

εἰς τὴν κατάπαυσιν αὐτοῦ καὶ αὐτὸς
into the rest   of him also [him]self

κατέπαυσεν ἀπὸ τῶν ἔργων αὐτοῦ,
rested   from the   works of him,

ὥσπερ ἀπὸ τῶν ἰδίων ὁ θεός. 11 Σπου-
as   from the(his) own - God [did].   Let us

δάσωμεν οὖν εἰσελθεῖν εἰς ἐκείνην τὴν
be eager therefore to enter into that   -

κατάπαυσιν, ἵνα μὴ ἐν τῷ αὐτῷ τις
rest,   lest   ³in ⁴the ⁵same ¹any-
                                    one

ὑποδείγματι πέσῃ τῆς ἀπειθείας. 12 Ζῶν
⁶example   ²falls - of dis-   [⁴is] ⁵living
                             obedience.

γὰρ ὁ λόγος τοῦ θεοῦ καὶ ἐνεργὴς
For ¹the ²word - ³of God and operative

καὶ τομώτερος ὑπὲρ πᾶσαν μάχαιραν
and sharper   beyond every   ²sword

δίστομον καὶ διϊκνούμενος ἄχρι μερισμοῦ
¹two-mouthed and passing through as far as division
(edged)

ψυχῆς καὶ πνεύματος, ἁρμῶν τε καὶ
of soul and of spirit,   ²of joints ¹both and

marrow, and discerning the thoughts and intentions of the heart. [13]And before him no creature is hidden, but all are open and laid bare to the eyes of him with whom we have to do.

14 Since then we have a great high priest who has passed through the heavens, Jesus, the Son of God, let us hold fast our confession. [15]For we have not a high priest who is unable to sympathize with our weaknesses, but one who in every respect has been tempted as we are, yet without sinning. [16]Let us then with confidence draw near to the throne of grace, that we may receive mercy and find grace to help in time of need.

μυελῶν,   καὶ   κριτικὸς   ἐνθυμήσεων   καὶ
of marrows,   and   able to judge   of thoughts   and

ἐννοιῶν   καρδίας·   13 καὶ   οὐκ ἔστιν   κτίσις
intentions   of a heart;   and   there is no   creature

ἀφανὴς   ἐνώπιον   αὐτοῦ,   πάντα δὲ   γυμνὰ
unmanifest   before   him,   but all things [are] naked

καὶ   τετραχηλισμένα   τοῖς   ὀφθαλμοῖς   αὐτοῦ,
and   having been laid open   to the   eyes   of him,

πρὸς   ὃν   ἡμῖν   ὁ   λόγος.
with   whom   to us [is]   the   word(account).[c]
       =is our account.

14 Ἔχοντες   οὖν   ἀρχιερέα   μέγαν   διεληλυ-
    Having   there-   high priest   a great   having gone
          fore

θότα   τοὺς   οὐρανούς,   Ἰησοῦν   τὸν   υἱὸν
through   the   heavens,   Jesus   the   Son

τοῦ   θεοῦ,   κρατῶμεν   τῆς   ὁμολογίας.   15 οὐ
--   of God,   let us hold   the   confession.   [1]not

γὰρ   ἔχομεν   ἀρχιερέα   μὴ   δυνάμενον
[1]For   [2]we have   a high priest   not   being able

συμπαθῆσαι   ταῖς   ἀσθενείαις   ἡμῶν,   πεπει-
to suffer with   the   weaknesses   of us,   [2]having

ρασμένον   δὲ   κατὰ   πάντα   καθ'   ὁμοιότητα
been tempted   [1]but   in all respects†   accord-   [our] likeness
                          ing to

χωρὶς   ἁμαρτίας.   16 προσερχώμεθα   οὖν
apart from   sin.   Let us approach   there-
                            fore

μετὰ   παρρησίας   τῷ   θρόνῳ   τῆς   χάριτος,
with   confidence   to the   throne   --   of grace,

ἵνα   λάβωμεν   ἔλεος   καὶ   χάριν   εὕρωμεν
in or-   we may   mercy   and   [2]grace   we [1]may
der that   receive   find

εἰς   εὔκαιρον   βοήθειαν.
for   timely   help.

CHAPTER 5

FOR every high priest chosen from among men is appointed to act on behalf of men in relation to God, to offer gifts and sacrifices for sins. [2]He can deal gently with the ignorant and wayward, since he him-

5 Πᾶς   γὰρ   ἀρχιερεὺς   ἐξ   ἀνθρώπων
For every   high priest   [2]out of   [3]men

λαμβανόμενος   ὑπὲρ   ἀνθρώπων   καθίσταται
[1]being taken   on behalf of   men   is appointed [in]

τὰ   πρὸς   τὸν   θεόν,   ἵνα   προσφέρῃ   δῶρά
the   in re-   --   God,   in order   he may offer   [2]gifts
things gard to   that

τε   καὶ   θυσίας   ὑπὲρ   ἁμαρτιῶν,   2 μετριο-
[1]both   and   sacrifices   on behalf of   sins,   [2]to feel in

παθεῖν   δυνάμενος   τοῖς   ἀγνοοῦσιν   καὶ
due measure   [1]being able   for the [ones] not knowing   and

πλανωμένοις,   ἐπεὶ   καὶ   αὐτὸς   περίκειται
being led astray,   since   also   he   is set round
                                [with]

self is beset with weakness. ³Because of this he is bound to offer sacrifice for his own sins as well as for those of the people. ⁴And one does not take the honor upon himself, but he is called by God, just as Aaron was.

5 So also Christ did not exalt himself to be made a high priest, but was appointed by him who said to him,

"Thou art my Son, today I have begotten thee";

⁶as he says also in another place,

"Thou art a priest for ever, after the order of Melchiz'edek."

7 In the days of his flesh, Jesus offered up prayers and supplications, with loud cries and tears, to him who was able to save him from death, and he was heard for his godly fear. ⁸Although he was a Son, he learned obedience through what he suffered; ⁹and being made perfect he became the source of eternal salvation to all who obey him, ¹⁰being designated by God a high priest after the order of Melchiz'edek.

ἀσθένειαν, 3 καὶ δι᾽ αὐτὴν ὀφείλει, καθὼς
weakness,   and because   it   he ought,   as
                of

περὶ τοῦ λαοῦ, οὕτως καὶ περὶ ἑαυτοῦ
concern- the   people,   so   also concerning himself
ing

προσφέρειν περὶ ἁμαρτιῶν. 4 καὶ οὐχ
to offer   concerning   sins.   And   ²not

ἑαυτῷ τις λαμβάνει τὴν τιμήν, ἀλλὰ
⁴to him- ¹anyone ²takes   the   honour,   but
self

καλούμενος ὑπὸ τοῦ θεοῦ, καθώσπερ καὶ
being called   by   -   God,   even as   indeed

᾽Ααρών. 5 Οὕτως καὶ ὁ Χριστὸς οὐχ
Aaron.   So   also   -   Christ   ²not

ἑαυτὸν ἐδόξασεν γενηθῆναι ἀρχιερέα, ἀλλ᾽
³himself ¹glorified   to become   a high priest,   but

ὁ λαλήσας πρὸς αὐτόν· υἱός μου εἶ
the [one] speaking   to   him: Son   of me   art

σύ, ἐγὼ σήμερον γεγέννηκά σε· 6 καθὼς
thou,   I   to-day   have begotten   thee;   as

καὶ ἐν ἑτέρῳ λέγει· σὺ ἱερεὺς εἰς τὸν
also   in   another   he says: Thou a priest   unto   the
                [psalm]   [art]

αἰῶνα κατὰ τὴν τάξιν Μελχισέδεκ. 7 ὃς
age   according   the   order   of Melchisedec.   Who
        to

ἐν ταῖς ἡμέραις τῆς σαρκὸς αὐτοῦ δεήσεις
in   the   days   of the   flesh   of him   ⁸petitions

τε καὶ ἱκετηρίας πρὸς τὸν δυνάμενον
⁹both ⁴and   ⁸entreaties   ¹¹to   ¹²the [one] ¹³being able

σῴζειν αὐτὸν ἐκ θανάτου μετὰ κραυγῆς
¹⁴to save ¹⁵him ¹⁶out of ¹⁷death   ⁶with   ⁵crying

ἰσχυρᾶς καὶ δακρύων προσενέγκας καὶ
⁷strong ⁸and ¹⁰tears   ¹offering   and

εἰσακουσθεὶς ἀπὸ τῆς εὐλαβείας, 8 καίπερ
being heard   from(for) the(his) devoutness,   though

ὢν υἱός, ἔμαθεν ἀφ᾽ ὧν ἔπαθεν τὴν
being a Son,   he   ²from ³[the] ⁴he suffered   -
                    learned   things which

ὑπακοήν, 9 καὶ τελειωθεὶς ἐγένετο πᾶσιν
¹obedience,   and being perfected he became   to all

τοῖς ὑπακούουσιν αὐτῷ αἴτιος σωτηρίας
the [ones]   obeying   him   [the] cause ²salvation

αἰωνίου, 10 προσαγορευθεὶς ὑπὸ τοῦ θεοῦ
¹of eternal,   being designated   by   -   God

ἀρχιερεὺς κατὰ τὴν τάξιν Μελχισέδεκ.
a high priest accord-   the   order   of Melchisedec.
            ing to

11 About this we have much to say which is hard to explain, since you have become dull of hearing. [12] For though by this time you ought to be teachers, you need some one to teach you again the first principles of God's word. You need milk, not solid food; [13] for every one who lives on milk is unskilled in the word of righteousness, for he is a child. [14] But solid food is for the mature, for those who have their faculties trained by practice to distinguish good from evil.

CHAPTER 6

THEREFORE let us leave the elementary doctrines of Christ and go on to maturity, not laying again a foundation of repentance from dead works and of faith toward God, [2] with instruction[h] about ablutions, the laying on of hands, the resurrection of the dead, and eternal judgment. [3] And this we will do if God permits.[i] [4] For it is impossible to

[h] Other ancient manuscripts read *of instruction*

[i] Other ancient manuscripts read *let us do this if God permits*

---

11 Περὶ οὗ πολὺς ἡμῖν ὁ λόγος καὶ
Concern- whom much to us the [1]word[e] [2]and
ing ＝we have much to say and hard ...

δυσερμήνευτος λέγειν, ἐπεὶ νωθροὶ γεγόνατε
[4]hard to interpret [3]to say, since dull ye have become

ταῖς ἀκοαῖς. 12 καὶ γὰρ ὀφείλοντες
in the hearings. For indeed owing*

εἶναι διδάσκαλοι διὰ τὸν χρόνον, πάλιν
to be teachers because of the time, [3]again

χρείαν ἔχετε τοῦ διδάσκειν ὑμᾶς τινα
[2]need [1]ye have ‒ [5]to teach[d] [6]you [4]someone

τὰ στοιχεῖα τῆς ἀρχῆς τῶν λογίων
the rudiments of the beginning of the oracles

τοῦ θεοῦ, καὶ γεγόνατε χρείαν ἔχοντες
‒ of God, and ye have become [2]need [1]having

γάλακτος, οὐ στερεᾶς τροφῆς. 13 πᾶς
of milk, not of solid food. every

γὰρ ὁ μετέχων γάλακτος ἄπειρος λόγου
For one partaking of milk [is] without of [the] word
experience

δικαιοσύνης, νήπιος γάρ ἐστιν· 14 τελείων δέ
of righteousness, for [2]an infant [1]he is; but [4]of mature men

ἐστιν ἡ στερεὰ τροφή, τῶν διὰ τὴν
[3]is the [1]solid [2]food, of the because the(ir)
[ones] of

ἕξιν τὰ αἰσθητήρια γεγυμνασμένα ἐχόντων
condition [2]the(ir) [3]faculties *having been* [4]exercised [1]having

πρὸς διάκρισιν καλοῦ τε καὶ κακοῦ.
for distinction [2]of good [1]both and of bad.

6 Διὸ ἀφέντες τὸν τῆς ἀρχῆς τοῦ Χριστοῦ
Wherefore leaving [1]the [2]of the [4]beginning ‒ [5]of Christ

λόγον ἐπὶ τὴν τελειότητα φερώμεθα, μὴ
[3]word [6]on to ‒ [7]maturity [8]let us be borne, not

πάλιν θεμέλιον καταβαλλόμενοι μετανοίας
again [2]a foundation [1]laying down of repentance

ἀπὸ νεκρῶν ἔργων, καὶ πίστεως ἐπὶ
from dead works, and of faith toward

θεόν, 2 βαπτισμῶν διδαχῆς, ἐπιθέσεώς τε
God, [2]of baptisms [1]of teaching, and of laying on

χειρῶν, ἀναστάσεως νεκρῶν, καὶ κρίματος
of hands, of resurrection of dead persons, and [3]judgment

αἰωνίου. 3 καὶ τοῦτο ποιήσομεν, ἐάνπερ
[2]of eternal. And this will we do, if indeed

ἐπιτρέπῃ ὁ θεός. 4 Ἀδύνατον γὰρ τοὺς
[2]permits ‒ [1]God. For [it is] impossible the [for] [ones]

* That is, " ye ought ... "

HEBREWS 6

865

restore again to repentance those who have once been enlightened, who have tasted the heavenly gift, and have become partakers of the Holy Spirit, ⁵and have tasted the goodness of the word of God and the powers of the age to come, ⁶if they then commit apostasy, since they crucify the Son of God on their own account and hold him up to contempt. ⁷For land which has drunk the rain that often falls upon it, and brings forth vegetation useful to those for whose sake it is cultivated, receives a blessing from God. ⁸But if it bears thorns and thistles, it is worthless and near to being cursed; its end is to be burned.

9 Though we speak thus, yet in your case, beloved, we feel sure of better things that belong to salvation. ¹⁰For God is not so unjust as to overlook your work and the love which you showed for his sake in serving the saints, as you still do. ¹¹And we desire each one of you to show the same earnestness in realizing the full assurance of hope until the

ἅπαξ φωτισθέντας γευσαμένους τε τῆς
once being enlightened and tasting of the

δωρεᾶς τῆς ἐπουρανίου καὶ μετόχους
²gift - ¹heavenly and sharers

γενηθέντας πνεύματος ἁγίου 5 καὶ καλὸν
becoming Spirit of [the] Holy and ²[the] good

γευσαμένους θεοῦ ῥῆμα δυνάμεις τε
¹tasting ⁴of God ³word and powerful deeds

μέλλοντος αἰῶνος, 6 καὶ παραπεσόντας, πάλιν
of a coming age, and falling away, again

ἀνακαινίζειν εἰς μετάνοιαν, ἀνασταυροῦντας
to renew to repentance, crucifying again

ἑαυτοῖς τὸν υἱὸν τοῦ θεοῦ καὶ παρα-
for them- the Son - of God and putting
selves

δειγματίζοντας. 7 γῆ γὰρ ἡ πιοῦσα
[him] to open shame. For earth - drinking

τὸν ἐπ' αὐτῆς ἐρχόμενον πολλάκις ὑετὸν
¹the ⁵upon ⁶it ²coming ⁴often ²rain

καὶ τίκτουσα βοτάνην εὔθετον ἐκείνοις
and bearing fodder suitable for those

δι' οὓς καὶ γεωργεῖται, μεταλαμβάνει
on ac- whom indeed it is farmed, receives
count of

εὐλογίας ἀπὸ τοῦ θεοῦ· 8 ἐκφέρουσα δὲ
blessing from - God; but bringing forth

ἀκάνθας καὶ τριβόλους ἀδόκιμος καὶ
thorns and thistles [it is] disapproved and

κατάρας ἐγγύς, ἧς τὸ τέλος εἰς καῦσιν.
²a curse ¹near, of which the end [is] for burning.

9 Πεπείσμεθα δὲ περὶ ὑμῶν, ἀγαπητοί,
But we have been concerning you, beloved,
persuaded

τὰ κρείσσονα καὶ ἐχόμενα σωτηρίας, εἰ
the better things and having salvation, if

καὶ οὕτως λαλοῦμεν. 10 οὐ γὰρ ἄδικος
indeed ²so ¹we speak. For ²not ³unjust

ὁ θεὸς ἐπιλαθέσθαι τοῦ ἔργου ὑμῶν
- ¹God [is] to be forgetful of the work of you

καὶ τῆς ἀγάπης ἧς ἐνεδείξασθε εἰς τὸ
and of the love which ye showed to the

ὄνομα αὐτοῦ, διακονήσαντες τοῖς ἁγίοις
name of him, having ministered to the saints

καὶ διακονοῦντες. 11 ἐπιθυμοῦμεν δὲ
and ministering. But we desire

ἕκαστον ὑμῶν τὴν αὐτὴν ἐνδείκνυσθαι
each one of you ³the ²same ¹to show

σπουδὴν πρὸς τὴν πληροφορίαν τῆς ἐλπίδος
eagerness to the full assurance of the hope

end, ¹²so that you may not be sluggish, but imitators of those who through faith and patience inherit the promises.

13 For when God made a promise to Abraham, since he had no one greater by whom to swear, he swore by himself, ¹⁴saying, "Surely I will bless you and multiply you." ¹⁵And thus Abraham, having patiently endured, obtained the promise. ¹⁶Men indeed swear by a greater than themselves, and in all their disputes an oath is final for confirmation. ¹⁷So when God desired to show more convincingly to the heirs of the promise the unchangeable character of his purpose, he interposed with an oath, ¹⁸so that through two unchangeable things, in which it is impossible that God should prove false, we who have fled for refuge might have strong encouragement to seize the hope set before us. ¹⁹We have this as a sure and steadfast anchor of the soul, a hope that enters into the inner shrine behind the curtain, ²⁰where Jesus has gone as a forerunner on our

ἄχρι   τέλους,   12 ἵνα   μὴ   νωθροὶ   γένησθε,
unto   [the] end,   lest   dull   ye become,

μιμηταὶ   δὲ   τῶν   διὰ   πίστεως   καὶ   μακρο-
but imitators   of the   through   faith   and   long-
                                    [ones]

θυμίας   κληρονομούντων   τὰς   ἐπαγγελίας.
suffering   inheriting   the   promises.

13 Τῷ   γὰρ   Ἀβραὰμ   ἐπαγγειλάμενος   ὁ
    -    For   ³to Abraham   ¹making promise   -

θεός,   ἐπεὶ   κατ'   οὐδενὸς   εἶχεν   μείζονος
¹God,   since   ¹by   no one   ¹he had   ⁴greater

ὀμόσαι,   ὤμοσεν   καθ'   ἑαυτοῦ,   14 λέγων·
to swear,   swore   by   himself,   saying:

εἰ   μὴν   εὐλογῶν   εὐλογήσω   σε   καὶ   πληθύνων
If   surely   blessing   I will bless   thee   and   multiplying

πληθυνῶ   σε·   15 καὶ   οὕτως   μακροθυμήσας
I will multiply thee;   and   so   being longsuffering

ἐπέτυχεν   τῆς   ἐπαγγελίας.   16 ἄνθρωποι   γὰρ
he obtained   the   promise.   For men

κατὰ   τοῦ   μείζονος   ὀμνύουσιν,   καὶ   πάσης
by   the   greater   swear,   and   ⁶of all

αὐτοῖς   ἀντιλογίας   πέρας   εἰς   βεβαίωσιν   ὁ
³[is] ⁴to   ⁷contradiction   ⁵an end   ⁵for   ⁸confirmation   ¹the
them

ὅρκος·   17 ἐν   ᾧ   περισσότερον   βουλόμενος
²oath;   wherein   ²more abundantly   ¹resolving

ὁ   θεὸς   ἐπιδεῖξαι   τοῖς   κληρονόμοις   τῆς
-    ¹God   to show   to the   heirs   of the

ἐπαγγελίας   τὸ   ἀμετάθετον   τῆς   βουλῆς
promise   the   unchangeableness   of the   resolve

αὐτοῦ   ἐμεσίτευσεν   ὅρκῳ,   18 ἵνα   διὰ
of him   interposed   by an   in or-   through
                        oath,   der that

δύο   πραγμάτων   ἀμεταθέτων,   ἐν   οἷς   ἀδύνατον
two   ²things   ¹unchangeable,   in which   impossible
                            [it was]

ψεύσασθαι   θεόν,   ἰσχυρὰν   παράκλησιν   ἔχωμεν
²to lie   ¹God,ᵇ   ²a strong   ³consolation   ¹we may
                                    have[,]

οἱ   καταφυγόντες   κρατῆσαι   τῆς   προκειμένης
the [ones] having fled   to lay hold   of the   ²set before [us]

ἐλπίδος·   19 ἣν   ὡς   ἄγκυραν   ἔχομεν   τῆς
¹hope;   which   as   an anchor   we have   of the

ψυχῆς   ἀσφαλῆ   τε   καὶ   βεβαίαν   καὶ
soul   ²safe   ¹both   and   firm   and

εἰσερχομένην   εἰς   τὸ   ἐσώτερον   τοῦ   κατα-
entering   into   the   inner [side]   of the   veil,

πετάσματος,   20 ὅπου   πρόδρομος   ὑπὲρ   ἡμῶν
where   a forerunner   on   us
                        behalf of

behalf, having become
a high priest for ever
after the order of
Melchiz'edek.

εἰσῆλθεν Ἰησοῦς, κατὰ τὴν τάξιν Μελχισέ-
entered[,]   Jesus,   ⁵according ¹the   ⁶order   ⁷of Melchise-
to

δεκ ἀρχιερεὺς γενόμενος εἰς τὸν αἰῶνα.
dec   ⁸a high priest ¹becoming ²unto ³the   ⁴age.

CHAPTER 7

FOR this Melchiz'-
edek, king of Salem,
priest of the most high
God, met Abraham re-
turning from the
slaughter of the kings
and blessed him; ²and
to him Abraham appor-
tioned a tenth part of
everything. He is first, by
translation of his name,
king of righteousness,
and then he is also king
of Salem, that is, king of
peace. ³He is without
father or mother or
genealogy, and has
neither beginning of days
nor end of life, but
resembling the Son of
God he continues a priest
for ever.

4 See how great he is!
Abraham the patriarch
gave him a tithe of the
spoils. ⁵And those de-
scendants of Levi who
receive the priestly office
have a commandment in
the law to take tithes
from the people, that is,
from their brethren,
though these also are
descended from Abra-
ham.

7 Οὗτος γὰρ ὁ Μελχισέδεκ, βασιλεὺς
For this   –   Melchisedec,   king

Σαλήμ, ἱερεὺς τοῦ θεοῦ τοῦ ὑψίστου,
of Salem,   priest   –   ³God ¹²of the ¹most high,

ὁ συναντήσας Ἀβραὰμ ὑποστρέφοντι ἀπὸ
the [one] meeting   Abraham   returning   from

τῆς κοπῆς τῶν βασιλέων καὶ εὐλογήσας
the   slaughter of the   kings   and   blessing

αὐτόν, 2 ᾧ καὶ δεκάτην ἀπὸ πάντων
him,   to whom indeed ³a tenth ⁴from   ⁵all

ἐμέρισεν Ἀβραάμ, πρῶτον μὲν ἑρμηνευ-
²divided ¹Abraham,   firstly   on one   being inter-
                                 hand

όμενος βασιλεὺς δικαιοσύνης, ἔπειτα δὲ καὶ
preted   King   of righteousness,   then   on the also
                                           other

βασιλεὺς Σαλήμ, ὅ ἐστιν βασιλεὺς εἰρήνης,
King   of Salem, which is   King   of peace,

3 ἀπάτωρ, ἀμήτωρ, ἀγενεαλόγητος, μήτε
without father, without mother,   without pedigree,   ⁵neither

ἀρχὴν ἡμερῶν μήτε ζωῆς τέλος ἔχων,
³beginning ⁴of days   ⁶nor   ⁷of life   ⁸end ¹having,

ἀφωμοιωμένος δὲ τῷ υἱῷ τοῦ θεοῦ, μένει
but *having been* made   *to* the   Son   –   of God, remains
like

ἱερεὺς εἰς τὸ διηνεκές. 4 Θεωρεῖτε δὲ
a priest   in   *the*   perpetuity.   Now behold ye

πηλίκος οὗτος, ᾧ δεκάτην Ἀβραὰμ
how great   this man   to   ⁴a tenth   ³Abraham
[was],   whom

ἔδωκεν ἐκ τῶν ἀκροθινίων ὁ πατριάρχης.
⁵gave ⁶of   ⁷the   ⁸spoils ¹the   ²patriarch.

5 καὶ οἱ μὲν ἐκ τῶν υἱῶν Λευὶ τὴν
And   ²the ¹on one ³of   ⁴the   ⁵sons   ⁶of Levi   ⁸the
[ones] hand

ἱερατείαν λαμβάνοντες ἐντολὴν ἔχουσιν
⁹priesthood   ⁷receiving   ¹¹a commandment   ¹⁰have

ἀποδεκατοῦν τὸν λαὸν κατὰ τὸν νόμον,
to take tithes   the   people   accord-   the   law,
from   ing to

τοῦτ᾽ ἔστιν τοὺς ἀδελφοὺς αὐτῶν, καίπερ
this   is   the   brothers   of them,   though

ἐξεληλυθότας ἐκ τῆς ὀσφύος Ἀβραάμ·
having come forth   out of   the   loin[s]   of Abraham;

⁶But this man who has not their genealogy received tithes from Abraham and blessed him who had the promises. ⁷It is beyond dispute that the inferior is blessed by the superior. ⁸Here tithes are received by mortal men; there, by one of whom it is testified that he lives. ⁹One might even say that Levi himself, who receives tithes, paid tithes through Abraham, ¹⁰for he was still in the loins of his ancestor when Melchiz'edek met him.

11 Now if perfection had been attainable through the Levit'ical priesthood (for under it the people received the law), what further need would there have been for another priest to arise after the order of Melchiz'edek, rather than one named after the order of Aaron? ¹²For when there is a change in the priesthood, there is necessarily a change in the law as well. ¹³For the one of whom these things are spoken belonged to another tribe, from which no one has ever served at the altar. ¹⁴For

6 ὁ δὲ μὴ γενεαλογούμενος ἐξ αὐτῶν
²the ¹on the not counting [his] pedigree from them
[one] other

δεδεκάτωκεν Ἀβραάμ, καὶ τὸν ἔχοντα
has tithed Abraham, and ²the [one] ³having

τὰς ἐπαγγελίας εὐλόγηκεν. 7 χωρὶς δὲ
⁴the ⁵promises ¹has blessed. And without

πάσης ἀντιλογίας τὸ ἔλαττον ὑπὸ τοῦ
all(any) contradiction the less ²by ³the

κρείττονος εὐλογεῖται. 8 καὶ ὧδε μὲν
⁴better ¹is blessed. And here on one
hand

δεκάτας ἀποθνήσκοντες ἄνθρωποι λαμβά-
⁴tithes ¹dying ²men ³re-

νουσιν, ἐκεῖ δὲ μαρτυρούμενος ὅτι ζῇ.
ceive, there on the being witnessed that he
other lives.

9 καὶ ὡς ἔπος εἰπεῖν, δι' Ἀβραὰμ
And as a word to say, through Abraham
=so to speak,

καὶ Λευὶς ὁ δεκάτας λαμβάνων δεδε-
indeed Levi ¹the [one] ²tithes ²receiving has

κάτωται· 10 ἔτι γὰρ ἐν τῇ ὀσφύϊ τοῦ
been tithed; for ²yet ³in ⁴the ⁵loin[s] ⁶of
the(his)

πατρὸς ἦν ὅτε συνήντησεν αὐτῷ Μελχισέ-
⁷father ¹he was ⁸when ¹⁰met ¹¹him ⁹Melchise-

δεκ. 11 Εἰ μὲν οὖν τελείωσις διὰ τῆς
dec. If – therefore perfection ¹through ²the

Λευιτικῆς ἱερωσύνης ἦν, ὁ λαὸς γὰρ
⁴Levitical ⁵priestly office ¹was, ⁴the ⁵people ¹for

ἐπ' αὐτῆς νενομοθέτηται, τίς ἔτι χρεία
²under* ³it has been furnished why yet need
with law,

κατὰ τὴν τάξιν Μελχισέδεκ ἕτερον
[was there ⁵the ⁶order ⁷of Melchisedec ¹another
for] ⁴accord-
ing to

ἀνίστασθαι ἱερέα καὶ οὐ κατὰ τὴν τάξιν
²to arise ³priest and not ²accord- ³the ⁴order
ing to

Ἀαρὼν λέγεσθαι; 12 μετατιθεμένης γὰρ
²of Aaron ¹to be said(named)? for ³being changed

τῆς ἱερωσύνης ἐξ ἀνάγκης καὶ νόμου
¹the ²priestly officeᵃ ⁴of ⁷necessity ⁵also ⁶of law

μετάθεσις γίνεται. 13 ἐφ' ὃν γὰρ λέγεται
³a change ⁴there ²[he] ³with ⁴whom ¹For ⁵is(are) said
occurs. respect to

ταῦτα, φυλῆς ἑτέρας μετέσχηκεν, ἀφ'
⁵these things, ³tribe ²of another ¹has partaken, from

ἧς οὐδεὶς προσέσχηκεν τῷ θυσιαστηρίῳ·
which no one has devoted himself to the altar;

* See note on ch. 9. 15.

it is evident that our Lord was descended from Judah, and in connection with that tribe Moses said nothing about priests.

15 This becomes even more evident when another priest arises in the likeness of Melchiz'edek, [16] who has become a priest, not according to a legal requirement concerning bodily descent but by the power of an indestructible life. [17] For it is witnessed of him, "Thou art a priest for ever, after the order of Melchiz'edek."

[18] On the one hand, a former commandment is set aside because of its weakness and uselessness [19] (for the law made nothing perfect); on the other hand, a better hope is introduced through which we draw near to God.

20 And it was not without an oath. [21] Those who formerly became priests took their office without an oath, but this one was addressed with an oath.

"The Lord has sworn
and will not change
his mind,
'Thou art a priest for
ever.' "

[22] This makes Jesus the

14 πρόδηλον γὰρ ὅτι ἐξ Ἰούδα ἀνατέταλκεν
for it is perfectly clear that out of Juda has risen

ὁ κύριος ἡμῶν, εἰς ἣν φυλὴν περὶ ἱερέων
the Lord of us, as to which tribe concerning priests

οὐδὲν Μωϋσῆς ἐλάλησεν. 15 καὶ περισ-
²nothing ¹Moses ³spoke. And more

σότερον ἔτι κατάδηλόν ἐστιν, εἰ κατὰ
abundantly still quite clear is it, if accord- ing to

τὴν ὁμοιότητα Μελχισέδεκ ἀνίσταται ἱερεὺς
the likeness of Melchisedec arises priest

ἕτερος, 16 ὃς οὐ κατὰ νόμον ἐντολῆς
another, who not accord- [the] law ²command- ing to ment

σαρκίνης γέγονεν ἀλλὰ κατὰ δύναμιν ζωῆς
¹of a fleshy has become but accord- [the] power life ing to

ἀκαταλύτου. 17 μαρτυρεῖται γὰρ ὅτι σὺ
of an indissoluble. For it is witnessed that Thou

ἱερεὺς εἰς τὸν αἰῶνα κατὰ τὴν τάξιν
a priest unto the age according to the order

Μελχισέδεκ. 18 ἀθέτησις μὲν γὰρ γίνεται
of Melchisedec. ⁴an annul- ²on one ¹For ³there ment hand comes about

προαγούσης ἐντολῆς διὰ τὸ αὐτῆς ἀσθενὲς
of [the] command- because ¹the ⁵of it ⁶weak[ness] preceding ment of

καὶ ἀνωφελές, 19 οὐδὲν γὰρ ἐτελείωσεν
²and ⁴unprofitable[ness], for ⁶nothing ⁵perfected

ὁ νόμος, ἐπεισαγωγὴ δὲ κρείττονος ἐλπίδος,
¹the ³law, ²a bringing in ¹on the of a better hope, other

δι' ἧς ἐγγίζομεν τῷ θεῷ. 20 καὶ καθ'
through we draw near – to God. And in pro- which

ὅσον οὐ χωρὶς ὁρκωμοσίας, — οἱ μὲν
portion not without oath-taking, ²the ²on one as (they) hand

γὰρ χωρὶς ὁρκωμοσίας εἰσὶν ἱερεῖς
¹for ⁷without ⁸oath-taking ⁴are ⁶priests

γεγονότες, 21 ὁ δὲ μετὰ ὁρκωμοσίας διὰ
⁵having the on the with oath-taking through become, (he) other

τοῦ λέγοντος πρὸς αὐτόν· ὤμοσεν κύριος,
the [one] saying to him: swore [The] Lord,

καὶ οὐ μεταμεληθήσεται· σὺ ἱερεὺς εἰς
and will not change [his] mind: Thou [art] a priest unto

τὸν αἰῶνα· — 22 κατὰ τοσοῦτο καὶ
the age;) by so much indeed

surety of a better covenant.

23 The former priests were many in number, because they were prevented by death from continuing in office; [24] but he holds his priesthood permanently, because he continues for ever. [25] Consequently he is able for all time to save those who draw near to God through him, since he always lives to make intercession for them.

26 For it was fitting that we should have such a high priest, holy, blameless, unstained, separated from sinners, exalted above the heavens. [27] He has no need, like those high priests, to offer sacrifices daily, first for his own sins and then for those of the people; he did this once for all when he offered up himself. [28] Indeed, the law appoints men in their weakness as high priests, but the word of the oath, which came later than the law, appoints a Son who has been made perfect for ever.

κρείττονος διαθήκης γέγονεν ἔγγυος Ἰησοῦς.
[4]of a better   [5]covenant   [2]has become   [3]surety   [1]Jesus.

23 καὶ οἱ μὲν πλείονές εἰσιν γεγονότες
And the on one [3]many   [1]are   [2]having become
(they) hand

ἱερεῖς διὰ τὸ θανάτῳ κωλύεσθαι παραμέ-
[4]priests because the [2]by death [1]to be prevented   [3]to con-
of   = being prevented by death from continuing;

νειν· 24 ὁ δὲ διὰ τὸ μένειν αὐτὸν εἰς
tinue;   the on the because the to remain   him[b]   unto
(he) other   of
              = because he remains

τὸν αἰῶνα ἀπαράβατον ἔχει τὴν ἱερωσύνην·
the   age   [3]intransmissible [1]has [2]the [4]priestly office;

25 ὅθεν καὶ σῴζειν εἰς τὸ παντελὲς
whence indeed [3]to save [2]to [4]the [5]entire

δύναται τοὺς προσερχομένους δι’ αὐτοῦ
[1]he is able the [ones] [1]approaching [2]through [4]him

τῷ θεῷ, πάντοτε ζῶν εἰς τὸ ἐντυγχάνειν
- [3]to God,   always living for the   to intercede

ὑπὲρ αὐτῶν. 26 τοιοῦτος γὰρ ἡμῖν καὶ
on be-   them.   For [1]such   [1]to us [2]indeed
half of

ἔπρεπεν ἀρχιερεύς, ὅσιος, ἄκακος, ἀμίαντος,
[4]was   [3]a high priest. holy,   harmless,   undefiled,
suitable

κεχωρισμένος ἀπὸ τῶν ἁμαρτωλῶν, καὶ
having been   from   -   sinners,   and
separated

ὑψηλότερος τῶν οὐρανῶν γενόμενος· 27 ὃς
higher [than] the   heavens   becoming;   who

οὐκ ἔχει καθ’ ἡμέραν ἀνάγκην, ὥσπερ
has not   [2]daily   [1]necessity,   as

οἱ ἀρχιερεῖς, πρότερον ὑπὲρ τῶν ἰδίων
the high priests,   firstly on behalf of the(his) own

ἁμαρτιῶν θυσίας ἀναφέρειν, ἔπειτα τῶν
sins   sacrifices   to offer up,   then the [sins]

τοῦ λαοῦ· τοῦτο γὰρ ἐποίησεν ἐφάπαξ
of the people;   for this   he did   once for all

ἑαυτὸν ἀνενέγκας. 28 ὁ νόμος γὰρ
himself   offering up.   For the law

ἀνθρώπους καθίστησιν ἀρχιερεῖς ἔχοντας
[2]men   [1]appoints   [3]high priests [3]having

ἀσθένειαν, ὁ λόγος δὲ τῆς ὁρκωμοσίας
[4]weakness,   but the word   of the   oath-taking

τῆς μετὰ τὸν νόμον υἱὸν εἰς τὸν αἰῶνα
-   after the   law   a Son [2]unto [3]the [4]age
[appoints]

τετελειωμένον.
[1]having been perfected.

CHAPTER 8

NOW the point in what we are saying is this: we have such a high priest, one who is seated at the right hand of the throne of the Majesty in heaven, [2]a minister in the sanctuary and the true tent[j] which is set up not by man but by the Lord. [3]For every high priest is appointed to offer gifts and sacrifices; hence it is necessary for this priest also to have something to offer. [4]Now if he were on earth, he would not be a priest at all, since there are priests who offer gifts according to the law. [5]They serve a copy and shadow of the heavenly sanctuary; for when Moses was about to erect the tent,[j] he was instructed by God, saying, "See that you make everything according to the pattern which was shown you on the mountain." [6]But as it is, Christ has obtained a ministry which is as much more excellent than the old as the covenant he mediates is better, since it is enacted on better promises. [7]For if that first covenant had been faultless, there would

---

8 Κεφάλαιον δὲ ἐπὶ τοῖς λεγομένοις,
Now a summary   over(of) the things   being said,

τοιοῦτον ἔχομεν ἀρχιερέα, ὃς ἐκάθισεν
[2]such   [1]we have   a high priest,   who   sat

ἐν δεξιᾷ τοῦ θρόνου τῆς μεγαλωσύνης
at [the] right of the   throne   of the   greatness

ἐν τοῖς οὐρανοῖς, 2 τῶν ἁγίων λειτουργὸς
in   the   heavens,   [1]of the [3]holy things   [1]a minister

καὶ τῆς σκηνῆς τῆς ἀληθινῆς, ἣν ἔπηξεν
and of the [2]tabernacle -   [1]true,   which [2]erected

ὁ κύριος, οὐκ ἄνθρωπος. 3 Πᾶς γὰρ
[1]the [2]Lord,   not   man.   For every

ἀρχιερεὺς εἰς τὸ προσφέρειν δῶρά τε
high priest   for   the [2]to offer   [4]gifts [5]both

καὶ θυσίας καθίσταται· ὅθεν ἀναγκαῖον
[3]and [6]sacrifices   [1]is appointed;   whence [it is] necessary

ἔχειν τι καὶ τοῦτον ὃ προσενέγκῃ. 4 εἰ
[2]to have [4]some- [2]also   [1]this   which he may offer.   If
thing   [priest]

μὲν οὖν ἦν ἐπὶ γῆς, οὐδ' ἂν ἦν ἱερεύς,
-   there- he   on   earth,   he would not be   a priest,
fore were

ὄντων τῶν προσφερόντων κατὰ νόμον
[there]   the [ones] offering[a]   [3]according to   [4]law
being

τὰ δῶρα· 5 οἵτινες ὑποδείγματι καὶ σκιᾷ
[1]the [2]gifts;   who   [3]an example [2]and [4]a
shadow

λατρεύουσιν τῶν ἐπουρανίων, καθὼς
[1]serve   of the   heavenly things,   as

κεχρημάτισται Μωϋσῆς μέλλων ἐπιτελεῖν
[2]has been warned   [1]Moses   being about   to complete

τὴν σκηνήν· ὅρα γάρ φησιν, ποιήσεις
the   tabernacle;   for See[,]   he says,   thou shalt
make

πάντα κατὰ τὸν τύπον τὸν δειχθέντα
all   according to   the   pattern -   shown
things

σοι ἐν τῷ ὄρει· 6 νῦν δὲ διαφορωτέρας
to thee in   the   mount;   but now   [2]a more excellent

τέτυχεν λειτουργίας, ὅσῳ καὶ κρείττονός
[1]he has   ministry,   by so indeed [4]of a better
obtained   much

ἐστιν διαθήκης μεσίτης, ἥτις ἐπὶ κρείττοσιν
[1][as] [5]covenant [3]mediator,   which [2]on [3]better
[2]he is

ἐπαγγελίαις νενομοθέτηται. 7 εἰ γὰρ ἡ
[4]promises   [1]has been enacted.   For if   -

πρώτη ἐκείνη ἦν ἄμεμπτος, οὐκ ἂν
[1]first [covenant] [1]that   was   faultless,   [2]would not

---

[j] Or tabernacle

have been no occasion for a second.

8 For he finds fault with them when he says: "The days will come, says the Lord, when I will establish a new covenant with the house of Israel and with the house of Judah;

⁹ not like the covenant that I made with their fathers on the day when I took them by the hand to lead them out of the land of Egypt; for they did not continue in my covenant, and so I paid no heed to them, says the Lord.

¹⁰ This is the covenant that I will make with the house of Israel after those days, says the Lord: I will put my laws into their minds, and write them on their hearts, and I will be their God, and they shall be my people.

¹¹ And they shall not teach every one his fellow or every one his brother, saying, 'Know the Lord,' for all shall know me, from the least of them to the greatest.

¹² For I will be merciful toward their iniquities,

δευτέρας ἐζητεῖτο τόπος. **8** μεμφόμενος
⁴of(for) a ᵃhave been ¹place. finding fault [with]
 second sought

γὰρ αὐτοὺς λέγει· ἰδοὺ ἡμέραι ἔρχονται,
For them he says: Behold[,] days are coming,

λέγει κύριος, καὶ συντελέσω ἐπὶ τὸν
says [the] Lord, and I will effect over the

οἶκον Ἰσραὴλ καὶ ἐπὶ τὸν οἶκον Ἰούδα
household of Israel and over the household of Juda

διαθήκην καινήν, **9** οὐ κατὰ τὴν διαθήκην
covenant a new, not accord- the covenant
    ing to

ἣν ἐποίησα τοῖς πατράσιν αὐτῶν ἐν
which I made with the fathers of them in

ἡμέρᾳ ἐπιλαβομένου μου τῆς χειρὸς αὐτῶν
[the] day taking meᵃ the hand of them
    =when I took

ἐξαγαγεῖν αὐτοὺς ἐκ γῆς Αἰγύπτου, ὅτι
to lead forth them out [the] of Egypt, because
    of land

αὐτοὶ οὐκ ἐνέμειναν ἐν τῇ διαθήκῃ μου,
they continued not in in the covenant of me,

κἀγὼ ἠμέλησα αὐτῶν, λέγει κύριος. **10** ὅτι
and I disregarded them, says [the] Lord. Because

αὕτη ἡ διαθήκη ἣν διαθήσομαι τῷ οἴκῳ
this [is] the covenant which I will with house-
    covenant the hold

Ἰσραὴλ μετὰ τὰς ἡμέρας ἐκείνας, λέγει
of Israel after those days, says

κύριος, διδοὺς νόμους μου εἰς τὴν διάνοιαν
[the] Lord, giving laws of me into the mind

αὐτῶν, καὶ ἐπὶ καρδίας αὐτῶν ἐπιγράψω
of them, and on hearts of them I will inscribe

αὐτούς, καὶ ἔσομαι αὐτοῖς εἰς θεὸν
them, and I will be to them for God

καὶ αὐτοὶ ἔσονταί μοι εἰς λαόν. **11** καὶ
and they shall be to me for a people. And

οὐ μὴ διδάξωσιν ἕκαστος τὸν πολίτην
by no means may they teach each man the citizen

αὐτοῦ καὶ ἕκαστος τὸν ἀδελφὸν αὐτοῦ,
of him and each man the brother of him,

λέγων· γνῶθι τὸν κύριον, ὅτι πάντες
saying: Know thou the Lord, because all

εἰδήσουσίν με ἀπὸ μικροῦ ἕως μεγάλου
will know me from little to great

αὐτῶν. **12** ὅτι ἵλεως ἔσομαι ταῖς ἀδικίαις
of them. Because merciful I will be to the unrighteous-
    nesses

αὐτῶν, καὶ τῶν ἁμαρτιῶν αὐτῶν οὐ μὴ
of them, and the sins of them by no means

and I will remember
their sins no more."
¹³ In speaking of a new
covenant he treats the
first as obsolete. And
what is becoming ob-
solete and growing old
is ready to vanish away.

μνησθῶ   ἔτι.   13 ἐν   τῷ   λέγειν   καινὴν
I may   more.   In   the   to say⁹   ' new '
remember   =When he says

πεπαλαίωκεν   τὴν   πρώτην·   τὸ   δὲ   παλαι-
he has made old   the   first;   and the thing   being

ούμενον   καὶ   γηράσκον   ἐγγὺς   ἀφανισμοῦ.
made old   and   growing aged   [is] near   vanishing.

CHAPTER 9

NOW even the first
covenant had regu-
lations for worship and
an earthly sanctuary.
² For a tent*ᵏ was pre-
pared, the outer one, in
which were the lamp-
stand and the table and
the bread of the
Presence;ˡ it is called
the Holy Place. ³ Behind
the second curtain stood
a tent*ᵏ called the Holy
of Holies, ⁴ having the
golden altar of incense
and the ark of the
covenant covered on all
sides with gold, which
contained a golden urn
holding the manna,
Aaron's rod that budded,
and the tables of the
covenant; ⁵ above it
were the cherubim of
glory overshadowing the
mercy seat. Of these
things we cannot now
speak in detail.

6 These preparations
having thus been made,
the priests go continually
into the outer tent,*ᵏ

9 Εἶχε   μὲν   οὖν   καὶ   ἡ   πρώτη   δικαι-
⁵had   ¹So then   ⁶both   ³the   ⁴first   ordin-
                                                [covenant]

ώματα   λατρείας   τό   τε   ἅγιον   κοσμικόν.
ances   of service   ²the   ¹and   ⁴holy place   ⁵worldly.

2 σκηνὴ   γὰρ   κατεσκευάσθη   ἡ   πρώτη,
For a tabernacle   was prepared[,]   the   first,

ἐν   ᾗ   ἥ   τε   λυχνία   καὶ   ἡ   τράπεζα   καὶ
in which   ²the   ¹both   lampstand   and   the   table   and
[were]

ἡ   πρόθεσις   τῶν   ἄρτων,   ἥτις   λέγεται
the   setting forth   of the   loaves,   which   is called

Ἅγια·   3 μετὰ   δὲ   τὸ   δεύτερον   καταπέτασμα
Holy;   and after   the   second   veil

σκηνὴ   ἡ   λεγομένη   Ἅγια   Ἁγίων,   4 χρυσοῦν
a taber-   the   being called   Holy   of Holies,   ²a golden
nacle   [one]

ἔχουσα   θυμιατήριον   καὶ   τὴν   κιβωτὸν   τῆς
¹having   altar   and   the   ark   of the

διαθήκης   περικεκαλυμμένην   πάντοθεν   χρυσίῳ,
covenant   having been covered round   on all sides   with gold,

ἐν   ᾗ   στάμνος   χρυσῆ   ἔχουσα   τὸ   μάννα
in   which   pot   a golden   having   the   manna
[were]

καὶ   ἡ   ῥάβδος   Ἀαρὼν   ἡ   βλαστήσασα
and   the   rod   of Aaron   –   budded

καὶ   αἱ   πλάκες   τῆς   διαθήκης,   5 ὑπεράνω
and   the   tablets   of the   covenant,   ²above

δὲ   αὐτῆς   Χερουβὶν   δόξης   κατασκιάζοντα
¹and   it   cherubim   of glory   overshadowing

τὸ   ἱλαστήριον·   περὶ   ὧν   οὐκ   ἔστιν   νῦν
the   mercy-seat;   concern-   which   there is not   now
                              ing   things   [?time]

λέγειν   κατὰ   μέρος.   6 τούτων   δὲ   οὕτως
to speak   in detail.   These things   now   thus
                                    =Now when these things had

κατεσκευασμένων   εἰς   μὲν   τὴν   πρώτην
having been prepared⁵   ⁴into   ¹on one   ³the   ⁵first
been thus prepared   hand

σκηνὴν   διὰ   παντὸς   εἰσίασιν   οἱ   ἱερεῖς
⁵tabernacle   ⁴at all times   ⁶go in   ¹the   ²priests

ᵏ Or tabernacle
ˡ Greek the presentation of the
loaves

performing their ritual duties; ⁷but into the second only the high priest goes, and he but once a year, and not without taking blood which he offers for himself and for the errors of the people. ⁸By this the Holy Spirit indicates that the way into the sanctuary is not yet opened as long as the outer tent*ᵏ* is still standing ⁹(which is symbolic for the present age). According to this arrangement, gifts and sacrifices are offered which cannot perfect the conscience of the worshiper, ¹⁰but deal only with food and drink and various ablutions, regulations for the body imposed until the time of reformation.

11 But when Christ appeared as a high priest of the good things that have come,*ᵐ* then through the greater and more perfect tent*ᵏ* (not made with hands, that is, not of this creation) ¹²he entered once for all into the Holy Place, taking not the blood of goats and calves but his own blood, thus securing an eternal redemption.

ᵏ Or *tabernacle*
ᵐ Other manuscripts read *good things to come*

τὰς   λατρείας   ἐπιτελοῦντες,   7 εἰς   δὲ   τὴν
¹¹the   ¹²services   ¹⁰accomplishing,   ²into ¹on the   ²the
                                             other

δευτέραν   ἅπαξ   τοῦ   ἐνιαυτοῦ   μόνος   ὁ
⁴second   ⁵once   ⁶of(in) the   ¹⁰year   [goes]   ⁴the
                                            ⁷alone

ἀρχιερεύς,   οὐ   χωρὶς   αἵματος   ὃ   προσφέρει
⁶high priest,   not   without   blood   which   he offers

ὑπὲρ   ἑαυτοῦ   καὶ   τῶν   τοῦ   λαοῦ   ἀγνοημά-
on be-   himself   and   ¹the   ²of the   ⁴people   ²ignor-
half of

των,   8 τοῦτο   δηλοῦντος   τοῦ   πνεύματος
ances,   ⁵this   ⁴showing   ¹the   ²Spirit

τοῦ   ἀγίου,   μήπω   πεφανερῶσθαι   τὴν   τῶν
–   ²Holy,³   ⁵not yet   ⁴to have been   ¹the   ²of the
                     manifested

ἀγίων   ὁδὸν   ἔτι   τῆς   πρώτης   σκηνῆς
⁴holies   ⁹way   ¹⁰still   ⁷the   ⁸first   ³tabernacle

ἐχούσης   στάσιν,   9 ἥτις   παραβολὴ   εἰς   τὸν
¹¹having³   ¹²standing,   which [was] a parable   for   the

καιρὸν   τὸν   ἐνεστηκότα,   καθ᾽   ἣν   δωρά
time   –   present,   accord- which   ²gifts
                              ing to

τε   καὶ   θυσίαι   προσφέρονται   μὴ   δυνάμεναι
¹both and   sacrifices   are being offered   not   being able

κατὰ   συνείδησιν   τελειῶσαι   τὸν   λατρεύοντα,
in respect conscience   to perfect   the [one]   serving,
of

10 μόνον   ἐπὶ   βρώμασιν   καὶ   πόμασιν   καὶ
   only   on   foods   and   drinks   and

διαφόροις   βαπτισμοῖς,   δικαιώματα   σαρκὸς
various   washings,   ordinances   of flesh

μέχρι   καιροῦ   διορθώσεως   ἐπικείμενα.
²until   ³a time   ⁴of amendment   ¹*being* imposed.

11 Χριστὸς   δὲ   παραγενόμενος   ἀρχιερεὺς
   But Christ   having appeared   a high priest

τῶν   γενομένων   ἀγαθῶν,   διὰ   τῆς   μείζονος
¹of the   ²having come   ²good things, through the   greater
      about

καὶ   τελειοτέρας   σκηνῆς   οὐ   χειροποιήτου,
and   more perfect   tabernacle   not   made by hand,

τοῦτ᾽   ἔστιν   οὐ   ταύτης   τῆς   κτίσεως,
this   is   not   of this   –   creation,

12 οὐδὲ   δι᾽   αἵματος   τράγων   καὶ   μόσχων,
  nor   through   blood   of goats   and   *of* calves,

διὰ   δὲ   τοῦ   ἰδίου   αἵματος   εἰσῆλθεν   ἐφάπαξ
but   the   own   blood   entered   once for
through   (his)   all

εἰς   τὰ   ἅγια,   αἰωνίαν   λύτρωσιν   εὑράμενος.
into   the   holies,   eternal   redemption   having found.

¹³ For if the sprinkling of defiled persons with the blood of goats and bulls and with the ashes of a heifer sanctifies for the purification of the flesh, ¹⁴ how much more shall the blood of Christ, who through the eternal Spirit offered himself without blemish to God, purify yourⁿ conscience from dead works to serve the living God.

15 Therefore he is the mediator of a new covenant, so that those who are called may receive the promised eternal inheritance, since a death has occurred which redeems them from the transgressions under the first covenant.^o ¹⁶ For where a will^o is involved, the death of the one who made it must be established. ¹⁷ For a will^o takes effect only at death, since it is not in force as long as the one who made it is alive. ¹⁸ Hence even the first covenant was not ratified without blood. ¹⁹ For when every commandment of the law had been declared by Moses to all the people, he took the blood of calves and

13 εἰ γὰρ τὸ αἷμα τράγων καὶ ταύρων
For if the blood of goats and of bulls

καὶ σποδὸς δαμάλεως ῥαντίζουσα τοὺς
and ashes of a heifer sprinkling the [ones]

κεκοινωμένους ἁγιάζει πρὸς τὴν τῆς
having been polluted sanctifies to ¹the ²of the

σαρκὸς καθαρότητα, 14 πόσῳ μᾶλλον τὸ
³flesh ²cleanness, by how much more the

αἷμα τοῦ Χριστοῦ, ὃς διὰ πνεύματος
blood - of Christ, who through ¹Spirit

αἰωνίου ἑαυτὸν προσήνεγκεν ἄμωμον τῷ
¹[the] eternal ⁴himself ⁵offered unblemished -

θεῷ, καθαριεῖ τὴν συνείδησιν ἡμῶν ἀπὸ
to God, will cleanse the conscience of us from

νεκρῶν ἔργων εἰς τὸ λατρεύειν θεῷ
dead works for the to serve ²God

ζῶντι. 15 καὶ διὰ τοῦτο διαθήκης καινῆς
¹[the] living. And therefore ⁴covenant ⁵of a new

μεσίτης ἐστίν, ὅπως θανάτου γενομένου
¹mediator ¹he is, so as death having occurred⁸

εἰς ἀπολύτρωσιν τῶν ἐπὶ τῇ πρώτῃ
for redemption ¹of the ⁹under * ⁴the ⁵first

διαθήκῃ παραβάσεων τὴν ἐπαγγελίαν
⁶covenant ⁹transgressions ¹⁰the ¹¹promise

λάβωσιν οἱ κεκλημένοι τῆς αἰωνίου
⁹may receive ⁷the ⁸having been ¹²of the ¹³eternal
   [ones] called

κληρονομίας. 16 Ὅπου γὰρ διαθήκη,
¹⁴inheritance. For where [there is] a covenant,

θάνατον ἀνάγκη φέρεσθαι τοῦ διαθεμένου·
²[the] death ¹[there is] ³to be offered ⁴of the ⁵making
   necessity [one] covenant;

17 διαθήκη γὰρ ἐπὶ νεκροῖς βεβαία, ἐπεὶ
for a covenant over dead [? bodies] [is] firm, since

μήποτε ἰσχύει ὅτε ζῇ ὁ διαθέμενος.
never has it when ³lives ¹the ²making
   strength [one] covenant.

18 ὅθεν οὐδὲ ἡ πρώτη χωρὶς αἵματος
Whence neither the first [covenant] ²without ³blood

ἐγκεκαίνισται. 19 λαληθείσης γὰρ πάσης
¹has been dedicated. For ³having been spoken ¹every

ἐντολῆς κατὰ τὸν νόμον ὑπὸ Μωϋσέως
²command- ³accord- ¹⁰the ¹¹law ⁴by ⁵Moses
ment⁸ ing to

παντὶ τῷ λαῷ, λαβὼν τὸ αἷμα τῶν
⁶to all ⁷the ⁸people, taking the blood of the

ⁿ Other manuscripts read *our*
^o The Greek word here used means *covenant* and *will*

* It may seem strange to translate a preposition which means "on" or "over" by "under"; but ἐπί has the meaning of "during the time of" (see Mark 2. 26; I. Tim. 6. 13).

goats, with water and scarlet wool and hyssop, and sprinkled both the book itself and all the people, 20 saying, "This is the blood of the covenant which God commanded you." 21 And in the same way he sprinkled with the blood both the tent[k] and all the vessels used in worship. 22 Indeed, under the law almost everything is purified with blood, and without the shedding of blood there is no forgiveness of sins.

23 Thus it was necessary for the copies of the heavenly things to be purified with these rites, but the heavenly things themselves with better sacrifices than these. 24 For Christ has entered, not into a sanctuary made with hands, a copy of the true one, but into heaven itself, now to appear in the presence of God on our behalf. 25 Nor was it to offer himself repeatedly, as the high priest enters the Holy Place yearly with blood not his own; 26 for then he would have had to suffer repeatedly since the foundation of the

μόσχων καὶ τῶν τράγων μετὰ ὕδατος
calves and of the goats with water

καὶ ἐρίου κοκκίνου καὶ ὑσσώπου, αὐτό
and ²wool ¹scarlet and hyssop, ⁴it[self]

τε τὸ βιβλίον καὶ πάντα τὸν λαὸν
³both ³the ⁴scroll ⁵and ⁶all ⁷the ⁸people

ἐρράντισεν, 20 λέγων· τοῦτο τὸ αἷμα τῆς
¹he sprinkled, saying: This [is] the blood of the

διαθήκης ἧς ἐνετείλατο πρὸς ὑμᾶς ὁ
covenant which ²enjoined ³to ⁴you –

θεός. 21 καὶ τὴν σκηνὴν δὲ καὶ πάντα
¹God. ²both ³the ⁴tabernacle ¹And and all

τὰ σκεύη τῆς λειτουργίας τῷ αἵματι
the vessels of the service with the blood

ὁμοίως ἐρράντισεν. 22 καὶ σχεδὸν ἐν
likewise he sprinkled. And ⁶almost ⁷by

αἵματι πάντα καθαρίζεται κατὰ τὸν νόμον,
⁸blood ⁴all things ⁵is(are) cleansed ¹accord- ²the ³law,
ing to

καὶ χωρὶς αἱματεκχυσίας οὐ γίνεται
and without bloodshedding there becomes no

ἄφεσις. 23 ἀνάγκη οὖν τὰ μὲν ὑπο-
remission. [There was] therefore ²[for] ¹on one ⁴ex-
necessity ³the hand

δείγματα τῶν ἐν τοῖς οὐρανοῖς τούτοις
amples of the in the heavens ²by these
things

καθαρίζεσθαι, αὐτὰ δὲ τὰ ἐπουράνια
¹to be cleansed, ²[them]- ¹on the ²[for] ⁴heavenly
selves other ³the things

κρείττοσιν θυσίαις παρὰ ταύτας. 24 οὐ
by better sacrifices than these. not

γὰρ εἰς χειροποίητα εἰσῆλθεν ἅγια Χριστός,
For into ⁴made by hand ⁴entered ¹holies ³Christ,

ἀντίτυπα τῶν ἀληθινῶν, ἀλλ' εἰς αὐτὸν
figures of the true things, but into ²[it]self

τὸν οὐρανόν, νῦν ἐμφανισθῆναι τῷ προσώπῳ
¹the ³heaven, now to appear in the presence

τοῦ θεοῦ ὑπὲρ ἡμῶν· 25 οὐδ' ἵνα πολ-
– of God on behalf of us; nor in order that often

λάκις προσφέρῃ ἑαυτόν, ὥσπερ ὁ ἀρχιερεὺς
he should offer himself, even as the high priest

εἰσέρχεται εἰς τὰ ἅγια κατ' ἐνιαυτὸν
enters into the holies year by year†

ἐν αἵματι ἀλλοτρίῳ, 26 ἐπεὶ ἔδει αὐτὸν
with blood belonging to others, since it behoved him

πολλάκις παθεῖν ἀπὸ καταβολῆς κόσμου·
often to suffer from [the] foundation of [the]
world;

---

[k] Or tabernacle

world. But as it is, he has appeared once for all at the end of the age to put away sin by the sacrifice of himself. [27] And just as it is appointed for men to die once, and after that comes judgment, [28] so Christ, having been offered once to bear the sins of many, will appear a second time, not to deal with sin but to save those who are eagerly waiting for him.

νυνὶ δὲ ἅπαξ ἐπὶ συντελείᾳ τῶν αἰώνων
but now   once   at [the] completion of the   ages

εἰς ἀθέτησιν τῆς ἁμαρτίας διὰ τῆς θυσίας
for   annulment   -   of sin   through   the   sacrifice

αὐτοῦ πεφανέρωται. 27 καὶ καθ᾽ ὅσον
of him   he has been manifested.   And   as

ἀπόκειται τοῖς ἀνθρώποις ἅπαξ ἀποθανεῖν,
it is reserved   -   to men   once   to die,

μετὰ δὲ τοῦτο κρίσις, 28 οὕτως καὶ
and after   this   judgment,   so   also

ὁ Χριστός, ἅπαξ προσενεχθεὶς εἰς τὸ
-   Christ,   once   having been offered   for   the

πολλῶν ἀνενεγκεῖν ἁμαρτίας, ἐκ δευτέρου
[2]of many   [1]to bear   [3]sins,   [4]a second [time]

χωρὶς ἁμαρτίας ὀφθήσεται τοῖς αὐτὸν
[3]without   [4]sin   [1]will appear   [5]to the [ones]   [7]him

ἀπεκδεχομένοις εἰς σωτηρίαν.
[6]expecting   for   salvation.

CHAPTER 10

FOR since the law has but a shadow of the good things to come instead of the true form of these realities, it can never, by the same sacrifices which are continually offered year after year, make perfect those who draw near. [2] Otherwise, would they not have ceased to be offered? If the worshipers had once been cleansed, they would no longer have any consciousness of sin. [3] But in these sacrifices there is a reminder of sin year after year. [4] For it is impossible that the blood of bulls and goats should take away sins.

5 Consequently, when Christ came into the world, he said,
  "Sacrifices and offerings thou hast not desired,
  but a body hast thou prepared for me;

10 Σκιὰν γὰρ ἔχων ὁ νόμος τῶν
For [4]a shadow [3]having [1]the [2]law of the

μελλόντων ἀγαθῶν, οὐκ αὐτὴν τὴν εἰκόνα
coming   good things,   not   [2][it]self   [1]the   [3]image

τῶν πραγμάτων, κατ᾽ ἐνιαυτὸν ταῖς αὐταῖς
of the   matters,   [2]every [3]year†   [1]by the   [4]same

θυσίαις ἃς προσφέρουσιν εἰς τὸ διηνεκὲς
[5]sacrifices [6]which   [7]they offer   [10]continually†

οὐδέποτε δύναται τοὺς προσερχομένους
[2]never   [1]can   [12]the [ones]   [13]approaching

τελειῶσαι· 2 ἐπεὶ οὐκ ἂν ἐπαύσαντο
[11]to perfect;   since   would not they have ceased

προσφερόμεναι, διὰ τὸ μηδεμίαν ἔχειν
being offered,   because of the   [2]no   [1]to have

ἔτι συνείδησιν ἁμαρτιῶν τοὺς λατρεύοντας
[3]still   [2]conscience   [4]of sins   [1]the [ones]   [5]serving

ἅπαξ κεκαθαρισμένους; 3 ἀλλ᾽ ἐν αὐταῖς
[3]once   [4]having been cleansed ?   But   in them [there

ἀνάμνησις ἁμαρτιῶν κατ᾽ ἐνιαυτόν·
is] a remembrance   of sins   yearly†;

4 ἀδύνατον γὰρ αἷμα ταύρων καὶ τράγων
for [it is] impossible   blood   of bulls   and   of goats

ἀφαιρεῖν ἁμαρτίας. 5 Διὸ εἰσερχόμενος εἰς
to take away   sins.   Wherefore   entering   into

τὸν κόσμον λέγει· θυσίαν καὶ προσφορὰν
the   world   he says: Sacrifice   and   offering

οὐκ ἠθέλησας, σῶμα δὲ κατηρτίσω μοι·
thou didst not wish,   but a body   thou didst prepare for me;

⁶in burnt offerings and sin offerings thou hast taken no pleasure.
⁷Then I said, 'Lo, I have come to do thy will, O God,' as it is written of me in the roll of the book."
⁸When he said above, "Thou hast neither desired nor taken pleasure in sacrifices and offerings and burnt offerings and sin offerings" (these are offered according to the law), ⁹then he added, "Lo, I have come to do thy will." He abolishes the first in order to establish the second. ¹⁰And by that will we have been sanctified through the offering of the body of Jesus Christ once for all.

11 And every priest stands daily at his service, offering repeatedly the same sacrifices, which can never take away sins. ¹²But when Christ had offered for all time a single sacrifice for sins, he sat down at the right hand of God, ¹³then

6 ὁλοκαυτώματα καὶ περὶ ἁμαρτίας οὐκ
   burnt offerings   and concerning   sins   not
                           [sacrifices]

εὐδόκησας. 7 τότε εἶπον· ἰδοὺ ἥκω,
thou wast well   Then   I said: Behold   I have
pleased [with].   come,

ἐν κεφαλίδι βιβλίου γέγραπται περὶ ἐμοῦ,
in   a heading   of a scroll   it has been concerning me,
                         written

τοῦ ποιῆσαι ὁ θεὸς τὸ θέλημά σου.
–   to do[,]ᵈ   –   God[,]*   the   will   of thee.

8 ἀνώτερον λέγων ὅτι θυσίας καὶ προσ-
   Above   saying   that   sacrifices   and   offer-

φορὰς καὶ ὁλοκαυτώματα καὶ περὶ ἁμαρτίας
ings   and   burnt offerings   and [sacrifices]   sins
                              concerning

οὐκ ἠθέλησας οὐδὲ εὐδόκησας, αἵτινες
thou didst not wish   nor   thou wast well   which
                      pleased [with],

κατὰ νόμον προσφέρονται, 9 τότε εἴρηκεν·
accord-   law   are offered,   then   he has said:
ing to

ἰδοὺ ἥκω τοῦ ποιῆσαι τὸ θέλημά σου.
Behold I have   –   to doᵈ   the   will   of thee.
come

ἀναιρεῖ τὸ πρῶτον ἵνα τὸ δεύτερον
He takes   the   first   in order   the   second
away   that

στήσῃ· 10 ἐν ᾧ θελήματι ἡγιασμένοι ἐσμὲν
he may   by which   will   ²having been   ¹we are
set up;   sanctified

διὰ τῆς προσφορᾶς τοῦ σώματος Ἰησοῦ
through the   offering   of the   body   of Jesus

Χριστοῦ ἐφάπαξ. 11 Καὶ πᾶς μὲν ἱερεὺς
Christ   once for all.   And   ²every ¹on one   ³priest
                        hand

ἕστηκεν καθ' ἡμέραν λειτουργῶν καὶ τὰς
stands   daily†   ministering   and   ³the

αὐτὰς πολλάκις προσφέρων θυσίας, αἵτινες
⁴same   ¹often   ²offering   ⁵sacrifices,   which

οὐδέποτε δύνανται περιελεῖν ἁμαρτίας· 12 οὗτος
never   can   to take away   sins;   ³this
                           [priest]

δὲ μίαν ὑπὲρ ἁμαρτιῶν προσενέγκας
¹on the   ⁴one   ⁶on behalf of   ⁷sins   ³having offered
other

θυσίαν εἰς τὸ διηνεκὲς ἐκάθισεν ἐν δεξιᾷ
⁵sacrifice   ⁹in   –   ¹⁰perpetuity   ⁸sat   at [the] right
                               [hand]

τοῦ θεοῦ, 13 τὸ λοιπὸν ἐκδεχόμενος ἕως
–   of God,   henceforth   expecting   till

* The "articular vocative"; cf. 1. 8, 9.

to wait until his enemies should be made a stool for his feet. [14] For by a single offering he has perfected for all time those who are sanctified. [15] And the Holy Spirit also bears witness to us; for after saying,

[16] "This is the covenant that I will make with them

after those days, says the Lord:

I will put my laws on their hearts,

and write them on their minds,"

[17] then he adds,

"I will remember their sins and their misdeeds no more."

[18] Where there is forgiveness of these, there is no longer any offering for sin.

[19] Therefore, brethren, since we have confidence to enter the sanctuary by the blood of Jesus, [20] by the new and living way which he opened for us through the curtain, that is, through his flesh, [21] and since we have a great priest over the house of God, [22] let us draw near with a true heart in full assurance of faith, with our hearts sprinkled clean from an evil conscience and our bodies

τεθῶσιν   οἱ   ἐχθροὶ   αὐτοῦ   ὑποπόδιον   τῶν
[4]are put   [1]the   [2]enemies   [3]of him   a footstool   of the

ποδῶν   αὐτοῦ.   14 μιᾷ   γὰρ   προσφορᾷ
feet   of him.   For by one   offering

τετελείωκεν   εἰς   τὸ   διηνεκὲς   τοὺς   ἁγιαζ-
he has perfected   in   –   perpetuity   the [ones]   being

ομένους.   15 Μαρτυρεῖ   δὲ   ἡμῖν   καὶ
sanctified.   And [3]witnesses   [1]to us   [4]indeed

τὸ   πνεῦμα   τὸ   ἅγιον·   μετὰ   γὰρ   τὸ
[1]the   [3]Spirit   –   [2]Holy;   for after   the

εἰρηκέναι·   16 αὕτη   ἡ   διαθήκη   ἣν   δια-
to have said: This [is]   the   covenant   which   I will
=having said:

θήσομαι   πρὸς   αὐτοὺς   μετὰ   τὰς   ἡμέρας
covenant   to   them   after   –   days

ἐκείνας,   λέγει   κύριος·   διδοὺς   νόμους   μου
those,   says [the] Lord: Giving   laws   of me

ἐπὶ   καρδίας   αὐτῶν,   καὶ   ἐπὶ   τὴν   διάνοιαν
on   hearts   of them,   also   on   the   mind

αὐτῶν   ἐπιγράψω   αὐτούς,   17 καὶ   τῶν
of them   I will inscribe   them,   and   the

ἁμαρτιῶν   αὐτῶν   καὶ   τῶν   ἀνομιῶν   αὐτῶν
sins   of them   and   the   iniquities   of them

οὐ   μὴ   μνησθήσομαι   ἔτι.   18 ὅπου   δὲ
by no means   I will remember   still.   Now where

ἄφεσις   τούτων,   οὐκέτι   προσφορὰ   περὶ
forgiveness   of these [is],   no longer   offering   concerning
[there is]

ἁμαρτίας.
sins.

19 Ἔχοντες   οὖν,   ἀδελφοί,   παρρησίαν   εἰς
Having   therefore,   brothers,   confidence   for

τὴν   εἴσοδον   τῶν   ἁγίων   ἐν   τῷ   αἵματι
the   entering   of the   holies   by   the   blood

Ἰησοῦ,   20 ἣν   ἐνεκαίνισεν   ἡμῖν   ὁδὸν
of Jesus,   which   he dedicated   for us[,]   a way

πρόσφατον   καὶ   ζῶσαν   διὰ   τοῦ   κατα-
fresh   and   living   through   the   veil,

πετάσματος,   τοῦτ᾽   ἔστιν   τῆς   σαρκὸς   αὐτοῦ,
this   is   the   flesh   of him,

21 καὶ   ἱερέα   μέγαν   ἐπὶ   τὸν   οἶκον   τοῦ
and   priest   a great   over   the   household   –

θεοῦ,   22 προσερχώμεθα   μετὰ   ἀληθινῆς
of God,   let us approach   with   a true

καρδίας   ἐν   πληροφορίᾳ   πίστεως,   ῥεραν-
heart   in   full assurance   of faith,   having been

τισμένοι   τὰς   καρδίας   ἀπὸ   συνειδήσεως
sprinkled   [as to] the   hearts   from   [2]conscience

washed with pure water. ²³Let us hold fast the confession of our hope without wavering, for he who promised is faithful; ²⁴and let us consider how to stir up one another to love and good works, ²⁵not neglecting to meet together, as is the habit of some, but encouraging one another, and all the more as you see the Day drawing near.

26 For if we sin deliberately after receiving the knowledge of the truth, there no longer remains a sacrifice for sins, ²⁷but a fearful prospect of judgment, and a fury of fire which will consume the adversaries. ²⁸A man who has violated the law of Moses dies without mercy at the testimony of two or three witnesses. ²⁹How much worse punishment do you think will be deserved by the man who has spurned the Son of God, and profaned the blood of the covenant by which he was sanctified, and outraged the Spirit

πονηρᾶς   καὶ   λελουσμένοι   τὸ   σῶμα   ὕδατι
¹an evil   and   having been   [as to]   body   ²water
                   bathed   the

καθαρῷ·   23 κατέχωμεν   τὴν   ὁμολογίαν   τῆς
¹in clean;   let us hold fast   the   confession   of the
                                                (our)

ἐλπίδος   ἀκλινῆ,   πιστὸς   γὰρ   ὁ   ἐπαγ-
hope   unyieldingly,   for faithful [is]   the [one] pro-

γειλάμενος,   24 καὶ   κατανοῶμεν   ἀλλήλους
mising,   and   let us consider   one another

εἰς   παροξυσμὸν   ἀγάπης   καὶ   καλῶν   ἔργων,
to   incitement   of love   and   of good   works,

25 μὴ   ἐγκαταλείποντες   τὴν   ἐπισυναγωγὴν
not   forsaking   the   coming together

ἑαυτῶν,   καθὼς   ἔθος   τισίν,   ἀλλὰ   παρα-
of [our]selves,   as   custom   with some [is], but   ex-

καλοῦντες,   καὶ   τοσούτῳ   μᾶλλον   ὅσῳ
horting,   and   by so much   more   as

βλέπετε   ἐγγίζουσαν   τὴν   ἡμέραν.   26 Ἑκουσίως
ye see   ³drawing near   ¹the   ²day.   wilfully

γὰρ   ἁμαρτανόντων   ἡμῶν   μετὰ   τὸ   λαβεῖν
For   sinning   usª   after   the   to receive
=when we sin wilfully   =receiving

τὴν   ἐπίγνωσιν   τῆς   ἀληθείας,   οὐκέτι   περὶ
the   full knowledge   of the   truth,   ⁵no more   ²con-
                                                cerning

ἁμαρτιῶν   ἀπολείπεται   θυσία,   27 φοβερὰ
²sins   ¹remains   ¹a sacrifice,   ³fearful

δέ   τις   ἐκδοχὴ   κρίσεως   καὶ   πυρὸς   ζῆλος
¹but   ²some expectation   of judgment   and   ²of fire   ¹zeal

ἐσθίειν   μέλλοντος   τοὺς   ὑπεναντίους.
⁴to consume   ³being about   the   adversaries.

28 ἀθετήσας   τις   νόμον   Μωϋσέως   χωρὶς
¹Disregarding   ¹anyone   ³law   ⁴of Moses   ⁵without

οἰκτιρμῶν   ἐπὶ   δυσὶν   ἢ   τρισὶν   μάρτυσιν
⁷compassions   ⁸on [the   ⁹two   ¹⁰or   ¹¹three   ¹²witnesses
            word of]

ἀποθνῄσκει·   29 πόσῳ   δοκεῖτε   χείρονος
⁶dies;   by how much   think ye   ²of worse

ἀξιωθήσεται   τιμωρίας   ὁ   τὸν   υἱὸν   τοῦ
¹will be thought   ³punishment   ⁴the   ⁶the   ⁷Son   –
worthy   [one]

θεοῦ   καταπατήσας   καὶ   τὸ   αἷμα   τῆς
⁸of God   ⁹having trampled   and   ²the   ⁴blood   ⁵of the
            [on]

διαθήκης   κοινὸν   ἡγησάμενος,   ἐν   ᾧ   ἡγιάσθη,
⁶covenant   ²common   ¹having   by which   he was
                    deemed,   sanctified,

καὶ   τὸ   πνεῦμα   τῆς   χάριτος   ἐνυβρίσας.
and   ³the   ³Spirit   –   ⁴of grace   ¹having insulted.

of grace? [30] For we know him who said, "Vengeance is mine, I will repay." And again, "The Lord will judge his people." [31] It is a fearful thing to fall into the hands of the living God.

[32] But recall the former days when, after you were enlightened, you endured a hard struggle with sufferings, [33] sometimes being publicly exposed to abuse and affliction, and sometimes being partners with those so treated. [34] For you had compassion on the prisoners, and you joyfully accepted the plundering of your property, since you knew that you yourselves had a better possession and an abiding one. [35] Therefore do not throw away your confidence, which has a great reward. [36] For you have need of endurance, so that you may do the will of God and receive what is promised.

[37] "For yet a little while, and the coming one shall come and shall not tarry;

[38] but my righteous one shall live by faith, and if he shrinks back,

---

30 οἴδαμεν γὰρ τὸν εἰπόντα· ἐμοὶ
For we know the [one] having said: To me
= Vengeance

ἐκδίκησις, ἐγὼ ἀνταποδώσω· καὶ πάλιν·
vengeance,[c] I will repay; and again:
is mine,

κρινεῖ κύριος τὸν λαὸν αὐτοῦ. **31** φοβερὸν
[2]will judge [1The] the people of him. A fearful
Lord thing [it is]

τὸ ἐμπεσεῖν εἰς χεῖρας θεοῦ ζῶντος.
the to fall in into [the] hands [2]God [1]of a living.

32 Ἀναμιμνήσκεσθε δὲ τὰς πρότερον ἡμέρας,
But remember ye the [2]formerly [1]days,

ἐν αἷς φωτισθέντες πολλὴν ἄθλησιν
in which being enlightened [2]a much(great) [1]struggle

ὑπεμείνατε παθημάτων, **33** τοῦτο μὲν
[1]ye endured [4]of sufferings, this on one hand

ὀνειδισμοῖς τε καὶ θλίψεσιν θεατριζόμενοι,
[2]to reproaches [3]both [4]and [5]to afflictions [1]being exposed,

τοῦτο δὲ κοινωνοὶ τῶν οὕτως ἀναστρεφ-
this on the [2]sharers [3]of the [6]thus [4]liv-
other [ones]

ομένων γενηθέντες. **34** καὶ γὰρ τοῖς
ing [1]having become. For indeed in the

δεσμίοις συνεπαθήσατε, καὶ τὴν ἁρπαγὴν
bonds ye suffered together, and [4]the [5]seizure

τῶν ὑπαρχόντων ὑμῶν μετὰ χαρᾶς
[6]of the [7]possessions [8]of you [1]with [2]joy

προσεδέξασθε, γινώσκοντες ἔχειν ἑαυτοὺς
[3]ye accepted, knowing [2]to have [1][your]selves

κρείσσονα ὕπαρξιν καὶ μένουσαν. **35** Μὴ
[2]a better [3]possession [4]and [5]remaining. not

ἀποβάλητε οὖν τὴν παρρησίαν ὑμῶν, ἥτις
Cast ye away therefore the confidence of you, which

ἔχει μεγάλην μισθαποδοσίαν. **36** ὑπομονῆς
has a great recompence. [2]of endurance

γὰρ ἔχετε χρείαν ἵνα τὸ θέλημα τοῦ
For [1]ye have [2]need in order [3]the [4]will –
that

θεοῦ ποιήσαντες κομίσησθε τὴν ἐπαγγελίαν.
[4]of God [1]having ye may obtain the promise.
done

37 ἔτι γὰρ μικρὸν ὅσον ὅσον, ὁ ἐρχόμενος
For yet [3]little [1]a very,* the coming [one]

ἥξει καὶ οὐ χρονίσει· **38** ὁ δὲ δίκαιός
will come and will not delay; but the just man

μου ἐκ πίστεως ζήσεται, καὶ ἐὰν ὑπο-
of me by faith will live, and if he

---

* Cf. our "so so".

my soul has no
pleasure in him."
[39] But we are not of
those who shrink back
and are destroyed, but
of those who have faith
and keep their souls.

στείληται,   οὐκ   εὐδοκεῖ   ἡ   ψυχή   μου
withdraws,   [4]is not well pleased   [1]the   [2]soul   [3]of me

ἐν   αὐτῷ.   39 ἡμεῖς   δὲ   οὐκ   ἐσμὲν   ὑποστολῆς
in   him.   But we   are not   of withdrawal

εἰς   ἀπώλειαν,   ἀλλὰ   πίστεως   εἰς   περιποίησιν
to   destruction,   but   of faith   to   possession

ψυχῆς.
of soul.

CHAPTER 11

NOW faith is the
assurance of things
hoped for, the conviction
of things not seen. [2] For
by it the men of old
received divine approval.
[3] By faith we understand
that the world was
created by the word of
God, so that what is
seen was made out of
things which do not
appear.

4 By faith Abel
offered to God a more
acceptable sacrifice than
Cain, through which he
received approval as
righteous, God bearing
witness by accepting his
gifts; he died, but
through his faith he is
still speaking. [5] By faith
Enoch was taken up so
that he should not see
death; and he was not
found, because God had
taken him. Now before
he was taken he was
attested as having pleased
God. [6] And without faith
it is impossible to please
him. For whoever would
draw near to God must

11 "Εστιν   δὲ   πίστις   ἐλπιζομένων   ὑπό-
    Now [5]is   [1]faith   [6]of things being hoped   [3][the]

στασις,   πραγμάτων   ἔλεγχος   οὐ   βλεπομένων.
reality,   [5]of things   [1][the] proof   not   being seen.

2 ἐν   ταύτῃ   γὰρ   ἐμαρτυρήθησαν   οἱ
by   this   For   [5]obtained witness   [1]the

πρεσβύτεροι.   3 Πίστει   νοοῦμεν   κατηρτίσθαι
[2]elders.   By faith we understand   [5]to have been
                                                    adjusted

τοὺς   αἰῶνας   ῥήματι   θεοῦ,   εἰς   τὸ   μὴ
[1]the   [2]ages   by a word   of God,   so as†   [2]not

ἐκ   φαινομένων   τὸ   βλεπόμενον   γεγονέναι.
[3]out   appearing   [1]the   [5]being seen   [4]to have
of   thing   become.

4 Πίστει   πλείονα   θυσίαν   "Αβελ   παρὰ
By faith   [4]a greater(? better)   [3]sacrifice   [1]Abel   [5]than

Κάϊν   προσήνεγκεν   τῷ   θεῷ,   δι'   ἧς
[7]Cain   [2]offered   -   [6]to God,   through which

ἐμαρτυρήθη   εἶναι   δίκαιος,   μαρτυροῦντος   ἐπὶ
he obtained   to be   just,   [2]witnessing   [3]over
witness

τοῖς   δώροις   αὐτοῦ   τοῦ   θεοῦ,   καὶ   δι'
[4]the   [5]gifts   [6]of him   -   [1]God,[3]   and through

αὐτῆς   ἀποθανὼν   ἔτι   λαλεῖ.   5 Πίστει
it   having died   still   he speaks.   By faith

Ἐνὼχ   μετετέθη   τοῦ   μὴ   ἰδεῖν   θάνατον,
Enoch   was removed   -   not   to see[d]   death,

καὶ   οὐχ   ηὑρίσκετο   διότι   μετέθηκεν   αὐτὸν
and   was not found   because   [2]removed   [3]him

ὁ   θεός.   6 πρὸ   γὰρ   τῆς   μεταθέσεως
-    [1]God.   For before   the(his)   removal

μεμαρτύρηται   εὐαρεστηκέναι   τῷ   θεῷ·   χωρὶς
he has obtained   to have been well-   -   to God; [2]without
witness   pleasing

δὲ   πίστεως   ἀδύνατον   εὐαρεστῆσαι·   πιστεῦσαι
[1]but faith [it is] impossible to be well-pleasing [to God]; [4]to believe

γὰρ   δεῖ   τὸν   προσερχόμενον   [τῷ]   θεῷ,
[1]for   [3]it   the [one]   [5]approaching   -   [2]to God,
            behoves

believe that he exists and
that he rewards those
who seek him. ⁷By faith
Noah, being warned by
God concerning events
as yet unseen, took heed
and constructed an ark
for the saving of his
household; by this he
condemned the world
and became an heir of
the righteousness which
comes by faith.

8 By faith Abraham
obeyed when he was
called to go out to a
place which he was to
receive as an inheritance;
and he went out, not
knowing where he was
to go. ⁹By faith he
sojourned in the land of
promise, as in a foreign
land, living in tents with
Isaac and Jacob, heirs
with him of the same
promise. ¹⁰For he looked
forward to the city which
has foundations, whose
builder and maker is God.
¹¹By faith Sarah herself received power to conceive,
even when she was past the
age, since she considered
him faithful who had
promised. ¹²Therefore
from one man, and him
as good as dead, were
born descendants as
many as the stars of

ὅτι   ἔστιν   καὶ   τοῖς   ἐκζητοῦσιν   αὐτὸν
that he is   and ³to the [ones] ⁴seeking ⁵out ¹him

μισθαποδότης   γίνεται.   7 Πίστει   χρηματισ-
²a rewarder   ¹becomes.   By faith   ⁷having been
                                        warned [by

θεὶς   Νῶε   περὶ   τῶν   μηδέπω   βλεπομένων,
God*] ¹Noah concerning the things not yet   being seen,

εὐλαβηθεὶς   κατεσκεύασεν   κιβωτὸν   εἰς
being devout   prepared   an ark   for

σωτηρίαν   τοῦ   οἴκου   αὐτοῦ,   δι'   ἧς
[the] salvation of the household of him, through which

κατέκρινεν   τὸν   κόσμον,   καὶ   τῆς   κατὰ
he condemned the   world,   and ³of the ⁵accord-
                                             ing to

πίστιν   δικαιοσύνης   ἐγένετο   κληρονόμος.
⁶faith ⁴righteousness ¹became ²heir.

8 Πίστει   καλούμενος   Ἀβραὰμ   ὑπήκουσεν
By faith ⁵being called ¹Abraham ¹¹obeyed

ἐξελθεῖν   εἰς   τόπον   ὃν   ἤμελλεν   λαμβάνειν
²to go forth ⁴to ⁵a place ⁶which ⁷he was about ⁸to receive

εἰς   κληρονομίαν,   καὶ   ἐξῆλθεν   μὴ   ἐπιστάμε-
⁹for ¹⁰an inheritance, and went forth not   understand-

νος   ποῦ   ἔρχεται.   9 Πίστει   παρῴκησεν
ing   where he goes(went). By faith he sojourned

εἰς   γῆν   τῆς   ἐπαγγελίας   ὡς   ἀλλοτρίαν,
in   a land   -   of promise   as   a foreigner,

ἐν   σκηναῖς   κατοικήσας,   μετὰ   Ἰσαὰκ   καὶ
in   tents   dwelling,   with   Isaac   and

Ἰακὼβ   τῶν   συγκληρονόμων   τῆς   ἐπαγ-
Jacob   the   co-heirs   of the   ³pro-

γελίας   τῆς   αὐτῆς·   10 ἐξεδέχετο   γὰρ   τὴν
mise   -   ¹same;   for he expected   the

τοὺς   θεμελίους   ἔχουσαν   πόλιν,   ἧς   τεχνίτης
³the ⁴foundations ²having ¹city, of which ⁵artificer

καὶ   δημιουργὸς   ὁ   θεός.   11 Πίστει   καὶ
⁶and ⁷maker   - ⁸God ⁹[is].   By faith   also

αὐτὴ   Σάρρα   δύναμιν   εἰς   καταβολὴν
²[her]self ¹Sara   ⁴power   ⁵for   ⁶conception

σπέρματος   ἔλαβεν   καὶ   παρὰ   καιρὸν   ἡλικίας,
⁷of seed ³received even beyond   time   of age,

ἐπεὶ   πιστὸν   ἡγήσατο   τὸν   ἐπαγγειλάμενον.
since   ²faithful ¹she deemed the [one]   having promised.

12 διὸ   καὶ   ἀφ'   ἑνὸς   ἐγενήθησαν,   καὶ
Wherefore indeed from one   there became,   and

ταῦτα   νενεκρωμένου,   καθὼς   τὰ   ἄστρα
that too† [he] having died,*   as   the   stars

---

*This must be understood, as the word always (or at
least generally) has reference to a divine communication.

heaven and as the innumerable grains of sand by the seashore.

13 These all died in faith, not having received what was promised, but having seen it and greeted it from afar, and having acknowledged that they were strangers and exiles on the earth. [14] For people who speak thus make it clear that they are seeking a homeland. [15] If they had been thinking of that land from which they had gone out, they would have had opportunity to return. [16] But as it is, they desire a better country, that is, a heavenly one. Therefore God is not ashamed to be called their God, for he has prepared for them a city.

17 By faith Abraham, when he was tested, offered up Isaac, and he who had received the promises was ready to offer up his only son, [18] of whom it was said, "Through Isaac shall your descendants be named." [19] He considered that God was able to raise men even from the dead; hence, figuratively speaking, he did receive him back. [20] By faith

τοῦ οὐρανοῦ τῷ πλήθει καὶ ὡς ἡ ἄμμος
of the heaven   – in multitude and   as the [3]sand

ἡ παρὰ τὸ χεῖλος τῆς θαλάσσης ἡ
– [3]by [1]the [5]lip [4]of the [2]sea   –

ἀναρίθμητος. 13 Κατὰ πίστιν ἀπέθανον
[1]innumerable.   [4]By way of [5]faith [3]died

οὗτοι πάντες, μὴ κομισάμενοι τὰς ἐπαγ-
[1]these [2]all,   not   having obtained   the   pro-

γελίας, ἀλλὰ πόρρωθεν αὐτὰς ἰδόντες καὶ
mises,   but   [3]from afar [4]them [1]seeing [2]and

ἀσπασάμενοι, καὶ ὁμολογήσαντες ὅτι ξένοι
[3]greeting,   and   confessing   that [2]strangers

καὶ παρεπίδημοί εἰσιν ἐπὶ τῆς γῆς.
[1]and [3]sojourners [1]they are   on   the   earth (? land).

14 οἱ γὰρ τοιαῦτα λέγοντες ἐμφανίζουσιν
For the [ones] [2]such things [1]saying   make manifest

ὅτι πατρίδα ἐπιζητοῦσιν. 15 καὶ εἰ μὲν
that [2]a fatherland [1]they seek.   And   if   on one hand

ἐκείνης ἐμνημόνευον ἀφ' ἧς ἐξέβησαν,
[2]that [1]they remembered   from   which they came out,

εἶχον ἂν καιρὸν ἀνακάμψαι· 16 νῦν
they might   time(opportunity)   to return;   now
have had

δὲ κρείττονος ὀρέγονται, τοῦτ' ἔστιν
on the [2]a better [1]they aspire to,   this   is
other

ἐπουρανίου. διὸ οὐκ ἐπαισχύνεται αὐτοὺς
a heavenly.   Wherefore [2]is not ashamed [of]   [3]them

ὁ θεὸς θεὸς ἐπικαλεῖσθαι αὐτῶν· ἡτοίμασεν
– [1]God [5]God [4]to be called [6]of them; [1]he prepared

γὰρ αὐτοῖς πόλιν. 17 Πίστει προσενήνοχεν
[1]for [2]for them   a city.   By faith [2]has offered up

Ἀβραὰμ τὸν Ἰσαὰκ πειραζόμενος, καὶ
[1]Abraham   – [4]Isaac [3]being tested,   and

τὸν μονογενῆ προσέφερεν ὁ τὰς ἐπαγγελίας
[5]the [6]only begotten [3]was [1]the [2]the [4]promises
(his)   offering up [one]

ἀναδεξάμενος, 18 πρὸς ὃν ἐλαλήθη ὅτι
[2]having undertaken,   as to   whom it was spoken[,]   –

ἐν Ἰσαὰκ κληθήσεταί σοι σπέρμα,
In   Isaac   shall be called   to thee   a seed,°
                                 =thy seed,

19 λογισάμενος ὅτι καὶ ἐκ νεκρῶν ἐγείρειν
reckoning   that [4]even [5]from [3]dead [5]to raise

δυνατὸς ὁ θεός· ὅθεν αὐτὸν καὶ ἐν
[2][was] [3]able   – [1]God;   whence [6]him [1]indeed [2]in

παραβολῇ ἐκομίσατο. 20 Πίστει καὶ περὶ
[3]a parable [4]he obtained.   By faith   also   [2]concerning

Isaac invoked future blessings on Jacob and Esau. ²¹ By faith Jacob, when dying, blessed each of the sons of Joseph, bowing in worship over the head of his staff. ²² By faith Joseph, at the end of his life, made mention of the exodus of the Israelites and gave directions concerning his burial.

23 By faith Moses, when he was born, was hid for three months by his parents, because they saw that the child was beautiful; and they were not afraid of the king's edict. ²⁴ By faith Moses, when he was grown up, refused to be called the son of Pharaoh's daughter, ²⁵ choosing rather to share ill-treatment with the people of God than to enjoy the fleeting pleasures of sin. ²⁶ He considered abuse suffered for the Christ greater wealth than the treasures of Egypt, for he looked to the reward. ²⁷ By faith he left Egypt, not being afraid of the anger of the king; for he endured as seeing him who is invisible. ²⁸ By faith he kept the Passover and sprinkled the blood, so that the

μελλόντων   εὐλόγησεν   ʼΙσαὰκ   τὸν   ʼΙακὼβ
²coming things   ³blessed   ¹Isaac   -   ⁴Jacob

καὶ   τὸν   ʼΗσαῦ.   **21**   Πίστει   ʼΙακὼβ
⁵and   -   ⁶Esau.   By faith   Jacob

ἀποθνήσκων   ἕκαστον   τῶν   υἱῶν   ʼΙωσὴφ
dying   ¹each   ²of the   ⁴sons   ⁵of Joseph

εὐλόγησεν,   καὶ   προσεκύνησεν   ἐπὶ   τὸ   ἄκρον
¹blessed,   and   worshipped   on   the   tip

τῆς   ῥάβδου   αὐτοῦ.   **22**   Πίστει   ʼΙωσὴφ
of the   rod   of him.   By faith   Joseph

τελευτῶν   περὶ   τῆς   ἐξόδου   τῶν   υἱῶν
dying   ²concerning   ³the   ⁴exodus   ⁵of the   ⁶sons

ʼΙσραὴλ   ἐμνημόνευσεν   καὶ   περὶ   τῶν
⁷of Israel   ¹remembered   and   ²concerning   ³the

ὀστέων   αὐτοῦ   ἐνετείλατο.   **23**   Πίστει
⁴bones   ⁵of him   ¹gave orders.   By faith

Μωϋσῆς   γεννηθεὶς   ἐκρύβη   τρίμηνον   ὑπὸ
Moses   having been born   was hidden   three months   by

τῶν   πατέρων   αὐτοῦ,   διότι   εἶδον   ἀστεῖον
the   parents   of him,   because   they saw   ²[to be] fine

τὸ   παιδίον,   καὶ   οὐκ   ἐφοβήθησαν   τὸ
¹the   ²child,   and   they did not fear   the

διάταγμα   τοῦ   βασιλέως.   **24**   Πίστει   Μωϋσῆς
decree   of the   king.   By faith   Moses

μέγας   γενόμενος   ἠρνήσατο   λέγεσθαι   υἱὸς
²great   ¹having become   denied   to be said(called)   son

θυγατρὸς   Φαραώ,   **25**   μᾶλλον   ἑλόμενος
of [the] daughter of Pharaoh,   rather   choosing

συγκακουχεῖσθαι   τῷ   λαῷ   τοῦ   θεοῦ   ἢ
to be ill treated with   the   people   -   of God   than

πρόσκαιρον   ἔχειν   ἁμαρτίας   ἀπόλαυσιν,
for a time   to have   ²of sin   ¹enjoyment,

26   μείζονα   πλοῦτον   ἡγησάμενος   τῶν
⁵greater   ⁶riches   ¹deeming   ⁷[than]   ⁸the

Αἰγύπτου   θησαυρῶν   τὸν   ὀνειδισμὸν   τοῦ
¹⁰of Egypt   ⁹treasures   ²the   ³reproach   -

Χριστοῦ·   ἀπέβλεπεν   γὰρ   εἰς   τὴν   μισθ-
⁴of Christ;   for he was looking away   to   the   recom-

ἀποδοσίαν.   **27**   Πίστει   κατέλιπεν   Αἴγυπτον,
pence.   By faith   he left   Egypt,

μὴ   φοβηθεὶς   τὸν   θυμὸν   τοῦ   βασιλέως·
not   fearing   the   anger   of the   king;

τὸν   γὰρ   ἀόρατον   ὡς   ὁρῶν   ἐκαρτέρησεν.
for   ³the   ⁴unseen [one]   ²as   ⁵seeing   ¹he endured.

28   Πίστει   πεποίηκεν   τὸ   πάσχα   καὶ   τὴν
By faith   he *has* made   the   passover   and   the

πρόσχυσιν   τοῦ   αἵματος,   ἵνα   μὴ   ὁ
affusion   of the   blood,   lest   the

Destroyer of the first-born might not touch them.

ὀλεθρεύων   τὰ   πρωτότοκα   θίγῃ   αὐτῶν.
[one] destroying ²the   ²firstborns   ¹should   ⁴of them.
                                                      touch

29 By faith the people crossed the Red Sea as if on dry land; but the Egyptians, when they attempted to do the same, were drowned.

29 Πίστει   διέβησαν   τὴν   ἐρυθρὰν   θάλασσαν
   By faith   they went   the   Red   Sea
              through

ὡς   διὰ   ξηρᾶς   γῆς,   ἧς   πεῖραν   λαβόντες
as   through   dry   land,   which   ⁴trial   ²taking

οἱ   Αἰγύπτιοι   κατεπόθησαν.   30 Πίστει
¹the   ²Egyptians   were swallowed up.   By faith

30 By faith the walls of Jericho fell down after they had been encircled for seven days.

τὰ   τείχη   Ἰεριχὼ   ἔπεσαν   κυκλωθέντα   ἐπὶ
the   walls   of Jericho   fell   having been   during
                                      encircled

ἑπτὰ   ἡμέρας.   31 Πίστει   Ῥαὰβ   ἡ   πόρνη
seven   days.   By faith   Rahab   the prostitute

31 By faith Rahab the harlot did not perish with those who were disobedient, because she had given friendly welcome to the spies.

οὐ   συναπώλετο   τοῖς   ἀπειθήσασιν,   δεξαμένη
did not perish with   the [ones]   disobeying,   having received

τοὺς   κατασκόπους   μετ'   εἰρήνης.   32 Καὶ
the   spies   with   peace.   And

32 And what more shall I say? For time would fail me to tell of Gideon, Barak, Samson, Jephthah, of David and Samuel and the prophets—

τί   ἔτι   λέγω;   ἐπιλείψει   με   γὰρ   διηγούμενον
what more may   ⁴will fail   ⁵me   ¹for   ⁶recounting
        I say?

ὁ   χρόνος   περὶ   Γεδεών,   Βαράκ,   Σαμψών,
²the   ³time   concerning   Gedeon,   Barak,   Samson,

Ἰεφθάε,   Δαυίδ   τε   καὶ   Σαμουὴλ   καὶ
Jephthae,   ¹David   ²both   and   Samuel   and

33 who through faith conquered kingdoms, enforced justice, received promises, stopped the mouths of lions,

τῶν   προφητῶν,   33 οἳ   διὰ   πίστεως
the   prophets,   who   through   faith

κατηγωνίσαντο   βασιλείας,   ἠργάσαντο   δι-
overcame   kingdoms,   wrought   right-

καιοσύνην,   ἐπέτυχον   ἐπαγγελιῶν,   ἔφραξαν
eousness,   obtained   promises,   stopped

34 quenched raging fire, escaped the edge of the sword, won strength out of weakness, became mighty in war, put foreign armies to flight.

στόματα   λεόντων,   34 ἔσβεσαν   δύναμιν
mouths   of lions,   quenched   [the] power

πυρός,   ἔφυγον   στόματα   μαχαίρης,   ἐδυναμώ-
of fire,   escaped   mouths(edges) of [the] sword,   were em-

θησαν   ἀπὸ   ἀσθενείας,   ἐγενήθησαν   ἰσχυροὶ
powered   from   weakness,   became   strong

ἐν   πολέμῳ,   παρεμβολὰς   ἔκλιναν   ἀλλοτρίων.
in   battle,   ²armies   ³made to yield   ¹of foreigners.

35 Women received their dead by resurrection. Some were tortured, refusing to accept release, that they might rise again to a better life.

35 ἔλαβον   γυναῖκες   ἐξ   ἀναστάσεως   τοὺς
²received   ¹women   ⁴by   ⁵resurrection   ³the

νεκροὺς   αὐτῶν·   ἄλλοι   δὲ   ἐτυμπανίσθησαν,
⁴dead   ⁵of them;   but others   were beaten to death,

οὐ   προσδεξάμενοι   τὴν   ἀπολύτρωσιν,   ἵνα
not   accepting   -   deliverance,   in or-
                                              der that

κρείττονος   ἀναστάσεως   τύχωσιν·   36 ἕτεροι
²a better   ²resurrection   ¹they might   others
                              obtain;

³⁶Others suffered mock-ing and scourging, and even chains and im-prisonment. ³⁷They were stoned, they were sawn in two,ᵖ they were killed with the sword; they went about in skins of sheep and goats, desti-tute, afflicted, ill-treated —³⁸of whom the world was not worthy— wandering over deserts and mountains, and in dens and caves of the earth.

39 And all these, though well attested by their faith, did not re-ceive what was promised, ⁴⁰since God had foreseen something better for us, that apart from us they should not be made perfect.

δὲ ἐμπαιγμῶν καὶ μαστίγων πεῖραν ἔλαβον,
and ³of mockings ⁴and ⁵of scourgings ²trial ¹took,

ἔτι δὲ δεσμῶν καὶ φυλακῆς· 37 ἐλιθάσ-
and more of bonds and of prison; they were

θησαν, ἐπειράσθησαν, ἐπρίσθησαν, ἐν φόνῳ
stoned, they were tried, they were ²by ³murder
                                sawn asunder,

μαχαίρης ἀπέθανον, περιῆλθον ἐν μηλωταῖς,
⁴of sword ¹they died, they went about in sheepskins,

ἐν αἰγείοις δέρμασιν, ὑστερούμενοι,
in goatskins, being in want,

θλιβόμενοι, κακουχούμενοι, 38 ὧν οὐκ ἦν
being afflicted, being ill treated, of whom was not

ἄξιος ὁ κόσμος, ἐπὶ ἐρημίαις πλανώμενοι
worthy the world, ²over ³deserts ¹wandering

καὶ ὄρεσιν καὶ σπηλαίοις καὶ ταῖς ὀπαῖς
and mountains and caves and the holes

τῆς γῆς. 39 Καὶ οὗτοι πάντες μαρτυρη-
of the earth. And these all having obtained

θέντες διὰ τῆς πίστεως οὐκ ἐκομίσαντο
witness through the(ir) faith obtained not

τὴν ἐπαγγελίαν, 40 τοῦ θεοῦ περὶ ἡμῶν
the promise, - God ⁴concerning ⁵us

κρεῖττόν τι προβλεψαμένου, ἵνα μὴ χωρὶς
³better ²some- ¹having foreseen,ᵃ in or- not without
       thing   der that

ἡμῶν τελειωθῶσιν.
us they should be perfected.

CHAPTER 12

THEREFORE, since we are surrounded by so great a cloud of witnesses, let us also lay aside every weight, and sin which clings so closely, and let us run with perseverance the race that is set before us, ²looking to Jesus the pioneer and perfecter of our faith, who for the joy that was set before him endured the cross, despising the shame, and is seated at the right hand of the throne of God.

12 Τοιγαροῦν καὶ ἡμεῖς, τοσοῦτον ἔχοντες
So therefore ²also ¹we, ²such ¹having

περικείμενον ἡμῖν νέφος μαρτύρων, ὄγκον
⁵lying around ⁴us ²a cloud ⁶of witnesses, ²encum-
                                          brance

ἀποθέμενοι πάντα καὶ τὴν εὐπερίστατον
¹putting away ¹every ²and ³the ⁷most besetting

ἁμαρτίαν, δι' ὑπομονῆς τρέχωμεν τὸν
⁶sin, through endurance let us run ¹the

προκείμενον ἡμῖν ἀγῶνα, 2 ἀφορῶντες εἰς
²set before ⁵us ²contest(race), looking away to

τὸν τῆς πίστεως ἀρχηγὸν καὶ τελειωτὴν
¹the ²of the ³faith ²author ²and ⁴finisher

Ἰησοῦν, ὃς ἀντὶ τῆς προκειμένης αὐτῷ
Jesus, who against ¹the ²set before ⁴him

χαρᾶς ὑπέμεινεν σταυρὸν αἰσχύνης κατα-
³joy endured a cross ³shame ¹de-

φρονήσας, ἐν δεξιᾷ τε τοῦ θρόνου τοῦ
spising, ²at ⁴[the] ¹and ⁵of the ⁶throne -
              right [hand]

ᵖ Other manuscripts add they were tempted

3 Consider him who endured from sinners such hostility against himself, so that you may not grow weary or faint-hearted. ⁴In your struggle against sin you have not yet resisted to the point of shedding your blood. ⁵And have you forgotten the exhortation which addresses you as sons?—

"My son, do not regard lightly the discipline of the Lord,

nor lose courage when you are punished by him.

⁶For the Lord disciplines him whom he loves,

and chastises every son whom he receives."

⁷It is for discipline that you have to endure. God is treating you as sons; for what son is there whom his father does not discipline? ⁸If you are left without discipline, in which all have participated, then you are illegitimate children and not sons. ⁹Besides this, we have had earthly fathers to discipline us and we respected them. Shall we not much more be subject to the Father of spirits and live? ¹⁰For they disciplined us for a short time at their pleasure, but he disciplines us for our good,

θεοῦ κεκάθικεν. 3 ἀναλογίσασθε γὰρ τὸν
²of   ²has taken   For consider ye   ¹the
God   [his] seat.   [one]

τοιαύτην ὑπομεμενηκότα ὑπὸ τῶν ἁμαρτω-
³such   ⁴having endured   ⁵by   -   ⁶of sin-

λῶν εἰς ἑαυτὸν ἀντιλογίαν, ἵνα μὴ κάμητε
ners ⁷against ⁸himself ⁴contradiction,   lest   ye grow
                                                   weary

ταῖς ψυχαῖς ὑμῶν ἐκλυόμενοι. 4 Οὔπω
²in the   ³souls   ⁴of you   ¹fainting.   Not yet

μέχρις αἵματος ἀντικατέστητε πρὸς τὴν
¹until   ²blood   ¹ye resisted   ²against   -

ἁμαρτίαν ἀνταγωνιζόμενοι, 5 καὶ ἐκλέλησθε
⁶sin   ⁴struggling against,   and   ye have
                                        forgotten

τῆς παρακλήσεως, ἥτις ὑμῖν ὡς υἱοῖς
the   exhortation,   which ²with you ¹as ⁴with sons

διαλέγεται· υἱέ μου, μὴ ὀλιγώρει παιδείας
¹discourses: Son of me, do not make   [the]
                                 light of   discipline

κυρίου, μηδὲ ἐκλύου ὑπ᾽ αὐτοῦ ἐλεγχόμενος·
of [the] nor faint ³by   ²him   ¹being reproved;
Lord,

6 ὃν γὰρ ἀγαπᾷ κύριος παιδεύει, μαστιγοῖ
for whom ²loves ¹[the] Lord he disciplines, ²scourges

δὲ πάντα υἱὸν ὃν παραδέχεται. 7 εἰς
¹and every   son whom he receives.   For

παιδείαν ὑπομένετε· ὡς υἱοῖς ὑμῖν
discipline endure ye; ⁴as ⁵with sons ¹with you

προσφέρεται ὁ θεός· τίς γὰρ υἱὸς ὃν
²is dealing   - ¹God; for what son whom
                                   [is there]

οὐ παιδεύει πατήρ; 8 εἰ δὲ χωρίς ἐστε
³disciplines not ¹a father? But if ¹without ¹ye are

παιδείας, ἧς μέτοχοι γεγόνασιν πάντες,
discipline, of which ³sharers ²have become ¹all,

ἄρα νόθοι καὶ οὐχ υἱοί ἐστε. 9 εἶτα
then bastards and not sons ye are. Furthermore

τοὺς μὲν τῆς σαρκὸς ἡμῶν πατέρας
the   - ³of the ⁴flesh ⁵of us ²fathers

εἴχομεν παιδευτὰς καὶ ἐνετρεπόμεθα· οὐ
¹we had ⁶correctors and we respected [them]: ²not

πολὺ μᾶλλον ὑποταγησόμεθα τῷ πατρὶ
¹much ²more ¹shall ²we ⁶be ²subject to the Father

τῶν πνευμάτων καὶ ζήσομεν; 10 οἱ μὲν
  - of spirits and we shall live? ¹they ²indeed

γὰρ πρὸς ὀλίγας ἡμέρας κατὰ τὸ δοκοῦν
¹for for a few days accord- the seeming
                          ing to thing [good]

αὐτοῖς ἐπαίδευον, ὁ δὲ ἐπὶ τὸ συμφέρον
to them disciplined [us], but he for the(our) profit

that we may share his holiness. ¹¹For the moment all discipline seems painful rather than pleasant; later it yields the peaceful fruit of righteousness to those who have been trained by it.

12 Therefore lift your drooping hands and strengthen your weak knees, ¹³and make straight paths for your feet, so that what is lame may not be put out of joint but rather be healed. ¹⁴Strive for peace with all men, and for the holiness without which no one will see the Lord. ¹⁵See to it that no one fail to obtain the grace of God; that no "root of bitterness" spring up and cause trouble, and by it the many become defiled; ¹⁶that no one be immoral or irreligious like Esau, who sold his birthright for a single meal. ¹⁷For you know that afterward, when he desired to inherit the blessing, he was rejected, for he found no chance to repent, though he sought it with tears.

18 For you have not

εἰς τὸ μεταλαβεῖν τῆς ἁγιότητος αὐτοῦ.
for the to partake of the sanctity of him.

11 πᾶσα μὲν παιδεία πρὸς μὲν τὸ παρὸν
²All ¹on ³discipline ⁴for ⁷in- ⁵the ⁶present
one hand deed

οὐ δοκεῖ χαρᾶς εἶναι ἀλλὰ λύπης, ὕστερον
seems not ²of joy ¹to be but of grief, ²later

δὲ καρπὸν εἰρηνικὸν τοῖς δι᾽ αὐτῆς
¹on the ⁵fruit ⁶peaceable ⁷to the ⁸through ¹⁰it
other [ones]

γεγυμνασμένοις ἀποδίδωσιν δικαιοσύνης.
⁹having been exercised ³it gives back ⁴of righteousness.

12 Διὸ τὰς παρειμένας χεῖρας καὶ τὰ
Where- ²the ³having been ⁴hands ⁵and ⁶the
fore wearied

παραλελυμένα γόνατα ἀνορθώσατε, 13 καὶ
⁷having been paralysed ⁸knees ¹straighten ye, and

τροχιὰς ὀρθὰς ποιεῖτε τοῖς ποσὶν ὑμῶν,
tracks straight make for the feet of you,

ἵνα μὴ τὸ χωλὸν ἐκτραπῇ, ἰαθῇ δὲ
lest the lame be turned ³may ¹but
aside, be cured

μᾶλλον. 14 Εἰρήνην διώκετε μετὰ πάντων,
²rather. Peace follow with all men,

καὶ τὸν ἁγιασμόν, οὗ χωρὶς οὐδεὶς
and – sanctification, ²which ¹without no one

ὄψεται τὸν κύριον, 15 ἐπισκοποῦντες μή
will see the Lord, observing not(lest)

τις ὑστερῶν ἀπὸ τῆς χάριτος τοῦ θεοῦ,
anyone failing from the grace – of God,

μή τις ῥίζα πικρίας ἄνω φύουσα ἐνοχλῇ
not any root of bitterness ²up ¹growing disturb
(lest)

καὶ διὰ ταύτης μιανθῶσιν οἱ πολλοί,
and through this ²be defiled the ¹many,

16 μή τις πόρνος ἢ βέβηλος ὡς Ἡσαῦ,
not(lest) any fornicator or profane man as Esau,

ὃς ἀντὶ βρώσεως μιᾶς ἀπέδοτο τὰ
who against ²eating ¹one gave up the

πρωτοτόκια ἑαυτοῦ. 17 ἴστε γὰρ ὅτι
rights of of himself. For ye know that
the firstborn

καὶ μετέπειτα θέλων κληρονομῆσαι τὴν
indeed afterwards wishing to inherit the

εὐλογίαν ἀπεδοκιμάσθη, μετανοίας γὰρ
blessing he was rejected, for ⁴of repentance

τόπον οὐχ εὗρεν, καίπερ μετὰ δακρύων
²place ²not ¹he found, though with tears

ἐκζητήσας αὐτήν. 18 Οὐ γὰρ προσεληλύθατε
seeking out it. For ²not ¹ye ³have ⁴approached

come to what may be touched, a blazing fire, and darkness, and gloom, and a tempest, [19]and the sound of a trumpet, and a voice whose words made the hearers entreat that no further messages be spoken to them. [20]For they could not endure the order that was given, "If even a beast touches the mountain, it shall be stoned." [21]Indeed, so terrifying was the sight that Moses said, "I tremble with fear." [22]But you have come to Mount Zion and to the city of the living God, the heavenly Jerusalem, and to innumerable angels in festal gathering, [23]and to the assembly[q] of the first-born who are enrolled in heaven, and to a judge who is God of all, and to the spirits of just men made perfect, [24]and to Jesus, the mediator of a new covenant, and to the sprinkled blood that speaks more graciously than the blood of Abel.

[25] See that you do not refuse him who is speaking. For if they did not escape when they refused him who warned them on earth, much less shall we escape if we reject him who warns from

---

ψηλαφωμένῳ   καὶ   κεκαυμένῳ   πυρὶ   καὶ
to [a mountain]   and   having been   with   and
                            being felt   ignited   fire

γνόφῳ   καὶ   ζόφῳ   καὶ   θυέλλῃ   19 καὶ
to darkness and *to* deep gloom and   *to* whirlwind   and

σάλπιγγος   ἤχῳ   καὶ   φωνῇ   ῥημάτων,   ἧς
²of trumpet ¹*to* a sound and *to* a voice   of words,   which

οἱ   ἀκούσαντες   παρῃτήσαντο   μὴ   προστεθῆναι
the [ones] hearing   entreated   not   to be added

αὐτοῖς   λόγον·   20 οὐκ   ἔφερον   γὰρ   τὸ
to them   a word;   ³not   ²they bore   ¹for   the
                                                          thing

διαστελλόμενον·   κἂν   θηρίον   θίγῃ   τοῦ ὄρους,
being charged: If even   a beast   touches   the mountain,

λιθοβοληθήσεται·   21 καὶ,   οὕτω   φοβερὸν   ἦν
it shall be stoned;   and,   so   fearful   was

τὸ   φανταζόμενον,   Μωϋσῆς   εἶπεν·   ἔκφοβός
the thing appearing,   Moses   said: ²Terrified

εἰμι   καὶ   ἔντρομος·   22 ἀλλὰ   προσεληλύθατε
¹I am   and   trembling;   but   ye have approached

Σιὼν   ὄρει   καὶ   πόλει   θεοῦ   ζῶντος,
²Zion   ¹*to* mount   and   *to* a city   ²God ³of [the] living,

Ἱερουσαλὴμ   ἐπουρανίῳ,   καὶ   μυριάσιν
²Jerusalem   ¹*to* a heavenly,   and   *to* myriads

ἀγγέλων,   23 πανηγύρει   καὶ   ἐκκλησίᾳ
of angels,   *to* an assembly   and   a church

πρωτοτόκων   ἀπογεγραμμένων   ἐν   οὐρανοῖς,
of firstborn [ones]   having been enrolled   in   heavens,

καὶ   κριτῇ   θεῷ   πάντων,   καὶ   πνεύμασι
and   ²judge   ¹*to* God   of all men,   and   *to* spirits

δικαίων   τετελειωμένων,   24 καὶ   διαθήκης
of just men   having been made   and   ⁴covenant
                    perfect,

νέας   μεσίτῃ   Ἰησοῦ,   καὶ   αἵματι   ῥαντισμοῦ
³of a   ²mediator   ¹*to* Jesus,   and   *to* blood   of sprinkling
new

κρεῖττον   λαλοῦντι   παρὰ   τὸν   "Ἀβελ.
²a better thing   ¹speaking   than   –   Abel.

25 Βλέπετε   μὴ   παραιτήσησθε   τὸν λαλοῦντα·
Look ye [that]   ²not   ¹ye refuse   the [one] speaking;

εἰ   γὰρ   ἐκεῖνοι   οὐκ   ἐξέφυγον   ἐπὶ   γῆς
for if   those   escaped not   ²on   ¹earth

παραιτησάμενοι   τὸν   χρηματίζοντα,   πολὺ
¹refusing   ²the [one]   ³warning,   much

μᾶλλον   ἡμεῖς   οἱ   τὸν   ἀπ'   οὐρανῶν
more   we*   ¹the   ²the [one]   ⁵from   ⁶heavens
                     [ones] ⁴[warning]

---

[q] Or angels, and to the festal gathering and assembly

* That is, "much more [shall] we [not escape]"; or, putting it in another way, "much less shall we escape."

heaven. [26] His voice then shook the earth; but now he has promised, "Yet once more I will shake not only the earth but also the heaven." [27] This phrase, "Yet once more," indicates the removal of what is shaken, as of what has been made, in order that what cannot be shaken may remain. [28] Therefore let us be grateful for receiving a kingdom that cannot be shaken, and thus let us offer to God acceptable worship, with reverence and awe; [29] for our God is a consuming fire.

ἀποστρεφόμενοι·
[1]turning from;

26 οὗ ἡ φωνὴ τὴν γῆν
of whom the voice [3]the [4]earth

ἐσάλευσεν τότε, νῦν δὲ ἐπήγγελται λέγων·
[2]shook [1]then, but now he has promised saying:

ἔτι ἅπαξ ἐγὼ σείσω οὐ μόνον τὴν
Yet once I will shake not only the

γῆν ἀλλὰ καὶ τὸν οὐρανόν. **27** τὸ δὲ
earth but also *the* heaven.   Now the [phrase]

ἔτι ἅπαξ δηλοῖ τὴν τῶν σαλευομένων
'Yet once' declares [1]the [3]of the things [4]being shaken

μετάθεσιν ὡς πεποιημένων, ἵνα μείνῃ τὰ
[2]removal as of things having in or- [4]may [1]the
                          been made, der that remain things

μὴ σαλευόμενα. **28** Διὸ βασιλείαν ἀσάλευτος
[2]not [3]being shaken. Wherefore [3]kingdom [2]an unshakable

παραλαμβάνοντες ἔχωμεν χάριν, δι᾽ ἧς
[1]receiving let us have grace, through which

λατρεύωμεν εὐαρέστως τῷ θεῷ, μετὰ
we may serve [2]well-pleasingly – [1]God,   with

εὐλαβείας καὶ δέους· **29** καὶ γὰρ ὁ θεὸς
devoutness and awe;   for indeed the God

ἡμῶν πῦρ καταναλίσκον.
of us [is] fire a consuming.

CHAPTER 13

LET brotherly love continue. [2]Do not neglect to show hospitality to strangers, for thereby some have entertained angels unawares. [3]Remember those who are in prison, as though in prison with them; and those who are ill-treated, since you also are in the body. [4]Let marriage be held in honor among all, and let the marriage bed be undefiled; for God will judge the immoral and adulterous. [5]Keep your life free from love of money, and be content with what you have; for

13 Ἡ φιλαδελφία μενέτω. **2** τῆς
  – [2]brotherly love [1]Let *it* [3]remain. –

φιλοξενίας μὴ ἐπιλανθάνεσθε· διὰ ταύτης
of hospitality Be ye not forgetful; [2]through [1]this

γὰρ ἔλαθόν τινες ξενίσαντες ἀγγέλους.
[3]for [5]unconsciously† [4]some [6]entertaining(ed) [7]angels.

3 μιμνῄσκεσθε τῶν δεσμίων ὡς συνδεδεμένοι,
Be ye mindful of the prisoners as *having been* bound
                                         with [them],

τῶν κακουχουμένων ὡς καὶ αὐτοὶ ὄντες
of the *being* ill treated as also [your]selves being
[ones]

ἐν σώματι. **4** Τίμιος ὁ γάμος ἐν πᾶσιν
in [the] body. [4]honourable – [2]marriage in all
                  [1][Let]   [3][be]

καὶ ἡ κοίτη ἀμίαντος· πόρνους γὰρ
and the bed undefiled;   for fornicators

καὶ μοιχοὺς κρινεῖ ὁ θεός. **5** Ἀφιλάργυρος
and adulterers [2]will judge – [1]God.   [6]without love of
                                                   money

ὁ τρόπος, ἀρκούμενοι τοῖς παροῦσιν·
[1][Let] [3]way of being satisfied the things present;
[2]the life [4][be], with
(your)

he has said, "I will never fail you nor forsake you." ⁶Hence we can confidently say,

"The Lord is my helper,
I will not be afraid;
what can man do to me?"

7 Remember your leaders, those who spoke to you the word of God; consider the outcome of their life, and imitate their faith. ⁸Jesus Christ is the same yesterday and today and for ever. ⁹Do not be led away by diverse and strange teachings; for it is well that the heart be strengthened by grace, not by foods, which have not benefited their adherents. ¹⁰We have an altar from which those who serve the tentʳ have no right to eat. ¹¹For the bodies of those animals whose blood is brought into the sanctuary by the high priest as a sacrifice for sin are burned outside the camp. ¹²So Jesus also suffered outside the gate in order to sanctify the people through his own blood. ¹³Therefore let us go

αὐτὸς γὰρ εἴρηκεν· οὐ μή σε ἀνῶ οὐδ'
for he has said: By no means thee will I nor
                                          leave

οὐ μή σε ἐγκαταλίπω· 6 ὥστε θαρροῦντας
by no(any) thee I forsake; so as being of good
means   cheer

ἡμᾶς λέγειν· κύριος ἐμοὶ βοηθός, οὐ
us to sayᵇ: [The] Lord to meᶜ [is] a helper, not

φοβηθήσομαι· τί ποιήσει μοι ἄνθρωπος;
I will fear; what ¹will ²do ⁴to me ²man?

7 Μνημονεύετε τῶν ἡγουμένων ὑμῶν,
Remember the [ones] leading of you,

οἵτινες ἐλάλησαν ὑμῖν τὸν λόγον τοῦ
who spoke to you the word of

θεοῦ, ὧν ἀναθεωροῦντες τὴν ἔκβασιν τῆς
of God, ⁵of ¹looking at ²the ³result ⁴of
whom   the

ἀναστροφῆς μιμεῖσθε τὴν πίστιν. 8 Ἰησοῦς
⁵conduct imitate ye the(ir) faith. Jesus

Χριστὸς ἐχθὲς καὶ σήμερον ὁ αὐτὸς
Christ ⁴yesterday ⁵and ⁶to-day ¹[is] ²the ³same

καὶ εἰς τοὺς αἰῶνας. 9 Διδαχαῖς ποικίλαις
and unto the ages. ⁵teachings ⁴by various

καὶ ξέναις μὴ παραφέρεσθε· καλὸν γὰρ
²and ⁴strange ¹Do not be carried away; for [it is] good

χάριτι βεβαιοῦσθαι τὴν καρδίαν, οὐ
⁴by grace ³to be confirmed ¹the ²heart,ᵇ not

βρώμασιν, ἐν οἷς οὐκ ὠφελήθησαν οἱ
by foods, by which ³were not profited ¹the

περιπατοῦντες. 10 ἔχομεν θυσιαστήριον ἐξ
²[ones] walking. We have an altar of

οὗ φαγεῖν οὐκ ἔχουσιν ἐξουσίαν οἱ τῇ
which ⁷to eat ⁵have not ⁶authority ¹the ²the
                                       [ones]

σκηνῇ λατρεύοντες. 11 ὧν γὰρ εἰσφέρεται
⁴tabernacle ²serving. For ³of what ¹is brought in

ζώων τὸ αἷμα περὶ ἁμαρτίας εἰς τὰ
⁴animals ¹the ²blood ³concerning ⁵sins into the

ἅγια διὰ τοῦ ἀρχιερέως, τούτων τὰ
holies through the high priest, of these the

σώματα κατακαίεται ἔξω τῆς παρεμβολῆς.
bodies is(are) burned outside the camp.

12 διὸ καὶ Ἰησοῦς, ἵνα ἁγιάσῃ διὰ
Where- in- Jesus, in order he might ³through
fore deed   that sanctify

τοῦ ἰδίου αἵματος τὸν λαόν, ἔξω τῆς
⁴the(his) ⁵own ⁶blood ¹the ²people, outside the

πύλης ἔπαθεν. 13 τοίνυν ἐξερχώμεθα πρὸς
gate suffered. So let us go forth to

ʳ Or tabernacle

forth to him outside the camp, bearing abuse for him. ¹⁴For here we have no lasting city, but we seek the city which is to come. ¹⁵Through him then let us continually offer up a sacrifice of praise to God, that is, the fruit of lips that acknowledge his name. ¹⁶Do not neglect to do good and to share what you have, for such sacrifices are pleasing to God.

17 Obey your leaders and submit to them; for they are keeping watch over your souls, as men who will have to give account. Let them do this joyfully, and not sadly, for that would be of no advantage to you.

18 Pray for us, for we are sure that we have a clear conscience, desiring to act honorably in all things. ¹⁹I urge you the more earnestly to do this in order that I may be restored to you the sooner.

20 Now may the God of peace who brought again from the dead our Lord Jesus, the great shepherd of the sheep,

---

αὐτὸν ἔξω τῆς παρεμβολῆς τὸν ὀνειδισμὸν
him outside the camp the reproach

αὐτοῦ φέροντες· **14** οὐ γὰρ ἔχομεν ὧδε
of him bearing; for ²not ¹we have here

μένουσαν πόλιν, ἀλλὰ τὴν μέλλουσαν
a continuing city, but the [one] coming

ἐπιζητοῦμεν. **15** Δι᾿ αὐτοῦ οὖν ἀναφέρωμεν
we seek. Through him therefore let us offer up

θυσίαν αἰνέσεως διὰ παντὸς τῷ θεῷ,
a sacrifice of praise always – to God,

τοῦτ᾿ ἔστιν καρπὸν χειλέων ὁμολογούντων
this is fruit of lips confessing

τῷ ὀνόματι αὐτοῦ. **16** τῆς δὲ εὐποιΐας
to the name of him. But of the doing good

καὶ κοινωνίας μὴ ἐπιλανθάνεσθε· τοιαύταις
and sharing be ye not forgetful; ²with such

γὰρ θυσίαις εὐαρεστεῖται ὁ θεός. **17** Πεί-
¹for sacrifices ²is well pleased – ¹God. Obey

θεσθε τοῖς ἡγουμένοις ὑμῶν καὶ ὑπείκετε·
ye the[ones] leading of you and submit to [them];

αὐτοὶ γὰρ ἀγρυπνοῦσιν ὑπὲρ τῶν ψυχῶν
for they watch on behalf of the souls

ὑμῶν ὡς λόγον ἀποδώσοντες· ἵνα μετὰ
of you as ²account ¹rendering*; in order that with

χαρᾶς τοῦτο ποιῶσιν καὶ μὴ στενάζ-
joy ²this ¹they may do and not groan-

οντες· ἀλυσιτελὲς γὰρ ὑμῖν τοῦτο.
ing; for profitless to you this [would be].

18 Προσεύχεσθε περὶ ἡμῶν· πειθόμεθα
Pray ye concerning us; ²we are persuaded

γὰρ ὅτι καλὴν συνείδησιν ἔχομεν, ἐν
¹for that a good conscience we have, ⁴in

πᾶσιν καλῶς θέλοντες ἀναστρέφεσθαι.
¹all [respects] ³well ¹wishing ²to behave.

19 περισσοτέρως δὲ παρακαλῶ τοῦτο
And more abundantly I beseech [you] this

ποιῆσαι, ἵνα τάχιον ἀποκατασταθῶ ὑμῖν.
to do, in order that sooner I may be restored to you.

20 Ὁ δὲ θεὸς τῆς εἰρήνης, ὁ ἀναγαγὼν
Now the God – of peace, the having led up [one]

ἐκ νεκρῶν τὸν ποιμένα τῶν προβάτων
out of [the] dead the ²shepherd ³of the ⁴sheep

* In the future.

by the blood of the eternal covenant, [21]equip you with everything good that you may do his will, working in you* that which is pleasing in his sight, through Jesus Christ; to whom be glory for ever and ever. Amen.

[22] I appeal to you, brethren, bear with my word of exhortation, for I have written to you briefly. [23]You should understand that our brother Timothy has been released, with whom I shall see you if he comes soon. [24]Greet all your leaders and all the saints. Those who come from Italy send you greetings. [25]Grace be with all of you. Amen.

τὸν μέγαν ἐν αἵματι διαθήκης αἰωνίου,
the   ¹great   in (? with) blood   ²covenant   ¹of an eternal,

τὸν κύριον ἡμῶν Ἰησοῦν, 21 καταρτίσαι
the   Lord   of us   Jesus,   may he adjust

ὑμᾶς ἐν παντὶ ἀγαθῷ εἰς τὸ ποιῆσαι
you   in   every   good thing   for   the   to do

τὸ θέλημα αὐτοῦ, ποιῶν ἐν ἡμῖν τὸ
the   will   of him,   doing   in   us   the [thing]

εὐάρεστον ἐνώπιον αὐτοῦ διὰ Ἰησοῦ
wellpleasing   before   him   through   Jesus

Χριστοῦ, ᾧ ἡ δόξα εἰς τοὺς αἰῶνας
Christ,   to [be]   glory   unto   the   ages
    whom the

τῶν αἰώνων· ἀμήν. 22 Παρακαλῶ δὲ
of the   ages: Amen.   And I beseech

ὑμᾶς, ἀδελφοί, ἀνέχεσθε τοῦ λόγου τῆς
you.   brothers,   endure   the   word

παρακλήσεως· καὶ γὰρ διὰ βραχέων
of beseeching;   for indeed   through   few [words]

ἐπέστειλα ὑμῖν. 23 Γινώσκετε τὸν ἀδελφὸν
I wrote   to you.   Know ye   the   brother

ἡμῶν Τιμόθεον ἀπολελυμένον, μεθ' οὗ
of us   Timothy   having been released,   with whom

ἐὰν τάχιον ἔρχηται ὄψομαι ὑμᾶς.
if   sooner   I come   I will see   you.

24 Ἀσπάσασθε πάντας τοὺς ἡγουμένους
Greet ye   all   the [ones] leading

ὑμῶν καὶ πάντας τοὺς ἁγίους. Ἀσπάζονται
of you   and   all   the   saints.   ²greet

ὑμᾶς οἱ ἀπὸ τῆς Ἰταλίας.
¹you   ¹The [ones]   ²from   -   ³Italy.

25 Ἡ χάρις μετὰ πάντων ὑμῶν.
-   Grace [be]   with   all   you.

JAMES 1
CHAPTER 1

JAMES, a servant of God and of the Lord Jesus Christ,
To the twelve tribes in the Dispersion:
Greeting.

* Other ancient authorities read *us*

ΙΑΚΩΒΟΥ ΕΠΙΣΤΟΛΗ
²Of James ¹Epistle

1 Ἰάκωβος θεοῦ καὶ κυρίου Ἰησοῦ
James   ²of God   ³and   ⁴of [the] Lord   ⁵Jesus

Χριστοῦ δοῦλος ταῖς δώδεκα φυλαῖς ταῖς
⁶Christ   ¹a slave   to the   twelve   tribes   -

ἐν τῇ διασπορᾷ χαίρειν.*
in   the   dispersion   greeting.*

* See note on Phil. 3.16 in Introduction.

2 Count it all joy, my brethren, when you meet various trials, [3]for you know that the testing of your faith produces steadfastness. [4]And let steadfastness have its full effect, that you may be perfect and complete, lacking in nothing.

5 If any of you lacks wisdom, let him ask God, who gives to all men generously and without reproaching, and it will be given him. [6]But let him ask in faith, with no doubting, for he who doubts is like a wave of the sea that is driven and tossed by the wind. [7],[8]For that person must not suppose that a double-minded man, unstable in all his ways, will receive anything from the Lord.

9 Let the lowly brother boast in his exaltation, [10]and the rich in his humiliation, because like the flower of the grass he will pass away. [11]For the sun rises with its scorching heat and withers the grass; its flower falls, and its beauty perishes.

2 Πᾶσαν χαρὰν ἡγήσασθε, ἀδελφοί μου,
All   joy   deem [it],   brothers of me,

ὅταν πειρασμοῖς περιπέσητε ποικίλοις,
whenever [3]trials [1]ye fall   [2]into various,

3 γινώσκοντες ὅτι τὸ δοκίμιον ὑμῶν τῆς
knowing   that the approved part [3]of you [1]of the
                     =that which is approved in your faith

πίστεως κατεργάζεται ὑπομονήν. 4 ἡ δὲ
[2]faith   works   endurance. – And

ὑπομονὴ ἔργον τέλειον ἐχέτω, ἵνα ἦτε
endurance [3]work [2]perfect [1]let it in or- ye may
                              have, der that be

τέλειοι καὶ ὁλόκληροι, ἐν μηδενὶ λειπόμενοι.
perfect and entire,   in nothing   wanting.

5 Εἰ δέ τις ὑμῶν λείπεται σοφίας, αἰτείτω
if But any- of you wants   wisdom, let him
     one   ask

παρὰ τοῦ διδόντος θεοῦ πᾶσιν ἁπλῶς
from [2]the [1]giving [1]God to all   unre-
      [one]   men   servedly

καὶ μὴ ὀνειδίζοντος, καὶ δοθήσεται αὐτῷ.
and not reproaching, and it will be given to him.

6 αἰτείτω δὲ ἐν πίστει, μηδὲν διακριν-
But let him ask in faith,   nothing doubt-

όμενος· ὁ γὰρ διακρινόμενος ἔοικεν κλύδωνι
ing;   for the [one] doubting   is like a wave

θαλάσσης ἀνεμιζομένῳ καὶ ῥιπιζομένῳ.
of [the] sea being driven by wind and being tossed.

7 μὴ γὰρ οἰέσθω ὁ ἄνθρωπος ἐκεῖνος
For let not [3]suppose [1]that [2]man

ὅτι λήμψεταί τι παρὰ τοῦ κυρίου, 8 ἀνὴρ
that he will any- from the Lord,   a man
         receive thing

δίψυχος, ἀκατάστατος ἐν πάσαις ταῖς
two-souled,   unsettled   in   all   the

ὁδοῖς αὐτοῦ. 9 Κανχάσθω δὲ ὁ ἀδελφὸς
ways of him.   But let [4]boast [1]the [3]brother

ὁ ταπεινὸς ἐν τῷ ὕψει αὐτοῦ, 10 ὁ δὲ
– [2]humble in the height of him,   and the

πλούσιος ἐν τῇ ταπεινώσει αὐτοῦ, ὅτι
rich one   in the humiliation of him, because

ὡς ἄνθος χόρτου παρελεύσεται. 11 ἀνέτειλεν
as a flower of grass he will pass away. [4]rose

γὰρ ὁ ἥλιος σὺν τῷ καύσωνι καὶ ἐξήρανεν
[1]For [2]the [3]sun with the hot wind and dried

τὸν χόρτον, καὶ τὸ ἄνθος αὐτοῦ ἐξέπεσεν
the grass,   and the flower of it   fell out

καὶ ἡ εὐπρέπεια τοῦ προσώπου αὐτοῦ
and the comeliness of the appearance of it

So will the rich man fade away in the midst of his pursuits.

12 Blessed is the man who endures trial, for when he has stood the test he will receive the crown of life which God has promised to those who love him. 13 Let no one say when he is tempted, "I am tempted by God"; for God cannot be tempted with evil and he himself tempts no one; 14 but each person is tempted when he is lured and enticed by his own desire. 15 Then desire when it has conceived gives birth to sin; and sin when it is full-grown brings forth death.

16 Do not be deceived, my beloved brethren. 17 Every good endowment and every perfect gift is from above, coming down from the Father of lights with whom there is no variation or shadow due to change.[a] 18 Of his own will he brought us forth by the word of truth that we should be a kind of first fruits of his creatures.

19 Know this, my beloved brethren. Let

[a] Other ancient authorities read *variation due to a shadow of turning*

ἀπώλετο· οὕτως καὶ ὁ πλούσιος ἐν ταῖς
perished; thus also the rich man in the

πορείαις αὐτοῦ μαρανθήσεται. 12 Μακάριος
goings of him will fade away. Blessed

ἀνὴρ ὃς ὑπομένει πειρασμόν, ὅτι δόκιμος
[the] who endures trial, because [2]approved

γενόμενος λήμψεται τὸν στέφανον τῆς
[1]having become he will receive the crown –

ζωῆς, ὃν ἐπηγγείλατο τοῖς ἀγαπῶσιν αὐτόν.
of life, which he promised to the [ones] loving him.

13 Μηδεὶς πειραζόμενος λεγέτω ὅτι ἀπὸ
[2]no man [3]being tempted [1]Let [4]say[,] – From

θεοῦ πειράζομαι· ὁ γὰρ θεὸς ἀπείραστός
God I am tempted; – for God [3]untempted

ἐστιν κακῶν, πειράζει δὲ αὐτὸς οὐδένα.
[1]is of(with) and [2]tempts [1]he no man.
evil things,

14 ἕκαστος δὲ πειράζεται ὑπὸ τῆς ἰδίας
But each man is tempted by the(his) own

ἐπιθυμίας ἐξελκόμενος καὶ δελεαζόμενος·
lusts being drawn out and *being* enticed;

15 εἶτα ἡ ἐπιθυμία συλλαβοῦσα τίκτει
then – lust having conceived bears

ἁμαρτίαν, ἡ δὲ ἁμαρτία ἀποτελεσθεῖσα
sin, – and sin having been
fully formed

ἀποκύει θάνατον. 16 Μὴ πλανᾶσθε, ἀδελφοί
brings forth death. Do not err, [2]brothers

μου ἀγαπητοί.
[3]of me [1]beloved.

17 Πᾶσα δόσις ἀγαθὴ καὶ πᾶν δώρημα
Every [2]giving [1]good and every [3]gift

τέλειον ἄνωθέν ἐστιν καταβαῖνον ἀπὸ τοῦ
[1]perfect [4]from above [3]is coming down from the

πατρὸς τῶν φώτων, παρ' ᾧ οὐκ ἔνι
Father of the lights, with whom [5]has no place

παραλλαγὴ ἢ τροπῆς ἀποσκίασμα. 18 βου-
[1]change [2]or [4]of turning [3]shadow. Having

ληθεὶς ἀπεκύησεν ἡμᾶς λόγῳ ἀληθείας,
purposed he brought forth us by a word of truth,

εἰς τὸ εἶναι ἡμᾶς ἀπαρχήν τινα τῶν
for the to be us[b] [2]firstfruit [1]a certain [3]of
=that we should be the

αὐτοῦ κτισμάτων.
[5]of him [4]creatures.

19 Ἴστε, ἀδελφοί μου ἀγαπητοί. ἔστω
Know ye, [2]brothers [3]of me [1]beloved. [2]let be

every man be quick to
hear, slow to speak,
slow to anger, 20for the
anger of man does not
work the righteousness
of God. 21Therefore put
away all filthiness and
rank growth of wicked-
ness and receive with
meekness the implanted
word, which is able to
save your souls.

22 But be doers of
the word, and not
hearers only, deceiving
yourselves. 23For if any
one is a hearer of the
word and not a doer, he
is like a man who
observes his natural face
in a mirror; 24for he
observes himself and goes
away and at once forgets
what he was like. 25But
he who looks into the
perfect law, the law of
liberty, and perseveres,
being no hearer that
forgets but a doer that
acts, he shall be blessed
in his doing.

26 If any one thinks
he is religious, and does
not bridle his tongue but
deceives his heart, this
man's religion is vain.
27Religion that is pure
and undefiled before God

δὲ πᾶς ἄνθρωπος ταχὺς εἰς τὸ ἀκοῦσαι,
1But every   man   swift   for the   to hear,

βραδὺς εἰς τὸ λαλῆσαι, βραδὺς εἰς ὀργήν·
slow   for the   to speak,   slow   to   wrath;

20 ὀργὴ γὰρ ἀνδρὸς δικαιοσύνην θεοῦ
for [the] wrath   of a man   2[the] righteousness 3of God

οὐκ ἐργάζεται.   21 διὸ ἀποθέμενοι πᾶσαν
1works not.   Wherefore putting away   all

ῥυπαρίαν καὶ περισσείαν κακίας ἐν πραΰ-
filthiness   and   superfluity   of evil   in   meek-

τητι δέξασθε τὸν ἔμφυτον λόγον τὸν
ness   receive ye   the   implanted   word   -

δυνάμενον σῶσαι τὰς ψυχὰς ὑμῶν. 22 γίν-
being able   to save   the   souls   of you.   be-

εσθε δὲ ποιηταὶ λόγου, καὶ μὴ ἀκροαταὶ
come ye And   doers   of [the] word,   and   not   hearers

μόνον παραλογιζόμενοι ἑαυτούς. 23 ὅτι
only   misleading   yourselves.   Because

εἴ τις ἀκροατὴς λόγου ἐστὶν καὶ οὐ
if anyone   2a hearer   3of [the] word   1is   and   not

ποιητής, οὗτος ἔοικεν ἀνδρὶ κατανοοῦντι
a doer,   this one   is like   a man   perceiving

τὸ πρόσωπον τῆς γενέσεως αὐτοῦ ἐν
the   face   of the   birth   of him   in

ἐσόπτρῳ· 24 κατενόησεν γὰρ ἑαυτὸν καὶ
a mirror;   for he perceived   himself   and

ἀπελήλυθεν, καὶ εὐθέως ἐπελάθετο ὁποῖος
has gone away,   and   straightway   forgot   what sort

ἦν. 25 ὁ δὲ παρακύψας εἰς νόμον
he was.   But the [one] having looked into   into   1law

τέλειον τὸν τῆς ἐλευθερίας καὶ παραμείνας,
2perfect   1the   -   of freedom   and   remaining,

οὐκ ἀκροατὴς ἐπιλησμονῆς γενόμενος ἀλλὰ
not   2a hearer   3of forgetfulness*   1becoming   but

ποιητὴς ἔργου, οὗτος μακάριος ἐν τῇ
a doer   of [the] work,   this one   2blessed   3in   4the

ποιήσει αὐτοῦ ἔσται. 26 Εἴ τις δοκεῖ
5doing   6of him   1will be.   If anyone   thinks

θρησκὸς εἶναι, μὴ χαλιναγωγῶν γλῶσσαν
2religious   1to be,   not   bridling   tongue

ἑαυτοῦ ἀλλὰ ἀπατῶν καρδίαν ἑαυτοῦ,
of himself   but   deceiving   heart   of himself,

τούτου μάταιος ἡ θρησκεία. 27 θρησκεία
of this one   vain   the   religion.   Religion

καθαρὰ καὶ ἀμίαντος παρὰ τῷ θεῷ
clean   and   undefiled   before   the   God

* Genitive of quality: " a forgetful hearer."

and the Father is this: to visit orphans and widows in their affliction, and to keep oneself unstained from the world.

καὶ   πατρὶ   αὕτη   ἐστίν,   ἐπισκέπτεσθαι
and   Father   ²this   ¹is,   to visit
ὀρφανοὺς   καὶ   χήρας   ἐν   τῇ   θλίψει   αὐτῶν,
orphans   and   widows   in   the   affliction   of them,
ἄσπιλον   ἑαυτὸν   τηρεῖν   ἀπὸ   τοῦ   κόσμου.
unspotted   himself   to keep   from   the   world.

CHAPTER 2

MY brethren, show no partiality as you hold the faith of our Lord Jesus Christ, the Lord of glory. ²For if a man with gold rings and in fine clothing comes into your assembly, and a poor man in shabby clothing also comes in, ³and you pay attention to the one who wears the fine clothing and say, "Have a seat here, please," while you say to the poor man, "Stand there," or, "Sit at my feet," ⁴have you not made distinctions among yourselves, and become judges with evil thoughts? ⁵Listen, my beloved brethren. Has not God chosen those who are poor in the world to be rich in faith and heirs of the kingdom which he has promised to those who love him? ⁶But you have dishonored the poor man. Is it not the rich who oppress you, is it not they who drag you into court? ⁷Is it not

2 Ἀδελφοί   μου,   μὴ   ἐν   προσωπολημψίαις
Brothers   of me,   not   in   respects of persons
ἔχετε   τὴν   πίστιν   τοῦ   κυρίου   ἡμῶν   Ἰησοῦ
have ye   the   faith   of the   Lord   of us   Jesus
Χριστοῦ   τῆς   δόξης.   2 ἐὰν   γὰρ   εἰσέλθῃ
Christ[,]   of the   glory.*   For if   [there] enters
εἰς   συναγωγὴν   ὑμῶν   ἀνὴρ   χρυσοδακτύλιος
into   a synagogue   of you   a man   gold-fingered
ἐν   ἐσθῆτι   λαμπρᾷ,   εἰσέλθῃ   δὲ   καὶ   πτωχὸς
in   ²clothing   ¹splendid,   and [there] enters   also   a poor man
ἐν   ῥυπαρᾷ   ἐσθῆτι,   3 ἐπιβλέψητε   δὲ   ἐπὶ
in   shabby   clothing,   and ye look on   on
τὸν   φοροῦντα   τὴν   ἐσθῆτα   τὴν   λαμπρὰν
the [one]   wearing   the   clothing   —   splendid
καὶ   εἴπητε·   σὺ   κάθου   ὧδε   καλῶς,   καὶ
and   say: ²thou   ¹Sit   here   well,   and
τῷ   πτωχῷ   εἴπητε·   σὺ   στῆθι   ἐκεῖ   ἢ
to the poor man   ye say: ²thou   ¹Stand   there   or
κάθου   ὑπὸ   τὸ   ὑποπόδιόν   μου,   4 οὐ
sit   under   the   footstool   of me,   not
διεκρίθητε   ἐν   ἑαυτοῖς   καὶ   ἐγένεσθε   κριταὶ
did ye dis-   among yourselves   and   became   judges
criminate
διαλογισμῶν   πονηρῶν;   5 Ἀκούσατε,   ἀδελφοί
²thoughts   ¹of evil ?§   Hear ye,   brothers
μου   ἀγαπητοί.   οὐχ   ὁ   θεὸς   ἐξελέξατο
of me   beloved.   ²not   —   ³God   ¹Chose
τοὺς   πτωχοὺς   τῷ   κόσμῳ   πλουσίους   ἐν
the   poor   in the   world   rich   in
πίστει   καὶ   κληρονόμους   τῆς   βασιλείας
faith   and   heirs   of the   kingdom
ἧς   ἐπηγγείλατο   τοῖς   ἀγαπῶσιν   αὐτόν;
which   he promised   to the [ones]   loving   him?
6 ὑμεῖς   δὲ   ἠτιμάσατε   τὸν   πτωχόν.   οὐχ
But ye   dishonoured   the   poor man.   [Do] not
οἱ   πλούσιοι   καταδυναστεύουσιν   ὑμῶν,   καὶ
the   rich men   oppress   you,   and
αὐτοὶ   ἕλκουσιν   ὑμᾶς   εἰς   κριτήρια;   7 οὐκ
they   drag   you   to   tribunals ?   [Do] not

* That is, taking "the glory" as in apposition to "Jesus Christ"; see Luke 2. 32b.

§ Genitive of quality: "evil-thinking judges."

they who blaspheme that honorable name by which you are called?

8 If you really fulfil the royal law, according to the scripture, "You shall love your neighbor as yourself," you do well. 9 But if you show partiality, you commit sin, and are convicted by the law as transgressors. 10 For whoever keeps the whole law but fails in one point has become guilty of all of it. 11 For he who said, "Do not commit adultery," said also, "Do not kill." If you do not commit adultery but do kill, you have become a transgressor of the law. 12 So speak and so act as those who are to be judged under the law of liberty. 13 For judgment is without mercy to one who has shown no mercy; yet mercy triumphs over judgment.

14 What does it profit, my brethren, if a man says he has faith but has not works? Can his faith save him? 15 If a brother or sister is ill-clad and in lack of daily food, 16 and one of you says to them, "Go in

αὐτοὶ βλασφημοῦσιν τὸ καλὸν ὄνομα τὸ
they blaspheme the good name

ἐπικληθὲν ἐφ᾽ ὑμᾶς; 8 εἰ μέντοι νόμον
called on on you? If indeed ³law

τελεῖτε βασιλικὸν κατὰ τὴν γραφήν·
¹ye fulfil ²a royal according to the scripture:

ἀγαπήσεις τὸν πλησίον σου ὡς σεαυτόν,
Thou shalt love the neighbour of thee as thyself,

καλῶς ποιεῖτε· 9 εἰ δὲ προσωπολημπτεῖτε,
²well ¹ye do; but if ye respect persons,

ἁμαρτίαν ἐργάζεσθε, ἐλεγχόμενοι ὑπὸ τοῦ
²sin ¹ye work, being reproved by the

νόμου ὡς παραβάται. 10 ὅστις γὰρ
law as transgressors. For ¹[he] who

ὅλον τὸν νόμον τηρήσῃ, πταίσῃ δὲ ἐν
³all ⁴the ⁵law ²keeps, yet stumbles in

ἑνί, γέγονεν πάντων ἔνοχος. 11 ὁ γὰρ
one he has ²of all ¹guilty. For the
thing, become [one]

εἰπών· μὴ μοιχεύσῃς, εἶπεν καὶ· μὴ
saying: Do not commit adultery, said also: not

φονεύσῃς· εἰ δὲ οὐ μοιχεύεις, φονεύεις
Do murder; now if thou dost not ²murderest
commit adultery,

δέ, γέγονας παραβάτης νόμου. 12 οὕτως
¹but, thou hast a transgressor of [the] So
become law.

λαλεῖτε καὶ οὕτως ποιεῖτε ὡς διὰ νόμου
speak ye and so do ye as ²through ⁴a law

ἐλευθερίας μέλλοντες κρίνεσθαι. 13 ἡ γὰρ
¹of freedom ¹being about ¹to be judged. For the

κρίσις ἀνέλεος τῷ μὴ ποιήσαντι ἔλεος·
judg- [will unmerci- to the not do(show)ing mercy;
ment be] ful [one]

κατακαυχᾶται ἔλεος κρίσεως. 14 Τί τὸ
²exults over ¹mercy of judgment. What [is] the

ὄφελος, ἀδελφοί μου, ἐὰν πίστιν λέγῃ
profit, brothers of me, if ⁴faith ²says

τις ἔχειν ἔργα δὲ μὴ ἔχῃ; μὴ δύναται
¹any- to have ⁴works ⁵but ³not ⁶has? not can
one

ἡ πίστις σῶσαι αὐτόν; 15 ἐὰν ἀδελφὸς
the faith to save him? If a brother

ἢ ἀδελφὴ γυμνοὶ ὑπάρχωσιν καὶ λειπόμενοι
or a sister ¹naked ²are and lacking

τῆς ἐφημέρου τροφῆς, 16 εἴπῃ δέ τις
of the daily food, and ⁴says ¹anyone

αὐτοῖς ἐξ ὑμῶν· ὑπάγετε ἐν εἰρήνῃ,
⁵to them ²of ³you: Go ye in peace,

peace, be warmed and filled," without giving them the things needed for the body, what does it profit? [17]So faith by itself, if it has no works, is dead.

18 But some one will say, "You have faith and I have works." Show me your faith apart from your works, and I by my works will show you my faith. [19]You believe that God is one; you do well. Even the demons believe —and shudder. [20]Do you want to be shown, you foolish fellow, that faith apart from works is barren? [21]Was not Abraham our father justified by works, when he offered his son Isaac upon the altar? [22]You see that faith was active along with his works, and faith was completed by works, [23]and the scripture was fulfilled which says, "Abraham believed God, and it was reckoned to him as righteousness"; and he was called the friend of God. [24]You see that a man is justified by works and not by faith alone. [25]And in the same way

θερμαίνεσθε   καὶ   χορτάζεσθε,   μὴ   δῶτε
be warmed   and   filled,   ²not   ²ye give
δὲ   αὐτοῖς   τὰ   ἐπιτήδεια   τοῦ   σώματος,
¹but   ³them   the   necessaries   of the   body,
τί   τὸ   ὄφελος;   17 οὕτως   καὶ   ἡ   πίστις,
what [is] the   profit ?   So   indeed –   faith,
ἐὰν   μὴ   ἔχῃ   ἔργα,   νεκρά   ἐστιν   καθ'
if   it has not   works,   ³dead   ¹is   by
ἑαυτήν.   18 ἀλλ'   ἐρεῖ   τις·   σὺ   πίστιν
itself.   But   ³will say ¹someone: Thou   ²faith
ἔχεις,   κἀγὼ   ἔργα   ἔχω·   δεῖξόν   μοι   τὴν
¹hast,   and I   ²works   ²have;   show   me   the
πίστιν   σου   χωρὶς   τῶν   ἔργων,   κἀγώ
faith   of thee   without   the   works,   and I
σοι   δείξω   ἐκ   τῶν   ἔργων   μου   τὴν   πίστιν.
thee will show ⁴by   ⁵the   ⁶works   ²of me ¹the   ²faith.
19 σὺ   πιστεύεις   ὅτι   εἷς   ἐστιν   ὁ   θεός;
Thou   believest   that   ²one   ²is – ¹God ?
καλῶς   ποιεῖς·   καὶ   τὰ   δαιμόνια   πιστεύουσιν
²well   ¹thou doest;   also   the   demons   believe
καὶ   φρίσσουσιν.   20 θέλεις   δὲ   γνῶναι,
and   shudder.   But art thou willing   to know,
ὦ   ἄνθρωπε   κενέ,   ὅτι   ἡ   πίστις   χωρὶς
O   ¹man   ¹vain,   that – faith   without
τῶν   ἔργων   ἀργή   ἐστιν;   21 Ἀβραὰμ   ὁ
–   works   barren   is ?   Abraham   the
πατὴρ   ἡμῶν   οὐκ   ἐξ   ἔργων   ἐδικαιώθη,
father   of us   not   by   works   was justified,
ἀνενέγκας   Ἰσαὰκ   τὸν   υἱὸν   αὐτοῦ   ἐπὶ
offering up   Isaac   the   son   of him   on
τὸ   θυσιαστήριον;   22 βλέπεις   ὅτι   ἡ   πίστις
the   altar ?   Thou seest that – faith
συνήργει   τοῖς   ἔργοις   αὐτοῦ,   καὶ   ἐκ
worked with   the   works   of him,   and   by
τῶν   ἔργων   ἡ   πίστις   ἐτελειώθη,   23 καὶ
the   works   the   faith   was perfected,   and
ἐπληρώθη   ἡ   γραφὴ   ἡ   λέγουσα·   ἐπίστευσεν
was fulfilled   the   scripture – saying: believed
δὲ   Ἀβραὰμ   τῷ   θεῷ,   καὶ   ἐλογίσθη   αὐτῷ
And   Abraham – God,   and   it was reckoned   to him
εἰς   δικαιοσύνην,   καὶ   φίλος   θεοῦ   ἐκλήθη.
for   righteousness,   and   ²friend   ²of God   ¹he was
                                                          called.
24 ὁρᾶτε   ὅτι   ἐξ   ἔργων   δικαιοῦται   ἄνθρωπος
Ye see   that   by   works   ²is justified   ¹a man
καὶ   οὐκ   ἐκ   πίστεως   μόνον.   25 ὁμοίως
and   not   by   faith   only.   likewise

was not also Rahab the harlot justified by works when she received the messengers and sent them out another way? ²⁶For as the body apart from the spirit is dead, so faith apart from works is dead.

δὲ καὶ ῾Ραὰβ ἡ πόρνη οὐκ ἐξ ἔργων
And also Rahab the prostitute not by works
ἐδικαιώθη, ὑποδεξαμένη τοὺς ἀγγέλους καὶ
was justified, entertaining the messengers and
ἑτέρᾳ ὁδῷ ἐκβαλοῦσα; 26 ὥσπερ γὰρ τὸ
by a way sending [them] For as the
different forth?
σῶμα χωρὶς πνεύματος νεκρόν ἐστιν, οὕτως
body without spirit ²dead ¹is, so
καὶ ἡ πίστις χωρὶς ἔργων νεκρά ἐστιν.
also - faith without works ²dead ¹is.

CHAPTER 3

LET not many of you become teachers, my brethren, for you know that we who teach shall be judged with greater strictness. ²For we all make many mistakes, and if any one makes no mistakes in what he says he is a perfect man, able to bridle the whole body also. ³If we put bits into the mouths of horses that they may obey us, we guide their whole bodies. ⁴Look at the ships also; though they are so great and are driven by strong winds, they are guided by a very small rudder wherever the will of the pilot directs. ⁵So the tongue is a little member and boasts of great things. How great a forest is set ablaze by a small fire!

6 And the tongue is a fire. The tongue is an unrighteous world among our members, staining

3 Μὴ πολλοὶ διδάσκαλοι γίνεσθε, ἀδελφοί
²not ³many ⁴teachers ¹Become ye, brothers
μου, εἰδότες ὅτι μεῖζον κρίμα λημψόμεθα.
of me, knowing that greater judgment we shall receive.
2 πολλὰ γὰρ πταίομεν ἅπαντες· εἴ τις
For [in] many [respects] we stumble all; if anyone
ἐν λόγῳ οὐ πταίει, οὗτος τέλειος ἀνήρ,
²in ³word ¹stumbles not, this [is] a perfect man,
δυνατὸς χαλιναγωγῆσαι καὶ ὅλον τὸ σῶμα.
able ²to bridle ¹indeed all the body.
3 εἰ δὲ τῶν ἵππων τοὺς χαλινοὺς εἰς
Now if - ⁶of horses - ⁵bridles ³into
τὰ στόματα βάλλομεν εἰς τὸ πείθεσθαι
⁴the ⁵mouths ¹we put for the to obey
＝to make them obey us,
αὐτοὺς ἡμῖν, καὶ ὅλον τὸ σῶμα αὐτῶν
themᵇ to us, and ²all ³the ⁴body ⁵of them
μετάγομεν. 4 ἰδοὺ καὶ τὰ πλοῖα, τηλικαῦτα
¹we direct. Behold also the ships, ¹so great
ὄντα καὶ ὑπὸ ἀνέμων σκληρῶν ἐλαυνόμενα,
¹being ²and ⁵by ⁷winds ⁶hard(strong) ⁴being driven,
μετάγεται ὑπὸ ἐλαχίστου πηδαλίου ὅπου
is(are) directed by a very little helm where
ἡ ὁρμὴ τοῦ εὐθύνοντος βούλεται· 5 οὕτως
the impulse of the [one] steering resolves; so
καὶ ἡ γλῶσσα μικρὸν μέλος ἐστὶν καὶ
also the tongue ²a little ³member ¹is and
μεγάλα αὐχεῖ. ἰδοὺ ἡλίκον πῦρ ἡλίκον
great things boasts. Behold how little a fire ²how great
ὕλην ἀνάπτει· 6 καὶ ἡ γλῶσσα πῦρ,
³wood ¹kindles; and the tongue [is] a fire,
ὁ κόσμος τῆς ἀδικίας, ἡ γλῶσσα καθίστα-
the world - of iniquity, the tongue is
ται ἐν τοῖς μέλεσιν ἡμῶν, ἡ σπιλοῦσα
set among the members of us, - spotting

the whole body, setting on fire the cycle of nature,[b] and set on fire by hell. [7]For every kind of beast and bird, of reptile and sea creature, can be tamed and has been tamed by human-kind, [8]but no human being can tame the tongue—a restless evil, full of deadly poison. [9]With it we bless the Lord and Father, and with it we curse men, who are made in the likeness of God. [10]From the same mouth come blessing and cursing. My brethren, this ought not to be so. [11]Does a spring pour forth from the same opening fresh water and brackish? [12]Can a fig tree, my brethren, yield olives, or a grapevine figs? No more can salt water yield fresh.

13 Who is wise and understanding among you? By his good life let him show his works in the meekness of wisdom. [14]But if you have bitter jealousy and selfish am-bition in your hearts, do

ὅλον　τὸ　σῶμα　καὶ　φλογίζουσα　τὸν
all　the　body　and　inflaming　the

τροχὸν　τῆς　γενέσεως　καὶ　φλογιζομένη
course　-　of nature　and　being inflamed

ὑπὸ　τῆς　γεέννης.　7 πᾶσα　γὰρ　φύσις
by　-　gehenna.　For every　nature

θηρίων　τε　καὶ　πετεινῶν,　ἑρπετῶν　τε
[2]of beasts　[1]both　and　of birds,　[2]of reptiles　[1]both

καὶ　ἐναλίων　δαμάζεται　καὶ　δεδάμασται
and　of marine　is tamed　and　has been tamed
　　creatures

τῇ　φύσει　τῇ　ἀνθρωπίνῃ,　8 τῇ　δὲ
by the　[2]nature　-　[1]human,　but the

γλῶσσαν　οὐδεὶς　δαμάσαι　δύναται　ἀνθρώπων·
tongue　[1]no one　[4]to tame　[3]is able　[2]of men;

ἀκατάστατον　κακόν,　μεστὴ　ἰοῦ　θανατηφόρου.
an unruly　evil,　full　[2]poison　[1]of death-dealing.

9 ἐν　αὐτῇ　εὐλογοῦμεν　τὸν　κύριον　καὶ
By　this　we bless　the　Lord　and

πατέρα,　καὶ　ἐν　αὐτῇ　καταρώμεθα　τοὺς
Father,　and　by　this　we curse

ἀνθρώπους　τοὺς　καθ᾽　ὁμοίωσιν　θεοῦ
men　-　[2]according to　[3]likeness　[4]of God

γεγονότας·　10 ἐκ　τοῦ　αὐτοῦ　στόματος　ἐξέρχεται
[1]having become;　out of the　same　mouth　comes forth

εὐλογία　καὶ　κατάρα.　οὐ　χρή,　ἀδελφοί
blessing　and　cursing.　It is not fitting,　brothers

μου,　ταῦτα　οὕτως　γίνεσθαι.　11 μήτι
of me,　these things　so　to be.　Not

ἡ　πηγὴ　ἐκ　τῆς　αὐτῆς　ὀπῆς　βρύει　τὸ
the fountain　out of　the　same　hole　sends forth　the

γλυκὺ　καὶ　τὸ　πικρόν;　12 μὴ　δύναται,
sweet　and　the　bitter?　Not　can,

ἀδελφοί　μου,　συκῆ　ἐλαίας　ποιῆσαι　ἢ
brothers　of me,　a fig-tree　[2]olives　[1]to produce　or

ἄμπελος　σῦκα;　οὔτε　ἁλυκὸν　γλυκὺ
a vine　figs?　neither　[2]salt　[1]sweet

ποιῆσαι　ὕδωρ.　13 Τίς　σοφὸς　καὶ　ἐπιστήμων
[2]to make　[1]water.　Who [is] wise　and　knowing

ἐν　ὑμῖν;　δειξάτω　ἐκ　τῆς　καλῆς　ἀναστροφῆς
among you?　let him show　by the(his)　good　conduct

τὰ　ἔργα　αὐτοῦ　ἐν　πραΰτητι　σοφίας.
the　works　of him　in　meekness　of wisdom.*

14 εἰ　δὲ　ζῆλον　πικρὸν　ἔχετε　καὶ　ἐριθείαν
But if　[2]jealousy　[3]bitter　[1]ye have　and　rivalry

ἐν　τῇ　καρδίᾳ　ὑμῶν,　μὴ　κατακαυχᾶσθε
in　the　heart　of you,　do not exult over

* Genitive of quality : " a wise meekness."

not boast and be false to the truth. ¹⁵This wisdom is not such as comes down from above, but is earthly, unspiritual, devilish. ¹⁶For where jealousy and selfish ambition exist, there will be disorder and every vile practice. ¹⁷But the wisdom from above is first pure, then peaceable, gentle, open to reason, full of mercy and good fruits, without uncertainty or insincerity. ¹⁸And the harvest of righteousness is sown in peace by those who make peace.

καὶ ψεύδεσθε κατὰ τῆς ἀληθείας. 15 οὐκ
and lie against the truth. ⁴not

ἔστιν αὕτη ἡ σοφία ἄνωθεν κατερχομένη,
³is ¹This – ²wisdom ⁶from above ⁵coming down,

ἀλλὰ ἐπίγειος, ψυχική, δαιμονιώδης· 16 ὅπου
but [is] earthly, natural, demon-like; ²where

γὰρ ζῆλος καὶ ἐριθεία, ἐκεῖ ἀκαταστασία
¹for jealousy and rivalry [are], there [is] tumult

καὶ πᾶν φαῦλον πρᾶγμα. 17 ἡ δὲ ἄνωθεν
and every worthless practice. But ¹the ²from
above

σοφία πρῶτον μὲν ἁγνή ἐστιν, ἔπειτα
²wisdom ⁵firstly – ⁶pure ⁴is. then

εἰρηνική, ἐπιεικής, εὐπειθής, μεστὴ ἐλέους
peaceable, forbearing, compliant, full of mercy

καὶ καρπῶν ἀγαθῶν, ἀδιάκριτος, ἀνυπό-
and ²fruits ¹of good, without uncertainty, un-

κριτος. 18 καρπὸς δὲ δικαιοσύνης ἐν
feigned. And [the] fruit of righteousness ²in

εἰρήνῃ σπείρεται τοῖς ποιοῦσιν εἰρήνην.
²peace ¹is sown for the [ones] making peace.

CHAPTER 4

WHAT causes wars, and what causes fightings among you? Is it not your passions that are at war in your members? ²You desire and do not have; so you kill. And you covet[c] and cannot obtain; so you fight and wage war. You do not have, because you do not ask. ³You ask and do not receive, because you ask wrongly, to spend it on your passions. ⁴Unfaithful creatures! Do you not know that friendship with the world is enmity with God? Therefore who-

4 Πόθεν πόλεμοι καὶ πόθεν μάχαι ἐν
Whence wars and whence fights among

ὑμῖν; οὐκ ἐντεῦθεν, ἐκ τῶν ἡδονῶν
you? not thence, out of the pleasures

ὑμῶν τῶν στρατευομένων ἐν τοῖς μέλεσιν
of you – soldiering in the members

ὑμῶν; 2 ἐπιθυμεῖτε, καὶ οὐκ ἔχετε·
of you? Ye desire, and have not;

φονεύετε καὶ ζηλοῦτε, καὶ οὐ δύνασθε
ye murder and are jealous, and are not able

ἐπιτυχεῖν· μάχεσθε καὶ πολεμεῖτε. οὐκ
to obtain; ye fight and ye war. not

ἔχετε διὰ τὸ μὴ αἰτεῖσθαι ὑμᾶς· 3 αἰτεῖτε
Ye have be- the not to ask you[b]; ye ask
cause of
=because ye ask not;

καὶ οὐ λαμβάνετε, διότι κακῶς αἰτεῖσθε,
and receive not, because ²ill ¹ye ask,

ἵνα ἐν ταῖς ἡδοναῖς ὑμῶν δαπανήσητε.
in or- in the pleasures of you ye may spend.
der that

4 μοιχαλίδες, οὐκ οἴδατε ὅτι ἡ φιλία
Adulteresses, know ye not that the friendship

τοῦ κόσμου ἔχθρα τοῦ θεοῦ ἐστιν; ὃς
of the world ²enmity – ²of God ¹is? Who-

---

[c] Or you kill and you covet

ever wishes to be a friend of the world makes himself an enemy of God. [5]Or do you suppose it is in vain that the scripture says, "He yearns jealously over the spirit which he has made to dwell in us"? [6]But he gives more grace; therefore it says, "God opposes the proud, but gives grace to the humble." [7]Submit yourselves therefore to God. Resist the devil and he will flee from you. [8]Draw near to God and he will draw near to you. Cleanse your hands, you sinners, and purify your hearts, you men of double mind. [9]Be wretched and mourn and weep. Let your laughter be turned to mourning and your joy to dejection. [10]Humble yourselves before the Lord and he will exalt you.

[11]Do not speak evil against one another, brethren. He that speaks evil against a brother or judges his brother, speaks evil against the law and judges the law. But if you judge the law, you are not a doer of the law but a judge. [12]There is one lawgiver and judge, he who is able to save

ἐὰν οὖν βουληθῇ φίλος εἶναι τοῦ κόσμου,
ever therefore ¹resolves ²a friend ²to be of the world,

ἐχθρὸς τοῦ θεοῦ καθίσταται. 5 ἢ δοκεῖτε
²an enemy – ²of God ¹is constituted. Or think ye

ὅτι κενῶς ἡ γραφὴ λέγει· πρὸς φθόνον
that vainly the scripture says: ⁸to ⁹envy

ἐπιποθεῖ τὸ πνεῦμα ὃ κατῴκισεν ἐν
⁷yearns ¹The ²Spirit ³which ⁴dwelt ⁵in

ἡμῖν; 6 μείζονα δὲ δίδωσιν χάριν· διὸ
⁶you? But ²greater ¹he gives ³grace; wherefore

λέγει· ὁ θεὸς ὑπερηφάνοις ἀντιτάσσεται,
it* says: – God ²arrogant men ¹resists,

ταπεινοῖς δὲ δίδωσιν χάριν. 7 ὑποτάγητε
but to humble men he gives grace. Be ye subject

οὖν τῷ θεῷ· ἀντίστητε δὲ τῷ διαβόλῳ,
there- – to God; but oppose the devil,
fore

καὶ φεύξεται ἀφ' ὑμῶν· 8 ἐγγίσατε τῷ
and he will flee from you; draw near –

θεῷ, καὶ ἐγγίσει ὑμῖν. καθαρίσατε
to God, and he will draw near to you. Cleanse ye

χεῖρας, ἁμαρτωλοί, καὶ ἁγνίσατε καρδίας,
hands, sinners, and purify hearts,

δίψυχοι. 9 ταλαιπωρήσατε καὶ πενθήσατε
two-souled Be ye distressed and mourn
(double-minded).

καὶ κλαύσατε· ὁ γέλως ὑμῶν εἰς πένθος
and weep; the laughter of you to mourning

μετατραπήτω καὶ ἡ χαρὰ εἰς κατήφειαν.
let it be turned and the joy to dejection.

10 ταπεινώθητε ἐνώπιον κυρίου, καὶ ὑψώσει
Be ye humbled before [the] Lord, and he will exalt

ὑμᾶς. 11 Μὴ καταλαλεῖτε ἀλλήλων, ἀδελφοί.
you. Speak not against one another, brothers.

ὁ καταλαλῶν ἀδελφοῦ ἢ κρίνων τὸν
The speaking a brother or judging the
[one] against

ἀδελφὸν αὐτοῦ καταλαλεῖ νόμου καὶ κρίνει
brother of him speaks against law and judges

νόμον· εἰ δὲ νόμον κρίνεις, οὐκ εἶ
law; and if law thou judgest, thou art not

ποιητὴς νόμου ἀλλὰ κριτής. 12 εἷς ἐστιν
a doer of law but a judge. One is

νομοθέτης καὶ κριτής, ὁ δυνάμενος
lawgiver and judge, the [one] being able

---

* That is, " the scripture " (as ver. 5).

and to destroy. But who are you that you judge your neighbor?

13 Come now, you who say, "Today or tomorrow we will go into such and such a town and spend a year there and trade and get gain"; ¹⁴whereas you do not know about tomorrow. What is your life? For you are a mist that appears for a little time and then vanishes. ¹⁵Instead you ought to say, "If the Lord wills, we shall live and we shall do this or that." ¹⁶As it is, you boast in your arrogance. All such boasting is evil. ¹⁷Whoever knows what is right to do and fails to do it, for him it is sin.

σῶσαι   καὶ   ἀπολέσαι·   σὺ   δὲ   τίς   εἶ,   ὁ
to save   and   to destroy;   ⁴thou   ¹and   ²who   ³art,   the
κρίνων   τὸν   πλησίον;
[one] judging the(thy)   neighbour?

13 "Ἄγε   νῦν   οἱ   λέγοντες·   σήμερον   ἢ
Come   now   the [ones]   saying: To-day   or
αὔριον   πορευσόμεθα   εἰς   τήνδε   τὴν   πόλιν
to-morrow   we will go   into   this   —   city
καὶ   ποιήσομεν   ἐκεῖ   ἐνιαυτὸν   καὶ   ἐμπορευ-
and   we will do   there   a year   and   we will
σόμεθα   καὶ   κερδήσομεν·   14 οἵτινες   οὐκ
trade   and   we will make a profit;   who   not
ἐπίστασθε   τῆς   αὔριον   ποία   ἡ   ζωὴ   ὑμῶν.
ye know   ⁵of the   ⁶morrow   ¹what   ²the   ³life   ⁴of you
[will be].

ἀτμὶς   γάρ   ἐστε   ἡ   πρὸς   ὀλίγον   φαινομένη,
For   ²a vapour   ¹ye are   —   ⁴for   ⁵a little while   ³appearing,
ἔπειτα   καὶ   ἀφανιζομένη·   15 ἀντὶ   τοῦ
thereafter   indeed   disappearing;   instead of   the
λέγειν   ὑμᾶς·   ἐὰν   ὁ   κύριος   θελήσῃ,   καὶ
to say   youᵇ: If   the   Lord   wills,   both
=your saying:

ζήσομεν   καὶ   ποιήσομεν   τοῦτο   ἢ   ἐκεῖνο.
we will live   and   we will do   this   or   that.

16 νῦν   δὲ   καυχᾶσθε   ἐν   ταῖς   ἀλαζονείαις
But now   ye boast   in   the   vauntings
ὑμῶν·   πᾶσα   καύχησις   τοιαύτη   πονηρά
of you;   all   ²boasting   ¹such   ⁴evil
ἐστιν.   17 εἰδότι   οὖν   καλὸν   ποιεῖν   καὶ
³is.   ²to [one]   ¹There-   ⁴good   ⁵to do   and
fore   knowing*
μὴ   ποιοῦντι,   ἁμαρτία   αὐτῷ   ἐστιν.
not   doing,   ³sin   ¹to him   ²it is.

CHAPTER 5

COME now, you rich, weep and howl for the miseries that are coming upon you. ²Your riches have rotted and your garments are motheaten. ³Your gold and silver have rusted, and their rust will be evidence against you and will eat

5 "Ἄγε   νῦν   οἱ   πλούσιοι,   κλαύσατε
Come   now   the   rich men,   weep ye
ὀλολύζοντες   ἐπὶ   ταῖς   ταλαιπωρίαις   ὑμῶν
crying aloud   over   the   hardships   of you
ταῖς   ἐπερχομέναις.   2 ὁ   πλοῦτος   ὑμῶν
—   coming upon.   The   riches   of you
σέσηπεν,   καὶ   τὰ   ἱμάτια   ὑμῶν   σητόβρωτα
have become and   the   garments   of you   moth-eaten
corrupted,
γέγονεν,   3 ὁ   χρυσὸς   ὑμῶν   καὶ   ὁ   ἄργυρος
have become,   the   gold   of you   and   the   silver
κατίωται,   καὶ   ὁ   ἰὸς   αὐτῶν   εἰς   μαρτύριον
has become   and   the   poison of them   for   a testimony
rusted over,
ὑμῖν   ἔσται   καὶ   φάγεται   τὰς   σάρκας
to(against)   will   and   will eat   the   fleshes
you   be

* See note on page xviii.

your flesh like fire. You
have laid up treasure[d]
for the last days.
[4] Behold, the wages of
the laborers who mowed
your fields, which you
kept back by fraud, cry
out; and the cries of the
harvesters have reached
the ears of the Lord of
hosts. [5] You have lived
on the earth in luxury
and in pleasure; you
have fattened your hearts
in a day of slaughter.
[6] You have condemned,
you have killed the
righteous man; he does
not resist you.

7 Be patient, therefore,
brethren, until the com-
ing of the Lord. Behold,
the farmer waits for the
precious fruit of the
earth, being patient over
it until it receives the
early and the late rain.
[8] You also be patient.
Establish your hearts,
for the coming of the
Lord is at hand. [9] Do
not grumble, brethren,
against one another, that
you may not be judged;
behold, the Judge is
standing at the doors.
[10] As an example of
suffering and patience,
brethren, take the
prophets who spoke in
the name of the Lord.
[11] Behold, we call those

ὑμῶν   ὡς   πῦρ.   ἐθησαυρίσατε   ἐν   ἐσχάταις
of you   as   fire.   Ye treasured   in   [the] last

ἡμέραις.   4 ἰδοὺ   ὁ   μισθὸς   τῶν   ἐργατῶν
days.   Behold[,] the   wages   of the   workmen

τῶν   ἀμησάντων   τὰς   χώρας   ὑμῶν   ὁ
-      having reaped   the   lands   of you   -

ἀφυστερημένος   ἀφ'   ὑμῶν   κράζει,   καὶ   αἱ
being kept back   from(by)   you   cries,   and   the

βοαὶ   τῶν   θερισάντων   εἰς   τὰ   ὦτα   κυρίου
cries   of the   having reaped   [2]into   [3]the   [4]ears   [5]of [the] Lord

σαβαὼθ   εἰσελήλυθαν.   5 ἐτρυφήσατε   ἐπὶ
[6]of hosts   [1]have entered.   Ye lived daintily   on

τῆς   γῆς   καὶ   ἐσπαταλήσατε,   ἐθρέψατε   τὰς
the   earth   and   lived riotously,   ye nourished   the

καρδίας   ὑμῶν   ἐν   ἡμέρᾳ   σφαγῆς.   6 κατε-
hearts   of you   in   a day   of slaughter.   Ye

δικάσατε,   ἐφονεύσατε   τὸν   δίκαιον·   οὐκ
condemned,   ye murdered   the   righteous man;   not

ἀντιτάσσεται   ὑμῖν.
he resists   you.

7 Μακροθυμήσατε   οὖν,   ἀδελφοί,   ἕως   τῆς
Be ye longsuffering   therefore,   brothers,   until   the

παρουσίας   τοῦ   κυρίου.   ἰδοὺ   ὁ   γεωργὸς
presence   of the   Lord.   Behold[,] the   farmer

ἐκδέχεται   τὸν   τίμιον   καρπὸν   τῆς   γῆς,
awaits   the   precious   fruit   of the   earth,

μακροθυμῶν   ἐπ'   αὐτῷ   ἕως   λάβῃ   πρόϊμον
being   over   it   until he receives   early
longsuffering

καὶ   ὄψιμον.   8 μακροθυμήσατε   καὶ   ὑμεῖς,
and   latter [rain].   Be [3]longsuffering   [2]also   [1]ye,

στηρίξατε   τὰς   καρδίας   ὑμῶν,   ὅτι   ἡ
establish   the   hearts   of you,   because   the

παρουσία   τοῦ   κυρίου   ἤγγικεν.   9 μὴ
presence   of the   Lord   has drawn near.   not

στενάζετε,   ἀδελφοί,   κατ'   ἀλλήλων   ἵνα   μὴ
Murmur ye,   brothers,   against   one another   lest

κριθῆτε·   ἰδοὺ   ὁ   κριτὴς   πρὸ   τῶν   θυρῶν
ye be   behold[,] the   judge   [2]before   [3]the   [4]doors
judged;

ἕστηκεν.   10 ὑπόδειγμα   λάβετε,   ἀδελφοί,
[1]stands.   [5]an example   [1]Take ye,   [3]brothers,

τῆς   κακοπαθίας   καὶ   τῆς   μακροθυμίας
-    [6]of suffering ill   [7]and   -   [8]of longsuffering

τοὺς   προφήτας,   οἳ   ἐλάλησαν   ἐν   τῷ
[3]the   [4]prophets,   who   spoke   in   the

ὀνόματι   κυρίου.   11 ἰδοὺ   μακαρίζομεν   τοὺς
name   of [the] Lord.   Behold   we count blessed   the

[d] Or will eat your flesh, since
you have stored up fire

happy who were stead-
fast. You have heard of
the steadfastness of Job,
and you have seen the
purpose of the Lord,
how the Lord is com-
passionate and merciful.

12 But above all, my
brethren, do not swear,
either by heaven or by
earth or with any other
oath, but let your yes be
yes and your no be no,
that you may not fall
under condemnation.

13 Is any one among
you suffering? Let him
pray. Is any cheerful?
Let him sing praise. 14 Is
any among you sick?
Let him call for the elders
of the church, and let
them pray over him,
anointing him with oil
in the name of the Lord;
15 and the prayer of faith
will save the sick man,
and the Lord will raise
him up; and if he has
committed sins, he will
be forgiven. 16 Therefore
confess your sins to one
another, and pray for one
another, that you may
be healed. The prayer of
a righteous man has
great power in its effects.
17 Eli′jah was a man of
like nature with our-
selves and he prayed
fervently that it might
not rain, and for three

ὑπομείναντας· τὴν ὑπομονὴν Ἰὼβ ἠκούσατε,
[ones] enduring;   ²the   ³endurance   ⁴of Job ¹ye heard [of],

καὶ τὸ τέλος κυρίου εἴδετε, ὅτι πολύ-
and ²the   ³end ⁴of [the] Lord ¹ye saw,   that   ⁴very

σπλαγχνός ἐστιν ὁ κύριος καὶ οἰκτίρμων.
compassionate ³is   ¹the ²Lord   and   pitiful.

12 Πρὸ πάντων δέ, ἀδελφοί μου, μὴ
²before ²all things ¹But,   brothers   of me,   not

ὀμνύετε, μήτε τὸν οὐρανὸν μήτε τὴν
swear ye, neither   by the   heaven   nor   by the

γῆν μήτε ἄλλον τινὰ ὅρκον· ἤτω δὲ
earth   nor   ²other   ¹any   oath;   but let be

ὑμῶν τὸ ναὶ ναί, καὶ τὸ οὒ οὔ, ἵνα μὴ
of you the Yes yes, and   the No no,   lest

ὑπὸ κρίσιν πέσητε. 13 Κακοπαθεῖ τις
²under ³judgment ¹ye fall.   Suffers ill   anyone

ἐν ὑμῖν; προσευχέσθω· εὐθυμεῖ τις;
among you?   let him pray;   is cheerful anyone?

ψαλλέτω. 14 ἀσθενεῖ τις ἐν ὑμῖν;
let him sing a psalm. Is weak anyone among   you?

προσκαλεσάσθω τοὺς πρεσβυτέρους τῆς
let him summon   the   elders   of the

ἐκκλησίας, καὶ προσευξάσθωσαν ἐπ᾽ αὐτὸν
church,   and   let them pray   over   him

ἀλείψαντες ἐλαίῳ ἐν τῷ ὀνόματι τοῦ
having anointed with oil ın   the   name   of the
[him]

κυρίου. 15 καὶ ἡ εὐχὴ τῆς πίστεως
Lord.   And the   prayer   –   of faith

σώσει τὸν κάμνοντα, καὶ ἐγερεῖ αὐτὸν
will heal the [one] being sick, and ²will raise ¹him

ὁ κύριος· κἂν ἁμαρτίας ᾖ πεποιηκώς,
¹the ²Lord;   and if ³sins   ¹he   ²having done,
may be

ἀφεθήσεται αὐτῷ. 16 ἐξομολογεῖσθε οὖν
it will be forgiven him.   Confess ye therefore

ἀλλήλοις τὰς ἁμαρτίας, καὶ προσεύχεσθε
to one   the(your) sins,   and   pray ye
another

ὑπὲρ ἀλλήλων, ὅπως ἰαθῆτε. πολὺ
on be-   one another,   so as   ye may ⁵much(very)
half of   be cured.

ἰσχύει δέησις δικαίου ἐνεργουμένη.
⁴is ⁵strong ¹a petition   ²of a   ³being made effective.
righteous man

17 Ἠλίας ἄνθρωπος ἦν ὁμοιοπαθὴς ἡμῖν,
Elias   ²a man   ¹was   of like feeling   to us,

καὶ προσευχῇ προσηύξατο τοῦ μὴ βρέξαι,
and ²in prayer ¹he prayed   –   not to rain,ᵈ
=that it should not rain,

years and six months it
did not rain on the earth.
¹⁸Then he prayed again
and the heaven gave rain,
and the earth brought
forth its fruit.

19 My brethren, if any
one among you wanders
from the truth and some
one brings him back,
²⁰let him know that
whoever brings back a
sinner from the error of
his way will save his
soul from death and will
cover a multitude of sins.

καὶ   οὐκ   ἔβρεξεν   ἐπὶ   τῆς   γῆς   ἐνιαυτοὺς
and   it rained not   on   the   earth   ¹years
τρεῖς   καὶ   μῆνας   ἕξ·   18 καὶ   πάλιν   προσ-
¹three   and   ²months   ¹six;   and   again   he
ηύξατο,   καὶ   ὁ   οὐρανὸς   ὑετὸν   ἔδωκεν   καὶ
prayed,   and   the   heaven   ¹rain   ¹gave   and
ἡ   γῆ   ἐβλάστησεν   τὸν   καρπὸν   αὐτῆς.
the   earth   brought forth   the   fruit   of it.
19 Ἀδελφοί   μου,   ἐάν   τις   ἐν   ὑμῖν   πλανηθῇ
Brothers   of me,   if   anyone among you   errs
ἀπὸ   τῆς   ἀληθείας   καὶ   ἐπιστρέψῃ   τις
from   the   truth   and   ²turns   ¹anyone
αὐτόν,   20 γινώσκετε   ὅτι   ὁ   ἐπιστρέψας
him,   know ye   that   the [one]   turning
ἁμαρτωλὸν   ἐκ   πλάνης   ὁδοῦ   αὐτοῦ   σώσει
a sinner   out of [the] error of way   of him   will save
ψυχὴν   αὐτοῦ   ἐκ   θανάτου   καὶ   καλύψει
soul   of him   out of   death   and   will hide
πλῆθος   ἁμαρτιῶν.
a multitude   of sins.

I. PETER 1

CHAPTER 1

PETER, an apostle of
Jesus Christ,
To the exiles of the
Dispersion in Pontus,
Galatia, Cappado'cia,
Asia, and Bithyn'ia,
²chosen and destined by
God the Father and
sanctified by the Spirit
for obedience to Jesus
Christ and for sprinkling
with his blood:
May grace and peace
be multiplied to you.
3 Blessed be the God
and Father of our Lord
Jesus Christ! By his

1 Πέτρος   ἀπόστολος   Ἰησοῦ   Χριστοῦ
Peter   an apostle   of Jesus   Christ
ἐκλεκτοῖς   παρεπιδήμοις   διασπορᾶς   Πόντου,
to [the] chosen   sojourners   of [the] dispersion   of Pontus,
Γαλατίας,   Καππαδοκίας,   Ἀσίας   καὶ
of Galatia,   of Cappadocia,   of Asia   and
Βιθυνίας,   2 κατὰ   πρόγνωσιν   θεοῦ   πατρός,
of Bithynia,   according   [the]   of God   Father,
to   foreknowledge
ἐν   ἁγιασμῷ   πνεύματος,   εἰς   ὑπακοὴν   καὶ
in   sanctification   of spirit,   to   obedience   and
ῥαντισμὸν   αἵματος   Ἰησοῦ   Χριστοῦ·   χάρις
sprinkling   of [the] blood   of Jesus   Christ·   Grace
ὑμῖν   καὶ   εἰρήνη   πληθυνθείη.
to you   and   peace   may it be multiplied.
3 Εὐλογητὸς   ὁ   θεὸς   καὶ   πατὴρ   τοῦ
Blessed [be]   the   God   and   Father   of the
κυρίου   ἡμῶν   Ἰησοῦ   Χριστοῦ,   ὁ   κατὰ   τὸ
Lord   of us   Jesus   Christ,   the   accord-   the
[one]   ing to

great mercy we have been born anew to a living hope through the resurrection of Jesus Christ from the dead, [4]and to an inheritance which is imperishable, undefiled, and unfading, kept in heaven for you, [5]who by God's power are guarded through faith for a salvation ready to be revealed in the last time. [6]In this you rejoice,[a] though now for a little while you may have to suffer various trials, [7]so that the genuineness of your faith, more precious than gold which though perishable is tested by fire, may redound to praise and glory and honor at the revelation of Jesus Christ. [8]Without having seen[b] him you[c] love him; though you do not now see him you[c] believe in him and rejoice with unutterable and exalted joy. [9]As the outcome of your faith you obtain the salvation of your souls.

10 The prophets who prophesied of the grace that was to be yours searched and inquired about this salvation; [11]they inquired what person or time was indicated by the Spirit of Christ

πολὺ αὐτοῦ ἔλεος ἀναγεννήσας ἡμᾶς εἰς
much of him mercy having regenerated us to
(great)

ἐλπίδα ζῶσαν δι' ἀναστάσεως Ἰησοῦ
[1]hope [1]a living through [the] resurrection of Jesus

Χριστοῦ ἐκ νεκρῶν, 4 εἰς κληρονομίαν
Christ from [the] dead, to an inheritance

ἄφθαρτον καὶ ἀμίαντον καὶ ἀμάραντον,
incorruptible and undefiled and unfading,

τετηρημένην ἐν οὐρανοῖς εἰς ὑμᾶς 5 τοὺς
having been kept in heavens for you the [ones]

ἐν δυνάμει θεοῦ φρουρουμένους διὰ πίστεως
[2]by [3][the] power [4]of God [1]being guarded through faith

εἰς σωτηρίαν ἑτοίμην ἀποκαλυφθῆναι ἐν
to a salvation ready to be revealed at

καιρῷ ἐσχάτῳ. 6 ἐν ᾧ ἀγαλλιᾶσθε,
[2]time [1][the] last. In which ye exult,

ὀλίγον ἄρτι εἰ δέον λυπηθέντες ἐν
a little [while] yet if necessary grieving by

ποικίλοις πειρασμοῖς, 7 ἵνα τὸ δοκίμιον
manifold trials, in order that the proving

ὑμῶν τῆς πίστεως πολυτιμότερον χρυσίου
[3]of you [1]of the [2]faith[,] much more precious [than] [4]gold

τοῦ ἀπολλυμένου, διὰ πυρὸς δὲ δοκιμαζ-
- [1]of perishing, [3]through [4]fire [1]yet [2]being

ομένου, εὑρεθῇ εἰς ἔπαινον καὶ δόξαν
proved, may be found to praise and glory

καὶ τιμὴν ἐν ἀποκαλύψει Ἰησοῦ Χριστοῦ·
and honour at [the] revelation of Jesus Christ;

8 ὃν οὐκ ἰδόντες ἀγαπᾶτε, εἰς ὃν ἄρτι
whom not having seen ye love, in whom yet

μὴ ὁρῶντες πιστεύοντες δὲ ἀγαλλιᾶσθε
not seeing [2]believing [1]but ye exult

χαρᾷ ἀνεκλαλήτῳ καὶ δεδοξασμένῃ,
with joy unspeakable and having been glorified,

9 κομιζόμενοι τὸ τέλος τῆς πίστεως
obtaining the end of the(your) faith

σωτηρίαν ψυχῶν. 10 περὶ ἧς σωτηρίας
[the] salvation of [your] souls. Concerning which salvation

ἐξεζήτησαν καὶ ἐξηρεύνησαν προφῆται οἱ
[2]sought out [10]and [11]searched out [1]prophets [2]the

περὶ τῆς εἰς ὑμᾶς χάριτος προφητεύσαντες,
[4]con- [3]the [7]for [5]you [6]grace [2][ones] prophesying,
cerning

11 ἐρευνῶντες εἰς τίνα ἢ ποῖον καιρὸν
searching for what or what sort of time

ἐδήλου τὸ ἐν αὐτοῖς πνεῦμα Χριστοῦ
[6]made clear [1]the [4]in [5]them [2]Spirit [3]of Christ

[a] Or Rejoice in this
[b] Other ancient authorities read known
[c] Or omit you

within them when predicting the sufferings of Christ and the subsequent glory. ¹²It was revealed to them that they were serving not themselves but you, in the things which have now been announced to you by those who preached the good news to you through the Holy Spirit sent from heaven, things into which angels long to look.

13 Therefore gird up your minds, be sober, set your hope fully upon the grace that is coming to you at the revelation of Jesus Christ. ¹⁴As obedient children, do not be conformed to the passions of your former ignorance, ¹⁵but as he who called you is holy, be holy yourselves in all your conduct; ¹⁶since it is written, "You shall be holy, for I am holy." ¹⁷And if you invoke as Father him who judges each one impartially according to his deeds, conduct yourselves with fear throughout the time of your exile. ¹⁸You know that you were ransomed from the futile

προμαρτυρόμενον τὰ εἰς Χριστὸν παθήματα
⁷forewitnessing ⁸the ¹⁰for ¹¹Christ ⁹sufferings

καὶ τὰς μετὰ ταῦτα δόξας. 12 οἷς
¹²and ¹³the ¹⁵after ¹⁶these ¹⁴glories. To whom

ἀπεκαλύφθη ὅτι οὐχ ἑαυτοῖς ὑμῖν δὲ
it was revealed that not to themselves ²to you ¹but

διηκόνουν αὐτά, ἃ νῦν ἀνηγγέλη ὑμῖν
they the same which now were to you
ministered things, announced

διὰ τῶν εὐαγγελισαμένων ὑμᾶς ἐν
through the [ones] having evangelized you by

πνεύματι ἁγίῳ ἀποσταλέντι ἀπ' οὐρανοῦ,
²Spirit ¹[the] Holy sent forth from heaven,

εἰς ἃ ἐπιθυμοῦσιν ἄγγελοι παρακύψαι.
into ¹which ²long ³angels ⁴to look into.
things

13 Διὸ ἀναζωσάμενοι τὰς ὀσφύας τῆς
Wherefore girding up the loins of the

διανοίας ὑμῶν, νήφοντες, τελείως ἐλπίσατε
mind of you, being sober, perfectly hope

ἐπὶ τὴν φερομένην ὑμῖν χάριν ἐν
on ¹the ²being brought ⁴to you ³grace at

ἀποκαλύψει Ἰησοῦ Χριστοῦ. 14 ὡς τέκνα
[the] revelation of Jesus Christ. As children

ὑπακοῆς, μὴ συσχηματιζόμενοι ταῖς πρότε-
of obedience,* not fashioning yourselves to the ⁸form-

ρον ἐν τῇ ἀγνοίᾳ ὑμῶν ἐπιθυμίαις, 15 ἀλλὰ
erly ³in ¹the ⁴ignorance ⁵of you ¹longings, but

κατὰ τὸν καλέσαντα ὑμᾶς ἅγιον καὶ
according to ²the ³having called ⁴you ²holy [one] ⁷also
ing to

αὐτοὶ ἅγιοι ἐν πάσῃ ἀναστροφῇ γενήθητε,
⁶[your]- ⁸holy ⁹in ¹⁰all ¹¹conduct ⁵become ye,
selves

16 διότι γέγραπται· [ὅτι] ἅγιοι ἔσεσθε,
because it has been written: – Holy ye shall be,

ὅτι ἐγὼ ἅγιος. 17 καὶ εἰ πατέρα
because I [am] holy. And if ²Father

ἐπικαλεῖσθε τὸν ἀπροσωπολήμπτως κρίνοντα
¹ye invoke [as] ³the [one] ⁵without respect to persons ⁴judging

κατὰ τὸ ἑκάστου ἔργον, ἐν φόβῳ τὸν
accord- the ²of each man ¹work, ²in ³fear ⁴the
ing to

τῆς παροικίας ὑμῶν χρόνον ἀναστράφητε,
⁶of the ⁷sojourning ⁸of you ⁵time ¹pass,

18 εἰδότες ὅτι οὐ φθαρτοῖς, ἀργυρίῳ ἢ
knowing that not with corruptible silver or
things,

* Genitive of quality: " obedient children."

ways inherited from your fathers, not with perishable things such as silver or gold, [19]but with the precious blood of Christ, like that of a lamb without blemish or spot. [20]He was destined before the foundation of the world but was made manifest at the end of the times for your sake. [21]Through him you have confidence in God, who raised him from the dead and gave him glory, so that your faith and hope are in God.[d]

[22]Having purified your souls by your obedience to the truth for a sincere love of the brethren, love one another earnestly from the heart. [23]You have been born anew, not of perishable seed but of imperishable, through the living and abiding word of God; [24]for

"All flesh is like grass and all its glory like the flower of grass. The grass withers, and the flower falls, [25]but the word of the Lord abides for ever."

That word is the good news which was preached to you.

CHAPTER 2

SO put away all malice and all guile and insincerity and envy and all slander. [2]Like new-

[d] Or so that your faith is hope in God

χρυσίῳ, ἐλυτρώθητε ἐκ τῆς ματαίας ὑμῶν
gold,   ye were redeemed from the   vain   [2]of you

ἀναστροφῆς πατροπαραδότου, 19 ἀλλὰ τιμίῳ
[1]conduct   delivered from   but   with
             [your] fathers,   precious

αἵματι ὡς ἀμνοῦ ἀμώμου καὶ ἀσπίλου
blood[,] as of a lamb unblemished and unspotted[,]

Χριστοῦ, 20 προεγνωσμένου μὲν πρὸ κατα-
of Christ,   having been foreknown on one from [the]
                                           hand

βολῆς κόσμου, φανερωθέντος δὲ ἐπ' ἐσχάτου
founda- of [the]   manifested   on the in [the] last
tion   world,   other

τῶν χρόνων δι' ὑμᾶς 21 τοὺς δι' αὐτοῦ
of the times because of you the ones through him

πιστοὺς εἰς θεὸν τὸν ἐγείραντα αὐτὸν
believing in God the [one] having raised him

ἐκ νεκρῶν καὶ δόξαν αὐτῷ δόντα, ὥστε
from [the] dead and [2]glory [3]to him [1]having given, so as

τὴν πίστιν ὑμῶν καὶ ἐλπίδα εἶναι εἰς
the [1]faith [4]of you [2]and [3]hope to be in

θεόν. 22 Τὰς ψυχὰς ὑμῶν ἡγνικότες
God.   [2]The [3]souls [4]of you [1]having purified

ἐν τῇ ὑπακοῇ τῆς ἀληθείας εἰς φιλαδελφίαν
by - obedience of(to) the truth to [2]brotherly love

ἀνυπόκριτον, ἐκ καρδίας ἀλλήλους ἀγαπήσατε
[1]unfeigned, [4]from [5][the] heart [3]one another [1]love ye

ἐκτενῶς, 23 ἀναγεγεννημένοι οὐκ ἐκ σπορᾶς
[2]earnestly,   having been regenerated not by [2]seed

φθαρτῆς ἀλλὰ ἀφθάρτου, διὰ λόγου ζῶντος
[1]corruptible but incorruptible, through [4]word [1][the] living

θεοῦ καὶ μένοντος. 24 διότι πᾶσα σὰρξ
[5]of God [2]and [3]remaining. Because all flesh [is]

ὡς χόρτος, καὶ πᾶσα δόξα αὐτῆς ὡς
as grass, and all [the] glory of it as

ἄνθος χόρτου· ἐξηράνθη ὁ χόρτος, καὶ
a flower of grass; was dried the grass, and

τὸ ἄνθος ἐξέπεσεν· 25 τὸ δὲ ῥῆμα κυρίου
the flower fell out; but the word of [the] Lord

μένει εἰς τὸν αἰῶνα. τοῦτο δέ ἐστιν
remains unto the age. And this is

τὸ ῥῆμα τὸ εὐαγγελισθὲν εἰς ὑμᾶς.
the word - preached [as good news] to you.

2 Ἀποθέμενοι οὖν πᾶσαν κακίαν καὶ
  Putting away therefore all malice and

πάντα δόλον καὶ ὑποκρίσεις καὶ φθόνους
all guile and hypocrisies and envies

καὶ πάσας καταλαλιάς, 2 ὡς ἀρτιγέννητα
and all detractions, as new born

born babes, long for the pure spiritual milk, that by it you may grow up to salvation; ³for you have tasted the kindness of the Lord.

4 Come to him, to that living stone, rejected by men but in God's sight chosen and precious; ⁵and like living stones be yourselves built into a spiritual house, to be a holy priesthood, to offer spiritual sacrifices acceptable to God through Jesus Christ. ⁶For it stands in scripture:

"Behold, I am laying in Zion a stone, a cornerstone chosen and precious,
and he who believes in him will not be put to shame."

⁷To you therefore who believe, he is precious, but for those who do not believe,

"The very stone which the builders rejected
has become the head of the corner,"

⁸and

"A stone that will make men stumble, a rock that will make them fall";

for they stumble because they disobey the word, as they were destined to do.

9 But you are a chosen race, a royal priesthood, a holy nation, God's own people, that you may declare the wonderful

---

βρέφη   τὸ   λογικὸν   ἄδολον   γάλα   ἐπιποθήσατε,
babes   ²the ³spiritual ⁴pure   ⁵milk   ¹desire ye,

ἵνα   ἐν   αὐτῷ   αὐξηθῆτε   εἰς   σωτηρίαν,
in or- by   it   ye may grow   to   salvation,
der that

3 εἰ   ἐγεύσασθε   ὅτι   χρηστὸς   ὁ   κύριος.
  if   ye tasted   that ³good   ¹the ²Lord [is].

4 πρὸς   ὃν   προσερχόμενοι,   λίθον   ζῶντα,
  to whom   approaching,   ²stone   ¹a living,

ὑπὸ   ἀνθρώπων   μὲν   ἀποδεδοκιμασμένον   παρὰ
by   men   on one   having been rejected   ³by
              hand

δὲ   θεῷ   ἐκλεκτὸν   ἔντιμον,   5 καὶ
¹on the ⁴God ²chosen[,]   precious,   ²also
other

αὐτοὶ   ὡς   λίθοι   ζῶντες   οἰκοδομεῖσθε   οἶκος
¹[your]- ³as ²stones ⁴living   are being built   ⁵house
selves

πνευματικὸς   εἰς   ἱεράτευμα   ἅγιον,   ἀνενέγκαι
¹a spiritual   for ²priesthood ¹a holy, to offer

πνευματικὰς   θυσίας   εὐπροσδέκτους   θεῷ   διὰ
spiritual   sacrifices   acceptable   to through
                                        God

Ἰησοῦ   Χριστοῦ· 6 διότι   περιέχει   ἐν   γραφῇ·
Jesus   Christ;   because it is   in scripture:
                          contained

ἰδοὺ   τίθημι   ἐν   Σιὼν   λίθον   ἐκλεκτὸν
Behold I lay   in   Sion ²stone   ¹a chosen

ἀκρογωνιαῖον   ἔντιμον,   καὶ   ὁ   πιστεύων
²corner foundation ¹precious, and the [one] believing

ἐπ'   αὐτῷ   οὐ   μὴ   καταισχυνθῇ.   7 ὑμῖν
on   it(him) by no means will be shamed.   To you
                                            = Yours

οὖν   ἡ   τιμὴ   τοῖς   πιστεύουσιν·   ἀπιστοῦσιν
there- ³[is] ⁶honour ¹the [ones]   ²believingᶜ;   ²to unbelieving
fore   ⁴the   [ones]
therefore who believe is the honour;

δὲ   λίθος   ὃν   ἀπεδοκίμασαν   οἱ   οἰκοδομοῦντες,
¹but a stone which ³rejected   ¹the [ones] ²building,

οὗτος   ἐγενήθη   εἰς   κεφαλὴν   γωνίας   8 καὶ
this   came to be for   head   of [the] corner   and

λίθος   προσκόμματος   καὶ   πέτρα   σκανδάλου·
a stone   of stumbling   and a rock   of offence;

οἱ   προσκόπτουσιν   τῷ   λόγῳ   ἀπειθοῦντες,
who   stumble   at the word   disobeying,

9 εἰς   ὃ   καὶ   ἐτέθησαν·   ὑμεῖς   δὲ   γένος
  to   which indeed   they were   but ye [are] ²race
                    appointed;

ἐκλεκτόν,   βασίλειον   ἱεράτευμα,   ἔθνος   ἅγιον,
¹a chosen,   a royal   priesthood,   nation   a holy,

λαὸς   εἰς   περιποίησιν,   ὅπως   τὰς   ἀρετὰς
a people for   possession,   so as   ²the   ³virtues

deeds of him who called you out of darkness into his marvelous light. 10 Once you were no people but now you are God's people; once you had not received mercy but now you have received mercy.

11 Beloved, I beseech you as aliens and exiles to abstain from the passions of the flesh that wage war against your soul. 12 Maintain good conduct among the Gentiles, so that in case they speak against you as wrongdoers, they may see your good deeds and glorify God on the day of visitation.

13 Be subject for the Lord's sake to every human institution,* whether it be to the emperor as supreme, 14 or to governors as sent by him to punish those who do wrong and to praise those who do right. 15 For it is God's will that by doing right you should put to silence the ignorance of foolish men. 16 Live as free men, yet without using your freedom as a pretext for evil; but live as servants of God. 17 Honor all

* Or every institution ordained for men

ἐξαγγείλητε τοῦ ἐκ σκότους ὑμᾶς καλέ-
¹ye may tell out ⁴of the ⁷out ⁸darkness ⁶you ⁵having
                  [one] of

σαντος εἰς τὸ θαυμαστὸν αὐτοῦ φῶς·
called into the marvellous ³of him ¹light;

10 οἳ ποτε οὐ λαός, νῦν δὲ λαὸς θεοῦ,
who then not a but [are] a of
     [were] people, now people God,

οἱ οὐκ ἠλεημένοι, νῦν δὲ ἐλεηθέντες.
the not having been pitied, but now pitied.
[ones]

11 Ἀγαπητοί, παρακαλῶ ὡς παροίκους
Beloved, I exhort [you] as sojourners

καὶ παρεπιδήμους ἀπέχεσθαι τῶν σαρκικῶν
and aliens to abstain from – fleshly

ἐπιθυμιῶν, αἵτινες στρατεύονται κατὰ τῆς
lusts, which war against the

ψυχῆς· 12 τὴν ἀναστροφὴν ὑμῶν ἐν τοῖς
soul; ²the ²conduct ⁴of you ⁵among ⁶the

ἔθνεσιν ἔχοντες καλήν, ἵνα ἐν ᾧ κατα-
⁷nations ¹having ⁸good, in order while they
                                that

λαλοῦσιν ὑμῶν ὡς κακοποιῶν, ἐκ τῶν
speak against you as evildoers, by the
                                    (your)

καλῶν ἔργων ἐποπτεύοντες δοξάσωσιν τὸν
good works observing they may glorify –

θεὸν ἐν ἡμέρᾳ ἐπισκοπῆς.
God in a day of visitation.

13 Ὑποτάγητε πάσῃ ἀνθρωπίνῃ κτίσει
Submit to every human ordinance

διὰ τὸν κύριον· εἴτε βασιλεῖ ὡς ὑπερέχοντι,
be- the Lord: whether to a king as being supreme,
cause of

14 εἴτε ἡγεμόσιν ὡς δι' αὐτοῦ πεμπομένοις
or to governors as through him being sent

εἰς ἐκδίκησιν κακοποιῶν ἔπαινον δὲ
for vengeance of(on) evildoers ²praise ¹but

ἀγαθοποιῶν· 15 ὅτι οὕτως ἐστὶν τὸ
of welldoers; because so is the

θέλημα τοῦ θεοῦ, ἀγαθοποιοῦντας φιμοῦν
will – of God, doing good to silence

τὴν τῶν ἀφρόνων ἀνθρώπων ἀγνωσίαν·
¹the – ³of foolish ⁴men ²ignorance;

16 ὡς ἐλεύθεροι, καὶ μὴ ὡς ἐπικάλυμμα
as free, and not ³as ⁴a cloak

ἔχοντες τῆς κακίας τὴν ἐλευθερίαν, ἀλλ'
¹having the ⁵of evil the ²freedom, but

ὡς θεοῦ δοῦλοι. 17 πάντας τιμήσατε,
as of God slaves. ²All men ¹honour ye,

men. Love the brotherhood. Fear God. Honor the emperor.

18 Servants, be submissive to your masters with all respect, not only to the kind and gentle but also to the overbearing. [19] For one is approved if, mindful of God, he endures pain while suffering unjustly. [20] For what credit is it, if when you do wrong and are beaten for it you take it patiently? But if when you do right and suffer for it you take it patiently, you have God's approval. [21] For to this you have been called, because Christ also suffered for you, leaving you an example, that you should follow in his steps. [22] He committed no sin; no guile was found on his lips. [23] When he was reviled, he did not revile in return; when he suffered, he did not threaten; but he trusted to him who judges justly. [24] He himself bore our sins in his body on the tree,[f] that we might die to sin and live to righteousness. By his wounds you have been healed. [25] For you

τὴν   ἀδελφότητα   ἀγαπᾶτε,   τὸν   θεὸν
²the   ²brotherhood   ¹love,   -   ²God

φοβεῖσθε,   τὸν   βασιλέα   τιμᾶτε.   18 Οἱ
¹fear,   ²the   ³king   ¹honour.   -

οἰκέται,   ὑποτασσόμενοι   ἐν   παντὶ   φόβῳ
House   submitting yourselves   in   all   fear
servants,

τοῖς   δεσπόταις,   οὐ   μόνον   τοῖς   ἀγαθοῖς
to the(your) masters,   not   only   to the   good

καὶ   ἐπιεικέσιν   ἀλλὰ   καὶ   τοῖς   σκολιοῖς.
and   forbearing   but   also   to the   perverse.

19 τοῦτο   γὰρ   χάρις   εἰ   διὰ   συνείδησιν
For this   [is] a favour   if   because of   conscience

θεοῦ   ὑποφέρει   τις   λύπας   πάσχων   ἀδίκως.
of God   ²bears   ¹anyone   griefs   suffering   unjustly.

20 ποῖον   γὰρ   κλέος   εἰ   ἁμαρτάνοντες   καὶ
For what   glory [is it] if   sinning   and

κολαφιζόμενοι   ὑπομενεῖτε;   ἀλλ'   εἰ   ἀγαθο-
being buffeted   ye endure ?   but   if   doing

ποιοῦντες   καὶ   πάσχοντες   ὑπομενεῖτε,   τοῦτο
good   and   suffering   ye endure,   this [is]

χάρις   παρὰ   θεῷ.   21 εἰς   τοῦτο   γὰρ
a favour   with   God.   ²to   ³this   ¹For

ἐκλήθητε,   ὅτι   καὶ   Χριστὸς   ἔπαθεν   ὑπὲρ
ye were   because   indeed   Christ   suffered   on be-
called,   half of

ὑμῶν,   ὑμῖν   ὑπολιμπάνων   ὑπογραμμὸν   ἵνα
you,   ²to you   ¹leaving behind   an example   in order that

ἐπακολουθήσητε   τοῖς   ἴχνεσιν   αὐτοῦ·   22 ὃς
ye should follow   the   steps   of him;   who

ἁμαρτίαν   οὐκ   ἐποίησεν   οὐδὲ   εὑρέθη   δόλος
³sin   ¹not   ²did   nor   was ²found   ¹guile

ἐν   τῷ   στόματι   αὐτοῦ·   23 ὃς   λοιδορούμενος
in   the   mouth   of him;   who   being reviled

οὐκ   ἀντελοιδόρει,   πάσχων   οὐκ   ἠπείλει,
reviled not in return,   suffering   he threatened not,

παρεδίδου   δὲ   τῷ   κρίνοντι   δικαίως·   24 ὃς
but delivered   to the   judging   righteously;   who
[himself]   [one]

τὰς   ἁμαρτίας   ἡμῶν   αὐτὸς   ἀνήνεγκεν   ἐν
³the   ⁴sins   ⁵of us   ¹[him]self   ²carried up   in

τῷ   σώματι   αὐτοῦ   ἐπὶ   τὸ   ξύλον,   ἵνα
the   body   of him   onto   the   tree,   in order that

ταῖς   ἁμαρτίαις   ἀπογενόμενοι   τῇ   δικαιοσύνῃ
-    to sins   ¹dying   -   ⁴to righteousness

ζήσωμεν·   οὗ   τῷ   μώλωπι   ἰάθητε.
²we might live;   ³of   ¹by   bruise   ye were cured.
whom   the

f Or *carried up . . . to the tree*

were straying like sheep, but have now returned to the Shepherd and Guardian of your souls.

25 ἦτε γὰρ ὡς πρόβατα πλανώμενοι,
    ye were   ¹For   ⁴as   ⁵sheep   ³wandering,

ἀλλὰ ἐπεστράφητε νῦν ἐπὶ τὸν ποιμένα
but   ye turned   now   to   the   shepherd

καὶ ἐπίσκοπον τῶν ψυχῶν ὑμῶν.
and   bishop   of the   souls   of you.

CHAPTER 3

LIKEWISE you wives, be submissive to your husbands, so that some, though they do not obey the word, may be won without a word by the behavior of their wives, ²when they see your reverent and chaste behavior. ³Let not yours be the outward adorning with braiding of hair, decoration of gold, and wearing of robes, ⁴but let it be the hidden person of the heart with the imperishable jewel of a gentle and quiet spirit, which in God's sight is very precious. ⁵So once the holy women who hoped in God used to adorn themselves and were submissive to their husbands, ⁶as Sarah obeyed Abraham, calling him lord. And you are now her children if you do right and let nothing terrify you.

7 Likewise you husbands, live considerately with your wives, bestowing honor on the woman as the weaker

3 Ὁμοίως γυναῖκες, ὑποτασσόμεναι τοῖς
  Likewise   wives,   submitting yourselves   to the
                                   (your)

ἰδίοις ἀνδράσιν, ἵνα καὶ εἴ τινες ἀπειθοῦσιν
own   husbands,   in or-   even   if   any   disobey
                   der that

τῷ λόγῳ, διὰ τῆς τῶν γυναικῶν ἀναστροφῆς
the   word, through ¹the   ⁵of   ⁴wives   ²conduct
                   the(ir)

ἄνευ λόγου κερδηθήσονται, 2 ἐποπτεύσαντες
without a word   they will(may) be gained,   observing

τὴν ἐν φόβῳ ἁγνὴν ἀναστροφὴν ὑμῶν.
¹the   ⁵in   ⁶fear   ²pure   ³conduct   ⁴of you.

3 ὧν ἔστω οὐχ ὁ ἔξωθεν ἐμπλοκῆς
Of whom let it be   not   ¹the   ²outward   ⁴of plaiting

τριχῶν καὶ περιθέσεως χρυσίων ἢ ἐνδύσεως
⁵of hairs   ⁶and   ⁷of putting   ⁸of gold   ⁹or   ¹⁰of clothing
            round(on)   [ornaments]

ἱματίων κόσμος, 4 ἀλλ' ὁ κρυπτὸς τῆς
¹¹of(with)   ³adorning,   but   ¹the   ²hidden   ⁴of the
garments

καρδίας ἄνθρωπος ἐν τῷ ἀφθάρτῳ τοῦ
⁵heart   ³man   in(?by) the   incorruptible of the
                          [adorning]

πραέος καὶ ἡσυχίου πνεύματος, ὅ ἐστιν
meek   and   quiet   spirit,   which   is

ἐνώπιον τοῦ θεοῦ πολυτελές. 5 οὕτως
before   –   God   of great value.   so

γάρ ποτε καὶ αἱ ἅγιαι γυναῖκες αἱ
For   then   indeed   the   holy   women   –

ἐλπίζουσαι εἰς θεὸν ἐκόσμουν ἑαυτάς,
hoping   in   God   adorned   themselves,

ὑποτασσόμεναι τοῖς ἰδίοις ἀνδράσιν, 6 ὡς
submitting themselves to the(ir)   own   husbands,   as

Σάρρα ὑπήκουσεν τῷ Ἀβραάμ, κύριον
Sara   obeyed   –   Abraham,   ³lord

αὐτὸν καλοῦσα· ἧς ἐγενήθητε τέκνα
²him   ¹calling;   of whom   ye became   children

ἀγαθοποιοῦσαι καὶ μὴ φοβούμεναι μηδεμίαν
doing good   and   not   fearing   no(any)

πτόησιν. 7 Οἱ ἄνδρες ὁμοίως, συνοικοῦντες
terror.   –   Husbands   likewise,   dwelling together

κατὰ γνῶσιν ὡς ἀσθενεστέρῳ σκεύει τῷ
accord-   knowledge   as   with a weaker   vessel   the
ing to

sex, since you are joint heirs of the grace of life, in order that your prayers may not be hindered.

8 Finally, all of you, have unity of spirit, sympathy, love of the brethren, a tender heart and a humble mind. 9 Do not return evil for evil or reviling for reviling; but on the contrary bless, for to this you have been called, that you may obtain a blessing. 10 For

"He that would love life

and see good days,

let him keep his tongue from evil

and his lips from speaking guile;

11 let him turn away from evil and do right;

let him seek peace and pursue it.

12 For the eyes of the Lord are upon the righteous,

and his ears are open to their prayer.

But the face of the Lord is against those that do evil."

13 Now who is there to harm you if you are zealous for what is right? 14 But even if you do suffer for righteousness' sake, you will be blessed. Have no fear of them, nor be troubled, 15 but in your hearts

γυναικείῳ, ἀπονέμοντες τιμὴν ὡς καὶ
female,   assigning   honour   as   indeed

συγκληρονόμοις χάριτος ζωῆς, εἰς τὸ μὴ
co-heirs   of [the] grace   of life,   for   the   not

ἐγκόπτεσθαι τὰς προσευχὰς ὑμῶν. 8 Τὸ δὲ
to be hindered   the   prayers   of you.b   Now the

τέλος πάντες ὁμόφρονες, συμπαθεῖς,
end[,]   [be ye] all   of one mind,   sympathetic,

φιλάδελφοι, εὔσπλαγχνοι, ταπεινόφρονες,
loving [the] brothers, compassionate,   humble-minded,

9 μὴ ἀποδιδόντες κακὸν ἀντὶ κακοῦ ἢ
not   giving back   evil   instead of   evil   or

λοιδορίαν ἀντὶ λοιδορίας, τοὐναντίον δὲ
reviling   instead of   reviling,   but on the contrary

εὐλογοῦντες, ὅτι εἰς τοῦτο ἐκλήθητε ἵνα
blessing,   because to   this   ye were called in order that

εὐλογίαν κληρονομήσητε. 10 ὁ γὰρ θέλων
blessing   ye might inherit.   For the [one] wishing

ζωὴν ἀγαπᾶν καὶ ἰδεῖν ἡμέρας ἀγαθάς,
¹life   ¹to love   and   to see   ²days   ¹good,

παυσάτω τὴν γλῶσσαν ἀπὸ κακοῦ καὶ
let him   the(his)   tongue   from   evil   and
restrain

χείλη τοῦ μὴ λαλῆσαι δόλον, 11 ἐκκλινάτω
[his] lips   -   not   to speakd   guile,   ¹let him turn aside

δὲ ἀπὸ κακοῦ καὶ ποιησάτω ἀγαθόν,
¹and from   evil   and   let him do   good,

ζητησάτω εἰρήνην καὶ διωξάτω αὐτήν·
let him seek   peace   and   pursue   it;

12 ὅτι ὀφθαλμοὶ κυρίου ἐπὶ δικαίους καὶ
because [the] eyes   of [the]   [are] on   [the]   and
          Lord   righteous

ὦτα αὐτοῦ εἰς δέησιν αὐτῶν, πρόσωπον
[the]   of him [open] to   [the]   of them,   ²[the] face
ears   petition

δὲ κυρίου ἐπὶ ποιοῦντας κακά.
¹but   of [the]   [is]   [ones] doing   evil things.
      Lord   against

13 Καὶ τίς ὁ κακώσων ὑμᾶς ἐὰν τοῦ
And   who the   harming   you   if   ³of the
      [is] [one]

ἀγαθοῦ ζηλωταὶ γένησθε; 14 ἀλλ' εἰ καὶ
⁴good   ²zealots   ¹ye become?   but   if indeed

πάσχοιτε διὰ δικαιοσύνην, μακάριοι. τὸν
ye suffer because of righteousness, blessed [are ye].   ²the

δὲ φόβον αὐτῶν μὴ φοβηθῆτε μηδὲ
¹But   ⁴fear   ⁵of them   ²fear ye not   nor

ταραχθῆτε, 15 κύριον δὲ τὸν Χριστὸν
be ye troubled,   ¹but   ⁴[as] ⁵Lord   -   ³Christ

reverence Christ as Lord. Always be prepared to make a defense to any one who calls you to account for the hope that is in you, yet do it with gentleness and reverence; [16]and keep your conscience clear. so that, when you are abused, those who revile your good behavior in Christ may be put to shame. [17]For it is better to suffer for doing right, if that should be God's will, than for doing wrong. [18]For Christ also died[g] for sins once for all, the righteous for the unrighteous, that he might bring us to God, being put to death in the flesh but made alive in the spirit; [19]in which he went and preached to the spirits in prison, [20]who formerly did not obey, when God's patience waited in the days of Noah, during the building of the ark, in which a few, that is, eight persons, were saved through water. [21]Baptism, which corresponds to this, now saves you, not as a removal of dirt from the body but as an appeal to God for a clear conscience, through the

ἁγιάσατε ἐν ταῖς καρδίαις ὑμῶν, ἕτοιμοι
²sanctify   in   the   hearts   of you,   ready
ἀεὶ πρὸς ἀπολογίαν παντὶ τῷ αἰτοῦντι
always for   defence   to every one   asking
ὑμᾶς λόγον περὶ τῆς ἐν ὑμῖν ἐλπίδος,
you   a word concerning ¹the ³in ⁴you   ²hope,
16 ἀλλὰ μετὰ πραΰτητος καὶ φόβου,
but   with   meekness   and   fear,
συνείδησιν ἔχοντες ἀγαθήν, ἵνα ἐν ᾧ
²conscience ¹having ²a good, in order that while
καταλαλεῖσθε καταισχυνθῶσιν οἱ ἐπηρεάζον-
ye are spoken against ²may be shamed [by] ¹the [ones] ²abusing
τες ὑμῶν τὴν ἀγαθὴν ἐν Χριστῷ
[you] ⁷of you ⁴the ⁵good ³in ⁶Christ
ἀναστροφήν.   17 κρεῖττον γὰρ ἀγαθοποι-
⁶conduct.   For [it is] better   doing
οῦντας, εἰ θέλοι τὸ θέλημα τοῦ θεοῦ,
good,   if ⁴wills ¹the ²will — ³of God,
πάσχειν ἢ κακοποιοῦντας. 18 ὅτι καὶ
to suffer than   doing evil.   Because indeed
Χριστὸς ἅπαξ περὶ ἁμαρτιῶν ἀπέθανεν,
Christ   once ²concerning ³sins   ¹died,
δίκαιος ὑπὲρ ἀδίκων, ἵνα ὑμᾶς προσαγάγῃ
a righteous on be- unrighteous in or- ²you ¹he might
man   half of   ones,   der that   bring
τῷ θεῷ, θανατωθεὶς μὲν σαρκὶ ζωοποιηθεὶς
— to   being put to on one in [the] quickened
God,   death   hand flesh[,]
δὲ πνεύματι· 19 ἐν ᾧ καὶ τοῖς ἐν
on the in [the]   in which indeed ²to the ⁴in
other   spirit;
φυλακῇ πνεύμασιν πορευθεὶς ἐκήρυξεν,
¹prison ³spirits   ²going   he proclaimed,
20 ἀπειθήσασίν ποτε ὅτε ἀπεξεδέχετο ἡ
to disobeying ones then when   ⁴waited   ¹the
τοῦ θεοῦ μακροθυμία ἐν ἡμέραις Νῶε
— ³of God ²longsuffering in [the] days of Noe
κατασκευαζομένης κιβωτοῦ, εἰς ἣν ὀλίγοι,
²being prepared ¹an ark,³ in which a few,
τοῦτ᾽ ἔστιν ὀκτὼ ψυχαί, διεσώθησαν δι᾽
this   is   eight   souls,   were through
                              quite saved
ὕδατος. 21 ὃ καὶ ὑμᾶς ἀντίτυπον νῦν
water.   ¹Which ²also ⁴us   ³figure   ⁴now
σῴζει βάπτισμα, οὐ σαρκὸς ἀπόθεσις
⁵saves [even] baptism, not ³of [the] ¹a putting
                              flesh   away
ῥύπου ἀλλὰ συνειδήσεως ἀγαθῆς ἐπερώτημα
²of [the] but ³conscience ²of a good ¹an answer
filth

[g] Other ancient authorities read suffered

resurrection of Jesus Christ, [22] who has gone into heaven and is at the right hand of God, with angels, authorities, and powers subject to him.

εἰς θεόν, δι' ἀναστάσεως Ἰησοῦ Χριστοῦ,
toward God, through [the] resurrection of Jesus Christ,

22 ὅς ἐστιν ἐν δεξιᾷ θεοῦ, πορευθεὶς
who is at [the] right of God, having gone
[hand]

εἰς οὐρανόν, ὑποταγέντων αὐτῷ ἀγγέλων
into heaven, [6]being subjected [7]to him [1]angels

καὶ ἐξουσιῶν καὶ δυνάμεων.
[2]and [3]authorities [4]and [5]powers[a].

CHAPTER 4

4 Χριστοῦ οὖν παθόντος σαρκὶ καὶ ὑμεῖς
[3]Christ [1]there-   having   in [the]   [2]also   [1]ye
fore   suffered[b]   flesh

SINCE therefore Christ suffered in the flesh,[h] arm yourselves with the same thought, for whoever has suffered in the flesh has ceased from sin, [2]so as to live for the rest of the time in the flesh no longer by human passions but by the will of God. [3]Let the time that is past suffice for doing what the Gentiles like to do, living in licentiousness, passions, drunkenness, revels, carousing, and lawless idolatry. [4]They are surprised that you do not now join them in the same wild profligacy, and they abuse you; [5]but they will give account to him who is ready to judge the living and the dead. [6]For this is why the gospel was preached even to the dead, that though judged in the flesh like men, they might live in the spirit like God.

τὴν αὐτὴν ἔννοιαν ὁπλίσασθε, ὅτι ὁ
[4]the   [5]same   [6]mind   [3]arm your-   because the
selves [with],   [one]

παθὼν σαρκὶ πέπαυται ἁμαρτίας, 2 εἰς
having   in [the] flesh   has ceased   from sin,   for
suffered

τὸ μηκέτι ἀνθρώπων ἐπιθυμίαις ἀλλὰ
the   [1]no longer   [6]of men   [4]in [the] lusts   [10]but

θελήματι θεοῦ τὸν ἐπίλοιπον ἐν σαρκὶ
[11]in [the] will   [12]of God   [3]the   [4]remaining   [5]in [7][the] flesh

βιῶσαι χρόνον. 3 ἀρκετὸς γὰρ ὁ παρεληλυ-
[2]to live   [8]time.   For [5]sufficient   [1]the [4]having passed

θὼς χρόνος τὸ βούλημα τῶν ἐθνῶν
away   [2]time [is] [7]the   [6]purpose   [9]of the   [10]nations

κατειργάσθαι, πεπορευμένους ἐν ἀσελγείαις,
[8]to have worked out,   having gone [on]   in licentiousnesses,

ἐπιθυμίαις, οἰνοφλυγίαις, κώμοις, πότοις
lusts,   debaucheries,   carousals,   drinking
bouts

καὶ ἀθεμίτοις εἰδωλολατρίαις. 4 ἐν ᾧ
and   unlawful   idolatries.   While

ξενίζονται μὴ συντρεχόντων ὑμῶν εἰς
they are surprised [2]not   [3]running with   [1]you[a]   to

τὴν αὐτὴν τῆς ἀσωτίας ἀνάχυσιν, βλασ-
the   same   –   [2]of profligacy   [3]excess,   blas-

φημοῦντες· 5 οἳ ἀποδώσουσιν λόγον τῷ
pheming;   who   will render   account to the
[one]

ἑτοίμως ἔχοντι κρῖναι ζῶντας καὶ νεκρούς.
readily   having   to judge   living   and   dead.
= who is ready

6 εἰς τοῦτο γὰρ καὶ νεκροῖς εὐηγγελίσθη,
[2]for   [3]this   [1]For indeed   [2]to   [1]good news
dead men   was preached,

ἵνα κριθῶσι μὲν κατὰ ἀνθρώπους
in order   [2]they might   [1]on one   according to   men
that   be judged   hand

σαρκί, ζῶσι δὲ κατὰ θεὸν πνεύματι.
in [the]   [2]might   [1]on the according   God   in [the] spirit.
flesh,   live   other   to

[h] Other ancient authorities add for us; some for you

7 The end of all things is at hand; therefore keep sane and sober for your prayers. [8]Above all hold unfailing your love for one another, since love covers a multitude of sins. [9]Practice hospitality ungrudgingly to one another. [10]As each has received a gift, employ it for one another, as good stewards of God's varied grace: [11]whoever speaks, as one who utters oracles of God; whoever renders service, as one who renders it by the strength which God supplies; in order that in everything God may be glorified through Jesus Christ. To him belong glory and dominion for ever and ever. Amen.

12 Beloved, do not be surprised at the fiery ordeal which comes upon you to prove you, as though something strange were happening to you. [13]But rejoice in so far as you share Christ's sufferings, that you may also rejoice and be glad when his glory is revealed. [14]If you are reproached for the name of Christ, you are blessed, because the spirit of glory[f] and of

[f] Other ancient authorities insert *and of power*

7 Πάντων δὲ τὸ τέλος ἤγγικεν.
Now of all things   the   end   has drawn near.

σωφρονήσατε οὖν καὶ νήψατε εἰς
Be ye soberminded therefore and be *ye* sober unto

προσευχάς· 8 πρὸ πάντων τὴν εἰς ἑαυτοὺς
prayers;   before all things   –   [4]to [5]yourselves

ἀγάπην ἐκτενῆ ἔχοντες, ὅτι ἀγάπη
[3]love   [2]fervent [1]having,   because   love

καλύπτει πλῆθος ἁμαρτιῶν· 9 φιλόξενοι εἰς
covers a multitude of sins;   [be] hospitable to

ἀλλήλους ἄνευ γογγυσμοῦ· 10 ἕκαστος καθὼς
one another without murmuring;   each one as

ἔλαβεν χάρισμα, εἰς ἑαυτοὺς αὐτὸ διακον-
he received a gift,   [3]to [4]yourselves [2]it [1]minister-

οῦντες ὡς καλοὶ οἰκονόμοι ποικίλης χάριτος
ing   as good   stewards of [the] manifold grace

θεοῦ· 11 εἴ τις λαλεῖ, ὡς λόγια θεοῦ·
of God;   if anyone speaks, as [the] of God;
                                       oracles

εἴ τις διακονεῖ, ὡς ἐξ ἰσχύος ἧς χορηγεῖ
if anyone ministers, as by strength which [3]supplies

ὁ θεός· ἵνα ἐν πᾶσιν δοξάζηται ὁ θεὸς
– [1]God; in or- in all things [2]may be glorified – [1]God
          der that

διὰ Ἰησοῦ Χριστοῦ, ᾧ ἐστιν ἡ δόξα
through Jesus   Christ, to whom is[c] the   glory
                           =whose is

καὶ τὸ κράτος εἰς τοὺς αἰῶνας τῶν
and the might unto the   ages   of the

αἰώνων· ἀμήν.
ages :   Amen.

12 Ἀγαπητοί, μὴ ξενίζεσθε τῇ ἐν ὑμῖν
   Beloved, be not surprised [at] [1]the [4]among [5]you

πυρώσει πρὸς πειρασμὸν ὑμῖν γινομένῃ,
[2]fiery trial [3]for [7]trial [6]to you [3]happening,

ὡς ξένου ὑμῖν συμβαίνοντος, 13 ἀλλὰ
as a surprising [2]to you [1]occurring[a], but
    thing

καθὸ κοινωνεῖτε τοῖς τοῦ Χριστοῦ
[2]as [3]ye share [4]the – [6]of Christ

παθήμασιν χαίρετε, ἵνα καὶ ἐν τῇ ἀπο-
[5]sufferings [1]rejoice, in order also at the reve-
                          that

καλύψει τῆς δόξης αὐτοῦ χαρῆτε ἀγαλ-
lation of the glory of him ye may exult-
                                rejoice

λιώμενοι. 14 εἰ ὀνειδίζεσθε ἐν ὀνόματι
ing.   If ye are reproached in [the] name

Χριστοῦ, μακάριοι, ὅτι τὸ τῆς δόξης
of Christ, blessed [are ye], because [1]the – [5]of glory

God rests upon you. ¹⁵But let none of you suffer as a murderer, or a thief, or a wrongdoer, or a mischief-maker; ¹⁶yet if one suffers as a Christian, let him not be ashamed, but under that name let him glorify God. ¹⁷For the time has come for judgment to begin with the household of God; and if it begins with us, what will be the end of those who do not obey the gospel of God? ¹⁸And

"If the righteous man is scarcely saved, where will the impious and sinner appear?"

¹⁹Therefore let those who suffer according to God's will do right and entrust their souls to a faithful Creator.

καὶ τὸ τοῦ θεοῦ πνεῦμα ἐφ' ὑμᾶς
⁴and ⁵the(?that) – ⁶of God ²spirit ⁸on ⁹you

ἀναπαύεται. **15** μὴ γάρ τις ὑμῶν πασχέτω
⁷rests. ³Not ¹for ⁴anyone ⁵of you ²let ²suffer

ὡς φονεὺς ἢ κλέπτης ἢ κακοποιὸς ἢ
as a murderer or a thief or an evildoer or

ὡς ἀλλοτριεπίσκοπος· **16** εἰ δὲ ὡς
as a pryer into other men's affairs; but if as

Χριστιανός, μὴ αἰσχυνέσθω, δοξαζέτω δὲ
a Christian, let him not be shamed, but let him glorify

τὸν θεὸν ἐν τῷ ὀνόματι τούτῳ. **17** ὅτι
– God by this name. Because

[ὁ] καιρὸς τοῦ ἄρξασθαι τὸ κρίμα ἀπὸ
the time – to begin^d the judgment from
[?has come]

τοῦ οἴκου τοῦ θεοῦ· εἰ δὲ πρῶτον ἀφ'
the household – of God; and if firstly from

ἡμῶν, τί τὸ τέλος τῶν ἀπειθούντων
us, what [will be] the end of the [ones] disobeying

τῷ τοῦ θεοῦ εὐαγγελίῳ; **18** καὶ εἰ ὁ
the – ²of God ¹gospel? and if the

δίκαιος μόλις σῴζεται, ὁ [δὲ] ἀσεβὴς
righteous man scarcely is saved, ²the – ¹impious

καὶ ἁμαρτωλὸς ποῦ φανεῖται; **19** ὥστε
⁴and ⁵sinner ¹where ²will ³appear? so as

καὶ οἱ πάσχοντες κατὰ τὸ θέλημα τοῦ
indeed the suffering accord- the will –
[ones] ing to

θεοῦ πιστῷ κτίστῃ παρατιθέσθωσαν τὰς
of God ⁴to a ⁵Creator ¹let them commit ²the
faithful

ψυχὰς αὐτῶν ἐν ἀγαθοποιΐᾳ.
³souls ⁴of them in welldoing.

CHAPTER 5

SO I exhort the elders among you, as a fellow elder and a witness of the sufferings of Christ as well as a partaker in the glory that is to be revealed. ²Tend the flock of God that is your charge,^j not by constraint but willingly,^k

^j Other ancient authorities add *exercising the oversight*
^k Other ancient authorities add *as God would have you*

5 Πρεσβυτέρους οὖν ἐν ὑμῖν παρακαλῶ
Elders there- among you I exhort
fore

ὁ συμπρεσβύτερος καὶ μάρτυς τῶν τοῦ
the co-elder and witness ¹of the –

Χριστοῦ παθημάτων, ὁ καὶ τῆς μελλούσης
²of Christ ³sufferings. ¹the ²also ⁴of the ⁶being about

ἀποκαλύπτεσθαι δόξης κοινωνός· **2** ποιμάνατε
⁷to be revealed ⁵glory ³sharer: shepherd

τὸ ἐν ὑμῖν ποίμνιον τοῦ θεοῦ, μὴ
¹the ⁴among ⁵you ³flock ²of God, not

ἀναγκαστῶς ἀλλὰ ἑκουσίως κατὰ θεόν,
by way of but willingly accord- God,
compulsion ing to

not for shameful gain but eagerly, ³not as domineering over those in your charge but being examples to the flock. ⁴And when the chief Shepherd is manifested you will obtain the unfading crown of glory. ⁵Likewise you that are younger be subject to the elders. Clothe yourselves, all of you, with humility toward one another, for "God opposes the proud, but gives grace to the humble."

6 Humble yourselves therefore under the mighty hand of God, that in due time he may exalt you. ⁷Cast all your anxieties on him, for he cares about you. ⁸Be sober, be watchful. Your adversary the devil prowls around like a roaring lion, seeking some one to devour. ⁹Resist him, firm in your faith, knowing that the same experience of suffering is required of your brotherhood throughout the world. ¹⁰And after you have suffered a little while, the God of all grace, who has called you to his eternal glory in Christ, will himself restore, establish, and strengthen*l* you. ¹¹To

μηδὲ αἰσχροκερδῶς ἀλλὰ προθύμως, 3 μηδ'
nor from eagerness for but eagerly, nor
base gain

ὡς κατακυριεύοντες τῶν κλήρων ἀλλὰ
as exercising lordship over the lots* but

τύποι γινόμενοι τοῦ ποιμνίου· 4 καὶ
²examples ¹becoming of the flock; and

φανερωθέντος τοῦ ἀρχιποίμενος κομιεῖσθε
appearing the chief shepherdᵃ ye will receive
=when the chief shepherd appears

τὸν ἀμαράντινον τῆς δόξης στέφανον.
the unfading – ²of glory ¹crown.

5 Ὁμοίως, νεώτεροι, ὑποτάγητε πρεσβυτέ-
Likewise, younger men, submit yourselves to older

ροις· πάντες δὲ ἀλλήλοις τὴν ταπεινοφρο-
men; and all ²to one another – ²humil-

σύνην ἐγκομβώσασθε, ὅτι ὁ θεὸς ὑπερηφάνοις
ity ¹gird ye on, because – God ²arrogant men

ἀντιτάσσεται, ταπεινοῖς δὲ δίδωσιν χάριν.
¹resists, but to humble men he gives grace.

6 Ταπεινώθητε οὖν ὑπὸ τὴν κραταιὰν
Be ye humbled therefore under the mighty

χεῖρα τοῦ θεοῦ, ἵνα ὑμᾶς ὑψώσῃ ἐν
hand – of God, in order ²you ¹he may exalt in
that

καιρῷ, 7 πᾶσαν τὴν μέριμναν ὑμῶν
time, ²all ³the ⁴anxiety ⁵of you

ἐπιρίψαντες ἐπ' αὐτόν, ὅτι αὐτῷ μέλει
¹casting on him, because ²to him ¹it matters

περὶ ὑμῶν. 8 Νήψατε, γρηγορήσατε. ὁ
concerning you. Be ye sober, watch ye. The

ἀντίδικος ὑμῶν διάβολος ὡς λέων ὠρυόμενος
adversary of you [the] devil as a lion roaring

περιπατεῖ ζητῶν τινα καταπιεῖν· 9 ᾧ
walks about seeking whom to devour; whom

ἀντίστητε στερεοὶ τῇ πίστει, εἰδότες τὰ
oppose firm in the faith, knowing the

αὐτὰ τῶν παθημάτων τῇ ἐν τῷ κόσμῳ
same of the sufferings ²in ⁵in ⁴the ⁷world
things the

ὑμῶν ἀδελφότητι ἐπιτελεῖσθαι. 10 Ὁ δὲ
⁶of you ³brotherhood ¹to be accomplished. ²the ¹Now

θεὸς πάσης χάριτος, ὁ καλέσας ὑμᾶς
God of all grace, the [one] having called you

εἰς τὴν αἰώνιον αὐτοῦ δόξαν ἐν Χριστῷ,
to the ¹eternal ²of him ²glory in Christ,

ὀλίγον παθόντας αὐτὸς καταρτίσει, στηρίξει,
¹[you] ²having [him]self will adjust, confirm,
²a little suffered

l Other ancient authorities read *restore, establish, strengthen and settle*

* That is, the various spheres assigned to the elders.

him be the dominion for
ever and ever. Amen.
  12 By Silva′nus, a
faithful brother as I
regard him, I have
written briefly to you,
exhorting and declaring
that this is the true
grace of God; stand fast
in it. [13]She who is at
Babylon, who is likewise
chosen, sends you greet-
ings; and so does my son
Mark. [14]Greet one
another with the kiss of
love.
  Peace to all of you
that are in Christ.

σθενώσει,   θεμελιώσει.   11 αὐτῷ   τὸ   κράτος
strengthen,   found.   To him [is][c] the   might
                                            =His is*

εἰς   τοὺς   αἰῶνας   τῶν   αἰώνων·   ἀμήν.
unto   the   ages   of the   ages: Amen.

  12 Διὰ   Σιλουανοῦ   ὑμῖν   τοῦ   πιστοῦ
     Through   Silvanus   to you   the   faithful

ἀδελφοῦ,   ὡς   λογίζομαι,   δι᾿   ὀλίγων   ἔγραψα,
brother,   as   I reckon,   by   a few   I wrote,
                                 means of [words]

παρακαλῶν   καὶ   ἐπιμαρτυρῶν   ταύτην   εἶναι
exhorting   and   witnessing   this   to be

ἀληθῆ   χάριν   τοῦ   θεοῦ,   εἰς   ἣν   στῆτε.
[the] true   grace   –   of God,   in   which ye stand.

  13 Ἀσπάζεται   ὑμᾶς   ἡ   ἐν   Βαβυλῶνι
     [10]greets   [11]you   [1]The   [3]in   [4]Babylon

συνεκλεκτὴ   καὶ   Μᾶρκος   ὁ   υἱός   μου.
[2]co-chosen   [5]and   [6]Mark   [7]the   [8]son   [9]of me.
[? church]

  14 ἀσπάσασθε   ἀλλήλους   ἐν   φιλήματι   ἀγάπης.
     Greet ye   one another   with   a kiss   of love.

  Εἰρήνη   ὑμῖν   πᾶσιν   τοῖς   ἐν   Χριστῷ.
  Peace   to you   all   the ones   in   Christ.

II. PETER 1

CHAPTER 1

SIMON   Peter, a
servant and apostle
of Jesus Christ,
  To those who have
obtained a faith of equal
standing with ours in the
righteousness of our
God and Savior Jesus
Christ:[a]
  2 May grace and
peace be multiplied to
you in the knowledge of
God and of Jesus our
Lord.
  3 His divine power has
granted to us all things

1 Συμεὼν   Πέτρος   δοῦλος   καὶ   ἀπόστολος
   Symeon   Peter   a slave   and   an apostle

Ἰησοῦ   Χριστοῦ   τοῖς   ἰσότιμον   ἡμῖν
of Jesus   Christ   [1]to the   [3]equally   [4]with
                    [ones]   precious   us

λαχοῦσιν   πίστιν   ἐν   δικαιοσύνῃ   τοῦ   θεοῦ
[2]having   [4]faith   in   righteousness   of the   God
obtained   [the]

ἡμῶν   καὶ   σωτῆρος   Ἰησοῦ   Χριστοῦ·
of us   and   Saviour   Jesus   Christ :

2 χάρις   ὑμῖν   καὶ   εἰρήνη   πληθυνθείη   ἐν
   Grace   to you   and   peace   may it be multiplied   by

ἐπιγνώσει   τοῦ   θεοῦ   καὶ   Ἰησοῦ   τοῦ
a full knowledge   –   of God   and   of Jesus   the

κυρίου   ἡμῶν.
Lord   of us.

3 Ὡς   τὰ   πάντα   ἡμῖν   τῆς   θείας   δυνάμεως
   As   –   all things   to us   the   divine   power
              =his divine power has given us all things . . .

[a] Or of our God and the
Savior Jesus Christ

* Cf. 4. 11 (a statement of fact, not a wish).

that pertain to life and
godliness, through the
knowledge of him who
called us to[b] his own
glory and excellence, [4] by
which he has granted to
us his precious and very
great promises, that
through these you may
escape from the cor-
ruption that is in the
world because of passion,
and become partakers of
the divine nature. [5] For
this very reason make
every effort to supple-
ment your faith with
virtue, and virtue with
knowledge, [6] and know-
ledge with self-control,
and self-control with
steadfastness, and stead-
fastness with godliness,
[7] and godliness with
brotherly affection, and
brotherly affection with
love. [8] For if these things
are yours and abound,
they keep you from being
ineffective or unfruitful
in the knowledge of our
Lord Jesus Christ. [9] For
whoever lacks these
things is blind and short-
sighted and has for-
gotten that he was
cleansed from his old
sins. [10] Therefore, brethren, be the more zealous

αὐτοῦ τὰ πρὸς ζωὴν καὶ εὐσέβειαν δεδωρημένης
of him - [belong- life and piety having given[a]
ing] to

διὰ τῆς ἐπιγνώσεως τοῦ καλέσαντος ἡμᾶς
through the full knowledge of the [one] having called us

ἰδίᾳ δόξῃ καὶ ἀρετῇ, 4 δι' ὧν τὰ τίμια
to [his] glory and virtue, through which the [3]precious
own things

καὶ μέγιστα ἡμῖν ἐπαγγέλματα δεδώρηται,
[4]and [5]very great [2]to us [6]promises [1]he has given,

ἵνα διὰ τούτων γένησθε θείας κοινωνοὶ
in or- through these ye might [3]of a divine [1]sharers
der that become

φύσεως, ἀποφυγόντες τῆς ἐν τῷ κόσμῳ
[3]nature, escaping from [1]the [3]in [4]the [5]world

ἐν ἐπιθυμίᾳ φθορᾶς. 5 καὶ αὐτὸ τοῦτο
[6]by [7]lust [2]corruption. [2]also [3]for this very thing
(reason)

δὲ σπουδὴν πᾶσαν παρεισενέγκαντες
[1]But [4]diligence [5]all [6]bringing in

ἐπιχορηγήσατε ἐν τῇ πίστει ὑμῶν τὴν
supply in the faith of you -

ἀρετήν, ἐν δὲ τῇ ἀρετῇ τὴν γνῶσιν,
virtue, and in - virtue - knowledge,

6 ἐν δὲ τῇ γνώσει τὴν ἐγκράτειαν,
and in - knowledge - self-control,

ἐν δὲ τῇ ἐγκρατείᾳ τὴν ὑπομονήν, ἐν
and in - self-control - endurance, [2]in

δὲ τῇ ὑπομονῇ τὴν εὐσέβειαν, 7 ἐν δὲ
[1]and - endurance - piety, and in

τῇ εὐσεβείᾳ τὴν φιλαδελφίαν, ἐν δὲ
- piety - brotherly friendship, and in

τῇ φιλαδελφίᾳ τὴν ἀγάπην. 8 ταῦτα
- brotherly friendship - love. these things

γὰρ ὑμῖν ὑπάρχοντα καὶ πλεονάζοντα
For [2]in you [1]being and abounding

οὐκ ἀργοὺς οὐδὲ ἀκάρπους καθίστησιν
[3]not [4]barren [5]nor [6]unfruitful [1]makes [2][you]

εἰς τὴν τοῦ κυρίου ἡμῶν Ἰησοῦ Χριστοῦ
in [1]the [2]of the [4]Lord [5]of us [6]Jesus [7]Christ

ἐπίγνωσιν· 9 ᾧ γὰρ μὴ πάρεστιν ταῦτα,
[3]full knowledge; for [he] [3]not [2]is(are) [1]these
in whom [4]present things,

τυφλός ἐστιν μυωπάζων, λήθην λαβὼν
[3]blind [1]is being short-sighted, forgetfulness taking
= being forgetful

τοῦ καθαρισμοῦ τῶν πάλαι αὐτοῦ ἁμαρτιῶν.
of the cleansing of the [2]in time [3]of him [1]sins.
past

10 διὸ μᾶλλον, ἀδελφοί, σπουδάσατε
Wherefore rather, brothers, be ye diligent

[b] Or by

to confirm your call and
election, for if you do
this you will never fall;
[11] so there will be richly
provided for you an
entrance into the eternal
kingdom of our Lord
and Savior Jesus Christ.

12 Therefore I intend
always to remind you of
these things, though you
know them and are
established in the truth
that you have. [13] I think
it right, as long as I am
in this body,[c] to arouse
you by way of reminder,
[14] since I know that the
putting off of my body[c]
will be soon, as our Lord
Jesus Christ showed me.
[15] And I will see to it
that after my departure
you may be able at any
time to recall these
things.

16 For we did not
follow cleverly devised
myths when we made
known to you the power
and coming of our Lord
Jesus Christ, but we
were eyewitnesses of his
majesty. [17] For when he
received honor and glory
from God the Father
and the voice was borne
to him by the Majestic

βεβαίαν ὑμῶν τὴν κλῆσιν καὶ ἐκλογὴν
[2]firm [7]of you [3]the [4]calling [5]and [6]choice
ποιεῖσθαι· ταῦτα γὰρ ποιοῦντες οὐ μὴ
[1]to make; for these things doing by no means
πταίσητέ ποτε. 11 οὕτως γὰρ πλουσίως
ye will fail ever. For so [2]richly
ἐπιχορηγηθήσεται ὑμῖν ἡ εἴσοδος εἰς τὴν
[1]will be supplied [2]to you the entrance into the
αἰώνιον βασιλείαν τοῦ κυρίου ἡμῶν καὶ
eternal kingdom of the Lord of us and
σωτῆρος Ἰησοῦ Χριστοῦ.
Saviour Jesus Christ.

12 Διὸ μελλήσω ἀεὶ ὑμᾶς ὑπομιμνήσκειν
Wherefore I *will* intend always you to remind
περὶ τούτων, καίπερ εἰδότας καὶ
concerning these things, though knowing and
ἐστηριγμένους ἐν τῇ παρούσῃ ἀληθείᾳ.
having been confirmed in the present truth.
13 δίκαιον δὲ ἡγοῦμαι, ἐφ᾽ ὅσον εἰμὶ
And [2]right [1]I deem [it], so long as† I am
ἐν τούτῳ τῷ σκηνώματι, διεγείρειν ὑμᾶς
in this - tabernacle, to rouse you
ἐν ὑπομνήσει, 14 εἰδὼς ὅτι ταχινή ἐστιν
by a reminder, knowing that soon is
ἡ ἀπόθεσις τοῦ σκηνώματός μου, καθὼς
the putting off of the tabernacle of me, as
καὶ ὁ κύριος ἡμῶν Ἰησοῦς Χριστὸς
indeed the Lord of us Jesus Christ
ἐδήλωσέν μοι· 15 σπουδάσω δὲ καὶ
made clear to me; and I will be diligent also
ἑκάστοτε ἔχειν ὑμᾶς μετὰ τὴν ἐμὴν
[6]always [7]to have [5]you [8]after - [4]my
ἔξοδον τὴν τούτων μνήμην ποιεῖσθαι.
[5]exodus [1]the [10]of these things [2]memory [1]to cause.

16 οὐ γὰρ σεσοφισμένοις μύθοις ἐξακολου-
For not [3]having been [2]fables [1]follow-
cleverly devised
θήσαντες ἐγνωρίσαμεν ὑμῖν τὴν τοῦ κυρίου
ing we made known to you [1]the [5]of the [6]Lord
ἡμῶν Ἰησοῦ Χριστοῦ δύναμιν καὶ
[7]of us [8]Jesus [9]Christ [2]power [3]and
παρουσίαν, ἀλλ᾽ ἐπόπται γενηθέντες τῆς
[4]presence, but [2]eyewitnesses [1]having become [3]of the
ἐκείνου μεγαλειότητος. 17 λαβὼν γὰρ
[5]of that one [4]majesty. For receiving
παρὰ θεοῦ πατρὸς τιμὴν καὶ δόξαν
from God [the] Father honour and glory
φωνῆς ἐνεχθείσης αὐτῷ τοιᾶσδε ὑπὸ τῆς
[2]a voice [3]being borne[=] [4]to him [1]such by the

Glory, "This is my beloved Son,[d] with whom I am well pleased," [18]we heard this voice borne from heaven, for we were with him on the holy mountain. [19]And we have the prophetic word made more sure. You will do well to pay attention to this as to a lamp shining in a dark place, until the day dawns and the morning star rises in your hearts. [20]First of all you must understand this, that no prophecy of scripture is a matter of one's own interpretation, [21]because no prophecy ever came by the impulse of man, but men moved by the Holy Spirit spoke from God.[e]

μεγαλοπρεποῦς   δόξης·   ὁ   υἱός   μου   ὁ
magnificent   glory :   The Son   of me the

ἀγαπητός   μου   οὗτός   ἐστιν,   εἰς   ὃν   ἐγὼ
beloved   of me   this   is,   in whom   I

εὐδόκησα,   —   18 καὶ   ταύτην   τὴν   φωνὴν
was wellpleased,—   and   this   -   voice

ἡμεῖς   ἠκούσαμεν   ἐξ   οὐρανοῦ   ἐνεχθεῖσαν
we   heard   ²out of ³heaven   ¹being borne

σὺν   αὐτῷ   ὄντες   ἐν   τῷ   ἁγίῳ   ὄρει.   19 καὶ
⁵with ⁶him ⁴being in the   holy mountain.   And

ἔχομεν   βεβαιότερον   τὸν   προφητικὸν   λόγον,
we have   more firm   the   prophetic   word,

ᾧ   καλῶς   ποιεῖτε   προσέχοντες   ὡς   λύχνῳ
to ²well   ¹ye do   taking heed   as to a lamp
which

φαίνοντι   ἐν   αὐχμηρῷ   τόπῳ,   ἕως   οὗ
shining   in   a murky   place,   until

ἡμέρα   διαυγάσῃ   καὶ   φωσφόρος   ἀνατείλῃ
day   dawns   and [the] daystar   rises

ἐν   ταῖς   καρδίαις   ὑμῶν·   20 τοῦτο   πρῶτον
in   the   hearts   of you;   ²this   ³firstly

γινώσκοντες,   ὅτι   πᾶσα   προφητεία   γραφῆς
¹knowing,   that   every   prophecy   of scripture
                                           =no . . . is . . .

ἰδίας   ἐπιλύσεως   οὐ   γίνεται·   21 οὐ   γὰρ
of [its] own solution   not becomes;   for not

θελήματι   ἀνθρώπου   ἠνέχθη   προφητεία
by will   of man   ²was borne   ¹prophecy

ποτέ,   ἀλλὰ   ὑπὸ   πνεύματος   ἁγίου   φερόμενοι
at any   but   ⁶by   ⁸Spirit   ⁷[the]   ⁵being borne
time,   Holy

ἐλάλησαν   ἀπὸ   θεοῦ   ἄνθρωποι.
²spoke   ³from   ⁴God   ¹men.

CHAPTER 2

BUT false prophets also arose among the people, just as there will be false teachers among you, who will secretly bring in destructive heresies, even denying the Master who bought them, bringing upon themselves swift destruction. [2]And many

2 Ἐγένοντο   δὲ   καὶ   ψευδοπροφῆται   ἐν
But there were   also   false prophets   among

τῷ   λαῷ,   ὡς   καὶ   ἐν   ὑμῖν   ἔσονται
the people,   as   indeed among you there will be

ψευδοδιδάσκαλοι,   οἵτινες   παρεισάξουσιν
false teachers,   who   will secretly bring in

αἱρέσεις   ἀπωλείας,   καὶ   τὸν   ἀγοράσαντα
opinions   of destruction,* and ²the   ⁴having bought

αὐτοὺς   δεσπότην   ἀρνούμενοι,   ἐπάγοντες
⁵them   ³Master   ¹denying,   bringing on

ἑαυτοῖς   ταχινὴν   ἀπώλειαν·   2 καὶ   πολλοὶ
themselves   swift   destruction;   and   many

[d] Or my Son, my (or the) Beloved

[e] Other authorities read moved by the Holy Spirit holy men of God spoke

---

* Genitive of quality : " destructive opinions."

will follow their licentiousness, and because of them the way of truth will be reviled. ³And in their greed they will exploit you with false words; from of old their condemnation has not been idle, and their destruction has not been asleep.

4 For if God did not spare the angels when they sinned, but cast them into hell and committed them to pits of nether gloom to be kept until the judgment; ⁵if he did not spare the ancient world, but preserved Noah, a herald of righteousness, with seven other persons, when he brought a flood upon the world of the ungodly; ⁶if by turning the cities of Sodom and Gomor'rah to ashes he condemned them to extinction and made them an example to those who were to be ungodly; ⁷and if he rescued righteous Lot, greatly distressed by the licentiousness of the wicked ⁸(for by what that righteous man saw and heard as he lived among them, he was vexed in his righteous soul day after day with their lawless deeds), ⁹then the Lord knows how to rescue the godly from

ἐξακολουθήσουσιν αὐτῶν ταῖς ἀσελγείαις,
will follow   ³of them ¹the ²licentiousnesses,

δι᾽ οὓς ἡ ὁδὸς τῆς ἀληθείας βλασφημη-
be- whom the way of the truth   will be
cause of

θήσεται·   3 καὶ ἐν πλεονεξίᾳ πλαστοῖς
blasphemed; and by covetousness with fabricated

λόγοις ὑμᾶς ἐμπορεύσονται· οἷς τὸ κρίμα
words ²you ¹they will make for the judg-
merchandise of; whom   ment

ἔκπαλαι οὐκ ἀργεῖ, καὶ ἡ ἀπώλεια
of old   lingers not,   and the destruction

αὐτῶν οὐ νυστάζει. 4 εἰ γὰρ ὁ θεὸς
of them slumbers not.   For if – God

ἀγγέλων ἁμαρτησάντων οὐκ ἐφείσατο, ἀλλὰ
²angels   ³sinning   ¹spared not, but

σιροῖς ζόφου ταρταρώσας παρέδωκεν
²in pits ³of gloom ¹consigning to Tartarus ⁴delivered [them]

εἰς κρίσιν τηρουμένους, 5 καὶ ἀρχαίου
⁵to ⁷judgment ⁶being kept,   and ²[the] ancient

κόσμου οὐκ ἐφείσατο, ἀλλὰ ὄγδοον Νῶε
³world   ¹spared not,   but ³[the] ³Noe
                               eighth man

δικαιοσύνης κήρυκα ἐφύλαξεν, κατακλυσμὸν
⁵of righteousness ⁴a herald ¹guarded, ²a flood

κόσμῳ ἀσεβῶν ἐπάξας, 6 καὶ πόλεις
⁴a world ⁵of impious men ¹bringing ³on, and ²[the] cities

Σοδόμων καὶ Γομόρρας τεφρώσας
⁴of Sodom ³and ⁵Gomorra ¹covering [them]
                          with ashes

καταστροφῇ κατέκρινεν, ὑπόδειγμα μελ-
⁷by an overthrow ³condemned, ²an example ³of men

λόντων ἀσεβεῖν τεθεικώς, 7 καὶ δίκαιον
intending ⁴to live ¹having set(made), and ²righteous
         impiously

Λὼτ καταπονούμενον ὑπὸ τῆς τῶν ἀθέσμων
³Lot ⁴being oppressed ⁵by ⁸the ¹⁰of the ¹¹lawless

ἐν ἀσελγείᾳ ἀναστροφῆς ἐρρύσατο· 8 βλέ-
⁹in ⁹licentiousness ⁷conduct ¹delivered;   ²in

ματι γὰρ καὶ ἀκοῇ ὁ δίκαιος ἐγκατοικῶν
seeing ¹for and in hear- the righteous dwelling
                  ing (that) man

ἐν αὐτοῖς ἡμέραν ἐξ ἡμέρας ψυχὴν
among them day   after† day ²[his] ³soul

δικαίαν ἀνόμοις ἔργοις ἐβασάνιζεν·
¹righteous ⁴with [their] lawless ⁵works ¹tormented·

9 οἶδεν κύριος εὐσεβεῖς ἐκ πειρασμοῦ
⁵knows* ¹[the] Lord ⁴pious men ⁶out of ⁶trial

* That is, " the Lord can deliver "; see note on page xviii.

trial, and to keep the
unrighteous under pun-
ishment until the day of
judgment, ¹⁰and espec-
ially those who indulge
in the lust of defiling
passion and despise
authority.

Bold and wilful, they
are not afraid to revile
the glorious ones,
¹¹whereas angels, though
greater in might and
power, do not pro-
nounce a reviling judg-
ment upon them before
the Lord. ¹²But these,
like irrational animals,
creatures of instinct,
born to be caught and
killed, reviling in
matters of which they
are ignorant, will be
destroyed in the same
destruction with them,
¹³suffering wrong for
their wrongdoing. They
count it pleasure to
revel in the daytime.
They are blots and
blemishes, reveling in
their dissipation,ᶠ carousing with you. ¹⁴They have
eyes full of adultery,
insatiable for sin. They
entice unsteady souls.
They have hearts trained
in greed. Accursed
children! ¹⁵Forsaking the
right way they have gone
astray; they have
followed the way of
Balaam, the son of
Be'or, who loved gain

ῥύεσθαι, ἀδίκους δὲ εἰς ἡμέραν κρίσεως
²to deliver, ³unjust men ¹but ⁵for ⁶a day ⁷of judgment

κολαζομένους τηρεῖν, 10 μάλιστα δὲ τοὺς
⁴being punished ²to keep, and most of all ¹the

ὀπίσω σαρκὸς ἐν ἐπιθυμία μιασμοῦ
³after ⁴flesh ⁵in ⁶lust ⁷of defilement*

πορευομένους καὶ κυριότητος καταφρονοῦντας.
²[ones] going ⁸and ¹⁰dominion ⁹despising.

τολμηταὶ αὐθάδεις, δόξας οὐ τρέμουσιν
²darers ¹Self-satisfied, glories they do not tremble [at]

βλασφημοῦντες, 11 ὅπου ἄγγελοι ἰσχύϊ καὶ
blaspheming, where angels ²in strength ⁴and

δυνάμει μείζονες ὄντες οὐ φέρουσιν κατ'
⁵in power ²greater ¹being do not bring against

αὐτῶν παρὰ κυρίῳ βλάσφημον κρίσιν.
them before [the] Lord railing judgment.

12 οὗτοι δέ, ὡς ἄλογα ζῷα γεγεννημένα
But these ¹as ⁴without ³animals ⁵having been
men, reason born

φυσικὰ εἰς ἅλωσιν καὶ φθοράν, ἐν οἷς
²natural for capture and corruption, ²in ³things
which

ἀγνοοῦσιν βλασφημοῦντες, ἐν τῇ φθορᾷ
⁴they are ¹railing, in the corruption
ignorant [of]

αὐτῶν καὶ φθαρήσονται, 13 ἀδικούμενοι
of them indeed they will be corrupted, suffering wrong

μισθὸν ἀδικίας· ἡδονὴν ἡγούμενοι τὴν
[as] wages of wrong; [to be] pleasure ¹deeming

ἐν ἡμέρα τρυφήν, σπίλοι καὶ μῶμοι
²in ⁴[the] day ¹luxury, spots and blemishes

ἐντρυφῶντες ἐν ταῖς ἀπάταις αὐτῶν
revelling in the deceits of them

συνευωχούμενοι ὑμῖν, 14 ὀφθαλμοὺς ἔχοντες
feasting along with you, ¹eyes ¹having

μεστοὺς μοιχαλίδος καὶ ἀκαταπαύστους
full of an adulteress and not ceasing from

ἁμαρτίας, δελεάζοντες ψυχὰς ἀστηρίκτους,
sin, alluring ²souls ¹unsteady,

καρδίαν γεγυμνασμένην πλεονεξίας ἔχοντες,
²a heart ³having been exercised ⁴of(in) covetousness ¹having,

κατάρας τέκνα· 15 καταλείποντες εὐθεῖαν
³of curse ¹children; forsaking a straight

ὁδὸν ἐπλανήθησαν, ἐξακολουθήσαντες τῇ
way they erred, following the

ὁδῷ τοῦ Βαλαὰμ τοῦ Βεώρ, ὃς μισθὸν
way - of Balaam the [son] of who ²[the]
Beor, wages

ᶠ Other ancient authorities
read *love feasts*

* Genitive of quality: " defiling lust."

from wrongdoing, ¹⁶but was rebuked for his own transgression; a dumb ass spoke with human voice and restrained the prophet's madness.

17 These are waterless springs and mists driven by a storm; for them the nether gloom of darkness has been reserved. ¹⁸For, uttering loud boasts of folly, they entice with licentious passions of the flesh men who have barely escaped from those who live in error. ¹⁹They promise them freedom, but they themselves are slaves of corruption; for whatever overcomes a man, to that he is enslaved. ²⁰For if, after they have escaped the defilements of the world through the knowledge of our Lord and Savior Jesus Christ, they are again entangled in them and overpowered, the last state has become worse for them than the first. ²¹For it would have been better for them never to have known the way of righteousness than after knowing it to turn back from the holy commandment delivered to them. ²²It has happened to them according to the true proverb, The dog

ἀδικίας   ἠγάπησεν,   16 ἔλεγξιν   δὲ   ἔσχεν
²of wrong   ¹loved,   and ²reproof   ¹had

ἰδίας   παρανομίας·   ὑποζύγιον   ἄφωνον   ἐν
of [his] own transgression;   ²ass   ¹a dumb   ⁴with

ἀνθρώπου   φωνῇ   φθεγξάμενον   ἐκώλυσεν
⁶of a man   ⁵voice   ³speaking   restrained

τὴν   τοῦ   προφήτου   παραφρονίαν.   17 οὗτοί
¹the   ²of the   ⁴prophet   ³madness.   These men

εἰσιν   πηγαὶ   ἄνυδροι   καὶ   ὁμίχλαι   ὑπὸ
are   ²springs   ¹waterless   and   mists   ³by

λαίλαπος   ἐλαυνόμεναι,   οἷς   ὁ   ζόφος   τοῦ
³storm   ¹being driven,   for whom the   gloom   of the

σκότους   τετήρηται.   18 ὑπέρογκα   γὰρ
darkness   has been kept.   For ²immoderate [words]

ματαιότητος   φθεγγόμενοι   δελεάζουσιν   ἐν
³of vanity   ¹speaking   they allure   by

ἐπιθυμίαις   σαρκὸς   ἀσελγείαις   τοὺς   ὀλίγως
[the] lusts   of [the] flesh   in excesses   the [ones]   almost

ἀποφεύγοντας   τοὺς   ἐν   πλάνῃ   ἀναστρε-
escaping   ¹the [ones]   ³in   ⁴error   ²liv-

φομένους,   19 ἐλευθερίαν   αὐτοῖς   ἐπαγγελ-
ing,   ²freedom   ³to them   ¹promis-

λόμενοι,   αὐτοὶ   δοῦλοι   ὑπάρχοντες   τῆς
ing,   [them]selves   ²slaves   ¹being

φθορᾶς·   ᾧ   γάρ   τις   ἥττηται,   τούτῳ
of corrup-   for by whom   anyone   has been   to this
tion;   defeated,   man

δεδούλωται.   20 εἰ   γὰρ   ἀποφυγόντες   τὰ
he has been enslaved.   For if   having escaped   the

μιάσματα   τοῦ   κόσμου   ἐν   ἐπιγνώσει   τοῦ
defilements   of the   world   by a full knowledge of the

κυρίου   καὶ   σωτῆρος   Ἰησοῦ   Χριστοῦ,
Lord   and   Saviour   Jesus   Christ,

τούτοις   δὲ   πάλιν   ἐμπλακέντες   ἡττῶνται,
yet by these   again   having been   have been
entangled   defeated,

γέγονεν   αὐτοῖς   τὰ   ἔσχατα   χείρονα   τῶν
²have become ⁴to them   ¹the   ³last things   worse [than] the

πρώτων.   21 κρεῖττον   γὰρ   ἦν   αὐτοῖς
first.   For better   it was   for them

μὴ   ἐπεγνωκέναι   τὴν   ὁδὸν   τῆς   δικαιοσύνης,
not to have fully known   the   way   –   of righteousness,

ἢ   ἐπιγνοῦσιν   ὑποστρέψαι   ἐκ   τῆς   παρα-
than   fully knowing   to turn   from   ¹the   ⁴de-

δοθείσης   αὐτοῖς   ἁγίας   ἐντολῆς.   22 συμβέ-
livered   ⁵to them   ²holy   ³commandment.   ¹has

βηκεν   αὐτοῖς   τὸ   τῆς   ἀληθοῦς   παροιμίας·
happened   ⁶to them   ¹The   ²of the   ³true   ⁴proverb:
thing

turns back to his own vomit, and the sow is washed only to wallow in the mire.

κύων ἐπιστρέψας ἐπὶ τὸ ἴδιον ἐξέραμα,
[The] dog turning upon the(its) own vomit,
καὶ· ὗς λουσαμένη εἰς κυλισμὸν βορβόρου.
and: [The] sow washed to wallowing of mud.

CHAPTER 3

THIS is now the second letter that I have written to you, beloved, and in both of them I have aroused your sincere mind by way of reminder; ²that you should remember the predictions of the holy prophets and the commandment of the Lord and Savior through your apostles. ³First of all you must understand this, that scoffers will come in the last days with scoffing, following their own passions ⁴and saying, "Where is the promise of his coming? For ever since the fathers fell asleep, all things have continued as they were from the beginning of creation." ⁵They deliberately ignore this fact, that by the word of God heavens existed long ago, and an earth formed out of water and by means of water, ⁶through which the world that then existed was deluged with water

3 Ταύτην ἤδη, ἀγαπητοί, δευτέραν ὑμῖν
¹This ¹now, ²beloved, ²second ²to you
γράφω ἐπιστολήν, ἐν αἷς διεγείρω ὑμῶν
¹I write ³epistle, in [both] which I rouse ⁴of you
ἐν ὑπομνήσει τὴν εἰλικρινῆ διάνοιαν,
⁵by ⁶reminder ¹the ²sincere ³mind,
2 μνησθῆναι τῶν προειρημένων ῥημάτων
to remember the ²having been ¹words
previously spoken
ὑπὸ τῶν ἁγίων προφητῶν καὶ τῆς τῶν
by the holy prophets and ¹the ²of the
ἀποστόλων ὑμῶν ἐντολῆς τοῦ κυρίου καὶ
³apostles ⁴of you ²commandment of the Lord and
σωτῆρος, 3 τοῦτο πρῶτον γινώσκοντες, ὅτι
Saviour, ³this ²firstly ¹knowing, that
ἐλεύσονται ἐπ' ἐσχάτων τῶν ἡμερῶν ἐν
there will come during [the] last of the days ³in
ἐμπαιγμονῇ ἐμπαῖκται κατὰ τὰς ἰδίας
⁴mocking ¹mockers ²according to ⁵the(ir) ⁶own
ἐπιθυμίας αὐτῶν πορευόμενοι 4 καὶ λέγοντες·
³lusts of them ²going and saying :
ποῦ ἐστιν ἡ ἐπαγγελία τῆς παρουσίας
Where is the promise of the presence
αὐτοῦ; ἀφ' ἧς γὰρ οἱ πατέρες ἐκοι-
of him? ²from ³which [day] ¹for the fathers fell
=for from the day when . . .
μήθησαν, πάντα οὕτως διαμένει ἀπ'
asleep, all things so remains from
ἀρχῆς κτίσεως. 5 λανθάνει γὰρ αὐτοὺς
[the] of creation. For ²is concealed ³them
beginning [from]
τοῦτο θέλοντας ὅτι οὐρανοὶ ἦσαν ἔκπαλαι
¹this wishing* that heavens were of old
καὶ γῆ ἐξ ὕδατος καὶ δι' ὕδατος
and earth by water and through water
συνεστῶσα τῷ τοῦ θεοῦ λόγῳ, 6 δι'
¹having been ²by - ⁴of God ³word, through
held together the
ὧν ὁ τότε κόσμος ὕδατι κατακλυσθεὶς
which the then§ world ²by water ¹being inundated
things

---

* That is, they wish it to be so.

§ This is allowable English : *cf.* " the then Prime Minister."

and perished. ⁷But by the same word the heavens and earth that now exist have been stored up for fire, being kept until the day of judgment and destruction of ungodly men.

8 But do not ignore this one fact, beloved, that with the Lord one day is as a thousand years, and a thousand years as one day. ⁹The Lord is not slow about his promise as some count slowness, but is forbearing toward you,*ᵍ* not wishing that any should perish, but that all should reach repentance. ¹⁰But the day of the Lord will come like a thief, and then the heavens will pass away with a loud noise, and the elements will be dissolved with fire, and the earth and the works that are upon it will be burned up.

11 Since all these things are thus to be dissolved, what sort of persons ought you to be in lives of holiness and godliness, ¹²waiting for and hastening*ʰ* the coming of the day of God, because of which the heavens will be kindled and dissolved, and the elements will melt with

---

ἀπώλετο·   7 οἱ   δὲ   νῦν   οὐρανοὶ   καὶ   ἡ
perished;   but the   now   heavens   and   the

γῆ   τῷ   αὐτῷ   λόγῳ   τεθησαυρισμένοι   εἰσὶν
earth by the   same   word   ²*having been* stored up   ¹are

πυρὶ   τηρούμενοι   εἰς   ἡμέραν   κρίσεως   καὶ
²for fire   ¹being kept   in   a day   of judgment   and

ἀπωλείας   τῶν   ἀσεβῶν   ἀνθρώπων.   8 ᵃἘν
destruction   of *the*   impious   men.   ²one

δὲ   τοῦτο   μὴ   λανθανέτω   ὑμᾶς,   ἀγαπητοί,
But   ¹this   let not be concealed   you,   beloved,
    ²thing   [from]

ὅτι   μία   ἡμέρα   παρὰ   κυρίῳ   ὡς   χίλια
that   one   day   with [the] Lord [is]   as a thousand

ἔτη   καὶ   χίλια   ἔτη   ὡς   ἡμέρα   μία.   9 οὐ
years   and a thousand years   as   ²day   ¹one.   ²not

βραδύνει   κύριος   τῆς   ἐπαγγελίας,   ὥς   τινες
³is ⁴slow   ¹[The]   of the   promise,   as   some
       Lord   (his)

βραδύτητα   ἡγοῦνται,   ἀλλὰ   μακροθυμεῖ   εἰς
²slowness   ¹deem,   but   is longsuffering toward

ὑμᾶς,   μὴ   βουλόμενός   τινας   ἀπολέσθαι
you,   not   purposing   any   to perish

ἀλλὰ   πάντας   εἰς   μετάνοιαν   χωρῆσαι.
but   all men   ³to   ²repentance   ¹to come.

10 ᵃἭξει   δὲ   ἡμέρα   κυρίου   ὡς   κλέπτης,
   But will come   [the] day   of [the] Lord as   a thief,

ἐν   ᾗ   οἱ   οὐρανοὶ   ῥοιζηδὸν   παρελεύσονται,
in   which the   heavens   ²with rushing   ¹will pass away,
          sound

στοιχεῖα   δὲ   καυσούμενα   λυθήσεται,   καὶ
and [the] elements   burning   will be dissolved,   and

γῆ   καὶ   τὰ   ἐν   αὐτῇ   ἔργα   εὑρεθήσεται.
[the]   and   ¹the   ³in   ⁴it   ²works   will be
earth   discovered.

11 Τούτων   οὕτως   πάντων   λυομένων
¹these things   ²thus   ¹All   ⁴being dissolvedᵃ

ποταποὺς   δεῖ   ὑπάρχειν   [ὑμᾶς]   ἐν   ἁγίαις
what sort   it be-   ²to be   ¹you   in   holy
of men   hoves

ἀναστροφαῖς   καὶ   εὐσεβείαις,   12 προσδοκῶντας
conduct*   and   piety,*   awaiting

καὶ   σπεύδοντας   τὴν   παρουσίαν   τῆς   τοῦ
and   hastening   the   presence   ¹of the   –

θεοῦ   ἡμέρας,   δι᾽   ἣν   οὐρανοὶ   πυρούμενοι
²of God   ¹day,   on ac- which   [the]   being set on fire
       count of   heavens

λυθήσονται   καὶ   στοιχεῖα   καυσούμενα
will be dissolved   and   [the] elements   burning

ᵍ Other ancient authorities read *on your account*

ʰ Or *earnestly desiring*

* The Greek plurals cannot be literally reproduced in English.

fire! [13]But according to his promise we wait for new heavens and a new earth in which righteousness dwells.

14 Therefore, beloved, since you wait for these, be zealous to be found by him without spot or blemish, and at peace. [15]And count the forbearance of our Lord as salvation. So also our beloved brother Paul wrote to you according to the wisdom given him, [16]speaking of this as he does in all his letters. There are some things in them hard to understand, which the ignorant and unstable twist to their own destruction, as they do the other scriptures. [17]You therefore, beloved, knowing this beforehand, beware lest you be carried away with the error of lawless men and lose your own stability. [18]But grow in the grace and knowledge of our Lord and Savior Jesus Christ. To him be the glory both now and to the day of eternity. Amen.

τήκεται.   13 καινοὺς   δὲ   οὐρανοὺς   καὶ
melts.   But new   heavens   and

γῆν   καινὴν   κατὰ   τὸ   ἐπάγγελμα   αὐτοῦ
²earth ¹a new   accord- the   promise   of him
               ing to

προσδοκῶμεν,   ἐν οἷς δικαιοσύνη κατοικεῖ.
we await,   in which righteousness   dwells.

14 Διό,   ἀγαπητοί,   ταῦτα   προσδοκῶντες
Wherefore, beloved,   ²these things   ¹awaiting

σπουδάσατε   ἄσπιλοι καὶ   ἀμώμητοι   αὐτῷ
be diligent   ⁵spotless ⁶and   ⁷unblemished ²by him

εὑρεθῆναι   ἐν   εἰρήνῃ,   15 καὶ   τὴν   τοῦ
¹to be found   ²in   ⁴peace,   and   ⁴the ⁵of the

κυρίου ἡμῶν μακροθυμίαν σωτηρίαν ἡγεῖσθε,
⁵Lord   ⁶of us   ³longsuffering ⁷salvation   ¹deem,

καθὼς   καὶ   ὁ   ἀγαπητὸς   ἡμῶν   ἀδελφὸς
as   indeed the   beloved   ²of us   ¹brother

Παῦλος   κατὰ   τὴν   δοθεῖσαν   αὐτῷ   σοφίαν
Paul   accord- ¹the   ²given   ⁴to him   ³wisdom
        ing to

ἔγραψεν   ὑμῖν,   16 ὡς   καὶ   ἐν   πάσαις
wrote   to you,   as   also   in   all [his]

ἐπιστολαῖς λαλῶν ἐν αὐταῖς περὶ τούτων,
epistles   speaking in   them   concerning these
                                          things,

ἐν αἷς ἐστιν δυσνόητά τινα, ἃ οἱ
in which is(are) ²hard to   ¹some   which the
                 understand things,

ἀμαθεῖς καὶ ἀστήρικτοι στρεβλοῦσιν ὡς
unlearned and   unsteady   twist   as

καὶ   τὰς λοιπὰς γραφὰς πρὸς τὴν ἰδίαν
also the remaining scriptures   to   the(ir) own

αὐτῶν ἀπώλειαν. 17 Ὑμεῖς οὖν, ἀγαπητοί,
of them   destruction.   Ye   therefore, beloved,

προγινώσκοντες   φυλάσσεσθε   ἵνα   μὴ   τῇ
knowing before   guard   lest   ²by the

τῶν ἀθέσμων πλάνῃ συναπαχθέντες ἐκπέ-
⁴of the ⁵lawless   ¹error ¹being led away with ye fall

σητε τοῦ ἰδίου στηριγμοῦ,   18 αὐξάνετε
from the(your)   own   stability,   ²grow ye

δὲ ἐν χάριτι καὶ γνώσει τοῦ κυρίου
¹but in   grace   and knowledge of the   Lord

ἡμῶν καὶ σωτῆρος Ἰησοῦ Χριστοῦ.
of us   and   Saviour   Jesus   Christ.

αὐτῷ   ἡ   δόξα   καὶ   νῦν   καὶ   εἰς
To himᵉ [is] the glory   both   now   and   unto
=His is*   =for ever.

ἡμέραν αἰῶνος.
a day   of age. §

* See note on I. Pet. 5. 11.   § ? "An age-lasting (i.e. eternal) day."

CHAPTER 1

THAT which was from the beginning, which we have heard, which we have seen with our eyes, which we have looked upon and touched with our hands, concerning the word of life—²the life was made manifest, and we saw it, and testify to it, and proclaim to you the eternal life which was with the Father and was made manifest to us—³that which we have seen and heard we proclaim also to you, so that you may have fellowship with us; and our fellowship is with the Father and with his Son Jesus Christ. ⁴And we are writing this that our*a* joy may be complete.

5 This is the message we have heard from him and proclaim to you, that God is light and in him is no darkness at all. ⁶If we say we have fellowship with him while we walk in darkness, we lie and do not

1 Ὁ   ἦν   ἀπ'   ἀρχῆς,   ὃ   ἀκηκόαμεν,
What was from [the]   what we have heard,
                beginning,

ὃ   ἑωράκαμεν   τοῖς   ὀφθαλμοῖς   ἡμῶν,   ὃ
what we have seen with the   eyes   of us, what

ἐθεασάμεθα   καὶ   αἱ   χεῖρες   ἡμῶν   ἐψηλάφησαν,
we beheld   and the hands   of us   touched,

περὶ   τοῦ   λόγου   τῆς   ζωῆς,   —   2 καὶ
concern- the word   –   of life, —   and
ing

ἡ   ζωὴ   ἐφανερώθη,   καὶ   ἑωράκαμεν   καὶ
the life was manifested, and we have seen   and

μαρτυροῦμεν   καὶ   ἀπαγγέλλομεν   ὑμῖν   τὴν
we bear witness and   we announce   to you the

ζωὴν   τὴν   αἰώνιον,   ἥτις   ἦν   πρὸς   τὸν
life   –   eternal,   which was with   the

πατέρα   καὶ   ἐφανερώθη   ἡμῖν,   —   3 ὃ
Father   and   was manifested to us, —   what

ἑωράκαμεν   καὶ   ἀκηκόαμεν,   ἀπαγγέλλομεν
we have seen   and   we have heard,   we announce

καὶ   ὑμῖν,   ἵνα   καὶ   ὑμεῖς   κοινωνίαν   ἔχητε
also   to you, in order ²also   ¹ye   ⁴fellowship   ³may
            that   have

μεθ'   ἡμῶν.   καὶ   ἡ   κοινωνία   δὲ   ἡ   ἡμετέρα
with   us.   ³indeed the ⁴fellowship ¹And –   ²our

μετὰ   τοῦ   πατρὸς   καὶ   μετὰ   τοῦ   υἱοῦ
[is] with the   Father   and   with   the   Son

αὐτοῦ   Ἰησοῦ   Χριστοῦ.   4 καὶ   ταῦτα
of him   Jesus   Christ.   And these things

γράφομεν   ἡμεῖς   ἵνα   ἡ   χαρὰ   ἡμῶν   ᾖ
write   we   in order the joy   of us   may
                  that   be

πεπληρωμένη.
having been fulfilled.

5 Καὶ   ἔστιν   αὕτη   ἡ   ἀγγελία   ἦν
   And   ²is   ¹this   the   message   which

ἀκηκόαμεν   ἀπ'   αὐτοῦ   καὶ   ἀναγγέλλομεν
we have heard from   him   and   we announce

ὑμῖν,   ὅτι   ὁ   θεὸς   φῶς   ἐστιν   καὶ   σκοτία
to you, that   –   God   ²light   ¹is   and   ³darkness

ἐν   αὐτῷ   οὐκ   ἔστιν   οὐδεμία.   6 Ἐὰν
¹in   ³him   ⁴not   ²is   none.   If

εἴπωμεν   ὅτι   κοινωνίαν   ἔχομεν   μετ'   αὐτοῦ
we say   that   ²fellowship   ¹we have with   him

καὶ   ἐν   τῷ   σκότει   περιπατῶμεν,   ψευδόμεθα
and   ²in ³the ⁴darkness   ¹we walk,   we lie

---

a Other ancient authorities read *your*

live according to the truth; [7] but if we walk in the light, as he is in the light, we have fellowship with one another, and the blood of Jesus his Son cleanses us from all sin. [8] If we say we have no sin, we deceive ourselves, and the truth is not in us. [9] If we confess our sins, he is faithful and just, and will forgive our sins and cleanse us from all unrighteousness. [10] If we say we have not sinned, we make him a liar, and his word is not in us.

καὶ   οὐ   ποιοῦμεν   τὴν   ἀλήθειαν·   7 ἐὰν
and   are not doing   the   truth;   [1]if

δὲ   ἐν   τῷ   φωτὶ   περιπατῶμεν   ὡς   αὐτός
[1]but [4]in [5]the [6]light [2]we walk   as   he

ἐστιν   ἐν   τῷ   φωτί,   κοινωνίαν   ἔχομεν
is   in   the   light,   [2]fellowship [1]we have

μετ’   ἀλλήλων   καὶ   τὸ   αἷμα   Ἰησοῦ   τοῦ
with   each other   and   the   blood   of Jesus   the

υἱοῦ   αὐτοῦ   καθαρίζει   ἡμᾶς   ἀπὸ   πάσης
Son   of him   cleanses   us   from   all

ἁμαρτίας.   8 ἐὰν   εἴπωμεν   ὅτι   ἁμαρτίαν
sin.   If   we say   that   sin

οὐκ   ἔχομεν,   ἑαυτοὺς   πλανῶμεν   καὶ   ἡ
we have not,   [2]ourselves [1]we deceive   and   the

ἀλήθεια   οὐκ   ἔστιν   ἐν   ἡμῖν.   9 ἐὰν
truth   is not   in   us.   If

ὁμολογῶμεν   τὰς   ἁμαρτίας   ἡμῶν,   πιστός
we confess   the   sins   of us,   faithful

ἐστιν   καὶ   δίκαιος,   ἵνα   ἀφῇ   ἡμῖν   τὰς
he is   and   righteous,   in order   he may   us   the
                            that   forgive

ἁμαρτίας   καὶ   καθαρίσῃ   ἡμᾶς   ἀπὸ   πάσης
sins   and   he may cleanse   us   from   all

ἀδικίας.   10 ἐὰν   εἴπωμεν   ὅτι   οὐχ
iniquity.   If   we say   that   not

ἡμαρτήκαμεν,   ψεύστην   ποιοῦμεν   αὐτὸν
we have sinned,   a liar   we make   him

καὶ   ὁ   λόγος   αὐτοῦ   οὐκ   ἔστιν   ἐν   ἡμῖν.
and   the   word   of him   is not   in   us.

CHAPTER 2

MY little children, I am writing this to you so that you may not sin; but if any one does sin, we have an advocate with the Father, Jesus Christ the righteous; [2] and he is the expiation for our sins, and not for ours only but also for the sins of the whole world. [3] And by this we may be sure that we know him, if we keep his commandments. [4] He

2 Τεκνία   μου,   ταῦτα   γράφω   ὑμῖν   ἵνα
Little children   of me,   these things   I write   to you   in order
                                                      that

μὴ   ἁμάρτητε.   καὶ   ἐάν   τις   ἁμάρτῃ,
ye sin not.   And   if   anyone   sins,

παράκλητον   ἔχομεν   πρὸς   τὸν   πατέρα,
an advocate   we have   with   the   Father,

Ἰησοῦν   Χριστὸν   δίκαιον·   2 καὶ   αὐτὸς
Jesus   Christ   [the] righteous;   and   he

ἱλασμός   ἐστιν   περὶ   τῶν   ἁμαρτιῶν   ἡμῶν,
[2]a propitiation [1]is   concerning   the   sins   of us,

οὐ   περὶ   τῶν   ἡμετέρων   δὲ   μόνον   ἀλλὰ
[2]not [3]concerning –   [4]ours   [1]but   only   but

καὶ   περὶ   ὅλου   τοῦ   κόσμου.   3 καὶ   ἐν
also   concerning   all   the   world.   And   by

τούτῳ   γινώσκομεν   ὅτι   ἐγνώκαμεν   αὐτόν,
this   we know   that   we have known   him,

ἐὰν   τὰς   ἐντολὰς   αὐτοῦ   τηρῶμεν.   4 ὁ
if   [2]the   [3]command-   [4]of him   [1]we keep.   The
                ments   [one]

who says "I know him" but disobeys his commandments is a liar, and the truth is not in him; [5]but whoever keeps his word, in him truly love for God is perfected. By this we may be sure that we are in him: [6]he who says he abides in him ought to walk in the same way in which he walked.

7 Beloved, I am writing you no new commandment, but an old commandment which you had from the beginning; the old commandment is the word which you have heard. [8]Yet I am writing you a new commandment, which is true in him and in you, because[b] the darkness is passing away and the true light is already shining. [9]He who says he is in the light and hates his brother is in the darkness still. [10]He who loves his brother abides in the light, and in it[c] there is no cause for stumbling. [11]But he who hates his brother is in the

λέγων ὅτι ἔγνωκα αὐτόν, καὶ τὰς ἐντολὰς
saying[,] – I have known him, and [1]the [1]commandments
αὐτοῦ μὴ τηρῶν, ψεύστης ἐστίν, καὶ
[2]of him [1]not [3]keeping, [2]a liar [1]is, and
ἐν τούτῳ ἡ ἀλήθεια οὐκ ἔστιν· 5 ὃς δ'
in this man the truth is not; but who-
ἂν τηρῇ αὐτοῦ τὸν λόγον, ἀληθῶς ἐν
ever keeps [3]of him [1]the [2]word, truly in
τούτῳ ἡ ἀγάπη τοῦ θεοῦ τετελείωται.
this man the love – of God has been perfected.
ἐν τούτῳ γινώσκομεν ὅτι ἐν αὐτῷ ἐσμεν.
By this we know that [2]in [3]him [1]we are.
6 ὁ λέγων ἐν αὐτῷ μένειν ὀφείλει καθὼς
The [one] saying in him to remain ought as
ἐκεῖνος περιεπάτησεν καὶ αὐτὸς οὕτως
that [one]* walked also [him]self so
περιπατεῖν.
to walk.

7 Ἀγαπητοί, οὐκ ἐντολὴν καινὴν γράφω
Beloved, [2]not [4]commandment [3]a new [1]I write
ὑμῖν, ἀλλ' ἐντολὴν παλαιὰν ἣν εἴχετε
to you, but [2]commandment [1]an old which ye had
ἀπ' ἀρχῆς· ἡ ἐντολὴ ἡ παλαιά ἐστιν
from [the] the [2]command- – [1]old is
beginning; ment
ὁ λόγος ὃν ἠκούσατε. 8 πάλιν ἐντολὴν
the word which ye heard. Again [2]command-
ment
καινὴν γράφω ὑμῖν, ὅ ἐστιν ἀληθὲς
[1]a new I write to you, what is true
ἐν αὐτῷ καὶ ἐν ὑμῖν, ὅτι ἡ σκοτία
in him and in you, because the darkness
παράγεται καὶ τὸ φῶς τὸ ἀληθινὸν
is passing and the [2]light – [1]true
ἤδη φαίνει. 9 ὁ λέγων ἐν τῷ φωτὶ
already shines. The [one] saying in the light
εἶναι καὶ τὸν ἀδελφὸν αὐτοῦ μισῶν
to be and the brother of him hating
ἐν τῇ σκοτίᾳ ἐστὶν ἕως ἄρτι. 10 ὁ
in the darkness is until now. The
ἀγαπῶν τὸν ἀδελφὸν αὐτοῦ ἐν τῷ φωτὶ
[one] loving the brother of him in the light
μένει, καὶ σκάνδαλον ἐν αὐτῷ οὐκ ἔστιν·
remains, and offence in him is not;
11 ὁ δὲ μισῶν τὸν ἀδελφὸν αὐτοῦ ἐν
but the [one] hating the brother of him in

[b] Or that
[c] Or him

* In a number of places John uses this demonstrative adjective as a substitute for " Christ " : " the remoter antecedent." See also John 2. 21.

darkness and walks in the darkness, and does not know where he is going, because the darkness has blinded his eyes.

12 I am writing to you, little children, because your sins are forgiven for his sake. 13 I am writing to you, fathers, because you know him who is from the beginning. I am writing to you, young men, because you have overcome the evil one. I write to you, children, because you know the Father. 14 I write to you, fathers, because you know him who is from the beginning. I write to you, young men, because you are strong, and the word of God abides in you, and you have overcome the evil one.

15 Do not love the world or the things in the world. If any one loves the world, love for the Father is not in him. 16 For all that is in the world, the lust of the flesh and the lust of the eyes and the pride of life, is not of the Father but is of the world. 17 And

---

τῇ σκοτίᾳ ἐστὶν καὶ ἐν τῇ σκοτίᾳ
the darkness is and in the darkness

περιπατεῖ, καὶ οὐκ οἶδεν ποῦ ὑπάγει,
walks, and knows not where he is going,

ὅτι ἡ σκοτία ἐτύφλωσεν τοὺς ὀφθαλμοὺς
be- the darkness blinded the eyes
cause

αὐτοῦ. 12 Γράφω ὑμῖν, τεκνία, ὅτι
of him. I write to you, little because
children,

ἀφέωνται ὑμῖν αἱ ἁμαρτίαι διὰ τὸ ὄνομα
have been to you the sins on ac- the name
forgiven (your) count of

αὐτοῦ. 13 γράφω ὑμῖν, πατέρες, ὅτι
of him. I write to you, fathers, because

ἐγνώκατε τὸν ἀπ᾽ ἀρχῆς. γράφω ὑμῖν,
ye have the from [the] I write to
known [one] beginning. you,

νεανίσκοι, ὅτι νενικήκατε τὸν πονηρόν.
young men, because ye have overcome the evil one.

14 ἔγραψα ὑμῖν, παιδία, ὅτι ἐγνώκατε
I wrote to you, young because ye have
children, known

τὸν πατέρα. ἔγραψα ὑμῖν, πατέρες,
the Father. I wrote to you, fathers,

ὅτι ἐγνώκατε τὸν ἀπ᾽ ἀρχῆς. ἔγραψα
be- ye have the from [the] I wrote
cause known [one] beginning.

ὑμῖν, νεανίσκοι, ὅτι ἰσχυροί ἐστε καὶ
to you, young men, because strong ye are and

ὁ λόγος τοῦ θεοῦ ἐν ὑμῖν μένει καὶ
the word – of God in you remains and

νενικήκατε τὸν πονηρόν. 15 Μὴ ἀγαπᾶτε
ye have overcome the evil one. Love ye not

τὸν κόσμον μηδὲ τὰ ἐν τῷ κόσμῳ.
the world nor the things in the world.

ἐάν τις ἀγαπᾷ τὸν κόσμον, οὐκ ἔστιν
If anyone loves the world, ⁶not ⁵is

ἡ ἀγάπη τοῦ πατρὸς ἐν αὐτῷ· 16 ὅτι
¹the ²love ³of the ⁴Father in him; because

πᾶν τὸ ἐν τῷ κόσμῳ, ἡ ἐπιθυμία τῆς
all that in the world, the lust of the
which† [is]

σαρκὸς καὶ ἡ ἐπιθυμία τῶν ὀφθαλμῶν
flesh and the lust of the eyes

καὶ ἡ ἀλαζονεία τοῦ βίου, οὐκ ἔστιν
and the vainglory – of life, is not

ἐκ τοῦ πατρός, ἀλλὰ ἐκ τοῦ κόσμου
of the Father, but of the world

the world passes away, and the lust of it; but he who does the will of God abides for ever.

18 Children, it is the last hour; and as you have heard that antichrist is coming, so now many antichrists have come; therefore we know that it is the last hour. [19]They went out from us, but they were not of us; for if they had been of us, they would have continued with us; but they went out, that it might be plain that they all are not of us. [20]But you have been anointed by the Holy One, and you all know.[d] [21]I write to you, not because you do not know the truth, but because you know it, and know that no lie is of the truth. [22]Who is the liar but he who denies that Jesus is the Christ? This is the antichrist, he who denies the Father and the Son. [23]No one who denies the Son has the Father. He who confesses the Son has the Father also. [24]Let what you heard from the beginning abide in you.

ἐστίν. 17 καὶ ὁ κόσμος παράγεται καὶ
is.   And the world   is passing away and

ἡ ἐπιθυμία αὐτοῦ· ὁ δὲ ποιῶν τὸ θέλημα
the lust   of it; but the [one] doing the will

τοῦ θεοῦ μένει εἰς τὸν αἰῶνα.
– of God remains unto the age.

18 Παιδία,   ἐσχάτη   ὥρα   ἐστίν,   καὶ
Young children, a last hour it is, and

καθὼς ἠκούσατε ὅτι ἀντίχριστος ἔρχεται,
as   ye heard that antichrist is coming,

καὶ νῦν   ἀντίχριστοι   πολλοὶ   γεγόνασιν·
even now [3]antichrists [1]many have arisen;

ὅθεν γινώσκομεν ὅτι ἐσχάτη ὥρα ἐστίν·
whence we know that a last hour it is.

19 ἐξ ἡμῶν ἐξῆλθαν, ἀλλ' οὐκ ἦσαν
From us they went out, but they were not

ἐξ ἡμῶν· εἰ γὰρ ἐξ ἡμῶν ἦσαν, μεμενή-
of   us; for if of   us they were, they would

κεισαν ἂν μεθ' ἡμῶν· ἀλλ' ἵνα φανερω-
have remained with   us; but in order it might be
                                          that

θῶσιν ὅτι οὐκ εἰσὶν πάντες ἐξ ἡμῶν.
manifested that they are not all of   us.

20 καὶ ὑμεῖς χρῖσμα ἔχετε ἀπὸ τοῦ
And ye an anointing have from the

ἁγίου, καὶ οἴδατε πάντες. 21 οὐκ ἔγραψα
Holy One, and [1]ye [3]know [1]all.   I wrote not

ὑμῖν ὅτι οὐκ οἴδατε τὴν ἀλήθειαν, ἀλλ'
to you because ye know not the truth,   but

ὅτι οἴδατε αὐτήν, καὶ ὅτι πᾶν ψεῦδος
because ye know it, and because every lie
                                  =no lie is . . .

ἐκ τῆς ἀληθείας οὐκ ἔστιν. 22 Τίς
of the truth   is not.   Who

ἐστιν ὁ ψεύστης εἰ μὴ ὁ ἀρνούμενος
is   the liar except the [one] denying

ὅτι Ἰησοῦς οὐκ ἔστιν ὁ χριστός; οὗτός
that Jesus not is   the Christ? this

ἐστιν ὁ ἀντίχριστος, ὁ ἀρνούμενος τὸν
is   the antichrist, the [one] denying the

πατέρα καὶ τὸν υἱόν. 23 πᾶς ὁ ἀρνούμενος
Father and the Son. Everyone denying

τὸν υἱὸν οὐδὲ τὸν πατέρα ἔχει· ὁ
the Son [2]neither [3]the [4]Father [1]has; the

ὁμολογῶν τὸν υἱὸν καὶ τὸν πατέρα ἔχει.
[one] confessing the Son [3]also [2]the [4]Father [1]has.

24 ὑμεῖς ὃ ἠκούσατε ἀπ' ἀρχῆς, ἐν
[1]Ye [1]what heard from [the] beginning, in

[d] Other ancient authorities read you know everything

If what you heard from the beginning abides in you, then you will abide in the Son and in the Father. ²⁵And this is what he has promised us,[e] eternal life.

26 I write this to you about those who would deceive you; ²⁷but the anointing which you received from him abides in you, and you have no need that any one should teach you; as his anointing teaches you about everything, and is true, and is no lie, just as it has taught you, abide in him.

28 And now, little children, abide in him, so that when he appears we may have confidence and not shrink from him in shame at his coming. ²⁹If you know that he is righteous, you may be sure that every one who does right is born of him.

CHAPTER 3

SEE what love the Father has given us, that we should be called children of God; and so we are. The reason why the world does not know

[e] Other ancient authorities read *you*

ὑμῖν μενέτω. ἐὰν ἐν ὑμῖν μείνῃ ὃ ἀπ'
you let it remain. If ⁶in ⁷you ⁵remains ¹what ²from

ἀρχῆς ἠκούσατε, καὶ ὑμεῖς ἐν τῷ υἱῷ
⁴[the] ²ye heard, ⁸both ¹ye ⁴in ⁵the ⁶Son
beginning

καὶ [ἐν] τῷ πατρὶ μενεῖτε.   25 καὶ
⁷and ⁸in ⁹the ¹⁰Father ⁹will remain.   And

αὕτη ἐστὶν ἡ ἐπαγγελία ἣν αὐτὸς ἐπηγ-
this is the promise which he pro-

γείλατο ἡμῖν, τὴν ζωὴν τὴν αἰώνιον.
mised us, the life – eternal.

26 Ταῦτα ἔγραψα ὑμῖν περὶ τῶν πλανών-
These I wrote to you concern- the leading
things ing [ones]

των ὑμᾶς.   27 καὶ ὑμεῖς τὸ χρῖσμα
²astray ¹you.   And ⁴ye ¹the ²anointing

ὃ ἐλάβετε ἀπ' αὐτοῦ μένει ἐν ὑμῖν,
³which received from him remains in you,

καὶ οὐ χρείαν ἔχετε ἵνα τις διδάσκῃ
and ²no ³need ¹ye have *in order* anyone should
that teach

ὑμᾶς· ἀλλ' ὡς τὸ αὐτοῦ χρῖσμα διδάσκει
you; but as the ²of him ¹anointing teaches

ὑμᾶς περὶ πάντων, καὶ ἀληθές ἐστιν
you concerning all things, and ²true ¹is

καὶ οὐκ ἔστιν ψεῦδος, καὶ καθὼς ἐδίδαξεν
and is not a lie, and as he/it taught

ὑμᾶς, μένετε ἐν αὐτῷ.
you, remain ye in him.

28 Καὶ νῦν, τεκνία, μένετε ἐν αὐτῷ,
And now, little children, remain ye in him,

ἵνα ἐὰν φανερωθῇ σχῶμεν παρρησίαν καὶ
in or- if he is manifested we may confidence and
der that have

μὴ αἰσχυνθῶμεν ἀπ' αὐτοῦ ἐν τῇ παρουσίᾳ
not be shamed from him in the presence

αὐτοῦ. 29 ἐὰν εἰδῆτε ὅτι δίκαιός ἐστιν,
of him. If ye know that ²righteous ¹he is,

γινώσκετε ὅτι καὶ πᾶς ὁ ποιῶν τὴν
know ye that also every one doing –

δικαιοσύνην ἐξ αὐτοῦ γεγέννηται.
righteousness ²of ³him ¹has been born.

3 Ἴδετε ποταπὴν ἀγάπην δέδωκεν ἡμῖν
See ye what manner of love ²has given ¹to us

ὁ πατὴρ ἵνα τέκνα θεοῦ κληθῶμεν,
¹the ²Father in order ³children ⁵of God ¹we may be
that called,

καὶ ἐσμέν. διὰ τοῦτο ὁ κόσμος οὐ
and we are. Therefore the world ²not

us is that it did not know him. ²Beloved, we are God's children now; it does not yet appear what we shall be, but we know that when he appears we shall be like him, for we shall see him as he is. ³And every one who thus hopes in him purifies himself as he is pure.

4 Every one who commits sin is guilty of lawlessness; sin is lawlessness. ⁵You know that he appeared to take away sins, and in him there is no sin. ⁶No one who abides in him sins; no one who sins has either seen him or known him. ⁷Little children, let no one deceive you. He who does right is righteous, as he is righteous. ⁸He who commits sin is of the devil; for the devil has sinned from the beginning. The reason the Son of God appeared was to destroy the works of the devil. ⁹No one born of God commits sin;

γινώσκει   ἡμᾶς,   ὅτι   οὐκ   ἔγνω   αὐτόν.
knows   ¹us,   because   it knew not   him.

2 ἀγαπητοί,   νῦν   τέκνα   θεοῦ   ἐσμεν,   καὶ
Beloved,   ²now   ³children   ⁴of God   ¹we are,   and

οὔπω   ἐφανερώθη   τί   ἐσόμεθα.   οἴδαμεν
not yet   was it manifested   what   we shall be.   We know

ὅτι   ἐὰν   φανερωθῇ   ὅμοιοι   αὐτῷ   ἐσόμεθα,
that   if   he(?it) is manifested   like   him   we shall be,

ὅτι   ὀψόμεθα   αὐτὸν   καθώς   ἐστιν.   3 καὶ
be-   we shall see   him   as   he is.   And
cause

πᾶς   ὁ   ἔχων   τὴν   ἐλπίδα   ταύτην   ἐπ'
everyone   having   this hope   on

αὐτῷ   ἁγνίζει   ἑαυτὸν   καθὼς   ἐκεῖνος   ἁγνός
him   purifies   himself   as   that one*   ²pure

ἐστιν.   4 πᾶς   ὁ   ποιῶν   τὴν   ἁμαρτίαν
¹is.   Everyone   doing   -   sin

καὶ   τὴν   ἀνομίαν   ποιεῖ,   καὶ   ἡ   ἁμαρτία
²also   -   ³lawlessness   ¹does,   and   -   sin

ἐστὶν   ἡ   ἀνομία.   5 καὶ   οἴδατε   ὅτι   ἐκεῖνος
is   -   lawlessness.   And ye know   that   that one*

ἐφανερώθη   ἵνα   τὰς   ἁμαρτίας   ἄρῃ,   καὶ
was manifested   in order   -   sins   he might   and
                  that   bear,

ἁμαρτία   ἐν   αὐτῷ   οὐκ   ἔστιν.   6 πᾶς   ὁ
sin   ²in   ³him   ¹is not.   Everyone

ἐν   αὐτῷ   μένων   οὐχ   ἁμαρτάνει·   πᾶς   ὁ
²in   ³him   ¹remaining   sins not;   everyone

ἁμαρτάνων   οὐχ   ἑώρακεν   αὐτὸν   οὐδὲ
sinning   has not seen   him   nor

ἔγνωκεν   αὐτόν.   7 Τεκνία,   μηδεὶς   πλανάτω
has known   him.   Little   ²no man   ¹let ³lead
               children,   ²astray

ὑμᾶς·   ὁ   ποιῶν   τὴν   δικαιοσύνην   δίκαιός
⁴you;   the [one] doing   -   righteousness   ²righteous

ἐστιν,   καθὼς   ἐκεῖνος   δίκαιός   ἐστιν·   8 ὁ
¹is,   as   that one*   ²righteous   ¹is;   the

ποιῶν   τὴν   ἁμαρτίαν   ἐκ   τοῦ   διαβόλου
[one] doing   -   sin   ⁵of   ³the   ⁴devil

ἐστίν,   ὅτι   ἀπ'   ἀρχῆς   ὁ   διάβολος   ἁμαρτάνει.
¹is,   because   ⁴from   ⁵[the]   ¹the   ²devil   ³sins.
                        beginning

εἰς   τοῦτο   ἐφανερώθη   ὁ   υἱὸς   τοῦ   θεοῦ,
For   this   was manifested   the   Son   -   of God,

ἵνα   λύσῃ   τὰ   ἔργα   τοῦ   διαβόλου.
in or-   he might   the   works   of the   devil.
der that   undo

9 Πᾶς   ὁ   γεγεννημένος   ἐκ   τοῦ   θεοῦ
Everyone   having been begotten   of   -   God

* See ch. 2. 6.

for God's nature abides in him, and he cannot sin because he is[f] born of God. [10]By this it may be seen who are the children of God, and who are the children of the devil: whoever does not do right is not of God, nor he who does not love his brother.

[11] For this is the message which you have heard from the beginning, that we should love one another, [12]and not be like Cain who was of the evil one and murdered his brother. And why did he murder him? Because his own deeds were evil and his brother's righteous. [13]Do not wonder, brethren, that the world hates you. [14]We know that we have passed out of death into life, because we love the brethren. He who does not love remains in death. [15]Any one who hates his brother is a murderer, and you know that no murderer has eternal life abiding in

ἁμαρτίαν οὐ ποιεῖ, ὅτι σπέρμα αὐτοῦ
²sin   ²not ¹does, because seed of him

ἐν αὐτῷ μένει· καὶ οὐ δύναται ἁμαρτάνειν,
in him remains; and he cannot to sin,

ὅτι ἐκ τοῦ θεοῦ γεγέννηται.   10 ἐν
because of - God he has been begotten. By

τούτῳ φανερά ἐστιν τὰ τέκνα τοῦ θεοῦ
this ¹manifest ¹is(are) the children - of God

καὶ τὰ τέκνα τοῦ διαβόλου· πᾶς ὁ
and the children of the devil; everyone

μὴ ποιῶν δικαιοσύνην οὐκ ἔστιν ἐκ
not doing righteousness is not of

τοῦ θεοῦ, καὶ ὁ μὴ ἀγαπῶν τὸν ἀδελφὸν
- God, and the not loving the brother
[one]

αὐτοῦ.   11 ὅτι αὕτη ἐστὶν ἡ ἀγγελία
of him. Because this is the message

ἣν ἠκούσατε ἀπ᾽ ἀρχῆς, ἵνα ἀγαπῶμεν
which ye heard from [the] in order we should love
beginning, that

ἀλλήλους·   12 οὐ καθὼς Κάϊν ἐκ τοῦ
one another; not as Cain ²of ¹the

πονηροῦ ἦν καὶ ἔσφαξεν τὸν ἀδελφὸν
⁴evil one ¹was and slew the brother

αὐτοῦ· καὶ χάριν τίνος ἔσφαξεν αὐτόν;
of him; and for the what slew he him?
       sake of

ὅτι τὰ ἔργα αὐτοῦ πονηρὰ ἦν, τὰ δὲ
be- the works of him ²evil ¹was(were). but the
cause   [works]

τοῦ ἀδελφοῦ αὐτοῦ δίκαια.   13 μὴ
of the brother of him righteous.   not

θαυμάζετε, ἀδελφοί, εἰ μισεῖ ὑμᾶς ὁ
Marvel ye, brothers, if ³hates ⁴you ¹the

κόσμος.   14 ἡμεῖς οἴδαμεν ὅτι μεταβεβή-
²world. We know that we have re-

καμεν ἐκ τοῦ θανάτου εἰς τὴν ζωήν,
moved out of the death into the life,

ὅτι ἀγαπῶμεν τοὺς ἀδελφούς· ὁ μὴ
because we love the brothers; the [one] not

ἀγαπῶν μένει ἐν τῷ θανάτῳ.   15 πᾶς
loving remains in - death. Every-

ὁ μισῶν τὸν ἀδελφὸν αὐτοῦ ἀνθρωποκτόνος
one hating the brother of him ¹a murderer

ἐστίν, καὶ οἴδατε ὅτι πᾶς ἀνθρωποκτόνος
¹is, and ye know that every murderer
                           =no murderer has ...

[f] Or for the offspring of God abide in him, and they cannot sin because they are

οὐκ ἔχει ζωὴν αἰώνιον ἐν αὐτῷ μένουσαν.
has not life eternal in him remaining.

him. ¹⁶By this we know love, that he laid down his life for us; and we ought to lay down our lives for the brethren. ¹⁷But if any one has the world's goods and sees his brother in need, yet closes his heart against him, how does God's love abide in him? ¹⁸Little children let us not love in word or speech but in deed and in truth.

19 By this we shall know that we are of the truth, and reassure our hearts before him ²⁰whenever our hearts condemn us; for God is greater than our hearts, and he knows everything. ²¹Beloved, if our hearts do not condemn us, we have confidence before God; ²²and we receive from him whatever we ask, because we keep his commandments and do what pleases him. ²³And this is his commandment, that we should believe in the name of his Son Jesus

---

16 ἐν τούτῳ ἐγνώκαμεν τὴν ἀγάπην, ὅτι
By this we have known — love, because

ἐκεῖνος ὑπὲρ ἡμῶν τὴν ψυχὴν αὐτοῦ
that one* on behalf of us the life of him

ἔθηκεν· καὶ ἡμεῖς ὀφείλομεν ὑπὲρ τῶν
laid down; and we ought on behalf of the

ἀδελφῶν τὰς ψυχὰς θεῖναι. **17** ὃς δ'
brothers the(our) lives to lay down. Who-

ἂν ἔχῃ τὸν βίον τοῦ κόσμου καὶ θεωρῇ
ever has the means of the world and beholds
        of life

τὸν ἀδελφὸν αὐτοῦ χρείαν ἔχοντα καὶ
the brother of him ²need ¹having and

κλείσῃ τὰ σπλάγχνα αὐτοῦ ἀπ' αὐτοῦ,
shuts the bowels of him from him,

πῶς ἡ ἀγάπη τοῦ θεοῦ μένει ἐν αὐτῷ;
how ²the ³love — ⁴of God ¹remains in him?

18 Τεκνία, μὴ ἀγαπῶμεν λόγῳ μηδὲ τῇ
Little children, let us not love in word nor in the

γλώσσῃ, ἀλλὰ ἐν ἔργῳ καὶ ἀληθείᾳ.
tongue, but in work and truth.

19 ἐν τούτῳ γνωσόμεθα ὅτι ἐκ τῆς ἀληθείας
By this we shall know that ³of ⁴the ⁴truth

ἐσμέν, καὶ ἔμπροσθεν αὐτοῦ πείσομεν
¹we are, and before him shall persuade

τὴν καρδίαν ἡμῶν **20** ὅτι ἐὰν καταγινώσκῃ
the heart of us that if ⁴blames [us]

ἡμῶν ἡ καρδία, ὅτι μείζων ἐστὶν ὁ
²of us ¹the ²heart, that greater is —

θεὸς τῆς καρδίας ἡμῶν καὶ γινώσκει
God [than] the heart of us and knows

πάντα. **21** Ἀγαπητοί, ἐὰν ἡ καρδία
all things. Beloved, if the(our) heart

μὴ καταγινώσκῃ, παρρησίαν ἔχομεν πρὸς
does not blame [us], confidence we have with

τὸν θεόν, **22** καὶ ὃ ἐὰν αἰτῶμεν λαμβάν-
— God, and whatever we ask we re-

ομεν ἀπ' αὐτοῦ, ὅτι τὰς ἐντολὰς αὐτοῦ
ceive from him, because ²the ³command- ⁴of him
        ments

τηροῦμεν καὶ τὰ ἀρεστὰ ἐνώπιον αὐτοῦ
¹we keep and ²the ³pleasing ⁴before ⁵him
        things

ποιοῦμεν. **23** καὶ αὕτη ἐστὶν ἡ ἐντολὴ
¹we do. And this is the command-
        ment

αὐτοῦ, ἵνα πιστεύσωμεν τῷ ὀνόματι τοῦ
of him, in order we should believe the name of the
      that

---

* See ch. 2. 6, 3. 3, 5, 7.

Christ and love one another, just as he has commanded us. [24]All who keep his commandments abide in him, and he in them. And by this we know that he abides in us, by the Spirit which he has given us.

υἱοῦ αὐτοῦ Ἰησοῦ Χριστοῦ καὶ ἀγαπῶμεν
Son of him Jesus Christ and love

ἀλλήλους καθὼς ἔδωκεν ἐντολὴν ἡμῖν.
one another as he gave commandment to us.

24 καὶ ὁ τηρῶν τὰς ἐντολὰς αὐτοῦ ἐν
And the keeping [one] the command-ments of him in

αὐτῷ μένει καὶ αὐτὸς ἐν αὐτῷ· καὶ
him remains and he in him; and

ἐν τούτῳ γινώσκομεν ὅτι μένει ἐν ἡμῖν,
by this we know that he remains in us,

ἐκ τοῦ πνεύματος οὗ ἡμῖν ἔδωκεν.
by the Spirit whom to us he gave.

CHAPTER 4

BELOVED, do not believe every spirit, but test the spirits to see whether they are of God; for many false prophets have gone out into the world. [2]By this you know the Spirit of God: every spirit which confesses that Jesus Christ has come in the flesh is of God, [3]and every spirit which does not confess Jesus is not of God. This is the spirit of antichrist, of which you heard that it was coming, and now it is in the world already. [4]Little children, you are of God, and have overcome them; for he who is in you is greater than he who is in the world. [5]They are of the world, therefore

4 Ἀγαπητοί, μὴ παντὶ πνεύματι
Beloved, [2]not [3]every [4]spirit

πιστεύετε, ἀλλὰ δοκιμάζετε τὰ πνεύματα
[1]believe ye, but prove the spirits

εἰ ἐκ τοῦ θεοῦ ἐστιν, ὅτι πολλοὶ
if of – God they are, because many

ψευδοπροφῆται ἐξεληλύθασιν εἰς τὸν
false prophets have gone forth into the

κόσμον. 2 ἐν τούτῳ γινώσκετε τὸ πνεῦμα
world. By this know ye the Spirit

τοῦ θεοῦ· πᾶν πνεῦμα ὃ ὁμολογεῖ Ἰησοῦν
– of God: every spirit which confesses Jesus

Χριστὸν ἐν σαρκὶ ἐληλυθότα ἐκ τοῦ
Christ [2]in [the] flesh [1]having come [4]of –

θεοῦ ἐστιν, 3 καὶ πᾶν πνεῦμα ὃ μὴ
[3]God [5]is, and every spirit which not

ὁμολογεῖ τὸν Ἰησοῦν ἐκ τοῦ θεοῦ οὐκ
confesses – Jesus [3]of – [4]God [1]not

ἔστιν· καὶ τοῦτό ἐστιν τὸ τοῦ ἀντιχρίστου,
[2]is; and this is the of the antichrist,
[spirit]

ὃ ἀκηκόατε ὅτι ἔρχεται, καὶ νῦν ἐν
which ye have that it is coming, and [2]now [4]in
heard

τῷ κόσμῳ ἐστὶν ἤδη. 4 ὑμεῖς ἐκ τοῦ
[5]the [6]world [1]is [3]already. Ye of –

θεοῦ ἐστε, τεκνία, καὶ νενικήκατε αὐτούς,
God are, little and have overcome them,
children,

ὅτι μείζων ἐστὶν ὁ ἐν ὑμῖν ἢ ὁ ἐν
because greater is the in you than the in
[one] [one]

τῷ κόσμῳ. 5 αὐτοὶ ἐκ τοῦ κόσμου
the world. [1]They [3]of [4]the [5]world

what they say is of the world, and the world listens to them. [6] We are of God. Whoever knows God listens to us, and he who is not of God does not listen to us. By this we know the spirit of truth and the spirit of error.

7 Beloved, let us love one another; for love is of God, and he who loves is born of God and knows God. [8] He who does not love does not know God; for God is love. [9] In this the love of God was made manifest among us, that God sent his only Son into the world, so that we might live through him. [10] In this is love, not that we loved God but that he loved us and sent his Son to be the expiation for our sins. [11] Beloved, if God so loved us, we also ought to love one another. [12] No man has ever seen God; if we love one another, God

εἰσίν· διὰ τοῦτο ἐκ τοῦ κόσμου λαλοῦσιν
[2]are;   therefore   [2]of [3]the   [4]world   [1]they speak

καὶ ὁ κόσμος αὐτῶν ἀκούει. 6 ἡμεῖς
and   the   world   them   hears.   [1]We

ἐκ τοῦ θεοῦ ἐσμεν· ὁ γινώσκων τὸν
[2]of   –   [4]God   [2]are;   the [one] knowing   –

θεὸν ἀκούει ἡμῶν, ὃς οὐκ ἔστιν ἐκ
God   hears   us,   [he] who   is not   of

τοῦ θεοῦ οὐκ ἀκούει ἡμῶν. ἐκ τούτου
–   God   hears not   us.   From   this

γινώσκομεν τὸ πνεῦμα τῆς ἀληθείας καὶ
we know   the   spirit   –   of truth   and

τὸ πνεῦμα τῆς πλάνης.
the   spirit   –   of error.

7 Ἀγαπητοί, ἀγαπῶμεν ἀλλήλους, ὅτι
Beloved,   let us love   one another,   because

ἡ ἀγάπη ἐκ τοῦ θεοῦ ἐστιν, καὶ πᾶς ὁ
–   love   [2]of   –   [3]God   [1]is,   and everyone

ἀγαπῶν ἐκ τοῦ θεοῦ γεγέννηται καὶ
loving   [2]of   –   [3]God   [1]has been begotten   and

γινώσκει τὸν θεόν. 8 ὁ μὴ ἀγαπῶν
knows   –   God.   The [one] not   loving

οὐκ ἔγνω τὸν θεόν, ὅτι ὁ θεὸς ἀγάπη
knew not   –   God,   because   –   God   [2]love

ἐστίν. 9 ἐν τούτῳ ἐφανερώθη ἡ ἀγάπη
[1]is.   By   this   was manifested   the   love

τοῦ θεοῦ ἐν ἡμῖν, ὅτι τὸν υἱὸν αὐτοῦ
–   of God   in(to)   us,   because   [3]the   [5]Son   [6]of him

τὸν μονογενῆ ἀπέσταλκεν ὁ θεὸς εἰς
–   [4]only begotten   [2]has sent   –   [1]God   into

τὸν κόσμον ἵνα ζήσωμεν δι’ αὐτοῦ.
the   world   in order   we might live   through   him.
    that

10 ἐν τούτῳ ἐστὶν ἡ ἀγάπη, οὐχ ὅτι
In   this   is   –   love,   not   that

ἡμεῖς ἠγαπήκαμεν τὸν θεόν, ἀλλ’ ὅτι
we   have loved   –   God,   but   that

αὐτὸς ἠγάπησεν ἡμᾶς καὶ ἀπέστειλεν τὸν
he   loved   us   and   sent   the

υἱὸν αὐτοῦ ἱλασμὸν περὶ τῶν ἁμαρτιῶν
Son   of him a propitiation concerning   the   sins

ἡμῶν. 11 ἀγαπητοί, εἰ οὕτως ὁ θεὸς
of us.   Beloved,   if   so   –   God

ἠγάπησεν ἡμᾶς, καὶ ἡμεῖς ὀφείλομεν
loved   us,   [2]also   [1]we   [3]ought

ἀλλήλους ἀγαπᾶν. 12 θεὸν οὐδεὶς πώποτε
[2]one another   [4]to love.   [4]God   [1]no man   [2]ever

τεθέαται· ἐὰν ἀγαπῶμεν ἀλλήλους, ὁ θεὸς
[3]has beheld;   if   we love   one another,   –   God

abides in us and his love is perfected in us.

13 By this we know that we abide in him and he in us, because he has given us of his own Spirit. 14And we have seen and testify that the Father has sent his Son as the Savior of the world. 15Whoever confesses that Jesus is the Son of God, God abides in him, and he in God. 16So we know and believe the love God has for us. God is love, and he who abides in love abides in God, and God abides in him. 17In this is love perfected with us, that we may have confidence for the day of judgment, because as he is so are we in this world. 18There is no fear in love, but perfect love casts out fear. For fear has to do with punishment, and he who fears is not perfected in love. 19We love, because he first

ἐν   ἡμῖν   μένει   καὶ   ἡ   ἀγάπη   αὐτοῦ
in   us   remains   and   the   · love   of him

τετελειωμένη   ἐν   ἡμῖν   ἐστιν.   13 Ἐν
²having been perfected ³in   ⁴us   ¹is.   By

τούτῳ   γινώσκομεν   ὅτι   ἐν   αὐτῷ   μένομεν
this   we know   that   in   him   we remain

καὶ   αὐτὸς   ἐν   ἡμῖν,   ὅτι   ἐκ   τοῦ   πνεύματος
and   he   in   us,   because ²of   ³the   ⁵Spirit

αὐτοῦ   δέδωκεν   ἡμῖν.   14 καὶ   ἡμεῖς
⁶of him   ¹he has given   ²us.   And   we

τεθεάμεθα   καὶ   μαρτυροῦμεν   ὅτι   ὁ   πατὴρ
have beheld   and   bear witness   that   the   Father

ἀπέσταλκεν   τὸν   υἱὸν   σωτῆρα   τοῦ   κόσμου.
has sent   the   Son [as] Saviour   of the   world.

15 ὃς   ἐὰν   ὁμολογήσῃ   ὅτι   Ἰησοῦς   ἐστιν
Whoever   confesses   that   Jesus   is

ὁ   υἱὸς   τοῦ   θεοῦ,   ὁ   θεὸς   ἐν   αὐτῷ   μένει
the   Son   — of God,   —   God   in   him   remains

καὶ   αὐτὸς   ἐν   τῷ   θεῷ.   16 καὶ   ἡμεῖς
and   he   in   —   God.   And   we

ἐγνώκαμεν   καὶ   πεπιστεύκαμεν   τὴν   ἀγάπην
have known   and   have believed   the   love

ἣν   ἔχει   ὁ   θεὸς   ἐν   ἡμῖν.   Ὁ   θεὸς   ἀγάπη
which ²has   — ¹God   in(to) us.   God   ²love

ἐστίν,   καὶ   ὁ   μένων   ἐν   τῇ   ἀγάπῃ   ἐν
¹is,   and   the remaining in   —   love   ²in
                             [one]

τῷ   θεῷ   μένει   καὶ   ὁ   θεὸς   ἐν   αὐτῷ
—   ²God   ¹remains   and   —   God   ²in   ³him

μένει.   17 Ἐν   τούτῳ   τετελείωται   ἡ   ἀγάπη
¹remains.   By   this   ²has been perfected   ¹love

μεθ'   ἡμῶν,   ἵνα   παρρησίαν   ἔχωμεν   ἐν
with   us,   in order that ²confidence ¹we may have   in

τῇ   ἡμέρᾳ   τῆς   κρίσεως,   ὅτι   καθὼς   ἐκεῖνός
the   day   —   of judgment, because   as   that one*

ἐστιν   καὶ   ἡμεῖς   ἐσμεν   ἐν   τῷ   κόσμῳ
is   ³also   ¹we   ²are   in   —   world

τούτῳ.   18 φόβος   οὐκ   ἔστιν   ἐν   τῇ   ἀγάπῃ,
this.   Fear   is not   in   —   love,

ἀλλ'   ἡ   τελεία   ἀγάπη   ἔξω   βάλλει   τὸν
but   —   perfect   love   ²out   ¹casts   the

φόβον,   ὅτι   ὁ   φόβος   κόλασιν   ἔχει,   ὁ   δὲ
fear,   because the fear   ²punishment ¹has,   and the

φοβούμενος   οὐ   τετελείωται   ἐν   τῇ   ἀγάπῃ.
[one] fearing   has not been perfected   in   —   love.

19 ἡμεῖς   ἀγαπῶμεν,   ὅτι   αὐτὸς   πρῶτος
We   love,   because   he   first

* See ch. 2. 6, 3. 3, 5, 7, 16.

loved us. ²⁰If any one says, "I love God," and hates his brother, he is a liar; for he who does not love his brother whom he has seen, cannot[f] love God whom he has not seen. ²¹And this commandment we have from him, that he who loves God should love his brother also.

ἠγάπησεν   ἡμᾶς.   **20** ἐάν   τις   εἴπη   ὅτι
loved   us.   If anyone says[,]

ἀγαπῶ   τὸν   θεόν,   καὶ   τὸν   ἀδελφὸν   αὐτοῦ
I love   -   God,   and ²the   ³brother   ⁴of him

μισῇ,   ψεύστης   ἐστίν·   ὁ   γὰρ   μὴ   ἀγαπῶν
¹hates, ²a liar   ¹he is; for the [one] not loving

τὸν   ἀδελφὸν   αὐτοῦ   ὃν   ἑώρακεν,   τὸν
the   brother   of him whom he has seen,

θεὸν   ὃν   οὐχ   ἑώρακεν   οὐ   δύναται   ἀγαπᾶν.
³God ⁴whom ⁵he has not seen ¹he cannot ²to love.

21 καὶ   ταύτην   τὴν   ἐντολὴν   ἔχομεν   ἀπ'
       And   this   -   commandment we have   from

αὐτοῦ,   ἵνα   ὁ   ἀγαπῶν   τὸν   θεὸν   ἀγαπᾷ
him,   in order the loving   -   God   loves
       that [one]

καὶ   τὸν   ἀδελφὸν   αὐτοῦ.
also   the   brother   of him.

CHAPTER 5

EVERY one who believes that Jesus is the Christ is a child of God, and every one who loves the parent loves the child. ²By this we know that we love the children of God, when we love God and obey his commandments. ³For this is the love of God, that we keep his commandments. And his commandments are not burdensome. ⁴For whatever is born of God overcomes the world; and this is the victory that overcomes the world, our faith. ⁵Who

5 Πᾶς   ὁ   πιστεύων   ὅτι   Ἰησοῦς   ἐστιν
   Everyone   believing   that   Jesus   is

ὁ   χριστὸς   ἐκ   τοῦ   θεοῦ   γεγέννηται,   καὶ
the Christ   ²of   -   ³God ¹has been begotten, and

πᾶς   ὁ   ἀγαπῶν   τὸν   γεννήσαντα   ἀγαπᾷ
everyone loving the [one] begetting   loves

τὸν   γεγεννημένον   ἐξ   αὐτοῦ.   **2** ἐν   τούτῳ
the having been begotten of him.   By   this
[one]

γινώσκομεν   ὅτι   ἀγαπῶμεν   τὰ   τέκνα   τοῦ
we know   that we love   the children   -

θεοῦ,   ὅταν   τὸν   θεὸν   ἀγαπῶμεν   καὶ   τὰς
of God, whenever -   ³God   ¹we love   and ²the

ἐντολὰς   αὐτοῦ   ποιῶμεν.   **3** αὕτη   γάρ
²command- ⁴of him ¹we do.   For this
ments

ἐστιν   ἡ   ἀγάπη   τοῦ   θεοῦ,   ἵνα   τὰς   ἐντολὰς
is   the love   -   of in order ²the ³command-
              God,   that   ments

αὐτοῦ   τηρῶμεν·   καὶ   αἱ   ἐντολαὶ   αὐτοῦ
⁴of him ¹we keep; and the commandments of him

βαρεῖαι   οὐκ   εἰσίν,   **4** ὅτι   πᾶν   τὸ   γεγεν-
heavy   are not,   because everything having

νημένον   ἐκ   τοῦ   θεοῦ   νικᾷ   τὸν   κόσμον·
been begotten of -   God overcomes the   world;

καὶ   αὕτη   ἐστὶν   ἡ   νίκη   ἡ   νικήσασα   τὸν
and   this   is   the victory - overcoming the

κόσμον,   ἡ   πίστις   ἡμῶν.   **5** Τίς   ἐστιν
world,   the   faith   of us.   ²Who   ³is

---

[f] Other ancient authorities read *how can he*

is it that overcomes the world but he who believes that Jesus is the Son of God?

6 This is he who came by water and blood, Jesus Christ, not with the water only but with the water and the blood. 7And the Spirit is the witness, because the Spirit is the truth. 8There are three witnesses, the Spirit, the water, and the blood; and these three agree. 9If we receive the testimony of men, the testimony of God is greater; for this is the testimony of God that he has borne witness to his Son. 10He who believes in the Son of God has the testimony in himself. He who does not believe God, has made him a liar, because he has not believed in the testimony that God has borne to his Son. 11And this is the testimony, that God gave us eternal life, and this life is in his Son. 12He

[δὲ] ὁ νικῶν τὸν κόσμον εἰ μὴ ὁ
¹and the overcoming the world except the
   [one]

πιστεύων ὅτι 'Ιησοῦς ἐστιν ὁ υἱὸς τοῦ
[one] believing that Jesus is the Son –

θεοῦ; 6 οὗτός ἐστιν ὁ ἐλθὼν δι' ὕδατος
of God? This is the coming through water
   [one]

καὶ αἵματος, 'Ιησοῦς Χριστός· οὐκ ἐν
and blood, Jesus Christ; not by

τῷ ὕδατι μόνον, ἀλλ' ἐν τῷ ὕδατι καὶ
the water only, but by the water and

ἐν τῷ αἵματι· καὶ τὸ πνεῦμά ἐστιν τὸ
by the blood; and the Spirit is the

μαρτυροῦν, ὅτι τὸ πνεῦμά ἐστιν ἡ ἀλήθεια.
[one] bearing be- the Spirit is the truth.
witness, cause

7 ὅτι τρεῖς εἰσιν οἱ μαρτυροῦντες, 8 τὸ
Because three there are the bearing witness, the
   [ones]

πνεῦμα καὶ τὸ ὕδωρ καὶ τὸ αἷμα, καὶ
Spirit and the water and the blood, and

οἱ τρεῖς εἰς τὸ ἕν εἰσιν. 9 εἰ τὴν
the three ²in the ³one ¹are. If ²the

μαρτυρίαν τῶν ἀνθρώπων λαμβάνομεν, ἡ
³witness – ⁴of men ¹we receive, the

μαρτυρία τοῦ θεοῦ μείζων ἐστιν, ὅτι
witness – of God ²greater ¹is, because

αὕτη ἐστὶν ἡ μαρτυρία τοῦ θεοῦ, ὅτι
this is the witness – of God, because

μεμαρτύρηκεν περὶ τοῦ υἱοῦ αὐτοῦ. 10 ὁ
he has borne concern- the Son of him. The
witness ing

πιστεύων εἰς τὸν υἱὸν τοῦ θεοῦ ἔχει
[one] believing in the Son – of God has

τὴν μαρτυρίαν ἐν αὐτῷ. ὁ μὴ πιστεύων
the witness in him. The not believing
   [one]

τῷ θεῷ ψεύστην πεποίηκεν αὐτόν, ὅτι
– God ²a liar ¹has made ³him, because

οὐ πεπίστευκεν εἰς τὴν μαρτυρίαν ἣν
he has not believed in the witness which

μεμαρτύρηκεν ὁ θεὸς περὶ τοῦ υἱοῦ
²has borne witness – ¹God concerning the Son

αὐτοῦ. 11 καὶ αὕτη ἐστὶν ἡ μαρτυρία,
of him. And this is the witness,

ὅτι ζωὴν αἰώνιον ἔδωκεν ὁ θεὸς ἡμῖν,
that ⁵life ⁴eternal ²gave – ¹God ³to us,

καὶ αὕτη ἡ ζωὴ ἐν τῷ υἱῷ αὐτοῦ
and this – life ²in ³the ⁴Son ⁵of him

who has the Son has life; he who has not the Son of God has not life.

13 I write this to you who believe in the name of the Son of God, that you may know that you have eternal life. [14]And this is the confidence which we have in him, that if we ask anything according to his will he hears us. [15]And if we know that he hears us in whatever we ask, we know that we have obtained the requests made of him. [16]If any one sees his brother committing what is not a mortal sin, he will ask, and God will give him life for those whose sin is not mortal. There is sin which is mortal; I do not say that one is to pray for that. [17]All wrong-doing is sin, but there is sin which is not mortal.

18 We know that any one born of God does not sin, but He who was born of God keeps him, and the evil one does not touch him.

19 We know that we

ἐστιν.   12 ὁ   ἔχων   τὸν   υἱὸν   ἔχει   τὴν
[1]is.   The [one] having   the   Son   has   the

ζωήν·   ὁ   μὴ   ἔχων   τὸν   υἱὸν   τοῦ   θεοῦ
life;   the   not   having   the   Son   –   of God
        [one]

τὴν   ζωὴν   οὐκ   ἔχει.
the   life   has not.

13 Ταῦτα   ἔγραψα   ὑμῖν   ἵνα   εἰδῆτε   ὅτι
These   I wrote   to you in order   ye may   that
things   know

ζωὴν   ἔχετε   αἰώνιον,   τοῖς   πιστεύουσιν
[3]life   [1]ye have   [2]eternal,   to the [ones]   believing

εἰς   τὸ   ὄνομα   τοῦ   υἱοῦ   τοῦ   θεοῦ.   14 Καὶ
in   the   name   of the Son   –   of God.   And

αὕτη   ἐστὶν   ἡ   παρρησία   ἣν   ἔχομεν   πρὸς
this   is   the   confidence   which we have   toward

αὐτόν,   ὅτι   ἐάν   τι   αἰτώμεθα   κατὰ   τὸ
him,   that   if   [2]anything   [1]we ask   according to the

θέλημα   αὐτοῦ   ἀκούει   ἡμῶν.   15 καὶ
will   of him   he hears   us.   And

ἐὰν   οἴδαμεν   ὅτι   ἀκούει   ἡμῶν   ὃ   ἐὰν
if   we know   that   he hears   us   whatever

αἰτώμεθα,   οἴδαμεν   ὅτι   ἔχομεν   τὰ   αἰτήματα
we ask,   we know   that   we have   the   requests

ἃ   ᾐτήκαμεν   ἀπ᾿   αὐτοῦ.   16 Ἐάν   τις
which   we have   from   him.   If   anyone
        asked

ἴδῃ   τὸν   ἀδελφὸν   αὐτοῦ   ἁμαρτάνοντα
sees   the   brother   of him   sinning

ἁμαρτίαν   μὴ   πρὸς   θάνατον,   αἰτήσει,   καὶ
a sin   not   unto   death,   he shall ask,   and

δώσει   αὐτῷ   ζωήν,   τοῖς   ἁμαρτάνουσιν
he will give to him   life,   to the [ones]   sinning

μὴ   πρὸς   θάνατον.   ἔστιν   ἁμαρτία   πρὸς
not   unto   death.   There is   a sin   unto

θάνατον·   οὐ   περὶ   ἐκείνης   λέγω   ἵνα
death;   not   concerning   that   do I say in order
                            that

ἐρωτήσῃ.   17 πᾶσα   ἀδικία   ἁμαρτία   ἐστίν,
he should inquire.   All   iniquity   [1]sin   [1]is,

καὶ   ἔστιν   ἁμαρτία   οὐ   πρὸς   θάνατον.
and   there is   a sin   not   unto   death.

18 Οἴδαμεν   ὅτι   πᾶς   ὁ   γεγεννημένος   ἐκ
We know   that   everyone   having been begotten   of

τοῦ   θεοῦ   οὐχ   ἁμαρτάνει,   ἀλλ᾿   ὁ   γεννηθεὶς
–   God   sins not,   but   the [one] begotten

ἐκ   τοῦ   θεοῦ   τηρεῖ   αὐτόν,   καὶ   ὁ   πονηρὸς
of   –   God   keeps   him,   and the   evil one

οὐχ   ἅπτεται   αὐτοῦ.   19 οἴδαμεν   ὅτι   ἐκ
does not touch   him.   We know   that   of

are of God, and the whole world is in the power of the evil one.

20 And we know that the Son of God has come and has given us understanding, to know him who is true; and we are in him who is true, in his Son Jesus Christ. This is the true God and eternal life. ²¹Little children, keep yourselves from idols.

τοῦ θεοῦ ἐσμεν, καὶ ὁ κόσμος ὅλος ἐν
the - God we are, and the ³world ¹whole in

τῷ πονηρῷ κεῖται. 20 οἴδαμεν δὲ ὅτι
the evil one lies. ¹we know ¹And that

ὁ υἱὸς τοῦ θεοῦ ἥκει, καὶ δέδωκεν
the Son - of God is come, and has given

ἡμῖν διάνοιαν ἵνα γινώσκωμεν τὸν
to us an understanding in order we might know the
that

ἀληθινόν· καὶ ἐσμεν ἐν τῷ ἀληθινῷ,
true [one]; and we are in the true [one],

ἐν τῷ υἱῷ αὐτοῦ Ἰησοῦ Χριστῷ. οὗτός
in the Son of him Jesus Christ. This

ἐστιν ὁ ἀληθινὸς θεὸς καὶ ζωὴ αἰώνιος.
is the true God and life eternal.

21 Τεκνία, φυλάξατε ἑαυτὰ ἀπὸ τῶν
Little children, guard yourselves from the

εἰδώλων.
idols.

II. JOHN

ΙΩΑΝΝΟΥ Β
Of John 2

THE elder to the elect lady and her children, whom I love in the truth, and not only I but also all who know the truth, ²because of the truth which abides in us and will be with us for ever:

3 Grace, mercy, and peace will be with us, from God the Father and from Jesus Christ the Father's Son, in truth and love.

1 Ὁ πρεσβύτερος ἐκλεκτῇ κυρίᾳ καὶ
The elder to [the] chosen lady and

τοῖς τέκνοις αὐτῆς, οὓς ἐγὼ ἀγαπῶ ἐν
to the children of her, whom I love in

ἀληθείᾳ, καὶ οὐκ ἐγὼ μόνος ἀλλὰ καὶ
truth, and not I alone but also

πάντες οἱ ἐγνωκότες τὴν ἀλήθειαν, 2 διὰ
all the having known the truth, because of
[ones]

τὴν ἀλήθειαν τὴν μένουσαν ἐν ἡμῖν,
the truth - remaining among us,

καὶ μεθ' ἡμῶν ἔσται εἰς τὸν αἰῶνα.
and with us will be unto the age.

3 ἔσται μεθ' ἡμῶν χάρις ἔλεος εἰρήνη
⁴will be ³with ⁵us ¹Grace[,] ²mercy[,] ³peace

παρὰ θεοῦ πατρός, καὶ παρὰ Ἰησοῦ
from God [the] Father, and from Jesus

Χριστοῦ τοῦ υἱοῦ τοῦ πατρός, ἐν ἀληθείᾳ
Christ the Son of the Father, in truth

καὶ ἀγάπῃ.
and love.

4 I rejoiced greatly to find some of your children following the truth, just as we have been commanded by the Father. ⁵And now I beg you, lady, not as though I were writing you a new commandment, but the one we have had from the beginning, that we love one another. ⁶And this is love, that we follow his commandments; this is the commandment, as you have heard from the beginning, that you follow love. ⁷For many deceivers have gone out into the world, men who will not acknowledge the coming of Jesus Christ in the flesh; such a one is the deceiver and the antichrist. ⁸Look to yourselves, that you may not lose what youᵃ have worked for, but may win a full reward. ⁹Any one who goes ahead and does not abide in the doctrine of Christ does not have God; he who abides in the doctrine has both the Father and the Son. ¹⁰If any one comes to you and does not bring this

ᵃ Other ancient authorities read *we*

---

4 Ἐχάρην λίαν ὅτι εὕρηκα ἐκ τῶν
I rejoiced greatly because I have of the
                                 found [some]

τέκνων σου περιπατοῦντας ἐν ἀληθείᾳ,
children of thee walking in truth,

καθὼς ἐντολὴν ἐλάβομεν παρὰ τοῦ πατρός.
as command- we received from the Father.
      ment

5 καὶ νῦν ἐρωτῶ σε, κυρία, οὐχ ὡς
And now I request thee, lady, not as

ἐντολὴν γράφων σοι καινήν, ἀλλὰ ἥν
²command- ¹writing ⁴to thee ³a new, but which
ment

εἴχομεν ἀπ' ἀρχῆς, ἵνα ἀγαπῶμεν
we had from [the] in order we should
             beginning, that love

ἀλλήλους. **6** καὶ αὕτη ἐστὶν ἡ ἀγάπη,
one another. And this is - love,

ἵνα περιπατῶμεν κατὰ τὰς ἐντολὰς
in order we should walk accord- the command-
that   ing to ments

αὐτοῦ· αὕτη ἡ ἐντολή ἐστιν, καθὼς
of him; this ³the ²commandment ¹is, as

ἠκούσατε ἀπ' ἀρχῆς, ἵνα ἐν αὐτῇ
ye heard from [the] in order ²in ³it
            beginning, that

περιπατῆτε. **7** ὅτι πολλοὶ πλάνοι ἐξῆλθον
¹ye should walk. Because many deceivers went forth

εἰς τὸν κόσμον, οἱ μὴ ὁμολογοῦντες
into the world, the not confessing
                [ones]

Ἰησοῦν Χριστὸν ἐρχόμενον ἐν σαρκί·
Jesus Christ coming in [the] flesh;

οὗτός ἐστιν ὁ πλάνος καὶ ὁ ἀντίχριστος.
this is the deceiver and the antichrist.

8 βλέπετε ἑαυτούς, ἵνα μὴ ἀπολέσητε
See yourselves, lest ye lose

ἃ ἠργασάμεθα, ἀλλὰ μισθὸν πλήρη
[the] we wrought, but ⁴reward ³a full
things which

ἀπολάβητε. **9** πᾶς ὁ προάγων καὶ μὴ
¹ye may receive. Everyone going forward and not

μένων ἐν τῇ διδαχῇ τοῦ Χριστοῦ θεὸν
remaining in the teaching - of Christ ³God

οὐκ ἔχει· ὁ μένων ἐν τῇ διδαχῇ, οὗτος
²not ¹has; the remaining in the teaching, this one
            [one]

καὶ τὸν πατέρα καὶ τὸν υἱὸν ἔχει.
³both ⁵the ⁴Father ⁵and ⁶the ⁷Son ¹has.

10 εἴ τις ἔρχεται πρὸς ὑμᾶς καὶ ταύτην
If anyone comes to you and this

doctrine, do not receive him into the house or give him any greeting; [11]for he who greets him shares his wicked work.

12 Though I have much to write to you, I would rather not use paper and ink, but I hope to come to see you and talk with you face to face, so that our joy may be complete.

13 The children of your elect sister greet you.

τὴν   διδαχὴν   οὐ   φέρει,   μὴ   λαμβάνετε
 -      teaching   brings not,   do not ye receive

αὐτὸν   εἰς   οἰκίαν,   καὶ   χαίρειν   αὐτῷ   μὴ
him   into [your]   and   ⁴to rejoice ³him ⁵not
              house,

λέγετε·   11 ὁ   λέγων   γὰρ   αὐτῷ   χαίρειν
¹tell ye·;   ³the ²telling ¹for   him   to rejoice
         [one]

κοινωνεῖ   τοῖς   ἔργοις   αὐτοῦ   τοῖς   πονηροῖς.
shares   in the ⁴works   ³of him   -   ²evil.

12 Πολλὰ   ἔχων   ὑμῖν   γράφειν   οὐκ
¹Many things ²having ⁴to you ³to write   ⁶not

ἐβουλήθην   διὰ   χάρτου   καὶ   μέλανος,   ἀλλὰ
⁵I purpose by means paper   and   ink,   but
            of

ἐλπίζω   γενέσθαι   πρὸς   ὑμᾶς   καὶ   στόμα
I am hoping to be   with   you   and   ²mouth

πρὸς   στόμα   λαλῆσαι,   ἵνα   ἡ   χαρὰ   ἡμῶν
²to   ⁴mouth   ¹to speak, in or- the   joy   of us
                          der that

πεπληρωμένη   ᾖ.   13 Ἀσπάζεταί   σε   τὰ
having been   may be.   ²greets   ¹thee ¹The
fulfilled

τέκνα   τῆς   ἀδελφῆς   σου   τῆς   ἐκλεκτῆς.
²children ³of the ⁴sister ⁵of thee -   ⁶chosen.

III. JOHN

ΙΩΑΝΝΟΥ Γ
Of John 3

THE elder to the beloved Ga′ius, whom I love in the truth.

2 Beloved, I pray that all may go well with you and that you may be in health; I know that it is well with your soul. [3]For I greatly rejoiced when some of the brethren arrived and testified to the truth of your life, as

1 Ὁ   πρεσβύτερος   Γαΐῳ   τῷ   ἀγαπητῷ,
The   elder   to Gaius the   beloved,

ὃν   ἐγὼ   ἀγαπῶ   ἐν   ἀληθείᾳ.
whom I   love   in   truth.

2 Ἀγαπητέ,   περὶ   πάντων   εὔχομαί   σε
Beloved,   concerning all things I pray   thee
                                         =that

εὐοδοῦσθαι   καὶ   ὑγιαίνειν,   καθὼς   εὐοδοῦταί
to prosper   and   to be in health, as   ⁴prospers
thou mayest prosper ...

σου   ἡ   ψυχή.   3 ἐχάρην   γὰρ   λίαν   ἐρχομένων
²of   ¹the ³soul.   For I rejoiced greatly coming
thee   =when [some]

ἀδελφῶν   καὶ   μαρτυρούντων   σου   τῇ
brothers   and   bearing witness*   of thee in the
brothers came and bore witness

* That is, "do not greet him."

indeed you do follow the truth. **4** No greater joy can I have than this, to hear that my children follow the truth.

5 Beloved, it is a loyal thing you do when you render any service to the brethren, especially to strangers, **6** who have testified to your love before the church. You will do well to send them on their journey as befits God's service. **7** For they have set out for his sake and have accepted nothing from the heathen. **8** So we ought to support such men, that we may be fellow workers in the truth.

9 I have written something to the church; but Diot'rephes, who likes to put himself first, does not acknowledge my authority. **10** So if I come, I will bring up what he is doing, prating against me with evil words. And not content with that, he refuses himself to welcome the brethren, and also stops those who want to welcome them and puts them out of the church.

11 Beloved, do not imitate evil but imitate

ἀληθείᾳ,   καθὼς   σὺ   ἐν   ἀληθείᾳ   περιπατεῖς.
truth,   as   thou in   truth   walkest.

4 μειζοτέραν   τούτων   οὐκ   ἔχω   χαράν,   ἵνα
²greater ⁶[than] ⁵these   ¹I have no   ³joy,   *in or-*
               things   *der* that

ἀκούω   τὰ   ἐμὰ   τέκνα   ἐν   τῇ   ἀληθείᾳ
I hear   –   my   children   ²in   ³the   ⁴truth

περιπατοῦντα.   **5** Ἀγαπητέ,   πιστὸν   ποιεῖς
¹walking.   Beloved,   faithfully   thou
                                           doest

ὃ   ἐὰν   ἐργάσῃ   εἰς   τοὺς   ἀδελφοὺς   καὶ
whatever thou workest   for   the   brothers   and

τοῦτο   ξένους,   **6** οἳ   ἐμαρτύρησάν   σου   τῇ
this   strangers,   who   bore witness   of thee   –

ἀγάπῃ   ἐνώπιον   ἐκκλησίας,   οὓς   καλῶς
in love   before   [the] church,   whom   well

ποιήσεις   προπέμψας   ἀξίως   τοῦ   θεοῦ·
thou wilt do   sending forward   worthily   –   of God;

7 ὑπὲρ   γὰρ   τοῦ   ὀνόματος   ἐξῆλθαν   μηδὲν
for on behalf of   the   name   they went forth ²nothing

λαμβάνοντες   ἀπὸ   τῶν   ἐθνικῶν.   **8** ἡμεῖς
¹taking   from   the   Gentiles.   We

οὖν   ὀφείλομεν   ὑπολαμβάνειν   τοὺς   τοιούτους,
there-   ought   to entertain   –   such men,
fore

ἵνα   συνεργοὶ   γινώμεθα   τῇ   ἀληθείᾳ.
in or-   ²co-workers   ¹we may become   in the   truth.
der that

9 Ἔγραψά   τι   τῇ   ἐκκλησίᾳ·   ἀλλ'   ὁ
I wrote   some-   to the   church;   but   the
          thing   [one]

φιλοπρωτεύων   αὐτῶν   Διοτρέφης   οὐκ
loving to be first   of them   Diotrephes   not

ἐπιδέχεται   ἡμᾶς.   **10** διὰ   τοῦτο,   ἐὰν
receives   us.   Therefore,   if

ἔλθω,   ὑπομνήσω   αὐτοῦ   τὰ   ἔργα   ἃ   ποιεῖ
I come,   I will remember   ²of him   ¹the   ³works which he does

λόγοις   πονηροῖς   φλυαρῶν   ἡμᾶς,   καὶ   μὴ
⁴words   ³with evil   ¹prating against   ²us,   and   not

ἀρκούμενος   ἐπὶ   τούτοις   οὔτε   αὐτὸς
being satisfied   on(with)   these   ²neither   ¹he

ἐπιδέχεται   τοὺς   ἀδελφοὺς   καὶ   τοὺς
³receives   the   brothers   and   the

βουλομένους   κωλύει   καὶ   ἐκ   τῆς   ἐκκλησίας
[ones] purposing   he prevents   and   ²out of   ³the   ⁴church

ἐκβάλλει.
¹puts out.

11 Ἀγαπητέ,   μὴ   μιμοῦ   τὸ   κακὸν   ἀλλὰ
     Beloved,   imitate not   the   bad   but

good. He who does good is of God; he who does evil has not seen God. [12] Deme'trius has testimony from every one, and from the truth itself; I testify to him too, and you know my testimony is true.

13 I had much to write to you, but I would rather not write with pen and ink; [14] I hope to see you soon, and we will talk together face to face.

15 Peace be to you. The friends greet you. Greet the friends, every one of them.

τὸ ἀγαθόν. ὁ ἀγαθοποιῶν ἐκ τοῦ θεοῦ
the good. The [one] doing good [2]of — [3]God

ἐστιν· ὁ κακοποιῶν οὐχ ἑώρακεν τὸν
[1]is; the [one] doing ill has not seen

θεόν. 12 Δημητρίῳ μεμαρτύρηται ὑπὸ
God. To Demetrius witness has been borne by

πάντων καὶ ὑπὸ αὐτῆς τῆς ἀληθείας·
all and by [3][it]self [1]the [2]truth;

καὶ ἡμεῖς δὲ μαρτυροῦμεν, καὶ οἶδας
[3]also [2]we [1]and bear witness, and thou knowest

ὅτι ἡ μαρτυρία ἡμῶν ἀληθής ἐστιν.
that the witness of us [2]true [1]is.

13 Πολλὰ εἶχον γράψαι σοι, ἀλλ' οὐ
[2]Many things [1]I had to write to thee, but not

θέλω διὰ μέλανος καὶ καλάμου σοι
I wish [2]by means of [4]ink [3]and [6]pen [5]to thee

γράφειν· 14 ἐλπίζω δὲ εὐθέως σε ἰδεῖν,
[1]to write; but I am hoping [2]immediately [3]thee [1]to see,

καὶ στόμα πρὸς στόμα λαλήσομεν.
and [2]mouth [3]to [4]mouth [1]we will speak.

15 Εἰρήνη σοι. ἀσπάζονταί σε οἱ φίλοι.
Peace to thee. [2]greet [4]thee [1]The [3]friends.

ἀσπάζου τοὺς φίλους κατ' ὄνομα.
Greet thou the friends by name.

JUDE

JUDE, a servant of Jesus Christ and brother of James,

To those who are called, beloved in God the Father and kept for Jesus Christ:

2 May mercy, peace, and love be multiplied to you.

3 Beloved, being very

ΙΟΥΔΑ
Of Jude

1 Ἰούδας Ἰησοῦ Χριστοῦ δοῦλος, ἀδελφὸς
Jude of Jesus Christ a slave, [2]brother

δὲ Ἰακώβου, τοῖς ἐν θεῷ πατρὶ
[1]and of James, [2]to the [ones] [4]by [5]God [6][the] Father

ἠγαπημένοις καὶ Ἰησοῦ Χριστῷ
[3]having been loved [7]and [8]for Jesus [10]Christ

τετηρημένοις κλητοῖς. 2 ἔλεος ὑμῖν καὶ
[9]having been kept [1]called. Mercy to you and

εἰρήνη καὶ ἀγάπη πληθυνθείη.
peace and love may it be multiplied.

3 Ἀγαπητοί, πᾶσαν σπουδὴν ποιούμενος
Beloved, [2]all [3]haste [1]making

eager to write to you of
our common salvation, I
found it necessary to
write appealing to you to
contend for the faith
which was once for all
delivered to the saints.
⁴ For admission has been
secretly gained by some
who long ago were
designated for this con-
demnation, ungodly per-
sons who pervert the
grace of our God into
licentiousness and deny
our only Master and
Lord, Jesus Christ.ᵃ

5 Now I desire to
remind you, though you
were once for all fully
informed, that heᵇ who
saved a people out of the
land of Egypt, afterward
destroyed those who did
not believe. ⁶ And the
angels that did not keep
their own position but
left their proper dwelling
have been kept by him
in eternal chains in the
nether gloom until the
judgment of the great
day; ⁷ just as Sodom and
Gomor'rah and the
surrounding cities, which
likewise acted immorally
and indulged in un-
natural lust, serve as an
example by undergoing a
punishment of eternal
fire.

8 Yet in like manner

γράφειν	ὑμῖν	περὶ	τῆς	κοινῆς	ἡμῶν
to write	to you	concerning	the	common	³of us

σωτηρίας,	ἀνάγκην	ἔσχον	γράψαι	ὑμῖν
¹salvation,	necessity	I had	to write	to you

παρακαλῶν	ἐπαγωνίζεσθαι	τῇ	ἅπαξ
exhorting	to contend for	¹the	²once

παραδοθείσῃ	τοῖς	ἁγίοις	πίστει.	4 παρεισε-
⁴delivered	⁵to the	⁶saints	³faith.	⁶crept

δύησαν	γάρ	τινες	ἄνθρωποι,	οἱ	πάλαι
in	For	¹certain	²men,	the [ones]	of old

προγεγραμμένοι	εἰς	τοῦτο	τὸ	κρίμα,
having been previously written	for	this	–	judgment,

ἀσεβεῖς,	τὴν	τοῦ	θεοῦ	ἡμῶν	χάριτα
impious men,	³the	⁴of the	⁵God	⁶of us	³grace

μετατιθέντες	εἰς	ἀσέλγειαν	καὶ	τὸν	μόνον
¹making ²a pretext for		wantonness	and	⁸the	⁹only

δεσπότην	καὶ	κύριον	ἡμῶν	Ἰησοῦν	Χριστὸν
¹⁰Master	⁸and	⁶Lord	⁷of us	¹Jesus	²Christ

ἀρνούμενοι.	5 Ὑπομνῆσαι	δὲ	ὑμᾶς	βούλομαι,
¹denying.	But ²to remind		³you	¹I purpose,

εἰδότας	ἅπαξ	πάντα,	ὅτι	κύριος	λαὸν
⁵knowing	¹once	all things,	that	[the] Lord	²[the] people

ἐκ	γῆς	Αἰγύπτου	σώσας	τὸ	δεύτερον
⁶out of	⁴[the]	⁵of Egypt	¹having saved	in the second place	

τοὺς	μὴ	πιστεύσαντας	ἀπώλεσεν,	6 ἀγγέλους
³the [ones]	²not	⁴believing	¹destroyed,	¹angels

τε	τοὺς	μὴ	τηρήσαντας	τὴν	ἑαυτῶν
²and	–	not	having kept	the	⁵of themselves

ἀρχὴν	ἀλλὰ	ἀπολιπόντας	τὸ	ἴδιον
¹rule	but	having deserted	the(ir)	⁶own

οἰκητήριον	εἰς	κρίσιν	μεγάλης	ἡμέρας
habitation	⁶for ⁷[the] judgment		⁸of [the] great	⁹day

δεσμοῖς	ἀϊδίοις	ὑπὸ	ζόφον	τετήρηκεν·
³bonds	²in everlasting	⁴under	⁵gloom	¹he has kept;

7 ὡς	Σόδομα	καὶ	Γόμορρα	καὶ	αἱ	περὶ
as	Sodom	and	Gomorra	and	¹the	²round

αὐτὰς	πόλεις,	τὸν	ὅμοιον	τρόπον	τούτοις
⁴them	³cities,	in the	like	manner	to these

ἐκπορνεύσασαι	καὶ	ἀπελθοῦσαι	ὀπίσω	σαρκὸς
committing fornication	and	going away	after	²flesh

ἑτέρας,	πρόκεινται	δεῖγμα	πυρὸς	αἰωνίου
¹different,	are set forth	an example	⁴fire	³of eternal

δίκην	ὑπέχουσαι.	8 Ὁμοίως	μέντοι	καὶ
²ven-geance	¹undergoing.	Likewise	indeed	also

ᵃ Or the only Master and our
Lord Jesus Christ
ᵇ Ancient authorities read
Jesus or the Lord or God

these men in their dreamings defile the flesh, reject authority, and revile the glorious ones. [9]But when the archangel Michael, contending with the devil, disputed about the body of Moses, he did not presume to pronounce a reviling judgment upon him, but said, "The Lord rebuke you." [10]But these men revile whatever they do not understand, and by those things that they know by instinct as irrational animals do, they are destroyed. [11]Woe to them! For they walk in the way of Cain, and abandon themselves for the sake of gain to Balaam's error, and perish in Korah's rebellion. [12]These are blemishes[c] on your love feasts, as they boldly carouse together, looking after themselves; waterless clouds, carried along by winds; fruitless trees in late autumn, twice dead, uprooted; [13]wild waves of the sea, casting up the foam of their own shame; wandering stars for whom the nether gloom of darkness has been reserved for ever.

[c] Or reefs

οὗτοι ἐνυπνιαζόμενοι σάρκα μὲν μιαίνουσιν,
these dreaming [ones] [3]flesh [1]on one hand [4]defile,

κυριότητα δὲ ἀθετοῦσιν, δόξας δὲ
[2]lordship [1]on the other [3]despise, and [2]glories

βλασφημοῦσιν. 9 Ὁ δὲ Μιχαὴλ ὁ ἀρχάγ-
[1]rail at. - But Michael the arch-

γελος, ὅτε τῷ διαβόλῳ διακρινόμενος
angel, when [3]with the [4]devil [1]contending

διελέγετο περὶ τοῦ Μωϋσέως σώματος,
he argued about [1]the [2]of Moses [3]body,

οὐκ ἐτόλμησεν κρίσιν ἐπενεγκεῖν βλασφημίας,
durst not [2]a judgment [1]to bring on of railing,

ἀλλὰ εἶπεν· ἐπιτιμήσαι σοι κύριος. 10 οὗτοι
but said : [2]rebuke [3]thee [1][The] Lord. these men

δὲ ὅσα μὲν οὐκ οἴδασιν βλασφημοῦσιν,
But what on one they know not they rail at,
things hand

ὅσα δὲ φυσικῶς ὡς τὰ ἄλογα ζῷα
what on the [3]naturally [2]as [4]the [5]without [6]animals
things other reason

ἐπίστανται, ἐν τούτοις φθείρονται. 11 οὐαὶ
[1]they understand, by these they are corrupted. Woe

αὐτοῖς, ὅτι τῇ ὁδῷ τοῦ Κάϊν ἐπορεύθησαν,
to them, because in the way - of Cain they went,

καὶ τῇ πλάνῃ τοῦ Βαλαὰμ μισθοῦ
and [2]to the [3]error - [4]of Balaam [5]of(for) reward

ἐξεχύθησαν, καὶ τῇ ἀντιλογίᾳ τοῦ Κόρε
[1]gave themselves and [2]in the [3]dispute - [4]of Korah
up,

ἀπώλοντο. 12 Οὗτοί εἰσιν οἱ ἐν ταῖς
[1]perished. These men are [1]the [2]in [3]the

ἀγάπαις ὑμῶν σπιλάδες συνευωχούμενοι
[5]love feasts [4]of you [6]rocks feasting together

ἀφόβως, ἑαυτοὺς ποιμαίνοντες, νεφέλαι
without fear, [2]themselves [1]feeding, [2]clouds

ἄνυδροι ὑπὸ ἀνέμων παραφερόμεναι, δένδρα
[1]waterless [4]by [5]winds [3]being carried away, [2]trees

φθινοπωρινὰ ἄκαρπα δὶς ἀποθανόντα
[1]autumn without fruit twice dying

ἐκριζωθέντα, 13 κύματα ἄγρια θαλάσσης
having been uprooted, [2]waves [1]fierce [3]of [the] sea

ἐπαφρίζοντα τὰς ἑαυτῶν αἰσχύνας, ἀστέρες
[4]foaming up [1]the [2]of themselves [3]shames, [1]stars

πλανῆται, οἷς ὁ ζόφος τοῦ σκότους
[1]wandering, for whom the gloom - of darkness

εἰς αἰῶνα τετήρηται. 14 Ἐπροφήτευσεν
unto [the] age has been kept. [1]prophesied

14 It was of these also that Enoch in the seventh generation from Adam prophesied, saying, "Behold, the Lord came with his holy myriads, ¹⁵to execute judgment on all, and to convict all the ungodly of all their deeds of ungodliness which they have committed in such an ungodly way, and of all the harsh things which ungodly sinners have spoken against him." ¹⁶These are grumblers, malcontents, following their own passions, loud-mouthed boasters, flattering people to gain advantage.

17 But you must remember, beloved, the predictions of the apostles of our Lord Jesus Christ; ¹⁸they said to you, "In the last time there will be scoffers, following their own ungodly passions." ¹⁹It is these who set up divisions, worldly people, devoid of the Spirit. ²⁰But you, beloved, build yourselves up on your most holy faith; pray in the Holy Spirit; ²¹keep yourselves in the love of

δέ   καὶ   τούτοις   ἕβδομος   ἀπὸ   'Αδὰμ
¹And   ²also   ³to these men   ⁴[the] seventh   ⁵from   ⁶Adam

'Ενὼχ   λέγων·   ἰδοὺ   ἦλθεν   κύριος   ἐν
²Enoch   saying :   Behold   came   [the] Lord   with

ἁγίαις   μυριάσιν   αὐτοῦ,   15 ποιῆσαι   κρίσιν
saints   ten thousands   of him,   to do   judgment

κατὰ   πάντων   καὶ   ἐλέγξαι   πάντας   τοὺς
against   all men   and   to rebuke   all   the

ἀσεβεῖς   περὶ   πάντων   τῶν   ἔργων   ἀσεβείας
impious   concerning   all   the   works   of impiety

αὐτῶν   ὧν   ἠσέβησαν   καὶ   περὶ   πάντων
of them   which they impiously did and   concerning   all

τῶν   σκληρῶν   ὧν   ἐλάλησαν   κατ'   αὐτοῦ
the   hard things   which   ³spoke   ⁴against   ⁵him

ἁμαρτωλοὶ   ἀσεβεῖς.   16 Οὗτοί   εἰσιν   γογ-
²sinners   ¹impious.   These men   are   ¹mur-

γυσταὶ   μεμψίμοιροι,   κατὰ   τὰς   ἐπιθυμίας
murers   ¹querulous,   ²according to   ³the   ⁴lusts

αὐτῶν   πορευόμενοι,   καὶ   τὸ   στόμα   αὐτῶν
⁵of them   ¹going,   and   the   mouth   of them

λαλεῖ   ὑπέρογκα,   θαυμάζοντες   πρόσωπα
speaks   arrogant things,   admiring   faces

ὠφελείας   χάριν.
²advantage   ¹for the sake of.

17 'Υμεῖς   δέ,   ἀγαπητοί,   μνήσθητε   τῶν
But ye,   beloved,   be mindful of   the

ῥημάτων   τῶν   προειρημένων   ὑπὸ   τῶν
words   –   previously spoken   by   the

ἀποστόλων   τοῦ   κυρίου   ἡμῶν   'Ιησοῦ
apostles   of the   Lord   of us   Jesus

Χριστοῦ,   18 ὅτι   ἔλεγον   ὑμῖν·   ἐπ'   ἐσχάτου
Christ,   because   they told   you: At   [the] last

τοῦ   χρόνου   ἔσονται   ἐμπαῖκται   κατὰ   τὰς
of the   time   will be   mockers   ²according to   ³the

ἑαυτῶν   ἐπιθυμίας   πορευόμενοι   τῶν   ἀσεβειῶν.
⁵of them-   ⁴lusts   ¹going   –   ⁶of impious
selves   things.

19 Οὗτοί   εἰσιν   οἱ   ἀποδιορίζοντες,   ψυχικοί,
These men   are the [ones] making separations,   natural,

πνεῦμα   μὴ   ἔχοντες.   20 ὑμεῖς   δέ,   ἀγαπητοί,
³spirit   ¹not   ²having.   But ye,   beloved,

ἐποικοδομοῦντες   ἑαυτοὺς   τῇ   ἁγιωτάτῃ   ὑμῶν
building up   yourselves in the   most holy   ³of you

πίστει,   ἐν   πνεύματι   ἁγίῳ   προσευχόμενοι,
¹faith,   ²in   ⁴Spirit   ³[the] Holy   ¹praying.

21 ἑαυτοὺς   ἐν   ἀγάπῃ   θεοῦ   τηρήσατε,
²yourselves   ³in   ⁴[the] love   ⁵of God   ¹keep,

God; wait for the mercy of our Lord Jesus Christ unto eternal life. [22]And convince some, who doubt; [23]save some, by snatching them out of the fire; on some have mercy with fear, hating even the garment spotted by the flesh.[d]

24 Now to him who is able to keep you from falling and to present you without blemish before the presence of his glory with rejoicing, [25]to the only God, our Savior through Jesus Christ our Lord, be glory, majesty, dominion, and authority, before all time and now and for ever. Amen.

προσδεχόμενοι τὸ ἔλεος τοῦ κυρίου ἡμῶν
awaiting   the mercy of the Lord of us

Ἰησοῦ Χριστοῦ εἰς ζωὴν αἰώνιον. 22 καὶ
Jesus Christ to life eternal.   And

οὓς μὲν ἐλεᾶτε διακρινομένους 23 σώζετε
some ¹pity ye ¹[who are] wavering   ¹save

ἐκ πυρὸς ἁρπάζοντες, οὓς δὲ ἐλεᾶτε
²out of ⁴fire ¹seizing,   others pity

ἐν φόβῳ, μισοῦντες καὶ τὸν ἀπὸ τῆς
with fear, hating   even ¹the ⁴from ⁵the

σαρκὸς ἐσπιλωμένον χιτῶνα.
⁶flesh ³having been spotted ²tunic.

24 Τῷ δὲ δυναμένῳ φυλάξαι ὑμᾶς
   Now to the [one] being able to guard you

ἀπταίστους καὶ στῆσαι κατενώπιον τῆς
without   and to set [you] before the
stumbling

δόξης αὐτοῦ ἀμώμους ἐν ἀγαλλιάσει,
glory of him unblemished with exultation,

25 μόνῳ θεῷ σωτῆρι ἡμῶν διὰ Ἰησοῦ
   to [the] only God Saviour of us through Jesus

Χριστοῦ τοῦ κυρίου ἡμῶν δόξα μεγαλωσύνη
Christ   the Lord of us [be] glory[,] greatness[,]

κράτος καὶ ἐξουσία πρὸ παντὸς τοῦ
might[,] and authority before all   the

αἰῶνος καὶ νῦν καὶ εἰς πάντας τοὺς
age   and now and unto all   the

αἰῶνας· ἀμήν.
ages: Amen.

[d] The Greek text in this sentence is uncertain at several points

CHAPTER 1

THE revelation of Jesus Christ, which God gave him to show to his servants what must soon take place; and he made it known by sending his angel to his servant John, ²who bore witness to the word of God and to the testimony of Jesus Christ, even to all that he saw. ³Blessed is he who reads aloud the words of the prophecy, and blessed are those who hear, and who keep what is written therein; for the time is near.

4 John to the seven churches that are in Asia:

Grace to you and peace from him who is and who was and who is to come, and from the seven spirits who are before his throne, ⁵and from Jesus Christ the faithful witness, the firstborn of the dead, and the ruler of kings on earth.

To him who loves us and has freed us from our sins by his blood

1 Ἀποκάλυψις   Ἰησοῦ   Χριστοῦ,   ἣν
A revelation   of Jesus   Christ,   which

ἔδωκεν   αὐτῷ   ὁ   θεός,   δεῖξαι   τοῖς   δούλοις
²gave   ³to him   –   ¹God,   to show   to the   slaves

αὐτοῦ   ἃ   δεῖ   γενέσθαι   ἐν   τάχει,   καὶ
of him   things   it be-   to occur   with   speed,   and
        which hoves

ἐσήμανεν   ἀποστείλας   διὰ   τοῦ   ἀγγέλου
he signified   sending   through   the   angel

αὐτοῦ   τῷ   δούλῳ   αὐτοῦ   Ἰωάννῃ,   2 ὃς
of him   to the   slave   of him   John,   who

ἐμαρτύρησεν   τὸν   λόγον   τοῦ   θεοῦ   καὶ
bore witness [of]   the   word   –   of God   and

τὴν   μαρτυρίαν   Ἰησοῦ   Χριστοῦ,   ὅσα   εἶδεν.
the   witness   of Jesus   Christ,   as many   he saw.
                things as

3 Μακάριος   ὁ   ἀναγινώσκων   καὶ   οἱ
Blessed [is]   the [one]   reading   and   the

ἀκούοντες   τοὺς   λόγους   τῆς   προφητείας
[ones] hearing   the   words   of the   prophecy

καὶ   τηροῦντες   τὰ   ἐν   αὐτῇ   γεγραμμένα·
and   keeping   the things   ²in   ³it   ¹having been written;

ὁ   γὰρ   καιρὸς   ἐγγύς.
²the   ¹for   time [is]   near.

4 Ἰωάννης   ταῖς   ἑπτὰ   ἐκκλησίαις   ταῖς
John   to the   seven   churches   –

ἐν   τῇ   Ἀσίᾳ·   χάρις   ὑμῖν   καὶ   εἰρήνη
in   –   Asia: Grace   to you   and   peace

ἀπὸ   ὁ   ὢν   καὶ   ὁ   ἦν   καὶ   ὁ   ἐρχόμενος,
from   the   being   and   the   was   and   the [one] coming,
    [one]   [one who]
    = the one who is

καὶ   ἀπὸ   τῶν   ἑπτὰ   πνευμάτων   ἃ   ἐνώπιον
and   from   the   seven   spirits   which   before
                    [are]

τοῦ   θρόνου   αὐτοῦ,   5 καὶ   ἀπὸ   Ἰησοῦ
the   throne   of him,   and   from   Jesus

Χριστοῦ,   ὁ   μάρτυς   ὁ   πιστός,   ὁ   πρωτότοκος
Christ,   the   ²witness   –   ¹faithful,   the   firstborn

τῶν   νεκρῶν   καὶ   ὁ   ἄρχων   τῶν   βασιλέων
of the   dead   and   the   ruler   of the   kings

τῆς   γῆς.   Τῷ   ἀγαπῶντι   ἡμᾶς   καὶ   λύσαντι
of the earth.   To   loving   us   and   having
        the [one]   loosed

ἡμᾶς   ἐκ   τῶν   ἁμαρτιῶν   ἡμῶν   ἐν   τῷ
us   out of   the   sins   of us   by   the

⁶and made us a kingdom, priests to his God and Father, to him be glory and dominion for ever and ever. Amen. ⁷Behold, he is coming with the clouds, and every eye will see him, every one who pierced him; and all tribes of the earth will wail on account of him. Even so. Amen.

8 "I am the Alpha and the Omega," says the Lord God, who is and who was and who is to come, the Almighty.

9 I John, your brother, who share with you in Jesus the tribulation and the kingdom and the patient endurance, was on the island called Patmos on account of the word of God and the testimony of Jesus. ¹⁰I was in the Spirit on the Lord's day, and I heard behind me a loud voice like a trumpet ¹¹saying, "Write what you see in a book and send it to the seven churches, to

αἵματι	αὐτοῦ,	6 καὶ		ἐποίησεν	ἡμᾶς
blood	of him,	and		made	us

βασιλείαν,	ἱερεῖς	τῷ	θεῷ	καὶ	πατρὶ
a kingdom,	priests	to the	God	and	Father

αὐτοῦ,	αὐτῷ	ἡ	δόξα	καὶ	τὸ	κράτος
of him,	to him² [is] the = his is	the	glory	and	the	might

εἰς	τοὺς	αἰῶνας	τῶν	αἰώνων·	ἀμήν.
unto	the	ages	of the	ages:	Amen.

7 Ἰδοὺ	ἔρχεται	μετὰ	τῶν	νεφελῶν,
Behold,	he comes	with	the	clouds,

καὶ	ὄψεται	αὐτὸν	πᾶς	ὀφθαλμὸς	καὶ
and	³will see	⁴him	¹every	²eye	and

οἵτινες	αὐτὸν	ἐξεκέντησαν,	καὶ	κόψονται
[those] who	²him	¹pierced,	and	³will wail

ἐπ'	αὐτὸν	πᾶσαι	αἱ	φυλαὶ	τῆς γῆς.
⁷over	⁸him	¹all	²the	³tribes	⁴of the ⁵land.

ναί,	ἀμήν.
Yes,	amen.

8 Ἐγώ	εἰμι	τὸ	ἄλφα	καὶ	τὸ ὦ,	λέγει
I	am	the	alpha	and	the omega,	says

κύριος	ὁ	θεός,	ὁ ὢν	καὶ	ὁ ἦν
[the] Lord	–	God,	the [one] being = the one who is	and	the was [one who]

καὶ	ὁ ἐρχόμενος,	ὁ παντοκράτωρ.
and	the [one] coming,	the Almighty.

9 Ἐγὼ	Ἰωάννης,	ὁ	ἀδελφὸς	ὑμῶν	καὶ
I	John,	the	brother	of you	and

συγκοινωνὸς	ἐν	τῇ	θλίψει	καὶ βασιλείᾳ
co-sharer	in	the	affliction	and kingdom

καὶ	ὑπομονῇ	ἐν	Ἰησοῦ,	ἐγενόμην	ἐν
and	endurance	in	Jesus,	came to be	in

τῇ	νήσῳ	τῇ	καλουμένῃ	Πάτμῳ διὰ
the	island	–	being called	Patmos on account of

τὸν	λόγον	τοῦ	θεοῦ	καὶ	τὴν μαρτυρίαν
the	word	–	of God	and	the witness

Ἰησοῦ.	10 ἐγενόμην	ἐν	πνεύματι	ἐν
of Jesus.	I came to be	in	[the] spirit	on

τῇ	κυριακῇ	ἡμέρᾳ,	καὶ	ἤκουσα ὀπίσω
the	imperial*	day,	and	heard behind

μου	φωνὴν	μεγάλην	ὡς	σάλπιγγος
me	²voice	¹a great(loud)	as	of a trumpet

11 λεγούσης·	ὃ βλέπεις	γράψον	εἰς	βιβλίον
saying:	What thou seest	write	in	a scroll

καὶ	πέμψον	ταῖς	ἑπτὰ	ἐκκλησίαις,	εἰς
and	send	to the	seven	churches,	to

* See I. Cor. 11. 20.

Ephesus and to Smyrna and to Per'gamum and to Thyati'ra and to Sardis and to Philadelphia and to La-odice'a."

12 Then I turned to see the voice that was speaking to me, and on turning I saw seven golden lampstands, [13] and in the midst of the lampstands one like a son of man, clothed with a long robe and with a golden girdle round his breast; [14] his head and his hair were white as white wool, white as snow; his eyes were like a flame of fire, [15] his feet were like burnished bronze, refined as in a furnace, and his voice was like the sound of many waters; [16] in his right hand he held seven stars, from his mouth issued a sharp two-edged sword, and his face was like the sun shining in full strength.

17 When I saw him, I fell at his feet as though dead. But he laid his right hand upon me, saying, "Fear not, I am the first and the last,

---

Ἔφεσον καὶ εἰς Σμύρναν καὶ εἰς Πέργαμον
Ephesus and to Smyrna and to Pergamum

καὶ εἰς Θυάτιρα καὶ εἰς Σάρδεις καὶ
and to Thyatira and to Sardis and

εἰς Φιλαδέλφειαν καὶ εἰς Λαοδίκειαν.
to Philadelphia and to Laodicea.

12 Καὶ ἐπέστρεψα βλέπειν τὴν φωνὴν
And I turned to see the voice

ἥτις ἐλάλει μετ᾽ ἐμοῦ· καὶ ἐπιστρέψας
which spoke with me; and having turned

εἶδον ἑπτὰ λυχνίας χρυσᾶς, **13** καὶ ἐν
I saw seven ²lampstands ¹golden, and in

μέσῳ τῶν λυχνιῶν ὅμοιον υἱὸν ἀνθρώπου,*
[the] of the lampstands [one] like a son of man,*
midst

ἐνδεδυμένον ποδήρη καὶ περιεζωσμένον
having been clothed to the feet and *having been* girdled round

πρὸς τοῖς μαστοῖς ζώνην χρυσᾶν· **14** ἡ
at the breasts ²girdle ¹[with] a golden; ²the

δὲ κεφαλὴ αὐτοῦ καὶ αἱ τρίχες λευκαὶ
¹and head of him and the hairs white

ὡς ἔριον λευκὸν ὡς χιών, καὶ οἱ ὀφθαλμοὶ
as wool white as snow, and the eyes

αὐτοῦ ὡς φλὸξ πυρός, **15** καὶ οἱ πόδες
of him as a flame of fire, and the feet

αὐτοῦ ὅμοιοι χαλκολιβάνῳ ὡς ἐν καμίνῳ
of him like *to* burnished brass as ²in ¹a furnace

πεπυρωμένης, καὶ ἡ φωνὴ αὐτοῦ ὡς
¹having been fired, and the voice of him as

φωνὴ ὑδάτων πολλῶν, **16** καὶ ἔχων ἐν
a sound waters of many, and having in

τῇ δεξιᾷ χειρὶ αὐτοῦ ἀστέρας ἑπτά,
the right hand of him ²stars ¹seven,

καὶ ἐκ τοῦ στόματος αὐτοῦ ῥομφαία
and out of the mouth of him ⁴sword

δίστομος ὀξεῖα ἐκπορευομένη, καὶ ἡ ὄψις
³two- ²a sharp ¹proceeding, and the face
mouthed(edged)

αὐτοῦ ὡς ὁ ἥλιος φαίνει ἐν τῇ δυνάμει
of him as the sun shines in the power

αὐτοῦ. **17** Καὶ ὅτε εἶδον αὐτόν, ἔπεσα
of it. And when I saw him, I fell

πρὸς τοὺς πόδας αὐτοῦ ὡς νεκρός· καὶ
at the feet of him as dead; and

ἔθηκεν τὴν δεξιὰν αὐτοῦ ἐπ᾽ ἐμὲ λέγων·
he placed the right [hand] of him on me saying:

μὴ φοβοῦ· ἐγώ εἰμι ὁ πρῶτος καὶ
Fear not: I am the first and

---

* Anarthrous; see also ch. 14. 14 and John 5. 27, and *cf.* Heb. 2. 6.

[18]and the living one; I died, and behold I am alive for evermore, and I have the keys of Death and Hades. [19]Now write what you see, what is and what is to take place hereafter. [20]As for the mystery of the seven stars which you saw in my right hand, and the seven golden lampstands, the seven stars are the angels of the seven churches and the seven lampstands are the seven churches.

ὁ ἔσχατος **18** καὶ ὁ ζῶν, καὶ ἐγενόμην
the   last   and the living [one], and I became

νεκρὸς καὶ ἰδοὺ ζῶν εἰμι εἰς τοὺς
dead   and behold [2]living [1]I am unto the

αἰῶνας τῶν αἰώνων, καὶ ἔχω τὰς κλεῖς
ages   of the ages,   and I have the keys

τοῦ θανάτου καὶ τοῦ ᾅδου. **19** γράψον
-    of death   and -   of hades.   Write thou

οὖν ἃ εἶδες καὶ ἃ εἰσὶν καὶ ἃ
there- [the] thou and [the] are and [the]
fore things sawest   things   things
      which   which   which

μέλλει   γενέσθαι   μετὰ   ταῦτα.   **20** τὸ
(is)are about to occur after these things.   The

μυστήριον τῶν ἑπτὰ ἀστέρων οὓς εἶδες
mystery   of the seven stars   which thou
                                              sawest

ἐπὶ τῆς δεξιᾶς μου, καὶ τὰς ἑπτὰ
on   the right [hand] of me, and the seven

λυχνίας τὰς χρυσᾶς· οἱ ἑπτὰ ἀστέρες
[2]lampstands - [1]golden: the seven stars

ἄγγελοι τῶν ἑπτὰ ἐκκλησιῶν εἰσιν, καὶ
messengers* of the seven churches   are,   and

αἱ λυχνίαι αἱ ἑπτὰ ἑπτὰ ἐκκλησίαι εἰσίν.
the [2]lampstands - [1]seven [4]seven [5]churches [3]are.

CHAPTER 2

"TO the angel of the church in Ephesus write: 'The words of him who holds the seven stars in his right hand, who walks among the seven golden lampstands. 2 "I know your works, your toil and your patient endurance, and how you cannot bear evil men but have tested those who call themselves apostles but are not, and found them to be false;

2 Τῷ ἀγγέλῳ τῆς ἐν Ἐφέσῳ ἐκκλησίας
To the messenger [1]of the [3]in [4]Ephesus [2]church

γράψον·
write thou:

Τάδε   λέγει   ὁ   κρατῶν   τοὺς   ἑπτὰ
These things says the [one] holding   the   seven

ἀστέρας ἐν τῇ δεξιᾷ αὐτοῦ, ὁ περιπατῶν
stars   in the right [hand] of him, the [one] walking

ἐν μέσῳ τῶν ἑπτὰ λυχνιῶν τῶν
in [the] midst of the seven [2]lampstands -

χρυσῶν· **2** οἶδα τὰ ἔργα σου καὶ τὸν
[1]golden: I know the works of thee and the

κόπον καὶ τὴν ὑπομονήν σου, καὶ ὅτι
labour and the endurance of thee, and that

οὐ δύνῃ βαστάσαι κακούς, καὶ ἐπείρασας
thou canst not to bear bad men,   and didst try

τοὺς λέγοντας ἑαυτοὺς ἀποστόλους καὶ
the [ones] say(call)ing themselves   apostles   and

οὐκ εἰσίν, καὶ εὗρες αὐτοὺς ψευδεῖς·
are not,   and didst find them   liars;

* This, of course, is the prime meaning of the word: whether these beings were "messengers" from the churches, or supernatural beings, "angels" as usually understood, is a matter of exegesis.

³I know you are enduring patiently and bearing up for my name's sake, and you have not grown weary. ⁴But I have this against you, that you have abandoned the love you had at first. ⁵Remember then from what you have fallen, repent and do the works you did at first. If not, I will come to you and remove your lampstand from its place, unless you repent. ⁶Yet this you have, you hate the works of the Nicola'itans, which I also hate. ⁷He who has an ear, let him hear what the Spirit says to the churches. To him who conquers I will grant to eat of the tree of life, which is in the paradise of God.'

8 "And to the angel of the church in Smyrna write: 'The words of the first and the last, who died and came to life.

9 " 'I know your tribulation and your poverty (but you are rich) and the slander of those who say that they are Jews and are not, but are a synagogue of Satan.

3 καὶ ὑπομονὴν ἔχεις, καὶ ἐβάστασας
and ¹endurance ¹thou hast, and didst bear

διὰ τὸ ὄνομά μου, καὶ οὐ κεκοπίακας.
be- the name of me, and hast not grown weary.
cause of

4 ἀλλὰ ἔχω κατὰ σοῦ ὅτι τὴν ἀγάπην
But I have against thee that ³the ⁴love

σου τὴν πρώτην ἀφῆκας. 5 μνημόνευε
⁶of thee – ³first ¹thou didst leave. Remember

οὖν πόθεν πέπτωκας, καὶ μετανόησον
therefore whence thou hast fallen, and repent

καὶ τὰ πρῶτα ἔργα ποίησον· εἰ δὲ
and ²the ³first ⁴works ¹do; and if

μή, ἔρχομαί σοι καὶ κινήσω τὴν λυχνίαν
not, I am coming to thee and will move the lampstand

σου ἐκ τοῦ τόπου αὐτῆς, ἐὰν μὴ
of thee out of the place of it, unless

μετανοήσῃς. 6 ἀλλὰ τοῦτο ἔχεις, ὅτι
thou repentest. But this thou hast, that

μισεῖς τὰ ἔργα τῶν Νικολαϊτῶν, ἃ
thou hatest the works of the Nicolaitans, which

κἀγὼ μισῶ. 7 Ὁ ἔχων οὖς ἀκουσάτω
I also hate. The [one] having an ear let him hear

τί τὸ πνεῦμα λέγει ταῖς ἐκκλησίαις.
what the Spirit says to the churches.

Τῷ νικῶντι δώσω αὐτῷ φαγεῖν ἐκ
To overcoming I will give to him to eat of
the [one]

τοῦ ξύλου τῆς ζωῆς, ὅ ἐστιν ἐν τῷ
the tree – of life, which is in the

παραδείσῳ τοῦ θεοῦ.
paradise – of God.

8 Καὶ τῷ ἀγγέλῳ τῆς ἐν Σμύρνῃ
And to the messenger ¹of the ²in ⁴Smyrna

ἐκκλησίας γράψον·
³church write thou:

Τάδε λέγει ὁ πρῶτος καὶ ὁ ἔσχατος,
These things says the first and the last,

ὃς ἐγένετο νεκρὸς καὶ ἔζησεν· 9 οἶδά
who became dead and lived [again]: I know

σου τὴν θλῖψιν καὶ τὴν πτωχείαν, ἀλλὰ
⁶of thee ¹the ²affliction ³and ⁴the ⁵poverty, but

πλούσιος εἶ, καὶ τὴν βλασφημίαν ἐκ
rich thou art, and the railing of

τῶν λεγόντων Ἰουδαίους εἶναι ἑαυτούς,
the [ones] say(call)ing ³Jews ²to be ¹themselves,

καὶ οὐκ εἰσὶν ἀλλὰ συναγωγὴ τοῦ σατανᾶ.
and they are not but a synagogue – of Satan.

¹⁰ Do not fear what you are about to suffer. Behold, the devil is about to throw some of you into prison, that you may be tested, and for ten days you will have tribulation. Be faithful unto death, and I will give you the crown of life. ¹¹ He who has an ear, let him hear what the Spirit says to the churches. He who conquers shall not be hurt by the second death.'

12 "And to the angel of the church in Per'ga-mum write: 'The words of him who has the sharp two-edged sword.

13 " 'I know where you dwell, where Satan's throne is; you hold fast my name and you did not deny my faith even in the days of An'tipas my witness, my faithful one, who was killed among you, where Satan dwells. ¹⁴ But I have a few things against you: you have some there who hold the teaching of Balaam, who taught Balak to put a stumbling block before the sons of

10 μὴ φοβοῦ ἃ μέλλεις πάσχειν. ἰδοὺ
Do not fear [the] thou art to suffer. Behold[.]
things which about

μέλλει βάλλειν ὁ διάβολος ἐξ ὑμῶν
²is about ⁴to cast ¹the ³devil [some] of you

εἰς φυλακὴν ἵνα πειρασθῆτε, καὶ ἕξετε
into prison in order that ye may be tried, and ye will have

θλῖψιν ἡμερῶν δέκα. γίνου πιστὸς ἄχρι
affliction ²days ¹ten. Be thou faithful until

θανάτου, καὶ δώσω σοι τὸν στέφανον
death, and I will give thee the crown

τῆς ζωῆς. 11 Ὁ ἔχων οὖς ἀκουσάτω
- of life. The [one] having an ear let him hear

τί τὸ πνεῦμα λέγει ταῖς ἐκκλησίαις.
what the Spirit says to the churches.

Ὁ νικῶν οὐ μὴ ἀδικηθῇ ἐκ τοῦ θανάτου
The over- by no will be by the ²death
[one] coming means hurt

τοῦ δευτέρου.
- ¹second.

12 Καὶ τῷ ἀγγέλῳ τῆς ἐν Περγάμῳ
And to the messenger ¹of the ³in ⁴Pergamum

ἐκκλησίας γράψον·
²church write thou:

Τάδε λέγει ὁ ἔχων τὴν ῥομφαίαν τὴν
These things says the having the ²sword -
[one]

δίστομον τὴν ὀξεῖαν· 13 οἶδα ποῦ κατοικεῖς·
¹two-mouthed - ²sharp: I know where thou
[edged] dwellest;

ὅπου ὁ θρόνος τοῦ σατανᾶ· καὶ κρατεῖς
where the throne - of Satan [is]; and thou holdest

τὸ ὄνομά μου, καὶ οὐκ ἠρνήσω τὴν
the name of me, and didst not deny the

πίστιν μου καὶ ἐν ταῖς ἡμέραις Ἀντιπᾶς
faith of me even in the days of Antipas

ὁ μάρτυς μου ὁ πιστός μου, ὃς
¹the ²witness ⁴of me the ³faithful of me, who

ἀπεκτάνθη παρ' ὑμῖν, ὅπου ὁ σατανᾶς
was killed among you, where - Satan

κατοικεῖ. 14 ἀλλ' ἔχω κατὰ σοῦ ὀλίγα,
dwells. But I have against thee a few
things,

ὅτι ἔχεις ἐκεῖ κρατοῦντας τὴν διδαχὴν
be- thou there [ones] holding the teaching
cause hast

Βαλαάμ, ὃς ἐδίδασκεν τῷ Βαλὰκ βαλεῖν
of Balaam, who taught - Balak to cast

σκάνδαλον ἐνώπιον τῶν υἱῶν Ἰσραήλ,
a stumbling-block before the sons of Israel,

Israel, that they might eat food sacrificed to idols and practice immorality. ¹⁵ So you also have some who hold the teaching of the Nicola'itans. ¹⁶ Repent then. If not, I will come to you soon and war against them with the sword of my mouth. ¹⁷ He who has an ear, let him hear what the Spirit says to the churches. To him who conquers I will give some of the hidden manna, and I will give him a white stone, with a new name written on the stone which no one knows except him who receives it.'

18 "And to the angel of the church in Thyati'ra write: 'The words of the Son of God, who has eyes like a flame of fire, and whose feet are like burnished bronze.

19 "'I know your works, your love and faith and service and patient endurance, and that your latter works exceed the first. ²⁰ But I have this against you, that you tolerate the woman Jez'ebel, who calls herself a prophetess and is teaching and beguiling my servants to

---

φαγεῖν εἰδωλόθυτα καὶ πορνεῦσαι. 15 οὕτως
to eat　idol sacrifices　and to commit fornication.　So

ἔχεις καὶ σὺ κρατοῦντας τὴν διδαχὴν
²hast　²also ¹thou　[ones] holding　the　teaching

τῶν Νικολαϊτῶν ὁμοίως. 16 μετανόησον
of the　Nicolaitans　likewise.　Repent thou

οὖν· εἰ δὲ μή, ἔρχομαί σοι ταχὺ καὶ
therefore; otherwise,　I am coming to thee quickly and

πολεμήσω μετ' αὐτῶν ἐν τῇ ῥομφαίᾳ
will fight　with　them　with the　sword

τοῦ στόματός μου. 17 Ὁ ἔχων οὖς
of the　mouth　of me.　The [one] having an ear

ἀκουσάτω τί τὸ πνεῦμα λέγει ταῖς
let him hear what the　Spirit　says　to the

ἐκκλησίαις. Τῷ νικῶντι δώσω αὐτῷ
churches.　To the [one] overcoming I will give　to him

τοῦ μάννα τοῦ κεκρυμμένου, καὶ δώσω
of the ²manna　—　¹having been hidden,　and I will give

αὐτῷ ψῆφον λευκήν, καὶ ἐπὶ τὴν ψῆφον
him　²stone ¹a white,　and　on　the　stone

ὄνομα καινὸν γεγραμμένον, ὃ οὐδεὶς οἶδεν
²name　¹a new　having been written, which no man knows

εἰ μὴ ὁ λαμβάνων.
except the [one] receiving [it].

18 Καὶ τῷ ἀγγέλῳ τῆς ἐν Θυατίροις
And to the messenger ¹of the ²in ⁴Thyatira

ἐκκλησίας γράψον·
¹church　write thou:

Τάδε λέγει ὁ υἱὸς τοῦ θεοῦ, ὁ ἔχων
These things says　the　Son　—　of God,　the having
[one]

τοὺς ὀφθαλμοὺς [αὐτοῦ] ὡς φλόγα πυρός,
the　eyes　of him　as　a flame　of fire,

καὶ οἱ πόδες αὐτοῦ ὅμοιοι χαλκολιβάνῳ·
and the　feet　of him　like　to burnished brass:

19 οἶδά σου τὰ ἔργα καὶ τὴν ἀγάπην
I know of thee the works and　the　love

καὶ τὴν πίστιν καὶ τὴν διακονίαν καὶ
and　the　faith　and　the　ministry　and

τὴν ὑπομονήν σου, καὶ τὰ ἔργα σου
the　endurance　of thee, and　the　²works ³of thee

τὰ ἔσχατα πλείονα τῶν πρώτων. 20 ἀλλὰ
the　¹last　more [than] the　first.　But

ἔχω κατὰ σοῦ ὅτι ἀφεῖς τὴν γυναῖκα
I have against thee that thou permittest the　woman

Ἰεζάβελ, ἡ λέγουσα ἑαυτὴν προφῆτιν,
Jezabel, the [one] say(call)ing　herself　a prophetess,

καὶ διδάσκει καὶ πλανᾷ τοὺς ἐμοὺς
and　she teaches and　deceives　—　my

practice immorality and
to eat food sacrificed to
idols. ²¹I gave her time
to repent, but she refuses
to repent of her im-
morality. ²²Behold, I will
throw her on a sickbed,
and those who commit
adultery with her I will
throw into great tribula-
tion, unless they repent
of her doings; ²³and I
will strike her children
dead. And all the
churches shall know that
I am he who searches
mind and heart, and I
will give to each of you
as your works deserve.
²⁴But to the rest of you
in Thyati'ra, who do
not hold this teaching,
who have not learned
what some call the deep
things of Satan, to you I
say, I do not lay upon
you any other burden;
²⁵only hold fast what
you have, until I come.
²⁶He who conquers and
who keeps my works
until the end, I will give
him power over the
nations, ²⁷and he shall
rule them with a rod of
iron, as when earthen
pots are broken in
pieces, even as I myself
have received power
from my Father; ²⁸and
I will give him the

δούλους   πορνεῦσαι   καὶ   φαγεῖν   εἰδωλόθυτα·
slaves to commit fornication and to eat   idol sacrifices;

21 καὶ   ἔδωκα   αὐτῇ   χρόνον   ἵνα   μετανοήσῃ,
and   I gave   her   time in order   she might
                           that   repent,

καὶ   οὐ   θέλει   μετανοῆσαι   ἐκ   τῆς   πορνείας
and she wishes not to repent   of   the fornication

αὐτῆς·   22 ἰδοὺ   βάλλω   αὐτὴν   εἰς   κλίνην,
of her.   Behold[,] I am casting her   into a bed,

καὶ   τοὺς   μοιχεύοντας   μετ'   αὐτῆς   εἰς
and the [ones] committing adultery with   her   into

θλῖψιν   μεγάλην,   ἐὰν   μὴ   μετανοήσουσιν
¹affliction ¹great, unless   they shall repent

ἐκ   τῶν   ἔργων   αὐτῆς·   23 καὶ   τὰ   τέκνα
of   the   works   of her;   and   the   children

αὐτῆς   ἀποκτενῶ   ἐν   θανάτῳ·   καὶ   γνώσονται
of her   I will kill   with   death;   and   ⁴will know

πᾶσαι   αἱ   ἐκκλησίαι   ὅτι   ἐγώ   εἰμι   ὁ
¹all   ²the   ³churches   that   I   am   the
                                        [one]

ἐρευνῶν   νεφροὺς   καὶ   καρδίας,   καὶ   δώσω
searching   kidneys   and   hearts,   and I will give

ὑμῖν   ἑκάστῳ   κατὰ   τὰ   ἔργα   ὑμῶν.
to you   each one according to the   works   of you.

24 ὑμῖν   δὲ   λέγω   τοῖς   λοιποῖς   τοῖς   ἐν
But to you   I say   to the   rest   -   in

Θυατίροις,   ὅσοι   οὐκ   ἔχουσιν   τὴν   διδαχὴν
Thyatira, as many as have not   -   teaching

ταύτην,   οἵτινες   οὐκ   ἔγνωσαν   τὰ   βαθέα
this,   who   knew not   the deep things

τοῦ   σατανᾶ,   ὡς   λέγουσιν·   οὐ   βάλλω
-   of Satan,   as   they say: I am not casting

ἐφ'   ὑμᾶς   ἄλλο   βάρος·   25 πλὴν   ὃ   ἔχετε
on   you   another burden; nevertheless what ye have

κρατήσατε   ἄχρι   οὗ   ἂν   ἥξω.   26 Καὶ
hold   until   I shall come.   And

ὁ   νικῶν   καὶ   ὁ   τηρῶν   ἄχρι   τέλους   τὰ
the over-   and the keeping until   [the]   the
[one] coming   [one]   end

ἔργα   μου,   δώσω   αὐτῷ   ἐξουσίαν   ἐπὶ
works   of me, I will give   him   authority   over

τῶν   ἐθνῶν,   27 καὶ   ποιμανεῖ   αὐτοὺς   ἐν
the   nations,   and he will shepherd them with

ῥάβδῳ   σιδηρᾷ,   ὡς   τὰ   σκεύη   τὰ   κεραμικὰ
²staff   ¹an iron,   as   the   ²vessels   -   ¹clay

συντρίβεται,   ὡς   κἀγὼ   εἴληφα   παρὰ
is(are) broken,   as   I also   have received   from

τοῦ   πατρός   μου, 28 καὶ   δώσω   αὐτῷ   τὸν
the   Father   of me,   and   I will give   him   the

morning star. ²⁹He who has an ear, let him hear what the Spirit says to the churches.'

ἀστέρα τὸν πρωϊνόν. 29 Ὁ ἔχων οὖς
¹star   –   ¹morning.   The [one] having an ear

ἀκουσάτω τί τὸ πνεῦμα λέγει ταῖς
let him hear what the Spirit says to the

ἐκκλησίαις
churches.

CHAPTER 3

"AND to the angel of the church in Sardis write: 'The words of him who has the seven spirits of God and the seven stars.

" 'I know your works; you have the name of being alive, and you are dead. ²Awake, and strengthen what remains and is on the point of death, for I have not found your works perfect in the sight of my God. ³Remember then what you received and heard; keep that, and repent. If you will not awake, I will come like a thief, and you will not know at what hour I will come upon you. ⁴Yet you have still a few names in Sardis, people who have not soiled their garments; and they shall walk with me in white, for they are worthy. ⁵He who conquers shall be clad thus in white garments, and I will not blot his

3 Καὶ τῷ ἀγγέλῳ τῆς ἐν Σάρδεσιν
   And to the messenger ¹of the ²in ⁴Sardis

ἐκκλησίας γράψον·
³church   write thou:

Τάδε λέγει ὁ ἔχων τὰ ἑπτὰ πνεύματα
These things says the having the seven Spirits
         [one]

τοῦ θεοῦ καὶ τοὺς ἑπτὰ ἀστέρας· οἶδά
– of God and the seven stars: I know

σου τὰ ἔργα, ὅτι ὄνομα ἔχεις ὅτι ζῇς,
³of ¹the ²works, that a name thou that thou
thee   hast   livest,

καὶ νεκρὸς εἶ. 2 γίνου γρηγορῶν, καὶ
and [yet] ²dead ¹thou art. Be thou watching, and

στήρισον τὰ λοιπὰ ἃ ἔμελλον ἀποθανεῖν·
establish the remain- which were to die;
        things ing   about

οὐ γὰρ εὕρηκά σου ἔργα πεπληρωμένα
for I have not found of thee works *having been* fulfilled

ἐνώπιον τοῦ θεοῦ μου· 3 μνημόνευε οὖν
before the God of me; remember therefore

πῶς εἴληφας καὶ ἤκουσας, καὶ τήρει
how thou hast received and didst hear, and keep

καὶ μετανόησον. ἐὰν οὖν μὴ γρηγορήσῃς,
and repent. If therefore thou dost not watch,

ἥξω ὡς κλέπτης, καὶ οὐ μὴ γνῷς ποίαν
I will as a thief, and by no thou at what
come   means knowest

ὥραν ἥξω ἐπὶ σέ. 4 ἀλλὰ ἔχεις ὀλίγα
hour I will come on thee. But thou hast a few

ὀνόματα ἐν Σάρδεσιν ἃ οὐκ ἐμόλυναν τὰ
names in Sardis which did not defile the

ἱμάτια αὐτῶν, καὶ περιπατήσουσιν μετ'
garments of them, and they shall walk with

ἐμοῦ ἐν λευκοῖς, ὅτι ἄξιοί εἰσιν. 5 Ὁ
me in white because ²worthy ¹they are. The
      [garments],   [one]

νικῶν οὕτως περιβαλεῖται ἐν ἱματίοις
overcoming ²thus ¹shall be clothed in ³garments

λευκοῖς, καὶ οὐ μὴ ἐξαλείψω τὸ ὄνομα
¹white, and by no means will I blot *out* the name

name out of the book of
life; I will confess his
name before my Father
and before his angels.
[6] He who has an ear, let
him hear what the Spirit
says to the churches.'

7 "And to the angel of
the church in Philadel-
phia write: 'The words of
the holy one, the true
one, who has the key of
David, who opens and
no one shall shut, who
shuts and no one opens.
8 " 'I know your
works. Behold, I have
set before you an open
door, which no one is
able to shut; I know
that you have but little
power, and yet you have
kept my word and have
not denied my name.
[9] Behold, I will make
those of the synagogue of
Satan who say that they
are Jews and are not, but
lie—behold, I will make
them come and bow
down before your feet,
and learn that I have
loved you. [10] Because you
have kept my word of

αὐτοῦ   ἐκ   τῆς   βίβλου   τῆς   ζωῆς,   καὶ
of him   out of   the   scroll   –   of life,   and

ὁμολογήσω   τὸ   ὄνομα   αὐτοῦ   ἐνώπιον   τοῦ
I will confess   the   name   of him   before   the

πατρός   μου   καὶ   ἐνώπιον   τῶν   ἀγγέλων
Father   of me   and   before   the   angels

αὐτοῦ.   6 Ὁ   ἔχων   οὖς   ἀκουσάτω   τί   τὸ
of him.   The [one]   having   an ear   let him hear   what   the

πνεῦμα   λέγει   ταῖς   ἐκκλησίαις.
Spirit   says   to the   churches.

7 Καὶ   τῷ   ἀγγέλῳ   τῆς   ἐν   Φιλαδελφείᾳ
And   to the   messenger   [1]of the   [3]in   [4]Philadelphia

ἐκκλησίας   γράψον·
[2]church   write thou:

Τάδε   λέγει   ὁ   ἅγιος,   ὁ   ἀληθινός,   ὁ
These   says   the   holy   the   true   the
things   [one],   [one],   [one]

ἔχων   τὴν   κλεῖν   Δαυίδ,   ὁ   ἀνοίγων   καὶ
having   the   key   of David,   the [one]   opening   and

οὐδεὶς   κλείσει,   καὶ   κλείων   καὶ   οὐδεὶς
no one   shall shut,   and   shutting   and   no one

ἀνοίγει·   8 οἶδά   σου   τὰ   ἔργα·   ἰδοὺ
opens: I know   of the   the   works;   behold[,]
    thee

δέδωκα   ἐνώπιόν   σου   θύραν   ἠνεῳγμένην,
I have given   before   thee   a door   having been opened,

ἣν   οὐδεὶς   δύναται   κλεῖσαι   αὐτήν·   ὅτι
which   no one   can   to shut   it;   because

μικρὰν   ἔχεις   δύναμιν,   καὶ   ἐτήρησάς   μου
[2]a little   [1]thou hast   power,   and   didst keep   of me

τὸν   λόγον   καὶ   οὐκ   ἠρνήσω   τὸ   ὄνομά
the   word   and   didst not deny   the   name

μου.   9 ἰδοὺ   διδῶ   ἐκ   τῆς   συναγωγῆς
of me.   Behold[,]   I may   [some]   the   synagogue
    (will) give of

τοῦ   σατανᾶ,   τῶν   λεγόντων   ἑαυτοὺς
–   of Satan,   the [ones]   say(call)ing   themselves

Ἰουδαίους   εἶναι,   καὶ   οὐκ   εἰσὶν   ἀλλὰ
Jews   to be,   and   they are not   but

ψεύδονται·   ἰδοὺ   ποιήσω   αὐτοὺς   ἵνα
they lie;   behold[,]   I will make   them   in order
    that

ἥξουσιν   καὶ   προσκυνήσουσιν   ἐνώπιον   τῶν
they shall   and   they shall worship   before   the
come

ποδῶν   σου,   καὶ   γνῶσιν   ὅτι   ἐγὼ   ἠγάπησά
feet   of thee,   and   they   that   I   loved
    shall know

σε.   10 ὅτι   ἐτήρησας   τὸν   λόγον   τῆς
thee.   Because thou didst keep   the   word   of the

patient endurance, I will keep you from the hour of trial which is coming on the whole world, to try those who dwell upon the earth. ¹¹I am coming soon; hold fast what you have, so that no one may seize your crown. ¹²He who conquers, I will make him a pillar in the temple of my God; never shall he go out of it, and I will write on him the name of my God, and the name of the city of my God, the New Jerusalem which comes down from my God out of heaven, and my own new name. ¹³He who has an ear, let him hear what the Spirit says to the churches.'

14 "And to the angel of the church in La-odice′a write: 'The words of the Amen, the faithful and true witness, the beginning of God's creation.

15 " 'I know your works: you are neither cold nor hot. Would that you were cold or hot! ¹⁶So, because you are lukewarm, and neither cold nor hot, I will spew

---

ὑπομονῆς μου, κἀγώ σε τηρήσω ἐκ
endurance of me, I also ²thee ¹will keep out of

τῆς ὥρας τοῦ πειρασμοῦ τῆς μελλούσης
the hour – of trial – being about

ἔρχεσθαι ἐπὶ τῆς οἰκουμένης ὅλης, πειράσαι
to come on ²the ²inhabited [earth] ¹all, to try

τοὺς κατοικοῦντας ἐπὶ τῆς γῆς. 11 ἔρχομαι
the [ones] dwelling on the earth. I am coming

ταχύ· κράτει ὃ ἔχεις, ἵνα μηδεὶς λάβῃ
quickly; hold what thou in order no one takes
      hast, that

τὸν στέφανόν σου. 12 Ὁ νικῶν, ποιήσω
the crown of thee. The [one] overcoming, I will make

αὐτὸν στῦλον ἐν τῷ ναῷ τοῦ θεοῦ
him a pillar in the shrine of the God

μου, καὶ ἔξω οὐ μὴ ἐξέλθῃ ἔτι, καὶ
of me, and out by no he will [any] and
              means go forth longer,

γράψω ἐπ' αὐτὸν τὸ ὄνομα τοῦ θεοῦ
I will write on him the name of the God

μου καὶ τὸ ὄνομα τῆς πόλεως τοῦ
of me and the name of the city of the

θεοῦ μου, τῆς καινῆς Ἰερουσαλὴμ ἡ
God of me, of the new Jerusalem –

καταβαίνουσα ἐκ τοῦ οὐρανοῦ ἀπὸ τοῦ
descending out of – heaven from the

θεοῦ μου, καὶ τὸ ὄνομά μου τὸ καινόν.
God of me, and ¹the ²name ⁴of me – ²new.

13 Ὁ ἔχων οὓς ἀκουσάτω τί τὸ πνεῦμα
The [one] having an ear let him hear what the Spirit

λέγει ταῖς ἐκκλησίαις.
says to the churches.

14 Καὶ τῷ ἀγγέλῳ τῆς ἐν Λαοδικείᾳ
And to the messenger ¹of the ²in ⁴Laodicea

ἐκκλησίας γράψον·
²church write thou:

Τάδε λέγει ὁ ἀμήν, ὁ μάρτυς ὁ
These things says the Amen, the ⁴witness –

πιστὸς καὶ ἀληθινός, ἡ ἀρχὴ τῆς κτίσεως
¹faithful ²and ³true, the chief of the creation

τοῦ θεοῦ· 15 οἶδά σου τὰ ἔργα, ὅτι
– of God: I know of thee the works, that

οὔτε ψυχρὸς εἶ οὔτε ζεστός. ὄφελον
neither cold art thou nor hot. I would that†

ψυχρὸς ἦς ἢ ζεστός. 16 οὕτως ὅτι
cold thou wast or hot. So because

χλιαρὸς εἶ, καὶ οὔτε ζεστὸς οὔτε ψυχρός,
lukewarm thou art, and neither hot nor cold,

you out of my mouth. ¹⁷For you say, I am rich, I have prospered, and I need nothing; not knowing that you are wretched, pitiable, poor, blind, and naked. ¹⁸Therefore I counsel you to buy from me gold refined by fire, that you may be rich, and white garments to clothe you and to keep the shame of your nakedness from being seen, and salve to anoint your eyes, that you may see. ¹⁹Those whom I love, I reprove and chasten; so be zealous and repent. ²⁰Behold, I stand at the door and knock; if any one hears my voice and opens the door, I will come in to him and eat with him, and he with me. ²¹He who conquers, I will grant him to sit with me on my throne, as I myself conquered and sat down with my Father on his throne.

μέλλω σε ἐμέσαι ἐκ τοῦ στόματός μου.
I am ²thee ¹to vomit out of the mouth of me.
about*

17 ὅτι λέγεις ὅτι πλούσιός εἰμι καὶ
Because thou sayest[,] – ²rich ¹I am and

πεπλούτηκα καὶ οὐδὲν χρείαν ἔχω, καὶ
I have become rich and ²no ³need ¹I have, and

οὐκ οἶδας ὅτι σὺ εἶ ὁ ταλαίπωρος
knowest not that thou art the [one] wretched

καὶ ἐλεεινὸς καὶ πτωχὸς καὶ τυφλὸς
and pitiable and poor and blind

καὶ γυμνός, 18 συμβουλεύω σοι ἀγοράσαι
and naked, I counsel thee to buy

παρ' ἐμοῦ χρυσίον πεπυρωμένον ἐκ πυρὸς
from me gold *having been* refined by fire
by fire

ἵνα πλουτήσῃς, καὶ ἱμάτια λευκὰ ἵνα
in or- thou mayest and ²garments ¹white in order
der that be rich, that

περιβάλῃ καὶ μὴ φανερωθῇ ἡ αἰσχύνη
thou mayest and ²may not be ¹the ²shame
be clothed manifested

τῆς γυμνότητός σου, καὶ κολλύριον
²of the ³nakedness ¹of thee, and eyesalve

ἐγχρῖσαι τοὺς ὀφθαλμούς σου ἵνα βλέπῃς.
to anoint the eyes of in order thou
thee that mayest see.

19 ἐγὼ ὅσους ἐὰν φιλῶ ἐλέγχω καὶ
¹I ¹as many as love I rebuke and

παιδεύω· ζήλευε οὖν καὶ μετανόησον.
I chasten; be hot therefore and repent thou.

20 Ἰδοὺ ἕστηκα ἐπὶ τὴν θύραν καὶ
Behold[,] I stand at the door and

κρούω· ἐάν τις ἀκούσῃ τῆς φωνῆς μου
I knock; if anyone hears the voice of me

καὶ ἀνοίξῃ τὴν θύραν, εἰσελεύσομαι πρὸς
and opens the door, I will enter to

αὐτὸν καὶ δειπνήσω μετ' αὐτοῦ καὶ
him and I will dine with him and

αὐτὸς μετ' ἐμοῦ. 21 Ὁ νικῶν, δώσω
he with me. The overcoming, I will
[one] give

αὐτῷ καθίσαι μετ' ἐμοῦ ἐν τῷ θρόνῳ
him to sit with me in the throne

μου, ὡς κἀγὼ ἐνίκησα καὶ ἐκάθισα
of me, as I also overcame and sat

μετὰ τοῦ πατρός μου ἐν τῷ θρόνῳ
with the Father of me in the throne

---

* As so often (see also ch. 1. 19, 2. 10), this verb does not necessarily connote imminence, but only simple futurity.

²²He who has an ear, let him hear what the Spirit says to the churches.' "

αὐτοῦ.
of him.

22 Ὁ ἔχων οὖς ἀκουσάτω τί
The [one] having an ear let him hear what

τὸ πνεῦμα λέγει ταῖς ἐκκλησίαις.
the Spirit says to the churches.

CHAPTER 4

AFTER this I looked, and lo, in heaven an open door! And the first voice, which I had heard speaking to me like a trumpet, said, "Come up hither, and I will show what must take place after this." ²At once I was in the Spirit, and lo, a throne stood in heaven, with one seated on the throne! ³And he who sat there appeared like jasper and carnelian, and a round the throne was a rainbow that looked like an emerald. ⁴Round the throne were twenty-four thrones, and seated on the thrones were twenty-four elders, clad in white garments, with golden crowns upon their heads. ⁵From the throne issue flashes of lightning, and voices and peals of thunder, and before the throne burn seven torches of fire, which are the seven spirits of God; ⁶and

4 Μετὰ ταῦτα εἶδον, καὶ ἰδοὺ θύρα
After these things I saw, and behold[,] a door

ἠνεῳγμένη ἐν τῷ οὐρανῷ, καὶ ἡ φωνὴ
having been in – heaven, and the ¹voice
opened

ἡ πρώτη ἣν ἤκουσα ὡς σάλπιγγος
– ¹first which I heard as of a trumpet

λαλούσης μετ' ἐμοῦ, λέγων· ἀνάβα ὧδε,
speaking with me, saying: Come up here,

καὶ δείξω σοι ἃ δεῖ γενέσθαι μετὰ
and I will thee things it be- to occur after
show which hoves

ταῦτα. εὐθέως ἐγενόμην ἐν πνεύματι·
these things. Immediately I became in spirit;

2 καὶ ἰδοὺ θρόνος ἔκειτο ἐν τῷ οὐρανῷ,
and behold[,] a throne was set in – heaven,

καὶ ἐπὶ τὸν θρόνον καθήμενος, **3** καὶ
and on the throne a sitting [one], and

ὁ καθήμενος ὅμοιος ὁράσει λίθῳ ἰάσπιδι
the [one] sitting [was] like in appearance ⁴stone ¹to a jasper

καὶ σαρδίῳ, καὶ ἶρις κυκλόθεν τοῦ
²and ³a sardius, and a rain- round the
[there was] bow

θρόνου ὅμοιος ὁράσει σμαραγδίνῳ. **4** καὶ
throne like in appearance to an emerald. And

κυκλόθεν τοῦ θρόνου θρόνους εἴκοσι
round the throne [I saw] ²thrones ¹twenty-

τέσσαρας, καὶ ἐπὶ τοὺς θρόνους εἴκοσι
four, and on the thrones twenty-

τέσσαρας πρεσβυτέρους καθημένους περι-
four elders sitting having been

βεβλημένους ἐν ἱματίοις λευκοῖς, καὶ ἐπὶ
clothed in garments white, and on

τὰς κεφαλὰς αὐτῶν στεφάνους χρυσοῦς·
the heads of them ²crowns ¹golden.

5 καὶ ἐκ τοῦ θρόνου ἐκπορεύονται ἀστραπαὶ
And out of the throne come forth lightnings

καὶ φωναὶ καὶ βρονταί· καὶ ἑπτὰ λαμπάδες
and voices* and thunders; and seven lamps

πυρὸς καιόμεναι ἐνώπιον τοῦ θρόνου, ἅ
of fire [are] burning before the throne, which

εἰσιν τὰ ἑπτὰ πνεύματα τοῦ θεοῦ· **6** καὶ
are the seven Spirits – of God; and

* Or "sounds"; and so elsewhere.

before the throne there is as it were a sea of glass, like crystal.

And round the throne, on each side of the throne, are four living creatures, full of eyes in front and behind: ⁷the first living creature like a lion, the second living creature like an ox, the third living creature with the face of a man, and the fourth living creature like a flying eagle. ⁸And the four living creatures, each of them with six wings, are full of eyes all round and within, and day and night they never cease to sing,

"Holy, holy, holy, is the Lord God Almighty, who was and is and is to come!"

⁹And whenever the living creatures give glory and honor and thanks to him who is seated on the throne, who lives for ever and ever, ¹⁰the twenty-four elders fall down before him who is seated on the throne and

ἐνώπιον	τοῦ	θρόνου	ὡς	θάλασσα	ὑαλίνη
before	the	throne	as	²sea	¹a glassy

ὁμοία	κρυστάλλῳ·	καὶ	ἐν	μέσῳ	τοῦ
like	to crystal;	and	in	[the] midst	of the

θρόνου	καὶ	κύκλῳ	τοῦ	θρόνου	τέσσερα
throne	and	round	the	throne	four

ζῷα	γέμοντα	ὀφθαλμῶν	ἔμπροσθεν	καὶ
living creatures	filling(full)	of eyes	before	and

ὄπισθεν.	7 καὶ	τὸ	ζῷον	τὸ	πρῶτον
behind.	And	the	²living creature	–	¹first

ὅμοιον	λέοντι,	καὶ	τὸ	δεύτερον	ζῷον
[was] like	to a lion,	and	the	second	living creature

ὅμοιον	μόσχῳ,	καὶ	τὸ	τρίτον	ζῷον	ἔχων
like	to a calf,	and	the	third	living creature	having

τὸ	πρόσωπον	ὡς	ἀνθρώπου,	καὶ	τὸ
the(its)	face	as	of a man,	and	the

τέταρτον	ζῷον	ὅμοιον	ἀετῷ	πετομένῳ.
fourth	living creature	like	eagle	to a flying.

8 καὶ	τὰ	τέσσερα	ζῷα,	ἓν	καθ'	ἓν
And	the	four	living creatures,	one	by	one

αὐτῶν	ἔχων	ἀνὰ	πτέρυγας	ἕξ,	κυκλόθεν
of them	having	each	²wings	¹six,	around

καὶ	ἔσωθεν	γέμουσιν	ὀφθαλμῶν·	καὶ
and	within	are full	of eyes;	and

ἀνάπαυσιν	οὐκ	ἔχουσιν	ἡμέρας	καὶ	νυκτὸς
respite	they have not		day	and	night

λέγοντες·	ἅγιος	ἅγιος	ἅγιος	κύριος	ὁ
saying:	Holy[,]	holy[,]	holy[,]	Lord	–

θεὸς	ὁ	παντοκράτωρ,	ὁ	ἦν	καὶ	ὁ	ὢν
God	the	Almighty,	the [one who]	was	and	the [one]	being

= the one who is

καὶ	ὁ	ἐρχόμενος.	9 Καὶ	ὅταν	δώσουσιν
and	the	coming [one].	And	whenever	³shall give

τὰ	ζῷα	δόξαν	καὶ	τιμὴν	καὶ	εὐχαριστίαν
¹the	²living creatures	glory	and	honour	and	thanks

τῷ	καθημένῳ	ἐπὶ	τῷ	θρόνῳ	τῷ	ζῶντι
to the [one]	sitting	on	the	throne[,]	to the [one]	living

εἰς	τοὺς	αἰῶνας	τῶν	αἰώνων,	10 πεσοῦνται
unto	the	ages	of the	ages,	⁴will fall

οἱ	εἴκοσι	τέσσαρες	πρεσβύτεροι	ἐνώπιον
¹the	²twenty-four		³elders	before

τοῦ	καθημένου	ἐπὶ	τοῦ	θρόνου,	καὶ
the [one]	sitting	on	the	throne,	and

worship him who lives for ever and ever; they cast their crowns before the throne, singing, 11 "Worthy art thou, our Lord and God, to receive glory and honor and power, for thou didst create all things, and by thy will they existed and were created."

προσκυνήσουσιν τῷ ζῶντι εἰς τοὺς αἰῶνας
they will worship   the [one] living   unto   the   ages

τῶν αἰώνων, καὶ βαλοῦσιν τοὺς στεφάνους
of the   ages,   and   will cast   the   crowns

αὐτῶν ἐνώπιον τοῦ θρόνου, λέγοντες·
of them   before   the   throne,   saying:

11 ἄξιος εἶ, ὁ κύριος καὶ ὁ θεὸς ἡμῶν,
Worthy art thou, the Lord   and the   God   of us,

λαβεῖν τὴν δόξαν καὶ τὴν τιμὴν καὶ
to receive   the   glory   and   the   honour   and

τὴν δύναμιν, ὅτι σὺ ἔκτισας τὰ πάντα,
the   power,   because thou createdst   – all things,*

καὶ διὰ τὸ θέλημά σου ἦσαν καὶ
and   on ac-   the   will   of thee they were   and
     count of

ἐκτίσθησαν.
they were created.

CHAPTER 5

AND I saw in the right hand of him who was seated on the throne a scroll written within and on the back, sealed with seven seals; ²and I saw a strong angel proclaiming with a loud voice, "Who is worthy to open the scroll and break its seals?" ³And no one in heaven or on earth or under the earth was able to open the scroll or to look into it, ⁴and I wept much that no one was found worthy to open the scroll or to look into it. ⁵Then one of the elders said to me, "Weep

5 Καὶ εἶδον ἐπὶ τὴν δεξιὰν τοῦ
And   I saw   on   the   right   of the
                     [hand]   [one]

καθημένου ἐπὶ τοῦ θρόνου βιβλίον
sitting   on   the   throne   a scroll

γεγραμμένον ἔσωθεν καὶ ὄπισθεν,
having been written   within   and on the reverse side,

κατεσφραγισμένον σφραγῖσιν ἑπτά. 2 καὶ
having been sealed   with ²seals   ¹seven.   And

εἶδον ἄγγελον ἰσχυρὸν κηρύσσοντα ἐν
I saw   angel   a strong   proclaiming   in

φωνῇ μεγάλῃ· τίς ἄξιος ἀνοῖξαι τὸ
¹voice   ¹a great(loud):   Who [is] worthy   to open   the

βιβλίον καὶ λῦσαι τὰς σφραγῖδας αὐτοῦ;
scroll   and to loosen   the   seals   of it ?

3 καὶ οὐδεὶς ἐδύνατο ἐν τῷ οὐρανῷ
And   no one   was able   in   –   heaven

οὐδὲ ἐπὶ τῆς γῆς οὐδὲ ὑποκάτω τῆς
nor   on   the   earth   nor   underneath   the

γῆς ἀνοῖξαι τὸ βιβλίον οὔτε βλέπειν
earth   to open   the   scroll   nor to see(look at)

αὐτό. 4 καὶ ἔκλαιον πολύ, ὅτι οὐδεὶς
it.   And   I wept   much, because   no one

ἄξιος εὑρέθη ἀνοῖξαι τὸ βιβλίον οὔτε
worthy   was found   to open   the   scroll   nor

βλέπειν αὐτό. 5 καὶ εἷς ἐκ τῶν πρεσ-
to look at   it.   And   one   of   the   el-

βυτέρων λέγει μοι· μὴ κλαῖε· ἰδοὺ
ders   says   to me: Weep not;   behold[,]

* τὰ πάντα = the universe.

not; lo, the Lion of the tribe of Judah, the Root of David, has conquered, so that he can open the scroll and its seven seals."

6 And between the throne and the four living creatures and among the elders, I saw a Lamb standing, as though it had been slain, with seven horns and with seven eyes, which are the seven spirits of God sent out into all the earth; [7]and he went and took the scroll from the right hand of him who was seated on the throne. [8]And when he had taken the scroll, the four living creatures and the twenty-four elders fell down before the Lamb, each holding a harp, and with golden bowls full of incense, which are the prayers of the saints; [9]and they sang a new song, saying,

"Worthy art thou to take the scroll and to open its seals, for thou wast slain and by thy blood didst ransom men for God from every tribe and tongue and people and nation, [10]and hast made them a kingdom and priests to our God,

ἐνίκησεν ὁ λέων ὁ ἐκ τῆς φυλῆς Ἰούδα,
[10]overcame [1]the [3]Lion – [5]of [4]the [6]tribe [3]Juda,

ἡ ῥίζα Δαυίδ, ἀνοῖξαι τὸ βιβλίον καὶ
[7]the [8]root [9]of David, to open the scroll and

τὰς ἑπτὰ σφραγῖδας αὐτοῦ. 6 Καὶ εἶδον
the seven seals of it.   And I saw

ἐν μέσῳ τοῦ θρόνου καὶ τῶν τεσσάρων
in [the] midst of the throne and of the four

ζῴων καὶ ἐν μέσῳ τῶν πρεσβυτέρων
living and in [the] of the elders
creatures   midst

ἀρνίον ἑστηκὸς ὡς ἐσφαγμένον, ἔχων
a Lamb standing as having been slain, having

κέρατα ἑπτὰ καὶ ὀφθαλμοὺς ἑπτά, οἵ
[3]horns [1]seven and [2]eyes [1]seven, which

εἰσιν τὰ ἑπτὰ πνεύματα τοῦ θεοῦ
are the seven Spirits – of God

ἀπεσταλμένοι εἰς πᾶσαν τὴν γῆν. 7 καὶ
having been sent forth into all the earth.   And

ἦλθεν καὶ εἴληφεν ἐκ τῆς δεξιᾶς τοῦ
he came and has taken out of the right [hand] of the

καθημένου ἐπὶ τοῦ θρόνου. 8 Καὶ ὅτε
[one] sitting on the throne.   And when

ἔλαβεν τὸ βιβλίον, τὰ τέσσερα ζῷα
he took the scroll, the four living
creatures

καὶ οἱ εἴκοσι τέσσαρες πρεσβύτεροι ἔπεσαν
and the twenty-four elders fell

ἐνώπιον τοῦ ἀρνίου, ἔχοντες ἕκαστος
before the Lamb, having each one

κιθάραν καὶ φιάλας χρυσᾶς γεμούσας
a harp and [1]bowls [1]golden being full

θυμιαμάτων, αἵ εἰσιν αἱ προσευχαὶ τῶν
of incenses, which are the prayers of the

ἁγίων. 9 καὶ ᾄδουσιν ᾠδὴν καινὴν
saints.   And they sing [2]song [1]a new

λέγοντες· ἄξιος εἶ λαβεῖν τὸ βιβλίον
saying: Worthy art thou to receive the scroll

καὶ ἀνοῖξαι τὰς σφραγῖδας αὐτοῦ, ὅτι
and to open the seals of it, because

ἐσφάγης καὶ ἠγόρασας τῷ θεῷ ἐν τῷ
thou wast slain and didst purchase – to God by the

αἵματί σου ἐκ πάσης φυλῆς καὶ γλώσσης
blood of thee out of every tribe and tongue

καὶ λαοῦ καὶ ἔθνους, 10 καὶ ἐποίησας
and people and nation,   and didst make

αὐτοὺς τῷ θεῷ ἡμῶν βασιλείαν καὶ
them to the God of us a kingdom and

and they shall reign on earth."

[11] Then I looked, and I heard around the throne and the living creatures and the elders the voice of many angels, numbering myriads of myriads and thousands of thousands, [12] saying with a loud voice, "Worthy is the Lamb who was slain, to receive power and wealth and wisdom and might and honor and glory and blessing!" [13] And I heard every creature in heaven and on earth and under the earth and in the sea, and all therein, saying, "To him who sits upon the throne and to the Lamb be blessing and honor and glory and might for ever and ever!" [14] And the four living creatures said, "Amen!" and the elders fell down and worshiped.

ἱερεῖς,   καὶ   βασιλεύσουσιν   ἐπὶ   τῆς   γῆς.
priests,   and   they will reign   on(? over) the   earth.

11 καὶ   εἶδον,   καὶ   ἤκουσα   φωνὴν   ἀγγέλων
And   I saw,   and   I heard   a sound   [2]angels

πολλῶν   κύκλῳ   τοῦ   θρόνου   καὶ   τῶν
[1]of many   round   the   throne   and   the

ζῴων   καὶ   τῶν   πρεσβυτέρων,   καὶ   ἦν
living   and   the   elders,   and   [4]was
creatures

ὁ   ἀριθμὸς   αὐτῶν   μυριάδες   μυριάδων   καὶ
[1]the   [2]number   [3]of them   myriads   of myriads   and

χιλιάδες   χιλιάδων,   12 λέγοντες   φωνῇ
thousands   of thousands,   saying   [2]voice

μεγάλῃ·   ἄξιός   ἐστιν   τὸ   ἀρνίον   τὸ
[1]with a great   Worthy   is   the   Lamb   –
(loud):

ἐσφαγμένον   λαβεῖν   τὴν   δύναμιν   καὶ   πλοῦτον
having been slain   to receive   the   power   and   riches

καὶ   σοφίαν   καὶ   ἰσχὺν   καὶ   τιμὴν   καὶ
and   wisdom   and   strength   and   honour   and

δόξαν   καὶ   εὐλογίαν.   13 καὶ   πᾶν   κτίσμα
glory   and   blessing.   And   every   creature

ὃ   ἐν   τῷ   οὐρανῷ   καὶ   ἐπὶ   τῆς   γῆς   καὶ
which [2]in –   [3]heaven   [4]and   [5]on   [6]the   [7]earth   [8]and

ὑποκάτω   τῆς   γῆς   καὶ   ἐπὶ   τῆς   θαλάσσης
[9]underneath   [10]the   [11]earth   [12]and   [13]on   [14]the   [15]sea

[ἐστίν],   καὶ   τὰ   ἐν   αὐτοῖς   πάντα,   ἤκουσα
[1]is,   and   –   [2]in   [3]them   [1]all things,   I heard

λέγοντας·   τῷ   καθημένῳ   ἐπὶ   τῷ   θρόνῳ
saying·   To the [one] sitting   on   the   throne

καὶ   τῷ   ἀρνίῳ   ἡ   εὐλογία   καὶ   ἡ   τιμὴ
and   to the   Lamb   the   blessing   and   the   honour

καὶ   ἡ   δόξα   καὶ   τὸ   κράτος   εἰς   τοὺς
and   the   glory   and   the   might   unto   the

αἰῶνας   τῶν   αἰώνων.   14 καὶ   τὰ   τέσσερα
ages   of the   ages.   And   the   four

ζῷα   ἔλεγον·   ἀμήν,   καὶ   οἱ   πρεσβύτεροι
living   said: Amen,   and   the   elders
creatures

ἔπεσαν   καὶ   προσεκύνησαν.
fell   and   worshipped.

CHAPTER 6

NOW I saw when the Lamb opened one of the seven seals, and I heard one of the four living creatures say, as

6 Καὶ   εἶδον   ὅτε   ἤνοιξεν   τὸ   ἀρνίον
And   I saw   when   [3]opened   [1]the   [2]Lamb

μίαν   ἐκ   τῶν   ἑπτὰ   σφραγίδων,   καὶ   ἤκουσα
one   of   the   seven   seals,   and   I heard

ἑνὸς   ἐκ   τῶν   τεσσάρων   ζῴων   λέγοντος
one   of   the   four   living creatures   saying

with a voice of thunder, "Come!" ²And I saw, and behold, a white horse, and its rider had a bow; and a crown was given to him, and he went out conquering and to conquer.

3 When he opened the second seal, I heard the second living creature say, "Come!" ⁴And out came another horse, bright red; its rider was permitted to take peace from the earth, so that men should slay one another; and he was given a great sword.

5 When he opened the third seal, I heard the third living creature say, "Come!" And I saw, and behold, a black horse, and its rider had a balance in his hand; ⁶and I heard what seemed to be a voice in the midst of the four living creatures saying, "A quart of wheat for a denarius, and three quarts of barley for a denarius; but do not harm oil and wine!"

7 When he opened the fourth seal, I heard the

ὡς φωνῇ βροντῆς· ἔρχου. **2** καὶ εἶδον,
as with a sound of thunder: Come. And I saw,

καὶ ἰδοὺ ἵππος λευκός, καὶ ὁ καθήμενος
and behold[,] ²horse ¹a white, and the [one] sitting

ἐπ' αὐτὸν ἔχων τόξον, καὶ ἐδόθη αὐτῷ
on it having a bow, and ²was given ³to him

στέφανος, καὶ ἐξῆλθεν νικῶν καὶ ἵνα
¹a crown, and he went forth overcoming and in order that

νικήσῃ. **3** Καὶ ὅτε ἤνοιξεν τὴν σφραγῖδα
he might And when he opened the ²seal
overcome.

τὴν δευτέραν, ἤκουσα τοῦ δευτέρου ζῴου
– ¹second, I heard the second living
creature

λέγοντος· ἔρχου. **4** καὶ ἐξῆλθεν ἄλλος
saying: Come. And ⁴went forth ¹another

ἵππος πυρρός, καὶ τῷ καθημένῳ ἐπ'
²horse[,] ³red, and to the [one] sitting on

αὐτὸν ἐδόθη αὐτῷ λαβεῖν τὴν εἰρήνην
it was given to him to take – peace

ἐκ τῆς γῆς καὶ ἵνα ἀλλήλους σφάξουσιν,
out the earth and in order ²one ¹they
of that another shall slay,

καὶ ἐδόθη αὐτῷ μάχαιρα μεγάλη. **5** Καὶ
and ²was given ⁴to him ³sword ¹a great. And

ὅτε ἤνοιξεν τὴν σφραγῖδα τὴν τρίτην,
when he opened the ²seal – ¹third,

ἤκουσα τοῦ τρίτου ζῴου λέγοντος· ἔρχου.
I heard the third living saying: Come.
creature

καὶ εἶδον, καὶ ἰδοὺ ἵππος μέλας, καὶ
And I saw, and behold[,] ²horse ¹a black, and

ὁ καθήμενος ἐπ' αὐτὸν ἔχων ζυγὸν
the [one] sitting on it having a balance

ἐν τῇ χειρὶ αὐτοῦ. **6** καὶ ἤκουσα ὡς
in the hand of him. And I heard as

φωνὴν ἐν μέσῳ τῶν τεσσάρων ζῴων
a voice in [the] of the four living
midst creatures

λέγουσαν· χοῖνιξ σίτου δηναρίου, καὶ τρεῖς
saying: A of of(for) and three
chœnix wheat a denarius,

χοίνικες κριθῶν δηναρίου· καὶ τὸ ἔλαιον
chœnixes of barley of(for) and ³the ²oil
a denarius;

καὶ τὸν οἶνον μὴ ἀδικήσῃς. **7** Καὶ
⁴and ⁵the ⁶wine ¹do not harm. And

ὅτε ἤνοιξεν τὴν σφραγῖδα τὴν τετάρτην,
when he opened the ²seal – ¹fourth,

voice of the fourth living creature say, "Come!" [8]And I saw, and behold, a pale horse, and its rider's name was Death, and Hades followed him; and they were given power over a fourth of the earth, to kill with sword and with famine and with pestilence and by wild beasts of the earth.

9 When he opened the fifth seal, I saw under the altar the souls of those who had been slain for the word of God and for the witness they had borne; [10]they cried out with a loud voice, "O Sovereign Lord, holy and true, how long before thou wilt judge and avenge our blood on those who dwell upon the earth?" [11]Then they were each given a white robe and told to rest a little longer, until the number of their fellow servants and their brethren should be complete, who were to be killed as they themselves had been.

12When he opened the

ἤκουσα φωνὴν τοῦ τετάρτου ζῴου λέγοντος·
I heard [the] voice of the fourth living creature saying:

ἔρχου.   8 καὶ εἶδον, καὶ ἰδοὺ ἵππος
Come.   And   I saw, and behold[,] [3]horse

χλωρός, καὶ ὁ καθήμενος ἐπάνω αὐτοῦ,
[1]a pale green, and the [one] sitting upon   it,

ὄνομα   αὐτῷ [ὁ] θάνατος, καὶ ὁ ᾅδης
name to him[c] – death, and – hades

ἠκολούθει μετ' αὐτοῦ, καὶ ἐδόθη αὐτοῖς
followed with him, and [3]was [2]to them
                                          given

ἐξουσία   ἐπὶ   τὸ   τέταρτον   τῆς   γῆς,
[1]authority over the fourth [part] of the earth,

ἀποκτεῖναι ἐν ῥομφαίᾳ καὶ ἐν λιμῷ
to kill with sword and with famine

καὶ ἐν θανάτῳ καὶ ὑπὸ τῶν θηρίων
and with death and by the wild beasts

τῆς γῆς.   9 Καὶ ὅτε ἤνοιξεν τὴν πέμπτην
of the earth. And when he opened the   fifth

σφραγῖδα, εἶδον ὑποκάτω τοῦ θυσιαστηρίου
seal,   I saw underneath the altar

τὰς ψυχὰς τῶν ἐσφαγμένων διὰ τὸν
the souls of the having been on account the
        [ones]   slain   of

λόγον τοῦ θεοῦ καὶ διὰ τὴν μαρτυρίαν
word – of God and on the witness
                    account of

ἣν εἶχον.   10 καὶ ἔκραξαν φωνῇ μεγάλῃ
which they had. And they cried [2]voice [1]with a
                                          great(loud)

λέγοντες· ἕως πότε, ὁ δεσπότης ὁ ἅγιος
saying: Until when, the Master – holy

καὶ ἀληθινός, οὐ κρίνεις καὶ ἐκδικεῖς
and true, judgest thou not and avengest

τὸ αἷμα ἡμῶν ἐκ τῶν κατοικούντων
the blood of us of the [ones] dwelling

ἐπὶ τῆς γῆς; 11 καὶ ἐδόθη αὐτοῖς ἑκάστῳ
on the earth? And [3]was [4]to them [5]each one
                          given

στολὴ λευκή, καὶ ἐρρέθη αὐτοῖς ἵνα
[2]robe [1]a white, and it was said to them in order
                                          that

ἀναπαύσωνται ἔτι χρόνον μικρόν, ἕως
they should rest yet [2]time [1]a little, until

πληρωθῶσιν καὶ οἱ σύνδουλοι αὐτῶν καὶ
should be fulfilled also the fellow-slaves of them and

οἱ ἀδελφοὶ αὐτῶν οἱ μέλλοντες ἀποκτέν-
the brothers of them the [ones] being about to be

νεσθαι ὡς καὶ αὐτοί.   12 Καὶ εἶδον
killed as also they.   And I saw

sixth seal, I looked, and
behold, there was a great
earthquake; and the sun
became black as sack-
cloth, the full moon
became like blood, [13] and
the stars of the sky fell to
the earth as the fig tree
sheds its winter fruit
when shaken by a gale;
[14] the sky vanished like a
scroll that is rolled up,
and every mountain and
island was removed from
its place. [15] Then the
kings of the earth and the
great men and the
generals and the rich
and the strong, and every
one, slave and free, hid in
the caves and among the
rocks of the mountains,
[16] calling to the mountains
and rocks, "Fall on us
and hide us from the
face of him who is seated
on the throne, and from
the wrath of the Lamb;
[17] for the great day of
their wrath has come,
and who can stand
before it?"

ὅτε ἤνοιξεν τὴν σφραγῖδα τὴν ἕκτην,
when he opened the ²seal – ¹sixth,

καὶ σεισμὸς μέγας ἐγένετο, καὶ ὁ ἥλιος
and ²earthquake ¹a great occurred, and the sun

ἐγένετο μέλας ὡς σάκκος τρίχινος, καὶ
became black as sackcloth made of hair, and

ἡ σελήνη ὅλη ἐγένετο ὡς αἷμα, 13 καὶ
the ²moon ¹whole became as blood, and

οἱ ἀστέρες τοῦ οὐρανοῦ ἔπεσαν εἰς τὴν
the stars – of heaven fell to the

γῆν, ὡς συκῆ βάλλει τοὺς ὀλύνθους
earth, as a fig-tree casts the unripe figs

αὐτῆς ὑπὸ ἀνέμου μεγάλου σειομένη,
of it ²by ⁴wind ³a great(strong) ¹being shaken,

14 καὶ ὁ οὐρανὸς ἀπεχωρίσθη ὡς βιβλίον
and the heaven departed as a scroll

ἑλισσόμενον, καὶ πᾶν ὄρος καὶ νῆσος
being rolled up, and every mountain and island

ἐκ τῶν τόπων αὐτῶν ἐκινήθησαν. 15 καὶ
out of the places of them were moved. And

οἱ βασιλεῖς τῆς γῆς καὶ οἱ μεγιστᾶνες
the kings of the earth and the great men

καὶ οἱ χιλίαρχοι καὶ οἱ πλούσιοι καὶ
and the chiliarchs and the rich men and

οἱ ἰσχυροὶ καὶ πᾶς δοῦλος καὶ ἐλεύθερος
the strong men and every slave and free man

ἔκρυψαν ἑαυτοὺς εἰς τὰ σπήλαια καὶ
hid themselves in the caves and

εἰς τὰς πέτρας τῶν ὀρέων, 16 καὶ
in the rocks of the mountains, and

λέγουσιν τοῖς ὄρεσιν καὶ ταῖς πέτραις·
they say to the mountains and to the rocks:

πέσετε ἐφ᾽ ἡμᾶς καὶ κρύψατε ἡμᾶς
Fall ye on us and hide us

ἀπὸ προσώπου τοῦ καθημένου ἐπὶ τοῦ
from [the] face of the [one] sitting on the

θρόνου καὶ ἀπὸ τῆς ὀργῆς τοῦ ἀρνίου,
throne and from the wrath of the Lamb,

17 ὅτι ἦλθεν ἡ ἡμέρα ἡ μεγάλη τῆς
because ⁷came ¹the ³day – ²great ⁴of the

ὀργῆς αὐτῶν, καὶ τίς δύναται σταθῆναι;
⁵wrath ⁶of them, and who can to stand ?

CHAPTER 7

AFTER this I saw
four angels standing
at the four corners of the

7 Μετὰ τοῦτο εἶδον τέσσαρας ἀγγέλους
After this I saw four angels

ἑστῶτας ἐπὶ τὰς τέσσαρας γωνίας τῆς
standing on the four corners of the

earth, holding back the four winds of the earth, that no wind might blow on earth or sea or against any tree. ²Then I saw another angel ascend from the rising of the sun, with the seal of the living God, and he called with a loud voice to the four angels who had been given power to harm earth and sea, ³saying, "Do not harm the earth or the sea or the trees, till we have sealed the servants of our God upon their foreheads." ⁴And I heard the number of the sealed, a hundred and forty-four thousand sealed, out of every tribe of the sons of Israel, ⁵twelve thousand sealed out of the tribe of Judah, twelve thousand of the tribe of Reuben, twelve thousand of the tribe of Gad, ⁶twelve thousand of the tribe of Asher, twelve thousand of the tribe of Naph'tali, twelve thousand of the tribe of Manas'seh, ⁷twelve thousand of the tribe of Simeon, twelve thousand of the tribe of Levi, twelve thousand of

γῆς, κρατοῦντας τοὺς τέσσαρας ἀνέμους
earth, holding the four winds

τῆς γῆς, ἵνα μὴ πνέῃ ἄνεμος ἐπὶ τῆς
of the earth, in order ³not ²should ¹wind on the
that ⁴blow

γῆς μήτε ἐπὶ τῆς θαλάσσης μήτε ἐπὶ
earth nor on the sea nor on

πᾶν δένδρον. 2 καὶ εἶδον ἄλλον ἄγγελον
every(any) tree. And I saw another angel

ἀναβαίνοντα ἀπὸ ἀνατολῆς ἡλίου, ἔχοντα
coming up from [the] rising of [the] sun, having

σφραγῖδα θεοῦ ζῶντος, καὶ ἔκραξεν φωνῇ
a seal God of [the] living, and he cried ²voice

μεγάλῃ τοῖς τέσσαρσιν ἀγγέλοις οἷς
¹with a to the four angels to whom
great(loud)

ἐδόθη αὐτοῖς ἀδικῆσαι τὴν γῆν καὶ
it was given to them to harm the earth and

τὴν θάλασσαν, 3 λέγων· μὴ ἀδικήσητε
the sea, saying: Do not harm

τὴν γῆν μήτε τὴν θάλασσαν μήτε τὰ
the earth nor the sea nor the

δένδρα, ἄχρι σφραγίσωμεν τοὺς δούλους
trees, until we may seal the slaves

τοῦ θεοῦ ἡμῶν ἐπὶ τῶν μετώπων αὐτῶν.
of the God of us on the foreheads of them.

4 Καὶ ἤκουσα τὸν ἀριθμὸν τῶν ἐσφραγισ-
And I heard the number of the [ones] having been

μένων, ἑκατὸν τεσσεράκοντα τέσσαρες
sealed, a hundred [and] forty-four

χιλιάδες ἐσφραγισμένοι ἐκ πάσης φυλῆς
thousands having been sealed out of every tribe

υἱῶν Ἰσραήλ· 5 ἐκ φυλῆς Ἰούδα δώδεκα
of sons of Israel: of [the] tribe Juda twelve

χιλιάδες ἐσφραγισμένοι, ἐκ φυλῆς Ῥουβὴν
thousands having been sealed, of [the] tribe Reuben

δώδεκα χιλιάδες, ἐκ φυλῆς Γὰδ δώδεκα
twelve thousands, of [the] tribe Gad twelve

χιλιάδες, 6 ἐκ φυλῆς Ἀσὴρ δώδεκα
thousands, of [the] tribe Aser twelve

χιλιάδες, ἐκ φυλῆς Νεφθαλὶμ δώδεκα
thousands, of [the] tribe Nephthalim twelve

χιλιάδες, ἐκ φυλῆς Μανασσῆ δώδεκα
thousands, of [the] tribe Manasse twelve

χιλιάδες, 7 ἐκ φυλῆς Συμεὼν δώδεκα
thousands, of [the] tribe Symeon twelve

χιλιάδες, ἐκ φυλῆς Λευὶ δώδεκα χιλιάδες,
thousands, of [the] tribe Levi twelve thousands,

the tribe of Is'sachar, [8] twelve thousand of the tribe of Zeb'ulun, twelve thousand of the tribe of Joseph, twelve thousand sealed out of the tribe of Benjamin.

9 After this I looked, and behold, a great multitude which no man could number, from every nation, from all tribes and peoples and tongues, standing before the throne and before the Lamb, clothed in white robes, with palm branches in their hands, [10] and crying out with a loud voice, "Salvation belongs to our God who sits upon the throne, and to the Lamb!" [11] And all the angels stood round the throne and round the elders and the four living creatures, and they fell on their faces before the throne and worshiped God, [12] saying, "Amen! Blessing and glory and wisdom and thanksgiving and honor and power and might be to our God for ever and ever! Amen."

13 Then one of the

ἐκ   φυλῆς   'Ισσαχὰρ   δώδεκα   χιλιάδες,
of [the]   tribe   Issachar   twelve   thousands,

8 ἐκ   φυλῆς   Ζαβουλὼν   δώδεκα   χιλιάδες,
of [the]   tribe   Zabulon   twelve   thousands,

ἐκ   φυλῆς   'Ιωσὴφ   δώδεκα   χιλιάδες,   ἐκ
of [the]   tribe   Joseph   twelve   thousands,   of

φυλῆς   Βενιαμὶν   δώδεκα   χιλιάδες   ἐσφραγισ-
[the] tribe   Benjamin   twelve   thousands   having been

μένοι.   9 Μετὰ   ταῦτα   εἶδον,   καὶ   ἰδοὺ   ὄχλος
sealed.   After these things   I saw,   and behold[,]   [2]crowd

πολύς,   ὃν   ἀριθμῆσαι   αὐτὸν   οὐδεὶς   ἐδύνατο,
[1]a much   which   [3]to number   it   [1]no one   [2]was able,
(great),

ἐκ   παντὸς   ἔθνους   καὶ   φυλῶν   καὶ   λαῶν
out of   every   nation   and   tribes   and   peoples

καὶ   γλωσσῶν,   ἑστῶτες   ἐνώπιον   τοῦ   θρόνου
and   tongues,   standing   before   the   throne

καὶ   ἐνώπιον   τοῦ   ἀρνίου,   περιβεβλημένους
and   before   the   Lamb,   having been clothed [with]

στολὰς   λευκάς,   καὶ   φοίνικες   ἐν   ταῖς
[2]robes   [1]white,   and   palms   in   the

χερσὶν   αὐτῶν·   10 καὶ   κράζουσιν   φωνῇ
hands   of them;   and   they cry   [2]voice

μεγάλη   λέγοντες·   ἡ   σωτηρία   τῷ   θεῷ
[1]with a great(loud)   saying: –   Salvation   to the   God[e]

ἡμῶν   τῷ   καθημένῳ   ἐπὶ   τῷ   θρόνῳ   καὶ
of us   –   sitting   on   the   throne   and

τῷ   ἀρνίῳ.   11 καὶ   πάντες   οἱ   ἄγγελοι
to the   Lamb.[e]   And   all   the   angels

εἱστήκεισαν   κύκλῳ   τοῦ   θρόνου   καὶ   τῶν
stood   round   the   throne   and   the

πρεσβυτέρων   καὶ   τῶν   τεσσάρων   ζώων,
elders   and   the   four   living
                                                                    creatures,

καὶ   ἔπεσαν   ἐνώπιον   τοῦ   θρόνου   ἐπὶ
and   fell   before   the   throne   on

τὰ   πρόσωπα   αὐτῶν   καὶ   προσεκύνησαν
the   faces   of them   and   worshipped

τῷ   θεῷ,   12 λέγοντες·   ἀμήν,   ἡ   εὐλογία
–   God,   saying: Amen,   –   blessing

καὶ   ἡ   δόξα   καὶ   ἡ   σοφία   καὶ   ἡ   εὐχαριστία
and   –   glory   and   –   wisdom   and   –   thanks

καὶ   ἡ   τιμὴ   καὶ   ἡ   δύναμις   καὶ   ἡ   ἰσχὺς
and   –   honour   and   –   power   and   –   strength

τῷ   θεῷ   ἡμῶν   εἰς   τοὺς   αἰῶνας   τῶν
to the   God[e]   of us   unto   the   ages   of the

αἰώνων·   ἀμήν.   13 Καὶ   ἀπεκρίθη   εἷς
ages: Amen.   And   [2]answered   [1]one

elders addressed me, saying, "Who are these, clothed in white robes, and whence have they come?" ¹⁴I said to him, "Sir, you know." And he said to me, "These are they who have come out of the great tribulation; they have washed their robes and made them white in the blood of the Lamb.

¹⁵Therefore are they before the throne of God, and serve him day and night within his temple; and he who sits upon the throne will shelter them with his presence.

¹⁶They shall hunger no more, neither thirst any more; the sun shall not strike them, nor any scorching heat.

¹⁷For the Lamb in the midst of the throne will be their shepherd, and he will guide them to springs of living water; and God will wipe away every tear from their eyes."

ἐκ τῶν πρεσβυτέρων λέγων μοι· οὗτοι
²of ³the ⁴elders saying to me: These

οἱ περιβεβλημένοι τὰς στολὰς τὰς
the having been clothed the ²robes -
[ones] [with]

λευκὰς τίνες εἰσὶν καὶ πόθεν ἦλθον;
¹white who are they and whence came they?

14 καὶ εἴρηκα αὐτῷ· κύριέ μου, σὺ
And I have said to him: Lord of me, thou

οἶδας. καὶ εἶπέν μοι· οὗτοί εἰσιν οἱ
knowest. And he told me: These are the

ἐρχόμενοι ἐκ τῆς θλίψεως τῆς μεγάλης
[ones] coming out of the ²affliction - ¹great

καὶ ἔπλυναν τὰς στολὰς αὐτῶν καὶ
and washed the robes of them and

ἐλεύκαναν αὐτὰς ἐν τῷ αἵματι τοῦ
whitened them in the blood of the

ἀρνίου. 15 διὰ τοῦτό εἰσιν ἐνώπιον τοῦ
Lamb. Therefore are they before the

θρόνου τοῦ θεοῦ, καὶ λατρεύουσιν αὐτῷ
throne - of God, and serve him

ἡμέρας καὶ νυκτὸς ἐν τῷ ναῷ αὐτοῦ,
day and night in the shrine of him,

καὶ ὁ καθήμενος ἐπὶ τοῦ θρόνου σκηνώσει
and the [one] sitting on the throne will spread
[his] tent

ἐπ᾽ αὐτούς. 16 οὐ πεινάσουσιν ἔτι οὐδὲ
over them. They will not hunger longer nor

διψήσουσιν ἔτι, οὐδὲ μὴ πέσῃ ἐπ᾽ αὐτοὺς
will they thirst longer, nor not fall on them

ὁ ἥλιος οὐδὲ πᾶν καῦμα, 17 ὅτι τὸ
the sun nor every(any) heat, because the

ἀρνίον τὸ ἀνὰ μέσον τοῦ θρόνου ποιμανεῖ
Lamb - in the midst of the throne will shepherd

αὐτοὺς καὶ ὁδηγήσει αὐτοὺς ἐπὶ ζωῆς
them and will lead them upon ²of life

πηγὰς ὑδάτων· καὶ ἐξαλείψει ὁ θεὸς
¹fountains ²of waters; and ²will wipe off - ¹God

πᾶν δάκρυον ἐκ τῶν ὀφθαλμῶν αὐτῶν.
every tear out of the eyes of them.

CHAPTER 8

WHEN the Lamb opened the seventh seal, there was silence in heaven for about half an hour. ²Then I saw the

8 Καὶ ὅταν ἤνοιξεν τὴν σφραγῖδα τὴν
And whenever he opened the ²seal

ἐβδόμην, ἐγένετο σιγὴ ἐν τῷ οὐρανῷ
¹seventh, occurred a silence in - heaven

ὡς ἡμίωρον. 2 Καὶ εἶδον τοὺς ἑπτα
about a half-hour. And I saw the seven

seven angels who stand before God, and seven trumpets were given to them. ³And another angel came and stood at the altar with a golden censer; and he was given much incense to mingle with the prayers of all the saints upon the golden altar before the throne; ⁴and the smoke of the incense rose with the prayers of the saints from the hand of the angel before God. ⁵Then the angel took the censer and filled it with fire from the altar and threw it on the earth; and there were peals of thunder, loud noises, flashes of lightning, and an earthquake.

6 Now the seven angels who had the seven trumpets made ready to blow them.

7 The first angel blew his trumpet, and there followed hail and fire, mixed with blood, which fell on the earth; and a third of the earth was burnt up, and a third of

ἀγγέλους	οἱ	ἐνώπιον	τοῦ θεοῦ	ἑστήκασιν,
angels	who	before	– God	stood,

καὶ	ἐδόθησαν	αὐτοῖς	ἑπτὰ	σάλπιγγες.
and	there were given	to them	seven	trumpets.

3 Καὶ ἄλλος ἄγγελος ἦλθεν καὶ ἐστάθη
And another angel came and stood

ἐπὶ τοῦ θυσιαστηρίου ἔχων λιβανωτὸν
on the altar having ²censer

χρυσοῦν, καὶ ἐδόθη αὐτῷ θυμιάματα πολλά,
¹a golden, and there was to him incenses many
                        given   (much),

ἵνα δώσει ταῖς προσευχαῖς τῶν ἁγίων
in order he will with the prayers of ²the ³saints
that give [it]

πάντων ἐπὶ τὸ θυσιαστήριον τὸ χρυσοῦν
¹all on the ²altar – ¹golden

τὸ ἐνώπιον τοῦ θρόνου. **4** καὶ ἀνέβη
– before the throne. And went up

ὁ καπνὸς τῶν θυμιαμάτων ταῖς προσευχαῖς
the smoke of the incenses with the prayers

τῶν ἁγίων ἐκ χειρὸς τοῦ ἀγγέλου ἐνώπιον
of the saints out of [the] hand of the angel before

τοῦ θεοῦ. **5** καὶ εἴληφεν ὁ ἄγγελος
– God. And ²has taken ¹the ²angel

τὸν λιβανωτόν, καὶ ἐγέμισεν αὐτὸν ἐκ
the censer, and filled it from

τοῦ πυρὸς τοῦ θυσιαστηρίου καὶ ἔβαλεν
the fire of the altar and cast

εἰς τὴν γῆν· καὶ ἐγένοντο βρονταὶ καὶ
into the earth; and there occurred thunders and

φωναὶ καὶ ἀστραπαὶ καὶ σεισμός.
sounds and lightnings and an earthquake.

6 Καὶ οἱ ἑπτὰ ἄγγελοι οἱ ἔχοντες
And the seven angels – having

τὰς ἑπτὰ σάλπιγγας ἡτοίμασαν αὐτοὺς
the seven trumpets prepared themselves

ἵνα σαλπίσωσιν. **7** Καὶ ὁ πρῶτος
in order they might And the first
that trumpet.

ἐσάλπισεν· καὶ ἐγένετο χάλαζα καὶ πῦρ
trumpeted; and there occurred hail and fire

μεμιγμένα ἐν αἵματι καὶ ἐβλήθη εἰς
having been in blood and it was cast to
mixed (with)

τὴν γῆν· καὶ τὸ τρίτον τῆς γῆς
the earth; and the third [part] of the earth

κατεκάη, καὶ τὸ τρίτον τῶν δένδρων
was burnt and the third [part] of the trees
down(up),

the trees were burnt up, and all green grass was burnt up.

8 The second angel blew his trumpet, and something like a great mountain, burning with fire, was thrown into the sea; 9 and a third of the sea became blood, a third of the living creatures in the sea died, and a third of the ships were destroyed.

10 The third angel blew his trumpet, and a great star fell from heaven, blazing like a torch, and it fell on a third of the rivers and on the fountains of water. 11 The name of the star is Wormwood. A third of the waters became wormwood, and many men died of the water, because it was made bitter.

12 The fourth angel blew his trumpet, and a third of the sun was struck, and a third of the moon, and a third of the stars, so that a third of their light was darkened; a third of the day was kept from shining, and likewise a third of the night.

κατεκάη, καὶ πᾶς χόρτος χλωρὸς κατεκάη.
was burnt and all ²grass ¹green was burnt
down(up), down(up).

8 Καὶ ὁ δεύτερος ἄγγελος ἐσάλπισεν·
And the second angel trumpeted;

καὶ ὡς ὄρος μέγα πυρὶ καιόμενον ἐβλήθη
and as ²mountain ¹a great ⁴with fire ³burning was cast

εἰς τὴν θάλασσαν· καὶ ἐγένετο τὸ τρίτον
into the sea; and ⁵became ¹the ²third [part]

τῆς θαλάσσης αἷμα, 9 καὶ ἀπέθανεν τὸ
³of the ⁴sea ⁶blood, and ¹⁰died ¹the

τρίτον τῶν κτισμάτων τῶν ἐν τῇ θαλάσσῃ,
²third ³of the ⁴creatures – ⁵in ⁶the ⁷sea,
[part]

τὰ ἔχοντα ψυχάς, καὶ τὸ τρίτον τῶν
– ⁸having ⁹souls, and the third [part] of the

πλοίων διεφθάρησαν. 10 Καὶ ὁ τρίτος
ships were destroyed. And the third

ἄγγελος ἐσάλπισεν· καὶ ἔπεσεν ἐκ τοῦ
angel trumpeted; and fell out of –

οὐρανοῦ ἀστὴρ μέγας καιόμενος ὡς
heaven star a great burning as

λαμπάς, καὶ ἔπεσεν ἐπὶ τὸ τρίτον τῶν
a lamp, and it fell onto the third [part] of the

ποταμῶν καὶ ἐπὶ τὰς πηγὰς τῶν ὑδάτων.
rivers and onto the fountains of the waters.

11 καὶ τὸ ὄνομα τοῦ ἀστέρος λέγεται
And the name of the star is said(called)

ὁ Ἄψινθος. καὶ ἐγένετο τὸ τρίτον τῶν
– Wormwood. And ⁵became ¹the ²third ³of the
[part]

ὑδάτων εἰς ἄψινθον, καὶ πολλοὶ τῶν
⁴waters into wormwood, and many of the

ἀνθρώπων ἀπέθανον ἐκ τῶν ὑδάτων ὅτι
men died from the waters because

ἐπικράνθησαν. 12 Καὶ ὁ τέταρτος ἄγγελος
they were made bitter. And the fourth angel

ἐσάλπισεν· καὶ ἐπλήγη τὸ τρίτον τοῦ
trumpeted; and ⁵was struck ¹the ²third [part] ³of the

ἡλίου καὶ τὸ τρίτον τῆς σελήνης καὶ
⁴sun and the third [part] of the moon and

τὸ τρίτον τῶν ἀστέρων, ἵνα σκοτισθῇ
the third of the stars, in order ⁴might be
[part] that darkened

τὸ τρίτον αὐτῶν καὶ ἡ ἡμέρα μὴ φάνῃ
¹the ²third [part] ³of them and the day might not appear

τὸ τρίτον αὐτῆς, καὶ ἡ νὺξ ὁμοίως.
the third [part] of it, and the night likewise.

13 Then I looked, and I heard an eagle crying with a loud voice, as it flew in midheaven, "Woe, woe, woe to those who dwell on the earth, at the blasts of the other trumpets which the three angels are about to blow!"

13 Καὶ εἶδον, καὶ ἤκουσα ἑνὸς ἀετοῦ
And   I saw,   and   I heard   one   eagle

πετομένου ἐν μεσουρανήματι λέγοντος φωνῇ
flying   in   mid-heaven   saying   [1]voice

μεγάλῃ· οὐαὶ οὐαὶ οὐαὶ τοὺς κατοικοῦν-
[1]with a   Woe[,]   woe[,]   woe   to the [ones]   dwell-
great(loud):

τας ἐπὶ τῆς γῆς ἐκ τῶν λοιπῶν φωνῶν
ing   on   the   earth   from   the   remaining   voices

τῆς σάλπιγγος τῶν τριῶν ἀγγέλων τῶν
of the   trumpet   of the   three   angels   –

μελλόντων σαλπίζειν.
being about   to trumpet.

CHAPTER 9

AND the fifth angel blew his trumpet, and I saw a star fallen from heaven to earth, and he was given the key of the shaft of the bottomless pit; [2]he opened the shaft of the bottomless pit, and from the shaft rose smoke like the smoke of a great furnace, and the sun and the air were darkened with the smoke from the shaft. [3]Then from the smoke came locusts on the earth, and they were given power like the power of scorpions of the earth; [4]they were told not to harm the grass of the earth or any green growth or any tree, but only those of mankind who have not the seal of God upon their fore-

9 Καὶ ὁ πέμπτος ἄγγελος ἐσάλπισεν·
And the   fifth   angel   trumpeted;

καὶ εἶδον ἀστέρα ἐκ τοῦ οὐρανοῦ πεπτω-
and   I saw   a star   out of   –   heaven   having

κότα εἰς τὴν γῆν, καὶ ἐδόθη αὐτῷ
fallen   onto   the   earth,   and   was given   to it

ἡ κλεὶς τοῦ φρέατος τῆς ἀβύσσου. 2 καὶ
the   key   of the   shaft   of the   abyss.   And

ἤνοιξεν τὸ φρέαρ τῆς ἀβύσσου· καὶ
he opened   the   shaft   of the   abyss;   and

ἀνέβη καπνὸς ἐκ τοῦ φρέατος ὡς
went up   a smoke   out of   the   shaft   as

καπνὸς καμίνου μεγάλης, καὶ ἐσκοτώθη
smoke   [2]furnace   [1]of a great,   and   [1]was darkened

ὁ ἥλιος καὶ ὁ ἀὴρ ἐκ τοῦ καπνοῦ
[1]the [2]sun   [3]and [4]the [5]air   by   the   smoke

τοῦ φρέατος. 3 καὶ ἐκ τοῦ καπνοῦ
of the   shaft.   And out of   the   smoke

ἐξῆλθον ἀκρίδες εἰς τὴν γῆν, καὶ ἐδόθη
came forth   locusts   to   the   earth,   and [3]was given

αὐτοῖς ἐξουσία ὡς ἔχουσιν ἐξουσίαν οἱ
[2]to them   [1]authority   as   [5]have   [4]authority   [1]the

σκορπίοι τῆς γῆς. 4 καὶ ἐρρέθη αὐτοῖς
[2]scorpions   [3]of the [4]earth.   And   it was said   to them

ἵνα μὴ ἀδικήσουσιν τὸν χόρτον τῆς
in order   they shall not harm   the   grass   of the
that

γῆς οὐδὲ πᾶν χλωρὸν οὐδὲ πᾶν δένδρον,
earth   nor   every   greenstuff   nor   every   tree,
(any)   (any)

εἰ μὴ τοὺς ἀνθρώπους οἵτινες οὐκ ἔχουσιν
except   the   men   who   have not

τὴν σφραγῖδα τοῦ θεοῦ ἐπὶ τῶν μετώπων.
the   seal   –   of God   on   the(ir)   foreheads.

heads; ⁵they were allowed to torture them for five months, but not to kill them, and their torture was like the torture of a scorpion, when it stings a man. ⁶And in those days men will seek death and will not find it; they will long to die, and death will fly from them.

7 In appearance the locusts were like horses arrayed for battle; on their heads were what looked like crowns of gold; their faces were like human faces, ⁸their hair like women's hair, and their teeth like lions' teeth; ⁹they had scales like iron breastplates, and the noise of their wings was like the noise of many chariots with horses rushing into battle. ¹⁰They have tails like scorpions, and stings, and their power of hurting men for five months lies in their tails. ¹¹They have as king over them the angel of the bottom-

5 καὶ ἐδόθη αὐτοῖς ἵνα μὴ ἀποκτείνωσιν
   And it was to them in order they should not kill
       given that

αὐτούς, ἀλλ' ἵνα βασανισθήσονται μῆνας
   them, but in order they shall be tormented ²months
           that

πέντε· καὶ ὁ βασανισμὸς αὐτῶν ὡς
   ¹five; and the torment of them [is] as

βασανισμὸς σκορπίου, ὅταν παίσῃ ἄνθρωπον.
   [the] torment of a scorpion, whenever it stings a man.

6 καὶ ἐν ταῖς ἡμέραις ἐκείναις ζητήσουσιν
   And in those days ²will seek

οἱ ἄνθρωποι τὸν θάνατον καὶ οὐ μὴ
   - ¹men - death and by no means

εὑρήσουσιν αὐτόν, καὶ ἐπιθυμήσουσιν
   will they find it, and they will long

ἀποθανεῖν καὶ φεύγει ὁ θάνατος ἀπ'
   to die and flees - ¹death from

αὐτῶν. 7 καὶ τὰ ὁμοιώματα τῶν ἀκρίδων
   them. And the likenesses of the locusts

ὅμοιοι ἵπποις ἡτοιμασμένοις εἰς πόλεμον,
   like to horses having been prepared for war,

καὶ ἐπὶ τὰς κεφαλὰς αὐτῶν ὡς στέφανοι
   and on the heads of them as crowns

ὅμοιοι χρυσῷ, καὶ τὰ πρόσωπα αὐτῶν
   like to gold, and the faces of them

ὡς πρόσωπα ἀνθρώπων, 8 καὶ εἶχον
   as faces of men, and they had

τρίχας ὡς τρίχας γυναικῶν, καὶ οἱ
   hairs as hairs of women, and the

ὀδόντες αὐτῶν ὡς λεόντων ἦσαν, 9 καὶ
   teeth of them ²as ³of lions ¹were, and

εἶχον θώρακας ὡς θώρακας σιδηροῦς,
   they had breastplates as ²breastplates ¹iron,

καὶ ἡ φωνὴ τῶν πτερύγων αὐτῶν ὡς
   and the sound of the wings of them as

φωνὴ ἁρμάτων ἵππων πολλῶν τρεχόντων
   sound ²chariots ³of horses ¹of many running

εἰς πόλεμον. 10 καὶ ἔχουσιν οὐρὰς ὁμοίας
   to war. And they have tails like

σκορπίοις καὶ κέντρα, καὶ ἐν ταῖς οὐραῖς
   to scorpions and stings, and ⁵with ⁷the ⁸tails

αὐτῶν ἡ ἐξουσία αὐτῶν ἀδικῆσαι τοὺς
   ⁹of them ¹the ²authority ³of them ⁴[is] to harm -

ἀνθρώπους μῆνας πέντε. 11 ἔχουσιν ἐπ'
   ⁵men ¹¹months ¹⁰five. They have over

αὐτῶν βασιλέα τὸν ἄγγελον τῆς ἀβύσσου,
   them a king the angel of the abyss,

less pit; his name in
Hebrew is Abad'don,
and in Greek he is called
Apol'lyon.[a]
12 The first woe has
passed; behold, two
woes are still to come.

13 Then the sixth
angel blew his trumpet,
and I heard a voice from
the four horns of the
golden altar before God,
[14] saying to the sixth
angel who had the
trumpet, "Release the
four angels who are
bound at the great river
Eu-phra'tes." [15] So the
four angels were re-
leased, who had been
held ready for the hour,
the day, the month, and
the year, to kill a third
of mankind. [16] The
number of the troops of
cavalry was twice ten
thousand times ten
thousand; I heard their
number. [17] And this was
how I saw the horses in
my vision: the riders
wore breastplates the
color of fire and of
sapphire[b] and of sulphur,
and the heads of the
horses were like lions'
heads, and fire and smoke
and sulphur issued from

ὄνομα αὐτῷ ‘Εβραϊστὶ ’Αβαδδών, καὶ
name to him[e] in Hebrew Abaddon, and
ἐν τῇ ‘Ελληνικῇ ὄνομα ἔχει ’Απολλύων.
in the Greek [2][the] name [1]he has Apollyon.
12 ‘Η οὐαὶ ἡ μία ἀπῆλθεν· ἰδοὺ ἔρχεται
The [2]woe – [1]one(first) passed away; behold [4]comes
ἔτι δύο οὐαὶ μετὰ ταῦτα.
[1]yet [3]two [2]woes after these things.

13 Καὶ ὁ ἕκτος ἄγγελος ἐσάλπισεν·
And the sixth angel trumpeted;
καὶ ἤκουσα φωνὴν μίαν ἐκ τῶν τεσσάρων
and I heard [2]voice [1]one out of the four
κεράτων τοῦ θυσιαστηρίου τοῦ χρυσοῦ
horns of the [2]altar – [1]golden
τοῦ ἐνώπιον τοῦ θεοῦ, 14 λέγοντα τῷ
the before – God, saying to the
ἕκτῳ ἀγγέλῳ, ὁ ἔχων τὴν σάλπιγγα·
sixth angel, – having the trumpet:
λῦσον τοὺς τέσσαρας ἀγγέλους τοὺς
Loose the four angels –
δεδεμένους ἐπὶ τῷ ποταμῷ τῷ μεγάλῳ
having been bound at the [2]river – [1]great
Εὐφράτῃ. 15 καὶ ἐλύθησαν οἱ τέσσαρες
Euphrates. And were loosed the four
ἄγγελοι οἱ ἡτοιμασμένοι εἰς τὴν ὥραν
angels – having been prepared for the hour
καὶ ἡμέραν καὶ μῆνα καὶ ἐνιαυτόν,
and day and month and year,
ἵνα ἀποκτείνωσιν τὸ τρίτον τῶν ἀνθρώπων.
in or- they should kill the third – of men.
der that [part]
16 καὶ ὁ ἀριθμὸς τῶν στρατευμάτων τοῦ
And the number of the bodies of soldiers of the
ἱππικοῦ δισμυριάδες μυριάδων· ἤκουσα τὸν
cavalry [was] two myriads of myriads; I heard the
ἀριθμὸν αὐτῶν. 17 καὶ οὕτως εἶδον
number of them. And thus I saw
τοὺς ἵππους ἐν τῇ ὁράσει καὶ τοὺς
the horses in the vision and the
καθημένους ἐπ’ αὐτῶν, ἔχοντας θώρακας
[ones] sitting on them, having breastplates
πυρίνους καὶ ὑακινθίνους καὶ θειώδεις·
fire-coloured and dusky red and sulphurous;
καὶ αἱ κεφαλαὶ τῶν ἵππων ὡς κεφαλαὶ
and the heads of the horses as heads
λεόντων, καὶ ἐκ τῶν στομάτων αὐτῶν
of lions, and out of the mouths of them
ἐκπορεύεται πῦρ καὶ καπνὸς καὶ θεῖον.
proceeds fire and smoke and sulphur.

---

[a] Or Destroyer
[b] Greek hyacinth

their mouths. [18] By these three plagues a third of mankind was killed, by the fire and smoke and sulphur issuing from their mouths. [19] For the power of the horses is in their mouths and in their tails; their tails are like serpents, with heads, and by means of them they wound.

20 The rest of mankind, who were not killed by these plagues, did not repent of the works of their hands nor give up worshiping demons and idols of gold and silver and bronze and stone and wood, which cannot either see or hear or walk; [21] nor did they repent of their murders or their sorceries or their immorality or their thefts.

18 ἀπὸ τῶν τριῶν πληγῶν τούτων ἀπεκτάν-
From   the   ²three   ³plagues   ¹these   were

θησαν τὸ τρίτον τῶν ἀνθρώπων, ἐκ
killed   the   third [part]   –   of men.   by

τοῦ πυρὸς καὶ τοῦ καπνοῦ καὶ τοῦ
the   fire   and   the   smoke   and   the

θείου τοῦ ἐκπορευομένου ἐκ τῶν στομάτων
sulphur   –   proceeding   out of   the   mouths

αὐτῶν. 19 ἡ γὰρ ἐξουσία τῶν ἵππων
of them.   For the   authority   of the   horses

ἐν τῷ στόματι αὐτῶν ἐστιν καὶ ἐν
¹in   ²the   ⁴mouth   ⁵of them   ³is   and   in

ταῖς οὐραῖς αὐτῶν· αἱ γὰρ οὐραὶ αὐτῶν
the   tails   of them;   for the   tails   of them

ὅμοιαι ὄφεσιν, ἔχουσαι κεφαλάς, καὶ ἐν
[are] like   to serpents,   having   heads,   and with

αὐταῖς ἀδικοῦσιν. 20 καὶ οἱ λοιποὶ τῶν
them   they do harm.   And   the   rest   –

ἀνθρώπων, οἳ οὐκ ἀπεκτάνθησαν ἐν ταῖς
of men,   who   were not killed   by   –

πληγαῖς ταύταις, οὐδὲ μετενόησαν ἐκ
plagues   these,   not even   repented   of

τῶν ἔργων τῶν χειρῶν αὐτῶν, ἵνα μὴ
the   works   of the   hands   of them,   in order not
                                                            that

προσκυνήσουσιν τὰ δαιμόνια καὶ τὰ εἴδωλα
they will worship   –   demons   and   –   idols

τὰ χρυσᾶ καὶ τὰ ἀργυρᾶ καὶ τὰ χαλκᾶ
–   golden   and   –   silver   and   –   bronze

καὶ τὰ λίθινα καὶ τὰ ξύλινα, ἃ οὔτε
and   –   stone   and   –   wooden,   which ²neither

βλέπειν δύνανται οὔτε ἀκούειν οὔτε
³to see   ¹can   nor   to hear   nor

περιπατεῖν, 21 καὶ οὐ μετενόησαν ἐκ τῶν
to walk,   and   they repented not   of   the

φόνων αὐτῶν οὔτε ἐκ τῶν φαρμακειῶν
murders   of them   nor   of   the   sorceries

αὐτῶν οὔτε ἐκ τῆς πορνείας αὐτῶν
of them   nor   of   the   fornication   of them

οὔτε ἐκ τῶν κλεμμάτων αὐτῶν.
nor   of   the   thefts   of them.

CHAPTER 10

THEN I saw another mighty angel coming down from heaven, wrapped in a cloud, with a rainbow over his head,

10 Καὶ εἶδον ἄλλον ἄγγελον ἰσχυρὸν
And   I saw   another   ²angel   ¹strong

καταβαίνοντα ἐκ τοῦ οὐρανοῦ, περιβεβλημέ-
coming down   out of   –   heaven,   having been clothed

νον νεφέλην, καὶ ἡ ἶρις ἐπὶ τὴν κεφαλὴν
[with]   a cloud,   and   the rainbow   on   the   head

and his face was like the sun, and his legs like pillars of fire. ²He had a little scroll open in his hand. And he set his right foot on the sea, and his left foot on the land, ³and called out with a loud voice, like a lion roaring; when he called out, the seven thunders sounded. ⁴And when the seven thunders had sounded, I was about to write, but I heard a voice from heaven saying, "Seal up what the seven thunders have said, and do not write it down." ⁵And the angel whom I saw standing on sea and land lifted up his right hand to heaven ⁶and swore by him who lives for ever and ever, who created heaven and what is in it, the earth and what is in it, and the sea and what is in it, that there should be no more delay, ⁷but that in the days of the trumpet call to be sounded by the seventh angel, the

αὐτοῦ, καὶ τὸ πρόσωπον αὐτοῦ ὡς ὁ
of him, and the face of him as the

ἥλιος, καὶ οἱ πόδες αὐτοῦ ὡς στῦλοι
sun, and the feet of him as pillars

πυρός, 2 καὶ ἔχων ἐν τῇ χειρὶ αὐτοῦ
of fire, and having in the hand of him

βιβλαρίδιον ἠνεῳγμένον. καὶ ἔθηκεν τὸν
a little scroll *having been* opened. And he placed ¹the

πόδα αὐτοῦ τὸν δεξιὸν ἐπὶ τῆς θαλάσσης,
²foot ⁴of him – ³right on the sea,

τὸν δὲ εὐώνυμον ἐπὶ τῆς γῆς, 3 καὶ
and the left on the land, and

ἔκραξεν φωνῇ μεγάλῃ ὥσπερ λέων μυκᾶται.
cried ²voice ¹with a as a lion roars.
great(loud)

καὶ ὅτε ἔκραξεν, ἐλάλησαν αἱ ἑπτὰ
And when he cried, ⁴spoke(uttered) ¹the ²seven

βρονταὶ τὰς ἑαυτῶν φωνάς. 4 Καὶ ὅτε
³thunders ⁵the ⁷of themselves ⁶voices. And when

ἐλάλησαν αἱ ἑπτὰ βρονταί, ἤμελλον
spoke the seven thunders, I was about

γράφειν· καὶ ἤκουσα φωνὴν ἐκ τοῦ
to write; and I heard a voice out of –

οὐρανοῦ λέγουσαν· σφράγισον ἃ ἐλάλησαν
heaven saying: Seal thou [the] ⁴spoke
things which

αἱ ἑπτὰ βρονταί, καὶ μὴ αὐτὰ γράψῃς.
¹the ²seven ³thunders, and ³not ²them *thou mayest*
¹write.

5 Καὶ ὁ ἄγγελος, ὃν εἶδον ἑστῶτα
And the angel, whom I saw standing

ἐπὶ τῆς θαλάσσης καὶ ἐπὶ τῆς γῆς,
on the sea and on the land,

ἦρεν τὴν χεῖρα αὐτοῦ τὴν δεξιὰν εἰς
lifted ¹the ³hand ⁴of him – ²right to

τὸν οὐρανόν, 6 καὶ ὤμοσεν ἐν τῷ ζῶντι
– heaven, and swore by the [one] living

εἰς τοὺς αἰῶνας τῶν αἰώνων, ὃς ἔκτισεν
unto the ages of the ages, who created

τὸν οὐρανὸν καὶ τὰ ἐν αὐτῷ καὶ τὴν
the heaven and the things in it and the

γῆν καὶ τὰ ἐν αὐτῇ καὶ τὴν θάλασσαν
earth and the in it and the sea
things

καὶ τὰ ἐν αὐτῇ, ὅτι χρόνος οὐκέτι
and the things in it, that time ²no longer

ἔσται, 7 ἀλλ' ἐν ταῖς ἡμέραις τῆς
¹shall be, but in the days of the

φωνῆς τοῦ ἑβδόμου ἀγγέλου, ὅταν μέλλῃ
voice of the seventh angel, whenever he is about

mystery of God, as he announced to his servants the prophets, should be fulfilled.

8 Then the voice which I had heard from heaven spoke to me again, saying, "Go, take the scroll which is open in the hand of the angel who is standing on the sea and on the land." 9 So I went to the angel and told him to give me the little scroll; and he said to me, "Take it and eat; it will be bitter to your stomach, but sweet as honey in your mouth." 10 And I took the little scroll from the hand of the angel and ate it; it was sweet as honey in my mouth, but when I had eaten it my stomach was made bitter. 11 And I was told, "You must again prophesy about many peoples and nations and tongues and kings."

CHAPTER 11

THEN I was given a measuring rod like a staff, and I was told: "Rise and measure the temple of God and the altar and those who worship there, 2 but do

---

σαλπίζειν,   καὶ   ἐτελέσθη   τὸ   μυστήριον
to trumpet,   even   was finished   the   mystery

τοῦ   θεοῦ,   ὡς   εὐηγγέλισεν   τοὺς   ἑαυτοῦ
-    of God,   as   he preached [to]   the   ²of himself

δούλους   τοὺς   προφήτας.   8 Καὶ   ἡ   φωνὴ
¹slaves   the   prophets.   And   the   voice

ἣν   ἤκουσα   ἐκ   τοῦ   οὐρανοῦ,   πάλιν
which   I heard   out of -   heaven,   again

λαλοῦσαν   μετ᾽   ἐμοῦ   καὶ   λέγουσαν·   ὕπαγε
speaking   with   me   and   saying: Go thou

λάβε   τὸ   βιβλίον   τὸ   ἠνεῳγμένον   ἐν   τῇ
take   the   scroll   - having been opened   in   the

χειρὶ   τοῦ   ἀγγέλου   τοῦ   ἑστῶτος   ἐπὶ
hand   of the   angel   -   standing   on

τῆς   θαλάσσης   καὶ   ἐπὶ   τῆς   γῆς.   9 καὶ
the   sea   and   on   the   land.   And

ἀπῆλθα   πρὸς   τὸν   ἄγγελον,   λέγων   αὐτῷ
I went away   toward   the   angel,   telling   him

δοῦναί   μοι   τὸ   βιβλαρίδιον.   καὶ   λέγει
to give   me   the   little scroll.   And   he says

μοι·   λάβε   καὶ   κατάφαγε   αὐτό,   καὶ
to me: Take   and   devour   it,   and

πικρανεῖ   σου   τὴν   κοιλίαν,   ἀλλ᾽   ἐν   τῷ
it will embitter   ²of thee   ¹the   ²stomach,   but   in   the

στόματί   σου   ἔσται   γλυκὺ   ὡς   μέλι.
mouth   of thee   it will be   sweet   as   honey.

10 καὶ   ἔλαβον   τὸ   βιβλαρίδιον   ἐκ   τῆς
And   I took   the   little scroll   out of   the

χειρὸς   τοῦ   ἀγγέλου   καὶ   κατέφαγον   αὐτό,
hand   of the   angel   and   devoured   it,

καὶ   ἦν   ἐν   τῷ   στόματί   μου   ὡς   μέλι
and   it was in   the   mouth   of me   as   ³honey

γλυκύ·   καὶ   ὅτε   ἔφαγον   αὐτό,   ἐπικράνθη
¹sweet;   and   when   I ate   it,   ⁴was made bitter

ἡ   κοιλία   μου.   11 καὶ   λέγουσίν   μοι·
¹the   ²stomach   ³of me.   And   they say   to me:

δεῖ   σε   πάλιν   προφητεῦσαι   ἐπὶ   λαοῖς
It behoves thee   again   to prophesy   before   peoples

καὶ   ἔθνεσιν   καὶ   γλώσσαις   καὶ   βασιλεῦσιν
and   nations   and   tongues   and   ²kings

πολλοῖς.   11 Καὶ   ἐδόθη   μοι   κάλαμος   ὅμοιος
¹many.   And   was given to me   a reed   like

ῥάβδῳ,   λέγων·   ἔγειρε   καὶ   μέτρησον   τὸν   ναὸν
to a staff,   saying: Rise   and   measure   the   shrine

τοῦ   θεοῦ   καὶ   τὸ   θυσιαστήριον   καὶ   τοὺς
-    of God   and   the   altar   and   the

προσκυνοῦντας   ἐν   αὐτῷ.   2 καὶ   τὴν
[ones] worshipping   in   it.   And   the

not measure the court outside the temple; leave that out, for it is given over to the nations, and they will trample over the holy city for forty-two months. ³And I will grant my two witnesses power to prophesy for one thousand two hundred and sixty days, clothed in sackcloth."

4 These are the two olive trees and the two lampstands which stand before the Lord of the earth. ⁵And if any one would harm them, fire pours from their mouth and consumes their foes; if any one would harm them, thus he is doomed to be killed. ⁶They have power to shut the sky, that no rain may fall during the days of their prophesying, and they have power over the waters to turn them into blood, and to smite the earth with every plague, as often as they desire. ⁷And when they have finished their testimony, the beast that ascends from the bottomless pit will make war upon them

αὐλὴν	τὴν	ἔξωθεν	τοῦ	ναοῦ	ἔκβαλε
⁴court	–	¹outside	of the	shrine	cast *out*

ἔξωθεν	καὶ	μὴ	αὐτὴν	μετρήσῃς, ὅτι
outside	and	³not	²it	*thou mayest* because ¹measure,

ἐδόθη	τοῖς	ἔθνεσιν,	καὶ	τὴν πόλιν	τὴν
it was given to the	nations,	and	the	²city	–

ἁγίαν	πατήσουσιν	μῆνας	τεσσεράκοντα
¹holy	they will trample	²months	¹forty-

[καὶ]	δύο.	3 καὶ	δώσω	τοῖς	δυσὶν
and	²two.	And	I will give	to the	two

μάρτυσίν	μου,	καὶ προφητεύσουσιν	ἡμέρας
witnesses	of me,	and they will prophesy	²days

χιλίας	διακοσίας	ἑξήκοντα	περιβεβλημένοι
¹a thousand	²two hundred	³[and] ⁴sixty	*having been* clothed

σάκκους.	4 οὗτοί	εἰσιν	αἱ δύο	ἐλαῖαι
[in] sackclothes.	These	are	the two	olive-trees

καὶ	αἱ δύο	λυχνίαι	αἱ ἐνώπιον	τοῦ
and	the two	lampstands	– ²before	³the

κυρίου	τῆς γῆς	ἑστῶτες.	5 καὶ	εἴ τις
⁴Lord	⁵of the ⁶earth	¹standing.	And	if anyone

αὐτοὺς	θέλει	ἀδικῆσαι,	πῦρ ἐκπορεύεται·
³them	¹wishes	²to harm,	fire proceeds

ἐκ τοῦ	στόματος	αὐτῶν καὶ	κατεσθίει
out of the	mouth	of them and	devours

τοὺς	ἐχθροὺς	αὐτῶν· καὶ	εἴ τις θελήσῃ
the	enemies	of them; and	if anyone should wish

αὐτοὺς	ἀδικῆσαι,	οὕτως	δεῖ αὐτὸν
²them	¹to harm,	thus	it behoves him

ἀποκτανθῆναι.	6 οὗτοι	ἔχουσιν τὴν	ἐξουσίαν
to be killed.	These	have the	authority

κλεῖσαι	τὸν	οὐρανόν,	ἵνα μὴ ὑετὸς
to shut	the	heaven,	in order that ²not ¹rain

βρέχῃ	τὰς ἡμέρας	τῆς προφητείας	αὐτῶν,
¹may ⁴rain(fall)	the days	of the prophecy	of them,

καὶ	ἐξουσίαν	ἔχουσιν	ἐπὶ τῶν	ὑδάτων
and	authority	they have	over the	waters

στρέφειν	αὐτὰ	εἰς αἷμα	καὶ πατάξαι
to turn	them	into blood	and to strike

τὴν γῆν	ἐν πάσῃ	πληγῇ	ὁσάκις ἐὰν
the earth	with every	[kind of] plague	as often as

θελήσωσιν.	7 Καὶ	ὅταν τελέσωσιν	τὴν
they may wish.	And	whenever they finish	the

μαρτυρίαν	αὐτῶν,	τὸ θηρίον	τὸ ἀναβαῖνον
witness	of them,	the beast	– coming up

ἐκ τῆς	ἀβύσσου	ποιήσει	μετ' αὐτῶν
out of the	abyss	¹will make	²with ⁴them

and conquer them and
kill them, [8] and their
dead bodies will lie in the
street of the great city
which is allegorically
called Sodom and Egypt,
where their Lord was
crucified. [9] For three days
and a half men from the
people and tribes and
tongues and nations gaze
at their dead bodies and
refuse to let them be
placed in a tomb, [10] and
those who dwell on the
earth will rejoice over
them and make merry
and exchange presents,
because these two
prophets had been a
torment to those who
dwell on the earth. [11] But
after the three and a half
days a breath of life
from God entered them,
and they stood up on
their feet, and great fear
fell on those who saw
them. [12] Then they heard
a loud voice from heaven
saying to them, "Come
up hither!" And in the
sight of their foes they
went up to heaven in a
cloud. [13] And at that

πόλεμον καὶ νικήσει αὐτοὺς καὶ ἀποκτενεῖ
[1]war and will overcome them and will kill

αὐτούς. 8 καὶ τὸ πτῶμα αὐτῶν ἐπὶ
them. And the corpse of them on

τῆς πλατείας τῆς πόλεως τῆς μεγάλης,
the open street of the [2]city – [1]great,

ἥτις καλεῖται πνευματικῶς Σόδομα καὶ
which is called spiritually Sodom and

Αἴγυπτος, ὅπου καὶ ὁ κύριος αὐτῶν
Egypt, where indeed the Lord of them

ἐσταυρώθη. 9 καὶ βλέπουσιν ἐκ τῶν
was crucified. And [10]see [1][some] of [2]the

λαῶν καὶ φυλῶν καὶ γλωσσῶν καὶ
[3]peoples [4]and [5]tribes [6]and [7]tongues [8]and

ἐθνῶν τὸ πτῶμα αὐτῶν ἡμέρας τρεῖς
[9]nations the corpse of them [4]days [1]three

καὶ ἥμισυ, καὶ τὰ πτώματα αὐτῶν
[2]and [3]a half, and [1]the [2]corpses [4]of them

οὐκ ἀφίουσιν τεθῆναι εἰς μνῆμα. 10 καὶ
[1]they do not allow to be placed in a tomb. And

οἱ κατοικοῦντες ἐπὶ τῆς γῆς χαίρουσιν
the [ones] dwelling on the earth rejoice

ἐπ' αὐτοῖς καὶ εὐφραίνονται, καὶ δῶρα
over them and are glad, and [2]gifts

πέμψουσιν ἀλλήλοις, ὅτι οὗτοι οἱ δύο
[1]they will send to one another, because these – two

προφῆται ἐβασάνισαν τοὺς κατοικοῦντας
prophets tormented the [ones] dwelling

ἐπὶ τῆς γῆς. 11 Καὶ μετὰ [τὰς] τρεῖς
on the earth. And after the [1]three

ἡμέρας καὶ ἥμισυ πνεῦμα ζωῆς ἐκ τοῦ
[4]days [2]and [3]a half a spirit of life out of –

θεοῦ εἰσῆλθεν ἐν αὐτοῖς, καὶ ἔστησαν
God entered in[to] them, and they stood

ἐπὶ τοὺς πόδας αὐτῶν, καὶ φόβος μέγας
on the feet of them, and [2]fear [1]great

ἐπέπεσεν ἐπὶ τοὺς θεωροῦντας αὐτούς.
fell on on the [ones] beholding them.

12 καὶ ἤκουσαν φωνῆς μεγάλης ἐκ τοῦ
And they heard [2]voice [1]a great(loud) out of –

οὐρανοῦ λεγούσης αὐτοῖς· ἀνάβατε ὧδε·
heaven saying to them: Come ye up here;

καὶ ἀνέβησαν εἰς τὸν οὐρανὸν ἐν τῇ
and they went up to – heaven in the

νεφέλῃ, καὶ ἐθεώρησαν αὐτοὺς οἱ ἐχθροὶ
cloud, and [4]beheld [3]them [1]the [2]enemies

αὐτῶν. 13 Καὶ ἐν ἐκείνῃ τῇ ὥρᾳ ἐγένετο
[5]of them. And in that – hour [2]occurred

hour there was a great earthquake, and a tenth of the city fell; seven thousand people were killed in the earthquake, and the rest were terrified and gave glory to the God of heaven.

14 The second woe has passed; behold, the third woe is soon to come.

15 Then the seventh angel blew his trumpet, and there were loud voices in heaven, saying, "The kingdom of the world has become the kingdom of our Lord and of his Christ, and he shall reign for ever and ever." 16 And the twenty-four elders who sit on their thrones before God fell on their faces and worshiped God, 17 saying,

"We give thanks to thee, Lord God almighty, who art and who wast, that thou hast taken thy great power and begun to reign.

18 The nations raged, but thy wrath came, and the time for the dead to be judged,

---

σεισμὸς μέγας, καὶ τὸ δέκατον τῆς
²earthquake ¹a great, and the tenth [part] of the

πόλεως ἔπεσεν, καὶ ἀπεκτάνθησαν ἐν τῷ
city fell, and ⁵were killed ⁶in ⁷the

σεισμῷ ὀνόματα ἀνθρώπων χιλιάδες ἑπτά,
⁸earthquake ³names ⁴of men ²thousands ¹seven,

καὶ οἱ λοιποὶ ἔμφοβοι ἐγένοντο καὶ
and the rest ²terrified ¹became and

ἔδωκαν δόξαν τῷ θεῷ τοῦ οὐρανοῦ.
gave glory to the God – of heaven.

14 Ἡ οὐαὶ ἡ δευτέρα ἀπῆλθεν· ἰδοὺ
The ²woe – ¹second passed away; behold[,]

ἡ οὐαὶ ἡ τρίτη ἔρχεται ταχύ.
the ²woe – ¹third is coming quickly.

15 Καὶ ὁ ἕβδομος ἄγγελος ἐσάλπισεν·
And the seventh angel trumpeted;

καὶ ἐγένοντο φωναὶ μεγάλαι ἐν τῷ
and there were voices great(loud) in –

οὐρανῷ, λέγοντες· ἐγένετο ἡ βασιλεία
heaven, saying: ⁵became ¹The ²kingdom

τοῦ κόσμου τοῦ κυρίου ἡμῶν καὶ τοῦ
²of the ⁴world of the Lord of us and of the
⁶[the kingdom]

χριστοῦ αὐτοῦ, καὶ βασιλεύσει εἰς τοὺς
Christ of him, and he shall reign unto the

αἰῶνας τῶν αἰώνων. 16 καὶ οἱ εἴκοσι
ages of the ages. And the twenty-

τέσσαρες πρεσβύτεροι, οἱ ἐνώπιον τοῦ
four elders, – ²before –

θεοῦ καθήμενοι ἐπὶ τοὺς θρόνους αὐτῶν,
³God ¹sitting on the thrones of them,

ἔπεσαν ἐπὶ τὰ πρόσωπα αὐτῶν καὶ
fell on the faces of them and

προσεκύνησαν τῷ θεῷ, 17 λέγοντες·
worshipped – God, saying:

εὐχαριστοῦμέν σοι, κύριε ὁ θεὸς ὁ
We thank thee, [O] Lord – God the

παντοκράτωρ, ὁ ὢν καὶ ὁ ἦν, ὅτι
Almighty, the [one] being and the was, because
= the one who is [one who]

εἴληφας τὴν δύναμίν σου τὴν μεγάλην
thou hast taken ¹the ³power ⁴of thee – ²great

καὶ ἐβασίλευσας· 18 καὶ τὰ ἔθνη ὠργίσ-
and didst reign; and the nations were

θησαν, καὶ ἦλθεν ἡ ὀργή σου καὶ ὁ
wrathful, and ⁴came ¹the ²wrath ³of thee and the

καιρὸς τῶν νεκρῶν κριθῆναι καὶ δοῦναι
time of the dead to be judged and to give

for rewarding thy servants, the prophets and saints, and those who fear thy name, both small and great, and for destroying the destroyers of the earth."

τὸν μισθὸν τοῖς δούλοις σου τοῖς προφήταις
the reward to the slaves of thee *to* the prophets
καὶ τοῖς ἁγίοις καὶ τοῖς φοβουμένοις
and to the saints and to the [ones] fearing
τὸ ὄνομά σου, τοῖς μικροῖς καὶ τοῖς
the name of thee, to the small and to the
μεγάλοις, καὶ διαφθεῖραι τοὺς διαφθείροντας
great, and to destroy the [ones] destroying

19 Then God's temple in heaven was opened, and the ark of his covenant was seen within his temple; and there were flashes of lightning, loud noises, peals of thunder, an earthquake, and heavy hail.

τὴν γῆν. 19 καὶ ἠνοίγη ὁ ναὸς τοῦ
the earth. And was opened the shrine –
θεοῦ ὁ ἐν τῷ οὐρανῷ, καὶ ὤφθη ἡ
of God – in – heaven, and was seen the
κιβωτὸς τῆς διαθήκης αὐτοῦ ἐν τῷ
ark of the covenant of him in the
ναῷ αὐτοῦ, καὶ ἐγένοντο ἀστραπαὶ καὶ
shrine of him, and occurred lightnings and
φωναὶ καὶ βρονταὶ καὶ σεισμὸς καὶ
voices and thunders and an earthquake and
χάλαζα μεγάλη.
³hail ¹a great.

CHAPTER 12

AND a great portent appeared in heaven, a woman clothed with the sun, with the moon under her feet, and on her head a crown of twelve stars; ²she was with child and she cried out in her pangs of birth, in anguish for delivery. ³And another portent appeared in heaven; behold a great red dragon, with seven heads and ten horns, and seven diadems upon his heads. ⁴His tail swept down a third of the stars of heaven, and cast them to the earth. And the

12 Καὶ σημεῖον μέγα ὤφθη ἐν τῷ
And ²sign ¹a great was seen in –
οὐρανῷ, γυνὴ περιβεβλημένη τὸν ἥλιον,
heaven, a woman *having been* clothed [with] the sun,
καὶ ἡ σελήνη ὑποκάτω τῶν ποδῶν αὐτῆς,
and the moon underneath the feet of her,
καὶ ἐπὶ τῆς κεφαλῆς αὐτῆς στέφανος
and on the head of her a crown
ἀστέρων δώδεκα, 2 καὶ ἐν γαστρὶ ἔχουσα,
²stars ¹of twelve, and in womb having,
= being pregnant,
καὶ κράζει ὠδίνουσα καὶ βασανιζομένη
and she cries suffering birth-pains and being distressed
τεκεῖν. 3 καὶ ὤφθη ἄλλο σημεῖον
to bear. And was seen another sign
ἐν τῷ οὐρανῷ, καὶ ἰδοὺ δράκων μέγας
in – heaven, and behold[,] ²dragon ¹a great
πυρρός, ἔχων κεφαλὰς ἑπτὰ καὶ κέρατα
²red, having ²heads ¹seven and ³horns
δέκα καὶ ἐπὶ τὰς κεφαλὰς αὐτοῦ ἑπτὰ
¹ten and on the heads of him seven
διαδήματα, 4 καὶ ἡ οὐρὰ αὐτοῦ σύρει
diadems, and the tail of him draws
τὸ τρίτον τῶν ἀστέρων τοῦ οὐρανοῦ,
the third [part] of the stars – of heaven,
καὶ ἔβαλεν αὐτοὺς εἰς τὴν γῆν. Καὶ
and cast them to the earth. And

dragon stood before the woman who was about to bear a child, that he might devour her child when she brought it forth; [5] she brought forth a male child, one who is to rule all the nations with a rod of iron, but her child was caught up to God and to his throne, [6] and the woman fled into the wilderness, where she has a place prepared by God, in which to be nourished for one thousand two hundred and sixty days.

7 Now war arose in heaven, Michael and his angels fighting against the dragon; and the dragon and his angels fought, [8] but they were defeated and there was no longer any place for them in heaven. [9] And the great dragon was thrown down, that ancient serpent, who is called the Devil and Satan, the deceiver of the whole world—he was thrown down to the earth, and his angels were thrown down with him. [10] And I heard a loud voice in heaven,

ὁ	δράκων	ἔστηκεν	ἐνώπιον	τῆς	γυναικὸς
the	dragon	stood	before	the	woman

τῆς	μελλούσης	τεκεῖν,	ἵνα	ὅταν	τέκῃ
-	being about	to bear,	in order	whenever	she bears that

τὸ	τέκνον	αὐτῆς	καταφάγῃ.	5 καὶ
[2]the	[3]child	[4]of her	[1]he might devour.	And

ἔτεκεν	υἱὸν	ἄρσεν,	ὃς	μέλλει	ποιμαίνειν
she bore	a son[,]	a male,	who	is about	to shepherd

πάντα	τὰ	ἔθνη	ἐν	ῥάβδῳ	σιδηρᾷ·	καὶ
all	the	nations	with	[2]staff	[1]an iron;	and

ἡρπάσθη	τὸ	τέκνον	αὐτῆς	πρὸς	τὸν
[4]was seized	[1]the	[2]child	[3]of her	to	-

θεὸν	καὶ	πρὸς	τὸν	θρόνον	αὐτοῦ.	6 καὶ
God	and	to	the	throne	of him.	And

ἡ	γυνὴ	ἔφυγεν	εἰς	τὴν	ἔρημον,	ὅπου
the	woman	fled	into	the	desert,	where

ἔχει	ἐκεῖ	τόπον	ἡτοιμασμένον	ἀπὸ
she has	there	a place	having been prepared	from

τοῦ	θεοῦ,	ἵνα	ἐκεῖ	τρέφωσιν	αὐτὴν
-	God,	in order that there	they might nourish	her

ἡμέρας	χιλίας	διακοσίας	ἑξήκοντα.
[5]days	[1]a thousand	[2]two hundred	[3][and] [4]sixty.

7 Καὶ	ἐγένετο	πόλεμος	ἐν	τῷ	οὐρανῷ,
And	occurred	war	in	-	heaven,

ὁ	Μιχαὴλ	καὶ	οἱ	ἄγγελοι	αὐτοῦ	τοῦ
-	Michael	and	the	angels	of him	-

πολεμῆσαι	μετὰ	τοῦ	δράκοντος.	καὶ	ὁ
to make war[d]	with	the	dragon.	And	the

δράκων	ἐπολέμησεν	καὶ	οἱ	ἄγγελοι	αὐτοῦ,
dragon	warred	and	the	angels	of him,

8 καὶ	οὐκ	ἴσχυσεν,	οὐδὲ	τόπος	εὑρέθη
and	prevailed not,		not even	place	was found

αὐτῶν	ἔτι	ἐν	τῷ	οὐρανῷ.	9 καὶ	ἐβλήθη
of them	still	in	-	heaven.	And	was cast

ὁ	δράκων	ὁ	μέγας,	ὁ	ὄφις	ὁ	ἀρχαῖος,
[1]the	[3]dragon	-	[2]great,	[4]the	[5]serpent	-	[6]old,

ὁ	καλούμενος	Διάβολος	καὶ	ὁ	Σατανᾶς,
-	being called	Devil	and	the	Satan,

ὁ	πλανῶν	τὴν	οἰκουμένην	ὅλην,	ἐβλήθη
the deceiving [one]		the	[2]inhabited [earth]	[1]whole,	was cast

εἰς	τὴν	γῆν,	καὶ	οἱ	ἄγγελοι	αὐτοῦ	μετ'
to	the	earth,	and	the	angels	of him	with

αὐτοῦ	ἐβλήθησαν.	10 καὶ	ἤκουσα	φωνὴν
him	were cast.	And	I heard	[2]voice

μεγάλην	ἐν	τῷ	οὐρανῷ	λέγουσαν	ἄρτι
[1]a great(loud)	in	-	heaven	saying:	Now

saying, "Now the salvation and the power and the kingdom of our God and the authority of his Christ have come, for the accuser of our brethren has been thrown down, who accuses them day and night before our God. ¹¹And they have conquered him by the blood of the Lamb and by the word of their testimony, for they loved not their lives even unto death. ¹²Rejoice then, O heaven and you that dwell therein! But woe to you, O earth and sea, for the devil has come down to you in great wrath, because he knows that his time is short!

13 And when the dragon saw that he had been thrown down to the earth, he pursued the woman who had borne the male child. ¹⁴But the woman was given the two wings of the great eagle that she might fly from the serpent into the wilderness, to the place where she is to be nourished for a time, and times, and half a time. ¹⁵The serpent poured water like a river out of his mouth after the

ἐγένετο ἡ σωτηρία καὶ ἡ δύναμις καὶ
became   the   salvation   and   the   power   and

ἡ βασιλεία τοῦ θεοῦ ἡμῶν καὶ ἡ ἐξουσία
the kingdom of the God   of us   and the authority

τοῦ χριστοῦ αὐτοῦ, ὅτι ἐβλήθη ὁ κατήγωρ
of the   Christ   of him, because ²was cast ¹the   ²accuser

τῶν ἀδελφῶν ἡμῶν, ὁ κατηγορῶν αὐτοὺς
³of the ⁴brothers   ⁵of us, the [one] accusing   them

ἐνώπιον τοῦ θεοῦ ἡμῶν ἡμέρας καὶ
before   the   God   of us   day   and

νυκτός.   11 καὶ αὐτοὶ ἐνίκησαν αὐτὸν
night.   And   they   overcame   him

διὰ τὸ αἷμα τοῦ ἀρνίου καὶ διὰ τὸν
be-   the   blood   of the Lamb   and because the
cause of   of

λόγον τῆς μαρτυρίας αὐτῶν, καὶ οὐκ
word   of the   witness   of them,   and   not

ἠγάπησαν τὴν ψυχὴν αὐτῶν ἄχρι θανάτου.
they loved   the   life   of them   until   death.

12 διὰ τοῦτο εὐφραίνεσθε, οὐρανοὶ καὶ
    Therefore   be ye glad,   heavens   and

οἱ ἐν αὐτοῖς σκηνοῦντες· οὐαὶ τὴν
the ²in   ³them   ¹tabernacling;   woe [to]   the
[ones]

γῆν καὶ τὴν θάλασσαν, ὅτι κατέβη ὁ
earth   and   the   sea,   because ²came down ¹the

διάβολος πρὸς ὑμᾶς ἔχων θυμὸν μέγαν,
²devil   to   you   having   ²anger   ¹great,

εἰδὼς ὅτι ὀλίγον καιρὸν ἔχει.   13 Καὶ
knowing that ²few(short) ¹time   ¹he has.   And

ὅτε εἶδεν ὁ δράκων ὅτι ἐβλήθη εἰς
when ²saw ¹the ²dragon   that   he was cast   to

τὴν γῆν, ἐδίωξεν τὴν γυναῖκα ἥτις
the   earth,   he pursued   the   woman   who

ἔτεκεν τὸν ἄρσενα.   14 καὶ ἐδόθησαν
bore   the   male.   And   were given

τῇ γυναικὶ αἱ δύο πτέρυγες τοῦ ἀετοῦ
to the woman   the   two   wings   of the   ²eagle

τοῦ μεγάλου, ἵνα πέτηται εἰς τὴν ἔρημον
-    ¹great,   in order she might   to   the   desert
                 that   fly

εἰς τὸν τόπον αὐτῆς, ὅπου τρέφεται
to   the   place   of her,   where she is nourished

ἐκεῖ καιρὸν καὶ καιροὺς καὶ ἥμισυ καιροῦ
there   a time   and   times   and   half   of a time

ἀπὸ προσώπου τοῦ ὄφεως.   15 καὶ ἔβαλεν
from   [the] face   of the   serpent.   And   ²cast

ὁ ὄφις ἐκ τοῦ στόματος αὐτοῦ ὀπίσω
¹the ²serpent out of the   mouth   of him   behind

woman, to sweep her away with the flood. [16] But the earth came to the help of the woman, and the earth opened its mouth and swallowed the river which the dragon had poured from his mouth. [17] Then the dragon was angry with the woman, and went off to make war on the rest of her offspring, on those who keep the commandments of God and bear testimony to Jesus. And he stood[c] on the sand of the sea.

τῆς γυναικὸς ὕδωρ ὡς ποταμόν, ἵνα
the woman water as a river, in order that

αὐτὴν ποταμοφόρητον ποιήσῃ.   16 καὶ
[2]her [3]carried off by [the] river [1]he might make.   And

ἐβοήθησεν ἡ γῆ τῇ γυναικί, καὶ ἤνοιξεν
[2]helped [1]the [2]earth the woman, and [1]opened

ἡ γῆ τὸ στόμα αὐτῆς καὶ κατέπιεν
[1]the [2]earth the mouth of it and swallowed

τὸν ποταμὸν ὃν ἔβαλεν ὁ δράκων ἐκ
the river which [1]cast [1]the [2]dragon out of

τοῦ στόματος αὐτοῦ.   17 καὶ ὠργίσθη
the mouth of him.   And [3]was enraged

ὁ δράκων ἐπὶ τῇ γυναικί, καὶ ἀπῆλθεν
[1]the [2]dragon over the woman, and went away

ποιῆσαι πόλεμον μετὰ τῶν λοιπῶν τοῦ
to make war with the rest of the

σπέρματος αὐτῆς, τῶν τηρούντων τὰς
seed of her, the [ones] keeping the

ἐντολὰς τοῦ θεοῦ καὶ ἐχόντων τὴν
commandments – of God and having the

μαρτυρίαν Ἰησοῦ· (18) καὶ ἐστάθη ἐπὶ τὴν
witness of Jesus;   and he stood on the

ἄμμον τῆς θαλάσσης.
sand of the sea.

CHAPTER 13

AND I saw a beast rising out of the sea, with ten horns and seven heads, with ten diadems upon its horns and a blasphemous name upon its heads. [2]And the beast that I saw was like a leopard, its feet were like a bear's, and its mouth was like a lion's mouth. And to it the

13 Καὶ εἶδον ἐκ τῆς θαλάσσης θηρίον
    And I saw out of [4]the [5]sea [1]a beast

ἀναβαῖνον, ἔχον κέρατα δέκα καὶ κεφαλὰς
[2]coming up, having [2]horns [1]ten and [2]heads

ἑπτά, καὶ ἐπὶ τῶν κεράτων αὐτοῦ δέκα
[1]seven, and on the horns of it* ten

διαδήματα, καὶ ἐπὶ τὰς κεφαλὰς αὐτοῦ
diadems, and on the heads of it

ὀνόματα βλασφημίας.   2 καὶ τὸ θηρίον
names of blasphemy.   And the beast

ὃ εἶδον ἦν ὅμοιον παρδάλει, καὶ οἱ
which I saw was like to a leopard, and the

πόδες αὐτοῦ ὡς ἄρκου, καὶ τὸ στόμα
feet of it as of a bear, and the mouth

αὐτοῦ ὡς στόμα λέοντος. καὶ ἔδωκεν
of it as [the] mouth of a lion.   And [3]gave

---

* αὐτοῦ, of course, may be neuter or masculine—" of it " or " of him". δράκων being masculine (=Satan), we have kept to the masculine. But θηρίον is neuter. Yet if it stands for a person, as δρκίον certainly does, it too should be treated, as to the pronoun, as a masculine. However, not to enter the province of interpretation, we have rendered αὐτοῦ by " of it ", though it will be seen that αὐτόν (him) is used in ver. 8, τίς (who?) in ver. 4, and ὅς (who) in ver. 14. See also ch. 17. 11.

[c] Other ancient authorities read *And I stood*, connecting the sentence with 13. 1

dragon gave his power and his throne and great authority. ³One of its heads seemed to have a mortal wound, but its mortal wound was healed, and the whole earth followed the beast with wonder. ⁴Men worshiped the dragon, for he had given his authority to the beast, and they worshiped the beast, saying, "Who is like the beast, and who can fight against it?"

5 And the beast was given a mouth uttering haughty and blasphemous words, and it was allowed to exercise authority for forty-two months; ⁶it opened its mouth to utter blasphemies against God, blaspheming his name and his dwelling, that is, those who dwell in heaven ⁷Also it was allowed to make war on the saints and to conquer them.ᵈ And authority was given it over every tribe and people and tongue and nation, ⁸and all who dwell on earth will worship it, every one whose name has not been

αὐτῷ ὁ δράκων τὴν δύναμιν αὐτοῦ καὶ
⁴to it   ¹the   ²dragon   the   power   of it   and

τὸν θρόνον αὐτοῦ καὶ ἐξουσίαν μεγάλην.
the   throne   of it   and   ²authority   ¹great.

3 καὶ μίαν ἐκ τῶν κεφαλῶν αὐτοῦ ὡς
And   one   of   the   heads   of it   as

ἐσφαγμένην εἰς θάνατον, καὶ ἡ πληγὴ
having been slain to   death,   and   the   stroke

τοῦ θανάτου αὐτοῦ ἐθεραπεύθη. καὶ
of the   death   of it   was healed.   And

ἐθαυμάσθη ὅλη ἡ γῆ ὀπίσω τοῦ θηρίου,
⁴wondered   ¹all   ¹the   ²earth   after   the   beast,

4 καὶ προσεκύνησαν τῷ δράκοντι, ὅτι
and   they worshipped   the   dragon,   because

ἔδωκεν τὴν ἐξουσίαν τῷ θηρίῳ, καὶ
he gave   the   authority   to the   beast,   and

προσεκύνησαν τῷ θηρίῳ λέγοντες· τίς
they worshipped   the   beast   saying: Who

ὅμοιος τῷ θηρίῳ, καὶ τίς δύναται
[is] like   to the   beast,   and   who   can

πολεμῆσαι μετ᾽ αὐτοῦ; 5 καὶ ἐδόθη αὐτῷ
to make war   with   it ?   And was given   to it

στόμα λαλοῦν μεγάλα καὶ βλασφημίας,
a mouth   speaking   great things   and   blasphemies,

καὶ ἐδόθη αὐτῷ ἐξουσία ποιῆσαι μῆνας
and   was given   to it   authority   to act   ¹months

τεσσεράκοντα [καὶ] δύο. 6 καὶ ἤνοιξεν
    ¹forty-two.   And   it opened

τὸ στόμα αὐτοῦ εἰς βλασφημίας πρὸς
the   mouth   of it   in   blasphemies   against

τὸν θεόν, βλασφημῆσαι τὸ ὄνομα αὐτοῦ
-   God,   to blaspheme   the   name   of him

καὶ τὴν σκηνὴν αὐτοῦ, τοὺς ἐν τῷ
and   the   tabernacle   of him,   ¹the [ones]   ²in   -

οὐρανῷ σκηνοῦντας. 7 καὶ ἐδόθη αὐτῷ
⁴heaven   ²tabernacling.   And it was given   to it

ποιῆσαι πόλεμον μετὰ τῶν ἁγίων καὶ
to make   war   with   the   saints   and

νικῆσαι αὐτούς, καὶ ἐδόθη αὐτῷ ἐξουσία
to overcome   them,   and   ²was given   ³to it   ¹authority

ἐπὶ πᾶσαν φυλὴν καὶ λαὸν καὶ γλῶσσαν
over   every   tribe   and   people   and   tongue

καὶ ἔθνος. 8 καὶ προσκυνήσουσιν αὐτὸν
and   nation.   And   ⁷will worship   ⁸him

πάντες οἱ κατοικοῦντες ἐπὶ τῆς γῆς,
¹all   ²the [ones]   ³dwelling   ⁴on   ⁵the   ⁶earth,

οὗ οὐ γέγραπται τὸ ὄνομα αὐτοῦ ἐν
²of   ⁴has not been written   ¹the   ²name   of him   in
    whom

ᵈ Other ancient authorities omit this sentence

written before the
foundation of the world
in the book of life of the
Lamb that was slain. ⁹If
any one has an ear, let
him hear:

¹⁰If any one is to be
taken captive,
to captivity he
goes;
if any one slays with
the sword,
with the sword
must he be slain.

Here is a call for the
endurance and faith of
the saints.

11 Then I saw another
beast which rose out of
the earth; it had two
horns like a lamb and it
spoke like a dragon. ¹²It
exercises all the
authority of the first
beast in its presence, and
makes the earth and its
inhabitants worship the
first beast, whose mortal
wound was healed. ¹³It
works great signs, even
making fire come down
from heaven to earth in
the sight of men; ¹⁴and
by the signs which it is
allowed to work in the
presence of the beast, it
deceives those who dwell

τῷ βιβλίῳ τῆς ζωῆς τοῦ ἀρνίου τοῦ
the   scroll   -   of life   of the   Lamb

ἐσφαγμένου ἀπὸ καταβολῆς κόσμου.
having been slain   from   [the] foundation   of [the] world.

9 Εἴ τις ἔχει οὖς ἀκουσάτω.   **10** εἴ
If   anyone   has   an ear   let him hear.   If

τις εἰς αἰχμαλωσίαν, εἰς αἰχμαλωσίαν
anyone [is] for   captivity,   to   captivity

ὑπάγει· εἴ τις ἐν μαχαίρῃ ἀποκτενεῖ,
he goes;   if   anyone   by   a sword   will kill,

δεῖ αὐτὸν ἐν μαχαίρῃ ἀποκτανθῆναι.
it behoves him   by   a sword   to be killed.

ʽΩδέ ἐστιν ἡ ὑπομονὴ καὶ ἡ πίστις
Here   is   the   endurance   and   the   faith

τῶν ἁγίων.
of the   saints.

11 Καὶ εἶδον ἄλλο θηρίον ἀναβαῖνον
And   I saw   another   beast   coming up

ἐκ τῆς γῆς, καὶ εἶχεν κέρατα δύο
out of the   earth,   and   it had   ²horns   ¹two

ὅμοια ἀρνίῳ, καὶ ἐλάλει ὡς δράκων.
like   to a lamb,   and   spoke   as   a dragon.

12 καὶ τὴν ἐξουσίαν τοῦ πρώτου θηρίου
And   ³the   ⁴authority   ⁵of the   ⁶first   ⁷beast

πᾶσαν ποιεῖ ἐνώπιον αὐτοῦ. καὶ ποιεῖ
²all   ¹it does(exercises) before   it.   And   it makes

τὴν γῆν καὶ τοὺς ἐν αὐτῇ κατοικοῦντας
the   earth   and   ¹the [ones]   ²in   ⁴it   ³dwelling

ἵνα προσκυνήσουσιν τὸ θηρίον τὸ πρῶτον,
in order   they shall worship   the   ²beast   -   ¹first,
der that

οὗ ἐθεραπεύθη ἡ πληγὴ τοῦ θανάτου
of which   ⁴was healed   ¹the   ²stroke   -   ³of death

αὐτοῦ.   **13** καὶ ποιεῖ σημεῖα μεγάλα,
of it.   And   it does   ²signs   ¹great,

ἵνα καὶ πῦρ ποιῇ ἐκ τοῦ οὐρανοῦ
in or-   ³even   ⁴fire   ²it ¹makes   ⁵out of   -   ⁶heaven
der that

καταβαίνειν εἰς τὴν γῆν ἐνώπιον τῶν
⁷to come down   onto   the   earth   before   -

ἀνθρώπων.   **14** καὶ πλανᾷ τοὺς κατοι-
men.   And   it deceives the [ones]   dwell-

κοῦντας ἐπὶ τῆς γῆς διὰ τὰ σημεῖα
ing   on   the   earth because of the   signs

ἃ ἐδόθη αὐτῷ ποιῆσαι ἐνώπιον τοῦ
which it was given   to it   to do   before   the

θηρίου, λέγων τοῖς κατοικοῦσιν ἐπὶ τῆς
beast,   telling   to the   [ones] dwelling   on   the

on earth, bidding them make an image for the beast which was wounded by the sword and yet lived; ¹⁵and it was allowed to give breath to the image of the beast so that the image of the beast should even speak, and to cause those who would not worship the image of the beast to be slain. ¹⁶Also it causes all, both small and great, both rich and poor, both free and slave, to be marked on the right hand or the forehead, ¹⁷so that no one can buy or sell unless he has the mark, that is, the name of the beast or the number of its name. ¹⁸This calls for wisdom: let him who has understanding reckon the number of the beast, for it is a human number, its number is six hundred and sixty-six.[e]

γῆς   ποιῆσαι   εἰκόνα   τῷ   θηρίῳ,   ὃς   ἔχει
earth   to make   an image   to the   beast,   who   has

τὴν   πληγὴν   τῆς   μαχαίρης   καὶ   ἔζησεν.
the   stroke   of the   sword   and lived [again].

15 καὶ   ἐδόθη   αὐτῷ   δοῦναι   πνεῦμα   τῇ
And   it was given   to it   to give   spirit   to the

εἰκόνι   τοῦ   θηρίου,   ἵνα   καὶ   λαλήσῃ   ἡ
image   of the   beast,   in order   ⁸even   ⁵might   ¹the
that   ⁷speak

εἰκὼν   τοῦ   θηρίου,   καὶ   ποιήσῃ   [ἵνα]
²image   ⁸of the   ⁴beast,   and   might make   in order
that

ὅσοι   ἐὰν   μὴ   προσκυνήσωσιν   τῇ   εἰκόνι
as many as   might not worship   the   image

τοῦ   θηρίου   ἀποκτανθῶσιν.   **16** καὶ   ποιεῖ
of the   beast   should be killed.   And   it makes

πάντας,   τοὺς   μικροὺς   καὶ   τοὺς   μεγάλους,
all men,   the   small   and   the   great,

καὶ   τοὺς   πλουσίους   καὶ   τοὺς   πτωχούς,
both   the   rich   and   the   poor,

καὶ   τοὺς   ἐλευθέρους   καὶ   τοὺς   δούλους,
both   the   free men   and   the   slaves,

ἵνα   δῶσιν   αὐτοῖς   χάραγμα   ἐπὶ   τῆς
in order   they   to them   a mark   on   the
that   should give

χειρὸς   αὐτῶν   τῆς   δεξιᾶς   ἢ   ἐπὶ   τὸ
²hand   ³of them   -   ¹right   or   on   the

μέτωπον   αὐτῶν,   **17** [καὶ]   ἵνα   μή   τις
forehead   of them,   and   lest   anyone

δύνηται   ἀγοράσαι   ἢ   πωλῆσαι   εἰ   μὴ
could   to buy   or   to sell   except

ὁ   ἔχων   τὸ   χάραγμα   τὸ   ὄνομα   τοῦ
the   having   the   mark[,]   the   name   of the
[one]

θηρίου   ἢ   τὸν   ἀριθμὸν   τοῦ   ὀνόματος
beast   or   the   number   of the   name

αὐτοῦ.   **18** Ὧδε   ἡ   σοφία   ἐστίν.   ὁ   ἔχων
of it.   Here   -   ²wisdom   ¹is.   The   having
[one]

νοῦν   ψηφισάτω   τὸν   ἀριθμὸν   τοῦ   θηρίου·
reason   let him count   the   number   of the   beast;

ἀριθμὸς   γὰρ   ἀνθρώπου   ἐστίν.   καὶ   ὁ
for   ²[the]   ³number   ⁴of a man   ¹it is.   And   the

ἀριθμὸς   αὐτοῦ   ἑξακόσιοι   ἑξήκοντα   ἕξ.
number   of it   [is]   six hundreds   [and]   sixty-six.

CHAPTER 14

^THEN I looked, and lo, on Mount Zion stood the Lamb, and with him a hundred and

14 Καὶ   εἶδον,   καὶ   ἰδοὺ   τὸ   ἀρνίον
And   I saw,   and   behold[,]   the   Lamb

ἑστὸς   ἐπὶ   τὸ   ὄρος   Σιών,   καὶ   μετ'   αὐτοῦ
standing on   the   mount   Sion,   and   with   him

[e] Other   ancient   authorities read six hundred and sixteen

forty-four thousand who had his name and his Father's name written on their foreheads. ²And I heard a voice from heaven like the sound of many waters and like the sound of loud thunder; the voice I heard was like the sound of harpers playing on their harps, ³and they sing a new song before the throne and before the four living creatures and before the elders. No one could learn that song except the hundred and forty-four thousand who had been redeemed from the earth. ⁴It is these who have not defiled themselves with women, for they are chaste;ᶠ it is these who follow the Lamb wherever he goes; these have been redeemed from mankind as first fruits for God and the Lamb, ⁵and in their mouth no lie was found, for they are spotless.

6 Then I saw another angel flying in mid-heaven, with an eternal gospel to proclaim to those who dwell on

ἑκατὸν τεσσεράκοντα τέσσαρες χιλιάδες
a hundred [and] forty-four thousands

ἔχουσαι τὸ ὄνομα αὐτοῦ καὶ τὸ ὄνομα
having the name of him and the name

τοῦ πατρὸς αὐτοῦ γεγραμμένον ἐπὶ τῶν
of the Father of him having been written on the

μετώπων αὐτῶν. 2 καὶ ἤκουσα φωνὴν
foreheads of them. And I heard a sound

ἐκ τοῦ οὐρανοῦ ὡς φωνὴν ὑδάτων πολλῶν
out of - heaven as a sound ¹waters ¹of many

καὶ ὡς φωνὴν βροντῆς μεγάλης, καὶ
and as a sound ²thunder ¹of great(loud), and

ἡ φωνὴ ἣν ἤκουσα ὡς κιθαρῳδῶν
the sound which I heard [was] as of harpers

κιθαριζόντων ἐν ταῖς κιθάραις αὐτῶν.
harping with the harps of them.

3 καὶ ᾄδουσιν ᾠδὴν καινὴν ἐνώπιον τοῦ
And they sing ²song ¹a new before the

θρόνου καὶ ἐνώπιον τῶν τεσσάρων ζῴων
throne and before the four living creatures

καὶ τῶν πρεσβυτέρων· καὶ οὐδεὶς ἐδύνατο
and the elders; and no man could

μαθεῖν τὴν ᾠδὴν εἰ μὴ αἱ ἑκατὸν
to learn the song except the hundred

τεσσεράκοντα τέσσαρες χιλιάδες, οἱ
[and] forty-four thousands, the

ἠγορασμένοι ἀπὸ τῆς γῆς. 4 οὗτοί εἰσιν
[ones] having from the earth. These are
been purchased

οἳ μετὰ γυναικῶν οὐκ ἐμολύνθησαν·
[those] ²with ²women ¹were not defiled;
who

παρθένοι γάρ εἰσιν. οὗτοι οἱ ἀκολουθοῦντες
for ²celibates ¹they are. These the [ones] following
[are]

τῷ ἀρνίῳ ὅπου ἂν ὑπάγῃ. οὗτοι ἠγοράσ-
the Lamb wherever he may go. These were

θησαν ἀπὸ τῶν ἀνθρώπων ἀπαρχὴ τῷ
purchased from - men firstfruit -

θεῷ καὶ τῷ ἀρνίῳ, 5 καὶ ἐν τῷ στόματι
to God and to the Lamb, and in the mouth

αὐτῶν οὐχ εὑρέθη ψεῦδος· ἄμωμοί εἰσιν.
of them was not found a lie; ²unblemished ¹they are.

6 Καὶ εἶδον ἄλλον ἄγγελον πετόμενον
And I saw another angel flying

ἐν μεσουρανήματι, ἔχοντα εὐαγγέλιον
in mid-heaven, having ²gospel

αἰώνιον εὐαγγελίσαι ἐπὶ τοὺς καθημένους
¹an eternal to preach over the [ones] sitting

ᶠ Greek virgins

earth, to every nation and tribe and tongue and people; [7]and he said with a loud voice, "Fear God and give him glory, for the hour of his judgment has come; and worship him who made heaven and earth, the sea and the fountains of water."

8 Another angel, a second, followed, saying, "Fallen, fallen is Babylon the great, she who made all nations drink the wine of her impure passion."

9 And another angel, a third, followed them, saying with a loud voice, "If any one worships the beast and its image, and receives a mark on his forehead or on his hand, [10]he also shall drink the wine of God's wrath, poured unmixed into the cup of his anger, and he shall be tormented with fire and brimstone in the presence of the holy angels and in the presence of the Lamb. [11]And the smoke of their torment goes up for ever and ever; and they have no rest, day or night, these

ἐπὶ τῆς γῆς καὶ ἐπὶ πᾶν ἔθνος καὶ
on   the   earth   and   over   every   nation   and

φυλὴν καὶ γλῶσσαν καὶ λαόν, 7 λέγων
tribe   and   tongue   and   people,   saying

ἐν φωνῇ μεγάλῃ· φοβήθητε τὸν θεὸν
in   [2]voice   [1]a great(loud):   Fear ye   –   God

καὶ δότε αὐτῷ δόξαν, ὅτι ἦλθεν ἡ ὥρα
and   give   [2]to him   [1]glory,   because   came   the   hour

τῆς κρίσεως αὐτοῦ, καὶ προσκυνήσατε
of the   judgment   of him,   and   worship

τῷ ποιήσαντι τὸν οὐρανὸν καὶ τὴν γῆν
the [one] having made   the   heaven   and   the   earth

καὶ θάλασσαν καὶ πηγὰς ὑδάτων. 8 Καὶ
and   sea   and   fountains   of waters.   And

ἄλλος ἄγγελος δεύτερος ἠκολούθησεν λέγων·
another   angel   a second   followed   saying:

ἔπεσεν ἔπεσεν Βαβυλὼν ἡ μεγάλη, ἣ
Fell[,]   fell   Babylon   the   great,   which

ἐκ τοῦ οἴνου τοῦ θυμοῦ τῆς πορνείας
of   the   wine   of the   anger   of the   fornication

αὐτῆς πεπότικεν πάντα τὰ ἔθνη. 9 Καὶ
of her   has made to drink   all   the   nations.   And

ἄλλος ἄγγελος τρίτος ἠκολούθησεν αὐτοῖς
another   angel   a third   followed   them

λέγων ἐν φωνῇ μεγάλῃ· εἴ τις προσκυνεῖ
saying   in   [2]voice   [1]a great(loud):   If   anyone   worships

τὸ θηρίον καὶ τὴν εἰκόνα αὐτοῦ, καὶ
the   beast   and   the   image   of it,   and

λαμβάνει χάραγμα ἐπὶ τοῦ μετώπου αὐτοῦ
receives   a mark   on   the   forehead   of him

ἢ ἐπὶ τὴν χεῖρα αὐτοῦ, 10 καὶ αὐτὸς
or   on   the   hand   of him,   even   he

πίεται ἐκ τοῦ οἴνου τοῦ θυμοῦ τοῦ
shall drink   of   the   wine   of the   anger   –

θεοῦ τοῦ κεκερασμένου ἀκράτου ἐν τῷ
of God   –   having been mixed   undiluted   in   the

ποτηρίῳ τῆς ὀργῆς αὐτοῦ, καὶ βασανισθήσε-
cup   of the   wrath   of him,   and   will be torment-

ται ἐν πυρὶ καὶ θείῳ ἐνώπιον ἀγγέλων
ed   by   fire   and   sulphur   before   [2]angels

ἁγίων καὶ ἐνώπιον τοῦ ἀρνίου. 11 καὶ
[1]holy   and   before   the   Lamb.   And

ὁ καπνὸς τοῦ βασανισμοῦ αὐτῶν εἰς
the   smoke   of the   torment   of them   unto

αἰῶνας αἰώνων ἀναβαίνει, καὶ οὐκ ἔχουσιν
ages   of ages   goes up,   and   they have not

ἀνάπαυσιν ἡμέρας καὶ νυκτὸς οἱ προσκυ-
rest   day   and   night   the [ones] wor-

worshipers of the beast and its image, and whoever receives the mark of its name."

12 Here is a call for the endurance of the saints, those who keep the commandments of God and the faith of Jesus.

13 And I heard a voice from heaven saying, "Write this: Blessed are the dead who die in the Lord henceforth." "Blessed indeed," says the Spirit, "that they may rest from their labors, for their deeds follow them!"

14 Then I looked, and lo, a white cloud, and seated on the cloud one like a son of man, with a golden crown on his head, and a sharp sickle in his hand. [15]And another angel came out of the temple, calling with a loud voice to him who sat upon the cloud, "Put in your sickle, and reap, for the hour to reap has come, for the harvest of the earth is fully ripe." [16]So he who sat upon the cloud swung his sickle

νοῦντες	τὸ	θηρίον	καὶ	τὴν	εἰκόνα	αὐτοῦ,
shipping	the	beast	and	the	image	of it,

καὶ	εἴ	τις	λαμβάνει	τὸ	χάραγμα	τοῦ
and	if	anyone	receives	the	mark	of the

ὀνόματος	αὐτοῦ.	**12**	*Ὧδε	ἡ	ὑπομονὴ
name	of it.		[1]Here	[2]the	[4]endurance

τῶν	ἁγίων	ἐστίν,	οἱ	τηροῦντες	τὰς
[3]of the	[5]saints	[2]is,	the [ones]	keeping	the

ἐντολὰς	τοῦ	θεοῦ	καὶ	τὴν	πίστιν	Ἰησοῦ.
command- ments	–	of God	and	the	faith	of Jesus.

13 Καὶ ἤκουσα φωνῆς ἐκ τοῦ οὐρανοῦ
And I heard a voice out of – heaven

λεγούσης·	γράψον·	μακάριοι	οἱ	νεκροὶ
saying:	Write thou:	Blessed [are]	the	dead

οἱ	ἐν	κυρίῳ	ἀποθνήσκοντες	ἀπ᾽	ἄρτι.
[1]the [ones]	[2]in	[4][the] Lord	[3]dying	from	now.

ναί,	λέγει	τὸ	πνεῦμα,	ἵνα	ἀναπαήσονται
Yes,	says	the	Spirit,	in order that	they shall rest

ἐκ	τῶν	κόπων	αὐτῶν·	τὰ	γὰρ	ἔργα
from	the	labours	of them;	for the		work-

αὐτῶν ἀκολουθεῖ μετ᾽ αὐτῶν.
of them follows with them.

14 Καὶ εἶδον, καὶ ἰδοὺ νεφέλη λευκή,
And I saw, and behold[,] [2]cloud [1]a white,

καὶ	ἐπὶ	τὴν	νεφέλην	καθήμενον	ὅμοιον
and	on	the	cloud	[one] sitting	like

υἱὸν	ἀνθρώπου,	ἔχων	ἐπὶ	τῆς	κεφαλῆς
a son	of man,*	having	on	the	head

αὐτοῦ	στέφανον	χρυσοῦν	καὶ	ἐν	τῇ	χειρὶ
of him	crown	a golden	and	in	the	hand

αὐτοῦ δρέπανον ὀξύ. **15** καὶ ἄλλος ἄγγελος
of him sickle a sharp. And another angel

ἐξῆλθεν	ἐκ	τοῦ	ναοῦ,	κράζων	ἐν	φωνῇ
went forth	out of	the	shrine,	crying	in	[2]voice

μεγάλη	τῷ	καθημένῳ	ἐπὶ	τῆς	νεφέλης·
[1]a great (loud)	to the	sitting [one]	on	the	cloud:

πέμψον	τὸ	δρέπανόν	σου	καὶ	θέρισον,
Send(Thrust)	the	sickle	of thee	and	reap thou,

ὅτι	ἦλθεν	ἡ	ὥρα	θερίσαι,	ὅτι	ἐξηράνθη
because	came	the	hour	to reap,	because	was dried

ὁ	θερισμὸς	τῆς	γῆς.	**16**	καὶ	ἔβαλεν
the	harvest	of the	earth.		And	[2]thrust

ὁ	καθήμενος	ἐπὶ	τῆς	νεφέλης	τὸ	δρέπανον
[1]the [one]	[2]sitting	[3]on	[4]the	[5]cloud	the	sickle

* See also ch. 1. 13 and John 5. 27.

on the earth, and the earth was reaped.

17 And another angel came out of the temple in heaven, and he too had a sharp sickle. 18 Then another angel came out from the altar, the angel who has power over fire, and he called with a loud voice to him who had the sharp sickle, "Put in your sickle, and gather the clusters of the vine of the earth, for its grapes are ripe." 19 So the angel swung his sickle on the earth and gathered the vintage of the earth, and threw it into the great wine press of the wrath of God; 20 and the wine press was trodden outside the city, and blood flowed from the wine press, as high as a horse's bridle, for one thousand six hundred stadia.*

αὐτοῦ ἐπὶ τὴν γῆν, καὶ ἐθερίσθη ἡ
of him   over   the   earth,   and   ²was reaped ¹the

γῆ.   17 Καὶ   ἄλλος   ἄγγελος   ἐξῆλθεν ἐκ
²earth.   And   another   angel   went forth out of

τοῦ ναοῦ τοῦ ἐν τῷ οὐρανῷ, ἔχων καὶ
the   shrine   –   in   –   heaven,   ¹having   ²also

αὐτὸς δρέπανον ὀξύ. 18 καὶ ἄλλος ἄγγελος
¹he   ⁵sickle   ⁴a sharp.   And another   angel

ἐξῆλθεν ἐκ τοῦ θυσιαστηρίου, [ὁ] ἔχων
went forth out of   the   altar,   the [one] having

ἐξουσίαν ἐπὶ τοῦ πυρός, καὶ ἐφώνησεν
authority   over   the   fire,   and   he spoke

φωνῇ μεγάλῃ τῷ ἔχοντι τὸ δρέπανον
²voice   ¹in a great   to the   having   the   ³sickle
    (loud)   [one]

τὸ ὀξὺ λέγων· πέμψον σου τὸ δρέπανον
–   ¹sharp   saying: Send(Thrust) ⁴of thee ¹the   ³sickle

τὸ ὀξὺ καὶ τρύγησον τοὺς βότρυας τῆς
–   ²sharp   and   gather   the   clusters of the

ἀμπέλου τῆς γῆς, ὅτι ἤκμασαν αἱ
vine   of the   earth,   because   ⁴ripened   ¹the

σταφυλαὶ αὐτῆς. 19 καὶ ἔβαλεν ὁ ἄγγελος
²grapes   ³of it.   And ³thrust ¹the   ²angel

τὸ δρέπανον αὐτοῦ εἰς τὴν γῆν, καὶ
the   sickle   of him   into   the   earth,   and

ἐτρύγησεν τὴν ἄμπελον τῆς γῆς καὶ
gathered   the   vine   of the   earth   and

ἔβαλεν εἰς τὴν ληνὸν τοῦ θυμοῦ τοῦ
cast   into   the   winepress ³of the   ²anger   –

θεοῦ τὸν μέγαν. 20 καὶ ἐπατήθη ἡ
⁵of God   –   ¹great.   And ²was trodden ¹the

ληνὸς ἔξωθεν τῆς πόλεως, καὶ ἐξῆλθεν
winepress   outside   the   city,   and   ³went out

αἷμα ἐκ τῆς ληνοῦ ἄχρι τῶν χαλινῶν
¹blood   out of   the   winepress as far as the   bridles

τῶν ἵππων, ἀπὸ σταδίων χιλίων ἑξακοσίων.
of the   horses,   from   ²furlongs ¹a thousand ³six hundred.

CHAPTER 15

THEN I saw another portent in heaven, great and wonderful, seven angels with seven plagues, which are the last, for with them the wrath of God is ended.

2 And I saw what appeared to be a sea of glass mingled with fire.

15 Καὶ εἶδον ἄλλο σημεῖον ἐν τῷ
And   I saw   another   sign   in   –

οὐρανῷ μέγα καὶ θαυμαστόν, ἀγγέλους
heaven[,]   great   and   wonderful,   ²angels

ἑπτὰ ἔχοντας πληγὰς ἑπτὰ τὰς ἐσχάτας,
¹seven   having   ²plagues ¹seven   the   last,

ὅτι ἐν αὐταῖς ἐτελέσθη ὁ θυμὸς τοῦ
because in   them   ⁴was finished ¹the   ²anger   –

θεοῦ. 2 Καὶ εἶδον ὡς θάλασσαν ὑαλίνην
³of God.   And   I saw   as   ²sea   ¹a glassy

*About two hundred miles

and those who had conquered the beast and its image and the number of its name, standing beside the sea of glass with harps of God in their hands. ³And they sing the song of Moses, the servant of God, and the song of the Lamb, saying,

"Great and wonderful
are thy deeds,
O Lord God the
Almighty!
Just and true are thy
ways,
O King of the ages![h]
⁴Who shall not fear
and glorify thy
name, O Lord?
For thou alone art
holy.
All nations shall
come and worship
thee,
for thy judgments
have been re-
vealed."

5 After this I looked, and the temple of the tent of witness in heaven was opened, ⁶and out of the temple came the seven angels with the seven plagues, robed in pure bright linen, and their breasts girded with golden girdles. ⁷And one of the four living creatures gave the seven angels seven golden

---

μεμιγμένην πυρί, καὶ τοὺς νικῶντας
having been mixed with fire, and the [ones] overcoming

ἐκ τοῦ θηρίου καὶ ἐκ τῆς εἰκόνος αὐτοῦ
of the beast and of the image of it

καὶ ἐκ τοῦ ἀριθμοῦ τοῦ ὀνόματος αὐτοῦ
and of the number of the name of it

ἑστῶτας ἐπὶ τὴν θάλασσαν τὴν ὑαλίνην,
standing on the ²sea – ¹glassy,

ἔχοντας κιθάρας τοῦ θεοῦ. 3 καὶ ᾄδουσιν
having harps – of God. And they sing

τὴν ᾠδὴν Μωϋσέως τοῦ δούλου τοῦ
the song of Moses the slave –

θεοῦ καὶ τὴν ᾠδὴν τοῦ ἀρνίου, λέγοντες·
of God and the song of the Lamb, saying:

μεγάλα καὶ θαυμαστὰ τὰ ἔργα σου,
Great and wonderful the works of thee,

κύριε ὁ θεὸς ὁ παντοκράτωρ· δίκαιαι
[O] Lord – God the Almighty; righteous

καὶ ἀληθιναὶ αἱ ὁδοί σου, ὁ βασιλεὺς
and true the ways of thee, the king

τῶν ἐθνῶν· 4 τίς οὐ μὴ φοβηθῇ, κύριε,
of the nations; who will not fear, [O] Lord,

καὶ δοξάσει τὸ ὄνομά σου; ὅτι μόνος
and *will* glorify the name of thee? because [thou] only

ὅσιος, ὅτι πάντα τὰ ἔθνη ἥξουσιν καὶ
[art] holy, because all the nations will come and

προσκυνήσουσιν ἐνώπιόν σου, ὅτι τὰ
will worship before thee, because the

δικαιώματά σου ἐφανερώθησαν. 5 Καὶ
ordinances of thee were made manifest. And

μετὰ ταῦτα εἶδον, καὶ ἠνοίγη ὁ ναὸς
after these things I saw, and was opened the shrine

τῆς σκηνῆς τοῦ μαρτυρίου ἐν τῷ οὐρανῷ,
of the tabernacle of the testimony in – heaven,

6 καὶ ἐξῆλθον οἱ ἑπτὰ ἄγγελοι οἱ ἔχοντες
and ²came forth ¹the ²seven ³angels – ⁴having

τὰς ἑπτὰ πληγὰς ἐκ τοῦ ναοῦ, ἐνδεδυμένοι
⁵the ⁶seven ⁷plagues out of the shrine, *having been* clothed [in]

λίνον καθαρὸν λαμπρὸν καὶ περιεζωσμένοι
²linen ¹clean ²bright and *having been* girdled

περὶ τὰ στήθη ζώνας χρυσᾶς. 7 καὶ
round the breasts [with] ²girdles ¹golden. And

ἓν ἐκ τῶν τεσσάρων ζώων ἔδωκεν τοῖς
one of the four living creatures gave to the

ἑπτὰ ἀγγέλοις ἑπτὰ φιάλας χρυσᾶς
seven angels seven ²bowls ¹golden

---

[h] Other ancient authorities read *the nations*

bowls full of the wrath of God who lives for ever and ever; ⁸and the temple was filled with smoke from the glory of God and from his power, and no one could enter the temple until the seven plagues of the seven angels were ended.

CHAPTER 16

THEN I heard a loud voice from the temple telling the seven angels, "Go and pour out on the earth the seven bowls of the wrath of God."

2 So the first angel went and poured his bowl on the earth, and foul and evil sores came upon the men who bore the mark of the beast and worshiped its image.

3 The second angel poured his bowl into the sea, and it became like the blood of a dead man, and every living thing died that was in the sea.

4 The third angel poured his bowl into the rivers and the fountains of water, and they became blood. ⁵And I heard the angel of water say,

---

γεμούσας τοῦ θυμοῦ τοῦ θεοῦ τοῦ ζῶντος
being filled of(with) anger – of – living
the God

εἰς τοὺς αἰῶνας τῶν αἰώνων. 8 καὶ
unto the ages of the ages. And

ἐγεμίσθη ὁ ναὸς καπνοῦ ἐκ τῆς δόξης
was filled the shrine of(with) smoke of the glory

τοῦ θεοῦ καὶ ἐκ τῆς δυνάμεως αὐτοῦ,
– of God and of the power of him,

καὶ οὐδεὶς ἐδύνατο εἰσελθεῖν εἰς τὸν
and no one could to enter into the

ναὸν ἄχρι τελεσθῶσιν αἱ ἑπτὰ πληγαὶ
shrine until should be finished the seven plagues

τῶν ἑπτὰ ἀγγέλων. 16 Καὶ ἤκουσα
of the seven angels. And I heard

μεγάλης φωνῆς ἐκ τοῦ ναοῦ λεγούσης τοῖς
a great(loud) voice out of the shrine saying to the

ἑπτὰ ἀγγέλοις· ὑπάγετε καὶ ἐκχέετε τὰς ἑπτὰ
seven angels: Go ye and pour out the seven

φιάλας τοῦ θυμοῦ τοῦ θεοῦ εἰς τὴν γῆν.
bowls of the anger – of God onto the earth.

2 Καὶ ἀπῆλθεν ὁ πρῶτος καὶ ἐξέχεεν τὴν
And ²went away ¹the ³first and poured out the

φιάλην αὐτοῦ εἰς τὴν γῆν· καὶ ἐγένετο
bowl of him onto the earth; and ⁴came

ἕλκος κακὸν καὶ πονηρὸν ἐπὶ τοὺς ἀνθρώπους
⁴sore ¹a bad ²and ³evil on the men

τοὺς ἔχοντας τὸ χάραγμα τοῦ θηρίου καὶ
– having the mark of the beast and

τοὺς προσκυνοῦντας τῇ εἰκόνι αὐτοῦ. 3 Καὶ
– worshipping the image of it. And

ὁ δεύτερος ἐξέχεεν τὴν φιάλην αὐτοῦ
the second poured out the bowl of him

εἰς τὴν θάλασσαν· καὶ ἐγένετο αἷμα
onto the sea; and it became blood

ὡς νεκροῦ, καὶ πᾶσα ψυχὴ ζωῆς ἀπέθανεν,
as of a dead and every soul of life died,
man,

τὰ ἐν τῇ θαλάσσῃ. 4 Καὶ ὁ τρίτος
the in the sea. And the third
things

ἐξέχεεν τὴν φιάλην αὐτοῦ εἰς τοὺς
poured out the bowl of him onto the

ποταμοὺς καὶ τὰς πηγὰς τῶν ὑδάτων·
rivers and the fountains of the waters;

καὶ ἐγένετο αἷμα. 5 Καὶ ἤκουσα τοῦ
and it became blood. And I heard the

ἀγγέλου τῶν ὑδάτων λέγοντος· δίκαιος
angel of the waters saying: Righteous

"Just art thou in these
thy judgments,
thou who art and
wast, O Holy One.
⁶For men have shed
the blood of saints
and prophets,
and thou hast given
them blood to
drink.
It is their due!"
⁷And I heard the altar
cry,
"Yea, Lord God the
Almighty,
true and just are thy
judgments!"
8 The fourth angel
poured his bowl on the
sun, and it was allowed
to scorch men with fire;
⁹men were scorched by
the fierce heat, and they
cursed the name of God
who had power over
these plagues, and they
did not repent and give
him glory.
10 The fifth angel
poured his bowl on the
throne of the beast, and
its kingdom was in dark-
ness; men gnawed their
tongues in anguish ¹¹and
cursed the God of heaven
for their pain and sores,
and did not repent of
their deeds.
12 The sixth angel
poured his bowl on the
great river Euphra′tes,

εἶ, ὁ ὢν καὶ ὁ ἦν, ὁ ὅσιος, ὅτι
art the being and the was, the holy because
thou, [one] [one who] [one],
=the one who is

ταῦτα ἔκρινας, 6 ὅτι αἷμα ἁγίων
¹these ¹thou judgedst, because ²[the] blood ²of saints
things

καὶ προφητῶν ἐξέχεαν, καὶ αἷμα αὐτοῖς
⁴and ⁵of prophets ¹they shed, and blood to them

δέδωκας πεῖν· ἄξιοί εἰσιν. 7 Καὶ ἤκουσα
thou hast to drink; ²worthy ¹they are. And I heard
given

τοῦ θυσιαστηρίου λέγοντος· ναί, κύριε
the altar saying: Yes, [O] Lord

ὁ θεὸς ὁ παντοκράτωρ, ἀληθιναὶ καὶ
- God the Almighty, true and

δίκαιαι αἱ κρίσεις σου. 8 Καὶ ὁ τέταρτος
righteous the judgments of thee. And the fourth

ἐξέχεεν τὴν φιάλην αὐτοῦ ἐπὶ τὸν ἥλιον·
poured out the bowl of him onto the sun;

καὶ ἐδόθη αὐτῷ καυματίσαι τοὺς
and it was given to him to burn

ἀνθρώπους ἐν πυρί. 9 καὶ ἐκαυματίσθησαν
men with fire. And ²were burnt [with]

οἱ ἄνθρωποι καῦμα μέγα, καὶ ἐβλασ-
- ¹men ²heat ¹great, and they blas-

φήμησαν τὸ ὄνομα τοῦ θεοῦ τοῦ ἔχοντος
phemed the name - of God the [one] having

τὴν ἐξουσίαν ἐπὶ τὰς πληγὰς ταύτας,
the authority over these plagues,

καὶ οὐ μετενόησαν δοῦναι αὐτῷ δόξαν.
and they repented not to give ²to him ¹glory.

10 Καὶ ὁ πέμπτος ἐξέχεεν τὴν φιάλην
And the fifth poured out the bowl

αὐτοῦ ἐπὶ τὸν θρόνον τοῦ θηρίου· καὶ
of him onto the throne of the beast; and

ἐγένετο ἡ βασιλεία αὐτοῦ ἐσκοτωμένη,
⁴became ¹the ²kingdom ³of it having been darkened,

καὶ ἐμασῶντο τὰς γλώσσας αὐτῶν ἐκ
and they(men) gnawed the tongues of them from

τοῦ πόνου, 11 καὶ ἐβλασφήμησαν τὸν θεὸν
the pain, and they blasphemed the God

τοῦ οὐρανοῦ ἐκ τῶν πόνων αὐτῶν καὶ
- of heaven from the pains of them and

ἐκ τῶν ἑλκῶν αὐτῶν, καὶ οὐ μετενόησαν
from the sores of them, and they repented not

ἐκ τῶν ἔργων αὐτῶν. 12 Καὶ ὁ ἕκτος
of the works of them. And the sixth

ἐξέχεεν τὴν φιάλην αὐτοῦ ἐπὶ τὸν ποταμὸν
poured out the bowl of him onto the ²river

and its water was dried up, to prepare the way for the kings from the east. ¹³And I saw, issuing from the mouth of the dragon and from the mouth of the beast and from the mouth of the false prophet, three foul spirits like frogs; ¹⁴for they are demonic spirits, performing signs, who go abroad to the kings of the whole world, to assemble them for battle on the great day of God the Almighty. ¹⁵("Lo, I am coming like a thief! Blessed is he who is awake, keeping his garments that he may not go naked and be seen exposed!") ¹⁶And they assembled them at the place which is called in Hebrew Armaged′don.

17 The seventh angel poured his bowl into the air, and a great voice came out of the temple, from the throne, saying, "It is done!" ¹⁸And there were flashes of lightning, loud noises, peals of thunder, and a great earthquake such as had

τὸν μέγαν Εὐφράτην· καὶ ἐξηράνθη τὸ
– ¹great Euphrates; and ⁴was dried ¹the

ὕδωρ αὐτοῦ, ἵνα ἑτοιμασθῇ ἡ ὁδὸς τῶν
²water ³of it, in order ⁵might be ¹the ²way ³of the
           that prepared

βασιλέων τῶν ἀπὸ ἀνατολῆς ἡλίου. 13 Καὶ
⁴kings – ⁵from ⁶[the] rising ⁷of [the] sun. And

εἶδον ἐκ τοῦ στόματος τοῦ δράκοντος
I saw out of the mouth of the dragon

καὶ ἐκ τοῦ στόματος τοῦ θηρίου καὶ
and out of the mouth of the beast and

ἐκ τοῦ στόματος τοῦ ψευδοπροφήτου
out of the mouth of the false prophet

πνεύματα τρία ἀκάθαρτα ὡς βάτραχοι·
²spirits ¹three ²unclean [coming] as frogs;

14 εἰσὶν γὰρ πνεύματα δαιμονίων ποιοῦντα
for they are spirits of demons doing

σημεῖα, ἃ ἐκπορεύεται ἐπὶ τοὺς βασιλεῖς
signs, which goes forth unto the kings

τῆς οἰκουμένης ὅλης, συναγαγεῖν αὐτοὺς
of the ²inhabited [earth] ¹whole, to assemble them

εἰς τὸν πόλεμον τῆς ἡμέρας τῆς μεγάλης
to the war of the ²day – ¹great

τοῦ θεοῦ τοῦ παντοκράτορος. 15 Ἰδοὺ
– of God of the Almighty. Behold

ἔρχομαι ὡς κλέπτης· μακάριος ὁ γρηγορῶν
I am coming as a thief: blessed [is] the [one] watching

καὶ τηρῶν τὰ ἱμάτια αὐτοῦ, ἵνα μὴ
and keeping the garments of him, lest

γυμνὸς περιπατῇ καὶ βλέπωσιν τὴν
naked he walk and they (men) see the

ἀσχημοσύνην αὐτοῦ. 16 Καὶ συνήγαγεν
shame of him. And [t]he[y] assembled

αὐτοὺς εἰς τὸν τόπον τὸν καλούμενον
them in the place – being called

Ἑβραϊστὶ Ἁρμαγεδών. 17 Καὶ ὁ ἕβδομος
in Hebrew Harmagedon. And the seventh

ἐξέχεεν τὴν φιάλην αὐτοῦ ἐπὶ τὸν ἀέρα·
poured out the bowl of him on the air;

καὶ ἐξῆλθεν φωνὴ μεγάλη ἐκ τοῦ ναοῦ
and ²came out ¹voice ¹a great(loud) out of the shrine

ἀπὸ τοῦ θρόνου λέγουσα· γέγονεν. 18 καὶ
from the throne saying: It has occurred. And

ἐγένοντο ἀστραπαὶ καὶ φωναὶ καὶ βρονταί,
there were lightnings and voices and thunders,

καὶ σεισμὸς ἐγένετο μέγας, οἷος οὐκ
and ²earthquake ³occurred ¹a great, such as not

never been since men were on the earth, so great was that earthquake. ¹⁹The great city was split into three parts, and the cities of the nations fell, and God remembered great Babylon, to make her drain the cup of the fury of his wrath. ²⁰And every island fled away, and no mountains were to be found; ²¹and great hailstones, heavy as a hundredweight, dropped on men from heaven, till men cursed God for the plague of the hail, so fearful was that plague.

ἐγένετο ἀφ' οὗ ἄνθρωπος ἐγένετο ἐπὶ
did occur from when† man was on
τῆς γῆς, τηλικοῦτος σεισμὸς οὕτω μέγας.
the earth, such an earthquake so great.

19 καὶ ἐγένετο ἡ πόλις ἡ μεγάλη εἰς
And ⁴became ¹the ²city – ³great into
τρία μέρη, καὶ αἱ πόλεις τῶν ἐθνῶν
three parts, and the cities of the nations
ἔπεσαν. καὶ Βαβυλὼν ἡ μεγάλη ἐμνήσθη
fell. And Babylon the great was remembered
ἐνώπιον τοῦ θεοῦ δοῦναι αὐτῇ τὸ ποτήριον
before – God to give to her/it* the cup
τοῦ οἴνου τοῦ θυμοῦ τῆς ὀργῆς αὐτοῦ.
of the wine of the anger of the wrath of him.

20 καὶ πᾶσα νῆσος ἔφυγεν, καὶ ὄρη
And every island fled, and mountains
οὐχ εὑρέθησαν. **21** καὶ χάλαζα μεγάλη
were not found. And ¹hail ¹a great
ὡς ταλαντιαία καταβαίνει ἐκ τοῦ οὐρανοῦ
as a talent in size comes down out of – heaven
ἐπὶ τοὺς ἀνθρώπους· καὶ ἐβλασφήμησαν
on – men; and ²blasphemed
οἱ ἄνθρωποι τὸν θεὸν ἐκ τῆς πληγῆς
the ¹men – God from the plague
τῆς χαλάζης, ὅτι μεγάλη ἐστὶν ἡ πληγὴ
of the hail, because ²great ⁴is ¹the ³plague
αὐτῆς σφόδρα.
²of it ⁵exceeding.

CHAPTER 17

THEN one of the seven angels who had the seven bowls came and said to me, "Come, I will show you the judgment of the great harlot who is seated upon many waters, ²with whom the kings of the earth have committed fornication, and with the wine of whose fornication the dwellers on earth have become drunk." ³And he carried

17 Καὶ ἦλθεν εἷς ἐκ τῶν ἑπτὰ ἀγγέλων
And came one of the seven angels
τῶν ἐχόντων τὰς ἑπτὰ φιάλας, καὶ
– having the seven bowls, and
ἐλάλησεν μετ' ἐμοῦ λέγων· δεῦρο, δείξω
spoke with me saying: Come, I will show
σοι τὸ κρίμα τῆς πόρνης τῆς μεγάλης
thee the judgment of the ²harlot – ¹great
τῆς καθημένης ἐπὶ ὑδάτων πολλῶν, **2** μεθ'
– sitting on ²waters ¹many, with
ἧς ἐπόρνευσαν οἱ βασιλεῖς τῆς γῆς,
whom ²practised ¹the ²kings ³of the ⁴earth,
fornication
καὶ ἐμεθύσθησαν οἱ κατοικοῦντες τὴν γῆν
and ²became drunk ¹the ³dwelling [on] ²the ⁴earth
[ones]
ἐκ τοῦ οἴνου τῆς πορνείας αὐτῆς. **3** καὶ
from the wine of the fornication of her. And

* Even in English a city is often personified as feminine.

me away in the Spirit into a wilderness, and I saw a woman sitting on a scarlet beast which was full of blasphemous names, and it had seven heads and ten horns. [4] The woman was arrayed in purple and scarlet, and bedecked with gold and jewels and pearls, holding in her hand a golden cup full of abominations and the impurities of her fornication; [5] and on her forehead was written a name of mystery: "Babylon the great, mother of harlots and of earth's abominations." [6] And I saw the woman, drunk with the blood of the saints and the blood of the martyrs of Jesus.

When I saw her I marveled greatly. [7] But the angel said to me, "Why marvel? I will tell you the mystery of the woman, and of the beast with seven heads and ten horns that carries her. [8] The beast that you saw was, and is not, and is to

ἀπήνεγκέν   με   εἰς   ἔρημον   ἐν   πνεύματι.
he carried away   me   into   a desert   in   spirit.

καὶ   εἶδον   γυναῖκα   καθημένην   ἐπὶ   θηρίον
And   I saw   a woman   sitting   on   [3]beast

κόκκινον,   γέμοντα   ὀνόματα   βλασφημίας,
[1]a scarlet,   being filled [with]   names   of blasphemy,

ἔχοντα   κεφαλὰς   ἑπτὰ   καὶ   κέρατα   δέκα.
having   [3]heads   [1]seven   and   [2]horns   [1]ten.

4 καὶ   ἡ   γυνὴ   ἦν   περιβεβλημένη   πορφυροῦν
And   the   woman   was   having been clothed [in]   purple

καὶ   κόκκινον,   καὶ   κεχρυσωμένη   χρυσίῳ
and   scarlet,   and   having been gilded   with gold

καὶ   λίθῳ   τιμίῳ   καὶ   μαργαρίταις,   ἔχουσα
and   [2]stone   [1]precious and   pearls,   having

ποτήριον   χρυσοῦν   ἐν   τῇ   χειρὶ   αὐτῆς
[2]cup   [1]a golden   in   the   hand   of her

γέμον   βδελυγμάτων   καὶ   τὰ   ἀκάθαρτα
being filled   of(with)   and   the   unclean things
             abominations

τῆς   πορνείας   αὐτῆς,   **5** καὶ   ἐπὶ   τὸ
of the   fornication   of her,   and   on   the

μέτωπον   αὐτῆς   ὄνομα   γεγραμμένον,
forehead   of her   a name   having been written,

μυστήριον,   *ΒΑΒΥΛΩΝ   Η   ΜΕΓΑΛΗ,*
a mystery,   BABYLON   THE   GREAT,

Η   ΜΗΤΗΡ   ΤΩΝ   ΠΟΡΝΩΝ   ΚΑΙ
The   Mother   of the   Harlots   and

ΤΩΝ   ΒΔΕΛΥΓΜΑΤΩΝ   ΤΗΣ   ΓΗΣ.
of the   Abominations   of the   Earth.

6 καὶ   εἶδον   τὴν   γυναῖκα   μεθύουσαν   ἐκ
And   I saw   the   woman   being drunk   from

τοῦ   αἵματος   τῶν   ἁγίων   καὶ   ἐκ   τοῦ
the   blood   of the   saints   and   from   the

αἵματος   τῶν   μαρτύρων   Ἰησοῦ.   Καὶ
blood   of the   witnesses   of Jesus.   And

ἐθαύμασα   ἰδὼν   αὐτὴν   θαῦμα   μέγα.   **7** καὶ
[1]I wondered   [2]seeing [3]her   [4][with] [4]wonder [3]a great.   And

εἶπέν   μοι   ὁ   ἄγγελος·   διὰ   τί   ἐθαύμασας;
[3]said   [4]to me [1]the [2]angel: Why   didst thou wonder?

ἐγὼ   ἐρῶ   σοι   τὸ   μυστήριον   τῆς   γυναικὸς
I   will tell   thee   the   mystery   of the   woman

καὶ   τοῦ   θηρίου   τοῦ   βαστάζοντος   αὐτὴν
and   of the   beast   –   carrying   her

τοῦ   ἔχοντος   τὰς   ἑπτὰ   κεφαλὰς   καὶ   τὰ
–   having   the   seven   heads   and   the

δέκα   κέρατα.   **8** Τὸ   θηρίον   ὃ   εἶδες   ἦν
ten   horns.   The   beast   which   thou   wa▪
                                                         sawest

ascend from the bottomless pit and go to perdition; and the dwellers on earth whose names have not been written in the book of life from the foundation of the world, will marvel to behold the beast, because it was and is not and is to come. [9]This calls for a mind with wisdom: the seven heads are seven hills on which the woman is seated; [10]they are also seven kings, five of whom have fallen, one is, the other has not yet come, and when he comes he must remain only a little while. [11]As for the beast that was and is not, it is an eighth but it belongs to the seven, and it goes to perdition. [12]And the ten horns that you saw are ten kings who have not yet received royal power, but they are to receive authority as kings for one hour, together with the beast. [13]These are of one mind and give over their power and authority to the beast; [14]they will make war on the Lamb, and the Lamb

καὶ οὐκ ἔστιν, καὶ μέλλει ἀναβαίνειν
and is not, and is about to come up

ἐκ τῆς ἀβύσσου καὶ εἰς ἀπώλειαν ὑπάγει·
out of the abyss and [2]to [3]destruction [1]goes;

καὶ θαυμασθήσονται οἱ κατοικοῦντες ἐπὶ
and [4]will wonder [1]the [ones] [2]dwelling [3]on

τῆς γῆς, ὧν οὐ γέγραπται τὸ ὄνομα
[4]the [5]earth, of whom [3]has not been written [1]the [2]name

ἐπὶ τὸ βιβλίον τῆς ζωῆς ἀπὸ καταβολῆς
on the scroll – of life from [the] foundation

κόσμου, βλεπόντων τὸ θηρίον ὅτι ἦν
of [the] world, seeing the beast that it was

καὶ οὐκ ἔστιν καὶ παρέσται. 9 ὧδε
and is not and is present. Here [is]

ὁ νοῦς ὁ ἔχων σοφίαν. αἱ ἑπτὰ
the mind – having wisdom. The seven

κεφαλαὶ ἑπτὰ ὄρη εἰσίν, ὅπου ἡ γυνὴ
heads [2]seven [3]mountains [1]are, where the woman

κάθηται ἐπ᾽ αὐτῶν, καὶ βασιλεῖς ἑπτά
sits on them, and [2]kings [2]seven

εἰσιν· 10 οἱ πέντε ἔπεσαν, ὁ εἷς ἔστιν,
[1]are: the five fell, the one is,

ὁ ἄλλος οὔπω ἦλθεν, καὶ ὅταν ἔλθῃ
the other not yet came, and whenever he comes

ὀλίγον αὐτὸν δεῖ μεῖναι. 11 καὶ τὸ
[4]a little [3]him [1]it behoves [2]to And the
[while] remain.

θηρίον ὃ ἦν καὶ οὐκ ἔστιν, καὶ αὐτὸς
beast which was and is not, even he

ὄγδοός ἐστιν, καὶ ἐκ τῶν ἑπτά ἐστιν,
[3]an eighth [1]is, and [2]of [3]the [4]seven [1]is,

καὶ εἰς ἀπώλειαν ὑπάγει. 12 καὶ τὰ
and to destruction goes. And the

δέκα κέρατα ἃ εἶδες δέκα βασιλεῖς
ten horns which thou [2]ten [1]kings
sawest

εἰσιν, οἵτινες βασιλείαν οὔπω ἔλαβον,
[1]are, who a kingdom not yet received,

ἀλλὰ ἐξουσίαν ὡς βασιλεῖς μίαν ὥραν
but [2]authority [3]as [4]kings [1]one [5]hour

λαμβάνουσιν μετὰ τοῦ θηρίου. 13 οὗτοι
[1]receive with the beast. These

μίαν γνώμην ἔχουσιν, καὶ τὴν δύναμιν
one mind have, and the power

καὶ ἐξουσίαν αὐτῶν τῷ θηρίῳ διδόασιν.
and authority of them to the beast they give.

14 οὗτοι μετὰ τοῦ ἀρνίου πολεμήσουσιν
These [2]with [3]the [4]Lamb [1]will make war

willconquer them, for he is
Lord of lords and King of
kings, and those with him
are called and chosen
and faithful."

15 And he said to me,
"The waters that you
saw, where the harlot is
seated, are people and
multitudes and nations
and tongues. ¹⁶And the
ten horns that you saw,
they and the beast will
hate the harlot; they will
make her desolate and
naked, and devour her
flesh and burn her up
with fire, ¹⁷for God has
put it into their hearts to
carry out his purpose by
being of one mind and
giving over their royal
power to the beast, until
the words of God shall
be fulfilled. ¹⁸And the
woman that you saw is
the great city which has
dominion over the kings
of the earth."

καὶ   τὸ   ἀρνίον   νικήσει   αὐτούς,   ὅτι   κύριος
and   the   Lamb   will overcome   them,   because   ³Lord

κυρίων   ἐστὶν   καὶ   βασιλεὺς   βασιλέων,   καὶ
²of lords   ¹he is   and   King   of kings,   and

οἱ   μετ'   αὐτοῦ   κλητοὶ   καὶ   ἐκλεκτοὶ   καὶ
the   with   him [are] called   and   chosen   and
[ones]

πιστοί.   15 Καὶ   λέγει   μοι·   τὰ   ὕδατα
faithful.   And   he says   to me: The   waters

ἃ   εἶδες,   οὗ   ἡ   πόρνη   κάθηται,   λαοὶ
which thou   where the   harlot   sits,   peoples
sawest,

καὶ   ὄχλοι   εἰσὶν   καὶ   ἔθνη   καὶ   γλῶσσαι.
and   crowds   are   and   nations   and   tongues.

16 καὶ   τὰ   δέκα   κέρατα   ἃ   εἶδες   καὶ
And   the   ten   horns   which thou sawest   and

τὸ   θηρίον,   οὗτοι   μισήσουσιν   τὴν   πόρνην,
the   beast,   these   will hate   the   harlot,

καὶ   ἠρημωμένην   ποιήσουσιν   αὐτὴν   καὶ
and   ²having been desolated   ¹will make   ²her   and

γυμνήν,   καὶ   τὰς   σάρκας   αὐτῆς   φάγονται,
naked,   and   ³the   ²flesh es   ⁴of her   ¹will eat,

καὶ   αὐτὴν   κατακαύσουσιν   [ἐν]   πυρί· 17 ὁ
and   ²her   ¹will consume   with   fire;

γὰρ   θεὸς   ἔδωκεν   εἰς   τὰς   καρδίας   αὐτῶν
for   God   gave   into   the   hearts   of them

ποιῆσαι   τὴν   γνώμην   αὐτοῦ,   καὶ   ποιῆσαι
to do   the   mind   of him,   and   to make

μίαν   γνώμην   καὶ   δοῦναι   τὴν   βασιλείαν
one   mind   and   to give   the   kingdom

αὐτῶν   τῷ   θηρίῳ,   ἄχρι   τελεσθήσονται   οἱ
of them   to the   beast,   until   ⁴shall be accomplished   ¹the

λόγοι   τοῦ   θεοῦ.   18 καὶ   ἡ   γυνὴ   ἣν
²words   –   ³of God.   And   the   woman   whom

εἶδες   ἔστιν   ἡ   πόλις   ἡ   μεγάλη   ἡ   ἔχουσα
thou   is   the   ²city   –   ¹great   –   having
sawest

βασιλείαν   ἐπὶ   τῶν   βασιλέων   τῆς   γῆς.
a kingdom   over   the   kings   of the   earth.

CHAPTER 18

A FTER this I saw
another angel com-
ing down from heaven,
having great authority;
and the earth was made
bright with his splendor.
²And he called out with a
mighty voice,

18 Μετὰ   ταῦτα   εἶδον   ἄλλον   ἄγγελον
After   these things   I saw   another   angel

καταβαίνοντα   ἐκ   τοῦ   οὐρανοῦ,   ἔχοντα
coming down   out of   –   heaven,   having

ἐξουσίαν   μεγάλην,   καὶ   ἡ   γῆ   ἐφωτίσθη
²authority   ¹great,   and   the   earth was enlightened

ἐκ   τῆς   δόξης   αὐτοῦ.   2 καὶ   ἔκραξεν
from the   glory   of him.   And   he cried

"Fallen, fallen is Babylon the great! It has become a dwelling place of demons, a haunt of every foul spirit, a haunt of every foul and hateful bird;

ἐν ἰσχυρᾷ φωνῇ λέγων· ἔπεσεν ἔπεσεν
in a strong voice saying: Fell[,] fell

Βαβυλὼν ἡ μεγάλη, καὶ ἐγένετο κατοικητή-
Babylon the great, and became a dwelling-

ριον δαιμονίων καὶ φυλακὴ παντὸς
place of demons and a prison of every

πνεύματος ἀκαθάρτου καὶ φυλακὴ παντὸς
²spirit ¹unclean and a prison of every

³for all nations have drunk[i] the wine of her impure passion, and the kings of the earth have committed fornication with her, and the merchants of the earth have grown rich with the wealth of her wantonness."

ὀρνέου ἀκαθάρτου καὶ μεμισημένον, 3 ὅτι
⁴bird ¹unclean ²and ³having been hated, because

ἐκ τοῦ οἴνου τοῦ θυμοῦ τῆς πορνείας
⁶of ⁵the ⁷wine ⁸of the ⁹anger ¹⁰of the ¹¹fornication

αὐτῆς πέπωκαν πάντα τὰ ἔθνη, καὶ
¹²of her ⁴have drunk ¹all ²the ³nations, and

οἱ βασιλεῖς τῆς γῆς μετ' αὐτῆς ἐπόρνευσαν,
the kings of the earth with her practised fornication,

καὶ οἱ ἔμποροι τῆς γῆς ἐκ τῆς δυνάμεως
and the merchants of the earth ²from ¹the ⁴power

⁴Then I heard another voice from heaven saying,

τοῦ στρήνους αὐτῆς ἐπλούτησαν. 4 Καὶ
³of the ⁵luxury ⁶of her ⁷became rich. And

"Come out of her, my people, lest you take part in her sins, lest you share in her plagues;

ἤκουσα ἄλλην φωνὴν ἐκ τοῦ οὐρανοῦ
I heard another voice out of – heaven

λέγουσαν· ἐξέλθατε ὁ λαός μου ἐξ αὐτῆς,
saying: Come ye out[,] the people of me[,] out of her,

ἵνα μὴ συγκοινωνήσητε ταῖς ἁμαρτίαις
lest ye share in the sins

⁵for her sins are heaped high as heaven, and God has remembered her iniquities;

αὐτῆς, καὶ ἐκ τῶν πληγῶν αὐτῆς ἵνα
of her, and ³of ⁴the ⁵plagues ⁶of her ¹lest

μὴ λάβητε· 5 ὅτι ἐκολλήθησαν αὐτῆς αἱ
²ye receive; because ³joined together ²of her ¹the

ἁμαρτίαι ἄχρι τοῦ οὐρανοῦ, καὶ ἐμνημό-
⁴sins up to – heaven, and ²remem-

⁶Render to her as she herself has rendered, and repay her double for her deeds; mix a double draught for her in the cup she mixed.

νευσεν ὁ θεὸς τὰ ἀδικήματα αὐτῆς.
bered – ¹God the misdeeds of her.

6 ἀπόδοτε αὐτῇ ὡς καὶ αὐτὴ ἀπέδωκεν,
Give ye back to her as indeed she gave back,

καὶ διπλώσατε τὰ διπλᾶ κατὰ τὰ ἔργα
and double ye the double according to the works

⁷As she glorified herself and played the wanton, so give her a like measure of torment and mourning.

αὐτῆς· ἐν τῷ ποτηρίῳ ᾧ ἐκέρασεν
of her; in the cup in which she mixed

κεράσατε αὐτῇ διπλοῦν· 7 ὅσα ἐδόξασεν
mix ye to her double; by what she glorified
    things

αὐτὴν καὶ ἐστρηνίασεν, τοσοῦτον δότε
her[self] and luxuriated, by so much give ye

ⁱ Other ancient authorities read *fallen by*

αὐτῇ βασανισμὸν καὶ πένθος. ὅτι ἐν
to her torment and sorrow. Because in

Since in her heart she says, 'A queen I sit,

I am no widow, mourning I shall never see,'

[8]so shall her plagues come in a single day,

pestilence and mourning and famine,

and she shall be burned with fire; for mighty is the Lord God who judges her."

9 And the kings of the earth, who committed fornication and were wanton with her, will weep and wail over her when they see the smoke of her burning; [10]they will stand far off, in fear of her torment, and say,

"Alas! alas! thou great city,

thou mighty city, Babylon!

In one hour has thy judgment come."

11 And the merchants of the earth weep and mourn for her, since no one buys their cargo any more, [12]cargo of gold, silver, jewels and pearls, fine linen, purple, silk and scarlet, all kinds of scented wood, all articles of ivory, all articles of costly wood,

τῇ	καρδίᾳ	αὐτῆς	λέγει ὅτι	κάθημαι
the	heart	of her	she says[,] –	I sit

βασίλισσα καὶ χήρα οὐκ εἰμὶ καὶ πένθος
a queen and a widow I am not and sorrow

οὐ μὴ ἴδω· 8 διὰ τοῦτο ἐν μιᾷ ἡμέρᾳ
by no means I see; therefore in one day

ἥξουσιν αἱ πληγαὶ αὐτῆς, θάνατος καὶ
will come the plagues of her, death and

πένθος καὶ λιμός, καὶ ἐν πυρὶ κατακαυ-
sorrow and famine, and with fire she will be

θήσεται· ὅτι ἰσχυρὸς κύριος ὁ θεὸς ὁ
consumed; because strong [is] [the] Lord – God the

κρίνας αὐτήν. 9 καὶ κλαύσουσιν καὶ
[one] judging her. And [1]will weep [2]and

κόψονται ἐπ' αὐτὴν οἱ βασιλεῖς τῆς
[3]wail [4]over [5]her [1]the [2]kings [3]of the

γῆς οἱ μετ' αὐτῆς πορνεύσαντες καὶ
[4]earth [16]the [12]with [13]her [11]having practised and
[ones] fornication

στρηνιάσαντες, ὅταν βλέπωσιν τὸν καπνὸν
having luxuriated, whenever they see the smoke

τῆς πυρώσεως αὐτῆς, 10 ἀπὸ μακρόθεν
of the burning of her, [2]from [3]afar

ἑστηκότες διὰ τὸν φόβον τοῦ βασανισμοῦ
[1]standing because of the fear of the torment

αὐτῆς, λέγοντες· οὐαὶ οὐαί, ἡ πόλις
of her, saying: Woe[,] woe, the [2]city

ἡ μεγάλη, Βαβυλὼν ἡ πόλις ἡ ἰσχυρά,
– [1]great, Babylon the [2]city – [3]strong,

ὅτι μιᾷ ὥρᾳ ἦλθεν ἡ κρίσις σου. 11 καὶ
be- in hour came the judgment of thee. And
cause one

οἱ ἔμποροι τῆς γῆς κλαίουσιν καὶ
the merchants of the earth weep and

πενθοῦσιν ἐπ' αὐτήν, ὅτι τὸν γόμον
sorrow over her, because [4]the [2]cargo

αὐτῶν οὐδεὶς ἀγοράζει οὐκέτι, 12 γόμον
[5]of them [1]no one [3]buys [2]any more, cargo

χρυσοῦ καὶ ἀργύρου καὶ λίθου τιμίου
of gold and of silver and [2]stone [1]of valuable

καὶ μαργαριτῶν καὶ βυσσίνου καὶ πορφύρας
and of pearls and of fine linen and of purple

καὶ σηρικοῦ καὶ κοκκίνου, καὶ πᾶν
and of silk and of scarlet, and all

ξύλον θύϊνον καὶ πᾶν σκεῦος ἐλεφάντινον
[2]wood [1]thyine and every [2]vessel [1]ivory

καὶ πᾶν σκεῦος ἐκ ξύλου τιμωτάτου
and every vessel of [2]wood [1]very valuable

bronze, iron and marble,
¹³cinnamon, spice, incense, myrrh, frankincense, wine, oil, fine flour and wheat, cattle and sheep, horses and chariots, and slaves, that is, human souls.

¹⁴"The fruit for which thy soul longed has gone from thee, and all thy dainties and thy splendor are lost to thee, never to be found again!"

¹⁵The merchants of these wares, who gained wealth from her, will stand far off, in fear of her torment, weeping and mourning aloud,

¹⁶"Alas, alas, for the great city that was clothed in fine linen, in purple and scarlet, bedecked with gold, with jewels, and with pearls!

¹⁷In one hour all this wealth has been laid waste."

And all shipmasters and seafaring men, sailors and all whose trade is on the sea, stood

καὶ χαλκοῦ καὶ σιδήρου καὶ μαρμάρου,
and of bronze and of iron and of marble,

13 καὶ κιννάμωμον καὶ ἄμωμον καὶ
and cinnamon and spice and

θυμιάματα καὶ μύρον καὶ λίβανον καὶ
incenses and ointment and frankincense and

οἶνον καὶ ἔλαιον καὶ σεμίδαλιν καὶ σῖτον
wine and oil and fine meal and corn

καὶ κτήνη καὶ πρόβατα, καὶ ἵππων
and beasts of burden and sheep, and of horses

καὶ ῥεδῶν καὶ σωμάτων, καὶ ψυχὰς
and of carriages and of bodies, and souls

ἀνθρώπων. 14 καὶ ἡ ὀπώρα σου τῆς
of men. And the fruit ⁴of thee ²of the

ἐπιθυμίας τῆς ψυχῆς ἀπῆλθεν ἀπὸ σοῦ,
²lust ³of the ⁴soul went away from thee,

καὶ πάντα τὰ λιπαρὰ καὶ τὰ λαμπρὰ
and all the sumptuous and the bright
things things

ἀπώλετο ἀπὸ σοῦ, καὶ οὐκέτι οὐ μὴ
perished from thee, and no more by no(any) means

αὐτὰ εὑρήσουσιν. 15 οἱ ἔμποροι τούτων,
²them ¹shall they find. The merchants of these things,

οἱ πλουτήσαντες ἀπ' αὐτῆς, ἀπὸ μακρόθεν
the having been rich from her, ²from ¹afar
[ones]

στήσονται διὰ τὸν φόβον τοῦ βασανισμοῦ
¹will stand because of the fear of the torment

αὐτῆς κλαίοντες καὶ πενθοῦντες, 16 λέγοντες·
of her weeping and sorrowing, saying:

οὐαὶ οὐαί, ἡ πόλις ἡ μεγάλη, ἡ περι-
Woe[,] the ¹city ²great, having

βεβλημένη βύσσινον καὶ πορφυροῦν καὶ
been clothed [with] fine linen and purple and

κόκκινον, καὶ κεχρυσωμένη ἐν χρυσίῳ
scarlet, and having been gilded with gold

καὶ λίθῳ τιμίῳ καὶ μαργαρίτῃ, 17 ὅτι
and ²stone ¹valuable and pearl, because

μιᾷ ὥρᾳ ἠρημώθη ὁ τοσοῦτος πλοῦτος.
in one hour ²was made ¹such great ³wealth.
desolate

καὶ πᾶς κυβερνήτης καὶ πᾶς ὁ ἐπὶ
And every steersman and ¹every ²one ⁴to

τόπον πλέων καὶ ναῦται καὶ ὅσοι τὴν
³a place ²sailing and sailors and as many as ⁵the

θάλασσαν ἐργάζονται, ἀπὸ μακρόθεν ἔστησαν
²sea ¹work, ²from ³afar ¹stood

far off ¹⁸and cried out as they saw the smoke of her burning,
"What city was like the great city?"

¹⁹And they threw dust on their heads, as they wept and mourned, crying out,
"Alas, alas, for the great city
where all who had ships at sea grew rich by her wealth!
In one hour she has been laid waste.
²⁰Rejoice over her, O heaven,
O saints and apostles and prophets,
for God has given judgment for you against her!"

21 Then a mighty angel took up a stone like a great millstone and threw it into the sea, saying,
"So shall Babylon the great city be thrown down with violence,
and shall be found no more;
²²and the sound of harpers and minstrels, of flute players and trumpeters,
shall be heard in thee no more;
and a craftsman of any craft
shall be found in thee no more;
and the sound of the millstone
shall be heard in thee no more;
²³and the light of a lamp
shall shine in thee no more;

---

18 καὶ   ἔκραζον   βλέποντες   τὸν   καπνὸν
and   cried out   seeing   the   smoke

τῆς   πυρώσεως   αὐτῆς   λέγοντες·   τίς   ὁμοία
of the   burning   of her   saying: Who(What) [is] like

τῇ   πόλει   τῇ   μεγάλῃ;   **19** καὶ   ἔβαλον
to the   ²city   –   ¹great ?   And   they cast

χοῦν   ἐπὶ   τὰς   κεφαλὰς   αὐτῶν   καὶ   ἔκραζον
dust   on   the   heads   of them   and   cried out

κλαίοντες   καὶ   πενθοῦντες,   λέγοντες·   οὐαὶ
weeping   and   sorrowing,   saying: Woe[,]

οὐαί,   ἡ   πόλις   ἡ   μεγάλη,   ἐν   ᾗ   ἐπλούτησαν
woe,   the   ²city   –   ¹great,   by which   ⁰were rich

πάντες   οἱ   ἔχοντες   τὰ   πλοῖα   ἐν   τῇ
¹all   ²the [ones]   ³having   ⁴the   ⁵ships   ⁶in   ⁷the

θαλάσσῃ   ἐκ   τῆς   τιμιότητος   αὐτῆς,   ὅτι
⁵sea   from   the   worth   of her, because

μιᾷ   ὥρᾳ   ἠρημώθη.   **20** Εὐφραίνου   ἐπ᾽
in one   hour   she was made desolate.   Be thou glad   over

αὐτῇ,   οὐρανὲ   καὶ   οἱ   ἅγιοι   καὶ   οἱ   ἀπό-
her,   heaven   and   the   saints   and   the   apost-

στολοι   καὶ   οἱ   προφῆται,   ὅτι   ἔκρινεν   ὁ
les   and   the   prophets,   because   ²judged   –

θεὸς   τὸ   κρίμα   ὑμῶν   ἐξ   αὐτῆς.   **21** Καὶ
¹God   the   judgment   of you   by   her.   And

ἦρεν   εἷς   ἄγγελος   ἰσχυρὸς   λίθον   ὡς
⁴lifted   ¹one   ²angel   ³strong   a stone   as

μύλινον   μέγαν,   καὶ   ἔβαλεν   εἰς   τὴν   θά-
³millstone   ¹a great,   and   threw   into   the   sea

λασσαν   λέγων·   οὕτως   ὁρμήματι   βληθήσεται
saying: Thus   with a rush   ⁵shall be thrown

Βαβυλὼν   ἡ   μεγάλη   πόλις,   καὶ   οὐ   μὴ
¹Babylon   ³the   ²great   ⁴city,   and by no means

εὑρεθῇ   ἔτι.   **22** καὶ   φωνὴ   κιθαρῳδῶν
[shall] be   longer.   And   sound   of harpers
found

καὶ   μουσικῶν   καὶ   αὐλητῶν   καὶ   σαλπιστῶν
and   of musicians   and   of flutists   and   of trumpeters

οὐ   μὴ   ἀκουσθῇ   ἐν   σοὶ   ἔτι,   καὶ   πᾶς
by no means [shall] be heard in   thee   longer,   and   every

τεχνίτης   πάσης   τέχνης   οὐ   μὴ   εὑρεθῇ
craftsman   of every   craft   by no means   [shall]
be found

ἐν   σοὶ   ἔτι,   καὶ   φωνὴ   μύλου   οὐ   μὴ
in   thee   longer,   and   sound   of a mill by no means

ἀκουσθῇ   ἐν   σοὶ   ἔτι,   **23** καὶ   φῶς
[shall] be heard in   thee   longer,   and   light

λύχνου   οὐ   μὴ   φάνῃ   ἐν   σοὶ   ἔτι,   καὶ
of a   by no means   [shall]   in   thee   longer,   and
lamp   shine

and the voice of bridegroom and bride shall be heard in thee no more; for thy merchants were the great men of the earth, and all nations were deceived by thy sorcery.

φωνὴ	νυμφίου	καὶ	νύμφης	οὐ μὴ
voice	of bridegroom	and	of bride	by no means

ἀκουσθῇ	ἐν σοὶ	ἔτι·	ὅτι [οἱ]	ἔμποροί
[shall] be heard in	thee	longer;	because the	merchants

σου	ἦσαν οἱ	μεγιστᾶνες	τῆς γῆς, ὅτι
of thee	were the	great ones	of the earth, because

ἐν τῇ	φαρμακείᾳ	σου ἐπλανήθησαν	πάντα
by the	sorcery	of thee ⁴were deceived	¹all

24 And in her was found the blood of prophets and of saints, and of all who have been slain on earth."

τὰ	ἔθνη, 24 καὶ	ἐν αὐτῇ	αἷμα προφητῶν
²the	³nations, and in	her	³blood ²of prophets

καὶ	ἁγίων	εὑρέθη	καὶ πάντων τῶν
⁴and	⁵of saints	¹was found	and of all the [ones]

ἐσφαγμένων	ἐπὶ	τῆς	γῆς.
having been slain	on	the	earth.

CHAPTER 19

AFTER this I heard what seemed to be the mighty voice of a great multitude in heaven, crying, "Hallelujah! Salvation and glory and power belong to our God, ²for his judgments are true and just; he has judged the great harlot who corrupted the earth with her fornication, and he has avenged on her the blood of his servants."

³Once more they cried, "Hallelujah! The smoke from her goes up for ever and ever."

⁴And the twenty-four elders and the four living creatures fell down and worshipped God who is seated on the throne,

19 Μετὰ	ταῦτα	ἤκουσα	ὡς	φωνὴν
After	these things	I heard	as	²voice

μεγάλην	ὄχλου	πολλοῦ	ἐν τῷ	οὐρανῷ
³a great (loud)	⁴crowd	⁵of a much (great)	in –	heaven

λεγόντων·	ἀλληλουϊά· ἡ	σωτηρία καὶ ἡ
saying:	Halleluia: The	salvation and the

δόξα	καὶ ἡ	δύναμις	τοῦ θεοῦ	ἡμῶν,
glory	and the	power	of the God	of us,

2 ὅτι	ἀληθιναὶ	καὶ	δίκαιαι αἱ κρίσεις
because	true	and	righteous the judgments

αὐτοῦ·	ὅτι	ἔκρινεν	τὴν πόρνην τὴν
of him;	because	he judged	the ²harlot –

μεγάλην	ἥτις	ἔφθειρεν	τὴν γῆν	ἐν τῇ
¹great	who	defiled	the earth	with the

πορνείᾳ	αὐτῆς,	καὶ ἐξεδίκησεν	τὸ αἷμα
fornication	of her,	and he avenged	the blood

τῶν	δούλων	αὐτοῦ ἐκ	χειρὸς αὐτῆς.
of the	slaves	of him out of	[the] hand of her.

3 καὶ	δεύτερον	εἴρηκαν·	ἀλληλουϊά· καὶ
And	secondly	they have said:	Halleluia; and

ὁ	καπνὸς	αὐτῆς	ἀναβαίνει εἰς τοὺς
the	smoke	of her	goes up unto the

αἰῶνας	τῶν	αἰώνων.	4 καὶ ἔπεσαν οἱ
ages	of the	ages.	And ³fell ¹the

πρεσβύτεροι	οἱ	εἴκοσι	τέσσαρες καὶ τὰ
²elders	–	³twenty-four	⁴and ⁵the

τέσσερα	ζῷα,	καὶ	προσεκύνησαν τῷ θεῷ
⁶four	⁷living creatures,	and	worshipped – God

τῷ	καθημένῳ	ἐπὶ	τῷ θρόνῳ λέγοντες·
–	sitting	on	the throne saying:

saying, "Amen. Hallelu-
jah!" [5]And from the
throne came a voice
crying,
  "Praise our God, all
    you his servants,
    you who fear him,
    small and great."
[6]Then I heard what
seemed to be the voice of
a great multitude, like
the sound of many
waters and like the
sound of mighty
thunderpeals, crying,
  "Hallelujah! For the
    Lord our God the
    Almighty reigns.
[7]Let us rejoice and
    exult and give him
    the glory,
  for the marriage of
    the Lamb has
    come,
  and his Bride has
    made herself ready;
[8]it was granted her to
be clothed with
fine linen, bright
and pure"—
for the fine linen is the
righteous deeds of the
saints.

9 And the angel said
to me, "Write this:
Blessed are those who
are invited to the
marriage supper of the
Lamb." And he said to
me, "These are true
words of God." [10]Then I
fell down at his feet to
worship him, but he said
to me, "You must not do
that! I am a fellow
servant with you and
your brethren who hold

ἀμὴν ἀλληλουϊά.   5 καὶ   φωνὴ   ἀπὸ   τοῦ
Amen[,] halleluia.   And   a voice [2]from   [3]the

θρόνου ἐξῆλθεν λέγουσα· αἰνεῖτε τῷ θεῷ
[4]throne [1]came out saying: Praise ye the God

ἡμῶν,   πάντες   οἱ   δοῦλοι   αὐτοῦ,   οἱ
of us,   all   the   slaves   of him,   the

φοβούμενοι αὐτόν, οἱ μικροὶ καὶ οἱ
[ones] fearing him,   the   small   and   the

μεγάλοι.   6 Καὶ ἤκουσα ὡς φωνὴν ὄχλου
great.   And   I heard   as   a sound [2]crowd

πολλοῦ καὶ ὡς φωνὴν ὑδάτων πολλῶν
[1]of a   and   as   a sound [2]waters [1]of many
much(great)

καὶ ὡς φωνὴν βροντῶν ἰσχυρῶν, λεγόντων·
and   as   a sound [2]thunders [1]of strong saying:
                                              (loud),

ἀλληλουϊά, ὅτι ἐβασίλευσεν κύριος ὁ θεὸς
Halleluia, because [2]reigned   [1][the] Lord [1]the [2]God

ἡμῶν ὁ παντοκράτωρ.   7 χαίρωμεν καὶ
[3]of us [4]the Almighty.   Let us rejoice and

ἀγαλλιῶμεν, καὶ δώσομεν τὴν δόξαν αὐτῷ,
let us exult,   and we will give the   glory   to him,

ὅτι ἦλθεν ὁ γάμος τοῦ ἀρνίου, καὶ
because [2]came [1]the [2]marriage [3]of the [4]Lamb, and

ἡ γυνὴ αὐτοῦ ἡτοίμασεν ἑαυτήν, 8 καὶ
the wife of him   prepared   herself,   and

ἐδόθη αὐτῇ ἵνα περιβάληται βύσσινον
it was   to her in order she might be [2]fine linen
given   that   clothed [with]

λαμπρὸν καθαρόν· τὸ γὰρ βύσσινον τὰ
[3]bright   [4]clean;   for the   fine linen   [1]the

δικαιώματα τῶν ἁγίων ἐστίν.   9 Καὶ
[2]righteous deeds [4]of the [3]saints [1]is.   And

λέγει μοι· γράψον· μακάριοι οἱ εἰς τὸ
he tells me: Write thou; blessed [1]the [ones] [2]to [4]the

δεῖπνον τοῦ γάμου τοῦ ἀρνίου κεκλημένοι.
[5]supper [6]of   [7]marriage [8]of [9]Lamb [3]having been
              the   the   called.

καὶ λέγει μοι· οὗτοι οἱ λόγοι ἀληθινοὶ
And he says to me: [1]These – [2]words [3]true

τοῦ θεοῦ εἰσιν.   10 καὶ ἔπεσα ἔμπροσθεν
–   [5]of God [4]are.   And   I fell   before

τῶν ποδῶν αὐτοῦ προσκυνῆσαι αὐτῷ.
the   feet   of him   to worship   him.

καὶ λέγει μοι· ὅρα μή· σύνδουλός σου
And he says to me: See thou not; [2]a fellow- [3]of
                      [do it]   slave   thee

εἰμι καὶ τῶν ἀδελφῶν σου τῶν ἐχόντων
[1]I am and of the brothers of thee – having

the testimony of Jesus. Worship God." For the testimony of Jesus is the spirit of prophecy.

11 Then I saw heaven opened, and behold, a white horse! He who sat upon it is called Faithful and True, and in righteousness he judges and makes war. ¹²His eyes are like a flame of fire, and on his head are many diadems; and he has a name inscribed which no one knows but himself. ¹³He is clad in a robe dipped in* blood, and the name by which he is called is The Word of God. ¹⁴And the armies of heaven, arrayed in fine linen, white and pure, followed him on white horses. ¹⁵From his mouth issues a sharp sword with which to smite the nations, and he will rule them with a rod of iron; he will tread the wine press of the fury of the wrath of God the Almighty. ¹⁶On his robe and on his

τὴν μαρτυρίαν Ἰησοῦ· τῷ θεῷ προσκύνησον.
the   witness   of Jesus;   – ²God ¹worship thou.

ἡ γὰρ μαρτυρία Ἰησοῦ ἐστιν τὸ πνεῦμα
For the   witness   of Jesus   is   the   spirit

τῆς προφητείας.
   of prophecy.

11 Καὶ εἶδον τὸν οὐρανὸν ἠνεῳγμένον,
   And   I saw   –   heaven   having been opened,

καὶ ἰδοὺ ἵππος λευκός, καὶ ὁ καθήμενος
and behold[,] ²horse ¹a white, and the [one] sitting

ἐπ' αὐτὸν πιστὸς καλούμενος καὶ ἀληθινός,
on   it   ²faithful ¹being called   and   true,

καὶ ἐν δικαιοσύνῃ κρίνει καὶ πολεμεῖ.
and   in   righteousness he judges and makes war.

12 οἱ δὲ ὀφθαλμοὶ αὐτοῦ φλὸξ πυρός,
   And the   eyes   of him [are as] a flame   of fire,

καὶ ἐπὶ τὴν κεφαλὴν αὐτοῦ διαδήματα
and   on   the   head   of him   ²diadems

πολλά, ἔχων ὄνομα γεγραμμένον ὃ οὐδεὶς
¹many, having a name having been written which no one

οἶδεν εἰ μὴ αὐτός, 13 καὶ περιβεβλημένος
knows except [him]self,   and   having been
                                   clothed [with]

ἱμάτιον βεβαμμένον αἵματι, καὶ κέκληται
a garment having been in blood, and ⁴has been
            dipped   called

τὸ ὄνομα αὐτοῦ ὁ λόγος τοῦ θεοῦ.
¹the ²name ³of him The Word – of God.

14 καὶ τὰ στρατεύματα τὰ ἐν τῷ οὐρανῷ
   And the   armies   –   in   –   heaven

ἠκολούθει αὐτῷ ἐφ' ἵπποις λευκοῖς, ἐνδεδυμένοι
followed   him   on   ²horses ¹white,   having been
                                          dressed [in]

βύσσινον λευκὸν καθαρόν. 15 καὶ ἐκ
²fine linen ¹white ³clean.   And out of

τοῦ στόματος αὐτοῦ ἐκπορεύεται ῥομφαία
the   mouth   of him   proceeds   ²sword

ὀξεῖα, ἵνα ἐν αὐτῇ πατάξῃ τὰ ἔθνη·
¹a sharp, in order with it he may the nations;
          that   smite

καὶ αὐτὸς ποιμανεῖ αὐτοὺς ἐν ῥάβδῳ
and   he   will shepherd them with ²staff

σιδηρᾷ· καὶ αὐτὸς πατεῖ τὴν ληνὸν
¹an iron; and   he   treads the winepress

τοῦ οἴνου τοῦ θυμοῦ τῆς ὀργῆς τοῦ
of the wine of the anger[,] of the wrath –

θεοῦ τοῦ παντοκράτορος. 16 καὶ ἔχει
of God of the Almighty.   And he has

ἐπὶ τὸ ἱμάτιον καὶ ἐπὶ τὸν μηρὸν
on the garment and on the thigh

thigh he has a name inscribed, King of kings and Lord of lords.

17 Then I saw an angel standing in the sun, and with a loud voice he called to all the birds that fly in midheaven, "Come, gather for the great supper of God, [18]to eat the flesh of kings, the flesh of captains, the flesh of mighty men, the flesh of horses and their riders, and the flesh of all men, both free and slave, both small and great." [19]And I saw the beast and the kings of the earth with their armies gathered to make war against him who sits upon the horse and against his army. [20]And the beast was captured, and with it the false prophet who in its presence had worked the signs by which he deceived those who had received the mark of the beast and those who worshiped its image. These two were thrown

αὐτοῦ   ὄνομα   γεγραμμένον·   *ΒΑΣΙΛΕΥΣ*
of him   a name   *having been* written: KING

ΒΑΣΙΛΕΩΝ   ΚΑΙ   ΚΥΡΙΟΣ   ΚΥΡΙΩΝ.
OF KINGS   AND   LORD   OF LORDS.

17 Καὶ   εἶδον   ἕνα   ἄγγελον   ἑστῶτα   ἐν
And   I saw   one   angel   standing   in

τῷ   ἡλίῳ,   καὶ   ἔκραξεν   ἐν   φωνῇ   μεγάλῃ
the   sun,   and   he cried out in   [1]voice   [1]a great
(loud)

λέγων   πᾶσιν   τοῖς   ὀρνέοις   τοῖς   πετομένοις
saying   to all   the   birds   –   flying

ἐν   μεσουρανήματι·   δεῦτε   συνάχθητε   εἰς
in   mid-heaven: Come ye[.]   assemble ye   to

τὸ   δεῖπνον   τὸ   μέγα   τοῦ   θεοῦ,   18 ἵνα
the   [2]supper   –   [1]great   –   of God,   in order that

φάγητε   σάρκας   βασιλέων   καὶ   σάρκας
ye may eat   fleshes   of kings   and   fleshes

χιλιάρχων   καὶ   σάρκας   ἰσχυρῶν   καὶ   σάρκας
of chiliarchs   and   fleshes   of strong men and   fleshes

ἵππων   καὶ   τῶν   καθημένων   ἐπ᾽   αὐτῶν,
of horses   and   of the [ones] sitting   on   them,

καὶ   σάρκας   πάντων   ἐλευθέρων   τε   καὶ
and   fleshes   of all   [1]free men   [1]both   and

δούλων   καὶ   μικρῶν   καὶ   μεγάλων.   19 Καὶ
slaves   both   small   and   great.   And

εἶδον   τὸ   θηρίον   καὶ   τοὺς   βασιλεῖς   τῆς
I saw   the   beast   and   the   kings   of the

γῆς   καὶ   τὰ   στρατεύματα   αὐτῶν   συνηγμένα
earth   and the   armies   of them   *having been assembled*

ποιῆσαι   τὸν   πόλεμον   μετὰ   τοῦ   καθημένου
to make   the   war   with the [one]   sitting

ἐπὶ   τοῦ   ἵππου   καὶ   μετὰ   τοῦ   στρατεύματος
on   the   horse   and   with   the   army

αὐτοῦ.   20 καὶ   ἐπιάσθη   τὸ   θηρίον   καὶ
of him.   And   [3]was seized   [1]the   [2]beast   and

μετ᾽   αὐτοῦ   ὁ   ψευδοπροφήτης   ὁ   ποιήσας
with   it   the   false prophet   the [one]   having done

τὰ   σημεῖα   ἐνώπιον   αὐτοῦ,   ἐν   οἷς   ἐπλάνη-
the   signs   before   it,   by which   he de-

σεν   τοὺς   λαβόντας   τὸ   χάραγμα   τοῦ
ceived the [ones]   having received   the   mark   of the

θηρίου   καὶ   τοὺς   προσκυνοῦντας   τῇ   εἰκόνι
beast   and   the [ones]   worshipping   the   image

αὐτοῦ·   ζῶντες   ἐβλήθησαν   οἱ   δύο   εἰς
of it;   [4]living   [3]were cast   [1]the   [2]two   into

alive into the lake of fire that burns with brimstone. ²¹And the rest were slain by the sword of him who sits upon the horse, the sword that issues from his mouth; and all the birds were gorged with their flesh.

τὴν λίμνην τοῦ πυρὸς τῆς καιομένης
the lake — of fire — burning*

ἐν θείῳ. 21 καὶ οἱ λοιποὶ ἀπεκτάνθησαν
with sulphur. And the rest were killed

ἐν τῇ ῥομφαίᾳ τοῦ καθημένου ἐπὶ τοῦ
with the sword of the [one] sitting on the

ἵππου τῇ ἐξελθούσῃ ἐκ τοῦ στόματος
horse — proceeding§ out of the mouth

αὐτοῦ, καὶ πάντα τὰ ὄρνεα ἐχορτάσθησαν
of him, and all the birds were filled

ἐκ τῶν σαρκῶν αὐτῶν.
by the fleshes of them.

CHAPTER 20

THEN I saw an angel coming down from heaven, holding in his hand the key of the bottomless pit and a great chain. ²And he seized the dragon, that ancient serpent, who is the Devil and Satan, and bound him for a thousand years, ³and threw him into the pit, and shut it and sealed it over him, that he should deceive the nations no more, till the thousand years were ended. After that he must be loosed for a little while.

4 Then I saw thrones, and seated on them were those to whom judgment was committed. Also I saw the souls of those who had been beheaded for their testimony to Jesus and for the word of

20 Καὶ εἶδον ἄγγελον καταβαίνοντα ἐκ
And I saw an angel coming down out of

τοῦ οὐρανοῦ, ἔχοντα τὴν κλεῖν τῆς
— heaven, having the key of the

ἀβύσσου καὶ ἅλυσιν μεγάλην ἐπὶ τὴν χεῖρα
abyss and ²chain ¹a great on the hand

αὐτοῦ. 2 καὶ ἐκράτησεν τὸν δράκοντα,
of him. And he laid hold [of] the dragon,

ὁ ὄφις ὁ ἀρχαῖος, ὅς ἐστιν Διάβολος
the ²serpent — ¹old, who is Devil

καὶ ὁ Σατανᾶς, καὶ ἔδησεν αὐτὸν χίλια
and — Satan, and bound him a thousand

ἔτη, 3 καὶ ἔβαλεν αὐτὸν εἰς τὴν ἄβυσσον,
years, and cast him into the abyss,

καὶ ἔκλεισεν καὶ ἐσφράγισεν ἐπάνω αὐτοῦ,
and shut and sealed over him,

ἵνα μὴ πλανήσῃ ἔτι τὰ ἔθνη, ἄχρι
in or- he should not deceive longer the nations, until
der that

τελεσθῇ τὰ χίλια ἔτη· μετὰ ταῦτα
⁴are finished ¹the ²thousand ³years; after these things

δεῖ λυθῆναι αὐτὸν μικρὸν χρόνον.
it be- ²to be ¹him a little time.
hoves loosed

4 Καὶ εἶδον θρόνους, καὶ ἐκάθισαν ἐπ'
And I saw thrones, and they sat on

αὐτούς, καὶ κρίμα ἐδόθη αὐτοῖς, καὶ
them, and judgment was given to them, and

τὰς ψυχὰς τῶν πεπελεκισμένων διὰ τὴν
the souls of the having been because of
[ones] beheaded

μαρτυρίαν Ἰησοῦ καὶ διὰ τὸν λόγον
witness of Jesus and because of the word

---

* Feminine, agreeing with λίμνη, not with the neuter πῦρ.

§ Agreeing, of course, with ῥομφαίᾳ.

God, and who had not worshiped the beast or its image and had not received its mark on their foreheads or their hands. They came to life and reigned with Christ a thousand years. ⁵The rest of the dead did not come to life until the thousand years were ended. This is the first resurrection. ⁶Blessed and holy is he who shares in the first resurrection! Over such the second death has no power, but they shall be priests of God and of Christ, and they shall reign with him a thousand years.

7 And when the thousand years are ended, Satan will be loosed from his prison ⁸and will come out to deceive the nations which are at the four corners of the earth, that is Gog and Magog, to gather them for battle; their number is like the sand of the sea. ⁹And they marched up over the broad earth and surrounded the camp of the saints and the beloved

τοῦ θεοῦ, καὶ οἵτινες οὐ προσεκύνησαν
\- of God, and who did not worship

τὸ θηρίον οὐδὲ τὴν εἰκόνα αὐτοῦ καὶ
the beast nor the image of it and

οὐκ ἔλαβον τὸ χάραγμα ἐπὶ τὸ μέτωπον
did not receive the mark on the forehead

καὶ ἐπὶ τὴν χεῖρα αὐτῶν· καὶ ἔζησαν
and on the hand of them; and they lived
[again]

καὶ ἐβασίλευσαν μετὰ τοῦ Χριστοῦ χίλια
and reigned with \- Christ a thousand

ἔτη. 5 οἱ λοιποὶ τῶν νεκρῶν οὐκ ἔζησαν
years. The rest of the dead did not live [again]

ἄχρι τελεσθῇ τὰ χίλια ἔτη. Αὕτη ἡ
until were finished the thousand years. This [is] the

ἀνάστασις ἡ πρώτη. 6 μακάριος καὶ
²resurrection ¹first. Blessed and

ἅγιος ὁ ἔχων μέρος ἐν τῇ ἀναστάσει
holy [is] the [one] having part in the ²resurrection

τῇ πρώτῃ· ἐπὶ τούτων ὁ δεύτερος θάνατος
\- ¹first; over these the second death

οὐκ ἔχει ἐξουσίαν, ἀλλ' ἔσονται ἱερεῖς
has not authority, but they will be priests

τοῦ θεοῦ καὶ τοῦ Χριστοῦ, καὶ βασιλεύ-
\- of God and \- of Christ, and will

σουσιν μετ' αὐτοῦ [τὰ] χίλια ἔτη.
reign with him the thousand years.

7 Καὶ ὅταν τελεσθῇ τὰ χίλια ἔτη,
And whenever are finished the thousand years,

λυθήσεται ὁ σατανᾶς ἐκ τῆς φυλακῆς
²will be loosed \- ¹Satan out of the prison

αὐτοῦ, 8 καὶ ἐξελεύσεται πλανῆσαι τὰ
of him, and will go forth to deceive the

ἔθνη τὰ ἐν ταῖς τέσσαρσιν γωνίαις τῆς
nations \- in the four corners of the

γῆς, τὸν Γὼγ καὶ Μαγώγ, συναγαγεῖν
earth, \- Gog and Magog, to assemble

αὐτοὺς εἰς τὸν πόλεμον, ὧν ὁ ἀριθμὸς
them to the war, of whom the number

αὐτῶν ὡς ἡ ἄμμος τῆς θαλάσσης. 9 καὶ
of them as the sand of the sea. And
[is]

ἀνέβησαν ἐπὶ τὸ πλάτος τῆς γῆς, καὶ
they went up over the breadth of the land, and

ἐκύκλευσαν τὴν παρεμβολὴν τῶν ἁγίων
encircled the camp of the saints

καὶ τὴν πόλιν τὴν ἠγαπημένην· καὶ
and the ²city \- having been ¹loved; and

city; but fire came down from heaven[k] and consumed them, [10]and the devil who had deceived them was thrown into the lake of fire and brimstone where the beast and the false prophet were, and they will be tormented day and night for ever and ever.

11 Then I saw a great white throne and him who sat upon it; from his presence earth and sky fled away, and no place was found for them. [12]And I saw the dead, great and small, standing before the throne, and books were opened. Also another book was opened, which is the book of life. And the dead were judged by what was written in the books, by what they had done. [13]And the sea gave up the dead in it, Death and Hades gave up the dead in them, and all were judged by what they had done. [14]Then Death and Hades were thrown into the lake of fire. This

κατέβη πῦρ ἐκ τοῦ οὐρανοῦ καὶ κατέφαγεν
²came ¹fire out - heaven and devoured
down of

αὐτούς· 10 καὶ ὁ διάβολος ὁ πλανῶν αὐτοὺς
them; and the Devil - deceiving them

ἐβλήθη εἰς τὴν λίμνην τοῦ πυρὸς καὶ
was cast into the lake - of fire and

θείου, ὅπου καὶ τὸ θηρίον καὶ ὁ
sulphur, where [were] also the beast and the

ψευδοπροφήτης, καὶ βασανισθήσονται ἡμέρας
false prophet, and they will be tormented day

καὶ νυκτὸς εἰς τοὺς αἰῶνας τῶν αἰώνων.
and night unto the ages of the ages.

11 Καὶ εἶδον θρόνον μέγαν λευκὸν καὶ
And I saw ²throne ¹a great ³white and

τὸν καθήμενον ἐπ' αὐτὸν οὗ ἀπὸ τοῦ
the sitting on it ⁴of ¹from ²the
[one] whom

προσώπου ἔφυγεν ἡ γῆ καὶ ὁ οὐρανός,
²face ³fled ¹the ²earth ³and ⁴the ⁵heaven,

καὶ τόπος οὐχ εὑρέθη αὐτοῖς. 12 καὶ
and a place was not found for them. And

εἶδον τοὺς νεκρούς, τοὺς μεγάλους καὶ
I saw the dead, the great and

τοὺς μικρούς, ἑστῶτας ἐνώπιον τοῦ θρόνου,
the small, standing before the throne,

καὶ βιβλία ἠνοίχθησαν· καὶ ἄλλο βιβλίον
and scrolls were opened; and another scroll

ἠνοίχθη, ὅ ἐστιν τῆς ζωῆς· καὶ ἐκρίθησαν
was which is [the - of life; and ²were judged
opened, scroll]

οἱ νεκροὶ ἐκ τῶν γεγραμμένων ἐν τοῖς
¹the ²dead by the having been in the
things written

βιβλίοις κατὰ τὰ ἔργα αὐτῶν. 13 καὶ
scrolls accord- the works of them. And
ing to

ἔδωκεν ἡ θάλασσα τοὺς νεκροὺς τοὺς
²gave ¹the ²sea the dead -

ἐν αὐτῇ, καὶ ὁ θάνατος καὶ ὁ ἄδης
in it, and - death and - hades

ἔδωκεν τοὺς νεκροὺς τοὺς ἐν αὐτοῖς,
gave the dead - in them,

καὶ ἐκρίθησαν ἕκαστος κατὰ τὰ ἔργα
and they were judged each one according to the works

αὐτῶν. 14 καὶ ὁ θάνατος καὶ ὁ ἄδης
of them. And - death and - hades

ἐβλήθησαν εἰς τὴν λίμνην τοῦ πυρός.
were cast into the lake - of fire.

[k] Other ancient authorities read *from God, out of heaven,* or *out of heaven from God*

is the second death, the lake of fire; [15] and if any one's name was not found written in the book of life, he was thrown into the lake of fire.

οὗτος ὁ θάνατος ὁ δεύτερός ἐστιν, ἡ
This *the ⁴death – ²second ¹is, the

λίμνη τοῦ πυρός. 15 καὶ εἴ τις οὐχ
lake – of fire. And if anyone not

εὑρέθη ἐν τῇ βίβλῳ τῆς ζωῆς γεγραμ-
was found ²in ³the ³scroll – ⁴of life ¹having been

μένος, ἐβλήθη εἰς τὴν λίμνην τοῦ πυρός.
written, he was cast into the lake – of fire.

CHAPTER 21

THEN I saw a new heaven and a new earth; for the first heaven and the first earth had passed away, and the sea was no more. [2] And I saw the holy city, new Jerusalem, coming down out of heaven from God, prepared as a bride adorned for her husband; [3] and I heard a great voice from the throne saying, "Behold, the dwelling of God is with men. He will dwell with them, and they shall be his people,[l] and God himself will be with them;[m] [4] he will wipe away every tear from their eyes, and death shall be no more, neither shall there be mourning nor crying nor pain any more, for the former things have passed away."

5 And he who sat upon the throne said, "Behold, I make all things new." Also he said, "Write this, for

21 Καὶ εἶδον οὐρανὸν καινὸν καὶ γῆν
And I saw ²heaven ¹a new and ²earth

καινήν· ὁ γὰρ πρῶτος οὐρανὸς καὶ ἡ
¹a new; for the first heaven and the

πρώτη γῆ ἀπῆλθαν, καὶ ἡ θάλασσα
first earth passed away, and the sea

οὐκ ἔστιν ἔτι. 2 καὶ τὴν πόλιν τὴν
is not longer. And ²the ⁴city –

ἁγίαν Ἰερουσαλὴμ καινὴν εἶδον κατα-
³holy ⁵Jerusalem ⁶new ¹I saw coming

βαίνουσαν ἐκ τοῦ οὐρανοῦ ἀπὸ τοῦ θεοῦ,
down out of heaven from – God,

ἡτοιμασμένην ὡς νύμφην κεκοσμημένην
having been prepared as a bride having been adorned

τῷ ἀνδρὶ αὐτῆς. 3 καὶ ἤκουσα φωνῆς
for the husband of her. And I heard ³voice

μεγάλης ἐκ τοῦ θρόνου λεγούσης· ἰδοὺ
¹a great(loud) out of the throne saying: Behold[,]

ἡ σκηνὴ τοῦ θεοῦ μετὰ τῶν ἀνθρώπων,
the tabernacle – of God [is] with – men,

καὶ σκηνώσει μετ' αὐτῶν, καὶ αὐτοὶ
and he will tabernacle with them, and they

λαοὶ αὐτοῦ ἔσονται, καὶ αὐτὸς ὁ θεὸς
²peoples ³of him ¹will be, and ²[him]self – ¹God

μετ' αὐτῶν ἔσται, 4 καὶ ἐξαλείψει πᾶν
with them will be, and will wipe off every

δάκρυον ἐκ τῶν ὀφθαλμῶν αὐτῶν, καὶ
tear out of the eyes of them, and

ὁ θάνατος οὐκ ἔσται ἔτι, οὔτε πένθος
– death will not be longer, nor sorrow

οὔτε κραυγὴ οὔτε πόνος οὐκ ἔσται ἔτι·
nor clamour nor pain will *not* be longer;

ὅτι τὰ πρῶτα ἀπῆλθαν. 5 καὶ εἶπεν
because the first things passed away. And ⁴said

ὁ καθήμενος ἐπὶ τῷ θρόνῳ· ἰδοὺ καινὰ
¹the [one] ²sitting ³on ⁴the ⁵throne: Behold ²new

ποιῶ πάντα. καὶ λέγει· γράψον, ὅτι
¹I make ³all things. And he says: Write thou, because

[l] Other ancient authorities read *peoples*

[m] Other ancient authorities add *and be*

these words are trust-worthy and true." ⁶And he said to me, "It is done! I am the Alpha and the Omega, the beginning and the end. To the thirsty I will give water without price from the fountain of the water of life. ⁷He who conquers shall have this heritage, and I will be his God and he shall be my son. ⁸But as for the cowardly, the faithless, the polluted, as for murderers, fornicators, sorcerers, idolaters, and all liars, their lot shall be in the lake that burns with fire and brimstone, which is the second death."

9 Then came one of the seven angels who had the seven bowls full of the seven last plagues, and spoke to me, saying, "Come, I will show you the Bride, the wife of the Lamb." ¹⁰And in the Spirit he carried me away to a great, high mountain, and showed me the holy city Jerusalem coming down out of heaven from God, ¹¹having the glory of

οὗτοι οἱ λόγοι πιστοὶ καὶ ἀληθινοί εἰσιν.
these – words faithful and true are.

6 καὶ εἶπέν μοι· γέγοναν. ἐγὼ τὸ ἄλφα
And he said to me: It has occurred.* I [am] the alpha

καὶ τὸ ὦ, ἡ ἀρχὴ καὶ τὸ τέλος. ἐγὼ
and the omega, the beginning and the end. *I

τῷ διψῶντι δώσω ἐκ τῆς πηγῆς
¹to the[one]²thirsting ⁴will give out of the fountain

τοῦ ὕδατος τῆς ζωῆς δωρεάν. 7 ὁ νικῶν
of the water – of life freely. The over-[one] coming

κληρονομήσει ταῦτα, καὶ ἔσομαι αὐτῷ
shall inherit these things, and I will be to him

θεὸς καὶ αὐτὸς ἔσται μοι υἱός. 8 τοῖς δὲ
God and he shall be to me a son. But for the

δειλοῖς καὶ ἀπίστοις καὶ ἐβδελυγμένοις
cowardly and unbelieving and *having become* foul

καὶ φονεῦσιν καὶ πόρνοις καὶ φαρμακοῖς
and murderers and fornicators and sorcerers

καὶ εἰδωλολάτραις καὶ πᾶσιν τοῖς ψευδέσιν
and idolaters and all the false [ones]

τὸ μέρος αὐτῶν ἐν τῇ λίμνῃ τῇ καιομένῃ
the part of them in the lake – burning

πυρὶ καὶ θείῳ, ὅ ἐστιν ὁ θάνατος ὁ
with fire and *with* which is the *death –

δεύτερος.
¹second [, shall be].

9 Καὶ ἦλθεν εἷς ἐκ τῶν ἑπτὰ ἀγγέλων
And came one of the seven angels

τῶν ἐχόντων τὰς ἑπτὰ φιάλας, τῶν
– having the seven bowls, –

γεμόντων τῶν ἑπτὰ πληγῶν τῶν ἐσχάτων,
being filled of(with) seven *plagues – ¹last,
the

καὶ ἐλάλησεν μετ᾽ ἐμοῦ λέγων· δεῦρο,
and spoke with me saying: Come,

δείξω σοι τὴν νύμφην τὴν γυναῖκα
I will show you the bride[,] the wife

τοῦ ἀρνίου. 10 καὶ ἀπήνεγκέν με ἐν
of the Lamb. And he bore away me in

πνεύματι ἐπὶ ὄρος μέγα καὶ ὑψηλόν,
spirit onto ⁴mountain ¹a great ²and ³high,

καὶ ἔδειξέν μοι τὴν πόλιν τὴν ἁγίαν
and showed me the ²city – ¹holy

Ἰερουσαλὴμ καταβαίνουσαν ἐκ τοῦ οὐρανοῦ
Jerusalem coming down out of – heaven

ἀπὸ τοῦ θεοῦ, 11 ἔχουσαν τὴν δόξαν
from – God, having the glory

* Collective neuter plural; *cf.* ch. 16. 17.

God, its radiance like a most rare jewel, like a jasper, clear as crystal. [12]It had a great, high wall, with twelve gates, and at the gates twelve angels, and on the gates the names of the twelve tribes of the sons of Israel were inscribed; [13]on the east three gates, on the north three gates, on the south three gates, and on the west three gates. [14]And the wall of the city had twelve foundations, and on them the twelve names of the twelve apostles of the Lamb.

15 And he who talked to me had a measuring rod of gold to measure the city and its gates and walls. [16]The city lies foursquare, its length the same as its breadth; and he measured the city with his rod, twelve thousand stadia;[n] its length and breadth and height are equal. [17]He also measured its wall, a hundred and forty-four cubits by a man's

τοῦ θεοῦ· ὁ φωστὴρ αὐτῆς ὅμοιος λίθῳ
– of God; the light of it [was] like to a stone

τιμιωτάτῳ, ὡς λίθῳ ἰάσπιδι κρυσταλλίζοντι·
very valuable, as ²stone ¹to a jasper being clear as crystal;

12 ἔχουσα τεῖχος μέγα καὶ ὑψηλόν,
having ⁴wall ¹a great ²and ³high,

ἔχουσα πυλῶνας δώδεκα, καὶ ἐπὶ τοῖς
having ²gates ¹twelve, and at the

πυλῶσιν ἀγγέλους δώδεκα, καὶ ὀνόματα
gates ²angels ¹twelve, and names

ἐπιγεγραμμένα, ἅ ἐστιν τῶν δώδεκα
having been inscribed, which is(are) of the twelve

φυλῶν υἱῶν Ἰσραήλ. 13 ἀπὸ ἀνατολῆς
tribes of sons of Israel. From east

πυλῶνες τρεῖς, καὶ ἀπὸ βορρᾶ πυλῶνες
²gates ¹three, and from north ²gates

τρεῖς, καὶ ἀπὸ νότου πυλῶνες τρεῖς,
¹three, and from south ²gates ¹three,

καὶ ἀπὸ δυσμῶν πυλῶνες τρεῖς. 14 καὶ
and from west ²gates ¹three. And

τὸ τεῖχος τῆς πόλεως ἔχων θεμελίους
the wall of the city having ²foundations

δώδεκα, καὶ ἐπ᾽ αὐτῶν δώδεκα ὀνόματα
¹twelve, and on them twelve names

τῶν δώδεκα ἀποστόλων τοῦ ἀρνίου. 15 Καὶ
of the twelve apostles of the Lamb. And

ὁ λαλῶν μετ᾽ ἐμοῦ εἶχεν μέτρον κάλαμον
the speak- with me had ²measure ³reed
[one] ing

χρυσοῦν, ἵνα μετρήσῃ τὴν πόλιν καὶ
¹a golden, in order he might the city and
that measure

τοὺς πυλῶνας αὐτῆς καὶ τὸ τεῖχος αὐτῆς.
the gates of it and the wall of it.

16 καὶ ἡ πόλις τετράγωνος κεῖται, καὶ
And the city ²square ¹lies, and

τὸ μῆκος αὐτῆς ὅσον τὸ πλάτος. καὶ
the length of it [is] as much as the breadth. And

ἐμέτρησεν τὴν πόλιν τῷ καλάμῳ ἐπὶ
he measured the city with the reed at

σταδίων δώδεκα χιλιάδων· τὸ μῆκος καὶ
²furlongs ¹twelve ³thousands; the length and

τὸ πλάτος καὶ τὸ ὕψος αὐτῆς ἴσα ἐστίν.
the breadth and the height of it ²equal ¹is(are).

17 καὶ ἐμέτρησεν τὸ τεῖχος αὐτῆς ἑκατὸν
And he measured the wall of it of a hundred

τεσσεράκοντα τεσσάρων πηχῶν, μέτρον
[and] forty-four cubits, a measure

[n] About fifteen hundred miles

measure, that is, an angel's. ¹⁸The wall was built of jasper, while the city was pure gold, clear as glass. ¹⁹The foundations of the wall of the city were adorned with every jewel; the first was jasper, the second sapphire, the third agate, the fourth emerald, ²⁰the fifth onyx, the sixth carnelian, the seventh chrysolite, the eighth beryl, the ninth topaz, the tenth chrysoprase, the eleventh jacinth, the twelfth amethyst. ²¹And the twelve gates were twelve pearls, each of the gates made of a single pearl, and the street of the city was pure gold, transparent as glass.

22 And I saw no temple in the city, for its temple is the Lord God the Almighty and the Lamb. ²³And the city has no need of sun or moon to shine upon it, for the glory of God is its light, and its lamp is the Lamb. ²⁴By its light shall

ἀνθρώπου, ὅ ἐστιν ἀγγέλου. **18** καὶ
of a man, which is of an angel. And

ἡ ἐνδώμησις τοῦ τείχους αὐτῆς ἴασπις,
the coping of the wall of it [was] jasper,

καὶ ἡ πόλις χρυσίον καθαρὸν ὅμοιον
and the city [was] ²gold ¹clean(pure) like

ὑάλῳ καθαρῷ. **19** οἱ θεμέλιοι τοῦ τείχους
²glass ¹to clean(pure). The foundations of the wall

τῆς πόλεως παντὶ λίθῳ τιμίῳ κεκοσμημένοι·
of the city ¹with ⁴stone ³precious ¹having been adorned;
   every

ὁ θεμέλιος ὁ πρῶτος ἴασπις, ὁ δεύτερος
the foundation – first jasper, the second

σάπφιρος, ὁ τρίτος χαλκηδών, ὁ τέταρτος
sapphire, the third chalcedony, the fourth

σμάραγδος, **20** ὁ πέμπτος σαρδόνυξ, ὁ
emerald, the fifth sardonyx, the

ἕκτος σάρδιον, ὁ ἕβδομος χρυσόλιθος,
sixth sardius, the seventh chrysolite,

ὁ ὄγδοος βήρυλλος, ὁ ἔνατος τοπάζιον,
the eighth beryl, the ninth topaz,

ὁ δέκατος χρυσόπρασος, ὁ ἐνδέκατος
the tenth chrysoprasus, the eleventh

ὑάκινθος, ὁ δωδέκατος ἀμέθυστος. **21** καὶ
hyacinth, the twelfth amethyst. And

οἱ δώδεκα πυλῶνες δώδεκα μαργαρῖται·
the twelve gates [were] twelve pearls;

ἀνὰ εἷς ἕκαστος τῶν πυλώνων ἦν ἐξ
respec- ²one ¹each of the gates was of
tively†

ἑνὸς μαργαρίτου. καὶ ἡ πλατεῖα τῆς
one pearl. And the street of the

πόλεως χρυσίον καθαρὸν ὡς ὕαλος διαυγής.
city [was] ²gold ¹clean(pure) as ²glass ¹transparent.

22 Καὶ ναὸν οὐκ εἶδον ἐν αὐτῇ· ὁ γὰρ
And a shrine I saw not in it; for the

κύριος ὁ θεὸς ὁ παντοκράτωρ ναὸς αὐτῆς
Lord – God the Almighty shrine of it

ἐστιν, καὶ τὸ ἀρνίον. **23** καὶ ἡ πόλις
is, and the Lamb. And the city

οὐ χρείαν ἔχει τοῦ ἡλίου οὐδὲ τῆς
not need has of the sun nor of the

σελήνης, ἵνα φαίνωσιν αὐτῇ· ἡ γὰρ
moon, in order they might in it; for the
   that shine

δόξα τοῦ θεοῦ ἐφώτισεν αὐτήν, καὶ
glory of God enlightened it, and

ὁ λύχνος αὐτῆς τὸ ἀρνίον. **24** καὶ
the lamp of it [is] the Lamb. And

the nations walk; and the kings of the earth shall bring their glory into it, ²⁵and its gates shall never be shut by day—and there shall be no night there; ²⁶they shall bring into it the glory and the honor of the nations. ²⁷But nothing unclean shall enter it, nor any one who practices abomination or falsehood, but only those who are written in the Lamb's book of life.

περιπατήσουσιν   τὰ   ἔθνη   διὰ   τοῦ   φωτὸς
³shall walk about   ¹the   ²nations   through   the   light

αὐτῆς,   καὶ   οἱ   βασιλεῖς   τῆς   γῆς   φέρουσιν
of it,   and   the   kings   of the earth   bring

τὴν   δόξαν   αὐτῶν   εἰς   αὐτήν·   25 καὶ   οἱ
the   glory   of them   into   it;   and   the

πυλῶνες   αὐτῆς   οὐ   μὴ   κλεισθῶσιν   ἡμέρας,
gates   of it   by no means   may be shut   by day,

νὺξ   γὰρ   οὐκ   ἔσται   ἐκεῖ·   26 καὶ   οἴσουσιν
for night   shall not be   there;   and   they will bring

τὴν   δόξαν   καὶ   τὴν   τιμὴν   τῶν   ἐθνῶν
the   glory   and   the   honour   of the   nations

εἰς   αὐτήν.   27 καὶ   οὐ   μὴ   εἰσέλθῃ   εἰς
into   it.   And   by no means   may enter   into

αὐτὴν   πᾶν   κοινὸν   καὶ   [ὁ]   ποιῶν
it   every(any)   profane thing   and   the [one]   making

βδέλυγμα   καὶ   ψεῦδος,   εἰ   μὴ   οἱ   γεγραμ-
an abomination   and   a lie,   except   the [ones]   *having been*

μένοι   ἐν   τῷ   βιβλίῳ   τῆς   ζωῆς   τοῦ   ἀρνίου.
written   in   the   scroll   –   of life   of the   Lamb.

CHAPTER 22

THEN he showed me the river of the water of life, bright as crystal, flowing from the throne of God and of the Lamb ²through the middle of the street of the city; also, on either side of the river, the tree of life° with its twelve kinds of fruit, yielding its fruit each month; and the leaves of the tree were for the healing of the nations. ³There shall no more be anything accursed, but the throne of God and of the Lamb shall be in it, and his servants shall worship

22 Καὶ   ἔδειξέν   μοι   ποταμὸν   ὕδατος
And   he showed   me   a river   of water

ζωῆς   λαμπρὸν   ὡς   κρύσταλλον,   ἐκπορευόμε-
of life   bright   as   crystal,   proceed-

νον   ἐκ   τοῦ   θρόνου   τοῦ   θεοῦ   καὶ   τοῦ
ing   out of   the   throne   –   of God   and of the

ἀρνίου.   2 ἐν   μέσῳ   τῆς   πλατείας   αὐτῆς
Lamb.   In [the] midst   of the   street   of it

καὶ   τοῦ   ποταμοῦ   ἐντεῦθεν   καὶ   ἐκεῖθεν
and   of the   river   hence   and   thence

ξύλον   ζωῆς   ποιοῦν   καρποὺς   δώδεκα,
a tree   of life   producing   fruits   twelve,

κατὰ   μῆνα   ἔκαστον   ἀποδιδοῦν   τὸν   καρπὸν
according to   ²month   ¹each   rendering   the   fruit

αὐτοῦ,   καὶ   τὰ   φύλλα   τοῦ   ξύλου   εἰς
of it,   and   the   leaves   of the tree   [will be] for

θεραπείαν   τῶν   ἐθνῶν.   3 καὶ   πᾶν   κατάθεμα
healing   of the nations.   And   every   curse
        = no curse will be any

οὐκ   ἔσται   ἔτι.   καὶ   ὁ   θρόνος   τοῦ   θεοῦ
will not be   longer.   And   the   throne   –   of God

καὶ   τοῦ   ἀρνίου   ἐν   αὐτῇ   ἔσται,   καὶ   οἱ
and   of the Lamb   ²in   ³it   ¹will be,   and   the

δοῦλοι   αὐτοῦ   λατρεύσουσιν   αὐτῷ,   4 καὶ
slaves   of him   will do service   to him,   and

° Or *the Lamb. In the midst of the street of the city, and on either side of the river, was the tree of life*, etc.

him; [4]they shall see his face, and his name shall be on their foreheads. [5]And night shall be no more; they need no light of lamp or sun, for the Lord God will be their light, and they shall reign for ever and ever.

6 And he said to me, "These words are trustworthy and true. And the Lord, the God of the spirits of the prophets, has sent his angel to show his servants what must soon take place. [7]And behold, I am coming soon."

Blessed is he who keeps the words of the prophecy of this book.

8 I John am he who heard and saw these things. And when I heard and saw them, I fell down to worship at the feet of the angel who showed them to me; [9]but he said to me, "You must not do that! I am a fellow servant with you and your brethren the prophets, and with those who keep the words of this book. Worship God."

10 And he said to me, "Do not seal up the words of the prophecy

ὄψονται   τὸ   πρόσωπον   αὐτοῦ,   καὶ   τὸ
they will see   the   face   of him,   and   the

ὄνομα   αὐτοῦ   ἐπὶ   τῶν   μετώπων   αὐτῶν.
name   of him [will be] on   the   foreheads   of them.

5 καὶ   νὺξ   οὐκ   ἔσται   ἔτι,   καὶ   οὐκ
And   night   will not be   longer,   and   not

ἔχουσιν   χρείαν   φωτὸς   λύχνου   καὶ   φωτὸς
they have   need   of light   of lamp   and   of light

ἡλίου,   ὅτι   κύριος   ὁ   θεὸς   φωτίσει   ἐπ᾽
of sun,   because [the] Lord   the   God   will shed light   on

αὐτούς,   καὶ   βασιλεύσουσιν   εἰς   τοὺς
them,   and   they will reign   unto   the

αἰῶνας   τῶν   αἰώνων.
ages   of the   ages.

6 Καὶ   εἶπέν   μοι·   οὗτοι   οἱ   λόγοι   πιστοὶ
And   he said   to me: These   -   words [are] faithful

καὶ   ἀληθινοί,   καὶ   ὁ   κύριος   ὁ   θεὸς   τῶν
and   true,   and   the   Lord   the   God   of the

πνευμάτων   τῶν   προφητῶν   ἀπέστειλεν   τὸν
spirits   of the   prophets   sent   the

ἄγγελον   αὐτοῦ   δεῖξαι   τοῖς   δούλοις   αὐτοῦ
angel   of him   to show   to the   slaves   of him

ἃ   δεῖ   γενέσθαι   ἐν   τάχει.   7 καὶ   ἰδοὺ
things it be-   to occur   quickly.   And   behold
which hoves

ἔρχομαι   ταχύ.   μακάριος   ὁ   τηρῶν   τοὺς
I am coming quickly.   Blessed [is] the [one] keeping   the

λόγους   τῆς   προφητείας   τοῦ   βιβλίου   τούτου.
words   of the   prophecy   of this scroll.

8 Κἀγὼ   Ἰωάννης   ὁ   ἀκούων   καὶ   βλέπων
And I   John [am] the [one] hearing   and   seeing

ταῦτα.   καὶ   ὅτε   ἤκουσα   καὶ   ἔβλεψα,
these things.   And   when   I heard   and   I saw,

ἔπεσα   προσκυνῆσαι   ἔμπροσθεν   τῶν   ποδῶν
I fell   to worship   before   the   feet

τοῦ   ἀγγέλου   τοῦ   δεικνύοντός   μοι   ταῦτα.
of the   angel   -   showing   me these things.

9 καὶ   λέγει   μοι·   ὅρα   μή·   σύνδουλός
And   he tells   me: See thou [do] not;   [a] fellow-slave

σού   εἰμι   καὶ   τῶν   ἀδελφῶν   σου   τῶν
[of thee] [I am   and   of the   brothers   of thee   the

προφητῶν   καὶ   τῶν   τηρούντων   τοὺς   λόγους
prophets   and of the [ones] keeping   the   words

τοῦ   βιβλίου   τούτου·   τῷ   θεῷ   προσκύνησον.
of this scroll: -   [2]God   [1]worship thou.

10 Καὶ   λέγει   μοι·   μὴ   σφραγίσῃς   τοὺς
And   he tells   me: Seal not   the

λόγους   τῆς   προφητείας   τοῦ   βιβλίου   τούτου·
words   of the   prophecy   of this scroll;

of this book, for the time is near. [11] Let the evil-doer still do evil, and the filthy still be filthy, and the righteous still do right, and the holy still be holy."

[12] "Behold, I am coming soon, bringing my recompense, to repay every one for what he has done. [13] I am the Alpha and the Omega, the first and the last, the beginning and the end."

[14] Blessed are those who wash their robes,[p] that they may have the right to the tree of life and that they may enter the city by the gates. [15] Outside are the dogs and sorcerers and fornicators and murderers and idolaters, and every one who loves and practices falsehood.

[16] "I Jesus have sent my angel to you with this testimony for the churches. I am the root and the offspring of David, the bright morning star."

[17] The Spirit and the Bride say, "Come." And

ὁ καιρὸς γὰρ ἐγγύς ἐστιν
the ²time ¹for ⁴near ⁴is.

[11] ὁ ἀδικῶν
The acting [one] unjustly

ἀδικησάτω ἔτι, καὶ ὁ ῥυπαρὸς ῥυπανθήτω
let him act unjustly still, and the filthy [one] let him act filthily

ἔτι, καὶ ὁ δίκαιος δικαιοσύνην ποιησάτω
still, and the righteous [one] ²righteousness ¹let him do

ἔτι, καὶ ὁ ἅγιος ἁγιασθήτω ἔτι.
still, and the holy [one] let him be hallowed still.

[12] Ἰδοὺ ἔρχομαι ταχύ, καὶ ὁ μισθός
Behold I am coming quickly, and the reward

μου μετ' ἐμοῦ, ἀποδοῦναι ἑκάστῳ ὡς
of me [is] with me, to render to each man as

τὸ ἔργον ἐστὶν αὐτοῦ. [13] ἐγὼ τὸ ἄλφα
the work ²is ¹of him. I [am] the alpha

καὶ τὸ ὦ, ὁ πρῶτος καὶ ὁ ἔσχατος,
and the omega, the first and the last,

ἡ ἀρχὴ καὶ τὸ τέλος. [14] μακάριοι οἱ
the beginning and the end. Blessed [are] [ones]

πλύνοντες τὰς στολὰς αὐτῶν, ἵνα ἔσται
washing the robes of them, in order that ⁴will be

ἡ ἐξουσία αὐτῶν ἐπὶ τὸ ξύλον τῆς
¹the ²authority ⁵of them over the tree –

ζωῆς καὶ τοῖς πυλῶσιν εἰσέλθωσιν εἰς
of life and ²by the ³gates ¹they may enter into

τὴν πόλιν. [15] ἔξω οἱ κύνες καὶ οἱ φαρμακοὶ
the city. Outside [are] the dogs and the sorcerers

καὶ οἱ πόρνοι καὶ οἱ φονεῖς καὶ οἱ
and the fornicators and the murderers and the

εἰδωλολάτραι καὶ πᾶς φιλῶν καὶ ποιῶν
idolaters and everyone loving and making

ψεῦδος.
a lie.

[16] Ἐγὼ Ἰησοῦς ἔπεμψα τὸν ἄγγελόν
I Jesus sent the angel

μου μαρτυρῆσαι ὑμῖν ταῦτα ἐπὶ ταῖς
of me to witness to you these things over(in) the

ἐκκλησίαις. ἐγώ εἰμι ἡ ῥίζα καὶ τὸ
churches. I am the root and the

γένος Δαυίδ, ὁ ἀστὴρ ὁ λαμπρὸς ὁ
offspring of David, the ²star – ¹bright –

πρωϊνός.
¹morning.

[17] Καὶ τὸ πνεῦμα καὶ ἡ νύμφη λέγουσιν·
And the Spirit and the bride say:

---

[p] Other ancient authorities read *do his commandments*

let him who hears say' "Come." And let him who is thirsty come, let him who desires take the water of life without price.

18 I warn every one who hears the words of the prophecy of this book: if any one adds to them, God will add to him the plagues described in this book, [19] and if any one takes away from the words of the book of this prophecy, God will take away his share in the tree of life and in the holy city, which are described in this book.

20 He who testifies to these things says, "Surely I am coming soon." Amen. Come, Lord Jesus!

21 The grace of the Lord Jesus be with all the saints.[q] Amen.

ἔρχου.   καὶ ὁ ἀκούων εἰπάτω·   ἔρχου.
Come.   And the [one] hearing   let him say: Come.

καὶ ὁ διψῶν ἐρχέσθω, ὁ θέλων λαβέτω
And the thirsting   let him   the wishing   let him
[one]   come,   [one]   take

ὕδωρ ζωῆς δωρεάν.
[the] of life freely.
water

18 Μαρτυρῶ ἐγὼ παντὶ τῷ ἀκούοντι
   [2]witness   [1]I   to everyone   hearing

τοὺς λόγους τῆς προφητείας τοῦ βιβλίου
the   words   of the   prophecy   -   [2]scroll

τούτου· ἐάν τις ἐπιθῇ ἐπ' αὐτά, ἐπιθήσει
[1]of this: If anyone adds upon(to) them,*   [2]will add

ὁ θεὸς ἐπ' αὐτὸν τὰς πληγὰς τὰς
-   [1]God   upon   him   the   plagues   -

γεγραμμένας ἐν τῷ βιβλίῳ τούτῳ· 19 καὶ
having been written in   this scroll;   and

ἐάν τις ἀφέλῃ ἀπὸ τῶν λόγων τοῦ
if   anyone takes away from   the   words   of the

βιβλίου τῆς προφητείας ταύτης, ἀφελεῖ
scroll   of this prophecy,   [2]will take
                                  away

ὁ θεὸς τὸ μέρος αὐτοῦ ἀπὸ τοῦ ξύλου
-   [1]God   the   part   of him   from   the   tree

τῆς ζωῆς καὶ ἐκ τῆς πόλεως τῆς ἁγίας,
-    of life   and out of the   [2]city   -   [1]holy,

τῶν γεγραμμένων ἐν τῷ βιβλίῳ τούτῳ.
of the   having been   in   this scroll.
things   written

20 Λέγει ὁ μαρτυρῶν ταῦτα· ναί, ἔρχομαι
   Says the   witnessing   these   Yes,   I am
       [one]   things: coming

ταχύ. Ἀμήν, ἔρχου κύριε Ἰησοῦ.
quickly.   Amen,   come[,]   Lord   Jesus.

21 Ἡ χάρις τοῦ κυρίου Ἰησοῦ μετὰ
   The   grace   of the   Lord   Jesus [be]   with

πάντων.
all.

* Neuter plural; see last clause of ver. 19.

[q] Other ancient authorities omit *all*; others omit *the saints*